1999 WRITER'S MARKET

8,000 EDITORS WHO BUY WHAT YOU WRITE

EDITOR
KIRSTEN C. HOLM

ASSISTANT EDITORS
DONYA DICKERSON
&
DON PRUES

WRITER'S DIGEST BOOKS
CINCINNATI, OHIO

Praise for *Writer's Market*

"Ever bigger and better, *Writer's Market*, as always, is every bit as essential to a writer's tool kit as a good dictionary and a good word processor."
—James Rettig, "Rettig on Reference" at Gale.com

"If you're serious about selling what your write and submit material regularly, you need a new copy every year." ***—Freelance Writer's Report***

"The preeminent tool for authors publishing their work."
—American Reference Books Annual

"A massive tome of excellence . . . a serious-sized book for writers seriously intent on being published." ***—Amazon.com Recommends***

"An invaluable resource that lays out the nuts and bolts of getting published."
—Library Journal

"No serious freelance writer should be without this resource. It's an excellent starting place for writers of all stripes." ***—Calliope***

Managing Editor, Annuals Department: Cindy Laufenberg
Supervisory Editor: Mark Garvey
Production Editor: Andrew Lucyszyn

Writer's Digest Website: http://www.writersdigest.com

Library of Congress Catalog Number 31-20772
International Standard Serial Number 0084-2729
International Standard Book Number 0-89879-850-7

Special thanks to SRDS for allowing us to use their editorial descriptions for publications that did not respond to our request for information.

Attention Booksellers: This is an annual directory of F&W Publications. Return deadline for this edition is December 31, 1999.

contents at a glance

Contents

From the Editors ***1***

Using Your *Writer's Market* to Sell Your Writing ***2***

Important Listing Information ***4***

Getting Published

Before Your First Sale ***5***

The basics of writing for publication, with Insider Reports offering insights for new writers. The writing team of ***John and Cathie Celestri*** *share what they learned when they decided to go the self-publishing route for their culinary mystery series on* ***page 9****. Writer* ***Ken Lamberton*** *describes on* ***page 16*** *how his personal interests in the natural world led him to take up writing in prison. After successfully selling dozens of magazine articles, he now has a book to his credit.*

Develop your ideas, then target the markets.......5
Query and cover letters 6
Book proposals 7
A word about agents.......8
Professionalism and courtesy 8
Writing tools 11
Manuscript format 13
Estimating word count.......13
Photographs and slides 14
Photocopies.......14
Mailing submissions 14
Recording submissions.......19

Writer' Digest, Writer's Market**'s Constant Companion,** **by Thomas Clark** ***20***

The former editor of ***Writer's Digest*** *magazine reveals how to use the monthly magazine's Markets column to keep your* Writer's Market *up-to-date and current all year long.*

Query Letter Clinic, by Don Prues ***22***

Eight new, real-life examples of queries that succeeded and queries that failed, with plenty of comments to help you understand why. A quick checklist of items a good query should contain is also included. ***Caitlyn Dlouhy****, editor at Laura Geringer Books (HarperCollins), discusses what makes a query hard to resist on* ***page 33****.*

Book Proposals Made Easy, by Sheree Bykofsky ***35***

A literary agent shows you how to craft a winning proposal that shows your book to its best advantage ***Judith McCarthy****, editor at John Wiley & Sons, outlines proposals that make an editor say "I do" on* ***page 40****.*

The Library on Your Desktop: Effective Research on the Web, by Jacqueline Justice, Ph.D. ***42***

A basic guide to online sources helps you expand your online research skills. Includes a list of popular search engines with addresses.

Personal Views

The Business of Writing

Literary Agents

Looking for a literary agent? Here's where to start your search, with 50 reputable literary agents that are open to new and previously published writers.

How to Find (and Keep) the Right Agent, by Lori Perkins *103*

An insider's look at what agents do . . . and how to get one to do it for you.

Literary Agents: The Listings *108*

Literary Agents Subject Index 124

The Markets

Book Publishers *130*

From A&B Publishers to Zondervan, hundreds of places to sell your book ideas. The introduction to this section helps you refine your approach to publishers. Writer ***Pearl Cleage*** *encourages writers to find their own voice and trust their writing instincts on* ***page 136.***

Canadian & International Book Publishers *338*

The introduction to this section covers how to submit your work to international markets.

Small Presses *358*

Companies publishing three or fewer books per year are listed here. Small presses often have narrowly tailored subjects—be sure to read each listing closely.

Book Producers *376*

Book producers, or packagers as they are sometimes called, assemble the elements of books (writers, editors, designers and illustrators) for publishers.

Consumer Magazines *381*

This section offers plentiful opportunities for writers with hundreds of listings for magazines on nearly every subject under the sun. ***Randy Johnson*** *of the inflight magazine* Hemispheres *discusses the global writing market on* ***page 554****, and how U.S. writers need to change their thinking when pitching to that market.* ***Michelle Alfano****, of the Canadian literary magazine* B&A: New Fiction*, discusses how newer writers can make the most of the opportunities on* ***page 575.***

Trade, Technical & Professional Journals *806*

Magazines listed in this section serve a wide variety of trades and professions. The introduction tells how to break in and establish yourself in the trades.

COMPLAINT PROCEDURE

If you feel you have not been treated fairly by a listing in ***Writer's Market***, we advise you to take the following steps:

- First try to contact the listing. Sometimes one phone call or a letter can quickly clear up the matter.
- Document all your correspondence with the listing. When you write to us with a complaint, provide the details of your submission, the date of your first contact with the listing and the nature of your subsequent correspondence.
- We will enter your letter into our files and attempt to contact the listing.
- The number and severity of complaints will be considered in our decision whether or not to delete the listing from the next edition.

From the Editors

When I moved to Cincinnati, I had a list of needs and wants to look for when house-hunting. High on the list was space to set up my husband's long-dormant woodshop. He spent long hours setting up his space, situating the band saw, the table saw and the planer just so. His clamp collection was hung from the overhead pipes with care (you can never have too many clamps, he says). When the shop was finally set up he went shopping for some odds and ends.

He returned, breathless with the news. "There's been a revolution in clamps!" Needless to say, he had to get his hands on the newly redesigned, better-than-ever tool. And the revolutionary clamps have proven to be just as wonderful as they promised to be (he says), allowing him to quickly tighten in on his project, without a lot of manual turning and twisting, freeing up his time for more important things.

I've always felt that *Writer's Market* was an essential part of a writer's toolbox. As with any tool, its effectiveness is largely influenced by the user's skill. The skills you bring to your project will determine how well the *Writer's Market* tool works for you.

Our job is to design the tool to be as effective as possible. While we may not have effected a revolution, we have made a number of significant changes aimed to make this tool easier to use, without a lot of turning and twisting, freeing *you* up to pursue more important things.

Find the important information fast. New symbols in the book publisher and magazine listings help you zero in quickly on key facts. New listings, magazine pay rates, publishers accepting only agented submissions and more are easily identified at a glance.

In Book Publishers we've highlighted royalty rates and advances, how many first-time and unagented writers the house has published in the last year, and the number of books published and manuscripts received. In Magazines we've highlighted the contact person, how much of the magazine is freelance-written, how many articles they purchase and how much they pay.

Find a literary agent. To help you pursue those publishers who accept only agented submissions, we've included a new section with 50 literary agents who are open to both new and previously published writers.

Find new skills. The articles this year will help you develop new skills, from crafting query letters and basic online research to negotiating higher pay rates and photography.

Find inspiration. Anna Quindlen, Sebastian Junger, Arthur Golden and Jack Canfield talk about how they developed the skills they needed and used the tools they had to become successful.

We want your *Writer's Market* to be the indispensable tool in your writer's toolbox, the tool you can't live without because it does the job you need it to do, allowing you to do the work you want to do.

Let us know how we're doing. If you're working on a project and think of a way that this tool could help you more, **write us.** We frequently survey our readers about how they use our books. If you would like to participate in a future survey, **write us.**

kirsten campbell holm

Kirsten Campbell Holm, Editor
writersmarket@fwpubs.com

Donya Dickerson

Donya Dickerson, Assistant Editor
literaryagents@fwpubs.com

P.S. Check out our new website, **http://www.writersdigest.com.** From the "Market of the Day" to the searchable database of over 1,000 writer's guidelines and many other features, we're looking for ways to give you more of what you need to get writing.

Using Your *Writer's Market* to Sell Your Writing

Writer's Market is here to help you decide where and how to submit your writing to appropriate markets. Each listing contains information about the editorial focus of the market, how it prefers material to be submitted, payment information and other helpful tips.

WHAT'S NEW THIS YEAR?

We've continued to search out improvements to help you use the book more efficiently.

Symbols. The most immediately noticeable new feature is the symbols preceding many, if not most, of the book publisher and magazine listings. These symbols will let you know, at a glance, whether a listing is new, a book publisher accepts only agented writers, comparative pay rates for a magazine, and more. A key to the symbols appears on the front and back inside covers.

Literary agents. Recognizing the increasing importance of literary agents in the book publishing field, we've researched and included 50 literary agents in a special section beginning on page 102. All of these agents have indicated a willingness to work with new, previously unpublished writers as well as more established authors. Most are members of the Association of Authors Representataives (AAR), a voluntary professional organization with a stringent code of ethics. Those who are not members of AAR have considerable editorial experience at major book publishing houses.

More names, royalty rates and advances highlighted. Last year in the U.S. Book Publishers section we added the word **Acquisitions:** and dug deeper for editors' names to help you get your manuscript to the right person. We've continued to probe for acquisitions editors' names and specific interests at each publisher and include many more this year. In addition, we've highlighted royalty rates and advances in boldface, as well as important information on the percentage of first-time writers, unagented writers, the number of books published and manuscripts received.

Names, pay rates and percentage freelance-written highlighted. This year in the Consumer Magazine section we've identified who to send your article to at each magazine by boldfacing the word **Contact:** followed by their name(s). In addition, the percentage of a magazine that is freelance written, the number of articles and pay rates for features, columns and departments, and fillers are also highlighted, quickly identifying the information you need to know when considering whether or not to submit your work.

New articles. Be sure to check out the new articles geared to more experienced writers in Minding the Details. In The Art of Negotiating, Greg Levoy gives you some tips and techniques for increasing your freelance rates. Gordon Burgett offers tips on boosting your article rates by including side material in Make More Money With Sidebars. And Abigail Seymour advises you on how to add photography to your arsenal of writerly weapons in Make More Money With Photos.

Interviews with bestselling authors. Personal Views, a new section this year, offers interviews with bestselling authors on writing and success. Veteran journalist and novelist Anna Quindlen, hot newcomers Sebastian Junger and Arthur Golden, and *Chicken Soup* serial phenom Jack Canfield offer insights into their writing life and advice for yours.

As always, all of the listings have been checked and verified, with more e-mail addresses and websites added.

IF *WRITER'S MARKET* IS NEW TO YOU . . .

A quick look at the Table of Contents will familiarize you with the arrangement of *Writer's Market*. The three largest sections of the book are the market listings of Book Publishers; Consumer Magazines; and Trade, Technical and Professional Journals. You will also find other sections of market listings for Scriptwriting, Syndicates, Greeting Cards and Contests and Awards. The section introductions contain specific information about trends, submission methods and other helpful resources for the material included in that section.

The articles in the first section, Getting Published, are included with you in mind. Query Letter Clinic showcases "good" and "bad" letters with comments straight from the editors' mouths about what attracted and what distracted. Literary agent Sherree Bykofsky offers her practiced advice on how to put together a winning book proposal. And basic online research "for the rest of us" is the topic of Jacqueline Justice's The Library on Your Desktop.

NARROWING YOUR SEARCH

After you've identified the market categories you're interested in, you can begin researching specific markets within each section.

Book Publishers are categorized, in the Book Publishers Subject Index, according to types of books they are interested in. If, for example, you plan to write a book on a religious topic, simply turn to the Book Publishers Subject Index and look under the Religion subhead in Nonfiction for the names and page numbers of companies that publish such books.

Consumer Magazines and Trade, Technical and Professional Journals are categorized by subject to make it easier for you to identify markets for your work. If you want to publish an article dealing with some aspect of retirement, you could look under the Retirement category of Consumer Magazines to find an appropriate market. You would want to keep in mind, however, that magazines in other categories might also be interested in your article (for example, women's magazines publish such material as well). Keep your antennae up while studying the markets: less obvious markets often offer the best opportunities.

INTERPRETING THE MARKETS

Once you've identified companies or publications that cover the subjects you're interested in, you can begin evaluating specific listings to pinpoint the markets most receptive to your work and most beneficial to you.

In evaluating an individual listing, first check the location of the company, the types of material it is interested in seeing, submission requirements, and rights and payment policies. Depending upon your personal concerns, any of these items could be a deciding factor as you determine which markets you plan to approach. Many listings also include a reporting time, which lets you know how long it will typically take for the publisher to respond to your initial query or submission. (We suggest that you allow an additional month for a response, just in case your submission is under further review or the publisher is backlogged.)

Check the Glossary at the back of the book for unfamiliar words. Specific symbols and abbreviations are explained in the key appearing on the front and back inside covers. The most important abbreviation is SASE—self-addressed, stamped envelope. Always enclose one when you send unsolicited queries, proposals or manuscripts. This requirement is not included in most of the individual market listings because it is a "given" that you must follow if you expect to receive a reply.

A careful reading of the listings will reveal that many editors are very specific about their needs. Your chances of success increase if you follow directions to the letter. Often companies do not accept unsolicited manuscripts and return them unread. Read each listing closely, heed the tips given, and follow the instructions. Work presented professionally will normally be given more serious consideration.

Whenever possible, obtain writer's guidelines before submitting material. You can usually obtain them by sending a SASE to the address in the listing. You should also familiarize yourself with the company's publications. Many of the listings contain instructions on how to obtain sample copies, catalogs or market lists. The more research you do upfront, the better your chances of acceptance, publication and payment.

ADDITIONAL HELP

The book contains many articles on a variety of helpful topics. Insider Reports—interviews with writers, editors and publishers—offer advice and an inside look at publishing. Some listings contain editorial comments, indicated by a bullet (●), that provide additional information discovered during our compilation of this year's *Writer's Market*. E-mail addresses and websites have been included for many markets. Publications of Interest in the Resources section includes some, but by no means all, trade magazines, directories and sources of information on writing-related topics. The Websites of Interest section points you to writing-related material on the Web.

Newer or unpublished writers should be sure to read Before Your First Sale. Minding the Details offers valuable information about rights, taxes and other practical matters. There is also a helpful section titled How Much Should I Charge? that offers guidance for setting your freelance fees.

IMPORTANT LISTING INFORMATION

• Listings are based on editorial questionnaires and interviews. They are not advertisements; publishers do not pay for their listings. The markets are not endorsed by *Writer's Market* editors. F&W Publications, Inc., Writer's Digest Books and its employees go to great effort to ascertain the validity of information in this book. However, transactions between users of the information and individuals and/or companies listed herein are strictly between those parties.

• All listings have been verified before publication of this book. If a listing has not changed from last year, then the editor told us the market's needs have not changed and the previous listing continues to accurately reflect its policies. We require documentation in our files for each listing.

• *Writer's Market* reserves the right to exclude any listing.

• When looking for a specific market, check the index. A market may not be listed for one of these reasons.

1. It doesn't solicit freelance material.
2. It doesn't pay for material.
3. It has gone out of business.
4. It has failed to verify or update its listing for the 1999 edition.
5. It was in the middle of being sold at press time, and rather than disclose premature details, we chose not to list it.
6. It hasn't answered *Writer's Market* inquiries satisfactorily. (To the best of our ability, and with our readers' help, we try to screen out fraudulent listings.)
7. It buys few manuscripts, constituting a very small market for freelancers.

• Individual markets that appeared in last year's edition but are not listed in this edition are included in the general index, with a notation giving the basis for their exclusion.

Getting Published

Before Your First Sale

Many writers new to the craft feel that achieving publication—and getting paid for their work—is an accomplishment so shrouded in mystery and magic that there can be little hope it will ever happen to *them.* Of course, that's nonsense. All writers were newcomers once. Getting paid for your writing is not a matter of insider information or being handed the one "key" to success. There's not even a secret handshake.

Making money from your writing will require three things of you:

- Good writing
- Knowledge of writing markets (magazines and book publishers) and how to approach them professionally
- Persistence

Good writing without marketing know-how and persistence might be art, but who's going to know if it never sells? A knowledge of markets without writing ability or persistence is pointless. And persistence without talent and at least a hint of professionalism is simply irksome. But a writer who can combine the above-mentioned virtues stands a good chance of not only selling a piece occasionally, but enjoying a long and successful writing career.

You may think a previously unpublished writer has a difficult time breaking into the field. As with any profession, experience is valued, but that doesn't mean publishers are closed to new writers. While it is true some editors prefer working with established writers, most are open to professional submissions and good ideas from any writer, and quite a few magazine editors like to feature different styles and voices.

In nonfiction book publishing, experience in writing or in a particular subject area is valued by editors as an indicator of the author's ability and expertise in the subject. As with magazines, the idea is paramount, and new authors break in every year with good, timely ideas.

As you work in the writing field, you may read articles or talk to writers and editors who give conflicting advice. There are some norms in the business, but they are few. You'll probably hear as many different routes to publication as writers you talk to.

The following information on submissions has worked for many writers, but it's not the *only* method you can follow. It's easy to get wrapped up in the specifics of submitting (should my name go at the top left or right of the manuscript?) and fail to consider weightier matters (is this idea appropriate for this market?). Let common sense and courtesy be your guides as you work with editors, and eventually you'll develop your own most effective submission methods.

DEVELOP YOUR IDEAS, THEN TARGET THE MARKETS

Writers often think of an interesting story, complete the manuscript and then begin the search for a suitable publisher or magazine. While this approach is common for fiction, poetry and screenwriting, it reduces your chances of success in many other writing areas. Instead, try choosing categories that interest you and study those sections in *Writer's Market.* Select several listings that you consider good prospects for your type of writing. Sometimes the individual listings will even help you generate ideas.

Next, make a list of the potential markets for each idea. Make the initial contact with markets using the method stated in the market listings. If you exhaust your list of possibilities, don't give up. Reevaluate the idea, revise it or try another angle. Continue developing ideas and approaching markets with them. Identify and rank potential markets for an idea and continue the process.

As you submit to the various periodicals listed in *Writer's Market*, it's important to remember that every magazine is published with a particular slant and audience in mind. Probably the number one complaint we hear from editors is that writers often send material and ideas that are completely wrong for their magazines. The first mark of professionalism is to know your market well. That knowledge starts here in *Writer's Market*, but you should also search out back issues of the magazines you wish to write for and learn what specific subjects they have published in past issues and how those subjects have been handled.

Prepare for rejection and the sometimes lengthy wait. When a submission is returned, check your file folder of potential markets for that idea. Cross off the market that rejected the idea and immediately mail an appropriate submission to the next market on your list. If the editor has given you suggestions or reasons as to why the manuscript was not accepted, you might want to incorporate these when revising your manuscript.

About rejection. Rejection is a way of life in the publishing world. It's inevitable in a business that deals with such an overwhelming number of applicants for such a limited number of positions. Anyone who has published has lived through many rejections, and writers with thin skin are at a distinct disadvantage. The key to surviving rejection is to remember that it is not a personal attack—it's merely a judgment about the appropriateness of your work for that particular market at that particular time. Writers who let rejection dissuade them from pursuing their dream or who react to each editor's "No" with indignation or fury do themselves a disservice. Writers who let rejection stop them do not publish. Resign yourself to facing rejection now. You will live through it, and you will eventually overcome it.

QUERY AND COVER LETTERS

A query letter is a brief but detailed letter written to interest an editor in your manuscript. It is a tool for selling both nonfiction magazine articles and nonfiction books. With a magazine query you are attempting to interest an editor in buying your article for her periodical. A book query's job is to get an editor interested enough to ask you for either a full proposal or the entire manuscript. (Note: Some book editors accept proposals on first contact. Refer to individual listings for contact guidelines.) Some beginners are hesitant to query, thinking an editor can more fairly judge an idea by seeing the entire manuscript. Actually, most nonfiction editors prefer to be queried.

There is no query formula that guarantees success, but there are some points to consider when you begin. Queries should:

- Be limited to one page, single-spaced, and address the editor by name (Mr. or Ms. and the surname).
- Grab the editor's interest with a strong opening. Some magazine queries begin with a paragraph meant to approximate the lead of the intended article.
- Indicate how you intend to develop the article or book. Give the editor some idea of the work's structure and content.
- Let the editor know if you have photos available to accompany your magazine article (never send original photos—send photocopies or duplicates).
- Mention any expertise or training that qualifies you to write the article or book. If you've published before, mention it; if not, don't.
- End with a direct request to write the article (or, if you're pitching a book, ask for the go-ahead to send in a full proposal or the entire manuscript). Give the editor an idea of the expected length and delivery date of your manuscript.

Some writers state politely in their query letters that after a specified date (slightly beyond the listed reporting time), they will assume the editor is not currently interested in their topic and will submit the query elsewhere. It's a good idea to do this only if your topic is a timely one that will suffer if not considered quickly.

A brief single-spaced cover letter enclosed with your manuscript is helpful in personalizing a submission. If you have previously queried the editor on the article or book, the cover letter should be a brief reminder, not a sales pitch. "Here is the piece on goat herding, which we discussed previously. I look forward to hearing from you at your earliest convenience."

If you are submitting to a market that considers unsolicited complete manuscripts, your cover letter should tell the editor something about your manuscript and about you—your publishing history and any particular qualifications you have for writing the enclosed manuscript.

Once your manuscript has been accepted, you may offer to get involved in the editing process, but policy on this will vary from magazine to magazine. Most magazine editors don't send galleys to authors before publication, but if they do, you should review the galleys and return them as soon as possible. Book publishers will normally involve you in rewrites whether you like it or not.

The Query Letter Clinic on page 22 presents several specific real-life query letters, some that worked (and some that didn't), along with editors' comments on why the letter was successful or where the letter failed to garner an assignment. For more information about writing query letters, read *How To Write Attention-Grabbing Query & Cover Letters*, by John Wood (Writer's Digest Books).

Querying for fiction

Fiction is sometimes queried, but most fiction editors don't like to make a final decision until they see the complete manuscript. Most editors will want to see a synopsis and sample chapters for a book, or a complete short story manuscript. Consult individual listings for specific fiction guidelines. If a fiction editor does request a query, briefly describe the main theme and story line, including the conflict and resolution.

BOOK PROPOSALS

Most nonfiction books are sold by book proposal, a package of materials that details what your book is about, who its intended audience is, and how you intend to write it. Most fiction is sold either by complete manuscript, especially for first-time authors, or by two or three sample chapters. Take a look at individual listings to see what submission method editors prefer.

The nonfiction book proposal includes some combination of a cover or query letter, an overview, an outline, author's information sheet and sample chapters. Editors also want to see information about the audience for your book and about titles that compete with your proposed book.

If a listing does not specify, send as much of the following information as you can.

- The cover or query letter should be a short introduction to the material you include in the proposal.
- An overview is a brief summary of your book. For nonfiction, it should detail your book's subject and give an idea of how that subject will be developed. If you're sending a synopsis of a novel, cover the basic plot.
- An outline covers your book chapter by chapter. The outline should include all major points covered in each chapter. Some outlines are done in traditional outline form, but most are written in paragraph form.
- An author's information sheet should—as succinctly and clearly as possible—acquaint the editor with your writing background and convince her of your qualifications to write about the subject.
- Many editors like to see sample chapters, especially for a first book. In fiction it's essential. In nonfiction, sample chapters show the editor how well you write and develop the ideas from your outline.
- Marketing information—i.e., facts about how and to whom your book can be successfully

marketed—is now expected to accompany every book proposal. If you can provide information about the audience for your book and suggest ways the book publisher can reach those people, you will increase your chances of acceptance.

- Competitive title analysis is an integral part of the marketing information. Check the *Subject Guide* to *Books in Print* for other titles on your topic. Write a one- or two-sentence synopsis of each. Point out how your book differs and improves upon existing titles.

For more detailed information on what your book proposal should contain, see Book Proposals Made Easy, by literary agent Sheree Bykofsky, as well as the Insider Report with Judith McCarthy, editor at John Wiley & Sons.

A WORD ABOUT AGENTS

Recognizing the importance of literary agents in publishing today, with this edition of *Writer's Market* we've included a section of 50 agents beginning on page 102. We've selected agents who describe themselves as open to both previously published and newer writers and who do not charge a fee to look at work. The majority belong to the Association of Authors Representatives (AAR), a voluntary professional organization. We've also included a few who are not members of AAR but have come to agenting after a notable career in editing and publishing.

An agent represents a writer's work to publishers, negotiates publishing contracts, follows up to see that contracts are fulfilled and generally handles a writer's business affairs, leaving the writer free to write. Effective agents are valued for their contacts in the publishing industry, their savvy about which publishers and editors to approach with which ideas, their ability to guide an author's career, and their business sense. In How to Find (and Keep) The Right Agent, literary agent Lori Perkins offers an inside look at how an agent works and how to find one that will go to work for you.

While most book publishers listed in *Writer's Market* publish books by unagented writers, some of the larger ones are reluctant to consider submissions that have not reached them through a literary agent. Companies with such a policy are noted by a symbol (A) at the beginning of the listing, as well as in the submission information within the listing.

For more information about finding and working with a literary agent, as well as 500 listings of literary and script agents, see *Guide to Literary Agents* (Writer's Digest Books). The *Guide* offers listings similar to those presented here, as well as a wealth of informational articles on the author-agent relationship and publishing processes.

PROFESSIONALISM AND COURTESY

Publishers are as crunched for time as any other business professional. Between struggling to meet deadlines without exceeding budgets and dealing with incoming submissions, most editors find that time is their most precious commodity. This state of affairs means an editor's communications with new writers, while necessarily a part of his job, have to be handled efficiently and with a certain amount of bluntness.

But writers work hard, too. Shouldn't editors treat them nicely? Shouldn't an editor take the time to point out the *good* things about the manuscript he is rejecting? Is that too much to ask? Well, in a way, yes. It *is* too much to ask. Editors are not writing coaches; much less are they counselors or therapists. Editors are in the business of buying workable writing from people who produce it. This, of course, does not excuse editors from observing the conventions of common business courtesy. Good editors know how to be polite (or they hire an assistant who can be polite for them).

The best way for busy writers to get along with (and flourish among) busy editors is to develop professional business habits. Correspondence and phone calls should be kept short and to the point. Don't hound editors with unwanted calls or letters. Honor all agreements, and give every assignment your best effort. Pleasantness, good humor, honesty and reliability will serve you as well in publishing as they will in any other area of life.

INSIDER REPORT

Self-publishers make all the right moves

"The first deadly killer I ever confronted face to face was a lump I found hiding in my breast."

-Kate Cavanaugh

Cathie and John Celestri

After spending months submitting their manuscript to a number of agents and publishers, Cathie and John Celestri (writing together as Cathie John) decided to take the alternative route of self-publishing. Says John, "We quickly tired of getting rejections that said 'not interested in the idea,' 'it's hard to publish a first-time novelist,' or 'this only has regional appeal.' So we owe getting our book self-published to our impatience and need for self-control." Cathie adds a bit more seriously, "We also believed in what we were doing strongly enough to say, 'It doesn't matter what agents and publishers think, we think it should be out there.' "

Out there it is. Published by Journeybook Press/CC Publishing, it's called *Add One Dead Critic*, a culinary mystery showcasing amateur sleuth and breast cancer survivor Kate Cavanaugh. And at press time it had reached 13th on the Cincinnati TriState Bestseller list—pretty impressive for a self-published book.

That Kate is a breast cancer survivor is no coincidence. So is Cathie, and her experience with breast cancer inspired writing and self-publishing the book. "Dealing with breast cancer taught us that time is important, so why waste time waiting for others to do something we could do on our own?" she says.

Waste time they did not. It was in July of 1997 when the Celestris opted to self-publish, and 5 weeks later 750 copies of the book arrived hot off the press—just in time for the fall and holiday selling seasons. "We knew fall was the best time to have a book out, so we decided to find a printer who could give us a very quick turnaround. We found one who got it to us in five weeks and at a good price."

Immediately after receiving their books, the couple approached local independent bookstores and offered it on a consignment basis. They also tried the big chains—Barnes & Noble and Borders—but without a distributor or wholesaler none would carry it. That's a typical Catch 22 when self-publishing: to sell books you need a wholesaler but to get a wholesaler you must prove your book is saleable and worthy of the warehouse space. "For a month or so we were only in the local independent bookstores, which was actually a good place to start because we could then show those sales to a wholesaler. We could say, 'Look, people aren't just interested in buying this book. People *are buying* this book.' "

Not only did sales in local independent stores prove useful in convincing a wholesaler to carry *Add One Dead Critic*, but the Celestris gathered more leverage when Barnes & Noble actually approached them. That's right. Every year the chain has a "Local Writers Harvest" in which each store highlights local authors. Fortunately for the Celestris, their local Barnes & Noble was looking for local authors for the Harvest. The Celestris, of

INSIDER REPORT, *Celestris*

course, obliged and allowed Barnes & Noble to carry their book. The authors even gave a signing and sold a number of copies, which allowed them to approach a wholesaler. "We said, 'look, we're selling books in local independent stores *and* in Barnes & Noble, you should carry *Add One Dead Critic*.' " Not surprisingly, Ingram is now their wholesaler.

Although they spent "almost nothing" on advertising, the Celestris managed to get quite a bit of attention for *Add One Dead Critic*. They devised a calculated three-pronged attack: play up the book's regional aspect, target the mystery market, and let breast cancer survivors know about Kate Cavanaugh. "We sent information about the book and copies to local newspaper reviewers, to mystery bookstores and magazines, and to breast cancer organizations," says John. "But we were careful not to become pests. When we approached a media outlet we'd make sure there was something in it for them. We'd ask ourselves: 'Why should they want or care to say anything about our book?' "

The couple's first attempts to drum up reviews in local dailies failed because papers don't review self-published books. Nonetheless, the Celestris did manage to receive coverage in a small suburban paper, at just the right time. As Cathie says, "It was October, which also happened to be National Breast Cancer Awareness Month, and the paper decided to run an article focusing on how our experience with breast cancer spurred the mystery. Talk about lucky timing. Sure the article was more about our surviving breast cancer than our writing a book, but it gave us and the book some exposure."

While newspapers weren't interested in reviewing the book, the Celestris found other publications that were. According to John, "Mystery publications from various parts of the country started reviewing the book and reviewing it favorably. We didn't even know some of these reviewers had a copy. One person picked up a copy of the book at a mystery conference and turned out to be a reviewer for a mystery magazine. People get interested in something new and spread the word when they like it."

In addition to positive reviews in the mystery genre, word of mouth pushed *Add One Dead Critic*'s popularity in the regional market. But just how does one begin and sustain a strong word-of-mouth campaign? "You have to take advantage of circumstances and happenstance," says John. "For example, I walk my dog every morning, and found out a neighbor I regularly passed was married to the police chief in a local community. The chief and I got to talking one day and I asked him for feedback on dealing with a crime. Well, it turned out he's a mystery reader. I told him about *Add One Dead Critic*, and he passed the word along to the police reporter for the community paper. The reporter needed a story so he came to us. We had no idea we would make that connection."

No doubt the Celestris have encountered quite a bit of luck—but they didn't depend on it. Like most smart business people the Celestris had a strong business plan but allowed themselves some flexibility with it. "You can have a business plan," says John, "but at the same time there's a lot of broken field running and you have to go with that, because it's not a straight line from goal to goal."

Obviously, the couple has learned that self-publishing requires much more than just writing a book and printing it. One has to make smart business decisions as well. For instance, the Celestris intentionally avoided going to a vanity or subsidy publisher. "With a vanity publisher, you have to pay them to produce the book, you have to pay them for their time, and you have little control. By self-publishing, we got to pick a printer who had a reasonable price, printed the book on quality paper, offered us a number of attractive template cover designs, and let us do the typesetting. All this was only about as expensive as going on a good vacation or buying a new computer." Although the Celestris live in

INSIDER REPORT, *continued*

Cincinnati, they chose Morris Publishing in Nebraska to print the book.

Selecting a good printer was not the only wise printing move the Celestris made. They also chose to have an initial print run of only 750 copies. A small first printing allowed them to manipulate the text on the back cover for the second printing. Why would they want to do that? To let bookshelf browsers know what others have said about it. The first printing of *Add One Dead Critic* had no review quotes on the back jacket. But once that first printing circulated and received rave reviews, the Celestris showered the second edition's back panel with laudatory quotes—a sharp business decision. The second printing was 1,000 copies.

Many self-published authors try to make a smash with one book. Not the Celestris. Because they plan to publish a 10-title *Journals of Kate Cavanaugh* series and establish a strong backlist in the ensuing years, they were not looking to make a profit off the first book. "We looked at it more as, 'this is what we wanted to do and if we broke even it would be well worth it,' " says Cathie. "If it takes off, that's great, but using self-publishing as a business to make a lot of money is a bad idea. We're doing it because we feel compelled to do it. We have to enjoy the process, not just the end result. That way we appreciate each little victory along the way."

Their second "little victory" is already in print. It's called *Beat a Rotten Egg to the Punch* and is published by none other than Journeybook Press/CC Publishing.

—*Don Prues*

You will occasionally run up against editors and publishers who don't share your standard of business etiquette. It is easy enough to withdraw your submissions from such people and avoid them in the future.

WRITING TOOLS

Typewriters and computers. For many years, *the* tool of the writer's trade was the typewriter. While many writers continue to produce perfectly acceptable material on their manual or electric typewriters, more and more writers have discovered the benefits of writing on a computer. Editors, too, have benefited from the change; documents produced on a computer are less likely to present to the editor such distractions as typos, eraser marks or globs of white correction fluid. That's because writing composed on a computer can be corrected before it is printed out.

If you think computers are not for you, you should reconsider. A desktop computer, running a good word processing program, can be the greatest boon to your writing career since the dictionary. For ease of manipulating text, formatting pages and correcting spelling errors, the computer handily outperforms the typewriter. Many word processing programs will count words for you, offer synonyms from a thesaurus, construct an index and give you a choice of typefaces to print out your material. Some will even correct your grammar (if you want them to). When you consider that the personal computer is also a great way of tracking your submissions and staying on top of all the other business details of a writing career—and a handy way to do research if you have a modem—it's hard to imagine how we ever got along without them.

Many people considering working with a computer for the first time are under the mistaken impression that they face an insurmountable learning curve. That's no longer true. While learning computer skills once may have been a daunting undertaking, today's personal computers are much more user-friendly than they once were. And as prices continue to fall, good systems can be had for under $1,000.

Whether you're writing on a computer or typewriter, your goal should be to produce pages of clean, error-free copy. Stick to standard typefaces, avoiding such unusual styles as script or italic. Your work should reflect a professional approach and consideration for your reader. If you are printing from a computer, avoid sending material printed from a low-quality dot-matrix printer, with hard-to-read, poorly shaped characters. Many editors are unwilling to read these manuscripts. New laser and ink jet printers, however, produce high-quality pages that *are* acceptable to editors. Readability is the key.

Electronic submissions. Many publishers are accepting or even requesting that final manuscript submissions be made on computer disk. This saves the magazine or book publisher the expense of having your manuscript typeset, and can be helpful in the editing stage. The publisher will simply download your finished manuscript into the computer system they use to produce their product. Be sure to mention if you are able to submit the final manuscript on disk. The editors will let you know what computer format they use and how they would like to receive your material.

Some publishers who accept submissions on disk also will accept electronic submissions by modem. Modems are computer components that can use your phone line to send computerized files to other computers with modems. It is an extremely fast way to get your manuscript to the publisher. However, you must work out submission information with the editor *before* you send something via modem. Causing the editor's system to crash, or unwittingly infecting his system with a virus, does not make for a happy business relationship.

Fax machines and e-mail. Fax machines transmit copy across phone lines. E-mail addresses are for receiving and sending electronic mail over a computer network, most commonly the Internet. Those publishers who wanted to list their fax machine numbers and e-mail addresses have done so.

Between businesses, the fax has come into standard daily use for materials that have to be sent quickly. Fax machines are in airports, hotels, libraries and even grocery stores. Many libraries, schools, copy shops and even "cyber cafés" offer computer time for free or for a low hourly rate. However, do not fax or e-mail queries, proposals or entire manscripts to editors unless they specifically request it. A proposal on shiny fax paper curling into itself on the editor's desk makes an impression—but not the one you want. If your proposal is being considered, it will probably be routed to a number of people for their reactions. Fax paper won't stand up well to that amount of handling. Writers should continue to use traditional means for sending manuscripts and queries and use the fax number or e-mail address we list only when an editor asks to receive correspondence by this method.

Letters and manuscripts sent to an editor for consideration should be neat, clean and legible. That means typed (or computer-printed), double spaced, on 8½×11 inch paper. Handwritten materials will most often not be considered at all. The typing paper should be at least 16 lb. bond (20 lb. is preferred).

The first impression an editor has of your work is its appearance on the page. Why take the chance of blowing that impression with a manuscript or letter that's not as appealing as it could be?

You don't need fancy letterhead for your correspondence with editors. Plain bond paper is fine. Just type your name, address, phone number and the date at the top of the page—centered or in the right-hand corner. If you want letterhead, make it as simple and businesslike as possible. Keep the cute clip art for the family newsletter. Many quick print shops have standard typefaces and can supply letterhead stationery at a relatively low cost. Never use letterhead for typing your manuscripts. Only the first page of queries, cover letters and other correspondence should be typed on letterhead.

MANUSCRIPT FORMAT

When submitting a manuscript for possible publication, you can increase its chances of making a favorable impression by adhering to some fairly standard matters of physical format. Many professional writers use the format described here. Of course, there are no "rules" about what a manuscript must look like. These are just guidelines—some based on common sense, others more a matter of convention—that are meant to help writers display their work to best advantage. Strive for easy readability in whatever method you choose and adapt your style to your own personal tastes and those of the editors to whom you submit.

Most manuscripts do not use a cover sheet or title page. Use a paper clip to hold pages together, not staples. This allows editors to separate the pages easily for editing. Scripts should be submitted with plain cardstock covers front and back, held together by Chicago or Revere screws.

The upper corners of the first page of an article manuscript contain important information about you and your manuscript. This information should be single-spaced. In the upper *left* corner list your name, address and phone number. If you are using a pseudonym for your byline, your legal name still should appear in this space. In the upper *right* corner, indicate the approximate word count of the manuscript, the rights you are offering for sale and your copyright notice (© 1999 Ralph Anderson). A handwritten copyright symbol is acceptable. (For more information about rights and copyright, see Minding the Details on page 62.) For a book manuscript include the same information with the exception of rights. Do not number the first page of your manuscript.

Center the title in capital letters one-third of the way down the page. Set the spacing to double-space. Type "by" and your name or pseudonym centered one double-space beneath that.

After the title and byline, drop down two double-spaces, paragraph indent, and begin the body of your manuscript. Always double-space your manuscript and use standard paragraph indentations of five spaces. Margins should be about 1½ inches on all sides of each full page of the manuscript.

On every page after the first, type your last name, a dash and the page number in either the upper left or right corner. The title of your manuscript may, but need not, be typed on this line or beneath it. Page number two would read: Anderson—2. Follow this format throughout your manuscript.

If you are submitting novel chapters, leave the top one-third of the first page of each chapter blank before typing the chapter title. Subsequent pages should include the author's last name, the page number, and a shortened form of the book's title: Anderson—2—Skating. (In a variation on this, some authors place the title before the name on the left side and put the page number on the right-hand margin.)

When submitting poetry, the poems should be typed single-spaced (double-space between stanzas), one poem per page. For a long poem requiring more than one page, paper clip the pages together. You may want to write "continued" at the bottom of the page, so if the pages are separated, editors, typesetters and proofreaders won't assume your poem ends at the bottom of the first page.

ESTIMATING WORD COUNT

Many computers will provide you with a word count of your manuscript. Your editor will count again after editing the manuscript. Although your computer is counting characters, an editor or production editor is more concerned with the amount of space the text will occupy on a page. Several small headlines, or subheads, for instance, will be counted the same by your computer as any other word of text. An editor may count them differently to be sure enough space has been estimated for larger type.

For short manuscripts, it's often quickest to count each word on a representative page and multiply by the number of pages. You can get a very rough count by multiplying the number of pages in your manuscript by 250 (the average number of words on a double-spaced typewritten page). Do not count words for a poetry manuscript or put the word count at the top of the manuscript.

To get a more precise count, add the number of characters and spaces in an average line and divide by six for the average words per line. Then count the number of lines of type on a representative page. Multiply the words per line by the lines per page to find the average number of words per page. Then count the number of manuscript pages (fractions should be counted as fractions, except in book manuscript chapter headings, which are counted as a full page). Multiply the number of pages by the number of words per page you already determined. This will give you the approximate number of words in the manuscript.

PHOTOGRAPHS AND SLIDES

The availability of good quality photos can be a deciding factor when an editor is considering a manuscript. Many publications also offer additional pay for photos accepted with a manuscript. Check the magazine's listing when submitting black & white prints for the size an editor prefers to review. The universally accepted format for transparencies is 35mm; few buyers will look at color prints. Don't send any transparencies or prints with a query; wait until an editor indicates interest in seeing your photos.

On all your photos and slides, you should stamp or print your copyright notice and "Return to:" followed by your name, address and phone number. Rubber stamps are preferred for labeling photos since they are less likely to cause damage. You can order them from many stationery or office supply stores. If you use a pen to write this information on the back of your photos, be careful not to damage the print by pressing too hard or by allowing ink to bleed through the paper. A felt tip pen is best, but you should take care not to put photos or copy together before the ink dries.

Captions can be typed on a sheet of paper and taped to the back of the prints. Some writers, when submitting several transparencies or photos, number the photos and type captions (numbered accordingly) on a separate 8½×11 sheet of paper.

Submit prints rather than negatives or consider having duplicates made of your slides or transparencies. Don't risk having your original negative or slide lost or damaged when you submit it.

For more information and advice on adding photography to your article submissions, see Make More Money with Photos, by Abigail Seymour, on page 84.

PHOTOCOPIES

Make copies of your manuscripts and correspondence before putting them in the mail. Don't learn the hard way, as many writers have, that manuscripts get lost in the mail and that publishers sometimes go out of business without returning submissions. You might want to make several good quality copies of your manuscript while it is still clean and submit them while keeping the original manuscript as a file copy.

Some writers include a self-addressed postcard with a photocopied submission and suggest in the cover letter that if the editor is not interested in the manuscript, it may be tossed out and a reply returned on the postcard. This practice is recommended when dealing with international markets. If you find that your personal computer generates copies more cheaply than you can pay to have them returned, you might choose to send disposable manuscripts. Submitting a disposable manuscript costs the writer some photocopy or computer printer expense, but it can save on large postage bills.

MAILING SUBMISSIONS

No matter what size manuscript you're mailing, always include a self-addressed, stamped envelope (SASE) with sufficient return postage that is large enough to contain your manuscript if it is returned.

A manuscript of fewer than six pages may be folded in thirds and mailed as if it were a letter using a #10 (business-size) envelope. The enclosed SASE can be a #10 folded in thirds or a #9 envelope which will slip into the mailing envelope without being folded. Some editors also appreciate the convenience of having a manuscript folded into halves in a 6×9 envelope. For manuscripts of six pages or longer, use 9×12 envelopes for both mailing and return. The return SASE may be folded in half.

A book manuscript should be mailed in a sturdy, well-wrapped box. Enclose a self-addressed mailing label and paper clip your return postage to the label. Unfortunately, new mailing restrictions make it more difficult to mail packages of 12 ounces and over, causing some publishers to discontinue returning submissions.

Always mail photos and slides First Class. The rougher handling received by standard mail could damage them. If you are concerned about losing prints or slides, send them certified or registered mail. For any photo submission that is mailed separately from a manuscript, enclose a short cover letter of explanation, separate self-addressed label, adequate return postage and an envelope. Never submit photos or slides mounted in glass.

To mail up to 20 prints, you can buy photo mailers that are stamped "Photos—Do Not Bend" and contain two cardboard inserts to sandwich your prints. Or use a 9×12 manila envelope, write "Photos—Do Not Bend" and make your own cardboard inserts. Some photography supply shops also carry heavy cardboard envelopes that are reusable.

When mailing a number of prints, say 25-50 for a book with illustrations, pack them in a sturdy cardboard box. A box for typing paper or photo paper is an adequate mailer. If, after packing both manuscript and photos, there's empty space in the box, slip in enough cardboard inserts to fill the box. Wrap the box securely.

To mail transparencies, first slip them into protective vinyl sleeves, then mail as you would prints. If you're mailing a number of sheets, use a cardboard box as for photos.

Types of mail service

- First Class is an expensive way to mail a manuscript, but many writers prefer it. First Class mail generally receives better handling and is delivered more quickly. Mail sent First Class is also forwarded for one year if the addressee has moved, and is returned automatically if it is undeliverable.
- Priority mail reaches its destination within two to three days. To mail a package of up to 2 pounds costs $3, less than either United Parcel Service or Federal Express. First Class mail over 11 ounces is classified Priority.
- Standard mail rates are available for packages, but be sure to pack your materials carefully because they will be handled roughly. To make sure your package will be returned to you if it is undeliverable, print "Return Postage Guaranteed" under your address.
- Certified Mail must be signed for when it reaches its destination. If requested, a signed receipt is returned to the sender. There is a $1.35 charge for this service, in addition to the required postage, and a $1.10 charge for a return receipt.
- Registered Mail is a high-security method of mailing where the contents are insured. The package is signed in and out of every office it passes through, and a receipt is returned to the sender when the package reaches its destination. The cost depends on the weight, destination and whether you obtain insurance.
- If you're in a hurry to get your material to your editor, you have a lot of choices. In addition to fax and computer technologies mentioned earlier, overnight and two-day mail services are provided by both the U.S. Postal Service and several private firms. More information on next day service is available from the U.S. Post Office in your area, or check your Yellow Pages under "Delivery Services."

INSIDER REPORT

Ken Lamberton: Let your interests lead you to your niche

Ken Lamberton

For some people, the life of a sequestered writer may seem idyllic. Nature writer Ken Lamberton, whose isolation is not voluntary, would claim otherwise. Spending over a decade in an Arizona prison has not only limited the resources available to him as a writer but has greatly restricted his encounters with his favorite subject, nature. Nevertheless, he has made the best of his situation, finding wilderness in unexpected places. His unusual perspective on the surrounding landscape eventually formed the backbone of his forthcoming book, *Wilderness and Razor Wire* (Mercury House). Descriptive details of his "encounters with nature in an unnatural place" fill what Lamberton maintains "is a work about transformation and celebration despite tragic circumstances, and by writing it I hope to share my own sense of wonder and hope within these circumstances."

With a B.S. in biology from the University of Arizona, Lamberton has published over a hundred articles in nature magazines like *Bird Watcher's Digest*, *New Mexico Wildlife*, *Tucson Lifestyle*, *Arizona Highways* and *Cimarron Review*. He also assists in teaching classes for his fellow inmates. Despite his flourishing career as a writer, he claims, "It wasn't until after I came to prison that I got serious about writing. I had prepared for a career in teaching science, and writing became an expression of my desire to continue teaching. It's strange, I've been teaching in prison for ten years, but I consider myself a writer. It's the only career I want to pursue." And it's a career move that paid off with the recent acceptance of his book by Mercury House.

Before embarking on this profession, however, he had to find his niche and that meant discovering his true interests. This search, he says, came complete with false starts. "I first started writing religious articles. I published a few but spent more than two years working in that direction without much success. I know now that I made a classic mistake. It's cliché, but this doesn't make it less true: You have to write what you know. I wish I had started out by trying to find my niche first. I'm a naturalist. I write about nature." His earlier publications did, however, give him a few credits on his writing résumé.

Once he unearthed his true talents, he was able to explore fully the spectacle of his surroundings with poetic language and precise details. He illustrates every element of nature he encounters, including the lives of birds that nest in his building. "Only three pairs came to breed under the visitation ramada, hauling thousands of beak-sized adobe bricks one at a time to construct their pueblo nests." Subtle humor often creeps into his prose. While describing how a new sewage irrigation system at an overcrowded prison affected the migration patterns of swallows, he elegantly states, "Twenty-one hundred men flushing their toilets had turned the desert green."

INSIDER REPORT, *Lamberton*

Lamberton's concentration on the subject he knows best has helped him publish extensively, and he's now completing another book, *Desert Memoir*, which he describes as "a collection of nature essays about my experiences in the Southwest before coming to prison."

Key factors contributing to his accomplishments are the support of his wife, Karen, who often researches material for articles, and the help of author and poet Richard Shelton, who teaches the creative writing workshop Lamberton has attended for ten years. "He has had the greatest influence on me. He is both mentor and friend, and the soul of *Wilderness and Razor Wire*." Attending Shelton's workshops has been crucial to his growth as a writer, and he believes the classes have likewise benefited other prisoners. Lamberton says, "Many prisoners turn to writing because they have a strong desire toward creativity. I see it in the men here in their poetry and prose but also in their painting and drawing, music and woodworking, even tattoos. Prisons are artists' colonies, and writing is just one form of artistic expression."

In workshops, he was not only creatively inspired, but was able to perfect his craft. One editor said his work was distinctly different from other articles by prisoners which were "invariably bad." Nevertheless, Lamberton claims, "I can't say that my work stands out from others, only that I have found a niche that suits me, my background and my experiences. If other men write poorly it's because, as Shelton says, they have 'a strong creative impulse and very little else.' I'm fortunate to have the foundation of a college education in biology and many experiences with wilderness to draw upon. I've allowed prison to teach me to focus on the essentials, like the migrations of swallows. I notice things. I concern myself with details. I write them down."

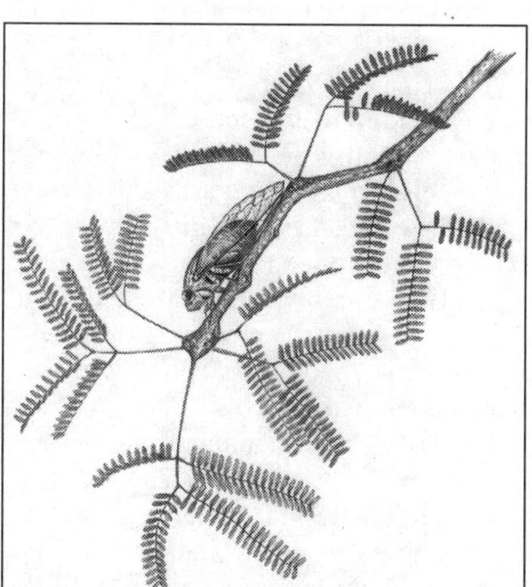

Detailed sketches of a cicada and a Sonoran desert toad exemplify Ken Lamberton's passion for the world around him. Inspired by nature writer Alison Deming's belief that as a culture we need to outgrow the childish notion that nature takes place only in wilderness, Lamberton claims, "My wilderness is a prison. It is a limited geographical area, not one bound by mountains or rivers or oceans, but by chain link and razor wire. Nature is here as much as it is in any natural park or forest or monument. One only has to notice it."

INSIDER REPORT, *continued*

Another way Lamberton profited from his workshops was by being exposed to markets for his work. He says, "From the beginning, I've used *Writer's Market* as my bible for publishing. I couldn't always get sample copies of magazines and had to target my articles according to the description given in *Writer's Market*. This wasn't a problem for the nature and hobbyist magazines. Many of them I saw for the first time when my article appeared in them. As I began to write literary essays, I found that styles and needs differed greatly between literary magazines. At this point, I had to rely more on the sample copies Richard Shelton brought to workshop."

Knowing the journals—as well as their editors—was essential to getting his essays published. "I've developed relationships with some editors to the point where they accept nearly every article I send them," Lamberton says, while on the other hand, "Book publishing is much more frustrating than article publishing for me. On a previous project—a book that remains unpublished—I had interested editors quit, get fired, and die before my manuscript made it into production. One editor was even jilted by her live-in co-editor and had to leave the press. Each time my manuscript went by the wayside."

He eventually made his way past these stumbling blocks, and *Wilderness and Razor Wire* was accepted. "The process for getting my book published began as I finished each chapter and submitted these to various literary journals. My first acceptances with the literary magazines *Oasis* and *Snowy Egret* encouraged me to continue until I had a complete manuscript." After polishing his manuscript, Lamberton wrote his proposal which introduced his book to publishers by describing his situation, which parallels the content of his book. "Here, where the migrations of barn swallows mark the passage of time, where horned owls restore faith in things supernatural, where the obstinance of a continued single mesquite tree stands for everything that takes advantage of difficult circumstances, the author finds healing, salvation."

When he felt his proposal was perfect, he sent sample chapters of his manuscript, including examples of his black and white illustrations, to Mercury House and one other press. "I chose these presses because they are literary and I like the nature books on their lists. Also, a writer friend of mine, Alison Deming, published her first book with Mercury House. Both responded positively and wanted to see the complete manuscript. It was Tom Christensen's enthusiasm about my work that finally brought me to Mercury House."

His success branched even further after Mercury House took his book. "The obvious benefit I've received with the acceptance of my book is a greater interest in my writing." *Puerto Del Sol* recently agreed to publish a chapter from his book, *The Wisdom of Toads*. The chapter "Raptors and Flycatchers," previously published in *Snowy Egret*, has also been accepted for inclusion in the *American Nature Writing 1999* anthology.

For writers, no matter their situation, he offers this advice: "Read, read, read. Read ten times as much as you write. If you write every day, read twice a day. Find authors who are writing in your genre and study them. It's a sure way to find inspiration if nothing else." For Lamberton, inspiration is found not only in books but in every aspect of the world around him. "Nature is a subject that has attracted me since childhood, and even in prison it calls me to watch and listen and participate . . . and in this I find healing."

—Donya Dickerson

Other correspondence details

Use money orders if you are ordering sample copies or supplies and do not have checking services. You'll have a receipt, and money orders are traceable. Money orders for up to $700 can be purchased from the U.S. Postal Service for an 85 cents service charge. Banks, savings and loans, and some commercial businesses also carry money orders; their fees vary. *Never* send cash through the mail for sample copies.

Insurance is available for items handled by the U.S. Postal Service but is payable only on typing fees or the tangible value of the item in the package—such as typing paper—so your best insurance when mailing manuscripts is to keep a copy of what you send. Insurance is 75 cents for $50 or less and goes up to a $45.70 plus postage maximum charge for $5,000.

When corresponding with publishers in other countries, International Reply Coupons (IRCs) must be used for return postage. Surface rates in other countries differ from those in the U.S., and U.S. postage stamps are of use only within the U.S. Currently, one IRC costs $1.05 and is sufficient for one ounce traveling at surface rate. Canadian writers pay $3.50 for an IRC which is redeemable for 46 cents in postage.

Because some post offices don't carry IRCs (or because of the added expense), many writers dealing with international mail send photocopies and tell the publisher to dispose of them if the manuscript is not appropriate. When you use this method, it's best to set a deadline for withdrawing your manuscript from consideration, so you can market it elsewhere.

International money orders are also available from the post office for a $3 charge or $7.50, depending on the destination.

RECORDING SUBMISSIONS

Once you begin submitting manuscripts, you'll need to manage your writing business by keeping copies of all manuscripts and correspondence, and by recording the dates of submissions.

One way to keep track of your manuscripts is to use a record of submissions that includes the date sent, title, market, editor and enclosures (such as photos). You should also note the date of the editor's response, any rewrites that were done, and, if the manuscript was accepted, the deadline, publication date and payment information. You might want to keep a similar record just for queries.

Also remember to keep a separate file for each manuscript or idea along with its list of potential markets. You may want to keep track of expected reporting times on a calendar, too. Then you'll know if a market has been slow to respond and you can follow up on your query or submission. It will also provide you with a detailed picture of your sales over time.

Writer's Digest: Writer's Market's Constant Companion

BY THOMAS CLARK

Think of *Writer's Digest* magazine as your monthly supplement to *Writer's Market*.

(It's a whole lot more than that, of course, but you're holding *Writer's Market* in your hands. And I have to start somewhere.)

Each month, the centerpiece of *Writer's Digest* magazine is The Markets, a compendium of news, reports and advice regarding the selling of your writing. By closely reading and noting the information you find there, you can continually refresh and update the information between the covers of this book.

Start in the market listings themselves. Each month The Markets features at least 50 reports on individual markets—magazines, book publishers, competitions, journals and more. These reports are similar in structure to the ones that fill this book; in fact, many of the opportunities featured in the magazine will be listed in *Writer's Market*. But the magazine's entries nearly always include additional information: perhaps it's the announcement of a new editor or a change in focus, or the addition of a new column or department. Or maybe it's simply additional comments from the editor about the types and styles of manuscripts she's looking for.

In the writing business, knowledge is marketing power, and each morsel of information you collect on a publisher can put you one step closer to that elusive sense of "knowing a market" that editors so desperately want in their writers.

Many writers I've met have shared their routines for updating into their *Writer's Market* with information they find in *Writer's Digest*'s market listings. Some create files—either on disk or on paper—and make note of the new information they glean from the magazine. They then make a note in their *Writer's Market* to indicate there's more information in this file. Others write out the facts on index cards that are clipped to the appropriate *Writer's Market* page. Or they jot the information in the margins of the book. If you own *Writer's Market: The Electronic Edition*, you can keep track of new markets and market updates on your computer.

One easy system is simply noting in the margins of *Writer's Market* the issue date and page number (6/99, p. 32, for instance) where the listing in *Writer's Digest* can be found, and then filing the magazines in a central location. Then again, I like anything that keeps the magazine on your office bookshelf!

If you read *WD*'s Markets section regularly, you'll be making notes in your *Writer's Market* about more than our market listings. Each month we feature a section of the marketplace, outlining the editorial customs and demands unique to that particular niche. (As I write this, we've recently covered Hispanic markets, gambling magazines, overseas English-language publications and Internet-related magazines—even journals specializing in literary erotica.) The publishing universe is vast, and each month's Close-Up piece shines a light into some corner of it for you.

Another light in an often-neglected area is the Contracts Watch report. Excerpted from the American Society of Journalists and Authors' newsletter, Contracts Watch talks about what

---

THOMAS CLARK *is the former Editor of* Writer's Digest *magazine, author of the book* Queries and Submissions *(Writer's Digest Books), and a frequent speaker at writers' conferences and seminars.*

publishers are doing in their contracts—and whether you need to negotiate those clauses out of your contracts. In an era when publishers and writers alike are trying to find some common ground in treating electronic rights (as well as foreign editions, windows of exclusivity and all manner of other clauses), Contracts Watch's timely, pull-no-punches reports are must additions to the information in *Writer's Market*.

Unless you have an open invitation to the inner sanctums of publishing, you may feel disconnected from the mainstream. Each month we combat that feeling by sitting down with some resident of the publishing universe for The Markets Q&A. Often our subject will be an editor or agent who's in a position to acquire your work—information that expands on his or her *Writer's Market* listing. Other times The Markets Q&A will introduce you to an observer of the industry (such as *Publishers Weekly* executive editor Daisy Maryles) or other players in this ever-changing field (such as the book buyer for the Home Shopping Network).

More voices are featured in exclusive trends reports from New York and Hollywood. In New York Observed, Jon Bing—a *Publishers Weekly* writer and editor—reports on such topics as the Random House/Bantam Doubleday Dell merger and the rise of the adventure narrative, and what these trends mean to you as an author looking to make a sale. Writer Pat H. Broeske has the same mission in the scriptwriting capital of the world, as Hollywood Observed charts the risings and wanings of film genres and practices.

Beyond The Markets department, *Writer's Digest* is a source of information, ideas and inspiration for all writers. Before you can sell your work, you must master the basics of your chosen styles of writing. Each month, *WD* examines aspects of both fiction and nonfiction writing and explains how to incorporate these techniques into your own bag of writing skills.

Writer's Digest also spotlights opportunities for you to exercise your talent. These opportunities may be a new niche in the magazine field, or a surging novel genre, or a freelance assignment just waiting for you. Combining these how-to pieces with your *Writer's Market* will increase your opportunities to see your byline in print—and your name on a check.

The book you hold in your hand is a powerful directory. Think of it as the *where to* source: It can point you to literally thousands of editors and publishers who want to publish the very finest writing they can find. Think of *Writer's Digest* as the *how to* source: a monthly dose of take-to-the-typewriter advice that will sharpen the words you send off to editors. Together, as writers have discovered for nearly 80 years, *Writer's Digest* and *Writer's Market* can form the cornerstone of the most profitable writing year you've ever enjoyed.

Query Letter Clinic

BY DON PRUES

The most indispensable companion to an unsold piece of writing is its query letter. Whether you're trying to sell a 100-word sidebar, a 4,000-word feature article, a 60,000-word nonfiction book or a 100,000-word novel, you need a darn good query letter to go with it. Period.

The *Writer's Encyclopedia* defines a query letter as "a sales letter to an editor that is designed to interest him in an article or book idea." The query is your opportunity to quickly convince an editor to buy your piece. With so many submissions to evaluate, editors tend to make fast judgments. So you must pitch a tight and concise query that explains the gist of your piece, why readers will want to read it, and why you're the perfect person to write it. Otherwise you're likely to sabotage your submission.

PRE-QUERY PROVISIONS

Identifying what to omit and what to include in your query can mean the difference between earning a sale or receiving a rejection. Before you end up making some serious query writing mistakes, take some precautions before submitting.

Trust the editor and suppress your paranoia. Some writers exclude important information from a query fearing the editor will "steal" their idea. Bad move. Editors aren't thieves, and leaving important information out of your query will only increase your chances of keeping yourself out of print. As will mentioning fees in your query; it will send your query straight to the can. If you're an unpublished writer, don't mention that either. Finally, never include a separate cover letter with your query letter. The query is your cover letter, your letter of inquiry, and your letter of intent—all packed into one tightly-wrapped, single-spaced page.

While some rules are meant to be broken, the rule of keeping a query to one page remains intact. Editors want to ensure it stays that way. The one-page query is not just a minor formality; it makes a lot of sense editorially. If you can't explain your idea in less than a page, you're probably not too clear about the idea itself.

Just because a query is simply one page don't assume it is simple to compose. A saleable query demands you include all the right information in a small space. Addressing your query to the appropriate editor is most important. Ensure this by calling the editorial office and asking who handles the type of material you're submitting. If you want to write a travel piece for a magazine, call and ask for the name and title of the travel editor. That's it. Don't ask to speak with the travel editor; merely get the correct spelling of his name. Always type or word process your query and put it on simple letterhead—editors want good ideas, not fancy fonts and cute clip art. Make your salutation formal; no "Dear Jim" or "Hello" (just today I saw two queries with these exact salutations!). And always offer an estimated word count and delivery date.

COMPOSING THE QUERY

You're ready to write your letter. Introduce your idea in a sentence or two that will make the editor curious, such as an interesting fact, an intriguing question, or maybe something humorous. Then state your idea in one crisp sentence to grab the editor's attention. But don't stop there. Reel in the editor with one or two paragraphs expounding upon your idea. Walk through the steps of your project and explain why you're the perfect person to write what you're proposing. List your sources, particularly if you have interviews lined up with specialists on your topic, as this will help establish the credibility of your work.

The Ten Query Commandments	The Ten Query Sins
Each query letter must be:	No query letter must ever be:
1. Professional (includes SASE, is error-free, is addressed to the right editor, etc.).	1. Wordy (text rambles; length exceeds one-and-a-half pages).
2. New (idea is fresh, set off, and up front).	2. Sketchy (idea isn't fleshed out enough).
3. Provocative (lead pulls you in).	3. Presumptuous (tone is too cocky).
4. Creative (presentation is offbeat).	4. Egotistical (topic is yourself).
5. Focused (story is narrowed down, length is kept to one page).	5. Reluctant (lame reason why you're doing it).
6. Customized (slanted to that magazine).	6. Loose-lipped (article is offered on spec).
7. Multifaceted (offers several options on how it could be done).	7. Stubborn (prior rejects from same editor haven't given you the hint).
8. Realistic (instills confidence that you're reliable and the project's doable).	8. Intrusive (phone call precedes or supplants query).
9. Accredited (includes your clips, credits, and qualifications).	9. Inappropriate (clips don't match the idea).
10. Conclusive (confirms that you're the best and only writer to do it).	10. Careless (faults are mentioned or major gaffe is made).

*From *How To Write Attention-Grabbing Query & Cover Letters*, by John Wood (Writer's Digest Books)

The tone of your writing is also important. Create a catchy query laden with confidence but devoid of cockiness. Include personal information only if it will help sell your piece, such as previous writing experience with the topic and relevant sample clips. And never forget a SASE. (Before sending your queries, use Andrew Scheer's Query Letter Checklist.)

Most questions about queries revolve around whether to send simultaneous submissions. There's no clear-cut way to wisdom here. Sending simultaneous queries to multiple editors is typically okay if you inform all editors you're doing so. But beware: Some editors refuse to read simultaneous queries (*Writer's Market* listings indicate an editor is not receptive to them) because they want an exclusive option to accept or reject your submission. This can be a problem if these editors do not respond quickly; it leaves you hanging and keeps you from submitting to other markets. The two clear advantages to sending simultaneous queries are that you have many lines in the water at once and it prompts a rapid reply—an editor excited by your query will be more apt to get back to you knowing the competition could get to you first.

WHAT THE CLINIC SHOWS YOU

Unpublished writers wonder how published writers break into print. It's not just a matter of luck; published writers construct compelling queries. What follows are eight actual queries submitted to editors (names and addresses have been altered). Four queries are strong; four are not. Detailed comments from the editors show what the writer did and did not do to secure a sale. As you'll see, there's no such thing as a boilerplate "good" query; every winning query works its own magic. Study the following examples so you can both avoid the pitfalls of those that failed and learn from those that went on to publication.

Bad

Tina Missedit
1234 Never Rd.
Stop Now, MO 33333

Jeff Ayers
Children's Better Health Institute
1100 Waterway Boulevard, P.O. Box 567
Indianapolis, IN 46206-0567

Dear Mr. Ayers,

Young children love to use their imagination. Wherever they are or whenever they are in need of a friend. They will block out the world and use their imaginations. The simplest toy or object begins to talk and come alive. The mind of a child is a open world of a fantasy adventure. When told to keep busy or take a bath, their world comes alive with fantasy.

Please find enclosed my manuscript fro a picture book, titled The Adventures of Sir Jerry In The Bath. When Jerry takes a bath and brings some toys with him. The waters and toys come alive. He becomes a fighter, protector and then the hero. He lets his imagination run wild. With a word count of about 500, this story is written for the three to seven age group. It uses playful, humorous language with the imagination of a young boy. It's off beat humor will appeal to children's sense of fantasy.

I have submitted seven simultaneous submissions. The other companies are: Arroyo Projects Studio, Boyds Mills Press, Children's Book Press, Dutton Children's Books, Farrar Straus & Giroux, Good Year Books, Greenwillow Books, Harper-Trophy Books. The magazines are Highlights for Children and Humpty Dumpty's Magazine. My story provides fun, fantasy and humor to young children.

Thank you for your consideration. I look forward to hearing from you.

Best wishes,

Tina Missedit

This is a dull, pointless opening. This statement is about as profound as saying, "Young children like to have fun." Duh.

An incomplete sentence. By now I've decided this submission will not be read.

Incorrect article; this looks bad. The entire opening paragraph is poorly constructed, repetitious, and tells me nothing other than that the author is not a professional writer.

Another incomplete sentence.

A typo. Again, the writer's lack of professionalism is showing.

Why is the author pitching a "picture book" to me, a magazine editor? This happens more frequently than one would think. Know the market and needs of the editor.

"Offbeat" is one word. All these errors kill any chance of actually having the manuscript read.

Why is the author telling me all this? The phrase "this is a simultaneous submission" is enough.

Overall, the poor quality of this query guarantees that the accompanying manuscript will not be read, let alone considered for publication. The only thing that could make it less professional would be some sort of statement that while the author has never been published before, her grandchildren love her stories. I get this all the time.

Comments provided by Jeff Ayers, editor of U.S. Kids.

Floyd Gotit
1234 Published Rd.
Sunny, FL 11111

Jeff Ayers
U.S. Kids
P.O. Box 567
Indianapolis, IN 46205

Dear Mr. Ayers,

Enclosed please find a 500-word nonfiction manuscript titled "The First Horse." I'd appreciate it if you'd consider it for publication. Since this is a printout, in the event of rejection you can discard it and respond via the SASE.

I'm a professional archeologist and freelance writer whose most recent publications include articles in the September 1994 and 1996 issues of *America's Civil War*, the June 1995 issue of *True West*, and the Autumn 1995 issue of *Persimmon Hill*, a publication of the National Cowboy Hall of Fame. I also have pieces appearing in forthcoming issues of *Florida Living and Military History*.

Thanks for your consideration. I look forward to hearing from you on this matter.

Sincerely,

Floyd Gotit

I know right up front that this article will fall within our word count requirements.

I might recommend putting sentence about responding via the SASE toward the end of the query, though it doesn't really bother me here.

Opening paragraph is straightforward and to the point. There are no details that I don't need since the manuscript is included (as specified in our writer's guidelines.) Also the author doesn't waste time telling me how much kids will enjoy reading his article.

I feel more comfortable with the reliability of the factual content of the article because the author has told me that he works in a related field.

Because the author lists his "most recent publications," I get the impression he has had success over a period of time, and is actively writing and being published at the present time.

The author has also told me that he has been published in other history-oriented publications. Again, my comfort level with the accuracy of the work is increased.

The ending is polite and business-like; I like that.

The only thing that should probably be added would be the author's name, address, tel. number, and the date at the top of the letter (though this was included on the manuscript.) Based on his query letter and the accompanying manuscript, this author received a "hold" letter explaining that we wanted to keep the piece for possible publication in a future issue.

Comments provided by Jeff Ayers, editor of *U.S. Kids*.

No way

February 9, 1998

Hasn't directed this to a person.

Editor
Random House, Inc.—Juvenile Books
201 E. 50th St.
New York, NY 10022

What is this? This is not the most relevant experience to sell me on her ability to write for children.

Assumption.

Dear Sir:

Awkward opener!

Being professionally involved in the funeral industry through contract work and having kids of my own has brought an interesting twist to my children's writing.

Very odd concept (but in no way the oddest I've ever been presented with).

These experiences have allowed me to approach the subject of death without being threatening to young readers (3/4-7). A series of stories has developed involving the interaction of different dogs with morticians and undertakers in a vast array of situations, including embalming, funeral planning, grief and mourning, etc.

Completely inappropriate subjects for children's books!

If you are interested in a manuscript copy of one of these stories, please contact me via the enclosed envelope.

All on its own? Poorly phrased.

Thank you for your time.

Sincerely,

Carol Quitnow

Why not simply enclose the materials? Am I going to take the extra step to request the manuscript? Never. I don't have the time or interest.

No return address. In the event the letter gets separated from the envelopes, she's out of luck!

Once again, no mention of format or any evidence that shows this writer understands how children's books are laid out.

Comments provided by Heidi Kilgras of Random House Books for Young Readers.

Tess Goodidea
P.O. Box 2170
Happy, Texas 78029

Heidi Kilgras
Random House
Books for Young Readers
201 E. 50th St.
New York, NY 10022

October 16, 1997

Dear Ms. Kilgras,

Good

I am a published author whose previous works include two time-travel romances, JEWELS OF TIME and CIRCLES IN TIME, one fantasy romance, ''The Fairy Bride'' for MIDSUMMER NIGHT'S MAGIC, an anthology, and one futuristic romance, TO TOUCH THE STARS, all for Leisure/Lovespell Books. My credits also include fiction published in *Highlights for Children.*

Since this is a children's book submission, it may have been better to state this first, but ok. More relevant.

Enclosed is a brief synopsis detailing a proposed science fiction book series, called MIND WARRIORS, for children ages 8 to 12. This idea has been formulated with the best possible source of input for such a project—my ten year old son, Jordan. He's my writing ''pardner,'' in as much as he has helped flesh out the characters and ideas for Mind Warriors and will continue to contribute to this series, hence the pseudonym which speaks for us both: J.C. Goodidea.

Great. Target audience is identified right away.

The series would consist, initially, of 7 books, each about 20,000 to 25,000 words written from the viewpoint of one of the Mind Warriors, including their pets, Galileo the dog, and Streak the cat. Future books, if the series attains the popularity I think possible, could feature the viewpoint of other characters, such as the good aliens who help the Mind Warriors battle the evil Mindbenders. Actually, the possibilities for new books from new viewpoints are limitless as the Mind Warriors' adventures lead them to make new friends—and new enemies.

This person clearly knows about book lengths and this information is helpful.

MIND WARRIORS will take 8 to 12 year olds on a journey not only into a fantasy of what might lie within our own world and universe, but on a journey inside themselves. Each character in the series will be placed in unusual situations and consequently be forced to deal with problems which will cause each one to draw upon his or her own individual strength, character, and sense of honor. Each character in MIND WARRIORS will also face regular, ''kid'' problems, and realize that it is possible to find the ''hero'' or ''heroine'' within themselves.

Overall series vision is stated clearly (and not overzealously).

With science-fiction continuing to soar in popularity, particularly in children's books for this age group, I believe this series could be a terrific success. I hope you enjoy the synopsis and other material enclosed. If you want to receive the first three chapters of the first book in the series, MIND WARRIORS: *THE BEGINNING*, I would be happy to send them to you. Thank you for your time.

Good. Just enough to whet the appetite. There's nothing worse than being overwhelmed by 80 pages of outlines, proposals, plot treatments, sample chapters, etc. It's not an efficient use of my time to have to slog through all that to see if the idea is at all interesting and whether the writer can actually write real narrative prose!

She is correct! She's done her research.

Sincerely,

Tess Goodidea (with Jordan Goodidea)
aka J.C. Goodidea

Comments provided by Heidi Kilgras, editor at Random House.

Bad

Mark Mistakes
1234 No No Way
Sorry, TX 86055

Jason Whitmarsh
Managing Editor
Transitions Abroad
P.O. Box 1300
Amherst, Massachusetts 01004-1300

Dear Mr Whitmarsh,

The enclosed article is an account of a trip my wife and I made on the Nile River in Egypt. I have 35mm slides to illustrate the aritcle. Let me know your needs.

I await your response.

Yours sincerely,

Mark Mistakes

No longer works here. Check the masthead of a current issue or call to confirm contact person before sending query.

No date!

No period after Mr. If he's this sloppy here, the article must be a mess!

Sent the article with his query! Did not send query and wait for a reply, and did not request the guidelines before sending!

No duh.

Color or black and white? If he'd read the guidelines he'd know we only accept black and white prints.

No! He should have requested the guidelines and topic schedules first, then tailored the query.

Amazing how many mistakes he made in so few lines. Overall, this query is far too short and tells us nothing of substance about this piece. Requesting and reading the guidelines first would have helped us all a great deal. And sending the piece without querying first was a big waste of postage—it went straight into the recycling bin unread.

Comments provided by David Cline, managing editor of *Transitions Abroad*.

Mykel Sold
P.O. Box 111
Published, NY 10012

October 26, 1997

David Cline
Managing Editor
Transitions Abroad
P.O. Box 1300
Amherst MA 01004

Dear Mr. Cline,

The closest I've come to Ivory Tower employment has been working as a cashier at the NYU bookstore. I heard about the mortarboard bureaucracy, but, until two years ago, never experienced it. Then I became a visiting professor, in the School of Foreign Service, at the most prestigious university in the weirdest country in the world: Mongolia.

My year in Mongolia was the strangest of my life. The best and the worst, it was a non-stop roller coaster from the ridiculous to the sublimep and back. I've written a book about that adventure. One chapter of that book specifically deals with my day-to-day teaching experience there. And it was wild!

As a longtime reader of "Transitions Abroad," I thought it might be time to contribute to it. I've edited the chapter, LIFE AT KAFKA U, specifically for the TA audience. Most of the articles in your magazine deal with the nuts and bolts of teaching, traveling and learning in other countries. Mine deals with the comedic adventures of someone actually doing it. Many readers will identify with the hilarious frustrations of day-to-day life in a place where you understand nothing.

I currently publish THE WORLD FOR FREE, a hospitality exchange bulletin with members in more than 20 countries. As a freelance writer, I've contributed to "New York Press," "The San Diego Union," "Newsday," and various small press books and magazines. I also have a long running non-music column in the San Francisco magazine, "Maximum Rock'n'Roll."

I'd like to send you the article for your consideration. Because of the formatting and type-face changes, it would be best to submit it via postal mail. If you can read WordPerfect 5.1 documents, I could also submit it as an attachment to an email message.

In any case, I'd like to hear from you whenever convenient. Thanks you for your time and consideration.

Sincerely,

Mykel Sold

Intriguing first line, encourages me to read on.

Great line! Now I'm hooked!

Low key and polite. Perfect.

This query was so good—funny, mellow, interesting—that we took a chance and agreed to look at a first-person narrative, which we usually don't run. The piece was terrific, and we ended up contracting with a photographer acquaintance of the author and running the piece as a feature in one of our more important issues.

Great to get an e-mail that is formatted like a traditional query letter. Most e-mail queries forget to include a postal address and phone/fax numbers. By including our complete postal address as well, he gives this e-mail the formality that a query demands.

Typo: frequent problem with e-mail. Get an e-mail spellchecker if you don't have one.

This paragraph is great. He obviously knows the magazine and what we like. Yet he's got the guts to try us with something that is within our interest but quite different from what we usually run.

Gives excellent qualifications without overdoing it.

Wow! Great to hear from someone who is sensitive to the problems of electronic submissions and actually ASKS FIRST.

Comments provided by David Cline, managing editor of *Transitions Abroad*.

Bad

Tom Notpublished
1234 Try Again Lane
Outta Print, OH 10001

James Gormbv, Editor
Better Nutrition Magazine
13th Floor, 5 Penn Plaza
New York City, NY 10001

March 10, 1997

Dear Mr. Gormbv:

I am a published freelance writer, closely associated with a group of highly successful Emu ranchers here, in the Ohio valley, and I would like to submit an article extolling the values of ''the other red meat''

According to a survey conducted by the Food Marketing Institute, 60% of the U.S. consumers were seeking a healthier diet, but were hestitant about giving up the flavor and taste of beef. Emu meat will fill the bill.

Although Emu and beef meat taste similar, there are nutritional facts that show a difference:

	Calories	Fat	Cholesterol
Emu	109	1.7 g	5.5 mg
Beef	225	15.6 g	65. mg
Chicken	110	1.2 g	64. mg
Turkey	104	1.6 g	73. mg

Serving size of 3.5 ozs.

If your readers had a choice of eating a red meat that tasted similar to beef, was 97% fat free, was higher in protein and Iron, lower in cholesterol, and low in calories, would they give it a try?

Emu meat has been recognized by the American Heart Association as being raised naturally, with no chemical additives or preservatives, and that it is high in iron and vitamin C. For better nutrition, consider a new experience of the rich flavor of this Ohio grown alternative, for Red Meat.

For more extensive information concerning this nutritional food: write to Emu, P.O. Box 1, Beaver, OH 22222, or call 1-800-111-0000, or their e-mail address: emu@eaddress.com.

The enclosed SASE is for your reply and for sending me a copy of your Writer's Guidelines, plus your AD Rate Card.

Sincerely,

Tom Notpublished

My name is misspelled.

Aberrant order of address elements.

No period.

Spelling errors in queries do not help.

Aberrant incorrect capitalization.

I am doubtful that the AHA would recognize that "Emu meat [is] raised naturally." The document should be cited.

Irregular indenting. Consistency is the key.

Sounds like an ad.

Why comma? Why caps?

"More" says it all.

Is he doing Public Relations and ad placement?

If you are with a PR/AD firm, say so and use appropriate letterhead. PR reps masquerading as independent freelancers is quite a turn off.

Comments provided by James Gormley, editor of *Better Nutrition Magazine.*

Patty Inprint
1000 Herbal Way
Seattle, WA 98334

February 20, 1997

James Gormley, Editor
Better Nutrition
13th Floor, 5 Penn Plaza
New York, NY 10001

A little long, but topics are right in line with our magazine, preliminary research was done and mini-proposals/descriptions are short and well-written.

Dear Mr. Gormley:

In the March 1997 issue of Writer's Digest Magazine, Better Nutrition was profiled in "The Markets" column. As a result, I have put together a brief resume and a few clips for your review.

I am interested in writing regular features or columns on a variety of natural health topics. Some Ideas I've been tossing around are:

- **Is the Herb Echinacea Better Than Antibiotics?**

The Bastyr University Research Institute just announced they will begin a clinical study of Echinacea and its effectiveness in treating respiratory infections. This article could include comments from Bastyr plus historical information and usage of this herb.

- **What to Include in a Natural First Aid Kit**

This could be written as a full-length feature with herbal first aid as well as homeopathics and essential oils for emergency use. Shorter pieces could be done on just homeopathic first aid or just aromatherapy first aid.

Proposes shorter articles.

- **Cleanse Your Body From the Outside In**

This topic would focus on dry skin body brushing as a healthy means of cleansing the body by opening the pores of the skin, allowing better elimination of waste. What could also be included is information on moisturizing after dry brushing and perhaps even a few "beauty" product home recipes.

Good sidebar possibilities.

- **Nature's Analgesics: Taking the Pain Away Without Drugs**
- **Suffering From Indigestion? Exploring Alternatives to Over-the-Counter Acid Blockers**

If you would like detailed queries on any of these ideas, I would be happy to elaborate. I have access to many highly qualified health professional resources including Bastyr University, which is practically in my back yard.

My writing is tight, informative, interesting and quick—I can usually produce a finished piece within 3-7 days of assignment.

I agree, on all counts.

Respectfully,

Sale? Yes, one sale, with probability of regular assignments.

Patty Inprint

Comments provided by James Gormley, editor of *Better Nutrition Magazine*.

ANDREW SCHEER'S QUERY LETTER CHECKLIST

CONTENT

1. Working title (to help editors grasp your idea quickly)
2. Summary of topic or theme
3. Intended reader application (takeaway value)
4. Approximate article length (e.g., 800 words, 1,500 words)
5. Sample paragraph: lead or key segment (a big help in assessing your writing)
6. Paragraph summarizing key supporting material (e.g., anecdotes, interviews)
7. Your qualifications to write on this topic (incl. writing experience, if applicable)

MECHANICS

1. Current magazine title
2. Current magazine address
3. Correct editor (when in doubt, ask first)
4. Correct spelling of editor's name
5. Neat, error-free typing
6. One page, single-spaced
7. Self-addressed, stamped envelope (SASE) (hint: fold it in thirds)
8. Mailed in #10 business envelope

INFORMATION ABOUT YOU

1. Your name
2. Your title (Miss, Ms., Mrs., Mr., Dr., etc.)
3. Your address
4. Your day phone number (fax, e-mail if available)

INFORMATION ABOUT YOUR ARTICLE

1. Approximate article length (e.g., 500 words, 1,200 words)
2. When article is available (e.g., immediately, in 4 weeks)
3. Rights available (first, one-time, or reprint)

OPTIONAL (in descending order of potential usefulness)

1. Samples (include only if applicable/impressive to this publication)
2. Reply Postcard
3. Letterhead (avoid unconventional stock or too many dingbats)
4. Business Card

DON'TS

1. Phone or fax (unless urgent article, e.g., L.A. earthquake story on 1/18/95)
2. Unrealistic deadline (''If I don't hear from you in one week . . .'')
3. Query for a topic that's just been given major coverage
4. Confess unfamiliarity with the magazine
5. Request guidelines as part of your query
6. ''Dear Editor''/''Occupant'' letter
7. Long or vague letter
8. Bad attitude (antagonistic, defeatist)
9. Query for type of articles the magazine doesn't print

There's no special format that results in a yes; let it reflect you and the nature of your topic.

Andrew Scheer is the managing editor of *Moody Magazine*.

INSIDER REPORT

Making queries hard to resist

Caitlyn Dlouhy

Creating a salable manuscript is only part of what makes the professional writer a success. Convincing a top-notch editor the work is a cut above the rest balances out that winning equation. But how? What makes one query letter stand out within a sea of submissions, while others miss the mark?

Considering she reviews as many as 100 would-be submissions each month, New York-based children's fiction editor Caitlyn Dlouhy of Laura Geringer Books (an imprint of HarperCollins) is well qualified to offer a few expert suggestions.

Several things make a query hard to resist, according to Dlouhy. First, a winning query reflects an author's willingness to do a little market research prior to submission. "If the person who's written the query has done their homework—if they know the kinds of books we publish—I'm impressed. If I get a query on a nonfiction manuscript, I'm not. We don't publish nonfiction, so I know that query is part of a blanket submission." Sending a query without first studying the market, according to Dlouhy, "is wasting the writer's time and mine."

For Dlouhy, basic market research is a matter of simple observation. "Look at your manuscript, and ask yourself, 'what does it remind me of?' " she says. "Then go to the bookstores or the library and look up those books. Look at your favorite books and see who publishes them." Dlouhy says that's the best way to find a publisher who might love your book as much as you do. And don't be afraid to call the publisher for suggestions as to which editor should review your manuscript. "Make sure the editor you're sending your query to is the right editor. What does not interest one editor might be just what another editor is looking for."

Once it's clear a query might be right for the Laura Geringer imprint, Dlouhy looks for personal electricity—an indication of who is writing the query and why she might have a little magic to sell. "I like queries with punch, something that gives me a peek into a writer's world. Remember, your query is an editor's first exposure to your writing style, and they will often base their decision to request your manuscript on that first look." Dlouhy also warns that writers should never consider sending a gift along with the query. "It makes me feel as though I'm being bought," she says. "It's very, very off-putting."

Concise, tightly written queries are more likely to get a close look. "If I open a query and it's two pages, I'm already groaning," Dlouhy says. "Which is why I'm thrilled *Writer's Market* is doing this report. I have to look at so much material, if I have to spend two pages just to review a query, it's time I'm not devoting to an actual manuscript. Half a page should do it—the shorter the better."

Several things should be included in that perfect query. "Give me a brief plot synopsis and a look at key characters," says Dlouhy. "Compare your manuscript to another book—this is Huck Finn with a twist because x, y and z happens. Show me why your book is

INSIDER REPORT, *Dlouhy*

different from anything else. List a few of your credits as a writer, if you have them. But you don't need to mention every place you've had a poem published.'' Editors are looking for strong manuscripts, not lengthy writers' histories.

So let's say you've taken Dlouhy's advice, crafted the perfect query and lovingly directed it into the hands of the editor best suited to consider the work. How long should you wait for a publisher's response? ''Figure on one to two months,'' she says. ''Please keep in mind, editors are only human. We do the best we can, but with more than 10,000 manuscripts a year and dozens of queries a week, there is often a staggering backlog. If two or three months go by and you still haven't heard back, feel free to follow up. But it's best to do that with a letter. We always get back to prospective authors.''

What one thing would Dlouhy like to say to prospective authors? ''I would like to tell them to read their manuscripts over carefully before they send them to us. Read them as if you're reading them for the first time. If you're thinking of another book when you read your manuscript, it's not going to create anything new in my mind. The manuscript that will catch my eye offers a different take on things. It's out of the ordinary. If a manuscript has me picturing incredible images in my head, that's a very good sign. If I'm imagining illustrations, I'm already seeing a book, not just a manuscript.''

Unagented authors often fear they are wasting their time querying prominent editors. Dlouhy admits, ''Some houses will only take agented submissions. But I am a writer as well as an editor. I know how difficult it is to get an agent. I don't think it's fair to deny people the chance to have their manuscripts seen just because they've yet to find an agent. So I always accept queries. Often, I'll then ask to see the entire manuscript, because it's frequently impossible to tell from a query. But even if we are flooded and aren't accepting unsolicited manuscripts, I'll still look at queries.''

—*Kelly Milner Halls*

Book Proposals Made Easy

BY SHEREE BYKOFSKY

When it comes to getting published, it may feel as though much of the process is out of your hands. But you probably have more control than you realize. And therein lies the secret: you must recognize what's within your control, then manipulate it to your best advantage. Do this, and more often than not things will go your way, especially with nonfiction. If you're a strong writer with an interesting and commercial idea, if you are considered an expert in your field, and if you are persistent, you will likely succeed in getting your book into print.

The first step in publishing your nonfiction book is to write a strong proposal that contains (among other things) at least one finished, polished, representative sample chapter of your proposed book. The book proposal is a blessing in several ways. Nearly all nonfiction books are contracted by publishers on the strength of the proposal itself and not the complete book, so you need not finish writing the book before submitting the proposal. In fact, a strong proposal is all you need to receive a substantial portion of the advance against royalties (usually half of the agreed amount). The proposal will also serve as a blueprint when the time comes to write the book.

Because most book proposals contain at least one sample chapter, putting together a proposal can be quite time-consuming. But your effort will not be wasted. You will get an idea of what it will feel like to write the book and be able to predict how long it will take to complete it. Furthermore, you will be able to use whatever representative chapters you include with the proposal in the final book.

Most importantly, the proposal is the author's chance to show the publisher how the proposed book will read. If, when the book is finished according to the plan and outline in the proposal, the publisher questions the final product, the author should be able to point to the proposal and say, "See. This is exactly what I told you I was writing." But be careful; this works both ways. If you turn in a book that is nothing like or only barely resembles the project you described in the proposal, the publisher can remind you that this is not the book he contracted for. It is therefore to everyone's benefit to begin with the most accurate and well-thought-out proposal possible.

Don't even think about approaching an agent or publisher until you have written your proposal. The more complete and solid your proposal, the better your chances of getting published. (If you're submitting fiction, you shouldn't send query letters to agents or publishers until you have written, edited, and polished the entire book.)

Begin your proposal by fleshing out your idea. If you have a terrific title that will attract the targeted audience, you're ahead of the game. If you don't, choose the most descriptive title you can think of and keep it as a working title until you or someone else comes up with something better. Be as focused as possible on what your book intends to accomplish. Nothing is in stone, so just start writing. You may find it easiest to begin with the descriptive portion of your book

---

For over seven years **SHEREE BYKOFSKY** *has led her own New York-based literary agency, Sheree Bykofsky Associates, Inc., which represents adult commercial and literary fiction and all areas of nonfiction. She is the author of a dozen books, including* The Complete Idiot's Guide to Getting Published (Macmillan, 1998), *and a member of both the American Society of Journalists and Authors and the Association of Authors' Representatives.*

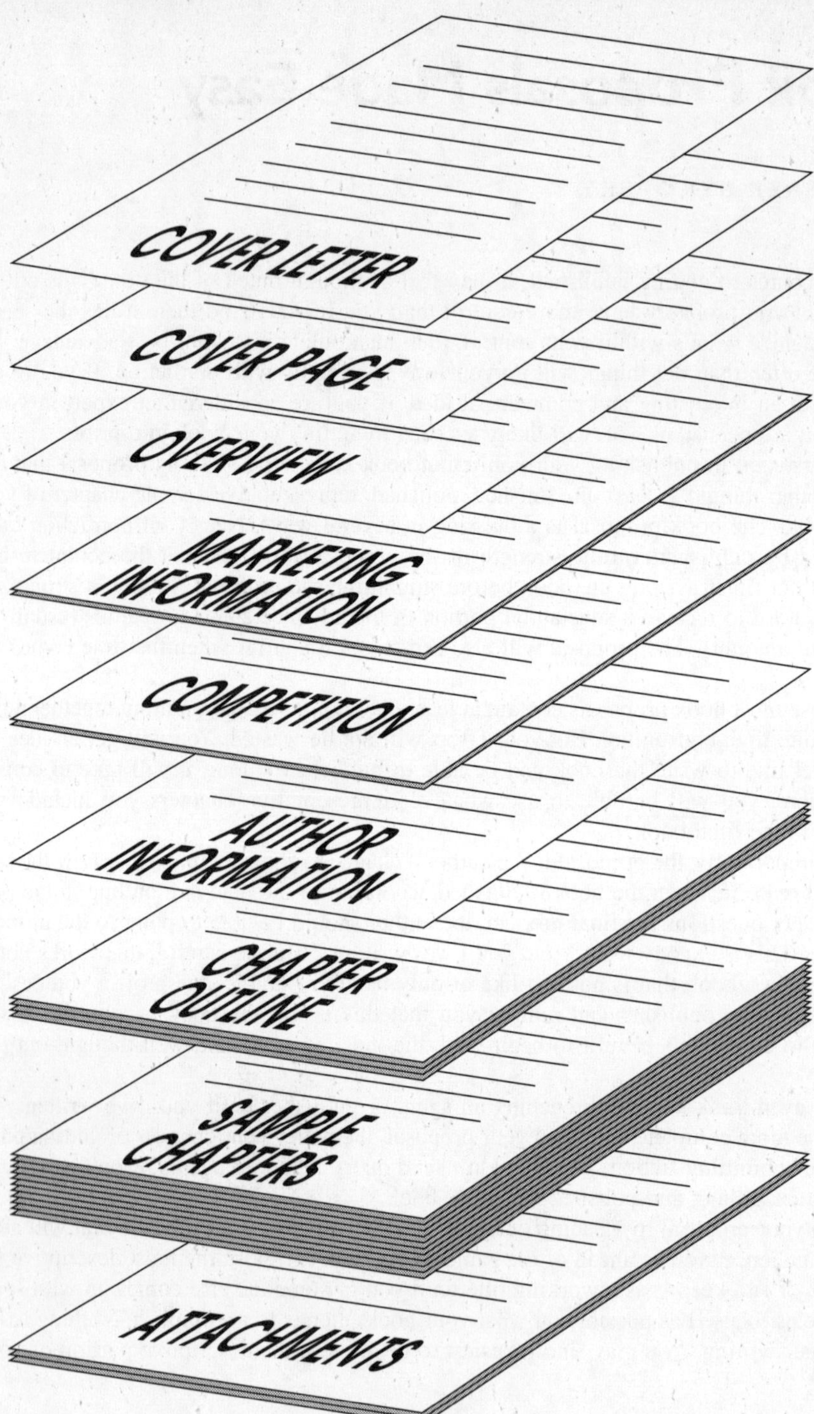

A nonfiction book proposal will usually consist of the elements illustrated above. Their order is less important than the fact that you have addressed each component.

proposal, or you may want to begin with the outline or by examining the competition.

If you're a quick study, use my Book Proposals at a Glance template. Ask yourself the questions it poses, and as you write your answers, your proposal will develop before your eyes. If you have the time and want more detailed guidelines, get one of the many excellent books on writing proposals from the writer's shelf at your library or local bookstore. I highly recommend Michael Larsen's *How to Write a Book Proposal* (Writer's Digest Books, 1996).

BOOK PROPOSALS AT A GLANCE

All good nonfiction book proposals should contain the following:

I. COVER LETTER

- Write this after you finish your proposal.
- Letter should contain (concisely) the relevant main points and the most compelling highlights of your book.

II. COVER PAGE WITH GREAT TITLE, YOUR NAME AND ADDRESS

III. THREE TO FIVE PAGE PITCH CONTAINING THESE FOUR PARTS

A. Overview

- Repeat title.
- Describe your book in one sentence.
- Elaborate on that in a paragraph or two. Describe the contents of your book enticingly and thoroughly.

B. Marketing Information

- Who is the audience? How big is the audience? Who will actually walk into the bookstore or library and request this book? Why will the audience need or desire the book? It's important that prospective readers won't be embarrassed to buy the book and that they can recognize their need for the book.
- Where will readers find it besides bookstores? General or specialized libraries? Catalogs? Garden supply stores? Gift stores? Hospitals? Hardware stores?
- What important, enticing and special points and features does this book have? For example, will there be sidebars, interviews, quotations?
- What do you envision the book looking like? Do you see it in paperback or hardcover or both? Does it require a special design? What trim size (width by height)? Number of pages? Number of entries? Number of essays? Will the book benefit from illustrations? If so, how many and what type? Line art? Photos? Do not prepare a cover to go with your proposal. The publisher's art department will handle that. But if your book is about your famous grandmother and you have an authentic reproducible photo of her square dancing with Abraham Lincoln, say so.
- What are your sources? How do you intend to do your research, if any? If special permissions or releases are required, think about how you will get them and what they will cost. Be certain this will not be a problem before you approach publishers.
- What is the book's genre? Visit a bookstore and imagine where on the shelf your book will go (or could go).

C. Competition

- What titles will your book sit next to when it is published? This is the competition. The competition analysis is perhaps the most important part of any book proposal and should be done before you get too far along with your proposal (or even before you start). Do a thorough search of *Books in Print* and read the books that are closest to yours in subject matter. How is your book different? How is your book better? Ask the bookstore owner or manager how these books are selling and work that information into the proposal in a way that will cast your book in the best light. It will backfire if you say that there is not now nor has there ever been another book that competes with yours. Publishers will usually be wary to publish such a book. They will either not believe you, or they will think it is therefore not a publishable topic. Perhaps, they may think, it is more suited to a magazine article or a TV movie.

- Are there special times of the year when this book can be promoted in a special way? Does it speak to a growing or renewable trend (such as turning 50) as opposed to a short-lived fad (remember pet rocks?)? If your book needs to be timed with an event (for example, the new millennium), make sure there is plenty of time to publish it and that you are ahead of others in the field.

D. Author Information

- Why are you the perfect author to write this book? Include your writing experience, publishing experience, work experience, educational experience, and special experience that makes you uniquely qualified to write this book.
- Are you a promotable author, i.e., if this is the kind of book that would benefit by a national author tour, do you and can you tour or speak in public? Do you have any other promotion ideas (that are not outlandish)?
- Have you already cultivated an audience that would buy the book (publishers refer to this as "having a platform")? Do you have other affiliations or contacts that could prove useful when marketing the book?
- Can you get glowing endorsements from famous writers or experts prominent in the field about which you are writing? If the book is written, it would be useful to get a quote or two in advance of marketing the manuscript to agents or publishers.
- What is your style? Work it in somewhere. What famous authors, if any, do you think your style can be compared to?

IV. CHAPTER OUTLINE (DETAILED TABLE OF CONTENTS)

- A short paragraph to describe each chapter or section should do the trick. It is more important that the headings be descriptive than clever.

V. REPRESENTATIVE SAMPLE CHAPTER/S OR ENTRIES

- Send at least one perfected sample chapter and more if they're convincing and interesting.

VI. ATTACHMENTS

- Recent major magazine articles about the topic.
- Sample articles you've written (particularly related to the topic).

By now you have put plenty of time, thought, creative energy and talent into writing your proposal, so you should be ready to start submitting it.

At this point I recommend researching and querying agents, particularly if you would like to place your manuscript with a large, commercial publishing company. The simple reason is that almost all commercial publishers prefer to work with agents, except under the rarest circumstances; nearly all agents deal almost exclusively with large publishers who can afford to pay high advances. But getting an agent to represent you can be difficult. For example, the agent might think your proposal is excellent but still refuse to represent it because she fears it will not command an advance high enough to cover her costs and the time spent shopping your work. Not having an agent isn't such a problem, though, if your book is suitable for a small, specialized or regional publisher. You're fine querying them directly rather than going through an agent. In fact, many small and even some medium-sized publishers are more interested in dealing directly with authors than with agents.

Assuming you're not using an agent, the next step is to research appropriate publishers, selecting a handful most suitable for your book. (Consult the Book Publishers section of *Writer's Market* and the *Literary Market Place* for information on book publishers.) Compose an engaging query letter that describes—as concisely as possible, on a single page—your book and your credentials to write it. Include in your letter any awards you have won or special ways to promote your book. If, for example, a best-selling author has agreed to endorse your book or has said glowing things about it, be sure to say so. Also, don't forget to include a SASE (self-addressed, stamped envelope). In your letter, state what you have available to send, namely, a book proposal and sample chapter or chapters or the whole book, and ask the agent or editor what he would like you to send. Let him know whether you are querying him exclusively or if you are sending out a multiple query—which is acceptable, so long as you so state in your letter. You may want to name a reasonable date when you expect a reply, but bear in mind that most publishers will likely ignore such a request and some will fail to respond altogether. So keep detailed records of whom you send your queries to and their responses, because you will probably see many rejections (even the best books do). If your proposal is rejected by several publishers and they all say the same thing, you may want to revise it accordingly before submitting it elsewhere.

If you do receive an offer to publish your book, seek the services of a literary agent or a lawyer to advise you or to represent you to the publisher—unless you have experience negotiating book contracts. If you wish to negotiate yourself, there are some good books on the subject, which you would be wise to study thoroughly. One such book is Mark Levine's *How to Negotiate a Book Contract* (Moyer-Bell). Many writers' organizations also offer valuable negotiating help to their members.

Best success getting your book published.

INSIDER REPORT

Proposals that make an editor say "I do"

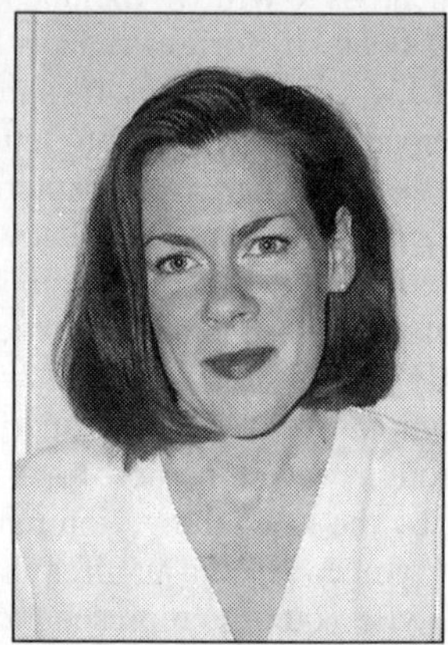
Judith McCarthy

Crisp, one-page query letters often open doors when it comes to matching fiction manuscripts with the editors who publish them. But if your destiny lies in facts, not fantasy, a sharp, well-crafted nonfiction book proposal just might be your golden key.

"I prefer agented submissions," says Judith McCarthy, nonfiction editor at John Wiley and Sons in New York, "because good agents help their authors prepare a professional proposal that will include all or most of what I need to know to sign a book."

How does a stellar proposal differ from a query? According to McCarthy (who fields better than 150 author submissions a month), "A query is just a letter with a brief pitch. A good nonfiction proposal is a detailed document with several key elements."

If you want your proposal to be well received, count on covering the following literary bases:

1) A broad summary or overview of the book.

2) An "About the Author" section that explains why the submitting author is the person best qualified to write the book.

3) The submitting author's past publishing history—including sales figures and reviews, if possible.

4) A section on how the author plans to help promote the book.

5) A complete analysis of how the proposed book fits in with, and how it stands apart from, the competition.

6) A table of contents including a description of exactly what will be included in each chapter.

7) At least one complete sample chapter.

While McCarthy prefers book proposals from agents, she will occasionally consider proposals from well-qualified authors. "A proposal is hard to resist if the person writing is an expert in the field or has teamed up with an expert, and if the book proposed truly seems to have something unique and valuable to offer."

But no matter how strong a proposal might be, McCarthy says a lack of market research will leave even good authors dead in the water. "The proposals I barely glance at are those clearly not focused on the areas I publish. People send me fiction queries, poetry, etc., when my company doesn't publish anything like that. I find it annoying, because I have to take the time to respond, even if they didn't take the time to research what we do."

Good proposals, according to McCarthy, reflect a sense of careful, advanced planning and professional strength. If you want to be taken seriously, research not only the publisher,

INSIDER REPORT, *McCarthy*

but the editors within the house. "Try to find out what kind of books each person publishes and get your proposal to the right editor. Find out the name and send it to that person, rather than submitting to a generic 'editor.' "

Once you've found the right editor, concentrate on polishing the proposal itself. And include a query letter with your proposal. McCarthy offers these simple suggestions as a guide to drafting a powerful query. "Be brief. Use fairly large type and good-sized margins. Get to the point quickly, and make it skimmable. Identify your book's market, your credentials for writing the book, and the basic topic. Do this in one or two sentences.

"Do not write too much," McCarthy warns. "The editor needs a quick pitch, not your life story. Do not send rejection letters from other publishers, even if they did compliment the book. That doesn't help your case. And do not say there is no competition. There is always competition, even if your book is very distinct."

If several weeks pass without a response to your submission, McCarthy says a brief follow-up letter is acceptable protocol. "I don't mind if an author follows up on a query, as long as it isn't too soon. And I prefer they do it in writing, not over the phone. Send a polite note to ask if I got the materials and asking to know the status." But choose your follow-up tone with the utmost of care. "If people contact me with real attitude, I usually figure I am probably better off passing on the project.

"I would like every would-be author to understand that editors truly do like books and want to publish the good ones," McCarthy says. "But we get so many submissions and have so much to do, we can't always give potential authors as much time as they would like. My first priority is to authors I have already signed." Writing a winning proposal could help you cross that well-defined line.

—Kelly Milner Halls

The Library on Your Desktop: Effective Research on the Web

BY JACQUELINE JUSTICE, PH. D.

It's time to face it—gone are the days when research meant strolling to your local library and browsing through long shelves of books, newspapers and periodicals. Although many of us may have been led to the writing life by our love of those dusty, musty books, to make a living as a writer in today's competitive and fast-paced market, we must each learn to complete effective research on the vast electronic library known as the Internet. What do you need to use this powerful research tool? Just a computer, a modem, a connection to the Internet, a Web browser (such as *Microsoft Internet Explorer* or *Netscape Navigator*), and a little know-how.

First, put aside any anxieties you might have about venturing into the Internet's virtual community. It is a friendlier place than you may have imagined; and for people who love words, it is a bottomless source of treasures. Second, don't assume that learning to complete research on the Internet will be a time-consuming task. The fact is, if you can complete research in a library, you already have the basic skills you need to successfully research any topic on the Internet. With these two fears firmly pushed aside, get ready to sound the depths of the largest library the world has ever known.

SELECTING THE RIGHT INDEX

Whether you are completing research on the Internet or at the library, the basic concepts of searching remain the same. You have a problem to solve, a question to answer, or a topic to explore. What do you do first? Most likely, you choose an index or catalog of publications to identify resources related to your topic. Just like your local library, the Internet makes many different types of catalogs and indexes available. Some indexes are focused; that is, they are not intended to be comprehensive. Instead, they are limited by subject or media type. For example, *Archie* (http://alpha.science.unitn.it/cgi-bin/archie) is an index that catalogs only files available for transfer on the Internet through a specific set of computer communication rules known as *FTP* (File Transfer Protocol), and *EDGAR* (http://www.sec.gov) is an index that catalogs only Securities and Exchange Commission filings that are available to the public.

Other indexes are intended to be comprehensive, to search all the information available to them regardless of media type or subject. Your public library's main catalog is comprehensive, cataloging all the resources available through the library. Similar indexes are available on the Internet. For instance, *AltaVista* is a popular comprehensive index on the World Wide Web (http://www.altavista.digital.com). *AltaVista* catalogs Internet materials on any subject and often crosses media types, listing gopher documents, FTP files, newsgroup postings, and World Wide Web pages. The most important difference between the comprehensive catalogs at your local library and those on the Internet is that the Internet's comprehensive catalogs are considerably

---

JACQUELINE JUSTICE *is managing editor of the* Internet Bulletin for CPAs. *In addition, she writes manuals and courses on technology topics for professionals in various fields. Her most recent publications include* CPA's Guide to Web Commerce *and* Running Start Guide to Windows 95, *both published by Kent Information Services, Inc., Kent, Ohio. Contact the author on the Internet at jj3858@aol.com.*

larger than your local library's catalog; *AltaVista*, for example, boasts a catalog that includes hundreds of millions of items!

Using these comprehensive Internet indexes (also known as "search engines") is the most common and efficient way to complete research on the Internet. Although these search engines may seem quite sophisticated (and even a little intimidating), they are simply computers running special software that creates and searches databases—just like the electronic catalogs available at your local library and the Find tool on your home computer. This search engine software (1) automatically "surfs" the Internet, collecting information resources, (2) catalogs information about the sites it visits, and (3) processes requests from users to list specific items included in its database.

USING AN INTERNET INDEX

Although you may choose from many different search engines when researching on the Internet (see the World Wide Web search engines sidebar at the end of this article for a list), using these search engines typically requires that you complete four simple steps:

1. Access the index by typing its Internet address into your Web browser software.
2. Enter a word or group of words related to the research topic into the search entry box.
3. Click the button that begins the search.
4. Review the list of results retrieved from the search engine's database.

While all search engines have these basic steps in common, you will find minor variations in the ways the software handles them. For instance, one engine's keyword entry box may be labeled "Search for" while another may call the same box "Query." Or the button that initiates the search in one engine may be labeled "Search" while in another, it's labeled "Go" or "Find."

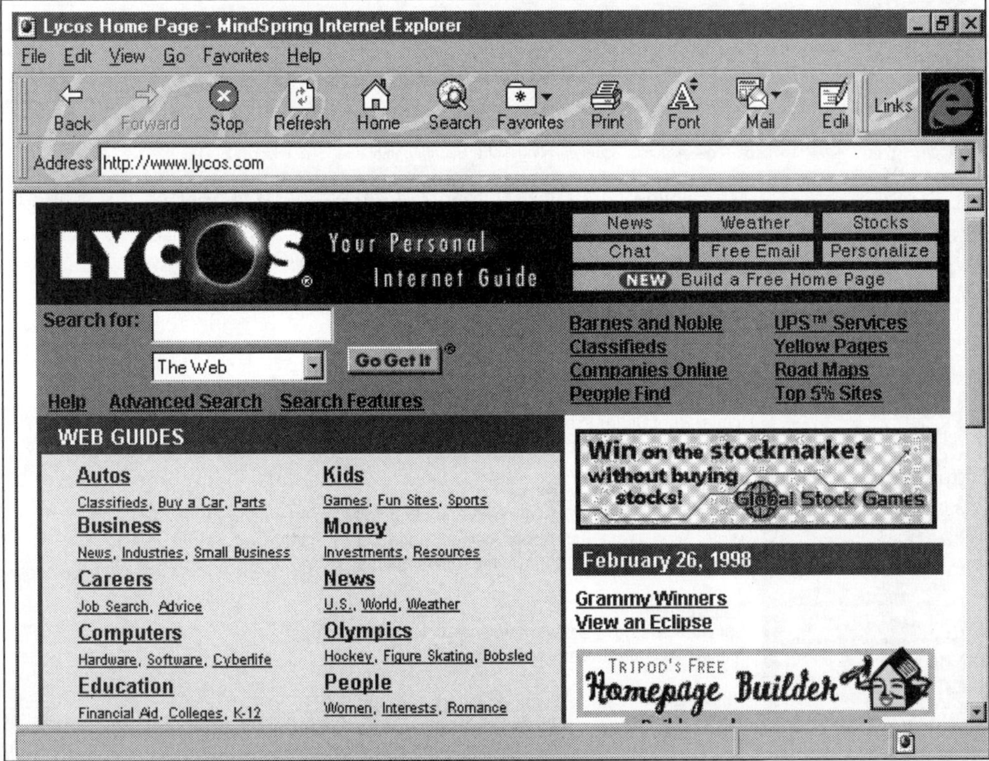

To begin an Internet search with Lycos, type a keyword in the "Search for" box and click the "Go Get It" button.

Don't let these minor differences throw you—in every case, you will find that the choices you need to make when you use these various sites will be quite intuitive now that you understand the tasks performed by these basic indexing/searching software programs.

Now let's take a look at another popular World Wide Web search engine, *Lycos*. To use this index to locate Internet resources, first type the *Lycos* Internet address (http://www.lycos.com) into the address box of your Web browser software. Your Web browser will then retrieve the opening screen of the *Lycos* search site.

Second, type a word or group of words related to your research topic (known as "keywords") into the "Search for" box. As in other kinds of research, remember that the keyword(s) you choose have an enormous bearing on the results of your search. It is a good idea to use several different keywords and to try multiple variations of those keywords. In general, keyword combinations constructed of more than one word (known as "search strings") result in more focused results, so enter two or three words related to your topic. Third, click the "Go Get It" button to launch the *Lycos* searching function. *Lycos* then uses the keyword(s) to screen its database for items that contain that keyword. Next *Lycos* displays listings of all documents that either contain the keyword(s) or have the keyword(s) cataloged in their index.

These matching documents, known as "hits," are typically listed as hyperlinks (text or graphics on a website that automatically connect to other documents) with some type of descriptive information. If a listed item interests you, simply use your mouse to click on the link and visit the website where the complete document is stored. When you are done reviewing the resource, click the "Back" button on your Web browser's toolbar to return to the listing of hits and select a new lead to follow.

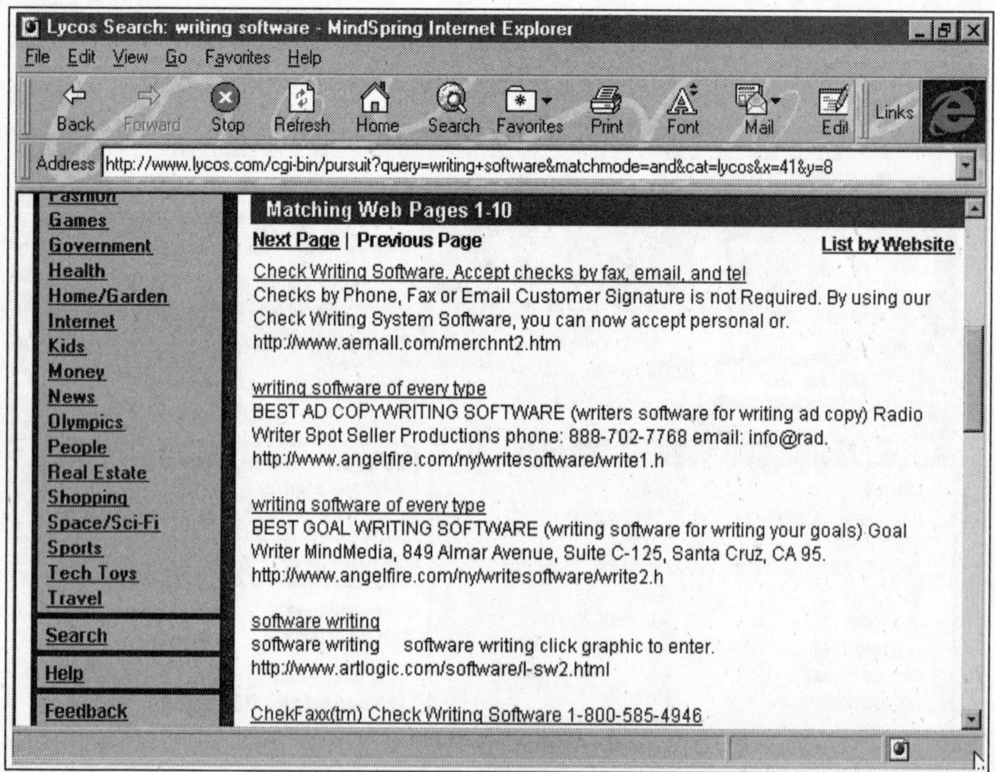

Explore Lycos search results by following hyperlinks to matching web documents.

FOCUSING YOUR SEARCH RESULTS

Sounds easy, yes? And it is. So what's the catch? Although you will likely never say, "I can't find any resources about this topic," you may often say, "There are so many hits, I don't know where to begin." In fact, it is not unusual to retrieve a listing of hits that includes thousands of items! Don't despair; most search engines use some system for ranking items according to relevance. Ranking systems vary in methodology, but most assign points for where and how frequently the keywords appear in a document. And items that the engine determines are most relevant will appear first in the listing of hits. These simple and automatic features will allow you to make sensible choices about items that are likely to be most useful to you. Even so, as you become a more experienced Internet researcher, you will want to begin using various strategies to restrict the hits that appear in your list of retrieved items.

The simplest way to restrict or expand the number of items you retrieve in a search is to use special words and symbols (sometimes known as "operators") to define the relationships between the words you type into the search engine's entry box. Although the specific symbols, words, and characters recognized by various search engines will differ, the most common, Boolean operators, are recognized by most. For example, the **OR** operator is useful for the first phases of a search, when you wish to see a broad range of related items. When typed between two words used in a keyword box, the **OR** operator instructs the search tool to retrieve any item containing either of the words. For instance, the keyword string **writing or software** will search for items containing either the word "writing" or the word "software." If you find that you need to focus the search more tightly, use the Boolean operator **AND**, which limits results to those items that contain both (or all) of the keywords. For example, the keyword string **writing and software** will search for only those items that contain both words. The last of the three most common Boolean operators is **NOT**. Use the **NOT** operator to eliminate items that contain a particular word or combination of words from your search results. For instance, when searching for writing software, you might wish to exclude items dealing with a particular software program. To make this exclusion, you could type this search string: **writing and software not WriterPro**. This search would return all items containing the words "writing" and "software," except for those that also contain the word "WriterPro."

Although the Boolean operators described above are the most commonly used method for restricting a search, there are many others you may wish to explore. For example, many search engines recognize that words placed within quotation marks should be treated as a phrase; in other words, in order for an item to qualify as a hit, the keywords must appear together. For example, the keywords **writing and software** will retrieve any items that contain the word "writing" and the word "software." But the search string **writing software** will retrieve only items in which the words "writing" and "software" appear together. Obviously, the results of these searches will be quite different.

To determine what symbols and characters are recognized by a search engine, read the engine's Help or Advanced Searching documents. (Typically you will find a button or link on the opening screen that will lead you to these important tips.) Each search engine offers different guidelines for using upper- and lower-case letters and for combining Boolean operators. Many even distinguish their software from other search engines by offering unique methods for refining searches. For example, in the *AltaVista* search engine, clicking on the **Help** option on the main screen opens a document from which we learn that *AltaVista* allows you to require or exclude certain words from your search strings, find pages that include specific graphic files or Internet addresses, sort results listings into various topic categories, and much more!

SEARCH THROUGH SEVERAL ENGINES FOR BEST RESULTS

Although you will quickly find engines that will become your personal favorites, remember that search engines and the databases they search are not identical. For example, although each World Wide Web search engine runs using a similar software program, one that automatically follows links and searches for items to add to the engine's database, the engines will not necessarily locate the same items or follow the same links. In addition, the databases used by these search engines are supplemented by entries submitted by Webmasters and Internet publishers, who may catalog their sites with several, but not all search engines. Finally, different engines support different types of operators and search-restricting devices. The bottom line is that keywords entered in one search engine will not necessarily retrieve the same results as the identical keywords entered in another search engine. As a result, when performing comprehensive research, it is a good idea to run your search on several engines. One way to economize on the time spent running multiple searches is to use a meta-search engine. Meta-search engines are special software programs that allow you to run your keywords through several search engines simultaneously. An additional benefit offered by the more sophisticated meta-search engines is the ability to manage and update searches that you repeat frequently. One meta-search engine you may wish to try is *WebFerret*. This program is available for free from the *FerretSoft* website at http://www.ferretsoft.com.

EVALUATING SEARCH RESULTS

Once you have located Internet resources on your research topic, you're in the home stretch, but your work is not over yet. As you know, the Internet is the largest resource for the distribution of information the world has ever seen. Unfortunately, not every report, article, and opinion posted on the Internet is reliable. Although this may seem obvious to most writers, according to Paul Gilster, author of *Digital Literacy*,

"*There's a lingering public perception . . . of the computer's ferocious accuracy: computers don't make mistakes. Couple that with the general public's sense of the Internet as having been developed by the academic-scientific community, under government auspices, as a high-level information source, and you do indeed have some people accepting far too quickly any information that appears on a computer screen simply because it does appear on a screen.*" ([November 1997] Available: http://208.4.153.2/diglit.htm)

To select authoritative and reliable Internet information resources, be certain that you have acceptable answers to the questions below before relying on the resources in your work.

Who wrote it?

The Internet is the largest source of information content in the world. It is also unmoderated. That means that anyone can post anything. Before using any resource that you find on the Internet, review the background and credentials of the author. Most authors provide either an online résumé or an e-mail address you can use to perform the necessary follow-up.

Who published it and why?

Individual authors and organizations often have very specific reasons for publishing materials on the Internet. For example, if you are contracted to write an article about 56K modems, you are likely to find many articles at the websites of 56K modem manufacturers, but these articles will likely place great emphasis on the particular products being promoted by these manufacturers. Before using any information you find on the Internet, be certain to evaluate the motives of the publisher (often known as a "content provider"). That is not to say that materials with a marketing or promotional agenda should be dismissed; many commercial organizations publish very informative and even-handed white papers and research articles that can be very useful research resources.

When was it published and/or updated?

Internet technology allows anyone to publish documents easily. And then, just as easily, those documents can be updated. Even so, much information published on the Internet is not frequently updated, if at all. Be certain to look for dates that indicate the currency of Internet materials before using them in your own research, because outdated information may not be accurate and may lead you to make embarrassing errors in your work.

USING WHAT YOU FIND

Once you have determined that a document found on the Internet is credible, depending on how and how much of the document you intend to use, you may need to consider copyright implications. As you probably know, copyright of electronic documents is currently a topic under hot debate. The safest way to proceed at this point is to treat any document you find online as a distinct publication. That means, whether or not a copyright notice appears on the document, it is owned by someone, and you are ethically and legally bound to (1) represent the work accurately, (2) give appropriate credits to the author and publisher, and (3) seek permissions for reprints when necessary.

The sudden influx of electronic texts has left many of us unsure about how to appropriately cite the resources we find published on the Internet. However, as with many other research steps described in this article, your past experiences can guide you here as well. When writing for a publication that follows a certain set of style guidelines, look to the style handbooks. Most provide some guidance for citing electronic resources. As you might imagine, many of these guidelines are available on the Internet. An excellent website to visit when looking for guides and manuals on how to cite electronic sources is the *Brandeis University Internet Fair* page at http://www.brandeis.edu/fair/citation.html. From this page you can access a lengthy descriptive listing of guides, many of which link to online versions that can provide you with quick answers to your citation questions.

So, gather up your notes and those long-delayed research projects. Now that you know a little about World Wide Web search engines and a few simple strategies for using them effectively, you are ready to use that library sitting right on your desktop. You are ready to ride the information superhighway to research and writing success.

World Wide Web Search Engines

The best way to learn about WWW search engines is to use them and begin to build an experiential sense of what works and what doesn't. A sampling of World Wide Web search engines and directories that you may want to try are listed below:

- *Aliweb*: http://web.nexor.co.uk/public/aliweb/search/doc/form.html
- *All4One*: http://www.all4one.com
- *All-in-One*: http://www.albany.net/allinone/
- *AltaVista*: http://www.altavista.digital.com
- *Archie*: http://alpha.science.unitn.it/cgi-bin/archie
- *CUSI*: http://web.nexor.co.uk/susi/cusi.html
- *Einet Galaxy*: http://www.einet.net
- *HotBot*: http://www.hotbot.com
- *Internet Sleuth*: http://www.isleuth.com
- *MetaCrawler*: http://www.metacrawler.com
- *Lycos*: http://www.lycos.com
- *UltraSeek*: http://ultra.infoseek.com
- *WebCrawler*: http://webcrawler.com
- *Yahoo*: http://www.yahoo.com

From Fact to Fiction: Anna Quindlen on Versatile Writing

BY ANNE BOWLING

Photo by Joyce Ravid

Anna Quindlen

"The very best training I could have had for a life as a novelist was a life as a reporter," says novelist Anna Quindlen, "because those things that lift prose off the page of one also lift prose off the page of another." Quindlen has had some practice perfecting her prose. For nearly 25 years, Quindlen has been paid to put words on paper, and during that time has written as a newspaper reporter and columnist, children's author, essayist and best-selling novelist. Her first two novels became bestsellers, followed by *Black and Blue* (Random House), her critically acclaimed 1998 novel, which hit the bestseller list less than a week after its release.

The Barnard-educated Pulitzer Prize winner began her professional writing life during college, when she sold the first short story she sent to *Seventeen* magazine for $350. "Seeing that check drop out of the envelope was maybe the most excited I've ever been in my professional life, until nearly 20 years later when I won the Pulitzer," Quindlen says. "Of course, selling that story spoiled me, because I assumed it was easy to sell short stories. Never happened again."

Quindlen was not to return to writing fiction professionally for many years. After graduating, she opted for newspaper work as a career, covering everything from the police beat to celebrity interviews, from City Hall to Fifth Avenue, as a general assignment reporter for *The New York Times*. After the birth of her first child, Quindlen left the newsroom for home, where she planned to begin her first novel, contribute a freelance column to the *Times*, and care for her son. But that column was so successful Quindlen was signed on for the weekly lifestyle column, "Life in the 30's." Writing as a reporter may have trained her eye for detail and her ear for dialogue, but it was in column writing that Quindlen first sank her teeth into what would become the heart of her novel writing—family relations.

Quindlen "occasionally tackles news issues, but she is more at home in the rocky emotional terrain of marriage, parenthood, secret desires and self-doubts," wrote Melinda Beck in *Newsweek* of Quindlen's lifestyle column. That slant would change with Quindlen's graduation to the op-ed page of the *Times* with her biweekly column "Public & Private," for which she won the 1992 Pulitzer Prize in commentary. "I think of a column as having a conversation with a person that it just so happens I can't see," Quindlen wrote in the *Times* after receiving the Pulitzer. "It's nice to know that my end of the conversation was heard."

ANNE BOWLING *is a production editor for Writer's Digest Books, who freelances interview/profiles in her spare time. Past interviews have included bestselling novelists Scott Turow, Jonathan Kellerman, Belva Plain, Ira Levin and Terry McMillan.*

It was as a stay-at-home mother and columnist that Quindlen also managed to write her first novel, *Object Lessons* (Random House, 1991), the story of a teen girl struggling to find her place in life beside a troubled mother. Her second novel, *One True Thing* (Random House), in which Quindlen examines one family's experience with euthanasia, was published in 1994. After that, the author, columnist and then mother of three was ready for a break. "When I decided to leave the *Times* to be a full-time novelist, many people said, 'Why can't you write the column and the novels?' " Quindlen recalls. "Let them try it. God."

Black and Blue, Quindlen's third and most successful book, was her first written as a full-time novelist, a position she plans to stay in for the foreseeable future. The story of nurse Fran Benedetto, who flees her violent and abusive husband to start a new life with their son, has been called "a heartbreaking tale . . . that works because it has the ring of truth" by *Time* magazine. The popularity of *Black and Blue* was boosted by its inclusion among Oprah Winfrey's reading selections.

While success seems to have pursued Quindlen persistently, she has not let it stand in the way of the requisite writer's insecurities: despite the Pulitzer, the bestsellers and her proven agility in shifting from writing form to writing form, Quindlen has her share of off days. "When I'm discouraged, I like to read bad reviews of great books," Quindlen says. "I have a bad review of *Catch 22*, and one of *The Age of Innocence*, that have gotten me over some rough times."

Here Quindlen discusses her craft as a writer of fiction and nonfiction, and offers some encouragement for writers having off days.

Where did you develop your love of writing?

I am the only writer in my family, but since on my father's side I am Irish, I come from a rich tradition of storytellers—and storytellers embroider the truth almost as a matter of honor. I like to think that I learned about revision by listening to my father and his brothers telling the same stories over and over, making them richer, fuller and more exciting each time. Never let truth stand in the way of a good story, they say in the newspaper business. I first learned that dictum in my grandparents' living room.

If you knew fiction writing was what you eventually wanted to do, why did you begin writing for newspapers?

I wanted to make money. I had read that you couldn't make money as a fiction writer. There certainly wasn't a steady paycheck in it. So I tormented the editor of a local paper with letters, calls and manuscripts until finally he gave me a job as a copy girl when I was 18.

As you moved from journalism to commentary to fiction, which elements of your writing grew stronger and why?

As a reporter at a time when more impressionistic renderings of events were beginning to creep into the news pages, I learned to always look for the telling detail: the baseball cap, the shards of broken glass, the neon sign in the club window, the striped towel on the deserted beach. Those things that—taken incrementally—make a convincing picture of real life. Those telling details are the essence of fiction that feels real. They are why Dickens remains so high in the pantheon.

I learned, from 25 years of writing down their words in notebooks, how real people really talk. I learned that syntax and rhythm were almost as individual as a fingerprint, and that one sentence, precisely transcribed, could effortlessly delineate a character in a way that five pages of exposition never could.

I also learned, in newspapers, to make every word count. All those years of being given 1,200 words, of having the 1,200 pared down to 900 at 3 o'clock, of having to take out another 100 to shoehorn it into the hole in the layout—it taught me to make the distinction between what was really necessary and illuminating and what was simply me in love with the sound of my own voice.

I don't write to space anymore. It's up to me to say when the story's done, but old habits die hard, so there's not a lot of fat in my prose. The most common shortcomings that I find in books I read nowadays is under-editing, not for sense but for excess. Many of them should be 50 to 100 pages shorter than they are. I do my own cutting. I learned that where cutting is commonplace, swift and Draconian.

Did the deadlines of newspaper writing help you learn early to handle writer's block?

Can you imagine being blocked on the police beat at five p.m.? I think the reason people have writer's block is not because they can't write, but because they despair of writing eloquently. Well, that's not the way it works, and one of the best places to learn that is a newspaper, which in its instant obsolescence is infinitely forgiving. Some days you plod, some days you soar. Often it's the same day, the same page, on which the next day you find a lot of chaff and a little bit of wheat so absolutely right the hair stands up on the back of your neck. People ask me the secret of writing a novel. Here it is: put your butt on the seat of a chair. Just do it, instead of talking about it. That's about 90 percent of it.

Did the fact that you had a widespread existing audience for your writing steady your nerves a bit when you set out to write your first novel, *Object Lessons*? Or was it difficult, in that you would be addressing your audience with a different voice?

I think you would have to be very foolish indeed not to be happy about the fact that you had a certain sort of instant name recognition with intelligent readers. I had no anxiety about that, quite the contrary. It seemed to me a luxurious cushion.

As a newcomer to fiction writing, what was the most difficult element of *Object Lessons*, and how did you overcome it?

The biggest problem with *Object Lessons* was that it essentially had no plot. I'm not being modest about this—it's true. My editor, Kate Medina, was extraordinarily complimentary about the writing and the characters, but she suggested strongly that I might want to have the characters do something. I snippily replied that in real life, there was little discernible plot. To which she replied—and I'll never forget this—"The difference between real life and a novel is that things happen in a novel." She is, by the way, the only fiction editor I've ever had, and a substantial chunk of my success as a novelist belongs to her. Sometimes I think her name should be on the cover too.

Tell us about the process of writing your first novel. Which came first, the characters or the story? Do you outline before you write or let your characters take you where they will as the story develops?

I am a completely character-driven novelist. I believe I've gotten better with each book, done things differently in each novel. But the extent to which character comes first for me has never changed. I feel quite strongly that if I am able to create real people from the ground up, plot will follow. Voice, style, are not as much of an issue for me anymore. I have a fairly idiosyncratic voice and writing style which has become sort of second nature. So it's all about the characters.

With three published novels under your belt, have you become a more confident fiction writer, trusting your ability more?

I think the confidence has to do with my relationship with Kate, my editor, which has matured on both our parts. My writing now needs much less massaging because I have learned to channel her editing voice while I work. And she speaks fluent Quindlen at this point, so there were some suggestions she might have made in the past—suggestions I would have decided not to implement—that she would not make today.

Obviously I have a certain level of confidence about sales of my work. Random House is committed to me, in large part because my books have been successful for them. And I know there are readers who buy my books simply because my name is on the cover. At this moment using sales as a measure of success would make me feel very, very secure, but that's not the way it works.

There comes a critical meeting of the minds, just before I've handed in a final manuscript, between Anna Quindlen the writer and Anna Quindlen the reader. It is an actual moment, at my desk, when the rereading is done and one says to the other, 'This is really good. This is good work.' It's a critical moment for me because it helps me get over both prepublication and the reviews. I think perhaps I've said that with a little more conviction to myself each time because I do think my work as a fiction writer has gotten better over the course of three books.

We have heard a lot about the books that made it into print, but have you had any false starts as a novelist while you were learning your craft?

Suffice it to say I have on the hard drive of my computer a 672-page manuscript of a novel I wrote in 1995, right after I left the *Times.* I still think it's some of the best work I've ever done, but I can't seem to revise it satisfactorily. I figured out my rewriting was making it flatter, not better. I admitted that to myself on a Tuesday. The following Monday I had lunch with my editor and my agent and told them I was starting a new book about a nurse who takes her kid and disappears somewhere in America to get away from her cop husband, who beats her. That book, of course, is *Black & Blue*, which has become the most successful book I've done. So writing is like anything else. You fall, you pick yourself up, and you try again. When you're discouraged, you eat ice cream.

Has it been a difficult transition, moving from speaking to your readers in the voice of a columnist to that of a novelist? Do readers still look to you for commentary on social issues such as euthanasia and spousal abuse?

I think I could write a novel about two women sitting at a kitchen table having a cup of tea for 400 pages and people would say that it reflected the ethos that post-feminist politics is essentially personal. Everything I do will doubtless be seen as political and polemical because of my past life. But why not? That's how I'd see myself were I the reader.

What have you got planned next?

Once I'm well launched on my new novel, I plan to write another book for children. I had a rather hectic spring, with a 15-city tour for *Black and Blue*, the Oprah brouhaha (bless her) and the delivery of the manuscript for the Library of Contemporary Thought book I did, *How Reading Changed My Life*. The end result was I had no time to work on the book I'd started once *Black and Blue* was done. Once I've broken the back of that new book, I'll start to think about another project for children.

First Book Anchors Writer's Career

BY DON PRUES

As a cultural anthropology major at Wesleyan University, Sebastian Junger had no idea he would become a journalist and best-selling author (*The Perfect Storm: A True Story of Men Against the Sea*) during his mid-thirties. "I was kind of a jock in college, not interested in journalism at all," Junger says. That changed when Junger—a long-distance runner himself—spent his senior summer on a Navajo reservation in Arizona researching and writing his senior anthropology thesis on Navajo long distance runners. "That was the first time I realized researching and writing could be such a high," he says. "I mean I was on fire writing that thing."

Photo by Dan Deitch

Sebastian Junger

TESTING THE WATERS

The jock turned journalist. After college Junger set out to freelance, initially landing articles with alternative weeklies in Washington, D.C. and Boston, but shortly thereafter he began traveling around the country, penning articles about tugboats, levees, bridge builders, crack dealers, and the smallest border town in Texas. Sounds like he scored some great assignments from editors, right? Not quite—Junger wasn't given any assignments by anyone, other than himself. "Throughout my twenties I would just assign topics to myself and go research and write about them and would peddle them afterward. It's a uniquely unsuccessful strategy," he teases. For almost ten years Junger wrote with such an agenda, finding it personally rewarding but financially strapping.

AN UNEXPECTED TURN

Unable to earn a living writing only about stories he sought out, Junger had to resort to other sources of income. First, he tried waiting tables. "That didn't really bolster my self-esteem," he says, "and as a man in my late twenties I felt like I was leading an existence that required no vigor or strength. I was writing stories at my desk and waiting tables, but that didn't do much for me physically or psychologically."

So he got a job climbing and cutting trees, a move that indelibly altered his writing career. "When I started doing tree work, I loved that it was this robust, risky work, and doing it made me feel really good about myself in a sort of 'masculine' way, however outdated the term. That job helped my writing career more than any Harvard extension course in writing could've because making good money doing something that exhausted and challenged me made me feel so pumped and proud." Cutting trees was, as Junger says, "a steroid injection." Until he gashed his leg with a chainsaw.

THE DANGEROUS IDEA

Injuring himself did more for Junger than put him on crutches and out of employment. It gave him an idea: to write a book about dangerous jobs. So off he went, westward to Idaho to write about forest fire-fighting, back east to Massachusetts to dive into commercial fishing, overseas to Bosnia to give war journalism a try.

Why was he so compelled to write about those who worked on the edge? One primary reason, according to Junger, is that these people exercise some fundamental parts of their brains that most of us aren't forced to use. "Humans didn't evolve to work indoors and at desks, to never be frightened or feel out of control," he says. "Think about why people take risks. They do it because taking risks feels right, and it feels right because we've evolved to deal with risk. We have all these structures in our brains that deal with it so well, and for most of us those parts languish. I'm interested in people who—because of their jobs—can't let risk rest."

However interesting a book on dangerous jobs was to Junger, the idea was no treasure trove to a literary agent. Says Junger, "I found a good agent through a connection I'd made, but the agent told me, 'look, a book like you're proposing isn't going to sell.' I said, 'Who cares if it sells. I'm 31 and I've been writing for years but my writing career doesn't really exist. I want to get a book written and published, which would be a huge step for me, even if nobody buys it." In effect, Junger uttered precisely what a literary agent does *not* want to hear.

MAKING HIS OWN WAVES

But Junger decided to follow his convictions and write the book anyway. Figuring he'd write the first chapter on parachuters who try to contain forest fires, Junger got in his car, went out West and spent the summer with these "smoke-jumpers." As he tells it, "I slept in the back of my car or camped out and cooked on a small camping stove. Of course I had no advance or book contract but I still wanted to write the book."

Next, Junger wanted to write his chapter about commercial fishing. He remembered when he witnessed the Halloween Gale of 1991 (called "the storm of the century") and read a newspaper account of how "the storm" devoured the *Andrea Gail*, a swordfishing boat that left Gloucester, Massachusetts early that October and never returned. All six crew members perished at sea. Junger opted to use this story as a starting point for his chapter on the dangers of commercial fishing, but the more he researched the tragedy the more obsessed he became with learning more about it. After much research, he wrote a chapter on the event and thought maybe he could produce a magazine article out of it as well. Fortunately, *Outside Magazine* wanted his article, a condensed version (5,000 words) of what he thought would become his book's second chapter (20,000 words).

Both to pursue material for his book's third chapter and to earn a living overseas, Junger decided to spend time as a war journalist. So in 1993 and 1994 he went to Bosnia and did freelance radio reports, experiencing first hand what it's like to be a war correspondent. Before Junger departed for Bosnia, though, his agent called and told him he might be able to sell Junger's story of the "the storm" to a publisher, if Junger would expand that one chapter into a full-length book. Junger said he could do it but was doubtful the idea would fly—after all, who would want to read an entire book about a fishing boat lost at sea?

LIGHTNING STRIKES

Although Junger's article on "the storm" was well received by *Outside* readers, he was still quite shocked when his agent faxed him in Bosnia to let him know W.W. Norton wanted to buy the book. "I'd been in Bosnia a few months and was kind of set into going into hard news," he says. "I was really starting to realize my professional goals as a writer, that I was drawn to the purity of strict reporting, just relaying the facts. As horrible as the situation was in Bosnia, professionally it was an incredible drug. I was so revved up and thrilled that I could participate in this news-gathering machine. I had almost forgotten about the book idea." But that phone call—with a $35,000 advance attached to it—jolted Junger's memory in no time. He flew back to the States and immersed himself into two and one-half years of researching and writing what became *The Perfect Storm.*

THE EYE OF THE STORM

Junger finished the book and delivered it to Norton in July of 1996, exactly one year late. But such tardiness didn't hurt Junger's reputation or the book's reception. "For some reason," he says, "the book quickly became a big hit with salespeople for Norton and then a buzz about it started in Hollywood." A loud buzz it must have been, because that October Warner Brothers purchased film rights for $500,000. A year later, paperback rights went to HarperCollins for $1.2 million.

Not surprisingly, with all this money and buzz around *The Perfect Storm*, Norton put Junger on a whirlwind book tour in the U.S. and abroad. If you think that's an author's dream-come-true, think again. "I hated the book tour," Junger says, "And I feel a little indulgent saying that, but it was brutal. Anything I did in Bosnia, anything I did in treework, any other story can't compare to the exhaustion I felt on the book tour. It was so difficult psychologically. I'd get up early and have 4 or 5 interviews a day, starting with the morning talk shows, then lunch with a newspaper reporter, then a couple of hours to return an average of 30 phone calls a day, then maybe a half hour for a nap, and then dinner and straight to a reading—which would last until 9:00 or 10:00—and then at almost every bookstore they're like 'Hey, we'd like to take you out after the reading.' "

Based on his experience, Junger is convinced that anyone who would like being an author would also hate going on a book tour. "They're just two diametrically opposed, totally contradictory states of mind," he says. "Either you're miserable doing one or you're miserable doing the other. I'm just insanely happy when I'm working alone, which means I'm almost insanely unhappy when on a book tour. I don't think one person's personality can really encompass both."

A DISTANT PERSPECTIVE

In an age of popular first-person memoirs and confessionals—which typically demand lots of memory but little research—Junger insists that most writers do themselves a favor by selecting subjects they're somewhat detached from. Not only does such detachment lend itself to more objective journalism; it also forces the writer to delve into research that might not have been required (or even considered) otherwise.

Take, for example, an article Junger wrote about the world's last whale harpooner, a 74-year-old man in Bequia, an island in the South Caribbean. Calling it "one of the best stories I've written," Junger says the article came out so well because nothing actually happened—no whale was harpooned—while he was in Bequia researching the piece. "It would have been terrible for me if a whale would've been caught while I was there, because all the attention—on the island and in my article—inevitably would have been about the event. That would've squashed the history, the character portraits, the research I had to do about the island and harpooning—the things that made the story so interesting."

The same is true of Junger's experience with—and the success of—*The Perfect Storm*. If one of the crew members would have survived the *Andrea Gail* and Junger knew exactly what happened, *The Perfect Storm* would've been just another adventure-at-sea tale. As Junger says, "Sure, there's no way it could have been the book it is. I wouldn't have had to write in all the meteorology, what it's like to drown, the Coast Guard and Air National Guard rescue operations, the history of commercial fishing. There would have been no sense of uncertainty or conjecture. All the stuff people like about the book I wouldn't have been able to put in [because it would've seemed superfluous]. I just would've had this straight narrative from the survivor's perspective. Sometimes, fortunately, a writer has to fall back on all this interesting material that's not a direct part of the story, as weird as that sounds."

CHARTING HIS OWN COURSE

Junger's finest feat thus far in his writing career is not his stellar writing, not his tough-and-smart-boy image, not his bestselling first book, not his millionaire status. It's that he has managed to actualize what most of us—writers and non-writers alike—never quite figure out: he's defined himself as a writer. Junger has outlined his parameters, and editors know what he can and wants to write about. "The more writers focus their area of expertise the better," he says.

Of course, you don't want to make your niche too narrow and limit your opportunities, but defining yourself does work to your advantage. As soon as Junger became known as "the guy who writes about dangerous jobs," his assignments picked up. "When magazine editors needed a story that had something to do with dangerous work—which, of course, does not describe the whole spectrum of my interests—my name popped in their heads and they'd call me," he says. "I think I found a handle that fit just right—not too broad, not too narrow, but recognizably mine."

Junger's point is a good one. Droves of writers will write about almost anything, thinking the more they write about the more and better work they will get. Not so, in Junger's world. "I've found that being a generalist doesn't bring more work," he says. "It just guarantees you're thrown in this huge crowd of people, making you indistinguishable. The way to distinguish yourself is to write what you love, what interests you. At least that's how it's worked for me, and I can't imagine an alternative way to go about writing."

Success is Golden: A First Novel Becomes a Bestseller

BY JOANNE MILLER

Photo by Jerry Bauer

Arthur Golden

Every author dreams of writing a bestseller. The dream became reality for Arthur Golden when his first published work garnered international acclaim within weeks of its debut, and remained on the *New York Times* bestseller list for more than six months. His novel, *Memoirs of a Geisha* (Alfred A. Knopf), spans 60 years in the life of a Japanese woman, Sayuri; as a child, she is sold by her impoverished father, grows up to become a celebrated geisha, and leaves Japan to spend her final years in New York City.

This emotionally rich, skillfully crafted novel proves that Arthur Golden has paid his dues to become a writer of substance. "I suppose *Memoirs of a Geisha* could be construed as my first, second and third novel, since I wrote it three times before it was published," he says. Indeed, during Golden's 15-year apprenticeship as a full-time fiction writer, the act of rewriting *Memoirs of a Geisha* was Golden's teacher and classroom—he worked on the novel almost exclusively. Golden credits this single-minded devotion to one story as responsible for his confident ability to evaluate his own work, separating the good from the not-good-enough, a skill he considers crucial for any successful author.

Many reviewers have made much of the fact that *Memoirs of a Geisha* is written in the first person by a white American male. Golden seems slightly astonished by all the attention. "Isn't that what writers do?" he says. "They put themselves into the minds of other people." He talked with us about the genesis of the book, about writing and marketing his work, and about success.

So how *did* a white American male become so thoroughly conversant with all things Japanese and with the world of the geisha in particular?

I majored in art history, with an emphasis in Japanese art. I spent a year in Japan, traveled to China, and learned some Mandarin, too. I became interested in certain aspects of Asian life, and eventually in the rarefied world of geisha. These women are professional entertainers who cater to the male elite in Japanese business, wear stylized make-up and clothing, and are highly trained in several arts. In retrospect, knowing the cadences of the Japanese language helped me select words and phrases as I wrote *Memoirs of a Geisha*. If you want to write dialogue that expresses cultural attitudes and nuances outside your native experience, learning the language is an absolute necessity, especially in first person narration.

JOANNE MILLER *has interviewed Isabel Allende and Ron Carlson for* 1998 Novel & Short Story Writer's Market, *and is the author of* Pennsylvania Handbook, *a comprehensive guide to the beauty, history and attractions of the Keystone State.*

You invested a tremendous amount of time in writing and rewriting this novel. Tell us how the project began and what the process was like.

Since I'm of an analytical turn of mind, I felt comfortable breaking fiction down into separate elements and approaching them one element at a time. I went to the library and read everything I could find, then worked on dialogue, setting scenes, creating characters. Four or five years into my apprenticeship, I began to understand what some of these things meant—then *structure* reared its ugly head. Structure is much more than plot. For instance, the Sherlock Holmes stories have whodunit plots with returning characters, but they can't be told from the point of view of Holmes, because he already knows who the culprit is early on . . . not much of a mystery. So Arthur Conan Doyle used Dr. Watson, a first-person narrator who's not too bright. Holmes has to explain things to him; Watson's character and existence in the story serve a structural aim.

When I started writing *Memoirs of a Geisha,* I made an acceptable first draft using a third-person point of view, though I didn't show it around. That took about two years. Shortly after that, I met Mineko, a woman who had been a geisha for many years in the Gion district. I interviewed her and followed her around Kyoto; what I learned from her took my understanding of a geisha's daily existence and stood it on its head. I threw out my entire 750-page draft and started from scratch. I wrote for another few years.

I thought I had done a good job. I called a friend and got names of agents, but before I could call them, my friend met with a few of them, and they called me and asked to read the manuscript. No one was interested, and I got word that the readers (including three friends of mine who were experienced writers) found the manuscript "dry." I realized that I had been holding Sayuri at arm's length, emotionally, and that was the problem. I started over again in May, 1994, writing in the first person this time.

What persistence! What was it that made you stick with this project for so long?

I found the patience not only to completely rewrite the book twice but to continue to have faith in it partly because I recognized that I was learning, so each draft was better than the one before, and partly because I believed in myself as a writer. A writer has to write really well, and work very hard, to enable the reader to care. You have to think not just about the words you're choosing, but about the pieces you're putting together—all the elements: settings, point of view, yearnings of your characters. The words aren't nearly as important as the elements of the story. My advice is, be careful to choose and create situations and characters that spark your imagination as you write. Even the best writer can't do very much with dull material.

As your drafts improved and the novel neared completion, how did you make the transition from writing to marketing the book?

When I started to rewrite the book for the third time, I decided to go a different route marketing it; I sent the manuscript to a friend in Los Angeles who was involved in the movie business. She liked the manuscript very much and recommended I send it to Liz Darhansoff, a literary agent in New York, who in turn gave it to Leigh Feldman. With enormous patience and kindness, Leigh waited over a year for me to complete the rewrite. Finally, perhaps fearing that *Memoirs of a Geisha* might be one of those books that never gets finished, she said, "Let's send it out half-done." So on a Friday, Leigh sent 350 pages to ten publishers. She said, "Don't expect to hear from me for two weeks. Try to get on with your life."

I had already begun to pace by the following Monday when Leigh called and said Knopf was interested. I later learned that Robin Desser, my editor at Knopf, had received the manuscript on Friday afternoon, and said something like, "There's no way an American man can pull this off!" She took the work home, planning to read 15 or so pages before she went out with friends for the evening—just to convince herself that the book was as bad as she thought it was going to be. She ended up canceling her date, spending the entire weekend with the book, and calling Leigh on Monday morning.

Robin then went to the other decision-makers at Knopf to work out a hard-soft deal, which meant they would offer to publish the book in both hardcover and softcover. A week and a half later, Knopf made me a preemptive offer. Preempting is designed to eliminate a bidding war by offering the highest bid the publisher would pay immediately, a take-it-or-leave-it proposition. Leigh called me and told me their offer. I accepted on the spot. I had no experience in this at all, so I called a few friends and asked if what was happening was normal. One—my cousin Eric Lax, who has written a number of biographies—told me, "It happens about as often as burning bushes talk to pedestrians." Within days, Knopf began selling foreign rights to my book all over the world at the Frankfurt book fair. It was a stunning week.

Did you have any idea that *Memoirs of a Geisha* would receive the kind of attention it has?

I never expected it to be such a massive hit. I loved the subject matter, and I knew if I did a good job, the book would be published and have at least a small audience. I didn't expect it to be a bestseller. Everyone daydreams about it a little bit, but I never believed it would happen. I called myself a writer for ten years: a writer tries to write. When Knopf preempted the book and generated a bidding war in Frankfurt, I felt, for the first time, like someone who makes a living from writing . . . in other words, a novelist.

What project are you working on now?

I have ideas, a story in mind, but I'm not sure where or when to set it. Setting and characters are very important to me. Writing on speculation, as when I wrote *Memoirs of a Geisha*, is very different from having had a novel published, especially when it does so well. Putting together the second novel will be very different from the first. I want to keep in mind what it was like to write my first book, and to shut out the voices of critics so I don't write to them. I want to address my faults as I see them, not as they see them. One of my greatest strengths has been the ability to judge for myself what was right and wrong for me, and I want to keep doing that. I'm trying very hard to block all expectations and write from what I believe.

Jack Canfield: Taking *Chicken Soup* to the Top

BY DEE PORTER

Jack Canfield, renowned speaker, author and co-creator of the *Chicken Soup for the Soul* series, has spent his life inspiring millions of people. One may ask what motivated the motivator?

Jack Canfield started his career as a high school teacher motivated by the Civil Rights Movement. He ended up teaching history in an all-black school in Chicago. "I realized that I was more interested in why kids weren't learning than in teaching history. I met a man, W. Clements Stone, who was a famous motivator and president of *Success* magazine. He became my mentor, and I went to work for his foundation. He was a self-made multi-millionaire who taught me the basic principles of success: the importance of taking personal responsibility for one's life and for one's own happiness. He taught me how to motivate myself and others and the importance of being of service to others. Soon we were training teachers on how to motivate kids to achieve on higher levels, to fulfill their potential."

Jack Canfield

Photo by Elliott DePicciotto

Canfield's first book, *100 Ways to Enhance Self-Concept in the Classroom*, was a bestseller in educational circles and sold about 400,000 copies within a few years. "It was kind of neat, writing the book, seeing it in print and getting letters back proving that it was a useful tool."

He then wrote two more books, *101 Ways to Develop Self-Esteem and Responsibility* and the accompanying curriculum guide, as well as dozens of articles for education, parenting and teen magazines. On the basis of his expertise, Canfield stayed busy speaking at workshops.

At one of the workshops, he met his soon-to-be business partner, Mark Victor Hansen. They were both fond of using stories in their speeches, having learned early in their careers that people remember a story more easily than they remember a concept and that if you illustrate a concept with a story, people will remember the concept better as well. "I'd steal from him, he'd steal from me, and we'd both use stories we'd read in *Reader's Digest*, *Guideposts* and other inspirational publications. We'd use these uplifting and inspirational stories to illustrate the points in our talks—that basically people should have high self-esteem, be better parents, overcome obstacles and not let anything stop that process.

"People began to come up to us after the seminars and say, 'You have the best stories! I wish my son had been here to hear the *Puppies for Sale* story' or 'I wish all my employees had been here to hear the *Monty Roberts* story.' We collected stories that covered a wide range of human behavior. We never thought of putting them in a book until one day someone said, 'Those stories you use are pretty cool, you ought to put them in a book.' We thought, 'Yeah right! thought, 'Yeah right! Who'd buy it?' It took us three years of hearing that to finally put them in a book."

DEE PORTER *is been involved in a variety of creative interests which include writing nonfiction, fiction and screenplays. She is the co-author of* Gangs, A Handbook for Community Awareness *(Facts On File). She interviewed Olivia Goldsmith and Mary Higgins Clark for the* 1999 Novel & Short Story Writer's Market.

The first *Chicken Soup for the Soul* book contained stories the two men had been using for 24 years in their lectures. "We chose the goal of 101 stories. At first we only had 68, so we asked some of our friends who were speakers to write some stories, people like Les Brown, Gloria Steinem, Tony Robbins and many more. We ended up with 120 stories and didn't know how to say no to more, and then there was the question of which ones to use."

To solve that problem, Canfield and Hansen created a panel of 15 people who read and gave final scores which determined what stories made it into the book. Today, every story that comes in is graded by the panel, which now includes about 40 people.

Finding a publisher was the first major obstacle. Hansen and Canfield worked hard at promoting the books. "We lived the principles we teach in our workshops. Most people don't know this, but when we completed writing the first *Chicken Soup for the Soul* book, we almost didn't get it published. We discovered that we had worked for three years on a book that no one thought would sell in today's world. We took it with an agent to every publishing house in New York and got over 100 rejections from the larger publishers. They told us the book was too nice, that what people wanted to read contained more violence and more sex; they just didn't think a book that was this positive and idealistic would sell. The agent gave it back to us, said he couldn't sell it. So we said, 'Fine, *we'll* sell it.' "

Rather than give up, Canfield and Hansen made 3-ring binders containing 40 stories and a proposal, and took them to the American Booksellers Association convention. "We decided to walk up and down the aisles and give a copy to every single publisher there until we found one that would give us a chance. After a day and a half of being rejected 111 times, we finally found a very small publisher from Florida, Health Communications, Inc., that said they would take a look at the book and give us a call. Well, they called us the very next day and said they absolutely loved it and they were going to take a chance and publish it. We asked about an advance, and they said, 'No advance. We're taking a chance, but we'll give you 20% across the board.' It's turned out to be a very good deal."

Finally, *Chicken Soup for the Soul* was published. Then came their next obstacle. "Once the book was printed we had to get the word out so people would come into the bookstore to buy it. We gave away literally thousands of free books. We sent them all over the country.

"We did everything we could to promote the book. We asked hundreds of famous people to give us testimonial quotes. We called all of the major newspapers and asked them to print articles about and stories from the book. We hired Deepak Chopra's public relations person to help us. We tried to get on every TV show we could—especially national shows. We did mailings to thousands of people to advertise our book and gave away thousands of free review copies. We wrote articles for every newspaper, magazine and newsletter we could. We sent review copies to all of the people that contributed to the book and asked them to sell it whenever they were out speaking. We did book signings in every bookstore we could get to. We did radio talk shows by phone at all hours of the day and night. We sold the books in nontraditional places like gas stations, beauty salons, food stores and other places where people are not used to seeing books. We felt if it was the only book in the store they would buy it! And they did.

"Eventually, word of mouth took off, and we finally made the *New York Times* bestseller list. We were number one on that list for over two years. Our latest book, *Chicken Soup for the Woman's Soul*, is also number one on the list and is currently selling over 10,000 copies a day in America."

To get material for the second book, they created several innovations. "On the last page of the book, we invited readers to send in their own stories for future books. Within 5 or 6 months we had an average of 50-60 stories coming in every day, sometimes even as high as 100. These stories were personal pieces, printed pieces cut out from newspapers, magazines, church letters. Now, we put ads in *Writer's Digest* looking for specific subjects. We post ads on Internet writers' chat rooms and also in specific niche places."

What accounts for their phenomenal success? "Marketing and promotion are very important, but not enough to make a bad book successful. Word of mouth is the best way. I think several things account for the success of the *Chicken Soup for the Soul* series. First, I think the world is hungry for hope and inspiration. Most people in the world are living in a state of resignation, cynicism and hopelessness. They believe that it is impossible for their lives to get better. They have settled for less than they really want. They are in desperate need of models of people who have opened their hearts, dared to live with passion and compassion, trusted their inner guidance, followed their hearts, pursued their dreams, persevered in the face of obstacles and made a difference in the lives of others. Our books give people hundreds of examples of ordinary people who have chosen to live extraordinary lives.

"I believe the second reason for the success of the books is that no story is over five pages long. Most people today are too busy to sit down and read a 500-page novel, but they can find 15 minutes a day to read several short inspirational stories.

"Next, I think our books have been so successful because we have a panel of over 40 people who read each story we consider publishing and grade each story on a scale of 1-10. A 10 means 'it gave me goosebumps,' 'it made me cry,' 'it inspired me,' or 'it made me want to get up and take action.' We have never published a story with an average score of less than 9.5. That means every story has been proven to have universal appeal. They are short stories with a 'barrel of laughter and a bucket of tears.'

"Another problem is that some of the books have a tremendous number of submissions to read. For instance, *Chicken Soup for the Kid's Soul* had 7,200 stories submitted; there were 6,000 stories for *Chicken Soup for the Christian Soul* and 2,500 submissions for *Chicken Soup for the Teenage Soul*. Each book is still 101 stories each. That's a lot of reading and editing. We keep learning how to improve the process. We've now hired 'stay at home' moms to read for us. It's 80% more efficient."

The authors encourage writers to send their stories, three to five pages double-spaced, to the Santa Barbara address listed below. Writers are paid, starting at $300 and going up to $1,000, depending on the story and the writer's experience. The writers retain their rights. "We aren't in the 'resale' business. We even copyright each story in the writer's name if they don't. We do have some media projects coming up from which the writers would also benefit, including a syndicated newspaper column and *Campbell's Soup for the Soul Minute*."

How have the *Chicken Soup* books changed Canfield's life? "I have a much greater appreciation for all I have been blessed with," he says. "I also have a much deeper appreciation for the wonderful generosity of spirit most people possess."

If you have a story that would fit in the *Chicken Soup* series, send it to

The Canfield Group
Chicken Soup for the Soul
P.O. Box 30880
Santa Barbara CA 93130

Fax: (805)563-2945; E-mail: soup4soul@aol.com; Website: http://www.chickensoup.com

In addition, Jennifer Read Hawthorne and Marcy Shimmel, co-editors with Canfield and Hansen of *Chicken Soup for the Woman's Soul* and *Chicken Soup for the Mother's Soul*, are seeking stories for additional helpings of those books as well as the new *Chicken Soup for the Single Soul*. See the Women's category in Consumer Magazines for more information.

The Business of Writing

Minding the Details

Writers who have had some success in placing their work know that the effort to publish requires an entirely different set of skills than does the act of writing. A shift in perspective is required when you move from creating your work to selling it. Like it or not, successful writers—*career* writers—have to keep the business side of the writing business in mind as they work.

Each of the following sections discusses a writing business topic that affects anyone selling his writing. We'll take a look at contracts and agreements—the documents that license a publisher to use your work. We'll consider your rights as a writer and sort out some potentially confusing terminology. We'll cover the basics of copyright protection—a topic of perennial concern for writers. And for those of you who are already making money with your writing, we'll offer some tips for keeping track of financial matters and staying on top of your tax liabilities.

Our treatment of the business topics that follow is necessarily limited. Look for complete information on each subject at your local bookstore or library—both in books (some of which we mention) and periodicals aimed at writers. Information is also available from the federal government, as indicated later in this article.

CONTRACTS AND AGREEMENTS

If you've been freelancing even a short time, you know that contracts and agreements vary considerably from one publisher to another. Some magazine editors work only by verbal agreement; others have elaborate documents you must sign in triplicate and return before you begin the assignment. As you evaluate any contract or agreement, consider carefully what you stand to gain and lose by signing. Did you have another sale in mind that selling all rights the first time will negate? Does the agreement provide the publisher with a number of add-ons (advertising rights, reprint rights, etc.) for which they won't have to pay you again?

In contract negotiations, the writer is usually interested in licensing the work for a particular use but limiting the publisher's ability to make other uses of the work in the future. It's in the publisher's best interest, however, to secure rights to use the work in as many ways as possible, both now and later on. Those are the basic positions of each party. The negotiation is a process of compromise and capitulation on questions relating to those basic points—and the amount of compensation to be given the writer for his work.

A contract is rarely a take-it-or-leave-it proposition. If an editor tells you that his company will allow *no* changes on the contract, you will then have to decide how important the assignment is to you. But most editors are open to negotiation, and you should learn to compromise on points that don't matter to you while maintaining your stand on things that do.

When it's not specified, most writers assume that a magazine publisher is buying first rights. Some writers' groups can supply you with a sample magazine contract to use when the publisher doesn't supply one, so you can document your agreement in writing. Members of The Authors

Guild are given a sample book contract and information about negotiating when they join. For more information about contracts and agreements, see *Business and Legal Forms for Authors & Self-Publishers*, by Tad Crawford (Allworth Press, 1990); *From Printout to Published*, by Michael Seidman (Carroll & Graf, 1992) or *The Writer's Guide to Contract Negotiations*, by Richard Balkin (Writer's Digest Books, 1985), which is out of print but should be available in libraries.

RIGHTS AND THE WRITER

A creative work can be used in many different ways. As the originator of written works, you enjoy full control over how those works are used; you are in charge of the rights that your creative works are "born" with. When you agree to have your work published, you are giving the publisher the right to use your work in one or more ways. Whether that right is simply to publish the work for the first time in a periodical or to publish it as many times as he likes and in whatever form he likes is up to you—it all depends on the terms of the contract or agreement the two of you arrive at. As a general rule, the more rights you license away, the less control you have over your work and the more money you should be paid for the license. We find that writers and editors sometimes define rights in different ways. For a classification of terms, read Types of Rights, below.

Sometimes editors don't take the time to specify the rights they are buying. If you sense that an editor is interested in getting stories but doesn't seem to know what his and the writer's responsibilities are regarding rights, be wary. In such a case, you'll want to explain what rights you're offering (preferably one-time or first serial rights only) and that you expect additional payment for subsequent use of your work.

You should strive to keep as many rights to your work as you can from the outset, otherwise, your attempts to resell your writing may be seriously hampered.

The Copyright Law that went into effect January 1, 1978, said writers were primarily selling one-time rights to their work unless they—and the publisher—agreed otherwise in writing. Book rights are covered fully by the contract between the writer and the book publisher.

TYPES OF RIGHTS

- First Serial Rights—First serial rights means the writer offers a newspaper or magazine the right to publish the article, story or poem for the first time in any periodical. All other rights to the material remain with the writer. The qualifier "North American" is often added to this phrase to specify a geographical limit to the license.

  When material is excerpted from a book scheduled to be published and it appears in a magazine or newspaper prior to book publication, this is also called first serial rights.
- One-Time Rights—A periodical that licenses one-time rights to a work (also known as simultaneous rights) buys the *nonexclusive* right to publish the work once. That is, there is nothing to stop the author from selling the work to other publications at the same time. Simultaneous sales would typically be to periodicals without overlapping audiences.
- Second Serial (Reprint) Rights—This gives a newspaper or magazine the opportunity to print an article, poem or story after it has already appeared in another newspaper or magazine. Second serial rights are nonexclusive—that is, they can be licensed to more than one market.
- All Rights—This is just what it sounds like. If you license away all rights to your work, you forfeit the right to ever use it again. If you think you'll want to use the material later, you must avoid submitting to such markets or refuse payment and withdraw your material. Ask the editor whether he is willing to buy first rights instead of all rights before you agree to an assignment or sale. Some editors will reassign rights to a writer after a given period, such as one year. It's worth an inquiry in writing.
- Electronics Rights—These rights cover usage in a broad range of electronic media, from

online magazines and databases to CD-ROM magazine anthologies and interactive games. The magazine contract should specify if—and which—electronic rights are included. The presumption is that unspecified rights are kept by the writer.

- Subsidiary Rights—These are the rights, other than book publication rights, that should be covered in a book contract. These may include various serial rights; movie, television, audiotape and other electronic rights; translation rights, etc. The book contract should specify who controls these rights (author or publisher) and what percentage of sales from the licensing of these sub rights goes to the author.
- Dramatic, Television and Motion Picture Rights—This means the writer is selling his material for use on the stage, in television or in the movies. Often a one-year option to buy such rights is offered (generally for 10% of the total price). The interested party then tries to sell the idea to other people—actors, directors, studios or television networks, etc. Some properties are optioned over and over again, but most fail to become dramatic productions. In such cases, the writer can sell his rights again and again—as long as there is interest in the material. Though dramatic, TV and motion picture rights are more important to the fiction writer than the nonfiction writer, producers today are increasingly interested in nonfiction material; many biographies, topical books and true stories are being dramatized.

SELLING SUBSIDIARY RIGHTS

The primary right in the world of book publishing is the right to publish the book itself. All other rights (such as movie rights, audio rights, book club rights, electronic rights and foreign rights) are considered secondary, or subsidiary, to the right to print publication. In contract negotiations, authors and their agents traditionally try to avoid granting the publisher subsidiary rights that they feel capable of marketing themselves. Publishers, on the other hand, typically hope to obtain control over as many of the sub rights as they can. Philosophically speaking, subsidiary rights will be best served by being left in the hands of the person or organization most capable of—and interested in—exploiting them profitably. Sometimes that will be the author and her agent, and sometimes that will be the publisher.

Larger agencies have experience selling foreign rights, movie rights and the like, and many authors represented by such agents prefer to retain those rights and let their agents do the selling. Book publishers, on the other hand, have subsidiary rights departments, which are responsible for exploiting all sub rights the publisher was able to retain during the contract negotiation.

That job might begin with a push to sell foreign rights, which normally bring in advance money which is divided among author, agent and publisher. Further efforts then might be made to sell the right to publish the book as a paperback (although many book contracts now call for hard/soft deals, in which the original hardcover publisher buys the right to also publish the paperback version).

Any other rights which the publisher controls will be pursued, such as book clubs and magazines. Publishers usually don't control movie rights to a work, as those are most often retained by author and agent.

The marketing of electronic rights to a work, in this era of rapidly expanding capabilities and markets for electronic material, can be tricky. With the proliferation of electronic and multimedia formats, publishers, agents and authors are going to great pains these days to make sure contracts specify exactly *which* electronic rights are being conveyed (or retained).

Compensation for these rights is a major source of conflict between writers and publishers, as many book publishers seek control of them and many magazines routinely include electronic rights in the purchase of all rights, often with no additional payment. Alternative ways of handling this issue include an additional 15% added to the amount to purchase first rights to a royalty system or a flat fee for use within a specified time frame, usually one year.

COPYRIGHT

Copyright law exists to protect creators of original works. It is engineered to encourage creative expression and aid in the progress of the arts and sciences by ensuring that artists and authors hold the rights by which they can profit from their labors.

Copyright protects your writing, unequivocally recognizes you (its creator) as its owner, and grants you all the rights, benefits and privileges that come with ownership. The moment you finish a piece of writing—whether it is a short story, article, novel or poem—the law recognizes that only you can decide how it is to be used.

The basics of copyright law are discussed here. More detailed information can be obtained from the Copyright Office and in the books mentioned at the end of this section.

Copyright law gives you the right to make and distribute copies of your written works, the right to prepare derivative works (dramatizations, translations, musical arrangements, etc.—any work based on the original) and the right to perform or publicly display your work. With very few exceptions, anything you write today will enjoy copyright protection for your lifetime plus 50 years. Copyright protects "original works of authorship" that are fixed in a tangible form of expression. Titles, ideas and facts can *not* be copyrighted.

Some people are under the mistaken impression that copyright is something they have to send away for, and that their writing is not properly protected until they have "received" their copyright from the government. The fact is, you don't have to register your work with the Copyright Office in order for your work to be copyrighted; any piece of writing is copyrighted the moment it is put to paper. Registration of your work does, however, offer some additional protection (specifically, the possibility of recovering punitive damages in an infringement suit) as well as legal proof of the date of copyright.

Registration is a matter of filling out a form (for writers, that's generally form TX) and sending the completed form, a copy of the work in question and a check for $20 to the Register of Copyrights, Library of Congress, Washington DC 20559. If the thought of paying $20 each to register every piece you write does not appeal to you, you can cut costs by registering a group of your works with one form, under one title for one $20 fee.

Most magazines are registered with the Copyright Office as single collective entities themselves; that is, the individual works that make up the magazine are *not* copyrighted individually in the names of the authors. You'll need to register your article yourself if you wish to have the additional protection of copyright registration. It's always a good idea to ask that your notice of copyright (your name, the year of first publication, and the copyright symbol ©) be appended to any published version of your work. You may use the copyright notice regardless of whether or not your work has been registered.

One thing writers need to be wary of is "work for hire" arrangements. If you sign an agreement stipulating that your writing will be done as work for hire, you will not control the copyright of the completed work—the person or organization who hired you will be the copyright owner. Work for hire arrangements and transfers of exclusive rights must be in writing to be legal, but it's a good idea to get every publishing agreement in writing before the sale.

You can obtain more information about copyright from the Copyright Office, Library of Congress, Washington DC 20559. To get answers to specific questions about copyright, call the Copyright Public Information Office at (202)707-3000 weekdays between 8:30 a.m. and 5 p.m. eastern standard time. To order copyright forms by phone, call (202)707-9100. Forms can also be downloaded from the Library of Congress website at http://lcweb.loc.gov/copyright. The website also includes information on filling out the forms, general copyright information and links to other websites related to copyright issues. A thorough (and thoroughly enjoyable) discussion of the subject of copyright law as it applies to writers can be found in Stephen Fishman's *The Copyright Handbook: How to Protect and Use Written Works* (Nolo Press, 1994). A shorter but no less enlightening treatment is Ellen Kozak's *Every Writer's Guide to Copyright & Publishing Law* (Henry Holt, 1990).

FINANCES AND TAXES

As your writing business grows, so will your obligation to keep track of your writing-related finances and taxes. Keeping a close eye on these details will help you pay as little tax as possible and keep you apprised of the state of your freelance business. A writing business with no systematic way of tracking expenses and income will soon be no writing business at all. If you dislike handling finance-related tasks, you can always hire someone else to handle them for a fee. If you do employ a professional, you must still keep the original records with an eye to providing the professional with the appropriate information.

If you decide to handle these tasks yourself—or if you just want to know what to expect of the person you employ—consider these tips:

Accurate records are essential, and the easiest way to keep them is to separate your writing income and expenses from your personal ones. Most professionals find that separate checking accounts and credit cards help them provide the best and easiest records.

Get in the habit of recording every transaction (both expenses and earnings) related to your writing. You can start at any time; you don't need to begin on January 1. Because you're likely to have expenses before you have income, start keeping your records whenever you make your first purchase related to writing—such as this copy of *Writer's Market.*

Any system of tracking expenses and income will suffice, but the more detailed it is, the better. Be sure to describe each transaction clearly—including the date; the source of the income (or the vendor of your purchase); a description of what was sold or bought; whether the payment was by cash, check or credit card; and the amount of the transaction.

The other necessary component of your financial record-keeping system is an orderly way to store receipts related to your writing. Check stubs, receipts for cash purchases, credit card receipts and similar paperwork should all be kept as well as recorded in your ledger. Any good book about accounting for small business will offer specific suggestions for ways to track your finances.

Freelance writers, artists and photographers have a variety of concerns about taxes that employees don't have, including deductions, self-employment tax and home office credits. Many freelance expenses can be deducted in the year in which they are incurred (rather than having to be capitalized, or depreciated, over a period of years). For details, consult the IRS publications mentioned later. Keep in mind that to be considered a business (and not a hobby) by the IRS you need to show a profit in three of the past five years. Hobby losses are deductible only to the extent of income produced by the activity.

There also is a home office deduction that can be claimed if an area in your home is used *exclusively* and *regularly* for business. Contact the IRS for information on requirements and limitations for this deduction. If your freelance income exceeds your expenses, regardless of the amount, you must declare that profit. If you make $400 or more after deductions, you must pay Social Security tax and file Schedule SE, a self-employment form, along with your Form 1040 and Schedule C tax forms.

While we cannot offer you tax advice or interpretations, we can suggest several sources for the most current information.

- Check the IRS website, http://www.irs.ustreas.gov/. Full of helpful tips and information, the site also provides instant access to important IRS forms and publications.
- Call your local IRS office. Look in the white pages of the telephone directory under U.S. Government—Internal Revenue Service. Someone will be able to respond to your request for IRS publications and tax forms or other information. Ask about the IRS Tele-tax service, a series of recorded messages you can hear by dialing on a touch-tone phone. If you need answers to complicated questions, ask to speak with a Taxpayer Service Specialist.

- Obtain the basic IRS publications. You can order them by phone or mail from any IRS office; most are available at libraries and some post offices. Start with *Your Federal Income Tax* (Publication 17) and *Tax Guide for Small Business* (Publication 334). These are both comprehensive, detailed guides—you'll need to find the regulations that apply to you and ignore the rest. There are many IRS publications relating to self-employment and taxes; Publication 334 lists many of these publications—such as *Business Use of Your Home* (Publication 587) and *Self-Employment Tax* (Publication 533).
- Consider other information sources. Many public libraries have detailed tax instructions available on tape. Some colleges and universities offer free assistance in preparing tax returns. And if you decide to consult a professional tax preparer, the fee is a deductible business expense on your tax return.

The Art of Negotiation

BY GREGG LEVOY

Many years ago, one of the magazine editors I regularly sold to left his spot on the masthead to become a fellow freelance writer—an irony only a writer can fully appreciate.

He was now considerably easier to reach, and during a phone conversation he told me something he never would have revealed while an editor: "You should have been asking for more money, more often, especially once you began writing for us consistently. You always took whatever we offered."

When breaking into a magazine, he said, writers *should* take whatever terms are offered. Continuing this practice after breaking in, however, is like turning down raises.

I was guilty as charged. My views on asking editors for more money, or more anything, could best be described as approach-avoidance: If I didn't approach the subject of negotiation, I could avoid rejection (which I'd already had plenty of, thank you).

I'd also thought of negotiation as something only for J.R. Ewing types. I didn't realize that the very qualities that make me a writer and made me think I'd be eaten alive at the bargaining table—sensitivity, thoughtfulness, creativity—are also typical (when combined with a bit of assertiveness) of the best negotiators.

But the former editor's remarks fired me with both insight and indignation. I began experimenting. When a trade magazine editor asked to reprint one of my stories for $75, I screwed up my courage and said, "How about $125?" He said, "How about $100? I said, "OK."

I made $25 for less than ten seconds of talking! That would make a dandy hourly wage.

Not all negotiations have been this easy, but each time I managed some success I was emboldened. Within a year I was negotiating with some of the buck-a-word magazines for money and rights that would eventually double my income. I learned three lessons in short order:

- *What you can get if you ask is astonishing*. One editor I know told me that nine out of ten writers never ask for anything, and she almost always says yes to the one who does.
- *The worst thing an editor will do is say no.* Not 1 editor in 20 years has hung up on me because I asked for more money.
- *Everything is negotiable*, from money and rights to deadline, expenses, payment schedule, kill fee, length, tone and editing.

COLLABORATIVE BARGAINING

There are more than a few writers who feel they couldn't warm up to editors if they were burned at the stake together. They approach negotiating in an atmosphere of trust not unlike that surrounding two nations exchanging captured spies at the border.

Editors, however, aren't our enemies. They are hardworking people trying to be recognized for their efforts. They're also not people you're selling used cars to. You want to develop long-term relationships with them, because the more steady customers you have, the more steady

---

GREGG LEVOY, *author of* Callings: Finding and Following An Authentic Life *and* This Business of Writing, *is a former adjunct professor of journalism at the University of New Mexico. His articles and essays have appeared in the* New York Times Magazine, Washington Post, Omni, Psychology Today *and many others. He currently lives in Tucson, Arizona.*

income you have. Your negotiations must be collaborative, with both sides feeling good about what they get.

So how do you manage a win-win outcome when editors have all the power?

First, understand that editors *don't* have all the power. It's a buyer's market for some writers, and a seller's market for others, as determined by the law of supply and demand. If most writers offer roughly the same thing—passably good writing, fairly good ideas, occasional reliability, a modest stamina for rewrites and a deep-seated fear of asking for anything more than editors offer—it's a buyer's market, and editors will buy the cheapest work available.

But when you begin giving editors what they want most—bang-up writing, imaginative ideas, a firm grasp of the audience, punctuality and a product that sells magazines—and when you then ask for payment commensurate with that quality of performance, it turns into a seller's market, with editors favorably disposed to negotiating to keep you.

USING YOUR BARGAINING POWER

Negotiating is not an event, but a process. It's more than just a quick pitch; it's the whole sales campaign.

It begins not when you pick up the phone, but when you pick up the professional relationship; bargaining power is the cumulative effect of everything you do in that relationship. Most writers don't recognize this and badly underestimate their bargaining power.

These five "power tools" will help you build a strong negotiation position.

1. Performance. Several years ago, I told one of my regular buyers of short pieces, Allied Publications, that I wanted to renegotiate my fee, which had held steady at $25 per piece for two years. He told me to put it in writing and let him think about it. I wrote the following letter:

> Dear Richard:
>
> It was nice chatting with you on the phone yesterday. I look forward to putting together more pieces for Allied. As for the business: After having written eight or ten pieces for Allied over the course of two years, at $25 each, I am hoping we can consider a higher fee, $50 each. I hope that given the consistent quality, fast turnaround and minimal editing my articles require, this will seem like a fair price. Give me a ring and we can discuss it.

His reply: He raised my rate to $35 and suggested we could discuss another adjustment in six months. Meanwhile, 45 percent raise.

When you deliver the goods and give editors more than they bargained for, don't let the fact go unnoticed at negotiating time.

2. Presentation. From the first impression on, your presence should communicate enthusiasm, self-motivation, attention to detail, resourcefulness, humor, patience and, above all, confidence (fake it if you must; it has a way of becoming a self-fulfilling prophecy anyway). How you present yourself is conveyed, whether you know it or not, through your phone manner, correspondence, query letters, stationery and writing.

3. Professionalism. During the negotiation that led to my first piece for *Pursuits Magazine*, the editor wanted me to pay expenses up front for a trip to Seattle to do the article, for which she would reimburse me.

I explained, though, that I was currently on assignment for two other national magazines, both of which wanted me to pay out-of-pocket expenses for trips (one to South America) and doing so was fast depleting my savings account. I asked her to reconsider her request and send me a check before the trip to cover my expenses. I also offered to send her an itemized list of exactly what I anticipated spending.

She sent a check for $600 that week.

I had, in this case by implication, demonstrated that I was a professional with credibility and competence, that I was *worth* sending not just to Seattle but to South America, but that I nonetheless had a limited bank account. Bringing self-esteem into your business and writing affairs can have a commanding effect.

"Professional" writers, for instance, are those most likely to succeed at changing "pays-on-publication" clauses to "pays-on-acceptance," simply because they know that in no other business do people, professional or not, stand for not being paid their wages on time. At the least these writers appeal to an editor's sense of logic, fairness and business principles by pointing out the time-honored tradition, common to all deferred-payment plans (such as credit card payments), that a buyer pays a higher price for delayed payment, and a seller gets a higher price for waiting.

4. Polish. Go the extra mile for editors: burn the midnight oil to give a story that extra shine; help them track down photos; do your own editing; double-check your facts; oblige all reasonable requests for rewrites; get work in *before* deadline. Then remind your editors of these facts at negotiating time.

5. Personal contact. People enjoy doing business with those they identify with. So give editors lots of opportunities to identify with you. Drop them notes, call with updates on stories, go visit them and break bread. And once you've broken into the stable of writers, cultivate your editorial relationships as if your livelihood depended on it. Remember: The stable is usually not far from the pasture.

THINK BIG

Several years ago, a *Vogue* editor called to buy a story idea from me. Not the story, just the idea. "How much do you want for it?" she asked.

Now what is a story idea worth? They're a dime a dozen—$100? I did save them time, though, by already doing the outline—$200? And now they wouldn't have to pay me to write—$300? "How about $400?" I finally said, thinking big. "Sold!" she said. There was a moment's silence, during which I thought to myself, *Damn*.

Anytime a buyer accepts your first offer, you've blown it. You've undersold yourself. Your writing is worth whatever someone will pay for it, and that is determined by how much they need it, how valuable they perceive it to be, the going rate, the budget and your bargaining power. But set high aspirations. Come in with a price before the editor does, one that is perhaps a third to a half higher than you expect to receive, or expect them to offer. Often your expectations of both are too low.

Remember, aspirations can always be lowered. Once stated, they can't be raised.

APPROACHING YOUR NEGOTIATIONS

You just asked an editor to pay you on acceptance instead of on publication. She flatly said no, sorry, company policy. Quick, what's your response?

You don't want to be reduced to responses like "Well, it doesn't hurt to ask, huh?" You need instead studied comebacks that grow out of planning your negotiations. Do not go into them thinking you'll just see what happens. Rely on homework, practicing what you'll preach, knowing what you'll say if an editor invokes "company policy." Script it out if need be. Above all, know what you want out of the negotiation, and what you're willing to settle for.

Another form of planning I undertake is keeping notes on all my conversations with editors. Several years ago, an editor at *Health* mentioned to me that rates were probably going down for shorter pieces and up to a dollar a word for longer features. I jotted it down. Four months later she called with a go-ahead on a query and offered me $1,500 for a 2,000-word piece.

I pulled out my file and there was the note about a probable rate change. I asked her about it. After much squirming, she finally offered me $1,800 for 1,800 words. Less work, more money.

You can also brainstorm advance solutions to potential negotiation deadlocks. For example, both sides usually want more money, and conventional wisdom suggests that more for you means less for them, and vice versa. Not necessarily. The pie can be expanded.

When I travel on assignment to a city where I have friends, I offer to stay with them instead of at a hotel, if the editor will kick back half the savings into my fee.

If the deadlock is over editors taking all rights, denying you the chance to make extra income from your writing, try this: Offer to retain "syndication rights." You can sell your pieces again, but only to newspaper syndicates that agree to put at the top of the story "Originally appeared in *XYZ Magazine*." The magazine gets its exclusivity; you get your extra income.

But you must think of these *before you begin to negotiate.*

EIGHT MORE NEGOTIATION TACTICS

All of these strategies are based on collaborative principles (or at least aren't contrary to them):

1. Listen. Sometimes the cheapest concession you can make in a negotiation is simply letting an editor know he's been heard. And remember, listening is not necessarily agreeing.

2. Be quiet. Nature abhors a vacuum. People will naturally rush in to fill silences, but if that silence is going to be broken with a compromise, let it be theirs, not yours.

During the negotiation with an inflight magazine editor about his pays-on-publication policy, I mentioned that as a business practice it didn't seem fair, and then I shut up for a moment. In the awkward silence that ensued, the urge to blurt out something—anything—to ease the tension, was excruciating. He broke first, and he did so with a compromise, effectively talking himself right out of his position.

3. Attack problems, not people. In the inflight negotiation, I made sure to focus my attention and displeasure on the issue, not the editor. It was the policy that was unfair, not the person trying to uphold it even against his own principles.

4. Ask open-minded questions. The more information you have about an editor's needs, interests and dilemmas, the better your bargaining position. So get them talking (before and during the negotiation) by asking questions that do not elicit *yes* or *no* answers: "Why do you have a pays-on-publication policy?" or "Are there improvements I could make in my writing that would make it work better for you?"

5. Have a concession strategy. Acrobats are the only people who make any sort of a living bending over backwards. Don't give in just to avoid conflict (but don't dig your heels in either, biting when a simple growl would do). If you come in with a price of $900 and your editor counters with $500, don't immediately whittle away at your initial offer by suggesting $700. Tell him why you believe you're worth $900.

When conceding, make small concessions. Don't jump from offering $1,000 to backing off to $500 in one giant step. It will appear you can be bought for even cheaper than *that.*

6. Discuss fees last. Fee is the area you're most likely to disagree about, so start, if you can, discussing more easily agreeable areas. If an editor suggests a three-month deadline, say you can get it done in two and a half. If she says $50 is all she can give you for phone expenses, say you'll make your calls in the evenings and weekends and save her $20. Then, once you've built up common ground and warmed the editor's heart with your conciliatory nature, talk price.

7. When you stop negotiating, stop. Make sure you discuss all negotiables in one session, not piecemeal. And once you've made your final agreements, don't try to better them.

8. Get it in writing. When you finish negotiating, make sure you commit your agreements to paper, be it a written contract or a simple letter of agreement. If an editor suggests you forego a written contract and just leave it at a friendly handshake, politely tell him that you'd like to *keep* the relationship friendly, so you would much prefer to work with a written contract—you can even tell him that's *your* company policy.

How Much Should I Charge?

BY ROBIN GEE

More and more writers are making the switch from a full-time job to a combination of a part-time job and freelance work or a full-time freelance career. Economic factors play a part, of course, as employers continue to downsize, but many choose the freelance life for a variety of reasons—for more freedom, to have more time with their families, to have more control over their careers, and, simply, because they want to make a living doing what they love.

One of the first questions new freelancers ask is, "How much should I charge?" Unfortunately, there is not one set of standard, agreed-upon rates. Many factors play a part in how fees are set. Freelancers must take into account their overhead and the costs of doing business, their level of experience, area of expertise and the kind of work they do. Sometimes location plays a part, as does the nature and size of a client's business.

PRICING IN THE FREELANCE MARKET

The information supplied in this section is designed to give new freelancers and those interested in trying other areas of freelance an idea of what other freelancers are charging. Based on research—surveys and interviews with freelancers, clients and writers' organizations in the U.S. and Canada—we've compiled a list of typical freelance projects or services and typical ranges. Some of the ranges are quite broad because fees vary widely depending on location (generally more on either coast), the nature of the client (nonprofits and small businesses pay less than large corporations) and the size or complexity of the job (highly skilled or technical tasks pay more than more generalized work).

Knowing what the market will bear is an important part of establishing a viable fee schedule. The most common mistake freelancers make is selling themselves short, underestimating the value of good writing and editing skills to business and others in need of such services. On the other hand, you don't want to price yourself out of the market.

Networking with other writers in your area is the best way to learn how much to charge for your level of expertise and location. Not only can talking to other writers help you determine how much you can charge for a particular service, it can also help you learn of new opportunities as well as combat the isolation that can come from working alone. The grapevine is also very useful in identifying problem clients and areas of concern.

FREELANCERS' ORGANIZATIONS

Most freelancers belong to at least one writers' or freelancers' organization. The National Writers Association and the Freelance Editorial Association are two national groups working for the best interests of freelance writers and editors. If you specialize in a particular area such as translation or indexing there are a number of professional organizations for those working in these areas. Check the Organizations of Interest section in *Writer's Market* or in the *Literary Market Place* publishing trade directory for names and addresses of writers' organizations. Just as important are regional and local associations—not just for writers and editors—but also chambers of commerce and business groups in which you are likely to meet potential contacts.

ROBIN GEE *is former editor of* Novel & Short Story Writer's Market *and is currently a freelance writer and editor in Madison, Wisconsin.*

"At least 25 percent of my new business comes from networking," says Colorado-based freelancer Carole Williams, who went from a full-time career as the director of information for a nonprofit organization to freelancing. Williams is a member of the National Writers Association, her local Chamber of Commerce, the Denver Women's Press Club and the Colorado Independent Publishers Association, where she meets many self-publishers looking for help with promotion.

"I've also received many wonderful referrals from graphic designers and other writers," she says. In fact, she and other writers sometimes subcontract work on large jobs to each other. "In this business it's better to be open to working with and referring others rather than to be highly competitive."

SETTING YOUR FEES

Take what you've learned from others in the field and the ranges provided here as starting points for establishing your own fees. You must also assess how much your particular client is willing or able to pay. In general, working in advertising or for businesses pays better than writing for magazines or editing books. Yet many freelancers prefer to work in the publishing industry because it can be steady and interesting. If, after you've studied the market, you are still unsure about a particular client, try to find out what the budget is for a project and work from there.

Location used to play a larger part in influencing fees. Although East and West Coast clients still tend to pay more, the rest of the country is catching up. Thanks to fax machines, e-mail and other technology, where you live is less important for many businesses. You may live in the South or Midwest and end up working for an East Coast publisher accustomed to paying higher rates. On the other hand, living near a small business or publisher may give you the edge and create a steady income even though your clients may not pay as much as those far away.

While you can quote flat fees for various projects, experienced freelancers say the best way to start out is to charge hourly rates until you are certain how long a particular type of job should take. Still, there are surprises. Before taking on any new project, it's best to take a good look at it first. Ask if you can do a sample—a few pages—so you and the client can be certain you understand exactly what the job entails, and you can get a feel for how long it is likely to take.

One way to determine an hourly fee is to determine how much a company might pay per hour for someone on staff to do the same job. If, for example, you think a client would have to pay a staff person $26,000/year, divide that by 2,000 (approximately 40 hours a week for 50 weeks) and you would get $13/hour.

Next, add another 33 percent to cover the cost of fringe benefits that an employer would normally pay in Social Security, unemployment insurance, hospitalization, retirement funds, etc. This figure varies from employer to employer but the U.S. Chamber of Commerce reports that the U.S. average paid by employers is 37.6 percent of an employee's salary.

Then add a dollars-per-hour figure to cover your actual overhead expenses for office space, equipment, supplies plus time spent for professional meetings, research and soliciting new business. (To get this figure, add one year's expenses and divide by the number of hours per year you have been freelancing.) In the beginning (when you have large investments such as a computer) you may have to adjust this amount to avoid pricing yourself out of the market. Finally, you may wish to figure in a profit percentage to be useful for capital investments or future growth.

It's useful to take this figure and compare it to the ranges provided here or those suggested by the different freelance organizations. Many freelancers temper the figure from the above formula with what they've learned from suggested ranges and networking. Keep in mind, too, that few full-time freelancers bill 2,000 hours per year. Most who consider themselves full-time bill about half that many hours. Some freelancers start with the amount they'd like to make in a year and work down to determine how many projects they need to do and what rate to charge.

Here's an example:

$26,000 (salary) ÷ 2,000 (hours) = $13.00 per hour
+ 4.29 (33% to cover fringe benefits, taxes, etc.)
+ 2.50 (overhead based on annual expenses of $5,000)
+ 1.30 (10% profit margin)
$21.09 per hour charge

No matter how you determine your fees initially, you will need to consider your experience, your client's budget and the current market value of your service.

Once you and your client have come to an agreement on how much to charge and the details of your assignment, make sure you follow up with a written contract or letter of agreement signed by both parties outlining exactly what is to be done. Experienced freelancers say this is the best way to avoid misunderstandings down the line. If there is any question about how long a job should take, be sure the agreement indicates that you are estimating the time and that your project fee is based on a certain number of hours. If you quote a flat fee, you should stipulate in the agreement that a higher rate might be charged for overtime hours or late changes in the project.

Communication is important in dealing with clients. Make sure they know right away if you find the project is more complex and will take more time than you anticipated. Leave yourself open to renegotiation and, again, be sure to put any renegotiated fees in writing. On big jobs, some freelancers ask for partial payment at different stages of the project.

Freelancers who deal with businesses (especially those working in public relations and advertising) are careful to outline additional expenses that might be charged. Some figure this into their flat fees, but if you require reimbursement for extensive photocopying, postage, gas mileage, etc., it's best to make sure your client knows upfront and that you get it in writing that these expenses will be paid. The bottom line: clear communication and mutual respect between you and your client is an important factor in building your credibility and your business.

FREELANCE TRENDS

"How Much Should I Charge?" has become a regular feature in this book and you will notice we've streamlined and reorganized some of the categories to better reflect changes in the field. We've noticed a few trends worth mentioning, too. Several freelance writers and editors have come to think of themselves as consultants. Writing consultants used to deal mostly with training others to improve their writing and editing skills. This is still a primary focus of many consultants, but others have added editing, manuscript evaluation and various writing projects to their list of services. In fact, the Professional Writing Consultants organization recently changed its name to the Association of Professional Communications Consultants to better reflect the growing diversity in their field.

Consultant Dan Dieterich says consulting is well suited to writers or editors who are comfortable working in front of a group and who enjoy teaching others how to improve their writing skills. Some beginning consultants fear selling themselves as trainers. Yet, he says, keep in mind that if you develop a good program you will be benefiting a large group of people as well as yourself.

"Many consultants get into the business through academia, a place where we teach for the love of learning, so we tend to undercharge for our services. Good communication skills can make the difference between success and failure in business and many organizations are willing to pay for help in these areas accordingly," he says. Deiterich has done a variety of work for various businesses including business communication development and proposal evaluation, but he enjoys teaching others best. Some of the training he's done includes helping school teachers eliminate sexist language from their communications, business people assess their needs in order to write better proposals, and businesses develop their own inhouse training programs.

Another growing area is technical writing. Ever since computers became commonplace there has been a need for writers and editors who can help develop clear training manuals and documentation, but the World Wide Web and an explosion in software has added even more opportunities for those with computer savvy. Indexing skills are needed for computer database archiving, and editors or writers who can identify key words and write clearly may find a number of projects developing online help programs for various software.

Writers and designers are needed for webpage development and editing for almost every type of business. Since this is such a new area, we took the average rate range, but have heard of freelancers receiving everything from $10-12/hour for a small organization's webpage to charging more than $10,000 for a large corporate site.

This type of work, however, usually requires expertise in writing in the HTML computer language and jobs often include graphic-design skills. Training in this area is becoming more available. Kurt Foss, professor of journalism at the University of Wisconsin, teaches a multimedia publishing course designed to prepare students for changes in technology. He says businesses are beginning to understand that they may need to hire writers and designers separately for webpage jobs. Yet, even if design is not included, writers will have to learn new skills to write effectively for webpages and software programs.

"There's a whole new area called multimedia reporting. Writers need to write in a nonlinear fashion," says Foss. People using websites and CD-ROM programs can start at different places and move about at random within the program so writing must be self-contained on each subject. Writers also need to think in terms of a variety of media. When interviewing, Foss thinks of sound clips from his taped interviews and possibilities for visuals.

Even in established areas of freelancing there have been some changes. In the public relations field more and more companies are outsourcing all their PR services. They may hire on an as-needed basis or hire someone who works on a retainer. Many former public relations employees are taking their skills into the freelance marketplace.

Again, keep in mind that reading the ranges in this book or looking at those provided by some of the professional organizations is only a first step in determining how much you should charge. Networking and studying the ever-changing market will help you remain competitive and motivated.

ADVERTISING, COPYWRITING & PR

Advertising copywriting: $35-100/hour; $250 and up per day; $500 and up per week; $1,000-$2,000 as a monthly retainer. Flat-fee-per-ad rates could range from $100 and up per page depending on the size and kind of client. In Canada rates range from $40-80/hour.

Advertorials: $25-35/hour; up to $1/word or by flat fee ($300 for about 700 words is typical). In Canada, 40-80¢/word; $35-75/hour.

Book jacket copywriting: $100-600 for front cover jacket plus flaps and back jacket copy summarizing content and tone of the book.

Catalog copywriting: $25-$45/hour or $85 and up per project.

Copyediting for advertising: $25-35/hour.

Direct-mail copywriting: $25-45/hour; $75 and up per item or $60-1,000/page.

Direct-mail packages: This includes copywriting direct mail letter, response card and advertising materials. Up to $85/hour or $500-3,000/project, depending on complexity of the project. Additional charges for production such as desktop publishing, addressing, etc.

Direct mail response card for a product: $250-500/project.

Fundraising campaign brochure: $50-75 for research (20 hours) and copywriting (30 hours);

up to $5,000 for major campaign brochure, including research, writing and production (about 50 hours of work).

New product release: $20-35/hour or $300-500/release.

News release: *See Press release.*

Political campaigns, public relations: Small town or state campaigns, $10-50/hour; congressional, gubernatorial or other national campaigns, $25-100/hour or up to 10 percent of campaign budget.

Promotion for events: $20-30/hour. For conventions and longer events, payment may be per diem or a flat fee of $500-2,500. *See also Press release.*

Press kits: $500-3,000/project.

Press release: $20-30/hour or $200-500/release.

Print advertisement: $200-500/project. In Canada, $100-200/concept. *See also Advertising copywriting*

Product information: $30-60/hour; $400-500/day or $100-300/page. *See also Sales and services brochures and fliers for smaller projects.*

Promotion for tourism, museums, art shows, etc.: $20-$50 and up per hour for writing or editing promotion copy. Additional charges for production, mailings, etc.

Public relations for businesses: $250-600/day plus expenses average—more for large corporations.

Public relations for government: $25-50/hour or a monthly retainer based on number of hours per period. Lower fees for local government agencies, higher for state-level and above.

Public relations for organizations or nonprofits: $15-35/hour. If working on a monthly retainer, $100-500/month.

Public relations for schools or libraries: $15-20/hour for small districts or libraries; up to $35 for larger districts.

Radio advertisement: $50-100/script; $200-400/week for part-time positions writing radio ads, depending on the size of the city (and market).

Sales and services brochures and fliers: $20-$600/published page or from $100 to $7,500/project depending on size and type of business (small nonprofit organization to a large corporation) and on the number of pages (usually from 1-16) and complexity of the job.

Sales letters: $350-1,000 for 1-2 pages.

Speech editing or evaluation: $20/hour and up.

Speechwriting (general): $30-85/hour. In Canada, $75-125/hour or $70-100/minute of speech.

Speechwriting for business owners or executives: Up to $80/hour or a flat fee of about $100 for a short (6- or 7- minute speech); $500-3,000 for up to 30 minutes. Rates also depend on size of the company and the event.

Speechwriting for government officials: $4,000 for 20 minutes plus up to $1,000 for travel and expenses.

Speechwriting for political candidates: $250 and up for local candidates (about 15 minutes); $375-800 for statewide candidates and $1,000 or more for national congressional candidates.

TV commercial: $60-375/finished minute; $1,000-2,000/finished project. In Canada, $60-130/minute of script (CBC pays Writers Guild rates, CTV pays close to that and others pay less. For example, TV Ontario pays $70-100/script minute).

AUDIOVISUALS & ELECTRONIC COMMUNICATIONS

Audiocassette scripts: $10-50/scripted minute, assuming written from existing client materials, with no additional research or meetings; otherwise $75-100/minute, $750 minimum.

Audiovisuals: For writing, $250-350/requested scripted minute; includes rough draft, editing conference with client, and final shooting script. For consulting, research, producing, directing, soundtrack oversight, etc. $400-600/day plus travel and expenses. Writing fee is sometimes 10% of gross production price as billed to client. Some charge flat fee of $1,500-2,100/package.

Book summaries for film producers: $50-100/book. *Note: You must live in the area where the business is located to get this kind of work.*

Business film scripts (training and information): $200-250/day.

Copyediting audiovisuals: $20-25/hour.

Industrial product film: $125-150/minute; $500 minimum flat fee.

Novel synopsis for film producer: $150 for 5-10 pages typed, single spaced.

Radio continuity writing: $5/page to $150/week, part-time. In Canada, $40-80/minute of script; $640/show for a multi-part series.

Radio copywriting: *See Advertising, Copywriting & PR.*

Radio documentaries: $258 for 60 minutes, local station.

Radio editorials: $10-30 for 90-second to two-minute spots.

Radio interviews: For National Public Radio, up to 3 minutes, $25; 3-10 minutes, $40-75; 10-60 minutes, $125 to negotiable fees. Small radio stations would pay approximately 50% of the NPR rate; large stations, double the NPR rate.

Script synopsis for business: $40/hour.

Script synopsis for agent or film producer: $75 for 2-3 typed pages, single-spaced.

Scripts for nontheatrical films for education, business, industry: Prices vary among producers, clients, and sponsors and there is no standardization of rates in the field. Fees include $75-120/minute for one reel (10 minutes) and corresponding increases with each successive reel; approximately 10% of the production cost of films that cost the producer more than $1,500/release minute.

Screenwriting: $6,000 and up per project.

Slide presentation: Including visual formats plus audio, $150-600 for 10-15 minutes.

Slide/single image photos: $75 flat fee.

Slide/tape script: $75-100/minute, $750 minimum.

TV commercial: *See Advertising, Copywriting & PR.*

TV documentary: 30-minute 5-6 page proposal outline, $1,839 and up; 15-17 page treatment, $1,839 and up; less in smaller cities. In Canada research for a documentary runs about $6,500.

TV editorials: $35 and up for 1-minute, 45 seconds (250-300 words).

TV filmed news and features: From $10-20/clip for 30-second spot; $15-25 for 60-second clip; more for special events.

TV information scripts: Short 5- to 10-minute scripts for local cable TV stations, $10-15/hour.

TV news film still photo: $3-6 flat fee.

TV news story: $16-25 flat fee.

TV, national and local public stations: For programs, $35-100/minute down to a flat fee of $5,000 and up for a 30- to 60-minute script.

TV scripts: (Teleplay only), 60 minutes; network prime time, Writers Guild rates: $14,048; 30 minutes, $10,414. In Canada, $60-130/minute of script.

BOOK PUBLISHING

Abstracting and abridging: Up to $75/hour for nonfiction; $30-35/hour for reference and professional journals.

Anthology editing: Variable advance plus 3-15 percent of royalties. Advance should cover reprint fees or fees are handled by the publisher. Flat-fee-per-manuscript rates range from $500-5,000 and up.

Book proposal consultation: $20-75/hour or a flat rate of $100-250.

Book proposal writing: Up to $150/page or a flat rate of $175-3,000 depending on length and whether the client provides full information or the writer must do research, and whether a sample chapter is required.

Book query critique: $50 for critique of letter to the publisher and outline.

Book summaries for book clubs: $50-100/book.

Content editing: $20-50/hour or $600-5,000/manuscript, based on the size and complexity of the project.

Copyediting: $16-40/hour or $2-4/page. Lower-end rates charged for light copyedit (3-10 pages per hour) of general, trade material. Higher-end rates charged for substantive copyediting or for textbooks and technical material (2-5 pages per hour).

Ghostwriting, as told to: This is writing for a celebrity or expert either for a self-published book or for a publisher. Author gets full advance plus 50 percent of royalties. Hourly rates for subjects who are self-publishing are $25-80/hour. In Canada, author also gets full advance and 50 percent of royalties or $10,000-20,000 flat fee per project. Research time is charged extra.

Ghostwriting, no credit: Projects may include writing for an individual planning to self publish or for a book packager, book producer, publisher, agent or corporation. Rates range from $5,000-35,000 and up (plus expenses) per project; packagers pay flat fee or combination of advance plus royalties. For self-published clients, ask for one-fourth down payment, one-fourth when book is half-finished, one-fourth at the three-quarters mark and one-fourth upon completion.

Indexing: $20-40/hour; charge higher hourly rate if using a computer index program that takes fewer hours. Also can charge $2-6/indexable page; 40-70 cents per line of index or a flat fee of $250-500 depending on length.

Jacket copywriting: *See Advertising, Copywriting & PR.*

Manuscript evaluation and critique: $150-200 for outline and first 20,000 words; $300-500 for up to 100,000 words. Also $15-35/hour for trade books, slightly less for nonprofits. Page rates run from $1.50-2.50/page.

Movie novelization: $3,500-15,000, depending on writer's reputation, amount of work to be done and amount of time writer is given.

Novel synopsis for a literary agent: $150 for 5-10 pages typed, single-spaced.

Page layout (desktop publishing): $20-35/hour or $5-15/page. Higher per page rates may be charged if material involves complex technical material and graphics.

Production editing/project management: This is overseeing the production of a project, coordinating editing and production stages, etc. $25-50/hour.

Proofreading: $12-30/hour or $1.50-3.50/page. High-end rates are charged for technical, scientific and reference material.

Research for writers or book publishers: $20-40/hour and up; $150 and up per day plus expenses. A flat rate of $300-500 may be charged, depending on complexity of the job.

Rewriting: $18-50/hour; $5-7/page. Some writers receive royalties on book projects.

Translation (literary): $30-35/hour; also $95-125 per 1,000 English words.

Typesetting: $20-35/hour or $4-7/page.

BUSINESS

Annual reports: A brief report with some economic information and an explanation of figures, $25-60/hour; 12- to 16-page report, $600-1,500 flat fees for editing. If extensive research and/or writing is involved in a large project, rates could go as high as $5,000-10,000/project. A report that must meet Securities and Exchange Commission (SEC) standards and reports requiring legal language could bill $40-85/hour. Bill separately if desktop publication (typesetting, page layout, etc.) is involved (some smaller firms and nonprofits may ask for writing/production packages).

Associations and organizations (writing for): $15-25/hour for small organizations; up to $50/hour for larger associations or a flat fee depending on the length and complexity of the project.

For example, $500-1,000 for association magazine article (2,000 words) or $1,000-1,800 for a 10-page informational booklet.

Audiovisuals/audiocassette scripts: *See Audiovisuals & Electronic Communications.*

Book summaries for businesses: $25-50/page or $20-35/hour.

Brochures, fliers, booklets for business: $25-40/hour for writing or from $500-$4,000 and up per project (12-16 pages and more). Additional charges for desktop publishing, usually $20-40/hour; $20-30/page or a flat fee per project. *See also Copyediting for business or Manuscript editing/evaluation for business in this section.*

Business editing (general): $25-50/hour.

Business letters: For letters such as form letters designed to improve customer relations or interoffice communications, $100-500/letter depending on the size of the business and the length/complexity of the material.

Business plan: $1/word; $200/manuscript page or up to $1,500/project. High-end rates are charged if extensive research is involved. Sometimes research is charged separately per hour or per day.

Business writing (general): $30-80/hour. In Canada, $1-2/word or $50-100/hour. *See other entries in this section and in Advertising, Copywriting & PR for specific projects such as brochures, copywriting, speechwriting, brochures or business letters. For business film scriptwriting see Audiovisuals & Electronic Communications.*

Business writing seminars: $500 for a half-day seminar, plus travel expenses or $1,000-5,000/day. Rates depend on number of participants as well as duration. Average per-person rate is $50/person for a half-day seminar. *See also Educational and Literary Services.*

Catalogs for business: $25-40/hour or $25-600/printed page; more if tables or charts must be reworked for readability or consistency. Additional charges for desktop publishing ($20-40/hour is average).

Collateral materials for business: *See individual pieces (brochures, catalogs, etc.) in this section and in Advertising, Copywriting & PR.*

Commercial reports for business, insurance companies, credit agencies: $6-15/page.

Consultation on communications: $300-2,000/day. Lower-end fees charged to nonprofits and small businesses.

Consumer complaint letters (answering): $25-30/letter.

Copyediting for business: $20-40/hour or $20-50/manuscript page, up to $40/hour for business proposals. Charge lower-end fees ($15-25/hour) to nonprofits and very small businesses.

Corporate histories: $1,000-2,000 flat fee.

Corporate periodicals, editing: $30-75/hour.

Corporate periodicals, writing: $30-100/hour, depending on size and nature of the corporation. Also 50¢ to $1/word. In Canada, $1-2/word or $40-90/hour.

Corporate profile: $1,250-2,500 flat fee for up to 3,000 words or charge on a per word basis, up to $1/word.

Financial presentation: $1,500-4,500 for a 20-30 minute presentation.

Fundraising campaign brochure: *See Advertising, Copywriting & PR.*

Ghostwriting for business (usually trade magazine articles or business columns): $25-100/hour; $200 or more per day plus expenses (depending on amount of research involved, length of project).

Government research: $35-50/hour.

Government writing: $30-50/hour. In Canada, $50-80/hour.

Grant proposal writing for nonprofits: $30-100/hour or flat fee.

Indexing for professional journals: $20-40/hour.

Industrial/service business training manual: $25-40/hour; $50-100/manuscript page or a flat fee, $1,000-4,000, depending on number of pages and complexity of the job.

Industry training film scripts: *See Business film scripts in Audiovisuals & Electronic Communications.*
Industrial product film script: *See Audiovisuals & Electronic Communications.*
Job application letters: $20-40/letter.
Manuals/documentation: $25-60/hour. *See also Computers, Science and Technical Writing.*
Manuscript editing/evaluation for trade journals: $20-40/hour.
Market research survey reports: $25-50/hour or $500-1,500/day; also flat rates of $500-2,000/project.
Newsletters, abstracting: $30/hour.
Newsletters, desktop publishing/production: $20-60/hour. Higher-end rates for scanning photographs, advertising layout, illustration or design. Editing charged extra.
Newsletters, editing: $25-45/hour; $50-500/issue. Higher-end fees charged if writing or production is included. Editors who produce a regular newsletter on a monthly or quarterly basis tend to charge per month or per issue—and find them easier to do after initial set up.
Newsletters, writing: $25-45/hour; 25¢ to $1/word; $25-300/page; $35-2,500/story or $375-2,500/issue. In Canada, $45-70/hour.
Programmed instruction consultation fees: *See Educational & Literary Services.*
Programmed instruction materials for business: *See Educational & Literary Services.*
Proofreading for business: $15-50/hour; low-end fees for nonprofits.
Public relations: *See Advertising, Copywriting and PR.*
Retail newsletters for customers: Charge regular newsletter rates or $175-300 per 4-page project. Additional charges for desktop publishing.
Sales brochures, fliers, letters, other advertising materials: *See Advertising, Copywriting & PR.*
Scripts for business/training films: *See Audiovisuals & Electronic Communications.*
Translation, commercial: $30-45/hour; $115-125 per 1,000 words. Higher-end fees for non-European languages into English.
Translation for government agencies: $30-45; up to $125 per 1,000 words. Higher-end fees for non-European languages into English.
Translation through translation agencies: Agencies by 33⅓ percent average less than end-user clients and mark up translator's prices by as much as 100 percent or more.
Translation, technical: $30-45/hour; $125 and up per 1,000 words, depending on complexity of the material.

COMPUTER, SCIENTIFIC & TECHNICAL

Computer documentation, general (hard copy): $30-75/hour; $20-30/page. *See also Software manual writing in this section.*
Computer documentation (online): $30-35/hour; $15-25/screen.
Demonstration software: $70 and up per hour.
Legal/government editing: $20-65/hour.
Legal/government writing: $30-65/hour.
Medical and science editing: $20-65/hour, depending on the complexity of the material and the expertise of the editor.
Medical and science proofreading: $15-30/hour.
Medical and science writing: $30-65/hour; $20-30/page, depending on the complexity of the project and the writer's expertise.
Online editing: $30-35/hour.
Software manual writing: $35-50/hour for research and writing.
Technical editing: $20-60/hour or $150-1,000/day.
Technical typesetting: $4-7/page; $25-35/hour; more for inputting of complex material.

Technical writing: $30-75/hour; $20-30/page. *See Computer documentation and Software manual writing in this section.*
Technical translation: *See item in Business section.*
Webpage design: $50-100/page.
Webpage editing: $30/page and up.

EDITORIAL/DESIGN PACKAGES

Business catalogs: *See Business.*
Desktop publishing: For 1,000 dots-per-inch type, $5-15/camera-ready page of straight type; $30/camera-ready page with illustrations, maps, tables, charts, photos; $100-150/camera-ready page for oversize pages with art. Also $20-40/hour depending on graphics, number of photos, and amount of copy to be typeset. Packages often include writing, layout/design, and typesetting services.
Greeting cards ideas (with art included): Anywhere from $30-300, depending on size of company.
Newsletters: *See Desktop Publishing (this section) and Newsletters (Business).*
Picture editing: $20-40.
Photo brochures: $700-15,000 flat fee for photos and writing.
Photo research: $15-30/hour.
Photography: $10-150/b&w photo; $25-300/color photo; also $800/day.

EDUCATIONAL & LITERARY SERVICES

Business writing seminars: *See Business.*
Consultation for individuals (in business): $250-1,000/day.
Consultation on communications: *See Business.*
Developing and designing courses for business or adult education: $250-$1,500/day or flat fee.
Editing for individual clients: $10-50/hour or $2-7/page.
Educational consulting and educational grant and proposal writing: $250-750/day or $30-75/hour.
Lectures at national conventions by well-known authors: $2,500-20,000 and up, plus expenses; less for panel discussions.
Lectures at regional writers' conferences: $300 and up, plus expenses.
Lectures to local groups, librarians or teachers: $50-150.
Lectures to school classes: $25-75; $150/day; $250/day if farther than 100 miles.
Manuscript evaluation for theses/dissertations: $15-30/hour.
Poetry manuscript critique: $25 per 16-line poem.
Programmed instruction consultant fees: $300-1,000/day, $50-75/hour.
Programmed instruction materials for business: $50/hour for inhouse writing and editing; $500-1,000/day plus expenses for outside research and writing. Alternate method: $2,000-5,000/hour of programmed training provided depending on technicality of subject.
Public relations for schools: *See Advertising, Copywriting & PR.*
Readings by poets, fiction writers: $25-600 depending on author.
Scripts for nontheatrical films for education: *See Audiovisuals & Electronic Communications.*
Short story manuscript critique: 3,000 words, $40-60.
Teaching adult education course: $10-60/class hour; fee usually set by school, not negotiated by teachers.
Teaching adult seminar: $400 plus mileage and per diem for a 6- or 7-hour day; plus 40% of the tuition fee beyond the sponsor's break-even point. In Canada, $35-50/hour.
Teaching business writing to company employees: *See Consultation on communications in Business section.*

Teaching college course or seminar: $15-70/class hour.

Teaching creative writing in school: $15-70/hour of instruction, or $1,500-2,000 per 12-15 week semester; less in recessionary times.

Teaching elementary and middle school teachers how to teach writing to students: $75-150 for a 1- to 1½ hour session.

Teaching home-bound students: $5-15/hour.

Tutoring: $25 per 1- to 1½ hour private session.

TV instruction taping: $150 per 30-minute tape; $25 residual each time tape is sold.

Writer-in-schools: Arts council program, $130/day; $650/week. Personal charges plus expenses vary from $25/day to $100/hour depending on school's ability to pay.

Writer's workshop: Lecturing and seminar conducting, $50-150/hour to $750/day plus expenses; local classes, $35-50/student for 10 sessions.

Writing for individual clients: $25-100/hour, depending on the situation. *See also Business writing in Business section.*

Writing for scholarly journals: $75/hour.

MAGAZINES & TRADE JOURNALS

Abstracting: $20-30/hour for trade and professional journals; $8 per abstract for scholarly journals.

Article manuscript critique: 3,000 words, $40.

Arts reviewing: $35-100 flat fee or 20-30¢/word, plus admission to events or copy of CD (for music).

Book reviews: $50-300 flat fee and copy of book.

Consultation on magazine editorial: $1,000-1,500/day plus expenses.

Copyediting magazines: $16-30/hour.

Editing: General, $25-500/day or $250-2,000/issue; Religious publications, $200-500/month or $15-30/hour.

Fact checking: $17-25/hour or 75¢ to $1/item.

Feature articles: Anywhere from 20¢ to $4/word; or $200-2,000 per 2,000 word article, depending on size (circulation) and reputation of magazine.

Ghostwriting articles (general): Up to $2/word; or $300-3,000/project.

Indexing: $15-40/hour.

Magazine, city, calendar of events column: $50-150/column.

Magazine column: 200 words, $40; 800 words, $400. Also $1/word. Larger circulation publications pay fees related to their regular word rate.

Manuscript consultation: $25-50/hour.

Manuscript criticism: $40-60 per article or short story of up to 3,000 words. Also $20-25/hour.

Picture editing: *See Editorial/Design Packages.*

Permission fees to publishers to reprint article or story: $75-500; 10-15¢/word; less for charitable organizations.

Production editing: $15-30/hour.

Proofreading: $12-25/hour.

Research: $20-25/hour.

Rewriting: Up to $80/manuscript page; also $100/published page.

Science writing for magazines: $2,000-5,000/article. *See also Computer, Scientific & Technical Writing.*

Special news article: For a business's submission to trade publication, $250-500 for 1,000 words. In Canada, 25-45¢/word.

Stringing: 20¢ to $1/word based on circulation. Daily rate: $150-250 plus expenses; weekly rate: $900 plus expenses. Also $10-35/hour plus expenses; $1/column inch.

Trade journal ad copywriting: *See Advertising, Copywriting & PR.*

Trade journal feature article: For business client, $400-1,000. Also $1-2/word.

NEWSPAPERS

Ads for small business: $25 for a small, one-column ad, or $10/hour and up. *See also Advertising, Copywriting & PR.*

Arts reviewing: For weekly newspapers, $15-35 flat fee; for dailies, $45 and up; for Sunday supplements, $100-400. Also admission to event or copy of CD (for music).

Book reviews: For small newspapers, byline and the book only; for larger publications, $35-200. Also copy of the book.

Column, local: $10-20 for a weekly; $15-30 for dailies of 4,000-6,000 circulation; $35-50 for 7,000-10,000 dailies; $40-75 for 11,000-25,000 dailies; and $100 and up for larger dailies. Also 15-80¢/word depending on circulation.

Copyediting: $10-30/hour; up to $40/hour for large daily paper.

Copywriting: *See Advertising, Copywriting & PR.*

Dance criticism: $25-400/article.

Drama criticism: Local, newspaper rates; non-local, $50 and up per review.

Editing/manuscript evaluation: $25/hour.

Fact checking: *See Magazines & Trade Journals.*

Feature: $25-35/article plus mileage for a weekly; $40-500 for a daily (depending on size of paper). Also 10-30¢/word. In Canada $15-40/word, but rates vary widely.

Obituary copy: Where local newspapers permit lengthier than normal notices paid for by the funeral home (and charged to the family), $15-25. Writers are engaged by funeral homes.

Picture editing: *See Editorial/Design Packages.*

Proofreading: $16-20/hour.

Science writing for newspapers: *See Computer, Scientific & Technical Writing.*

Stringing: Sometimes flat rate of $20-35 to cover meeting and write article; sometimes additional mileage payment.

Syndicted column, self-promoted: $5-10 each for weeklies; $10-25/week for dailies, based on circulation.

MISCELLANEOUS

Comedy writing for night club entertainers: Gags only, $5-25 each. Routines, $100-1,000 per minute. Some new comics may try to get a 5-minute routine for $150; others will pay $2,500 for a 5-minute bit from a top writer.

Comics writing: $35-50/page and up for established comics writers.

Contest judging: Short manuscripts, $10/entry; with one-page critique, $15-25. Overall contest judging: $100-500.

Corporate comedy skits: $300-800 for half-hour skit (used at meetings, conventions).

Craft ideas with instructions: $50-200/project.

Encyclopedia articles: Entries in some reference books, such as biographical encyclopedias, 500-2,000 words; pay ranges from $60-80 per 1,000 words. Specialists' fees vary.

Family histories: Fees depend on whether the writer edits already prepared notes or does extensive research and writing; and the length of the work, $500-15,000.

Institutional (church, school) history: $200-1,000 for 15-50 pages, or $20-35/hour.

Manuscript typing: Depending on manuscript length and delivery schedule, $1.25-2/page with one copy; $15/hour.

Party toasts, limericks, place card verses: $1.50/line.

Research for individuals: $5-30/hour, depending on experience, geographic area and nature of work.

Special occasion booklet: Family keepsake of a wedding, anniversary, Bar Mitzvah, etc., $120 and up.

Double Threat: Make More Money with Photographs

BY ABIGAIL SEYMOUR

"Normally we wouldn't buy a story like this, but we like your photographs, so we'll assign it to you. How about 1,500 words?" So read my golden first acceptance letter from a magazine, which I held with trembling hands after ripping open the envelope and scanning it for that dreaded word, "unfortunately" which, fortunately, I didn't find.

For that first story, a profile of a Spanish painter at work in his studio, I was paid $200 for the text—and $300 each for four black and white photographs.

It wasn't my writing that got me started as a writer, but my photographs, and I learned that not only can taking pictures be a profitable sideline to freelance writing, but it can be the deciding factor in whether an editor will hire you to do the story. With very little expense you can add a nice accessory to your writer's toolbox, one that can double or even triple your income—and turn an unsold story into a clip.

BUT FIRST, THE TOOLS

I once heard that being an actor is easy, as long as you stick to three rules: "Talk loud enough so they can hear you, stand where the light is, and don't knock the stuff over." Taking photographs is really not much different: Take the lens cap off before you press the button, point the viewfinder at what you want to shoot, and don't jiggle around too much. Fine-tuning those rules is easier than most people think

Most modern point and shoot cameras come with fully automated focus and exposure, so even the most novice photographer can produce quality images. The least expensive point and shoot cameras (called SLR, for Single Lens Reflex) sell for about $100 and are completely idiot-proof, excellent for beginners. The primary danger with fully automatic cameras is that they focus on what is in the dead center of the viewfinder, and this can limit your composition or allow you to accidentally focus on something other than your subject. So if you're not careful you might end up with a perfectly focused elbow but a blurry face.

You can, however, avoid this catastophe if, once you focus on your subject, you then hold the shutter-release button down halfway and move the camera to recompose the shot. This will lock the focus on your subject.

If you really want to add photography to your repertoire, it's worth the investment to move up into the mid-range, where you have the option of manual settings (flash, focus, exposure and shutter speed can all be turned off for more control) and automatic features (auto focus, auto flash, auto aperature and shutter speed control). You can get one of these cameras for about $400-700. At the highest end of the price spectrum, cameras go for about $3,000, not including the lens, which will run another $700-800. For the purposes of supplementing writer's income and not launching a full-time career in photography, however, my suggestion would be to spend

---

ABIGAIL SEYMOUR *is the associate editor of* Attaché, *the inflight magazine for US Airways. After earning a degree from New York University in Photography, she worked as a freelance writer and photographer in Spain for three years. Her articles and photographs have appeared in numerous publications, including* US Air Magazine, Hope, Attaché, *and* Variety.

such money elsewhere. You can also buy digital cameras from $300-1,000, but the resolution is not yet perfected; you typically get a better digital photo by actually using a regular, nondigital camera and then scanning the slide or print.

Assuming you're not using a digital camera, film is your second-most important piece of equipment. Slide film is best because it keeps longer, and you can go from color to black and white but not the other way around when reproducing the image, which is why most editors prefer you to submit slides. The film I prefer is Fujichrome 100, which is full of very rich blues and greens, and also works well for bright daylight settings. If you do decide to use black and white film, I suggest Kodak T-Max 400 or Kodak Tri-X Pan 400.

A local commercial lab will probably take good care of your images, but since quality and color balance varies greatly from lab to lab, you should run some test prints to find the lab most suitable for your purposes. Of course, professional private labs do great work, too, but they're processing charges can be quite expensive.

SHOOT THE WAY YOU WRITE

Who knows which images will best illustrate your story better than the person who wrote it—you? You actually have a great advantage over a photographer hired separately who has scant information on the story. Use your strengths as a writer—paying attention, finding the essence of the story, connecting with your subject—to make your photographs as strong as your words. The photograph happens in your mind and not in the camera, so think in advance about what you envision the final image will look like and how it will complement your article.

If you're interviewing someone and need a portrait, conduct the interview first, then shoot the photos. Be sure the interview is over and that you've established a rapport with your subject, because nothing makes for a better photo shoot than a connection and trust between the photographer and the subject. I find my best shots, like the best answers to questions, come at the end of the session, when we're officially "done" and the subject (and the photographer) is more relaxed. "Just one more" might be the publishable image, so it's worth it to ask for it.

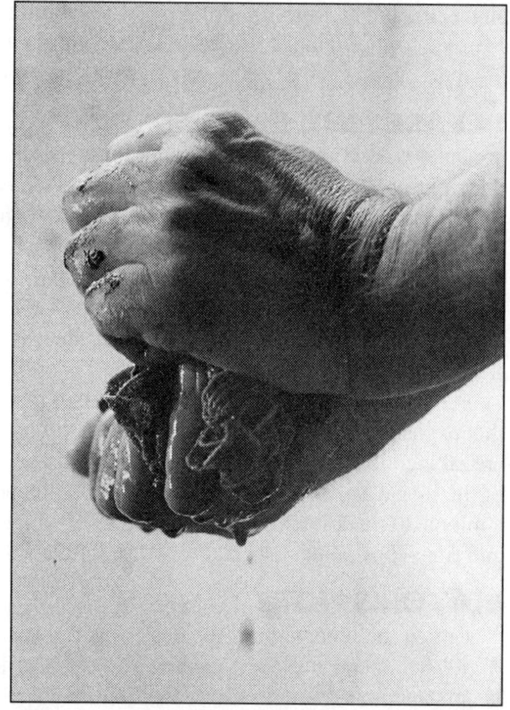

Interesting photographs that capture the essence of your subject can help sell your articles to editors. This sensitive close-up of an artist's hands wringing a paint-soaked rag, along with three other photos, convinced a reluctant editor to run a profile—and earned an extra $1,200.

MANY SHOTS WILL BE PORTRAITS

The most important thing about taking portraits is to shoot them in natural light, either near a window or outdoors in the shade. There is a famous portraitist in London who was once asked how she did her luminous photographs. "Simple," she replied. "I just sit them in front of a dark background and open the aperture all the way up." I couldn't get consistent quality with my portraits until I took her advice, and now I swear by it. A dark background makes skin look supple and tends to forgive blemishes, splotchy skin, and even erases bags under eyes. I always shoot in indirect light, and avoid harsh sunlight on faces, which tends to make us all look haggard and tired.

After you find a suitable light source, it's time to find a pose that best conveys the mood of the piece, as well as the character of your subject. Instead of standing directly in front of your subject, which can make her look like she is standing in a police line up, ask her to sit down. Imagine how you would like to be photographed, and then take that picture of someone else. We all want to look as natural and lovely as possible. Try a few with their chins resting on their hands (this tends to make people look instantly like Pulitzer-prize winning authors on a glossy book jacket). Watch out for wrinkled skin when people lean on their hands. It gives a nice angle to the shot and can add character to the composition.

OTHER MENTIONABLES

Now that you're actually taking photos, remember to take three of each shot, "bracketing" each exposure plus one and minus one. This way you're sure to get a usable image. Film is relatively cheap, but going back in a few weeks and reshooting isn't.

It's always courteous to make sure you have the person's name and address, and I send a copy of the best shots as a thank-you. Also, if it's for a news feature and the person is a "man on the street," it's equally nice (not to mention journalistically correct) to get their name and address to send them a copy of the image.

If you're doing a story that requires more informational shots than portraits, try to stay away from shots that don't support the story or are simply factual. The closer you are to whatever you're photographing, the more interesting the images are. When I shot my first pictures of the painter at work in his studio, I made sure to focus on things that expressed the essence of who he is instead of just a wide-angle shot of the studio with him at the easel. The published images included a still life of his brushes in a coffee can; a lily stem in water on his table; his hands squeezing water from a paint-soaked rag, so close up that you could see the veins in his arm. My worst photographs are ones taken when I was too timid to approach a subject or too far away to capture the essence of what was going on.

PLEASE FIND ENCLOSED . . .

Once you've taken your photographs, the way in which you get them packaged and sent to the right publication is as important as the kinds of images you've taken. As you would when pitching an article idea, study the kinds of photographs your target magazines publish. Check for composition, style, captions, color usage, whether or not they tend to use images with people in them, or whether they prefer landscapes, or use horizontals, verticals, etc.

Choose the best of your images, and don't send every shot you took, especially when you have been "bracketing." Send slides in plastic sleeves, and put them between two pieces of cardboard. It's also a good idea to send images via Federal Express so you can have a tracking number.

Put your name and address on the back of the contact sheets or prints. I enclose a caption sheet that explains each image, so the editor doesn't have to do any guessing. Take copious notes as you are taking the photographs to avoid confusion or vagueness later on. I also write down the number of the image as I'm shooting in a reporter's notebook, and as soon as I'm done with the roll I take a minute to mark it with a Sharpie pen as to which assignment it is. Doing it later can be confusing and time-consuming, especially with multiple rolls for several publications.

EDITOR'S NOTE

I'm on the other side of the desk now, as associate editor at U.S. Airways' inflight magazine, *Attaché*. I spend my days reading through the kinds of queries I also send as a writer, and I understand now more than ever the importance of a well-researched and targeted idea. Publishing is more competitive than ever, and we editors are increasingly on the prowl for "double threats"—contributors who deliver a complete package of quality copy *and* quality images. Time, as always, is in short supply. If the bulk of an editor's work can be done before the assignment is made by selecting the writer who can deliver, benefits. In today's market, adding a skill like photography to your list of "can provide" is a wise and profitable move.

Make More Money with Sidebars

BY GORDON BURGETT

Sidebars aren't the meat and potatoes of selling, but tasty side dishes that enhance the overall flavor of the meal and increase its value.

They do deserve special attention, though, particularly if you want to earn a healthy income from writing. You must know how they fit into the larger scheme of selling, when they can make the difference to a sale, and how and when they can or should be offered or provided.

WHEN SHOULD YOU USE SIDEBARS?

Sometimes you need more than a simple, self-contained article to make the sale or to explain the topic fully. Sidebars accompany perhaps a third of the magazine articles sold, so you must know what they are and how they enhance your salability to editors. The good news: They usually earn you more money!

You may hear sidebars referred to as bars or boxes. They're the same thing; secondary information linked to an article and contained in a box or sidebar.

Time and *Newsweek* use them frequently, often shaded a different color to set them off. If the main story is about welfare change, the box will probably contain an in-depth account of how the changes affect one welfare family or a list of changes in the law.

If you're writing about the turnip festival in Tulip, Michigan, your box might be (1) other town activities this year, (2) other points of interest to see within 40 miles of Tulip, (3) a thumbnail history of the town and township, (4) six national figures born in Tulip.

You get the idea: If the main article covers the broad theme (taxation, life on Mars, illegal immigrants), the sidebar zeroes in (a state that lowers taxes annually, how microbes can exist in hostile environments, one family living in three countries). Macro/micro.

Or the reverse: The article is about type B blood and the difficulty of matching donors in Finland, Spain and Bolivia; the box tells how the mutant blood type began and spread. Or the article is a biography of Sandy Koufax; the box tells of Jewish ball players in the major leagues. Micro/macro.

WHICH EDITORS USE SIDEBARS?

Most do, but you must study the publication to see if the one you want to buy your masterpiece is in the majority. Newspaper editors are the most likely buyers, particularly if the box is short and tucks up in an empty hole near the article.

Sidebars create more problems for magazine editors, who are cramped for space. So they are more likely to break the article into components, the body and a box or two (before or after) only if they know in advance the total space needed and why the sidebar adds appreciably to the article's content.

HOW DO YOU SELL SIDEBARS?

You really only have two means to get the additional copy accepted and bought.

The best is probably just to write the box at the same time you write the article, create and print

---

GORDON BURGETT *is the author of* The Travel Writer's Guide, Publishing the Niche Market, How to Sell More Than 75% of Your Writing, *and* Sell & Resell Your Magazine Articles. *He lives in Santa Maria, California.*

up each manuscript separately, and on the top of the sidebar, write in large letters "SIDEBAR" so the editor knows it is supplementary material. Then the editor has four choices: (1) buy the article alone, (2) buy the article and the sidebar, (3) buy only the sidebar or (4) send you packing, sans sale.

You won't sell the article/sidebar package if you don't send in a good sidebar that adds significantly to the original piece. Often enough, an editor will buy an article and not the accompanying sidebar. It's a rare day that an editor buys only a sidebar, although not so rare to kindly refuse the article for some reason but ask you to expand the sidebar into another article with a new slant.

Those are the positives, that sidebars can not only increase your income, sometimes doubling it, but also offer sales opportunities in addition to the main article.

The negative is the loss of time writing sidebars that are unbought.

An example might help clarify the process. Some years back I became interested in gray whales and their near extinction in California, where I had recently moved. In researching the topic, I discovered that one could take a three-hour boat trip from the San Pedro harbor, near Los Angeles, to see the giant critters up close, or as close as they want you to be.

I bobbed and exclaimed in awe with other fair-weather gawkers as the whales appeared, blew mist, breathed and gracefully disappeared. After interviewing the captain and first mate, I found my land legs and spoke to the founder of the Whale Watch program at the nearby Maritime Museum, which had an excellent exhibit about the oldest and largest extant mammals. The result was an article about how one could see gray whales by ship off the southern California coast.

My choice was either to cram another thousand words of details into that magic prose about precisely which cities had wharves housing ships that took the public on such excursions, where the wharves were, the names of the ships, their whale-watching schedules, the costs, phone numbers for amplification and other particulars—or set those aside in a box and let the editors decide if the box, all or part, was wanted for their pages.

As it turned out, six newspaper editors bought the article. All paid extra and bought the sidebar too. More often, a few buy it all but most have room only for the main offering.

Another way to handle this problem is to suggest, in the cover note accompanying the finished manuscript, that you could write a sidebar, then explain what it would say and why it would add significantly to the article. (Savvy editors would ask themselves why, if it's so valuable, you didn't just write and send it.)

There are distinct drawbacks to this method. One, there is too little room as it is in the cover note, and what there is should be used to sell the article itself and to explain the availability of photos. Two, the editors must put the article aside, contact you about the sidebar, wait until it arrives and then pump up their enthusiasm a second time about the article, if they can still find it. The newspaper world spins too quickly for that many variables; too many sales will be lost. Better to take the chance, write a sidebar if it's needed, and get something bought at the first reading.

For magazines, you are far less likely to lose time writing unbought boxes. Mention the possibility of a sidebar in your query letter first, and only if the editor encourages its creation and submission will you invest the extra effort needed.

Thinking about what you can put in a sidebar will also better guide you when you prepare the article itself. With a sidebar you can focus on one aspect of the topic and leave the other details or uncovered critical points to the article. Without it, you must touch every base in the text.

Another cetaceous example, a bit convoluted, shows what I mean. I had just sent a finished manuscript to *Dynamic Years* about "Whale Watching in the United States" when, in an airplane seat next to mine, I met a sea captain who had been contracted to capture the only gray whale in existence, Gigi, kept in San Diego's Sea World. Since he too was captive, I interviewed Frank Mason and asked if he minded if I shared his adventure with the world.

The next morning I called the editor of *Dynamic Years*, explained my good fortune and suggested that the core of the interview might make an interesting sidebar. He agreed. I wrote it up that afternoon, mailed it (during the era when a fax was presumably a female fox), and the article and sidebar suddenly became the lead piece and required a cover photo to match!

The order was reversed—95 percent of the sidebars I've sold to magazines were suggested in the query letter and developed as a result of the editor's interest—but the end result was the same: a better writing product, more complete with more facts, quotes and anecdotes. A subject better developed, balanced between two angles. And a fatter paycheck for not a whole lot more work.

A last point: How and where do you suggest a sidebar in a query letter?

If at all, I like to do it dead last, after I've sold the idea. My last paragraph might read: "If interested, I can also provide a sidebar about Frank Mason, the only sea captain who ever captured a gray whale (Gigi, for San Diego's Sea World). Since you required those interviewed to be 45+, Frank, at 63, is fair game. Just let me know."

If you have two possible sidebars, use the same format: "I can also provide sidebars about (A), with a quick explanation, and/or (B), with an explanation, if interested. Just let me know." Three is too many. One, if too long, is too many. Keep the focus in a query on the primary topic, and only suggest a sidebar if it's an interesting, valuable addition that adds a second dimension.

How much are sidebars worth?

Certainly less than the article itself. Sometimes the editor won't pay a penny extra, thinking that the text is all part of a larger article, however divided. But that's rare.

Newspapers might pay you from $25 to $100 or more. Magazines often increase the pay from 10 to 50 percent depending on the amount of work or research required. The truth is, you are often left to the mercy or charity of the editor.

Often the real payment doesn't became apparent until later. A well-structured article that includes a sidebar, even two, convinces the editor you are the kind of professional who should write often for her pages—main pieces, usually on assignment, travel paid. The payback is delayed but will amount to considerably more over the long run than the few extra bucks earned now from a single sale.

Can sidebars be sold any other way?

Sell your words any way you can. You can break an epic into 100 short poems and sell each to a different editor, if you wish. Sidebars can be sold as add-ons to an article, then rewritten and sold as a short article or a filler to another magazine. If you can find 40 different ways the same facts can be resorted into clearly distinct items, you have 40 different products to sell.

But note the word *rewrite*. You get hopelessly enmeshed in the rights issue unless you change the title, the lead, the conclusion and the order—that is, decidedly reslant each version. Once reslanted, go to it. You may even need a sidebar to go alongside your reformulated sidebar. If so, follow the process above!

Sunset Editors Speak to Writers

BY JOANNE MILLER

"I know freelancing is difficult—I've done it, and it takes a lot of work. Freelancers have to play the odds, but those increase substantially if writers are more aware of the magazine they're pitching to. Know your market, and make your query specific."
—Peter Fish, travel editor

Analyzing the tone, style, editorial content, article type and length, and use of sidebars in a publication is an important part of approaching a potential market. If the publication happens to be *Sunset*, one of America's oldest and liveliest shelter magazines, knowledge is the first step in building relationships with editors and getting assignments. As Senior Food Editor Jerry Anne DiVeccio says, "We give out specific information in a very stylized way."

The magazine's tone is friendly without being folksy. The style is concise and information-packed. The editorial divisions—Travel, Garden, Food, Home/Style (interior decor, home furnishing) and Home/Special Projects (architecture)—are divided into feature articles and shorts. Features may focus on any of the topics above, and are placed among five discrete sections in the magazine; the remainder of each section is filled with short articles. *Sunset*'s sidebars, which accompany both features and shorts, are an art in themselves: the style, content, and length vary with each section and type of article.

Sunset is unusual in two ways: It's a regional publication concentrating on 13 western states and southern British Columbia; and, it's published in five "zones": the Mountain Edition (Montana, Utah, Idaho, Wyoming, Nevada, Colorado); Southwest Edition (Arizona, New Mexico); Southern California (including Hawaii); Northern California; and Northwest Edition (Oregon, Washington, Alaska and southern British Columbia). Each zone receives information specific to the area in addition to all-zone articles. Because of this need for regionality, and a new expansiveness in editorial policy, freelancers now have more opportunity than ever to appear on the pages of this leading publication. *Sunset* is enjoying a circulation of nearly 1.5 million, in addition to its highest newsstand sales in 20 years.

Sunset organization

Though *Sunset* maintains staff in northern and southern California, and Seattle, Washington, the magazine's zoning divisions create a need for freelancers who are familiar with the outlying states. In one editor's opinion, "Freelancers make economic sense—we don't have to maintain a branch office—and they're far more accurate than someone who's just visiting."

Each of *Sunset*'s five editorial sections carry equal weight. All have their own senior editors who not only read and place freelance material but also coordinate in-house and freelance staff to photograph, illustrate and design the concept, look and premise of each issue's stories. The amount of space in the magazine devoted to each section varies with the season. Not all sections are open to freelancers—nearly all Home/Special Projects articles are written inhouse, and many projects are generated by the Western Home Awards, an annual contest for architects. Each issue

---

JOANNE MILLER *has interviewed Isabel Allende and Ron Carlson for* 1997 Novel & Short Story Writer's Market, *and is the author of* Pennsylvania Handbook, *a comprehensive guide to the beauty, history and attractions of the Keystone State.*

has an Events Calendar, Travel Guides section and Gear section that are largely staff-written.

Queries for articles for each section should be sent to the senior editor of that section. If an editor likes the story, it's brought to Editor-in-Chief Rosalie Muller Wright, who makes the final decision and creates the "mix" that makes up each issue. Section editors generally prefer a one-page query with related clips, plus "scouting snapshots." These photos don't have to be of publishable quality but should give an idea of the vista, food item, garden, etc. in the query. Ms. Wright says, "For me, snapshots help to sell the story idea." Articles may be chosen or rejected based on a number of factors, including amount of space and focus of each issue. In the paragraphs that follow, individual editors talk about what they want from freelancers.

THE EDITORS:

Travel, Senior Editor Peter Fish

Travel has traditionally used the largest number of freelancers—largely because *Sunset* zones much of its travel coverage to provide close-to-home travel ideas for each of its five regional editions. What Fish looks for from freelancers is expertise and surprise. "We want to offer our readers a real sense of authority—the sense that we know every corner of the West better than anybody else. We want to tell them things about the West they didn't know before, in prose that is vivid, vigorous and eloquent." For that reason, he urges writers to submit proposals only about places and experiences they know well and can make come alive on the page. Fish plans feature articles anywhere from 4 to 14 months ahead of time, depending on the need for seasonal photography. Features are always assigned to writers he has worked with in the past. The best way for freelancers to make themselves known is to aim for one of the shorter travel pieces, 200-1,000 words, that make up the body of the travel section.

Travel sidebars are service-oriented, making it easier for the reader to find specific information related to the story (phone numbers, addresses). In feature articles, sidebars often have more of a presence, featuring recipes or related places to visit. In one issue, a story on oysters in the Northwest was made almost entirely of sidebars—restaurants, oyster barbecue, oyster farming—while the short main body of the story related a personal experience.

Fish asks for travel queries of no more than one page. "You should be able to tell the story in a paragraph," he says. "I have to tell my editor-in-chief in a sentence." He suggests summing up a story by creating a "cover line" for it. "The few words that appear on the cover of a magazine must speak to a reader immediately and accurately." Include one or two clips maximum.

Garden, Senior Editor Kathleen Norris Brenzel

Though much of the Garden section is written inhouse, Kathleen Norris Brenzel says, "I'm always on the lookout for regionally based cutting-edge gardens, new plants, gardening techniques, solutions to regional garden problems and quick projects, such as new ways to dress up container pots." The Garden section is heavily zone-specific, and because of that, offers good opportunity for freelancers.

Garden has a bonus section (requiring more articles) four times a year. "I listen to my readers and plan the articles I buy for this bonus section accordingly; garden color is the primary theme at present; it's a favorite subject with our readers," Brenzel says. She generally plans one year ahead, due to the necessity of seasonal photography for features and bonus issues. Feature articles, up to 1,500 words, are occasionally assigned to freelancers.

Garden uses numerous sidebars, often two or three on subjects related to each article. Sidebars may contain loosely related items, such as a recipe for herbal vinegar in an article on growing herbs, or directly related, such as specific buying information.

Brenzel prefers a query, clips (make sure they're garden related) and snapshots, when appropriate. Freelancers are most likely to break in by querying short articles, 150-300 words, for the Garden Guides column.

Food, Senior Editor Jerry Anne DiVeccio

"We use fresh ideas and fresh food," says Jerry Anne DiVeccio. The Food section is often the same in all zones but shows a clear awareness of what's in the markets of each zone. "I'm interested in regional specialties," she says, "but people have to be able to buy the ingredients all over the West."

Sunset has a distinct way of presenting recipes, and all recipes that end up in print are thoroughly tested in *Sunset*'s kitchens. "It's about food," says DiVeccio. "We often get queries about personalities in the food industry, but that's not our focus. We need very tight and concentrated information in a relaxed style. Style is paramount! Study the magazine!" Text is brief and the focus is on recipes. In most food stories, the recipes form the bulk of the article while sidebars carry additional information—history, ingredient background, purchasing specifics. Some food articles such as the Food Guide are composed of small segments. A feature food story dictates its own sidebars. For instance, a recent story on breadmakers had one sidebar on the origins of sourdough bread and another on making and keeping bread dough starter. DiVeccio says, "If it can be headlined, it may be used as a sidebar."

Writers have the best chance of breaking in by composing recipes for the Low-Fat and/or Quick Cook columns. *Sunset* pays $50 per recipe. DiVeccio works with a flexible quarterly calendar, and has most of the year's recipes by June. The Food section is allotted much more space during the holidays: "Our November-December issues are the recipe issues." The best time to send new food ideas is in the fall and early winter. DiVeccio likes to see the entire article including recipes, plus snapshots of the completed dishes.

Home/Style, Senior Editor Ann Bertelsen

The Home/Style section goes to all zones; articles, which average 500 words, must have wide appeal. Ann Bertelsen looks for fresh story ideas that readers can emulate, not only in interior decorating (projects have included multiple uses for center islands, storage innovations, unusual window treatments), but also in sophisticated craft how-tos such as new materials for topiaries, painted glassware, and novel uses for table napkins. *Sunset* style is elegant and comfortable, personal and adaptable. "Think Pottery Barn," says Bertelsen. Crafts and seasonal tabletop decorating ideas are in demand. The editor normally plans six months to one year ahead, due to photographic requirements. "I want to develop a network of writers throughout the western states, preferably outside California—we're well-covered here," she says. Writers who focus on interior design should be aware of current trends and materials. Craftspeople and artists should avoid anything too "country-cutesy"—"We don't want welcome mats and bisque bunnies." For crafts projects, materials have to be commonly available, or everyday items that can be used uniquely. The project can't be so specialized that it requires a high level of artistic skill. "Ideally," says Bertelsen, "the project utilizes a familiar object in a highly inventive way, taking it to a new artistic level." Because of the nature of crafts projects, writers and artists outside the western states are welcome to submit their ideas.

Home/Style sidebars usually contain service information (contact names, address) at the end of a project. The Home/Style section often runs short articles on several individual projects. Send queries with a specific story idea accompanied by snapshots or a sketch, and include clips. Bertelsen assigns major feature stories and pays up to $300 for ideas.

Break in with short pieces

Sunset offers writers—in the region and beyond—ample opportunity to break in with short pieces and to enhance articles with sidebars. With any new market, beginning with short articles makes sense. Editors often face hard deadlines and shifting requirements; they want to work with writers who have delivered on time, as promised, in the past. However, any query that's presented without knowledge of a periodical's focus and style in articles and sidebars is doomed to failure. *Sunset* is, above all, a service magazine. As Rosalie Muller Wright says, "If it doesn't work for the readers, it doesn't belong in *Sunset*."

Tips for Tapping Online Writing Markets

BY ANTHONY TEDESCO

I know, I know. The Internet is basically a big hype sandwich. It's projected to be projecting infinite everything within the nearly foreseeable and almost certainly probably forthcoming future of the new world, millennium millennium, and a virtual hoorah to boot.

But I hereby do solemnly swear: There's nothing virtual or pending about online writing markets. They're here now and they're real. Featuring real editors with real checks which can really be cashed for money. (Real money.) You just need to know how to adapt your plenitude of print writing skills to the online publishing world.

So I contacted the online publishing world (at least a few of its more deft and debonair experts), and requested some of the online-writing wisdom that it/they have amassed on the way to expertdom. Turns out they're deft, debonair, and good sharers, too. Here's a healthy headstart for your online-writing and (real) check-cashing pleasure. (Enjoy.)

DEBBIE RIDPATH OHI
Online Editor of *Inklings* (www.inkspot.com/inklings)

"*Inklings* is a free electronic newsletter for writers, and part of the writers' Web resource, Inkspot (www.inkspot.com). To subscribe, send e-mail to subscribe@inkspot.com."

Tips for online writers:

• Most writers don't realize how many online writing opportunities are available to them. Not just writing for zines, but also writing for content-rich sites, electronic newsletters, news and service websites, press releases, writing courses, online books . . . and these are just a few. There are also many sources of market information online, places where you can find publisher guidelines and news about the publishing industry as well as job opportunities for writers. I have some listed at: http://www.inkspot.com/market/.

• The Internet has enormous networking and research potential; invest the time to explore the possibilities. Check out newsgroups, discussion mailing lists, online writing groups and live chats. Learn proper "netiquette" and always read guidelines before posting a message that will be read by many people. If you're surfing the Web for research information, be efficient. Take the time to learn how to properly use several good search engines. Also, don't assume that all information you find online is accurate: always verify the source.

• When querying by e-mail, remember to follow the same rules you would when sending a

---

ANTHONY TEDESCO *(anthony@crispzine.com) is cofounder/editorial director of the Crisp Website Network (www.crispzine.com) and author of the book-in-progress,* Writer's Online Markets: Where and How to Sell Your Writing on the Internet.

regular query. Don't assume it's okay to be informal just because you're using e-mail. Some editors may be fine with this, but many editors have only recently made the transition from traditional print to electronic media and are still used to traditional methods. In short, be as professional in your electronic communication as you would be in any other form. Also, don't assume online editors have lower standards than editors of print publications. Send only your best.

• If you're using URLs or specific Internet information in your article (e.g., names of mailing lists, newsgroups), be sure to double check spellings before submitting the final copy. Websites and other Internet-based sources frequently move and disappear, and editors are likely to be unimpressed if they receive an article in which half the URLs prove to be defunct. They're bound to wonder how much other information in your article is also outdated.

Christina Tourigny
Online writer, e-mail: ctourigny@xtalwind.net

"Let's classify my genre as nonfiction—travel, sports, interviews, health, etc. I've written for *First Books* (Travel Guide), *Essence*, *Cigar Lifestyles* and other print publications, as well as such online markets as Internetwork Publishing (www.ipcc.com/publications.html), Travelocity (www.travelocity.com), Fitnesslink (www.fitnesslink.com) and Beckett Online (www.beckett.com)."

Tips on writing for online markets:

• You do not have to write online for free. It's your work, and if you want to make writing your livelihood, you need to be paid. If you're trying to build up your credit list, start out with online markets that pay very little and work up—even if it's only a penny or two a word the first few times or maybe $15-20 dollars for your whole piece. If you build up your credit list with free markets, editors will take notice of it and offer you a fraction of what you could have gotten or offer you a credit like the others. New writers need to be aware that there are plenty of paying online markets out there for them to break into. Don't just shoot for the big guns. Go after the smaller ones too—they're almost always your bread-and-butter makers. All nonpaying markets have survived this long because new writers are misguided and don't realize they can negotiate with magazines. Don't sell yourself short.

• If you can work with a company that owns, or is hired out by, multiple online publications, it's better than hitting one big market sometimes. I have a lot of regular work from four different companies like this that call me up and ask me to write for them for both online and print (e.g., Beckett's online at www.beckett.com). Most of these group publishers don't advertise in writer's markets, so you've got to ask around in newsgroups such as alt.writing and peruse writing newsletters.

• Know your rights when it comes to online contracts; there is negotiating room with almost all contracts. National Writers Union (NWU) (www.nwu.org/nwu/index.htm) and The American Society of Journalists and Authors (www.asja.org) have lots of copyright information. Other sites writers should know about: The Copyright Website (www.benedict.com) and Books A To Z Copyright Basics (www.booksatoz.com/copyrigh/whatis.htm).

Alice Bradley
Editor-in-Chief of *Charged* (www.charged.com)

"*Charged* is the extreme leisure authority. Whether you want to snowboard, breakdance, or wander the streets wearing nothing but oven mitts, *Charged* will give you the where, when and how. Our goal is to provide expert advice and information on action sports, urban activities and unusual travel options. And we're funny, too."

Tips for online writers:

• When you're writing for the Web, you have to be hyper-aware of your audience's lack of patience. Think of your text in terms of short bites. Web surfers are allergic to scrolling. Usually when I receive a story, I go through it and see how I can break it up into smallish paragraphs—it's just less overwhelming than having a page full of text to scroll through. Often I'm amazed by how much I have to reorganize and rewrite someone else's story. And if I'm not able to spend a lot of time on it, I might not be able to accept it.

• Putting in subheads is always a good idea. It helps the writer (and the editor/producer) organize the story.

• You should have a general sense of what the design for the story will be. Think of how the text will look on the site. What should be hyperlinked? Should it have simultaneous narratives? A left-side frame with links to specific paragraphs? Could it be a choose-your-own-adventure piece? It obviously depends on what piece you're talking about, but the format should direct your story to some extent. Ideally, you and a producer would determine together what kind of format fits the story, and you would write it accordingly. Long, linear stories will make for a boring design—or a story that has been totally rewritten by an editor.

• Instead of e-mailing clips or URLs with your initial query, it's better to just send your pitch and then offer to send clips, and ask how the editor would like the clips to be sent. Some editors feel strongly about their preferred method, and there's really no set standard. Do you attempt to make nice color printouts of your story and mail them? Do you e-mail attached stories (and then they look terrible because of the HTML, or if you look at them in Netscape, the images are missing), or do you just send URLs? As an editor, I prefer the last alternative; Web stories are Web stories and should be read as such. But some editors say it's not their job to go looking for your clips at a URL. The only way to know an editor's preference is to ask beforehand.

Gary Welz
Online writer, e-mail: gary@welz.com

"My writing topics range from advertising and personalities to publishing and technology, for both print and online publications, including Internet World, Web Week, Webdeveloper.com (www.webdeveloper.com), Crisp (www.crispzine.com), and The X Advisor."

Tips on writing for online markets:

• Although writers need to be compensated accordingly, it can be quite beneficial to have your online articles archived by the publication and available to readers forever. It's even worth setting up your own web page with your clips and credentials—whether or not you've ever been published online. Print articles run for their month and then that's usually it—they're out of the public eye. But I've received so many opportunities from editors and companies who came across a past online article of mine, or who did an Internet search on a certain subject and my name and article came up—even for articles that I wrote a long time ago. With archived articles, I'm also able to query new online markets with URLs pointing to my previous clips.

• Indulge your loquacity. Yes, some editors prefer your articles to be short, but as long as you can break the writing into short sections, there's no real limit to space in online magazines. They don't have any printing costs. My regular column for Webdeveloper.com had a 600-word minimum. Maximum? Almost anything I wanted. For columns conducive to personality, really let your personality show through.

• It always helps to include some URLs/links in your articles.

• If you want to write for the Internet, know what's on the Internet. Search engines are probably the greatest tool for online writers. Search on your topic to see what's already out there so you don't have to reinvent the wheel—and you don't have to submit a story that's already been written. Find source material so you can give it a new perspective. And remember not to rely on just one search engine.

• Get out and meet editors. Sure, you could conduct business entirely through e-mail, but meeting people face-to-face is still extremely important. Build some rapport. Go to events and conferences, and introduce yourself to people. It's a huge advantage to have an editor put a face with your name.

Melissa Weiner
Managing Editor of *Swoon* (www.swoon.com)

"*Swoon* is the Web's premier relationship site for the twenty-something generation. It is also the online home of *Details*, *GQ*, *Mademoiselle* and *Glamour*."

Tips for online writers:

• Investigate each site and pitch accordingly. Don't conduct a mass e-mailing campaign. It's obvious, annoying and a complete turn-off. Make your pitch site-specific. Keep in mind that every successful online publication provides a unique user experience that your piece should help create. Convince the editor that your idea is vital to her site.

• The Web's interactivity is what distinguishes it from print. For example, you can search for inexpensive airline fares in seconds or check out your investments at a glance. While you are not going to produce a database of inexpensive airline fares or stock market feeds, you can come up with short, interactive and easy-to-implement features. Depending on the site, quizzes, games, forums, links or interactive polls might be the way to go. Each content site has its own idea of interactivity and user experience. Keep the value of the Web's immediate return in mind when you are developing your pitches, and determine the focus of the site you are pitching so your stories fit accordingly.

• Since a good website is not simply an electronic version of your favorite print magazine, coming up with pieces for an online publication requires a different thought process. Take a step back and think about what *you* would go online to read.

Publishers and Their Imprints: A Breakdown

Keeping up with the heavy wave of buying, selling, merging, consolidating and dissolving among publishers and their imprints over the last few years can leave even the most devout *Publishers Weekly* ready dizzy. To help curious writers sort it out, we offer this breakdown of major publishers, who owns whom, and which imprints are under which umbrella. Remember, this list is just a snapshot of how things are shaped at our press time—due to the dynamic nature of the publishing world, it's subject to change at any moment.

BANTAM DOUBLEDAY DELL (Bertelsmann Book Group)

Bantam Books
Bantam Classics
Bantam Crime Line
Bantam Fanfare
Bantam Spectra

Bantam Doubleday Dell Books for Young Readers
Delacorte
Doubleday Books for Young Readers
Laurel Leaf
Picture Yearling
Skylark
Starfire
Yearling

BDD Audio

Broadway Books

Dell
Delacorte Press
Dell Books
Delta Books
Dial Press
DTP
Island Books
Laurel Books

Doubleday
Anchor
Currency
Doubleday
Image Books
Main Street Books
Nan A. Talese

RANDOM HOUSE (Bertelsmann Book Group)

The Ballantine Publishing Group
Ballantine Books
Columbine
Del Rey
Fawcett
House of Collectibles
Ivy
Library of Contemporary Thought
One World

Fodor's Travel Publications

The Crown Publishing Group
Bell Tower
Clarkson Potter
Crown Publishers Inc.
Custom Publishing
Harmony Books
Living Language
Three Rivers Press

Knopf Publishing Group
Everyman's Library
Alfred A. Knopf Inc.
Pantheon Books
Random House AudioBooks
Random House Large Print Publishing
Schocken Books
Vintage Books

Random House International
Knopf
Random House of Canada
Random House UK

Random House Trade Group
The Modern Library
Random House Adult Trade Books
Villard Books
Random House Information Group
- Princeton Review
- Random House Reference & Information Publishing
- Times Books
- Times Business Books

Random House Children's Publishing
Bullseye Books
Children's Media
Crown Books for Young Readers
Dragonfly Books
Knopf Books for Young Readers
Knopf Paperbacks
Random House
Random House Entertainment

Random House New Media

Random House Value Publishing
Children's Classics
Crescent
Derrydale
Gramercy Books
Gramercy Park Gift & Stationery
JellyBean Press
Wings

PENGUIN PUTNAM INC. (Pearson)

Penguin USA

Viking Penguin
Penguin Studio
Viking

Dutton Signet
DAW Books
Dutton
Mentor
NAL
Obelisk
Onyx
Plume
ROC
Signet
Topaz

The Putnam Berkley Group
Ace
Berkley Books
Berkley Prime Crime
Boulevard
Jove
Perigee
Price Stern Sloan, Inc.
G.P. Putnam's Sons
Riverhead
Jeremy P. Tarcher

Children's Division
Dial Books for Young Readers
Dutton Children's Books
Grosset & Dunlap
Philomel Books
Planet Dexter
Price Stern Sloan, Inc.
Puffin
G.P. Putnam's Sons
Viking Children's Books
Frederick Warne

SIMON & SCHUSTER (Viacom, Inc.)

(Note: Parts of Simon & Schuster were recently sold, notably the publisher's reference and textbook divisions. Imprints gathered under the company's Consumer Group remain the property of Viacom, and are represented here.)

Pocket Books
Archway Paperbacks
Minstrel Books
MTV Books
Pocket Books Hardcover
Pocket Books Trade Paperbacks
Washington Square Press

Simon & Schuster Children's Publishing
Aladdin Paperbacks
Atheneum Books for Young Readers
Little Simon
Margaret K. McElderry Books
Simon & Schuster Books for Young Readers
Simon Spotlight
Simon & Schuster Interactive

Simon & Schuster Audio

Simon & Schuster Trade
Fireside
The Free Press
Scribner
  Lisa Drew Books
  Rawson Associates
Simon & Schuster
Simon & Schuster Editions
Simon & Schuster Libros en Espanol
Touchstone

HARPERCOLLINS (Rupert Murdoch)

Cliff Street Books
HarperActive
HarperAudio
HarperBusiness
HarperCollins
HarperCollins Children's Books
HarperEdge
HarperEntertainment
HarperFlamingo
HarperHorizon
HarperPaperbacks
HarperPerennial
HarperPrism
HarperResource
HarperSanFrancisco
HarperTrophy
Regan Books
Voyager
Zondervan Publishing House

HarperCollinsAustralia
HarperCollinsCanada
HarperCollinsUK

TIME WARNER

Warner Books
Mysterious Press
Warner Aspect
Warner Romance
Warner Vision

Little, Brown and Company
Back Bay Books
Bullfinch Press
Little, Brown Books for Children

Time Life Inc.

Time Warner Audiobooks

HOLTZBRINCK

St. Martin's

Bedford Books
Buzz Books
Dead Letter
Tom Doherty Associates, Inc.
- TOR
- Forge

Thomas Dunne Books
Griffin
Let's Go
Picador
St. Martin's Paperbacks
St. Martin's Press
St. Martin's Scholarly & Reference
Stonewall Inn
Truman Talley Books

Farrar Straus & Giroux

Faber & Faber Inc.
Farrar Straus & Giroux Books for Young Readers
- Aerial Fiction
- Francis Foster Books
- Mirasol/Libros Juveniles
- R and S Books
- Sunburst Paperbacks

Hill and Wang
Noonday Press
North Point Press
Sunburst Books

Henry Holt & Co.

Henry Holt & Co. Books for Young Readers
- Edge Books

Henry Holt Reference Books
John Macrae Books
Metropolitan Books
Owl Books
Marian Wood Books

HEARST BOOKS

Avon

Avon Eos
Avon Flare
Bard
Camelot
Mass Market
Trade Paperback
Twilight

William Morrow

Beech Tree Books
Greenwillow Books
Lothrop, Lee & Shepard Books
William Morrow Books
Morrow Junior Books
Mulberry Books
Quill Trade Paperbacks
Tupelo Books
Rob Weisbach Books

Literary Agents

The publishing world is never static. There's the quiet ebb and flow of imprints expanding and editors moving, and then there's the cataclysmic explosion when two publishing giants collide to become one. Through it all, the literary agent has become an increasingly important mediator, connecting writers, ideas and publishers to form new books. Almost 50,000 books a year, as a matter of fact.

With an increasing emphasis on profit margins, many of the larger publishers have eliminated the entry level editorial assistants who were primarily responsible for reading manuscripts sent in by writers—"over the transom" to the "slush pile," in the jargon. As a result, agents have taken over some of this task, separating the literary wheat from the chaff and forwarding the promising manuscripts on to possible publishers. Most publishers remain open to receiving at least query letters directly from authors, but some of the largest publishers will accept submissions only from agents.

As you look through the Book Publishers section of *Writer's Market*, you will see the symbol (A) at the beginning of certain listings. This symbol denotes publishers that accept submissions only from agents. If you find a book publisher that is a perfect market for your work but only reads agented manuscripts, contacting an agent is your next logical step.

Finding an agent is *not* easier than finding a publisher. It may even be harder, since there are far fewer agents than publishing companies. However, if you do secure representation, your "reach" into the publishing world has extended to include everyone that agent knows.

CHOOSING AND USING AN AGENT

Literary agents, like authors, come in all shapes and sizes, with different areas of interest and expertise. It's to your advantage to take the time and choose an agent who is most closely aligned to your interests and your manuscript's subject.

The 50 agents listed in this section have all indicated that they are open to working with new, previously unpublished writers as well as published writers. None of these agents charge a "reading fee," which is money paid to an agent to cover the time and effort in reading a manuscript or a few sample chapters. While there is nothing wrong with charging a reading fee (after all, agents have to make a living too), we encourage writers to first try agents that do not.

Literary agent Lori Perkins's article, How to Find (and Keep) the Right Agent, will arm you with the basics of choosing and using a literary agent. From query protocol to typical activities in her day, she outlines what you can expect in seeking representation and what to do after you've secured it.

The listings that follow Perkins's article contain the information you need to determine if an agent is suitable for your work. Read each listing carefully to see if an agency specializes in your subject areas. Or go straight to the Literary Agent Subject Index found after the listings to obtain a list of agencies specifically interested in the subjects you write. To make your search as easy as possible, we've broken the Subject Index into two main categories: nonfiction and fiction.

How to Find (and Keep) the Right Agent

BY LORI PERKINS

I have always wanted to get published.

Before I became an agent, I was a journalist, and before that I was an aspiring writer. After nearly two decades of working with words for a living, I am finally the author of two books of my very own. I can honestly say that I would not be published, and published well, without the guidance of my agent. So I write this article from both sides of the fence.

Before I became a literary agent, I used to think New York literary agents were mystical beings who would change my life with one phone call, if only they would respond to my query letters. When I finally left the news business and became a literary agent, I was honestly surprised to find that agents were mere mortals with no super powers, only high-powered rolodexes and a nearly insane desire to get people published.

Now I know that a good literary agent receives at least a thousand query letters a month, so your work as a writer has to be exceptional (and professional) from the beginning. As someone who has been on the outside looking in and now as an insider looking out, I write this article to give you an insider's view on how to get and keep the right agent for you.

WHAT IS AN AGENT?

You'd be surprised at the number of writers who think an agent is an editor, business manager, lawyer, publicist, banker, mother, new best friend, fairy godmother—the list is endless.

A synonym for agent is "author's representative," and that really is a perfect definition of the agent's role. An agent is your representative to the publishing industry, whom you hire to negotiate in your best interests. What this entails can differ slightly from agent to agent, but it generally falls into the following tasks (assuming your material is ready for submission):

- knowing who to send your work to;
- helping you chose the right publisher/editor (should more than one be interested);
- negotiating the terms of your contract;
- representing the foreign and subsidiary rights to your book (film, magazine, audio, etc.);
- making sure your publisher keeps you informed of your book's progress before and after publication;
- preparing your next project for submission and negotiating those terms;
- keeping on top of the financial and legal matters related to your books after publication.

DO YOU REALLY NEED AN AGENT?

Look at the list of things an agent does and tell me you have the time, ability and inclination to handle it all without making mistakes that could set back your career in ways you can't even

---

LORI PERKINS *is a partner in Perkins, Rabiner, Rubie & Associates. She has been a literary agent for 15 years. Prior to that she was the publisher of* The Uptown Dispatch, *a Manhattan newspaper, and an adjunct journalism professor at NYU. She is the author of* The Cheapskate's Guide to Entertaining: How to Throw Fabulous Parties on a Modest Budget *(Carol Publishing) and is currently working on* How to Find the Right Agent for You *(Writer's Digest Books).*

imagine. Or let me put it to you another way: only a fool has himself for a client.

That's not to say authors don't sell books themselves, but there's much more to being an agent than making a sale. Often, when an author sells his own book, the editor will refer him to an agent to guide him through the contract and production process and fill him in on all the publishing details the editor doesn't have the time to explain. Editors edit.

Agents know what the industry norms are (such as how much the industry is paying right now for certain kinds of books, what rights are selling, where a house is flexible on contract terms, etc.); they know the history of the publisher with your kind of book, as well as the strengths and weaknesses of your editor.

And agents have clout. When your publisher (and editor) does a deal with your agent, the entire agency roster is on your side. They don't want to upset your agent because it might affect another book they have under contract or their chances of getting one of your agent's really hot writers when their next book comes up.

But that's not the only reason you need an agent. When I entered the publishing business, I was stunned at the sheer number of books published every year (about 50,000). Only someone who eats (we lunch professionally), sleeps, and schmoozes books for a living could possibly keep up with who's buying what for how much and why. Writers write. If you're spending the amount of time necessary to keep up with the publishing business, than you are either working for *Publishers Weekly* or not as serious about writing as you should be.

WHAT DOES AN AGENT REALLY DO?

When I go to writers' conferences, authors are always amazed that I don't read manuscripts in the office and that I read at the same speed they do. One author actually thought I had some special ability to read manuscripts at super-human speed.

The best way to tell you what agents really do is to describe a typical work day. I start at 10:00 a.m. because editors straggle into their office late, and I work until 6:00 p.m. The first thing I do is call all the editors who have promised to respond to me by that day and check up on projects. Most of the time I leave a message, and the editors get back to me after lunch.

I then prepare the day's multiple submissions (three to five copies for a novel, five to ten copies for a nonfiction proposal), which includes writing pitch letters, calling all the editors and pitching the book, and then getting everything packaged by 5:00 p.m. for UPS.

Lunch is an extremely important part of my business. It's where I get to know an individual editor's taste, learn what they and their publishing house are buying right now, hear industry gossip, and pitch my agency for future projects. A good, productive lunch can net me up to ten book sales over a year. Lunch is therefore sacred, and I do it seriously. I usually have lunch at 12:30 p.m., which means I leave my office at noon to travel. Lunch lasts about two hours, and I'm always back at my desk by 3:00 p.m. I tell you this because you should never call an agent between noon and 3:00 New York time. We should be out to lunch, and if we are in our office answering phone calls, we're not doing our job.

The afternoon I spend getting back to editors who have returned my calls, going through the mail, perhaps reading over a contract or preparing a foreign mailing (I have 11 foreign agents who represent my books throughout the world and I send them monthly bulletins about my books along with a mailing). From 5:00 to 6:00 p.m., I call my authors because I don't have to worry about being interrupted by editors since their work day is over. I can devote my full attention to my authors this way. I also return phone calls from the West Coast at this time, because they are just returning from their lunches.

I get home, have dinner, put the kid to sleep, unwind, and try to read at least an hour each weeknight and five hours over the weekend. I average about one novel and four or five proposals a week.

I represent about 50 writers, each of whom writes at least 1 book a year; some write as many as 4. My stable of writers takes up most of my reading time. The same is true of my partner,

Peter Rubie, although he reads more unsolicited query letters than I do.

Most agents represent between 50 and 75 writers. If an agent is established, she is quite busy with the authors she has already made a commitment to and will relegate responding to query letters as a lesser priority. Most agents assign this task to the lowliest person in their office or wait until the pile is so high you can cut through it with a scythe.

Right now, we receive about 1,000 query letters a month, so it takes a while to respond to all the mail. We have hired a college English student whose job it is to sift through our unsolicited mail and call our attention to those letters that fit our tastes. She's very good at it. My partner and I then read through this material when we have a free moment. This is why it often takes up to three months to get a form rejection in your self-addressed stamped envelope (SASE). This is also why it's so important for you to include that SASE in your mailing.

HOW DO I FIND THE RIGHT AGENT?

The best way to get an agent is to be informed, and that doesn't mean clipping the *USA Today* article about how much John Grisham got for his latest book. It means buying a book like this one, using a specialized directory such as the *Guide to Literary Agents* (Writer's Digest Books) or going to the library, and doing a little research. You will quickly learn that there are about 1,000 literary agents throughout the country and, just like writers, they are all different.

You could do a mass mailing to all agents listed, but that's not a wise investment. The best thing to do is to narrow your field of submission by finding out what areas the agents specialize in and matching them to your type of book.

All books fall into a category or genre, and "fiction," "nonfiction," "mainstream," or "best-seller" are not specific enough. All agents specialize in some area of publishing. It's impossible nowadays to be a generalist, although most of us are open to new areas. For instance, my areas of interest are horror, thrillers, dark literary fiction and books about popular culture. My partner specializes in literate science fiction, fantasy, thrillers, crime novels and narrative nonfiction. Recently, I found that the market for adult horror was shrinking, but the young adult market was booming, so I now sell young adult and middle grade horror. I also found that I was good at selling to niche markets, so I've begun selling gay and Latino books (both fiction and nonfiction), and have added them to my areas of representation.

Just as the publishing market changes, a good agent changes her taste and skills with the market. Although I represent both fiction and nonfiction, nearly all the agency's clients have been, or still are, journalists. So when one market declines, we often move a client into another area of that market (from adult to young adult fiction or to nonfiction) while their genre is in a slump, so they can continue to publish.

Because my partner and I were both journalists before we became agents, we also come up with ideas for our clients when their own ideas don't sell. We've received quite a reputation for coming up with book ideas, and now editors often call us with books they're looking for. We represent the author, not just the book. About a third of our business is now done this way.

The book on agenting I am writing for Writer's Digest Books is the perfect example of the difference a good agent can make to a writer's success. I had written a book proposal the editor liked but could not get his publisher to buy. He came back to my agent apologetically, saying he'd like to work with me on something else. My agent quickly made a few suggestions (knowing my interests and abilities) and when my editor said he wanted to see a proposal on one of them, I quickly responded. We had an offer within weeks.

The single most frequent reason I reject query letters is because I don't handle the material I am being queried on. You can save yourself postage and aggravation if you do this research ahead of time.

Once you know the kind of book you are writing, you should join the professional organization that supports those writers. All genres have associations (Romance Writers of America, Science Fiction Writers of America, etc.), as do professions (The Society of Journalists and Authors).

Many of these organizations compile a list of agents representing their kind of book. Some charge non-members for access to this list, others do not.

HOW DO I GET THE RIGHT AGENT TO REPRESENT ME?

Don't try to dazzle or impress a prospective agent with gimmicks. Be direct. In a one-page query letter, tell me what your book is about and who you are. Let your work speak for itself. Don't tell me how your wife, kids, aunt and high school English teacher think you are the next Stephen King. I only want to know if you were a high school track star or Honda Salesman of the Year if it relates directly to your book. The only background information I want in a query letter is your relevant publishing history, educational information (writing workshops, who you've studied with/under, etc.) and maybe some biographical information that relates directly to your book (such as the fact that you're a doctor and you've written a medical thriller).

Don't overwhelm me. If you've been writing unpublished for 16 years and have 17 novels in the closet, don't try to pitch all of them to me at once. Just send a query about the one you think is best, with a brief line about how you have other completed manuscripts, should I be interested in seeing something else. Show me that you've done some research. If you took the time to go to *Writer's Market*, and chose me from that listing, tell me so in your letter. You might even want to start your letter off that way. It will definitely get my attention.

If you've joined a writer's organization, tell me. If they gave you my name, tell me that. If you got my name from one of my clients, definitely tell me that, because if a client of mine asks me to look at something from a new writer, it moves to the top of my pile. If you think your book is similar to a book you know I've represented, tell me that as well.

Below is a basic example of a query letter that would grab my interest:

"Dear Ms. Perkins:

I read your article on agents in the *1999 Writer's Market* and I thought you might be interested in seeing an outline and sample chapters of my novel, (title). It's about (brief description).

For your information, I am a member of (professional organization) and I have attended (University writing program). My short stories have appeared in (publications).

I've enclosed an SASE for your response."

The only other thing you should do is to make sure your presentation to me is professional. That means typed, double-spaced on 8½×11 nonerasable paper with a SASE with the proper postage. Your query letter should be free of typographical and grammatical errors.

Because of the sheer volume of queries our agency receives and the hours it takes to go through everything, I prefer to receive a simple query letter first and additional material only if I ask for it. The less material you send, the sooner someone will respond to you.

Many agents are now on the Internet and some welcome e-mail queries, though my partner and I do not accept queries this way. You can also fax a query letter, especially if the book you want to write is timely, but you may not get any response at all from an e-mail or fax query, which is why I prefer an SASE. Do not query about sending a query letter. Do not send disks unsolicited. Never send your whole novel, even over the Internet.

HOW DOES THE AGENT/WRITER RELATIONSHIP WORK?

Okay, let's assume you receive a letter from me requesting sample chapters and an outline. Take your time and send me the most polished material you can. Send me the first three chapters of your novel or representative chapters of nonfiction, or published articles about that topic.

Then be patient. I will endeavor to get back to you within six weeks, but life often gets in the way. For instance, things slow down over the Thanksgiving to New Year's holiday season, as well as in the summer. If you haven't heard from me in six weeks, feel comfortable in giving me a polite phone call asking me for an estimate of when I should be able to get to your work. Don't e-mail me or fax me.

Let's assume I like what you've sent and I've read the whole novel or proposal. I might ask you to make some changes that I feel will help sell the book or make it more commercial. Trust my judgment. I don't get paid until I sell your work, and that's the only reason I am asking for these changes. When an agent agrees to work with you, you are a negative asset until your work is sold. We are gambling on you because we see something in you and your work we believe in.

You send me the work, and we agree it's ready to go out. You then become my client with a verbal handshake over the phone.

Some literary agencies have agency contracts, but I do not. When I sell a book, the publishing contract includes a clause that insures I am the agent of record for that title until the rights revert.

I then go over the terms of our representation, which are pretty standard. We take a 15% commission on domestic sales, 20% on foreign sales and charge only for photocopying. The older (established prior to 1975) and bigger agencies take a 10% commission, and some agencies charge for expenses such as phone calls, faxes, postage, etc., but most also charge for copying.

Your material is then sent out to multiple editors and we wait. A sale can be made in a week (more likely for nonfiction) and it has taken me up to 3 years to sell a novel (rejected by 33 publishers).

If your work is under submission and you haven't heard from me in six weeks, by all means give me a call to ask what's happening. However, if you haven't heard from me it means that no one has gotten back to me, or I've only had rejections. You will definitely hear from me if I've got an offer for your book. Sometimes, I send an author copies of relevant rejection letters (maybe the editor had something to say that was thought-provoking), but it's not a regular procedure, unless you request it.

Once I have an offer for your book, I go over it with you. We discuss everything from how much money you get and how you get it to when you will deliver the manuscript. Once the terms of the agreement are made, I usually get you and your editor together over the phone.

It usually takes four to six weeks for me to receive the contract, which I go over with the publisher's contracts department and then send on to you for your signature. You return it to me, and we wait another four to six weeks for the signing payment.

You then write the book, or make the changes that the editor requested. All editorial matters go directly to your editor, but you should keep me informed of your progress on the book, especially if you are having problems with your editor.

Sometimes I have to interfere on your behalf.

Let's say you deliver your manuscript and your editor loves it. I then write a letter requesting your delivery and acceptance payment, and we wait at least another six weeks for that.

I then begin asking you about your next book. You draw up an outline and sample chapters (whether it's fiction or nonfiction), and I send it to your editor. We then wait for her response.

TIPS TO IMPROVE THE AUTHOR/AGENT RELATIONSHIP

Be mindful of your agent's schedule. Don't call during lunch hours. Don't call more than once a day. Remember that during the summer, publishers and agents close at noon on Fridays.

Be mindful of your agent's workload. Remember that we have many clients (and many books to read). If we don't get to something right away, it is not a comment on our love for you or your work. It just means we are overwhelmed.

Say "Thank You" once in awhile. You can't imagine how nice it is to hear those words or see them in a letter or a card. Yes, it's my job, but it's nice to know that you think I did it well.

Literary Agents: The Listings

This section consists of 50 individual agency listings, followed by a Subject Index of nonfiction and fiction book categories followed by the names of agencies that have expressed an interest in manuscripts on that subject.

You can approach this information in two ways. You can skim through the listings and see if an agent stands out as particularly right for your manuscript and proceed from there. Or you can check the Literary Agent Subject Index that follows these listings to focus your search more narrowly. Cross-referencing categories and concentrating on those agents interested in two or more aspects of your manuscript might increase your chances of success.

Either way, it is important to carefully read the information contained in the listing. Each agency has different interests, submission requirements and response times. They'll tell you what they want, what they don't want, and how they want to receive it. Try to follow their directions as closely as possible. For these agents in particular, time is extremely important, and wasting theirs won't help your case.

There are several sections to each listing. The first paragraph lists the agency's name, address and contact information. It also includes when the agency was established, how many clients it represents and what percentage of those clients are new/previously unpublished writers. It offers the agency's self-described areas of specialization and a breakdown of the different types of manuscripts it handles (nonfiction, fiction, movie scripts, etc.).

The first subsection is **Member Agents**, which lists the individuals who work at the agency. The next is **Handles**, which outlines the different nonfiction and fiction categories an agency will look at. **Needs** identifies subjects they are particularly interested in seeing, as well as what they definitely do not handle and will not look at. **Recent Sales** is pretty self-explanatory. **Terms** offers information on the commission an agent takes (domestic and foreign), if a written contract is offered, and whether and what miscellaneous expenses are charged to an author's account. **Writers' Conferences** identifies conferences that agent attends. And **Tips** presents any last words of advice an agent might want to give prospective authors.

FOR MORE ON THE SUBJECT . . .

The *Guide to Literary Agents* (Writer's Digest Books) offers 500 agent listings and a wealth of informational articles on the author/agent relationship and other related topics.

N **AGENCY ONE**, 87 Hamilton St., S. Portland ME 04106. (207)799-5689. E-mail: mmccutc642@aol.com. Contact: Marc McCutcheon. Estab. 1997. Member of Authors Guild. Specializes in popular nonfiction and reference titles with long shelf lives, and popular science fiction along the lines of Michael Crichton. Also really likes seeing quality historical novels in any genre and in any period. Currently handles: 50% nonfiction books; 50% novels.

- Prior to opening his agency, Mr. McCutcheon authored numerous books, including *Building Believable Characters*, *Writer's Guide to Everyday Life in the 1800s*, *Writer's Guide to Everyday Life From Prohibition through World War II*, *Roget's Super Thesaurus* (all published by Writer's Digest Books) and *Descriptionary*.

Handles: Nonfiction books, novels. Considers these nonfiction areas: agriculture/horticulture; anthropology/archaeology; biography/autobiography; business; child guidance/parenting; cooking/food/nutrition; current affairs; government/politics/law; health/medicine; history; how-to; humor; military/war; money/finance/economics; nature/environment; popular culture; psychology; religious/inspirational; science/technology; self-help/personal improvement; sociology; sports; true crime/investigative; women's issues/women's studies; true adventure and "slice of life" stories. Considers these fiction areas: action/adventure; detective/police/crime; family saga; fantasy; glitz; historical; horror; mystery/suspense; romance (historical); science fiction. Query or send outline/proposal. Reports in 2 weeks on queries; 3 weeks on mss.

Needs: Actively seeking "popular reference, nonfiction, popular science fiction and quality historical novels." Does not want to receive "textbooks, coffeetable books, juveniles, biographies of Uncle Ed." Obtains new clients through recommendations from others and solicitation.

Recent Sales: New agency with no reported sales.

Terms: Agent receives 15% commission on domestic sales; 20% on foreign sales. No written contract. Works on a book-by-book agreement. Authors are free to leave at any time. "In addition to offering full agenting services (Plan A) at the standard rates, I also offer a second tier of service (Plan B) for a one-time fee, payable on a sale only. With this plan, I land an acceptable publisher but leave the contract negotiation and maintenance to the author. I provide the author with a free info sheet to show them what to ask for and what to avoid in the contract. Plan B can get authors' manuscripts through the doors of publishers who would not otherwise consider the material without an agent. The plan recognizes that not every author needs or wants full agenting services." Charges for photocopies, approximately 5¢ per page or asks client to send photocopies.

Tips: "Always go the extra mile in your writing, in your research, and in your query and proposal presentation."

N **LORETTA BARRETT BOOKS INC.**, 101 Fifth Ave., New York NY 10003. (212)242-3420. Fax: (212)691-9418. President: Loretta A. Barrett. Estab. 1990. Represents 70 clients. Specializes in general interest books. Currently handles: 25% fiction; 75% nonfiction.

- Prior to opening her agency, Ms. Barrett was vice president and executive editor at Doubleday for 25 years.

Handles: Considers all areas of nonfiction. Considers these fiction areas: action/adventure; cartoon/comic; confessional; contemporary issues; detective/police/crime; ethnic; experimental; family saga; fantasy; feminist; gay; glitz; historical; humor/satire; lesbian; literary; mainstream; mystery/suspense; psychic/supernatural; religious/inspirational; romance; sports; thriller/espionage. Query first with SASE. Reports in 4-6 weeks on queries.

Recent Sales: Sold about 20 titles in the last year. Prefers not to share info. on specific sales.

Terms: Agent receives 15% commission on domestic sales; 20% on foreign sales. Offers written contract. Charges for shipping and photocopying.

Writers' Conferences: San Diego State University Writers' Conference (January); Maui Writers Conference.

N **THE BEDFORD BOOK WORKS, INC.**, 194 Katonah Ave., Katonah NY 10536. (914)242-6262. Fax: (914)242-5232. Contact: Joel E. Fishman (president), Lucy Herring Chambers (agent). Estab. 1993. Represents 30 clients. 50% of clients are new/previously unpublished writers. Currently handles: 80% nonfiction books, 20% novels.

- Prior to becoming agents, Mr. Fishman served as senior editor at Doubleday; Ms. Chambers was an editor at Doubleday; and Mr. Lang worked as Doubleday's foreign rights director.

Member Agents: Joel E. Fishman (narrative nonfiction, category nonfiction and commercial fiction); Lucy H. Chambers (children's books); Kevin Lang (commercial fiction, humor, nonfiction).

Handles: Nonfiction books, novels. Considers these nonfiction areas: biography/autobiography; business; current affairs; health/medicine; history; how-to; humor; money/finance/economics; popular culture; psychology; science/technology; sports; women's issues/women's studies. Considers these fiction areas: contemporary issues; detective/police/crime; literary; mainstream; mystery/suspense; thriller/espionage. Query. Reports in 2 weeks on queries; 2 months on mss.

Needs: Obtains new clients through recommendations and solicitation.

Recent Sales: *Pour Your Heart Into It: How Starbucks Built a Company One Cup at a Time*, by Howard Schultz with Doris Jones Yang (Hyperion); *Plundering America*, by Bill Lerach with Patrick Dillon (HarperCollins).

Terms: Agent receives 15% commission on domestic sales; 20% on foreign sales. Offers written contract, binding for 1 year with 60 day cancellation clause. Charges for postage and photocopying.

Tips: "Grab my attention right away with your query—not with gimmicks, but with excellent writing."

N **DAVID BLACK LITERARY AGENCY, INC.**, 156 Fifth Ave., New York NY 10001. (212)242-5080. Fax: (212)924-6609. Contact: David Black, owner. Estab. 1990. Member of AAR. Represents 150 clients. Specializes in sports, politics, novels. Currently handles: 80% nonfiction; 20% novels.

Member Agents: Susan Raihofer, Gary Morris.

Handles: Nonfiction books, literary and commercial fiction. Considers these nonfiction areas: politics; sports. Query with outline and SASE. Reports in 2 months on queries.

Recent Sales: Sold 18 titles in the last year. *The Other Side of the River*, by Alex Kotlogitz (Nan Talese-Doubleday); *The Temple Bombing*, by Melissa Fay Greene (Addison-Wesley); *Like Judgement Day*, by Michael Dorso (Grosset); *Turning Stones*, by Marc Parent (Harcourt Brace).

Terms: Agent receives 15% commission. Charges for photocopying and books purchased for sale of foreign rights.

N **BOOK DEALS, INC.**, Civic Opera Bldg., 20 N. Wacker Dr., Suite 1928, Chicago IL 60606. (312)372-0227. Contact: Caroline Carney. Estab. 1996. Represents 35 clients. 25% of clients are new/previously unpublished writers. Specializes in highly commercial and literary fiction and nonfiction. Currently handles: 50% nonfiction books, 50% fiction.

- Prior to opening her agency, Ms. Carney was editorial director for a consumer book imprint within Times Mirror and held senior editorial positions in McGraw-Hill and Simon & Schuster.

Handles: Narrative nonfiction, how-to, novels. Considers these nonfiction areas: animals; biography/autobiography; business; cooking/food/nutrition; current affairs; ethnic/cultural interests; government/politics/law; health/medicine; history; money/finance/economics; nature/environment; popular culture; science/technology; sports; translations. Considers these fiction areas: contemporary issues; ethnic; feminist; humor/satire; literary; mainstream; sports; white-collar crime stories; urban literature. Send synopsis, outline/proposal with SASE. Reports in 1-2 weeks on queries; 3-4 weeks on mss.

Needs: Actively seeking well-crafted fiction and nonfiction. Does not want to receive fantasy, science fiction or westerns.

Recent Sales: Prefers not to share info.

Terms: Agent receives 15% commission on domestic sales; 20% on foreign sales. Offers a written contract. Charges for photocopying and postage.

N **CURTIS BROWN LTD.**, 10 Astor Place, New York NY 10003-6935. (212)473-5400. Member of AAR; signatory of WGA. Perry Knowlton, chairman & CEO. Peter L. Ginsberg, president. Queries to Laura Blake Peterson.

Member Agents: Laura Blake Peterson; Ellen Geiger; Emilie Jacobson, vice president; Maureen Walters, vice president; Virginia Knowlton; Timothy Knowlton, COO (film, screenplays, plays); Marilyn Marlow, executive vice president; Jess Taylor (film, screenplays, plays); Jennifer MacDonald; Clyde Taylor; Mitchell Waters.

Handles: Nonfiction books, juvenile books, novels, novellas, short story collections, poetry books. All categories of nonfiction and fiction considered. Query. Reports in 3 weeks on queries; 3-5 weeks on mss (only if requested).

Needs: Obtains new clients through recommendations from others, solicitation, at conferences and query letters.

Recent Sales: Did not respond.

Terms: Offers written contract. Charges for photocopying, some postage.

Also Handles: Movie scripts (feature film), TV scripts (TV mow), stage plays. Considers these script subject areas: action/adventure; comedy; detective/police/crime; ethnic; feminist; gay; historical; horror; lesbian; mainstream; mystery/suspense; psychic/supernatural; romantic comedy and drama; thriller; westerns/frontier.

N **SHEREE BYKOFSKY ASSOCIATES, INC.**, 11 E. 47th St., Box WD, New York NY 10017. Website: http://www.users.interport.net/~sheree. Estab. 1984. Incorporated 1991. Member of AAR, ASJA, WNBA. Represents "a limited number of" clients. Specializes in popular reference nonfiction. Currently handles: 80% nonfiction; 20% fiction.

- Prior to opening her agency, Ms. Bykofsky served as executive editor of The Stonesong Press and managing editor of Chiron Press. She is also the author of 10 books.

Handles: Nonfiction, commercial and literary fiction. Considers all nonfiction areas, especially biography/autobiography; business; child guidance/parenting; cooking/foods/nutrition; current affairs; ethnic/cultural interests; gay/lesbian issues; health/medicine; history; how-to; humor; music/dance/theater/film; popular culture; psychology; inspirational; self-help/personal improvement; true crime/investigative; women's issues/women's studies. "I have wide-ranging interests, but it really depends on quality of writing, originality, and how a particular project appeals to me (or not). I take on very little fiction unless I completely love it—it doesn't matter what area or genre." Query with SASE. No unsolicited mss or phone calls. Reports in 1 week on short queries; 1 month on solicited mss.

Needs: Does not want to receive poetry, children's, screenplays. Obtains new clients through recommendations from others.

Recent Sales: Sold 50 titles in the last year. *How Not to Make Love to a Woman*, by G. Gaynor McTigue (St. Martin's); *Breast Cancer Survival Manual*, by John Link, M.D. (Holt); *The Smoky Mountain Cage Bird Society and Other Magical Tales of Everyday Life*, by John Skoyles (Kodansha); and *Christmas Miracles*, by Jamie Miller, Jennifer Basye Sander and Laura Lewis (Morrow).

Terms: Agent receives 15% commission on domestic sales; 15% on foreign sales. Offers written contract, binding for 1 year "usually." Charges for postage, photocopying and fax.

Writers' Conferences: ASJA Annual Writers' Conference East (New York NY, May); Asilomar (Pacific Grove CA); Kent State; Southwest Writers Workshop Conference (Albuquerque NM, August); Willamette Writers Conference (Portland, August); Dorothy Canfield Fisher Writers Conference (San Diego); Maui Writers Conference (Maui HI, August); Pacific Northwest Writers Conference (Seattle, February and July); IWWG; and many others.

Tips: "Read the agent listing carefully and comply with guidelines."

N **MARIA CARVAINIS AGENCY, INC.**, 235 West End Ave., New York NY 10023. (212)580-1559. Fax: (212)877-3486. Contact: Maria Carvainis. Estab. 1977. Member of AAR, Authors Guild, American Booksellers Association, Mystery Writers of America, Romance Writers of America, signatory of WGA. Represents 30 clients. 10% of clients are new/previously unpublished writers. Currently handles: 29% nonfiction books; 15% juvenile books; 55% novels; 1% poetry books.

- Prior to opening her agency, Ms. Carvainis spent more than ten years in the publishing industry as a senior editor with Macmillan Publishing, Basic Books, Avon Books, where she worked closely with Peter Mayer and Crown Publishers. Maria Carvainis is also a member of the AAR Board of Directors and AAR Treasurer.

Handles: Nonfiction books, novels. Considers these nonfiction areas: political and film biographies; business; health/medicine; finance; psychology; travel; women's health; popular science. Considers these fiction areas: fantasy; historical; literary; mainstream; mystery/suspense; romance; thriller; children's; young adult. Query first with SASE. Reports within 2-3 weeks on queries; within 3 months on solicited mss.

Needs: Does not want to receive science fiction. "60% of new clients derived from recommendations or conferences. 40% of new clients derived from letters of query."

Recent Sales: *Silent Melody*, by Mary Balogh (Berkley); *The Guru Guide*, by Joseph H. Boyett and Jimmie T. Boyett (John Wiley and Sons); *Fat Tuesday*, by Sandra Brown (Warner Books); *Sheer Gall*, by Michael Kahn (Dutton/Signet). Other clients include Candace Camp, Pam Conrad, Catherine Hart, Samantha James, Gerrit Verschaur and Jose Yglesias.

Terms: Agent receives 15% commission on domestic sales; 20% on foreign sales. Offers written contract, binding for 2 years "on a book-by-book basis." Charges for foreign postage and bulk copying.
Writers' Conferences: BEA (Chicago, June); Romance Writers of America National Conference (Houston, July/August); Frankfurt Book Fair; Novelists, Inc. Conference (Denver, October).

N **CASTIGLIA LITERARY AGENCY**, 1155 Camino Del Mar, Suite 510, Del Mar CA 92014. (619)755-8761. Fax: (619)755-7063. Contact: Julie Castiglia. Estab. 1993. Member of AAR, PEN. Represents 50 clients. Currently handles: 60% nonfiction books; 35% novels.

- Prior to opening her agency, Ms. Castiglia served as an agent with Waterside Productions, as well as working as a freelance editor and published writer of three books.

Handles: Nonfiction books, novels. Considers these nonfiction areas: animals; anthropology/archaeology; biography/autobiography; business; child guidance/parenting; cooking/food/nutrition; current affairs; ethnic/cultural interests; finance; health/medicine; history; language/literature/criticism; nature/environment; New Age/metaphysics; psychology; religious/inspirational; science/technology; self-help/personal improvement; sociology; women's issues/women's studies. Considers these fiction areas: contemporary issues; ethnic; glitz; literary; mainstream; mystery/suspense; women's fiction especially. Send outline/proposal plus 2 sample chapters; send synopsis with 2 chapters for fiction. Reports in 6-8 weeks on mss.
Needs: Does not want to receive horror, science fiction or Holocaust novels. No screenplays or academic nonfiction. Obtains new clients through solicitations, conferences, referrals.
Recent Sales: *The Power of Positive Prophecy*, by Laurie Beth Jones (Hyperion/Disney); *7 Miracles of Management*, by Alan Downs (Prentice-Hall); *150 Ways to Help Your Child Succeed*, by Karin Ireland (Berkley); *Wild Turkey Moon*, by April Cristofferson (TOR/Forge).
Terms: Agent receives 15% commission on domestic sales; 20% on foreign sales. Offers written contract, 6 week termination. Charges for excessive postage and copying.
Writers' Conferences: Southwest Writers Workshop Conference (Albuquerque NM, August); National Writers Association Conference (Denver, June); Willamette Writers Conference (Portland OR, August); San Diego State University Writers' Conference (January); Writers at Work Fellowship Competition Conference (UT, July).
Tips: "Be professional with submissions. Attend workshops and conferences before you approach an agent."

N **RUTH COHEN, INC. LITERARY AGENCY**, P.O. Box 7626, Menlo Park CA 94025. (650)854-2054. Contact: Ruth Cohen or associates. Estab. 1982. Member of AAR, Authors Guild, Sisters in Crime, Romance Writers of America, SCBWI. Represents 75 clients. 20% of clients are new/previously unpublished writers. Specializes in "quality writing in mysteries, juvenile fiction, adult women's fiction." Currently handles: 15% nonfiction books; 40% juvenile books; 45% novels.

- Prior to opening her agency, Ms. Cohen served as directing editor at Scott Foresman & Company (now HarperCollins).

Handles: Adult novels, juvenile books. Considers these nonfiction areas: ethnic/cultural interests; juvenile nonfiction; women's issues/women's studies. Considers these fiction areas: detective/police; ethnic; historical; juvenile; literary; mainstream; mystery/suspense; picture books; romance (historical, long contemporary); young adult. *No unsolicited mss.* Send outline plus 2 sample chapters. Must include SASE. Reports in 1 month on queries.
Needs: Obtains new clients through recommendations from others.
Recent Sales: Did not respond.
Terms: Agent receives 15% commission on domestic sales; 20% on foreign sales, "if a foreign agent is involved." Offers written contract, binding for 1 year "continuing to next." Charges for foreign postage and photocopying for submissions.
Tips: "A good writer cares about the words she uses—so do I. Also, if no SASE is included, material will not be read."

N **COLUMBIA LITERARY ASSOCIATES, INC.**, 7902 Nottingham Way, Ellicott City MD 21043-6721. (410)465-1595. Fax: Call for number. Contact: Linda Hayes. Estab. 1980. Member of AAR, IACP, RWA, WRW. Represents 40 clients. 10% of clients are new/previously unpublished writers. Specializes in women's commercial contemporary fiction (mainstream/genre), commercial nonfiction, especially cookbooks. Currently handles: 40% nonfiction books; 60% novels.
Handles: Nonfiction books, novels. Considers these nonfiction areas: cooking/food/nutrition; health/medicine; self-help. Considers these fiction areas: mainstream; commercial women's fiction; suspense; contemporary romance; psychological/medical thrillers. Reports in 2-4 weeks on queries; 6-8 weeks on mss; "rejections faster."
Recent Sales: Sold 20-30 titles in the last year. *Eyes of Night*, by Beth Amos (HarperPaperbacks); *Nowhere Man*, by Rebecca York (Harlequin Intrigue); *Pacific Light Cookbook*, by Ruth Law (Penguin/Fine); Right Bride, Wrong Groom series, by Metsy Hingle (Silhouette Desire); *What Love Sees*, by Susan Vreeland (Rosemont Productions).
Terms: Agent receives 15% commission on domestic sales. Offers single- or multiple-book written contract, binding for 6-month terms. "Standard expenses are billed against book income (e.g., books for subrights exploitation, toll calls, express mail)."
Writers' Conferences: Romance Writers of America National Conference (Houston, July/August); International Association of Culinary Professionals; Novelists, Inc. Conference (Denver, October).
Tips: "CLA's list is very full; we're able to accept only a rare few top-notch projects." Submission requirements: "For fiction, send a query letter with author credits, narrative synopsis, first chapter or two, manuscript word count and

submission history (publishers/agents); self-addressed, stamped mailer mandatory for response/manuscript return. (When submitting romances, note whether manuscript is mainstream or category—if category, say which line(s) manuscript is targeted to.) Same for nonfiction, plus include table of contents and note audience, how project is different and better than competition (specify competing books with publisher and publishing date). Please note that we do *not* handle: historical or literary fiction, westerns, science fiction/fantasy, military books, poetry, short stories or screenplays."

N **ROBERT CORNFIELD LITERARY AGENCY**, 145 W. 79th St., New York NY 10024-6468. (212)874-2465. Fax: (212)874-2641. Contact: Robert Cornfield. Estab. 1979. Member of AAR. Represents 60 clients. 20% of clients are new/previously unpublished writers. Specializes in film, art, literary, music criticism, food, fiction. Currently handles: 60% nonfiction books; 20% scholarly books; 20% novels.

- Prior to opening his agency, Mr. Cornfield was an editor at Holt and Dial Press.

Handles: Nonfiction books, novels. Considers these nonfiction areas: animals; anthropology/archaeology; art/architecture/design; biography/autobiography; cooking/food/nutrition; history; language/literature/criticism; music/dance/theater/film. Considers literary fiction. Query. Reports in 2-3 weeks on queries.
Needs: Obtains new clients through recommendations.
Recent Sales: Sold 15-20 titles in the last year. Prefers not to share info on specific sales.
Terms: Agent receives 10% commission on domestic sales; 20% on foreign sales. No written contract. Charges for postage, excessive photocopying.

N **DARHANSOFF & VERRILL LITERARY AGENTS**, 179 Franklin St., 4th Floor, New York NY 10013. (212)334-5980. Estab. 1975. Member of AAR. Represents 100 clients. 10% of clients are new/previously unpublished writers. Specializes in literary fiction. Currently handles: 25% nonfiction books; 60% novels; 15% short story collections.
Member Agents: Liz Darhansoff, Charles Verrill, Leigh Feldman.
Handles: Nonfiction books, novels, short story collections. Considers these nonfiction areas: anthropology/archaeology; biography/autobiography; current affairs; health/medicine; history; language/literature/criticism; nature/environment; science/technology. Considers literary and thriller fiction. Query letter only. Reports in 2 weeks on queries.
Needs: Obtains new clients through recommendations from others.
Recent Sales: *Cold Mountain*, by Charles Frazier (Atlantic Monthly Press); *At Home in Mitford*, by Jan Karon (Viking).

N **DH LITERARY, INC.**, P.O. Box 990, Nyack NY 10960-0990. (212)753-7942. E-mail: dhendin@aol.com. Contact: David Hendin. Estab. 1993. Member of AAR. Represents 50 clients. 20% of clients are new/previously unpublished writers. Specializes in trade fiction, nonfiction and newspaper syndication of columns or comic strips. Currently handles: 60% nonfiction books; 10% scholarly books; 20% fiction; 10% syndicated material.

- Prior to opening his agency, Mr. Hendin served as president and publisher for Pharos Books/World Almanac as well as senior VP and COO at sister company United Feature Syndicate.

Handles: Nonfiction books, scholarly books, novels, syndicated material. Considers these nonfiction areas: animals; anthropology/archaeology; biography/autobiography; business; child guidance/parenting; current affairs; education; ethnic/cultural interests; gay/lesbian issues; government/politics/law; health/medicine; history; how-to; language/literature/criticism; military/war; money/finance/economics; music/dance/theater/film; nature/environment; popular culture; psychology; science/technology; self-help/personal improvement; sociology; sports; true crime/investigative; women's issues/women's studies. Considers these fiction areas: literary; mainstream; mystery; thriller/espionage. Reports in 4-6 weeks on queries.
Needs: Obtains new clients through referrals from others (clients, writers, publishers).
Recent Sales: Sold 20 titles in the last year. *Nobody's Angels*, by Leslie Haynesworth and David Toomey (William Morrow); *Backstab*, by Elaine Viets (Dell); *The Created Self*, by Robert Weber (Norton); *The Books of Jonah*, by R.O. Blechman (Stewart, Tabori and Chang); *Eating the Bear*, by Carole Fungaroli (Farrar, Straus & Giroux); *Miss Manners Basic Training: Eating*, by Judith Martin (Crown); *Do Unto Others*, by Abraham Twerski, M.D. (Andrews & McMeel).
Terms: Agent receives 15% commission on domestic sales; 20% on foreign sales. Offers written contract, binding for 1 year. Charges for out-of-pocket expenses for postage, photocopying manuscript, and overseas phone calls specifically related to a book.
Tips: "Have your project in mind and on paper before you submit. Too many writers/cartoonists say 'I'm good . . . get me a project.' Publishers want writers with their own great ideas and their own unique voice. No faxed submissions."

N **ANITA DIAMANT LITERARY AGENCY, THE WRITER'S WORKSHOP, INC.**, 310 Madison Ave., New York NY 10017-6009. (212)687-1122. Contact: Robin Rue. Estab. 1917. Member of AAR. Represents 125 clients. 25% of clients are new/previously unpublished writers. Currently handles: 20% nonfiction books; 80% novels.
Member Agents: Robin Rue (fiction and nonfiction); John Talbott (agent); Mark Chelius (associate).
Handles: Nonfiction books, young adult, novels. Considers these nonfiction areas: animals; art/architecture/design; biography/autobiography; business; child guidance/parenting; cooking/food/nutrition; crafts/hobbies; current affairs; government/politics/law; health/medicine; history; juvenile nonfiction; money/finance/economics; nature/environment; New Age/metaphysics; psychology; religious/inspirational; science/technology; self-help/personal improvement; sports; true crime/investigative; women's issues/women's studies. Considers these fiction areas: action/adventure; contemporary issues; detective/police/crime; experimental; family saga; feminist; gay; historical; juvenile; literary; mainstream; mystery/suspense; psychic/supernatural; religious/inspirational; romance; thriller/espionage; westerns/frontier; young adult. Query with SASE. Reports "at once" on queries; 2 months on mss.

Needs: Obtains new clients through "recommendations from publishers and clients, appearances at writers' conferences, and through readers of my written articles."
Recent Sales: *All That Glitters*, by V.C. Andrews (Pocket); *Why Smart People Do Dumb Things*, by John Tarrand (Fireside); *Jacqueline Kennedy Onassis*, by Lester David (Carol); *Old Ways in the New World*, by Richard Conroy (St. Martin's); *Death of Love*, by Bartholomew Gill (Morrow).
Terms: Agent receives 15% commission on domestic sales; 20% on foreign sales. Offers written contract.
Writers' Conferences: Romance Writers of America National Conference (Houston, July/August); BEA (Chicago, June).

N **SANDRA DIJKSTRA LITERARY AGENCY**, 1155 Camino del Mar, #515, Del Mar CA 92014. (619)755-3115. Contact: Sandra Zane. Estab. 1981. Member of AAR, Authors Guild, PEN West, Poets and Editors, MWA. Represents 100 clients. 30% of clients are new/previously unpublished writers. "We specialize in a number of fields." Currently handles: 60% nonfiction books; 5% juvenile books; 35% novels.
Member Agents: Sandra Dijkstra.
Handles: Nonfiction books, novels. Considers these nonfiction areas: anthropology; biography/autobiography; business; child guidance/parenting; nutrition; current affairs; ethnic/cultural interests; government/politics; health/medicine; history; literary studies (trade only); military/war (trade only); money/finance/economics; nature/environment; psychology; science/technology; self-help/personal improvement; sociology; sports; true crime/investigative; women's issues/women's studies. Considers these fiction areas: contemporary issues; detective/police/crime; ethnic; family saga; feminist; literary; mainstream; mystery/suspense; thriller/espionage. Send "outline/proposal with sample chapters for nonfiction, synopsis and first 50 pages for fiction and SASE." Reports in 4-6 weeks on queries and mss.
Needs: Obtains new clients primarily through referrals/recommendations, but also through queries and conferences and often by solicitation.
Recent Sales: *The Mistress of Spices*, by Chitra Divakaruni (Anchor Books); *The Flower Net*, by Lisa See (HarperCollins); *Outsmarting the Menopausal Fat Cell*, by Debra Waterhouse (Hyperion); *Verdi*, by Janell Cannon (children's, Harcourt Brace); *The Nine Secrets of Women Who Get Everything They Want*, by Kate White (Harmony).
Terms: Agent receives 15% commission on domestic sales; 20% on foreign sales. Offers written contract, binding for 1 year. Charges for expenses from years we are *active* on author's behalf to cover domestic costs so that we can spend time selling books instead of accounting expenses. We also charge for the photocopying of the full manuscript or nonfiction proposal and for foreign postage."
Writers' Conferences: "Have attended Squaw Valley, Santa Barbara, Asilomar, Southern California Writers Conference, Rocky Mountain Fiction Writers, to name a few. We also speak regularly for writers groups such as PEN West and the Independent Writers Association."
Tips: "Be professional and learn the standard procedures for submitting your work. Give full biographical information on yourself, especially for a nonfiction project. Always include SASE with correct return postage for your own protection of your work. Query with a 1 or 2 page letter first and always include postage. Nine page letters telling us your life story, or your book's, are unprofessional and usually not read. Tell us about your book and write your query well. It's our first introduction to who you are and what you can do! Call if you don't hear within a reasonable period of time. Be a regular patron of bookstores and study what kind of books are being published. READ. Check out your local library and bookstores—you'll find lots of books on writing and the publishing industry that will help you! At conferences, ask published writers about their agents. Don't believe the myth that an agent has to be in New York to be successful—we've already disproved it!"

N **JANE DYSTEL LITERARY MANAGEMENT**, One Union Square West, New York NY 10003. (212)627-9100. Fax: (212)627-9313. Website: http://www.dystel.com. Contact: Miriam Goderich. Estab. 1994. Member of AAR. Presently represents 200 clients. 50% of clients are new/previously unpublished writers. Specializes in commercial and literary fiction and nonfiction plus cookbooks. Currently handles: 65% nonfiction books; 25% novels; 10% cookbooks.
- Prior to opening her agency, Ms. Dystel was a principal agent in Acton, Dystel, Leone and Jaffe.

Handles: Nonfiction books, novels, cookbooks. Considers these nonfiction areas: animals; anthropology/archaeology; biography/autobiography; business; child guidance/parenting; cooking/food/nutrition; current affairs; education; ethnic/cultural interests; gay/lesbian issues; government/politics/law; health/medicine; history; humor; military/war; money/finance/economics; New Age/metaphysics; popular cultures; psychology; religious/inspirational; science/technology; true crime/investigative; women's issues/women's studies. Considers these fiction areas: action/adventure; contemporary issues; detective/police/crime; ethnic; family saga; gay; lesbian; literary; mainstream; thriller/espionage. Query. Reports in 3 weeks on queries; 6 weeks on mss.
Needs: Obtains new clients through recommendations from others, solicitation, at conferences.
Recent Sales: *What the Deaf Mute Heard*, by Dan Gearino (Simon & Schuster). *Tiger's Tail*, by Gus Lee (Knopf); *I Never Forget A Meal*, by Michael Tucker (Little, Brown); *The Sparrow*, by Mary Russell (Villard); *A Tavola con Lidia*, by Lidia Bastianich (William Morrow); *Simplify Your Life*, by Elaine St. James (Hyperion).
Terms: Agent receives 15% commission on domestic sales; 19% of foreign sales. Offers written contract on a book-to-book basis. Charges for photocopying. Galley charges and book charges from the publisher are passed on to the author.
Writers' Conferences: West Coast Writers Conference (Whidbey Island WA, October); Iowa Summer Writing Festival (Iowa City); Maui Writer's Conference (August); Pike's Peak Writer's Conference; Santa Barbara Writer's Conference.

N **FELICIA ETH LITERARY REPRESENTATION**, 555 Bryant St., Suite 350, Palo Alto CA 94301-1700. (650)375-1276. Fax: (650)375-1277. E-mail: feliciaeth@aol.com. Contact: Felicia Eth. Estab. 1988. Member of AAR. Represents 25-35 clients. Works with established and new writers; "for nonfiction, established expertise is certainly a plus, as is magazine publication—though not a prerequisite. I specialize in provocative, intelligent, thoughtful nonfiction on a wide array of subjects which are commercial and high-quality fiction, preferably mainstream and contemporary. I am highly selective, but also highly dedicated to those projects I represent." Currently handles: 85% nonfiction; 15% adult novels.

Handles: Nonfiction books, novels. Considers these nonfiction areas: animals; anthropology; biography; business; child guidance/parenting; current affairs; ethnic/cultural interests; gay/lesbian issues; government/politics/law; health/medicine; history; nature/environment; popular culture; psychology; science/technology; sociology; true crime/investigative; women's issues/women's studies. Considers these fiction areas: ethnic; feminist; gay; lesbian; literary; mainstream; thriller/espionage. Query with outline. Reports in 3 weeks on queries; 1 month on proposals and sample pages.

Recent Sales: Sold 8 titles in the last year. *Weight Training for Dummies*, by Schlossberg and Neponent (IDG Books); *Hand Me Down Dreams*, by Mary Jacobsen (Crown Publishers); *Java Joe & the March of Civilization*, by Stewart Allen (Soho Press); *The Charged Border*, by Jim Nolman (Henry Holt & Co.).

Terms: Agent receives 15% commission on domestic sales; 20% on dramatic sales; 20% on foreign sales. Charges for photocopying, express mail service—extraordinary expenses.

Writers' Conferences: Independent Writers of (LA); Conference of National Coalition of Independent Scholars (Berkeley CA); IWWG.

N **JEANNE FREDERICKS LITERARY AGENCY, INC.**, 221 Benedict Hill Rd., New Canaan CT 06840. Phone/fax: (203)972-3011. E-mail: jflainc@ix.netcom.com. Contact: Jeanne Fredericks. Estab. 1997. Represents 70 clients. 10% of clients are new/unpublished writers. Specializes in quality adult nonfiction by authorities in their fields. Currently handles: 95% nonfiction books; 3% juvenile books; 2% novels.

• Prior to opening her agency, Ms. Fredericks was an agent with the Susan P. Urstadt Agency Inc.

Handles: Nonfiction books. Considers these nonfiction areas: animals; anthropology/archaeology; art/architecture; biography/autobiography; business; child guidance/parenting; cooking/food/nutrition; crafts/hobbies; current affairs; education; health/medicine; history; horticulture; how-to; interior design/decorating; money/finance/economics; nature/environment; New Age/metaphysics; photography; psychology; science/technology; self-help/personal improvement; sports; women's issues/women's studies. Considers these fiction areas: family saga; historical; literary. Query first with SASE, then send outline/proposal or outline and 1-2 sample chapters with SASE. Reports in 3 weeks on queries; 4-6 weeks on mss.

Needs: Obtains new clients through referrals, submissions to agency, conferences.

Recent Sales: *The Ultimate House Hunting Book*, by Carolyn Janik (Kiplinger); *Altitude Superguide to Colorado*, by Dan Klinglesmith and Patrick Soran (Altitude); *The Art of the Kitchen Garden*, by Michael and Jan Gettley (Taunton); *Cooperstown*, by Kathleen Quigley (Simon & Schuster).

Terms: Agent receives 15% commission on domestic sales; 20% on foreign sales; 25% with foreign co-agent. Offers written contract, binding for 9 months. 2 months notice must be given to terminate contract. Charges for photocopying of whole proposals and mss, overseas postage, express mail.

Writers' Conferences: PEN Women Conference (Williamsburg VA, February); Connecticut Press Club Biennial Writers' Conference (Stamford CT, April); ASJA Annual Writers' Conference East (New York NY, May); BEA (Chicago, June).

Tips: "Be sure to research the competition for your work and be able to justify why there's a need for it. I enjoy building an author's career, particularly if she is professional, hardworking, and courteous. Aside from seven years of agenting experience, I've had ten years of editorial experience in adult trade book publishing that enables me to help an author polish a proposal so that it's more appealing to prospective editors. My MBA in marketing also distinguishes me from other agents."

N **SANFORD J. GREENBURGER ASSOCIATES, INC.**, 55 Fifth Ave., New York NY 10003. (212)206-5600. Fax: (212)463-8718. Contact: Heide Lange. Estab. 1945. Member of AAR. Represents 500 clients.

Member Agents: Heide Lange, Faith Hamlin, Beth Vesel, Theresa Park, Elyse Cheney, Dan Mandel.

Handles: Nonfiction books, novels. Considers all nonfiction areas. Considers these fiction areas: action/adventure; contemporary issues, detective/police/crime; ethnic; family saga; feminist; gay; glitz; historical; humor/satire; lesbian; literary; mainstream; mystery/suspense; psychic/supernatural; regional; sports; thriller/espionage. Query first. Reports in 3 weeks on queries; 2 months on mss.

Needs: Does not want to receive romances or westerns.

Recent Sales: Sold 200 titles in the last year. Prefers not to share info. on specific sales. Clients include Andrew Ross, Margaret Cuthbert, Nicholas Sparks, Mary Kurcinke, Edy Clarke and Peggy Claude Pierre.

Terms: Agent receives 15% commission on domestic sales; 20% on foreign sales. Charges for photocopying, books for foreign and subsidiary rights submissions.

N **HEACOCK LITERARY AGENCY, INC.**, 1523 Sixth St., Suite #14, Santa Monica CA 90401-2514. (310)393-6227. Contact: Rosalie Grace Heacock. Estab. 1978. Member of AAR, Authors Guild, SCBWI. Represents 60 clients. 10% of clients are new/previously unpublished writers. Currently handles: 90% nonfiction books; 10% novels.

Handles: Adult nonfiction and fiction books, children's picture books. Considers these nonfiction areas: anthropology;

art/architecture/design; biography (contemporary celebrity); business; child guidance/parenting; cooking/food/nutrition; crafts/hobbies; ethnic/cultural interests; health/medicine (including alternative health); history; how-to; language/literature/criticism; money/finance/economics; music; nature/environment; popular culture; psychology; religious/inspirational; science/technology; self-help/personal improvement; sociology; spirituality/metaphysics; women's issues/women's studies. Considers limited selection of top children's book authors; no beginners. "No multiple queries, please." Query with sample chapters. Reports in 3 weeks on queries; 2 months on mss.

Needs: Does not want to receive scripts. Obtains new clients through "referrals from present clients and industry sources as well as mail queries."

Recent Sales: Did not respond.

Terms: Agent receives 15% commission on domestic sales; 25% on foreign sales "if foreign agent used; if sold directly, 15%." Offers written contract, binding for 1 year. Charges for actual expenses for telephone, postage, packing, photocopying. We provide copies of each publisher submission letter and the publisher's response." 95% of business is derived from commission on ms sales.

Writers' Conferences: Maui Writers Conference (August); Santa Barbara City College Annual Writer's Workshop; Pasadena City College Writer's Forum; UCLA Symposiums on Writing Nonfiction Books; Society of Children's Book Writers and Illustrators.

Tips: "Take time to write an informative query letter expressing your book idea, the market for it, your qualifications to write the book, the 'hook' that would make a potential reader buy the book. Always enclose SASE; we cannot respond to queries without return postage. Our primary focus is upon books which make a contribution."

N **RICHARD HENSHAW GROUP**, 264 W. 73rd St., New York NY 10023. (212)721-4721. Fax: (212)721-4208. E-mail: rhgagents@aol.com. Contact: Rich Henshaw. Estab. 1995. Member of AAR, SinC, MWA, HWA, SFWA. Represents 35 clients. 20% of clients are new/previously unpublished writers. Specializes in thrillers, mysteries, science fiction, fantasy and horror. Currently handles: 20% nonfiction books; 10% juvenile books; 70% novels.

- Prior to opening his agency, Mr. Henshaw served as an agent with Richard Curtis Associates, Inc.

Handles: Nonfiction books, juvenile books, novels. Considers these nonfiction areas: animals; biography/autobiography; business; child guidance/parenting; computers/electronics; cooking/food/nutrition; current affairs; gay/lesbian issues; government/politics/law; health/medicine; how-to; humor; juvenile nonfiction; military/war; money/finance/economics; music/dance/theater/film; nature/environment; New Age/metaphysics; popular culture; psychology; science/technology; self-help/personal improvement; sociology; sports; true crime/investigative; women's issues/women's studies. Considers these fiction areas: action/adventure; detective/police/crime; ethnic; family saga; fantasy; glitz; historical; horror; humor/satire; juvenile; literary; mainstream; psychic/supernatural; science fiction; sports; thriller/espionage; young adult. Query. Reports in 3 weeks on queries; 6 weeks on mss.

Needs: Obtains new clients through recommendations from others, solicitation, at conferences and query letters.

Recent Sales: Sold 17 titles in the last year. *Out For Blood*, by Dana Stabenow (Dutton/Signet); *Deadstick*, by Megan Mallory Rust (Berkley); *And Then There Were None*, by Stephen Solomita (Bantam); *The Well-Trained Mind*, by Susan Wise Bauer and Jessie Wise (W.W. Norton).

Terms: Agent receives 15% commission on domestic sales; 20% on foreign sales. No written contract. Charges for photocopying manuscripts and book orders. 100% of business is derived from commission on sales.

Tips: "Always include SASE with correct return postage."

N **THE JEFF HERMAN AGENCY INC.**, 140 Charles St., Suite 15A, New York NY 10014. (212)941-0540. Contact: Jeffrey H. Herman. Estab. 1985. Member of AAR. Represents 100 clients. 10% of clients are new/previously unpublished writers. Specializes in adult nonfiction. Currently handles: 85% nonfiction books; 5% scholarly books; 5% textbooks; 5% novels.

- Prior to opening his agency, Mr. Herman served as a public relations executive.

Member Agents: Deborah Levine (vice president, nonfiction book doctor); Jamie Forbes (fiction).

Handles: Considers these nonfiction areas: business, computers; health; history; how-to; politics; popular psychology; popular reference; recovery; self-help; spirituality. Query. Reports in 2 weeks on queries; 1 month on mss.

Recent Sales: *Joe Montana on the Magic of Making Quarterback*, by Joe Montana (Henry Holt); *The Aladdin Factor*, by Jack Canfield and Mark Victor Hansen (Putnam); *The I.Q. Myth*, by Bob Sternberg (Simon & Schuster); *All You Need to Know About the Movie and TV Business*, by Gail Resnick and Scott Trost (Fireside/Simon & Schuster).

Terms: Agent receives 15% commission on domestic sales. Offers written contract.

N **BARBARA S. KOUTS, LITERARY AGENT**, P.O. Box 560, Bellport NY 11713. (516)286-1278. Contact: Barbara Kouts. Estab. 1980. Member of AAR. Represents 50 clients. 10% of clients are new/previously unpublished writers. Specializes in adult fiction and nonfiction and children's books. Currently handles: 20% nonfiction books; 60% juvenile books; 20% novels.

Handles: Nonfiction books, juvenile books, novels. Considers these nonfiction areas: biography/autobiography; child

N **INDICATES THAT** the listing is new to this edition. New markets are often more receptive to freelance submissions.

guidance/parenting; current affairs; ethnic/cultural interests; health/medicine; history; juvenile nonfiction; music/dance/theater/film; nature/environment; psychology; self-help/personal improvement; women's issues/women's studies. Considers these fiction areas: contemporary issues; family saga; feminist; historical; juvenile; literary; mainstream; mystery/suspense; picture book; young adult. Query. Reports in 2-3 days on queries; 4-6 weeks on mss.

Needs: Obtains new clients through recommendations from others, solicitation, at conferences, etc.

Recent Sales: *Voice Lessons*, by Nancy Mairs (Beacon); *The Faithful Friend*, by Robert San Souci (Simon & Schuster).

Terms: Agent receives 10% commission on domestic sales; 20% on foreign sales. Charges for photocopying.

Tips: "Write, do not call. Be professional in your writing."

N **SABRA ELLIOTT LARKIN**, Bly Hollow Rd., Cherry Plain NY 12040-0055. Phone/fax: (518)658-3065. E-mail: becontree@taconic.net. Contact: Sabra Larkin. Estab. 1996. Represents 10 clients. 90% of clients are new/unpublished writers. Currently handles: 70% nonfiction books; 10% juvenile books; 20% novels.

- Prior to opening her agency, Ms. Larkin worked for over 30 years in publishing: 5 years in editorial at Dutton; 7 years at Ballantine Books in publicity and advertising; 10 years at Avon Books; and 10 years at Putnam Berkley as vice president of Publicity, Promotion, Advertising and Public Relations

Handles: Nonfiction books, scholarly books, novels, illustrated books/(adult) art and photography. Considers these nonfiction areas: agriculture/horticulture; animals; anthropology/archaeology; art/architecture/design; biography/autobiography; business; cooking/food/nutrition; current affairs; education; ethnic/cultural interests; government/politics/law; health/medicine; history; how-to; interior design/decorating; language/literature/criticism; money/finance/economics; music/dance/theater/film; nature/environment; photography; popular culture; psychology; religious/inspirational; science/technology; self-help/personal improvement; true crime/investigative; women's issues/women's studies. Considers these fiction areas: action/adventure; contemporary issues; detective/police/crime; ethnic; experimental; family saga; glitz; historical; horror; humor/satire; literary; mainstream; mystery/suspense; regional; romance (contemporary, historical); thriller/espionage; young adult. Query. Send outline and 2-3 sample chapters with return postage. Reports in 2 weeks on queries; 1 month on mss.

Needs: Obtains new clients through recommendations from others.

Recent Sales: Sold 2 titles in the last year. *Water Rat*, by Marnie Laird (Winslow Press); *Winter Soups*, by Lisa Fosburgh (Country Roads Press). Other clients include Dorsey Fiske, Steve Stargen, Gretchen McKenzie, Ernest Barker.

Terms: Agent receives 15% commission on domestic sales; 20% on foreign sales. Offers written contract, binding for 5 years. 60 days notice must be given to terminate contract. Charges for postage and photocopying of mss. "Copies of receipts for dollar amounts are supplied to clients. Not applicable to contracted clients."

N **MICHAEL LARSEN/ELIZABETH POMADA LITERARY AGENTS**, 1029 Jones St., San Francisco CA 94109-5023. (415)673-0939. Website: http://www.Larsen-Pomada.com. Contact: Mike Larsen or Elizabeth Pomada. Estab. 1972. Members of AAR, Authors Guild, ASJA, NWA, PEN, WNBA, California Writers Club. Represents 100 clients. 40-45% of clients are new/unpublished writers. Eager to work with new/unpublished writers. "We have very diverse tastes. We look for fresh voices and new ideas. We handle literary, commercial and genre fiction, and the full range of nonfiction books." Currently handles: 70% nonfiction books; 30% novels.

- Prior to opening their agency, both Mr. Larsen and Ms. Pomada were promotion executives for major publishing houses. Mr. Larsen worked for Morrow, Bantam and Pyramid (now part of Berkley), Ms. Pomada worked at Holt, David McKay, and The Dial Press.

Member Agents: Michael Larsen (nonfiction), Elizabeth Pomada (fiction, books of interest to women).

Handles: Adult nonfiction books, novels. Considers these nonfiction areas: anthropology/archaeology; art/architecture/design; biography/autobiography; business; cooking/food/nutrition; crafts/hobbies; current affairs; ethnic/cultural interests; futurism; gay/lesbian issues; government/politics/law; health/medicine; history; how-to; humor; interior design/decorating; language/literature/criticism; memoirs; money/finance/economics; music/dance/theater/film; nature/environment; New Age/metaphysics; parenting; photography; popular culture; psychology; religious/inspirational; science/technology; self-help/personal improvement; sociology; sports; travel; true crime/investigative; women's issues/women's studies. Considers these fiction areas: action/adventure; contemporary issues; detective/police/crime; ethnic; experimental; family saga; fantasy; feminist; gay; glitz; historical; horror; humor/satire; lesbian; literary; mainstream; mystery/suspense; psychic/supernatural; religious/inspirational; romance (contemporary, gothic, historical, regency). Query with synopsis and first 30 pages of completed novel. Reports in 2 months on queries. For nonfiction, "please read Michael's book *How to Write a Book Proposal* (Writer's Digest Books) and then send the title of your book and your promotion plan." Always include SASE. Send SASE for brochure.

Needs: Actively seeking commercial and literary fiction. "Fresh voices with new ideas from authors 'ready to pop' onto the bestseller lists. Does not want to receive children's books, plays, short stories, screenplays, pornography.

Recent Sales: Sold 15 titles in the last year. *Armor of Lies*, by Katharine Kerr (TOR); *Catch Your Dog Doing Something Right: How to Train Any Dog in Five Minutes*, by Krista Cantrell (Plume); *Guerrilla Marketing with Technology*, by Jay Conrad Levinson (A-W); *I'm Not as Old as I Used to Be*, by Frances Weaver (Hyperion).

Terms: Agent receives 15% commission on domestic sales; 15% on dramatic sales; 20% on foreign sales. May charge writer for printing, postage for multiple submissions, foreign mail, foreign phone calls, galleys, books, and legal fees.

Writers' Conferences: BEA (Chicago, June); Santa Barbara Writer's Conference (Santa Barbara); Maui Writers Conference (August); ASJA (Los Angeles, February).

N LEVANT & WALES, LITERARY AGENCY, INC., 108 Hayes St., Seattle WA 98109-2808. (206)284-7114. Fax: (206)284-0190. E-mail: bizziew@aol.com. Contact: Elizabeth Wales or Adrienne Reed. Estab. 1988. Member of AAR, Pacific Northwest Writers' Conference, Book Publishers' Northwest. Represents 65 clients. We are interested in published and not-yet-published writers. Especially encourages writers living in the Pacific Northwest, West Coast, Alaska and Pacific Rim countries. Specializes in mainstream nonfiction and fiction, as well as narrative nonfiction and literary fiction. Currently handles: 60% nonfiction books; 40% novels.

- Prior to becoming an agent, Ms. Wales worked at Oxford University Press and Viking Penguin.

Handles: Nonfiction books, novels. Considers these nonfiction areas: animals; anthropology/archaeology; art/architecture/design; biography/autobiography; business; child guidance/parenting; current affairs; education; ethnic/cultural interests; gardening; gay/lesbian issues; health; language/literature/criticism; lifestyle; memoirs; nature; New Age/metaphysics; popular culture; psychology; science; self-help/personal improvement; sports; women's issues/women's studies—open to creative or serious treatments of almost any nonfiction subject. Considers these fiction areas: cartoon/comic/women's; ethnic; experimental; feminist; gay; lesbian; literary; mainstream (no genre fiction). Query first. Reports in 3 weeks on queries; 6 weeks on mss.
Recent Sales: Sold 15 titles in the last year. *Into the Forest*, by Jean Hegland (Bantam); *Animals as Teachers & Healers*, by Susan Chernak McElroy (Ballantine); *Six Seasons in the Minnesota Woods with Little Bit the Bear*, by Jack Becklund (Hyperion); *Be an Outrageous Older Woman*, by Ruth Harriet Jacobs (HarperCollins).
Terms: Agent receives 15% commission on domestic sales. "We make all our income from commissions. We offer editorial help for some of our clients and help some clients with the development of a proposal, but we do not charge for these services. We do charge, after a sale, for express mail, manuscript photocopying costs, foreign postage and outside USA telephone costs."
Writers' Conferences: Pacific Northwest Writers Conference (Seattle, July).

N JAMES LEVINE COMMUNICATIONS, INC., 307 Seventh Ave., Suite 1906, New York NY 10001. (212)337-0934. Fax: (212)337-0948. E-mail: levineja@aol.com. Estab. 1989. Represents 150 clients. 33⅓% of clients are new/previously unpublished writers. Specializes in business, psychology, parenting, health/medicine, narrative nonfiction. Currently handles: 90% nonfiction books; 10% fiction. Member agents: James Levine; Daniel Greenberg (sports, history, fiction); Arielle Eckstut (narrative nonfiction, psychology, spirituality, religion, women's issues).

- Prior to opening his agency, Mr. Levine served as vice president of the Bank Street College of Education.

Handles: Nonfiction books, novels. Considers these nonfiction areas: animals; art/architecture/design; biography/autobiography; business; child guidance/parenting; computers/electronics; cooking/food/nutrition; gardening; gay/lesbian issues; health/medicine; money/finance/economics; nature/environment; New Age/metaphysics; psychology; religious/inspirational; science/technology; self-help/personal improvement; sociology; sports; women's issues/women's studies. Considers these fiction areas: contemporary issues; literary; mainstream. Send outline/proposal plus 1 sample chapter. Reports in 2 weeks on queries; 1 month on mss.
Needs: Obtains new clients through client referrals.
Recent Sales: *All I Really Need to Know in Business I Learned at Microsoft*, by Julie Bick (Pocket/Simon & Schuster); *We Can Do It When . . .*, by John Stanford and Robin Simons (Bantam); *The Energy Break*, by Bradford Keeney, Ph.D. (Golden Books); *Lipshtick*, by Gwen Macsai (HarperCollins); *Working Wounded*, by Bob Rosner (Warner).
Terms: Agent receives 15% commission on domestic sales; 20% on foreign sales. Offers written contract; length of time varies per project. Does not charge reading fee. Charges for out-of-pocket expenses—telephone, fax, postage and photocopying—directly connected to the project.
Writers' Conferences: ASJA Annual Writers' Conference East (New York, May); BEA (Chicago, June).
Tips: "We work closely with clients on editorial development and promotion. We work to place our clients as magazine columnists and have created columnists for *McCall's* and *Child*. We work with clients to develop their projects across various media—video, software, and audio."

N ELLEN LEVINE LITERARY AGENCY, INC., 15 E. 26th St., Suite 1801, New York NY 10010. (212)889-0620. Fax: (212)725-4501. Contact: Ellen Levine, Elizabeth Kaplan, Diana Finch, Louise Quayle. Estab. 1980. Member of AAR. Represents over 100 clients. 20% of clients are new/previously unpublished writers. "My three younger colleagues at the agency (Louise Quayle, Diana Finch and Elizabeth Kaplan) are seeking both new and established writers. I prefer to work with established writers, mostly through referrals." Currently handles: 60% nonfiction books; 8% juvenile books; 30% novels; 2% short story collections.
Handles: Nonfiction books, juvenile books, novels, short story collections. Considers these nonfiction areas: anthropology; biography; current affairs; health; popular culture; psychology; science; women's issues/women's studies; books by journalists. Considers these fiction areas: literary; women's fiction; thrillers. Query. Reports in 3 weeks on queries, if SASE provided; 6 weeks on mss, if submission requested.
Needs: Obtains new clients through recommendations from others.
Recent Sales: *Cloudsplitter*, by Russell Banks (HarperCollins); *The Aquero Sisters*, by Cristina Garcia (Knopf); *Shaking the Money Tree: Women's Hidden Fear of Supporting Themselves*, by Colette Dowling (Little, Brown).
Terms: Agent receives 15% commission on domestic sales; 20% on foreign sales. Charges for overseas postage, photocopying, messenger fees, overseas telephone and fax, books ordered for use in rights submissions.

N LINDSTROM LITERARY GROUP, 871 N. Greenbrier St., Arlington VA 22205-1220. (703)522-4730. Fax: (703)527-7624. E-mail: lindlitgrp@aol.com. Contact: Kristin Lindstrom. Estab. 1994. Represents 22 clients. 40% of

clients are new/previously unpublished writers. Currently handles: 20% nonfiction books; 80% novels.
Handles: Nonfiction books; novels. Considers these nonfiction areas: biography/autobiography; current affairs; ethnic/cultural interests; history; memoirs; popular culture; psychology; science/technology. Considers these fiction areas: action/adventure; contemporary issues; detective/police/crime; ethnic; family saga; fantasy; historical; mainstream; science fiction; thriller/espionage. For fiction, send 3 chapters and outline with SASE to cover return of ms if desired. For nonfiction, send outline/proposal with SASE. Reports in 1 month on queries; 6 weeks on mss.
Needs: Obtains new clients through references, guide listing.
Recent Sales: Sold 4 titles in the last year. *Shelter from the Storm*, by Tony Dunbar (G.P. Putnam & Sons); *Triple Play*, by Elizabeth Gunn (Walker & Co.); *Tyrants & Kings*, by John Marco (Bantam Spectra); *The Last Family*, by John Ramsey Miller (Hallmark Television). Other clients include Scott Gier.
Terms: Agent receives 15% commission on domestic sales; 20% on foreign sales; 20% on performance rights sales. Offers written contract. Charges for marketing and mailing expense, express mail, etc.
Tips: "Include biography of writer. Send enough material for an overall review of project scope."

N **WENDY LIPKIND AGENCY**, 165 E. 66th St., New York NY 10021. (212)628-9653. Fax: (212)628-2693. Contact: Wendy Lipkind. Estab. 1977. Member of AAR. Represents 60 clients. Specializes in adult nonfiction. Currently handles: 80% nonfiction books; 20% novels.
Handles: Nonfiction, novels. Considers these nonfiction areas: biography; current affairs; health/medicine; history; science; social history, women's issues/women's studies. Considers mainstream and mystery/suspense fiction. No mass market originals. For nonfiction, query with outline/proposal. For fiction, query with SASE only. Reports in 1 month.
Needs: Usually obtains new clients through recommendations from others.
Recent Sales: *Where's The Baby* and *Animal's Lullaby*, both by Tom Paxton (Morrow Junior Books), *Methyl Magic*, by Dr. Craig Cooney (Andrews-McMeel).
Terms: Agent receives 15% commission on domestic sales; 20% on foreign sales. Sometimes offers written contract. Charges for foreign postage and messenger service.
Tips: "Send intelligent query letter first. Let me know if you sent to other agents."

N **LOWENSTEIN ASSOCIATES, INC.**, 121 W. 27th St., Suite 601, New York NY 10001. (212)206-1630. Fax: (212)727-0280. President: Barbara Lowenstein. Estab. 1976. Member of AAR. Represents 150 clients. 20% of clients are new/unpublished writers. Specializes in multicultural books (fiction and nonfiction), medical experts, commercial fiction, especially suspense, crime and women's issues. Currently handles: 60% nonfiction books; 40% novels.
Member Agents: Barbara Lowenstein (serious nonfiction, multicultural issues); Nancy Yost (commercial fiction, commercial nonfiction).
Handles: Nonfiction books, novels. Considers these nonfiction areas: animals; anthropology/archaeology; art/architecture/design; biography/autobiography; business; child guidance/parenting; craft/hobbies; current affairs; education; ethnic/cultural interests; gay/lesbian issues; government/politics/law; health/medicine; history; how-to; humor; language/literature/criticism/; memoirs; money/finance/economics; music/dance/theater/film; nature/environment; New Age/metaphysics, popular culture; psychology; religious/inspirational; science/technology; self-help/personal improvement; sociology; sports; travel; true crime/investigative; women's issues/women's studies. Considers these fiction areas: contemporary issues; detective/police/crime; erotica; ethnic; feminist; gay; historical; humor/satire; lesbian; mainstream; mystery/suspense; romance (contemporary, historical, regency); medical thrillers. Send query with SASE, "otherwise will not respond." For fiction, send outline and 1st chapter. No unsolicited mss. Reports in 6 weeks on queries.
Needs: Obtains new clients through recommendations from others.
Recent Sales: Sold approximately 75 titles in the last year. *In the Life of a Child*, by Barbara Meltz (Delacorte); *Kissed a Sad Goodbye*, by Deborah Armbie (Bantam); *Stealing Time*, by Leslie Glass (Dutton); *Take Care of Your House*, by Don Vandervert (Addison-Wesley).
Terms: Agent receives 15% commission on domestic and dramatic sales; 20% on foreign sales. Offers written contract, binding for 2 years, with 60 day cancellation clause. Charges for photocopying, foreign postage, messenger expenses.
Writer's Conference: Malice Domestic; Bouchercon.
Tips: "Know the genre you are working in and READ!"

N **MARGRET MCBRIDE LITERARY AGENCY**, 7744 Fay Ave., Suite 201, La Jolla CA 92037. (619)454-1550. Fax: (619)454-2156. Contact: Lys Chard. Also: 11684 Ventura Blvd., Suite 956, Studio City CA 91604. (818)508-0031. Contact: Kimberly Sauer (associate agent). Estab. 1980. Member of AAR, Authors Guild. Represents 50 clients. 15% of clients are new/unpublished writers. Specializes in mainstream fiction and nonfiction.

- Prior to opening her agency, Ms. McBride served in the marketing departments of Random House and Ballantine Books and the publicity departments of Warner Books and Pinnacle Books.

Member Agents: Winifred Golden (associate agent); Kim Sauer (submissions manager); Stacy Horne; Lys Chard (submissions manager); Jason Cabassi (assistant).
Handles: Nonfiction books, novels, audio, video film rights. Considers these nonfiction areas: biography/autobiography; business; child guidance/parenting; cooking/food/nutrition; current affairs; ethnic/cultural interests; gay/lesbian issues; government/politics/law; health/medicine; history; how-to; money/finance/economics; music/dance/theater/film; popular culture; psychology; religious/inspirational; science/technology; self-help/personal improvement; sociology; sports; true crime/investigative; women's issues/women's studies. Considers these fiction areas: action/adventure; detective/police/crime; ethnic; historical; humor; literary; mainstream; mystery/suspense; thriller/espionage; westerns/frontier.

Query with synopsis or outline. No unsolicited mss. Reports in 6 weeks on queries.
Needs: No screenplays.
Recent Sales: *Do They Hear You When You Cry*, by Fauziya Kasinga with Layli Miller-Bashir (Dell); *The Unimaginable Life*, by Kenny and Julia Loggins; *Healing Anxiety With Herbs*, by Harold H. Bloomfield, M.D. (HarperCollins); *Ain't Gonna Be The Same Fool Twice*, by April Sinclair; *Weddings*, by Collin Cowel.
Terms: Agent receives 15% commission on domestic sales; 10% on dramatic sales; 25% on foreign sales. Charges for express mail and photocopying.

N **CAROL MANN AGENCY**, 55 Fifth Ave., New York NY 10003. (212)206-5635. Fax: (212)675-4809. Contact: Carol Mann. Estab. 1977. Member of AAR. Represents over 100 clients. 25% of clients are new/previously unpublished writers. Specializes in current affairs, self-help, psychology, parenting, history. Currently handles: 70% nonfiction books; 30% novels.
Member Agents: Gareth Esersky (contemporary nonfiction); Christy Fletcher (literary fiction, nonfiction).
Handles: Nonfiction books. Considers these nonfiction areas: anthropology/archaeology; art/architecture/design; biography/autobiography; business; child guidance/parenting; current affairs; ethnic/cultural interests; government/politics/law; health/medicine; history; money/finance/economics; psychology; self-help/personal improvement; sociology; women's issues/women's studies. Considers literary fiction. Query with outline/proposal and SASE. Reports in 3 weeks.
Needs: Actively seeking "nonfiction: pop culture, business and health; fiction: literary fiction." Does not want to receive "genre fiction (romance, mystery, etc.)."
Recent Sales: Sold approximately 30 titles in the last year. *The Making of a Classic: Hitchcock's Vertigo*, by Dan Aviler (St. Martin's); *Radical Healing*, by Rudolph Ballentine, M.D. (Harmony); *Hand to Mouth*, by Paul Auster (Holt); *Stopping Cancer Before It Starts*, by American Institute for Cancer Research (Golden). Other clients include Dr. William Julius Wilson, Barry Sears (*Mastering The Zone*) and Dr. Judith Wallerstein.
Terms: Agent receives 15% commission on domestic sales; 20% on foreign sales. Offers written contract.
Tips: No phone queries. Must include SASE for reply.

N **THE DENISE MARCIL LITERARY AGENCY, INC.**, 685 West End Ave., New York NY 10025. (212)932-3110. Contact: Denise Marcil. Estab. 1977. Member of AAR. Represents 70 clients. 40% of clients are new/previously unpublished authors. Specializes in women's commercial fiction, business books, popular reference, how-to and self-help. Currently handles: 30% nonfiction books; 70% novels.

- Prior to opening her agency, Ms. Marcil served as an editorial assistant with Avon Books and as an editor with Simon & Schuster.

Member Agents: Jeffrey Rutherford (thrillers, mysteries, alternative health, pop culture, popular reference).
Handles: Nonfiction books, novels. Considers these nonfiction areas: business; child guidance/parenting; ethnic/cultural interests; nutrition; alternative health/medicine; how-to; inspirational; money/finance/economics; psychology; self-help/personal improvement; spirituality; women's issues/women's studies. Considers these fiction areas: mystery/suspense; romance (contemporary); thrillers/espionage. Query with SASE *only*! Reports in 3 weeks on queries. "Does not read unsolicited manuscripts."
Needs: Actively seeking "big, commercial books with solid plotting, in-depth characters, and suspense. Cyberthrillers may be the next hot topic." Does not want to receive "cozies or British-style mysteries." Obtains new clients through recommendations from other authors. "35% of my list is from query letters!"
Recent Sales: Sold 67 titles in the last year. *Good News for Bad Days*, by Father Paul Keenan (Warner Books); *Stepping Out With Attitude: Sister Sell Your Dream*, by Anita Bunkley (HarperCollins); *His Flame*, by Arnette Lamb (Pocket Books); *Crossing the Line*, by Laura Parker (Kensington Publishers).
Terms: Agent receives 15% commission on domestic sales; 20% on foreign sales. Offers written contract, binding for 2 years. Charges $100/year for postage, photocopying, long-distance calls, etc. 100% of business is derived from commissions on ms sales.
Writers' Conferences: Maui Writers Conference (August); Pacific Northwest Writers Conference (Seattle, February and July); Romance Writers America National Conference (Houston, July/August).
Tips: "Only send a one-page query letter. I read them all and ask for plenty of material; I find many of my clients this way. *Always* send a SASE."

N **ELAINE MARKSON LITERARY AGENCY**, 44 Greenwich Ave., New York NY 10011. (212)243-8480. Estab. 1972. Member of AAR. Represents 200 clients. 10% of clients are new/unpublished writers. Specializes in literary fiction, commercial fiction, trade nonfiction. Currently handles: 35% nonfiction books; 55% novels; 10% juvenile books.
Member Agents: Geri Thoma, Sally Wofford-Girand, Elaine Markson.
Handles: Quality fiction and nonfiction. Query with outline (must include SASE). SASE is required for the return of any material.
Recent Sales: *The Genesis Code*, by John Case (Ballantine); *Girls*, by Fred Busch (Harmony); *Life and Death*, by Andrea Dworkin (Free Press).
Terms: Agent receives 15% commission on domestic sales; 20% on foreign sales. Charges for postage, photocopying, foreign mailing, faxing, long-distance telephone and other special expenses. "Please make sure manuscript weighs no more than one pound."

N THE BETSY NOLAN LITERARY AGENCY, 224 W. 29th St., 15th Floor, New York NY 10001. (212)967-8200. Fax: (212)967-7292. President: Betsy Nolan. Estab. 1980. Represents 200 clients. 10% of clients are new/unpublished writers. Works with a small number of new/unpublished authors. Currently handles: 90% nonfiction books; 10% novels.

Member Agents: Donald Lehr, Carla Glasser, Ellen Morrissey.

Handles: Nonfiction books. Query with outline. Reports in 3 weeks on queries; 2 months on mss.

Recent Sales: Sold 30 titles in the last year. *Desperation Dinners*, by Beverly Mills and Alicia Koss (Workman); *Your Oasis on Flame Lake*, by Lorna Landvik (Ballantine); *The Olives Table*, by Todd English and Sally Sampson (Simon & Schuster); *My First White Friend*, by Patricia Raybon (Viking Penguin).

Terms: Agent receives 15% commission on domestic sales; 20% on foreign sales.

N ALICE ORR AGENCY, INC., 305 Madison Ave., Suite 1166, New York NY 10165. (718)204-6673. Fax: (718)204-6023. E-mail: orragency@aol.com. Website: http://www.romanceweb.com/aorr/aorr.html. Contact: Alice Orr. Estab. 1988. Member of AAR. Represents 20 clients. Specializes in commercial ("as in nonliterary") fiction and nonfiction. Currently handles: 5% nonfiction books; 5% juvenile books; 90% novels.

- Prior to opening her agency, Ms. Orr was an editor of mystery/suspense and romance fiction; a national lecturer on how to write and get that writing published; and was a published popular fiction novelist.

Handles: Considers commercial nonfiction. Considers these fiction areas: family saga; glitz; mainstream; romance (contemporary, historical); mystery/suspense. Send SASE for synopsis/proposal guidelines. Send outline and 3 sample chapters. Reports in 6-8 weeks on ms.

Needs: Actively seeking "absolutely extraordinary, astounding, astonishing work." Does not want to receive "science fiction and fantasy, horror fiction, literary nonfiction, literary fiction, poetry, short stories, children's fiction and nonfiction (for younger than middle grade readers)." Obtains new clients through recommendations from others, writers' conferences, meetings with authors and submissions.

Terms: Agent receives 15% commission on domestic sales; 20% on foreign sales. No written contract.

Recent Sales: Sold over 20 titles in the last year. Prefers not to share info on specific sales.

Writers' Conferences: Edgar Allen Poe Awards; Novelists, Inc. Conference (Denver, October); IWWG Summer Conference (Saratoga Springs NY, August); Romance Writers of America National Conference (Houston, July/August); Romantic Times Booklovers Convention.

N PERKINS, RABINER, RUBIE & ASSOCIATES, 240 W. 35th St., New York NY 10001. (718)543-5344. Fax: (212)569-8188. Contact: Lori Perkins, Peter Rubie, Susan Rabiner. Estab. 1997. Member of AAR, HWA. Represents 130 clients. 15% of clients are new/previously unpublished writers. Perkins specializes in horror, dark thrillers, literary fiction, pop culture, Latino and gay issues (fiction and nonfiction). Rubie specializes in crime, science fiction, fantasy, off-beat mysteries, history, literary fiction, dark thrillers, narrative nonfiction. Rabiner specializes in narrative and serious nonfiction as well as commercial fiction. Currently handles: 60% nonfiction books; 40% novels.

- Mr. Rubie is the author of *The Elements of Storytelling* (John Wiley) and *Story Sense*. Prior to becoming an agent, Ms. Rabiner was recently editorial director of Basic Books at HarperCollins. She also taught nonfiction at Yale and authored *Thinking Like Your Editor: A Guide to Writing Serious Nonfiction*.

Handles: Nonfiction books, novels. Considers these nonfiction areas: art/architecture/design; current affairs; commercial academic material; ethnic/cultural interests; music/dance/theater/film; science; "subjects that fall under pop culture—TV, music, art, books and authors, film, current affairs, etc." Considers these fiction areas: detective/police/crime; ethnic; fact-based historical fiction; fantasy; horror; literary; mainstream; mystery/suspense; psychic/supernatural; science fiction; dark thriller. Query with SASE. Reports in 3-6 weeks on queries with SASE; 10 weeks on mss.

Needs: Obtains new clients through recommendations from others, solicitation, at conferences, etc.

Recent Sales: *Song of the Banshee*, by Greg Kihn (Forge); *Light & Shadow*, by K. Ramsland (Harper); *Godzilla: The Unofficial Biography*, by S. Ryfle (Delta); *Keeper*, by Gregory Rucka (Bantam); *Witchunter*, by C. Lyons (Avon); *How the Tiger Lost Its Stripes*, by C. Meacham (Harcourt Brace).

Terms: Agent receives 15% commission on domestic sales; 20% on foreign sales. Offers written contract, only "if requested." Charges for photocopying.

Tips: "Sometimes I come up with book ideas and find authors (*Coupon Queen*, for example). Be professional. Read *Publishers Weekly* and genre-related magazines. Join writers' organizations. Go to conferences. Know your market and learn your craft."

N PINDER LANE & GARON-BROOKE ASSOCIATES, LTD., (formerly Jay Garon-Brooke Assoc. Inc.), 159 W. 53rd St., Suite 14E, New York NY 10019. (212)489-0880. Vice President: Jean Free. Member of AAR, signatory of WGA. Represents 80 clients. 20% of clients are new/previously unpublished writers. Specializes in mainstream fiction and nonfiction. "With our literary and media experience, our agency is uniquely positioned for the current and future direction publishing is taking." Currently handles: 25% nonfiction books; 75% novels.

Member Agents: Nancy Coffey, Dick Duane, Robert Thixton.

Handles: Nonfiction books, novels. Considers these nonfiction areas: biography/autobiography; child guidance/parenting; gay/lesbian issues; health/medicine; history; memoirs; military/war; music/dance/theater/film; psychology; self-help/personal improvement; true crime/investigative. Considers these fiction areas: contemporary issues; detective/police/crime; family saga; fantasy; gay; literary; mainstream; mystery/suspense; romance; science fiction. Query with SASE. Reports in 3 weeks on queries; 2 months on mss.

Needs: Does not want to receive screenplays, TV series teleplays or dramatic plays. Obtains new clients through referrals and from queries.
Recent Sales: Sold 15 titles in the last year. *The Gemini Man*, by Richard Steinberg (Doubleday); *Shattered Bone*, by Chris Stewart (M. Evans); *Return to Christmas*, by Chris Heimerdinger (Ballantine); *Reaper*, by Ben Mezrich (HarperCollins).
Terms: Agent receives 15% on domestic sales; 30% on foreign sales. Offers written contract, binding for 3-5 years.
Tips: "Send query letter first giving the essence of the manuscript and a personal or career bio with SASE."

N **AARON M. PRIEST LITERARY AGENCY**, 708 Third Ave., 23rd Floor, New York NY 10017. (212)818-0344. Contact: Aaron Priest or Molly Friedrich. Member of AAR. Currently handles: 25% nonfiction books; 75% fiction.
Member Agents: Lisa Erbach Vance, Paul Cirone.
Handles: Nonfiction books, fiction. Query only (must be accompanied by SASE). Unsolicited mss returned unread.
Recent Sales: *Absolute Power*, by David Baldacci (Warner); *Three to Get Deadly*, by Janet Evanovich (Scribner); *How Stella Got Her Groove Back*, by Terry McMillan (Viking); *Day After Tomorrow*, by Allan Folsom (Little, Brown); *Angela's Ashes*, by Frank McCourt (Scribner); *M as in Malice*, by Sue Grafton (Henry Holt).
Terms: Agent receives 15% commission on domestic sales. Charges for photocopying, foreign postage expenses.

N **SUSAN ANN PROTTER LITERARY AGENT**, 110 W. 40th St., Suite 1408, New York NY 10018. (212)840-0480. Contact: Susan Protter. Estab. 1971. Member of AAR. Represents 40 clients. 10% of clients are new/unpublished writers. Writer must have book-length project or ms that is ready to be sold. Works with a very small number of new/unpublished authors. Currently handles: 40% nonfiction books; 60% novels; occasional magazine article or short story (for established clients only).

• Prior to opening her agency, Ms. Potter was associate director of subsidiary rights at Harper & Row Publishers.

Handles: Nonfiction books, novels. Considers these nonfiction areas: biography; child guidance/parenting; health/medicine; memoirs; psychology; science. Considers these fiction areas: detective/police/crime; mystery; science fiction, thrillers. Send short query with brief description of project/novel, publishing history and SASE. Reports in 3 weeks on queries; 2 months on solicited mss. "Please do not call; mail queries only."
Needs: Actively seeking psychological thrillers, mysteries, science fiction, true crime, self-help, parenting, psychology, biography, medicine/science. Does not want to receive westerns, romance, fantasy, children's books, young adult novels, screenplays, plays, poetry, Star Wars or Star Trek.
Recent Sales: Sold 13 titles in the last year. *Einstein's Bridge*, by John Cramer (Avon); *The Gift*, by Patrick O'Leary (TOR); *Saucer Wisdom*, by Rudy Rucker (Hardwired); *Science Fiction Century*, edited by David G. Hartwell (TOR/BOMC).
Terms: Agent receives 15% commission on domestic sales; 15% on TV, film and dramatic sales; 25% on foreign sales. "There is a $10 handling fee requested with submission to cover cost of returning materials should they not be suitable." Charges for long distance, photocopying, messenger, express mail, airmail expenses.
Tips: "Please send neat and professionally organized queries. Make sure to include an SASE or we cannot reply. We receive up to 100 queries a week and read them in the order they arrive. We usually reply within two weeks to any query. Do not call. If you are sending a multiple query, make sure to note that in your letter."

N **HELEN REES LITERARY AGENCY**, 308 Commonwealth Ave., Boston MA 02115-2415. (617)262-2401. Fax: (617)236-0133. Contact: Joan Mazmanian. Estab. 1981. Member of AAR. Represents 50 clients. 50% of clients are new/previously unpublished writers. Specializes in general nonfiction, health, business, world politics, autobiographies, psychology, women's issues. Currently handles: 60% nonfiction books; 40% novels.
Handles: Nonfiction books, novels. Considers these nonfiction areas: biography/autobiography; business; current affairs; government/politics/law; health/medicine; history; money/finance/economics; women's issues/women's studies. Considers these fiction areas: contemporary issues; detective/police/crime; glitz; historical; literary; mainstream; mystery/suspense; thriller/espionage. Query with outline plus 2 sample chapters. Reports in 2 weeks on queries; 3 weeks on mss.
Needs: Obtains new clients through recommendations from others, solicitation, at conferences, etc.
Recent Sales: *Shiny Water*, by Anna Salter (fiction); *Jackie and Ari, The Onassis Years* (tentative title), by Kiki Moutsatsos and Phyllis Karas (biography); *Precedents*, (tentative title), by Jim Champy (business).
Terms: Agent receives 15% commission on domestic sales; 20% on foreign sales.

N **THE DAMARIS ROWLAND AGENCY**, 510 E. 23rd St., #8-G, New York NY 10010-5020. (212)475-8942. Fax: (212)358-9411. Contact: Damaris Rowland or Steve Axelrod. Estab. 1994. Member of AAR. Represents 40 clients. 10% of clients are new/previously unpublished writers. Specializes in women's fiction. Currently handles: 75% novels, 25% nonfiction.
Handles: Nonfiction books, novels. Considers these nonfiction areas: animals; cooking/food/nutrition; health/medicine; nature/environment; New Age/metaphysics; religious/inspirational; women's issues/women's studies. Considers these fiction areas: detective/police/crime; historical; literary; mainstream; psychic/supernatural; romance (contemporary, gothic, historical, regency). Send outline/proposal. Reports in 6 weeks.
Needs: Obtains new clients through recommendations from others, at conferences.
Recent Sales: *The Perfect Husband*, by Lisa Gardner (Bantam); *Falling in Love Again*, by Cathy Maxwell (Avon); *Soul Dating to Soul Mating: On the Path to Spiritual Partnership*, by Basha Kaplan and Gail Prince (Putnam Books).

Terms: Agent receives 15% commission on domestic sales; 20% on foreign sales. Offers written contract, with 30 day cancellation clause. Charges only if extraordinary expenses have been incurred, e.g., photocopying and mailing 15 mss to Europe for a foreign sale. 100% of business is derived from commissions on sales.
Writers' Conferences: Novelists, Inc. (Denver, October); Romance Writers of America National Conference (Houston, July/August).

N RUSSELL & VOLKENING, 50 W. 29th St., #7E, New York NY 10001. (212)684-6050. Fax: (212)889-3026. Contact: Joseph Regal or Jennie Dunham. Estab. 1940. Member of AAR. Represents 140 clients. 10% of clients are new/previously unpublished writers. Specializes in literary fiction and narrative nonfiction. Currently handles: 40% nonfiction books; 15% juvenile books; 2% short story collections; 40% novels; 2% novellas; 1% poetry.
Member Agents: Timothy Seldes (nonfiction, literary fiction); Joseph Regal (literary fiction, thrillers, nonfiction); Jennie Dunham (literary fiction, nonfiction, children's books).
Handles: Nonfiction books, juvenile books, novels, novellas, short story collections. Considers these nonfiction areas: anthropology/archaeology; art/architecture/design; biography/autobiography; business; cooking/food/nutrition; current affairs; education; ethnic/cultural interests; gay/lesbian issues; government/politics/law; health/medicine; history; juvenile nonfiction; language/literature/criticism; military/war; money/finance/economics; music/dance/theater/film; nature/environment; photography; popular culture; psychology; science/technology; sociology; sports; true crime/investigative; women's issues/women's studies. Considers these fiction areas: action/adventure; detective/police/crime; ethnic; juvenile; literary; mainstream; mystery/suspense; picture book; sports; thriller/espionage; young adult. Query. Reports in 1 week on queries; 1 month on mss.
Needs: Obtains new clients through "recommendations of writers we already represent.
Recent Sales: *Ladder of Years*, by Anne Tylor (Knopf); *Guide My Feet*, by Marian Wright Edelman (Beacon Press); *Writing & Being*, by Nadine Gordimer (Harvard University Press); *The Chatham School Affair*, by Thomas H. Cook (Bantam); *Liliane*, by Ntozake Shange (St. Martin's); *White Widow*, by Jim Lehrer (Random House).
Terms: Agent receives 10% commission on domestic sales; 20% on foreign sales. Charges for "standard office expenses relating to the submission of materials of an author we represent, e.g., photocopying, postage."
Tips: "If the query is cogent, well-written, well-presented and is the type of book we'd represent, we'll ask to see the manuscript. From there, it depends purely on the quality of the work."

N VICTORIA SANDERS LITERARY AGENCY, 241 Avenue of the Americas, New York NY 10014-4822. (212)633-8811. Fax: (212)633-0525. Contact: Victoria Sanders and/or Diane Dickensheid. Estab. 1993. Member of AAR, signatory of WGA. Represents 50 clients. 25% of clients are new/previously unpublished writers. Currently handles: 50% nonfiction books; 50% novels.
Handles: Nonfiction, novels. Considers these nonfiction areas: biography/autobiography; current affairs; ethnic/cultural interests; gay/lesbian issues; government/politics/law; history; humor; language/literature/criticism; music/dance/theater/film; popular culture; psychology; translations; women's issues/women's studies. Considers these fiction areas: action/adventure; contemporary issues; ethnic, family saga; feminist; gay; lesbian; literary; thriller/espionage. Query and SASE. Reports in 1 week on queries; 1 month on mss.
Needs: Obtains new clients through recommendations, "or I find them through my reading and pursue."
Recent Sales: *Whatever Happened to Daddy's Little Girl: The Effect of Fatherlessness on Black Women*, by Jonetta Rose Barras (Ballantine/One World); *Food and Whine*, by Jennifer Moses (Simon & Schuster); *Straight From the Ghetto*, by Dr. Bertice Berry and Joan Coker, M.D. (St. Martin's Press).
Terms: Agent receives 15% commission on domestic sales; 20% on foreign sales. Offers written contract binding at will. Charges for photocopying ms, messenger, express mail and extraordinary fees. If in excess of $100, client approval is required.
Also Handles: Movie scripts (feature film); TV scripts (TV mow, miniseries). Considers these script areas: action/adventure; comedy; contemporary issues; family saga; romantic comedy and drama; thriller. Query. Reports in 1 week on queries; 1 month on scripts.
Tips: "Limit query to letter, no calls and give it your best shot. A good query is going to get good responses."

N IRENE SKOLNICK, 121 W. 27th St., Suite 601, New York NY 10001. (212)727-3648. Fax: (212)727-1024. E-mail: sirene35@aol.com. Contact: Irene Skolnick. Estab. 1993. Member of AAR. Represents 45 clients. 75% of clients are new/previously unpublished writers.
Handles: Adult nonfiction books, adult fiction. Considers these nonfiction areas: biography/autobiography; current affairs. Considers these fiction areas: contemporary issues; historical; literary. Query with SASE, outline and sample chapter. No unsolicited mss. Reports in 2-4 weeks on queries.
Recent Sales: Did not respond.
Terms: Agent receives 15% commission on domestic sales; 20% on foreign sales. Sometimes offers criticism service. Charges for international postage, photocopying over 40 pages.

N ROBIN STRAUS AGENCY, INC., 229 E. 79th St., New York NY 10021. (212)472-3282. Fax: (212)472-3833. E-mail: springbird@aol.com. Contact: Robin Straus. Estab. 1983. Member of AAR. Specializes in high-quality fiction and nonfiction for adults. Currently handles: 65% nonfiction books; 35% novels.

- Prior to becoming an agent, Robin Straus served as a subsidiary rights manager at Random House and Doubleday and worked in editorial at Little, Brown.

Handles: Nonfiction, novels. Considers these nonfiction areas: animals; anthropology/archaeology; art/architecture/design; biography/autobiography; business; child guidance/parenting; cooking/food/nutrition; current affairs; ethnic/cultural interests; government/politics/law; health/medicine; history; language/literature/criticism; music/dance/theater/film; nature/environment; popular culture; psychology; science/technology; sociology; women's issues/women's studies. Considers these fiction areas: contemporary issues; family saga; historical; literary; mainstream; thriller/espionage. Query with sample pages. SASE ("stamps, not metered postage") required. Reports in 1 month on queries and mss.
Needs: Obtains new clients through recommendations from others.
Recent Sales: Prefers not to share info.
Terms: Agent receives 15% commission on domestic sales; 20% on foreign sales. Offers written contract when requested. Charges for "photocopying, express mail, messenger and foreign postage, etc., as incurred."

N **SUSAN TRAVIS LITERARY AGENCY**, 1317 N. San Fernando Blvd., #175, Burbank CA 91504-4236. (818)557-6538. Fax: (818)557-6549. Contact: Susan Travis. Estab. 1995. Represents 10 clients. 60% of clients are new/previously unpublished writers. Specializes in mainstream fiction and nonfiction. Currently handles: 70% nonfiction books; 30% novels.

- Prior to opening her agency, Ms. Travis served as an agent with the McBride Agency and prior to that worked in the Managing Editors Department of Ballantine Books.

Handles: Nonfiction books, novels. Considers these nonfiction areas: agriculture/horticulture; biography/autobiography; business; child guidance/parenting; cooking/food/nutrition; crafts/hobbies; ethnic/cultural interests; gay/lesbian issues; health/medicine; how-to; interior design/decorating; money/finance/economics; nature/environment; popular culture; psychology; religious/inspirational; self-help/personal improvement; women's issues/women's studies. Considers these fiction areas: action/adventure; contemporary issues; erotica; ethnic; feminist; gay; historical; lesbian; literary; mainstream; mystery/suspense; romance (historical); thriller/espionage. Query. Reports in 3 weeks on queries; 4-6 weeks on mss.
Needs: Actively seeking mainstream nonfiction. Does not want to receive science fiction. Obtains new clients through referrals from existing clients, and mss requested from query letters.
Recent Sales: Sold 1 title in the last year. Prefers not to share info. on specific sales.
Terms: Agent receives 15% commission on domestic sales; 20% on foreign sales. Offers written contract, binding for 1 year, with 60 day cancellation clause. Charges for photocopying of mss and proposals if copies not provided by author. 100% of business is derived from commissions on sales.

N **SUSAN ZECKENDORF ASSOC. INC.**, 171 W. 57th St., New York NY 10019. (212)245-2928. Contact: Susan Zeckendorf. Estab. 1979. Member of AAR. Represents 35 clients. 25% of clients are new/previously unpublished writers. "We are a small agency giving lots of individual attention. We respond quickly to submissions." Currently handles: 50% nonfiction books; 50% fiction.

- Prior to opening her agency, Ms. Zeckendorf was a counseling psychologist.

Handles: Nonfiction books, novels. Considers these nonfiction areas: art/architecture/design; biography/autobiography; child guidance/parenting; health/medicine; history; memoirs; music/dance/theater/film; psychology; science; sociology; true crime/investigative; women's issues/women's studies. Considers these fiction areas: action/adventure; contemporary issues; detective/police/crime; ethnic; family saga; glitz; historical; literary; mainstream; mystery/suspense; thriller/espionage. Query. Reports in 10 days on queries; 3 weeks mss.
Needs: Actively seeking mysteries, literary fiction, mainstream fiction, thrillers, social history, parenting, classical music, biography. Does not want to receive science fiction, romance. Obtains new clients through recommendations, listings in writer's manuals.
Recent Sales: Sold 10 titles in the last year. *Muscle Memory Magic*, by Marjorie Jaffe (M. Evans); *Dark Passions* and *The Second Skin*, both by Una-Mary Parker (Headline); *The Biography of Bill Wilson—Founder of AA*, by Francis Harrigan (St. Martin's).
Terms: Agent receives 15% commission on domestic sales; 20% on foreign sales. Charges for photocopying, messenger services.
Writers' Conferences: Central Valley Writers Conference; Tucson Publishers Association Conference; Writer's Connection (San Jose CA, June); Frontiers in Writing Conference (Amarillo TX); Golden Triangle Writers Conference (Beaumont TX, October); Oklahoma Festival of Books (Claremont OK); Mary Mount Writers Conference.

Literary Agents Subject Index

LITERARY AGENTS/FICTION

NONFICTION

The Markets

Book Publishers

The book business, for the most part, runs on hunches. Whether the idea for a book comes from a writer, an agent or the imagination of an acquiring editor, it is generally expressed in these terms: "This is a book that I *think* people will like. People will *probably* want to buy it." The decision to publish is mainly a matter of the right person, or persons, agreeing that those hunches are sound.

THE PATH TO PUBLICATION

Ideas reach editors in a variety of ways. They arrive unsolicited every day through the mail. They come by phone, sometimes from writers but most often from agents. They arise in the editor's mind because of his daily traffic with the culture in which he lives. The acquisitions editor, so named because he is responsible for securing manuscripts for his company to publish, sifts through the deluge of possibilities, waiting for a book idea to strike him as extraordinary, inevitable, profitable.

In some companies, acquisitions editors possess the authority required to say, "Yes, we will publish this book." In most publishing houses, though, the acquisitions editor must prepare and present the idea to a proposal committee made up of marketing and administrative personnel. Proposal committees are usually less interested in questions of extraordinariness and inevitability than they are in profitability. The editor has to convince them that it makes good business sense to publish this book.

Once a contract is signed, several different wheels are set in motion. The author, of course, writes the book if he hasn't done so already. While the editor is helping to assure that the author is making the book the best it can be, promotion and publicity people are planning mailings of review copies to influential newspapers and review periodicals, writing catalog copy that will help sales representatives push the book to bookstores, and plotting a multitude of other promotional efforts (including interview tours and bookstore signings by the author) designed to dangle the book attractively before the reading public's eye.

When the book is published, it usually receives a concerted promotional push for a month or two. After that, the fate of the book—whether it will "grow legs" and set sales records or sit untouched on bookstore shelves—rests in the hands of the public. Publishers have to compete with all of the other entertainment industries vying for the consumer's money and limited leisure time. Successful books are reprinted to meet the demand. Unsuccessful books are returned from bookstores to publishers and are sold off cheaply as "remainders" or are otherwise disposed of.

THE STATE OF THE BUSINESS

The book publishing industry is beginning to recover from the difficulties experienced in the last few years. Publishers sell their products to bookstores on a returnable basis, which means the stores usually have 120 days to either pay the bill or return the order. With independent bookstores continuing to close and superstores experiencing setbacks as well, many publishers were hit with staggering returns. This has slowed somewhat, but continues to be a concern. While there are many more outlets to *buy* books, including online bookstores such as Amazon.com,

Borders.com and Barnesandnoble.com, this doesn't necessarily translate into more books being *bought*. Some feel the superstore phenomenon has proved a mixed blessing. The greater shelf area means there are more materials available, but also drives a need for books as "wallpaper" that is continually refreshed by returning older books and restocking with newer ones.

But that's not to say publishers are rushing to bring esoteric or highly experimental material to the marketplace. The blockbuster mentality—publishing's penchant for sticking with "name brand" novelists—still drives most large publishers. It's simply a less risky venture to continue publishing authors whom they know readers like. On the other hand, the prospects for nonfiction authors are perhaps better than they have been for years. The boom in available shelf space has provided entree to the marketplace for books on niche topics that heretofore would not have seen the light of day in most bookstores. The superstores position themselves as one-stop shopping centers for readers of every stripe. As such, they must carry books on a wide range of subjects.

Paper costs continue to be an area of concern for publishers, although prices are predicted to remain relatively stable and supply is estimated to grow slightly yet steadily over the next several years. Most publishers have laid in a supply that would get them through any price increases without upsetting their budgets.

The publishing community as a whole is stepping back from the multimedia hype and approaching the market more cautiously, if not abandoning it entirely. While the possibilities offered by CD-ROM technology still exist, publishers realize that marrying format and content are crucial for a successful, profitable product. Online publishing seems to offer promise, if only publishers can figure out how to make money from this new and different format.

HOW TO PUBLISH YOUR BOOK

The markets in this year's Book Publishers section offer opportunities in nearly every area of publishing. Large, commercial houses are here as are their smaller counterparts; large and small "literary" houses are represented as well. In addition, you'll find university presses, industry-related publishers, textbook houses and more.

The Book Publishers Subject Index is the place to start. You'll find it in the back of the book, before the General Index. Subject areas for both fiction and nonfiction are broken out for the over 1,200 total book publisher listings. Not all of them buy the kind of book you've written, but this Index will tell you which ones do.

When you have compiled a list of publishers interested in books in your subject area, read the detailed listings. Pare down your list by cross-referencing two or three subject areas and eliminating the listings only marginally suited to your book. When you have a good list, send for those publishers' catalogs and any manuscript guidelines available or check publishers' websites, which often contain catalog listings, manuscript preparation guidelines, current contact names and other information helpful to prospective authors. You want to make sure your book idea is in line with a publisher's list but is not a duplicate of something already published. Visit bookstores and libraries to see if their books are well represented. When you find a couple of books they have published that are similar to yours, write or call the company to find out who edited these books. This last, extra bit of research could be the key to getting your proposal to precisely the right editor.

Publishers prefer different kinds of submissions on first contact. Most like to see a one-page query with SASE, especially for nonfiction. Others will accept a brief proposal package that might include an outline and/or a sample chapter. Some publishers will accept submissions from agents only. Virtually no publisher wants to see a complete manuscript on initial contact, and sending one when they prefer another method will signal to the publisher "this is an amateur's submission." Editors do not have the time to read an entire manuscript, even editors at small presses who receive fewer submissions. Perhaps the only exceptions to this rule are children's picture book manuscripts and poetry manuscripts, which take only as much time to read as an outline and sample chapter anyway.

In your one-page query, give an overview of your book, mention the intended audience, the competition (check *Books in Print* and local bookstore shelves), and what sets your book apart. Detail any previous publishing experience or special training relevant to the subject of your book. All of this information will help your cause; it is the professional approach.

Only one in a thousand writers will sell a book to the first publisher they query, especially if the book is the writer's first effort. Make a list of a dozen or so publishers that might be interested in your book. Try to learn as much about the books they publish and their editors as you can. Research, knowing the specifics of your subject area, and a professional approach are often the difference between acceptance and rejection. You are likely to receive at least a few rejections, however, and when that happens, don't give up. Rejection is as much a part of publishing, if not more, than signing royalty checks. Send your query to the next publisher on your list. Multiple queries can speed up the process at this early stage.

Personalize your queries by addressing them individually and mentioning what you know about a company from its catalog or books you've seen. Never send a form letter as a query. Envelopes addressed to "Editor" or "Editorial Department" end up in the dreaded slush pile.

If a publisher offers you a contract, you may want to seek advice before signing and returning it. An author's agent will very likely take 15% if you employ one, but you could be making 85% of a larger amount. Some literary agents are available on an hourly basis for contract negotiations only. For more information on literary agents, contact the Association of Author's Representatives, 10 Astor Place, 3rd Floor, New York NY 10003, (212)353-3709. Also check the current edition of *Guide to Literary Agents* (Writer's Digest Books). Attorneys will only be able to tell you if everything is legal, not if you are getting a good deal, unless they have prior experience with literary contracts. If you have a legal problem, you might consider contacting Volunteer Lawyers for the Arts, 1 E. 53rd St., 6th Floor, New York NY 10022, (212)319-2787.

AUTHOR-SUBSIDY PUBLISHER'S LISTINGS ELIMINATED

Writer's Market is a reference tool to help you sell your writing, and we encourage you to work with publishers that pay a royalty. Subsidy publishing involves paying money to a publishing house to publish a book. The source of the money could be a government, foundation or university grant, or it could be the author of the book. Publishers offering nonauthor-subsidized arrangements have been included in the appropriate section. If one of the publishers listed here offers you an author-subsidy arrangement (sometimes called "cooperative publishing," "co-publishing" or "joint venture"), asks you to pay for all or part of the cost of any aspect of publishing (printing, advertising, etc.) or to guarantee the purchase of any number of the books yourself, we would like you to let us know about that company immediately.

Sometimes newer publishers will offer author-subsidy contracts to get a leg up in the business and plan to become royalty-only publishers once they've reached a firm financial footing. Some publishers feel they must offer subsidy contracts to expand their lists beyond the capabilities of their limited resources. This may be true, and you may be willing to agree to it, but we choose to list only those publishers paying a royalty without requiring a financial investment from the author. In recent years, several large subsidy publishers have suddenly gone out of business, leaving authors without their money, their books, and in some cases, without the copyright to their own manuscripts.

WHAT'S NEW THIS YEAR

We've added several features to make *Writer's Market* even more helpful in your search for the right publisher for your work, features you won't find in any other writer's guide.

Information at a glance

Most immediately noticeable, we've added a number of symbols at the beginning of each listing to quickly convey certain information at a glance. In the Book Publisher sections, these symbols identify new listings (N), "opportunity" markets that buy at least 50 percent from unagented or first-time writers (✪), and publishers that accept agented submissions only (A). Different sections of *Writer's Market* include other symbols; check the front and back inside covers for an explanation of all the symbols used throughout the book.

How much money? What are my odds?

We've also highlighted important information in boldface, the "quick facts" you won't find in any other market guide but should know before you submit your work. This includes: how many manuscripts a publisher buys per year; how many from first-time authors; how many from unagented writers; the royalty rate a publisher pays; and how large an advance is offered.

Publishers, their imprints and how they are related

In this era of big publishing—and big mergers—the world of publishing has grown even more intertwined. A "family tree" on page 98 lists the imprints and often confusing relationships of the eight largest conglomerate publishers.

In the listings, "umbrella" listings for these larger houses list the imprints under the company name. Imprint names in boldface indicate a separate, individual listing, easily located alphabetically, which provides much more detailed information about that imprints specific focus, needs and contacts.

Each listing includes a summary of the editorial mission of the house, an overarching principle that ties together what they publish. Under the heading **Acquisitions:** we list many more editors, often with their specific areas of expertise. We have also increased the number of recent titles to help give you an idea of the publishers' scope. We have included the royalty rates for those publishers willing to disclose them, but contract details are closely guarded and a number of larger publishers are reluctant to publicly state these terms. Standard royalty rates for paperbacks generally range from 7½ to 12½ percent, for hardcovers from 10 to 15 percent. Royalty rates for children's books are often lower, generally ranging from 5 to 10 percent.

Finally, we have listed a number of publishers who only accept agented submissions. This benefits the agents who use *Writer's Market*, those writers with agents who use the book themselves, and those as yet unagented writers who want to know more about a particular company.

For a list of publishers according to their subjects of interest, see the nonfiction and fiction sections of the Book Publishers Subject Index. Information on book publishers and producers listed in the previous edition of *Writer's Market* but not included in this edition can be found in the General Index.

A&B PUBLISHERS GROUP, 1000 Atlantic Ave., Brooklyn NY 11238. (718)783-7808. **Acquisitions:** Maxwell Taylor, editor. Publishes hardcover originals and trade paperback originals and reprints. **Publishes 12 titles/year. Receives 180 queries and 75 mss/year. 20% of books from first-time authors; 40% from unagented writers. Pays 5-12% royalty on retail price. Offers $500-2,500 advance.** Publishes book 1 year after acceptance of ms. Accepts simultaneous submissions. Reports in 2 months on queries and proposals, 5 months on mss. Book catalog free.

Nonfiction: Children's/juvenile, coffee table book, cookbook, illustrated book. Subjects include cooking/foods/nutrition, history. Query. Reviews artwork/photos as part of ms package. Send photocopies.

Fiction: "We have published no fiction, but may start in fall '99." Query.

Tips: Audience is children and adult African-Americans. "Read, read, read. The best writers are developed from good reading. There is not enough attention to quality."

ABBEVILLE PRESS, Abbeville Publishing Group, 22 Cortland St., New York NY 10007. (212)577-5555. Fax: (212)577-5579. Website: http://www.abbeville.com. **Acquisitions:** Susan Costello, editorial director/editor-in-chief. Abbeville publishes high-quality illustrated trade nonfiction. Publishes hardcover and trade paperback originals. **Publishes 100 titles/year. 5% of books from first-time authors; 75% from unagented writers. Pays royalty. Advance varies.**

Publishes book 18 months after acceptance of ms. Accepts simultaneous submissions. Reports in 3 months on queries. Book catalog free; call customer service.

Nonfiction: Coffee table book, cookbook, gift book, illustrated book. Subjects include art/architecture, cooking/food, gardening, fashion, interior design, decorative arts, lifestyle, history, photography. Rarely publishes unsolicited material. Query with outline, TOC, list of competing books, CV, cover letter describing scope of project and SASE. Reviews artwork/photos (photocopies or duplicates only) as part of the ms package. Send photocopies.

Recent Title(s): *The New Father: A Dad's Guide to the Toddler Years*, by Armin Brott.

ABBEVILLE PUBLISHING GROUP, 22 Cortland St., New York NY 10007. (212)577-5555. Fax: (212)577-5579. Website: http://www.abbeville.com **Acquisitions:** Susan Costello, editorial director and editor-in-chief; Nancy Grubb, executive editor; Jacqueline Decter, senior editor. Publishes illustrated hardcover and trade paperback originals. **Pays royalty.** Publishes book 18 months after acceptance of ms. Accepts simultaneous submissions. Reports in 3 months on queries. Book catalog and ms guidelines free; call customer service.

Imprint(s): Abbeville Press, Abbeville Kids, Artabras (promotional books), Cross River Press, Modern Masters.

ABBOTT, LANGER & ASSOCIATES, 548 First St., Crete IL 60417-2199. (708)672-4200. **Acquisitions:** Dr. Steven Langer, president. Estab. 1967. Publishes trade paperback originals, loose-leaf books. **Publishes 25 titles/year, mostly prepared inhouse. Receives 25 submissions/year. 10% of books from first-time authors; 90% of books from unagented writers. Pays 10-15% royalty. Offers advance.** Publishes book 18 months after acceptance. Book catalog for 6×9 SAE with 2 first-class stamps. Reports in 1 month on queries, 3 months on mss.

Nonfiction: How-to, reference, technical on some phase of human resources management, security, sales management, etc. Especially needs "a very limited number (3-5) of books dealing with very specialized topics in the field of human resource management, wage and salary administration, sales compensation, recruitment, selection, etc." Publishes for human resources directors, wage and salary administrators, sales/marketing managers, security directors, etc. Query with outline. Reviews artwork/photos.

Recent Title(s): *Fire Safety & High Rise Buildings*, by Harry Azoni.

Tips: "A writer has the best chance selling our firm a how-to book in human resources management, sales/marketing management or security management."

ABC-CLIO, INC., 501 S. Cherry St., Suite 350, Denver CO 80246. (303)333-3003. Fax: (303)333-4037. Subsidiaries include ABC-CLIO Ltd. **Acquisitions:** Gary Kuris, senior developmental editor. Estab. 1955. ABC-CLIO publishes "easy-to-use, authoritative sources on high-interest topics." Publishes hardcover originals. **Publishes 45 titles/year. Receives 500 submissions/year. 20% of books from first-time authors; 95% from unagented writers. Pays royalty on net receipts. Offers advance.** Publishes ms 10 months after acceptance. Reports in 2 months on queries. Book catalog and ms guidelines free.

Nonfiction: Reference. Subjects include art/architecture, education, environmental issues, government/politics, history, literary studies, multicultural studies, mythology, science, women's issues/studies. No monographs or textbooks. Query or submit outline and sample chapters.

Recent Title(s): *Encyclopedia of Satirical Literature*, by Mary Ellen Snodgrass.

THE ABERDEEN GROUP, 426 S. Westgate St., Addison IL 60101. (630)543-0870. Fax: (630)543-3112. Website: http//www.wocnet.com/mags/as.htm. **Acquisitions:** Mark DiCicco, publisher; Kari Moosmann, managing editor. "We seek to strengthen and grow the concrete and masonry industries worldwide by striving to be the world's foremost information provider for these industries." **Publishes 6 titles/year. Receives 75 queries and 12 mss/year. 10% of books from first-time authors; 100% from unagented writers. Pays 6-18% royalty on retail price. Offers $1,000-2,000 advance.** Publishes book 6 months after acceptance of ms. Accepts simultaneous submissions. Reports in 1 month on queries and proposals, 2 months on mss. Book catalog free.

Nonfiction: How-to, technical (primarily in the concrete and masonry fields.) Subjects include architecture, construction, general engineering and construction business. Query with outline, 2-3 sample chapters, definition of topic, features, market analysis.

Recent Title(s): *Epoxy Injection*, by John Treat.

ABINGDON PRESS, The United Methodist Publishing House, P.O. Box 801, Nashville TN 37202-0801. (615)749-6301. Fax: (615)748-6512. Website: http://www.abingdon.org. President/Publisher: Neil M. Alexander. Vice President/ Editorial Director: Harriett Jane Olson. **Acquisitions:** Michael E. Lawrence, director, academic/professional unit; Mary Catherine Dean, director (general interest books); Ulrike Guthrie, senior editor (academic books); J. Richard Peck, senior editor, United Methodist Newscope; Robert Ratcliff, senior editor (professional products); Jack Keller, director (reference books); Gary A. Smith, senior editor (music). Estab. 1789. "Abingdon Press, America's oldest theological publisher, provides an ecumenical publishing program dedicated to serving the Christian community—clergy, scholars, church leaders, musicians and general readers—with quality resources in the areas of Bible study, the practice of ministry, theology, devotion, spirituality, inspiration, prayer, music and worship, reference, Christian education and church supplies." Publishes hardcover and paperback originals and reprints; church supplies. **Publishes 130 titles/year. Receives 2,500 submissions/year. Few books from first-time authors; 90-95% of books from unagented writers. Pays royalty.** Publishes book 2 years after acceptance. Manuscript guidelines for SASE. Reports in 3 months.

Imprint(s): Dimensions for Living, Cokesbury.

Nonfiction: Religious-lay and professional, children's religious books, academic texts. Length: 32-300 pages. Query with outline and samples only.
Recent Title(s): *God in Pain*, by Barbara Brown Taylor.

N **ABIQUE**, 1700 Amelia Court, #423, Plano TX 75075. E-mail: abique@lycosmail.com. Website: http://www.cmpu.net/public/abique. **Acquisitions:** Tom Kyle, editorial director. "We are somewhat like a university press in that we seek books with too narrow an audience for other publishers to consider." Publishes hardcover and trade paperback originals. **Publishes 20 titles/year.** "We hope to publish 40 titles this coming year. This will be our first full year of publishing. Our small print runs mean we need to do lots of titles." **Pays 10% royalty on retail price.** Publishes book 3 months after acceptance of ms. Accepts simultaneous submissions. Reports in 1 month on queries.
Nonfiction: Reference, technical, textbook, academic disciplines. Subjects include anthropology/archaeology, business and economics, computers and electronics, education, government/politics, health/medicine, history, music/dance, nature/environment, philosophy, psychology, science, sociology. Query first with SASE. Reviews artwork/photos as part of the ms package. Send photocopies.
Recent Title(s): *The Body's Use and Disposal of Energy*, by Sybrand G. Boersma (physiology).
Tips: "We specialize in books aimed directly at a small specialized audience. This can be people in a narrow discipline or students using a textbook compiled for use in a limited number of schools. Our authors are experts who write for a limited audience. We rely on them to direct us to that audience and to know what that audience wants to read."

HARRY N. ABRAMS, INC., Groupe Latingy, 100 Fifth Ave., New York NY 10011. (212)206-7715. President/Publisher/Editor-in-Chief: Paul Gottlieb. **Acquisitions:** Margaret Chase, managing editor. Estab. 1949. "We publish *only* high-quality illustrated art books, i.e., art, art history, museum exhibition catalogs, written by specialists and scholars in the field." Publishes hardcover and "a few" paperback originals. **Publishes 100 titles/year. Pays royalty. Offers variable advance.** Publishes book 2 years after acceptance. Reports in 3 months. Book catalog for $5.
Nonfiction: Art, nature and science, outdoor recreation. Requires illustrated material for art and art history, museums. Submit outline, sample chapters and illustrations. Reviews artwork/photos as part of ms package.
Tips: "We are one of the few publishers who publish almost exclusively illustrated books. We consider ourselves the leading publishers of art books and high-quality artwork in the U.S. Once the author has signed a contract to write a book for our firm the author must finish the manuscript to agreed-upon high standards within the schedule agreed upon in the contract."

ABSEY & CO., 5706 Root Rd., Suite #5, Spring TX 77389. (281)257-2340. E-mail: abseyandco@aol.com. **Acquisitions:** Trey Hall, editor-in-chief. "Our goal is to publish original, creative works of literary merit. We work closely and attentively with authors and their work." Publishes hardcover, trade paperback and mass market paperback originals. **Publishes 6-10 titles/year. 50% of books from first-time authors; 50% from unagented writers. Royalty and advance vary.** Publishes book 1 year after acceptance of ms. Accepts simultaneous submissions. No e-mail submissions. Reports in 3 months on queries, 6 months on mss. Manuscript guidelines for #10 SASE.

- Two Absey books, *Just People* and *Poetry After Lunch* were named 1998 Best Books for Young Adults by the American Library Association and to the New York Public Library's 1998 Best Books for the Teen Age.

Nonfiction: Educational subjects and language arts, as well as essay collections on history behind fictional works. Query with SASE.
Fiction: "Since we are a small, new press, we are looking for book-length manuscripts with a firm intended audience." Query with SASE.
Poetry: Publishes the "Writers and Young Writers Series." Interested in thematic poetry collections of literary meit. Query with SASE.
Recent Title(s): *Just People*, by Kathi Appelt (original poems and invitations to write); *Jesus Didn't Use Worksheets*, by Joyce A. Carroll and Ron Habermas (teaching).

ACCENT ON LIVING, Cheever Publishing, Inc., P.O. Box 700, Bloomington IL 61702. (309)378-2961. Fax: (309)378-4420. **Acquisitions:** Betty Garee, editor. Accent on Living publishes books pertaining to the physically disabled. **Publishes 4 titles/year. Receives 300 queries and 150 mss/year. 50% of books from first-time authors; 95% from unagented writers. Makes outright purchase.** Publishes book 3 months after acceptance of ms. Accepts simultaneous submissions. Reports on queries in 1 month. Book catalog for 8×10 SAE with 2 first-class stamps. Manuscript guidelines for #10 SASE.
Nonfiction: How-to, humor, self-help. Subjects include business/economics, child guidance/parenting, cooking/foods/nutrition, education, gardening, money/finance, recreation, religion, travel. All pertaining to physically disabled. Query. Reviews artwork/photos as part of ms package. Send snapshots or slides.

ACCENT PUBLICATIONS, Cook Communications Ministries, P.O. Box 36640, Colorado Springs CO 80936-3664. (719)536-0100, ext. 3337. **Acquisitions:** Cheryl Crews. Estab. 1947. Publishes evangelical church resource products. **Publishes 6-8 titles/year. 100% of books from unagented writers. Pays royalty on retail price or makes outright purchase.** Publishes book within 1 year of acceptance. Reports in 3 months. Manuscript guidelines for #10 SASE.
Nonfiction: "We are currently soliciting only Church Resources for the programmed ministries of the local church such as VBS, clubs, and children's church (no children's sermons). We would consider Bible study series and ancillary curriculum programs, or children's programs for the King James Version church market. We do not consider games,

INSIDER REPORT

Pearl Cleage: Find your own voice, trust your vision

Pearl Cleage isn't worried about being typecast, either as a person, or an author. But she refuses to accept restrictions on her politics, her personal life, or the way she writes. "Too many authors get caught up in finding the right formula," says the playwright-turned-essayist and first-time novelist. "But if you have something to say, you'll find the right form."

Cleage, a nationally known playwright, is accustomed to crossing boundaries to make her point. Many of her works, including *Flyin' West*, *Blues for an Alabama Sky*, and *Bourbon at the Border*, show the struggles facing women, especially African-American women. Her 1994 book of essays, *Deals with the Devil: And Other Reasons to Riot* (One World/Ballantine Books), confronted those issues in a more personal voice. When she sat down to write what became her first novel, *What Looks Like Crazy on an Ordinary Day* (Avon Books), she had some specific objectives.

"I wanted to tell a love story," she says. But the novel is hardly a cookie-cutter romance. Cleage's heroine is HIV positive, a woman who plans a brief trip to her hometown before moving on to the more supportive environment of San Francisco. "I wanted to show that becoming HIV-positive doesn't mean your world comes to an end," Cleage says. And while AIDS is an issue, the novel also tackles joblessness, teenage motherhood, family relationships and problems that are increasingly commonplace in America. The novel is set in Idlewild, Michigan, a former all-black resort town. Cleage says Idlewild is a small rural town, facing all the big-city pressures of nearby Detroit—the perfect place to describe what she sees happening around her.

Cleage also deliberately chose the novel as a format for her message because she wanted to focus on her characters' thoughts and emotions. "With plays, you can show interactions," she says, "but it's more difficult to show the inner workings." Despite her experience as an author, Cleage confesses she made some false starts in the new format.

"I sat down and wrote 30 pages that were awful," she says. "It's very different from writing for the theater." Cleage says writing plays is a communal experience because the work is made real by the interaction of the actors. But novels are a one-to-one communication between reader and author. Cleage says it took her some time to find her feet in the new format, but even the false starts were helpful. And she found the format made some things easier. "In a play you have to use stage directions and lighting cues and suggestions to let the audience know it's morning in Atlanta," Cleage notes. "But in a novel, you simply say, 'it's morning in Atlanta.' "

Cleage wrote the bulk of her novel before taking it to an editor. Although many of her friends have an editor review work as they write, Cleage prefers to work on her own. There is no right or wrong way to write, she says, but writers have to find a style they are comfortable with. "The important thing is to be authentic," she says. While an editor can

INSIDER REPORT, *Cleage*

help fine-tune a project, Cleage says it's no substitute for "finding your own voice." And she says writers need to have the confidence to stand behind their work.

When Cleage took the manuscript for *What Looks Like Crazy* to her editor at Ballantine, the editor recommended several major changes. So Cleage decided to go to another publisher. "That can be a little scary," she admits, especially for first-time authors who are reluctant to disagree with editors. But she says writing is a solo pursuit, and a good piece, whether it's a play, an essay or a novel, needs to have a single vision. Learning to trust yourself is the most important lesson an author can learn. "You have to be confident of your voice, in what you have to say," Cleage says.

Cleage has found herself part of a growing wave of African-American women writers, like Alice Walker and Terri McMillan. She says publishers are paying more attention to these women, in part to capture a new reader's market. But she isn't worried about being lumped in some category. "I certainly don't mind being grouped with writers like Alice Walker," she laughs. And she thinks there is enough diversity of message, method and approach to go around. "This is a segment of the population that traditionally hasn't been heard from," she says. "And we have a lot to say." Regardless of publishers' motivations, she says it's refreshing to see a wider range of people being published.

It's still not an easy market, Cleage warns. And even though publishers are considering a wider range of authors, the market as a whole is shrinking. "You have a situation where publishers are reluctant to take a chance," she says. She advises authors to be open to criticism and to new ideas. "What works for one writer won't necessarily work for another," she says, "and you need to keep working at it, to find what works for you, for your voice."

Cleage says writers need to be persistent and patient. But she hopes more people will find their voice and share their vision with others. "There's a million stories about people in this country," she says. "And we need to eliminate barriers and extend our vision."

—Alison Holm

puzzles, puppet books, fiction for children, youth, or adults. We do not consider devotionals, poetry, biographies, autobiographies, personal experience stories, manuscripts with a charismatic emphasis, or general Christian living." Query with brief synopsis and chapter outline. Do not submit full ms unless requested. No phone calls, please.
Recent Title(s): *Celebrating the Heart of Marriage*, by Kathy Collard Miller (Women's Bible study).

[A] **ACE SCIENCE FICTION AND FANTASY**, The Berkley Publishing Group, Penguin Putnam Inc., 375 Hudson St., New York NY 10014. (212)366-2000. E-mail: ace.books@genie.com. Website: http//www.penguinputnam.com. **Acquisitions:** Anne Sowards, editor. Estab. 1953. Ace publishes exclusively science fiction and fantasy. Publishes hardcover, paperback and trade paperback originals and reprints. **Publishes 75 titles/year.** Reports in 6 months. Manuscript guidelines for #10 SASE.
Fiction: Science fiction, fantasy. *Agented submissions only;* query first with SASE.
Recent Title(s): *The Night Watch*, by Sean Stewart.

ACROPOLIS BOOKS, INC., 747 Sheridan Blvd., #1A, Lakewood CO 80214-2551. (303)231-9923. Fax: (303)235-0492. E-mail: acropolisbooks@worldnet.att.net. Website: http://www.acropolisbooks.com. **Acquisitions:** Constance J. Wilson, vice president of editorial operations. "It is the mission of Acropolis Books to publish books at the highest level of consciousness, commonly referred to as mysticism. This was the consciousness demonstrated by revelators of every religion in the world. Our commitment is the publication of mystical literature—the spiritual principles of Omnipresence, Omnipotence and Omniscience and its expression." Publishes hardcover and trade paperback originals and reprints. **Publishes 20 titles/year. Imprint publishes 5-10 titles/year. Receives 150 queries and 80 mss/year. 30% of books from first-time authors; 90% from unagented writers. Royalties or outright purchases negotiable.**

Advances negotiable. Publishes book an average of 1 year after acceptance of ms. Reports in 1 month on queries and proposals, 2 months on mss. Book catalog and ms guidelines for #10 SASE.
Imprint(s): I-Level, Awakening, Flashlight, Acropolis, Acropolis Classic.
Nonfiction: Inspirational. Subjects include philosophy, religion and mysticism. "We publish books of higher consciousness and books that are a bridge to higher consciousness. Writers must understand our focus." Submit 4 sample chapters with SASE. Reviews artwork/photos as part of ms package. Send photocopies.
Fiction: Mysticism/inspirational. "Our books encompass the spiritual principles of Omnipresence, Omnipotence and Omniscience; and further bring home the mystical realization that everyone in this world is an individual instrument of God in expression." Submit 4 sample chapters with SASE.
Poetry: Submit complete ms.
Recent Title(s): *Living Joyfully with Children*, by Win and Bill Sweet (parenting); *Bunny Bu*, by Dianne Baker (children's fiction).
Tips: "Clearly understand our focus by reading or understanding books that we have published."

ACTA PUBLICATIONS, 4848 N. Clark St., Chicago IL 60640-4711. Fax: (773)271-7399. E-mail: acta@one.org. **Acquisitions:** Gregory F. Augustine Pierce, Thomas R. Artz, co-publishers. Estab. 1958. "We publish non-academic, practical books aimed at the mainline religious market." Publishes trade paperback originals. **Publishes 10 titles/year. Receives 50 queries and 15 mss/year. 50% of books from first-time authors; 90% from unagented writers. Pays 10-12½% royalty on wholesale price.** Publishes book 1 year after acceptance of ms. Reports in 2 months on proposals. Book catalog and author guidelines for SASE.
Nonfiction: Religion. Submit outline and 1 sample chapter. Reviews artwork/photos. Send photocopies.
Recent Title(s): *Daily Meditations (with Scripture), for Busy Moms*, by Patricia Robertson (spirituality).
Tips: "Don't send a submission unless you have read our catalog or one of our books."

ADAMS MEDIA CORPORATION, 260 Center St., Holbrook MA 02343. (781)767-8100. Fax: (781)767-0994. Website: http://www.adamsmedia.com. Editor-in-Chief: Edward Walters. **Acquisitions:** Anne Weaver; Pam Liflander; Jere Calmes, senior business editor. "We publish commercial nonfiction, not scholarly or literary material." Publishes hardcover originals, trade paperback originals and reprints. **Publishes 100 titles/year. Receives 1,500 queries and 500 mss/year. 25% of books from first-time authors; 25% from unagented writers. Pays standard royalty or makes outright purchase. Offers variable advance.** Publishes book 1 year after acceptance of ms. Accepts simultaneous submissions. Reports in 3 months.
Nonfiction: Biography, children's/juvenile, cookbook, gift book, how-to, humor, illustrated book, reference, self-help. Subjects include Americana, animals, business/economics, child guidance/parenting, cooking/foods/nutrition, gardening, government/politics, health/medicine, history, hobbies, language/literature, military/war, money/finance, nature/environment, psychology, regional, science, sports, women's issues/studies. Submit outline.
Recent Title(s): *Raising a Happy, Confident, Successful Child*, by Trish Magee (parenting).

ADAMS-BLAKE PUBLISHING, 8041 Sierra St., Fair Oaks CA 95628. (916)962-9296. Website: http//www.adams-blake.com. Vice President: Paul Raymond. **Acquisitions:** Monica Blane, senior editor. "We are looking for business, technology and finance titles as well as data that can be bound/packaged and sold to specific industry groups at high margins. We are especially looking for 'high ticket' items that sell to the corporate market for prices between $100-300." Publishes trade paperback originals and reprints. **Publishes 10-15 titles/year. Receives 150 queries and 90 mss/year. 90% of books from first-time authors; 90% from unagented writers. Pays 15% royalty on wholesale price.** Publishes book 6 months after acceptance of ms. Accepts simultaneous submissions. Reports in 1 month on mss. *Writer's Market* recommends allowing 2 months for reply.
Nonfiction: How-to, technical. Subjects include business/economics, computers/electronics, health/medicine, money/finance, software. Query with sample chapters or complete ms. Reviews artwork/photos as part of ms package. Send photocopies.
Fiction: "For a possible new imprint, we are also looking for mainstream fiction that we can develop, initially market, and then sell to a larger house or to the electronic media. Interested in authors who write literature, not pulp thrillers. Looking for contemporary works with wide appeal, such as the *Forrest Gump*, *Christmas Box*, *Bridges of Madison County* type of stories. NOT interested in genre fiction such as romance, spy, mystery, gothic, western, sci-fi, etc."
Recent Title(s): *Manage IT: Training Manual for Managing a Small Computer Network*, by Mary Kelly.
Tips: "We will take a chance on material the big houses reject. Since we sell the majority of our material directly, we can publish material for a very select market. This year we seek niche market material that we can Douctech™ and sell direct to the corporate sector. Author should include a marketing plan. Sell us on the project!"

ADDICUS BOOKS, INC., P.O. Box 45327, Omaha NE 68145. **Acquisitions:** Rod Colvin, president. E-mail: addicusbks@aol.com Website: http://www.addicusbooks.com. Seeks high-quality mss with national or strong regional appeal. Publishes trade paperback originals. **Publishes 8-10 titles/year. 70% of books from first-time authors; 60% from unagented writers. Pays royalty on retail price.** Publishes book 9 months after acceptance of ms. Accepts simultaneous submissions. Reports in 1 month on proposals. Guidelines for #10 SASE.
Nonfiction: How-to, self-help. Subjects include Americana, business/economics, health/medicine, psychology, regional, true-crime. Query with outline and 3-4 sample chapters.
Recent Title(s): *The Stroke Recovery Book*, by Kip Burkman, M.D. (health).

Tips: "With health titles, we're looking for high-quality manuscripts from authors who have done their market research. In addition to books with national appeal, we will consider titles with strong regional appeal, such as true-crime. Here, we're looking for well-written, well-researched manuscripts with interesting stories behind the crimes."

ADDISON WESLEY LONGMAN, INC., One Jacob Way, Reading MA 01867. (781)944-3700. Fax: (781)944-8243. Website: http://www.aw.com.

- Addison Wesley Longman is owned by Pearson, which also owns Penguin Putnam Inc. The General Publishing Group, including the imprints Helix Books and Merloyd Lawrence, was purchased by The Perseus Book Group. The Planet Dexter imprint was shifted to the Penguin children's division. Editorial plans for the remainder of the company have not been finalized.

N **ADVANTAGE PUBLISHERS GROUP**, AMS, 5880 Oberlin Dr., San Diego CA 92121. (619)457-2500. Managing Editor: JoAnn Padgett. Publishes hardcover and trade paperback originals and reprints. Publishes 120 titles/year.
Imprint(s): Laurel Glen Publishing, Silver Dolphin Books, Thunder Bay Press.

AEGIS PUBLISHING GROUP, 796 Aquidneck Ave., Newport RI 02842-7246. (401)849-4200. Fax: (401)849-4231. E-mail: aegis@aegisbooks.com. Website: http//www.aegisbooks.com. **Acquisitions:** Robert Mastin, publisher. Estab. 1992. "Our specialty is telecommunications books targeted to small businesses, entrepreneurs and telecommuters—how they can benefit from the latest telecom products and services." Publishes trade paperback originals and reprints. **Publishes 5 titles/year. Pays 12% royalty on net sales. Offers $1,000-4,000 advance.** Reports in 2 months on queries.
Nonfiction: Reference, business. Subjects include telecommunications, data networking. "Author must be an experienced authority in the subject, and the material must be very specific with helpful step-by-step advice." Query with outline and SASE.
Recent Title(s): *Getting the Most from Your Yellow Pages Advertising*, by Barry Maher.

AHA PRESS, (formerly American Hospital Publishing, Inc.), American Hospital Association, 737 N. Michigan Ave., Chicago IL 60611-2615. (312)440-6800. Fax: (312)440-4001. E-mail: hill@aha.org. Website: http://www.ahapress.com. **Acquisitions:** Editorial Director. Estab. 1979. "We publish books for senior and middle management of health care institutions to improve health through information." Publishes hardcover and trade paperback originals. **Publishes 35-40 titles/year. Receives 150-200 submissions/year. 20% of books from first-time authors; 100% from unagented writers. Pays 10-12% royalty on retail price. Offers $1,000 average advance.** Publishes book 1 year after acceptance. Reports in 3 months. Book catalog and ms guidelines for 9×12 SAE with 7 first-class stamps.
Nonfiction: Reference, technical, textbook. Subjects include business/economics (specific to health care institutions); health/medicine (never consumer oriented). Need field-based, reality-tested responses to changes in the health care field directed to hospital CEO's, planners, boards of directors, or other senior management. No personal histories, untested health care programs or clinical texts. Query with SASE.
Recent Title(s): *Health Information Management*, by Skwika.
Tips: "The successful proposal demonstrates a clear understanding of the needs of the market and the writer's ability to succinctly present practical knowledge of demonstrable benefit that comes from genuine experience that readers will recognize, trust and accept."

AKTRIN FURNITURE INFORMATION CENTER, 164 S. Main St., P.O. Box 898, High Point NC 27261. (336)841-8535. Fax: (336)841-5435. E-mail: aktrin@aktrin.com. Website: http://www.aktrin.com. **Acquisitions:** Carlene Damba, director of operations. "AKTRIN is a full-service organization dedicated to the furniture industry. Our focus is on determining trends, challenges and opportunities, while also identifying problems and weak spots." Publishes trade paperback originals. **Publishes 8 titles/year. Receives 5 queries/year. 20% of books from first-time authors; 20% from unagented writers. Makes outright purchase of $1,500 minimum. Offers $300-600 advance.** Publishes book 2 months after acceptance. Accepts simultaneous submissions. Reports in 1 month. *Writer's Market* recommends allowing 2 months for reply. Book catalog free.
Imprint(s): AKTRIN Furniture Information Center-Canada (151 Randall St., Oakville, Ontario L6J 1P5 Canada. (905)845-3474. Contact: Stefan Wille).
Nonfiction: Reference. Business/economics subjects. "Have an understanding of business/economics. We are writing only about the furniture industry." Query.
Recent Title(s): *The American Demand for Office Furniture and Trends*, by Andrew McCormick (in-depth analysis of American office furniture market).
Tips: Audience is executives of furniture companies (manufacturers and retailers) and suppliers to the furniture industry.

ALBA HOUSE, 2187 Victory Blvd., Staten Island NY 10314-6603. (718)761-0047. **Acquisitions:** Edmund C. Lane, S.S.P., editor. Alba House is the North American publishing division of the Society of St. Paul, an International Roman Catholic Missionary Religious Congregation dedicated to spreading the Gospel message. Publishes hardcover, trade paperback and mass market paperback originals. **Publishes 24 titles/year. Receives 300 queries and 150 mss/year. 20% of books from first-time authors; 100% from unagented writers. Pays 7-10% royalty. No advance.** Publishes book 9 months after acceptance of ms. Reports in 1 month on queries and proposals, 2 months on mss. Book catalog and ms guidelines free.
Nonfiction: Reference, textbook. Religious subjects. Manuscripts which contribute, from a Roman Catholic perspec-

tive, to the personal, intellectual and spiritual growth of individuals in the following areas: Scripture, theology and the Church, saints-their lives and teachings, spirituality and prayer, religious life, marriage and family life, liturgy and homily preparation, pastoral concerns, religious education, bereavement, moral and ethical concerns, philosophy, psychology. Reviews artwork/photos as part of ms package. Send photocopies.
Recent Title(s): *Living The Truth In Love*, by Benedict Ashley, O.P. (moral theology textbook).

N **THE ALBAN INSTITUTE**, 7315 Wisconsin Ave., Suite 1250 W., Bethesda MD 20814-3211. (301)718-4407. Fax: (301)718-1958. **Acquisitions:** Linda Marie Delloff, director of publishing. Publishes trade paperback originals. **Publishes 10 titles/year. Receives 100 submissions/year. 100% of books from unagented writers. Pays 7-10% royalty on books;** makes outright purchase of $50-100 on publication for 450-2,000 word articles relevant to congregational life—practical—ecumenical. Publishes book 1 year after acceptance. Reports in 4 months. Book catalog and ms guidelines for 9×12 SAE with 3 first-class stamps.
Nonfiction: Religious—focus on local congregation—ecumenical. Must be accessible to general reader. Research preferred. Needs mss on the task of the ordained leader in the congregation, the career path of the ordained leader in the congregation, problems and opportunities in congregational life, and ministry of the laity in the world and in the church. No sermons, devotional, children's titles, novels, inspirational or prayers. Query for guidelines. Proposals only, no unsolicited mss.
Tips: "Our audience is comprised of intelligent, probably liberal mainline Protestant and Catholic clergy and lay leaders, executives and seminary administration/faculty—people who are concerned with the local church at a practical level and new approaches to its ministry. We are looking for titles on congregations, the clergy role, calling and career; visions, challenges, how-to's; and the ministry of the laity in the church and in the world."

N **ALBURY PUBLISHING**, P.O. Box 470406, Tulsa OK 74147. **Acquisitions:** Elizabeth Sherman, editorial development manager. "We are a Christian publisher with an upbeat presentation. We also publish charismatic material." Publishes hardcover and trade paperback originals and reprints. **Publishes 20 titles/year. Receives 200 queries and 45 mss/year. 1% of books from first-time authors; 80% from unagented writers. Pays royalty or makes outright purchase.** Publishes book 1 year after acceptance of ms. Reports in 6 months on proposals. Book catalog for 9×12 SAE and 5 first-class stamps. Manuscript guidelines for #10 SASE.
Nonfiction: Biography, humor, self-help, compilations of historic Christian leaders. Subjects include religion. "Most of our authors are established ministers and friends of the house. In order to break into our market, writers must exhibit a clearly defined, well-focused, professionally presented proposal that shows people know/understand our market." Submit outline, 3 sample chapters and author bio with SASE.
Recent Title(s): *Smith Wigglesworth: The Complete Collection of His Life Teachings*, compiled by Roberts Liardon (compilation of sermons).

N **ALEF DESIGN GROUP**, Torah Aura Productions, 4423 Fruitland Ave., Los Angeles CA 90058. (213)585-7312. Website: http://www.torahaura.com. **Acquisitions**: Jane Golub. "We publish books of Judaic interest only." Publishes hardcover and trade paperback originals. **Firm publishes 25 titles/year. Imprint publishes 10 titles/year. Receives 30 queries and 30 mss/year. 80% of books from first-time authors; 100% from unagented writers. Pays 10% royalty.** Publishes book 3 years after acceptance of ms. Accepts simultaneous submissions. Reports in 6 months on mss. Book catalog for 9×12 SAE and 10 first-class stamps..
Nonfiction: Children's/juvenile, textbook. Subjects include language/literature (Hebrew), religion (Jewish). Query with SASE. Reviews artwork/photos as part of ms package. Send photocopies.
Fiction: Juvenile, picture books, religious, young adult. "We publish books of Judaic interest only." Query with SASE.
Recent Title(s): *Sing Time*, by Bruce Sigel, illustrated by Joshua Sigel (middle reader fiction); *40 Things You Can Do to Save the Jewish People*, by Joel Lurie Grishaver (education).

ALEXANDER BOOKS, Creativity, Inc., 65 Macedonia Rd., Alexander NC 28701. (828)252-9515. Fax: (828)255-8719. E-mail: sales@abooks.com. Website: http//www.abooks.com. **Acquisitions:** Barbara Blood, acquisitions editor. Alexander Books is mostly nonfiction national titles, both new and reprints. Farthest Star reprints classic science fiction (very few new titles). Mountain Church prints mainline Protestant material. Publishes hardcover originals and trade paperback and mass market paperback originals and reprints. **Publishes 15-20 titles/year. Receives 200 queries and 100 mss/year. 10% of books from first-time authors; 75% from unagented writers. Pays 12-15% royalty on wholesale price. Advances seldom given (minimum $100).** Publishes book 18 months after acceptance of ms. Book catalog and ms guidelines for 9×12 SASE with $1.01 postage.
Imprint(s): Farthest Star, Mountain Church.
Nonfiction: Biography, how-to, reference, self-help. Subjects include computers/electronics, government/politics, collectibles, history, regional, religion, travel."We are interested in large niche markets." Query or submit 3 sample chapters and proposal package, including marketing plans with SASE. Reviews artwork/photos as part of ms package. Send photocopies.
Fiction: Historical, mainstream/contemporary, mystery, science fiction, western. "We prefer local or well-known authors or local interest settings". Query or submit synopsis and 3 sample chapters with SASE.
Recent Title(s): *Is It Antique Yet?*, by Frank Farmer Loomis IV (hobby); *Six-Gun Ladies*, by Talmage Powell.
Tips: "Send well-proofed manuscripts in final form. We will not read first rough drafts. Know your market."

ALGONQUIN BOOKS OF CHAPEL HILL, Workman Publishing, P.O. Box 2225, Chapel Hill NC 27515-2225. (919)967-0108. Fax: (919)933-0272. E-mail: shannonr@workman.com. Website: http://www.workman.com. **Acquisitions:** Editorial Department. "We're a very small company that tries to give voice to new writers." Publishes hardcover originals, trade paperback originals and reprints of own titles. **Publishes 24 titles/year.** Prefers not to share information.

ALLWORTH PRESS, 10 E. 23rd St., Suite 210, New York NY 10010-4402. Fax: (212)777-8261. E-mail: pub@allworth.com. Website: http://www.allworth.com. **Acquisitions:** Ted Gachot, editor. Tad Crawford, publisher. Estab. 1989. "Allworth Press publishes business and self-help information for artists, designers, photographers, authors and film and performing artists, as well as books about business, money and the law for the general public. The press also publishes the best of classic and contemporary writing in art and graphic design." Publishes hardcover and trade paperback originals. **Publishes 26 titles/year. Pays 6-7½% royalty (for paperback) on retail price.** Reports in 1 month on queries and proposals. Book catalog and ms guidelines free on request.
Nonfiction: How-to, reference. Subjects include the business aspects of art, design, photography, performing arts, writing, as well as business and legal guides for the public. Query.
Recent Title(s): *Historic Photographic Process: A Guide to Creating Handmade Photographic Images*, by Richard Farber (how to use 19th Century processes to create stunning effects).
Tips: "We are trying to give ordinary people advice to better themselves in practical ways—as well as helping creative people in the fine and commercial arts."

ALLYN & BACON, 160 Gould St., Needham Heights MA 02194-2310. (781)455-1200. Website: http://www.abacon.com. **Acquisitions:** Nancy Forsyth, editorial director. *Education:* Virginia Lanigan, editor (educational technology, curriculum, reading/emergent literacy, language arts, children's literature, ESL/bilingual methods, vocational-ed methods); Frances Helland, editor (C&L, social studies, multicultural ed, math & science, early childhood); Sean Wakely, editor (ed psych); Ray Short, editor (special ed, counseling, ed administration); Steve Dragin, editor (special-path, aud, deaf study/ed, higher ed, foundations of education). *English:* Joe Opiela, editor (English comp plus developmental, authors with last name A-K and all developmental authors); Eben Ludlow, editor (English comp, authors with last name L-Z). *Communication:* Karen Bowers, editor (mass communication, speech communication, journalism, drama). *Political Science:* Paul Smith, editor. *Psychology:* Carolyn Merrill, editor (intro, developmental, physio, clinical psych, assessment, professional psych, statistics/methods); Joe Burns, editor (health, phys ed, dance, human sexuality). *Sociology:* Karen Hanson, editor (sociology/intro, crime, criminal justice); Judy Fifer, editor (social work, family therapy); Sarah Kelbaugh, editor (advanced sociology, anthropology). *First-year Orientation:* Virginia Lanigan, editor. Allyn & Bacon publishes college texts, freshman through graduate level, and professional reference books. Publishes hardcover and trade paperback originals. Publishes 300 titles/year. 5-10% of books from first-time authors; 95% from unagented writers. Pays 10-15% royalty on net price. Advance varies. Publishes book 1-3 years after acceptance of ms. Accepts simultaneous submissions. Reports in 2 months on queries. Book catalog and ms guidelines free; also available online.

- Allyn & Bacon was recently acquired by Hicks Muse Tate & Furst, a Dallas-based investment firm.

Nonfiction: Reference, technical, textbook; primarily college texts; some titles for professionals. Subjects include education, government/politics, health/medicine, psychology, sociology, criminal justice, social work, speech, mass communication. "We focus on a few areas and cover them thoroughly; publishing vertically, from freshman level through graduate level. We also publish a number of titles within each discipline, same area but different approach. So, just because we have titles in an area already, it doesn't mean we aren't interested in more." Query with outline, 2-3 sample chapters, table of contents, author's vita and SASE. Reviews artwork/photos as part of ms package. Send photocopies.
Recent Title(s): *Educational Psychology*, by Anita Woolfolk (textbook).

ALMAR PRESS, 4105 Marietta Dr., Vestal NY 13850-4032. (607)722-0265. Fax: (607)722-3545. Editor-in-Chief: A.N. Weiner. **Acquisitions:** M.F. Weiner, managing editor. Estab. 1977. "*Almar Reports* are business and technology subjects published for management use and prepared in 8½×11 book format. Reprint publications represent a new aspect of our business. We are expanding our books on avoiding crime problems in business and personal life, and books covering unusual business topics—*not* the usual 'How to succeed in business,' or 'How I made a fortune in business.' " Publishes hardcover and paperback originals and reprints. **Publishes 8 titles/year. Receives 200 submissions/year. 75% of books from first-time authors; 100% from unagented writers. Pays 10% royalty. No advance.** Publishes book 6 months after acceptance. Prefers exclusive submissions; however, accepts simultaneous submissions, if so noted. Reports within 2 months. Book catalog for #10 SAE with 2 first-class stamps.
Nonfiction: Publishes business, technical, regional, consumer books and reports. Main subjects include general business, financial, travel, career, technology, personal help, Northeast regional, hobbies, general medical, general legal, how-to. Submit outline and sample chapters with SASE. Submissions *must* include SASE for reply. Reviews artwork/photos as part of ms package.
Recent Title(s): *How to Reduce Business Losses From Employee Theft and Customer Fraud.*
Tips: "We are open to any suggested topic. This type of book will be important to us. We look for timely subjects. The type of book the writer has the best chance of selling to our firm is something different or unusual—*no* poetry or fiction, also *no* first-person travel or family history. The book must be complete and of good quality."

N **ALYSON PUBLICATIONS, INC.**, 6922 Hollywood Blvd., Suite 1000, Los Angeles CA 90028. (213)871-1225. Fax: (213)467-6805. **Acquisitions:** Greg Constante, publisher. Estab. 1979. Publishes trade paperback originals and

reprints. **Publishes 40 titles/year. Receives 1,500 submissions/year. 40% of books from first-time authors; 80% from unagented writers. Pays 8-15% royalty on net price. Offers $1,500-15,000 advance.** Publishes book 15 months after acceptance. Reports in 1 month. Book catalog and ms guidelines for 6×9 SAE with 3 first-class stamps.
Imprint(s): Alyson Wonderland, Alyson Classics Library.
Nonfiction: Gay/lesbian subjects. "We are especially interested in nonfiction providing a positive approach to gay/lesbian/bisexual issues." Accepts nonfiction translations. Submit 2-page outline with SASE. No dissertations. Reviews artwork/photos as part of ms package.
Fiction: Gay novels. Accepts fiction translations. No short stories, poetry. Submit 1-2 page synopsis with SASE.
Recent Title(s): *Gay Old Girls*, by Zsa Zsa Gershick (nonfiction); *Looking Glass Lives*, by Felice Picano (fiction).
Tips: "We publish many books by new authors. The writer has the best chance of selling to our firm well-researched, popularly written nonfiction on a subject (e.g., some aspect of gay history) that has not yet been written about much. With fiction, create a strong storyline that makes the reader want to find out what happens. With nonfiction, write in a popular style for a non-academic audience. We also look at manuscripts aimed at kids of lesbian and gay parents."

☆ **AMACOM BOOKS**, American Management Association, 1601 Broadway, New York NY 10019-7406. (212)903-8081. Fax: (212)903-8083. Website: http://www.amanet.org. Managing Director: Weldon P. Rackley. Publisher: Hank Kennedy. **Acquisitions:** Adrienne Hickey, executive editor (management, human resources development, training); Ellen Kadin, senior acquisitions editor (marketing, sales, customer service, personal development); Ray O'Connell, senior acquisitions editor (manufacturing finance, technology, project management). Estab. 1923. "We publish books on business issues, strategies and tasks to enhance organizational and individual effectiveness." Publishes hardcover and trade paperback originals, professional books in various formats, multimedia and self-study courses. **Publishes 75 titles/year. Receives 500 submissions/year. 50% of books from first-time authors; 80% from unagented writers. Pays 10-15% royalty on net receipts by the publisher. Publishes book 9 months after acceptance. Reports in 2 months. Book catalog and proposal guidelines free.**
Nonfiction: Publishes business books of all types, including management, marketing, training, technology applications, finance, career, professional skills. Retail, direct mail, college, corporate markets. Query or submit outline/synopsis, sample chapters, résumé/vita with SASE.
Recent Title(s): *The Ultimate Business Library*, by Stuart Crainer.

☆ **AMERICA WEST PUBLISHERS**, P.O. Box 2208, Carson City NV 89702-2208. (702)585-0700. Fax: (702)891-0704. **Acquisitions:** George Green, president. Estab. 1985. America West seeks research and proof of the "other side of picture," political cover-ups and new health alternatives. Publishes hardcover and trade paperback originals and reprints. **Publishes 20 titles/year. Receives 150 submissions/year. 90% of books from first-time authors; 90% from unagented writers. Pays 10% on wholesale price. Offers $300 average advance.** Publishes book 6 months after acceptance. Accepts simultaneous submissions. Reports in 1 month. Book catalog and ms guidelines free.
Imprint(s): Bridger House Publishers, Inc.
Nonfiction: Subjects include economic, health/medicine (holistic self-help), political (including cover-up), UFO—metaphysical. Submit outline/synopsis and sample chapters. Reviews artwork/photos as part of ms package.
Recent Title(s): *The Cholesterol Hoax*, by Sheldon Zerdon (cholesterol lies).
Tips: "We currently have materials in all bookstores that have areas of UFOs; also political and economic nonfiction."

AMERICAN ASTRONAUTICAL SOCIETY, Univelt, Inc., Publisher, P.O. Box 28130, San Diego CA 92198. (760)746-4005. Fax: (760)746-3139. Website: http://univelt.staigerland.com. **Acquisitions:** Robert H. Jacobs, editorial director. Estab. 1970. "Our books must be space-oriented or space-related. They are meant for technical libraries, research establishments and the aerospace industry worldwide." Publishes hardcover originals. **Publishes 8 titles/year. Receives 12-15 submissions/year. 5% of books from first-time authors; 5% from unagented writers. Pays 10% royalty on actual sales.** Publishes book 4 months after acceptance. Accepts simultaneous submissions. Reports in 1 month. *Writer's Market* recommends allowing 2 months for reply. Book catalog and ms guidelines for 9×12 SAE with 3 first-class stamps.
Nonfiction: Proceedings or monographs in the field of astronautics, including applications of aerospace technology to Earth's problems. Call first, then submit outline and 1-2 sample chapters. Reviews artwork/photos as part of ms package.
Recent Title(s): *History of Rocketry and Astronautics, Vol. 21*, edited by Philippe Jung.

AMERICAN ATHEIST PRESS, P.O. Box 140195, Austin TX 78714-0195. (512)458-1244. Fax: (512)467-9525. E-mail: editor@atheists.org. Website: http://www.atheists.org. **Acquisitions:** Frank Zindler, editor. Estab. 1959. "We are interested in hard-hitting and original books expounding the lifestyle of atheism and criticizing religion." Publishes trade paperback originals and reprints. **Publishes 12 titles/year. Receives 200 submissions/year. 40-50% of books from first-time authors; 100% from unagented writers. Pays 5-10% royalty on retail price.** Publishes book 2 years after acceptance. Accepts simultaneous submissions. Reports in 4 months on queries. Book catalog for 6½×9½ SAE. Writer's guidelines for 9×12 SAE.
Imprint(s): Gustav Broukal Press.
Nonfiction: Biography, reference, general. Subjects include history (of religion and atheism, of the effects of religion historically); philosophy and religion (from an atheist perspective, particularly criticism of religion); politics (separation of state and church, religion and politics); atheism (particularly the lifestyle of atheism; the history of atheism; applications of atheism). "We would like to see more submissions dealing with the histories of specific religious sects, such

as the L.D.S., the Worldwide Church of God, etc." Submit outline and sample chapters. Reviews artwork/photos.
Fiction: Humor (satire of religion or of current religious leaders); anything of particular interest to atheists. "We rarely publish any fiction. But we have occasionally released a humorous book. No mainstream. For our press to consider fiction, it would have to tie in with the general focus of our press, which is the promotion of atheism and free thought." Submit outline/synopsis and sample chapters.
Recent Title(s): *The Legend of Saint Peter*, by Arthur Drews (history of religion/Bible criticism).
Tips: "We will need more how-to types of material—how to argue with creationists, how to fight for state/church separation, etc. We have an urgent need for literature for young atheists."

AMERICAN BAR ASSOCIATION BOOK PUBLISHING, 750 N. Lake Shore Dr., Book Publishing 8.1, Chicago IL 60611. Fax: (312)988-6030. E-mail: jweintraub@staff.abanet.org. Website: http://www.abanet.org/abapubs/. **Acquisitions:** J. Weintraub, director of publishing. Jane L. Johnston, executive editor. "We are interested in books that will help lawyers practice law more effectively whether it's help in handling clients, structuring a real estate deal or taking an antitrust case to court." Publishes hardcover and trade paperback originals. **Publishes 100 titles/year. Receives 50 queries/year. 20% of books from first-time authors; 95% from unagented writers. Pays 5-15% royalty on wholesale or retail price.** Publishes book 18 months after acceptance of ms. Accepts simultaneous submissions. Reports in 1 months on queries and proposals, 3 months on mss. Book catalog for $5.95. Manscript guidelines free.

- "The Association also publishes over 50 major national periodicals in a variety of legal areas. Write to Susan Yessne, executive editor, at the above address for guidelines"

Nonfiction: How-to (in the legal market), reference, technical. Subjects include business/economics, computers/electronics, money/finance, software, legal practice. "Our market is not, generally, the public. Books need to be targeted to lawyers who are seeking solutions to their practice problems. We rarely publish scholarly treatises." Query with SASE.
Recent Title(s): *Freedom of Speech in the Public Workplace* (municipal law).

AMERICAN COLLEGE OF PHYSICIAN EXECUTIVES, (ACPE PUBLICATIONS), 4890 W. Kennedy Blvd., Suite 200, Tampa FL 33609. (813)287-2000. E-mail: wcurry@acpe.org. Website: http://www.acpe.org. **Acquisitions:** Wesley Curry, managing editor. "Our books are aimed at physicians in their roles as managers within the health care delivering and financing system." Publishes hardcover and trade paperback originals. **Publishes 12-15 titles/year. Receives 6 queries and 3 mss/year. 80% of books from first-time authors; 100% from unagented writers. Pays 10-15% royalty on wholesale price or makes outright purchase of $1,000-4,000.** Publishes book 8 months after acceptance of ms. Reports in 1 month on queries and ms, 2 months on proposals. Book catalog and ms guidelines free.
Nonfiction: Technical, textbook. Subjects include business/economics, health/medicine. Query and submit outline. Reviews artwork/photos as part of ms package. Send photocopies.
Recent Title(s): *Making Sense of Managed Care*, edited by Kimball Austin Miller, M.D., MHSA, and Elaine King Miller, Ph.D.
Tips: Audience is physicians in management and physicians interested in management.

AMERICAN CORRECTIONAL ASSOCIATION, 4380 Forbes Blvd., Lanham MD 20706. (301)918-1800. Fax: (301)918-1896. E-mail: afins@aca.com. Website: http://www.corrections.com/aca. **Acquisitions:** Alice Fins, managing editor. Estab. 1870. American Correctional Association provides practical information on jails, prisons, boot camps, probation, parole, community corrections, juvenile facilities and rehabilitation programs, substance abuse programs and other areas of corrections. Publishes hardcover and trade paperback originals. **Publishes 18 titles/year. Receives 40 submissions/year. 90% of books from first-time authors; 100% from unagented writers. Pays 10% royalty on net sales.** Publishes book 6-12 months after acceptance. Reports in 4 months. Book catalog and ms guidelines free.

- This publisher advises out-of-town freelance editors, indexers and proofreaders to refrain from requesting work from them.

Nonfiction: How-to, reference, technical, textbook, correspondence courses. "We are looking for practical, how-to texts or training materials written for the corrections profession. No autobiographies or true-life accounts by current or former inmates or correctional officers, theses, or dissertations." No fiction. No poetry. Query with SASE. Reviews artwork/photos as part of ms package.
Recent Title(s): *No Time to Play: Youthful Offenders in Adult Correctional Systems*, by Barry Glick, Ph.D., William Sturgeon with Charles Venator-Santiago.
Tips: Authors are professionals in the field and corrections. "Our audience is made up of corrections professionals and criminal justice students. No books by inmates or former inmates."

N **AMERICAN COUNSELING ASSOCIATION**, 5999 Stevenson Ave., Alexandria VA 22304-3300. (703)823-9800. **Acquisitions:** Carolyn C. Baker, director of acquisitions. "The American Counseling Association is dedicated to promoting public confidence and trust in the counseling profession." Scholarly paperback originals. **Publishes 10-15 titles/year. Receives 200 queries and 125 mss/year. 5% of books from first-time authors; 90% from unagented writers. Pays 10-15% royalty on net sales.** Publishes book within 7 months after acceptance of final draft. Accepts simultaneous submissions. Reports in 2 months on queries and proposals, 4 months on mss. Manuscript guidelines free.
Nonfiction: Reference, textbooks for professional counselors. Subjects include education, gay/lesbian, health/medicine, psychology, religion, sociology, women's issues/studies. ACA does not publish self-help books or autobiographies. Query with proposal package, including outline, 2 sample chapters and vitae and SASE.
Recent Title(s): *Tough Kids, Cool Counseling: User Friendly Approaches with Challenging Youth*, by John and Rita

Sommers-Flanagan.
Tips: "Target your market. Your books will not be appropriate for everyone across all disciplines."

AMERICAN DIABETES ASSOCIATION, 1660 Duke St., Alexandria VA 22314. (703)549-1500. Website: http://www.diabetes.org. **Acquisitions:** Robert J. Anthony, acquisitions editor. "The mission of the American Diabetes Association is to prevent and cure diabetes and to improve the lives of all people affected by diabetes." Publishes hardcover originals and trade paperback originals. **Publishes 15 titles/year. Receives 60 queries and 20 mss/year. 10% of books from first-time authors; 80% from unagented writers. Pays royalty on retail price.** Publishes book 9 months after acceptance of final ms. Reports in 2 months. Book catalog free.
Nonfiction: Cookbook, how-to, reference, self-help. Subjects include child guidance/parenting, cooking/foods/nutrition, health/medicine, psychology. "Our books are written for people with diabetes and their families. We are interested in the medical, nutritional and psychosocial aspects of living with diabetes." Query with outline and 2 sample chapters with SASE. Reviews artwork/photos as part of ms package. Send photocopies.
Recent Title(s): *Robyn Webb's Memorable Menus Made Easy* (cookbook).
Tips: "Our audience consists primarily of consumers with diabetes who want to better manage their illness. Obtain a few of our books to better understand our target audience and appropriate reading level."

AMERICAN EAGLE PUBLICATIONS INC., P.O. Box 1507, Show Low AZ 85901. Phone/fax: (520)367-1621. E-mail: ameagle@whitemtns.com. **Acquisitions:** Mark Ludwig, publisher. Estab. 1988. Publishes scholarly hardcover and trade paperback originals and reprints. **Publishes 8 titles/year. 50% of books from first-time authors; 100% from unagented writers. Pays 7-15% royalty on retail price. Offers $1,000 average advance.** Publishes book 6 months after acceptance of ms. Accepts simultaneous submissions. Reports in 2 months. Catalog for #10 SASE.
• American Eagle reports no interest in seeing military or other autobiographies.
Nonfiction: Historical biography, technical. Subjects include computers/electronics (security), military/war and science (computers and artificial intelligence). "We have recently established a line of patriot/political books. Writers should call and discuss what they have first." Query. Reviews artwork/photos as part of freelance ms package. Send photocopies.
Recent Title(s): *The Happy Hacker*, by C. Meinel (computers/technical).
Tips: Audience is "scholarly, university profs (some used as textbooks), very technical programmers and researchers, military, very international. No autobiographies."

AMERICAN FEDERATION OF ASTROLOGERS, P.O. Box 22040, Tempe AZ 85285. (602)838-1751. Fax: (602)838-8293. E-mail: afa@msn.com. **Acquisitions:** Kris Brandt Riske, publications manager. American Federation of Astrologers publishes only astrology books, software, calendars, charts and related aids. Publishes trade paperback originals and reprints. **Publishes 10-15 titles/year. Receives 10 queries and 20 mss/year. 50% of books from first-time authors; 100% from unagented writers. Pays 10% royalty.** Publishes book 10 months after acceptance of ms. Accepts simultaneous submissions. Reports in 6 months on mss. Book catalog for $2. Manuscript guidelines free.
Nonfiction: Astrology. Submit complete ms.
Recent Title(s): *The Astrologer's Forecasting Workbook*, by Lloyd Cope.

AMERICAN INSTITUTE OF CERTIFIED PUBLIC ACCOUNTANTS, Harborside Financial Center, 201 Plaza Three, Jersey City NJ 07711-3881. Fax: (201)938-3780. E-mail: mbareille@aicpa.org. Website: http://www.aicpa.org. Senior Manager: Marie Bareille. **Acquisitions:** Laura Inge (CPA firm management); Murray Schwartzberg (taxes, personal finance planning); Philip Rossman (computer technology and management accounting). "We produce high-quality, advanced or cutting edge information for financial professionals." Publishes hardcover and trade paperback originals. **Publishes 104 titles/year. Receives 5 queries/year; 3 mss/year. 10% of books are from first-time authors; 100% from unagented writers. Pays 10-15% royalty on retail price. Offers $500-2,000 advance.** Publishes book 5 months after acceptance of ms. Reports in 1 month on queries, 3 months on proposals and mss. Book catalog and ms guidelines free.
Nonfiction: Technical. Subjects include business/economics, computers/electronics, accounting, taxation, personal financial planning. "We are interested in expanding in topics for corporate accountants, consultants and computers." Submit proposal package including table of contents and outline.
Recent Title(s): *What Every CPA Needs to Know About the New IRAs; Solving the Year 2000 Dilemma*, by Sandi Smith (computer technology).
Tips: Audience is CPAs in public accounting firms and corporate accountants.

AMERICAN NURSES PUBLISHING, American Nurses Foundation, an affiliate of the American Nurses Association, 600 Maryland Ave. SW, #100 West, Washington DC 20024-2571. (202)651-7213. Fax: (202)651-7003. **Acquisitions:** Rosanne O'Connor, publisher. American Nurses publishes books designed to help professional nurses in their work and careers. "Through the publishing program, the Foundation fulfills one of its core missions—to provide nurses in all practice settings with publications that address cutting-edge issues and form a basis for debate and exploration of this century's most critical health care trends." Publishes professional and trade paperback originals and reprints. **Publishes 15-20 titles/year. Receives 40 queries and 10 mss/year. 75% of books from first-time authors; 100% from unagented writers. Pays 10% royalty on retail price.** Publishes book 4-6 months after acceptance of ms. Reports in 4-6 months on proposals and mss. Catalog and ms guidelines free.
Nonfiction: Reference, technical and textbook. Subjects include business/economics, education, health/medicine,

money/finance, psychology, science, women's issues/studies pertaining to nursing. Submit outline and 1 sample chapter. Reviews artwork/photos as part of ms package. Send photocopies.
Recent Title(s): *The Acute Care Nurse in Transition.*

AMERICAN PRESS, 520 Commonwealth Ave., Boston MA 02215-2605. **Acquisitions:** Jane Kirk, editor. Publishes college textbooks. **Publishes 25 titles/year. Receives 350 queries and 100 mss/year. 50% of books from first-time authors; 90% from unagented writers. Pays 5-15% royalty on wholesale price.** Publishes book 9 months after acceptance of ms. Reports in 3 months. Book catalog free.
Nonfiction: Technical, textbook. Subjects include agriculture/horticulture, anthropology/archaeology, art/architecture, business/economics, education, government/politics, health/medicine, history, music/dance, psychology, science, sociology, sports. "We prefer that our authors actually teach courses for which the manuscripts are designed." Query or submit outline with tentative table of contents. No complete mss.

THE AMERICAN PSYCHIATRIC PRESS, INC., 1400 K St. NW, Washington DC 20005. (202)682-6231. **Acquisitions:** Carol C. Nadelson, editor-in-chief. Estab. 1981. American Psychiatric Press publishes professional, authoritative reference books and general nonfiction on psychiatry only. Publishes hardcover and trade paperback originals and hardcover reprints. **Publish 50 titles/year. Receives 200 queries/year. 25% of books from first-time authors; 90% from unagented writers. Pays 10-15% royalty on net sales. Offers $3,000 advance.** Publishes book 1 year after acceptance of ms. Accepts simultaneous submissions, but this must be mentioned in the submission. Reports in 1 month on queries, 2 months on proposals. Book catalog, author questionnaire and proposal guidelines free.
Nonfiction: Reference (psychiatry), textbook (psychiatry), handbooks, manuals, study guides, assessment/interview booklets, clinical and research aspects. All psychiatry-related. "Projects with significant clinical applications in psychiatry will be given the highest priority. We are also interested in authoritative books that interpret the scientific and medical aspects of serious mental illness for the lay public. Request and submit a completed author questionnaire. Do not submit an entire manuscript. American Psychiatric press prefers to consider proposals." Submit outline and 1 sample chapter and proposal package, including Author Questionnaire, table of contents, author's curriculum vitae with SASE. Reviews artwork/photos as part of the proposal package. Send photocopies.
Recent Title(s): *The Selfish Brain: Learning from Addiction*, by Robert L. Dupont, M.D. (trade).
Tips: "Primary audience is psychiatrists and other mental health professionals. Secondary audience is primary care physicians and other health care professionals.

AMERICAN SOCIETY OF CIVIL ENGINEERS PRESS, 1801 Alexander Bell Dr., Reston VA 20191-4400. (703)295-6275. Fax: (703)295-6278. E-mail: lehmer@asce.org. Website: http://www.asce.org. **Acquisitions:** Lisa Ehmer, acquisitions editor: . Estab. 1988. "We publish books by individual authors to advance the civil engineering profession." **Publishes 15-20 titles/year. 50% of books from first-time authors; 100% from unagented writers. Pays 10% royalty. No advance.** Accepts simultaneous submissions. Request proposal guidelines.
Nonfiction: Civil engineering. "We are looking for topics that are useful and instructive to the engineering practitioner." Query with outline, sample chapters and cv.
Recent Title(s): *Historic American Covered Bridges*, by McKee (engineering history).
Tips: "ASCE is a not-for-profit organization, so we've always been cost conscious. We produce inexpensive professional books on a tight budget. We have increased the number of new books that we are producing by about 50-100%."

AMERICAN WATER WORKS ASSOCIATION 6666 W. Quincy Ave., Denver CO 80235. (303)794-7711. Manager of Business and Product Development, Mead L. Noss. **Acquisitions:** Colin Murcray, acquisitions editor (youth educational materials); Mindy Burke, senior technical editor; Bill Cobban, technical editor (technical operations handbooks). "AWWA strives to advance and promote the safety and knowledge of drinking water and related issues to all audiences—from kindergarten through post-doctorate." Publishes hardcover and trade paperback originals. **Publishes 100 titles/year. Receives 200 queries and 35 mss/year. 30% of books from first-time authors; 100% from unagented writers. Pays 15% royalty on wholesale or retail price. No advance.** Publishes book 1 year after acceptance of ms. Book catalog and manuscript guidelines free.
Nonfiction: Multimedia (Windows format), technical. Subjects include nature/environment, science, software, drinking water-related topics. Query or submit outline, 3 sample chapters and author biography. Reviews artwork/photos as part of ms package. Send photocopies.
Recent Title(s): *The Changing Water Utility*, by Garret P. Westerhoff, et al.

AMHERST MEDIA, INC., 155 Rand St., Suite 300, Buffalo NY 14207. (716)874-4450. Fax: (716)874-4508. Publisher: Craig Alesse. **Acquisitions:** Craig Alesse. Estab. 1974. "We publish how-to photography books." Publishes trade paperback originals and reprints. **Publishes 10 titles/year. Receives 50 submissions/year. 80% of books from first-time authors; 100% from unagented writers. Pays 8% royalty on retail price.** Publishes book 1 year after acceptance. Accepts simultaneous submissions. Reports in 2 months. Book catalog and ms guidelines free.
Nonfiction: Photography how-to. Looking for well-written and illustrated photo books. Query with outline, 2 sample chapters and SASE. Reviews artwork/photos as part of ms package.
Recent Title(s): *Handcoloring Photographs Step-by-Step*, by Sandra Laird and Carey Chambers.
Tips: "Our audience is made up of beginning to advanced photographers. If I were a writer trying to market a book today, I would fill the need of a specific audience and self-edit in a tight manner."

THE AMWELL PRESS, P.O. Box 5385, Clinton NJ 08809-0385. (908)537-6888. President: James Rikhoff. **Acquisitions:** Monica Sullivan, vice president. Corporate Secretary: Genevieve Symonds. Estab. 1976. Publishes hardcover originals. **Publishes 6 titles/year.** Publishes book 18 months after acceptance. Reports in 2 months on queries.
Nonfiction: Hunting and fishing stories/literature (not how-to). No fiction. Mostly limited editions. Query with SASE.
Recent Title(s): *Taking Your Chances in the High Country*, anthology compiled by Jim Rikhoff.

ANCESTRY INCORPORATED, 266 W. Center St., Orem UT 84057. (801)426-3500. Fax: (801)426-3501. E-mail: mattg@ancestry.com. Book Editor: Matt Grove. *Ancestry* magazine Editor: Alyssa Hickman. **Acquisitions:** Loretto Szucs, executive editor. Estab. 1983. "Our publications are aimed exclusively at the genealogist. We consider everything from short monographs to book length works on immigration, migration, record collections and heraldic topics." Publishes hardcover, trade and paperback originals and *Ancestry* magazine. **Publishes 12-20 titles/year. Receives over 100 submissions/year. 70% of books from first-time authors; 100% from unagented writers. Pays 8-12% royalty or makes outright purchase. No advance.** Publishes book 1 year after acceptance. Accepts simultaneous submissions for books. Reports in 2 months. Book catalog for 9×12 SAE with 2 first-class stamps.
Nonfiction: How-to, reference, genealogy. Subjects include Americana, historical methodology and genealogical research techniques. No mss that are not genealogical or historical. Query, or submit outline/synopsis and sample chapters with SASE. Reviews artwork/photos.
Recent Title(s): *Printed Sources*, by Kory L. Meyerink.
Tips: "Genealogical and historical reference, how-to, and descriptions of source collections have the best chance of selling to our firm. Be precise in your description. Please, no family histories or genealogies."

ANCHORAGE PRESS, INC., P.O. Box 8067, New Orleans LA 70182-8067. (504)283-8868. Fax: (504)866-0502. **Acquisitions:** Orlin Corey, editor. Publishes hardcover originals. Estab. 1935. "We are an international agency for plays for young people. First in the field since 1935." **Publishes 10 titles/year. Receives 450-900 submissions/year. 50% of books from first-time authors; 80% from unagented writers. Pays 10-15% royalty on retail price. Playwrights also receive 50-75% royalties.** Publishes book 1-2 years after acceptance. Reports in 1 month on queries, 4 months on mss. Book catalog and ms guidelines free.
Nonfiction: Textbook, plays. Subjects include education, language/literature, plays. "We are looking for play anthologies; and texts for teachers of drama/theater (middle school and high school.)" Query. Reviews artwork/photos.
Fiction: Plays of juvenile/young people's interest. Query.
Recent Title(s): *The Theater of Aurand Harris*, by Lowell Swortzell.

[N] WILLIAM ANDREW, INC., Plastics Design Library, 13 Eaton Ave., Norwich NY 13815. (607)337-5000. Fax: (607)337-5090. E-mail: publishing@williamandrew.com. Website: http://www.williamandrew.com. **Acquisitions**: George Wypych, editorial director (plastics, additives); William Woishnis, editor (welding); Sasha Gurke, vice president technology (CD-ROM, Web software). Publishes hardcover originals. **Publishes 11 titles/year. Receives 100 queries and 20 mss/year. 40% of books from first-time authors; 100% from unagented writers. Pays 8-15% royalty on wholesale price or uses in-house authors. Offers $1,000-5,000 advance.** Publishes book 6 months after acceptance of ms. Accepts simultaneous submissions. Reports in 1 month on queries, 2 months on proposals and mss. Book catalog and ms guidelines free.
Imprint(s): Plastics Design Library, (contact Bill Woishnis, publisher); Rover (contact Chris Forbes, president).
Nonfiction: Reference, technical, textbook. Subjects include science, engineering, materials science. Submit outline and SASE. Reviews artwork/photos as part of ms package. Send photocopies.
Recent Title(s): *Medical Plastics*, by George Wypych (all reference).

[A] ANDREWS McMEEL UNIVERSAL, 4520 Main St., Kansas City MO 64111-7701. **Acquisitions:** Christine Schillig, vice president/editorial director. (816)932-6700. Andrews McMeel publishes general trade books, humor books, miniature gift books, calendars, greeting cards, and stationery products. Publishes hardcover and paperback originals. **Publishes 300 titles/year. Pays royalty on retail price. Offers advance.**
Nonfiction: General trade, humor, how-to, journalism, juvenile, consumer reference books. Also produces gift books, posters and kits. Query only. *Agented submissions only.*
Recent Title(s): *24 Years of Housework . . . and the Place is Still a Mess*, by Pat Schroeder.

[N] ANGELINES® PRODUCTIONS, Multiple Corporation, 361 Post Rd. W., Wesport CT 06880. Website: http://www.angelines.com. **Acquisitions:** J. Anne Weber, editor-in-chief. Publishes trade paperback originals. "AngeLines publishes for metaphysically and spiritually aware adults." **Publishes 6 titles/year. Receives 20 queries and 10 mss/year. 10% of books from first-time authors; 75% from unagented writers. Royalty on retail price varies. Advance varies.** Publishes book 1 year after publication of ms. Accepts simultaneous submissions if so noted. Reports in 2 months on proposals. Manuscript guidelines for #10 SASE.
Nonfiction: Self-help, self-actualization. Subjects include money/finance, psychology, metaphysics, spirituality. "We currently are producing a 14-volume series of articles, *ACP Oracles*™, by psychic/channel Amie Angeli. Most of our books published/contracted are channeled material." Submit proposal, chapter outline and 1-3 sample chapters with SASE. Reviews artwork/photos as part of the ms package. Send photocopies.
Recent Title(s): *Conversations with an Unseen Friend*, by Amie Angeli.
Tips: "Our ideal author is an advanced metaphysician with journalist experience, previously published; international

experience is a real plus—our books are sold internationally. Check our website!"

ANTIQUE TRADER BOOKS, Landmark Specialty Publications, 150 W. Brambleton Ave., Norfolk VA 23510-2075. Website: http://www.collect.com. **Acquisitions**: Allan Miller, managing editor; Tony Lillis, acquisitions editor. "Antique Trader Books publishes annuals, reference books, collector's guides and price guides for all areas of collecting." Publishes hardcover and trade paperback originals. **Firm publishes 30 titles/year; imprint publishes 5 titles/year. Receives 58 queries and 20 mss/year. 60% of books from first-time authors; 100% from unagented writers. Pays 10-15% royalty on wholesale price. Offers $2,000-8,000 advance.** Publishes book 6 months after acceptance of ms. Accepts simultaneous submissions. Reports in 2-3 months on proposals. Book catalog and ms guidelines free.
Imprint(s): Tuff Stuff Books.
Nonfiction: Price guides. Subjects include hobbies (antiques and collectibles). Query or submit outline and 2 sample chapters and SASE. Reviews artwork/photos as part of ms package. Send duplicate prints or transparencies.
Recent Title(s): *Beanie Family Album*, by Shawn Brecka.
Tips: "Audience is collectors of just about everything and anything."

APPALACHIAN MOUNTAIN CLUB BOOKS, 5 Joy St., Boston MA 02108. (617)523-0636. Fax: (617)523-0722. Website: http://www.outdoors.org. **Acquisitions:** Mark Russell, acquisitions. "We publish hiking guides, water-recreation guides (non-motorized), nature, conservation and mountain-subject guides for America's Northeast. We connect recreation to conservation." Publishes trade paperback originals. **Publishes 6-10 titles/year. Receives 200 queries and 20 mss/year. 30% of books from first-time authors; 90% from unagented writers. Pays 6-10% royalty on retail price. Offers modest advance.** Publishes book 10 months after acceptance of ms. Accepts simultaneous submissions. Reports in 3 months on proposals. Book catalog for 8½×11 SAE with 4 first-class stamps. Manuscript guidelines for #10 SASE.
Nonfiction: How-to, guidebooks. Subjects include history (mountains, Northeast), nature/environment, recreation, regional (Northeast outdoor recreation). Writers should avoid submitting: proposals on Appalachia (rural southern mountains); not enough market research; too much personal experience—autobiography." Query. Reviews artwork/photos as part of ms package. Send photocopies and transparencies "at your own risk."
Recent Title(s): *Classic Northeast Whitewater Guide.*
Tips: "Our audience is outdoor recreationalists, conservation-minded hikers and canoeists, family outdoor lovers, armchair enthusiasts. Our guidebooks have a strong conservation message."

A-R EDITIONS, INC., 801 Deming Way, Madison WI 53717. (608)836-9000. Fax: (608)831-8200. Website: http://www.areditions.com. **Acquisitions:** Paul Corneilson, managing editor, Recent Researches music editions; James L. Zychowicz, managing editor, Computer Music and Digital Audio Series. Estab. 1962. "A-R Editions publishes modern critical editions of music based on current musicological research. Each edition is devoted to works by a single composer or to a single genre of composition. The contents are chosen for their potential interest to scholars and performers, then prepared for publication according to the standards that govern the making of all reliable, historical editions." **Publishes 20 titles/year. Receives 40 queries and 24 mss/year. 50% of books from first-time authors; 100% from unagented writers. Pays royalty or honoraria.** Reports in 1 month on queries, 3 months on proposals and 6 months on mss. Book catalog and newsletter free. Manuscript guidelines free (check website).
Nonfiction: Historical music editions, computers and electronics, software; also titles related to computer music and digital audio. Query or submit outline with SASE.
Recent Title(s): *Celestial Airs of Antiquity: Music of the Seven-String Zither of China*, edited by Bell Yung.

ARABESQUE, Kensington, 850 Third Ave., 16th Floor, New York NY 10022. (212)407-1500. Website: http://www.kensington.com/arabesque. **Acquisitions:** Karen Thomas, editor. "Arabesque publishes contemporary romances about African-American couples." Publishes mass market paperback originals. **Publishes 48 titles/year. 30-50% of books from first-time authors; 50% from unagented writers. Pays royalty on retail price, varies by author. Advance varies by author.** Publishes book 18 months after acceptance of ms. Accepts simultaneous submissions. Reports in 3 months on mss. Book catalog for #10 SASE.
Fiction: Multicultural romance. Query with synopsis and SASE. *No unsolicited mss.*
Recent Title(s): *Silken Betrayal*, by Francis Ray.

ARCADE PUBLISHING, 141 Fifth Ave., New York NY 10010. (212)475-2633. **Acquisitions:** Cal Barksdale, senior editor; Timothy Bent, senior editor; Sean McDonald; Richard Seaver, publisher; Jeannette Seaver, associate publisher. Arcade prides itself on publishing top-notch commercial nonfiction and literary fiction. Publishes hardcover originals, trade paperback originals and reprints. **Publishes 40 titles/year. 5% of books from first-time authors. Pays royalty on retail price. Offers $3,000-50,000 advance.** Publishes book within 18 months after acceptance of ms. Reports in 3 months on queries.
Nonfiction: Biography, cookbook, general nonfiction. Subjects include cooking/foods/nutrition, government/politics, history, nature/environment and travel. *Agented submissions only.* Reviews artwork/photos. Send photocopies.
Fiction: Ethnic, historical, humor, literary, mainstream/contemporary, mystery, short story collections, suspense. *Agented submissions only.*
Recent Title(s): *The Laundrymen: I Made Money Laundering the World's Third Largest Business*, by Jeffrey Robinson (nonfiction); *The File on H.*, by Tomail Kadare (fiction).

ARCHWAY PAPERBACKS, Pocket Books for Young Readers, Simon & Schuster, 1230 Avenue of the Americas, New York NY 10020. (212)698-7669. Website: http://www.simonsayskids.com. Vice President/Editorial Director: Patricia MacDonald. **Acquisitions:** send all submissions Attn: Manuscript Proposals. Archway Paperbacks publishes fiction and current nonfiction for young adult readers ages 12-18. Publishes mass market paperback originals and reprints. Publishes 80 titles/year. Receives over 1,000 submissions/year. Pays 6-8% royalty on retail price. Publishes book 2 years after acceptance. Reports in 3 months.

Nonfiction: Young adult, ages 12-18. Subjects include current popular subjects or people, sports. Query with outline/synopsis, 2 sample chapters and SASE. SASE for all material necessary or query not answered. Reviews artwork/photos as part of ms package. Send photocopies.

Fiction: Young adult horror, mystery, suspense thrillers, contemporary fiction, romances for YA, ages 12-18. Query with outline/synopsis, sample chapters and SASE.

Recent Title(s): *Aliens Ate My Homework*, by Bruce Coville.

ARDEN PRESS INC., P.O. Box 418, Denver CO 80201-0418. (303)697-6766. **Acquisitions:** Susan Conley, publisher. Estab. 1980. "We publish nonfiction on women's subjects and sell to general and women's bookstores and public and academic libraries. Many of our titles are adopted as texts for college courses." Publishes hardcover and trade paperback originals and reprints. 95% of books are originals; 5% are reprints. **Publishes 4-6 titles/year. Receives 600 submissions/year. 20% of books from first-time authors; 80% from unagented writers. Pays 8-15% royalty on wholesale price. Offers $2,000 average advance.** Publishes book 6 months after acceptance. Accepts simultaneous submissions. Reports in 2 months on queries. Manuscript guidelines free.

Nonfiction: Practical guides in many subjects, biography, reference, textbooks. Subjects include women's issues/studies and video selection guides. No personal memoirs or autobiographies. Query with outline/synopsis and sample chapters.

Recent Title(s): *Whatever Happened to the Year of the Woman?*, by Handlin (politics/women's studies).

Tips: "Writers have the best chance selling us nonfiction on women's subjects. If I were a writer trying to market a book today, I would learn as much as I could about publishers' profiles *then* contact those who publish similar works."

ARDSLEY HOUSE PUBLISHERS, INC., 320 Central Park West, New York NY 10025. (212)496-7040. **Acquisitions:** Ellissa Morris. "We publish only college-level textbooks—particularly in the areas of music, philosophy, history, and film." Publishes hardcover and trade paperback originals and reprints. **Publishes 5-8 titles/year. 25% of books from first-time authors; 100% from unagented writers (all are college professors). Pays generally by royalty. No advance.** Publishes book 15 months after acceptance of ms. Reports in 1 month on queries, 2 months on proposals, 3 months on mss. Book catalog free.

Nonfiction: Textbook (college). Subjects include Americana, history, music/dance, philosophy, film. "We don't accept any other type of manuscript." Query with proposal package, including outline, 2-3 sample chapters, prospectus, author's résumé and SASE. Reviews artwork/photos as part of ms package. Send photocopies.

Recent Title(s): *Functional Hearing: A Contextual Method for Ear Training*, by Arthur Gottschalk, Phillip Kloeckner.

ARKANSAS RESEARCH, P.O. Box 303, Conway AR 72033. (501)470-1120. Fax: (501)470-1120. E-mail: desmond@ipa.net. **Acquisitions:** Desmond Walls Allen, owner. "Our company opens a world of information to researchers interested in the history of Arkansas." Publishes hardcover originals and trade paperback originals and reprints. **Publishes 20 titles/year. 90% of books from first-time authors; 100% from unagented writers. Pays 5-10% royalty on retail price. Offers no advance.** Publishes book 2 months after acceptance of ms. Reports in 1 month. Book catalog for $1. Manuscript guidelines free.

Imprint(s): Research Associates.

Nonfiction: How-to (genealogy), reference, self-help. Subjects include Americana, ethnic, history, hobbies (genealogy), military/war, regional, all Arkansas-related. "We don't print autobiographies or genealogies about one family." Query with SASE. Reviews artwork/photos as part of ms package. Send photocopies.

Recent Title(s): *Civil War Soldiers Buried in Arkansas' National Cemeteries*, by Rena Knight.

JASON ARONSON, INC., 230 Livingston St., Northvale NJ 07647-1726. (201)767-4093. Fax: (201)767-4330. Website: http://www.aronson.com. Editor-in-chief: Arthur Kurzweil. **Acquisitions:** Michael Moskowitz (psychology); Arthur Kurzweil (Judaica). Estab. 1967. "We are looking for high quality books in two fields: psychotherapy and Judaica." Publishes hardcover and trade paperback originals and reprints. **Publishes 250 titles/year. 50% of books from first-time authors; 95% from unagented writers. Pays 10-15% royalty on retail price. Offers $250-$2500 advance.** Publishes book an average of 1 year after acceptance. Reports in 1 month. *Writer's Market* recommends allowing 2 months for reply. Catalog and ms guidelines free.

Nonfiction: Subjects include history, philosophy, psychology, religion translation. Query or submit outline and sample chapters. Reviews artwork/photos as part of ms packages. Send photocopies.

Recent Title(s): *Talmudic Images*, by Adin Steinsaltz (Judaica).

ART DIRECTION BOOK COMPANY, INC., 456 Glenbrook Rd., Glenbrook CT 06096-1800. (203)353-1441. Fax: (203) 353-1371. **Acquisitions:** Don Barron, editorial director. "We are interested in books for the professional advertising art field—books for art directors, designers, etc.; also entry level books for commercial and advertising art students in such fields as typography, photography, paste-up, illustration, clip-art, design, layout and graphic arts."

Publishes hardcover and paperback originals. **Publishes 6 titles/year. Pays 10% royalty on retail price. Offers average $1,000 advance.** Publishes book 1 year after acceptance. Reports in 3 months. Book catalog for 6×9 SASE.
Imprint(s): Infosource Publications.
Nonfiction: Commercial art, ad art how-to and textbooks. Query with outline and 1 sample chapter. Reviews artwork/photos as part of ms package.

ARTE PUBLICO PRESS, University of Houston, Houston TX 77204-2090. (713)743-2841. Fax (713)743-2847. **Acquisitions:** Nicolas Kanellos, editor. Estab. 1979. "We are a showcase for Hispanic literary creativity, arts and culture. Our endeavor is to provide a national forum for Hispanic literature." Publishes hardcover originals, trade paperback originals and reprints. **Publishes 36 titles/year. Receives 1,000 queries and 500 mss/year. 50% of books from first-time authors; 80% from unagented writers. Pays 10% royalty on wholesale price. Offers $1,000-3,000 advance.** Publishes book 2 years after acceptance of ms. Accepts simultaneous submissions. Reports in 1 month on queries and proposals; 4 months on mss. Book catalog free. Manuscript guidelines for #10 SASE.
Imprint(s): Pinata Books.
Nonfiction: Children's/juvenile, reference. Subjects include ethnic, language/literature, regional, translation, women's issues/studies. "Nonfiction is definitely not our major publishing area." Query with outline/synopsis, 2 sample chapters and SASE. "Include cover letter explaining why your manuscript is unique and important, why we should publish it, who will buy it, etc."
Fiction: Ethnic, literary, mainstream/contemporary. Query with synopsis, 2 sample chapters and SASE.
Poetry: Submit 10 sample poems.
Recent Title(s): *Chicano! The History of the Mexican American Civil Rights Movement*, by F. Arturo Rosales (history/nonfiction); *Project Death*, by Richard Bertematti (novel/mystery); *I Used to Be a Superwoman*, by Gloria Velasquez (poetry collection/inspirational).

ASA, AVIATION SUPPLIES & ACADEMICS, 7005 132nd Place SE, Newcastle WA 98059. (425)235-1500. Director of Operations: Mike Lorden. Editor: Jennifer Trerise. **Acquisitions:** Fred Boyns, controller. "ASA is an industry leader in the development and sales of aviation supplies, publications, and software for pilots, flight instructors, flight engineers and aviation technicians. All ASA products are developed by a team of researchers, authors and editors." **Publishes 25-40 titles/year. 100% of books from unagented writers.** Publishes book 9 months or more after acceptance. Book catalog free.
Nonfiction: How-to, technical, education. All subjects must be related to aviation education and training. "We are primarily an aviation publisher. Educational books in this area are our specialty; other aviation books will be considered." Query with outline. Send photocopies.
Recent Title(s): *Dictionary of Aeronautical Terms, Third Edition*, by Dale Crane (aviation reference).
Tips: "Two of our specialty series include ASA's *Focus Series*, and ASA *Aviator's Library*." Books in our Focus Series concentrate on single-subject areas of aviation knowledge, curriculum and practice. The Aviator's Library is comprised of titles of known and/or classic aviation authors or established instructor/authors in the industry, and other aviation specialty titles."

ASIAN HUMANITIES PRESS, Jain Publishing Co., P.O. Box 3523, Fremont CA 94539. (510)659-8272. Fax: (510)659-0501. E-mail: mail@jainpub.com. Website: http://www.jainpub.com. **Acquisitions:** M.K. Jain, editor-in-chief. Estab. 1989. Asian Humanities Press publishes in the areas of Asian religions, philosophies and literature. Publishes hardcover and trade paperback originals and reprints. **Publishes 6 titles/year. Receives 200 submissions/year. 100% of books from unagented authors. Pays up to 15% royalty on net sales. Offers occasional advance.** Publishes book 1-2 years after acceptance. Reports in 3 months on mss if interested. Book catalog for 6×9 SAE. Manuscript guidelines for #10 SAE and on website.

- Publisher reports an increased emphasis on undergraduate-level textbooks.

Nonfiction: Reference, textbooks, general trade books. Subjects include Asian classics, language/literature (Asian), philosophy/religion (Asian and East-West), psychology/spirituality (Asian and East-West), art/culture (Asian and East-West). Submit proposal package, including vita, list of prior publications. Reviews artwork/photos as part of ms package. Send photocopies. Does not return proposal materials.
Recent Title(s): *Windows Into the Infinite: A Guide to the Hindu Scriptures*, by Barbara Powell (textbook).

ASPHODEL PRESS, Moyer Bell, Kymbolde Way, Wakefield RI 02879. (401)789-0074. Fax: (401)789-3793. **Acquisitions:** Jennifer Moyer, editor. "Asphodel publishes fine art and literary titles." Publishes trade paperback originals. **Publishes 4 titles/year. 1% of books from first-time authors; 90% from unagented writers. Pays royalty on retail price. No advance.** Publishes book 1-2 years after acceptance of ms. Reports in 1 month on queries, 6 months on mss. Book catalog for #10 SASE.
Nonfiction: Biography, reference, literary criticism. Subjects include art/architecture. Query with 1-2 sample chapters and SASE.
Recent Title(s): *Directory of Literary Magazines*, edited by The Council of Literary Magazines and Presses (reference); *The Turning*, by Hilda Morley (poetry).

N **ASTRAGAL PRESS**, P.O. Box 239, Mendham NJ 07945. (973)543-3045. **Acquisitions:** Lisa Pollak, president. Publishes hardcover and trade paperback originals and reprints. **Publishes 10-15 titles/year. Receives 50 queries/year.**

Pays 10% royalty on net sales or 25% after direct costs (paid by Astragal Press) are recovered. Publishes book 6-12 months after acceptance of ms. Reports in 1 month. Book catalog and ms guidelines free.
Nonfiction: Books on early tools, trades or technology. Query. Reviews artwork/photos as part of ms package. Send photocopies.
Recent Title(s): *Price Guide of Antique Tools*, by Herbert Kear.
Tips: "We sell to niche markets. We are happy to work with knowledgeable amateur authors in developing titles."

[N] **ASTRO COMMUNICATIONS SERVICES**, 5521 Ruffin Rd., San Diego CA 92123. (619)492-9919. Fax: (619)492-9917. E-mail: maritha@astrocom.com. Website: http://www.astrocom.com. **Acquisitions**: Maritha Pottenger, editorial director. "ACS publishes astrology titles for professionals, serious students and general public interested in astrology, as well as people who want to improve themselves and their lives." Publishes trade paperback originals and reprints and mass market paperback originals and reprints. **Publishes 4-5 titles/year. Receives 100 queries and 15 mss/year. 20% of books from first-time authors; 95% from unagented writers. Pays 10-15% royalty.** Publishes book 1 year after acceptance of ms. Accepts simultaneous submissions. Reports in 3 months on queries and proposals, 6 months on mss. Book catalog and ms guidelines for 9×12 SAE with 3 first-class stamps.
Nonfiction: Astrology only. Query with SASE. Reviews artwork/photos as part of ms package. Send photocopies.
Recent Title(s): *Millennium Fears, Fantasies & Facts*, foreword by Marion March.
Tips: "Make sure the publisher does work such as you're submitting. (Send to the right firms!) We do *astrology* only and emphasize personal responsibility and power."

ATHENEUM BOOKS FOR YOUNG READERS, Simon & Schuster, 1230 Avenue of the Americas, New York NY 10020. (212)698-7000. Associate Publisher, Vice President/Editorial Director: Jonathan J. Lanman. **Acquisitions:** Marcia Marshall, executive editor; Anne Schwartz, editorial director, Anne Schwartz Books; and Jean Karl, editor of Jean Karl books. Estab. 1960. "Our books are aimed at children from pre-school age, up through high school." Publishes hardcover originals. Publishes 70 titles/year. Receives 15,000 submissions/year. 8-12% of books from first-time authors; 50% from unagented writers. Pays 10% royalty on retail price. Offers $2,000-3,000 average advance. Publishes book 18 months after acceptance. Reports within 3 months. Manuscript guidelines for #10 SASE.
Nonfiction: Biography, history, science, humor, self-help, all for juveniles. Subjects include: Americana, animals, art, business/economics, health, music, nature, photography, politics, psychology, recreation, religion, sociology, sports and travel. "Do remember, most publishers plan their lists as much as two years in advance. So if a topic is 'hot' right now, it may be 'old hat' by the time we could bring it out. It's better to steer clear of fads. Some writers assume juvenile books are for 'practice' until you get good enough to write adult books. Not so. Books for young readers demand just as much professionalism in writing as adult books. So save those 'practice' manuscripts for class, or polish them before sending them." *Query only for all submissions.*
Fiction: Adventure, ethnic, experimental, fantasy, gothic, historical, horror, humor, mainstream, mystery, science fiction, suspense, western, all in juvenile versions. "We have few specific needs except for books that are fresh, interesting and well written. Again, fad topics are dangerous, as are works you haven't polished to the best of your ability. (The competition is fierce.) We've been inundated with dragon stories (misunderstood dragon befriends understanding child), unicorn stories (misunderstood child befriends understanding unicorn), and variations of 'Ignatz the Egg' (Everyone laughs at Ignatz the egg [giraffe/airplane/accountant] because he's square [short/purple/stupid] until he saves them from the eggbeater [lion/storm/I.R.S. man] and becomes a hero). Other things we don't need at this time are safety pamphlets, ABC books, coloring books, board books, and rhymed narratives. In writing picture book texts, avoid the coy and 'cutesy,' such as stories about characters with alliterative names." *Query only for all submissions.* Reviews artwork as part of ms package. Send photocopies.
Recent Title(s): *Where You Belong*, by Mary Ann McGuigan.
Poetry: "At this time there is a growing market for children's poetry. However, we don't anticipate needing any for the next year or two, especially rhymed narratives."

[N] **ATL PRESS, INC.**, P.O. Box 4563, Shrewsbury MA 01545. (508)898-2290. Website: http://www.bookzone.com/atlpress. **Acquisitions**: Paul Lucio. "ATL specializes in science and technology publications for both the professional and the popular audience. We are committed to produce authoritative and thought-provoking titles that are distinguished both in their contract and appearance." Publishes hardcover and trade paperback originals. **Publishes 8-12 titles/year. Receives 100 queries/year. 25% of books from first-time authors. Pays royalty on retail price.** Publishes book 3 months after acceptance of ms. Reports in 1-2 months on queries. Book catalog and ms guidelines for #10 SASE.
Nonfiction: Children's/juvenile, multimedia (CD-ROM), reference, technical, textbook. Subjects include business and economics, education, health/medicine, money/finance, nature/environment, science. "We look for well-written manuscripts in subjects with either broad, general interest topics of leading-edge professional topics. Avoid too narrow a focus." Submit outline and 3-4 sample chapters with SASE.
Recent Title(s): *The Comet Hale-Bopp Book*, by T. Hockey (science); *Fidelity Select Money*, by D. and S. Pickenpaugh (business).
Tips: "Audience is educated, open-minded adults, juveniles, parents, educators, professionals. Realistically evaluate your manuscript against competition. We publish only titles for which there is an actual demand."

AUGSBURG BOOKS, Augsburg Fortress Publishers, P.O. Box 1209, Minneapolis MN 55440-1209. (612)330-3433. Director of Publications: Henry French. **Acquisitions:** Robert Klausmeier and Ronald Klug, acquisitions editors. "We

publish for the mainline Christian market." Publishes trade and mass market paperback originals and reprints. **Publishes 30 titles/year. 2-3% of books from first-time authors. Pays royalty.** Publishes book 18 months after acceptance of ms. Reports in 3 months. Book catalog for 8½×11 SAE with 3 first-class stamps. Manuscript guidelines for #10 SASE.
Nonfiction: Children's/juvenile, self-help. Subjects include religion, adult spirituality, healing/wholeness, interactive books for children and families, seasonal and picture books. Submit outline and 1-2 sample chapters if requested. Overstocked in children's book mss.
Recent Title(s): *Love, Dad: Letters of Faith to My Children*, by Herbert Browning.

AUTONOMEDIA, P.O. Box 568, Williamsburgh Station, Brooklyn NY 11211. (718)963-2603. **Acquisitions:** Jim Fleming, editor (Semiotext(e)); Peter Lamborn Wilson, editor (New Autonomy). Autonomedia publishes radical and marginal books on culture and politics. Publishes trade paperback originals and reprints. **Publishes 25 titles/year. Receives 350 queries/year. 30% of books from first-time authors; 90% from unagented writers. Pays variable royalty. Offers $100 advance.** Publishes book 6 months after acceptance of ms. Accepts simultaneous submissions. Reports in 2 months. Book catalog for $1.
Imprint(s): Semiotext(e); New Autonomy.
Nonfiction: Subjects include anthropology/archaeology, art/architecture, business/economics, gay/lesbian, government/politics, history, nature/environment, philosophy, religion, translation, women's issues/studies. Submit outline with SASE. Reviews artwork/photos as part of ms package. Send photocopies.
Fiction: Erotica, experimental, feminist, gay/lesbian, literary, mainstream/contemporary, occult, science fiction, short story collections. Submit synopsis with SASE.
Poetry: Submit sample poems.
Recent Title(s): *Foucault Live*, by Michel Foucault (interviews); *Cutmouth Lady*, by Romy Ashby (contemporary).

AVALON BOOKS, Thomas Bouregy & Co., Inc., 401 Lafayette St., New York NY 10003-7014. **Acquisitions:** Marcia Markland, vice president/publisher. Estab. 1950. "We publish wholesome fiction. We're the 'Family Channel' of publishing. We try to make what we publish suitable for anybody in the family." **Publishes 60 titles/year. 10% of books from unagented writers. Pays royalty; contracts negotiated on an individual basis.** Publishes book 6 months after acceptance. Reports in 6 months. Manuscript guidelines for #10 SASE.
Fiction: "We publish wholesome romances, mysteries, westerns. Our books are read by adults as well as teenagers, and their characters are all adults. All the romances and mysteries are contemporary; all the westerns are historical." Length: 40,000-50,000 words. Submit first chapter, a brief, but complete summary of the book and SASE.
Recent Title(s): *Hannah and the Horseman*, by Johnny D. Boggs (western).
Tips: "We are looking for love stories, heroines who have interesting professions, and we are actively seeking ethnic fiction. We do accept unagented manuscripts, and we do publish first novels. Right now we are concentrating on finding talented new mystery and romantic suspense writers."

AVANYU PUBLISHING INC., P.O. Box 27134, Albuquerque NM 87125. (505)266-6128. **Acquisitions:** J. Brent Ricks, president. Estab. 1984. Avanyu publishes highly-illustrated, history-oriented books and contemporary Indian/Western art. "Our audience consists of libraries, art collectors and history students." Publishes hardcover and trade paperback originals and reprints. **Publishes 4 titles/year. Receives 40 submissions/year. 30% of books from first-time authors; 90% from unagented writers. Pays 8% maximum royalty on wholesale price.** Publishes book 1 year after acceptance. Reports in 2 months. Book catalog for #10 SASE.
Nonfiction: Biography, illustrated book, reference, Southwest Americana. Subjects include Americana, anthropology/archaeology, art/architecture, ethnic, history, photography, regional, sociology. Query with SASE. Reviews artwork/photos as part of ms package.

AVERY PUBLISHING GROUP, INC., 120 Old Broadway, Garden City Park NY 11040. (516)741-2155. Fax: (516)742-1892. E-mail: averyedit@aol.com. **Acquisitions:** Rudy Shur, managing editor. "Avery specializes in alternative medicine, natural medicine, health, healthy cooking, health reference, childcare and childbirth." Publishes trade paperback originals. **Publishes 50 titles/year. Receives 3,000 queries and 1,000 mss/year. 70% of books from first-time authors; 90% from unagented writers. Pays royalty. Conservative advances offered.** Publishes book 1 year after acceptance of ms. Accepts simultaneous submissions. Reports in 2 weeks on queries, 3 weeks on proposals and manuscripts. *Writer's Market* recommends allowing 2 months for reply. Book catalog and ms guidelines free.
Nonfiction: Cookbook, reference, self-help. Subjects include business/economics, child guidance/parenting, cooking, foods and nutrition, gardening, health/medicine, money/finance. "We generally do not publish personal accounts of health topics unless they outline a specific plan that covers all areas of the topic." Submit outline with proposal package, including cover letter, author biography, table of contents, preface with SASE.
Recent Title(s): *Secrets of Fat-Free Chinese Cooking*, by Ying-Chang Compestine.

AVIATION PUBLISHERS, Markowski International Publishers, 1 Oakglade Circle, Hummelstown PA 17036-9525. (717)566-0468. Fax: (717)566-6423. E-mail: avipub@aol.com. **Acquisitions**: Michael A. Markowski, editor-in-chief. "Our mission is to help people learn more about aviation and model aviation through the written word. We want to help youth get started and enhance everyone's enjoyment of the hobby." Guidelines for #10 SASE with 2 first-class stamps.
Nonfiction: How-to and historical. Subjects include radio control, free flight, indoor models, electric flight, rubber

powered flying models, micro radio control, aviation history, homebuilt aircraft, ultralights and hang gliders.
Recent Title(s): *Amelia Earhart—Case Closed?*, by Roessler and Gomez (aviation history).
Tips: "Our focus is on books of short to medium length that will serve the emerging needs of the hobby."

AVIATION PUBLISHING, INC., P.O. Box 5674, Destin FL 32540-5634. (850)654-4696. Fax: (850)654-1542. E-mail: destina@cybertron.com. **Acquisitions**: Wallace Kemper, president (general aviation history). Aviation specializes in aviation-related nonfiction and fiction. Publishes mass market paperback originals and reprints. **Publishes 20 titles/year. Receives 60 queries/year. 30% of books from first-time authors. Pays 10% royalty on retail price.** Publishes book 6 months after acceptance of ms. Accepts simultaneous submissions. Reports in 1 month on queries. Book catalog for #10 SASE.
Nonfiction: General aviation history. Subjects include military/war, recreation. Query or submit 2 sample chapters and SASE. Reviews artwork/photos as part of ms package. Send photocopies.
Fiction: In an aviation setting. Submit synopsis and 2 sample chapters and SASE.
Recent Title(s): *Worldwide Directory of Racing Aircraft*, by Don Berliner; *Ace*, by Nick Bloom (adventure fiction).
Tips: "Audience is older men who have pilots licenses and flew in World War II or Korea."

AVISSON PRESS, INC., 3007 Taliaferro Rd., Greensboro NC 27408. **Acquisitions:** M.L. Hester, editor. "Avisson Press publishes helpful nonfiction for senior citizens, minority topics and young adult biographies (African-American, women)." Publishes hardcover originals and trade paperback originals and reprints. **Publishes 9-10 titles/year. Receives 600 queries and 400 mss/year. 5% of books from first-time authors; 90% from unagented writers. Pays 8-10% royalty on wholesale price. Offers occasional small advance.** Publishes book 9-15 months after acceptance of ms. Accepts simultaneous submissions if so noted. Reports in 1 week on queries and proposals, 1-3 months on mss. Book catalog for #10 SASE.

- Avission Press no longer accepts fiction or poetry.

Nonfiction: Biography, reference, self-help (senior citizens and teenagers), regional or North Carolina, textbook (creative writing text). Subjects include history (Southeast or North Carolina), language/literature, psychology, regional, sports, women's issues/studies. Query or submit outline and 1-3 sample chapters.
Recent Title(s): *Hunting the Snark*, by Robert Peters (criticism/textbook).
Tips: Audience is primarily public and school libraries.

AVON BOOKS, The Hearst Corp., 1350 Avenue of the Americas, New York NY 10019. Website: http://www.avonbooks.com. **Acquisitions:** Editorial Submissions. Estab. 1941. Publishes hardcover, trade and mass market paperback originals and reprints. **Publishes 400 titles/year. Royalty and advance negotiable.** Publishes ms 2 years after acceptance. Accepts simultaneous submissions. Reports in 3 months. Guidelines for SASE.
Imprint(s): Avon Eos, Avon Flare, **Bard**, **Camelot**, Twilight.
Nonfiction: How-to, popular psychology, self-help, health, history, war, sports, business/economics, biography, politics. No textbooks. Query only with SASE.
Fiction: Romance (contemporary, historical), science fiction, fantasy, men's adventure, suspense/thriller, mystery, western. Query only with SASE.
Recent Title(s): *A Gift of Irish Wisdom*, by Cyril and Renee Reilly (nonfiction); *So Worthy My Love*, by Kathleen Woodwiss (fiction).

AVON EOS, (formerly Avon Science Fiction), Avon Books, The Hearst Corp., 1350 Avenue of the Americas, New York NY 10019. (212)261-6800. Website: http://www.avonbooks.com/eos. **Acquisitions:** Jennifer Brehl, senior editor. "We are a 'small big company.' We can't be all things to all people. We put out a cutting-edge, literary, science fiction/fantasy line that appeals to people who want to read good books." Publishes hardcover originals, trade paperback and mass market paperback originals and reprints. **Publishes 70 titles/year. Receives 2,500 queries and 800 mss/year. 25% of books from first-time authors; 5% from unagented writers. Pays royalty on retail price, range varies.** Publishes book 18 months after acceptance of ms. Accepts simultaneous submissions, if so noted. Reports in 6 months. Book catalog for 9×12 SAE with 7 first-class stamps. Manuscript guidelines for #10 SASE.
Fiction: Fantasy, science fiction. No horror or juvenile topics. "We look for cutting-edge, original work that will break traditional boundaries of this genre." Query with full synopsis of book, 3 sample chapters and SASE.
Recent Title(s): *Prisoner of Conscience*, by Susan R. Matthews (science fiction).
Tips: "We strongly advise submitting via a literary agent. If you make an unsolicited, unagented submission, follow our guidelines (i.e., do not send an entire manuscript; send query, synopsis and sample chapters only)."

AVON FLARE BOOKS, Avon Books, The Hearst Corp., 1350 Avenue of the Americas, New York NY 10019. (212)261-6800. Fax: (212)261-6895. **Acquisitions:** Elise Howard, executive editor; Ruth Katcher, senior editor. Publishes mass market paperback originals and reprints for young adults. **Imprint publishes 24 new titles/year. 25% of books from first-time authors; 15% from unagented writers. Pays 6-8% royalty. Offers $2,500 minimum advance.** Publishes book 2 years after acceptance. Accepts simultaneous submissions. Reports in 4 months. Book catalog and ms guidelines for 8×10 SAE with 5 first-class stamps.
Nonfiction: General. Submit outline/synopsis and sample chapters. "*Very* selective with young adult nonfiction."
Fiction: Adventure, ethnic, humor, mainstream, mystery, romance, suspense, contemporary. "Very selective with mystery." Manuscripts appropriate to ages 12-18. Query with sample chapters and synopsis.

Recent Title(s): *Help! My Heart is Breaking*, by Meg Schneider (nonfiction); *Hearts and Dreams* series, by Cameron Dokey (fiction).
Tips: "The YA market is not as strong as it was five years ago. We are very selective with young adult fiction. *Avon does not publish picture books,* nor do we use freelance readers."

N **AZTEX CORP.**, P.O. 50046, Tucson AZ 85703-1046. (520)882-4656. Website: http://www.aztexcorp.com. **Acquisitions:** Elaine Jordan, editor. Estab. 1976. Publishes hardcover and paperback originals. **Publishes 10 titles/year. Receives 250 submissions/year. 100% of books from unagented writers. Pays 10% royalty.** Publishes book 18 months after acceptance. Reports in 3 months. "Queries without return envelopes or postage are not responded to."

- This company received the Thomas McKean Award from the Antique Automobile Club of America for outstanding research for *Tire Wars: Racing With Goodyear.*

Nonfiction: "We specialize in transportation subjects (how-to and history)." Accepts nonfiction translations. Submit outline and 2 sample chapters. Reviews artwork/photos as part of ms package.
Tips: "We look for accuracy, thoroughness and interesting presentation."

BACKCOUNTRY PUBLICATIONS, The Countryman Press, W.W. Norton & Co., P. O. Box 748, Woodstock VT 05091-0748. (802)457-4826. Fax: (802)457-1678. E-mail: countrymanpress@wwnorton.com. Website: http://www.countrymanpress.com. **Acquisitions:** Ann Kraybill, managing editor. "Our aim is to publish guidebooks of the highest quality that encourage physical fitness and appreciation for and understanding of the natural world, self-sufficiency and adventure." Publishes trade paperback originals. **Publishes 15 titles/year. Receives 1,000 queries and a few mss/year. 25% of books from first-time authors; 75% from unagented writers. Pays 7-10% royalty on retail price. Offers $1,500-2,500 advance.** Publishes book 18 months after acceptance of ms. Accepts simultaneous submissions. Returns submissions only with SASE. Reports in 2 months on proposals. Book catalog free. Ms guidelines for #10 SASE.
Nonfiction: Subjects include nature/environment, outdoor, recreation: bicycling, hiking, canoeing, kayaking, fly fishing, walking, guidebooks and series. "Look at existing series of guidebooks to see how your proposal fits in." Query with outline, 50 sample pages and proposal package including market analysis and SASE.
Recent Title(s): *50 More Hikes in New Hampshire*, by Daniel Doan and Ruth Doan MacDougall (outdoor recreation).

BAEN PUBLISHING ENTERPRISES, P.O. Box 1403, Riverdale NY 10471-0671. (718)548-3100. Website: http://baen.com. **Acquisitions:** Toni Weisskopf, executive editor. Estab. 1983. "We publish books at the heart of science fiction and fantasy." Publishes hardcover, trade paperback and mass market paperback originals and reprints. **Publishes 120 titles/year. Receives 5,000 submissions/year. 5% of books from first-time authors; 50% from unagented writers. Pays royalty on retail price.** Reports in 6-8 months on queries and proposals, 9-12 months on complete mss. Book catalog free. Manuscript guidelines for #10 SASE.
Fiction: Fantasy, science fiction. Submit outline/synopsis and sample chapters or complete ms.
Recent Title(s): *Glenraven*, by Marion Zimmer-Bradley and Holly Lisle.
Tips: "See our books before submitting. Send for our writers' guidelines."

BAKER BOOK HOUSE COMPANY, P.O. Box 6287, Grand Rapids MI 49516-6287. (616)676-9185. Fax: (616)676-9573. Website: http://www.bakerbooks.com.
Imprint(s): Baker Academic, **Baker Books**, Baker Bytes, **Chosen**, **Fleming H. Revell**.

BAKER BOOKS, Baker Book House Company, P.O. Box 6287, Grand Rapids MI 49516-6287. (616)676-9185. Fax: (616)676-9573. E-mail: tbennett@bakerbooks.com. Website: http://www.bakerbooks.com. Director of Publications: Allan Fisher. **Acquisitions:** Rebecca Cooper, editorial assistant. Estab. 1939. "Baker Books publishes popular religious nonfiction and fiction, children's books, academic and reference books, and professional books for church leaders." Publishes hardcover and trade paperback originals. **Publishes 120 titles/year. 10% of books from first-time authors; 85% from unagented writers. Pays 14% royalty on net receipts.** Publishes book within 1 year after acceptance. Accepts simultaneous submissions, if so noted. Reports in 2 months on proposals. Book catalog for 9×12 SAE with 6 first-class stamps. Manuscript guidelines for #10 SASE, also online.
Imprint(s): Hamewith, Hourglass, Labyrinth, Raven's Ridge, Spire Books.
Nonfiction: Contemporary issues, women's concerns, parenting, singleness, seniors' concerns, self-help, children's books, Bible study, Christian doctrine, reference books, books for pastors and church leaders, textbooks for Christian colleges and seminaries. Query with proposal, including chapter summaries or outlines, 1-2 sample chapters, cv, letter of recommendation and SASE. *No unsolicited mss.* Reviews artwork as part of ms package. Send 1-2 photocopies.
Fiction: Literary novels focusing on women's concerns, mainstream/contemporary, religious, mysteries. Query with synopsis/outline, 1-2 sample chapters, résumé and SASE. *No unsolicited mss.*
Recent Title(s): *Excuse Me? I'll Take My Piece of the Planet Now*, by Joey O'Connor (grad book); *Praise Jerusalem*, by Augusta Trobaugh (fiction).
Tips: "Most of our authors and readers are evangelical Christians, and our books are purchased from Christian bookstores, mail-order retailers, and school bookstores."

BALE BOOKS, Bale Publications, P.O. Box 2727, New Orleans LA 70176. **Acquisitions:** Don Bale, Jr, editor-in-chief. Estab. 1963. "Our mission is to educate numismatists about coins, coin collecting and investing opportunities." Publishes hardcover and paperback originals and reprints. **Publishes 10 titles/year. Receives 25 submissions/year. 50%**

of books from first-time authors; 90% from unagented writers. Offers standard 10-12½-15% royalty contract on wholesale or retail price; sometimes makes outright purchases of $500. No advance. Publishes book 3 years after acceptance. Reports in 3 months. Book catalog for #10 SAE with 2 first-class stamps.

Nonfiction: Numismatics. "Our specialties are coin and stock market investment books; especially coin investment books and coin price guides. Most of our books are sold through publicity and ads in the coin newspapers. We are open to any new ideas in the area of numismatics. Write for a teenage through adult level. Lead the reader by the hand like a teacher, building chapter by chapter. Our books sometimes have a light, humorous treatment, but not necessarily. We look for good English, construction and content, and sales potential." Submit outline and 3 sample chapters.

Recent Title(s): *How To Invest in Uncirculated Singles.*

BALLANTINE BOOKS, Random House, Inc., 201 E. 50th St., New York NY 10022. (212)572-4910. Publishes wide variety of nonfiction and fiction. Publishes hardcover and trade paperback originals. **Acquisitions**: Doug Grad, editor (sports and business nonfiction, historical and thriller fiction); Leona Nevler, editor (all kinds of fiction and nonfiction); Peter Borland, executive editor (commercial fiction, pop culture); Elisa Wares, senior editor (romance, health, parenting, mystery); Joe Blades, associate publisher (mystery); Susan Randol, senior editor (business, narrative motivational, true medicine, true crime, mystery); Elizabeth Zack, editor (motivational, inspirational, women's sports; career, seasonal tie-ins); Joanne Wyckoff, senior editor (religion, spirituality, nature/pets, psychology); Andrea Schulz, editor (literary fiction, travel, women's studies, narrative nonfiction); Shauna Summers, senior editor (historical and contemporary romance, commercial women's fiction, general fiction, thrillers/suspense); Ginny Faber, senior editor (health, psychology, spirituality, travel, general nonfiction); Sarah Glazer, assistant editor (historical fiction, commercial fiction, arm-chair travel, animals). Publishes hardcover, trade paperback, mass market paperback originals.

- Also see the listing for Random House, Inc.

Nonfiction: How-to, humor, illustrated book, reference, self-help. Subjects include animals, child guidance/parenting, cooking/foods/nutrition, health/medicine. Submit proposal and 100 ms pages with SASE. Reviews artwork/photos as part of ms package. Send photocopies.

Fiction: Historical fiction, women's mainstream, multicultural and general fiction.

Recent Title(s): *Rookery Blues*, by Jon Hassler (fiction); *Guilty By Reason of Insanity: A Psychiatrist Probes the Minds of Killers*, by Dorothy Otnow Lewis, M.D. (nonfiction);

BANTAM BOOKS, Bantam Doubleday Dell, Dept. WM, 1540 Broadway, New York NY 10036. (212)354-6500. Senior Vice President/Deputy Publisher: Nita Taublib. **Acquitisions:** Toni Burbank, Ann Harris, executive editors. Publishes hardcover, trade paperback and mass market paperback originals, trade paperback; mass market paperback reprints and audio. **Publishes 350 titles/year.** Publishes book an average of 1 year after ms is accepted. Accepts simultaneous submissions from agents.

Imprint(s): Bantam Classics (reprints); Crime Line (Kate Miciak, associate publisher); **Fanfare** (Beth DeGuzman, Wendy McCurdy), **Spectra** (Pat LoBrutto, Anne Groell).

Nonfiction: Biography, how-to, humor, self-help. Subjects include Americana, business/economics, child care/parenting, diet/fitness, education, cooking/foods/nutrition, gay/lesbian, government/politics, health/medicine, history, language/literature, military/war, mysticism/astrology, nature, philosophy/mythology, psychology, religion/inspiration, science, sociology, spirituality, sports, true crime, women's studies. Query or submit outline/synopsis. *All unsolicited mss returned unopened.*

Fiction: Adventure, fantasy, feminist, gay/lesbian, historical, horror, literary, mainstream/contemporary, mystery, romance, science fiction, suspense. Query or submit outline/synopsis. *All unsolicited mss returned unopened.*

BANTAM DOUBLEDAY DELL, 1540 Broadway, New York NY 10036. (212)354-6500. Publishes hardcover originals and reprints, trade paperback originals and reprints, mass market paperback originals and reprints.

Imprint(s): Divisions include: *Bantam Books* (**Bantam Books**, Crime Line, **Fanfare, Spectra**); **Bantam Doubleday Dell Books for Young Readers** (Delacorte Books for Young Readers, Doubleday Books for Young Readers, Laurel Leaf, Picture Yearling, Skylark, Starfire, Yearling); *Dell Publishing* (**Delacorte Press, Dell Books, Delta Books, Dial Press**, DTP, Island Books, **Laurel**); **Broadway Books**; *Doubleday* (Anchor Books, **Currency, Doubleday, Image Books, Main Street Books, Nan A. Talese**).

BANTAM DOUBLEDAY DELL BOOKS FOR YOUNG READERS, Bantam Doubleday Dell, 1540 Broadway, New York NY 10036. (212)354-6500. Fax: (212)302-7985. Website: http://www.bdd.com. **Contact:** Editorial Director. "Bantam Doubleday Dell Books for Young Readers publishes award-winning books by distinguished authors and the most promising new writers." Publishes hardcover, trade paperback and mass market paperback originals, trade paperback reprints. **Publishes 300 titles/year. Receives thousands of queries/year. 10% of books from first-time authors; none from unagented writers. Pays royalty. Advance varies.** Publishes book 2 years after acceptance of ms. Reports in 4 months. Book catalog free.

Imprint(s): Delacorte Press Books for Young Readers, Doubleday Books for Young Readers, Laurel Leaf, Picture Yearling, Skylark, Starfire, Yearling.

- The best way to break in to this market is through its two contests, the Marguerite de Angeli contest and the Delacorte Press Contest for a First Young Adult novel, listed in the Contests & Awards section of this book.

Nonfiction: "Bantam Doubleday Dell Books for Young Readers publishes a very limited number of nonfiction titles."
Fiction: Adventure, fantasy, humor, juvenile, mainstream/contemporary, mystery, picture books, suspense, young adult. Query with SASE. *No unsolicited material.*
Recent Title(s): *The Lizard and the Sun*, by Alma Flor Ada (folktale picture book).

BARNEGAT LIGHT PRESS, P.O. Box 305, Barnegat Light NJ 08006. (609)494-3154. Fax: (609)494-6092. **Acquisitions:** R. Marilyn Schmidt, publisher. "We are a regional publisher emphasizing the mid-Atlantic region. Areas concerned are gardening and cooking." Publishes trade paperback originals. **Publishes 8 titles/year. Receives 12 queries and 10 mss/year. 0% of books from first-time authors; 100% from unagented writers. Makes outright purchase.** Publishes book 6 months after acceptance of ms. Reports in 1 month. *Writer's Market* recommends allowing 2 months for reply. Book catalog free.
Imprint(s): Pine Barrens Press.
Nonfiction: Cookbook, how-to. Subjects include cooking/foods/nutrition, gardening, regional, travel, all New Jersey-oriented. Query.
Recent Title(s): *Seashore Gardening with Native Plants*, by R. Marilyn Schmidt.

BARRICADE BOOKS INC., 150 Fifth Ave., Suite 700, New York NY 10011-4311. **Acquisitions:** Carole Stuart, publisher. "We look for nonfiction, mostly of the controversial type, and books we can promote with authors who can talk about their topics on radio and television and to the press." Publishes hardcover and trade paperback originals and trade paperback reprints. **Publishes 30 titles/year. Receives 200 queries and 100 mss/year. 80% of books from first-time authors; 50% from unagented writers. Pays 10-12% royalty on retail price for hardcover. Advance varies.** Publishes book 18 months after acceptance of ms. Reports in 1 month on queries. Book catalog for $3.
Nonfiction: Biography, how-to, reference, self-help. Subjects include business/economics, child guidance/parenting, ethnic, gay/lesbian, government/politics, health/medicine, history, nature/environment, psychology, sociology, women's issues/studies. Query with outline and 1-2 sample chapters with SASE or material will not be returned. Reviews artwork/photos as part of ms package. Send photocopies.
Recent Title(s): *Grave Exodus*, by Xavier Cronin (dealing with death in the 20th Century).
Tips: "Do your homework. Visit bookshops to find publishers who are doing the kinds of books you want to write. Always submit to a *person*—not just 'editor.' *Always enclose SASE.*"

BARRON'S EDUCATIONAL SERIES, INC., 250 Wireless Blvd., Hauppauge NY 11788. Fax: (516)434-3217. Website: http://barronseduc.com. **Acquisitions:** Grace Freedson, managing editor/director of acquisitions. "Barron's tends to publish series of books, both for adults and children." Publishes hardcover and paperback originals and software. **Publishes 400 titles/year. Reviews 1,000 queries and 600 mss/year. 40% of books from first-time authors; 75% from unagented writers. Pays royalty on both wholesale and retail price.** Publishes book 1 year after acceptance. Accepts simultaneous submissions. Reports in 8 months. Book catalog free.
Nonfiction: Adult education, art, business, cookbooks, crafts, foreign language, review books, guidance, pet books, travel, literary guides, parenting, health, juvenile, young adult sports, test preparation materials and textbooks. Reviews artwork/photos as part of ms package. Query or submit outline/synopsis and 2-3 sample chapters. Accepts nonfiction translations.
Recent Title(s): *Painless Grammar*, by Rebecca Eliott (grammar).
Tips: "Audience is mostly educated self-learners and hobbyists. The writer has the best chance of selling us a book that will fit into one of our series. SASE must be included for the return of all materials."

BATTELLE PRESS, Battelle Memorial Institute, 505 King Ave., Columbus OH 43201. (614)424-6393. Fax: (614)424-3819. E-mail: press@battelle.org. Website: http://www.battelle.org/bookstore. **Acquisitions:** Joe Sheldrick. "Battelle Press strives to be a primary source of books and software on science and the management of science." Publishes hardcover and paperback originals and markets primarily by direct mail. **Publishes 10 titles/year. Pays 10% royalty on retail price. No advance.** Publishes book 6 months after acceptance of ms. Accepts simultaneous submissions. Reports in 1 month. Book catalog free.
Nonfiction: "We are looking for management, leadership, project management and communications books specifically

targeted to engineers and scientists." Query. Reviews artwork/photos as part of ms package. Send photocopies. Returns submissions with SASE only by writer's request.
Recent Title(s): *Risk Communication, 2nd Edition*, by R. Lundgren.
Tips: Audience consists of engineers, researchers, scientists and corporate researchers and developers.

BAYWOOD PUBLISHING CO., INC., 26 Austin Ave., Amityville NY 11701. (516)691-1270. Fax: (516)691-1770. E-mail: baywood@baywood.com. Website: http://www.baywood.com. **Acquisitions:** Stuart Cohen, managing editor. "We publish original and innovative books in the humanities and social sciences, including areas such as health sciences, gerontology, death and bereavement, psychology, technical communications and archaeology." **Publishes 25 titles/year. Pays 7-15% royalty on retail price.** Publishes book within 1 year after acceptance of ms. Catalog and ms guidelines free.
Nonfiction: Technical, scholarly. Subjects include anthropology/archaeology, computers/electronics, gerontology, imagery, labor relations, education, death/dying, drugs, nature/environment, psychology, public health/medicine, sociology, technical communications, women's issues/studies. Submit outline/synopsis and sample chapters.
Recent Title(s): *The Political Economy of AIDS*, edited by Merrill Singer.

BEACHWAY PRESS, 9201 Beachway Lane, Springfield VA 22153. **Acquisitions:** Scott Adams, publisher. "Our books are designed to open up new worlds of experiences for those anxious to explore, and to provide the detailed information necessary to get them started." **Publishes 10-15 titles/year. Pays 10-15% royalty on wholesale price. Offers $1,500 advance.** Publishes book 1 year after acceptance of ms. Reports in 2 months on queries and proposals. Manuscript guidelines for #10 SASE.
Nonfiction: Innovative outdoor adventure and travel guidebooks. "We welcome ideas that explore the world of adventure and wonder; from day hikes to mountain bikes, from surf to skis." Query with outline, 2 sample chapters, methods of research and SASE. Reviews artwork/photos as part of ms package. Send proof prints.
Recent Title(s): *Mountain Bike Vermont*, by Jen Mynter (guidebook).
Tips: "Someone interested in writing for us should be both an avid outdoors person and an expert in their area of interest. This person should have a clear understanding of maps and terrain and should enjoy sharing their adventurous spirit and enthusiasm with others."

BEACON HILL PRESS OF KANSAS CITY, Nazarene Publishing House, P.O. Box 419527, Kansas City MO 64141. Fax: (816)753-4071. E-mail: bjp@bhillkc.com. **Acquisitions:** Kelly Gallagher, director. Estab. 1912. "Beacon Hill Press is a Christ-centered publisher that provides authentically Christian resources that are faithful to God's word and relevant to life." Publishes hardcover and paperback originals. **Publishes 30 titles/year. Standard contract is 12% royalty on net sales for first 10,000 copies and 14% on subsequent copies. (Sometimes makes flat rate purchase.)** Publishes book within 1 year after acceptance. Reports within 3 months.
Nonfiction: Inspirational, Bible-based. Doctrinally must conform to the evangelical, Wesleyan tradition. No autobiography, poetry, short stories or children's picture books. Contemporary issues acceptable. Accent on holy living; encouragement in daily Christian life. Query or proposal preferred. Average ms length: 30,000-60,000 words.
Recent Title(s): *This is a Story About God*, by Ann Kiemel.

BEACON PRESS, 25 Beacon St., Boston MA 02108-2892. (617)742-2110. Fax: (617)723-3097. E-mail: candrews@beacon.org. Website: http://www.beacon.org/Beacon. Director: Helene Atwan. **Acquisitions:** Editorial Director (African-American, Asian-American, Latino, Native American, Jewish and gay and lesbian studies, anthropology); Deanne Urmy, executive editor, (child and family issues, environmental concerns); Micah Kleit, editor (education, current affairs, philosophy, religion). Estab. 1854. "Beacon Press publishes general interest books that promote the following values: the inherent worth and dignity of every person; justice, equity, and compassion in human relations; acceptance of one another; a free and responsible search for truth and meaning; the goal of world community with peace, liberty and justice for all; respect for the interdependent web of all existence." Publishes hardcover originals and paperback reprints. **Publishes 60 titles/year. Receives 4,000 submissions/year. 10% of books from first-time authors. Pays royalty. Advance varies.** Accepts simultaneous submissions. Reports in 3 months.
Imprint(s): Bluestreak Series (contact Deb Chasman, editor) (innovative literary writing by women of color).
Nonfiction: General nonfiction including works of original scholarship, religion, women's studies, philosophy, current affairs, anthropology, environmental concerns, African-American, Asian-American, Native American, Latino and Jewish studies, gay and lesbian studies, education, legal studies, child and family issues, Irish studies. Query with outline/synopsis, cv or résumé and sample chapters with SASE. *Strongly prefers agented submissions.*
Recent Title(s): *The Opening of the American Mind: Canons, Culture, and History*, by Lawrence W. Levine (history/education).
Tips: "We probably accept only one or two manuscripts from an unpublished pool of 4,000 submissions per year. No fiction, children's book, or poetry submissions invited. Authors should have academic affiliation."

N **BEAVER POND PUBLISHING**, P.O. Box 224, Greenville PA 16125. (724)588-3492. **Acquisitions**: Rich Faler, publications director. "Beaver Pond is primarily a publisher of outdoor-oriented books and magazines." Publishes trade paperback originals and reprints. **Publishes 6 titles/year. Receives 30 queries and 20 mss/year. 50% of books from first-time authors; 100% from unagented writers. Pays 8% royalty on net sales or makes outright purchase.**

Publishes book 1 year after acceptance of ms. Accepts simultaneous submissions. Reports in 1 month. Book catalog and ms guidelines free.

Nonfiction: Outdoor how-to. Subjects include photography (outdoor), hunting, fishing. "We are actively seeking shorter length manuscripts suitable for 20-40 page booklets, in addition to longer length books. Don't offer too general a title with no 'meat.' " Query or submit outline and 2 sample chapters with SASE. Reviews artwork/photos as part of ms package.

Recent Title(s): *Deer Hunting Strategies for Whitetails*, by Terry Soderberg.

Tips: "Audience is active outdoor people that want to excel at their craft. Write the book that you would have wanted when you first began a specific outdoor activity. The manuscript needs to completely cover a narrow topic indepth."

BEHRMAN HOUSE INC., 235 Watchung Ave., West Orange NJ 07052-9827. (973)669-0447. Fax: (973)669-9769. E-mail: webmaster@behrmanhouse.com. Website: http://www.behrmanhouse.com. **Acquisitions:** Send to Attn: Acquisitions Department. Estab. 1921. "Behrman House publishes quality books of Jewish content—history, Bible, philosophy, holidays, ethics, Israel, Hebrew—for children and adults." **Publishes 20 titles/year. Receives 200 submissions/year. 20% of books from first-time authors; 95% from unagented writers. Pays 2-10% on wholesale price or retail price or makes outright purchase of $500-10,000. Offers $1,000 average advance.** Publishes book 18 months after acceptance. Accepts simultaneous submissions. Reports in 2 months. Book catalog free.

Nonfiction: Juvenile (ages 1-18), reference, textbook. Religious subjects. "We want Jewish textbooks for the el-hi market." Query with outline and sample chapters.

Recent Title(s): *Living As Partners with God*, by Gila Gevirtz (theology).

FREDERIC C. BEIL, PUBLISHER, INC., 609 Whitaker St., Savannah GA 31401. Phone/fax: (912)233-2446. E-mail: beilbook@beil.com. Website: http://www.beil.com. **Acquisitions:** Mary Ann Bowman, editor. "Our objectives are (1) to offer to the reading public carefully selected texts of lasting value; (2) to adhere to high standards in the choice of materials and in bookmaking craftsmanship; (3) to produce books that exemplify good taste in format and design; and (4) to maintain the lowest cost consistent with quality." Publishes hardcover originals and reprints. **Publishes 7 titles/year. Receives 700 queries and 9 mss/year. 15% of books from first-time authors; 80% from unagented writers. Pays 7½% royalty on retail price.** Publishes book 20 months after acceptance. Accepts simultaneous submissions. Reports in 1 month on queries. Book catalog free.

Imprint(s): The Sandstone Press.

Nonfiction: Biography, general trade, illustrated book, juvenile, reference. Subjects include art/architecture, history, language/literature, book arts. Query. Reviews artwork/photos as part of ms package. Send photocopies.

Fiction: Historical and literary. Query.

Recent Title(s): *The Transcendental Saunterer: Thoreau and the Search for Self*, by David C. Smith (nonfiction); *A Master of the Century Past*, by Robert Metzger (fiction).

N THE BENEFACTORY, INC., 1 Post Rd., Fairfield CT 06430. (203)255-7744. Fax: (203)255-6200. E-mail: benfactry@aol.com. **Acquisitions**: Cynthia A. Germain, senior manager, product development. "Our mission is to foster animal protection, motivate reading, teach core values and encourage children to become creative, responsible individuals." Publishes hardcover and trade paperback originals and reprints. **Publishes 9 titles/year. Receives 15 queries and 10 mss/year. 50% of books from first-time authors; 50% from unagented writers. Pays 3-5% royalty on wholesale price. Offers $3,000-5,000 advance.** Publishes book 1 year after acceptance of ms. Accepts simultaneous submissions. Reports in 2 months on queries and proposals, 4 months on mss. Book catalog and ms guidelines free.

Nonfiction: Children's/juvenile. Subjects include animals, nature/environment. "Each story must be a true story about a real animal. Both prose and verse are accepted." Submit outline and SASE. Reviews artwork/photos as part of ms package. Send photocopies.

Recent Title(s): *Condor Magic*, by Lyn Littlefield Hoopes.

ROBERT BENTLEY, INC., Automotive Publishers, 1734 Massachusetts Ave., Cambridge MA 02138-1804. (617)547-4170. **Acquisitions:** Michael Bentley, publisher. Estab. 1949. Robert Bentley publishes books for automotive enthusiasts. Publishes hardcover and trade paperback originals and reprints. **Publishes 15-20 titles/year. 20% of books are from first-time authors; 95% from unagented writers. Pays 10-15% royalty on net price or makes outright purchase. Advance negotiable.** Publishes book 1 year after acceptance. Reports in 6 weeks. Book catalog and ms guidelines for 9×12 SAE with 4 first-class stamps.

Nonfiction: How-to, technical, theory of operation, coffee table. Automotive subjects only; this includes motor sports. Query or submit outline and sample chapters. Reviews artwork/photos as part of ms package.

Recent Title(s): *Race Car Aerodynamics*, by Joe Katz.

Tips: "Our audience is composed of serious, intelligent automobile, sports car, and racing enthusiasts, automotive technicians and high-performance tuners."

THE BERKLEY PUBLISHING GROUP, Penguin Putnam, Inc., 375 Hudson St., New York NY 10014. (212)366-2000. Website: http://www.penguinputnam.com. **Acquisitions:** Denise Silvestro, senior editor (general nonfiction, business); Judith Stern Palais, senior editor (women's general, literary and romance fiction); Tom Colgan, senior editor (history, business, inspiration, biography, suspense/thriller, mystery, adventure); Gail Fortune, senior editor (women's fiction, romance, mystery); Lisa Considine, senior editor. Estab. 1954. "The Berkley Publishing Group publishes a

variety of general nonfiction and fiction including the traditional categories of romance, mystery and science fiction. We run the gamut." Publishes paperback and mass market originals and reprints. **Publishes approximately 800 titles/year. Few books from first-time authors; 1% from unagented writers. Pays 4-15% royalty on retail price. Offers advance.** Publishes book 2 years after acceptance. Reports in 6 weeks on queries.
Imprint(s): Ace Science Fiction, Berkley, Boulevard, Jove, Prime Crime.
Nonfiction: Biography, reference, self-help, how-to. Subjects include business management, job-seeking communication, positive thinking, gay/lesbian, health/fitness, psychology/self-help, women's issues/studies, general commercial publishing. No memoirs or personal stories. Query with SASE. Prefers agented submissions.
Fiction: Mystery, romance, western, young adult. No adventure or occult fiction. Prefers agented material. Query with SASE.
Recent Title(s): *Tom Clancy's Power Plays: Politika*, by Tom Clancy (novel); *Meditations from Conversations with God*, by Neale Donald Walsch (inspiration).

BERKSHIRE HOUSE PUBLISHERS, INC., 480 Pleasant St., Suite #5, Lee MA 01238. (413)243-0303. Fax: (413)243-4737. President: Jean J. Rousseau. **Acquisitions:** Philip Rich, managing editor. Estab. 1989. "Our books have a strong Berkshires, New England or Northeast orientation—no others, please." **Publishes 12-15 titles/year. Receives 100 queries and 6 mss/year. 50% of books from first-time authors; 80% from unagented writers. Pays 5-10% royalty on retail price. Offers $500-5,000 advance.** Publishes book 18 months after acceptance. Accepts simultaneous submissions. Reports in 1 month on proposals. Book catalog free.
Nonfiction: Subjects include US travel, Americana, history, nature/environment, recreation (outdoors), wood crafts, regional cookbooks. "To a great extent, we choose our topics then commission the authors, but we don't discourage speculative submissions. We just don't accept many. Don't overdo it; a well-written outline/proposal is more useful than a full manuscript. Also, include a cv with writing credits."
Recent Title(s): *Old Barns in the New World*, by Richard Babcock and Lauren Stevens.
Tips: "Our readers are literate, active, prosperous, interested in travel, especially in selected 'Great Destinations' areas and outdoor activities and cooking."

BETTERWAY BOOKS, F&W Publications, 1507 Dana Ave., Cincinnati OH 45207. (513)531-2690. **Acquisitions:** William Brohaugh (genealogy, reference books and handbooks, theater and the performing arts); Adam Blake (home decorating and remodeling, lifestyle (including home organization), woodworking, small business and personal finance, hobbies and collectibles). Estab. 1982. "Betterway books are instructional books that are to be *used*. We like specific step-by-step advice, charts, illustrations, and clear explanations of the activities and projects the books describe." Publishes hardcover and trade paperback originals, trade paperback reprints. **Publishes 30 titles/year. Pays 10-20% royalty on net receipts. Offers $3,000-5,000 advance.** Accepts simultaneous submissions, if so noted. Publishes book an average of 18 months after acceptance. Reports in 1 month. Book catalog for 9×12 SAE with 6 first-class stamps.
Nonfiction: How-to, illustrated book, reference and self-help in 7 categories. "Genealogy and family traditions are topics that we're particularly interested in. We are interested mostly in original material, but we will consider republishing self-published nonfiction books and good instructional or reference books that have gone out of print before their time. Send a sample copy, sales information, and reviews, if available. If you have a good idea for a reference book that can be updated annually, try us. We're willing to consider freelance compilers of such works." No cookbooks, diet/exercise, psychology self-help, health or parenting books. Query with outline and sample chapters. Reviews artwork/photos as part of ms package.
Recent Title(s): *Family History Logbook*, by Reinhard Klein (genealogy).
Tips: "Keep the imprint name well in mind when submitting ideas to us. What is the 'better way' you're proposing? How will readers benefit *immediately* from the instruction and information you're giving them?"

BIRCH BROOK PRESS, P.O. Box 81, Delhi NY 13753. **Acquisitions**: Tom Tolnay, editor. "Birch Brook Press is a popular culture and literary publisher of handcrafted books and art, featuring letterpress editions produced at its own printing, typesetting and binding facility." Publishes hardcover and trade paperback originals. **Publishes 4-6 titles/year. Receives hundreds of queries and mss/year. 95% of books from unagented writers. Royalty varies. Offers modest advance.** Publishes book 1 year after acceptance of ms. Accepts simultaneous submissions. Reports in 1 month on queries, 2 months on mss. Book catalog free. Manuscript guidelines for #10 SASE.
Imprint(s): Birch Brook Impressions.
Nonfiction: Literary. Subjects include literature, books on books, baseball, fly fishing. "We have a very limited nonfiction publishing program, mostly generated inhouse in anthologies." Query with SASE. Reviews artwork/photos as part of ms package. Send photocopies to Frank C. Eckmair, art director.
Fiction: Literary, popular culture. "Mostly we do anthologies around a particular theme generated inhouse." Query with synopsis with SASE.
Poetry: Submit complete ms.
Recent Titles: *Baseball and the Game of Ideas: Essays for the Serious Fan* (nonfiction essays); *Kilimanjaro Burning*, by John B. Robinson (novella); *The Melancholy of Yorick*, by Joel Chace (classical poetry).
Tips: "Audience is college educated, readers and collectors. Our books are mostly letterpress editions with metal type and therefore tend to be short and suitable to antique printing methods."

BIRCH LANE PRESS, Carol Publishing, 120 Enterprise Ave., Secaucus NJ 07094. (201)866-0490. Fax: (201)866-8159. **Acquisitions:** Hillel Black, executive editor. Birch Lane publishes general interest nonfiction for an adult audience. Publishes hardcover originals. **Publishes 100 titles/year. 10% of books first-time authors; 10% from unagented writers. Pays 5-15% royalty on retail price. Offers $10,000-20,000 advance.** Publishes book 1 year after acceptance of ms. Accepts simultaneous submissions. Reports in 2 months on proposals.
Nonfiction: Subjects include business/economics, cooking/foods/nutrition, government/politics, history, humor, music/dance, popular culture. Query with outline, 2-3 sample chapters and SASE. Reviews artwork/photos as part of ms package. Send photocopies.
Recent Title(s): *The Financially Independent Woman*, by Barbara Lee (investment).

BLACKBIRCH PRESS, INC., P.O. Box 3573, Woodbridge CT 06525. E-mail: staff@blackbirch.com. Website: http://www.blackbirch.com. **Acquisitions:** Bruce Glassman, editorial director. Senior Editor: Deborah Kops. Blackbirch Press publishes juvenile and young adult nonfiction and fiction titles. Publishes hardcover and trade paperback originals. **Publishes 30-40 titles/year. Receives 400 queries and 75 mss/year. 100% of books from unagented writers. Pays 4-8% royalty on wholesale price or makes outright purchase. Offers $1,000-5,000 advance.** Publishes book 1 year after acceptance of ms. Accepts simultaneous submissions. Reports in 2 months. Manuscript guidelines free. "We cannot return submissions or send guidelines/replies without an enclosed SASE."
Nonfiction: Children's/juvenile: biography, illustrated books, reference. Subjects include animals, anthropology/archeology, art/architecture, education, health/medicine, history, nature/environment, science, sports, travel, women's issues/studies. "No proposals for adult readers, please." Publishes in series—6-8 books at a time. Query with SASE. *No unsolicited mss or proposals.* Cover letters and résumés are useful for identifying new authors. Reviews artwork/photos as part of ms package. Send photocopies.
Fiction: Children's/juvenile rhyming and other picture books. Look for fiction books that tie into school (usually grades K-8) curriculum, including books on Native American and African-American approaches. Query with SASE.
Recent Title(s): *Madeline Albright: U.S. Secretary of State*, by Rose Blue and Corrine J. Naden (biography); *Monsieur Thermidor*, by Richard Kidd (fiction).

JOHN F. BLAIR, PUBLISHER, 1406 Plaza Dr., Winston-Salem NC 27103-1470. (336)768-1374. Fax: (336)768-9194. **Acquisitions:** Carolyn Sakowski, editor. Estab. 1954. "John F. Blair publishes hardcover and trade paperback fiction and nonfiction originals in the areas of travel, history, folklore and the outdoors for a general trade audience, most of whom live or travel in the southeastern U.S." Publishes hardcover originals and trade paperbacks." **Publishes 15 titles/year. Receives 5,000 submissions/year. 20-30% of books from first-time authors; 90% from unagented writers. Royalty negotiable.** Publishes book 18 months after acceptance. Reports in 3 months. Book catalog and ms guidelines for 9×12 SAE with 5 first-class stamps.
Nonfiction: Especially interested in travel guides dealing with the Southeastern US. Also interested in Civil War, outdoors, travel and Americana; query on other nonfiction topics. Looks for utility and significance. Submit outline and first 3 chapters. Reviews artwork/photos as part of ms package.
Fiction: "We publish one work of fiction per year relating to the Southeastern U.S." No category fiction, juvenile fiction, picture books or poetry. *Writer's Market* recommends sending a query with SASE first.

BLOOMBERG PRESS, Bloomberg L.P., 100 Business Park Dr., P.O. Box 888, Princeton NJ 08542-0888. Website: http://www.bloomberg.com. **Acquisitions:** Jared Kieling, editorial director; Jacqueline Murphy, senior editor (Bloomberg Professional Library). "Bloomberg Press publishes professional books for practitioners in the financial markets and finance and investing for informed personal investors, entrepreneurs and consumers. We publish commercially successful books of impressively high quality that stand out clearly from the competition by their brevity, ease of use, sophistication, and abundance of practical tips and strategies; books readers need, will use and appreciate." Publishes hardcover and trade paperback originals. **Publishes 12-18 titles/year. Receives 90 queries and 17 mss/year. 45% of books from unagented writers. Pays negotiable, competitive royalty on net receipts. Offers negotiable advance.** Publishes book 9 months after acceptance of ms. Accepts simultaneous submissions. Reports in 1 month on queries. Book catalog for 10×13 SAE with 5 first-class stamps.
Imprint(s): Bloomberg Personal Bookshelf, Bloomberg Professional Library, Bloomberg Small Business.
Nonfiction: How-to, reference, technical. Subjects include small business, current affairs, money/finance, personal finance and investing for consumers, professional books on finance, investment and financial services. "We are looking for authorities and experienced service journalists who know their subjects and beats cold. We are looking for original solutions to widespread problems and books offering fresh investment opportunities. Do not send us management books—we don't publish them—or unfocused books containing general information already covered by one or more well-established backlist books in the marketplace." Submit outline, sample chapters and SAE with sufficient postage.
Recent Title(s): *A Commonsense Guide to Your 401(k)*, by Mary Rowland (personal finance).
Tips: "*Bloomberg Professional Library*: Audience is upscale financial professionals—traders, dealers, brokers, financial managers, money managers, company executives, sophisticated investors, such as people who lease a BLOOMBERG system. *Bloomberg Personal Bookshelf:* audience is upscale consumers and individual investors, as well as all categories listed for the Professional Library—readers of our magazine *Bloomberg Personal*. Authors are experienced business and financial journalists and/or financial professionals nationally prominent in their specialty for some time who have proven an ability to write a successful book. Research Bloomberg and look at our specially formatted books in a library or bookstore, read *Bloomberg Personal* and *Bloomberg* magazines and peruse our website."

BLUE MOON BOOKS, INC., Avalon Publishing Group, 841 Broadway, New York NY 10003. (212)614-7880. Fax: (212)614-7887. E-mail: tmpress@aol.com. **Acquisitions:** Barney Rosset, editor. "Blue Moon Books is strictly an erotic press; largely fetish-oriented material, B&D, S&M, etc." Publishes trade paperback and mass market paperback originals. Publishes 30-40 titles/year. Receives 1,000 queries and 500 mss/year. Pays 7½-10% royalty on retail price. Offers $500 and up advance. Publishes book 1 year after acceptance of ms. Reports in 2 months. Book catalog free.
Nonfiction: Trade erotic and sexual nonfiction. Query. *No unsolicited mss.*
Fiction: Erotica. Query *No unsolicited mss.*
Recent Title(s): *Patong Sisters: An American Woman's View of the Bangkok Sex World*, by Cleo Odzer; *J and Seventeen*, by Kenzaburo Oe.

BLUE POPPY PRESS, 3450 Penrose Place, Suite 110, Boulder CO 80301. (303)447-8372. Fax: (303)245-8362. E-mail: bluepp@compuserve.com. Website: http://www.bluepoppy.com. **Acquisitions:** Bob Flaws, editor-in-chief. "Blue Poppy Press is dedicated to expanding and improving the English language literature on acupuncture and Asian medicine for both professional practitioners and lay readers." Publishes hardcover and trade paperback originals. **Publishes 9-12 titles/year. Receives 50-100 queries and 20 mss/year. 40-50% of books from first-time authors; 100% from unagented writers. Pays 10-15% royalty "of sales price at all discount levels."** Publishes book 1 year after acceptance. Reports in 1 month. Book catalog and ms guidelines free.
Nonfiction: Self-help, technical, textbook related to acupuncture and Oriental medicine. "We only publish books on acupuncture and Oriental medicine by authors who can read Chinese and have a minimum of five years clinical experience. We also require all our authors to use Wiseman's *Glossary of Chinese Medical Terminology* as their standard for technical terms." Query or submit outline, 1 sample chapter and SASE.
Recent Title(s): *Curing Arthritis Naturally with Chinese Medicine*, by Doug Frank.
Tips: Audience is "practicing acupuncturists, interested in alternatives in healthcare, preventive medicine, Chinese philosophy and medicine."

THE BLUE SKY PRESS, Scholastic Inc., 555 Broadway, New York NY 10012. (212)343-6100. Fax: (212)343-4535. Website: http://www.scholastic.com. Editorial Director: Bonnie Verburg. **Acquisitions:** The Editors. Blue Sky Press publishes primarily juvenile picture books. Publishes hardcover originals. **Publishes 15-20 titles/year. Receives 2,500 queries/year. 1% of books from first-time authors; 75% from unagented writers. Pays 10% royalty on wholesale price, between authors and illustrators.** Publishes book 2 1/2 years after acceptance of ms. Reports in 6 months on queries.

- Because of a large backlog of books, The Blue Sky Press is not accepting unsolicited submissions.

Fiction: Juvenile: adventure, fantasy, historical, humor, mainstream/contemporary, picture books, multicultural, folktales. Query with SASE.
Recent Title(s): *When Birds Could Talk & Bats Could Sing*, by Virginia Hamilton (folktales).

BLUE STAR PRODUCTIONS, Bookworld, Inc., 9666 E. Riggs Rd., #194, Sun Lakes AZ 85248. (602)895-7995. Fax: (602)895-6991. E-mail: bkworld@aol.com. Website: http://www.bkworld.com. **Acquisitions:** Barbara DeBolt, editor. Blue Star Productions publishes metaphysical fiction and nonfiction titles on specialized subjects. For "the spiritual growth of mankind." Publishes trade and mass market paperback originals. **Publishes 10-12 titles/year. Receives 500 queries and 400-500 mss/year. 75% of books from first-time authors; 99% from unagented writers. Pays 10% royalty on wholesale or retail price. No advance.** Reports in 1 month on queries, 2 months on proposals, 6 months on mss. Book catalog free. Manuscript guidelines for #10 SASE.
Nonfiction: Subjects include philosophy, ufology, spiritual (metaphysical), self-help. Query with SASE. No response without SASE. No phone queries. Reviews artwork/photos as part of the ms package. Send photocopies.
Fiction: Fantasy, spiritual (metaphysical), UFO's. Query or submit synopsis and the first 3 chapters. SASE a must.
Recent Title(s): *Cataclysms*, by Norma Hickox (Earth changes/nonfiction); *Me 'n God in the Coffee Shop*, by Rene Donovan (spiritual fantasy).
Tips: "Know our guidelines. We are now accepting manuscripts on disk using WordPerfect 6.0 and higher."

BLUE/GRAY BOOKS, Creativity, Inc., 65 Macedonia Rd., Alexander NC 28701. (828)252-9515. **Acquisitions:** Barbara Blood, acquisitions editor. Blue/Gray Books specializes in Civil War history. Publishes trade paperback originals and reprints. **Publishes 4 titles/year. Pays 12-15% royalty on wholesale price. Seldom offers advance.** Publishes book 18 months after acceptance of ms. Book catalog and ms guidelines for 9×12 SASE with $1.01 postage.
Nonfiction: Civil War subjects include Americana, government/politics, biography, history, military/war. Query or submit proposal package, including original book if wanting reprint with SASE. Reviews artwork/photos as part of ms package. Send photocopies. Query or submit synopsis and 3 sample chapters with SASE.

BNA BOOKS, The Bureau of National Affairs, Inc., 1250 23rd St. NW, Washington DC 20037-1165. (202)833-7470. Fax: (202)833-7490. E-mail: books@bna.com. Website: http://www.bna.com. **Acquisitions:** Tim Darby, acquisitions manager; Jim Fattibene (environment and intellectual property). Estab. 1929. "BNA Books publishes professional reference books written by lawyers, for lawyers." Publishes hardcover and softcover originals. **Publishes 35 titles/year. Receives 200 submissions/year. 20% of books from first-time authors; 95% from unagented writers. Pays 5-15% royalty on net cash receipts. Offers $500 average advance.** Publishes book 1 year after acceptance. Accepts simultaneous submissions. Reports in 3 months on queries. Book catalog and ms guidelines free.

Nonfiction: Reference, professional/scholarly. Subjects include labor and unemployment law, environmental law, legal practice, labor relations and intellectual property law. No biographies, bibliographies, cookbooks, religion books, humor or trade books. Submit detailed table of contents or outline.
Recent Title(s): *Equal Employment Law Updates*, by Richard T. Seymour and Barbara Beris Brown.
Tips: "Our audience is made up of practicing lawyers and business executives; managers, federal, state, and local government administrators; unions; and law libraries. We look for authoritative and comprehensive works that can be supplemented or revised every year or two on subjects of interest to those audiences."

BOA EDITIONS, LTD., 260 East Ave., Rochester NY 14604. (716)546-3410. Fax: (716)546-3913. E-mail: boaedit@frontiernet.net. Website: http://www.boaeditions.org. **Acquisitions:** Steven Huff, publisher/managing editor. "BOA Editions publishes frontlist and backlist collections of poetry and poetry in translation." Publishes hardcover and trade paperback originals. **Publishes 8 titles/year. Receives 1,000 queries and 700 mss/year. 15% of books from first-time authors; 90% from unagented writers. Pays 7½-10% royalty on retail price. Advance varies, usually $500.** Publishes book 18 months after acceptance of ms. Accepts simultaneous submissions. Reports in 1 month on queries, 4 months on mss. Book catalog and ms guidelines free.
Poetry: Accepting mss for publication in 2000 and beyond. Query or submit 10 sample poems with SASE.
Recent Title(s): *The Quicken Tree*, by Bill Knott.
Tips: "Readers who, like Whitman, expect of the poet to 'indicate more than the beauty and dignity which always attach to dumb real objects . . . they expect him to indicate the path between reality and their souls,' are the audience of BOA's books."

N **THE BOLD STRUMMER LTD.**, 20 Turkey Hill Circle, P.O. Box 2037, Westport CT 06880-2037. (203)259-3021. Fax: (203)259-7369. **Acquisitions:** Nicholas Clarke. "The Bold Strummer Ltd., or our associate publisher Pro/Am Music resources, publishes most good quality work that is offered in our field(s). BSL publishes guitar and related instrument books (guitar, violin, drums)." Publishes hardcover and trade paperback originals and reprints. **Publishes 6-8 titles/year. Receives 5 queries and 2 mss/year. 50% of books from first-time authors; 100% from unagented writers. Pays 10% royalty on retail price.** Publishes book 9-12 months after acceptance of ms. Book catalog and ms guidelines free.
Nonfiction: Music with an emphasis on guitar and piano-related books. Query. Reviews artwork as part of ms package. Send photocopies.
Tips: "Bold Strummer has also become a leading source of books about Flamenco. Pro/AM specializes in piano books, composer biography, etc. Very narrow niche publishers."

BONUS BOOKS, INC., Precept Press, 160 E. Illinois St., Chicago IL 60611. (312)467-0580. Fax: (312)467-9271. Website: http://www.bonus-books.com. Managing Editor: Andrea Rackel. **Acquisitions:** Aili Breshnahow, assistant editor. Estab. 1985. Bonus Books is a publishing and audio/video company featuring subjects ranging from human interest to sports to gambling. Publishes hardcover and trade paperback originals and reprints. **Publishes 30 titles/year. Receives 400-500 submissions/year. 40% of books from first-time authors; 60% from unagented writers. Royalties vary. Rarely offers advance.** Publishes book 8 months after acceptance. Accepts simultaneous submissions, if so noted. Reports in 2 months on queries. Book catalog for 9×11 SASE. Manuscript guidelines for #10 SASE.
Nonfiction: Subjects include automotive/self-help, biography/current affairs, broadcasting, business/self-help, Chicago people and places, collectibles, cookbooks, education/self-help, fund raising, handicapping winners, home and health, humor, entertainment, regional, sports and women's issues/studies. Query with outline, sample chapters and SASE. Reviews artwork/photos as part of ms package. All submissions and queries must include SASE.
Recent Title(s): *Paul Simon Autobiography*, by Paul Simon.

BOOKCRAFT, INC., 2405 W. Orton Circle, West Valley UT 84119. (801)908-3400. **Acquisitions:** Cory H. Maxwell, editorial manager. Estab. 1942. Publishes hardcover and trade paperback originals. "Our mission is to publish well-written, accessible, inspirational books that help the reader understand, appreciate, and follow the principles of the Gospel of Jesus Christ." **Publishes 40-45 titles/year. Receives 800-1,000 submissions/year. 20% of books from first-time authors; virtually 100% from unagented writers. Pays standard 7½-10-12½-15% royalty on retail price. Rarely gives advance.** Publishes book 6 months after acceptance. Accepts simultaneous submissions. Reports in about 2 months. Book catalog and ms guidelines for #10 SASE.
Imprint: Parliament.
Nonfiction: "We publish for members of The Church of Jesus Christ of Latter-Day Saints (Mormons) and our books are closely oriented to the faith and practices of the LDS church, and we will be glad to review such mss. Those which have merely a general religious appeal are not acceptable. Ideal book lengths range from about 100-300 pages or so, depending on subject, presentation, and age level. We look for a fresh approach—rehashes of well-known concepts or doctrines not acceptable. Manuscripts should be anecdotal unless truly scholarly or on a specialized subject. We do not publish anti-Mormon works. We also publish short and moderate length books for children and young adults, and fiction as well as nonfiction. These reflect LDS principles without being 'preachy'; must be motivational. 50,000-100,000 words is about the right length, though good, longer manuscripts are not ruled out. We publish only 5 or 6 new juvenile titles annually. No poetry, plays, personal philosophizings, or family histories." Biography, childrens/juvenile, coffee table book, how-to, humor, reference, self-help. Subjects include: child guidance/parenting, history, religion. Query with

full ms and SASE. *Writer's Market* recommends sending a query with SASE first. Reviews artwork/photos as part of ms package. Send photocopies.

Fiction: Should be oriented to LDS faith and practices. Adventure, historical, juvenile, literary, mainstream/contemporary, mystery, religious, romance, short story collections, suspense, western, young adult. Submit full ms with SASE. *Writer's Market* recommends sending a query with SASE first.

Recent Title(s): *The Fire of Faith* by John H. Groberg (nonfiction); *A Shawl and a Violin*, by Randall Hall (hisorical fiction for middle grade readers).

Tips: "The competition in the area of fiction is much more intense than it has ever been before. We receive two or three times as many quality fiction manuscripts as we did even as recently as five years ago."

BOOKS IN MOTION, 9212 E. Montgomery, #501, Spokane WA 99206. (509)922-1646. **Acquisitions:** Gary Challender, president. Publishes unabridged audiobook originals. **Publishes 70-80 titles/year. 25% of books from first-time authors; 90% from unagented writers. Pays 10% royalty on wholesale or retail price.** Publishes book 3 months after acceptance of ms. Accepts simultaneous submissions. Reporting time varies. Book catalog and ms guidelines on request.

Fiction: Adventure, fantasy, historical, horror, humor, mainstream/contemporary, mystery, religious, science fiction, suspense, western. "Minimal profanity and no gratuitous sex. We like series using the same charismatic character." Query with synopsis and first chapter.

Recent Title(s): *Timegap*, by Loren Robinson (science fiction).

Tips: "Our audience is 20% women, 80% men. Many of our audience are truck drivers, who want something interesting to listen to."

THE BORGO PRESS, P.O. Box 2845, San Bernardino CA 92406-2845. (909)884-5813. Fax: (909)888-4942. E-mail: borgopr@gte.net. Website: http://www.borgopress.com. **Acquisitions:** Robert Reginald, Mary A. Burgess, publishers. Estab. 1975. "We publish quality books on literature, the theater and related topics for the library and academic market." Publishes hardcover and paperback originals. **Publishes 15 new titles/year. Receives 100 submissions/year. 50% of books from first-time authors; 90% of books from unagented writers. Pays 10% royalty on retail price. No advance.** Publishes book 3 years after acceptance. "99% of our sales go to the academic library market; we do not sell to the trade (i.e., bookstores)." Reports in 3 months.

Imprint(s): Brownstone Books, St. Willibrod's Press.

- This publisher says they are currently backlogged and buying only a handful of new books.

Nonfiction: Publishes literary critiques, bibliographies, theatrical research, scholarly literary biographies and reference works for the academic library market only. Query with letter or outline/synopsis, 1 sample chapter and SASE.

Recent Title(s): *Scaring Us to Death*, by Collings.

Tips: "All of our proprietary books, without exception, are published in open-ended, numbered, monographic series. Do not submit proposals until you have looked at actual copies of recent Borgo Press publications (*not our catalog*). We are *not* a market for fiction, poetry, popular nonfiction, artwork, or anything else except scholarly monographs in the humanities. We discard unsolicited manuscripts from outside of our subject fields that are not accompanied by SASE. The vast majority of proposals we receive are clearly unsuitable and are a waste of both our time and the prospective author's."

BOWLING GREEN STATE UNIVERSITY POPULAR PRESS, Bowling Green State University, Bowling Green OH 43403-1000. (419)372-7866. Fax: (419)372-8095. Website: http://www.bgsu.edu/colleges/library/press/press.html. **Acquisitions:** (Ms.) Pat Browne. Estab. 1967. Publishes hardcover originals and trade paperback originals and reprints. **Publishes 25 titles/year. Receives 400 submissions/year. 50% of books from first-time authors; 100% from unagented writers. Pays 5-12% royalty on wholesale price or makes outright purchase.** Publishes book 9 months after acceptance. Reports in 3 months. Book catalog and ms guidelines free.

Nonfiction: Biography, reference, textbook. Subjects include Americana, art/architecture, ethnic, history, language/literature, regional, sports, women's issues/studies. Submit outline and 3 sample chapters.

Recent Title(s): *Stephen King's America*, by Jonathan Davis.

Tips: "Our audience includes university professors, students, and libraries."

BOYDS MILLS PRESS, *Highlights for Children*, 815 Church St., Honesdale PA 18431-1895. (717)253-1164. Publisher: Kent L. Brown. **Acquisitions:** Beth Troop, manuscript coordinator. Estab. 1990. "We publish a wide range of children's books of literary merit, from preschool to young adult." Publishes hardcover originals and trade paperback originals and reprints. **Publishes 50 titles/year. Imprint publishes 10-20 titles/year. Receives 10,000 queries and mss/year. 20% of books are from first-time authors; 20% from unagented writers. Pays 8-15% royalty on retail price. Advance varies.** Accepts simultaneous submissions. Reports in 3 months. Book catalog and ms guidelines free.

Imprint(s): Wordsong (poetry).

Nonfiction: Juvenile subjects include agriculture/horticulture, animals, ethnic, history, hobbies, nature/environment, regional, religion, sports, travel. "Nonfiction should be accurate, tailored to young audience. Accompanying art is preferred, as is simple, narrative style, but in compelling, evocative language. Too many overwrite for the young audience and get bogged down in minutia. Boyds Mills Press is not interested in manuscripts depicting violence, explicit sexuality, racism of any kind or which promote hatred. We also are not the right market for self-help books." Query with proposal package, including outline, 1 sample chapter, some art samples (photos, drawings), with SASE.

Fiction: Adventure, confession, ethnic, fantasy, historical, humor, juvenile, mainstream/contemporary, mystery, picture books, religious, science fiction, short story collections, suspense, western, young adult. "Don't let a personal agenda dominate to the detriment of plot. In short, tell a good story. Too many writers miss the essence of a good story: beginning, middle, end; conflict and resolution because they're more interested in making a sociological statement." Submit outline/synopsis and 3 sample chapters for novel or complete ms for picture book.
Poetry: "Poetry should be appropriate for young audiences, clever, fun language, with easily understood meaning. Too much poetry is either too simple and static in meaning or too obscure." Submit 10 sample poems.
Recent Title(s): *Everybody Has a Bellybutton*, by Laurence Pringle (nonfiction); *Nellie Bishop*, by Clara Gillow Clark (historical novel).
Tips: "Our audience is pre-school to young adult. Concentrate first on your writing. Polish it. Then—and only then—select a market. We need primarily picture books with fresh ideas and characters—avoid worn themes of 'coming-of-age,' 'new sibling,' and self-help ideas. We are always interested in multicultural settings. Please—no anthropomorphic characters."

BRANDEN PUBLISHING CO., INC., 17 Station St., Box 843, Brookline Village MA 02147. Fax: (617)734-2046. Website: http://www.branden.com. **Acquisitions:** Adolph Caso, editor. Estab. 1965. "Branden publishes books by or about women, children, military, Italian-American, or African-American themes." Subsidiaries include International Pocket Library and Popular Technology, Four Seas and Brashear. Publishes hardcover and trade paperback originals, reprints and software. **Publishes 15 titles/year. Receives 1,000 submissions/year. 80% of books from first-time authors; 90% from unagented writers. Pays 5-10% royalty on net. Offers $1,000 maximum advance.** Publishes book 10 months after acceptance. Reports in 1 month. *Writer's Market* recommends allowing 2 months for reply.
Nonfiction: Biography, illustrated book, juvenile, reference, technical, textbook. Subjects include Americana, art, computers, health, history, music, photography, politics, sociology, software, classics. Especially looking for "about 10 manuscripts on national and international subjects, including biographies of well-known individuals." No religion or philosophy. Paragraph query only with author's vita and SASE. *No unsolicited mss.* No telephone, e-mail or fax inquiries. Reviews artwork/photos as part of ms package.
Fiction: Ethnic (histories, integration); religious (historical-reconstructive). No science, mystery or pornography. Paragraph query only with author's vita and SASE. *No unsolicited mss.* No telephone, fax or e-mail inquiries.
Recent Title(s): *Abenaki Warrior*, by Alfred Kayworth (Native American history); *Blood Games*, by Woody Tanger (medical thriller).

BRASSEY'S, INC., Brassey's Ltd. (London), 22883 Quicksilver Dr., Dulles VA 20166. (703)260-0602. Fax: (703)260-0701. E-mail: brasseys@aol.com. Website: http://www.brasseys.com. **Acquisitions:** Don McKeon, editorial director. Brassey's is a US publisher specializing in national and international affairs, military history, biography, intelligence, foreign policy, defense and sports. Publishes hardcover and trade paperback originals and reprints. **Publishes 40 titles/year. Receives 900 queries/year. 30% of books from first-time authors; 80% from unagented writers. Pays 6-12% royalty on wholesale price. Offers $50,000 maximum advance.** Publishes book 1 year after acceptance of ms. Accepts simultaneous submissions. Reports in 2 months on proposals. Book catalog and ms guidelines for 9×12 SASE.
Nonfiction: Biography, coffee-table book, reference, textbook. Subjects include government/politics, national and international affairs, history, military/war, intelligence studies and sports. "We are seeking to build our biography, military history and national affairs lists and have also created a new imprint, Brassey's Sports." When submitting nonfiction, be sure to include sufficient biographical information (e.g., track records of previous publications), and "make clear in proposal how your work might differ from other such works already published and with which yours might compete." Submit proposal package, including outline, 1 sample chapter, bio, analysis of book's competition, return postage and SASE. Reviews artwork/photos as part of ms package. Send photocopies.
Recent Title(s): *Freedom's Voice: The Perilous Present and Uncertain Future of the First Amendment*, by Robert D. Richards.
Tips: "Our audience consists of military personnel, government policymakers, and general readers with an interest in military history, biography, national and international affairs, defense issues, intelligence studies and sports." Brassey's does not consider fiction.

GEORGE BRAZILLER, INC., 171 Madison Ave., Suite 1103, New York NY 10016. (212)889-0909. Publisher: George Braziller. **Acquisitions:** Mary Taveros, production editor. Publishes hardcover originals, trade paperback originals and reprints. **Publishes 25 titles/year. Receives 300 queries and 60 mss/year. 2% of books from first-time authors; 80% from unagented writers. Pays standard royalty: 8% paperback, 10-15% hardcover.** Publishes book 10 months after acceptance of ms. Reports in 3 months on proposals. Book catalog and ms guidelines free.
Nonfiction: Art books. Subjects include art/architecture, history, language/literature. "We do very little nonfiction but, as we don't publish in specific categories only, we are willing to consider a wide range of subjects." Submit outline with 4 sample chapters and SASE. Reviews artwork/photos as part of ms package. Send photocopies.
Fiction: Ethnic, gay/lesbian, literary. "We rarely do fiction but when we have published novels, they have mostly been literary novels." Submit 4-6 sample chapters with SASE.
Recent Title(s): *Michelangelo: The Sistine Chapel Ceiling, Rome*, by Loren Partridge (art).

BREVET PRESS, INC., P.O. Box 1404, Sioux Falls SD 57101. **Acquisitions:** Donald P. Mackintosh, publisher (business); Peter E. Reid, managing editor (technical); A. Melton, editor (Americana); B. Mackintosh, editor (history).

Estab. 1972. Brevet Books seeks nonfiction with "market potential and literary excellence." Publishes hardcover and paperback originals and reprints. **Publishes 15 titles/year. Receives 40 submissions/year. 50% of books from first-time authors; 100% from unagented writers. Pays 5% royalty. Offers $1,000 average advance.** Publishes book 1 year after acceptance. Accepts simultaneous submissions. Reports in 2 months. Book catalog free.
Nonfiction: Specializes in business management, history, place names, and historical marker series. Americana, business, history, technical books. Query with SASE. "After query, detailed instructions will follow if we are interested." Reviews artwork/photos as part of ms package. Send photocopies.
Tips: "Keep sexism out of the manuscripts."

BREWERS PUBLICATIONS, Association of Brewers, 736 Pearl St., Boulder CO 80302. (303)447-0816. Fax: (303)447-2825. E-mail: bp@aob.org. Website: http://beertown.org. **Acquisitions:** Toni Knapp, publisher. Estab. 1986. "Brewers Publications is the largest publisher of books on beer-related subjects." Publishes hardcover and trade paperback originals. **Publishes 12 titles/year. 50% of books from first-time authors; 75% from unagented writers. Pays royalty on net receipts. Advance negotiated.** Publishes book within 18 months of acceptance of ms. Accepts simultaneous submissions. Reports in 3 months. Book catalog free.
Nonfiction: "We publish books on history, art, culture, literature, brewing and science of beer. In a broad sense, this also includes biographies, humor and cooking." Query first with brief proposal and SASE.
Recent Title(s): *Beer for Pete's Sake*, by Pete Slosberg (biography/business).

BRIDGE WORKS PUBLISHING CO., Box 1798, Bridge Lane, Bridgehampton NY 11932. (516)537-3418. Fax: (516)537-5092. **Acquisitions:** Barbara Phillips, editor/publisher. "We are a very small press dedicated to quality fiction and nonfiction. We are not interested in mass market material, but look for writing that is original and inventive, as well as entertaining." Publishes hardcover originals and reprints. **Publishes 4-6 titles/year. Receives 1,000 queries and mss/year. 50% of books from first-time authors; 80% from unagented writers. Pays 10% royalty on retail price. Offers $1,000 advance.** Publishes book 1 year after acceptance of ms. Reports in 1 month on queries and proposals, 2 months on mss. Book catalog and ms guidelines for #10 SASE.
Nonfiction: Biography, history, language/literature, philosophy, psychology, sociology. "We *do not* accept multiple submissions. We prefer a query first, and the subjects should have either a national or universal significance." Query or submit outline and proposal package with SASE. Reviews artwork/photos as part of ms package. Send photocopies.
Fiction: Historical, literary, mystery, short story collections. "Query with SASE before submitting ms. First-time authors should have manuscripts vetted by freelance editors before submitting. We do not accept or read multiple submissions." Query or submit synopsis and 2 sample chapters with SASE.
Poetry: "We publish only *one* collection every 5 years." Query and submit sample poems.
Recent Title(s): *Fair Seafarer*, by Nancy Allen (adventure, nonfiction); *Boondocking*, by Tricia Bauer (fiction).
Tips: "Query letters should be one page, giving general subject or plot of the book and stating who the writer feels is the audience for the work. In the case of novels or poetry, a portion of the work could be enclosed."

BRISTOL FASHION PUBLICATIONS, P.O. Box 20, Enola PA 17025. **Acquisitions:** John Kaufman, publisher; Robert "Bob" Lollo, managing editor. Publishes hardcover and trade paperback originals. **Publishes 6-8 titles/year. Receives 20 queries and 4 mss/year. 80% of books from first-time authors; 100% from unagented writers. Pays 7-11% royalty on retail price. Splits royalty or makes outright purchase for portions to be included with other's work. Offers $500-2,500 advance based on writer and project. Usually offers no advance to unpublished authors.** Publishes books 6 months after acceptance of ms. Accepts simultaneous submissions. Reports in 1 month on queries and proposals, 2 months on mss. Book catalog for 9½×12 SAE and $1.01 postage. Ms guidelines for #10 SASE.
Nonfiction: How-to, reference. Nautical/marine subjects only. "All titles are how to repair, maintain and restore boats over 25 feet. Query for specific needs with a list of your ideas. Include phone number. This is a fast changing market. We make no long range title plans. We prefer good technical knowledge with simple to understand, step-by-step writing. K.I.S.S." Query first, then submit proposal package, including outline, writing samples, tearsheets, with SASE. Reviews artwork/photos as part of the ms package. Send photocopies of b&w prints and/or line art.
Recent Title(s): *Boat Repair Made Easy* series: *Systems*, *Haul Out*, *Engines*, *Troubleshooting*, *Finishes*.
Tips: "Audience is boaters with vessels over 25 feet who want to learn how to do their own work, new boaters, boaters who have recently purchased a larger vessel, cruising boaters or in general, the non-handy. No agents. Period!!! Keep it simple and easy to follow. Use nautical terms where appropriate. Do not use complicated technical terms or formulas. Start from the very basic and work towards the larger projects. Write for guidelines and include any ideas you may have for a title. Use good craftsman as a resource."

N **BRISTOL PUBLISHING ENTERPRISES**, 14692 Wicks Blvd., San Leandro CA 94577. (800)346-4889. (510)895-4461. **Acquisitions:** Jennifer L. Newens, managing editor. "Our readers may not be very experienced or 'hip' to the current trends in cooking and entertaining, but are eager to learn. Our books educate without intimidating." Publishes hardcover and trade paperback originals. **Firm publishes 18-30 titles/year; each imprint publishes 4-12 titles/year. Receives 50-75 queries/year. 50% of books from first-time authors; 100% from unagented writers. Pays 6% royalty on wholesale price or makes varying outright purchase.** Publishes book 6 months after acceptance of ms. Accepts simultaneous submissions. Reports in 4 months. Book catalog free. Manuscript guidelines for #10 SASE.
Imprint(s): Nitty Gritty cookbooks, The Best 50 Recipe Series, Indoor Gardening for Brown Thumbs.
Nonfiction: Cookbook, how-to. Subjects include cooking/foods/nutrition, gardening, entertaining. "Send a proposal

or query first; editor will contact if interested in seeing manuscript. Most cookbooks are related to housewares products and/or hot culinary trends. Readers are novice cooks who want to know more about what is going on. Don't send family recipe collections; research our company before submitting." Query with outline and 1-2 samples chapters
Recent Title(s): *Cooking with Fresh Herbs*, by Lou Seibert Pappas.
Tips: "We do not work with agents."

BROADMAN & HOLMAN PUBLISHERS, 127 Ninth Ave. N., Nashville TN 37234. Publisher: Kenneth Stephens. **Acquisitions:** Richard Rosenbaum, editorial director. "Broadman & Holman will be the best provider of distinctive, relevant, high-quality products and services that lead individuals toward: a personal faith in Jesus Christ, a lifestyle of practical discipleship, a world view that is consistent with the historic, Christian Faith. We will accomplish this in a manner that glorifies God and serves His Kingdom while making a positive financial contribution." Publishes hardcover and paperback originals. **Publishes 48 titles/year. Pays negotiable royalty.** Reports in 2 months. Writer's guidelines for #10 SAE with 2 first-class stamps.
Nonfiction: Religion. "We are open to freelance submissions in all areas. Materials in these areas must be suited for an evangelical Christian readership." No poetry, biography, sermons, or art/gift books. Query with outline/synopsis and sample chapters with SASE.
Fiction: Religious. "We publish a limited number of fiction titles. We want not only a very good story, but also one that sets forth Christian values. Nothing that lacks a positive Christian emphasis; nothing that fails to sustain reader interest." Query with SASE.
Recent Title(s): *The Father Connection*, by Josh McDowell (parenting); *Anonymous Tip*, by Michael Farris (current issues/fiction).
Tips: "Please study competing titles and be able to identify the unique, compelling features of your proposed book."

[A] **BROADWAY BOOKS**, Bantam Doubleday Dell, 1540 Broadway, New York NY 10036. (212)354-6500. Website: http://www.bdd.com. Publisher: William Shinker. Editor-in-Chief: John Sterling. **Acquisitions:** Harriet Bell, executive editor (cookbooks); John Sterling, vice president and editor-in-chief (literary fiction, nonfiction); Lauren Marino, editor (pop culture, entertainment, spirituality); Suzanne Oaks, editor (business); Tracy Behar, managing editor and special projects editor (illustrated books, family issues, consumer reference, health); Charles Conrad, vice president and executive editor (general nonfiction). Broadway publishes general interest nonfiction and fiction for adults. Publishes hardcover and trade paperback originals and reprints.
Nonfiction: General interest adult books. Subjects include biography/memoirs, business, child care/parenting, cookbooks, current affairs, diet/nutrition, health, history, illustrated books, New Age/spirituality, money/finance, politics, popular culture, psychology, women's studies, multicultural studies, gay and lesbian, sex/erotica, consumer reference, golf. Agented submissions only.
Fiction: Publishes commercial literary fiction.
Recent Title(s): *Costas on Baseball*, by Bob Costas with Buzz Bissinger; *Freedomland*, by Richard Price (fiction).

BROOKLINE BOOKS, P.O. Box 1047, Cambridge MA 02238. (617)868-0360. Fax: (617)868-1772. E-mail: brooklinebks@delphi.com. Website: http://people.delphi.com/brooklinebks. **Acquisitions:** Sadi Ranson, executive editor. "Brookline publishes books for parents, families and professionals whose lives were affected by disabilities, and the need for special education." Publishes trade and professional paperback originals and reprints. **Publishes 8-12 titles/year. Receives 50-100 queries and 30-50 mss/year. 30% of books from first-time authors; majority from unagented writers. Pays 10-15% royalty on wholesale price.** Publishes book 8 months after acceptance of ms. Accepts simultaneous submissions. Reports in 1 month on queries, 2 months on proposals and mss. Book catalog and ms guidelines free.
Imprint(s): Lumen Editions, Nitelight (children's books).
Nonfiction: Reference, technical, textbook, professional. Subjects include child guidance/parenting, education, health/medicine, language/literature, psychology, translation, special needs/disabilities. Query or submit outline, 3 sample chapters and SASE. Reviews artwork/photos as part of ms package. Send photocopies.
Fiction: First time translations of Latin American, European and Asian literary fiction and nonfiction. Query or submit synopsis, 3 sample chapters and SASE.
Recent Title(s): *New Voices*, by G. Dybwad and H. Bersani (self-advocacy among persons with mental retardation); *Urban Oracles*, by Mayra Santos-Febres (fictional stories of lives of Puerto Rican women); *Dialogues for Left and Right Hand*, by Steven Cramer (poetry).

BRYANT & DILLON PUBLISHERS, INC., P.O. Box 39, Orange NJ 07050. (973)763-1470. Fax: (973)675-8443. **Acquisitions:** Gerri Dillon. "We publish books that speak to an African-American audience." Publishes hardcover and trade paperback originals. **Publishes 8-10 titles/year. Receives 500 queries and 700 mss/year. 100% of books from first-time authors; 90% from unagented writers. Pays 6-10% royalty on retail price.** Publishes book 1 year after acceptance of ms. Accepts simultaneous submissions. Reports in 3 months on proposals.

- Bryant & Dillon no longer publishes fiction.

Nonfiction: Biography, how-to, self-help. Subjects include Black studies, business/economics, education, ethnic, film, government/politics, history, language/literature, money/finance, women's issues/studies. "Must be on subjects of interest to African-Americans." Submit cover letter, author's information sheet, marketing information, outline and 3 sample chapters with SASE (envelope large enough for contents sent). "No faxes or phone calls!" No poetry or children's books.

Recent Title(s): *Breaking the Glass Ceiling*, by Anthony Stith (business).

BUCKNELL UNIVERSITY PRESS, Lewisburg PA 17837. (717)524-3674. Fax: (717)524-3797. E-mail: clingham@bucknell.edu. Website: http://www.bucknell.edu/departments/library/bupress. **Acquisitions:** Greg Clingham, director. Estab. 1969. "In all fields, our criteria are scholarly excellence, critical originality, and interdisciplinary and theoretical expertise and sensitivity." Publishes hardcover originals. **Publishes 30-35 titles/year. Receives 400 inquiries and submissions/year. 20% of books from first-time authors; 99% from unagented writers. Pays royalty.** Publishes accepted works within 2 years of delivery of finished ms. Reports in 1 month on queries. Book catalog free.

Nonfiction: English and American literary criticism, literary theory and cultural studies, historiography (including the history of law, medicine and science), art history, modern languages, classics, philosophy, anthropology, ethnology, psychology, sociology, religion, political science, cultural and political geography, and interdisciplinary combinations of the aforementioned. Series: Bucknell Studies in Eighteenth-Century Literature and Culture, Bucknell Studies in Latin American Literature and Theory, Bucknell Studies in Historiography, Bucknell Series in Contemporary Poetry; Biannual Journal: The Bucknell Review: A Scholarly Journal of Letters, Arts, and Sciences. Query with SASE.

Recent Title(s): *Intertextual Pursuits: Literary Mediations in Modern Spanish Narrative*, edited by Jeanne P. Brownlow and John W. Kronik.

Tips: "An original work of high-quality scholarship has the best chance. We publish for the scholarly community."

BULFINCH PRESS, Little, Brown & Co., 3 Center Plaza, Boston MA 02108. (617)263-2797. Fax: (617)263-2857. Website: http://www.littlebrown.com. Publisher: Carol Judy Leslie. **Acquisitions:** Melissa Lotfy, department assistant. "Bulfinch Press publishes large format art books using the finest quality production." Publishes hardcover and trade paperback originals. **Publishes 60-70 titles/year. Receives 500 queries/year. Pays variable royalty on wholesale price. Advance varies.** Publishes book 18 months after acceptance of ms. Accepts simultaneous submissions. Reports in 2 months on proposals.

Nonfiction: Coffee table book, gift book, illustrated book. Subjects include art/architecture, gardening, photography. Query with outline, sample artwork and SASE. Send color photocopies or laser prints.

Recent Title(s): *Half Past Autumn*, by Gordon Parks (photography).

THE BUREAU FOR AT-RISK YOUTH, P.O. Box 760, Plainview NY 11803-0760. **Acquisitions:** Sally Germain, editor-in-chief. Publishes booklets, pamphlets, curriculum and other educational materials for educators, parents, mental health and juvenile justice professionals. **Publishes 25-50 titles/year. Receives hundreds of submissions/year. Most books from first-time authors; 100% from unagented writers. Pays royalty of 10% maximum on selling price. Advance varies.** Publication 1 year after acceptance of ms. Accepts simultaneous submissions. Reports in 1-8 months. Book catalog free if appropriate after communication with author.

Nonfiction: Educational materials for parents, educators and other professionals who work with youth. Subjects include child guidance/parenting, education. "The materials we publish are curriculum, book series, workbook/activity books or how-to-oriented pieces tailored to our audience. They are generally not single book titles and are rarely book length." Query.

Recent Title(s): *C.O.L.O.R.S: Crossing Over Lines of Racial Stereotypes*, by Michelle Jackson, Ph.D. (race relations curriculum).

Tips: "Publications are sold exclusively through direct mail catalog. We do not publish book-length pieces. Writers whose expertise is appropriate to our customers should send query or proposal since we tailor everything very specifically to meet our audience's needs."

N **BURFORD BOOKS**, P.O. Box 388, Short Hills NJ 07078. (973)258-0960. Fax: (973)258-0113. **Acquisitions:** Peter Burford, publisher. "We publish books on all aspects of the outdoors, from gardening to sports, practical and literary." Publishes hardcover originals, trade paperback originals and reprints. **Publishes 15 titles/year. Receives 150 queries and 100 mss/year. 30% of books from first-time authors; 60% from unagented writers. Pays royalty on wholesale price.** Accepts simultaneous submissions. Publishes book 18 months after acceptance of ms. Reports in 1 month on queries and proposals, 2 months on mss. Book catalog and ms guidelines free.

Nonfiction: How-to, illustrated book. Subjects include horticulture, animals, cooking/foods/nutrition, gardening, hobbies, military/war, nature/environment, recreation, sports, travel. Query with outline with SASE. Reviews artwork/photos as part of the ms package. Send photocopies.

Recent Title(s): *Golf: An Album of Its History*, by Robert McCord (illustrated/sports).

BUSINESS & LEGAL REPORTS, INC., 39 Academy St., Madison CT 06443-1513. (203)318-0000. Fax: (203)245-0483. **Acquisitions:** Daniel Schwartz, executive editor. Estab. 1978. Business & Legal Reports publishes administrative and management titles for business. Publishes loose leaf and soft cover originals. **Averages 20 titles/year. Receives 100 submissions/year. Pays 2½-5% royalty on retail price, or makes outright purchase for $1,000-5,000. Offers $3,000 average advance.** Publishes book an average of 6 months after acceptance. Accepts simultaneous submissions. Book catalog free.

Nonfiction: Reference. Subjects include human resources, management, safety, environmental management. Query.

- Publisher reports a special interest in "how-to" compliance guides.

BUSINESS McGRAW-HILL, The McGraw Hill Companies, 11 W. 19th St., New York NY 10011. (212)337-4098. Fax: (212)337-5999. Publisher: Philip Ruppel. **Acquisitions:** Betsy Brown, senior editor; Nancy Caraccilo. "McGraw Hill's business division is the world's largest business publisher, offering nonfiction trade and paperback originals in more than ten areas, including management, sales and marketing, careers, self-help, training, finance, personal finance and manufacturing operations." **Publishes 100 titles/year. Receives 1,200 queries and 1,200 mss/year. 30% of books from first-time authors; 60% from unagented writers. Pays 5-17% royalty on net price. Offers $1,000-100,000 advance.** Publishes book 6 months after acceptance of ms. Accepts simultaneous submissions. Reports in 3 months. Book catalog and ms guidelines free on request with SASE.

Nonfiction: How-to, reference, self-help, technical. Subjects include business/economics, government/politics, money/finance. "Current, up-to-date, original ideas are needed. Good self-promotion is key." Submit proposal package, including outline, table of contents, concept.

Recent Nonfiction Title(s): *Informed Consent*, by John Byrne (general interest).

N BUTTE PUBLICATIONS, INC., P.O. Box 1328, Hillsboro OR 97123-1328. (503)648-9791. Fax: (503)693-9526. **Acquisitions**: M. Brink, president. Butte publishes books related to deafness and education. **Publishes 6-8 titles/year. Receives 30 queries and 20 mss/year. 50% of books from first-time authors; 100% from unagented writers. Pays 8-12% royalty on net receipts.** Publishes book 1 year after acceptance of ms. Accepts simultaneous submissions. Reports in 1 month on queries, 4 months on proposals, 6 months on mss. Book catalog and ms guidelines free.

Nonfiction: Children's/juvenile, textbook. Subjects include education, all related to field of deafness and education. Submit proposal package, including author bio, synopsis, market survey and complete ms, if completed. Reviews artwork/photos as part of ms package (if essential to the educational value of the work). Send photocopies.

Fiction: Adventure, historical, mystery, young adult (deaf characters). All must deal with hearing loss or include deaf characters. Submit complete ms and SASE. *Writer's Market* recommends sending a query with SASE first.

Recent Title(s): *Living Legends*, by Toole (biographies); *Balancing Act*, by Scott (young adult novel).

Tips: "Audience is students, teachers, parents and professionals in the arena dealing with deafness and hearing loss."

BUTTERWORTH-HEINEMANN, Reed-Elsevier, 225 Wildwood Ave., Woburn MA 01801-2041. Website: http://www.bh.com. **Acquisitions:** Karen Speerstra, publishing director (books on transforming business); Marie Lee, publisher (Focal Press); Liz McCarthy, editor (Digital Press); Susan Pioli, publishing director (Medical); Laurel DeWolf, senior editor (Security Criminal Justice); Jo Gilmore, senior editor (Newnes). "Butterworth-Heinemann has been serving professionals and students for over five decades. We remain committed to publishing materials that forge ahead of rapidly changing technology and reinforce the highest professional standards. Our goal is to give you the competitive advantage in this rapidly changing digital age." Publishes hardcover and trade paperback originals. **Publishes 150 titles/year. Each imprint publishes 25-30 titles/year. 25% of books from first-time authors; 95% from unagented writers. Pays 10-12% royalty on wholesale price. Offers modest advance.** Publishes book 9 months after acceptance of ms. Reports in 1 month on proposals. Book catalog and ms guidelines free.

Imprint(s): Butterworth-Heinemann, Medical, Digital Press (computing), **Focal Press**, Medical, Newnes (electronics), Security & Criminal Justice.

Nonfiction: How-to (in our selected areas), reference, technical, textbook. Subjects include business, computers/electronics, health/medicine, photography, security/criminal justice, audio-video broadcast, communication technology. "We publish technical professional and academic books; no fiction." Submit outline, 1-2 sample chapters, competing books and how yours is different/better, with SASE. Reviews artwork/photos as part of ms package. Send photocopies.

CADDO GAP PRESS, 3145 Geary Blvd., Suite 275, San Francisco CA 94118. (415)392-1911. Fax: (415)392-8748. E-mail: caddogap@aol.com. **Acquisitions:** Alan H. Jones, publisher. Caddo Gap publishes works on education. Estab. 1989. Publishes trade paperback originals and educational journals and newsletters. **Publishes 4 titles/year. Receives 20 queries and 10 mss/year. 50% of books from first-time authors; 100% from unagented writers. Pays 10% royalty on wholesale price.** Publishes book 1 year after acceptance of ms. Accepts simultaneous submissions. Reports in 2 months on proposals.

Nonfiction: Subjects limited to teacher education, social foundations of education, and multicultural education. Query.

Recent Title(s): *Empowering the Second-Language Classroom*, by Huberto Molina.

N CADENCE JAZZ BOOKS, Cadence Building, Redwood NY 13679. (315)287-2852. Fax: (315)287-2860. **Acquisitions**: Bob Rusch, Carl Ericson. Cadence publishes jazz histories and discographies. Publishes trade paperback and mass market paperback originals. **Publishes 15 titles/year. Receives 10 queries and 10 mss/year. 90% of books from first-time authors; 100% from unagented writers. Pays royalty or makes outright purchase.** Publishes book 6 months after acceptance of ms. Reports in 1 month.

Nonfiction: Jazz music biographies, discographies and reference works. Submit outline and sample chapters and SASE. Reviews artwork/photos as part of ms package. Send photocopies.

Recent Title(s): *The Earthly Recordings of Sun Ra*, by Robert L. Campbell (discography).

CAMBRIDGE EDUCATIONAL, P.O. Box 2153, Charleston WV 25328-2153. (800)468-4227. Fax: (304)744-9351. Subsidiaries include: Cambridge Parenting and Cambridge Job Search. President: Edward T. Gardner, Ph.D. **Acquisitions:** Amy Pauley, managing editor. Estab. 1981. Publishes supplemental educational products. "We are known in the education industry for guidance-related and career search programs." **Publishes 30-40 titles/year. Receives 200**

submissions/year. 20% of books from first-time authors; 90% from unagented writers. Makes outright purchase of $1,500-4,000. Occasional royalty arrangement. Publishes book 8 months after acceptance. Accepts simultaneous submissions.

• Cambridge Educational reports a greater focus on social studies and science.

Nonfiction: Subjects include child guidance/parenting, cooking/foods/nutrition, education, health/medicine, money/finance, career guidance, social studies and science. "We are looking for scriptwriters in the same subject areas and age group. We only publish books written for young adults and primarily sold to libraries, schools, etc. We do not seek books targeted to adults or written at high readability levels." Query or submit outline/synopsis and sample chapters. Reviews artwork/photos as part of ms package. No response unless interested.

Recent Title(s): *Job Search Tactics.*

Tips: "We encourage the submission of high-quality books on timely topics written for young adult audiences at moderate to low readibility levels. Call and request a copy of all our current catalogs, talk to the management about what is timely in the areas you wish to write on, thoroughly research the topic, and write a manuscript that will be read by young adults without being overly technical. Low to moderate readibility yet entertaining, informative and accurate."

CAMELOT BOOKS, Avon Books, The Hearst Corp., 1350 Avenue of the Americas, New York NY 10019. (212)261-6800. Fax: (212)261-6895. **Acquisitions**: Elise Howard, executive editor; Ruth Katcher, senior editor. Camelot publishes fiction for children ages 8-12. Publishes hardcover and paperback originals and reprints. **Publishes 80 titles/year. Pays 6-8% royalty on retail price. Offers $2,000 minimum advance.** Publishes book 2 years after acceptance. Reports back in 4 months. Book catalog and ms guidelines for 8×10 SAE with 5 first-class stamps.

Fiction: Subjects include adventure, humor, juvenile (ages 8-12) mainstream, mystery, suspense. *No picture books.* Submit query letter *only.*

Recent Title(s): *Angela & Diabola*, by Lynne Reid Banks.

CAMINO BOOKS, INC., P.O. Box 59026, Philadelphia PA 19102. (215)732-2491. Fax: (215)732-8288. Website: http://www.caminobooks.com. **Acquisitions**: E. Jutkowitz, publisher. Estab. 1987. Camino publishes nonfiction of regional interest to the Mid-Atlantic states. Publishes hardcover and trade paperback originals. **Publishes 8 titles/year. Receives 500 submissions/year. 20% of books from first-time authors. Pays 6-12% royalty on net price. Offers $1,000 average advance.** Publishes book 1 year after acceptance. Reports in 2 weeks on queries. *Writer's Market* recommends allowing 2 months for reply.

Nonfiction: Biography, cookbook, how-to, juvenile. Subjects include agriculture/horticulture, Americana, art/architecture, child guidance/parenting, cooking/foods/nutrition, ethnic, gardening, government/politics, history, regional, travel. Query with outline/synopsis and sample chapters with SASE.

Tips: "The books must be of interest to readers in the Middle Atlantic states, or they should have a clearly defined niche, such as cookbooks."

[A] **CANDLEWICK PRESS**, Walker Books Ltd. (London), 2067 Massachusetts Ave., Cambridge MA 02140. (617)661-3330. Fax: (617)661-0565. **Acquisitions:** Liz Bicknell, editor-in-chief; Mary Lee Donovan, senior editor (nonfiction/fiction); Gale Pryor, editor (nonfiction/fiction); Amy Ehrlich, editor-at-large (picture books); Liz Gavril, assistant editor. Candlewick Press publishes high-quality, illustrated children's books for ages infant through young adult. "We are a truly child-centered publisher." Estab. 1991. Publishes hardcover originals, trade paperback originals and reprints. **Publishes 200 titles/year. Receives 1,000 queries and 1,000 mss/year. 5% of books from first-time authors; 20% from unagented writers. Pays 10% royalty on retail price. Advance varies.** Publishes book 3 years after acceptance of ms for illustrated books, 1 year for others. Accepts simultaneous submissions, if so noted. Reports in 10 weeks on mss.

Nonfiction: Children's/juvenile. "Good writing is essential; specific topics are less important than strong, clear writing." *Agented submissions only.*

Fiction: Juvenile. *Agented submissions only.*

Recent Title(s): *The Explorer's News*, (history in newspaper format); *What Do Fish Have To Do With Anything*, by Avi (fiction).

C&T PUBLISHING, 1651 Challenge Dr., Concord CA 94520. Fax: (510)677-0374. E-mail: ctinfo@ctpub.com. Website: http://www.ctpub.com. **Acquisitions:** Liz Aneloski, editor. Estab. 1983. "C&T publishes well-written, beautifully designed quilting and needlework books." Publishes hardcover and trade paperback originals. **Publishes 12-18 titles/year. Receives 60 submissions/year. 10% of books from first-time authors; 100% from unagented writers. Pays 5-10% royalty on retail price. Offers $1,000 average advance.** Accepts simultaneous submissions. Reports in 2 months. Free book catalog and proposal guidelines. No SASE required.

Nonfiction: Quilting books, primarily how-to, occasional quilt picture books, children's books relating to quilting, quilt-related crafts, wearable art, needlework, fiber and surface embellishments, other books relating to fabric crafting. "Please call or write for proposal guidelines." Extensive proposal guidelines are also available on their website.

Recent Title(s): *Art & Inspirations*, by Ruth B. McDowell.

Tips: "In our industry, we find that how-to books have the longest selling life. Quiltmakers, sewing enthusiasts, needle artists and fiber artists are our audience. We like to see new concepts or techniques. Include some great examples and you'll get our attention quickly. Dynamic design is hard to resist, and if that's your forté, show us what you've done."

CARDOZA PUBLISHING, 132 Hastings St., Brooklyn NY 11235. Website: http://www.cardozapub.com. **Acquisitions:** Rose Swann, acquisitions editor. "Cardoza is the world's foremost publisher of gaming and gambling books." Publishes trade paperback originals, mass market paperback originals and reprints. **Publishes 175 titles/year. Receives 175 queries and 70 mss/year. 50% of books from first-time authors; 90% from unagented writers. Pays 5% royalty on retail price. Offers $500-2,000 advance.** Publishes book 6 months after acceptance of ms. Accepts simultaneous submissions. Reports in 2 months on queries.
Imprint(s): Gambling Research Institute, Word Reference Library.
Nonfiction: How-to, reference. Subjects include gaming, gambling, health/fitness, publishing, reference/word, travel. "We are expanding into how-to books by qualified and knowledgeable writers." We're also actively seeking travel guides for our sister company Open Road Publishing and multimedia and software titles on all subjects for our sister company, Cardoza Entertainment." Submit outline, table of contents and 2 sample chapters.
Recent Title(s): *Standard Chess Openings*, by Eric Schiller.

THE CAREER PRESS, INC., Box 687, 3 Tice Rd., Franklin Lakes NJ 07417. (201)848-0310. Fax: (201)848-1727. President: Ronald Fry. **Acquisitions:** Betsy Sheldon, editor-in-chief. Career Press publishes primarily paperback and some hardcover nonfiction originals in the areas of job hunting and career improvement, including reference and education; as well as management philosophy titles for a small business and management audience. Career Press also offers a line of personal finance titles for a general readership. **Publishes 50 titles/year. Receives 100 queries and 200 mss/year. 50% of books from first-time authors; 50% from unagented writers. Pays royalty on retail price.** Publishes book 6 months after acceptance of ms. Accepts simlultaneous submissions. Reports in 2 months on queries, 3 months on mss. Book catalog and ms guidelines free.
Nonfiction: Coffee table book, how-to, reference, self-help. Subjects include business/economics, money/finance, recreation, financial planning/careers. "Look through our catalog; become familiar with our publications. We like to select authors who are specialists on their topic." Query with outline, 1-2 sample chapters and SASE.
Recent Title(s): *How to Soar Beyond Your Expectations*, by Danny Cox (self-help/business).

CAROL PUBLISHING, 120 Enterprise Ave., Secaucus NJ 07094. (201)866-0490. Fax: (201)866-8159. Publisher: Steven Schragis. **Acquisitions:** Hillel Black (Birch Lane Press); Jim Ellison (University Books, Citadel Press); Michael Lewis (Citadel Press); Monica Harris (Citadel Press); Carrie Cantor (Birch Lane Press). Carol has a reputation for publishing celebrity biographies for a general audience. Publishes hardcover originals, trade paperback originals and mass market paperback reprints. **Publishes 180 titles/year. Receives 2,000 submissions/year. 10% of books from first-time authors; 10% from unagented writers. Pays 5-15% royalty on retail price. Offers $5,000-25,000 advance.** Publishes book 1 year after acceptance. Accepts simultaneous submissions. Reports in 2 months.
Imprint(s): Birch Lane Press; Citadel Press.
Nonfiction: Biography, cookbook, gift book, how-to, humor, self-help. Subjects include Americana, animals, art/architecture, business/economics, cooking/foods/nutrition, education ethnic, film, gay/lesbian, government/politics, health/medicine, history, hobbies, language/literature, military/war, money/finance, music/dance, nature/environment, philosophy, psychology, recreation, regional, science, sports, travel, women's issues/studies. Submit outline/synopsis, sample chapters and SASE. Reviews artwork as part of ms package. Send photocopies.
Recent Title(s): *Sinatra*, by J. Randy Taraborrelli.

CAROLRHODA BOOKS, INC., Lerner Publications Co., 241 First Ave. N., Minneapolis MN 55401. (612)332-3344. Fax: (612)332-7615. Website: http://www.lernerbooks.com. **Acquisitions:** Rebecca Poole, submissions editor. Estab. 1969. "Carolrhoda Books is a children's publisher focused on producing high-quality, socially conscious nonfiction and fiction books with unique and well-developed ideas and angles for young readers that help them learn about and explore the world around them." Publishes hardcover originals. **Publishes 50-60 titles/year. Receives 2,000 submissions/year. 10% of books from first-time authors; 90% from unagented writers. Pays royalty on wholesale price, makes outright purchase or negotiates payments of advance against royalty. Advance varies.** Publishes book 18 months after acceptance. Accepts simultaneous submissions. Reports in 3 months on queries, 5 months on mss. Book catalog and ms guidelines for 9×12 SASE with $3 in postage. No phone calls.
Nonfiction: Children's/juvenile (pre-kindergarten to 3rd grade). Subjects include biography, ethnic, nature/environment, science, sports. Carolrhoda Books seeks creative children's nonfiction "We are always interested in adding to our biography series. Also seeking books on math and hard sciences." Query with SASE for return of ms. Reviews artwork/photos as part of ms package. Send photocopies.
Fiction: Juvenile, historical, picture books. "We continue to add fiction for middle grades and one picture book per year. Not looking for folktales or anthropomorphic animal stories." Query with SASE, send complete ms for picture books.
Recent Title(s): *Wildlife Watching with Charles Eastman*, by Michael Elsohn Ross (Naturalist's Apprentice nonfiction series); *The Flight of the Union*, by Tekla White (easy reader historical fiction).
Tips: "Our audience consists of children ages four to eleven. We publish very few picture books. Nonfiction science topics, particularly nature, do well for us, as do biographies, photo essays, and easy readers. We prefer manuscripts that can fit into one of our series. Spend time developing your idea in a unique way or from a unique angle; avoid trite, hackneyed plots and ideas."

CARROLL & GRAF PUBLISHERS INC., 19 W. 21st St., Suite 601, New York NY 10010. (212)627-8590. Fax: (212)627-8490. **Acquisitions:** Kent Carroll, publisher/executive editor. Estab. 1983. "Carroll and Graf Publishers offers quality hardcover, trade paperback, and mass market fiction and nonfiction for a general readership. Carroll and Graf is one of the few remaining independent trade publishers and is therefore able to publish successfully and work with first-time authors and novelists." Publishes hardcover and trade paperback originals. **Publishes 120 titles/year. 10% of books from first-time authors. Pays 10-15% royalty on retail price for hardcover, 7½% for paperback. Offers $5,000-100,000 advance.** Publishes book 9 months after acceptance of ms. Reports in 1 month on queries. Book catalog free.

Nonfiction: Biography, reference, self-help. Subjects include business/economics, history, contemporary culture, true crime. Publish general trade listings; are interested in developing long term relations with authors. Query. *Agented submissions only.*

Fiction: Erotica, literary, mystery, science fiction, suspense, thriller. Query. *Agented submissions only.*

Recent Title(s): *Master Georgie*, by Beryl Bainbridge (fiction); *Faust's Metropolis: A History of Berlin*, by Alexandria Richie (history).

CARSTENS PUBLICATIONS, INC., Hobby Book Division, P.O. Box 700, Newton NJ 07860-0700. (201)383-3355. Fax: (204)383-4064. Website: http://www.carstens-publications.com. **Acquisitions:** Harold H. Carstens, publisher. Estab. 1933. Carstens specializes in books about railroads, model railroads and airplanes for hobbyists. Publishes paperback originals. **Averages 8 titles/year. 100% of books from unagented writers. Pays 10% royalty on retail price. Offers advance.** Publishes book 1 year after acceptance. *Writer's Market* recommends allowing 2 months for reply. Book catalog for SASE.

Nonfiction: Model railroading, toy trains, model aviation, railroads and model hobbies. "Authors must know their field intimately because our readers are active modelers. Writers cannot write about somebody else's hobby with authority. If they do, we can't use them. Our railroad books presently are primarily photographic essays on specific railroads." Query. Reviews artwork/photos as part of ms package.

Recent Title(s): *Track Design*, by H. Carstens (model railroading).

Tips: "We need lots of good photos. Material must be in model, hobby, railroad and transportation field only."

CARTWHEEL BOOKS, Scholastic, Inc., 555 Broadway, New York NY 10012. (212)343-6100. Fax: (212)343-4444. Website: http://www.scholastic.com. Vice President/Editorial Director: Bernette Ford. **Acquisitions:** Grace Maccarone, executive editor; Gina Shaw, editor; Sonia Black, editor; Diane Muldrow, editor; Kimberly Weinberger, associate editor. Estab. 1991. "Cartwheel Books publishes innovative books for children, ages 3-9. We are looking for 'novelties' that are books first, play objects second. Even without its gimmick, a Cartwheel Book should stand alone as a valid piece of children's literature." Publishes hardcover originals. **Publishes 85-100 titles/year. Receives 250 queries/year; 1,200 mss/year. 1% of books from first-time authors; 50% from unagented writers. Pays royalty on retail price. Offers advance.** Publishes book 2 years after acceptance of ms. Accepts simultaneous submissions. Reports in 2 months on queries; 3 months on proposals; 6 months on mss/ Book catalog for 9×12 SAE. Manuscript guidelines free.

Nonfiction: Children's/juvenile. Subjects include animals, history, music/dance, nature/environment, recreation, science, sports. "Cartwheel Books publishes for the very young, therefore nonfiction should be written in a manner that is accessible to preschoolers through 2nd grade. Often writers choose topics that are too narrow or 'special' and do not appeal to the mass market. Also, the text and vocabulary are frequently too difficult for our young audience." *Agented submissions or previously published authors only.* Reviews artwork/photos as part of ms package.

Fiction: Fantasy, humor, juvenile, mystery, picture books, science fiction. "Again, the subject should have mass market appeal for very young children. Humor can be helpful, but not necessary. Mistakes writers make are a reading level that is too difficult, a topic of no interest or too narrow, or manuscripts that are too long." *Agented submissions or previously published authors only.*

Recent Title(s): *Tonka® Photo Board Books*, by James Levin (nonfiction); *Little Bill*, by Bill Cosby (picture book series).

Tips: Audience is young children, ages 3-9. "Know what types of books the publisher does. Some manuscripts that don't work for one house may be perfect for another. Check out bookstores or catalogs to see where your writing would 'fit' best."

CATBIRD PRESS, 16 Windsor Rd., North Haven CT 06473-3015. (203)230-2391. **Acquisitions:** Robert Wechsler, publisher. Estab. 1987. Catbird publishes sophisticated, humorous, literary fiction and nonfiction with fresh styles and approaches. Publishes hardcover and trade paperback originals and trade paperback reprints. **Publishes 4-5 titles/year. Receives 1,000 submissions/year. 5% of books from first-time authors; 100% from unagented writers. Pays 2½-10% royalty on retail price. Offers $2,000 average advance.** Publishes book 1 year after acceptance. Accepts simultaneous submissions, if so noted. Reports in 1 month on queries if SASE is included. *Writer's Market* recommends allowing 2 months for reply. Book catalog free. Manuscript guidelines for #10 SASE.

Imprint(s): Garrigue Books (Czech works in translation).

Nonfiction: Humor, law, general. "We are looking for up-market prose humorists. No joke or other small gift books. We are also interested in very well-written general nonfiction that takes fresh, sophisticated approaches." Submit outline, sample chapters and SASE.

Fiction: Literary, humor, translations. "We are looking for writers of well-written literature who have a comic vision,

take a fresh approach, and have a fresh, sophisticated style. No genre, wacky, or derivative mainstream fiction." Submit outline/synopsis, sample chapter and SASE.
Recent Title(s): *Performing Without a Stage: The Art of Literary Translation*, by Robert Wechsler (nonfiction); *It Came with the House*, by Jeffrey Shaffer (humorous fiction).
Tips: "First of all, we want writers, not books. Second, we only are interested in writing that is not like what is out there already. The writing should be highly sophisticated, but not obscure; the approach or, better, approaches should be fresh and humorous. If a writer is more interested in content than in style, that writer should look elsewhere."

CATHOLIC UNIVERSITY OF AMERICA PRESS, 620 Michigan Ave. NE, Washington DC 20064. (202)319-5052. Fax: (202)319-4985. E-mail: cua-press@cua.edu. Website: http://www.cua.edu/cupr. **Acquisitions:** Dr. David J. McGonagle, director. Estab. 1939. "The Catholic University of America Press publishes in the fields of history (ecclesiastical and secular), literature and languages, philosophy, political theory, social studies, and theology. We have interdisciplinary emphasis on patristics, medieval studies and Irish studies. Our principal interest is in works of original scholarship intended for scholars and other professionals and for academic libraries, but we will also consider manuscripts whose chief contribution is to offer a synthesis of knowledge of the subject which may be of interest to a wider audience or suitable for use as supplementary reading material in courses." **Publishes 15-20 titles/year. Receives 100 submissions/year. 50% of books from first-time authors; 100% from unagented writers. Average print order for a first book is 750. Pays variable royalty on net receipts.** Publishes book 1 year after acceptance. Reports in 3 months. Book catalog for SASE.
Nonfiction: History, languages and literature, philosophy, religion, church-state relations, political theory. No unrevised doctoral dissertations. Length: 80,000-200,000 words. Query with outline, sample chapter, cv and list of previous publications.
Recent Title(s): *Ancient Faith and Modern Freedom in John Dryden's "The Hind and the Panther,"* by Anne B. Gardiner (literature).
Tips: "Scholarly monographs and works suitable for adoption as supplementary reading material in courses have the best chance."

CATO INSTITUTE, 1000 Massachusetts Ave. NW, Washington DC 20001. (202)842-0200. **Acquisitions:** David Boaz, executive vice president. Estab. 1977. "We publish books on public policy issues from a free-market or libertarian perspective." Publishes hardcover originals, trade paperback originals and reprints. **Publishes 12 titles/year. Receives 50 submissions/year. 25% of books from first-time authors; 90% from unagented writers. Makes outright purchase of $1,000-10,000.** Publishes book 9 months after acceptance. Accepts simultaneous submissions. Reports in 3 months. Book catalog free.
Nonfiction: Public policy *only*. Subjects include foreign policy, economics, education, government/politics, health/medicine, monetary policy, sociology. Query.

THE CAXTON PRINTERS, LTD., 312 Main St., Caldwell ID 83605-3299. (208)459-7421. Fax: (208)459-7450. Website: http://caxtonprinters.com. President: Gordon Gipson. **Acquisitions:** Wayne Cornell, editor. Estab. 1907. "Western Americana nonfiction remains our focus. We define Western Americana as almost any topic that deals with the people or culture of the west, past and present." Publishes hardcover and trade paperback originals. **Publishes 6-10 titles/year. Receives 250 submissions/year. 50% of books from first-time authors; 60% from unagented writers. Pays royalty. Offers $500-2,000 advance.** Publishes book 18 months after acceptance. Accepts simultaneous submissions. Reports in 3 months. Book catalog for 9×12 SASE.
Nonfiction: Coffee table, Americana, Western Americana. "We need good Western Americana, especially the Northwest, preferably copiously illustrated with unpublished photos." Query. Reviews artwork/photos as part of ms package.
Recent Title(s): *Hatchet, Hands & Hoe*, by Erica Calkins (heritage gardening/history).
Tips: "Books to us never can or will be primarily articles of merchandise to be produced as cheaply as possible and to be sold like slabs of bacon or packages of cereal over the counter. If there is anything that is really worthwhile in this mad jumble we call the twentieth century, it should be books."

CCC PUBLICATIONS, 9725 Lurline Ave., Chatsworth CA 91311. (818)718-0507. **Acquisitions:** Cliff Carle, editorial director. Estab. 1983. "CCC publishes humor that is 'today' and will appeal to a wide demographic." Publishes trade paperback and mass market paperback originals. **Publishes 40-50 titles/year. Receives 1,000 mss/year. 50% of books from first-time authors; 50% of books from unagented writers. Pays 7-12% royalty on wholesale price.** Publishes book 6 months after acceptance. Accepts simultaneous submissions. Reports in 3 months. Catalog for 10×13 SAE with 2 first-class stamps.

- CCC is looking for short, punchy pieces with *lots* of cartoon illustrations.

Nonfiction: Humorous how-to/self-help. "We are looking for *original*, *clever* and *current* humor that is not too limited in audience appeal or that will have a limited shelf life. All of our titles are as marketable five years from now as they are today. No rip-offs of previously published books, or too special interest manuscripts." Query or send complete ms with SASE. Reviews artwork/photos as part of ms package.
Recent Title(s): *Retirement: The Get Even Years*, by Fred Sahnger (over-the-hill humor).
Tips: "Humor—we specialize in the subject and have a good reputation with retailers and wholesalers for publishing super-impulse titles. SASE is a must!"

CELESTIAL ARTS, Ten Speed Press, P.O. Box 7123, Berkeley CA 94707. (510)559-1600. Fax: (510)524-1052. Publisher: David Hinds. **Acquisitions**: Veronica Randall, managing editor. Publishes hardcover and trade paperback originals, trade paperback reprints. "Celestial Arts publishes nonfiction for a forward-thinking, open-minded audience interested in psychology, self-help, spirituality, health and parenting." **Publishes 40 titles/year. Receives 500 queries and 200 mss/year. 30% of books from first-time authors; 10% from unagented writers. Pays 15% royalty on wholesale price. Offers modest advance.** Publishes book 6 months after acceptance of ms. Accepts simultaneous submissions. Reports in 6 weeks on queries, 3 months on proposals and mss. Book catalog and ms guidelines free.
Nonfiction: Cookbook, how-to, reference, self-help. Subjects include child guidance/parenting, cooking/foods/nutrition, education, gay/lesbian, health/medicine, New Age, psychology, women's issues/studies. "We specialize in parenting, women's issues, health and family/parenting. On gay/lesbian topics, we publish nonfiction only. And please, no poetry!" Submit proposal package, including: outline, 1-2 sample chapters, author background and SASE. Reviews artwork/photos as part of ms package. Send photocopies.
Recent Title(s): *Raising A Family: Living on Planet Parenthood*, by Don and Jeanne Elium (parenting).
Tips: Audience is fairly well-informed, interested in psychology and sociology related topics, open-minded, innovative, forward-thinking. "The most completely thought-out (developed) proposals earn the most consideration."

CENTENNIAL PUBLICATIONS, 256 Nashua Ct., Grand Junction CO 81503. (970)243-8780. **Acquisitions:** Dick Spurr, publisher. Publishes hardcover and trade paperback originals and reprints. **Publishes 4-5 titles/year. Receives 20 queries and 10 mss/year. 80% of books from first-time authors; 100% from unagented writers. Pays 8-10% royalty on retail price. Offers average of $1,000 advance.** Publishes book 8 months after acceptance of ms. Reports in 1 week on queries, 2 weeks on proposals, 1 month on mss.
Nonfiction: Biography, how-to. Subjects include Americana, history, hobbies, fishing. "A phone call is easiest way to determine suitability of topic. No poorly researched topics." Submit proposal package, including outline and sample chapters. Reviews artwork/photos as part of the ms package. Send photocopies.
Fiction: Humor, mystery. "We are very selective in this market." Submit synopsis.
Recent Title(s): *Bamboo Rod Restoration*, by Michael Sinclair (how-to); *In Over My Waders*, by Jack Sayer (humor).

CENTERSTREAM PUBLICATIONS, P.O. Box 17878, Anaheim Hills CA 92807. (714)779-9390. Fax: (714)779-9390. E-mail: centerstrm@aol.com. **Acquisitions:** Ron Middlebrook, Cindy Middlebrook, owners. Estab. 1980. Centerstream publishes music history and instructional books. Publishes hardcover and mass market paperback originals, trade paperback and mass market paperback reprints. **Publishes 12 titles/year. Receives 15 queries and 15 mss/year. 80% of books from first-time authors; 100% from unagented writers. Pays 10-15% royalty on wholesale price. Offers $300-3,000 advance.** Publishes book 8 months after acceptance of ms. Accepts simultaneous submissions. Reports in 3 months on queries. Book catalog and ms guidelines for #10 SASE.
Nonfiction: Music history and music instructional book. Query with SASE.
Recent Title(s): *Sunburst Alley, Gibson Les Paul Guitars* by Vic DaPra.

CHANDLER HOUSE PRESS, (formerly Databooks), Rainbow New England Corp., 335 Chandler St., Worcester MA 01602. (508)756-7644. Fax: (508)756-9425. E-mail: databooks@tatnuck.com. Website: http://www.tatnuck.com. President: Lawrence J. Abramoff. Publisher: Richard J. Staron. Vice President of Sales: Irene S. Bergman. **Acquisitions:** Jennifer Goguen, editorial/production manager. Chandler House Press is a general interest nonfiction publisher. "We publish useful and timely books that are tools for living better personal and professional lives." Publishes hardcover and trade paperback originals and reprints. **Publishes 12-15 titles/year. Receives 200 queries and 50 mss/year. 50% of books from first-time authors; 70% from unagented writers. Pays royalty on net sales.** Publishes book 1 year after acceptance of ms. Accepts simultaneous submissions. Reports in 1 month. *Writer's Market* recommends allowing 2 months for reply. Book catalog and manuscript guidelines free.
Imprint(s): Tatnuck Bookseller Press, Professional Development Press.
Nonfiction: Biography, gift book, how-to, illustrated book, reference, self-help. Subjects include Americana, business, history, parenting, personal finance, recreation, regional, relationships, sports, women's issues. Submit outline, 1-3 sample chapters and SASE. Reviews artwork/photos as part of ms package. Send photocopies.
Recent Title(s): *For All Our Daughters: How Mentoring Helps Young Women and Girls Master the Art of Growing Up*, by Pegine Echevarria, MSW (women's issues/parenting).

CHARIOT CHILDREN'S BOOKS, Chariot Victor Publishing, 4050 Lee Vance View, Colorado Springs CO 80918. (719)536-3271. Fax: (719)536-3269. **Acquisitions:** Liz Duckworth, managing editor. "Chariot Children's Books publishes works of children's inspirational titles, ages 1-12, with a strong underlying Christian theme or clearly stated Biblical value." Publishes hardcover and trade paperback originals. **Publishes 40 titles/year. Receives 200 queries and 1,500-2,000 mss/year. 10% of books from first-time authors; 80% from unagented writers. Pays variable royalty on retail price or flat fee depending on the project.** Publishes book 2 years after acceptance of ms. Accepts simultaneous submissions if so noted. Reports in 4 months on queries. Book catalog on request. Manuscript guidelines for #10 SASE.

● Chariot Children's Books is not accepting unsolicited submissions at this time.

Nonfiction: Biography, children's/juvenile. Subjects include religion. Query with SASE.
Fiction: Historical, juvenile, picture books, religious. No teen fiction; currently overwhelmed with contemporary fiction. Accepts queries with SASE from previously published authors *only*.

Recent Title(s): *Volcanoes and Earthquakes*, written and illustrated by Michael Carroll (nonfiction); *Dance of Darkness*, by Sigmund Brouwer (Winds of Light fiction series).

CHARIOT/VICTOR PUBLISHING, Cook Communications Ministries, 4050 Lee Vance View, Colorado Springs CO 80918. (719)536-3271. Fax: (719)536-3269. **Acquisitions**: Cindy Simon, administrative assistant. Chariot/Victor publishes children's and family spiritual growth books. Books "must have strong underlying Christian themes or clearly stated Biblical value." Publishes hardcover and trade paperback originals, both children's and adult, fiction and nonfiction. **Publishes 150 titles/year. 10% of books from first-time authors; 50% from unagented writers. Pays variable royalty on net price. Advance varies.** Publishes book 1-2 years after acceptance of ms. Accepts simultaneous submissions, if so noted. Reports in 2 months on queries. Manuscript guidelines for #10 SASE.
Imprint(s): Rainfall (contact Judith Barnes), **Chariot Children's Books**, **Lion Publishing**.
Nonfiction: Biography, children's/juvenile. Child guidance/parenting, history, religion. Query with SASE.
Fiction: Historical, mainstream/contemporary, religious. Query with SASE.
Recent Title(s): *The Reflective Life*, by Ken Gire (nonfiction); *Peacemakers*, by Jack Cavanaugh (fiction).
Tips: "All books must in some way be Bible-related by authors who themselves are evangelical Christians with a platform. Chariot Victor, therefore, is not a publisher for everybody. Only a small fraction of the manuscripts received can be seriously considered for publication. Most books result from contacts that acquisitions editors make with qualified authors, though from time to time an unsolicited proposal triggers enough excitement to result in a contract. A writer has the best chance of selling Chariot Victor a well-conceived and imaginative manuscript that helps the reader apply Christianity to her life in practical ways. Christians active in the local church and their children are our audience."

N **THE CHARLES PRESS, PUBLISHERS**, The Oxbridge Corporation, P.O. Box 15715, Philadelphia PA 19103. (215)545-8933. Fax: (215)545-8937. E-mail: chsprspub@aol.com. Website: http://www.charlespresspub.com. **Acquisitions**: Lauren Meltzer, editor-in-chief. "Our main areas of interest are counseling, bereavement, death and dying, criminology and self-help." Publishes hardcover and trade paperback originals. **Publishes 10 titles/year. Receives 1,000 queries and 300 mss/year. Pays 7½-12% royalty. Offers $1,000-25,000 advance.** Publishes book 10 months after acceptance of ms. Accepts simultaneous submissions. Reports in 1 month on queries, 2 months on proposals, 3 months on mss. Book catalog ms guidelines free.
Nonfiction: How-to, reference, self-help, textbook. Subjects include child guidance/parenting, health/medicine, psychology, religion, sociology, spirituality, true crime. Query or submit proposal package, including description of book, intended audience, reasons people will buy it and SASE. Reviews artwork/photos as part of the ms package. Send photocopies or transparencies.
Recent Title(s): *How Different Religions View Death & Afterlife*, 2nd ed., by Christopher Johnson, Ph.D. and Marsha McGee, Ph.D.
Fiction: Horror, humor, literary, mainstream/contemporary, mystery, short story collections, suspense. No poetry. Query with synopsis and SASE.

CHARLES RIVER PRESS, 427 Old Town Court, Alexandria VA 22314-3544. (703)519-9197. **Acquisitions**: Lynn Page Whittaker, editor-in-chief. "Charles River Press is a small, independent publishing house committed to bringing to readers the personal stories that illustrate and illuminate historical events and current issues. Our accent is on narrative nonfiction in the areas of race relations, women and multi-cultural history from U.S. and global perspectives." Publishes trade paperback originals and reprints. Publishes 5 titles/year. Pays 5-15% royalty on wholesale price. Offers $0-1,000 advance. Reports in 1 month on proposals. *Writer's Market* recommends allowing 2 months for reply.
Nonfiction: Biography and general nonfiction. Subjects include Americana, ethnic, history (especially African-American), women's issues/studies (especially women's stories), travel memoirs, race relations. Submit proposal package, including outline, 1 sample chapter, letter saying why you have written the book, audience for it, bio and SASE. No phone calls, please.
Recent Title(s): *I Have Arrived Before My Words: Autobiographical Writing of Homeless Women*, by Deborah Pugh and Jeanie Tietjen.
Tips: "I'm interested in personal stories by writers who have achieved deep understanding and insights into those stories and their meaning. I am especially interested in stories of individuals that illustrate historical events and social issues and in academic work that can be adapted to a general audience. In 1998 we will publish an author that came to us through *Writer's Market*. What stood out? An original story (the author was with the Peace Corp in the Ukraine), a good sense of narrative structure, and fabulous writing."

N **CHARLESBRIDGE PUBLISHING**, Trade and School Divisions, 85 Main St., Watertown MA 02472. (617)926-0329. Fax: (617)926-5720. Estab. 1980. Publishes hardcover and trade paperback nonfiction (80%) and fiction for the trade and library markets, as well as school programs and supplementary materials. The Trade Division is "always interested in innovative approaches to a difficult genre, the nonfiction picture book." No novels or nonfiction for older children. The School Division is "looking for fiction to use as literature in the math curriculum and kids activity books (not coloring)." Senior Editor: Harold Underdown. **Acquisitions:** *Trade Division:* Submissions Editor. *School Division:* Elena Dworkin Wright, school division editorial director. **Publishes 20-24 trade books, 2-4 school titles plus school materials and curriculum. Receives 2,500 submissions/year. 10-20% from first-time authors; 80% from unagented writers.** Publishes books 2-4 years after acceptance of ms.
Imprint(s): Talewinds (2 fiction titles/season for Trade Division).

Nonfiction: *Trade Division:* Strong interest in nature, environment, social studies and other topics for trade and library markets. *School Division:* School or craft books that involve problem solving, building, projects, crafts are written with humor and expertise in the field. Submit complete ms with cv and SASE. Exclusive submissions only.
Fiction: *Trade Division:* "Strong, realistic stories with enduring themes." *School Division:* Math concepts in non-rhyming story.
Recent Title(s): *Trade Division:* COW!, by Jules Older (cows); *School Division: Building a Wells Fargo Stagecoach,* by Richard Mansir (nonfiction).

CHATHAM PRESS, Box A, Old Greenwich CT 06870. Fax: (203)531-7755. **Acquisitions:** Jane Andrassi. Estab. 1971. Chatham Press publishes "books that relate to the U.S. coastline from Maine to the Carolinas and which bring a new insight, visual or verbal, to the non-fiction topic." Publishes hardcover and paperback originals, reprints and anthologies. **Publishes 10 titles/year. Receives 50 submissions/year. 25% of books from first-time authors; 75% from unagented writers. Nonauthor subsidy publishes 10% of books, mainly poetry or ecological topics. "Standard book contract does not always apply if the book is heavily illustrated. Average advance is low."** Publishes book 6 months after acceptance. Reports in 2 months. Book catalog and ms guidelines for 6×9 SAE with 6 first-class stamps.

- Chatham Press indicates its need for freelance material has lessened.

Nonfiction: Illustrated books subjects include regional history (Northeast seaboard), natural history, nature/environment, recreation. Accepts nonfiction translations from French and German. Query with outline and 3 sample chapters. Reviews artwork/photos as part of ms package.
Recent Title(s): *Exploring Old Martha's Vineyard.*
Tips: "Illustrated New England-relevant titles have the best chance of being sold to our firm. We have a slightly greater (15%) skew towards cooking and travel titles."

N **CHELSEA HOUSE PUBLISHERS**, Main Line Book Co., 1974 Sprout Rd., Suite 400, Broomall PA 19008. (610)353-5166. Fax: (610)353-5191. E-mail: chelseahouse@worldnet.att.net. **Acquisitions**: Jim Gallagher, editor-in-chief. Chelsea House publishes nonfiction series for young adults and children. Publishes hardcover originals and trade paperback originals and reprints. **Publishes 250 titles/year. Receives 400 queries and 200 mss/year. Makes outright purchase of $3,000.** Publishes book 7 months after acceptance of ms. Book catalog and ms guidelines for #10 SASE.
Nonfiction: Biography, children's/juvenile, reference. Subjects include Americana, animals, art/architecture, business/economics, child guidance/parenting, gay/lesbian, government/politics, health/medicine, history, money/finance, nature/environment, regional, science, sports, travel. "We publish our nonfiction for young adults and children in a series format. If the title fits in an exisitng series it's more likely to be accepted." Query with SASE.
Recent Title(s): *Bill Clinton* (Overcoming Adversity series).

N **CHEMICAL PUBLISHING COMPANY, INC.**, 192 Lexington Ave., Suite 1201, New York NY 10016-6823. (212)779-0090. Fax: (212)889-1537. E-mail: chempub@aol.com. Website: http://www.chemicalpublishing.com. **Acquisitions**: Ms. S. Soto-Galicia, publisher. Chemical publishes professional chemistry titles. Publishes hardcover originals. **Publishes 8 titles/year. Receives 20 queries/year. 50% of books from first-time authors; 100% from unagented writers. Pays 10% royalty on retail price or makes negotiable outright purchase. Offers negotiable advance.** Publishes book 8 months after acceptance of ms. Reports in 3 weeks on queries, 5 weeks on proposals, 2 months on mss. Book catalog and ms guidelines free.
Nonfiction: How-to, reference, applied chemical technology. Subjects include agriculture, analytical methods, chemical technology, cosmetics, dictionaries, engineering, environmental science, food technology, formularies, industrial technology, medical, metallurgy, textiles. Submit outline and a few pages of 3 sample chapters and SASE. Reviews artwork/photos as part of ms package.
Recent Title(s): *Food Proteins*, edited by Nakai and Modler (food technology).
Tips: Audience is professionals in various fields of chemistry, corporate and public libraries, college libraries.

CHESS ENTERPRISES, 107 Crosstree Rd., Caraopolis PA 15108-2607. Fax: (412)262-2138. E-mail: dudley@robert-morris.edu. **Acquisitions:** Bob Dudley, owner. Estab. 1981. Chess Enterprises publishes books on how to play the game of chess. Publishes trade paperback originals. **Publishes 10 titles/year. Receives 20 queries and 12 mss/year. 10% of books from first-time authors; 100% from unagented writers. Makes outright purchase of $500-3,000. No advance.** Publishes book 4 months after acceptance of ms. Accepts simultaneous submissions. Reports in 1 month.
Nonfiction: Game of chess only. Query.
Recent Title(s): *The King in the Endgame*, by Edmar Mednis (complicated endgame play).
Tips: "Books are targeted to chess tournament players, book collectors."

CHICAGO REVIEW PRESS, 814 N. Franklin, Chicago IL 60610-3109. **Acquisitions**: Cynthia Sherry, editorial director. Estab. 1973. Chicago Review Press publishes intelligent nonfiction on timely subjects for educated readers with special interests. Publishes hardcover and trade paperback originals and trade paperback reprints. **Publishes 25 titles/year. Receives 300 queries and 300 manuscripts/year. 30% of books from first-time authors; 50% from unagented writers. Pays 7½-12½% royalty. Offers $1,500 average advance.** Publishes book 15 months after acceptance. Accepts simultaneous submissions. Reports in 2 months. Book catalog for 9×12 SAE with 10 first-class stamps. Manuscript guidelines for #10 SASE.

Nonfiction: Children's/juvenile (activity books only), cookbooks (specialty only), how-to, child guidance/parenting/pregnancy, education, gardening (regional), history, hobbies, regional. Submit outline and 1-2 sample chapters or proposal package (see our guidelines). Reviews artwork/photos.
Recent Title(s): *On Stage! Theater Games and Activities for Kids*, by Lisa Bany-Winters.
Tips: "Please send for our guidelines and read them carefully."

CHILD WELFARE LEAGUE OF AMERICA, 440 First St. NW, Third Floor, Washington DC 20001. (202)638-2952. Fax: (202)638-4004. E-mail: books@cwla.org. Website: http://www.cwla.org. **Acquisitions:** Susan Brite, director, publications. "CWLA is a privately supported, nonprofit, membership-based organization committed to preserving, protecting and promoting the well-being of all children and their families." Publishes hardcover and trade paperback originals. **Publishes 10-12 titles/year. Receives 60-100 submissions/year. 95% of books from unagented writers. 50% of books are nonauthor-subsidy published. Pays 0-10% royalty on net domestic sales.** Publishes book 1 year after acceptance. Reports on queries in 3 months. Book catalog and ms guidelines free.
Imprint(s): CWLA Press (child welfare professional publications), Child & Family Press (children's books and parenting books for the general public).
Nonfiction: Child welfare. Subjects include children's books, child guidance/parenting, sociology. Submit outline and sample chapters.
Recent Title(s): *Peace in the Streets: Breaking the Cycle of Gang Violence*, by Arturo Hernandez (gang and youth violence/education); *Sassafras*, by Audrey Penn (children's picture book on self-esteem/fiction).
Tips: "Our audience is child welfare workers, administrators, agency executives, parents, children, etc. We also publish training curricula, including videos."

CHILDREN'S PRESS, Grolier Publishing, Sherman Turnpike, Danbury CT 06816. (203)797-6802. Fax: (203)797-6986. Website: http://www.grolier.com. **Acquisitions**: Mark Friedman, executive editor; Melissa Stewart, senior editor (science); Dana Rau, associate editor. "Children's Press publishes nonfiction for the school and library market. Our books support textbooks and closely relate to the elementary and middle-school curriculum." Publishes nonfiction hardcover originals. **Publishes 200 titles/year. Makes outright purchase for $500-1,000. No advance.** Publishes book 20 months after acceptance. Book catalog available.
Nonfiction: Children's/juvenile. Subjects include animals, anthropology/archaeology, art/architecture, ethnic, health/medicine, history, hobbies, music/dance, nature/environment, science and sports. Query with SASE. "We publish nonfiction books that supplement the elementary school curriculum."
Recent Title(s): *Extraordinary Jewish Americans*, by Phillip Brooks; *Messey Bessey's School Desk*, by Patricia McKissack (fiction).

CHINA BOOKS & PERIODICALS, INC., 2929 24th St., San Francisco CA 94110-4126. (415)282-2994. Fax: (415)282-0994. Website: http://www.chinabooks.com. **Acquisitions:** Greg Jones, editor. Estab. 1960. "China Books is the main importer and distributor of books and magazines from China, providing an ever-changing variety of useful tools for travelers, scholars and others interested in China and Chinese culture. We are not publishing fiction at this time." Publishes hardcover and trade paperback originals. **Averages 5 titles/year. Receives 300 submissions/year. 10% of books from first-time authors; 95% from unagented writers. Pays 6-8% royalty on net receipts. Offers $1,000 average advance.** Publishes book 1 year after acceptance. Accepts simultaneous submissions. Reports in 3 months on queries. Book catalog free. Manuscript guidelines for #10 SASE.
Nonfiction: "*Important*: *All* books *must* be on topics related to China or East Asia, or Chinese-Americans. Books on China's history, politics, environment, women, art, architecture; language textbooks, acupuncture and folklore." Query with outline and sample chapters. Reviews artwork/photos as part of ms package.
Tips: "We are looking for original ideas, especially in language study, children's education, adoption of Chinese babies, or health issues relating to traditional Chinese medicine. See our website for author guidelines."

CHOSEN BOOKS PUBLISHING CO., LTD., Baker Book House Company, 3985 Bradwater St., Fairfax VA 22031-3702. (703)764-8250. Fax: (703)764-3995. E-mail: jecampbell@aol.com. Website: http://www.bakerbooks.com. **Acquisitions:** Jane Campbell, editor. Estab. 1971. "We publish well-crafted books that recognize the gifts and ministry of the Holy Spirit, and help the reader live a more empowered and effective life for Jesus Christ." Publishes hardcover and trade paperback originals. **Publishes 8 titles/year. Receives 500 submissions/year. 15% of books from first-time authors; 99% from unagented writers. Pays royalty on net receipts.** Publishes book 18 months after acceptance. Accepts simultaneous submissions. Reports in 3 months. Manuscript guidelines for #10 SASE. Catalogs not available.
Nonfiction: Expositional books on narrowly focused themes. "We publish books reflecting the current acts of the Holy Spirit in the world, books with a charismatic Christian orientation." No New Age, poetry, fiction, autobiographies, Bible studies, booklets, academic or children's books. Submit synopsis, chapter outline, résumé, 2 sample chapters and SASE. No response without SASE. No e-mail submissions; query only by e-mail. *No complete mss.*
Recent Title(s): *Beyond Imagination*, by Dick Eastman (world evangelization).
Tips: "We look for solid, practical advice for the growing and maturing Christian from authors with professional or personal experience platforms. No conversion accounts or chronicling of life events, please. State the topic or theme of your book clearly in your cover letter."

N **CHRISTIAN ED. PUBLISHERS**, P.O. Box 26639, San Diego CA 92196. (619)578-4700. Fax: (619)578-2431. E-mail: BibleClubs@cepub.com. Website: http://www.cepub.com. **Acquisitions:** Dr. Lon Ackelson, senior editor. "Christian Ed. Publishers is an independent, non-denominational, evangelical company founded nearly 50 years ago to produce Christ-centered curriculum materials based on the Word of God for thousands of churches of different denominations throughout the world. Our mission is to introduce children, teens and adults to a personal faith in Jesus Christ and to help them grow in their faith and service to the Lord. We publish materials that teach moral and spiritual values while training individuals for a lifetime of Christian service." **Publishes 64 titles/year. Makes outright purchase of 3¢/word.** Reports in 3 months on queries, 5 months on proposals. Book catalog for 9×12 SASE and 5 first-class stamps. Manuscript guidelines for #10 SASE.

Nonfiction: Bible Club curriculum. "All subjects are on assignment." Query with SASE.

Fiction: "All writing is done on assignment." Query with SASE.

Recent Title(s): *A Church Family Celebration*, by Laverne Stroup (Christmas program for all ages).

Tips: "Read our guidelines carefully before sending us a manuscript. All writing is done on assignment only and must be age appropriate (preschool-6th grade)."

CHRISTIAN LITERATURE CRUSADE, 701 Pennsylvania Ave., P.O. Box 1449, Fort Washington PA 19034-8449. (215)542-1242. Fax: (215)542-7580. **Acquisitions:** Willard Stone, publications coordinator. "Publications are carefully selected to conform to our constitutional statement of only producing and distributing books which are true to the inerrant Word of God and the fundamentals of the faith as commonly held by all evangelical believers." Publishes mass market and trade paperback originals and reprints. **Publishes 6-8 titles/year. Receives 50-100 queries and 80-100 mss/year. 90% of books from first-time authors; 100% from unagented writers. Pays 5-10% on retail price.** Publishes book 1 year after acceptance of ms. Accepts simultaneous submissions. Reports in 3 months on proposals. Book catalog free. Manuscript guidelines for #10 SASE.

Nonfiction: Biography. Subjects include religion. Query or submit outline with 3 sample chapters with SASE. Writers must send query before submitting ms.

Recent Title(s): *The Marriage Ring*, by D. Talmadge (marriage, morality, family).

Tips: "We publish books which deal with the following areas: Evangelism, Discipleship, Deeper Spiritual Life and Mission. Our audience consists of 'Deeper Life' readers; missions, adults, and junior high students."

CHRISTIAN PUBLICATIONS, INC., 3825 Hartzdale Dr., Camp Hill PA 17011. (717)761-7044. Fax: (717)761-7273. E-mail: editors@cpi-horizon.com. Website: http://www.cpi-horizon.com. Managing Editor: David E. Fessenden. **Acquisitions:** George McPeek, editorial director. "Our purpose is to propagate the gospel of Jesus Christ through evangelistic, deeper life and other publishing, serving our denomination and the wider Christian community." Publishes hardcover originals and trade paperback originals and reprints. **Publishes 48 titles/year (about 50% are reprints of classic authors). Receives 600 queries and 800 mss/year. 25% of books from first-time authors; 80% from unagented writers. Pays 5-10% royalty on retail price or makes outright purchase. Advance varies.** Publishes book 18 months after acceptance of ms. Accepts simultaneous submissions; "We do *not* reprint other publishers' material." Book catalog for 9×12 SAE with 7 first-class stamps. Manuscript guidelines for #10 SASE.

Imprint(s): Christian Publications, Inc., Horizon Books.

Nonfiction: Biography, gift book, how-to, humor, reference (reprints *only*), self-help. Subjects include religion (Evangelical Christian perspective), Americana. Submit proposal package, including chapter synopsis, 2 sample chapters (including chapter 1), audience and market ideas, author bio.

Fiction: Historical, humor, mainstream/contemporary, mystery, religious, spiritual, young adult. "All books must have an evangelical Christian slant. No poetry." Query with SASE. *All unsolicited ms returned unopened.*

Recent Title(s): *Joy Comes in the Mourning*, by David Johnson (nonfiction); *The Flame and the Fury*, by Esther Vogt (fiction).

Tips: "We are owned by The Christian and Missionary Alliance denomination; while we welcome and publish authors from various denominations, their theological perspective must be compatible with The Christian and Missionary Alliance. We are especially interested in fresh, practical approaches to deeper life—sanctification with running shoes on. Readers are evangelical, regular church-goers, mostly female, usually leaders in their church. Take time with your proposal—make it thorough, concise, complete. Authors who have done their homework regarding our message and approach have a much better chance of being accepted."

CHRONICLE BOOKS, Chronicle Publishing Co., 85 Second St., 6th Floor, San Francisco CA 94105. (415)537-3730. Fax: (415)537-4440. E-mail: frontdesk@chronbooks.com. Website: http://www.chronbooks.com. President: Jack Jensen. Publishing Director: Caroline Herter. **Acquisitions:** Jay Schaefer, editor (fiction); Bill LeBlond, editor (cookbooks); Sarah Putnam, editor (general); Victoria Rock, editor (children's); Debra Lande, editor (ancillary products); (Mr.) Nion McEvoy, editor (general); Leslie Jonath, editor (gardening); Joni Owens, editor (regional); Alan Rapp, (popular culture); Sarah Malarky (popular culture). "Chronicle Books specializes in high-quality, reasonably priced illustrated books for adults and children. Our titles include best-selling cookbooks; fine art, design, photography, and architecture titles; full-color nature books; award-winning poetry and literary fiction; regional and international travel guides; and gift and stationery items." Publishes hardcover and trade paperback originals. **Publishes 200 titles/year. Receives 22,500 submissions/year. 20% of books from first-time authors. 15% from unagented writers.** Publishes book 18 months after acceptance. Accepts simultaneous submissions. Reports in 3 months on queries. Book catalog for 11×14 SAE with 5 first-class stamps. Guidelines available on website.

Imprint(s): Chronicle Books for Children, GiftWorks (ancillary products, such as stationery, gift books).
Nonfiction: Coffee table book, cookbook, regional California, architecture, art, design, gardening, gift, health, nature, nostalgia, photography, recreation, travel. Query or submit outline/synopsis with artwork and sample chapters.
Fiction: Novels, novellas, short story collections. Submit complete ms and synopsis; do not query.
Recent Title(s): *Star Wars Chronicles*, by Deborah Fine and Aeon Inc. (film/popular culture); *The Loneliest Road in America*, by Roy Parrin (short story collection).

CHRONIMED PUBLISHING, P.O. Box 50932, Minneapolis MN 55459-0032. (612)979-3600. Fax: (612)979-3870. Website: http://www.chronimed.com. **Acquisitions**: Jeff Braun, editorial manager. Estab. 1986. Chronimed Publishing publishes authoritative health and disease management titles. Publishes hardcover originals and trade paperback originals and reprints. **Publishes 30-40 titles/year. Receives 600 submissions/year. 30% of books are from first-time authors; 60% from unagented writers. Pays 7-12% royalty on retail price. Offers $1,000-5,000 advance.** Publishes ms an average of 1 year after acceptance of ms. Accepts simultaneous submissions. Reports in 2 months on queries, 3 months on proposals and mss. Book catalog free. Manuscript guidelines free or on website.
Nonfiction: Cookbook, how-to, reference, self-help. Subjects include child guidance/parenting, cooking/foods/nutrition, health/medicine. "We are seeking manuscripts relating to health and chronic disease management from authoritative sources. No New Age material." Query or submit proposal including outline and 1-2 sample chapters. Reviews artwork/photos as part of ms package. Send photocopies.
Recent Title(s): *Quick Meals for Healthy Kids and Busy Parents*, by Sandra Nissenberg.
Tips: Audience is "general consumers concerned about overall good health and people with a chronic illness interested in specific information from medical professionals. Be clear about your book's topic—better to be specific when it comes to writing about health-related issues. Cookbook authors be sure to tell what your recipe-testing process is."

CHURCH GROWTH INSTITUTE, P.O. Box 7000, Forest VA 24551. (804)525-0022. Fax: (804)525-0608. **Acquisitions**: Cindy Spear, director of resource development. Estab. 1984. "Our mission is to provide cutting-edge seminars and publish practical resources to help pastors, churches and individuals reach their potential for Christ; to promote spiritual and numerical growth in churches, thereby leading Christians to maturity and lost people to Christ; and to equip pastors so they can equip their church members to do the work of the ministry." Publishes trade paperback originals. **Publishes 10 titles/year. Pays 5% royalty on retail price.** Publishes book 1 year after acceptance of ms. Accepts simultaneous submissions. Reports in 3 months on queries. Resource catalog for 9×12 SAE with 4 first-class stamps. Manuscript guidelines given after query and outline is received.
Nonfiction: How-to manuals. Subjects include religious education (church-growth related). "Material should originate from a conservative Christian view and cover topics that will help churches grow, through leadership training, new attendance or stewardship programs, and new or unique ministries, or enhancing existing ministries. Accepted manuscripts will be adapted to our resource packet format. All material must be practical and easy for the *average* Christian to understand." Query or submit outline and brief explanation of what the packet will accomplish in the local church and whether it is leadership or lay-oriented. Reviews artwork/photos as part of ms package. Send photocopies or transparencies.
Recent Title(s): *Stop Child Abuse Before It Happens*, by Bill Harper.
Tips: "We are not publishing many *textbooks*. Concentrate on how-to manuals, video curriculum for small group studies and complete resource packets (planning a campaign, program or ministry, step-by-step agenda, resource list, etc., plus audio- or video-cassettes)."

CIRCLET PRESS INC., 1770 Massachusetts Ave., #278, Cambridge MA 02140. E-mail: circlet-info@circlet.com. Website: http://www.circlet.com/circlet/home.html. **Acquisitions:** Cecilia Tan, publisher/editor. "Circlet Press publishes science fiction/fantasy which is too erotic for the mainstream and to promote literature with a positive view of sex and sexuality, which celebrates pleasure and diversity. We also publish other books celebrating sexuality and imagination with our imprints—The Ultra Violet Library and Circumflex." Publishes hardcover and trade paperback originals. **Publishes 6-10 titles/year. Receives 50-100 queries and 500 mss/year. 50% of stories from first-time authors; 90% from unagented writers. Pays 4-12% royalty on retail price or makes outright purchase (depending on rights); also pays in books if author prefers.** Publishes stories 12-18 months after acceptance. Accepts simultaneous submissions. Reports in 1 month on queries, 6-18 months on mss. Book catalog and ms guidelines for #10 SASE.

- Circlet Press currently accepts manuscripts only between April 15 and August 31. Manuscripts received outside this reading period are discarded.

Imprint(s): The Ultra Violet Library (gay and lesbian science fiction and fantasy. "These books will not be as erotic as our others."); Circumflex (erotic and sexual nonfiction titles, how-to and essays).
Fiction: Erotic science fiction and fantasy short stories only. Gay/lesbian stories needed but all persuasions welcome. "Fiction must combine both the erotic and the fantastic. The erotic content needs to be an integral part of a science fiction story, and vice versa. Writers should not assume that any sex is the same as erotica." Submit full short stories up to 10,000 words. *Writer's Market* recommends sending a query with SASE first. Queries only via e-mail.
Recent Title(s): *Things Invisible to See*, edited by Lawrence Schimel (science fiction/fantasy short stories).
Tips: "Our audience is adults who enjoy science fiction and fantasy, especially the works of Anne Rice, Storm Constantine, Samuel Delany, who enjoy vivid storytelling and erotic content. Seize your most vivid fantasy, your deepest dream and set it free onto paper. That is at the heart of all good speculative fiction. Then if it has an erotic theme as well as a science fiction one, send it to me. No horror, rape, death or mutilation! I want to see stories that *celebrate* sex and

sexuality in a positive manner. Please write for our guidelines as each year we have a specific list of topics we seek."

CITADEL PRESS, Carol Publishing Group, 120 Enterprise, Secaucus NJ 07094. Fax: (201)866-8159. E-mail: info@citadelpublishing.com. Website: http://www.citadelpublishing.com. **Acquisitions**: Alan Wilson, executive editor; Hillel Black, executive editor. Estab. 1945. "We concentrate on biography, film, how-to, new age and gaming." Publishes hardcover originals and paperback reprints. **Publishes 60-80 titles/year. Receives 800-1,000 submissions/year. 7% of books from first-time authors; 50% from unagented writers. Pays 10% royalty on hardcover, 6-7½% on paperback. Offers average $7,000 advance.** Publishes book 1 year after acceptance. Accepts simultaneous submissions. Reports in 2 months. Book catalog for $1.

Nonfiction: Biography, film, psychology, humor, history. Also seeks "off-beat material, but no fiction, poetry, religion, politics." Accepts nonfiction translations. Query or submit outline/synopsis and 3 sample chapters. Reviews artwork/photos as part of ms package. Send photocopies with SASE.

Recent Title(s): *Making of Schindler's List*, by F. Palowski (Schindler and Spielberg's vision and how the film was made; rare photographs).

CLARION BOOKS, Houghton Mifflin Company, 215 Park Ave. S., New York NY 10003. Clarion is a strong presence when it comes to books for young readers. Publishes hardcover originals. Publishes 50 titles/year.

- Clarion is swamped with submissions and is not accepting manuscripts at this time.

CLEAR LIGHT PUBLISHERS, 823 Don Diego, Santa Fe NM 87501-4224. (505)989-9590. E-mail: clpublish@aol.com. **Acquisitions:** Harmon Houghton, publisher. Estab. 1981. Publishes hardcover and trade paperback originals. **Publishes 18 titles/year. Receives 100 queries/year. 10% of books from first-time authors; 50% from unagented writers. Pays 10% royalty on wholesale price. Offers advance, a percent of gross potential.** Publishes book 1 year after acceptance of ms. Accepts simultaneous submissions. Reports in 3 months on queries. Book catalog free.

Nonfiction: Biography, coffee table book, cookbook. Subjects include Americana, anthropology/archaelogy, art/architecture, cooking/foods/nutrition, ethnic, history, nature/environment, philosophy, photography, regional (Southwest). Query with SASE. Reviews artwork/photos as part of ms package. Send photocopies (no originals).

Recent Title(s): *Best of Dee Brown-West*, by Dee Brown.

CLEIS PRESS, P.O. Box 14684, San Francisco CA 94114-0684. Fax: (415)864-3385. **Acquisitions:** Frederique Delacoste. Estab. 1980. Cleis Press specializes in feminist and lesbian fiction and nonfiction for the progressive and feminist bookstore market. Publishes trade paperback originals and reprints. **Publishes 12 titles/year. 20% of books are from first-time authors; 75% from unagented writers. Pays variable royalty on retail price.** Publishes book 1 year after acceptance. Accepts simultaneous submissions "only if accompanied by an original letter stating where and when ms was sent." Reports in 2 months. Book catalog for #10 SAE with 2 first-class stamps.

Nonfiction: Subjects include feminist, gay/lesbian and human rights. "We are interested in books that will sell in feminist and progressive bookstores and will sell in Europe (translation rights). We are interested in books by and about women in Latin America; on lesbian and gay rights; on sexuality; and other feminist topics which have not already been widely documented. We do not want religious/spiritual tracts; we are not interested in books on topics which have been documented over and over, unless the author is approaching the topic from a new viewpoint." Query or submit outline and sample chapters.

Fiction: Feminist, gay/lesbian, literary. "We are looking for high quality fiction by women and men. No romances." Submit complete ms. *Writer's Market* recommends sending a query with SASE first.

Recent Title(s): *Annie Sprinkle Post-Porn Modernist: My 25 Years as a Multimedia Whore* (nonfiction); *The Assignment*, by B.R. Johnson (fiction).

Tips: "If I were trying to market a book today, I would become very familiar with the presses serving my market. More than reading publishers' catalogs, I think an author should spend time in a bookstore whose clientele closely resembles her intended audience; be absolutely aware of her audience; have researched potential market; present fresh new ways of looking at her topic; avoid 'PR' language in query letter."

CLIFFS NOTES, INC., P.O. Box 80728, Lincoln NE 68501. (402)423-5050. Website: http://www.cliffs.com. General Editor: Michele Spence. **Acquisitions**: Gary Carey, notes editor. Estab. 1958. "We publish self-help study aids directed to junior high through graduate school audience. Publications include *Cliffs Notes, Cliffs Test Preparation Guides, Cliffs Quick Reviews* and other study guides." Publishes trade paperback originals. **Publishes 20 titles/year. 100% of books from unagented writers. Pays royalty on wholesale price. Buys majority of mss outright; "full payment on**

**FOR EXPLANATIONS OF THESE SYMBOLS,
SEE THE INSIDE FRONT AND BACK COVERS OF THIS BOOK**

acceptance of ms." Publishes book 1 year after acceptance. Reports in 1 month. "We provide specific guidelines when a project is assigned."
Nonfiction: Self-help, textbook. "Most authors are experienced teachers, usually with advanced degrees. Some books also appeal to a general lay audience." Query.
Recent Title(s): Cliffs *Quick Review Microbiology.*

COFFEE HOUSE PRESS, 27 N. Fourth St., Suite 400, Minneapolis MN 55401. Fax: (612)338-4004. Publisher/Editor: Allan Kornblum. **Acquisitions:** Chris Fischbach, managing editor. Estab. 1984. Publishes hardcover and trade paperback originals. **Publishes 14 titles/year. Receives 5,000 queries and mss/year. 95% of books are from unagented writers. Pays 8% royalty on retail price.** Publishes book 18-24 months after acceptance. Reports in 1 month on queries or samples, 4-6 months on mss. Book catalog and ms guidelines for #10 SAE with 2 first-class stamps.
Fiction: Literary novels, short story collections, short-short story collections. No genre. Query first with samples and SASE.
Recent Title(s): *The Cockfighter*, by Frank Monley (fiction); *Avalanche*, by Quincy Troupe (poetry).
Tips: "Look for our books at stores and libraries to get a feel for what we like to publish. No phone calls or faxes."

N **COLLECTORS PRESS, INC.**, P.O. Box 230986, Portland OR 97281-0986. (503)684-3030. Fax: (503)684-3777. Website: http://www.collectorspress.com. **Acquisitions**: Lisa Perry, managing editor. Publishes hardcover and trade paperback originals. **Publishes 8-10 titles/year. Receives 10 queries and 20 mss/year. 75% of books from first-time authors; 90% from unagented writers. Pays 2-10% royalty on wholesale price.** Publishes book 1 year after acceptance of ms. Reports in 1 month on proposals, 3 months on mss. Book catalog and ms guidelines free.
Nonfiction: Biography, coffee table book, gift book, illustrated book, reference. Subjects include art/architecture. Submit proposal package, including market research, outline, 2 sample chapters and SASE. Reviews artwork/photos as part of ms package. Send transparencies or *very* clear photos.
Fiction: Fantasy, historical, mainstream/contemporary, mystery, picture books, science fiction.
Recent Title(s): *James Montgomery Flagg: Uncle Sam and Beyond*, by Nicholas Steward.
Tips: "Your professional package must be typed. No computer disks accepted."

THE COLLEGE BOARD, College Entrance Examination Board, 45 Columbus Ave., New York NY 10023-6992. (212)713-8000. Website: http://www.collegeboard.org. **Acquisitions:** Carolyn Trager, director of publications. "We publish guidance information for college-bound students." Publishes trade paperback originals. **Publishes 30 titles/year; imprint publishes 12 titles/year. Receives 50-60 submissions/year. 25% of books from first-time authors; 50% from unagented writers. Pays royalty on retail price. Offers advance.** Publishes book 9 months after acceptance. Reports in 2 months on queries. Book catalog free.
Nonfiction: Education-related how-to, reference, self-help. Subjects include college guidance, education, language/literature, science. "We want books to help students make a successful transition from high school to college." Query or send outline and sample chapters with SASE.
Recent Title(s): *The College Application Essay*, by Sarah Myers McGinty.

N **COLLEGE PRESS PUBLISHING COMPANY**, P.O. Box 1132, Joplin MO 64802. (417)673-6280. Website: http://www.collegepress.com. **Acquisitions:** John Hunter, managing editor. "College Press is an organization dedicated to support the mission and work of the church. Its mission is the production and distribution of materials which will facilitate the discipling of the nations as commanded by our Lord Jesus Christ." Publishes hardcover and trade paperback originals and reprints. **Publishes 25-30 titles/year. Receives 400 queries and 300 mss/year. 25% of books from first-time authors; 90% from unagented writers. Pays 5-15% royalty on wholesale price. Offers $50-500 advance.** Publishes book 6 months after acceptance of ms. Accepts simultaneous submissions. Reports in 3 months on proposals. Book catalog for 9×12 SAE and 5 first-class stamps. Manuscript guidelines for #10 SASE.
Nonfiction: Textbook, Christian textbooks and small group studies. Subjects include religion, Christian Apologetics. "We seek textbooks used in Christian colleges and universities—leaning toward an Arminian and an amillennial mindset. Do not send unsolicited manuscripts, not realizing our connection to Christian Churches/Churches of Christ." Query with proposal package, including synopsis, author bio, 3 sample chapters with SASE.
Recent Title(s): *Servant-Driven Church*, by Ray Fulenwider (church growth).
Tips: "Our core market is Christian Churches/Churches of Christ and conservative evangelical Christians. Have your material critically reviewed prior to sending it. Make sure that it is non-Calvinistic and that it leans more amillennial (if it is apocolyptic writing)."

N **COMBINED BOOKS, INC**, 476 W. Elm St., P.O. Box 307, Conshohocken PA 19428. (610)828-2595. Fax: (610)828-2603. **Acquisitions:** Kenneth S. Gallagher, senior editor. Publishes hardcover originals and trade paperback reprints. **Publishes 12-14 titles/year. 30% of books from first-time authors; 100% from unagented writers. Pays 8-10% royalty on wholesale price. Offers $1,000-1,500 advance.** Publishes book 1 year after acceptance of ms. Reports in 4 months. Book catalog free.
Nonfiction: Military history. "We publish a series called Great Campaigns. Authors should be aware of the editorial formula of this series." Submit outline, 1 sample chapter and SASE. Reviews artwork/photos as part of ms package. Send photocopies only.

COMMUNE-A-KEY PUBLISHING, P.O. Box 58637, Salt Lake City UT 84158. (801)581-9191. Fax: (801)581-9196. E-mail: keypublish@lgcy.com. **Acquisitions:** Caryn Summers, editor-in-chief. Commune-A-Key's mission statement is: "Communicating Keys to Growth and Empowerment." Publishes trade paperback originals. **Publishes 4-6 titles/year. 40% of books from first-time authors; 75% from unagented writers. Pays 7-8% royalty on retail price.** Publishes book 1 year after acceptance of ms. Accepts simultaneous submissions. Reports in 1 month on queries and proposals, 2 months on mss. Book catalog and ms guidelines with SASE.

Nonfiction: Gift book/inspirational, humor, self-help/psychology, spiritual. Subjects include health/medicine, psychology, men's or women's issues/studies, recovery, Native American. Query with SASE. Reviews artwork/photos as part of ms package. Send photocopies.

Recent Title(s): *Seeking the Silent Stranger: Drawing Your Way Into the Deeper Self*, by Lidia Everett, M.D. and Hyacinthe Kuller-Baron (art/self-improvement/psychology).

COMPANION PRESS, P.O. Box 2575, Laguna Hills CA 92654. Fax: (714)362-4489. E-mail: sstewart@companionpress.com. **Acquisitions**: Steve Stewart, publisher. "We are interested in gay erotic books written for the general reader, rather than the academic." Publishes trade paperback originals. **Publishes 6 titles/year. Receives 50 queries and 25 mss/year. 50% of books from first-time authors; 100% from unagented writers. Pays 6-8% royalty on retail price or makes outright purchase. Offers $500-750 advance.** Publishes book 9 months after acceptance of ms. Reports in 1 month. *Writer's Market* recommends allowing 2 months for reply. Book catalog and ms guidelines for #10 SASE.

Fiction and Nonfiction: Biographies, anthologies, photobooks, video guidebooks. Subjects include: adult, bisexuality, fetishes, homosexuality, nudity, sex symbols and sexual taboos. Query. Reviews artwork/photos as part of ms package. Send photocopies.

Recent Title(s): *Coming of Age*, by Don Lort (sexuality in movies).

COMPASS AMERICAN GUIDES INC., Fodor's, Random House. 5332 College Ave., Suite 201, Oakland CA 94618. **Acquisitions:** Kit Duane, managing editor; Christopher Burt, creative director. "We publish guides to U.S. and Canadian states, provinces or cities." Publishes trade paperback originals. **Publishes 10 titles/year. Receives 50 queries and 5 mss/year. 5% of books from first-time authors; 90% from unagented writers. Makes outright purchase of $5,000-10,000. Offers $1,500-3,000 advance.** Publishes book an average of 8 months after acceptance of ms. Accepts simultaneous submissions. Reports in 6 months. Book catalog for $1.

Nonfiction: Travel guides. "We cannot guarantee the return of any submissions." Query this publisher about its specific format. Reviews artwork/photos as part of ms package. Photographers should send duplicate slides.

COMPUTER SCIENCE PRESS, W.H. Freeman and Company, 41 Madison Ave., New York NY 10010. (212)576-9451. Fax: (212)689-2383. E-mail: rjbonacci@whfreeman.com. Website: http://www.whfreeman.com. **Acquisitions:** Richard J. Bonacci, publisher. Estab. 1974. "Computer Science Press publishes technical books in all aspects of computer science, computer engineering, information systems and telecommunications." Publishes hardcover and paperback originals. **Publishes 5 titles/year. 25% of books from first-time authors; 98% of books from unagented writers. All authors are recognized subject area experts. Pays royalty on net price.** Publishes book 6-9 months after acceptance. Reports ASAP.

Nonfiction: Primarily textbooks. Subjects include computer science, computer engineering, information systems and telecommunications. Also considers public appeal 'trade' books in computer science, manuscripts and diskettes." Query or submit sample chapters of ms. Looks for "technical accuracy of the material and an explanation of why this approach was taken. We would also like a covering letter stating what the author sees as the competition for this work and why this work is superior or an improvement on previous available material."

Recent Title(s): *Programming Visual Basic*, by Gersting (textbook).

Tips: "We are looking for more trade titles on technology's effect on society, politics or business."

COMPUTING McGRAW-HILL, McGraw-Hill Publishing Group, 11 W. 19th St., New York NY 10011. (212)337-4098. Website: http://www.mcgraw-hill.com. **Acquisitions:** Braudon Nordin, editor. Estab. 1992. "Computing McGraw-Hill publishes computer titles for professionals. We're especially strong in emerging technologies." Publishes hardcover and trade paperback originals. **Publishes 120 titles/year. Receives 500 queries/year. 25% of books from first-time writers. 25% from unagented writers. Pays 7½-15% royalty on net price. Advance varies.** Publishes book 9 months after acceptance of ms. Accepts simultaneous submissions. Reports in 1 month on proposals. Book catalog and ms guidelines not available.

Nonfiction: Reference, textbook. Subjects include computers/electronics, data communications. "Writers should keep two things in mind. First: what is the purpose of this book, as distinct from the topic. Second: a clear statement of who the book is intended for." Query with outline, 1 sample chapter and SASE.

Recent Title(s): *Novelle CNA CNE*, by Mueller (programming).

CONARI PRESS, 2550 Ninth St., Suite 101, Berkeley CA 94710. (510)649-7175. Fax: (510)649-7190. E-mail: conari@ix.netcom.com. Website: http://www.readersndex.com/conari. **Acquisitions:** Claudia Schaab, managing editor. Estab. 1987. "Conari Press publishes books that make a difference. We value integrity, process, compassion and receptivity, both in the books we publish and in our internal workings." Publishes hardcover and trade paperback originals. **Publishes 30 titles/year. Receives 1,000 submissions/year. 50% of books from first-time authors; 50% from unagented writers. Pays 12-16% royalty on net price. Offers $5,000 average advance. Publishes book 1-3 years after accep-**

tance. Accepts simultaneous submissions. Reports in 3 months. Manuscript guidelines for 6×9 SASE.
Nonfiction: Psychology, spirituality, women's issues, parenting. No poetry or fiction! Submit outline and sample chapters, attn: Claudia Schaab. Reviews artwork/photos as part of ms package.
Recent Title(s): *Simple Pleasures of the Garden*, by Susannah Seton.
Tips: "Writers should send us well-targeted, specific and focused manuscripts. No recovery issues."

CONCORDIA PUBLISHING HOUSE, 3558 S. Jefferson Ave., St. Louis MO 63118-3968. (314)268-1000. Fax: (314)268-1329. E-mail: Jadoubek@cphnet.org. Website: http://www.cph.org. **Acquisitions:** Rachel Hoyer, editor (adult and youth nonfiction and drama); Jane Wilke, associate editor (children's and teaching resources); Dawn Weinstock, managing editor (devotional collections). Estab. 1869. "We publish Protestant, inspirational, theological, family and juveniles. All manuscripts must conform to the doctrinal tenets of The Lutheran Church—Missouri Synod." Publishes hardcover and trade paperback originals. **Publishes 80-100 titles/year. Receives 3,000 submissions/year. 10% of books from first-time authors; 95% from unagented writers. Pays royalty or makes outright purchase.** Publishes book 1 year after acceptance. Simultaneous submissions discouraged. Reports in 2 months on queries. Manuscript guidelines for #10 SASE.
Nonfiction: Juvenile, adult. Subjects include child guidance/parenting (in Christian context), inspirational, how-to, religion. Query with SASE first.
Fiction: Juvenile. "We will consider preteen and children's fiction and picture books. All books must contain Christian content. No adult Christian fiction." Query with SASE first.
Recent Title(s): *501 Practical Ways to Teach Your Children Values*, by Dr. Bobbie Reed (parenting); *Invasion From Planet X*, by Paul Buchanan and Rod Randall (fiction).
Tips: "Our needs have broadened to include writers of books for lay adult Christians."

CONGRESSIONAL QUARTERLY, INC., 1414 22nd St. NW, Washington DC 20037. (202)887-8640 or 8645. Fax: (202)822-6583. E-mail: swagger@cqalert.com or dtarr@cqalert.com. Website: http://www.books.cq.com. **Acquisitions:** David Tarr, Shana Wagger (CQ Reference), Brenda Carter (CQ Press), acquisitions editors. CQ seeks "to educate the public by publishing authoritative works on American and international government and politics." **Publishes 50-70 hardcover and paperback titles/year. 95% of books from unagented writers. Pays college or reference royalties or fees. Sometimes offers advance.** Publishes book an average of 1 year after acceptance. Accepts simultaneous submissions. Reports in 3 months. Book catalog free.
Imprint(s): CQ Press, CQ Reference.
Nonfiction: All levels of college political science texts. "We are interested in American government, public administration, comparative government, and international relations." Academic reference books, information directories on federal and state governments, national elections, international/state politics and governmental issues. Submit proposal, outline and bio.
Recent Title(s): *Guide to the Presidency*, edited by Nelson (government/law).
Tips: "Our books present important information on American government and politics, and related issues, with careful attention to accuracy, thoroughness and readability."

N **CONSORTIUM PUBLISHING**, 640 Weaver Hill Rd., W. Greenwich RI 02817-2261. (401)397-9838. Fax: (401)392-1926. **Acquisitions**: John M. Carlevale, chief of publications. Consortium publishes books for all levels of the education market. Publishes trade paperback originals and trade paperback reprints. **Publishes 12 titles/year. Receives 150 queries and 50 mss/year. 50% of books from first-time authors; 95% from unagented writers. Pays 10-15% royalty.** Publishes book 3 months after acceptance of ms. Reports in 2 months. Book catalog and ms guidelines for #10 SASE.
Nonfiction: How-to, humor, illustrated book, reference, self-help, technical, textbook. Subjects include business/economics, child guidance/parenting, education, government/politics, health/medicine, history, music/dance, nature/environment, psychology, science, sociology, women's issues/studies. Query or submit proposal package, including table of contents, outline, 1 sample chapter and SASE. Reviews artwork/photos as part of ms package. Send photocopies.
Recent Title(s): *Teaching the Child Under Six, 4th edition*, by James L. Hymes, Jr. (education).
Tips: Audience is college and high school students and instructors, elementary school teachers and other trainers.

CONSUMER PRESS, 13326 SW 28 St., Suite 102, Ft. Lauderdale FL 33330. **Acquisitions**: Joseph Pappas, editorial director. Publishes trade paperback originals. **Publishes 2-5 titles/year. Receives 1,000 queries and 700 mss/year. 50% of books from first-time authors; 70% from unagented writers. Pays royalty on wholesale price or on retail price, as per agreement.** Publishes book 6 months after acceptance of ms. Accepts simultaneous submissions. Book catalog free.
Imprint(s): Women's Publications.
Nonfiction: How-to, self-help. Subjects include homeowner guides, building/remodeling, child guidance/parenting, health/medicine, money/finance, women's issues/studies. Query with SASE.
Recent Title(s): *The Ritalin Free Child*, by Diana Hunter.

N **CONSUMER REPORTS SPECIAL PUBLICATIONS**, (formerly Consumer Reports Books), Consumers Union, 101 Truman Ave., Yonkers NY 10703-1057. Fax: (914)378-2904. **Acquisitions:** Andrea Scott, director. Estab. 1936. Publishes hardcover and trade paperback originals and reprints. Publishes annuals based on material in *Consumer*

Reports magazine. "Titles focus on consumer issues (retirement, money planning, baby products)." **Publishes 10 titles/year. Makes outright purchase.**

Nonfiction: How-to, reference, self-help, automotive. Subjects include health and medicine, automotive, consumer guidance, home owners reference, money and finance. Submit outline/synopsis and 1-2 sample chapters.

Recent Title(s): *The Consumer Reports Money Book* (personal finance).

COPPER CANYON PRESS, P.O. Box 271, Port Townsend WA 98368. (360)385-4925. **Acquisitions:** Sam Hamill, editor. "Copper Canyon Press has remained dedicated to publishing poetry in a wide range of styles and from a full range of the world's many cultures." Publishes trade paperback originals and occasional clothbound editions. **Publishes 10 titles/year. Receives 1,500 queries/year and 500 mss/year. 10% of books from first-time authors; 95% from unagented writers. Pays 7-10% royalty on retail price.** Publishes book 18 months after acceptance of ms. Reports in 1 month. Book catalog free.

Poetry: *No unsolicited mss.* Query with 5-7 sample poems and SASE.

Recent Title(s): *Scrambled Eggs & Whiskey*, by Hayden Carruth.

CORNELL MARITIME PRESS, INC., P.O. Box 456, Centreville MD 21617-0456. (410)758-1075. Fax: (410)758-6849. **Acquisitions:** Charlotte Kurst, managing editor. Estab. 1938. "Cornell Maritime Press publishes books for the merchant marine and a few recreational boating books." Publishes hardcover originals and quality paperbacks for professional mariners and yachtsmen. **Publishes 7-9 titles/year. Receives 150 submissions/year. 41% of books from first-time authors; 99% from unagented writers. "Payment is negotiable but royalties do not exceed 10% for first 5,000 copies, 12½% for second 5,000 copies, 15% on all additional. Royalties for original paperbacks are invariably lower. Revised editions revert to original royalty schedule."** Publishes book 1 year after acceptance. Reports in 2 months. Book catalog for 10×13 SAE with 5 first-class stamps.

Imprint: Tidewater (regional history, folklore and wildlife of the Chesapeake Bay and the Delmarva Peninsula).

Nonfiction: Marine subjects (highly technical), manuals, how-to books on maritime subjects. Query first, with writing samples and outlines of book ideas.

Recent Title(s): *Auxiliary Sail Vessel Operations*, by G. Andy Chase.

[N] **CORNELL UNIVERSITY PRESS**, Sage House, 510 E. State St., Ithaca NY 14850. (607)277-2338. **Acquisitions:** Frances Benson, editor-in-chief. "Cornell University Press is the oldest university press in the country. From our beginnings in 1869, we have grown to be a major scholarly publishers, offering 150 new titles a year in many disciplines." Publishes hardcover originals. **Pays 0-15% royalty. Offers $0-5,000 advance.** Publishes book 1 year after acceptance of ms. Sometimes accepts simultaneous submissions.

Imprint(s): Comstock (Contact: Peter J. Prescott, science editor), **ILR Press**.

Nonfiction: Biography, reference, textbook. Subjects include agriculture/horticulture, anthropology/archaeology, art/architecture, business and economics, education, ethnic, gay/lesbian, government/politics, health/medicine, history, language/literature, military/war, music/dance, philosophy, psychology, regional, religion, science, sociology, translation, women's issues/studies. Submit outline.

Recent Title(s): *Seeking the Spiritual: The Paintings of Marsden Hartley*, by Townsend Ludington (art/art history).

[N] **CORNERSTONE PRESS CHICAGO**, 939 W. Wilson Ave., Suite 202A, Chicago IL 60640. **Acquisitions:** Tom Montgomery, acquisitions editor. "We are evangelical Christians with a wide range of interests. Not all of our books deal directly with religion, but they all must be compatible with an evangelical Christian worldview." Publishes trade paperback originals and reprints. **Publishes 4-6 titles/year. Receives 60 queries and 210 mss/year. 25% of books from first-time authors; 100% from unagented writers. Pays 0-14% royalty on wholesale price.** Publishes book 1-2 years after acceptance of ms. Accepts simultaneous submissions. Reports in 6 months on mss. Book catalog for 6×9 SAE and 2 first-class stamps. Manuscript guidelines for #10 SASE.

Nonfiction: Biography, children's/juvenile, humor. Subjects include art, music, religion. Submit outline and 4 sample chapters with SASE. Reviews artwork/photos as part of the ms package. Send photocopies.

Fiction: Adventure, ethnic, fantasy, historical, horror, humor, juvenile, literary, mainstream/contemporary, mystery, religious, romance, science fiction, short story collections, suspense, young adult. "We have not published much fiction, but we are always looking for new authors. We want to penetrate the secular market place with thoughtful books reflecting a Christian worldview. Christian truth should arise in the story naturally rather than be superimposed. Please, no more romances where a midwestern woman falls in love and marries a pastor." Submit synopsis, 3 sample chapters, an author bio and a cover letter stating what the author hopes to accomplish through his/her work with SASE.

Poetry: "We have published many poetry chapbooks in the past, but we are currently re-evaluating the chapbook format. We may consider doing an anthology of contemporary poetry sometime in the future." Submit 10 sample poems.

Recent Title(s): *C.S. Lewis: Mere Christian*, by Kathryn Lindskoog (theology/literature); *My Son, My Brother, My Friend*, by Dale Willard (fiction).

Tips: "Our fiction titles are aimed at anyone looking for a good story. Our nonfiction titles are aimed at thoughtful adults interested in contemporary social issues, art, music and the Christian life."

CORWIN PRESS, INC., 2455 Teller Rd., Thousand Oaks CA 91320. (805)499-9734. Fax: (805)499-5323. E-mail: jay_whitney@corwinpress.com. **Acquisitions:** Jay Whitney, director of acquisitions. Corwin Press, Inc. publishes leading-edge, user-friendly publications for education professionals. Publishes hardcover and paperback originals. **Publishes**

70 titles/year. Pays 10% royalty on net sales. Publishes book 7 months after acceptance of ms. Reports in 1 month on queries. Manuscript guidelines for #10 SASE.

Nonfiction: Curriculum activities and professional-level publications for administrators, teachers, school specialists, policymakers, researchers and others involved with early childhood-12 education. Seeking fresh insights, conclusions and recommendations for action. Prefers theory or research based books that provide real-world examples and practical, hands-on strategies to help busy educators be successful. No textbooks that simply summarize existing knowledge or mass-market books. Query.

COTTONWOOD PRESS, INC., 305 W. Magnolia, Suite 398, Fort Collins CO 80521. Fax: (970)204-0761. Website: http://www.verinet.com/cottonwood. **Acquisitions:** Cheryl Thurston, editor. "We believe English should be everyone's favorite subject. We publish creative and practical materials for English and language arts teachers, grades 5-12." Publishes trade paperback originals. **Publishes 2-8 titles/year. Receives 50 queries and 400 mss/year. 50% of books from first-time authors; 100% from unagented writers. Pays 10-12% royalty on net sales.** Publishes book 1 year after acceptance. Accepts simultaneous submissions, if so noted. Reports in 1 month on queries and proposals, 3 months on mss. Book catalog for 6×9 SAE with 2 first-class stamps. Manuscript guidelines for #10 SASE.

Nonfiction: Textbook. Subjects include education, language/literature. "We publish *only* supplemental textbooks for English/language arts teachers, grades 5-12, with an emphasis upon middle school and junior high materials. Don't assume we publish educational materials for all subject areas. We do not. Never submit anything to us before looking at our catalog. We have a very narrow focus and a distinctive style. Writers who don't understand that are wasting their time." Query with outline and 1-3 sample chapters. "We are always looking for truly original, creative materials for teachers."

Recent Title(s): *Abra Vocabra—The Amazingly Sensible Approach to Teaching Vocabulary.*

[A] **COUNTERPOINT**, Perseus Book Group, 1627 I St. NW, Suite 850, Washington DC 20006. (202)887-0363. Fax: (202)887-0562. **Acquisitions**: Jack Shoemaker, editor-in-chief. "Counterpoint publishes serious literary work, with particular emphasis on natural history, science, philosophy and contemporary thought, history, art, poetry and fiction." Publishes hardcover and trade paperback originals and reprints. **Publishes 20-25 titles/year. Receives 10 queries/week, 250 mss/year. 2% of books from first-time authors; 2% from unagented writers. Pays 7½-15% royalty on retail price.** Publishes book 18 months after acceptance of ms. Accepts simultaneous submissions. Reports in 2 months.

Nonfiction: Biography, coffee table book, gift book. Subjects include agriculture/horticulture, art/architecture, history, language/literature, nature/environment, philosophy, religion, science, translation. *Agented submissions only.*

Fiction: Historical, humor, literary, mainstream/contemporary, religious, short story collections. *Agented submissions only.*

Recent Title(s): *Tube: The Invention of Television*, by David E. Fisher and Marshall John Fisher (history of science); *Women in Their Beds*, by Gina Berriault (short stories).

THE COUNTRYMAN PRESS, W.W. Norton & Co., Inc., P.O. Box 748, Woodstock VT 05091-0748. (802)457-4826. Fax: (802)457-1678. E-mail: countrymanpress@wwnorton.com. Website: http://www.countrymanpress.com. Editor-in-Chief: Helen Whybrow. **Acquisitions:** Ann Kraybill, managing editor. "We aim to publish books of the highest quality that encourage physical fitness and appreciation for and understanding of the natural world, self-sufficiency and adventure." Publishes hardcover originals, trade paperback originals and reprints. **Publishes 25 titles/year. Receives 1,000 queries/year. 30% of books from first-time authors; 70% from unagented writers. Pays 5-15% royalty on retail price. Offers $1,000-5,000 advance.** Publishes book 18 months after acceptance of ms. Accepts simultaneous submissions. Reports in 2 months on proposals. Book catalog free. Manuscript guidelines for #10 SASE.

Imprint(s): Backcountry Publications.

Nonfiction: How-to, guidebooks, general nonfiction. Subjects include gardening, nature/environment, recreation, regional, travel, country living. "We publish several series of regional recreation guidebooks—hiking, bicycling, walking, fly-fishing—and are looking to expand them. We're also looking for books of national interest on travel, gardening, rural living, nature and fly-fishing." Submit proposal package including outline, 3 sample chapters, market information, author bio with SASE. Reviews artwork/photos as part of ms package. Send photocopies.

Recent Title(s): *Nine Months to Gettysburg*, by Howard Coffin (history).

COUNTRYSPORT PRESS, Building 116, Craig Industrial Park, Selma AL 36701. Fax: (334)872-6443. E-mail: countrysport@tomnet.com. Website: http://www.countrysport.com. **Acquisitions:** Bob Hunter, publisher. "Our audience is upscale sportsmen with interests in wingshooting, fly fishing, fine guns and other outdoor activities." Publishes hardcover originals and reprints. **Publishes 12 titles/year. 20% of books from first-time authors; 90% from unagented writers. Pays royalty on wholesale price. Advance varies by title.** Publishes book 1 year after acceptance of ms. Accepts simultaneous submissions. Reports in 1 month on queries; 3 months on proposals and mss. Book catalog free.

Nonfiction: Coffee table book, how-to, illustrated book, other. Subjects include wingshooting, fly fishing, fine guns, outdoor-related subjects. "We are looking for high-quality writing that is often reflective, anecdotal, and that offers a complete picture of an outdoor experience." Query with outline and 3 sample chapters.

Recent Title(s): *Hunting Upland Birds*, by Charley Waterman (how-to).

CRAFTSMAN BOOK COMPANY, 6058 Corte Del Cedro, Carlsbad CA 92009-9974. (760)438-7828 or (800)829-8123. Fax: (760)438-0398. E-mail: ld-jacobs@msn.com. Website: http://www.craftsman-book.com. **Acquisitions:** Laurence D. Jacobs, editorial manager. Estab. 1957. "Our books must be step-by-step instructions on topics for the professional builder. We do not sell to the do-it-youselfer." Publishes paperback originals. **Publishes 12 titles/year. Receives 50 submissions/year. 85% of books from first-time authors; 98% from unagented writers. Pays 7½-12½% royalty on wholesale price or retail price.** Publishes book 2 years after acceptance. Accepts simultaneous submissions. Reports in 2 months. Book catalog and ms guidelines free.

Nonfiction: How-to, technical. All titles are related to construction for professional builders. Query with SASE. Reviews artwork/photos as part of ms package.

Recent Title(s): *Masonry & Concrete Construction*, by Ken Nolan (professional masonry work).

Tips: "The book should be loaded with step-by-step instructions, illustrations, charts, reference data, forms, samples, cost estimates, rules of thumb, and examples that solve actual problems in the builder's office and in the field. The book must cover the subject completely, become the owner's primary reference on the subject, have a high utility-to-cost ratio, and help the owner make a better living in his chosen field."

N **CREATIVE HOMEOWNER PRESS**, 24 Park Way, Upper Saddle River NJ 07458. (201)934-7100. Fax: (201)934-7541. E-mail: chpress@sprynet.com. **Acquisitions**: Mike McClintock, senior editor (home improvement/DIY); Neil Soderstrom, senior editor (gardening); Kathie Robits, editor (home decorating/design). "Creative Homeowner Press is the one course for the largest selection of quality how-to books, booklets and project plans." Publishes trade paperback originals. **Publishes 12-16 titles/year. Receives 10 queries and 10 mss/year. 50% of books from first-time authors; 98% from unagented writers. Makes outright purchase of $8,000-35,000.** Publishes book 16 months after acceptance of ms. Reports in 6 months on queries. Book catalog free.

Nonfiction: How-to, illustrated book. Subjects include gardening, hobbies, home remodeling/building, home repairs, home decorating/design. Query or submit proposal package, including competitive books (short analysis) and outline and SASE. Reviews artwork/photos as part of ms package.

Recent Title(s): *Color in the American Home*, by Margaret Sabo Wills (home design).

THE CROSSING PRESS, 97 Hangar Way, Watsonville CA 95019. (408)722-0711. Fax: (408)772-2749. Website: http://www.crossingpress.com. **Acquisitions:** Jill Schettler, acquisitions editor. Elaine Goldman Gill, publisher. The Crossing Press publishes titles on a theme of "tools for personal change" with an emphasis on health, spiritual growth, healing and empowerment. Publishes trade paperback originals. **Publishes 40-50 titles/year. Receives 2,000 submissions/year. 10% of books from first-time authors; 75% from unagented writers. Pays royalty.** Publishes book 18 months after acceptance. Accepts simultaneous submissions. Reports in 2 months on queries. Book catalog free.

Nonfiction: Natural and alternative health, spirituality/New Age, empowerment, self-help, cookbooks. Submit detailed outline, sample chapter and credentials.

Recent Title(s): *Recurring Dreams: A Journey to Wholeness*, by Kathleen Sullivan.

Tips: "Simple intelligent query letters do best. No come-ons, no cutes. It helps if you have credentials. Authors should research the press first to see what sort of books we currently publish."

CROSS CULTURAL PUBLICATIONS, INC., P.O. Box 506, Notre Dame IN 46556. Fax: (219)273-5973. E-mail: crosscult@crossculturalpub.com. Website: http://www.crossculturalpub.com. **Acquisitions**: Cyriac Pullapilly, general editor. "We publish to promote intercultural and interfaith understanding." Publishes hardcover and softcover originals. **Publishes 15-20 titles/year. Receives 3,000 queries and 1,000 mss/year. 25% of books from first-time authors; 99% from unagented writers. Pays 10% royalty on wholesale price.** Publishes book 6 months after acceptance of ms. Accepts simultaneous submissions. Reports in 1 month on queries. *Writer's Market* recommends allowing 2 months for reply. Book catalog free.

Nonfiction: Biography. Subjects include government/politics, history, philosophy, religion, sociology, scholarly. "We publish scholarly books that deal with intercultural topics—regardless of discipline. Books pushing into new horizons are welcome, but they have to be intellectually sound and balanced in judgement." Query.

Recent Title(s): *Hidden Immigrants: Legacies of Growing Up Abroad*, by Linda Bell (multicultural).

CROSSWAY BOOKS, Good News Publishers, 1300 Crescent St., Wheaton IL 60187-5800. Fax: (630)682-4785. **Acquisitions:** Jill Carter. Editorial Director: Marvin Padgett. Estab. 1938. " 'Making a difference in people's lives for Christ' as its maxim, Crossway Books lists titles written from an evangelical Christian perspective. Both its expansive fiction line and its nonfiction list present a Christian worldview." Publishes hardcover and trade paperback originals. **Publishes 60 titles/year. Receives 2,500 submissions/year. 2% of books from first-time authors; 75% from unagented writers. Pays negotiable royalty. Offers negotiable advance.** Publishes book 18 months after acceptance. Reports in up to 2 months. Book catalog for 9×12 SAE with 6 first-class stamps. Manuscript guidelines for #10 SASE.

Nonfiction: "Books that provide fresh understanding and a distinctively Christian examination of questions confronting Christians and non-Christians in their personal lives, families, churches, communities and the wider culture. The main types include: (1) Issues books that typically address critical issues facing Christians today; (2) Books on the deeper Christian life that provide a deeper understanding of Christianity and its application to daily life; and, (3) Christian academic and professional books directed at an audience of religious professionals. Be sure the books are from an evangelical Christian worldview. Writers often give sketchy information on their book's content." Query with SASE. No phone queries.

Fiction: "We publish fiction that falls into these categories: (1) Christian realism, or novels set in modern, true-to-life settings as a means of telling stories about Christians today in an increasingly post-Christian era; (2) Supernatural fiction, or stories typically set in the 'real world' but that bring supernatural reality into it in a way that heightens our spiritual dimension; (3) Historical fiction, using historical characters, times and places of interest as a mirror for our own times; (4) Some genre-technique fiction (mystery, western); and (5) Children's fiction. "We are not interested in romance novels, horror novels, biblical novels (i.e., stories set in Bible times that fictionalize events in the lives of prominent biblical characters), issues novels (i.e., fictionalized treatments of contemporary issues), and end times/prophecy novels. We do not accept full manuscripts or electronic submissions." Submit synopsis with 2 sample chaptes and SASE.
Recent Title(s): *A Hunger for God*, by John Piper (Christian living); *The Stain*, by Harry Lee Kraus, Jr. (medical thriller).
Tips: "All of our fiction must have 'Christian' content—combine the Truth of God's Word with a passion to live it out. Writers often submit without thinking about what a publisher actually publishes. They also send full manuscripts without a synopsis. Without a synopsis, the manuscript does not get read."

CUMBERLAND HOUSE PUBLISHING, 431 Harding Industrial Dr., Nashville TN 37211. (615)832-1171. Fax: (615)832-0633. E-mail: cumbhouse@aol.com. **Acquisitions:** Ron Pitkin, president; Julia M. Pitkin (cooking/lifestyle). "We look for unique titles with clearly defined audiences." Publishes hardcover and trade paperback originals, and hardcover and trade paperback reprints. **Publishes 35 titles/year. Imprint publishes 5 titles/year. Receives 1,000 queries and 400 mss/year. 30% of books from first-time authors; 80% from unagented writers. Pays 10-20% royalty on wholesale price. Offers $1,000-10,000 advance.** Publishes book an average of 8 months after acceptance. Accepts simultaneous submissions. Reports in 2 months on queries and proposals, 4 months on mss. Book catalog for 8×10 SAE and 4 first-class stamps. Manuscript guidelines free.
Imprint(s): Cumberland House Hearthside: Julia M. Pitkin, editor-in-chief.
Nonfiction: Cookbook, gift book, how-to, humor, illustrated book, reference. Subjects include Americana, cooking/foods/nutrition, government/politics, history, military/war, recreation, regional, sports, travel. Query or submit outline. Reviews artwork/photos as part of ms package. Send photocopies.
Fiction: Mystery. Writers should know "the odds are really stacked against them." Query.
Recent Title(s): *The Abbott & Costello Story*, by Stephen Cox and John Lofflin (entertainment); *Questionable Remains*, by Beverly Connor (mystery).
Tips: Audience is "adventuresome people who like a fresh approach to things. Writers should tell what their idea is, why it's unique and why somebody would want to buy it—but don't pester us."

[A] **CURRENCY**, Doubleday, 1540 Broadway, New York NY 10036. (212)354-6500. Fax: (212)782-8911. **Acquisitions:** Roger Scholl, senior editor. Estab. 1989. Currency publishes "business books for people who want to make a difference, not just a living." Pays 7½-15% royalty on retail price. Offers advance. Publishes book 1 year after acceptance of ms.
Nonfiction: Business/economics subjects. *Agented submissions only.*
Recent Title(s): *Intellectual Capital*, by Thomas Stewart.

CURRENT CLINICAL STRATEGIES PUBLISHING, 27071 Cabot Rd., Suite 126, Laguna Hills CA 92653. E-mail: info@ccspublishing.com. Website: http://www.ccspublishing.com. **Acquisitions:** Camille deTonnancour, editor. CCS is a medical publisher for healthcare professionals. Publishes trade paperback originals. **Publishes 20 titles/year. Receives 10 queries and 10 mss/year. 50% of books from first-time authors; 80% from unagented writers. Pays royalty.** Publishes book 6 months after acceptance of ms.
Nonfiction: Technical. Health/medicine subjects. Submit 6 sample chapters. Reviews artwork/photos as part of ms package. Send photocopies.
Recent Title(s): *Current Clinical Strategies, Gynecology and Obstetrics, 3rd ed.*, by Paul D. Chan and Christopher R. Winkle (medical reference).

[N] **CYPRESS PUBLISHING GROUP**, 11835 ROE #187, Leawood KS 66211. (913)681-9875. Fax: (913)341-5158. Vice President Marketing: Carl Heintz. **Acquisitions:** William S. Noblitt, JoAnn Heinz. "We are an innovative niche publisher with expertise in direct marketing." Publishes hardcover and trade paperback originals. **Publishes 10 titles/year. 80% of books from first-time authors; 90% from unagented writers. Pays 10-15% royalty on wholesale price.** Publishes book 8 months after acceptance of ms. Reports in 2 weeks on queries, 1 month on proposals and mss. *Writer's Market* recommends allowing 2 months for reply. Book catalog free. Manuscript guidelines for #10 SASE.
Nonfiction: How-to, illustrated book, self-help, technical, textbook. Subjects include business/economics, computers/electronics (business related), hobbies (amateur radio, antique radio), money/finance, psychology (business related), software (business related). Query with proposal package, including outline, 1-3 sample chapters, overview of book. Send photocopies.
Recent Title(s): *The Edison Effect*, by Ron Ploof (adapting to technological change).
Tips: "We use America Online and CompuServe extensively. Our editorial plans change—we are always looking for outstanding submissions. Many writers fail to consider what other books on the topics are available. The writer must think about the fundamental book marketing question: Why will a customer *buy* the book?"

DANCE HORIZONS, Princeton Book Co., Publishers, P.O. Box 831, 614 Route 130, Hightstown NJ 08520. (609)426-0602. Fax: (609)426-1344. Publicity Manager: Naomi Mindlin. **Acquisitions:** Charles Woodford, president. Estab. 1976. Publishes hardcover and paperback originals, paperback reprints. **Publishes 10 titles/year. Receives 25-30 submissions/year. 50% of books from first-time authors; 98% of books from unagented writers. Pays 10% royalty on net receipts. No advance.** Publishes book 10 months after acceptance. Accepts simultaneous submissions. Reports in 3 months. Book catalog free.
Nonfiction: Dance and children's movement subjects only. Query with SASE.
Recent Nonfiction Title(s): *Lugi's Jazz Warm Up*, by Lugi Loraine Kriegel and Francis Roach.
Tips: "We're very careful about the projects we take on. They have to be, at the outset, polished, original and cross-marketable."

DANCING JESTER PRESS, 3411 Garth Rd., Suite 208, Baytown TX 77521. (713)427-9560. E-mail: djpress@aol.com. **Acquisitions:** Ms. Shiloh Daniel, acquisitions editor; Alex Roman (Dancing Dagger Mystery); Dorothy Lawson (Dancing Jester Poetry); Lawrence Jacob, nonfiction editor; Glenda Daniel, fiction editor. "The Dancing Jester Press publishes in order to promote understanding, cooperation, and tolerance." Publishes hardcover and trade paperback originals and reprints. **Publishes 10 titles/year. Imprints publish 5 titles/year. 15% of books from first-time authors; 100% from unagented writers. Pays 4-20% royalty on retail price or makes outright purchase. No advance.** Publishes book 18 months after acceptance of ms. Accepts simultaneous submissions. Reports in 6 months. Book catalog for $2. Manuscript guidelines for #10 SASE and $1.
Imprint(s): Dancing Dagger (mystery); Dancing Jester Press.

- Dancing Jester Press also sponsors the "Dancing Jester Poetry. One Night in Paris Should Be Enough" prize. See the Contests and Awards section for more information.

Nonfiction: Autobiography, children's/juvenile, coffee table book, cookbook, how-to, humor, illustrated book, multimedia (CD-ROM), reference, self-help, textbook. Subjects include animals (rights), anthropology/archaeology, art/architecture, cooking/foods/nutrition (vegan/low-fat only), ethnic, lesbian, government/politics, health/medicine, history (of censorship), language/literature/criticism/theory, music/dance, nature/environment, philosophy, photography, psychology, recreation, religion, science, sociology, software, translation, women's issues/studies. Query with outline and SASE. Does not return submissions. Reviews artwork/photos as part of ms package. Send photocopies or transparencies.
Fiction: Adventure, erotica, ethnic, experimental, feminist, gay/lesbian, historical, humor, juvenile, literary, mainstream/contemporary, mystery, picture books, plays, short story collections, suspense, western, young adult. "For children's mystery imprint we will consider 100-page manuscripts of books easily expandable into series." Query with synopsis, 3 sample chapters and SASE. Does not return submissions. Send a copy only.
Recent Title(s): *Solace of the Aging Male*, by Dan Starky (nonfiction); *Mystery of the Blue Heron*, by Nile Lienad (fiction).

DANTE UNIVERSITY OF AMERICA PRESS, INC., P.O. Box 843, Brookline Village MA 02147-0843. Fax: (617)734-2046. E-mail: danteu@usa1.com. Website: http://www.danteuniversity.org/dpress.html. **Acquisitions**: Adolph Caso, president. "The Dante University Press exists to bring quality, educational books pertaining to our Italian heritage as well as the historical and political studies of America. Profits from the sale of these publications benefit the Foundation, bringing Dante University closer to a reality." Estab. 1975. Publishes hardcover and trade paperback originals and reprints. **Publishes 5 titles/year. Receives 50 submissions/year. 50% of books from first-time authors; 50% from unagented writers. Pays royalty. Negotiable advance.** Publishes book 10 months after acceptance. Reports in 2 months.
Nonfiction: Biography, reference, reprints, translations from Italian and Latin. Subjects include general scholarly nonfiction, Renaissance thought and letter, Italian language and linguistics, Italian-American history and culture, bilingual education. Query first with SASE. Reviews artwork/photos as part of ms package.
Fiction: Translations from Italian and Latin. Query first with SASE.
Poetry: "There is a chance that we would use Renaissance poetry translations."
Recent Title(s): *Trapped in Tuscany*, by Tullio Bertini (World War II nonfiction); *Rogue Angel*, by Carol Damioli (mystery).

MAY DAVENPORT, PUBLISHERS, 26313 Purissima Rd., Los Altos Hills CA 94022. (415)948-6499. Fax: (650)947-1373. E-mail: robertd@whidbey.com. Website: http://www.maydavenportpublishers.com. **Acquisitions:** May Davenport, editor/publisher. Estab. 1976. May Davenport publishes "literature for teenagers (before they graduate from high schools) as supplementary literary material in English courses nationwide." Publishes hardcover and trade paperback originals. **Publishes 4 titles/year. Receives 1,500 submissions/year. 95% of books from first-time authors; 100% from unagented writers. Pays 15% royalty on retail price. No advance.** Publishes book 1 year after acceptance. Reports in 1 month. *Writer's Market* recommends allowing 2 months for reply. Book catalog and ms guidelines for #10 SASE.
Imprint: md Books (nonfiction and fiction).
Nonfiction: Subjects include: Americana, language/literature, humorous memoirs for children/young adults. "For children ages 6-8: stories to read with pictures to color in 500 words. For preteens and young adults: exhibit your writing skills and entertain them with your literary tools." Query with SASE.
Fiction: Humor, literary. Novels: "We want to focus on novels junior and senior high school teachers can share with their reluctant readers in their classrooms."

Recent Title(s): *Just a Little Off the Top*, by Linda Ropes (beautician's humorous essays) *The Ghost, the Gold and the Whippoorwill*, by Frank J. Nuckols (juvenile literature).
Tips: "We prefer books which can be *used* in high schools as supplementary readings in English or creative writing courses. Reading skills have to be taught, and novels by humorous authors can be more pleasant to read than Hawthorne's or Melville's novels, war novels, or novels about past generations. Humor has a place in literature. Since the TV-oriented youth in schools today do not like to read or to write, why not create books for that impressionable and captive audience? Great to work with talented writers especially when writers are happy and inspired within themselves."

JONATHAN DAVID PUBLISHERS, INC., 68-22 Eliot Ave., Middle Village NY 11379-1194. (718)456-8611. Fax: (718)894-2818. E-mail: info@jonathandavidonline.com. Website: http://www.jonathandavidonline.com. **Acquisitions:** Alfred J. Kolatch, editor-in-chief. Estab. 1948. Jonathan David publishes "popular Judaica." Publishes hardcover and trade paperback originals and reprints. **Publishes 20-25 titles/year. 50% of books from first-time authors; 90% from unagented writers. Pays royalty or makes outright purchase.** Publishes book 18 months after acceptance of ms. Reports in 2 months on queries. Book catalog for 6×9 SAE with 4 first-class stamps.

- This publisher has expressed an interest in seeing more projects geared toward children.

Nonfiction: Cookbook, how-to, reference, self-help. Submit outline, 1 sample chapter and SASE.
Recent Title(s): *The New Baseball Catalog*, by Dan Schlossberg.

HARLAN DAVIDSON, INC., 773 Glenn Ave., Wheeling IL 60090-6000. (847)541-9720. Fax: (847)541-9830. E-mail: harlandavidson@harlandavidson.com. Website: http://www.harlandavidson.com. **Acquisitions:** Andrew J. Davidson, publisher. Harlan Davidson publishes college textbooks in American history, women's and European history, and political science. Estab. 1972. Publishes college texts, both hardcover and paperback. **Publishes 6-15 titles/year. Receives 100 queries and 15 mss/year. 100% of books from unagented writers. Manuscripts contracted as work for hire. Pays royalty on net.** Publishes book 10 months after acceptance of ms. Accepts simultaneous submissions. Reports in 3 months on proposals. Book catalog free.
Imprint(s): Forum Press, Inc., Crofts Classics.
Nonfiction: Textbooks. Subjects include business, ethnic history, government, history (main list), regional and state histories, women's issues/studies. "Because we are a college textbook publisher, academic credentials are extremely important. We usually find our own authors for a need in the field that we identify, but we are also receptive to ideas brought to us by qualified professionals, in history, especially." Submit proposal package, including outline, brief description of proposed book, its market and competition and a recent vita.
Recent Title(s): *"We Are Still Here:" American Indians in the Twentieth Century*, by Peter Iverson.

DAW BOOKS, INC., Penguin Putnam Inc., 375 Hudson St., 3rd Floor, New York NY 10014-3658. Publishers: Elizabeth Wollheim and Sheila Gilbert. **Acquisitions:** Peter Stampfel, submissions editor. Estab. 1971. Publishes science fiction and fantasy hardcover and paperback originals and reprints. Publishes 60-80 titles/year. Pays in royalties with an advance negotiable on a book-by-book basis. Sends galleys to author. Simultaneous submissions "returned unread at once, unless prior arrangements are made by agent." Reports in 6 weeks "or longer, if a second reading is required." Book catalog free.
Fiction: "We are interested in science fiction and fantasy novels. We need science fiction more than fantasy right now, but we're still looking for both. We like character-driven books with attractive characters. We're not looking for horror novels, but we are looking for mainstream suspense thrillers. We accept both agented and unagented manuscripts. Long books are absolutely not a problem. We are not seeking collections of short stories or ideas for anthologies. We do not want any nonfiction manuscripts." Submit complete ms. *Writer's Market* recommends sending a query with SASE first.
Recent Title(s): *River of Blue Fire*, by Tad Williams (science fiction).

DAWN PUBLICATIONS, 14618 Tyler Foote Rd., Nevada City CA 95959. (800)545-7475. Fax: (530)478-7541. E-mail: Dawnpub@oro.net. Website: http://www.dawnpub.com. **Acquisitions:** Glenn J. Hovemann, editor. "Dawn Publications is dedicated to inspiring in children a sense of appreciation for all life on earth." Publishes hardcover and trade paperback originals. **Publishes 6 titles/year. Receives 250 queries and 1,500 mss/year. 35% of books from first-time authors; 100% from unagented writers. Pays royalty on wholesale price.** Publishes book 1 year after acceptance of ms. Accepts simultaneous submissions. Reports in 2 months. Book catalog and ms guidelines for #10 SASE.
Nonfiction: Children's/juvenile. Nature awareness and inspiration. Query with SASE.
Fiction: Children's juvenile. Nature awareness and inspiration. Query with SASE.
Recent Title(s): *A Drop Around the World*, by Barbara Shaw McKinney (explores the water cycle); *Walking with Mama*, by Barbara Stynes (fiction/nature).

DAYBREAK BOOKS, Rodale Press, Inc., 733 Third Ave., 15th Floor, New York NY 10017-3204. **Acquisitions:** Karen Kelly, editorial director. "Daybreak Books explore all aspects of spirituality and humanity through a variety of voices, viewpoints and approaches." Publishes hardcover and trade paperback originals. **Publishes 9-12 titles/year. Pays 6-15% royalty on retail price.** Publishes book 12-18 months after acceptance of ms. Accepts simultaneous submissions. Reports in 1 month on queries, 2 months on proposals and mss. Book catalog and ms guidelines free.
Nonfiction: Spirituality, inspirational. Query with proposal package including outline, 1-2 sample chapters and author's résumé. Prefers agented submissions.
Recent Title(s): *Love Yourself Thin*, by Victoria Moran.

DEAD LETTER, St. Martin's Press, 175 Fifth Ave., New York NY 10010. (212)674-5151. **Acquisitions:** Joe Veltre, editor. Publishes mass market paperback originals and reprints. **Publishes 36 titles/year. 15% of books from first-time authors; 7% from unagented writers. Pays variable royalty on net price. Advance varies.** Accepts simultaneous submissions. Book catalog and ms guidelines not available.
Fiction: Mystery. Query with synopsis, 3 sample chapters and SASE.
Recent Title(s): *A Stiff Risotto*, by Lou Jane Temple.

DEARBORN FINANCIAL PUBLISHING, INC., 155 N. Wacker Dr., Chicago IL 60606-1719. (312)836-4400. Fax: (312)836-1021. Website: http://www.dearborn.com. **Acquisitions:** Diana Faulhaber (real estate); Cynthia Zigmund (finance); Anne Shropshire (insurance). Estab. 1959. "We provide products and services for information, education and training globally. We are highly focused in niche markets and expect to be a recognized leader in each market segment we serve." Publishes hardcover and paperback originals. **Publishes 200 titles/year. Receives 200 submissions/year. 50% of books from first-time authors; 50% from unagented writers. Pays 1-15% royalty on wholesale price.** Publishes book 6 months after acceptance. Accepts simultaneous submissions. Reports in 1 month. Book catalog and ms guidelines free.

- Dearborn was purchased by Kaplan Educational Centers, a subsidiary of the Washington Post Company.

Imprint(s): Upstart Publishing Co.
Nonfiction: How-to, reference, textbooks. Subjects include small business, real estate, insurance, banking, securities, money/finance. Query.
Recent Title(s): *Modern Real Estate Practice, 14th edition*, by Galaty, Allaway, Kyle.
Tips: "People seeking real estate, insurance, broker's licenses are our audience; also professionals in these areas. Additionally, we publish for those interested in managing their finances or people in starting and running a small business."

IVAN R. DEE, INC., 1332 N. Halsted St., Chicago IL 60622-2637. (312)787-6262. Fax: (312)787-6269. E-mail: elephant@ivanrdee.com. Website: http://www.ivanrdee.com. **Acquisitions:** Ivan R. Dee, president. Estab. 1988. Ivan R. Dee publishes serious nonfiction for general informed readers. Publishes hardcover originals and trade paperback originals and reprints. **Publishes 35 titles/year. 10% of books from first-time authors; 75% from unagented writers. Pays royalty.** Publishes book 9 months after acceptance. Reports in 1 month on queries. *Writer's Market* recommends allowing 2 months for reply. Book catalog free.
Imprint(s): Elephant Paperbacks.
Nonfiction: History, literature and letters, biography, politics, contemporary affairs, theater. Submit outline and sample chapters. Reviews artwork/photos as part of ms package.
Recent Title(s): *Chekov*, by Philip Callow (biography).
Tips: "We publish for an intelligent lay audience and college course adoptions."

DEL REY BOOKS, Ballantine Books, 201 E. 50th St., New York NY 10022-7703. (212)572-2677. E-mail: delrey@randomhouse.com. Website: http://www.randomhouse.com/delrey/. Executive Editor: Shelly Shapiro. Senior Editor: Veronica Chapman. **Acquisitions:** Jill Benjamin. Estab. 1977. Del Rey publishes top level fantasy and science fiction. "In terms of mass market, we basically created the field of fantasy bestsellers. Not that it didn't exist before, but we put the mass into mass market." Publishes hardcover, trade paperback, and mass market originals and mass market paperback reprints. **Publishes 60 titles/year. Receives 1,900 submissions/year. 10% of books from first-time authors; 40% from unagented writers. Pays royalty on retail price. Offers competitive advance.** Publishes book 1 year after acceptance. Reports in 6 months, occasionally longer. Writer's guidelines for #10 SASE.
Fiction: Fantasy ("should have the practice of magic as an essential element of the plot"), science fiction ("well-plotted novels with good characterization, exotic locales, and detailed alien cultures"). Query first to Jill Benjamin with detailed outline and synopsis of story from beginning to end. *No unsolicited mss.*
Recent Title(s): *First King of Shamara*, by Terry Brooks.
Tips: "Del Rey is a reader's house. Pay particular attention to plotting and a satisfactory conclusion. It must be/feel believable. That's what the readers like."

DELACORTE PRESS, Bantam Doubleday Dell, 1540 Broadway, New York NY 10036. (212)354-6500. Editor-in-Chief: Leslie Schnur. **Acquisitions:** (Ms.) Jackie Cantor (women's fiction); Steve Ross (commercial nonfiction and fiction). Publishes hardcover and trade paperback originals. **Publishes 36 titles/year. Pays 7½-12½% royalty. Advance varies.** Publishes book 2 years after acceptance, but varies. Accepts simultaneous submissions. Reports in 4 months. Guidelines for 9×12 SASE.
Nonfiction and Fiction: Query with outline, first 3 chapters or brief proposal. No children's, young adult or poetry.
Recent Title(s): *A Day in the Life: The Music and Artistry of the Beatles*, by Mark Hetsgaard; *The Horse Whisperer*, by Nicholas Evans.

DELL PUBLISHING ISLAND, Bantam Doubleday Dell, 1540 Broadway, New York NY 10036. (212)354-6500. **Acquisitions**: Leslie Schnur, editor-in-chief. Publishes trade paperback originals and reprints. Publishes bestseller fiction and nonfiction. **Publishes 12 titles/year. 15% of books from first-time authors; 5% from unagented writers. Pay 7½-12½% royalty on retail price. Advance varies.** Publishes book 1 year after acceptance of ms. Accepts simultaneous submissions. Reports in 6 months on queries. Book catalog for 9×12 SAE and 3 first class stamps.

Nonfiction: subjects include government/politics, health/medicine, history, psychology. Query with synopsis, 2-3 sample chapters and SASE.
Fiction: Mystery, romance, suspense.
Recent Title(s): *Runaway Jury*, by John Grisham (suspense).

DELL TRADE PAPERBACKS, Dell Publishing, Bantam Doubleday Dell, 1540 Broadway, New York NY 10036. (212)354-6500. **Acquisitions**: Leslie Schnur, editor-in-chief. Publishes trade paperback originals, mostly light, humorous material and books on pop culture. **Publishes 36 titles/year. 15% of books from first-time authors; 5% from unagented writers. Pays 7½-12½% royalty on retail price. Advance varies.** Publishes book 1 year after acceptance of ms. Accepts simultaneous submissions. Reports in 4-6 months on queries. Book catalog for 9×12 SAE and 3 first class stamps.
Nonfiction: Humor, self-help, pop culture. Query with synopsis, 2-3 sample chapters and SASE.
Recent Title(s): *Seven Weeks to Better Sex*, by Domeena Renshan.

DELTA TRADE PAPERBACKS, Dell Publishing, Bantam Doubleday Dell, 1540 Broadway, New York NY 10036. (212)354-6500. **Acquisitions**: Leslie Schnur, editor-in-chief. Publishes trade paperback originals, mostly light, humorous material and books on pop culture. **Publishes 36 titles/year. 15% of books from first-time authors; 5% from unagented writers. Pays 7½-12½% royalty on retail price. Advance varies.** Publishes book 1 year after acceptance of ms. Accepts simultaneous submissions. Reports in 4-6 months on queries. Book catalog for 9×12 SAE and 3 first class stamps.
Nonfiction: Biography, memoir. Subjects include child guidance/parenting, ethnic, health/medicine, music/dance. Query with synopsis, 2-3 sample chapters and SASE.
Fiction: Erotica, literary, short story collections. Query with synopsis, 2-3 sample chapters or complete ms and SASE.
Recent Title(s): *Oasis: What's the Story*, by Ian Robertson (nonfiction/music); *Fast Greens*, by Turk Pipkin (fiction).

THE DENALI PRESS, P.O. Box 021535, Juneau AK 99802-1535. (907)586-6014. Fax: (907)463-6780. E-mail: denalipr@alaska.net. Website: http://www.alaska.net/~denalipr/index.html. **Acquisitions:** Alan Schorr, editorial director. Editorial Associate: Sally Silvas-Ottumwa. Estab. 1986. The Denali Press looks for reference works suitable for the educational, professional and library market. Publishes trade paperback originals. **Publishes 5 titles/year. Receives 120 submissions/year. 50% of books from first-time authors; 80% from unagented writers. Pays 10% royalty on wholesale price or makes outright purchase.** Publishes book 1 year after acceptance. Accepts simultaneous submissions. Reports in 1 month. *Writer's Market* recommends allowing 2 months for reply. Query. Book catalog free.
Nonfiction: Reference. Subjects include Americana, Alaskana, anthropology, ethnic, government/politics, history, recreation. "We need reference books—ethnic, refugee and minority concerns." Query with outline and sample chapters. All unsolicited mss are tossed. Author must contact prior to sending ms.
Recent Title(s): *An Ocean of Oil: A Century of Political Struggle Over Petroleum*, by Robert Sollen.

T.S. DENISON & CO., INC., 9601 Newton Ave. S., Minneapolis MN 55431-2590. (612)888-6404. Fax: (612)888-6318. Director of Product Development: Sherrill B. Flora. **Acquisitions:** Danielle de Gregory, acquisitions editor. Estab. 1876. T.S. Denison publishes supplemental educational materials; teacher aid materials. **Receives 1,500 submissions/year. 20% of books from first-time authors; 100% from unagented writers. No advance. Makes outright purchase.** Publishes book 2 years after acceptance. Reports in 2 months. Book catalog and ms guidelines for 9×12 SASE with 3 first-class stamps.
Nonfiction: Specializes in early childhood, elementary and middle school teaching aids. Submit complete ms. *Writer's Market* recommends query with SASE first. Reviews artwork/photos as part of ms package. Send prints if photos are to accompany ms.
Recent Title(s): *Teaching Real Painting*, by Darry Bell-Myers (art projects for elementary students).

DIAL BOOKS FOR YOUNG READERS, Penguin Putnam Inc., 345 Hudson St., 3rd Floor, New York NY 10014. (212)366-2800. Editorial Assistant: Victoria Wells. **Acquisitions:** Submissions Editor. Dial publishes quality picture books for ages 18 months-8 years, lively, believable novels for middle readers and young adults, and well-researched manuscripts for young adults and middle readers. Publishes hardcover originals. **Publishes 80 titles/year. Receives 8,000 submissions/year. 10% of books from first-time authors. Pays variable royalty and advance.** Reports in 4 months.
Nonfiction: Juvenile picture books, middle grade and young adult books. Especially looking for "quality picture books and well-researched young adult and middle-reader manuscripts that lend themselves to attractive illustration." Not interested in alphabet books, riddle and game books, and early concept books. Responds to query letters outlining book and giving writer's credentials. Include SASE. *No unsolicited mss.*
Fiction: Juvenile picture books, young adult books. Adventure, fantasy, historical, humor, mystery, contemporary romance, suspense. Especially looking for "lively and well written novels for middle grade and young adult children involving a convincing plot and believable characters. The subject matter or theme should not already be overworked in previously published books. The approach must not be demeaning to any minority group, nor should the roles of female characters (or others) be stereotyped, though we don't think books should be didactic, or in any way message-y. No topics inappropriate for the juvenile, young adult, and middle grade audiences. No plays." *Agented mss only.* Responds to query letter with SASE outlining book and author's credentials only. *No unsolicited mss.*

Recent Title(s): *I Am Rosa Parks*, by Rosa Parks (easy-to read autobiography); *I Did It, I'm Sorry*, by Caralyn and Mark Buehner (picture book).
Tips: "Our readers are anywhere from preschool age to teenage. Picture books must have strong plots, lots of action, unusual premises, or universal themes treated with freshness and originality. Humor works well in these books. A very well thought out and intelligently presented book has the best chance of being taken on. Genre isn't as much of a factor as presentation."

[A] **DIAL PRESS**, Dell Publishing, 1540 Broadway, New York NY 10036. (212)354-6500. Fax: (212)782-9698. Website: http://www.bbd.com. **Acquisitions:** Susan Kamil, vice president, editorial director. Estab. 1924. "Dial Press publishes quality fiction and nonfiction." **Publishes 6 titles/year. Receives 200 queries and 450 mss/year. 75% of books from first-time authors. Pays royalty on retail price. Offers $25,000-500,000 advance.** Publishes book 1-2 years after acceptance of ms. Accepts simultaneous submissions. Reports in 2 months.
Nonfiction: Biography, memoirs, serious nonfiction, cultural criticism. Subjects include Americana, art/architecture, government/politics, health/medicine, history, psychology, women's issues/studies. *Agented submissions only;* query by letter with SASE.
Fiction: Ethnic, literary. *Agented submissions only;* query with SASE.
Recent Title(s): *The Last Gift of Time*, by Carolyn Heilbrun (essays); *Drinking: A Love Story*, by Caroline Knapp (memoir).

DIMI PRESS, 3820 Oak Hollow Lane, SE, Salem OR 97302-4774. (503)364-7698. Fax: (503)364-9727. E-mail: dickbook@aol.com. Website: http://www.open.org/dicklutz/DIMI_PRESS.html. **Acquisitions:** Dick Lutz, president. "We provide accurate information about unusual things in nature." Publishes trade paperback originals. **Publishes 5 titles/year. Receives 100-150 queries and 20-25 mss/year. 80% of books from first-time authors; 90% from unagented writers. Pays 10% royalty on net receipts. No advance.** Publishes book 9 months after acceptance of ms. Accepts simultaneous submissions. Reports in 2 weeks on queries and proposals, 1 month on mss. *Writer's Market* recommends allowing 2 months for reply. Book catalog and ms guidelines for #10 SASE.
Nonfiction: "Soliciting manuscripts on unusual things in nature, such as unusual animals or natural formations. Also natural disasters such as volcanic eruptions, earthquakes, or floods. Preferably of the world's 'worst.' Also related manuscripts on nature/travel/environment. No travel guides." Query with outline and 1 sample chapter and SASE, if answer is desired. Reviews artwork/photos as part of ms package. Send photocopies.
Recent Title(s): *Hidden Amazon*, by Lutz.
Tips: "Audience is adults who wish to learn something and are interested in unusual travel excursions. Please send for guidelines before submitting."

[N] **DO-IT-YOURSELF LEGAL PUBLISHERS**, 60 Park Place, Suite 103, Newark NJ 07102. (973)639-0400. Fax: (973)639-1801. **Acquisitions:** Dan Benjamin, associate editor; Anne Torrey, editorial assistant. Publishes trade paperback originals. **Publishes 6 titles/year. Imprint publishes 2 titles/year. Receives 25 queries/year. Pays 15-20% royalty on wholesale price. No advance.** Publishes book 1 year after acceptance of ms. Accepts simultaneous submissions. Reports in 1 month on queries and proposals, 3 months on mss.
Imprint(s): Selfhelper Law Press of America.
Nonfiction: How-to (law topics), self-help (law topics). Subject matter should deal with self-help law topics that instruct the lay person on how to undertake legal tasks without the use of attorney or other high cost experts. Query.
Recent Title(s): *Peaceful Divorce* or *Separation: How to Draw up Your Settlement Agreement With Your Spouse*, by Benji O. Anosike.
Tips: "The fundamental premise underlying our works is that the simplest problems can be effectively handled by anyone with average common sense and a competent guidebook."

DORAL PUBLISHING, INC., 8560 SW Salish Lane, #300, Wilsonville OR 97070-9612. (503)682-3307. Fax: (503)682-2648. E-mail: doralpub@easystreet.com. Website: http://www.doralpubl.com. **Acquisitions:** Mark Anderson, executive editor; Joan Bailey, editor (Swan Valley Press). "We publish only books about dogs and dog-related topics, mostly geared for pure-bred dog owners and showing." Publishes hardcover and trade paperback originals. **Publishes 7 titles/year. Receives 30 queries and 15 mss/year. 60% of mss from first-time authors, 85% from unagented writers. Pays 10% royalty on wholesale price.** Publishes book 6 months after acceptance of ms. *Writer's Market* recommends allowing 2 months for reply. Book catalog free. Manuscript guidelines for #10 SASE.
Imprint(s): Swan Valley Press.
Nonfiction: How-to, children's/juvenile, reference. Subjects must be dog-related (showing, training, agility, search and rescue, health, nutrition, etc.). "We are looking for new ideas. No flowery prose. Manuscripts should be literate, intelligent, but easy to read." Query first or submit outline and 2 sample chapters with SASE. Reviews artwork/photos as part of the ms package. Send photocopies.
Fiction: Children's/juvenile. Subjects must center around dogs. Either the main character should be a dog or a dog should play an integral role. Query with SASE.
Recent Title(s): *The Newfoundland*, by Dr. Emmy Bruno (Newfoundland breed); *How Willy Got His Wheels* (children's).
Tips: "We are currently expanding and are looking for new topics and fresh ideas while staying true to our niche. While we will steadfastly maintain that market—we are always looking for excellent breed books—we also want to

explore more 'mainstream' topics. We have a new children's book coming out that looks to do very well and we could be expanding into that market."

DORCHESTER PUBLISHING CO., INC., 276 Fifth Ave., Suite 1008, New York NY 10001-0112. (212)725-8811. Fax: (212)532-1054. E-mail: timdy@aol.com.
Imprint(s): Love Spell (romance), **Leisure Books**.

DOUBLEDAY ADULT TRADE, Bantam Doubleday Dell, 1540 Broadway, New York NY 10036. (212)782-9911. Fax: (212)782-9700. Website: http://www.bdd.com. **Acquisitions:** Patricia Mulcahy, vice president/editor-in-chief. Estab. 1897. "Doubleday publishes the best in quality fiction and nonfiction." Publishes hardcover and trade paperback originals and reprints. **Publishes 200 titles/year. Receives thousands of queries and mss/year. 30% of books from first-time authors. Pays royalty on retail price. Advance varies.** Publishes book 1 year after acceptance of ms. Reports in 6 months on queries.
Imprint(s): Anchor Press (contact Martha Lewis); **Currency**; **Doubleday Religious Division** (contact Eric Major); **Image Books**; **Main Street** (contact Gerald Howard); **Nan A. Talese**.
Nonfiction: Biography, cookbook, gift book, how-to, humor, illustrated book, self-help. Subjects include agriculture/horticulture, Americana, animals, anthropology, art/architecture, business/economics, child guidance/parenting, computers/electronics, cooking/foods/nutrition, education, ethnic, gardening, gay/lesbian, government/politics, health/medicine, history, hobbies, language/literature, military/war, money/finance, music/dance, nature/environment, philosophy, photography, psychology, recreation, regional, religion, science, sociology, software, sports, translation, travel, women's issues/studies. *Agented submissions only.*
Fiction: Adventure, confession, erotica, ethnic, experimental, feminist, gay/lesbian, historical, horror, humor, literary, mainstream/contemporary, mystery, picture books, religious, short story collections, suspense. *Agented submissions only.*
Recent Title(s): *The Street Lawyer*, by John Grisham (fiction); *Xena: Warrior Princess: The Official Guide to the Xenaverse*, by Robert Weisbrot (entertainment).

DOUBLEDAY RELIGIOUS DIVISION, Doubleday Books, Bantam Doubleday Dell, 1540 Broadway, New York NY 10036. Fax: (212)782-8911. Website: http://www.bdd.com. **Acquisitions**: Eric Major, vice president, religious division; Mark Fretz, senior editor; Trace Murphy, editor. Estab. 1897. "Doubleday's diverse religious booklist offers breadth and strength in depth that gives it its unique place in religious publishing. Publishes hardcover originals and reprints, trade paperback originals and reprints, mass market paperback originals and reprints. **Publishes 36 titles/year; each imprint publishes 12 titles/year. Receives 700 queries/year; receives 500 mss/year. 5% of books are from first-time authors; 1% from unagented writers. Pays 7½-15% royalty on net price. Advance varies.** Publishes book 13 months after acceptance of ms. Accepts simultaneous submissions. Reports in 3 months on proposals. Book catalog for SAE with 3 first-class stamps.
Imprint(s): Image, Culilee, Doubleday Bible Commentary, Anchor Bible Commentary, Anchor Bible Reference, Anchor Bible Dictionary.
Nonfiction: Biography, cookbook, gift book, how-to, humor, illustrated book, reference, self-help. Subjects include child guidance/parenting, history, language/literature, religion. *Agented submissions only.*
Recent Title(s): *Introduction to the New Testament*, by Prof. Raymond Braun.

DOVER PUBLICATIONS, INC., 31 E. 2nd St., Mineola NY 11501. **Acquisitions:** Mary Carolyn Waldrep, crafts editor. Publishes trade paperback originals and reprints. **Publishes 500 titles/year. Makes outright purchase.** Book catalog free.
Nonfiction: Biography, children's/juvenile, coffee table book, cookbook, how-to, humor, illustrated book, textbook. Subjects include agriculture/horticulture, Americana, animals, anthropology/archaeology, art/architecture, cooking, food & nutrition, health/medicine, history, hobbies, language/literature, music/dance, nature/environment, philosophy, photography, religion, science, sports, translation, travel. Publishes mostly reprints. Accepts original paper doll collections, game books, coloring books (juvenile). Query. Reviews artwork/photos as part of ms package.
Recent Title(s): *Medieval Knights Paper Soldiers*, by A.G. Smith (toy).

DOWLING PRESS, INC., 1110 17th Ave. S., #4, Nashville TN 37212. (615)340-0967. **Acquisitions:** Maryglenn McCombs. Publishes hardcover, trade paperback and mass market paperback originals. **Publishes 5 titles/year. Receives 150 queries and 100 mss/year. Pays 10% royalty on retail price. No advance.** Reports in 3 months on queries and proposals, 6 months on mss. Manuscript guidelines free.
Nonfiction: Biography, cookbook, gift book, how-to, humor, self-help. Subjects include Americana, cooking/foods/nutrition, gardening, gay/lesbian, hobbies, music/dance, women's issues/studies. Query with SASE.
Recent Title(s): *The Walrus Was Paul: The Great Beatle Death Clues of 1969*, by R. Gary Patterson (music/mystery).
Tips: Audience is 18-40 year olds, middle class. "Please proofread! There is nothing worse than carelessness (especially in a cover letter). Don't call us a day after we've received the manuscript to ask what we think! Be patient."

DOWN EAST BOOKS, Down East Enterprise, Inc., P.O. Box 679, Camden ME 04843-0679. Fax: (207)594-7215. E-mail: adevine@downeast.com. Senior Editor: Karin Womer. **Acquisitions:** Acquisitions Editor. Estab. 1967. "Down East Books is committed to publish books, videos, calendars and other products of above-average quality, to offer our products at a fair market price and make a fair profit and to treat our authors, customers, suppliers, and

coworkers with fairness, respect, and a high standard of ethics." Publishes hardcover and trade paperback originals, trade paperback reprints. **Publishes 20-24 titles/year. Receives 600 submissions/year. 50% of books from first-time authors; 90% from unagented writers. Pays 10-15% on receipts. Offers $200 average advance.** Publishes book 1 year after acceptance. Accepts simultaneous submissions. Reports in 2 months. Manuscript guidelines for 9×12 SAE with 3 first-class stamps.
Imprint(s): Silver Quill (fishing and hunting market), Chris Cornell, editor (E-mail: ccornell@downeast.com.)
Nonfiction: Books about the New England region, Maine in particular. Subjects include Americana, history, nature, guide books, crafts, recreation. "All of our regional books must have a Maine or New England emphasis." Query. Reviews artwork/photos as part of ms package.
Fiction: "We publish 1-2 juvenile titles/year (fiction and non-fiction), and 1-2 adult fiction titles/year." *Writer's Market* recommends sending a query with SASE first.
Recent Title(s): *Night Train at Wiscasset Station*, photographs by Kosti Ruohomaa, text by Lew Dietz (nonfiction); *My Brothers' Keeper*, by Nancy Johnson (Civil War fiction story for ages 9-12).

[A] **LISA DREW BOOKS**, Simon & Schuster, 1230 Avenue of the Americas, New York NY 10020. (212)698-7000. **Acquisitions:** Lisa Drew, publisher. "We publish *reading* books; nonfiction that tells a story, not '14 ways to improve your marriage.' " Publishes hardcover originals. **Publishes 10-14 titles/year. Receives 600 queries/year. 10% of books from first-time authors. Pays royalty on retail price, varies by author and project. Advance varies.** Publishes book 1 year after acceptance of ms. Accepts simultaneous submissions, if so noted. Reports in 1 month on queries. Book catalog free through Scribner (same address).
Nonfiction: Subjects include government/politics, history, women's issues/studies, law, entertainment. *Agented submissions only.* No unsolicited material.

[N] **DUFOUR EDITIONS**, P.O. Box 7, Chester Springs PA 19425. (610)458-5005. **Acquisitions**: Thomas Lavoie, associate publisher. "We're a small literary house and distribute a number of quality fiction, poetry and nonfiction titles from the U.K. and Irish publishers as well." Publishes hardcover originals, trade paperback originals and reprints. **Publishes 5-7 titles/year. Receives 100 queries and 15 mss/year. 2-3% of books from first-time authors; 50% from unagented writers. Pays 6-10% royalty on net receipts. Offers $500-1,000 advance.** Publishes book 18 months after acceptance of ms. Accepts simultaneous submissions. Reports in 3 months on queries and proposals, 6 months on mss. Book catalog and ms guidelines free.
Nonfiction: Biography. Subjects include history, translation. Query with SASE. Reviews artwork/photos as part of ms package. Send photocopies.
Fiction: Ethnic, historical, literary, short story collections. Query with SASE.
Poetry: Query.
Recent Title(s): *Ireland: Our Island Home*, by K. Dwyer (nonfiction); *The Carriage Stone*, by Sigbjorn Holmebakk (Norwegian fiction translation).
Tips: "Audience is sophisticated, literate readers especially interested in foreign literature and translations, and a strong Irish-Celtic focus. Check to see if the publisher is really a good match for your subject matter."

DUKE PRESS, Duke Communications International, 221 E. 29th St., Loveland CO 80538. (970)663-4700. Fax: (970)203-2756. E-mail: mcconnta@duke.com. Website: http://www.dukepress.com. **Acquisitions:** Tricia McConnell, acquisitions editor, (AS/400); Mick Gusinde-Duffy, acquisitions editor (Windows NT). "Readers are MIS managers, students, programmers, and system operators working on an IBM AS/400 midrange computer or a Windows NT platform; financial controllers." Publishes trade paperback originals. **Publishes 20-25 titles/year. Receives 20 queries and 5 mss/year. 75% of books from first-time authors; 90% from unagented writers. Pays 10-15% royalty on wholesale price. Offers no advance.** Publishes book 4 months after acceptance of complete ms. Accepts simultaneous submissions. Reports in 1 month on proposals. Book catalog and ms guidelines free.
Nonfiction: Technical, textbook, multimedia (CD-ROM). Subjects include IBM AS/400 midrange computer, accounting software and Windows NT operating system. Submit proposal package including overview, table of contents, sample chapter, schedule, target audience, competing products, marketing plan, personal information, résumé, list of previous publications.
Recent Title(s): *Data Warehousing and the AS/400*, by Scott Steinacher (data warehousing/midrange computing).
Tips: "Authors must have technical knowledge and experience on an IBM AS/400 or Windows NT."

[A] **DUMMIES TRADE PRESS**, IDG Books, 645 N. Michigan Ave., Chicago IL 60611. (312)482-8460. Fax: (312)482-8561. E-mail: kwelton@idgbooks.com. Website: http://www.dummies.com. **Acquisitions**: Kathleen A. Welton, vice president/publisher. "Dummies Trade Press dedicates itself to publishing innovative, high-quality "For Dummies™" titles on the most popular business and general reference topics." Publishes trade paperback originals. **Pays 10-15% royalty. Offers $0-25,000 advance.** Publishes book 3 months after acceptance of ms. Reports in 2 months. Manuscript guidelines free.
Nonfiction: Cookbook, gift book, how-to, illustrated book, reference, self-help. Subjects include animals, art/architecture, business/economics, child guidance/parenting, cooking/food/nutrition, diet/health/medical, gardening, government/politics, hobbies, money/finance, music/dance, nature/environment, photography, recreation, sports, travel. *Agented submissions only.*
Recent Title(s): *Wine for Dummies*, by Ed McCarthy and Mary Ewing-Mulligan.

THOMAS DUNNE BOOKS, St. Martin's Press, 175 Fifth Ave., New York NY 10010. (212)674-5151. **Acquisitions:** Tom Dunne. Publishes wide range of fiction and nonfiction. Publishes hardcover originals, trade paperback originals and reprints. **Publishes 90 titles/year. Receives 1,000 queries/year. 20% of books from first-time authors; less than 5% from unagented writers. Pays 10-15% royalty on retail price for hardcover, 7½% for paperback. Advance varies with project.** Publishes book 1 year after acceptance of ms. Accepts simultaneous submissions. Reports in 2 months on queries. Ms guidelines for #10 SASE.

Nonfiction: Biography. Subjects include government/politics, history, political commentary. "Author's attention to detail is important. We get a lot of manuscripts that are poorly proofread and just can't be considered." Query or submit outline and 100 sample pages with SASE. Reviews artwork/photos as part of ms package. Send photocopies.

Fiction: Mainstream/contemporary, thrillers, suspense, women's. Query or submit synopsis and 100 sample pages with SASE.

Recent Title(s): *Beyond The Wild Blue: A History of The United States Air Force*, by Walter Boyne (military history); *Brandenburg*, by Glenn Meade (thriller).

DUQUESNE UNIVERSITY PRESS, 600 Forbes Ave., Pittsburgh PA 15282-0101. (412)396-6610. Fax: (412)396-5984. Website: http://www.duq.edu/dupress.html. **Acquisitions:** Susan Wadsworth-Booth, editor-in-chief. Publishes hardcover and trade paperback originals. **Publishes 8-12 titles/year. Receives 500 queries and 75 mss/year. 30% of books from first-time authors; 95% from unagented writers. Pays royalty on net price.** Publishes book 1 year after acceptance of ms. Reports in 1 month on proposals, 3 months on mss. Book catalog and ms guidelines free.

Nonfiction: Creative nonfiction, scholarly/academic. Subjects include language/literature, philosophy, religion. "Duquesne publishes scholarly monographs in the fields of literary studies (medieval & Renaissance), philosophy, ethics, religious studies and psychology. We look for quality of scholarship. We also publish a series, *Emerging Writers in Creative Nonfiction*, for first-time authors of creative nonfiction for a general readership. For this series, two copies of the manuscript are required for submissions." For scholarly books, query or submit outline, 1 sample chapter and SASE.

Recent Title(s): *"Renaissance" Talk: Ordinary Language and the Mystique of Critical Problems*, by Stanley Stewart (literary criticism/theory).

[A] **DUTTON**, Penguin Putnam Inc., 375 Hudson St., New York NY 10014. (212)366-2000. Publisher: Clare Ferrar. **Acquisitions:** Rosemary Ahern, senior editor (scholarly books, literary fiction); Matthew Carnicelli, editor (general nonfiction, business); Joe Pittman, editor (mystery); Diedre Mullane, senior editor (nonfiction, science, multicultural literary fiction); Audrey LaFehr, executive editor (women's fiction); Micheala Hamilton, editorial director (psychology, true crime, fiction). Estab. 1852. Dutton publishes hardcover, original, mainstream, and contemporary fiction and nonfiction in the areas of biography, self-help, politics, psychology, and science for a general readership. **Publishes 500 titles/year. Receives 20,000 queries and 10,000 mss/year. 30-40% of books from first-time authors; 2% from unagented writers. Royalty and advance negotiable.** Publishes book 18 months after acceptance. Reports in 6 months.

Imprint(s): Signet, Onyx, Topaz, NAL, Plume.

Nonfiction: Biography, cookbook, gift book, how-to, humor, reference, self-help. Subjects include agriculture/horticulture, Americana, animals, anthropology/archaeology, art/architecture, business/economics, child guidance/parenting, cooking/foods/nutrition education, ethnic, gardening, gay/lesbian, government/politics, health/medicine, history, hobbies, language/literature, military/war, money/finance, music/dance, nature/environment, philosophy, photography, psychology, recreation, regional, religion, science, sociology, sports, translation, women's issues/studies. "Author's credentials are essential. Many writers don't know the difference between a good book idea and a good idea for a magazine article. *Agented submissions only.*

Fiction: Adventure, erotica, ethnic, fantasy, gay/lesbian, historical, horror, literary, mainstream/contemporary, mystery, occult, romance, science fiction, short story collections, suspense, western. "We are looking for novelists who can write a book a year with consistent quality." *Agented submissions only.*

Recent Title(s): *Foster Child: A Biography of Jodie Foster*, by Buddy Foster and Leon Wagener (celebrity biography); *Ordeal*, by Deanie Francis Mills (suspense).

Tips: "Write the complete manuscript and submit it to an agent or agents. We publish The Trailsman, Battletech and other western and science fiction series—all by ongoing authors. Receptive to ideas for new series in commercial fiction."

DUTTON CHILDREN'S BOOKS, Penguin Putnam Inc., 375 Hudson St., New York NY 10014. (212)366-2000. **Acquisitions:** Lucia Monfried, editor-in-chief. Estab. 1852. Dutton Children's Books publishes fiction and nonfiction for readers ranging from preschoolers to young adults on a variety of subjects. Publishes hardcover originals. Publishes 70 titles/year. 15% from first-time authors. Pays royalty on retail price.

Nonfiction: For preschoolers to middle-graders; including animals/nature, U.S. history, science and photo essays. Query with SASE.

Fiction: Dutton Children's Books has a complete publishing program that includes picture books; easy-to-read books; and fiction for all ages, from "first-chapter" books to young adult readers. Query with SASE.

Recent Title(s): *Our Journey From Tibet*, by Laurie Dolphin; *The Iron Ring*, by Lloyd Alexander.

EAGLE'S VIEW PUBLISHING, 6756 N. Fork Rd., Liberty UT 84310. Fax: (801)745-0903. E-mail: Eglcrafts@aol.com. **Acquisitions:** Denise Knight, editor-in-chief. Estab. 1982. "We publish nonfiction only. Primarily how-to craft books with a subject related to historical or contemporary Native American/Mountain Man/frontier crafts." Publishes trade paperback originals. **Publishes 4-6 titles/year. Receives 40 queries and 20 mss/year. 90% of books from first-time authors; 100% from unagented writers. Pays 8-10% royalty on net selling price.** Publishes book 1 year or more after acceptance of ms. Accepts simultaneous submissions. Reports in 1 year on proposals. Book catalog and ms guidelines for $3.

Nonfiction: How-to, Indian, mountain man and American frontier (history and craft). Subjects include anthropology/archaeology (Native American crafts), ethnic (Native American), history (American frontier historical pattern books), hobbies (crafts, especially beadwork, earrings). "We are expanding from our Indian craft base to more general but related crafts." Submit outline and 1-2 sample chapters. Reviews artwork/photos as part of ms package. Send photocopies or sample illustrations. "We prefer to do photography in house."

Recent Title(s): *Voices of Native America*, by Douglas Spotted Eagle (Native American music and instruments).

Tips: "We will not be publishing any new beaded earrings books for 1 to 2 years. We are interested in other craft projects using seed beads, especially books that feature a variety of items, not just different designs for one item."

EAKIN PRESS/SUNBELT MEDIA, INC., P.O. Box 90159, Austin TX 78709-0159. (512)288-1771. Fax: (512)288-1813. **Acquisitions:** Edwin M. Eakin, editorial director; Virginia Messer, associate publisher. Estab. 1978. Eakin specializes in Texana and Western Americana for adults and juveniles. Publishes hardcover and paperback originals and reprints. **Publishes 45 titles/year. Receives 1,500 submissions/year. 50% of books from first-time authors; 90% from unagented writers. Pays 10-12-15% royalty on net sales.** Publishes book 18 months after acceptance. Accepts simultaneous submissions. Reports in 3 months. Book catalog for $1.25. Manuscript guidelines for #10 SASE.

Imprint(s): Eakin Press, Nortex Press.

Nonfiction: Adult nonfiction: Western Americana, African American studies, business, sports, biographies, Civil War, regional cookbooks, Texas history, World War II. Juvenile nonfiction: includes biographies of historic personalities, prefer with Texas or regional interest, or nature studies; and easy-read illustrated books for grades 1-3. Query with SASE.

Fiction: No adult fiction. Juvenile fiction for grades 4-7, preferably relating to Texas and the Southwest or contemporary. Query or submit outline/synopsis and sample chapters.

Recent Title(s): *Historic Ranches of the Old West*, by Bill O'Neal (history); *The Burro & the Basket*, by Lloyd Mandis, illustrated by Scott Arbuckle (picture book).

EASTERN NATIONAL ASSOCIATION, 470 Maryland Dr., Fort Washington PA 19034. (610)832-0555. Fax: (610)832-0308. **Acquisitions:** Patti Plummer, production coordinator. Estab. 1948. "Our mission is to continue to strengthen our relationship with the National Park Service and other partners." Publishes trade paperback originals and reprints. **Publishes 50-60 titles/year. Receives 20 queries and 10 mss/year. 5% of books from first-time authors; 50% from unagented writers. Pays 1-10% royalty on retail price or makes outright purchase of $6,000 maximum.** Publishes book 2 years after acceptance of ms. Reports in 1 month on queries. *Writer's Market* recommends allowing 2 months for reply. Book catalog free.

Imprint(s): Eastern Acorn Press.

Nonfiction: Biography, children's/juvenile. Subjects include Americana, history, military/war and nature/environment. "Requests for editorial plans are only accepted from member agencies." Query. *All unsolicited mss returned unopened.*

Recent Title(s): *Life in Civil War America*, by Catherine Clinton.

EASTLAND PRESS, P.O. Box 99749, Seattle WA 98199. (206)217-0204. Fax: (206)217-0205. Website: http://www.eastlandpress.com. **Acquisitions:** John O'Connor, managing editor. "We are primarily interested in textbooks for practitioners of alternative medical therapies." Publishes hardcover and trade paperback originals. **Publishes 4-6 titles/year. Receives 25 queries/year. 30% of books from first-time authors; 90% from unagented writers. Pays 10-15% royalty on receipts. Offers $500-1,500 advance.** Publishes book 18 months after acceptance of ms. Accepts simultaneous submissions. Reports in 1 month. Book catalog free.

Nonfiction: Reference, textbook, alternative medicine (Chinese and physical therapies and related bodywork). "We prefer that a manuscript be completed or close to completion before we will consider publication. Proposals are rarely considered, unless submitted by a published author or teaching institution." Submit outline and 2-3 sample chapters. Reviews artwork/photos as part of ms package. Send photocopies.

Recent Title(s): *Patterns & Practice in Chinese Medicine*, by Zhao Jingyi.

THE ECCO PRESS, 100 W. Broad St., Hopewell NJ 08525. (609)466-4748. Website: http://www.wwnorton.com/ecco/welcome.htm. Editor-in-Chief: Daniel Halpern. **Acquisitions:** address queries to Submissions Editor. "For the past twenty-six years, The Ecco Press has been publishing finely crafted books of high literary merit, establishing a reputation as one of the most important literary publishers worldwide." Publishes hardcover and trade paperback originals and reprints. **Publishes 60 titles/year. Receives 3,000 queries/year. Pays royalty. Offers advance.** Publishes book 1 year after acceptance of ms. Book catalog and ms guidelines free.

Nonfiction: Biography/autobiography, cookbook. Subjects include cooking/foods, literature, sports, translations. Query with SASE.

Fiction: Literary, short story collections. Query with SASE.

Poetry: "We are not accepting unsolicited poetry."

Recent Title(s): *Hell*, by Kathryn David (fiction); *Shroud of the Gnome*, by James Tate (poetry).

EDGE BOOKS, Henry Holt & Co., 115 W. 18th St., New York NY 10011. (212)886-9200. **Acquisitions:** Marc Aronson, executive editor. "Our titles are international or multicultural coming-of-age fiction and nonfiction." Publishes hardcover originals. **Publishes 2-3 titles/year. 80% of books from first-time authors. Pays 8-10% royalty on retail price. Advance varies.** Publishes book 18 months after acceptance of ms. Reports in 4 months on queries. Book catalog free from Henry Holt (same address).
Nonfiction: Young adult. Query with outline, 1 sample chapter, market analysis and SASE.
Fiction: Young adult. Query or submit complete ms.
Recent Title(s): *Forbidden Love*, by Gary Nash (groundbreaking history); *The Long Season of Rain*, by Helen Kim (novel); *Earth-Shattering Poems*, by Liz Rosenberg (poetry).
Tips: "We are very open to new authors, but because we publish so few titles, the standards are very high. The emphasis is on voice and literary quality, rather than subject."

N EDUCATIONAL TECHNOLOGY PUBLICATIONS, 700 Palisade Ave., Englewood Cliffs NJ 07632. (201)871-4007. **Acquisitions:** Lawrence Lipsitz, publisher. Educational Technology publishes books on the use of technology in eductaion. Publishes hardcover and trade paperback originals. **Publishes 12-15 titles/year. Receives 100 queries and 50 mss/year. 33% of books from first-time authors; 100% from unagented writers. Pays 10-15% royalty on wholesale or retail price. No advance.** Publishes book 1 year after acceptance of ms. Reports in 1 month.
Nonfiction: Technical, textbook, professional books on education technology. "No other topics, please. We are not a general purpose publisher." Query with outline and SASE. Reviews artwork/photos as part of ms package.
Recent Title(s): *Web-Based Instruction*, edited by Badurl H. Khan.
Tips: "Audience is sophisticated educators interested in all areas of technology in education. We desire only very expert authors, able to do high-level work—not P.R. 'flacks.' Only leading-edge, up-to-date material will be considered."

N EDUCATOR'S INTERNATIONAL PRESS, INC., 18 Colleen Rd., Troy NY 12180. (518)271-9886. **Acquisitions**: Sarah J. Biondello, publisher. "Educator's International publishes books in all aspects of education, broadly conceived, from pre-kindergarten to postgraduate. We specialize in texts, professional books, videos and other materials for students, faculty, practitioners and researchers. We also publish a full list of books in the areas of women's studies, social and behavioral sciences, and nursing and health." Publishes hardcover and trade paperback originals and reprints. **Publishes 10-12 titles/year. Receives 50 queries and 50 mss/year. 50% of books from first-time authors; 98% from unagented writers. Pays 3-15% royalty on wholesale price.** Publishes book 1 year after acceptance of ms. Accepts simultaneous submissions. Reports in 2 months on queries and proposals, 3 months on mss. Book catalog and ms guidelines free.
Nonfiction: Textbook, supplemental texts, conference proceedings. Subjects include education, gay/lesbian, health/medicine, language/literature, philosophy, psychology, software, women's issues/studies. Submit table of contents, outline, 2-3 chapters, résumé with SASE. Reviews artwork/photos as part of ms package.
Recent Title(s): *An Introduction to Educational Administration: Social, Legal, and Ethical Perspectives*, by Haller and Strike.
Tips: Audience is professors, students, researchers, individuals, libraries.

N EDUCATORS PUBLISHING SERVICES, INC., 31 Smith Place, Cambridge MA 02138-1089. (617)547-6706. Fax: (617)547-0412. Website: http://www.epsbooks.com. **Acquisitions:** Dorothy Miller, executive editor. "EPS is looking for supplementary materials for the regular K-12 classroom. We are particularly interested in workbook series, but will gladly consider any proposals for high-quality material that is useful to teachers and students." **Publishes 20 titles/year. Receives 250 queries and 250 mss/year. 50% of books come from first-time authors; 100% from unagented writers. Pays 5-12% royalty on retail price.** Publishes book 8 months after acceptance of ms. Accepts simultaneous submissions. Reports in 1 month on queries and 3 months on proposals and mss. Book catalog and ms guidelines free on request.
Nonfiction: Workbooks (language arts and math) and some professional books. Language/literature subjects. Query. Reviews artwork/photos as part of ms package. Send photocopies.
Recent Title(s): *Bookwise Literature Guides,* by various authors (guides to children's literature).
Tips: Teacher, students (K-adult) audiences.

N EDUPRESS, 1140-A Calle Cordillera, San Clemente CA 92673. (714)366-9499. **Acquisitions**: Kathy Rogers. Edupress publishes classroom resources. Publishes trade paperback originals. **Publishes 40 titles/year. Receives 20 queries and 20 mss/year. 25% of books from first-time authors. Makes outright purchase.** Publishes book 1 year after acceptance of ms. Reports in 2 months on queries, 5 months on mss. Book catalog and ms guidelines free.
Nonfiction: Educational resources for pre-school through middle school. Submit proposal package, including ms copy, outline, 1 sample chapter and SASE. Reviews artwork/photos as part of ms package. Send photocopies. "We use inhouse artists, but will consider submitted art."
Recent Title(s): *Fun With Fingerpuppets*, by Judie Bertolino.
Tips: Audience is classroom teachers and home-school parents.

N EERDMANS BOOKS FOR YOUNG READERS, William B. Eerdmans Publishing Co., 255 Jefferson Ave. SE, Grand Rapids MI 49503. (616)459-4591. Fax: (616)459-6540. **Acquisitions**: Judy Zylstra, editor. "We seek manuscripts that nurture children's faith in God and help them understand and explore life in God's world—its wonder and joy, but also its challenges." Publishes picture books and middle reader and young adult fiction and nonfiction. **Publishes 12-15 titles/year. Receives 3,000 submissions/year. Pays 5-7½% royalty on retail price.** Publishes middle reader and YA books 1 year after acceptance. Publishes picture books 2-3 years after acceptance. Accepts simultaneous submissions if noted. Reports in 6 weeks on queries. Book catalog for SASE.

Nonfiction and Fiction: Children's books. Picture books, middle reader, young adult fiction and nonfiction. Submit complete mss for picture books and middle readers under 200 pages with SASE. For longer books, send query letter and 3 or 4 sample chapters with SASE. "Do not send illustrations unless you are a professional illustrator." Send color photocopies rather than original art.

Recent Title(s): *Silent Night: The Song and Its Story*, by Margaret Hodges, illustrated by Tim Ladwig.

WILLIAM B. EERDMANS PUBLISHING CO., 255 Jefferson Ave. SE, Grand Rapids MI 49503. (616)459-4591. Fax: (616)459-6540. **Acquisitions:** Jon Pott, editor-in-chief; Charles Van Hof, managing editor (history); Judy Zylstra, children's book editor. Estab. 1911. "Approximately 80% of our adult publications are religious and most of these are academic or semi-academic in character (as opposed to inspirational or celebrity books), though we also publish books on the Christian life. Our nonreligious titles, most of them in regional history or on social issues, aim, similarly, at an educated audience." Publishes hardcover and paperback originals and reprints. **Publishes 120-130 titles/year. Receives 3,000-4,000 submissions/year. 10% of books from first-time authors; 95% from unagented writers. Pays 7½-10% royalty on retail price.** Publishes book 1 year after acceptance. Accepts simultaneous submissions if noted. Reports in 6 weeks on queries. Book catalog free.

Imprint(s): Eerdmans Books for Young Readers (Judy Zylstra, editor).

Nonfiction: Religious, reference, textbooks, monographs, children's books. Subjects include biblical studies, theology, ethics, literature, religious history, philosophy of religion, psychology, sociology, regional history. "We prefer that writers take the time to notice if we have published anything at all in the same category as their manuscript before sending it to us." Accepts nonfiction translations. Query with outline, 2-3 sample chapters and SASE for return of ms. Reviews artwork/photos.

Recent Title(s): *Malcolm Muggeridge: A Biography*, by Gregory Wolfe.

N ELDER BOOKS, P.O. Box 490, Forest Knolls CA 94933. (415)488-9002. Website: http://www.nbn.com/~elder/alzheimer.html. **Acquisitions:** Carmel Sheridan, director. "Elder Books is dedicated to publishing practical, hands-on guidebooks for family and professional caregivers of persons with Alzheimer's." Publishes trade paperback originals. **Publishes 6-10 titles/year. Receives 200 queries and 50 mss/year. 50% of books from first-time authors; 50% from unagented writers. Pays .7% royalty on retail price. No advance.** Publishes book 9 months after acceptance of ms. Reports in 3 months on queries. Book catalog free.

Nonfiction: Gift book, how-to, self-help. Subjects include parenting, education, health/medicine, money/finance, psychology, senior issues, Alzheimer's disease, women's issues/studies. Submit outline, 2 sample chapters. Reviews artwork/photos as part of ms package. Send photocopies.

Recent Title(s): *Coping With Caring: Daily Reflections for Alzheimer's Caregivers*, by Lyn Roche.

Tips: "Our books are written in a style that is user-friendly and non-technical, presenting key information on caregiver concerns including: how to keep the person engaged through meaningful activities, prevent caregiver burnout, cope with wandering and organize a search in the event the person disappears, deal with difficult behaviors."

ELEMENT BOOKS, Element Books Ltd. (UK), 160 N. Washington St., 4th Floor, Boston MA 01966. (617)248-9494. Fax: (617)248-0909. E-mail: element@cove.com. **Acquisitions:** Roberta Scimone, editorial director. Estab. 1975. "We publish high-quality, accessible books on spiritual traditions, complimentary health and inner wisdom." Publishes hardcover originals. **Publishes 15-20 titles/year. Receives 600 queries/year. 50% of books from first-time authors; 80% from unagented writers. Pays 15-20% royalty on retail price. Offers $3,000 average advance.** Publishes book 1 year after acceptance of ms. Accepts simultaneous submissions. Reports in 2 months on proposals. Book catalog and ms guidelines free.

Imprint(s): One World (UK), Element Children's Books.

Nonfiction: Reference, self-help. Subjects include business/economics, health/medicine, philosophy, psychology, regional. Query with outline, 2-3 sample chapters, table of contents, author's bio and SASE. Reviews artwork/photos as part of ms package. Send photocopies.

Recent Title(s): *My Father, My Self*, by Dr. Masa Aiba Goetz (self-help).

ELEPHANT BOOKS, Creativity, Inc., 65 Macedonia Rd., Alexander NC 28701. (828)252-9515. Fax: (828)255-8719. E-mail: sales@abooks.com. Website: http://www.abooks.com. **Acquisitions:** Barbara Blood, executive editor. Publishes trade paperback originals and reprints. **Publishes 8 titles/year. Receives 20 queries and 15 mss/year. 90% of books from first-time authors; 80% from unagented writers. Pays 12-15% royalty on wholesale price. Seldom offers advance.** Publishes book 18 months after acceptance of ms. Book catalog and manuscript guidelines for 9×12 SASE with $1.01 postage.

Imprint(s): Blue/Gray Books (contact Ralph Roberts, Civil War history).

Nonfiction: Cookbooks, history subjects. Interested in Civil War and innovative cookbooks. Query or submit outline with 3 sample chapters and proposal package, including potential marketing plans with SASE. Reviews artwork/photos as part of ms package. Send photocopies.

Recent Title(s): *Women of the War*, by Frank Moore.

ENGINEERING & MANAGEMENT PRESS, 25 Technology Park/Atlanta, Norcross GA 30092. (770)449-0461. Fax: (770)263-8532. E-mail: gcacioppo@iienet.org. Website: http://www.iienet.org. **Acquisitions:** Eric Torrey, publisher; Gabrielle Cacioppo, book editor. "Engineering & Management Press publishes quality books that cover timely, crucial topics of importance to engineering and management professionals and businesses today." Publishes hardcover and trade paperback originals. **Publishes 6-10 titles/year. Receives 60-80 queries and 40-50 mss/year. 75% of books from first-time authors; 100% from unagented writers. Pays 10-15% royalty. Offers up to $1,000 advance.** Publishes book 1 year after acceptance of ms. Accepts simultaneous submissions. Reports in 3 months on mss. Book catalog and ms guidelines for SASE or on website.

Nonfiction: All books relate to industrial engineering disciplines. Reference, technical, textbook. Subjects include business, computers/electronics, health/medicine (healthcare administration), industrial engineering and related topics. Submit proposal package, including outline, 2 sample chapters, competitive analysis and what makes your book unique. Reviews artwork/photos as part of ms package. Send photocopies.

Recent Title(s): *You're Fired!*, by Eileen Berman.

ENSLOW PUBLISHERS INC., 44 Fadem Rd., P.O. Box 699, Springfield NJ 07081. (201)379-8890. Website: http://www.enslow.com. **Acquisitions:** Brian D. Enslow, editor. Estab. 1977. Enslow publishes nonfiction for children and young adults in a variety of subjects including science, history, reference and biographies. Publishes hardcover originals. **Publishes 120 titles/year. 30% require freelance illustration. Pays royalty on net price. Offers advance.** Publishes book 1 year after acceptance. Reports in 1 month. *Writer's Market* recommends allowing 2 months for reply. Book catalog for $2 and 9×12 SAE with 3 first-class stamps. Writer's guidelines for SASE.

- Enslow Publishers is especially interested in ideas for series. It does not publish fiction, fictionalized history or educational materials.

Nonfiction: Interested in nonfiction mss for young adults and children. Some areas of special interest are science, social issues, biography, reference topics, recreation. Query with information on competing titles and writer's résumé.

Recent Title(s): *Bizarre Insects*, by Margaret J. Anderson (science).

EPICENTER PRESS, INC., P.O. Box 82368, Kenmore WA 98028. (425)485-6822. Fax: (425)481-8253. E-mail: cummel@aol.com. **Acquisitions:** Christine Ummel, acquisitions editor; Kent Sturgis, publisher. "We are a regional press founded in Alaska whose interests include but are not limited to the arts, history, environment, and diverse cultures and lifestyles of the North Pacific and high latitudes." Publishes hardcover and trade paperback originals. **Publishes 10 titles/year. Receives 200 queries and 100 mss/year. 90% of books from first-time authors; 90% from unagented writers. Advance negotiable.** Publishes book 2 years after acceptance of ms. Reports in 2 months on queries. Book catalog and ms guidelines free.

Imprint(s): Umbrella Books.

Nonfiction: Biography, coffee table book, gift books, humor. Subjects include animals, art/architecture, ethnic, history, nature/environment, photography, recreation, regional, travel, women's issues/studies. "Our focus is the Pacific Northwest and Alaska. We do not encourage nonfiction titles from outside Alaska and the Pacific Northwest, nor travel from beyond Alaska, Washington, Oregon and California." Submit outline and 3 sample chapters. Reviews artwork/photos as part of ms package. Send photocopies.

Recent Title(s): *Seven Words for Wind*, by Sumner MacLeish.

EPM PUBLICATIONS, INC., Box 490, McLean VA 22101. **Acquisitions:** Evelyn P. Metzger, editor/publisher. Publishes hardcover and trade paperback originals and reprints. **Publishes 8-10 titles/year. Nearly all books from unagented writers. Pays 6-15% royalty on retail price.** Publishes book 4 months after acceptance of ms. Reports within 1 month on queries, 1-2 months on mss.

Nonfiction: Biography, cookbook, gift book, how-to, humor, illustrated book, self-help. Subjects include Americana, art/architecture, child guidance/parenting, cooking/foods/nutrition, education, gardening, history, hobbies, language/literature, military/war (Civil War), nature/environment, recreation, regional, sports, travel, women's issues/studies. Query with outline and SASE. Reviews artwork/photos as part of ms package. Send photocopies.

ERICA HOUSE, P.O. Box 1109, Frederick MD 21702. (301)631-0747 or (301)631-9073. E-mail: eribooks@fred.net. **Contact:** Willem Meiners, publisher; Aida Matic-Chaffee, senior editor. "Our books are for and about people who face great challenges in life and who are determined to overcome them by turning their stumbling blocks into stepping stones." Publishes hardcover and trade paperback originals. **Publishes 20 titles/year. Receives 600 queries and 500 mss/year. 75% of books from first-time authors; 50% from unagented writers. Pays 8-15% royalty on retail price.** Publishes book 1 year after acceptance of ms. Accepts simultaneous submissions. Reports in 1 months on queries, 4 months on mss. Book catalog and ms guidelines free.

Imprint(s): Baughman Press.

Nonfiction: Biography, children's/juvenile, self-help. Subjects include anthropology/archaeology, child guidance/parenting, government/politics, history, philosophy, psychology, religion, sociology, motivational, inspirational. Submit proposal package, including outline, bio and ms with SASE.

Fiction: Adventure, confession, fantasy, historical, literary, mainstream/contemporary, religious, romance, motivational, inspirational. "We are especially looking for novels about overcoming hardships/challenges." Send complete ms, bio and outline with SASE.

Recent Title(s): *The Waltz King*, by Andre Riev (classics star talks about his music); *Madame President*, by Gene

McCreary (first female president faces scandals and election).
Tips: "Our readers are looking for upbeat inspirational titles with a positive outlook. We encourage new talent."

PAUL S. ERIKSSON, PUBLISHER, P.O. Box 62, Forest Dale VT 05745-4210. (802)247-4210. Fax: (802)247-4256. **Acquisitions:** Paul S. Eriksson, publisher/editor; Peggy Eriksson, associate publisher/co-editor. Estab. 1960. "We look for intelligence, excitement and saleability." Publishes hardcover and paperback trade originals, paperback trade reprints. **Publishes 5 titles/year. Receives 1,500 submissions/year. 25% of books from first-time authors; 95% from unagented writers. Pays 10-15% royalty on retail price. Offers advance if necessary.** Publishes book 6 months after acceptance. *Writer's Market* recommends allowing 2 months for reply. Catalog for #10 SASE.
Nonfiction: Americana, birds (ornithology), art, biography, business/economics, cooking/foods/nutrition, health, history, hobbies, how-to, humor, nature, politics, psychology, recreation, self-help, sociology, sports, travel. Query with SASE.
Recent Title(s): *The Revenge of the Fishgod*, by Carl von Essen, M.D. (fishing).
Fiction: Serious, literary. Query with SASE.

ETC PUBLICATIONS, 700 E. Vereda Sur, Palm Springs CA 92262-4816. (760)325-5352. Fax: (760)325-8841. **Acquisitions:** Dr. Richard W. Hostrop, publisher (education and social sciences); Lee Ona S. Hostrop, editorial director (history and works suitable below the college level). Estab. 1972. ETC publishes works that "further learning as opposed to entertainment." Publishes hardcover and paperback originals. **Publishes 6-12 titles/year. Receives 100 submissions/year. 75% of books from first-time authors; 90% from unagented writers. Offers 5-15% royalty, based on wholesale and retail price.** Publishes book 9 months after acceptance. *Writer's Market* recommends allowing 2 months for reply.
Nonfiction: Educational management, gifted education, futuristics, textbooks. Accepts nonfiction translations in above areas. Submit complete ms with SASE. *Writer's Market* recommends query first with SASE. Reviews artwork/photos as part of ms package.
Recent Title(s): *Corresponding With History*, by John E. Schlimm II (art and benefits of autograph collecting).
Tips: "ETC will seriously consider textbook manuscripts in any knowledge area in which the author can guarantee a first-year adoption of not less than 500 copies. Special consideration is given to those authors who are capable and willing to submit their completed work in camera-ready, typeset form. We are particularly interested in works suitable for *both* the Christian school market and homeschoolers; e.g., state history texts below the high school level with a Christian-oriented slant."

M. EVANS AND CO., INC., 216 E. 49th St., New York NY 10017-1502. Fax: (212)486-4544. **Acquisitions:** George C. deKay, editor-in-chief. Estab. 1960. "We publish a general trade list of adult nonfiction, cookbooks and semi-reference works. The emphasis is on selectivity, publishing commercial works with quality." Publishes hardcover and trade paperback originals. Pays negotiable royalty. **Publishes 30-40 titles/year. 5% of books from unagented writers. Publishes book 8 months after acceptance.** Reports in 2 months. Book catalog for 9×12 SAE with 3 first-class stamps.
Nonfiction: "Our most successful nonfiction titles have been related to health and the behavioral sciences. No limitation on subject." Query. *No unsolicited mss.*
Fiction: "Our very small general fiction list represents an attempt to combine quality with commercial potential. We publish no more than one novel per season." Query. *No unsolicited mss.*
Recent Title(s): *Dr. Atkins' New Diet Revolution* (health); *A Fine Italian Hand*, by William Murray (mystery).
Tips: "A writer should clearly indicate what his book is all about, frequently the task the writer performs least well. His credentials, although important, mean less than his ability to convince this company that he understands his subject and that he has the ability to communicate a message worth hearing. Writers should review our book catalog before making submissions."

EXCALIBUR PUBLICATIONS, P.O. Box 36, Latham NY 12110-0036. **Acquisitions:** Alan M. Petrillo, editor. Excalibur publishes works on military history, strategy and tactics, history of battles, firearms, arms and armour. Publishes trade paperback originals. **Publishes 6-8 titles/year. Pays royalty or makes outright purchase.** Reports in 2 months on mss.
Nonfiction Military history, strategy and tactics, as well as the history of battles, firearms, arms and armour. "We are seeking well-researched and documented works. Unpublished writers are welcome." Query with outline, first and any 2 additional consecutive chapters with SASE. Include notes on photos, illustrations and maps.
Recent Title(s): *British .22RF Training Rifles*, by Dennis Lewis and Robert Washburn.

EXCELSIOR CEE PUBLISHING, P.O. Box 5861, Norman OK 73070. (405)329-3909. Fax: (405)329-6886. **Acquisitions:** J.C. Marshall. Publishes hardcover and trade paperback originals. **Publishes 8 titles/year. Receives 100 queries/**

FOR INFORMATION on book publishers' areas of interest, see the nonfiction and fiction sections in the Book Publishers Subject Index.

year. **Pays royalty or makes outright purchase (both negotiable). Offers no advance.** Publishes book 1 year after acceptance of ms. Accepts simultaneous submissions. Reports in 1 month. *Writer's Market* recommends allowing 2 months for reply. Book catalog for #10 SASE.

Nonfiction: Biography, coffee table book, how-to, humor, self-help, textbook. Subjects include Americana, education, history, hobbies, language/literature, women's issues/studies, writing. Query with SASE.

Recent Title(s): *How to Record Your Family History*, by Jimmie Blaine Marshall.

Tips: "We have a general audience, book store browser interested in nonfiction reading. We publish titles that have a mass appeal and can be enjoyed by a large reading public. We publish very few unsolicited manuscripts, and our publishing calendar is 75% full up to 1 year in advance."

⊘ FABER & FABER, INC.

● Farrar Straus & Giroux purchased a majority stake in Faber & Faber, Inc., the US subsidiary of the British publisher Faber & Faber Ltd. Faber & Faber Inc. no longer originates its own titles, but will publish and distribute titles acquired on the British side by Faber & Faber Ltd.

FACTS ON FILE, INC., 11 Penn Plaza, New York NY 10001. (212)967-8800. Fax: (212)967-9196. E-mail: pkatzman.factsonfile.com. Website: http://www.factsonfile.com. **Acquisitions:** Laurie Likoff, editorial director (science, music, history); Eleanora Von Dehsen (science, nature, multi-volume reference); Nicole Bowen, senior editor (American history, women's studies, young adult reference); James Chambers, trade editor (health, pop culture, sports); Pam Katzman, editorial assistant. Estab. 1941. "We produce high-quality reference materials for the school library market and the general nonfiction trade." Publishes hardcover originals and reprints. **Publishes 135 titles/year. Receives approximately 2,000 submissions/year. 25% of books from unagented writers. Pays 10-15% royalty on retail price. Offers $10,000 average advance.** Accepts simultaneous submissions. Reports in 2 months on queries. Book catalog free.

Imprint(s): Checkmark Books.

Nonfiction: Reference. Informational books on careers, education, health, history, entertainment, natural history, philosophy, psychology, recreation, religion, language, sports, multicultural studies, science, popular culture. "We publish serious, informational books for a targeted audience. All our books must have strong library interest, but we also distribute books effectively to the book trade. Our library books fit the junior and senior high school curriculum." No computer books, technical books, cookbooks, biographies (except YA), pop psychology, humor, fiction or poetry. Query or submit outline and sample chapter with SASE. No submissions returned without SASE.

Recent Title(s): *Smart Start*, by Marian Borden.

Tips: "Our audience is school and public libraries for our more reference-oriented books and libraries, schools and bookstores for our less reference-oriented informational titles."

FAIRVIEW PRESS, 2450 Riverside Ave. S., Minneapolis MN 55454. (800)544-8207. Fax: (612)672-4980. Website: http://www.press.fairview.org. Publisher: Edward A. Wedman. **Acquisitions:** Lane Stiles, senior editor; Stephanie Billecke, assistant editor; Jessica Thorson, children's editor. "Fairview Press publishes books and related materials that educate families and individuals about their physical and emotional health, and motivate them to seek positive changes in themselves and their communities." Publishes hardcover and trade paperback originals and reprints. **Publishes 24-30 titles/year. Receives 3,000 queries and 500 mss/year. 40% of books from first-time authors; 65% from unagented writers. Pays 8-12% royalty on wholesale price. Offers $500-2,500 advance.** Publishes book 1 year after acceptance of ms. Accepts simultaneous submissions. Reports in 3 months on proposals. Book catalog and manuscript guidelines free.

Imprint(s): Growing & Reading with Bob Keeshan (contact Jessica Thoreson, children's book editor).

Nonfiction: Children's/juvenile, how-to, reference, self-help. Subjects include child guidance/parenting, psychology, sociology, social and family issues. "We publish books on issues that impact families and the communities in which they live. Manuscripts that are essentially one person's story are rarely saleable." Submit proposal package, including outline, 2 sample chapters, author information, marketing ideas and SASE. Reviews artwork/photos as part of ms package. Send photocopies.

Recent Title(s): *The Therapy Answer Book*, by Kathleen L. Papantola, Ph.D. (psychology/self-help).

Tips: Audience is general reader, especially families. "Tell us what void your book fills in the market; give us an angle. Tell us who will buy your book. We have moved away from recovery books and have focused on social, community and family issues."

FAITH PUBLISHING COMPANY, P.O. Box 237, Milford OH 45150. Fax: (513)576-0022. **Acquisitions:** Mary Ann Liming, president. "Faith publishes works written to draw the reader to a deeper love for God." Publishes trade paperback originals and reprints. **Publishes 2-7 titles/year. Receives 100 queries and 30 mss/year. 50% of books from first-time authors; 100% from unagented writers.** Publishes book 6 months after acceptance of ms. Accepts simultaneous submissions. Reports in 3 months on mss. Book catalog and ms guidelines for #10 SASE.

Nonfiction: Biography, reference, devotional. Religious (Roman Catholic) subjects. Submit entire ms with SASE. *Writer's Market* recommends query with SASE. Reviews artwork/photos as part of ms package. Send photocopies.

Fiction: Religious, short story collections, both with Roman Catholic emphasis. Submit entire ms with SASE.

Recent Title(s): *After Life*, by Michael H. Brown (journalistic devotional); *God in a Box*, by Frank Callison (inspirational fiction).

FALCON PUBLISHING, INC., Landmark Communications, Box 1718, Helena MT 59624. (406)442-6597. Fax: (406)442-2995. E-mail: falconbk@ix.netcom. Website: http://www.falconguide.com. **Acquisitions:** Molly Jay, editorial assistant. Estab. 1978. "Falcon Press is primarily interested in ideas for recreational guidebooks and books on regional outdoor subjects." Publishes hardcover and trade paperback originals. **Publishes 80 titles/year. Receives 350 queries and 30 mss/year. 20% of books from first-time authors; 95% from unagented writers. Pays royalty on net sales.** Publishes book 1-2 years after acceptance of ms. Accepts simultaneous submissions. Reports in 2 months on queries. Book catalog for $2.50.
Imprint(s): Chockstone, Falcon Guide, Insiders', Sky House, **Two Dot**.
Nonfiction: Illustrated book, guide books. Subjects include nature/environment, recreation, travel. Query with SASE. "We can only respond to queries submitted on the topics listed above. No fiction, no poetry." Reviews artwork/photos as part of the ms package. Send transparencies.
Recent Title(s): *Hiking Pennsylvania*; *Mountain Biking Moab.*

FANFARE, Bantam Books, Bantam Doubleday Dell, 1540 Broadway, New York NY 10036. (212)354-6500. Fax: (212)782-9523. Website: http://www.bdd.com. **Acquisition:** Beth de Guzman, senior editor; Wendy McCurdy, senior editor; Stephanie Kip, editor; Cassie Goddard, associate editor. Fanfare "publishes a range of the best voices in women's fiction from brand new to established authors." **Published 30 titles/year. 10-15% of books from first-time authors; less than 5% from unagented writers. Royalty and advance negotiable.** Publishes book 18 months after acceptance of ms. Accepts simultaneous submissions. Reports in 3 months on queries; 4 months on requested proposals and mss.
Fiction: Publishes romance and women's contemporary fiction only. Adventure/romance, historical/romance, suspense/romance, western/romance. Length: 90,000-120,000 words. Query with SASE. *No unsolicited mss.*
Recent Title(s): *Stolen Hearts*, by Michelle Martin (contemporary romance).
Tips: "We advise that writers review the titles we have published in the past several years to get an idea of what we are looking for. Be aware of our needs in terms of length and content of manuscripts."

FARRAR STRAUS & GIROUX BOOKS FOR YOUNG READERS, Farrar Straus Giroux, Inc., 19 Union Square West, New York NY 10003. (212)741-6900. Fax: (212)633-2427. **Acquisitions:** Margaret Ferguson, editor-in-chief. Estab. 1946. "We publish original and well-written material for all ages." Publishes hardcover and trade paperback originals. **Publishes 50 titles/year. Receives 6,000 queries and mss/year. 10% of books from first-time authors; 50% from unagented writers. Pays 6% royalty on retail price for paperbacks, up to 10% for hardcovers. Offers $3,000-15,000 advance.** Publishes book 18 months after acceptance of ms. Accepts simultaneous submissions, if informed. Reports in 2 months on queries, 3 months on mss. Book catalog for 9×12 SASE with 3 first-class stamps. Manuscript guidelines for #10 SASE.
Imprint(s): Aerial Fiction, Francis Foster Books, Mirasol/Libros Juveniles, R and S Books, Sunburst Paperbacks.
Fiction: Juvenile, picture books, young adult. Query with SASE; considers complete ms. "We still look at unsolicited manuscripts, but for novels we prefer synopsis and sample chapters. Always enclose SASE for any materials author wishes returned. Query status of submissions in writing—no calls, please."
Recent Title(s): *Belle Prater's Boy*, by Ruth White—won Newbery Honor (novel, ages 9-12).
Tips: Audience is full age range, preschool to young adult. Specializes in literary fiction.

FARRAR, STRAUS & GIROUX, INC., 19 Union Square West, New York NY 10003. Fax: (212)633-2427. **Acquisitions:** Jonathan Galassi, editor-in-chief (fiction, poetry, arts, biography, general nonfiction); Elisabeth Sifton, publisher (Hill & Wang: European history, literary criticism, historical biography, European literature, German literature in translation); John Glusman, executive editor (literary fiction, popular science, literary biography, belles lettres); Rebecca Saletan, editorial director (North Point Press: literary nonfiction, food writing, memoir); Elizabeth Dyssegaard, executive editor (Noonday: Scandinavian literature in translation, health, women's issues, education); Lauren Osborne, editor (Hill & Wang: American history, cultural studies, law, philosophy); Paul Elie, editor (literary nonfiction, poetry, religion, music); Ethan Nosowsky, editor (literary fiction, nature writing, biography, cultural history); Rebecca Kurson, assistant editor (natural history, anthropology, Jucaica, fiction, sports). Farrar, Straus & Giroux is one of the most respected publishers of top-notch commercial-literary fiction and specialized nonfiction, as well as cutting-edge poetry. Publishes hardcover originals. **Publishes 120 titles/year. Receives 5,000 submissions/year. Pays royalty. Offers advance.** Publishes book 18 months after acceptance. Reports in 3 months. Catalog for 9×12 SAE with 3 first-class stamps.
Imprint(s): Faber & Faber Inc., Farrar Straus & Giroux Books for Young Readers, Hill & Wang, Noonday Press, **North Point Press**, Sunburst Books.
Nonfiction and Fiction: Submit outline/synopsis, sample chapters. Reviews artwork/photos as part of ms package.
Recent Title(s): *Slaves in the Family*, by Edward Ball (nonfiction); *Gain*, by Richard Powers (fiction); *Birthday Letters*, by Ted Hughes (poetry).

FAWCETT JUNIPER, Ballantine Books, 201 E. 50th St., New York NY 10022. (212)751-2600. **Acquisitions:** Leona Nevler, editor. **Publishes 24 titles/year. Pays royalty. Offers advance.** Publishes book 1 year after acceptance. Accepts simultaneous submissions. Reports in 6 months on queries.
Nonfiction: Adult books.
Fiction: Mainstream/contemporary, young adult (12-18). No children's books. Query.
Recent Title(s): *My Life: Magic Johnson*, by Magic Johnson; *The Genesis Code*, by John Case.

THE FEMINIST PRESS AT THE CITY UNIVERSITY OF NEW YORK, Wingate Hall, City College/CUNY, Convent Ave. at 138th St., New York NY 10031. (212)650-8890. Fax: (212)650-8893. Executive Director: Susan Cozzi. **Acquisitions:** Jean Casella, senior editor; Denise Maynard, assistant editor (juvenile). Estab. 1970. "Our primary mission is to publish works of fiction by women which preserve and extend women's literary traditions. We emphasize work by multicultural/international women writers." Publishes hardcover and trade paperback originals and reprints. **Publishes 22 titles/year. Receives 1,000 submissions/year. 20% of books from first-time authors; 80% from unagented writers. Pays royalty on net price. Offers $250 average advance.** Accepts simultaneous submissions. Reports in 4 months on proposals. Book catalog for 8½×11 SASE. Ms guidelines for #10 SASE.

Nonfiction: "We look for nonfiction work which challenges gender-role stereotypes and documents women's historical and cultural contributions. No monographs. Note that we generally publish for the college classroom as well as the trade." Children's (ages 8 and up)/juvenile, primary materials for the humanities and social science classroom and general readers, with a special emphasis on multicultural and international characters and settings. Subjects include ethnic, gay/lesbian, government/politics, health/medicine, history, language/literature, music, sociology, translation, women's issues/studies and peace, memoir, international. Send proposal package, including materials requested in guidelines. Reviews artwork/photos as part of ms package. Send photocopies and SASE.

Fiction: "The Feminist Press publishes fiction reprints only. No original fiction is considered."

Recent Title(s): *A Cross and a Star*, by Marjorie Agosin (memoirs of a Jewish girl in Chile).

FERGUSON PUBLISHING COMPANY, (formerly J.G. Ferguson Publishing Company), 200 W. Madison, Suite 300, Chicago IL 60606. Website: http://www.fergpubco.com. **Acquisitions:** Holli Cosgrove, editorial director. Estab. 1940. "We are primarily a career education publisher that publishes for schools and libraries." Publishes hardcover originals. **Publishes 15 titles/year. Reports in 3 months on queries. Pays by project.**

Nonfiction: Reference. "We publish work specifically for the junior high/high school/college library reference market. Works are generally encyclopedic in nature. Our current focus is career encyclopedias. No mass market, scholarly, or juvenile books, please." Query or submit outline and 1 sample chapter.

Recent Title(s): *Career Discovery Encyclopedia*, edited by Holli Cosgrove.

Tips: "We like writers who know the market—former or current librarians or teachers or guidance counselors."

FILTER PRESS, P.O. Box 95, Palmer Lake CO 80133-0095. (719)481-2420. Fax: (719)481-2420. E-mail: filter.press@mci2000.com. **Acquisitions:** Doris Baker, president. Estab. 1956. Filter Press specializes in nonfiction of the West. Publishes trade paperback originals and reprints. **Publishes 4-6 titles/year. Pays 10-12% royalty on wholesale price.** Publishes ms an average of 8 months after acceptance.

Nonfiction: Subjects include Americana, anthropology/archaeology, cooking/foods/nutrition, crafts and crafts people of the Southwest, women writers of the West. "We're interested in the history and natural history of the West." Query with outline and SASE. Reviews artwork/photos as part of ms package.

Recent Title(s): *The Glorious Quest of Chief Washakie*, by R. Tillman (biography).

FIREBRAND BOOKS, 141 The Commons, Ithaca NY 14850. (607)272-0000. **Acquisitions:** Nancy K. Bereano, publisher. Estab. 1985. "Our audience includes feminists, lesbians, ethnic audiences, and other progressive people." Publishes hardcover and trade paperback originals. **Publishes 6-8 titles/year. Receives 400-500 submissions/year. 50% of books from first-time authors; 90% from unagented writers. Pays 7-9% royalty on retail price, or makes outright purchase.** Publishes book 18 months after acceptance. Accepts simultaneous submissions, if so noted. Reports in 1 month on queries. *Writer's Market* recommends allowing 2 months for reply. Book catalog free.

Nonfiction: Personal narratives, essays. Subjects include feminism, lesbianism. Submit complete ms.

Fiction: Considers all types of feminist and lesbian fiction.

Recent Title(s): *Don't Explain*, by Jewelle Gomez.

FISHER BOOKS, 4239 W. Ina Road, Suite 101, Tucson AZ 85741. (520)744-6110. Fax: (520)744-0944. Website: http://www.fisherbooks.com. **Acquisitions:** Sarah Trotta, managing editor. Estab. 1987. Publishes trade paperback originals and reprints. **Publishes 16 titles/year. 25% of books from first-time authors; 75% from unagented writers. Pays 10-15% royalty on wholesale price.** Accepts simultaneous submissions. Book catalog for 8½×11 SAE with 3 first-class stamps.

Nonfiction: Subjects include automotive, business, cooking/foods/nutrition, regional gardening, family health, self-help. Submit outline and sample chapter with SASE. *No unsolicited mss.*

Recent Title(s): *Your Pregnancy After 30*, by Glade B. Curtis, M.D. (health).

FJORD PRESS, INC., P.O. Box 16349, Seattle WA 98116. (206)935-7376. Fax: (206)938-1991. E-mail: fjord@halcyon.com. Website: http://www.fjordpress.com/fjord. **Acquisitions:** Steven T. Murray, editor-in-chief. "We publish only literary novels of the highest quality." Publishes trade paperback originals and reprints. **Publishes 4-6 titles/year. Receives 1,500 queries and 200 mss/year. 10% of books from first-time authors; 80% from unagented writers. Pays 8-10% royalty on retail price or small advance and royalty. Offers $250-1,000 advance.** Publishes book 7-24 months after acceptance of ms. Accepts simultaneous submissions. Reports in 2 months on queries. Book catalog and ms guidelines for #10 SASE.

- Fjord Press also sponsors the Fjord Discoveries First Novel Award. Guidelines for SASE and on website. Charges $20 fee. Prize: $1,000 and possible publication.

Fiction: Ethnic, feminist (but not anti-male), literary, mainstream/contemporary, mystery, suspense (no military or techno), literature in translation. "Topics we do not do: WWII, historical, child abuse, anything medical or religious, fantasy or science fiction, romance, gore, kinky sex, recovering anything." Query or submit 1 sample chapter (not over 20 pages) and SASE.
Recent Title(s): *Plenty Good Room*, by Teresa McClain-Watson (African American novel).
Tips: Audience is literate readers looking for something different and willing to take a chance on an unfamiliar author. "If your fiction isn't as good as what's out there on the market, save your postage and keep practicing. If you expect to get rich by selling your book to Hollywood, write a screenplay instead. We want serious and entertaining novels (50,000-90,000 words) with well-rounded characters we can remember. Looking for new voices from both the African-American and white, Gen-X, angst communities, especially writers who love music and have a sense of rhythm in their prose. Some of our favorite writers are: Kafka, E. Leonard, Mosley, Morrison, Stegner, T. Wolff—get the idea?"

N **FLORICANTO PRESS**, Inter American Corp., 650 Castro St., Suite 120-331, Mountain View CA 94041. (415)552-1879. Fax: (415)793-2662. E-mail: floricanto@msn. Website: http://www.floricantopress.com. Publishes hardcover and trade paperback originals and reprints. **Publishes 6 titles/year. Receives 200 queries/year. 60% of books from first-time authors; 5% from unagented writers. Pays 5% royalty on wholesale price. Offers $500-1,500 advance.** Rejected mss destroyed. Reports in 3 months on queries, 7 months on mss. Book catalog for #10 SASE.
Nonfiction: Biography, cookbook, reference. Subjects include anthropology/archaeology, ethnic (Hispanic), health/medicine, history, language/literature, psychology, women's issues/studies. "We are looking primarily for nonfiction popular (but serious) titles that appeal the general public on Hispanic subjects: history, language, psychology, biography, cookbooks. Submit outline and sample chapter(s).
Fiction: Adventure, erotica, ethnic (Hispanic), literary, occult, romance, short story collections. "On fiction we prefer contemporary works and themes." Submit synopsis and 1 sample chapter.
Recent Title(s): *Far from My Mother's Home*, by Barbara Jujica (short stories); *Cinco de Mayo: A Symbol of Mexican Resistance* (nonfiction).
Tips: Audience is general public interested in Hispanic culture. "Submit material as described, on DOS disk, graphic art for cover. We need authors that are willing to promote heavily their work."

FOCAL PRESS, Butterworth Heinemann, Reed Elsevier (USA) Inc., 275 Wildwood Ave., Woburn MA 01801-2041. Fax: (781)904-2640. E-mail: marie.lee@bhusa.com. Website: http://www.bh.com/fp/. **Acquisitions:** Marie Lee, senior editor. Estab. US, 1981; UK, 1938. "Focal Press is based on over 50 years of quality publishing in all areas of the media, from audio, broadcasting, and cinematography, through to journalism, radio, television, video, and writing. Focal Press books provide a comprehensive library of reference material for anyone involved in these varied fields." Publishes hardcover and paperback originals and reprints. **Publishes 40-45 UK-US titles/year; entire firm publishes 200 titles/year. Receives 500-700 submissions/year. 25% of books from first-time authors; 90% from unagented writers. Pays 10-12% royalty on wholesale price. Offers modest advance.** Publishes book 9 months after acceptance. Accepts simultaneous submissions. Reports in 2 months. Book catalog and ms guidelines for SASE.
Nonfiction: How-to, reference, technical and textbooks in media arts: photography, film and cinematography, broadcasting, theater and performing arts and audio, sound and media technology. High-level scientific/technical monographs are also considered. "We do not publish collections of photographs or books composed primarily of photographs. Our books are text-oriented, with artwork serving to illustrate and expand on points in the text." Query preferred, or submit outline and sample chapters. Reviews artwork/photos as part of ms package.
Recent Title(s): *Practical Recording Techniques*, by Bruce Bartlett and Jenny Bartlett.
Tips: "We are publishing fewer photography books. Our advances and royalties are more carefully determined with an eye toward greater profitability for all our publications."

FOCUS PUBLISHING, INC., 1375 Washington Ave. S., Bemidji MN 56601. (218)759-9817. Fax: (218)751-2183. E-mail: focus@paulbunyan.net. Website: http://www.paulbunyan.net/focus. **Acquisitions:** Jan Haley, vice president. "Focus Publishing is a small press primarily devoted to Christian books and appropriate to children and home-schooling families." Publishes hardcover and trade paperback originals and reprints. **Publishes 4-6 titles/year. Receives 250 queries and 100 mss/year. 90% of books from first-time authors; 100% from unagented writers. Pays 7-10% royalty on retail price.** Publishes book 1 year after acceptance of ms. Reports in 2 months. Book catalog free.
Nonfiction: Children's/juvenile. Subjects include religion, women's issues/studies. Submit proposal package, including marketing ideas with SASE. Reviews artwork/photos as part of the ms package. Send photocopies.
Fiction: Juvenile, picture books, religious, young adult. "We are looking for Christian books for men and young adults. Be sure to list your target audience." Query and submit synopsis.
Poetry: "We are not especially interested in poetry at this time." Query.
Recent Title(s): *Three to Get Ready*, by Dr. Howard Eyrich (Christian Marriage counseling); *The Gift*, by Jan Haley (children's picture book).
Tips: "I prefer SASE inquiries, synopsis and target markets. Please don't send 5 lbs. of paper with no return postage. Our focus is on Christian living books for adults and children. Only Biblically-sound proposals considered."

N **FODOR'S TRAVEL PUBLICATIONS, INC.**, Random House, 201 E. 50th, New York NY 10022. **Acquisitions**: Karen Cure, editorial director. Publishes trade paperback originals. **Publishes 150 titles/year. Receives 100 queries and 4 mss/year. Most titles are collective works, with contributions as works for hire. Most contributions are**

updates of previously published volumes. Publishes book 1 year after acceptance of ms. Accepts simultaneous submissions. Reports in 2 months on queries. Book catalog free.

Nonfiction: Travel guides, some illustrated. "We're not interested in travel literature or in proposals for general travel guidebooks. We are interested in unique approaches to favorite destinations. Writers seldom review our catalog or our list and often query about books on topics that we're already covering. Beyond that, it's important to review competition and to say what the proposed book will add." Query or submit outline, sample chapter(s) and proposal package, including competition review and review of market with SASE. "Do not send originals without first querying as to our interest in the project."

Recent Title(s): *France '98*, by Fodor's (travel guide).

Tips: Audience is travelers who buy and use guidebooks. "In preparing your query or proposal, remember that it's the only argument Fodor's will hear about why your book will be a good one and why you think it will sell; and it's also best evidence of your ability to create the book you propose. Craft your proposal well and carefully so that it puts your best foot forward."

N **FOGHORN PRESS**, 340 Bodega Ave., Petaluma CA 94952. (707)521-3300. Fax: (707)521-3361. Website: http://www.foghorn.com. **Acquisitions:** Dave Morgan, publisher; Vicki De Armon, marketing director; Donna Leverenz, editor-in-chief. Publishes trade paperback originals and reprints. Publishes outdoor recreation guidebooks. **Publishes 30 titles/year. Receives 500 queries and 200 mss/year. 30% of books from first-time authors; 98% from unagented writers. Pays 12% royalty on wholesale price; occasional work-for-hire.** Publishes book 18 months after acceptance of ms. Accepts simultaneous submissions. Reports in 1 month on queries, 2 months on proposals and mss. Book catalog and ms guidelines free.

Nonfiction: Outdoor recreation guidebooks. Subjects include nature/environment, recreation (camping, hiking, fishing), sports, outdoors, leisure. Submit proposal package, including outline or chapter headings, résumé, 2 or more sample chapters, marketing plan, author information.

Recent Title(s): *California Camping*, by Tom Stienstra.

Tips: "We are expanding our list nationally in the formats we already publish (camping, hiking, fishing, dogs) as well as developing new formats to test California."

FORGE, Tom Doherty Associates, Inc., St. Martin's Press, 175 Fifth Ave., 14th Floor, New York NY 10010. (212)388-0100. Fax: (212)388-0191. Website: http://www.tor.com. **Acquisitions:** David G. Hartwell, senior editor (science fiction and fantasy, western/historical, thriller, suspense); Patrick Nielsen Hayden, senior editor (science fiction and fantasy, technological, thriller, alternate history); Melissa Ann Singer, senior editor (western/historical, medical or biotechnological thriller, contemporary mysteries, contemporary women's fiction, historical, women's or health issues, horror/occult); Natalia Aponte, editor (Western/historical, women of the west, contemporary mystery, contemporary women's fiction, suspense/thriller, historical); Claire Eddy, editor (science fiction and fantasy, contemporary and historical mystery, historical suspense); Stephen de las Heras, editor (science fiction, western/historical); Jenna Felice, editor (science fiction and fantasy). "TDA publishes the best of past, present, and future—meaning that we cover all ground in fiction from historicals set in prehistory to the sharpest contemporary fiction to the acknowledged best in science fiction and fantasy." Publishes hardcover, trade paperback and mass market paperback originals, trade and mass market paperback reprints. **Receives 5,000 mss/year. 2% of books from first-time authors; a few from unagented writers. Royalties: paperback, 6-8% first-time authors, 8-10% established authors; hardcover, 10% first 5,000, 12½% second 5,000, 15% thereafter. Offers $7,500 and up advance.** Reports in 4 months on proposals. Book catalog for 9×12 SASE with 2 first-class stamps.

Imprint(s): TOR Books (science fiction, fantasy and horror); Orb (reprint science fiction, fantasy and horror).

Nonfiction: Subjects include health/medicine, women's issues/studies. Query with outline and 3 sample chapters.

Fiction: Historical, horror, mainstream/contemporary, mystery, suspense, thriller; general fiction of all sorts. "We handle a wide range of books; if you're not sure if a project is right for us, phone us and ask." Query with synopsis and 3 sample chapters.

Recent Title(s): *Windy City*, by Hugh Holton (mystery).

FORTRESS PRESS, Augsburg Fortress Publishers. Box 1209, Minneapolis MN 55440. (612)330-3300. Fax: (612)330-3455. Website: http://www.augsburgfortress.org. **Acquisitions**: Dr. Henry F. French, editorial director; Dr. K.C. Hanson, acquisitions editor; J. Michael West, senior editor. Estab. 1855. Fortress Press publishes academic books in Biblical studies, theology, Christian ethics, church history. Publishes hardcover and trade paperback originals. **Publishes 45 titles/year. Receives 500-700 queries/year. 5-10% of books from first-time authors. Pays royalty on retail price. No advance.** Publishes book 1 year after acceptance of ms. Accepts simultaneous submissions. Reports in 3 months on proposals. Book catalog free (call 1-800-328-4648). Manuscript guidelines available online.

Nonfiction: Subjects include government/politics, history, religion, women's issues/studies, African-American studies. Query with annotated toc, brief cv, sample chapter (introduction) and SASE. Please study guidelines before submitting.

Recent Title(s): *Women and Redemption*, by Rosemary Ruether.

FORUM, Prima Publishing, 3875 Atherton Rd., Rocklin CA 95765. (916)632-4400. Fax: (916)632-4403. **Acquisitions:** Steven Martin, editorial director. "Forum publishes business books that contribute to the marketplace of ideas." Publishes hardcover and trade paperback originals and reprints. **Publishes 10-15 titles/year. 25% of books from first-time authors; 5% from unagented writers. Pays variable advance and royalty.** Publishes book 1 year after acceptance

of ms. Accepts simultaneous submissions. Reports in 1 month on queries and proposals, 2 months on mss.
Nonfiction: Subjects include libertarian/conservative thought, business/economics, government/politics, history, religion, current affairs, individual empowerment. Query with outline, 1 sample chapter and SASE.
Recent Title(s): *Reagan on Leadership*, by James Strock (business).

FORWARD MOVEMENT PUBLICATIONS, 412 Sycamore St., Cincinnati OH 45202. Fax: (513)721-0729. E-mail: forward.movement@ecunet.org. Website: http://www.dfms.org/forward-movement. **Acquisitions:** Edward S. Gleason, editor and director. "Forward Movement was established in 1934 'to help reinvigorate the life of the church.' Many titles focus on the life of prayer, where our relationship with God is centered, death, marriage, baptism, recovery, joy, the Episcopal Church and more." Publishes trade paperback originals. **Publishes 12 titles/year. 50% of books from first-time authors; 100% from unagented writers. Pays one-time honorarium.** Reports in 1 month on queries and proposals, 2 months on mss. Book catalog for 9×12 SAE with $1.47 postage.

- The editor notes that this publisher is just beginning to seek middle school (ages 8-12) fiction in their subject area.

Nonfiction: Essays. Religious subjects. "We publish a variety of types of books, but they all relate to the lives of Christians. We are an agency of the Episcopal Church." Query with SASE.
Fiction: Episcopal for middle school (ages 8-12) readers. Query with SASE.
Recent Title(s): *Ecumenism 101*, by Alton Motter (Ecumenical movement).
Tips: Audience is primarily members of mainline Protestant churches.

WALTER FOSTER PUBLISHING, INC., A Quarto Group Company, 23062 La Cadena Dr., Laguna Hills CA 92653. **Acquisitions:** Sheena Needham, creative director. "We publish instructional 'how to' art/craft instruction only." Publishes trade paperback originals. **Publishes 40-100 titles/year. Receives 10-20 queries/year. 50% of books from first-time authors; 100% from unagented writers. Makes outright purchase. No advance.** Publishes book 1-2 years after acceptance of ms. Accepts simultaneous submissions. Reports in 2 months on queries, 6 months on proposals and mss. "Don't call us, we'll call you." Book catalog free.
Nonfiction: How-to. Arts and crafts subjects. Submit proposal package, including query letter, color photos/examples of artwork. Reviews artwork/photos as part of ms package. Send color photocopies or color photos. "Send enough samples of your artwork to prove your qualifications."
Recent Title(s): *Papier-Mâché* (art instruction).

FOUL PLAY, W.W. Norton, 500 Fifth Ave., New York NY 10110. (212)354-5500. Fax: (212)869.0856. Website: http://www.wwnorton.com. **Acquisitions:** Candace Watt, editor. Estab. 1996. "We publish a broad range of mysteries, from cozies to hard-boiled to traditional." Publishes hardcover originals and reprints. **Publishes 6 titles/year. Receives hundreds of queries/year. A small percentage of books from first-time authors; 10% from unagented writers. Pays royalty on retail price. Advance varies.** Publishes book 6 months after acceptance of ms. Reporting time varies. Book catalog free from W.W. Norton (same address).
Fiction: Mystery, suspense. Query with synopsis, 1 sample chapter and SASE.
Recent Title(s): *Death of a Sunday Writer*, by Eric Wright.

FOUR WALLS EIGHT WINDOWS, 39 W. 14th St., Room 503, New York NY 10011. Fax: (212)206-8799. E-mail: eightwind@aol.com. Website: http://www.fourwallseightwindows.com. Publisher: John Oakes. **Acquisitions.** Acquisitions Editor. Estab. 1987. "Emphasizing fine literature and quality nonfiction, Four Walls Eight Windows has a reputation for carefully edited and distinctive books." Publishes hardcover originals, trade paperback originals and reprints. **Publishes 20 titles/year. Receives 3,000 submissions/year. 15% of books from first-time authors; 50% from unagented writers. Pays royalty on retail price. Advance varies widely.** Publishes book 1-2 years after acceptance. Reports in 2 months on queries. Book catalog for 6×9 SAE with 3 first-class stamps.
Nonfiction: Political, investigative. Subjects include art/architecture, government/politics, history, language/literature, nature/environment, science. No New Age. Query with outline and SASE. All mss without SASE discarded.
Fiction: Feminist, literary, science fiction. "No romance, popular." Query first with outline/synopsis and SASE.
Recent Title(s): *Genesis: The Story of Apollo 8*, by Robert Zimmerman (science); *Arcade*, by Gordon Lish (fiction).

FOX CHAPEL PUBLISHING, 1970 Broad St., East Petersburg PA 17520. **Acquisitions:** John Alan. Fox Chapel publishes woodworking and woodcarving titles for professionals and hobbyists. Publishes hardcover and trade paperback originals and trade paperback reprints. **Publishes 12-20 titles/year. 80% of books from first-time authors; 100% from unagented writers. Pays royalty or makes outright purchase. Advance varies.** Publishes book 6-18 months after acceptance of ms. Accepts simultaneous submissions. Reports in 2 months on queries.
Nonfiction: Woodworking, woodcarving and related titles. Query. Reviews artwork/photos as part of ms package. Send photocopies.
Recent Title(s): *Making Classic Chairs: A Chippendale Reference*, by Ron Clarkson.
Tips: "We're looking for knowledgeable artists, woodworkers first, writers second to write for us. Our market is for avid woodworking hobbyists and professionals."

FRANCISCAN UNIVERSITY PRESS, University Blvd., Steubenville OH 43952. Fax: (614)283-6427. Website: http://esoptron.umd.edu/fusfolder/press.html. **Acquisitions:** James Fox, executive director. "We seek to further the

Catholic and Franciscan mission of Franciscan University of Steubenville by publishing quality popular-level Catholic apologetics and biblical studies. In this manner we hope to serve Pope John Paul II's call for a new evangelization of today's Catholics." Publishes trade paperback originals and reprints. **Publishes 7 titles/year. 5% of books from first-time authors; 100% from unagented writers. Pays 5-15% royalty on retail price.** Publishes book 1 year after acceptance of ms. Reports in 3 months on proposals. Book catalog and ms guidelines free.
Nonfiction: Popular level Catholic theology. Subjects include catechetics, scripture, Catholic apologetics. Query with cv and SASE.
Recent Title(s): *If Your Mind Wanders at Mass*, by Thomas Howard (religion/liturgy).
Tips: "95% of our publications are solicited from authors who have already been published."

THE FREE PRESS, Simon & Schuster, 1230 Avenue of the Americas, New York NY 10020. (212)698-7000. Fax: (212)632-4989. **Acquisitions:** Liz Maguire, editorial director; Paul Golob; Adam Bellow; Robert Wallace, senior editor (business); Bruce Nichols, senior editor (history); Paul Golob (current events/politics); Philip Rapapport, editor (psychology/social work/self-help); Steven Morrow, editor (science, math, literature, art). Estab. 1947. The Free Press publishes serious adult nonfiction. **Publishes 120 titles/year. Receives 3,000 submissions/year. 15% of books from first-time authors; 50% of books from unagented writers. Pays variable royalty.** Publishes book 1 year after acceptance of ms. Reports in 2 months.
Nonfiction: professional books and college texts in the social sciences, humanities and business. Reviews artwork/photos as part of ms package. "We look for an identifiable target audience, evidence of writing ability." Accepts nonfiction translations. Query with 1-3 sample chapters, outline before submitting mss.

FREE SPIRIT PUBLISHING INC., 400 First Ave. N., Suite 616, Minneapolis MN 55401-1730. (612)338-2068. Fax: (612)337-5050. E-mail: help4kids@freespirit.com. Publisher: Judy Galbraith. **Acquisitions:** Caryn Pernu, acquisitions editor. "We believe passionately in empowering kids to learn to think for themselves and make their own good choices." Publishes trade paperback originals and reprints. **Publishes 20 titles/year. 10% of books from first-time authors; 90% from unagented writers. Offers advance.** Book catalog and ms guidelines free.
Imprint(s): Self-Help for Kids®, Free Spirited Classroom® Series.
Nonfiction: Self-Help for Kids ®. Subjects include child guidance/parenting, education (pre-K-12, but not textbooks or basic skills books like reading, counting, etc.), health (mental/emotional health—*not* physical health—for/about children), psychology (for/about children), sociology (for/about children). Query with outline, 2 sample chapters and SASE. Send photocopies. "Many of our authors are teachers, counselors or others involved in helping kids."
Recent Title(s): *The Right Moves, A Girl's Guide to Getting Fit and Feeling Good*, by Tina Schwager and Michelle Schleger.
Tips: "Our audience is children, teens, teachers, parents and youth counselors. We are concerned with kids' mental/emotional well-being. We are not looking for academic or religious materials, nor books that analyze problems with the nation's school systems. Instead we want books that offer practical, positive advice so kids can help themselves."

FRIENDS UNITED PRESS, 101 Quaker Hill, Richmond IN 47374. (765)962-7573. Fax: (765)966-1293. Website: http://www.fum.org. **Acquisitions:** Barbara Bennett Mays, editor/manager. Estab. 1968. "Friends United Press commits itself to energize and equip Friends and others through the power of the Holy Spirit to gather people into fellowship where Jesus Christ is known, loved and obeyed as teacher and Lord." **Publishes 5 titles/year. Receives 100 queries and 80 mss/year. 50% of books from first-time authors; 99% from unagented writers. Pays 7½% royalty.** Publishes ms 1 year after acceptance of ms. Accepts simultaneous submissions. Reports in 3 months. Book catalog and ms guidelines free.
Nonfiction: Biography, humor, children's/juvenile, reference, textbook. Religious subjects. "Authors should be Quaker and should be familiar with Quaker history, spirituality and doctrine." Submit proposal package. Reviews artwork/photos as part of ms package. Send photocopies.
Fiction: Historical, juvenile, religious. "Must be Quaker-related." Query.
Recent Title(s): *The Fairest Isle*, by Mary Langford (history of Friends in Jamaica).
Tips: "Spirituality manuscripts must be in agreement with Quaker spirituality."

FROMM INTERNATIONAL PUBLISHING CORPORATION, 560 Lexington Ave., New York NY 10022. **Acquisitions:** Fred Jordan, executive director; Matthew McGowan, assistant editor. Publishes hardcover originals, trade paperback originals and reprints. **Publishes 20-25 titles/year. Receives 200 mss/year. 10% of books from first-time authors; 10% from unagented writers. Pays 10-15% royalty. Offers $2,500 advance.** Publishes book 1 year after acceptance of ms. Accepts simultaneous submissions. Reports in 1 month on queries and proposals, 2 months on mss. Book catalog free.
Nonfiction: Biography, illustrated book, reference. Subjects include Americana, art/architecture, health/medicine, history, language/literature, psychology, popular culture. Submit 3 sample chapters and table of contents with SASE. Reviews artwork/photos as part of ms package. Send photocopies.
Recent Title(s): *The Story of Britain*, by Roy Strong (history).
Tips: Audience is the general trade, both popular and "high brow."

GATF PRESS, Graphic Arts Technical Foundation, 200 Deer Run Rd., Sewickley PA 15143-2600. (412)741-6860. Fax: (412)741-2311. E-mail: poresick@gatf.com. Website: http://www.gatf.org. **Acquisitions:** Peter Oresick, director

of publications; Tom Destree, editor in chief; Pamela J. Groff, technical editor. Estab. 1924. "GATF's mission is to serve the graphic communications community as the major resource for technical information and services through research and education." Publishes trade paperback originals and hardcover reference texts. **Publishes 15 titles/year. Receives 25 submissions/year. 50% of books from first-time authors; 100% from unagented writers. Pays 5-15% royalty on retail price.** Publishes book 6 months after acceptance. Reports in 1 month on queries. *Writer's Market* recommends allowing 2 months for reply. Book catalog for 9×12 SAE with 2 first-class stamps. Manuscript guidelines for #10 SASE.
Nonfiction: How-to, reference, technical, textbook. Subjects include printing/graphic communications and electronic publishing. "We primarily want textbook/reference books about printing and related technologies. However, we are expanding our reach into general computing and electronic communications." Query with SASE or submit outline, sample chapters and SASE. Reviews artwork/photos as part of ms package.
Recent Title(s): *PDF Bible: A Complete Guide to Acrobat 3.0*, by Mark Witkowski (computers).
Tips: "We are publishing titles that are updated more frequently, such as *Understanding Electronic Communications*. Our scope now includes reference titles geared toward general audiences interested in computers, imaging, and Internet as well as print publishing."

GAY SUNSHINE PRESS and LEYLAND PUBLICATIONS, P.O. Box 410690, San Francisco CA 94141-0690. **Acquisitions:** Winston Leyland, editor. Estab. 1970. "We seek innovative literary nonfiction and fiction depicting gay themes and lifestyles." Publishes hardcover originals, trade paperback originals and reprints. **Publishes 6-8 titles/year. Pays royalty or makes outright purchase.** Reports in 6 weeks on queries. Book catalog for $1.
Nonfiction: How-to and gay lifestyle topics. "We're interested in innovative literary nonfiction which deals with gay lifestyles." No long personal accounts, academic or overly formal titles. Query. "After we respond positively to your query, submit outline and sample chapters with SASE." *All unsolicited mss are returned unopened.*
Fiction: Erotica, ethnic, experimental, historical, mystery, science fiction, translation. "Interested in well-written novels on gay themes; also short story collections. We have a high literary standard for fiction." Query. "After we respond positively to your query, submit outline/synopsis and sample chapters with SASE." All unsolicited mss returned unopened.
Recent Title(s): *Partings at Dawn: An Anthology of Japanese Gay Literature.*

GEM GUIDES BOOK COMPANY, 315 Cloverleaf Dr., Suite F, Baldwin Park CA 91706-6510. (626)855-1611. Fax: (626)855-1610. **Acquisitions**: Kathy Mayerski, editor. "Gem Guides prefers nonfiction books for the hobbyist in rocks and minerals; lapidary and jewelry-making; travel and recreation guide books for the West and Southwest; and other regional local interest." **Publishes 6-8 titles/year. Receives 40 submissions/year. 30% of books from first-time authors; 100% from unagented writers. Pays 6-10% royalty on retail price.** Publishes book 1 year after acceptance. Accepts simultaneous submissions. Reports in 3 months.
Imprint(s): Gembooks.
Nonfiction: Gem Guides specializes in books on earth sciences, lapidary and jewelry-making, nature books, also travel/local interest titles for the Western US. Subjects include hobbies, Western history, nature/environment, recreation, travel. Query with outline/synopsis and sample chapters with SASE. Reviews artwork/photos as part of ms package.
Recent Title(s): *Free Mining Adventures & Rock Hunting Expeditions in the U.S.*, by Monaco & Monaco.
Tips: "We have a general audience of people interested in recreational activities. Publishers plan and have specific book lines in which they specialize. Learn about the publisher and submit materials compatible with that publisher's product line."

GENERAL PUBLISHING GROUP, 2701 Ocean Park Blvd., Suite 140, Santa Monica CA 90405. (310)314-4000. Fax: (310)314-8080. E-mail: gpgedit@aol.com. **Acquisitions:** Peter Hoffman, editorial director. General Publishing Group specializes in popular culture, entertainment, politics and humor titles. Publishes hardcover and trade paperback originals. **Publishes 50 titles/year. Pays royalty.** Publishes ms 8 months after acceptance. Accepts simultaneous submissions. Reports in 4 months on queries. Book catalog free.
Nonfiction: Biography, coffee table book, gift book, humor, illustrated book. Subjects include Americana, art/architecture, music/dance, photography, entertainment/media, politics. Query with proposal package, including sample chapters, toc and SASE. Reviews artwork as part of ms package. Send photocopies.
Recent Title(s): *Stoked: A History of Surf Culture.*

LAURA GERINGER BOOKS, HarperCollins Children's Books, 10 E. 53rd St., New York NY 10022. (212)207-7000. Website: http://www.harpercollins.com. **Acquisitions:** Laura Geringer, editorial director; Caitlyn Dlouhy, senior editor. "We look for books that are out of the ordinary, authors who have their own definite take, and artists that add a sense of humor to the text." Publishes hardcover originals. **Publishes 15-20 titles/year. 5% of books from first-time authors; 25% from unagented writers. Pays 10-12½% on retail price. Advance varies.** Publishes ms 6-12 months after acceptance of ms for novels, 1-2 years after acceptance of ms for picture books. Reports in 2 weeks on queries, 1 month on proposals, 4 months on mss. Book catalog for 8×10 SAE with 3 first-class stamps. Manuscript guidelines for #10 SASE.
Fiction: Children's, adventure, fantasy, historical, humor, literary, picture books, young adult. "A mistake writers often make is failing to research the type of books an imprint publishes, therefore sending inappropriate material." Query with SASE for picture books; submit complete ms with SASE for novels.

Recent Title(s): *Zip: Wolfbay Wings*, by Bruce Brooks (novel).

GESSLER PUBLISHING CO., INC., 10 E. Church Ave., Roanoke VA 24011. (540)345-1429. Fax: (540)342-7172. E-mail: gesslerco@aol.com. Website: http://www.gessler.com. **Acquisitions:** Richard Kurshan, CEO. Estab. 1932. "We provide high-quality language-learning materials for the education market." Publishes trade paperback originals and reprints. **Publishes 75 titles/year. Receives 50 queries and 25 mss/year. 5% of books from first-time authors; 90% from unagented writers, "very few, if any, are agented." Pays 10-20% royalty on retail price. Offers $250-500 advance.** Publishes book 9 months after acceptance of ms. Accepts simultaneous submissions. Reports in 3 days on queries, 3 weeks on mss. *Writer's Market* recommends allowing 2 months for reply. Book catalog free.
Nonfiction: Textbook. Subjects include education, language/literature, multicultural. "We publish supplementary language learning materials. Our products assist teachers with foreign languages, ESL, and multicultural activities." Query first, then submit outline/synopsis with 2-3 sample chapters or complete ms with cover letter and SASE. Reviews artwork/photos as part of ms package. Send photocopies.
Recent Title(s): *Buenviaje*, by Maria Koonce (Spanish workbook).
Tips: Middle school/high school audience. "Writers need to be more open-minded when it comes to understanding not everyone learns the same way. They may have to be flexible when it comes to revising their work to accommodate broader teaching/learning methods."

N **GIFTED EDUCATION PRESS**, 10201 Yuma Court, P.O. Box 1586, Manassas VA 20109. (703)369-5017. **Acquisitions**: Maurice Fisher, publisher. "We publish books on humanities education for gifted children and how to parent gifted children." Publishes mass market paperback originals. **Publishes 10 titles/year. Receives 75 queries and 25 mss/year. 90% of books from first-time authors; 100% from unagented writers. Pays 10-12% royalty on retail price.** Publishes book 3 months after acceptance of ms. Accepts simultaneous submissions. Reports in 1 month. Book catalog free. Manuscript guidelines for #10 SASE.
Nonfiction: Reference, textbook, teacher's guides. Subjects include child guidance/parenting, computers and electronics, education, language/literature, philosophy, psychology, science. "Writers must indicate their expertise in the subject and propose challenging topics for teachers and gifted students." Query or submit outline with SASE. All unsolicited mss returned. Reviews artwork/photos as part of ms package.
Recent Title(s): *Quotations for Creative Insights & Inspiration*, by Ross Butchart (text for teachers and students).
Tips: Audience is parents and teachers of gifted students, university professors and graduate students. "We are looking for clear, straight forward and well-organized writing. Expertise in the topical areas is required."

GLENBRIDGE PUBLISHING LTD., 6010 W. Jewell Ave., Denver CO 80232-7106. Fax: (303)987-9037. **Acquisitions:** James A. Keene, editor. Estab. 1986. "Glenbridge has an eclectic approach to publishing. We look for titles that have long-term capabilities." Publishes hardcover originals and reprints, trade paperback originals. **Publishes 6-8 titles/year. Pays 10% royalty.** Publishes book 1 year after acceptance. Accepts simultaneous submissions. Reports in 2 months on queries. Book catalog for 6×9 SASE. Manuscript guidelines for #10 SASE.
Nonfiction: Subjects include Americana, business/economics, history, music, philosophy, politics, psychology, sociology, cookbooks. Query with outline/synopsis, sample chapters and SASE.
Recent Title(s): *Three Minute Therapy: Change Your Thinking, Change Your Life*, by Dr. Michael Edelstein (psychology).

N **THE GLENLAKE PUBLISHING COMPANY, LTD.**, 1261 W. Glenlake, Chicago IL 60660. (773)262-9765. Fax: (773)262-9436. E-mail: glenlake@ix.netcom.com. Website: http://www.glenlake.com. **Acquisitions**: Barbara Craig, editor. "Glenlake is an independent book publisher whose primary objective is to promote the advancement of current thinking in the areas of business, finance, economics, applied statistics, computer applications to business and statistics, and environmental science and engineering." Publishes hardcover originals. **Publishes 20 titles/year. Receives 50 queries and 5 mss/year. 25% of books from first-time authors; 100% from unagented writers. Pays 10-15% royalty on wholesale price. Offers $1,500 average advance.** Publishes book 2 months after acceptance of ms. Accepts simultaneous submissions. Reports in 1 month on queries. Book catalog free.
Nonfiction: Subjects include business/economics, computers/electronics, money/finance. Submit proposal package, including author's bio, outline, 1 sample chapter and SASE.
Recent Title(s): *International Handbook of Corporate Finance*, by Brian Terry.

THE GLOBE PEQUOT PRESS, INC., P.O. Box 833, Old Saybrook CT 06475-0833. (860)395-0440. Fax: (203)395-1418. President/Publisher: Linda Kennedy. **Acquisitions:** Elizabeth Taylor, submissions editor. Estab. 1947. "Globe Pequot is among the top sources for travel books in the United States and offers the broadest selection of travel titles of any vendor in this market." Publishes hardcover originals, paperback originals and reprints. **Publishes 130 titles/year. Receives 1,500 submissions/year. 30% of books from first-time authors; 70% from unagented writers. Average print order for a first book is 4,000-7,500. Makes outright purchase or pays 10% royalty on net price. Offers advance.** Publishes book 1 year after acceptance. Accepts simultaneous submissions. Reports in 3 months. Book catalog for 9×12 SASE.
Nonfiction: Travel guidebooks (regional OK) and outdoor recreation. No doctoral theses, fiction, genealogies, memoirs, poetry or textbooks. Submit outline, table of contents, sample chapter and résumé/vita. Reviews artwork/photos.
Recent Title(s): *Hostels U.S.A.*, by Evan Halper and Paul Karr.

DAVID R. GODINE, PUBLISHER, INC., 9 Hamilton Place, Boston MA 02108. Website: http://www.godine.com. **Acquisitions:** Mark Polizzotti, editorial director. Estab. 1970. "We publish books that matter for people who care." Publishes hardcover and trade paperback originals and reprints. **Publishes 25 titles/year. Pays royalty on retail price.** Publishes book 3 years after acceptance of ms. Book catalog for 5×8 SAE with 3 first-class stamps.
Nonfiction: Biography, coffee table book, cookbook, illustrated book, children's/juvenile. Subjects include Americana, art/architecture, gardening, nature/environment, photography, literary criticism and current affairs. *No unsolicited mss.*
Fiction: Literary, novel, short story collection, children's/juvenile. *No unsolicited manuscripts.*
Recent Title(s): *Tyranny of the Normal*, by Leslie Fiedler (essays); *Last Trolley from Beethovenstraat*, by Grete Weil (novel).

GOLDEN WEST PUBLISHERS, 4113 N. Longview, Phoenix AZ 85014. (602)265-4392. Fax: (602)279-6901. **Acquisitions:** Hal Mitchell, editor. Estab. 1973. "We seek to provide quality, affordable cookbooks and books about the Southwest to the marketplace." Publishes trade paperback originals. **Publishes 15-20 titles/year. Receives 200 submissions/year. 50% of books from first-time authors; 100% from unagented writers. Prefers mss on work-for-hire basis. No advance.** Publishes book an average of 6 months after acceptance. Accepts simultaneous submissions. Reports in 1 month on queries, 2 months on mss.
Nonfiction: Cookbooks, books on the Southwest and West. Subjects include cooking/foods, Southwest history and outdoors, travel. Query. Reviews artwork/photos as part of ms package.
Recent Title(s): *Kokopelli's Cook Book*, by Cunkle (southwest cookbook).
Tips: "We are interested in Arizona and Southwest material, and regional and state cookbooks for the entire country, and welcome material in these areas."

GOVERNMENT INSTITUTES/ABS., 4 Research Place, Suite 200, Rockville MD 20850-3226. (301)921-2355. Fax: (301)921-0373. E-mail: giinfo@govinst.com. Website: http://www.govinst.com. **Acquisitions:** Russ Bahorsky, acquisitions editor (occupational safety and health, quality, ISO 9000, the Internet); Charlene Ikonomou (environmental compliance and sciences, telecommunications), editors. Estab. 1973. "Our mission is to be the leading global company providing practical, accurate, timely and authoritative information desired by people concerned with environment, health and safety, telecommunications, and other regulatory and technical topics." Publishes hardcover and softcover originals and CD-ROM/disk products. **Publishes 45 titles/year. Receives 100 submissions/year. 50% of books from first-time authors; 100% from unagented writers. Pays royalty or makes outright purchase.** Publishes book 2 months after acceptance. Accepts simultaneous submissions, if so noted. Reports in 2 months. Book catalog free.
Nonfiction: Reference, technical. Subjects include environmental law, occupational safety and health, environmental engineering, telecommunications, employment law, FDA matters, industrial hygiene and safety, real estate with an environmental slant, management systems, Quality, ISO 9000, Internet business. Needs professional-level titles in those areas. Also looking for international environmental topics. Submit outline and at least 1 sample chapter.
Recent Title(s): *Environmental Law Handbook*, Thomas F.P. Sullivan.
Tips: "We also conduct courses. Authors are frequently invited to serve as instructors."

THE GRADUATE GROUP, P.O. Box 370351, West Hartford CT 06137-0351. **Acquisitions:** Mara Whitman, president; Robert Whitman, vice president. "The Graduate Group helps college and graduate students better prepare themselves for rewarding careers and helps people advance in the workplace." Publishes trade paperback originals. **Publishes 50 titles/year. Receives 100 queries and 70 mss/year. 60% of books from first-time authors; 85% from unagented writers. Pays 20% royalty on retail price.** Publishes book 3 months after acceptance of ms. Accepts simultaneous submissions. Reports in 1 month. Book catalog and ms guidelines free.
Nonfiction: Reference. Subjects include career/internships, law, medicine, law enforcement, corrections, how to succeed, self-motivation, education, professional development, building self-esteem, learning networking skills, working with the disabled and gifted, summer/year round opportunities for students assisting the elderly. Send complete ms and SASE with sufficient postage.
Recent Title(s): *The Stripped Down, Do It Now, I Want a Job, Complete Job Search Workbook*, by Greg Tzinberg.
Tips: Audience is career planning offices; college, graduate school and public libraries. "We are open to all submissions, especially those involving career planning, internships and other nonfiction titles. Looking for books on law enforcement, books for prisoners and reference books on subjects/fields students would be interested in. We want books on helping students to interview, pass tests, gain opportunity, understand the world of work, networking, building experience, preparing for advancement, preparing to enter business, improving personality and building relationships."

GRAYWOLF PRESS, 2402 University Ave., Suite 203, St. Paul MN 55114. (612)641-0077. Fax: (612)641-0036. Website: http://www.graywolfpress.org. Editor/publisher: Fiona McCrae. Executive Editor: Anne Czarniecki. **Acquisitions:** Jeffrey Shotts. Estab. 1974. "Graywolf Press is an independent, nonprofit publisher dedicated to the creation and promotion of thoughtful and imaginative contemporary literature essential to a vital and diverse culture." Publishes trade cloth and paperback originals and reprints. **Publishes 16 titles/year. Receives 2,500 queries/year. 20% of books from first-time authors; 50% from unagented writers. Pays royalty on retail price. Offers $1,000-6,000 advance on average.** Publishes book 18 months after acceptance of ms. Reports in 3 months on queries. Book catalog free. Manuscript guidelines for #10 SASE.
Nonfiction: Language/literature/culture. Query with SASE.
Fiction: Literary. "Familiarize yourself with our list first." Query with SASE.

Poetry: "We are interested in linguistically challenging work." Query sample with SASE.
Recent Title(s): *Otherwise: New & Selected Poems*, by Jane Kenyon; *The Apprentice*, by Lewis Libby (novel).

GREAT QUOTATIONS PUBLISHING, 1967 Quincy Ct., Glendale Heights IL 60139. (630)582-2800. Fax: (630)582-2813. **Acquisitions:** Patrick Caton, acquisitions editor. Estab. 1991. "Great Quotations seeks original material for the following general categories: humor, inspiration, motivation, success, romance, tributes to mom/dad/grandma/grandpa, etc." **Publishes 30 titles/year. Receives 1,500 queries and 1,200 mss/year. 50% of books from first-time authors; 80% from unagented writers. Pays 3-10% royalty on net sales or makes outright purchase of $300-3,000. Offers $200-1,200 advance.** Publishes book 6 months after acceptance of ms. "We publish new books twice a year, in July and in January." Accepts simultaneous submissions. Reports in 6 months. Book catalog for $1.50. Manuscript guidelines for #10 SASE.
Nonfiction: Humor, illustrated book, self-help, quotes. Subjects include business/economics, child guidance/parenting, nature/environment, religion, sports, women's issues/studies. "We look for subjects with identifiable markets, appeal to the general public. We do not publish children's books or others requiring multicolor illustration on the inside. Nor do we publish highly controversial subject matter." Submit outline and 2 sample chapters. Reviews artwork/photos as part of ms package. Send photocopies, transparencies.
Poetry: "We would be most interested in upbeat and juvenile poetry."
Recent Title(s): *Secret Language of Men*, by Shearer Weaver (gift book).
Tips: "Our books are physically small, and generally a very quick read. They are available at gift shops and book shops throughout the country. We are very aware that most of our books are bought on impulse and given as gifts. We need very strong, clever, descriptive titles; beautiful cover art and brief, positive, upbeat text. Be prepared to submit final manuscript on computer disk, according to our specifications. (It is not necessary to try to format the typesetting of your manuscript to look like a finished book.)"

GREENE BARK PRESS, P.O. Box 1108, Bridgeport CT 06601. (203)372-4861. Fax: (203)371-5856. Website: http://www.bookworld.com/greenebark. **Acquisitions:** Thomas J. Greene, Michele Hofbauer, associate publishers. "We only publish children's fiction—all subjects—but in reading picture book format appealing to ages 3-9 or all ages." Publishes hardcover originals. **Publishes 5 titles/year. Receives 100 queries and 6,000 mss/year. 60% of books from first-time authors; 100% from unagented writers. Pays 10-15% royalty on wholesale price.** Publishes book 1 year after acceptance of ms. Accepts simultaneous submissions. Reports in 3 months on mss. Book catalog and ms guidelines with SASE.
Fiction: Juvenile. Submit entire ms with SASE. No queries or ms by e-mail.
Recent Title(s): *Molly Meets Mona & Friends*, by Gladys Walker (a magical day at an art museum).
Tips: Audience is "children who read to themselves and others. Mothers, fathers, grandparents, godparents who read to their respective children, grandchildren. Include SASE, be prepared to wait, do not inquire by telephone."

GREENHAVEN PRESS, INC., P.O. Box 289009, San Diego CA 92198-9009. (619)485-7424. Fax: (619)485-9549. **Acquisitions:** Brenda Stalcup, managing editor. Estab. 1970. "Publishes hard and softcover educational supplementary materials and (nontrade) nonfiction anthologies on contemporary issues, literary criticism and history for high school and college readers. Generally does not publish single-author manuscripts except for titles in the *Opposing Viewpoints Digests Series*, which must conform to strict guidelines." **Publishes approximately 100 anthologies/year; all anthologies are works for hire. Makes outright purchase of $1,000-3,000.** Publishes ms 1 year after acceptance. Book catalog for 9×12 SAE with 3 first-class stamps.
Nonfiction: "We produce tightly formatted anthologies on contemporary issues, literary criticism, and history for high school- and college-level readers. We are looking for freelance book editors to research and compile these anthologies; we are not interested in submissions of single-author manuscripts. Each series has specific requirements. Potential book editors should familiarize themselves with our catalog and anthologies." Query. No unsolicited mss.
Recent Title(s): *Tobacco and Smoking* (Opposing Viewpoints Series).

GREENWILLOW BOOKS, William Morrow & Co., The Hearst Corp., 1350 Avenue of the Americas, New York NY 10019. (212)261-6500. Website: http://www.williammorrow.com. **Acquisitions:** Editorial Department, Greenwillow Books. Estab. 1974. "Greenwillow Books publishes quality picture books and fiction for young readers of all ages, and nonfiction primarily for children under seven years of age." Publishes hardcover originals and reprints. **Publishes 70-80 titles/year. 1% of books from first-time authors; 30% from unagented writers. Pays 10% royalty on wholesale price for first-time authors. Advance varies.** Publishes ms 2 years after acceptance of ms. Accepts simultaneous submissions, if so noted. Reports in 3 months on mss. Book catalog for 9×12 SAE with $2 postage. Manuscript guidelines for #10 SASE.
Fiction: Juvenile, picture books: fantasy, historical, humor, literary, mystery. Send complete ms with SASE. Reviews artwork with submissions. Send photocopies.
Recent Title(s): *Lilly's Purple Plastic Purse*, by Kevin Henkes.

GREENWOOD PRESS, Greenwood Publishing Group, 88 Post Rd. W., Westport CT 06881. (203)226-3571. Fax: (203)222-1502. Website: http://www.greenwood.com. **Acquisitions:** Peter Kracht, executive editor. "Greenwood Press publishes reference materials for the entire spectrum of libraries, as well as scholarly monographs in the humanities and the social and behavioral sciences." Publishes hardcover and trade paperback originals. **Publishes 300 titles/year.**

Receives 1,000 queries/year. 50% of books from first-time authors. Pays variable royalty on net price. Offers advance rarely. Publishes book 1 year after acceptance of ms. Accepts simultaneous submissions. Reports in 6 months on queries. Book catalog and ms guidelines online.
Nonfiction: Reference. Query with proposal package, including scope, organization, length of project, whether a complete ms is available or when it will be, CV or résumé and SASE. *No unsolicited mss.*
Recent Title(s): *John Grisham: A Critical Companion*, by Mary Beth Pringle.

GROLIER PUBLISHING, Grolier Inc., 90 Sherman Turnpike, Danbury CT 06816. (203)797-3500. Fax: (203)797-3197. Estab. 1895. "Grolier Publishing is a leading publisher of reference, educational and children's books. We provide parents, teachers and librarians with the tools they need to enlighten children to the pleasure of learning and prepare them for the road ahead." Publishes hardcover and trade paperback originals. **5% of books from first-time authors; 95% from unagented writers. Prefers to work with unagented authors. Pays royalty for established authors; makes outright purchase for others. Advance and fees vary.** Accepts simultaneous submissions. Reports in 3 months on proposals. Book catalog for 9×12 SAE and $3 postage. Manuscript guidelines free.
Imprint(s): Children's Press, Franklin Watts.
Nonfiction: Children's/juvenile, illustrated book, reference. Query with outline and SASE.
Recent Title(s): *Muhammad Ali*, by John Tessitore.

[A] **GROSSET & DUNLAP PUBLISHERS**, Penguin Putnam Inc., 345 Hudson St., New York NY 10014. Associate Publisher: Ronnie Ann Herman. **Acquisitions:** Jane O'Connor, president. Estab. 1898. Grosset & Dunlap publishes children's books that examine new ways of looking at the world of a child. Publishes hardcover (few) and paperback originals. **Publishes 100 titles/year.** Publishes book 18 months after acceptance. Reports in 2 months.
Imprint(s): Tuffy Books, Platt & Munk.
Nonfiction: Juveniles. Subjects include nature, science. *Agented submissions only.*
Fiction: Juveniles. *Agented submissions only.*
Recent Title(s): *The Clear and Simple Thesaurus.*
Tips: "Nonfiction that is particularly topical or of wide interest in the mass market; new concepts for novelty format for preschoolers; and very well-written easy readers on topics that appeal to primary graders have the best chance of selling to our firm."

GROUP PUBLISHING, INC., 1515 Cascade Ave., Loveland CO 80538. Fax: (970)669-1994. E-mail: kloesche@aol.com. Website: http://www.grouppublishing.com. **Acquisitions:** Kerri Loesche, editorial assistant; Paul Woods (curriculum); David Thorton (adult acquisitions); Lori Haynes Niles (children's acquisitions); Amy Simpson (youth books). "Our mission is to encourage Christian growth in children, youth and adults." Publishes trade paperback originals. **Publishes 20-30 titles/year. Receives 200-400 queries and 300-500 mss/year. 30% of books from first-time authors; 95% from unagented writers. Pays up to 10% royalty on wholesale price or makes outright purchase. Offers up to $1,000 advance.** Publishes book 18 months after acceptance of ms. Accepts simultaneous submissions. Reports in 2 months on queries, 6 months on proposals. Book catalog for 9×12 SAE with 2 first-class stamps. Manuscript guidelines for #10 SASE.
Imprint(s): Group (contact Amy Simpson or Lori Haynes Niles), Vital Ministry (contact David Thornton).
Nonfiction: How-to, adult, youth and children's ministry resources. Subjects include education, religion and any subjects pertinent to adult, youth or children's ministry in a church setting. "We're an interdenominational publisher of resource materials for people who work with adults, youth or children in a Christian church setting. We also publish materials for use directly by youth or children (such as devotional books, workbooks or Bibles stories). Everything we do is based on concepts of active and interactive learning as described in *Why Nobody Learns Much of Anything at Church: And How to Fix It*, by Thom and Joani Schultz. We need new, practical, hands-on, innovative, out-of-the-box ideas—things that no one's doing . . . yet." Submit proposal package, including outline, 2 sample chapters, introduction to the book (written as if the reader will read it), and sample activities if appropriate.
Recent Title(s): *Fun Friend-Making Activities for Adult Groups*, by Dockrey (adult programming ideas).
Tips: "We're seeking proposals for CD-ROM projects. Submit same as proposal package above."

GROVE/ATLANTIC, INC., 841 Broadway, New York NY 10003. (212)614-7850, 7860. Fax: (212)614-7886, 7915. Publisher: Morgan Entrekin. Editor-in-Chief: Ira Silverberg. Senior Editor: Anton Muller. **Acquisitions:** Joan Bingham, executive editor. "Grove/Atlantic publishes serious nonfiction and literary fiction." Publishes hardcover originals, trade paperback originals and reprints. **Publishes 60-70 titles/year. Receives 1000s queries/year. 10-15% of books from first-time authors; "very few" from unagented writers. Pays 7½-15% royalty on retail price. Advance varies considerably.** Publishes book 1 year after acceptance of ms. Accepts simultaneous submissions. "Because of volume of queries, Grove/Atlantic can only respond when interested—though SASE might generate a response." Book catalog free.
Imprint(s): Grove Press (estab. 1952), Atlantic Monthly Press (estab. 1917).
Nonfiction: Biography. Subjects include art/architecture, cooking/foods/nutrition, government/politics, history, language/literature, travel. Query with SASE. *No unsolicited mss.*
Fiction: Experimental, literary. Query with SASE. *No unsolicited mss.*
Poetry: "We try to publish at least one volume of poetry every list." Query. *No unsolicited mss.*
Recent Title(s): *Ship of Gold in the Deep Blue Sea*, by Gary Kinder; *Cold Mountain*, by Charles Frazier (fiction).

ALDINE DE GRUYTER, Walter de Gruyter, Inc., 200 Saw Mill River Rd., Hawthorne NY 10532. **Acquisitions**: Dr. Richard Koffler, executive editor. Aldine de Gruyter is an academic nonfiction publisher. Publishes hardcover and academic paperback originals. **Publishes 15-25 titles/year. Receives several hundred queries and 100 mss/year. 15% of books from first-time authors; 99% from unagented writers. Pays 7½-10% royalty on net sales.** Publishes book 9 months after acceptance of ms. Accepts simultaneous submissions. Reports in 2 months on proposals. Book catalog free. Manuscript guidelines only after contract.

Nonfiction: Textbook (rare), course-related monographs and edited volumes. Subjects include anthropology/archaeology (biological); sociology, human services. "Aldine's authors are academics with Ph.D's and strong publication records." Submit 1-2 sample chapters, proposal package, including c.v., market, competing texts, etc., reviews of earlier work.

Recent Title(s): *Targeting Guns*, by Gary Keeck (criminology).

Tips: Audience is professors and upper level and graduate students.

GRYPHON HOUSE, INC., P.O. Box 207, Beltsville MD 20704. (301)595-9500. Fax: (301)595-0051. Website: http://www.ghbooks.com. **Acquisitions:** Kathy Charner, editor-in-chief. Gryphon House publishes books of creative educational activities for parents and teachers to do with children ages 1-5. Publishes trade paperback originals. **Publishes 6 titles/year. Pays royalty on wholesale price.** Reports in 3 months.

Nonfiction: How-to, education. Submit outline, 2-3 sample chapters and SASE.

Recent Title(s): *Cooking Art*, by Maryann Kohl and Jean Potter (open-ended art activities for young children).

GRYPHON PUBLICATIONS, P.O. Box 209, Brooklyn NY 11228. **Acquisitions:** Gary Lovisi, owner/publisher. Publishes trade paperback originals and reprints. **Publishes 10 titles/year. Receives 500 queries and 1,000 mss/year. 60% of books from first-time authors; 90% from unagented writers. No advance.** Makes outright purchase by contract, price varies. Publishes book 2 years after acceptance of ms. Reports in 1 month on queries. *Writer's Market* recommends allowing 2 months for reply. Book catalog and ms guidelines for #10 SASE.

Imprint(s): Paperback Parade Magazine, Hardboiled Magazine, Other Worlds Magazine, Gryphon Books, Gryphon Doubles.

Nonfiction: Reference, bibliography. Subjects include hobbies, literature and book collecting. "We need well-written, well-researched articles, but query first on topic and length. Writers submit material that is not fully developed/researched." Query with SASE. Reviews artwork/photos as part of ms package. Send photocopies (slides, transparencies may be necessary later).

Fiction: Mystery, science fiction, suspense, urban horror, hardboiled fiction. "We want cutting-edge fiction, under 3,000 words with impact!" For short stories, query or submit complete ms. For novels, send 1-page query letter with SASE.

Tips: "We are very particular about novels and book-length work. A first-timer has a better chance with a short story or article. On anything over 6,000 words *do not* send manuscript, send *only* query letter with SASE."

GULF PUBLISHING COMPANY, P.O. Box 2608, Houston TX 77252-2608. (713)520-4465. Fax: (713)520-4438. Website: http://www.gulfpub.com. **Acquisitions:** Phil Carmical, performance manager. (science/technical, business, children's's); Kim Kilmer, performance manager (field guides, cookbooks, Texana, self-help). "Gulf has always been and continues to be a major publisher of technical and Texana titles, but we are expanding to publish books for a more general nonfiction audience. The titles include, but are not necessarily limited to, outdoor field guides, general cookbooks, business books, self-help books, and books on human resources and training." Publishes hardcover and trade paperback originals and reprints. **Publishes 60-65 titles/year. Receives 1,000 queries and 400 mss/year. 50% of books from first-time authors; 90% from unagented writers. Pays royalty.** Publishes book 18 months after acceptance of ms. Accepts simultaneous submissions. Reports in 1 month on queries, 3 months on proposals and mss. Book catalog and ms guidelines free.

Imprint(s): Maverick (Hank the Cowdog).

Nonfiction: Children's/juvenile, cookbook, how-to, reference, self-help, technical, Texana. Subjects include business/economics, child guidance/parenting, cooking/foods/nutrition, money/finance, nature/environment, regional. Submit proposal package, including cover letter, outline, résumé, sample chapters and SASE. Reviews artwork/photos as part of ms package. Send color copies, slides or actual photos.

Fiction: Juvenile, picture books. "Primarily, we are interested in picture books for young readers and short novels for older children (ages 8-13)." Submit synopsis, sample chapter and SASE.

Recent Title(s): *The Power of 360° Feedback*, by Waldman/Atwater (business/human resources); *Hank the Cowdog #30: Case of the Haystack Kitties.*

Tips: "We are also expanding our line of children's fiction to include more than our very successful 'Hank the Cowdog' series, published under the Maverick imprint. Children's fiction, like all of our books, must be of very high quality."

HACHAI PUBLISHING, 156 Chester Ave., Brooklyn NY 11218. (718)633-0100. Website: http://www.hachai.com. **Acquisitions**: Dina Rosenfeld, editor. "Hachai is dedicated to producing high quality Jewish children's litearture." Publishes hardcover originals. **Publishes 6 titles/year. Makes $1,000 outright purchase.** Accepts simultaneous submissions. Reports in 2 months on mss. Book catalog free. Manuscript guidelines for #10 SASE.

Nonfiction: Children's/juvenile. Jewish religious subjects. Submit complete ms with SASE. Reviews artwork/photos as part of ms package. Send photocopies.

Recent Title(s): *I Go To School*, by Rikki Benenfeld (nonfiction); *One of a Kind Yanky*, by Pia Dolcowitz, illustrated by Vitaly Romanenko (fiction).

HALF HALT PRESS, INC., P.O. Box 67, Boonsboro MD 21713. (301)733-7119. Fax: (301)733-7408. **Acquisitions:** Elizabeth Carnes, publisher. Estab. 1986. "We publish high-quality nonfiction on equestrian topics, books that help riders and trainers do something better." Publishes 90% hardcover and trade paperback originals and 10% reprints. **Publishes 15 titles/year. Receives 150 submissions/year. 25% of books from first-time authors; 50% from unagented authors. Pays 10-12½% royalty on retail price. Offers advance by agreement.** Publishes book 1 year after acceptance. Reports in 1 month on queries. *Writer's Market* recommends allowing 2 months for reply. Book catalog for 6×9 SAE with 2 first-class stamps.
Nonfiction: Instructional: horse and equestrian-related subjects only. "We need serious instructional works by authorities in the field on horse-related topics, broadly defined." Query with SASE. Reviews artwork/photos as part of ms package.
Recent Title(s): *The Art of Training*, by The Baron Hans von Blixen-Finecke (classical training principles for horses).
Tips: "Writers have the best chance selling us well-written, unique works that teach serious horse people how to do something better. If I were a writer trying to market a book today, I would offer a straightforward presentation, letting work speak for itself, without hype or hard sell. Allow publisher to contact writer, without frequent calling to check status. They haven't forgotten the writer but may have many different proposals at hand; frequent calls to 'touch base,' multiplied by the number of submissions, become an annoyance. As the publisher/author relationship becomes close and is based on working well together, early impressions may be important, even to the point of being a consideration in acceptance for publication."

ALEXANDER HAMILTON INSTITUTE, 70 Hilltop Rd., Ramsey NJ 07446-1119. (201)825-3377. Fax: (201)825-8696. Website: http://www.ahipubs.com. **Acquisitions:** Brian L.P. Zevnik, editor-in-chief. Estab. 1909. Alexander Hamilton Institute publishes "non-traditional" management books for upper-level managers and executives. Publishes 3-ring binder and paperback originals. **Publishes 10-15 titles/year. Receives 50 queries and 10 mss/year. 25% of books from first-time authors; 95% from unagented writers. Pays 5-8% royalty on retail price or makes outright purchase ($3,500-7,000). Offers $3,500-7,000 advance.** Publishes book 10 months after acceptance. Accepts simultaneous submissions. Reports in 1 month on queries, 2 months on mss.
Nonfiction: Executive/management books. The first audience is overseas, upper-level managers. "We need how-to and skills building books. *No* traditional management texts or academic treatises." The second audience is US personnel executives and high-level management. Subject is legal personnel matters. "These books combine court case research and practical application of defensible programs." Submit outline, 3 paragraphs on each chapter, examples of lists, graphics, cases.
Recent Title(s): *The Employee Problem Solver.*
Tips: "We sell exclusively by direct mail to managers and executives around the world. A writer must know his/her field and be able to communicate practical systems and programs."

N **HAMPTON ROADS PUBLISHING COMPANY, INC.**, 134 Burgess Lane, Charlottesville VA 22902. (804)296-2772. Fax: (804)296-5096. E-mail: hrpc@hrpub.com. Website: http://hrpub.com. **Acquisitions:** Frank De Marco, chief editor (metaphysical/visionary fiction); Robert S. Friedman, president (metaphysical/alternative medicine); Ken Eagle Feather, marketing director (spiritual paths/Toltec). "Our reason for being is to impact, uplift and contribute to positive change in the world." Publishes hardcover and trade paperback originals. **Publishes 25-30 titles/year. Receives 1,000 queries and 1,500 mss/year. 50% of books from first-time authors; 70% from unagented writers. Pays royalty. Offers $1,000-100,000 advance.** Publishes book 1 year after acceptance of ms. Accepts simultaneous submissions. Reports in 1 month on queries and proposals, 5 months on mss. Book catalog free. Ms guidelines free.
Nonfiction: How-to, illustrated book, self-help. Spirituality subjects. Submit 3 sample chapters. Reviews artwork/photos as part of the ms package. Send photocopies.
Fiction: Spiritual, visionary fiction. "Fiction should have one or more of the following themes: spiritual, inspirational, metaphysical, i.e., past life recall, out of body experiences, near death experience, paranormal." Query or submit synopsis with 3 sample chapters and SASE.
Recent Title(s): *Conversations with God, Book 2*, by Neale Donald Walsch (inspirational/spiritual nonfiction); *Naked Into the Night*, by Monty Joynes (fiction).

HANCOCK HOUSE PUBLISHERS, 1431 Harrison Ave., Blaine WA 98230-5005. (604)538-1114. Fax: (604)538-2262. E-mail: hancock@uniserve.com. **Acquisitions:** David Hancock, publisher; Nancy Miller, editor. Estab. 1971. Hancock House Publishers, seeks aviculture, natural history, animal husbandry, conservation and popular science titles with a regional (Pacific Northwest), national or international focus. Publishes hardcover and trade paperback originals and reprints. **Publishes 14 titles/year. Receives 300 submissions/year. 50% of books from first-time authors; 90% from unagented writers. Pays 10% royalty.** Accepts simultaneous submissions. Publishes book up to 1 year after acceptance. Book catalog free. Manuscript guidelines for #10 SASE.
Nonfiction: Biography, how-to, reference, technical. Pacific Northwest history and biography, nature guides, native culture, and international natural history. "Centered around Pacific Northwest, local history, nature guide books, international ornithology and Native Americans." Submit outline, 3 sample chapters and proposal package, including selling points with SASE. Reviews artwork/photos as part of ms package. Send photocopies.

Recent Title(s): *Bushplanes of the North*, by Robert Grant (aviation/history).

HANSER GARDNER PUBLICATIONS, 6915 Valley Ave., Cincinnati OH 45244. (513)527-8977. Fax: (513)527-8950. Website: http://www.gardnerweb.com. **Acquisitions:** Woody Chapman. Hanser Gardner publishes training and practical application titles for metalworking, machining and finishing shops/plants. Publishes hardcover and paperback originals and reprints. **Publishes 5-10 titles/year. Receives 40-50 queries and 5-10 mss/year. 75% of books from first-time authors; 100% from unagented writers. Pays 10-15% royalty on net receipts. No advance.** Publishes book 10 months after acceptance of ms. Accepts simultaneous submissions. Reports in 2 weeks on queries, 1 month on proposals and mss. Book catalog and ms guidelines free.

Nonfiction: How-to, technical, textbook. Subjects include metalworking and finishing processes, and related management topics. "Our books are primarily basic introductory-level training books, and books that emphasize practical applications. Strictly deal with subjects shown above." Query with résumé, preface, outline, sample chapter, comparison to competing or similar titles. Reviews artwork/photos as part of ms package. Send photocopies.

Recent Title(s): *Industrial Painting*, by Norman R. Roobol (industrial reference).

Tips: "Our readers and authors occupy various positions within small and large metalworking, machining and finishing shops/plants. We prefer that interested individuals write, call, or fax us with their queries first, so we can send them our proposal guideline form."

HARCOURT BRACE & COMPANY, Children's Books Division, 525 B St., Suite 1900, San Diego CA 92101. (619)231-6616. Fax: (619)699-6777. Website: http://www.harcourtbooks.com/Childrens/childrn.html. Publisher: Louise Phelan. **Acquisitions:** Manuscript Submissions. "Harcourt Brace & Company owns some of the world's most prestigious publishing imprints—imprints which distinguish quality products for the juvenile, educational, scientific, technical, medical, professional and trade markets worldwide." Publishes hardcover originals and trade paperback reprints.

Imprint(s): Browndeer Press, Gulliver Books, Gulliver Green, Magic Carpet, Red Wagon, Silver Whistle, Voyager Paperbacks, Jane Yolen Books.

Nonfiction and Fiction: Agented submissions or query letters only with SASE. *No unsolicited mss.* No phone calls.

Recent Title(s): *I Want to Be an Astronaut*, by Stephanie Maze and Catherine O'Neill Grace (nonfiction picture book); *Tangerine*, by Edward Bloor (young adult fiction).

HARCOURT BRACE & COMPANY, Trade Division, 525 B St., Suite 1900, San Diego, CA 92101. (619)699-6560. Website: http://www.harcourtbooks.com. **Acquisitions**: Marsha Brubaker. "Harcourt Brace & Company owns some of the world's most prestigious publishing imprints—imprints which distinguish quality products for the juvenile, educational, scientific, technical, medical, professional and trade markets worldwide."

Nonfiction: Publishes all categories *except* business/finance (university texts), cookbooks, self-help, sex. Agented submissions or query letters only with SASE. *No unsolicited mss.*

Recent Title(s): *In Light of India*, by Octavio Paz (memoir); *Ingenious Pain*, by Andrew Miller (fiction).

HARPERACTIVE, HarperCollins Publishers, 10 E. 53rd St., New York NY 10022. (212)207-7000. Editorial Director/ Vice President: Hope Innelli. **Acquisitions:** Marco Parra, editor. Estab. 1997. "A newly formed imprint, HarperActive is dedicated to publishing the hottest properties in biographies, sports, movie and TV tie-ins, anything that reflects trends in pop culture." **40% of books from first-time authors. Pays royalty or makes outright purchase. Advance varies.** Reports in 3-12 months on mss. Book catalog and mss guidelines not available.

Nonfiction: Children's/juvenile, biographies, spoofs, movie and TV-tie ins. "The bulk of our work is done by experienced writers for hire, but we are open to original ideas." Query with outline and SASE.

Fiction: Humor, juvenile, movie and TV tie-ins. Query with synopsis and SASE.

Recent Title(s): *The Backstreet Boys*, by Rodriguez (biography of the band); *Patrick's Pals*, by Robb Armstrong (middle grade).

HARPERBUSINESS, HarperCollins Publishers, 10 E. 53rd St., New York NY 10036. (212)207-7006. Website: http://www.harpercollins.com. **Acquisitions:** Adrian Zackheim, senior vice president/publisher. Estab. 1991. Harper Business publishes "the inside story on ideas that will shape business practices and thinking well into the next millenium, with cutting-edge information and visionary concepts." Publishes hardcover, trade paperback and mass market paperback originals, hardcover and trade paperback reprints. **Publishes 50-55 titles/year. Receives 500 queries and mss/year. 1% of books from first-time authors; 10% from unagented writers. Pays royalty on retail price; varies. Offers $15,000 and up advance.** Publishes book 1 year after acceptance of ms. Accepts simultaneous submissions. Reports in 2 months on proposals and mss. Book catalog free.

Nonfiction: Biography (economics); business/economics, marketing subjects. "We don't publish how-to, textbooks or things for academic market; no reference (tax or mortgage guides), our reference department does that. Proposals need to be top notch, especially for unagented writers. We tend not to publish people who have no business standing. Must have business credentials." Submit proposal package with SASE.

Recent Title(s): *The Dilbert Principle*, by Scott Adams (business/humor).

Tips: Business audience: managers, CEOs, consultants, some academics. "We accept more unagented proposals, but they tend to come from authors who are already well established in their fields."

HARPERCOLLINS CHILDREN'S BOOKS, HarperCollins Publishers, 10 E. 53rd St., New York NY 10022. (212)207-7000. Website: http://www.harpercollins.com. Editor-in-Chief: Kate Morgan Jackson. **Acquisitions:** Sally Doherty, executive editor; Robert Warren, executive editor; Phoebe Yeh, executive editor. "We have no rules for subject matter, length or vocabulary, but look instead for ideas that are fresh and imaginative, good writing that involves the reader is essential." Publishes hardcover originals. **Publishes 350 titles/year. Receives 200 queries and 5,000 mss/year. 5% of books from first-time authors; 25% from unagented writers. Pays 10-12½% royalty on retail price. Advance varies.** Publishes novel 1 year, picture books 2 years after acceptance of ms. Accepts simultaneous submissions. Reports in 1 month on queries and proposals, 4 months on mss. Book catalog for 8×10 SASE with 3 first-class stamps. Manuscript guidelines for #10 SASE.

Imprint(s): Joanna Cotler Books (Joanna Cotler, editorial director); Michael DiCapua Books (Michael DiCapua, editorial director); **Laura Geringer Books** (Laura Geringer, editorial director); Harper Festival (Mary Alice Moore, editorial director); Harper Trophy (Stephanie Spinner, editorial director).

Fiction: Adventure, fantasy, historical, humor, juvenile, literary, picture books, young adult. Query *only* with SASE. no unsolicited mss.

Recent Title(s): *The Leaf Men*, by William Joyce (picture book).

[A] **HARPERCOLLINS PUBLISHERS**, 10 E. 53rd St., New York NY 10022. (212)207-7000. Website: http://www.harpercollins.com. **Acquisitions**: Joelle Del Bourgo, vice president/editorial director. "HarperCollins, one of the largest English language publishers in the world, is a broad-based publisher with strengths in academic, business and professional, children's, educational, general interest, and religious and spiritual books, as well as multimedia titles." Publishes hardcover and paperback originals and paperback reprints. **Trade publishes more than 500 titles/year. Pays standard royalties. Advance negotiable.** Reports on solicited queries in 6 weeks.

Imprint(s): Cliff Street Books (Diane Reverand), Harper Adult Trade; **HarperActive**, Harper Audio, **HarperBusiness**, HarperCollins, **HarperCollins Children's Books**, HarperEdge, HarperEntertainment, HarperFlamingo (Susan Weinberg), HarperHorizon, **HarperLibros**, Harper Paperback, **HarperPerennial**, HarperPrism, HarperResource, **HarperSanFrancisco**, HarperTrophy, **Regan Books**, **Zondervan Publishing House**.

Nonfiction: Americana, animals, art, biography, business/economics, current affairs, cookbooks, health, history, how-to, humor, music, nature, philosophy, politics, psychology, reference, religion, science, self-help, sociology, sports, travel. *Agented submissions only. No unsolicited queries or mss.*

Fiction: Adventure, fantasy, gothic, historical, mystery, science fiction, suspense, western, literary. "We look for a strong story line and exceptional literary talent." *Agented submissions only. No unsolicited queries or mss.*

Recent Title(s): *10 Stupid Things Men Do to Mess Up Their Lives*, by Dr. Laura Schlessinger (psychology); *Monkey King*, by Patricia Chao.

HARPERLIBROS, HarperCollins Publishers, 10 E. 53rd St., New York NY 10022. (212)207-7000. Fax: (212)207-7145. Website: http://www.harpercollins.com. **Acquisitions:** Terry Karten, editorial director. Estab. 1994. "Harper Libros offers Spanish language editions of selected HarperCollins titles, sometimes reprints, sometimes new books that are published simultaneously in English and Spanish. The list mirrors the English-language list of HarperCollins in that we publish both literary and commercial fiction and nonfiction titles including all the different HarperCollins categories, such as self-help, spirituality, etc." Publishes hardcover and trade paperback originals. **Publishes 10 titles/year. Receives 250 queries/year. 30% of books from first-time authors. Pays variable royalty on net price. Advance varies.** Publishes book 1 year after acceptance of ms.

Imprint(s): Harper Arco Iris (contact Jennifer Pasanen) (children's).

Nonfiction: How-to, self-help. Subjects include business/economics, ethnic, spirituality, women's health. Query. *No unsolicited mss.*

Fiction: Literary. Query. *No unsolicited mss.*

Recent Title(s): *Salud: A Latina's Guide to Total Health*, by Jane Delgado, MD (women's health).

[A] **HARPERPERENNIAL**, HarperCollins Publishers, 10 E. 53rd St., New York NY 10036. (212)207-7000. Website: http://www.harpercollins.com. **Acquisitions:** Susan Weinberg, senior vice president/publisher. Estab. 1963. "Harper Perennial publishes a broad range of adult fiction and nonfiction paperbacks." Publishes trade paperback originals and reprints. **Publishes 100 titles/year. Receives 500 queries/year. 5% of books from first-time authors; 2% from unagented writers. Pays 5-7½% royalty. Advance varies.** Publishes book 6 months after acceptance of ms. Reports in 2 weeks on queries, 1 month on mss. Book catalog free.

Nonfiction: Biography, cookbook, how-to, humor, illustrated book, reference, self-help. Subjects include Americana, animals, art/architecture, business/economics, child guidance/parenting, computers/electronics, education, ethnic, gardening, gay/lesbian,history, hobbies/antiques/collectibles, language/literature, mental health, military/war, money/finance, music/dance, nature/environment, philosophy, psychology/self-help psychotherapy, recreation, regional, religion/spirituality, science, sociology, sports, translation, travel, women's issues/studies. "Our focus is ever-changing, adjusting to the marketplace. Mistakes writers often make are not giving their background and credentials—why they are qualified to write the book. A proposal should explain why the author wants to write this book; why it will sell; and why it is better or different from others of its kind." *Agented submissions only.*

Fiction: Ethnic, feminist, literary. "Don't send us novels—go through hardcover." *Agented submissions only.*

Poetry: "Don't send poetry unless you have been published in several established literary magazines already." *Agented submissions only.* Query with 10 sample poems.

Recent Title(s): *Downsize This!*, by Michael Moore (current affairs/humor); *Bird Girl and the Man Who Followed the Sun*, by Velma Wallis (fiction/native American studies); *Selected Poems*, by Allen Ginsberg.

HARPERSANFRANCISCO, HarperCollins Publishers, 353 Sacramento St., Suite 500, San Francisco CA 94111-3653. (415)477-4400. Fax: (415)477-4444. E-mail: hcsanfrancisco@harpercollins.com. Publisher: Diane Gedymin. **Acquisitions:** Mark Chimsky, executive editor (religious studies, popular spirituality, popular culture); Patricia Klein, senior editor (Christian life, spirituality, devotional); John Loudon, executive editor (religious studies, psychology/personal growth, Eastern religions); Caroline Pincus, senior editor (personal growth, Jewish culture, alternative medicine and health, multicultural studies). Estab. 1977. HarperSanFrancisco publishes books that "nurture the mind, body and spirit; support readers in their ongoing self-discovery and personal growth; explore the essential religious and philosophical issues of our time; and present the rich and diverse array of the wisdom traditions of the world to a contemporary audience." Publishes hardcover originals, trade paperback originals and reprints. **Publishes 125 titles/year. Receives about 10,000 submissions/year. 5% of books from first-time authors. Pays royalty.** Publishes book within 18 months after acceptance.

- HarperSanFrancisco no longer accepts unsolicited manuscripts.

Nonfiction: Biography, how-to, reference, self-help. Subjects include psychology, religion, self-help, spirituality. Query. *No unsolicited mss.*
Recent Title(s): *Cash*, by Johnny Cash.

HARVARD BUSINESS SCHOOL PRESS, Harvard Business School Publishing Corp., 60 Harvard Way, Boston MA 02163. (617)495-6700. Fax: (617)496-8066. Website: http://www.hbsp.harvard.edu. Director: Carol Franco. **Acquisitions:** Marjorie Williams, executive editor; Kirsten Sandberg, senior editor; Hollis Heimbouch, senior editor; Janet Coleman, senior editor; Nikki Sabin editor. "The Harvard Business School Press publishes books for an audience of senior and general managers and business scholars. HBS Press is the source of the most influential ideas and conversation that shape business worldwide." Publishes hardcover originals. **Publishes 35-45 titles/year. Receives 500 queries and 300 mss/year. 20% of books from first-time authors; 10% from unagented writers. Pays escalating royalty on retail price. Advances vary widely depending on author and market for the book.** Publishes book 9 months after acceptance of ms. Accepts simultaneous submissions. Reports in 1 month on proposals and mss. Book catalog and ms guidelines free.
Nonfiction: Business/economics subjects. Submit proposal package, including outline with sample chapters.
Recent Title(s): *Net Gain*, by John Hagel and Arthur Armstrong.
Tips: "Take care to really look into the type of business books we publish. They are generally not handbooks, how-to manuals, policy-oriented, dissertations, edited collections, or personal business narratives."

THE HARVARD COMMON PRESS, 535 Albany St., Boston MA 02118-2500. (617)423-5803. Fax: (617)423-0679 or (617)695-9794. **Acquisitions:** Bruce P. Shaw, president/publisher. Associate Publisher: Dan Rosenberg. Estab. 1976. "We want strong, practical books that help people gain control over a particular area of their lives." Publishes hardcover and trade paperback originals and reprints. **Publishes 10 titles/year. Receives 1,000 submissions/year. 40% of books from first-time authors; 70% of books from unagented writers. Pays royalty. Offers average $4,000 advance.** Publishes book 1 year after acceptance. Accepts simultaneous submissions. Reports in 2 months. Book catalog for 9×12 SAE with 3 first-class stamps. Manuscript guidelines for SASE.
Imprint(s): Gambit Books.
Nonfiction: Subjects include cooking, childcare/parenting, travel. "An increasing percentage of our list is made up of books about cooking, child care and parenting; in these areas we are looking for authors who are knowledgeable, if not experts, and who can offer a different approach to the subject. We are open to good nonfiction proposals that show evidence of strong organization and writing, and clearly demonstrate a need in the marketplace. First-time authors are welcome." Accepts nonfiction translations. Submit outline and 1-3 sample chapters. Reviews artwork/photos.
Recent Title(s): *The Vegetarian Grill*, by Andrea Cheeman (cooking).
Tips: "We are demanding about the quality of proposals; in addition to strong writing skills and thorough knowledge of the subject matter, we require a detailed analysis of the competition."

HARVARD UNIVERSITY PRESS, 79 Garden St., Cambridge MA 02138. (617)495-2600. Fax: (617)495-5898. Website: http://www.hup.harvard.edu. **Acquisitions:** Aïda D. Donald, assistant director/editor-in-chief (history, contemporary affairs, sociology with historical emphasis, women's studies with historical emphasis); Lindsay Waters, executive editor for the humanities (literary criticism, philosophy, multicultural studies); Michael G. Fisher, executive editor for science and medicine (medicine, neuroscience, science, astronomy); Joyce Seltzer, senior executive editor (history, contemporary affairs); Michael Aronson, senior acquisitions editor for social sciences (sociology, economics, law, political science); Margaretta Fulton, general editor for the humanities (classics, religion, music, art, Jewish studies, women's studies); Elizabeth Knoll, senior editor for the behavioral sciences (behavioral sciences, neuroscience, education). "Harvard University Press publishes scholarly books and works of general interest in the humanities, the social and behavioral sciences, the natural sciences, and medicine. Does not normally publish poetry, fiction, festschriften, memoirs, symposia, or unrevised doctoral dissertations." **Publishes 130 titles/year.**
Imprint(s): The Belknap Press.
Nonfiction: Reference. Subjects include art/architecture, business/economics, ethnic, government/politics, history, language/literature, music, philosophy, psychology, religion, science, sociology, women's issues/studies. Query with SASE.

Recent Title(s): *Florence: A Portrait*, by Michael Levey (history).

HASTINGS HOUSE, Eagle Publishing Corp., United Publishers Group, 50 Washington St., 7th Floor, Norwalk CT 06854. (203)838-4083. Fax: (203)838-4084. Editor/Publisher: Henno Lohmeyer. **Acquisitions:** Hy Steirman. "We are looking for books that address consumer needs." Publishes hardcover and trade paperback originals and reprints. **Publishes 30 titles/year. Receives 700 queries and 750 mss/year. 5% of books from first-time authors; 40% from unagented writers. Pays 8-10% royalty on retail price on trade paperbacks. Offers $1,000-10,000 advance.** Publishes book 10 months after acceptance of ms. Reports in 1 month.
Nonfiction: Biography, coffee table book, cookbook, how-to, humor, reference, self-help, consumer. Subjects include business/economics, cooking/foods/nutrition, health/medicine, psychology, travel, writing. Query or submit outline.
Recent Title(s): *Lincoln's Unknown Private Life*.

HATHERLEIGH PRESS, 1114 First Ave., New York NY 10021. (212)832-1584. Fax: (212)308-7930. E-mail: info@hatherleigh.com. Website: http://www.hatherleigh.com. Editor-In-Chief: Frederic Flach, M.D. **Acquisitions:** Adam Cohen, managing editor. Hatherleigh Press publishes general self-help titles and reference books for mental health professionals. Publishes hardcover originals, trade paperback originals and reprints. **Publishes 10-12 titles/year. Receives 20 queries and 20 mss/year. Pays 5-15% royalty on retail price or makes outright purchase. Offers $500-5,000 advance.** Publishes book 6 months after acceptance of ms. Reports in 2 months on queries. Book catalog free.
Imprint(s): Red Brick Books—new fiction imprint (Kevin J. Moran, acquisitions editor); Five Star Fitness Publishing.
Nonfiction: Reference, self-help, technical. Subjects include health/medicine, psychology. Submit outline and 1 sample chapter with SASE. Reviews artwork/photos as part of ms package. Send photocopies.
Recent Title(s): *Climb A Fallen Ladder: How to Survive (And Thrive!) in a Downsized America*, by Rochelle H. Gordon, M.D. and Catherine E. Harold.
Tips: Audience is mental health professionals. Submit a clear outline, including market and audience for your book.

THE HAWORTH PRESS, INC., 10 Alice St., Binghamton NY 13904. Website: http://www.haworthpressinc.com. **Acquisitions:** Bill Palmer, managing editor. The Haworth Press is primarily a scholarly press. Publishes hardcover and trade paperback originals. **Publishes 100 titles/year. Receives 500 queries and 250 mss/year. 60% of books from first-time authors; 98% from unagented writers. Pays 7½-15% royalty on wholesale price. Offers $500-1,000 advance.** Publishes book 1 year after acceptance of ms. Reports in 2 months on proposals. Manuscript guidelines free.
Imprint(s): The Harrington Park Press, Haworth Pastoral Press, Haworth Food Products Press.
Nonfiction: Reference, textbook. Subjects include agriculture/horticulture, business/economics, child guidance/parenting, cooking/foods/nutrition, gay/lesbian, health/medicine, money/finance, psychology, sociology, women's issues/studies. "No 'pop' books." Submit proposal package, including outline and 1-3 sample chapters and author bio. Reviews artwork/photos as part of ms package. Send photocopies.
Recent Title(s): *Reviving the Tribe*, by Eric Rofes (gay & lesbian).

HAY HOUSE, INC., P.O. Box 5100, Carlsbad CA 92018-5100. (760)431-7695. Fax: (760)431-6948. Website: http://www.hayhouse.com. **Acquisitions:** Jill Kramer, editorial director. Estab. 1985. "We publish books, audios and videos that help heal the planet." Publishes hardcover and trade paperback originals. **Publishes 30 titles/year. Receives 1,200 submissions/year. 10% of books are from first-time authors; 25% from unagented writers. Pays standard royalty.** Publishes book 10-15 months after acceptance. Accepts simultaneous submissions. Reports in 3 weeks. *Writer's Market* recommends allowing 2 months for reply. Book catalog free. Does not respond or return mss without SASE.
Imprint(s): Astro Room.
Nonfiction: Primarily self-help, Subjects include relationships, mind/body health, nutrition, education, astrology, environment, health/medicine, money/finance, nature, philosophy/New Age, psychology, spiritual, sociology, women's and men's issues/studies. "Hay House is interested in a variety of subjects as long as they have a positive self-help slant to them. No poetry, children's books or negative concepts that are not conducive to helping/healing ourselves or our planet." Query or submit outline, sample chapters and SASE.
Recent Title(s): *Heal Your Life with Home Remedies and Herbs*, by Hanna Kroeger.
Tips: "Our audience is concerned with our planet, the healing properties of love, and general self-help principles. If I were a writer trying to market a book today, I would research the market thoroughly to make sure that there weren't already too many books on the subject I was interested in writing about. Then I would make sure that I had a unique slant on my idea. SASE a must!"

HEALTH COMMUNICATIONS, INC., 3201 SW 15th St., Deerfield Beach FL 33442. (954)360-0909. Website: http://www.hci-online.com. **Acquisitions:** Christine Belleris, editorial director; Matthew Diener, senior editor; Allison Janse, associate editor; Lisa Drucker, associate editor. "We are the Life Issues Publisher. Health Communications, Inc., strives to help people grow mentally, emotionally and spiritually." Publishes hardcover and trade paperback originals. **Publishes 40 titles/year. 20% of books from first-time authors; 90% from unagented writers. Pays 15% royalty on net price.** Publishes book 9 months after acceptance of ms. Accepts simultaneous submissions. Reports in 1 month on queries, 3 months on proposals and mss. Book catalog for 8½×11 SASE. Manuscript guidelines for #10 SASE.
Nonfiction: Gift book, self-help. Subjects include child guidance/parenting, inspiration, psychology, spirituality, women's issues/studies, recovery. Submit proposal package, including outline, 2 sample chapters, vitae, marketing study and SASE. No phone calls. Reviews artwork/photos as part of ms package. Send photocopies.

Recent Title(s): *A Child Called "It,"* by Dave Pelzer (self-help/inspiration).
Tips: Audience is composed primarily of women, aged 25-60, interested in personal growth and self-improvement. "Please do your research in your subject area. We publish general self-help books and are expanding to include new subjects such as business self-help and possibly alternative healing. We need to know why there is a need for your book, how it might differ from other books on the market and what you have to offer to promote your work."

HEALTH INFORMATION PRESS (HIP), PMIC (Practice Management Information Corp.), 4727 Wilshire Blvd., Los Angeles CA 90010. (213)954-0224. Fax: (213)954-0253. E-mail: pmiceditor@aol.com. Website: http://medicalbookstore.com. **Acquisitions:** Kathryn Swanson, managing editor. "Audience is consumers who are interested in taking an active role in their health care." Publishes hardcover originals, trade paperback originals and reprints. **Publishes 8-10 titles/year. Receives 100 queries and 50 mss/year. 10% of books from first-time authors; 90% from unagented writers. Pays 10-15% royalty on net receipts. Offers $1,500-5,000 average advance.** Publishes books 18 months after acceptance of ms. Reports in 6 months. Book catalog and ms guidelines for #10 SASE.
Nonfiction: How-to, illustrated book, reference, self-help. Subjects include health/medicine, psychology, science. "We seek to simplify health and medicine for consumers." Submit proposal package, including outline, 3-5 sample chapters, curriculum vitae or résumé and letter detailing who would buy the book and the market/need for the book. Reviews artwork/photos as part of the ms package.
Recent Title(s): *Living Longer with Heart Disease*, by Howard Wayne, M.D.

HEALTH PRESS, P.O. Box 1388, Santa Fe NM 87504. (505)982-9373. Fax: (505)983-1733. E-mail: hthprs@trail.com. Website: http://www.healthpress.com. **Acquisitions:** Corie Conwell, editor. "Health Press publishes books by health care professionals on cutting-edge patient education topics." Publishes hardcover and trade paperback originals. **Publishes 4 titles/year. 90% of books from first-time authors; 90% from unagented writers. Pays standard royalty on wholesale price.** Publishes book 1 year after acceptance of ms. Accepts simultaneous submissions. Reports in 2 months on proposals. Book catalog free.
Nonfiction: Subjects include health/medicine, patient education. Submit proposal package, including résumé, outline and 3 complete chapters. Reviews artwork/photos as part of ms package. Send photocopies.
Recent Title(s): *Blueberry Eyes*, by Monica Dorscoll Beatty, illustration by Peg Michel (children's book concerning eye treatment).

N **HEALTHWISE PUBLICATIONS**, Piccadilly Books, P.O. Box 25203, Colorado Springs CO 80936-5203. (719)550-9887. **Acquisitions**: Submissions Department. "Healthwise specializes in the publication of books on health and fitness written with a holistic or natural health viewpoint." Publishes hardcover and trade paperback originals and trade paperback reprints. **Pays 15-10% royalty on retail price.** Publishes book 1 year after acceptance of ms. Accepts simultaneous submissions. Reports only if interested.
Nonfiction: Diet, nutrition, exercise, alternative medicine and related topics. Query with sample chapters.
Recent Title(s): *Panic Free: Eliminate Anxiety/Panic Attacks Without Drugs*, by Lynne Freeman, Ph.D. (health/psychology).

N **HEARTSFIRE BOOKS**, 500 N. Guadalupe St., G-465, Santa Fe NM 87501. (505)988-5160. **Acquisitions**: Claude Saks, publisher. Publishes hardcover and trade paperback originals. **Publishes 4-6 titles/year. Receives 150 queries and mss/year. 95% of books from first-time authors; 98% from unagented writers. Pays 5-10% royalty. Offers $500-3,000 advance.** Publishes book 12-18 months after acceptance of ms. Accepts simultaneous submissions. Reports in 2 months on mss. Book catalog and ms guidelines free.
Nonfiction: Self-help. Subjects include health, psychology, religion, spiritual/metaphysical, "complementary" healing. "Writers must give readers specific information or revelation for the reader's own life process. Writers can be too focused on themselves, and the message is often too loose, too broad." Query or send complete ms. Reviews artwork/photos as part of ms package. Send photocopies.
Recent Title(s): *The Alchemy of Love*, by Robert Boldman (men's spirituality).
Tips: "Readers are on the path of discovery and healing. Submit double-spaced ms, a biography, and why your book is different from the competition."

HEINEMANN, Reed Elsevier, 361 Hanover St., Portsmouth NH 03801. Fax: (603)431-7840. Website: http://www.heinemann.com. **Acquisitions:** Leigh Peake, executive editor (education); Lisa Barnett, senior editor (performing arts); William Varner, acquisitions editor; Jim Lance, African editor. Heinemann specializes in theater, world literature and education titles. "Our goal is to offer a wide selecton of books that satisfy the needs and interests of educators from kindergarten to college." Publishes hardcover and trade paperback originals. **Publishes 80-100 titles/year. 50% of books from first-time authors; 75% from unagented writers. Pays royalty on wholesale price. Advance varies widely.** Publishes book 9 months after acceptance of ms. Accepts simultaneous submissions. Reports in 3 months on proposals. Book catalog free. Manuscript guidelines for #10 SASE.
Imprint(s): Boynton/Cook Publishers, Beeline Books.
Nonfiction: How-to, reference. Subjects include parenting as it relates to school education, education, gay/lesbian issues, language arts, women's issues/studies, African studies, drama. "Our goal is to provide books that represent leading ideas within our niche markets. We publish very strictly within our categories. We do not publish classroom textbooks." Query. Submit proposal package, including table of contents, outline, 1-2 sample chapters.

Recent Title(s): *It Begins with Tears*, by Opal Palmer Adisa (Caribbean literature); *The African Novel in English*, by M. Keith Booker (African studies).
Tips: "Keep your queries (and manuscripts!) short, study the market, be realistic and prepared to promote your book!"

HELIX BOOKS, Perseus Book Group, One Jacob Way, Reading MA 01867 (781)944-3700, ext. 2853. Fax: (781)944-8243. Website: http://www.aw.com. **Acquisitions**: Jeffrey Robbins, executive editor; Heather Mimnaugh, assistant editor. Estab. 1992. "Helix Books presents the world's top scientists and science writers sharing with the general public the latest discoveries and their human implications, across the full range of scientific disciplines. Publishes hardcover and trade paperback originals and reprints. **Publishes 30 titles/year. Receives 160 queries/year. 50% of books from first-time authors; 60% from unagented writers. Pays 7½-15% royalty on retail price "sliding scale based on number of copies sold." Offers $5,000 and up advance.** Publishes book 6 months after acceptance of ms. Accepts simultaneous submissions but prefer exclusive. Reports in 1 month on queries. Book catalog free.
Nonfiction: Science. Query or submit outline, 2 sample chapters and proposal package, including market analysis, competition analysis, audience description, chapter outlines/table of contents, why topic is hot, why author is the one to write this book, 25-word synopsis that explains why the proposed book will be the best ever written about this topic.
Recent Title(s): *Six Not So Easy Pieces: Einstein's Relativity, Symmetry, and Space-Time*, by Richard P. Feynman (physics).

HELLGATE PRESS, PSI Research, 300 N. Valley Dr., Grants Pass OR 97526. (503)479-9464. Fax: (503)476-1479. Website: http://www.psi-research.com/hellgate.htm. **Acquisitions:** Emmett Ramey, president. Estab. 1996. "Hellgate Press specializes in military history and other military topics." **Publishes 6-8 titles/year. Pays royalty.** Publishes books 6 months after acceptance of ms. Accepts simultaneous submissions. Reports in 2 months on queries. Book catalog and ms guidelines for #10 SASE.
Nonfiction: Subjects include history, military/war, travel. Query with outline, sample chapter and SASE. Reviews artwork/photos as part of the ms package. Send photocopies.
Recent Title(s): *Gulf War Debriefing Book*, by Andrew Leyden.

HENDRICK-LONG PUBLISHING CO., INC., P.O. Box 25123, Dallas TX 75225-1123. (214)358-4677. Fax: (214)352-4768. E-mail: hendrick-long@worldnet.att.net. **Acquisitions:** Joann Long. Estab. 1969. Hendrick-Long publishes historical fiction and nonfiction primarily about Texas and the Southwest for children and young adults. Publishes hardcover and trade paperback originals and hardcover reprints. **Publishes 8 titles/year. Receives 500 submissions/year. 90% of books from unagented writers. Pays royalty on selling price.** Publishes book 18 months after acceptance. Reports in 1 month on queries, 2 months if more than query sent. Book catalog for 8½×11 or 9×12 SAE with 4 first-class stamps. Manuscript guidelines for #10 SASE.
Nonfiction: Biography, history. Texas and Southwest-focused material for children and young adults. Query or submit outline and 2 sample chapters. Reviews artwork/photos as part of ms package; send photocopies. Do not send original art.
Fiction: Texas and the Southwest-focused material for kindergarten through young adult. Query or submit outline/synopsis and 2 sample chapters.
Recent Title(s): *Lone Star Justice: Supreme Court Justice Tom C. Clark*, by Evan Young (young adult); *I Know an Old Texan Who Swallowed a Fly*, by Donna Cooner, illustrated by Ann Rife (fiction ages 4-8).

HENDRICKSON PUBLISHERS, INC., 140 Summit St., P.O. Box 3473, Peabody MA 01961-3473. Fax: (508)531-8146. E-mail: DPenwell@hendrickson.com or PAlexander@hendrickson.com. **Acquisitions:** Dan Penwell, manager of products; Patrick Alexander, editorial director (academic). Estab. 1983. Hendrickson publishes "books that give insight into Bible understanding (academically) and encourage spiritual growth (popular trade)." Publishes hardcover and trade paperback originals and reprints. **Publishes 35 titles/year. Receives 200 submissions/year. 10% of books from first-time authors; 100% from unagented writers.** Publishes book an average of 1 year after acceptance. Accepts simultaneous submissions (if so notified). Reports in 2 months. Book catalog and ms guidelines for SASE.
Nonfiction: Religious subjects. "We will consider any quality manuscript specifically related to biblical studies and related fields. Also, nonfiction books in a more popular vein that give a hunger to studying, understanding and applying Scripture; books that encourage spiritual growth, such as personal devotionals." Submit outline and sample chapters.
Recent Title(s): *The Bible Made Easy*, by Mark Water.

VIRGIL HENSLEY PUBLISHING, 6116 E. 32nd St., Tulsa OK 74135-5494. (918)664-8520. E-mail: neal@vwhp.com. Website: http://www.vwhp.com. **Acquisitions:** Terri Kalfas, editor. Estab. 1965. "We serve an interdenominational market—all Christian persuasions. Our goal is to get readers back into studying their Bible instead of studying about the Bible." Publishes hardcover and paperback originals. **Publishes 5-10 titles/year. Receives 800 submissions/year. 50% of books from first-time authors; 50% from unagented writers. Pays 5% minimum royalty on gross sales or makes outright purchase of $250 minimum for study aids.** Publishes ms 18 months after acceptance. Reports in 2 months on queries. Manuscript guidelines for #10 SASE.
Nonfiction: Bible study curriculum. Subjects include child guidance, parenting, money/finance, men's and women's Christian education, prayer, prophecy, Christian living, large and small group studies, discipleship, adult development, parenting, personal growth, pastoral aids, church growth, family. "We do not want to see anything non-Christian." No New Age, poetry, plays, sermon collections. Query with synopsis and sample chapters.

Recent Title(s): *Couples in the Bible: Examples to Live By*, by Sylvia Charles (Bible).
Tips: "Submit something that crosses denominational lines directed toward the large Christian market, not small specialized groups."

HERITAGE BOOKS, INC., 1540-E Pointer Ridge Place, Bowie MD 20716-1859. (301)390-7708. Fax: (301)390-7193. **Acquisitions:** Leslie Towle, editorial supervisor. Estab. 1978. "We particularly desire to publish nonfiction titles dealing with history and genealogy." Publishes hardcover and paperback originals and reprints. **Publishes 100 titles/year. Receives 300 submissions/year. 25% of books from first-time authors; 100% from unagented writers. Pays 10% royalty on list price.** Accepts simultaneous submissions. Reports in 1 month. *Writer's Market* recommends allowing 2 months for reply. Book catalog for SAE.
Nonfiction: History and genealogy including how-to and reference works, as well as conventional histories and genealogies. "Ancestries of contemporary people are not of interest. The titles should be either of general interest or restricted to Eastern U.S. and Midwest, United Kingdom, Germany. Material dealing with the present century is usually not of interest." Query or submit outline with SASE. Reviews artwork/photos.
Tips: "The quality of the book is of prime importance; next is its relevance to our fields of interest."

HEYDAY BOOKS, Box 9145, Berkeley CA 94709-9145. Fax: (510)549-1889. E-mail: heyday@heydaybooks.com. **Acquisitions:** Malcolm Margolin, publisher. Estab. 1974. "Heyday Books publishes nonfiction books with a strong California focus." Publishes hardcover originals, trade paperback originals and reprints. **Publishes 8-10 titles/year. Receives 200 submissions/year. 50% of books from first-time authors; 90% of books from unagented writers. Pays 8-15% royalty on net price.** Publishes book 8 months after acceptance. Reports in 1 week on queries, 5 weeks on mss. *Writer's Market* recommends allowing 2 months for reply. Book catalog for 7×9 SAE with 2 first-class stamps.
Nonfiction: Books about California only. Subjects include Americana, history, nature, travel. "We publish books about native Americans, natural history, history, and recreation, with a strong California focus." Query with outline and synopsis. Reviews artwork/photos.
Recent Title(s): *Fine Art of California Indian Basketry*, by Brian Bibby (basket weaving).
Tips: "Give good value, and avoid gimmicks."

HIGH PLAINS PRESS, P.O. Box 123, 539 Cassa Rd., Glendo WY 82213. Fax: (307)735-4590. **Acquisitions:** Nancy Curtis, publisher. "What we sell best is history of the Old West, focusing on Wyoming. We also publish one book of poetry a year in our Poetry of the American West series." Publishes hardcover and trade paperback originals. **Publishes 4 titles/year. Receives 300 queries and 200 mss/year. 80% of books from first-time authors; 95% from unagented writers. Pays 10% royalty on wholesale price. Offers $100-600 advance.** Publishes book 2 years after acceptance. Accepts simultaneous submissions. Reports in 1 month on queries and proposals, 3 months on mss. Book catalog and ms guidelines for 8½×10 SASE.
Nonfiction: Biography, Western Americana, Americana, art/architecture, history, nature/environment, regional. "We focus on books of the American West, particularly history." Submit outline. Reviews artwork/photos as part of ms package. Send photocopies.
Poetry: "We only seek poetry closely tied to the Rockies. Do not submit single poems." Query with complete ms.
Recent Title(s): *I See By Your Outfit: Historic Cowboy Gear of the Northern Plains*, by Steve Mount and Tom Lindmer (history); *Glass-Eyed Paint in the Rain*, by Laurie Wagner Buyer (poetry).

HIGHSMITH PRESS, P.O. Box 800, Fort Atkinson WI 53538-0800. (920)563-9571. Fax: (920)563-4801. E-mail: hpress@highsmith.com. Website: http://www.hpress.highsmith.com. **Acquisitions:** Donald J. Sager, publisher. "Highsmith Press emphasizes library reference and professional books that meet the practical needs of librarians, educators and the general public." Publishes hardcover and paperback originals. **Publishes 20 titles/year. Receives 500-600 queries and 400-500 mss/year. 30% of books from first-time authors; 100% from unagented writers. Pays 10-12% royalty on net sales price. Offers $250-1,000 advance.** Publishes book 6 months after acceptance of ms. Accepts simultaneous submissions. Reports in 1 month on queries, 2 months on proposals, 3 months on mss. Book catalog and ms guidelines free.
Imprint(s): Alleyside Press (creative and low cost resources, designed to save time for teachers and librarians).
Nonfiction: Reference, professional. Subjects include education, language/literature, multicultural, professional (library science), teacher activity. "We are primarily interested in reference and library professional books, multicultural resources for youth, library and study skills, curricular and activity books for teachers and others who work with preschool through high school youth." Query with outline and 1-2 sample chapters. Reviews artwork/photos as part of ms package. Send transparencies.
Fiction: No longer accepting children's picture book mss. "Our current emphasis is on storytelling collections for preschool-grade 6. We prefer stories that can be easily used by teachers and children's librarians, multicultural topics,

ALWAYS ENCLOSE a self-addressed, stamped envelope (SASE) with all your queries and correspondence.

and manuscripts that feature fold and cut, flannelboard, tangram, or similar simple patterns that can be reproduced."
Recent Title(s): *How to Get a Job If You're a Teenager*, by Cindy Pervola and Debby Hobgood; *Great Asian Stories*, by Cathy Spagnoli (fiction).

HILL AND WANG, Farrar Straus & Giroux, Inc., 19 Union Square W., New York NY 10003. (212)741-6900. Fax: (212)633-9385. **Acquisitions:** Elisabeth Sifton, publisher; Lauren Osborne, editor. "We publish serious nonfiction books, primarily in history and the social sciences." Publishes hardcover and trade paperback originals. **Publishes 12 titles/year. Receives 1,500 queries/year. 5% of books from first-time authors; 50% from unagented writers. Pays 7½% royalty on retail price. Advances "vary widely from a few hundred to several thousand dollars."** Publishes book 1 year after acceptance of ms. Accepts simultaneous submissions. Reports in 2 months. Book catalog free.
Nonfiction: Cross-over academic and trade books. Subjects include government/politics, history (primarily American, some European and African history), public policy, sociology, women's issues, some drama. Submit outline, sample chapters, letter explaining rationale for book and SASE. Reviews artwork/photos as part of ms package. Send samples.
Fiction: *Not* considering new fiction.
Recent Title(s): *A Place for Us: How to Make Society Civil and Democracy Strong*, by Benjamin R. Barber.

HIPPOCRENE BOOKS INC., 171 Madison Ave., New York NY 10016. (212)685-4371. Fax: (212)779-9338. E-mail: hippocre@ix.netcom.com. Website: http://www.hippocrenebooks.com. **Acquisitions:** George Blagowidow, president/editorial director. Publisher: Jacek Galazka. Estab. 1971. "We publish reference books of international interest, often bilingual, in the fields of cookery, travel, language and literature." Publishes hardcover and trade paperback originals. **Publishes 100 titles/year. Receives 250 submissions/year. 10% of books from first-time authors; 95% from unagented writers. Pays 6-10% royalty on retail price. Offers $2,000 advance.** Publishes book 16 months after acceptance. Accepts simultaneous submissions. Reports in 2 months. Book catalog for 9×12 SAE with 5 first-class stamps. Manuscript guidelines for #10 SASE.
Nonfiction: Reference. Subjects include foreign language, Judaic reference, ethnic and special interest travel, military history, bilingual love poetry, bilingual proverbs, international cookbooks, Polish interest, foreign language, dictionaries and instruction. Submit outline, 2 sample chapters, toc.
Recent Title(s): *Polish Folk Dances & Songs*, by Ada Dziewanowska (nonfiction).
Tips: "Our recent successes in publishing general books considered midlist by larger publishers is making us more of a general trade publisher. We continue to do well with reference books like dictionaries, atlases and language studies. We ask for proposal, sample chapter, and table of contents. We then ask for material if we are interested."

HOHM PRESS, P.O. Box 2501, Prescott AZ 86302. Fax: (520)717-1779. E-mail: pinedr@goodnet.com. **Acquisitions:** Regina Sara Ryan, managing editor. "Our offerings include a range of titles in the areas of psychology and spirituality, herbistry, alternative health methods and nutrition." Publishes hardcover and trade paperback originals. **Publishes 6-8 titles/year. 50% of books from first-time authors. Pays 10-15% royalty on net sales. No advance.** Publishes book 18 months after acceptance of ms. Accepts simultaneous submissions. Reports in 3 months on queries. Book catalog for $1.50.
Nonfiction: Self-help. Subjects include child guidance/parenting, health/medicine, philosophy, religious (Hindu, Buddhist, Sufi or translations of classic texts in major religious traditions). "We look for writers who have an established record in their field of expertise. The best buy of recent years came from two women who fully substantiated how they could market their book. We believed they could do it. We were right." Query with SASE.
Poetry: "We are not accepting poetry at this time except for translations of recognized religious/spiritual classics." Query.
Recent Title(s): *Conscious Parenting*, by Lee Lozowick (child-raising).

HOLLIS PUBLISHING COMPANY, Puritan Press, Inc., 95 Runnells Bridge Rd., Hollis NH 03049. (603)889-4500. Fax: (603)889-6551. E-mail: books@hollispublishing.com. Website: http://www.hollispublishing.com. **Acquisitions:** Rebecca Shannon, editor (history, sociology, politics, NE authors); Fred Lyford, editor (education, business, American studies). "We primarily publish supported titles aimed at college professors for use in university libraries/courses." Publishes hardcover and trade paperback originals. **Publishes 5 titles/year. Receives 25 queries and 15 mss/year. 50% of books from first-time authors; 100% from unagented writers. Pays 5-10% royalty on retail price.** Publishes book within 6 months of acceptance of ms. Accepts simultaneous submissions. Reports in 1 month on queries and proposals, 2 months on mss. Book catalog free. Manuscript guidelines for #10 SASE.
Nonfiction: Biography, textbook, scholarly. Subjects include Americana, anthropology/archaeology, education, ethnic, government/politics, history, memoirs, nature/environment, regional, sociology, travel. Query with outline and 2 sample chapters with SASE.
Recent Title(s): *Canoeing the Charles*, by Ralph Perry (regional/family memoir).

HOLMES & MEIER PUBLISHERS, INC., East Building, 160 Broadway, New York NY 10038. (212)374-0100. Fax: (212)374-1313. **Acquisitions:** Katharine Turok, executive editor. Publisher: Miriam H. Holmes. Estab. 1969. "We are noted as an academic publishing house and are pleased with our reputation for excellence in the field. However, we are also expanding our list to include books of more general interest." Publishes hardcover and paperback originals. **Publishes 20 titles/year. Pays royalty.** Publishes book an average of 18 months after acceptance. Reports in up to 6 months. Query with SASE. Book catalog free.

Imprint(s): Africana Publishing Co.
Nonfiction: Africana, art, biography, business/economics, history, Judaica, Latin American studies, literary criticism, politics, reference and women's studies. Accepts translations. Query first with outline, sample chapters, cv and idea of intended market/audience.

HOLMES PUBLISHING GROUP, P.O. Box 623, Edmonds WA 98020. E-mail: jdh@jdh.seanet.com. CEO: J.D. Holmes. **Acquisitions:** L.Y. Fitzgerald. Holmes publishes informative spiritual health titles on philosophy, metaphysical and religious subjects. Publishes hardcover and trade paperback originals and reprints. **Publishes 40 titles/year. Receives 120 queries and 80 mss/year. 20% of books from first-time authors; 20% from unagented writers. Pays 10% royalty on wholesale price.** Publishes book 4 months after acceptance of ms. Reports in 2 months.
Imprint(s): Alchemical Press, Sure Fire Press, Contra/Thought, Alexandrian Press.
Nonfiction: Self-help. Subjects include health/medicine, occult, philosophy, religion, metaphysical. "We do not publish titles that are more inspirational than informative." Query only with SASE.
Fiction: Metaphysical, occult. Query with SASE.
Recent Title(s): *Age of Lucifer: Predatory Spirituality & The Quest for Godhood*, by Robert Tucker (nonfiction).

HENRY HOLT & COMPANY BOOKS FOR YOUNG READERS, Henry Holt & Co., Inc., 115 W. 18th St., New York NY 10011. (212)886-9200. Associate Publisher: Laura Godwin (picture books, chapter books and middle grade). Senior Editor: Marc Aronson (young adult). Senior Editor: Christy Ottaviano (picture books, chapter books and middle grade). Associate Editor: Margaret Garrou. **Acquisitions:** BYR Submissions. Estab. 1866 (Holt). "Henry Holt Books for Young Readers publishes highly original and cutting-edge fiction and nonfiction for all ages, from the very young to the young adult." Publishes hardcover originals. **Publishes 70-80 titles/year. 5% of books from first-time authors; 50% from unagented writers. Pays royalty on retail price. Offers $3,000 and up advance.** Publishes book 18 months after acceptance of ms. Reports in 5 months on queries and mss. Book catalog and ms guidelines free with SASE.
Imprint(s): Edge Books (cutting-edge young adult books); Red Feather Books (chapter books for ages 7-10).
Nonfiction: Children's/juvenile, illustrated book. Query with SASE.
Fiction: Juvenile: adventure, animal, contemporary, fantasy, history, humor, multicultural, religion, sports, suspense/mystery. Picture books: animal, concept, history, humor, multicultural, religion, sports. Young adult: contemporary, fantasy, history, multicultural, nature/environment, problem novels, sports. Query with SASE.
Recent Title(s): *Robber and Me*, by Josef Holub (juvenile fiction).

HENRY HOLT & COMPANY, INC., 115 W. 18th St., New York NY 10011. (212)886-9200. Editor-in-Chief: William Strachan. **Acquisitions**: Sara Bershtel, editorial director (Metropolitan Books); Bryan Oettel, editor (nonfiction); Elizabeth Crossman, editor (cooking); Allen Peacock, senior editor (fiction); David Sobel, senior editor (science, culture, history, health). General interest publisher of both fiction and nonfiction. Query before submitting.

- This publisher informs us that they receive too many inappropriate submissions. Check their catalog to make sure your work fits into their publishing program.

Imprint(s): Edge Books, John Macrae Books, Metropolitan Books, **Owl Books**, Marian Wood Books, **Henry Holt & Company Books for Young Readers** (Books by Michael Hague, Books by Bill Martin Jr. and John Archambault, Owlet Paperbacks, Redfeather Books, W5 Reference).

[N] **HOLY CROSS ORTHODOX PRESS**, Hellenic College, 50 Goddard Ave., Brookline MA 02146. Fax: (617)566-9075. **Acquisitions:** Anton C. Vrame, Ph.D., managing editor. "Holy Cross publishes titles that are rooted in the tradition of the Eastern Orthodox Church." Publishes trade paperback originals. **Publishes 8 titles/year. Imprint publishes 2 titles/year. Receives 10-15 queries and 10-15 mss/year. 85% of books from first-time authors; 100% from unagented writers. Pays 8-12% royalty on retail price.** Publishes book 18 months after acceptance of ms. Accepts simultaneous submissions. Reports in 6 months on mss. Book catalog free.
Imprint(s): Hellenic College Press.
Nonfiction: Academic. Subjects include ethnic, religion (Greek Orthodox). "Holy Cross Orthodox Press publishes scholarly and popular literature in the areas of Orthodox Christian theology and Greek letters. Submissions are often far too technical usually with a very limited audiences." Submit outline and complete ms. Reviews artwork/photos as part of the manuscript package. Send photocopies.
Recent Title(s): *Love, Sexuality & Marriage*, by Chryssavgis (spirituality).

HONOR BOOKS, P.O. Box 55388, Tulsa OK 74155. (918)496-9007. **Acquistions:** Mark Gilroy, director of product development and editorial services. "We are a Christian publishing house with a mission to inspire and encourage people to draw near to God and to enjoy His love and grace." Publishes hardcover and trade paperback originals. **Publishes 60 titles/year. Receives 1,000 queries and 500 mss/year. 2% of books from first-time authors. 90% of books from unagented writers. Pays royalty on wholesale price, makes outright purchase or assigns work for hire. Offers small advance.** Publishes book 1 year after acceptance of ms. Accepts simultaneous submissions. Reports in 1 month on queries, 3 months on proposals. Ms guidelines for #10 SASE.
Nonfiction: Devotional gift book, humor, seasonal/holiday gift books, "portable" inspiration. Subjects include hobbies (devotional or inspirational in format), religion, devotional. "We aren't looking for testimony books, but we do welcome personal experience stories that illustrate specific principles that are central to the theme of the book and which accom-

plish our publishing mission." Query with outline, writing sample and proposal package, including table of contents, synopsis and author bio, SASE. Reviews artwork/photos as part of the ms package. Send photocopies.
Recent Title(s): *How to Be an Up Person in a Down World* (devotional).
Tips: "Our books are for busy, achievement-oriented people who are looking for balance between reaching their goals and knowing that God loves them unconditionally. Our books should challenge spiritual growth, victorious living and an intimate knowledge of God. Write about what you are for and not what you are against. We look for scripts that are biblically correct and which edify the reader."

HOUGHTON MIFFLIN BOOKS FOR CHILDREN, Houghton Mifflin Company, 222 Berkeley St., Boston MA 02116. (617)351-5959. Fax: (617)351-1111. Website: http://www.hmco.com. **Acquisitions:** Sarah Hines-Stephens, submissions coordinator. "Houghton Mifflin gives shape to ideas that educate, inform, and above all, delight." Publishes hardcover and trade paperback originals and reprints. **Firm publishes 100 titles/year. Receives 5,000 queries and 12,000 mss/year. 10% of books from first-time authors; 70% from unagented writers. Pays 5-10% royalty on retail price. Advance dependent on many factors.** Publishes book 18 months after acceptance of ms. Accepts simultaneous submissions. Reports in 4 months. Book catalog for 9×12 SASE with 3 first-class stamps. Manuscript guidelines for #10 SASE.
Imprint(s): Sandpiper Paperback Books (Eden Edwards, editor).
Nonfiction: Biography, children's/juvenile, humor, illustrated book. Subjects include agriculture/horticulture, Americana, animals, anthropology, art/architecture, ethnic, gardening, history, language/literature, music/dance, nature/environment, recreation, regional, science, sports, travel. Interested in "innovative science books, especially about scientists 'in the field' and what they do." Submit outline and 2 sample chapters with SASE. Mss not returned without appropriate-sized SASE. Reviews artwork/photos as part of ms package. Send photocopies.
Fiction: Adventure, ethnic, historical, humor, juvenile (early readers), literary, mystery, picture books, suspense, young adult, board books. Submit full ms with appropriate-sized SASE.
Recent Title(s): *Art Around the World: Loo-Loo, Boo, & More Art You Can Do*, by Denis Roche (art); *Distant Feathers*, by Tim Egan (humorous picture book).
Tips: "Faxed manuscripts and proposals are not considered."

HOUGHTON MIFFLIN COMPANY, 222 Berkeley St., Boston MA 02116. (617)351-5000. Fax: (617)351-1202. Website: http://www.hmco.com. **Acquisitions:** Submissions Editor. Estab. 1832. "Houghton Mifflin gives shape to ideas that educate, inform and delight. In a new era of publishing, our legacy of quality thrives as we combine imagination with technology, bringing you new ways to know." Publishes hardcover and trade paperback originals and reprints. **Publishes 60 hardcovers, 30-40 paperbacks/year. 10% of books from first-time authors; 20% from unagented writers. Hardcover: pays 10-15% royalty on retail price, sliding scale or flat rate based on sales; paperback: 7½% flat fee, but negotiable. Advance varies.** Publishes book 1-2 years after acceptance of ms. Accepts simultaneous submissions. Reports in 3 months. Book catalog and ms guidelines free.
Imprint(s): Chapters Publishing Ltd., Clarion Books, Peter Davison Books, Walter Lorraine Books, **Houghton Mifflin Books for Children**, Mariner Paperbacks, Sandpiper Paperbacks, Frances Tenenbaum Books.
Nonfiction Biography, childrens/juvenile, language/literature, military/war, money/finance, music/dance, nature/environment, philosophy, photography, psychology, recreation, regional, religion, science, sociology, sports, travel, women's issues/studies. "We are not a mass market publisher. Our main focus is serious nonfiction. We do practical self-help but not pop psychology self-help." Query with outline, 1 sample chapter and SASE. Reviews artwork/photos as part of ms package. Send photocopies.
Fiction: Adventure, confession, ethnic, fantasy, feminist, gay/lesbian, historical, humor, literary, mainstream/contemporary, mystery, short story collections, suspense. "We are not a mass market publisher. Study the current list." Query with 3 sample chapters or complete mss and SASE.
Poetry: "At this point we have an established roster of poets we use. It is hard for first-time poets to get published by Houghton Mifflin."
Recent Title(s): *Bogart: A Life in Hollywood*, by Jeffrey Meyers (biography); *American Pastoral*, by Philip Roth (literary novel).

HOUSE OF COLLECTIBLES, Ballantine Publishing, 201 E. 50th St., New York NY 10022. Website: http://www.randomhouse.com. **Acquisitions:** Randy Ladenheim-Gil, editor. "One of the premier publishing companies devoted to books on a wide range of antiques and collectibles, House of Collectibles publishes books for the seasoned expert and the beginning collector alike. We have been publishing price guides and other books on antiques and collectibles for over 35 years and plan to meet the needs of collectors, dealers and appraisers well into the 21st century." Publishes trade and mass market paperback originals. **Publishes 25-28 titles/year. Receives 200 queries/year. 1% of books from first-time authors; 85% from unagented writers. Pays royalty on retail price, varies. Offers advance against royalties, varies.** Publishes book 6 months after acceptance of ms. Accepts simultaneous submissions, if so noted. Reports in 3 months on queries. Book catalog free from Ballantine.
Imprint(s): Official Price Guide series.
Nonfiction: Coffee table book, how-to (related to collecting antiques and coins), reference books. Subjects include hobbies, recreation. "We are happy to hear from collectors with a particular expertise. Something may strike us, or be timely. We are expanding beyond price guides." Query or submit outline, 3 sample chapters with SASE.
Recent Title(s): *How to Buy Jewelry Wholesale*, by Frank J. Adler.

HOWELL BOOK HOUSE, Macmillan General Reference, 1633 Broadway, New York NY 10019. (212)654-8500. **Acquisitions**: Sean Frawley, publisher; Don Stevens, associate publisher; Seymour Weiss, editor; Madeleine Larsen, equine editor. "Our mission is to publish the highest quality and most useful information and reference books on pet and animal subjects." Publishes hardcover originals, trade paperback originals and reprints. **Publishes 60-100 titles/year. Receives 3,000 queries/year. 15% of books from first-time authors; 40% from unagented writers. Pays royalty on retail price or net sales, or makes outright purchase or work-for-hire assignments. Offers variable advance.** Publishes book 1 year after acceptance of ms. Accepts simultaneous submissions. Reports in 2 months on queries and mss, 1 month on proposals.

Nonfiction: How-to, reference. Subjects include animals, recreation. Submit outline with 1 sample chapter and proposal package, including table of contents, author's credentials, target audience and market analysis. Reviews artwork/photos as part of ms package. Send photocopies. SASE for returns.

Recent Title(s): *Dressage by the Letter*, by Moira C. Harris.

HOWELL PRESS, INC., 1147 River Rd., Suite 2, Charlottesville VA 22901-4172. (804)977-4006. Fax: (804)971-7204. E-mail: howellpres@aol.com. Website: http://www.howellpress.com. **Acquisitions:** Ross A. Howell, president. Estab. 1985. "Howell Press publishes and distributes books in the categories of history, transportation, gardening, cooking and regional (Mid-Atlantic and Southeastern U.S.) interest." **Publishes 6-8 titles/year. Receives 500 submissions/year. 10% of books from first-time authors; 80% from unagented writers. Pays 5-7% royalty on net retail price. "We generally offer an advance, but amount differs with each project and is generally negotiated with authors on a case-by-case basis."** Publishes book 18 months after acceptance. Reports in 2 months. Book catalog for 9×12 SAE with 4 first-class stamps. Manuscript guidelines for #10 SASE.

Nonfiction: Illustrated books, historical texts. Subjects include aviation, military history, cooking, maritime history, motorsports, gardening. "Generally open to most ideas, as long as writing is accessible to average adult reader. Our line is targeted, so it would be advisable to look over our catalog before querying to better understand what Howell Press does." Query with outline and sample chapters with SASE. Reviews artwork/photos as part of ms package. Does not return mss without SASE.

Recent Title(s): *Black Brass: Black Generals and Admirals in the Armed Forces of the United States*, by Dabbs.

Tips: "Focus of our program has been illustrated books, but we will also consider nonfiction manuscripts that would not be illustrated. Selections limited to history, transportation, cooking and gardening."

HOWELLS HOUSE, P.O. Box 9546, Washington DC 20016-9546. (202)333-2182. **Acquisitions:** W.D. Howells, publisher. Estab. 1988. "Our interests are institutions and institutional change." Publishes hardcover and trade paperback originals and reprints. **Publishes 4 titles/year; each imprint publishes 2-3 titles/year. Receives 2,000 queries and 300 mss/year. 50% of books from first-time authors; 60% from unagented writers. Pays 15% net royalty or makes outright purchase. May offer advance.** Publishes book 8 months after ms development completed. Reports in 2 months on proposals.

Imprint(s): The Compass Press, Whalesback Books.

Nonfiction: Biography, illustrated book, textbook. Subjects include Americana, anthropology/archaeology, art/architecture, business/economics, education, government/politics, history, military/war, photography, science, sociology, translation. Query.

Fiction: Historical, literary, mainstream/contemporary. Query.

HUMANICS CHILDREN'S HOUSE, Humanics Publishing, 1482 Mecaslin St. NW, Atlanta GA 30309. (404)874-2176. **Acquisitions:** Chris Walker, editor. Estab. 1977. "We publish picture books for young children that incorporate a small message about self-development." Publishes hardcover and trade paperback originals and reprints. **Publishes 8 titles/year. Receives 1,200 queries and 1,300 mss/year. 90% of books from unagented writers. Pays 5-13% royalty on net receipts. Offers $500-1,000 advance.** Publishes book 6-24 months after acceptance of ms. Accepts simultaneous submissions, if so noted. Reports in 1 month. Book catalog for 9×12 SAE with 7 first-class stamps. Manuscript guidelines for #10 SASE.

Fiction: Picture books. "We do not publish many unsolicited manuscripts." Query or submit ms with SASE.

Recent Title(s): *Giggle E. Goose*, by Al Newman.

Tips: Audience is young children who need to be read to, or are beginning to read a little. "No phone calls, please."

HUMANICS LEARNING, Humanics Publishing Group, 1482 Mecaslin St. NW, Atlanta GA 30309. (404)874-2176. Fax: (404)874-1976. **Acquisitions:** Chris Walker, editor. Estab. 1977. "Our goal is to furnish teachers, home schoolers, daycare facilitators and other instructors with the best teacher resource guides available to help improve curriculum." Publishes hardcover and trade paperback originals and reprints. **Publishes 8 titles/year. Receives 1,500 queries and 1,300 mss/year. 90% of books from unagented writers. Pays 5-13% royalty on net receipts. Offers $500-1,000 advance.** Publishes book 1-6 months after acceptance of ms. Accepts simultaneous submissions, if so noted. Reports in 1 month. Book catalog for 9×12 SAE with 7 first-class stamps. Manuscript guidelines for #10 SASE.

Nonfiction: How-to, teacher resource guides. Subjects include child guidance/parenting, education, ethnic, health, language, music/dance, nature/environment, psychology, self-esteem, science. "Know our focus." Query and/or submit outline and 3 sample chapters with SASE. Reviews artwork/photos as part of ms package. Send photocopies.

Recent Title(s): *Pre-K Science*, by Cynthia Marthy (teacher resource).

Tips: "Request a catalog."

HUMANICS PUBLISHING GROUP, 1482 Mecaslin St. NW, Atlanta GA 30309. (404)874-2176. Fax: (404)874-1976. E-mail: humanics@mindspring.com. **Acquisitions:** Chris Walker, editor. Estab. 1976. Humanics Trade publishes "books for the mind, body and spirit." Publishes hardcover and trade paperback originals. **Publishes 22 titles/year; imprints: Humanics Trade, 2; Humanics Children's House, 2; Humanics Learning, 10. Receives 5,000 queries/year. 70% of books from first-time authors. Pays 10% royalty on wholesale price. Offers $500-3,000 advance.** Publishes book 1-12 months after acceptance of ms. Accepts simultaneous submissions, if so noted. Responds only if interested. Book catalog free. Manuscript guidelines for #10 SASE.
Imprint(s): Humanics Trade, **Humanics Learning**, **Humanics Children's House**.
Nonfiction: Children's/juvenile, illustrated book, self-help. Subjects include child guidance/parenting, philosophy, spirituality (e.g., taoism). Query with outline, 1 sample chapter and SASE.
Recent Title(s): *Zen of Magic*, by Inez Stein.
Tips: "For our activity books, audience is parents and educators looking for books which will enrich their children's lives. For our trade books, audience is anyone interested in positive, healthy self-development. We are looking for quality and creativity. As a small publisher, we don't waste our time or an author's time on books that are not of lasting importance or value. Taoism and Zen high interest."

HUMANITIES PRESS INTERNATIONAL INC., 165 First Ave., Atlantic Highlands NJ 07716. (732)872-1441. Website: http://www.humanitiespress.com. **Acquisitions:** Keith Ashfield, publisher. "We publish books suitable for use in college courses." Publishes hardcover originals and trade paperback originals and reprints. **Publishes 35 titles/year. 25% of books from first-time authors; 99% from unagented writers. Pays 5-10% royalty on retail price. Offers $0-1,000 advance.** Publishes book 15 months after acceptance of ms. Reports in 1 month on queries and proposals, 3 months on mss. Book catalog and ms guidelines free.
Nonfiction: Textbook (college level). Subjects include political theory, history, philosophy, religion, sociology. "Junior/senior undergrad level and up. All authors will be post doctoral, holding a current academic position." Query.
Recent Title(s): *The Scientific Revolution*, by James R. Jacob (history).

HUNGRY MIND PRESS, 1648 Grand Ave., St. Paul MN 55105. Fax: (612)699-7190. E-mail: hmindpress@aol.com. **Acquisitions:** Pearl Kilbride. "We publish adult-level, literary fiction and nonfiction." Publishes hardcover originals, trade paperback originals and reprints. **Publishes 8-10 titles/year. Receives 200 queries and 300 mss/year. 25% of books from unagented writers. Royalties and advances vary.** Publishes book 10 months after acceptance of ms. Accepts simultaneous submissions. Reports in 2 months on proposals. Book catalog for 6×9 SAE and 2 first-class stamps. Manuscript guidelines for #10 SASE.
Nonfiction and Fiction: Literary, adult fiction and nonfiction. No how-to or self-help/instructional mss. Submit proposal package, including letter, outline and at least one sample chapter with SASE.
Recent Title(s): *Crossing the Moon*, by Paulette Bates Alden (memoir/infertility).

HUNTER HOUSE, P.O. Box 2914, Alameda CA 94501. Website: http://www.hunterhouse.com. **Acquisitions:** Editorial Coordinator. "We are interested in proposals that reflect our motto 'Books for health, family and community.' " Publishes hardcover and trade paperback originals and reprints. **Publishes 10-12 titles/year. Receives 200-300 queries and 100 mss/year. 50% of books from first-time authors; 80% from unagented writers. Pays 12-15% royalty on net receipts, defined as selling price. Offers $250-2,500 advance.** Publishes book 1-2 years after acceptance of final ms. Accepts simultaneous submissions. Reports in 2 months on queries, 3 months on proposals, 6 months on mss. Book catalog and ms guidelines for 8½×11 SAE with 3 first-class stamps.
Nonfiction: Reference, (only health reference); self-help, social issues. "Health books (especially women's health) should focus on emerging health issues or current issues that are inadequately covered and be written for the general population. Family books: Our current focus is sexuality and couple relationships, and alternative lifestyles to high stress. Community topics include violence prevention, violence intervention and human rights. We also publish specialized curricula for counselors and educators in the areas of violence prevention and trauma in children." Query with proposal package, including synopsis, table of contents and chapter outline, sample chapter, target audience information, competition and what distinguishes the book. Send photocopies, proposals generally not returned, requested mss returned with SASE. Reviews artwork/photos as part of ms package.
Recent Title(s): *Her Healthy Heart*, by Linda Ojeda, Ph.D.
Tips: Audience is concerned people who are looking to educate themselves and their community about real-life issues that affect them. "Please send as much information as possible about *who* your audience is, *how* your book addresses their needs, and *how* you reach that audience in you ongoing work."

HUNTER PUBLISHING, INC., 130 Campus Dr., Edison NJ 08818. Fax: (561)546-8040. E-mail: hunterpub@emi.net. Website: http://www.hunterpublishing.com. **Acquisitions:** Kim André, editor; Lissa Dailey. President: Michael Hunter. Estab. 1985. "We publish practical guides for travelers." **Publishes 100 titles/year. Receives 300 submissions/year. 10% of books from first-time authors; 75% from unagented writers. Pays royalty. Offers negotiable advance.** Publishes book 5 months after acceptance. Accepts simultaneous submissions. Reports in 3 weeks on queries, 1 month on ms. *Writer's Market* recommends allowing 2 months for reply. Book catalog for #10 SAE with 4 first-class stamps.
Imprint(s): Adventure Guides, Romantic Weekends Guides, Alive Guides.

Nonfiction: Reference, travel guides. "We need travel guides to areas covered by few competitors: Caribbean Islands, South and Central America, regional U.S. from an active 'adventure' perspective." No personal travel stories or books not directed to travelers. Query or submit outline/synopsis and sample chapters. Reviews artwork/photos as part of ms package.
Recent Title(s): *Romantic Weekends in Virginia and Washington D.C.*, by Renouf.
Tips: "Guides should be destination-specific, rather than theme-based alone. Thus, 'travel with kids' is too broad; 'Florida with Kids' is OK. Make sure the guide doesn't duplicate what other guide publishers do. We need active adventure-oriented guides and more specialized guides for travelers in search of the unusual."

⊘ **HYPERION** does not accept freelance submissions.

⊘ **HYPERION BOOKS FOR CHILDREN** does not accept freelance submissions.

ICC PUBLISHING, INC., International Chamber of Commerce, 156 Fifth Ave., Suite 308, New York NY 10010. (212)206-1150. Fax: (212)633-6025. E-mail: iccpub@interport.net. Website: http://www.iccwbo.org. **Acquisitons:** Rachelle Bijou, director. "We publish essential books and reference materials on all facets of international banking and business including letters of credit, collections, law and arbitration and environmental business matters." Publishes paperback originals. **Publishes 10 titles/year. Pays royalty or makes outright purchase.** Publishes book 1 year after acceptance of ms. Accepts simultaneous submissions. Reports in 1 month. Book catalog and ms guidelines free.
Nonfiction: Reference, technical. Subjects include international trade and business. Query or submit proposal package, including outline, table of contents and 3 sample chapters with SASE.
Recent Title(s): *ICC Guide to Bank-to-Bank Reimbursements Under Documentary Credits*, by Dan Taylor.

ICON EDITIONS, Westview Press, Perseus Book Gorup, 10 E. 53rd St., New York NY 10036. (212)207-7282. **Acquisitions:** Cass Canfield, Jr., editor. Estab. 1973. "Icon Editions focuses on books in architecture, art history and art criticism for the academic and semi-academic market, college and university market." Publishes hardcover and trade paperback originals and reprints. **Publishes 6-8 titles/year. Receives hundreds of queries/year. 25% of books from first-time authors; 80% from unagented writers. Royalty and advance vary.** Publishes book 18 months after acceptance of ms. Accepts simultaneous submissions, if so noted. Returns submissions with SASE if author requests. Book catalog free.
Nonfiction: Books for academic and semi-academic market. Subjects include art/architecture, art history. Query with SASE. Reviews artwork/photos as part of ms package "if we're interested." Send photocopies.
Recent Title(s): *Titian and Venetian Painting*, by Bruce Cole (art history).

ICS PUBLICATIONS, Institute of Carmelite Studies, 2131 Lincoln Rd. NE, Washington DC 20002. (202)832-8489. Fax: (202)832-8967. Website: http://www.ocd.or.at/ics. **Acquisitions:** Steven Payne, O.C.D., editorial director. "Our audience consists of those interested in the Carmelite tradition or in developing their life of prayer and spirituality." Publishes hardcover and trade paperback originals and reprints. **Publishes 8 titles/year. Receives 10-20 queries and 10 mss/year. 10% of books from first-time authors; 90-100% from unagented writers. Pays 2-6% royalty on retail price or makes outright purchase. Offers $500 advance.** Publishes book 2 years after acceptance. Accepts simultaneous submissions, if so noted. Reports in 2 months on proposals. Book catalog for 7×10 SAE with 2 first-class stamps. Writer's guidelines for #10 SASE.
Nonfiction: Religious (should relate to Carmelite spirituality and prayer). "We are looking for significant works on Carmelite history, spirituality, and main figures (Saints Teresa, John of the Cross, Therese of Lisieux, etc.). Too often we receive proposals for works that merely repeat what has already been done, are too technical for a general audience, or have little to do with the Carmelite tradition and spirit." Query or submit outline and 1 sample chapter.
Recent Title(s): *Carmelite Spirituality in the Teresian Tradition*, by Paul-Marie of the Cross.

IDE HOUSE PUBLISHERS, 4631 Harvey Dr., Mesquite TX 75150-1609. (214)686-5332. Website: http://www.idehouse.com. **Acquistions:** Ryan Idol, senior editor (gay/lesbian studies); Geofferoi de Struckette, liberal studies coordinator; Nalinda Downs, senior editor (women's studies); David Ashford, associate editor (US politics); Mary Meeks, associate editor (Third World politics); James Davidson, associate editor (European politics). "We publish books that reflect choice for mortals and reject all religious and political interference in the evolution of life and instill the reality of people's obligation to live with nature." Publishes hardcover and trade paperback originals. **Publishes 10 titles/year. Receives 300 queries and 500 mss/year. 70% of books from first-time authors; 100% from unagented writers. Pays 4-7% royalty on retail price.** Publishes book 1 year after acceptance of ms. Reports in 1 month on queries and proposals, 4 months on mss. Book catalog for 6×9 SAE with 5 first-class stamps. Manuscript guidelines for #10 SASE.
Imprint(s): Hercules Press (Bryan Estevez, executive senior vice president/editor).
Nonfiction: Women's history. Subjects include gay/lesbian, government/politics (liberal only), history, women's issues/studies. "We accept only nonsexist/nonhomophobic scholarly works." Query with outline and 2 sample chapters. All unsolicited mss returned unopened.
Recent Title(s): *What America Wants, America Gets*, by Joe Sharpnack (politics/humor); *Darvik*, by Tim Oates (3rd world poetry/epic).
Tips: "Inaugurating poetry branch. We are emphasizing a quest for liberal politics and have budgeted for 100 titles in 1996-1998."

IDEALS CHILDREN'S BOOKS, Hambleton-Hill Publishing, Inc., 1501 County Hospital Rd., Nashville TN 37218. **Acquisitions:** Bethany Snyder, copy editor. Ideals Children's Books publishes fiction and some nonfiction for toddlers to 8-year-olds. Publishes children's hardcover and trade paperback originals. **Publishes 40 titles/year. Receives 300 queries and 2,000-2,500 mss/year. 10% of books from first-time authors; 80% from unagented writers. Pay determined by individual contract.** Publishes book up to 2 years after acceptance of ms. Reports in 6 months on queries, proposals and mss. Manuscript guidelines for #10 SASE.

- This publisher accepts only unsolicited manuscripts from agents, members of the Society of Children's Book Writers & Illustrators, and previously published book authors who may submit with a list of writing credits.

Nonfiction: Children's. Subjects include Americana, animals, art/architecture, nature/environment, science, sports. No middle-grade or young adult novels. Submit proposal package. Reviews artwork/photos as part of ms package. Send photocopies.

Fiction: Submit complete ms with SASE.

Recent Title(s): *What Do Animals Do in Winter?*, by Melvin and Gilda Berger (easy reader nonfiction); *The Littlest Tree*, by Charles Tazewell (fiction).

Tips: Audience is children in the toddler to 8-year-old range. "We are seeking original, child-centered fiction for the picture book format."

IDEALS PUBLICATIONS INC., 535 Metroplex Dr., Suite 250, Nashville TN 37211. (615)333-0478. Publisher: Patricia Pingry. Editor: Lisa Ragan. **Acquisitions:** Michelle Burke, copy editor. Estab. 1944. Publishes highly-illustrated seasonal and nostalgic hardbound books. Uses short prose and poetry. Also publishes *Ideals* magazine. **Publishes 4 hardbound books, 6 *Ideals*,** 1-2 others titles/year. Payment varies. Accepts simultaneous submissions. Accepts previously published material. Send information about when and where the piece previously appeared. Reports in 2 months. Manuscript guidelines free with SASE.

IDYLL ARBOR, INC., P.O. Box 720, Ravensdale WA 98051. (425)432-3231. Fax: (425)432-3726. E-mail: idyarbor@ix.netcom.com. **Acquisitions:** Tom Blaschko. "Our books provide practical information on the current state and art of health care practice." Publishes hardcover and trade paperback originals and trade paperback reprints. **Publishes 6 titles/year. 50% of books from first-time authors; 100% from unagented writers. Pays 8-15% royalty on wholesale price or retail price.** Publishes book 1 year after acceptance of ms. Accepts simultaneous submissions. Reports in 1 month on queries, 2 months on proposals, 4 months on mss. Book catalog and ms guidelines free.

Nonfiction: Technical, textbook. Subjects include agriculture/horticulture (used in long term care activities or health care—therapy), health/medicine (for therapists, social service providers and activity directors), recreation (as therapy). "Idyll Arbor is currently developing a line of *Personal Health* books where each one explains a condition or a closely related set of medical or psychological conditions. The target audience is the person or the family of the person with the condition. We want to publish a book that explains a condition at the level of detail expected of the average primary care physician so that our readers can address the situation intelligently with specialists. We look for manuscripts from authors with recent clinical experience. Good grounding in theory is required, but practical experience is more important." Query preferred with outline and 1 sample chapter. Reviews artwork as part of ms package. Send photocopies.

Recent Title(s): *Idyll Arbor's Glossary for Therapists*, by Joan Burlingame and Thomas K. Skalko (health care reference).

Tips: "We currently emphasize therapies (recreational, occupational, music, horticultural), activity directors in long term care facilities, and social service professionals. The books must be useful for the health practitioner who meets face to face with patients *or* the books must be useful for teaching undergraduate and graduate level classes. We are especially looking for therapists with a solid clinical background to write on their area of expertise."

ILR PRESS, Cornell University Press, Sage House, 512 E. State St., Ithaca NY 14850. (607)277-2338 ext. 232. Fax: (607)277-2374. **Acquisitions:** F. Benson, editor. Estab. 1945. "We are interested in manuscripts with innovative perspectives on current workplace issues that concern both academics and the general public." Publishes hardcover and trade paperback originals and reprints. **Publishes 12-15 titles/year. Pays royalty.** Reports in 2 months on queries. Book catalog free.

Nonfiction: All titles relate to industrial relations and/or workplace issues including relevant work in the fields of history, sociology, political science, economics, human resources, and organizational behavior. Needs for the next year include mss on workplace problems, employment policy, immigration, current history, and dispute resolution for academics and practitioners. Query or submit outline and sample chapters.

Recent Title(s): *Finding Time*, by Leslie A. Perlow.

Tips: "Manuscripts must be well documented to pass our editorial evaluation, which includes review by academics in related fields."

IMAGE BOOKS, Doubleday Books, Bantam Doubleday Dell, 1540 Broadway, New York NY 10036. (212)354-6500. Fax: (212)782-8911. Website: http://www.bdd.com. **Acquisitions:** Trace Murphy, editor. Estab. 1956. "Image Books has grown from a classic Catholic list to include a variety of current and future classics, maintaining a high standard of quality as the finest in religious paperbacks." Publishes hardcover originals and reprints, trade paperback originals and reprints, mass market paperback originals and reprints. **Publishes 12 titles/year. Receives 500 queries/year; receives 300 mss/year. 10% of books from first-time writers; no unagented writers. Pays royalty on net price.**

Advance varies. Publishes book 18 months after acceptance of ms. Accepts simultaneous submissions. Reports in 3 months on proposals. Book catalog for 9×12 SAE with 3 first-class stamps.
Nonfiction: Biography, cookbook, gift book, how-to, humor, illustrated book, reference, self-help. Subjects include philosophy, psychology, religious/inspirational, world wisdom traditions, women's issues/studies. Query. Prefers agented submissions. Reviews artwork as part of ms package. Send photocopies.
Recent Title(s): *The Inner Voice of Love*, by Henri J.M. Nouwen (inspirational).

N **IMPACT PUBLISHERS, INC.**, P.O. Box 910, San Luis Obispo CA 93406-0910. (805)543-5911. Fax: (805)543-4093. **Acquisitions**: Melissa Froehner, assistant publisher. "Our purpose is to make the best human services expertise available to the widest possible audience: children, teens, parents, couples, individuals seeking self-help and personal growth, and human service professionals." Publishes trade paperback originals. **Publishes 6 titles/year. Receives 250 queries and 250 mss/year. 40% of books from first-time authors; 60% from unagented writers. Pays 10% royalty on net receipts.** Publishes book 12-18 months after acceptance of ms. Accepts simultaneous submissions. Reports in 5 months on proposals. Book catalog and ms guidelines free.
Imprint(s): Little Imp Books, American Source Books.
Nonfiction: Children's/juvenile, self-help. Subjects include child guidance/parenting, health/medicine, psychology (professional), caregiving/eldercare. "All our books are written by qualified human service professionals and are in the fields of mental health, personal growth, relationships, aging, families, children and professional psychology. We are currently seeking to expand our professional list." Submit proposal package, including short résumé or vita, book description, audience description, outline, 1-3 sample chapters and SASE.
Recent Title(s): *Master Your Panic and Take Back Your Life!*, by Denise F. Beckfield, Ph.D. (self-help/psychology).
Tips: "Don't call to see if we have received your submission. Include a self-addressed, stamped postcard if you want to know if manuscript arrived safely. We prefer a non-academic, readable style. We publish only popular psychology and self-help materials written in 'everyday language' by professionals with advanced degrees and significant experience in the human services."

INCENTIVE PUBLICATIONS, INC., 3835 Cleghorn Ave., Nashville TN 37215-2532. (615)385-2934. Fax: (615)385-2967. E-mail: incentiv@nashville.net. Website: http://www.nashville.net./~incentiv. **Acquisitions:** Catherine Aldy, assistant to the president. Editor: Anna Quinn. Estab. 1970. "Incentive publishes developmentally appropriate instructional aids for grades K-8." Publishes paperback originals. **Publishes 25-30 titles/year. Receives 350 submissions/year. 25% of books from first-time authors; 95% from unagented writers. Pays royalty or makes outright purchase.** Publishes book an average of 1 year after acceptance. Reports in 1 month on queries.
Nonfiction: Teacher resource books in pre-K through 8th grade. Query with synopsis and detailed outline.
Recent Title(s): *BASIC/Not Boring Series,* by Forte and Frank (basic skill mastery).

INDEX PUBLISHING GROUP, INC., 3368 Governor Dr., Suite 273, San Diego CA 92122. (619)455-6100. Fax: (619)552-9050. E-mail: ipgbooks@indexbooks.com. Website: http://www.electriciti.com/ipgbooks. **Acquisitions:** Linton M. Vandiver, publisher (casino gambling, privacy, identity changes); Henry L. Eisenson, vice president, editorial (radios and electronics). "We publish nonfiction, for both trade and special markets, with emphasis on casino gambling, communication electronics (scanners, ham radio, cellular telephones), and gray areas (e.g., identity, privacy, etc.)." Publishes hardcover and trade paperback originals. **Publishes 25 titles/year. Receives 100 queries and 40 mss/year. 40% of books from first-time authors; 100% from unagented writers. Pays 6-20% royalty on price.** Publishes book 4 months after acceptance. Accepts simultaneous submissions. Reports in 1 week on queries, 2 weeks on proposals. Book catalog and ms guidelines free and on website.
Nonfiction: Reference, technical, trade nonfiction. Subjects include gambling, computers/electronics, hobbies (consumer electronics: ham radio, scanners), electronic crime: cellular telephones, computer hacking, etc. "Index Publishing specializes in trade nonfiction (paper and hardcover) in three broad areas: (1) communication electronics, especially ham radio, scanning and radio monitoring, cellular telephones, computer hacking, etc.; (2) controversial topics such as eavesdropping, cable and satellite TV signal piracy, identity changes, electronic crime prevention; (3) gambling, especially casino gambling and gaming theory." Query.
Recent Title(s): *Credit Power! Rebuild Your Credit in 90 Days or Less*, by Trent Sands.

INDIANA UNIVERSITY PRESS, 601 N. Morton St., Bloomington IN 47404-3797. (812)855-4203. Fax: (812)855-8507. E-mail: iupress@indiana.edu. Website: http://www.indiana.edu/~iupress/. **Acquisitions:** Robert J. Sloan (civil war, classical studies, drama/performance, paleontology, history, medical/ethics, philanthropy, politics, science and religion), Janet Rabinowitch (art, African studies, Jewish studies, philosopohy, Middle East studies, Russian and East European studies), John Gallman (Asian studies, politics), Joan Catopano (dance, film studies, gay/lesbian/gender studies, Black studies, film, women's studies), Jeffrey Ankrom (music). Estab. 1951. Publishes hardcover originals, paperback originals and reprints. **Publishes 175 titles/year. 30% of books from first-time authors; 98% from unagented writers. Nonauthor subsidy publishes 9% of books. Pays maximum 10% royalty on retail price. Offers occasional advance.** Publishes book 1 year after acceptance. Reports in 2 months. Book catalog and ms guidelines free.
Nonfiction: Scholarly books on humanities, history, philosophy, religion, Jewish studies, Black studies, criminal justice, translations, semiotics, public policy, film, music, philanthropy, social sciences, regional materials, African studies, Russian Studies, women's studies, and serious nonfiction for the general reader. Also interested in textbooks and works with course appeal in designated subject areas. Query with prospectus, sample chapter, CV, book length and discussion

of the market. "Queries should include as much descriptive material as is necessary to convey scope and market appeal to us." Reviews artwork/photos.

Recent Title(s): *The Making of a Conservative Environmentalist*, by Gordon Durnil.

INFO NET PUBLISHING, 34188 Coast Highway, Suite C, Dana Point CA 92629. (714)489-9292. Fax: (714)489-95495. E-mail: infonetpub@aol.com Website: http://www.infonetpublishing.com. **Acquisitions:** Herb Wetenkamp, president. "Info Net publishes for easily identified niche markets; specific markets with some sort of special interest, hobby, avocation, profession, sport or lifestyle." Publishes hardcover and trade paperback originals. **Publishes 6 titles/year. Receives 50 queries and 20 mss/year. 80% of books from first-time authors; 85% from unagented writers. Pays 7-10% royalty on wholesale price or makes outright purchase of $1,000-10,000. Offers $1,000-2,000 advance in some cases.** Publishes book 10 months after acceptance of ms. Accepts simultaneous submissions. Reports in 2 months. Book catalog for 10×12 SAE and 2 first-class stamps. Manuscript guidelines for #10 SASE.

Nonfiction: Biography, children's/juvenile, gift book, how-to, reference, self-help, technical. Subjects include Americana and collectibles, aviation/aircraft archaeology, business and economics (retailing), history, hobbies, military/war, nature/environment, recreation, regional, science, sports, travel, women's issues/studies. "We are looking for specific niche market books, not general titles, other than self-help. Do not repeat same formula as other books. Offer something new, in other words." Submit outline, 3 sample chapters, proposal package, including demographics, marketing plans/data with SASE. Reviews artwork/photos as part of the ms package. Send photocopies.

Recent Title(s): *The Survival Guide for Today's Career Woman*, by Rayner (women's issues/self help).

Tips: "Please check to be sure similar titles are not already published covering the exact same subject matter. Research the book you are proposing."

INNER TRADITIONS INTERNATIONAL, P.O. Box 388, 1 Park St., Rochester VT 05767. (802)767-3174. Fax: (802)767-3726. E-mail: info@gotoit.com. Website: http://www.gotoit.com. Managing Editor: Rowan Jacobsen. **Acquisitions:** Jon Graham, editor. Estab. 1975. "Inner Traditions publishes works representing the spiritual, cultural and mythic traditions of the world and works on alternative medicine and holistic health that combine contemporary thought with the knowledge of the world's great healing traditions." Publishes hardcover and trade paperback originals and reprints. **Publishes 40 titles/year. Receives 3,000 submissions/year. 10% of books from first-time authors; 20% from unagented writers. Pays 8-10% royalty on net receipts. Offers $1,000 average advance.** Publishes book 1 year after acceptance. Reports in 3 months on queries, 6 months on mss. Book catalog and ms guidelines free.

Imprint(s): Inner Traditions, Destiny Books, Healing Arts Press, Park Street Press, Destiny Recordings, Destiny Audio Editions, Inner Traditions En Español, Inner Traditions India.

Nonfiction: Subjects include anthropology/archaeology, natural foods, cooking, nutrition, health/alternative medicine, history and mythology, indigenous cultures, music/dance, nature/environment, esoteric philosophy, psychology, world religions, women's issues/studies, New Age. "We are interested in the relationship of the spiritual and transformative aspects of world cultures." Query or submit outline and sample chapters with SASE. Does not return mss without SASE. Reviews artwork/photos as part of ms package.

Recent Title(s): *Return of the Tribal*, by Rufus C. Camphausen (indigenous/pop culture).

Tips: "We are not interested in autobiographical stories of self-transformation. We do not accept any electronic submissions (via e-mail). We are not currently looking at fiction."

INNISFREE PRESS, 136 Roumfort Rd., Philadelphia PA 19119. (215)247-4085. Fax: (215)247-2343. E-mail: InnisfreeP@aol.com. **Acquisitions:** Marcia Broucek, publisher. "Innisfree's mission is to publish books that nourish individuals both emotionally and spiritually; to offer books that 'call to the deep heart's core' " Publishes trade paperback originals. **Publishes 6-8 titles/year. Receives 500 queries and 300 mss/year. 50% of books from first-time authors; 90% from unagented writers. Pays 10-15% royalty on wholesale price.** Publishes book 1 year after acceptance of ms. Accepts simultaneous submissions. Reports in 1 month on queries; 2 months on proposals; 3 months on mss. Book catalog and ms guidelines free.

Nonfiction: Spiritually focused self-help and personal growth. Subjects include child guidance/parenting, health/medicine, holistic body/mind/spirit, nature/environment, psychology, religion, women's issues/studies. No poetry or children's material or "survival" manuscripts, please. Query with proposal package, including outline, 2 sample chapters, potential audience, and what makes the book unique, with SASE. Reviews artwork as part of ms package. Send photocopies.

Recent Title(s): *Sabbath Sense: A Spiritual Antidote for the Overworked*, by Donna Schaper.

INSIGHT BOOKS TRADE, Plenum Publishing Corp., 233 Spring St., New York NY 10013-1578. (212)620-8000. Fax: (212)463-0742. E-mail: frankd@plenum.com. Website: http://www.plenum.com. **Acquisitions:** Frank K. Darmstadt, editor. Plenum estab. 1946. "Insight Books are to-the-point, unafraid to address important or controversial issues, and its authors are qualified to promote their work." Publishes trade nonfiction hardcover and sometimes paperback originals. **Publishes 12 titles/year. Receives 1,000 submissions/year. 50% of books from first-time authors; 75% from unagented writers. Prefers proposals from agents. Pays royalty. Advance varies.** Publishes book 1-2 years after acceptance. Accepts simultaneous submissions. Reports in 2 months. Book catalog free for #10 SASE.

Nonfiction: Self-help, how-to, treatises. Subjects include anthropology, business/economics, education, ethnic, gay and lesbian studies, government/politics, health/medicine, money/finance, nature/environment, psychology, science, sociology, women's issues/studies. Submit outline, sample chapters and résumé. "Please don't e-mail proposals!"

Recent Title(s): *Conquering High Blood Pressure*, by Wood and Griffith.

Tips: "Insight Books cater to the needs and interests of the professional and lay readers. We encourage authors who are passionate about their work! Writers have the best chance selling authoritative, well-written, serious information in areas of health, mental health, social sciences, education and contemporary issues. Our audience consists of informed general readers as well as professionals and students in human, life and social sciences. If I were a writer trying to market a book today, I would say something interesting, important and useful, and say it well."

INSIGNIA PUBLISHING, 1429 G St. NW, Washington DC 20005. (301)540-4413. Fax: (301)540-3795. E-mail: InsigniaPC@aolcom. Website: http://www.InsigniaUSA.com. **Acquisitions:** Bruce W. Kletz, president. "Insignia is an independent publisher of books on current and historical geopolitical and military topics. Insignia seeks to inform inspire and enrich those with an interest in the defense of our country and the profession of arms." Publishes hardcover and trade paperback originals. **50% of books from first-time authors; 100% from unagented writers. Pays 8-15% royalty on retail price.** Reports in 2 months on proposals. Manuscript guidelines free.
Nonfiction: Biography, coffee table book, reference. Subjects include government/politics, history, military/war. "We're looking for current debates on national security issues, historical perspectives on military affairs, Gulf War topics, historical/military biography, professional military education." Query with outline (annotated), 1 sample chapter or writing sample for new authors and SASE. Reviews artwork/photos as part of ms package. Send photocopies.
Recent Title(s): *Gassed in the Gulf: The Inside Story of the Pentagon-CIA Cover-Up of Gulf War Syndrome*, by Patrick E. Eddington.

INSTITUTE OF POLICE TECHNOLOGY AND MANAGEMENT, University of North Florida, 4567 St. Johns Bluff Rd. S., Jacksonville FL 32224-2645. (904)646-2722. **Acquisitions:** Richard C. Hodge, editor. "Our publications are principally for law enforcement. Our authors are almost all present or retired law enforcement officers with excellent, up-to-date knowledge." Publishes trade paperback originals. **Publishes 8 titles/year. Receives 30 queries and 12 mss/year. 50% of books from first-time authors; 100% from unagented writers. Pays 25% royalty on retail price or makes outright purchase of $300-2,000 (may be some combination of above). No advance.** Publishes book 2 months after acceptance of ms. Accepts simultaneous submissions. Reports in 2 months.
Nonfiction: Illustrated book, reference, technical, textbook. Subjects pertain to law enforcement. "Our authors are not necessarily persons whose works have been published. Manuscripts should *not* be submitted until the author has talked with the editor on the telephone. The best procedure is to have this talk before beginning to write. Articles and short handbooks are acceptable as well as longer manuals." Query by phone first. Reviews artwork/photos as part of ms package. Send photocopies.
Recent Title(s): *Legal Application of Mobile Videotaping to Criminal Interdiction Patrol*, by Jim Kuboviak.
Tips: Audience is law enforcement, private investigators, personal injury attorneys, insurance investigators and adjustors.

INTERCULTURAL PRESS, INC., P.O. Box 700, Yarmouth ME 04096. (207)846-5168. Fax: (207)846-5181. E-mail: interculturalpress@internetmci.com. Website: http://www.bookmasters.com/interclt/index.htm. **Acquisitions:** Judy Carl-Hendrick, managing editor. Estab. 1980. "Intercultural Press publishes materials related to intercultural relations, including the practical concerns of living and working in foreign countries, the impact of cultural differences on personal and professional relationships and the challenges of interacting with people from unfamiliar cultures, whether at home or abroad." Publishes hardcover and trade paperback originals. **Publishes 10-15 titles/year. Receives 50-80 submissions/year. 50% of books from first-time authors; 95% of books from unagented writers. Pays royalty. Offers small advance occasionally.** Publishes book within 2 years after acceptance. Accepts simultaneous submissions. Reports in 2 months. Book catalog and ms guidelines free.
Nonfiction: Reference, textbook and theory. "We want books with an international or domestic intercultural or multicultural focus, especially those on business operations (how to be effective in intercultural business activities), education (textbooks for teaching intercultural subjects, for instance) and training (for Americans abroad or foreign nationals coming to the United States). Our books are published for educators in the intercultural field, business people engaged in international business, managers concerned with cultural diversity in the workplace, and anyone who works in an occupation where cross-cultural communication and adaptation are important skills. No manuscripts that don't have an intercultural focus." Accepts nonfiction translations. Query with outline or proposal. *No unsolicited mss.*
Recent Title(s): *Pathways to Culture*, by Paula Heusinkveld (teaching culture in the foreign language class).

INTERLINK PUBLISHING GROUP, INC., 46 Crosby St., Northampton MA 01060. (413)582-7054. Fax: (413)582-7057. E-mail: interpg@aol.com. **Acquisitions**: Michel Moushabeck, publisher. "Interlink publishes a general trade list of adult fiction and nonfiction with an emphasis on books that have a wide appeal while also meeting high intellectual and literary standards." Publishes hardcover and trade paperback originals. **Publishes 40 titles/year. Receives 600 submissions/year. 30% of books from first-time authors; 50% from unagented writers. Pays 5-7% royalty on retail price.** Publishes book 18 months after acceptance. Accepts simultaneous submissions. Reports in 1 month on queries. *Writer's Market* recommends allowing 2 months for reply. Book catalog and ms guidelines free.
Imprint(s): Interlink Books; Crocodile Books, USA; Olive Branch Press.
Nonfiction: World travel, world history and politics, ethnic cooking. Submit outline and sample chapters.
Fiction: Ethnic, international feminist. "Adult fiction—We are looking for translated works relating to the Middle East, Africa or Latin America. Juvenile/Picture Books—Our list is full for the next two years. No science fiction, romance, plays, erotica, fantasy, horror. Submit outline/synopsis and sample chapters.
Recent Title(s): *A Traveller's Wine Guide to France*, by Christopher Felden; *Samarkand*, by Amin Maalouf (translated

fiction).
Tips: "Any submissions that fit well in our publishing program will receive careful attention. Visit your local bookstore or library to look at some of our books before you send in your submission is recommended."

INTERNATIONAL FOUNDATION OF EMPLOYEE BENEFIT PLANS, P.O. Box 69, Brookfield WI 53008-0069. (414)786-6700. Fax: (414)786-8670. E-mail: books@ifebp.org. Website: http://www.ifebp.org. **Acquisitions:** Dee Birschel, senior director of publications. Estab. 1954. "We publish general and technical monographs on all aspects of employee benefits—pension plans, health insurance, etc." Publishes hardcover and trade paperback originals. **Publishes 10 titles/year. Receives 20 submissions/year. 15% of books from first-time authors; 80% from unagented writers. Pays 5-15% royalty on wholesale and retail price.** Publishes book 1 year after acceptance. Reports in 3 months on queries. Book catalog free. Manuscript guidelines for SASE.
Nonfiction: Reference, technical, consumer information, textbook. Subjects limited to health care, pensions, retirement planning, and employee benefits. Query with outline.
Recent Title(s): *Health Care Cost Management—A Basic Guide, Third Edition*, by Madelon Lubin.
Tips: "Be aware of interests of employers and the marketplace in benefits topics, for example, how AIDS affects employers, health care cost containment."

INTERNATIONAL MEDICAL PUBLISHING, P.O. Box 479, McLean VA 22101-0479. (703)519-0807. Fax: (703)519-0806. E-mail: masterso@patriot.net. **Acquisitions:** Thomas Masterson, MD, editor. Publishes mass market paperback originals. **Publishes 11 titles/year. Receives 20 queries and 2 mss/year. 5% of books from first-time authors; 100% from unagented writers. Pays royalty on gross receipts.** Publishes book 8 months after acceptance. Reports in 2 months on queries. Book catalog free.
Nonfiction: Reference, textbook. Health/medicine subjects. "We distribute only through medical and scientific bookstores. Look at our books. Think about practical material for doctors-in-training. We are interested in handbooks. Keep prose simple when dealing with very technical subjects." Query with outline.
Recent Title(s): *How to Be a Truly Excellent Medical Student*, by Robert Lederman (medical).

N **INTERNATIONAL SCHOLARS PUBLICATIONS, INC.**, 7831 Woodmont Ave., #345, Bethesda MD 20814. (301)654-7335. E-mail: austinisp1@aol.com. Website: http://www.interscholars.com. **Acquisitions**: Dr. Robert West. "International Scholars Publications is an independent publishing house founded by scholars from a variety of traditions united by the goal of affirming the richness and diversity of contemporary scholarship." Publishes hardcover and trade paperback originals, hardcover reprints. **Publishes 120 titles/year. Receives 1,720 queries and 800 mss/year. 80% of books from first-time authors; 100% from unagented writers. Pays 8-12% royalty on wholesale price.** Publishes book 8 months after acceptance of ms. Accepts simultaneous submissions. Reports in 2 months on queries and mss, 1 month on proposals. Book catalog and ms guidelines for #10 SASE.
Imprint(s): Christian Universities Press, Catholic Scholars Publications, University Press for West Africa.
Nonfiction: Biography, reference, scholarly, textbook. Subjects include art/architecture, education, ethnic, government/politics, history, language/literature, military/war, money/finance, philosophy, psychology, religion, science, sociology, women's issues/studies, Africa. "Research monographs and revised dissertations welcome. Some submissions do not contain enough information or have work condition problems." Query with outline, 2 sample chapters, cv and SASE.
Recent Title(s): *Youth Street Gangs*, by Vernon Harlan (criminal justice).
Tips: "Audience are upscale readers who enjoy an intellectual challenge. Focus on concept, contents, size of work and why it should be released."

INTERNATIONAL WEALTH SUCCESS, P.O. Box 186, Merrick NY 11570-0186. (516)766-5850. Fax: (516)766-5919. **Acquisitions:** Tyler G. Hicks, editor; Steven D. Hicks, associate editor. Estab. 1967. "We publish nonfiction books and periodicals to help Beginning Wealth Builders choose, start, finance, and succeed in their own home-based or externally-quartered small business. These publications present a wide range of business opportunities while providing practical, hands-on, step-by-step instructions aimed at helping readers achieve their personal goals in as short a time as possible while adhering to ethical and professional business standards." **Publishes 10 titles/year. Receives 100 submissions/year. 100% of books from first-time authors; 100% from unagented writers. Pays 10% royalty on wholesale or retail price. Buys all rights. Offers usual advance of $1,000, but this varies depending on author's reputation and nature of book.** Publishes book 4 months after acceptance. Reports in 1 month. Book catalog and ms guidelines for 9×12 SAE with 3 first-class stamps.
Nonfiction: Self-help, how-to. "Techniques, methods, sources for building wealth. Highly personal, how-to-do-it with plenty of case histories. Books are aimed at wealth builders and are highly sympathetic to their problems." Financing, business success, venture capital, etc. Length: 60,000-70,000 words. Query. Reviews artwork/photos.
Recent Title(s): *How to Start and Finance a Business That Works for You.*
Tips: "With the mass layoffs in large and medium-size companies there is an increasing interest in owning your own business. So we will focus on more how-to hands-on material on owning—and becoming successful in—one's own business of any kind. Our market is the BWB—Beginning Wealth Builder. This person has so little money that financial planning is something they never think of. Instead, they want to know what kind of a business they can get into to make some money without a large investment. Write for this market and you have millions of potential readers. Remember—there are a lot more people *without* money than *with* money."

N INTERSTATE PUBLISHERS, INC., 510 N. Vermilion St., P.O. Box 50, Danville IL 61834-0050. (217)446-0500. Fax: (217)446-9706. E-mail: info-ipp@ippinc.com. Website: http://www.ippinc.com. **Acquisitions**: Ronald L. McDaniel, vice president, editorial. "Our company specializes in textbooks and related materials that infuse science concepts into agricultural education." Publishes hardcover originals. **Publishes 20 titles/year. Receives 100 queries and 25 mss/year. 50% of books from first-time authors; 100% from unagented writers. Pays 10% royalty on actual money received from sales.** Publishes book 6 months after acceptance of ms. Accepts simultaneous submissions, if so noted. Reports in 2 months on proposals. Book catalog (specify high school or college) for 9×12 SAE with 4 first-class stamps for high school, 2 first-class stamps for college.
Nonfiction: Textbook, ancillary materials for each textbook. Subjects include agriculture/horticulture education (middle school, high school, college). Submit proposal package, including prospectus, outline, 2 sample chapters and SASE. Reviews artwork/photos as part of ms package. Send photocopies.
Recent Title(s): *Introduction to Horticulture: Science and Technology, 2nd ed.*, by Charles B. Schroeder, et al.
Tips: "Our audience is students who are interested in agriculture. They may simply want to become literate on the subject, or they may be preparing for a career in the new science-oriented agriculture. The career may well be off the farm and in areas such as landscaping, food technology, biotechnology, plant and soil science, etc. It is essential that all educational texts demonstrate fair and balanced treatment of the sexes, minorities, and persons with disabilities."

N INTERVARSITY PRESS, P.O. Box 1400, Downers Grove IL 60515. (630)887-2500. Fax: (630)887-2520. E-mail: mail@iupress.com. Website: http://www.iupress.com. **Acquisitions:** David Zimmerman, editorial assistant. "InterVarsity Press publishes a full line of books from an evangelical Christian perspective targeted to an open-minded audience." Publishes hardcover originals, trade paperback and mass market paperback originals. **Publishes 70-80 titles/year. Receives 1,500 queries and 1,000 mss/year. 15% of books from first-time authors; 85% from unagented writers. Pays negotiable flat fee or royalty on retail price. Offers negotiable advance.** Publishes book 2 years after acceptance. Accepts simultaneous submissions. Reports in 2 months on proposals. Book catalog for 9×12 SAE and 5 first-class stamps. Manuscript guidelines for #10 SASE.
Imprint(s): Academic (contact: Rodney Clapp); Reference (contact Dan Reid); Bible Study; Popular; General.
Nonfiction: Religious subjects. Writers need cv/résumé and detailed table of contents with query and SASE.
Recent Title(s): *Adopting for Good*, by Jorie Kincaid (Christian living).

INTERWEAVE PRESS, 201 E. Fourth St., Loveland CO 80537. (667)669-7672. Fax: (970)669-8317. **Acquisitions:** Judith Durant, craft book editor; Doree Pitkin, herb book editor. Estab. 1975. Interweave Press publishes instructive and inspirational titles relating to the fiber arts and herbal topics. Publishes hardcover and trade paperback originals. **Publishes 10-15 titles/year. Receives 50 submissions/year. 60% of books from first-time authors; 98% from unagented writers. Pays 10% royalty on net receipts.** Publishes book 1 year after acceptance. Accepts simultaneous submissions, if so noted. Reports in 2 months. Book catalog and ms guidelines free.
Nonfiction: How-to, technical. Subjects limited to fiber arts—basketry, spinning, knitting, dyeing and weaving—and herbal topics—gardening, cooking, and lore. Submit outline/synopsis and sample chapters. Reviews artwork/photos as part of ms package.
Recent Title(s): *Slip Stitch Knitting*, by Roxana Bartlett (crafts/how-to).
Tips: "We are looking for very clear, informally written, technically correct manuscripts, generally of a how-to nature, in our specific fiber and herb fields only. Our audience includes a variety of creative self-starters who appreciate inspiration and clear instruction. They are often well educated and skillful in many areas."

ITALICA PRESS, 595 Main St., Suite 605, New York NY 10044-0047. (212)935-4230. Fax: (212)838-7812. E-mail: italica@aol.com. **Acquisitions:** Ronald G. Musto and Eileen Gardiner, publishers. Estab. 1985. Italica Press publishes English translations of modern Italian fiction and medieval and Renaissance nonfiction. Publishes trade paperback originals. **Publishes 6 titles/year. Receives 75 queries and 20 mss/year. 50% of books from first-time authors; 100% from unagented writers. Pays 7-15% royalty on wholesale price.** Publishes book 1 year after acceptance of ms. Accepts simultaneous submissions. Reports in 1 month on queries. Book catalog free.
Nonfiction: "We publish *only* English translations of medieval and Renaissance source materials and English translations of modern Italian fiction." Query. Reviews artwork/photos as part of ms package. Send photocopies.
Tips: "We are interested in considering a wide variety of medieval and Renaissance topics (not historical fiction), and for modern works we are only interested in translations from Italian fiction."

JAIN PUBLISHING CO., P.O. Box 3523, Fremont CA 94539. (510)659-8272. Fax: (510)659-0501. E-mail: mail@jainpub.com. Website: http://www.jainpub.com. **Acquisitions:** M.K. Jain, editor-in-chief. Estab. 1989. "Our goal is to provide quality reading material at reasonable prices." Publishes hardcover and trade paperback originals and reprints. **Publishes 10 titles/year. Receives 500 queries/year. 20% of books from first-time authors; 100% from unagented writers. Pays up to 15% royalty on net sales. Offers occasional advance.** Publishes book 1-2 years after acceptance. Reports in 3 months on mss if interested. Book catalog for 6×9 SAE. Manuscript guidelines for #10 SASE. Also available on website."
Imprint(s): Asian Humanities Press.
Nonfiction: Self-help, motivational/inspirational, how-to, foods/nutrition (vegetarian), health/healing (alternative), philosophies/religions (Asian), business/management, reference, textbooks. "Manuscripts should be thoroughly researched and written in an 'easy to read' and understandable format. Preferably between 60,000-100,000 words." Submit proposal

package, including cv and list of prior publications. Reviews artwork/photos as part of ms package. Send photocopies. Does not return submissions.
Recent Title(s): *Menopause: A Basic Guide for Women*, by Alan J. Silverstein, M.D. (health/healing).
Tips: Jain is putting more emphasis on books dealing with health/healing and business/management. Continued emphasis on undergraduate textbooks. "We're interested more in user-oriented books than general treatises."

JAMESON BOOKS INC., 722 Columbus St., P.O. Box 738, Ottawa IL 61350. (815)434-7905. Fax: (815)434-7907. **Acquisitions:** Jameson G. Campaigne, publisher/editor. Estab. 1986. "Jameson Books publishes conservative politics and economics; Chicago area history; and biographies." **Publishes hardcover originals. Publishes 12 titles/year. Receives 500 queries/year; 300 mss/year. 33% of books from first-time authors; 33% from unagented writers. Pays 6-15% royalty on retail price. Offers $1,000-25,000 advance.** Publishes book 1 year after acceptance. Accepts simultaneous submissions. Reports in 6 months on queries. Book catalog for 8×10 SASE.
Nonfiction: Biography. Subjects include business/economics, history, politics, regional (Chicago area). Query with sample chapter and SASE (essential). *Submissions not returned without SASE.*
Fiction: Interested in pre-cowboy frontier fiction. Query with 1 sample chapter and SASE.
Recent Title(s): *Politics as a Noble Calling*, by F. Clifton White (memoirs); *Yellowstone Kelly: Gentleman and Scout*, by Peter Bowen (fiction).

JEWISH PUBLICATION SOCIETY, 1930 Chestnut St., Philadelphia PA 19103. (215)564-5925. Fax: (215)564-6640. E-mail: jewishbook@aol.com. Website: http://www.jewishpub.org. **Acquisitions**: Dr. Ellen Frankel, editor-in-chief; Bruce Black, children's editor. "The Jewish Publication Society is a nonprofit educational association formed for the purpose of promoting Jewish culture by disseminating a wide variety of religious and secular works in the U.S. and abroad." Publishes hardcover and trade paperback originals, trade paperback reprints. **Publishes 12 titles/year. 20% of books from first-time authors; 75% from unagented writers. Pays 10% royalty on wholesale price. Offers $1,000-4,000 advance.** Publishes book 18 months after acceptance. Accepts simultaneous submissions, if noted. Reports in 3 months on proposals. Book catalog free.
Nonfiction: Children's/juvenile, reference, trade books. Subjects include history, language/literature, religion, women's issues/studies. "No monographs or textbooks. We do not accept memoirs, biographies, art books, coffee-table books, fiction or poetry." Children's books include picture books, biography, history, religion, young middle readers; young adult include biography, history, religion, sports. Query with proposal package including outline, description and proposed table of contents, cv and SASE.
Recent Title(s): *Heeding the Call: Jewish Voices in America's Civil Rights Struggle*, by Norman Finkelstein.
Tips: "Our audience is college-educated Jewish readers interested in Bible, Jewish history or Jewish practice, as well as young readers."

JIST WORKS, INC., 720 N. Park Ave., Indianapolis IN 46202-3431. (317)264-3720. Fax: (317)264-3763. E-mail: jistworks@aol.com. Website: http://www.jistworks.com. **Acquisitions:** Marta Partington, associate publisher. Estab. 1981. "Our purpose is to provide quality career, job search, and other living skills information, products, and services that help people manage and improve their lives—and the lives of others." Publishes trade paperback originals and reprints. **Publishes 40 titles/year. Receives 300 submissions/year. 60% of books from first time authors; majority from unagented writers. Pays 5-12% royalty on wholesale price or makes outright purchase (negotiable).** Publishes book 1 year after acceptance. Accepts simultaneous submissions. Reports in 3 months on queries. Book catalog and ms guidelines for 9×12 SAE with 6 first-class stamps.
Imprint(s): Park Avenue Publications (business and self-help that falls outside of the JIST topical parameters).
Nonfiction: How-to, career, reference, self-help, software, video, textbook. Specializes in job search, self-help and career related topics. "We want text/workbook formats that would be useful in a school or other institutional setting. We also publish trade titles, all reading levels. Will consider books for professional staff and educators, appropriate software and videos." Query with SASE. Reviews artwork/photos as part of ms package.
Recent Title(s): *Networking for Everyone*, by Michelle Tullier.
Tips: "Institutions and staff who work with people of all reading and academic skill levels, making career and life decisions or people who are looking for jobs are our primary audience, but we're focusing more on business and trade topics for consumers."

JOHNSON BOOKS, Johnson Publishing Co., 1880 S. 57th Court., Boulder CO 80301. (303)443-9766. Fax: (303)443-1106. **Acquisitions:** Stephen Topping, editorial director. Estab. 1979. Johnson Books specializes in books on the American West, primarily outdoor, "useful" titles that will have strong national appeal. Publishes hardcover and paperback originals and reprints. **Publishes 10-12 titles/year. Receives 500 submissions/year. 30% of books from first-time authors; 90% from unagented writers. Royalties vary.** Publishes book 1 year after acceptance. Reports in 3 months. Book catalog and ms guidelines for 9×12 SAE with 5 first-class stamps.
Imprint(s): Spring Creek Press.
Nonfiction: General nonfiction, books on the West, environmental subjects, natural history, paleontology, geology, archaeology, travel, guidebooks, outdoor recreation. Accepts nonfiction translations. "We are primarily interested in books for the informed popular market, though we will consider vividly written scholarly works." Submit outline/synopsis and 3 sample chapters. Looks for "good writing, thorough research, professional presentation and appropriate style. Marketing suggestions from writers are helpful."

Recent Title(s): *Army Wives on the American Frontier*, by Anne B. Eales (western history).

JOSSEY-BASS/PFEIFFER, 350 Sansome St., San Francisco CA 94104. (415)433-1740.Fax: (415)433-1711. E-mail: mholt@jbp.com. Website: http://www.pfeiffer.com. **Acquisitions**: Matthew Holt, editor. "Jossey-Bass/Pfeiffer specializes in human resource development titles in the fields of business, management and training." **Publishes 25-50 titles/year. 25% of books from first-time authors; 95% of books from unagented writers. Pays 10% average royalty.** Publishes book 1 year after acceptance of manuscript. Accepts simultaneous submissions. Reports in 1-2 months on queries.
Nonfiction: Subjects include management, human resource development, training, both books and instruments. Query with SASE.
Recent Title(s): *The Business of Consulting*, by Elaine Biech.

JOURNEY BOOKS, (formerly Bob Jones University Press Books for Young Readers), Bob Jones University Press, 1700 Wade Hampton Blvd., Greenville SC 29614-0001. **Acquisitions:** Gloria Repp, acquisitions editor. Estab. 1974. Journey Books publishes nonfiction and fiction "reflecting a Christian perspective." Publishes trade paperback originals and reprints. **Publishes 11 titles/year. Receives 180 queries and 480 mss/year. 40% of books from first-time authors; 100% from unagented writers. Makes outright purchase of $500-1,250; royalties to established authors.** Publishes book 18 months after acceptance. Accepts simultaneous submissions. Reports in 2 months on mss. Book catalog and ms guidelines free.
Nonfiction: Biography (for teens), children's/juvenile. Subjects include animals, gardening, health/medicine, history, nature/environment, sports. "We're looking for concept books on almost any subject suitable for children. We also like biographies." Submit outline and 3 sample chapters.
Fiction: Juvenile, young adult. "We're looking for well-rounded characters and plots with plenty of action suitable for a Christian audience. Avoid being preachy." Submit synopsis and 5 sample chapters or complete ms.
Recent Title(s): *Dust of the Earth*, by Donna Hess (biographical fiction ages 12+).
Tips: "Our readers are children ages two and up, teens and young adults. We're looking for high-quality writing that reflects a Christian perspective and features well-developed characters in a convincing plot. Most open to: first chapter books, adventure, biography."

JUDAICA PRESS, 123 Ditmas Ave., Brooklyn NY 11218. Fax: (718)972-6204. E-mail: judaicapr@aol.com. **Acquisitions:** Bonnie Goldman, senior editor. "We cater to the traditional, Orthodox Jewish market." Publishes hardcover and trade paperback originals and reprints. **Publishes 8 titles/year. No advance.** Reports in 3 months on queries.
Nonfiction: "Looking for very traditional Judaica, especially children's books." Query with outline, 1 sample chapter.
Recent Title(s): *Not By Chance.*

JUDSON PRESS, P.O. Box 851, Valley Forge PA 19482-0851. (610)768-2128. Fax: (610)768-2441. E-mail: judsonpress@juno.com. Website: http://www.judsonpress.com. Publisher: Kristy Arnesen Pullen. **Acquisitions:** Randy Frame, senior editor; Mary Nicol. Estab. 1824. "Our audience is mostly church members and leaders who seek to have a more fulfilling personal spiritual life and want to serve Christ in their churches and other relationships." Publishes hardcover and paperback originals. **Publishes 20-30 titles/year. Receives 750 queries/year. Pays royalty or makes outright purchase.** Publishes book 15 months after acceptance. Accepts simultaneous submissions. Reports in 3 months. Enclose return postage. Book catalog for 9×12 SAE with 4 first-class stamps. Manuscript guidelines for #10 SASE.

- Judson Press also publishes a quarterly journal, *The African American Pulpit*; call for submission guidelines.

Nonfiction: Adult religious nonfiction of 30,000-80,000 words. Query with outline and sample chapter.
Recent Title(s): *Finding God Between the Lines*, by Jody Seymour (inspirational).
Tips: "Writers have the best chance selling us practical books assisting clergy or laypersons in their ministry and personal lives. Our audience consists of Protestant church leaders and members. Be sensitive to our workload and adapt to the market's needs. Books on multicultural issues are very welcome."

KALMBACH PUBLISHING CO., 21027 Crossroads Circle, P.O. Box 1612, Waukesha WI 53187-1612. Fax: (414)798-6468. E-mail: tspohn@kalmbach.com. Website: http://books.kalmbach.com. **Acquisitions:** Terry Spohn, senior acquisitions editor (railroading, astronomy, scale modeling, miniatures, radio control); Kent Johnson, acquisitions editor (model railroading, toy trains); Roger Carp, acquisitions editor (toy trains, toys). Estab. 1934. "Kalmbach publishes books covering hobby, special interest, and leisure-time subjects." Publishes hardcover and paperback originals, paperback reprints. **Publishes 15-20 titles/year. Receives 100 submissions/year. 85% of books from first-time authors; 100% from unagented writers. Pays 10% royalty on net. Offers $1,500 average advance.** Publishes book 18 months after acceptance. Reports in 2 months.
Nonfiction: Hobbies, how-to, amateur astronomy, railroading. "Our book publishing effort is in amateur astronomy, railroading and hobby how-to-do-it titles *only*." Query first. "I welcome telephone inquiries. They save me a lot of time, and they can save an author a lot of misconceptions and wasted work." In written query, wants detailed outline of 2-3 pages and a complete sample chapter with photos, drawings, and how-to text. Reviews artwork/photos as part of ms package.
Recent Title(s): *Through the Eyes of Hubble: The Birth, Life, and Violent Death of Stars*, by Robert Naeye.
Tips: "Our books are about half text and half illustrations. Any author who wants to publish with us must be able to furnish good photographs and rough drawings before we'll consider contracting for his book."

KAYA PRODUCTION, 132 W. 22nd St., 4th Floor, New York NY 10011. (212)352-9220. Fax: (212)352-9221. E-mail: kaya@kaya.com. Website: http://www.kaya.com. **Acquisitions:** Sunyoung Lee, associate editor. "Kaya is a small independent press dedicated to the publication of innovative literature from the Asian diaspora." Publishes hardcover originals and trade paperback originals and reprints. Accepts simultaneous submissions. Reports in 6 months on mss. Book catalog free. Manuscript guidelines for #10 SASE.

Nonfiction: "Kaya publishes Asian, Asian-American and Asian diasporic materials. We are looking for innovative writers with a commitment to quality literature." Submit proposal package, including outline, sample chapters, previous publications with SASE. Reviews artwork/photos as part of ms package. Send photocopies.

Fiction: Submit synopsis and 2-4 sample chapters with SASE.

Poetry: Submit complete ms.

Recent Title(s): *Oriental Girls Desire Romance*, by Catherine Lia (novel); *City Terrace Field Manual*, by Sesshu Foster (prose poetry collection).

Tips: Audience is people interested in a high standard of literature and who are interested in breaking down easy approaches to multicultural literature.

KENSINGTON, 850 Third Ave., 16th Floor, New York NY 10022. (212)407-1500. Fax: (212)935-0699. **Acquisitions:** Ann LaFarge, executive editor (romance, fiction); Tracy Bernstein, executive editor (pop culture, spiritual, New Age, parenting, health); Paul Dinas, editor-in-chief (nonfiction, thrillers); Kate Duffy, senior editor (historical, regency, romance); John Scognamiglio, senior editor (romance, mystery); Hillary Sares, editor (Precious Gem romances); Karen Thomas, editor (Arabesque multicultural romances); Diane Stockwell, editor (En Canto, Hispanic romances). "Kensington focuses on profitable niches and uses aggressive marketing techniques to support its books." Publishes hardcover originals, trade paperback originals and reprints. **Kensington publishes 300 titles/year; Pinnacle 60; Zebra 140-170; Arabesque 48. Receives 6,000 queries/year. 3-5% of books from first-time authors. Pays royalty on retail price, varies by author and type of book.** Advance varies by author and type of book. Publishes book 18 months after acceptance of ms. Accepts simultaneous submissions. Reports in 1 month on queries; 3 months on mss. Book catalog for #10 SASE.

Imprint(s): Zebra, Pinnacle, Arabesque.

Nonfiction: Self-help. Subjects include health/medicine, pop culture. Query with outline and SASE. *No unsolicited mss. No unagented writers.* Reviews artwork/photos as part of the ms package, if integral to project. Send photocopies.

Fiction: Mystery, romance, suspense, women's. Query with synopsis and SASE. *No unsolicited mss. No unagented writers.*

KENT STATE UNIVERSITY PRESS, P.O. Box 5190, Kent OH 44242-0001. (330)672-7913. Fax: (330)672-3104. **Acquisitions:** John T. Hubbell, director (history, regional); Julia Morton, editor-in-chief (literary criticism). Estab. 1965. Kent State publishes primarily scholarly works and titles of regional interest. Publishes hardcover and paperback originals and some reprints. **Publishes 30-35 titles/year. Nonauthor subsidy publishes 20% of books. Standard minimum book contract on net sales. Offers advance rarely.** Reports in 3 months. Book catalog free.

Nonfiction: Especially interested in "scholarly works in history and literary studies of high quality, any titles of regional interest for Ohio, scholarly biographies, archaeological research, the arts, and general nonfiction. Always write a letter of inquiry before submitting manuscripts. We can publish only a limited number of titles each year and can frequently tell in advance whether or not we would be interested in a particular manuscript. This practice saves both our time and that of the author, not to mention postage costs. If interested we will ask for complete manuscript. Decisions based on inhouse readings and two by outside scholars in the field of study." Enclose return postage.

Recent Title(s): *The Life and Death of Pretty Boy Floyd*, by Jeffery S. King (history); *She Loved Me Once and Other Stories*, by Lester Goran (original short stories).

Tips: "We are cautious about publishing heavily-illustrated manuscripts."

MICHAEL KESEND PUBLISHING, LTD., 1025 Fifth Ave., New York NY 10028. (212)249-5150. Publisher: Michael Kesend. **Acquisitions:** Judy Wilder, editor. Estab. 1979. Michael Kesend publishes guidebooks and other nonfiction titles for sale in bookstore chains and independents, in museum stores, parks or similar outlets. Publishes hardcover and trade paperback originals and reprints. **Publishes 4-6 titles/year. Receives 300 submissions/year. 20% of books from first-time authors; 40% from unagented writers. Pays 6% royalty on wholesale price. Advance varies.** Publishes book 18 months after acceptance. Reports in 2 months on queries. Guidelines for #10 SASE.

Nonfiction: Biography, how-to, illustrated book, self-help, sports, travel guides (regional and national). Subjects include animals, health, history, hobbies, nature, sports, travel, the environment, guides to several subjects. Needs sports, health self-help and environmental awareness guides. No photography mss. Submit outline and sample chapters. Reviews artwork/photos as part of ms package.

Recent Title(s): *A Guide to the Sculpture Parks and Gardens of America*, by McCarthy & Epstein (national guidebook).

Tips: "Looking for national guides, outdoor travel guides, sports nonfiction, art or garden-related guides and/or others suitable for museum stores, natural history and national or state park outlets."

KINSEEKER PUBLICATIONS, P.O. Box 184, Grawn MI 49637-0184. (616)276-7653. E-mail: kinseeker6@aol.com. Website: http://www.angelfire.com/biz/Kinseeker/index.html. **Acquisitions:** Victoria Wilson, editor. Estab. 1986. "We publish books to help people researching their family histories." Publishes trade paperback originals. **Publishes 6 titles/year. 95% of books from unagented writers. Pays 10-25% royalty on retail price. No advance.** Publishes book 8

months after acceptance. Reports in 3 months. Book catalog and ms guidelines for #10 SASE.
Imprint(s): Roundsky Press.
Nonfiction: How-to, reference books. Subjects are local history and genealogy. Query or submit outline and sample chapters. Reviews artwork/photos as part of ms package.
Recent Title(s): *Tickling Your Ancestral Funnybone*, by Janet Elaine Smith (genealogy).

KITCHEN SINK PRESS, Disappearing, Inc., 76 Pleasant St., Northampton MA 01060. (413)586-9525. Fax: (413)586-7040. Website: http://www.kitchensink.com. Publisher: Denis Kitchen. **Acquisitions**: N.C. Christopher Couch, senior editor; Robert Boyd, editor; Catherine Garnier, associate editor. Estab. 1969. "Kitchen Sink Press publishes graphic novels and comics. It also publishes historical and analytical works on comics, artists, film and animation." Publishes trade paperback originals. **Publishes 20 titles/year. Receives 1,000 queries/year and 500 mss/year. 10% of books from first-time authors; 90% from unagented writers. Authors paid royalty on original work; stories based on licensed characters treated as work-for-hire.** Publishes book 18 months after acceptance of ms. Accepts simultaneous submissions. Reports in 3 months on queries. For book catalog call (800)672-7862 or fax request to (413)582-7116. Manuscript guidelines for #10 SASE.
Imprint(s): Kitchen Sink Comix (comic books), Kitchen Sink Kids (children's titles).
Nonfiction: Illustrated book. Subjects include comics, film, animation. Query with SASE. Reviews artwork/photos as part of the ms package. Send photocopies.
Fiction: Graphic novels, comics. Holds license for Will Eisner's *The Spirit*, J. O'Barr's *The Crow*. "We are not interested in superheroes. Check current catalog and works by Will Eisner, Alan Moore to get a feel for what we want." Query with sample chapter for graphic novels, several pages for comics, and SASE.
Recent Title(s): *Understanding Comics*, by Scott McCloud (art); *The Spirit: The New Adventures*, by Eisner, et al.

N **B. KLEIN PUBLICATIONS**, P.O. Box 6578, Delray Beach FL 33482. (561)496-3316. Fax: (561)496-5546. **Acquisitions:** Bernard Klein, editor-in-chief. Estab. 1946. Publishes hardcover and paperback originals. Specializes in directories, annuals, who's who books, bibliography, business opportunity, reference books. **Publishes 5 titles/year. Pays 10% royalty on wholesale price, "but we're negotiable. Advance depends on many factors."** Markets books by direct mail and mail order. Accepts simultaneous submissions. Reports in 2 months. Book catalog for #10 SASE.
Nonfiction: Business, hobbies, how-to, reference, self-help, directories and bibliographies. Query or submit outline and sample chapters.
Recent Title(s): *Guide to American Directories*, by Bernard Klein.

ALFRED A. KNOPF AND CROWN BOOKS FOR YOUNG READERS, Random House, 201 E. 50th St., New York NY 10022. (212)751-2600. Website: http://www.randomhouse.com/knopf/index. Publishing Director: Simon Boughton. Senior Editor: Tracy Gates. Associate Publisher: Andrea Cascardi. **Acquisitions:** send mss to Crown/Knopf Editorial Department. "Knopf is known for high quality literary fiction, and is willing to take risks with writing styles. It publishes for children ages 5 and up. Crown is known for books young children immediately use and relate to. It publishes work for children ages 2-5." Publishes hardcover originals, trade paperback reprints. **Publishes 60 titles/year. 10% of books from first-time authors; 40% from unagented writers. Pays 4-10% royalty on retail price. Offers advance of $3,000 and up.** Publishes book 1-2 years after acceptance of ms. Accepts simultaneous submissions. Reports in 3 months on mss. Book catalog for 9×12 SASE. Manuscript guidelines free.
Imprint(s): Alfred A. Knopf Books for Young Readers (Andrea Cascardi), Crown Books for Young Readers (Andrea Cascardi), Knopf Paperbacks (Joan Slattery, executive editor), Dragonfly (Joan Slattery, executive editor).
Nonfiction: Children's/juvenile, biography. Subjects include ethnic, history, nature/environment, science. Query with entire ms and SASE.
Fiction: Juvenile, literary, picture books, young adult. Query with entire ms and SASE.
Recent Title(s): *Me On the Map*, by Joan Sweeney (science—Crown); *My Little Sister Ate One Hair*, by Bill Grossman (picture book—Crown).

ALFRED A. KNOPF, INC., Random House, 201 E. 50th St., New York NY 10022. (212)751-2600. **Acquisitions:** Senior Editor or Children's Book Editor. Vice President: Judith Jones. Publishes hardcover and paperback originals. **Averages 200 titles/yearly. 15% of books from first-time authors; 30% from unagented writers. Royalty and advance vary.** Publishes book 1 year after acceptance. Accepts simultaneous submissions, if so noted. Reports in 3 months. Book catalog for 7½×10½ SAE with 5 first-class stamps.
Nonfiction: Book-length nonfiction, including books of scholarly merit. Preferred length: 50,000-150,000 words. "A good nonfiction writer should be able to follow the latest scholarship in any field of human knowledge, and fill in the abstractions of scholarship for the benefit of the general reader by means of good, concrete, sensory reporting." Query. Reviews artwork/photos as part of ms package.
Fiction: Publishes book-length fiction of literary merit by known or unknown writers. Length: 40,000-150,000 words. Query with sample chapters.
Recent Title(s): *River*, by Colin Fletcher; *I Was Amelia Earhart*, by Jane Mendelsohn.

KREGEL PUBLICATIONS, Kregel, Inc., P.O. Box 2607, Grand Rapids MI 49501. E-mail: kregelpub@aol.com. Website: http://www.gospelcom.net/kregel. **Acquisitions:** Dennis R. Hillman, publisher. "Our mission as an evangelical Christian publisher is to provide—with integrity and excellence—trusted, biblically-based resources that challenge and encourage individuals in their Christian lives." Publishes hardcover and trade paperback originals and reprints. **Publishes 80 titles/year. Receives 150 queries and 100 mss/year. 5% of books from first-time authors; 100% from unagented writers. Pays 8-14% royalty on wholesale price or makes outright purchase of $500-1,000. Offers negotiated advance.** Publishes book 1 year after acceptance of ms. Accepts simultaneous submissions. Reports in 1 month on queries and proposals, 3 months on mss. Book catalog for 9×12 SAE with 3 first-class stamps. Manuscript guidelines for #10 SASE.

Imprint(s): Kregel Classics.

Nonfiction: Biography (Christian), reference, textbook. Religious subjects. "We serve evangelical Christian readers and those in career Christian service." Query with outline, 2 sample chapters, bio and market comparison.

Recent Title(s): *Suicide: A Christian Response*, by Gary Stewart and Timothy Demy.

Tips: "Looking for titles with broad appeal in the area of biblical studies and spiritual living."

KRIEGER PUBLISHING CO., P.O. Box 9542, Melbourne FL 32902-9542. (407)724-9542. Fax: (407)951-3671. E-mail: info@krieger-pub.com. **Acquisitions:** Elaine Harland (natural history); Michael W. Galbraith (Professional Practices Series); Gordon Patterson (Open Forum Series); Donald M. Waltz (Orbit Series); Hans Trefousse (Anvil Series). "We provide accurate and well documented titles for text and reference use, college level and higher." Publishes hardcover and paperback originals and reprints. **Publishes 60 titles/year. Receives 50-60 submissions/year. 30% of books from first-time authors; 100% from unagented writers. Pays royalty on net price.** Publishes book 8 months after acceptance. Reports in 1 month. *Writer's Market* recommends allowing 2 months for reply. Book catalog free.

Imprint(s): Orbit Series, Anvil Series and Public History.

Nonfiction: College reference, technical, textbook. Subjects include history, music, philosophy, psychology, space science, herpetology, chemistry, physics, engineering, medical. Query. Reviews artwork/photos as part of ms package.

Recent Title(s): *Tales of Giant Snakes: A Historical Natural History of Anacondas and Pythons*, by John C. Murphy and Robert W. Henderson.

KROSHKA BOOKS, 6080 Jericho Turnpike, Suite 207, Commack NY 11725-2808. (516)499-3103. Fax: (516)499-3146. E-mail: novascience@earthlink.net. **Acquisitions:** Frank Columbus, editor-in-chief; Nadya Columbus, editor. "Virtually all areas of human endeavor fall within our scope of interest." Publishes hardcover and paperback originals. **Publishes 150 titles/year. Receives 1,000 queries/year. Pays royalty.** Publishes book 6-12 months year after acceptance. Accepts simultaneous submissions. Reports in 1 month.

Imprint: Troitsa Books.

Nonfiction: Biography, novels, self-help, technical, textbook. Subjects includc Americana, anthropology, business/economics, computers/electronics, nutrition, education, government/politics, health/medicine, history, money/finance, nature/environment, philosophy, poetry, psychology, recreation, religion, science, sociology, software, sports, childhood development. Query. Reviews artwork/photos as part of ms package. Send photocopies.

Recent Title(s): *Firemania*, by Carl Chiarelli; *Tests of Being*, by Nur Cheyenne (poetry).

KUMARIAN PRESS, INC., 14 Oakwood Ave., West Hartford CT 06119-2127. (860)233-5895. Fax: (860)233-6072. E-mail: kpbooks@aol.com. Website: http://www.kpbooks.com. **Acquisitions:** Acquisitions Editor. "We publish books for professionals, academics, students interested in global affairs." Publishes hardcover and trade paperback originals. **Publishes 8-12 titles/year. Pays royalty of 7-10% of net.** Accepts simultaneous submissions, if so noted. Reports in 1 month on queries and proposals. Book catalog and ms guidelines free.

Nonfiction: Professional, academic. Subjects include economics, government/politics, nature/environment, sociology, women's issues/studies, microenterprise, globalization, international development, sustainability. "Kumarian Press looks for mss that address world issues and promote change. Areas of interest include, but are not limited to: international development, peace and conflict resolution, gender, NGOs, Third World studies, environment and works that link the shared problems faced by both the North and the South." Submit proposal package including outline, 1-2 sample chapters, cv or résumé, intended readership, detailed table of contents and projected word count with SASE.

Recent Title(s): *Rethinking Tourism*, by Deborah McLaren (ecotourism).

PETER LANG PUBLISHING, Peter Lang AG, 275 Seventh Ave., New York NY 10001. (212)647-7700. Fax: (212)647-7707. Website: http://www.peterlang.com. Managing Director: Christopher S. Myers. Senior Editor: Heidi Burns, Ph.D. **Acquisitions:** Owen Lancer, editor. Estab. 1952. "We publish scholarly monographs in the humanities and social sciences." Publishes mostly hardcover originals. **Publishes 300 titles/year. 75% of books from first-time authors; 98% from unagented writers. Pays 10-20% royalty on net price. No advance.** Publishes book 1 year after acceptance. Reports in 3 months. Book catalog free.

Nonfiction: Reference works, scholarly monographs. Subjects include literary criticism, Germanic and Romance languages, art history, business/economics, American and European political science, history, music, philosophy, psychology, religion, sociology, biography. All books are scholarly monographs, textbooks, reference books, reprints of historic texts, critical editions or translations. "We do not publish original fiction or poetry. We seek scholarly and critical editions only." No mss shorter than 200 pages. Query with cv and synopsis or sample chapter. Fully refereed review process.

Recent Title(s): *American Indian Studies*, edited by Dane Morrison.

Tips: "Besides our commitment to specialist academic monographs, we are one of the few US publishers who publish books in most of the modern languages. A major advantage for Lang authors is international marketing and distribution of all titles. Translation rights sold for many titles."

LANGENSCHEIDT PUBLISHING GROUP, 46-35 54th Rd., Maspeth NY 11378. (800)432-MAPS. Fax: (718)784-0640. E-mail: kroche@langenscheidt.com. **Acquisitions:** Christine Cardone, editor. "We publish maps, travel guides and foreign language dictionary products." Publishes hardcover and trade paperback. **Publishes over 100 titles/year; imprint publishes 20 titles/year. Receives 25 queries and 15 mss/year. 100% of books from unagented writers. Pays royalty or makes outright purchase.** Publishes book 6 months after acceptance of ms. Accepts simultaneous submissions. Reports in 2 months on proposals. Book catalog free.
Imprint(s): Hagstrom Map, American Map, Trakker Map, Arrow Map, Creative Sales.
Nonfiction: Reference. Foreign language subjects. "Any foreign language that fills a gap in our line is welcome." Submit outline and 2 sample chapters (complete ms preferred.)
Recent Title(s): *Diccionario Universal* (foreign language).
Tips: "Any item related to our map, foreign language dictionary and travel products could have potential for us."

LARK BOOKS, Altamont Press, 50 College St., Asheville NC 28801. E-mail: carol.taylor@larkbooks.com. Website: http://www.larkbooks.com. **Acquisitons:** President: Rob Pulleyn. Estab. 1976. "We publish high quality, highly illustrated books, primarily in the crafts/leisure markets celebrating the creative spirit. We work closely with bookclubs. Our books are either how-to, 'gallery' or combination books." Publishes hardcover and trade paperback originals and reprints. **Publishes over 50 titles/year. Receives 300 queries and 100 mss/year. 80% of books from first-time authors; 100% from unagented writers. Offers up to $2,500 advance.** Publishes book 1 year after acceptance of ms. Accepts simultaneous submissions. Reports in 2 months.
Nonfiction: Coffee table book, cookbook, how-to, illustrated book, children's/juvenile. Subjects include cooking, gardening, hobbies, nature/environment, crafts. Submit outline and 1 sample chapter, sample projects, table of contents. Reviews artwork/photos as part of ms package. Send transparencies if possible.
Recent Title(s): *Making Glass Beads*, by Cindy Jenkins (beads).

N **LATIN AMERICAN LITERARY REVIEW PRESS**, 121 Edgewood Ave., Pittsburgh PA 15218. (412)371-9023. Fax: (412)371-9025. E-mail: lalrp@aol.com. Website: http://www.lalrp.org. **Acquisitions**: K.M. Ballew, assistant editor (Latin American fiction). "We focus on English translations of works that were originally written in Spanish or Portuguese." Publishes trade paperback originals. **Publishes 12 titles/year. Receives 40 queries and 50 mss/year. 25% of books from first-time authors; 75% from unagented writers. Pays 7-10% royalty on wholesale price or makes outright purchase.** Publishes book 14 months after acceptance of ms. Accepts simultaneous submissions. Reports in 6 months on mss. Book catalog and ms guidelines free.
Nonfiction: Subjects include language/literature (Latin American), translation, women's issues/studies. Query with SASE. Reviews artwork/photos as part of ms package. Send photocopies.
Fiction: Literary, multicultural, short story collections, translation. Send complete ms with SASE.
Poetry: Poetry, poetry in translation. "Translated poetry should be by a recognized name." Submit complete ms.
Recent Title(s): *Cruel Fictions, Cruel Realities: Short Stories by Latin American Women Writers*, edited and translated by Kathy S. Leonard (fiction); *Ceremonial Songs*, by Pablo Neruda (poetry).
Tips: Publishes for the general adult and college level audiences.

LAUREL BOOKS, Dell Publishing, Bantam Doubleday Dell, 1540 Broadway, New York NY 10036. (212)354-6500. **Acquisitions:** Leslie Schnur, editor-in-chief. Publishes trade paperback originals, mostly light, humorous material and books on pop culture. **Publishes 4 titles/year. 15% of books from first-time authors; less than 5% from unagented writers. Pay 7½-12½% royalty on retail price. Advance varies.** Publishes book 1 year after acceptance of ms. Accepts simultaneous submissions. Reports in 4-6 months on queries. Book catalog for 9x12 SAE and 3 first class stamps.
Nonfiction: Textbook. Subjects include education, government/politics, history, philosophy, psychology, science, sociology. Query with synopsis, 2-3 sample chapters and SASE.
Fiction: Literary. Query with synopsis, 2-3 sample chapters or complete ms and SASE.

N **LAUREL GLEN PUBLISHING**, Advantage Publishers Group, 5880 Oberlin Dr., San Diego CA 92121. (619)457-2500. **Acquisitions**: JoAnn Padgett, managing editor. "Laurel Glen publishes unique, high-design concept, well-written books by authors who are authorities in their fields. We will initially concentrate our effort on creating highly illustrated books on carefully selected nonfiction subjects in the areas of art, cooking, home decorating and nature." Publishes hardcover and trade paperback originals and reprints. **Publishes 30 titles/year. Receives 175 queries and 75 mss/year. Pays 10-15% royalty on wholesale price or makes outright purchase. Offers $1,000 advance.** Publishes book 1 year after acceptance. Accepts simultaneous submissions. Reports in 1 month on queries, 4 months on proposals, 6 months on mss. Book catalog for $1 and 9×12 SASE with 5 first-class stamps. Manuscript guidelines for #10 SASE.
Nonfiction: Publishes highly illustrated books. Subjects include art, cooking, home decorating, nature. "As we grow, we will move to include narrative nonfiction on business, self-help, family and other topics related to personal growth." Submit cover letter, outline, table of contents, sample chapters or complete ms, estimated length or word count, author bio or résumé, and marketing information, including a clear statement of the work's purpose, target audience and

comparison with competition. Include SASE with sufficient postage for return of materials. Reviews artwork/photos as part of ms package. Send transparencies.
Recent Title(s): *Tuscan Food & Folklore*, by Jeni Wright (cooking).
Tips: Audience is "the sophisticated reader with an upscale lifestyle. Try to present a unique topic or a topic treated from a unique angle."

MERLOYD LAWRENCE BOOKS, Perseus Book Group, 102 Chestnut St., Boston MA 02108. **Acquisitions:** Merloyd Lawrence, president. Estab. 1982. Publishes hardcover and trade paperback originals. **Publishes 7-8 titles/year. Receives 400 submissions/year. 25% of books from first-time authors; 20% from unagented writers. Pays royalty on retail price.** Publishes book 1 year after acceptance. Accepts simultaneous submissions.
Nonfiction: Biography, child development, health/medicine, nature/environment, psychology. Query with SASE. *All queries with SASE read and answered.* No unsolicited mss read.
Recent Title(s): *Living Downstream: An Ecologist Looks at Cancer and the Environment*, by Sandra Steingraber (health/science).

LAWYERS & JUDGES PUBLISHING CO., P.O. Box 30040, Tucson AZ 85751-0040. (520)323-1500. Fax: (520)323-0055. E-mail: lj_publ@azstarnet.com. Website: http://www.azstarnet.com/~lj_publ/. **Acquisitions:** Steve Weintraub, president. "We are a highly specific publishing company, reaching the legal and insurance fields and accident reconstruction." Publishes professional hardcover originals. **Publishes 15 titles/year. Receives 200 queries and 30 mss/year. 5% of books from first-time authors; 100% from unagented writers. Pays 7-10% royalty on retail price.** Publishes book 5 months after acceptance of ms. Accepts simultaneous submissions. Reports in 2 months. Book catalog free.
Nonfiction: Reference. Legal/insurance subjects. "Unless a writer is an expert in the legal/insurance areas, we are not interested." Submit proposal package, including full or *very* representative portion of ms.
Recent Title(s): *Forensic Aspects of Vision and Highway Safety*, by Allen, Abrams, Ginsburg and Weintraub.

LEE & LOW BOOKS, 95 Madison Ave., New York NY 10016. (212)779-4400. Fax: (212)683-1894. Website: http://www.leeandlow.com. Publisher: Philip Lee. **Acquisitions:** Elizabeth Szabla, editor-in-chief. Estab. 1991. "Our goals are to meet a growing need for books that address children of color, and to present literature that all children can identify with. We only consider multicultural children's picture books. **Publishes 12 titles/year.** Send complete ms with SASE. Reports in 5 months. Encourages new writers.

- Lee & Low offers extensive writer's guidelines on their website.

Recent Title(s): *A House by the River*, by William Miller, illustrated by Cornelius Van Wright and Ying-Hwa Hu (fiction); *In Daddy's Arms I Am Tall: African Americans Celebrating Fathers (poetry).*
Tips: "Of special interest are stories set in contemporary America. We are interested in fiction as well as nonfiction. We do not consider folktales, fairy tales or animal stories."

J & L LEE CO., P.O. Box 5575, Lincoln NE 68505. **Acquisitions:** James L. McKee, publisher. "Virtually everything we publish is of a Great Plains nature." Publishes trade paperback originals and reprints. **Publishes 5 titles/year. Receives 25 queries and 5-10 mss/year. 20% of books from first-time authors; 60% from unagented writers. Pays 10% royalty on retail price or makes outright purchase of $100 minimum. Rarely offers advance.** Publishes book 10 months after acceptance of ms. Accepts simultaneous submissions. Reports in 6 months on queries and mss, 1 month on proposals. Book catalog free.
Imprint(s): Salt Creek Press, Young Hearts.
Nonfiction: Biography, reference. Subjects include Americana, history, regional. Query.
Recent Title(s): *Nebraska Place Names*, by Elton Perkey (history).

LEHIGH UNIVERSITY PRESS, Linderman Library, 30 Library Dr., Lehigh University, Bethlehem PA 18015-3067. (610)758-3933. Fax: (610)974-2823. E-mail: inlup@lehigh.edu. **Acquisitions:** Philip A. Metzger, director. Estab. 1985. Publishes hardcover originals. **Publishes 10 titles/year. Receives 30 queries and 25 mss/year. 70% of books from first-time authors; 100% from unagented writers. Pays royalty.** Publishes book 18 months after acceptance of ms. Accepts simultaneous submissions. Reports in 3 months. Book catalog and ms guidelines free.
Nonfiction: Biography, reference, academic. Subjects include Americana, art/architecture, history, language/literature, science. Submit 1 sample chapter and proposal package.
Recent Title(s): *A World of Crisis and Progress: The American YMCA in Japan, 1890-1930*, by Jon Thares Davidann.
Tips: "We are an academic press publishing scholarly monographs. We are especially interested in works on 18th century studies and the history of technology, but consider works of quality on a variety of subjects."

LEISURE BOOKS, 276 Fifth Ave., Suite 1008, New York NY 10001-0112. (212)725-8811. Fax: (212)532-1054. E-mail: timdy@aol.com. **Acquisitions:** Jennifer Bonnell, editorial assistant; Gretchen Comba, editorial assistant; Alicia Condon, editorial director; Gwen Jones, managing editor; Don D'Auria, editor (Westerns, technothrillers, horror); Christopher Keeslar, editor. Estab. 1970. Leisure Books is seeking time-travel or futuristic romances, westerns, horror and techno-thrillers. Publishes mass market paperback originals and reprints. **Publishes 160 titles/year. Receives thousands of submissions/year. 20% of books from first-time authors; 20% from unagented writers. Pays royalty on retail**

price. Advance negotiable. Publishes book 18 months after acceptance. Reports in 4 months on queries. Book catalog and ms guidelines for #10 SASE.

Imprint(s): Love Spell (romance), **Leisure** (romance, western, techno, horror).

Fiction: Historical romance (90,000-120,000 words); time-travel romance (90,000 words); futuristic romance (90,000 words); westerns (75,000-115,000 words); horror (90,000 words); techno-thrillers (90,000 words). "We are strongly backing historical romance. No sweet romance, gothic, science fiction, erotica, contemporary women's fiction, mainstream or action/adventure." Query or submit outline/synopsis and sample chapters. "No material returned without SASE."

Recent Title(s): *Viking!*, by Connie Mason (historical romance).

LERNER PUBLISHING GROUP, 241 First Ave. N., Minneapolis MN 55401. (612)332-3344. Website: http://www.lernerbooks.com. **Acquisitions:** Jennifer Martin, editor. Estab. 1959. "Our goal is to publish books that educate, stimulate and stretch the imagination, foster global awareness, encourage critical thinking and inform, inspire and entertain." Publishes hardcover originals, trade paperback originals and reprints. **Publishes 150-175 titles/year; First Avenue Edition, 30; Carolrhoda, 50-60; Runestone Press, 3. Receives 1,000 queries and 300 mss/year. 20% of books from first-time authors; 95% from unagented writers. Pays 3-8% royalty on retail price (approximately 60% of books) or makes outright purchase of $1,000-3,000 (for series and work-for-hire). Offers $1,000-3,000 advance.** Publishes book 2 years after acceptance of ms. Accepts simultaneous submissions. Reports in 4 months on proposals. Catalog for 9×12 SAE with 6 first-class stamps. Manuscript guidelines for #10 SASE.

Imprint(s): Runestone Press, First Avenue Editions (paperback reprints for hard/soft deals only); **Carolrhoda Books**; Lerner Publications.

Nonfiction: Children's/juvenile (grades 3-10). Subjects include art/architecture, ethnic, history, nature/environment, science, sports, aviation, geography. Query with outline, 1-2 sample chapters, SASE.

Fiction: Juvenile (middle grade). "We are not actively pursuing fiction titles." Query with synopsis, 1-2 sample chapters and SASE.

Recent Title(s): *Songs from the Loom: A Navajo Girl Learns to Weave*, by Monty Ruessel (cultural studies); *Mystery in Miami Beach*, by Harriet Feder (mystery).

LIBRARIES UNLIMITED, INC., P.O. Box 6633, Englewood CO 80155. (303)770-1220. Fax: (303)220-8843. E-mail: lu-editorial@lu.com. Website: http://www.lu.com. **Acquisitions:** Susan Zernial, editor. Betty Morris, acquisitions editor (school library titles); Ron Maas, general manager (academic/reference titles). Libraries Unlimited publishes resources for libraries, librarians and educators. Publishes hardcover originals. **Publishes 75 titles/year; Ukranian, 45; Teacher Ideas, 30. Receives 400 queries and 100 mss/year. 50% of books from first-time authors; 100% from unagented writers. Pays 8-15% royalty on wholesale price.** Publishes book 1 year after acceptance of ms. Accepts simultaneous submissions. Reports in 1 month on queries, 2 months on proposals and mss. Book catalog and manuscript guidelines free.

Imprint(s): Teacher Ideas Press (Susan Zernial, acquisitions editor); Ukrainian Academic Press.

Nonfiction: Reference, textbook, teacher resource and activity books. Reference books on these topics for libraries: agriculture/horticulture, anthropology/archaeology, art/architecture, business/economics, education, ethnic, health/medicine, history, language/literature, military/war, music/dance, philosophy, psychology, religion, science, sociology, women's issues/studies. Interested in reference books of all types (annotated bibliographies, sourcebooks and handbooks; curriculum enrichment/support books for teachers K-12 and school librarians). Submit proposal package, including brief description of book, outline, 1 sample chapter, author credentials, comparison with competing titles, audience and market. Reviews artwork/photos as part of ms package. Send photocopies.

Recent Title(s): *The Magic Egg*, by Barbara J. Suwyn (folktales from Ukraine).

Tips: "We welcome any ideas that combine professional expertise, writing ability, and innovative thinking. Audience is librarians (school, public, academic and special) and teachers (K-12)."

LIFETIME BOOKS, INC., 2131 Hollywood Blvd., Hollywood FL 33020. (954)925-5242. Fax: (954)925-5244. E-mail: lifetime@shadow.net. Website: http://www.lifetimebooks.com. **Acquisitions:** Callie Rucker, senior editor. "Lifetime Books is committed to inspiring readers to improve all aspects of their lives by providing how-to and self-help information which can help them obtain such a goal." Publishes hardcover and trade paperback originals. **Publishes 20 titles/year. Receives 500 queries and 1,000 mss/year. 95% of books from first-time authors; 95% from unagented writers. Pays 6-15% royalty on retail price. Offers advance of $0-10,000.** Publishes book 1 year after acceptance. Accepts simultaneous submissions. Reports in 1 month on queries, 2 months on proposals and mss. Book catalog and ms guidelines free.

Imprint(s): Fell Publishers; Compact Books (contact Donald Lessne); Lifetime Periodicals.

Nonfiction: Biography, coffee table books, cookbooks, giftbooks, reference, how-to, self-help. Subjects include business and sales, psychology, child guidance/parenting, education, ethnic, health/medicine, history, religion, sports, medical, hobbies, Hollywood bio/exposé, money/finance. "We are interested in material on business, health and fitness, self-improvement and reference. We will not consider topics that only appeal to a small, select audience." Submit outline, author bio, publicity ideas, proposals and 3 sample chapters. Reviews artwork as part of ms package. Send photocopies. No poetry, no fiction, no short stories, no children's.

Recent Title(s): *Sales Dragon*, by John Scevola (business/inspiration).

Tips: "We are most interested in well-written, timely nonfiction with strong sales potential. Our audience is very general. Learn markets and be prepared to help with sales and promotion. Show us how your book is unique, different or better than the competition."

LIGUORI PUBLICATIONS, One Liguori Dr., Liguori MO 63057. (314)464-2500. Fax: (314)464-8449. E-mail: 104626.1563@compuserve.com. Website: http://www.liguori.org. Publisher: Thomas M. Santa, C.SS.R. **Acquisitions:** Anthony Chiffolo, managing editor (Trade Group); Patricia Kossman, executive editor (Trade Group, New York office 718/229-8001, ext. 231 or 232, Fax: 718/631-5339.); Kass Dotterweich and Elsie McGrath, managing editors (Catechetical and Pastoral Resources Group); Scott Guillot, software engineer (Electronic Publishing). "Liguori Publications, faithful to the charism of Saint Alphonsus, is an apostolate within the mission of the Denver Province. Its mission, a collaborative effort of Redemptorists and laity, is to spread the gospel of Jesus Christ primarily through the print and electronic media. It shares in the Redemptorist priority of giving special attention to the poor and the most abandoned." The Trade Group publishes hardcover and trade paperback originals and reprints under the Liguori and Liguori/Triumph imprints; publishes 30 titles/year. The Catechetical and Pastoral Resources Group publishes paperback originals and reprints under the Liguori and Libros Liguori imprints: **Publishes 50 titles/year, including Spanish-language titles.** The Electronic Publishing Division publishes 4 titles/year under the Faithware® imprint. **Royalty varies or purchases outright. Advance varies.** Publishes 2 years after acceptance of ms. Prefers no simultaneous submissions. Reports in 2 months on queries and proposals, 3 months on mss. Author guidelines on request.
Imprint(s): Liguori Books, Libros Liguori, Faithware®, Liguori/Triumph.
Nonfiction: Inspirational, devotional, prayer, Christian-living, self-help books. Religious subjects. Mostly adult audience; limited children/juvenile. Query with annotated outline, 1 sample chapter, SASE. Query for CD-ROM and Internet publishing. Publishes very few electronic products received unsolicited.
Recent Title(s): *Simple Truths* by Fulton J. Sheen (spirituality).

LIMELIGHT EDITIONS, Proscenium Publishers, Inc., 118 E. 30th St., New York NY 10016. Fax: (212)532-5526. E-mail: jjlmlt@haven.ios.com. **Acquisitions:** Melvyn B. Zerman, president; Roxanna Font, assistant publisher. "We are committed to publishing books on film, theater, music and dance that make a strong contribution to their fields and deserve to remain in print for many years." Publishes hardcover and trade paperback originals, trade paperback reprints. **Publishes 14 titles/year. Receives 150 queries and 40 mss/year. 15% of books from first-time authors; 20% from unagented writers. Pays 7½ (paperback)-10% (hardcover) royalty on retail price. Offers $500-2,000 advance.** Publishes book 10 months after acceptance of ms. Reports in 1 month on queries and proposals, 3 months on mss. Book catalog and ms guidelines free.
Nonfiction: Biography, historical, humor, instructional—most illustrated—on music/dance or theater/film. "All books are on the performing arts *exclusively.*" Query with proposal package, including 2-3 sample chapters, outline with SASE. Reviews artwork/photos as part of ms package. Send photocopies.
Recent Title(s): *The Four Voices of Man*, by Jerome Hines (opera singing).

LION BOOKS, Sayre Ross Co., 210 Nelson Rd., Scarsdale NY 10583. (914)725-2280. Fax: (914)725-3572. **Acquisitions:** Harriet Ross, editor. Publishes hardcover originals and reprints, trade paperback reprints. **Publishes 14 titles/year. Receives 60-150 queries and 100 mss/year. 60% of books from first-time authors. Pays 7-15% royalty on wholesale price or makes outright purchase of $500-5,000.** Publishes book 5 months after acceptance of ms. Reports in 1 week on queries, 1 month on mss.
Nonfiction: Biography, how-to. Subjects include Americana, ethnic, government/politics, history, recreation, sports. No fiction, please! Submit complete mss with SASE. *Writer's Market* recommends query with SASE first.

LION PUBLISHING, Chariot Victor Publishing, 4050 Lee Vance View, Colorado Springs CO 80918-7102. (719)536-3271. Fax: (719)536-3269. Managing Editor: Liz Duckworth. Executive Editor: Greg Clouse. **Acquisitions**: Lee Hough, senior acquisitions editor. "Lion Publishing's books are more 'seeker-sensitive' than Chariot; more accessible to the 'unchurched.' Lion seeks to lead the way with Spiritual Growth products." Publishes hardcover and trade paperback originals. **Published 10 titles/year. Pays variable royalty on wholesale price. Advance varies.** Publishes book 18 months after acceptance of ms. Accepts simultaneous submissions, if so noted. Reports in 3 months on queries.

- Lion Publishing originates and distributes books in the United Kingdom and the United States. The numbers listed above do not include titles originating in and distributed solely in U.K.

Nonfiction: Biography, gift book, devotional. Subjects include child guidance/parenting, religion, marriage/family, inspirational, Christian living. Query or submit outline, 1 sample chapter with SASE.
Fiction: Religious. Query with complete ms. *Writer's Market* recommends query with SASE first.
Recent Title(s): *What Happens When Women Pray*, by E. Christenson (prayer); *Riversong*, by R. Elwood (fiction).
Tips: "All Lion books are written from a Christian perspective. However, they must speak primarily to a general audience. Half of our titles are children's books, yet we receive few manuscripts of publishable quality and almost no

nonfiction of *any* kind. In short, we need high-quality nonfiction of all types that fit our guidelines."

LIPPINCOTT, Lippincott-Raven Publishers, Subsidiary of Wolters Kluwer, 227 E. Washington Square, Philadelphia PA 19106.(215)238-4200. Fax:(215)238-4411. Website: http://www.lrpub.com. **Acquisitions:** Donna Hilton, vice president, publisher. Estab. 1792. Lippincott publishes high-quality nursing and allied health texts and reference books for healthcare students and practitioners. Publishes hardcover and trade paperback originals and reprints. **Publishes 50 titles/year. Receives 500 queries and 20 proposals/year. 75% of books from first-time authors; 100% from unagented writers. Pays 10-18% royalty on wholesale price. Offers $2,000-10,000 advance.** Publishes book 1 year after acceptance of ms (2 years from initiation of project and development of ms). Accepts simultaneous submissions. Reports in 2 months on proposals. Book catalog and ms guidelines free.
Nonfiction: Reference, textbook, healthcare practitioner books. Subjects include health/medicine, science, women's issues/studies. Query or submit outline, 2 sample chapters and proposal package, including purpose, market and table of contents with SASE. Reviews artwork/photos as part of ms package. Send originals.
Recent Title(s): *Handbook of Nursing Diagnosis*, by Linda Carpenito.

LIPPINCOTT-RAVEN PUBLISHERS, Wolters Kluwer, 227 E. Washington Sq., Philadelphia PA 19106. (215)238-4200. Fax: (215)238-4227. Website: http://www.LRPUB.com. **Acquisitions:** Kathey Alexander, vice president/editor-in-chief, medical; Donna Hilton, vice president/editor-in-chief, nursing. Estab. 1792. "The mission of Lippincott-Raven is to disseminate healthcare information, including basic science, for medical and nursing students and ongoing education for practicing clinicians." Publishes hardcover originals. **Publishes 180 titles/year. Pay rates vary depending on type of book, whether the author is the principal or contributing author and amount of production necessary.** Accepts simultaneous submissions, if so noted. Reports in 3 months on proposals.
Imprint(s): Lippincott.
Nonfiction: Reference, textbook, manuals, atlases on health/medicine subjects. "We do not publish for the layperson." Query with proposal package including outline, table of contents, cv, proposed market and how your ms differs, estimate number of trim size pages and number and type of illustrations (line drawing, half-tone, 4-color).
Recent Title(s): *Cancer: Principles and Practice of Oncology, 5th Ed.*, by Devita Hellman and Rosenberg.
Tips: Audience is medical and nursing students, medical students and practicing clinicians.

LITTLE, BROWN AND CO., INC., Time Warner Inc., 1271 Avenue of the Americas, New York NY 10020. (212)522-8700. **Acquisitions:** Editorial Department, Trade Division. Estab. 1837. "The general editorial philosophy for all divisions continues to be broad and flexible, with high quality and the promise of commercial success as always the first considerations." Publishes hardcover originals and paperback originals and reprints. **Publishes 100 titles/year. "Royalty and advance agreements vary from book to book and are discussed with the author at the time an offer is made."**
Imprint(s): Back Bay Books; **Bulfinch Press; Little, Brown and Co. Children's Books.**
Nonfiction: "Issue books, autobiography, biographies, culture, cookbooks, history, popular science, nature, and sports." Query *only. No unsolicited mss or proposals.*
Fiction: Contemporary popular fiction as well as fiction of literary distinction. Query *only. No unsolicited mss.*
Recent Title(s): *Naked*, by David Sedaris (nonfiction); *Blood Work*, by Michael Connelly (fiction).

LITTLE, BROWN AND CO., CHILDREN'S BOOKS, 34 Beacon St., Boston MA 02108. (617)227-0730. Website: http://www.littlebrown.com. Editor-in-Chief: Maria Modugno. Senior Editor: Megan Tingley. Editor: Stephanie Peters. **Acquisitions:** Amy Kaiser. Estab. 1837. "We publish books on a wide variety of nonfiction topics which may be of interest to children and are looking for strong writing and presentation, but no predetermined topics." Publishes hardcover originals, trade paperback originals and reprints. **Firm publishes 60-70 titles/year. Pays royalty on retail price. Offers advance to be negotiated individually.** Publishes book 2 years after acceptance of ms. Accepts simultaneous submissions, if so noted. Reports in 1 month on queries, 2 months on proposals and mss.
Nonfiction: Children's/juvenile, middle grade and young adult. Subjects include animals, art/architecture, ethnic, gay/lesbian, history, hobbies, nature/environment, recreation, science, sports. Writers should avoid "looking for the 'issue' they think publishers want to see, choosing instead topics they know best and are most enthusiastic about/inspired by." *Agented submissions only.*
Fiction: All juvenile/young adult; picture books. Categories include adventure, ethnic, fantasy, feminist, gay/lesbian, historical, humor, mystery, science fiction and suspense. "We are looking for strong fiction for children of all ages in any area, including multicultural. We always prefer full manuscripts for fiction." *Agented submissions only.*
Recent Title(s): *The Girls' Guide to Life: How to Take Charge of the Issues that Affect You*, by Catherine Dee (nonfiction); *Revenge of the Snob Squad*, by Julie Ann Peters (fiction).
Tips: "Our audience is children of all ages, from preschool through young adult. We are looking for quality material that will work in hardcover—send us your best."

LITTLE SIMON, Simon & Schuster Children's Publishing Division, Simon & Schuster, 1230 Avenue of the Americas, New York NY 10020. (212)698-7200. Website: http://www.simonandschuster.com. **Acquisitions:** Submissions Editor. "Our goal is to provide fresh material in an innovative format for pre-school to age eight. Our books are often, if not exclusively, illustrator driven." Publishes novelty books only. **Publishes 120 titles/year. 5% of books from first-time**

authors; 5% from unagented writers. Pays 2-5% royalty on retail price for original, non-licensed mss. Publishes book 6 months after acceptance of ms. Reports on queries in 8 months.

Nonfiction: Children's/juvenile novelty books. "Novelty books include many things that do not fit in the traditional hardcover or paperback format, like pop-up, board book, scratch and sniff, glow in the dark, open the flap, etc." Query only with SASE. *All unsolicited mss returned unopened.*

Recent Title(s): *Bugs in Space*, by David Carter (pop-up).

LITTLE TIGER PRESS, % XYZ Group, N16 W23390 Stoneridge Dr., Waukesha WI 53188. (414)544-2001. Fax: (414)544-2022. **Acquisitions**: Jody A. Linn. Publishes hardcover originals. "We focus on bringing new talent into the field of children's books and publishing appealing, funny, and memorable titles. Our goal is to provide books that will win the hearts of adults as well as children." **Publishes 20-25 titles/year. Receives 300 queries and 1,800 mss/year. 75% of books from first-time authors; 85% from unagented writers. Pays 7½-10% royalty on retail price or for first-time authors makes outright purchase of $800-2,500. Offers $2,000 minimum advance.** Publishes book 1 year after acceptance of ms. Accepts simultaneous submissions. Reports in 2 months on queries and proposals, 3 months on mss. Book catalog for #10 SASE with 3 first-class stamps. Manuscript guidelines for #10 SASE.

Fiction: Humor, juvenile, picture books. "Humorous stories, stories about animals, children's imagination, or realistic fiction are especially sought." Send ms with SASE.

Recent Title(s): *Counting Leopard's Spots*, by Hiawyn Oram, illustrated by Tim Warnes.

Tips: "Audience is children 3-8 years old. We are looking for simple, basic picture books, preferably humorous, that children will enjoy again and again. We do not have a multicultural or social agenda."

LIVING THE GOOD NEWS, The Morehouse Group, 600 Grant St., Suite #400. Denver CO 80203. Fax: (303)832-4971. **Acquisitions:** Liz Riggleman, editorial administrator. "Living The Good News is looking for books on practical, personal, spiritual growth for children, teens, families and faith communities." Publishes hardcover and trade paperback originals. **Publishes 15 titles/year. Pays royalty.** Publishes book 1 year after acceptance of ms. Accepts simultaneous submissions. Reports in 2 months on proposals. Book catalog for 9×12 SAE and 4 first-class stamps. Manuscript guidelines for #10 SASE.

Imprint(s): Spindle Press (children's materials; contact Liz Riggleman, editorial director).

Nonfiction: Children's/juvenile, gift book, how-to, illustrated book, self-help. Subjects include child guidance/parenting, grandparenting, education, religion (prayer, scripture, saints, ritual and celebration), storytelling, contemporary issues. No poetry or drama. Submit proposal package, including cover letter, chapter outline, sample chapter, author information and SASE. Reviews artwork/photos as part of ms package. Send photocopies.

Recent Title(s): *Our Family Book of Days: A Record Through the Years*, by Kathy Finley.

Fiction: Juvenile, picture books, religious, young adult. Query or submit synopsis with SASE.

Tips: Audience is those seeking to enrich their spiritual journey, typically from mainline and liturgical church backgrounds. "We look for original, creative ways to build connectedness with self, others, God and the earth."

LLEWELLYN PUBLICATIONS, Llewellyn Worldwide, Ltd., P.O. Box 64383, St. Paul MN 55164-0383. (612)291-1970. Fax: (612)291-1908. E-mail: lwlpc@llewellyn.com. Website: http://www.llewellyn.com. **Acquisitions:** Nancy J. Mostad, acquisitions manager. Estab. 1901. Llewellyn publishes New Age fiction and nonfiction exploring "new worlds of mind and spirit." Publishes trade and mass market paperback originals. **Publishes 100 titles/year. Receives 500 submissions/year. 30% of books from first-time authors; 90% from unagented writers. Pays 10% royalty on moneys received both wholesale and retail.** Accepts simultaneous submissions. Reports in 3 months. Book catalog for 9×12 SAE with 4 first-class stamps. Manuscript guidelines for SASE.

- Llewellyn has had a 20% growth rate in sales each year for the past seven years.

Nonfiction: How-to, self-help. Subjects include nature/environment, health and nutrition, metaphysical/magic, psychology, women's issues/studies. Submit outline and sample chapters. Reviews artwork/photos as part of ms package.

Fiction: Metaphysical/occult, which is authentic and educational, yet entertaining.

Recent Title(s): *The Magick of Aromatherapy*, by Gwydion O'Hara (nonfiction); *Warrior of Shadows*, by D.J. Conway (fiction).

LOCUST HILL PRESS, P.O. Box 260, West Cornwall CT 06796-0260. (860)672-0060. Fax: (860)672-4968. **Acquisitions:** Thomas C. Bechtle, publisher. Locust Hill Press specializes in scholarly reference and bibliography works for college and university libraries worldwide, as well as monographs and essay collections on literary subjects. Publishes hardcover originals. **Publishes 12 titles/year. Receives 150 queries and 20 mss/year. 100% of books from unagented writers. Pays 12-18% royalty on retail price.** Publishes book 6 months after acceptance of ms. Accepts simultaneous submissions. Reports in 1 month. *Writer's Market* recommends allowing 2 months for reply. Book catalog free.

Nonfiction: Reference. Subjects include ethnic, language/literature, women's issues/studies. "Since our audience is exclusively college and university libraries (and the occasional specialist), we are less inclined to accept manuscripts in 'popular' (i.e., public library) fields. While bibliography has been and will continue to be a specialty, our Locust Hill Literary Studies is gaining popularity as a series of essay collections and monographs in a wide variety of literary topics." Query.

Recent Title(s): *Aldous Huxley and W.H. Auden: On Language*, by David G. Izzo.

Tips: "Remember that this is a small, very specialized academic publisher with no distribution network other than mail contact with most academic libraries worldwide. Please shape your expectations accordingly. If your aim is to reach the world's scholarly community by way of its libraries, we are the correct firm to contact. But *please*: no fiction, poetry, popular religion, or personal memoirs."

LONE EAGLE PUBLISHING CO., 2337 Roscomare Rd., Suite 9, Los Angeles CA 90077-1851. (310)471-8066 or 1-800-FILMBKS. Fax: (310)471-4969. E-mail: info@loneeagle.com. Website: http://www.loneeagle.com. **Acquisitions:** Jeff Black, editor. Estab. 1982. "Lone Eagle Publishing Company is one of the premier publishing companies servicing the entertainment community. Lone Eagle publishes reference directories that contain comprehensive and accurate credits, personal data and contact information for every major entertainment industry craft. Lone Eagle also publishes many 'how-to' books for the film production business, including books on screenwriting, directing, budgeting and producing, acting, editing, etc." Publishes perfectbound and trade paperback originals. **Publishes 15 titles/year. Receives 100 submissions/year. 80% of books from unagented writers. Pays 10% royalty minimum on net income wholesale and retail. Offers $500-1,000 average advance.** Publishes book 1 year after acceptance. Accepts simultaneous submissions. Reports quarterly on queries. Book catalog free.
Nonfiction: Technical, how-to, reference. Film and television subjects. "We are looking for technical books in film and television, related topics or biographies." Submit outline and sample chapters. Reviews artwork/photos as part of ms package.
Recent Title(s): *Filmmaker's Dictionary*, by Ralph Singleton.
Tips: "A well-written, well-thought-out book on some technical aspect of the motion picture (or video) industry has the best chance: for example, script supervising, editing, special effects, costume design, production design. Pick a subject that has not been done to death, make sure you know what you're talking about, get someone well-known in that area to endorse the book and prepare to spend a lot of time publicizing the book."

LONELY PLANET PUBLICATIONS, 150 Linden St., Oakland CA 94607-2538. (510)893-8555. Fax: (510)893-8563. E-mail: info@lonelyplanet.com. Website: http://www.lonelyplanet.com. **Acquisitions:** Publishing Manager. Estab. 1973. Publishes trade paperback originals. **Publishes 30 titles/year. Receives 500 queries and 100 mss/year. 5% of books from first-time authors; 50% from unagented writers. Makes outright purchase or negotiated fee—⅓ on contract, ⅓ on submission, ⅓ on approval.** Publishes book 2 years after acceptance of ms. Accepts simultaneous submissions. Reports in 3 months on queries. Book catalog free.
Nonfiction: Travel guides, phrasebooks atlases and travel literature exclusively. "Request our catalog first to make sure we don't already have a similar book or call and see if a similar book is on our production schedule." Submit outline or proposal package. Reviews artwork/photos as part of ms package. Send photocopies.
Recent Title(s): *The Gates of Damascus*, by Lieve Joris.

LONGSTREET PRESS, INC., 2140 Newmarket Parkway, Suite 122, Marietta GA 30067. (770)980-1488. Fax: (770)859-9894. President/Editor: Chuck Perry. **Acquisitions**: Editorial Department. Estab. 1988. "We want serious journalism-oriented nonfiction on subjects appealing to a broad, various audience or popular fiction that's exceptionally well done. The audience for our books has a strong sense of intellectual curiosity and a functioning sense of humor." Publishes hardcover and trade paperback originals. **Publishes 45 titles/year. Receives 2,500 submissions/year. 10% of books from first-time authors. Pays royalty.** Publishes book 1 year after acceptance. Accepts simultaneous submissions. Reports in 3 months. Book catalog for 9×12 SAE with 4 first-class stamps. Manuscript guidelines for #10 SASE.
Nonfiction: Biography, coffee table book, cookbook, humor, illustrated book, reference. Subjects include Americana, cooking/foods/nutrition, gardening, history, language/literature, nature/environment, photography, regional, sports, women's issues/studies. "No poetry, how-to, religious, scientific or highly technical, textbooks of any kind, erotica." Query or submit outline and sample chapters. Reviews artwork as part of ms package.
Fiction: Literary, mainstream/contemporary. *Agented fiction only.*
Recent Title(s): *Too Blue To Fly*, by Judith Richards (fiction).
Tips: "Midlist books have a harder time making it. The nonfiction book, serious or humorous, with a clearly defined audience has the best chance. If I were a writer trying to market a book today, I would do thorough, professional work aimed at a clearly defined and reachable audience."

LOOMPANICS UNLIMITED, P.O. Box 1197, Port Townsend WA 98368-0997. Fax: (360)385-7785. E-mail: loompanx@olympus.net. Website: http://www.loompanics.com. President: Michael Hoy. **Acquisitions:** Dennis P. Eichhorn, editorial director. Estab. 1975. The mission statement offered by Loompanics is "no more secrets—no more excuses—no more limits!" Publishes trade paperback originals. **Publishes 15 titles/year. Receives 500 submissions/year. 40% of books from first-time authors; 100% from unagented writers. Pays 10-15% royalty on wholesale or retail price or makes outright purchase of $100-1,200. Offers $500 average advance.** Publishes book 1 year after acceptance. Accepts simultaneous submissions. Reports in 2 months. Author guidelines free. Book catalog for $5, postpaid.
Nonfiction: How-to, reference, self-help. "In general, works about outrageous topics or obscure-but-useful technology written authoritatively in a matter-of-fact way." Subjects include the underground economy, crime, drugs, privacy, self-sufficiency, anarchism and "beat the system" books. "We are looking for how-to books in the fields of espionage, investigation, the underground economy, police methods, how to beat the system, crime and criminal techniques. We are also looking for similarly-written articles for our catalog and its supplements. No cookbooks, inspirational, travel, management or cutesy-wutesy stuff." Query or submit outline/synopsis and sample chapters. Reviews artwork/photos.
Recent Title(s): *101 Things to Do 'Til the Revolution*, by Claire Wolfe.
Tips: "Our audience is young males looking for hard-to-find information on alternatives to 'The System.' Your chances

for success are greatly improved if you can show us how your proposal fits in with our catalog."

LOTHROP, LEE & SHEPARD BOOKS, William Morrow & Co., The Hearst Corp., 1350 Avenue of the Americas, New York NY 10019. (212)261-6640. Fax: (212)261-6648. **Acquisitions:** Susan Pearson, editor-in-chief; Melanie Donovan, senior editor. Estab. 1859. Lothrop, Lee & Shepard publishes children's books only and is currently emphasizing picture books. Publishes hardcover originals only. Royalty and advance vary according to type of book. **Publishes 30 titles/year. Fewer than 2% of books from first-time authors; 25% of books from unagented writers.** Publishes book within 2 years of acceptance of artwork. Reports in 3 months.
Fiction and Nonfiction: Publishes picture books, general nonfiction, and novels. Emphasis is on picture books. Looks for "organization, clarity, creativity, literary style." Query with samples. *No unsolicited mss.*
Recent Title(s): *African Beginnings*, by Jane Haskins and Kathleen Benson, illustrated by Floyd Cooper (nonfiction); *My Life With the Wave*, by Catherine Cowan, illustrated by Mark Buehner (fiction); *Keepers*, by Alice Schertle (poetry).

N **LOUISIANA STATE UNIVERSITY PRESS**, P.O. Box 250537, Baton Rouge LA 70894-5053. (504)388-6294. Fax: (504)388-6461. **Acquisitions:** L.E. Phillabaum, director; Maureen G. Hewitt, assistant director and editor-in-chief; John Easterly, executive editor; Sylvia Frank, acquisitions editor. Estab. 1935. Publishes hardcover originals, hardcover and trade paperback reprints. **Publishes 70-80 titles/year. Receives 800 submissions/year. 33% of books from first-time authors. 95% from unagented writers. Pays royalty on net and wholesale price.** Publishes book 1-2 years after acceptance. Reports in 6 weeks on queries. *Writer's Market* recommends allowing 2 months for reply. Book catalog and ms guidelines free.
Nonfiction: Biography and literary poetry collections. Subjects include anthropology/archaeology, art/architecture, ethnic, government/politics, history, language/literature, military/war, music/dance, philosophy, photography, regional, sociology, women's issues/studies. Query or submit outline and sample chapters.
Recent Title(s): *Lee Smith, Annie Dillard, and the Hollins Group: A Genesis of Writers*, by Nancy C. Parrish (literary women's studies); *Fields of Praise*, by Marilyn Nelson (poetry).
Tips: "Our audience includes scholars, intelligent laymen, general audience."

N **THE LOVE AND LOGIC PRESS, INC.**, Cline/Fay Institute, Inc., 2207 Jackson St., Golden CO 80401. Fax: (303)278-3894. Website: http://www.loveandlogic.com. **Acquisitions:** Nancy Henry, president/publisher. "We publish titles which help empower parents, teachers and others who help young people, and which help these individuals become more skilled and happier in their interactions with children. Our titles stress building personal responsibility in children and helping them become prepared to function well in the world." Publishes hardcover and trade paperback originals. **Publishes 5-12 titles/year. 10% of books from first-time authors; 100% from unagented writers. Pays 7½-12% royalty on wholesale price. Offers $500-5,000 advance.** Publishes book 18 months after acceptance of ms. Accepts simultaneous submissions. Reports in 1 month on queries and proposals; 3 months on mss. Book catalog free.
Nonfiction: Self-help. Subjects include child guidance/parenting, education, health/medicine, psychology, sociology, current social issue trends. "We consider any queries/proposals falling into the above categories (with the exception of parenting) but especially psychology/sociology and current social issues and trends." No mss or proposals in New Age category, personal recovery stories, i.e., experiences with attempted suicide, drug/alcohol abuse, institutionalization or medical experiences. Query with SASE. Reviews artwork/photos as part of ms package. Send photocopies.
Recent Title(s): *Teaching With Love and Logic: Taking Control of the Classroom*, by Jim Fay and David Funk (education).

LOVE SPELL, Leisure Books, Dorchester Publishing Co., Inc., 276 Fifth Ave., Suite 1008, New York NY 10001-0112. (212)725-8811. **Acquisitions**: Jennifer Bonnell, editorial assistant; Gretchen Comba, editorial assistant; Christopher Kesslar, editor. "Love Spell publishes the quirky sub-genres of romance: time-travel, paranormal, futuristic. Despite the exotic settings, we are still interested in character-driven plots." Publishes mass market paperback originals. **Publishes 48 titles/year. Receives 1,500-2,000 queries and 150-500 mss/year. 30% of books from first-time authors; 25-30% from unagented writers. Pays 4% royalty on retail price for new authors. Offers $2,000 average advance for new authors.** Publishes book 1 year after acceptance of ms. Reports in 6 months on mss. Book catalog free (800)481-9191. Manuscript guidelines for #10 SASE.
Fiction: Romance: historical, time travel, paranormal, futuristic, legendary lover. Query with synopsis, 3 sample chapters and SASE. "Books industry-wide are getting shorter; we're interested in 90,000 words."
Recent Title(s): *The Highwayman's Daughters*, by Anne Avery (Legendary Lovers).

N **LOWELL HOUSE**, NTC/Contemporary, 2020 Avenue of the Stars, Suite 300, Los Angeles CA 90067. **Acquisitions**: B. Sperry or M. Magallanes. "Lowell House publishes reference titles in the health, parenting and adult education." Publishes hardcover originals, trade paperback originals and reprints. **Publishes 120 titles/year. 60% of books from first-time authors; 75% from unagented writers. Pays royalty on retail price.** Publishes book 20 months after acceptance of ms. Accepts simultaneous submissions. Reports in 3 months on proposals. Book catalog for 9×12 SAE with $3 postage.

- Lowell House was purchased by NTC/Contemporary Group.

Imprint(s): Anodyne, Extension Press, Legacy Press, Woman to Woman, Gifted & Talented, 50 Nifty, Classics, Draw Science.
Nonfiction: Reference. Subjects include child guidance/parenting, cooking/foods/nutrition, education, health/medicine,

money/finance, psychology, recreation, sports, women's issues/studies. "Juvenile division does not accept outside submissions." Query or submit outline, 1 sample chapter and SASE.
Recent Title(s): *The Dream Sourcebook*, by Phyllis Koch-Sheras and Amy Lemley (reference).
Tips: "Submit a well-constructed proposal that clearly delineates the work's audience, its advantages over previously published books in the area, a detailed outline, and synopsis and the writer's cv or background.

N LOYOLA PRESS, 3441 N. Ashland Ave., Chicago IL 60657-1397. (773)281-1818 ext. 300. Fax: (773)281-4129. E-mail: schroeder@loyolapress.com. **Acquisitions:** Austin Tighe, chief editor. Estab. 1912. Publishes hardcover and trade paperback originals and reprints. **Publishes 20 titles/year. Receives 500 submissions/year. 10% of books from first-time authors; 60% from unagented writers. Pays variable royalty as percentage of net sales. Small advance.** Publishes book 1 year after acceptance of ms. Accepts simultaneous submissions. Reports in 2 months. Book catalog for 8½×11 SASE.
Imprint(s): Jesuit Way, Wild Onion, Seeker's Guides.
Nonfiction: Practical spirituality with Catholic Christian flavor. Subjects include prayer and meditation, personal relationships, spiritual wisdom for everyday life, culture and faith, scripture study for nonspecialists, the Catholic tradition. *Jesuit Way* books focus on Jesuit history, biography, and spirituality. *Seeker's Guides* are short introductions to various aspects of Christian living. *Wild Onion* books highlight religion in Chicago. Query before submitting ms.
Recent Title(s): *The Gift of Peace*.
Tips: "We need authors who are experts in their field, yet who can communicate their knowledge to beginners without talking down; authors who love the Catholic spiritual tradition and can open up its riches to others; authors who write simply and clearly—and with style. The winning combination is expertise + spirituality + style."

LUCENT BOOKS, P.O. Box 289011, San Diego CA 92198-9011. (619)485-7424. Fax: (619)485-9549. **Acquisitions:** Bonnie Szumski, editorial director; Lori Shein, David M. Haugen, editors. Estab. 1988. "Lucent publishes nonfiction for a middle school audience providing students with resource material for academic studies and for independent learning." Publishes hardcover educational supplementary materials and (nontrade) juvenile nonfiction. **Publishes 105 books/year. 5% of books from first-time authors; 95% from unagented writers. Makes outright purchase of $2,500-3,000.** Query for book catalog and ms guidelines; send 9×12 SAE with 3 first-class stamps.
Nonfiction: Juvenile. "We produce tightly-formatted books for middle grade readers. Each series has specific requirements. Potential writers should familiarize themselves with our material." Series deal with history, current events, social issues. Submit outline and first chapter with SASE. All are works for hire, on assignment only. No unsolicited mss.
Recent Title(s): *The Fall of the Roman Republic*, by Don Nardo (history).
Tips: "We expect writers to do thorough research using books, magazines and newspapers. Biased writing—whether liberal or conservative—has no place in our books. We prefer to work with writers who have experience writing nonfiction for middle grade students."

THE LYONS PRESS, 31 W. 21st St., New York NY 10010. (212)620-9580. Fax: (212)929-1836. **Acquisitions:** Lilly Golden, senior editor (sports, cooking); Bryan Oettel, senior editor, (all subjects); Anja Schmidt, associate editor (gardening, adventure); Christopher Pavone, managing editor (food, fiction); Christina Rudofstei, assistant editor (reprints). Estab. 1984. "The Lyons Press publishes practical and literary books, chiefly centered on outdoor subjects—natural history, all sports, gardening, horses, fishing." Publishes hardcover and trade paperback originals and reprints. **Publishes 75-85 titles/year. 30% of books from first-time authors; 75% from unagented writers. Pays varied royalty on retail price.** Publishes book 1 year after acceptance. Accepts simultaneous submissions. Reports in 3 weeks on queries. *Writer's Market* recommends allowing 2 months for reply. Book catalog free.
Nonfiction: Subjects include Americana, animals, art/architecture, cooking/foods/nutrition, gardening, hobbies, nature/environment, science, sports, travel. Query.
Recent Title(s): *North of Now*, by W.D. Wetherell (memoir).

M & T BOOKS, IDG Books Worldwide, Inc., 599 Lexington Ave., New York NY 10022. (212)745-1122. Fax: (212)745-1136. Website: http://www.mispress.com, http://www.idgbooks.com. Associate Publisher: Paul Farrell. **Acquisitions:** Ann Lush, assistant editor; Laura Lewin, editor. Estab. 1984. M & T Books provides high-level guides to advanced programmers and networking professionals using commercial developing environments and the latest technological innovations. Publishes trade paperback originals and reprints. **Publishes 25 titles/year. Receives 250 queries/year. 20% of books from first-time authors; 50% of books from unagented writers. Pays 5-12% royalty on net receipts. Offers $8,000 average advance.** Publishes book 4 months after acceptance of ms. Reports in 2 months on queries. Book catalog free.
Nonfiction: How-to, technical, networking, programming, databases, operating systems. Computer books for advanced users. "We are not about 'business management theory,' but we are about the practical and usable. Beware of poor grammar, spelling and writing in proposals." Query with idea and topic only. *No unsolicited mss.*
Recent Title(s): *XML: A Primer*, by Simon St. Laurent (web development).

MACMILLAN BOOKS, Macmillan General Reference, 1633 Broadway, New York NY 10019. (212)654-8500. **Acquisitions**: Natalie Chapman, publisher (popular reference, history, social sciences, arts, illustrated reference, atlases); Bob Kerler (sports); Betsy Thorpe, editor (health, psychology, parenting, self-help, popular reference); Michelle Tupper, assistant editor (illustrated reference, arts and music, popular culture, history, social sciences). "Our mission is to publish the highest quality and most useful information and consumer reference books." Publishes hardcover originals, trade paperback originals and reprints. **Publishes 30-50 titles/year. Receives 3,000 queries/year. 15% of books from first-time authors; 5% from unagented writers. Pays royalty on retail price or net sales, makes outright purchase or work-for-hire assignments. Offers wide-ranging advance.** Publishes book 1 year after acceptance of ms. Accepts simultaneous submissions. Reports in 2 months on queries and mss, 1 month on proposals.

● Macmillan Books strongly urges writers to submit to them through agents.

Nonfiction: How-to, reference, self-help. Subjects include child guidance/parenting, nutrition, health/medicine, history, language/literature, psychology, recreation, science, sports, writing, atlases. Authors must have interesting and original ideas, top credentials and writing skills and an understanding of their market and audience. *Agented submissions preferred.* Submit outline, 1 sample chapter and proposal package, including table of contents, author credentials, target audience and market analysis. Reviews artwork/photos as part of ms package. Send photocopies.

Recent Title(s): *The People's Medical Society Men's Health and Wellness Encyclopedia*, edited by Charles Inlander.

MACMILLAN BRANDS, Macmillan General Reference, 1633 Broadway, New York NY 10019. (212)654-8500. Website: http://www.mgr.com. **Acquisitions**: Susan Clarey, publisher; Anne Ficklen, executive editor (Weight Watchers, Betty Crocker); Barbara Berger, associate editor (Burpee gardening); Emily Nolan, editor (Weight Watchers, Betty Crocker); Jennifer Griffin, senior editor (cooking); James Willhite, assistant editor (cooking, gardening). MacMillan Brands publishes cooking and gardening reference titles. Publishes hardcover originals, trade paperback originals and reprints. **Publishes 60-100 titles/year. Receives 3,000 queries/year. 15% of books from first-time authors; 5% from unagented writers. Pays royalty on retail price or net sales, or makes outright purchase or work-for-hire assignments. Offers variable advance.** Publishes book 1 year after acceptance of ms. Accepts simultaneous submissio ns. Reports in 2 months on queries and mss, 1 month on proposals.

Nonfiction: Cookbook, how-to, reference. Subjects include cooking/foods/nutrition, gardening. Submit outline, 1 sam ple chapter and proposal package, including table of contents, author credentials, target audience and market analysis. Reviews artwork/photos as part of ms package. Send photocopies.

Recent Title(s): *American Brasserie*, by Rick Tramonto and Gale Gand with Julie Moir Messervy.

MACMILLAN COMPUTER PUBLISHING, 201 W. 103rd St., Indianapolis IN 46290. (317)581-3500. Website: http://www.mcp.com.

Imprint(s): Adobe Press, Brady Games (by invitation), Cisco Press, Hayden Books, Lycos Press, Macmillan Digital Publishing USA, Macmillan Technical Publishing, New Riders Publishing, **Que Publishing** (EarthWeb Press, Que Education & Training), **Sams Publishing** (Borland Press, Red Hat Press, Sams.net), Waite Group Press, Ziff-Davis Press.

MACMILLAN GENERAL REFERENCE, 1633 Broadway, New York NY 10019. (212)654-8500. Fax: (212)654-4850. Website: http://www.mcp.com/mgr. **Acquisitions**: Natalie Chapman, publisher. "We publish popular reference in travel, pet books, consumer information, careers, test preparation, tax guides, cooking, gardening, sports, health, history, psychology, parenting, writing guides, atlases, dictionaries, music, the arts, business, parenting, science, religion." Publishes hardcover originals, trade paperback originals and reprints. **Publishes 400-500 titles/year. Receives 10,000 queries/year. 15% of books from first-time authors; 5% from unagented writers. Pays royalty on retail price or net sales or makes outright purchase or work-for-hire assignments. Offers $1,000-1,000,000 advance depending on imprint.** Publishes book 1 year after acceptance of ms. Accepts simultaneous submissions. Reports in 2 months on queries and mss, 1 month on proposals.

Imprint(s): Macmillan Books, Macmillan Travel (Mike Spring, publisher), **Macmillan Brands and Cookbooks** (Susan Clarey, publisher), **Howell Book House**, (Sean Frawley, publisher); **Arco** (Chuck Wall, publisher); Macmillan Lifestyle Guides (Kathy Nebenhaus, publisher).

Nonfiction: Biography, cookbook, gift book, how-to, illustrated book, multimedia (disk/CD-ROM/cassette with book), reference, self-help. Subjects include Americana, animals, anthropology/archaeology, art/architecture, business/economics, child guidance/parenting, computers/electronics, cooking/foods/nutrition, education, ethnic, gardening, gay/lesbian, government/politics, health/medicine, history, hobbies, language/literature, military/war, money/finance, music/dance, nature/environment, psychology, recreation, religion, science, sociology, software, sports, travel, women's issues/studies, pets, consumer affairs. Submissions must have an original and interesting idea, good credentials and writing skills and an understanding of the market, and audience. Submit outline, 1 sample chapter and proposal package, including table of contents, author credentials, market competition and audience assessment. Reviews artwork/photos as part of ms package. Send photocopies.

Tips: Audience is "people who want practical information."

[A] **MACMILLAN TRAVEL**, Macmillan General Reference, 1633 Broadway, New York NY 10019. (212)654-8500. Website: http://www.frommers.com **Acquisitions**: Michael Spring, publisher. "Macmillan Travel publishes regional travel guides that fit destination-specific formats or series." Publishes trade paperback originals and reprints. **Publishes 60-100 titles/year. Receives 3,000 queries/year. 15% of books from first-time authors. Pays royalty on retail price or net sales, or makes outright purchase or work-for-hire assignments. Offers variable advance.** Publishes book 1 year after acceptance of ms. Accepts simultaneous submissions. Reports in 2 months on queries and mss, 1 month on proposals.

Nonfiction: Subjects include regional, travel. *Agented submissions only.*

Recent Title(s): *Frommer's San Francisco from $60 a Day*, by Erika Genkert (budget travel).

MACMURRAY & BECK, 1649 Downing St., Denver CO 80218. Fax: (303)832-2158. E-mail: ramey@macmurraybeck.com. Website: http://www.macmurraybeck.com. **Acquisitions:** Frederick Ramey, executive editor; Greg Michelson, fiction. "We are interested in reflective personal narrative of high literary quality both fiction and nonfiction." Publishes hardcover and trade paperback originals. **Publishes 5-8 titles/year. 90% of books from first-time authors; 20% from unagented writers. Pays 8-12% royalty on retail price. Offers $2,000-5,000 advance.** Publishes book 18 months after acceptance of ms. Accepts simultaneous submissions. Reports in 3 months on queries and proposals, 4 months on mss. Book catalog $2. Manuscript guidelines free.
Imprint(s): Divina—a speculative imprint (contact Leslie Koffler).
Nonfiction: "We are looking for personal narratives and extraordinary perspectives." Submit outline and 2 sample chapters with SASE. Reviews artwork/photos as part of ms package. Send photocopies.
Fiction: Literary. "We are most interested in debut novels of life in the contemporary West, but we select for voice and literary merit far more than for subject or narrative." Writers often make the mistake of "submitting genre fiction when we are in search of strong literary fiction." Submit synopsis and 3 sample chapters with SASE.
Recent Title(s): *Reeling & Writhing*, by Candida Lawrence (memoir); *Horace Afoot*, by Frederick Reuss (fiction).

MADISON BOOKS, University Press of America, 4720 Boston Way, Lanham MD 20706. (301)459-3366. Fax: (301)459-2118. **Acquisitions:** Nancy Ulrich, acquisitions editor; Julie Kirsch, managing editor. Estab. 1984. Publishes hardcover originals, trade paperback originals and reprints. **Publishes 40 titles/year. Receives 1,200 submissions/year. 15% of books from first-time authors; 65% from unagented writers. Pays 10-15% royalty on net price.** Publishes ms 1 year after acceptance. *Writer's Market* recommends allowing 2 months for reply. Book catalog and ms guidelines for 9×12 SAE with 4 first-class stamps.
Nonfiction: History, biography, contemporary affairs, trade reference. Query or submit outline and sample chapter. *No unsolicited mss.*

MAGE PUBLISHERS INC., 1032 29th St. NW, Washington DC 20007. Fax: (202)342-9269. E-mail: mage1@access.digex.com. Website: http://www.mage.com. **Acquisitions:** Amin Sepehri, assistant to publisher. "We publish books relating to Persian/Iranian culture." Publishes hardcover originals and reprints, trade paperback originals. **Publishes 4 titles/year. Receives 40 queries and 20 mss/year. 10% of books from first-time authors; 95% from unagented writers. Pays variable royalty. Offers $250-1,500 advance.** Publishes book 8-16 months after acceptance of ms. Accepts simultaneous submissions. Reports in 1 month on queries and proposals, 3 months on mss. Book catalog free.
Nonfiction: Biography, children's/juvenile, coffee table book, cookbook, gift book, illustrated book. Subjects include anthropology/archaeology, art/architecture, cooking/foods/nutrition, ethnic, history, language/literature, music/dance, sociology, translation. Query. Reviews artwork/photos as part of ms package. Send photocopies.
Fiction: Ethnic, feminist, historical, literary, mainstream/contemporary, short story collections. Must relate to Persian/Iranian culture. Query.
Poetry: Must relate to Persian/Iranian culture. Query.
Recent Title(s): *Lost Treasures of Persia*, by V. Lukonin (Persian art); *The Lion and the Throne*, by Ferdowsi (mythology).
Tips: Audience is the Iranian-American community in America and Americans interested in Persian culture.

MAIN STREET BOOKS, Doubleday, 1540 Broadway, New York NY 10036. (212)354-6500. **Acquisitions:** Gerald Howard, editor-in-chief. Estab. 1992. "Main Street Books continues the tradition of Dolphin Books of publishing backlists, but we are focusing more on 'up front' books and big sellers in the areas of self-help, fitness and popular culture." Publishes hardcover originals, trade paperback originals and reprints. **Publishes 20-30 titles/year. Receives 600 queries, 200 mss/year. 25% of books from first-time authors. Offers advance and royalties.** Publishes book 18 months after acceptance of ms. Accepts simultaneous submissions, if so noted. Reports in 1 month on queries, 6 months on mss. Doubleday book catalog and ms guidelines free.
Nonfiction: Cookbook, gift book, how-to, humor, illustrated book, self-help. Subjects include Americana, animals, business/economics, child guidance/parenting, cooking/foods/nutrition, education, ethnic, gay/lesbian, health/fitness, money/finance, music/dance, nature/environment, pop psychology, pop culture. Query with SASE, but agented submissions only of manuscripts. Reviews artwork/photos as part of ms package, "but never send unless requested."
Fiction: Literary, pop and commercial. *Agented submissions only.*
Recent Title(s): *Checklist for Your First Baby*, by Susan Kagen Podell, M.S., R.D. (parenting/childcare); *Beeperless Remote*, by Van Whitfield (fiction).

MARCH STREET PRESS, 3413 Wilshire, Greensboro NC 27408. E-mail: rbixby@aol.com. Website: http://users.aol.com/marchst. **Acquisitions:** Robert Bixby, editor/publisher. "We want to support good work by drawing attention to it and to help poets create a lasting legacy beyond reading." Publishes literary chapbooks. **Publishes 6-10 titles/year. Receives 12 queries and 30 mss/year. 50% of books from first-time authors; 100% from unagented writers. Pays 15% royalty. Offers advance of 10 copies.** Publishes book 6 months after acceptance of ms. Accepts simultaneous submissions. Reports in 3 months on mss. Book catalog and ms guidelines for #10 SASE.
Poetry: "My plans are based on the submissions I receive, not vice versa." Submit complete ms.
Recent Title(s): *Everything I Need*, by Keith Taylor.

Tips: "Audience is extremely sophisticated, widely read graduates of M.A., M.F.A. and Ph.D. programs in English and fine arts. Also lovers of significant, vibrant and enriching verse regardless of field of study or endeavor. Most beginning poets, I have found, think it beneath them to read other poets. This is the most glaring flaw in their work. My advice is to read ceaselessly. Otherwise, you may be published, but you will never be accomplished."

MARINER BOOKS, Houghton Mifflin, 222 Berkeley St., Boston MA 02116. (617)351-5000. Fax: (617)351-1202. Website: http://www.hmco.com. **Acquisitions:** John Radziewicz. Estab. 1997. "Houghton Mifflin books give shape to ideas that educate, inform and delight. Mariner is an eclectic list that notably embraces fiction." Publishes trade paperback originals and reprints. **Advance and royalty vary.** Accepts simultaneous submissions. Reports in 2 months on mss.
Nonfiction: Subjects include biography, business/economics, education, government/politics, history, military/war, philosophy, political thought, sociology. Query with SASE.
Fiction: Literary, mainstream/contemporary. Submit synopsis with SASE. *Prefers agented submissions.*
Recent Title(s): *Waiting for Fidel*, by Christopher Hunt (travel); *Kowloon Tong*, by Paul Theroux (fiction).

MARIPOSA, Scholastic, Inc., 555 Broadway, New York NY 10012. (212)343-6100. Website: http://www.scholastic.com. **Acquisitions:** Susana Pasternac, editor. "There is a great need for children's Spanish-language literature, work that is well done and authentic, that fills a *need*, not just a space." Publishes trade paperback originals and reprints. **Publishes 20-25 titles/year (2-3 original titles/year). Receives 40 queries/year. Pays royalty on retail price, varies.** Publishes book 1 year after acceptance of ms. Accepts simultaneous submissions. Reports in 3 months on mss. Book catalog for #10 SASE.
Nonfiction: Children's/juvenile, all areas. "We are introducing more nonfiction; looking for titles that don't have nationalities, that are interesting to everybody." Query with completed ms and SASE. Reviews artwork/photos as part of ms package if important to ms. Send photocopies.
Fiction: Juvenile, picture books, young adult. Query with completed ms and SASE. "We do Spanish-language translations of the Magic School Bus, Clifford, and Goosebumps series."
Recent Title(s): *Gracias, el Pavo de Thanksgiving*, by Joy Cowley, illustrated by Joe Cepeda (fiction).

MARLOR PRESS, INC., 4304 Brigadoon Dr., St. Paul MN 55126. (612)484-4600. Fax: (612)490-1182. **Acquisitions:** Marlin Bree, publisher. Estab. 1981. "We publish quality nonfiction trade paperback books that fit a perceived market need." Publishes trade paperback originals. **Publishes 6 titles/year. Receives 100 queries and 25 mss/year. Pays 8-10% royalty on wholesale price.** Publishes book 8 months after final acceptance. Reports in 1 month. Book catalog for 6×9 SAE with 2 first-class stamps. Manuscript guidelines for #10 SASE.
Nonfiction: Travel, boating, children's and gift books. "Primarily how-to stuff. No anecdotal reminiscences or biographical materials." Query first; submit outline with sample chapters only when requested. *No unsolicited mss.* Do not send full ms. Reviews artwork/photos as part of ms package.
Recent Title(s): *Guest Afloat: The Essential Guide to Being a Welcome Guest on Board a Boat*, by Barbara Branfield and Sara Slater.
Tips: "We only look for nonfiction titles and want more general interest boating and how-to travel books."

MARLOWE & COMPANY, Avalon Publishing Group, 841 Broadway, 4th Floor, New York NY 10003. (212)614-7880. Publisher: Neil Ortenberg. **Acquisitions:** Jeri T. Smith, acquisitions editor. "We feature challenging, entertaining and topical titles in our extensive publishing program." Publishes hardcover and trade paperback originals and reprints. **Publishes 60 titles/year. Receives 800 queries/year. 5% of books from first-time authors; 5% from unagented writers. Pays 10% royalty on retail price for hardcover, 6% for paperback. Offers advance of 50% of anticipated first printing.** Publishes book 1 year after acceptance of ms. Reports in 2 months on queries. Book catalog free.
Nonfiction: Health/medicine, New Age, history. Query with SASE. *No unsolicited submissions.*
Fiction: Literary. "We are looking for literary, rather than genre fiction." Query with SASE. *No unsolicited submissions.*
Recent Title(s): *Dog Soldiers: Societies of the Plains*, by Thomas Mails (history); *Amistad*, by David Pesci (fiction).

N **MASQUERADE BOOKS**, Crescent Publishing, 801 Second Ave., New York NY 10017. (212)661-7878. Fax: (212)986-7355. E-mail: masqbks@aol.com. **Acquisitions**: Marti Hohmann, editor-in-chief (short stories, writing by women, avant-garde fiction); Jennifer Rent, managing editor. Masquerade is "the world's largest publisher of erotica." Publishes hardcover, trade paperback and mass market paperback originals and reprints. **Publishes 120 titles/year. Receives 500 queries and 1,000 mss/year. 10% of books from first-time authors; 95% from unagented writers. Pays 5% royalty on retail price. Offers $1,500 advance.** Publishes book 6 months after acceptance of ms. Reports in 1 month on queries and proposals, 3 months on mss. Manuscript guidelines free.
Imprint(s): Masquerade (heterosexual, 50 titles/year), Rosebud (lesbian, 20 titles/year), Badboy (gay, 12 titles/year), Rhino*ceros* (heterosexual literary, 25 titles/year), Hard Candy (gay/lesbian literary, 13 titles/year).
Nonfiction: Subjects include gay/lesbian, self-help, sex, women's issues/studies. Submit proposal package, including cover letter with bio, outline, 3 sample chapters and SASE.
Fiction: Erotica, gay/lesbian, literary, short story collections, translation. Writing in all categories must be erotic or thematically concerned with sex and/or sexuality. Query or submit synopsis, 3 sample chapters, author bio and SASE.
Recent Title(s): *Taking Liberties: Gay Men's Essays on Politics, Culture & Sex*, edited by Michael Bronski; *White Stains*, by Anaïs Nin (short story collection).

Tips: "Our readers are long-time lovers of textual erotica and newcomers to the genre. Please do not send poorly-written material that is better placed in skin mags. We are always interested in well-done contemporary S&M and writing by women."

MASTERS PRESS, NTC/Contemporary Group, 1214 W. Boston Post Rd., #302, Mamaroneck NY 10543. (914)834-8284. Website: http://www.masterspress.com. Editorial Director: John T. Nolan. **Acquisitions:** Ken Samuelson, acquisitions editor. Estab. 1986. "Our audience is sports enthusiasts and participants, people interested in fitness." Publishes hardcover and trade paperback originals. **Publishes 45-50 titles/year; imprint publishes 20 titles/year. Receives 60 queries and 50 mss/year. 25% of books from first-time authors; 75% from unagented writers. Pays 10-15% royalty. Offers $1,000-5,000 advance.** Publishes book 1 year after acceptance. Accepts simultaneous submissions. Reports in 2 months on proposals. Book catalog free.
Imprint(s): Spalding Sports Library.
- Masters Press was purchased by NTC/Contemporary Group.

Nonfiction: Biography, how-to, reference, self-help. Subjects include recreation, sports, fitness. Submit outline, 2 sample chapters, author bio and marketing ideas.
Recent Title(s): *Cross Training for Fitness*, by Matt Brzycki.

MAYFIELD PUBLISHING COMPANY, 1280 Villa St., Mountain View CA 94041. Fax: (650)960-0826. Website: http://www.mayfieldpub.com. **Acquisitions:** Ken King, (philosophy, religion); Holly Allen, (communications); Frank Graham, (psychology, parenting); Jan Beatty, (anthropology, theater, art); Renee Deljon, (English); Michele Sordi, (health, physical eduction); Serina Beauparlant (sociology, women's studies). Mayfield Publishing Company publishers "books that solve teaching problems for college level courses in the humanities and social sciences." **Publishes 70-80 titles/year.** Accepts simultaneous submissions. Manuscript guidelines free.
Nonfiction: Textbook (*college only*). Subjects include anthropology/archaeology, art, child guidance/parenting, communications/theater, health/physical education, English composition, music/dance, philosophy, psychology, religion, sociology, women's studies. Submit proposal package including outline, table of contents, sample chapter, description of proposed market.

MBI PUBLISHING, (formerly Motorbooks International), 729 Prospect Ave., Osceola WI 54020. Fax: (715)294-4448. E-mail: mbibks@win.bright.net. Website: http://www.motorbooks.com. Publishing Director: Jack Savage. **Acquisitions:** Lee Klancher, acquisitions editor (tractors, stock car racing, American cars) Mike Haenggi, acquisitions editor (aviation, military history); Keith Mathiowetz, acquisitions editor (American cars, Americana, railroading); Anne McKenna, acquisitions editor (racing, bicycles); Paul Johnson, acquisitions editor (automotive how-to); Zack Miller, senior editor (foreign cars, racing, bicycles). Estab. 1973. "We are a transportation-related publisher: cars, motorcycles, racing, trucks, tractors—also Americana, aviation and military history." Publishes hardcover and paperback originals. **Publishes 125 titles/year. 95% of books from unagented writers. Pays 12% royalty on net receipts. Offers $3,000 average advance.** Publishes book 1 year after acceptance. Accepts simultaneous submissions. Reports in 3 months. Free book catalog. Manuscript guidelines for #10 SASE.
Imprint(s): Bicycle Books, Crestline, Zenith Books.
Nonfiction: History, how-to, photography (as they relate to cars, trucks, motorcycles, motor sports, aviation—domestic, foreign and military). Accepts nonfiction translations. Submit outline, 1-2 sample chapters and sample of illustrations. "State qualifications for doing book." Reviews artwork/photos as part of ms package.
Recent Title(s): *America's Special Forces*, by David Bohrer (modern military).

McBOOKS PRESS, 120 W. State St., Ithaca NY 14850. (607)272-2114. Website: http://www.mcbooks.com. Publisher: Alexander G. Skutt. **Acquisitions:** (Ms.) S.K. List, editorial director. "We are a growing publishing house interested in any nonfiction of substance." Publishes trade paperback and hardcover originals and reprints. **Publishes 12 titles/year. Pays 5-10% royalty on retail price. Offers $1,000-5,000 advance.** Reports in 1 month on queries, 2 months on proposals.
Nonfiction: Subjects include child guidance/parenting, cooking, nutrition (vegetarianism), regional (New York State), sports. "Authors' ability to promote a plus." Query or submit outline and 2 sample chapters with SASE.
Recent Title(s): *A+ Parents: Help Your Child Learn and Succeed in School*, by Adrienne Mack.

MARGARET K. McELDERRY BOOKS, Simon & Schuster Children's Publishing Division, Simon & Schuster, 1230 Sixth Ave., New York NY 10020. (212)698-7200. Fax: (212)698-2796. Editor-at-large: Margaret K. McElderry. **Acquisitions:** Emma D. Dryden, senior editor; Karen Riskin, assistant editor. Estab. 1971. Publishes quality material for preschoolers to 16-year-olds, but publishes only a few YAs. "We are more interested in superior writing and illustration than in a particular 'type' of book." Publishes hardcover originals. **Publishes 25 titles/year. Receives 5,000 queries/year. 10% of books from first-time authors; 66% from unagented writers. Average print order is 4,000-6,000 for a first teen book; 8,000-10,000 for a first picture book. Pays royalty on retail price: 10% fiction; picture book, 5% author, 5% illustrator. Offers $5,000-6,000 advance for new authors.** Publishes book 18 months after contract signing. Manuscript guidelines for #10 SASE.
Nonfiction: Children's/juvenile, adventure, biography, history. "Read. The field is competitive. See what's been done and what's out there before submitting. Looks for originality of ideas, clarity and felicity of expression, well-organized

plot and strong characterization (fiction) or clear exposition (nonfiction); quality. We will accept one-page query letters for picture books or novels." *No unsolicited mss.*

Fiction: Juvenile only. Adventure, fantasy, historical, mainstream/contemporary, mystery, science fiction. Query with SASE. *No unsolicited mss.*

Poetry: Query with 3 sample poems.

Recent Title(s): *How It Was with Dooms: A True Story from Africa*, by Carol Hopcraft (nonfiction); *The Boggart and the Monster*, by Susan Cooper (fiction).

Tips: "Freelance writers should be aware of the swing away from teen-age novels to books for younger readers and of the growing need for beginning chapter books for children just learning to read on their own."

McFARLAND & COMPANY, INC., PUBLISHERS, Box 611, Jefferson NC 28640. (336)246-4460. Fax: (336)246-5018. E-mail: mcfarland@skybest.com. Website: http://www.mcfarlandpub.com. **Acquisitions:** Robert Franklin, president and editor-in-chief; Steve Wilson, editor; Virginia Tobiassen, editor. Estab. 1979. Publishes reference books and scholarly, technical and professional monographs. "We will consider any scholarly book—with authorial maturity and competent grasp of subject." Publishes mostly hardcover and a few "quality" paperback originals; a non-"trade" publisher. **Publishes 150 titles/year. Receives 1,200 submissions/year. 70% of books from first-time authors; 95% from unagented writers. Pays 10-12½% royalty on net receipts. No advance.** Publishes book 10 months after acceptance. Reports in 2 weeks. *Writer's Market* recommends allowing 2 months for reply.

Nonfiction: Reference books and scholarly, technical and professional monographs. Subjects include African American studies (very strong), art, business, chess, Civil War, drama/theater, cinema/radio/TV (very strong), health, history, librarianship (very strong), music, pop culture, sociology, sports/recreation (very strong), women's studies (very strong), world affairs (very strong). Reference books are particularly wanted—fresh material (i.e., not in head-to-head competition with an established title). "We prefer manuscripts of 250 or more double-spaced pages. Our market is worldwide and libraries are an important part." No fiction, New Age, exposés, poetry, children's books, devotional/inspirational, Bible studies, works or personal essays. Query with outline and sample chapters. Reviews artwork/photos as part of ms package.

Recent Title(s): *Television Westerns Episode Guide: All United States Series, 1949-1996*, by Harris M. Lentz III; *The Cultural Encyclopedia of Baseball*, by Jonathan Fraser Light.

Tips: "We want well-organized knowledge of an area in which there is not information coverage at present, plus reliability so we don't feel we have to check absolutely everything."

McGRAW-HILL COMPANIES, 1221 Avenue of the Americas, New York NY 10020. Website: http://www.mcgraw-hill.com. Divisions include **Business McGraw Hill**; **Computing McGraw Hill**; Glencoe/McGraw Hill; McGraw-Hill Higher Education; McGraw Hill Inc./TAB Books; McGraw-Hill Ryerson (Canada), **Osborne/McGraw-Hill**, McGraw-Hill Professional Book Group. General interest publisher of nonfiction. Query before submitting.

McGREGOR PUBLISHING, 118 S. Westshore Blvd., Suite 233, Tampa FL 33609. (813)254-2665 or (888)405-2665. Fax: (813)254-6177. E-mail: mcgregpub@aol.com. **Acquisitions:** Dave Rosenbaum, acquisitions editor. "We publish nonfiction books that tell the story behind the story." Publishes hardcover and trade paperback originals. **Publishes 4-6 titles/year. Receives 20 queries and 12 mss/year. 75% of books from first-time authors; 100% from unagented writers. Pays 10-12% on retail price; 13-16% on wholesale price. Advances vary.** Publishes book 1 year after acceptance of ms. Accepts simultaneous submissions. Reports in 1 month on queries and proposals, 2 months on mss. Book catalog and ms guidelines free.

Nonfiction: Biography, how-to, self-help. Subjects include business/economics, ethnic, history, money/finance, regional, sports. "We're always looking for regional nonfiction titles, and especially for sports, biographies, true crime, self-help and how-to books." Query or submit outline with 2 sample chapters.

Fiction: Mystery, suspense. Query or submit synopsis with 2 sample chapters.

Recent Title(s): *The Canadian's Guide to Florida*, by Fred Wright (travel).

Tips: "We pride ourselves on working closely with an author and producing a quality product with strong promotional campaigns."

MEADOWBROOK PRESS, 5451 Smetana Dr., Minnetonka MN 55343. (612)930-1100. Fax: (612)930-1940. **Acquisitions:** Heather Hooper, submissions editor. Estab. 1975. "We are a family-oriented press which specializes in parenting books, party books, humorous quote books, humorous children's poetry books, children's activity books and juvenile fiction." Publishes trade paperback originals and reprints. **Publishes 15 titles/year. Receives 1,500 queries/year. 15% of books from first-time authors.** Publishes book 1 year after acceptance. Accepts simultaneous submissions. Reports in 3 months on queries. Book catalog and ms guidelines for #10 SASE.

- Meadowbrook needs parenting titles, humorous children's poetry and juvenile fiction.

Nonfiction: How-to, humor, reference. Subjects include baby and childcare, senior citizens, children's activities, relationships. No academic or autobiography. Query with outline and sample chapters. "We prefer a query first; then we will request an outline and/or sample material." Send for guidelines.

Recent Title(s): *No More Homework! No More Tests!*, selected by Bruce Lansky, illustrated by Stephen Carpenter (poetry); *The Kids' Pick-a-Party Book*, by Penny Warner.

Tips: "Always send for fiction and poetry guidelines before submitting material. We do not accept unsolicited picture book submissions."

MERCURY HOUSE, 785 Market St., Suite 1500, San Francisco CA 94103. (415)974-0729. Fax: (415)974-0832. Website: http://www.wenet.net/~mercury/. **Acquisitions:** Tom Christensen, executive director; K. Janene-Nelson, managing editor. "Mercury House is a nonprofit corporation guided by a dedication to literary values. It exists to promote professional publishing services to writers largely abandoned by market-driven commercial presses. Our purpose is to promote the free exchange of ideas, including minority viewpoints, by providing our writers with both an enduring format and the widest possible audience for their work." Publishes hardcover originals and trade paperbacks originals and reprints. **Averages 8 titles/year. Pays 10-15% royalty on retail price. Offers $3,000-5,000 advance.** Publishes book 1 year after acceptance of ms. Reports in 3 months. Catalog for 55¢ postage.

Nonfiction: Biography, essays, memoirs. Subjects include anthropology, ethnic, gay/lesbian, politics/current affairs, language/literature, literary current affairs, nature/environment, philosophy, translation, literary travel, women's issues/studies, human rights/indigenous peoples. "Within the subjects we publish, we are above all a literary publisher looking for high quality writing and innovative book structure, research, etc." Query with 1 sample chapter.

Fiction: Ethnic, experimental, feminist, gay/lesbian, historical, literary, short story collections, literature in translation. "Very limited spots. We prefer sample chapters to determine writing style. It's very important to submit only if the subject is appropriate (as listed), though we do enjoy mutations/blending of genres (high quality, thoughtful work!)." No mainstream, thrillers, sexy books." Query first.

Recent Title(s): *In Few Words/En Pocas Palabras*, by José Antonio Burciaga (Latino folk wit and wisdom); *Ledoyt*, by Emshwiller (fiction).

Tips: "Our reader is a person who is discriminating about his/her reading material, someone who appreciates the extra care we devote to design, paper, cover, and exterior excellence to go along with the high quality of the writing itself. Be patient with us concerning responses: it's easier to reject the manuscript of a nagging author than it is to decide upon it. The manner in which an author deals with us (via letter or phone) gives us a sense of how it would be to work with this person for a whole project; good books with troublesome authors are to be avoided."

MERIWETHER PUBLISHING LTD., 885 Elkton Dr., Colorado Springs CO 80907-3557. (719)594-4422. **Acquisitions:** Arthur Zapel, Theodore Zapel, Rhonda Wray, editors. Estab. 1969. Meriwether publishes theater books, games and videos; speech resources; plays, skits and musicals; and resources for gifted students. Publishes trade paperback originals and reprints. **Publishes 10-12 books/year; 50-60 plays/year. Receives 1,200 submissions/year. 50% of books from first-time authors; 90% from unagented writers. Pays 10% royalty on retail price or makes outright purchase.** Publishes book 6 months after acceptance. Accepts simultaneous submissions. Reports in 2 months. Book catalog and ms guidelines for $2.

- Meriwether is looking for books of short scenes and textbooks on directing, staging, make-up, lighting, etc.

Nonfiction: How-to, reference, educational, humor. Also textbooks. Subjects include art/theatre/drama, music/dance, recreation, religion. "We publish unusual textbooks or trade books related to the communication or performing arts and how-to books on staging, costuming, lighting, etc. We are not interested in religious titles with fundamentalist themes or approaches—we prefer mainstream religion titles." Query or submit outline/synopsis and sample chapters.

Recent Title(s): *Don't Give Up the Script*, by Robert Allen.

Fiction: Plays and musicals—humorous, mainstream, mystery, religious, suspense.

Tips: "Our educational books are sold to teachers and students at college and high school levels. Our religious books are sold to youth activity directors, pastors and choir directors. Our trade books are directed at the public with a sense of humor. Another group of buyers is the professional theatre, radio and TV category. We focus more on books of plays and theater texts."

THE MESSAGE COMPANY, 4 Camino Azul, Sante Fe NM 87505. (505)474-0998. **Acquisitions:** James Berry, president. The Message Company packages alternative topics for the mainstream market. Publishes trade paperback originals and reprints. **Publishes 6-8 titles/year. Receives 20 queries and 12 mss/year. 80% of books from first-time authors; 100% from unagented writers. Pays 6-8% royalty on retail price or makes outright purchase of $500-2,000. No advance.** Publishes book 3 months after acceptance of ms. Accepts simultaneous submissions. Book catalog for 6×9 SAE with 2 first-class stamps.

Nonfiction: How-to. Subjects include business/economics (spirituality in business-related only), government/politics (freedom/privacy issues only), science (new energy/new science only). Submit proposal package, including outline and sample chapters. Reviews artwork/photos as part of ms package. Send photocopies.

Recent Title(s): *Physics of Love*, by Dale Pond.

MEYERBOOKS, PUBLISHER, P.O. Box 427, Glenwood IL 60425-0427. (708)757-4950. **Acquisitions:** David Meyer, publisher. Estab. 1976. Imprint is David Meyer Magic Books. Publishes hardcover and trade paperback originals and reprints. **Publishes 5 titles/year. Pays 10-15% royalty on wholesale or retail price. No advance.** Reports in 3 months on queries.

Nonfiction: History, reference. Subjects include Americana, herbal studies, history of stage magic. Query with SASE.

Recent Title(s): *The Hanlon Brothers: Their Amazing Acrobatics, Pantomimes and Stage Specials*, by McKinven (theatrical history).

MICHIGAN STATE UNIVERSITY PRESS, 1405 S. Harrison Rd., Manly Miles Bldg., Suite 25, East Lansing MI 48823-5202. (517)355-9543. Fax: (800)678-2120; local/international (517)432-2611. E-mail: msp05@admin.msu.edu. Website: http://web.msu.edu/unit/msupress. **Acquisitions:** Martha Bates, acquisitions editor. Estab. 1947. "We publish

scholarly books that further scholarship in their particular field. In addition, we publish nonfiction that addresses, in a more contemporary way, social concerns, such as diversity, civil rights, the environment." Publishes hardcover and softcover originals. **Publishes 35 titles/year. Receives 1,000 submissions/year. 75% of books from first-time authors; 100% from unagented writers. Royalties vary.** Publishes ms 18 months after acceptance. Book catalog and ms guidelines for 9×12 SASE.
Imprint(s): Lotus, Colleagues.
Nonfiction: Scholarly, trade. Subjects include Afro-American studies, American regional history, American literature and criticism, American studies, business, Canadian studies, contemporary African studies, contemporary civil rights history, creative nonfiction, Great Lakes regional, labor studies, legal studies, Native American studies, women's studies. Series: Canadian Series, Lotus Poetry Series, Schoolcraft Series, Rhetoric and Public Affairs Series, Native American Series, Colleagues Books. Query with outline and sample chapters. Reviews artwork/photos.
Recent Title(s): *Profiles in Diversity: Women in the New South Africa*, by Patricia Romero.

N **MIDDLE ATLANTIC PRESS**, 10 Twosome Dr., Box 600, Moorestown NJ 08057. **Acquisitions**: Carol Hupping, acquisitions editor. Middle Atlantic Press is a regional publisher focusing on New York, New Jersey, Pennsylvania and Delaware. Publishes trade paperback originals and mass market paperback originals. **Publishes 4-6 titles/year. Receives 24 queries and 12 mss/year. 5% of books from first-time authors; 50% from unagented writers. Offers $3,000-5,000 advance.** Publishes book 3 months after acceptance of ms. Accepts simultaneous submissions. Reports in 1 week on queries, 1 month on proposals.
Imprint(s): Terence Doherty.
Nonfiction: Children's/juvenile, cookbook. Subjects include history, recreation, regional, sports. Submit proposal package, outline with 3 sample chapters and SASE. Sometimes reviews artwork/photos as part of ms package. Send photocopies.
Fiction: Young adult. Submit synopsis.
Recent Title(s): *Filling in the Seams*, by Chris Edwards (sports); *Julie and the Marigold Boy*, by Larona Homer (fiction).

MID-LIST PRESS, Jackson, Hart & Leslie, 4324 12th Ave S., Minneapolis MN 55407-3218. Website: http://www.midlist.org. Publisher: Marianne Nora. **Acquisitions:** Lane Stiles, senior editor. Estab. 1989. Mid-List Press is an independent press. "Mid-List Press publishes books of high literary merit and fresh artistic vision by new and emerging writers." In addition to publishing the annual winners of the Mid-List Press First Series Awards, Mid-List Press publishes fiction and creative nonfiction by first-time and established writers. Publishes hardcover and trade paperback originals. **Publishes minimum 4 titles/year. Pays 40-50% royalty of profits. Offers $500-1,000 advance.** Send SASE for First Series guidelines and/or general submission guidelines; also available online.
Recent Title(s): *The Mensch*, by David Weiss (fiction); *At the Bottom of the Sky*, by Donald Merrill (poetry).

N **MIDMARCH ARTS PRESS**, 300 Riverside Dr., New York NY 10025-5239. (212)666-6990. **Acquisitions**: S. Moore, editor (art/literature). Midmarch Arts Press publishes books on the arts, art history, criticism and poetry. Publishes hardcover and trade paperback originals. **Publishes 4-6 titles/year. Receives 60-100 queries and 15 mss/year. 1% of books from first-time authors; 100% from unagented writers. Pays 10% minimum royalty on retail price.** Publishes book 3 months after acceptance of ms. Reports in 3 months. Book catalog and ms guidelines for #10 SASE.
Nonfiction: Subjects include art/architecture, photography. Query. Reviews artwork/photos as part of ms package. Send photocopies.
Poetry: Query.
Recent Title(s): *Almost Lost to History: The Women Artists of Italian Futurism*, by Mirella Bentivoiglio and Franca Zoccoli (art history); *Sight Lines* by Charlotte Mandel (poetry).

N **MIDNIGHT MARQUEE PRESS, INC.**, 9721 Britinay Lane, Baltimore MD 21234. (410)665-1198. Fax: (410)665-9207. E-mail: mmarquee@aol.com. Website: http://www.midmar.com. **Acquisitions**: Gary J. Svehla, president. Midnight Marquee Press publishes film history and biographies. Publishes trade paperback originals. **Publishes 8 titles/year. Receives 20 queries and 15 mss/year. 50% of books from first-time authors; 100% from unagented writers. Pays 10-12½% royalty on wholesale price.** Accepts simultaneous submissions. Reports in 2 months on queries and proposals, 4 months on mss. Book catalog free. Manuscript guidelines for #10 SASE.
Nonfiction: Film history or biography. Query with SASE. Reviews artwork/photos as part of ms package. Send photocopies.
Recent Title(s): *Psychos! Sickos! Sequels! Horror Films of the 1980s*, by John Stell.

MILKWEED EDITIONS, 430 First Ave. N, Suite 400, Minneapolis MN 55401-1743. (612)332-3192. Website: http://www.milkweed.org. **Acquisitions:** Emilie Buchwald, publisher; Elisabeth Fitz, manuscript coordinator. Estab. 1980. "Milkweed Editions publishes with the intention of making a humane impact on society in the belief that literature is a transformative art uniquely able to convey the essential experiences of the human heart and spirit." Publishes hardcover originals and paperback originals and reprints. **Publishes 20 titles/year. Receives 2,000 submissions/year. 30% of books from first-time authors; 70% from unagented writers. Pays 7½% royalty on list price. Advance varies.** Publishes work 1-2 years after acceptance. Accepts simultaneous submissions. Reports in 6 months. Book catalog for $1.50. Manuscript guidelines for SASE.

Nonfiction: Literary. Subjects include language/literature, nature/environment. Query with 2-3 sample chapters and an SASE for our response.
Fiction: Literary. Novels for readers aged 8-14. High literary quality. Query with 2-3 sample chapters and SASE.
Recent Title(s): *Persistent Rumours*, by Lee Langley (fiction); *The Most Wonderful Books: Writers on Discovering the Pleasures of Reading*, edited by Michael Dorns and Emilie Buchwald.
Tips: "We are looking for excellent writing in fiction, nonfiction, poetry and children's novels, with the intent of making a humane impact on society. Send for guidelines. Acquaint yourself with our books in terms of style and quality before submitting. Many factors influence our selection process, so don't get discouraged. Nonfiction is taking a predominantly environmental focus. We no longer publish children's biographies. We read poetry in January and June only."

THE MILLBROOK PRESS INC., 2 Old New Milford Rd., Brookfield CT 06804. Fax: (203)775-5643. Senior Vice President/Publisher: Jean Reynolds. Editor: Laura Walsh. Senior Editor: Amy Shields. **Acquisitions:** Meghann Hall, manuscript coordinator. Estab. 1989. "Millbrook Press publishes quality children's books that educate and entertain." Publishes hardcover and paperback originals. **Publishes 150 titles/year. Pays varying royalty on wholesale price or makes outright purchase. Advance varies.** Publishes book 1 year after acceptance of ms. Reports in 1 month on queries and proposals. Book catalog for 9×12 SAE with 4 first-class stamps. Manuscript guidelines for #10 SASE.
Imprint(s): Twenty-First Century Books (Pat Culleton, publisher; Virginia Koeth, editor).
Nonfiction: Children's/juvenile. Subjects include animals, anthropology/archaeology, ethnic, government/politics, health/medicine, history, hobbies, nature/environment, science, sports. "We publish curriculum-related nonfiction for the school/library market. Mistakes writers most often make when submitting nonfiction are failure to research competing titles and failure to research school curriculum." Query or submit outline and 1 sample chapter.
Recent Title(s): *More Nature in Your Backyard*, by Susan Lang.

MINNESOTA HISTORICAL SOCIETY PRESS, Minnesota Historical Society, 345 Kellogg Blvd. W., St. Paul MN 55102-1906. (612)297-4457. Fax: (612)297-1345. Website: http://www.mnhs.org. **Acquisitions:** Ann Regan, managing editor. Minnesota Historical Society Press publishes both scholarly and general interest books that contribute to the understanding of Minnesota and Midwestern history. Publishes hardcover and trade paperback originals, trade paperback reprints. **Publishes 10 titles/year (5 for each imprint). Receives 100 queries and 25 mss/year. 50% of books from first-time authors; 100% from unagented writers. Royalties are negotiated.** Publishes book 14 months after acceptance. Reports in 1 month on queries. *Writer's Market* recommends allowing 2 months for reply. Book catalog free.

- Minnesota Historical Society Press is getting many inappropriate submissions from their listing. *A regional connection is required.*

Imprint(s): Borealis Books (reprints only); Midwest Reflections (memoir and personal history).
Nonfiction: Regional works only: biography, coffee table book, cookbook, illustrated book, reference. Subjects include anthropology/archaeology, art/architecture, history, memoir, photography, regional, women's issues/studies, Native American studies. Query with proposal package including letter, outline, vita, sample chapter. Reviews artwork/photos as part of ms package. Send photocopies.
Recent Title(s): *Twin Cities: Then and Now*, by Larry Millett, photography by Jerry Mathiason.

MINSTREL BOOKS, Pocket Books for Young Readers, Simon & Schuster, 1230 Avenue of the Americas, New York NY 10020. (212)698-7669. Website: http://www.simonsayskids.com. Editorial director: Patricia McDonald. **Acquisitions:**Attn: Manuscript proposals. Estab. 1986. "Minstrel publishes fun, kid-oriented books, the kinds kids pick for themselves, for middle grade readers, ages 8-12. " Publishes hardcover originals and reprints, trade paperback originals. **Publishes 125 titles/year. Receives 1,200 queries/year. Less than 25% from first-time authors; less than 25% from unagented writers. Pays 6-8% royalty on retail price. Advance varies.** Publishes book 2 years after acceptance of ms. Accepts simultaneous submissions. Reports in 3 months on queries. Book catalog and ms guidelines free.
Nonfiction: Children's/juvenile—middle grades, ages 8-12. Subjects include celebrity biographies and books about TV shows. Query with outline, sample chapters and SASE.
Fiction: Middle grade fiction for ages 8-12: animal stories, fantasy, humor, juvenile, mystery, suspense. No picture books. "Thrillers are very popular, and 'humor at school' books." Query with synopsis/outline, sample chapters and SASE.
Recent Title(s): *Nickelodeon® The Big Help™ Book: 365 Ways You Can Make a Difference Volunteering*, by Alan Goodman (nonfiction); *R.L. Stine's Ghosts of Fear Street*, by R.L. Stine (fiction).
Tips: "Hang out with kids to make sure your dialogue and subject matter are accurate."

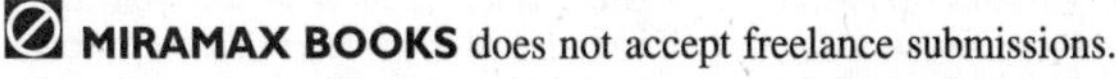
MIRAMAX BOOKS does not accept freelance submissions.

MIS PRESS, IDG Books Worldwide, Inc., 599 Lexington Ave., Suite 2300, New York NY 10022. (212)745-1122. Website: http://www.mispress.com., http://www.idgbooks.com. **Acquisitions:** Walter Bruce, associate publisher. "MIS Press provides practical guides to the general PC user on how to use their PC, including upgrading and maintaining hardware, how to use software packages and applications like Microsoft Office 97 and Windows 95, and guides to the Internet and the World Wide Web." Publishes trade paperback originals. **Publishes 50 titles/year. Receives 250 queries/year. 20% of books from first-time authors; 50% from unagented writers. Pays 5-15% royalty on net price received (receipts), or makes outright work-for-hire purchase of $5,000-20,000. Offers $5,000-10,000 advance.** Publishes book 4 months after acceptance. Accepts simultaneous submissions. Book catalog and ms guidelines free.

Nonfiction: Technical, computer, electronic, internet, World Wide Web. "MIS Press publishes titles related to computer software or hardware." Submit title ideas and cv. *No unsolicited mss.*
Recent Title(s): *The Windows 95 Registry*, by John Woram.
Tips: "Our audience consists of low-level, brand new computer users. Beginners. A more mass market appeal."

MITCHELL LANE PUBLISHERS, P.O. Box 200, Childs MD 21916-0200. Fax: (410)392-4781. **Acquisitions:** Barbara Mitchell, publisher. "We only publish multicultural biographies." Publishes hardcover and trade paperback originals. **Publishes 8-15 titles/year. 10% of books from first-time authors; 100% from unagented writers. Makes outright purchase on work-for-hire basis.** "Looking for freelancers to research, interview subjects and write multicultural biographies for children and young adults." **No advance.** Publishes book 1 year after acceptance of ms. Reports in 2 months. Book catalog free.
Nonfiction: Biography, multicultural. Ethnic subjects. Query with SASE.
Recent Title(s): *Rafael Palmeiro: Living the American Dream*, by E. Brandt (biography).

MODERN LANGUAGE ASSOCIATION OF AMERICA, Dept. WM, 10 Astor Pl., New York NY 10003. (212)475-9500. Fax: (212)477-9863. **Acquisitions:** Joseph Gibaldi, director of book acquisitions and development. Director of MLA Book Publications: Martha Evans. Estab. 1883. Publishes on current issues in literary and linguistic research and teaching of language and literature at postsecondary level. Publishes hardcover and paperback originals. **Publishes 15 titles/year. Receives 125 submissions/year. 100% of books from unagented writers. Pays 5-10% royalty on net proceeds.** Publishes book 1 year after acceptance. Reports in 2 months on mss. Book catalog free.
Nonfiction: Scholarly, professional. Language and literature subjects. No critical monographs. Query with outline.

MONACELLI PRESS, 10 E. 92nd St., New York NY 10128. (212)831-0248. **Acquisitions:** Andrea Monfried, editor. Estab. 1994. "Monacelli Press produces high-quality illustrated books in architecture, fine arts, decorative arts, landscape and photography." Publishes hardcover and trade paperback originals. **Publishes 25-30 titles/year. Receives over 100 queries and mss/year. 10% of books from first-time authors; 90% from unagented writers. Pays royalty on retail price. Offers occasional advance, amount negotiable.** Publishes book 18 months after acceptance of ms. Accepts simultaneous submissions. Reports in 3 months on queries. Book catalog free.
Nonfiction: Coffee table book. Subjects include art/architecture. Query with outline, 1 sample chapter and SASE. Reviews artwork/photos as part of ms package. Send transparencies, duplicate slides best. (Monacelli does not assume responsibility for unsolicited artwork; call if you are uncertain about what to send.)
Recent Title(s): *Henry Hobson Richardson: A Genius for Architecture*, by Margaret Henderson Floyd, photographs by Paul Warhol.

N **MONUMENT PRESS**, P.O. Box 140361, Las Colinas TX. 75014-0361. (214)686-5332. **Acquisitions:** Mary Markal. Publishes trade paperback originals. **Publishes 15 titles/year. Receives 300 queries and 50 mss/year. 100% of books from first-time authors; 100% from unagented writers. Pays 4% minimum royalty on retail price.** Publishes book 1-2 years after acceptance of ms. Reports in 4 months. Book catalog for 6×9 SAE with 6 first-class stamps. Manuscript guidelines for #10 SASE.
Nonfiction: Textbook. Subjects include gay/lesbian, government/politics, health/medicine, military/war, religion, women's issues/studies. Query with outline and 2 sample chapters. *All unsolicited mss returned unopened.*
Recent Title(s): *Military Secret*, by Robert Graham (homosexuality in Navy).

MOODY PRESS, Moody Bible Institute, 820 N. LaSalle Blvd., Chicago IL 60610. (312)329-2101. Fax: (312)329-2144. **Acquisitions:** Acquisitions Coordinator. Estab. 1894. "The mission of Moody Press is to educate and edify the Christian and to evangelize the non-Christian by ethically publishing conservative, evangelical Christian literature and other media for all ages around the world; and to help provide resources for Moody Bible Institute in its training of future Christian leaders." Publishes hardcover, trade and mass market paperback originals and hardcover and mass market paperback reprints. **Publishes 60 titles/year; imprint publishes 5-10 titles/year. Receives 1,500 queries and 2,000 mss/year. Less than 1% of books from first-time authors; 99% from unagented writers. Royalty varies. Offers $500-50,000 advance.** Publishes book 6 months after acceptance of ms. Accepts simultaneous submissions but prefers not to. Reports in 2 months. Book catalog for 9×12 SAE with 4 first-class stamps. Guidelines for #10 SASE.
Imprint(s): Northfield Publishing.
Nonfiction: Children's/juvenile, gift book, general Christian living. Subjects include child guidance/parenting, money/finance, religion, women's issues/studies. "Look at our recent publications, and convince us of what sets your book apart from all the rest on bookstore shelves and why it's consistent with our publications. Many writers don't do enough research of the market or of our needs." Query with outline, 3 sample chapters, table of contents, author's own market study showing why book will be successful and SASE.
Recent Nonfiction Title(s): *Growing Little Women*, by Donna J. Miller (women/family).
Fiction: Religious. "We are not currently accepting fiction submissions."
Tips: "Our audience consists of general, average Christian readers, not scholars. Know the market and publishers. Spend time in bookstores researching."

MOREHOUSE PUBLISHING CO., 4475 Linglestown Rd., Harrisburg PA 17112. Fax: (717)541-8130. Fax: (717)541-8136. Website: http://www.morehousegroup.com. **Acquisitions:** Debra K. Farrington, editorial director. Estab.

1884. Morehouse Publishing has traditionally published for the Episcopal Church and the Anglican Communion. Publishes hardcover and paperback originals. **Publishes 35 titles/year. 50% from first-time authors. Pays 10% net royalties. Offers small advance.** Publishes books within 18 months of acceptance. Accepts simultaneous submissions. Reports in 2 months. Guidelines available upon request.
Nonfiction: "In addition to its line of books for the Episcopal church, it also publishes books of practical value from within the Christian tradition for clergy, laity, academics, professionals, and seekers." Subjects include spirituality, biblical studies, liturgics, congregational resorces, women's issues, devotions and meditations, and issues around Christian life. Submit outline, 1-2 sample chapters, résumé or cv, and market analaysis.
Fiction: Christian children's picture books for ages 3-8. Submit entire ms (no more than 1,500 words) and résumé/cv.
Recent Title(s): *Living with Contradiction: An Introduction to Benedictine Spirituality*, by Esther de Waal; *No Toys on Sundays*, by Nancy Markham Alberts, illustrated by Erin McGonigle Brammer (fiction).

[A] **WILLIAM MORROW AND CO.**, The Hearst Corp., 1350 Avenue of the Americas, New York NY 10019. (212)261-6500. Fax: (212)261-6595. Website: http://www.williammorrow.com. Editorial Director: Betty Nichols Kelly. Managing Editor: Kim Lewis. **Acquisitions:** Pam Moenig, editorial director (Hearst Books, Hearst Marine Books); David Reuther, editor-in-chief (Beech Tree Books, Morrow Junior Books, Mulberry Books); Susan Pearson, editor-in-chief (Lothrop, Lee & Shepard Books); Toni Sciarra, editor (Quill Trade Paperbacks); Susan Hirschman (Greenwillow Books). Estab. 1926. Morrow publishes a wide range of titles that receive much recognition and prestige. A most selective house. **Publishes 200 titles/year. Receives 10,000 submissions/year. 30% of books from first-time authors; 5% from unagented writers. Pays standard royalty on retail price. Advance varies.** Publishes book 2 years after acceptance. Reports in 3 months.
Imprint(s): Beech Tree Books (juvenile); **Greenwillow Books** (juvenile); Hearst Books; Hearst Marine Books; **Lothrop, Lee & Shepard Books** (juvenile); **Morrow Junior Books** (juvenile); Mulberry Books (juvenile); Quill Trade Paperbacks, Tupelo Books; Rob Weisbach Books.
Nonfiction and Fiction: Publishes adult fiction, nonfiction, history, biography, arts, religion, poetry, how-to books, cookbooks. Length: 50,000-100,000 words. *Agented submissions only. No unsolicited mss or proposals.*
Recent Title(s): *The Last Party: The Life and Times of Studio 54*, by Anthony Haden-Guest (social history); *Van Gogh's Bad Cafe*, by Frederic Tuten.

MORROW JUNIOR BOOKS, William Morrow and Co., The Hearst Corp., 1350 Avenue of the Americas, New York NY 10019. (212)261-6691. Publisher: Barbara Lalicki. **Acquisitions:** Meredith Carpenter, executive editor; Andrea Curley, senior editor. "Morrow is one of the nation's leading publishers of books for children, including bestselling fiction and nonfiction." Publishes hardcover originals. **Publishes 50 titles/year. All contracts negotiated individually. Offers variable advance.** Book catalog and guidelines for 9×12 SAE with 3 first-class stamps.
Nonfiction: Juveniles (trade books). No textbooks. Query. *No unsolicited mss.*
Fiction: Juveniles (trade books). Query. *No unsolicited mss.*
Recent Title(s): *The Honey Makers*, by Gail Gibbons (nature); *Rumpelstiltskin's Daughter*, by Diane Stanley.

[N] **MOSAIC PRESS**, 85 River Rock Dr., Buffalo NY 14207. (800)387-8992. Fax: (800)387-8992. E-mail: cp507@freenet.toronto.on.ca. Publishes hardcover and trade paperback originals. **Publishes 20 titles/year. Pays 10% royalty on retail price.** Accepts simultaneous submissions. Manuscript guidelines free on request.
Nonfiction: Biography, humor. Subjects include art/architecture, business/economics, ethnic, government/politics, health/medicine, history, language/literature, music/dance, philosophy, psychology, religion, sociology, sports, translation, women's issues/studies. Submit proposal package including sample chapters.
Fiction: Ethnic, experimental, feminist, historical, horror, humor, literary, mainstream/contemporary, multicultural, mystery, plays, poetry, poetry in translation, religious, short story collections, sports, translation. Submit synopsis.
Poetry: Submit sample poems.

MOUNTAIN PRESS PUBLISHING COMPANY, P.O. Box 2399, Missoula MT 59806-2399. (406)728-1900. Fax: (406)728-1635. E-mail: mtnpress@montana.com. Website: http://www.mtnpress.com. **Acquisitions:** Kathleen Ort, editor-in-chief (natural history/science/outdoors); Gwen McKenna, editor (history); Jennifer Carey, assistant editor (Roadside Geology and Tumblweed Series). Estab. 1948. "We are expanding our Roadside Geology and Roadside History series (done on a state by state basis). We are interested in well-written regional field guides—plants, flowers and birds—and readable history and natural history." Publishes hardcover and trade paperback originals. **Publishes 15 titles/year. Receives 250 submissions/year. 50% of books from first-time authors; 90% from unagented writers. Pays 7-12% on wholesale price.** Publishes book 2 years after acceptance. Reports in 3 months. Book catalog free.
Nonfiction: Western history, nature/environment, regional, earth science, creative nonfiction. "No personal histories or journals." Query or submit outline and sample chapters. Reviews artwork/photos as part of ms package.
Recent Title(s): *South of Seattle: Notes on Life in the Northwest Woods*, by James LeMonds.
Tips: "If I were a writer trying to market a book today, I would find out what kind of books a publisher was interested in and tailor my writing to them; research markets and target my audience. Research other books on the same subjects. Make yours different. Don't present your manuscript to a publisher—*sell* it to him. Give him the information he needs to make a decision on a title. Please learn what we publish before sending your proposal. We are a 'niche' publisher."

THE MOUNTAINEERS BOOKS, 1001 SW Klickitat Way, Suite 201, Seattle WA 98134-1162. (206)223-6303. Fax: (206)223-6306. E-mail: mbooks@mountaineers.org. Executive Director: Art Freeman. Managing Editor: Cindy Bohn. **Acquisitions:** Margaret Foster, editor-in-chief; Thom Votteler, senior acquisitions editor. Estab. 1961. "We specialize in expert, authoritative books dealing with mountaineering, hiking, backpacking, skiing, snowshoeing, canoeing, bicycling, etc. These can be either how-to-do-it or where-to-do-it (guidebooks)." Publishes 95% hardcover and trade paperback originals and 5% reprints. **Publishes 40 titles/year. Receives 150-250 submissions/year. 25% of books from first-time authors; 98% from unagented writers. Pays royalty on net sales. Offers advance.** Publishes book 1 year after acceptance. Reports in 3 months. Book catalog and ms guidelines for 9×12 SAE with $1.47 postage.

- The Mountaineers Books is looking for manuscripts with more emphasis on regional conservation and natural history. See the Contests and Awards section for information on the Barbara Savage/"Miles From Nowhere" Memorial Award for outstanding adventure narrataives offered by Mountain Books.

Nonfiction: Guidebooks for national and international adventure travel, recreation, natural history, conservation/environment, non-competitive self-propelled sports, outdoor how-to, and some children's books. Does *not* want to see "anything dealing with hunting, fishing or motorized travel." Submit author bio, outline and minimum of 2 sample chapters. Accepts nonfiction translations. Looks for "expert knowledge, good organization." Also interested in nonfiction adventure narratives.

Recent Title(s): *Himalaya Alpine-Style: The Most Challenging Routes on the Highest Peaks*, by Andy Fashawe and Stephen Venables.

Tips: "The type of book the writer has the best chance of selling our firm is an authoritative guidebook (*in our field*) to a specific area not otherwise covered; or a how-to that is better than existing competition (again, *in our field*)."

MOYER BELL, Kymbolde Way, Wakefield RI 02879. (401)789-0074. Fax: (401)789-3793. Editor/Publisher: Britt Bell. **Acquisitions:** Jennifer Moyer, editor. Estab. 1984. "Moyer Bell was established to publish literature, reference and art books." Publishes hardcover originals, trade paperback originals and reprints. **Publishes 25 titles/year; imprint publishes 4 titles/year. Receives 500 queries and 1,500 mss/year. 1% of books from first-time authors; 90% from unagented writers. Pays royalty on retail price. No advance.** Publishes book 1-2 years after acceptance of ms. Accepts simultaneous submissions. Reports in 1 month on queries and proposals; 6 months on mss. Book catalog for #10 SASE.

Imprint(s): Asphodel Press.

Nonfiction: Biography, self-help. Subjects include art/architecture, current affairs, politics. Query with outline, 1-2 sample chapters and SASE.

Fiction: Literary. Query with synopsis, 1-2 sample chapters and SASE.

Recent Title(s): *Angels in Our Midst*, by Mary Fisher (nonfiction); *An Advent Calendar*, by Shena Mackay (novel).

JOHN MUIR PUBLICATIONS, Agora Inc., P.O. Box 613, Santa Fe NM 87504. (505)982-4078. Fax: (505)988-1680. **Acquisitions:** Cassandra Conyers, acquisitions editor. "We make the complex simple in the areas of independent travel and alternative health. We live in a busy time so our expert authors sort through time-sapping and money-wasting alternatives to offer our readers the best information for decision-making." Publishes trade paperback originals. **Publishes 60-70 titles/year. Receives 1,000 queries and 50 mss/year. 60% of books from first-time authors; 90% from unagented writers. Pays 3½-10% royalty on wholesale price or makes outright purchase occasionally. Offers $1,000-3,500 advance.** Publishes book 1 year after acceptance of ms. Accepts simultaneous submissions if noted in cover letter. Reports in 6 weeks on queries, 4 months on proposals. Book catalog for 9×12 SAE and 3 first-class stamps. Manuscript guidelines for #10 SASE.

Nonfiction: Adult travel and alternative health. "We are continuing our commitment to adult travel titles and are seeking unique travel-related manuscripts. We are refining our list, and we're particularly interested in alternative health. Do your homework to see what kinds of books we publish." Query or submit outline, 1-2 sample chapters and proposal package, including competition, résumé, marketing ideas with SASE. Reviews artwork/photos as part of ms package. Send photocopies or transparencies.

Recent Title(s): *Adventures in Nature: Alaska* (adventure and eco-travel).

Tips: "Audience is environmentally-minded, adults interested in independent travel and wanting to share enthusiasm with their children. They are somewhat adventurous and interested in multicultural themes. John Muir publishes nonfiction, so don't send us your great fiction idea. Check the competition. We don't want to see your idea if it's already on the store shelves. We are particularly interested in seeing niche travel proposals for the U.S. (domestic) traveler."

N MULTNOMAH PUBLISHERS, INC., P.O. Box 1720, Sisters OR 97759. (541)549-1144. E-mail: mjacobson@multnomahpubl.com. **Acquisitions:** Matt Jacobson, vice president, editorial; Alice Gray (gift books, women's); Louise Keffer (children's); Rod Morris (genre, men's fiction, theology, sports); Karen Ball (romance and women's fiction). "Multnomah publishes books on Christian living and family enrichment, devotional and gift books, fiction and children's books." Publishes hardcover and trade paperback originals. **Publishes 120 titles/year. Receives 2,400 queries and 1,200 mss/year. 2% of books from first-time authors; 50% from unagented writers. Pays royalty on wholesale price.** Publishes book 1-2 years after acceptance of ms. Accepts simultaneous submissions. Reports in 3 months on queries. Manuscript guidelines for #10 SASE.

Imprint(s): Alabaster, Multnomah Books, Gold'n'Honey Books, Palisades.

Nonfiction: Children, coffee table book, gift book, humor, illustrated book. Subjects include child guidance/parenting, religion, sports (Christian sports figures). Submit proposal package, including outline/synopsis, 3 sample chapters and market study with SASE. Reviews artwork/photos as part of ms package. Send photocopies.

Fiction: Adventure, historical, humor, mystery, religious, romance, suspense, western. Submit synopsis, 3 sample chapters with SASE.
Recent Title(s): *Stories for the Families*, by Alice Gray (nonfiction); *Publish & Perish*, by Sally Wright (mystery).

MUSTANG PUBLISHING CO., P.O. Box 3004, Memphis TN 38173-0004. (901)521-1406. **Acquisitions:** Rollin Riggs, editor. Estab. 1983. Mustang publishes general interest nonfiction for an adult audience. Publishes hardcover and trade paperback originals. **Publishes 10 titles/year. Receives 1,000 submissions/year. 50% of books from first-time authors; 90% of books from unagented writers. Pays 6-8% royalty on retail price.** Publishes book 1 year after acceptance. Accepts simultaneous submissions. Reports in 1 month. *Writer's Market* recommends allowing 2 months for reply. Book catalog for $2 and #10 SASE. No phone calls, please.
Nonfiction: How-to, humor, self-help. Subjects include Americana, hobbies, recreation, sports, travel. "Our needs are very general—humor, travel, how-to, etc.—for the 18-to 60-year-old market." Query or submit outline and sample chapters with SASE.
Recent Title(s): *How to Be a Way Cool Grandfather*, by Steen (how-to).
Tips: "From the proposals we receive, it seems that many writers never go to bookstores and have no idea what sells. Before you waste a lot of time on a nonfiction book idea, ask yourself, 'How often have my friends and I actually *bought* a book like this?' Know the market, and know the audience you're trying to reach."

[A] **THE MYSTERIOUS PRESS**, Warner Books, 1271 Avenue of the Americas, New York NY 10020. (212)522-5144. Fax: (212)522-7994. Website: http://www.twep.timeinc.com/twep/mysterious_press. **Acquisitions:** William Malloy, editor-in-chief; Sara Ann Freed, executive editor; Susanna Einstein, assistant editor. Estab. 1976. The Mysterious Press seeks "well-written crime/mystery/suspense fiction." Publishes hardcover and mass market editions. **Publishes 36 titles/year. No unagented writers. Pays standard, but negotiable, royalty on retail price. Amount of advance varies widely.** Publishes book an average of 1 year after acceptance. Reports in 2 months.
Fiction: Mystery, suspense, crime/detective novels. No short stories. Query. *Agented submissions only.*
Recent Title(s): *The Ax*, by Donald Westlake.

THE NAIAD PRESS, INC., P.O. Box 10543, Tallahassee FL 32302. (850)539-5965. Fax: (850)539-9731. Website: http://www.naiadpress.com. **Acquisitions:** Barbara Grier, editorial director. Estab. 1973. "We publish lesbian fiction, preferably lesbian/feminist fiction." Publishes paperback originals. **Publishes 31 titles/year. Receives over 1,500 submissions/year. 20% of books from first-time authors; 99% from unagented writers. Pays 15% royalty on wholesale or retail price. No advance.** Publishes book 2 years after acceptance. Reports in 4 months. Book catalog and ms guidelines for 6×9 SAE and $1.50 postage and handling
Fiction: "We are not impressed with the 'oh woe' school and prefer realistic (i.e., happy) novels. We emphasize fiction and are now heavily reading manuscripts in that area. We are working in a lot of genre fiction—mysteries, short stories, fantasy—all with lesbian themes, of course. We have instituted an inhouse anthology series, featuring short stories only by our own authors (authors who have published full length fiction with us or those signed to do so)." Query.
Recent Title(s): *City Lights, Country Candles*, by Penny Haves (lesbian romance).
Tips: "There is tremendous world-wide demand for lesbian mysteries from lesbian authors published by lesbian presses, and we are doing several such series. We are no longer seeking science fiction. Manuscripts under 50,000 words have twice as good a chance as over 50,000."

[N] **NARWHAL PRESS, INC.**, 1629 Meeting St., Charleston SC 29405-9408. (803)853-0510. Fax: (803)853-2528. E-mail: shipwrex@aol.com. Website: http://www.shipwrecks.com. **Acquisitions**: Dr. E. Lee Spence, chief editor (marine archaeology, shipwrecks); Dr. Terry Frazier, managing editor (novels, marine histories, military); Roni L. Smith, associate editor (novels, children's books). Narwhal Press specializes in books about shipwrecks and marine archaeology and history. Publishes hardcover and trade paperback originals. **Publishes 10 titles/year. Receives 100 queries and 50 mss/year. 75% of books from first-time authors; 100% from unagented writers. Pays 10-15% royalty on wholesale price. Offers $1,000-2,000 advance.** Publishes book 3 months after acceptance of ms. Accepts simultaneous submissions. Reports in 2 weeks on queries, 1 month on mss.
Nonfiction: Biography, children's/juvenile, how-to, reference. Subjects include anthropology/archaeology, history, memoirs, military/war. "We are constantly searching for titles of interest to shipwreck divers, marine archaeologists, Civil War buffs, etc., but we are expanding our titles to include novels, children's books, modern naval history and personal memoirs." Query or submit outline and 3 sample chapters and SASE. Reviews artwork/photos as part of ms package. Send photocopies.
Fiction: Historical, juvenile, mainstream/contemporary, military/war, young adult, dive-related. "We prefer novels with a strong historical context. We invite writers to submit fiction about undersea adventures. Best to call or write first." Query, then submit synopsis and 3 sample chapters and SASE.
Recent Title(s): *The Hunley: Submarines, Sacriface & Success in the Civil War*, by Mark Ragan (history); *Budapest Betrayal*, by Mimi Hallman (historical novel).
Tips: "Become an expert in your subject area. Polish and proofread your writing."

NASW PRESS, National Association of Social Workers, 750 First St. NE, Suite 700, Washington DC 20002-4241. Fax: (202)336-8312. E-mail: press@naswdc.org. Website: http://www.naswpress.org. Executive Editor: Paula Delo. **Acquisitions**: Chanté Lampton, acquisitions associate. Estab. 1956. NASW Books "provides outstanding information tools for social workers and other human service professionals to advance the knowledge base in social work and social welfare." **Publishes 10-15 titles/year. Receives 100 submissions/year. 20% of books from first-time authors; 100% from unagented writers. Pays 10-15% royalty on net prices.** Publishes book 8 months after acceptance of ms. Reports within 4 months on submissions. Book catalog and ms guidelines free.

• NASW will be putting more emphasis on publishing health, policy, substance abuse and aging books.

Nonfiction: Textbooks of interest to professional social workers. "We're looking for books on social work in health care, mental health, multicultural competence and substance abuse. Books must be directed to the professional social worker and build on the current literature." Submit outline and sample chapters with SASE. Rarely reviews artwork/photos as part of ms package.

Recent Title(s): *Issues in International Social Work*, edited by M.C. Hokestad and James Midgley.

Tips: "Our audience includes social work practitioners, educators, students and policy makers. They are looking for practice-related books that are well grounded in theory. The books that do well have direct application to the work our audience does. New technology, AIDS, welfare reform and health policy will be of increasing interest to our readers. We are particularly interested in manuscripts for fact-based practice manuals that will be very user-friendly."

[N] **NATIONAL PRESS BOOKS, INC.**, 1925 K St., Suite 100, Washington DC 20006. (202)833-2021. Fax: (202)822-6062. **Acquisitions:** G. Edward Smith, editorial director. Estab. 1984. "National Press publishes 'America's most talked-about books' about how to improve the world in policy or by helping people." Publishes hardcover and trade paperback originals. Publishes 6 titles/year. **Receives 1,500 submissions/year. 20% of books are from first-time authors; 80% from unagented writers. Pays 5-10% royalty on wholesale or retail price or makes outright purchases. Offers variable advance.** Publishes book 8 months after acceptance. Accepts simultaneous submissions. Reports in 4 months.

Nonfiction: Biography, cookbook, self-help. Subjects include business/economics, child guidance/parenting, government/politics, health/medicine, history, money/finance, psychology. Submit outline and sample chapters.

Recent Title(s): *Tapped Out*, by Sen. Paul Simon (the world's drinking water shortage).

NATIONAL TEXTBOOK CO., NTC/Contemporary Publishing Group, 4255 W. Touhy Ave., Lincolnwood IL 60646. (847)679-5500. Fax: (847)679-2494. President/CEO: Mark R. Pattis. Editorial Director: Cindy Krejcsi. **Acquisitions:** N. Keith Fry, director of foreign language publishing (world languages and ESL); Fitzgerald Higgins, executive editor (language arts); Betsy Lancefield (VGM Career Horizons); Lynn Mooney (NTC Business Books). "We are a niche-oriented educational publisher of supplementary and core curricular materials." Publishes original textbooks for education and trade market, and software. **Publishes 100-150 titles/year. Receives 1,000 submissions/year. 10% of books from first-time authors. 75% from unagented writers. Manuscripts purchased on either royalty or fee basis.** Publishes book 1 year after acceptance. Reports in 3 months. Book catalog and ms guidelines for 6×9 SAE and 2 first-class stamps.

Nonfiction: Textbooks. Major emphasis being given to world language and languages arts classroom texts, especially secondary level material, and business and career subjects (marketing, advertising, sales, etc.). Send sample chapter and outline or table of contents.

Recent Title(s): *Hammer's German Grammar and Usage*; *Theatre—Art in Action*; *Advertising Principles*.

[N] **NATURE PUBLISHING HOUSE**, 6399 Wilshire Blvd., Suite 412, Los Angeles CA 90048. (213)651-2540. E-mail: naturehouse@sprynet.com. **Acquisitions:** Jon Thibault, editor. Publishes trade paperback originals. **Publishes 30-50 titles/year. Publishes 50% of books from first-time authors; 50% from unagented writers. Royalties and advances negotiated on project-by-project basis.** Accepts simultaneous submissions. Reports in 1 month on queries and proposals; 2 months on mss. Book catalog and ms guidelines for #10 SASE with 1 first-class stamp.

Nonficition: Children's/juvenile, illustrated book. Subjects included animals, anthropology/archaeology, education, nature/environment, science. "Our unique books are fully color illustrated. An educational blend of fantasy and adventure with science & nature." Query with outline and 3 sample chapters. Reviews artwork/photos as part of ms package. Send photocopies.

Fiction: Adventure, comic books, fantasy, historical, juvenile, science fiction, young adult. "Our unique, full-color illustrated books are an educational blend of fantasy and adventure with science & nature." Query, submit synopsis with 3 sample chapters or complete ms.

Recent Title(s): *Wildlife Adventure, Volcano Adventure,* by Stu Duval (science comic book).

NATUREGRAPH PUBLISHERS, INC., P.O. Box 1047, Happy Camp CA 96039. (530)493-5353. Fax: (530)493-5240. E-mail: naturgraph@aol.com. Website: http://members.aol.com/naturegraph/homepage.htm. **Acquisitions**: Barbara Brown, editor-in-chief; Keven Brown, editor. Estab. 1946. Naturegraph publishes "books for a better world. Within our niches of nature and Indian subjects, we hope the titles we choose to publish will benefit the world in some way." Publishes trade paperback originals. **Publishes 5 titles/year. Pays 8-10% royalty on wholesale price. No advance.** Reports in 1 month on queries, 2 months on proposals and mss.

Nonfiction: Primarily publishes nonfiction for the layman in natural history (biology, geology, ecology, astronomy); American Indian (historical and contemporary); outdoor living (backpacking, wild edibles, etc.); land and gardening (modern homesteading); crafts and how-to. "Our primary niches are nature and Native American subjects with adult level, non-technical language and scientific accuracy. First, send for our free catalog. Study what kind of books we have already published." Submit outline and 2 sample chapters with SASE.

Recent Title(s): *Tricks of the Trail: Modern Backpacking*, by Roy Santoro (outdoor).
Tips: "Please—always send a stamped reply envelope. Publishers get hundreds of manuscripts yearly; not just yours."

THE NAUTICAL & AVIATION PUBLISHING CO., 8 W. Madison St., Baltimore MD 21201. (410)659-0220. Fax: (410)539-8832. President/Publisher: Jan Snouck-Hurgronje. **Acquisitions:** Rebecca Irish, editor. Estab. 1979. "We are publishers of military history." Publishes hardcover originals and reprints. **Publishes 10-12 titles/year. Receives 125 submissions/year. Pays 10-15% royalty on net selling price. Rarely offers advance.** Accepts simultaneous submissions. Book catalog free.
Nonfiction: Reference. Subjects include history, military/war. Query with synopsis and 3 sample chapters. Reviews artwork/photo as part of package.
Fiction: Historical. Submit outline/synopsis and sample chapters.
Recent Title(s): *The Battle for Baltimore: 1814*, by Joseph A. Whitehorne (War of 1812 on the Chesapeake Bay); *The Black Flower: A Novel of the Civil War*, by Howard Bahr.
Tips: "We are primarily a nonfiction publisher, but will review historical fiction of military interest."

NAVAL INSTITUTE PRESS, US Naval Institute, 118 Maryland Ave., Annapolis MD 21402-5035. Fax: (410)269-7940. E-mail: esecunda@usni.org. Website: http://www.usni.org. Press Director: Ronald Chambers. **Acquisitions:** Paul Wilderson, executive editor; Mark Gatlin, senior acquisitions editor; Scott Belliveau, acquisitions editor. Estab. 1873. The U.S. Naval Institute Press publishes general and scholarly books of professional, scientific, historical and literary interest to the naval and maritime community. **Publishes 80 titles/year. Receives 400-500 submissions/year. 50% of books from first-time authors; 85% from unagented writers. Pays 5-10% royalty on net sales.** Publishes book 1 year after acceptance. Book catalog free with 9×12 SASE. Manuscript guidelines for #10 SASE.
Imprint(s): Bluejacket Books (paperback reprints).
Nonfiction: "We are interested in naval and maritime subjects and in broad military topics, including government policy and funding. Specific subjects include: tactics, strategy, navigation, history, biographies, aviation, technology and others." Query letter strongly recommended.
Fiction: Limited fiction on military and naval themes.
Recent Title(s): *Wolf: U-Boat Commanders in World War II*, by Jordan Vause (nonfiction); *Rising Wind*, by Dick Couch (modern military thriller).

NEAL-SCHUMAN PUBLISHERS, INC., 100 Varick St., New York NY 10013. (212)925-8650. Fax: (212)219-8916. E-mail: ctharmon@aol.com. Website: http://www.neal-schuman.com. **Acquistions:** Charles Harmon, editorial director. "Neal-Schuman publishes books about libraries, information science and the use of information technology, especially in education and libraries." Publishes hardcover and trade paperback originals. **Publishes 30 titles/year. Receives 300 submissions/year. 75% of books from first-time authors; 90% from unagented writers. Pays 10% royalty on net sales. Offers advances infrequently.** Publishes book 1 year after acceptance. Reports in 1 month on proposals. *Writer's Market* recommends allowing 2 months for reply. Book catalog and ms guidelines free.
Nonfiction: Reference, Internet guides, textbook, texts and professional books in library and information science. "We are looking for many books about the Internet." Submit proposal package, including vita, outline, preface and sample chapters.
Recent Title(s): *Securing PCs and Data in Schools and Libraries*, by Allen Benson.

NEGATIVE CAPABILITY, 62 Ridgelawn Dr. E., Mobile AL 36608. Fax: (334)344-8478. Editor/Publisher: Sue Walker. Publishes hardcover and trade paperback originals. **Publishes 4 titles/year. Negotiates royalty.** Publishes book 10 months after acceptance of ms. Reports in 2 months. Manuscript guidelines free.
Nonfiction: Self-help. Subjects include education, health/medicine, language/literature, women's issues/studies.
Fiction: Feminist, historical, literary, short story collections. Query with SASE.
Poetry: Submit 5 sample poems.
Recent Title(s): *Wake Up Laughing*, by Pat Schneider (autobiography); *Little Dragons*, by Michael Bugeja (short story collection).

THOMAS NELSON PUBLISHERS, Box 141000, Nashville TN 37214-1000. Corporate address does not accept unsolicited mss; no phone queries. **Acquisitions:** Janet Thoma (Janet Thoma Books, 1157 Molokai, Tega Cay SC 29715, fax: 803/548-2684); Victor Oliver (Oliver-Nelson Books, 1360 Center Dr., Suite 102-B, Atlanta GA 30338, fax: 770/391-9784); Mark Roberts, (reference, academic, professional), P.O. Box 141000, Nashville TN 37214, fax: 615/391-5225). Publishes Christian lifestyle nonfiction and fiction. **Publishes 150-200 titles/year. Pays royalty on net sales with rates negotiated for each project.** Publishes books 1-2 years after acceptance. Reports in 3 months. Accepts simultaneous submissions if so stated in cover letter.
Imprint(s): Janet Thoma Books, Oliver-Nelson Books, **Tommy Nelson**.
Nonfiction: Adult inspirational, motivational, devotional, self-help, Christian living, prayer and evangelism, reference/Bible study. Query with SASE, then send brief, prosaic résumé, 1-page synopsis and 1 sample chapter to one of the acquisitions editors at the above locations with SASE.
Fiction: Seeking successfully published commercial fiction authors who write for adults from a Christian perspective. Send brief, prosaic résumé, 1-page synopsis and 1 sample chapter to one of the acquisitions editors at the above locations with SASE.

Recent Title(s): *Spine Chillers*, by Fred E. Katz (thriller series); *The Treasury of David, Updated Edition*, by Charles H. Spurgeon, updated by Ron H. Clarke (nonfiction).

TOMMY NELSON, Thomas Nelson, Inc., 404 BNA Dr., Bldg. 200, Suite 508, Nashville TN 37217. Fax: (615)902-2415. Website: http://www.tommynelson.com. **Acquisitions**: Laura Minchew, acquisitions editor. Tommy Nelson publishes children's Christian nonfiction and fiction for boys and girls up to age 14. "We honor God and serve people through books, videos, software and Bibles for children that improve the lives of our customers." Publishes hardcover and trade paperback originals. **Publishes 50-75 titles/year. Receives 200 queries and 1,000 mss/year. 5% of books from first-time authors; 50% from unagented writers. Pays royalty on wholesale price or makes outright purchase. Pays $1,000 minimum advance.** Publishes book 18 months after acceptance of ms. No simultaneous submissions. Reports in 1 month on queries, 3 months on proposals and mss. Guidelines for #10 SASE.
Imprint(s): Word Kids.
Nonfiction: Children's/juvenile. Religious subjects (Christian evangelical). Submit outline and 3 sample chapters with SASE.
Fiction: Adventure, juvenile, mystery, picture books, religious. "No stereotypical characters without depth." Submit synopsis with 3 sample chapters.
Recent Title(s): *50 Money Making Ideas for Kids*, by Allen & Lauree Burkett (money making projects); *Butterfly Kisses*, by Bob Carlisle (father's reflections on daughter).
Tips: "Know the CBA market. Check out the Christian bookstores to see what sells and what is needed." Note: Nelson Children's Books and Word Children's books are now Tommy Nelson.

NELSON-HALL PUBLISHERS, 111 N. Canal St., Chicago IL 60606. (312)930-9446. Senior Editor: Richard O. Meade. **Acquisitions:** Editorial Director. Estab. 1909. Nelson-Hall publishes college textbooks and general scholarly books in the social sciences. Publishes hardcover and paperback originals. **Publishes 30 titles/year. Receives 200 queries and 20 mss/year. 90% of books submitted by unagented writers. Pays 5-15% royalty on wholesale price.** Publishes book 1 year after acceptance. Accepts simultaneous submissions. Reports in 1 month on queries.
Nonfiction: Subjects include anthropology/archaeology, government/politics, music/dance, psychology, sociology. Query with outline, 2 sample chapters, cv.
Recent Title(s): *The Rich Get Richer*, by Denny Braun, Ph.D.

THE NEW ENGLAND PRESS, INC., P.O. Box 575, Shelburne VT 05482. (802)863-2520. Fax: (802)863-1510. E-mail: nep@together.net. Website: http://www.nepress.com. **Acquisitions:** Mark Wanner, managing editor. "The New England Press publishes high-quality trade books of regional northern New England interest." Publishes hardcover and trade paperback originals. **Publishes 6-8 titles/year. Receives 500 queries and 200 mss/year. 50% of books from first-time authors; 90% from unagented writers. Pays royalty on wholesale price. No advance.** Publishes book 15 months after acceptance of ms. Accepts simultaneous submissions. Reports in 3 months. Book catalog free.
Nonfiction: Biography, children's/juvenile, illustrated book. Subjects include gardening, history, regional, Vermontiana. "Nonfiction submissions must be based in Vermont and have northern New England topics. No memoirs or family histories. Identify potential markets and ways to reach them in cover letter." Submit outline and 2 sample chapters with SASE. Reviews artwork/photos as part of the ms package. Send photocopies.
Fiction: "We look for very specific subject matters based on Vermont history and heritage. We are also interested in historical novels for young adults based in New Hampshire and Maine. We do not publish contemporary adult fiction of any kind." Submit synopsis and 2 sample chapters with SASE.
Recent Title(s): *Spanning Time: Vermont's Covered Bridges*, by Joseph Nelson (travel); *The Black Bonnet*, by Louella Bryant (young adult/Vermont history).
Tips: "Our readers are interested in all aspects of Vermont and northern New England, including hobbyists (railroad books) and students (young adult fiction and biography). No agent is needed, but our market is extremely specific and our volume is low, so send a query or outline and writing samples first. Sending the whole manuscript is discouraged. We will not accept projects that are still under development or give advances."

NEW HARBINGER PUBLICATIONS, 5674 Shattuck Ave., Oakland CA 94609. Fax: (510)652-5472. E-mail: nhhelp@newharbinger.com. Website: http://www.newharbinger.com. **Acquisitions:** Kristin Beck, acquisitions editor; Catharine Sutker, acquisitions assistant. "We look for psychology and health self-help books that teach the average reader how to master essential skills. Our books are also read by mental health professionals who want simple, clear explanations of important psychological techniques and health issues." **Publishes 30 titles/year. Receives 750 queries**

FOR EXPLANATIONS OF THESE SYMBOLS,
SEE THE INSIDE FRONT AND BACK COVERS OF THIS BOOK

and 200 mss/year. 60% of books from first-time authors; 95% from unagented writers. Pays 12% royalty on wholesale price. Offers $0-3,000 advance. Publishes book 1 year after acceptance of ms. Accepts simultaneous submissions. Reports in 1 month on queries and proposals, 2 months on mss. Book catalog and ms guidelines free.
Nonfiction: Self-help (psychology/health), textbooks. Subjects include anger management, anxiety, coping, health/ medicine, psychology. "Authors need to be a qualified psychotherapist or health practitioner to publish with us." Submit proposal package, including outline, 3 sample chapters, competing titles and why this one is special.
Recent Title(s): *Being, Belonging, Doing*, by Ronald T. Potter-Efron (balancing needs).
Tips: Audience includes psychotherapists and lay readers wanting step-by-step strategies to solve specific problems. "Our definition of a self-help psychology or health book is one that teaches essential life skills. The primary goal is to train the reader so that, after reading the book, he or she can deal more effectively with problems."

NEW HOPE PUBLISHERS, Division of Woman's Missionary Union, P.O. Box 12065, Birmingham AL 35202-2065. (205)991-8100. Fax: (205)991-4990. Website: http://www.newhopepubl.com. **Acquisitions:** Jennifer Law, editor. "Our goal is to provide resources to motivate and equip women to share the hope of Christ." **Publishes 15 titles/year. Receives 100 queries and 60 mss/year. 25% of books from first-time authors; 98% from unagented writers. Pays 7-10% royalty on retail price or makes outright purchase.** Publishes book 2 years after acceptance of ms. Reports in 6 months on mss. Book catalog for 9×12 SAE with 3 first-class stamps. Manuscript guidelines for #10 SASE.
Imprint(s): New Hope, Woman's Missionary Union.
Nonfiction: How-to, children's/juvenile (religion), personal spiritual growth. Subjects include child guidance/parenting (from Christian perspective), education (Christian church), religion (Christian faith—must relate to missions work, culture and multicultural issues, Christian concerns, Christian ethical issues, spiritual growth, etc.), women's issues/ studies from Christian perspective. "We publish Christian education materials that focus on missions work or educational work in some way. Teaching helps, spiritual growth material, ideas for working with different audiences in a church, etc.—missions work overseas or church work in the U.S., women's spiritual issues, guiding children in Christian faith." Submit outline and 3 sample chapters for review. Submit complete ms for acceptance decision.
Recent Title(s): *God's Heart, God's Hands*, by Daniel George.

NEW LEAF PRESS, INC., P.O. Box 726, Green Forest AR 72638-0726. Fax: (870)438-5120. Editor: Jim Fletcher. **Acquisitions:** Editorial Board. Estab. 1975. "We are known for our prophecy books, Christian living books and our inspirational gift line." Publishes hardcover and paperback originals. **Publishes 15-20 titles/year. Receives 500 submissions/year. 15% of books from first-time authors; 90% from unagented writers. Pays variable royalty once per year. No advance.** Publishes book 10 months after acceptance. Accepts simultaneous submissions. Reports in 3 months. Book catalog and ms guidelines for 9×12 SAE with 5 first-class stamps.
Nonfiction: How to live the Christian life, humor, self-help, devotionals. Length: 100-400 pages. Submit complete ms. *Writer's Market* recommends sending a query with SASE first. Reviews artwork/photos as part of ms package. Send photos and illustrations to accompany ms.
Recent Title(s): *Signs of His Coming*, by David Allan Lewis.

NEW RIVERS PRESS, 420 N. Fifth St., Suite 910, Minneapolis MN 55401. **Acquisitions**: James Cihlar, managing editor. "New Rivers publishes the best poetry, fiction and creative nonfiction from new and emerging writers from the upper Midwest." Publishes trade paperback originals and occasional jacketed cloth editions. **Publishes 8-10 titles/year. Receives 500 queries and 1,000 mss/year. 95% of books from first-time authors; 99.9% from unagented writers. Pays royalty; pays $500 honoraria for contest winners.** Publishes book 2 years after acceptance. Book catalog free. Send SASE for manuscript guidelines to the Minnesota Voices Project (Minnesota authors only), and the Headwaters Literary Competition (writers from Illinois, Iowa, Michigan, North Dakota, South Dakota, and Wisconsin).
Nonfiction: Creative prose. "We publish memoirs, essay collections, and other forms of creative nonfiction." Query.
Fiction: Literary and short story collections. Query with synopsis and 2 sample chapters.
Poetry: Submit 10-15 sample poems.
Recent Title(s): *The Dirty Shame Hotel*, by Ron Block (short stories); *Sermon on a Perfect Spring Day*, by Philip Bryant.

NEW VICTORIA PUBLISHERS, P.O. Box 27, Norwich VT 05055-0027. Phone/fax: (802)649-5297. E-mail: newvic @aol.com. Website: http://www.opendoor.com/NewVic/. **Acquisitions:** Claudia Lamperti, editor; ReBecca Béguin, editor. Estab. 1976. "New Victoria is a nonprofit literary and cultural organization producing the finest in lesbian fiction and nonfiction." Publishes trade paperback originals. **Publishes 8-10 titles/year. Receives 100 submissions/year. 50% of books from first-time authors; most books from unagented writers. Pays 10% royalty.** Publishes book 1 year after acceptance. Reports on queries in 1 month. Book catalog free.
Nonfiction: History. "We are interested in feminist history or biography and interviews with or topics relating to lesbians. No poetry." Submit outline and sample chapters.
Fiction: Adventure, erotica, fantasy, historical, humor, mystery, romance, science fiction, western. "We will consider most anything if it is well written and appeals to lesbian/feminist audience." Submit outline/synopsis and sample chapters. "Hard copy only—no disks."
Recent Title(s): *Barbie Unbound*, by Sarah Strohmeyer (humor); *Backstage Pass: Interviews with Women in Music*, by Laura Post (women musicians).
Tips: "Try to appeal to a specific audience and not write for the general market. We're still looking for well-written,

hopefully humorous, lesbian fiction and well-researched biography or nonfiction."

NEW WORLD LIBRARY, Whatever Publishing, Inc., 14 Pamaron Way, Novato CA 94949. (415)884-2100. Fax: (415)884-2199. E-mail: escort@nwlib.com. Website: http://www.nwlib.com. Publisher: Marc Allen. **Acquisitions:** Becky Benenate, editorial director. "NWL is dedicated to publishing books and cassettes that inspire and challenge us to improve the quality of our lives and our world." Publishes hardcover and trade paperback originals and reprints. **Publishes 35 titles/year. 10% of books from first-time authors; 50% from unagented writers. Pays 12-16% royalty on wholesale price. Offers $0-200,000 advance.** Publishes book 18 months after acceptance of ms. Accepts simultaneous submissions. Reports in 2 months. Book catalog and ms guidelines free.
Imprint(s): Nataraj.
Nonfiction: Gift book, self-help. Subjects include business/prosperity, cooking/foods/nutrition, ethnic (African-American, Native American), money/finance, nature/environment, personal growth, psychology, religion, women's issues/studies. Query or submit outline, 1 sample chapter and author bio with SASE. Reviews artwork/photos as part of ms package. Send photocopies.
Recent Title(s): *No Greater Love*, by Mother Teresa (inspiration/religion); *Papa's Angels*, by Collin Wilcox-Paxton (Christmas); *Legends*, by J. Miller (photography/women's studies).

NEW YORK UNIVERSITY PRESS, 70 Washington Square S., New York NY 10012. (212)998-2575. Fax: (212)995-3833. Website: http://www.nyupress.nyu.edu. **Acquisitions:** Tim Bartlett (psychology, literature); Eric Zinner (cultural studies, media, anthropology, psychology/religion); Jennifer Hammer (Jewish studies, women's studies); Niko Pfund (business, history, law); Stephen Magro (social sciences). Estab. 1916. "New York University Press embraces ideological diversity. We often publish books on the same issue from different poles to generate dialogue, engender and resist pat categorizations." Hardcover and trade paperback originals. **Publishes 150 titles/year. Receives 800-1,000 queries/year. 30% of books from first-time authors; 90% from unagented writers. Advance and royalty on net receipts varies by project.** Publishes book 8 months after acceptance of ms. Accepts simultaneous submissions. Reports in 1 month on proposals (peer reviewed).
Nonfiction: Subjects include anthropology/archaeology, art/architecture, business/economics, computers/electronics, education, ethnic, gay/lesbian, government/politics, health/medicine, history, language/literature, military/war, money/finance, music/dance, nature/environment, philosophy, photography, psychology, regional, religion, sociology, sports, travel, women's issues/studies. Submit proposal package, including outline, 1 sample chapter and with SASE. Reviews artwork/photos as part of the ms package. Send photocopies.
Fiction: Literary. "We publish only 1 fiction title per year and don't encourage fiction submissions." Submit synopsis and 1 sample chapter with SASE.
Poetry: "We publish only 1 poetry title per year and don't encourage poetry submissions." Submit 3-5 sample poems.
Recent Title(s): *Black Rage Confronts The Law*, by Paul Harris (social history); *The Ruins*, by Trace Farrell (fiction); *Long Like a River*, by Nancy Schoenberger (poetry).

N **NEWCASTLE PUBLISHING CO., INC.**, 13419 Saticoy, N. Hollywood CA 91605. (818)787-4378. Fax: (213)780-2007. Editor-in-Chief: Alfred Saunders. **Acquisitions:** Daryl Jacoby, editor; Jodi Grossblatt, assistant editor. Estab. 1970. "Newcastle publishes quality paperbacks for the discerning reader." Publishes trade paperback originals and reprints. **Publishes 10 titles/year. Receives 300 submissions/year. 70% of books from first-time authors; 95% of books from unagented writers. Pays 5-10% royalty on retail price. No advance.** Publishes book an average of 8 months after acceptance. Accepts simultaneous submissions. Reports in 1 month. *Writer's Market* recommends allowing 2 months for reply. Free book catalog. Manuscript guidelines for SASE.
Nonfiction: How-to, self-help, metaphysical, New Age and practical advice for older adults. Subjects include health (physical fitness, diet and nutrition), psychology and religion. No biography, travel, children's books, poetry, cookbooks or fiction. Query or submit outline and sample chapters. Looks for "something to grab the reader so that he/she will readily remember that passage."
Recent Title(s): *Celtic Mythology.*
Tips: "Check the shelves in the larger bookstores on the subject of the manuscript being submitted. A book on life extension, holistic health, or stress management has the best chance of selling to our firm along with books geared for older adults on personal health issues, etc."

NEWJOY PRESS, P.O. Box 3437, Ventura CA 93006. (800)876-1373. Fax: (805)984-0503. E-mail: njpublish@aol.com. **Acquisitions**: Joy Nyquist, publisher. "Our plan is to publish quality books in an easy-to-read style. We publish traveler's help books, recover books (focus on relapse prevention) and self-help books (focus on women's issues)." Publishes trade paperback originals. **Publishes 7-10 titles/year. Pays 10-15% royalty on retail price.** Reports in 4 months.
Nonfiction: Publishes chemical dependency relapse prevention books; self-help books with focus on women's issues; traveler's help books. Submit (by mail only) a proposal with outline, sample chapter and author's qualifications. Previous marketing experience and a strong marketing plan along with a commitment to marketing is very important.
Recent Title(s): *Travel Light: How to Go Anywhere in the World With Only One Suitcase*, by Joy Nyquist.
Tips: "Newjoy Press is looking for books written by qualified persons who offer relevant information based on research and expertise on their subject. In addition, the authors must have a strong marketing plan and marketing skills such as public speaking."

N **A** **NEWSTAR PRESS**, (formerly Dove Books), NewStar Media, 8955 Beverly Blvd., Los Angeles CA 90048. Website: http://www.doveaudio.com. **Acquisitions**: Beth Lieberman, editorial director. NewStar Press publishes a diverse list of fiction and nonfiction titles. Publishes hardcover originals, trade paperback originals and reprints. **Publishes 25 titles/year. Receives 1,000 queries and 250 mss/year. 5% of books from first-time authors; 1% from unagented writers. Pays royalty on retail price. Advance varies.** Publishes book 1 year after acceptance of ms. Accepts simultaneous submissions. Reports in 2 months.

Nonfiction: Biography, how-to, reference, self-help. Subjects include Americana, business and economics, child guidance/parenting, cooking/foods/nutrition, government/politics, health/medicine, money/finance, psychology, regional, science. *Agented submissions only.* All unsolicited mss returned unopened.

Fiction: *Agented submissions only.*

Recent Title(s): *On Selling*, by Mark McCormack (business); *The 50 Greatest Mysteries of All Times*, by Otto Penzler (fiction anthology).

NIGHTSHADE PRESS, P.O. Box 76, Troy ME 04987. (207)948-3427. Fax: (207)948-5088. E-mail: potatoeyes@unin ets.net. Website: http://www.maineguide.com/giftshop/potatoeyes. Publishes hardcover and trade paperback originals. **Publishes 4-5 titles/year. Pays royalty on retail price. No advance.** Reports in 2 months on queries and proposals, 3 months on mss.

- Nightshade Press also publishes the literary magazine *Potato Eyes*.

Fiction: Contemporary, feminist, humor/satire, literary, mainstream, regional. No religious, romance, preschool, juvenile, young adult, psychic/occult. Query with SASE.

Poetry: Submit 3-5 poems with SASE.

Recent Title(s): *Every Day A Visitor*, by Richard Abrons (short story collection); *Bone Music*, by Howard Nelson.

NOLO PRESS, 950 Parker St., Berkeley CA 94710. (510)549-1976. Fax: (510)548-5902. E-mail: info@nolo.com. Website: http://www.nolo.com. **Acquisitions:** Barbara Kate Repa, senior editor. Estab. 1971. "Our goal is to publish 'plain English' self-help law books for the average consumer." Publishes trade paperback originals. **Publishes 10 titles/year. 25% of books from first-time authors; 98% from unagented writers. Pays 10-12% royalty on net sales.** Accepts simultaneous submissions. Reports within 2 weeks on queries.

Nonfiction: How-to, reference, self-help. Subjects include law, business/economics, money/finance, legal guides. "We do some business and finance titles, but always from a legal perspective, i.e., bankruptcy law." Query with outline, 1 sample chapter and SASE. Welcome queries but majority of titles are produced inhouse.

Recent Title(s): *Safe Homes, Safe Neighborhoods: Stopping Crime Where You Live*, by Stephanie Mann with M.C. Blakeman.

NOONDAY PRESS, Farrar Straus & Giroux, Inc., 19 Union Square W., New York NY 10003. (212)741-6900. Fax: (212)633-9385. **Acquisitions:** Elisabeth Dyssegaard, executive editor. Noonday emphasizes literary nonfiction and fiction, as well as fiction and poetry reprints. Publishes trade paperback originals and reprints. **Publishes 70 titles/year. Receives 1,500-2,000 queries/mss per year. Pays 6% royalty on retail price. Advance varies.** Publishes book 1 year after acceptance of ms. Accepts simultaneous submissions. Reports in 2 months on queries and proposals. Book catalog and ms guidelines free.

Nonfiction: Biography. Subjects include child guidance/parenting, education, language/literature. Query with outline, 2-3 sample chapters, cv, cover letter discribing project and SASE. *No unsolicited mss.*

Fiction: Literary. Mostly reprints of classic authors.

Recent Title(s): *Message from My Father*, by Calvin Trillin (memoir); *Enemies: A Love Story*, by Isaac Bashevis Singer (fiction).

NORTH LIGHT BOOKS, F&W Publications, 1507 Dana Ave., Cincinnati OH 45207. Editorial Director: Greg Albert.**Acquisitions:** Acquisitions Coordinator. North Light Books publishes art, craft and design books, including watercolor, drawing, colored pencil and decorative painting titles that emphasize how-to art instruction. Publishes hardcover and trade paperback how-to books. **Publishes 40-45 titles/year. Pays 10-20% royalty on net receipts. Offers $4,000 advance.** Accepts simultaneous submissions. Reports in 1 month. Book catalog for 9×12 SAE with 6 first-class stamps.

Nonfiction: Watercolor, drawing, colored pencil, decorative painting, craft and graphic design instruction books. Interested in books on watercolor painting, basic drawing, pen and ink, colored pencil, airbrush, crafts, decorative painting, basic design, computer graphics, layout and typography. Do not submit coffee table art books without how-to art instruction. Query or submit outline and examples of artwork (transparencies and photographs).

Recent Title(s): *Painting Beautiful Watercolors from Photographs*, by Jan Kunz.

NORTH POINT PRESS, Farrar Straus & Giroux, Inc., 19 Union Square W., New York NY 10003. (212)741-6900. Fax: (212)633-9385. Editorial Director: Rebecca Saletan. Editor: Ethan Nosowsky. **Acquisitions:** Katrin Wilde. Estab. 1980. "We are a broad-based literary trade publisher—high quality writing only." Hardcover and trade paperback originals. **Publishes 25 titles/year. Receives hundreds of queries and hundreds of mss/year. 20% of books from first-time authors; 90% from unagented writers. Pays standard royalty rates. Advance varies.** Publishes book 18 months after acceptance of ms. Accepts simultaneous submissions. Reports in 2 months on queries and proposals, 3 months on mss. Manuscript guidelines for #10 SASE.

Nonfiction: Subjects include nature/environment, food/gardening, history, religion (no New Age), music, memoir/biography, sports, travel. "Be familiar with our list. No genres." Query with outline, 1-2 sample chapters and SASE.
Recent Title(s): *Olives: Life & Love of a Noble Fruit*, by Mort Rosenblum.

N **NORTHEASTERN UNIVERSITY PRESS**, 360 Huntington Ave., 416CP, Boston MA 02115. (617)373-5480. Fax: (617)373-5483. Website: http://www.neu.edu/nupress. **Acquisitions**: William Frohlich, director (music, criminal justice); John Weingartner, senior editor (history, law and society); Terri Teleen, editor (women's studies). Publishes hardcover originals and trade paperback originals and reprints. **Publishes 40 titles/year. Receives 500 queries and 100 mss/year. 50% of books from first-time authors; 90% from unagented writers. Pays 5-15% royalty on wholesale price. Offers $500-5,000 advance.** Publishes book 1 year after acceptance of ms. Accepts simultaneous submissions. Reports in 1 month. Book catalog and ms guidelines free.
Nonfiction: Biography, adult trade scholarly monographs. Subjects include Americana, creative nonfiction, criminal justice, ethnic, history, language/literature, law & society, memoirs, music/dance, regional, women's issues/studies. Query or submit proposal package, outline and 1-2 sample chapters and SASE. Reviews artwork/photos as part of ms package. Send photocopies.
Fiction: Literary. Majority of fiction titles are reissues. Query.
Recent Title(s): *Public Heroes, Private Felons*, by Jeff Benedict (athletes and crimes against women).

NORTHERN ILLINOIS UNIVERSITY PRESS, DeKalb IL 60115-2854. (815)753-1826/753-1075. Fax: (815)753-1845. **Acquisitions**: Mary L. Lincoln, director/editor-in-chief. Estab. 1965. "Our mission is to facilitate the advancement of knowledge and disseminate the results of scholarly inquiry. In carrying out its role, the press publishes both specialized scholarly work and books of general interest to the informed public." **Publishes 18-20 titles/year. Pays 10-15% royalty on wholesale price.** Book catalog free.
Nonfiction: "Publishes mainly history, political science, social sciences, philosophy, literary criticism and regional studies. No collections of previously published essays, no unsolicited poetry." Accepts nonfiction translations. Query with outline and 1-3 sample chapters.
Recent Title(s): *Chicago Transit: An Illustrated History*, by David M. Young.

NORTHFIELD PUBLISHING, Moody Press, 820 N. LaSalle Dr., Chicago IL 60610. (312)329-2101. Fax: (312)329-2144. **Acquisitions:** Acquisitions Coordinator. "Northfield publishes a line of books for non-Christians or those exploring the Christian faith. While staying true to Biblical principles, we eliminate some of the Christian wording and scriptual references to avoid confusion." **Publishes 5-10 titles/year. Less than 1% of books from first-time authors; 95% from unagented writers. Pays royalty on retail price. Offers $500-50,000 advance.** Publishes books 6 months after acceptance of ms. Accepts simultaneous submissions, but prefers not to. Reports in 2 months on queries. Book catalog for 9×12 SAE with 2 first-class stamps. Manuscript guidelines for #10 SASE.
Nonfiction: Biographies (classic). Subjects include business/economics, child guidance/parenting, finance. Query with outline, 2-3 sample chapters, table of contents, author's market study of why this book will be successful and SASE.
Recent Title(s): *Loving Solutions*, by Gary Chapman (marriage helps).

NORTHLAND PUBLISHING CO., INC., P.O. Box 1389, Flagstaff AZ 86002-1389. (520)774-5251. Fax: (520)774-0592. E-mail: emurphy@northlandpub.com. Website: http://www.northlandpub.com. **Acquisitions:** Erin Murphy, editor-in-chief. Estab. 1958. "Northland is well regarded in the publishing industry as a publisher of quality nonfiction books on the material culture and indigenous peoples of the American West, including fine art, history, natural history and cookbooks. Under our new imprint, Rising Moon, we publish picture books for children and novels for older readers." Publishes hardcover and trade paperback originals. **Publishes 25 titles/year. Imprint publishes 10 titles/year. Receives 4,000 submissions/year. 75% of books from first-time authors; 80% from unagented writers. Pays 5-12% royalty on net receipts, depending upon terms. Offers $4,000-5,000 advance.** Publishes book 2 years after acceptance. Accepts simultaneous submissions. Reports in 3 months. Book catalog for 9×12 SAE with $1.24 in postage. Manuscript guidelines for #10 SASE.

- This publisher has received the following awards in the past year: National Cowboy Hall of Fame Western Heritage Award for Outstanding Juvenile Book (*The Night the Grandfathers Danced*); Colorado Book Awards—Best Children's Book (*Goose and the Mountain Lion*); Reading Rainbow Book (*It Rained on the Desert Today*).

Imprint(s): Rising Moon (books for young readers).
Nonfiction: Biography, children's/juvenile, coffee table book, cookbook, gift book, illustrated book (picture books). Subjects include animals (children's and adult natural history), anthropology/archaeology (Native America), art/architecture (multi-author/artist only), cooking/foods/nutrition (cookbooks, Southwest), ethnic (Native Americans, Hispanic), history (natural and Native America), hobbies (collecting/arts), nature/environment (picture books), regional (Southwestern and Western US). "Please know the kinds of books we are looking for by reading our guidelines and catalogs. Do not submit materials inappropriate for our market or topics that are for too narrow." Submit outline and 2-3 sample chapters with SASE. No fax or e-mail submissions. Reviews artwork/photos as part of the ms package. "Artwork should be sent to the Art Director unless it is critical to understanding the proposal."
Fiction: Middle reader, young adult, picture books. "Please review our submission guidelines and catalogs to know what we're looking for. We do *not* publish adult fiction. Do not submit children's fiction that is inappropriate for our market." Submit synopsis and 3 sample chapters with SASE. "No dummy books! For picture books, send complete manuscript with SASE."

Recent Title(s): *One Woman's West: The Life of Mary-Russell Ferrell Colton*, by Richard and Sherry Mangum (biography); *A Campfire for Cowboy Billy*, by Wendy K. Ulmer, illustrated by Kenneth Spengler (fiction).
Tips: "Our audience is composed of general interest readers and those interested in specialty subjects such as Native American culture and crafts. It is not necessarily a scholarly market, but it is sophisticated."

[A] **NORTH-SOUTH BOOKS**, Nord-Sud Verlag AG, 1123 Broadway, Suite 800, New York NY 10010. (212)463-9736. **Acquisitions:** Julie Amper. Website: http://www.northsouth.com. Estab. 1985. "The aim of North-South is to build bridges—bridges between authors and artists from different countries and between readers of all ages. We believe children should be exposed to as wide a range of artistic styles as possible with universal themes." **Publishes 100 titles/year. Receives 5,000 queries/year. 5% of books from first-time authors. Pays royalty on retail price.** Publishes book an average of 2 years after acceptance of ms. Returns submissions accompanied by SASE. "But is very low priority." Does not respond unless interested.
Fiction: Picture books, easy-to-read. "We are currently accepting only picture books; all other books are selected by our German office." *Agented submissions only. All unsolicited mss returned unopened.*
Recent Title(s): *The Rainbow Fish & the Big Blue Whale*, by Marcus Pfister (picture).

NORTHWORD PRESS, Cowles Creative Publishing, 5900 Green Oak Dr., Minnetonka MN 55343. (612)936-4700. Fax: (612)933-1456. **Acquisitions:** Barbara K. Harold, editorial director. Estab. 1984. Publishes hardcover and trade paperback originals. "We publish exclusively nature and wildlife titles for adults, teens, and children." **Publishes 15-20 titles/year. Receives 600 submissions/year. 50% of books are from first-time authors; 90% are from unagented writers. Pays 10-15% royalty on wholesale price. Offers $2,000-20,000 advance.** Publishes book 1 year after acceptance. Accepts simultaneous submissions. Reports in 3 months on queries. Book catalog for 9×12 SASE with 7 first-class stamps. Manuscript guidelines for SASE.
Nonfiction: Coffee table books, introductions to wildlife and natural history, guidebooks, children's illustrated books; nature and wildlife subjects exclusively. Query with outline, sample chapters and SASE.
Recent Title(s): *Children of the Earth. . . Remember*, by Schim Schimmel (children's).
Tips: "No poetry, fiction or memoirs. We have expanded to include exotic and non-North American topics."

W.W. NORTON CO., INC., 500 Fifth Ave., New York NY 10110. Fax: (212)869-0856. Website: http://www.wwnorton.com. **Acquisitions**: "The Editors." General trade publisher of fiction, poetry and nonfiction, educational and professional books. "W. W. Norton & Company strives to carry out the imperative of its founder to 'publish books not for a single season, but for the years' in the areas of fiction, nonfiction, and poetry." Publishes hardcover and paperback originals and reprints. **Publishes 300 titles/year. Pays royalty.** Reports in 2 months.
Imprint(s): Backcountry Publishing, Countryman Press, Foul Play Press, W.W. Norton.
Nonfiction and Fiction: Subjects include antiques and collectibles, architecture, art/design, autobiography/memoir, biography, business, child care, cooking, current affairs, family, fiction, games, health, history, law, literature, music, mystery, nature, photography, poetry, politics/political science, reference, religion, sailing, science, self-help, transportation, travel. *College Department:* Subjects include biological sciences, economics, psychology, political science, and computer science. *Professional Books* specializes in psychotherapy. "We are not interested in considering books from the following categories: juvenile or young adult, religious, occult or paranormal, genre fiction (formula romances, sci-fi or westerns), and arts and crafts. Please give a brief description of your submission, your writing credentials, and any experience, professional or otherwise, which is relevant to your submission. Submit 2 or 3 sample chapters, one of which should be the first chapter, with SASE. No phone calls. Address envelope and letter to The Editors."
Recent Title(s): *The Perfect Storm*, by Sebastian Junger (nonfiction); *Oyster*, by Janette Turner Hospital.

NOVA PRESS, 11659 Mayfield Ave., Suite 1, Los Angeles CA 90049. (310)207-4078. Fax: (310)571-0908. E-mail: novapress@aol.com. Website: http://www.mrcybermall.com/novapress. **Acquisitions:** Jeff Kolby, president. "We publish only test prep books for college entrance exams, and closely related reference books, such as college guides and vocabulary books." Publishes trade paperback originals. **Publishes 10 titles/year. Pays 10-22½% royalty on net price.** Publishes book 6 months after acceptance of ms. Book catalog free.
Nonfiction: Test prep books for college entrance exams. How-to, self-help, technical. Education, software subjects.
Recent Title(s): *The MCAT Biology Book*, by Nancy Morvillo.

NOYES DATA CORP., 369 Fairview Ave., Westwood NJ 07675. (201)666-2121. Fax: (201)666-5111. **Acquisitions**: Editorial Department. Noyes publishes technical books primarily of interest to business executives, research scientists and research engineers. Estab. 1959. Publishes hardcover originals. **Publishes 30 titles/year. Pays 12% royalty on net proceeds. Advance varies, depending on author's reputation and nature of book.** Reports in 2 weeks. Book catalog free.
Nonfiction: Technical. Subjects include industrial processing, science, economic books pertaining to chemistry, chemical engineering, food, textiles, energy, electronics, pollution control, material science, semi-conductor material and process technology. Length: 50,000-250,000 words.

NTC/CONTEMPORARY PUBLISHING GROUP, 4255 W. Touhy Ave., Lincolnwood IL 60646-1975. (847)679-5500. Fax: (847)679-2494. E-mail: ntcpub2@aol.com. Editorial Director: John T. Nolan. **Acquisitions:** Linda Gray, senior editor. Estab. 1947. "We are midsize, niche-oriented, backlist-oriented publisher. We publish exclusively nonfiction in general interest trade categories plus travel, reference and quilting books." Publishes hardcover originals and trade paperback originals and reprints. **Publishes 400 titles/year. Receives 9,000 submissions/year. 10% of books from first-time authors; 25% of books from unagented writers. Pays 6-15% royalty on retail price.** Publishes book 10 months after acceptance. Accepts simultaneous submissions. Reports in 2 months. Manuscript guidelines for SASE.

Imprint(s): Contemporary Books, Country Roads Press, **Lowell House**, **Masters Press**, NTC Business Books, **NTC Publishing Group**, **National Textbook Company** (Anne Knudsen, editor), Passport Books, **The Quilt Digest Press**, **VGM Career Horizons** (Betsy Lancefield, editor).

Nonfiction: Biography, cookbook, how-to, humor, reference, self-help. Subjects include business, careers, child guidance/parenting, crafts (especially quilting), finance, cooking, health/fitness, nutrition, popular culture, psychology, real estate, sports, travel, women's studies. Submit outline, sample chapters and SASE. Reviews artwork/photos as part of ms package.

Recent Title(s): *Mad as Hell*, by Mike Lupica (sports).

OASIS PRESS, Imprint of PSI Research, 300 N. Valley Dr. Grants Pass OR 97526, Grants Pass OR 97526. (503)479-9464. Fax: (503)476-1479. **Acquisitions:** Emmett Ramey, president. Estab. 1975. Oasis Press publishes books for small business or individuals who are entrepreneurs or owners or managers of small businesses (1-300 employees). Publishes hardcover, trade paperback and binder originals. **Publishes 20-30 books/year. Receives 90 submissions/year. 60% of books from first-time authors; 90% from unagented writers. Pays 10% royalty on the net received, except wholesale sales. No advance.** Publishes book 1 year after acceptance. Accepts simultaneous submissions. Reports in 2 months (initial feedback) on queries. Book catalog and ms guidelines for SASE.

Imprint(s): Hellgate Press.

Nonfiction: How-to, reference, textbook. Subjects include business/economics, computers, education, money/finance, retirement, exporting, franchise, finance, marketing and public relations, relocations, environment, taxes, business start up and operation. Needs information-heavy, readable mss written by professionals in their subject fields. Interactive where appropriate. Authorship credentials less important than hands-on experience qualifications. Query for unwritten material or to check current interest in topic and orientation. Submit outline/synopsis and sample chapters. Reviews artwork/photos as part of ms package.

Recent Title(s): *Smile Training Isn't Enough*, by Gallagher (customer service).

Tips: "Best chance is with practical, step-by-step manuals for operating a business, with worksheets, checklists. The audience is made up of entrepreneurs of all types: small business owners and those who would like to be; attorneys, accountants and consultants who work with small businesses; college students; dreamers. Make sure your information is valid and timely for its audience, also that by virtue of either its content quality or viewpoint, it distinguishes itself from other books on the market."

[N] **OCEANA PUBLICATIONS, INC.**, 75 Main St., Dobbs Ferry NY 10522. (914)693-8100. Website: http://www.oceanalaw.com. **Acquisitions:** M.C. Susan De Maio, vice-president, product development. "With 50 years of experience, Oceana Publications, Inc., is recognized as the premier publisher of international legal texts." **Publishes 200 looseleaf and clothbound titles/year. Receives 250 queries and 150 mss/year. 85% of books from first-time authors; 100% from unagented writers. Pays 10-15% royalty.** Publishes book 3 months after acceptance of ms. Accepts simultaneous submissions. Reports in 1 month. Book catalog and ms guidelines free.

Nonfiction: Reference. Subjects include international law, business. "We pride ourselves on our long-standing partnerships with the world's leading experts in international trade and commercial law; banking, investment and financial law; the law of arbitration and dispute settlement; environmental law treaties; intellectual property law. Most of Oceana's titles are looseleaf in format and should be structured accordingly." Query with outline, table of contents and 2 sample chapters.

Recent Title(s): *Comparative Environmental Law and Regulation*, edited by Nicholas A. Robinson.

OCTAMERON ASSOCIATES, 1900 Mt. Vernon Ave., Alexandria VA 22301. (703)836-5480. E-mail: stokstad@octameron.com. Websites: http://www.octameron.com. **Acquisitions:** Karen Stokstad, editorial director. Estab. 1976. Octameron publishes college and career reference books. They emphasize college admission and financial aid titles. Publishes trade paperback originals. **Publishes 15 titles/year. Receives 100 submissions/year. 10% of books from first-time authors; 100% from unagented writers. Pays 7½% royalty on retail price.** Publishes book 6 months after acceptance. Accepts simultaneous submissions. Reports in 2 months. Book catalog for #10 SAE with 2 first-class stamps.

Nonfiction: Reference, career, post-secondary education subjects. Especially interested in "paying-for-college and college admission guides." Query with outline and 2 sample chapters. Reviews artwork/photos as part of ms package.

Recent Title(s): *College.edu: On-line Resources for the Cyber-Savvy Student*, by Lisa Guernsey.

OHIO STATE UNIVERSITY PRESS, 1070 Carmack Rd., Columbus OH 43210. (614)292-6930. Fax: (614)292-2065. E-mail: ohiostatepress@osu.edu. Website: http://www.sbs.ohio-sate.edu/osu-press. **Acquisitions:** Charlotte Dihoff, assistant director/editor-in-chief; Barbara Hanrahan, director. Ohio State University Press publishes scholarly nonfiction, fiction and poetry. **Publishes 30 titles/year. Pays royalty.** Reports in 3 months; ms held longer with author's permission.

Imprint(s): Sandstone Books.

Nonfiction: Scholarly studies with special interests in African American studies, business and economic history,

criminology, literary criticism, political science regional studies, teaching and higher education, Victorian studies, women's and gender studies, women's health. Query with outline and sample chapters and SASE.
Recent Title(s): *Fallout: A Historian Reflects on America's Half-Century Encounter With Nuclear Weapons*, by Paul Boyer (history/culture); *Radiance: Ten Stories*, by John J. Clayton (fiction).
Tips: "Publishes some poetry and fiction. Query first."

OHIO UNIVERSITY PRESS, Scott Quadrangle, Athens OH 45701. (740)593-1155. **Acquisitions:** Gillian Berchowitz, senior editor. "Ohio University Press publishes and disseminates the fruits of research and creative endeavor, specifically in the areas of literary studies, regional works, philosophy, contemporary history, African studies and frontier Americana. Its charge to produce books of value in service to the academic community and for the enrichment of the broader culture is in keeping with the university's mission of teaching, research and service to its constituents." Publishes hardcover and trade paperback originals and reprints. **Publishes 40-45 titles/year. Receives 500 queries and 50 mss/year. 20% of books from first-time authors; 95% from unagented writers. Pays 7-10% royalty on net sales. No advance.** Publishes book 1 year after acceptance of ms. Reports in 1 month on queries and proposals, 2 months on mss. Book catalog free. Manuscript guidelines for #10 SASE.
Imprint(s): Swallow Press (David Sanders, director); Ohio University Monographs in International Studies (Gillian Berchowitz).
Nonfiction: Biography, reference, scholarly. Subjects include African studies, agriculture/horticulture, Americana, animals, anthropology/archaeology, art/architecture, ethnic, gardening, government/politics, history, language/literature, military/war, nature/environment, philosophy, regional, sociology, travel, women's issues/studies. Query with proposal package, including outline, sample chapter and SASE. "We prefer queries or detailed proposals, rather than manuscripts, pertaining to scholarly projects that might have a general interest. Proposals should explain the thesis and details of the subject matter, not just sell a title." Reviews artwork/photos as part of ms package. Send photocopies.
Recent Title(s): *Hired Pens: Professional Writers in America's Golden Age of Print*, by Ronald Weber; *Frozen in Silver: The Life and Frontier Photography of P.E. Larson*, by Ronald T. Bailey.
Tips: "Rather than trying to hook the editor on your work, let the material be compelling enough and well-presented enough to do it for you."

N **THE OLIVER PRESS, INC.**, 5707 W. 36th St., Minneapolis MN 55416-2510. (612)926-8981. Fax: (612)926-8965. E-mail: theoliverpress@mindspring.com. Website: http://www.mindspring.com/~theoliverpress. **Acquisitions**: Teresa Faden, editor. "We publish collective biographies for ages 10 and up. Although we cover a wide array of subjects, all are published in this format." Publishes hardcover originals. **Publishes 8 titles/year. Receives 100 queries and 20 mss/year. 10% of books from first-time authors; 100% from unagented writers. Makes outright purchase of $800-2,000.** Publishes book 1 year after acceptance of ms. Accepts simultaneous submissions. Reports in 2 months on queries. Book catalog for 6×9 SAE with 3 first-class stamps. Manuscript guidelines for #10 SASE.
Nonfiction: Children's/juvenile, collective biographies only. Subjects include business/economics, ethnic, government/politics, health/medicine, military/war, nature/environment, science. Query with SASE.
Recent Title(s): *Treacherous Traitors*, by Nathan Aaseng (American traitors and spies).
Tips: "Audience is primarily junior and senior high school students writing reports."

ONE WORLD, Ballantine Publishing, 201 E. 50th St., New York NY 10022. (212)572-2620. Fax: (212)940-7539. Website: http://www.randomhouse.com. **Acquisitions:** Cheryl Woodruff, associate publisher; Gary Brozek, associate editor. Estab. 1992. "One World's list includes books written by and focused on African Americans, Native Americans, Asian Americans and Latino Americans. We concentrate on *American* multicultural experiences." Publishes hardcover and trade paperback originals, trade and mass market paperback reprints. **Publishes 8-10 titles/year. Receives 1,200 queries and mss/year. 25% of books from first-time authors; 5% from unagented writers. Pays 8-12% royalty on retail price, varies from hardcover to mass market. Advance varies.** Publishes book 2 years after acceptance of ms. Accepts simultaneous submissions, if so noted. Reports in 4 months. Book catalog and ms guidelines for #10 SASE.
Nonfiction: Biography, cookbook, memoir, relationships. Subjects include business/economics, child guidance/parenting, cooking/foods/nutrition, ethnic, gay/lesbian, health/medicine, religion/inspirational, sociology, women's issues/studies. "We are dealing with American people of color." Query or submit proposal package including 200 pages with SASE. Reviews artwork/photos as part of ms package, where germane. Send photocopies.
Fiction: Historical. "We are looking for good contemporary fiction. In the past, topics have mostly been 'pre-Civil rights era and before.' " Query with synopsis, 3 sample chapters (100 pages) and SASE.
Recent Title(s): *Native Wisdom for White Minds*, by Ann Wilson Shaef (inspirational); *Kinfolks*, by Kristin Hunter Lattany (novel).
Tips: "For first-time authors, have a completed manuscript. You won't be asked to write on speculation."

ORCHARD BOOKS, Grolier Publishing, 95 Madison Ave., New York NY 10016. (212)951-2650. President/Publisher: Judy V. Wilson. **Acquisitions:** Sarah Caguiat, editor; Dominic Barth, associate editor. Orchard specializes in children's picture books. Publishes hardcover and trade paperback originals. **Publishes 60-70 titles/year. Receives 1,600 queries/year. 25% of books from first-time authors; 50% from unagented writers. Pays 6-10% royalty on retail price. Advance varies.** Publishes book 1 year after acceptance of ms. Reports in 3 months on queries.
Nonfiction: Children's/juvenile, illustrated book. Subjects include animals, history, nature/environment. Query with

SASE. "*No unsolicited mss at this time*. Queries only! Be as specific and enlightening as possible about your book." Reviews artwork/photos as part of the ms package. Send photocopies.

Fiction: Picture books, young adult, middle reader, board book, novelty. Query with SASE. *No unsolicited mss, please.*

Recent Title(s): *Tale of a Tadpole*, Porte and Cannon (nonfiction); *Mysterious Thelonius*, by Raschka (fiction).

Tips: "Go to a bookstore and read several Orchard Books to get an idea of what we publish. Write what you feel and query us if you think it's 'right.' It's worth finding the right publishing match."

ORCHISES PRESS. P.O. Box 20602, Alexandria VA 22320-1602. (703)683-1243. E-mail: rlathbur@osfl.gmu.edu. Website: http://mason.gmu.edu/~rlathbur. **Acquisitions:** Roger Lathbury, editor-in-chief. Estab. 1983. Orchises Press publishes professional, literate and academic nonfiction and poetry based on literary and commercial merit. It prides itself on the attractiveness of its volumes. Publishes hardcover and trade paperback originals and reprints. **Publishes 4-5 titles/year. Receives 600 queries and 200 mss/year. 1% of books from first-time authors; 95% from unagented writers. Pays 36% of receipts after Orchises has recouped its costs.** Publishes book 1 year after acceptance. Accepts simultaneous submissions. Reports in 3 months. Book catalog for #10 SASE.

Nonfiction: Biography, how-to, humor, reference, technical, textbook. No real restrictions on subject matter. Query. Reviews artwork/photos as part of the ms package. Send photocopies.

Poetry: Poetry must have been published in respected literary journals. Publishes free verse, but has strong formalist preferences. Query or submit 5 sample poems.

Recent Title(s): *Notes on Grammar*, by DeeAnn Holisky (linguistics); *What She Knew*, by Peter Filkins.

Tips: "Show some evidence of appealing to a wider audience than simply people you know."

ORYX PRESS, 4041 N. Central Ave., Suite 700, Phoenix AZ 85012. (602)265-2651. Fax: (602)265-6250. E-mail: info@oryxpress.com. Website: http://www.oryxpress.com/. President: Phyllis B. Steckler. **Acquisitions:** Donna Sanzone, Henry Rasof, Jake Goldberg, acquisitions editors; Martha Wilke (submission). Estab. 1975. Publishes print and/or electronic reference resources for public, college and university, K-12 school, business and medical libraries, and professionals. **Publishes 50 titles/year. Receives 500 submissions/year. 40% of books from first-time authors; 80% from unagented writers. Pays 10% royalty on net receipts. Offers moderate advances.** Publishes book 9 months after acceptance of manuscript. Proposals via Internet welcomed. Reports in 1 month. Book catalog and author guidelines free.

Nonfiction: Directories, dictionaries, encyclopedias, in print and electronic formats (online and CD-ROM), and other general reference works; special subjects: business, education, consumer health care, government information, gerontology, social sciences. Query or submit outline/rationale and samples. Queries/mss may be routed to other editors in the publishing group.

Recent Title(s): *Storytelling Encyclopedia: Historical, Cultural and Multiethnic Approaches to Oral Traditions Around the World*, edited by David Leeming (reference).

Tips: "We are accepting and promoting more titles over the Internet. We are also looking for up-to-date, relevant ideas to add to our established line of print and electronic works."

OSBORNE/MCGRAW-HILL, The McGraw-Hill Companies, 2600 10th St., Berkeley CA 94710. (510)548-2805. (800)227-0900. **Acquisitions:** Scott Rogers, editor-in-chief. Estab. 1979. Osborne publishes technical computer books and software. Publishes computer trade paperback originals. **Publishes 100 titles/year. Receives 120 submissions/year. 30% of books from first-time authors; 95% from unagented writers. Pays 8-12% royalty on wholesale price. Offers $5,000 average advance.** Publishes book an average of 6 months after acceptance. Accepts simultaneous submissions. Reports in 2 months. Book catalog free.

Nonfiction: Software, technical. Computer subjects. Query with outline and sample chapters. Reviews artwork/photos as part of ms package.

Recent Title(s): *Microsoft Office 97: The Complete Reference*, by Stephen L. Nelson and Peter Weverka.

OUR SUNDAY VISITOR, INC., 200 Noll Plaza, Huntington IN 46750-4303. (219)356-8400. Fax: (219)359-9117. President/Publisher: Robert Lockwood. Editor-in-Chief: Greg Erlandson. **Acquistions:** James Manney or Jackie Lindsey, acquisitions editors. Estab. 1912. "We are a Catholic publishing company seeking to educate and deepen our readers in their faith." Publishes paperback and hardbound originals. **Publishes 20-30/year. Receives over 100 submissions/year. 10% of books from first-time authors; 90% from unagented writers. Pays variable royalty on net receipts. Offers $1,000 average advance.** Publishes book 1 year after acceptance. Reports in 3 months. Author's guide and catalog for SASE.

Nonfiction: Catholic viewpoints on current issues, reference and guidance, family, prayer and devotional books, and Catholic heritage books. Prefers to see well-developed proposals as first submission with annotated outline and definition of intended market. Reviews artwork/photos as part of ms package.

Recent Title(s): *A Priest Forever*, by Father Benedict Groeschel.

Tips: "Solid devotional books that are not first-person, well-researched church histories or lives of the saints and catechetical books have the best chance of selling to our firm. Make it solidly Catholic, unique, without pious platitudes."

N A **THE OVERLOOK PRESS**, Distributed by Penguin Putnam, 386 W. Broadway, New York NY 10012. **Acquisitions:** Editorial Department. Publishes hardcover and trade paperback originals and hardcover reprints. **Publishes**

40 titles/year. Receives 300 submissions/year. Pays 3-15% royalty on wholesale or retail price. Reports in 5 months. Book catalog free.
Imprint(s): Tusk Books.
Nonfiction: Art, architecture, design, film, history, biography, current events, popular culture, New York State regional. No pornography. *Agented submissions only.*
Fiction: Literary fiction, fantasy, foreign literature in translation. *Agented submissions only.*

RICHARD C. OWEN PUBLISHERS INC., P.O. Box 585, Katonah NY 10536. Fax: (914)232-3977. Website: http://www.rcowen.com. **Acquisitions:** Janice Boland, director of children's books; Amy Haggblom, project editor (professional books). "Our focus is literacy education with a meaning-centered perspective. We believe students become enthusiastic, independent, life-long learners when supported and guided by skillful teachers. The professional development work we do and the books we publish support these beliefs." Publishes hardcover and paperback originals. **Publishes 23 titles/year. Receives 150 queries and 1,000 mss/year. 99% of books from first-time authors; 100% from unagented writers. Pays 5% royalty on wholesale price.** Publishes book 3 years after acceptance of ms. Accepts simultaneous submissions, if so noted. Reports in 1 month on queries and proposals, 2 months on mss. Manuscript guidelines for SASE with 52¢ postage.

- "We are also seeking manuscripts for our new collection of short, snappy stories for children. Subjects include humor, careers, mysteries, science fiction, folktales, women, fashion trends, sports, music, myths, journalism, history, inventions, planets, architecture, plays, adventure, technology, vehicles."

Nonfiction: Children's/juvenile humor, illustrated book. Subjects include animals, nature/environment, gardening, music/dance, recreation, science, sports. "Our books are for 5-7-year-olds. The stories are very brief—under 100 words—yet well structured and crafted with memorable characters, language and plots." Send for ms guidelines, then submit complete ms with SASE.
Fiction: Picture books. "Brief, strong story line, believable characters, natural language, exciting—child-appealing stories with a twist. No lists, alphabet or counting books." Send for ms guidelines, then submit full ms with SASE.
Poetry: Poems that excite children, fun, humorous, fresh. No jingles. Must rhyme without force or contrivance. Send for ms guidelines, then submit complete ms with SASE.
Recent Title(s): *The Changing Caterpillar*, by Sherry Shahan (science/nature); *Jump the Broom*, by Candy Helmso (fiction).
Tips: "We don't respond to queries. Because our books are so brief it is better to send entire ms. We publish books with intrinsic value for young readers—books they can read with success, books with supports and challenges to take them to the next learning point."

OWL BOOKS, Henry Holt & Co., Inc., 115 W. 18th St., New York NY 10011. (212)886-9200. Website: http://www.hholt.com. Associate Publisher: Wendy Sherman. **Acquisitions:** David Sobel, senior editor. Estab. 1996. "We are looking for original, great ideas that have commercial appeal, but that you can respect." Publishes trade paperback originals. **Firm publishes 135-140 titles/year; imprint publishes 50-60 titles/year. 30% of books from first-time authors; 5% from unagented writers. Pays 6-7½% royalty on retail price. Advance varies.** Publishes book 1 year after acceptance of ms. Accepts simultaneous submissions. Reports in 3 months on proposals.
Nonfiction: "Broad range." Subjects include art/architecture, biography, cooking/foods/nutrition, gardening, health/medicine, history, language/literature, nature/environment, regional, sociology, sports, travel. Query with outline, 1 sample chapter and SASE.
Fiction: Literary fiction. Query with synopsis, 1 sample chapter and SASE.
Recent Title(s): *White Boy Shuffle*, by Paul Beatty; *The Debt to Pleasure*, by John Lanchester.

OWL CREEK PRESS, 2693 SW Camano Dr., Camano Island WA 98292. **Acquisitions:** Rich Ives, editor. "Owl Creek Press exists to support literary art regardless of commercial considerations." Publishes hardcover originals, trade paperback originals and reprints. **Publishes 4-6 titles/year. 50% of books from first time authors; 95% from unagented writers. Pays 10-15% royalty, makes outright purchase or with a percentage of print run.** Publishes book 2 years after acceptance. Reports in 3 months. Book catalog for #10 SASE.

- Owl Creek Press has discontinued its three contests, the Owl Creek Poetry Prize, the Owl Creek Press Fiction Prize and the Green Lake Chapbook Prize.

Fiction: Literary, short story collections and novels. "We publish selections of artistic merit only."
Recent Title(s): *Beasts of the Forest, Beasts of the Field*, by Matt Pavelich (fiction); *The Wedding Boat*, by Sue Ellen Thompson (poetry).

N **OXFORD UNIVERSITY PRESS**, 198 Madison Ave., New York NY 10016. (212)726-6000. Website: http://www.oup-usa.org/. **Acquisitions:** Joan Bossert, editorial director (humanities and science); Laura Brown, director (trade publishing). "We publish books that make a significant contribution to the literature and research in a number of disciplines, which reflect the departments at the University of Oxford." Publishes hardcover and trade paperback originals and reprints. **Publishes 1,500 titles/year. 40% of books from first-time authors; 80% from unagented writers. Pays 0-15% royalty on wholesale price or retail price. Offers $0-40,000 advance.** Publishes book 10 months after acceptance of ms. Accepts simultaneous submissions. Reports in 3 months on proposals. Book catalog free.
Nonfiction: Biography, children's/juvenile, reference, technical, textbook. Subjects include anthropology/archaeology, art/architecture, business/economics, computers/electronics, gay/lesbian, government/politics, health/medicine, history,

language/literature, law, military/war, music/dance, nature/environment, philosophy, psychology and psychiatry, religion, science, sociology, women's issues/studies. Oxford is an academic, scholarly press. Submit outline, sample chapters and cv. Reviews artwork/photos as part of ms package (but not necessary).
Recent Title(s): *On the Air: The Encyclopedia of Old-Time Radio*, by John Dunning (entertainment/reference).

PACIFIC BOOKS, PUBLISHERS, P.O. Box 558, Palo Alto CA 94302-0558. (650)965-1980. **Acquisitions:** Henry Ponleithner, editor. "We publish general interest and scholarly nonfiction including professional and technical books, and college textbooks since 1945." **Publishes 6-12 titles/year. Pays 7½-15% royalty. No advance.** Reports in 1 month. *Writer's Market* recommends allowing 2 months for reply. Book catalog and guidelines for 9×12 SASE.
Nonfiction: General interest, professional, technical and scholarly nonfiction trade books. Specialties include western Americana and Hawaiiana. Looks for "well-written, documented material of interest to a significant audience." Also considers text and reference books for high school and college. Accepts artwork/photos and translations. Query with outline and SASE.
Recent Title(s): *Issei Women: Echoes From Another Frontier*, by Eileen Sunada Sarasohn (history/women's studies).

PACIFIC PRESS PUBLISHING ASSOCIATION, Book Division, P.O. Box 5353, Nampa ID 83653-5353. (208)465-2570. Fax: (208)465-2531. E-mail: kenwad@pacificpress.com. Website: http://www.pacificpress.com. **Acquisitions:** Jerry Thomas. Estab. 1874. "We are an exclusively religious publisher of the Seventh-Day Adventist denominations. We are looking for practical, how-to oriented manuscripts on religion, health, and family life that speak to human needs, interests and problems from a Biblical perspective." Publishes hardcover and trade paperback originals and reprints. **Publishes 35 titles/year. Receives 600 submissions and proposals/year. Up to 35% of books from first-time authors; 100% from unagented writers. Pays 8-16% royalty on wholesale price. Offers $300-1,500 average advance depending on length.** Publishes book 10 months after acceptance. Reports in 3 months. Manuscript guidelines for #10 SASE.
Nonfiction: Biography, cookbook (vegetarian), how-to, juvenile, self-help. Subjects include cooking/foods (vegetarian only), health, nature, religion, family living. "We can't use anything totally secular or written from other than a Christian perspective." Query or request information on how to submit a proposal. Reviews artwork/photos.
Recent Title(s): *Stand at the Cross*, by Lonnie Melashenko and John McClarty; *Prayer Warriors*, by Celeste Perrino Walker.
Tips: "Our primary audiences are members of the Seventh-Day Adventist denomination, the general Christian reading market, and the secular or nonreligious reader. Books that are doing well for us are those that relate the Biblical message to practical human concerns and those that focus more on the experiential rather than theoretical aspects of Christianity. We are assigning more titles, using less unsolicited material—although we still publish manuscripts from freelance submissions and proposals."

PALADIN PRESS, P.O. Box 1307, Boulder CO 80306-1307. (303)443-7250. Fax: (303)442-8741. E-mail: editorial@paladin-press.com. Website: http://www.paladin-press.com. President/Publisher: Peder C. Lund. **Acquisitions:** Jon Ford, editorial director. Estab. 1970. Paladin Press publishes the "action library" of nonfiction in military science, police science, weapons, combat, personal freedom, self-defense, survival, "revenge humor." Publishes hardcover and paperback originals and paperback reprints. **Publishes 50 titles/year. 50% of books from first-time authors; 100% from unagented writers. Pays 10-12-15% royalty on net sales.** Publishes book 1 year after acceptance. Accepts simultaneous submissions. Reports in 2 months. Book catalog free.
Imprint(s): Sycamore Island Books.
Nonfiction: "Paladin Press primarily publishes original manuscripts on military science, weaponry, self-defense, personal privacy, financial freedom, espionage, police science, action careers, guerrilla warfare, fieldcraft and 'creative revenge' humor. How-to manuscripts are given priority. If applicable, send sample photographs and line drawings with complete outline and sample chapters." Query with outline and sample chapters.
Recent Title(s): *Ultimate Internet Terrorist*, by Robert Merkle (hackers on the Internet).
Tips: "We need lucid, instructive material aimed at our market and accompanied by sharp, relevant illustrations and photos. As we are primarily a publisher of 'how-to' books, a manuscript that has step-by-step instructions, written in a clear and concise manner (but not strictly outline form) is desirable. No fiction, first-person accounts, children's, religious or joke books. We are also interested in serious, professional videos and video ideas (contact Michael Janich)."

PANTHEON BOOKS, Random House, Inc., 201 E. 50th St., 25th Floor, New York NY 10022. (212)751-2600. Fax: (212)572-6030. Editorial Director: Dan Frank. Editor: Claudine O'Hearn. Senior Editor: Shelley Wagner. Executive Editor: Erroll McDonald. **Acquisitions:** Adult Editorial Department. "Pantheon Books, which Kurt and Helen Wolff established in 1942 to introduce intellectual European writers to American readers, publishes both Western and non-Western authors of literary fiction and important nonfiction." **Pays royalty. Offers advance.**
Nonfiction: History, politics, autobiography, biography, interior design. Query.
Recent Title(s): *Bad Land*, by Jonathan Raban; *Crooked Little Heart*, by Anne Lamott.

PAPIER-MACHE PRESS, 627 Walker St., Watsonville CA 95076. (408)763-1420. Fax: (408)763-1422. Website: http://www.ReadersNdex.com/papiermache. **Acquisitions:** Shirley Coe, acquisitions editor. "Our goal is to produce attractive, accessible books that deal with contemporary personal, social and political issues. We focus primarily on midlife women and aging and have a national reputation for 'gentle consciousness raising.' " **Publishes 4-6 titles/year.**

Pays royalty. Accepts simultaneous submissions. Book catalog and ms guidelines free.
Fiction: Feminist, mainstream/contemporary (women), short story collections (women), aging. "We publish theme anthologies that include fiction and poetry." Write for submission guidelines.
Recent Title(s): *One Small Step: Moving Beyond Trauma and Therapy to a Life of Joy*, by Yvonne Dolan, MA (self-help); *Grow Old Along with Me—The Best Is Yet to Be*, edited by Sandra Haldeman Martz (fiction).
Tips: Audience is women, 35-55 years old. Always request submission guidelines before submitting.

N **PARACLETE PRESS**, P.O. Box 1568, Orleans MA 02653. (508)255-4685. **Acquisitions:** William Miao, CEO. Publishes hardcover and trade paperback originals. **Publishes 10 titles/year. Receives 156 queries and 60 mss/year. 80% of books from unagented writers. Pays 10-12% royalty. Offers $1000-1500 advance.** Publishes book 12 months after acceptance of ms. Accepts simultaneous submissions. Reports in 2 months on queries, proposals and mss. Book catalog and ms guidelines for 8½×11 SASE and 3 first-class stamps.
Nonfiction: Spirituality. religious subjects. No poetry or children books. Submit outline with sample chapters.
Recent Title(s): *Awake My Heart-Psalms for Life,* edited by Frederick Bassett (Psalms paperback); *Creative Prayer,* by Brigid Herman (paperback); *Reader's Companion to Crossing the Threshold of Hope,* by various authors (hardcover).
Fiction: Religious.

PARADIGM PUBLISHING INC., EMC Corporation, 875 Montreal Way, St. Paul MN 55102. (612)290-2800. Fax: (612)290-2828. E-mail: publish@emcp.com. Website: http://www.emcp.com. **Acquisitions:** Mel Hecker, publisher. "We focus on textbooks for business and office, computer information systems, and allied health education marketed to proprietary business schools and community colleges. textbooks enhanced by technology for existing full semester courses." **Publishes 50 titles/year. Receives 60 queries and 35 mss/year. 20% of books from first-time authors; 100% from unagented writers. Pays 6-10% royalty on net. Offers $1,000-2,500 advance.** Publishes book 1 year after acceptance of ms. Accepts simultaneous submissions. Reports in 2 months on proposals. Book catalog for 8×12 SAE with 4 first-class stamps. Manuscript guidelines free.
Nonfiction: Textbook, multimedia. Subjects include business and office, communications, computers, psychology, allied health and accounting. Submit outline and 2 sample chapters.
Recent Title(s): *Microsoft Office Professional 97*, by Nita Rutkosky.
Tips: "We are looking more seriously at materials for distributive education. Let us know what ideas you have."

PARKWAY PUBLISHERS, INC., Box 3678, Boone NC 28607. Phone/fax: (704)265-3993. E-mail: aluri@netins.net. Website: http://www.netins.net/showcase/alurir. **Acquisitions:** Rao Aluri, president. "Publishes books on the local history and culture of Western North Carolina; prefers manuscripts suitable for tourism industry/market." Publishes hardcover and trade paperback originals. **Publishes 4-6 titles/year. Receives 15-20 queries and 10 mss/year. 75% of books from first-time authors; 100% from unagented writers. Pays 10-15% royalty on retail price. No advance.** Publishes book 8 months after acceptance. Reports in 1 month on queries, 2 months on mss. Book catalog on website.
Nonfiction: Reference, technical. Subjects include history, culture and tourism of western North Carolina. Prefers complete ms with SASE. *Writer's Market* recommends sending a query with SASE first.
Recent Title(s): *Living with Autism: The Parents' Stories*, by Kathleen Dillon (psychology).

PASSEGGIATA PRESS, P.O. Box 636, Pueblo CO 81002. (719)544-7889. **Acquisitions:** Donald E. Herdeck, publisher/editor-in-chief; Harold Ames, Jr., general editor. Estab. 1973. "We search for books that will make clear the complexity and value of non-Western literature and culture." Publishes hardcover and paperback originals and reprints. **Publishes 10-20 titles/year. Receives 200 submissions/year. 15% of books from first-time authors; 99% from unagented writers. Nonauthor-subsidy publishes 5% of books. Pays 10% royalty. Offers advance "only on delivery of complete manuscript which is found acceptable; usually $300."** Accepts simultaneous submissions. Reports in 2 months.
Nonfiction: Specializes in African, Caribbean, Middle Eastern (Arabic and Persian) and Asian-Pacific literature, criticism and translation, Third World literature and history, fiction, poetry, criticism, history and translations of creative writing, including bilingual texts (Arabic language/English translations). Query with outline, table of contents. Reviews artwork/photos as part of ms package. State availability of photos/illustrations.
Fiction: Query with synopsis, plot summary (1-3 pages).
Poetry: Submit 5-10 sample poems.
Recent Title(s): *Where Land is Mostly Sky*, by Dr. Richard Fleck (nonfiction); *Four Seasons by Fan Chengda*, translated by Lois Baker (bilingual poetry).
Tips: "We are always interested in genuine contributions to understanding non-Western culture. We need a *polished* translation, or original prose or poetry by non-Western authors *only*. Critical and cross-cultural studies are accepted from any scholar from anywhere."

PASSPORT PRESS, P.O. Box 1346, Champlain NY 12919-1346. **Acquisitions:** Jack Levesque, publisher. Estab. 1975. Passport Press publishes practical travel guides on specific countries. Publishes trade paperback originals. **Publishes 4 titles/year. 25% of books from first-time authors; 100% from unagented writers. Pays 6% royalty on retail price.** Publishes book 9 months after acceptance.
Imprint(s): Travel Line Press.
Nonfiction: Travel books only, not travelogues. Especially looking for mss on practical travel subjects and travel

guides on specific countries. Send 1-page query only. Reviews artwork/photos as part of ms package.
Recent Title(s): *Nicaragua Guide*, by Paul Glassman.

PAULINE BOOKS & MEDIA, Daughters of St. Paul, 50 St. Paul's Ave., Jamaica Plain MA 02130-3491. (617)522-8911. Fax: (617)541-9805. Website: http://www.pauline.org. **Acquisitions:** Sister Mary Mark Wickenheiser, FSP, acquisitions (adult); Sister Patricia Edward Jablonski, acquisitions (children). Estab. 1948. "As a Catholic publishing house, Pauline Books & Media communicates the Gospel message through all available forms of media. We serve the Church by responding to the hopes and needs of all people with the Word of God, in the spirit of St. Paul." Publishes trade paperback originals and reprints. **Publishes 25-35 titles/year. Receives approximately 1,300 proposals/year. Pays authors 8-12% royalty on net sales.** Publishes ms 2-3 years after acceptance. Reports in 3 months. Book catalog for 9×12 SAE with 4 first-class stamps.
Nonfiction: Saints' biographies, juvenile, spiritual growth and faith development. Subjects include child guidance/parenting, religion teacher resources, Scripture. No strictly secular mss. Query with SASE. *No unsolicited mss.*
Fiction: Juvenile. Query only with SASE. *No unsolicited mss.*
Recent Title(s): *The Christmas Creche: Treasure of Faith, Art & Theater*, by Matthew Powell, O.P. (gift book); *The Mystery*, by Dan Montgomery (novel).
Tips: "We are interested in books concerning faith and moral values, as well as works on spiritual growth and development and religious instruction for young adults and adults. Always interested in books of Christian formation for families. No New Age books, poetry, adult fiction or autobiographies—all works must be consonant with Catholic theology."

PAULIST PRESS, 997 Macarthur Blvd., Mahwah NJ 07430. (201)825-7300. Fax: (201)825-8345. **Acquisitions:** Lawrence E. Boadt, president/editorial director. Managing Editor: Donald Brophy. Children's and Juvenile Books: Karen Schilabba. Estab. 1865. Paulist Press publishes Christian and Catholic theology, spirituality and religion titles. Publishes hardcover and paperback originals and paperback reprints. **Publishes 90-100 titles/year. Receives 500 submissions/year. 5-8% of books from first-time authors; 95% from unagented writers. Nonauthor subsidy publishes 1-2% of books. Pays royalty on retail price. Usually offers advance.** Publishes book 10 months after acceptance. Reports in 2 months.
Nonfiction: Philosophy, religion, self-help, textbooks (religious). Accepts nonfiction translations from German, French and Spanish. "We would like to see theology (Catholic and ecumenical Christian), popular spirituality, liturgy, and religious education texts." Submit outline and 2 sample chapters. Reviews artwork/photos as part of ms package.
Recent Title(s): *Trappist*, by Michael Downey.

PBC INTERNATIONAL INC., 1 School St., Glen Cove NY 11542. (516)676-2727. Fax: (516)676-2738. Website: http://www.dir-dd.com/pbc.html. Publisher: Mark Serchuck. **Acquisitions:** Lisa Maruca, acquisitions and marketing development manager. Estab. 1980. "PBC International is the publisher of full-color visual idea books for the design, marketing and graphic arts professional." Publishes hardcover and paperback originals. **Publishes 18 titles/year. Recei ves 100-200 submissions/year. Most of books from first-time authors and unagented writers done on assignment. Pays royalty and/or flat fees.** Accepts simultaneous submissions. Reports in 2 months. Book catalog for 9×12 SASE.
Nonfiction: Subjects include design, graphic art, architecture/interior design, packaging design, marketing design, product design. No submissions not covered in the above listed topics. Query with outline and sample chapters with SASE. Reviews artwork/photos as part of ms package.
Recent Title(s): *Restaurant 2000: Dining Design III*, by Christy Casamassima.

PEACHTREE CHILDREN'S BOOKS, Imprint of Peachtree Publishers, Ltd. 494 Armour Circle NE, Atlanta GA 30324. (404)876-8761. Fax: (404)875-2578. E-mail: peachtree@mindspring.com. Website: http://peachtreebooks.com. President/Publisher: Margaret Quinlin. **Acquisitions:** Helen Harriss, submissions editor; "We publish a broad range of subjects and perspectives, with emphasis on innovative plots and strong writing." Publishes hardcover and trade paperback originals. **Publishes 18-20 titles/year. 25% of books from first-time authors; 25% from unagented writers. Pays royalty on retail price. Advance varies.** Publishes book 18 months after acceptance of ms. Accepts simultaneous submissions. Reports in 3 months on queries, 4 months on manuscripts. Book catalog for $1.35 first-class postage. Manuscript guidelines for #10 SASE.
Imprint(s): Peachtree Jr., Free Stone.
Nonfiction: Children's/juvenile. Subjects include health, history, regional. Submit complete ms with SASE. *Writer's Market* recommends sending a query with SASE first.
Fiction: Juvenile, picture books, young adult. Submit ms with SASE.
Recent Title(s): *About Mammals*, by Sills & Sills (children's picture book).

PEACHTREE PUBLISHERS, LTD., 494 Armour Circle NE, Atlanta GA 30324-4888. (404)876-8761. Fax: (404)875-2578. **Acquisitions:** Sarah Helyar Smith, Amy Sproul (regional/outdoors). Estab. 1977. Peachtree Publishers prefers to work with Southern writers and professional storytellers. They specialize in children's books, juvenile chapter books, young adult, regional guidebooks, parenting and self-help. Publishes hardcover and trade paperback originals. **Publishes 15-20 titles/year; 1 fiction book/year.** Approximately 65% of Peachtree's list consists of children's books. **Receives up to 18,000 submissions/year. 25% of books from first-time authors; 75% from unagented writers. Prefers to work with previously published authors. Pays 7½-15% royalty.** Publishes book 2 years after acceptance. Reports in 6 months on queries. Book catalog for 9×12 SAE with 3 first-class stamps.

Imprint(s): Peachtree Children's Books (Peachtree Jr., Free Stone).

Nonfiction: General. Subjects include children's titles and juvenile chapter books, cooking/foods, history, health, humor, gardening, biography, general gift, recreation, self-help. No technical or reference. Submit outline and sample chapters. Reviews artwork/photos as part of ms package. Send photocopies.

Fiction: Literary, juvenile, mainstream. No fantasy, science fiction, mystery or romance. Submit sample chapters.

Recent Title(s): *Food Gifts for All Seasons*, by Anne Byrn (cooking/gift); *Over What Hill? (Notes from the Pasture)*, by Effie Leland Wilder.

PELICAN PUBLISHING COMPANY, 200 Newton St., P.O. Box 3110, Gretna LA 70053. (504)368-1175. Website: http://www.pelicanpub.com. President/Publisher: Milburn Calhoun. **Acquisitions:** Nina Kooij, editor-in-chief. Estab. 1926. "We seek writers on the cutting edge of ideas. We believe ideas have consequences. One of the consequences is that they lead to a bestselling book. We publish books to improve and uplift the reader." Publishes hardcover, trade paperback and mass market paperback originals and reprints. **Publishes 70 titles/year. Receives 5,000 submissions/year. 15% of books from first-time authors; 95% from unagented writers. Pays royalty on actual receipts.** Publishes book 18 months after acceptance. Reports in 1 month on queries. Writer's guidelines for SASE.

Nonfiction: Biography, coffee table book (limited), popular history, sports, architecture, illustrated book, juvenile, motivational, inspirational, Scottish, Irish, editorial cartoon. Subjects include Americana (especially Southern regional, Ozarks, Texas, Florida and Southwest); business (popular motivational, if author is a speaker); history; music (American artforms: jazz, blues, Cajun, R&B); politics (special interest in conservative viewpoint); religion (for popular audience mostly, but will consider others). *Travel*: Regional and international. *Motivational*: with business slant. *Inspirational*: author must be someone with potential for large audience. *Cookbooks*: "We look for authors with strong connection to restaurant industry or cooking circles, i.e., someone who can promote successfully." Query with SASE. "We require that a query be made first. This greatly expedites the review process and can save the writer additional postage expenses." No multiple queries or submissions. Reviews artwork/photos as part of ms package. Send photocopies only.

Fiction: Historical, Southern, juvenile. "We publish maybe one novel a year, usually by an author we already have. Almost all proposals are returned. We are most interested in historical Southern novels." No young adult, romance, science fiction, fantasy, gothic, mystery, erotica, confession, horror, sex or violence. Submit outline/synopsis and 2 sample chapters with SASE.

Recent Title(s): *Civil War in Texas and New Mexico Territory*, by Steve Cottrell (history); *A Redneck Night Before Christmas*, by David Davis (poem parody).

Tips: "We do extremely well with cookbooks, travel and popular histories. We will continue to build in these areas. The writer must have a clear sense of the market and knowledge of the competition. A query letter should describe the project briefly, give the author's writing and professional credentials, and promotional ideas."

PENCIL POINT PRESS, INC., 277 Fairfield Rd., Fairfield NJ 07004. **Acquisitions:** Gene Garone, publisher. Publishes educational supplemental materials for teachers of all levels. Publishes 12 titles/year. **Receives 12 queries and 12 mss/year. 100% of books from first-time authors. Pays 5-16% royalty on retail price or makes outright purchase of $25-50/page. No advance.** Publishes book 1 year after acceptance. Accepts simultaneous submissions. Reports in 2 months on proposals. Book catalog free.

Nonfiction: Reference, technical, textbook. Subjects include education, music, science, mathematics, language arts, ESL and special needs. Prefers supplemental resource materials for teachers grades K-12 and college (especially mathematics). Submit proposal package, including outline, 2 sample chapters and memo stating rationale and markets.

Recent Title(s): *Rhythm and Melody Concepts: A Sequential Approach for Children*, by Michon Rozmajzl and Rosalie Castleberry.

Tips: Audience is K-8 teachers, 9-12 teachers and college-level supplements. No children's trade books or poetry.

PENGUIN PUTNAM INC., 375 Hudson St., New York NY 10014. Website: http://www.penguinputnam.com. President: Phyllis Grann. General interest publisher of both fiction and nonfiction.

Imprint(s): Viking Penguin: Viking, Penguin, **Penguin Studio. Dutton/Signet: DAW Books, Dutton,** Mentor, Meridian, New American Library, Obelisk, Onyx, Plume, **ROC, Signet**, Topaz. **The Putnam Berkley Publishing Group: The Berkley Publishing Group (Ace**, Berkley Books, Berkley Prime Crime, Boulevard, Jove), **Perigee Books, Price Stern Sloan, G.P. Putnam's Sons**, Riverhead Books, **Jeremy P. Tarcher. Children's Division: Dial Books for Young Readers, Dutton Children's Books, Grosset & Dunlap**, Lady Bird Books, **Philomel Books,** Planet Dexter, **Price Stern Sloan, Puffin Books, G.P. Putnam's Sons, Viking Children's Books**, Frederick Warne.

[A] **PENGUIN STUDIO**, Penguin Putnam, Inc., 375 Hudson St., New York NY 10014. (212)366-2191. Website: http://www.penguinputnam.com. **Acquisitions:** Michael Fragnito, publisher (nonfiction general interest); Christopher Sweet, executive editor (art, music, history, photography, sports); Cyril Nelson, senior editor (arts & crafts, decorative arts); Marie Timell, senior editor (nonfiction general interest, astrology, New Age); Rachel Tsutsumi, associate editor, (art, architecture, photography, fashion, design, travel). "We publish high-quality nonfiction, illustrated hardcover/trade books." Publishes hardcover originals. **Publishes 35-40 titles/year. Receives 300 submissions/year. Less than 10% of books are from first-time authors; less than 5% from unagented writers.** Publishes book 1 year after acceptance. Accepts simultaneous submissions. Reports in 2 months.

Nonfiction: Coffee table book, gift book, illustrated book. Subjects include Americana, military/war, music/dance, photography, New Age/metaphysics, art, photography, popular culture, music, sports, military history, astrology, architec-

ture, crafts, collectibles, fashion. *Agented submissions only.* Reviews artwork as part of ms package. Send photocopies.
Recent Title(s): *Infinite Worlds*, by V. Difate (art); *Chocolate Bible*, by C. Teuguer (culinary).

PENNSYLVANIA HISTORICAL AND MUSEUM COMMISSION, Imprint of the Commonwealth of Pennsylvania, P.O. Box 1026, Harrisburg PA 17108-1026. (717)787-8099. Fax: (717)787-8312. Website: http://www.state.pa.us. **Acquisitions:** Diane B. Reed, chief, publications and sales division. Estab. 1913. "We have a tradition of publishing scholarly and reference works, as well as more popularly styled books that reach an even broader audience interested in some aspect of Pennsylvania." Publishes hardcover and paperback originals and reprints. **Publishes 6-8 titles/year. Receives 25 submissions/year. Pays 5-10% royalty on retail price. Makes outright purchase or sometimes makes special assignments.** Publishes book 18 months after acceptance. Accepts simultaneous submissions. Reports in 4 months. Prepare mss according to the *Chicago Manual of Style*.
Nonfiction: All books must be related to Pennsylvania, its history or culture: biography, illustrated books, reference, technical and historic travel. "The Commission seeks manuscripts on Pennsylvania, specifically on archaeology, history, art (decorative and fine), politics and biography." Query or submit outline and sample chapters. Guidelines and proposal forms available.
Recent Title(s): *Prehistoric Cultures of Eastern Pennsylvania*, by Jay Custer (archaeology).
Tips: "Our audience is diverse—students, specialists and generalists—all of them interested in one or more aspects of Pennsylvania's history and culture. Manuscripts must be well researched and documented (footnotes not necessarily required depending on the nature of the manuscript) and interestingly written. Manuscripts must be factually accurate, but in being so, writers must not sacrifice style."

N PERFECTION LEARNING CORPORATION, 10520 New York Ave., Des Moines IA 50322-3775. (515)278-0133. Fax: (515)278-2245. Website: http://www.plconline.com. **Acquisitions:** Sue Thies, senior elementary editor (grades K-6); Terry Ofner, senior secondary editor (grades 7-12). "Perfection Learning is dedicated to publishing literature-based materials that enhance teaching and learning in Pre K-12 classrooms and libraries." Publishes hardcover and trade paperback originals. **Publishes 50-60 fiction and informational; 150 teacher's resources titles/year. Pays 5-8% royalty on retail price. Offers $300-500 advance.** Reports in 5 months on proposals.
Imprint(s): Magic Key.
Nonfiction: Publishes supplemental educational material for grades K-12. "We are publishing hi-lo informational books for students in grades 2-8, reading levels 1-4. We would be interested in biographies at this level as well." Query or submit outline with SASE.
Fiction: "We are publishing hi-lo fiction in a variety of genres for students in grades 2-8, reading levels 1-3." Submit 2-3 sample chapters with SASE.
Recent Title(s): *The Rattlesnake Necklace*, by Linda Baxter (hi-lo historical fiction); *The Iditarod*, by Monica Devine (hi-lo informational book in a narrative style).

N PERIGEE BOOKS, Penguin Putnam Inc., 375 Hudson St., New York NY 10014. (212)366-2000. **Acquisitions:** John Duff, editor. Publishes trade paperback originals and reprints. **Publishes 12-15 titles/year. Receives hundreds of queries/year; 30 proposals/year. 30% first-time authors; 10% unagented writers. Pays 7½-15% royalty. Offers $5,000-150,000 advance.** Publishes book 18 months after acceptance of ms. Reports in 2 months. Catalog free. Manuscript guidelines given on acceptance of ms.
Nonfiction: Prescriptive books. Subjects include health/fitness, child care, spirituality. Query with outline. Prefers agented mss, but accepts unsolicited queries.

THE PERMANENT PRESS/SECOND CHANCE PRESS, 4170 Noyac Rd., Sag Harbor NY 11963. (516)725-1101. Website: http://www.thepermanentpress.com. **Acquisitions:** Judith Shepard, editor. Estab. 1978. "We endeavor to publish quality writing—primarily fiction—without regard to authors' reputations or track records." Permanent Press publishes literary fiction. Second Chance Press devotes itself exclusively to re-publishing fine books that are out of print and deserve continued recognition. Publishes hardcover originals. **Publishes 12 titles/year. Receives 7,000 submissions/year. 60% of books from first-time authors; 60% from unagented writers. Pays 10-15% royalty on wholesale price. Offers $1,000 advance for Permanent Press books; royalty only on Second Chance Press titles.** Publishes book 18 months after acceptance. Accepts simultaneous submissions. Reports in 6 months on queries. Book catalog for 8×10 SAE with 7 first-class stamps. Manuscript guidelines for #10 SASE.

- Permanent Press does not employ readers and the number of submissions it receives has grown. If the writer sends a query or manuscript that the press is not interested in, a reply may take six weeks. If there is interest, it may take 3 to 6 months.

Nonfiction: Biography, autobiography, historical. No scientific and technical material, academic studies. Query.
Fiction: Literary, mainstream, mystery. Especially looking for high line literary fiction, "artful, original and arresting." No genre fiction, poetry or short stories. Query with first 20 pages.
Recent Title(s): *Hotline Heaven*, by Frances Park (fiction).
Tips: "Audience is the silent minority—people with good taste. We are interested in the writing more than anything and long outlines are a turn-off. The SASE is vital to keep track of things, as we are receiving ever more submissions. No fax queries will be answered. We aren't looking for genre fiction but a compelling, well-written story."

PERSPECTIVES PRESS, P.O. Box 90318, Indianapolis IN 46290-0318. (317)872-3055. E-mail: ppress@iquest.net. Website: http://www.perspectivespress.com. **Acquisitions:** Pat Johnston, publisher. Estab. 1982. "Our purpose is to promote understanding of infertility issues and alternatives, adoption and closely-related child welfare issues, and to educate and sensitize those personally experiencing these life situations, professionals who work with such clients, and the public at large." Publishes hardcover and trade paperback originals. **Averages 4 titles/year. Receives 200 queries/year. 95% of books from first-time authors; 95% from unagented writers. Pays 5-15% royalty on net sales.** Publishes book 1 year after acceptance. Reports in 1 month on queries to schedule a full reading. *Writer's Market* recommends allowing 2 months for reply. Book catalog and writer's guidelines for #10 SAE with 2 first-class stamps. Available on the website.

Nonfiction: How-to, juvenile and self-help books on health, psychology and sociology. Must be related to infertility, adoption, alternative routes to family building."No adult fiction!" Query with SASE.

Recent Title(s): *Toddler Adoption: The Weaver's Craft*, by Mary Hopkins Best.

Tips: "For adults, we are seeking infertility and adoption decision-making materials, books dealing with adoptive or foster parenting issues, books to use with children, books to share with others to help explain infertility, adoption, foster care, third party reproductive assistance, special programming or training manuals, etc. For children, we will consider adoption or foster care-related fiction manuscripts that are appropriate for preschoolers and early elementary school children. We do not consider YA. Nonfiction manuscripts are considered for all ages. No autobiography, memoir or adult fiction. While we would consider a manuscript from a writer who was not personally or professionally involved in these issues, we would be more inclined to accept a manuscript submitted by an infertile person, an adoptee, a birthparent, an adoptive parent or a professional working with any of these."

PETER PAUPER PRESS, INC., 202 Mamaroneck Ave., White Plains NY 10601-5376. Fax: (914)681-0389. **Acquisitions:** Solomon M. Skolnick, creative director. Estab. 1928. PPP publishes only small format illustrated gift books. "We focus on small format, illustrated gifts for occasions and in celebration of specific relationships such as Mom, Dad, sister, teacher, grandmother." Publishes hardcover originals. **Publishes 70-80 titles/year. Receives 700 queries and 300 mss/year. 40% of books from first-time authors; 100% from unagented writers. Makes outright purchase only.** Publishes ms 1 year months after acceptance. Reports in 1 month. *Writer's Market* recommends allowing 2 months for reply. Manuscript guidelines for #10 SASE.

Nonfiction: Subjects include specific relationships or special events and occasions (graduation, Mother's Day, Christmas, etc.). "We do not publish narrative works. We publish collections of brief, original quotes, aphorisms, and wise sayings or brief prescriptive works for specific people, i.e., Mom, babysitter, teacher. *Please do not send us other people's quotes*." Submit outline with SASE.

Recent Title(s): *Mom Relief: Stress-Reducing Ideas*, by Kara Leverte Farley.

Tips: "Our readers are primarily female, age 20 and over, who are likely to buy a 'gift' book in a stationery, gift, book or boutique store. Writers should become familiar with our previously published work. We publish only small-format illustrated hardcover gift books of between 750-4,000 words."

A.K. PETERS, LTD., 289 Linden St., Wellesley MA 02181. (781)235-2210. Fax: (781)235-2404. E-mail: editorial@akpeters.com. Website: http://www.akpeters.com. **Acquisitions:** Alice and Klaus Peters, publishers. "AK Peters, Ltd. publishes scientific/technical/medical books and popular nonfiction titles related to science and technology." Publishes hardcover originals and reprints. **Publishes 15 titles/year. Receives 50 queries and 30 mss/year. 75% of books from first-time authors; 100% from unagented writers. Pays 15-20% royalty on net price.** Publishes book 4 months after acceptance of ms. Accepts simultaneous submissions. Reports in 3 months. Book catalog and ms guidelines free.

Nonfiction: Biography, multimedia (format: CD-ROM), technical, textbook. Subjects include computers/electronics, health/medicine, science, software, mathematics. "We are predominantly a publisher of mathematics and computer science, but we are very interested in expanding our list in robotics and health/medicine as well. Stories of people behind the science are also of interest. Proposals for nonfiction should be well organized and well written, clearly noting its audience and purpose." Submit proposal package, including outline or table of contents with sample chapters or full ms. Description of target audience also helpful. Reviews artwork/photos as part of the ms package. Send photocopies.

Recent Title(s): *Logical Dilemmas: The Life & Work of Kurt Gödel*, by Dawson (mathematical biography).

PETERSON'S, P.O. Box 2123, Princeton NJ 08543-2123. (800)338-3282. Fax: (609)243-9150. Website: http://www.petersons.com. **Acquisitions:** Eileen Fiore, executive assistant, editorial. Estab. 1966. "Peterson's is the country's largest educational information/communications company, providing the academic, consumer, and professional communities with books, software and online services in support of lifelong education access and career choice. Peterson's publishes well-known references as its annual guides to graduate and professional programs, colleges and universities, financial aid, private schools, standardized test-prep, summer programs, international study, executive education, job hunting and career opportunities, as well as a full line of software offering career guidance and information for adult learners. Many of Peterson's reference works are updated annually. Peterson's is a Thomson company. Peterson's markets strongly to libraries and institutions, as well as to the corporate sector." Publishes trade and reference books. **Publishes 55-75 titles/year. Receives 250-300 submissions/year. 60% of books from first-time authors; 90% from unagented writers. Pays 7½-12% royalty on net sales. Offers advance.** Publishes book 1 year after acceptance. Reports in 3 months. Book catalog free.

Nonfiction: Careers, education, authored titles, as well as education and career directories. Submit complete ms or table of contents, introduction and 2 sample chapters with SASE. *Writer's Market* recommends query with SASE first.

Looks for "appropriateness of contents to our markets, author's credentials, and writing style suitable for audience."
Recent Title(s): *The Ultimate College Survival Guide*, by Janet Farrar Worthington and Ronald Farrar.

PHI DELTA KAPPA EDUCATIONAL FOUNDATION, P.O. Box 789, Bloomington IN 47402. (812)339-1156. Fax: (812)339-0018. E-mail: special.pubs@pdkintl.org. Website: http://www.pdkintl.org. **Acquisitions:** Donovan R. Walling, editor of special publications. "We publish books for educators—K-12 and higher education. Our professional books are often used in college courses but are never specifically designed as textbooks." Publishes hardcover and trade paperback originals. **Publishes 24-30 titles/year. Receives 100 queries and 50-60 mss/year. 50% of books from first-time authors; 100% from unagented writers. Pays honorarium of $500-5,000.** Publishes book 6-9 months after acceptance of ms. Reports in 3 months on proposals. Book catalog and ms guidelines free.
Nonfiction: How-to, reference, essay collections. Subjects include child guidance/parenting, education, legal issues. Query with outline and 1 sample chapter. Reviews artwork/photos as part of ms package.
Recent Title(s): *The Truth about America's Schools: The Bracey Reports, 1991-97*, by Gerald W. Bracey (school performance, evaluation and reform).

PHILOMEL BOOKS, Penguin Putnam Inc., 345 Hudson St., New York NY 10014. (212)414-3610. **Acquisitions:** Patricia Lee Gauch, editorial director; Michael Green, editor. Estab. 1980. "We look for beautifully written, engaging manuscripts for children and young adults." Publishes hardcover originals. **Publishes 20-25 titles/year. Receives 2,600 submissions/year. 15% of books from first-time authors; 30% from unagented writers. Pays standard (7½-15%) royalty. Advance negotiable.** Publishes book 2 years after acceptance. Reports in 2 months on queries, 3 months on unsolicited mss. Book catalog for 9×12 SAE with 4 first-class stamps. Request book catalog from marketing department of Putnam Publishing Group.
Fiction: Children's picture books (ages 3-8); middle-grade fiction and illustrated chapter books (ages 7-10); young adult novels (ages 10-15). Particularly interested in picture book mss with original stories and regional fiction with a distinct voice. Historical fiction OK. Unsolicited mss accepted for picture books only; query first for long fiction. Always include SASE. No series or activity books.
Recent Title(s): *In Enzo's Splendid Gardens*, by Patricia Polacco.
Tips: "We prefer a very brief synopsis that states the basic premise of the story. This will help us determine whether or not the manuscript is suited to our list. If applicable, we'd be interested in knowing the author's writing experience or background knowledge. We try to be less influenced by the swings of the market than in the power, value, essence of the manuscript itself."

PHILOSOPHY DOCUMENTATION CENTER, Bowling Green State University, Bowling Green OH 43403-0189. (419)372-2419, (800)444-2419. Fax: (419)372-6987. E-mail: pdc@mailserver.bgsu.edu. Website: http://www.bgsu.edu/pdc/. **Acquisitions:** Dr. George Leaman, director. The Philosophy Documentation Center "works in cooperation with publishers, database producers, software developers, journal editors, authors, librarians and philosophers to create an electronic clearinghouse for philosophical publishing." **Publishes 4 titles/year. Receives 4-6 queries and 4-6 mss/year. 50% of books from first-time authors. Pays 2½-10% royalty.** Publishes book 1 year after acceptance. Reports in 2 months. Book catalog free.
Nonfiction: Textbook, software, guidebooks, directories in the field of philosophy. "We want to increase our range of philosophical titles and are especially interested in electronic publishing." Query with outline.
Recent Title(s): *The Collaborative Bibliography of Women in Philosophy*, by Noël Huchings and William Rumsey.

PICADOR USA, St. Martin's Press, 175 Fifth Ave., New York NY 10010. **Acquisitions:** George Witte. Estab. 1994. "We publish high-quality literary fiction and nonfiction. We are open to a broad range of subjects, well written by authoritative authors." Publishes hardcover originals and trade paperback originals and reprints. **Publishes 40-50 titles/year. 30% of books from first-time authors. Publishes "few" unagented writers. Pays 7½-12½% royalty on retail price. Advance varies.** Publishes book 18 months after acceptance of ms. Accepts simultaneous submissions. Reports in 2 months on queries. Book catalog for 9×12 SASE and $2.60 postage. Manuscript guidelines for #10 SASE.
Nonfiction: Subjects include language/literature, philosophy, biography/memoir, pop culture, narative books with a point of view on a particular subject. "When submitting queries, be aware of things outside the book, including credentials, that may affect our decision." Query only with SASE. No phone queries.
Fiction: Literary. Query only with SASE.
Recent Title(s): *As If*, by Blake Morrison (current affairs); *Dewey Defeats Truman*, by Thomas Mallon (fiction).

PICCADILLY BOOKS, P.O. Box 25203, Colorado Springs CO 80936-5203. (719)550-9887. **Acquisitions:** Submissions Department. Estab. 1985. "Experience has shown that those who order our books are either kooky or highly intelligent or both. If you like to laugh, have fun, enjoy games, or have a desire to act like a jolly buffoon, we've got the books for you." Publishes hardcover and trade paperback originals and trade paperback reprints. **Publishes 3-8 titles/year. Receives 300 submissions/year. 70% of books from first-time authors; 95% from unagented writers. Pays 5-10% royalty on retail price.** Publishes book 1 year after acceptance. Accepts simultaneous submissions. Responds only if interested.
Nonfiction: How-to books on entertainment, humor and performing arts. "We have a strong interest in subjects on clowning, magic, puppetry and related arts, including comedy skits and dialogs." Query with sample chapters.
Recent Title(s): *The Gospel in Greasepaint*, by Mark Stucky.

PICTON PRESS, Picton Corp., P.O. Box 250, Rockport ME 04856-0250. (207)236-6565. Fax: (207)236-6713. E-mail: picton@midcoast.com. Website: http://www.pictonpress.com. **Acquisitions:** Candy McMahan Perry, office manager. "Picton Press is one of America's oldest, largest and most respected publishers of genealogical and historical books specializing in research tools for the 17th, 18th and 19th centuries." Publishes hardcover and mass market paperback originals and reprints. **Publishes 30 titles/year. Receives 30 queries and 15 mss/year. 50% of books from first-time authors; 100% from unagented writers. Pays 0-10% royalty on wholesale price or makes outright purchase.** Publishes book 6 months after acceptance of ms. Reports in 2 months on queries and proposals, 3 months on mss. Book catalog free.

Imprint(s): Picton Press, Penobscot Press, Cricketfield Press, New England History Press.

Nonfiction: Reference, textbook. Subjects include Americana, genealogy, history, vital records. Query with outline.

Recent Title(s): *18th Century Emigrants from Baden and Württemberg*, by Brigitte Burkett.

THE PILGRIM PRESS, United Church Board for Homeland Ministries, 700 Prospect Ave. E., Cleveland OH 44115-1100. (216)736-3715. Fax: (216)736-3703. E-mail: stavet@ucc.org. **Acquisitions:** Timothy G. Staveteig, editorial director. Publishes hardcover and trade paperback originals. **Publishes 40 titles/year. 30% of books from first-time authors; 80% from unagented writers. Pays standard royalties and advances where appropriate.** Publishes book an average of 18 months after acceptance. Reports in 3 months on queries. Book catalog and ms guidelines free.

Nonfiction: Ethics, social issues with a strong commitment to justice—addressing such topics as public policy, sexuality and gender, economics, medicine, gay and lesbian concerns, human rights, minority liberation and the environment—primarily in a Christian context, but not exclusively.

Recent Title(s): *Amistad*, by Helen Kromer.

Tips: "We are concentrating more on academic and trade submissions. Writers should send books about contemporary social issues. Our audience is liberal, open-minded, socially aware, feminist, church members and clergy, teachers and seminary professors."

PILOT BOOKS, 127 Sterling Ave., P.O. Box 2102, Greenport NY 11944. (516)477-1094. Fax: (516)477-0978. E-mail: feedback@pilotbooks@aol.com. Website: http://www.pilotbooks.com. **Acquisitions:** Robert Ungerleider, publisher; Ruth Gruen, editor. Estab. 1959. "Pilot Books offers readers well-organized, well-written 'how' and 'where'-to books on a variety of timely topics." Publishes paperback originals. **Publishes 10-15 titles/year. Receives 200-300 submissions/year. 30% of books from first-time authors; 90% from unagented writers. Offers standard royalty contract based on retail price. Offers $250 usual advance, but this varies.** Publishes book an average of 8 months after acceptance. Reports in 2 months. Book catalog and guidelines for #10 SASE.

Nonfiction: Publishes "personal, business and career guides, senior and budget travel information and books on new ideas and trends for today's older adult. We prefer authors with credentials in the field they're writing about." Length: 25,000-50,000 words. Send outline with SASE. Reviews artwork/photos as part of ms package.

Recent Title(s): *Have Grandchildren, Will Travel*, by Spurlock (travel with grandchildren).

PIÑATA BOOKS, Arte Publico Press, University of Houston, Houston TX 77204-2090. (713)743-2841. Fax: (713)743-2847. **Acquisitions:** Nicolas Kanellos, president. Estab. 1994. "We are dedicated to the publication of children's and young adult literature focusing on U.S. Hispanic culture." Publishes hardcover and trade paperback originals. **Publishes 10-15 titles/year. 60% of books from first-time authors. Pays 10% royalty on wholesale price. Offers $1,000-3,000 advance.** Publishes book 2 years after acceptance of ms. Accepts simultaneous submissions. Reports in 1 month on queries, 6 months on mss. Book catalog free. Manuscript guidelines for #10 SASE.

Nonfiction: Children's/juvenile. Ethnic subjects. "Pinata Books specializes in publication of children's and young adult literature that authentically portrays themes, characters and customs unique to U.S. Hispanic culture." Query with outline/synopsis, 2 sample chapters and SASE.

Fiction: Adventure, juvenile, picture books, young adult. Query with synopsis, 2 sample chapters and SASE.

Poetry: Appropriate to Hispanic theme. Submit 10 sample poems.

Recent Title(s): *Silent Dancing: A Partial Remembrance of a Puerto Rican Childhood*, by Judith Ortiz-Cofer (memoir, ages 11-adult); *Tun-ta-ca-tun*, edited by Sylvia Pena (children's poetry, preschool to young adult).

Tips: "Include cover letter with submission explaining why your manuscript is unique and important, why we should publish it, who will buy it, etc."

PINEAPPLE PRESS, INC., P.O. Box 3899, Sarasota FL 34230. (941)953-2797. **Acquisitions:** June Cussen, editor. Estab. 1982. "We are seeking quality nonfiction on diverse topics for the library and book trade markets." Publishes hardcover and trade paperback originals. **Publishes 20 titles/year. Receives 1,500 submissions/year. 20% of books from first-time authors; 80% from unagented writers. Pays 6½-15% royalty on retail price. Seldom offers advance.** Publishes book 18 months after acceptance. Accepts simultaneous submissions. Reports in 3 months. Book catalog for 9×12 SAE with $1.24 postage.

Nonfiction: Biography, how-to, reference, regional (Florida), nature. Subjects include animals, history, gardening, nature. "We will consider most nonfiction topics. Most, though not all, of our fiction and nonfiction deals with Florida." No pop psychology or autobiographies. Query or submit outline/brief synopsis, sample chapters and SASE.

Fiction: Literary, historical, mainstream, regional (Florida). No romance, science fiction, children's. Submit outline/brief synopsis and sample chapters.

Recent Title(s): *Art Lover's Guide to Florida*, by Anne Jeffrey and Aletta Dreller; *Myra Sims*, by Janis Owens

(literature).
Tips: "If I were trying to market a book today, I would learn everything I could about book publishing and publicity and agree to actively participate in promoting my book. A query on a novel without a brief sample seems useless."

[A] **PINNACLE BOOKS**, Kensington, 850 Third Ave., 16th Floor, New York NY 10022. (212)407-1500. **Acquisitions:** Paul Dinas, editor. "Pinnacle features bestselling commercial fiction, and also humor." Publishes hardcover, trade paperback and mass market paperback originals and reprints. **Publishes 60 titles/year. 3-5% of books from first-time authors; 30% from unagented writers. Pays royalty on retail price, varies by author and type of book. Advance varies, by author and type of book.** Publishes book 18 months after acceptance of ms. Accepts simultaneous submissions. Reports in 1 month on queries, 3 months on ms. Book catalog for #10 SASE.
Nonfiction: Male-oriented, humor. True crime subjects. Query with outline and SASE. *Agented submissions only.* Reviews artwork/photos as part of the ms package, if integral to project. Send photocopies.
Fiction: General, male-oriented. Query with synopsis and SASE. *Agented submissions only.*

PIPPIN PRESS, 229 E. 85th St., P.O. Box 1347, Gracie Station, New York NY 10028. (212)288-4920. Fax: (732)225-1562. **Acquisitions:** Barbara Francis, president and editor-in-chief; Joyce Segal, senior editor. Estab. 1987. Pippin publishes general nonfiction and fiction for children ages 4-11. Publishes hardcover originals. **Publishes 4-6 titles/year. Receives 1,500 queries/year. 80% of queries from unagented writers. Pays royalty.** Publishes book 2 years after acceptance. Reports in 3 weeks on queries. *Writer's Market* recommends allowing 2 months for reply. Book catalog for 6×9 SASE. Manuscript guidelines for #10 SASE.
Nonfiction: Children's books: biography, humor, picture books. Subjects include animals, history, language/literature, nature, science. General nonfiction for children ages 4-10. Query with SASE only. *No unsolicited mss.* Reviews artwork/photos as part of ms package. Send photocopies.
Fiction: Historical fiction, humor, mystery, picture books, "We're especially looking for small chapter books for 7- to 11-year olds, especially by people of many cultures." Also interested in humorous fiction for ages 7-11. Query with SASE only.
Recent Title(s): *James Madison and Dolly Madison and Their Times*, by Robert Quackenbush (biography); *Abigail's Drum*, by John A. Minahan, illustrated by Robert Quackenbush (historical fiction).
Tips: "Read as many of the best children's books published in the last five years as you can. We are looking for multi-ethnic fiction and nonfiction for ages 7-10, as well as general fiction for this age group. I would pay particular attention to children's books favorably reviewed in *School Library Journal*, *The Booklist*, *The New York Times Book Review*, and *Publishers Weekly*."

PLANNERS PRESS, American Planning Association, 122 S. Michigan Ave., Chicago IL 60603. Fax: (312)431-9985. E-mail: slewis@planning.org. Website: http://www.planning.org. **Acquisitions:** Sylvia Lewis, director of publications. "Our books have a narrow audience of city planners and often focus on the tools of city planning." Publishes hardcover and trade paperback originals. **Publishes 4-6 titles/year. Receives 20 queries and 6-8 mss/year. 50% of books from first-time authors; 100% from unagented writers. Pays 7½-12% royalty on retail price.** Publishes book 1 year after acceptance. Reports in 1 month on queries, 2 months on proposals and mss. Book catalog and ms guidelines free.
Nonfiction: Technical (specialty-public policy and city planning). Government/political subjects. Submit 2 sample chapters and table of contents. Reviews artwork/photos as part of ms package. Send photocopies.
Recent Title(s): *Urban Planning & Politics*, by William C. Johnson (textbook).

PLANNING/COMMUNICATIONS, 7215 Oak Ave., River Forest IL 60305. (708)366-5200. E-mail: dl@jobfindersonline.com. Website: http://jobfindersonline.com. **Acquisitions:** Daniel Lauber, president. "Planning Communications seeks to help people find jobs and get hired, and to address national issues and to illuminate the world." Publishes hardcover, trade and mass market paperback originals, trade paperback reprints. **Publishes 3-8 titles/year. Receives 30 queries and 3 mss/year. 50% of books from first-time authors; 100% from unagented writers. Pays 15-20% royalty on net sales.** Publishes book 1 year after acceptance of ms. Accepts simultaneous submissions. Reports in 2 months on queries, 3 months on proposals and mss. Book catalog for $2. Manuscript guidelines for #10 SASE.
Nonfiction: Careers, self-help, résumés, cover letters, interviewing. Subjects include business/economics (careers), education, government/politics, money/finance, sociology, software. Submit outline and 3 sample chapters with SASE. Reviews artwork/photos as part of ms package. Send photocopies.
Recent Title(s): *National Job Hotline Directory*, by Marcia Williams and Sue Cubbage.

PLAYERS PRESS, INC., P.O. Box 1132, Studio City CA 91614-0132. (818)789-4980. **Acquisitions:** Robert W. Gordon, vice president, editorial. Estab. 1965. "We publish quality plays, musicals and performing arts books for theater, film and television." Publishes hardcover and trade paperback originals, and trade paperback reprints. **Publishes 35-70 titles/year. Receives 200-1,000 submissions/year. 15% of books from first-time authors; 80% from unagented writers. Pays royalty on wholesale price.** Publishes book within 2 years of acceptance. Reports on queries in 1 month, up to 1 year on mss. Book catalog and guidelines for 9×12 SAE with 5 first-class stamps.
Nonfiction: Juvenile and theatrical drama/entertainment industry. Subjects include the performing arts, costume, theater and film crafts. Needs quality plays and musicals, adult or juvenile. Query. Reviews artwork/photos as part of package.
Plays: Plays. Subject matter includes adventure, confession, ethnic, experimental, fantasy, historical, horror, humor, mainstream, mystery, religious, romance, science fiction, suspense, western. Submit complete ms for theatrical plays

only. Plays must be previously produced. "No novels or story books are accepted."
Recent Title(s): *Silly Soup*, by Carol Corty (drama, young audiences).
Tips: "Plays, entertainment industry texts, theater, film and TV books have the only chances of selling to our firm."

PLEASANT COMPANY PUBLICATIONS, 8400 Fairway Pl., Middleton WI 53562. Fax: (608)836-1999. Website: http://www.americangirl.com. **Acquistions:** Jennifer Hirsch, submissions editor. "Pleasant Company publishes fiction and nonfiction for girls 7-12 under its two imprints. The American Girls Collection© and American Girl Library©. The company relies primarily on its own team of writers, editors, and designers to produce its books and print products." Publishes hardcover and trade paperback originals. **Publishes 8-25 title/year. Receives 400 queries and 400 mss/year. 90% of books from unagented writers. "Payment varies extremely depending on the nature of the work." Advance varies.** Accepts simultaneous submissions. Reports in 2 months. Book catalog for SASE.

- Mattel Inc., manufacturers of Barbie, purchased Pleasant Company.

Imprint(s): The American Girls Collection, American Girl Library.
Nonfiction: Children's/juvenile for girls, ages 7-12. Subjects include contemporary lifestyle, activities, how-to. Query.
Fiction: Juvenile for girls, ages 7-12. Subjects include contemporary and historical fiction, mysteries. "We are seeking high-quality contemporary fiction about girls ages 9-12 for new, non-series imprint. No romance, fantasy, picture books, rhyme or stories about talking animals." Query.
Recent Title(s): *Oops! The Manners Guide for Girls*, by Nancy Holyoke (nonfiction); *Meet Josefina, An American Girl*, by Valerie Tripp (fiction).

PLENUM PUBLISHING, Wolters Kluwer, 233 Spring St., New York NY 10013-1578. (212)620-8000. **Acquisitions:** Linda Greenspan Regan, executive editor, trade books. Estab. 1946. "Plenum publishes expertly-written, marketable books on contemporary topics in the sciences and social sciences for the scientifically curious reader." Publishes hardcover originals. **Publishes 350 titles/year; Plenum Trade publishes 20-30 titles/year. Receives 1,000 submissions/year. 20% of books from first-time authors; 20% from unagented writers. Offers standard royalty contract.** Publishes book 2 years after acceptance. Accepts simultaneous submissions. Reports in 8 months.
Nonfiction: Subjects include trade science, criminology, anthropology, mathematics, sociology, psychology, health. "We are seeking high quality, popular books in the sciences and social sciences." Query only.
Recent Title(s): *Mathematical Mysteries*, by Calvin Clawson.
Tips: "Our audience consists of intelligent laymen and professionals. Authors should be experts on subject matter of book. Compare your book with competitive works, explain how it differs, and define the market for your books."

POCKET BOOKS, Simon & Schuster, Dept. WM, 1230 Avenue of the Americas, New York NY 10020. **Acquisitions:** Emily Bestler, vice president/editorial director. Pocket Books publishes general interest nonfiction and adult fiction. Publishes paperback originals and reprints, mass market and trade paperbacks and hardcovers. **Publishes 250 titles/year. Receives 2,500 submissions/year. 25% of books from first-time authors; less than 25% from agented writers. Pays 6-8% royalty on retail price.** Publishes book an average of 2 years after acceptance. Book catalog free. Manuscript guidelines for #10 SASE.
Nonfiction: History, biography, reference and general nonfiction, humor, calendars. Query with SASE.
Fiction: Adult (mysteries, thriller, psychological suspense, Star Trek ® novels, romance, westerns). Query with SASE.
Recent Title(s): *All I Really Need to Know in Business I Learned at Microsoft*, by Julie Brick (nonfiction); *Star Trek Avenger*, by William Shatner (fiction).

N POLYCHROME PUBLISHING CORPORATION, 4509 N. Francisco, Chicago IL 60625. (312)478-4455. **Acquisitions:** Editorial Board. Publishes hardcover originals and reprints. **Publishes 4 titles/year. Receives 3,000 queries and 7,500-8,000 mss/year. 50% of books from first-time authors; 100% from unagented writers. Pays royalty, "usually a combination of fee plus royalties." Advance.** Publishes book 2 years after acceptance. Accepts simultaneous submissions. Reports in 8 months on mss. Book catalog and ms guidelines for #10 SASE.
Nonfiction: Children's/juvenile. Subjects emphasize ethnic, particularly multicultural/Asian-American. Submit outline and 3 sample chapters. Reviews artwork/photos as part of ms package, but not necessary. Send photocopies.
Fiction: Multicultural, particularly Asian-American. Ethnic, juvenile, picture books, young adult. "We do not publish fables, folktales, fairytales or anthropomorphic animal stories." Submit synopsis and 3 sample chapters; for picture books, submit whole ms.
Recent Title(s): *Thanksgiving at Obachan's*, by Janet Mitsui Brown (fiction/picture book).

POPULAR CULTURE INK, P.O. Box 1839, Ann Arbor MI 48106. (734)677-6351. **Acquisitions:** Tom Schultheiss, publisher. Popular Culture Ink publishes directories and reference books for radio, TV, music and other entertainment subjects. Publishes hardcover originals and reprints. **Publishes 4-6 titles/year. Receives 50 queries and 20 mss/year. 100% of books from first-time authors; 100% from unagented writers. Pays variable royalty on wholesale price. Offers variable advance.** Publishes book 2 years after acceptance. Accepts simultaneous submissions. Reports in 1 month. *Writer's Market* recommends allowing 2 months for reply. Book catalog and ms guidelines free.
Nonfiction: Reference. Subjects include music, popular entertainment. Query with SASE.
Recent Title(s): *Surfin' Guitars*, by Robert Dalley (1960s surf music).
Tips: Audience is libraries, avid collectors. "Know your subject backwards. Make sure your book is unique."

N **POPULAR WOODWORKING BOOKS**, F&W Publications, 1507 Dana Ave., Cincinnati OH 45207. (513)531-2690. **Acquisitions**: R. Adam Blake, acquisitions editor. Publishes hardcover and trade paperback originals and reprints. **Publishes 10-12 titles/year. Receives 30 queries and 10 mss/year. 50% of books from first-time authors; 95% from unagented writers. Pays 10-20% royalty on net receipts. Offers $3,000-5,000 advance.** Publishes book 1 year after acceptance of ms. Accepts simultaneous submissions. Reports in 1 month. Book catalog and ms guidelines for 9×12 SAE with 6 first-class stamps.
Nonfiction: How-to, illustrated book, woodworking/wood crafts. "We publish heavily illustrated how-to woodworking books that show, rather than tell, our readers how to accomplish their woodworking goals." Query with proposal package, including outline, transparencies and SASE. Reviews artwork/photos as part of ms package. Send transparencies. "Always submit copies of transparencies. We will not be responsible for lost or stolen transparencies!"
Recent Title(s): *Beautiful Wooden Gifts You Can Make in a Weekend*, by Alan & Gill Bridgewater (woodworking).

CLARKSON POTTER, The Crown Publishing Group, Random House, 201 E. 50th St., New York NY 10022. Website: http://www.randomhouse.com. Editor: Roy Finamore. Senior Editors: Annetta Hanna, Katie Workman. Executive Editor: Pam Krauss. **Acquisitions**: Lauren Shakely, editorial director. Clarkson Potter specializes in publishing cooking books, decorating and other around-the-house how-to subjects. Publishes hardcover and trade paperback originals. **Publishes 55 titles/year. 15% of books from first-time authors.** Reports in 3 months on queries and proposals.
Nonfiction: Publishes art/architecture, biography, child guidance/parenting, crafts, cooking and foods, decorating, design gardening, how-to, humor, photography, and popular psychology. Query or submit outline and sample chapter with tearsheets from magazines and artwork copies (e.g.—color photocopies or duplicate transparencies).

PPI PUBLISHING, P.O. Box 292239, Kettering OH 45429. (937)294-5057. **Acquisitions:** Shary Price, managing editor. "PPI Publishing seeks to provide top-quality, well researched, up to the-minute information on the 'hot' issues for teens." Publishes age-specific paperback originals and distributes them mostly to schools and public libraries. **Publishes 10-15 titles/year. Receives 200 queries and 50 mss/year. 90% of books from first-time authors; 100% from unagented writers. Pays 10% royalty on retail price.** Publishes book 10 months after acceptance of ms. Accepts simultaneous submissions. Reports in 2 months on queries, 3 months on proposals, 2 months on mss. Catalog and guidelines for 9×12 SASE and 2 first-class stamps. Manuscript guidelines for #10 SASE.
Nonfiction: Children/young adult, how-to, self-help. Subjects include motivational; social issues such as AIDS, abortion, teenage drinking; environmental issues such as the Rainforest and the ozone layer; teen sexuality, "hot youth topics," career guidance. Publishes books in the Fall. Query or submit outline with 3 sample chapters with SASE. Reviews artwork/photos as part of the ms package. Send photocopies.
Recent Title(s): *AIDS: Facts, Issues, Choices*, by Faith H. Brynie, Ph.D.
Tips: Readers are students in grades 7-12 and their teachers. "We're looking for quality material on 'hot' topics that will appeal to middle school/high school students. Submit fresh topics with logical thought and writing."

PRACTICE MANAGEMENT INFORMATION CORP. (PMIC), 4727 Wilshire Blvd., Los Angeles CA 90010. (213)954-0224. Fax: (213)954-0253. E-mail: pmiceditor@aol.com. Website: http://www.medicalbookstore.com. **Acquisitions:** Kathryn Swanson, managing editor. "We seek to help doctors with the business of medicine." Publishes hardcover originals. **Publishes 21 titles/year. Receives 100 queries and 50 mss/year. 10% of books from first-time authors; 90% from unagented writers. Pays 12½% royalty on net receipts. Offers $1,000-5,000 advance.** Publishes book 18 months after acceptance of ms. Reports in 6 months on queries. Book catalog and ms guidelines for #10 SASE.
Imprint(s): PMIC, Health Information Press.
Nonfiction: Reference, technical, textbook, medical practice management, clinical, nonfiction. Subjects include business/economics, health/medicine, science. Submit outline and proposal package, including letter stating who is the intended audience, the need/market for such a book, as well as outline, 3-5 sample chapters and curriculum vitae/résumé.
Recent Title(s): *Clinical Research Opportunities*, by Matthew Heller, M.D., and Tony Boyle, M.D.
Tips: Audience is doctors, medical office and hospital staff, medical managers, insurance coding/billing personnel.

PRAIRIE OAK PRESS, 821 Prospect Place, Madison WI 53703. (608)255-2288. **Acquisitions:** Jerry Minnich, president; Kristin Visser, vice president. Estab. 1991. Prairie Oak publishes exclusively Upper Great Lakes regional nonfiction. Publishes hardcover originals, trade paperback originals and reprints. **Publishes 6-8 titles/year. Pays royalty or makes outright purchase. Offers $500-1,000 advance.** Reports in 3 months on proposals.
Imprint: Prairie Classics.
Nonfiction: History, folklore, gardening, sports, travel, architecture, other general trade subjects. "Any work considered must have a strong tie to Wisconsin and/or the Upper Great Lakes region." Query or submit outline and 1 sample chapter with SASE.
Recent Title(s): *Wisconsin with Kids*, by Visser (family travel guide).
Tips: "When we say we publish regional works only, we mean Wisconsin, Minnesota, Michigan, Illinois. Please do not submit books of national interest. We cannot consider them."

PRECEPT PRESS, Bonus Books, 160 E. Illinois St., Chicago IL 60611. (312)467-0424. Fax: (312)467-9271. E-mail: elena@bonus-books.com. Website: http://www.bonus-books.com. **Acquisitions:** Andrea Lacko, managing editor. "Precept Press features a wide variety of books for the technical community." Publishes hardcover and trade paperback

originals. **Publishes 20 titles/year. Receives 300 queries and 100 mss/year. 25% of books from first-time authors; 90% from unagented writers. Pays royalty.** Publishes book 8 months after acceptance. Accepts simultaneous submissions if so noted. Reports in 3 months on proposals. Manuscript guidelines for #10 SASE.
Nonfiction: Reference, technical, clinical, textbook. Subjects include business, CD-ROM, medical and oncology texts. Query with SASE.
Recent Title(s): *Nutrition Manual for At-Risk Infants and Toddlers*, by Janice Hovasi Cox, M.S., R.N.

PRESIDIO PRESS, 505B San Marin Dr., Suite 300, Novato CA 94945-1340. (415)898-1081 ext. 125. Fax: (415)898-0383. **Acquisitions:** E.J. McCarthy, executive editor. Estab. 1974. "We publish the finest and most accurate military history and military affairs nonfiction, plus entertaining and provocative fiction related to military affairs." Publishes hardcover originals and reprints. **Averages 24 titles/year. Receives 1,600 submissions/year. 35% of books from first-time authors; 65% from unagented writers. Pays 15-20% royalty on net receipts. Advance varies.** Publishes book 12-18 months after acceptance. Reports within 1 month on queries. Book catalog and ms guidelines for 7½×10½ SAE with 4 first-class stamps.
Imprint(s): Lyford Books.
Nonfiction: Subjects include military history and military affairs. Query with SASE. Reviews artwork/photos as part of ms package. Send photocopies.
Fiction: Men's action-adventure, thriller, mystery, military, historical. Query with SASE.
Recent Title(s): *The Biographical History of World War II*, by Mark M. Boatner III; *Blood Tells*, by Ray Saunders (military fiction).
Tips: "If I were a writer trying to market a book today, I would study the market. Find out what publishers are publishing, what they say they want and so forth. Then write what the market seems to be asking for, but with some unique angle that differentiates the work from others on the same subject. We feel that readers of hardcover fiction are looking for works of no less than 80,000 words."

PRICE STERN SLOAN, INC., Penguin Putnam Inc., 345 Hudson, New York NY 10014. (212)951-8700. Fax: (212)951-8694. Editorial Director: Lara Bergen. **Acquisitions:** Submissions Editor (juvenile submissions); Calendars Editor (calendar submissions). Estab. 1963. Price Stern Sloan publishes mass market novelty series for juveniles and adult page-a-day calendars. **Publishes 80 titles/year (95% children's). Receives 3,000 submissions/year. 20% of books from first-time authors; 30% from unagented writers. Pays royalty on net retail or makes outright purchase. Offers advance.** Reports in 3 months. Catalog for 9×12 SAE with 5 first-class stamps. Manuscript guidelines for SASE. Address to "Catalog Request" or "Manuscript Guidelines."
Imprint(s): Troubador Press, Wee Sing®, Doodle Art®, Mad Libs®, Mad Mysteries®, Serendipity®, Plugged In®, Travel Games to Go, I Can Read Comics, Mr. Men & Little Miss.
Nonfiction and Fiction: Mass market juvenile series and adult page-a-day calendars only. Do not send *original* artwork or ms. "Most of our titles are unique in concept as well as execution."
Recent Title(s): The *Bang on the Door* series; *Fabric Painting*, by Melanie Williams, illustrated by Paula Turnbull; *Murphy's Law 1998 Desk Calendar*, by Arthur Bloch.
Tips: "Price Stern Sloan has a unique, humorous, off-the-wall feel. Know our history before you submit to us."

PRIDE & IMPRINTS, (formerly Pride Publications), 7419 Ebbert Dr. SE, Port Orchard WA 98367. E-mail: pridepblsh@aol.com. Website: http://members.aol.com/PridePblsh/Pride.html. **Acquisitions:** Cris Newport, senior editor. "We publish work that is revolutionary in content, sheds light on misconceptions and challenges stereotypes." Publishes trade paperback originals and reprints. **Publishes 10 titles/year. Receives 75 queries and 100 mss/year. 50% of books from first-time authors; 50% from unagented writers. Pays 10-15% royalty on wholesale price.** Publishes book 1 year after acceptance of ms. Accepts simultaneous submissions. Reports in 3 months on mss. Book catalog and ms guidelines for #10 SASE and 2 first class stamps.
Imprint(s): RAMPANT Gaming, Little Blue Works, Keystone Agencies.
Nonfiction: Biography, children's/juvenile, cookbook, how-to, humor, illustrated book, reference, self-help. Subjects include business/economics, cooking/foods/nutrition, education, gay/lesbian, history, language/literature, money/finance, philosophy, psychology. Submit synopsis and first 50 pages with SASE. Reviews artwork/photos as part of the ms package. Send photocopies.
Fiction: Adventure, cyberfiction, erotica, ethnic, experimental, fantasy, feminist, future fiction, gay/lesbian, gothic, historical, horror, humor, juvenile, literary, mainstream/contemporary, mystery, occult, plays, romance, science fiction, suspense, young adult. "We look for work that challenges the way we see the world." Submit general synopsis, chapter-by-chapter synopsis and first 50 pages with SASE.
Poetry: "We look for poetry that others might consider 'too wild, too risky, too truthful.' A collection must have at least 100 poems for us to consider it." Submit complete ms.
Recent Title(s): *1000 Reasons You Might Think Is She My Lover*, by Angela Costa (fiction/erotica); *Still Life with Buddy*, by Lesleá Newman (NEA award-winning poems).
Tips: "We publish for almost every audience. Read one of our books before sending anything."

PRIMA PUBLISHING, P.O. Box 1260, Rocklin CA 95677-1260. (916)632-4400. Website: http://www.primapublishing.com. Publisher: Ben Dominitz. **Acquisitions:** *Lifestyles Division:* Steven Martin, editorial director; Susan Silva, acquisitions editor; Jamie Miller, acquisitions editor; Denise Sternad, acquisitions; Lorna Dolley, acquisitions; Julie

McDonald, acquisitions. *Entertainment Division:* Debra Kempker, publisher; Stacy DeFoe, product manager; Amy Raynor, product manager. *Computers & Technology Division:* Matthew Carleson, publisher; Dan J. Foster, managing editor; Deborah F. Abshier, acquisitions editor; Jenny Watson, acquisitions editor. "Books for the way we live, work and play." Publishes hardcover originals and trade paperback originals and reprints. **Publishes 300 titles/year. Receives 750 queries/year. 10% of books from first-time authors; 30% from unagented writers. Pays 15-20% royalty on wholesale price. Advance varies.** Publishes book 18 months after acceptance. Accepts simultaneous submissions. Reports in 3 months. Catalog for 9×12 SAE with 8 first-class stamps. Writer's guidelines for #10 SASE.

Nonfiction: Business, parenting, education, alternative and traditional health, entertainment, writing, biography, self-help. Subjects include cooking/foods, crafts, history, pets, politics, psychology, relationships, sports, current affairs, network marketing. "We want books with originality, written by highly qualified individuals. No fiction at this time." Query with SASE.

Tips: "Prima strives to reach the primary and secondary markets for each of its books. We are known for promoting our books aggressively. Books that genuinely solve problems for people will always do well if properly promoted. Try to picture the intended audience while writing the book. Too many books are written to an audience that doesn't exist."

PROMETHEUS BOOKS, 59 John Glenn Dr., Buffalo NY 14228. (716)691-0133. Fax: (716)564-2711. E-mail: SLMPBBOOKS@aol.com. Website: http://www.prometheusbooks.com. Managing Editor: Dr. Mark Hall. **Acquisitions:** Steven Mitchell, editorial director. Estab. 1969. "We are a niche, or specialized, publisher that focuses in the area of *critiquing* the paranormal, religious extremism and right wing fundamentalism. We are one of the largest independent publishers of philosophy in the country. We focus on free thought, critical thinking and scientific method." Publishes hardcover originals, trade paperback originals and reprints. **Publishes 75-80 titles/year. Receives 2,500 queries and mss/year. 25% of books from first-time authors; 50% from unagented writers. Pays 10-15% royalty on wholesale price; other for paper. Offers $1,000-3,000 advance; advance rare, if ever, for children's books.** Publishes book 1 year after acceptance of ms. Accepts simultaneous submissions, if so noted. Reports in 2 weeks on queries and proposals, 4 months on mss. Book catalog free. Manuscript guidelines for #10 SASE.

Nonfiction: Biography, children's/juvenile, reference. Subjects include education, government/politics, health/medicine, history, language/literature, philosophy, psychology, religion (not religious, but critiquing), critiques of the paranormal and UFO sightings, etc. "Ask for a catalog, go to the library, look at our books and others like them to get an idea of what our focus is." Submit proposal package including outline, synopsis and a well-developed query letter with SASE. Reviews artwork/photos as part of ms package. Send photocopies.

Recent Title(s): *The Real Roswell Crashed Saucer Coverup*, by Philip J. Klass (paranormal).

Tips: "Audience is highly literate with multiple degrees. An older, but not 'old' audience that is intellectually mature and knows what it wants. They are aware, and we try to provide them with new information on topics of interest to them in mainstream and related areas."

PROMPT PUBLICATIONS, Howard W. Sams & Co., 2647 Waterfront Parkway E. Dr., Indianapolis IN 46214-2041. (317)298-5400. Fax: (317)298-5604. E-mail: cdrake@in.net. Website: http://www.hwsams.com. **Acquisitions:** Candace Drake Hall, managing editor. "Our mission is to produce quality and reliable electronics technology publications to meet the needs of the engineer, technician, hobbyist and average consumer." Publishes trade paperback originals and reprints. **Publishes 30 titles/year. Receives 50-75 queries and 30 mss/year. 40% of books from first-time authors; 90% from unagented writers. Pays royalty on retail price based on author's experience. Advance varies.** Publishes book 1 year after acceptance of ms. Reports in 2 months on queries, 4 months on proposals, 6 months or more on mss. Book catalog free.

Nonfiction: How-to, reference, technical, textbook. Subjects include audio/visual, computers/electronics, electronics repair, energy, science (electricity). "Books should be written for beginners *and* experts, hobbyists *and* professionals. We do not publish books about software. We like manuscripts about household electronics, professional electronics, troubleshooting and repair, component cross-references and how to create or assemble various electronic devices." Established authors query; new authors send complete ms with SASE. Reviews artwork/photos as part of ms package. Send photocopies or sketches ("we have technicians to produce illustrations if necessary").

Recent Title(s): *Computer Monitor Troubleshooting and Repair*, by Joe Desposito.

Tips: Audience is electronics/technical hobbyists, professionals needing reference books, and technical schools. "Please keep in mind that most technical books have a short shelf life, and write accordingly. Remember, also, that it takes a while for a book to be published, so keep notes on updating your material when the book is ready to print. When submitting, above all, *be patient*. It can take up to a year for a publisher to decide whether or not to publish your book."

PRUETT PUBLISHING, 2928 Pearl St., Boulder CO 80301. (303)449-4919. Fax: (303)443-9019. E-mail: pruettbks@aol.com. Publisher: Jim Pruett. **Acquisitions:** Marykay Scott, editor. Estab. 1959. "Pruett Publishing strives to convey to our customers and readers a respect of the American West, in particular the spirit, traditions, and attitude of the region. We publish books in the following subject areas: outdoor recreation, regional history, environment and nature travel and culture." Publishes hardcover paperback and trade paperback originals and reprints. **Publishes 10-15 titles/year. 60% of books are from first-time authors; 100% from unagented writers. Pays 10-12% royalty on net income.** Publishes book 18 months after acceptance. Accepts simultaneous submissions. Reports in 2 months on queries. Book catalog and ms guidelines free.

Nonfiction: Regional history, guidebooks, nature, biography. Subjects include Western Americana, archaeology (Native American), Western history, nature/environment, recreation (outdoor), regional/ethnic cooking/foods (Native American,

Mexican, Spanish), regional travel, regional sports (cycling, hiking, fishing). "We are looking for nonfiction manuscripts and guides that focus on the Rocky Mountain West." Submit proposal package. Reviews artwork/photos and formal proposal as part of ms package.

Recent Title(s): *Colorado Nature Almanac: A Month-by-Month Guide to the State's Wildlife and Wild Places*, by Stephen R. Jones and Ruth Carol Cusman.

Tips: "There has been a movement away from large publisher's mass market books and towards small publisher's regional interest books, and in turn distributors and retail outlets are more interested in small publishers. Authors don't need to have a big name to have a good publisher. Look for similar books that you feel are well produced—consider design, editing, overall quality and contact those publishers. Get to know several publishers, and find the one that feels right—trust your instincts."

PRUFROCK PRESS, P.O. Box 8813, Waco TX 76714. (254)756-3337. Fax: (254)756-3339. E-mail: prufrock@prufrock.com or joel_mcintosh@prufrock.com. Website: http://www.prufrock.com. **Acquisitions:** Joel McIntosh, publisher. "Prufrock Press provides exciting, innovative and current resources supporting the education of gifted and talented learners." Publishes trade paperback originals and reprints. **Publishes 15 titles/year. Receives 150 queries and 50 mss/year. 50% of books from first-time authors; 100% from unagented writers. Pays 10% royalty on sale price.** Publishes book 9 months after acceptance of ms. Reports in 2 months. Book catalog and ms guidelines free.

Nonfiction: Children's/juvenile, how-to, textbook. Subjects include child guidance/parenting, education. "We publish for the education market. Our readers are typically teachers or parents of gifted and talented children. Many authors send us classroom activity books. Our product line is built around professional development books for teachers. While some of our books may include activities, many are included to illustrate a teaching concept on strategies, or strategy in use at an application level." Request query package from publisher.

Recent Title(s): *Coping for Capable Kids*, by Dr. Leonora M. Cohen and Dr. Erica Frydenberg.

Tips: "We are one of the larger independent education publishers; however, we have worked hard to offer authors a friendly, informal atmosphere. Authors should feel comfortable calling up and bouncing an idea off of us or writing us to get our opinion of a new project idea."

PUBLISHERS ASSOCIATES, P.O. Box 140361, Las Colinas TX 75014-0361. (972)686-5332. Senior Editor: Belinda Buxjom. **Acquisitions:** Mary Markal, manuscript coordinator. Estab. 1974. "Publishers Associates publishes liberal academic studies titles emphasizing gay/lesbian history, pro-choice/feminist studies and liberal politics." Publishes trade paperback originals. **Publishes 20 titles/year. Receives 1,500 submissions/year. 60% of books from first-time authors; 100% from unagented writers. Pays 4% and up royalty on retail price.** Publishes book 1 year after acceptance. Reports in 4 months. Book catalog for 6×9 SAE with 4 first-class stamps. Manuscript guidelines for #10 SAE with 2 first-class stamps.

Imprint(s): Hercules Press, The Liberal Press, Liberal Arts Press, Minuteman Press, **Monument Press**, Nichole Graphics, Scholars Books, Tagelwüld.

Nonfiction: Textbook (scholarly). Subjects include gay/lesbian, government/politics (liberal), history, religion (liberation/liberal), women's issues/studies. "Quality researched gay/lesbian history will pay beginning royalty of 7% and up. Academics are encouraged to submit. No biographies, evangelical fundamentalism/Bible, conservative politics, New Age studies or homophobic. No fiction or poetry." Query. Reviews artwork/photos as part of ms package.

Recent Title(s): *Harvest of Contempt*, by Joe Armey (liberal politics).

Tips: "Writers have the best chance with gender-free/nonsexist, liberal academic studies. We sell primarily to libraries and scholars. Our audience is highly educated, politically and socially liberal, if religious they are liberational. If I were a writer trying to market a book today, I would compare my manuscript with books already published by the press I am seeking to submit to."

PUFFIN BOOKS, Penguin Putnam Inc., 375 Hudson St., New York NY 10014-3657. (212)366-2000. Website: http://www.penguin.com/childrens. President/Publisher: Tracy Tang. **Acquisitions:** Sharyn November, senior editor; Joy Peskin, editorial assistant. "Puffin Books publishes high-end trade paperbacks and paperback reprints for preschool children, beginning and middle readers, and young adults." Publishes trade paperback originals and reprints. **Publishes 175-200 titles/year. Receives 300 queries and mss/year. 1% of books by first-time authors; 5% from unagented writers. Royalty and advance vary.** Publishes book 1 year after acceptance of ms. Accepts simultaneous submissions, if so noted. Reports in 1 month on mss. Book catalog for 9×12 SASE with 7 first-class stamps; send request to Marketing Department.

Nonfiction: Biography, children's/juvenile, illustrated book, young children's concept books (counting, shapes, colors). Subjects include education (for teaching concepts and colors, not academic), women in history. " 'Women in history' books interest us." Query. *No unsolicited mss.*

Fiction: Picture books, young adult novels, middle grade and easy-to-read grades 1-3. "We publish mostly paperback reprints. We do few original titles." Query. *No unsolicited mss.*

Tips: "Our audience ranges from little children 'first books' to young adult (ages 14-16). An original idea has the best luck."

N **PURA VIDA PUBLISHING COMPANY**, P.O. Box 379, Mountlake Terrace WA 98043-0379. (425)670-1346. **Acquisitions:** Michele Rogalin, president. Publishes hardcover and trade paperback originals. **Publishes 4 titles/year.**

Pays 6-15% royalty on retail price. Offers up to $1,000 advance. Publishes book 6 months after acceptance of ms. Accepts simultaneous submissions. Reports in 2 months on queries.
Nonfiction: Children's/juvenile, illustrated children's book, self-help, spirituality. Subjects include child guidance/parenting, cooking, foods & nutrition, health/medicine, nature/environment, spirituality/new age. "No religious submissions. Looking for new, fresh material with mind-body-spirit unification as theme. Environmental twist a plus." Query or submit outline and 2 sample chapters and introduction with SASE. Reviews artwork/photos as part of ms package.
Fiction: New age/spirituality. "We don't plan to publish any fiction until 1999 at the earliest. Then we'll be seeking fiction with mind-body-spirit unification theme. Environmental twist a plus." Query or submit synopsis and 2 sample chapters with SASE.
Recent Title(s): *Living the Dream: It's Time*, by Conrad and Varnum (spiritual nonfiction).
Tips: "Those seeking to change the world through internal transformation. If your intuition guides you, send us material."

PURDUE UNIVERSITY PRESS, 1532 South Campus Courts, Bldg. E, West Lafayette IN 47907-1532. (317)494-2038. **Acquisitions:** Thomas Bacher, director; Margaret Hunt, managing editor. Estab. 1960. "Dedicated to excellence in scholarship and the advancement of critical thought that continually expands the horizons of knowledge." Publishes hardcover and trade paperback originals and trade paperback reprints. **Publishes 14-20 titles/year. Receives 600 submissions/year. Pays 7½-15% royalty.** Publishes book 9 months after acceptance. Reports in 2 months. Book catalog and ms guidelines for 9×12 SASE.
Nonfiction: "We publish work of quality scholarship and titles with regional (Midwest) flair. Especially interested in innovative contributions to the social sciences and humanities that break new barriers and provide unique views on current topics. Expanding into veterinary medicine, engineering and business topics. Always looking for new authors who show creativity and thoroughness of research." Print and electronic projects accepted. Query before submitting.
Poetry: One book selected each year by competition. Send SASE for guidelines.
Recent Title(s): *Possum in the Pawpaw Tree: A Seasonal Guide to Midwestern Gardening*, by Lerner and Netzhammer.

G.P. PUTNAM'S SONS, (Adult Trade), Penguin Putnam, Inc., 345 Hudson, New York NY 10014. (212)951-8405. Fax: (212)951-8694. Website: http://www.putnam.com. **Acquisitions:** Acquisitions Editor. Publishes hardcover and trade paperback originals. **5% of books from first-time authors; none from unagented writers. Pays variable advance on retail price.** Accepts simultaneous submissions. Reports in 6 months on queries. Request book catalog through mail order department. Manuscript guidelines free.
Imprint(s): Perigee, Price Stern Sloan, Putnam (children's), **Jeremy P. Tarcher**.
Nonfiction: Biography, celebrity-related topics, contemporary affairs, cookbook, self-help. Subjects include animals, business/economics, child guidance/parenting, cooking/foods/nutrition, health/medicine, military/war, nature/environment, religion/inspirational, science, sports, travel, women's issues/studies. Query with SASE. *No unsolicited mss.*
Fiction: Adventure, literary, mainstream/contemporary, mystery, suspense, women's. Query with synopsis, *brief* writing sample (the shorter the better) and SASE. Prefers agented submissions.
Recent Title(s): *Lindbergh*, by A. Scott Berg (nonfiction); *Rainbow Six*, by Tom Clancy (adventure).

N **G.P. PUTNAM'S SONS BOOKS FOR YOUNG READERS**, Penguin Putnam Books for Young Readers, Penguin Putnam Inc., 345 Hudson St., New York NY 10014. (212)414-3610. **Acquisitions:** Manuscript editor. Publishes hardcover originals. **Publishes 40 titles/year. Receives 2,500 submissions/year. 20% of books from first-time authors; 30% from unagented writers. Pays standard royalty. Advance negotiable.** Publishes book 2 years after acceptance of ms. Reports in 2 months on queries and unsolicited mss.
Fiction: Children's picture books (ages 3-8); middle-grade fiction and illustrated chapter books (ages 7-10); older middle-grade fiction (ages 10-14) some young adult (ages 14-18). Particularly interested in middle-grade fiction with strong voice, literary quality, high interest for audience, poignancy, humor, unusual settings or plots. Historical fiction OK. Unsolicited mss accepted for picture books only; query first for fiction. Always include SASE or no response. No science fiction, no series or activity books, no board books.
Recent Title(s): *Cowboy Bunnies*, by Christine Loomis, illustrated by Ora Eitan (picture book); *Rules of the Road*, by Joan Bauer (middle-grade novel).

QUE BOOKS, Macmillan Computer Publishing, 201 W. 103rd St., Indianapolis IN 46290. (317)581-3500. Website: http://www.mcp.com/que/. Publisher: Richard Swadley **Acquisitions:** Andi Richter, executive assistant. Publishes hardcover, trade paperback and mass market paperback originals and reprints. **Publishes 200 titles/year. 85% of books from unagented writers. Pays variable royalty on wholesale price or makes work-for-hire arrangements. Advance varies.** Accepts simultaneous submissions. Reports in 1 month on proposals. Catalog and ms guidelines free.
Nonfiction: How-to, illustrated book, reference, technical. Subjects include computers/electronics, hardware, software. Query with outline, marketing analysis and SASE. Reviews artwork/photos as part of ms package. Reviews PCX files (uses Collage software).
Recent Title(s): *Using the Internet, 4th edition.*

QUEST BOOKS, Theosophical Publishing House, P.O. Box 270, Wheaton IL 60189. (630)665-0130. Fax: (630)665-8791. E-mail: questbooks@aol.com. Website: htpp://www.theosophica.org. **Acquisitions:** Brenda Rosen, executive editor. "TPH is dedicated to the promotion of the unity of humanity and the encouragement of the study of religion, philosophy and science, to the end that we may better understand ourselves and our place in the universe." Publishes hardcover originals and trade paperback originals and reprints. **Publishes 12-15 titles/year. Receives 500 queries and 100 mss/year. 50% of books from first-time authors; 75% from unagented writers. Pays 10-13% on wholesale price. Offers $3,000-10,000 advance.** Publishes book 20 months after acceptance of ms. Accepts simultaneous submissions. Reports in 1 month on queries, 2 months on proposals, 3 months on mss. Book catalog and ms guidelines free.

● Quest gives preference to writers with established reputations/successful publications.

Nonfiction: Biography, illustrated book, self-help. Subjects include anthropology/archaeology, art/architecture, health/medicine, music/dance, nature/environment, travel, self-development, self-help, philosophy (holistic), psychology (transpersonal), Eastern and Western religions, theosophy, comparative religion, men's and women's spirituality, Native American spirituality, holistic implications in science, health and healing, yoga, meditation, astrology. "Our speciality is high-quality spiritual nonfiction with a self-help aspect. Great writing is a must. We seldom publish 'personal spiritual awakening' stories. No submissions accepted that do not fit the needs outlined above." Accepts nonfiction translations. Query or submit proposal package, including author bio, contents, sample chapter and SASE. Reviews artwork/photos as part of ms package. Send photocopies.

Recent Title(s): *Getting in Touch*, by Christine Caldwell (psychology).

Tips: Our audience includes the 'New Age' community, seekers in all religions, general public, professors, and health professionals. Read a few recent Quest titles. Know our books and our company goals. Explain how your book or proposal relates to other Quest titles."

QUILL DRIVER BOOKS/WORD DANCER PRESS, 8386 N. Madsen Ave., Clovis CA 93611. (209)322-5917. Fax: (209)322-5967. E-mail: sbm12@csufresno.edu. **Acquisitions:** Stephen Blake Mettee, publisher. "We publish a modest number of books per year, each of which, we hope, makes a worthwhile contribution to the human community, and we have a little fun along the way." Publishes hardcover and trade paperback originals and reprints. **Publishes 10-12 titles/year. (Quill Driver Books: 4/year, Word Dancer Press: 6-8/year). 20% of books from first-time authors; 95% from unagented writers. Pays 4-10% royalty on retail price. Offers $500-5,000 advance.** Publishes book 9 months after acceptance. Accepts simultaneous submissions. Reports in 1 month on queries and proposals, 3 months on mss. Book catalog and ms guidelines for #10 SASE.

Nonfiction: Biography, how-to, reference, general nonfiction. Subjects include Americana, regional, fund-raising, writing. Query with proposal package. Reviews artwork/photos as part of ms package. Send photocopies.

Recent Title(s): *Feminine Wiles: Creative Techniques for Writing Women's Feature Articles That Sell*, by Donna Elizabeth Boetig (writing).

THE QUILT DIGEST PRESS, NTC/Contemporary Publishing Group, 4255 W. Touhy, Lincolnwood IL 60646. (847)679-5500. Fax: (847)679-2494. **Acquisitions**: Anne Knudsen, senior editor. Quilt Digest Press publishes quilting and sewing craft books. Publishes hardcover and trade paperback originals. **Publishes 10-12 titles/year. Receives 100 queries and 30 mss/year. 20% of books from first-time authors; 80% from unagented writers. Pays royalty on wholesale price.** Publishes book 1 year after acceptance of ms. Accepts simultaneous submissions. Reports in 2 months. Book catalog and ms guidelines free.

Nonfiction: How-to. Subjects include hobbies, crafts/quilting. Submit outline, bio, sample, photos and SASE. Reviews artwork/photos as part of ms package. Send color photocopies.

Recent Title(s): *Quilts! Quilts!! Quilts!!!*, by Diana McClun/Laura Nownes.

QUITE SPECIFIC MEDIA GROUP LTD., (formerly Drama Publishers) 260 Fifth Ave., Suite 703, New York NY 10001. (212)725-5377. Fax: (212)725-8506. E-mail: info@quitespecificmedia.com. Website: http://www.quitespecificmedia.com. **Acquisitions:** Ralph Pine, editor-in-chief. Estab. 1967. "Quite Specific Media Group is an umbrella company of five imprints specializing in costume and fashion, theater and design." Publishes hardcover originals, trade paperback originals and reprints. **Publishes 12 titles/year. Receives 300 queries/year and 100 mss/year. 75% of books from first-time authors; 85% from unagented writers. Pays royalty on wholesale price. Advance varies.** Publishes book 18 months after acceptance. Accepts simultaneous submissions. Reports "as quickly as possible." Book catalog and ms guidelines free.

Imprint(s): Costume & Fashion Press, Drama Publishers, By Design Press, Entertainment Pro, Jade Rabbit

Nonfiction: Texts, guides, manuals, directories, reference and multimedia—for and about performing arts theory and practice: acting, directing; voice, speech, movement; makeup, masks, wigs; costumes, sets, lighting, sound; design and execution; technical theater, stagecraft, equipment; stage management; producing; arts management, all varieties; business and legal aspects; film, radio, television, cable, video; theory, criticism, reference; playwriting; theater and performance history; costume and fashion. Accepts nonfiction and technical works in translations also. Query with 1-3 sample chapters and SASE; no complete mss. Reviews artwork/photos as part of ms package.

Recent Title(s): *The Articulate Body: The Physical Training for the Actor*, by Anne Dennis.

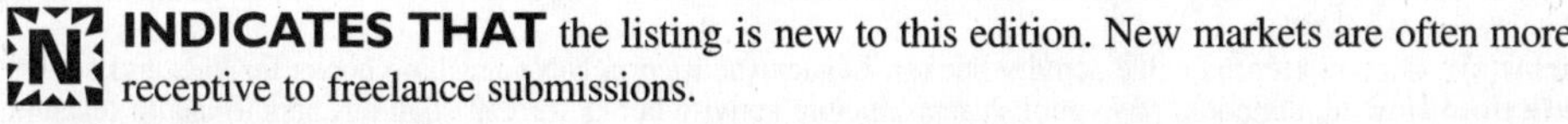

INDICATES THAT the listing is new to this edition. New markets are often more receptive to freelance submissions.

QUIXOTE PRESS, 3544 Blakeslee St., Wever IA 52658. (319)372-7480. Fax: (319)372-7480. **Acquisitions:** Bruce Carlson, president. Quixote Press specializes in humorous regional folklore and special interest cookbooks. Publishes trade paperback originals and reprints. **Publishes 20 titles/year. Receives 500-600 queries and 300-400 mss/year. 90% of books from first-time authors; 95% from unagented writers. Pays 10% royalty on wholesale price. No advance.** Publishes book 1 week to 1 year after acceptance of ms. Accepts simultaneous submissions. Reports in 2 months. Book catalog and manuscript guidelines for #10 SASE.

Imprint(s): Blackiron Cooking Co., Hearts & Tummies Cookbook Co.

Nonfiction: Children's/juvenile, cookbook, humor, self-help. Subjects include agriculture/horticulture, Americana, cooking/foods/nutrition, regional, travel, folklore. "We must be in on ground floor of the product design." Submit outline, 2 sample chapters and SASE. Reviews artwork/photos as part of ms package. Send photocopies.

Fiction: Adventure, ethnic, experimental, humor, short story collections, children's. Query with synopsis and SASE.

Recent Title(s): *Peaches! Peaches! Peaches!*, by M. Mosley (cookbook); *Out Behind the Barn*, by B. Carlson (rural folklore).

Tips: Carefully consider marketing considerations. Audience is women in gift shops, on farm site direct retail outlets.

RAGGED MOUNTAIN, International Marine/The McGraw-Hill Companies, P.O. Box 220, Camden ME 04843-0220. (207)236-4837. Fax: (207)236-6314. **Acquisitions:** Jeffery Serena, acquisitions editor; Jonathan Eaton, editorial director. Estab. 1969. Ragged Mountain Press publishes "books that take you off the beaten path." Publishes hardcover and trade paperback originals and reprints. **Publishes 40 titles/year; imprint publishes 15, remainder are International Marine. Receives 200 queries and 100 mss/year. 30% of books from first-time authors; 90% from unagented writers. Pays 10-15% royalty on net price. Offers advance.** Publishes book 1 year after acceptance of ms. Accepts simultaneous submissions. Reports in 1 month on queries. *Writer's Market* recommends allowing 2 months for reply. Book catalog for 9×12 SAE with 10 first-class stamps. Manuscript guidelines for #10 SASE.

Nonfiction: Outdoor-related how-to, guidebooks, essays. Subjects include camping, fly fishing, snowshoeing, backpacking, canoeing, outdoor cookery, skiing, snowboarding, survival skills and wilderness know-how, birdwatching, natural history, climbing and kayaking. "Raged Mountain publishes nonconsumptive outdoor and environmental issues books of literary merit or unique appeal. Be familiar with the existing literature. Find a subject that hasn't been done or has been done poorly, then explore it in detail and from all angles." Query with outline and 1 sample chapter. Reviews artwork/photos as part of ms package. Send photocopies.

Recent Title(s): *The Ragged Mountain Press Pocket Pocket Guide to Wilderness Medicine and First Aid*, by Paul G. Gill, Jr., M.D.

RAINBOW BOOKS, INC., P.O. Box 430, Highland City FL 33846. (941)648-4420. Fax: (941)648-4420. E-mail: naip@aol.com. **Acquisitons:** Betsy A. Lampe, editorial director. "We want to provide answers to problems and issues that concern today's readers, both adults and children ages 8-14." Publishes hardcover and trade paperback originals. **Publishes 12-15 titles/year. Receives 300 queries and 100 mss/year. 90% of books from first-time authors; 80% from unagented writers. Pays 6-12% royalty on retail price. Offers $500-1,000 advance.** Publishes book 1 year after acceptance of ms. Accepts simultaneous submissions. Reports in 1 month on queries and proposals, 2 months on mss. Book catalog and ms guidelines for #10 SASE.

- This publisher is now accepting fiction.

Nonfiction: Biography, children's/juvenile, gift book, how-to, humor, self-help. Subjects include animals, business/economics, child guidance/parenting, education, gardening, hobbies, money/finance, nature/environment, philosophy, psychology, recreation, science, sociology, sports, women's issues/studies. "We want books that provide authoritative answers to questions in layman language. We have also begun a list of 3rd-to-8th grade titles for young people along the same lines as our adult general nonfiction. Writers must include background credentials for having written the book they propose." Query with SASE. Reviews artwork/photos as part of ms package. Send photocopies.

Fiction: "We published 2 fiction titles in 1998: a science-oriented mystery and a somewhat mainstream romance/adventure title. That does not mean we won't be interested in other categories. Mainly, we're looking for well-written books that deserve to be published." Submit synopsis and complete ms and SASE with sufficient postage.

Recent Title(s): *6 Steps to Reforming America's Schools*, by Sim O. Wilde (how to); *Pharmacology Is Murder*, by Dirk Wyle (murder mystery).

Tips: "We are addressing an adult population interested in answers to questions, and also 8- to 14-year-olds of the same mindset. Be professional in presentation of queries and manuscripts, and always provide a return mailer with proper postage attached in the event the materials do not fit our list."

RAINBOW PUBLISHERS, P.O. Box 261129, San Diego CA 92196. (619)271-7600. **Acquisitions:** Christy Allen, editor. "Rainbow Publishers strives to publish Bible-based materials that contribute to, inspire spiritual growth and development in children and adults and meet the needs of readers in the Christian realm, preferably evangelical." **Publishes 20 titles/year. Receives 250 queries and 100 mss/year. 50% of books from first-time authors. Pays royalty based on wholesale price.** Publishes book 18 months after acceptance of ms. Accepts simultaneous submissions. Reports in 3 months on queries, proposals and mss. Book catalog for 9×12 SAE with 2 first-class stamps. Manuscript guidelines for #10 SASE.

Imprint(s): Rainbow (reproducible activity books); Legacy (nonfiction Bible-teaching books for kids and adults).

Nonfiction: How-to, textbook. "We publish reproducible activity books for Christian teachers to use in teaching the Bible to children ages 2-12 and Bible-teaching books for children and adults." Query with outline, sample pages, age

level, introduction. "We use freelance artists. Send a query and photocopies of art samples."
Recent Title(s): *Make & Learn Bible Toys*, by Nancy Kline (craft books series).
Tips: "We are seeking manuscripts for *both* the children's and adult Christian book market, focusing on Christian education. We plan a much more aggressive publishing schedule than in the past."

RANDOM HOUSE, 201 E. 50th St., New York NY 10022. (212)751-2600.
Imprint(s): *Ballantine Publishing*: **Ballantine**, Columbine, **Del Rey**, **Fawcett**, **House of Collectibles**, Ivy Books, **One World**; *Crown Publishing Group:* **Clarkson Potter**, Crown Books, Harmony Books; *Knopf Publishing Group:* **Alfred A. Knopf, Pantheon, Schocken, Vintage Books**; *Random House:* Modern Library; **Random House, Times Books, Times Business Books, Villard Books**, *Random House Children's*: Dragonfly, **Knopf and Crown Books for Young Readers**, Random House Books for Young Readers.

RANDOM HOUSE, ADULT BOOKS, Random House, Inc., 201 E. 50th St., 11th Floor, New York NY 10022. (212)751-2600. **Acquisitions:** Sandy Fine, submissions coordinator. Estab. 1925. "Random House is the world's largest English-language general trade book publisher. It includes an array of prestigious imprints that publish some of the foremost writers of our time—in hardcover, trade paperback, mass market paperback, electronic, multimedia and other formats." **Publishes 120 titles/year. Receives 3,000 submissions/year. Pays royalty on retail price.** Accepts simultaneous submissions. Reports in 2 months. Book catalog free. Manuscript guidelines for #10 SASE.
Imprint(s): Ballantine, Crown, Del Rey, Fawcett, Harmony, **Alfred A. Knopf**, Modern Library, **Pantheon, Clarkson N. Potter, Random House, Villard, Vintage.**
Nonfiction: Biography, cookbook, humor, illustrated book, self-help. Subjects include Americana, art, business/economics, classics, cooking and foods, health, history, music, nature, politics, psychology, religion, sociology and sports. No juveniles or textbooks (separate division). Query with outline, 3 sample chapters and SASE.
Fiction: Adventure, confession, experimental, fantasy, historical, horror, humor, mainstream, mystery, and suspense. Submit outline/synopsis, 3 sample chapters and SASE.
Recent Title(s): *Sex On Campus*, by Elliott and Brantley; *The Gospel According to the Son*, by Norman Mailer.

[A] **RANDOM HOUSE CHILDREN'S PUBLISHING**, Random House, Inc., 201 E. 50th St., New York NY 10022. (212)751-2600. Fax: (212)940-7685. Website: http://www.randomhouse/com/kids. Publishing Director: Kate Klimo. **Acquisitions:** Ruth Koeppel, senior editor/licensing director (Stepping Stones); Heidi Kilgras, editor (Step into Reading); Stephanie St. Pierre, senior editor (Picturebacks). Estab. 1935. Publishes hardcover, trade paperback, and mass market paperback originals and reprints. "Random House Books aim to create books that nurture the hearts and minds of children, providing and promoting quality books and a rich variety of media that entertain and educate readers from 6 months to 12 years." **Publishes 200 titles/year. Receives 1,000 queries/year. Pays 1-6% royalty or makes outright purchase. Advance varies.** Publishes book 1 year after acceptance of ms. Accepts simultaneous submissions. Reports in 3 weeks-6 months. Book catalog free.
Imprint(s): Random House Books for Young Readers, **Alfred A. Knopf and Crown Children's Books**, Dragonfly Paperbacks.
Nonfiction: Children's/juvenile. Subjects include animal, history, nature/environment, popular culture, science, sports. Agented submissions only. *No unsolicited mss.*
Fiction: Humor, juvenile, mystery, picture books, young adult. "Familiarize yourself with our list. We look for original, unique stories. Do something that hasn't been done." Agented submissions only. *No unsolicited mss.*
Recent Title(s): *Shooting Stars: The Women of Pro Basketball*, by Bill Gutman; *The Mermaids' Lullaby*, by Kate Spohn, (glitter book about mermaids).

RAWSON ASSOCIATES, Simon & Schuster, 1230 Avenue of the Americas, New York NY 10020. (212)698-7000. **Acquisitions:** Eleanor Rawson, publisher. Rawson Associates publishes nonfiction. "We are interested in original concepts that deal with issues of concern to many people." Publishes hardcover originals. **Publishes 5 titles/year. Receives "hundreds" of queries/year. Less than 10% of books from first-time authors.** *Writer's Market* recommends allowing 2 months for a reply.
Nonfiction: Subjects include business, contemporary lifestyle concerns, health/medicine, psychology. "We are looking for author's with strong credentials and ability to assist in marketing work." Query or submit outline with 1 sample chapter and credentials with SASE. Reviews artwork/photos as part of the ms package. Send photocopies.
Recent Nonfiction Title(s): *The Power of Hope*, by Maurice Lamm.

[N] **RED HEN PRESS**, Valentine Publishing Group, P.O. Box 902582, Palmdale CA 93590-2582. Phone/fax: (818)831-0649. E-mail: redhen@vpg.net. Website: http://www.vpg.net. **Acquisitions**: Mark E. Cull, publisher/editor (fiction); Katherine Gale, poetry editor (poetry, literary fiction). Red Hen Press specializes in literary fiction and poetry. Publishes trade paperback originals. **Publishes 6 titles/year. Receives 2,000 queries and 500 mss/year. 10% of books from first-time authors; 90% from unagented writers. Pays 10% royalty on retail price.** Publishes book 1 year after acceptance of ms. Accepts simultaneous submissions. Reports in 1 month on queries, 2 months on proposals, 3 months on mss. Book catalog and ms guidelines free.
Nonfiction: Biography, children's/juvenile, cookbooks. Subjects include anthropology/archaeology, ethnic, gay/lesbian, language/literature, travel, women's issues/studies. Query with SASE. Reviews artwork/photos as part of ms package. Send photocopies.

Fiction: Ethnic, experimental, feminist, gay/lesbian, historical, literary, mainstream/contemporary, poetry, poetry in translation, short story collections. "We prefer high-quality literary fiction." Query with SASE.
Poetry: Query with 5 sample poems.
Recent Titles: *Highway Trade*, by John Domini (short story collection); *The Sun Takes Us Away*, by Benjamin Sultam (lyric poetry).
Tips: "Audience reads poetry, literary fiction, intelligent nonfiction. If you have an agent, we may be too small since we don't pay advances. Write well. Send queries first. Be willing to help promote your own book."

REFERENCE PRESS INTERNATIONAL, P.O. Box 4126, Greenwich CT 06830. (203)622-6860. Fax: (203)622-5983. E-mail: ml2626@aol.com. **Acquisitions:** Cheryl Lacoff, senior editor. Reference Press specializes in instructional, reference and how-to titles. Publishes hardcover and trade paperback originals. **Publishes 6 titles/year. Receives 50 queries and 20 mss/year. 75% of books from first-time authors; 100% from unagented writers. Pays royalty or makes outright purchase. Advance determined by project.** Publishes book 6 months after acceptance. Accepts simultaneous submissions. Reports in 3 months. Book catalog for #10 SASE.
Nonfiction: How-to, illustrated book, multimedia (audio, video, CD-ROM), reference, technical, educational, instructional. Subjects include Americana, art/architecture, business/economics, hobbies, money/finance, gardening, photography, anything related to the arts or crafts field. "Follow the guidelines as stated concerning subjects and types of books we're looking for." Query with outline, 1-3 sample chapters and SASE. Reviews artwork/photos as part of ms package. Send photocopies.
Recent Title(s): *Who's Who in the Peace Corps*, (alumni directory).

REFERENCE SERVICE PRESS, 5000 Windplay Dr., Suite 4, El Dorado Hills CA 95762. (916)939-9620. Fax: (916)939-9626. E-mail: findaid@aol.com. Website: http://www.rspfunding.com. **Acquisitions:** Stuart Hauser, acquisitions editor. Estab. 1977. "We are interested only in directories and monographs dealing with financial aid." Publishes hardcover originals. **Publishes 5-10 titles/year. 100% of books from unagented writers. Pays 10% or higher royalty.** Publishes book 6 months after acceptance. Accepts simultaneous submissions. Reports in 2 months. Book catalog for #10 SASE.

- This publisher maintains databases on America Online.

Nonfiction: Reference for financial aid seekers. Subjects include education, ethnic, military/war, women's issues/studies, disabled. Submit outline and sample chapters.
Recent Title(s): *College Students' Guide to Merit Funding and Other No-Need Scholarships*, by Gail Ann Schlachter and R. David Weber.
Tips: "Our audience consists of librarians, counselors, researchers, students, re-entry women, scholars and other fund-seekers."

[A] **REGAN BOOKS**, HarperCollins, 10 E. 53rd St., New York NY 10022. (212)207-7400. Fax: (212)207-6951. Website: http://www.harpercollins.com. **Acquisitions:** Judith Regan, president/publisher. Estab. 1994. "Regan Books publishes general fiction and nonfiction: biography, self-help, style and gardening books." Regan Books is known for contemporary topics and controversial authors and titles. Publishes hardcover and trade paperback originals. **Publishes 30 titles/year. Receives 7,500 queries and 5,000 mss/year. Pays royalty on retail price. Advance varies.** Publishes book 1 year after acceptance of ms. Accepts simultaneous submissions. Reports in 3 months on proposals.
Nonfiction: Biography, coffee table book, cookbook, gift book, illustrated book, reference, self-help. All subjects. *Agented submissions only. No unsolicited mss.* Reviews artwork as part of ms package. Send photocopies.
Fiction: All categories. *Agented submissions only. No unsolicited mss.*
Recent Title(s): *Recapturing the Joys of Victorian Life*, by Linda S. Lichter (inspirational/women's studies); *Girlfriend in a Coma*, by Douglas Coupland (fiction).

REGNERY PUBLISHING, INC., Eagle Publishing, One Massachusetts Ave., NW, Washington DC 20003. Fax: (202)546-8759. Publisher: Alfred S. Regnery. Executive Editor: Harry Crocker. Associate Publisher: Richard Vigilante. Managing Editor: David Dortman. **Acquisitions:** Submissions Editor. Estab. 1947. "Regnery has been America's premier publisher of conservative books since its founding. Regnery's authors have been the intellectual leaders of American's conservative movment. Regnery publishes well-written, well-produced, sometimes controversial, but always provocative books." Publishes hardcover and paperback originals and reprints. **Publishes 30 titles/year. Pays 8-15% royalty on retail price. Offers $0-50,000 advance.** Publishes book 1 year after acceptance. Accepts simultaneous submissions. No fax submissions. Reports in 6 months on proposals. Guidelines for SASE. "Please request guidelines before submitting."
Imprint(s): Gateway Editions, Life Line Press.
Nonfiction: Biography, business/economics, current affairs, education, government/politics, health/medicine, history, military/war, nature/environment, philosophy, religion, science, sociology. Query with outline and 2-3 sample chapters. Does not accept full ms before proposal/query. Reviews artwork/photos as part of ms package. Send photocopies. Does not return submissions.
Recent Title(s): *Unlimited Access*, by Gary Aldrich (nonfiction); *Hannibal: A Novel*, by Ross Leckie (fiction).
Tips: "Currently we are looking for newsworthy, provactive and timely books—especially high-impact, headline-making, bestseller treatments of the most pressing current political, social and cultural issues, or profiles of the currently famous players in those fields. While we are seeking serious and important books, we are not looking for earnest or

scholarly public policy tracts with a limited audience. We welcome timely projects that are completed or are near completion. Please request manuscript guidelines before sumbitting."

N **RENAISSANCE BOOKS**, Renaissance Media, 5858 Wilshire Blvd., Suite 200, Los Angeles CA 90036. (213)939-1840. **Acquisitions:** Brenda Scott Royce, production coordinator; James Robert Parish, editor (show business); Richard F.X. O'Connor, editor (general nonfiction); Joe McNeely, editor (New Age/psychology). "Renaissance publishes a wide range of nonfiction trade books." Publishes hardcover and trade paperback originals. **Publishes 30 titles/year. Receives 300 queries/year. 10% of books from first-time authors; 30% from unagented writers. Pays royalty on retail price. Advance varies widely.** Publishes book 6 months after acceptance of ms. Accepts simultaneous submissions. Reports in 2 months on proposals. Book catalog free.

Nonfiction: Biography, cookbook, how-to, humor, reference, self-help. Subjects include Americana, animals, business and economics, child guidance/parenting, cooking/foods/nutrition, government/politics, health/medicine, history, hobbies, money/finance, psychology, recreation, sociology, sports, entertainment, show business. Submit outline and 2 sample chapter with SASE.

Recent Title(s): *Selling Goodness*, by Michael Levine (public relations).

Tips: "Include as much marketing information as possible in your proposal. Why will your book sell in today's marketplace?"

REPUBLIC OF TEXAS PRESS, Wordware Publishing, Inc., 2320 Los Rios Blvd., Suite 200, Plano TX 75074. (972)423-0090. Fax: (972)881-9147. E-mail: gbivona@wordwave.com. Website: http://www.wordware.com. **Acquisitions:** Ginnie Bivona, Diana Stultz and James S. Hill. "We publish books pertaining to Western history, outlaws and folklore, military history, ghost stories and humor." Publishes trade and mass market paperback originals. **Publishes 25-30 titles/year. Receives 400 queries and 300 mss/year. 80% of books from unagented writers. Pays 8-12% royalty on wholesale price.** Publishes book 9 months after acceptance of ms. Reports in 2 months. Book catalog and ms guidelines for SASE.

Nonfiction: History, Texana material, general interest. Subjects include Old West, Southwest, cookbooks, military, women of the West, ghost stories, humor, biography. Submit toc, 2 sample chapters, target audience and author bio.

Recent Title(s): *Texas Ranger Tales*, by Mike Wilcox.

RESOURCE PUBLICATIONS, INC., 160 E. Virginia St., Suite #290, San Jose CA 95112-5876. (408)286-8505. Fax: (408)287-8748. E-mail: orders@rpinet.com. Website: http://www.rpinet.com/ml/ml.html. **Acquisitions:** Nick Wagner, editorial director (religious books); Kenneth Guentert, editor (secular books). "We help liturgists and ministers make the imaginative connection between liturgy and life." Produces trade paperback originals. **Produces 20 titles/year. 30% of books from first-time authors; 95% from unagented writers. Pays 8% royalty (for a first project). Rarely offers advance.** Reports in 10 weeks. Catalog for 9×12 SAE with postage for 10 ozs. Manuscript guidelines for #10 SASE.

Nonfiction: How-to, self-help. Subjects include child guidance/parenting, education, music/dance, religion, professional ministry resources for worship, education, clergy and other leaders, for use in Roman Catholic and mainline Protestant churches. Submit proposal. Reviews artwork as part of freelance ms package.

Fiction: Fables, anecdotes, faith sharing stories, any stories useful in preaching or teaching. Query.

Recent Title(s): *Nun Better* (short stories); *Dreams That Help You Mourn*, by Lois Hendricks (dreams in grieving).

Tips: "We are publishers and secondarily we are book packagers. Pitch your project to us for publication first. If we can't take it on on that basis, we may be able to take it on as a packaging and production project."

RESURRECTION PRESS, LTD., P.O. Box 248, Williston Park NY 11596. (516)742-5686. Fax: (516)746-6872. **Acquisitions:** Emilie Cerar, publisher. Resurrection Press publishes religious, devotional and inspirational titles. Publishes trade paperback originals and reprints. **Publishes 6-8 titles/year; imprint publishes 4 titles/year. Receives 100 queries and 100 mss/year. 25% of books from first-time authors; 100% from unagented writers. Pays 5-10% royalty on retail price. Offers $250-2,000 advance.** Publishes book 1 year after acceptance of ms. Accepts simultaneous submissions. Reports in 1 month on queries and proposals, 2 months on mss. Book catalog and ms guidelines free.

Imprint(s): Spirit Life Series.

Nonfiction: Self-help. Religious subjects. Wants mss of no more than 200 double-spaced typewritten pages. Query with outline and 2 sample chapters. Reviews artwork/photos as part of ms package. Send photocopies.

Recent Title(s): *Surprising Mary: Meditations and Prayers on the Mother of Jesus*, by Mitch Finely.

FLEMING H. REVELL PUBLISHING, Baker Book House, P.O. Box 6287, Grand Rapids MI 49516. Fax: (616)676-2315. Website: http://www.bakerbooks.com. **Acquisitions:** Linda Holland, editorial director; Bill Petersen, senior acquisitions editor; Jane Campbell, senior editor (Chosen Books). "Revell publishes to the heart (rather than to the head). For 125 years, Revell has been publishing evangelical books for the personal enrichment and spiritual growth of general Christian readers." Publishes hardcover, trade paperback and mass market paperback originals and reprints. **Publishes 50 titles/year; imprint publishes 10 titles/year. Receives 750 queries and 1,000 mss/year. 10% of books from first-time authors; 75% from unagented writers. Pays 7½-15% royalty on wholesale price.** Publishes book 1 year after acceptance of ms. Accepts simultaneous submissions. Reports in 3 months. Manuscript guidelines for #10 SASE.

Imprint(s): Spire Books, **Chosen Books.**

Nonfiction: Biography, coffee table book, how-to, self-help. Subjects include child guidance/parenting, Christian

Living. Query with outline and 2 sample chapters.
Fiction: Religious. Submit synopsis and 2 sample chapters.
Recent Title(s): *God's Guidance*, by Elisabeth Elliot (nonfiction); *A Time of War*, by Gilbert Morris (fiction).

REVIEW AND HERALD PUBLISHING ASSOCIATION, 55 W. Oak Ridge Dr., Hagerstown MD 21740. (301)791-7000. **Acquisitions**: Jeannette R. Johnson, acquisitions editor. "Through print and electronic media, the Review and Herald Publishing Association nurtures a growing relationship with God by providing products that teach and enrich people spiritually, mentally, physically and socially as we near Christ's soon second coming. We belong to the Seventh Day Adventist denomination." Publishes hardcover, trade paperback and mass market paperback originals and reprints. **Publishes 40-50 titles/year. Receives 200 queries and 350 mss/year. 50% of books from first-time authors; 95% from unagented writers. Pays 7-15% royalty. Offers $500-1,000 advance.** Publishes book 18 months after acceptance of ms. Accepts simultaneous submissions. Reports in 1 month on queries and proposals, 2 months on mss. Book catalog for 10×13 SASE. Manuscript guidelines for #10 SASE.
Nonfiction: Biography, children's/juvenile, cookbook, gift book, humor, multimedia, reference, self-help, textbook, Christian lifestyle, inspirational. Subjects include animals, anthropology/archaeology, child guidance/parenting, cooking/foods/nutrition, education, health/medicine, history, nature/environment, philosophy, religion, women's issues/studies. Submit proposal package, including 3 sample chapters and cover letter with SASE.
Fiction: Adventure, historical, humor, juvenile, mainstream/contemporary, religious, all Christian-living related. Submit synopsis and or 3 sample chapters.
Recent Title(s): *The Appearing*, by Penny Estes Wheeler (inspirational); *Incredible Answers to Prayer*, by Roger Morneau.

MORGAN REYNOLDS PUBLISHING, 620 S. Elm St., Suite 384, Greensboro NC 27406. Fax: (336)275-1152. E-mail: morganreynolds@www.morganreynolds.com. Website: http://www.morganreynolds.com. **Acquisitions**: John Riley. "Our books focus on both well-known historical and contemporary figures and people and events too often left out of the textbooks. Our goal is to continue to publish lively, informative and original works of non-fiction." Publishes hardcover originals. **Publishes 10-12 titles/year. Receives 200-250 queries and 75-100 mss/year. 50% of books from first-time authors; 100% from unagented writers. Pays 8-12% royalty on wholesale price. Offers $500-1,000 advance.** Publishes book 8 months after acceptance of ms. Accepts simultaneous submissions. Reports in 2 months.
Nonfiction: Biography. Subjects include Americana, business/economics, government/politics, history, language/literature, military/war, money/finance, women's issues/studies, all young adult/juvenile oriented. No children's books. "We publish nonfiction for juvenile and young adult readers. We publish titles in our five series: Notable Americans, World Writers, Great Events, Champions of Freedom, Great Athletes—as well as high-quality non-series works. We plan to expand our biography lines. We are interested in well-written books on prominent women from ancient and medieval times." Submit outline, 3 sample chapters with SASE. Reviews artwork/photos as part of ms package. Send photocopies.
Recent Title(s): *The Ordeal of Olive Oatman: A True Story of the American West*, by Margaret Raer.
Tips: "Research the markets before submitting. We spend too much time dealing with manuscripts that shouldn't have been submitted."

THE RIEHLE FOUNDATION, P.O. Box 7, Milford OH 45150. Fax: (513)576-0022. **Acquisitions:** Mrs. B. Lewis, general manager. "We are only interested in materials which are written to draw the reader to a deeper love for God." Publishes trade paperback originals and reprints. **Publishes 6-7 titles/year. Receives 100 queries and 30 mss/year. 50% of books from first-time authors; 100% from unagented writers. Pays royalty.** Publishes book 6 months after acceptance of ms. Accepts simultaneous submissions. Reports in 3 months on mss. Book catalog and ms guidelines for #10 SASE.
Nonfiction: Biography, reference, devotional. Subjects include religion (Roman Catholic). Submit entire ms, curriculum vitae, a statement of your purpose and intentions for writing the book and your intended audience with SASE. Reviews artwork/photos as part of ms package. Send photocopies.
Fiction: Religious, short story collections; all with Roman Catholic subjects. Submit entire ms with SASE.
Recent Title(s): *Fire From Above*, by René-Kieda (autobiography); *Six Short Stories on the Via Dolorosa*, by Ernesto V. Laguette (devotional short stories).

RISING STAR PRESS, P.O. Box BB, Los Altos CA 94023. (650)966-8920. Fax: (650)968-2658. E-mail: rising.star.press@worldnet.att.net or histar@aol.com. Website: http://members.aol.com/HiStar/index.htm. **Acquisitions:** Editorial Director. Publishes hardcover originals and reprints, trade paperback originals and reprints. Rising Star publishes quality books that inform and inspire. "Rising Star selects manuscripts based on benefit to the reader. We are interested in a wide variety of nonfiction topics." **Publishes 4-8 titles/year. Pays 10-15% royalty on wholesale price. Offers $1,000-8,000 advance.** Publishes book 3-6 months after acceptance of ms. Accepts simultaneous submissions. Reports in 1 month on proposals.
Nonfiction: Biography, how-to, humor, reference, self-help, technical. Subjects include business/economics, computers/electronics, education, health/medicine, language/literature, philosophy, regional, religion, social issues, sociology, spirituality, sports. "Authors need to be able to answer these questions: Who will benefit from reading this? Why? Mistakes writers often make are not identifying their target market early and shaping the work to address it, and a lack of clarity regarding the writer's role—participant or reporter? If a participant, does the writer's presence in the narrative

truly add value (sometimes ego intrudes inappropriately)." Query with proposal package including outline, 2 sample chapters, target market, author's connection to market, and author's credentials, with SASE. "We do *not* publish fiction, children's books, or poetry."
Recent Title(s): *Azim's Bardo*, by Azim Khamisa (father's outreach after son's murder).

RISING TIDE PRESS, 3831 N. Oracle Rd., Tucson AZ 85705-3254. (520)888-1140. E-mail: rtpress@aol.com. **Acquisitions:** Alice Frier, senior editor (nonfiction, romance); Lee Boojamra, editor/publisher (fiction). Estab. 1991. "Our books are for, by and about lesbian lives. They change lives and help create a better society. We seek to promote social justice and equal rights for lesbians and gay men." Publishes trade paperback originals. **Publishes 10-15 titles/year. Receives 1,000 queries and 600 mss/year. 75% of books from first-time authors; 100% from unagented writers. Pays 10-15% royalty on wholesale price.** Publishes book 15 months after acceptance. *No* simultaneous submissions. Reports in 1 week on queries, 1 months on proposals, 3 months on mss. Book catalog for $1. Writer's guidelines for #10 SASE.
Nonfiction: Lesbian nonfiction. Query with outline, entire ms and *large* SASE. *Writer's Market* recommends sending a query with SASE first. Reviews artwork/photos as part of ms package. Send photocopies.
Fiction: "Lesbian fiction only." Adventure, erotica, fantasy, historical, horror, humor, literary, mainstream/contemporary, mystery, occult, romance, science fiction, suspense, mixed genres. "Major characters must be lesbian. Primary plot must have lesbian focus and sensibility." Query with synopsis or entire ms and SASE. *Writer's Market* recommends sending a query with SASE first.
Recent Title(s): *Feathering Your Nest: An Interactive Guide to a Loving Lesbian Relationship*, by Gwen Leonhard and Jenny Mast (self-help); *Deadly Gamble*, by Diane Davidson (fiction).
Tips: "We welcome unpublished authors. We do *not* consider agented authors. Any material submitted should be proofed. No multiple submissions."

ROC BOOKS, Penguin Putnam Inc., 375 Huron St., New York NY 10014. (212)366-2000. **Acquisitions:** Laura Anne Gilman, executive editor. Publishes mass market, trade and hardcover originals. "We're looking for books that are a good read, that people will want to pick up time and time again." **Publishes 36 titles/year. Receives 500 queries/year. Pays royalty. Advance negotiable.** Accepts simultaneous submissions. Report in 2-3 months on queries.
Fiction: Fantasy, horror, science fiction. "ROC tries to strike a balance between fantasy and science fiction." Query with synopsis and 1-2 sample chapters. *"We discourage unsolicited submissions."*
Recent Title(s): *Dragons of Argonath*, by Christopher Rowley.

ROCKBRIDGE PUBLISHING CO., P.O. Box 351, Berryville VA 22611-0351. (540)955-3980. Fax: (540)955-4126. E-mail: cwpub@visuallink.com. Website: http://rockbpubl.com. **Acquisitions**: Katherine Tennery, publisher. Estab. 1989. "We publish nonfiction books about the Civil War, Virginia tour guides, Virginia/Southern folklore and ghost stories." Publishes hardcover original and reprints, trade paperback originals. **Publishes 4-6 titles/year. Pays royalty on wholesale price. No advance.** Reports in 3 months on proposals. Writer's guidelines available on website.
Nonfiction: "We are developing a series of travel guides to the country roads in various Virginia counties. The self-guided tours include local history, identify geographic features, etc. We are also looking for material about the Civil War, especially biographies, and expanding interests from Virginia to other southern states, notably Georgia." Query with outline, 3 sample chapters, author credentials and SASE.
Recent Title(s): *Battlefield Ghosts*, by Keith Toney (ghost sightings).

RODALE BOOKS, Rodale Press, Inc., 400 S. Tenth St., Emmaus PA 18098. Website: http://www.rodalepress.com. Publisher: Carolyn Gavett. Editorial Director for Home and Garden Books: Maggie Lydic. Editorial Director for Health and Fitness Books: Deborah Yost. **Acquisitions:** Sally Reith, assistant acquisitions editor. Estab. 1932. "Our mission is to show people how they can use the power of their bodies and minds to make their lives better." Publishes hardcover originals, trade paperback originals and reprints. **Publishes 75-100 titles/year; imprint publishes 10-15 titles/year. Pays 6-15% royalty on retail price.** Publishes book 18 months after acceptance of ms. Accepts simultaneous submissions. Reports in 1 month on queries, 2 months on proposals and mss. Book catalog and ms guidelines free.
Imprint(s): Daybreak Books (Karen Kelly, editorial director).
Nonfiction: Cookbook, how-to, self-help. Subjects include cooking/foods/nutrition, gardening, health/medicine (men's, women's, alternative, African-American, seniors), quilting, sewing and woodworking. "Our publications focus on the individual and what you can do to make life more natural, more self-reliant and more healthful." Query or submit proposal package including 1-2 sample chapters, author's resume and SASE.
Recent Title(s): *Natural Landscaping*, by Sally Roth (gardening).
Tips: "We're looking for authors who can dig deeply for facts and details, report accurately and write with flair."

N **RONIN PUBLISHING, INC.**, P.O. Box 1035, Berkeley CA 94701. (510)540-6278. Fax: (510)548-7326. E-mail: roninpub@aol.com. Website: http://www.roninpub.com. **Acquisitions**: Beverly Potter, publisher; Dan Joy, editor. "Ronin publishes book as tools for personal development, visionary alternatives and expanded consciousness." Publishes hardcover and trade paperback originals and reprints. **Publishes 5 titles/year. Imprint publishes 1-2 titles/year. Receives 10 queries and 10 mss/year. Pays 2-6% royalty on retail price. Offers $250-500 advance.** Publishes book 1 year after acceptance of ms. Reports in 3 months on queries, 6 months on proposals and mss. Book catalog free.
Imprint(s): 20th Century Alchemist (Contact: Beverly Potter, editor-in-chief).

Nonfiction: Biography, reference, self-help. Subjects include agriculture/horticulture, business/economics, cooking/foods/nutrition, gardening, health/medicine, psychology, spirituality, counterculture/psychedelia. "Our publishing purview is highly specific, as indicated in our catalog. We have rarely if ever published a book which initially arrived as an unsolicited manuscript. Please send queries only." Query with SASE. Agented submissions only. *All unsolicited mss returned unopened.*
Recent Title(s): *The Illuminati Papers*, by Wilson (counterculture/future).
Tips: "Our audience is interested in hard information and often buys several books on the same subject. Please submit query only. If on the basis of the query, we are interested in seeing the proposal or manuscript, we will let you know. No response to the query indicates that we have no interest. Become familiar with our interests through our catalog."

THE ROSEN PUBLISHING GROUP, 29 E. 21st St., New York NY 10010. (212)777-3017. Fax: (212)777-0277. E-mail: rosened@erols.com. **Acquisitions:** Jane Kelly Kosek, executive editor. "The Rosen Publishing Group publishes young adult titles for sale to school and public libraries. Each book is aimed at teenage readers and addresses them directly." Publishes hardcover and trade paperback originals. **Publishes 300 titles/year. Receives 150 queries and 75 mss/year. 50% of books from first-time authors; 95% from unagented writers. Pays 6-10% royalty on retail price or makes outright purchase of $175-1,000. May offer $500-1,000 advance.** Publishes books about 9 months after acceptance of ms. Reports in 2 months on proposals. Book catalog and ms guidelines free.

- The Rosen Publishing Group's imprint, Power Kids Press, publishes nonfiction for grades K-4 that are supplementary to the curriculum. Topics include conflict resolution, character-building, health, safety, drug abuse prevention, history, self-help, religion, science and multicultural titles. Contact: Helen Packard or Caroline Levchuck, acquisitions editors.

Nonfiction: Juvenile, self-help, young adult, reference. Submit outline and 1 sample chapter. Books should be written at K-4 or 8th grade reading level. Areas of particular interest include multicultural ethnographic studies; careers; coping with social, medical and personal problems; values and ethical behavior; drug abuse prevention; self-esteem; social activism; religion.
Recent Title(s): *Narcotics: Dangerous Painkillers*, by George Glass.
Tips: "The writer has the best chance of selling our firm a book on vocational guidance or personal social adjustment, or high-interest, low reading-level material for teens."

FRED B. ROTHMAN & CO., 10368 W. Centennial Rd., Littleton CO 80127. (303)979-5657. Fax: (303)978-1457. E-mail: sjarrett@rothman.com. **Acquisitions:** Sheila Jarrett, editorial/production manager. Fred B. Rothman & Co., publishes references books for law librarians, legal researchers and those interested in legal writing. Publishes hardcover and trade paperback originals. **Publishes 12 titles/year. Receives 30 queries and 15 mss/year. 20% of books from first-time authors; 100% from unagented writers. Pays 10-20% royalty on net price.** Publishes book 9 months after acceptance of ms. Accepts simultaneous submissions. Does not return submissions. Reports in 3 months. Book catalog free.
Nonfiction: Reference. Subjects include law and librarianship. Submit proposal package, including outline, 3 sample chapters and intended audience.
Recent Title(s): *Courts Counselors & Correspondents: A Media Relations Analysis of the Legal System*, by Richard Stack (public relations/law).

N **ROUTLEDGE, INC.**, 29 W. 35th St., New York NY 10001-2299. (212)216-7800. **Acquisitions:** Kenneth Wright, vice president/associate publisher. The Routledge list includes humanities, social sciences, business/economics, reference. Monographs, reference works, hardback and paperback upper-level texts, academic general interest. **Publishes 175 titles/year in New York. 10% of books from first-time authors; 95% of books from unagented authors. Pays royalty.** Publishes book 1 year after acceptance. Accepts simultaneous submissions. Reports in 3 months on queries.
Imprint(s): Theatre Arts Books.
Nonfiction: Academic subjects include philosophy, literary criticism, psychoanalysis, social sciences, business/economics, history, psychology, women's studies, lesbian and gay studies, race and ethnicity, political science, anthropology, geography development, education, reference. Query with proposal package, including toc, intro, sample chapter, overall prospectus, cv and SASE.
Recent Title(s): *Teaching to Transgress*, by bell hooks.

ROXBURY PUBLISHING CO., P.O. Box 491044, Los Angeles CA 90049. (213)653-1068. **Acquisitions:** Claude Teweles, executive editor. Roxbury publishes college textbooks in the humanities and social sciences only. Publishes hardcover and paperback originals and reprints. **Publishes 15-25 titles/year. Pays royalty.** Accepts simultaneous submissions. Reports in 2 months.
Nonfiction: College-level textbooks *only.* Subjects include humanities, speech, developmental studies, social sciences, sociology, criminology, criminal justice. Query, submit outline/synopsis and sample chapters, or submit complete ms. *Writer's Market* recommends sending a query with SASE first.

RUNNING PRESS BOOK PUBLISHERS, 125 S. 22nd St., Philadelphia PA 19103. (215)567-5080. Fax: (215)568-2919. President/Publisher: Stuart Treacher. **Acquisitions:** Mary Ellen Lewis, assistant to the associate publisher/editorial director; Nancy Steele, director of acquisitions; Brian Perrin, associate publisher/editorial director; Mary McGuire Ruggiero, associate editorial director. Estab. 1972. Publishes hardcover originals, trade paperback originals and reprints.

Publishes 150 titles/year. Receives 600 queries/year. 50% of books from first-time authors; 30% from unagented writers. Payment varies. Advances varies. Publishes book 6-18 months after acceptance of ms. Accepts simultaneous submissions. Reports in 1 month on queries. Book catalog free. Manuscript guidelines for #10 SASE.
Imprint(s): Courage Books.
Nonfiction: Children's/juvenile, how-to, self-help. Subjects include art/architecture, cooking/foods/nutrition, recreation, science, craft, how-to. Query with outline, contents, synopsis and SASE. Reviews artwork/photos as part of the ms package. Send photocopies. "*No* originals, please!"
Recent Title(s): *Disney Miniature Editions*™ (Hercules, The Lion King, and others); *Georges Perrier Le Bec-fin Recipes*, by Georges Perrier with Aliza Green (cookbook).

RUSSIAN HILL PRESS, 1250 17th Street, 2nd Floor, San Francisco CA 94107. (415)487-0480. Fax: (415)487-0290. E-mail: editors@russianhill.com. Website: http://www.russianhill.com. **Acquisitions:** (Ms.) Kit Cooley, assistant editor. "We focus on an eclectic collection of West Coast writers with a message that is in turn hungry, angry, political, alternative and frightening. We want distinctive voices both fresh and well established with material that is urgent and relevant." Publishes hardcover originals. **Publishes 6-10 titles/year. Receives 1,000 queries and 60 mss/year. 25% of books from first-time authors; 10% from unagented writers. Pays 10-15% royalty on retail price. Advance varies.** Publishes book 8 months after acceptance of ms. Accepts simultaneous submissions. Reports in 2 months on queries. Book catalog for $2. Manuscript guidelines for #10 SASE.
Nonfiction: Biography (literary). Government/political subjects. Query with SASE. Prefers agented submissions. Reviews artwork as part of ms package. Send photocopies.
Fiction: Erotica, ethnic, feminist, gay/lesbian, humor, literary, mainstream/contemporary, mystery, suspense. Focuses on West Coast authors. "We're looking for angry, young, lively fiction." Query only with SASE. Prefers agented submissions.
Recent Title(s): *S.F. Comic Strip: Book of Big-Ass Mocha*, by Don Asmussen (humorous comics); *One Worm*, by Jim Kalin.

RUSSIAN INFORMATION SERVICES, 89 Main St., Suite 2, Montpelier VT 05602. (802)223-4955. Website: http://solar.ini.utk.edu/rispubs/ **Acquisitions:** Stephanie Ratmeyer, vice president. "Audience is business people and independent travelers to Russia and the former Soviet Union." Publishes trade paperback originals and reprints. **Publishes 5 titles/year. Receives 20-30 queries and 10 mss/year. 50% of books from first-time authors; 100% from unagented writers. Pays 8-12% royalty on retail price.** Publishes book 8 months after acceptance of ms. Accepts simultaneous submissions. Reports in 2 months on mss. Book catalog free.

- RIS also publishes *Russian Life*, a monthly magazine on Russian history, travel, culture and life. See the Ethnic/Minority section of Consumer Magazines.

Nonfiction: Reference, travel, business. Subjects include business/economics, language/literature, travel. "Our editorial focus is on Russia and the former Soviet Union." Submit proposal package, including ms, summary and cv. Reviews artwork/photos as part of ms package. Send photocopies.
Recent Title(s): *Survival Russian*, by Ivanov (language).

RUTGERS UNIVERSITY PRESS, 100 Joyce Kilmer Ave., Piscataway NJ 08854-8099. (732)445-7762. Fax: (732)445-7039. E-mail: marlie@rci.rutgers.edu. Website: http://info.rutgerspress.rutgers.edu. **Acquisitions**: Leslie Mitchner, editor-in-chief/associate director (humanities); Martha Heller, acquiring editor (social sciences); Helen Hsu, acquiring editor (science, regional books). "Our press aims to reach audiences beyond the academic community with accessible scholarly and regional books." Publishes hardcover originals and trade paperback originals and reprints. **Publishes 70 titles/year. Receives up to 1,500 queries and up to 300 books/year. Up to 30% of books from first-time authors; 70% from unagented writers. Pays 7½-15% royalty on retail or net price. Offers $1,000-10,000 advance.** Publishes book 1 year after acceptance of ms. Accepts simultaneous submissions, if so noted. Reports in 1 month on proposals. Book catalog free.
Nonfiction: Biography, textbook and books for use in undergraduate courses. Subjects include Americana, anthropology, African-American studies, education, gay/lesbian, government/politics, health/medicine, history, language/literature, multicultural studies, nature/environment, regional, religion, science, sociology, translation, women's issues/studies. Submit outline and 2-3 sample chapters. Reviews artwork/photos as part of the ms package. Send photocopies.
Recent Title(s): *Feminisms*, by Warhol and Herndl (feminist theory).
Tips: Both academic and general audiences. "Many of our books have potential for undergraduate course use. We are more trade-oriented than most university presses. We are looking for intelligent, well-written and accessible books. Avoid overly narrow topics."

RUTLEDGE HILL PRESS, 211 Seventh Ave. N., Nashville TN 37219-1823. (615)244-2700. Fax: (615)244-2978. **Acquisitions:** Mike Towle, executive editor. Estab. 1982. "We are a publisher of market-specific books, focusing on particular genres or regions." Publishes hardcover and trade paperback originals and reprints. **Publishes 60 titles/year. Receives 1,500 submissions/year. 25% of books from first-time authors; 60% from unagented writers. Pays 10-20% royalty on net price.** Publishes book 1 year after acceptance. Reports in 2 months. Book catalog for 9×12 SAE with 4 first-class stamps.
Nonfiction: Biography, cookbook, humor, travel, Civil War history, quilt books, sports. "The book should have a unique marketing hook other than the subject matter itself. Books built on new ideas and targeted to a specific U.S.

region are welcome. Please, no fiction, children's, academic, poetry or religious works, and we won't even look at *Life's Little Instruction Book* spinoffs or copycats." Submit cover letter that includes brief marketing strategy and author bio, outline and sample chapters. Reviews artwork/photos as part of ms package.

Recent Title(s): *Fairways and Dreams*, by Micahel Arkush (golf).

SAE INTERNATIONAL, Society of Automotive Engineers, 400 Commonwealth Dr., Warrendale PA 15096. (724)776-4841. **Acquisitions**: Jeff Worsinger, product manager; Edward Manns, product manager. "Automotive means anything self-propelled. We are a professional society serving this area, which includes aircraft, spacecraft, marine, rail, automobiles, trucks and off-highway vehicles." Publishes hardcover and trade paperback originals. **Publishes 15-20 titles/year. Receives 250 queries and 75 mss/year. 30-40% of books from first-time authors; 100% from unagented writers. Pays royalty with possible advance.** Publishes book 1 year after acceptance of ms. Accepts simultaneous submissions. Reports in 1 month. Book catalog and ms guidelines free.

Imprint(s): STS Press.

Nonfiction: Biography, multimedia (CD-ROM), reference, technical, textbook. Automotive and aerospace subjects. "Request submission guidelines. Clearly define your book's market or angle." Query with SASE. Reviews artwork/photos as part of ms package. Send photocopies.

Recent Title(s): *Creating the Customer-Driven Car Company*, by Karl Ludvigsen (business/how-to).

Tips: "Audience is automotive engineers, technicians, car buffs, aerospace engineers, technicians and historians."

SAFARI PRESS INC., 15621 Chemical Lane, Building B, Huntington Beach CA 92649-1506. (714)894-9080. Fax: (714)894-4949. E-mail: info@safaripress.com. Website: http://www.safaripress.com. **Acquisitions:** Jacqueline Neufeld, editor. "We publish books only on big-game hunting, firearms and wingshooting; this includes African, North American, European, Asian, and South American hunting and wingshooting." Publishes hardcover originals and reprints and trade paperback reprints. **Publishes 6-15 titles/year. 50% of books from first-time authors; 99% from unagented writers. Pays 8-15% royalty on wholesale price.** No simultaneous submissions. Book catalog for $1. "Request our 'Notice to Prospective Authors.' "

Nonfiction: Biography, how-to, adventure stories. Subjects include hunting, firearms, wingshooting—"nothing else. We discourage autobiographies, unless the life of the hunter or firearms maker has been exceptional. We routinely reject manuscripts along the lines of 'Me and my buddies went hunting for . . . and a good time was had by all!' No fishing." Query with outline and SASE.

Recent Title(s): *American Man-Killers*, by Don Zaidle.

ST. ANTHONY MESSENGER PRESS, 1615 Republic St., Cincinnati OH 45210-1298. (513)241-5615. Fax: (513)241-0399. E-mail: stanthony@americancatholic.org. Website: http://www.americancatholic.org. Publisher: The Rev. Jeremy Harrington, O.F.M. **Acquisitions:** Kathleen Carroll, editor (children's books and spirituality); Diane Houdek, editor (liturgy, scripture); Lisa Biedenbach, managing editor. Estab. 1970. "St. Anthony Messenger Press/Franciscan Communications seeks to communicate the word that is Jesus Christ in the styles of Saints Francis and Anthony. Through print and electronic media marketed in North America and worldwide, we endeavor to evangelize, inspire and inform those who search for God and seek a richer Catholic, Christian, human life. Our efforts help support the life, ministry and charities of the Franciscan Fathers of St. John the Baptist Province, who sponsor our work." Publishes trade paperback originals. **Publishes 12-16 titles/year. Receives 200 queries and 50 mss/year. 5% of books from first-time authors; 100% from unagented writers. Pays 10-12% royalty on net receipts of sales. Offers $1,000 average advance.** Publishes book 18 months after acceptance. Reports in 1 month on queries, 2 months on proposals and mss. Book catalog for 9×12 SAE with 4 first-class stamps. Manuscript guidelines free.

- St. Anthony Messenger Press especially seeks books which will sell in bulk quantities to parishes, teachers, pastoral ministers, etc. They expect to sell at least 5,000 to 7,000 copies of a book.

Nonfiction: History, religion, Catholic identity and teaching, prayer and spirituality resources, scripture study. Children's books with Catholic slant, family-based religious education programs. Query with outline and SASE. Reviews artwork/photos as part of ms package.

Recent Title(s): *Paths to Prayer*, by Robert F. Morneau.

Tips: "Our readers are ordinary 'folks in the pews' and those who minister to and educate these folks. Writers need to know the audience and the kind of books we publish. Manuscripts should reflect best and current Catholic theology and doctrine."

ST. BEDE'S PUBLICATIONS, St. Scholastica Priory, P.O. Box 545, Petersham MA 01366-0545. (508)724-3407. Fax: (508)724-3574. **Acquisitions:** Acquisitions Editor. Estab. 1978. "St. Bede's Publications is owned and operated by the Roman Catholic nuns of St. Scholastica Priory. The publications are seen as as apostolic outreach. The mission is to make available to everyone quality books on spiritual subjects such as prayer, scripture, theology and the lives of holy people." Publishes hardcover originals, trade paperback originals and reprints. **Publishes 8-12 titles/year. Receives 100 submissions/year. 30-40% of books from first-time authors; 98% from unagented writers. Nonauthor subsidy publishes 10% of books. Pays 5-10% royalty on wholesale price or retail price. No advance.** Publishes book 2 years after acceptance. Accepts simultaneous submissions. Reports in 2 months. Book catalog and ms guidelines for 9×12 SAE and 2 first-class stamps.

Nonfiction: Textbook (theology), religion, prayer, spirituality, hagiography, theology, philosophy, church history, related lives of saints. "We are always looking for excellent books on prayer, spirituality, liturgy, church or monastic

history. Theology and philosophy are important also. We publish English translations of foreign works in these fields if we think they are excellent and worth translating." No submissions unrelated to religion, theology, spirituality, etc. Query or submit outline and sample chapters with SASE. Does not return submissions without adequate postage.
Recent Title(s): *Contemplation 2000*, by James Kinn.
Tips: "There seems to be a growing interest in monasticism among lay people and we will be publishing more books in this area. For our theology/philosophy titles our audience is scholars, colleges and universities, seminaries, etc. For our other titles (i.e. prayer, spirituality, lives of saints, etc.) the audience is above-average readers interested in furthering their knowledge in these areas."

ST. MARTIN'S PRESS, 175 Fifth Ave., New York NY 10010. Publishes hardcover, trade paperback and mass market originals. **Publishes 1,500 titles/year.** General interest publisher of both fiction and nonfiction.
Imprint(s): Bedford Books, Buzz Books, **Dead Letter, Thomas Dunne Books, Forge, Picador USA, St. Martin's Press Scholarly & Reference, Stonewall Inn Editions, TOR Books.**
Nonfiction: General nonfiction, reference, scholarly, textbook. Biography, business/economics, contemporary culture, cookbooks, self-help, sports, true crime.
Fiction: General fiction. Fantasy, historical, horror, literary, mainstream, mystery, science fiction, suspense, thriller, Western (contemporary).
Recent Title(s): *El Sid*, by David Dalton (music/biography); *Chocolate Star*, by Sheila Copeland.

ST. MARTIN'S PRESS, SCHOLARLY & REFERENCE DIVISION, St. Martin's Press, 257 Park Ave. S., New York NY 10010. (212)982-3900. Fax: (212)777-6359. Website: http://www.stmartins.com. **Acquisitions:** Michael Flamini, senior editor (history, politics, education, religion); Karen Wolny, editor (politics); Maura Burnett, associate editor (literature, cultural studies). "We remain true to our origin as a scholarly press . . . with the backing of St. Martin's Press we are able to make books more accessible." Publishes hardcover and trade paperback originals. **Firm publishes 500 titles/year. Receives 500 queries and 600 mss/year. 25% of books from first-time authors; 75% from unagented writers. Pays royalty: trade, 7-10% list; other, 7-10% net. Advance varies.** Publishes book 7 months after acceptance of ms. Accepts simultaneous submissions. Reports in 1 month on proposals. Book catalog and ms guidelines free.
Nonfiction: Reference, scholarly. Subjects include business/economics, government/politics, history, language/literature, philosophy, religion, sociology, women's issues/studies, humanities, social studies. "We are looking for good solid scholarship." Query with proposal package including outline, 3-4 sample chapters, prospectus, cv and SASE. "We like to see as much completed material as possible." Reviews artwork/photos as part of ms package.
Recent Title(s): *I May Be Some Time*, by F. Spufford (travel/cultural studies).

SAMS PUBLISHING, Macmillan Computer Publishing, 201 W. 103rd St., Indianapolis IN 46290. (317)581-3500. Website: http://www.mcp.com/sams/. Publisher: Richard Swadley. **Acquisitions:** Andi Richter, executive assistant. Estab. 1951. "Sams Publishing has made a major commitment to publishing books that meet the needs of computer users, programmers, administrative and support personnel, and managers." Publishes trade paperback originals. **Publishes 160 titles/year. 30% of books from first-time authors; 95% from unagented writers. Pays royalty on wholesale price, negotiable. Advance negotiable.** Publishes book 1 year after acceptance of ms. Accepts simultaneous submissions if noted; "however, once contract is signed, Sams Publishing retains first option rights on future works on same subject." Reports in 6 weeks on queries. Manuscript guidelines free.
Nonfiction: Computer subjects. Also contracts with first-time authors for chapters, especially in series. Query with SASE.
Recent Title(s): *Teach Yourself Java in 21 Days*, by Laura Lemay (computers).
Tips: "*Teach Yourself Java in 21 Days* is one of the bestselling computer books of all time and the author's first book."

J.S. SANDERS & COMPANY, INC., P.O. Box 50331, Nashville TN 37205. Fax: (615)790-2594. **Acquisitions:** John Sanders, publisher. "In addition to our Southern Classic series of reprints of works by important Southern writers of the 19th and 20th centuries, we are interested in new fiction of quality by Southern writers or with a Southern setting; and in works of Southern history, belles-lettres and on general cultural themes." Publishes hardcover originals and trade paperback originals and reprints. **Publishes 5 titles/year. Receives 300 queries and 25 mss/year. 75% of books from unagented writers. Pays 6-8% royalty.** Publishes book 9 months after acceptance of ms. Accepts simultaneous submissions. Reports in 2 months on queries. Book catalog free.

- J.S. Sanders & Company discourages novice writers.

Imprint(s): Caliban Books.
Nonfiction: Biography, humor. Subjects include Americana, government/politics, history, language/literature, military/war, regional, travel. Query with SASE. Reviews artwork/photos as part of ms package. Send photocopies.
Fiction: Historical, literary. Submit 1 sample chapter with SASE.
Recent Title(s): *Dear Harp of My Country: The Irish Melodies of Thomas Moore*, by James W. Flannery (Irish music); *The Women on the Porch*, by Caroline Gordon (literary reprint).

SANTA MONICA PRESS LLC, P.O. Box 1076, Santa Monica CA 90406. **Acquisitions:** Rick Baker, editorial manager. "Santa Monica Press Publishes two lines of books: general how-to books written in simple, easy-to-understand terms; and books which explore sports and arts and entertainment from an offbeat perspective." Publishes trade paperback originals. **Publishes 6-10 titles/year. Receives 200-300 queries and mss/year. 75% of books from first-time**

authors; 100% from unagented writers. Pays 6-12% royalty on wholesale price. Offers $500-2,500 advance. Publishes book 6-12 months after acceptance of ms. Accepts simultaneous submissions. Reports in 2 months on proposals. Book catalog and ms guidelines for #10 SASE.

Nonfiction: Gift book, how-to, illustrated book reference. Subjects include Americana, pop culture, health/medicine, music/dance, sports, theater, film, general how-to. Submit proposal package, including outline, 2-3 sample chapters, biography, marketing potential of book with SASE. All unsolicited mss returned unopened. Reviews artwork/photos as part of the ms package. Send photocopies.

Recent Title(s): *Letter Writing Made Easy! Volume 2*, by Margaret McCarthy (how-to).

Tips: "Our how-to books provide readers with practical guidance in a wide variety of subjects, from letter writing to health care. These handy guides are written in simple, easy-to-understand terms. Our offbeat books explore popular culture from an offbeat perspective. These large format books feature hundreds of graphics and photos and are written for the naturally curious reader who possesses a healthy sense of humor."

N **SARABANDE BOOKS, INC.**, 2234 Dundee Rd., Suite 200, Louisville KY 40205. (502)458-4028. Fax: (502)458-4065. E-mail: sarabandeb@aol.com. Website: http://www.sarabandebooks.org. **Acquisitions**: Sarah Gorham, editor-in-chief. Publishes hardcover and trade paperback originals. **Publishes 7 titles/year. Receives 500 queries and 2,000 mss/year. 35% of books from first-time authors; 75% from unagented writers. Pays 10% royalty on actual income received. Offers $500-2,000 advance.** Publishes book 18 months after acceptance of ms. Accepts simultaneous submissions. Reports in 3 months on queries, 6 months on mss. Book catalog free. Manuscript guidelines for #10 SASE.

Fiction: Literary, novellas, short story collections. "We do not publish novels." Query with 1 sample story, 1 page bio, listing of publishing credits and SASE. Submissions in September only.

Poetry: "Poetry of superior artistic quality. Otherwise no restraints or specifications." Query and submit 10 sample poems. Submissions in September only.

Recent Title(s): *The Least You Need to Know*, by Lee Martin (short story collection); *Dark Blonde*, by Belle Waring.

Tips: Sarabande publishes for a general literary audience. "Know your market. Read—and buy—books of literature."

N **SARPEDON PUBLISHERS**, 49 Front St., Rockville Centre NY 11570. **Acquisitions:** Susan Walker. Publishes hardcover originals and trade paperback reprints. **Publishes 6 titles/year. Receives 100 queries/year. 14% of books from first-time authors; 20% from unagented writers. Pays royalty. Offers $250-1,250 advance.** Publishes book 6-9 months after acceptance of ms. Accepts simultaneous submissions. Reports in 1 months on queries, 2 months on proposals, 3 months on mss. Book catalog and ms guidelines for #10 SASE.

Nonfiction: "We specialize in military history." Biography. Subjects include Americana, government, history, military/war. Submit outline, 2 sample chapters and synopsis. Reviews artwork/photos as part of ms package. Send photocopies.

SAS INSTITUTE INC., SAS Campus Dr., Cary NC 27513-2414. (919)677-8000. Fax: (919)677-4444. E-mail: sasbbu @unx.sas.com. Website: http://www.sas.com. **Acquisitions:** David D. Baggett, editor-in-chief. Estab. 1976. "Our readers are SAS software users, both new and experienced." Publishes hardcover and trade paperback originals. **Publishes 40 titles/year. Receives 10 submissions/year. 50% of books from first-time authors; 100% from unagented writers. Payment negotiable. Offers negotiable advance.** Reports in 2 weeks on queries. Book catalog and ms guidelines free.

Nonfiction: Software, technical, textbook, statistics. "SAS Institute's Publications Division publishes books developed and written inhouse. Through the Books by Users program, we also publish books by SAS users on a variety of topics relating to SAS software. We want to provide our users with additional titles to supplement our primary documentation and to enhance the users' ability to use the SAS System effectively. We're interested in publishing manuscripts that describe or illustrate using any of SAS Institute's software products. Books must be aimed at SAS software users, either new or experienced. Tutorials are particularly attractive, as are descriptions of user-written applications for solving real-life business, industry or academic problems. Books on programming techniques using the SAS language are also desirable. Manuscripts must reflect current or upcoming software releases, and the author's writing should indicate an understanding of the SAS System and the technical aspects covered in the manuscript." Query. Submit outline/synopsis and sample chapters. Reviews artwork/photos as part of ms package.

Recent Title(s): *SAS Programming by Example*, by Ron Cody and Ray Pass.

Tips: "If I were a writer trying to market a book today, I would concentrate on developing a manuscript that teaches or illustrates a specific concept or application that SAS software users will find beneficial in their own environments or can adapt to their own needs."

SASQUATCH BOOKS, 615 Second Ave., Suite 260, Seattle WA 98104. (206)467-4300. Fax: (206)467-4301. E-mail: books@sasquatchbooks.com. Website: http://www.sasquatchbooks.com. President: Chad Haight. **Acquisitions:** Gary Luke, editorial director; Kate Rogers, editor (travel). Estab. 1986. Sasquatch Books publishes adult nonfiction from the Northwest, specializing in travel, cooking, gardening, history and nature. Publishes regional hardcover and trade paperback originals. **Publishes 30 titles/year. 20% of books from first-time authors; 75% from unagented writers. Pays authors royalty on cover price. Offers wide range of advances.** Publishes ms 6 months after acceptance. Reports in 3 months. Book catalog for 9×12 SAE with 2 first-class stamps.

Nonfiction: Subjects include regional art/architecture, cooking, foods, gardening, history, nature/environment, recreation, sports, travel and outdoors. "We are seeking quality nonfiction works about the Pacific Northwest and West Coast regions (including Alaska to California). In this sense we are a regional publisher, but we do distribute our books nationally." Query first, then submit outline and sample chapters with SASE.

Recent Title(s): *Watertrail*, by Joel Rogers..
Tips: "We sell books through a range of channels in addition to the book trade. Our primary audience consists of active, literate residents of the West Coast."

SCARECROW PRESS, INC., University Press of America, 4720 Boston Way, Lanham MD 20706. (301)459-3366. Fax: (301)459-2118. Website: http://www.scarecrowpress.com. **Acquisitions:** Shirley Lambert, editorial director; Amanda Irwin, assistant editor. Estab. 1950. "We consider any scholarly title likely to appeal to libraries. Emphasis is on reference material." Scarecrow Press publishes several series: The Historical Dictionary series, which includes countries, religious, international organizations; and Composers of North America. Publishes hardcover originals. **Publishes 165 titles/year. Receives 600-700 submissions/year. 70% of books from first-time authors; 99% from unagented writers. Pays 8% royalty on net of first 1,000 copies; 10% of net price thereafter. No advance.** Publishes book 18 months after receipt of ms. Reports in 2 months. Book catalog for 9×12 SAE and 4 first-class stamps.
Nonfiction: Reference books and meticulously prepared annotated bibliographies, indices and books on women's studies, ethnic studies, music, movies, stage. library and information science, parapsychology, fine arts and handicrafts, social sciences, religion, sports, literature and language. Query.
Recent Title(s): *Orchestral Music*, by David Daniels.

N **SCHENKMAN BOOKS, INC.**, 118 Main Street, Rochester VT 05767. (802)767-3702. Fax: (802)767-9528. E-mail: schenkma@sover.net. Website: http://www.sover.net/~schenkma/. **Acquisitions:** Tepin Thoenen, editor. "Schenkman Books specializes in publishing scholarly monographs for the academic community. For almost forty years we have brought revolutionary works to the public to fuel discourse on important issues. It is our hope that the material we make available contributes to the efforts toward peace and humanitarianism throughout the world." Publishes hardcover and trade paperback originals and reprints. **Publishes 6 titles/year. Receives 100 queries and 25 mss/year. 80% of books from first-time authors; 95% from unagented writers. Pays 10% royalty on net receipts.** Accepts simultaneous submissions. Book catalog and ms guidelines free.
Nonfiction: Biography, self-help, textbook, scholarly monographs. Subjects include anthropology, ethnic, government/politics, history, music, philosophy, psychology, sociology, women's issues/studies, African studies, African-American studies, Asian studies, Caribbean studies. Query with outline. Reviews art as part of the package. Send photocopies.
Recent Title(s): *Work Abuse*, by Judith Wyatt and Chauncey Hare (self-help/management relations).

SCHIRMER BOOKS, Macmillan Reference, 1633 Broadway, New York NY 10019-6785. (212)654-8414. Fax: (212)654-4745. **Acquisitions:** Richard Carlin, executive editor. Schirmer publishes scholarly and reference books on the performing arts. Publishes hardcover and paperback originals, related CDs, CD-ROMs, audiocassettes. **Publishes 50 books/year. Receives 250 submissions/year. 25% of books from first-time authors; 75% of books from unagented writers.** Publishes book 1 year after acceptance. Reports in 4 months. Book catalog and ms guidelines for SASE.

- Schirmer Books reports more interest in popular music, including rock and jazz.

Nonfiction: Publishes college texts, biographies, scholarly, reference, and trade on the performing arts specializing in music, film and theatre. Submit outline/synopsis, sample chapters and current vita. Reviews artwork/photos as part of ms package. "Submit only if central to the book, not if decorative or tangential."
Recent Title(s): *Billboard's American Rock and Roll in Review*, by Jay Warner.
Tips: "The writer has the best chance of selling our firm a music book with a clearly defined, reachable audience, either scholarly or trade. Must be an exceptionally well-written work of original scholarship prepared by an expert who has a thorough understanding of correct manuscript style and attention to detail (see the *Chicago Manual of Style*)."

SCHOCKEN, Knopf Publishing Group, Random House, 201 E. 50th St., New York NY 10022. (212)572-2559. Fax: (212)572-6030. Website: http://www.randomhouse.com/knopf. **Acquisitions:** Arthur Samuelson, editorial director; Cecelia Cancellaro, editor. Estab. 1933. "Schocken publishes a broad nonfiction list of serious, solid books with commercial appeal, as well as reprints of classics." Publishes hardcover originals and reprints, trade paperback originals and reprints. **Publishes 24 titles/year. A small percentage of books are from first-time writers; small percentage from unagented writers. Pays royalty on net price. Advance varies.** Accepts simultaneous submissions. Book catalog free.
Nonfiction: Subjects include education, ethnic, government/politics, health/medicine, history, Judaica, nature/environment, philosophy, religion, women's issues/studies. Submit proposal package, including "whatever is necessary to make the case for your book."
Recent Title(s): *The Five Books of Moses: The Schocken Bible, Volume 1*, translation/commentary by Everett Fox.
Fiction: Reprints classics.

SCHOLASTIC INC., Book Group, 555 Broadway, New York NY 10012. (212)343-6100. Estab. 1920. Publishes trade paperback originals for children ages 4-young adult. "We are proud of the many fine, innovative materials we have created—such as classroom magazines, book clubs, book fairs, and our new literacy and technology programs. But we are most proud of our reputation as 'The Most Trusted Name in Learning.' " Publishes juvenile hardcover picture books, novels and nonfiction. **All divisions: Pays advance and royalty on retail price.** Reports in 6 months. Manuscript guidelines for #10 SASE.
Imprint(s): Blue Sky Press, Cartwheel Books, Arthur Levine Books, **Mariposa, Scholastic Press**, Scholastic Reference & Gallimard (contact Wendy Barish), Scholastic Trade Paperback (contact Craig Walker).

Nonfiction: Publishes nonfiction for children ages 4 to teen. Query.
Fiction: Hardcover—open to all subjects suitable for children. Paperback—family stories, mysteries, school, friendships for ages 8-12, 35,000 words. YA fiction, romance, family and mystery for ages 12-15, 40,000-45,000 words for average to good readers. Queries welcome. Unsolicited manuscripts discouraged.
Recent Title(s): *The Great Fire*, by Jim Murphy (Newbery Honor Book); *Out of the Dust*, by Karen Hesse (Newbery Medal Book).
Tips: New writers for children should study the children's book field before submitting.

[A] **SCHOLASTIC PRESS**, Scholastic Inc., 555 Broadway, New York NY 10012. (212)343-6100. Website: http://www.scholastic.com. **Acquisitions:** Heather Dietz, editor. Scholastic Press publishes a range of picture books, middle grade and young adult novels. Publishes hardcover originals. **Publishes 60 titles/year. Receives 2,500 queries/year. 5% of books from first-time authors. Pays royalty on retail price. Royalty and advance vary.** Publishes book 18 months after acceptance of ms. Reports in 6 months on queries.
Nonfiction: Children's/juvenile, general interest. *Agented submissions only.*
Fiction: Juvenile, picture books. *Agented submissions only.*
Recent Title(s): *The Great Fire*, by Jim Murphy (history); *Slam*, by Walter Dean Myers.

SCHOLASTIC PROFESSIONAL PUBLISHING, Scholastic, Inc., 555 Broadway, New York NY 10012. Website: http://www.scholastic.com. Vice President/Editor-in-Chief: Terry Cooper. **Acquisitions**: Shawn Richardson, managing editor. **Publishes 80-100 books/year. Offers standard contract.** Reports in 2 months. Book catalog for 9×12 SAE.
Nonfiction: Elementary and middle-school level enrichment—all subject areas, including math and science and theme units, integrated materials, writing process, management techniques, teaching strategies based on personal/professional experience in the classroom and technology ideas. Production is limited to printed matter: resource and activity books, professional development materials, reference titles. Length: 6,000-12,000 words. Query with table of contents, outline and sample chapter.
Recent Titles(s): *Science See-Throughs That Teach.*
Tips: "Writer should have background working in the classroom with elementary or middle school children, teaching pre-service students, and/or solid background in developing supplementary educational materials for these markets."

[N] **D&F SCOTT PUBLISHING, INC.**, P.O. Box 821653, North Richland Hills TX 76182. (817)788-2280. Fax: (817)788-9232. E-mail: bibal@pu.net. Website: http://www.cmpu.net/public/bibal. **Acquisitions:** Dr. William R. Scott, president. Publishes hardcover and trade paperback originals. **Publishes 20 titles/year. Receives 50 queries/year, 15 mss/year. 10% of books from first-time authors; 100% from unagented writers. Pays 10-20% royalty on wholesale price. No advance.** Publishes book 6 months after acceptance of ms. Accepts simultaneous submissions. Reports in 3 months. Book catalog and ms guidelines free.
Imprints: BIBAL Press.
Nonfiction: How-to, reference, textbook. Subjects include anthropology/archaeology, religion. Submit proposal package, including table of contents, 2 sample chapters and SASE. Reviews artwork/photos as part of the ms package. Send photocopies.
Recent Title(s): *A Study Guide to Mark's Gospel*, by Scott Sinclair.

[A] **SCRIBNER**, Simon & Schuster, 1230 Avenue of the Americas, New York NY 10020. (212)698-7000. **Acquisitions:** Jillian Blake, associate editor. Publishes hardcover originals. **Publishes 70-75 titles/year. Receives thousands of queries/year. 20% of books from first-time authors; none from unagented writers. Pays 7½-12½% royalty on wholesale price. Advance varies.** Publishes book 9 months after acceptance of ms. Accepts simultaneous submissions. Reports in 3 months on queries.
Imprint(s): Rawson Associates (contact Eleanor Rawson); **Lisa Drew Books** (contact Lisa Drew); Scribner Classics (reprints only); Scribner Poetry (by invitation only).
Nonfiction: Subjects include education, ethnic, gay/lesbian, health/medicine, history, language/literature, nature/environment, philosophy, psychology, religion, science, biography, criticism. *Agented submissions only.*
Fiction: Literary, mystery, suspense. *Agented submissions only.*
Poetry: Publishes few titles; by invitation only.
Recent Title(s): *Angela's Ashes*, by Frank McCourt (memoir, National Book Award and Pulitzer Prize winner); *Underworld*, by Don DeLillo.

SEAL PRESS, 3131 Western Ave., Suite 410, Seattle WA 98121. Fax: (206)285-9410. E-mail: sealprss@scn.org. Website: http://www.sealpress.com. **Acquisitions**: Faith Conlon, editor/publisher. Jennie Goode, managing editor. "Seal Press is an independent feminist book publisher interested in original, lively, radical, empowering and culturally diverse nonfiction by women addressing contemporary issues from a feminist perspective or speak positively to the experience of being female." Publishes hardcover and trade paperback originals. **Publishes 14 titles/year. Receives 500 queries and 250 mss/year. 25% of books from first-time authors; 80% from unagented writers. Pays 6-10% royalty on retail price. Offers $500-1,000 advance.** Publishes book 18 months after acceptance of ms. Accepts simultaneous submissions. Reports in 2 months on queries. Book catalog and ms guidelines free.
Imprint(s): Adventura Books; Live Girls, Djuna Books.
Nonfiction: Self-help, literary nonfiction essays. Subjects include child guidance/parenting, ethnic, gay/lesbian, health/

medicine, nature/outdoor writing, travel, women's issues/studies, popular culture. "We do not publish poetry." Query with SASE. Reviews artwork/photos as part of ms package. Send photocopies.
Fiction: Ethnic, feminist, gay/lesbian, literary. "We are interested in alternative voices that aren't often heard from." Query with synopsis and SASE. *No unsolicited mss.*
Recent Title(s): *The Lesbian Health Book*, edited by Marissa C. Martinez and Jocelyn White; *Exit to Reality*, by Edith Forbes (fiction).
Tips: "Our audience is generally composed of women interested in reading about contemporary issues addressed from a feminist perspective."

SEASIDE PRESS, Wordware Publishing, Inc., 2320 Los Rios Blvd., Suite 200, Plano TX 77574. (972)423-0090. Fax: (972)881-9147. E-mail: sales@wordware.com. Website: http://www.wordware.com. President: Russell A. Stultz. **Acquisitions:** Mary Goldman, publisher. "Seaside Press publishes in the areas of travel, travel/history, pet care, humor and general interest." Publishes trade paperback originals. **Publishes 7-10 titles/year. Receives 50-60 queries and 20-30 mss/year. 40% of books from first-time authors; 95% from unagented writers. Pays 8-12% royalty on net.** Publishes book 1 year after acceptance of ms. Accepts simultaneous submissions. Reports in 2 months. Book catalog and ms guidelines with SASE.
Nonfiction: How-to, pet care, humor. Subjects include travel/history (family guides for exploring cities). Submit proposal package, including table of contents, 2 sample chapters, target audience summation, competing products.
Recent Title(s): *Your Kitten's First Year*, by Shawn Messonnier (pet care).
Tips: "We are not currently taking submissions for children's books."

SEAWORTHY PUBLICATIONS, INC., 507 Sunrise Dr., Port Washington WI 53074. (414)268-9250. Fax: (414)268-9208. E-mail: publisher@seaworthy.com. Website: http://www.seaworthy.com. **Acquisitions:** Joseph F. Janson, publisher. "Seaworthy Publications is a nautical book publisher that primarily publishes books of interest to recreational boaters and serious bluewater cruisers." Publishes trade paperback originals and reprints. **Publishes 6 titles/year. Receives 60 queries and 20 mss/year. 60% of books from first-time authors; 100% from unagented writers. Pays 15% royalty on wholesale price. Offers $1,000 advance.** Publishes book 6 months after acceptance of ms. Reports in 1 month. Book catalog and ms guidelines for #10 SASE.
Nonfiction: Regional guide books, first-person adventure, illustrated book, reference, technical—all dealing with boating. Subjects include cooking/foods/nutrition, nautical history, hobbies of sailing and boating, regional boating guide books, sport sail racing, world travel. Query with 3 sample chapters and SASE. Reviews artwork/photos as part of ms package. Send photocopies or color prints.
Fiction: Nautical adventure, historical. "Our focus is clearly nonfiction. However, we will consider high quality fiction with a nautical theme." Query with 3 sample chapters and SASE.
Poetry: "Our focus is clearly nonfiction. However, we will consider high quality poetry with a nautical theme." Query with 5 sample poems and SASE.
Recent Title(s): *Chasing the Long Rainbow*, by Hal Roth (single-handed, sailboat race around the world).
Tips: "Our audience is sailors, boaters, and those interested in the sea, sailing or long distance cruising and racing."

★ **SEEDLING PUBLICATIONS, INC.**, 4079 Overlook Dr. E, Columbus OH 43214-2931. Phone/fax: (614)451-2412 or (614)792-0796. E-mail: sales@seedlingpub.com. Website: http://www.seedlingpub.com. **Acquisitions:** Josie Stewart, vice president. Seedling publishes books for young children to "keep young readers growing." Publishes in an 8-, 12-, or 16-page format for beginning readers. **Publishes 8-10 titles/year. Receives 10 queries and 200 mss/year. 80% of books from first-time authors; 100% from unagented writers. Pays royalty or makes outright purchase.** Publishes book 1 year after of acceptance of ms. Accepts simultaneous submissions. Reports in 6 months. Book catalog for #10 SAE and 2 first-class stamps. Manuscript guidelines for #10 SASE.
Nonfiction: Children's/juvenile. Animal subjects. Submit outline with SASE. Reviews artwork/photos as part of ms package. Send photocopies.
Fiction: Juvenile. Submit outline with SASE. Reviews artwork/photos as part of ms package. Send photocopies.
Recent Title(s): *Free to Fly*, by Kathleen Gibson (nonfiction in a story setting); *Dinosaurs Galore*, by Audrey Eaton and Jane Kennedy (fiction).
Tips: "Follow our guidelines. Do not submit full-length picture books or chapter books. Our books are for children, ages 5-7, who are just beginning to read independently. Try a manuscript with young readers. Listen for spots in the text that don't flow when the child reads the story. Rewrite until the text sounds natural to beginning readers."

SERENDIPITY SYSTEMS, P.O. Box 140, San Simeon CA 93452. (805)927-5259. E-mail: bookware@thegrid.net. Website: http://www.thegrid.net/bookware/bookware.htm. **Acquisitions:** John Galuszka, publisher. "Since 1986 Serendipity Systems has promoted and supported electronic publishing with electronic books for IBM-PC compatible computers." **Publishes 6-12 titles/year; each imprint publishes 0-6 titles/year. Receives 600 queries and 150 mss/year. 95% of books from unagented writers. Pays 25-33% royalty on wholesale price or on retail price, "depending on how the book goes out."** Publishes book 2 months after acceptance of ms. Accepts simultaneous submissions. Electronic submissions required. Reports in 1 month on mss. *Writer's Market* recommends allowing 2 months for reply. Book catalog available online. Manuscript guidelines for #10 SASE, or on the Internet.

• The publishers note: "We are reorganizing. Check our guidelines on the Internet for the latest information."

Imprint(s): Books-on-Disks™, Bookware™.

Nonfiction: "We only publish reference books on literature, writing and electronic publishing." Query first with SASE. Submit entire ms on disk in ASCII or HTML files. Queries by e-mail; mss, summaries with sample chapters and long documents should be sent by postal mail.
Fiction: "We want to see *only* works which use (or have a high potential to use) hypertext, multimedia, interactivity or other computer-enhanced features. No romance, religious, occult, New Age, fantasy, or children's mss. Submit entire ms on disk in ASCII or HTML files. Query first.
Recent Title(s): *The Electronic Publishing Forum* (nonfiction); *Sideshow*, by Marian Allen.

SERVANT PUBLICATIONS, P.O. Box 8617, Ann Arbor MI 48107. (734)677-6490. **Acquisitions:** Anne Bannan. Estab. 1972. "Servant is a communications company whose materials spread the Gospel of Jesus Christ, help Christians live in accordance with that Gospel, promote renewal in the church and bear witness to Christian unity." Publishes hardcover, trade and mass market paperback originals and trade paperback reprints. **Publishes 50 titles/year. 5% of books from first-time authors; 90% from unagented writers. Offers standard royalty contract.** Publishes book 1 year after acceptance. Reports in 2 months. Book catalog for 9×12 SASE.
Imprint(s): Vine Books ("especially for evanglical Protestant readers"); Charis Books ("especially for Roman Catholic readers").
Nonfiction: "We look for practical Christian teaching, devotionals, scripture, current problems facing the Christian church, and inspiration." No heterodox or non-Christian approaches. Query only. *All unsolicited mss returned unopened.*
Fiction: Accepts unsolicited queries only, from published authors or their agents. *All unsolicited mss returned unopened.*
Recent Title(s): *God Thinks You're Positively Awesome*, by Andrea Stephens (teenage guide to inner beauty); *Copper Hill*, by Stephen and Janet Bly.

SEVEN STORIES PRESS, 140 Watts St., New York NY 10013. (212)995-0908. Website: http://www.sevenstories.com. **Acquisitions:** Daniel Simon. Seven Stories Press publishes general, contemporary fiction and nonfiction for a well-educated, progressive, mainstream audience. Publishes hardcover and trade paperback originals. **Publishes 20-25 titles/year. 15% of books from first-time authors; 15% from unagented writers. Pays 7-15% royalty on retail price.** Publishes book 1-3 years after acceptance. Accepts simultaneous submissions. Reports in 3 months. Book catalog and manuscript guidelines free.
Nonfiction: Biography. Subjects include general nonfiction. Query only. No unsolicited ms. Responds only if interested.
Fiction: Contemporary. Query only. *No unsolicited mss.* Responds only if interested.
Recent Title(s): *The More You Watch, The Less You Know*, by Danny Schechter (media studies); *I Who Have Never Known Men*, by Jacqueline Harpman (translation).

HAROLD SHAW PUBLISHERS, 388 Gundersen Dr., P.O. Box 567, Wheaton IL 60189. (630)665-6700. **Acquisitions:** Lori McCullough, editorial assistant. Estab. 1967. "We publish a wide range (full circle) of books from a Christian perspective for use by a broad range of readers." Publishes mostly trade paperback originals and reprints. **Publishes 40 titles/year. Receives 1,000 submissions/year. 10-20% of books from first-time authors; 90% from unagented writers. Offers 5-10% royalty on retail price. Offers $500-1,000 advance. Sometimes makes outright purchase of $375-2,500 for Bible studies and compilations.** Publishes book 18 months after acceptance of ms. Reports in 3-6 months. Guidelines for #10 SASE. Catalog for 9×12 SAE with 5 first-class stamps.
Nonfiction: Subjects include marriage, family and parenting, self-help, mental health, spiritual growth, Bible study and literary topics. "We are looking for adult general nonfiction with different twists—self-help manuscripts with fresh insight and colorful, vibrant writing style. No autobiographies or biographies accepted. Must have a Christian perspective for us even to review the manuscript." Query with SASE.
Recent Title(s): *Bright Evening Star*, by Madeleine L'Engle.
Tips: "Get an editor who is not a friend or a spouse who will tell you honestly whether your book is marketable. It will save a lot of your time and money and effort. Then do an honest evaluation. Who would read the book other than yourself? If it won't sell 5,000 copies, it's not very marketable and most publishers wouldn't be interested."

SIERRA CLUB BOOKS, Dept. WM, 85 Second, San Francisco CA 94105. (415)977-5500. Fax: (415)291-1602. Executive Director: Carl Pope. **Acquisitions:** James Cohee, senior editor. Estab. 1962. "The Sierra Club was founded to help people to explore, enjoy and preserve the nation's forests, waters, wildlife and wilderness. The books program looks to publish quality trade books about the outdoors and the protection of natural resources." Publishes hardcover and paperback originals and reprints. **Publishes 30 titles/year. Receives 1,000 submissions/year. 50% of books from unagented writers. Royalties vary by project. Offers $3,000-15,000 average advance.** Publishes book 18 months after acceptance. Reports in 2 months. Book catalog free.
Imprint(s): Sierra Club Books for Children.
Nonfiction: A broad range of environmental subjects: outdoor adventure, descriptive and how-to, women in the outdoors; landscape and wildlife pictorials; literature, including travel and works on the spiritual aspects of the natural world; travel and trail; natural history and current environmental issues, including public health and uses of appropriate technology; gardening; general interest; and children's books. "Specifically, we are interested in literary natural history, environmental issues such as nuclear power, self-sufficiency, politics and travel, and juvenile books with an ecological theme." Does *not* want "proposals for large color photographic books without substantial text; how-to books on building things outdoors; books on motorized travel; or any but the most professional studies of animals." Query first, then submit outline and sample chapters. Reviews artwork/photos as part of ms package. Send photocopies.

Recent Title(s): *Still Wild, Always Wild*, by Ann Zwinger (nature).

SIERRA CLUB BOOKS FOR CHILDREN is currently not accepting submissions.

SIGNET, Penguin Putnam Inc., 375 Hudson St., New York NY 10014. (212)366-2000. Website: http://www.penguin.com Michaela Hamilton, editor-in-chief. **Acquisitions:** Danielle Perez, senior editor (New Age, inspirational); Hugh Rowson, director of reference publishing (reference); Deb Brody, senior editor (health/diet); Audrey LaFehr, executive editor (women's fiction); Joe Pittman, senior editor (suspense). Signet publishes commercial fiction and nonfiction for the popular audience." Publishes mass market paperback originals and reprints. **Publishes 500 titles/year. Receives 20,000 queries and 10,000 mss/year. 30-40% of books from first-time authors; 5% from unagented writers. Advance and royalty negotiable.** Publishes book 18 months after acceptance of ms. Reports in 6 months.
Imprint(s): Mentor, Onyx, **ROC**, Signet Classic, Topaz, Signet Reference.
Nonficzntion: Biography, how-to, reference, self-help. Subjects include animals, child guidance/parenting, cooking/foods/nutrition, ethnic, health/medicine, language/literature, military/war, money/finance, psychology, sports. "Looking for reference and annual books." *Agented submission only.*
Fiction: Erotica, ethnic, fantasy, historical, horror, literary, mainstream/contemporary, mystery, occult, romance, science fiction, suspense, western. "Looking for writers who can deliver a book a year (or faster) of consistent quality." Agented submissions only.
Recent Title(s): *Down at the End of Lonely Street*, by Peter Harry Brown and Pat H. Broeske (biography of Elvis Presley); *Mortal Fear*, by Greg Iles (thriller).

SILHOUETTE BOOKS, 300 E. 42nd St., New York NY 10017. (212)682-6080. Fax: (212)682-4539. Website: http://www.romance.net. Editorial Manager, Silhouette Books, Harlequin Historicals: Tara Gavin. **Acquisitions:** Joan Marlow Golan, senior editor (Silhouette Romance); Tara Gavin, senior editor (Silhouette Special Editions); Melissa Senate, senior editor (Silhouette Desire); Leslie Wainger, executive senior editor/editorial coordinator (Silhouette Intimate Moments and Silhouette Yours Truly); Tracy Farrell, senior editor (Harlequin Historicals). Estab. 1979. Silhouette publishes contemporary adult romances. Publishes mass market paperback originals. **Publishes 350 titles/year. Receives 4,000 submissions/year. 10% of books from first-time authors; 50% from unagented writers. Pays royalty.** Publishes book 1-3 years after acceptance. Manuscript guidelines for #10 SASE.
Imprint(s): *Silhouette Romances* (contemporary adult romances, 53,000-58,000 words); *Silhouette Special Editions* (contemporary adult romances, 75,000-80,000 words); *Silhouette Desires* (contemporary adult romances, 55,000-60,000 words); *Silhouette Intimate Moments* (contemporary adult romances, 80,000-85,000 words); *Silhouette Yours Truly* (contemporary adult romances, 53,000-58,000 words); *Harlequin Historicals* (adult historical romances, 95,000-105,000 words).
Fiction: Romance (contemporary and historical romance for adults). "We are interested in seeing submissions for all our lines. No manuscripts other than the types outlined. Manuscript should follow our general format, yet have an individuality and life of its own that will make it stand out in the readers' minds." Send query letter, 2 page synopsis and SASE to head of imprint. *No unsolicited mss.*
Recent Title(s): *Montana Mavericks Weddings*, collection by Diana Palmer, Ann Major and Susan Mallery.
Tips: "The romance market is constantly changing, so when you read for research, read the latest books and those that have been recommended to you by people knowledgeable in the genre. We are actively seeking new authors for all our lines, contemporary and historical."

SILVER BURDETT PRESS, Macmillan Children's Reference, 1633 Broadway, New York NY 10019.

- Silver Burdett Press has become part of Macmillan Children's Reference and moved to Macmillan's New York City offices. It, along with other Simon & Schuster reference, business and professional imprints, were sold to a Dallas-based investment firm, Hicks Muse Tate & Furst. Editorial plans have not been finalized.

Imprint(s): Crestwood House, Dillon Press, Julian Messner, New Discovery, Silver Press.

SILVER DOLPHIN BOOKS, Advantage Publishers Group, 5880 Oberlin Dr., San Diego CA 92121. (619)457-2500. **Acquisitions**: JoAnn Padgett, managing editor. "Silver Dolphin publishes trade children's books that are bold, colorful and striking with a broad appeal. All our books are educational and developemental in an innovative, creative way. Children not only read and learn, but interact and play with our books." Publishes hardcover and trade paperback originals and reprints. **Publishes 30 titles/year. Receives 175 queries and 75 mss/year. Pays 10-15% royalty on wholesale price or makes outright purchase on a project basis. Offers $1,000 advance.** Publishes book 1 year after acceptance of ms. Accepts simultaneous submissions. Reports in 1 month on queries, 4 months on proposals, 6 months on mss. Book catalog for $1 and 9×12 SAE with 5 first-class stamps. Manuscript guidelines for #10 SASE.
Nonfiction: Juvenile. Publishes "preschool novelty books for toddlers through five years of age and educational nonfiction for children 6-12 years of age." Submit cover letter, outline, table of contents, sample chapters or complete ms., estimated length or word count, author bio or résumé, and marketing information, including a clear statement of the work's purpose, target audience and comparison with competition. Include SASE with sufficient postage for return of materials. Reviews artwork/photos as part of ms package. Send transparencies.
Recent Title(s): *Let's Start* series (art activity books).
Tips: Audience is "parents who want fun, educational books for their children. Try to present a unique topic or a topic treated from a unique angle."

SIMON & SCHUSTER, 1230 Avenue of the Americas, New York NY 10020. Website: http://www.simonsays.com. Simon & Schuster Trade (**Scribner** [**Lisa Drew**, **Rawson Associates**, Scribner], Fireside, **The Free Press**, Simon & Schuster, Touchstone), Simon & Schuster Children's Publishing (Aladdin Paperbacks, **Atheneum Books for Young Readers**, **Margaret K. McElderry Books**), Simon Spotlight [**Little Simon**], **Simon & Schuster Books for Young Readers**); Simon & Schuster New Media; **Pocket Books** (MTV Books, Star Trek, Washington Square Press, Pocket Books for Young Adults [**Archway Paperbacks**, **Minstrel Books**, Pocket Books for Young Adults]).

SIMON & SCHUSTER BOOKS FOR YOUNG READERS, Simon & Schuster Children's Publishing Division, 1230 Avenue of the Americas, New York NY 10020. (212)698-2851. Website: http://www.simonandschuster.com. or http://www.simonsayskids.com. Executive Editor: Virginia Duncan (picture books, nonfiction, fiction). Senior Editor: David Gale (middle grade and YA fiction). Andrea Davis Pinckney, editor (picture books, nonfiction, fiction). Rebecca Davis (picture books, poetry, fiction). **Acquisitions:** Acquisitions Editor. "We publish mainly for the bookstore market, and are looking for books that will appeal directly to kids." Publishes hardcover originals. **Publishes 80-90 titles/year. Receives 2,500 queries and 10,000 mss/year. 5-10% of books from first-time authors; 40% from unagented writers. Pays 4-12% royalty on retail price. Advance varies.** Publishes book 1-3 years after acceptance of ms. Accepts simultaneous submissions. Reports in 2 months on queries. Manuscript guidelines for #10 SASE.
Nonfiction: Children's/juvenile. Subjects include animals, ethnic, history, nature/environment. "We're looking for innovative, appealing nonfiction especially for younger readers. Please don't submit education or textbooks." Query with SASE only. *All unsolicited mss returned unread.*
Fiction: Fantasy, historical, humor, juvenile, mystery, picture books, science fiction, young adult. "Fiction needs to be fresh, unusual and compelling to stand out from the competition. We're not looking for problem novels, stories with a moral, or rhymed picture book texts." Query only, include SASE. *All unsolicited mss returned unread.*
Poetry: "Most of our poetry titles are anthologies; we publish very few stand-alone poets." No picture book ms in rhymed verse. Query.
Recent Title(s): *The Space Between Our Footsteps*, by Naomi Shihab Nye (young adult).
Tips: "We're looking for fresh, original voices and unexplored topics. Don't do something because everyone else is doing it. Try to find what they're *not* doing."

N **SKIDMORE-ROTH PUBLISHING, INC.**, 400 Inverness Dr., S. #260, Englewood CO 80112. (800)825-3150. Fax: (303)306-1460. E-mail: info@skidmore-roth. com. Website: http://www.skidmore-roth.com. **Acquisitions**: Molly Sullivan, editor (nursing); Rae Robertson, editor (allied health and medical). "Skidmore-Roth is dedicated to providing quality medical books and material to medical professionals worldwide." Publishes trade paperback originals. **Publishes 24 titles/year. Receives 10 queries and 24 mss/year. 50% of books from first-time authors; 100% from unagented writers. Pays 4-8% royalty on wholesale price or makes outright purchase of $2,500-10,000.** Publishes book 9 months after acceptance of ms. Accepts simultaneous submissions. Reports in 2 weeks on proposals.
Nonfiction: Reference, textbook. Health/medicine subjects . "We are looking for proposals in areas where there is currently a lack of publication."
Recent Title(s): *Long Term Care: A Skills Handbook for Nurse Assistants*, by Barbara Vitale.
Tips: "Audience is licensed nurses working in hospitals, long term care facilities, subacute centers, home health, HMO's and medical clinics, nurse assistants and nurse aides, nursing students and other allied health professions."

SKY PUBLISHING CORP., 49 Bay State Rd., Cambridge MA 02138. (617)864-7360. Fax: (617)864-6117. E-mail: postmaster@skypub.com. Website: http://www.skypub.com. President/Publisher: Richard Tresch Fienberg. **Acquisitions:** J. Kelly Beatty, senior editor; Carolyn Collins Petersen, editor, books and products; Sally MacGilliray, publications manager. Estab. 1941. "Sky Publishing Corporation will be an advocate of astronomy and space science through its products and services and will aggressively promote greater understanding of these disciplines among laypeople." **Publishes 6 titles/year.** Publishes hardcover and trade paperback originals on topics of interest to serious amateur astronomers as well as *Sky & Telescope: The Essential Magazine of Astronomy* and *Skywatch: Your Guide to Stargazing and Space Exploration.* Nonfiction only. Magazine articles: pays 20¢/word. **Books: pays 10% royalty on net sales.** Magazine author and book proposal guidelines available. Catalog free.
Recent Title(s): *The Modern Amateur Astronomer*, edited by Patrick Moore.

N **SLACK INC.**, 6900 Grove Rd., Thorofare NJ 08086. (609)848-1000. Fax: (609)853-5991. E-mail: adrummond@slackinc.com. Website: http://www.slackinc.com. **Acquisitions:** Amy E. Drummond, editorial director. Publishes hardcover and softcover originals. **Publishes 24 titles/year. Receives 80 queries and 23 mss/year. 75% of books from first-time authors; 100% from unagented writers. Pays 10% royalty.** Publishes book 8 months after acceptance. Accepts simultaneous submissions. Reports in 4 months on queries, 1 month on proposals, 3 months on mss. Book catalog and ms guidelines free.
Nonfiction: Textbook (medical). Subjects include ophthalmology, athletic training, physical therapy, occupational therapy. Submit proposal package, including outline, 2 sample chapters, market profile and cv. Reviews artwork/photos as part of ms package. Send photocopies.
Recent Title(s): *Occupational Therapy: Enabling Function and Well Being*, by Christiansen and Baum.

THE SMITH, The Generalist Association, Inc., 69 Joralemon St., Brooklyn NY 11201-4003. (718)834-1212. **Acquisitions:** Harry Smith, publisher/editor; Michael McGrinder, associate editor. Estab. 1964. The Smith publishes literature of "outstanding artistic quality." Publishes hardcover and trade paperback originals. **Publishes 3-5 titles/year. Receives 2,500 queries/year. 50% of books from first-time authors; more than 90% from unagented writers. Pays royalty. Offers $500-1,000 advance.** Publishes book 9 months after acceptance. Accepts simultaneous submissions. Reports in 3 months. Guidelines for #10 SASE.

Nonfiction: Literary essays, language and literature. "The 'how' is as important as the 'what' to us. Don't bother to send anything if the prose itself is not outstanding. We don't publish anything about how to fix your car or your soul." Query with proposal package including outline and sample chapter. Reviews artwork/photos as part of ms package. Send photocopies. No registered mail.

Fiction: Experimental, literary, short story collections. "Emphasis is always on artistic quality. A synopsis of almost any novel sounds stupid." Query with 1 sample chapter. *No complete mss. No registered mail.*

Poetry: "No greeting card sentiments, no casual jottings." Submit 7-10 sample poems. No complete ms. Do not send registered mail.

Recent Title(s): *Crank Letters*, by Kirby Congdon (letters); *A Visit to Pinky Ryder's*, by Marshall Brooks (humor/art).

N **SMITH AND KRAUS PUBLISHERS, INC.**, One Main St., P.O. Box 127, Lyme NH 03768. (603)643-6431. **Acquisitions:** Marisa Smith, president/publisher. Publishes hardcover and trade paperback originals. **Publishes 35-40 books/year. 10% of books from first-time authors; 10-20% from unagented writers. Pays 10% royalty of net on retail price. Offers $500-2,000 advance.** Publishes book 1 year after acceptance. Reports in 1 month on queries, 2 months on proposals, 4 months on mss. Book catalog free.

Nonfiction and Fiction: Drama, theater. Query with SASE. Does not return submissions.

Recent Title(s): *Horton Foote: Collected Plays Volume III*; *Plays of Fairy Tales (Grades K-3)*, by L.E. McCullough.

GIBBS SMITH, PUBLISHER, P.O. Box 667, Layton UT 84041. (801)544-9800. Fax: (801)544-5582. Website: http://www.gibbs~smith.com. **Acquistions:** Madge Baird, editorial director (humor, western, gardening, architecture); Gail Yngve, editor (fiction, personal development, interior decorating, poetry); Theresa Desmond, editor (children's); Estab. 1969. "We publish books that make a contribution to the culture of our time." Publishes hardcover and trade paperback originals. **Publishes 50 titles/year. Receives 1,500-2,000 submissions/year. 8-10% of books from first-time authors; 50% from unagented writers. Pays 6-15% royalty on net receipts. Offers $2,000-3,000 advance.** Publishes book 1-2 years after acceptance of ms. Accepts simultaneous submissions, if so noted. Reports in 1 month on queries, 10 weeks on proposals and mss. Book catalog for 9×12 SAE and $2.13 in postage. Manuscript guidelines free.

Imprint(s): Peregrine Smith Books.

Nonfiction: Children's/juvenile, illustrated book, textbook. Subjects include Americana, art/architecture, humor, interior design, nature/environment, regional. Query or submit outline, several completed sample chapters and author's cv. Reviews artwork/photos as part of the ms package. Send sample illustrations if applicable.

Fiction: Literary, mainstream/contemporary. "We publish fewer than 3 novels a year." Submit synopsis and 3 sample chapters, with sample illustration if applicable.

Poetry: "Our annual poetry contest accepts entries only in April. Charges $15 fee. Prize: $500." Submit complete ms.

Recent Title(s): *Retreats*, by Lawson Drinkard III (nonfiction); *Cypher*, by Brad Teave (fiction).

SOCIAL SCIENCE EDUCATION CONSORTIUM, P.O. Box 21270, Boulder CO 80308-4270. (303)492-8154. Fax: (303)449-3925. E-mail: singletl@stripe.colorado.edu. **Acquisitions:** Laurel R. Singleton, managing editor. Estab. 1963. "The mission of the SSEC is threefold: (1) to provide leadership for social science education, (2) to promote a larger role for the social sciences in the curriculum, and (3) to close the gap between frontier thinking in the social sciences and the curriculum." Publishes trade paperback originals. **Publishes 8 titles/year. 25% of books from first-time authors; 100% from unagented writers. Pays 8-12% royalty on net sales (retail price minus average discount).** Publishes book 6 months after acceptance. Accepts simultaneous submissions. Reports in 1 month on proposals.

Nonfiction: Teacher resources. Subjects include education, government/politics, history; must include teaching applications. "We publish titles of interest to social studies teachers particularly; we do not generally publish on such broad educational topics as discipline, unless there is a specific relationship to the social studies/social sciences." Submit outline and 1-2 sample chapters.

Recent Title(s): *A New Look at the American West*, by Eastman & Miller.

SOHO PRESS, INC., 853 Broadway, New York NY 10003. (212)260-1900. Website: http://www.sohopress.com. **Acquisitions:** Juris Jurjevics, publisher/editor-in-chief; Laura Hruska, associate publisher; Melanie Fleishman, director of marketing. Estab. 1986. "Soho Press publishes discerning authors for discriminating readers, finding the strongest possible writers and publishing them." Publishes hardcover and trade paperback originals. **Publishes 25 titles/year. Receives 5,000 submissions/year. 75% of books from first-time authors; 50% from unagented writers. Pays 7½-15% royalty on retail price. Offers advance.** Publishes book within 1 year after acceptance. Accepts simultaneous submissions. Reports in 1 month. Book catalog for 6×9 SAE with 2 first-class stamps.

- Soho Press also publishes two book series: Hera ("historical fiction with accurate and strong female lead characters") and Soho Crime (mysteries, noir, procedurals).

Nonfiction: Literary nonfiction: travel, autobiography, biography, etc. "No self-help." Submit outline and sample chapters.

Fiction: Adventure, ethnic, feminist, historical, literary, mainstream/contemporary, mystery, suspense. Submit complete ms with SASE. *Writer's Market* recommends query with SASE first.
Recent Title(s): *A Dublin Girl*, by Elaine Crowley (autobiography); *A Much Younger Man*, by Diane Highbridge.

SOUNDPRINTS, The Trudy Corp., 353 Main Ave., Norwalk CT 06851. Fax: (203)846-1776. E-mail: sndprnts@ix.net com.com. Website: http://www.soundprints.com. **Acquisitions**: Cassia Farkas, editor. "Soundprints takes you on an Odyssey of discovery, exploring an historical event or a moment in time that affects our every day lives. Each Odyssey is approved by a Smithsonian Institution curator, so readers experience the adventures as if they were really there." Publishes hardcover originals. **Publishes 10-14 titles/year. Receives 200 queries/year. 20% of books from first-time authors; 90% of books from unagented writers. Makes outright purchase. No advance.** Publishes book 2 years after acceptance of ms. Accepts simultaneous submissions. Reports on queries in 3 months. Book catalog for 9×12 SAE with $1.05 postage. Manuscript guidelines for #10 SASE.

- "We are getting ready to launch a new multinational series in 1999. All authors and illustrators must be native to the country represented in each book. We accept résumés and samples."

Nonfiction: Children's/juvenile, animals. "We focus on North American wildlife and ecology. Subject animals must be portrayed realistically and must not be anthropomorphic. Meticulous research is required." Query with SASE. Does not review artwork/photos. (All books are now illustrated in full color.)
Fiction: Juvenile. "Most of our books are under license from the Smithsonian or The Nature Conservancy, and are closely curated fictional stories based on fact. We never do stories of anthropomorphic animals. When we publish juvenile fiction, it will be about wildlife or history and all information in the book *must* be accurate." Query.
Recent Title(s): *Handshake in Space: The Appolo-Soyuz Test Project*, by Sheri Tan, illustrated by Higgins Bond.
Tips: "Our books are written for children from ages four through eight. Our most successful authors can craft a wonderful story which is derived from authentic wildlife or historic facts. First inquiry to us should ask about our interest in publishing a book about a specific animal or habitat. Stories about historical events must be represented by exhibits in the Smithsonian Institution's museums."

SOURCEBOOKS, INC., P.O. Box 372, Naperville IL 60566. (630)961-3900. Fax: (630)961-2168. Publisher: Dominique Raccah. **Acquisitions:** Todd Stocke, managing editor; Mark Warda (Legal Survival Guides self-help/law series). Estab. 1987. "Our goal is to provide customers with terrific, innovative books at reasonable prices." Publishes hardcover and trade paperback originals. **Publishes 70 titles/year. 50% of books from first-time authors; 75% from unagented writers. Pays 6-15% royalty on wholesale price.** Publishes book 1 year after acceptance. Accepts simultaneous submissions. Reports in 3 months on queries. Book catalog and ms guidelines for 9×12 SASE.
Imprint(s): Casablanca Press, Legal Survival Guides, Sphinx Publishing.
Nonfiction: *Small Business Sourcebooks:* books for small business owners, entrepreneurs and students. "A key to submitting books to us is to explain how your book helps the reader, why it is different from the books already out there (please do your homework) and the author's credentials for writing this book." *Sourcebooks Trade:* gift books, self-help, general business, and how to. "Books likely to succeed with us are self-help, art books, parenting and childcare, psychology, women's issues, how-to, house and home, gift books or books with strong artwork." Query or submit outline and 2-3 sample chapters (not the first). *No complete mss.* Reviews artwork/photos as part of ms package.
Recent Title(s): *Unstoppable*, by Cynthia Kersey (self-improvment).
Tips: "We love to develop books in new areas or develop strong titles in areas that are already well developed."

SOUTH END PRESS, 7 Brookline St., Cambridge MA 02139. (617)547-4002. Fax: (617)547-1333. **Acquisitions:** Loie Hayes (feminist/gay/lesbian studies, education); Anthony Arnove (African-American studies, labor, history, political theory, economics); Lynn Lu (cultural studies, media, Latin American studies); Dionne Brooks (African-American studies, global politics); Sonia Shah (global politics, creative nonfiction, Asian-American studies). "We publish nonfiction political books with a new left/feminist/multicultural perspective." Publishes hardcover and trade paperback originals and reprints. **Publishes 15 titles/year. Receives 400 queries and 100 mss/year. 50% of books from first-time authors; 95% from unagented writers. Pays 11% royalty on wholesale price. Occasionally offers $500-2,500 advance.** Publishes book 9 months after acceptance. Accepts simultaneous submissions. Reports in up to 3 months on queries and proposals. Book catalog and ms guidelines free.
Nonfiction: Subjects include economics, education, ethnic, gay/lesbian, government/politics, health/medicine, history, nature/environment, philosophy, science, sociology, women's issues/studies, political. Query or submit 2 sample chapters including intro or conclusion and annotated toc. Reviews artwork as part of ms package. Send photocopies.
Recent Title(s): *Black Liberation in Conservative America*, by Manning Marable (Black studies).

N **SOUTHERN ILLINOIS UNIVERSITY PRESS**, P.O. BOX 3697, Carbondale IL 62902-3697. (618)453-2680. Fax: (618)453-1221. **Acquisitions**: Jim Simmons, editorial director (film, theater, American history); John Gehner, sponsoring editor (composition, rhetoric, criminology). Publishes hardcover and trade paperback originals and reprints. **Publishes 50-60 titles/year. Imprint publishes 4-6 titles/year. Receives 800 queries and 300 mss/year. 45% of books from first-time authors; 100% from unagented writers. Pays 5-10% royalty on wholesale price. Rarely offers advance.** Publishes book 1 year after acceptance of ms. Reports in 3 months. Book catalog and ms guidelines free.
Imprint(s): Shawnee Books (contact Lisa Bayer, director of marketing).
Nonfiction: Biography, reference, textbook. Subjects include Americana, history, regional, sports, women's issues/studies. Query with proposal package, including synopsis, table of contents, author's vita with SASE.

Recent Title(s): *The English Department*, by W. Ross Winterowd (rhetoric/composition).

SOUTHERN METHODIST UNIVERSITY PRESS, P.O. Box 415, Dallas TX 75275. Fax: (214)768-1432. Website: http://www.smu.edu/~press. **Acquisitions:** Kathryn Lang, senior editor. Estab. 1937. Southern Methodist University publishes in the fields of literary fiction, ethics and human values, film and theater, regional studies and theological studies. Publishes hardcover and trade paperback originals and reprints. **Publishes 10-15 titles/year. Receives 500 queries and 500 mss/year. 75% of books from first-time authors; 95% from unagented writers. Pays up to 10% royalty on wholesale price. Offers $500 advance.** Publishes book 1 year after acceptance. Reports in 1 month on queries and proposals, 6-12 months on mss.
Nonfiction: Subjects include medical ethics/human values, film/theater, regional history, theology. Query with outline, 3 sample chapters, table of contents and author bio. Reviews artwork/photos as part of the ms package. Send photocopies.
Fiction: Literary novels and short story collections. Query.
Recent Title(s): *Mexicano Resistance in the Southwest*, by Robert Rosenbaum (history); *The Light Possessed*, by Alan Cheuse.

SOUTHFARM PRESS, Haan Graphic Publishing Services, Ltd., P.O. Box 1296, Middletown CT 06457. (860)346-8798. Fax: (860)347-9931. E-mail: haan/southfarm@usa.net. Publisher: Walter J. Haan. **Acquisitions:** Wanda P. Haan, editor-in-chief. Estab. 1983. Southfarm publishes primarily history and military/war nonfiction. Publishes trade hardcover and paperback originals. **Publishes 5 titles/year. 90% from first-time authors; 100% from unagented writers. Pays 5-10% royalty on retail price. No advance.** Publishes book 1 year after acceptance of ms. Accepts simultaneous submissions. Reports in 1 month. *Writer's Market* recommends allowing 2 months for reply.
Nonfiction: Subjects include history, military/war and dog breeds. Submit outline/synopsis and sample chapters.
Recent Title(s): *Janey: A Little Plane in a Big War*, by Alfred W. Schultz.

SPECTRA, Bantam Books, Bantam Doubleday Dell, 1540 Broadway, New York NY 10036. (212)782-9418. Fax: (212)782-9523. Website: http://www.bdd.com. **Acquisitions:** Anne Lesley Groell, editor. Estab. 1984. "Spectra has a high-quality list, but we buy across the board. If we like something, we'll try it." Publishes hardcover, trade and mass market paperback originals and reprints. **Receives hundreds of queries and 500 mss/year. 20% of books from first-time authors. Pays 8-10% royalty on wholesale price. Pays $5,000 and up advance.** Publishes book 1 year after acceptance of ms. Accepts simultaneous submissions, if so noted. Reports in 6 months. Manuscript guidelines for #10 SASE.
Fiction: Fantasy, humor (fantasy, science fiction), science fiction. "We try to have a high-quality list. If we love and are passionate about what we're reading, we'll do what we can to work with it." Submit synopsis, 3 sample chapters with SASE.
Recent Title(s): *Antarctica*, by Kim Stanley Robinson (science fiction).
Tips: "We publish books for an adult audience. Market does not rule our list. We like to bring new authors in."

THE SPEECH BIN, INC., 1965 25th Ave., Vero Beach FL 32960-3062. (561)770-0007. **Acquisitions:** Jan J. Binney, senior editor. Estab. 1984. Publishes professional materials for specialists in rehabilitation, particularly speech-language pathologists and audiologists, special educators, occupational and physical therapists and parents and caregivers of children and adults with developmental and post-trauma disabilities." Publishes trade paperback originals. **Publishes 10-20 titles/year. Receives 500 mss/year. 50% of books from first-time authors; 90% from unagented writers. Pays negotiable royalty on wholesale price.** Publishes ms 1 year after acceptance if SASE included. Reports in up to 3 months. Book catalog for 9×12 SASE and $1.48 postage.

- The Speech Bin is increasing their number of books published per year and is especially interested in reviewing treatment materials for adults and adolescents.

Nonfiction: How-to, illustrated book, juvenile (preschool-teen), reference, textbook, educational material and games for both children and adults. Subjects include health, communication disorders and education for handicapped persons. Query or submit outline and sample chapters with SASE. Reviews artwork as part of ms package. Send photocopies.
Fiction: "Booklets or books for children and adults about handicapped persons, especially with communication disorders." Query or submit outline/synopsis and sample chapters. "This is a potentially new market for The Speech Bin."
Recent Title(s): *The Breakfast Club: A Treatment Protocol for Treating Dementia*, by Mary Jo Santo Pietro and Faerella Boczcho.
Tips: "Books and materials must be clearly presented, well written and competently illustrated. We have added books and materials for use by other allied health professionals. We are also looking for more materials for use in treating adults and very young children with communication disorders. Please do not fax manuscripts to us."

SPINSTERS INK, 32 E. First St., #330, Duluth, MN 55802. (218)727-3222. Fax: (218)727-3119. E-mail: spinsters@spinsters-ink.com. Website: http://www.lesbian.org/spinsters-ink. **Acquisitions:** Nancy Walker. Estab. 1978. "We are interested in books that not only name the crucial issues in women's lives, but show and encourage change and growth from a feminine perspective." Publishes trade paperback originals and reprints. **Publishes 6 titles/year. Receives 400 submissions/year. 50% of books from first-time authors; 95% from unagented writers. Pays 7-11% royalty on retail price.** Publishes book 18 months after acceptance. Reports in 4 months. Book catalog free. Manuscript guidelines for SASE.
Nonfiction: Feminist analysis for positive change. Subjects include women's issues. "We do not want to see work by

men or anything that is not specific to women's lives (humor, children's books, etc.)." Query. Reviews artwork/photos as part of ms package.

Fiction: Ethnic, women's, lesbian. "We do not publish poetry or short fiction. We are interested in fiction that challenges, women's language that is feminist, stories that treat lifestyles with the diversity and complexity they deserve. We are also interested in genre fiction, especially mysteries." Submit outline/synopsis and sample chapters.

Recent Title(s): *Look Me in the Eye: Old Women, Aging and Ageism*, by Barbara MacDonald and Cynthia Rich (nonfiction); *Silent Words*, by Joan Drury (Edgar Award-nominated mystery).

STACKPOLE BOOKS, 5067 Ritter Rd., Mechanicsburg PA 17055. Fax: (717)796-0412. E-mail: stackpoleedit@paonline.com. Website: http://www.stackpolebooks.com. **Acquisitions:** William C. Davis, editor (history); Mark Allison, editor (sports, photography); Judith Schnell, editor (fly fishing, carving); Ed Skender, editor (military guides); Jane Devlin (nature); Kyle Weaver (Pennsylvania, woodworking, gardening). Estab. 1935. "Stackpole maintains a growing and vital publishing program by featuring authors who are experts in their fields, from outdoor activities to Civil War history." Publishes hardcover and paperback originals and reprints. **Publishes 75 titles/year. Pays industry standard royalty.** Publishes book 1 year after acceptance. Reports in 1 month. *Writer's Market* recommends allowing 2 months for reply.

Nonfiction: Outdoor-related subject areas—nature, wildlife, outdoor skills, outdoor sports, fly fishing, paddling, climbing, crafts and hobbies, gardening, decoy carving, photography, woodworking, history especially Civil War and military guides. Query. Does not return unsolicited mss. Reviews artwork/photos as part of ms package.

Recent Title(s): *Exploring the Appalachian Trail Guides* (5-book hiking series).

Tips: "Stackpole seeks well-written, authoritative manuscripts for specialized and general trade markets. Proposals should include chapter outline, sample chapter and illustrations and author's credentials."

STANFORD UNIVERSITY PRESS, Stanford CA 94305-2235. (415)723-9598. Website: http://www.sup.org. Managing Editor: Pamela Holway. Senior Editor: Muriel Bell. Assistant Director: Helen Tartar. **Acquisitions:** Norris Pope, director. Estab. 1925. Stanford University Press publishes scholarly books in the humanities, social sciences and natural history, high-level textbooks and some books for a more general audience. **Publishes 120 titles/year. Receives 1,500 submissions/year. 40% of books from first-time authors; 95% from unagented writers. Pays up to 15% royalty ("typically 10%, often none"). Sometimes offers advance.** Publishes book 14 months after receipt of final ms. Reports in 6 weeks.

Nonfiction: History and culture of China, Japan and Latin America; literature, criticism, and literary theory; political science and sociology; European history; anthropology, linguistics and psychology; archaeology and geology; medieval and classical studies. Query with prospectus and an outline. Reviews artwork/photos as part of ms package.

Recent Title(s): *History in a Grotesque Key: Russian Literature and the Idea of Revolution*, by Kevin M.F. Platt.

Tips: "The writer's best chance is a work of original scholarship with an argument of some importance."

STARBURST PUBLISHERS, P.O. Box 4123, Lancaster PA 17604. (717)293-0939. Fax: (717)293-1945. E-mail: starburst@starburstpublishers.com. Website: http://www.starburstpublishers.com. **Acquisitions:** David A. Robie, editor-in-chief. Estab. 1982. "We seek to publish helpful books that will be accepted by both the ABA and CBA markets." Publishes hardcover and trade paperback originals. **Publishes 10-15 titles/year. Receives 1,000 queries and mss/year. 50% of books from first-time authors, 75% from unagented writers. Pays 6-16% royalty on wholesale price. Advance varies.** Publishes book 1 year after acceptance of ms. Accepts simultaneous submissions. Reports in 1 month on queries. *Writer's Market* recommends allowing 2 months for reply. Book catalog for 9×12 SASE with 4 first-class stamps. Manuscript guidelines for #10 SASE.

Nonfiction: General nonfiction, cookbook, gift book, how-to, self-help, Christian. Subjects include business/economics, child guidance/parenting, cooking/foods/nutrition, counseling/career guidance, education, gardening, health/medicine, money/finance, nature/environment, psychology, real estate, recreation, religion. "We are looking for contemporary issues facing Christians and today's average American." Submit proposal package including outline, 3 sample chapters, author's biography and SASE. Reviews artwork/photos as part of ms package. Send photocopies.

Fiction: Inspirational. "We are only looking for good wholesome fiction that inspires or fiction that teaches self-help principles." Submit outline/synopsis, 3 sample chapters, author's biography and SASE.

Recent Title(s): *The Miracle of the Sacred Scroll*. by Johan Christian (self-help/inspirational); *Frazzled Working Woman*, by Lyon (parenting).

Tips: "Fifty percent of our line goes into the Christian marketplace, fifty percent into the general marketplace. We have direct sales representatives in both the Christian and general (bookstore, library, health and gift) marketplace. Write on an issue that slots you on talk shows and thus establishes your name as an expert and writer."

STEEPLE HILL, Harlequin Enterprises, 300 E. 42nd St., New York NY 10017. Website: http://www.romance.net. **Acquisitions**: Tara Gavin, editorial manager; Melissa Jeglinski, editor; Anne Canadeo, freelance editor. "This series of contemporary, inspirational love stories portrays Christian characters facing the many challenges of life, faith and love in today's world." Publishes mass market paperback originals. **Pays royalty.** Manuscript guidelines for #10 SASE.

Imprint(s): Love Inspired.

Fiction: Christian romance (70,000 words). Query or submit synopsis and 3 sample chapters with SASE.

Recent Title(s): *With Baby in Mind*, by Arlene James.

Tips: "Drama, humor and even a touch of mystery all have a place in this series. Subplots are welcome and should further the story's main focus or intertwine in a meaningful way. Secondary characters (children, family, friends, neighbors, fellow church members, etc.) may all contribute to a substantial and satisfying story. These wholesome tales of romance include strong family values and high moral standards. While there is no premarital sex between characters, a vivid, exciting romance that is presented with a mature perspective, is essential. Although the element of faith must clearly be present, it should be well integrated into the characterizations and plot. The conflict between the main characters should be an emotional one, arising naturally from the well-developed personalities you've created. Suitable stories should also impart an important lesson about the powers of trust and faith."

STENHOUSE PUBLISHERS, Highlights for Children, P.O. Box 360, York ME 03909. (207)363-9198. Fax: (207)363-9730. E-mail: philippa@stenhouse.com. Website: http://www.stenhouse.com. **Acquisitions:** Philippa Stratton, editorial director. "Stenhouse publishes books that support teachers' professional growth by connecting theory and practice in an accessible manner." Publishes paperback originals. **Publishes 15 titles/year. Receives 300 queries/year. 30% of books from first-time authors; 99% from unagented writers. Pays royalty on wholesale price. Offers "very modest" advance.** Publishes book 6 months after delivery of final ms. Reports in 1 month on queries, 2 months on proposals, 3 months on mss. Book catalog and ms guidelines free or on website.
Nonfiction: Exclusively education. "All our books are a combination of theory and practice." Query with outline. Reviews artwork/photos as part of ms package. Send photocopies.
Recent Title(s): *Peer Mediation*, by Judith Ferrara.

STERLING PUBLISHING, 387 Park Ave. S., New York NY 10016. (212)532-7160. Fax: (212)213-2495. **Acquisitions:** Sheila Anne Barry, acquisitions manager. Estab. 1949. "Publishes highly illustrated, accessible, hands-on, practical books for adults and children." Publishes hardcover and paperback originals and reprints. **Publishes 350 titles/year. Pays royalty. Offers advance.** Publishes book 1 year after acceptance. Reports in 2 months. Guidelines for SASE.
Imprint(s): Sterling/Chapelle; Sterling/Tamos.
Nonfiction: Alternative lifestyle, fiber arts, games and puzzles, health, how-to, hobbies, children's humor, children's science, nature and activities, pets, recreation, reference, sports, wine, gardening, art, home decorating, dolls and puppets, ghosts, UFOs, woodworking, crafts, history, medieval, Celtic subjects, alternative health and healing, new consciousness. Query or submit detailed outline and 2 sample chapters with photos if applicable.
Recent Title(s): *Illustrated Dream Dictionary*, by Russell Grant (dreams).

STILL WATERS POETRY PRESS, 459 Willow Ave., Galloway Township NJ 08201. Website: http://www2.netcom.com/~salake/stillwaterspoetry.html. **Acquisitions**: Shirley A. Lake, editor. "Dedicated to significant poetry for, by or about women, we want contemporary themes and styles set on American soil. We don't want gay, patriarchal religion, lesbian, simple rhyme or erotic themes." Publishes trade paperback originals and chapbooks. **Publishes 4 titles/year. Receives 50 queries and 500 mss/year. 80% of books from first-time authors; 100% from unagented writers. Pays in copies for first press run; 10% royalty for additional press runs. No advance.** Publishes book 4 months after acceptance of ms. Accepts simultaneous submissions. Reports in 1 month on queries and proposals, 3 months on mss. Book catalog and ms guidelines for #10 SASE.
Fiction: Literary, women's interests. "We seldom publish fiction. Don't send the same old stuff." No long books, no novels. Short stories only with SASE.
Poetry: "We publish chapbooks only, 20-30 pages, one author at a time. Do not expect publication of a single poem. Enclose SASE. Query then submit complete ms.
Recent Title(s): *The End* by Shirley A. Lake; *Grain Pie*, by Anne Lawrence (chapbook).
Tips: "Don't send manuscripts via certified mail. It wastes your money and my time."

STIPES PUBLISHING CO., 10-12 Chester St., Champaign IL 61824-9933. (217)356-8391. Fax: (217)356-5753. E-mail: stipes@soltec.com. **Acquisitions:** Benjamin H. Watts, (engineering, science, business); Robert Watts (agriculture, music and physical education). Estab. 1925. Stipes Publishing is "oriented towards the education market and educational books with some emphasis in the trade market." **Publishes hardcover and paperback originals. Publishes 15-30 titles/year. Receives 150 submissions/year. 50% of books from first-time authors; 95% from unagented writers. Pays 15% maximum royalty on retail price.** Publishes book 4 months after acceptance. Reports in 2 months.
Nonfiction: Technical (some areas), textbooks on business/economics, music, chemistry, CADD, AUTO-CADD, agriculture/horticulture, environmental education, and recreation and physical education. "All of our books in the trade area are books that also have a college text market. No books unrelated to educational fields taught at the college level." Submit outline and 1 sample chapter.
Recent Title(s): *Keyboard Musianship, Book One*, by James Lykeetal (music).

STOEGER PUBLISHING COMPANY, 5 Mansard Court, Wayne NJ 07470. (973)872-9500. Fax: (973)872-2230. **Acquisitions:** David Perkins, vice president. Estab. 1925. "For hunting, shooting sports, fishing, cooking, nature and wildlife, Stoeger books lead the industry in outstanding quality, content and unprecedented sales and profits, year after year." Publishes trade paperback originals. **Publishes 12-15 titles/year. Royalty varies, depending on ms.** Accepts simultaneous submissions. Reports in 1 month. Book catalog for #10 SAE with 2 first-class stamps.
Nonfiction: Specializing in reference and how-to books that pertain to hunting, fishing and appeal to gun enthusiasts. Submit outline and sample chapters.
Recent Title(s): *Advanced Black Powder Hunting*, by Toby Bridges.

STONE BRIDGE PRESS, P.O. Box 8208, Berkeley CA 94707. (510)524-8732. Fax: (510)524-8711. E-mail: sbp@stonebridge.com. Website: http://www.stonebridge.com/. **Acquisitions:** Peter Goodman, publisher. Strives "to publish and distribute high-quality informational tools about Japan." Publishes hardcover and trade paperback originals. **Publishes 6 titles/year; imprint publishes 2 titles/year. Receives 100 queries and 75 mss/year. 15-20% of books from first-time authors; 90% from unagented writers. Pays royalty on wholesale price. Advance varies.** Publishes book 2 years after acceptance. Accepts simultaneous submissions. Reports in 1 month on queries and proposals, 4 months on mss. Book catalog free.
Imprint(s): The Rock Spring Collection of Japanese Literature.
Nonfiction: How-to, reference. Subjects include art/architecture, business/economics, government/politics, language/literature, philosophy, translation, travel, women's issues/studies. "We publish Japan- (and some Asia-) related books only." Query with SASE. Reviews artwork/photos as part of ms package. Send photocopies.
Recent Title(s): *Little Adventures in Tokyo*, by Rick Kennedy (travel).
Tips: Audience is "intelligent, worldly readers with an interest in Japan based on personal need or experience. No children's books or commercial fiction. Realize that interest in Japan is a moving target. Please don't submit yesterday's trends or rely on a view of Japan that is outmoded. Stay current!"

STONEWALL INN, St. Martin's Press, 175 Fifth Ave., New York NY 10010. (212)674-5151. Website: http://www.stonewallinn.com. **Acquisitions:** Keith Kahla, general editor. "Stonewall Inn is the only gay and lesbian focused imprint at a major house . . . and is more inclusive of gay men than most small presses." Publishes trade paperback originals and reprints. **Publishes 20-23 titles/year. Receives 3,000 queries/year. 40% of books from first-time authors; 25% from unagented writers. Pays standard royalty on retail price. Advance varies.** Publishes book 1 year after acceptance of ms. Accepts simultaneous submissions. Reports in 6 months on queries. Book catalog free.
Nonfiction: Subjects include nearly every aspect of gay/lesbian studies. "We are looking for well-researched sociological works; author's credentials count for a great deal." Query with SASE.
Fiction: Gay/lesbian, literary, mystery. "Anybody who has any question about what a gay novel is should go out and read half a dozen. For example, there are hundreds of 'coming out' novels in print." Query with SASE.
Recent Title(s): *Now That I'm Out, What Do I Do?*, by Brian McNaught (nonfiction); *Buddies*, by Ethan Mordden (fiction).

STONEYDALE PRESS, 523 Main St., Stevensville MT 59870. (406)777-2729. Fax: (406)777-2521. **Acquisitions:** Dale A. Burk, publisher. Estab. 1976. "We seek to publish the best available source books on big game hunting, historical reminiscence and outdoor recreation in the Northern Rocky Mountain region." Publishes hardcover and trade paperback originals. **Publishes 4-6 titles/year. Receives 40-50 queries and 6-8 mss/year. 90% of books from unagented writers. Pays 12-15% royalty.** Publishes book 18 months after acceptance of ms. Reports in 2 months. Book catalog available.
Nonfiction: How-to hunting books. "We are interested only in hunting books." Query.
Recent Title(s): *The Woodsman and His Hatchet*, by Bud Cheff (wilderness survival).

STOREY PUBLISHING, Schoolhouse Rd., Pownal VT 05261. (802)823-5200. Fax: (802)823-5819. Website: http://www.storey.com. **Acquisitions:** Gwen Steege, editorial director; Deborah Balmuth (crafts, herbs); Elizabeth McHale (animals, horses, beer, building); Deb Burns (gardening). Estab. 1983. "We publish practical information that encourages personal independence in harmony with the environment." Publishes hardcover and trade paperback originals and reprints. **Publishes 45 titles/year. Receives 350 queries and 150 mss/year. 25% of books from first-time authors; 80% from unagented writers. Pays royalty or makes outright purchase.** Publishes book within 2 years of acceptance. Accepts simultaneous submissions. Reports in 1 month on queries, 3 months on proposals and mss. Book catalog and ms guidelines free.
Nonfiction: Cookbook, how-to. Subjects include agriculture/horticulture, animals, building, beer, cooking/foods/nutrition, crafts, gardening, hobbies, nature/environment. Submit proposal package, including outline, sample chapter, competitive books, author résumé. Occasionally reviews artwork/photos as part of the ms package.
Recent Title(s): *A Guide to Raising Pigs*, by Kelly Klober (animals).

STORY LINE PRESS, P.O. Box 1108, Ashland OR 97520. (541)512-8792. Fax: (541)512-8793. **Acquisitions:** Robert McDowell, publisher/editor. "Story Line Press exists to publish the best stories of our time in poetry, fiction and nonfiction. Seventy-five percent of our list includes a wide range of poetry and books about poetry. Our books are intended for the general and academic reader. We are working to expand the audience for serious literature." Publishes hardcover and trade paperback originals. **Publishes 12-16 titles/year. Receives 500 queries and 1,000 mss/year. 10% of books from first-time authors; most from unagented writers. Pays 10-15% royalty on retail price or makes**

outright purchase of $250-1,500. Offers $0-2,000 advance. Publishes book 1-2 years after acceptance of ms. Accepts simultaneous submissions. Reports in 1 month on queries, 3 months on mss. Book catalog free. Manuscript guidelines for #10 SASE.

- See the Contests & Awards section for details on the Nicholas Roerich Poetry Prize.

Nonfiction: Literary. Subjects include authors/literature. Query with SASE.
Fiction: Literary, no popular genres. "We currently have a backlist through the year 2000. Please send query letter first." Query with SASE.
Poetry: "Backlist for publication is through the year 2000.
Recent Title(s): *Oh Jackie*, by Mandy Benz (fiction); *The Muse Strikes Back* (poetry anthology).
Tips: "We strongly recommend that first-time poetry authors submit their book-length manuscript in the Nicholas Roerich Poetry Contest."

STYLUS PUBLISHING, LLC, 22883 Quicksilver Dr., Sterling VA 20166. **Acquisitions:** John von Knorring, publisher. Stylus specializes in trade and academic titles. Publishes hardcover and trade paperback originals. **Publishes 6-10 titles/year. Receives 20 queries and 6 mss/year. 50% of books from first-time authors; 100% from unagented writers. Pays 5-10% royalty on wholesale price.** Publishes book 6 months after acceptance of ms. Reports in 1 month. Book catalog and ms guidelines free.
Nonfiction: Subjects include business and training, education. Query or submit outline, 1 sample chapter with SASE. Reviews artwork/photos as part of ms package. Send photocopies.
Recent Title(s): *Using Presentations in Training and Development*, by Leslie Rae.

SUCCESS PUBLISHERS, One Oakglade Circle, Hummelstown PA 17036-9525. (717)566-0468. Fax: (717)566-6423. **Acquisitions:** Mike Markowski, president (Aviation Publishers); Marjorie L. Markowski, editor-in-chief (Success Publishers). Estab. 1981. "Our mission is to help the people of the world grow and become the best they can be, through the written and spoken word. We strive to make a difference in people's lives and make the world a better place to live." Publishes trade paperback originals. **Publishes 10 titles/year. Receives 1,000 submissions/year. 90% of books from first-time authors; 100% from unagented writers. Royalties vary.** Publishes book 1 year or less after acceptance. Reports in 2 months. Manuscript guidelines for #10 SAE and 2 first-class stamps.
Imprint(s): Aviation Publishers, Health Publishers, **Success Publishers.**
Nonfiction: How-to, self-help. Subjects include business, current significant events, pop-psychology, success/motivation, inspiration, entrepreneurship, sales marketing, network marketing and homebased business topics, and human interest success stories.
Recent Title(s): *Reject Me—I Love It!*, by John Furhman.
Tips: "Our focus is on creating and publishing bestsellers written by authors who speak and consult. We're looking for authors who are serious about making a difference in the world."

SUCCESS PUBLISHING, 3419 Dunham Rd., Warsaw NY 14569-9735. (716)786-5663. President: Allan H. Smith. **Acquisitions:** Robin Garretson, submission manager. Estab. 1982. Publishes trade paperback originals. **Publishes 6 titles/year. Receives 200 submissions/year. 75% of books from first-time authors; 100% from unagented writers. Pays 7% royalty.** Publishes book 3 months after acceptance. Accepts simultaneous submissions. Reports in 2 months on queries. Book catalog and ms guidelines for #10 SAE with 2 first-class stamps.

- Success Publishing is looking for ghostwriters.

Nonfiction: How-to, humor, self-help. Subjects include business/economics, hobbies, money/finance. "We are looking for books on how-to subjects such as home business and sewing." Query.
Recent Title(s): *50 Ways to Find a Date/Mate*, by Herbison.
Tips: "Our audience is made up of housewives, hobbyists and owners of home-based businesses."

THE SUMMIT PUBLISHING GROUP, 2000 E. Lamar Blvd., Suite 600, Arlington TX 76006. (817)588-3013. **Acquisitions:** Jill Bertolet, publisher. Summit Publishing Group seeks contemporary books with a nationwide appeal. Publishes hardcover originals, trade paperback originals and reprints. **Publishes 35 titles/year. 40% of books from first-time authors; 80% from unagented writers. Pays 5-20% royalty on wholesale price. Offers $2,000 and up advance.** Publishes book 6 months after acceptance of ms. Accepts simultaneous submissions. Reports in 1 month on queries and proposals, 3 months on mss.
Imprints: Legacy Books (corporate private label organizational publications).
Nonfiction: Biography, children's/juvenile, coffee table book, cookbook, gift book, how-to, humor, self-help. Subjects include art/architecture, business/economics, cooking, ethnic, gardening, government/politics, health/medicine, history, hobbies, military/war, money/finance, nature/environment, recreation, regional, religion, science, sociology, sports, women's issues/studies. Submit proposal package including outline, 2 sample chapters, table of contents, proposal marketing letter and résumé with SASE. Reviews artwork/photos as part of ms package. Send photocopies.
Recent Title(s): *Love and War: 250 Years of Wartime Love Letters*, by Susan Besze Wallace (history).
Tips: "Books should have obvious national-distribution appeal, be of a contemporary nature and be marketing-driven: author's media experience and contacts a strong plus."

SUNSTONE PRESS, P.O. Box 2321, Santa Fe NM 87504-2321. (505)988-4418. **Acquisitions:** James C. Smith, Jr., president. Estab. 1971. "Sunstone Press has traditionally focused on Southwestern themes, especially for nonfiction.

However, in the past 18 months, general fiction titles have become very successful nationwide." Publishes paperback and hardcover originals. **Publishes 25 titles/year. Receives 400 submissions/year. 70% of books from first-time authors; 100% from unagented writers. Pays 7½-15% royalty on wholesale price.** Publishes book 18 months after acceptance. Reports in 1 month.

• This publisher's focus is the Southwestern US but it receives many, many submissions outside this subject.

Imprint(s): Sundial Publications.

Nonfiction: How-to series craft books. Books on the history, culture and architecture of the Southwest. "Looks for strong regional appeal (Southwestern)." Query with SASE. Reviews artwork/photos as part of ms package.

Fiction: Publishes material with Southwestern theme. Query with SASE.

Recent Title(s): *Silvio: Congressman for Everyone*, by Peter Lynch; *Goldtown*, by Rita Cleary.

SURREY BOOKS, 230 E. Ohio St., Suite 120, Chicago IL 60611. Fax: (312)751-7334. E-mail: surreybks@aol.com. Website: http://www.surreybooks.com. **Acquisitions:** Susan Schwartz, publisher. "Surrey publishes books for the way we live today." Publishes hardcover and trade paperback originals. **Publishes 10-15 titles/year. Receives 150 queries and 20 mss/year. 5% of books from first-time authors; 80% from unagented writers. Pays 10-15% on wholesale price. Offers $500-5,000 advance.** Publishes book 1 year after acceptance of ms. Accepts simultaneous submissions. Reports in 1 month on queries, 3 months on proposals if interested. Book catalog free.

Nonfiction: Cookbook, how-to, self-help. Subjects include business, child guidance/parenting, cooking/foods/nutrition, gardening, health/medicine, recreation, sports, travel. "Books must be marketable to a distinct audience—not everyone. Don't submit topics we don't publish." Query or proposal package, including sample chapters, outline and marketing ideas. Does not return submissions. *All unsolicited mss returned unopened.*

Recent Title(s): *Simply Casseroles*, by Kim Lila (cooking).

N **SYRACUSE UNIVERSITY PRESS**, 1600 Jamesville Ave., Syracuse NY 13244-5160. (315)443-5534. Fax: (315)443-5545. **Acquisitions:** Robert A. Mandel, director. Estab. 1943. **Averages 80 titles/year. Receives 600-700 submissions/year. 25% of books from first-time authors; 75% from unagented writers. Nonauthor subsidy publishes 20% of books. Pays royalty on net sales.** Publishes book an average of 15 months after acceptance. Simultaneous submissions discouraged. Book catalog and ms guidelines for 9×12 SAE with 3 first-class stamps.

Nonfiction: "Special opportunity in our nonfiction program for freelance writers of books on New York state, sports history, Jewish studies, the Middle East, religious studies, television and popular culture. We have published regional books by people with limited formal education, but authors were thoroughly acquainted with their subjects, and they wrote simply and directly about them. Provide precise descriptions of subjects, along with background description of project. The author must make a case for the importance of his or her subject." Query with outline and at least 2 sample chapters. Reviews artwork/photos as part of ms package.

SYSTEMS CO., INC., P.O. Box 339, Carlsborg WA 98324. (360)683-6860. **Acquisitions:** Richard H. Peetz, Ph.D., president. "We publish succinct and well-organized technical and how-to-do-it books with minimum filler." Publishes hardcover and trade paperback originals. **Publishes 3-5 titles/year. 50% of books from first-time authors; 100% from unagented writers. Pays 20% royalty on wholesale price after costs.** Publishes book 6 months after acceptance of ms. Accepts simultaneous submissions. Reports in 2 months. Book catalog free. Manuscript guidelines for $1.

Nonfiction: How-to, self-help, technical, textbook. Subjects include business/economics, automotive, health/medicine, money/finance, nature/environment, science/engineering. "In submitting nonfiction, writers often make the mistake of picking a common topic with lots of published books in print." Submit outline, 2 sample chapters and SASE. Reviews artwork/photos as part of ms package. Send photocopies.

Recent Title(s): *ABC's of Retiring Early* (how to retire early).

Tips: "Our audience consists of people in technical occupations, people interested in doing things themselves."

A **NAN A. TALESE**, Doubleday, 1540 Broadway, New York NY 10036. (212)782-8918. Fax: (212)782-9261. Website: http://www.bdd.com. **Acquisitions:** Nan A. Talese, editorial director. "Nan A. Talese publishes nonfiction with a powerful guiding narrative and relevance to larger cultural trends and interests, and literary fiction of the highest quality." Publishes hardcover originals. **Publishes 15 titles/year. Receives 400 queries and mss/year. Pays variable royalty on retail price. Advance varies.** Publishes book 8 months after acceptance of ms. Accepts simultaneous submissions. Reports in 1 week on queries, 1 month on proposals and mss.

Nonfiction: Biography, gift book, select. Subjects include art/architecture, history, philosophy, current trends. *Agented submissions only.*

Fiction: Literary. "We're interested in everything literary. No genre fiction or low-market stuff." *Agented submissions only.*

Recent Title(s): *The Gifts of the Jews*, by Thomas Cahill (history); *Enduring Love*, by Ian McEwan (novel).

Tips: "Audience is highly literate people interested in literary books. We want well-written material."

JEREMY P. TARCHER, INC., Penguin Putnam, Inc., 375 Hudson St., New York NY 10014. (212)414-3610. E-mail: jptarcher@aol.com. Website: http://www.penguin.com. Publisher: Joel Fotinos. **Acquisitions**: Mitch Hoffman, senior editor; Wendy Hubbert, editor; David Groff, associate editor; Joel Fotinos, publisher (nonfiction). "Although Tarcher is not a religion imprint per se, Jeremy Tarcher's vision was to publish ideas and works about human consciousness that were large enough to include matters of spirit and religion." Publishes hardcover and trade paperback originals and reprints. **Publishes 30-40 titles/year. Receives 500 queries and 500 mss/year. 10% of books from first-time authors; 5% from unagented writers. Pays 5-8% royalty on retail price. Offers advance.** Accepts simultaneous submissions. Reports in 1 month. Book catalog free.

Nonfiction: How-to, self-help. Subjects include business/economics, child guidance/parenting, gay/lesbian, health/medicine, nature/environment, philosophy, psychology, religion, women's issues/studies. Query with SASE.

Recent Title(s): *Sweat Your Prayers*, by Gabrielle Roth (spirituality, psychology).

Tips: "Audience seeks personal growth through books. Understand the imprint's focus and categories. We stick with the tried and true."

TAYLOR PUBLISHING COMPANY, 1550 W. Mockingbird Lane, Dallas TX 75235. (214)819-8560. Fax: (214)819-8580. Website: http://www.taylorpub.com. President: Maurice Dake. Publisher/Editorial Director: Lynn Brooks. **Acquisitions:** Editorial Department, Trade Books Division. Estab. 1981. "We publish solid, practical books that should backlist well. We look for authors who are expert authors in their field and already have some recognition, i.e., magazine articles, radio appearances or their own show, speaker or educator, etc." Publishes hardcover and softcover originals. **Publishes 35 titles/year. Receives 1,500 submissions/year. 5% of books from first-time authors; 25% from unagented writers.** Publishes book 1-2 years after acceptance. Accepts simultaneous submissions. Reports in 2 months. Book catalog and ms guidelines for 10×13 SASE.

• Taylor Publishing is no longer seeking true crime, cookbooks, humor, self-help, trivia or business.

Nonfiction: Gardening, sports, popular culture, parenting, health, home improvement, how-to, popular history, spiritual/inspiration, celebrity biography, miscellaneous nonfiction. Submit outline, sample chapter, an overview of the market and competition and an author bio as it pertains to proposed subject matter. Reviews artwork as part of ms package.

Recent Title(s): *The Organic Rose Garden*, by Liz Druitt (gardening).

TEACHERS COLLEGE PRESS, 1234 Amsterdam Ave., New York NY 10027. (212)678-3929. Fax: (212)678-4149. Website: http://www.tc.columbia.edu/tcpress. Director: Carole P. Saltz. **Acquisitions:** Brian Ellerbeck, executive acquisitions editor. Estab. 1904. Teachers College Press publishes a wide range of educational titles for all levels of students: early childhood to higher education. "Publishing books that respond to, examine and confront issues pertaining to education, teacher training and school reform." Publishes hardcover and paperback originals and reprints. **Publishes 40 titles/year. Pays industry standard royalty.** Publishes book 1 year after acceptance. Reports in 2 months. Catalog free.

Nonfiction: "This university press concentrates on books in the field of education in the broadest sense, from early childhood to higher education: good classroom practices, teacher training, special education, innovative trends and issues, administration and supervision, film, continuing and adult education, all areas of the curriculum, computers, guidance and counseling and the politics, economics, philosophy, sociology and history of education. We have recently added women's studies to our list. The Press also issues classroom materials for students at all levels, with a strong emphasis on reading and writing and social studies." Submit outline and sample chapters.

Recent Title(s): *How Schools Might Be Governed and Why*, by Seymour Sarason.

N **TEACHING & LEARNING COMPANY**, 1204 Buchanan St., P.O. Box 10, Carthage IL 62321-0010. (217)357-2591. Fax: (217)357-6789. E-mail: tandlcom@adams.net. Website: http://www.teachinglearning.com. **Acquisitions:** Jill Eckhardt, managing editor. Teaching & Learning Company publishes teacher resources (supplementary activity/idea books) for grades pre K-8. **Publishes 60 titles/year. Receives 25 queries and 200 mss/year. 25% of books from first-time authors; 98% from unagented writers. Pays royalty.** Accepts simultaneous submissions. Reports in 3 months on queries, 9 months on proposals and mss. Book catalog and ms guidelines free.

Nonfiction: Subjects include teacher resources: language arts, reading, math, science, social studies, arts and crafts, responsibility education. No picture books or storybooks. Submit table of contents, introduction, 3 sample chapters with SASE. Reviews artwork/photos as part of ms package. Send photocopies.

Recent Title(s): *Listen Up! MATH*, by Ann Richmond Fisher (language arts/math).

Tips: "Our books are for teachers and parents of pre K-8th grade children."

TEMPLE UNIVERSITY PRESS, USB, 1601 N. Broad St., Philadelphia PA 19122-6099. (215)204-8787. Fax: (215)204-4719. E-mail: tempress@astro.ocis.temple.edu. Website: http://www.temple.edu. **Acquisitions:** Michael Ames, consulting editor; Janet Francendese, editor-in-chief; Doris Braendel, senior acquisitions editor. "Temple University Press has been publishing useful books on Asian-Americans, law, gender issues, film, women's studies and other interesting areas for nearly 30 years for the goal of social change." **Publishes 60 titles/year. Pays royalty of up to 10% on wholesale price.** Publishes book 10 months after acceptance. Reports in 2 months. Book catalog free.

Nonfiction: American history, sociology, women's studies, health care, ethics, labor studies, photography, urban studies, law, Latin American studies, African-American studies, Asian-American studies, public policy and regional (Philadelphia area). "No memoirs, fiction or poetry." Uses *Chicago Manual of Style*. Reviews artwork/photos. Query.

Recent Title(s): *Workin' It*, by Leon Pettiway (women's studies).

TEN SPEED PRESS, P.O. Box 7123, Berkeley CA 94707. (510)559-1600. Fax: (510)524-1052. E-mail: info@tenspeed.com. Publisher: Kirsty Melville. **Acquisitions:** Address submissions to "Acquisitions Department." Estab. 1971. Ten Speed Press publishes authoritative books with a long shelf life for an audience interested in innovative, proven ideas. Publishes trade paperback originals and reprints. **Firm publishes 100 titles/year; imprint averages 70 titles/year. 25%**

of books from first-time authors; 50% from unagented writers. Pays 8-12% royalty on retail price. Offers $2,500 average advance. Publishes book 1 year after acceptance. Accepts simultaneous submissions. Reports in 3 months on queries. Book catalog for 9×12 SAE with 6 first-class stamps. Manuscript guidelines for #10 SASE.

Imprint(s): Celestial Arts, Tricycle Press.

Nonfiction: Cookbook, how-to, reference, self-help. Subjects include business and career, child guidance/parenting, cooking/foods/nutrition, gardening, health/medicine, money/finance, nature/environment, recreation, science. "We mainly publish innovative how-to books. We are always looking for cookbooks from proven, tested sources—successful restaurants, etc. *Not* 'Grandma's favorite recipes.' Books about the 'new science' interest us. No biographies or autobiographies, first-person travel narratives, fiction or humorous treatments of just about anything." Query or submit outline and sample chapters.

Recent Title(s): *The Joy of Not Working*, by Ernie Zelinski.

Tips: "We like books from people who really know their subject, rather than people who think they've spotted a trend to capitalize on. We like books that will sell for a long time, rather than nine-day wonders. Our audience consists of a well-educated, slightly weird group of people who like food, the outdoors and take a light but serious approach to business and careers. If I were a writer trying to market a book today, I would study the backlist of each publisher I was submitting to and tailor my proposal to what I perceive as their needs. Nothing gets a publisher's attention like someone who knows what he or she is talking about, and nothing falls flat like someone who obviously has no idea who he or she is submitting to."

TEXAS A&M UNIVERSITY PRESS, College Station TX 77843-4354. (409)845-1436. Fax: (409)847-8752. E-mail: fdl@tampress.tamu.edu. Website: http://www.tamu.edu/upress. **Acquisitions:** Noel Parsons, editor-in-chief (military, eastern Europe, natural history, agriculture, nautical archeaology); Mary Lenn Dixon, managing editor (political science, presidential studies, anthropology, borderlands, western history); Dennis Lynch, associate editor (nautical archaeology). Estab. 1974. Texas A&M University Press publishes a wide range of nonfiction of regional and national interest. **Publishes 40 titles/year. Nonauthor-subsidy publishes 25% of books. Pays in royalties.** Publishes book 1 year after acceptance. Reports in 1month. *Writer's Market* recommends allowing 2 months for reply. Book catalog free.

Nonfiction: "Texas A&M University Press's editorial program consists of books on Texas and the Southwest, military studies, American and western history, Texas and western literature, Mexican-U.S. borderlands studies, nautical archaeology, women's studies, ethnic studies, natural history, the environment, presidential studies, economics, business history, architecture, Texas and western art and photography, and veterinary medicine." Query.

Recent Title(s): *Now Hiring: The Feminization of Work in the United States, 1900-1995*, by Julia Kirk Blackwelder (American history, women's history).

Tips: New publishing fields of Eastern European studies, US-Mexican borderlands studies and agriculture.

TEXAS CHRISTIAN UNIVERSITY PRESS, P.O. Box 298300, TCU, Fort Worth TX 76129. (817)257-7822. Fax: (817)257-7333. **Acquisitions:** Tracy Row, editor. Judy Alter, director (fiction). Estab. 1966. Texas Christian publishes "scholarly monographs, other serious scholarly work and regional titles of significance focusing on the history and literature of the American West." Publishes hardcover originals, some reprints. **Publishes 12 titles/year. Receives 100 submissions/year. 10% of books from first-time authors; 75% from unagented writers. Nonauthor-subsidy publishes 10% of books. Pays 10% royalty on net price.** Publishes book 16 months after acceptance. Reports in 3 months on queries.

Nonfiction: American studies, literature and criticism. Query. Reviews artwork/photos as part of ms package.

Fiction: Regional fiction, by invitation only. *Please do not query.*

Recent Title(s): *The Trinity River: Photographs*, by Luther Smith; *Tales from the Sunday House*, by Minetta Altgelt Goyne (history).

Tips: "Regional and/or Texana nonfiction has best chance of breaking into our firm."

TEXAS STATE HISTORICAL ASSOCIATION, 2.306 Richardson Hall, University Station, Austin TX 78712. (512)471-1525. **Acquisitions:** George B. Ward, assistant director. "We are interested in scholarly historical articles and books on any aspect of Texas history." Publishes hardcover and trade paperback originals and reprints. **Publishes 8 titles/year. Receives 50 queries and 50 mss/year. 10% of books from first-time authors; 95% from unagented writers. Pays 10% royalty on net cash proceeds.** Publishes book 1 year after acceptance. Reports in 2 months on mss. Catalog and ms guidelines free.

Nonfiction: Biography, coffee table book, illustrated book, reference. Historical subjects. Query. Reviews artwork/photos as part of ms package. Send photocopies.

Recent Title(s): *El Llano Estacado: Exploration and Imagination on the High Plains of Texas and New Mexico, 1536-1860*, by John Miller Morris (history).

N **THIRD WORLD PRESS**, P.O. Box 19730, Chicago IL 60619. (773)651-0700. Fax: (773)651-7286. Publisher: Haki R. Madhubuti. **Acquisitions:** Gwendolyn Mitchell, editor. Publishes hardcover and trade paperback originals and reprints. **Publishes 20 titles/year. Receives 200-300 queries and 200 mss/year. 20% of books from first-time authors; 80% from unagented writers. Pays 7% royalty on retail price.** Publishes book 18 months after acceptance of ms. Accepts simultaneous submissions. Reports in 6 months. Book catalog and ms guidelines free.

- Third World Press is open to submissions in January and July only.

Nonfiction: African-centered and African-American materials: illustrated book, children's/juvenile, reference, self-

help, textbook. Subjects include anthropology/archaeology, Black studies, education, ethnic, government/politics, health/medicine, history, language/literature, literary criticism, philosophy, psychology, regional, religion, sociology, women's issues/studies. Query with outline and 5 sample chapters. Reviews artwork as part of ms package. Send photocopies.
Fiction: African-centered and African American materials: Ethnic, feminist, historical, juvenile, literary, mainstream/contemporary, picture books, plays, short story collections, young adult. Query with synopsis and 5 sample chapters.
Poetry: African-centered and African-American materials. Submit complete ms.
Recent Title(s): *Intellectual Warfare*, by Jacob Carruthers (social science); *Arolantica Legacies*, by Derrick Bell.

N **THUNDER BAY PRESS**, Advantage Publishers Group, 5880 Oberlin Dr., San Diego CA 92121. (619)457-2500. **Acquisitions**: JoAnn Padgett, managing editor. "Thunder Bay publishes highly illustrated, well-written, creatively designed books in subject areas of high-demand, strong marketability or historical precedent." Publishes hardcover and trade paperback originals and reprints. **Publishes 60 titles/year. Receives 175 queries and 75 mss/year. Pays 10-15% royalty on wholesale price or makes outright purchase on a project basis. Offers $1,000 advance.** Publishes book 1 year after acceptance of ms. Accepts simultaneous submissions. Reports in 1 month on queries, 4 months on proposals, 6 months on mss. Book catalog for $1 and 9×12 SAE with 5 first-class stamps. Manuscript guidelines for #10 SASE.
Nonfiction: Publishes highly illustrated books. Subjects include art/architecture, automobiles, cooking, history, home decorating, nature. Submit cover letter, outline, table of contents, sample chapters or complete ms, estimated length or word count, author bio or résumé and marketing information, including a clear statement of the work's purpose, target audience and comparison with competition. Include SASE with sufficient postage for return of materials. Reviews artwork/photos as part of ms package. Send transparencies.
Recent Title(s): *Customizing Your Harley-Davidson*, by Patrick Hook.
Tips: "Try to present a unique topic or a topic treated from a unique angle."

THUNDER'S MOUTH PRESS, Avalon Publishing Group, 841 Broadway, 4th Floor, New York NY 10003. (212)614-7880. Publisher: Neil Ortenberg. **Acquisitions:** (Ms.) Jeri T. Smith, acquisitions editor. Estab. 1982. Publishes hardcover and trade paperback originals and reprints, almost exclusively nonfiction. **Publishes 70-80 titles/year. Receives 1,000 submissions/year. 15% of books from unagented writers. Pays 7-10% royalty on retail price. Offers $15,000 average advance.** Publishes book 8 months after acceptance. Reports in 2 months on queries.
Nonfiction: Biography, politics, popular culture. Query with SASE. *No unsolicited mss.*
Recent Title(s): *Sweet Swing Blues*, by Wynton Marsalis.

TIARE PUBLICATIONS, P.O. Box 493, Lake Geneva WI 53147-0493. Fax: (414)249-0299. E-mail: info@tiare.com. Website: http://www.tiare.com. **Acquisitions:** Gerry L. Dexter, president. Estab. 1986. "Tiare Publications specializes in books for radio communications hobbyists." Publishes trade paperback originals. **Publishes 6-12 titles/year. Receives 25 queries and 10 mss/year. 40% of books from first-time authors; 100% from unagented writers. Pays 15% royalty on retail/wholesale price.** Publishes book 3 months after acceptance. Reports in 1 month on queries. *Writer's Market* recommends allowing 2 months for reply. Book catalog for $1.
Imprint(s): Limelight Books, Balboa Books.
Nonfiction: Technical, general nonfiction, mostly how-to, (Limelight); jazz/big bands (Balboa). Query.
Recent Title(s): *Stan Kenton: The Studio Sessions*, by Michael Sparke.

TIDE-MARK PRESS, P.O. Box 280311, East Hartford CT 06128-0311. (860)289-0363. Fax: (860)289-3654. **Book Acquisitions:** Carol Berto, editor; Trish Reynolds, editor (calendars). "Focus is on illustrations and text about journeys of discovery into the natural world." Publishes hardcover originals. **Publishes 2-3 titles/year and 44 calendars. Receives 50-100 queries/year. 50% of books from first-time authors; most from unagented writers. Pays 10% on net sales. Advances vary with projects.** Publishes book 18 months after acceptance of ms. Reports in 1 month.
Nonfiction: Coffee table book, gift book, calendars. "The explorer/illustrator can be a scientist with a camera, a perceptive traveler, or someone thoroughly grounded in a particular landscape or region." Reviews artwork/photos as part of the ms package. Call for proposal guidelines.
Recent Title(s): *Beneath the North Atlantic*, by Jonathan Bird (marine biology).

TIDEWATER PUBLISHERS, Cornell Maritime Press, Inc., P.O. Box 456, Centreville MD 21617-0456. (410)758-1075. Fax: (410)758-6849. **Acquisitions:** Charlotte Kurst, managing editor. Estab. 1938. "Tidewater Publishers issues adult nonfiction works related to the Chesapeake Bay area, Delmarva or Maryland in general. The only fiction we handle is juvenile and must have a regional focus." Publishes hardcover and paperback originals. **Publishes 7-9 titles/year. Receives 150 submissions/year. 41% of books from first-time authors; 99% from unagented writers. Pays 7½-15% royalty on retail price.** Publishes book 1 year after acceptance. Reports in 2 months. Book catalog for 10×13 SAE with 5 first-class stamps.
Nonfiction: Cookbook, history, illustrated book, juvenile, reference. Regional subjects only. Query or submit outline and sample chapters. Reviews artwork/photos as part of ms package.
Fiction: Regional juvenile fiction only. Query or submit outline/synopsis and sample chapters.
Recent Title(s): *From Colts to Ravens: A Behind-the-Scenes Look at Baltimore Professional Football*; *Sam: The Tale of a Chesapeake Rockfish*, by Kristina Henry, illustrated by Jeff Dombek.
Tips: "Our audience is made up of readers interested in works that are specific to the Chesapeake Bay and Delmarva Peninsula area."

TIMES BOOKS, Random House, Inc., 201 E. 50th St., New York NY 10022. (212)751-2600. Website: www.randomhouse.com. Vice President/Publisher: Peter Bernstein. Vice President/Associate Publisher: Carie Freimuth. **Acquisitions**: Elizabeth Rapoport (health, family, education); Karl Weber (business); John Mahaney (business); Geoffrey Shandler (current events, history); Stanley Newman (crossword puzzles); Tracy Smith (technology, business). "Times Books is noted for its books on current affairs and political commentary, as well as a popular line of puzzles and games." Publishes hardcover and paperback originals and reprints. **Publishes 50-60 titles/year. Pays royalty. Offers average advance.** Publishes book 1 year after acceptance. *Writer's Market* recommends allowing 2 months for reply.
Nonfiction: Business/economics, science and medicine, history, biography, women's issues, the family, cookbooks, current affairs. Query. Solicited mss only. Reviews artwork/photos as part of ms package.
Recent Title(s): *Living Faith*, by Jimmy Carter (inspiration).

TIMES BUSINESS, Random House, Inc., 201 E. 50th St., New York NY 10022. (212)572-8104, 751-2600. Fax: (212)572-4949. Website: http://www.randomhouse.com. **Acquisitions:** John Mahaney, executive editor. Estab. 1995. Publishes hardcover and trade paperback originals. **Publishes 20-25 titles/year. 50% of books from first-time authors; 15% from unagented writers. Pays negotiable royalty on list price; hardcover on invoice price. Advance negotiable.** Publishes book 9 months after acceptance of ms. Accepts simultaneous submissions. Reports in 1 month on proposals. Book catalog free from Random House (same address). Manuscript guidelines for #10 SASE.
Nonfiction: Subjects include business/economic, money/finance, management, technology and business. Query with proposal package including outline, 1-2 sample chapters, market analysis and SASE.
Recent Title(s): *Profit Zone*, by Adrian Zlywotzky and David Morrison.

TOR BOOKS, Tom Doherty Associates, Inc., St. Martin's Press, 175 Fifth Ave., New York NY 10010. **Acquisitions**: Patrick Nielsen Hayden, senior editor; Melissa Singer (Forge Books). "TOR Books publishes what is arguably the largest and most diverse line of science fiction and fantasy ever produced by a single English-language publisher." Publishes hardcover originals and trade and mass market paperback originals and reprints. **Publishes 150-200 books/year. 2-3% of books from first-time authors; 3-5% from unagented writers. Pays royalty on retail price.** Publishes book 1-2 years after acceptance. No simultaneous submissions. "No queries please." Reports in 2-6 months on proposals and mss. Book catalog for 9×12 SAE with 2 first-class stamps; ms guidelines for SASE.
Fiction: Adventure, fantasy, historical, horror, science fiction. Submit synopsis and 3 sample chapters.
Recent Title(s): *A Crown of Swords*, by Robert Jordan (fantasy).
Tips: "We're never short of good sci-fi or fantasy, but we're always open to solid, technologically knowledgeable hard science fiction or thrillers by writers with solid expertise."

[N] TORAH AURA PRODUCTIONS, 4423 Fruitland Ave., Los Angeles CA 90058. (213)585-7312. Website: http://www.torahaura.com. **Acquisitions**: Jane Golub. "We publish mostly educational materials for Jewish classrooms." Publishes hardcover and trade paperback originals. **Publishes 25 titles/year. Imprint publishes 10 titles/year. Receives 5 queries and 10 mss/year. 2% of books from first-time authors; 100% from unagented writers. Pays 10% royalty on wholesale price.** Publishes book 3 years after acceptance of ms. Accepts simultaneous submissions. Reports in 6 months on mss. Book catalog free.
Imprint(s): Alef Design Group.
Nonfiction: Children's/juvenile, textbook. Subjects include language/literature (Hebrew), religion (Jewish). Query with SASE. Reviews artwork/photos as part of ms package. Send photocopies.
Fiction: Juvenile, picture books, religious, young adult. All fiction must have Jewish interest. Query with SASE.
Recent Title(s): *The Alef Parent Folders*; *Kindergarten: The Gan Curriculum.*

[N] TOTEM BOOKS, Icon Books PLC, P.O. Box 223, Canal St., Station, New York NY 10013. (212)431-9368. Fax: (212)966-5768. E-mail: totem@theliteraryagency.com. **Acquisitions**: Richard Appignanesi, editorial director (nonfiction, psychology, philosophy); Duncan Heath, executive editor (science, music, language). Totem Books publishes graphic study guides for high school and junior college students. Publishes trade paperback originals. **Publishes 12 titles/year. Receives 10 queries and 2 mss/year. 30% of books from first-time authors; 75% from unagented writers. Pays 4% royalty on retail price.** Publishes book 15 months after acceptance of ms. Reports in 2 months on queries. Book catalog free.
Imprint(s): The Introducing Series.
Nonfiction: Biography, reference, graphic study guides. Subjects include anthropology, language/literature, music, philosophy, psychology, religion, science, sociology, women's issues/studies. Query with SASE.
Recent Title(s): *Introducing Cultural Studies* (high school/junior college graphic study guide).
Tips: "Study our books and recognize that we only publish collaborations of author and illustrator."

TOTLINE PUBLICATIONS, Frank Schaffer Publications, Inc., P.O. Box 2250, Everett WA 98203-0250. (206)353-3100. E-mail: totline@gte.net. **Acquisitions:** Kathleen Cubley, managing editor (book mss); Submissions Editor (single activity ideas). Estab. 1975. "All the products we publish must be educationally and developmentally appropriate for 2-, 3-5-, or 6-year-olds." Publishes educational activity books and parenting books for teachers and parents of 2-6-year-olds. **Publishes 50-60 titles/year. 100% from unagented writers. Makes outright purchase plus copies of book/newsletter author's material appears in.** Book catalog and ms guidelines free on written request.
Nonfiction: Illustrated activity books for parents and teachers of 2-6-year-olds. Subjects include animals, art, child

guidance/parenting, cooking with kids, foods and nutrition, education, ethnic, gardening, hobbies, language/literature, music, nature/environment, science. Considers activity book and single activity submissions from early childhood education professionals. Considers parenting activity mss from parenting experts. Query with SASE. No children's storybooks, fiction or poetry.
Recent Title(s): *Multisensory Theme-A-Saurus*, edited by Gayle Bittinger.
Tips: "Our audience is teachers and parents who work with children ages 2-6. Write for submission requirements. We are especially interested in parent-child activities for 0- to 3-year-olds and teacher-child activities for toddler groups."

TOWER PUBLISHING, 588 Saco Rd., Standish ME 04084. (207)642-5400. Fax: (207)642-5463. E-mail: tower@ime.net. Website: http://www.towerdata.com. **Acquisitions:** Michael Lyons, president. Estab. 1972. "Tower Publishing has proven itself to be one of the most comprehensive business information resources available." They specialize in business and professional directories. Publishes hardcover originals and reprints, trade paperback originals. **Publishes 15 titles/year. Receives 60 queries and 30 mss/year. 10% of books from first-time authors; 90% from unagented writers. Pays royalty on net receipts. No advance.** Publishes book 6 months after acceptance of ms. Accepts simultaneous submissions. Reports in 1 month on queries, 2 months on proposals and mss. Book catalog and guidelines free.
Nonfiction: Reference. Subjects include business/economics. Looking for legal books of a national stature. Query with outline.

TRAFALGAR SQUARE PUBLISHING, P.O. Box 257, N. Pomfret VT 05053-0257. (802)457-1911.Fax: (802)457-1913. E-mail: tsquare@sover.net. Publisher: Caroline Robbins. **Acquisitions:** Martha Cook, managing editor. "We publish high quality instructional books for horsemen and horsewomen, always with the horse's welfare in mind." Publishes hardcover and trade paperback originals and reprints. **Publishes 8 titles/year. Pays royalty.** Reports in 1 month on queries and proposals, 2 months on mss.
Nonfiction: Books about horses. "We publish books for intermediate to advanced riders and horsemen. No stories, children's books or horse biographies." Query with proposal package, including outline, 1-2 sample chapters, letter of writer's qualifications and audience for book's subject.
Recent Title(s): *For the Good of the Horse*, Mary Wanless (alternative horse care).

N **TRANS-ATLANTIC PUBLICATIONS, INC.**, 311 Bainbridge St., Philadelphia PA 19147. Fax: (215)925-7412. E-mail: rsmolin@lx.netcom. com. Website: http://www.transatlanticpub.com. **Acquisitions**: Ron Smolin. Trans-Atlantic publishes a wide variety of nonfiction and fiction and distributes a wide variety of business books published in England. Publishes hardcover, trade paperback and mass market paperback originals. **Publishes 100 titles/year. Imprint publishes 20 titles/year. Receives 100 queries and 100 mss/year. 15% of books from first-time authors; 20% from unagented writers. Pays 7½-12% royalty on retail price. Offers $2,500-10,000 advance.** Publishes book 11 months after acceptance of ms. Accepts simultaneous submissions.
Imprint(s): Bainbridge Books.
Nonfiction: Biography, coffee table book, illustrated book, reference. Subjects include animals, art/architecture, nutrition, creative nonfiction, gay/lesbian, government/politics, health/medicine, history, nature/environment, philosophy, photography, science, sex, sociology, sports. Query with SASE. Reviews artwork/photos as part of ms package. Send photocopies.
Fiction: Adventure, experimental, humor, literary, mainstream/contemporary, mystery, plays, science fiction, suspense, young adult. Query with 2 sample chapters and SASE.
Recent Title(s): *Bella Mafia*, by La Plante (mystery); *Food Combining 2-Day Detox*, by Marsden (diet and nutrition).

TRANSNATIONAL PUBLISHERS, INC., 411 Saw Mill River Rd., Ardsley NY 10502. (914)693-5100. Fax: (914)693-4430. E-mail: transbooks@aol.com. Editor: Maria Angelini. **Acquisitions**: Adriana Maida, acquisitions editor. "We provide specialized publications for the teaching of law and law-related subjects in law school classroom, clinic and continuing legal education settings." Publishes hardcover and trade paperback originals. **Publishes 15-20 titles/year. Receives 40-50 queries and 30 mss/year. 60% of books from first-time authors; 95% from unagented writers. Pays 15% royalty of net revenue. Offers no advance.** Publishes book 9 months after acceptance of ms. Accepts simultaneous submissions. Reports in 1 month. Book catalog and ms guidelines free.
Imprint(s): Bridge Street Books.
Nonfiction: Reference, technical, textbook. Subjects include business/economics, government/politics, women's issues/studies. Query or submit proposal package, including table of contents, introduction, sample chapter with SASE.
Recent Title(s): *International Commercial Arbitration*, by Jack Coe.

TREASURE LEARNING SYSTEMS, Treasure Publishing, 1133 Riverside St., Fort Collins CO 80524. (970)484-8483. Fax: (970)495-6700. E-mail: treasure@webaccess.net. Website: http://www.treasurepub.com. **Acquisitions**: Mark A. Steiner, senior editor. "Treasure Learning Systems exists to help the Church fulfill the Great Commission. We create and distribute Christian education resources which feature excellence in biblical content, educational methodology and product presentation. Our primary responsibility is to serve the local and international Church." Publishes hardcover originals. **Publishes 4 titles/year. Receives 150 queries and 150 mss/year. 50% of books from first-time authors; 80% from unagented writers. Pays royalty on retail price or makes outright purchase. Offers $5,000 advance.** Publishes book 6 months after acceptance of ms. Accepts simultaneous submissions. Reports in 1 month on queries and mss, 2 months on proposals. Book catalog and ms guidelines free.

Nonfiction: Children's/juvenile, illustrated book. Subjects include education, Bible stories. All books are Christian oriented. "No novels or shallow content." Query with SASE. Reviews artwork/photos. Send photocopies.
Poetry: Must be Christian oriented.
Recent Title(s): *Discipleland* (elementary Bible study).

TRICYCLE PRESS, Ten Speed Press, P.O. Box 7123, Berkeley CA 94707. (510)559-1600. Fax: (510)524-1052. **Acquisitions:** Nicole Geiger, managing editor/acquisitions editor. "Tricycle Press looks for something outside the mainstream; books that encourage children to look at the world from a possibly alternative angle." Publishes hardcover and trade paperback originals. **Publishes 10-12 titles/year. 20% of books from first-time authors; 60% from unagented authors. Pays 15% royalty on wholesale price (lower if book is illustrated). Offers $0-9,000 advance.** Publishes book 1 year after acceptance of ms. Accepts simultaneous submissions. Reports in 3 months on queries. Book catalog for 9×12 SAE and $1.01 in postage; ms guidelines for #10 SASE; or one large envelope for both.
Nonfiction: Children's/juvenile, how-to, self-help, picture books, activity books. Subjects include art/architecture, gardening, health/medicine, nature/environment, science, geography. Submit complete ms for activity books; 2-3 chapters or 20 pages for others. Reviews artwork/photos as part of ms package. Send photocopies.
Fiction: Picture books. Submit complete ms for picture books. Query with synopsis and SASE for all others.
Recent Title(s): *Raptors, Fossils, Fins & Fangs*, by Ray Troll and Brad Matsen (science/natural history); *Toes Are To Tickle*, by Shen Roddie and Katie MacDonald-Denton.

TRILOGY BOOKS, 50 S. DeLacey Ave., Suite 201, Pasadena CA 91105. (626)440-0669. Fax: (626)585-9441. E-mail: 72274,44@compuserve.com. **Acquisitions:** Marge Wood, publisher. "We publish women's studies, self-help and psychology that have both mainstream and scholarly appeal." Publishes trade paperback originals. **Publishes 4 titles/year. Pays 10% royalty on net revenues. Advance varies.** Publishes book 1 year after acceptance of ms. Accepts simultaneous submissions. Reports in 1 month on queries. Book catalog and ms guidelines free.
Nonfiction: Subjects include women's history, women's issues/studies, self-help, psychology. Query.
Recent Title(s): *Beauty Bites Beast: Awakening the Warrior in Women and Girls*, by Ellen Snortland

N **TRINITY PRESS INTERNATIONAL**, The Morehouse Group, P.O. Box 1321, Harrisburg PA 17105. **Acquisitions:** Harold Rast, publisher. "Trinity Press International is an ecumenical publisher of serious books on theology and the Bible for the religious academic community, religious professionals, and serious book readers." Publishes trade paperback originals and reprints. **Publishes 40 titles/year. Pays 10% royalty on wholesale price.** Publishes book 6 months after acceptance of ms. Accepts simultaneous submissions. Book catalog free.
Nonfiction: Textbook, Christian/theological studies. Subjects include history (as relates to the Bible), translation (biblical/Christian texts). Submit outline and 1 sample chapter.
Recent Title(s): *Seeing Through the Media*, by Michael Warren.

N **TROITSA BOOKS**, Kroshka Books, 6080 Jericho Turnpike, Suite 207, Commack NY 11725-2808. (516)499-3103. Fax: (516)499-3146. E-mail: novascience@earthlink.net. **Acquisitions**: Frank Columbus, editor-in-chief; Nadya Columbus, editor. "This imprint is devoted to all aspects of Christianity." Publishes hardcover and paperback originals. Publishes book up to 1 year after acceptance of ms. Accepts simultaneous submissions. Reports in 1 month.
Nonfiction: Christianity. Subjects include biography, history, inspirational, sermons, prayer books, memoirs. Query with SASE. Reviews artwork/photos as part of ms package. Send photocopies.
Recent Title(s): *In His Own Words: The Beliefs and Teachings of Jesus*, by Albert Kirby Griffin.

TSR, INC., Wizards of the Coast, P.O. Box 707, Renton WA 98057-0707. (425)226-6500. Estab. 1975. Executive Editor: Mary Kirchoff. **Acquisitions:** Novel Submissions Editor. TSR publishes science fiction and fantasy titles. Publishes hardcover and trade paperback originals and trade paperback reprints. **Publishes 40-50 titles/year. Receives 600 queries and 300 mss/year. 10% of books from first-time authors; 20% from unagented authors. Pays 4-8% royalty on retail price. Offers $4,000-6,000 average advance.** Publishes book 1 year after acceptance. Accepts simultaneous submissions. Reports in 2 months on queries. Guidelines for #10 SASE.
Imprint(s): Dragonlance® Books, Forgotten Realms® Books, Magic: The Gathering® Books, Ravenloft® Books, Star*-Drive Books.
Nonfiction: "All of our nonfiction books are generated inhouse."
Fiction: Fantasy, gothic, humor, science fiction short story collections. "We currently publish only work-for-hire novels set in our trademarked worlds. No violent or gory fantasy or science fiction." Request guidelines, then query with outline/synopsis and 3 sample chapters.
Recent Title(s): *The Silent Blade*, by R.H. Salvatore, in *The Forgotten Realms* series.
Tips: "Our audience largely is comprised of highly imaginative 12-40 year-old males."

TURTLE PRESS, S.K. Productions Inc., P.O. Box 290206, Wethersfield CT 06129-0206. (860)529-7770. Fax: (860)529-7775. E-mail: editorial@turtlepress.com. Website: http://www.turtlepress.com. **Acquisitions:** Cynthia Kim, editor. Turtle Press publishes sports and martial arts nonfiction and juvenile fiction for a specialty niche audience. Publishes hardcover originals, trade paperback originals and reprints. **Publishes 4-6 titles/year. Pays 8-10% royalty. Offers $500-1,000 advance.** Reports in 1 month on queries. *Writer's Market* recommends allowing 2 months for reply.
Nonfiction: How-to, martial arts, philosophy, self-help, sports. "We prefer tightly targeted topics on which there is

little or no information available in the market, particularly for our sports and martial arts titles." Query with SASE
Fiction: "We have just begun a line of children's martial arts adventure stories and are very much interested in submissions to expand this line." Query with SASE.
Recent Title(s): *Martial Arts for Women*, by Jennifer Lawler (martial arts); *A Part of the Ribbon*, by Ruth Hunter and Debra Fritsch (children's chapter book).

CHARLES E. TUTTLE CO., 153 Milk St., 5th Floor, Boston MA 02109. **Acquisitions:** Michael Lewis, acquisitions editor. Isabelle Bleeker, senior editor (cooking and gardening). "Tuttle is America's leading publisher of books on Japan and Asia." Publishes hardcover and trade paperback originals and reprints. **Publishes 60 titles/year. Receives more than 1,000 queries/year. 20% of books from first-time authors; 60% from unagented writers. Pays 5-10% royalty on retail price, depending on format.** Publishes book 18 months after acceptance of ms. Accepts simultaneous submissions. Reports in 6 weeks on proposals. Book catalog free.
Nonfiction: Self-help, Eastern philosophy, alternative health. Subjects include cooking/foods/nutrition (Asian related), philosophy, Buddhist, Taoist, religion (Eastern). Submit query, outline and SASE. Cannot guarantee return of ms.
Recent Title(s): *Japanese Garden Design*, by Marc P. Keane.

N **TV BOOKS, INC.**, 1619 Broadway, 9th Floor, New York NY 10019. **Acquisitions:** Peter B. Kaufman, president/publisher; Sommer Hixson, associate editor. "Our plans include more books based on original television documentaries, as well as anthologies and reference books on categories related to current or vintage TV programming. More humor, too!" Publishes hardcover and trade paperback originals and reprints. **Firm publishes 10-15 titles/year, each imprint publishes 5-7 titles/year. Receives 20 queries and 10 mss/year. 10% of books from first-time authors; 25% from unagented writers. Outright purchase $6,000-20,000.** Publishes book 6 months after acceptance of ms. Accepts simultaneous submissions. Reports in 2 months on proposals. Book catalog free.
Imprint(s): TV Books, Viewer Books.
Nonfiction: Biography, coffee table book, humor, illustrated book, reference. Subjects include government/politics, history, military/war, science, travel, TV tie-in books. "We will not consider manuscripts that are not inspired by TV programming or books on films that are not based on television programming or original teleplays." Submit outline with 1 sample chapter and SASE. Reviews artwork/photos as part of the ms package. Send photocopies.
Recent Title(s): *TV Weddings: An Illustrated Guide*, by Marisa Keller and Mike Mashon.
Tips: "TV Books targets educated, media-savvy adults interested in history, social sciences and popular culture. We most often acquire manuscripts written by scholars and historians; however, we prefer texts that are engaging and accessible and serve well as illustrated volumes."

TWENTY-FIRST CENTURY BOOKS, Millbrook Press, 274 Madison Ave., Suite 1406, New York NY 10016. (212)481-6432. Publisher: Pat Culleton. Editor: Virginia Koeth. **Acquisitions:** Editorial Department. Twenty-First Century Books publishes only nonfiction current events or social issues titles for children and young adults. Publishes hardcover originals. **Publishes 40 titles/year. Receives 200 queries and 50 mss/year. 20% of books from first-time writers; 75% from unagented writers. Pays 5-8% royalty on net price.** Publishes book 18 months after acceptance of ms. Accepts simultaneous submissions. Reports in 3 months on proposals.
Nonfiction: Children's and young adult nonfiction. Subjects include government/politics, health/medicine, history, military/war, nature/environment, science, current events and social issues. "We publish primarily in series of four or more titles, for ages 10 and up, grades 5-8 (middle grade), and single titles for grades 7 and up. No picture books, fiction or adult books." Submit proposal package including outline, sample chapter and SASE. Does not review artwork.
Recent Title(s): *Tracking Dinosaurs in the Gobi.*
Tips: "We are now accepting single titles for both middle grade and young adult readers."

TWO DOT, Falcon Publishing Co. Inc., Box 1718, Helena MT 59624. (406)442-6597. Fax: (406)442-0384. E-mail: falcon@desktop.org. Website: http://www.falconguide.com. **Acquisitions:** Megan Hiller, editor. "Two Dot looks for lively writing for a popular audience, well-researched, on western themes." Publishes hardcover and trade paperback originals. **Publishes 6 titles/year. 30% of books from first-time authors; 100% from unagented writers. Pays 8-12½% on net. Offers minimal advance.** Publishes book 1 year after acceptance of ms. Accepts simultaneous submissions. Reports in 4 months. Book catalog for 9×12 SASE with 3 first-class stamps. Manuscript guidelines free.
Nonfiction: Subjects include Americana (western), cooking/foods/nutrition, history, regional. Two state by state series of interest: *More Than Petticoats*, on notable women; and *It Happened In* . . . state histories. Submit outline, 1 sample chapter and SASE. Reviews artwork/photos as part of the ms package. Send photocopies.
Recent Title(s): *The Champion Buffalo Hunter: The Frontier Memoirs of Yellowstone Vic Smith*, by Victor Grant Smith, edited by Jeanette Prodgers (history).

TYNDALE HOUSE PUBLISHERS, INC., 351 Executive Dr., P.O. Box 80, Wheaton IL 60189-0080. (630)668-8300. Website: http://www.tyndale.com. Vice President, Editorial: Ronald Beers. **Acquisitions:** Manuscript Review Committee. Estab. 1962. Tyndale House publishes "practical, user-friendly Christian books for the home and family." Publishes hardcover and trade paperback originals and mass paperback reprints. **Publishes 100 titles/year. 5-10% of books from first-time authors. Average first print order for a first book is 5,000-10,000. Royalty and advance negotiable.** Publishes book 18 months after acceptance. Reports in up to 2 months. Book catalog and ms guidelines for 9×12 SAE with 9 first-class stamps.

Nonfiction: Christian growth/self-help, devotional/inspirational, theology/Bible doctrine, children's nonfiction, contemporary/critical issues." Send query or synopsis with SASE. *No unsolicited mss.*
Fiction: "Biblical, historical and other Christian themes. No short story collections. Youth books: character building stories with Christian perspective. Especially interested in ages 10-14." Send query or synopsis with SASE. *No unsolicited mss.*
Recent Title(s): *7 Habits of a Healthy Home*, by Bill Carmichael; *The Treasure of Zanzibar*, by Catherine Palmer (Christian romance).

ULI, THE URBAN LAND INSTITUTE, 1025 Thomas Jefferson St. N.W., Washington DC 20007-5201. (202)624-7000. Fax: (202)624-7140. **Acquisitions**: Rachelle Levitt, vice president/publisher. Estab. 1936. ULI publishes technical books on real estate development and land planning. Publishes hardcover and trade paperback originals. **Publishes 15-20 titles/year. Receives 20 submissions/year. No books from first-time authors; 100% of books from unagented writers. Pays 10% royalty on gross sales. Offers $1,500-2,000 advance.** Publishes book 6 months after acceptance. Book catalog and ms guidelines for 9×12 SAE.
Nonfiction: "The majority of manuscripts are created inhouse by research staff. We acquire two or three outside authors to fill schedule and subject areas where our list has gaps. We are not interested in real estate sales, brokerages, appraisal, making money in real estate, opinion, personal point of view, or manuscripts negative toward growth and development." Query. Reviews artwork/photos as part of ms package.
Recent Title(s): *America's Real Estate.*

N **ULYSSES PRESS**, P.O. Box 3440, Berkeley CA 94703. (510)601-8301. Fax: (510)601-8307. E-mail: ulypress@aol.com. **Acquisitions:** Ray Riegert, editorial director. Estab. 1982. Publishes trade paperback originals. **Publishes 40 titles/year. 25% of books from first-time authors; 75% from unagented writers. Pays 12-16% royalty on wholesale price. Offers $2,000-8,000 advance.** Publishes book 6 months after acceptance. Accepts simultaneous submissions. Reports in 2 months on proposals. Book catalog free.

- Ulysses is rapidly expanding its lines of travel, spirituality and health books and is very interested in looking at proposals in these areas.

Nonfiction: Travel, spirituality, health. Submit proposal package including outline, 2 sample chapters and market analysis. Reviews artwork/photos as part of ms package. Send photocopies.
Recent Title(s): *Jesus and Buddha: The Parallel Sayings*, by Marcus Borg and Jack Kornfield (spirituality).

UNITY BOOKS, Unity School of Christianity, 1901 NW Blue Parkway, Unity Village MO 64065-0001. (816)524-3550 ext. 3190. Fax: (816)251-3552. E-mail: sprice@unityworldhq.org. Website: http://www.unityworldhq.org. **Acquisitions**: Michael Maday, editor; Raymond Teague, associate editor. "We are a bridge between traditional Christianity and New Age spirituality. Unity School of Christianity is on Christian principles, spiritual values and the healing power of prayer as a resource for daily living." Publishes hardcover and trade paperback originals and reprints. **Publishes 16 titles/year. Receives 100 queries and 500 mss/year. 30% of books from first-time authors; 95% from unagented writers. Pays 10-15% royalty on net receipts.** Publishes book 13 months after acceptance of final ms. Reports in 1 month on queries and proposals, 2 months on mss. Book catalog and ms guidelines free.
Nonfiction: Inspirational, self-help, reference (spiritual/metaphysical). Subjects include health (holistic), philosophy (perennial/New Thought), psychology (transpersonal), religion (spiritual/metaphysical Bible interpretation/modern Biblical studies). "Writers should be familiar with principles of metaphysical Christianity but not feel bound by them. We are interested in works in the related fields of holistic health, spiritual psychology and the philosophy of other world religions." Book proposal and/or query with outline and sample chapter. Reviews artwork/photos as part of ms package. Send photocopies.
Recent Title(s): *Wisdom for a Lifetime*, by Alden Studebaker.

UNIVELT, INC., P.O. Box 28130, San Diego CA 92198. (760)746-4005. Fax: (760)746-3139. Website: http://univelt.staigerland.com. **Acquisitions:** Robert H. Jacobs, publisher. Estab. 1970. Univelt publishes astronautics, spaceflight, aerospace technology and history titles. Publishes hardcover originals. **Publishes 8 titles/year. Receives 20 submissions/year. 5% of books from first-time authors; 5% from unagented writers. Nonauthor-subsidy publishes 10% of books. Pays 10% royalty on actual sales. No advance.** Publishes book 4 months after acceptance. Reports in 1 month. Book catalog and ms guidelines for SASE.
Imprint(s): American Astronautical Society, National Space Society.
Nonfiction: Publishes in the field of aerospace, especially astronautics, including application of aerospace technology to Earth's problems. Call and then submit outline and 1-2 chapters. Reviews artwork/photos as part of ms package.
Recent Title(s): *Strategies for Mars: A Guide to Human Exploration, Volume 86*, edited by Carol Stoker and Carter Emmart.
Tips: "Writers have the best chance of selling manuscripts on the history of astronautics (we have a history series) and astronautics/spaceflight subjects. We publish for the American Astronautical Society."

N **UNIVERSITY OF ALABAMA PRESS**, P.O. Box 870380, Tuscaloosa AL 35487-0380. Fax: (205)348-9201. Website: http://www.uapress.ua.edu. **Acquisitions:** Nicole Mitchell, director. Estab. 1945. Publishes hardcover and paperbound originals. **Averages 40 titles/year. Receives 200 submissions/year. 80% of books from first-time authors;**

100% from unagented writers. Publishes book 1 year after acceptance. Book catalog free. Manuscript guidelines for SASE.

• University of Alabama Press responds to an author immediately upon receiving the manuscript. If they think it is unsuitable for Alabama's program, they tell the author at once. If the manuscript warrants it, they begin the peer-review process, which may take two to four months to complete. During that process, they keep the author fully informed.

Nonfiction: Considers upon merit almost any subject of scholarly interest, but specializes in speech communication, political science and public administration, literary criticism and biography, history, and archaeology of the Southeastern United States. Accepts nonfiction translations. Reviews artwork/photos as part of ms package.

UNIVERSITY OF ALASKA PRESS, P.O. Box 756240, 1st Floor Gruening Bldg., UAF, Fairbanks AK 99775-6240. (907)474-5831. Fax: (907)474-5502. E-mail: fypress@uaf.edu. Manager: Debbie Van Stone. **Acquisitions:** Pam Odom. Estab. 1967. "The mission of the University of Alaska Press is to encourage, publish and disseminate works of scholarship that will enhance the store of knowledge about Alaska and the North Pacific Rim, with a special emphasis on the circumpolar regions." Publishes hardcover originals, trade paperback originals and reprints. **Publishes 5-10 titles/year. Receives 100 submissions/year. Pays 7½-10% royalty on net sales.** Publishes book within 2 years after acceptance. Reports in 2 months. Book catalog free.

Imprint(s): Ramuson Library Historical Translation Series, LanternLight Library, Oral Biographies, Classic Reprints.

Nonfiction: Biography, reference, technical, textbook, scholarly nonfiction relating to Alaska-circumpolar regions. Subjects include agriculture/horticulture, Americana (Alaskana), animals, anthropology/archaeology, art/architecture, education, ethnic, government/politics, health/medicine, history, language, military/war, nature/environment, regional, science, translation. Nothing that isn't northern or circumpolar. Query or submit outline. Reviews copies of artwork/photos as part of ms package.

Recent Title(s): *Two Years in the Klondike and Alaskan Gold-Fields 1896-1898*, by William B. Haskell (history).

Tips: "Writers have the best chance with scholarly nonfiction relating to Alaska, the circumpolar regions and North Pacific Rim. Our audience is made up of scholars, historians, students, libraries, universities, individuals."

UNIVERSITY OF ARIZONA PRESS, 1230 N. Park Ave., #102, Tucson AZ 85719-4140. (520)621-1441. Fax: (520)621-8899. E-mail: uapress@uapress.arizona.edu. Website: http://www.uapress.arizona.edu. **Acquisitions**: Stephen Cox, director; Christine Szuter, editor-in-chief. Estab. 1959. "University of Arizona is a publisher of scholarly books and books of the Southwest." Publishes hardcover and paperback originals and reprints. **Publishes 50 titles/year. Receives 300-400 submissions/year. 30% of books from first-time authors; 95% from unagented writers. Average print order is 1,500. Royalty terms vary; usual starting point for scholarly monograph is after sale of first 1,000 copies.** Publishes book 1 year after acceptance. Reports in 3 months. Book catalog for 9×12 SASE. Manuscript guidelines for #10 SASE.

• *Blue Horses Rush In*, by Luci Tapahonso was the winner of the 1998 MPBA Regional Poetry Award.

Nonfiction: Scholarly books about anthropology, Arizona, American West, archaeology, behavioral sciences, Chicano studies, environmental science, global change, Latin America, Native Americans, natural history, space sciences and women's studies. Query with outline, sample chapter and current curriculum vitae or résumé. Reviews artwork/photos as part of ms package.

Recent Title(s): *Speaking for the Generations*, edited by Simon Ortiz (Native American studies).

Tips: "Perhaps the most common mistake a writer might make is to offer a book manuscript or proposal to a house whose list he or she has not studied carefully. Editors rejoice in receiving material that is clearly targeted to the house's list, 'I have approached your firm because my books complement your past publications in . . .,' presented in a straightforward, businesslike manner."

THE UNIVERSITY OF ARKANSAS PRESS, 201 Ozark Ave., Fayetteville AR 72701-1201. (501)575-3246. Fax: (501)575-6044. E-mail: uaprinfo@cavern.uark.edu. Website: http://www.uark.edu/~uaprinfo. Director: John Coghland, acting director. **Acquisitions:** Kevin Brock, acquisitions editor. Estab. 1980. "Regional awareness, national impact . . . through books." Publishes hardcover and trade paperback originals and reprints. **Publishes 32 titles/year. Receives 1,000 submissions/year. 30% of books from first-time authors; 95% from unagented writers. Pays 10% royalty on net receipts from hardcover; 6% on paper.** Publishes book 1 year after acceptance. Accepted mss must be submitted on disk. Reports in up to 3 months. Book catalog for 9×12 SAE with 5 first-class stamps. Manuscript guidelines for #10 SASE.

Nonfiction: Arkansas and regional studies, African-American studies, Southern history and literature, Modernist studies (literature). "Our current needs include literary criticism and history. We won't consider manuscripts for texts, juvenile or religious studies, fiction or anything requiring a specialized or exotic vocabulary." Query or submit outline and sample chapters.

Recent Title(s): *Arkansas and the New South*, by Carl Moneyhan (history).

Poetry: Arkansas Poetry Award suspended for 1998.

UNIVERSITY OF CHICAGO PRESS, 5801 Ellis Ave., Chicago IL 60637. (773)702-7700. Fax: (773)702-9756. **Acquisitions**: Editorial Department. Estab. 1891. "We are a scholarly and academic press that also publishes books for a wider audience." Publishes hardcover originals, trade paperback originals and reprints. **Publishes 260 titles/year. 10% of books from first-time authors; 85% from unagented writers. Pays 5-10% royalty on hardcover, 7½%**

for paperback on net receipts for first-time authors. Advance varies. Publishes book 1 year after acceptance of ms. Accepts simultaneous submissions. Reports in 3 weeks on proposals. Catalog and guidelines free; "call marketing department."

Imprint(s): Midway Reprints (reprints only), Phoenix Books (poetry and fiction by invitation only).

Nonfiction: Subjects include anthropology/archaeology, art/architecture, business/economics, education, ethnic, gay/lesbian, government/politics, history, language/literature, money/finance, music/dance, philosophy, psychology, religion, science, sociology, translation, women's issues/studies, law, physical sciences, linguistics. Prefers authors with established credentials. Query or submit proposal package, including prospectus, table of contents, 2-3 sample chapters and author's cv with SASE. Reviews artwork/photos as part of ms package. Send photocopies.

Poetry: Publishes 4 titles/year by invitation. *No unsolicited submissions.*

Recent Title(s): *Scientific Revolution*, by Steven Shapin (history/technology); *Confession*, by Susan Han.

UNIVERSITY OF IDAHO PRESS, 16 Brink Hall, Moscow ID 83844-1107. (208)885-5939. Fax: (208)885-9059. E-mail: uipress@uidaho.edu. **Acquisitions**: Peggy Pace, director. Estab. 1972. The University of Idaho specializes in regional history and natural history, Native American studies, literature and literary criticism, and Northwest folklore. Publishes hardcover and trade paperback originals and reprints. **Publishes 10-12 titles/year. Receives 150-250 queries and 25-50 mss/year. 100% of books from unagented writers. Pays up to 10% royalty on net sales.** Publishes book 1 year after acceptance of ms. Reports in 6 months. Book catalog free. Manuscript guidelines $3.

Imprint(s): Northwest Folklife; Idaho Yesterdays; Northwest Naturalist Books; Living the West.

Nonfiction: Biography, reference, technical, textbook. Subjects include agriculture/horticulture, Americana, anthropology/archaeology, ethnic, folklore, history, language/literature, nature/environment, recreation, regional, women's issues/studies. "Writers should contact us to discuss projects in advance and refer to our catalog to become familiar with the types of projects the press publishes. Be aware of the constraints of scholarly publishing, and avoid submitting queries and manuscripts in areas in which the press doesn't publish." Query or submit proposal package, including sample chapter, contents, vita. Reviews artwork/photos as part of ms package. Send photocopies.

Recent Title(s): *The Milwaukee Revisited*, by Stanley W. Johnson.

UNIVERSITY OF ILLINOIS PRESS, 1325 S. Oak St., Champaign IL 61820-6903. (217)333-0950. Fax: (217)244-8082. E-mail: uipress@uiuc.edu. Website: http://www.uiuc.edu/providers/uipress. **Acquisitions:** Richard Wentworth, director/editor-in-chief. Estab. 1918. University of Illinois Press publishes "scholarly books and serious nonfiction" with a wide range of study interests. Publishes hardcover and trade paperback originals and reprints. **Publishes 100-110 titles/year. 50% of books from first-time authors; 95% from unagented writers. Nonauthor-subsidy publishes 10% of books. Pays 0-10% royalty on net sales; offers $1,000-1,500 average advance (rarely).** Publishes book 1 year after acceptance. Reports in 1 month. Book catalog for 9×12 SAE with 2 first-class stamps.

Nonfiction: Biography, reference, scholarly books. Subjects include Americana, history (especially American history), music (especially American music), politics, sociology, philosophy, sports, literature. Always looking for "solid, scholarly books in American history, especially social history; books on American popular music, and books in the broad area of American studies." Query with outline.

Recent Title(s): *Last Cavalier: The Life and Times of John A. Lomax, 1867-1948*, by Nolan Porterfield.

Tips: "Serious scholarly books that are broad enough and well-written enough to appeal to nonspecialists are doing well for us in today's market."

UNIVERSITY OF IOWA PRESS, 119 W. Park Rd., Iowa City IA 52242-1000. (319)335-2000. Fax: (319)335-2055. Website: http://www.uiowa.edu/~uipress. Editor/Associate Director: Holly Carver. **Acquisitions:** Holly Carver, interim director. Estab. 1969. "We publish authoritative, original nonfiction that we market mostly by direct mail to groups with special interests in our titles and by advertising in trade and scholarly publications." Publishes hardcover and paperback originals. **Publishes 35 titles/year. Receives 300-400 submissions/year. 30% of books from first-time authors; 95% from unagented writers. Pays 7-10% royalty on net price.** Publishes book 1 year after acceptance. Reports within 4 months. Book catalog and ms guidelines free.

Nonfiction: Publishes anthropology, archaeology, British and American literary studies, history (Victorian, U.S., regional Latin American), jazz studies, history of photography and natural history. Looks for evidence of original research; reliable sources; clarity of organization; complete development of theme with documentation, supportive footnotes and/or bibliography; and a substantive contribution to knowledge in the field treated. Query or submit outline. Use *Chicago Manual of Style*. Reviews artwork/photos as part of ms package.

Fiction and Poetry: Currently publishes the Iowa Short Fiction Award selections and winners of the Iowa Poetry Prize Competition. Query regarding poetry or fiction before sending ms.

Recent Title(s): *Race and Excellence: My Dialogue with Chester Pierce*, by Ezra Griffith.

Tips: "Developing a series in creative nonfiction."

UNIVERSITY OF MASSACHUSETTS PRESS, P.O. Box 429, Amherst MA 01004-0429. (413)545-2217. Fax: (413)545-1226. Website: http://www.umass.edu/umpress. Director: Bruce Wilcox. **Acquisitions**: Clark Dougan, senior editor. Estab. 1963. "Our mission is to publish first-rate books, design them well and market them vigorously. In so doing, the Press enhances the visibility and stature of the university." Publishes hardcover and paperback originals, reprints and imports. **Publishes 40 titles/year. Receives 600 submissions/year. 20% of books from first-time authors; 90% from unagented writers. Royalties generally begin at 10% of net income. Advance sometimes offered.**

Publishes book 1 year after acceptance. Preliminary report in 1 month. Book catalog free.
Nonfiction: Publishes African-American studies, art and architecture, biography, criticism, history, natural history, philosophy, poetry, public policy, sociology and women's studies in original and reprint editions. Accepts nonfiction translations. Submit outline and 1-2 sample chapters. Reviews artwork/photos as part of ms package.
Recent Title(s): *The Lesbian Menace: Ideology, Identity and the Representation of Lesbian Life*, by Sherrie A. Inness (gay/lesbian studies).

UNIVERSITY OF MISSOURI PRESS, 2910 LeMone Blvd., Columbia MO 65201. (573)882-7641. Fax: (573)884-4498. Website: http://www.system.missouri.edu/press. Director: Beverly Jarrett. **Acquisitions:** Mr. Clair Willcox, acquisitions editor. University of Missouri Press publishes primarily scholarly nonfiction in the social sciences and also some short fiction collections. Publishes hardcover and paperback originals and paperback reprints. **Publishes 50 titles/year. Receives 500 submissions/year. 25-30% of books from first-time authors; 90% from unagented writers. Pays up to 10% royalty on net receipts. No advance.** Publishes book 1 year after acceptance of ms. Reports in 6 months. Book catalog free.
Nonfiction: Scholarly publisher interested in history, literary criticism, political science, journalism, social science, some art history. Also regional books about Missouri and the Midwest. No mathematics or hard sciences. Query or submit outline and sample chapters. Consult *Chicago Manual of Style*.
Fiction: "Collections of short fiction are considered throughout the year; the press does not publish novels. Queries should include sample story, a table of contents and a brief description of the manuscript that notes its length."
Recent Title(s): *Quakers and Nazis*, by Hans A. Schmitt (WWII history); *The Buddha in Malibu*, by William Harrison.

UNIVERSITY OF NEVADA PRESS, MS 166, Reno NV 89557. (702)784-6573. Fax: (702)784-6200. E-mail: dalrympl@scs.unr.edu. Director: Ronald E. Latimer. Editor-in-Chief: Margaret F. Dalrymple. **Acquisitions:** Trudy McMurrin, acquisitions editor. Estab. 1961. "We are the first university press to sustain a sound series on Basque studies—New World and Old World." Publishes hardcover and paperback originals and reprints. **Publishes 35 titles/year. 20% of books from first-time authors; 99% from unagented writers. Pays average of 10% royalty on net price.** Publishes book 1 year after acceptance of ms. Preliminary report in 2 months. Book catalog and ms guidelines free.
Nonfiction: Specifically needs regional history and natural history, literature, current affairs, ethnonationalism, gambling and gaming, anthropology, biographies, Basque studies. No juvenile books. Submit complete ms. *Writer's Market* recommends query with SASE first. Reviews photocopies of artwork/photos as part of ms package.
Recent Title(s): *Old Heart of Nevada*, by Shawn Hall.

UNIVERSITY OF NEW MEXICO PRESS, 1720 Lomas Blvd. NE, Albuquerque NM 87131-1591. (505)277-2346. E-mail: unmpress@unm.edu. **Acquisitions:** "Write or call the managing editor for more information." Estab. 1929. "The Press is well known as a publisher in the fields of anthropology, archaeology, Latin American studies, photography, architecture and the history and culture of the American West, fiction, some poetry, Chicano/a studies and works by and about American Indians." Publishes hardcover originals and trade paperback originals and reprints. **Publishes 100 titles/year. Receives 600 submissions/year. 12% of books from first-time authors; 90% from unagented writers. Royalty varies.** *Writer's Market* recommends allowing 2 months for reply. Book catalog free.
Nonfiction: Biography, illustrated book, scholarly books. Subjects include anthropology/archaeology, art/architecture, ethnic, history, photography. "No how-to, humor, juvenile, self-help, software, technical or textbooks." Query. Reviews artwork/photos as part of ms package. Send photocopies.

UNIVERSITY OF NORTH TEXAS PRESS, P.O. Box 311336, Denton TX 76203-1336. Fax: (940)565-4590. E-mail: vick@acad.admin.unt.edu or wright@acad.admin.unt.edu. Website: accessible through http://www.tamu.edu/upress. **Acquisitions**: Frances B. Vick, director. Charlotte Wright, editor. Estab. 1987. "We have series called War and the Southwest; Practical Guide Series; Texas Folklore Society Publications series; the Western Life Series; Literary Biographies of Texas Writers series." Publishes hardcover and trade paperback originals and reprints. **Publishes 15-20 titles/year. Receives 400 queries and mss/year. 95% of books from unagented writers. Pays 7½-10% royalty of net.** Publishes book 2 years after acceptance of ms. Reports in 3 months on queries. Book catalog for 8½×11 SASE.
Nonfiction: Biography, reference. Subjects include agriculture/horticulture, Americana, ethnic, government/politics, history, language/literature, military/war, regional. Query with SASE. Reviews artwork/photos as part of ms package. Send photocopies.
Poetry: Offers the Vassar Miller Prize in Poetry, an annual, national competition resulting in the publication of a winning manuscript each fall. Query first with SASE.
Recent Title(s): *Cowboy Fiddler in Bob Wills' Band*, by Frankie McWhorter as told to John R. Erickson (music/ranching).

UNIVERSITY OF OKLAHOMA PRESS, 1005 Asp Ave., Norman OK 73019-0445. (405)325-5111. Fax: (405)325-4000. E-mail: rlewis@ou.edu. **Acquisitions:** Randall Lewis, acquisitions editor (American Indian studies, western history); Ron Chrisman, acquisitions editor (paperbacks); Kimberly Wiar, senior editor (American Indian literature, political science, natural history, literary criticism, classics). Estab. 1928. University of Oklahoma Press publishes books for both a scholarly and general audience. Publishes hardcover and paperback originals and reprints. **Publishes 100 titles/year. Pays royalty comparable to those paid by other publishers for comparable books.** Publishes book 12-18 months after acceptance. Reports in 3 months. Book catalog for $1 and 9×12 SAE with 6 first-class stamps.

Imprint(s): Oklahoma Paperbacks.
Nonfiction: Publishes American Indian studies, Western US history, political science, literary theory, natural history, women's studies, classical studies. No unsolicited poetry or fiction. Query with outline, 1-2 sample chapters and author résumé. Use *Chicago Manual of Style* for ms guidelines. Reviews artwork/photos as part of ms package.
Recent Title(s): *The Mythology of Native North America*, by Leeming and Page (American Indian literature).

N **UNIVERSITY OF PENNSYLVANIA PRESS**, 4200 Pine St., Philadelphia PA 19104-4011. (215)898-6261. Fax: (215)898-0404. Director: Eric Halpern. **Acquisitions:** Jerome Singerman, humanities editor; Patricia Smith, social sciences editor; Jo Joslyn, art and architecture editor. Estab. 1890. Publishes hardcover and paperback originals and reprints. **Publishes 70 titles/year. Receives 650 submissions/year. 10-20% of books from first-time authors; 99% from unagented writers. Royalty determined on book-by-book basis.** Publishes book 10 months after delivery of final ms. Reports in 3 months or less. Book catalog for 9×12 SAE with 6 first-class stamps.
Nonfiction: Publishes American history, literary criticism, women's studies, cultural studies, ancient studies, medieval studies, business, economics, history, law, anthropology, folklore, art history, architecture. "Serious books that serve the scholar and the professional, student and general reader." Follow the *Chicago Manual of Style*. Query with outline, résumé or vita. *No unsolicited mss.* Reviews artwork as part of ms package. Send photocopies.
Recent Title(s): *ABC of Architecture*, by James F. O'Gorman.

UNIVERSITY OF SCRANTON PRESS, University of Scranton, Scranton PA 18510-4660. (717)941-4228. Fax: (717)941-4309. E-mail: rousseaur1@uofs.edu. Website: http://www.uofs.edu.uofspress/uofspress.html. **Acquisitions:** Richard Rousseau, director. Estab. 1981. The University of Scranton Press, a member of the Association of Jesuit University Presses, publishes primarily scholarly monographs in theology, philosophy and the culture of northeast Pennsylvania. Publishes hardcover and paperback originals. **Publishes 5 titles/year. Receives 200 queries and 45 mss/year. 60% of books from first-time authors; 100% from unagented writers. Pays 10% royalty.** Publishes book 1 year after acceptance. Reports in 1 month on queries. Book catalog and ms guidelines free.
Imprint(s): Ridge Row Press.
Nonfiction: Scholarly monographs. Subjects include art/architecture, language/literature, philosophy, religion, sociology. Looking for clear editorial focus: theology/religious studies; philosophy/philosophy of religion; scholarly treatments; the culture of northeast Pennsylvania. Query or submit outline and 2 sample chapters.
Poetry: Only poetry related to northeast Pennsylvania.
Recent Title(s): *Coalseam, 2nd edition*, edited by K. Blomain; *Religious Values of the Terminally Ill: A Handbook for Healthcare Professionals*, by Delfi Mondragón.

N **UNIVERSITY OF SOUTH CAROLINA PRESS**, 937 Assembly St., 8th Floor, Columbia SC 29208. **Acquisitions:** Fred Kameny, editor-in-chief. "We focus on scholarly monographs and regional trade of lasting merit." Publishes hardcover originals, trade paperback originals and reprints. **Publishes 50 titles/year. Receives 1,000 queries/year and 250 mss/year. 30% of books from first-time authors; 90% from unagented writers. Pays 7½-20% royaltyon wholesale price. Offers $1,000-5,000 advance.** Publishes book 13 months after acceptance of ms. Accepts simultaneous submissions. Reports in 3 months on mss. Book catalog and ms guidelines free on request.
Nonfiction: Biography, illustrated book, reference, monograph. Subjects include art/architecture, business and economics, history, language/literature, military/war, regional, religion, international relations. "Do not submit entire unsolicited manuscripts or projects with little scholarly value." Submit outline, 2 samples chapters, proposal package, including C.V., résumé with SASE. Reviews artwork/photos as part of the ms package. Send photocopies.
Poetry: "All poetry is published as part of the James Dickey Contemporary Poetry Series and should be submitted directly to the series editor, Richard Howard." Submit "some" sample poems.
Recent Title(s): *The Buildings of Charleston*, by Jonathan Poston (architectural guide); *Errors and Angels*, by Maureen Bloomfield.

THE UNIVERSITY OF TENNESSEE PRESS, 293 Communications Bldg., Knoxville TN 37996-0325. Fax: (423)974-3724. E-mail: utpress2@utk.edu. Website: http://www.sunsite.utk.edu/utpress/. **Acquisitions:** Joyce Harrison, acquisitions editor (scholarly books); Jennifer Siler, director (Civil War, regional trades, fiction). Estab. 1940. "Our mission is to stimulate scientific and scholarly research in all fields; to channel such studies, either in scholarly or popular form, to a larger number of people; and to extend the regional leadership of the University of Tennessee by stimulating research projects within the South and by non-university authors." **Publishes 30 titles/year. Receives 450 submissions/year. 35% of books from first-time authors; 99% from unagented writers. Nonauthor-subsidy publishes 10% of books. Pays negotiable royalty on net receipts.** Book catalog for 12×16 SASE with 2 first-class stamps. Manuscript guidelines for SASE.
Nonfiction: American studies *only*, in the following areas: African American studies; Appalachian studies, religion (history, sociology, anthropology, biography only), folklore/folklife, history, literary studies, vernacular architecture, historical archaeology, and material culture. Submissions in other fields, and submissions of poetry, textbooks, plays and translations, are not invited. Prefers "scholarly treatment and a readable style. Authors usually have Ph.D.s." Submit outline, author vita and 2 sample chapters. Reviews artwork/photos as part of ms package.
Fiction: Regional. Query with synopsis and author biographical information.
Recent Title(s): *On Being Female, Black, and Free: Essays by Margaret Walker, 1932-1992*, edited by Maryemma Graham (African American studies, literary studies); *Sharpshooter: A Novel of the Civil War*, by David Madden.

Tips: "Our market is in several groups: scholars; educated readers with special interests in given scholarly subjects; and the general educated public interested in Tennessee, Appalachia and the South. Not all our books appeal to all these groups, of course, but any given book must appeal to at least one of them."

UNIVERSITY OF TEXAS PRESS, P.O. Box 7819, Austin TX 78713-7819. Fax: (512)320-0668. E-mail: castiron@mail.utexas.edu. Website: http://www.utexas.edu/utpress/. **Acquisitions:** Theresa May, assistant director/executive editor (social sciences, Latin American studies); James Burr, acquisition editor (humanities, classics); Shannon Davies, acquisitions editor (science). Estab. 1952. "The mission of the University of Texas Press is to advance and disseminate knowledge through the publication of books. In addition to publishing the results of advanced research for scholars worldwide, UT Press has a special obligation to the people of its state to publish authoritative books on Texas." **Publishes 80 titles/year. Receives 1,000 submissions/year. 50% of books from first-time authors; 99% from unagented writers. Pays royalty usually based on net income. Offers advance occasionally.** Publishes book 18 months after acceptance of ms. Reports in up to 3 months. Book catalog and ms guidelines free.
Nonfiction: General scholarly subjects: natural history, American, Latin American, Native American, Chicano and Middle Eastern studies, classics and the ancient world, film, contemporary regional architecture, archaeology, anthropology, geography, ornithology, environmental studies, biology, linguistics, women's literature, literary biography (Modernist period). Also uses specialty titles related to Texas and the Southwest, national trade titles and regional trade titles. Accepts nonfiction translations related to above areas. Query or submit outline and 2 sample chapters. Reviews artwork/photos as part of ms package.
Fiction: Latin American and Middle Eastern fiction only in translation.
Recent Title(s): *Latina Adolescent Childbearing in East Los Angeles*, by Pamela I. Erickson; *Houses Behind the Trees*, by Mohamed El-Bisatie.
Tips: "It's difficult to make a manuscript over 400 double-spaced pages into a feasible book. Authors should take special care to edit out extraneous material. We look for sharply focused, in-depth treatments of important topics."

N **UNIVERSITY PRESS OF AMERICA, INC.**, 4720 Boston Way, Lanham MD 20706. (301)459-3366. **Acquisitions:** Jon Sisk, associate publisher. University Press of America publishes scholarly books on a variety of nonfiction subjects. Publishes hardcover and trade paperback originals and reprints. **Publishes 600 titles/year. Receives 2,000 queries and 1,000 mss/year. 95% from unagented writers. Pays 5-15% royalty on wholesale price. Advance depends on imprint.** Publishes book 6 months after acceptance of ms. Accepts simultaneous submissions.
Imprint(s): Rowman & Littlefield (contact Jon Sisk), **Madison Books** (contact Nancy Ulrich), **Scarecrow Press**.
Nonfiction: Biography, reference, textbook, scholarly. Subjects include anthropology/archaeology, business and economics, child guidance/parenting, education, ethnic, gay/lesbian, government/politics, history, language/literature, military/war, money/finance, music/dance, philosophy, psychology, religion, sociology, translations, women's issues/studies.

UNIVERSITY PRESS OF COLORADO, 4699 Nautilus Court, Suite 403, Boulder CO 80301. (303)530-5337. Fax: (303)530-5306. Director: Luther Wilson. **Acquisitions:** Yashka Hallein, acquisitions editor. Estab. 1965. "We are a university press. Books should be solidly researched and from a reputable scholar." Publishes hardcover and paperback originals. **Publishes 40 titles/year. Receives 1,000 submissions/year. 50% of books from first-time authors; 95% from unagented writers. Pays 7½-15% royalty contract on net price.** Publishes book 2 years after acceptance of ms. Reports in 6 months. Book catalog free.
Nonfiction: Scholarly, regional and environmental subjects. Length: 250-500 pages. Query first with table of contents, preface or opening chapter and SASE. Reviews artwork/photos as part of ms package.
Fiction: Limited fiction series; works of fiction on the trans-Mississippi West, by authors residing in the region. Query with SASE.
Recent Title(s): *When the Dogs Ate Candles: A Time in El Salvador*, by Bill Hutchinson (Latin America); *The Circle Leads Home*, by Mary Anderson Parks (Women's West series).
Tips: "We have series on the Women's West and on Mesoamerican worlds."

UNIVERSITY PRESS OF FLORIDA, 15 NW 15th St., Gainesville FL 32611. (352)392-1351. **Acquisitions:** Meredith Morris-Babb, editor-in-chief. "The Press seeks to maintain the professional excellence of American university presses in general and to present the finest national and international scholarship in those academic areas in which we publish. In recognition of the State University System's educational mission and public role, the Press also publishes books of interest and significance for our region and state." Publishes hardcover and trade paperback originals and reprints. **Publishes 85-90 titles/year. Receives 600 queries and 85 mss/year. 30% of books from first-time quthors; 100% from unagented writers. Pays 5-10% royalty on wholesale price. No advance.** Publishes book 10 months after acceptance of ms. Accepts simultaneous submissions. Reports in 2 weeks on queries, 1 month on proposals, 2 months on mss.
Nonfiction: Academic and regional interest. Subjects include natural histories, African-American studies, Floridiana, archaeology, architecture, history, language/literature, photography, international relations: Latin America, Middle East.
Recent Title(s): *Celebrating Florida: Works of Art from the Vickers Collection*, edited by Gary R. Libley.

N **UNIVERSITY PRESS OF KANSAS**, 2501 W. 15th St., Lawrence KS 66049-3905. (785)864-4154. Fax: (785)864-4586. E-mail: upkansas@kuhub.cc.ukans.edu. **Acquisitions:** Michael J. Briggs, editor-in-chief (military history, political science, law); Nancy Scott Jackson, acquisitions editor (western history, environmental studies, women's studies, philosophy); Fred M. Woodward, director, (political science, presidency, regional). "The University Press of Kansas publishes scholarly books that advance knowledge and regional books that contribute to the understanding of Kansas, the Great Plains and the Midwest." Publishes hardcover originals, trade paperback originals and reprints. **Publishes 50 titles/year. Receives 600 queries/year. 20% of books from first-time authors; 98% from unagented writers. Pays 5-15% royalty on net price.** Publishes book 10 months after acceptance of ms. Reports in 1 month on proposals. Book catalog and ms guidelines free.

Nonfiction: Biography. Subjects include Americana, anthropology/archaeology, government/politics, history, military/war, nature/environment, philosophy, regional, sociology, women's issues/studies. "We are looking for books on topics of wide interest based on solid scholarship and written for both specialists and informed general readers. Do not send unsolicited complete manuscripts." Submit cover letter, cv, and prospectus, outline or sample chapter. Reviews artwork/photos as part of the ms package. Send photocopies.

Recent Title(s): *The Dark Side of the Left*, by Richard J. Ellis (political science).

UNIVERSITY PRESS OF KENTUCKY, 663 S. Limestone, Lexington KY 40508-4008. (606)257-2951. Fax: (606)257-2984. Website: http://www.uky.edu/UniversityPress/. **Acquisitions**: Nancy Grayson Holmes, editor-in-chief. Estab. 1951. "We are a scholarly publisher, publishing chiefly for an academic and professional audience." Publishes hardcover and paperback originals and reprints. **Publishes 60 titles/year. Payment varies. No advance.** Publishes ms 1 year after acceptance. Reports in 2 months on queries. Book catalog free.

Nonfiction: Biography, reference, monographs. "Strong areas are American history, literature, women's studies, film studies, American and African-American studies, folklore, Kentuckiana and regional books, Appalachian studies, Irish studies and military history. No textbooks, genealogical material, lightweight popular treatments, how-to books or books unrelated to our major areas of interest." The Press does not consider original works of fiction or poetry. Query.

Recent Title(s): *Pickford: The Woman Who Made Hollywood*, by Eileen Whitfield.

UNIVERSITY PRESS OF MISSISSIPPI, 3825 Ridgewood Rd., Jackson MS 39211-6492. (601)982-6205. Fax: (601)982-6217. E-mail: press@ihl.state.ms.us. Director: Richard Abel. Associate Director/Editor-in-Chief: Seetha Srinivasan. **Acquisitions:** Acquisitions Editor. Estab. 1970. "University Press of Mississippi publishes scholarly and trade titles, as well as special series, including: American Made Music; Author and Artist; Comparative Diaspora Studies; Faulkner and Yoknapatawpha; Fiction Series; Folk Art and Artists; Folklife in the South; Literary Conversations; Natural History; Performance Studies in Culture; Studies in Popular Culture; Understanding Health and Sickness; Writers and Their Work." Publishes hardcover and paperback originals and reprints. **Publishes 55 titles/year. Receives 750 submissions/year. 20% of books from first-time authors; 90% from unagented writers. "Competitive royalties and terms."** Publishes book 1 year after acceptance. Reports in 3 months. Catalog for 9×12 SAE with 3 first-class stamps.

Imprint(s): Muscadine Books (regional trade), Banner Books (literary reprints).

Nonfiction: Americana, biography, history, politics, folklife, literary criticism, ethnic/minority studies, art, photography, music, health, popular culture with scholarly emphasis. Interested in southern regional studies and literary studies. Submit outline, sample chapters and cv. "We prefer a proposal that describes the significance of the work and a chapter outline." Reviews artwork/photos as part of ms package.

Fiction: Commissioned trade editions by prominent writers.

Recent Title(s): *After the Machine: Visual Arts and the Erasing of Cultural Boundaries*, by Miles Orvell; *Me: A Book of Remembrance*, by Winnifred Eaton.

UNIVERSITY PRESS OF NEW ENGLAND, (includes Wesleyan University Press), 23 S. Main St., Hanover NH 03755-2048. (603)643-7100. Fax: (603)643-1540. E-mail: university.press@dartmouth.edu. Website: http://www.dartmouth.edu/acad-inst/upne/. Acting Director: Peter Gilbert. **Acquisitions:** Phil Pochoda, editorial director; Phyllis Deutsch, editor; April Ossmann, assistant editor. Estab. 1970. "University Press of New England is a consortium of university presses. Some books—those published for one of the consortium members—carry the joint imprint of New England and the member: Wesleyan, Dartmouth, Brandeis, Tufts, University of New Hampshire and Middlebury College." Publishes hardcover and trade paperback originals, trade paperback reprints. **Publishes 75-80 titles/year. Pays standard royalty. Offers advance occasionally.** Reports in 2 months. Book catalog and guidelines for 9×12 SAE with 5 first-class stamps.

Nonfiction: Americana (New England), art, biography, music, nature, American studies, Jewish studies, performance studies, regional (New England). No festschriften, unrevised doctoral dissertations, or symposium collections. Submit outline, 1-2 sample chapters with SASE. *No* electronic submissions.

Fiction: *Only* New England novels and reprints.

Recent Title(s): *The Measure of My Days*, by David Loxterkamp (medicine/memoir); *Judgment Hill*, by Castle Freeman, Jr.

UPSTART PUBLISHING CO., Dearborn Publishing Group, 155 N. Wacker Dr., Chicago IL 60606. (312)836-4400. Website: http://www.dearborn.com. **Acquisitions:** Danielle Egan-Miller, acquisitions editor (trade small business); Robin Nominelli, product manager (adult learning and educational products); Cynthia Zigmund, executive editor (finance). Estab. 1979. "It's an attitude. Upstart Publishing Company produces hands-on, how-to titles on entrepreneurship and all aspects of small business operations and management. Our books are friendly, accessible and real-life oriented and are often written by seasoned entrepreneurs and business owners." **Publishes 20 titles/year. Publishes 95% trade paperback originals, 5% hardcover. 50% of books from new authors, 50% from unagented writers. Pays royalty on wholesale price and offers advances.** Publishes book 6-12 months after acceptance of ms. Accepts simultaneous submissions. Reports in 2 months on queries. Book catalog and ms guidelines free.

Nonfiction: Trade small business subjects, including Small Office/Home Office topics. Textbooks, adult learning, training and educational products cover all aspects of entrepreneurship and small business management and operations. Query with proposal package including 2 chapters, author information ("any unusual credentials, seminar experience, etc. is useful") and SASE.

Recent Title(s): *Going Public*, by James Arkebauer and Ron Schultz.

UTAH STATE UNIVERSITY PRESS, 7800 University Blvd., Logan UT 84322-7800. (801)797-1362. Fax: (801)797-0313. Website: http://www.usu/edu/~usupress. Director: Michael Spooner. **Acquisitions:** John Alley, editor. Estab. 1972. "Particularly interested in book-length scholarly manuscripts dealing with folklore, western history, western literature or composition studies." Publishes hardcover and trade paperback originals and reprints. **Publishes 15 titles/year. Receives 170 submissions/year. 8% of books from first-time authors. Pays royalty on net price. No advance.** Publishes book 18 months after acceptance. Reports in 1 month on queries. Book catalog free. Manuscript guidelines for SASE.

- Utah State University Press is especially interested in supporting Native American writers with scholarly or creative manuscripts.

Nonfiction: Biography, reference and textbook on folklore, Americana (history and politics). Query with SASE. Reviews artwork/photos as part of ms package.

Recent Title(s): *Worth Their Salt*, edited by Colleen Whitley.

VALLEY OF THE SUN PUBLISHING, P.O. Box 38, Malibu CA 90265. President: Richard Sutphen.

- At press time it was learned that Valley of the Sun will discontinue publishing books and concentrate on producing audio and video tapes.

[N] **VAN DER PLAS PUBLICATIONS**, 1282 Seventh Ave., San Francisco CA 94122. (415)665-8214. Fax: (415)753-8572. **Acquisitions:** Rob van der Plas, publisher/editor. Estab. 1997. Publishes hardcover and trade paperback originals. **Averages 6 titles/year. Receives 20 submissions/year. 20% of books from first-time authors. 50% from unagented writers. Pays 12% of net royalty.** Publishes book an average of 1 year after acceptance. Accepts simultaneous submissions. Reports in 2 months. Book catalog free.

Nonfiction: How-to, technical. Submit complete ms. Artwork/photos essential as part of the ms package.

Tips: "Writers have a good chance selling us books with better and more illustrations and a systematic treatment of the subject. First check what is on the market and ask yourself whether you are writing something that is not yet available and wanted."

VANDERBILT UNIVERSITY PRESS, Box 1813, Station B, Nashville TN 37235. (615)322-3585. Fax: (615)343-8823. E-mail: vupress@vanderbilt.edu. Website: http://www.vanderbilt.edu/VUPress. **Acquisitions:** Charles Backus, director. Among other titles, publishes Vanderbilt Library of American Philosophy (Herman J. Saatkamp, editor); Vanderbilt Issues in Higher Education (John Braxton, editor) and Innovations in Applied Mathematics (Larry Schumacher, editor). Also distributes for and co-publishes with the Country Music Foundation. "Vanderbilt University Press, the publishing arm of the nation's leading research university, has maintained a strong reputation as a publisher of distinguished titles in the humanities, social sciences, education, medicine and regional studies, for both academic and general audiences, responding to rapid technological and cultural changes, while upholding high standards of scholarly publishing excellence." Publishes hardcover originals and trade paperback originals and reprints. **Publishes 15-20 titles/year. Receives 200-250 queries/year. 25% of books from first-time authors; 90% from unagented writers. Pays 15% maximum royalty on net income. Sometimes offers advance.** Publishes book 10 months after acceptance of ms. Accepts simultaneous submissions. Reports in 3 months on proposals. Book catalog and ms guidelines free.

Nonfiction: Biography, textbook, scholarly. Subjects include Americana, anthropology/archaeology, education, government/politics, health/medicine, history, language/literature, music and popular culture, nature/environment, philosophy, regional, religion, translation, women's issues/studies. Submit outline, 1 sample chapter and cv. Reviews artwork/photos as part of ms package. Send photocopies.

Recent Title(s): *His Glassy Essence: An Autobiography of Charles S. Pierce*, by Kenneth Laine Ketner (biography/philosophy).

ALWAYS SUBMIT unsolicited manuscripts or queries with a self-addressed, stamped envelope (SASE) within your country or a self-addressed envelope with International Reply Coupons (IRC) purchased from the post office for other countries.

Tips: "Our audience consists of scholars and educated general readers."

VERSO, 180 Varick St., 10th Fl., New York NY 10014. Website: http://www.verso-nlr.com. **Acquisitions**: Colin Robinson, managing director. "Our books cover politics, culture, and history (among other topics), but all come from a critical, Leftist viewpoint, on the border between trade and academic." Publishes hardcover and trade paperback originals. **Publishes 40-60 titles/year. Receives 300 queries and 150 mss/year. 10% of mss from first-time authors, 95% from unagented writers. Pays royalty.** Publishes book 1 year after acceptance of ms. Accepts simultaneous submissions. Reports in 5 months. Book catalog free.
Nonfiction: Illustrated book. Subjects include economics, government/politics, history, philosophy, sociology and women's issues/studies. "We are loosely affiliated with *New Left Review* (London). We are not interested in academic monographs." Submit proposal package, including at least 1 sample chapter.
Recent Title(s): *Wall Street*, by Doug Henwood (politics/economics).

VGM CAREER HORIZONS, NTC/Contemporary Publishing Group, 4255 W. Touhy Ave., Lincolnwood IL 60646-1975. (847)679-5500. Fax: (847)679-2494. Editorial Group Director: John Nolan. **Acquisitions:** Betsy Lancefield, editor. Estab. 1963. Publishes career-focused titles for job seekers, career planners, job changers, students and adults in education and trade markets. Publishes hardcover and paperback originals. **Publishes 100 titles/year. Receives 250-300 submissions/year. 15% of books from first-time authors; 95% from unagented writers. Pays royalty or makes outright purchase. Advance varies.** Publishes book 1 year after acceptance of ms. Accepts simultaneous submissions. Reports in 3 months. Book catalog and ms guidelines for 9×12 SAE with 5 first-class stamps.
Nonfiction: Textbook and general trade on careers in medicine, business, environment, etc. Query or submit outline and sample chapters.
Recent Title(s): *The Guide to Internet Job Searching*, 2nd Edition.
Tips: VGM also hires revision authors to handle rewrites and new editions of existing titles.

VIKING, Penguin Putnam Inc., 375 Hudson St., New York NY 10014. (212)366-2000. **Acquisitions:** Barbara Grossman, publisher. Publishes a mix of academic and popular fiction and nonfiction. Publishes hardcover and trade paperback originals. **Pays 10-15% royalty on retail price. Advance negotiable.** Publishes book 1 year after acceptance of ms. Accepts simultaneous submissions. Report in 6 months on queries.
Nonfiction: Subjects include biography, business/economics, child guidance/parenting, cooking/foods/nutrition, health/medicine, history, language/literature, music/dance, philosophy, women's issues/studies. *Agented submissions only.*
Fiction: Literary, mainstream/contemporary, mystery, suspense. "Looking for writers who can deliver a book a year (or faster) of consistent quality. *Agented submissions only.*
Recent Title(s): *Without a Doubt*, by Marcia Clark (popular culture); *Out to Canaan*, by John Karon (novel).

VIKING CHILDREN'S BOOKS, Penguin Putnam Inc., 375 Hudson St., New York NY 10014. (212)366-2000. Editor-in-Chief: Elizabeth Law. **Acquisitions:** Submissions Editors. "Viking Children's Books publishes the highest quality trade books for children including fiction, nonfiction, and novelty books for pre-schoolers through young adults." Publishes hardcover originals. **Publishes 80 books/year. Receives 7500 queries/year. 25% of books from first-time authors; 33% from unagented writers. Pays 10% royalty on retail price.** Advance negotiable. Publishes book 1 year after acceptance of ms. Report in 4 months on queries.
Nonfiction: Children's books. Query with outline, 3 sample chapters and SASE.
Fiction: Juvenile, young adult. Submit complete ms for novels, picture books and chapter books with SASE.
Recent Title(s): *See Through History*, series by various authors (history); *The Awful Aardvarks Go to School*, by Reeve Lindbergh (picture book).
Tips: Mistakes often made is that "authors disguise nonfiction in a fictional format."

VILLARD BOOKS, Random House, 201 E. 50th St., New York NY 10022. (212)572-2878. Publisher: Brian DeFiore. Director of Publicity: Adam Rothberg. **Acquisitions**: Acquisitions Editor. Estab. 1983. "Villard Books is the publisher of savvy and sometimes quirky bestseller hardcovers and trade paperbacks." Publishes hardcover and trade paperback originals. **Publishes 55-60 titles/year. 95% of books are agented submissions. Advances and royalties; negotiated separately.** Accepts simultaneous submissions.
Nonfiction and Fiction: Commercial nonfiction and fiction. *Agented submissions only.* Submit outline/synopsis and up to 50 pages in sample chapters. *No unsolicited submissions.*
Recent Title(s): *Marriage Shock: The Emotional Transformation of Women Into Wives*, by Dalma Heyn (relationships).

VINTAGE, Knopf Publishing Group, Random House, 201 E. 50th St., New York NY 10020. Vice President: LuAnn Walther. Editor-in-Chief: Martin Asher. **Acquisitions:** Linda Rosenberg, managing editor. Publishes trade paperback originals and reprints. **Imprint publishes 200 titles/year. Receives 600-700 mss/year. 5% of books from first time-authors; less than 1% from unagented writers. Pays 4-8% on retail price. Offers $2,500 and up advance.** Publishes book 1 year after acceptance of ms. Accepts simultaneous submissions. Reports in 6 months.
Nonfiction: Subjects include anthropology/archaeology, biography, business/economics, child guidance/parenting, education, ethnic, gay/lesbian, government/politics, health/medicine, history, language/literature, military/war, nature/environment, philosophy, psychology, regional, science, sociology, translation, travel, women's issues/studies. Submit outline and 2-3 sample chapters. Reviews artwork as part of ms package. Send photocopies.

Fiction: Literary, mainstream/contemporary, short story collections. Submit synopsis with 2-3 sample chapters.
Recent Title(s): *A Civil Action*, by Harr (current affairs); *Snow Falling on Cedars*, by Guterson (contemporary).

VISIONS COMMUNICATIONS, 205 E. 10th St., 2D, New York NY 10003. **Acquisitions:** Beth Bay. Visions specializes in technical and reference titles. Publishes hardcover originals and trade paperback originals and reprints. **Publishes 5 titles/year. Receives 20 queries and 10 mss/year. 50% of books from first-time authors; 75% from unagented writers. Pays 5-20% royalty on retail price.** Publishes book 6 months after acceptance of ms. Accepts simultaneous submissions. Reports in 1 month on queries, 2 months on proposals, 3 months on mss. Manuscript guidelines free.
Nonfiction: Children's/juvenile, how-to, self-help, reference, technical, textbook. Subjects include art/architecture, business/economics, health/medicine, psychology, religion, science, women's issues/studies. Submit outline, 3 sample chapters and proposal package.
Recent Title(s): *Ten Minute Marketing*, by Patricia Brenna.

VISTA PUBLISHING, INC., 422 Morris Ave., Suite #1, Long Branch NJ 07740. (732)229-6500. Fax: (732)229-9647. E-mail: czagury@vistapubl.com. Website: http://www.vistapubl.com. **Acquisitions**: Carolyn Zagury, president. Vista publishes books by nurses and allied health professionals. Publishes trade paperback originals. **Publishes 12 titles/year. Receives 200 queries and 125 mss/year. 75% of books from first-time authors; 100% from unagented writers. Pays 50% royalty on wholesale or retail price.** Publishes book 2-3 years after acceptance of ms. Accepts simultaneous submissions. Reports in 3 months on mss. Book catalog and ms guidelines free.
Nonfiction: Nursing and career related. Subjects include business, child guidance/parenting, creative nonfiction, health/medicine, women's issues/studies, specific to nursing and allied health professionals. Submit full ms and SASE. *Writer's Market* recommends querying with SASE first. Reviews artwork/photos as part of ms package. Send photocopies.
Fiction: Horror, multicultural, mystery, poetry, short story collections, nursing medical. "We specialize in nurse and allied health professional authors." Submit full ms and SASE.
Poetry: Nursing-related. Submit complete ms.
Recent Title(s): *Sunshine at the End of Life*, by Dr. Peggy Merkel (dealing with death); *Yesterday's Nightmare*, by Donna Harland (mystery).
Tips: "It's always worth the effort to submit your manuscript."

VOLCANO PRESS, INC., P.O. Box 270, Volcano CA 95689-0270. (209)296-3445. Fax: (209)296-4515. E-mail: ruth@volcanopress.com. Website: http://www.volcanopress.com. **Acquisitions:** Ruth Gottstein, publisher. "We believe that the books we are producing today are of even greater value than the gold of yesteryear and that the sybolism of the term 'Mother Lode' is still relevant to our work." Publishes trade paperback originals. **Publishes 4-6 titles/year. Pays royalties on net price. Offers $500-1,000 advance.** Reports in 1 month on queries. Book catalog free.
Nonfiction: "We publish women's health and social issues, particularly in the field of domestic violence, and multicultural books for children that are non-racist and non-sexist." Query with brief outline and SASE by mail; no e-mail or fax submissions.
Recent Title(s): *Family Violence and Religion.*
Tips: "Look at our titles on the Web or in our catalog, and submit materials consistent with what we already publish."

VOYAGEUR PRESS, 123 N. Second St., Stillwater MN 55082. (612)430-2210. Fax: (612)430-2211. E-mail: mdregni@voyageurpress.com or tberger@voyageurpress.com. **Acquisitions:** Todd R. Berger (regional travel and photography. Michael Dregni, editorial director. "Voyageur Press is internationally known as a leading publisher of quality natural history, wildlife, sports/recreation, travel and regional books." Publishes hardcover and trade paperback originals. **Publishes 30 titles/year. Receives 1,200 queries and 500 mss/year. 10% of books from first-time authors; 90% from unagented writers. Pays royalty.** Publishes book 1 year after acceptance of ms. Accepts simultaneous submissions. Reports in 3 months. Book catalog and ms guidelines free.
Nonfiction: Coffee table book (and smaller format photographic essay books), cookbook. Subjects include natural history, nature/environment, Americana, collectibles, history, outdoor recreation, regional, travel. Query or submit outline. Reviews artwork/photos. Send transparencies—duplicates and tearsheets only.
Recent Title(s): *Love of Labs* (Labrador retriever coffee table book).
Tips: "We publish books for a sophisticated audience interested in natural history and cultural history of a variety of subjects. Please present as focused an idea as possible in a brief submission (one page cover letter; two page outline or proposal). Note your credentials for writing the book. Tell all you know about the market niche and marketing possibilities for proposed book."

WADSWORTH PUBLISHING COMPANY, International Thomson Publishing, Inc., 10 Davis Dr., Belmont CA 94002. (650)595-2350. Fax: (650)637-7544. Website: http://www.thomson.com/wadsworth.html. **Acquisitions:** Rob Zwettler, editorial director. Estab. 1956. "We publish books and media products that use fresh teaching approaches to all courses taught at schools of higher education throughout the U.S. and Canada." Publishes hardcover and paperback originals and software. **Publishes 240 titles/year. 35% of books from first-time authors; 99% of books from unagented writers. Pays 5-15% royalty on net price. Advances not automatic policy.** Publishes ms 1 year after acceptance. Accepts simultaneous submissions. Book catalog (by subject area) and ms guidelines available.
Nonfiction: Textbooks and multimedia products: higher education only. Subjects include biology, astronomy, earth

science, music, social sciences, philosophy, religious studies, speech and mass communications, broadcasting, TV and film productions, college success multimedia. Query or submit outline/synopsis and sample chapters.
Recent Title(s): *Production and Operations Management*, 7th edition, by Norman Gaither.

WAKE FOREST UNIVERSITY PRESS, P.O. Box 7333, Winston-Salem NC 27109. (910)759-5448. **Acquisitions:** Dillon Johnston, director. Manager: Candide Jones. Estab. 1976. "We publish exclusively the poetry of Ireland and have discontinued our bilingual series of French poetry." Publishes hardcover and trade paperback originals. **Publishes 5 titles/year. Receives 80 submissions/year. Pays 10% on retail price. Offers $500 average advance.** Publishes book 6 months after acceptance of ms. Reports in 2 months on queries. Book catalog free.
Poetry: Language/literature subjects. Query.
Recent Title(s): *Selected Poems*, by Medbh McGuckian.
Tips: "Readers of contemporary poetry and of books of Irish interest are our audience."

J. WESTON WALCH, PUBLISHER, P.O. Box 658, Portland ME 04104-0658. (207)772-2846. Fax: (207)774-7167. Website: http://www.walch.com. Vice President: Joan E. Whitney. **Acquisitions:** Lisa French, editor-in-chief; Kate O'Halloran, editor; Margaret Cleveland, editor; Pam O'Neil, editor; Julie Mazur, editor; Lisa Chmelecki, assistant editor. Estab. 1927. Publishes educational softcover originals for grades 6-adult in the US and Canada. **Publishes 100 titles/year. Receives 300 submissions/year. 10% of books from first-time authors; 95% from unagented writers. Offers 8-12% royalty on gross receipts. Advances negotiable.** Publishes book 18 months after acceptance of ms. Reports in 4 months. Book catalog for 9×12 SAE with 5 first-class stamps. Manuscript guidelines for #10 SASE.
Nonfiction: Subjects include art, business, technology, economics, English, geography, government, history, literacy, mathematics, middle school, psychology, science, social studies, sociology, special education. "We publish only supplementary educational material for grades six to adult in the U.S. and Canada. Formats include books, posters, blackline masters, cassettes, and mixed packages. Most titles are assigned by us, though we occasionally accept an author's unsolicited submission. We have a great need for author/artist teams and for authors who can write at third- to tenth-grade levels. We do *not* want basic texts or anthologies. Most of our authors—but not all—have secondary teaching experience. *Query first.* Looks for sense of organization, writing ability, knowledge of subject, skill of communicating with intended audience." Reviews artwork/photos as part of ms package.
Recent Title(s): *Langston Hughes: An Interdisciplinary Biography*, by Fred Lown.

WALKER AND CO., Walker Publishing Co., 435 Hudson St., New York NY 10014. Fax: (212)727-0984. Publisher: George Gibson. Editors: Jacqueline Johnson, Michael Seidman. Juvenile editor: Soyung Pak. **Acquisitions:** Submissions Editor or Submisions Editor-Juvenile. Estab. 1959. Walker publishes general nonfiction on a variety of subjects as well as mysteries, children's books and large print religious reprints. Publishes hardcover and trade paperback originals. **Publishes 70 titles/year. Receives 3,500 submissions/year. Pays royalty on retail price, 7½-12% on paperback, 10-15% on hardcover. Offers competitive advances.** Material without SASE will not be returned. Reports in 3 months. Book catalog and ms guidelines for 9×12 SAE with 3 first-class stamps.
Nonfiction: Biography, history, science and natural history, health, juvenile, music, nature and environment, reference, popular science, sports/baseball, and self-help books. Query with SASE. No phone calls.
Fiction: Adult mystery, juvenile fiction and picture books. Query with SASE.
Recent Title(s): *What Jazz Is*, by Johnny King (music); *Devil's Den*, by Susan Beth Pfeffer (juvenile).

[A] **WARNER ASPECT**, Warner Books. 1271 Avenue of the Americas, New York NY 10020. Editor-in-Chief: Betsy Mitchell. "We're looking for 'epic' stories in both fantasy and science fiction." Publishes hardcover, trade paperback, mass market paperback originals and mass market paperback reprints. **Publishes 30 titles/year. Receives 500 queries and 350 mss/year. 5-10% of books from first-time authors; 1% from unagented writers. Pays royalty on retail price. Offers $5,000-up advance.** Publishes book 1 year after acceptance of ms. Reports in 3 months on mss.
Fiction: Fantasy, science fiction. "Sample our existing titles—we're a fairly new list and pretty strongly focused." Mistake writers often make is "hoping against hope that being unagented won't make a difference. We simply don't have the staff to look at unagented projects."
Recent Title(s): *The Reality Dysfunction*, by Peter F. Hamilton (science fiction).

WARNER BOOKS, Time & Life Building, 1271 Avenue of the Americas, New York NY 10020. (212)522-7200. Warner publishes general interest fiction and nonfiction. Publishes hardcover, trade paperback and mass market paperback originals and reprints. **Publishes 350 titles/year.**
Imprint(s): Mysterious Press, Warner Aspect, Warner Romance, Warner Vision.
Nonfiction: Biography, business, cooking, current affairs, health, history, home, humor, popular culture, psychology, reference, self-help, sports. Query with SASE.
Fiction: Fantasy, horror, mainsteam, mystery, romance, science fiction, suspense, thriller.
Recent Title(s): *Brain Longevity*, by Dharma Singh Khalsa, M.D. (health); *Mail*, by Mameve Medwed.

WASHINGTON STATE UNIVERSITY PRESS, Pullman WA 99164-5910. (800)354-7360. Fax: (509)335-8568. E-mail: pkeithc@wsu.edu. Website: http://www.publications.wsu.edu/wsupress. Director: Thomas H. Sanders. Editor: Glen Lindeman. **Acquisitions:** Keith Petersen, editor. Estab. 1928. WSU Press publishes books on the history, prehistory, culture, and politics of the West, particularly the Pacific Northwest. Publishes hardcover originals, trade paperback originals and reprints. **Publishes 10 titles/year. Receives 300-400 submissions/year. 50% of books from first-time writers; mostly unagented authors. Pays 5% minimum royalty, graduated according to sales.** Publishes book 18 months after acceptance of ms. Reports on queries in 2 months.

Nonfiction: Subjects include Americana, art, biography, environment, ethnic studies, history (especially of the American West and the Pacific Northwest), politics, essays. "We seek manuscripts that focus on the Pacific Northwest as a region. No romance novels, how-to books, gardening books or books used specifically as classroom texts. We welcome innovative and thought-provoking titles in a wide diversity of genres, from essays and memoirs to history, anthropology and political science." Submit outline and sample chapters. Reviews artwork/photos as part of ms package.

Recent Title(s): *My Heart on the Yukon River*, by Monique Dykstra.

Tips: "We have developed our marketing in the direction of regional and local history and have attempted to use this as the base upon which to expand our publishing program. In regional history, the secret is to write a good narrative—a good story—that is substantiated factually. It should be told in an imaginative, clever way. Have visuals (photos, maps, etc.) available to help the reader envision what has happened. Tell the regional history story in a way that ties it to larger, national, and even international events. Weave it into the large pattern of history. We have published our first book of essays and a regional cookbook and will do more in these and other fields if we get the right manuscript."

FRANKLIN WATTS, INC., Grolier, Inc., Sherman Turnpike, Danbury CT 06816. (203)797-6802. Website: http://publishing.grolier.com/publishing.html. Publisher: John Selfridge. **Acquisitions:** Mark Friedman, executive editor; Melissa Stewart, senior editor (science); Halley Gatenby, senior editor (geography); Douglas Hill, senior editor (reference); Dana Rau, associate editor. Estab. 1942. Franklin Watts publishes curriculum materials and books and teacher's materials (K-12) to supplement textbooks. Publishes both hardcover and softcover originals. **Publishes 150 titles/year. 5% of books from first-time authors; 95% from unagented writers. Advance varies.** Publishes book 18 months after acceptance of ms. Accepts simultaneous submissions. Reports in 4 months on queries. Book catalog for $3.

Nonfiction: History, science, social issues, biography. Subjects include education, language/literature, American and world history, politics, natural and physical sciences, sociology. Multicultural, curriculum-based nonfiction lists published twice a year. Strong also in the area of contemporary problems and issues facing young people. No humor, coffee table books, fiction, poetry, cookbooks or gardening books. Query with outline and SASE. *No unsolicited mss.* No phone calls. Prefers to work with unagented authors.

Recent Title(s): *A Young Man's Journey With AIDS*, by Luellen Reese.

Tips: Most of this publisher's books are developed inhouse; less than 5% come from unsolicited submissions. However, they publish several series for which they always need new books. Study catalogs to discover possible needs.

WEATHERHILL, INC., 568 Broadway, Suite 705, New York NY 10012. **Acqusitions:** Raymond Furse, editorial director. Weatherhill publishes exclusively Asia-related nonfiction and Asian fiction and poetry in translation. Publishes hardcover and trade paperback originals and reprints. **Publishes 36 titles/year. Receives 250 queries and 100 mss/year. 20% of books from first-time authors; 95% from unagented writers. Pays 12-18% royalty on wholesale price. Offers advances up to $10,000. Publishes books 8 months after acceptance of ms.** Accepts simultaneous submissions. Reports in 1 month on proposals. Book catalog and ms guidelines free.

Imprint(s): Weatherhill, Tengu Books.

Nonfiction: Asia-related topics only. Biography, coffee table book, cookbook, gift book, how-to, humor, illustrated book, reference, self-help. Subjects include anthropology/archaeology, art/architecture, cooking/foods/nutrition, gardening, history, language/literature, music/dance, nature/environment, photography, regional, religion, sociology, translation, travel. Submit outline, 2 sample chapters and sample illustrations (if applicable). Reviews artwork/photos as part of ms package. Send photocopies.

Fiction: "We publish only important Asian writers in translation. Asian fiction is a hard sell. Authors should check funding possibilities from appropriate sources: Japan Foundation, Korea Foundation, etc." Query with synopsis.

Poetry: Only Asian poetry in translation. Query.

Recent Title(s): *Healthy Japanese Cooking*, by Fukuhara; *The Fugu Plan*, by Marvin Tokayer and Mary Swarty (historical fiction).

WEIDNER & SONS PUBLISHING, P.O. Box 2178, Riverton NJ 08077. (609)486-1755. Fax: (609)486-7583. E-mail: weidner@waterw.com. Website: http://www.waterw.com/~weidner. **Acquisitions:** James H. Weidner, president. Estab. 1967. "We publish primarily science, text and reference books for scholars, college students and researchers." Publishes hardcover and trade paperback originals and reprints. **Publishes 10-20 titles/year; imprint publishes 10 titles/year. Receives hundreds of queries and 50 mss/year. 100% of books from first-time authors; 90% from unagented writers. Pays 10% maximum royalty on wholesale price.** Accepts simultaneous submissions. Reports in 1 month on queries.

Imprint(s): Hazlaw Books, Medlaw Books, Bird Sci Books, Delaware Estuary Press, Tycooly Publishing USA, Pulse Publications.

Nonfiction: Reference, technical, textbook. Subjects include agriculture/horticulture, animals, business/economics, child guidance/parenting, computers/electronics, education, gardening, health/medicine, hobbies (electronic), language/literature, nature/environment, psychology, science and ecology/environment. "We rarely publish fiction; never poetry. No topics in the 'pseudosciences': occult, astrology, New Age and metaphysics, etc." Query or submit outline and sample chapters. Return postage and SASE required for all. Include e-mail address for faster response. Reviews artwork/

photos as part of ms package. Send photocopies. "Suggest 2 copies of ms, double spaced, along with PC disk in Word, Word Perfect, Write or Pagemaker."
Recent Title(s): *International Guide to Educational Standards.*

SAMUEL WEISER, INC., P.O. Box 612, York Beach ME 03910-0612. (207)363-4393. Fax: (207)363-5799. E-mail: weiserbooks@worldnet.att.net. **Acquisitions:** Eliot Stearns, editor. Estab. 1956. "We look for strong books in oriental philosophy, metaphysics, esoterica of all kinds (tarot, astrology, qabalah, magic, etc.) written by teachers and people who know the subject." Publishes hardcover originals and trade paperback originals and reprints. **Publishes 18-20 titles/year. Receives 200 submissions/year. 50% of books from first-time authors; 98% from unagented writers. Pays 10% royalty on wholesale and retail price. Offers $500 average advance.** Publishes book 18 months after acceptance of ms. Reports in 3 months. Book catalog free.
Nonfiction: How-to, self-help. Subjects include health, music, philosophy, psychology, religion. "We don't want a writer's rehash of all the astrology books in the library, only texts written by people with strong backgrounds in the field. No poetry or novels." Submit complete ms. *Writer's Market* recommends query with SASE first. Reviews artwork/photos as part of ms package.
Recent Title(s): *Sophia-Maria: A Holistic Vision of Creation*, by Father Thomas Schipflinger.
Tips: "Most new authors do not check permissions, nor do they provide proper footnotes. If they did, it would help. We look at all manuscripts submitted to us. We are interested in seeing freelance art for book covers."

WESCOTT COVE PUBLISHING CO., P.O. Box 130, Stamford CT 06904. (203)322-0998. **Acquisitions:** Julius M. Wilensky, president. Estab. 1968. "We publish the most complete cruising guides, each one an authentic reference for the area covered." Publishes trade paperback originals and reprints. **Publishes 4 new titles/year. Receives 15 queries and 10 mss/year. 25% of books from first-time authors; 95% from unagented writers. Pays 5-10% royalty on retail price. Offers $1,000-1,500 advance.** Publishes book 1 year after acceptance of ms. Accepts simultaneous submissions. Reports in 1 month on queries. Book catalog free.
Nonfiction: How-to, humor, illustrated book, reference, nautical books. Subjects include history, hobbies, regional, travel. "All titles are nautical books; half of them are cruising guides. Mostly we seek out authors knowledgeable in sailing, navigation, cartography and the area we want covered. Then we commission them to write the book." Query with outline, 1-2 sample chapters, author's credentials and SASE.
Recent Title(s): *First Time Around*, by Jamie Bryson.

WESLEYAN UNIVERSITY PRESS, 110 Mount Vernon St., Middletown CT 06459. (860)685-2420. **Acquisitions:** Suzanna Tamminen, editor. "We are a scholarly press with a focus on cultural studies." Publishes hardcover originals and paperbacks. **Publishes 25-30 titles/year. Receives 1,500 queries and 1,000 mss/year. 10% of books from first-time authors; 80% from unagented writers. Pays 0-10% royalty. Offers up to $3,000 advance.** Publishes book 1 year after acceptance of ms. Accepts simultaneous submissions. Reports in 1 month on queries, 2 months on proposals, 3 months on mss. Book catalog free. Manuscript guidelines for #10 SASE.
Nonfiction: Biography, textbook, scholarly. Subjects include art/architecture, ethnic, gay/lesbian, history, language/literature, music/dance, philosophy, sociology, theater, film. Submit outline, proposal package, including: introductory letter, curriculum vitae, table of contents. Reviews artwork/photos as part of ms package. Send photocopies.
Fiction: Science fiction. "We publish very little fiction, less than 3% of our entire list."
Poetry: "Writers should request a catalog and guidelines." Submit 5-10 sample poems.
Recent Title(s): *Historiography of the Twentieth Century*, by Georg Iggers (scholarly); *Loose Sugar*, by Brenda Hillman (poetry).

WESTCLIFFE PUBLISHERS, P.O. Box 1261, Englewood CO 80150. (303)935-0900. Fax: (303)935-0903. E-mail: westclif@westcliffepubishers.com. **Acquisitions:** Linda Doyle, director of marketing. "Westcliffe Publishers produces the highest quality in regional photography and essays for our coffee table-style books and calendars. As an eco publisher our mission is to foster environmental awareness by showing the beauty of the natural world." Publishes hardcover originals, trade paperback originals and reprints. **Publishes 23 titles/year. Receives 100 queries and 10 mss/year. 75% of books from first-time authors; 100% from unagented writers. Pays 3-15% royalty on retail price. Offers advance of 50% of the first year's royalties.** Publishes book 18 months after acceptance of ms. Accepts simultaneous submissions. Reports in 1 month. Book catalog and ms guidelines free.
Nonfiction: Coffee table book, gift book, illustrated book, reference. Subjects include Americana, animals, gardening, nature/environment, photography, regional, travel. "Writers need to do their market research to justify a need in the marketplace." Submit outline with proposal package. Westcliffe will contact you for photos, writing samples.
Recent Title(s): *A Tennessee Christmas*, by Jan Kiefer (Americana).
Tips: Audience are nature and outdoors enthusiasts and photographers. "Just call us!"

WESTERNLORE PRESS, P.O. Box 35305, Tucson AZ 85740. Fax: (520)297-1722. **Acquisitions:** Lynn R. Bailey, editor. Publishes Western Americana of a scholarly and semischolarly nature. **Publishes 6-12 titles/year. Pays standard royalties on retail price "except in special cases."** Reports in 2 months.
Nonfiction: Subjects include anthropology, history, biography, historic sites, restoration, and ethnohistory pertaining to the American West. Re-publication of rare and out-of-print books. Length: 25,000-100,000 words. Query with SASE.
Recent Title(s): *The Apache Kid*, by de la Gaza (western history).

N **WESTMINSTER JOHN KNOX**, 100 Witherspoon St., Louisville KY 10202-1396. (800)277-2872. Fax: (502)569-5113. E-mail: pcusa@org/ppc. Website: http://pcusa.org/ppc/wjkcatlg/wik.htm. "All WJK books have a religious/spiritual angle, but are written for various markets—scholarly, professional, and the general reader." Westminster John Knox is affiliated with the Presbyterian Church USA. **Acquisitions:** Stephanie Egnotovich, managing editor; Nick Street, editor; Cynthia Thompson, editor. Publishes hardcover and trade paperback originals. **Publishes 70 titles/year. Receives 1,000 queries per year; 500 mss/year. 25% of books from first-time authors. Pays royalty on retail price.** Publishes book 1-2 years after acceptance of ms. No simultaneous submissions. Does not return mss. Book catalog and manuscript guidelines on request. Book catalog also on website.
Nonfiction: Biography, children's juvenile, coffee table book, gift book, how-to, humor, reference, self-help, textbook, professional books. Subjects include Christian education, ethnic, gay/lesbian, government/politics, history, memoirs, philosophy, psychology, religion, sociology, spirituality, women's issues/studies, Bible studies, ethics, theology. Submit proposal according to WJK book proposal guidelines. Reviews artwork/photos as part of ms package. Send photocopies.
Fiction: Literary, mainstream/contemporary, mystery, religious, spiritual. Send complete ms with SASE.
Recent Title(s): *What Christians Really Believe—And Why*, by Stanley Grenz (nonfiction); *Dark the Night, Wild the Sea*, by Robert McAfee Brown (fiction).

WESTVIEW PRESS, Perseus Book Group, 5500 Central Ave., Boulder CO 80301-2877. (303)444-3541. Fax: (303)449-3356. Website: http://www.hcacademic.com. Executive Editor: Leo Wigman. Senior Acquisitions Editors: Karl Yambert, Katherine Murphy. **Acquisitions:** Marcus Boggs, publisher. Estab. 1975. "Westview Press publishes a wide range of general interest and scholarly nonfiction (including undergraduate and graduate-level textbooks) in the social sciences and humanities. Our mission is to publish 'books that matter.' " Publishes hardcover and trade paperback originals and reprints. **Publishes 250 titles/year. Receives 1,000 queries and 500 mss/year. 25% of books from first-time authors; 90% from unagented writers. Pays 8-15% royalty on net receipts. Advance varies, $0-20,000 and up.** Publishes book 1 year after acceptance of ms. Accepts simultaneous submissions, if so noted. Reports in 1 week on queries, 6 weeks on proposals and mss. Book catalog available on Website. Manuscript guidelines free.
Imprint(s): Icon Editions (Cass Canfield).
Nonfiction: Biography, reference, textbook, trade, monograph. Subjects include anthropology, art/architecture (criticism and history), education, ethnic (cultural studies), government/politics, history, military/war (history), psychology, religious studies, sociology, women's issues/studies. "Know our focus. We publish books of original scholarship. To gain our interest, write a book that is both original and interesting." Query or submit proposal package including outline, 3 sample chapters, table of contents with SASE. Reviews artwork/photos as part of ms package, if germane. Send photocopies.
Recent Title(s): *International Encyclopedia of Public Administration*, by Shafritz.

WHISPERING COYOTE PRESS, L.P., 300 Crescent Court, Suite 860, Dallas TX 75201. Fax: (214)871-5577 or (214)319-7298. **Acquisitions**: Mrs. Lou Alpert, editor. "Our focus is on children's picture books ages 4-11. We try to publish a product that is child-friendly and will encourage children to love reading." **Publishes 6 titles/year. 20% of books from first-time authors; 90% from unagented writers. Pays 8% royalty on retail price of first 10,000 copies, 10% after (combined author and illustrator). Offers $2,000-8,000 advance (combined author, illustrator).** Publishes book 2 years after acceptance of ms. Accepts simultaneous submissions. Reports in 3 months. Book catalog and ms guidelines for #10 SAE with 55¢ postage.
Fiction: Juvenile picture books, adventure, fantasy. "We only do picture books." Submit complete ms. If author is illustrator also, submit sample art. Send photocopies, no original art. No holiday-specific books.
Poetry: "We like poetry—if it works in a picture book format. We are not looking for poetry collections."
Recent Title(s): *The First Starry Night*, by Jann Shaddox Isom (fiction); *Hey Diddle Diddle*, by Kin Eagle (extended rhyme).

WHITE PINE PRESS, 10 Village Square, Fredonia NY 14063. (716)672-5743. Fax: (716)672-4724. E-mail: wpine@netsync.net. Website: http://www.netsync.net/users/wpine/. **Acquisitions:** Dennis Maloney, editor/publisher (nonfiction); Elaine LaMattina, managing director (fiction). "White Pine Press is your passport to a world of voices, emphasizing literature from around the world." Publishes hardcover and trade paperback originals. **Publishes 10 titles/year. Receives 400 queries and 150 mss/year. 20% of books from first-time authors; 99% from unagented writers. Pays 5-10% royalty on wholesale price. Offers $250 and up advance.** Publishes book 18 months after acceptance of ms. Accepts simultaneous submissions. Reports in 2 months on queries. Book catalog free.
Imprint(s): Springhouse Editions.
Nonfiction: Subjects include ethnic, language/literature, translation, women's issues/studies. Query.
Fiction: Ethnic, literary, short story collections. Interested in strong novels. Query with synopsis and 2 chapters.
Poetry: "We do a large amount of poetry in translation. We award the White Pine Press Poetry Prize annually. Write for details. We read manuscripts of American poetry only as part of our annual competition." Query.
Recent Title(s): *An Albanian Journal*, by Edmund Keeley; *Lost Chronicles of Terra Firma*, by Rosario Aguilar.

ALBERT WHITMAN AND CO., 6340 Oakton St., Morton Grove IL 60053-2723. (847)581-0033. **Acquisitions**: Kathleen Tucker, editor-in-chief. Estab. 1919. Albert Whitman publishes "good books for children." Publishes hardcover originals and paperback reprints. **Averages 30 titles/year. Receives 5,000 submissions/year. 20% of books from first-time authors; 70% from unagented writers. Pays 10% royalty for novels; 5% for picture books.** Publishes book

an average of 18 months after acceptance. Simultaneous submissions OK. Reports in 5 months. Book catalog for 8×10 SAE and 2 first-class stamps. Manuscript guidelines for #10 SASE.
Nonfiction: "All books are for ages 2-12." Concept books about special problems children have, easy science, social studies, math. Query.
Fiction: "All books are for ages 2-12." Adventure, ethnic, fantasy, historical, humor, mystery, picture books and concept books (to help children deal with problems). "We need easy historical fiction and picture books. No young adult and adult books." Submit outline/synopsis and sample chapters (novels) and complete ms (picture books).
Recent Title(s): *Sugar Was My Best Food: Diabetes and Me*, by Carol Peacock, Adair Gregory and Kyle Gregory (autobiography); *Missing: One Stuffed Rabbit*, by Maryann Cocca-Leffler.
Tips: "There is a trend toward highly visual books. The writer can most easily sell us strong picture book text that has good illustration possibilities. We sell mostly to libraries, but our bookstore sales are growing."

THE WHITSTON PUBLISHING CO., P.O. Box 958, Troy NY 12181-0958. Phone/fax: (518)283-4363. E-mail: whitson@capital.net. Website: http://www.capital.net/com/whitston. **Acquisitions:** Jean Goode, editorial director. Estab. 1969. "We are concentrating mostly on American literture." Publishes hardcover originals. **Averages 15 titles/year. Receives 100 submissions/year. 50% of books from first-time authors; 100% from unagented writers. Pays 10% royalty on price of book (wholesale or retail) after sale of 500 copies.** Publishes book 1 year after acceptance. Reports in up to 6 months. Book catalog for $1.
Nonfiction: "We publish scholarly and critical books in the arts, humanities and some of the social sciences. We will consider author bibliographies. We are interested in scholarly monographs and collections of essays." Query. Reviews artwork/photos as part of ms package.
Recent Title(s): *The Ghost Dance Anthology*, edited by Hugh Fox; *One Million Words of Book Notes*, by Richard Kostelantz (literary criticism).

N **MARKUS WIENER PUBLISHERS INC.**, 231 Nassau St., Princeton NJ 08542. (609)971-1141. **Acquisitions:** Shelley Frisch, editor-in-chief. Markus Wiener publishes textbooks in history subjects and regional world history. Publishes hardcover originals and trade paperback originals and reprints. **Publishes 20-25 titles/year; imprint publishes 5 titles/year. Receives 50-150 queries and 50 mss/year. Pays 10% royalty on net sales.** Publishes book 1 year after acceptance. Reports in 2 months on queries and proposals. Book catalog free.
Imprint(s): Topics in World History.
Nonfiction: Textbook. History subjects, Caribbean studies, Middle East, Africa.
Recent Title(s): *Challenges to Democracy* (Middle East studies).

MICHAEL WIESE PRODUCTIONS, 11288 Ventura Blvd., Suite 821, Studio City CA 91604. (818)379-8799. Website: http://www.mwp.com. **Acquisitions:** Ken Lee, vice president. Michael Wiese publishes how-to books for professional film or video makers, film schools and bookstores. Publishes trade paperback originals. **Publishes 4-6 titles/year. Receives 10-15 queries/year. 90% of books from first-time authors. Pays 7-10% royalty on retail price. Offers $500-1,000 advance.** Publishes book 10 months after acceptance of ms. Accepts simultaneous submissions. Reorts in 1 month on queries and proposals, 2 months on mss. Book catalog free.
Nonfiction: How-to. Subjects include professional film and videomaking. Call before submitting nonfiction; submit outline with 3 sample chapters.
Recent Title(s): *Producer to Producer, 2nd Edition.*
Tips: Audience is professional filmmakers, writers, producers, directors, actors and university film students.

WILD FLOWER PRESS, Blue Water Publishing, P.O. Box 190, Mill Spring NC 28756. (704)894-8444. Fax: (704)894-8454. E-mail: bluewaterp@aol.com. Website: http://www.5thworld.com or http://bluewater.com. President: Pam Meyer. **Acquisitions:** Brian Crissey; Julie Sherar, editor. "Wild Flower Press strives to preserve the Earth by publishing books that develop new wisdom about our emerging planetary citizenship, bringing information from the outerworlds to our world." Publishes hardcover originals and trade paperback originals and reprints. **Publishes 6 titles/year. Receives 50 queries and 25 mss/month. 80% of books from first-time authors; 90% from unagented writers. Pays 7½-15% royalty.** Publishes book 16 months after acceptance of ms. Accepts simultaneous submissions. Reports in 2 months on mss. Book catalog and ms guidelines for SASE with 55¢ postage.
Nonfiction: Books about extraterrestrial research and experiences. Submit outline. Reviews artwork/photos as part of ms package. Send photocopies.
Recent Title(s): *The Voice of the Infinite in the Small*, by Joanne Lauck.

WILDER PUBLISHING CENTER, 919 Lafond Ave., St. Paul MN 55104. (612)659-6013. Fax: (612)642-2061. E-mail: vlh@wilder.org. Website: http://www.wilder.org. **Acquisitions:** Vincent Hyman, editorial director. Wilder Publishing Center emphasizes community and nonprofit organization management and development. Publishes trade paperback originals. **Publishes 4-6 titles/year. Receives 30 queries and 15 mss/year. 75% of books from first-time authors; 100% from unagented writers. Pays 10% royalty on net. Books are sold through direct mail; average discount is 15%. Offers $1,000-3,000 advance.** Publishes book 1 year after acceptance of ms. Accepts simultaneous submissions, if so noted. Reports in 1 month on queries and proposals, 3 months on mss. Book catalog and ms guidelines free.
Nonfiction: Nonprofit management, organizational development, community organizing. Subjects include government/politics, sociology. "We are in a growth mode and welcome proposals in these areas. We are seeking manuscripts that

report 'best practice' methods using handbook or workbook formats." Phone query OK before submitting proposal with detailed chapter ouline, 1 sample chapter and SASE.
Recent Title(s): *Coping with Cutbacks: The Nonprofit Guide to Success When Times Are Tight.*
Tips: "Writers must be practitioners with a passion for their work and experience presenting their techniques at conferences. Freelance writers with an interest in our niches could do well searching out and teaming up with such practitioners as our books sell very well to a tightly-targeted market."

WILDERNESS PRESS, 2440 Bancroft Way, Berkeley CA 94704-1676. (510)843-8080. Fax: (510)548-1355. E-mail: wpress@ix.netcom.com. Website: http://www.wildernesspress.com. **Acquisitions:** Caroline Winnett, publisher. Estab. 1967. "We seek to publish the most accurate, reliable and useful outdoor books and maps for self-propelled outdoor activities." Publishes paperback originals. **Publishes 10 titles/year. Receives 150 submissions/year. 20% of books from first-time authors; 95% from unagented writers. Pays 8-10% royalty on retail price. Offers $1,000 average advance.** Publishes book 8 months after acceptance of ms. Reports in 1 month. *Writer's Market* recommends allowing 2 months for reply. Book catalog free.
Nonfiction: "We publish books about the outdoors. Most are trail guides for hikers and backpackers, but we also publish how-to books about the outdoors. The manuscript must be accurate. The author must thoroughly research an area in person. If he is writing a trail guide, he must walk all the trails in the area his book is about. The outlook must be strongly conservationist. The style must be appropriate for a highly literate audience." Request proposal guidelines.
Recent Title(s): *50 Best Short Hikes in California's Central Coast*, by John Krist (hiking guide).

JOHN WILEY & SONS, INC., 605 Third Ave., New York NY 10158. Associate Publisher/Editor-in-Chief of General Interest Publishing: Carole Hall. **Acquisitions**: Editorial Department. "The General Interest group publishes books for the consumer market." Publishes hardcover originals, trade paperback originals and reprints. **Pays "competitive royalty rates."** Accepts simultaneous submissions. Book catalog free.
Nonfiction: Biography, how-to, children's/juvenile, reference, self-help. Subjects include child guidance/parenting, current affairs, health/medicine, history, hospitality, military/war, psychology, science, women's issues/studies, African American interest. Query.
Recent Title(s): *The New York Public Library Business Desk Reference.*

WILLIAMSON PUBLISHING CO., P.O. Box 185, Church Hill Rd., Charlotte VT 05445. Website: http://www.williamsonbooks.com. President: Jack Williamson. **Acquisitions**: Susan Williamson, editorial director. Estab. 1983. "Our mission is to help every child fulfull his/her potential and experience personal growth." Publishes trade paperback originals. **Publishes 15 titles/year. Receives 1,500 queries and 2,000 mss/year. 75% of books from first-time authors; 90% from unagented writers. Pays 7½-15% royalty on retail price. Advance negotiable.** Publishes book 18 months after acceptance. Accepts simultaneous submissions, but prefers 1 year exclusivity. Reports in 4 months with SASE. Book catalog for 8½×11 SAE with 4 first-class stamps.

- Williamson's big success is its *Kids Can!®* series books like *Super Science Concoctions. The Kids' Multicultural Art Book* won the Parents' Choice Gold Award; *Tales Alive* won Benjamin Franklin best juvenile fiction.

Nonfiction: Children's/juvenile, children's creative learning books on subjects ranging from science, art, to early learning skills. Adult books include cookbook, how-to, self-help. "Williamson has four very successful children's book series: *Little Hands®* (ages 2-6), *Kids Can!®* (ages 5-10), *Tales Alive®* (folktales plus activities, age 4-10) and *Kaleidoscope Kids®* (96-page, single subject, ages 7-12). They must incorporate learning through doing. *No picture books or fiction please!* Please don't call concerning your submission. It never helps your review, and it takes too much of our time. With an SASE, you'll hear from us." Submit outline, 2-3 sample chapters and SASE.
Recent Title(s): *Alphabet Art*, by Judy Press.
Tips: "Our children's books are used by kids, their parents, and educators. They encourage self-discovery, creativity and personal growth. Our books are based on the philosophy that children learn best by doing, by being involved. Our authors need to be excited about their subject area and equally important, excited about kids."

WILLOW CREEK PRESS, P.O. Box 147, 9931 Highway 70 W., Minocqua WI 54548. (715)358-7010. Fax: (715)358-2807. E-mail: ljevert@newnorth.net. Website: http://www.willowcreekpress.com. **Acquisitions:** Laura Evert, managing editor. Willow Creek specializes in nature, outdoor and animal books, calendars and videos with high-quality photography. Publishes hardcover and trade paperback originals and reprints. **Publishes 25 titles/year. Receives 400 queries and 150 mss/year. 15% of books from first-time authors; 50% from unagented writers. Pays 6-15% royalty on wholesale price. Offers $2,000-5,000 advance.** Publishes book 10 months after acceptance of ms. Accepts simultaneous submissions. Reports in 2 months. Book catalog for $1.
Nonfiction: Coffee table book, cookbook, how-to, humor, illustrated book. Subjects include wildlife, pets, cooking/foods/nutrition, gardening, hobbies, nature/environment, photography, recreation, sports. Submit outline and 1 sample chapter. Must include SASE for return of materials. Reviews artwork/photos as part of ms package. Send photocopies.
Fiction: Adventure, humor, picture books, short story collections. Submit synopsis and 2 sample chapters.
Recent Title(s): *Cats Have No Masters . . . Just Friends*, by Karen Anderson (cat behavior); *Poetry for Guys*, by Kathy Schmook.

WILSHIRE BOOK CO., 12015 Sherman Rd., North Hollywood CA 91605-3781. (818)765-8579. Publisher: Melvin Powers. **Acquisitions:** Marcia Grad, senior editor. Estab. 1947. "You are not only what you are today, but also what you choose to become tomorrow." Publishes trade paperback originals and reprints. **Publishes 25 titles/year. Receives 3,000 submissions/year. 80% of books from first-time authors; 75% from unagented writers. Pays standard royalty.** Publishes book 6 months after acceptance of ms. Reports in 2 months. Welcomes telephone calls to discuss mss or book concepts.

Nonfiction: Self-help, motivation/inspiration/spiritual, psychology, recovery, how-to. Subjects include personal success, entrepreneurship, marketing on the Internet, mail order, horsemanship. Min. 60,000 words. Requires detailed chapter outline, 3 sample chapters and SASE. Accepts queries and complete mss. Reviews artwork/photos as part of ms package. Send photocopies.

Fiction: Allegories that teach principles of psychological/spiritual growth or offer guidance in living. Min. 30,000 words. Requires synopsis, 3 sample chapters and SASE. Accepts complete mss.

Recent Title(s): *Guide to Rational Living*, by Albert Ellis, Ph.D. and Robert Harper, Ph.D.; *The Knight in Rusty Armor*, by Robert Fisher.

Tips: "We are vitally interested in all new material we receive. Just as you hopefully submit your manuscript for publication, we hopefully read every one submitted, searching for those that we believe will be successful in the marketplace. Writing and publishing must be a team effort. We need you to write what we can sell. We suggest that you read the successful books mentioned above or others that are similar to the manuscript you want to write. Analyze them to discover what elements make them winners. Duplicate those elements in your own style, using a creative new approach and fresh material, and you will have written a book we can catapult onto the bestseller list."

WINDSOR BOOKS, Windsor Marketing Corp., P.O. Box 280, Brightwaters NY 11718-0280. (516)321-7830. Website: http://www.ison.com/windsor/index.html. **Acquisitions:** Jeff Schmidt, managing editor. Estab. 1968. "Our books are for serious investors." Publishes hardcover and trade paperback originals, reprints, and very specific software. **Publishes 8 titles/year. Receives approximately 40 submissions/year. 60% of books from first-time authors; 90% from unagented writers. Pays 10% royalty on retail price; 5% on wholesale price (50% of total cost). Offers variable advance.** Publishes book an average of 6 months after acceptance of ms. Simultaneous submissions OK. Reports in 2 weeks on queries. *Writer's Market* recommends allowing 2 months for reply. Book catalog and ms guidelines free.

Nonfiction: How-to, technical. Subjects include business/economics (investing in stocks and commodities). Interested in books on strategies, methods for investing in the stock market options market and commodity markets. Query or submit outline and sample chapters. Reviews artwork/photos as part of ms package.

Tips: "We sell through direct mail to our mailing list and other financial lists. Writers must keep their work original; this market tends to have a great deal of information overlap among publications."

WINDWARD PUBLISHING, INC., P.O. Box 371005, Miami FL 33137-1005. (305)576-6232. **Acquisitions**: Jack Zinzow, vice president. Estab. 1973. Windward publishes illustrated natural history and recreation books. Publishes trade paperback originals. **Publishes 6 titles/year. Receives 50 queries and 10 mss/year. 35% of books from first-time authors; 100% from unagented writers. Pays 10% royalty on wholesale price.** Publishes book 14 months after acceptance of ms. Accepts simultaneous submissions. Reports in 2 weeks. *Writer's Market* recommends allowing 2 months for reply.

Nonfiction: Illustrated books, natural history, handbooks. Subjects include agriculture/horticulture, animals, gardening, nature/environment, recreation (fishing, boating, diving, camping), science. Query with SASE. Reviews artwork/photos as part of the ms package.

Recent Title(s): *Mammals of Florida.*

WISDOM PUBLICATIONS, 199 Elm St., Somerville MA 02144. (617)776-7416, ext. 25. Fax: (617)776-7844. E-mail: editorial@wisdompubs.org. Website: http://www.widsompubs.org. Publisher: Timothy McNeill. **Acquisitions:** Editorial Director. "Wisdom Publications is dedicated to making available authentic Buddhist works for the benefit of all. We publish translations, commentories and teachings of past and contemporary Buddhist masters and original works by leading Buddhist scholars." Publishes hardcover originals, trade paperback originals and reprints. **Publishes 12-15 titles/year. Receives 240 queries/year. 50% of books from first-time authors; 95% from unagented writers. Pays 4-8% royalty on wholesale price (net).** Publishes book within 2 years after acceptance of ms. Book catalog and ms guidelines free on website.

Nonfiction: Subjects include philosophy (Buddhist or comparative Buddhist/Western), Buddhism, Buddhist texts and Tibet. Query with SASE. Reviews artwork/photos as part of ms package. Send photocopies.

Poetry: Buddhist.

Recent Title(s): *The Tibet Guide: Central and Western Tibet*, by Stephen Batchelor; *The Clouds Should Know Me By Now: Buddhist Poet Monks of China*, edited by Mike O'Connor and Red Pine.

Tips: "We are basically a publisher of Buddhist books—all schools and traditions of Buddhism. Please see our catalog or our website *before* you send anything to us to get a sense of what we publish."

WOODBINE HOUSE, 6510 Bells Mill Rd., Bethesda MD 20817. (301)897-3570. Fax: (301)897-5838. E-mail: info@woodbinehouse.com. **Acquisitions**: Susan Stokes, editor. Estab. 1985. "We publish books for or about individuals with disabilities that will, in our judgment, help those individuals and their families live fulfilling and satisfying lives in their communities." Publishes hardcover and trade paperback originals and reprints. **Publishes 8 titles/year. 90% of books from unagented writers. Pays 10-12% royalty.** Publishes book 18 months after acceptance of ms. Accepts

simultaneous submissions. Reports in 2 months. Book catalog and ms guidelines for 6×9 SAE with 3 first-class stamps.
Nonfiction: Publishes books for and about children and adults with disabilities. No personal accounts or general parenting guides. Submit outline and 3 sample chapters with SASE. Reviews artwork/photos as part of ms package.
Fiction: Children's picture books. Submit entire ms with SASE.
Recent Title(s): *Views From Our Shores: Growing Up With a Brother or Sister With Special Needs*, by Donald Meyer; *Zipper, the Kid with ADHD*, by Caroline Janover.
Tips: "Do not send us a proposal on the basis of this description. Examine our catalog and a couple of our books to make sure you are on the right track. Put some thought into how your book could be marketed (aside from in bookstores). Keep cover letters concise and to the point; if it's a subject that interests us, we'll ask to see more."

N **WOODHOLME HOUSE PUBLISHERS**, 1829 Reisterstown Rd., #130, Baltimore MD 21208. (410)653-7903. Fax: (410)653-7904. **Acquisitions**: Gregg A. Wilhelm, director. "We are a regional-interest publisher (mid-Atlantic/Chesapeake Bay area) covering a variety of genres." Publishes hardcover and trade paperback originals. **Publishes 5 titles/year. Receives 100 queries and 50 mss/year. 50% of books from first-time authors; 80% from unagented writers. Pays 5-15% royalty on retail price.** Publishes book 9 months after acceptance of ms. Accepts simultaneous submissions. Reports in 1 month on queries, 3 months on mss. Manuscript guidelines for #10 SASE.
Nonfiction: Biography, cookbook, guidebooks, history, memoir. Regional subjects. Submit proposal package, including cover letter, outline/synopsis, author bio and SASE. Reviews artwork/photos as part of ms package. Send photocopies.
Fiction: Short story collections, regional interest. "Setting/people/place should have regional flavor. We are impressed with work that possesses a strong sense of place." Query or submit synopsis with 1 sample chapter and SASE.
Recent Title(s): *KAL Draws a Crowd*, by Kevin Kallaugher (political cartoons).
Tips: "Audience is interested in the Chesapeake Bay and Mid-Atlantic area, from Baltimore, Maryland, out."

WORDWARE PUBLISHING, INC., 1506 Capitol Ave., Plano TX 75074. (214)423-0090. Fax: (214)881-9147. E-mail: jhill@wordware.com. Website: http://www.wordware.com. President: Russell A. Stultz. **Acquisitions:** Mary Goldman, editor. Wordware publishes computer/electronics books covering a broad range of technologies for professional programmers and developers. Publishes trade paperback and mass market paperback originals. **Publishes 40-50 titles/year. Receives 100-150 queries and 50-75 mss/year. 40% of books from first-time authors; 95% from unagented writers. Pays 10-14% royalty on wholesale price. Offers $3,000-5,000 advance.** Publishes book 6 months after acceptance of ms. Acccpts simultaneous submissions. Reports in 2 months. Book catalog and ms guidelines free.
Imprint(s): Iron Castle Productions (George Baxter, acquisitions editor), **Republic of Texas Press, Seaside Press.**
Nonfiction: Reference, technical, textbook. Subjects include computers, electronics. "Wordware publishes advanced titles for developers and professional programmers." Submit proposal package, including table of contents, 2 sample chapters, target audience summation, competing books.
Recent Title(s): *Learn Microsoft Office 97*, by Russell A. Stultz (software).

WORKMAN PUBLISHING CO., 708 Broadway, New York NY 10003. (212)254-5900. Fax: (212)254-8098. Website: http://www.workman.com. **Acquisitions:** Sally Kovalchik, editor-in-chief (gardening, popular reference, humor); Suzanne Rafer, executive editor (cookbook, child care, parenting, teen interest); Ruth Sullivan, senior editor (humor, fashion, health); Anne Kostick, senior editor (crafts, children, computers); Michaela Muntean, senior editor (children's). Estab. 1967. "We are a trade paperback house specializing in a wide range of popular nonfiction. We publish no adult fiction and very little children's fiction. We also publish a full range of full color wall and Page-A-Day® calendars." Publishes hardcover and trade paperback originals. **Publishes 40 titles/year. Receives thousands of queries/year. Open to first-time authors. Pays variable royalty on retail price. Advance varies.** Publishes book 1 year after acceptance of ms. Accepts simultaneous submissions. Reports in 4 months. Book catalog free.
Imprint(s): Algonquin Books of Chapel Hill, Artisan.
Nonfiction: Cookbooks, gift books, how-to, humor. Subjects include child guidance/parenting, gardening, health/medicine, sports, travel. Query with sample chapters and SASE. Reviews artwork/photos as part of ms package "if relevant to project. Don't send anything you can't afford to lose."
Recent Title(s): *Children's Letters to God*, by Stuart Hample (children write to God).

WORLD LEISURE, P.O. Box 160, Hampstead NH 03841. (617)569-1966. Fax: (617)561-7654. E-mail: wleisure@aol.com. **Acquisitions:** Charles Leocha, president. World Leisure specializes in travel books, activity guidebooks and self-help titles. Publishes trade paperback originals. **Publishes 6-8 titles/year. Pays royalty or makes outright purchase. No advance.** Reports in 2 months on proposals.
Nonfiction: "We will be publishing annual updates to *Ski Europe* and *Skiing America*. Writers planning any ski stories should contact us for possible add-on assignments at areas not covered by our staff. We also will publish general travel titles such as Travelers' Rights, Family travel guides, guidebooks about myths and legends, the *Cheap Dates* (affordable activity guidebooks) series and self/help books such as *Getting To Know You*, and *A Woman's ABCs of Life*." Submit outline, intro chapter and annotated table of contents with SASE.
Recent Title(s): *Seababies and Their Friends*, by Cathleen Arone.

WRITE WAY PUBLISHING, 10555 E. Dartmouth, Suite 210, Aurora CO 80014 Website: http://www.writewaypub.com. **Acquisitions**: Dorrie O'Brien, owner/editor. "Write Way is a fiction-only small press concentrating on genre publications such as mysteries, soft science fiction, fairy tale/fantasy and horror/thrillers." Publishes hardcover and trade paperback originals. **Publishes 10-15 titles/year. Receives 1,000 queries and 350 mss/year. 50% of books from first-time authors; 95% from unagented writers. Pays 8-10% royalty on wholesale price. No advance.** Publishes book within 3 years after acceptance of ms. Accepts simultaneous submissions. Reports in 1 month on queries and proposals; 6 months on mss. Book brochure and ms guidelines free for SASE.

Fiction: Fantasy, horror, mystery, science fiction, suspense. Query with short synopsis, 1-2 sample chapters and postage with proper-sized box or envelope. "We only consider completed works."

Recent Title(s): *For the Time Being*, by M. DesJardin.

Tips: "We find that lengthy outlines and/or synopsis are unnecessary and much too time-consuming for our editors to read. We prefer a very short plot review and one to two chapters to get a feel for the writer's style. If we like what we read, then we'll ask for the whole manuscript."

WRITER'S DIGEST BOOKS, F&W Publications, 1507 Dana Ave., Cincinnati OH 45207. Website: http://www.writersdigest.com. Editor: Jack Heffron. **Acquisitions:** Acquisitions Coordinator. Estab. 1920. Writer's Digest Books is the premiere source for books about writing, publishing instructional and reference books for writers that concentrate on the creative technique and craft of writing rather than the marketing of writing. Publishes hardcover and paperback originals. **Publishes 28 titles/year. Pays 10-20% royalty on net receipts.** Accepts simultaneous submissions, if so noted. Publishes book 18 months after acceptance of ms. Reports in 2 months. Book catalog for 9×12 SAE with 6 first-class stamps.

Nonfiction: Instructional and reference books for writers. "Our instruction books stress results and how specifically to achieve them. Should be well-researched, yet lively and readable. Our books concentrate on writing techniques over marketing techniques. We do *not* want to see books telling readers how to crack specific nonfiction markets: *Writing for the Computer Market* or *Writing for Trade Publications*, for instance. Concentrate on broader writing topics. In the offices here we refer to a manuscript's 4T value—manuscripts must have information writers can Take To The Typewriter. We are continuing to grow our line of reference books for writers, such as *Modus Operandi* and *Malicious Intent* in our Howdunit series, and *A Writer's Guide to Everyday Life in the Middle Ages*. References must be usable, accessible, and, of course, accurate." Query or submit outline and sample chapters with SASE. "Be prepared to explain how the proposed book differs from existing books on the subject." *No fiction or poetry.* "Writer's Digest Books also publishes instructional books for photographers and songwriters, but the main thrust is on writing books. The same philosophy applies to songwriting and photography books: they must instruct about the creative craft, as opposed to instructing about marketing."

Recent Title(s): *Dynamic Characters*, by Nancy Kress.

WRITERS PRESS, 5278 Chinden Blvd., Boise ID 83714. (208)327-0566. Fax: (208)327-3477. E-mail: writers@cyberhighway.net. Website: http://www.writerspress.com. Publisher: John Ybarra. **Acquisitions:** Crickett Syes, acquisitions. "Our philosophy is to show children how to help themselves and others. By publishing high-quality children's literature that is both fun and educational, we are striving to make a difference in today's educational world." Publishes hardcover and trade paperback originals. **Publishes 6 titles/year. Receives 50 queries and 30 mss/year. 60% of books from first-time authors; 100% from unagented writers. Pays 4-12% royalty or makes outright purchase of up to $1,500.** Publishes book 6 months after acceptance of ms. Catalog and ms guidelines free.

Nonfiction: Children's/juvenile. Subjects include education, history, inclusion, special education. Query. Reviews artwork/photos as part of ms package. Send photocopies.

Fiction: Adventure, historical, juvenile, picture books, young adult, inclusion, special education. Query.

Recent Title(s): *Alpha*, by Kevin Boos.

YALE UNIVERSITY PRESS, 302 Temple St., New Haven CT 06520. (203)432-0960. Fax: (203)432-0948. Website: http://www.yale.edu/yup. **Acquisitions:** Jonathan Brent, editorial director (literature, philosophy); Charles Grench, editor-in-chief (anthropology, history, Judaic studies, religion, women's studies); Jean E. Thomson Black, editor (science, medicine); John S. Covell, senior editor (economics, law, political science); Harry Haskell, editor (music, classics, archaeology, performing arts); Richard Miller, assistant editor, (poetry); Judy Metro, senior editor (art, art history, architecture, geography); Gladys Topkis, senior editor (education, psychiatry, psychology, sociology). Estab. 1908. "We publish scholarly and general interest books." Publishes hardcover and trade paperback originals. **Publishes 225 titles/year. Receives 8,000 queries and 400 mss/year. 15% of books from first-time authors; 85% from unagented writers. Pays 0-15% royalty on net price. Offers $500-50,000 advance (based on expected sales).** Publishes book 1 year after acceptance of ms. Accepts simultaneous submissions, if so noted. Reports in 1 month on queries, 2 months on proposals, 3 months on mss. Book catalog and ms guidelines for #10 SASE.

Nonfiction: Biography, illustrated book, reference, textbook, scholarly works. Subjects include Americana, anthropology/archaeology, art/architecture, economics, education, history, language/literature, medicine, military/war, music/dance, philosophy, psychology, religion, science, sociology, women's issues/studies. "Our nonfiction has to be at a very high level. Most of our books are written by professors or journalists, with a high level of expertise." Query by letter with SASE. "We'll ask if we want to see more. No unsolicited manuscripts. We won't return them." Reviews artwork/photos as part of ms package. Send photocopies, not originals.

Poetry: Publishes 1 book each year. Submit complete ms to Yale Series of Younger Poets Competition. Open to poets under 40 who have not had a book previously published. Submit ms of 48-64 pages in February. Entry fee: $15. Send SASE for rules and guidelines.

Recent Title(s): *Diplomacy for the Next Century*, by Abba Eban (politics).

Tips: "Audience is scholars, students and general readers."

YMAA PUBLICATION CENTER, 38 Hyde Park Ave., Jamaica Plain MA 02130. (800)669-8892. Fax: (617)524-4184. **Acquisitions:** Andrew Murray, editor. Estab. 1982. "We are a well-established publisher of books on Chinese Chi Kung (Qigong) and Chinese martial arts. We are expanding our focus to include books on healing, wellness, meditation and subjects related to Chinese culture and Chinese medicine." Publishes hardcover and trade paperback originals and reprints. **Publishes 6 titles/year. Pays royalty on retail price. No advance.** Reports in 2 months on proposals.
Nonfiction: "We are most interested in Chinese martial arts, Chinese medicine and Chinese Qigong. We publish Chinese philosophy, health, meditation, massage and martial arts. We no longer publish or solicit books for children. We also produce instructional videos to accompany our books on traditional Chinese martial arts, meditation, massage and Chi Kung." Send proposal with outline, 1 sample chapter and SASE.
Recent Title(s): *Back Pain—Chinese Qigong for Healing and Prevention*, by Dr. Yang Jwing-Ming.
Tips: "If you are submitting health-related material (Qigong/Chinese medicine etc.) please list *specific benefits* readers can expect."

ZEBRA BOOKS, Kensington, 850 Third Ave., 16th Floor, New York NY 10022. (212)407-1500. **Acquisitions**: Ann Lafarge, editor; Kate Duffy, senior editor (historical, regency, romance); John Scognamiglio, senior editor (romance, mystery, thrillers, pop culture); Hillary Sares (Precious Gem romances). "Zebra Books is dedicated to women's fiction, which includes, but is not limited to romance." Publishes hardcover originals, trade paperback and mass market paperback originals and reprints. **Publishes 140-170 titles/year. 5% of books from first-time authors; 30% from unagented writers. Pays variable royalty and advance.** Publishes book 18 months after acceptance of ms. Accepts simultaneous submissions. Reports in 1 month on queries, in 3 months on mss. Book catalog for #10 SASE.
Fiction: Romance, women's fiction. Query with synopsis and SASE. *No unsolicited submissions.*

ZOLAND BOOKS, INC., 384 Huron Ave., Cambridge MA 02138. (617)864-6252. Fax: (617)661-4998. **Acquisitions:** Stephen Hull, editor (nonfiction); Roland Pease, Jr., publisher/editor (fiction). Estab. 1987. "Zoland Books is an independent publishing company producing fiction, poetry and art books of literary interest." Publishes hardcover and trade paperback originals. **Publishes 8-12 titles/year. Receives 400 submissions/year. 15% of books from first-time authors; 60% from unagented writers. Pays 7½% royalty on retail price.** Publishes book 18 months after acceptance of ms. Reports in 4 months. Book catalog for 6½×9½ SAE with 2 first-class stamps.
Nonfiction: Biography, art book. Subjects include art/architecture, language/literature, nature/environment, photography, regional, translation, travel, women's issues/studies. Query. Reviews artwork/photos as part of ms package.
Fiction: Literary, short story collections. Submit complete ms. *Writer's Market* recommends querying with SASE first.
Recent Title(s): *Reinventing a Continent*, by Brink (politics); *The Old World*, by Jonathan Strong; *Human Rights*, by Joseph Lease.
Tips: "We are most likely to publish books which provide original, thought-provoking ideas, books which will captivate the reader and are evocative."

ZONDERVAN PUBLISHING HOUSE, HarperCollins Publishers, 5300 Patterson Ave. SE, Grand Rapids MI 49530-0002. (616)698-6900. E-mail: zpub@zph.com. Website: http://www.zondervan.com. Publisher: Scott Bolinder. Editors: David Lambert, Sandy Vander Zeicht. **Acquisitions:** Manuscript Review Editor. Estab. 1931. "Our mission is to be the leading Christian communications company meeting the needs of people with resources that glorify Jesus Christ and promote biblical principles." Publishes hardcover and trade paperback originals and reprints. **Publishes 120 titles/year. Receives 3,000 submissions/year. 20% of books from first-time authors; 80% from unagented writers. Pays 14% royalty on net amount received on sales of cloth and softcover trade editions; 12% royalty on net amount received on sales of mass market paperbacks. Offers variable advance.** Reports in 3 months on proposals. SASE required. Guidelines for #10 SASE. To receive a recording about submissions call (616)698-6900.
Nonfiction and Fiction: Biography, autobiography, self-help, devotional, contemporary issues, Christian living, Bible study resources, references for lay audience; some adult fiction; youth and children's ministry, teens and children. Academic and Professional Books: college and seminary textbooks (biblical studies, theology, church history); preaching, counseling, discipleship, worship, and church renewal for pastors, professionals and lay leaders in ministry; theological and biblical reference books. All from religious perspective (evangelical). Submit outline/synopsis, 1 sample chapter, and SASE for return of materials.
Recent Title(s): *Perennial: Meditations for the Seasons of Life*, by Twila Paris; *Every Hidden Thing*, by Athol Dickson (mystery).

MARKETS THAT WERE listed in the 1998 edition of *Writer's Market* but do not appear this year are listed in the General Index with a notation explaining why they were omitted.

Canadian & International Book Publishers

Canadian book publishers share the same mission as their U.S. counterparts—publishing timely books on subjects of concern and interest to a targetable audience. Most of the publishers listed in this section, however, differ from U.S. publishers in that their needs tend toward subjects that are specifically Canadian or intended for a Canadian audience. Some are interested in submissions from Canadian writers only. There are many regional Canadian publishers that concentrate on region-specific subjects, and many Quebec publishers will consider only works in French.

U.S. writers hoping to do business with Canadian publishers should take pains to find out as much about their intended markets as possible. The listings will inform you about what kinds of books the companies publish and tell you whether they are open to receiving submissions from non-Canadians. To further target your markets and see very specific examples of the books they are publishing, send for catalogs from publishers or check their websites.

There has always been more government subsidy of publishing in Canada than in the U.S. However, with continued cuts in such subsidies, government support is on the decline. There are a few author-subsidy publishers in Canada and writers should proceed with caution when they are made this offer.

Publishers offering author subsidy arrangements (sometimes referred to as "joint venture," "co-publishing" or "cooperative publishing") are not listed in *Writer's Market*. If one of the publishers in this section offers you an author-subsidy arrangement or asks you to pay for all or part of the cost of any aspect of publishing (printing, marketing, etc.) or asks you to guarantee the purchase of a number of books yourself, please let us know about that company immediately.

Despite a healthy book publishing industry, Canada is still dominated by publishers from the U.S. Two out of every three books found in Canadian bookstores are published in the U.S. These odds have made some Canadian publishers even more determined to concentrate on Canadian authors and subjects. Writers interested in additional Canadian book publishing markets should consult *Literary Market Place* (R.R. Bowker & Co.), *The Canadian Writer's Guide* (Fitzhenry & Whiteside) and *The Canadian Writer's Market* (McClelland & Stewart).

INTERNATIONAL MAIL

U.S. postage stamps are useless on mailings originating outside of the U.S. When enclosing a self-addressed envelope for return of your query or manuscript from a publisher outside the U.S., you must include International Reply Coupons (IRCs). IRCs are available at your local post office and can be redeemed for stamps of any country. You can cut a substantial portion of your international mailing expenses by sending disposable proposals and manuscripts (i.e., photocopies or computer printouts which the recipient can recycle if she is not interested), instead of paying postage for the return of rejected material. Please note that the cost for items such as catalogs is expressed in the currency of the country in which the publisher is located.

For a list of publishers according to their subjects of interest, see the nonfiction and fiction sections of the Book Publishers Subject Index. Information on book publishers and producers listed in the previous edition of *Writer's Market* but not included in this edition can be found in the General Index.

THE ALTHOUSE PRESS, U.W.O., Faculty of Education, 1137 Western Rd., London, Ontario N6G 1G7 Canada. (519)661-2096. Fax: (519)661-3833. E-mail: press@edu.uwo.ca. Website: http://www.uwo.ca./edu/press. **Acquisitions:** Katherine Butson, editorial assistant. Publishes trade paperback originals and reprints. **Publishes 1-5 titles/year. Receives 30 queries and 19 mss/year. 100% of books from unagented writers. Pays 10% royalty on net price. Offers $300 advance.** Accepts simultaneous submissions. Reports in 2 weeks on queries, 4 months on mss. Book catalog and manuscript guidelines free.
Nonfiction: Education subjects. Query. Reviews artwork/photos as part of ms package. Send photocopies.
Recent Title(s): *Not Wanted in the Classroom*, by Vera C. Pletsch (the mentally challenged in the 1960s).
Tips: Audience is practicing teachers and graduate education students.

ANVIL PRESS, 204-A E. Broadway, Vancouver, British Columbia V5T 1W2 Canada. (604)876-8710. Fax: (604)879-2667. E.-mail: subter@pinc.com. Website: http://www.anvilpress.com. **Acquisitions:** Brian Kaufman. "Anvil Press publishes contemporary adult fiction, poetry and drama, giving voice to up-and-coming Canadian writers, exploring all literary genres, discovering, nurturing and promoting new Canadian literary talent." Publishes trade paperback originals. **Publishes 4 titles/year. Receives 100 queries/year. 80% of books from first-time authors; 70% from unagented writers. Pays 10-15% on wholesale price. Offers $200-400 advance.** Publishes ms 8 months after acceptance of ms. Reports in 2 months on queries and proposals, 6 months on mss. Book catalog for 9×12 SAE with 2 first-class stamps. Manuscript guidelines for #10 SASE.

- Anvil Press also publishes the literary magazine *sub-Terrain* and sponsors several contests, including the 3-Day Novel Writing Contest, the *sub-Terrain* Short Story Contest, the Last Poems Contest and the Creative Nonfiction Contest.

Fiction: Literary, plays, short story collections. Contemporary, modern literature—no formulaic or genre. Query with 2 sample chapters and SASE.
Poetry: "Get our catalog, look at our poetry, read *sub-Terrain* magazine (our quarterly literary magazine). We do very little poetry in book form—maybe 1 title per year." Query with 12 sample poems.
Recent Title(s): *Ivanhoe Station*, by Lyle Neff (poetry); *The Underwood*, by P.G. Tarr (3-Day Novel Contest winner).
Tips: Audience is young, informed, educated, aware, with an opinion, culturally active (films, books, the performing arts). "No U.S. authors, unless selected as the winner of our 3-Day Novel Contest. Research the appropriate publisher for your work."

ARSENAL PULP PRESS, 103, 1014 Homer St., Vancouver, British Columbia V6B 2W9 Canada. (604)687-4233. **Acquisitions**: Linda Field, editor. Estab. 1980. Publishes hardcover and trade paperback originals, trade paperback reprints. **Publishes 12-15 titles/year. Receives 400 queries and 200 mss/year. 25% of books from first-time authors; 100% from unagented writers. Pays 15% royalty on wholesale price. Advance varies.** Publishes book 1 year after acceptance of ms. Reports in 4 months, with exceptions. Book catalog and ms guidelines free with 9×12 SASE. *Publishes only Canadian writers.*
Imprint(s): Tillacum Library.
Nonfiction: Humor. Subjects include ethnic (Canadian, aboriginal issues), gay/lesbian, popular music, history (cultural), literature, regional (British Columbia), sociology, women's issues/studies. Submit outline and 2-3 sample chapters.
Fiction: Experimental, feminist, gay/lesbian, literary and short story collections. Submit synopsis and 2-3 sample chapters.
Recent Title(s): *American Whiskey Bar*, Michael Turner (novel); *You're Not As Good As You Think You Are*, by Chris Gudgean (humor/nonfiction).

BEACH HOLME PUBLISHERS LTD., 226-2040 W. 12th Ave., Vancouver, British Columbia V6J 2G2 Canada. (604)773-4868. Fax: (604)733-4860. E-mail: bhp@beachholme.bc.ca. Website: http://www.beachholme.bc.ca. **Acquisitions:** Joy Gugeler, managing editor; Teresa Bubela, editor. Estab. 1971. Beach Holme seeks "to publish excellent, emerging Canadian fiction and poetry and to contribute to Canadian materials for children with quality young adult historical novels." Publishes trade paperback originals. **Publishes 10 titles/year. Receives 1,000 submissions/year. 40% of books from first-time authors; 75% from unagented writers. Pays 10% royalty on retail price. Offers $500 average advance.** Publishes ms 1 year after acceptance. Accepts simultaneous submissions, if so noted. Reports in 2 months. Manuscript guidelines free.
Imprint(s): Porcepic Books (literary imprint); Sandcastle Book (children's/YA imprint).

- Beach Holme no longer publishes nonfiction.

Fiction: Adult literary fiction and poetry from authors published in Canadian literary magazines. Young adult (Canada historical/regional). "Interested in excellent quality, imaginative writing. *Accepting only Canadian submissions.* Send cover letter, SASE, outline and two chapters.
Recent Title(s): *The Dream King*, by Gregor Robinson.
Tips: "Make sure the manuscript is well written. We see so many that only the unique and excellent can't be put down. Prior publication is a must. This doesn't necessarily mean book length manuscripts, but a writer should try to publish his or her short fiction."

BOREALIS PRESS, LTD., 9 Ashburn Dr., Nepean, Ontario K2E 6N4 Canada. Fax: (613)829-7783. Editorial Director: Frank Tierney. E-mail: borealis@istar.ca. **Acquisitions:** Glenn Clever, senior editor. Estab. 1972. Publishes hardcover and paperback originals. **Publishes 10-12 titles/year. Receives 400-500 submissions/year. 80% of books from first-**

time authors; 95% from unagented writers. Pays 10% royalty on list price. No advance.** Publishes book 18 months after acceptance. "No multiple submissions or electronic printouts on paper more than 8½ inches wide." Reports in 2 months. Book catalog for $3 and SASE.

Imprint(s): Tecumseh Press.

Nonfiction: "Only material Canadian in content." Biography, children's/juvenile, reference. Subjects include government/politics, history, language/literature. Query with outline, 2 sample chapters and SASE. No unsolicited mss. Reviews artwork/photos as part of ms package. Looks for "style in tone and language, reader interest and maturity of outlook."

Fiction: "Only material Canadian in content and dealing with significant aspects of the human situation." Adventure, ethnic, historical, juvenile, literary, romance, short story collections, young adult. Query with synopsis, 1-2 sample chapters and SASE. No unsolicited mss.

Recent Title(s): *A Critical Edition*, edited by Elizabeth Thompson (fiction); *How Parliament Works*, by John Beiermi.

THE BOSTON MILLS PRESS, 132 Main St., Erin, Ontario N0B 1T0 Canada. (519)833-2407. Fax: (519)833-2195. E-mail: books@boston-mills.on.ca. Website: http://www.boston-mills.on.ca. President: John Denison. **Acquisitions**: Noel Hudson, managing editor. Estab. 1974. Boston Mills Press publishes specific market titles of Canadian and American interest including history, transportation and regional guidebooks. Publishes hardcover and trade paperback originals. **Publishes 20 titles/year. Receives 200 submissions/year. 75% of books from first-time authors; 90% from unagented writers. Pays 10% royalty on retail price. Offers small advance.** Publishes book 1 year after acceptance. Accepts simultaneous submissions. Reports in 2 months. Book catalog free.

Nonfiction: Illustrated books. Subjects include history, nature, guidebooks. "We're interested in anything to do with Canadian or American history—especially transportation." No autobiographies. Query. Reviews artwork/photos as part of ms package.

Recent Title(s): *Superior*, by Gary and Joan McGuffin (Lake Superior).

Tips: "We can't compete with the big boys so we stay with short-run specific market books that bigger firms can't handle. We've done well this way so we'll continue in the same vein."

BROWN BEAR PRESS, 122a Felbrigg Ave., Toronto, Ontario M5M 2M5 Canada. E-mail: ruthbear@istar.ca. **Acquisitions**: Ruth Bradley-St-Cyr, publisher. Publishes trade paperback original nonfiction from Canadian authors only and reprints of Canadian classics. "We do not publish new fiction." **Publishes 4 titles/year. Pays 8-10% royalty on retail price. Offers $100-300 advance.** Publishes books 1 year after acceptance of ms. Reports in 2 months on proposals. Submission guidelines free with Canadian SASE or via e-mail.

Nonfiction: Canadian social, political and family issues. Query with SASE first.

Fiction: Reprints only. Canadian literature for adults and children.

BUTTERWORTHS CANADA, 75 Clegg Rd., Markham, Ontario L6G 1A1 Canada. (905)479-2665. Fax: (905)479-2826. E-mail: info@butterworths.ca. Website: http://www.butterworths.ca. **Acquisitions:** Caryl Young, publishing director. Butterworths publishes professional reference material for the legal, business and accounting markets. **Publishes 100 titles/year. Receives 100 queries and 10 mss/year. 50% of books from first-time authors; 100% from unagented writers. Pays 5-15% royalty on wholesale price; occasionally by fee. Offers $1,000-5,000 advance.** Publishes book 6 months after acceptance of ms. Accepts simultaneous submissions. Reports in 1 month. Book catalog free.

Nonfiction: Multimedia (disk and CD-Rom), reference, looseleaf. Subjects include health/medicine (medical law), legal and business reference. Query with SASE.

Recent Title(s): *The Law of Corporate Finance in Canada*, by Edmund Kwaw.

Tips: Audience is legal community, business, medical, accounting professions.

THE CANADIAN INSTITUTE OF STRATEGIC STUDIES, Box 2321, 2300 Yonge St., Suite 402, Toronto, Ontario M4P 1E4 Canada. (416)322-8128. Fax: (416)322-8129. E-mail: info@ciss.ca. Website: http://www.ciss.ca. **Acquisitions**: Alex Morrison, president; David Rudd, executive director; Jim Hanson, associate executive director; Peter Hammerschmidt, research officer. "The CISS is dedicated to the research, analysis and discussion of national and international strategic issues in a Canadian context. Many of our books deal with military history." Publishes hardcover and trade paperback originals. **Publishes 3-4 books/year. Receives 10 queries and 10 mss/year. 50% of books from first-time authors; 100% of books from unagented writers. Negotiates payment in advance.** Publishes book approximately 6 months after acceptance of ms. Accepts simultaneous submissions.

Imprint(s): The Peacekeeping Press, The Pearson Peacekeeping Centre.

Nonfiction: "The subject should fall within the area of national security of Canada or military history, strategic studies/analysis." *Writer's Market* recommends sending a query with SASE first.

Recent Title(s): *Maritime Defence of Canada*, by Roger Sarty (military history).

CANADIAN PLAINS RESEARCH CENTER, University of Regina, Regina, Saskatchewan S4S 0A2 Canada. (306)585-4795. Fax: (306)585-4699. **Acquisitions**: Brian Mlazgar, coordinator. Estab. 1973. Publishes scholarly paperback originals and some casebound originals. Publishes research on the Canadian plains. **Publishes 5-6 titles/year. Receives 10-15 submissions/year. 35% of books from first-time authors. Nonauthor-subsidy publishes 80% of books.** Publishes book 2 years after acceptance. Reports in 2 months. Book catalog and ms guidelines free. Also publishes *Prairie Forum*, a scholarly journal.

Nonfiction: Biography, illustrated book, technical, textbook, scholarly. Subjects include business and economics,

history, nature, politics, sociology. "The Canadian Plains Research Center publishes the results of research on topics relating to the Canadian Plains region, although manuscripts relating to the Great Plains region will be considered. Material *must* be scholarly. Do not submit health, self-help, hobbies, music, sports, psychology, recreation or cookbooks unless they have a scholarly approach. For example, we would be interested in acquiring a pioneer manuscript cookbook, with modern ingredient equivalents, if the material relates to the Canadian Plains/Great Plains region." Submit complete ms. *Writer's Market* recommends query with SASE first. Reviews artwork/photos as part of ms package.
Recent Title(s): *Discover Saskatchewan*, by Nilson (guide to historic sites and markers).
Tips: "Pay attention to manuscript preparation and accurate footnoting, according to *Chicago Manual of Style*."

CARSWELL THOMSON PROFESSIONAL PUBLISHING, The Thomson Corp., One Corporate Plaza, 2075 Kennedy Rd., Scarborough, Ontario M1T 3V4 Canada. (416)298-5024. Fax: (416)298-5094. E-mail: rfreeman@carswell .com. Website: http://www.carswell.com. **Acquisitions**: Robert Freeman, vice president, publishing. "Carswell Thomson is Canada's national resource of information and legal interpretations for law, accounting, tax and business professionals." Publishes hardcover originals. **Publishes 150-200 titles/year. 30-50% of books from first-time authors. Pays 5-15% royalty on wholesale price. Offers $1,000-5,000 advance.** Publishes book 6 months after acceptance of ms. Accepts simultaneous submissions. Reports in 3 months. Book catalog and ms guidelines free.
Nonfiction: Legal, tax and business reference. "Canadian information of a regulatory nature is our mandate." Submit proposal package, including résumé and outline.
Recent Title(s): *The Internet Handbook for Canadian Lawyers*, by M. Drew Jackson and Timothy L. Taylor.
Tips: Audience is Canada and persons interested in Canadian information; professionals in law, tax, accounting fields; business people interested in regulatory material.

N **CHA PRESS**, Canadian Healthcare Association, 17 York St., Ottawa, Ontario K1N 9J6 Canada. (613)241-8005, ext. 264. **Acquisitions:** Eleanor Sawyer, director of publishing. "CHA's mission is to improve the delivery of health services in Canada through policy development, advocacy and leadership." Publishes softcover specialty textbooks. **Publishes 8-10 titles/year. Receives 7 queries and 3 mss/year. 60% from first-time authors, 90% from unagented writers. Pays 10-17% royalty on retail price or makes outright purchase $250-1,000. Offers $500-1,500 advance.** Publishes book 8 months after acceptance of ms. Accepts simultaneous submissions. Reports in 3 months. Book catalog and ms guidelines free.
Nonfiction: How-to, textbook. Subjects include health/medicine, history, management, healthcare policy, healthcare administration. "CHA Press is looking to expand its frontlist for 1999-2000 on issues specific to Canadian healthcare system reform; continuum of care issues; integrated health delivery. Don't underestimate amount of time it will take to write or mistake generic 'how-to' health for mass media as appropriate for CHA's specialty press." Query with outline and with SASE.
Tips: "Audience is healthcare facility managers (senior/middle); policy analysts/researchers; nurse practitioners and other healthcare professionals; trustees."

CHEMTEC PUBLISHING, 38 Earswick Dr., Toronto-Scarborough, Ontario M1E 1C6 Canada. (416)265-2603. Fax: (416)265-1399. E-mail: chemtec@io.org. Website: http://www.io.org/~chemtec. **Acquisitions**: Anna Wypych, president. Publishes hardcover originals. **Publishes 5 titles/year. Receives 10 queries and 7 mss/year. 20% of books from first-time authors. Pays 5-15% royalty on retail price.** Publishes book 6 months after acceptance of ms. Accepts simultaneous submissions. Reports in 2 months on queries, 4 months on mss. Book catalog and ms guidelines free.
Nonfiction: Technical, textbook. Subjects include nature/environment, science, chemistry, polymers. Submit outline or sample chapter(s).
Recent Title(s): *Concepts in Polymer Thermodynamics*, by M.A. van Dijk and K. Wakker.
Tips: Audience is industrial research and universities.

COTEAU BOOKS, 2206 Dewdney Ave., Suite 401, Regina, Saskatchewan S4R 1H3 Canada. (306)777-0170. Fax: (306)522-5152. E-mail: coteau@coteau.unibase.com. Website: http://coteau.unibase.com. **Acquisitions**: Geoffrey Ursell, publisher; Barbara Sapergia, acquisitions editor. Estab. 1975. "Coteau Books publishes the finest Canadian fiction, poetry, drama and children's literature, with an emphasis on Saskatchewan and prairie writers." Publishes Canadian writers only. **Publishes 14 titles/year. Receives approximately 1,000 queries and mss/year. 10% of books from first-time authors; 95% from unagented writers. Pays 10% royalty on retail price or makes outright purchase of $50-200 for anthology contributors.** Publishes book 18 months after acceptance. Reports in 1 month on queries, 4 months on mss. Book catalog for SASE.
Nonfiction: Reference, desk calendars. Subjects include language/literature, regional studies. "*We publish only Canadian authors.*" Query with SASE first.
Fiction: Ethnic, feminist, humor, juvenile, literary, mainstream/contemporary, plays, short story collections. Submit complete ms. Query with SASE first. "We publish fiction and poetry from Canadian authors only."
Recent Title(s): *In the Misleading Absence of Light*, by Joanne Gerber (short stories); *On Glassy Wings*, by Anne Szumigalski (poetry).
Tips: "We do not publish picture books, but are interested in juvenile and YA fiction from Canadian authors."

N **CRESCENT MOON PUBLISHING**, P.O. Box 393, Maidstone Kent ME14 5XU United Kingdom. **Acquisitions:** Jeremy Robinson, director. Publishes hardcover and trade paperback originals. **Publishes 25 titles/year. Imprints**

publish 10 titles/year. Receives 100 queries and 400 mss/year. 2% of books from first-time authors; 2% from unagented writers. Royalty and advance negotiable. Publishes book 18 months after acceptance of ms. Accepts simultaneous submissions. Reports in 2 months on queries, 4 months on proposals and mss. Book catalog and ms guidelines free.

Imprint(s): Joe's Press, Pagan America Magazine, Passion Magazine.

Nonfiction: Biography, children's/juvenile, illustrated book, reference, textbook. Subjects include Americana, art/architecture, gardening, language/literature, music/dance, philosophy, religion, travel, women's issues/studies. "Dont send too much material. Include SASE and return address." Query with outline and 2 sample chapters with SASE. Reviews artwork/photos as part of the ms package. Send photocopies.

Fiction: Erotica, experimental, feminist, literary. "We do not publish much fiction at present, but will consider high quality new work." Submit synopsis and 2 sample chapters with SASE.

Poetry: "We prefer a small selection of the poet's very best work at first. We prefer non-rhyming poetry. Do not send too much material." Query with 6 sample poems.

Recent Title(s): *Paul Bowles and Bernardo Bertolucci*, by B.D. Bamede; *Rainer Maria Rilke: Selected Poems.*

Tips: "Our audience is interested in new contemporary writing."

CULTURE CONCEPTS PUBLISHERS, INC., 69 Ashmount Crescent, Toronto, Ontario M9R 1C9 Canada. (416)245-8119. Fax: (416)245-3383. E-mail: cultureconcepts@sympatico.ca. Website: http://www3.sympatico.ca/cultureconcepts. **Acquisitions**: Thelma Barer-Stein, Ph.D., publisher. Publishes hardcover and trade paperback originals. **Publishes 3-4 titles/year. Receives 40 queries and 10 mss/year. 50% of books from first-time authors; 95% from unagented writers. Pays 6-12% royalty. Offers $200-2,000 advance.** Publishes book within 2 years after acceptance of ms. Accepts simultaneous submissions. Reports in 1 month. Book catalog and ms guidelines free.

Nonfiction: Cookbook, how-to, humor, reference. Subjects include cooking, foods & nutrition, education (adult). "Contact us before sending any mss." Query with SASE.

Recent Title(s): *To Life*, by Barerstein, Schwartz, Vandersluis (kosher cookbook).

Tips: Audience is university-educated adults. "Culture Concepts publishes books that won't stay on the shelf."

ECRITS DES FORGES, C.P. 335, 1497 Laviolette, Trois-Rivières, Quebec G9A 5G4 Canada. (819)379-9813. Fax: (819)376-0774. E-mail: ecrits.desforges@aiqnet.com. **Acquisitions**: Gaston Bellemare, president. Publishes hardcover originals. **Publishes 40 titles/year. Receives 30 queries and 1,000 mss/year. 10% of books from first-time authors; 90% from unagented writers. Pays 10-30% royalty. Offers 50% advance.** Publishes book 9 months after acceptance of ms. Accepts simultaneous submissions. Reports in 9 months. Book catalog free.

Poetry: Poetry only and written in *French.* Submit 20 sample poems.

Recent Title(s): *Écrits profanes*, by Sor Juana Ines de la Cruz.

ECW PRESS, 2120 Queen St. E., Suite 200, Toronto, Ontario M4E 1E2 Canada. (416)694-3348. Fax: (416)698-9906. E-mail: ecw@sympatico.ca. President: Jack David. Estab. 1979. Publishes hardcover and trade paperback originals. **Publishes 20 titles/year. Receives 400 submissions/year. 50% of books from first-time authors; 80% from unagented writers. Nonauthor-subsidy publishes up to 5% of books. Pays 10% royalty on retail price.** Accepts simultaneous submissions. Reports in 2 months. Book catalog free.

Nonfiction: "ECW is particularly interested in popular biography, sports books and general trade books." Query. Reviews artwork/photos as part of ms package.

Recent Title(s): Unauthorized biography of *Godzilla.*

Tips: "ECW does not accept unsolicited fiction or poetry manuscripts. We are looking for sports books and music biographies; please query first."

N EDGE SCIENCE FICTION AND FANTASY PUBLISHING, Box 75064 Cambrian PO, Calgary, Alberta T2K 6J8 Canada. (403)282-5206. Fax: (403)254-0456. E-mail: editor@cadivision.com. Website: http://www.trickster.com/edge. **Acquisitions**: Jessie Tambay/Katherine Lockhart, acquisitions editors. Editorial Manager: Lynn Jennyc. Publishes hardcover and trade paperback originals. **Publishes 3-12 titles/year. Receives 40 queries and 400 mss/year. 50% of books from first-time authors; 75% from unagented writers. Pays 10% royalty on wholesale price. Offers $500-1000 advance.** Publishes book 1 year after acceptance of ms. Accepts simultaneous submissions. Reports in 2 months on queries and proposals; 2-6 months on mss. Book catalog not available. Manuscript guidelines for #10 SASE. (If from US, use IRCs, not US stamps.)

Fiction: Fantasy, science fiction. "We are looking for all types of fantasy and science fiction, except juvenile/young adult." Submit synopsis and 3 sample chapters with SASE.

Recent Title(s): *The Black Chalice*, by Marie Jakober (historical fantasy); *Keeper's Child*, by Leslie Davis (science fiction).

Tips: "Audience would be anyone who enjoys a well written science fiction or fantasy novels. Polish your manuscript before you submit it. Get your manuscript critiqued by others before you submit it."

N ÉDITIONS LOGIQUES/LOGICAL PUBLISHING, P.O. Box 10, Station D, Montreal, Quebec H3K 3B9 Canada. (514)933-2225. Fax: (514)933-8823. E-mail: logique@cam.org. Website: http://www.logique.com. **Acquisitions**: Roger Des Roches, chief editor. "Les Éditions Logiques will only publish books translated or written in French." Publishes hardcover, trade and mass market paperback originals and reprints. **Publishes 30 titles/year. Receives 100**

queries and 75 mss/year. 40% of books from first-time authors; 100% from unagented writers. Pays 6-10% royalty on retail price. Offers advance up to $1,000. Publishes book 6 months after acceptance of ms. Reports in 2 months. Book catalog free.

Nonfiction: Biography, coffee table book, cookbook, how-to, humor, illustrated book, children's/juvenile, reference, self-help, technical, textbook and computer books. "We aim to the contemporary adult: technology, environment, learning, trying to cope and live a happy life. Writers should offer some insight on the reality of today." Submit outline, 2-3 sample chapters and pictures if required. Reviews artwork as part of the ms package. Send photocopies.

Fiction: Erotica, experimental, fantasy, literary, mainstream/contemporary and science fiction. "Be modern." Submit complete ms only. *Writer's Market* recommends query with SASE first.

Recent Title(s): *Les 4 Clés de l'Équilibre Personnel*, (self-help, health); *Les Bouquets de Noces* (romance).

Tips: "Our audience consists of contemporary men and women. French manuscripts only, please, or a copy of English book if already published and French rights are available."

EDITIONS PHIDAL, 5740 Ferrier, Mont-Royal, Quebec H4P 1M7 Canada. (514) 738-0202. Chief Editor: Lionel Soussan. Publishes hardcover and mass market paperback originals. **Publishes 50-70 titles/year. Receives 50 queries and 20 mss/year. 5% of books from first-time authors; 5% from unagented writers.** Publishes book 6 months after acceptance. Accepts simultaneous submissions. Reports in 2 months on mss.

Fiction: Juvenile. "We specialize in children's books ages three and up. Illustrations are very helpful." Submit synopsis and 3-5 sample chapters.

Tips: Audience is children, both in English and French languages. Ages 3 and up.

EMPYREAL PRESS, P.O. Box 1746, Place Du Parc, Montreal, Quebec HZW 2R7 Canada. **Acquisitions**: Geof Isherwood, publisher. "Our mission is the publishing of Canadian and other literature which doesn't fit into any standard 'mold'—writing which is experimental yet grounded in discipline, imagination." Publishes trade paperback originals. **Publishes 1-4 titles/year. 50% of books from first-time authors; 90% from unagented writers. Pays 10% royalty on wholesale price. Offers $300 (Canadian) advance.** Book catalog for #10 SASE.

Fiction: Experimental, feminist, gay/lesbian, literary, short story collections. No unsolicited mss, due to heavy backlog.

Recent Title(s): *The Space*, by Patrick Borden (novel); *1941 Diary*, by Louis Dudek (literary nonfiction).

N **FERNWOOD PUBLISHING LTD.**, P.O. Box 9409, Station A, Halifax, Nova Scotia B3K 5S3 Canada. (902)422-3302. **Acquisitions**: Errol Sharpe, publisher. "Fernwood's objective is to publish critical works which challenge existing scholarship." Publishes trade paperback originals. **Publishes 12-15 titles/year. Receives 80 queries and 30 mss/year. 40% of books from first-time authors; 100% from unagented writers. Pays 7-10% royalty on wholesale price.** Publishes book 1 year after acceptance of ms. Accepts simultaneous submissions. Reports in 6 weeks on proposals. Book catalog and ms guidelines free.

Nonfiction: Biography, reference, textbook. Subjects include anthropology/archaeology, education, ethnic, gay/lesbian, government/politics, health/medicine, history, language/literature, nature/environment, philosophy, sociology, sports, translation, women's issues/studies, Canadaiana. "Our main focus is in the social sciences and humanities, emphasizing labor studies, women's studies, gender studies, critical theory and research, political economy, cultural studies and social work—for use in college and university courses." Submit proposal package, including outline, table of contents, sample chapters. Reviews artwork/photos as part of ms package. Send photocopies.

Recent Title(s): *Blaming Children: Youth Crime, Moral Panics and the Politics of Hate*, by Bernard Schissel.

FITZHENRY & WHITESIDE, LTD., 195 Allstate Parkway, Markham, Ontario L3R 4T8 Canada. (905)477-9700. Fax: (905)477-9179. **Acquisitions:** Richard Dionne, editor. Estab. 1966. Publishes hardcover and paperback originals and reprints. **Publishes 20 titles/year, text and trade. Royalty contract varies. Advance negotiable.** Enclose return postage.

Nonfiction: "Interested only in topics of interest to Canadians, and by Canadians," history, nature, Native studies, reference, children's, young adult. Submit outline and 1 sample chapter. Length: open.

Fiction: Children's, young adult only. Query with SASE.

Recent Title(s): *Canadian Facts and Dates*, by Jay Myers and James Musson; *Project Puffin*, by Stephen Kress and Pete Sulmansohn (fiction).

GOOSE LANE EDITIONS, 469 King St., Fredericton, New Brunswick E3B 1E5 Canada. (506)450-4251. **Acquisitions**: Laurel Boone, editorial director. Estab. 1956. Goose Lane publishes fiction and nonfiction from well-read authors with finely crafted literary writing skills. **Publishes 12-14 titles/year. Receives 500 submissions/year. 20% of books from first-time authors; 75-100% from unagented writers. Pays royalty on retail price.** Reports in 6 months. Manuscript guidelines for SASE (Canadian stamps or IRCs).

Nonfiction: Biography, illustrated book, literary history (Canadian). Subjects include art/architecture, history, language/literature, nature/environment, translation, women's issues/studies. No crime, confessional, how-to, self-help, medical, legal or cookbooks. Query first.

Fiction: Experimental, feminist, historical, literary, short story collections. "Our needs in fiction never change: substantial, character-centred literary fiction. No children's, YA, mainstream, mass market, genre, mystery, thriller, confessional or sci-fi fiction." Query with SASE first.

Recent Title(s): *Phantom Islands of the Atlantic*, by Donald S. Johnson (history of exploration and cartography);

English Lessons, by Shauna Singh Baldwin (short stories).
Tips: "Writers should send us outlines and samples of books that show a very well-read author who has thought long and deeply about the art of writing and, in either fiction or nonfiction, has something of Canadian relevance to offer. We almost never publish books by non-Canadian authors, and we seldom consider submissions from outside the country. Our audience is literate, thoughtful and well-read. If I were a writer trying to market a book today, I would contact the targeted publisher with a query letter and synopsis, and request manuscript guidelines. Purchase a recent book from the publisher in a relevant area, if possible. Never send a complete manuscript blindly to a publisher. *Never* send a manuscript or sample without an SASE with IRC's or sufficient return postage in Canadian stamps."

GUERNICA EDITIONS, Box 117, Station P, Toronto, Ontario M5S 2S6 Canada. (416)658-9888. Fax: (416)657-8885. **Acquisitions**: Antonio D'Alfonso, editor/publisher. Estab. 1978. Publishes trade paperback originals, reprints and software. **Publishes 20 titles/year. Receives 1,000 submissions/year. 5% of books from first-time authors. "Subvention in Canada is received only when the author is established, Canadian-born and active in the country's cultural world. The others we subsidize ourselves." Pays 10% royalty on retail price or makes outright purchase of $200-5,000. Offers 10¢/word advance for translators.** IRCs required. "American stamps are of no use to us in Canada." Reports in 3 months. Book catalog for SASE.
Nonfiction: Biography, art, film, history, music, philosophy, politics, psychology, religion, literary criticism, ethnic history, multicultural comparative literature.
Fiction: Original works and translations. "We wish to open up into the fiction world and focus less on poetry. Also specialize in European, especially Italian, translations." Query.
Poetry: "We wish to have writers in translation. Any writer who has translated Italian poetry is welcomed. Full books only. Not single poems by different authors, unless modern, and used as an anthology. First books will have no place in the next couple of years." Submit samples.
Recent Title(s): *Daughters For Sale*, by Gianna Patriarca (poetry).
Tips: "We are seeking less poetry, more prose, essays, novels, and translations into English."

N **GYNERGY BOOKS**, Ragweed Press, P.O. Box 2023, Charlottetown, Prince Edward Island C1A 7N7 Canada. (902)566-5750. Fax: (902)566-4473. E-mail: editor@gynergy.com. **Acquisitions**: Sibyl Frei, managing editor. Publishes trade paperback originals. **Publishes 10 titles/year. Imprint publishes 5 titles/year. Receives 200 queries and 1,500-2,000 mss/year. 25% of books from first-time authors; 95% from unagented writers. Pays 8-10% royalty on wholesale or retail price. Advance amount confidential.** Publishes book 1-2 years after acceptance of ms. Accepts simultaneous submissions. Reports in 6 months on mss. Book catalog free. Manuscript guidelines for #10 SASE.
Nonfiction: Gift book, humor, illustrated book, feminist, lesbian. Subjects include child guidance/parenting, creative nonfiction, gay/lesbian, women's issues/studies. "For nonfiction, we prefer to review proposals and, if accepted, work with the author or editor on developing the book from concept through to final manuscript." Submit proposal package, including authority on subject and samples of writing, outline and SASE.
Fiction: Gay/lesbian, mystery. "We are interested in series, looking to add line of feminist/lesbian fantasy or science fiction." Send complete ms and SASE.
Recent Title(s): *Hot Licks: Lesbian Musicians of Note*, edited by Lee Fleming; *Last Resort*, by Jackie Manthorne (mystery).

HARPERCOLLINS PUBLISHERS LTD., 55 Avenue Rd., Suite 2900, Toronto, Ontario M5R 3L2 Canada. (416) 975-9334. **Acquisitions:** Iris Tupholme, vice president/publisher/editor-in-chief. Publishes hardcover and trade paperback originals and reprints, mass market paperback reprints. **Publishes 40-60 titles/year. Pays 8-15% royalty on retail price. Offers from $1,500 to over six figures advance.** Publishes book 18 months after acceptance.
Nonfiction: Biography, children's/juvenile, self-help. Subjects include business and economics, gardening, gay/lesbian, government/politics, health/medicine, history, language/literature, money/finance, nature/environment, religion, travel, women's issues/studies. "We do not accept unsolicited mss. Query first with SASE and appropriate Canadian Postage or international postal coupons."
Fiction: Ethnic, experimental, feminist, juvenile, literary, mainstream/contemporary, picture books, religious, short story collections, young adult. "We do not accept unsolicited mss. Query first with SASE and appropriate Canadian Postage or international postal coupons."
Recent Title(s): *A Place Called Heaven: The Meaning of Being Black in Canada*, by Cecil Foster (nonfiction); *Any Known Blood*, by Lawrence Hill (novel).

N **F.P. HENDRIKS PUBLISHING**, 4806-53 St., Stettler, Alberta T0C 2L2 Canada. (403)742-6483. **Acquisitions**: Faye Boer, managing editor. "Primary focus—teacher's resources in English/language arts and sciences including lessons and activities with solid theoretical background." **Publishes 3-5 titles/year. Receives 30 queries and 20 mss/year. 80% of books from first-time authors; 100% from unagented writers. Pays 10% royalty. Offers $250-1,000 advance depending on author.** Publishes book 18 months after acceptance of ms. Accepts simultaneous submissions. Reports in 2 months on queries, 3 months on proposals, 6 months on mss. Book catalog free.
Nonfiction: Teacher's resources, self-help, textbook. Subjects include child guidance/parenting, education, health/medicine, language/literature, science, sports. Submit outline with SASE. Reviews artwork/photos as part of ms package. Send photocopies.
Fiction: Adventure, fantasy, humor, juvenile, mystery, science fiction, young adult. "We plan to publish young adult

fiction in the above categories to commence 1999-2000. Must include accompanying teacher resources. Beware of lack of attention to intended audience; lack of attention to elements of plot." Submit synopsis with SASE.
Recent Title(s): *From Your Child's Teacher*, by David Platt, Robin Bright, Lisa McMullin.
Tips: "Audience is teachers of elementary, middle school, junior high in English/language arts and science."

HERITAGE HOUSE PUBLISHING CO. LTD., 17921 55th Ave., Unit 8, Surrey, British Columbia V3S 6C4 Canada. Fax: (250)468-5318. E-mail: herhouse@island.net. Website: http://www.heritagehouse.ca. **Acquisitions**: Rodger Touchie, publisher/president. Heritage House is primarily a regional publisher of Western Canadiana and the Pacific Northwest. "We aim to publish and distribute good books that entertain and educate our readership regarding both historic and contemporary Western Canada and Pacific Northwest." Publishes trade paperback originals. **Publishes 10-12 titles/year. Receives 200 queries and 60 mss/year. 50% of books from first-time authors; 100% from unagented writers. Pays 10-12% royalty.** Publishes book 1 year after acceptance. Reports in 2 months. Book catalog for SASE.
Nonfiction: Biography, cookbook, how-to, illustrated book. Subjects include animals, anthropology/archaeology, cooking/foods/nutrition, history, nature/environment, recreation, regional, sports, western Canadiana. "Writers should include a sample of their writing, an overview sample of photos or illustrations to support the text and a brief letter describing who they are writing for." Query with outline, 2-3 sample chapters and SASE. Reviews artwork/photos as part of ms package. Send photocopies.
Fiction: Very limited. Only author/illustrator collaboration.
Recent Title(s): *The Mulligan Affair*, by O'Keefe/Macdonald (police history); *Orca's Family & More Northwest Coast Stories*, by Jim Challenger (children's fiction).
Tips: "Our books appeal to residents and visitors to the northwest quadrant of the continent. Present your material after you have done your best. Double space. Don't worry about getting an agent if yours is a one-shot book. Write for the love it. The rest will take care of itself."

HIPPOPOTAMUS PRESS, 22 Whitewell Rd., Frome, Somerset BA11 4EL United Kingdom. 0173-466653. Fax: 01373-466653. **Acquisitions**: R. John, editor. Hippopotamus Press publishes literary poetry and nonfiction. Publishes hardcover and trade paperback originals. Publishes 6-12 titles/year. 90% of books from first-time authors; 90% from unagented writers. **Pays 7½-10% royalty on retail price. Rarely offers advance.** Publishes book 10 months after acceptance of ms. Accepts simultaneous submissions. Reports in 1 month. *Writer's Market* recommends allowing 2 months for reply. Book catalog free.
Imprint(s): Hippopotamus Press, *Outposts* Poetry Quarterly; distributor for University of Salzburg Press.
Nonfiction: Essays, literary criticism. Subjects include language/literature, translation. Submit complete ms. *Writer's Market* recommends sending a query with SASE first.
Poetry: "Read one of our authors! Poets often make the mistake of submitting poetry not knowing the type of verse we publish." Submit complete ms.
Recent Title(s): *Mystic Bridge*, by Edward Lowbury; *Immigrants of Loss*, by G.S.Sharat Chandra (selected poems).
Tips: "We publish books for a literate audience. Read what we publish."

HORSDAL & SCHUBART PUBLISHERS LTD., 623-425 Simcoe St., Victoria, British Columbia V8V 4T3 Canada. Fax: (250)360-0829. **Acquisitions**: Marlyn Horsdal, editor. "We concentrate on Western and Northern Canada and nautical subjects." Publishes hardcover originals and trade paperback originals and reprints. **Publishes 8-10 titles/year. 50% of books from first-time authors; 100% from unagented writers. Pays 15% royalty on wholesale price. Negotiates advance.** Publishes books 6 months after acceptance of ms. Accepts simultaneous submissions. Reports in 1 month on queries. Book catalog free.
Nonfiction: Subjects include anthropology/archaeology, art/architecture, biography, government/politics, history, nature/environment, recreation, regional. Query with outline, 2-3 sample chapters and SASE or SAE with IRCs. Reviews artwork/photos as part of ms package. Send photocopies.
Recent Title(s): *Warped Rods and Squeaky Reels*, by Robert Jones (fishing).

HOUSE OF ANANSI PRESS, Stoddart Publishing, 34 Lesmill Rd., Toronto, Ontario M3B 2T6 Canada. (416)445-3333. E-mail: anansi@irwin-pub.com. Website: http://www.irwin-pub.com/irwin/anansi/. **Acquisitions:** Martha Sharpe, publisher. "Our mission is to publish the best new literary writers in Canada and to continue to grow and adapt along with the Canadian literary community, while maintaining Anansi's rich history." Publishes hardcover and trade paperback originals. **Publishes 10-15 titles/year. Receives 750 queries/year. 5% of books from first-time authors; 99% from unagented writers. Pays 8-15% royalty on retail price. Offers $500-2,000 advance.** Publishes book 9 months after acceptance of ms. Accepts simultaneous submissions. Reports in 2 months on queries, 3 months on proposals, 4 months on mss.
Nonfiction: Biography, critical thought, literary criticism. Subjects include anthropology, gay/lesbian, government/

THE MAPLE LEAF symbol indicates publishers which consider book proposals by Canadian authors only.

politics, history, language/literature, philosophy, science, sociology, women's issues/studies, only Canadian writers. "Our nonfiction list is literary, but not overly academic. Some writers submit academic work better suited for university presses or pop-psychology books, which we do not publish." Submit outline with 2 sample chapters and SASE. Send photocopies of artwork/photos.

Fiction: "We publish literary fiction by Canadian authors." Experimental, feminist, gay/lesbian, literary, short story collections. "Authors must have been published in established literary magazines and/or journals. We only want to consider sample chapters." Submit synopsis, 2 sample chapters with SASE.

Poetry: "We only publish book-length works by Canadian authors. Poets must have a substantial résumé of published poems in literary magazines or journals. We only want samples from a ms." Submit 10-15 sample poems or 15 pages.

Recent Title(s): *The Tracey Fragments*, by Maureen Medved (fiction); *The Elsewhere Community*, by Hugh Kenner (1997 Massey lectures).

Tips: "Submit often to magazines and journals. Read and buy other writers' work. Know and be a part of your writing community."

INSTITUTE OF PSYCHOLOGICAL RESEARCH, INC./INSTITUT DE RECHERCHES PSYCHOLOGIQUES, INC., 34 Fleury St. W., Montréal, Québec H3L 1S9 Canada. (514)382-3000. Fax: (514)382-3007. **Acquisitions**: Marie-Paule Chevrier, president. Estab. 1958. Institute of Psychological Research publishes psychological tests and science textbooks for a varied professional audience. Publishes hardcover and trade paperback originals and reprints. **Publishes 12 titles/year. Receives 15 submissions/year. 10% of books from first-time authors, 100% from unagented writers. Pays 10-12% royalty.** Publishes book 6 months after acceptance of ms. Reports in 2 months.

Nonfiction: Textbooks, psychological tests. Subjects include philosophy, psychology, science, translation. "We are looking for psychological tests in French or English." Submit complete ms. *Writer's Market* recommends query with SASE first.

Recent Title(s): *Épreuve individuelle d'habileté mentale*, by Jean-Marc Chevrier (intelligence test).

Tips: "Psychologists, guidance counsellors, professionals, schools, school boards, hospitals, teachers, government agencies and industries comprise our audience."

[A] **KEY PORTER BOOKS LTD.**, 70 The Esplanade, Toronto, Ontario M5E 1R2 Canada. (416)862-7777. Fax: (416)862-2304. Website: http://www.keyporter.com. **Acquisitions**: Michael Mouland, senior editor (nonfiction); Barbara Berson, senior editor (fiction); Susan Renouf, president/editor-in-chief (nonfiction, nature, health) . Publishes hardcover originals and trade paperback originals and reprints. "Key Porter Books, founded in Toronto in 1979, is one of Canada's largest independent trade book publishers, enjoying an international reputation as a producer of quality books in a broad range of categories." **Publishes 80 titles/year. Imprint publishes 10 titles/year. Receives hundreds of queries and mss/year. 10% of books from first-time authors; 5% from unagented writers. Pays 10-12½% royalty on retail price. Offers $2,000-50,000 advance.** Publishes book 1 year after acceptance of ms. Reports in 6 months on proposals. Book catalog for #10 SASE.

Imprint(s): Firefly Books, L&OD.

Nonfiction: Biography, coffee table book, illustrated book, reference, technical. Subjects include animals, art/architecture, business and economics, child guidance/parenting, cooking/foods/nutrition, creative nonfiction, gardening, health/medicine, history, hobbies, language/literature, memoirs, military/war, money/finance, nature/environment, photography, regional, sociology. Query with SASE. *No unsolicited mss. Agented submissions only.*

Recent Title(s): *BRE-X: The Inside Story*, by Diane Francis (business).

KINDRED PRODUCTIONS, 4-169 Riverton Ave., Winnipeg, Manitoba R2L 2E5 Canada. (204)669-6575. Fax: (204)654-1865. E-mail: kindred@cdnmbconf.ca. Website: http://www.mbconf.org/mbc/kp/kindred.htm. **Acquisitions**: Marilyn Hudson, manager. "Kindred Productions publishes, promotes and markets print and nonprint resources that will shape our Christian faith and discipleship from a Mennonite Brethren perspective." Publishes trade paperback originals and reprints. **Publishes 3 titles/year. 1% of books from first-time authors; 100% from unagented writers. Non-author subsidy publishes 20% of books. Pays 10-15% royalty on retail price.** Publishes book 18 months after acceptance of ms. Accepts simultaneous submissions. Reports in 3 months on queries, 5 months on proposals. Book catalog and ms guidelines free.

Nonfiction: Biography (select) and Bible study. Religious subjects. "Our books cater primarily to our Mennonite Brethren denomination readers." Query with outline, 2-3 sample chapters and SASE.

Fiction: Historical (religious), juvenile, religious. "All our publications are of a religious nature with a high moral content." Submit synopsis, 2-3 sample chapters and SASE.

Recent Title(s): *Saints, Sinners and Angels*, by Danny Unrau (nonfiction).

Tips: "Most of our books are sold to churches, religious bookstores and schools. We are concentrating on devotional and inspirational books. We are accepting *very* few children's manuscripts."

LAURIER BOOKS, LTD., P.O. Box 2694, Station D, Ottawa, Ontario K1P 5W6 Canada. (613)738-2163. **Acquisitions:** M. Lalwani. Publishes hardcover and trade paperback originals and reprints. **Publishes 10 titles/year. Receives 40 queries and 5 manuscripts/year. 10% of books from first-time authors. Makes outright purchase.** Publishes book 4 months after acceptance of ms. Accepts simultaneous submissions. Reports in 1 month. Book catalog and manuscript guidelines free.

Nonfiction: How-to, reference, self-help. Subjects include ethnic, language/literature, Native Americans. Query with

proposal and SASE. Reviews artwork/photos as part of manuscript package. Send photocopies.
Recent Title(s): *Eskimo Dictionary.*
Tips: Audience is libraries, universities, colleges and schools.

LE LOUP DE GOUTTIÈRE, 347 Rue Saint-Paul, Quebec, Quebec G1K 3X1 Canada. (418)694-2224. Fax: (418)694-2225. **Acquisitions**: Francine Vernac, directrice générale. **Publishes 16 titles/year. Receives 150 queries/year. 15% of books from first-time authors. Pays 10% royalty. Offers no advance.** Publishes book 1 year after acceptance of ms. Reports in 1 year on mss. Book catalog free.
Imprint(s): Littérature Veunesse.
Nonfiction: Subjects include art/architecture, literature, philosophy, psychology.
Fiction: Literary, short story collections. Submit 3 sample chapters in French.
Poetry: Submit complete ms in French.
Recent Title(s): *Les Aventures Mathématiques de Mathilde et David*, by Marie-France Daniel, Louise Lafortune, Richard Pallascio and Pierre Sykes (nonfiction); *Mémoire d'Hiver*, by Louis-Jean Thibault (poetry).

LONE PINE PUBLISHING, 10426 81st Ave., #206, Edmonton, Alberta T6E 1X5 Canada. (403)433-9333. Fax: (403)433-9646. Website: http://www.lonepinepublishing.com. **Acquisitions**: Nancy Foulds, senior editor. Estab. 1980. "We publish recreational and natural history titles, and some poular history." Publishes trade paperback originals and reprints. **Publishes 12-20 titles/year. Receives 800 submissions/year. 75% of books from first-time authors; 95% from unagented writers. Pays royalty.** Reports in 2 months on queries. Book catalog free.
Imprint(s): Lone Pine, Home World, Pine Candle and Pine Cone.
Nonfiction: Nature/recreation guide books. Subjects include animals, anthropology/archaeology, botany/ethnobotany, gardening, history, nature/environment ("this is where most of our books fall"), travel ("another major category for us"). The list is set for the next year and a half, but we are interested in seeing new material. Submit outline and sample chapters. Reviews artwork/photos as part of ms package. Do not send originals. Send SASE with sufficient international postage if you want your ms returned.
Recent Title(s): *Wildflowers of Washington*, by C.P. Lyons (plant guide).
Tips: "Writers have their best chance with recreational or nature guidebooks and popular history. Most of our books are strongly regional in nature."

LYNX IMAGES, INC., 104 Scollard St., Toronto, Ontario M5R 1G2 Canada. (416)925-8422. Fax: (925)952-8352. E-mail: lynximag@interlog.com. Website: http://www.lynximages.com. **Acquisitions**: Russell Floren, president; Andrea Gutsche, editor; Barbara Chesholm, editor. Publishes hardcover and trade paperback originals. **Publishes 6 titles/year. Receives 100 queries and 50 mss/year. 80% of books from first-time authors; 80% from unagented writers. Makes outright purchase of $6,000-15,000. Offers 40% advance.** Publishes book 6 months-1 year after acceptance of ms. Accepts simultaneous submissions. Reports in 6 months on mss. Book catalog free.
Nonfiction: Coffee table book, gift book, multimedia (video). Subjects include history, nature/environment, travel. Submit proposal package, including sample chapter. Reviews artwork/photos as part of ms package. Send photocopies or other formats.
Recent Title(s): *Canada's Train Stations*, by R. Brown (history, travel).

McGRAW-HILL RYERSON LIMITED, The McGraw-Hill Companies, 300 Water St., Whitby, Ontario L1N 9B6 Canada. Fax: (416)430-5020. Website: http://www.mcgrawhill.ca. **Acquisitions**: Joan Homewood, publisher. McGraw-Hill Ryerson, Ltd., publishes books on Canadian business and personal finance for the Canadian market. Publishes hardcover and trade paperback originals and reprints. **Publishes 20 new titles/year. 75% of books are originals; 25% are reprints. 15% of books from first-time authors; 85% from unagented writers. Pays 7½-10% royalty on retail price. Offers $2,000 average advance.** Publishes book 1 year after acceptance. Accepts simultaneous submissions. Reports in 6 months on queries.
Nonfiction: How-to, reference, professional. Subjects include business, management, personal finance, Canadian military history, training for business skills. "No books and proposals that are American in focus. We publish primarily for the Canadian market, but work with McGraw-Hill U.S. on business, management and training titles." Query. Submit outline and sample chapters.
Recent Title(s): *Digital Property*, by Lesley Ellen Harris (understanding intellectual property in the digital world).
Tips: "Writers have the best chance of selling us nonfiction business and personal finance books. Proposal guidelines are available. Thorough market research on competitive titles increases chances of your proposal getting serious consideration, as does endorsement by or references from relevant professionals."

MARCUS BOOKS, P.O. Box 327, Queensville, Ontario L0G 1R0 Canada. (905)478-2201. Fax: (905)478-8338. **Acquisitions**: Tom Rieder, president. Publishes trade paperback originals and reprints. **Publishes 3-4 titles/year. Receives 12 queries and 6 mss/year. 90% of books from first-time authors; 100% from unagented writers. Pays 10% royalty on retail price.** Publishes book 6 months after acceptance of ms. Reports in 4 months on mss. Book catalog for $1.
Nonfiction: "Interested in alternative health and esoteric topics." Submit outline and 3 sample chapters.

MARITIMES ARTS PROJECTS PRODUCTIONS, Box 596, Station A, Fredericton, New Brunswick E3B 5A6 Canada. (506)454-5127. Fax: (506)454-5127. E-mail: jblades@nbnet.nb.ca. **Acquisitions**: Joe Blades, publisher. "We are a small literary and regional Canadian publishing house." Publishes Canadian-authored trade paperback originals and reprints. **Publishes 8-12 titles/year. 50% of books from first-time authors; 100% from unagented writers. Pays 10% royalty on retail price or 10% of print run. Offers $0-100 advance.** Publishes book 1-1½ year after acceptance of ms. Reports in 6-12 months on mss. Book catalog for 9×12 SAE with 2 first-class Canadian stamps in Canada. Manuscript guidelines for #10 SASE (Canadian postage or IRC).

Imprint(s): Broken Jaw Press, Book Rat, SpareTime Editions, Dead Sea Physh Products.

Nonfiction: Illustrated book. Subjects include history, language/literature, nature/environment, regional, women's issues/studies, criticism, culture. Query with SASE (Canadian postage or IRC). Reviews artwork/photos as part of ms package. Send photocopies, transparencies.

Fiction: Literary. Query with bio and SASE.

Poetry: Submit complete ms for annual New Muse Award with $15 fee. Guidelines for SASE. Deadline: March 31.

Recent Title(s): *Rum River*, by Raymond Faser (fiction); *The Dark—Poets of Publishing*, by Joe Blades.

MEKLER & DEAHL, PUBLISHERS, (formerly Unfinished Monument Press), 237 Prospect St. S., Hamilton, Ontario L8M 2Z6 Canada. (905)312-1779. Fax: (905)312-8285. E-mail: meklerdeahl@globalserve.net. **Acquisitions:** Gilda Mekler, editor (nonfiction); James Deahl, editor (fiction). "Books must be very well written, and have a marekt for us to be interested. We will shift our focus from poetry to nonfiction." Publishes trade paperback originals and reprints. **Publishes 4-6 titles/year. No books from first-time authors; 100% from unagented writers. Pays 10-12% royalty on retail price.** Publishes book 10 months after acceptance. Accepts simultaneous submissions. Reports in 1 month on queries. *Writer's Market* recommends allowing 2 months for reply. Book catalog and ms guidelines free.

Imprint(s): Unfinished Monument Press (literature); Hamilton Haiku Press.

Nonfiction: Medical books, biography. Query with SASE.

Fiction: Plays. "We hope to get into short stories soon." Query with SASE.

Poetry: "We have a special interest in people's poetry." Query with SASE.

Recent Title(s): *Sing for the Inner Ear*, edited by Al Purdy (poetry); *I Wish It Were Fiction: Memories, 1939-1945*, by Elsa Thon.

Tips: "American authors can use our U.S. address: P.O. Box 4279, Pittsburgh PA 15203."

NEWEST PUBLISHERS LTD., 201, 8540- 109 St., Edmonton, Alberta T6G 1E6 Canada. (403)432-9427. Fax: (403)433-3179. E-mail: newest@planet.eon.net. **Acquisitions**: Liz Grieve, managing editor. Estab. 1977. "We only publish Western Canadian authors. Our audience consists of people interested in the west and north of Canada; teachers, professors." Publishes trade paperback originals. **Publishes 8 titles/year. Receives 200 submissions/year. 40% of books from first-time authors; 90% from unagented writers. Pays 10% royalty.** Publishes book 2 years after acceptance. Accepts simultaneous submissions. Reports in 6 months on queries. Book catalog for 9×12 SAE with 4 first-class Canadian stamps or IRCs.

Nonfiction: Literary/essays (Western Canadian authors). Subjects include ethnic, government/politics (Western Canada), history (Western Canada), Canadiana. Query.

Fiction: Literary. Submit outline/synopsis and sample chapters.

Recent Title(s): *Mothertalk: Life Stories of Mary Kiyoshi Kiyooka*, by Roy Kiyooka (biography of Japanese-Canadian).

Tips: "Trend is towards more nonfiction submissions. Would like to see more full-length literary fiction."

NORTHSTONE PUBLISHING INC., Woodlake Books, Inc., 9025 Jim Bailey Rd., Kelowna, British Columbia V4V 1R2 Canada. E-mail: info@woodlake.com. Website: http://www.joinhands.com. **Acquisitions:** Michael Schwartzentruber, editorial director. "Northstone publishes books that provide high quality products promoting positive social and spiritual value. No academia." Publishes hardcover and trade paperback originals. **Publishes 14 titles/year. Receives 100 queries/year. 30% of books from first-time writers; 100% from unagented writers. Pays 8% royalty on retail price.** Publishes book 18 months after acceptance of ms. Accepts simultaneous submissions. Reports in 2 months on proposals. Book catalog for $2 (Canadian) and 9×12 SAE; ms guidelines for #10 SASE.

Nonfiction: Self-help. Subjects include health/medicine (healing, holistic approach, spiritual), philosophy (voluntary simplicity/lifestyle), spirituality (grounded in everyday life), sociology (social issues). Submit outline with SASE; all unsolicited mss returned unopened. Reviews artwork/photos as part of ms package. Send photocopies.

Recent Title(s): *Speaking of Sex*, by Meg Hickling (information on sex education for youth).

Tips: "Our audience is primarily women, baby boomers, spiritually interested though not necessarily connected to institutional religion; inner-directed with strong interests in social issues, ecology and justice."

OOLICHAN BOOKS, P.O. Box 10, Lantzville, British Columbia V0R 2H0 Canada. Phone/fax: (250)390-4839. E-mail: oolichan@mail.island.net. Website: sland.net/~oolichan. **Acquisitions**: Ron Smith, publisher. Oolichan publishes literary fiction, short story collections and poetry. Publishes hardcover and trade paperback originals and reprints. **Publishes 6 titles/year. Receives 300 queries/year. 25% of books from first-time authors. Pays 6-10% royalty on retail price.** Publishes book 6 months after acceptance of ms. Accepts simultaneous submissions. Reports in 1 month on queries, 6 months on mss. Book catalog for #10 SASE. Manuscript guidelines free.

Fiction: Literary, poetry, short story collections. Query with SASE.

Poetry: "We publish contemporary verse. Writers should be aware of current aesthetic. No doggerel, card verse, or verse that proselytizes." Query with 10 sample poems.

Recent Title(s): *The Unhinging of Wings*, by Margo Button (poetry); *Crossing The Gulf*, by Keith Harrison (short fiction).

ORCA BOOK PUBLISHERS LTD., P.O. Box 5626 Station B, Victoria, British Columbia V8R 6S4 Canada. (250)380-1229. Fax: (250)380-1892. E-mail: orca@pinc.com. Website: http://www.swiftly.com/orca. Publisher: R. Tyrrell. **Acquisitions**: Ann Featherstone, children's book editor; R. Tyrell (young adult and adult submissions). Estab. 1984. Publishes hardcover and trade paperback originals. **Publishes 20-25 titles/year. Receives 600-800 submissions/year. 50% of books from first-time authors; 80% from unagented writers. Pays 10-12½% royalty on retail price. Offers $1,000 average advance.** Publishes book 1 year after acceptance. Reports in 2 months on queries. Book catalog for 9×12 SAE and $2 postage (Canadian). Manuscript guidelines for SASE or IRCs. No fax or e-mailed queries or submissions.
Nonfiction: Biography, illustrated book, travel guides, children's. Subjects include history, nature/environment, recreation, sports, travel. Needs history (*West Coast Canadian*) and young children's book. Query or submit outline and sample chapters. Reviews artwork/photos as part of ms package. *Publishes Canadian material only.*
Fiction: Juvenile, illustrated children's books, 4-8-year-old range older juvenile and YA. Query or submit outline/synopsis and sample chapters.
Recent Title(s): *Gray Whales, Wandering Giants*, by Robert H. Busch (natural history/photography); *Brad's Universe*, by Mary Woodbury (young adult novel).

OWL BOOKS, 179 John St., Suite 500, Toronto, Ontario M5T 3G5 Canada. Fax: (416)340-9769. E-mail: owlbooks@owl.on.ca. Website: http://www.owl.on.ca. **Acquisitions**: Sheba Meland, publishing director. Estab. 1976. Publishes hardcover and trade paperback originals. **Publishes 10 titles/year. Receives 100 queries and 500 mss/year. 15% of books from first-time authors; 80% from unagented writers. Pays royalty on retail price.** Publishes book 18 months after acceptance of ms. Accepts simultaneous submissions. Reports in 3 months. Catalog and ms guidelines for #10 SAE with IRC. (No US stamps).
Nonfiction: Children's/juvenile. Subjects include animals, hobbies, nature/environment, science and science activities. "We are closely affiliated with the discovery-oriented children's magazines *Owl* and *Chickadee*, and concentrate on fresh, innovative nonfiction and picture books with nature/science themes, and quality children's craft/how-to titles." Submit proposal package, including outline, vita and 3 sample chapters. Reviews artwork/photos as part of ms package. Send photocopies or transparencies (not originals).
Fiction: Picture books. Submit complete ms. *Writer's Market* recommends sending a query with SASE first.
Recent Title(s): *Lights, Cameria, Action!*, by Lisa O'Brien (motion pictures); *Don't Dig So Deep, Nicholas*, by Troon Harrison (fiction).
Tips: "To get a feeling for our style of children's publishing, take a look at some of our recent books and at *Owl* and *Chickadee* magazines. We publish Canadian authors in the main but will occasionally publish a work from outside Canada if it strikingly fits our list."

PACIFIC EDUCATIONAL PRESS, Faculty of Education, University of British Columbia, Vancouver, British Columbia V6T 1Z4 Canada. Fax: (604)822-6603. E-mail: cedwards@interchange.ubc.ca. **Acquisitions:** Catherine Edwards, director. Publishes trade paperback originals. **Publishes 6-8 titles/year. Receives 200 submissions/year. 15% of books from first-time authors; 100% from unagented writers.** Accepts simultaneous submissions, if so noted. Reports in 6 months on mss. Book catalog and ms guidelines for 9×12 SAE with IRCs.

- Pacific Educational Press no longer publishes childrens' titles, and now focuses on educational titles. "We now publish for the teacher education market, that is: books on curriculum and instruction in school subjects; books in the foundations of education: philosophy and history of education, educational administration, sociology and psychology of education; plus books for general readers on current topics and issues in education."

Recent Title(s): *Trends and Issues in Canadian Social Studies*, by Wrights and Sears (education); *How to Read a Dinosaur and Other Musuem Tales*, by Sale and Dubinsky (fiction/museum literacy and education).

PENGUIN BOOKS CANADA LTD., The Penguin Group, 10 Alcorn Ave., Suite 300, Toronto, Ontario M4V 3B2 Canada. (416)925-0068. **Acquisitions**: Jackie Kaiser, senior editor (cooking, biography, native); Meg Masters, executive editor (sports, biography, business); Cynthia Good, president/publisher (crime).
Nonfiction: Sports, true crime and any Canadian subject by Canadian authors. No unsolicited mss.
Recent Title(s): *Mr. Doyle & Dr. Bell*, by Howard Engel (crime fiction); *Mrs. King*, by Charlotte Gray (biography).

N PINTER PUBLISHERS LTD., Cassell plc, Wellington House, 125 Strand, London WC2R OBB England. (71)420-5555. Potential authors in North America should contact: Pinter Cassell Academic, P.O. Box 605, Herndon VA 20172. (800)561-7704 or (703)661-1589. Fax: (703)661-1501. **Acquisitions:** Janet Joyce, publisher (academic reference); Gillian Paterson, publisher (religious books); Ruth McCurry, publisher (professional books); Stephen Butcher, managing director. "Cassell Academic publishes textbooks, monographs and reference works in the humanities, arts and social sciences for students, teachers and professionals worldwide." Publishes hardcover originals and paperback textbooks. **Publishes 100 titles/year. Receives 1,000 queries and 100 mss/year. 10% of books from first-time authors; 99% from unagented writers. Pays 0-10% royalty.** Publishes books 9 months after acceptance of ms. No simultaneous submissions. Reports in 1 month on proposals. *Writer's Market* recommends allowing 2 months for reply. Book catalog and ms guidelines free.

Imprint(s): Cassell Academic, Pinter, Leicester University Press, Geoffrey Chapman, Mowbray, Mansell.
Nonfiction: Reference, technical, textbook. Subjects include anthropology/archaeology, business and economics, government/politics, history, religion/theology, sociology, linguistics. Submit outline.
Recent Title(s): *Western Primitivism, African Ethnicity*, by Aidan Campbell (anthropology).

PLAYWRIGHTS CANADA PRESS, Playwrights Union of Canada, 54 Wolseley St., 2nd Floor, Toronto, Ontario M5T 1A5 Canada. (416)703-0201. Fax: (416)703-0059. E-mail: cdplays@interlog.com. Website: http://www.puc.ca. **Acquisitions**: Angela Rebeiro, publisher. Estab. 1972. Publishes paperback originals and reprints of plays by Canadian citizens or landed immigrants. "Playwrights Canada Press publishes only drama which has received professional production." **Receives 100 member submissions/year. 50% of plays from first-time authors; 50% from unagented authors. Pays 10% royalty on list price.** Publishes 1 year after acceptance. Reports in up to 1 year. Play catalog for $5. Manuscript guidelines free. Non-members should query. Accepts children's plays.
Recent Title(s): *A View From the Roof*, by Dave Carley.

N THE PRAIRIE PUBLISHING CO., P.O. Box 2997, Winnipeg, Manitoba R3C 4B5 Canada. (204)837-7499. **Acquisitions**: Ralph E. Watkins, publisher. "The mission of The Prarie Publishing Company is that of any other publishing company in the world: to obtain the best manuscripts in its field and to publish those works.".
Nonfiction: Query with SASE.
Fiction: Query with SASE.
Recent Title(s): *High Times With Stewart MacPherson*, by John Robertson (biography); *Reflections From a Basement Window*, by Brian Richardson (a collection of poems of reflections and hope).

PRENTICE-HALL CANADA INC., 1870 Birchmount Rd., Scarborough, Ontario M1P 2J7 Canada. (416)293-3621. Fax: (416)293-3625. **Acquisitions**: Dean Hannaford, acquisitions editor. Estab. 1960. Publishes hardcover and trade paperback originals. **Publishes 40 titles/year. Receives 750-900 submissions/year. 15% of books from first-time authors; 50% from unagented writers. Pays negotiable royalty. Offers advance.** Publishes book 9 months after acceptance. Reports in 3 months. Manuscript guidelines for #10 SAE with 1 IRC.
Nonfiction: Subjects of Canadian and international interest: politics and current affairs, technology, self-help, pop culture, business, finance, health, food. Submit outline and sample chapters. Reviews artwork/photos as part of ms package.
Recent Title(s): *Get Wired, You're Hired: Canadian Guide to Job Hunting Online*, by Mark Swartz (technology and self-help).
Tips: "Present a clear, concise thesis, well-argued with a thorough knowledge of existing works with strong Canadian orientation. Need general interest nonfiction books on topical subjects."

PRESSES DE L'UNIVERSITÉ DE MONTRÉAL, (formerly University of Montreal Press), P.O. Box 6128, Station Downtown, Montreal H3C 3J7 Canada. (514)343-6929. Fax: (514)343-2232. E-mail: pumedit@ere.umontreal.ca. Webs ite: http://www.pum.umontreal.ca/pum/. **Acquisitions**: Marise Labrecque, editor-in-chief. Publishes hardcover and trade paperback originals. **Publishes 20-25 titles/year. Nonauthor-subsidy publishes 25% of books. Pays 8-12 % royalty on net price.** Publishes book 6 months after acceptance of ms. Reports in 1 month on queries and proposals, 3 months on mss. Book catalog and ms guidelines free.
Nonfiction: Reference, textbook. Subjects include anthropology, education, health/medicine, history, language/literature, philosophy, psychology, religion, sociology, translation. Submit outline and 2 sample chapters.

PRODUCTIVE PUBLICATIONS, P.O. Box 7200 Station A, Toronto, Ontario M5W 1X8 Canada. (416)483-0634. Fax: (416)322-7434. **Acquisitions**: Iain Williamson, owner. Estab. 1985. "Productive publishes books to help readers succeed." Publishes trade paperback originals. **Publishes 24 titles/year. Receives 160 queries and 40 mss/year. 80% of books from first-time authors; 100% from unagented writers. Pays 10-15% royalty on wholesale price.** Publishes book 3 months after acceptance of ms. Reports in 1 month on queries and proposals, 3 months on mss. Accepts simultaneous submissions. Book catalog free.

- Productive Publications is also interested in books on business computer software, the Internet for business purposes, investment, stock market and mutual funds, etc.

Nonfiction: How-to, reference, self-help, technical. Subjects include business and economics, computers and electronics, health/medicine, hobbies, money/finance, software (business). "We are interested in small business/entrepreneurship/employment/self-help (business)/how-to/health and wellness—100 to 300 pages." Submit outline. Reviews artwork as part of ms package. Send photocopies.
Recent Title(s): *The Internet Job Search Guide*, by Cathy and Dave Noble.
Tips: "We are looking for books written by *knowledgeable, experienced experts* who can express their ideas *clearly* and *simply*."

PURICH PUBLISHING, Box 23032, Market Mall Post Office, Saskatoon, Saskatchewan S7J 5H3 Canada. (306)373-5311. Fax: (306)373-5315. E-mail: purich@sk.sympatico.ca. **Acquisitions**: Donald Purich, publisher. "We are a specialized publisher focusing on law, Aboriginal issues and western history for the education and professional trade reference market." Publishes trade paperback originals. **Publishes 3-5 titles/year. 20% of books from first-time authors. Pays 8-12% royalty on retail price or makes outright purchase. Offers $100-1,500 advance.** Publishes book 4 months

after acceptance of ms. Accepts simultaneous submissions. Reports in 1 month on queries, 3 months on mss. Book catalog free.
Nonfiction: Reference, technical, textbook. Subjects include agriculture/horticulture, government/politics, history, law, Aboriginal issues. "We are a specialized publisher and only consider work in our subject areas." Query.
Recent Title(s): *Tom Three Persons*, by Hugh A. Dempsey (biography of Indian rodeo star).

QUINTET PUBLISHING LIMITED, The Fitzpatrick Bldg., 188-195 York Way, London, England N7 9QR. Tel: 011.44.171.700.2001. Fax: 011.44.171.700.5785. **Acquisitions**: Anna Southgate, new titles acquisitions editor. "We are a distinguished international illustrated book packager, and proposals must show the promise of broad appeal in many countries on all continents." Publishes hardcover and trade paperback originals and reprints. **Publishes 70 titles/year. 50% of books from first-time authors; 100% from unagented writers. Makes outright purchase of $1,000-8,000 (US). Offers 33% advance.** Publishes book 9 months after acceptance. Reports in 1 month.
Nonfiction: Coffee table book, cookbook, gift book, how-to, reference, technical. Subjects include: Americana, animals, anthropology/archaeology, art/architecture, child guidance/parenting, cooking/foods/nutrition, gardening, history, hobbies, military/war, music/dance, nature/environment, photography, recreation, sports. Writers should show a thorough awareness, reflected in their market analysis, of previously published titles in the subject area for which they are making a proposal. Query with proposal package including 1 sample chapter and/or marketing analysis. "Include a synopsis of all the elements of the book, so that we can consider how to make a flat-plan for an illustrated title." Reviews artwork/photos as part of ms package. Send transparencies.
Recent Title(s): *Simple Tarts*, by Elizabeth Wolf Cohen.

N **RAGWEED PRESS**, P.O. Box 2023, Charlottetown, Prince Edward Island C1A 7N7 Canada. (902)566-5750. Fax: (902)566-4473. E-mail: editor@ragweed.com. **Acquisitions**: Sibyl Frei, managing editor. Publishes hardcover and trade paperback originals. **Publishes 10 titles/year. Imprint publishes 5 titles/year. Receives 200 queries and 1,500-2,000 mss/year. 25% of books from first-time authors; 95% from unagented writers. Pays 8-10% royalty on wholesale or retail price. Advance amount confidential.** Publishes book 1-2 years after acceptance of ms. Accepts simultaneous submissions. Reports in 6 months on mss. Book catalog free. Manuscript guidelines for #10 SASE.
Imprint(s): gynergy books.
Nonfiction: Biography, children's/juvenile, coffee table book, cookbook, gift book, humor, illustrated book. Subjects include cooking/foods/nutrition, government/politics, history, music/dance, nature/environment, photography, recreation, regional. "Have a good look at our catalog to see if your subject matter might fit our diverse but specific publishing program." Submit proposal package, including draft of ms if available with SASE.
Fiction: Adventure, historical, juvenile, literary, multicultural, picture books, poetry, young adult. "Our children's, juvenile and young adult fiction features girl heroes (no rhyming stories for children). Our adult fiction must be written in or about the Atlantic Canada region." Submit complete ms and SASE.
Poetry: "Must be writers in the Atlantic Canada region." Submit complete ms.
Recent Title(s): *Rock, Rhythm & Reels: Canada's East Coast Musicians on Stage*, edited by Lee Fleming (gift book/music); *A Marriage of Masks*, by M.T. Dohaney (contemporary).

A **RANDOM HOUSE OF CANADA LIMITED**, Random House, Inc., Suite 210, 33 Yonge St., Toronto, Ontario M5E 1G4 Canada. Publishes hardcover and trade paperback originals. Publishes 75 titles/year. *No unsolicited mss. Agented submissions only. All unsolicited mss returned unopened.*

RED DEER COLLEGE PRESS, Box 5005, 56th Ave. and 32nd St., Red Deer, Alberta T4N 5H5 Canada. (403)342-3321. Fax: (403)357-3639. E-mail: vmix@admin.rdc.ab.ca. **Acquisitions:** Dennis Johnson, managing editor; Peter Carver, childrens' acquisitions editor. Publishes trade paperback originals and occasionally reprints. **Publishes 14-17 titles/year. Receives 1,700 queries and 2,000 mss/year. 20% of books from first-time authors; 90% from unagented writers. Pays 8-10% royalty on retail price.** Publishes book 1 year after acceptance of ms. Accepts simultaneous submissions. Reports in 6 months.
Imprint(s): Northern Lights Books for Children, Northern Lights Young Novels, Discovery Books, Roundup Books, Writing West.
Nonfiction: Children's/juvenile, cookbook, humor, illustrated books. Subjects include anthropology/archaeology/paleontology, cooking/foods/nutrition, gardening, history (local/regional), nature/environment (local/regional), regional, travel. Nonfiction list focuses on regional history, paleontology, and some true crime, travel, gardening—much with a regional (Canadian) emphasis. "Writers should assess their competition in the marketplace and have a clear understanding of their potential readership." Query with SASE. Reviews artwork/photos as part of ms package. Send photocopies.
Fiction: Adventure, ethnic, experimental, historical, humor, juvenile, literary, mainstream/contemporary, picture books, plays (occasionally), short story collections (occasionally), western, young adult. Adult fiction list includes well-established Canadian writers writing literary fiction, though the press is open to accepting other forms if tastefully and skillfully done. Query.
Poetry: Query.
Recent Title(s): *Mamie's Children*, by Judy Schultz (fiction); *Alaska and Yukon History Along the Highway*, by Ted Stone (history/guidebook).
Tips: Audience varies from imprint to imprint. "Know as much as you can about the potential market/readership for your book and indicate clearly how your book is different from or better than others in the same genre." Accepts very

few unsolicited manuscripts each year. Prefers Canadian authors with proven track record.

REIDMORE BOOKS INC., 18228-102 Ave., Edmonton, Alberta T5S 1S7 Canada. (403)424-4420. Fax: (403)441-9919. E-mail: reidmore@compusmart.ab.ca. Website: http://www.reidmore.com. **Acquisitions**: Leah-Ann Lymer, senior editor. Estab. 1979. "Publishes social studies for kindergarten to grade 12." Publishes hardcover originals. **Publishes 10-12 titles/year. Receives 18-20 submissions/year. 60% of books from first-time authors; 100% from unagented writers. Subsidy publishes 5% of books. Pays royalty.** Publishes book 1 year after acceptance. Reports in 3 months on queries. Book catalog free.
Nonfiction: Textbook. Subjects include ethnic, government/politics, history, elementary mathematics and social studies. Query. Most manuscripts are solicited by publisher from specific authors.
Recent Title(s): *Century of Change: Europe from 1789 to 1918*, by Mitchner and Tuffs (grades 10-12).

ROCKY MOUNTAIN BOOKS, #4 Spruce Centre SW, Calgary, Alberta T3C 3B3 Canada. (403)249-9490. Fax: (403)249-2968. E-mail: tonyd@rmbooks.com. Website: http://www.rmbooks.com. **Acquisitions**: Tony Daffern, publisher. "We are focused on Western Canada and also mountaineering." **Publishes trade paperback originals. Publishes 5 titles/year. Receives 30 queries/year. 75% of books from first-time authors; 100% from unagented writers. Pays 10% royalty. Offers $1,000-2,000 advance.** Publishes book 1 year after acceptance. Reports in 1 month on queries. *Writer's Market* recommends allowing 2 months for reply. Book catalog and ms guidelines free.
Nonfiction: How-to. Subjects include nature/environment, recreation, travel. "Our main area of publishing is outdoor recreation guides to Western and Northern Canada." Query.
Recent Title(s): *GPS Made Easy*, by Lawrence Letham (how-to).

🍁 **RONSDALE PRESS**, 3350 W. 21st Ave., Vancouver, British Columbia V6S 1G7 Canada. Website: http://www.ronsdalepress.com. **Acquisitions:** Ronald B. Hatch, director. "We aim to publish the best Canadian writers. We are particularly interested in books that help Canadians know one another better." Publishes trade paperback originals. **Publishes 8 titles/year. Receives 100 queries and 200 mss/year. 60% of books from first-time authors; 95% from unagented writers. Pays 10% royalty on retail price.** Publishes book 1 year after acceptance of ms. Accepts simultaneous submissions. Reports in 1 week on queries, 1 month on proposals, 3 months on mss. Book catalog for #10 SASE. Writers *must* be Canadian citizens or landed immigrants.
Nonfiction: Biography, children's/juvenile. No picture books. Subjects include history, language/literature, nature/environment, regional.
Fiction: Novels, short story collections, children's literature. Query with at least 80 pages.
Poetry: "Poets should have published some poems in magazines/journals and should be well-read in contemporary masters." Submit complete ms.
Recent Poetry Title(s): *Take My Words*, by Howard Richler (uses of language); *Hong Kong Poems*, by A. Parkin and L. Wong (about Hong Kong in English and Chinese).

SELF-COUNSEL PRESS, 1481 Charlotte Rd., North Vancouver, British Columbia V7J 1H1 Canada. (604)986-3366. Also 1704 N. State Street, Bellingham, WA 98225. (360)676-4530. **Acquisitions:** Lori Ledingham, managing editor. Estab. 1970. "We look for manuscripts full of useful information that will allow readers to take the solution to their needs or problems into their own hands and succeed. We do not want personal self-help accounts, however." Publishes trade paperback originals. **Publishes 15-20 titles/year. Receives 1,000 submissions/year. 80% of books from first-time authors; 95% from unagented writers. Pays 10% royalty on net receipts.** Publishes book 9 months after acceptance. Accepts simultaneous submissions. Reports in 2 months. Book catalog and ms guidelines for 9×12 SAE.
Nonfiction: How-to, self-help. Subjects include business, law, reference. Query or submit outline and sample chapters.
Recent Title(s): *Computer Crisis 2000*, by W. Michael Fletcher.
Tips: "The Self-Counsel author is an expert in his or her field and capable of conveying practical, specific information to those who are not."

[A] **SEVERN HOUSE PUBLISHERS**, 9-15 High St., Sutton, Surrey SM1 1DF United Kingdom. (0181)770-3930. Fax: (0181)770-3850. **Acquisitions**: Sara Short, editorial director. Publishes hardcover and trade paperback originals and reprints. **Publishes 120 titles/year. Receives 250 queries and 50 mss/year. 0.5% of books from first-time authors; 0.5% from unagented writers. Pays 7½-15% royalty on retail price. Offers $750-2,500.** Accepts simultaneous submissions. Reports in 3 months on proposals. Book catalog free.
Fiction: Adventure, fantasy, historical, horror, mainstream/contemporary, mystery, romance, science fiction, short story collections, suspense. Submit synopsis and 3 sample chapters. *Agented submissions only.*
Recent Title(s): *Blood and Honor*, by W.E.B. Griffin (war fiction).

ALWAYS SUBMIT unsolicited manuscripts or queries with a self-addressed, stamped envelope (SASE) within your country or a self-addressed envelope with International Reply Coupons (IRC) purchased from the post office for other countries.

SHORELINE, Ste.-Anne, Ste.-Anne-de-Bellevue 23, Quebec H9X 1L1 Canada. Phone/fax: (514)457-5733. **Acquisitions:** Judy Isherwood, editor. "Our mission is to support new authors by publishing literary works of considerable merit." Publishes trade paperback originals. **Publishes 3 titles/year. Pays 10% royalty on retail price.** Publishes book 1 year after acceptance. Reports in 1 month on queries, 4 months on ms. Book catalog for 50¢ postage.
Nonfiction: Biography, essays, humour, illustrated book, reference. Subjects include: America, art, Canada, education, ethnic, health/mental health, history, mediation, regional, religion, Mexico, Spain, the Arctic, travel, women's studies.
Recent Title(s): *Alaska Burning*, by Jerry Nelson.
Tips: Audience is "adults and young adults who like their nonfiction personal, different and special. Beginning writers welcome, agents unnecessary. Send your best draft (not the first!), make sure your heart is in it."

SNOWAPPLE PRESS, Box 66024, Heritage Postal Outlet, Edmonton, Alberta T6J 6T4 Canada. **Acquisitions**: Vanna Tessier, editor. "We focus on topics that are interesting, unusual and controversial." Publishes hardcover originals, trade paperback originals and reprints, mass market paperback originals and reprints. **Publishes 5-6 titles/year. Receives 300 queries/year. 50% of books from first-time authors; 100% from unagented writers. Pays 10-50% royalty on retail price or makes outright purchase of $100 or pays in copies. Offers $100-200 advance.** Publishes book 2 years after acceptance. Accepts simultaneous submissions. Reports in 1 month on queries, 3 months on proposals and mss.
Fiction: Adventure, ethnic, experimental, fantasy, feminist, historical, literary, mainstream/contemporary, mystery, picture books, short story collections, young adult. Query with SASE.
Poetry: Query with SASE or SAE and IRC.
Recent Title(s): *Salamander Moon*, by Cecelia Frey (nonfiction); *A Windburnt Girl*, by Vanna Tessier (poetry).
Tips: Audience is educated readers. "We are a small press that will publish original, interesting and entertaining fiction and poetry."

SOUND AND VISION PUBLISHING LIMITED, 359 Riverdale Ave., Toronto, Ontario M4J 1A4 Canada. (416)465-2828. Fax: (416)465-0755. Website: http://www.soudandvision.com. **Acquisitions:** Geoff Savage. Sound and Vision specializes in books on music with a humorous slant. Publishes trade paperback originals. **Publishes 2 titles/year.** Reports in 3 months on proposals.
Nonfiction: Music/humor subjects. Submit outline and SASE.
Recent Title(s): *A Working Musician's Joke Book.*

STODDART PUBLISHING CO., LTD., General Publishing Co., Ltd., 34 Lesmill Rd., Toronto, Ontario M3B 2T6 Canada. **Acquisitions:** Donald G. Bastian, managing editor. Stoddart publishes "important Canadian books" for a general interest audience. Publishes hardcover, trade paperback and mass market paperback originals and trade paperback reprints. **Publishes 100 titles/year. Receives 1,200 queries and mss/year. 10% of books from first-time authors; 50% from unagented writers. Pays 8-10% royalty on retail price.** Publishes book 1 year after acceptance of ms. Accepts simultaneous submissions. Reports in 2 months. Book catalog and ms guidelines for #10 SASE.
Imprint(s): Stoddart Kids (Kathryn Cole, publisher).
Nonfiction: Biography, children's/juvenile, coffee table book, cookbook, gift book, how-to, humor, illustrated book, self-help. Subjects include art/architecture, business and economics, child guidance/parenting, computers and electronics, cooking/foods/nutrition, gardening, government/politics, health/medicine, history, language/literature, military/war, money/finance, nature/environment, psychology, science, sociology, sports. Submit outline, 2 sample chapters, outline, résumé, with SASE.
Recent Title(s): *The Pig and the Python*, by David Cork, Susan Lightstone (financial planning).

THISTLEDOWN PRESS, 633 Main St., Saskatoon, Saskatchewan S7H 0J8 Canada. (306)244-1722. Fax: (306)244-1762. E-mail: thistle@sk.sympatico.ca. Website: http://www.thistledown.sk.ca. Editor-in-Chief: Patrick O' Rourke. **Acquisitions**: Jesse Stothers. Estab. 1975. Publishes trade paperback originals by resident Canadian authors *only.* **Publishes 10-12 titles/year. Receives 350 submissions/year. 10% of books from first-time authors; 90% from unagented writers. Pays standard royalty on retail price.** Publishes book 2 years after acceptance. Reports in 2 months. Book catalog and guidelines for #10 SASE.
Fiction: Juvenile (ages 8 and up), literary. Minimum of 30,000 words. *No unsolicited mss.* Query first.
Poetry: "The author should make him/herself familiar with our publishing program before deciding whether or not his/her work is appropriate." Prefers poetry ms that has had some previous exposure in literary magazines. No unsolicited ms. Query first.
Recent Title(s): *The Lavender Child*, by Harriet Richards (fiction); *Zhivago's Fire*, by Andrew Wreggitt (poetry).
Tips: "We prefer to receive a query letter first before a submission. We're looking for quality, well-written literary fiction—for children and young adults and for our adult fiction list as well. Increased emphasis on fiction (short story collections and novels) for young adults, aged 12-18 years."

THOMPSON EDUCATIONAL PUBLISHING INC., 14 Ripley Ave., Suite 104, Toronto, Ontario M6S 3N9 Canada. (416)766-2763. Fax: (416)766-0398. E-mail: thompson@canadabooks.ingenia.com. Website: http://canadabooks.ingenia.com. **Acquisitions:** Keith Thompson, president. Thompson Educational specializes in high-quality educational texts in the social sciences and humanities." **Publishes 10 titles/year. Receives 15 queries and 10 mss/year. 80% of books from first-time authors; 100% from unagented writers. Pays 10% royalty on net price.** Publishes book 1 year after acceptance. Reports in 1 month. Book catalog free.

Nonfiction: Textbook. Subjects include business and economics, education, government/politics, sociology, women's issues/studies. Submit outline and 1 sample chapter and résumé.
Recent Title(s): *Learning for Life*, edited by Sue Scott, Bruce Spencer and Alan Thomas (adult education).

N **THORSONS**, Imprint of HarperCollins, 77-85 Fulham Palace Rd., Hammersmith, London W6 8JB England. Fax: 081-307-4440. **Acquisitions**: Eileen Campbell, managing director. Estab. 1930. Publishes paperback originals. **Publishes 150 titles/year. Pays 7½-10% royalty.** Reports in 2 months. Book catalog free.
Nonfiction: Publishes books on health and lifestyle, environmental issues, business, popular psychology, self-help and positive thinking, therapy, religion and spirituality, philosophy, new science, psychic awareness, astrology, divination, and Western tradition.

TITAN BOOKS LTD., 42-44 Dolben St., London SE1 OUP England. Fax: (0171)620-0032. E-mail: 101447.2455@compuserve.can. **Acquisitions**: D. Barraclough, editorial manager. Publishes trade and mass market paperback originals and reprints. **Publishes 60-90 titles/year. Receives 1,000 queries and 500 mss/year. Less than 1% of books from first-time authors; 50% from unagented writers. Pays royalty of 6-8% on retail price. Advance varies.** Publishes books 1 year after acceptance of ms. Accepts simultaneous submissions. Reports in 1 month on queries, 3 months on proposals, 6 months on mss. Manuscript guidelines for SASE with IRC.
Nonfiction: Subjects include music, film and TV. Send synopsis and sample chapter with SASE.
Recent Title(s): *Mondo Macabro: Bizarre World Cinema*, by Pete Tambs (cinema).

N **TRILOBYTE PRESS**, 1486 Willowdown Rd., Oakville, Ontario L6L 1X3 Canada. (905)847-7366. Fax: (905)847-3258. E-mail: doday@credit.erin.utoronto.ca. Website: http://www.successatschool.com. Publisher: Danton H. O'Day, Ph.D. Publishes trade paperback originals. **Publishes 3-4 titles/year. Receives 50 queries and 20 mss/year. 50% of books from first-time authors; 100% from unagented writers. Pays 10% royalty on wholesale price. No advance.** Publishes book 8 months after acceptance of ms. Accepts simultaneous submissions. Reports in 1 month on queries, 2 months on proposals, 3 months on mss. Book catalog free.
Nonfiction: How-to, reference, self-help, textbook. Subjects include education, health/medicine, science. "We are continually looking for guides to help students succeed in school and in their careers." Query with proposal package, including outline, 2 sample chapters, qualifications of author and SASE. Reviews artwork/photos as part of ms package. Send photocopies.
Recent Title(s): *Stressed Out! Taking Control of Student Stress*, by David C. Rainham, M.D. (self-help).
Tips: Audience is "young people from high school through college age who want to do their best and get the job they want. Think about your submission—why us and why is your book worth publishing? Who will read it and why."

TURNSTONE PRESS, 607-100 Arthur St., Winnipeg, Manitoba R3B 1H3 Canada. (204)947-1555. Fax: (204)942-1555. E-mail: editor@turnstonepress.mb.ca. Website: http://www.turnstonepress.com. **Acquisitions:** Manuela Dias, managing editor. Estab. 1971. "Turnstone Press is a literary press that publishes Canadian writers with an emphasis on writers from, and writing on, the Canadian west." Publishes trade paperback originals by Canadians and permanent residents only. **Publishes 10-12 titles/year. Receives 1,000 mss/year. 25% of books from first-time authors; 75% from unagented writers. Pays 10% royalty on retail price. Offers $100-500 advance.** Publishes book 1 year after acceptance of ms. Reports in 4 months. Book catalog free.
Imprint(s): Raven's Stone (literary genre fiction).
Nonfiction: Turnstone Press would like to see more nonfiction books, particularly travel, memoir, women's writing. Query with SASE.
Fiction: Adventure, ethnic, experimental, feminist, gothic, humor, literary, mainstream/contemporary, mystery, short story collections, women's. Would like to see more novels. Query with SASE (Canadian postage) first.
Poetry: Submit complete ms.
Recent Fiction Title(s): *Kabloona in the Yellow Kayak*, by Victoria Jason (kayaking through Northwest Passage); *What Birds Can Only Whisper*, by Julie Brickman (recovered memory).
Tips: "Writers are encouraged to view our list and check if submissions are appropriate. Would lke to see more women's writing, travel, memoir, life-writing as well as eclectic novels. Would like to see 'non-formula' genre writing, especially *literary* mystery, gothic and noir for our new imprint."

UMBRELLA PRESS, 56 Rivercourt Blvd., Toronto, Ontario M4J 3A4 Canada. (416)696-6665. Fax: (416)696-9189. E-mail: umbpress@interlog.com. Website: http://www.interlog.com/~umbpress. **Acquisitions:** Ken Pearson, publisher. "We focus on books for young people directed to schools and libraries as supplemental and reference. The emphasis is on issues of multiculturalism." Publishes hardcover and softbound originals. **Publishes 6 titles/year. Receives 10 queries and 5 mss/year. 75% of books from first-time authors; 100% from unagented writers. Pays 10-15% royalty on wholesale price for education, on retail price for trade. Offers $250-500 advance.** Publishes book 18 months after acceptance of ms. Accepts simultaneous submissions. Reports in 1 month on queries; 2 months on proposals; 3 months on mss. Book catalog and ms guidelines free.
Nonfiction: Biography, reference, library/education supplement. Subjects include multiculturalism, education, history, women's issues/studies. Submit outline with 2 sample chapters.
Recent Title(s): *Arctic Awakening*, by Stephen Ward.

THE UNITED CHURCH PUBLISHING HOUSE (UCPH), 3250 Bloor St. W., 4th Floor, Etobicoke, Ontario M8X 2Y4 Canada. (416)231-5931. Fax: (416)232-6004. E-mail: bookpub@uccan.org. Website: http://www.uccan.org/ucph. **Acquisitions:** Ruth Bradley-St-Cyr, managing editor. "We are committed to publishing books and resources that help people to engage in Christian ministry. We are further committed to engaging readers, regardless of denomination or faith, in consideration of the spiritual aspects of their lives." Publishes trade paperback originals from Canadian authors only. **Publishes 12-16 titles/year. Receives 80 queries and 30 mss/year. 80% of books from first-time authors; 99% from unagented writers. Pays 10% royalty on retail price. Offers $100-300 advance.** Publishes book 1 year after acceptance. Reports in 2-4 months on proposals. Proposal guidelines free with SASE.
Nonfiction: Subjects relate to United Church of Canada interests only, in the following areas: history, religion, sociology, women's issues/studies, theology and biblical studies. "Complete ms not welcome. Please query before submitting any material."
Recent Title(s): *Circle of Grace: Worship and Prayer in the Everyday*, by Keri K. Wehlander.

THE UNIVERSITY OF ALBERTA PRESS, 141 Athabasca Hall, Edmonton, Alberta T6G 2E8 Canada. (403)492-3662. Fax: (403)492-0719. E-mail: uap@gpu.srv.ualberta.ca. Website: http://www.ualberta.ca/~uap. **Acquisitions**: Glenn Rollans, director. Estab. 1969. "For more than a quarter-century, the University of Alberta Press has steadily built its reputation for publishing important scholarly works and fine books for broad audiences." Publishes hardcover and trade paperback originals and trade paperback reprints. **Publishes 18-25 titles/year. Receives 200 submissions/year. 60% of books from first-time authors; majority from unagented writers. Pays 10% royalty on net price.** Publishes book within 1 year after acceptance. Reports in 3 months. Book catalog and ms guidelines free.
Nonfiction: "Our interests include the Canadian West, the North, multicultural studies, health science and native studies." Submit table of contents, 1-2 chapters, sample illustrations and cv.
Recent Title(s): *Shredding the Public Interest*, by Kevin Taft (Canadian politics); *Sightlines: Printmaking and Image Culture*, edited by Walter Jule (art/history).
Tips: "Since 1969, the University of Alberta Press has earned recognition and awards from the Association of American University Presses, the Alcuin Society, the Book Publishers Association of Alberta and the Bibliographical Society of Canada, among others. Now we're growing—in the audiences we reach, the numbers of titles we publish, and our energy for new challenges. But we're still small enough to listen carefully, to work closely with our authors, to explore possibilities. Our list is strong in Canadian, western and northern topics, but it ranges widely."

N **UNIVERSITY OF CALGARY PRESS**, 2500 University Dr. NW, Calgary, Alberta T2N 1N4 Canada. (403)220-7578. Fax: (403)282-0085. E-mail: 75001@aoss.ucalgary.ca. Website: http://www.ucalgary.ca/ucpress. **Acquisitions:** Shirley A. Onn, director. "University of Calgary Press is committed to the advancement of scholarship through the publication of first-rate monographs and academic and scientific journals." Publishes hardcover and trade paperback originals and reprints. **Publishes 12-15 titles/year. Pays 4-6% royalty on wholesale price.** Publishes book 12-18 months after acceptance of ms. Reports in 1 month on queries, 2 months on proposals, 4 months on mss. Book catalog and ms guidelines free.
Nonfiction: Subjects include art/architecture, business/economics, creative nonfiction, health/medicine, philosophy, travel, women's issues/studies, Canadian studies, post-modern studies, international relations. Submit outline and 2 sample chapters with SASE. Reviews artwork/photos of the ms package. Send photocopies.
Recent Title(s): *Financing Growth in Canada*, edited by Paul Halpern (economics/public policy).
Tips: "If I were trying to interest a scholarly publisher, I would prepare my manuscript on a word processor and submit a completed prospectus, including projected market, to the publisher."

UNIVERSITY OF MANITOBA PRESS, 15 Gillson St., #244, University of Manitoba, Winnipeg, Manitoba R3T 5V6 Canada. Website: http://www.umanitoba.ca/publications/uofmpress. **Acquisitions**: David Carr, director. Estab. 1967. "Western Canadian focus or content is important." Publishes nonfiction hardcover and trade paperback originals. **Publishes 4-6 titles/year. Pays 5-15% royalty on wholesale price.** Reports in 3 months.
Nonfiction: Scholarly. Subjects include Western Canadian history, women's issues/studies, Native history. Query.
Recent Title(s): *In Her Own Voice*, by Martens and Harms (women/Manitoba).

UNIVERSITY OF OTTAWA PRESS, 542 King Edward, Ottawa, Ontario K1N 6N5 Canada. (613)562-5246. Fax: (613)562-5247. E-mail: press@uottawa.ca. Website: http://www.uopress.uottawa.ca. **Acquisitions:** Vicki Bennett, editor. Estab. 1936. The University Press publishes books for the scholarly and educated general audiences. They were "the first *officially* bilingual publishing house in Canada." **Publishes 22 titles/year; 10 titles/year in English. Receives 250 submissions/year. 20% of books from first-time authors; 95% from unagented writers. Determines nonauthor subsidy by preliminary budget. Pays 5-10% royalty on net price.** Publishes book 4 months after acceptance. Reports in 2 months on queries, 4 months on mss. Book catalog and author's guide free.
Nonfiction: Reference, textbook, scholarly. Subjects include criminology, education, Canadian government/politics, Canadian history, language/literature, nature/environment, philosophy, religion, sociology, translation, women's issues/studies. Submit outline/synopsis and sample chapters.
Recent Title(s): *Women and Political Representation in Canada*, edited by Manon Tremblay and Caroline Andrew.
Tips: "Envision audience of academic specialists and (for some books) educated public."

THE UNIVERSITY OF WESTERN ONTARIO, 1137 Western Rd., London, Ontario N6G 1G7 Canada. (519)661-2096. Fax: (519)661-3833. E-mail: press@edu.uwo.ca. Website: http://www.uwo.ca/edu/press. **Acquisitions:** Dr. David

Radcliff, director. "We publish scholarly books for teachers and graduate students in education." Publishes trade paperback originals. **Publishes 3 titles/year. Receives 12 queries and 12 mss/year. 50% of books from first-time authors; 100% from unagented writers. Pays 10% royalty on wholesale price. No advance.** Publishes book 6 months after acceptance of ms. Reports in 1 month on queries and proposals, 3 months on mss. Manuscript guidelines free.
Imprint(s): The Althouse Press.
Nonfiction: Education (scholarly) subjects. "We publish scholarly books for teachers and graduate students in education. Beware of sending incomplete manuscripts that are only marginally apt to our market and limited mandate." Query or submit outline or proposal package including completed ms. Reviews artwork/photos as part of ms package. Send photocopies.
Recent Title(s): *Not Wanted In the Classroom*, by Pletsch.

UPNEY EDITIONS, 19 Appalachian Crescent, Kitchener, Ontario N2E 1A3 Canada. **Acquisitions**: Gary Brannon, managing editor. Publishes trade paperback originals. **Publishes 2-4 titles/year. Receives 200 queries and 100 mss/year. 33% of books from first-time authors; 100% from unagented writers. Pays 10% royalty on wholesale price.** Publishes book 9 months after acceptance. Reports in 1 month. Book catalog for #10 SASE (Canadian).
Nonfiction: Biography, reference. Subjects include Americana, art/architecture, history (with Canada/USA connections or Canadian history), language/literature, military/war, nature/environment, regional, travel. "Remember that we are a Canadian small press, and our readers are mostly Canadians! We are specifically interested in popular history with cross-border U.S. Canada connection; also, popular travel literature (Europe or specific locations), but it must be witty and critically honest. No travel guides, cycling, hiking or driving tours! We prefer words to paint pictures rather than photographs, but line art will be considered. Queries or submissions that dictate publishing terms turn us right off. So do submissions with no SASE or submissions with return U.S.postage stamps. Enclose sufficient IRCs or we cannot return material." Length: 50,000 words maximum. Query with outline, 2 sample chapters and SASE for Canada. "We prefer to see manuscripts well thought out chapter by chapter, not just a first chapter and a vague idea of the rest." Reviews artwork/photos as part of ms package. Send photocopies.
Recent Title(s): *An Awful Grandeur*, edited by Robert Higgins.
Tips: "Although our titles are directed to a general audience, our sales and marketing are focused on libraries (public, high school, college) 70% and 30% on bookstores. We are dismayed by the 'pushy' attitude of some submissions. We will not even look at 'finished package, ready-to-print' submissions, which seem to be growing in number. The authors of these instant books clearly need a printer and/or investor and not a publisher. Electronic, preformatted submissions on disk are preferred—we are a Mac environment."

VANWELL PUBLISHING LIMITED, 1 Northrup Crescent, P.O. Box 2131, St. Catharines, Ontario L2M 6P5 Canada. (905)937-3100. Fax: (905)937-1760. **Acquisitions:** Angela Dobler, general editor; Simon Kooter, editor (military). Estab. 1983. "Vanwell is considered Canada's leading naval heritage publisher. We also publish military aviation, biography, WWII and WWI histories. Recently publishing children's fiction and nonfiction, but not picture books." Publishes trade originals and reprints. **Publishes 5-7 titles/year. Receives 100 submissions/year. Publishes Canadian authors only. 85% of books from first-time authors; 100% from unagented writers. Pays 8-15% royalty on wholesale price. Offers $200 average advance.** Publishes book 1 year after acceptance of ms. Reports in 3 months on queries. Book catalog free.

- Vanwell Publishing Ltd. has received awards from Canadian Libraries Association, Education Children's Book Centre and Notable Education Libraries Association. It is seeing increased demand for biographical nonfiction for ages 10-14.

Nonfiction: All military/history related. Query with SASE. Reviews artwork/photos as part of ms package.
Recent Title(s): *Wings of a Hero: Wop May*, by Sheila Reid (aviation biography); *Incident at North Point*, by Marc Milner (adult fiction).
Tips: "The writer has the best chance of selling a manuscript to our firm which is in keeping with our publishing program, well written and organized. Our audience: older male, history buff, war veteran; regional tourist; students. *Canadian* only military/aviation, naval, military/history and children's nonfiction have the best chance with us."

WALL & EMERSON, INC., 6 O'Connor Dr., Toronto, Ontario M4K 2K1 Canada. (416)467-8685. Fax: (416)696-2460. E-mail: wall@wallbooks.com. Website: http://www.wallbooks.com. **Acquisitions:** Byron E. Wall, president; Martha Wall, vice president. Estab. 1987. "We are most interested in textbooks for college courses that meet well-defined needs and are targeted to their audiences." Publishes hardcover and trade paperback originals and reprints. **Publishes 3 titles/year. 50% of books from first-time authors; 100% from unagented writers. Pays royalty of 8-15% on wholesale price.** Publishes book 2 years after acceptance. Accepts simultaneous submissions. Reports in 3 months.
Nonfiction: Reference, textbook. Subjects include adult education, health/medicine, philosophy, science, mathematics. "We are looking for any undergraduate college text that meets the needs of a well-defined course in colleges in the U.S. and Canada." Submit outline and sample chapters.
Recent Title(s): *Principles of Real-Time Software Engineering*, by Michael Moore and André Pruitt (engineering).
Tips: "Our audience consists of college undergraduate students and college libraries. Our ideal writer is a college professor writing a text for a course he or she teaches regularly. If I were a writer trying to market a book today, I would identify the audience for the book and write directly to the audience throughout the book. I would then approach a publisher that publishes books specifically for that audience."

N **WARWICK PUBLISHING INC.**, #111, 388 King St. W, Toronto, Ontario M5V 1K2 Canada. (416)596-1555. Fax: (416)596-1520. **Acquisitions**: Nick Pitt, publisher. Publishes hardcover originals and trade paperback originals and reprints. **Publishes 30 titles/year. Receives 200 queries and 30 mss/year. 20% of books from first-time authors; 80% from unagented writers. Pays 7-12% royalty on retail price. No advance.** Publishes book 1 year after acceptance of ms. Accepts simultaneous submissions. Reports in 4 months. Book catalog for 8x10 SASE. Manuscript guidelines for #10 SASE.

Nonfiction: Biography, coffee table book, cookbook, gift book, how-to, illustrated book, multimedia (CD-ROM), reference, self-help. Subjects include art/architecture, business/economics, child guidance/parenting, cooking/food/nutrition, education, gardening, history, money/finance, nature/environment, photography, recreation, sports, travel. Query or submit proposal package, including marketing information, outline and 1 sample chapters with SASE. Reviews artwork/photos as part of ms package. Send photocopies.

Fiction: Adventure, sports, young adult. Query.

Recent Title(s): *Generation Eats*, by Amy Rosen (cookbook); *The Youngest Goalie*, by Brian McFarlane (YA).

Tips: "Be patient, we are overworked."

WHITECAP BOOKS LTD., 351 Lynn Ave., North Vancouver, British Columbia V7J 2C4 Canada. (604)980-9852. Fax: (604)980-8197. E-mail: bkwiz@pinc.com. Website: http://www.whitecap.ca. **Acquisitions**: Robin Rivers, editorial director. Whitecap Books publishes a wide range of nonfiction with a Canadian and international focus. Publishes hardcover and trade paperback originals. **Publishes 24 titles/year. Receives 150 queries and 200 mss/year. 20% of books from first-time authors; 90% from unagented writers. Royalty and advance negotiated for each project.** Publishes book 12-18 months after acceptance. Accepts simultaneous submissions. Reports in 2 months on proposals.

Nonfiction: Coffee table book, cookbook, children's/juvenile. Subjects include animals, gardening, history, nature/environment, recreation, regional, travel. "We require an annotated outline. Writers should also take the time to research our list." Submit outline, 1 sample chapter, table of contents and SASE with international postal voucher for submission from the U.S. Send photocopies, not original material.

Recent Title(s): *Messing About in Boats*, byWill Millar (memoir).

Tips: "We want well-written, well-researched material that presents a fresh approach to a particular topic."

WORDSTORM PRODUCTIONS INC., Box 49132, 7740 18th St. SE, Calgary, Alberta T2C 3W5 Canada. Phone/fax: (403)236-1275. E-mail: perry@perryrose.com. Website: http://www.perryrose.com. **Acquisitions:** Perry P. Rose, president; Eileen A. Rose, vice president. "Wordstorm seeks to provide the highest quality books on the most important subjects of humour to adults and positive resolution of childhood trauma to children." Publishes trade and mass market paperback originals. **Publishes 5-7 titles/year. 90% of books from first-time authors; 95% from unagented writers. Pays 10-12% royalty on retail price. (Works released in USA paid 66% of above.)** Publishes book 1 year after acceptance of ms. Reports in 2 months on queries, 4 months on proposals, 6 months on mss. Manuscript guidelines for #10 SASE.

Nonfiction: Humor. Query with outline, 3 sample chapters and SASE or SAE and IRCs. Reviews artwork/photos as part of ms package. Send photocopies.

Fiction: Humor, children's books. Query with synopsis, 3 sample chapters and SASE or SAE and IRCs. All unsolicited mss returned unopened.

Recent Title(s): *Tales From the Police Locker Room, Volumes 1 & 2* (nonfiction); *The Secret Days of Sydney and Cassidy Jewel* (fiction).

Tips: When sending self-addressed return envelope, please remember to use an international postal coupon if mailing is originating outside Canada. U.S. stamps cannot be used to mail "from" Canada.

MARKETS THAT WERE listed in the 1998 edition of *Writer's Market* but do not appear this year are listed in the General Index with a notation explaining why they were omitted.

Small Presses

"Small press" is a relative term. Compared to the dozen or so conglomerates, the rest of the book publishing world may seem to be comprised of small presses. A number of the publishers listed in the Book Publishers section consider themselves small presses and cultivate the image. For our classification, small presses are those that publish three or fewer books per year.

The publishing opportunities are slightly more limited with the companies listed here than with those in the Book Publishers section. Not only are they publishing fewer books, but small presses are usually not able to market their books as effectively as larger publishers. Their print runs and royalty arrangements are usually smaller. It boils down to money, what a publisher can afford, and in that area, small presses simply can't compete with conglomerates.

However, realistic small press publishers don't try to compete with Penguin Putnam or Random House. They realize everything about their efforts operates on a smaller scale. Most small press publishers get into book publishing for the love of it, not solely for the profit. Of course, every publisher, small or large, wants successful books. But small press publishers often measure success in different ways.

Many writers actually prefer to work with small presses. Since small publishing houses are usually based on the publisher's commitment to the subject matter, and since they necessarily work with far fewer authors than the conglomerates, small press authors and their books usually receive more personal attention than the larger publishers can afford to give them. Promotional dollars at the big houses tend to be siphoned toward a few books each season that they have decided are likely to succeed, leaving hundreds of "midlist" books underpromoted, and, more likely than not, destined for failure. Since small presses only commit to a very small number of books every year, they are vitally interested in the promotion and distribution of each one.

Just because they publish three or fewer titles per year does not mean small press editors have the time to look at complete manuscripts on spec. In fact, the editors with smaller staffs often have even less time for submissions. The procedure for contacting a small press with your book idea is exactly the same as it is for a larger publisher. Send a one-page query with SASE first. If the press is interested in your proposal, be ready to send an outline or synopsis, and/or a sample chapter or two. Be patient with their reporting times; small presses can be slower to respond than larger companies. You might consider simultaneous queries, as long as you note this, to compensate for the waiting game.

For more information on small presses, see *Novel & Short Story Writer's Market* and *Poet's Market* (Writer's Digest Books), and *Small Press Review* and *The International Directory of Little Magazines and Small Presses* (Dustbooks).

For a list of publishers according to their subjects of interest, see the nonfiction and fiction sections of the Book Publishers Subject Index. Information on book publishers and producers listed in the previous edition of *Writer's Market* but not included in this edition can be found in the General Index.

N **ACADA BOOKS**, 1850 Union St., Suite 1216, San Francisco CA 94123. President: Brian Romer. Publishes trade paperback originals. **Publishes 3 titles/year. Receives 30 queries/year; 15 mss/year. 50% of books from first-time authors; 100% from unagented writers. Royalty and advances vary.** Publishes book 6 months after acceptance of ms. Accepts simultaneous submissions. Reports in 2 months on proposals. Manuscript guidelines free.

Nonfiction: Textbook. Subjects include business and economics, communications, government/politics, history, nature/environment, psychology, sociology. "Author must have current or previous college teaching experience." Submit proposal package with SASE. Reviews artwork/photos as part of the ms package. Send photocopies. Recent title(s):

Gifts from the Heart and *Discovering the Leader Within*, by Randy Fujishin (communications).

ACME PRESS, P.O. Box 1702, Westminster MD 21158-1702. (410)848-7577. Managing Editor: Ms. E.G. Johnston. Estab. 1991. Publishes hardcover and trade paperback originals. **Publishes 1-2 titles/year. Pays 50% of profits. Offers small advance.** Reports in 2 months on mss.

Fiction: Humor. "We accept submissions on any subject as long as the material is humorous; prefer full-length novels. No cartoons or art (text only). No pornography, poetry, short stories or children's material." Submit outline, first 50-75 pages and SASE. Recent title(s): *Hearts of Gold*, by James Magorian (comic mystery).

Tips: "We are always looking for the great comic novel."

ADAMS-HALL PUBLISHING, 11661 San Vincente Blvd., Suite 210, Los Angeles CA 90049. (800)888-4452. Editorial Director: Sue Ann Bacon. Publishes hardcover and trade paperback originals and reprints. **Publishes 3-4 titles/year. Pays 10% royalty on net receipts to publisher. Advance negotiable.** Reports in 1 month on queries. *Writer's Market* recommends allowing 2 months for reply. Accepts simultaneous submissions, if so noted.

Nonfiction: Quality business and personal finance books. Small, successful house that aggressively promotes select titles. Only interested in business or personal finance titles with broad appeal. Query first with proposed book idea, a listing of current, competitive books, author qualifications, how book is unique and the market(s) for book. Then submit outline and 2 sample chapters with SASE. Recent title(s): *The Generation X Money Book.*

N **AFRIMAX, Inc.**, 703 Shannon Lane, Kirksville MO 63501. (660)665-0757. President: Emmanuel Nnadozie. Publishes trade paperback originals. **Publishes 4 titles/year. Pays 8% royalty. No advance.** Reports in 5 months on queries, 1 month on proposals, 3 months on mss. Manuscript guidelines free on request.

Nonfiction: How-to and textbook. Subjects include business and economics, ethnic, money/finance, regional, travel. "International business & African business related interests. They do not carefully consider the audience and present the materials in the most appropriate way." Query. Recent title(s): *African Culture & American Business in Africa*, by Emmanuel Nnadozie (business/how-to).

Tips: Audience includes business managers, business educators, students.

ALETHEIA PUBLICATIONS, 38-15 Corporal Kennedy St., Bayside NY 11361. Publisher: Carolyn Smith. Imprint: Social Change Press. "We specialize in books for and about Americans who have lived or are living overseas in the Foreign Service, the military and other contexts. We also publish books about freelance editing and writing." Publishes trade paperback originals and reprints. **Publishes 3 titles/year. Imprint publishes 2 titles/year. Receives 10 queries and 3 mss/year. 90% of books from first-time authors; 100% from unagented writers. Pays 10% royalty on retail price. No advance.** Publishes book 8 months after acceptance of ms. Accepts simultaneous submissions. Reports in 1 month on queries, 2 months on proposals, 3 months on mss.

Nonfiction: Subjects include sociology, editing. Submit proposal package, including rationale, sample chapters, table of contents and SASE. Recent title(s): *Editorial Freelancing*, by Trumbull Rogers.

Tips: Audience is Americans who have lived overseas and freelance editors and writers. Audience for Social Change Press is sociologists interested in urban problems and culture.

ALLEN PUBLISHING CO., 7324 Reseda Blvd., Reseda CA 91335. (818)344-6788. Owner/Publisher: Michael Wiener. Estab. 1979. "Our books are primarily aimed at opportunity seekers—people who are looking for an opportunity (usually a business) to improve their financial condition. Our books are not aimed at sophisticated entrepreneurs." Publishes mass market paperback originals. **Publishes 4 titles/year. Receives 50-100 submissions/year. 50% of books from first-time authors; 90% from unagented writers. Makes outright purchase for negotiable sum.** Publishes book 6 months after acceptance. Accepts simultaneous submissions. Reports in 2 weeks. *Writer's Market* recommends allowing 2 months for reply. Book catalog and writer's guidelines for #10 SASE.

- This publisher reports having received many manuscripts outside its area of interest. Writers are encouraged to follow the publisher's subject matter guidelines.

Nonfiction: How-to, self-help. Subjects include how to start various businesses and how to improve your financial condition. "We want self-help material, 25,000 words approximately, aimed at wealth-builders, opportunity seekers, aspiring entrepreneurs. We specialize in material for people who are relatively inexperienced in the world of business and have little or no capital to invest. Material must be original and authoritative, not rehashed from other sources. All our books are marketed exclusively by mail, in soft-cover, 8½×11 format. We are a specialty publisher and will not consider anything that does not exactly meet our needs." Query. Reviews artwork/photos as part of ms package. Recent title(s): *How to Make Money Working at Home.*

Tips: "We are a specialty publisher, as noted above. If your subject does not match our specialty, do not waste your time and ours by submitting a query we cannot possibly consider."

AMERICAN CATHOLIC PRESS, 16565 S. State St., South Holland IL 60473. (312)331-5845. Editorial Director: Rev. Michael Gilligan, Ph.D. Estab. 1967. Publishes hardcover originals and hardcover and paperback reprints. "Most of our sales are by direct mail, although we do work through retail outlets." **Publishes 4 titles/year. Pays by outright purchase of $25-100. No advance.**

Nonfiction: "We publish books on the Roman Catholic liturgy—for the most part, books on religious music and educational books and pamphlets. We also publish religious songs for church use, including Psalms, as well as choral and instrumental arrangements. We are interested in new music, meant for use in church services. Books, or even pamphlets, on the Roman Catholic Mass are especially welcome. We have no interest in secular topics and are not interested in religious poetry of any kind."

AMIGADGET PUBLISHING COMPANY, P.O. Box 1696, Lexington SC 29071. (803)957-1106. Fax: (803)957-7495. E-mail: jaygross@calweb.com. Website: http://www.calweb.com/~jaygross. Editor-in-Chief: Jay Gross. Publishes hardcover and trade paperback originals. **Publishes 2 titles/year. Pays royalty or makes outright purchase. Advance negotiable.** Reports in 6 months.
Nonfiction: "Niche markets are our specialty. Do not send manuscript. Queries only. No books on Windows." Query only with SASE. Recent title(s): *How to Start Your Own Underground Newspaper*, by J. Gross (how-to).

ARIADNE PRESS, 4817 Tallahassee Ave., Rockville MD 20853-3144. (301)949-2514. President: Carol Hoover. Estab. 1976. "Our purpose is to promote the publication of emerging fiction writers." Publishes hardcover and trade paperback originals. **Publishes 1 book/year. Pays 10% royalty on retail price. No advance.** Reports in 1 month on queries, 3 months on mss.
Fiction: Adventure, feminist, historical, humor, literary, mainstream/contemporary. "We look for exciting and believable plots, strong themes, and non-stereotypical characters who develop in fascinating and often unpredictable directions." Query with 1-2 page plot summary, bio and SASE. "Send brief plot summary. Please do not send sample chapters unless requested." Recent title(s): *Steps of the Sun*, by Eva Thaddeus, winner of Ariadne Prize for best first novel, 1997.

ARTEMIS CREATIONS PUBLISHING, 3395 Nostrand Ave., 2-J, Brooklyn NY 11229. President: Shirley Oliveira. Imprints are FemSuprem, Matriarch's Way. Publishes trade paperback and mass market paperback originals. **Publishes 4 titles/year. Pays 5-10% royalty on retail price or makes outright purchase of $300 minimum (30,000 words). No advance.** Publishes book 18 months after acceptance of ms. Accepts simultaneous submissions. Reports in 1 week. Book catalog and ms guidelines for #10 SASE.
Nonfiction: Subjects include women's issues/studies. "Strong feminine archetypes, subjects only. Query or submit outline, 3 sample chapters, author bio, marketing plan and SASE. Reviews artwork/photos as part of the ms package. Send photocopies. Recent title(s): *Gospel of Goddess*, by Bond and Suffield (metaphysical).
Fiction: Erotica, experimental, fantasy, feminist, gothic, horror, mystery, occult, religious, science fiction. Query or submit synopsis and 3 sample, marketing plan and SASE. Recent title(s): *Lady Killer: Tale of Horror and the Erotic*, by Tony Malo.
Tips: "Our readers are looking for strong, powerful feminie archetypes in fiction and nonfiction. Graphic sex and language are OK."

AUSTEN SHARP, P.O. Box 12, Newport RI 02840. (401)846-9884. President: Eleyne Austen Sharp. Estab. 1996. Children's imprint is Blue Villa. Publishes hardcover and trade paperback originals. **Publishes 1-2 titles/year. Pays up to 40% royalty on wholesale price.** Reports in 2 months on queries, 3 months on mss.
Nonfiction: Children's picture books and travel. "Currently, we have a special interest in New England travel books. Submissions should be well-researched and creative, not your run-of-the-mill history or guidebook." Query only. Recent title(s): *Haunted Newport*, by Eleyne Austen Sharp.
Tips: "Query with a one-page cover letter first. Phone queries are not accepted. If we are interested in seeing the manuscript, we will notify you. Book publishing is extremely competitive, so know the market! What you think is an original idea may be published already."

AUTO BOOK PRESS, P.O. Bin 711, San Marcos CA 92079-0711. (760)744-3582. Editorial Director: William Carroll. Estab. 1955. Publishes hardcover and paperback originals. **Publishes 2-4 titles/year. Pays negotiated royalty on wholesale price. Advance varies.** Reports in 1 month on queries.
Nonfiction: Automotive material only: technical or definitive how-to. Query with SASE. Recent title(s): *Two Wheels to Panama.*

BALCONY PRESS, 512 E. Wilson, Suite 306, Glendale CA 91206. (818)956-5313. Publisher: Ann Gray. Publishes hardcover and trade paperback originals. **Publishes 2-4 titles/year. Pays 10% royalty on wholesale price. No advance.** Reports in 1 month on queries and proposals; 3 months on mss. Book information free.
Nonfiction: Biography, coffee table books and illustrated books. Subjects include art/architecture, ethnic, gardening, history (relative to design, art and architecture) and regional. "We are interested in the human side of design as opposed to technical or how-to. We like to think our books will be interesting to the general public who might not otherwise select an architecture or design book." Query by telephone or letter. Submit outline and 2 sample chapters with introduction if applicable. Recent title(s): *The Last Remaining Seats: Movie Palaces of Tinseltown*, by Steven M. Silverman.
Tips: Audience consists of architects, designers and the general public who enjoy those fields. "Our books typically cover California subjects but that is not a restriction. It's always nice when an author has strong ideas about how the book can be effectively marketed. We are not afraid of small niches if a good sales plan can be devised."

N **BANDANNA BOOKS**, 319-B Anacapa St., Santa Barbara CA 93101. (805)564-3559. Fax: (805)564-3278. Publisher: Sasha Newborn. Editor: Joan Blake. Publishes trade paperback originals and reprints. **Publishes 3 titles/year. Receives 300 queries and 100 mss/year. 50% of books from first-time authors; 90% from unagented writers.**

Pays 5-10% royalty on retail price (a few books gratis). Offers $50-200 advance. Publishes book 6-12 months after acceptance. Accepts simultaneous submissions. Reports in 4 months on proposals.
Nonfiction: Textbooks for college students, some illustrated. Subjects include history, literature, language. "Bandanna Books seeks to humanize the classics, history, language in non-sexist, modernized translations, using direct and plain language." Submit query letter, table of contents and first chapter. Reviews artwork/photos as part of ms package. Send photocopies. Recent title(s): *Don't Panic: The Procrastinator's Guide to Writing an Effective Term Paper*, by Steven Posusta.
Tips: "Our readers have a liberal arts orientation. Inventive, professional, well-thought-out presentations, please. Always include a SASE for reply."

BAYLOR UNIVERSITY PRESS, P.O. Box 97363, Waco TX 76798. (254)710-3164. Acquisitions: J. David Holcomb. Imprint is Markham Press Fund. Publishes hardcover and trade paperback originals. **Publishes 2 titles/year. Pays 10% royalty on wholesale price.** Publishes book 6 months after acceptance of ms. Reports in 2 months on proposals. Book catalog free.
Nonfiction: Scholarly. Subjects include anthropology/archaeology, history, regional, religion, women's issues/studies. Submit outline and 1-3 sample chapters. Recent title(s): *Thomas Robinson's New Cithaven Lessons (1609)*, by Colman and Casey (Renaissance music transcription).

N **BERKELEY HILLS BOOKS, INC.**, P.O. Box 9877, Berkeley CA 94709. General Manager: John Strohmeler. Berkeley Hills Books is looking for "serious" nonfiction. Publishes hardcover and trade paperback originals and reprints. **Publishes 4 titles/year. Receives 20 queries and 10 mss/year. 50% of books from first-time authors; 75% from unagented writers. Pays 10-15% royalty on wholesale price. Offers $0-1,500 advance.** Publishes book 1 year after acceptance of ms. Accepts simultaneous submissions. Reports in 2 months.
Nonfiction: Biography. Subjects include Americana, art/architecture, cooking/foods/nutrition, history, nature/environment, philosophy, religion. "We are looking for serious work." Submit outline. No unsolicited ms are returned. Reviews artwork/photos as part of the ms package. Send photocopies. Recent title(s): *Sharing The Universe*, by Seth Shostak (popular science).

N **BICK PUBLISHING HOUSE**, 307 Neck Rd., Madison CT 06443. (203)245-0073. President: Dale Carlson. "Bick publishes professional information for the general audience." Publishes trade paperback originals and reprints. **Publishes 2-6 titles/year. Receives 60 submissions/year. 10% of books from first-time authors; 10% from unagented writers. Pays 10-15% royalty on retail price. Offers $1,000-2,000 advance.** Publishes book 1 year after acceptance of ms. Reports in 2 months on queries, 3 months on proposals and mss. Book catalog and ms guidelines free.
Nonfiction: Biography, children's/juvenile, special needs/disabilities, wildlife rehabilitation. Subjects include animals, child guidance/parenting, health/medicine, psychology, women's issues/studies. Submit outline, 3 sample chapters, cv with SASE. Reviews artwork/photos as part of ms/package. Send photocopies. Recent title(s): *Psychology for Teenagers Series*.
Tips: "We are interested in animals, young people, people with disabilities/special needs, general nonfiction. Learn to outline, learn to write clearly, simply, intelligently on the subject."

BLACK HERON PRESS, P.O. Box 95676, Seattle WA 98145. Publisher: Jerry Gold. Publishes hardcover and trade paperback originals. **Publishes 4 titles/year. Pays 8-10% royalty on retail price.** Reports in 3 months on queries, 6 months on proposals and mss.

- Black Heron Press is not looking at new material until 1999.

Fiction: High quality, innovative fiction. Query with outline, 3 sample chapters and SASE. Recent title(s): *The Rat and The Rose*, by Arnold Rabin (surrealistic humorous novel).
Tips: "Readers should look at some of Black Heron's Books before submitting—they are easily available. Most submissions we see are competently done but have been sent to the wrong press. We do not publish self-help books."

BLISS PUBLISHING CO., P.O. Box 920, Marlborough MA 01752. (508)779-2827. Publisher: Stephen H. Clouter. Publishes hardcover and trade paperback originals. **Publishes 2-4 titles/year. Pays 10-15% royalty on wholesale price. No advance.** Reports in 2 months.
Nonfiction: Biography, illustrated book, reference, textbook. Subjects include government/politics, history, music/dance, nature/environment, recreation, regional. Submit proposal package, including outline, table of contents, 3 sample chapters, brief author biography, table of contents, SASE. Recent title(s): *Ninnuock, The Algonkian People of New England*, by Steven F. Johnson.

BLUE SKY MARKETING, INC., P.O. Box 21583, St. Paul MN 55121. (612)456-5602. President: Vic Spadaccini. Publishes hardcover and trade paperback originals. **Publishes 3 titles/year. Pays royalty on wholesale price.** Reports in 3 months. Manuscript guidelines for 6×9 SAE with 4 first-class stamps.
Nonfiction: Gift book, how-to. Subjects include gardening, hobbies, regional, travel, house and home. "Ideas must be unique. If it's been done, we're not interested!" Submit proposal package, including outline, 1 sample chapter, author bio, intended market, analysis comparison to competing books with SASE. Recent title(s): *31 Days to Increase Your Stress*, by Tricia Seymour (self-help/humor).
Tips: "Our books are primarily 'giftbooks,' sold to women in specialty stores, gift shops and bookstores."

BOTTOM DOG PRESS, %Firelands College of BGSU, Huron OH 44839. (419)433-5560. Director: Dr. Larry Smith. "We are Midwest focused and somewhat literary." Publishes hardcover, trade paperback and mass market paperback originals, hardcover and trade paperback reprints. **Publishes 4 titles/year. Receives 300 queries and 250 mss/year. 30% of books from first-time authors, 90% from unagented writers. Pays 7-15% royalty on wholesale price. Offers $100-300 advance.** Publishes book 1 year after acceptance of ms. Accepts simultaneous submissions (if notified). Reports in 1 months on queries and proposals, 4 months on mss. Books catalog and ms guidelines free.
Nonfiction: Biography. Subjects include writing, nature/environment, photography, regional (Midwest), women's issues/studies, working class issues. Query then submit outline and 2 sample chapters with SASE. Reviews artwork/photos as part of ms package. Send photocopies. Recent title(s): *In Buckeye Country*, edited by John Moor and Larry Smith (Ohio land and people).
Fiction: Ethnic, literary, mainstream/contemporary, working class. "We do one fiction book/year, Midwest based with author on locale." Query then submit synopsis, 2 sample chapters and SASE. Recent title(s): *Beyond Rust*, by Larry Smith (novels and stories).
Poetry: Midwest, working class focus. "Read our books before submitting." Query first then submit 10 sample poems.
Tips: "We publish for broad yet literate public. Do not get an agent—try the small presses first."

BRETT BOOKS, INC., P.O. Box 290-637, Brooklyn NY 11229-0637. Publisher: Barbara J. Brett. Estab. 1993. Publishes hardcover originals. **Publishes 1-2 titles/year. Pays 5-15% royalty on retail price. Offers advance beginning at $1,000. Reports in 2 months on queries.**
Nonfiction: General interest nonfiction books on timely subjects. "We are looking for general-interest inspirational nonfiction. Minimum length is 40,000 words; maximum is 50,000. Query with SASE. Recent title(s): *Friendships in the Dark: A Blind Woman's Story of the People and Pets Who Light Up Her World*, by Phyllis Campbell (inspirational).
Tips: "Send a query letter of no more than two pages in which you briefly state your professional background and summarize your book or book proposal in two to four paragraphs. Queries without SASE aren't answered or returned."

BRIDGE LEARNING SYSTEMS, INC., 351 Los Altos Place, American Canyon CA 94589. (510)228-3177. Publisher: Alfred J. Garrotto. Publishes trade paperback originals. **Publishes 1-3 titles/year. Receives 5-10 queries and 1 mss/year. 5% of books from first-time authors; 100% from unagented writers. Pays 15% royalty on publisher's selling price. Offers no advance.** Publishes book 6 months after acceptance of ms. Accepts simultaneous submissions. Reports in 1 month. Book catalog and ms guidelines free.
Nonfiction: How-to, technical. Subjects include computers and electronics (tutorials), religion, software. "We are looking for keystroke-by-keystroke tutorials of software and hardware products." Query. Reviews artwork/photos as part of ms package. Send photocopies. Recent title(s): *Jump Start*, by James Potter and Alfred Garrotto (tutorial).
Tips: Audience ranges from middle schools to university and vocational schools.

BRIGHT MOUNTAIN BOOKS, INC., 138 Springside Rd., Asheville NC 28803. (704)684-8840. Editor: Cynthia F. Bright. Imprint is Historical Images. Publishes hardcover originals and trade paperback originals and reprints. **Publishes 3 titles/year. Pays 5-10% royalty on retail price. No advance.** Reports in 1 month on queries; 3 months on mss.
Nonfiction: "Our current emphasis is on regional titles set in the Southern Appalachians and Carolinas, which can include nonfiction by local writers." Query with SASE. Recent title(s): *Mountain Fever*, by Tom Alexander (regional autobiography).

BRIGHT RING PUBLISHING, INC., P.O. Box 31338, Bellingham WA 98228-3338. (360)734-1601. Owner: Mary Ann Kohl. Publishes trade paperback originals on creative ideas for children. **Publishes 1 title/year. Pays 3-5% royalty on net price. Offers $500 advance.** Reports in 2 months. Ms guidelines for SASE.
Nonfiction: "Only books which specifically fit our format will be considered: art or creative activities with 1) materials 2) procedure 3) variations/extensions. One idea per page, about 150 ideas total. No crafts, fiction, picture books, poetry." Query with 1-2 sample chapters or submit proposal package, including complete book, with SASE. *Writer's Market* recommends sending a query with SASE first. Recent title(s): *Great Artists: Hands-On Art for Children in the Styles of the Great Masters.*
Tips: "Send for guidelines first. Check out books at the library or bookstore to see what style the publisher likes. Submit only ideas that specifically relate to the company's list."

CADMUS EDITIONS, P.O. Box 126, Tiburon CA 94920. Director: Jeffrey Miller. Publishes hardcover and trade paperback originals. **Publishes 3-4 titles/year. Pays negotiated royalty. No advance.** Reports in 1 month. *Writer's Market* recommends allowing 2 months for reply.
Fiction: Literary fiction. "We seek only truly distinguished work." Query with SASE. Recent title(s): *The Pelcari Project*, by R. Rey Rusa (novel about Guatemalan abuse of human rights).
Poetry: Query with SASE. Recent title(s): *Wandering into the Wind*, by Sāntoka, translated by Cid Corman (Haiku poetry of last wandering itinerant monk in Japan).
Tips: "Do not submit unless work is truly distinguished and will fit well in our short but carefully selected title list."

CALYX BOOKS, P.O. Box B, Corvallis OR 97339-0539. (541)753-9384. Also publishes *Calyx, A Journal of Art & Literature by Women.* Director: Margarita Donnelly. Managing Editor: Micki Reaman. Estab. 1986 for Calyx Books; 1976 for Calyx, Inc. Publishes fine literature by women, fiction, nonfiction and poetry. **Publishes 3 titles/year. Pays**

10% royalty on net price; amount of advance depends on grant support. Reports in 1 year.

• Calyx is open to submissions from January 1-March 15, 1999 *only.*

Nonfiction: Outline, 3 sample chapters and SASE. Recent title(s): *Natalie on the Street*, by Ann Nietzke (story of author's friendship with elderly homeless woman living in her neighborhood).

Fiction: Five literary fiction by women. "Please do not query." Send sample chapters during open book ms period only. Recent title(s): *Into the Forest*, by Jean Hegland.

Poetry: "We only publish 1 poetry book a year." Submit 10 samples, table of contents and bio.

Tips: "Please be familiar with our publications."

CAROUSEL PRESS, P.O. Box 6038, Berkeley CA 94706-0038. (510)527-5849. Editor and Publisher: Carole T. Meyers. Estab. 1976. Publishes trade paperback originals and reprints. **Publishes 1-2 titles/year. Pays 10-15% royalty on wholesale price. Offers $1,000 advance.** Reports in 1 month on queries. *Writer's Market* recommends allowing 2 months for reply.

Nonfiction: Family-oriented travel and other travel books. Query with outline, 1 sample chapter and SASE. Recent title(s): *The Zoo Book: A Guide to America's Best*, by A. Nyhius (guide).

CASSANDRA PRESS, P.O. Box 868, San Rafael CA 94915. (415)382-8507. President: Gurudas. Estab. 1985. Publis hes trade paperback originals. **Publishes 3 titles/year. Receives 200 submissions/year. 50% of books from first-time authors; 50% from unagented writers. Pays 6-8% maximum royalty on retail price. Advance rarely offered.** Publishes book 1 year after acceptance. Accepts simultaneous submissions. Reports in 3 weeks on queries, 3 months on mss. Book catalog and ms guidelines free.

Nonfiction: New Age, how-to, self-help. Subjects include cooking/foods/nutrition, health/medicine (holistic health), philosophy, psychology, religion (New Age), metaphysical, political tyranny. "We like to do around 3 titles a year in the general New Age, metaphysical and holistic health fields so we continue to look for good material. No children's books or novels." Submit outline and sample chapters. Reviews artwork/photos as part of ms package. Recent title(s): *Treason the New World Order*, by Gurudas (political).

Tips: "Not accepting fiction or children's book submissions."

CLARITY PRESS INC., 3277 Roswell Rd. NE, #469, Atlanta GA 30305. (404)231-0649. Fax: (404)231-3899. E-mail: clarity@islandnet.com. Website: http://www.bookmasters.com/clarity. Contact: Annette Gordon. Estab. 1984. Publishes mss on minorities, human rights in U.S., Middle East and Africa. Publishes hardcover and trade paperback originals. **Publishes 4 titles/year.** Reports in 3 months on queries only if interested.

Nonfiction: Human rights/minority issues. No fiction. Query with author's bio, synopsis and endorsements. Responds *only* if interested, so do *not* enclose SASE. Recent title(s): *The Legacy of IBO Landing: Gullah Roots of African American Culture*, by M.L. Goodwine (anthology).

Tips: "Check our titles on website."

CLEVELAND STATE UNIVERSITY POETRY CENTER, R.T. 1813, Cleveland State University, Cleveland OH 44115-2440. (216)687-3986. Fax: (216)687-6943. E-mail: poetrycenter@popmail.csuohio.edu. Editors: David Evett and Ted Lardner. Estab. 1962. Publishes trade paperback and hardcover originals. **Publishes 4 titles/year. Receives 500 queries and 1,000 mss/year. 60% of books from first-time authors; 100% from unagented writers. 30% of titles subsidized by CSU, 20% by government subsidy. CSU Poetry Series pays one-time, lump-sum royalty of $200-400, plus 50 copies; Cleveland Poetry Series (Ohio poets only) pays 100 copies. $1,000 prize for best ms each year. No advance.** Publishes book within 18 months of acceptance. Accepts simultaneous submissions. Reports in 1 month on queries, 8 months on mss. Book catalog for 6×9 SAE with 2 first-class stamps. Manuscript guidelines for SASE. Manuscripts are not returned.

Poetry: No light verse, inspirational, or greeting card verse. ("This does not mean that we do not consider poetry with humor or philosophical/religious import.") Query; ask for guidelines. Submit only December-February. Charges $15 reading fee. Reviews artwork/photos if applicable (e.g., concrete poetry). Recent title(s): *The Door Open to the Fire*, by Judith Vollmer.

Tips: "Our books are for serious readers of poetry, i.e. poets, critics, academics, students, people who read *Poetry, Field, American Poetry Review*, etc. Trends include movement away from 'confessional' poetry; greater attention to form and craftsmanship. Project an interesting, coherent personality; link poems so as to make coherent unity, not just a miscellaneous collection. Especially need poems with *mystery*, i.e., poems that suggest much, but do not tell all."

N **CROSSQUARTER BREEZE**, P.O. Box 8756, Santa Fe NM 87504. (505)438-9846. Owner: Therese Francis. "We emphasize personal sovereignty, self responsibility and growth with pagan or pagan-friendly emphasis for young adults and adults." Publishes trade paperback originals and reprints. **Publishes 3-5 titles/year. Receives 8 queries/year. 90% of books from first-time authors. Pays 8-10% royalty on wholesale or retail price.** Publishes book 6 months after acceptance of ms. Accepts simultaneous submissions. Reports in 2 months on queries. Book catalog for $1.75.

Nonfiction: Children's/juvenile, how-to, self-help. Subjects include health/medicine, nature/environment, philosophy, religion (pagan only). Query with SASE. Reviews artwork/photos as part of the ms package. Send photocopies. Recent title(s): *Age of Aquarius Astrology*, by Therese Francis and Estelle Daniels (astrology).

Tips: "Audience is earth-conscious people looking to grow into balance of body, mind, emotion and spirit."

DA CAPO PRESS, Plenum Publishing, 233 Spring St., New York NY 10013. Fax: (212)647-1898. Senior Editor: Michael Dorr. Editor: Soo Mee Kwon. Da Capo Press specializes in reissuing hard-to-find nonfiction books in inexpensive quality paperback format. Publishes trade paperback reprints. **Publishes 66 titles/year. Pays 6% royalty on wholesale price. Offers $1,500-2,000 advance.** Publishes book 1 year after acceptance of ms. Accepts simultaneous submissions. Reports in 4 months on queries. Book catalog free.

• Da Capo Press publishes only four or six paperback originals per year; the rest are reprints.

Nonfiction: Biography, history. Subjects include art/architecture, gay/lesbian, government/politics, military/war, music/dance, psychology, science, sports. Query. Recent title(s): *Sinatra!* by Will Friedwald (music).

DAWBERT PRESS, INC., Box 2758, Duxbury MA 023331. (617)934-7202. E-mail: dawbert@thecia.net. Website: http://www.dawbert.com. Submission Editor: Will Morris. Publishes mass market paperback originals. **Publishes 3 titles/year. Pays 5-10% royalty on retail price.** Publishes book 6 months after acceptance of ms. Accepts simultaneous submissions.

Nonfiction: Reference. Subjects include recreation, travel. "We only publish travel and recreation books." Submit outline. Reviews artwork/photos as part of ms package. Send photocopies. Recent title(s): *On the Road Again with Man's Best Friend*, by Habgood (travel).

DEPTH CHARGE, P.O. Box 7037, Evanston IL 60201. (847)864-6258. Assistant Editor: R. Matthew Sonnenberg. Publishes trade paperback originals. **Publishes 2-4 titles/year. Pays 10% royalty on retail price.** Book catalog for 9×12 SAE with 2 first-class stamps. Manuscript guidelines for #10 SASE.

Fiction: Experimental, literary fiction. "Familiarize yourselves with our publications and be aware that we publish 'subterficial' fiction. Be aware of what subterficial is." Recent title(s): *Ring In a River*, by Eckhard Gerdes.

Poetry: "The only poetry we publish is that which meets subterficial fiction at their interface area." Submit ms.

N DICKENS PUBLICATIONS, 1703 Taylor St. NW, Washington DC 20011-5312. President: Nathaniel A. Dickens. Estab. 1982. Publishes nonfiction related to education, history, finance and various forms of fiction. Send query letter initially with SASE; manuscript only upon request.

N DRY BONES PRESS, P.O. Box 640345, San Francisco CA 94164. (415)252-7341. Website: http://www.drybones.com. Editor/Publisher: J. Rankin. Publishes hardcover and trade paperback originals and reprints and mass market paperback originals. **Publishes 2-4 titles/year. Receives 25 queries and 15 mss/year. 100% from first-time authors, 100% from unagented writers. Pays 6-10% royalty on retail price.** Publishes book 1-2 years after acceptance of ms. Accepts simultaneous submissions, "if we are told." Reports in 2 months. Book catalog for #10 SASE.

Nonfiction: California Gold Rush, reference, technical. Subjects include health/medicine, history, philosophy, regional, religion, translation, nursing patient writing. "We have much to catch up with, already—but would still like to receive proposals. Do last-minute polishing!" Submit outline, 1-2 sample chapters and proposal package, including marketing ideas with SASE. Reviews artwork/photos as part of the ms package. Send "cheap copies." Recent title(s): *Coming Home*, by Grace Elizabeth Skye (sex abuse survivor account).

Fiction: Historical, humor/satire, mainstream/contemporary, mystery, plays, religious, science fiction. "Looking for unique items, with solid quality. No maudlin sentimentality or failure to develop insight or characters." Submit synopsis, 1-2 sample chapters with SASE. Recent title(s): *Aquarius*, by Richard Epstein (satire/social commentary).

Poetry: "Poetry doesn't make money. We do it as possible, between other projects, as time and money allow. We've mostly received good material, but people who write 'religious' poetry don't usually send material we'd publish (we'd like to see some good religious poetry, too)." Dry Bones Press pays only in copies for publication of poetry. Query with 1-5 sample poems.

Tips: Audience is "quite varied depending on work. Some specially items, including 13th century Caralan works, religions of current humor/satire. Mainly nursing and patient issues. If you believe in yourself—keep on writing, no matter what. We receive many excellent works. But religious writers, develop your skills—faith and devotion (however sincere) do not justify all sins!"

EARTH-LOVE PUBLISHING HOUSE LTD., 3440 Youngfield St., Suite 353, Wheat Ridge CO 80033. (303)233-9660. Fax: (303)233-9354. Director: Laodeciae Augustine. Publishes trade paperback originals. **Publishes 1-2 books/year. Pays 6-10% royalty on wholesale price.** Reports in 1 month on queries and proposals, 3 months on mss.

Nonfiction: Metaphysics and minerals. Query with SASE. Recent title(s): *Love Is In The Earth—Kaleidoscope Pictorial Supplement*, by Melody (metaphysical reference).

ECOPRESS, 1029 NE Kirsten Place, Corvallis OR 97330. (541)758-7545. E-mail: ecopress@peak.org. Editor-in-Chief: Christopher Beatty. Publishes hardcover originals, trade paperback originals and reprints. **Publishes 2-4 titles/year. Pays 6-15% royalty on publisher's receipts. Offers $0-5,000 advance.** Reports in 1 month on queries and proposals, 3 months on mss. Manuscript guidelines for #10 SASE or submit electronically.

Nonfiction: How-to, multimedia. Subjects include agriculture/horticulture, animals, education, gardening, nature/environment, recreation (outdoor, hiking), science, sports (outdoor, fishing). "The work must have some aspect that enhances environmental awareness. Do a competitive analysis and create a marketing plan for your book or proposal." Query with SASE by electronic or regular mail. Recent title(s): *The Trinity Alps Companion*, by Wayne Moss.

Tips: "A major focus of Ecopress is outdoor guides, especially river and hiking guides. Other nonfiction will be considered. All Ecopress books must have an environmental perspective."

ELLIOTT & CLARK PUBLISHING, Imprint of Black Belt Publishing, P.O. Box 551, Montgomery AL 36101. (334)265-6752. Fax: (334)269-6210. E-mail: jeff_slaton@black-belt.com. Editor: Jeff Slaton. Elliott & Clark specializes in illustrated histories. Publishes hardcover and trade paperback originals. **Publishes 3 titles/year. 50% of books from first-time authors; 90% from unagented writers. Pays royalty on wholesale price. Offers variable advance.** Accepts simultaneous submissions. Reports in 3 months on proposals. Manuscript guidelines free.
Nonfiction: Subjects include Americana, art/architecture, biography, history, nature/environment, photography. "We specialize in illustrated histories—need to think of possible photography/illustration sources to accompany manuscript. Submit an analysis of audience or a discussion of possible sales avenues beyond traditional book stores (such as interest groups, magazines, associations, etc.)." Submit proposal package, including possible illustrations (if applicable), outline, sales avenues. Reviews artwork/photos as part of ms package. Send transparencies. SASE must be included for response and returned materials. Recent title(s): *Outlaws*, by Marley Brandt (James/Younger Gang, Jesse James et. al.).
Tips: "We prefer proactive authors who are interested in providing marketing and the right leads."

EMERALD WAVE, Box 969, Fayetteville AR 72702. Contact: Maya Harrington. Publishes trade paperback originals. **Publishes 1-3 titles/year. Pays 7-10% royalty. No advance.** Reports in 1 month on queries, 3 months on mss.
Nonfiction: Spiritual/metaphysical New Age. Subjects include health, environment, philosophy, psychology. "We publish thoughtful New Age books which relate to everyday life and/or the environment on this planet with enlightened attitudes. Nothing poorly written, tedious to read or too 'out there.' It's got to have style too." Submit outline and 3 sample chapters with SASE. Reviews artwork/photos as part of ms package. Send photocopies. Recent title(s): *Spirit at Work*, by Lois Grant (angels/healing).

EMIS, INC., (formerly Essential Medical Information Systems, Inc.), P.O. Box 1607, Durant OK 74702. President: Linda Blake. Publishes trade paperback originals. **Publishes 2 titles/year. Pays 12-25% royalty on retail price.** Reports in 1 month. Book catalog and manuscript guidelines free.
Nonfiction: Reference. Subjects include health/medicine and psychology. Submit 3 sample chapters with SASE. Recent title(s): *Medical Management of Depression, 2nd edition*, by DeBattista.
Tips: Audience is medical professionals and medical product manufacturers and distributors.

THE FAMILY ALBUM, Rt. 1, Box 42, Glen Rock PA 17327. (717)235-2134. Fax: (717)235-8765. E-mail: ronbiblio@delphi.com. Contact: Ron Lieberman. Estab. 1969. Publishes hardcover originals and reprints and software. **Publishes 2 titles/year. Pays royalty on wholesale price.**
Nonfiction: "Significant works in the field of (nonfiction) bibliography. Worthy submissions in the field of Pennsylvania history, folk art and lore. We are also seeking materials relating to books, literacy, and national development. Special emphasis on Third World countries, and the role of printing in international development." No religious material or personal memoirs. Submit outline and sample chapters.

FIESTA CITY PUBLISHERS, ASCAP, P.O. Box 5861, Santa Barbara CA 93150. (805)681-9199. President: Frank E. Cooke. Publishes hardcover and mass market paperback originals. **Publishes 2-3 titles/year. Pays 5-20% royalty on retail price. No advance.** Reports in 1 month on queries, 2 months on proposals. Book catalog and ms guidelines for #10 SASE.
Nonfiction: "Seeking originality." Children's/juvenile, cookbook, how-to, humor nonfiction and musical plays. "Prefers material appealing to young readers, especially related to music: composing, performing, etc." Query with outline and SASE. Recent title(s): *The Piano*, by Philip Gurlik, R.T.T. (technician's guide for piano owners).
Fiction: Musical plays only. "Must be original, commercially viable, preferably short, with eye-catching titles. Must be professionaly done and believable. Avoid too much detail." Query with 1 or 2 sample chapters and SASE. Recent title(s): *Break Point*, by Frank Cooke a.k.a. Eddie Franck (young people's musical).
Tips: "Looking for material which would appeal to young adolescents in the modern society. Prefer little or no violence with positive messages. Carefully-constructed musical plays always welcome for consideration."

FLOWER VALLEY PRESS, INC., 7851-C Beechcraft Ave., Gaithersburg MD 20879. (301)654-1996. Editor: Seymour Bress. Publishes hardcover and trade paperback originals. **Publishes 2-3 titles/year. Pays 5.83-10% royalty on retail price. Offers $500-1,000 advance.** Reports in 2 months on queries, 3 months on proposals and mss. Book catalog for #10 SASE.
Nonfiction: Art how-to. Subjects include art, crafts and jewelry made with Polymer clay. "We look for new and unique work of high quality (all our recent books have been completely illustrated in color) and where the market for the book is relatively easy to identify and reach. For craft books, make certain that directions are clear and complete so the reader can actually finish a project by simply following instructions. Include color photographs, clear and understandable diagrams where needed and many examples of finished pieces (color photos)." Query with SASE or submit outline and 2 sample chapters. Reviews artwork/photos as part of ms package. Send transparencies. Recent title(s): *Great Impressions: The Art & Technique of Rubber Stamping*, by Pat Gryner Berlin.
Fiction: "We have no specific plans for fiction and have only accepted two fiction titles so far. We are most likely to accept fiction that would most appeal to a specific audience and one which can easily be reached." Submit synopsis with query letter. Recent title(s): *Adventures of Charles the Well-Traveled Bear*, by Gemma Dubaldo (adult hardcover).

Tips: "We look for niche markets. The author should be able to tell us the kinds of people who would be interested in the book and how we can reach them."

FRONT ROW EXPERIENCE, 540 Discovery Bay Blvd., Byron CA 94514-9454. Phone/fax: (510)634-5710. Contact: Frank Alexander. Estab. 1974. Imprint is Kokono. Publishes trade paperback originals and reprints. **Publishes 1-2 titles/year. Pays 10% royalty on income received. No advance.** Reports in 1 month.
Nonfiction: Teacher/educator edition paperback originals. "We're always focused on movement education advitities and lesson plans for pre-k to the 6th grade. Recent title(s): *School Based Home Developmental P.E. Program*, by Barbara Wood (movement education book 1st grade).
Tips: "Be on target—find out what we want and only submit queries."

GAMBLING TIMES, INC., 16140 Valerio St., Suite B, Van Nuys CA 91406-2916. (818)781-9355. Fax: (818)781-3125. Publisher: Stanley R. Suudikoff. Publishes hardcover and trade paperback originals. **Publishes 2-4 titles/year. Pays 4-11% royalty on retail price.** Reports in 2 months on queries, 3 months on proposals, 6 months on mss.
Nonfiction: How-to and reference books on gambling. Submit proposal package, including ms and SASE. *Writer's Market* recommends sending a query with SASE first. Recent title(s): *Book of Tells*, by Caro (poker).
Tips: "All of our books serve to educate the public about some aspect of gambling."

N **GODDESSDEAD PUBLICATIONS**, P.O. Box 46277, Los Angeles CA 90046. (213)850-0067. Publisher: Tracy Lee Williams. "We strive to be the Starbucks of books, offering you some of the freshest-ground, bravest, in-your-face literature, featuring the best of the up-and-coming new writers on the planet." Publishes trade paperback originals. **Publishes 4-5 titles/year. Receives 20 queries and 10 mss/year. Pays 7-15% royalty on gross receipts.** Publishes book 1 year after acceptance of ms. Accepts simultaneous submissions. Reports in 2 months on proposals. Book catalog free. Manuscript guidelines for #10 SASE.
Nonfiction: Biography, humor, memoir. Subjects include language/literature. Query with 1-2 sample chapters with SASE. Recent title(s): *The Pajama Years*, by Tracey Lee Williams (memoir).
Fiction: Confession, erotica, feminist, humor, literary, mainstream/contemporary, short story collections. Query or submit synopsis, 1-2 sample chapters with SASE.
Poetry: Query. Submit 20 sample poems. Recent title(s): *Duckwalking through the Apocalypse*, by SA Griffin.
Tips: Audience is the "18-35 Generation-X crowd, but appeals to varying audience. We are for the writer. If we like your work, and you don't have an agent, that's okay. We want to find the needle in the haystack."

GOOD BOOK PUBLISHING COMPANY, P.O. Box 959, Kihei HI 96753-0959. Phone/fax: (808)874-4876. E-mail: dickb@dickb.com. Publisher: Richard G. Burns. Publishes trade paperback originals and reprints. **Publishes 4 titles/year. Pay 10% royalty. No advance.** Reports in 2 months.
Nonfiction: Spiritual roots of Alcoholics Anonymous. Query with SASE. Recent title(s): *The Good Book and the Big Book: A.A.'s Roots in the Bible*, by Dick B. (history of early AA's spiritual roots and successes).

HEMINGWAY WESTERN STUDIES SERIES, Boise State University, 1910 University Dr., Boise ID 83725. (208)385-1999. Fax: (208)385-4373. E-mail: ttrusky@bsu.idbsu.edu. Editor: Tom Trusky. Publishes multiple edition artists' books which deal with Rocky Mountain political, social and environmental issues. Write for author's guidelines and catalog.

HERBAL STUDIES LIBRARY, 219 Carl St., San Francisco CA 94117. (415)564-6785. Fax: (415)564-6799. Owner: J. Rose. Publishes trade paperback originals. **Publishes 3 titles/year. Pays 5-10% royalty on retail price. Offers $500 advance.** Reports in 1 month on mss with SASE. *Writer's Market* recommends allowing 2 months for reply.
Nonfiction: How-to, reference, self-help. Subjects include gardening, health/medicine, herbs and aromatherapy. No New Age. Query with sample chapter and SASE. Recent title(s): *Guide to Essential Oils*, by Jeanne Rose (scientific information about essential oils).

HI-TIME PUBLISHING CORP., 12040-L W. Feerick St., Milwaukee WI 53222-2136. (414)466-2420. Fax: (800)370-4450. Senior Editor: Lorraine M. Kukulski. **Publishes 4 titles/year. Receives 20 queries, 5 mss/year. Payment method may be outright purchase, royalty or down payment plus royalty.** Book catalog and ms guidelines free.
Nonfiction: Textbook, religion. "We publish religious education material for Catholic junior high through adult programs. Most of our material is contracted in advance and written by persons with theology or religious education backgrounds." Query with SASE. Recent title(s): *Catholics and Fundamentalists*, by Martin Pable, O.F.M.

N **ILLUMINATION ARTS**, P.O. Box 1865, Bellevue WA 98009. (425)646-4144. Editorial Director: Ruth Thompson. Illumination Arts publishes inspirational/spiritual children's nonfiction and fiction. Publishes hardcover originals. **Publishes 1-3 titles/year. Receives 200-250 queries and 100 mss/year. 50% of books from first-time authors; 100% from unagented writers. Pays royalty.** Publishes book 1-2 years after acceptance of ms. Accepts simultaneous submissions. Reports in 2 weeks on queries and proposals, 1 month on mss. Book catalog free. Manuscript guidelines for #10 SASE.
Nonfiction: Children's/juvenile. Subjects include child guidance/parenting. "Our books are all high quality, inspirational/spiritual. Send for our guidelines. Stories need to be exciting and inspirational for children." Query with complete

ms and SASE. Reviews artwork/photos as part of the ms package. Send photocopies. Recent title(s): *The Right Touch*, by Sandy Kleven (book to help children avoid sexual abuse).

Fiction: Juvenile, picture books. "All are inspirational/spiritual. No full-length novels. Send for guidelines. Some writers do not include sufficient postage to return manuscripts. A few writers just do not have a grasp of correct grammar. Some are dull or uninteresting." Query with complete ms and SASE. Recent title(s): *The Sai Prophecy*, by Barbara Gardner (a saga of five generations).

Tips: "Audience is looking for a spiritual message and children who enjoy stories that make them feel self assured. All of our stories have inspirational, spiritual messages."

IN PRINT PUBLISHING, 6770 W. State Route 89A, 346, Sedona AZ 86336-9758. (520)282-4589. Fax: (520)282-4631. Publisher/Editor: Tomi Keitlen. Estab. 1991. Publishes trade paperback originals. **Publishes 3-5 titles/year. Pays 6-10% royalty on retail price. Offers $250-500 advance.** Reports in 2 months on queries and proposals, 3 months on mss.

Nonfiction: "We are an eclectic publisher interested in books that have current impact: political, spiritual, financial, medical, environmental problems. We are interested in books that will leave a reader with hope. We are also interested in books that are metaphysical, books that give ideas and help for small business management and books that have impact in all general subjects. No violence, sex or poetry." Query with SASE. Recent title(s): *Spirituality, Sex & Silliness*, by Chandler Everett.

Tips: "We are interested in books about Angels. We are also interested in short books that will be part of a Living Wisdom Series™. These books must be no more than 18,000-20,000 words. We are not interested in any books that are over 300 pages—and are more likely interested in 75,000 words or less. Find areas that are not overdone and offer new insight to help others."

INDIANA HISTORICAL SOCIETY, 315 W. Ohio St., Indianapolis IN 46202-3299. (317)232-1882. Fax: (317)233-3109. Director of Publications: Thomas A. Mason. Estab. 1830. Publishes hardcover originals. **Publishes 3 titles/year. Pays 6% royalty on retail price.** Reports in 1 month.

Nonfiction: "We seek book-length manuscripts that are solidly researched and engagingly written on topics related to the history of Indiana." Query with SASE. Recent title(s): *Sherman Minton: New Deal Senator, Cold War Justice*, by Linda C. Gugin and James E. St. Clair.

N **INVERLOCHEN PRESS**, P.O. Box 7878, Fredricksburg VA 22404. Fax: (804)493-9156. Senior Editor/Publisher: Patrick Harrigan. Contact: Maggie MacKinnon. Publishes hardcover and paperback originals. **Publishes 4 titles/year. Pays royalty.** Publishes book 5 months after acceptance of ms. Accepts simultaneous submissions if notified. Reports in 2 weeks on queries, 1 week on faxed queries, 1 month on mss.

Nonfiction: Historical, biography, music, politics, Irish politics, humor, military/war, art/architecture, general, some coffee table books, No technical. Query with SASE. Reviews artwork/photos as part of ms package.

Fiction: Juvenile, adult, general. Action/espionage, especially maritime and military/war, historical—especially British, Irish, and American, humor, Irish political, literary—most subjects. "We will consider novels of any subject, any lenth, if they are well-written, conservative and polished. Accuracy, morality and a solid grounding in traditional values are a plus." Query with SASE.

Tips: "We are truly an authors' press—no agents please. We prefer to work one on one with the author. Each manuscript receives a critique; authors will not receive form letters. Any book with clear, solid writing and a good, working plot will be considered. We accept fax queries. Tell us a good story—we'll listen."

IVY LEAGUE PRESS, INC., P.O. Box 3326, San Ramon CA 94583-8326. 1-(800)IVY-PRESS or (510)736-0601. Fax: (510)736-0602. E-mail: ivyleaguepress@worldnet.att.net. Editor: Maria Thomas. Publishes hardcover, trade paperback and mass market paperback originals. Reports in 3 months.

- Ivy League is focusing more on medical thrillers, although it still welcomes Judaica and other submissions.

Nonfiction: Subjects include health/medicine, Judaica and self-help nonfiction. Query with SASE. Recent title(s): *Jewish Divorce Ethics*, by Bulka.

Fiction: Medical suspense. Query with SASE. Recent title(s): *Allergy Shots*, by Litman.

JELMAR PUBLISHING CO., INC., P.O. Box 488, Plainview NY 11803. (516)822-6861. President: Joel J. Shulman. Publishes hardcover and trade paperback originals. **Publishes 2-5 titles/year. Pays 25% royalty after initial production and promotion expenses of first and successive printings.** Reports in 1 week. *Writer's Market* recommends allowing 2 months for reply.

Nonfiction: How-to and technical subjects on the packaging, package printing and printing fields. "The writer must be a specialist and recognized expert in the field." Query with SASE. Recent title(s): *Graphic Design for Corrugated Packaging*, by Donald G. McCaughey Jr. (graphic design).

JOHNSTON ASSOCIATES, INTERNATIONAL (JASI), P.O. Box 313, Medina WA 98039. (425)454-3490. Fax: (425)462-1355. E-mail: iasibooks@aol.com. Publisher: Ann Schuessler. Publishes trade paperback originals. **Publishes 3-5 titles/year. Receives 40 queries and 8 ms/year. Pays 10-15% royalty on wholesale price. Advance varies.** Publishes book 1-3 years after acceptance of ms. Accepts simultaneous submissions. Reports in 3 months. Book catalog and ms guidelines for #10 SASE.

Nonfiction: Recreation, regional (any region), travel and other nonfiction. "We are interested in books that hit unique niches or look at topics in new, unique ways." Query with proposal package, including outline, sample chapter, target market, competition, reason why the book is different and SASE. Recent title(s): *Discover the Poconos with Kids* by Marynell Strunk.
Tips: "We are interested in books that fit unique niches or look at a topic in a unique way."

KALI PRESS, P.O. Box 2169, Pagosa Springs CO 81147. (970)264-5200. E-mail: kalipres@rmi.net. Contact: Cynthia Olsen. Publishes trade paperback originals. **Publishes 3 titles/year. Pays 8-10% royalty on net price. No advance.** Reports in 1 month on queries, 6 weeks on proposals, 2 months on mss.
Nonfiction: Natural health and spiritual nonfiction. Subjects include education (on natural health issues). Query with 2 sample chapters and SASE. Reviews artwork/photos as part of ms package. Send photocopies. Recent title(s): *Don't Drink the Water*, by Lono A'o.

LAHONTAN IMAGES, 210 S. Pine St., Susanville CA 96130. (916)257-6747. Fax: (916)251-4801. Owner: Tim I. Purdy. Estab. 1986. Publishes hardcover and trade paperback originals. **Publishes 2 titles/year. Pays 10-15% royalty on wholesale or retail price. No advance.** Reports in 2 months.
Nonfiction: Publishes nonfiction books pertaining to northeastern California and western Nevada. Query with outline and SASE. Recent title(s): *Maggie Greeno*, by George McDow Jr. (biography).

N **LAUREATE PRESS**, 2710 Ohio St., Bangor ME 04401-1056. Editor/Publisher: Lance C. Lobo. Publishes trade paperback originals and reprints. **Publishes 3 titles/year. Pays 6-10% royalty on wholesale price. Offers $100 advance.** Reports in 2 months on queries.
Nonfiction: Fencing subjects only—how-to, technical. Fencing books must be authored by diplomaed fencing masters. Query with outline and SASE. Recent title(s): *The Science of Fencing*, by William Gaugler (fencing-technical).
Tips: Audience is recreational and competitive fencers worldwide.

LAWCO LTD., P.O. Box 2009, Manteca CA 95336-1209. (209)239-6006. Imprints are Money Tree and Que House. Senior Editor: Bill Thompson. **Publishes 3-6 titles/year. Pays 3-12% royalty on wholesale price or makes outright purchase of $500 minimum.** Reports in 1 month on queries, 4 months on mss.
Nonfiction: Books on billiards industry. "We are looking for business books targeting the small business. We will also consider sports-related books." Query with SASE. Recent title(s): *The Pool Player's Road Atlas*, by J.R. Lucas.
Tips: "Do your homework. Know the market, the sales potential, why the book is needed, who will buy it and why."

LINTEL, 24 Blake Lane, Middletown NY 10940. (212)674-4901. Editorial Director: Walter James Miller. Estab. 1978. Publishes hardcover originals and reprints and trade paperback originals. **Publishes 2 titles/year. Authors get 100 copies originally, plus royalties after all expenses are cleared.** Reports in 2 months on queries, 4 months on proposals, 6 months on ms.
Nonfiction: "So far all our nonfiction titles have been textbooks. Query with SASE. Recent title(s): *Writing a Television Play, Second Edition,* by Michelle Cousin (textbook).
Fiction: Publishes experimental fiction, art poetry and selected nonfiction. Query with SASE.
Poetry: Submit 5 sample poems. Recent title(s): *Mud River*, by Judy Aygildiz (hardcover with art work).

MADWOMAN PRESS, P.O. Box 690, Northboro MA 01532-0690. (508)393-3447. E-mail: 76620.460@compuserve.com. Editor/Publisher: Diane Benison. Publishes trade paperback originals. Estab. 1991. **Publishes 1-2 titles/year. Pays 15% royalty on revenues collected after production costs are recovered. No advance.** Reports in 2 months on queries, 4 months on mss.

- Madwoman Press is looking for more mystery novels.

Nonfiction: Lesbian nonfiction. Query with outline and SASE. Recent title(s): *On My Honor: Lesbians Reflect on Their Scouting Experience*, by Nancy Manahan.
Fiction: Lesbian fiction. "Primarily interested in mysteries." Query with synopsis (which must include an explanation of how the novel ends) and SASE. Recent title(s): *The Grass Widow*, by Nanci Little (historical novel).
Tips: "We hold ourselves out as a press that publishes *only* works by lesbian women. Please don't query if you don't meet the qualification. We make no exceptions to that policy."

MAGICKAL CHILDE INC., 35 W. 19th St., New York NY 10011. (212)242-7182. Manager/Buyer: Tony Passaro. Publishes nonfiction books on occult.

MANAGEMENT TECHNOLOGY INSTITUTE, 2919 E. Military Trail, Suite 155, West Palm Beach FL 33409. (561)791-1200. Editor: Margaret E. Haase. **Publishes 2 titles/year. 100% of books from first-time authors; 100% from unagented writers.** Publishes book 12-18 months after acceptance of ms. Accepts simultaneous submissions. Reports within 6 months on mss.
Nonfiction: How-to, self-help, textbook. Subjects include business management, motivation, leadership, empowerment, education, psychology, women's issues/studies. Submit chapter outlines and 1-3 sample chapters with SASE. Reviews artwork/photos as part of ms package. Send photocopies. Recent title(s): *Don't Buy the Lie (D.B.L.)*, by Jordan (management).

Poetry: Submit 3 sample poems. "We prefer free verse, any length, but welcome traditional or experimental work. Want substantial, well-crafted, and memorable poems. Special attention given to poetry about business and women's issues. No handwritten or dot matrix submissions."
Tips: Audience is college and university faculty, business students, business executives and upper-level managers, employees, supervisors and lower-level management.

MANGAJIN, INC., P.O. Box 77188, Atlanta GA 30357-1188. Publisher: V.P. Simmons. Publishes mass market paperback originals and reprints. **Publishes 2-3 titles/year. Pays 5-15% royalty on wholesale price.** Reports in 2 months on queries.
Nonfiction: Reference, textbook. Subjects include business and economics, government/politics, language/literature, religion, sociology, translation, travel. Mangajin publishes books about Japanese language and culture. Query. Recent title(s): *Mr. Benihana: The Rocky Aoki Story* (business/biography).
Tips: Audience is "people interested in Japanese language and culture."

N A **MARLTON PUBLISHERS, INC.**, P.O. Box 223, Severn MD 21144. President: Bruce Rory. Marlton publishes Christian suspense novels for adults. Publishes hardcover, trade paperback originals and mass market pocketbook originals. **Publishes 3 titles/year. Makes outright purchase of $500-1,500.**
Fiction: Ethnic, religious, romance, suspense. "Company plans to publish 3-10 Christian suspense novels per year; paperbacks less than 25,000 words." *Agented submissions only.* Recent title(s): *Extreme Flashbacks*, by Ralph Thomas (suspense).

N **MEDIA FORUM INTERNATIONAL, LTD.**, R.R. 1, P.O. Box 107, W. Danville VT 05873. (802)592-3444. Or P.O. Box 265, Peacham VT 05862-0265. Fax: (802)592-3001. Managing Director: D.K. Bognár. Estab. 1969. Imprints are: Media Forum Books. Publishes hardcover and trade paperback originals. **Publishes 2 titles/year. Pays 10% minimum royalty.** "We are consultants primarily."
Nonfiction: Biography, humor, reference. Subjects include ethnic, broadcast/film. "All mss are assigned." Recent title(s): *The Little Blue Book . . . 1998.*

MEGA MEDIA PRESS, 3838 Raymert Dr., #203, Las Vegas NV 89121. (702)433-5388. President: Lillian S. Payn. Publishes trade paperback originals. **Publishes 3 titles/year. Pay varies.** Reports in 1 month.
Nonfiction: Subjects include business and economics, software. Query. Recent title(s): *Consultant's Little Instruction Book*, Ray Payn (business).

MIDDLE PASSAGE PRESS INC., 5517 Secrest Dr., Los Angeles CA 90043. (213)298-0266. Publisher: Barbara Bramwell. Estab. 1992. Publishes trade and mass market paperback and hardcover originals. **Publishes 1 title/year. Pays 3-10% royalty on wholesale price. Offers $500-1,500 advance.** Reports in 3 months.
Nonfiction: "The emphasis is on contemporary issues that deal directly with the African-American Experience. No fiction, no poetry." Query with SASE. Recent title(s): *Outcast: My Journey From the White House to Homelessness*, by Michael A. Hobbs
Tips: "Don't include scripts in place of manuscripts. I prefer query with 2 written chapters as opposed to a proposal. I want to see how someone writes."

MILKWEEDS FOR YOUNG READERS, Imprint of Milkweed Editions, 430 First Ave. N., Suite 400, Minneapolis MN 55401-1743. (612)332-3192. Fax: (612)332-6248. Website: http://www.milkweed.org. Children's Reader: Elisabeth Fitz. Estab. 1984. "Milkweeds for Young Readers are works that embody humane values and contribute to cultural understanding." Publishes hardcover and trade paperback originals. **Publishes 1-2 titles/year. 25% of books from first-time authors; 70% from unagented writers. Pays 7½% royalty on retail price. Advance varies.** Publishes book 1 year after acceptance of ms. Accepts simultaneous submissions. Reports in 2 months on queries, 6 months on mss. Book catalog for $1.50. Manuscript guidelines for #10 SASE.
Fiction: For ages 8-12: adventure, animal, fantasy, historical, humor, environmental, mainstream/contemporary. Query with 2-3 sample chapters and SASE. Recent title(s): *The Gumma Wars*, by David Haynes.

MOSAIC PRESS MINIATURE BOOKS, 358 Oliver Rd., Cincinnati OH 45215-2615. (513)761-5977. Publisher: Miriam Irwin. Estab. 1977. **Publishes 1 nonfiction book/year.** "Subjects range widely. Please query."

N **MOUNT IDA PRESS**, 152 Washington Ave., Albany NY 12210. (518)426-5935. Fax: (518)426-4116. Publisher: Diana S. Waite. Publishes trade paperback original illustrated books on architecture and local history.

NEW ENGLAND CARTOGRAPHICS, INC., P.O. Box 9369, North Amherst MA 01059. (413)549-4124. Fax: (413)549-3621. President: Christopher Ryan. Publishes trade paperback originals and reprints. **Publishes 3 titles/year. Pays 5-15% royalty on retail price. No advance.** Reports in 2 months.
Nonfiction: Outdoor recreation nonfiction subjects include nature/environment, recreation, regional. "We are interested in specific 'where to' in the area of outdoor recreation guidebooks of the northeast U.S." Topics of interest are hiking/backpacking, skiing, canoeing etc. Query with outline, sample chapters and SASE. Reviews artwork/photos as part of ms package. Send photocopies. Recent title(s): *Golfing in New England*, by DaSilva.

N NEWSAGE PRESS, P.O. Box 607, Troutdale OR 97060-0607. (503)695-2211. Fax: (503)695-5406. E-mail: newsage@teleport.com. Website: http://www.teleport.com/~newsage. Publisher: Maureen R. Michelson. Editorial Assistant: Cindy McKechnie. "NewSage Press book address a myriad of social concerns, from environmental issues to women's issues to health issues." Estab. 1985. Publishes hardcover and trade paperback originals. Recent title(s): *The Wolf, the Woman, the Wilderness: A True Story of Returning Home*, by Teresa Tsimmu Martino.

NICOLAS-HAYS, Box 612, York Beach ME 03910. (207)363-4393. Publisher: B. Lundsted. Publishes hardcover originals and trade paperback originals and reprints. **Publishes 2-4 titles/year. Pays 15% royalty on wholesale price. Offers $200-500 advance.** Reports in 2 months.

Nonfiction: Publishes self-help; nonfiction. Subjects include philosophy (oriental), psychology (Jungian), religion (alternative), women's issues/studies. Query with outline, 3 sample chapters and SASE. Recent title(s): *Modern Woman In Search of Soul*, by June Singer (Jungian analyst).

Tips: "We only publish books that are the lifework of authors—our editorial plans change based on what the author writes."

OBERLIN COLLEGE PRESS, Rice Hall, Oberlin College, Oberlin OH 44074. (440)775-8408. Contact: Heather Smith. Editors: David Young, Alberta Turner, David Walker. Imprints are *Field Magazine: Contemporary Poetry & Poetics*, Field Translation Series, Field Poetry Series. Publishes hardcover and trade paperback originals. **Publishes 2-3 titles/year. Pays 7½-10% royalty on retail price. Offers $500 advance.** Reports in 1 month on queries and proposals, 2 months on mss.

Poetry: *Field Magazine*—submit up to 5 poems with SASE for response; *Field* Translation Series—Query with SASE and sample poems; *Field* Poetry Series—no unsolicited mss, enter mss in *Field* Poetry Prize held annually in December. Send SASE for guidelines after October 1st. Recent title(s): *A Stick That Breaks and Breaks*, by Marianne Boruch.

N OCEAN VIEW BOOKS, P.O. Box 102650, Denver CO 80250. Editor: Lee Ballentine. "Ocean View Books is an award-winning publisher of new speculative and slipstream fiction, poetry, criticism, surrealism and science fiction." Publishes hardcover originals and trade paperback originals. **Publishes 2 titles/year. 100% from unagented writers. Pays negotiable royalty.** Reports in 4 months on queries.

Fiction: Literary, science fiction, fiction about the 1960s. Query with SASE. Recent title(s): *All the Visions*, by Rudy Rucker.

C. OLSON & CO., P.O. Box 100-WM, Santa Cruz CA 95063-0100. (408)458-9004. E-mail: bttrsweett@aol.com. Owner: Clay Olson. Estab. 1981. Publishes trade paperback originals. **Publishes 1-2 titles/year. Royalty negotiable.** Reports in 2 months on queries.

Nonfiction: "We are looking for nonfiction manuscripts or books that can be sold at natural food stores and small independent bookstores on health and on how to live a life which improves the earth's environment. Also interested in a photo book for young children about the horrors and tragedy of wars." Query first with SASE. Recent title(s): *World Health, Carbon Dioxide & The Weather*, by J. Recklaw (ecology).

OMEGA PUBLICATIONS, 256 Darrow Rd., New Lebanon NY 12125-9801. (518)794-8183. Fax: (518)794-8187. E-mail: omegapub@wisdomschild.com. Website: http://www.omegapub@wisdomschild.com. Contact: Abi'l-Khayr. Estab. 1977. Publishes hardcover and trade paperback originals and reprints. **Publishes 2-3 titles/year. Pays 6-12% royalty on wholesale price. Offers $500-1,000 advance.** Reports in 3 months on mss.

Nonfiction: "We are interested in any material related to Sufism, and only that." Query with 2 sample chapters. Recent title(s): *Creating the Person*, by Khan (spirituality).

N PACE UNIVERSITY PRESS, One Pace Plaza, New York NY 10038. (212)346-1405. Contact: Mark Hussey. Publishes hardcover originals. **Publishes 2-3 titles/year. Pays 5-10% royalty on wholesale price. No advance.** Reports in 2 months on queries and proposals, 6 months on mss.

Nonfiction: "We publish scholarly work in the humanities, business, and social science fields." Query with outline, 1 sample chapter and SASE. Recent title(s): *Virginia Woolf & The Arts*, by Diane Gillespie and Leslie K. Hankins (conference proceedings).

PACIFIC VIEW PRESS, P.O. Box 2657, Berkeley CA 94702. (510)849-4213. President: Pam Zumwalt. Publishes hardcover and trade paperback originals. **Publishes 3 titles/year. Pays 5-10% royalty on wholesale price. Offers $500-2,000 advance.** Reports in 2 months. Book catalog free.

Nonfiction: Subjects include Asia-related business and economics, Asian current affairs, Chinese medicine, nonfiction Asian-American multicultural children's books. "We are only interested in Pacific Rim related issues. Do not send proposals outside our area of interest." Query with proposal package, including outline, 1 sample chapter, author background, audience info and SASE. No unsolicited mss. Recent title(s): *Tibet: Abode of the Gods, Pearl of the Motherland*, by Barbara Erickson (reportage).

PAIDEIA PRESS, P.O. Box 121303, Arlington TX 76012. (817)265-8215. Managing Editor: N.R. VanBoskirk. Publishes trade paperback originals. **Publishes 3 titles/year. 90% of books from first-time authors; 100% from unagented writers. Pays 5-15% royalty on retail price. No advance.** Publishes book 8 months after acceptance of ms. Accepts simultaneous submissions. Reports in 1 month on queries and proposals, 2 months on mss. Manuscript guidelines for #10 SASE.

Nonfiction: Theory and practice, multimedia (CD-ROM, software), textbook. Subjects include education and supplementary texts for education market (grades 8-college), women's issues/studies. "We are currently interested in works relating to ethical culture and social ecology." Query with SASE. Reviews artwork/photos as part of ms package. Send photocopies. Recent title(s): *Discovering the Essay*, by F. Andrew Wolf, Jr. (education/developmental writing).

Tips: Audience is education market; library. "We are only interested in hearing from writers regarding ethical culture and social ecology texts."

PARTNERS IN PUBLISHING, P.O. Box 50347, Tulsa OK 74150-0374. Phone/fax: (918)835-8258. Editor: P.M. Fielding. Estab. 1976. Publishes trade paperback originals. **Publishes 1-2 titles/year. Pays royalty on wholesale price. No advance.** Reports in 2 months on queries.

● This press reports being deluged with submissions having nothing to do with learning disabilities.

Nonfiction: "Understand that we are only interested in older teen and young adults with learning disabilities." Biography, how-to, reference, self-help, technical and textbooks on learning disabilities, special education for youth and young adults. Query with SASE. Recent title(s): *Enhancing Self-Esteem for Exceptional Learners*, by John R. Moss and Elizabeth Ragsdale (for parents and teachers who deal with exceptional youth and young adults).

PEEL PRODUCTIONS, INC., P.O. Box 546, Columbus NC 28722. Managing Editor: S. DuBosque. Estab. 1985. Publishes hardcover and trade paperback originals. **Publishes 3-5 titles/year. Publishes how-to draw and picture books. Pays royalty on wholesale price. Offers $300-500 advance.** Query first with outline/synopsis, sample chapters and SASE. Reports in 1 month. *Writer's Market* recommends allowing 2 months for reply.

Nonfiction: Looking for how-to-draw books. Recent title(s): *Draw Desert Animals*, by Doug DuBosque.

PIONEER INSTITUTE, 85 Devonshire St., 8th Floor, Boston MA 02109. (617)723-2277. Research Director: Gabriela MRAD. Publishes trade paperback originals. **Publishes 3-4 titles/year. Makes outright purchase or provides foundation grant.** Reports in 1 month. *Writer's Market* recommends allowing 2 months for reply. Book catalog free.

Nonfiction: "Our publications are only about Massachusetts public policy." Scholarly nonfiction. Subjects include business and economics, education, government/politics, health/medicine, sociology. "Pioneer Institute will generally make overtures to a chosen author. Queries and author introductions are preferred. Unsolicited manuscripts will not be reviewed or returned." Recent title(s): *Seducing the Samaritan*, by Joe Locente.

Tips: Audience is public policy makers in Massachusetts and nationally college professors and students.

POGO PRESS, INCORPORATED, 4 Cardinal Lane, St. Paul MN 55127-6406. E-mail: pogopres@minn.net. Vice President: Leo J. Harris. Publishes trade paperback originals. **Publishes 3 titles/year. Receives 20 queries and 20 mss/year. 100% of books from unagented writers. Pays royalty on wholesale price.** Publishes book 6 months after acceptance. Reports in 2 months. Book catalog free.

Nonfiction: "We limit our publishing to Breweriana, history, art, popular culture and travel odysseys. Our books are heavily illustrated." Query. Reviews artwork/photos as part of ms package. Send photocopies. Recent title(s): *Songs of Life—The Meaning of Country Music*, by Jennifer Lawler.

PRAKKEN PUBLICATIONS, INC., P.O. Box 8623, Ann Arbor MI 48107-8623. (313)975-2800. Fax: (313)975-2787. Publisher: George Kennedy. Book Editor: Susanne Peckman. Estab. 1934. Publishes educational hardcover and paperback originals as well as educational magazines. **Publishes 3 book titles/year. Receives 50 submissions/year. 20% of books from first-time authors; 95% from unagented writers. Pays 10% royalty on net sales (negotiable with production costs).** Publishes book within 1 year of acceptance. Accepts simultaneous submissions. Reports in 2 months if reply requested and SASE furnished. Book catalog for #10 SASE.

Nonfiction: Industrial, vocational and technology education and related areas; general educational reference. "We are currently interested in manuscripts with broad appeal in any of the specific subject areas of industrial arts, technology education, vocational-technical education, and reference for the general education field." Submit outline and sample chapters. Reviews artwork/photos as part of ms package. Recent title(s): *Winning Ways: Best Practices in Work-Based Learning*, edited by Albert J. Pawtler Jr. and Deborah Buffamanti.

Tips: "We have a continuing interest in magazine and book manuscripts which reflect emerging issues and trends in education, especially vocational, industrial and technological education."

PRIMER PUBLISHERS, 5738 N. Central Ave., Phoenix AZ 85012. (602)234-1574. Publishes trade paperback originals. **Publishes 4-5 titles/year. Pays royalty. No advance.** Reports in 1 month on queries.

Nonfiction: Mostly regional subjects; travel, outdoor recreation, history, etc. "We target Southwestern US parks, museum gift shops. We want to know how your book will sell in these retailers." Query first with SASE. Recent title(s): *Easy Field Guide to Fly-Fishing Terms & Tips*, by David Phares.

PUCKERBRUSH PRESS, 76 Main St., Orono ME 04473-1430. (207)581-3832 or 866-4808. Publisher/Editor: Constance Hunting. Estab. 1971. Publishes trade paperback originals and reprints of literary fiction and poetry. **Publishes 3-4 titles/year. Pays 10-15% royalty on wholesale price or makes outright purchase.** Reports in 1 month on queries; 2 months on proposals; 3 months on ms.

Nonfiction: Belles lettres, translations. Query with SASE. Recent title(s): *Reminiscences of Tolstoi*, by Gorky.
Fiction: Literary and short story collections. Recent title(s): *Young*, by Miriam Colwell (novel).
Poetry: Highest literary quality. Submit complete ms with SASE.

N **PUPPY HOUSE PUBLISHING COMPANY, LLC**, P.O. Box 1539, New York NY 10021. (212)661-9378. Publisher: Richard Hurowitz. "Puppy House seeks to publish exceptional books in all areas with an emphasis on talented young writers." Publishes hardcover and trade paperback originals. **Publishes 3 titles/year. Pay is negotiable, "varies from book to book."** Reports in 1 month.
Nonfiction: Biography, children's/juvenile, coffee table book, cookbook, gift book, humor. Subjects include Americana, animals, anthropology/archaeology, art/architecture, business/economics, creative nonfiction, government/politics, health/medicine, history, hobbies, language/literature, memoirs, military/war, money/finance, music/dance, nature/environment, philosophy, photography, psychology, recreation, regional, religion, science, sex, sociology, spirituality, sports, translation, travel. "We will consider any interesting proposals and seek manuscripts that are well written." Query with SASE.
Fiction: Adventure, confession, erotica, ethnic, experimental, gothic, historical, humor, juvenile, literary, mainstream/contemporary, military/war, multimedia, mystery, picture books, plays, poetry, poetry in translation, religious, romance, science fiction, short story collections, spiritual, sports, suspense, translation, western, young adult. "Puppy House publishes important new works from fresh and interesting voices. The company was founded to give expression to innovative writers." Query with SASE. Recent title(s): *Maiden Serenade*, by Richard Hurowitz.
Tips: "Puppy House seeks to publish important books from new and exceptional authors in all areas intended for a wide and general audience. Puppy House Publishing Company, LLC was founded in order to publish the finest literature by new young writers. Recognizing that many innovative books of literary quality, especially by untested authors, are often never given the chance for publication, and therefore that the marketplace and our culture are deprived of lively and important works, Puppy House Publishing hopes to fill this niche. It is the goal of the company to give voice to the next generation of great writers and to establish a catalog of remarkable works of all kinds."

RACE POINT PRESS, P.O. Box 770, Provincetown MA 02657. Vice President: Roselyn Callahan. Publishes trade paperback originals. **Publishes 5 titles/year. Pays 7-12% royalty on wholesale price or makes outright purchase.** Reports in 2 months on proposals.
Nonfiction: How-to, reference, self-help, technical. Subjects include art/architecture, health/medicine, aging. "Our focus is on books for the senior market which highlight available programs or practical advice on accessing needed services." Query or submit outline or proposal package, including 2 sample chapters and probable completion date; author biography. All unsolicited mss returned unopened. Recent title(s): *The Medicare Answer Book*, by Connacht Cash (technical).

RED EYE PRESS, INC., P.O. Box 65751, Los Angeles CA 90065. President: James Gordon. Publishes trade paperback originals. **Publishes 2 titles/year. Pays 8-12% royalty on retail price. Offers $1-2,000 advance.** Reports in 1 month on queries, 3 months on mss.
Nonfiction: How-to, gardening, reference books. Query with outline, 2 sample chapters and SASE. Recent title(s): *Almanac of Great Labor Quotations*, by P. Bollen (reference).

N **RED WHEELBARROW PRESS, INC.**, P.O. Box 33143, Austin TX 78764. President: L.C. Sajbel. "We are targeting readers who are looking for fresh, new writers and thought-provoking literature. For children and adults, we feel that literature should be fun and challenging." Publishes hardcover and trade paperback originals and reprints. **Publishes 1-5 titles/year. 90% of books from first-time authors; 90% for unagented writers. Pays 10% royalty on retail price.** Publishes book 1 year after acceptance of ms. Reports in 4 months on mss. Manuscript guidelines for #10 SASE.
Nonfiction: Children's/juvenile, humor. Subjects include Americana. "We hope to find manuscripts that deal with original non-fiction topics in which children ages 6-12 would be interested and from which they would learn, including (for example) local geography or biographies or obscure archeological finds that children could connect with their studies. Poor grammar or punctuation make it difficult to trust that the author has thoroughly checked other details in text." Submit 3-5 sample chapters and outline with SASE. Reviews artwork/photos as part of the ms package. Send photocopies and samples of medium used, if it enhances the illustration.
Fiction: Adventure, humor, juvenile, literary, short story collections. "We will be focusing on children's literature. Make me care about your characters! No one is interested in a story if they are not engaged by the protagonist. We also accept poetry for children *only*." Submit synopsis and 3-5 sample chapters with SASE. Recent title(s): *The Ambitious Baker's Batter*, by Wendy Seese (juvenile).

SANDPIPER PRESS, P.O. Box 286, Brookings OR 97415-0028. (541)469-5588. Editor: Marilyn Riddle. Estab. 1979. **Outright purchase varies.** Reports in 1 month.
Nonfiction: "Next book: Sayings; Quotes, uncommon, pro-peace, brotherhood, ecology and humor." Query with SASE. Recent title(s): *Physically Challenged Can-Do* (textbook).

SCOTTWALL ASSOCIATES, 95 Scott St., San Francisco CA 94117. (415)861-1956. Contact: James Heig, owner. Publishes hardcover and trade paperback originals. **Publishes 2-3 titles/year. Pays 5-7% royalty on wholesale price.**

No advance. Reports in 1 month on queries and proposals, 2 months on mss. Book catalog and ms guidelines free.
Nonfiction: California history and biography *only.* Query with SASE. Reviews artwork/photos as part of the ms package. Send photocopies. Recent title(s): *Alaska Gold,* by Jeff Kunkel (letters and photographs from Alaska to California, 1898-1906).

SOUND VIEW PRESS, 170 Boston Post Rd., Madison CT 06443. President: Peter Hastings Falk. Estab. 1985. Publishes hardcover and trade paperback originals, dictionaries, exhibition records, and price guides exclusive to fine art. All titles are related.

SPECTACLE LANE PRESS INC., P.O. Box 1237, Mt. Pleasant SC 29465-1237. Phone/fax: (843)971-9165. Editor: James A. Skardon. Publishes nonfiction hardcover and trade paperback originals. **Publishes 2-3 titles/year. Pays 6-10% royalty on wholesale price. Offers $500-1,000 advance.** Reports in 1 month on queries, 2 months on mss.
Nonfiction: "More celebrity and TV-oriented humor and sports and family-oriented life-style subjects holding closely to current trends. "Query first. Then send outline and 3 chapters with SASE if we are interested." Recent title(s): *Learning with Molly,* by Karen Zurheid (parenting/inspirational).

STA-KRIS, INC., 107 N. Center, Marshalltown IA 50158. (515)753-4139. President: Kathy Wagoner. Publishes hardcover and trade paperback originals. **Publishes 4 titles/year. Pays negotiated royalty on wholesale price or makes outright purchase. Advance negotiable.** Publishes book 1 year after acceptance. Accepts simultaneous submissions. Reports in 2 months on queries and proposals, 4 months on mss. Book catalog free.
Nonfiction: Coffee table book, gift book, illustrated book, self-help. "We publish nonfiction gift books that portray universal feelings, truths and values or have a special occasion theme, plus small format compilations of statements about professions, issues, attitudes, etc." Query with proposal package including synopsis, bio, published credits. Recent title(s): *Rhythm of the Season,* by Marilyn Adams (illustrated gift book).
Tips: "Our audience tends to be women ages 20 and older. We are an independent publisher who supports the marketing of their books with great energy and knowledge."

STEEL BALLS PRESS, P.O. Box 807, Whittier CA 90608. Owner: R. Don Steele. Website: http://steelballs.com. "We publish only controversial nonfiction." Publishes hardcover and trade paperback originals. **Publishes 2-3 titles/year. Pays 10% royalty on retail price after break-even. No advance.** Guidelines available on website.
Nonfiction: How-to, self-help. Subjects include business and economics, money/finance, psychology, sociology, women's issues/studies. No humor, homeless, incest/molestation, save-the-world. Query (1 page) *only* with SASE. Recent title(s): *Sex, Truth and Audiotape,* by Joanna B. Lopez (self-help for divorced men).
Tips: "Write a persuasive one-page query letter. Explain who will buy and why."

STORM PEAK PRESS, 157 Yesler Way, Suite 413, Seattle WA 98104. (206)223-0162. Publishes trade paperback originals and reprints. **Publishes 2 books/year. Pays royalty on retail price or net revenues.** Reports in 7 months.
Nonfiction: Memoirs. Subjects include Americana, health/medicine, history, travel. "We only consider high-quality, unique manuscripts." Query with SASE. Recent title(s): *Return to Chewelah, A Story of Innocence and Loss,* by Janet May (memoir).
Fiction: Juvenile adventure. Recent title(s): *The King of Messy Potatoes,* by John Dashney.
Tips: "Get editorial help before sending a manuscript. Be confident the material is well written."

STUDIO 4 PRODUCTIONS, P.O. Box 280400, Northridge CA 91328. (818)700-2522. Editor-in-Chief: Charlie Matthews. Publishes trade paperback originals. **Publishes 2-5 titles/year. Pays 10% royalty on retail price. Offers $500-1,000 advance.** Reports in 1 month on queries and proposals, 3 months on mss.
Nonfiction: Subjects include character education (values, ethics and morals), parenting, travel, self-help. "Writers should be familiar with the Character Education movement. We have recently entered the area of Senior publications. We will continue to publish in previously established areas as well." Query with outline and SASE. Recent title(s): *Airfare Secrets Exposed,* by Matt Wunder (travel).

THE SUGAR HILL PRESS, 216 Stoddard Rd., Hancock NH 03449-5102. Publisher: L. Bickford. Estab. 1990. Publishes trade paperback originals. **Publishes 1 title/year. Pays 15-20% royalty on publisher's revenues. No advance.** Reports in 2 months on proposals.
Nonfiction: "We publish technical manuals for users of school administrative software *only.* (These are supplemental materials, not the manuals which come in the box.) A successful writer will combine technical expertise with crystal-clear prose." Query with outline and 1 sample chapter. Recent title(s): *Perfect Attendance,* by Frances M. Kulak (technical manual).

TAMARACK BOOKS, INC., P.O. Box 190313, Boise ID 83719-0313. (800)962-6657. (208)387-2656. Fax: (208)387-2650. President/Owner: Kathy Gaudry. Publishes trade paperback originals and reprints. **Publishes 3-5 titles/year. Pays 5-15% royalty.** Reports in 4 months on queries, 6 months on mss.
Nonfiction: History and illustrated books on West for people living in or interested in the American West. "We are looking for manuscripts for popular audience, but based on solid research. We specialize in mountain man, women's issues and outlaw history prior to 1940 in the West, but will book at any good manuscript on Western history prior to

1940." Query with outline and SASE. Recent title(s): *When All Roads Led to Tombstone*, by John Plesent Gray, edited and annotated by W. Lane Rogers (Southwest history).
Tips: "We look for authors who want to actively participate in the marketing of their books."

TAMBRA PUBLISHING, P.O. Box 3044, Montclair CA 91763. E-mail: tambra_publishing@juno.com. Editor: Tambra Campbell. Publisher: Kathy Gulley. Publishes hardcover and trade paperback originals. Estab. 1985. Publishes how-to books on handwriting analysis; also accepts well-written screenplays and manuscripts with good storylines that can be adapted into screenplays, as well as being published. Will consider works on psychology and on family relations, love stories. **Pays royalty on retail price.** Reports in 2 months on queries, 4 months on mss.
Nonfiction: Query with SASE first, or send outline, 3-4 sample chapters and SASE. Recent title(s): *Handwriting Reveals Personality*, by Stevens.

THIRD SIDE PRESS, INC., 2250 W. Farragut, Chicago IL 60625. Editor/Publisher: Midge Stocker. Third Side Press publishes feminist books, with focus on women's health and lesbian fiction. **Publishes 1-2 titles/year. 30% of books from first-time authors; 100% from unagented writers. Pays 6% royalty and up on wholesale price.** Publishes book 18 months after acceptance of ms. Accepts simultaneous submissions (with nonfiction). Reports in 1 month on queries, 6 months on mss. Book catalog and manuscript guidelines for 9×12 SAE with 2 first-class stamps.
Nonfiction: Self-help. Subjects include health/medicine (women's only), lesbian, psychology, women's issues/studies. "We are looking for manuscripts that approach women's health issues from a feminist perspective." Query with SASE. Recent title(s): *Beyond Bedlam: Contemporary Women Psychiatric Surviors Speak Out*, edited by Jeanine Grobe.
Fiction: Contemporary, experimental, feminist, lesbian, literary. "We are not seeking collections of short stories by individual authors. We are seeking quality novels with lesbian main characters." Query with complete ms and SASE. Recent title(s): *The Mayor of Heaven*, by Lynn Kanter.

TIA CHUCHA PRESS, A Project of The Guild Complex, P.O. Box 476969, Chicago IL 60647. (773)377-2496. Fax: (773)252-5388. Director: Luis Rodriguez. Publishes trade paperback originals. **Publishes 2-4 titles/year. Receives 25-30 queries and 150 mss/year. Pays 10% royalty on wholesale price. Offers $500-1,000 advance.** Reports in 9 months on mss. Publishes book 1 year after acceptance. Book catalog and ms guidelines free.
Poetry: "No restrictions as to style or content. We do cross-cultural and performance-oriented poetry. It has to work on the page, however." Submit complete ms with SASE. Recent title(s): *Body of Life*, by Elizabeth Alexander.
Tips: Audience is "those interested in strong, multicultural, urban poetry—the best of bar-cafe poetry. Annual manuscript deadline is June 30. Send your best work. No fillers. We read in the summer; we decide in the fall what books to publish for the following year."

THE UNIVERSITY OF OKLAHOMA NATIONAL RESOURCE CENTER FOR YOUTH SERVICES, 202 W. Eighth St., Tulsa OK 74119. (918)585-2986. Fax: (918)592-1841. E-mail: mhightower@ou.edu. Editor: Michael J. Hightower. Publishes hardcover and trade paperback originals. "The National Resource Center for Youth Services, a division of the University of Oklahoma College of Continuing Education, aims to enhance the services provided to the nation's at-risk youth by improving the effectiveness of human services." **Publishes 2 titles/year. Pays 10-15% royalty on retail price.** Reports in 2 months on proposals, 4 months on mss. Book catalog and ms guidelines free.
Nonfiction: "All titles submitted must relate to at-risk youth." Children's/juvenile, reference. Subjects include child guidance/parenting, gay/lesbian. Query. Reviews artwork/photos as part of ms package. Recent title(s): *Toward a Gang Solution: The Redirectional Method*, by Rosen, Hingano and Spencer.
Tips: Audience consists of public and private nonprofit child welfare, juvenile justice, and youth services professionals.

VALIANT PRESS, INC., P.O. Box 330568, Miami FL 33233. (305)665-1889. President: Charity Johnson. Estab. 1991. Publishes hardcover and trade paperback originals. **Publishes 1-3 titles/year. Pays royalty on net receipts. Offers minimal advance.** Reports in 2 months.
Nonfiction: "We are interested in nonfiction books on Florida subjects." Submit proposal package, including outline, 2-3 sample chapters, author's background, marketing info with SASE. Recent title(s): *The Biltmore, Beacon for Miami, Revised and Expanded*, by Helen Muir.

N **VANDERWYK & BURNHAM**, P.O. Box 2789, Acton MA 01720. (978)263-5906. Fax: (978)263-7553. President: Meredith Rutter. Publishes hardcover and trade paperback originals. **Publishes 1-3 titles/year. 100% from first-time authors, 100% from unagented writers. Pays royalty on retail price. Offers $2,000 advance.** Reports in 3 months on queries. Book catalog and ms guidelines for #10 SASE.
Nonfiction: Self-help. Subjects include Americana, education, psychology, sociology, creative nonfiction, aging. Query with proposal package, including résumé, publishing history, clips with SASE. Recent title(s): *For the Love of Teaching: And Other Reasons Teachers Do What They Do.*

VISIONS COMMUNICATIONS, 205 E. Tenth St., Suite 2D, New York NY 10003. Publisher: Beth Bay. Publishes hardcover originals and trade paperback originals and reprints. **Publishes 4 titles/year. Pays 5-20% royalty on retail price.** Reports in 6 months.
Nonfiction: Children's/juvenile, how-to, reference, self-help, technical, textbook. Subjects include art/architecture, business and economics, computers and electronics, nature/environment, religion, science. Submit résumé, outline, 2

sample chapters with SASE. Recent title(s): *Restructuring Electricity Markets*, by Charles Cichetti.

N **VITESSE PRESS**, 4431 Lehigh Rd., #288, College Park MD 20740-3127. (301)772-5915. Fax: (301)772-5921. E-mail: dickmfield@aol.com. Website: http://www.Acornpub.com. Editor: Richard H. Mansfield. Estab. 1985. Publishes trade paperback originals. **Publishes 3 titles/year. Pays 7-10% royalty. No advance.** Reports in 1 month on queries.
Nonfiction: Regionanl mountain biking guides (Eastern), outdoor recreation books. Especially interested in cycling-related books. Recent title(s): *Cycling Health and Physiology*, by Ed Burke (self-help/fitness).

WAYFINDER PRESS, P.O. Box 217, Ridgway CO 81432-0217. (970)626-5452. Owner: Marcus E. Wilson. Estab. 1980. Publishes trade paperback originals. **Publishes 2 titles/year. Pays 8-10% royalty on retail price.** Accepts simultaneous submissions. Reports in 1 month. *Writer's Market* recommends allowing 2 months for reply.

- Wayfinder Press no longer accepts fiction or children manuscripts.

Nonfiction: Illustrated book, reference. Subjects include Americana, government/politics, history, nature/environment, photography, recreation, regional, travel. "We are looking for books on western Colorado: history, nature, recreation, photo, and travel. No books on subjects outside our geographical area of specialization." Query or submit outline/synopsis, sample chapters and SASE. Reviews artwork/photos as part of ms package. Recent title(s): *Hiking the Gunnison Basin*, by Bloomquist (hiking guide).
Tips: "Writers have the best chance selling us tourist-oriented books. The local population and tourists comprise our audience."

WHITE-BOUCKE PUBLISHING, P.O. Box 400, Lafayette CO 80026. (303)604-0661. Partner: Laurie Boucke. Publishes trade paperback originals. **Publishes 2-3 titles/year. Pays 0-10% royalty on retail price.** Reports in 1 month on queries and proposals, 2 months on mss.
Nonfiction: Humor, reference. Subjects include music, sports, travel (Europe). "Topical, lively works, preferably containing a strong element of humor." Query with outline, 3 sample chapters and SASE. Recent title(s): *People I Could Do Without*, by Donald G. Smith (lifestyles/humor).

WHITEHORSE PRESS, P.O. Box 60, North Conway NH 03860-0060. (603)356-6556. Fax: (603)356-6590. Publisher: Dan Kennedy. Estab. 1988. Publishes trade paperback originals. **Publishes 3-4 titles/year. Pays 10% maximum royalty on wholesale price. No advance.** Reports in 1 month on queries.
Nonfiction: "We are actively seeking nonfiction books to aid motorcyclists in topics such as motorcycle safety, restoration, repair and touring. We are especially interested in technical subjects related to motorcycling." Query. Recent title(s): *How to Set Up Your Motorcycle Workshop*, by Charlie Masi (trade paperback).
Tips: "We like to discuss project ideas at an early stage and work with authors to develop those ideas to fit our market."

N **WHITFORD PRESS**, Schiffer Publishing, Ltd., 4880 Lower Valley Rd., Atglen PA 19310. (610)593-1777. Managing Editor: Ellen Taylor. Estab. 1985. Publishes trade paperback originals. **Averages 1-3 titles/year. Receives 400-500 submissions/year. 20% of books from first-time authors; 90% from unagented writers. Pays royalty on wholesale price; no advances.** Publishes book 9-12 months after acceptance and receipt of complete ms. Accepts simultaneous submissions. Reports within 3 months. Book catalog free. Manuscript guidelines for SASE.
Nonfiction: How-to, self-help, reference. Subjects include astrology, metaphysics, New Age topics. "We are looking for well written, well-organized, original books on all metaphysical subjects (except channeling and past lives). Books that empower the reader or show him/her ways to develop personal skills are preferred. New approaches, techniques, or concepts are best. No personal accounts unless they directly relate to a general audience. No moralistic, fatalistic, sexist or strictly philosophical books." Query first or send outline with SASE large enough to hold your submission.
Tips: "Our audience is knowledgeable in metaphysical fields, well-read and progressive in thinking. Please check bookstores to see if your subject has already been covered thoroughly. Expertise in the field is not enough; your book must be clean, well written and well organized. A specific and unique marketing angle is a plus. No Sun-sign material; we prefer more advanced work. Please don't send entire manuscript unless we request it, and be sure to include SASE. Let us know if the book is available on computer diskette and what type of hardware/software. Manuscripts should be between 60,000 and 110,000 words."

MARKETS THAT WERE listed in the 1998 edition of *Writer's Market* but do not appear this year are listed in the General Index with a notation explaining why they were omitted.

Book Producers

Book producers provide services for book publishers, ranging from hiring writers to editing and delivering finished books. Most book producers possess expertise in certain areas and will specialize in producing books related to those subjects. They provide books to publishers who don't have the time or expertise to produce the books themselves (many produced books are highly illustrated and require intensive design and color-separation work). Some work with on-staff writers, but most contract writers on a per-project basis.

Most often a book producer starts with a proposal; contacts writers, editors and illustrators; assembles the book; and sends it back to the publisher. The level of involvement and the amount of work to be done on a book by the producer is negotiated in individual cases. A book publisher may simply require the specialized skill of a particular writer or editor, or a producer could put together the entire book, depending on the terms of the agreement.

Writers have a similar working relationship with book producers. Their involvement depends on how much writing the producer has been asked to provide. Writers are typically paid by the hour, by the word, or in some manner other than on a royalty basis. Writers working for book producers usually earn flat fees. Writers may not receive credit (a byline in the book, for example) for their work, either. Most of the contracts require work for hire, and writers must realize they do not own the rights to writing published under this arrangement.

The opportunities are good, though, especially for writing-related work, such as fact checking, research and editing. Writers don't have to worry about good sales. Their pay is secured under contract. Finally, writing for a book producer is a good way to broaden experience in publishing. Every book to be produced is different, and the chance to work on a range of books in a number of capacities may be the most interesting aspect of all.

Book producers most often want to see a query detailing writing experience. They keep this information on file and occasionally even share it with other producers. When they are contracted to develop a book that requires a particular writer's experience, they contact the writer. There are well over 100 book producers, but most prefer to seek writers on their own. The book producers listed in this section have expressed interest in being contacted by writers. For a list of more producers, contact the American Book Producers Association, 160 Fifth Ave., Suite 625, New York NY 10010, or look in *Literary Market Place* (R.R. Bowker).

For a list of publishers according to their subjects of interest, see the nonfiction and fiction sections of the Book Publishers Subject Index. Information on book publishers and producers listed in the previous edition of *Writer's Market* but not included in this edition can be found in the General Index.

A.G.S. INCORPORATED, P.O. Box 460313, San Francisco CA 94146. Contact: Mr. Yenne. Averages 10-12 titles/year. 15% of books from first-time authors; 100% from unagented writers. Makes outright purchase. Reports in 2 months.

• A.G.S. Incorporated does not work with out-of-area writers.

Nonfiction: Coffee table book, illustrated book, reference. Subjects include Americana, animals, history, military/war, photography, transportation. Query.

B&B PUBLISHING, INC., P.O. Box 96, Walworth WI 53184-0096. (414)275-9474. Fax: (414)275-9530. President: William Turner. Managing Director: Katy O'Shea. Produces supplementary educational materials for grades K-12. Produces 5-10 titles/year. 10% of books from first-time authors, 90% from unagented writers. Payment varies, mostly "work-for-hire" contracts. Reports in 3 months. Book catalog and ms guidelines for SASE.

Nonfiction: Especially interested in curriculum based material in social studies, reading, writing and math. Query.

Reviews artwork/photos as part of ms package.
Recent Title(s): *Geotrax* (geography).

BOOKWORKS, INC., P.O. Box 204, West Milton OH 45383. (937)698-3619. Fax: (937)698-3651. E-mail: bookworks@worldnet.att.net. President: Nick Engler. Produces hardcover originals. Produces 4 titles/year. 100% of books from unagented writers. Pays "on-staff salary." Reports in 1 month.
Nonfiction: How-to. Subjects include hobbies (woodworking). Query.
Recent Title(s): *Nick Engler's Woodworking Wisdom.*
Tips: "Query for short books, 128-320 pages in length."

ALISON BROWN CERIER BOOK DEVELOPMENT, INC., 815 Brockton Lane N., Plymouth MN 55410. (612)449-9668. Fax: (612)449-9674. "The vast majority of books start with our ideas or those of a publisher, not with proposals from writers. We do not act as authors' agents." Produces hardcover and trade paperback originals. Produces 4 titles/year. 50% of books from first-time authors; 90% from unagented writers. Payment varies with the project. Reports in 3 weeks. *Writer's Market* recommends allowing 2 months for reply.
Nonfiction: How-to, popular reference, self-help. Subjects include child guidance/parenting, cooking/foods/nutrition, health, sports, women's interest. Query with SASE.
Recent Title(s): *Family Traditions*, by Elizabeth Berg (Reader's Digest).
Tips: "I often pair experts with writers and like to know about writers and journalists with co-writing experience."

COURSE CRAFTERS, INC., 33 Low St., 2nd Floor, Newburyport MA 01950. (978)465-2040. Fax: (978)465-5027. E-mail: lise@coursecrafters.com. Website: http://www.coursecrafters.com. President: Lise B. Ragan. Produces textbooks, language materials (Spanish/ESL) and publishes packages for early childhood/family learning that feature storytelling and music. Makes outright purchase. Manuscript guidelines vary based upon project-specific requirements.
Nonfiction: Textbook. "We package materials that teach language. We are particularly looking for innovative approaches and visually appealing presentations." Subjects include language, education (preschool-adult), and early childhood. Submit résumé, publishing history and clips. Reviews artwork/photos as part of ms package.
Tips: "Mail (or fax) résumé with list of projects related to specific experience with ESL, bilingual and/or foreign language textbook development. Also interested in storytellers and musicians for our new audio/game packages."

N **DIMENSIONS & DIRECTIONS, LTD.**, 41 Old Rt. 6, RR #9, Brewster NY 10509. (914)279-7043 or 301 E. 21st St., New York NY 10010. (212)529-9569. Fax: (212)353-2984. President: Helena Frost. Estab. 1970. Packages approximately 20 titles/year. Receives approximately 100 queries/year. Authors paid by royalty, by flat or hourly fees on freelance assignments. Advance varies. Reports in 3 weeks. Manuscript guidelines available per project.
Nonfiction: Textbook ancillaries, some general trade titles. Subjects include business and economics, education, government/politics, health/medicine, history, language/literature, psychology. Query with résumé, publishing history and clips.
Recent Title(s): *Self-Esteem* (Globe, supplementary text).
Tips: "Although we are not interested in over-the-transom manuscripts, we do request writers' and editors' résumés with publication history and will review school-related proposals and outlines for submission to major publishers."

ERIAKO ASSOCIATES, 1380 Morningside Way, Venice CA 90291. (310)392-6537. Fax: (310)396-4307. Director: Erika Fabian. Produces hardcover and trade paperback originals. Produces 3-4 titles/year. 100% of books from unagented writers. Pays per contract agreement per individual artist. Reports in 2 months.
Nonfiction: Coffee table book, illustrated book, juvenile. Subjects include business and economics, ethnic, photography, travel. Query with résumé, publishing history and clips with SASE. Reviews artwork/photos as part of ms package.
Recent Title(s): *The Ph.D. Guide to Travel Photography.*

- Eriako Associates is not planning any fiction titles for the coming year.

Tips: "We're interested in travel writers/photographers with a proven track record in professional photojournalism, and ability to function in foreign countries under all types of circumstances."

N **GLEASON GROUP, INC.**, 6 Old Kings Hwy., Norwalk CT 06850. (203)847-6658. President: Gerald Gleason. Produces 4-8 titles/year. Work-for-hire.
Nonfiction: Textbooks about software with disks. Submitt résumé and published clips. *No unsolicited mss.*
Recent Title(s): *Word 97: A Professional Approach.*
Tips: "If writer is well versed in the most recent Microsoft office software (or the most recent version of Pagemaker), and has written technical or software-related material before, he/she can send us their résumé."

HILLER BOOK MANUFACTURING, 631 North 400 W., Salt Lake City UT 84103. (801)521-2411. Fax: (801)521-2420. President: Melvin Hiller. Produces hardcover originals. Produces 500 titles/year. 10% of books from first-time authors; 20% from unagented writers. Pays royalty on net receipts. Reports in 1 month. Book catalog free.
Nonfiction: Coffee table book, cookbook, illustrated book, juvenile, reference, journals, scrapbooks, seminar education materials. Subjects include cooking, education, religion. Submit proposal. Reviews artwork/photos as part of ms package.
Fiction: Historical, humor, juvenile, picture books, religious.

JENKINS GROUP, 121 E. Front St., 4th Floor, Traverse City MI 49684. (616)933-0445. Fax: (616)933-0448. E-mail: mdressler@smallpress.com. Website: http://www.smallpress.com. Vice President/Publisher: Mark Dressler. "We publish books about the people and heritage of the Great Lakes Region." Produces hardcover, trade paperback originals. Produces 20 titles/year. 50% of books from first-time authors; 75% from unagented writers. Makes outright purchase of $2,000-5,000. Reports in 1 month. *Writer's Market* recommends allowing 2 months for reply.
Imprint: Rhodes & Easton.
Nonfiction: Biography, coffee table book, corporate and premium books. Subjects include Americana, business and economics, hobbies, photography, recreation, regional, travel. Submit résumé, publishing history and clips.
Recent Title(s): *Great Lakes Good Times* (keepsake/travel).
Tips: "We look for situation-specific experience."

LOUISE B. KETZ AGENCY, 1485 First Ave., Suite 4B, New York NY 10021. (212)535-9259. President: Louise B. Ketz. Produces and agents hardcover and paperback originals. Averages 1-3 titles/year. 90% of books from unagented writers. Pays flat fees and honoraria to writers. Reports in 6-8 weeks.
Nonfiction: Biography, reference. Subjects include Americana, business and economics, history, military/war, science, sports. Submit proposal.
Recent Title(s): *Soccer for Juniors* revised edition (Macmillan).
Tips: "It is important for authors to list their credentials relevant to the book they are proposing (i.e., why they are qualified to write that nonfiction work). Also helps if author defines the market (who will buy the book and why)."

GEORGE KURIAN REFERENCE BOOKS, Box 519, Baldwin Place NY 10505. Phone/fax: (914)962-3287. President: George Kurian. "We seek to provide accurate information on issues of global interest." Produces hardcover originals. Produces 6 titles/year. 10% of books from first-time authors; 50% from unagented writers. Pays 10-15% royalty on net receipts. Reports in 3 months. Book catalog for 8½×11 SAE with 2 first-class stamps. Manuscript guidelines for #10 SASE.
Imprints: International Encyclopedia Society; UN Studies Forum.
Nonfiction: Biography, illustrated book, reference. Subjects include Americana, business and economics, education, ethnic, government/politics, history, military/war, philosophy, photography, science, religion, travel. Query or submit proposal.
Recent Title(s): *Political Market Place.*

LAING COMMUNICATIONS INC., 16250 NE 80th St., Redmond WA 98052-3821. (425)869-6313. Fax: (425)869-6318. E-mail: lci@laingpub.com. Vice President/Editorial Director: Christine Laing. Estab. 1985. Imprint is Laing Research Services (industry monographs) and The History Bank (Americana). Produces hardcover and trade paperback originals primarily for or in partnership with institutions and publishers. Produces 10-15 titles/year. 5% of books from first-time authors; 100% from unagented writers. Payment "varies dramatically since all work is sold to publishers as royalty-inclusive package." Reports in 1 month. *Writer's Market* recommends allowing 2 months for reply.
Nonfiction: Illustrated book, juvenile, medical, museum, reference, technical, textbook. Subjects include Americana, US history, baseball, computers/electronics. Query with SASE. Reviews artwork/photos as part of ms package.
Recent Title(s): *Beyond the Mississippi: Early Westward Expansion of the United States* (Lodestar Books).

LAMPPOST PRESS INC., 1172 Park Ave., New York NY 10128-1213. (212)876-9511. President: Roseann Hirsch. Estab. 1987. Produces hardcover, trade paperback and mass market paperback originals. Averages 25 titles/year. 50% of books from first-time authors; 85% from unagented writers. Pays 50% royalty or makes outright purchase.
Nonfiction: Biography, cookbook, how-to, humor, illustrated book, juvenile, self-help. Subjects include child guidance/parenting, cooking/foods/nutrition, gardening, health, money/finance, women's issues. Query or submit proposal. Reviews artwork/photos as part of ms package.

McCLANAHAN BOOK COMPANY INC., 23 W. 26th St., New York NY 10010. (212)725-1515. General Manager: Jean Firestone. Produces 50-60 titles/year. 5% of books from first-time authors; 90% from unagented writers. Makes outright purchase. Reports within 3 months to submissions with SASE.
Nonfiction: Juvenile. Submit proposal. Reviews artwork/photos as part of ms package.
Recent Title(s): *Crabs Grab*, by Kees Moerbeck (pop-up).
Fiction: Juvenile, picture books. Submit complete ms, proposal, résumé, publishing history and clips. Query with SASE first.

MEGA-BOOKS, INC., 240 E. 60th St., New York NY 10022. (212)355-6200. Fax: (212)355-6303. President: Pat Fortunato. Acquisitions: John Craddock. Produces trade paperback and mass market paperback originals and fiction and nonfiction for the educational market. Produces 45 titles/year. Works with first-time authors, established authors and unagented writers. Makes outright purchase for $3,000 and up. Offers 50% average advance.
Fiction: Juvenile, mystery, young adult. Submit résumé, publishing history and clips. *No unsolicited mss.*
Recent Title(s): *Nancy Drew* series.
Tips: "Please be sure to obtain a current copy of our writers' guidelines before writing."

MENASHA RIDGE PRESS, INC., P.O. Box 43059, Birmingham AL 35243. (205)322-0439. Fax: (205)326-1012. Publisher: R.W. Sehlinger. Acquisitions: Budd Zehmer, senior acquisitions editor (outdoors); Molly Burns (travel,

reference). Estab. 1982. Menasha Ridge publishes "distinctive books in the areas of outdoor sports, travel and diving. Our authors are among the best in their fields." Produces hardcover and trade paperback originals. Produces 35 titles/year. Receives 600-800 submissions/year. 30% of books from first-time authors; 85% of books from unagented writers. Average print order for a first book is 4,000. Royalty and advances vary. Publishes book 1 year after acceptance. Accepts simultaneous submissions. Reports in 2 months. Book catalog for 9×12 SAE with 4 first-class stamps.
Nonfiction: How-to, humor, outdoor recreation, travel guides. Subjects include regional, recreation, adventure sports, travel. No fiction, biography or religious copies. "Most publishing concepts originate in-house, although a few come from outside submissions." Submit proposal, résumé and clips. Reviews artwork/photos.
Recent Title(s): *Mountain Bike! Virginia*, by Randy Porter (mountain biking/travel).
Tips: "Audience: age 25-60, 14-18 years' education, white collar and professional, $30,000 median income, 75% male, 55% east of Mississippi River."

NEW ENGLAND PUBLISHING ASSOCIATES, INC., P.O. Box 5, Chester CT 06412. (860)345-READ. Fax: (860)345-3660. E-mail: nepa@nepa.com. President: Elizabeth Frost-Knappman; Vice President/Treasurer: Edward W. Knappman. Staff: Victoria Harlow, Ron Formica and Christopher Ceplenski. Estab. 1983. "Our mission is to provide personalized service to a select list of clients." NEPA develops adult and young adult reference and information titles and series for the domestic and international markets. Produces hardcover and trade paperback originals. 25% of books from first-time authors. Reports in 2 months.

- Elizabeth Frost-Knappman's *Women's Progress in America* was selected by *Choice* as Outstanding Reference Book of the Year.

Tips: "We are looking for writers in the area of women's history and political science."

N **NEWMARKET PRESS**, 18 E. 48th St., Suite 1501, New York NY 10017. (212)832-3575. Fax: (212)832-3629. Assistant Editor: Rachel Reiss. Produces hardcover and trade paperback originals. Produces 25-30 titles/year. Pays royalty. Catalog for SAE 9×12 and $1.01 postage. Manuscript guidelines for #10 SASE.
Nonfiction: General nonfiction, self-help. Subjects include child guidance/parenting, cooking/foods/nutrition, health, money/finance, psychology. Query with SASE or submit proposal.
Recent Title(s): *Bankroll on Your Future* (personal finance/retirement).
Tips: "Check out other Newmarket titles before submitting to get a sense of the kind of books we publish. Be patient!"

PUBLISHERS RESOURCE GROUP, INC. (PRG), 307 Camp Craft Rd., Suite 100, Austin TX 78746. (512)328-7007. Fax: (512)328-9480. Editorial Director: Claudia Capp. "We're a development house that does work for hire for educational publishers. We look for writers and editors with education background and publishing experience." Pays per project/per page.
Nonfiction: Teacher editions, student materials—textbook and ancillary for all major educational publishing companies, all elementary and secondary subject areas. Submit résumé, publishing history and writing samples.
Recent Title(s): *Chemistry*, for Prentice-Hall (teacher's edition, teaching resources/student materials).
Tips: "If they have written classroom instructional materials before—have taught and/or worked for an educational publisher, they are usually the best prepared to work for PRG."

SACHEM PUBLISHING ASSOCIATES, INC., P.O. Box 412, Guilford CT 06437-0412. (203)453-4328. Fax: (203)453-4320. E-mail: sachempublishing@guilfordct.com. President: Stephen P. Elliott. Estab. 1974. Produces hardcover originals for publishers. Produces 3 titles/year. 5% of books from first-time authors; 100% from unagented writers. Pays royalty or works for hire. Reports in 1 month. *Writer's Market* recommends allowing 2 months for reply.
Nonfiction: Reference. Subjects include Americana, government/politics, history, military/war. Submit résumé and publishing history.
Recent Title(s): *American Heritage Encyclopedia of American History*, by John Mack Faragher, general editor.

SILVER MOON PRESS, 160 Fifth Ave., New York NY 10010. (212)242-6499. Fax: (212)242-6799. E-mail: silvermp@aol.com. Website: http://www.silvermoonpress.com. Editorial Assistant: Karin Lillebo. Publisher: David Katz. "We publish mainly American historical fiction for age group 8-12." Produces hardcover originals. Produces 2-4 books/year. 10% of books from first-time authors; 90% from unagented writers. Book catalog free.
Nonfiction: Juvenile. Subjects include education, history, science, sports. Submit proposal. Reviews artwork/photos as part of ms package.
Fiction: Historical, juvenile, mystery. Submit sample chapters or synopsis along with SASE.
Recent Title(s): *Beauty Lab*, Mildred Dawson (science).

SOMERVILLE HOUSE BOOKS LIMITED, 3080 Yonge St., Suite 5000, Toronto Ontario M4N 3N1 Canada. Contact: Acquisition Department. Produces literary fiction and nonfiction. Produces 8 titles/year. 5% of books from first-time authors. Reports in 4 months. Manuscript guidelines for #10 SASE with postage (Canadian or IRC).
Nonfiction: Subjects include technology, politics, culture and metaphysics. Query.
Fiction: Literary novels and short story collections. Query.
Recent Title(s): *The Skin of Culture* (media/technology).
Tips: "Remember that we publish very few adult fiction and nonfiction a year. We do *not* accept manuscripts for children's books."

N **STOREY COMMUNICATIONS, INC., CUSTOM BOOK PACKAGING**, Schoolhouse Rd., Pownal VT 05261. (413)458-2711. Fax: (413)458-0965. Director of Custom Publishing: Deirdre Lynch. Produces hardcover originals and trade paperback originals. Produces 15-20 titles/year. 75% of books from first-time authors, 95% from unagented writers. Work for hire. Reports in 2 months. Book catalog free.
Nonfiction: Coffee table book, cookbook, how-to, illustrated book, reference. Subjects include animals, cooking/foods/nutrition, gardening, hobbies, recreation, lifestyle, nature, outdoor recreation, herbal, pets, do-it-yourself, home decorating. Submit résumé, publishing history and clips.
Recent Title(s): *Get Yard Smart* (Reader's Digest).

SUCCESS PUBLISHERS, One Oakglade Circle, Hummelstown PA 17036-9525. (717)566-0468. Fax: (717)566-6423. Editor-in-Chief: Marjorie L. Markowski. "Our mission is to help the people of the world grow and become the best they can be through the written and spoken word. We strive to make a difference in people's lives and make the world a better place to live." Guidelines for #10 SAE with 2 first-class stamps.
Imprint: Aviation Publishers.
Nonfiction: How-to, self-help. Subjects include business, pop-psychology, success/motivation, entrepreneurship, sales, marketing, network marketing and home-based business topics. Submit proposal with résumé, publishing history and clips.
Recent Title(s): *No Excuse! I'm Doing It (Abridged)*, by Jay Rifenbary (how to win with people and build your business).
Tips: "Our focus is on publishing bestsellers written by authors who speak and consult. We're looking for authors who are serious about making a difference in the world."

TENTH AVENUE EDITIONS, 625 Broadway, Suite 903, New York NY 10012. (212)529-8900. Fax: (212)529-7399. Managing Editor: Clive Giboire. Submissions Editor: Suzanne Cobban. Estab. 1984. Produces hardcover, trade paperback and mass market paperback originals. Produces 6 titles/year. Pays advance paid by publisher less our commission. Reports in 2 months.
Nonfiction: Biography, how-to, crafts, illustrated book, juvenile, catalogs. Subjects include music/dance, photography, women's issues/studies, art, children's. *Queries only.* Reviews artwork/photos as part of ms package.
Recent Title(s): *Waiter, There's a Fly in My Soup*, by Leslie N. Lewis (BookMark).
Tips: "Send query with publishing background. Return postage a must."

2M COMMUNICATIONS LTD., 121 W. 27th St., New York NY 10001. (212)741-1509. Fax: (212)691-4460. Editorial Director: Madeleine Morel. Produces hardcover, trade paperback and mass market paperback originals. Produces 15 titles/year. 50% of books from first-time authors. Reports in 2 weeks. *Writer's Market* recommends allowing 2 months for reply.
Nonfiction: Biography, cookbook, how-to, humor. Subjects include child guidance/parenting, cooking/foods/nutrition, ethnic, gay/lesbian, health, psychology, women's studies. Query or submit proposal with résumé and publishing history.

N **THE WONDERLAND PRESS**, 160 Fifth Ave., Suite 723, New York NY 10010. (212)989-2550. Fax: (212)989-2321. President: John Campbell. Produces hardcover and trade paperback originals and mass market paperback originals. Produces 50 titles/year. 80% of books from first-time authors, 90% from unagented writers. Payment depends on the book: sometimes royalty with advance, sometimes work-for-hire. Reports in 3 weeks.
Nonfiction: Biography, coffee table book, how-to, humor, illustrated book, reference, self-help. Subjects include business and economics, education, gardening, gay/lesbian, history, money/finance, photography, psychology, art. Submit proposal with sample chapter(s). Reviews artwork/photos as part of ms package.
Recent Title(s): *501 Great Things About Being Gay* (Andrews McMeel).
Tips: "Always submit in writing, never by telephone. Know your market intimately. Study the competition and decide whether there is a genuine need for your book, with a market base that will justify publication. Send us an enthused, authoritative, passionately written proposal that shows your mastery of the subject and that makes us say, 'Wow, we want that!' "

MARKETS THAT WERE listed in the 1998 edition of *Writer's Market* but do not appear this year are listed in the General Index with a notation explaining why they were omitted.

Consumer Magazines

Selling your writing to consumer magazines is as much an exercise of your marketing skills as it is of your writing abilities. Editors of consumer magazines are looking not simply for good writing, but for good writing which communicates pertinent information to a specific audience—their readers. Why are editors so particular about the readers they appeal to? Because it is only by establishing a core of faithful readers with identifiable and quantifiable traits that magazines attract advertisers. And with many magazines earning up to half their income from advertising, it is in their own best interests to know their readers' tastes and provide them with articles and features that will keep their readers coming back.

APPROACHING THE CONSUMER MAGAZINE MARKET

Marketing skills will help you successfully discern a magazine's editorial slant and write queries and articles that prove your knowledge of the magazine's readership to the editor. The one complaint we hear from magazine editors more than any other is that many writers don't take the time to become familiar with their magazine before sending a query or manuscript. Thus, editors' desks become cluttered with inappropriate submissions—ideas or articles that simply will not be of much interest to the magazine's readers.

You can gather clues about a magazine's readership—and thus establish your credibility with the magazine's editor—in a number of ways:

- Start with a careful reading of the magazine's listing in this section of *Writer's Market*. Most listings offer very straightforward information about their magazine's slant and audience.
- Send for a magazine's writer's guidelines, if available. These are written by each particular magazine's editors and are usually quite specific about their needs and their readership.
- If possible, talk to an editor by phone. Many will not take phone queries, particularly those at the higher-profile magazines. But many editors of smaller publications will spend the time to help a writer over the phone.
- Perhaps most important, read several current issues of the target magazine. Only in this way will you see firsthand the kind of stories the magazine actually buys.
- Check a magazine's website. Often writer's guidelines and a selection of articles are included in a publication's online version. A quick check of archived articles lets you know if ideas you want to propose have already been covered.

Writers who can correctly and consistently discern a publication's audience and deliver stories that speak to that target readership will win out every time over writers who simply write what they write and send it where they will.

AREAS OF CURRENT INTEREST

Today's consumer magazines reflect societal trends and interests. As baby boomers age and the so-called "Generation X" comes along behind, magazines arise to address their concerns, covering topics of interest to various subsets of both of those wide-ranging demographic groups. Some areas of special interest now popular among consumer magazines include gardening, health & fitness, family leisure, computers, travel, fashion and cooking.

As in the book publishing business, magazine publishers are experimenting with a variety of approaches to marketing their publications electronically, whether on the Internet, the World Wide Web or via CD-ROM. For tips from online writers and editors on writing for magazines in the electronic age, see page 94 by Anthony Tedesco.

WHAT EDITORS WANT

In nonfiction, editors continue to look for short feature articles covering specialized topics. They want crisp writing and expertise. If you are not an expert in the area about which you are writing, make yourself one through research.

Always query by mail before sending your manuscript package, and do not e-mail or fax a query unless an editor specifically mentions an openness to this in the listing. Publishing, despite all the electronic advancements, is still a very paper-oriented industry. Once a piece has been accepted, however, many publishers now prefer to receive your submission via disk or modem so they can avoid re-keying the manuscript. Some magazines will even pay an additional amount for disk submission.

Fiction editors prefer to receive complete short story manuscripts. Writers must keep in mind that marketing fiction is competitive and editors receive far more material than they can publish. For this reason, they often do not respond to submissions unless they are interested in using the story. Before submitting material, check the market's listing for fiction requirements to ensure your story is appropriate for that market. More comprehensive information on fiction markets can be found in *Novel & Short Story Writer's Market* (Writer's Digest Books).

Many writers make their articles do double duty, selling first or one-time rights to one publisher and second serial or reprint rights to another noncompeting market. The heading, **Reprints**, offers details when a market indicates they accept previously published submissions, with submission form and payment information if available.

When considering magazine markets, be sure not to overlook opportunities with Canadian and international publications. Many such periodicals welcome submissions from U.S. writers and can offer writers an entirely new level of exposure for their work.

Regardless of the type of writing you do, keep current on trends and changes in the industry. Trade magazines such as *Folio*, *Advertising Age* and *Writer's Digest* will keep you abreast of start-ups and shutdowns and other writing/business trends.

PAYMENT

Writers make their living by developing a good eye for detail. When it comes to marketing material, the one detail of interest to almost every writer is the question of payment. Most magazines listed here have indicated pay rates; some give very specific payment-per-word rates while others state a range. Any agreement you come to with a magazine, whether verbal or written, should specify the payment you are to receive and when you are to receive it. Some magazines pay writers only after the piece in question has been published. Others pay as soon as they have accepted a piece and are sure they are going to use it.

In *Writer's Market*, those magazines that pay on acceptance have been highlighted with the phrase **pays on acceptance** set in bold type. Payment from these markets should reach you faster than from markets who pay on publication. There is, however, some variance in the industry as to what constitutes payment "on acceptance"—some writers have told us of two- and three-month waits for checks from markets that supposedly pay on acceptance. It is never out of line to ask an editor when you might expect to receive payment for an accepted article.

So what is a good pay rate? There are no standards; the principle of supply and demand operates at full throttle in the business of writing and publishing. As long as there are more writers than opportunities for publication, wages for freelancers will never skyrocket. Rates vary widely from one market to the next, however, and the news is not entirely bleak. One magazine industry source puts the average pay rate for consumer magazine feature writing at $1.25 a word, with "stories that require extensive reporting . . . more likely to be priced at $2.50 a word." In our opinion, those estimates are on the high side of current pay standards. Smaller circulation magazines and some departments of the larger magazines will pay a lower rate.

Editors know that the listings in *Writer's Market* are read and used by writers with a wide range of experience, from those as-yet unpublished writers just starting out, to those with a successful, profitable freelance career. As a result, many magazines publicly report pay rates in the lower end of their actual pay ranges. Experienced writers will be able to successfully negotiate higher pay rates for their material. Newer writers should be encouraged that as your reputation grows (along with your clip file), you will be able to command higher rates. See the article by Greg Levoy, The Art of Negotiation, for techniques that will help you in negotiating higher pay rates for your work.

WHAT'S NEW THIS YEAR?

We've added several features to make *Writer's Market* even more helpful in your search for the right magazine markets, features you won't find in any other writer's guide.

Information at-a-glance

Most immediately noticeable, we've added a number of symbols at the beginning of each listing to quickly convey certain important information. In the Consumer Magazine section, symbols identify comparative payment rates ($); new listings (N); "opportunity" markets (★) that are at least 75% freelance written, appear quarterly or more frequently, and buy a high number of manuscripts; and magazines that do not accept freelance submissions (⊘). Different sections of *Writer's Market* include other symbols; check the front and back inside covers for an explanation of all the symbols used throughout the book.

Who do you query? How much money? What are my odds?

We've also highlighted important information in boldface, the "quick facts" you won't find in any other market book, but should know before you submit your work. To clearly identify the editorial "point person" at each magazine, we've boldfaced the word "**Contact:**" for each magazine. We also highlight what percentage of the magazine is freelance written, how many manuscripts a magazine buys per year of nonfiction, fiction, poetry and fillers and respective pay rates in each category.

Information on publications listed in the previous edition of *Writer's Market* but not included in this edition may be found in the General Index.

ANIMAL

The publications in this section deal with pets, racing and show horses, and other domestic animals and wildlife. Magazines about animals bred and raised for the market are classified in the Farm category of Trade, Technical and Professional Journals. Publications about horse racing can be found in the Sports section.

$ $ AKC GAZETTE, American Kennel Club, 51 Madison Ave., New York NY 10010-1603. (212)696-8222. Fax: (212)696-8272. Website: http://www.akc.org/akc/. Editor-in-Chief: Diane Vasey. **Contact:** George Burger, managing editor. **80% freelance written.** Monthly association publication "slanted to interests of fanciers of purebred dogs as opposed to commercial interests or pet owners." Estab. 1889. Circ. 58,000. **Pays on acceptance of final ms.** Publishes ms an average of 6 months after acceptance. Byline given. Buys first North American serial rights. Submit seasonal material 6 months in advance. Reports in up to 2 months. Writer's guidelines for #10 SASE.
Nonfiction: General interest, historical, how-to, humor, photo feature, profiles, dog art, travel, training and canine performance sports. No poetry, tributes to individual dogs, or fiction. **Buys 75 mss/year.** Query with or without published clips. Length: 1,000-2,000 words. **Pays $200-400.**
Photos: State availability of photos with submission. Reviews color transparencies and prints only. Offers $25-150/photo. Captions and identification of subjects required. Buys one-time rights. Photo contest guidelines for #10 SASE.
Fiction: Annual short fiction contest only. Guidelines for #10 SASE.
Tips: "Contributors should be involved in the dog fancy or expert in area they write about (veterinary, showing, field trialing, obedience, training, dogs in legislation, dog art or history or literature). All submissions are welcome but author must be a credible expert or be able to interview and quote the experts. Veterinary articles must be written by or with

veterinarians. Humorous features are personal experiences relative to purebred dogs that have broader applications. For features generally, know the subject thoroughly and be conversant with jargon peculiar to the sport of dogs."

$ AMERICA'S CUTTER, Published by GoGo Communications, Inc., 201 W. Moore, Suite 200, Terrell TX 75160. (972)563-7001. Fax: (972)563-7004. **Contact:** Carroll Brown Arnold, publisher/editor. **25% freelance written.** Works with a small number of new/unpublished writers each year. Monthly magazine covering cutting horses, their owners, trainers and riders. Estab. 1995. Circ. 6,500. Pays on publication. Publishes ms 2 months after acceptance. Buys one-time, North American serial rights or second (reprint) rights. Byline given. Reports in 1 month. Sample copy $2.95.
Nonfiction: Informational and historical articles on cutting horse competition and equipment; new products; interviews/profiles. Length: 250-2,000 words. **Pays $10-150.**
Reprints: Send photocopy of article, typed ms with rights for sale noted and information about when and where the article previously appeared.
Photos: Send photo with submission. Reviews 35mm slide transparencies, 5×7 and 8×10 photos, color and b&w. Pays $5-15/photo.
Poetry: Accepts some poetry geared toward cutters and cutting horse owners and trainers. **Pays $5-25.**
Tips: "We are interested only in cutting horse-related subjects. Writing style should show a deep interest in horses coupled with knowledge of the world of cutting."

$ $ APPALOOSA JOURNAL, Appaloosa Horse Club, 5070 Hwy. 8 West, P.O. Box 8403, Moscow ID 83843-0903. (208)882-5578. Fax: (208)882-8150. E-mail: journal@appaloosa.com. **Contact:** Robin Hirzel, editor. **20-40% freelance written.** Monthly magazine covering Appaloosa horses. Estab. 1946. Circ. 25,000. Pays on publication. Publishes ms an average of 3 months after acceptance. Byline given. Buys first North American serial rights. Reports in 1 month on queries; 2 months on mss. Sample copy and writer's guidelines free.

• *Appaloosa Journal* no longer accepts material for columns.

Nonfiction: Historical, interview/profile, photo feature. **Buys 15-20 mss/year.** Query with or without published clips, or send complete ms. Length: 1,000-3,000 words. **Pays $100-400.** Sometimes pays expenses of writers on assignment.
Photos: Send photos with submission. Payment varies. Captions and identification of subjects required.
Tips: "Articles by writers with horse knowledge, news sense and photography skills are in great demand. If it's a solid article about an Appaloosa, the writer has a pretty good chance of publication. A good understanding of the breed and the industry is helpful. Make sure there's some substance and a unique twist."

N $ BIRD TALK, Dedicated to Better Care for Pet Birds, Fancy Publications, P.O. Box 6050, Mission Viejo CA 92690. (714)855-8822. Fax: (714)855-3045. **Contact:** Melissa Kauffman, editor. **50% freelance written.** Monthly magazine covering the care and training of cage birds for men and women who own any number of pet or exotic birds. Pays latter part of month in which article appears. Byline given. Buys first North American serial rights. Submit seasonal material 7 months in advance. No simultaneous submissions. Reports in 6 weeks on queries, 2 months on mss. Sample copy for $4.50. Writer's guidelines for #10 SASE.
Nonfiction: General interest (anything to do with pet birds); historical/nostalgic (of bird breeds, owners, cages); how-to (build cages, aviaries, playpens and groom, feed, breed, tame); humor; interview/profile (of birds and bird owners); how-to (live with birds—compatible pets, lifestyle, apartment adaptability, etc.); personal experience (with your own bird); photo feature (humorous or informative); travel (with pet birds or to see exotic birds); and articles giving behavioral guidelines, medical information, legal information, and description of species. No juvenile or material on wild birds not pertinent to pet care; everything should relate to *pet* birds. **Buys 120 mss/year.** Query. Length: 500-3,000 words. **Pays 7-10¢/word.**
Photos: State availability of photos or include in ms. Reviews prints; prefers slides. Pays $50-150 for color transparencies. Model release and identification of subjects preferred. Buys one-time rights.

$ $ CAT FANCY, Fancy Publications, Inc., P.O. Box 6050, Mission Viejo CA 92690. (714)855-8822. Website: http://www.catfancy.com. **Contact:** Jane Calloway, editor. **80-90% freelance written.** Monthly magazine mainly for women ages 25-54 interested in all phases of cat ownership. Estab. 1965. Circ. 303,000. Pays on publication. Publishes ms an average of 6 months after acceptance. Buys first North American serial rights. Byline given. Absolutely no simultaneous submissions. Submit seasonal material 4 months in advance. Reports in 3 months. Sample copy for $5.50. Writer's guidelines for SASE.
Nonfiction: Historical, medical, how-to, humor, informational, personal experience, photo feature, technical; must be cat oriented. **Buys 5-7 mss/issue.** *Query first with published clips.* Length: 500-3,000 words. **Pays $35-400; special rates for photo/story packages.**
Photos: Photos purchased with or without accompanying ms. Pays $50 minimum for color prints; $50-200 for 35mm or 2¼×2¼ color transparencies; occasionally pays more for particularly outstanding or unusual work. Photo guidelines for SASE; then send prints and transparencies. Model release required.
Columns/Departments: Cat Newsline (news of national interest to cat lovers), 1,000 words maximum; Kids for Cats (short stories, how-to, crafts, puzzles for 10-16 year olds); Feline Friends (once or twice/year, readers' special cats).
Poetry: Short, cat-related poems. Submit any number but always with SASE.
Fiction: Not reviewing fiction at this time.
Fillers: Newsworthy or unusual; items with photos. Query first. Buys 5/year. Length: 500-1,000 words. Pays $35-100.
Tips: "Most of the articles we receive are profiles of the writers' own cats or profiles of cats that have recently died.

We reject almost all of these stories. What we need are well-researched articles that will give our readers the information they need to better care for their cats or to help them fully enjoy cats. Please review past issues and notice the informative nature of articles before querying us with an idea. *Please query first.*"

$ $ CATS MAGAZINE, P.O. Box 1790, Peoria IL 61656. (309)682-6626. Fax: (309)679-5454. E-mail: editor@catsmag.com. Website: http://www.catsmag.com. **Contact:** Annette Bailey, editor. **80% freelance written.** Monthly magazine for owners and lovers of cats. Estab. 1945. Circ. 127,000. **Pays on acceptance.** Byline given. Buys all rights. Editorial works 6 months in advance. Sample copy and writer's guidelines for $3 and 9×12 SAE.

Nonfiction: General interest (concerning cats); how-to (care, etc. for cats); health-related; personal experience; travel. Special issues: Nutrition (September 1998); Senior Cats (October 1998); Holidays (November 1998); Family (December 1998). Query with outline. Length 1,500-2,500 words. **Pays $50-500.**

Photos: State availability of photos with submissions. Reviews color slides, 2¼×2¼ transparencies. Identification of subjects required. Buys all rights.

Columns/Departments: Cat Tales (true and fictional cat-theme short stories), 250-1,000 words. **Pays $10-50.**

Tips: "Writer must show an affinity for cats. Extremely well-written, thoroughly researched, carefully thought out articles have the best chance of being accepted. Innovative topics or a new twist on an old subject are always welcomed."

N ★ $ CATS USA, Guide to Buying and Caring for Purebred Kittens, Fancy Publications, P.O. Box 6050, Mission Viejo CA 92690. (714)855-8822. Fax: (714)855-3045. **Contact:** Jane Calloway, editor. **90% freelance written.** "Annual magazine is aimed at first time purebred kitten buyers. It provides information about health care, nutrition and various cat breeds." Estab. 1993. Circ. 155,000. Pays on publication. Offers 50% kill fee. Buys first North American serial rights. Editorial lead time 6 months. Reports in 3 months on queries. Writer's guidelines free.

Nonfiction: Personal experience. **Buys 20 mss/year.** Query with published clips. Length: 500-2,500 words. **Pays $50 and up.** Sometimes pays the expenses of writers on assignment.

Photos: Send photos with submission. Reviews transparencies. Negotiates payment individually. Captions, model releases and identification of subjects required. Buys one-time rights.

Columns/Departmenst: Kids for Cats (for readers 10-16 years old, short stories, how-to pieces, word puzzles, quizzes and craft projects. Good-quality photographs are essential to craft projects. Query.

Poetry: Short, cat-related poems, used primarily as filler in the back of the magazine. "Straightforward poems that capture the essence of the cat or of what owning a cat means to our readers. We rarely go for esoteric poems with deep hidden meanings."

Tips: "Send well-written, well-researched queries. Read the magazine!"

N $ CATSUMER REPORT, Consumer Magazine for Cat Owners, Good Communications, P.O. Box 10069, Austin TX 78766-1069. (512)454-6090. Fax: (512)454-3420. E-mail: gooddogmag@aol.com. Website: http://www.prodogs.com/dmn/gooddog. Publisher: Ross Becker. **Contact**: Judi Becker, editor/managing editor. **90% freelance written.** Bimonthly magazine for consumers/laypeople. "*CATsumer Report* is fun, easy, conversational read, but the reader should also learn while enjoying the publication." Estab. 1994. Pays on publication. Byline given. Kill fee varies. Buys first North American serial rights. Editorial lead time 4 months. Submit seasonal material 4 months in advance. Accepts simultaneous submissions. Sample copy and writer's guidelines free.

Nonfiction: General interest, humor, interview/profile, new product, opinion, personal experience. No fiction or poetry. **Buys 30 mss/year.** Send complete ms. Length: 700-1,200 words. Rates negotiable.

Tips: "E-mail me a cover letter and include the manuscript (as an e-mail message, not an attached file). It's faster."

★ $ $ THE CHRONICLE OF THE HORSE, P.O. Box 46, Middleburg VA 20118. (540)687-6341. Fax: (540)687-3937. Website: http://www.chronofhorse.com. Editor: John Strassburger. Managing Editor: Nancy Comer. **Contact:** Beth Rasin, assistant editor. **80% freelance written.** Weekly magazine about horses. "We cover English riding sports, including horse showing, grand prix jumping competitions, steeplechase racing, foxhunting, dressage, endurance riding, handicapped riding and combined training. We are the official publication for the national governing bodies of many of the above sports. We feature news, how-to articles on equitation and horse care and interviews with leaders in the various fields." Estab. 1937. Circ. 22,000. **Pays for features on acceptance**; news and other items on publication. Publishes ms an average of 4 months after acceptance. Byline given. Buys first North American rights and makes work-for-hire assignments. Submit seasonal material 3 months in advance. Reports in 6 weeks. Sample copy for $2 and 9×12 SAE. Writer's guidelines for #10 SASE.

Nonfiction: General interest; historical/nostalgic (history of breeds, use of horses in other countries and times, art, etc.); how-to (trailer, train, design a course, save money, etc.); humor (centered on living with horses or horse people); interview/profile (of nationally known horsemen or the very unusual); technical (horse care, articles on feeding, injuries, care of foals, shoeing, etc.). Length: 6-7 pages. **Pays $125-200.** News of major competitions, "clear assignment with us first." Length: 1,500 words. **Pays $100-150.** Small local competitions, 800 words. **Pays $50-75.** Special issues: Steeplechase Racing (January); American Horse in Sport and Grand Prix Jumping (February); Horse Show (March); Intercollegiate (April); Kentucky 4-Star Preview (April); Junior and Pony (April); Combined Training (May); Dressage (June); Hunt Roster (September); Vaulting and Handicapped (November); Stallion (December). No Q&A interviews, clinic reports, Western riding articles, personal experience or wild horses. **Buys 300 mss/year.** Query or send complete ms. Length: 300-1,225 words. **Pays $25-200.**

Photos: State availability of photos. Accepts prints or color slides. Accepts color for b&w reproduction. Pays $25-30.

Identification of subjects required. Buys one-time rights.
Columns/Departments: Dressage, Combined Training, Horse Show, Horse Care, Racing over Fences, Young Entry (about young riders, geared for youth), Horses and Humanities, Hunting. Query or send complete ms. Length: 300-1,225 words. **Pays $25-200.**
Poetry: Light verse, traditional. No free verse. **Buys 30/year.** Length: 5-25 lines. **Pays $15.**
Fillers: Anecdotes, short humor, newsbreaks, cartoons. **Buys 300/year.** Length: 50-175 lines. **Pays $10-20.**
Tips: "Get our guidelines. Our readers are sophisticated, competitive horsemen. Articles need to go beyond common knowledge. Freelancers often attempt too broad or too basic a subject. We welcome well-written news stories on major events, but clear the assignment with us."

$ $ DOG FANCY, Fancy Publications, Inc., P.O. Box 6050, Mission Viejo CA 92690-6050. (714)855-8822. Fax: (714)855-3045. E-mail: HRizzo@fancypubs.com. Website: http://www.dogfancy.com. Editor: Betty Liddick. **Contact:** Holly Ocasio Rizzo, associate editor. **95% freelance written.** Monthly magazine for men and women of all ages interested in all phases of dog ownership. Estab. 1970. Circ. 286,000. Pays on publication. Publishes ms an average of 6 months after acceptance. Byline given. Buys first North American serial and electronic rights. Submit seasonal material 6 months in advance. Accepts simultaneous submissions. Reports in 2 months. Writer's guidelines for #10 SASE.
Nonfiction: Essays, general interest, how-to, humor, informational, inspirational, interview/profile, personal experience, photo feature, travel. **Buys 100 mss/year.** Query. Length: 350-1,200 words. **Pays $50-500.**
Photos: Send photos with submission. Reviews transparencies. Offers no additional payment for photos accepted with ms. Model release, identification of subjects required. Buys one-time and electronic rights.
Columns/Departments: Dogs on the Go (travel with dogs), 800 words; Dogs That Make a Difference (heroic dogs), 800 words. **Buys 24 mss/year.** Query. **Pays $150-350.**
Fiction: Occasionally publishes novel excerpts.
Tips: "We're looking for the unique experience that enhances the dog/owner relationship—with the dog as the focus of the story, not the owner. Medical articles are assigned to veterinarians. Note that we write for a lay audience (non-technical), but we do assume a certain level of intelligence."

N $ $ DOG MAGAZINE, Dogs International, P.O. Box 2270, Alpine CA 91903. (619)390-2424. (800)364-3282. Fax: (619)390-2425. E-mail: dogmag@juno.com. **Contact:** Vicki Lynn Samson, senior editor. **80% freelance written.** Bimonthly magazine covering "dogs (all aspects) and the people who love them. Our magazine's slogan is for every dog, for every dog lover. Readers range from those living with their first dog to professional trainers and fanciers." Estab. 1995. Circ. 40,000. Pays on publication. Publishes ms an average of 9 months after acceptance. Byline given. Buys first North American serial rights. Editorial lead time 1 year. Submit seasonal material 1 year in advance. Reports in 6 months on mss; 3 months on queries. Sample copy and writer's guidelines free.
Nonfiction: Book excerpts, essays, exposé, general interest, historical/nostalgic, how-to (training; outings with your dog), humor, interview/profile, opinion, personal experience, photo feature, travel (only destinations that welcome dogs), canine health/medical. **Buys 50 mss/year.** Send complete ms. Length: 600-1,800 words. **Pays 10-25¢/word.**
Reprints: Occasionally accepts previously published sumbissions. Send tearsheet of article or short story and information about when and where the article previously appeared.
Photos: Send photos with submission. Reviews contact sheets and any size prints. Negotiates payment individually. Model releases and identification of subjects required. Buys one-time rights.
Columns/Departments: Waggin' Tales (humor), 500 words; Reviews—books, videos, film (all aspects of dogs—health, training, "feel good" pieces), 500-600 words. **Buys 20-30 mss/year.** Send complete ms. **Pays 10¢/word.**
Fiction: Humorous, slice-of-life vignettes. **Buys 3 mss/year.** Send complete ms. Length: 600-1,200 words. **Pays 10¢/word.** Publishes novel excerpts.
Poetry: Avant-garde, free verse, haiku, light verse, traditional. **Buys 12 poems/year.** Submit 5 poems max. **Pays subscription-10¢/word.**
Fillers: Anecdotes, facts, gags to be illustrated by cartoonist, newsbreaks, short humor. "We solicit, but do not pay for, fillers. We publish 25-30 a year."
Tips: "Following specific instructions is always appreciated (e.g., including word count, double-spacing ms), as is awareness of the range of our audience."

N $ $ DOG WORLD, The World's Largest All-Breed Dog Magazine, Primedia Special Interest Publications, 29 N. Wacker Dr., Chicago IL 60606. (312)609-4340. Fax: (312)236-2413. E-mail: dogworld3@aol.com. Website: http://www.dogworldmag.com. **Contact:** Donna Marcel, editor. Sarah McCollum, associate editor. **70% freelance written.** Monthly magazine covering dogs. "We write for the serious dog enthusiasts, breeders, veterinarians, groomers, etc., as well as a general audience interested in in-depth information about dogs." Estab. 1915. Circ. 68,000. **Pays on acceptance.** Byline given. Editorial lead time 10 weeks. Submit seasonal material 4 months in advance. Accepts simultaneous submissions. Reports in 4-6 months. Writer's guidelines free.
Nonfiction: General interest on dogs including health care, veterinary medical research, grooming, legislation, responsible ownership, show awards, obedience training, show schedules, Junior Showmanship, kennel operations, dog sports, breed spotlights and histories, how-to, interview/profile, new products, personal experience, travel. No fluffy poems or pieces about dogs. Special issues: July (rare breed); February (puppy). **Buys approximately 80 mss/year.** Query with SASE. Pay negotiated on individual basis. Sometimes pays the expenses of writers on assignment.
Reprints: Rarely publishes reprints. Send tearsheet of article, typed ms with rights for sale noted, and information

about when and where the article previously appeared. Payment negotiated on individual basis.
Photos: State availability of photos with submission. Offers no additional payment for photos accepted with ms; occasionally negotiates payment individually for professional photos. Current rate for a cover photo is $300; inside color photo $50-100; b&w $25-50, depending on size used. Payment on publication. Buys one-time rights.
Tips: "Get a copy of editorial calendar, stay away from 'fluffy' pieces—we run very few. Be able to translate technical/medical articles into what average readers can understand. Mention accompanying art—very important."

$ DOGGONE, The Newsletter About Fun Places to Go And Cool Stuff to Do With Your Dog, P.O. Box 651155, Vero Beach FL 32965-1155. Fax: (561)569-8434. E-mail: doggonenl@aol.com. **Contact:** Wendy Ballard, publisher. "*DogGone* is a bimonthly travel and activity newsletter for dog owners. All destination pieces are written with a dog slant, including lodgings that accept pets, dog-allowed tourist attractions, parks, hiking trails, walking tours, even restaurants with outdoor seating that don't mind a pooch on the porch." Estab. 1993. Circ. 3,000. Pays on publication. Publishes ms an average of 4 months after acceptance. Buys first rights and electronic rights. Editorial lead time 4 months. Submit seasonal material 4 months in advance. Reports in 1 month. Sample copy for 9×12 SASE and 3 first-class stamps. Writer's guidelines for #10 SASE.
Nonfiction: Exposé, historical, how-to, personal experience, travel. "No poetry or 'My dog is the best because . . .' articles." Query with published clips or send complete ms. Length: 300-1,000 words. **Pays $34-100.** Writers may opt to accept subscription to *DogGone* as partial payment.
Reprints: Send photocopy of article and information about when and were it previously appeared. **Pays $34-100.**
Photos: Send photos with submission. Reviews prints or slides. Offers no additional payment for photos accepted with ms. Captions required. Buys rights with ms.
Columns/Departments: Beyond Fetch (creative activities to enjoy with dogs), 300-900 words; Parks Department (dogs-allowed national, state, regional parks), 300 words; Visiting Vet (travel-related), 300 words; Touring (walking or driving tours with pets-allowed stops), 600-900 words. Query with published clips or send complete ms. **Pays $34-100.**
Fillers: Facts, dogs-allowed events. Length: 50-200 words. **Pays $15.**

N $ $ DRESSAGE & CT, Cowles Enthusiast Media/Primedia, P.O. Box 530, Unionville PA 19375. (610)380-8977. Fax: (610)380-8304. E-mail: dressagect@aol.com. Website: http://www.esquiresource.com/Dressage_CT/. **Contact:** Jennifer O. Bryant. **20% freelance written**. Monthly magazine. "*Dressage & CT* is the official publication of the United States Dressage Federation. All content must be specific to the sport of dressage and/or combined training, with relevance to the North American enthusiast." Estab. 1971. Circ. 40,000. **Pays on acceptance**. Publishes ms 3 months after acceptance. Byline given. Offers 40% kill fee. Buys first North American serial rights or all rights. Editorial lead time 3 months. Submit seasonal material 6 months in advance. Reports in 1 month on queries; 2 months on mss. Sample copy for $5. Writer's guidelines for #10 SASE.
Nonfiction: Book excerpts, how-to (training), interview/profile, photo feature. **Buys 36 mss/year**. Query with published clips. Length: 600-2,500 words. **Pays $100-500 for assigned articles; $75-300 for unsolicited articles**. Pays expenses of writers on assignment.
Photos: State availability of photos with submission. Reviews transparencies, prints. Offers $25-150/photo. Captions, model releases, identification of subjects required. Buys one-time rights.
Columns/Departments: For the Record (news/event coverage), 250 words; Salute (important figure in the sport), 650 words. **Buys 24 mss/year**. Query with published clips. **Pays $50-250**.

N ☆ $ DRESSAGE TODAY, Fleet Street Publishing, 656 Quince Orchard Rd., Suite 600, Gaithersburg MD 20878. (301)977-3900. Fax: (301)990-9015. E-mail: dtletters@aol.com. Editorial Director: Mary Kay Kinnish. **Contact:** Stacey Wigmore, assistant editor. **70% freelance written.** Monthly. "*Dressage Today* presents national and international news and developments associated with the art and sport of dressage. Expands reader's knowledge of this classical, universal equestrian discipline. Serves as a conscience for good of sport, horses and riders; provides a forum for discussion and debate with respect to the sport. Enhances self-awareness and self-improvement through articles that address mental, physical and emotional aspects of the sport." Estab. 1994. Circ. 36,000. **Pays on acceptance**. Publishes ms an average of 6 months after acceptance. Byline given. Buys first North American serial rights and makes work-for-hire assignments. Offers 25% kill fee. Editorial lead time 3 months. Submit seasonal material 6 months in advance. Reports in 2 months. Sample copy free. Writer's guidelines for #10 SASE.
Nonfiction: Book excerpts, general interest, historical/nostalgic, how-to (dressage training for horse and/or rider, equine management), humor, interview/profile, opinion, personal experience, product reviews, technical. **Buys 36 mss/year.** Query or query with published clips. Length: 500-3,000 words. **Pays $150-300 for assigned articles, $100 maximum for unsolicited articles.** Sometimes pays expenses of writers on assignment.
Reprints: Sometimes accepts previously published submissions. Send photocopy of article or typed ms with rights for sale noted and information about when and where the article previously appeared. Negotiates payment individually.
Photos: State availability of photos with submission or send photos with submission. Reviews transparencies and 4×6 or 3×5 prints). Negotiates payment individually. Captions and identification of subjects required. Buys one-time rights.
Columns/Departments: The Arena (short, newsworthy items), 200-400 words; Reader to Reader (question, dilemma or practical solution posed and answered by readers), 600-1,200 words; Book/video reviews, 500 words. **Buys 12-24 mss/year.** Query. **Pays $25-50.**
Fiction: Humorous, slice-of-life vignettes. For example, "800-word articles that epitomize the relationship with dressage horses." No articles about horses dying. Query. Length: 650-1,000 words. **Pays $50 maximum.**

Tips: "Send résumé with relevant clips. Call on phone. Be willing to start out with a smaller piece."

N $ $ THE GAITED HORSE, The One Magazine for all Gaited Horses, 4 Cadence L.L.C., 8008 Elk-to-Hwy Rd., P.O. Box 259, Elk WA 99009. (509)292-2699. Fax: (509)292-8330. E-mail: editor hegaitedhorse.com. Website: http://www.thegaitedhorse.com. **Contact:** Rhonda Hart, editor. Quarterly magazine. "Subject matter must relate in some way to gaited horses." Estab. 1998. Circ. 5,000. Pays on publication. Publishes ms an average of 2 months after acceptance. Byline given. Buys first North American serial rights or makes work-for-hire assignments. Editorial lead time 4 months. Submit seasonal material 4 months in advance. Accepts simultaneous submissions. Reports in 6 weeks on queries; 1 month on mss. Sample copy for $3; writer's guidelines free.
Nonfiction: Book excerpts, essays, exposé, general interest (gaited horses), historical/nostalgic, how-to, humor, interview/profile, new product, personal experience, photo experience, photo features, travel, anything related to gaited horses, lifestyles, art, etc. "No 'My first horse' stories." **Buys 25 mss/year.** Query and/or send complete ms. Length: 1,000-2,500 words. **Pays $50-300.**
Photos: State availability of photos with submission or send photos with submission. Reviews prints (3×5 or larger). Negotiates payment individually. Captions, model releases and identification of subjects required. Buys one-time rights.
Columns/Departments: Through the Legal Paces (equine owners rights & responsibilities; Horse Cents (financial advice for horse owners); Vet Check (vet advice); Smoother Trails (trail riding); all 500-1,000 words. **Buys 24 mss/year.** Query. **Pays $100.**
Fillers: Anecdotes, newsbreaks, short humor. **Buys 20/year.** Length: 5-300 words. **Pays $10-50.**
Tips: "We are actively seeking to develop writers from within the various gaited breeds and equine disciplines. If you have a unique perspective on these horses, we would love to hear from you."

N $ GOOD DOG!, Consumer Magazine for Dog Owners, P.O. Box 10069, Austin TX 78766-1069. (512)454-6090. Fax: (512)454-3420. E-mail: gooddogmag@aol.com. Website: http://www.prodogs.com/dmn/gooddog. Publisher: Ross Becker. **Contact**: Judi Becker, editor/managing editor. **90% freelance written.** Bimonthly magazine for consumers/laypeople. "*Good Dog!* is a fun, easy, conversational read but the reader should also learn while enjoying the publication." Estab. 1988. Pays on publication. Byline given. Buys first North American serial rights. Editorial lead time 4 months. Submit seasonal material 4 months in advance. Accepts simultaneous submissions. Sample copy and writer's guidelines free.
Nonfiction: General interest, humor, interview/profile, new product, opinion, personal experience. No fiction or poetry. **Buys 30 mss/year.** Send complete ms. Length: 700-1,200 words. Rates negotiable.
Photos: Send photos with submission. Reviews 4×6 or larger prints. Negotiates payment individually. Identification of subjects required with label of photo owner/address.
Tips: "E-mail a cover letter and manuscript (as an e-mail message not an attached file). It's faster this way."

$ THE GREYHOUND REVIEW, P.O. Box 543, Abilene KS 67410-0543. (785)263-4660. Fax: (785)263-4689. E-mail: nga@jc.net. Website: http://www.nga.jc.net. Editor: Gary Guccione. **Contact:** Tim Horan, managing editor. **20% freelance written.** Monthly magazine covering greyhound breeding, training and racing. Estab. 1911. Circ. 4,000. **Pays on acceptance.** Byline given. Buys first rights. Submit seasonal material 2 months in advance. Reports in 2 weeks on queries; 1 month on mss. Sample copy for $3. Writer's guidelines free.
Nonfiction: How-to, interview/profile, personal experience. "Articles must be targeted at the greyhound industry: from hard news, special events at racetracks to the latest medical discoveries. Do not submit gambling systems." **Buys 24 mss/year.** Query. Length: 1,000-10,000 words. **Pays $85-150.** Sometimes pays the expenses of writers on assignment.
Reprints: Send photocopy of article. Pays 100% of the amount paid for an original article.
Photos: State availability of photos with submission. Reviews 35mm transparencies and 8×10 prints. Offers $10-50/photo. Identification of subjects required. Buys one-time rights.

$ $ THE HORSE, Your Guide To Equine Health Care, P.O. Box 4680, Lexington KY 40544-4680. (606)276-6771. Fax: (606)276-4450. E-mail: kherbert@thehorse.com. Website: http://www.thehorse.com. **Contact:** Kimberly S. Herbert, editor. **75% freelance written.** Monthly magazine covering equine health and care. *The Horse* is "an educational/news magazine geared toward the professional, hands-on horse owner." Estab. 1983. Circ. 36,000. Pays on publication. Publishes ms an average of 2 months after acceptance. Byline given. Reports in 2 months on queries. Sample copy for $2.95. Writer's guidelines free.
Nonfiction: How-to, technical, topical interviews. "No first-person experiences not from professionals; this is a technical magazine to inform horse owners." **Buys 90 mss/year.** Query with published clips. Length: 500-5,000 words. **Pays $75-650.**
Photos: Send photos with submission. Reviews transparencies. Offers $10-150/photo. Captions and identification of subjects required. Buys one-time rights.
Columns/Departments: Up Front (news on horse health), 100-500 words; Equinomics (economics of horse ownership), 2,500 words. **Buys 40 mss/year.** Query with published clips. **Pays $50-350.**
Tips: "We publish reliable horse health information from top industry professionals from around the world. Manuscript must be submitted electronically or on disk."

$ $ HORSE ILLUSTRATED, The Magazine for Responsible Horse Owners, Fancy Publications, Inc., P.O. Box 6050, Mission Viejo CA 92690-6050. (714)855-8822. Fax: (714)855-3045. E-mail: joltmann@fancypubs.com.

Website: http://www.horseillustrated.com. Contact: Jennifer Oltman, associate editor. **90% freelance written.** Prefers to work with published/established writers but will work with new/unpublished writers. Monthly magazine covering all aspects of horse ownership. "Our readers are adults, mostly women, between the ages of 18 and 40; stories should be geared to that age group and reflect responsible horse care." Estab. 1976. Circ. 190,000. Pays on publication. Publishes ms an average of 8 months after acceptance. Byline given. Buys one-time rights; requires first North American rights among equine publications. Submit seasonal material 6 months in advance. Reports in 3 months. Sample copy for $3.50. Writer's guidelines for #10 SASE.

Nonfiction: How-to (horse care, training, veterinary care), photo feature. No "little girl" horse stories, "cowboy and Indian" stories or anything not *directly* relating to horses. "We are looking for longer, more authoritative, in-depth features on trends and issues in the horse industry. Such articles must be queried first with a detailed outline of the article and clips. We rarely have a need for fiction." **Buys 20 mss/year.** Query or send complete ms. Length: 1,000-2,000 words. **Pays $100-300 for assigned articles; $50-300 for unsolicited articles.**

Photos: Send photos with submission. Reviews 35mm transparencies, medium format transparencies and 5×7 prints.

Tips: "Freelancers can break in at this publication with feature articles on Western and English training methods; veterinary and general care how-to articles; and horse sports articles. We rarely use personal experience articles. Submit photos with training and how-to articles whenever possible. We have a very good record of developing new freelancers into regular contributors/columnists. We are always looking for fresh talent, but certainly enjoy working with established writers who 'know the ropes' as well. We are accepting less freelance work—much is now assigned and contracted."

$ $ I LOVE CATS, I Love Cats Publishing, 450 Seventh Ave., Suite 1701, New York NY 10123. (212)244-2351. Fax: (212)244-2367. E-mail: yankee@dancom.com. Editor: Lisa Allmendinger. **85% freelance written.** Bimonthly magazine covering cats. "*I Love Cats* is a general interest cat magazine for the entire family. It caters to cat lovers of all ages. The stories in the magazine include fiction, nonfiction, how-to, humorous and columns for the cat lover." Estab. 1989. Circ. 200,000. Pays on publication. Publishes ms an average of 2 years after acceptance. Byline given. No kill fee. Buys all rights. Must sign copyright consent form. Submit seasonal material 9 months in advance. Reports in 2 months. Sample copy for $4. Writer's guidelines for #10 SASE.

Nonfiction: Essays, how-to, humor, inspirational, interview/profile, opinion, personal experience, photo feature. No poetry. **Buys 200 mss/year.** Send complete ms. Length: 100-1,000 words. **Pays $40-250, contributor copies or other premiums "if requested."** Sometimes pays expenses of writers on assignment.

Photos: Send photos with submission. Offers no additional payment for photos accepted with ms. Identification of subjects required. Buys all rights.

Fiction: Adventure, fantasy, historical, humorous, mainstream, mystery, novel excerpts, slice-of-life vignettes, suspense. "This is a family magazine. No graphic violence, pornography or other inappropriate material. *I Love Cats* is strictly 'G-rated.' " **Buys 50 mss/year.** Send complete ms. Length: 500-1,200 words. **Pays $40-250.**

Fillers: Quizzes and short humor. **Buys 20/year. Pays $10-35.**

Tips: "Please keep stories short and concise. Send complete ms with photos, if possible. I buy lots of first-time authors. Nonfiction pieces w/color photos are always in short supply. With the exception of the standing columns, the rest of the magazine is open to freelancers. Be witty, humorous or take a different approach to writing."

N $ $ MUSHING, Stellar Communications, Inc., P.O. Box 149, Ester AK 99725-0149. (907)479-0454. Fax: (907)479-3137. E-mail: editor@mushing.com. Website: http://www.mushing.com. Publisher: Todd Hoener. **Contact**: Diane Herrmann, managing editor. Bimonthly magazine on "all aspects of the growing sports of dogsledding, skijoring, carting, dog packing and weight pulling. *Mushing* promotes responsible dog care through feature articles and updates on working animal health care, safety, nutrition and training." Estab. 1987. Circ. 7,000. Pays on publication. Publishes ms an average of 4 months after acceptance. Byline given. Buys first serial and second serial (reprint) rights. Submit seasonal material 4 months in advance. Reports in 8 months. Sample copy for $5. Writer's guidelines free. Call or e-mail for information.

Nonfiction: Historical, how-to, humor, interview/profile, new product, personal experience, photo feature, technical, innovations, travel. "We consider articles on canine health and nutrition, sled dog behavior and training, musher profiles and interviews, equipment how-to's, trail tips, expedition and race accounts, innovations, sled dog history, current issues, personal experiences and humor." Themes: Iditarod and long-distance racing (January/February); Expeditions (March/April); health and nutrition (May/June); musher and dog profiles, summer activities (July/August); equipment, fall training (September/October); races and places (November/December). Query with or without published clips, or send complete ms and SASE. Length: 1,000-2,500 words. **Pays $50-250 for articles.** Payment depends on length, quality, deadlines, experience. Pays expenses of writers on assignment, if prearranged.

Photos: Send photos with submission. Reviews contact sheets, transparencies, prints. Prefers 8×10 glossy prints or negatives for b&w. Offers $20-165/photo. Captions, model releases, identification of subjects required. Buys one-time and second reprint rights. We look for good b&w and quality color for covers and specials.

Columns/Departments: Query with or without published clips and SASE or send complete ms with SASE. Length: 500-1,000 words.

Fiction: Considers well-written and relevant or timely fiction. Query or send complete ms with SASE. Pay varies.

Fillers: Anecdotes, facts, cartoons, newsbreaks, short humor, puzzles. Length: 100-250 words. **Pays $20-35.**

Tips: "Read our magazine. Know something about dog-driven, dog-powered sports."

[N] $ $ **PAINT HORSE JOURNAL**, American Paint Horse Association, P.O. Box 961023, Fort Worth TX 76161-0023. (817)439-3400, ext. 210. Fax: (817)439-3484. E-mail: dstreeter@apha.com. Website: http://www.apha.com. **Contact:** Dan Streeter, senior copy editor. **10% freelance written.** Works with a small number of new/unpublished writers each year. Monthly magazine for people who raise, breed and show Paint horses. Estab. 1966. Circ. 30,000. **Pays on acceptance.** Publishes ms an average of 3 months after acceptance. Buys first North American serial rights plus reprint rights occasionally. Pays negotiable kill fee. Byline given. Phone queries OK, but prefers written query. Submit seasonal material 3 months in advance. Reports in 1 month. Writers guidelines available upon request. Sample copy $4.

Nonfiction: General interest (personality pieces on well-known owners of Paints); historical (Paint horses in the past—particular horses and the breed in general); how-to (train and show horses); photo feature (Paint horses). Now seeking informative well-written articles on recreational riding. **Buys 4-5 mss/issue.** Send complete ms. Length: 1,000-2,000 words. **Pays $35-450.**

Reprints: Accepts previously published articles. Send typed ms with rights for sale noted and information about when and where the article previously appeared. For reprints, pays 30-50% of the amount paid for an original article.

Photos: Send photos with ms. Offers no additional payment for photos accepted with accompanying ms. Uses 3×5 or larger b&w or color glossy prints; 35mm or larger color transparencies. Captions required. Photos must illustrate article and must include Paint Horses.

Tips: "*PHJ* needs breeder-trainer articles, Paint horse marketing and timely articles from areas throughout the US and Canada. We are looking for more recreational and how-to articles. We are beginning to cover equine activity such as trail riding, orienteering and other outdoor events. Photos with copy are almost always essential. Well-written first person articles are welcomed. Submit items that show a definite understanding of the horse business. Be sure you understand precisely what a Paint horse is as defined by the American Paint Horse Association. Use proper equine terminology and proper grounding in ability to communicate thoughts."

$ $ **PETS MAGAZINE**, Moorshead Publications, Ltd., 10 Gateway Blvd., Suite 490, North York, Ontario M3C 3T4 Canada. (416)969-5488. Fax: (416)696-7395. E-mail: pets@moorshead.com. **Contact:** Edward Zapletal, editor. **40% freelance written.** Bimonthly magazine for "pet owners, primarily cat and dog owners, but we also cover rabbits, guinea pigs, hamsters, gerbils, birds and fish. Issues covered include: pet health care, nutrition, general interest, grooming, training humor, human-animal bond stories. No fiction! No poetry!" Estab. 1983. Circ. 51,000. Pays within 30 days of publication. Publishes ms an average of 2 months after acceptance. Byline given. Offers 50% kill fee. Buys first North American serial rights or other negotiable rights. Editorial lead time 3 months. Submit seasonal material 2 months in advance. Sample copy for #10 SAE with IRCs. Writer's guidelines for 9½×4 SAE with IRCs.

Nonfiction: General interest, humor, new product, personal experience, veterinary medicine, human interest (i.e., working animal), training and obedience. No fiction. **Buys 10 mss/year.** Query. Length: 500-1,500 words. **Pays 12-18¢/word (Canadian funds).**

Reprints: Considers reprints of previously published submissions. **Pays 6-9¢/word.**

Photos: Prefers good color pictures or slides. Reviews photocopies. Identification of subjects required. Buys one-time rights.

Columns/Departments: Grooming Your Pet (mostly dogs and cats), 300-400 words. **Buys 6-12 mss/year.** Query.

Fillers: Facts. **Buys 5/year.** Length: 20-100 words. **Pays $10-20.**

Tips: "Always approach with a query letter first. E-mail is good if you've got it. We'll contact you if we like what we see. I like writing to be friendly, informative, well-balanced with pros and cons. Remember, we're catering to pet owners, and they are a discriminating audience."

[N] $ $ **THE POINTING DOG JOURNAL**, Wildwood Press, P.O. Box 38, Adel IA 50003. E-mail: wpdogs@aol.com. **Contact**: Dave Meisner, editor/publisher. Managing Editor: Steve Smith. **65% freelance written.** "Our journal emphasizes the time-honored tradition of hunting with dogs and concentrates exclusively on the pointing breeds. We strive to give our readers informative features and columns, nostalgia, and humor, all written by talented and knowledgeable outdoor writers." Estab. 1993. Circ. 29,000. **Pays on acceptance**. Publishes ms an average of 8-12 months after acceptance. Byline given. Offers 33% kill fee. Buys first North American serial rights. Editorial lead time 1 year. Submit seasonal material 1 year in advance. Accepts simultaneous submissions. Reports in 6 weeks on queries; 3 months on mss. Sample copy for $6.50. Writer's guidelines for #10 SASE.

Nonfiction: Essays, general interest, how-to, humor, interview/profile, personal experience. **Buys 15-20 mss/year.** Query or send complete ms. Length: 1,500-2,200 words. **Pays $300-500 for assigned articles; $150-300 for unsolicited articles.** Sometimes pays expenses of writers on assignment.

Photos: State availability of photos with submission. Offers no additional payment for photos accepted with ms; negotiates payment individually for separate photos. Captions required. Buys one-time rights.

Fiction: Humorous, slice-of-life vignettes. No dead dog stories or stories from the dog's point of view. **Buys 6-8 mss/year.** Send complete ms. Length: 1,500-2,200 words. **Pays $300-400.**

Fillers: Newsbreaks, short humor. **Buys 1-3/year.** Length: 700-1,500 words. **Pays $125-300.**

Tips: "Feature stories of 1,800-2,800 words should focus on the use of pointing dogs in hunting, training techniques, trialing, and canine medicine. We especially need well-written nostalgia, humor, and features dealing with the traditions of hunting with pointing dogs. Features on shotguns and shotgunning, wildlife species, and conservation topics are also in demand, as are profiles of notable dogs, kennels, and trainers. There is an ongoing need for shorter featurettes and short filler pieces, such as training tips, vet tips, humor, dog-related news, product reviews, quotable quotes, and book reviews. These should be 150-1,000 words."

$ $ THE QUARTER HORSE JOURNAL, P.O. Box 32470, Amarillo TX 79120. (806)376-4811. Fax: (806)376-8364. E-mail: aqhajrnl@arnet. Website: http://www.aqha.com. Senior Director of Publications: Jim Jennings. **Contact:** Christi Huffman, editor. **20% freelance written.** Prefers to work with published/established writers. Monthly official publication of the American Quarter Horse Association. Estab. 1948. Circ. 75,000. **Pays on acceptance.** Publishes ms an average of 6 months after acceptance. Buys first North American serial rights. Submit seasonal material 6 months in advance. Reports in 2 months. Sample copy and writer's guidelines free.

Nonfiction: How-to (fitting, grooming, showing, or anything that relates to owning, showing, or breeding); informational (educational clinics, current news); interview (feature-type stories—must be about established horses or people who have made a contribution to the business); personal opinion; and technical (equine updates, new surgery procedures, etc.). **Buys 20 mss/year.** Length: 800-1,800 words. **Pays $150-300.**

Photos: Purchased with accompanying ms. Captions required. Send prints or transparencies. Uses 4×6 color glossy prints, 2¼×2¼, 4×5 or 35mm color transparencies. No additional pay for photos accepted with accompanying ms.

Tips: "Writers must have a knowledge of the horse business."

N ✪ $ $ REPTILE HOBBYIST, T.F.H. Publications, 211 W. Sylvania Ave., Neptune NJ 07753. (732)988-8400, ext. 235. E-mail: rephob@aol.com. **Contact:** Jerry G. Walls, editor. Managing Editor: Neal Pronek. **100% freelance written.** "Colorful, varied monthly covering reptiles and amphibians as pets aimed at beginning to intermediate hobbyists. Pet shop distribution. Writers must know their material, including scientific names, identification, general terrarium maintenance." Estab. 1995. Circ. 30,000. Pays 60 days after acceptance. Publishes ms 6 months after acceptance. Byline given. Buys all rights. Editorial lead time 2 months. Reports in 1 month on queries; 2 months on mss. Sample copy for $4.50. Writer's guidelines free.

Nonfiction: General interest, interview/profile, personal experience, photo feature, technical, travel. "No gushy iguana articles or macho snake experiences." **Buys 120 mss/year.** Query. Length: 1,500-2,000 words. **Pays $100-120.**

Photos: Send photos with submission. Reviews transparencies and prints. Offers $20/photo. Captions, model releases and identification of subjects required. Buys all rights.

Columns/Departments: Herp People (profiles herp-related personalities); In Review (book reviews); Invertebrate Corner (terrarium invertebrates), all 1,500 words. **Buys 45 mss/year.** Query. **Pays $75-100.**

Tips: "Talk to the editor before sending anything. A short telephone conversation tells more about knowledge of subject matter than a simple query. I'll read anything, but it is very easy to detect an uninformed author. Very willing to polish articles from new writers."

N $ $ THE RETRIEVER JOURNAL, Wildwood Press, P.O. Box 968, Traverse City MI 49685. E-mail: wpdogs@aol.com. Associate Editor: Bob Butz. **Contact:** Steve Smith, editor. **65% freelance written,** Bimonthly magazine covering retriever training and hunting with retrievers. "*The Retriever Journal* is geared to the retriever owner who hunts all game—upland and waterfowl—with a retriever. We cover major field trials and tests. We use some well-written 'how-to' and 'where-to' in each issue." Estab. 1995. Circ. 18,000. Pays on publication. Publishes ms an average of 1 year after acceptance. Byline given. Offers 33% kill fee. Buys first North American serial rights. Editorial lead time 8 months. Submit seasonal material 8 months in advance. Accepts simultaneous submissions. Reports in 1 month on queries; 2 months on mss. Sample copy for $6.50. Writer's guidelines for #10 SASE.

Nonfiction: Essays, how-to, humor, personal experience, photo feature. Feature stories should focus on the use of retrieving breeds in hunting, training techniques, trialing, and canine medicine. We especially need well-written nostalgia, humor, and features dealing with the traditions of hunting with retrievers. Features on shotguns and shotgunning, wildlife species, and conservation topics are also in demand, as are profiles of notable dogs, kennels, and trainers. "No 'dead dog' stories or stories from the animal's point of view." **Buys 10-20 mss/year.** Query or send complete ms. Length: 1,500-2,200 words. **Pays $300-500 for assigned articles; $250-400 for unsolicited articles.** Sometimes pays expenses of writers on assignment.

Photos: State availability of photos with submission. Reviews transparencies. Offers no additional payment for photos accepted with ms. Buys one-time rights.

Fiction: Humorous, slice-of-life vignettes. "Fiction is acceptable, but it must have the dog at the forefront of the story." **Buys 4-6 mss/year.** Send complete ms.

Fillers: Anecdotes, short humor. "There is an ongoing need for shorter featurettes and short filler pieces, such as training tips, vet tips, humor, dog-related news, product reviews, quotable quotes, and book reviews. These should be 150-1,000 words." **Buys 6-8/year.** Length: 700-1,500 words. **Pays $150-300.**

Tips: "Be familiar with past issues of *The Retriever Journal*. Since we only publish 6 times a year, submitting 'new' and 'fresh' material is important—don't send us a story similar to something we ran a year ago."

✪ $ $ TROPICAL FISH HOBBYIST MAGAZINE, "The World's Most Widely Read Aquarium Monthly," TFH Publications, Inc., One TFH Plaza, Neptune City NJ 07753. (732)988-8400. Fax: (732)988-9635. E-mail: editor@tfh.com. **Contact:** David E. Boruchowitz, editor. Managing Editor: Dominique DeVito. **90% freelance written.** Monthly magazine covering tropical fish. Estab. 1952. Circ. 50,000. **Pays on acceptance.** Byline given. Buys all rights. Editorial lead time 3 months. Submit seasonal material 6 months in advance. Reports immediately for electronic submissions, others much longer. Guidelines by e-mail to editor with subject line "submission guidelines."

Nonfiction: "We cover any aspect of aquarium science, aquaculture, and the tropical fish hobby. Our readership is diverse—from neophytes to mini reef specialists. We require well-researched, well-written, and factually accurate copy, preferably with photos." **Buys 100-150 mss/year.** Query. **Pays $100-250.**

Photos: State availability of photos with submission. Reviews 2×2 transparencies. Negotiates payment individually. Model releases and identification of subjects required. Buys multiple nonexclusive rights.
Tips: "With few exceptions all communication and submission must be electronic. We want factual, interesting, and relevant articles about the aquarium hobby written by people who are obviously knowledgeable. We publish an enormous variety of article types. Review several past issues to get an idea of the scope."

$ $ THE WESTERN HORSEMAN, World's Leading Horse Magazine Since 1936, Western Horseman, Inc., P.O. Box 7980, Colorado Springs CO 80933-7980. (719)633-5524. Fax: (719)633-1392. Website: http//www.westernhorseman.com. **Contact:** Pat Close, editor. **50% freelance written.** Works with a small number of new/unpublished writers each year. Monthly magazine for horse owners covering horse care and training. Estab. 1936. Circ. 220,000. **Pays on acceptance.** Publishes ms an average of 5 months after acceptance. Buys one-time and North American serial rights. Byline given. Submit seasonal material 6 months in advance. Reports in 3 weeks. Sample copy for $5. Writer's guidelines for #10 SASE.
Nonfiction: How-to (horse training, care of horses, tips, ranch/farm management, etc.), informational (on rodeos, ranch life, historical articles of the West emphasizing horses). **Buys 250 mss/year.** Query; no fax material. Length: 500-2,500 words. **Pays $35-500, "sometimes higher by special arrangement."**
Photos: Send photos with ms. Offers no additional payment for photos. Uses 5×7 or 8×10 b&w glossy prints and 35mm transparencies. Captions required.
Tips: "Submit clean copy, double spaced, with professional quality photos. Stay away from generalities. Writing style should show a deep interest in horses coupled with a wide knowledge of the subject."

ART & ARCHITECTURE

Listed here are publications about art, art history, specific art forms and architecture written for art patrons, architects, artists and art enthusiasts. Publications addressing the business and management side of the art industry are listed in the Art, Design and Collectibles category of the Trade section. Trade publications for architecture can be found in Building Interiors, and Construction and Contracting sections.

N $ $ THE AMERICAN ART JOURNAL, Kennedy Galleries, Inc., 730 Fifth Ave., New York NY 10019. (212)541-9600. Fax: (212)977-3833. **Contact:** Jayne A. Kuchna, editor-in-chief. Prefers to work with published/established writers; works with a small number of new/unpublished writers each year. "Annual scholarly magazine of American art history of the 17th, 18th, 19th and 20th centuries, including painting, sculpture, architecture, photography, cultural history, etc., for people with a serious interest in American art, and who are already knowledgeable about the subject. Readers are scholars, curators, collectors, students of American art, or persons with a strong interest in Americana." Circ. 2,000. **Pays on acceptance.** Publishes ms an average of 6 months after acceptance. Buys all rights, but will reassign rights to writer. Byline given. Reports in 2 months. Sample copy for $18.
Nonfiction: "All articles are about some phase or aspect of American art history. No how-to articles or reviews of exhibitions. No book reviews or opinion pieces. No human interest approaches to artists' lives. No articles written in a casual or "folksy" style. *Writing style must be formal and serious.*" **Buys 10-15 mss/year.** Submit complete ms "with good cover letter." No queries. Length: 2,500-8,000 words. **Pays $400-600.**
Photos: Purchased with accompanying ms. Captions required. Uses b&w only. Offers no additional payment for photos accepted with accompanying ms.
Tips: "Articles *must be* scholarly, thoroughly documented, well-researched, well-written and illustrated. Whenever possible, all manuscripts must be accompanied by b&w photographs, which have been integrated into the text by the use of numbers."

$ $ AMERICAN INDIAN ART MAGAZINE, American Indian Art, Inc., 7314 E. Osborn Dr., Scottsdale AZ 85251-6417. (602)994-5445. Fax: (602)945-9533. **Contact:** Roanne P. Goldfein, editor. **97% freelance written.** Works with many new/unpublished writers each year. Quarterly magazine covering Native American art, historic and contemporary, including new research on any aspect of Native American art north of the US/Mexico border. Estab. 1975. Circ. 30,000. Pays on publication. Publishes ms an average of 3 months after acceptance. Byline given. Buys one-time and first rights. Reports in 3 weeks on queries; 3 months on mss. Writer's guidelines for #10 SASE.
Nonfiction: New research on any aspect of Native American art. No previously published work or personal interviews with artists. **Buys 12-18 mss/year.** Query. Length: 1,000-2,500 words. **Pays $75-300.**
Tips: "The magazine is devoted to all aspects of Native American art. Some of our readers are knowledgeable about the field and some know very little. We seek articles that offer something to both groups. Articles reflecting original research are preferred to those summarizing previously published information."

N AMERICAN STYLE, The Art of Living Creatively, The Rosen Group, 3000 Chestnut Ave., Suite 304, Baltimore MD 21211. (410)889-3093. Fax: (410)243-7089. **Contact:** Hope Daniels, editor. **50% freelance written.** Quarterly magazine covering handmade American Crafts. Estab. 1994. Circ. 50,000. Pays on publication. Publishes ms an average of 6 months after acceptance. Byline given. Buys first North American serial rights. Editorial lead time 6-9 months.

Submit seasonal material 1 year in advance. Sample copy for $3. Writer's guidelines for #10 SASE.

● *American Style* is especially interested in travel articles on arts/resort destinations and profiles of contemporary craft collectors.

Nonfiction: Specialized arts/crafts interests. Query with published clips. Length: 300-2,500 words. **Pays $500-800.** Sometimes pays expenses of writers on assignment.

Photos: Send photos with submission. Reviews oversized transparencies and 35mm slides. Negotiates payment individually. Captions required.

Columns/Departments: Artist Profiles, Artful Dining, 700-1,000 words. Query with published clips. **Pays $300-500.**

Tips: "Contact editor about upcoming issues, article ideas. Concentrate on contemporary American craft art, such as ceramics, wood, fiber, glass, etc. No hobby crafts."

$ ART PAPERS, Atlanta Art Papers, Inc., P.O. Box 5748, Atlanta GA 31107. (404)588-1837. Fax: (404)588-1836. E-mail: mpittar@pd.org. **Contact:** Michael Pittari, editor. **75% freelance written**. Bimonthly magazine covering contemporary art and artists. "*Art Papers,* about regional and national contemporary art and artists, features a variety of perspectives on current art concerns. Each issue presents topical articles, interviews, reviews from across the US, and an extensive and informative artists' classified listings section. Our writers and the artists they cover represent the scope and diversity of the country's art scene." Estab. 1977. Circ. 5,000. Pays on publication. Publishes ms an average of 3 months after acceptance. Byline given. Buys all rights. Editorial lead time 2 months. Submit seasonal material 2 months in advance. Sample copy and writer's guidelines for $1.24 check.

Nonfiction: Feature articles and reviews. **Buys 240 mss/year. Pays $40-100, unsolicited articles are on spec.**

Photos: Send photos with submission. Reviews color slides, b&w prints. Offers no additional payment for photos accepted with ms. Identification of subjects required.

Columns/Departments: Postscripts and newsbriefs (current art concerns and news). **Buys 8-10 mss/year.** Query. **Pays $30.**

Tips: "Write for a copy of our writer's guidelines and request a sample copy of *Art Papers*. Interested writers should call Michael Pittari to discuss intents."

$ $ THE ARTIST'S MAGAZINE, F&W Publications, Inc., 1507 Dana Ave., Cincinnati OH 45207-1005. (513)531-2690, ext. 467. Fax: (513)531-2902. E-mail:TAMEDIT@aol.com. Editor: Sandra Carpenter. **Contact:** Jennifer King, associate editor. **80% freelance written.** Works with a small number of new/unpublished writers each year. Monthly magazine covering primarily two-dimensional art instruction for working artists. "Ours is a highly visual approach to teaching the serious amateur artist techniques that will help him improve his skills and market his work. The style should be crisp and immediately engaging." Circ. 250,000. Pays on publication. Publishes ms an average of 6 months after acceptance. Bionote given for feature material. Offers 25% kill fee. Buys first North American serial and second serial (reprint) rights. Reports in 3 months. Sample copy for $3 and 9×12 SAE with 3 first-class stamps. Writer's guidelines for #10 SASE.

● Writers must have working knowledge of art techniques. This magazine's most consistent need is for instructional feature articles written in the artist's voice.

Nonfiction: Instructional only—how an artist uses a particular technique, how he handles a particular subject or medium, or how he markets his work. "The emphasis must be on how the reader can learn some method of improving his artwork, or the marketing of it." No unillustrated articles; no seasonal material; no travel articles; no profiles. **Buys 60 mss/year.** Query first; all queries must be accompanied by slides, transparencies, prints or tearsheets of the artist's work as well as the artist's bio, and the writer's bio and clips. Length: 1,200-1,800 words. **Pays $200-350 and up.** Sometimes pays the expenses of writers on assignment.

Photos: "Transparencies are required with every accepted article since these are essential for our instructional format. Full captions must accompany these." Buys one-time rights.

Columns/Departments: "Two departments are open to freelance writers." Swipe File is a collection of tips and suggestions, including photos and illustrations. No query required. Length: up to 100 words. **Pays $10 and up.** Drawing Board is a monthly column that covers basic art or drawing skills. Query first with illustrations. Length: 1,200 words. **Pays $250 and up.**

Tips: "Look at several current issues and read the author's guidelines carefully. Submissions must include artwork. Remember that our readers are fine and graphic artists."

$ $ ARTNEWS, ABC, 48 W. 38th St., New York NY 10018. (212)398-1690. Fax: (212)768-4002. E-mail: goartnews@aol.com. **Contact:** Eric Gibson, executive editor. Monthly. "*Artnews* reports on the art, personalities, issues, trends and events that shape the international art world. Investigative features focus on art ranging from old masters to contemporary, including painting, sculpture, prints and photography. Regular columns offer exhibition and book reviews, travel destinations, investment and appreciation advice, design insights and updates on major art world figures." Estab. 1902. Circ. 9,877. Query before submitting.

$ $ $ ART-TALK, Box 8508, Scottsdale AZ 85252. (602)948-1799. Fax: (602)994-9284. Editor: Bill Macomber. **Contact:** Thom Romeo. **30% freelance written.** Newspaper published 9 times/year covering fine art. "*Art-Talk* deals strictly with fine art, the emphasis being on the Southwest. National and international news is also covered. All editorial is of current interest/activities and written for the art collector." Estab. 1981. Circ. 42,000. **Pays on acceptance**. Publishes ms an average of 2 months after acceptance. Byline given. Buys first North American serial rights and makes work-for-hire assignments. Editorial lead time 3 months. Submit seasonal material 4 months in advance. Accepts simultaneous submissions. Reports in 2 weeks on queries; 1 month on mss. Sample copy free.

Nonfiction: Exposé, general interest, humor, interview/profile, opinion, personal experience, photo feature. No articles on non-professional artists (e.g., Sunday Painters) or about a single commercial art gallery. **Buys 12-15 mss/year.** Query with published clips. Length: 500-4,000 words. **Pays $75-800 for assigned articles; $50-750 for unsolicited articles.** Sometimes pays expenses of writers on assignment.

Photos: State availability of photos with submission. Reviews transparencies, prints. Offers no additional payment for photos accepted with ms. Captions, identification of subjects required. Buys one-time rights.

Columns/Departments: Maintains 9 freelance columnists in different cities. **Buys 38 mss/year.** Query with published clips. **Pays $100-175.**

Tips: "Good working knowledge of the art gallery/auction/artist interconnections. Should be a part of the 'art scene' in an area known for art."

$ $ C, international contemporary art, C Arts Publishing and Production, Inc., P.O. Box 5, Station B, Toronto, Ontario M5T 2T2. (416)539-9495. E-mail: cmag@istar.ca. Website: http://www.CMagazine.com. **Contact:** Joyce Mason, editor/publisher. **80% freelance written.** Quarterly magazine covering international contemporary art. "*C* provides a vital and vibrant forum for the presentation of contemporary art and the discussion of issues surrounding art in our culture, including feature articles, dialogue, reviews and reports, as well as original artists' projects." Estab. 1983. Circ. 7,000. Pays on publication. Publishes ms an average of 4 months after acceptance. Byline given. Offers kill fee. Editorial lead time 3 months. Accepts simultaneous submissions, if so noted. Reports in 6 weeks on queries; 4 months on mss. Sample copy for $10 (US). Writer's guidelines free.

Nonfiction: Essays, general interest, opinion, personal experience. **Buys 50 mss/year.** Query. Length: 1,000-3,000 words. **Pays $150-500 (Canadian), ($105-350 US).**

Photos: State availability of photos with submission or send photos with submission. Reviews 4×5 transparencies or 8×10 prints. Offers no additional payment for photos accepted with ms. Captions required. Buys one-time rights.

Columns/Departments: Reviews (review of art exhibitions), 500 words. **Buys 30 mss/year.** Query. **Pays $100 (Canadian) ($170 US).**

$ $ FUSE MAGAZINE, A magazine about issues of art & culture, ARTONS Publishing, 401 Richmond St. W., #454, Toronto, Ontario M5V 3A8 Canada. (416)340-8026. Fax: (416)340-0494. E-mail: fuse@interlog.com. **Contact:** Petra Chevrier, managing editor. **100% freelance written.** Quarterly magazine covering art and art criticism; analysis of cultural and political events as they impact on art production and exhibition. Estab. 1976. Circ. 2,500. Pays on publication. Publishes ms an average of 4 months after acceptance. Byline given. Offers 50% kill fee for commissioned pieces only. Buys first North American serial rights all languages. Editorial lead time 4 months. Submit seasonal material 2 months in advance. Accepts simultaneous submissions. Sample copy for $5 (US funds if outside Canada). Writer's guidelines for #10 SAE with IRCs.

Nonfiction: Essays, interview/profile, opinion, art reviews. **Buys 50 mss/year.** Query with published clips and detailed proposal or send complete ms. Length: 800-6,000 words. **Pays 10¢/word or $100 for reviews (Canadian funds).**

Photos: State availability of photos with submission. Reviews 5×7 prints. Offers no additional payment for photos accepted with ms. Captions required.

Columns/Departments: Buys 10 mss/year. Pays 10¢/word.

Tips: Send detailed, but not lengthy, proposals or completed manuscripts for review by the editorial board.

N $ $ THE MAGAZINE ANTIQUES, Brant Publications, 575 Broadway, New York NY 10012. (212)941-2800. Fax: (212)941-2819. **Contact:** Allison Ledes, editor. **75% freelance written**. Monthly. "Articles should present new information in a scholarly format (with footnotes) on the fine and decorative arts, architecture, historic preservation and landscape architecture." Estab. 1922. Circ. 62,078. Pays on publication. Publishes ms an average of 6 months after acceptance. Byline given. Buys all rights. Editorial lead time 6 months. Submit seasonal material 6 months in advance. Reports in 3 weeks on queries; 6 months on mss. Sample copy for $10.50.

Nonfiction: Historical/nostalgic, scholarly. **Buys 50 mss/year**. Query with cv. Length: 2,850-3,000 words. **Pays $250-500**. Sometimes pays expenses of writers on assignment.

Photos: State availability of photos with submission. Reviews contact sheets, negatives, transparencies and prints. Captions and identification of subjects required. Buys one-time rights.

$ $ $ METROPOLIS, The Magazine of Architecture and Design, Bellerophon Publications, 177 E. 87th St., New York NY 10128. (212)722-5050. Fax: (212)427-1938. E-mail: kira@metropolismag.com. Website: http://www.metropolismag.com. Editor-in-Chief: Susan S. Szenasy. **Contact:** Kira Gould, managing editor. **80% freelance written.** Monthly magazine (combined issues February/March and August/September) for consumers interested in architecture and design. Estab. 1981. Circ. 48,000. **Pays on acceptance.** Publishes ms an average of 3 months after acceptance. Byline given. Makes work-for-hire assignments. Submit calendar material 6 weeks in advance. Reports in 8 months. Sample copy for $4.95.

Nonfiction: Contact: Susan S. Szenasy, editor-in-chief. Essays (design, architecture, urban planning issues and ideas), profiles (multi-disciplinary designers/architects). No profiles on individual architectural practices, information from public relations firms, or fine arts. **Buys 30 mss/year.** Length: 500-2,000 words. **Pays $100-1,000.**

Photos: State availability of or send photos with submission. Reviews contact sheets, 35mm or 4×5 transparencies, or 8×10 b&w prints. Payment offered for certain photos. Captions required. Buys one-time rights.
Columns/Departments: Insites (short takes on design and architecture), 100-600 words; **pays $50-150.** In Print (book review essays: focus on issues covered in a group of 2-4 books), 2,500-3,000 words; The Metropolis Observed (architecture and city planning news features and opinion), 750-1,500 words; **pays $200-500.** Visible City (historical aspects of cities), 1,500-2,500 words; **pays $600-800**; direct queries to Kira Gould, managing editor. By Design (the process of design), 1,000-2,000 words; **pays $600-800**; direct queries to Janet Rumble, senior editor. **Buys approximately 40 mss/year.** Query with published clips.
Tips: "We're looking for ideas, what's new, the obscure or the wonderful. Keep in mind that we are interested *only* in the consumer end of architecture and design. Send query with examples of photos explaining how you see illustrations working with article. Also, be patient and don't expect an immediate answer after submission of query."

"Avoid technical jargon. Keep in mind that at *Metropolis*, a firm's new work isn't a story—but the critical issues that their work brings to light might be a story. We do not cover conferences or seminars, though if such events offer new perspectives on contemporary issues in the world of art, architecture, design, graphics, urbanism, development, planning, or preservation, then an article could be framed that way."

$ $ MIX, The Magazine of Artist-Run Culture, Parallélogramme Artist-Run Culture and Publishing, Inc., 401 Richmond St. #446, Toronto, Ontario M5V 3A8 Canada. (416)506-1012. Fax: (416)340-8458. E-mail: mix@web.net. Website: http://www.mix.web.net/mix/. **Contact:** Peter Hudson, editor. Managing Editor: Jennifer Rudder. **90% freelance written.** Quarterly magazine covering artist-run gallery activities. "*Mix* represents and investigates contemporary artistic practices and issues, especially in the progressive Canadian artist-run scene." Estab. 1973. Circ. 3,500. Pays on publication. Publishes ms an average of 6 months after acceptance. Byline given. Offers 60% kill fee. Buys first North American serial rights. Editorial lead time 6 months. Submit seasonal material 4 months in advance. Reports in 2 months on queries; 3 months on mss. Sample copy for $6.50, 9×12 SASE and 6 first-class stamps. Writer's guidelines free.
Nonfiction: Essays, interview/profile. **Buys 12-20 mss/year.** Query with published clips. Length: 750-3,500 words. **Pays $100-500.** Sometimes pays expenses of writers on assignment.
Reprints: Send photocopy of article and information about when and where the article previously appeared.
Photos: State availability of photos with submission. Offers $25/photo. Captions and identification of subjects required. Buys one-time rights.
Columns/Departments: Extracts, 1,000-2,500 words; Artist's Texts, 2,000-3,000 words; Interviews, 2,000-3,000 words. Query with published clips. **Pays $100-300.**
Tips: "Read the magazine and other contemporary art magazines. Understand the idea 'artist-run.' "

$ $ SOUTHWEST ART, CBH Publishing, 5444 Westheimer #1440, Houston TX 77056. (713)296-7900. Fax: (713)850-1314. **Contact:** Margaret L. Brown, editor. **60% freelance written.** Monthly fine arts magazine "directed to art collectors interested in artists, market trends and art history of the American West." Estab. 1971. Circ. 60,000. **Pays on acceptance.** Publishes ms an average of 1 year after acceptance. Byline given. Offers $125 kill fee. Submit seasonal material 8 months in advance. Reports in 6 months. Writer's guidelines free.
Nonfiction: Book excerpts, interview/profile, opinion. No fiction or poetry. **Buys 70 mss/year.** Query with published clips. Length 1,400-1,600 words. **Pays $500.** Send photos with submission.
Photos: Reviews 35mm, 2¼, 4×5 transparencies and 8×10 prints. Captions and identification of subjects required. Negotiates rights.

$ $ U.S. ART: All the News That Fits Prints, MSP Communications, 220 S. Sixth St., Suite 500, Minneapolis MN 55402. (612)339-7571. Fax: (612)339-5806. E-mail: sgilbert@mspcommunications.com. Publisher: Frank Sisser. **Contact:** Sara Gilbert, editor. **40% freelance written.** Monthly magazine that reflects current events in the limited-edition-print market and educates collectors and the trade about the market's practices and trends. Circ. 55,000. **Pays on acceptance.** Publishes ms 3-4 months after acceptance. Distributed primarily through a network of 900 galleries as a free service to their customers. Writer byline given. Offers 25% kill fee. Departments/columns are staff-written.
Nonfiction: Two artist profiles per issue; an average of 6 features per issue including roundups of painters whose shared background of geographical region, heritage, or currently popular style illustrates a point; current events and exhibitions; educational topics on buying/selling practices and services available to help collectors purchase various print media. Length: 1,000-2,000 words. **Pays $400-550.**
Photos: Color transparencies are preferred. B&w photos considered for the staff-written columns. Returns materials after 2 months.
Tips: "We are open to writers whose background is not arts-specific. We generally do not look for art critics but prefer general-assignment reporters who can present factual material with flair in a magazine format. We also are open to opinion pieces from experts (gallery owners, publishers, consultants, show promoters) within the industry."

$ $ $ WILDLIFE ART, The Art Journal of the Natural World, Pothole Publications, Inc. 4725 Hwy. 7, P.O. Box 16246, St. Louis Park MN 55416-0246. (612)927-9056. Fax: (612)927-9353. E-mail: pbarry@mail.winternet.com. Website: http://www.wildlifeartmag.com. Editor-in-Chief: Robert Koenke. **Contact:** Rebecca Hakala Rowland, editor. **80% freelance written.** Bimonthly magazine. "*Wildlife Art* is the world's largest wildlife art magazine. Features cover interviews on living artists as well as wildlife art masters, illustrators and conservation organizations. Audience is publishers, collectors, galleries, museums, show promoters worldwide." Estab. 1982. Circ. 50,000. **Pays on acceptance.**

Publishes ms an average of 6 months after acceptance. Byline given. Negotiable kill fee. Buys second serial (reprint) rights. Reports in 4-6 months. Sample copy for 9×12 SAE with 10 first-class stamps. Writer's guidelines for #10 SASE.
Nonfiction: Buys 40 mss/year. Query with published clips; include samples of artwork. Length: 800-5,000 words. **Pays $150-900.**
Columns/Departments: Buys up to 6 mss/year. Pays $100-300.

ASSOCIATIONS

Association publications allow writers to write for national audiences while covering local stories. If your town has a Kiwanis, Lions or Rotary Club chapter, one of its projects might merit a story in the club's magazine. If you are a member of the organization, find out before you write an article if the publication pays members for stories; some associations do not. In addition, some association publications gather their own club information and rely on freelancers solely for outside features. Be sure to find out what these policies are before you submit a manuscript. Club-financed magazines that carry material not directly related to the group's activities are classified by their subject matter in the Consumer and Trade sections.

$ COMEDY WRITERS ASSOCIATION NEWSLETTER, P.O. Box 23304, Brooklyn NY 11202-0066. (718)855-5057. **Contact:** Robert Makinson, editor. **10% freelance written.** Semiannual newsletter on comedy writing for association members. Estab. 1989. **Pays on acceptance.** Publishes ms 3 months after acceptance. Byline given. Buys all rights. Reports in 2 weeks on queries; 1 month on mss. Sample copy for $5. Guidelines for #10 SASE.
Nonfiction: How-to, humor, opinion, personal experience. "No exaggerations about the sales that you make and what you are paid. Be accurate." Query. Length: 250-500 words. "You may submit articles and byline will be given if used, but at present payment is only made for jokes. Emphasis should be on marketing, not general humor articles."
Tips: "The easiest way to be mentioned in the publication is to submit short jokes. (Payment is $1-3 per joke.) Jokes for professional speakers preferred. Include SASE when submitting jokes."

$ $ THE ELKS MAGAZINE, 425 W. Diversey, Chicago IL 60614-6196. E-mail: JanellN@elks.org/elksmag. Website: http://www.elks.org/elksmag/. **Contact:** Janell Neal, editorial assistant. Editor: Fred D. Oakes. Managing Editor: Anne L. Idol. **25% freelance written.** Will work with published or unpbulished writers. Magazine published 10 times/year with basic mission of being the "voice of the Elks." All material concerning the news of the Elks is written in-house. Freelance, general interest articles are to be upbeat, wholesome, informative, with family appeal. Estab. 1922. Circ. 1,200,000. **Pays on acceptance.** Buys first North American serial rights, print only. Reports within 1 month. Sample copy and writer's guidelines for 9×12 SAE with 4 first-class stamps.
Nonfiction: "We're really interested in seeing manuscripts on business, technology, history, or just intriguing topics, ranging from science to sports." No fiction, politics, religion, controversial issues, travel, first person, fillers or verse. **Buys 2-3 mss/issue.** Prefer complete ms. Length: 1,500-3,000 words. **Pays 20¢ per word.**
Tips: "Check our website. Freelance articles are noted on the Table of Contents, but are not reproduced online, as we purchase only one-time print rights. If possible, please advise where photographs may be found. Photographs taken and submitted by the writer are paid for separately at $25 each. Please try us first. We'll get back to you soon."

N $ FEDCO REPORTER, A Publication Exclusively for FEDCO Members, Box 2605, Terminal Annex, Los Angeles CA 90051. (562)946-2511, ext. 3321. **Contact:** Anita McManes, editor. **90% freelance written.** Works with a small number of new/unpublished writers each year. Twice-monthly catalog/magazine for FEDCO department store members. Estab. 1940. Circ. 2,000,000. **Pays on acceptance.** Byline given. Buys all rights. Reports in 6 weeks. Sample copy for 9×12 SAE with 4 first-class stamps. Writer's guidelines for SASE.
Nonfiction: Events, personalities, anecdotes, little-known happenings of historical significance relating to Southern California. No first person narrative. **Buys 85 mss/year.** Query with or without published clips or send complete ms. Length: 450 words. **Pays $125.**
Photos: State availability of photos. Reviews b&w and color slides. **Pays $25.**
Tips: "We publish tightly written, well-researched stories relating to the history of Southern California."

$ $ $ KIWANIS, 3636 Woodview Trace, Indianapolis IN 46268-3196. Fax: (317)879-0204. E-mail: cjonak@kiwanis.org. Website: http://www.kiwanis.org. Managing Editor: Chuck Jonak. **80% freelance written.** Magazine published 10 times/year for business and professional persons and their families. Estab. 1917. Circ. 274,000. **Pays on acceptance.** Buys first serial rights. Offers 40% kill fee. Publishes ms an average of 6 months after acceptance. Byline given. Reports within 2 months. Sample copy and writer's guidelines for 9×12 SAE with 5 first-class stamps.
Nonfiction: Articles about social and civic betterment, small-business concerns, science, education, religion, family, youth, health, recreation, etc. Emphasis on objectivity, intelligent analysis and thorough research of contemporary issues. Positive tone preferred. Concise, lively writing, absence of clichés, and impartial presentation of controversy required. When applicable, include information and quotations from international sources. Avoid writing strictly to a US audience. "We have a continuing need for articles of international interest. In addition, we are very interested in proposals that

concern helping youth, particularly prenatal through age five: day care, developmentally appropriate education, early intervention for at-risk children, parent education, safety and health." **Buys 40 mss/year.** Length: 2,000-2,500 words. **Pays $600-1,000.** "No fiction, personal essays, profiles, travel pieces, fillers or verse of any kind. A light or humorous approach is welcomed where the subject is appropriate and all other requirements are observed." Usually pays the expenses of writers on assignment. Query first. Must include SASE for response.

Photos: "We accept photos submitted with manuscripts. Our rate for a manuscript with good photos is higher than for one without." Model release and identification of subjects required. Buys one-time rights.

Tips: "We will work with any writer who presents a strong feature article idea applicable to our magazine's audience and who will prove he or she knows the craft of writing. First, obtain writer's guidelines and a sample copy. Study for general style and content. When querying, present a detailed outline of proposed manuscript's focus and editorial intent. Indicate expert sources to be used as well as article's tone and length. Present a well-researched, smoothly written manuscript that contains a 'human quality' with the use of anecdotes, practical examples, quotations, etc."

$ $ THE LION, 300 22nd St., Oak Brook IL 60523-8842. (630)571-5466. Fax: (630)571-8890. E-mail: lions@lionsclubs.org. Website: http://www.lionsclubs.org. **Contact**: Robert Kleinfelder, editor. **35% freelance written.** Works with a small number of new/unpublished writers each year. Monthly magazine covering service club organization for Lions Club members and their families. Estab. 1918. Circ. 600,000. **Pays on acceptance.** Publishes ms an average of 5 months after acceptance. Buys all rights. Byline given. Reports in 6 weeks. Sample copy and writer's guidelines free.

Nonfiction: Informational (issues of interest to civic-minded individuals) and photo feature (must be of a Lions Club service project). No travel, biography or personal experiences. Welcomes humor, if sophisticated but clean; no sensationalism. Prefers anecdotes in articles. **Buys 4 mss/issue.** Query. Phone queries OK. Length: 500-2,200. **Pays $100-750.** Sometimes pays the expenses of writers on assignment.

Photos: Purchased with or without accompanying ms or on assignment. Captions required. Query for photos. B&w and color glossies at least 5×7 or 35mm color slides. Total purchase price for ms includes payment for photos accepted with ms. "Be sure photos are clear and as candid as possible."

Tips: "Incomplete details on how the Lions involved actually carried out a project and poor quality photos are the most frequent mistakes made by writers in completing an article assignment for us. We are geared increasingly to an international audience. Writers who travel internationally could query for possible assignments, although only locally-related expenses could be paid."

$ $ THE OPTIMIST, Optimist International, 4494 Lindell Blvd., St. Louis MO 63108. (314)371-6000. Fax: (314)371-6006. E-mail: magazine@optimist.org. Website: http://www.optimist.org. **Contact:** Dena Hull, managing editor. **10% freelance written.** Bimonthly magazine about the work of Optimist clubs and members for members of the Optimist clubs in the United States and Canada. Circ. 154,000. **Pays on acceptance.** Publishes ms an average of 4 months after acceptance. Buys first North American serial rights. Submit seasonal material 3 months in advance. Reports in 1 week. Sample copy and writer's guidelines for 9×12 SAE with 4 first-class stamps.

Nonfiction: Human interest, profiles, humor. "We want articles about the activities of local Optimist clubs. These volunteer community-service clubs are constantly involved in projects, aimed primarily at helping young people. With over 4,000 Optimist clubs in the US and Canada, writers should have ample resources. Some large metropolitan areas boast several dozen clubs. We are also interested in feature articles on individual club members who have in some way distinguished themselves, either in their club work or their personal lives. Good photos for all articles are a plus and can mean a bigger check." Will also consider short (200-400 word) articles that deal with self-improvement or a philosophy of optimism. **Buys 1-2 mss/issue.** Query. "Submit a letter that conveys your ability to turn out a well-written article and tells exactly what the scope of the article will be." Length: 800-1,200 words. **Pays $300 and up.**

Reprints: Send photocopy of article and information about when and where the article previously appeared. Pays 50% of amount paid for an original article.

Photos: State availability of photos. Payment negotiated. Captions preferred. Buys all rights. "No mug shots or people lined up against the wall shaking hands."

Tips: "Find out what the Optimist clubs in your area are doing, then find out if we'd be interested in an article on a specific club project. All of our clubs are eager to talk about what they're doing. Just ask them and you'll probably have an article idea. We would like to see short pieces on the positive effect an optimistic outlook on life can have on an individual. Examples of famous people who overcame adversity because of their positive attitude are welcome."

$ $ RECREATION NEWS, Official Publication of the Washington DC Chapter of the National Employee Services and Recreation Association, Icarus Publishers, Inc., P.O. Box 32335, Calvert Station, Washington DC 20007-0635. (202)965-6960. Fax: (202)965-6964. E-mail: recreation_news@mcimail.com. **Contact:** Henry T. Dunbar, editor. **85% freelance written.** Monthly guide to leisure-time activities for federal and private industry workers covering outdoor recreation, travel, fitness and indoor pastimes. Estab. 1979. Circ. 104,000. Pays on publication. Publishes ms an average of 8 months after acceptance. Byline given. Buys first rights and second serial (reprint) rights. Submit seasonal material 10 months in advance. Accepts simultaneous submissions. Reports in 2 months. Sample copy and writer's guidelines for 9×12 SAE with $1.05 in postage.

Nonfiction: Articles Editor. Leisure travel (mid-Atlantic travel only); sports; hobbies; historical/nostalgic (Washington-related); personal experience (with recreation, life in Washington). Special issues: skiing (December). Query with clips of published work. Length: 800-2,000 words. **Pays from $50-300.**

Reprints: Send photocopy of article or typed ms with rights for sale noted, and information about where and when article previously appeared. Pays $50.

Photos: Photo editor. State availability of photos with query letter or ms. Uses b&w prints. Pays $25. Uses color transparency on cover only. Pays $50-125 for transparency. Captions and identification of subjects required.

Tips: "Our writers generally have a few years of professional writing experience and their work runs to the lively and conversational. We like more manuscripts in a wide range of recreational topics, including the off-beat. The areas of our publication most open to freelancers are general articles on travel and sports, both participational and spectator, also historic in the DC area. In general, stories on sites visited need to include info on nearby places of interest and places to stop for lunch, to shop, etc."

$ $ $ THE ROTARIAN, Rotary International, 1560 Sherman Ave., Evanston IL 60201-1461. (847)866-3000. Fax: (847)866-9732. E-mail: 75457.3577@compuserve.com. Website: http://www.rotary.org. Editor-in-chief: Willmon L. White. **Contact:** Charles W. Pratt, editor. **40% freelance written.** Monthly magazine for Rotarian business and professional men and women and their families, schools, libraries, hospitals, etc. "Articles should appeal to an international audience and in some way help Rotarians help other people. The organization's rationale is one of hope, encouragement and belief in the power of individuals talking and working together." Estab. 1911. Circ. 514,565. **Pays on acceptance**. Byline sometimes given. Kill fee negotiable. Buys one-time or all rights. Reports in 2 weeks. Sample copy for 9×12 SAE with 6 first-class stamps. Writer's guidelines for #10 SASE.

- Ranked as one of the best markets for freelance writers in *Writer's Yearbook* magazine's annual "Top 100 Markets," January 1998.

Nonfiction: Essays, general interest, humor, inspirational, photo feature, travel, business, environment. No fiction, religious or political articles. Query with published clips. Length: 1,500 words maximum. Negotiates payment.

Reprints: Send tearsheet or photocopy of article or typed ms with rights for sale noted and information about when and where the article previously appeared. Negotiates payment.

Photos: State availability of photos. Reviews contact sheets and transparencies. Usually buys one-time rights.

Columns/Departments: Manager's Memo (business), Executive Health, Executive Lifestyle, Earth Diary, Travel Tips, Trends. Length: 800 words. Query.

Tips: "The chief aim of *The Rotarian* is to report Rotary International news. Most of this information comes through Rotary channels and is staff written or edited. The best field for freelance articles is in the general interest category. These run the gamut from humor pieces and 'how-to' stories to articles about such significant concerns as business management, world health and the environment."

$ $ THE SAMPLE CASE, The Order of United Commercial Travelers of America, 632 N. Park St., P.O. Box 159019, Columbus OH 43215-8619. (614)228-3276. Fax: (614)228-1898. Editor: Megan Woitovich. **Contact:** Linda Fisher, managing editor. Quarterly magazine covering news for members of the United Commercial Travelers emphasizing fraternalism for its officers and active membership. Estab. 1891. Circ. 150,000. Pays on publication. Buys one-time rights. Reports in 3 months. Submit seasonal material 6 months in advance. Accepts submissions.

Nonfiction: Articles on health/fitness/safety; family; hobbies/entertainment; fraternal/civic activities; business finance/insurance; travel in the US and Canada; food/cuisine. Length: 1,000-3,000 words. **Pays $200-300.**

Reprints: Send tearsheet or photocopy of article or typed ms with rights for sale noted and information about when and where the article previously appeared. Pays 100% of amount paid for an original article.

Photos: David Knapp, art director. State availability of photos with ms. Prefers color prints. Pay negotiable. Captions required.

$ $ SCOUTING, Boy Scouts of America, 1325 W. Walnut Hill Lane, P.O. Box 152079, Irving TX 75015-2079. (214)580-2367. Fax: (214)580-2079. E-mail: 103064.3363@compuserve.com. Website: http://www.bsa.scouting.org. **Contact**: Jon C. Halter, editor. Executive Editor: Scott Daniels. **90% freelance written.** Magazine published 6 times/year on Scouting activities for adult leaders of the Boy Scouts and Cub Scouts. Estab. 1913. Circ. 1,000,000. **Pays on acceptance**. Publishes ms an average of 6 months after acceptance. Byline given. Buys first North American serial rights. Submit seasonal material 9 months in advance. Reports in 2-3 weeks. Sample copy for $1 and 9×12 SAE with 4 first-class stamps. Writer's guidelines for #10 SASE.

- *Scouting* is looking for more articles about scouting families involved in interesting/unusual family-together activities/hobbies, i.e., caving, bicycle touring (they've done two), and profiles of urban/inner-city scout leaders and packs or troop with successful histories.

Nonfiction: Program activities; leadership techniques and styles; profiles; inspirational; occasional general interest for adults (humor, historical, nature, social issues, trends). **Buys 60 mss/year.** Query with published clips and SASE. Length: 500-1,200 words. **Pays $500-800 for major articles; $200-500 for shorter features.** Pays expenses of writers on assignment.

Reprints: Send photocopy of article and information about where and when the article previously appeared. "First-person accounts on Scouting experiences (previously published in local newspapers, etc.) are a popular subject."

Photos: State availability of photos with submission. Reviews contact sheets and transparencies. Identification of subjects required. Buys one-time rights.

Columns/Departments: Way it Was (Scouting history), 1,000 words; Family Talk (family—raising kids, etc.), 1,000 words. **Buys 6 mss/year.** Query. **Pays $200-400.**

Tips: "Because most volunteer Scout leaders are also parents of children of Scout age, *Scouting* is also considered a *family* magazine. We publish material we feel will help parents in strengthening families. (Because they often deal with communicating and interacting with young people, many of these features are useful to a reader in both roles as parent and Scout leader). Many of our best article ideas come from volunteer and professional Scouters, but most stories are written by staff members or professional writers assigned by us. We seldom publish unsolicited manuscripts (the exception being inspirational accounts or successful program ideas by individual Scouters). We rely heavily on regional writers to cover an event or activity in a particular part of the country."

$ $ THE TOASTMASTER, Toastmasters International, 23182 Arroyo Vista, Rancho Santa Margarita CA 92688 or P.O. Box 9052, Mission Viejo, CA 92690-7052. (714)858-8255. Fax: (714)858-1207. E-mail: sfrey@toastmasters.org. Website: http://www.toastmasters.org. **Contact:** Suzanne Frey, editor. Associate Editor: Mary Frances Conley. **50% freelance written.** Monthly magazine on public speaking, leadership and club concerns. "This magazine is sent to members of Toastmasters International, a nonprofit educational association of men and women throughout the world who are interested in developing their communication and leadership skills. Members range from novice speakers to professional orators and come from a wide variety of backgrounds." Estab. 1932. Circ. 170,000. **Pays on acceptance.** Publishes ms an average of 10 months after acceptance. Byline given. Buys second serial (reprint), first-time or all rights. Submit seasonal material 3 months in advance. Accepts simultaneous submissions. Reports in 6 weeks on queries; 1 month on mss. Sample copy for 9×12 SAE with 4 first-class stamps. Writer's guidelines for #10 SASE.
Nonfiction: Book excerpts, how-to (communications related), humor (only if informative; humor cannot be off-color or derogatory), interview/profile (only if of a very prominent member or former member of Toastmasters International or someone who has a valuable perspective on communication and leadership). **Buys 50 mss/year.** Query. Length: 1,000-2,500 words. **Pays $100-250.** Sometimes pays expenses of writers on assignment. "Toastmasters members are requested to view their submissions as contributions to the organization. Sometimes asks for book excerpts and reprints without payment, but original contribution from individuals outside Toastmasters will be paid for at stated rates."
Reprints: Send typed ms with rights for sale noted and information about when and where the article previously appeared. Pays 50-70% of amount paid for an original article.
Photos: Reviews b&w prints. No additional payment for photos accepted with ms. Captions required. Buys all rights.
Tips: "We are looking primarily for 'how-to' articles on subjects from the broad fields of communications and leadership which can be directly applied by our readers in their self-improvement and club programming efforts. Concrete examples are useful. Avoid sexist or nationalist language."

$ $ VFW MAGAZINE, Veterans of Foreign Wars of the United States, 406 W. 34th St., Kansas City MO 64111. (816)756-3390. Fax: (816)968-1169. Website: http://www.vfw.org. **Contact:** Rich Kolb, editor-in-chief. **40% freelance written.** Monthly magazine on veterans' affairs, military history, patriotism, defense and current events. "*VFW Magazine* goes to its members worldwide, all having served honorably in the armed forces overseas from World War II through Bosnia." Circ. 2,000,000. **Pays on acceptance.** Offers 50% kill fee on commissioned articles. Buys first rights. Submit seasonal material 6 months in advance. Submit detailed query letter, résumé and sample clips. Reports in 2 months. Sample copy for 9×12 SAE with 5 first-class stamps.

- *VFW Magazine* is becoming more current-events oriented.

Nonfiction: Veterans' and defense affairs; recognition of veterans and military service; current foreign policy; American armed forces abroad and international events affecting U.S. national security are in demand. Resolutions passed each August at VFW national convention; recent legislation and veteran concerns. **Buys 25-30 mss/year.** Query with 1-page outline and published clips. Length: 1,000 words. **Pays up to $500 maximum unless otherwise negotiated.**
Photos: Send photos with submission. Color transparencies (2¼×2¼) preferred; b&w prints (5×7, 8×10). Reviews contact sheets, negatives, transparencies and prints. Captions, model releases and identification of subjects required. Buys first North American rights.
Tips: "Absolute accuracy and quotes from relevant individuals are a must. Bibliographies useful if subject required extensive research and/or is open to dispute. Consult *The Associated Press Stylebook* for correct grammar and punctuation. Please enclose 3-sentence biography describing your military service in the field in which you are writing." Welcomes member and freelance submissions. No phone queries.

ASTROLOGY, METAPHYSICAL & NEW AGE

Magazines in this section carry articles ranging from shamanism to extraterrestrial phenomena. With the coming millennium, there is increased interest in spirituality, angels, near death experiences, mind/body healing and other New Age concepts and figures. The following publications regard astrology, psychic phenomena, metaphysical experiences and related subjects as sciences or as objects of serious study. Each has an individual personality and approach to these phenomena. If you want to write for these publications, be sure to read them carefully before submitting.

$ ☆ ASTROLOGY YOUR DAILY HOROSCOPE, Popular Magazine Group, 7002 W. Butler Pike, Ambler PA 19002. **Contact:** Arthur Ofner, associate editor. **90% freelance written.** Monthly magazine covering astrology and horoscopes. "*Astrology Your Daily Horoscope* is a monthly astrology magazine that covers all facets of astrology, including weekly and daily predictions, advice from astrologers, prophetic numerology, lunar forecasts, birthday horoscopes and forecasts about love, money and health issues. Feature articles relate to planetary transits, how astrology is used in individual lives and how-to articles. Publishes ms an average of 4 months after acceptance. Byline given. Buys all rights. Editorial lead time 4 months. Submit seasonal material 6 months in advance. Reports in 2 months. Sample copy for $4.95. Writer's guidelines for #10 SASE.

Nonfiction: Book excerpts, how-to (e.g., interpret a natal chart), chart analysis of celebrities. Special issue: Astrology Annual (Fall). **Buys 48 mss/year.** Send complete ms. Length: 1,200-3,000 words. **Pays $48-120.**

Photos: State availability of photos with submission. Reviews 4×6 prints. Offers no additional payment for photos accepted with ms. Captions, identification of subjects required. Rights purchased are negotiable.

$ $ FATE, Llewellyn Worldwide, Ltd., P.O. Box 64383, St. Paul MN 55164-0383. Fax: (612)291-1908. E-mail: fate@LLewellyn.com. Website: http://www.fatemag.com. **Contact:** Editor. **70% freelance written.** Estab. 1948. Circ. 65,000. Buys all rights. Byline given. Pays after publication. Sample copy and writer's guidelines for $3 and 9×12 SAE with 5 first-class stamps. Reports in 3 months or more.

Nonfiction and Fillers: Personal psychic and mystical experiences, 350-500 words. **Pays $25.** Articles on parapsychology, Fortean phenomena, cryptozoology, parapsychology, spiritual healing, flying saucers, new frontiers of science, and mystical aspects of ancient civilizations, 500-3,000 words. Must include complete authenticating details. Prefers interesting accounts of single events rather than roundups. "We very frequently accept manuscripts from new writers; the majority are individual's first-person accounts of their own psychic/mystical/spiritual experiences. We do need to have all details, where, when, why, who and what, included for complete documentation. We ask for a notarized statement attesting to truth of the article." Query first. **Pays 10¢/word.** Fillers are especially welcomed and must be be fully authenticated also, and on similar topics. Length: 50-300 words.

Photos: Buys slides. prints, or digital photos/illustrations with mss. Pays $10.

Tips: "We would like more stories about *current* paranormal or unusual events."

N $ FREE SPIRIT MAGAZINE, 107 Sterling Place, Brooklyn NY 11217. (718)638-3733. Fax: (718)230-3459. E-mail: fsny@fsmagazine.com. Managing Editor: Ceci Russell. **Contact:** Paul English, editor. Bimonthly tabloid covering New Age health, spirituality and personal growth. "We are an alternative New Age publication. Writers must have an open mind and be interested in New Age thinking." Circ. 300,000. **Pays on acceptance**. Publishes ms 3 months after acceptance. Byline given. Buys first rights. Editorial lead time 1 month. Accepts simultaneous submissions. Reports in 1 month. Sample copy for 8×10 SAE with 10 first-class stamps. Writer's guidelines free.

Nonfiction: Essays, how-to, humor, inspirational, interview/profile, new product, photo feature. **Buys 30 mss/year**. Query with or without published clips. Length: 1,000-3,500 words. **Pays $150 maximum**.

Reprints: Accepts previously published submissions.

Photos: State availability of photos with submission. Model releases required.

Columns/Departments: Fitness (new ideas in staying fit), 1,500 words (can be regional NY or LA); **Pays $150**. A-Z (recommendations for places, events, records, books, etc.), 100 words. Query or send complete ms. **Pays $6/word**.

Fiction: Humorous, inspirational, mainstream. **Buys 5 mss/year**. Query with published clips. Length: 1,000-3,500 words. **Pays $150.**

Tips: "Be vivid and descriptive. We are *very* interested in hearing from new writers."

✪ $ $ GNOSIS, A Journal of the Western Inner Traditions, Lumen Foundation, P.O. Box 14217, San Francisco CA 94114. (415)974-0600. Fax: (415)974-0366. E-mail: smoley@well.com (queries); gnosis@well.com (unsolicited mss). Website: http://www.lumen.org. **Contact:** Richard Smoley, editor. **75% freelance written.** Quarterly magazine covering esoteric spirituality. "*Gnosis* is a journal covering the esoteric, mystical, and occult traditions of Western civilization, including Judaism, Christianity, Islam, and Paganism." Estab. 1985. Circ. 16,000. Pays on publication. Publishes ms an average of 3 months after acceptance. Byline given. Buys first North American serial rights. Editorial lead time 5 months. Submit seasonal material 5 months in advance. Reports in 1 month on queries; 4 months on mss. Sample copy for $9. Writer's guidelines for #10 SASE.

Nonfiction: Book excerpts, essays, religious. Theme issue articles (esoteric traditions and practices, past and present); interviews with spiritual teachers, authors, and scholars. #51 theme, The Grail (Spring 1999, deadline November 1, 1998). **Buys 32 mss/year.** Query with published clips. Length: 1,000-5,000 words. **Pays $100-300 for assigned articles; $50-200 for unsolicited articles.** All contributors also receive 4 copies plus a year's subscription.

Reprints: Send information about when and where the article previously appeared. Pays 50% of amount paid for an original article.

Photos: State availability of photos with submissions. Reviews contact sheets, prints. Offers $50-125/photo. Captions, identification of subjects required. Buys one-time rights.

Columns/Departments: News & Notes (items of current interest in esoteric spirituality), 1,000 words. **Pays $100-250 per article.** Book Reviews (reviews of new books in the field), 250-1,000 words. **Pays $50 per book reviewed. Buys 45 mss/year.** Query with published clips.

Tips: "We give strong preference to articles related to our issue themes (available with writer's guidelines). No faxed submissions or queries, please."

✪ $ HOROSCOPE GUIDE, JBH Publishing Co., 7002 W. Butler Pike, Ambler PA 19002. **Contact:** Arthur Ofner, editor-in-chief. **90% freelance written.** "*Horoscope Guide* is a monthly astrology magazine with comprehensive daily forecasts for all signs of the zodiac, monthly forecasts on love, yearly prophesies, astrology advice columns, and feature articles dealing with any facet of astrology, from the mundane to the esoteric. Audience is 90% female, ages 25-55, with high school or above education level." Pays on publication. Publishes ms an average of 4 months after acceptance. Byline given. Buys all rights. Editorial lead time 4 months. Submit seasonal material 6 months in advance. Reports in 2 months. Sample copy for $3.95. Writer's guidelines for #10 SASE.

Nonfiction: Book excerpts, how-to (e.g. interpret a natal chart), chart analysis of celebrities. Special issues: True Astrology Forecast (Spring, Fall); Psychic Astrology Horoscope (Spring, Fall); Astro-Annual (Fall). **Buys 60 mss/year.** Send complete ms. Length: 1,200-3,000 words. **Pays $48-120.**

Photos: State availability of photos with submission. Reviews 4×6 prints. Offers no additional payment for photos accepted with ms. Captions, identification of subjects required. Rights purchased negotiable.

N ✪ $ $ LAPIS, The inner meaning of contemporary life, New York Open Center, 83 Spring St., New York NY 10012. (212)334-0210. Fax: (212)219-1347. E-mail: nyoc@aol.com. Website: http://www.opencenter.org. **Contact**: Cathy Mars, editorial assistant. Editor: Ralph White. Managing Editor: John Isaacs. **95% freelance written.** Magazine published 3 times/year. "*Lapis* contains the finest in holistic writing today. Articles by world leaders, scholars, philosophers, artists and adventurers provide in-depth exploration of new trends in consciousness and current affairs. Addressing both the inner world of soul and spirit and the outer world of politics, society, and ecology, *Lapis* occupies a unique niche in contemporary publications." Estab. 1995. Circ. 20,000. Pays on publication. Publishes ms an average of 2 months after acceptance. Byline given. Buys first rights or second serial (reprint) rights. Editorial lead time 3 months. Reports in 2 weeks on queries; 2 months on mss. Sample copy and writer's guidelines free.

Nonfiction: Book excerpts, essays, general interest, humor, inspirational, interview/profile, opinion, personal experience, photo feature, religious, travel. **Buys 50-60 mss/year.** Send complete ms. Length: 1,000-5,000 words. **Pays $100-500.**

Reprints: Send photocopy of article or short story or typed ms with rights for sale noted and information about when and where the article or story previously appeared. Negotiable payment.

Photos: State availability of photos with submission. Reviews contact sheets, transparencies, 8×10 prints. Negotiates payment individually. Identification of subjects required. Buys one-time rights.

Columns/Departments: The World, Traditions, Lovers of Wisdom, Society, Freedom and Poetry.

Fiction: Ethnic, historical, humorous, mystery, slice-of-life vignettes. **Buys 5 mss/year.** Send complete ms. Length: 1,000-5,000 words. **Pays $100-500.** Publishes novel excerpts.

Poetry: Avant-garde, free verse, haiku, spiritual. **Buys 3-5 poems/year.** Submit maximum 3 poems. **Pays $50-200.**

Tips: "Submissions should always be crisp, meaningful and enlightening. *Lapis* is a channel for deeper and more spiritual understanding of issues and experiences. We're looking for wise voices."

$ $ MAGICAL BLEND MAGAZINE, A Primer for the 21st Century, P.O. Box 600, Chico CA 95927. (916)893-9037. E-mail: magical@inreach.com. Website: http://www.magicalblend.com. **Contact:** Jerry Snider, managing editor. **50% freelance written.** Bimonthly magazine covering social and mystical transformation. "*Magical Blend* endorses no one pathway to spiritual growth, but attempts to explore many alternative possibilities to help transform the planet." Estab. 1980. Circ. 65,000. Pays on publication. Publishes ms an average of 2 months after acceptance. Byline given. Reports in 2 months. Sample copy free. Writer's guidelines for #10 SASE.

Nonfiction: Book excerpts, essays, general interest, inspirational, interview/profile, religious. "Articles must reflect our standards: see our magazine. No poetry or fiction." **Buys 24 mss/year.** Send complete ms. Length: 1,000-5,000 words. Pay varies. Contributor copies.

Photos: State availability of photos with submission. Reviews transparencies. Negotiates payment individually. Model releases, identification of subjects required. Buys all rights.

Fillers: Newsbreaks. **Buys 12-20/year.** Length: 300-450 words. Pay varies.

$ $ $ NEW AGE: The Journal for Holistic Living, (formerly *New Age Journal*), 42 Pleasant St., Watertown MA 02172. (617)926-0200. Fax: (617)924-2967. Executive Editor: Luise Light. Editor: Joan Duncan Oliver. **Contact:** Devra First, assistant editor. **35% freelance written.** Works with a small number of new/unpublished writers each year. Bimonthly magazine emphasizing "personal fulfillment and social change. The audience we reach is college-educated, social-service/hi-tech oriented, 25-55 years of age, concerned about social values, humanitarianism and balance in personal life." Estab. 1974. Cir. 275,000. Publishes ms 5 months after acceptance. Byline given. Offers 25% kill fee. Buys first North American serial and reprint rights. Submit seasonal material 6 months in advance. Accepts simultaneous submissions. Reports in 3 months on queries. Sample copy for $5 and 9×12 SAE. Guidelines for #10 SASE.

Nonfiction: Book excerpts, exposé, general interest, how-to (travel on business, select a computer, reclaim land, plant a garden), behavior, trend pieces, humor, inspirational, interview/profile, new product, food, sci-tech, music, media, nutrition, holistic health, education, personal experience. **Buys 60-80 mss/year.** Query with published clips. No phone calls. The process of decision making takes time and involves more than one editor. An answer cannot be given over the phone." Length: 200-4,000 words. **Pays $50-2,500.** Pays the expenses of writers on assignment.

Reprints: Send tearsheet or photocopy of article.

Photos: State availability of photos. Model releases, identification of subjects required. Buys one-time rights.

Columns/Departments: Body/Mind; Reflections; First Person, Upfront. **Buys 60-80 mss/year.** Query with published clips. Length: 250-1,500 words. **Pays $50-850.**

Tips: "Submit short, specific news items to the Upfront department. Query first with clips. A query is one to two paragraphs—if you need more space than that to *present* the idea, then you don't have a clear grip on it. The next open area is columns: First Person and Reflections often take first-time contributors. Read the magazine and get a sense of type of writing run in these two columns. In particular we are interested in seeing inspirational, first-person pieces that highlight an engaging idea, experience or issue. We are also looking for new cutting-edge thinking."

$ $ PARABOLA, The Magazine of Myth and Tradition, The Society for the Study of Myth and Tradition, 656 Broadway, New York NY 10012-2317. (212)505-9037. Fax: (212)979-7325. E-mail: parabola@panix.com. Website: http://www.parabola.org. **Contact:** Natalie Baan, managing editor. Quarterly magazine "devoted to the exploration of the quest for meaning as expressed in the myths, symbols, and tales of the religious traditions. Particular emphasis is on the relationship between this wisdom and contemporary life." Estab. 1976. Circ. 40,000. Pays on publication. Publishes ms 3 months after acceptance. Byline given. Offers kill fee for assigned articles only (usually $100). Buys first North American serial, first, one-time or second serial (reprint) rights. Editorial lead time 4 months. Accepts simultaneous submissions. Reports in 3 weeks on queries; on mss "variable—for articles directed to a particular theme, we usually respond the month of or the month after the deadline (so for an April 15 deadline, we are likely to respond in April or May). Articles not directed to themes may wait four months or more!" Sample copy for $6.95 current issue; $8.95 back issue. Writers guidelines and list of themes for SASE.

Nonfiction: Book excerpts, essays, photo feature. Send for current list of themes. No articles not related to specific themes. **Buys 4-8 mss/year.** Query. Length: 2,000-4,000 words. **Pays $100 minimum.** Sometimes pays expenses of writers on assignment.

Reprints: Send photocopy of article or short story (must include copy of copyright page) and information about when and where the article or short story previously appeared.

Photos: State availability of photos with submission. Reviews contact sheets, any transparencies and prints. Identification of subjects required. Buys one-time rights.

Columns/Departments: Tangents (reviews of film, exhibits, dance, theater, video, music relating to theme of issue), 2,000-4,000 words; Book Reviews (reviews of current books in religion, spirituality, mythology and tradition), 500 words; Epicycles (retellings of myths and folk tales of all cultures—no fiction or made-up mythology!), under 2,000 words. **Buys 2-6 unsolicited mss/year.** Query. **Pays $75.**

Fiction: "We *very* rarely publish fiction; must relate to upcoming theme." Query. Publishes novel excerpts.

Tips: "Each issue of *Parabola* is organized around a theme. Examples of themes we have explored in the past include Rite of Passage, Sacred Space, The Child, Ceremonies, Addiction, The Sense of Humor, Hospitalilty, The Hunter and The Stranger."

$ $ THE SANTA FE SUN, New Mexico's Newspaper for Wellness, Sustainability and Creative Community, New Mexico Sun, Ltd. Co., 1229 St. Francis, Suite C4, Santa Fe NM 87505. (505)989-8381. Fax: (505)989-4767. E-mail: editor@santafesun.com. **Contact:** Will Sims, publisher. **80% freelance written.** Monthly newspaper covering alternative/New Age, with a preference to articles with a northern New Mexico slant. Estab. 1988. Circ. 23,000. Pays on publication. Publishes ms an average of 2 months after acceptance. Byline given. Not copyrighted. Buys first rights. Editorial lead time 2 months. Submit seasonal material 1 month in advance. Accepts simultaneous submissions. Reports in 1 month on queries. Sample copy for $3. Writer's guidelines for #10 SASE.

Nonfiction: Book excerpts, essays, inspirational, interview/profile, opinion, personal experience, photo feature, religious, travel. **Buys 12 mss/year.** Query with published clips. Length: 600-2,200 words. **Pays $50-200 for assigned articles.**

Reprints: Send photocopy of article and information about when and where the article previously appeared. Pay negotiable.

Photos: State availability of photos with submission. Reviews contact sheets. Negotiates payment individually. Identification of subjects required. Buys one-time rights.

Columns/Departments: Pays 7¢/word.

Poetry: Avant-garde, free verse, haiku, light verse, traditional.

N $ UFO UNIVERSE, Global Communications, 11 E. 30th St., New York NY 10016. Phone/fax: (212)685-4080. **Contact**: T.G. Beckley, editor. Quarterly magazine covering UFOs. Pays on publication. Byline given. Buys first North American serial rights, second serial (reprint) rights or all rights or makes work-for-hire assignments. Editorial lead time 6 months. Accepts previously published submissions. Reports in 6 weeks on queries. Sample copy for $5 plus $2 postage. Writer's guidelines for #10 SASE.

Nonfiction: Book excerpts, exposé, how-to, inspirational, personal experience, travel. **Buys 100 mss/year.** Query. Length: 2,500-3,500 words. **Pays $100.**

Photos: State availability or send photos with submission. Reviews prints. Captions required.

Fillers: Length: 300-1,000 words. **Pays $25-40.**

$ WHOLE LIFE TIMES, P.O. Box 1187, Malibu CA 90265. (310)317-4200. Fax: (310)317-4206. E-mail: wholelifex @aol.com. **Contact:** S.T. Alcantara, senior editor. Monthly consumer tabloid covering holistic thinking. Estab. 1979. Circ. 55,000. Pays within 30 days after publication for feature stories only. Buys first North American serial rights. Sample copy for $3. Writer's guidelines for #10 SASE.

Nonfiction: Exposé, general interest, how-to, humor, inspirational, interview/profile, spiritual, technical, travel, leading-edge information, book excerpts. Special issues: Family (September), Healing Arts (October), Food & Nutrition (November), Spirituality (December), New Beginnings (January), Relationships (February). **Buys 25 mss/year.** Query

with published clips or send complete ms. Length: 1,200-1,500 words. **Pays 5-10¢/word for feature stories only.**
Reprints: E-mail, fax or mail typed ms or send Macintosh, Microsoft Word diskette of ms with rights for sale noted and information about when and where the article previously appeared. Pays 50% of amount paid for an original article.
Columns/Departments: Healing, Parenting, Finance, Food, Personal Growth, Relationships, Humor, Travel, Sexuality, Spirituality and Psychology. Length: 750-1,200 words. Query.
Tips: "Queries should show an awareness of current topics of interest in our subject area. We welcome investigative reporting and are happy to see queries that address topics in a political context. We are especially looking for articles on health and nutrition."

AUTOMOTIVE & MOTORCYCLE

Publications in this section detail the maintenance, operation, performance, racing and judging of automobiles and recreational vehicles. Publications that treat vehicles as means of shelter instead of as a hobby or sport are classified in the Travel, Camping and Trailer category. Journals for service station operators and auto and motorcycle dealers are located in the Trade Auto and Truck section.

$ AMERICAN MOTORCYCLIST, American Motorcyclist Association, 33 Collegeview Rd, Westerville OH 43081-6114. (614)891-2425. **Contact:** Greg Harrison, executive editor. Monthly magazine for "enthusiastic motorcyclists, investing considerable time and money in the sport. We emphasize the motorcyclist, not the vehicle." Estab. 1942. Circ. 220,000. Pays on publication. Rights purchased vary with author and material. Pays 25-50% kill fee. Byline given. Submit seasonal material 4 months in advance. Reports in 1 month. Writer's guidelines for SASE.
Nonfiction: How-to (different and/or unusual ways to use a motorcycle or have fun on one); historical (the heritage of motorcycling, particularly as it relates to the AMA); interviews (with interesting personalities in the world of motorcycling); photo feature (quality work on any aspect of motorcycling); technical articles. No product evaluations or stories on motorcycling events not sanctioned by the AMA. **Buys 20-25 mss/year.** Query with SASE. Length: 500 words minimum. **Pays minimum $7/published column inch.**
Photos: Purchased with or without accompanying ms or on assignment. Captions required. Query. Pays $40/photo minimum.
Tips: "Accuracy and reliability are prime factors in our work with freelancers. We emphasize the rider, not the motorcycle itself. It's always best to query us first and the further in advance the better to allow for scheduling."

$ AMERICAN WOMAN MOTORSCENE, American Woman Motorscene, 1510 11th St., Suite 201B, Santa Monica CA 90401. (310)260-0192. Fax: (310)260-0175. E-mail: courtney@americanwomanmag.com. Website: http://www.americanwomanmag.com. **Contact:** Courtney Caldwell, editor-in-chief. **80% freelance written.** Bimonthly automotive/adventure lifestyle and service-oriented magazine for women. Estab. 1988. Circ. 100,000. Pays on publication 2 months after acceptance. Byline always given. Buys first rights and second serial (reprint) rights or makes work-for-hire assignments. Submit seasonal material 4 months in advance. Reports in 2 months. Free sample copy.
Nonfiction: Humor, inspirational, interview/profile, new product, photo feature, travel, lifestyle. No articles depicting women in motorsports or professions that are degrading, negative or not upscale. Special issues: The Family Car Buyers Guide: Mid-Size for Middle America, How to Choose Tires and Wheels, Car Care: How to Maintain Your Looks (September/October 1998); 1999 Compact Pick-up Trucks, Christmas Gift Ideas, Express Service Centers (November/December 1998). **Buys 30 mss/year.** Send complete ms. Length 250-1,500 words. **Pays 10¢/word for assigned articles; 7¢ for unsolicited articles.** Sometimes pays expenses of writers on assignment.
Reprints: Send photocopy of article and information about when and where the article previously appeared.
Photos: Send photos with submission. Reviews contact sheets. Black and white or Kodachrome 64 preferred. Offers $10-50/photo. Captions, model releases and identification of subjects required. Buys all rights.
Columns/Departments: Tech Talk: (The Mall) new products; Tale End (News); 100-750 words. "Humor is best."
Fillers: Anecdotes, facts, gags to be illustrated by cartoonist, newsbreaks, short humor. **Buys 12/year.** Length: 25-100 words. Negotiable.
Tips: "The *AWM* reader is typically career and/or family oriented, independent, and adventurous. She demands literate, entertaining and useful information from a magazine enabling her to make educated buying decisions. It helps if the writer is into cars, trucks or motorcycles. It is a special sport. If he/she is not involved in motorsports, he/she should have a positive point of view of motorsports and be willing to learn more about the subject. We are a lifestyle type of publication more than a technical magazine. Positive attitudes wanted."

$ $ AUTOMOBILE QUARTERLY, The Connoisseur's Magazine of Motoring Today, Yesterday, and Tomorrow, Kutztown Publishing Co., P.O. Box 348, 15076 Kutztown Rd., Kutztown PA 19530-0348. (610)683-3169. Fax: (610)683-3287. Publishing Director: Jonathan Stein. **Contact:** Karla Rosenbusch, senior editor. Assistant Editor: Stuart Wells. **85% freelance written.** Quarterly hardcover magazine covering "automotive history, with excellent photography." Estab. 1962. Circ. 13,000. **Pays on acceptance.** Publishes ms an average of 1 year after acceptance. Byline given. Buys first international serial rights. Editorial lead time 9 months. Reports in 2 weeks on queries; 2 months on mss. Sample copy for $19.95.

Nonfiction: Essays, historical/nostalgic, photo feature, technical. **Buys 25 mss/year.** Query by mail or fax. Length: 3,500-8,000 words. **Pays approximately 30¢/word.** Sometimes pays expenses of writers on assignment.
Photos: State availability of photos with submission. Reviews 4×5, 35mm and 120 transparencies and historical prints. Buys one-time rights.
Tips: "Study the publication, and stress original research."

N $ $ $ $ **AUTOWEEK**, Crain Communications, 1400 Woodbridge, Detroit MI 48207. (313)446-6000. Fax: (313)446-0347. Website: http://www.autoweek.com. Editor: Dutch Mandel. Managing Editor: Larry Edsall. **Contact**: John Cortez, senior editor/features. **33% freelance written.** "*AutoWeek* is the country's only weekly magazine for the auto enthusiast." Estab. 1958. Circ. 300,000. Pays on publication. Publishes ms an average of 1 month after acceptance. Byline given. Buys first North American serial rights
Nonfiction: Historical/nostalgic, interview/profile, new product, travel. **Buys 100 mss/year.** Query. Length: 700-3,000 words. **Pays $1/word.** Sometimes pays expenses of writers on assignment.

$ $ **BRITISH CAR MAGAZINE**, 343 Second St., Suite H, Los Altos CA 94022-3639. (650)949-9680. Fax: (650)949-9685. E-mail: britcarmag@aol.com. **Contact:** Gary G. Anderson, editor and publisher. **50% freelance written.** Bimonthly magazine covering British cars. "We focus upon the cars built in Britain, the people who buy them, drive them, collect them, love them. Writers must be among the aforementioned. Written by enthusiasts for enthusiasts." Estab. 1985. Circ. 30,000. Pays on publication. Publishes ms an average of 3 months after acceptance. Byline given. Buys all rights, unless other arrangements made. Submit seasonal material 4 months in advance. Reports in 1 month. Sample copy for $5. Writer's guidelines for #10 SASE.

- The editor is looking for more technical and restoration articles by knowledgeable enthusiasts and professionals.

Nonfiction: Historical/nostalgic; how-to (repair or restoration of a specific model or range of models, new technique or process); humor (based upon a realistic nonfiction situation); interview/profile (famous racer, designer, engineer, etc.); photo feature; technical. **Buys 30 mss/year.** Send complete ms. "Include SASE if submission is to be returned." Length: 750-4,500 words. **Pays $2-5/column inch for assigned articles; $2-3/column inch for unsolicited articles.**
Photos: Send photos with submission. Reviews transparencies and prints. Offers $15-75/photo. Captions and identification of subjects required. Buys all rights, unless otherwise arranged.
Columns/Departments: Update (newsworthy briefs of interest, not too timely for bimonthly publication), approximately 50-175 words. **Buys 20 mss/year.** Send complete ms.
Tips: "Thorough familiarity of subject is essential. *British Car* is read by experts and enthusiasts who can see right through superficial research. Facts are important, and must be accurate. Writers should ask themselves 'I know I'm interested in this story, but will most of *British Car* readers appreciate it?' "

$ $ $ $ **CAR AND DRIVER**, Hachette Filipacchi Magazines, Inc., 2002 Hogback Rd., Ann Arbor MI 48105-9736. (313)971-3600. Fax: (313)971-3600. E-mail: editors@caranddriver.com. Website: http://www.caranddriver.com. **Contact:** Csaba Csere, editor-in-chief. Monthly magazine for auto enthusiasts; college-educated, professional, median 24-35 years of age. Estab. 1956. Circ. 1,200,000. **Pays on acceptance.** Byline given. Offers 25% kill fee. Rights purchased vary with author and material. Buys all rights or first North American serial rights. Reports in 2 months.
Nonfiction: Non-anecdotal articles about automobiles, new and old. Automotive road tests, informational articles on cars and equipment, some satire and humor and personalities, past and present, in the automotive industry and automotive sports. "Treat readers as intellectual equals. Emphasis on people as well as hardware." Informational, humor, historical, think articles and nostalgia. All road tests are staff-written. "Unsolicited manuscripts are not accepted. Query letters must be addressed to the Managing Editor. Rates are generous, but few manuscripts are purchased from outside." **Buys 1 freelance ms/year. Pays maximum $3,000/feature; $750-1,500/short piece.** Pays expenses of writers on assignment.
Photos: Color slides and b&w photos sometimes purchased with accompanying mss.
Tips: "It is best to start off with an interesting query and to stay away from nuts-and-bolts ideas because that will be handled in-house or by an acknowledged expert. Our goal is to be absolutely without flaw in our presentation of automotive facts, but we strive to be every bit as entertaining as we are informative."

⊘ **CAR CRAFT** does not accept freelance submissions.

N $ $ $ $ **CAR STEREO REVIEW, The Mobile Electronics Authority**, Hachette Filipacchi Magazines, 1633 Broadway, 45th Floor, New York NY 10019. (212)767-6000. Fax: (212)333-2434. E-mail: carsterev@aol.com. **Contact:** Mike Mettler, editor-in-chief. **45% freelance written.** Published 10 times/year (monthly except February/March and November/December). "*Car Stereo Review* is geared toward the mobile-electronics enthusiast, encompassing such things as sound-off competitions, product test reports, installation techniques, new technologies such as navigation, and music." Estab. 1987. Circ. 140,000. **Pays on acceptance.** Publishes ms an average of 3 months after acceptance. Byline given. Offers 25% kill fee. Buys first North American serial rights. Editorial lead time 3-4 months. Reports in 4-6 weeks on queries; 1-2 months on mss. Sample copy and writer's guidelines free.
Nonfiction: How-to (installation techniques), interview/profile, new product, technical. "As we are a highly specialized publication, we won't look at anything non-specific to our audience's needs." **Buys 10-20 ms/year.** Query with published clips. Length: 200-3,000 words. **Pays $40-5,000 for assigned articles; $40-2,000 for unsolicited articles.** Sometimes pays the expenses of writers on assignment.
Photos: State availability of photos with submission. Reviews contact sheets, negatives, transparencies. Negotiates

payment individually. Model releases and identification of subjects required. Buys one-time rights.
Columns/Department: Intersection (mobile-electronics news and unique car-stereo applications—in a plane, boat, golf cart, tractor, etc.), 200 words. **Buys 6-10 mss/year.** Query with published clips. **Pays $75-100.**
Tips: "As we are experts in our field, and looked to as being the 'authority,' writers *must* have some knowledge of electronics, car stereo applications, and theory, especially in relation to the car environment. Our readers are *not* greenhorns, and expect expert opinions."

$ $ CC MOTORCYCLE MAGAZINE, Motomag Corp., P.O. Box 1046, Nyack NY 10960. (914)353-MOTO. Fax: (914)353-5240. E-mail: motomag@aol.com. Website: http://www.moto-mag.com. **Contact:** Mark Kalan, publisher/editor. **90% freelance written.** Monthly magazine featuring "positive coverage of motorcycling in America—riding, travel, racing and tech." Estab. 1989 (as *CC Motorcycle Magazine*). Circ. 30,000. Pays on publication. Publishes ms an average of 2 months after acceptance. Byline given. Buys one-time rights. Editorial lead time 3 months. Submit seasonal material 3 months in advance. Accepts simultaneous submissions. Reports in 1 month. Sample copy for $3. Writer's guidelines for #10 SASE.
Nonfiction: Essays, general interest, historical/nostalgic, how-to, humor, inspirational, interview/profile, new product, personal experience, photo feature, technical, travel. Special issues: Annual Edition; Laconia's 75th Anniversary (racing at NIHS) Speedway; Daytona Beach Biketoberfest; Summer touring stories—travel. **Buys 12 mss/year.** Query with published clips. Length: 1,000-2,000 words. **Pays $50-250 for assigned articles; $25-125 for unsolicited articles.** Sometimes pays expenses of writers on assignment.
Reprints: Send tearsheet or photocopy of article or short story. No payment. Publishes novel excerpts.
Photos: State availability of photos with submission. Reviews contact sheets, transparencies. Negotiates payment individually. Captions, model releases, identification of subjects required. Buys one-time rights.
Fiction: Adventure, fantasy, historical, romance, slice-of-life vignettes. All fiction must be motorcycle related. **Buys 6 mss/year.** Query with published clips. Length: 1,500-2,500 words. **Pays $50-250.**
Poetry: Avant-garde, free verse, haiku, light verse, traditional. Must be motorcycle related. **Buys 6 poems/year.** Submit 12 maximum poems. Length: open. **Pays $10-50.**
Fillers: Anecdotes, cartoons. **Buys 12/year.** Length: 100-200 words. **Pays $10-50.**
Tips: "Ride a motorcycle and be able to construct a readable sentence!"

$ $ CLASSIC AUTO RESTORER, Fancy Publishing, Inc., P.O. Box 6050, Mission Viejo CA 92690-6050. (714)855-8822. Fax: (714)855-3045. **Contact:** Ted Kade, managing editor. **85% freelance written.** Monthly magazine on auto restoration. "Our readers own old cars and they work on them. We help our readers by providing as much practical, how-to information as we can about restoration and old cars." Estab. 1989. Pays on publication. Publishes ms an average of 3 months after acceptance. Buys first North American serial or one-time rights. Submit seasonal material 4 months in advance. Reports in 2 months. Sample copy for $5.50. Writer's guidelines free.
Nonfiction: How-to (auto restoration), new product, photo feature, technical, product evaluation. Buys 120 mss/year. Query with or without published clips. Length: 200-2,500 words. **Pays $150/published page, including photos and illustrations.**
Photos: Send photos with submission. Reviews contact sheets, transparencies and 5×7 prints. Technical drawings that illustrate articles in black ink are welcome. Offers no additional payment for photos accepted with ms.
Tips: "Query first. Interview the owner of a restored car. Present advice to others on how to do a similar restoration. Seek advice from experts. Go light on history and non-specific details. Make it something that the magazine regularly uses. Do automotive how-tos."

N $ $ CLASSIC TRUCKS, Primedia/McMullen Argus Publishing, 774 S. Placentia Ave., Placentia CA 92680. (714)572-2255. Fax: (714)572-1864. Website: http://www.mcmullenargus.com. **Contact:** Dan Sanchez, editor. Managing Editor: Mat Emery. Monthly magazine covering classic trucks from the 1930s to 1973. Estab. 1994. Circ. 60,000. Pays on publication. Byline given. Buys first North American serial rights. Editorial lead time 4 months. Submit seasonal material 4 months in advance. Writer's guidelines free.
Nonfiction: How-to, interview/profile, new product, technical, travel. Query. Length: 1,500-5,000 words. **Pays $75-200/page for assigned articles; $100/page maximum for unsolicited articles.**
Photos: Send photos with submission. Reviews transparencies and 5×7 prints. Negotiates payment individually. Captions, model releases, identification of subjects required. Buys one-time rights.
Columns/Departments: Buys 24 mss/year. Query.

$ $ CRUISING RIDER MAGAZINE, Motorcycling with Style, (formerly *BLVD Magazine*), Hansen Communications, 11435 N. Cave Creek Rd., Suite 101, Phoenix AZ 85020. (602)997-5887. Fax: (602)997-6567. E-mail: joshua@verdenet.com. **Contact:** Joshua Placa, editor (P.O. Box 1943, Sedona AZ 86336). **50% freelance written.** "Bimonthly coffee table magazine with national distribution for professional, affluent cruiser-style motorcycle enthusiasts. Crosses all brand lines in coverage. Query for events. Freestyle, technical, off-beat and humorous or travel (bike included) features." Estab. 1996. Circ. 200,000. Pays on publication. Publishes ms an average of 3 months after acceptance. Byline given. Buys all rights. Editorial lead time 2 months. Submit seasonal material 6 months in advance. Accepts simultaneous submissions. Reports as soon as possible. Sample copy and writer's guidelines free.
Nonfiction: General interest, how-to, humor, interview/profile, new product, personal experience, photo feature, techni-

cal, travel. **Buys 20-30 mss/year.** Query with published clips. Length: 500-2,500 words. **Pays $150-750.** Sometimes pays expenses of writers on assignment.
Photos: Send photos with submission. Negotiates payment individually. Buys all rights.
Columns/Departments: Street Scene (industry, insurance, legal news), words vary; Where It's At (events), 200 words; Fashion (motor clothes), 1,000 words; Training Wheels (riding safety), 1,000 words. **Buys 12 mss/year.** Query with published clips. **Pays $50-300.**
Fillers: Anecdotes, facts, gags to be illustrated by cartoonist, newsbreaks, short humor. Length: 50-200 words. **Pays $50-150.**

N $ $ **EASYRIDERS MAGAZINE**, Paisano Publications, Inc., P.O. Box 3000, Agoura Hills CA 91301. (818)889-8740. **Contact**: Nancy Trier, executive assistant. Editor: Keith R. Ball. Managing Editor: Lisa Pedicini. **50% freelance written.** Monthly magazine covering motorcycle events and articles for Harley-Davidson type audience." Estab. 1971. Pays on publication. Byline given. Buys first rights. Editorial lead time 3 months. Submit seasonal material 3 months in advance. Writer's guidelines free.
Nonfiction: Book excerpts, essays, exposé, general interest, historical/nostalgic, how-to, humor, inspirational, interview/profile, new product, opinion, personal experience, photo feature, technical, travel. Query. Length: 1,000-3,000 words. **Pays 25¢/word.** Sometimes pays expenses of writers on assignment.
Photos: Send photos with submission. Captions, model releases and identification of subjects required. Buys all rights.
Fiction: Adventure, erotica, experimental, fantasy, historical, humorous, suspense, western, motorcycle stories.

$ $ **FOUR WHEELER MAGAZINE**, 3330 Ocean Park Blvd., Santa Monica CA 90405. (310)392-2998. Fax: (310)392-1171. Website: http://www.fourwheeler.com. Editor: John Stewart. **20% freelance written.** Works with a small number of new/unpublished writers each year. Monthly magazine covering four-wheel-drive vehicles, back-country driving, competition and travel/adventure. Estab. 1963. Circ. 355,466. Pays on publication. Publishes ms an average of 4 months after acceptance. Buys all rights. Submit seasonal material at least 4 months in advance. Writer's guidelines for #10 SASE.
Nonfiction: 4WD competition and travel/adventure articles, technical, how-tos, and vehicle features about unique four-wheel drives. "We like the adventure stories that bring four wheeling to life in word and photo: mud-running deserted logging roads, exploring remote, isolated trails, or hunting/fishing where the 4×4 is a necessity for success." Query with photos before sending complete ms. Length: 1,200-2,000 words; average 4-5 pages when published. **Pays $200-300/feature vehicles; $350-600/travel and adventure; $100-800/technical articles.**
Photos: Requires professional quality color slides and b&w prints for every article. Captions required. Prefers Kodachrome 64 or Fujichrome 50 in 35mm or 2¼ formats. "Action shots a must for all vehicle features and travel articles."
Tips: "Show us you know how to use a camera as well as the written word. The easiest way for a new writer/photographer to break in to our magazine is to read several issues of the magazine, then query with a short vehicle feature that will show his or her potential as a creative writer/photographer."

$ $ **4-WHEEL DRIVE & SPORT UTILITY**, McMullen-Argus, 774 S. Placentia Ave., Placentia CA 92670. (714)572-2255. Fax: (714)572-7337. **Contact:** Trent Riddle, editor. **40% freelance written.** Monthly magazine covering outdoor automotive adventure travel for the enthusiast. Estab. 1985. Circ. 96,000. Pays on publication. Byline given. Buys all rights. Editorial lead time 4 months. Submit seasonal material 6 months in advance. Sample copy for $3.50. Writer's guidelines free.
Nonfiction: General interest, how-to, humor, new product, personal experience, photo feature, travel. No "How I Built My Truck," etc. **Buys 40 mss/year.** Query. **Pays $100-600.**
Photos: Send photos with submission. Reviews contact sheets, transparencies. Offers no additional payment for photos accepted with ms. Captions, model releases, identification of subjects required. Buys all rights.

N $ **HARLEY WOMEN/ASPHALT ANGELS MAGAZINE**, Zacharia Advertising & Publications, P.O. Box 227, Anamosa IA 52205. (319)462-4855. Fax: (319)462-2961. E-mail: aangels@netins.net. Website: http://www.asphaltangels.com. **Contact:** Angie Hanken, co-editor. **50% freelance written.** Bimonthly magazine for motorcycle and Harley female enthusiasts. Estab. 1985. Circ. 60,000. Pays on publication. Publishes ms an average of 2 months after acceptance. Byline given. Buys first rights. Editorial lead time 2 months. Submit seasonal material 2 months in advance. Accepts simultaneous submissions. Sample copy and writer's guidelines free.
Nonfiction: General interest, historical/nostalgic, how-to (technical motorcycle), humor, interview/profile, new product, personal experience, photo feature, technical. **Buys 35 mss/year.** Query with published clips. Length: 200-2,000 words. **Pays $5/100 words, up to 600 words.** Sometimes pays expenses of writers on assignment.
Reprints: Send photocopy of article or typed ms with rights for sale noted and information about when and where the article previously appeared. Pays 100% of amount paid for an original article.
Photos: Send photos. Captions, model releases, identification of subjects required. Buys one-time rights.
Poetry: Avant-garde, free verse, haiku, light verse, traditional. **Buys 6 poems/year. Pays $5¢/word, 600 words max.**
Fillers: Anecdotes, facts, gags to be illustrated by cartoonist, newsbreaks, short humor. No pay.

$ $ **IN THE WIND**, Paisano Publications, P.O. Box 3000, Agoura Hills CA 91376-3000. (818)889-8740. Fax: (818)889-1252. E-mail: ermagazine@aol.com. Editor: Kim Peterson. Managing Editor: Lisa Pedicini. **Contact:** Scott McCool, editoral assistant. **50% freelance written.** Bimonthly magazine "aimed at Harley-Davidson motorcycle riders and motorcycling enthusiasts, *In the Wind* is mainly a pictorial—action photos of bikes being ridden, and events, with a monthly travel piece—Travelin' Trails." Estab. 1978. Circ. 90,000. Pays on publication. Publishes ms an average of 9 months after acceptance. Byline given. Buys all rights. Editorial lead time 6 months. Submit seasonal material 8 months in advance. Reports in 2 weeks on queries; 2 months on mss. Writer's guidelines free.

Nonfiction: Photo feature, travel. No long-winded tech articles. **Buys 6 mss/year.** Query by mail or e-mail. Length: 1,000-2,000 words. **Pays $250-600.** Sometimes pays expenses of writers on assignment.

Photos: Send photos with submission. Reviews transparencies. Offers $30-100/photo. Model releases, identification of subjects required. Buys all rights.

Columns/Departments: Travelin' Trails (good spots to ride to, places to stay, things to do, history), 1,200 words. **Buys 6 mss/year.** Query. **Pays $250-600.**

Poetry: Free verse. Does not want to see graphic violence or drug use. **Buys 10 poems/year.** Submit maximum 3 poems with SASE. Length: 10-100 lines. **Pays $20-100.**

Tips: "Know the subject. Looking for submissions from people who ride their own bikes."

$ $ $ MOTOR TREND, Petersen Publishing Co., 6420 Wilshire Blvd., Los Angeles CA 90048. (213)782-2220. Fax: (213)782-2355. E-mail: mtletters@aol.com. Website: http://www.motortrend.com. **Contact:** C. Van Tune, editor. **5-10% freelance written.** Prefers to work with published/established writers. Monthly magazine for automotive enthusiasts and general interest consumers. Circ. 1,200,000. Publishes ms an average of 3 months after acceptance. Buys all rights. Reports in 1 month.

Nonfiction: "Automotive and related subjects that have national appeal. Emphasis on domestic and imported cars, road tests, driving impressions, auto classics, auto, travel, racing, and high-performance features for the enthusiast. Packed with facts. Freelancers should confine queries to photo-illustrated exotic drives and other feature material; road tests and related activity are handled inhouse. Fact-filled query suggested for all freelancers."

Columns/Departments: Car care (query Rik Paul, senior feature editor); Motorsport (query Mac DeMere, senior road test editor)

Photos: Buys photos, particularly of prototype cars and assorted automotive matter. Pays $25-500 for transparencies.

N $ $ MOTORCYCLE TOUR & CRUISER, TAM Communications, 1010 Summer St., Stamford CT 06905. (203)425-8775. Fax: (203)425-8775. **Contact:** George Depountis, senior editor. Editor: Buzz Kanter. **75% freelance written.** Bimonthly magazine covering touring and cruising motorcycles. Estab. 1993. Circ. 30,000. Pays on publication. Publishes ms an average of 6 months after acceptance. Byline given. Editorial lead time 4 months. Submit seasonal material 6 months in advance. Accepts simultaneous submissions. Writer's guidelines for #10 SASE.

Nonfiction: General interest, historical/nostalgic, how-to, interview/profile, new product, personal experience, technical, travel. No opinion pieces. Query with published clips. Length: 1,000-3,000 words. **Pays $100-400.**

Photos: Send photos with submission. Offers no additional payment for photos accepted with ms. Buys one-time rights.

Columns/Departments: Highway Help (roadside repairs), 600 words; Garage Tech (garage repairs), 600 words; Tours (bike tours), 2,000-2,500 words. Query with published clips.

N $ $ MUSTANG & FORDS MAGAZINE, Petersen Publishing Company, 6420 Wilshire Blvd., Los Angeles CA 90048. Fax: (213)782-2263. E-mail: smartj@petersenpub.com. **Contact:** Jim Smart, editor. **30% freelance written.** Monthly magazine covering vintage post-war Fords, Mercurys, Lincolns. "Anyone who writes to this audience better know Fords. Our audience is primarily early Ford performance buffs. Our typical reader is an aging baby boomer who loves old Fords. Most of them drive new Fords." Estab. 1980. Circ. 100,000 subscribers, plus 75,000 newsstand. Pays on publication. Byline given. Offers $100 kill fee. Buys all rights. Editorial lead time 4 months. Reports in 3 weeks on queries. Sample copy and writer's guidelines free.

Nonfiction: New product, photo feature, technical. Query. Length: 300-1,500 words. **Pays $100-250/page.** Sometimes pays expenses of writers on assignment.

Photos: Send photos with submission. Reviews contact sheets, negatives, transparencies. Offers no additional payment for photos accepted with ms. Captions, model releases, identification of subjects required. Buys one-time rights.

Columns/Departments: Buys 48 mss/year. Query with published clips. Pay varies.

$ $ OFF-ROAD, McMullen & Argus Publishing, Inc., 774 S. Placentia Ave., Placentia CA 92870-6846. (714)572-6801. Fax: (714)572-7337. **Contact:** Rick Shandley, editor. **50% freelance written.** Monthly magazine covering off-road vehicles, racing, travel. "Our audience is full-size, off-road truck enthusiasts." Estab. 1969. Circ. 100,000. Pays on publication. Publishes ms within 6 months after acceptance. Byline given. Buys first North American rights. Editorial lead time 6 months. Submit seasonal material 4-6 months in advance. Reports in 2 weeks on queries.

Nonfiction: How-to, interview/profile, photo feature, technical, travel. **Buys 50 mss/year.** Query or send complete ms with SASE. Length: 550-1,200 words. **Pays $150/published page for mss w/photos; $100/published without photos.** Sometimes pays expenses of writers on assignment.

Photos: Send photos with submission. Reviews contact sheets, negatives, transparencies, prints. Captions, model releases, identification of subjects required. Buys one-time rights.

Fiction: Adventure, historical, humorous. **Buys 1-2 mss/year.** Send complete ms. Length: 500-2,000 words. **Pays $100/page.**

Fillers: Facts, newsbreaks. **Buys 10/year.** Length: 50-500 words. **Pays $15/page.**

Tips: "Study magazine for style! We welcome fax queries. We'd like to see travel pieces that have full-size, four-wheel drive trucks in the story *and* photography."

$ RIDER, TL Enterprises, Inc., 2575 Vista Del Mar Dr., Ventura CA 93001. (805)667-4100. Managing Editor: Donya Carlson. **Contact:** Mark Tuttle, Jr., editor. **50% freelance written.** Monthly magazine on motorcycling. "*Rider* serves owners and enthusiasts of road and street motorcycling, focusing on touring, commuting, camping and general sport street riding." Estab. 1974. Circ. 140,000. Pays on publication. Publishes ms an average of 6-12 months after acceptance. Byline given. Offers 25% kill fee. Buys first North American serial rights. Editorial lead time 4 months. Submit seasonal material 6 months in advance. Reports in 2 months. Sample copy for $2.95. Writer's guidelines for #10 SASE.
Nonfiction: General interest, historical/nostalgic, how-to (re: motorcycling), humor, interview/profile, personal experience. Does not want to see "fiction or articles on 'How I Began Motorcycling.' " **Buys 30 mss/year.** Query. Length: 500-1,500 words. **Pays $100 minimum for unsolicited articles.**
Photos: Send photos with submission. Reviews contact sheets, transparencies and 5×7 prints (b&w only). Offers no additional payment for photos accepted with ms. Captions required. Buys one-time rights.
Columns/Departments: Rides, Rallies & Clubs (favorite ride or rally), 800-1,000 words. **Buys 15 mss/year.** Query. **Pays $150.**
Tips: "We rarely accept manuscripts without photos (slides or b&w prints). Query first. Follow guidelines available on request. We are most open to feature stories (must include excellent photography) and material for 'Rides, Rallies and Clubs.' Include information on routes, local attractions, restaurants and scenery in favorite ride submissions."

$ $ $ ROAD & TRACK, Hachette Filipacchi Magazines Inc., 1499 Monrovia Ave., Newport Beach CA 92663. (714)720-5300. Fax: (714)631-2757. Editor: Thomas L. Bryant. **Contact:** Ellida Maki, managing editor. **25% freelance written.** Monthly automotive magazine. Estab. 1947. Circ. 740,000. Pays on publication. Publishes ms an average of 6 months after acceptance. Kill fee varies. Buys first rights. Editorial lead time 3 months. Reports in 1 month on queries; 2 months on mss.
Nonfiction: Automotive interest. No how-to. Query. Length: 2,000 words. Pay varies. Pays expenses of writers on assignment.
Reprints: Send photocopy of article or short story or typed ms with rights for sale noted.
Photos: State availability of photos with submissions. Reviews transparencies, prints. Negotiates payment individually. Model releases required. Buys one-time rights.
Columns/Department: Reviews (automotive), 500 words. Query. Pay varies.
Fiction: Automotive. Query. Length: 2,000 words. Pay varies.
Tips: "Because mostly written by staff or assignment, we rarely purchase unsolicited manuscripts—but it can and does happen! Writers must be knowledgeable about enthusiast cars."

$ $ TRUCKIN', World's Leading Sport Truck Publication, McMullen & Yee Publishing, 774 S. Placentia Ave., Placentia CA 92670. (714)572-2255. Fax: (714)572-1864. **Contact:** Kevin Wilson, editor. Vice President Editorial: Steve Stillwell. 15% freelance written. Monthly magazine covering customized sport trucks. "We purchase events coverage, technical articles and truck features, all having to be associated with customized ½ ton pickups and mini-trucks." Estab. 1975. Circ. 200,000. Pays on publication. Buys all rights unless previously agreed upon. Editorial lead time 3 months. Submit seasonal material 6 months in advance. Reports in 2 weeks on queries; 1 month on mss. Sample copy for $4.50. Writer's guidelines free.
Nonfiction: How-to, new product, photo feature, technical, events coverage. **Buys 50 mss/year.** Query. Length: 1,000 words minimum. Pay negotiable. Sometimes pays expenses of writers on assignment.
Photos: Send photos with submission. Reviews contact sheets and transparencies. Captions, model releases, identification of subjects required. Buys all rights unless previously agreed upon.
Columns/Departments: Bill Blankenship. Insider (latest automotive/truck news), 2,000 words. **Buys 70 mss/year.** Send complete ms. **Pays $25 minimum.**
Fillers: Bill Blankenship. Anecdotes, facts, newsbreaks. **Buys 50/year.** Length: 600-1,000 words. Pay negotiable.
Tips: "Send all queries and submissions in envelopes larger than letter size to avoid being detained with a mass of reader mail. Send complete packages with transparencies and contact sheets (with negatives). Submit hard copy and a computer disc when possible. Editors purchase the materials that are the least complicated to turn into magazine pages! All materials have to be fresh/new and primarily outside of California."

N ✪ $ $ VETTE MAGAZINE, CSK Publishing, Inc., 299 Market St., Saddle Brook NJ 07663. (201)712-9300, ext. 617. Fax: (201)712-9899. **Contact:** Richard A. Lentinello, editor-in-chief. Managing Editor: Peter Easton. **75% freelance written.** Monthly magazine covering all subjects related to the Corvette automobile. "Our readership is extremely knowledgeable about the subject of Corvettes. Therefore, writers must know the subject thoroughly and be good at fact checking." Estab. 1976. Circ. 65,000. Offers 50% kill fee. Buys first North American serial rights. Submit seasonal material 4 months in advance. Query for electronic submissions. Reports in 6 weeks. Sample copy for 9×12 SAE with 6 first-class stamps. Writer's guidelines for #10 SASE.

Nonfiction: General interest, historical/nostalgic, how-to, interview/profile, new product, personal experience, photo feature, technical, travel. **Buys 120 mss/year.** Query with published clips. Length: 400-2,700 words. **Pays $150-750 for assigned articles; $100-350 for unsolicited articles.** Sometimes pays expenses of writers on assignment.

Photos: State availability of photos with submission. Reviews contact sheets. Offers no additional payment for photos accepted with ms. Captions and model releases required. Buys one-time rights.

Columns/Departments: Reviews (books/videos), 400-500 words. **Buys 12-20 mss/year.** Query. **Pays $75-200.**

N $ $ $ $ VIPER MAGAZINE, The Magazine for Dodge Viper Enthusiasts, (formerly *Viper Quarterly*), J.R. Thompson Co., 31670 W. 12 Mile Rd., Farmington Hills MI 48334-4459. (248)553-4566. Fax: (248)553-2138. E-mail: jrt@jrthompson.com. **Contact**: Daniel Charles Ross, editor-in-chief. Editorial Director: John Thompson. **40% freelance written.** Quarterly magazine covering "all Vipers—all the time." Also the official magazine of the Viper Club of America. "Speak to *VM* readers from a basis of Viper knowledge and enthusiasm. We take an honest, journalistic approach to all stories, but we're demonstrably and understandably proud of the Dodge Viper sports car, its manufacturer and employees." Estab. 1995. Circ. 15,000. **Pays on acceptance**. Publishes ms an average of 4 months after acceptance. Byline given. Buys first rights or second serial (reprint) rights. Editorial lead time 5 months. Submit seasonal material 6 months in advance. Reports in 1 week. Writer's guidelines for #10 SASE or by e-mail.

Nonfiction: Query. Length: 400-1,500 words. **Pays $1/word.** Sometimes pays expenses of writers on assignment.

Reprints: Send information about when and where the article previously appeared. Payment varies.

Photos: State availability or send photos with submission. Negotiates payment individually. Captions, model releases and identification of subjects required. Buys all rights.

Columns/Departments: SnakeBites (coverage of Viper Club of America events such as local chapter activities, fundraising, track days, etc.), under 200 words; Competition (competitive Viper events such as road-racing, drag-racing, etc.), under 200 words. **Pays $1/word.**

Fillers: Anecdotes, facts, gags to be illustrated by cartoonist, newsbreaks, short humor. Length: 25-100 words. **Pays $1/word.**

Tips: "Being a Viper owner is a good start, since you have been exposed to our 'culture' and probably receive the magazine. This is an even more specialized magazine than traditional auto-buff books, so knowing Vipers is essential."

AVIATION

Professional and private pilots and aviation enthusiasts read the publications in this section. Editors want material for audiences knowledgeable about commercial aviation. Magazines for passengers of commercial airlines are grouped in the Inflight category. Technical aviation and space journals and publications for airport operators, aircraft dealers and others in aviation businesses are listed under Aviation and Space in the Trade section.

$ $ $ $ AIR & SPACE/SMITHSONIAN MAGAZINE, 370 L'Enfant Promenade SW, 10th Floor, Washington DC 20024-2518. (202)287-3733. Fax: (202)287-3163. E-mail: airspacedt@aol.com. Website: http://www.airspacemag.com. Editor: George Larson. **Contact:** Linda Shiner, executive editor. **80% freelance written.** Prefers to work with published/established writers. Bimonthly magazine covering aviation and aerospace for a non-technical audience. "The emphasis is on the human rather than the technological, on the ideas behind the events. Features are slanted to a technically curious, but not necessarily technically knowledgeable audience. We are looking for unique angles to aviation/aerospace stories, history, events, personalities, current and future technologies, that emphasize the human-interest aspect." Estab. 1985. Circ. 284,000. **Pays on acceptance.** Byline given. Offers kill fee. Buys first North American serial rights. Adapts from soon to be published books. Reports in 3 months. Sample copy for $5. Guidelines free.

Nonfiction: Book excerpts, essays, general interest (on aviation/aerospace), historical/nostalgic, humor, photo feature, technical. **Buys 50 mss/year.** Query with published clips. Length: 1,500-3,000 words. **Pays $1,000-2,500 average.** Pays expenses of writers on assignment.

- The editors are actively seeking stories covering space and general or business aviation.

Photos: State availability of illustrations with submission. Reviews 35mm transparencies. Refuses unsolicited material.

Columns/Departments: Above and Beyond (first person), 1,500-2,000 words; Flights and Fancy (whimsy), approximately 800 words; From the Field (science or engineering in the trenches), 1,200 words; Collections (profiles of unique museums), 1,200 words. **Buys 25 mss/year.** Query with published clips. **Pays $1,000 maximum.** Soundings (brief items, timely but not breaking news), 500-700 words. **Pays $150-300.**

Tips: "Soundings is most open to freelancers. We continue to be interested in stories about space exploration."

$ $ AIR LINE PILOT The Magazine of Professional Flight Deck Crews, Air Line Pilots Association, 535 Herndon Parkway, P.O. Box 1169, Herndon VA 20172. (703)481-4460. Fax: (703)689-4370. E-mail: magazine@alpa.org. Website: http://www.alpa.org. **Contact:** Gary DiNunno, editor. **10% freelance written.** Prefers to work with published/established writers; works with a small number of new/unpublished writers each year. Monthly magazine for airline pilots covering commercial aviation industry information—economics, avionics, equipment, systems, safety—that affects a pilot's life in professional sense. Also includes information about management/labor relations trends, contract negotiations, etc. Estab. 1931. Circ. 72,000. **Pays on acceptance.** Publishes ms an average of 6 months after acceptance. Offers 50% kill fee. Buys all rights except book rights. Submit seasonal material 6 months in advance. Reports in 2 months. Sample copy for $2. Writer's guidelines for #10 SASE.

Nonfiction: Humor, inspirational, photo feature, technical. **Buys 20 mss/year.** Query with or without published clips, or send complete ms and SASE. Length: 700-3,000 words. **Pays $100-500 for assigned articles; pays $50-500 for unsolicited articles.**

Reprints: Send photocopy of article or typed ms with rights for sale noted and information about when and where the article previously appeared. Pay varies.

Photos: "Our greatest need is for strikingly original cover photographs featuring ALPA flight deck crew members and their airlines in their operating environment." Send photos with submission. Reviews contact sheets, 35mm transparencies and 8×10 prints. Offers $10-35/b&w photo, $20-50 for color used inside and $350 for color used as cover. For cover photography, shoot vertical rather than horizontal. Identification of subjects required. Buys all rights for cover photos, one-time rights for inside color.

Tips: "For our feature section, we seek aviation industry information that affects the life of a professional airline pilot from a career standpoint. We also seek material that affects a pilot's life from a job security and work environment standpoint. Any airline pilot featured in an article must be an Air Line Pilot Association member in good standing. Our readers are very experienced and require a high level of technical accuracy in both written material and photographs."

$ $ $ AOPA PILOT, Official Publication of: Aircraft Owners and Pilots Association, 421 Aviation Way, Frederick MD 21701. (301)695-2350. Fax: (301)695-2180. Website: http://www.aopa.org/pilot. Editor-in-Chief: Thomas B. Haines. Monthly. *AOPA Pilot* contains feature articles on both new and older aircraft, piloting techniques, safety issues and regulatory initiatives that affect Federal Aviation Regulations. Articles address special informational requirements for all pilots." This magazine did not respond to our request for information. Query before submitting.

$ BALLOON LIFE, Balloon Life Magazine, Inc., 2336 47th Ave. SW, Seattle WA 98116-2331. (206)935-3649. Fax: (206)935-3326. E-mail: tom@balloonlife.com. Website: http://www.balloonlife.com. **Contact:** Tom Hamilton, editor-in-chief. **75% freelance written.** Monthly magazine for sport of hot air ballooning. Estab. 1986. Circ. 4,000. Pays on publication. Byline given. Offers 50-100% kill fee. Buys non-exclusive all rights. Submit seasonal material 4 months in advance. Reports in 3 weeks on queries; 1 month on mss. Sample copy for 9×12 SAE with $2 postage. Writer's guidelines for #10 SASE.

Nonfiction: Book excerpts, general interest, events/rallies, safety seminars, balloon clubs/organizations, how-to (flying hot air balloons, equipment techniques), interview/profile, new product, letters to the editor, technical. **Buys 150 mss/year.** Query with or without published clips, or send complete ms. Length: 1,000-1,500 words. **Pays $50-75 for assigned articles; $25-50 for unsolicited articles.** Sometimes pays expenses of writers on assignment.

Reprints: Send photocopy of article or short story or typed ms with rights for sale noted and information about when and where the article or story previously appeared. Pays 100% of amount paid for an original article or story.

Photos: Send photos with submission. Reviews transparencies, prints. Offers $15/inside photo, $50/cover. Identification of subjects required. Buys non-exclusive all rights.

Columns/Departments: Hangar Flying (real life flying experience that others can learn from), 800-1,500 words; Crew Quarters (devoted to some aspect of crewing), 900 words; Preflight (a news and information column), 100-500 words; **pays $50.** Logbook (recent balloon events—events that have taken place in last 3-4 months), 300-500 words; **pays $20. Buys 60 mss/year.** Send complete ms.

Fiction: Humorous. **Buys 3-5 mss/year.** Send complete ms. Length: 800-1,500 words. **Pays $50.**

Tips: "This magazine slants toward the technical side of ballooning. We are interested in articles that help to educate and provide safety information. Also stories with manufacturers, important individuals and/or of historic events and technological advances important to ballooning. The magazine attempts to present articles that show 'how-to' (fly, business opportunities, weather, equipment). Both our Feature Stories section and Logbook section are where most manuscripts are purchased."

$ CESSNA OWNER MAGAZINE, Jones Publishing, Inc., N7450 Aanstad Rd., P.O. Box 5000, Iola WI 54945. (715)445-5000. Fax: (715)445-4053. E-mail: aircraft@aircraftownergroup.com. Website: http://www.aircraftownergroup.com. **Contact:** Bruce Loppnow, publisher and editor. **50% freelance written.** Monthly magazine covering Cessna single and twin engine aircraft. "*Cessna Owner Magazine* is the official publication of the Cessna Owner Organization (C.O.O.). Therefore, our readers are Cessna aircraft owners, renters, pilots, and enthusiasts. Articles should deal with buying/selling, flying, maintaining, or modifying Cessnas. The purpose of our magazine is to promote safe, fun, and affordable flying." Estab. 1975. Circ. 6,000. Pays on publication. Publishes ms an average of 3 months after acceptance. Byline given. Buys first, one-time or second serial (reprint) rights or makes work-for-hire assignment on occasion. Editorial lead time 1 month. Submit seasonal material 3 months in advance. Reports in 2 weeks on queries; 1 month on mss. Sample copy and writer's guidelines free.

Nonfiction: Historical/nostalgic (of specific Cessna models), how-to (aircraft repairs and maintenance), new product, personal experience, photo feature, technical (aircraft engines and airframes). "We are always looking for articles about Cessna aircraft modifications. We also need articles on Cessna twin-engine aircraft. April, July, and October are always big issues for us, because we attend various airshows during these months and distribute free magazines. Feature articles on unusual, highly-modified, or vintage Cessnas are especially welcome during these months. Good photos are also a must." Special issues: Engines (maintenance, upgrades; Avionics (purchasing, new products). **Buys 24 mss/year.** Query. Length: 1,500-3,500 words. **Pays 7-11¢/word.**

Reprints: Send typed ms with rights for sale noted and information about when and where the article previously appeared.

Photos: Send photos with submission. Reviews 3×5 and larger prints. Captions and identification of subjects required.

Tips: "Always submit a hard copy or ASCII formatted computer disk. Color photos mean a lot to us, and manuscripts stand a much better chance of being published when accompanied by photos. Freelancers can best get published by submitting articles on aircraft modifications, vintage planes, restorations, flight reports, twin-engine Cessnas, etc."

$ FLYER, (formerly *General Aviation News & Flyer*), N.W. Flyer, Inc., P.O. Box 39099, Tacoma WA 98439-0099. (253)471-9888. Fax: (253)471-9911. E-mail: comments@ganflyer.com. Website: http://www.ganflyer.com. **Contact:** Kirk Gormley, managing editor. **30% freelance written.** Prefers to work with published/established writers. Biweekly tabloid covering general, regional, national and international aviation stories of interest to pilots, aircraft owners and aviation enthusiasts. Estab. 1949. Circ. 35,000. Pays 1 month after publication. Publishes ms an average of 3 months after acceptance. Byline given. Buys one-time and first North American serial rights; on occasion second serial (reprint) rights. Submit seasonal material 2 months in advance. Reports in 2 months. Sample copy for $3.50. Writer's and style guidelines for #10 SASE.

Nonfiction: "We stress news. A controversy over an airport, a first flight of a new design, storm or flood damage to an airport, a new business opening at your local airport—those are the sort of projects that may get a new writer onto our pages, if they arrive here soon after they happen. We are especially interested in reviews of aircraft." Personality pieces involving someone who is using his or her airplane in an unusual way, and stories about aviation safety are of interest. Query first on historical, nostalgic features and profiles/interviews. Many special sections throughout the year; send SASE for list. **Buys 100 mss/year.** Query or send complete ms. Length: 500-2,000 words. **Pays up to $3/printed column inch maximum.** Rarely pays the expenses of writers on assignment.

Reprints: Accepts previously published submissions from noncompetitive publications, if so noted. Payment varies.

Photos: Shoot clear, up-close photos, preferably color prints or slides. Send photos with ms. Captions and photographer's ID required. Pays $10/b&w photo and $50/cover photo 1 month after publication.

Tips: "The longer the story, the less likely it is to be accepted. A 1,000-word story with good photos is the best way to see your name in print. If you are covering controversy, send us both sides of the story. Most of our features and news stories are assigned in response to a query."

$ $ $ FLYING, Hachette Filipacchi Magazines, Inc. 500 W. Putnam, Greenwich CT 06830. (203)622-2700. This magazine did not respond to our request for information. Query before submitting.

N $ MOUNTAIN PILOT MAGAZINE, Wiesnor Publishing, 7009 S. Potomac St., Englewood CO 80112. (303)397-7600, etx. 284. Fax: (303)397-7619. E-mail: ehuber@winc.usa.com. **Contact:** Edward Huber, editor. **50% freelance written.** Bimonthly. "*Mountain Pilot* is the only magazine that serves pilots operating or planning to operate in the mountainous states. Editorial material focuses on mountain performance—flying, safety and education." Estab. 1985. Circ. 15,000. Pays 30 days after publication. Byline sometimes given. Buys first rights. Editorial lead time 3 months. Submit seasonal material 6 months in advance. Reports in 3 weeks on queries. Writer's guidelines free.

Nonfiction: General interest, how-to, opinion, personal experience, technical (aircraft maintenance). "Regular features include: aviation experiences, technology, high altitude maintenance and flying, cold weather tips and pilot techniques." No fiction. **Buys 20-30 mss/year.** Query. Length: 700-2,000 words. **Pays $50 for assigned articles.**

Photos: Send photos with submission. Reviews slides, any size prints. Offers no additional payment for photos accepted with ms. Captions, model releases and identification of subjects required.

Columns/Departments: Buys 6 mss/year. Query. **Pays $50.**

$ $ PIPERS MAGAZINE, Jones Publishing, Inc., N7450 Aanstad Rd., P.O. Box 5000, Iola WI 54945. (715)445-5000. Fax: (715)445-4053. E-mail: aircraft@aircraftownergroup.com. Website: http://www.aircraftownergroup.com. **Contact:** Bruce Loppnow, publisher/editor. **50% freelance written.** Monthly magazine covering Piper single and twin engine aircraft. "*Pipers Magazine* is the official publication of the Piper Owner Society (P.O.S). Therefore, our readers are Piper aircraft owners, renters, pilots, mechanics and enthusiasts. Articles should deal with buying/selling, flying, maintaining or modifying Pipers. The purpose of our magazine is to promote safe, fun and affordable flying." Estab. 1988. Circ. 5,000. Pays on publication. Publishes ms an average of 3 months after acceptance. Buys first, one-time or second serial (reprint) rights or makes work-for-hire assignment on occasion. Editorial lead time 1 month. Submit seasonal material 3 months in advance. Reports in 2 weeks on queries; 1 month on mss. Sample copy and writer's guidelines free.

Nonfiction: Historical/nostalgic (of specific models of Pipers), how-to (aircraft repairs & maintenance), new product, personal experience, photo feature, technical (aircraft engines and airframes). "We are always looking for articles about Piper aircraft modifications. We also are in need of articles on Piper twin engine aircraft, and late-model Pipers. April, July, and October are always big issues for us, because we attend airshows during these months and distribute free magazines." Feature articles on unusual, highly-modified, vintage, late-model, or ski/float equipped Pipers are especially welcome. Good photos are a must. **Buys 24 mss/year.** Query. Length: 1,500-3,500 words. **Pays 7-11¢/word.**

Reprints: Send typed ms with rights for sale noted and information about when and where the article previously appeared.
Photos: Send photos with submissions. Reviews transparencies, 3×5 and larger prints. Offers no additional payment for photos accepted. Captions, identification of subjects required.
Tips: "Always submit a hard copy or ASCII formatted computer disk. Color photos mean a lot to us, and manuscripts stand a much greater chance of being published when accompanied by photos. Freelancers can best get published by submitting articles on aircraft modifications, vintage planes, late-model planes, restorations, twin-engine Pipers, etc."

$ $ PLANE AND PILOT, Werner Publishing Corp., 12121 Wilshire Blvd., Suite 1220, Los Angeles CA 90025. (310)820-1500. Fax: (310)826-5008. E-mail: editors@planeandpilot.com. Website: http://www.planeandpilotmag.com. Editor: Steve Werner. **Contact:** Jenny Shearer, managing editor. **100% freelance written.** Monthly magazine that covers general aviation. "We think a spirited, conversational writing style is most entertaining for our readers. We are read by private and corporate pilots, instructors, students, mechanics and technicians—everyone involved or interested in general aviation." Estab. 1964. Circ. 130,000. Pays on publication. Publishes ms an average of 3 months after acceptance. Byline given. Kill fee negotiable. Buys all rights. Submit seasonal material 4 months in advance. Reports in 2 months. Sample copy for $5.50. Writer's guidelines free.
Nonfiction: Book excerpts, essays, general interest, how-to, new product, personal experience, technical, travel, pilot proficiency and pilot reports on aircraft. **Buys 150 mss/year.** Submit query with idea, length and the type of photography you expect to provide. Length: 1,000-2,500 words. **Pays $200-500.** Rates vary depending on the value of the material as judged by the editors. Pays expenses of writers on assignment.
Reprints: Send photocopy of article or typed ms with rights for sale noted with information about when and where the article previously appeared. Pays 50% of amount paid for original article.
Photos: Submit suggested heads, decks and captions for all photos with each story. Submit b&w photos in proof sheet form with negatives or 8×10 prints with glossy finish. Submit color photos in the form of 2¼×2¼ or 4×5 or 35mm transparencies in plastic sleeves. Offers $50-300/photo. Buys all rights.
Columns/Departments: Readback (any newsworthy items on aircraft and/or people in aviation), 100-300 words; Flight To Remember (a particularly difficult or wonderful flight), 1,000-1,500 words; Jobs & Schools (a feature or an interesting school or program in aviation), 1,000-1,500 words; and Travel (any traveling done in piston-engine aircraft), 1,000-2,500 words. **Buys 30 mss/year.** Send complete ms. **Pays $200-500.** Rates vary depending on the value of the material as judged by the editors.

N $ $ $ PRIVATE PILOT, Y-Visionary, Inc., 265 S. Anita Dr., #120, Orange CA 92868. (714)939-9991. Fax: (714)939-9909. E-mail: aircrftdr@aol.com, stevewhitson@compuserve.com. **Contact**: Steve Whitson, editor; Bill Fedorko, executive editor' or Amy Maclean, managing editor. **85% freelance written.** Monthly magazine covering general aviation. Estab. 1965. Circ. 85,000. Pays on publication. Publishes ms an average of 4 months after acceptance. Byline given. Buys first North American serial rights. Editorial lead time 3 months. Submit seasonal material 6 months in advance. Reports in 6 weeks on queries; 2 months on mss. Writer's guidelines free.
Nonfiction: General interest, how-to, humor, personal experience, travel, aircraft types. **Buys 100 mss/year.** Query. Length: 1,000-2,500 words. **Pays $400-850. Sometimes pays expenses of writers on assignment.**
Photos: State availability of photos with submission. Reviews 35mm transparencies. Negotiates payment individually. Model releases and identification of subjects required. Buys one-time rights.
Tips: "Send good queries. Readers are pilots who want to read about aircraft, places to go and ways to save money."

$ WOMAN PILOT, Aviatrix Publishing, Inc., P.O. Box 485, Arlington Heights IL 60006-0485. **Contact:** Danielle Clarneaux, editor. **80% freelance written.** Bimonthly magazine covering women who fly all types of aircraft and careers in all areas of aviation. Personal profiles, historical articles and current aviation events. Estab. 1993. Circ. 5,000. Pays on publication. Publishes ms an average of 5 months after acceptance. Byline given. Buys first North American serial rights. Editorial lead time 4 months. Sample copy for $3. Writer's guidelines for #10 SASE.
Nonfiction: Book excerpts, historical/nostalgic, humor, interview/profile, new product, personal experience, photo feature. **Buys 35 mss/year.** Query with published clips or send complete ms. Length: 500-3,000 words. **Pays $20-55 for assigned articles; $20-40 for unsolicited articles; and contributor copies.**
Reprints: Send tearsheet or photocopy of article or short story or typed ms with rights for sale noted and information about when and where the article or short story previously appeared.
Photos: State availability or send photos/photocopies with submission. Negotiates payment individually. Captions, model releases, identification of subjects required. Buys one-time rights.
Fiction: Adventure, historical, humorous, slice-of-life vignettes. **Buys 4 mss/year.** Query with or without published clips. Length: 500-2,000 words. **Pays $20-35.**
Fillers: Cartoons. **Buys 6/year. Pays $10-20.**
Tips: "If a writer is interested in writing articles from our leads, she/he should send writing samples and explanation of any aviation background. Include any writing background."

BUSINESS & FINANCE

Business publications give executives and consumers a range of information from local business news and trends to national overviews and laws that affect them. National and regional publications are listed below in separate categories. Magazines that have a technical slant are in the Trade section under Business Management, Finance or Management and Supervision categories.

National

$ $ $ BLACK ENTERPRISE, ABC, 130 Fifth Ave., New York NY 10011. (212)242-8000. This magazine did not respond to our request for information. Query before submitting.

$ $ BUSINESS START-UPS, Entrepreneur Media, Inc., 2392 Morse Ave., Irvine CA 92614. (714)261-2325. Fax: (714)755-4211. Website: http://www.entrepreneurmag.com. **Contact:** Karen Axelton, managing editor. **90% freelance written.** Monthly magazine "provides how-to information for starting a small business, running a small business during the first year and profiles of entrepreneurs who have started successful small businesses." Estab. 1989. Circ. 250,000. **Pays on acceptance.** Byline given. Offers 20% kill fee. Buys first time international rights. Submit seasonal material 6 months in advance. Reports in 2 months on queries. Sample copy for $3 and $3 shipping. Writer's guidelines for SASE (please write: "Attn: Writer's Guidelines" on envelope).
Nonfiction: "Our readers want new business ideas. We're also looking for how-to articles about starting a business that focus precisely on one element of the process: marketing, PR, business plan writing, taxes, financing, selling, low-cost advertising, etc." Profiles of entrepreneurs. "We're also seeking psychological/motivational features. Please read the magazine and writer's guidelines before querying. Query by fax or mail only, please." Feature length: 1,200-1,500 words. **Pays $400-600 for features, $100 for briefs.**
Reprints: Send tearsheet of article and info about when and where the article previously appeared. Pay varies.
Photos: Daryl Hoopes, art director. State availability of photos with submission. Identification of subjects required.
Tips: "We're looking for articles that will appeal to two distinct groups: people who are eager to launch their own companies and people who run new companies." Articles should be lessons-oriented, to-the-point, and concrete, using specific real-world examples that avoid management theory. Write with self-reliance in mind. "Don't tell our readers how to hire someone to write their business plan. Tell them how they can do it themselves."

BUSINESS WEEK does not accept freelance submissions.

$ $ $ $ BUSINESS99, Success Strategies For Small Business, Group IV Communications, Inc., 125 Auburn Court, #100, Thousand Oaks CA 91362-3617. (805)496-6156. Editor: Daniel Kehrer. **Contact:** Maryann Hammers, managing editor. **75% freelance written.** Bimonthly magazine for small and independent business. "We publish only practical, mostly how-to, articles of interest to small business owners all across America." Estab. 1993. Circ. 610,000. **Pays on acceptance.** Publishes ms an average of 4 months after acceptance. Byline given. Offers 25% kill fee. First and non-exclusive reprint rights. Reports in 3-6 months. Sample copy for $6. Writer's guidelines for #10 SASE.

- All submissions will be considered for *Independent Business*, also published by Group IV.

Nonfiction: How-to articles for operating a small business. No "generic" business articles, articles on big business, articles on how to start a business or general articles on economic theory. **Buys 80-100 mss/year.** Query with résumé and published clips; do not send ms. Length: 1,500-2,500 words. **Pays $500-1,500.** Pays expenses of writers on assignment.
Columns/Departments: Smart Marketing, Your Employees, Ad-Vantage, Sales Savvy, Cutting Costs, Tax File, Business Basics, Managing Your Business; all 1,200-1,800 words. **Buys 40-50 mss/year.** Query with résumé and published clips. **Pays $500-1,500.**
Tips: "Talk to small business owners anywhere in America about what they want to read, what concerns or interests them in running a business. All areas open, but we use primarily professional business writers with top credentials in the field. Writers must use real small business examples (no "XYZ Company) examples" to illustrate points being made. Don't be afraid to have a sense of style—and a sense of humor—in your writing. Make it lively. No fax or e-mail queries, please."

$ $ $ DIVIDENDS, Imagination Publishing, 820 W. Jackson Blvd., Suite 450, Chicago IL 60607. (312)627-1020. Fax: (312)627-1105. E-mail: dividends@aol.com. **Contact:** Shannon Watts, editor. 40% freelance written. Custom bimonthly magazine for small and home-based business customers of Staples Office Super Store. "*Dividends* is a resource for small business owners. Articles should include general tips, specific contacts, resources, etc." Circ. 350,000. Pays on publication. Publishes ms an average of 3 months after acceptance. Byline given. Buys first North American serial rights.
Nonfiction: Interview/profile, sales, management, home/office, finance, customer service, human resources, legal, small business. **Buys 25 mss/year.** Query with published clips. Length: 1,200-1,800 words. **Pays 50¢/word.**
Photos: State availability of photos with submission.
Columns/Departments: Sales and marketing, management, technology, finance, legal and tax issues, home office. Length: 500-1,000 words. **Pays 50¢/word.**
Tips: "Our readers are more interested in lessons from their self-employed peers than advice from experts and pundits."

ENTREPRENEUR MAGAZINE, 2392 Morse Ave., Irvine CA 92614. Fax: (714)755-4211. E-mail: entmag@entrepreneurmag.com. Website: http://www.entrepreneurmag.com. **Contact:** Rieva Lesonsky, editor, or Peggy Bennett, articles editor. **40% freelance written.** "Readers are small business owners seeking information on running a better business. *Entrepreneur* readers already run their own businesses. They have been in business for several years and are seeking innovative methods and strategies to improve their business operations. They are also interested in new business ideas and opportunities, as well as current issues that affect their companies." **Pays on acceptance.** Publishes ms an average of 5 months after acceptance. Buys first international rights. Byline given. Submit seasonal material 6 months in advance of issue date. Reports in 3 months. Sample copy for $7 from Order Deaprtment. Writer's guidelines for #10 SASE (please write "Attn: Writer's Guidelines" on envelope).

- *Entrepreneur* publishes the bimonthly *Entrepreneur International* which covers the latest in U.S. trends and franchising for an international audience. (This is not written for a U.S. audience.) They encourage writers with expertise in this area to please query with ideas. Sample copy $6.50 from Order Department.

Nonfiction: How-to (information on running a business, dealing with the psychological aspects of running a business, profiles of unique entrepreneurs), current news/trends and their effect on small business. **Buys 10-20 mss/year.** Query with clips of published work and SASE or query by fax. Length: 2,000 words. Payment varies. Columns not open to freelancers.

Photos: "We use color transparencies to illustrate articles. Please state availability with query." Uses standard color transparencies. Buys first rights.

Tips: "Read several issues of the magazine! Study the feature articles versus the columns. Probably 75 percent of our freelance rejections are for article ideas covered in one of our regular columns. It's so exciting when a writer goes beyond the typical, flat 'business magazine query'—how to write a press release, how to negotiate with vendors, etc.—and instead investigates a current trend and then develops a story on how that trend affects small business."

N $ $ $ **ENTREPRENEUR'S HOME OFFICE**, Entrepreneur Group Inc., 2392 Morse Ave., Irvine CA 92614. Fax: (714)755-4211. E-mail: hoffice@entrepreneurmag.com. Website: http://www.entrepreneurmag.com. **Contact:** Janean Chun, articles editor. Editor: Rieva Lesonsky. Managing Editor: Maria Valdez Haubrich. **70% freelance written.** Bimonthly consumer magazine covering home based business. "Information and help for home based business owners who have been in business for 3 years or more." Estab. 1997. Circ. 150,000. Byline given. Offers 25% kill fee. Buys first rights. Editorial lead time 8 months. Submit seasonal material 8 months in advance. Accepts simultaneous submissions. Reports in 2 months on queries. Sample copy for $2.95 plus $3 shipping; writer's guidelines for #10 SASE.

Nonfiction: Book excerpts, essays, general interest, how-to, personal experience, technical. No start-up articles or profiles. **Buys 30 mss/year**. Length: 2,000-3,000 words. **Pays $500-1,000**. Sometimes pays expenses of writers on assignment.

Photos: State availability of photos with submissions.

Tips: "Keep in mind the reader has already been in business for at least three years and has specific needs as a home based business owners. Use real home based entrepreneurial examples."

FORBES, 60 Fifth Ave., New York NY 10011. (212)620-2200. Website: http://www.forbes.com. This magazine did not respond to our request for information. Query before submitting.

$ $ $ $ **FORTUNE**, Time Inc. Magazine Co. Time & Life Bldg., Rockefeller Center, 15th Floor, New York NY 10020. (212)522-1212. Website: http://www.pathfinder.com/fortune. This magazine did not respond to our request for information. Query before submitting.

$ $ $ **INDEPENDENT BUSINESS: America's Small Business Magazine**, Group IV Communications, Inc., 125 Auburn Ct., #100, Thousand Oaks CA 91362-3617. (805)496-6156, ext. 18. Fax: (805)496-5469. Website: http://www.yoursource.com. **Contact:** Maryann Hammers, managing editor. Editorial Director: Don Phillipson. **75% freelance written.** Bimonthly magazine for small and independent business. "We publish only practical 'how-to' articles of interest to small business owners all across America." Estab. 1989. Circ. 630,000. **Pays on acceptance.** Publishes ms an average of 4 months after acceptance. Byline given. Offers 25% kill fee. Buys first rights. Reports in 6 months. Sample copy for $4. Writer's guidelines for #10 SASE.

- All submissions will also be considered for *Business99*, also published by Group IV.

Nonfiction: How-to articles for operating a small business. No "generic" business articles, articles on big business, how to start a business or general economic theory. **Buys 80-100 mss/year.** Query with résumé and published clips; do not send mss. Length: 1,000-2,000 words. **Pays $500-1,500.** Pays expenses of writers on assignment.

Columns/Departments: Tax Tactics, Money Matters, Small Business Computing, Marketing Moves, Ad-visor, Your Employees, Managing Smart, Selling Smart, Business Cost-Savers, all 1,000-2,000 words. **Buys 40-50 mss/year.** Query with résumé and published clips. **Pays $500-1,500.**

Tips: "Talk to small business owners anywhere in America about what they want to read, what concerns or interests them in running a business. All areas open, but we use primarily professional business writers with top credentials in the field. Please read magazine before submitting query!"

☆ $ $ **PROFIT**, Investor Portfolio, Profit Publications, Inc., 69730 Highway 111, Suite 102, Rancho Mirage CA 92270. (760)202-1545. Fax: (760)202-1544. E-mail: profitpc@aol.com. Editor: Jayne Lanza. Managing Editor: Paula Carrick. **Contact:** Cynthia A. Rushton, staff writer. **40% freelance written.** Bimonthly magazine covering financial issues/lifestyle. "*Profit* is an upscale magazine with financial and lifestyle subject matter. Our reader base is upper income, educated and health conscious individuals." Estab. 1994. Circ. 50,000. Pays on publication. Publishes ms an average of 2 months after acceptance. Byline given. Buys one-time rights. Editorial lead time 2 months. Submit seasonal material 4 months in advance. Sample copy for $7. Writer's guidelines for #10 SASE.

Nonfiction: Book excerpts, exposé, inspirational, new product, travel. No religion, personal experience or pornography. **Buys 12-14 mss/year.** Query with published clips or send complete ms. Length: 500-3,000 words. **Pays $250-750.** Sometimes pays expenses of writers on assignment.

Reprints: Accepts previously published submissions.

Photos: State availability of photos with submission. Negotiates payment individually. Captions, model releases and identification of subjects required. Rights purchased vary.

Columns/Departments: Travel Guide, 600-1,200 words; Health & Medicine, 600-1,800 words; Editorial, 800-1,800 words. **Buys 12 mss/year.** Query. **Pays $150-500.**

Fiction: Novel excerpts. **Buys 6 mss/year.** No religion or pornography. Send complete ms. Length: 500-1,000 words. **Pays $250-750.**

Tips: "We're looking for a creative display of financial facts, new slants. We want to see variety and risky writing that is postitive overall. Submit query and manuscript or query and samples. We want to see your writing style."

N $ $ $ $ REPORT ON BUSINESS MAGAZINE, Globe and Mail, 444 Front St. W., Toronto Ontario M5V 2S9 Canada. (416)585-5499. Fax: (416)585-5705. E-mail: twilson@globeandmail.ca Website: http://www.robmagazine.com/. Editor: Patricia Best. **Contact:** Trish Wilson, managing editor. **50% freelance written.** Monthly "business magazine like *Forbes* or *Fortune* which tries to capture major trends and personalities." Circ. 300,000. **Pays on acceptance.** Publishes ms an average of 4 months after acceptance. Byline given. Offers 50% kill fee. Buys first North American serial rights. Query for electronic submissions. Reports in 3 weeks. Free sample copy.

Nonfiction: Book excerpts, exposé, interview/profile, new product, photo feature. Special issue: quaraterly technology report. **Buys 30 mss/year.** Query with published clips. Length: 2,000-4,000 words. **Pays $200-3,000.** Pays expenses of writers on assignment.

Tips: "For features send a one-page story proposal. We prefer to write about personalities involved in corporate events."

N ✪ $ $ SELF EMPLOYED PROFESSIONAL, Business Media Group, 462 Boston St., Topsfield MA 01983. (978)887-7900. Fax: (978)887-6117. E-mail: sepedit@aol.com. Editor-in-Chief: Barry Harrigan. Managing Editor: Peter Homan. **Contact**: Carole Matthews, senior editor. **95% freelance written.** Magazine published 9 times/year "providing advice on how to run a company of one to upwards of 50 employees more efficiently and profitably. Our readers are sophisticated, technologically savvy business owners with established companies. Our articles provide strategies and information in three main areas: finance, technology and marketing." Estab. 1995. Circ. 125,000. Pays 45 days after acceptance. Publishes ms an average of 1 month after acceptance. Byline given. Offers 10-20% kill fee. Not copyrighted. Buys all rights. Editorial lead time 1 month. Submit seasonal material 3 months in advance. Reports in 1 month on queries; 2 months on mss. Sample copy and writer's guidelines for #10 SASE.

Nonfiction: Book excerpts, essays, how-to (devise marketing strategies; communicate effectively, develop a business plan, find capital, grow a business, use new technology, invest wisely, etc.), humor, interview/profile, new product, personal experience, photo feature, technical. No articles about large firms (100 or more employees) or part-time home office businesses. **Buys 108 mss/year.** Query with published clips. Length: 700-2,500 words. **Pays 15-30¢/word.**

Photos: State availability of photos with submission. Reviews 1×1½ transparencies. Offers no additional payment for photos accepted with ms. Identification of subjects required.

Columns/Departments: Technology-hardware & software (practical application of new products), 1,200 words; Finance-banking, coping (subjects include cash flow, collections, investing, etc.), 1,200 words; Marketing (advice re: business growth, reaching customers, etc.), 1,200 words; Boss (management advice), 1,200 words; Profile (focuses on success or failure of a business person), 1,500 words; Cost Cutter (practical advice on cost containment, lowering overhead, etc.), 1,200 words; Insurance (strategies for life, health coverage), 1,200 words; Client Relations, 1,000 words; Up at Night (humorous look at running your own business), 1,000 words; Reviews (new products, hardware and software and how they help), 100 words. **Buys 72 mss/year.** Query with published clips. **Pays 15-30¢/word.**

Tips: "Queries are the best method; with clips attached. We welcome suggestions for articles that demonstrate successful business strategies and that answer the questions that arise daily for these busy professionals."

"We publish four types of articles: *Features*: Feature articles are the showcase pieces of each issue. Writers explore topics in greater depth and present them in a lively and informative manner. These stories may provide problem-solving tools (for instance, strategies for raising capital), instructions (how to produce effective direct mail), inspiration (a profile of a successful small-business owner and how he or she reached the top) or comparative information (the pros and cons of venture capital vs. private investors). *Technology*: Our technology articles run under a separate banner and feature the latest hardware and software for small businesses. While their main purpose is to inform our readers of new products and their features, we avoid straight product descriptions. Instead, we prefer articles be application driven. *Financial*: These also run under a separate banner and cover topics such as cash flow (collection and cash management strategies), personal investing, retirement options and banking options. Many financial topics apply to businesses of any size. Be sure to explain the implications and risks for a self-employed professional. *Departments*: Departments are short, meaty, informational or how-to articles interpreted for small businesses. Departments such as 'Boss' (management), 'Client Relations,' 'Marketing,' 'Marketing Mix,' 'Cost Cutter,' 'Employee Relations,' 'Insurance,' 'Lawyer,' 'Taxes,'

'Managing Technology,' and 'Up at Night' (last page) run on a rotating basis. Please read some departments in *Self Employed Professional* before you send us ideas."

$ $ $ $ SMART MONEY, Wall Street Journal Magazine of Personal Business, 1755 Broadway, 4th Floor, New York NY 10019. (212)492-1300. Fax:(212)245-7276. E-mail: editors@smartmoney.com. Website: http://www.smartmoney.com. **Contact:** Robert Sabat, managing editor. Editor-in-Chief: Steven Swartz. Monthly magazine. "*Smart Money* is a personal business magazine edited for discriminating investors, featuring practical and imaginative ideas for investing, spending and saving. Articles and features provide action-oriented information on investment opportunities and pitfalls." Estab. 1992. Circ. 750,000. Query before submitting. Accepts queries by mail and fax.

✪ $ $ TECHNICAL ANALYSIS OF STOCKS & COMMODITIES, The Trader's Magazine, Technical Analysis, Inc., 4757 California Ave. SW, Seattle WA 98116-4499. Fax: (206)938-1307. E-mail: editor@traders.com. Website: http://www.traders.com. Publisher: Jack K. Hutson. **Contact:** Thomas R. Hartle, editor. **75% freelance written.** Eager to work with new/unpublished writers. Magazine covers methods of investing and trading stocks, bonds and commodities (futures), options, mutual funds and precious metals. Estab. 1982. Circ. 56,000. Pays on publication. Publishes ms an average of 3 months after acceptance. Byline given. Buys all rights; however, second serial (reprint) rights revert to the author, provided copyright credit is given. Reports in 3 weeks on queries; 1 month on mss. Sample copy for $5. Writer's guidelines for #10 SASE or on website.

Nonfiction: Reviews (new software or hardware that can make a trader's life easier, comparative reviews of software books, services, etc.); how-to (trade); technical (trading and software aids to trading); utilities (charting or computer programs, surveys, statistics or information to help the trader study or interpret market movements); humor (unusual incidents of market occurrences, cartoons). "No newsletter-type, buy-sell recommendations. The article subject must relate to trading psychology, technical analysis, charting or a numerical technique used to trade securities or futures. Virtually requires graphics with every article." **Buys 150 mss/year.** Query with published clips if available or send complete ms. Length: 1,000-4,000 words. **Pays $100-500.** (Applies per inch base rate and premium rate—write for information). Sometimes pays expenses of writers on assignment.

Reprints: Send tearsheet or photocopy of article or typed ms with rights for sale noted and information about when and where the article appeared.

Photos: Christine M. Morrison, art director. State availability of art or photos. Pays $60-350 for b&w or color negatives with prints or positive slides. Captions, model releases and identification of subjects required. Buys one-time and reprint rights.

Columns/Departments: Buys 100 mss/year. Query. Length: 800-1,600 words. **Pays $50-300.**

Fillers: Karen Wasserman, fillers editor. Jokes and cartoons on investment humor. Must relate to trading stocks, bonds, options, mutual funds, commodities or precious metals. **Buys 20/year.** Length: 500 words. **Pays $20-50.**

Tips: "Describe how to use technical analysis, charting or computer work in day-to-day trading of stocks, bonds, commodities, options, mutual funds or precious metals. A blow-by-blow account of how a trade was made, including the trader's thought processes, is the very best received story by our subscribers. One of our primary considerations is to instruct in a manner that the layperson can comprehend. We are not hypercritical of writing style."

$ $ $ YOUR MONEY, Consumers Digest Inc., 8001 Lincoln Ave., Skokie IL 60077. (847)763-9200. Fax: (847)763-0200. E-mail: drogus@consumersdigest.com. **Contact**: Deborah Rogus, associate editor. **75% freelance written.** Bimonthly magazine on personal finance. "We cover the broad range of topics associated with personal finance—spending, saving, investing earning, etc." Estab. 1979. Circ. 500,000. **Pays on acceptance.** Publishes ms an average of 2 months after acceptance. Byline given. Offers 50% kill fee. Buys first rights and second serial (reprint) rights. Reports in 3 months (or longer) on queries. Do not send computer disks. Sample copy and writer's guidelines for 9×12 SAE with 4 first-class stamps. Writer's guidelines for #10 SASE.

- *Your Money* has been receiving more submissions and has less time to deal with them. Accordingly, they often need more than three months reporting time.

Nonfiction: How-to. "No first-person success stories or profiles of one company." Financial planning: debt management, retirement, funding education; investment: stocks and bonds, mutual funds, collectibles, treasuries, CDs; consumer-oriented topics: travel, car bargains, etc. **Buys 25 mss/year.** Send complete ms or query and clips. Include stamped, self-addressed postcard for more prompt response. Length: 1,500-2,500 words. **Pays 60¢/word.** Pays expenses of writers on assignment.

Tips: "Know the subject matter. Develop real sources in the investment community. Demonstrate a reader-friendly style that will help make the sometimes complicated subject of investing more accessible to the average person. Fill manuscripts with real-life examples of people who actually have done the kinds of things discussed—people we can later photograph. Although many of our readers are sophisticated investors, we provide jargon-free advice for people who may not be sophisticated."

Regional

$ $ ALASKA BUSINESS MONTHLY, Alaska Business Publishing, 501 W. Northern Lights Blvd., Suite 100, Anchorage AK 99503. (907)276-4373. Fax: (907)279-2900. E-mail: editor@akbizmag.com. **Contact:** Editor. **80%**

freelance written. Monthly magazine covering Alaska-oriented business and industry. "Our audience is Alaska business men and women who rely on us for timely features and up-to-date information about doing business in Alaska." Estab. 1985. Circ. 10,000. **Pays on acceptance.** Publishes ms an average of 2 months after acceptance. Byline given. Offers $50 kill fee. Buys first North American serial rights, first rights, one-time rights or makes work-for-hire assignments. Editorial lead time 2 months. Submit seasonal material 3 months in advance. Reports in 2 weeks on queries; 1 month on mss. Sample copy for 9×12 SAE and 6 first-class stamps. Writer's guidelines free.

Nonfiction: Humor, interview/profile, new product, opinion, technical, business. No fiction, poetry or anything not pertinent to Alaska. **Buys 45 mss/year.** Send complete ms. Length: 500-2,500 words. Pays $150-300. Sometimes pays expenses of writers on assignment.

Photos: Send photos with submission. Reviews 35mm or larger transparencies and 5×7 or larger prints. Offers $25-400/photo. Captions, model releases and identification of subjects required. Buys one-time rights.

Columns/Departments: Required Reading (business book reviews); Small Business Profile, 500 words. **Buys 12 mss/year.** Send complete ms. **Pays $100-150.**

Tips: "Send a well-written manuscript on a subject of importance to Alaska businesses. Include photos."

$ $ $ BC BUSINESS, Canada Wide Magazines & Communications Ltd., 4th Floor, 4180 Lougheed Highway, Burnaby, British Columbia V5C 6A7 Canada. (604)299-7311. Fax: (604)299-9188. **Contact:** Bonnie Irving, editor. **80% freelance written.** Monthly magazine "reports on significant issues and trends shaping the province's business environment. Stories are lively, topical and extensively researched." Circ. 26,000. Pays 2 weeks prior to publication. Publishes ms an average of 2 months after acceptance. Byline given. Kill fee varies. Buys first Canadian rights. Editorial lead time 4 months. Submit seasonal material 4 months in advance. Accepts simultaneous submissions. Reports in 6 weeks. Writer's guidelines free.

Nonfiction: Query with published clips. Length: 800-3,000 words. **Pays 40-60¢/word**, depending on length of story (and complexity). Sometimes pays expenses of writers on assignment.

Photos: State availability of photos with submission.

$ $ BOULDER COUNTY BUSINESS REPORT, 3180 Sterling Circle, Suite 200, Boulder CO 80301-2338. (303)440-4950. Fax: (303)440-8954. E-mail: jwlewis@bcbr.com. Website: http://www.bcbr.com. **Contact:** Jerry W. Lewis, editor. **75% freelance written.** Prefers to work with published/established writers; works with a small number of new/unpublished writers each year. Monthly newspaper covering Boulder County business issues. Offers "news tailored to a monthly theme and read primarily by Colorado businesspeople and by some investors nationwide. Philosophy: Descriptive, well-written articles that reach behind the scene to examine area's business activity." Estab. 1982. Circ. 18,000. Pays on publication. Publishes ms an average of 1 month after acceptance. Byline given. Buys one-time rights and second serial (reprint) rights. Reports in 1 month on queries; 2 weeks on mss. Sample copy for $1.44.

Nonfiction: Interview/profile, new product, examination of competition in a particular line of business. "All our issues are written around three or four monthly themes. No articles are accepted in which the subject has not been pursued in depth and both sides of an issue presented in a writing style with flair." **Buys 120 mss/year.** Query with published clips. Length: 250-2,000 words. **Pays $50-200.**

Photos: State availability of photos with query letter. Reviews b&w contact sheets. Pays $10 maximum for b&w contact sheet. Identification of subjects required. Buys one-time rights and reprint rights.

Tips: "Must be able to localize a subject. In-depth articles are written by assignment. The freelancer located in the Colorado area has an excellent chance here."

$ $ BUSINESS JOURNAL OF CENTRAL NY, CNY Business Review, Inc., 231 Wallton St., Syracuse NY 13202. (315)472-3104. Fax: (315)472-3644. E-mail: blrbmeistr@aol.com. Editor: Norm Poltenson. **Contact:** Mark Hadley, managing editor. **35% freelance written.** Biweekly newspaper covering "business news in a 16-county area surrounding Syracuse. The audience consists of owners and managers of businesses." Estab. 1985. Circ. 8,500. Pays on publication. Publishes ms an average of 2 months after acceptance. Byline given. Kill fee negotiable. Buys first rights. Editorial lead time 1 month. Sample copy and writer's guidelines free.

Nonfiction: Humor, opinion. **Buys 100 mss/year.** Query. Length: 750-2,000 words. **Pays $50-300.** Sometimes pays in copies. Sometimes pays expenses of writers on assignment.

Photos: State availability of photos with submission. Reviews contact sheets. Negotiates payment individually. Captions, model releases, identification of subjects required.

Columns/Departments: Buys 20 mss/year. Query with published clips.

Fillers: Facts, newsbreaks, short humor. **Buys 10/year.** Length: 300-600 words. **Pays $50-150.**

Tips: "The audience is comprised of owners and managers. Focus on their needs. Call or send associate editor story ideas: be sure to have a Central New York 'hook.' "

N $ $ BUSINESS LIFE MAGAZINE, Business Life, Inc., 4101-A Piedmont Pkwy., Greensboro NC 27410-8110. Fax: (336)812-8832. E-mail: lmbouchey@aol.com. Website: http://www.bizlife.com. **Contact:** Lisa M. Bouchey, editor. **30% freelance written**. Monthly consumer magazine covering business. "*Business Life* is a monthly, full-color magazine profiling businesses and business people that have ties to the Piedmont Triad, are headquartered here, or have an impact on the lines of local business people." Estab. 1989. Circ. 12,500. Pays on the 15th of the month of publication. Publishes ms 3 months after acceptance. Byline given. Offers ⅓ kill fee. Buys first rights and second serial (reprint) rights. Editorial lead time 2 months. Submit seasonal material 5 months in advance. Accepts simultaneous submissions.

Reports in 3 weeks on queries. Sample copy for 9×12 SASE and $3 postage. Guidelines free.

Nonfiction: Book excerpts, general interest, interview/profile, travel. No articles without ties to NC or the Piedmont Triad region (except travel). **Buys 45 mss/year**. Query with published clips. Length: 1,800-2,500 words. **Pays $200-250**.

Photos: State availability of photos with submission. Reviews transparencies (2×3). Negotiates payment individually. Captions and identification of subjects required. Buys one-time rights.

Tips: "Story should be of interest to readers in our area, either with a national angle that impacts people here or a more 'local' approach (a profile in the Piedmont Triad). We are primarily a regional publication."

N $ $ $ **BUSINESS NORTH CAROLINA**, McClatchy Newspapers, 5435 77-Center Dr., Charlotte NC 28217. (704)523-6987. Fax: (704)523-4211. Editor: David Kinney. **Contact:** Terry Noland, managing editor. **60% freelance written**. Monthly magazine covering business in North Carolina. "We seek to show not only trends and events but the human face of commerce." Estab. 1981. Circ. 30,000. **Pays on acceptance**. Publishes ms an average of 2 months after acceptance. Byline sometimes given. Offers 25% kill fee. Makes work-for-hire assignments. Editorial lead time 2 months. Reports in 2 weeks on queries; 2 months on mss. Sample copy for $3.50.

Nonfiction: Book excerpts, exposé, general interest, interview/profile, photo feature. No how-to, general trend stories or new product reviews. **Buys 25 mss/year**. Query with published clips. Length: 2,000-4,000 words. **Pays $400-800**. Pays expenses of writers on assignment.

Columns/Departments: People (profiles of business people), 500 words; Professions (issues dealing with a particular profession or unusual occupation), 1,300 words. **Buys 65 mss/year**. Query with published clips. **Pays $100-350**.

Tips: "The People department—short personality profiles—is the most common place for new freelancers to break in. If they can pitch us on an idea, that helps. Knowledge of North Carolina is a plus. Do not pitch how-to/service pieces. And only pitch issue stories that have a strong North Carolina tie."

$ $ **COLORADO BUSINESS**, Wiesner Inc., 7009 S. Potomac St., Englewood CO 80112. (303)397-7600. Fax: (303)397-7619. E-mail: bgold@winc.usa.com. Website: http://www.cobizmag.com. **Contact:** Bruce Goldberg, editor. **85% freelance written.** Monthly. "Our features focus on the big picture, on trends and overviews in Colorado business, and on successful businesses and business owners. Also, we offer solid business advice and strategy for our readers. We try to include businesses from around the state, not just the Front Range. Charts and graphs are welcome. Our readership is a high-end audience, with average salaries in six figures. Many are CEOs, business owners, or high-ranking executives or managers. Our readership is 75 percent male, but our female readership includes many successful women business owners and operators. They seek information on any business development that's new, interesting and useful to their business or personal life." Estab. 1973. Circ. 20,000. **Pays on acceptance.** Publishes ms an average of 3 months after acceptance. Byline given. Offers 33% kill fee. Buys first rights. Editorial lead time 5 months. Reports in 1 month on queries. Prefers Colorado writers. Writer's guidelines for #10 SASE.

Nonfiction: Business, health care, financials, telecommunications, how-to, interview/profile, photo feature, technical. **Buys 40 mss/year.** Query with published clips. Length: 1,200 words, including sidebars. **Pays 22¢/word.** Sometimes pays expenses of writers on assignment. Best bet: Follow the editorial calendar.

Photos: State availability of photos with submission. Reviews contact sheets, transparencies. Negotiates payment individually. Captions, identification of subjects required. Buys one-time rights.

Columns/Departments: "We created a new look in October 1997. We added many columns, but they are assigned on a beat basis to free-lancers."

Tips: "Know the magazine before you pitch me. Solid story ideas specifically geared to Colorado audience. No boring stories. No corporatese."

$ $ **CRAIN'S DETROIT BUSINESS**, Crain Communications Inc., 1400 Woodbridge Ave., Detroit MI 48207. (313)446-6000. Fax: (313)446-1687. E-mail: 75147.372@compuserve.com. Website: http://bizserve.com/crains/. Editor: Mary Kramer. Executive Editor: Cindy Goodaker. **Contact:** Julie Cantwell, special sections editor. **15% freelance written.** Weekly tabloid covering business in the Detroit metropolitan area—specifically Wayne, Oakland, Macomb, Washtenaw and Livingston counties. Estab. 1985. Circ. 150,000 readership. Pays on publication. Publishes ms an average of 1 month after acceptance. Byline given. Buys all rights and all electronic rights. Sample copy for $1.

- *Crain's Detroit Business* uses only area writers and local topics.

Nonfiction: New product, technical, business. **Buys 100 mss/year.** Query with published clips. Length: 30-40 words/column inch. **Pays $10/column inch.** Pays expenses of writers on assignment.

Photos: State availability of photos with submissions.

Tips: "Contact special sections editor in writing with background and, if possible, specific story ideas relating to our type of coverage and coverage area."

N ✩ $ $ **ILLINOIS BUSINESS, The Official Magazine of the Illinois Chamber of Commerce**, Progressive Publishing, Inc., 936 W. Lake St., Roseelle IL 60172. (630)582-8888. Fax: (630)582-8895. E-mail: Almanac123@aol.com. **Contact:** Juli Bridgers, editor. **80% freelance written.** Quarterly magazine covering Illinois business. Estab. 1995. Circ. 25,000. Pays on publication. Publishes ms an average of 4 months after acceptance. Byline given. Offers 25% kill fee. Buys first North American serial or one-time rights. Editorial lead time 2 months. Submit seasonal material 3 months in advance. Reports in 2 weeks on queries; 1 month on mss. Sample copy free. Writer's guidelines for #10 SASE.

Nonfiction: Exposé, interview/profile, technical, Illinois business. "Do not submit anything that does not pertain to business in Illinois; small business info/features." **Buys 25-30 mss/year.** Query with published clips. Length: 400-1,200 words. **Pays $75-200 for assigned articles; $50-100 for unsolicited articles.** Sometimes pays expenses of writers on assignment.
Photos: State availability of photos with submission or send photos with submission. Reviews transparencies. Offers $10-20/photo. Captions and identification of subjects required. Buys one-time rights.
Columns/Departments: Business Briefs, 200-300 words; Regional Report, 350-400 words. **Buys 4 mss/year.** Query. **Pays $50-100.**
Fillers: Facts, short humor. **Buys 25-30/year.** Length: 50-100 words. **Pays $15-20.**

$ $ $ INGRAM'S, Show-Me Publishing, Inc., 306 E. 12th St., Suite 1014, Kansas City MO 64106. (816)842-9994. Fax: (816)474-1111. **Contact:** Toni Carderella, managing editor. **50% freelance written.** Monthly magazine covering Kansas City business/executive lifestyle for "upscale, affluent business executives and professionals. Looking for sophisticated writing with style and humor when appropriate." Estab. 1989. Circ. 24,000. **Pays on acceptance.** Publishes ms an average of 2 months after acceptance. Byline given. Buys first rights and Internet rights. Editorial lead time 2 months. Submit seasonal material 3 months in advance. Reports in 6 weeks on queries. Sample copy for $3 current, $5 back. Writer's guidelines free.
Nonfiction: How-to (businesses and personal finance related), interview/profile (KC execs and politicians, celebrities), opinion. **Buys 30 mss/year.** Query with published clips. "All articles must have a Kansas City angle. We don't accept unsolicited manuscripts except for opinion column." Length: 500-3,000 words. **Pays $175-500 maximum.** Sometimes pays expenses of writers on assignment.
Columns/Departments: Say-So (opinion), 1,500 words. **Buys 12 mss/year. Pays $175 maximum.**
Tips: "Writers must understand the publication and the audience—knowing what appeals to a business executive, entrepreneur, or professional in Kansas City."

N $ $ JOHNSON COUNTY BUSINESS TIMES, Sun Publications Inc., 7373 W. 107th St., Overland Park KS 66212. (913)649-8778. Fax: (913)381-9889. E-mail: jcbt1@aol.com. **Contact:** Tony Cox, editor. **5% freelance written.** Weekly magazine covering Johnson County business news. "Our magazine is written for local CEOs." Estab. 1994. Circ. 15,000. **Pays on acceptance.** Publishes ms an average of 1 month after acceptance. Byline given. Offers 25% kill fee. Buys first rights. Editorial lead time 1 month. Submit seasonal material 3 months in advance. Reports in 2 weeks on queries. Sample copy for $1.50 plus postage. Writer's guidelines for $1.50 plus postage.
Nonfiction: How-to (business stories), interview/profile, business trend stories. Buys 10 mss/year. Query with published clips. Length: 600-3,000 words. **Pays $75-500.** Sometimes pays expenses of writers on assignment.
Photos: State availability of photos with submission. Reviews negatives. Negotiates payment individually. Identification of subjects required. Buys all rights.
Columns/Departments: Query with published clips. **Pays $75-100.**
Tips: "Propose specific, well-thought-out ideas that are a good fit for our audience."

N $ $ THE LANE REPORT, Lane Communications Group, 269 W. Main St., Lexington KY 40503. (606)244-3500. E-mail: lanereport@aol.com. **Contact:** Kevin Depew, editorial director. **75% freelance written.** Monthly magazine covering regional business. "We focus on the needs of small businesses and their owners." Estab. 1986. Circ. 9,000. **Pays on acceptance.** Byline given. Offers 50% kill fee. Buys one-time rights. Editorial lead time 6 weeks. Submit seasonal material 3 months in advance. Accepts simultaneous submissions. Reports in 1 month. Sample copy and guidelines free.
Nonfiction: Essays, exposé, interview/profile, new product, photo feature. No fiction. **Buys 30-40 mss/year.** Query with published clips. Length: 500-2,000 words. **Pays $100-375.** Sometimes pays expenses of writers on assignment.
Reprints: Accepts previously published submissions.
Photos: State availability of photos with submission. Reviews contact sheets, negatives, transparencies, prints. Negotiates payment individually. Identification of subjects required. Buys one-time rights.
Columns/Departments: Small Business, less than 750 words. **Buys 12 mss/year.** Send complete ms. **Pays $100.**

$ $ $ LONDON BUSINESS MAGAZINE, Bowes Publishers, Box 7400, London, Ontario N5Y 4X3 Canada. (519)472-7601. Editor: Janine Foster. **70% freelance written.** Monthly magazine covering London business. "Our audience is primarily small and medium businesses and entrepreneurs. Focus is on success stories and how to better operate your business." Estab. 1987. Circ. 14,000. Pays on publication. Publishes ms an average of 3 months after acceptance. Byline given. Offers 50% kill fee. Buys first rights. Editorial lead time 3 months. Reports in 3 months. Sample copy for #10 SASE. Guidelines free.
Nonfiction: How-to (business topics), humor, interview/profile, new product (local only), personal experience. Must have a London connection. **Buys 30 mss/year.** Query with published clips. Length: 250-1,500 words. **Pays $25-800.**
Photos: Send photos with submission. Reviews contact sheets, transparencies. Negotiates payment individually. Identification of subjects required. Buys one-time rights.
Tips: "Phone with a great idea. The most valuable thing a writer owns is ideas. We'll take a chance on an unknown if the idea is good enough."

N $ $ NC ENTREPENEUR, Entrepreneur Publications, Inc., 2627 Grimsley St., Greensboro NC 27403. (336)854-5711. Fax: (336)854-8566. E-mail: mitchell@ncentrepreneur.com. Website: http://www.NCEntrepreneur.com. Managing Editor: Pat Mitchell. **Contact**: Laura Juckett, production manager. **90% freelance written.** Bimonthly magazine covering "what North Carolina-based entrepreneurs have done to grow their business that readers can copy (or learn) and apply to their business. 'How-to' focused case studies." Estab. 1996. Circ. 20,000. **Pays on acceptance** when invoiced. Publishes ms an average of 2 months after acceptance. Byline sometimes given. Offers $100 kill fee. Buys all rights or makes work-for-hire assignments. Editorial lead time 4 months. Submit seasonal material 1 month in advance. Accepts simultaneous submissions. Sample copy and writer's guidelines free.

Nonfiction: How-to, interview/profile, personal experience. "No press release or public relations articles. No entrepreneur or company profiles! Must have practical, 'how to' lesson for the reader." **Buys 50 mss/year.** Query with published clips. Length: 800-1,200 words. **Pays $200-300.** Pays expenses of writers on assignment.

Photos: Send photos with submission. Negotiates payment individually. Captions and identification of subjects required. Buys all rights.

Tips: "Feature stories must include the following elements: High-quality (no Polaroids or passport photos) head and shoulders photograph of the entrepreneur or founder. Story Title & Platform which catches the reader's eye, draws interest and provides a very brief synopsis of the story's lesson. Side-bar showcasing key statistics, a process or resources relevant to the story. Network NCE: a call-out box which includes all contact information for the entrepreneur and any other important resources mentioned in the story. Artwork, company logos, additional photographs that will add to the story's look and feel. Relevant Web Links. Writers are asked to compile any relevant websites and e-mail addresses for key contacts and other points of interest to the reader."

N $ $ 128 NEWS, Rieder Communications, 382 Lowell St. #203, Wakefield MA 01880. (781)246-3883. Managing Editor: Judy McKinnon. **Contact**: Martin Rieder, publisher/editor. **50% freelance written.** Monthly business tabloid covering high technology, employee issues, entertainment. "We try to explain new developments in high technology and business in English—without the jargon—we try to help our readers make sense of a fascinating business and cultural area." Estab. 1985. Circ. 25,000. **Pays on acceptance**. Publishes ms an average of 1 month after acceptance. Byline given. Offers 100% kill fee. Buys first and second serial (reprint) rights. Editorial lead time 2 months. Accepts simultaneous submissions. Reports in 1 month on queries. Sample copy and writer's guidelines free.

Nonfiction: General interest, interview/profile, new product, opinion, technical, business. **Buys 40 mss/year.** Query with or without published clips. Length: 2,000 words maximum. **Pays $50-175.**

Photos: State availability of photos with submission. Reviews prints. Negotiates payment individually. Model releases and identification of subjects required. Buys one-time rights.

Tips: "All articles should be okayed in advance. Send a query letter, clips and a résumé—we'll follow up."

$ $ $ OREGON BUSINESS, Oregon Business Media, 610 SW Broadway, Suite 200, Portland OR 97205. (503)223-0304. Fax: (503)221-6544. Website: http://www.oregonbusiness.com. Editor: Kathy Dimond. **Contact:** Shirleen Holt, managing editor. 30% freelance written. Monthly magazine covering business in Oregon. "Our subscribers include owners of small and medium-sized businesses, government agencies, professional staffs of banks, insurance companies, ad agencies, attorneys and other service providers." **30% freelance written.** "We accept *only* stories about Oregon businesses, issues and trends." Estab. 1981. Circ. 19,490. Pays on publication. Byline given. Buys first North American serial and electronic rights. Editorial lead time 2 months. Sample copy $4. Writer's guidelines for #10 SASE.

Nonfiction: Service, trend pieces; interview/profile, new product. **Buys 40 mss/year.** Query with published clips. No unsolicited mss. Length: section stories 1,200 words; feature stories 2,000-4,000 words. **Pays average of $360 for a section story, $400-1,000 for a feature story**, depending on length and complexity.

Photos: State availability of photos with submission. Reviews 2×3 transparencies. Offers $85-450/photo. Identification of subjects required. Buys one-time rights.

Tips: "An *Oregon Business* story must meet at least two of the following criteria: Size and location: The topic must be relevant to Northwest businesses. Companies (including franchises) must be based in Oregon or Southwest Washington with at least five employees and annual sales above $250,000. Service: Our sections (1,200 words) are reserved largely for service pieces focusing on finance, marketing, management or other general business topics. These stories are meant to be instructional, emphasizing problem-solving by example. Trends: These are sometimes covered in a section piece, or perhaps a feature story. We aim to be the state's leading business publication, so we want to be the first to spot trends that affect Oregon companies. Exclusivity or strategy: of an event, whether it's a corporate merger, a dramatic turnaround, a marketing triumph or a PR disaster."

N $ $ PACIFIC BUSINESS NEWS, The Best Selling Business Publication in Hawaii, 863 Halekauwila, Honolulu HI 96813. (808)596-2021. Fax: (808)591-2321. E-mail: pbn@lava.net. **Contact**: Michelle Yamaguchi, editor. **5% freelance written.** Weekly business newspaper. Estab. 1963. Circ. 14,600. Pays on publication. Byline given. Offers 50% kill fee. Buys all rights. Editorial lead time 1 month. Reports in 2 weeks on queries. Sample copy free.

Nonfiction: Inspirational, interview/profile, opinion, personal experience. **Buys 12 mss/year.** Query with published clips. Length: 1,000-1,500 words. **Pays $200.**

Photos: State availability of photos with submission. Reviews negatives. Offers no additional payment for photos accepted with ms. Captions required. Buys all rights.

N ☆ $ $ PHILADELPHIA ENTERPRISER, Business Pursuits, Inc., 140 S. Village Ave., Suite 10, Exton PA 19341. (610)524-8877. Fax: (610)524-8884. E-mail: entrprser@aol.com. **Contact:** Marlene Prost, editor. **90% freelance written.** "Bimonthly conversational style magazine targeting practical advice for owners of emerging growth companies." Estab. 1994. Circ. 20,351. **Pays on acceptance.** Publishes ms an average of 1 month after acceptance. Byline given. Offers 50% kill fee. Buys first North American serial rights. Editorial lead time 1 month. Submit seasonal material 2 months in advance. Sample copy for $3.95.
Nonfiction: How-to, humor, inspirational, interview/profile, new product, travel. **Buys 56 mss/year.** Query with published clips. Length: 800-2,000 words. **Pays $265-660 for assigned articles; $160-400 for unsolicited articles.**
Photos: Send photos with submission. Reviews negatives. Offers no additional payment for photos accepted with ms. Captions and identification of subjects required. Buys all rights.
Columns/Departments: Buys 56 mss/year. Query with published clips. **Pays $800-2,000.**
Tips: "Send us article ideas with first right of refusal on new topics of interest to business owners."

N $ $ PITTSBURGH BUSINESS TIMES, American City Business Journals, Inc., 2313 E. Carson St., Suite 200, Pittsburgh PA 15203. (412)481-6397. Fax: (412)481-9956. E-mail: pittsburgh@amcity.com. Managing Editor: Betsy Benson. **Contact**: Paul Furiga, editor. **10% freelance written.** Weekly business journal. "*The Business Times* is the first and foremost source of business information for business executives in the Pittsburgh region and focuses on excellent reporting, fine writing and breaking news." Estab. 1981. Circ. 13,500. Pays on publication. Publishes ms an average of 1 month after acceptance. Byline given. Offers negotiable kill fee. Buys all rights. Editorial lead time 2 months. Reports in 1 week on queries; 2 weeks on mss. Sample copy and writer's guidelines free.
Nonfiction: Exposé, general interest, how-to, interview. "No first-person pieces; stories promoting any specific person/entity or company." **Buys 20-40 mss/year.** Query with published clips. Length: 200-2,000 words. **Pays $50-200.** Sometimes pays expenses of writers on assignment.
Photos: State availability of photos with submission. Reviews contact sheets. Negotiates payment individually. Identification of subjects required. Buys all rights.
Columns/Departments: John Berger, special reports editor. Strategies (how-to stories on business issues), 800 words. **Buys 10-15 mss/year.** Query with published clips. **Pays $50-200.**
Tips: "Understand the focus and audience of weekly business journals, which are written for a highly literate, information-hungry, sophisticated group of readers. Always query first. One-page letters with a focused, one-paragraph story description are best."

N $ $ THE RUSSIAN MAGAZINE, For the Adventure Capitalist, Russian Business Press, 6255 Sunset Blvd., #1007, Los Angeles CA 90028. (213)462-7005. Fax: (213)462-7017. E-mail: editor@mag.com. Website: http://www.rmag.com. **Contact:** Martha Little, managing editor. Editor: Leon Kopelevich. **100% freelance written.** Monthly consumer magazine covering western involvement in Russian business development. "No pieces should be analytical in nature. Always should serve the American or western business interested in Russia." Estab. 1994. Circ. 35,000. Pays 30 days following publication. Publishes ms an average of 2 months after acceptance. Byline given. Offers $100 kill fee. Buys first North American serial rights. Editorial lead time 2 months. Submit seasonal material 2 months in advance. Sample copy for $4.95; writer's guidelines free.
Nonfiction: General interest, interview/profile, opinion, technical. "No articles on culture, history, etc., unless they have a contemporary business angle." **Buys 130 mss/year**. Query with published clips. Length: 1,000-2,500 words. **Pays $150-500.**
Reprints: Accepts previously published submissions depending on place published.
Photos: State availability of photos with submission. Reviews negatives. Negotiates payment individually. Identification of subjects required. Buys one-time rights plus promotion.
Columns/Departments: Market Insights (humor, investment analysis), 1,000 words; Kremlin Commentary (politics, economics, inside intrigue), 2,000 words. **Buys 20 mss/year**. Send complete ms. **Pays $350-500.**
Tips: "Mail/fax article proposals along with clips and résumé."

N $ $ SACRAMENTO BUSINESS JOURNAL, American City Business Journals Inc., 1401 21st St., Suite 200, Sacramento CA 95814. (916)447-7661. E-mail: sbj@ns.net. **Contact**: Beth Davis, managing editor. Editor: Lee Wessman. **5% freelance written.** Weekly newspaper covering the Sacramento area's economy. "Our readers are decision makers. They own or manage companies, or are community leaders who want to know what's happening. They expect sophisticated, well-researched news. And they don't read fluff." Estab. 1984. Circ. 14,000. Pays on publication. Publishes ms an average of 1 month after acceptance. Byline sometimes given. Offers 50% kill fee. Buys all rights or makes work-for-hire assignments. Editorial lead time 2 months. Submit seasonal material 2 months in advance. Reports in 3 weeks on queries. Sample copy for $2 and SAE with 2 first-class stamps.
Nonfiction: Humor, interview/profile, new product, opinion, local business news and trends. "No public relations stories on behalf of specific companies or industries. No thinly sourced stories." **Buys 60 mss/year.** Query with published clips. Length: 500-1,500 words. **Pays $125-200.** Sometimes pays expenses of writers on assignment.
Photos: State availability of photos with submission. Reviews contact sheets, prints. Offers $25-50 maximum/photo. Captions and identification of subjects required. Buys one-time rights.
Columns/Departments: Robert Celaschi, associate editor. Small Biz (meaningful successes or failures), 750 words; Focus (industry trends), 1,200 words. **Buys 20 mss/year.** Query. **Pays $100-175.**
Tips: "Most of our freelance work is done on assignment with a three-week turnaround. We look for a regular stable

of writers who can get an assignment, do the research and produce a well-focused story that reflects the drama of business and doesn't avoid controversy."

N $ $ TAMPA BAY BUSINESS JOURNAL, American City Business Journals, 4350 W. Cypress St., Tampa FL 33607. (813)873-8225. Fax: (813)873-0219. E-mail: tbbj@tbbj.com. Editor: Dave Szymanski. **Contact:** Tyler E. Ward, managing editor. **10% freelance written.** Weekly regional business newspaper. Estab. 1980. Circ. 13,000. Pays on publication. Publishes ms an average of 1 month after acceptance. Byline given. Offers $50 kill fee. Buys first North American serial rights. Editorial lead time 1 month. Reports in 1 week. Sample copy and writer's guidelines free.

Nonfiction: Interview/profile. **Buys 100 mss/year.** Query with published clips. Length: 1,500-3,000 words. **Pays $100-200.**

Photos: State availability of photos with submission. Reviews negatives. Negotiates payment individually. Identification of subjects required. Buys one-time rights.

Columns/Departments: Dave Szymanski, editor. Opinion (local issues), 1,000 words. Does not pay for opinion columns. Query.

N ☆ $ $ UTAH BUSINESS, Olympus Publishers, 85 East Fort Union Blvd., Midvale UT 84047. (801)568-0114. Fax: (801)568-0812. E-mail: editor@utahbusiness.com. **Contact:** Matt Wright, associate editor. Editor: Brian Pittman. **80% freelance written.** "*Utah Business* is a monthly magazine focusing on the people, practices, and principles that drive Utah's economy. Audience is business owners and executives." Estab. 1983. Circ. 35,000. Pays on publication. Publishes ms an average of 2-3 months after acceptance. Byline given. Buys first rights and makes work-for-hire assignments. Editorial lead time 3 months. Submit seasonal material 2-3 months in advance. Accepts simultaneous submissions. Reports in 6 weeks on queries; 2 months on mss. Sample copy for 8½×11 SAE with 4 first-class stamps. Writer's guidelines for #10 SASE.

Nonfiction: How-to (business), interview/profile (business), new product, technical (business/technical), policy and politics. "No cake recipes. Nothing in first person. There is no self-only information." **Buys 200 mss/year.** Send complete ms. Length: 700-3,000 words. **Pays 25¢/word.** Sometimes pays expenses of writers on assignment.

Reprints: Accepts previously published submissions.

Photos: State availability of photos with submission. Reviews negatives. Offers no additional payment for photos accepted with ms. Identification of subjects required. Buys one-time rights.

Columns/Departments: Books/Travel/Money (direct, informative, advice, how-to), 650-700 words; In The News (business, Utah relevant news), 1,200 words; Features (Utah relevant conceptual stories), 2,000-3,000 words. **Buys 80 mss/year.** Send complete ms. **Pays 25¢/word.**

Fillers: Facts, newsbreaks. **Buys 20/year.** Length: 120-500 words. **Pays 25¢/word.**

Tips: "Use common sense; tailor your queries and stories to this market. Use AP style and colorful leads. Read the magazine first!"

$ $ VERMONT BUSINESS MAGAZINE, Lake Iroquois Publications, 2 Church St., Burlington VT 05401. (802)863-8038. Fax: (802)863-8069. E-mail: vtbizmag@together.net. **Contact:** Timothy McQuiston, editor. **80% freelance written.** Monthly tabloid covering business in Vermont. Circ. 8,000. Pays on publication. Publishes ms an average of 1 month after acceptance. Byline given. Buys one-time rights. Reports in 2 months. Sample copy for 11×14 SAE with 7 first-class stamps.

Nonfiction: Business trends and issues. **Buys 200 mss/year.** Query with published clips. Length: 800-1,800 words. **Pays $100-200.**

Reprints: Send tearsheet of article and information about when and where the article previously appeared.

Photos: Send photos with submission. Reviews contact sheets. Offers $10-35/photo. Identification of subjects required.

Tips: "Read daily papers and look for business angles for a follow-up article. We look for issue and trend articles rather than company or businessman profiles. Note: magazine accepts Vermont-specific material *only.* The articles *must* be about Vermont."

CAREER, COLLEGE & ALUMNI

Three types of magazines are listed in this section: university publications written for students, alumni and friends of a specific institution; publications about college life for students; and publications on career and job opportunities. Literary magazines published by colleges and universities are listed in the Literary and "Little" section.

☆ $ $ CAREER FOCUS, For Today's Rising Professional, Communications Publishing Group, Inc., 3100 Broadway, Suite 660, Kansas City MO 64111. (816)960-1988. Fax: (816)960-1989. **Contact:** Neoshia Michelle Paige, editor. **80% freelance written.** Bimonthly magazine "devoted to providing positive insight, information, guidance and motivation to assist Blacks and Hispanics (ages 21-40) in their career development and attainment of goals." Estab. 1988. Circ. 250,000. Pays on publication. Byline often given. Buys second serial (reprint) rights and makes work-for-hire assignments. Submit seasonal material 6 months in advance. Accepts simultaneous submissions. Reports in 2 months. Sample copy for 9×12 SAE with 4 first-class stamps. Writer's guidelines for #10 SASE.

• The editor notes that if the writer can provide the manuscript on 3.25 disk, saved in generic ASCII, pay is $10 higher and chance of acceptance is greater.

Nonfiction: Book excerpts, general interest, historical, how-to, humor, inspirational, interview/profile, personal experience, photo feature, technical, travel. Length: 750-2,000 words. **Pays $150-400 for assigned articles; 12¢/word for unsolicited articles.** Sometimes pays expenses of writers on assignment.

Reprints: Send tearsheet of article or short story and information about when and where the article previously appeared. Pays 6¢/word.

Photos: State availability of photos with submission. Reviews transparencies. Pays $20-25/photo. Captions, model releases and identification of subjects required. Buys all rights.

Columns/Departments: Profiles (striving and successful Black and Hispanic young adult, ages 21-40). **Buys 15 mss/year.** Send complete ms. Length: 500-1,000 words. **Pays $50-250.**

Fiction: Adventure, ethnic, historical, humorous, mainstream, slice-of-life vignettes. **Buys 3 mss/year.** Send complete ms. Length: 500-2,000 words. Pay varies.

Fillers: Anecdotes, facts, gags to be illustrated by cartoonist, newsbreaks, short humor. **Buys 10/year.** Length: 25-250 words. **Pays $25-100.**

Tips: For new writers: Submit full ms that is double-spaced; clean copy only. If available, send clips of previously published works and résumé. Should state when available to write. Most open to freelancers are profiles of successful and striving persons including photos. Profile must be of a Black or Hispanic adult living in the US. Include on first page of ms name, address, phone number, Social Security number and number of words in article.

$ $ CARNEGIE MELLON MAGAZINE, Carnegie Mellon University, Bramer House, Pittsburgh PA 15213-3890. (412)268-2132. Fax: (412)268-6929. Editor: Ann Curran. Estab. 1914. Quarterly alumni publication covering university activities, alumni profiles, etc. Circ, 67,000. **Pays on acceptance.** Byline given. Reports in 1 month. Sample copy for $2 and 9×12 SAE.

Nonfiction: Book reviews (faculty alumni), general interest, humor, interview/profile, photo feature. "We use general interest stories linked to Carnegie Mellon activities and research." No unsolicited mss. **Buys 10-15 features and 5-10 alumni profiles/year.** Query with published clips. Length: 800-2,000 words. **Pays $100-400 or negotiable rate.**

Poetry: Avant-garde, traditional. Poet or topic must be related to Carnegie Mellon University. No previously published poetry. **Pays $25.**

$ $ $ CAROLINA ALUMNI REVIEW, UNC General Alumni Association, P.O. Box 660, Chapel Hill NC 27514-0660. (919)962-1208. Fax: (919)962-0010. E-mail: alumni@unc.edu. Managing Editor/Art Director: Diana Palmer. **Contact:** Regina Oliver, editor. Bimonthly University of North Carolina alumni magazine seeking understanding of issues and trends in higher education. Estab. 1912. Circ. 55,000. **Pays on acceptance.** Publishes ms an average of 4 months after acceptance. Byline given. Offers 50% kill fee. Buys first North American serial rights and second serial (reprint) rights (for electronic republishing). Editorial lead time 9 months. Submit seasonal material 6 months in advance. Reports in 4 months on mss, 2 months on queries. Sample copy free.

Nonfiction: Interview/profile, photo feature. Nothing unrelated to UNC or higher education. **Buys 25 mss/year.** Query by mail, e-mail or fax with published clips. Length: 750-2,500 words. **Pays $200-1,000.** "We take very few unsolicited pieces." Pays the expenses of writers on assignment with limit agreed upon in advance.

Photos: State availability of photos with submission. Reviews contact sheets, negatives, transparencies or prints. Offers $25-700/photo. Identification of subjects required. Buys one-time and electronic republishing rights.

Tips: "Be familiar with *Chronicle of Higher Education* and other journals covering higher education, including other alumni magazines."

$ $ CIRCLE K MAGAZINE, 3636 Woodview Trace, Indianapolis IN 46268-3196. Fax: (317)879-0204. E-mail: ckimagazine@kiwanis.org. Website: http://www.kiwanis.org/circlek/. **Contact**: Nicholas K. Drake, executive editor. **60% freelance written.** "Our readership consists almost entirely of above-average college students interested in voluntary community service and leadership development. They are politically and socially aware and have a wide range of interests." Published 5 times/year. Circ. 15,000. **Pays on acceptance.** Buys first North American serial rights. Byline given. Reports in 2 months. Sample copy and writer's guidelines for large SAE with 3 first-class stamps.

Nonfiction: Articles published in *Circle K* are of 2 types—serious and light nonfiction. "We are interested in general interest articles on topics concerning college students and their lifestyles, as well as articles dealing with careers, community concerns and leadership development. No first person confessions, family histories or travel pieces." Query. Length: 1,500-2,000 words. **Pays $150-400.**

Photos: Purchased with accompanying ms. Captions required. Total purchase price for ms includes payment for photos.

Tips: "Query should indicate author's familiarity with the field and sources. Subject treatment must be objective and in-depth, and articles should include illustrative examples and quotes from persons involved in the subject or qualified to speak on it. We are open to working with new writers who present a good article idea and demonstrate that they've done their homework concerning the article subject itself, as well as concerning our magazine's style. We're interested in college-oriented trends, for example: entrepreneur schooling, high-tech classrooms, music, leisure and health issues."

$ COLLEGE BOUND, The Magazine for High School Students By College Students, Ramholtz Publishing Inc., 2071 Clove Rd., Suite 206, Staten Island NY 10304. (718)273-5700. Fax: (718)273-2539. E-mail: editorial@cbnet.com. Website: http://www.cbnet.com. **Contact**: Gina LaGuardia, editor-in-chief. **85% freelance written.** Bimonthly magazine "written by college students for high school students and is designed to provide an inside view of college life." Estab. 1987. Circ. 95,000. Pays on publication. Publishes ms an average of 4 months after acceptance. Byline given. Buys first and second rights. Editorial lead time 4 months. Submit seasonal material 4 months in advance. Accepts simultaneous submissions. Reports in 5 weeks. Sample copy and writer's guidelines for 9×12 SASE.

Nonfiction: How-to (apply for college, prepare for the interview, etc.), personal experience (college experiences). **Buys 30 mss/year.** Query with published clips. Length: 1,200-1,500 words. **Pays $50-75.** Sometimes pays expenses of writers on assignment.

Reprints: Send photocopy of article.

Photos: Send photos with submission. Reviews negatives, prints. Offers no additional payment for photos accepted with ms. Buys one time rights.

Columns/Departments: Campus Traditions (unique traditions from different colleges), 100-150 words; Clip Notes (admissions facts and advice, as well as interesting tidbits on "happenings" related to junior and senior students' lifestyles, 75-200 words); Books (reviews of books and guides to college life and preparation); Traditions (events on campus that are timeless or entertaining); Focus (indepth profile of a community organization, student-founded group or other group of interest); Campus Tours (walk the readers through a college campus); Applause! (schools that have won awards, big scholarship winners, etc.); Interview (a look at the college application process, presenting a profile of various college administrators, deans, teachers, career advisors, etc.); That's Life (issues outside the academic realm, i.e., money tips, current events, social commentary); all 500-1,000 words. **Buys 30 mss/year.** Query with published clips. **Pays $15-50.**

Fillers: Anecdotes, facts, gags to be illustrated, newsbreaks, short humor. **Buys 10/year.** Length: 50-200 words. **Pays $15-25.**

Tips: "College students from around the country are welcome to serve as correspondents to provide our teen readership with personal accounts on all aspects of college. Give us your expertise on everything from living with a roommate, choosing a major, and joining a fraternity or sorority, to college dating, interesting course offerings on your campus, how to beat the financial headache and other college application nightmares."

$ ▣ COLLEGE BOUND.NET, A Student's Interactive Guide to College Life, Ramholtz Publishing, Inc., 2071 Clove Rd., Staten Island NY 10304. (718)273-5700. Fax: (718)273-2539. E-mail: editorial@cbnet.com. Website: http://www.cbnet.com. **Contact**: Gina LaGuardia, editor-in-chief. **60% freelance written.** "Online magazine for students making the transition from high school to college." Estab. 1996. Pays on publication. Publishes ms 4 months after acceptance. Byline given. Buys first rights and second serial (reprint) rights. Editorial lead time 4 months. Submit seasonal material 4 months in advance. Reports in 2 months on queries. Writer's guidelines for #10 SASE.

Nonfiction: Essays, general interest, how-to, inspirational, interview/profile, new product, personal experience, student travel. Query. Length: 300-700 words. **Pays $15-65.** Sometimes pays the expenses of writers on assignment.

Reprints: Send photocopy of article.

Photos: State availability of photos with submission. Reviews transparencies and prints. Offers no additional payment for photos accepted with ms. Captions and identification of subjects required.

Columns/Departments: Digital Details (technology), Money, Food, Sports, Music, Shout!, Go Girl! Length: 300-500 words. **Buys 30 mss/year.** Query with published clips. **Pays $15-40.**

Fillers: Anecdotes, facts, gags to be illustrated by cartoonist, newsbreaks, short humor. Buys 10/year. Length: 50 words.

☆ $ $ COLLEGE PREVIEW, A Guide for College-Bound Students, Communications Publishing Group, 3100 Broadway, Suite 660, Kansas City MO 64110. (816)960-1988. Fax: (816)960-1989. **Contact:** Neoshia Michelle Paige, editor. **80% freelance written.** Quarterly educational and career source guide. "Contemporary guide designed to inform and motivate Black and Hispanic young adults, ages 16-21 years old about college preparation, career planning and life survival skills." Estab. 1985. Circ. 600,000. Pays on publication. Byline often given. Buys first serial and second serial (reprint) rights or makes work-for-hire assignments. Submit seasonal material 6 months in advance. Accepts simultaneous submissions. Reports in 2 months. Sample copy for 9×12 SAE with 4 first-class stamps. Writer's guidelines for #10 SASE.

- The editor notes that if the writer can provide the manuscript on 3.25 disk, saved in generic ASCII, pay is $10 higher and chance of acceptance is greater.

Nonfiction: Book excerpts or reviews, general interest, how-to (dealing with careers or education), humor, inspirational, interview/profile (celebrity or "up and coming" young adult), new product (as it relates to young adult market), personal experience, photo feature, technical, travel. Send complete ms. Length: 750-2,000 words. **Pays $150-400 for assigned articles; 12¢/word for unsolicited articles.** Sometimes pays expenses of writers on assignment.

Reprints: Send photocopy of article or short story or typed ms with rights for sale noted and information about when and where the article previously appeared. Pays 6¢/word.

Photos: State availability of photos with submission. Reviews transparencies. Offers $20-$25/photo. Captions, model releases and identification of subjects required. Will return photos—send SASE.

Columns/Departments: Profiles of Achievement (striving and successful minority young adults ages 16-35 in various careers). **Buys 30 mss/year.** Send complete ms. Length: 500-1,500. **Pays 10¢/word.**

Fiction: Adventure, ethnic, historical, humorous, mainstream, slice-of-life vignettes. **Buys 3 mss/year.** Send complete ms. Length: 500-2,000 words. Pay varies.

Fillers: Anecdotes, facts, gags to be illustrated by cartoonist, newsbreaks, short humor. **Buys 10/year.** Length: 25-250 words. **Pays $25-100.**

Tips: For new writers—send complete ms that is double spaced; clean copy only. If available, send clips of previously published works and résumé. Should state when available to write. Include on first page of ms name, address, phone, Social Security number, word count and SASE.

$ $ DIRECT AIM, For Today's Career Strategies, Communications Publishing Group, 3100 Broadway, Suite 660, Kansas City MO 64110. (816)960-1988. Fax: (816)960-1989. **Contact:** Neoshia Michelle Paige, editor. **80% freelance written.** Quarterly educational and career source guide for Black and Hispanic college students at traditional, non-traditional, vocational and technical institutions. "This magazine informs students about college survival skills and planning for a future in the professional world." Buys second serial (reprint) rights or makes work-for-hire assignments. Submit seasonal material 6 months in advance. Accepts simultaneous submissions. Reports in 2 months. Sample copy for 9×12 SAE with 4 first-class stamps. Writer's guidelines for #10 SASE.

- The editor notes that if the writer can provide the manuscript on 3.25 disk, saved in generic ASCII, pay is $10 higher and chance of acceptance is greater.

Nonfiction: Book excerpts or reviews, general interest, how-to (dealing with careers or education), humor, inspirational, interview/profile (celebrity or "up and coming" young adult), new product (as it relates to young adult market), personal experience, photo feature, technical, travel. Query or send complete ms. Length: 750-2,000 words. **Pays $150-400 for assigned articles; 12¢/word for unsolicited articles.** Sometimes pays expenses of writers on assignment.

Reprints: Send photocopy of article or typed ms with rights for sale noted and information about when and where the article previously appeared. Pays 6¢/word.

Photos: State availability of photos with submission. Reviews transparencies. Offers $20-25/photo. Captions, model releases and identification of subjects required. Will return photos.

Columns/Departments: Profiles of Achievement (striving and successful minority young adult age 18-35 in various technical careers). **Buys 25 mss/year.** Send complete ms. Length: 500-1,500. **Pays $50-250.**

Fiction: Publishes novel excerpts. Adventure, ethnic, historical, humorous, mainstream, slice-of-life vignettes. **Buys 3 mss/year.** Send complete ms. Length: 500-2,000 words. Pay varies.

Fillers: Anecdotes, facts, gags to be illustrated by cartoonist, newsbreaks, short humor. **Buys 30/year.** Length: 25-250 words. **Pays $25-100.**

Tips: For new writers—send complete ms that is double spaced; clean copy only. If available, send clips of previously published works and résumé. Should state when available to write. Include on first page of ms name, address, phone, Social Security number and word count. Photo availability is important."

$ $ EEO BIMONTHLY, Equal Employment Opportunity Career Journal, CASS Communications, Inc., 1800 Sherman Ave., Suite 300, Evanston IL 60201-3769. (847)475-8800. Fax: (847)475-8807. E-mail: casspubs@cassco m.com. Website: http://www.casscom.com. **Contact:** Robert Shannon, senior editor. **85% freelance written.** Bimonthly magazine covering career management, specifically for women, minorities and persons with disabilities. "Although our audience is specifically female and minority, much of our content applies to all white-collar professionals—career management tips, industry overviews and trends, and job search techniques. Anything job- or career-related (interviewing, résumé writing, relocating, communicating, automating, etc.) fits our publication." Estab. 1969. Circ. 7,500. **Pays on acceptance.** Publishes ms an average of 4 months after acceptance. Byline given. Buys multiple rights for use in smaller publications. Editorial lead time 3 months. Accepts simultaneous submissions. Reports in 3 weeks on queries; 1 month on mss. Sample copy for 10×12 SAE with 6 first-class stamps.

Nonfiction: General interest (career/workplace related), how-to (career planning related), interview/profile. **Buys 24-30 mss/year.** Query with published clips and SASE. Length: 1,800-3,000 words. **Pays $350-600 for assigned articles; $250-500 for unsolicited articles.**

Reprints: Send photocopy of and information about when and where the article previously appeared. Pay varies.

Photos: State availability of photos with submissions. Reviews contact sheets, transparencies, prints. Negotiates payment individually. Captions, model releases, identification of subjects required. Buys one-time rights.

Columns/Departments: Success Stories (profiles of successful individuals either female, minority or disabled—but not entrepreneurs; "we are looking for corporate types, especially in engineering and other technical fields"), Length: 2,000 words. **Buys 10-12 mss/year.** Query with published clips and SASE. **Pays $250-600.**

Tips: "Your queries can be informal outlines; just show us that you can write and that you know your subject."

$ $ EQUAL OPPORTUNITY, The Nation's Only Multi-Ethnic Recruitment Magazine for Black, Hispanic, Native American & Asian American College Grads, Equal Opportunity Publications, Inc., 1160 E. Jericho Turnpike, Suite 200, Huntington NY 11743. (516)421-9421. Fax: (516)421-0359. E-mail: info@aol.com. Website: http://www.eop.com. **Contact:** James Schneider, editor. **70% freelance written.** Prefers to work with published/established writers. Triannual magazine covering career guidance for minorities. "Our audience is 90% college juniors and seniors; 10% working graduates. An understanding of educational and career problems of minorities is essential." Estab. 1967. Circ. 15,000, distributed through college guidance and placement offices. Pays on publication. Publishes ms an average of 6 months after acceptance. Byline given. Buys first rights. Editorial lead time 6 months. Submit seasonal material 6 months in advance. Reports in 2 weeks on queries, 1 month on mss. Accepts simultaneous queries. Sample copy and writer's guidelines for 9×12 SAE with 5 first-class stamps.

Nonfiction: Book excerpts and articles (job search techniques, role models); general interest (specific minority concerns); how-to (job-hunting skills, personal finance, better living, coping with discrimination); humor (student or career related); interview/profile (minority role models); opinion (problems of minorities); personal experience (professional and student study and career experiences); technical (on career fields offering opportunities for minorities); travel (on overseas job opportunities); and coverage of Black, Hispanic, Native American and Asian American interests. **Buys 10 mss/year.** Query or send complete ms. Deadline dates: fall (June 10); winter (September 15); spring (January 1). Length: 1,000-2,000 words. **Pays 10¢/word.** Sometimes pays expenses of writers on assignment.

Reprints: Send information about when and where the article previously appeared. Pays 10¢/word.

Photos: Prefers 35mm color slides and b&w. Captions and identification of subjects required. Buys all rights. Pays $15/photo use.

Tips: "Articles must be geared toward questions and answers faced by minority and women students."

$ $ FIRST OPPORTUNITY, Today's Career Options, Communications Publishing Group, 3100 Broadway, Suite 660, Kansas City MO 64111. (816)960-1988. Fax: (816)960-1989. **Contact:** Neoshia Michelle Paige, editor. **80% freelance written.** Resource publication focusing on advanced vocational/technical educational opportunities and career preparation for Black and Hispanic young adults, ages 16-21. Circ. 500,000. Pays on publication. Byline sometimes given. Buys second serial (reprint) rights or makes work-for-hire assignments. Submit seasonal material 6 months in advance. Accepts simultaneous submissions. Reports in 2 months. Sample copy for 9×12 SAE with 4 first-class stamps. Writer's guidelines for #10 SASE.

- The editor notes that if the writer can provide the manuscript on 3.25 disk, saved in generic ASCII, pay is $10 higher and chance of acceptance is greater.

Nonfiction: Book excerpts or reviews, general interest, how-to (dealing with careers or education), humor, inspirational, interview/profile (celebrity or "up and coming" young adult), new product (as it relates to young adult market), personal experience, photo feature, technical, travel. Length: 750-2,000 words. **Pays $150-400 for assigned articles; 12¢/word for unsolicited articles.** Sometimes pays expenses of writers on assignment.

Reprints: Send photocopy of article or typed ms with rights for sale noted and information about when and where the article previously appeared. Pays 6¢/word.

Photos: State availability of photos with submission. Prefers transparencies. Offers $20-25/photo. Captions, model releases, identification of subjects required. Buys all rights.

Columns/Departments: Profiles of Achievement (striving and successful minority young adult, age 16-35 in various vocational or technical careers). **Buys 15 mss/year.** Send complete ms. Length: 500-1,500. **Pays $50-250.**

Fiction: Adventure, ethnic, historical, humorous, mainstream, slice-of-life vignettes. **Buys 3 mss/year.** Send complete ms. Length: 500-5,000 words. Pay varies.

Fillers: Anecdotes, facts, gags to be illustrated by cartoonist, newsbreaks, short humor. **Buys 10/year.** Length: 25-250 words. **Pays $25-100.**

Tips: For new writers—send complete ms that is double spaced; clean copy only. If available, send clip of previously published works and résumé. Should state when available to write. Include on first page of ms name, address, phone, Social Security number and word count. Photo availability is important.

$ FLORIDA LEADER (for college students), P.O. Box 14081, Gainesville FL 32604. (352)373-6907. Fax: (352)373-8120. E-mail: oxendine@compuserve.com. Publisher: W.H. "Butch" Oxendine, Jr. Managing Editor: Kay Quinn. **Contact**: Teresa Beard, assistant editor. **10% freelance written.** Triannual "college magazine, feature-oriented, especially activities, events, interests and issues pertaining to college students." Estab. 1981. Circ. 27,000. Publishes ms an average of 2 months after acceptance. Byline given. Submit seasonal material 6 months in advance. Reports in 2 months on queries. Sample copy and writer's guidelines for $3.50, 9×12 SAE and 5 first-class stamps.

Nonfiction: How-to, humor, interview/profile, feature—all multi-sourced and Florida college related. Special issues: Careers and Majors (January, June); Florida Leader high school edition (August, January, May); Transfer (for community college transfers, November, July); Returning Student (for nontraditional-age students, July); Back to School (September); Student Leader (October, March—pays double). Query with SASE. Length: 900 words. **Pays $35-75.** Sometimes pays expenses of writers on assignment.

Photos: State availability of photos with submission. Reviews negatives and transparencies. Captions, model releases, identification of subjects required.

N $ $ JOURNEY, A Success Guide for College and Career Bound Students, Communications Publishing Group, 3100 Broadway St., Suite 660, Kansas City MO 64111-2413. (816)960-1988. Fax: (816)960-1989. **Contact:** Neoshia Michelle Paige, editor. **40% freelance written.** Biannual educational and career source guide for Asian-American high school and college students (ages 16-25) who have indicated a desire to pursue higher education through college, vocational and technical or proprietary schools. Estab. 1982. Circ. 200,000. Pays on publication. Byline sometimes given. Buys second serial (reprint) rights or makes work-for-hire assignments. Submit seasonal material 6 months in advance. Accepts simultaneous submissions. Reports in 3 months. Sample copy for 9×12 SAE with 4 first-class stamps. Writer's guidelines for #10 SASE.

- The editor notes that if the writer can provide the manuscript on 3.25 disk, saved in generic ASCII, pay is $10 higher and chance of acceptance is greater.

Nonfiction: Book excerpts or reviews, general interest, how-to (dealing with careers or education), humor, inspirational, interview/profile (celebrity or "up and coming" young adult), new product (as it relates to young adult market), personal experience, photo feature, sports, technical, travel. First time writers with *Journey* must submit complete ms for consideration. Length: 750-2,000 words. **Pays $150-400 for assigned articles; 12¢/word for unsolicited articles.** Sometimes pays expenses of writers on assignment.

Reprints: Send typed ms with rights for sale noted and information about when and where the article previously appeared. Pays 10¢/word.
Photos: State availability of photos with submission. Prefers transparencies. Offers $20-25/photo. Captions, model releases and identification of subjects required. Buys all or one-time rights.
Columns/Departments: Profiles of Achievement (striving and successful minority young adult, age 16-35 in various careers). **Buys 15 mss/year.** Send complete ms. Length: 500-1,500. **Pays $50-200.**
Fiction: Publishes novel exerpts. Adventure, ethnic, historical, humorous, mainstream, slice-of-life vignettes. **Buys 3 mss/year.** Send complete ms. Length: 1,000-3,000 words. **Pays $100-400.**
Fillers: Anecdotes, facts, gags to be illustrated by cartoonist, newsbreaks, short humor. **Buys 10/year.** Length: 25-250 words. **Pays $25-100.**
Tips: For new writers—must submit complete ms that is double spaced; clean copy only. If available, send clippings of previously published works and résumé. Should state when available to write. Include on first page your name, address, phone, Social Security number and word count. Availability of photos enhances your chances. "We desperately need more material dealing with concerns of Asian-American students."

$ $ LINK MAGAZINE, The College Magazine, College Television Network, 110 Greene St., #407, New York NY 10012. (212)966-1100. Fax: (212)966-1380. E-mail: editor@linkmag.com. Website: http://www.linkmag.com. **Contact:** Peter Kraft. **95% of mss are solicited. Rarely accepts unsolicited materials.** Quarterly magazine covering college news, issues and lifestyle. Estab. 1993. Circ. 1,000,000. Pays on publication. Publishes ms an average of 6 months after acceptance. Byline given. Offers 25% kill fee. Buys first or one-time rights. Editorial lead time 4 months. Submit seasonal material 4 months in advance. Accepts simultaneous submissions. Reports in 2 months on queries, 3 months on mss. Writer's guidelines for #10 SASE.
Nonfiction: Book excerpts, essays, exposé, general interest, how-to (educational, financial, lifestyle, etc.), interview/profile, photo feature, travel. Special issues: Environmental, Job Hunting, Computers. **Buys 5 mss/year.** Query with published clips. Length: 400-3,000. **Pays $150-500 for assigned articles; $100-200 for unsolicited articles.** Pays expenses of writers on assignment.
Photos: Send photos with submission. Reviews contact sheets, transparencies, prints. Negotiates payment individually. Captions required. Buys one-time rights.
Columns/Departments: Get A Job (how-to job hunting), 700-800 words; It's Your Life (lifestyle articles), 700-800 words; Interview (national politicians and writers), 700-1,500 words. Buys 5 mss/year. Query with published clips. **Pays $200-250.**
Tips: "Research very informative, insightful or how-to articles and present completed ideas with clips in a query. Keep everything geared only to what college students would appreciate."

$ $ $ ☆ NOTRE DAME MAGAZINE, University of Notre Dame, 538 Grace Hall, Notre Dame IN 46556-5612. (219)631-5335. Fax: (219)631-6767. E-mail: ndmag.1@nd.edu. **Contact**: Kerry Temple, editor. Managing Editor: Carol Schaal. **75% freelance written.** Quarterly magazine covering news of Notre Dame and education and issues affecting contemporary society. "We are interested in the moral, ethical and spiritual issues of the day and how Christians live in today's world. We are universal in scope, Catholic in viewpoint and serve Notre Dame alumni, friends and other constituencies." Estab. 1972. Circ. 135,000. **Pays on acceptance.** Publishes ms an average of 1 year after acceptance. Byline given. Kill fee negotiable. Buys first serial and electronic rights. Reports in 1 month. Free sample copy.
Nonfiction: Opinion, personal experience, religion. **Buys 35 mss/year.** Query with clips of published work. Length: 600-3,000 words. **Pays $250-1,500.** Sometimes pays expenses of writers on assignment.
Photos: State availability of photos. Reviews b&w contact sheets, transparencies and 8×10 prints. Model releases and identification of subjects required. Buys one-time rights.
Columns/Departments: Perspectives (essays, often written in first-person, deal with a wide array of issues—some topical, some personal, some serious, some light). Query with published clips or submit ms.
Tips: "The editors are always looking for new writers and fresh ideas. However, the caliber of the magazine and frequency of its publication dictate that the writing meet very high standards. The editors value articles strong in storytelling quality, journalistic technique, and substance. They do not encourage promotional or nostalgia pieces, stories on sports, or essays which are sentimentally religious."

$ $ OREGON QUARTERLY, The Magazine of the University of Oregon, 5228 University of Oregon, Eugene OR 97403-5228. (541)346-5048. Fax: (541)346-5571. E-mail: gmaynard@oregon.uoregon.edu. Website: http://www.uoregon.edu/~oq. **Contact**: Guy Maynard, editor. Assistant Editor: Kathleen Holt. **50% freelance written.** Quarterly university magazine of people and ideas at the University of Oregon and the Northwest. Estab. 1919. Circ. 95,000. Pays on publication. Publishes ms an average of 3 months after acceptance. Byline given. Offers 20% kill fee. Buys first North American serial rights. Reports in 2 months. Sample copy for 9×12 SAE with 4 first-class stamps.
Nonfiction: Northwest issues and culture from the perspective of UO alumni and faculty. **Buys 30 mss/year.** Query with published clips. Length: 250-2,500 words. **Pays $50-500.** Sometimes pays expenses of writers on assignment.
Reprints: Send photocopy of article and information about when and where the article previously appeared. Pays 50% of the amount paid for an original article.
Photos: State availability of photos with submission. Reviews 8×10 prints. Offers $10-25/photo. Identification of subjects required. Buys one-time rights.
Fiction: Publishes novel excerpts.

Tips: "Query with strong, colorful lead; clips."

N $ $ $ THE OREGON STATER, Oregon State University Alumni Association, 204 CH2M Hill Alumni Center, Corvallis OR 97331-6303. (503)737-0780. E-mail: edmonstg@ccmail.orst.edu. **Contact**: George Edmonston Jr., editor. **20% freelance written.** Tabloid covering news of Oregon State University and its alumni. Estab. 1915. Circ. 16,000. **Pays on acceptance.** Byline given. Buys one-time rights. Editorial lead time 4 months. Submit seasonal material 3 months in advance. Reports in 2 weeks on queries; 3 months on mss. Sample copy and writer's guidelines free.
Nonfiction: General interest, historical/nostalgic, humor, inspirational, interview/profile, personal experience, photo feature. **Buys 40 mss/year.** Query with or without published clips. Length: 2,000 words maximum. **Pays $50-1,000.** Pays expenses of writers on assignment.
Photos: Send photos with submission. Offers no additional payment for photos accepted with ms. Captions, model releases and identification of subjects required. Buys one-time rights.

$ $ THE PENN STATER, Penn State Alumni Association, 11 Old Main, University Park PA 16802. (814)865-2709. Fax: (814)863-5690. E-mail: pennstater@psu.edu. Website: http://www.alumni.psu.edu. **Contact**: Tina Hay, editor. **75% freelance written.** Bimonthly magazine covering Penn State and Penn Staters. Estab. 1910. Circ. 120,000. **Pays on acceptance.** Publishes ms an average of 4 months after acceptance. Byline given. Offers 50% kill fee. Buys first North American serial rights or second serial (reprint) rights. Web rights negotiable. Editorial lead time 3 months. Submit seasonal material 6-8 months in advance. Accepts simultaneous submissions. Reports in 2 months on queries. Prefers no unsolicited mss. Sample copy and writer's guidelines free.
Nonfiction: Book excerpts (by Penn Staters), general interest, historical/nostalgic, humor (sometimes), interview/profile, personal experience (sometimes), book reviews, photo feature, science/research. Stories must have Penn State connection. **Buys 20 mss/year.** Query with published clips and SASE. Length: 400-2,500 words. Pays competitive rates. Pays expenses of writers on assignment.
Reprints: Send photocopy of article and information about when and where it previously appeared. Payment varies.
Photos: Send photos with submission. Reviews transparencies and prints. Negotiates payment individually. Captions required. Buys one-time rights.
Tips: "We are especially interested in attracting writers who are savvy in creative nonfiction/literary journalism. All stories must have a Penn State tie-in."

$ $ THE PURDUE ALUMNUS, Purdue Alumni Association, Purdue Memorial Union 160, 101 N. Grant St., West Lafayette IN 47906-6212. (765)494-5184. Fax: (765)494-9179. **Contact:** Tim Newton, editor. **50% freelance written.** Prefers to work with published/established writers; works with small number of new/unpublished writers each year. Bimonthly magazine covering subjects of interest to Purdue University alumni. Estab. 1912. Circ. 65,000. Pays on publication. Publishes ms an average of 2 months after acceptance. Byline given. Buys first rights and makes work-for-hire assignments. Submit seasonal material 6 months in advance. Accepts simultaneous submissions. Reports in 2 weeks on queries; 1 month on mss. Sample copy for 9×12 SAE with 2 first-class stamps.
Nonfiction: Book excerpts, general interest, historical/nostalgic, humor, interview/profile, personal experience. Focus is on alumni, campus news, issues and opinions of interest to 65,000 members of the Alumni Association. Feature style, primarily university-oriented. Issues relevant to education. **Buys 12-20 mss/year.** Length: 1,500-2,500 words. **Pays $250-500.** Pays expenses of writers on assignment.
Reprints: Accepts previously published submissions.
Photos: State availability of photos. Reviews b&w contact sheet or 5×7 prints.
Tips: "We have 300,000 living, breathing Purdue alumni. If you can find a good story about one of them, we're interested. We use local freelancers to do campus pieces."

$ $ RIPON COLLEGE MAGAZINE, P.O. Box 248, Ripon WI 54971-0248. (920)748-8364. Fax: (920)748-9262. E-mail: booneL@mac.ripon.edu. Website: http://www.ripon.edu. **Contact:** Loren J. Boone, editor. **15% freelance written.** Quarterly magazine that "contains information relating to Ripon College and is mailed to alumni and friends of the college." Estab. 1851. Circ. 14,000. Pays on publication. Publishes ms an average of 3 months after acceptance. Byline given. Not copyrighted. Makes work-for-hire assignments. Reports in 2 weeks.
Nonfiction: Historical/nostalgic, interview/profile. **Buys 4 mss/year.** Query with or without published clips, or send complete ms. Length: 250-1,000 words. **Pays $25-350.**
Photos: State availability of photos with submission. Reviews contact sheets. Offers additional payment for photos accepted with ms. Captions and model releases are required. Buys one-time rights.
Tips: "Story ideas must have a direct connection to Ripon College."

$ SUCCEED, The Magazine for Continuing Education, Ramholtz Publishing Inc., 2071 Clove Rd., Staten Island NY 10304. (718)273-5700. Fax: (718)273-2539. E-mail: ramholtz@intercall.com. **Contact**: Gina LaGuardia, editor-in-chief. **85% freelance written.** Triannual magazine. "*Succeed*'s readers are interested in continuing education, whether it be for changing careers or enhancing their current career." Estab. 1994. Circ. 155,000. Pays on publication. Publishes ms an average of 4 months after acceptance. Byline given. Buys first and second rights. Editorial lead time 4 months. Submit seasonal material 4 months in advance. Accepts simultaneous submissions. Reports in 5 weeks. Sample copy for $1.50. Writer's guidelines for 9×12 SASE.
Nonfiction: Essays, exposé, general interest, how-to (change careers), interview/profile (interesting careers); new

product, opinion, personal experience, technical. **Buys 25 mss/year.** Query with published clips. Length: 1,000-1,500 words. **Pays $75-125.** Sometimes pays expenses of writers on assignment.

Reprints: Send photocopy of article.

Photos: Send photos with submission. Reviews negatives, prints. Offers no additional payment for photos accepted with ms. Captions and identification of subjects required. Buys one-time rights.

Columns/Departments: Tech Zone (new media/technology), 300-700 words; To Be... (personality/career profile), 600-800 words; Financial Fitness (finance, money management), 100-300 words. **Buys 10 mss/year.** Query with published clips. **Pays $15-70.**

Fillers: Facts, newsbreaks. **Buys 5/year.** Length: 50-200 words.

Tips: "Here are some topics we're interested in covering for future issues: Finding a Career That Fits, Retirement Strategies, Ethics in the Business World, Returning to School: Portfolio Assessment."

$ U, The National College Magazine, American Collegiate Network Inc., 1800 Century Park E., #820, Los Angeles CA 90067. (310)551-1831. Fax: (310)551-1659. E-mail: editor@umagazine.com. Website: http://www.umagazine.com. **Contact**: Frances Huffman, editor. **70% freelance written.** Magazine published 6 times/year "for college students by college students covering news, lifestyle and entertainment that relates to college students and college life." Estab. 1987. Circ. 1.5 million. **Pays on acceptance.** Publishes ms an average of 3 months after acceptance. Byline given. Buys all rights. Editorial lead time 3 months. Submit seasonal material 3 months in advance. Reports in 2 months. Sample copy and writer's guidelines free.

Nonfiction: Exposé, general interest, historical/nostalgic, humor, interview/profile, opinion, photo feature, travel. No articles that do not relate to college students or college life. **Buys 150-200 mss/year.** Query with published clips. Length: 250-1,000 words. **Pays $25-100.** Sometimes pays expenses of writers on assignment.

Photos: Reviews transparencies, prints. Negotiates payment individually. Buys all rights.

Columns/Departments: U. News (college news), 300 words; U. Life (college lifestyle/trends), 400 words; 15 Minutes (profile of outstanding student), 300 words; Byte Me (technology), 300 words; U. Lose (wrongdoings of administration, organization or student); R&R (entertainment, reviews). **Buys 200 mss/year.** Query with published clips. **Pays $25-35.**

Tips: Contributors must be enrolled as a college student. "*U* is written in 'college speak.' The tone is conversational, lively, engaging, smart, hip, and a little irreverent. Write articles as if you were talking to your friends at school. *U* is a magazine, not a newspaper—no inverted pyramid stories please! Magazine style requires a punchy lead that grabs the reader, a compelling main body and a witty walk-off."

N $ $ US BLACK ENGINEER/HISPANIC ENGINEER, And Information Technology, Career Communications Group, Inc., 729 E. Pratt St., Suite 504, Baltimore MD 21202. (410)244-7101. Fax: (410)752-1837. Website: http://www.ccgmag.com. Managing Editor: Grady Wells. **Contact:** Garland L. Thompson, editorial director. **80% freelance written**. Quarterly magazine. "Both of our magazines are designed to bring technology issues home to people of color. We look at careers in technology and what affects career possibilities, including education. But we also look at how technology affects Black Americans and Latinos." Estab. 1976. Circ. 20,000. Pays on publication. Publishes ms an average of 1 month after acceptance. Byline given. Offers 50% kill fee. Makes work-for-hire assignments. Editorial lead time 2 months. Reports in 2 weeks. Sample copy and ms guidelines for #10 SASE.

Nonfiction: How-to (plan a career, get a first job, get a good job), interview/profile, new product, technical (new technologies and people of color involved with them (Capitol Hill/federal reportage on technology and EEO issues). No opinion pieces, first-person articles, routine profiles with no news peg or grounding in science/technology issues. Length: 650-1,800 words. **Pays $250-600**. Sometimes pays expenses of writers on assignment.

Photos: State availability of photos with submission. Negotiates payment individually. Captions, model releases, identification of subjects required. Buys all rights.

Columns/Departments: Color of Technology (did you know that . . .?), 800 words; Pros on the Move (Black/Hispanic career moves), 500 words; Greatest Challenge (up from the roots), 650 words; Surfing the Net (websites of interest), 650 words; New in Print (books), 350 words; Community News (relating to science and tech people), 650 words. **Buys 30 mss/year**. Query with published clips. **Pays $250-300**.

Tips: "Call or come see me. Also contact us about covering our conferences, Black Engineer of the Year Awards and Women of Color Technology Awards."

N $ $ WPI JOURNAL, Worcester Polytechnic Institute, 100 Institute Rd., Worcester MA 01609-2280. Fax: (508)831-6004. E-mail: wpi-journal@wpi.edu. Website: http://www.wpi.edu/+journal. **Contact:** Michael Dorsey, editor. **50% freelance written.** Quarterly alumni magazine covering science and engineering/education/business personalities for 20,000 alumni, primarily engineers, scientists, managers, national media. Estab. 1897. Circ. 25,000. Pays on publication. Publishes ms an average of 6 months after acceptance. Byline given. Buys one-time rights. Submit seasonal material 6 months in advance. Accepts simultaneous submissions. Query for electronic submissions. Requires hard copy also. Reports in 1 month on queries.

Nonfiction: Interview/profile (people in engineering, science); photo feature; features on science, engineering and management. Query with published clips. Length: 1,000-4,000 words. Pays negotiable rate. Sometimes pays the expenses of writers on assignment.

Reprints: Accepts previously published submissions.

Photos: State availability of photos with query or ms. Reviews b&w contact sheets. Pays negotiable rate. Captions required.

Tips: "Submit outline of story and/or ms of story idea or published work. Features are most open to freelancers. Keep in mind that this is an alumni magazine, so most articles focus on the college and its community."

CHILD CARE & PARENTAL GUIDANCE

Magazines in this section address the needs and interests of families with children. Some publications are national in scope, others are geographically specific. Some offer general advice for parents, while magazines such as *Black Child* or *Catholic Parent* answer the concerns of smaller groups. Other markets that buy articles about child care and the family are included in the Religious and Women's sections and in the Trade Education and Counseling section. Publications for children can be found in the Juvenile and Teen sections.

$ $ $ AMERICAN BABY MAGAZINE, For Expectant and New Parents, Primedia Communications, 249 W. 17th St., New York NY 10011. (212)462-3000. Fax: (212)367-8332. Website: http://www.enews.com.80/magazines/baby/. **Contact:** Jen Schroeder, editorial assistant. Editor-in-Chief: Edith Nolte. **70% freelance written.** Prefers to work with published/established writers; works with a small number of new/unpublished writers each year. Monthly magazine addressing health, medical and childcare concerns for expectant and new parents, particularly those having their first child or those whose child is between the ages of birth and 2 years old. Mothers are the primary readers, but fathers' issues are equally important. "A simple, straightforward, clear approach is mandatory." Estab. 1938. Circ. 1,650,000. **Pays on acceptance.** Publishes ms an average of 6 months after acceptance. Byline given. Offers 25% kill fee. Buys first North American serial rights. Editorial lead time 5 months. Submit seasonal material 6 months in advance. Accepts simultaneous submissions. Reports in 4 weeks on queries; 2 months on mss. Sample copy for 9×12 SAE with 6 first-class stamps. Writer's guidelines for #10 SASE.

- Ranked as one of the best markets for freelance writers in *Writer's Yearbook* magazine's annual "Top 100 Markets," January 1998.

Nonfiction: Book excerpts, essays, general interest, how-to (some aspect of pregnancy or baby care), humor, new product and personal experience. "No 'hearts and flowers' or fantasy pieces." Full-length articles should offer helpful expert information on some aspect of pregnancy or child care; should cover a common problem of child-raising, along with solutions; or should give expert advice on a psychological or practical subject. Articles about products, such as toys and nursery furniture, are not accepted, as these are covered by staff members. **Buys 60 mss/year.** Query with published clips or send complete ms. Length: 1,000-2,000 words. **Pays $750-1,200 for assigned articles; $600-800 for unsolicited articles.** Pays the expenses of writers on assignment.

Reprints: Send photocopy of article and information about when and where the article previously appeared. Pays 50% of amount paid for an original article.

Photos: State availability of photos with submission. Reviews transparencies and prints. Model release and identification of subjects required. Buys one-time rights.

Columns/Departments: Personal Experience, 900-1,200 words, **pays $500**; Short Items, Crib Notes (news and feature items) and Medical Update, 50-250 words, **pays $100.**

Tips: "Get to know our style by thoroughly reading the magazine. Don't send something we recently published. Our readers want to feel connected to other parents, both to share experiences and to learn from one another. They want reassurance that the problems they are facing are solvable and not uncommon. They want to keep up with the latest issues affecting their new family, particularly health and medical news, but they don't have a lot of spare time to read. We forgo the theoretical approach to offer quick-to-read, hands-on information that can be put to use immediately."

$ AT-HOME MOTHER, (formerly *At-Home Mothering*), At-Home Mothers' Resource Center, 406 E. Buchanan Ave., Fairfield IA 52556. (515)472-3202. Fax: (515)469-3068. E-mail: ahmrc@lisco.com. **Contact**: Jeanette Lisefski, editor. **100% freelance written.** Quarterly magazine. "*At-Home Mother* provides support for at-home mothers and features up-beat articles that reinforce their choice to stay at home with their children, helping them to find maximum fulfillment in this most cherished profession. Through education and inspiration, we also help those mothers who want to stay at home find ways to make this goal a reality." **Pays on acceptance.** Publishes ms an average of 3-12 months after acceptance. Byline given. Buys first North American serial rights or second serial (reprint) rights. Editorial lead time 3 months. Accepts simultaneous submissions. Reports in 1 month on queries; 2 months on mss. Sample copy for $4. Writer's guidelines for #10 SASE.

Nonfiction: Essays, how-to, humor, inspirational, interview/profile, personal experience, photo feature. Features and departments focus on: Choosing Home, Earning at Home, Earning by Saving at Home, Mothers' Self-Esteem and Happiness at Home, Managing at Home, Celebrating Motherhood, Heart-to-Heart Parenting, Flexible Work Options, Teaching at Home, Learning at Home. **Buys 100 mss/year.** Query with or without published clips. Length: 1,200-2,500 words. **Pays $25-150.**

Reprints: Send photocopy of article or typed ms with rights for sale noted and information about when and where the article previously appeared. Pays 50% of amount paid for an original article.

Photos: Send photos with submission. Reviews prints. Offers $10-150. Model releases required. Buys one-time rights.

Columns/Departments: Book reviews, 300-400 words. Query with or without published clips. **Pays $10-50.**

Poetry: Free verse, light verse, traditional. **Buys 8 poems/year.** Length: 4-50 lines. **Pays $10-50.**
Fillers: Anecdotes, facts, short humor. **Buys 12/year.** Length: 20-500 words. **Pays $10-50.**
Tips: "Follow our writer's guidelines. Write specifically to at-home mothers."

$ ATLANTA PARENT/ATLANTA BABY, Suite 506, 4330 Georgetown Square II, Atlanta GA 30338-6217. (770)454-7599. Fax: (770)454-7699. E-mail: atlparent@family.com. Website: http://www.atlantaparent.com. Editor: Liz White. **Contact**: Peggy Middendorf, managing editor. **50% freelance written.** *Atlanta Parent* is a monthly tabloid covering parenting of children from birth-16 years old. Offers "down-to-earth help for parents." Estab. 1983. Circ. 75,000. *Atlanta Baby* magazine is published 6 times/year for expectant and new parents. Circ. 30,000. Pays on publication. Publishes ms 3 months after acceptance. Byline given. Buys one-time rights. Submit seasonal material 6 months in advance. Reports in 4 months. Sample copy for $2.
Nonfiction: General interest, how-to, humor, interview/profile, travel. Special issues: Private school (January); Birthday parties (February); Camp (March/April); Maternity and Mothering (May); Childcare (July); Back-to-school (August); Drugs (October); Holidays (November/December). No first-person accounts or philosophical discussions. **Buys 60 mss/year.** Query with or without published clips, or send complete ms. Length: 700-2,100 words. **Pays $15-30.** Sometimes pays expenses of writers on assignment.
Reprints: Send tearsheet or photocopy of article or typed ms with rights for sale noted and information about when and where the article previously appeared. Pays $15-30.
Photos: State availability of photos with submission and send photocopies. Reviews 3×5 photos "b&w preferably." Offers $10/photo. Buys one-time rights.
Tips: "Articles should be geared to problems or situations of families and parents. Should include down-to-earth tips and be clearly written. No philosophical discussions or first-person narratives."

BABY MAGAZINE, Baby Publishing Group, 124 E. 40th St., Suite 1101, New York NY 10016. (212)986-1422. Fax: (212)338-9011. E-mail: thebabymag@aol.com. **Contact**: Jeanne Muchnick, editor. **40% freelance written.** Bimonthly magazine covering late pregnancy, birth, first year of baby's life. "*BaBY* is distributed by diaper services, doctor's offices and retail outlets. The primary recipients are women in the last trimester of pregnancy and new parents." Estab. 1994. Circ. 850,000. **Pays on acceptance.** Publishes ms an average of 2 months after acceptance. Byline given. Buys first North American serial rights. Editorial lead time 4 months. Submit seasonal material 4 months in advance. Reports in 1 month. Sample copy for 9×12 SAE with $1.01 postage.
Nonfiction: Essays (e.g. first-time dad), how-to (any topics of interest to new parents, e.g. baby care, photography, siblings, traveling, choosing doctor, breast feeding, etc.), personal experience, photo feature, professional or expert articles on baby care, family issues. "We do not include stories about toilet-training, preschool or anything related to children over age one." **Buys 22 mss/year.** Query.
Reprints: Send tearsheet of article and information about when and where the article previously appeared.
Columns/Departments: BaBY Briefs, Relationship Quiz, Worry Wart Guide, Confessions of a Rookie Dad, Best Buys.

N $ $ $ $ BABY TALK, Time Publishing Ventures, 1325 Avenue of the Americas, 27th Floor, New York NY 10019. (212)522-8080. Fax: (212)522-8750. **Contact:** Managing Editor. Editors-in-Chief: Trisha Thompson, Fred Levine. **Mostly freelance written**. Magazine published 10 times a year. "*Baby Talk* is written primarily for women who are considering pregnancy or who are expecting a child, and parents of children from birth through age one, with the emphasis on pregnancy through first six months of life." Estab. 1935. Circ. 1,500,000. Reports in 2 months.
Nonfiction: Features cover pregnancy, the basics of baby care, infant/toddler health, growth and development, juvenile equipment and toys, work and day care, marriage and sex, "approached from a how-to, service perspective. The message—Here's what you need to know and why—is delivered with smart, crisp style. The tone is confident and reassuring (and, when appropriate, humorous and playful), with the backing of experts. In essence, *Baby Talk* is a training manual of parents facing the day-to-day dilemmas of new parenthood." Query in writing with SASE. No phone calls, please. Length: 1,000-2,000 words. **Pays $500-2,000**, depending on length, degree of difficulty, and the writer's previous experience.
Columns/Departments: Several departments are written by regular contributors. Length: 100-1,000 words. **Pays $100-750.** Query in writing with SASE.
Tips: "Please familiarize yourself with the magazine before submitting a query. Take the time to focus your story idea; scattershot queries are a waste of everyone's time."

☆ $ $ BABY'S WORLD MAGAZINE, America's Baby Magazine, Baby's World Publications Inc., 16 Peniston Ave. E., Hanover NJ 07936. (973)503-0700. Fax: (973)887-6801. E-mail: info@babysworld.com. **Contact**: Taylor Scott, managing editor. **75% freelance written.** Quarterly magazine with "features, columns and stories for new and expectant parents of newborns-to-toddlers regarding health, medicine and nutrition for both baby and mother. Also includes safety, first aid and all-around fun reading." Estab. 1996. Circ. 25,000. Pays on publication. Publishes ms an average of 3 months after acceptance. Byline given. Buys first North American serial rights. Editorial lead time 2 months. Submit seasonal material 3 months in advance. Accepts simultaneous submissions. Reports in 2 months. Sample copy for 9×12 SAE and 5 first-class stamps. Writer's guidelines for #10 SASE.
Nonfiction: General interest, how-to, humor, inspirational, interview/profile, new product, opinion, personal experi-

ence, photo feature. **Buys 25 mss/year.** Query with or without published clips. Length: 250-3,000 words. **Pays $25-500 for assigned articles; $25-200 for unsolicited articles.**

Reprints: Send tearsheet or photocopy of article.

Columns/Departments: You Need To Know (bits and tips), 25 words; Celebrity Parenting, 250 words. Buys 10 mss/year. Query with or without published clips. **Pays $10-250.**

Fillers: Anecdotes, facts, gags to be illustrated by cartoonist, newsbreaks, short humor. **Buys 10/year.** Length: 25-50 words. **Pays $10-25.**

Tips: "We are looking for fresh, innovative writing on the latest in baby care, articles on the newest procedures, answers to new parents' most-asked questions, and fun reading for women expecting their new baby."

$ BAY AREA BABY, 401 Alberto Way, Suite A, Los Gatos CA 95032. (408)358-1414. Editor: Anne Chappell Belden. **Contact**: Mary Brence Martin, managing editor. Magazine published 3 times a year covering pregnancy and new parenthood (usually first-time). "*Bay Area Baby* targets pregnant couples and new (usually first-time) parents. We provide local, up-to-the minute information on pregnancy and babies." Estab. 1986. Circ. 60,000. Pays on publication. Publishes ms an average of 6 months after acceptance. Byline given. Buys first rights. Editorial lead time 4 months. Submit seasonal material 6 months in advance. Accepts simultaneous submissions. Reports in 2 months. Sample copy for 8½×11½ SAE with 5 first-class stamps. Writer's guidelines for #10 SASE.

Nonfiction: Book excerpts, essays, interview/profile, personal experience (must be related to pregnancy or new parenthood). **Buys 9 mss/year.** Send complete ms. Length: 600-1,400 words. **Pays 6¢/word.** Sometimes pays expenses of writers on assignment.

Reprints: Accepts previously published submissions.

Photos: State availability of photos with submission. Reviews contact sheets, transparencies, prints. Offers $10-15/photo. Buys one-time rights.

$ BIG APPLE PARENT/QUEENS PARENT, Family Communications, Inc., 36 E. 12th St., New York NY 10003. (212)533-2277. Fax: (212)475-6186. E-mail: parentspaper@mindspring.com. Website: bigappleparents.com. **Contact:** Helen Freedman, managing editor. **95% freelance written.** Monthly tabloids covering New York City family life. "*BAP* readers live in high-rise Manhattan apartments; it is an educated, upscale audience. Often both parents are working full time in professional occupations. Child-care help tends to be one-on-one, in the home. Kids attend private schools for the most part. While not quite a suburban approach, some of our *QP* readers do have backyards (though most live in high-rise apartments). It is a more middle-class audience in Queens. More kids are in day care centers; majority of kids are in public schools." Estab. 1985. *Big Apple* circ. 62,000, *Queens* circ. 40,000. Pays end of month following publication. Byline given. Offers 50% kill fee. Buys first New York City rights. Reserves the right to publish an article in either or both the Manhattan and Queens editions and online. Submit seasonal material 3 months in advance. Accepts simultaneous submissions. Reports immediately; however, request no submissions during the summer months. Sample copy and writer's guidelines free.

Nonfiction: Essays, exposé, general interest, how-to, inspirational, interview/profile, opinion, photo feature, family health, education. **Buys 60-70 mss/year.** Query by mail, fax or e-mail or send complete ms. Length: 600-1,000 words. **Pays $35-50.** Sometimes pays expenses of writers on assignment. "We are not buying any more humor or personal parenting essays through end of 1999, but we're *always* looking for news and coverage of controversial issues."

Reprints: Send tearsheet or photocopy of article or typed ms with rights for sale noted and information about when and where the article previously appeared. Pays same as article rate.

Photos: State availability of or send photos with submission. Reviews contact sheets, prints. Offers $20/photo. Captions required. Buys one-time rights.

Columns/Departments: Dads; Education; Family Finance. **Buys 50-60 mss/year.** Send complete ms.

Tips: "We have a very local focus; our aim is to present articles our readers cannot find in national publications. To that end, news stories and human interest pieces must focus on New York and New Yorkers. Child-raising articles must include quotes from New York and Queens' experts and sources. We are always looking for news and newsy pieces; we keep on top of current events, frequently giving issues that may relate to parenting a local focus so that the idea will work for us as well."

$ BLACK CHILD MAGAZINE, Heritage Publishing Group, P.O. Box 12048, Atlanta GA 30355. (404)350-7877. Fax: (404)350-0819. **Contact:** Candy Mills, editor. **80% freelance written.** Quarterly magazine "covering all concerns/issues relating to healthy parenting of African-American children from birth to early teens." Estab. 1995. Circ. 25,500. Pays on publication. Publishes ms an average of 3 months after acceptance. Byline given. Buys first, one- or second serial (reprint) rights. Submit seasonal material 4 months in advance. Reports in 1 month on queries; 2 months on mss. Sample copy for $2 and 9×12 SAE with 4 first-class stamps. Writer's guidelines for #10 SASE.

Nonfiction: Book excerpts, essays, exposé, general interest, historical/nostalgic, how-to, humor, inspirational, interview/profile, new product, opinion, personal experience, photo feature. **Buys 30 mss/year.** Send complete ms. No simultaneous submissions. Length: 800-2,000 words. **Pays 4¢/word.**

Reprints: Send photocopy of article and information about when and where the article previously appeared. Pays 4¢/word. Pays 75% of amount paid for an original article.

Photos: State availability of or send photos with submissions. Reviews contact sheets, negatives, transparencies, prints. Offers $25-50/photo. Model releases, identification of subjects required. Buys one-time rights.

Columns/Departments: Health/Fitness, Education, Discipline; all 700-1,400 words. **Buys 10 mss/year.** Query. **Pays**

4¢/word.

Tips: "Unique parental articles with hard hitting, no-nonsense approach always preferred. Empowering the parents to raise happy healthy African-American children is our goal! No fiction!"

$ CATHOLIC PARENT, Our Sunday Visitor, 200 Noll Plaza, Huntington IN 46750. (219)356-8400. **Contact:** Woodeene Koenig-Bricker, editor. **95% freelance written.** Bimonthly magazine. "We look for practical, realistic parenting articles written for a primarily Roman Catholic audience. They key is practical, not pious." Estab. 1993. Circ. 32,000. **Pays on acceptance**. Publishes ms an average of 6 months after acceptance. Byline given. Kill fee varies. Buys first North American serial rights. Editorial lead time 6 months. Submit seasonal material 6 months in advance. Accepts simultaneous submissions. Reports in 2 months. Sample copy for $3.

- *Catholic Parent* is extremely receptive to first-person accounts of personal experiences dealing with parenting issues that are moving, emotionally engaging and uplifting for the reader. Bear in mind the magazine's mission to provide practical information for parents.

Nonfiction: Essays, how-to, humor, inspirational, personal experience, religious. **Buys 50 mss/year.** Send complete ms. Length: 850-1,200 words. Pay varies. Sometimes pays expenses of writers on assignment.

Photos: State availability of photos with submissions.

Columns/Departments: This Works (parenting tips), 200 words. **Buys 50 mss/year.** Send complete ms. **Pays $15-25.**

$ $ CHICAGO PARENT, Connecting with families, Wednesday Journal, Inc., 141 S. Oak Park Ave., Oak Park IL 60302. Fax: (708)524-0447. E-mail: chiparent@wjinc.com. Website: http://chicagoparent.com. **Contact:** Sharon Bloyd-Peshkin, editor. **50% freelance written.** Monthly. "We are a highly local parenting publication with a strong preference for local writers, although we are open to others. We cover a gamut of issues, doing everything from investigative features and in-depth reporting to service pieces on child health and daycare issues." Estab. 1988. Circ. 125,000 in four zones. Publishes ms 1-2 months after acceptance. Pays on publication. Byline given. Offers 10% kill fee. Buys first rights; reprint rights at 20%, online at 10% of original ms payment. Editorial lead time 3-4 months. Submit seasonal material 4-5 months in advance. Reports in 1 month. Sample copy for $3 and SAE with $1.65 postage. Writer's guidelines for #10 SASE.

Nonfiction: Book excerpts, profiles, general parenting interest, how-to (parent-related), humor, investigative features. Few essays. Special issues include Healthy Woman, Chicago Baby, Healthy Child. **Buys 120 mss/year.** Query with published clips. Length: 800-3,000 words. **Pays $100-350 for assigned articles, $35-200 for unsolicited articles.** Sometimes pays expenses of writers on assignment.

Photos: State availability of photos with submission or send photos with submission. Reviews contact sheets, negatives, any transparencies, any prints. Offers $0-40/photo. Negotiates payment individually. Buys one-time rights.

Columns/Departments: Healthy Kids (kids' health issues); Single Parent (legal or other issues for single parents); Parent on the Payroll (issues of reconciling work and home life), all 850 words. **Buys 30 mss/year.** Query with published clips or send complete ms. **Pays $100.**

$ $ $ $ CHILD, Gruner + Jahr, 375 Lexington Ave., New York NY 10017-5514. (212)499-2004. Fax: (212)499-2038. E-mail: childmag@aol.com. Editor: Pamela Abrams. Managing Editor: Sylvia Barsotti. **Contact:** Julie Savacool, editorial assistant. **95% freelance written.** Monthly magazine for parenting. Estab. 1986. Circ. 930,000. **Pays on acceptance.** Byline given. Offers 25% kill fee. Buys first North American serial, first, one-time and second serial (reprint) rights. Editorial lead time 3 months. Submit seasonal material 6 months in advance. Reports in 2 months. Sample copy for $3.95. Writer's guidelines free.

- Ranked as one of the best markets for freelance writers in *Writer's Yearbook* magazine's annual "Top 100 Markets," January 1998.

Nonfiction: Book excerpts, general interest, interview/profile, new product, photo feature, travel. No poetry. **Buys 50 feature mss/year, 25-30 short pieces/year.** Query with published clips. Length: 650-2,500 words. **Pays $1/word.** Sometimes pays expenses of writers on assignment.

Photos: State availability of photos with submission. Reviews transparencies. Negotiates payment individually. Buys one-time rights.

Columns/Departments: First Person (mother's or father's perspective); Lesson Learned (experience mother or father learned from). Query with published clips. **Buys 100 mss/year.** Length: 1,500 words. **Pays $1/word.**

Tips: "Stories should include opinions from experts as well as anecdotes from parents to illustrate the points being made. Service is key."

FOR EXPLANATIONS OF THESE SYMBOLS,
SEE THE INSIDE FRONT AND BACK COVERS OF THIS BOOK

$ $ CHRISTIAN PARENTING TODAY, Good Family Magazines, 4050 Lee Vance View, Colorado Springs CO 80918. (719)531-7776. Fax: (719)535-0172. E-mail: cptmag@aol.com. Editor: Erin Healy. **Contact**: Kathy Davis, associate editor. **90% freelance written.** Bimonthly magazine "encourages and informs parents of children ages birth to 12 who want to build strong families and raise their children from a positive, authoritative Christian perspective. *CPT* strives to give parents practical tools in four areas: 1) encouraging the spiritual and moral growth of their children; 2) guiding the physical, emotional, social and intellectual development of their children; 3) enriching the reader's marriage; and 4) strengthening the reader's family relationships." Estab. 1988. Circ. 120,000. Pays on acceptance or publication. Byline given. Buys first North American serial or second serial (reprint) rights. Submit seasonal material 8 months in advance. Reports in 2 months. Sample copy for 9×12 SAE with $3 postage. Writer's guidelines for #10 SASE.

Nonfiction: Book excerpts, how-to, humor, inspirational, religious. Feature topics of greatest interest: practical guidance in spiritual/moral development and values transfer; practical solutions to everyday parenting issues; tips on how to enrich readers' marriages; ideas for nurturing healthy family ties; family activities that focus on parent/child interaction; humorous pieces about everyday family life. **Buys 50 mss/year.** Query. Length: 750-2,000 words. **Pays 15-25¢/word.** Sometimes pays expenses of writers on assignment.

Reprints: Send photocopy of article and typed ms with rights for sale noted and information about when and where the article previously appeared. **Pays $50.**

Photos: State availability of photos with submission. Do not submit photos without permission. Reviews transparencies. Model release required. Buys one-time rights.

Columns/Departments: Parent Exchange (family-tested parenting ideas from our readers), 25-100 words **(pays $40)**; Life In Our House (entertaining, true, humorous stories about your family), 25-100 words **(pays $25)**; Train Them Up (spiritual development topics from a Christian perspective), 600-650 words **(pays $125)**; Healthy & Safe (practical how-to articles that speak to parents' desire to provide their children with an emotionally and physically safe environment both at home and away), 600 words **(pays $125)**; The Lighter Side (humorous everyday family life), 600-700 words **(pays $125)**. Buys 120 mss/year. Submissions become property of *CPT*. Submissions to *Life In Our House* and *Parent Exchange* are not acknowledged or returned.

Tips: "Tell it like it is. Readers have a 'get real' attitude that demands a down-to-earth, pragmatic take on topics. Don't sugar-coat things. Give direction without waffling. If you've 'been there,' tell us. The first-person, used appropriately, is OK. Don't distance yourself from readers. They trust people who have walked in their shoes. Get reader friendly. Fill your article with nuts and bolts: developmental information, age-specific angles, multiple resources, sound-bite sidebars, real-life people and anecdotes and realistic, vividly explained suggestions."

$ DPX, Divorced Parents X-Change, Inc., P.O. Box 1127, Athens OH 45701-1127. (614)664-3030. E-mail: tuqbutfy@bright.net. **Contact:** Terri Andrews, editor/founder. **75% freelance written.** Monthly newsletter. "The *DPX* is a national publication devoted to supporting, informing, educating and assisting divorced- and step-parenting. We emphasize co-parenting, communication and positive parenting." Estab. 1993. Circ. 250. Pays on publication. Publishes ms an average of 3 months after acceptance. Buys one-time rights. Editorial lead time 3 months. Submit seasonal material 4 months in advance. Accepts simultaneous submissions. Reports in 6 weeks on queries; 1 month on mss. Sample copy $3. Manuscript guidelines for #10 SASE.

Nonfiction: Book excerpts, essays, general interest, how-to, humor, inspirational, interview/profile, personal experience, self-help. "No how-to-get-even-with-your-ex articles." **Buys 40 mss/year.** Send complete ms. Length: 200-1,000 words. **Pays 1¢/word.** Pays with contributor copies at writer's request.

Reprints: Send photocopy of article or typed ms with rights for sale noted and information about when and where the article previously appeared. Payment negotiable.

Poetry: Avant-garde, free verse, haiku, light verse, traditional. Submit maximum 5 poems. **Length: 6-20 lines. Pays 1¢/word.**

Fillers: Facts, short humor. Length: 10-100 words. **Pays 1¢/word.**

Tips: "Read our newsletter first. We focus on the positive side of co-parenting. We inspire and motivate parents—not add fuel to their anger."

N $ $ FAMILY DIGEST, The Black Mom's Best Friend!, Family Digest Association, 696 San Ramon Valley Blvd., #349, Danville CA 94526. Fax: (925)838-4948. **Contact:** Darryl Mobley, associate editor. **90% freelance written.** Quarterly magazine covering women's services. "Our mission: Help black moms/female heads-of-household get more out of their roles as wife, mother, homemaker. Editorial coverage includes parenting, health, love and marriage, travel, family finances, and beauty and style . . . All designed to appeal to black moms." Estab. 1997. Circ. 2,100,000. Pays on publication. Publishes ms an average of 6 months after acceptance. Byline sometimes given. Buys first North American serial rights, second serial (reprint) rights, or makes work-for-hire assignments. Editorial lead time 2 months. Submit seasonal material 3 months in advance. Accepts simultaneous submissions. Reports in 2 weeks on queries; 1 month on mss. Writer's guidelines free on request by e-mail or for SASE and 2 first-class stamps.

Nonfiction: Book excerpts, general interest (dealing with relationships), historical/nostalgic, how-to, humor, inspirational, interview/profile, personal experience. "We are not political. We do not want articles that blame others. We do want articles that improve the lives of our readers." Query with published clips. Length: 1,000-3,000 words. **Pays $100-500**. Sometimes pays expenses of writers on assignment.

Reprints: Accepts previously published submissions.

Photos: State availability of or send photos with submission. Reviews negatives, transparencies, prints. Offers no

additional payment for photos accepted with ms. Captions, model releases, identification of subjects required.
Columns/Departments: Parenting, love and marriage, health, family finances, beauty and style, A Better You! (personal development). **Buys 100 mss/year**. Query with published clips. **Pays $100-500.**
Fiction: Erotica, ethnic, historical, humorous, novel excerpts, romance. Query with published clips.
Fillers: Anecdotes, facts, gags to be illustrated by cartoonist, short humor. **Buys 100 mss/year**. Length: 50-250 words.

$ THE FAMILY DIGEST, P.O. Box 40137, Fort Wayne IN 46804. **Contact:** Corine B. Erlandson, editor. **95% freelance written.** Bimonthly digest-sized magazine. "*The Family Digest* is dedicated to the joy and fulfillment of the Catholic family and its relationship to the Catholic parish." Estab. 1945. Circ. 150,000. Pays within 1-2 months of acceptance. Publishes ms usually within 1 year after acceptance. Byline given. Buys first North American rights. Submit seasonal material 7 months in advance. Reports in 2 months. Sample copy and writer's guidelines for 6×9 SAE with 2 first-class stamps.
Nonfiction: Family life, parish life, how-to, seasonal, inspirational, prayer life, Catholic traditions. Send ms with SASE. No poetry or fiction. **Buys 60 unsolicited mss/year.** Length: 750-1,200 words. **Pays $40-60/article.**
Reprints: Prefers previously unpublished articles. Send typed ms with rights for sale noted and information about when and where the article previously appeared. Pays 5¢/word.
Fillers: Anecdotes, tasteful humor based on personal experience. **Buys 3/issue.** Length: 25-100 words maximum. **Pays $20 on acceptance.** Cartoons: Publishes 5 cartoons/issue, related to family and Catholic parish life. Pays $35/cartoon on acceptance.
Tips: "Prospective freelance contributors should be familiar with the publication, and the types of articles we accept and publish. We are especially looking for upbeat articles which affirm the simple ways in which the Catholic faith is expressed in daily life. Articles on family and parish life, including seasonal articles, how-to pieces, inspirational, prayer, spiritual life and Church traditions, will be gladly reviewed for possible acceptance and publication."

$ $ $ $ FAMILY LIFE, Hachette-Filipacchi Magazines, Inc., 1633 Broadway, 41st Floor, New York NY 10019. Fax: (212)489-4561. E-mail: familylife@aol.com. Editor-in-Chief: Peter Herbst. **Contact**: Ziona Hochbaum, editorial assistant. **90% freelance written.** Magazine published 10 times/year for parents of children ages 3-12. Estab. 1993. Circ. 400,000. **Pays on acceptance.** Publishes ms an average of 4 months after acceptance. Byline given. Offers 25% kill fee. Buys first North American rights. Editorial lead time 5 months. Submit seasonal material 8 months in advance. Accepts simultaneous submissions. Reports in 6 weeks on queries. Sample copy for $3, call (201)451-9420. Writer's guidelines for #10 SASE.
Nonfiction: Parenting book excerpts, essays, general interest, new product, photo feature, travel. Does not want to see articles about children under 3 or childbirth. Feature length: 2,000-3,500 words. Query with published clips. **Pays $1/word.** Pays expenses of writers on assignment.
Photos: State availability of photos with submission. Reviews transparencies. Negotiates payment individually. Buys one-time rights.
Columns/Departments: Family Matters section in the front of the book (newsy shorts on parenting topics, interesting travel destinations and the latest health issues), 150-250 words. Individual columns: Parent to Parent (story by a parent about life with his or her child that epitomizes one issue in child-rearing); Motherhood (changes and challenges that being a mother brings to a woman's life); Family Affairs (personal issues parents face as their children grow up); School Smart (today's educational issues); House Calls (health); Chip Chat (the latest in family computing). Length: 1,000-1,500 words. Query with published clips.
Tips: "Our readers are parents of children ages 3-12 who are interested in getting the most out of family life. Most are college educated and work hard at a full-time job. We want fresh articles dealing with the day-to-day issues that these families face, with personal insight and professional opinion on how to handle them."

$ FAMILY TIMES, Family Times, Inc., 1900 Superfine Lane, Wilmington DE 19802. (302)575-0935. Fax: (302)575-0933. E-mail: ftimes@family.com. Website: http://www.family.com. **Contact**: Denise Yearian, editor. **50% freelance written.** Monthly tabloid for parenting. "Our targeted distribution is to parents via a controlled network of area schools, daycares, pediatricians and places where families congregate. We only want articles related to parenting, children's issues and enhancing family life." Estab. 1990. Circ. 35,000. Pays on publication. Publishes ms an average of 2 months after acceptance. Byline given. Buys one-time or second serial (reprint) rights. Editorial lead time 2 months. Submit seasonal material 2 months in advance. Accepts simultaneous submissions. Reports in 3 months on mss. Sample copy for 3 first-class stamps.
Nonfiction: Book excerpts, how-to parenting, inspirational, interview/profile, new product, opinion, personal experience, photo feature, travel, children, parenting. Special issues: Technology/Education (January); Fitness (February); Summer Camps (March); Environment (April); Birthdays (May); Summer Fun (June); Pregnancy & Birth (July); After-School Activities (August); Back-To-School (September); Childcare Options (October); Health & Safety (November); Holiday Celebrations (December). **Buys 60 mss/year.** Send complete ms. Length: 750-1,000 words. **Pays $30 minimum for assigned articles; $25 for unsolicited articles.** Sometimes pays expenses of writers on assignment.
Reprints: Send tearsheet or photocopy of article or typed ms with rights for sale noted.
Photos: State availability of photos with submission. Negotiates payment individually. Identification of subjects required. Buys one-time rights.
Columns/Departments: Pays $25-50.
Tips: "Work with other members of PPA (Parenting Publications of America) since we all share our writers and watch

others' work. We pay little but you can sell the same story to 30 other publications in different markets. Online use offers additional author credit and payment based on accesses. We are most open to general features."

$ $ $ $ FAMILYFUN, Disney Magazine Publishing Inc., 244 Main St., Northampton MA 01060. Fax: (413)586-5724. Website: http://www.familyfun.com. **Contact:** Susan Claire Ellis, editor. Magazine published 10 times/year covering activities for families with kids ages 3-12. "*Family Fun* is about all the great things families can do together. Our writers are either parents or professionals in education." Estab. 1991. Circ. 1,000,000. **Pays on acceptance.** Publishes ms an average of 4 months after acceptance. Byline sometimes given. Offers 25% kill fee. Buys simultaneous rights or makes work-for-hire assignments. Editorial lead time 4 months. Submit seasonal material 6 months in advance. Accepts simultaneous submissions. Reports in 2 months. Sample copy and writer's guidelines for $3 (call (800)289-4849).

Nonfiction: Features Editor. Book excerpts, essays, general interest, how-to (crafts, cooking, educational activities), humor, interview/profile, personal experience, photo feature, travel. Special issues: Crafts, Holidays, Back to School, Summer Vacations. **Buys hundreds mss/year.** Query with published clips. No unsolicited mss. Length: 850-3,000 words. **Pays $1/word.** Sometimes pays expenses of writers on assignment.

Photos: State availability of photos with submissions. Reviews contact sheets, negatives, transparencies. Offers $75-500/photo. Model releases, identification of subjects required. Buys all rights (simultaneous).

Columns/Departments: Family Almanac, Cindy Littlefield, associate editor (simple, quick, practical, inexpensive ideas and projects—outings, crafts, games, nature activities, learning projects, and cooking with children), 200-600 words; query or send ms; **pays 50¢/word, also pays $75 for ideas.** Family Traveler, Deb Geigis Berry, senior editor (brief, newsy items about family travel, what's new, what's great, and especially, what's a good deal), 100-125 words; send ms; **pays $100, also pays $50 for ideas.** Family Ties, Ann Hallock, editor (first-person column that spotlights some aspect of family life that is humorous, inspirational, or interesting); 1,500 words; send ms; **pays $1,500**. My Great idea, Gret Lauzon, staff writer (explains fun and inventive ideas that have worked for writer's own family); 800-1,000 words; query or send letter letter or ms; **pays $750 on acceptance**; also publishes best letters from writers and readers following column, send to My Great Ideas editor, 100-150 words, **pays $25 on publication. Buys 20-25 mss/year.**

Tips: "Many of our writers break into *FF* by writing for Family Almanac or Family Traveler (front-of-the-book departments)."

N $ GRAND RAPIDS PARENT MAGAZINE, Gemini Publications, 549 Ottawa Ave. NW, Grand Rapids MI 49503. (616)459-4545. Fax: (616)459-4800 or (616)459-2004. **Contact**: Carole Valade, editor. Monthly magazine covering local parenting issues. "*Grand Rapids Parent Magazine* seeks to inform, instruct, amuse and entertain its readers and their families." Pays on publication. Byline given. Offers $25 kill fee. Buys first North American serial rights, simultaneous rights, all rights or makes work-for-hire assignments. Editorial lead time 2-3 months. Submit seasonal material 4 months in advance. Accepts simultaneous submissions. Reports in 2 months on queries; 6 months on mss. Writer's guidelines for #10 SASE.

Nonfiction: "The publication recognizes that parenting is a process that begins before conception/adoption and continues for a lifetime. The issues are diverse and ever changing. *Grand Rapids Parent* seeks to identify these issues and give them a local perspective, using local sources and resources." Query. **Pays $25-50.**

Photos: State availabililty of photos with submission. Reviews contact sheets. Offers $25/photo. Captions, model releases and identification of subjects required. Buys one-time or all rights.

Columns/Departments: All local: law, finance, humor, opinion, mental health. **Pays $25.**

N $ $ $ GREAT EXPECTATIONS, Today's Parent Group, 269 Richmond St. W, Toronto, Ontario M5V 1X1 Canada. Fax: (416)496-1991. Website: http://www.todaysparent.com. **Contact:** Susan Spicer, assistant editor. Editor: Holly Bennett. **100% freelance written**. Consumer magazine published 3 times a year. "*GE* helps, supports and encourages expectant and new parents with news and features related to pregnancy, birth, human sexuality and parenting." Estab. 1973. Circ. 200,000. **Pays on acceptance**. Publishes ms an average of 8 months after acceptance. Bylines given. Buys first North American serial rights. Editorial lead time 6 months. Reports in 6 weeks on queries. Sample copy and writer's guidelines for #10 SASE.

Nonfiction: Features about pregnancy, labor and delivery, post-partum issues. **Buys 12 mss/year**. Query with published clips. Length: 700-2,000 words. **Pays $400-1,200.** Sometimes pays expenses of writers on assignment.

Photos: State availability of photos with submission. Negotiates payment individually. Rights negotiated individually.

Tips: "Our writers are professional freelance writers with specific knowledge and/or experience in the childbirth field. *GE* is written for a Canadian audience using Canadian researchers and sources."

$ $ GROWING PARENT, Dunn & Hargitt, Inc., P.O. Box 620, Lafayette IN 47902-0620. (765)423-2624. Fax: (765)742-8514. **Contact:** Nancy Kleckner, editor. **40-50% freelance written.** Works with a small number of new/unpublished writers each year. "We do receive a lot of unsolicited submissions but have had excellent results in working with some unpublished writers. So, we're always happy to look at material and hope to find one or two jewels each year." Monthly newsletter which focuses on parents—the issues, problems, and choices they face as their children grow. "We want to look at the parent as an adult and help encourage his or her growth not only as a parent but as an individual." Estab. 1973. Pays on publication. Publishes ms an average of 6 months after acceptance. Byline given. Buys first North American serial rights; maintains exclusive rights for three months. Submit seasonal material 6 months in advance. Reports in 2 weeks. Sample copy and writer's guidelines for 5×8 SAE with 2 first-class stamps.

Nonfiction: "We are looking for informational articles written in an easy-to-read, concise style. We would like to see articles that help parents deal with the stresses they face in everyday life—positive, upbeat, how-to-cope suggestions. We rarely use humorous pieces, fiction or personal experience articles. Writers should keep in mind that most of our readers have children under two years of age." **Buys 15-20 mss/year.** Query. Length: 1,000-1,500 words; will look at shorter pieces. **Pays 10-15¢/word.**

Reprints: Send tearsheet of article and information about when and where it previously appeared.

Tips: "Submit a very specific query letter with samples."

$ $ $ $ HEALTHY KIDS, Primedia Publishing, 249 W. 17th St., New York NY 10011. (212)462-3300. Fax: (212)367-8332. Managing Editor: Laura Broadwell. **Contact:** Tova Eisner, editorial assistant. **90% freelance written.** Bimonthly magazine that addresses all elements that go into the raising of a healthy, happy child, from basic health care information to an analysis of a child's growing mind and behavior patterns. Extends the wisdom of the pediatrician into the home, and informs parents of young children (ages birth to 10 years) about proper health care. The only magazine produced for parents in association with the American Academy of Pediatrics, the nonprofit organization of more than 53,000 pediatricians dedicated to the betterment of children's health. To ensure accuracy, all articles are reviewed by an editorial advisory board comprised of distinguished pediatricians. Estab. 1989. Circ. 1,550,000. **Pays on acceptance.** Byline given. Buys first North American rights. Submit seasonal material at least 6 months in advance. Reports in 2 months. Writer's guidelines for #10 SASE.

- Ranked as one of the best markets for freelance writers in *Writer's Yearbook* magazine's annual "Top 100 Markets," January 1998.

Nonfiction: How-to help your child develop as a person, keep safe, keep healthy. No poetry, fiction, travel or product endorsement. Special issues: Good Eating!—A complete guide to feeding your family (February/March). Query. No unsolicited mss. Length: 2,000-2,500 words. **Pays $1,200-1,700.** Pays expenses of writers on assignment.

Columns/Departments: Focus On . . . (an informal conversation with a pediatrician, in a question-and-answer format, about a timely health issue); Let's Eat (advice on how to keep mealtimes fun and nutritious, along with some child-friendly recipes); Behavior Basics (a helpful article on how to deal with some aspect of a child's behavior—from first friendships to temper tantrums). **Buys 20 mss/year.** Query. Length: 1,500-1,800 words. **Pays $1,200.**

Tips: "A simple, clear approach is mandatory. Articles should speak with the voice of medical authority in children's health issues, while being helpful and encouraging, cautionary but not critical, and responsible but not preachy. All articles should include interviews with appropriate Academy-member pediatricians and other health care professionals."

$ HOME EDUCATION MAGAZINE, P.O. Box 1587, Palmer AK 99645. Fax: (907)746-1335. E-mail: homeedmag@aol.com. Website: http://www.home-ed-press.com. **Contact**: Helen E. Hegener, managing editor. **80% freelance written.** Bimonthly magazine covering home-based education. "We feature articles which address the concerns of parents who want to take a direct involvement in the education of their children—concerns such as socialization, how to find curriculums and materials, testing and evaluation, how to tell when your child is ready to begin reading, what to do when homeschooling is difficult, teaching advanced subjects, etc." Estab. 1983. Circ. 32,000. **Pays on acceptance.** Publishes ms an average of 4 months after acceptance. Byline given. ("Please include a 30-50 word credit with your article.") Buys first North American electronic, serial, first, one-time rights. Submit seasonal material 6 months in advance. Reports in 2 months. Sample copy for $4.50. Writer's guidelines for #10 SASE or via e-mail.

Nonfiction: Essays, how-to (related to home schooling), humor, interview/profile, personal experience, photo features, technical. **Buys 40-50 mss/year.** Query with or without published clips, or send complete ms. Length: 750-2,500 words. **Pays $25-50.** Sometimes pays expenses of writers on assignment.

Photos: Send photos with submission. Reviews enlargements, 35mm prints, b&w snapshots, CD-ROMs. Color transparencies for covers $50 each; inside b&w $10 each. Identification of subjects preferred. Buys one-time rights.

Tips: SASE. "We would like to see how-to articles (that don't preach, just present options); articles on testing, accountability, working with the public schools, socialization, learning disabilities, resources, support groups, legislation and humor. We need answers to the questions that homeschoolers ask. Please, no teachers telling parents how to teach. Personal experience with homeschooling is most preferred approach."

$ $ INDY'S CHILD, 836 E. 64, Indianapolis IN 46220. Fax: (317)722-8510. E-mail: indychild@family.com. **Contact:** Tom Wynne, co-editor. **100% freelance written.** Monthly magazine covering parenting. "*Indy's Child* is a parenting magazine circulated throughout Central Indiana. We cover topics ranging from maternity, camps, birthday parties, mental health, enrichment, education and discipline to finances and computers. Ninety-five percent of our readers are college-educated, middle to upperclass women ages 25-45." Estab. 1984. Circ. 70,000. Pays on publication. Publishes ms an average of 3 months after acceptance. Byline given. Buys first rights or second serial (reprint) rights. Editorial lead time 3 months. Submit seasonal material 3 months in advance. Reports in 2 months. Sample copy for 9×12 SAE with 4 first-class stamps. Writer's guidelines for #10 SASE.

Nonfiction: Essays, general interest, how-to (anything that deals with parenting. humor, inspirational, personal experience, travel. Nothing political or one sided. Special issue: Baby Guide. **Buys 36 mss/year.** Query by mail, e-mail or fax, or send complete ms. Length: 1,000-2,500 words. **Pays $50-175 for assigned articles; $25-135 for unsolicited articles.** Sometimes pays expenses of writers on assignment.

Reprints: Send tearsheet of article or short story or typed ms with rights for sale noted and information about when and where the article previously appeared.

Photos: State availability of photos with submission. Reviews 3×5 prints. Negotiates payment individually. Identifica-

tion of subjects required. Negotiates rights purchased.
Fiction: Humorous, life lesson. **Buys 2 mss/year.** Send complete ms. Length: 1,000-1,500 words. **Pays $50-150.**
Tips: "We tend to accept articles that are not only serious issues to parents but that also have great solutions or specific places to turn to for help. Everything needs a local slant."

N $ $ KIDS: ACTIVITIES FOR FAMILIES, Woman's Day Special Interest Publications, Hachette-Filipacchi Magazines, 1633 Broadway, New York NY 10019. Fax: (212)767-5612. E-mail: wdspecials@aol.com. **Contact:** Janice Wright, managing editor. Editor: Carolyn Gatto. "This semiannual magazine is a resource guide for parents who want to stimulate their child's creativity by exploring crafts, cooking, and other home-based leisure time activities, including holiday ideas. Complete how-to for crafts, games and activities are provided. Ideas should be of interest to children ages 3 to 13, but need not span the entire range. 95% of the readers are female, with a median age of 41." **Pays on acceptance**. Publishes ms an average of 3 months after acceptance. Offers up to 25% kill fee. Buys first North American serial or second serial (printing) rights. Editorial lead time 6 months. Submit seasonal material 10 months in advance. Reports in 2 months. Writer's guidelines for #10 SASE.
Nonfiction: How-to (crafts & activities for families), new products, reviews of children's books, videos, software, music & other media. **Buys 30 mss/year**. Query with published clips. Length: 250-1,000 words. Payment varies based on length, writer, importance. Sometimes pays expenses of writers on assignment.
Reprints: Accepts previously published submissions.
Photos: State availability of photos with submissions. Model releases required. Buys one-time rights.
Columns/Departments: Query with published clips. Payment varies based on length, writer, and level of amount of research required.
Tips: "Send a brief, clear query letter with relevant clips, and be patient. Potential reviewers must query, stating qualifications: Do not send unsolicited reviews."

$ $ L.A. PARENT, The Magazine for Parents in Southern California, P.O. Box 3204, Burbank CA 91504. (818)846-0400. Fax: (818)841-4964. E-mail: laparent@compuserve.com. Website: http://www.laparent.com. Editor: Jack Bierman. **Contact**: Christina Elston, managing editor. **80% freelance written.** Prefers to work with published/established writers, but works with a small number of new/unpublished writers each year. Monthly tabloid covering parenting. Estab. 1980. Circ. 200,000. **Pays on acceptance**. Publishes ms an average of 4 months after acceptance. Byline given. Buys first and reprint rights. Submit seasonal material 3 months in advance. Accepts simultaneous queries. Reports in 3 months. Sample copy and writer's guidelines for $2 and 11×14 SAE with 5 first-class stamps.

- *L.A. Parent* is looking for more articles pertaining to infants and early childhood.

Nonfiction: General interest, how-to. Special issues: High Potential Parenting and Nutrition of the Young Child. "We focus on generic parenting for ages 0-10 and Southern California activities for families, and do round-up pieces, i.e., a guide to private schools, art opportunities." **Buys 60-75 mss/year.** Query with clips of published work. Length: 700-1,200 words. **Pays $250-350 plus expenses.**
Reprints: Send photocopy of article or typed ms with rights for sale noted and information about when and where the article previously appeared. Pays $50 on average for reprints.
Tips: "We will be using more contemporary articles on parenting's challenges. If you can write for a 'city magazine' in tone and accuracy, you may write for us. The 'Baby Boom' has created a need for more generic parenting material. We look for a sophisticated tone in covering the joys and demands of being a mom or dad in the 90s."

N $ LEFTY KIDS, Lefthanders International, Inc., P.O. Box 8249, Topeka KS 66608. (785)234-2177. **Contact**: Kim Kipers, editor. **70% freelance written.** Quarterly magazine covering subjects relating to lefthanded children, 6-10. "All material must be about lefthandedness—a special child who is a lefty and what that means, school and life tips for lefties, stories that mean something to a lefthander." Estab. 1998. Pays on publication. Publishes ms an average of 4 months after acceptance. Byline sometimes given. Offers 20% kill fee. Buys all rights unless otherwise agreed. Editorial lead time 10 weeks. Submit seasonal material 3 months in advance. Accepts simultaneous submissions. Reports in 3 weeks on queries; 3 months on mss. Sample copy for $2 and 9×12 SAE with 4 first-class stamps. Writer's guidelines for #10 SASE.
Nonfiction: How-to (specific craft instructions for lefty kids), inspirational, interview/profile, new product (for kids). No personal experience, stories demeaning lefthandedness, stories not directly relating to kids and lefthandedness. Query. Length: 750-1,500 words. **Pays $50-150 for assigned articles; $25-85 for unsolicited articles.** Sometimes pays expenses of writers on assignment.
Photos: Send photos with submission. Offers no additional payment for photos accepted with ms. Buys one-time rights.
Columns/Departments: Crafts/hobbies (instructions for lefties), 500 words; Lefty Life Tips (helpful info for classwork, life), 750 words; Interviews (kids or figures who have done something special), 1,000-1,200 words. Query. **Pays $25-150.**
Fiction: Adventure, slice-of-life vignettes. Don't need just fantastic tales. Fiction stories need to be about lefthandedness and generally have a positive lefty slant or uplifting ending. Query. Length: 750-1,200 words. **Pays $50-100.**
Fillers: Anecdotes, facts. Length: 200-500 words. **Pays $25-50.**
Tips: "Write with children ages 6-10 in mind since they are the target audience. All stories must directly relate to lefthandedness. We like positive, helpful information that can aid kids, parents and teachers."

$ LONG ISLAND PARENTING NEWS, RDM Publishing, P.O. Box 214, Island Park NY 11558. (516)889-5510. Fax: (516)889-5513. E-mail: liparent@family.com. Website: http://www.LIPN.com. **Contact:** Pat Simms-Elias, editorial director. Director: Andrew Elias. **70% freelance written.** Free community newspaper published monthly "for concerned parents with active families and young children. Our slogan is: 'For parents who care to know.' " Estab. 1989. Circ. 57,000. Pays on publication. Publishes ms an average of 3 months after acceptance. Byline given (also 1-3 line bio, if appropriate). Buys one-time rights. Accepts simultaneous submissions. Reports in 3 months. Sample copy for $3 and 9×12 SAE with 5 first-class stamps. Writer's guidelines free.
Nonfiction: Essays, general interest, humor, interview/profile, travel. Needs articles covering childcare, childbirth/maternity, schools, camps and back-to-school. Special issues: Schools, Sleepaway Camps and Family Safety (January); Camps, Family Health (February); Sports and Fitness Programs (March); Swing Sets, Hospitals (April); Summer Programs and Camps, Summer Vacations (May); Maternity & Birthing, Childcare (June); Schools and Fall Programs, Special Needs (August); Dance, Music, Theater and Arts Programs, Children's Health (September); Women's Health, Halloween (October); Winter Vacations (November); Winter and Spring Programs, Family Skiing (December). **Buys 30-50 mss/year.** Query with or without published clips, or send complete ms. Length: 350-2,000 words. **Pays $25-150.** "Sometimes trade article for advertising space." Sometimes pays expenses of writers on assignment.
Reprints: Send photocopy of article or typed ms with rights for sale noted and information about when and where the article previously appeared. Negotiates fee.
Photos: Send photos, preferably b&w, with submission. Reviews 4×5 prints. Offers $5-50/photo. Captions required. Buys one-time rights.
Columns/Departments: On the Island (local, national and international news of interest to parents); Off The Shelf (book reviews); Fun & Games (toy and game reviews); KidVid (reviews of kids' video); The Beat (reviews of kids' music); Monitor (reviews of computer hardware and software for kids); The Big Picture (reviews of kids' films); Soon Come (for expectant parents); Educaring (parenting info and advice); Something Special (for parents of kids with special needs); Growing Up (family health issues); On the Ball (sports for kids); Family Matters (essays on family life); Words Worth (storytelling); Getaway (family travel); Teen Time (for parents of teenagers). **Buys 20-30 mss/year.** Send complete ms. Length: 500-1,000 words. **Pays $25-150.**
Fillers: Facts and newsbreaks. **Buys 1-10/year.** Length: 200-500. **Pays $10-25.**

N $ MAMA'S LITTLE HELPER, Turquoise Butterfly Press, P.O. Box 1127, Athens OH 45701-1127. (740)664-3030. E-mail: turqbutfly@bright.net. **Contact**: Terri Andrews, editor. "We are the only parenting support group via the mail for ADHD parents. We focus on all aspects of raising spirited children." Buys one-time rights. Sample copy for $3.50. Writer's guidelines for #10 SASE.
Nonfiction: "Our primary goal is to support and assist parents of hyperactive, ADHD, spirited and energetic children with guidance, information, tried and tested tips and medical information. Topics include: Ritalin, diet, positive discipline, stress-busting, car trips, restaurants, dealing with schools and siblings, recipes, ADHD history. Length: 900-1,500 words for features, 100-900 words for personal stories, interviews, humor, etc. Send complete ms with word count and SASE. Include researched citations. **Pays 1¢/word or contributor copies.**

$ METRO PARENT MAGAZINE, All Kids Considered, Ltd., 24567 Northwestern Hwy., Suite 150, Southfield MI 48075. (248)352-0990. Fax: (248)352-5066. E-mail: metparent@aol.com. Website: http://family.com. **Contact:** Liz Goldner, editor. **100% freelance written.** Monthly tabloid covering parenting/family issues. "*Metro Parent* is a local parenting publication geared toward parents with children under the age of 12. We look for sound, pertinent information for our readers, preferably using local experts as sources." Estab. 1986. Distributed throughout Oakland, Macomb and Wayne Counties and the city of Ann Arbor. Circ. 70,000. Pays on publication. Publishes ms an average of 2 months after acceptance. Byline given. Buys one-time rights. Editorial lead time 3 months. Submit seasonal material 4 months in advance. Accepts simultaneous submissions. Sample copy and writer's guidelines free.
Nonfiction: Book excerpts, general interest, how-to, humor, inspirational, interview/profile, new product, travel. Special issues: Metro Baby Magazine (geared for expectant parents, August, January); Camps (January-May); Birthdays (March); Back to School (August/September); and Holiday issues (October, November, December, February). **Buys 25 mss/year.** Query with published clips. Length: 500-3,000 words. **Pays $75-150 for assigned articles.**
Reprints: Send photocopy and information about when and where the article previously appeared. **Pays $35.**
Photos: State availability of photos with submission. Reviews 4×6 prints. Negotiates payment individually. Captions, model releases, identification of subjects required. Buys one-time rights.
Columns/Departments: Bits 'n' Pieces (new products) 100 words; Multi Media (video, movie, books, audio, software), 700 (total) words; Boredom Busters (craft ideas, games & activities), 700 words; Let's Party! (fun, unique ideas for parties and other celebrations), 700 words. **Buys 35 mss/year.** Query with published clips. **Pays $30-50.**

$ METROKIDS MAGAZINE, The Resource for Delaware Valley Families, Kidstuff Publications, Inc., 1080 N. Delaware Ave., #702, Philadelphia PA 19125-4330. (215)291-5560. Fax: (215)291-5563. E-mail: metrokid@family.com. Website: http://www.metrokids.com. **Contact**: Sharon Cohen, managing editor. **80% freelance written.** Monthly tabloid providing information for parents and kids in Philadelphia, South Jersey and surrounding counties. Estab. 1990. Circ. 90,000. Pays on publication. Byline given. Buys one-time rights. Submit seasonal material 4 months in advance. Reports in up to 8 months on queries. Sample copy for $2 and 9×12 SAE. Guidelines for #10 SASE.

• *MetroKids* welcomes query letters, e-mails or faxes. They especially want to hear from writers in their area.

Nonfiction: General interest, how-to, humor, new product, travel, parenting, nutrition. Special issues: Baby First

editions (April and November); Camps (January-May); Special Kids edition (October); Vacations and Theme Parks (May, June). **Buys 40 mss/year.** Query with or without published clips. Prefers mss to queries. Length: 800-1,200 words maximum. **Pays $1-50.** Sometimes pays expenses of writers on assignment.
Reprints: Send photocopy of article and information about when and where it previously appeared. **Pays $20-40.**
Photos: State availability of photos with submission. Captions required. Buys one-time rights.
Columns/Departments: Book Beat (book reviews); Bytesize, 500-800 words. "*MetroKids* also features monthly health columns on topics like breast cancer, insurance, women's health issues, children's health; travel to local destinations like the Poconos, the Shore and points in between." **Buys 25 mss/year.** Query. **Pays $1-50.**
Tips: "Send a query letter several months before a scheduled topical issue; then follow-up with a telephone call. We are interested in feature articles (on specified topics) or material for our regular columns (with a regional/seasonal base). Editorial calendar available on request. We are also interested in finding local writers for assignments."

N $ **MINNESOTA PARENT**, Stern Publishing, 401 N. Third St., Suite 550, Minneapolis MN 55401. (612)375-1203. Fax: (612)375-3782. E-mail: ppfeiffer@citypages.com. **Contact**: Paul Pfeiffer, associate editor. Editor: Jeannine Ouellette Howitz. **100% freelance written.** Monthly tabloid covering parenting. "We prefer strong, first-person accounts of the joys and struggles inherent in family life, and opinionated analyses of current issues facing parents." Estab. 1986. Circ. 65,000. Pays on publication. Publishes ms an average of 3 months after acceptance. Byline given. Buys first North American serial rights. Editorial lead time 6 months. Submit seasonal material 6 months in advance. Accepts simultaneous submissions. Reports in 2 months on mss. Sample copy for $3 and SASE. Writer's guidelines for #10 SASE.
Nonfiction: Book excerpts, essays, exposé, general interest, inspirational, interview/profile, opinion, personal experience. No how-to pieces. **Buys 60 mss/year.** Send complete ms. Length: 1,500-3,000 words. **Pays $150.** Sometimes pays expenses of writers on assignment.
Reprints: Send photocopy and information about when and where article or story previously appeared. Pays $15-200.
Photos: State availability of photos with submission. Offers no additional payment for photos accepted with ms or negotiates payment individually. Model releases and identification of subjects required. Buys one-time rights.
Fiction: Family oriented. **Buys 4 mss/year.** Send complete ms. Length: 1,500-3,000 words. **Pays $150.** Publishes novel excerpts.
Poetry: All types. **Buys 30 poems/year. Pays $10-30.**
Tips: "Send complete manuscripts. Don't call to check up (our small staff is overworked). Be personal, brilliant, literary, edgy, witty and original with your writing."

$ $ **MOTHERING**, P.O. Box 1690, Santa Fe NM 87504. (505)984-8116. Fax: (505)986-8335. E-mail: mother@ni.net. **Contact**: Ashisha, senior editor. Bimonthly magazine covering natural family living for mothers and fathers, as well as grandparents, educators and health care workers. Estab. 1975. Circ. 70,250. Pays on publication. Publishes ms 6-12 months after acceptance. Byline given. Buys one-time rights. Reports in 2 weeks. Sample copy for $3. Writer's guidelines for #10 SASE.
Nonfiction: Essays, general interest, how-to, inspirational, interview/profile, personal experience. "*Mothering* has 6 regular features: 'The Art of Mothering' (inspirational and spiritual side of nurturing); 'Health' (new approaches to health care for the whole family—we encourage articles on unconventional approaches to common childhood health questions); 'A Child's World' (reflecting the world as a child sees it. We especially like to feature activities, crafts, arts, music and stories for children); 'Pregnancy, Birth & Midwifery' (all aspects of pregnancy and birth as well as actual experiences and stories of childbirth. This section encompasses all types of noninterventionist birth attendance of use to midwives and of interest to parents, largely in an inspirational rather than a technical vein.); 'Ways of Learning' (innovative, multidimensional, people-centered approaches to education. This section focuses on how people learn rather than where they learn, and includes learning about traditional subjects as well as subjects usually thought of as outside the realm of education: responsibility, ethics, adventure, travel, intuition, spirituality. We want to know about new ways of learning and rediscovered old ways.); 'Family Living' (information sharing, general interest stories, helpful hints, practical suggestions and insights into the daily realities of parenting)." **Buys 100 mss/year.** Query. Length: 1,000-1,500 words. **Pays $175-500.**
Columns/Departments: Breastfeeding, Work & Family Life, Your Letters, Good News, Reflections, For the Children.
Photos: State availability of photos with submission. Reviews 5×7 or 8×10 b&w and color prints. Negotiates payment individually. Buys one-time rights. Photographer's/artist's guidelines available for #10 SASE.
Tips: "Be familiar with our magazine before submitting articles. We are more likely to publish your article if you are a *Mothering* reader and are familiar with the issues we discuss. Think about the subjects you know well and areas in which little information exists. The 'Your Letters' section of the magazine is a good place to find topics of interest to our readers. Our main goal is to be truly helpful, to provide information that empowers our readers to make changes or simply to get what they want from their lives. We like articles that have a strong point of view and come from the heart. We like articles that are moving or challenging. We publish articles in relation to other articles we have published on the subject, how new the topic is to us, and how unique the presentation is."

$ **NEW JERSEY FAMILY MAGAZINE**, 210 W. State St., Trenton NJ 08608. (609)695-5646. Fax: (609)695-5612. E-mail: njfamily@family.com. Website: http://www.njfamily.com. **Contact**: Barbara M. Gaeta, editor. **90% freelance written.** Monthly newspaper for parents and kids. Feature articles address current issues affecting families both nationally and regionally. Estab. 1993. Circ. 30,000. Pays 30 days after publication. Publishes ms an average of 6-12 months from submission. Byline and bio given. Buys first, one-time, second serial (reprint) rights or makes work-for-hire assignments. Editorial lead time 6 months. Submit seasonal material 3 months in advance. Accepts simultaneous submissions. Only responds when interested. Sample copy and writer's guidelines free.

- New Jersey Family Magazine is looking for more issue-oriented features, including topics highlighting social concerns: childcare reform, teen pregnancy, drug abuse, education reform and juvenile delinquency.

Nonfiction: Book excerpts, essays, general interest, historical/nostalgic, how-to, interview/profile, new product, photo feature, travel. No first person narratives about potty-training little Johnny or other "cute" stories. **Buys 40-60 mss/year.** Send complete ms. Length: 500-1,000 words. **Pays $30-75 for assigned articles; $10-75 for unsolicited articles.** Pays expenses of writers on assignment. Electronic rights negotiable.

Reprints: Send tearsheet of article or typed ms with rights for sale noted and information about when and where article previously appeared, only if within our competitive market. Pays $30-50.

Photos: Send photos with submission. Reviews prints. Offers no additional payment for photos accepted with ms. Identification of subjects required. Buys one-time rights.

Columns/Departments: Humor; length: 500-800 words. Published on a rotating basis both in the magazine and electronically on our website. Query with published clips. **Pays $10-35.**

Fiction: Will consider novel excerpts.

Tips: "Send well-written, informational articles with facts or resources documented, on any topics relevant to today's family environment. For all articles, keep in mind that 'family' has a broader definition than in years past."

$ NEW MOON NETWORK: FOR ADULTS WHO CARE ABOUT GIRLS, New Moon Publishing, Inc., P.O. Box 3620, Duluth MN 55803. (218)728-5507. Fax: (218)728-0314. E-mail: newmoon@cp.duluth.mn.us. Website: http://wwww. newmoon.org. **Contact:** Joe Kelly, editor. **10% freelance written.** Bimonthly magazine covering adults (parents, teachers, others) who work with girls age 8-14. "*New Moon Network* is the companion publication to *New Moon: The Magazine For Girls and Their Dreams*. It is written by and for adults—parents, teachers, counselors and others—who are working to raise healthy, confident girls. Its goal is to celebrate girls and support their efforts to hang onto their voices, strengths and dreams as they move from being girls to becoming women." Estab. 1992. Circ. 3,000. Pays on publication. Publishes ms an average of 2 months after acceptance. Byline given. Buys first rights and second serial (reprint) rights. Editorial lead time 3 months. Submit seasonal material 4 months in advance. Accepts simultaneous submissions. Reports in 1 month on queries; 2 months on mss. Sample copy for $6.50. Writer's guidelines free.

Nonfiction: Essays, general interest, historical/nostalgic, humor, inspirational, interview/profile, opinion, personal experience, photo feature, religious, technical, book reviews. Editorial calendar available. **Buys 6 mss/year.** Query. Length: 750-1,500 words. **Pays 4-8¢/word.**

Reprints: Send photocopy of article or short story and information about when and where the article previously appeared.

Photos: State availability of photos with submissions (prefers b&w). Reviews 4×5 prints. Negotiates payment individually. Captions, model releases, identification of subjects required. Buys one-time rights.

Columns/Departments: Mothering (personal experience), 900 words; Fathering (personal experience), 900 words; Current Research (girl-related), 900-1,800 words; Book Reviews, 900 words. **Buys 3 mss/year.** Query. **Pays 4-8¢/word.**

Fiction: Humorous, slice-of-life vignettes, multicultural/girl centered. **Buys 1 mss/year.** Query. Length: 900-1,800 words. **Pays 4-8¢/word.**

Tips: "Writers and artists who comprehend our goals have the best chance of publication. Refer to our guidelines and upcoming themes. We are not looking for advice columns or 'twelve tips for being a successful parent' formula articles. Write for clarity and ease of understanding, rather than in an 'academic' style."

N $ $ NEW YORK FAMILY, CONNECTICUT FAMILY, WESTCHESTER FAMILY, Family Publishing Group, Inc., 141 Halstead Ave., Mamaroneck NY 10543. (914)381-7474. Fax: (914)381-7672. E-mail: edit2@familygroup.com. Website: http://www.nyfamily.com; ctfamily.com; westchesterfam.com. **Contact:** Betsy F. Woolf, senior editor. **90% freelance written.** Monthly magazine "that serves as a local parenting resource." Estab. 1986. Circ. 155,000. Pays on publication. Publishes ms an average of 6 months after acceptance. Byline given. Offers $25 kill fee. Buys first or second serial (reprint) rights; prefers first rights. Editorial lead time 4 months. Submit seasonal material 4 months in advance. Writer's guidelines available online.

Nonfiction: How-to (home, raising kids), humor, personal experience, travel (for parenting market). Special issue: Baby Guide (2/year). No articles unrelated to parenting and the home. **Buys 100 mss/year.** Query with published clips. Length: 800-1,200 words. **Pays $50-200 for assigned articles; $50-125 for unsolicited articles.**

Reprints: Accepts previously published materials.

Photos: Send photos with submission. Reviews prints (5×7). Negotiates payment individually. Model releases required. Buys one-time rights.

$ $ $ $ PARENTING MAGAZINE, 1325 Avenue of the Americas, 27th Floor, New York NY 10019. (212)522-8989. Fax: (212)522-8699. Editor-in-Chief: Janet Chan. Executive Editor: Lisa Bain. **Contact:** Articles Editor. Magazine published 10 times/year "for parents of children from birth to twelve years old, with the most emphasis put on the under-sixes, and covering both the psychological and practical aspects of parenting." Estab. 1987. **Pays on acceptance.** Byline given. Offers 25% kill fee. Buys first rights. Reports in 2 months. Sample copy for $1.95 and 9×12 SAE with 5 first-class stamps. Writer's guidelines for #10 SASE.

- Ranked as one of the best markets for freelance writers in *Writer's Yearbook* magazine's annual "Top 100 Markets," January 1998.

Nonfiction: Articles editor. Book excerpts, humor, investigative reports, personal experience, photo feature. **Buys 20-30 features/year.** Query with or without published clips. No phone queries, please. Length: 1,000-3,000 words. **Pays $500-2,000.** Sometimes pays expenses of writers on assignment.
Columns/Departments: Family Reporter (news items relating to children/family), 100-400 words; Ages and Stages (health, nutrition, new products and service stories), 100-500 words. **Buys 50-60 mss/year.** Query to the specific departmental editor. **Pays $50-500.**
Tips: "The best guide for writers is the magazine itself. Please familiarize yourself with it before submitting a query."

$ $ $ $ PARENTS MAGAZINE, Gruner + Jahr, 375 Lexington Ave., New York NY 10017-5514. Website: http://www.parents.com. Editor-in-Chief: Ann Pleshette Murphy. **Contact:** Wendy Schuman or Sarah Mahoney, executive editors. **25% freelance written.** Monthly. Estab. 1926. Circ. 1,825,000. **Pays on acceptance.** Publishes ms an average of 8 months after acceptance. Usually buys first serial or first North American serial rights; sometimes buys all rights. Offers 25% kill fee. Reports in approximately 4 months. Sample copy for $2. Guidelines for #10 SASE.
Nonfiction: "We are interested in well-documented articles on the development and behavior of infants, preschool, school-age and pre-teen children and their parents; good, practical guides to the routines of baby care; articles that offer professional insights into family and marriage relationships; reports of new trends and significant research findings in education and in mental and physical health; articles encouraging informed citizen action on matters of social concern; and first-person true stories on aspects of parenthood. Especially need articles on women's issues, pregnancy, birth, baby care and early childhood. We're also interested in opinion essays on topics of interest to our readers such as education, interpersonal relationships. We prefer a warm, colloquial style of writing, one that avoids the extremes of either slang or technical jargon. Anecdotes and examples should be used to illustrate points which can then be summed up by straight exposition." Query. Length: 2,500 words maximum. **Pays approximately $1/word.** Pays the expenses of writers on assignment up to an agreed-upon limit.

$ $ PARENTS' PRESS, The Monthly Newspaper for Bay Area Parents, 1454 Sixth St., Berkeley CA 94710. (510)524-1602. Fax: (510)524-0912. E-mail: parentsprs@aol.com. Editor: Dixie M. Jordan. **Contact**: Patrick Totty, managing editor. **50% freelance written.** Monthly tabloid for parents. Estab. 1980. Circ. 75,000. Pays within 60 days of publication. Publishes ms an average of 4 months after acceptance. Kill fee varies (individually negotiated). Buys first rights, second serial (reprint) and almost always Northern California Exclusive rights. Submit seasonal material 6 months in advance. Reports in 3 months. Sample copy for $3. Writer's guidelines and editorial calendar for #10 SASE. Rarely considers simultaneous submissions.
Nonfiction: Book excerpts (family, children), how-to (parent, raise children, nutrition, health, etc.), humor (family life, children), interview/profile (of Bay Area residents, focus on their roles as parents), travel (family), family resources and activities. "Annual issues include Pregnancy and Birth, Travel, Back-to-School, Children's Health. Write for planned topic or suggest one. We require a strong Bay Area focus where appropriate. Please don't send 'generic' stories. While we publish researched articles which spring from personal experience, we do not publish strictly personal essays. Please, no birth stories." **Buys 30-50 mss/year.** Query with or without published clips, or send complete ms. Length: 300-3,000 words; 1,500-2,000 average. **Pays $50-500 for assigned articles; $25-250 for unsolicited articles.** Will pay more if photos accompany article. Negotiable. Will negotiate fees for special projects written by Bay Area journalists.
Reprints: Send photocopy of article with rights for sale noted and information about when and where the article previously appeared. Pays up to $50.
Photos: State availability of photos with submission. Reviews prints, any size, b&w only. Offers $10-15/photo. Model release and identification of subject required. Buys one-time rights.
Columns/Departments: "In My Life" column **pays $150** for first-person essays or reminiscences relating to parenthood." Sole criterion for acceptance: The manuscript must be superlatively written. 'Cute' doesn't make it."
Tips: "All sections of *Parents' Press* are open to freelancers, but we ask writers to query whether a topic has been addressed in the last three years. Best bets to break in are family activities, including "Places To Go/Things To Do" articles, education, nutrition, family dynamics and issues. While we prefer articles written by experts, we welcome well-researched journalism with quotes from experts and 'real life' parents."

$ $ PARENT.TEEN, The Magazine for Bay Area Families with Teens, Parents' Press, 1454 Sixth St., Berkeley CA 94710. (510)524-1602. Fax: (510)524-0912. E-mail: parentsprs@aol.com. Editor: Dixie M. Jordan. **Contact**: Patrick Totty, managing editor. **75% freelance written.** Bimonthly magazine for parents of teens. Estab. 1997. Circ. 60,000. Pays within 60 days of publication. Publishes ms an average of 3 months after acceptance. Kill fee varies (individually negotiated). Buys all rights, first rights, second serial (reprint) and almost always Northern California Exclusive rights. Submit seasonal material 6 months in advance. Reports in 2 months. Sample copy for $3. Writer's guidelines and editorial calendar for #10 SASE.
Nonfiction: Regular features, open to all, cover adolescent medicine, teen psychology, youth culture and trends, education, college preparation, work, sports, sex, gender roles, family relationships, legal topics, financial issues and profiles of interesting teens, colleges and programs. "We require a strong Bay Area focus in most articles. Use quotes from experts and Bay Area teens." **Buys 60 mss/year.** Query with clips or send complete ms on spec. "We pay for lively, information-packed content, not length." Length: 500-1,200 words. **Pays $150-500.**
Reprints: Send a photocopy of article with rights for sale noted and information about when and where the article previously appeared. Pays up to $50.
Photos: State availability of photos with submission. Payment rates higher for mss with photos. Photos only: $15-50

for one-time rights (b&w). Reviews color slides for cover; contact art director Renee Benoit before sending. Photos returned only if accompanied by SASE. Model releases and subject identification required.

Columns/Departments: Pays $5-10 for "grab bag" items, ranging from one sentence to one paragraph on "weird facts about teens" or teen-related Bay Area news item. Submissions must cite sources of information.

Tips: "We do not commission stories by writers who are unknown to us, so your best bet is to send us original articles on spec or already published articles offered for reprint rights. We are looking for writers who can pack a lot of information in as few words as possible in lively prose. No first-person 'How I Got My Kid Through Teenhood.' "

N $ $ PASTOR'S FAMILY, For Ministers at Home, Focus on the Family, 8605 Explorer Dr., Colorado Springs CO 80920. Fax: (719)531-3499. **Contact**: Simon J. Dahlman, editor. **70% freelance written.** Bimonthly magazine. "*Pastor's Family* supports, encourages and informs ministers, their spouses and children in the area of home life. Thus, we look for articles that address unique needs of the family, not church leadership or administration." Estab. 1996. Circ. 20,000. **Pays on acceptance**. Byline given. Offers 25% kill fee. Buys first North American serial rights. Editorial lead time 6 months. Submit seasonal material 6 months in advance. Reports in 1 month on queries; 2 months on mss. Sample copy and writer's guidelines free.

Nonfiction: How-to, humor, interview/profile, personal experience, religious, family issues. "No generic family topics; articles must pertain to ministry/pastorate. No church leadership/administration." **Buys 50 mss/year.** Query. Length: 400-2,000 words. **Pays $50-400 for assigned articles; $40-360 for unsolicited articles.** Sometimes pays expenses of writers on assignment.

Photos: State availability of photos with submission. Negotiate payment individually. Model releases and identification of subjects required. Buys one-time rights.

Columns/Departments: Susan Stevens, associate editor. After Church (roundtable discussion about life in ministry), 1,500 words. **Buys 6 mss/year.** Query. **Pays $180-300.**

Fillers: Susan Stevens, associate editor. Anecdotes, short humor. **Buys 24/year.** Length: 25-100 words. **Pays $15-25.**

$ SAN DIEGO FAMILY MAGAZINE, San Diego County's Leading Resource for Parents & Educators Who Care!, P.O. Box 23960, San Diego CA 92193-3960. E-mail: sandiegofamily@family.com. Website: http://sandiegofamily.com. **Contact:** Sharon Bay, editor. **75% freelance written.** Monthly magazine for parenting and family issues. "*SDFM* strives to provide informative, educational articles emphasizing positive parenting for our typical readership of educated mothers, ages 25-45, with an upper-level income. Most articles are factual and practical, a few are humor and personal experience. Editorial emphasis is uplifting and positive." Estab. 1982. Circ. 120,000. Pays on publication. Byline given. Buys first, one-time or second serial (reprint) rights. Editorial lead time 2 months. Submit seasonal material 3 months in advance. Reports in 2 months on queries; 3 months on mss. Sample copy and writer's guidelines for $3.50 with 9×12 SAE.

Nonfiction: How-to, parenting, new baby help, enhancing education, family activities, interview/profile (influential or noted persons or experts included in parenting or the welfare of children) and articles of specific interest to or regarding San Diego (for California) families/children/parents/educators. "No rambling, personal experience pieces." **Buys 75 mss/year.** Send complete ms. Length: 800 maximum words. **Pays $1.25/column inch.** "Byline and contributor copies if writer prefers."

Reprints: Send typed ms with rights for sale noted and information about when and where the article previously appeared.

Photos: State availability of photos with submission. Reviews contact sheets and 3½×5 or 5×7 prints. Negotiates payment individually. Identification of subjects preferred. Buys one-time rights.

Columns/Departments: Kids' Books (topical book reviews), 800 words. **Buys 12 mss/year.** Query with published clips. **Pays $1.25/column inch minimum.**

Fillers: Facts and newsbreaks (specific to the family market). **Buys 10/year.** Length: 50-200 words. **Pays $1.25/column inch minimum.**

$ $ SAN FRANCISCO PENINSULA PARENT, Peninsula Parent Newspaper Inc., 1480 Rollins Rd., Burlingame CA 94010. (650)342-9203. Fax: (650)342-9276. E-mail: sfpp@aol.com. Website: http://www.SFParent.com. **Contact**: Lisa Rosenthal, editor. **25% freelance written.** Monthly magazine geared to parents of children from birth to teens. "We provide articles that empower parents with the essential parenting skills they need and offer local resource information." Estab. 1984. Circ. 65,000. Pays on publication. Publishes ms 3-6 months after acceptance. Byline given. Offers 50% kill fee. Buys first and second serial (reprint) rights. Editorial lead time 5 months. Submit seasonal material 4 months in advance. Reports in 3 months on queries; 4 months on mss. Sample copy and writer's guidelines free.

Nonfiction: Humor, interview/profile, travel (family-related). No articles that preach to parents, no first-person memories. **Buys 8 mss/year.** Query with or without published clips. Length: 800-1,200 words. **Pays $100-200 for assigned articles; $25-100 for unsolicited articles.** Sometimes pays expenses of writers on assignment.

Reprints: Send tearsheet or photocopy of article or typed ms with rights for sale noted and information about when and where the article previously appeared. Pays $25-50.

Photos: State availability of photos with submission. Offers $25-$50/photo; negotiates payment individually. Captions and model releases required. Buys one-time rights.

Columns/Departments: Healthbeat (health news for families), 1,000 words; Parents of Teens Column, 1,000 words. **Buys 2 mss/year.** Query with or without published clips. **Pays $25-100.**

N $ $ SEATTLE'S CHILD/EASTSIDE PARENT, Northwest Parent Publishing, 2107 Elliott Ave., Suite 303, Seattle WA 98121. Fax: (206)441-4919. **Contact**: Virginia Smyth, managing editor. Editor: Ann Bergman. **70% freelance written.** Monthly tabloid "featuring practical, timely information about parenting and family issues." Estab. 1979. Circ. 75,000. Pays on publication. Publishes ms an average of 6 months after acceptance. Byline given. Buys one-time rights, all rights. Editorial lead time 3 months. Submit seasonal material 4 months in advance. Accepts simultaneous submissions. Reports in 3 weeks on queries; 1 month of mss. Sample copy for $3. Writer's guidelines free.

Nonfiction: Essays, general interest, how-to, humor, interview/profile, personal experience, travel. **Buys 70-80 mss/year.** Query with published clips. Length: 600-2,500 words. **Pays $75-600 for assigned articles; $75-200 for unsolicited articles.** Sometimes pays expenses of writers on assignment.

Reprints: Accepts previously published submissions.

Photos: State availability of photos with submission. Offers no additional payment for photos accepted with ms. Captions required. Buys one-time rights.

Tips: "New freelancers should be well aware of our market, and the local quality of our publication. Articles with local ties always get our attention. New writers must send published clips and/or be willing to work on a 'spec' basis."

$ $ $ $ SESAME STREET PARENTS, Children's Television Workshop, 1 Lincoln Plaza, New York NY 10023. (212)595-3456. Fax: (212)875-6105. Editor-in-Chief: Ira Wolfman. **Contact**: Aileen Love, assistant editor. **80% freelance written.** Magazine published 10 times/year for parents of preschoolers that accompanies every issue of Sesame Street Magazine. Circ. 1,000,000. **Pays on acceptance.** Byline given. Offers 33% kill fee. Buys varying rights. Submit seasonal material 7 months in advance. Reports in 2 months on queries. Sample copy for 9×12 SAE with 6 first-class stamps. Writer's guidelines for #10 SASE.

- Ranked as one of the best markets for freelance writers in *Writer's Yearbook* magazine's annual "Top 100 Markets," January 1998.

Nonfiction: Child development/parenting, how-to (practical tips for parents of preschoolers), interview/profile, personal experience, book excerpts, essays, photo feature, travel (with children). **Buys 100 mss/year.** Query with published clips or send complete ms. Length: 500-2,000 words. **Pays $300-2,000 for articles.**

Reprints: Send typed ms with rights for sale noted and information about when and where the article previously appeared. Negotiates payment.

Photos: State availability of photos with submission. Model releases, identification of subjects required. Buys one-time or all rights.

$ $ SOUTH FLORIDA PARENTING, 5555 Nob Hill Rd., Sunrise FL 33351. (954)747-3063. Fax: (954)747-3055. E-mail: kbochi@aol.com. Website: http://www.sfparenting.com. Managing Editor: KiKi Bochi. **90% freelance written.** Monthly magazine covering parenting, family. Estab. 1989. Circ. 100,000. Pays on publication. Publishes ms an average of 3 months after acceptance. Byline given. Buys one-time rights or second serial (reprint) rights. Editorial lead time 4 months. Submit seasonal material 4 months in advance. Accepts simultaneous submissions. Writer's guidelines for SASE.

Nonfiction: Family and children's issues, how-to, humor, interview/profile, new product, personal experience. Special issues: Education Issue/Winter Health Issue (January); Birthday Party Issue (February); Summer Camp Issue (March); Maternity Issue (April); Florida/Vacation Guide (May); Home & Decor (June); Healthy, from Head to Toe (July); Back to School (August); Education (September); Kid Crown Awards (October); Holiday (December). **Buys 30-40 mss/year.** Query with published clips or send complete ms with SASE. Length: 600-1,800 words. **Pays $75-350 for articles.** Sometimes pays expenses of writers on assignment.

Reprints: Accepts previously published submissions "if not published in our circulation area." Send photocopy of article and information about when and where the article appeared. **Pays $25-50.**

Photos: State availability of photos with submission. Sometimes offers additional payment for ms with photos.

Tips: "A unique approach to a universal parenting concern will be considered for publication. Profiles or interviews of courageous parents. Opinion pieces on child rearing should be supported by experts and research should be listed. First person stories should be fresh and insightful. All writing should be clear and concise. Submissions can be typewritten, double-spaced, but the preferred format is on diskette."

N $ $ $ SUCCESSFUL STUDENT, Imagination Publishing, 820 W. Jackson Blvd., Suite 450, Chicago IL 60607. (312)627-1020. Fax: (312)627-1105. Editor: Rebecca Rolfer. **Contact:** Eva Dienel, assistant editor. **30% freelance written**. Semiannual magazine published for customers of Sylvan Learning Centers covering education. "We focus on education-related issues and study habits and tips. We frequently use expert writers and/or sources." Circ. 550,000. Pays on publication. Publishes ms an average of 5 months after acceptance. Byline given. Offers 33% kill fee. Buys first North American serial rights. Editorial lead time 6 months. Accepts simultaneous submissions.

Nonfiction: Book excerpts, essays, how-to (tips on studying, etc.), inspriational, interview/profile, new product. No parenting stories. **Buys 2-4 mss/year**. Query with published clips and SASE. Length: 300-1,700 words. **Pays 50¢/word.** Pays expenses of writers on assignment.

Reprints: Accepts previously published submissions.

Photos: State availability of photos with submission. Negotiates payment individually. Buys one-time rights.

Tips: "We're looking for writers with strong voices and an understanding of our editorial categories, who have the ability to write clearly and concisely. Because many of our stories include expert sources, our writers have enough of an education background to recognize these people. We frequently ask writers to pull short facts or tips into sidebars to complement the main stories. Stories are carefully reviewed for accuracy and appropriateness by the editorial staff and an advisory board from Sylvan Learning Systems."

$ $ $ $ TODAY'S PARENT, Canada's Parenting Magazine, Professional Publishing Associates Ltd., 269 Richmond St. West, Toronto, Ontario M5V 1X1 Canada. (416)596-8680. Fax: (416)596-1991. E-mail: todaysparent.com. Website: http://www.todaysparent.com. **Contact**: Linda Lewis, editor-in-chief. **99% freelance written;** *Canadian writers only.* Magazine published 11 times/year; December/January double issue. "*Today's Parent* is a magazine for parents of children aged 0-12." Circ. 160,000. **Pays on acceptance**. Publishes ms an average of 5 months after acceptance. Byline given. Buys first North American serial rights. Reports in 6 weeks on queries. Sample copy for $5 (Canadian). Writer's guidelines for #10 SASE.

Nonfiction: Features: Exposé, general interest, how-to. Query with published clips by mail only; include SASE. Length: 1,000-3,000 words. **Pays $750-1,800 for assigned articles.** Sometimes pays expenses of writers on assignment.

Columns/Departments: Health, Behavior, Education, all 1,200-1,500 words. **Pays $750-900.** Slice of Life (humor), 750 words. **Pays $500.** Query with published clips.

$ $ TOLEDO AREA PARENT NEWS, Toledo Area Parent News, Inc., 1120 Adams St., Toledo OH 43624. (419)244-9859. Fax: (419)244-9871. E-mail: toledoparent@family.com. **Contact:** Veronica Hughes, editor. **50% freelance written.** Monthly tabloid for Northwest Ohio/Southeast Michigan parents. Estab. 1992. Circ. 50,000. Pays on publication. Publishes ms an average of 1 month after acceptance. Byline given. Makes work-for-hire assignments. Editorial lead time 2-3 months. Reports in 1 month. Sample copy for $1.50.

Nonfiction: "We use only local writers, by assignment only." General interest, interview/profile, opinion. "We accept queries and opinion pieces only. Send cover letter and clips to be considered for assignments." **Buys 30 mss/year.** Length: 1,000-2,500 words. **Pays $75-125.**

Photos: State availability of photos with submission. Negotiates payment individually. Identification of subjects required. Buys all rights.

N $ $ TUESDAY'S CHILD MAGAZINE, Parenting Kids of All Abilities, Lynn Martens-Publisher, P.O. Box 270046, Fort Collins CO 80527. (970)416-7416. E-mail: tueskid@frii.com. **Contact:** Sarah Asmus, editor. **60% freelance written**. Bimonthly consumer magazine covering parenting children with disabilities. Circ. 10,000. **Pays on acceptance**. Byline given. Offers 50% kill fee. Buys first North American serial rights. Editorial lead time 2 months. Submit seasonal material 3 months in advance. Sample copy and writer's guidelines free on request.

Nonfiction: General interest, how-to, humor, inspirational, interview/profile, new product, personal experience, photo feature, technical, travel, disability related issues. **Buys 20 mss/year**. Query or query with published clips. Length: 800-5,000 words. **Pays $100/magazine page**. Sometimes pays expenses of writers on assignment.

Reprints: Accepts previously published submissions.

Photos: State availability of photos with submissions. Offers no additional payment for photos accepted with ms. Buys one-time rights.

Columns/Departments: Parent's Place, Kid Ability, Feature. **Buys 20 mss/year**. Query. **Pays $100/magazine page.**

Poetry: Free verse, light verse, traditional. **Buys 1 poem/year**. Submit maximum 2 poems. Length: 5-25 words.

N $ $ TWINS, The Magazine for Parents of Multiples, The Business Word, Inc., 5350 S. Roslyn St., Suite 400, Englewood CO 80111. Fax: (303)290-9025. E-mail: twins.editor@businessword.com. **Contact**: Heather White, assistant editor. Editor-in-Chief: Susan J. Alt. Managing Editor: Marge D. Hansen. **80% freelance written.** Bimonthly magazine covering parenting multiples. "*TWINS* is an international publication that provides informational and educational articles regarding the parenting of twins, triplets and more. All articles must be multiple specific and have an upbeat, hopeful and/or positive ending." Estab. 1984. Circ. 55,000. Pays on publication. Byline given. Buys first North American serial rights. Editorial lead time 3 months. Submit seasonal material 5 months in advance. Accepts simultaneous submissions. Reporting time varies. Sample copy for $5. Writer's guidelines for #10 SASE.

Nonfiction: Inspirational (first person), personal experience (first-person parenting experience, experience as a twin). Nothing on cloning, potty training, pregnancy reduction, celebrity twins. **Buys 12 mss/year.** Query with or without published clips or send complete ms. Length: 1,300 words. **Pays $25-250 for assigned articles; $25-75 for unsolicited articles.**

Photos: State availability of photos with submission. Offers no additional payment for photos accepted with ms. Identification of subjects required.

Columns/Departments: On Being Parents (parenting multiples/personal essay), 800-850 words; On Being Twins (being a twin/personal essay), 800-850 words; Growing Stages (personal short observations), 100-150 words. **Buys 12-20 mss/year.** Query with or without published clips or send complete ms. **Pays $25-75.** "All department articles must have a happy ending, as well as teach a lesson or provide a moral that parents of multiples can learn from."

$ VALLEY PARENT MAGAZINE, Bay Area Publishing Group, Inc., 401 Alberto Way, Suite A, Los Gatos CA 95032. (408)358-1414. Associate Publisher: Lynn Berardo. **Contact:** Mary Brence Martin, managing editor. **43% freelance written.** Monthly magazine covering parenting children ages birth through early teens. "The information we are most likely to use is local, well-researched and geared to our readers." Estab. 1992. Circ. 55,000. Pays on publication. Publishes ms an average of 6 months after acceptance. Byline given. Buys first rights. Editorial lead time 4 months.

Submit seasonal material 4 months in advance. Accepts simultaneous submissions. Reports in 2 months. Sample copy for 8½×12 SAE with 5 first-class stamps. Writer's guidelines for #10 SASE.

Nonfiction: Book excerpts, interview/profile, opinion, personal experience (all parenting-related). Send complete ms with SASE. **Buys 22 mss/year.** Length: 900-2,000 words. **Pays 6-9¢/word.**

Reprints: Send tearsheet or photocopy of article or typed ms with rights for sale noted and information about when and where the article previously appeared. Pays 100% of amount paid for an original article.

Photos: State availability of photos with submission. Reviews contact sheets, negatives, transparencies, prints. Offers $10-15/photo. Buys one-time rights.

Columns/Departments: First Year, 950-1,000 words. Query with published clips or send complete ms with SASE. **Pays 6-9¢/word.**

N $ VALLEYKIDS PARENT NEWS, 355-H Woodridge Circle, South Elgin IL 60177. (847)608-8122. **Contact**: Vivian J. Nimmo, editor. **50% freelance written.** Monthly tabloid featuring "suggestions for busy parents who care about their children." Estab. 1992. Circ. 61,000. Pays on publication. Publishes ms an average of 2 months after acceptance. Byline given. Buys one-time rights and makes work-for-hire assignments. Editorial lead time 3 months. Submit seasonal material 3 months in advance. Accepts simultaneous submissions. Reports in 2 months on queries; 3 months on mss. Sample copy for $1. Writer's guidelines free.

Nonfiction: General interest, how-to, inspirational. No self-promotional pieces. **Buys 30 mss/year.** Send complete ms. Length: 600-1,200 words. **Pays $25-50.**

Reprints: Accepts previously published submissions.

Photos: State availability of photos with submission. Buys one-time rights.

$ $ $ $ WORKING MOTHER MAGAZINE, MacDonald Communications, 135 W. 50th St., New York NY 10020. (212)445-6100. Fax: (212)445-6174. E-mail: jculbreth@womweb.com. **Contact**: Judsen Culbreth, editor-in-chief. **90% freelance written.** Prefers to work with published/established writers; works with a small number of new/unpublished writers each year. Monthly magazine for women who balance a career with the concerns of parenting. Circ. 925,000. Publishes ms an average of 4 months after acceptance. Byline given. Buys all rights. Pays 20% kill fee. Submit seasonal material 6 months in advance. Sample copy for $4. Writer's guidelines for SASE.

Nonfiction: Service, humor, child development, material pertinent to the working mother's predicament. Query to *Working Mother Magazine*. **Buys 9-10 mss/issue.** Length: 1,500-2,000 words. Pays expenses of writers on assignment.

Tips: "We are looking for pieces that help the reader. In other words, we don't simply report on a trend without discussing how it specifically affects our readers' lives and how they can handle the effects. Where can they look for help if necessary?"

N $ $ $ YOUR BABY, Today's Parent Group, 269 Richmond St. W., Toronto, Ontario M5V 1X1 Canada. Fax: (416)496-1991. Website: http://www.todaysparent.com. **Contact:** Susan Spicer, assistant editor. Editor: Holly Bennett. **100% freelance written**. Magazine published 3 times a year covering parenting from birth to age 2. "Articles of interest to parents of young children about child development, care, health and parenting issues." **Pays on acceptance**. Publishes ms an average of 8 months after acceptance. Bylines given. Buys first North American serial rights. Editorial lead time 6 months. Reports in 6 weeks on queries. Sample copy and writer's guidelines for #10 SASE.

Nonfiction: Personal experience (occasionally), features about parenting young children. **Buys 12 mss/year**. Query with published clips. Length: 500-1,500 words. **Pays $400-1,000.** Sometimes pays expenses of writers on assignment.

COMIC BOOKS

Comic books aren't just for kids. Today, this medium also attracts a reader who is older and wants stories presented visually on a wide variety of topics. In addition, some instruction manuals, classics and other stories are being produced in a comic book format.

This doesn't mean you have to be an artist to write for comic books. Most of these publishers want to see a synopsis of one to two double-spaced pages. Be concise. Comics use few words and rely on graphics as well as words to forward the plot.

Once your synopsis is accepted, either an artist will draw the story from your plot, returning these pages to you for dialogue and captions, or you will be expected to write a script. Scripts run approximately 23 typewritten pages and include suggestions for artwork as well as dialogue. Try to imagine your story on actual comic book pages and divide your script accordingly. The average comic has six panels per page, with a maximum of 35 words per panel.

If you're submitting a proposal to Marvel, your story should center on an already established character. If you're dealing with an independent publisher, characters are often the property of their creators. Your proposal should be for a new series. Include a background sheet for main characters who will appear regularly, listing origins, weaknesses, powers or other information that will make your character unique. Indicate an overall theme or direction for your series. Submit story ideas for the first three issues. If you're really ambitious, you may also include a script for your first issue. As with all markets, read a sample copy before making a submission. The best markets may be those you currently read, so consider submitting to them even if they aren't listed in this section.

$ CARTOON WORLD, P.O. Box 1164, Kent WA 98035. E-mail: cartoonworld@usa.net. **Contact**: Vic Stredicke, editor. (253)854-6649. Monthly newsletter for professional and serious amateur cartoonists who want to find new places to sell their cartoons. Circ. 300. **Pays on acceptance.** Byline given. Offers counsel to new writers. Submit seasonal material 3 months in advance. Reports in 1 month. Sample copy free.
Nonfiction: "Want articles about the business of cartooning. Most features should be first-person accounts of cartoon editing, creating ideas, work habits." All cartoons run must have been published elsewhere. Length: 1,000 words. **Pays $5/page/feature.**
Reprints: Note where previously appeared. **Pays $5/page.**

N $ MIXXZINE, 100% Motionless Entertainment, Mixx Entertainment, Inc., 746 W. Adams Blvd., Los Angeles CA 90089-7725. (213)743-2519. Fax: (213)749-7199. E-mail: info@mixxonline.com. **Contact**: Ron Scovil, Jr., editor-in-chief. **95% freelance written.** Bimonthly magazine covering Japanese comics and animation (manga, anime). "*MixxZine* readers are the most up-to-date on Japanese comics and animation and are interested in learning more about Japanese culture." Estab. 1997. Circ. 100,000. Pays on publication. No byline. Makes work-for-hire assignments. Editorial lead time 3 months. Submit seasonal material 3 months in advance. Accepts simultaneous submissions. Sample copy for $2.50.
Nonfiction: New product. **Buys 3 mss/year.** Query with published clips. Length: 500-4,000 words. **Pays $100/feature articles.**
Photos: State availability of photos with submission. Reviews 8½×11 prints. Offers no additional payment for photos accepted with ms. Buys all rights.

N $ $ $ $ TARZAN, STAR WARS, BUFFY THE VAMPIRE SLAYER, STARSHIP TROOPERS, ALIENS, PREDATOR, DARK HORSE PRESENTS, Dark Horse Comics, Inc. 10956 SE Main St., Milwaukee OR 97222. E-mail: mikeh@dhorse.com. Website: http://www.dhorse.com. **Contact**: Mike Hansen, submissions editor. Editor: Jamie S. Rich. Managing Editor: Randy Stradley. **90-100% freelance written.** Monthly comic books (serialized graphic narratives). "Writers should have a strong grasp of the comics medium and be familiar/comfortable with storytelling in a medium where the images are as important as the words." Estab. 1986. Circ. all titles combined 3-4 million/year; individual titles 20,000-30,000/issue. **Pays on acceptance**. Publishes ms an average of 9 months after acceptance. Byline sometimes given. Buys first North American serial rights or makes work-for-hire assignments. Editorial lead time 9 months. Accepts simultaneous submissions. Reports in 2 months. Guidelines for 9×12 SASE.
Reprints: Send tearsheet or photocopy with information about when and where material previously appeared.
Fiction: Adventure, fantasy, horror, humorous, mystery, science fiction, serialized novels, suspense, Western. **Buys 25 mss/year.** Query with published clips. **Pays $75-110/page.**
Tips: "A request for submission guidelines will save much time. Writers should *not* submit samples based on licensed characters, as legal concerns keep us from being able to review them. Otherwise, just *know* comics."

N $ $ WIZARD: THE COMICS MAGAZINE, Wizard Entertainment, 151 Wells Ave., Congers NY 10920. (914)268-2000. Fax: (914)268-0053. E-mail: wizandrew@aol.com. Website: http://www.wizardpress.com. Editor: Brian Cunningham. Senior Editor: Joe Yanarella. **Contact**: Andrew Kardon, managing editor. **70% freelance written.** Monthly magazine covering comics and action figures. Estab. 1991. Circ. 300,000. Pays on publication. Publishes ms an average of 3 months after acceptance. Byline given. Offers 50% kill fee. Buys all rights. Editorial lead time 4 months. Sample copy and writer's guidelines free.
Nonfiction: Historical/nostalgic, how-to, humor, interview/profile, new product, personal experience, photo feature, first person diary. No columns or opinion pieces. **Buys 100 mss/year.** Query with or without published clips. Length: 250-4,000 words. **Pays 15-20¢/word.** Sometimes pays expenses of writers on assignment.
Photos: State availability of photos with submission. Negotiates payment individually. Identification of subjects required. Buys all rights.
Columns/Departments: Character Profile (profile of comic character), 750-900 words; Time Travel (classic moment in comic history), 500 words; Coming Attractions (comic book-related movies and TV shows), 150-500 words. Query with published clips. **Pays $75-500.**

CONSUMER SERVICE & BUSINESS OPPORTUNITY

Some of these magazines are geared to investing earnings or starting a new business; others show how to make economical purchases. Publications for business executives and consumers interested in business topics are listed under Business and Finance. Those on how to run specific businesses are classified by category in the Trade section.

N $ $ **AMERICAN VENTURE, For Entrepreneurs & Accredited Investors**, Fusion International, Inc., 621 SW Alder, Suite 415, Portland OR 97205. (503)221-9981. Fax: (503)221-9987. E-mail: avce@aol.com. Website: http://www.avce.com. **Contact**: Douglas Clements, editor-in-chief. **75% freelance written.** "Quarterly magazine contains articles written for individuals and companies that invest in new ventures and people that manage new ventures. Articles should *not* favor tax-funded programs or laws that restrict economic freedom. Articles should be consistent with free-market economics." Estab. 1997. Circ. 15,000. Pays on publication. Publishes ms an average of 2 months after acceptance. Byline given. Buys all rights. Editorial lead time 2 months. Submit seasonal material 2 months in advance. Accepts simultaneous submissions. Sample copy and writer's guidelines free on website.
Nonfiction: Essays, exposé, general interest, historical/nostalgic, how-to, inspirational, interview/profile, new product, opinion, personal experience. **Buys 15 mss/year.** Query with published clips. Length: 500-1,250 words. **Pays $50-300.**
Reprints: Accepts previously published submissions.
Photos: State availability of photos with submission. Reviews contact sheets. Negotiates payment individually. Buys one-time rights.
Columns/Departments: Investor's Perspective (investor talks about his philosophy, deals), 750 words; Success Against the Odds (entrepreneur who succeeded despite much adversity), 1,000 words; Secret of their Success (story of the early days of a famous company), 1,000 words; Innovators (a company with a revolutionary new product/service), 750 words. **Buys 10 mss/year.** Query with or without published clips. **Pays $50-300.**
Fillers: Anecdotes, facts, newsbreaks, short humor. **Buys 5/year.** Length: 100-300 words. **Pays $30-150.**
Tips: "Articles should contain interesting new information that venture capitalists and entrepreneurs can use. No boring, obvious tracts. We like 'war stories' from investors and entrepreneurs that are inspirational. Articles that illustrate the beauty of free-market capitalism are favored."

$ $ **JERRY BUCHANAN'S INFO MARKETING REPORT**, TOWERS Club Press, Inc., P.O. Box 2038, Vancouver WA 98668-2038. (360)574-3084. Fax: (360)576-8969. **Contact**: Jerry Buchanan, editor. **5-10% freelance written.** Works with a small number of unpublished writers each year. Monthly of 10 or more pages on entrepreneurial enterprises, reporting especially on self-publishing of how-to reports, books, audio and video tapes, seminars, etc. "By-passing big trade publishers and marketing your own work directly to consumer (mail order predominantly)." Estab. 1974. Circ. 10,000. Pays on publication. Publishes ms an average of 2 months after acceptance. Byline given. Buys one-time rights. Reports in 2 weeks. Sample copy for $15 and 6×9 SASE.
Nonfiction: Exposé (of mail order fraud); how-to (personal experience in self-publishing and marketing); book reviews of new self-published nonfiction how-to-do-it books (must include name and address of author). "Welcomes well-written articles of successful self-publishing/marketing ventures. Must be current, and preferably written by the person who actually did the work and reaped the rewards. There's very little we will not consider, *if* it pertains to unique money-making enterprises that can be operated from the home." **Buys 10 mss/year.** Send complete ms. Fax submissions accepted of no more than 3 pages. Length: 500-1,500 words. **Pays $150-250.** Pays extra for b&w photo and bonus for excellence in longer ms.
Reprints: Send tearsheet or photocopy of article or typed ms with rights for sale noted and information about when and where the article previously appeared. Pays 10% of the amount paid for an original article.
Tips: "The most frequent mistake made by writers in completing an article for us is that they think they can simply rewrite a newspaper article and be accepted. That is only the start. We want them to find the article about a successful self-publishing enterprise, and then go out and interview the principal for a more detailed how-to article, including names and addresses. We prefer that writer actually interview a successful self-publisher. Articles should include how idea first came to subject; how they implemented and financed and promoted the project; how long it took to show a profit and some of the stumbling blocks they overcame; how many persons participated in the production and promotion; and how much money was invested (approximately) and other pertinent how-to elements of the story. Glossy photos (b&w) of principals at work in their offices will help sell article."

$ $ $ $ **CONSUMERS DIGEST MAGAZINE, For People who Demand Value**, Consumers Digest, Inc., 8001 N. Lincoln Ave., Skokie IL 60077. (847)763-9200. Fax: (847)763-0200. E-mail: Jmanos@consumersdigest.com. Website: http://www.consumersdigest.com. **Contact**: John Manos, editor-in-chief. **70% freelance written.** Bimonthly magazine offering "practical advice on subjects of interest to consumers: products and services, automobiles, health, fitness, consumer legal affairs, personal money management, etc." Estab. 1959. Circ. 1,300,000. **Pays on acceptance.** Publishes ms an average of 3 months after acceptance. Byline given. Offers 50% kill fee. Buys first and second North American serial and electronic rights. Submit seasonal material 6 months in advance. Accepts simultaneous submissions. Reports in 2 months. Sample copy for 9×12 SAE with 6 first-class stamps. Writer's guidelines free.
Nonfiction: Exposé, general interest, how-to (financial, purchasing), new product, travel, health, fitness. **Buys 80 mss/year.** Query with published clips. Length: 1,000-3,000 words. **Pays $1,000-3,500 for assigned articles; $400-1,700 for unsolicited articles.** Pays phone expenses and sometimes other expenses of writers on assignment.
Photos: State availability of photos with submission.
Columns/Departments: Nikki Hopewell, column editor. Consumerscope (brief items of general interest to consum-

ers—auto news, travel tips, the environment, smart shopping, news you can use). **Buys 10 mss/year.** Query. Length: 200-500 words. **Pays $200-500.**

Tips: "Keep the queries brief and tightly focused. Read our writer's guidelines first and request an index of past articles for trends and to avoid repeating subjects. Focus on subjects of broad national appeal. Stress personal expertise in proposed subject area. We need expert advice to help consumers save money on all spending for products and services, from computer software to health care, or food processors to legal and investment advice. Our advice is always very specific—which model of any product offers the best value. Generalities are not useful without specific, hand-holding recommendations."

N $ $ CUTTING EDGE MEDIA, INC., 29 S. Market St., Elizabethtown PA 17022. Fax: (717)361-0860. E-mail: heather@cuttingedgemedia.com. **Contact**: Heather Leonard, managing editor. Editor: Dawn Josephson. **40% freelance written.** "Monthly magazine covering home businesses, network marketing, multi-level marketing for people who are looking to get into a home-based business." Estab. 1989. Circ. 135,000. Pays on publication. Publishes ms an average of 6 months after acceptance. Byline sometimes given. Buys one-time, second serial (reprint) or simultaneous rights. Editorial lead time 3 months. Submit seasonal material 3 months in advance. Accepts simultaneous submissions. Sample copy and writer's guidelines free.

- Cutting Edge Media publishes these magazines: *Home Business Connection*, *Network Marketing Connection* and *Cutting Edge Opportunities*.

Nonfiction: Book excerpts, general interest, how-to (build your business), inspirational, interview/profile, new product, technical (technology). Send complete ms. Length: 700-1,500 words. **Pays $25-200** or pays writers with contributor copies or other premiums for extensive bylines referencing books, seminars, etc.

Reprints: Accepts previously published submissions.

Photos: Send photos with submission. Reviews 3×5 prints. Negotiates payment individually.

Columns/Departments: Book Reviews, 100 words; Success Stories, 700-1,500 words; How-to, 700-1,500 words. Send complete ms. **Pays $25-200.**

Fillers: Anecdotes, facts, newsbreaks, short humor. Length: 75-150 words.

Tips: "Fax or send submissions with a cover letter explaining the outline of the article or filler. This is our first year buying submissions."

N $ $ HOME BUSINESS MAGAZINE, United Marketing & Research Company, Inc., 9582 Hamilton Ave. #368, Huntington Beach CA 92646. Fax: (714)962-7722. E-mail: henderso@ix.netcom.com. Website: http://www.homebusinessmag.com. **Contact**: Stacy Ann Henderson, editor-in-chief. **75% freelance written.** "*Home Business Magazine* covers every angle of the home-based business market including: cutting edge editorial by well-known authorities on sales and marketing, business operations, the home office, franchising, business opportunities, network marketing, mail order and other subjects to help readers choose, manage and prosper in a home-based business; display advertising, classified ads and a directory of home-based businesses; technology, the Internet, computers and the future of home-based business; home-office editorial including management advice, office set-up, and product descriptions; business opportunities, franchising and work-from-home success stories." Estab. 1993. Circ. 80,000. Pays on publication. Publishes ms an average of 4 months after acceptance. Byline given. Buys first, one-time, second serial (reprint) rights or makes work-for-hire assignments. Editorial lead time 2 months. Submit seasonal material 3 months in advance. Accepts simultaneous submissions. Sample copy for 9×12 SASE with 8 first-class stamps. Writer's guidelines for #10 SASE.

Nonfiction: Book excerpts, general interest, how-to (home business), inspirational, interview/profile, new product, personal experience, photo feature, technical, mail order, franchise, business management, Internet, finance network marketing. No non-home business related topics. **Buys 40 mss/year.** Send complete ms with 9×12 SASE with 8 first-class stamps. Length: 265-3,200 words. **Pays $67-500 for assigned articles; $0-200 for unsolicited articles.** Pays with contributor copies or other premiums on request or per pre-discussed arrangement with magazine.

Reprints: Accepts previously published submissions.

Photos: Send photos with submission. Offers no additional payment for photos accepted with ms. Identification of subjects required. Buys one-time rights.

Columns/Departments: Marketing & Sales; Money Corner; Home Office; Management; Technology; Working Smarter; Franchising; Network Marketing, all 265-1,200 words. Send complete ms. Pays $0-200.

Tips: "Send complete information by mail as per our writer's guidelines and e-mail if possible."

$ $ INCOME OPPORTUNITIES, NewsLinc, 5300 Citiplex Tower, 2448 E. 81st St., Tulsa OK 74137-4207. (918)491-6100. Fax: (918)491-9410. E-mail: ahinds@natcom-publications.com. **Contact:** André Hinds, executive editor. Managing Editor: Steven M Brown. **90% freelance written.** Monthly magazine covering small and home-based businesses and entrepreneurial concepts for 42 years. Estab. 1956. Circ. 300,000. **Pays on acceptance.** Publishes ms an average of 5 months after acceptance. Byline given. Offers 33% kill fee. Buys first North American serial rights. Reports in 2 months. Writer's guidelines for #10 SASE.

- "We won the 1996 National Press Club Consumer Journalism Award for magazines and are looking for more award-winning stories."

Nonfiction: "We need insightful, practical articles that help people starting or running a small or home-based business." Interested in how-to pieces on managing, financing and marketing a small business, and profiles of well-known entrepreneurs who started on a shoestring." No purely inspirational articles. **Buys 72 mss/year.** Query by mail or fax with published clips. Length: 1,000-2,000 words. **Pays $300-500.** Pays expenses of writers on assignment.

Photos: Send photos with submission if applicable. Offers no additional payment for photos accepted with ms. Identification of subjects required. Buys one-time rights.
Columns/Departments: Success Story and Tech Talk, 600-1,000 words. **Buys 130 mss/year.** Query with published clips. Pay varies.
Tips: "The bulk of published articles concern general money-making, small business or entrepreneurial concepts. Recent examples include 'Internet Marketing Without a Website,' 'Where to Find Next Year's Customers,' and 'Summer Businesses that Sizzle; pick up a copy and familiarize yourself with our style before you submit."

$ $ $ $ KIPLINGER'S PERSONAL FINANCE, 1729 H St. NW, Washington DC 20006. (202)887-6400. Fax: (202)331-1206. Website: http://www.kiplinger.com. Editor: Ted Miller. **Contact:** Margaret Ringer, senior editorial assistant. **Less than 10% freelance written.** Prefers to work with published/established writers. Monthly magazine for general, adult audience interested in personal finance and consumer information. "*Kiplinger's* is a highly trustworthy source of information on saving and investing, taxes, credit, home ownership, paying for college, retirement planning, automobile buying and many other personal finance topics." Estab. 1947. Circ. 1,300,000. **Pays on acceptance.** Publishes ms an average of 2 months after acceptance. Buys all rights. Reports in 1 month.
Nonfiction: "Most material is staff-written, but we accept some freelance. Thorough documentation is required for fact-checking." Query with clips of published work. Pays expenses of writers on assignment.
Tips: "We are looking for a heavy emphasis on personal finance topics."

N $ NO-DEBT LIVING NEWSLETTER, Financial Management with a Christian Perspective, No Debt Living, P.O. Box 282, Veradale WA 99037. E-mail: nodebt@gntech.net. Website: http://www.nodebtnews.com. **Contact:** Robert Frank, editor. **40% freelance written**. Monthly newsletter covering personal financial management with a Christian perspective. Estab. 1993. Circ. 2,000. Pays on publication. Publishes ms 2 months after acceptance. Byline given. Buys first North American serial rights or one-time rights. Editorial lead time 2 months. Submit seasonal material 2 months in advance. Reports in 2 weeks on queries. Sample copy and writer's guidelines for 6×9 SASE and 55¢. Writer's guidelines also available on website.
Nonfiction: Book excerpts, how-to, interview/profile, home management, medical/wellness, personal financial management, time management. Query with published clips or CV. Length: 300-1,200 words. **Pays $30-70.**
Reprints: Accepts previously published submissions.
Columns/Departments: Buys 2 mss/year. Query with background description. **Pays $30-40.**
Tips: "Write in good journalistic, AP style. Use fresh comments/quotes from recognized national experts."

N ☆ $ $ OPPORTUNITY MAGAZINE, 18 E. 41st St., New York NY 10017. Fax: (212)376-7723. E-mail: opptnty@aol.com. Website: htpp://www.ashlee.com. **Contact**: Michael Hyde, editor. **75% freelance written.** Monthly magazine on small business and money-making ideas. Provides "hands-on service to help small-business owners, home office workers and entrepreneurs successfully start up and run their enterprises." Estab. 1989. Circ. 150,000. Pays on publication. Byline given. Buys first North American serial or second serial rights. Sample copy for $2.50. Writer's guidelines for #10 SASE.
Nonfiction: Articles should be fact-filled: book excerpts, how-to (business, finance, home office, technical, start-up), interview/profile. **Buys 48 mss/year.** Query. Length: 900-2,000 words. **Pays $400-600 for assigned articles; $100-200 for unsolicited articles.** Pays expenses of writers on assignment.
Reprints: Accepts previously published submissions. Send tearsheet of article and information about when and where the article previously appeared.
Photos: State availability of photos with submission. Offers no additional payment for photos accepted with ms.
Columns/Departments: Small-Biz; Finance & Law; Trends; Publicity; Success Stories, 750-900 words. **Pays $100-150.**
Tips: Write for editorial calendar as well as ms guidelines. Submit via e-mail or computer disk.

$ $ ☆ SPARE TIME MAGAZINE, The Magazine of Money Making Opportunities, Kipen Publishing Corp., 5810 W. Oklahoma Ave., Milwaukee WI 53219. (414)543-8110. Fax: (414)543-9767. Email: editor@spare-time.com. Website: http://www.spare-time.com. **Contact**: Peter Abbott, editor. **75% freelance written.** Magazine published 11 times/year (monthly except July) covering affordable money-making opportunities. "We publish information the average person can use to begin and operate a spare-time business or extra income venture, with the possible goal of making it fulltime." Estab. 1955. Circ. 300,000. Pays on publication. Publishes ms an average of 3 months after acceptance. Byline given. Buys first North American serial rights. Editorial lead time 2 months. Submit seasonal material 3 months in advance. Accepts simultaneous submissions, query first. Reports in 1 month on queries; 2 months on mss. Sample copy for $2.50. Writer's guidelines and editorial calendar for #10 SASE.
Nonfiction: Book excerpts and reviews (small business related), how-to (market, keep records, stay motivated, choose opportunity), interview/profile and personal experience (small business related). Special issues: Starting a new business (January); Hobby businesses (February); Taxes (March); Low cost franchising (April); Sales and marketing (May/June); Education and training (August). **Buys 24-54 mss/year.** Query with SASE. Length: up to 1,100 words (cover story: 1,500-2,000 words; installment series; three parts up to 1,100 words each). **Pays 15¢/word upon publication.** Sometimes pays expenses of writers on assignment.
Reprints: Send photocopy of article or typed ms with information about when and where the article previously appeared. Pays 50% of amount paid for an original article.

Photos: State availability of photos with submission. Reviews contact sheets, 3×5 or larger prints. Pays $15/published photo. Captions, identification of subjects required. Buys one-time rights.
Tips: "It is always best to query. At all times keep in mind that the audience is the average person, not over-educated in terms of business techniques. The best pieces are written in lay language and relate to that type of person."

CONTEMPORARY CULTURE

These magazines often combine politics, current events and cultural elements such as art, literature, film and music, to examine contemporary society. Their approach to institutions is typically irreverent and investigative. Some, like *Swing Magazine*, report on alternative culture and appeal to a young adult "Generation X" audience. Others, such as *Mother Jones* or *Rolling Stone*, treat mainstream culture for a baby boomer generation audience.

N $ $ **THE AMERICAN SCHOLAR**, Phi Beta Kappa, 1811 Q St. NW, Washington DC 20009. (202)265-3808. Fax: (202)986-1601. Editor: Anne Fadiman. **Contact**: Jean Stipicevic, managing editor. **100% freelance written.** Quarterly journal. "Our intent is to have articles written by scholars and experts but written in nontechnical language for an intelligent audience. Material covers a wide range in the arts, sciences, current affairs, history and literature." Estab. 1932. Circ. 25,000. Pays on publication. Publishes ms an average of 1 year after acceptance. Byline given. Offers 50% kill fee. Buys first rights. Editorial lead time 6 months. Submit seasonal material 6 months in advance. Reports in 2 weeks on queries; 2 months on mss. Sample copy for $6.95. Writer's guidelines free.
Nonfiction: Essays, historical/nostalgic. **Buys 40 mss/year.** Query. Length: 3,000-5,000 words. **Pays $500 maximum.**
Poetry: Rob Farnsworth, poetry editor. "We have no special requirements of length, form or content for original poetry." **Buys 40 poems/year.** Submit 3-4 poems maximum. **Pays $50.**

$ $ **BUILD MAGAZINE A Magazine About Young People Building Communities, Do Something,** 423 W. 55th St., New York NY 10019. (212)523-1175. Fax: (212)582-1307. E-mail: daramay@aol.com. Website: http://www.dosomething.org. **Contact**: Dara Mayers, editor. **100% freelance written.** Quarterly magazine covering activism, youth leadership, social justice and entertainment. "The goal of *Build* is to inspire young people to take action in their communities. We also seek to provide issue-oriented information which may not otherwise be accessible to a young audience. *Build* also entertains while it educates." Estab. 1996. Circ. 100,000. Pays on publication. Byline given. Offers 15% kill fee. Makes work-for-hire assignments. Editorial lead time 6 weeks. Submit seasonal material 2 months in advance. Accepts simultaneous submissions. Sample copy and writer's guidelines for SASE.
Nonfiction: Essays, general interest, historical/nostalgic, how-to, inspirational, interview/profile, opinion, personal experience, photo feature, religious. "We are always looking for socially active celebrities and charismatic grass roots leaders. **Buys 20 mss/year.** Query with published clips. Length: 250-3,000 words. **Pays $100-400.** Sometimes pays expenses of writers on assignment.
Reprints: Accepts previously published material.
Photos: Send photos with submission. Reviews negatives. Negotiates payment individually. Captions, identification of subjects required. Buys one-time rights.
Columns/Departments: Kelly Chase, editorial assistant. Recommended Consumption (socially relevant reviews of movies, books and films), 100-150 words; Action Shots (actions taking place locally), 100-150 words; Protius (young activists personal histories), 1,500-2,000 words. **Buys 50 mss/year.** Query with published clips. **Pays $25-150.**
Tips: "Information should be presented in a way which appeals to 16- to 25-year-olds; hip, but not cynical."

N $ **CAFE EIGHTIES MAGAZINE, The Perfect Blend of Yesterday's Grinds and What's Brewing in Your Mind Today**, 1562 First Ave., Suite 180, New York NY 10028. Fax: (212)861-0588. **Contact**: Kimberly Brittingham, publisher/editor-in-chief. **90% freelance written.** Quarterly magazine. "*Cafe Eighties* is created by and for the mini-generation that 'came of age' in the early-to-mid 1980s. We want our stories to be told. We want *Cafe Eighties* to serve as a forum, a scrapbook, a storybook, a historical reference and an all-encompassing diary of who we are and the events and trends that lead us into today." Estab. 1993. Circ. 2,500. Pays on publication. Publishes ms 1 year after acceptance. Byline given. Buys one-time and second serial (reprint) rights and makes work-for-hire assignments. Submit seasonal material 9 months in advance. Accepts simultaneous submissions. Reports in 1 week on queries; 2 months on mss. Sample copy for $5. Writer's guidelines for #10 SASE.
Nonfiction: Essays, general interest, humor, interview/profile, new product, opinion, personal experience, photo feature, travel. "No subject matter that does not pertain to a 25-35 readership." **Buys 20 mss/year.** Query. Length: 300-2,000 words. **Pays $10-100.** Sometimes pays expenses of writers on assignment.
Reprints: Accepts previously published submissions.
Photos: State availability of photos with submission. Reviews contact sheets. Negotiates payment individually. Identification of subjects required. Buys one-time rights.
Columns/Departments: Books; Retro Reviews. **Buys 20 mss/year.** Query. **Pays $10-50.**
Fillers: Facts, gags to be illustrated by cartoonist, short humor. **Buys 20/year. Pays $5-20.**

$ CANADIAN DIMENSION, Dimension Publications Inc., 91 Albert St., Room 2-B, Winnipeg, Manitoba, R3B 1G5 Canada. Fax: (204)943-4617. E-mail: info@canadiandimension.mb.ca. Website: http://www.canadiandimension.mb.ca/cd/index.htm. **80% freelance written. Contact:** George Harris. Bimonthly magazine "that makes sense of the world. We bring a socialist perspective to bear on events across Canada and around the world. Our contributors provide in-depth coverage on popular movements, peace, labour, women, aboriginal justice, environment, third world and eastern Europe." Estab. 1963. Circ. 4,000. Pays on publication. Publishes ms an average of 6 months after acceptance. Copyrighted by *CD* after publication. Accepts simultaneous submissions. Reports in 6 weeks on queries. Sample copy for $2. Writer's guidelines for #10 SAE with IRC.

Nonfiction: Interview/profile, opinion, reviews, political commentary and analysis, journalistic style. **Buys 8 mss/year.** Length: 500-2,000 words. **Pays $25-100.**

Reprints: Sometimes accepts previously published submissions. Send typed ms with rights for sale noted (electronic copies when possible) and information about when and where the article previously appeared.

N ✪ $ CURIO, Curio Magazine, Inc., 81 Pondfield Rd., Suite 264, Bronxville NY 10708. (914)961-8649. Fax: (914)779-4033. E-mail: genm20b@prodigy.com. **Contact:** Mickey Z., editor. **80% freelance written.** Quarterly magazine covering politics, art, culture and photography. "Our readers are socially aware and independent with strong opinions and a definite sense of humor." Estab. 1996. Circ. 50,000. Pays on publication. Publishes ms an average of 3 months after acceptance. Byline given. Offers $25 kill fee. Buys first North American serial rights. Editorial lead time 3 months. Submit seasonal material 3 months in advance. Accepts simultaneous submissions. Sample copy for $6. Writer's guidelines for #10 SASE.

Nonfiction: Book excerpts, general interest, how-to (i.e., throw a movie punch), humor, interview/profile, new product, opinion, personal experience, travel. **Buys 20 mss/year.** Send complete ms. Length: 300-3,000 words. **Pays $140/page.** Pays writers with contributor copies or other premium for poetry or if specifically negotiated with writer.

Photos: "*Curio* offers photographers 6 pages to layout their own work for $300. Photo essay may be approved by art director." Captions, model releases and identification of subjects required. Buys one-time rights, plus use in future "best of" issues and for publicity, if needed.

Reprints: Send photocopy of article. Pays contributors copy only.

Columns/Departments: Interrogation (Q&A interviews); Reviews (film, art, music, television, video, photography, radio, food, restaurants, etc.), 300 words. **Buys 100 mss/year.** Send complete ms. **Pays $105-140/page.**

Fillers: Anecdotes, facts, gags to be illustrated by cartoonist, short humor. **Pays $0-25.**

Tips: "Send complete manuscript. Don't call us, we will call you. But, if you move, please give us your new address."

N ✪ $ $ FIRST THINGS, Institute on Religion & Public Life, 156 Fifth Ave., Suite 400, New York NY 10010. (212)627-1985. Fax: (212)627-2184. E-mail: ft@firstthings.com. Website: http://www.firstthings.com. **Contact**: James Nuechlerleir, editor. Editor-in-Chief: Richard John Neuhaus. Managing Editor: Matthew Berke. Associate Editor: Daniel Moloney. **70% freelance written.** "Intellectual journal published 10 times/year containing social and ethical commentary in broad sense, religious and ethical perspectives on society, culture, law, medicine, church and state, morality and mores." Estab. 1990. Circ. 32,000. Pays on publication. Publishes ms an average of 4 months after acceptance. Byline given. Kill fee varies. Buys all rights. Editorial lead time 2 months. Submit seasonal material 5 months in advance. Reports in 3 months on mss. Sample copy and writer's guidelines free.

Nonfiction: Essays, opinion. **Buys 60 mss/year.** Send complete double-spaced ms. Length: 1,500 words for Opinion; 4,000-6,000 words for long articles. **Pays $250-700.** Sometimes pays expenses of writers on assignment.

Poetry: Traditional. **Buys 25-30 poems/year.** Length: 4-40 lines. **Pays $50.**

Tips: "We prefer complete manuscripts (hard copy, double-spaced) to queries, but will reply if unsure."

$ $ FRANCE TODAY, FrancePress Inc., 1051 Divisadero St., San Francisco CA 94115. (415)921-5100. Fax: (415)921-0213. E-mail: fpress@hooked.net. Editor: Anne Prah-Perochon. **Contact**: Cara Ballard, assistant editor. **90% freelance written.** Bimonthly tabloid covering contemporary France. "*France Today* is a feature publication on contemporary France including sociocultural analysis, business, trends, current events and travel." Estab. 1989. Circ. 25,000. Pays on publication. Publishes ms an average of 3-5 months after acceptance. Byline given. Buys first North American and second serial (reprint) rights. Submit seasonal material 4 months in advance. Reports in 3 months. Sample copy for 10×13 SAE with 5 first-class stamps.

Nonfiction: Essays, exposé, general interest, historical, humor, interview/profile, personal experience, travel. "No travel pieces about well-known tourist attractions." Special issues: The Best of France in the US, French Around the World, France Adventure. **Buys 50 mss/year.** Query with or without published clips, or send complete ms. Length: 500-1,500 words. **Pays $150-250.** Pays expenses of writers on assignment.

Reprints: Send typed ms with rights for sale noted and information about when and where the article previously appeared. Pay varies.

Photos: Offers $25/photo. Identification of subjects required. Buys one-time rights.

N $ $ GADFLY MAGAZINE, Gadfly Productions, P.O. Box 7926, Charlottesville VA 22906-7482. (804)975-1652. Fax: (804)978-1789. E-mail: editor@gadfly.org. **Contact**: Amy I. Nickell, editor. Managing Editor: Tanya Stanciu. **30% freelance written.** Monthly. "*Gadfly Magazine* is devoted to cultural advancement in education, literature, television, music, film and the arts." Estab. 1997. Circ. 18,000. **Pays on acceptance**. Publishes ms an average of 3 months after acceptance. Byline given. Offers 50% kill fee. Buys all rights. Editorial lead time 4 months. Submit seasonal material 4 months in advance. Accepts simultaneous submissions. Reports in 3 months. Sample copy and writer's guidelines free.

Nonfiction: Essays, general interest, historical/nostalgic, interview/profile. "We are not interested in academic or technical articles." **Buys 25 mss/year.** Query with published clips. Length: 600-5,000 words. **Pays $75-700.** Sometimes pays expenses of writers on assignment.

Photos: State availability of photos with submission. Reviews contact sheets, negatives, transparencies and prints. Negotiates payment individually. Identification of subjects required. Buys one-time rights.

Columns/Departments: Arts & Culture (book, film, video, music, performance, art exhibit reviews), 200-1,200 words. **Buys 15 mss/year.** Query with published clips. **Pays $75-200.**

$ $ $ HIGH TIMES, Trans High Corp., 235 Park Ave. S., 5th Floor, New York NY 10003-1405. (212)387-0500. Fax: (212)475-7684. E-mail: hteditor@hightimes.com. Website: http://www.hightimes.com. Publisher: Mike Edison. News Editor: Dean Latimer. **Contact:** Paul DeRienzo. **30% freelance written.** Monthly magazine covering marijuana and the counterculture. Estab. 1974. Circ. 250,000. Pays on publication. Byline given. Offers 20% kill fee. Buys one-time or all rights or makes work-for-hire assignments. Submit seasonal material 6 months in advance. Reports in 1 month on queries; 4 months on mss. Sample copy for $5 and #10 SASE. Writer's guidelines for SASE.

Nonfiction: Book excerpts, exposé, humor, interview/profile, new product, personal experience, photo feature, travel. **Buys 30 mss/year.** Send complete ms. Length: 2,000-7,000 words. **Pays $300-1,000.** Sometimes pays expenses of writers on assignment.

Reprints: Send tearsheet of article or typed ms with rights for sale noted. Pays in ad trade.

Photos: Shirley Halperin, photo editor. Send photos with submission. Pays $25-400, $400 for cover photos, $350 for centerfold. Captions, model release, identification of subjects required. Buys all rights or one-time use.

Columns/Departments: Steve Bloom, music editor; Chris Simunek, cultivation editor; Steve Wishnia, views editor. Drug related books, news. Buys 10 mss/year. Query with published clips. Length: 100-2,000 words. Pays $25-300.

Fillers: Gags to be illustrated by cartoonist, newsbreaks, short humor. Buys 10 mss/year. Length: 100-500 words. Pays $10-50. Frank Max, cartoon editor.

Tips: "Although promoting the legalization and cultivation of medicinal plants, primarily cannabis, is central to our mission, *High Times* does not promote the indiscriminate use of such plants. We are most interested in articles on cannabis cultivation, the history of hemp, the rise of the modern hemp industry, the history of the counterculture and countercultural trends and events. The best way for new writers to break in is through our news section. We are always looking for regional stories involving the Drug War that have national significance. This includes coverage of local legal battles, political controversies, drug testing updates and legalization rally reports. All sections are open to good, professional writers."

☆ $ $ $ MOTHER JONES, Foundation for National Progress, 731 Market St., Suite 600, San Francisco CA 94103. (415)665-6637. Fax: (415)665-6696. E-mail: query@motherjones.com. Website: http://www.motherjones.com. Editor: Jeffrey Klein. **Contact:** Kerry Lauerman, investigative editor; John Cook, assistant managing editor. **80% freelance written.** Bimonthly national magazine covering politics, investigative reporting, social issues and pop culture. "*Mother Jones* is a 'progressive' magazine—but the core of its editorial well is reporting (i.e., fact-based). No slant required." Estab. 1976. Circ. 150,000. Pays on publication. Publishes ms an average of 4 months after acceptance. Byline given. Offers 33% kill fee. Buys first North American serial rights, first rights, one-time rights or online rights (limited). Editorial lead time 4 months. Submit seasonal material 6 months in advance. Reports in 2 months. Sample copy for $6 and 9×12 SAE. Writer's guidelines for #10 SASE.

Nonfiction: Book excerpts, essays, exposé, humor, interview/profile, opinion, personal experience, photo feature, current issues, policy. **Buys 70-100 mss/year.** Query with 2-3 published clips and SASE. Length: 2,000-5,000 words. **Pays 80¢/word.** Sometimes pays expenses of writers on assignment.

Columns/Departments: Colleen Quinn. Outfront (short, newsy and/or outrageous and/or humorous items), 200-500 words; Profiles of "Hellraisers," "Visionaries" (short interviews), 250 words. **Pays 80¢/word.**

Fiction: Publishes novel excerpts.

Tips: "We're looking for hard-hitting, investigative reports exposing government cover-ups, corporate malfeasance, scientific myopia, institutional fraud or hypocrisy; thoughtful, provocative articles which challenge the conventional wisdom (on the right or the left) concerning issues of national importance; and timely, people-oriented stories on issues such as the environment, labor, the media, health care, consumer protection, and cultural trends. Send a great, short query and establish your credibility as a reporter. Explain what you plan to cover and how you will proceed with the reporting. The query should convey your approach, tone and style, and should answer the following: What are your specific qualifications to write on this topic? What 'ins' do you have with your sources? Can you provide full documentation so that your story can be fact-checked?"

$ NEW HAVEN ADVOCATE, News & Arts Weekly, New Mass Media Inc., 1 Long Wharf Dr., New Haven CT 06511-5991. (203)789-0010. Fax: (203)787-1418. E-mail: editor@newhavenadvocate.com. Website: http://www.newhavenadvocate.com. **Contact**: Joshua Mamis, editor. **10% freelance written.** Weekly tabloid. "Alternative, investigative, cultural reporting with a strong voice. We like to shake things up." Estab. 1975. Circ. 55,000. Pays on publication. Byline given. Buys on speculation. Buys one-time rights. Editorial lead time 1 month. Submit seasonal material 2 months in advance. Accepts simultaneous submissions. Reports in 1 month.

Nonfiction: Book excerpts, essays, exposé, general interest, humor, interview/profile. **Buys 15-20 mss/year.** Query

with published clips. Length: 750-2,000 words. **Pays $50-150.** Sometimes pays expenses of writers on assignment.
Photos: Freelancers should state availability of photos with submission. Captions, model releases, identification of subjects required. Buys one-time rights.
Tips: "Strong local focus; strong literary voice, controversial, easy-reading, contemporary, etc."

$ $ ON THE ISSUES, The Progressive Woman's Quarterly, Merle Hoffman Enterprises, Ltd., 97-77 Queens Blvd., Suite 1120, Forest Hills NY 33174. Fax: (718)997-1206. E-mail: onissues@echonyc.com. Website: http://www.igc.apc.org/onissues. **Contact**: Jan Goodwin, editor. **90% freelance written.** "Quarterly magazine for 'thinking feminists'—women and men interested in progressive social change, advances in feminist thought, and coverage of politics, society, economics, medicine, relationships, the media and the arts from a range of feminist viewpoints." Estab. 1983. Circ. 18,000. **Pays on acceptance.** Publishes ms an average of 5 months after acceptance. Byline given. Offers 25% kill fee. Buys first North American serial rights or all rights. Editorial lead time 3 months. Accepts simultaneous submissions, if so notified. Reports in 2 months. Sample copy for $3.95. Writer's guidelines free.
Nonfiction: Book excerpts, essays, exposé, general interest, historical/nostalgic, humor, interview/profile, opinion, personal experience, photo feature. **Buys 40 mss/year.** Query with published clips. Length: 75-2,500 words. **Pays $25-400.** Sometimes pays expenses of writers on assignment.
Reprints: Accepts previously published submissions (occasionally). Send tearsheet or photocopy with information about when and where the article previously appeared. Pay varies.
Photos: State availability of photos with submissions. Negotiates payment individually. Captions, identification of subjects required. Buys all rights.
Columns/Departments: Talking Feminist (personal experience), 1,500 words; Book Reviews, 500 words. **Buys 15 mss/year.** Query with published clips. Payment varies.
Tips: "Always looking for investigative, newsworthy pieces. Query first. 'Talking Feminist' can be on any subject: a personal experience or editorial style essay."

ROLLING STONE, Wenner Media Inc., 1290 Avenue of the Americas, New York NY 10104. (212)484-1616. This magazine did not respond to our request for information. Query before submitting.

$ $ SHEPHERD EXPRESS, Alternative Publications, Inc., 1123 N. Water St., Milwaukee WI 53202. (414)276-2222. Fax: (414)276-3312. Website: http://www.shepherd-express.com. **Contact:** Joel McNally, editor. **50% freelance written.** Weekly tabloid covering "news and arts with a progressive news edge and a hip entertainment perspective." Estab. 1982. Circ. 58,000. Pays on publication. Publishes ms an average of 2 weeks after acceptance. Byline given. No kill fee. Buys first, one-time or all rights or makes work-for-hire assignments. Editorial lead time 2 weeks. Submit seasonal material 1 month in advance. Accepts simultaneous submissions. Sample copy for $3.
Nonfiction: Book excerpts, essays, exposé, opinion. **Buys 200 mss/year.** Query with published clips or send complete ms. Length: 900-2,500 words. **Pays $35-300 for assigned articles; $10-200 for unsolicited articles.** Sometimes pays expenses of writers on assignment.
Reprints: Accepts previously published submissions.
Photos: State availability of photos with submissions. Reviews prints. Negotiates payment individually. Captions, model releases, identification of subjects required. Buys one-time rights.
Columns/Departments: Opinions (social trends, politics, from progressive slant), 800-1,200 words; Books Reviewed (new books only: Social trends, environment, politics), 600-1,200 words. **Buys 10 mss/year.** Send complete ms.
Tips: "Include solid analysis with point of view in tight but lively writing. Nothing cute. Do not tell us that something is important, tell us why."

N $ $ THE SOURCE, The Magazine of Hip Hop Music, Culture and Politics, Source Publications, Inc., 215 Park Ave. S., 11th Floor, New York NY 10003. (212)253-3700. Fax: (212)253-9343. **Contact:** Paula T. Renfroe, assistant to the editor. Editor: Selwyn Seyfu Hinds. Managing Editor: Kim Jack Riley. **75% freelance written.** Monthly magazine covering hip hop music. culture and politics. Pays on publication. Byline given. Offers 25% kill fee. Buys first North American serial rights. Editorial lead time 2 months. Sample copy and writer's guidelines free.
Nonfiction: Interview/profile, new product, photo feature, entertainment news. Query with published clips and SASE to the attention of the executive editor. Length: 2,000-4,000 words. **Pays 45¢/word.** Sometimes pays expenses of writers on assignment.
Photos: State availability of photos with submission. Reviews transparencies. Negotiates payment individually. Caption, model releases, identification of subjects required.
Columns/Departments: Tracii McGregor, lifestyle editor. Video Game Review, Car Audio, Book & Film Review (African American); all 300 words. Query with published clips and SASE. **Pays 45¢/word.**
Tips: "Read the magazine. Familiarize yourself with each of the sections, especially the one(s) you want to write for. Please do not call to follow-up on your query. If your idea is not accepted, don't be discouraged. Try us again. Persistence is the key."

$ $ $ SWING MAGAZINE, The Swing Corporation, 342 Madison Ave., Suite 1402, New York NY 10017. (212)490-0525. Fax: (212)490-8073. E-mail: swingmag1@aol.com. Editor: David Lauren. Managing Editor: Lynne Sanford. **Contact**: Megan Liberman, executive editor. **70% freelance written.** Magazine published 10 times/year. "The reader of our magazine is usually 18- to 34-years-old and looking for pertinent, newsworthy information and features

on politics, sports, entertainment and technology that can guide twentysomethings in making decisions." Estab. 1994. Circ. 100,000. **Pays on acceptance**. Publishes ms an average of 3 months after acceptance. Byline given. Offers 25% kill fee. Makes work-for-hire assignments. Editorial lead time 3 months. Submit seasonal material 4 months in advance. Accepts simultaneous submissions. Reports in 3 weeks on queries; 2 months on mss. Writer's guidelines free.
Nonfiction: General interest, interview/profile, personal experience, service pieces on personal finance, careers, health, travel, relationships, technology. Special issues: The Most Powerful Twentysomethings in America (December/January); Love & Relationships (February); Jobs (June); Best Places to Live (July/August). **Buys 40-50 mss/year.** Query with published clips. Length: 1,500-3,500 words. **Pays 50¢-$1/word.** Pays expenses of writers on assignment.
Reprints: Accepts previously published submissions.
Photos: State availability of photos with submission. Reviews contact sheets, transparencies. Negotiates payment individually. Model releases, identification of subjects required. Buys one-time rights.
Columns/Departments: Health, Finance, Travel; all 800 words. **Buys 50 mss/year.** Query with published clips. **Pays 50-75¢/word.**
Tips: "Send specific queries with concrete names and ideas. The more general, the less chance."

UTNE READER, 1624 Harmon Place, Suite 330, Minneapolis MN 55403. Fax: (612)338-6043. E-mail: editor@utne.com. Website: http://www.utne.com. **Contact**: Craig Cox, managing editor. No unsolicited mss.
Reprints: Accepts previously published submissions only. Send tearsheet or photocopy of article or typed ms with rights for sale noted and information about when and where the article previously appeared.
- The *Utne Reader* has been a finalist three times for the National Magazine Award for general excellence.

$ $ $ XSeSS LIVING, CDZeene, ComEnt Media Group, Inc., 3932 Wilshire Blvd., #212, Los Angeles CA 90010. Fax: (213)383-1093. E-mail: popcultmag@aol.com. Website: http://www.allmediadist.com. **Contact**: Sean Perkin, editor. **80% freelance written.** Bimonthly lifestyles publication covering fashion, business, politics, music, entertainment, etc. Estab. 1992. Circ. 30,000. Pays within 2 weeks after publication. Publishes ms an average of 1 month after acceptance. Byline given. Buys one-time rights and makes work-for-hire assignments. Editorial lead time 3 months. Submit seasonal material 4 months in advance. Accepts simultaneous submissions. Sample copy for $12.50. Writer's guidelines provided only upon hiring.
Nonfiction: Exposé, interview/profile, new product, travel. Query. **Pays $50-800.**
Reprints: Send photocopy and information about when and where the article previously appeared. Payment varies.

$ YES! A Journal of Positive Futures, Positive Futures Network, P.O. Box 10818, Bainbridge Island WA 98110. (206)842-0216. Fax: (206)842-5208. E-mail: editors@futurenet.org. Website: http://www.futurenet.org. Editor: Sarah van Gelder. **Contact**: Tracy Rysavy, associate editor. Quarterly magazine emphasizing sustainability and community. "Interested in stories on building a positive future: sustainability, overcoming divisiveness, ethical business practices, etc." Estab. 1996. Circ. 14,000. Pays on publication. Byline given. Buys various rights. Editorial lead time 4 months. Accepts simultaneous submissions. Reports in 3 months on mss; 1 month on queries. Sample copy for $5. Writer's guidelines for #10 SASE.
Nonfiction: Book excerpts, essays, how-to, humor, interview/profile, personal experience, photo feature, technical, environmental. "No negativity or blanket prescriptions for changing the world." Query with published clips. "Please contact us for a detailed call for submission before each issue." Length: 200-3,500 words. Pays writers with 1-year subscription and 2 contributor copies. **May pay $20-50.** Sometimes pays expenses of writers on assignment.
Reprints: Send photocopy of article or typed ms with rights for sale noted and information about when and where the article previously appeared. Pays 100% of amount paid for an original article.
Photos: State availability of photos with submission. Reviews contact sheets, negatives, transparencies and prints. Offers $20-75/photo. Identification of subjects required. Buys one-time rights.
Columns/Departments: Query with published clips. **Pays $20-60.**
Poetry: Avant-garde, free verse, haiku, light verse, traditional. **Buys 2-3 poems/year.** Submit maximum 10 poems.
Tips: "Read and become familiar with the publication's purpose, tone and quality. We are about facilitating the creation of a better world. We are looking for writers who want to participate in that process. *Yes!* is less interested in bemoaning the state of our problems and more interested in highlighting promising solutions."

DETECTIVE & CRIME

Fans of detective stories want to read accounts of actual criminal cases, detective work and espionage. Markets specializing in crime fiction are listed under Mystery publications.

$ $ DETECTIVE CASES, Detective Files Group, Globe Communications Corp., 1350 Sherbrooke St. West, Suite 600, Montreal, Quebec H3G 2T4 Canada. (514)849-7733. **Contact:** Dominick A. Merle, editor-in-chief. Bimonthly magazine. See *Detective Files*.

$ $ DETECTIVE DRAGNET, Detective Files Group, Globe Communications Corp., 1350 Sherbrooke St. West, Suite 600, Montreal, Quebec H3G 2T4 Canada. (514)849-7733. **Contact:** Dominick A. Merle, editor-in-chief. Bimonthly 72-page magazine. See *Detective Files*.

$ $ DETECTIVE FILES, Detective Files Group, Globe Communications Corp., 1350 Sherbrooke St. West, Suite 600, Montreal, Quebec H3G 2T4 Canada. (514)849-7733. **Contact:** Dominick A. Merle, editor-in-chief. **100% freelance written.** Bimonthly magazine featuring "narrative accounts of true murder mysteries leading to arrests and convictions." **Pays on acceptance.** Publishes ms an average of 6 months after acceptance. Byline given. Buys all rights. Reports in 2 weeks on queries; 2 months on mss. Sample copy and writer's guidelines for SASE.
Nonfiction: True crime cases only; no fiction. Query. Length: 3,000-6,000 words. **Pays $250-350.**
Photos: Send photos with submission. Offers no additional payment for photos accepted with ms. Captions, identification of subjects required. Buys all rights.
Tips: "Build suspense and police investigation leading to arrest. No smoking gun or open and shut cases. Neatness, clarity and pace will help you make the sale."

$ $ HEADQUARTERS DETECTIVE, Detective Files Group, Globe Communications Corp., 1350 Sherbrooke St. West, Suite 600, Montreal, Quebec H3G 2T4 Canada. (514)849-7733. **Contact:** Dominick A. Merle, editor-in-chief. Bimonthly magazine; 72 pages. See *Detective Files*.

$ P. I. MAGAZINE, America's Private Investigation Journal, 755 Bronx, Toledo OH 43609. (419)382-0967. Fax: (419)382-0967. E-mail: pimag1@aol.com. Website: http://www.PIMALL.com. **Contact:** Bob Mackowiak, editor/publisher. **75% freelance written.** "Audience includes professional investigators and mystery/private eye fans." Estab. 1988. Circ. 4,000. Pays on publication. Publishes ms an average of 3 months after acceptance. Buys one-time rights. Submit seasonal material 3 months in advance. Accepts simultaneous submissions. Reports in 3 months on queries; 4 months on mss. Sample copy for $6.75.
Nonfiction: Interview/profile, personal experience and accounts of real cases. **Buys 4-10 mss/year.** Send complete ms. Length: 1,000 words and up. **Pays $75 minimum for unsolicited articles.**
Photos: Send photos with submission. May offer additional payment for photos accepted with ms. Model releases, identification of subjects required. Buys one-time rights.
Tips: "The best way to get published in *P.I.* is to write a detailed story about a professional P.I.'s true-life case. No fiction, please. Unsolicited fiction manuscripts will not be returned."

$ $ STARTLING DETECTIVE, Detective Files Group, Globe Communications Corp., 1350 Sherbrooke St. West, Suite 600, Montreal, Quebec H3G 2T4 Canada. (514)849-7733. **Contact:** Dominick A. Merle, editor-in-chief. Bimonthly 72-page magazine. See *Detective Files*.

$ $ TRUE POLICE CASES, Detective Files Group, Globe Communications Corp., 1350 Sherbrooke St. West, Suite 600, Montreal, Quebec H3G 2T4 Canada. (514)849-7733. **Contact:** Dominick A. Merle, editor-in-chief. Bimonthly 72-page magazine. Buys all rights. See *Detective Files*.

DISABILITIES

These magazines are geared toward disabled persons and those who care for or teach them. A knowledge of disabilities and lifestyles is important for writers trying to break in to this field; editors regularly discard material that does not have a realistic focus. Some of these magazines will accept manuscripts only from disabled persons or those with a background in caring for disabled persons.

$ $ ACCENT ON LIVING, P.O. Box 700, Bloomington IL 61702-0700. (309)378-2961. Fax: (309)378-4420. E-mail: acntlvg@aol.com. Website: http://www.blvd.com/accent. **Contact**: Betty Garee, editor. **75% freelance written.** Eager to work with new/unpublished writers. Quarterly magazine for physically disabled persons and rehabilitation professionals. Estab. 1956. Circ. 20,000. Buys first and second (reprint) rights. Byline usually given. Pays on publication. Publishes ms an average of 6 months after acceptance. Reports in 1 month. Sample copy and writer's guidelines $3.50 for #10 SAE with 7 first-class stamps. Writer's guidelines for #10 SASE.
Nonfiction: Articles about new devices that would make a disabled person with limited physical mobility more independent; should include description, availability and photos. Medical breakthroughs for disabled people. Intelligent discussion articles on acceptance of physically disabled persons in normal living situations; topics may be architectural barriers, housing, transportation, educational or job opportunities, organizations, or other areas. How-to articles concerning everyday living, giving specific, helpful information so the reader can carry out the idea himself/herself. News articles about active disabled persons or groups. Good strong interviews. Vacations, accessible places to go, sports, organizations, humorous incidents, self improvement and sexual or personal adjustment—all related to physically handicapped persons. "We are looking for upbeat material." **Buys 50-60 unsolicited mss/year.** Query with SASE. Length: 250-1,000 words. **Pays 10¢/word for published articles** (after editing and/or condensing by staff).
Reprints: Send tearsheet and information about when and where the article previously appeared. Pays 10¢/word.
Photos: Pays $10 minimum for b&w photos purchased with accompanying captions. Amount will depend on quality of photos and subject matter. Pays $50 and up for four-color cover photos. "We need good-quality color or b&w photos (or slides and transparencies)."

Tips: "Ask a friend who is disabled to read your article before sending it to *Accent*. Make sure that he/she understands your major points and the sequence or procedure."

$ $ ACTIVE LIVING, Disability Today Publishing Group, Inc., 132 Main St. E., Suite 1, Grimsby, Ontario L3M 1P1 Canada. (905)309-1639. Fax: (905)309-1640. E-mail: activliv@aol.com. **Contact**: Theresa MacInnis, managing editor. **70% freelance written.** Bimonthly magazine. "*Activeliving* is about how to improve health, fitness and mobility, where to enjoy accessible leisure and travel, and what to look for in new therapeutic, recreational and/or sporting activities for people with a disability." Estab. 1990. Circ. 45,000. Pays on publication. Publishes ms an average of 3 months after acceptance. Byline given. Buys one-time or second serial (reprint) rights. Editorial lead time 3 months. Submit seasonal material 6 months in advance. Sample copy $5.50. Writer's guidelines for #10 SAE and IRC.
Nonfiction: Book excerpts, health and fitness, humor, inspirational, interview/profile, new product, opinion, personal experience, photo feature, recreation, travel. Annual features: O&P feature section (February); Kids (December). **Buys 12 mss/year.** Query with SAE and IRC. Length: 1,000-2,500 words. **Pays $100-400.** Sometimes pays expenses of writers on assignment.
Reprints: Send tearsheet, photocopy or typed ms on disk with rights for sale noted and information about when and where the article previously appeared. Pay negotible.
Photos: Send photos with submission. Reviews 4×6 prints. Offers no additional payment for photos accepted with ms. Model releases and identification of subjects required. Buys one-time rights.
Columns/Departments: Sports (disabled sports), 800 words; Alternative Therapies, 600 words; Destinations (travel), 600 words; Nutrition, 600 words; Take Note (news), include 5-6 items of 200-300 words. Health; Fitness; Getting Started; O&P (orthotics & prosthetics); Ask the Experts; 750 words. **Buys 24 mss/year.** Query. **Pays $50-200.**
Fiction: Occasionally publishes novel excerpts.
Tips: "Provide outline for a series of contributions; identify experience in field of disability. Unsolicited manuscripts and photos will not be returned. No phone queries. Please avoid labeling or use of disparaging language like 'the disabled,' confined, crippled."

$ $ $ $ ARTHRITIS TODAY, Arthritis Foundation. 1330 W. Peachtree St., Atlanta GA 30309. (404)872-7100. Fax: (404)872-9559. E-mail: smorrow@arthritis.org. Website: http://www.arthritis.org. Editor: Cindy T. McDaniel. Managing Editor: Shelly Morrow. Executive Editor: Marcy O'Koon. **Contact**: Michele Taylor, editorial coordinator. **70% freelance written.** Bimonthly magazine about living with arthritis; latest in research/treatment. "*Arthritis Today* is written for the more than 40 million Americans who have arthritis and for the millions of others whose lives are touched by an arthritis-related disease. The editorial content is designed to help the person with arthritis live a more productive, independent and painfree life. The articles are upbeat and provide practical advice, information and inspiration." Estab. 1987. Circ. 600,000. **Pays on acceptance.** Offers 25% kill fee. Buys first North American serial rights but requires unlimited reprint rights in any Arthritis Foundation-affiliated endeavor. Submit seasonal material 6 months in advance. Considers simultaneous submissions. Reports in 6-8 weeks. Sample copy for 9×11 SAE with 4 first-class stamps. Writer's guidelines for #10 SASE.

- Ranked as one of the best markets for freelance writers in *Writer's Yearbook* magazine's annual "Top 100 Markets," January 1998.

Nonfiction: General interest, how-to (tips on any aspect of living with arthritis), service, inspirational, opinion, personal experience, photo feature, technical, nutrition, general health and lifestyle. **Buys 5-10 unsolicited mss/year.** Query with published clips or send complete ms. Length: 750-3,500. **Pays $450-1,800.** Pays expenses of writers on assignment.
Columns/Departments: Research Spotlight (research news about arthritis); LifeStyle (travel, leisure); Well Being (arthritis-specific medical news), 50-400 words. **Buys 10 mss/year.** Query with published clips. **Pays $150-400.**
Tips: "In addition to articles specifically about living with arthritis, we look for articles to appeal to an older audience on subjects such as hobbies, general health, lifestyle, etc."

$ $ ASTHMA MAGAZINE, Strategies For Taking Control, Lifelong Publications, 3 Bridge St., Newton MA 02158. (617)964-4910. Fax: (617)964-8095. E-mail: asthmamag@aol.com. **Contact:** Rachel Butler, editor-in-chief. **50% freelance written.** Bimonthly. "*Asthma Magazine* offers unbiased education for people with asthma. We are an independent publication (not sponsored by any drug company) and we provide indepth education to help the asthmatic manage his/her disease and live an active and healthy life." Estab. 1995. Circ. 30,000. Pays on publication. Publishes ms an average of 1 month after acceptance. Byline given. Offers 25% kill fee. Buys all rights. Editorial lead time 6 weeks. Submit seasonal material 3 months in advance. Sample copy and writer's guidelines free.
Nonfiction: How-to, humor, inspirational, interview/profile, new product (usually a news blurb, not a full article), personal experience, technical, travel—all related to the subject matter. **Buys 12-15 mss/year.** Query with published clips. Length: 800-1,200 words. **Pays $200-500.**
Photos: State availability of photos with submission. Reviews prints. Offers no additional payment for photos accepted with ms. Buys all rights.
Columns/Departments: Hear My Story (personal experience of a person with asthma or article about someone who has accomplished something significant despite their asthma, or someone in the asthma/medical field); 900 words. Query with published clips. **Pays $250.**
Tips: "We look for writers who have had experience writing for the medical community for either clinicians or patients. Writing must be clear, concise and easy to understand (7th-9th grade reading level), as well as thoroughly researched and medically accurate."

$ $ CAREERS & the disABLED, Equal Opportunity Publications, 1160 E. Jericho Turnpike, Suite 200, Huntington NY 11743. (516)421-9421. Fax: (516)421-0359. E-mail: info@aol.com. Website: http://www.eop.com. **Contact**: James Schneider, editor. **60% freelance written.** Quarterly magazine "offers role-model profiles and career guidance articles geared toward disabled college students and professionals and promotes personal and professional growth." Pays on publication. Publishes ms an average of 6 months after acceptance. Estab. 1967. Circ. 10,000. Byline given. Buys first North American serial rights. Editorial lead time 6 months. Submit seasonal material 6 months in advance. Accepts simultaneous submissions. Reports in 3 weeks. Sample copy and writer's guidelines for 9×12 SAE with 5 first-class stamps.
Nonfiction: Essays, general interest, how-to, interview/profile, new product, opinion, personal experience. **Buys 30 mss/year.** Query. Length: 1,000-2,500 words. **Pays 10¢/word, $350 maximum.** Sometimes pays the expenses of writers on assignment.
Reprints: Send information about when and where the article previously appeared.
Photos: State availability of or send photos with submission. Reviews transparencies, prints. Offers $15-50/photo. Captions, identification of subjects required.. Buys one-time rights.
Tips: "Be as targeted as possible. Role model profiles and specific career guidance strategies that offer advice to disabled college students are most needed."

$ $ DIABETES SELF-MANAGEMENT, R.A. Rapaport Publishing, Inc., 150 W. 22nd St., Suite 800, New York NY 10011-2421. (212)989-0200. Fax: (212)989-4786. **Contact**: James Hazlett, editor-in-chief. **20% freelance written.** Bimonthly. "We publish how-to health care articles for motivated, intelligent readers who have diabetes and who are actively involved in their own health care management. All articles must have immediate application to their daily living." Estab. 1983. Circ. 330,000. Pays on publication. Publishes ms an average of 3 months after acceptance. Byline given. Offers 20% kill fee. Buys all rights. Submit seasonal material 6 months in advance. Reports in 6 weeks. Sample copy for $3.50 and 9×12 SAE with 6 first-class stamps. Writer's guidelines for #10 SASE.
Nonfiction: How-to (exercise, nutrition, diabetes self-care, product surveys), technical (reviews of products available, foods sold by brand name, pharmacology), travel (considerations and prep for people with diabetes). **Buys 10-12 mss/year.** Query with published clips. Length: 1,500-2,500 words. **Pays $400-600 for assigned articles; $200-600 for unsolicited articles.**
Tips: "The rule of thumb for any article we publish is that it must be clear, concise, useful, and instructive, and it must have immediate application to the lives of our readers. If your query is accepted, expect heavy editorial supervision."

$ DIALOGUE, Blindskills, Inc., P.O. Box 5181, Salem OR 97301-0181. (800)860-4224; (503)581-4224. Fax: (503)581-0178. E-mail: blindskl@teleport.com. Website: http://www.teleport.com/blindskl. **Contact:** Carol M. McCarl, editor. **85% freelance written.** Quarterly journal covering the visually impaired. Estab. 1961. Circ. 1,100. Pays on publication. Publishes ms an average of 8 months after acceptance. Byline given. Buys first rights. Editorial lead time 3 months. Submit seasonal material 3 months in advance. Sample copy $6. Writer's guidelines free.
Nonfiction: Essays, general interest, historical/nostalgic, how-to, humor, interview/profile, new product, personal experience. Prefer material by visually impaired writers. No controversial, explicit sex or religious or political topics. **Buys 20 mss/year.** Send complete ms. Length: 500-1,200 words. **Pays $10-35 for assigned articles; $10-25 for unsolicited articles.**
Reprints: Send tearsheet or photocopy of article or short story or typed ms with rights for sale noted and information about when and where the article or story previously appeared.
Columns/Departments: All material should be relative to blind and visually impaired readers. Careers, 1,000 words; What's New & Where to Get It (resources, new product), 2,500 words; What Do You Do When . . . ? (dealing with sight loss), 1,000 words. **Buys 40 mss/year.** Send complete ms. **Pays $10-25.**
Fiction: Adventure, humorous, science fiction, slice-of-life vignettes, first person experiences. Prefer material by visually impaired writers. No controversial, explicit sex. No religious or political. **Buys 6-8 mss/year.** Query with complete ms. Length: 800-1,200 words. **Pays $15-25.**
Poetry: Free verse, light verse, traditional. Prefer material by visually impaired writers. No controversial, explicit sex or religious or political topics. **Buys 15-20 poems/year.** Submit maximum 5 poems. Length: 20 lines maximum. **Pays $10-15.**
Fillers: Anecdotes, facts, newsbreaks, short humor. Length: 50-150 words. No payment.
Tips: Send SASE for free writers guidelines, $6 for sample in Braille, cassette or large print.

$ $ HEARING HEALTH, Voice International Publications, Inc., P.O. Drawer V, Ingleside TX 78362-0500. Fax: (512)776-3278. **Contact**: Paula Bonillas, editor. **20% freelance written.** Bimonthly magazine covering issues and concerns pertaining to hearing and hearing loss. Estab. 1984. Circ. 20,000. Pays on publication. Byline given. Buys one-time rights. Editorial lead time 2 months. Submit seasonal material 4 months in advance. Accepts simultaneous submissions. Reports in 6 weeks on queries; 2 months on mss. Sample copy for $2. Writer's guidelines for #10 SASE.
Nonfiction: Books excerpts, essays, exposé, general interest, historical/nostalgic, humor, inspirational, interview/profile, new product, opinion, personal experience, photo feature, technical, travel. No self-pitying over loss of hearing. Query with published clips. Length: 500-2,000 words. **Pays $75-200.** Sometimes pays expenses of writers on assignment.
Reprints: Accepts previously published submissions, if so noted.
Photos: State availability of photos with submission. Reviews contact sheets. Negotiates payment individually. Captions, model releases, identification of subjects required. Buys one-time rights.

Columns/Departments: Kidink (written by kids with hearing loss), 300 words; People (shares stories of successful, everyday people who have loss of hearing), 300-400 words. **Buys 2 mss/year.** Query with published clips.
Fiction: Fantasy, historical, humorous, novel excerpts, science fiction. **Buys 2 mss/year.** Query with published clips. Length: 400-1,500 words.
Poetry: Avant-garde, free verse, light verse, traditional. **Buys 2/year.** Submit 2 poems max. Length: 4-50 lines.
Fillers: Anecdotes, facts, gags to be illustrated, newsbreaks, short humor. **Buys 6/year.** Length: 25-1,500 words.
Tips: "We look for fresh stories, usually factual but occasionally fictitious, about coping with hearing loss. A positive attitude is a must for *Hearing Health.* Unless one has some experience with deafness or hearing loss—whether their own or a loved one's—it's very difficult to 'break in' to our publication. Experience brings about the empathy and understanding—the sensitivity—and the freedom to write humorously about any handicap or disability."

$ KALEIDOSCOPE: International Magazine of Literature, Fine Arts, and Disability, Kaleidoscope Press, 701 S. Main St., Akron OH 44311-1019. (330)762-9755. Fax: (330)762-0912. **Contact**: Dr. Darshan Perusek, editor-in-chief. Subscribers include individuals, agencies and organizations that assist people with disabilities and many university and public libraries. Estab. 1979. Circ. 1,500. **75% freelance written.** Semiannual. Byline given. Rights return to author upon publication. Eager to work with new/unpublished writers; appreciates work by established writers as well. Especially interested in work by writers with a disability, but features writers both with and without disabilities. "Writers without a disability must limit themselves to our focus, while those with a disability may explore any topic (although we prefer original perspectives about experiences with disability)." Reports in 3 weeks, acceptance or rejection may take 6 months. Sample copy for $4 prepaid. Guidelines free for SASE.
Nonfiction: Personal experience essays, book reviews and articles related to disability. Special issues: Disability: Parents and Children (July, deadline March); The Created Environment (January, deadline August). Submit photocopies with SASE for return of work. Please type submissions. All submissions should be accompanied by an autobiographical sketch. May include art or photos that enhance works, prefer b&w with high contrast. **Publishes 8-14 mss/year.** Maximum 5,000 words. **Pays $10-125 plus 2 copies.**
Reprints: Send typed ms with rights for sale noted and information about when and where the article previously appeared.
Fiction: Short stories, novel excerpts. Traditional and experimental styles. Works should explore experiences with disability. Use people-first language. Maximum 5,000 words.
Poetry: Limit 5 poems/submission. **Publishes 12-20 poems/year.** Do not get caught up in rhyme scheme. High quality with strong imagery and evocative language. Reviews any style.
Tips: "Inquire about future themes of upcoming issues. Sample copy very helpful. Works should not use stereotyping, patronizing or offending language about disability. We seek fresh imagery and thought-provoking language."

$ MAINSTREAM, Magazine of the Able-Disabled, Exploding Myths, Inc., 2973 Beech St., San Diego CA 92102. (619)234-3138. Fax: (619)234-3155. E-mail: editor@mainstream-mag.com. Website: http://www.mainstream-mag.com. Publisher: Cyndi Jones. **Contact:** William Stothers, editor. **100% freelance written.** Eager to develop writers who have a disability. Magazine published 10 times/year (monthly except January and June) covering disability-related topics, written for active and upscale disabled consumers. Estab. 1975. Circ. 24,500. Pays on publication. Publishes ms an average of 3 months after acceptance. Byline given. Buys all rights. Submit seasonal material 4 months in advance. Reports in 4 months. Sample copy for $5, or 9×12 SAE and $4 with 6 first-class stamps. Guidelines for #10 SASE.
Nonfiction: Book excerpts, exposé, how-to (daily independent living tips), humor, interview/profile, personal experience (dealing with problems/solutions), photo feature, technology, computers, travel, politics and legislation. "All must be disability-related, directed to disabled consumers. No articles on 'my favorite disabled character,' 'my most inspirational disabled person,' 'poster child stories.' " **Buys 65 mss/year.** Query by mail or e-mail, with or without published clips or send complete ms. Length: 8-12 pages. **Pays $100-150.** May pay subscription if writer requests.
Photos: State availability of photos with submission. Reviews contact sheets, 1½×¾ transparencies and 5×7 or larger prints. Offers $20-25/b&w photo. Captions, identification of subjects required. Buys all rights.
Columns/Departments: "We are looking for disability rights cartoons."
Tips: "It seems that politics and disability are becoming more important. Please include your phone number on cover page. We accept 5.25 or 3.5 floppy disks—ASCII, Wordperfect, IBM."

$ SILENT NEWS, World's Most Popular Newspaper of the Deaf and Hard of Hearing People, Silent News, Inc., 133 Gaither Dr., Suite E, Mt. Laurel NJ 08054-1710. (609)802-1977 (voice) or (609)802-1978 (TTY). Fax: (609)802-1979. E-mail: silentnews@aol.com. **Contact**: Editorial staff. **50% freelance written.** Monthly newspaper covering news of deaf, hard of hearing and deaf-blind concerns, the "World's Most Popular Newspaper of the Deaf and Hard of Hearing." Estab. 1969. Circ. 15,000. Pays on publication. Byline given. Editorial lead time 2 months. Submit seasonal material 3 months in advance. Accepts simultaneous submissions. Reports in 2 weeks on queries; 2 months on mss.
Nonfiction: General interest, historical/nostalgic, humor, inspirational, interview/profile, new product, opinion, personal experience, photo feature, religious, technical, travel. All articles must concern deaf and hard of hearing or deaf-blind people. Special issues: Deaf Awareness (September); Holiday Shoppers Guide (November); Assistive Technology (March); Hard of Hearing Issues (May). **Buys 60 mss/year.** Query with published clips. Length: 100-500 words. **Pays $50.** Sometimes pays expenses of writers on assignment.
Reprints: Accepts previously published submissions.

Photos: Send photos with submission. Reviews negatives, 5×7 transparencies and prints. Negotiates payment individually. Identification of subjects required. Buys all rights.
Columns/Departments: National News, International News (both regarding hard of hearing and deaf); Sports (for the blind); all 500 words. **Buys 60 mss/year.** Query with published clips.
Fiction: "Presently we don't use fiction, but we would be interested in reviewing subject-appropriate material." Query.
Poetry: Light verse. "Nothing too deep!" **Buys 12 poems/year.** Submit maximum 2 poems. Length: 10-20 lines.
Fillers: Anecdotes, facts, gags to be illustrated, newsbreaks, short humor. **Buys 100/year.** Length: 50-100 words.
Tips: "Writers must have understanding of issues confronting deaf, hard of hearing, and deaf-blind people."

ENTERTAINMENT

This category's publications cover live, filmed or videotaped entertainment, including home video, TV, dance, theater and adult entertainment. In addition to celebrity interviews, most publications want solid reporting on trends and upcoming productions. Magazines in the Contemporary Culture and General Interest sections also use articles on entertainment. For those publications with an emphasis on music and musicians, see the Music section.

N $ $ **ANGLOFILE, British Entertainment & Pop Culture**, The Goody Press, P.O. Box 33515, Decatur GA 30033. (404)633-5587. Fax: (404)321-3109. Contact: William P. King, editor. Managing Editor: Leslie T. King. **15% freelance written.** Monthly newsletter. "News and interviews on British entertainment, past and present, from an American point of view." Circ. 3,000. Pays on publication. Publishes ms an average of 6 months after acceptance. Byline given. Buys all rights. Reports in 2 months. Free sample copy.
Nonfiction: Justin Stonehouse articles editor. Book excerpts, essays, historical/nostalgic, interview/profile, opinion, personal experience, photo feature, and travel. "No articles written for general audience." **Buys 5 mss/year.** Send complete ms. Length: 1,500 words. **Pays $25-250.**
Reprints: Send tearsheet or photocopy of story with information about when and where the article previously appeared. Payment negotiable.
Photos: Send photos with submission. Reviews prints. Offers $10-25/photo. Identification of subjects required. Buys all rights.

$ **CINEASTE, America's Leading Magazine on the Art and Politics of the Cinema**, Cineaste Publishers, Inc., 200 Park Ave. S., #1601, New York NY 10003. Phone/fax: (212)982-1241. E-mail: cineaste@cineaste.com. **Contact**: Gary Crowdus, editor. **30% freelance written.** Quarterly magazine covering motion pictures with an emphasis on social and political perspective on cinema. Estab. 1967. Circ. 10,000. Pays on publication. Publishes ms an average of 4 months after acceptance. Byline given. Offers 50% kill fee. Buys first North American serial rights. Editorial lead time 3 months. Submit seasonal material 4 months in advance. Reports in 1 month. Sample copy $5. Writer's guidelines for #10 SASE.
Nonfiction: Essays, historical/nostalgic, humor, interview/profile, opinion. **Buys 20-30 mss/year.** Query with published clips. Length: 2,000-5,000 words. **Pays $30-100.** Pays in contributor copies at author's request.
Photos: State availability of photos with submission. Reviews transparencies, 8×10 prints. Offers no additional payment for photos accepted with ms. Identification of subjects required. Buys one-time rights.
Columns/Departments: Homevideo (topics of general interest or a related group of films); A Second Look (new interpretation of a film classic or a reevaluation of an unjustly neglected release of more recent vintage); Lost and Found (film that may or may not be released or otherwise seen in the US but which is important enough to be brought to the attention of our readers); Festivals (film festivals of particular political importance); all 1,000-1,500 words. Query with published clips. **Pays $50 minimum.**

CINEFANTASTIQUE MAGAZINE, The Review of Horror, Fantasy and Science Fiction Films, P.O. Box 270, Oak Park IL 60303. (708)366-5566. Fax: (708)366-1441. **Contact:** Frederick S. Clarke, editor. **100% freelance written.** Willing to work with new/unpublished writers. Bimonthly magazine covering horror, fantasy and science fiction films. Estab. 1970. Circ. 30,000. Pays on publication. Publishes ms an average of 6 months after acceptance. Byline given. Buys all magazine rights. Reports in 2 months or longer. Sample copy for $7 and 9×12 SAE.
Nonfiction: Historical/nostalgic (retrospects of film classics); interview/profile (film personalities); new product (new film projects); opinion (film reviews, critical essays); technical (how films are made). **Buys 100-125 mss/year.** Query with published clips and SASE. "Enclose SASE if you want your manuscript back." Length: 1,000-10,000 words.
Photos: State availability of photos with query letter or ms.
Tips: "Study the magazine to see the kinds of stories we publish. Develop original story suggestions; develop access to film industry personnel; submit reviews that show a perceptive point of view."

$ $ $ **COUNTRY AMERICA**, Meredith Corporation, 1716 Locust, Des Moines IA 50309-3023. (515)284-3787. Fax: (515)284-3035. Editor: Richard Krumme. **Contact:** Bill Eftink, managing editor. Bimonthly magazine covering country entertainment/lifestyle. Estab. 1989. Circ. 900,000. **Pays on acceptance.** Buys all rights (lifetime). Submit seasonal material 8 months or more in advance. Reports in 3 months. Guidelines for #10 SASE.

Nonfiction: Food, general interest, historical/nostalgic, interview/profile (country music entertainers), photo feature, travel. Special issues: Christmas, travel, country music. **Buys 130 mss/year.** Query. **Pays $100-1,000.** Sometimes pays expenses of writers on assignment.
Photos: State availability of photos with submission. Reviews contact sheets, negatives, 35mm transparencies. Offers $50-500/photo. Captions, identification of subjects required. Buys all rights.
Tips: "Think visually. Our publication will be light on text and heavy on photos. Think country. Our publication is meant to be read by every member of the family interested in country music. We are a service-oriented publication; please stress how-to sidebars and include addresses and phone numbers to help readers find out more."

$ DANCE INTERNATIONAL, Vancouver Ballet Society, 1415 Barclay St., Vancouver, British Columbia V6G 1J6 Canada. (604)681-1525. Fax: (604)681-7732. Editor: Maureen Riches. **Contact**: Tamar Satov, contributing editor. **100% freelance written.** Quarterly magazine covering dance arts. "Articles and reviews on current activities in world dance, with occasional historical essays; reviews of dance films, video and books." Estab. 1973. Circ. 3,500. Pays on publication. Publishes ms an average of 3 months after acceptance. Byline given. Offers 50% kill fee. Buys one-time rights. Editorial lead time 3 months. Submit seasonal material 6 weeks in advance. Reports in 2 weeks on queries; 1 month on mss. Sample copy and writer's guidelines free.
Nonfiction: Book excerpts, essays, historical/nostalgic, interview/profile, personal experience, photo feature. **Buys 100 mss/year.** Query. Length: 1,200-2,200 words. **Pays $40-150.**
Reprints: Accepts previously published submissions.
Photos: Send photos with submission. Reviews prints. Offers no additional payment for photos accepted with ms. Identification of subjects required.
Columns/Departments: Kaija Pepper, copy editor. Dance Bookshelf (recent books reviewed), 1,200 words; Regional Reports (events in each region), 1,200-2,000 words. **Buys 100 mss/year.** Query. **Pays $60-70.**
Tips: "Send résumé and samples of recent writings."

$ $ DRAMATICS MAGAZINE, Educational Theatre Association, 3368 Central Pkwy., Cincinnati OH 45225-2392. (513)559-1996. Fax: (513)559-0012. E-mail: pubs@one.net. Website: http://www.etassoc.org. **Contact:** Donald Corathers, editor-in-chief. **70% freelance written.** Works with small number of new/unpublished writers. For theater arts students, teachers and others interested in theater arts education. Magazine published monthly, September-May. Estab. 1929. Circ. 38,000. **Pays on acceptance.** Publishes ms an average of 3 months after acceptance. Buys first North American serial rights. Byline given. Submit seasonal material 3 months in advance. Accepts simultaneous submissions. Reports in 3 months; longer on unsolicited mss. Sample copy for 9×12 SAE with 5 first-class stamps. Guidelines free.
Nonfiction: How-to (technical theater, directing, acting, etc.), informational, interview, photo feature, humorous, profile, technical. **Buys 30 mss/year.** Submit complete ms. Length: 750-3,000 words. **Pays $50-300.** Rarely pays expenses of writers on assignment.
Reprints: Send tearsheet or photocopy of article or play, or typed ms with rights for sale noted and information about when and where the article previously appeared. Pays 75% of amount paid for an original article.
Photos: Purchased with accompanying ms. Uses b&w photos and transparencies. Query. Total purchase price for ms usually includes payment for photos.
Fiction: Drama (one-act and full-length plays). "No plays for children, Christmas plays or plays written with no attention paid to the conventions of theater." Prefers unpublished scripts that have been produced at least once. **Buys 5-9 mss/year.** Send complete ms. **Pays $100-400.**
Tips: "The best way to break in is to know our audience—drama students, teachers and others interested in theater—and to write for them. Writers who have some practical experience in theater, especially in technical areas, have a leg-up here, but we'll work with anybody who has a good idea. Some freelancers have become regular contributors. Others ignore style suggestions included in our writer's guidelines."

$ EAST END LIGHTS, The Quarterly Magazine for Elton John Fans ,Voice Communications Corp., P.O. Box 760, New Baltimore MI 48047. (810)949-7900. Fax: (810)949-2217. E-mail: eastendlts@aol.com. **Contact**: Tom Stanton, editor. **90% freelance written.** Quarterly magazine covering Elton John. "In one way or another, a story must relate to Elton John, his activities or associates (past and present). We appeal to discriminating Elton fans. No gushing fanzine material. No current concert reviews." Estab. 1990. Circ. 1,700. Pays 3 weeks after publication. Publishes ms an average of 3 months after acceptance. Byline given. Offers 100% kill fee. Buys first rights and second serial (reprint) rights. Submit seasonal material 3 months in advance. Reports in 2 months. Sample copy $2.
Nonfiction: Book excerpts, essays, exposé, general interest, historical/nostalgic, humor and interview/profile. **Buys 20 mss/year.** Query with or without published clips or send complete ms. Length: 400-1,000 words. **Pays $50-200 for assigned articles; $40-150 for unsolicited articles.** Pays with contributor copies only if the writer requests.
Reprints: Send tearsheet or photocopy of article or typed ms with rights for sale noted and information about when and where the article previously appeared. Pays 50% of amount paid for an original article.
Photos: State availability of photos with submission. Reviews negatives and 5×7 prints. Offers $40-75/photo. Buys one-time rights and all rights.
Columns/Departments: Clippings (non-wire references to Elton John in other publications), maximum 200 words. **Buys 12 mss/year.** Send complete ms. Length: 50-200 words. **Pays $10-20.**
Tips: "Approach with a well-thought-out story idea. We'll provide direction. All areas equally open. We prefer inter-

views with Elton-related personalities—past or present. We are particularly interested in music/memorabilia collecting of Elton material."

$ $ $ EMMY MAGAZINE, Academy of Television Arts & Sciences, 5220 Lankershim Blvd., North Hollywood CA 91601-3109. (818)754-2800. Fax: (818)761-2827. E-mail: emmymag@emmys.org. Website: http://www.emmys.org/. Editor/Publisher: Hank Rieger. **Contact**: Gail Polevoi, managing editor. **90% freelance written.** Prefers to work with published established writers. Bimonthly magazine on television for TV professionals and enthusiasts. Circ. 12,000. Pays on publication or within 6 months. Publishes ms an average of 4 months after acceptance. Byline given. Offers 25% kill fee. Buys first North American serial rights. Reports in 1 month. Sample copy for 9×12 SAE with 6 first-class stamps.

Nonfiction: Articles on contemporary issues, trends, and VIPs (especially those behind the scenes) in broadcast and cable TV; programming and new technology. "We require TV industry expertise and clear, lively writing." Query with published clips. Length: 2,000 words. **Pay $800-1,000.** Pays some expenses of writers on assignment.

Columns/Departments: Most written by regular contributors, but newcomers can break into CloseUps or The Industry. Query with published clips. Length: 500-1,500 words, depending on department. **Pays $250-750.**

Tips: "Please review recent issues before querying us. Query in writing with published, television-related clips. No fanzine, academic or nostalgic approaches, please."

$ $ $ $ ENTERTAINMENT WEEKLY, Time Inc. Magazine Co., 1675 Broadway, New York NY 10016. (212)522-5600. Fax: (212)522-0074. President: John Squires. **Contact**: Jeannie Park, assistant managing editor. "*Entertainment Weekly* provides both a critical guide to popular culture and an informative inside look at the people, products, companies and ideas that shape the increasingly influential world of entertainment." Estab. 1990. Circ. 1,350,000. Pays on publication. Byline usually given. Offers 50% kill fee. Buys all rights. Accepts simultaneous submissions.

Nonfiction: Buys fewer than 5 mss/year. Query with published clips. Length: 1,500-3,000 words. **Pays $1-2/word.**

Columns/Departments: Length: 500-1,000 words. **Buys 10 mss/year.** Query with published clips. **Pays $1-2/word.**

Tips: "*EW* editors welcome story suggestions covering almost any aspect of entertainment news, with emphasis on the word 'news.' We are interested in news scoops about entertainment people and products; inside stories about the making of movies, TV, albums, etc.; entertainment trends; and entertainment-related or celebrity anecdotes (with quotes). We are generally not interested in ideas for celebrity profiles or other obvious entertainment-related stories. An *EW* editor's 'dream' article would be one that breaks news and makes news; is thoroughly researched and reported, with quotes from industry players; is written in a lively and accessible manner; and would never have been thought of by one of our own staffers. Writers wishing to work for *EW* must grasp our 'style' of approach, reporting, and writing. The best preparation for querying *EW* is to read it closely."

$ $ FANGORIA: Horror in Entertainment, Starlog Communications, Inc., 475 Park Ave. S., 8th Floor, New York NY 10016. (212)689-2830. Fax: (212)889-7933. **Contact:** Anthony Timpone, editor. **95% freelance written.** Works with a small number of new/unpublished writers each year. Magazine published 10 times/year covering horror films, TV projects, comics, videos and literature and those who create them. "We emphasize the personalities and behind-the-scenes angles of horror filmmaking." Estab. 1979. Pays on publication. Publishes ms an average of 3 months after acceptance. Byline given. Buys all rights. Submit seasonal material 4 months in advance. Reports in 6 weeks. "We provide an assignment sheet (deadlines, info) to writers, thus authorizing queried stories that we're buying." Sample copy for $6 and 10×13 SAE with 4 first-class stamps. Writer's guidelines for #10 SASE.

- *Fangoria* is looking for more articles on independent filmmakers and better-known horror novelists.

Nonfiction: Book excerpts; interview/profile of movie directors, makeup FX artists, screenwriters, producers, actors, noted horror/thriller novelists and others—with genre credits; special FX and special makeup FX how-it-was-dones (on filmmaking only). Occasional "think" pieces, opinion pieces, reviews, or sub-theme overviews by industry professionals. **Buys 100 mss/year.** Query by letter (never by phone) with ideas and published clips. Length: 1,000-3,500 words. **Pays $100-250.** Rarely pays expenses of writers on assignment. Avoids most articles on science fiction films—see listing for sister magazine *Starlog* in *Writer's Market* Science Fiction consumer magazine section.

Photos: State availability of photos. Reviews b&w and color prints and transparencies. "No separate payment for photos provided by film studios." Captions, identification of subjects required. Photo credit given.

Columns/Departments: Monster Invasion (exclusive, early information about new film productions; also mini-interviews with filmmakers and novelists). Query with published clips. Length: 300-500 words. **Pays $45-75.**

- *Fangoria* emphasizes that it does not publish fiction or poetry.

Tips: "Other than recommending that you study one or several copies of *Fangoria*, we can only describe it as a horror film magazine consisting primarily of interviews with technicians and filmmakers in the field. Be sure to stress the interview subjects' words—not your own opinions as much. We're very interested in small, independent filmmakers working outside of Hollywood. These people are usually more accessible to writers, and more cooperative. *Fangoria* is also sort of a *de facto* bible for youngsters interested in movie makeup careers and for young filmmakers. We are devoted only to *reel* horrors—the fakery of films, the imagery of the horror fiction of a Stephen King or a Clive Barker—*we do not* want nor would we *ever* publish articles on real-life horrors, murders, etc. A writer must *like* and *enjoy* horror films and horror fiction to work for us. If the photos in *Fangoria* disgust you, if the sight of (*stage*) blood repels you, if you feel 'superior' to horror (and its fans), you aren't a writer for us and we certainly aren't the market for you. We love giving new writers their *first* chance to break into print in a national magazine. We are currently looking for Vancouver-, Arizona- and Las Vegas-based correspondents."

$ $ FILM COMMENT, Film Society of Lincoln Center, 70 Lincoln Center Plaza, New York NY 10023. (212)875-5610. Fax: (212)875-5636. E-mail: rtjfc@aol.com. **Contact**: Richard T. Jameson, editor. **100% freelance written.** Bimonthly magazine covering film criticism and film history, "authoritative, personal writing (not journalism) reflecting experience of and involvement with film as an art form." Estab. 1962. Circ. 30,000. Pays on publication. Publishes ms an average of 2 months after acceptance. Byline given. Offers 50% kill fee (assigned articles only). Editorial lead time 6 weeks. Accepts simultaneous submissions. Reports in 2 weeks. Guidelines free.

Nonfiction: Essays, historical, interview, opinion. **Buys 100 mss/year.** Send complete ms. "We respond to queries, but rarely *assign* a writer we don't know." Length: 800-8,000 words. "We don't use a separate pay scale for solicited or unsolicited. **There is no fixed rate, but roughly based on 3 words/$1.**"

Photos: State availability of photos. No additional payment for photos accepted with ms. Buys one-time rights.

Tips: "We are more or less impervious to 'hooks,' don't worry a whole lot about 'who's hot who's not,' or tying in with next fall's surefire big hit (we think people should write about films they've seen, not films that haven't even been finished). We appreciate good writing (writing, not journalism) on subjects in which the writer has some personal investment and about which he or she has something noteworthy to say. Demonstrate ability and inclination to write *FC*-worthy articles. We read and consider everything we get, and we do print unknowns and first-timers. Probably the writer with a shorter submission (1,000-2,000 words) has a better chance than with an epic article that would fill half the issue."

N $ $ FILM THREAT, "Hollywood's Indie Voice," Gore Group Publications, 5042 Wilshire Blvd., Suite 150, Los Angeles CA 90036. E-mail: input@filmthreat.com. Editor: Chris Gore. **Contact**: F. Knowles, contributing editor. **50% freelance written.** Bimonthly magazine covering film. Estab. 1985. Circ. 100,000. Pays 30 days after publication. Publishes ms an average of 6 months after acceptance. Byline given. Buys all rights. Editorial lead time 6 months. Submit seasonal material 6 months in advance. Accepts simultaneous submissions. Reports in 1 month on queries; 2 months on mss. Sample copy free.

Nonfiction: Book excerpts, essays, exposé, how-to, interview/profile, opinion, personal experience, photo feature, technical. Special issues: film festivals, film schools. **Buys 15-20 mss/year.** Query with published clips. Length: 1,000-6,000 words. **Pays 10¢/word.** Sometimes pays expenses of writers on assignment.

Photos: State availability of photos with submission. Reviews contact sheets. Offers no additional payment for photos accepted with ms. Captions, model releases and identification of subjects required. Buys one-time rights.

$ $ GLOBE, A Globe Communications Corp. Publication, 5401 NW Broken Sound Blvd., Boca Raton FL 33487. (561)997-7733. This magazine did not respond to our request for information. Query before submitting.

$ $ $ $ HOME THEATER, Curt Co./Freedom Group, 29160 Heathercliff Rd., Malibu CA 90265. (310)589-3100. Fax: (310)589-3131. E-mail: peterb@curtco.com. Website: http://www.hometheatermag.com. **Contact:** Peter Barry, editorial director. Managing Editor: Monica James. **30% freelance written.** Monthly magazine covering audio/video hardware and software. Estab. 1994. Circ. 100,000. Pays on publication. Publishes ms an average of 1 month after acceptance. Byline given. Buys first North American serial, second serial and electronic rights. Editorial lead time 3 months. Reports in 2 months. Sample copy for $4.95.

Nonfiction: Interview/profile, new product, technical, general interest. Publishes quarterly buyer's guides. **Buys 50 mss/year.** Query with published clips. Length: 150-2,500 words. **Pays $100-1,000.** Sometimes pays expenses of writers on assignment.

Photos: State availability of photos with submission. Reviews contact sheets, negatives, transparencies, prints. Negotiates payment individually. Captions required. Buys all rights.

Columns/Departments: Tech Talk, 1,000 words. **Buys 12 mss/year.** Query. **Pays $500-1,000.**

Tips: "You must be highly experienced with audio and/or video gear or particularly knowledgeable about relevant new technologies, and preferably a published writer."

$ $ KPBS ON AIR MAGAZINE, San Diego's Guide to Public Broadcasting, KPBS Radio/TV, 5200 Campanile Dr., San Diego CA 92182-5400. (619)594-3766. Fax: (619)265-6417. **Contact**: Michael Good, editor. **15% freelance written.** Monthly magazine on public broadcasting programming and San Diego arts. "Our readers are very intelligent, sophisticated and rather mature. Your writing should be, too." Estab. 1970. Circ. 63,000. Pays on publication. Publishes ms an average of 1 month after acceptance. Byline given. Offers 50% kill fee. Not copyrighted. Buys first North American serial rights. Submit seasonal material 3 months in advance. Reports in 3 months. Sample copy for 9×12 SAE with 4 first-class stamps.

Nonfiction: Interview/profile of PBS personalities and/or artists performing in San Diego, opinion, profiles of public TV and radio personalities, backgrounds on upcoming programs. Nothing over 1,500 words. **Buys 60 mss/year.** Query with published clips. Length: 300-1,500 words. **Pays 20¢/word, 25¢/word if the article is received via modem or computer disk.** Sometimes pays expenses of writers on assignment.

Reprints: Rarely accepts reprints of previously published submissions. Send tearsheet or typed ms with rights for sale noted and information about when and where the article previously appeared. Pays 25¢/word.

Photos: State availability of photos with submission. Reviews transparencies, 5×7 prints. Offers $30-300/photo. Identification of subjects required. Buys one-time rights.

Columns/Departments: On the Town (upcoming arts events in San Diego), 800 words; Short Takes (backgrounds on public TV shows), 500 words; Radio Notes (backgrounders on public radio shows), 500 words. **Buys 35 mss/year.**

Query with or without published clips. **Pays 20¢/word; 25¢/word if the article is received via modem or disk.**
Tips: "Feature stories for national writers are most open to freelancers. Arts stories for San Diego writers are most open. Read the magazine, then talk to me."

N $ $ **MAD RHYTHMS**, College Entertainment Communications, 222 W. 21st St., Suite F-125, Norfolk VA 23517. Fax: (757)558-0762. E-mail: madrhythms@aol.com. **Contact:** Yasmin Shiraz, editor-in-chief. **50% freelance written.** "Quarterly magazine covering entertainment of interest to the urban market and college market. Most of our readers are African American—92%. Most of our readers are female—69%. This publication discusses entertainment with an educational and informative slant. It writes for a knowledgeable audience." Estab. 1994. Circ. 30,000. Pays on publication. Publishes ms an average of 3 months after acceptance. Byline given. Buys first rights and one-time rights. Editorial lead time 3 months. Submit seasonal material 4 months in advance. Accepts simultaneous submissions. Reports in 3 weeks on queries. Sample copy for SAE with 4 first-class stamps. Writer's guidelines for #10 SASE.
Nonfiction: Essays, interview/profile, opinion, personal experience, music. Special issue: End of the Entertainment Year: highlights; profiles on entertainers who have grown the most. No erotic, historical, how-to, technical. Query with published clips. Length: 500-1,500 words. **Pays $100-200 for assigned articles, $25-75 for unsolicited articles.** Pays writers with contributor copies or other premiums for music or concert reviews.
Photos: State availability of photos with submission or send photos with submission. Negotiates payment individually. Captions and identification of subjects required. Buys one-time rights.
Columns/Departments: MAD Sports (sports figure interview), 1,000 words; They Did That! (profile of behind the scenes entertainer), 750 words; Our Pulse! (issues affecting African American urban and college community), 1,000 words. **Buys 12 mss/year.** Query with published clips. **Pays $100-200.**
Fillers: Facts, newsbreaks, short humor. **Buys 3/year.** Length: 100-300 words. **Pays $10.**
Tips: "Write on a relatively unknown entertainer and make it so interesting that everyone wants to know them."

PEOPLE, Time Inc. Magazine Co., Time & Life Bldg., Rockefeller Center, New York NY 10020. (212)522-1212. Fax: (212)522-0536. Website: http://www.people.com. This magazine did not respond to our request for information. Query before submitting.

$ $ $ **PERFORMING ARTS MAGAZINE**, 3539 Motor Ave., Los Angeles CA 90034. (310)839-8000. Editor: Dana Kitaj. **100% freelance written.** Monthly magazine covering theater, music, dance, visual art. "We publish general pieces on the arts of a historical or 'current-events' nature." Estab. 1965. Circ. 700,000. Pays on publication. Publishes ms an average of 2 months after acceptance. Offers $150 kill fee. Buys one-time rights. Submit seasonal material 3 months in advance. Sample copy for 9×12 SASE.
Nonfiction: Book excerpts (on the Arts), general interest (theater, dance, opera), historical/nostalgic, interview/profile (performers, artists), travel. No critical texts, religious, political essays or reviews. **Buys 60 mss/year.** Query with published clips. Length: 1,500-3,000 words. **Pays $500-1,000.** Sometimes pays expenses of writers on assignment.
Reprints: Accepts previously published submissions.
Photos: State availability of photos with submission. Reviews transparencies. Offers no additional payment for photos accepted with ms. Buys one-time rights.
Tips: "Theater, dance and music on the West Coast are our main interests. Write broad information pieces or interviews."

$ $ $ $ **PREMIERE**, Hachette Filipacchi Magazines, 1633 Broadway, New York NY 10019. (212)767-5400. Fax: (212)767-5444. E-mail: frcohn@aol.com. Website: http://www.premieremag.com. Editor-in-Chief: James Meigs. Contact: Glenn Kenny, senior editor. Monthly magazine covering movies. "*Premiere* is a magazine for young adults that goes behind the scenes of movies in release and production. Feature articles include interviews, profiles plus film commentary and analysis. Monthly departments provide coverage of the movie business, video technology and hardware, home video, film and video reviews/releases, movie music/scoring and books." Estab. 1987. Circ. 617,000. **Pays on acceptance.** Byline given. Offers 25-33% kill fee. Buys all rights. Reports in 1 month. Writer's guidelines for #10 SASE.
Nonfiction: "Deeply reported, well-written pieces that focus on how movies are made." Query with published clips by mail or e-mail. Length: 2,000-4,000 words. Pays $1-2/word. Pays the expenses of writers on assignment.
Columns/Departments: Length: 750-2,000 words. Query with published clips by mail or e-mail. Pays $1/word. "A short front-of-the-book item is often the best way to break in to the magazine."
Tips: "We are not interested in queries that simply list the names of actors a writer would like to interview. Writers without specialized experience covering the film industry are generally not considered for freelance assignments."

$ $ **THE READERS SHOWCASE**, Suggitt Publishing, Ltd., 16511-116 Ave., Edmonton, Alberta T5M 3V1 Canada. (403)486-5802. Fax: (403)481-9276. E-mail: suggitt@planet.eon.net. **Contact**: Maureen Hutchison, senior editor. **80-100% freelance written.** Bimonthly magazine covering books available at SmithBooks and Coles bookstores. "*The Readers Showcase* consists of author interviews, book reviews, lifestyle pieces, industry news, contests, book-related editorials, etc." Estab. 1993. Circ. 400,000 (1,000,000 in November). Pays 30 days after publication. Publishes ms an average of 1 month after acceptance. Byline given. Offers 50% kill fee. Editorial lead time 2 months. Submit seasonal material 2 months in advance. Accepts simultaneous submissions. Sample copy and writer's guidelines free.
Nonfiction: Book excerpts, interview/profile, book reviews. **Buys 300 mss/year.** Query with published clips. Length: 400-2,000 words. **Pays 15¢/word.** Sometimes pays expenses of writers on assignment.

Reprints: Accepts previously published submissions.

$ $ RIGHT ON!, Sterling's Magazines, 233 Park Ave. S., New York NY 10003. (212)780-3519. **Contact**: Cynthia Horner, editorial director. **10% freelance written.** Monthly black entertainment magazine for teenagers and young adults. Circ. 250,000. Pays on publication. Publishes ms an average of 3 months after acceptance. Byline given. Buys all rights. Submit seasonal material 4 months in advance. Reports in 1 month on queries.
Nonfiction: Interview/profile. "We only publish entertainment-oriented stories or celebrity interviews." **Buys 15-20 mss/year.** Query with or without published clips, or send ms. Length: 500-4,000 words. **Pays $50-200.**
Photos: State availability of photos with submission. Reviews transparencies, 8×10 b&w prints. Offers no additional payment for photos accepted with ms. Identification of subjects required. Buys one-time or all rights.

$ $ $ SATELLITE ORBIT, Commtek Communications Corp., Suite 600, 8330 Boone Blvd., Vienna VA 22182. (703)827-0511. Fax: (703)827-0159. E-mail: satorbit@aol.com. Website: http://www.orbitmagazine.com. Publisher: Phillip Swann. **Contact:** Linda Casey, editor. **25% freelance written.** Monthly magazine on television available to owners of large satellite dishes. Estab. 1979. **Pays on acceptance.** Publishes an average of 2 months after acceptance. Kill fee varies. Reports in 1 month.
Nonfiction: "Wants to see articles on satellite programming, equipment, television trends, sports and celebrity interviews." Query with published clips and SASE. *No unsolicited mss.* Length: 700 words. **Pay 50¢/word.**
Reprints: Pays 20% of amount paid for an original article.

N ★ $ $ SCI-FI ENTERTAINMENT, Sovereign Media, 11305 Sunset Hills Rd., Reston VA 20190. (703)471-1556. E-mail: scottedelman@erols.com. **Contact**: Scott Edelman, editor. **100% freelance written**. Published 9 times/year. Magazine covering science fiction movies—old, new, upcoming fantasy. Estab. 1994. Circ. 70,000. Pays 30 days after acceptance. Publishes ms an average of 1 month after acceptance. Byline given. Offers 10% kill fee. Buys first world rights. Editorial lead time 1 month. Submit seasonal material 3 months in advance. Accepts simultaneous submissions. Reports in 2 weeks on queries; 1 month on mss. Sample copy for $4.95. Guidelines for #10 SASE.
Nonfiction: General interest, historical/nostalgic, interview/profile, new product (games), opinion, personal experience. photo feature. **Buys 100 mss/year**. Query. Length: 2,300 words. **Pays $200-500**. Sometimes pays expenses of writers on assignment.
Reprints: Accepts previously published submissions.
Photos: State availability of photos with submissions. Offers no additional payment for photos accepted with ms. Identification of subjects required. Buys one-time rights.
Columns/Departments: Infinite Channels (games), 2,300 words; Video (video reviews), 2,400 words; Books (books on movies), 2,500 words. **Buys 6 mss/year**. Query with published clips.

$ $ SOAP OPERA DIGEST, 261 Madison Ave., 10th Floor, New York NY 10016. (212)716-2700. Fax: (212)661-2560. E-mail: sodeditor@aol.com. Website: http://www.soapdigest.com. **Contact:** Carolyn Hinsey. **5% freelance written.** Bimonthly magazine covering soap operas. "Extensive knowledge of daytime and prime time soap operas is required." Estab. 1975. Circ. 107,276. **Pays on acceptance.** Publishes ms an average of 2 months after acceptance. Byline given. Offers 30% kill fee. Buys first North American serial and second serial (reprint) rights. Submit seasonal material 4 months in advance. Reports in 1 month.
Nonfiction: Interview/profile. No essays. **Buys 10 mss/year**. Query with published clips. Length: 1,000-2,000 words. **Pays $250-500 for assigned articles.** Pays meal expenses of writers on assignment.
Photos: Offers no additional payment for photos accepted with ms. Buys all rights.

$ $ SOAP OPERA MAGAZINE, American Media, Inc., 660 White Plains Rd., Tarrytown NY 10591. (914)332-5021. Fax: (800)331-4936. Editor-in-Chief: Garrett A. Foster. **Contact:** Lynne Dorsey, executive editor. **10% freelance written.** Weekly. "We cover TV soap operas from a storyline and off-camera standpoint." Estab. 1991. Circ. 350,000. Pays on publication. Publishes ms an average of 2 weeks after acceptance. Byline given. Buys first North American serial rights. Editorial lead time 2 weeks. Submit seasonal material 2 months in advance.
Nonfiction: No articles not pertaining to the field of soap opera-oriented material only. Buys 100 mss/year. Query with published clips. Length: 500-2,000 words. **Pays $250-750.** Sometimes pays expenses of writers on assignment.
Photos: Jeannine Boffa, photo editor. State availability of photos with submission. Negotiates payment individually. Captions, identification of subjects required. Buys one-time rights.
Columns/Departments: Buzz in the Biz (soap news), 100 words. **Buys 100 mss/year.** Query. **Pays $50-100.**
Tips: "You have to be interested in soap operas and be able to develop story ideas that will appeal to other soap fans. It's that simple. No phone queries. Fax queries OK."

$ $ SOAP OPERA UPDATE, Bauer Publishing, 270 Sylvan Ave., Englewood Cliffs NJ 07632. (201)569-6699. Fax: (201)569-2510. **Contact**: Richard Spencer, editor-in-chief. **25% freelance written.** Biweekly. "We cover daytime and prime time soap operas with preview information, in-depth interviews and exclusive photos, history, character sketches, events where soap stars are seen and participate." Estab. 1988. Circ. 288,000. Pays on publication. Byline given. Buys first North American serial rights. Submit seasonal material 3 months in advance. Reports in 1 month.
Nonfiction: Humor, interview/profile. "Only articles directly about actors, shows or history of a show." **Buys 100**

mss/year. Query with published clips. Length: 750-2,200 words. **Pays $400.** Sometimes pays expenses of writers on assignment.
Photos: State availability of photos with submission. Reviews transparencies. Offers $25. Captions and identification of subjects required. Buys all rights.
Tips: "Come up with fresh, new approaches to stories about soap operas and their people. Submit ideas and clips. Take a serious approach; don't talk down to the reader. All articles must be well written and the writer knowledgeable about his subject matter."

$ $ $ STAR MAGAZINE, 600 S. East Coast Ave., Lantana FL 33462. (916)332-5000. Editor-in-Chief: Phil Bunton. **Contact**: Dick Belsky. Weekly magazine covering celebrity news and lifestyles. Estab. 1973. Circ. 2,220,700. Pays on publication. Publishes ms 10 days after acceptance. Buys all rights. Responds in 1 day. Sample copy for $1.49.
Nonfiction: Expose, general interest, interview/profile, photo feature—all celebrity news-related. **Buys 2,000 mss/year.** Query with published clips. Length: 1,000 words. **Pays $300-1,000.**

N $ $ STEPPIN' OUT MAGAZINE, Collins Communications, Inc., 381 Broadway, Westwood NJ 07675. (201)358-2929. Fax: (201)358-2824. E-mail: stepoutmag@aol.com. Website: http://www.steppinoutmagazine.com. **Contact**: Chauncé Hayden, editor. **20% freelance written.** Weekly regional entertainment magazine. "*Steppin' Out* targets younger readers. Submissions should be hip and timely." Estab. 1988. Circ. 70,000. Pays on publication. Publishes ms an average of 1 month after acceptance. Byline given. Offers 20% kill fee. Buys one-time and second serial (reprint) rights. Editorial lead time 2 months. Submit seasonal material 2 months in advance. Accepts simultaneous submissions. Reports in 2 weeks on queries; 1 month on mss. Sample copy for $5.
Nonfiction: Exposé, general interest, humor, interview/profile, opinion, personal experience, photo feature, travel. **Buys 20 mss/year.** Query with published clips. Length: 500-2,000 words. **Pays $20-500 for assigned articles; $20-100 for unsolicited articles.** Sometimes pays expenses of writers on assignment.
Reprints: Accepts previously published submissions.
Photos: State availability of photos with submission. Reviews any size prints. Offers no additional payment for photos accepted with ms. Captions, model releases and identification of subjects required. Buys one-time rights.
Columns/Departments: More Music (music-national); 24-7 (opinion); Bar Fly (young adult), all 200 words. **Buys 10 mss/year.** Query with published clips. **Pays $20-100.**
Fiction: Humorous, slice-of-life vignettes.
Fillers: Anecdotes, facts, gags to be illustrated by cartoonist, newsbreaks, short humor. **Buys 20/year.** Length: 50-500 words. **Pays $20-100.**
Tips: "Keep it simple, write honestly and don't be afraid to voice your opinion."

$ $ $ US, Wenner Media Inc., 1290 Avenue of the Americas, 2nd Floor, New York NY 10104. (212)767-8205. This magazine did not respond to our request for information. Query before submitting.

N $ $ $ XXL MAGAZINE, Harris Publications, 1115 Broadway, 8th Floor, New York NY 10027. E-mail: annag@harris~pub.com. **Contact:** Anna Gebbie, managing editor. **50% freelance written.** Bimonthly. "*XXL* is hip-hop on a higher level, an upscale urban lifestyle magazine." Estab. 1997. Circ. 250,000. Pays on publication. Byline given. Offers 25% kill fee. Buys all rights. Editorial lead time 3-4 months. Submit seasonal material 3 months in advance.
Nonfiction: How-to, interview/profile, new product, personal experience, photo feature, technical, music, entertainment, luxury materialism, consumer info. Query with published clips. Length: 200-5,000 words. **Pays 50¢/word.** Pays expenses of writers on assignment.
Photos: State availability of photos with submission. Reviews contact sheets, transparencies, prints. Negotiates payment individually. Captions, model releases required. Buys "3 month no-see" rights.
Tips: "Please send clips, query and cover letter by mail or e-mail."

ETHNIC & MINORITY

Ideas and concerns of interest to specific nationalities and religions are covered by publications in this category. General interest lifestyle magazines for these groups are also included. Many ethnic publications are locally-oriented or highly specialized and do not wish to be listed in a national publication such as *Writer's Market*. Query the editor of an ethnic publication with which you're familiar before submitting a manuscript, but do not consider these markets closed because they are not listed in this section. Additional markets for writing with an ethnic orientation are located in the following sections: Career, College and Alumni; Juvenile; Literary and "Little"; Men's; Women's; and Teen and Young Adult.

$ AIM MAGAZINE, AIM Publishing Company, 7308 S. Eberhart Ave., Chicago IL 60619-0554. (773)874-6184. Managing Editor: Dr. Myron Apilado. **Contact**: Ruth Apilado, associate editor. Estab. 1975. **75% freelance**

written. Works with a small number of new/unpublished writers each year. Quarterly magazine on social betterment that promotes racial harmony and peace for high school, college and general audience. Circ. 10,000. Pays on publication. Publishes ms an average of 3 months after acceptance. Offers 60% kill fee. Not copyrighted. Buys one-time rights. Submit seasonal material 6 months in advance. Accepts simultaneous submissions. Reports in 2 months on queries. Sample copy and writer's guidelines for $4 and 9×12 SAE with $1.70 postage.
Nonfiction: Exposé (education); general interest (social significance); historical/nostalgic (Black or Indian); how-to (create a more equitable society); profile (one who is making social contributions to community); book reviews and reviews of plays "that reflect our ethnic/minority orientation." No religious material. **Buys 16 mss/year.** Send complete ms. Length: 500-800 words. **Pays $25-35.**
Photos: Reviews b&w prints. Captions, identification of subjects required.
Fiction: Ethnic, historical, mainstream, suspense. "Fiction that teaches the brotherhood of man." **Buys 20 mss/year.** Send complete ms. Length: 1,000-1,500 words. **Pays $25-35.**
Poetry: Avant-garde, free verse, light verse. No "preachy" poetry. **Buys 20 poems/year.** Submit maximum 5 poems. Length: 15-30 lines. **Pays $3-5.**
Fillers: Jokes, anecdotes, newsbreaks. **Buys 30/year.** Length: 50-100 words. **Pays $5.**
Tips: "Interview anyone of any age who unselfishly is making an unusual contribution to the lives of less fortunate individuals. Include photo and background of person. We look at the nations of the world as part of one family. Short stories and historical pieces about Blacks and Indians are the areas most open to freelancers. Subject matter of submission is of paramount concern for us rather than writing style. Articles and stories showing the similarity in the lives of people with different racial backgrounds are desired."

$ ALBERTA SWEETGRASS, Aboriginal Multi-Media Society of Alberta, 15001 112th Ave., Edmonton, Alberta T5M 2V6 Canada. (403)455-2945. Fax: (403)455-7639. E-mail: edsweet@ammsa.com. **Contact**: Rob McKinley, editor. Monthly tabloid newspaper. **50% freelance written.** "*Alberta Sweetgrass* is a community paper which focuses on people from within Alberta's first nations, métis and non-status aboriginal communities." Estab. 1993. Circ. 7,500. Pays 10th of month following publication. Sample copy free. Writer's guidelines and production schedule available upon request.
Nonfiction: Features, general interest, interview/profile, opinion, photo feature, travel, community-based stories, all with an Alberta angle (no exceptions). **Usually runs 2-3 focus sections/month.** Query. Length: 400-1,200 words. **Pays $3/published inch for one-source stories; $3.60 for multiple sources (less** for excess editorial work).
Reprints: Pays 50% of amount paid for an original article.
Photos: State availability of photos with submission. Offers $15/b&w photo; $50/color cover; $15/inside color.
Columns/Departments: Book/Film/Art Reviews (Alberta Aboriginal), 450-500 words; Briefs (community news shorts), 150-200 words.
Tips: "Aboriginal knowledge is definitely an asset in order to send us usable stories, but even if you aren't familiar with Aboriginal culture, but are still a good writer, bounce a story idea off the editor and do the interview. That way, you will begin to learn more about Aboriginal culture."

$ $ AMERICAN VISIONS, The Magazine of Afro-American Culture, 1156 15th St. NW, Suite 615, Washington DC 20005. (202)496-9593. Fax: (202)496-9851. E-mail: editor@avs.americanvisions.com. Website: http://www.americanvisions.com. **Contact:** Joanne Harris, editor. **75% freelance written.** Bimonthly. "Editorial is reportorial, current, objective, 'pop-scholarly.' Audience is ages 25-54, mostly black, college educated. The scope of the magazine includes the arts, history, literature, cuisine, genealogy and travel—all filtered through the prism of the African-American experience." Estab. 1986. Circ. 125,000. Pays 30 days after publication. Publishes ms an average of 2 months after acceptance. Byline given. Offers 25% kill fee. Buys all and second serial (reprint) rights. Submit seasonal material 5 months in advance. Accepts simultaneous submissions. Reports in 3 months. Sample copy and writer's guidelines with SASE.
Nonfiction: Book excerpts, general interest, historical, interview/profile, literature, photo feature, travel. Publishes travel supplements—domestic, Africa, Europe, Canada, Mexico. No fiction, poetry, personal experience or opinion. **Buys about 60-70 mss/year.** Query with or without published clips, or send complete ms. Accepts queries by mail, fax and e-mail. Length: 500-2,500 words. **Pays $100-600 for assigned articles; $100-400 for unsolicited articles.** Sometimes pays expenses of writers on assignment.
Reprints: Send tearsheet of article or short story or typed ms with rights for sale noted and information about when and where the article or story previously appeared. Pays $100 (flat fee).
Photos: State availability of photos with submission. Reviews contact sheets, 3×5 transparencies, and 3×5 or 8×10 prints. Offers $15 minimum. Identification of subjects required. Buys one-time rights.
Columns/Departments: Arts Scene, Books, Cuisine, Film, Music, Profile, Genealogy, Computers & Technology, Travel, 750-1,750 words. **Buys about 40 mss/year.** Query or send complete ms. **Pays $100-400.**
Fiction: Publishes novel excerpts.
Tips: "Little-known but terribly interesting information about black history and culture is desired. Aim at an upscale audience. Send ms with credentials. Looking for writers who are enthusiastic about their topics."

$ $ ARMENIAN INTERNATIONAL MAGAZINE, 207 S. Brand Blvd., Suite 205, Glendale CA 91204. (818)246-7979. Fax: (818)246-0088. E-mail: aim4m@well.com. **Contact:** Salpi H. Ghazarian, editor/publisher. **50% freelance written.** Monthly magazine about the Caucasus and the global Armenian diaspora. "Special reports and features about politics, business, education, culture, interviews and profiles. Each month, *AIM* is filled with essential news, situation analysis, and indepth articles with local and international coverage of events that affect Armenian life." Estab. 1989. Circ. 10,000. Pays on publication. Publishes ms an average of 3 months after acceptance. Byline given. Buys all rights. Reports in 2 weeks on queries; 6 weeks on mss.

Nonfiction: General interest, historical, interview/profile, photo feature and travel. Special issue: Armenian restaurants around the world. **Buys 60 mss/year.** Query by mail, fax or e-mail with published clips. Length: 600-1,200 words. **Pays $50-400 for assigned articles; $50-200 for unsolicited articles.** Sometimes pays expenses of writers on assignment.

Reprints: Send photocopy of article.

Photos: State availability of photos with submission. Reviews negatives, transparencies and prints. Offers $10-50/photo. Captions and identification of subjects required.

Fiction: Publishes novel excerpts upon approval.

$ $ BLACK DIASPORA MAGAZINE, Black Diaspora Communications Ltd., 298 Fifth Ave., 7th Floor, New York NY 10001. (212)268-8348. Fax: (212)268-8370. Executive Editor: Jerry King. **Contact:** Michelle Phipps, executive editor. **25% freelance written.** Published 7 times/year. "A general interest publication geared toward the global Black Diaspora population between ages 18-49." Estab. 1979. Circ. 250,000. Pays 30 days after acceptance. Byline given. Buys first North American serial and second serial (reprint) rights. Submit seasonal material 2 months in advance. Reports in 6 weeks. Sample copy for 9×12 SAE with 4 first-class stamps. Guidelines for #10 SASE.

Nonfiction: Exposé, general interest, historical/nostalgic, interview/profile, religious, sports, travel, international. Query with published clips. Length: 500-1,300 words. **Pays 10¢/word maximum.** Sometimes pays expenses of writers on assignment.

Photos: Send photos with submission. Offers no additional payment for photos accepted with ms. Captions, model releases, identification of subjects required. Buys all rights.

Columns/Departments: International (social, political or economic issues in the world, also culture and lifestyles; 1,500-2,000 words; payment negotiable); In Focus (similar to International, but geared more toward domestic issues; 1,000-1,500 words; payment negotiable). Business (national and international events or persons who encourage and assist economic development, readily considers personality profiles, but will increasingly cover developing entrepreneurial and financial trends; 800 words). Travel (consumer-oriented department, well-published retreats and sites that are off the beaten path; please include photographs and model releases where applicable; 800-1,000 words). Communication (personalities and trends within communications industry; 800 words). Arts and Entertainment (all facets of the arts, with focus on entertainment personalities as well as lesser known trend-setters within the artistic world; please include photography; 800-1,000 words). Sports and Hobbies (athletic personalities, amateur or professional and fitness activities for the working man or woman; 800 words). Health and Beauty (health-related and beauty trends, or "How To" approach; 800 words). Religion (spiritual concerns of the day, personalities who are making substantial contributions in the religious world, issues of a religious or spiritual nature; 500-800 words). Career & Education, Teen Scene, Consumer Awareness; Hair Care; Styles and Grooming, Images and History (800 words with photography, where applicable); **Pays 10¢/word maximum; or as noted.**

Poetry: Buys 10-20 poems/year. Submit maximum 5 poems. **Pays $15 maximum.**

Tips: "Features about culture, politics, arts and life-styles of the African Diaspora in general and 'how to' pieces that cater to the needs of minority consumers are always welcome."

$ $ THE B'NAI B'RITH INTERNATIONAL JEWISH MONTHLY, 1640 Rhode Island Ave. NW, Washington DC 20036. (202)857-2708. Fax: (202)296-1092. E-mail: sfreed@bnaibrith.org. Website: http://bnaibrith.org/ijm. **Contact:** Stacey Freed, managing editor. Editor: Eric Rozenman. **50% freelance written.** Bimonthly magazine covering Jewish affairs. Estab. 1886. Circ. 200,000. **Pays on acceptance.** Publishes ms an average of 3 months after acceptance. Byline given. Offers 20% kill fee. Buys first North American serial rights. Editorial lead time 3 months. Submit seasonal material 6 months in advance. Accepts simultaneous submissions. Reports in 1 month. Sample copy for $2 and 9×13 SAE with 2 first-class stamps. Writer's guidelines free.

Nonfiction: General interest pieces of relevance to the Jewish community of US and abroad; interview/profile, photo feature. **Buys 15-25 mss/year.** Query by mail, fax or e-mail with published clips. Length: 750-2,500 words. **Pays $400-750 for assigned articles; $400-600 for unsolicited articles.** Sometimes pays expenses of writers on assignment.

Photos: State availability of photos with submission. Reviews contact sheets, 2×3 transparencies and prints. Pays $150/page for color, $100/page for b&w. Identification of subjects required. Buys one-time rights.

Tips: "Know what's going on in the Jewish world. Look at other Jewish publications. Writers should submit clips with their queries. The best way to break into the *Jewish Monthly* is to submit a range of good story ideas accompanied by clips. We aim to establish relationships with writers and we tend to be loyal. We generally do not publish first-person essays, and we do not do book reviews.."

$ CONGRESS MONTHLY, American Jewish Congress, 15 E. 84th St., New York NY 10028. (212)879-4500. **Contact:** Maier Deshell, editor. **90% freelance written.** Bimonthly magazine. "*Congress Monthly*'s readership is popular, but well-informed; the magazine covers political, social, economic and cultural issues of concern to the Jewish community in general and to the American Jewish Congress in particular." Estab. 1933. Circ. 35,000. Pays on publication. No simultaneous submissions. Responds to queries in 1 month. Publishes ms an average of 3 months after acceptance. Byline given. Buys one-time rights. Submit seasonal material 2 months in advance. Reports in 2 months.

Nonfiction: General interest ("current topical issues geared toward our audience"). No technical material. Query only. *No unsolicited mss.* Length: 1,200-1,500 words. Book reviews, 750-1,000 words; author profiles, film and theater

reviews, travel. Payment amount determined by author experience and article length.
Photos: State availability of photos. Reviews b&w prints. "Photos are paid for with payment for ms."

$ $ DIMENSIONS, the Magazine of Jewish Lifestyle in South Florida, Skarco Press Inc., 1701 W. Hillsboro Blvd., Deerfield Beach FL 33442. (954)252-9393. E-mail: skarco@gate.net. **Contact:** Linda Janasz, editor. Quarterly magazine covering Jewish lifestyle in Southern Florida, geared toward 30-50-year-olds. Estab. 1995. Circ. 40,000. Pays on publication. Byline given. Buys first North American and second serial rights. Editorial lead time 4 months. Submit seasonal material 4 months in advance. Accepts simultaneous submissions. Reports in 2 months. Sample copy for $3 plus $1.24 postage.
Nonfiction: Book excerpts, general interest, interview/profile (with celebrity or well-known person), religious (Jewish), family matters, health and well-being, fashion, travel. **Buys 10 mss/year.** Query with published clips. Length: 600-2,000 words. **Pays $100-300.**
Photos: State availability of photos with submission. Negotiates payment individually. Captions, model releases, identification of subjects required.
Tips: "Writers should understand our market and readers' lifestyle: Jewish professionals, families and singles aged 30s-50s, affluent, upscale, living in South Florida. Very cosmopolitan."

⊘ **EBONY MAGAZINE** does not accept freelance writing.

$ $ $ EMERGE, Black America's Newsmagazine, Emerge Communications, Inc., 1 BET Plaza, 1900 W Place NE, Washington DC 20018. (202)608-2093. Fax: (202)608-2598. **Contact:** George E. Curry, editor. Managing Editor: Florestine Purnell. **80% freelance written.** African-American news monthly. "*Emerge* is a general interest publication reporting on a wide variety of issues from health to sports to politics, almost anything that affects Black Americans. Our audience is comprised primarily of African-Americans 25-49, individual income of $55,000, professional and college educated." Estab. 1989. Circ. 200,000. **Pays on acceptance.** Publishes ms an average of three months after acceptance. Byline given. Offers 25% kill fee. Buys first North American serial rights. Submit seasonal material 6 months in advance. Reports in 5 weeks. Sample copy for $3 and 9×12 SAE. Writer's guidelines for #10 SAE with 2 first-class stamps.

- Ranked as one of the best markets for freelance writers in *Writer's Yearbook* magazine's annual "Top 100 Markets," January 1998.

Nonfiction: Essays, exposé, general interest, historical/nostalgic, humor, interview/profile, technical, travel. "We are not interested in standard celebrity pieces that lack indepth reporting as well as analysis, or pieces dealing with interpersonal relationships." Query with published clips. Length: 600-2,000 words. **Pays 60-75¢/word.**
Photos: State availability of photos with submission. Reviews contact sheets. Negotiated payment. Captions, model releases, indentification of subjects required. Buys one-time rights.
Columns/Departments: Query.
Tips: "If a writer doesn't have a completed manuscript, then he should mail a query letter with clips. No phone calls. First-time authors should be extremely sensitive to the *Emerge* style and fit within these guidelines as closely as possible. We do not like to re-write or re-edit pieces. We are a news monthly so articles must be written with a 3-month lead time in mind. Writers must assist our research department during fact checking process and closing. Read at least six issues of the publication before submitting ideas."

$ $ ESTYLO MAGAZINE, Latina Lifestyle, Mandalay Publishing, 3660 Wilshire Blvd., Suite 530, Los Angeles CA 90010. (213)383-6300. Fax: (213)383-6499. E-mail: Estylo@aol.com. Editor: Juana I. Gallegos. **Contact:** Denise M. Castañon, managing editor. **75% freelance written.** "Quarterly fashion, beauty and entertainment magazine for the affluent and mobile Latina. It contains a wide variety of features and departments devoted to all areas of interest to Latinas: career, cuisine, travel, health, fitness, relationships, beauty, fashion and entertainment topics. Estab. 1997. Circ. 50,000. Pays on publication. Publishes ms an average of 2 months after acceptance. Byline given. Buys first rights. Editorial lead time 3 months. Submit seasonal material 3 months in advance. Accepts simultaneous submissions. Reports in 2 weeks on queries; 1 month on mss. Writer's guidelines free.
Nonfiction: Expose, general interest, how-to (career, fitness, health), humor, inspirational, interview/profile, new product, opinion, personal experience, photo feature, religious, technical, travel. **Buys 15-20 mss/year.** Query by mail, fax or e-mail with published clips. Length: 1,200-2,000 words. **Pays $100 minimum.** Sometimes pays expenses of writers on assignment.
Reprints: Send photocopy of article.
Photos: State availability of photos with submission. Reviews contact sheets. Negotiates payment individually. Captions, model releases, identificiation of subjects required. Buys all rights.
Columns/Departments: Buys 15-20 mss/year. Query with published clips. Length: 800-1,200 words. **Pays $100 minimum.**
Fillers: Anecdotes, facts, gags to be illustrated by cartoonist, newsbreaks, short humor. **Buys 5-10/year.** Length: open. **Pays $100 minimum.**

$ FILIPINAS, A magazine for All Filipinos, Filipinas Publishing, Inc., 655 Sutter St., Suite 333, San Francisco CA 94102. (415)563-5878. Fax: (415)292-5993. E-mail: filmagazin@aol.com. Website: http://www.filipinasmag.com. **Contact:** Rene Ciria-Cruz, editor. Monthly magazine focused on Filipino American affairs. "*Filipinas* answers the lack of mainstream media coverage of Filipinos in America. It targets both Filipino immigrants and American-born Filipinos, gives in-depth coverage of political, social, cultural events in The Philippines and in the Filipino American community. Features role models, history, travel, food and leisure, issues and controversies." Estab. 1992. Circ. 40,000. Pays on publication. Publishes ms an average of 3 months after acceptance. Byline given. Offers $10 kill fee. Buys first rights or all rights. Editorial lead time 2 months. Submit seasonal material 4 months in advance. Reports in 5 weeks on queries; 18 months on mss. Sample copy for $5. Writer's guidelines for 9½×4 SASE.

Nonfiction: Exposé, general interest, historical/nostalgic, how-to, humor, interview/profile, personal experience, travel. No academic papers. **Buys 80-100 mss/year.** Query with published clips. Length: 800-1,500 words. **Pays $50-100.** Sometimes pays writers other than cash payment by mutual agreement."

Photos: State availability of photos with submission. Reviews 2¼×2¼ and 4×5 transparencies. Offers $15-35/photo. Captions and model releases required. Buys one-time rights.

Columns/Departments: Entree (reviews of Filipino restaurants), 1,200 words; Cultural Currents (Filipino traditions, beliefs), 1,500 words. Query with published clips. **Pays $50-75.**

$ $ GERMAN LIFE, Zeitgeist Publishing Inc., 226 N. Adams St., Rockville MD 20850-1829. (301)294-9081. Fax: (301)294-9084. E-mail: editor@GermanLife.com. Website: http://www.GermanLife.com. **Contact**: Heidi L. Whitesell, editor. **50% freelance written.** Bimonthly magazine covering German-speaking Europe. "*German Life* is for all interested in the diversity of German-speaking culture, past and present, and in the various ways that the United States (and North America in general) has been shaped by its German immigrants. The magazine is dedicated to solid reporting on cultural, historical, social and political events." Estab. 1994. Circ. 50,000. Pays on publication. Publishes ms an average of 6 months after acceptance. Byline given. Buys first North American serial rights. Editorial lead time 4 months. Submit seasonal material 6 months in advance. Reports in 1 month on queries; 3 months on mss. Sample copy for $4.95 and SAE with 4 first-class stamps. Writer's guidelines free.

Nonfiction: Exposé, general interest, historical/nostalgic, how-to (German crafts, recipes, gardening), interview/profile, opinion (only for final column), photo feature, travel. Special issues: Oktoberfest-related (October); seasonal relative to Germany, Switzerland or Austria (December); travel to German-speaking Europe (April); education or politics in Germany (August). **Buys 50 mss/year.** Query with published clips. Length: 1,000-2,000 words. **Pays $200-500 for assigned articles; $200-350 for unsolicited articles.** Sometimes pays expenses of writers on assignment.

Photos: State availability of photos with submission. Reviews color transparencies, 5×7 color or b&w prints. Offers no additional payment for photos accepted with ms. Identification of subjects required. Buys one-time rights.

Columns/Departments: German-Americana (regards specific German-American communities, organizations and/or events past or present), 1,500 words; Profile (portrays prominent Germans, Americans, or German-Americans), 800 words; At Home (cuisine, home design, gardening, crafts, etc. relating to German-speaking Europe), 800 words; Library (reviews of books, videos, CDs, etc.), 300 words. **Buys 30 mss/year.** Query with published clips. **Pays $130-300.**

Fillers: Anecdotes, facts, newsbreaks, short humor. Length: 100-300 words. **Pays $50-150.**

Tips: "The best queries include several informative proposals. Ideally, clips show a background in a German-related topic, but more importantly, a flair for 'telling stories.' Majority of articles present a human interest angle. Even though *German Life* is a special interest magazine, writers should avoid overemphasizing autobiographical experiences/stories."

$ $ HADASSAH MAGAZINE, 50 W. 58th St., New York NY 10019. **Contact:** Alan M. Tigay, executive editor. **90% freelance written.** Works with small number of new/unpublished writers each year. Monthly (except combined issues June/July and August/September). "*Hadassah* is a general interest, Jewish feature and literary magazine. We speak to our readers on a vast array of subjects ranging from politics to parenting, to midlife crisis to Mideast crisis. Our readers want coverage on social and economic issues, the arts, travel and health." Circ. 334,000. Buys first rights (with travel and family articles, buys all rights). Sample copy and writer's guidelines for 9×13 SASE.

Nonfiction: Primarily concerned with Israel, Jewish communities around the world and American civic affairs as relates to the Jewish community. "We are also open to art stories that explore trends in Jewish art, literature, theater, etc. Will not assign/commission a story to a first-time writer for Hadassah." **Buys 10 unsolicited mss/year.** Send query and writing samples. No phone queries. Length: 1,500-2,000 words. **Pays $350 minimum, $75 for reviews.** Sometimes pays expenses of writers on assignment.

Photos: "We buy photos only to illustrate articles, with the exception of outstanding color photos from Israel which we use on our covers. We pay $175 and up for a suitable cover photo." Offers $50 for first photo; $35 for each additional. "Always interested in striking cover (color) photos, especially of Israel and Jerusalem."

Columns/Departments: "We have a Family column and a Travel column, but a query for topic or destination should be submitted first to make sure the area is of interest and the story follows our format."

Fiction: Joan Michel, fiction editor. Short stories with strong plots and positive Jewish values. No personal memoirs, "schmaltzy" or shelter magazine fiction. "We continue to buy very little fiction because of a backlog." Length: 1,500 words maximum. **Pays $300 minimum.** "Require proper size SASE."

Tips: "We are interested in reading articles that offer an American perspective on Jewish affairs (1,500 words). For example, a look at the presidential candidates from a Jewish perspective. Send query of topic first."

$ $ $ HERITAGE FLORIDA JEWISH NEWS, P.O. Box 300742, Fern Park FL 32730-0742. (407)834-8787. Fax: (407)831-0507. E-mail: heritagefl@aol.com. Publisher/Editor: Jeffrey Gaeser. **Contact:** Chris Allen, associate editor. **20% freelance written.** Weekly tabloid on Jewish subjects of local, national and international scope, except for special issues. "Covers news of local, national and international scope of interest to Jewish readers and not likely to be found in other publications." Estab. 1976. Circ. 3,500. Pays on publication. Publishes ms an average of 2 months after acceptance. Byline given. Buys first North American serial, first, one-time, second serial (reprint) or simultaneous rights. Submit seasonal material 3 months in advance. Reports in 1 month. Sample copy for $1 and 9×12 SASE.

Nonfiction: General interest, interview/profile, opinion, photo feature, religious, travel. "Especially needs articles for these annual issues: Rosh Hashanah, Financial, Chanukah, Celebration (wedding and bar mitzvah), Passover, Health and Fitness, Education, Travel. No fiction, poems, first-person experiences." **Buys 50 mss/year.** Send complete ms. Length: 500-1,000 words. **Pays 50¢/column inch.**

Reprints: Send typed ms with rights for sale noted.

Photos: State availability of photos with submission. Reviews b&w prints up to 8×10. Offers $5/photo. Captions, identification of subjects required. Buys one-time rights.

$ THE HIGHLANDER, Angus J. Ray Associates, Inc., P.O. Box 22307, Kansas City MO 64113. Fax: (816)523-7474. **Contact**: Crennan Wade, editor. **50% freelance written.** Works with a number of new/unpublished writers each year. Bimonthly magazine covering Scottish history, clans, genealogy, travel/history, and Scottish/American activities. Estab. 1961. Circ. 35,000. **Pays on acceptance.** Publishes ms an average of 6 months after acceptance. Byline given. Buys first North American serial and second serial (reprint) rights. Submit seasonal material 6 months in advance. Reports in 1 month. Sample copy for $5. Writer's guidelines free.

Nonfiction: Historical/nostalgic. "No fiction; no articles unrelated to Scotland." **Buys 100 mss/year.** Query. Length: 750-2,000 words. **Pays $75-150.**

Reprints: Send tearsheet or photocopy of article or typed ms with information about when and where the article previously appeared. Pays 50% of amount paid for an original article.

Photos: State availability. Prefers color photos, but include transparencies, maps, and/or line or historical drawings to illustrate your work. Identification of subjects required. Writer must provide one-time rights. Artwork returned after publication.

Tips: "Articles should be related to Scotland in a time span of roughly 1300 to 1900, although there is some flexibility in the time. We are not concerned with modern Scotland or with current problems or issues in Scotland."

$ $ HISPANIC, 98 San Jacinto Blvd., Suite 1150, Austin TX 78701. (512)476-5599. Fax: (512)320-1943. E-mail: editor@hisp.com. Website: http://www.hisp.com. Publisher: Alfredo J. Estrada. **Contact:** Katherine A. Diaz, managing editor. **80% freelance written.** Monthly English-language magazine for the US Hispanic community. "*Hispanic* is a general interest publication emphasizing political issues, business news, and cultural affairs." Estab. 1987. Circ. 250,000. Pays on publication. Publishes ms an average of 4 months after acceptance. Byline given. Offers 25% kill fee. Buys all rights, puts some features on the Internet (*Hispanic Online*). Editorial lead time 3 months.

Nonfiction: General interest, business news, career strategies, politics, investigative pieces, culture features, opinion, personal essays. **Buys 200 mss/year.** Query in writing or submit ms on spec. Length: 1,400-3,500 words. **Pays $200-450.** Pays phone expenses, "but these must be cleared with editors first."

Photos: State availability of photos with submission. Reviews transparencies. Offers $25-500/photo. Captions, model releases, identification of subjects required.

Columns/Departments: Forum (op-ed), portfolio (product coverage, travel destinations, book, film and music reviews, money tips, cars). **Pays $75.**

Tips: "We prefer a tone that doesn't overexplain the Hispanic perspective (such as not explaining Hispanic symbolism or translating Spanish words to English). Generally, the point of view should be inclusive: 'we' rather than 'they.' "

$ $ $ INSIDE, The Jewish Exponent Magazine, Jewish Federation of Greater Philadelphia, 226 S. 16th St., Philadelphia PA 19102. (215)893-5700. Fax: (215)546-3957. E-mail: expent@netaxs.com. **Contact**: Jane Biberman, editor. Managing Editor: Martha Ledger. **95% freelance written** (by assignment). Works with published/established writers and a small number of new/unpublished writers each year. Quarterly Jewish regional magazine for a sophisticated and upscale Jewish readership 25 years of age and older. Estab. 1979. Circ. 75,000. Pays on publication. Offers 20% kill fee. Publishes ms an average of 2 months after acceptance. Byline given. Buys first rights. Submit seasonal material 3 months in advance. Reports in 3 weeks on queries; 1 month on mss. Sample copy for $5 and 9×12 SAE. Writer's guidelines for #10 SASE.

Nonfiction: Book excerpts, general interest, historical/nostalgic, humor, interview/profile, personal experience, religious. Philadelphia angle desirable. **Buys 12 unsolicited mss/year.** Query. Length: 1,000-3,500 words. **Pays $100-1,000.**

Reprints: Send photocopy of article or short story. Pays $50-100.

Photos: State availability of photos with submission. Identification of subjects required. Buys first rights.

Fiction: Short stories. Rarely publishes novel excerpts.

Tips: "Personalities—very well known—and serious issues of concern to Jewish community needed."

$ INTERNATIONAL EXAMINER, 622 S. Washington, Seattle WA 98104. (206)624-3925. Fax: (206)624-3046. E-mail: tsojen@alumni.stanford.org. Website: http://www.xaminer.com. **Contact:** Eric T. Hsu, managing editor. **75% freelance written.** Biweekly journal of Asian-American news, politics and arts. "We write about Asian-American issues and things of interest to *Asian-Americans*. We do not want stuff about *Asian* things (stories on your trip to China, Japanese Tea Ceremony, etc. will be rejected). Yes, we are in English." Estab. 1974. Circ. 12,000. Pays on publication. Publishes ms an average of 1 month after acceptance. Buys one-time rights. Editorial lead time 1 month. Submit seasonal material 2 months in advance. Accepts simultaneous submissions. Sample copy, writer's guidelines and editorial calendar for #10 SASE.

Nonfiction: Essays, exposé, general interest, historical/nostalgic, humor, interview/profile, opinion, personal experience, photo feature. **Buys 100 mss/year.** Query by mail, fax or e-mail with published clips. Length: 750-5,000 words, depending on subject. **Pays $25-100.** Sometimes pays expenses of writers on assignment.

Reprints: Accepts previously published submissions (as long as not published in same area). Send typed ms with rights for sale noted and information about when and where the article previously appeared. Pay negotiable.

Photos: State availability of photos with submission. Reviews contact sheets. Negotiates payment individually. Captions, identification of subjects required, Buys one-time rights.

Fiction: Asian-American authored fiction. Publishes novel excerpts. **Buys 1-2 mss/year.** Query. Holiday fiction issue; fiction by or about Asian-Americans. Holiday fiction contest submissions due by December 1st.

Tips: "Write decent, suitable material on a subject of interest to Asian-American community. All submissions are reviewed; all good ones are contacted. It helps to call and run idea by editor before or after sending submissions."

$ $ $ ITALIAN AMERICA, Official Publication of the Order Sons of Italy in America, Order Sons of Italy in America, 219 E St. NE, Washington DC 20002. E-mail: markeditor@aol.com. **Contact**: Anthony Mark Dalessandro, editor. **50% freelance written.** Quarterly magazine. "*Italian America* strives to provide timely information about OSIA, while reporting on individuals, institutions, issues and events of current or historical significance in the Italian-American community." Estab. 1996. Circ. 75,000. Pays on publication. Publishes ms an average of 3 months after acceptance. Byline given. Offers 50% kill fee. Buys first North American serial rights. Editorial lead time 3 months. Accepts simultaneous submissions. Sample copy and writer's guidelines free.

Nonfiction: Essays, exposé, historical, current events, nostalgic, interview/profile, opinion, personal experience, travel. **Buys 10 mss/year.** Query with published clips. Length: 500-2,500 words. **Pays $150-1,000.** Sometimes pays expenses of writers on assignment.

Photos: State availability of photos with submission. Reviews contact sheets. Negotiates payment individually. Identification of subjects required. Buys one-time rights.

Columns/Departments: Community Notebook (Italian American life), 500 words; Postcard from Italy (life in Italy today), 750 words; Reviews (books, films by or about Italian Americans), 500 words. **Buys 5 mss/year.** Send complete ms. **Pays $100-500.**

$ $ JEWISH ACTION, Union of Orthodox Jewish Congregations of America, 333 Seventh Ave., 18th Floor, New York NY 10001-5072. (212)563-4000, ext. 146, 147. Fax: (212)564-9058. Editor: Charlotte Friedland. **Contact**: Elissa Epstein, assistant editor. **80% freelance written.** "Quarterly magazine offering a vibrant approach to Jewish issues, Orthodox lifestyle and values." Circ. 30,000. Pays 4-6 weeks after publication. Byline given. Submit seasonal material 4 months in advance. Reports in 3 months. Sample copy and guidelines for 9×12 SAE with 5 stamps.

Nonfiction: Current Jewish issues, history, biography, art, inspirational, humor, music and book reviews. Query with published clips. **Buys 30-40 mss/year.** Length: 1,000-3,000 words, including footnotes. **Pays $100-300 for assigned articles; $75-150 for unsolicited articles.**

Photos: Send photos with submission. Identification of subjects required.

Fiction: Must have relevance to Orthodox reader. Length: 1,000-2,000 words.

Poetry: Limited number accepted. **Pays $25-75.**

Columns/Departments: Student Voice (about Jewish life on campus), 1,000 words. **Buys 4 mss/year.** Just Between Us (personal opinion on current Jewish life and issues), 1,000 words. **Buys 4 mss/year.** Jewish Living (section pertaining to holidays, contemporary Jewish practices), 1,000-1,500 words. **Buys 10 mss/year.**

Tips: "Remember that your reader is well educated and has a strong commitment to Orthodox Judaism. Articles on the Holocaust, holidays, Israel and other common topics should offer a fresh insight. Because the magazine is a quarterly, we do not generally publish articles which concern specific timely events."

N $ JEWISH AFFAIRS, P.O. Box 87557, Houghton 872041 South Africa. Fax: 27+11+646+4940. E-mail: 071jos@muse.arts.wits.ac.za. **Contact**: Joseph Sherman, editor. **95% freelance written.** "*JA* is an intellectual quarterly devoted to issues that affect the Jewish community in South Africa and elsewhere. It is non-political and aims to promote an awareness of Jewish cultural, intellectual and social achievements past and present, and critically to examine the role Jews are playing in the world today." Estab. 1941. Circ. 2,000. **Pays on acceptance**. Publishes ms an average of 1 year after acceptance. Byline given. Buys first rights. Editorial lead time 1 year. Submit seasonal material 6 months in advance. Reports in 1 month. Sample copy for $10.

Nonfiction: Book excerpts, essays, historical/nostalgic, interview/profile, opinion, personal experience, religious. **Buys 100 mss/year.** Send complete ms. Length: 2,000-6,000 words. **Pays $50.** Pays writers with contributor copies.

Fiction: Ethnic, historical, humorous, mainstream, novel excerpts, religious. **Buys 6-20 mss/year.** Send complete ms. Length: 1,500-6,000 words. **Pays $50 maximum.**

Poetry: Accepts the following types of poetry: avant-garde, free verse, light verse, traditional. **Buys 25-35 poems/year.** Submit no more than 5 poems at one time. **Pays $5-10.**

Tips: "Research papers should show evidence of scholarly preparation and make a fresh contribution to the subject. Unusual or little known areas of Jewish cultural life, history, thought or current affairs will be especially favored. Welcomes potential articles and top quality fiction and poetry. *JA* has published Nadine Gordimer, Lionel Abrahams, Don Mattera and many leading scholars, so we're looking for the best."

$ $ MINORITY ADVANCEMENT PROFILE (MAP), 30 N. Raymond, Suite 211, Pasadena CA 91103. (626)577-1984. Fax: (626)577-1490. E-mail: info@mapnews.com. Website: http://www.mapnews.com. Publisher: Darrell R. Dansby. Senior Editor: Jeanetta M. Standefor. **Contact**: Editorial Staff. **40% freelance written.** Bimonthly business newsletter written for minority entrepreneurs and career professionals covering all aspects of business and careers. "We provide how-to information for starting and growing small businesses, profiles of successful entrepreneurs, career advancement advice and profiles of successful career professionals." Estab. 1996. Circ. 28,000. Pays on publication. Publishes ms an average of 2 months after acceptance. Byline given. Buys first rights and second serial (reprint) rights. Submit seasonal material 2 months in advance. Accepts simultaneous submissions. Reports in 2 months. Sample copy for $3. Writer's guidelines for #10 SASE with "Attn: Writer's Guidelines" on envelope.

Nonfiction: Book excerpts, how-to (business/career issues), humor, inspirational, interview/profile, new product, technical. No entertainment, travel, general interest. "We seek 'how-to-do-it-better' articles for starting and growing a small business or various aspects of career advancement. Please read the newsletter and writer's guidelines before querying. Articles covering up-to-date practical business and career information and interviews or profiles of successful entrepreneurs and career professionals are welcome." Query with published clips. Length: 300-1,000 words. **Pays $100-500.**

Reprints: Accepts previously published submissions.

Photos: State availability of photos with submission. Captions, model releases, identification of subjects required. Pays $5-20/photo. Buys one-time rights.

Columns/Departments: Entrepreneur/Career Profiles; MAP Hall of Shame (humorous personal, business or work experiences), 100 words; Entrepreneur Report (timely, professional, practical information for entrepreneurs), 500-700 words; Career Management (how-to advice and opportunities for career advancement), 500-700 words; Keeping You in the Know (personal, career, business advice and information), 200-300 words; Product Review and Recommendation (books, product and service reviews), 100-150 words; Just Ask Us . . . Q&A (business and career advice), 250-300 words. Query with published clips. **Pays $100-500.**

Fillers: Anecdotes, facts, gags to be illustrated, newsbreaks, short humor. Length: 100-500 words. **Pays $50-200.**

Tips: "MAP addresses the specific needs of minority entrepreneurs and career professionals. Each issue combines dual information, issues and events about and from the minority perspective. Profiles, departments and columns are most open to freelancers."

$ $ MODERNA MAGAZINE, The Latina Magazine, Hispanic Publishing Corp., 98 San Jacinto Blvd., Suite 1150, Austin TX 78701. (512)476-5599. E-mail: moderna@hisp.com. Website: http://www.hisp.com/moderna. **Contact:** Katharine Díaz, editor. **60% freelance written.** Quarterly magazine covering fashion, beauty and health for 18- 44-year-old college-educated Latinas, published bilingually. Estab. 1996. Circ. 150,000. Pays on publication. Byline given. Offers 25% kill fee. Buys all rights. Editorial lead time 2 months. Submit seasonal material 6 months in advance. Accepts simultaneous submissions. Reports in 3 months on queries. Sample copy for $3. Writer's guidelines free.

Nonfiction: General interest, how-to, humor, interview/profile, new product, opinion, personal experience, travel. Query with published clips. Length: 1,200-3,000 words. **Pays $200-300.** Sometimes pays expenses of writers on assignment.

Photos: Send photos with submission. Reviews contact sheets, negatives. Negotiates payment individually. Model releases, identification of subjects required. Buys one-time rights.

Columns/Departments: Que Pasa, 50-100 words; Sabor (food), 750-1,000 words; Travel, 75-1,000 words; Mi Vida, 750 words; Punto de Vista, 750 words; Su Dinero, 750 words; Hotline, 50-100 words; Cais, 750 words. Query with published clips. **Pays $50-100.**

Fillers: Facts, gags to be illustrated by cartoonist, newsbreaks. Length: 25-100 words. **Pays $25-50.**

Tips: "*Moderna* is bilingual, and publishes newsworthy, fashion-related stories, profiles of Latina personalties, and entertaining stories about health and fitness, relationships, parenting, food and recipes, travel, film and book reviews, and any other aspect of US society that affects Latinas. Moderna is a bilingual magazine with 1/3 of its articles published in Spanish. There are English translations of all Spanish articles published in the back section."

☆ $ $ $ MOMENT, The Magazine of Jewish Culture & Opinion, 4710 41st St. NW, Washington DC 20016. (202)364-3300. Fax: (202)364-2636. E-mail: basmom@clark.net. Publisher/Editor: Hershel Shanks. Managing Editor: Suzanne Singer. **Contact**: Amy Rassberg, assistant editor. **90% freelance written.** "*Moment* is an independent Jewish bimonthly general interest magazine that specializes in cultural, political, historical, religious and 'lifestyle' articles relating chiefly to the North American Jewish community and Israel." Estab. 1975. Circ. 70,000. Pays on publication. Publishes ms an average of 6 months after acceptance. Byline given. Buys first North American serial rights. Editorial lead time 3 months. Submit seasonal material 6 months in advance. Accepts simultaneous submissions. Reports within 1 month on queries; 3 months on mss. Sample copy for $4.50 and SAE. Writer's guidelines free.

Nonfiction: Book excerpts, essays, interview/profile, memoirs, opinion, religious. **Buys 60-80 mss/year.** Query with published clips. Writers of potentially lengthy articles are urged to send a detailed query letter first, either by regular mail or e-mail. Length: 2,500-4,000 words. **Pays $40-1,100 for assigned articles; $40-500 for unsolicited articles.** Sometimes pays expenses of writers on assignment.

Photos: State availability of photos with submission. Negotiates payment individually. Identification of subjects required. Buys one-time rights.

Columns/Departments: Guest Column (personal/opinion), 750-1,000 words; Holiday (seasonal celebrations), 750-1,500 words; Responsa (rabbinic response to contemporary dilemmas), 800-1,200 words; book reviews (fiction and nonfiction) are accepted but generally assigned, 400-800 words. **Buys 15 mss/year.** Query with published clips. **Pays $100-250.**

Tips: "Stories for *Moment* are usually assigned, but unsolicited manuscripts are often selected for publication. Successful features offer readers an in-depth journalistic treatment of an issue, phenomenon, institution, or individual. The more the writer can follow the principle of 'show, don't tell,' the better."

$ $ NATIVE PEOPLES MAGAZINE, The Arts and Lifeways, 5333 N. Seventh St., Suite C-224, Phoenix AZ 85014-2804. (602)252-2236. Fax: (602)265-3113. E-mail: editorial@nativepeoples.com. Website: http://www.nativepeoples.com. **Contact**: Priscilla Thomas, editorial coordinator or Ben Winton, associate editor. Quarterly full-color magazine on Native Americans. "The primary purpose of this magazine is to offer a sensitive portrayal of the arts and lifeways of native peoples of the Americas." Estab. 1987. Circ. 95,000. Pays on publication. Byline given. Buys one-time rights. Reports in 1 month on queries; 2 months on mss. Sample copy for 9×12 SAE with 7 first-class stamps. Writer's guidelines and sample copy free. "Extremely high quality reproduction with full-color throughout."

Nonfiction: Book excerpts (pre-publication only), historical/nostalgic, interview/profile, personal experience, photo feature. Special issue: Travel and Destination, January 1999. **Buys 35 mss/year.** Query with published clips. Length: 1,500-3,000 words. **Pays 25¢/word.**

Photos: State availability of photos with submission. Reviews transparencies (all formats) but prefers 35mm slides. Offers $45-150/page rates. Pays $250 for cover photos. Identification of subjects required. Buys one-time rights.

Columns/Departments: In the News (profiles of tribal members who achieved success in area of difficulty). Length: 300 words accompanied by b&w photo of individual. Byline given.

Tips: "We are extremely focused upon authenticity and a positive portrayal of present-day traditional and cultural practices. Our readership has been expanded to include Native American students in schools throughout the country. This is being done for the purpose of giving young people a sense of pride in their heritage and culture, to offer role models and potential career considerations. Therefore, it is extremely important that the Native American point of view be incorporated in each story."

N $ $ RUSSIAN LIFE, RIS Publications, 89 Main St., #2, Montpelier VT 05602. Phone/fax: (802)223-4955. E-mail: ruslifeispubs.com. Website: http://www.rispubs.com. Editor: Mikhail Ivanov. **Contact:** Paul Richardson, publisher. **40% freelance written.** Magazine published 10 times/year covering Russian culture, history, travel & business. "Our readers are informed Russophiles with an avid interest in all things Russian. But we do not publish personal travel journals or the like." Estab. 1956. Circ. 15,000. Pays on publication. Publishes ms 2 months after acceptance. Byline given. Offers $25 kill fee. Buys first rights. Editorial lead time 2 months. Submit seasonal material 3 months in advance. Accepts previously published submissions. Reports in 1 month. Sample copy for 9×12 SAE with 6 first-class stamps. Writer's guidelines for #10 SASE.

Nonfiction General interest, photo feature, travel. No personal stories, i.e., "How I came to love Russia." **Buys 15-20 mss/year**. Query. Length: 1,000-6,000 words. **Pays $100-300.**

Photos: Send photos with submission. Reviews contact sheets. Negotiates payment individually. Captions required. Buys one-time rights.

Tips: "A straightforward query letter with writing sample or manuscript (non-returnable) enclosed."

$ $ SCANDINAVIAN REVIEW, The American-Scandinavian Foundation, 725 Park Ave., New York NY 10021. (212)879-9779. Fax: (212)249-3444. **Contact:** Adrienne Gyongy, editor. **75% freelance written.** Triannual magazine for contemporary Scandinavia. Audience: members, embassies, consulates, libraries. Slant: popular coverage of contemporary affairs in Scandinavia. Estab. 1913. Circ. 4,000. Pays on publication. Publishes ms 2 months after acceptance. Byline given. Buys first North American serial and second serial (reprint) rights. Editorial lead time 3 months. Submit seasonal material 3 months in advance. Reports in 6 weeks on queries. Sample copy and writer's guidelines free.

Nonfiction: General interest, interview/profile, photo feature, travel (must have Scandinavia as topic focus). Special issue on Scandinavian travel. *No pornography.* **Buys 30 mss/year.** Query with published clips. Length: 1,500-2,000 words. **Pays $300 maximum.** Pays contributor's copies at writer's request.

Reprints: Accepts previously published submissions.

Photos: State availability or send photos with submission. Reviews 3×5 transparencies or prints. Pays $25-50/photo; negotiates payment individually. Captions required. Buys one-time rights.

$ $ UPSCALE MAGAZINE, The World's Finest African-American Magazine, Upscale Communications, Inc., 600 Bronner Brothers Way SW, Atlanta, GA 30310. (404)758-7467. Fax: (404)755-9892. E-mail: upscale8@mindspring.com. Website: http://www.upscale8@mindspring.com. Editor-in-Chief: Sheila Bronner. **Contact:** Norma Chappell, senior editor; Sylviette McGill, managing editor. **75-80% freelance written.** Monthly magazine covering topics that inspire, inform or entertain African-Americans. "*Upscale* is a general interest publication featuring a variety of topics—beauty, health and fitness, business news, travel, arts, relationships, entertainment and other issues that affect day-to-day lives of African-Americans." Estab. 1989. Circ. 242,000. Byline given. Offers 25% kill fee. Buys all rights in published form. Editorial lead time 3 months. Submit seasonal material 4 months in advance. Accepts simultaneous submissions. Sample copy for $2. Writer's guidelines free.

Nonfiction: Book excerpts/reviews, general interest, historical/nostalgic, inspirational, interview/profile, personal experience, religious, travel. **Buys 135 mss/year.** Query by mail or fax. Length varies. **Pays $150 minimum.** Sometimes pays expenses of writers.

Photos: State availability of photos with submission. Reviews contact sheets, transparencies, prints. Negotiates payment individually. Captions, model releases, identification of subjects required. Buys one-time or reprint rights.
Columns/Departments: Norma Chappell, senior editor. Positively You, Viewpoint, Perspective (personal inspiration/perspective). **Buys 50 mss/year.** Query by mail or fax. **Pays $75.**
Fiction: Publishes novel excerpts.
Tips: "No unsolicited fiction, poetry or essays. Unsolicited nonfiction is accepted for our Perspective, Positively You, and Viewpoint sections. Queries for exciting and informative nonfiction story ideas are welcomed."

N $ $ VISTA MAGAZINE, The Magazine for all Hispanics, Horizon, a U.S. Communications Company, 999 Ponce de Leon Blvd., Suite 600, Coral Gables FL 33134. (305)442-2462. Fax: (305)443-7650. E-mail: jlobaco@aol.com. Website: http://www.vistamagazine.com. **Contact:** Julia Bencomo Lobaco, editor. **50% freelance written.** Monthly, "Sunday supplement style magazine targeting Hispanic audience. Dual-language, Spanish/English, 30/70%. Stories appear in one language or another, not both. Topics of general interest, but with a Hispanic angle." Estab. 1985. Circ. 1,100,000. Pays on publication. Publishes ms an average of 2 months after acceptance. Byline given. Offers 25% kill fee. Buys first North American serial rights. Editorial lead time 2 months. Submit seasonal material 4 months in advance. Sample copy free.
Nonfiction: Exposé, general interest, historical/nostalgic, how-to (home improvement), inspirational, interview/profile, new product, opinion, personal experience, photo feature, travel. "No creative writing, poems, etc." **Buys 40-50 mss/year.** Query with published clips. Length: 500-1,600 words. **Pays $250-450.** Sometimes pays expenses of writers on assignment.
Photos: State availability of photos with submission.
Columns/Departments: Voices (personal opinion re: Hispanic-related theme), 500 words. **Pays $100.**
Tips: "Query by phone is usually best."

$ WINDSPEAKER, Aboriginal Multi-Media Society of Alberta, 15001-112 Ave., Edmonton Alberta T5M 2V6 Canada. (403)455-2700 or (800)661-5469. Fax: (403)455-7639. E-mail: edwind@ammsa.com. Website: http://www.ammsa.com. **Contact**: Debora Lockyer, managing editor. **75% freelance written.** Monthly tabloid covering native issues. "Focus on events and issues that affect and interest native peoples, national or local." Estab. 1983. Circ. 15,000. Pays on publication. Publishes ms an average of 1 month after acceptance. Byline given. Offers $25 kill fee. Buys first rights. Editorial lead time 1 month. Submit seasonal material 2 months in advance. Accepts simultaneous submissions. Sample copy and writer's guidelines free.
Nonfiction: Humor, interview/profile, opinion, personal experience, photo feature, travel, reviews: books, music, movies. Special issues: Powwow (June); Travel supplement (May). **Buys 200 mss/year.** Query with published clips and SASE or by phone with story ideas. Length: 500-800 words. **Pays $3-3.60/published inch.** Sometimes pays expenses of writers on assignment.
Photos: Send photos with submission. Reviews color negatives, prints. Offers $15-50/photo. Will pay for film and processing. Identification of subjects required. Buys one-time rights.
Columns/Departments: Arts reviews (Aboriginal artists), 300-500 words. Buys 25 mss/year. Query with published clips and SASE. **Pays $3-3.60/inch.**
Tips: "You don't have to be native to work for us."

FOOD & DRINK

Magazines appealing to gourmets, health-conscious consumers and vegetarians are classified here. Some publications emphasize "the art and craft" of cooking for food enthusiasts who enjoy developing these skills as a leisure activity. Another popular trend stresses healthy eating and food choices. Many magazines in the Health and Fitness category present a holistic approach to well-being through nutrition and fitness for healthful living. Magazines in General Interest and Women's categories also buy articles on food topics. Journals aimed at food processing, manufacturing and retailing are in the Trade section.

$ $ ALL ABOUT BEER MAGAZINE, Chautauqua, Inc., 1627 Marion Ave., Durham NC 27705. (919)490-0589. Fax: (919)490-0865. E-mail: allabtbeer@aol.com. Website: http://www.allaboutbeer.com. Editor: Daniel Bradford. **Contact:** Julie Johnson Bradford, managing editor. **10% freelance written.** "Bimonthly magazine that educates the beer-loving community about the breadth and variety of beers, the history and culture surrounding beer appreciation, the methods and traditions of beer making, and the political and social environments that affect the pursuit of beer pleasure." Estab. 1979. Circ. 40,000. Pays on publication. Byline given. Offers 50% kill fee. Buys first North American serial rights (includes electronic rights). Editorial lead time 4 months. Submit seasonal material 4 months in advance. Reports in 6 weeks on queries; 2 months on mss. Sample copy for $3.50. Writer's guidelines for #10 SASE.
Nonfiction: Essays, historical/nostalgic, interview/profile, new product, travel, book reviews. **Buys 5 mss/year.** Query with published clips. Length: 500-2,000 words. **Pays $100-350 for assigned articles; $50-250 for unsolicited articles.**

Photos: State availability of photos with submissions. Reviews contact sheets, transparencies. Pay negotiable. Captions, identification of subjects required. Buys one-time rights.
Columns/Departments: Stylistically Speaking (a look at a specific beer style) 700-900 words; Small Beers (news items) 200-500 words. **Buys 5 mss/year.** Query with published clips. **Pays $80-200.**
Fillers: Anecdotes, facts, newsbreaks. **Buys 14/year.** Length: 50-150 words. **Pays $25.**
Tips: "Unsolicited manuscripts without SASE will not be returned. Query first. A short story idea and some published clips have the best chance of success. Book reviews are a place where we try out new writers."

$ $ $ $ BEER CONNOISSEUR, The Guide to Beer and the Good Life, Adams Media, Inc., 1180 Sixth Ave., 11th Floor, New York NY 10036, (212)827-4732. Fax: (212)827-4720. E-mail: agiglio3@aol.com. **Contact:** Anthony Giglio, editor. Managing editor: Libe Goad. 75% freelance written. Magazine published 9 times/year. "*Beer Connoisseur* targets a young, affluent and mostly male audience (21 to 34 years old with incomes of $50,000+). It's about beer—and so much more. Lifestyle issues include topics today's young urban professionals have come to associate with the rewards of hard work. From style to sex, travel to tax tips, music to menus, *Beer Connoisseur* is a veritable handbook on how to live." Estab. 1996. Circ, 100,000.

• Beer Connoisseur is being restructured. Query before submitting.

$ $ $ $ BON APPETIT, America's Food and Entertaining Magazine, Condé Nast Publications, Inc., 6300 Wilshire Blvd., Los Angeles CA 90048. (213)965-3600. Fax: (213)937-1206. **Contact:** Barbara Fairchild, executive editor. Editor-in-Chief: William J. Garry. **10% freelance written.** Monthly magazine that covers fine food, restaurants and home entertaining. "*Bon Appetit* readers are upscale food enthusiasts and sophisticated travelers. They eat out often and entertain four to six times a month." Estab. 1975. Circ. 1,331,853. **Pays on acceptance**. Byline given. Negotiates rights. Submit seasonal material 1 year in advance. Reports in 6 weeks. Guidelines for #10 SASE.
Nonfiction: Travel (restaurant or food-related), food feature, dessert feature. "No cartoons, quizzes, poetry, historic food features or obscure food subjects." **Buys 45 mss/year.** Query with published clips; include list of 6-8 recipes with 2-3 sentence descriptions detailing ingredients, seasoning, garnish, size, shape, color. Length: 750-2,000 words. **Pays $500-1,800.** Pays expenses of writers on assignment.
Photos: Never send photos.
Tips: "We are most interested in receiving travel stories from freelancers. They must have a good knowledge of food (as shown in accompanying clips) and a light, lively style with humor. Nothing long and pedantic please."

$ $ CHILE PEPPER, The Magazine of Spicy Foods, Magnolia Media Group, 1227 W. Magnolia Ave., Ft. Worth TX 76104. Editor: Sharon Hudgins. **Contact:** Joel Gregory, editor-in-chief. **70-80% freelance written.** Bimonthly magazine on spicy foods. "The magazine is devoted to spicy foods, and most articles include recipes. We have a very devoted readership who love their food hot!" Estab. 1986. Circ. 85,000. Pays on publication. Buys first and second rights and first electronic rights. Submit seasonal material 6 months in advance. Sample copy for 9×12 SAE with 5 first-class stamps. Writer's guidelines for #10 SASE.

• *Chile Pepper* also publishes a trade journal, *Hot Times*, which debuted in April, 1997.

Nonfiction: Book excerpts (cookbooks), how-to (cooking and gardening with spicy foods), humor (having to do with spicy foods), new product (hot products), travel (having to do with spicy foods). **Buys 50 mss/year.** Query. Length: 1,000-3,000 words. **Pays $300 minimum for feature article.**
Reprints: Send tearsheet or photocopy of article and information about when and where the article previously appeared.
Photos: State availability of photos with submission. Reviews contact sheets, negatives, transparencies, prints. Offers $25/photo minimum. Captions, identification of subjects required. Buys one-time rights.
Tips: "We're always interested in queries from *food* writers. Articles about spicy foods with six to eight recipes are just right. No fillers. Need location travel/food pieces from inside the U.S. and Mexico."

$ $ $ CIGAR AFICIONADO, M. Shanken Community, Inc., 387 Park Ave. S., New York NY 10016. (212)684-4224. Fax: (212)684-5424. Website: http://www.cigaraficionado.com. Editor: Marvin Shanken. **Contact**: Gordon Mott, managing editor. **75% freelance written.** Bimonthly magazine covering cigars. Estab. 1992. Circ. 400,000. **Pays on acceptance.** Publishes ms an average of 9 months after acceptance. Byline given. Offers 25% kill fee. Buys all rights. Editorial lead time 3 months. Submit seasonal material 3 months in advance. Sample copy and writer's guidelines free.
Nonfiction: Query. Length: 2,000 words. Sometimes pays expenses of writers on assignment.

N $ CIGAR LIFESTYLES MAGAZINE, Made Ya Look! Inc., 1845 Oak St., #12, Northfield IL 60093. (847)446-1735. Fax: (847)446-1699. E-mail: yalook@aol.com. **Contact**: Editorial Department. Editor: Patrick Grady. Managing Editor: Roger Blackshaw. **90% freelance written.** Quarterly magazine covering cigars and male lifestyles. "*Cigar Lifestyles Magazine* offers a look at the good life and easy living." Estab. 1995. Circ. 300,000. Pays on publication. Byline sometimes given. Offers 25% kill fee. Buys all rights. Editorial lead time 1 month. Submit seasonal material 3 months in advance. Accepts simultaneous submissions. Reports in 1 month on queries; 2 months on mss. Sample copy and writer's guidelines for $3.50.
Nonfiction: Book excerpts, essays, exposé, humor, inspirational, interview/profile, new product, photo feature, travel. **Buys 50 mss/year.** Query with published clips. Length: 750-1,500 words. Sometimes pays expenses of writers on assignment. Pay varies.
Reprints: Accepts previously published submissions.

Photos: Send photos with submission. Reviews 5×10 prints. Offers no additional payment for photos accepted with ms. Model releases and identification of subjects required. Buys all rights.
Fillers: Anecdotes, facts, gags to be illustrated by cartoonist, newsbreaks, short humor. **Buys 75-100/year.** Length: 500-750 words. Pay varies.
Tips: "Call us and fax us information. Stories with photos are your best chance. Good photos help."

N $ $ $ COOKING & ENTERTAINING, Woman's Day Special Interest Publications, Hachette-Filipacchi Magazines, 1633 Broadway, New York NY 10019. Fax: (212)767-5612. E-mail: wdspecials@aol.com. **Contact:** Janice Wright, managing editor. Editor: Carolyn Gatto. Consumer magazine published 3 times a year covering food, cooking, entertaining. "This magazine is full of ideas for seasonal get-togethers for spring, summer and the holidays, from festive food (a major focus) to fanciful decorating to table settings. Helpful articles, from the best equipment to prepare-ahead strategies to highlights of seasonal foods are also included. The average reader is female and 43 years old." **Pays on acceptance**. Publishes ms an average of 3 months after acceptance. Byline given. Offers up to 25% kill fee. Buys first North American serial or second serial (printing) rights. Editorial lead time 6 months. Submit seasonal material 10 months in advance. Reports in 2 months. Sample copy not available; writer's guidelines for #10 SASE.
Nonfiction: How-to (party planning, cooking, cleanup, grocery shopping), new product, photo features (tabletop settings). **Buys 15 mss/year**. Query with published clips. Length: 250-1,000 words. Payment varies based on length, writer, importance. Sometimes pays expenses of writers on assignment.
Reprints: Accepts previously published submissions.
Photos: State availability of photos with submission. Model releases required. Buys one-time rights.
Columns/Departments: Query with published clips. Payment varies based on length, writer, and level/amount of research required.
Tips: "Send a brief, clear query letter with relevant clips, and be patient."

$ $ $ $ COOKING LIGHT, The Magazine of Food and Fitness, P.O. Box 1748, Birmingham AL 35201-1681. (205)877-6000. Fax: (205)877-6600. Website: http://cookinglight.com. Editor: Douglas Crichton. Executive Editor: Nathalie Dearing. **Contact:** Jill Melton, senior food editor (food); Lisa Delaney, senior health and fitness editor (fitness). 75% freelance written. Magazine published 10 times/year on healthy recipes and fitness information. "*Cooking Light* is a positive approach to a healthier lifestyle. It's written for healthy people on regular diets who are counting calories or trying to make calories count toward better nutrition. Moderation, balance and variety are emphasized. The writing style is fresh, upbeat and encouraging, emphasizing that eating a balanced, varied, lower-calorie diet and exercising regularly do not have to be boring." Estab. 1987. Circ. 1,350,000. **Pays on acceptance.** Publishes ms an average of 1 year after acceptance. Byline sometimes given. Offers 33% kill fee. Submit seasonal material 1 year in advance. Reports in 1 year.

- Ranked as one of the best markets for freelance writers in *Writer's Yearbook* magazine's annual "Top 100 Markets," January 1998.

Nonfiction: Personal experience on nutrition, healthy recipes, fitness/exercise. Back up material a must. Buys 150 mss/year. Query with published clips. Length: 400-2,000 words. Pays $250-2,000. Pays expenses of writers on assignment.
Tips: "Emphasis should be on achieving a healthier lifestyle through food, nutrition, fitness, exercise information. In submitting queries, include information on professional background. Food writers should include examples of healthy recipes which meet the guidelines of *Cooking Light*."

$ $ DRINK MAGAZINE, GulfStream Communications, P.O. Box 1794, Mt. Pleasant SC 29465. (803)971-9811. Fax: (803)971-0121. E-mail: drink@gulfstreamcom.com. Website: http://www.drinkonline.com. Editor: Aaron Sigmond. **Contact**: Dawn Chipman, managing editor. **90% freelance written.** Quarterly magazine covering beer, wine, spirits and cigars. "*Drink Magazine* is a lifestyle magazine for educated, affluent readers who have an appreciation for beer, spirits and life. *Drink* covers travel, music, food and other topics of interest to beer and spirits connoisseurs." Estab. 1995. Circ. 250,000. Pays 30 days after publication. Publishes ms an average of 6 months after acceptance. Byline given. Offers 25% kill fee. Buys first North American serial rights. Editorial lead time 3 months. Submit seasonal material 6 months in advance. Reports in 6 weeks. Sample copy for $2 and 9×12 SAE with 5 first-class stamps. Writer's guidelines for #10 SASE.
Photos: State availability of photos with submission. Reviews transparencies. Negotiates payment individually. Identification of subjects required. Buys one-time rights.
Columns/Departments: Destinations (travel features related to microbrews), length: 1,800-2,000 words; Entertainment (stylish, hip coverage of entertainment, primarily musical, with a microbrew twist), length: 1,000-2,000 words; Affordable Luxuries (hobbies, interests, and other passions of our readers, not necessarily related to drinks), length: 1,000-1,500 words; Beer Nuts (upbeat profiles of people especially interesting in their dedication to beer), length: 900-1,200 words; Smokes (cigars and the cigar craze), length: 1,200-1,500 words; The Buzz (short, beer-related items of interest), length: 200-400 words; Eats (food articles with a beer or spirits slant, such as pairing certain beers with particular foods or cooking with beer, including recipes), length: 1,000-1,200 words; Spirits (any aspect of liquor, including profiles of interesting people in the industry, the history of a particular liquor, and serving suggestions), length: 1,200-1,500 words; On the Label (profile of a microbrew's label, the artist who rendered it, and interesting tidbits about the brewery that makes the beer), length: 6-7 copy blocks of 50-75 words each.
Tips: "Query first with published clips. We're looking for clever writing and fresh angles. No beer-party stories or beer

festival reviews. Look for original ways to cover beer or spirits; for example, we did an article called 'America's Best 19th Holes.' "

N $ $ $ EATING LIGHT, Woman's Day Special Interest Publications, Hachette-Filipacchi Magazines, 1633 Broadway, New York NY 10019. Fax: (212)767-5612. E-mail: wdspecials@aol.com. **Contact:** Janice Wright, managing editor. Editor: Carolyn Gatto. Semiannual consumer magazine covering food, cooking, healthy eating. "This magazine provides today's busy, health-conscious cooks with recipes and menus for healthy family meals. Recipes featured range from snacks to entrees to desserts and are quick to make; many can be prepared in advance. Recipes must be clear and concise, and fat content must be 30 percent or less. Articles of approximately 500 words on relevant food news and trends are included. Median age of reader is 41, and 99 percent of readers are female." **Pays on acceptance**. Publishes ms an average of 3 months after acceptance. Byline given. Offers up to 25% kill fee. Buys first North American serial or second serial (printing) rights. Editorial lead time 6 months. Submit seasonal material 10 months in advance. Reports in 2 months. Sample copy not available; writer's guidelines for #10 SASE.

Nonfiction: How-to (cooking healthy), new product (related to eating healthy). **Buys 10 mss/year**. Query with published clips. Length: 250-1,000 words. Payment varies based on length, writer, importance. Sometimes pays expenses of writers on assignment.

Reprints: Accepts previously published submissions.

Photos: State availability of photos with submission. Model releases required. Buys one-time rights.

Columns/Departments: Query with published clips. Payment varies based on length, writer, and level/amount of research required.

Tips: "Send a brief, clear query letter with relevant clips, and be patient."

$ $ $ $ EATING WELL, The Smart Magazine of Food and Health, 823 A Ferry Rd., Charlotte VT 05445. (802)425-3961. Fax: (802)425-3675. E-mail: ewelledit@aol.com. Website: http://www.eatingwell.com. **Contact:** Marcelle DiFalco, editor. Food Editor: Patsy Jamieson. **90% freelance written.** Magazine published 8 times/year. Estab. 1989. Circ. 640,000. Pays 60 days after acceptance. Publishes ms an average of 6 months after acceptance. Byline given. Buys first North American serial rights. Submit seasonal material 1 year in advance. Reports in 2-6 months.

Nonfiction: Nutrition, cooking, interview/profile, food, travel. Query with published clips. Length: 2,000-3,000 words. **Pays $1,000-3,000.** Pays expenses of writers on assignment.

Columns/Departments: Caroline Crawford, assistant editor. Eating Well in America (current news in the food world), 150-400 words. Buys 60 mss/year. Query. **Pays $200-500.**

Tips: "We invite experienced, published science writers to do a broad range of in-depth, innovative food-health-nutrition features. Read the magazine first. No phone queries, please."

$ $ FAST AND HEALTHY MAGAZINE, Pillsbury Co., 200 S. Sixth St., M.S. 28M7, Minneapolis MN 55402. Fax: (612)330-4875. **Contact**: Betsy Wray, editor. **50% freelance written.** "*Fast and Healthy* is a family-oriented bimonthly food magazine with healthful recipes for active people. All recipes can be prepared in 30 minutes or less and meet the U.S. Dietary guidelines for healthful eating. The magazine's emphasis is on Monday through Friday cooking. Our readers are busy people who are looking for information and recipes that help them prepare healthy meals quickly." Estab. 1992. Circ. 200,000. **Pays on acceptance.** Publishes ms an average of 8 months after acceptance. Byline given. Offers 20% kill fee. Buys all rights. Editorial lead time 1 year. Submit seasonal material 18 months in advance. Reports in 6 weeks on queries. Sample copy for $3. Writer's guidelines for #10 SASE.

Nonfiction: Food topics related to health, nutrition, convenience. **Buys 6 mss/year.** Query with résumé and published clips. Length: 100-1,500 words. **Pays $50-500.**

Columns/Departments: Living Better (health, nutrition, healthy lifestyle news), 25-200 words. **Buys 25 mss/year.** Query with published clips. **Pays $25-200.**

$ $ $ $ FOOD & WINE, American Express Publishing Corp., 1120 Avenue of the Americas, New York NY 10036. (212)382-5618. Editor-in-Chief: Dana Cowin. Managing Editor: Mary Ellen Ward. Executive Editor: Craig Seligman. Food Editor: Tina Ujlaki. Monthly magazine for "active people for whom eating, drinking, entertaining, dining out and travel are central to their lifestyle." Estab. 1978. Circ. 855,286. **Pays on acceptance.** Byline given. Offers 25% kill fee. Buys first world rights. Submit seasonal material 9 months in advance. Reports in 3 weeks on queries; 2 weeks on mss. Sample copy for $5. Writer's guidelines for #10 SASE.

- *Food & Wine* notes that they are very selective in choosing outside freelance writers.

Nonfiction: Food trends and news, how-to, kitchen and dining room design, travel. Query with published clips. **Buys 125 mss/year.** Length: 1,000-3,000 words. **Pays $800-2,000.** Pays expenses of writers on assignment.

Photos: State availability of photos with submission. No unsolicited photos or art. Offers $100-450/photo. Model releases and identification of subjects required. Buys one-time rights.

Columns/Departments: Restaurants, Travel, Style, Food, Health, Cooking Openers/Well-being, Cooking Fast, Cooking Master. **Buys 120 mss/year.** Query with published clips. Length: 800-3,000 words. **Pays $800-2,000.**

Tips: "Good service, good writing, up-to-date information, interesting article approach and appropriate point of view for *F&W*'s audience are important elements to keep in mind. Look over several recent issues before writing query."

GOURMET, Condé Nast Publications, Inc., 560 Lexington Ave., New York NY 10022. (212)880-2712. Website: http://www.gourmet.com. Publisher: K. Hunsinger. Editor: Gina Sanders. Affluent monthly magazine emphasizing fine dining.

"*Gourmet, The Magazine of Good Taste*, encompasses fine dining and entertaining, world travel, cooking, including elegant table settings, wines and spirits, shopping, culture and history, art and antiques." This magazine did not respond to our request for information. Query before submitting.

N ★ **HOME COOKING**, House of White Birches, Publishers, 306 E. Parr Rd., Berne IN 46711. (219)589-8741, ext. 396. Fax: (219)589-8093. E-mail: home_cooking@whitebirches.com. **Contact**: Shelly Vaughan, editor. Managing Editor: Barb Sprunger. **60% freelance written.** "*Home Cooking* delivers dozens of kitchen-tested recipes from home cooks every month. Special monthly features offer recipes, tips for today's busy cooks, techniques for food preparation, nutritional hints and more. Departments cover topics to round out the cooking experience." Circ. 75,000. **Pays within 45 days after acceptance**. Publishes ms an average of 8 months after acceptance. Byline given. Buys all or first rights. occasionally one-time rights. Editorial lead time 6 months. Submit seasonal material 8 months in advance. Accepts simultaneous submissions. Reports in 1 month on queries; 2 months on mss. Sample copy for 6×9 SAE and 2 first-class stamps. Editorial calendar for #10 SASE.

Nonfiction: How-to, humor, interview/profile, new product, personal experience, recipes, book reviews, all in food/cooking area. No health/fitness or travel articles. **Buys 85 mss/year.** Query or send complete ms. Length: 250-750 words plus 6-8 recipes. **Pays $10-300 for assigned articles; $10-150 for unsolicited articles.** Sometimes pays expenses of writers on assignment.

Reprints: Accepts previously published submissions.

Photos: State availability of photos with submission. Reviews prints. Negotiates payment individually. Model releases and identification of subjects required. Buys one-time rights.

Columns/Departments: Dinner Tonight (complete 30-minute meal with preparation guide), 500 words; Invitation to Dinner (complete meal to serve 6-12 guests), 600 words; Last Bite (first-person essay), 250 words. **Buys 20 mss/year.** Query or send complete ms. **Pays $10-75.**

Fillers: Anecdotes, facts, newsbreaks, short humor. **Buys 10/year.** Length: 10-150 words. **Pays $5-20.**

Tips: "Departments are most open to new writers. All submissions should be written specifically for our publication. Be sure to check spelling, grammar and punctuation before mailing. If that means setting aside your manuscript for two weeks to regain your objectivity, do it. A sale two weeks later beats a rejection earlier. If you follow our style in your manuscript, we know you've read our magazine."

N $ $ **JOURNAL OF ITALIAN FOOD & WINE**, 609 W. 114th St., Suite 77, New York NY 10025. **Contact**: J. Mimser Woggins, managing editor. **80% freelance written.** Bimonthly magazine. Estab. 1991. Circ. 50,000. Pays on publication. Publishes ms 2-4 months after acceptance. Byline given. Offers 25% kill fee or $100. Buys all rights. Editorial lead time 2-6 months. Submit seasonal material 4 months in advance. Simultaneous submissions OK. Query for electronic submissions. Reports in 2 weeks on queries; 2 months on mss. Sample copy $5.

Nonfiction: Book excerpts, essays, historical, how-to (cooking Italian), humor, interview/profile, new product, photo feature and travel. Special Christmas issue. "No first person, 'I remember when the smell of my mother's cooking came wafting into my room,' or 'ethnic' humor." **Buys 12-18 mss/year.** Query. Length: 500-2,500 words. **Pays $350 min. for assigned articles; $250 min. for unsolicited articles.** Sometimes pays expenses of writers on assignment.

Photos: Send photos with submission. Reviews 5×7 prints. Offers $35-200 but negotiates payment individually. Captions, model releases and identification of subjects required. Buys all rights.

Columns/Departments: Nota Bene (short, short on Italian food or wine ideas), 125-250 words. **Buys 5-7 mss/year.** Send complete ms. **Pays $20-75.**

Fiction: Ethnic, historical, slice-of-life vignettes. Buys 6 mss/year. Query. Length: 500-1,500 words. Pays $100-300.

Poetry: Facts, gags to be illustrated by cartoonist, short humor, cartoons. **Buys 15/year.** Length: 50-200 words. **Pays $10-50.**

Tips: "Writers should ignore *all* other food magazines. Articles should be long on hard facts and well-edited *before* we get them. It costs too much in human resources to edit the basics. And, don't try to recycle old material to us. It will be tossed back immediately."

$ $ **KASHRUS MAGAZINE, The Bimonthly for the Kosher Consumer and the Trade**, Yeshiva Birkas Reuven, P.O. Box 204, Parkville Station, Brooklyn NY 11204. (718)336-8544. **Contact:** Rabbi Yosef Wikler, editor. **25% freelance written.** Prefers to work with published/established writers, but will work with new/unpublished writers. Bimonthly magazine covering kosher food industry and food production. Estab. 1980. Circ. 10,000. Pays on publication. Publishes ms an average of 2 months after acceptance. Byline given. Offers 50% kill fee. Buys first or second serial (reprint) rights. Submit seasonal material 2 months in advance. Accepts simultaneous submissions. Reports in 1 week on queries, 2 weeks on mss. *Writer's Market* recommends allowing 2 months for reply. Sample copy for $3. Professional discount on subscription: $18/10 issues (regularly $33).

Nonfiction: General interest, interview/profile, new product, personal experience, photo feature, religious, technical and travel. Special issues feature: International Kosher Travel (October); Passover (March). **Buys 8-12 mss/year.** Query with published clips. Length: 1,000-1,500 words. **Pays $100-250 for assigned articles; up to $100 for unsolicited articles.** Sometimes pays expenses of writers on assignment.

Reprints: Send tearsheet or photocopy of article and information about when and where the article previously appeared. Pays 25-50% of amount paid for an original article.

Photos: State availability of photos with submission. Offers no additional payment for photos accepted with ms. Acquires one-time rights.

Columns/Departments: Book Review (cook books, food technology, kosher food), 250-500 words; People in the News (interviews with kosher personalities), 1,000-1,500 words; Regional Kosher Supervision (report on kosher supervision in a city or community), 1,000-1,500 words; Food Technology (new technology or current technology with accompanying pictures), 1,000-1,500 words; Travel (international, national), must include Kosher information and Jewish communities, 1,000-1,500 words; Regional Kosher Cooking, 1,000-1,500 words. **Buys 8-12 mss/year.** Query with published clips. **Pays $50-250.**

Tips: "*Kashrus Magazine* will do more writing on general food technology, production, and merchandising as well as human interest travelogs and regional writing in 1999 than we have done in the past. Areas most open to freelancers are interviews, food technology, cooking and food preparation, dining, regional reporting and travel. We welcome stories on the availability and quality of Kosher foods and services in communities across the U.S. and throughout the world. Some of our best stories have been by non-Jewish writers about kosher observance in their region. We also enjoy humorous articles. Just send a query with clips and we'll try to find a storyline that's right for you, or better yet, call us to discuss a storyline."

$ $ ON THE GRILL, On The Grill, Inc., 11063 Topeka Pl., Cooper City FL 33026. (954)430-0282. Fax: (954)430-3430. E-mail: onthegrill@aol.com. **Contact:** Scott M. Fine, editor-in-chief. 80% freelance written. Bimonthly magazine, "the first and only magazine dedicated to outdoor grilling and BBQing." Estab. 1996. Circ. 60,000. Pays on publication. Publishes ms an average of 3 months after acceptance. Byline given. Buys first rights. Editorial lead time 10 weeks. Submit seasonal material 3 months in advance. Reports in 1 month. Sample copy $3.95.

Nonfiction: Related to outdoor cooking: trends, ethnic, barbeque, grilling. **Buys 18 mss/year.** Query with published clips and SASE. Length: 1,500-2,500 words. **Pays $350-600 for assigned articles.**

Photos: State availability of photos with submission. Reviews 2¼×2¼ transparencies. Offers no additional payment for photos accepted with ms. Captions required. Buys one-time rights.

Columns/Departments: Buys 18 mss/year. Query with published clips and SASE.

Tips: "Please send samples of work and a brief bio and résumé. We will not respond to queries unless you include published clips."

☆ $ $ RISTORANTE, Foley Publishing, P.O. Box 73, Liberty Corner NJ 07938. (908)766-6006. Fax: (908)766-6607. E-mail: barmag@aol.com. Website: http://www.bartender.com. Contact: Raymond Foley, publisher. **Contact:** Jaclyn Foley, editor. **75% freelance written.** Bimonthly magazine covering "Italian anything! *Ristorante—The magazine for the Italian Connoisseur.* For Italian restaurants and those who love Italian food, travel, wine and all things Italian!" Estab. 1994. Circ. 40,000. Pays on publication. Publishes ms an average of 3 months after acceptance. Byline sometimes given. Buys first North American and one-time rights. Editorial lead time 3 months. Submit seasonal material 3 months in advance. Reports in 1 month on queries; 2 months on mss. Sample copy and writer's guidelines for 9×12 SAE and 4 first-class stamps.

Nonfiction: Book excerpts, general interest, historical/nostalgic, how-to (prepare Italian foods), humor, new product, opinion, personal experience, travel. **Buys 25 mss/year.** Send complete ms. Length: 100-1,000 words. **Pays $100-350 for assigned articles; $75-300 for unsolicited articles.** Sometimes pays expenses of writers on assignment.

Reprints: Send tearsheet or photocopy of article and information about when and where the article previously appeared. Pays 25% of amount paid for an original article.

Photos: Send photos with submission. Reviews 3×5 prints. Negotiates payment individually. Captions, model releases required. Buys one-time rights.

Columns/Departments: Send complete ms. **Pays $50-200.**

Fillers: Anecdotes, facts, short humor. **Buys 10/year. Pays $10-50.**

☆ $ $ $ $ SHAPE COOKS, The Guide to Healthy Eating, Weider Publications, 21100 Erwin St., Woodland Hills CA 91367. Fax: (818)992-6895. E-mail: shapette@aol.com. Website: http://www.fitnessonline.com. Editor: Katherine M. Tomlinson. **Contact**: Maureen Healy, assistant editor. **80% freelance written.** Quarterly magazine covering healthful low-fat cooking and eating. "*Shape Cooks* provides cutting-edge, hands-on information for active people who want healthful eating to taste great." Estab. 1996. Circ. 300,000. **Pays on acceptance**. Publishes ms an average of 3 months after acceptance. Offers 30% kill fee. Editorial lead time 6 months. Submit seasonal material 8 months in advance. Reports in 6 weeks on queries. Sample copy not available. Writer's guidelines for #10 SASE.

Nonfiction: Book excerpts, general interest, how-to, humor, new product, travel. **Buys 35 mss/year.** Query with published clips. *No unsolicited manuscripts*. Length: 600-2,500 words. **Pays 70¢-$1.20/word.**

Columns/Departments: Nutrition (hands-on tips and info); Fitness (reports on how food and nutrition affect physical performance); Traveling Light (vacations/adventures with a healthy-eating slant); all 600-1,200 words. **Buys 25 mss/year.** Query with published clips. **Pays 70¢-$1.20/word.**

N $ $ SIMPLY SEAFOOD, Waterfront Press Co., 5305 Shilshole Ave. NW, Suite 200, Seattle WA 98107. (206)789-6506. Fax: (206)789-9193. E-mail: editor@simplyseafood.com. Website: http://www.simplyseafood.com. Editor: Peter Redmayne. **Contact**: Cynthia Nims, editor. **50% freelance written.** Quarterly magazine covering seafood. "We are a consumer food magazine aimed at amateur cooks who enjoy seafood or would like to learn more about it. Contributors must be able to write knowledgeably and provide excellent, tested recipes." Estab. 1991. Circ. 60,000. **Pays on acceptance.** Publishes ms an average of 6 months after acceptance. Byline given. Buys first North American serial rights and makes work-for-hire assignments. Editorial lead time 6 months. Submit seasonal queries 1 year in advance. Reports in 1 month on queries. Writer's guidelines for #10 SASE.

Nonfiction: How-to (cooking), interview/profile (chefs, celebrities), travel. **Buys 8 mss/year.** Length: 1,000-2,000 words. **Pays $100-600.**

Photos: State availability of photos with submission. Reviews transparencies (any format). Negotiates payment individually. Captions, identification of subjects required. Buys one-time rights.

Columns/Departments: Seafood City (tour of a city's great seafood restaurants), 700 words. **Buys 4 mss/year. Pays $100.**

Tips: "Read our magazine and writer's guidelines first. Then imagine a story idea that would compel a grocery shopper passing by the seafood counter to buy our magazine. Write from a standpoint of knowledge—you need to be skilled with seafood in your own kitchen."

N $ $ $ $ SMOKE MAGAZINE, Cigars, Pipes & Life's Other Burning Desires, Lockwood Publications, 130 W. 42nd St., New York NY 10036. (212)391-2060. Fax: (212)827-0945. E-mail: cigarbar@aol.com. Website: http://www.smokemag.com. **Contact:** Michael Malone, assistant editor. Editor: Alyson Boxman. Managing Editor: Andy Marinkovich. **75% freelance written**. Quarterly consumer magazine covering cigars and men's lifestyle issues. "A large majority of *Smoke's* readers are affluent men, ages 28-35; active, educated and adventurous." Estab. 1995. Circ. 200,000. Pays on publication. Publishes ms an average of 3 months after acceptance. Byline given. Offers 25% kill fee. Buys first rights. Editorial lead time 2 months. Submit seasonal material 6 months in advance. Accepts simultaneous submissions. Reports in 6 weeks on queries; 3 months on mss. Sample copy for $4.95; writer's guidelines for #10 SASE.

Nonfiction: Essays, exposé, general interest, historical/nostalgic, how-to, humor, interview/profile, opinion, personal experience, photo feature, travel. **Buys 25 mss/year**. Query with published clips. Length: 1,500-3,000 words. **Pays $500-2,500.** Sometimes pays expenses of writers on assignment.

Photos: State availability of photos with submission. Reviews transparencies (2¼×2¼). Negotiates payment individually. Identification of subjects required.

Columns/Departments: Romeo (men's humor); y Julieta (men's humor written by women); What Lew Says (cigar industry humor); all 1,500 words. **Buys 20 mss/year**. Query with published clips. **Pays $500-2,000.**

Fiction: Adventure, condensed novels, confession, experimental, fantasy, historical, humorous, mainstream, mystery, novel excerpts, serialized novels, slice-of-life vignettes, suspense, western. **Buys 4 mss/year**. Query with published clips. Length: 3,000-5,000 words. **Pays $2,500.**

Fillers: Anecdotes, facts, gags to be illustrated by cartoonist, newsbreaks, short humor. **Buys 12/year**. Length: 200-500 words. **Pays $200-500.**

Tips: "Send a short clear query with clips. Go with your field of expertise: cigars, sports, music, true crime, etc. . . ."

$ $ $ VEGETARIAN TIMES, 4 High Ridge Park, Stamford CT 06905. (708)848-8100. Fax: (203)322-1966. **Contact:** Donna Sapolin, editorial director. **50% freelance written.** Prefers to work with published/established writers; works with small number of new/unpublished writers each year. Monthly magazine. Circ. 320,000. Buys first serial or all rights. Byline given unless extensive revisions are required or material is incorporated into a larger article. **Pays on acceptance.** Publishes ms an average of 4 months after acceptance. Submit seasonal material 6 months in advance. Reports in 3 months. Writer's guidelines for #10 SASE.

Nonfiction: Features articles that inform readers about how vegetarianism relates to diet, cooking, lifestyle, natural health, consumer choices, natural foods, environmental concerns and animal welfare. "All material should be well-documented and researched, and written in a sophisticated and lively style." Informational, how-to, personal experience, interview, investigative. Query with published clips. Length: average 2,000 words. **Pays flat rate of $100-1,000**, sometimes higher, depending on length and difficulty of piece. Also uses 200-500-word items for news department. Sometimes pays expenses of writers on assignment.

Photos: Payment negotiated/photo.

Tips: "You don't have to be a vegetarian to write for *Vegetarian Times*, but it is vital that your article have a vegetarian perspective. The best way to pick up that slant is to read several issues of the magazine (no doubt a tip you've heard over and over). We are looking for stories that go beyond the obvious 'Why I Became a Vegetarian.' A well-written provocative query plus samples of your best writing will increase your chances of publication. No phone queries. Fax queries OK."

★ $ $ VEGGIE LIFE, Growing Green, Cooking Lean, Feeling Good, EGW Publishing, 1041 Shary Circle, Concord CA 94518. (510)671-9852. Fax: (510)671-0692. E-mail: veggieed@aol.com. Website: http://www.veggielife.com. Contact: Sharon Barcla, editor. **90% freelance written.** Bimonthly magazine covering vegetarian cooking, natural health, herbal healing and organic gardening. Estab. 1992. Circ. 260,000. **Pays half on acceptance**, half on publication. Publishes ms an average of 4 months after acceptance. Byline given. Offers 25% kill fee. Buys all rights or makes work-for-hire assignments. Editorial lead time 4-6 months. Submit seasonal material 4-6 months in advance. Reports in 2-4 months, no phone calls, please. E-mail OK. Writer's guidelines for #10 SASE.

Nonfiction: Vegetarian cooking/recipes, gardening how-to, natural health, herbal healing, nutrition, fitness, health and gardening. No animal rights issues/advocacy, religious/philosophical, personal opinion. **Buys 30-50 mss/year.** Query with published clips. Length: 1,500-2,000 words. **Pays 35¢/word.** More for credentialed professionals. Food features:

300-500 words plus 6-8 recipes. Recipes must be 30% or less in fat, no more than 10g per serving. **Pays 35¢/word plus $35/recipe.**

Photos: State availability of photos with submission. Negotiates payment individually. Captions, model releases and identification of subjects required. Buys one-time rights or makes work-for-hire assignments.

Columns/Departments: Quick Cuisine, 100-150 words followed by 6-8 recipes prepared in 45 minutes or less each; Cooking with Soy, 150-200 word introduction followed by 4-5 eggless, dairy-free recipes made with a soy product. Remakes of old favorites encouraged. **Pays 35¢/published word plus $35/published recipe.**

Tips: "Research back issues; be authoritative; no 'Why I Became a Vegetarian . . .' stories. Please state why you are qualified to write particular subject matter—a *must* on health/herbal mss. No article will be considered without sufficient fact verification information. Gender specific and age specific (i.e., children, adolescents, seniors) topics are encouraged. Photographs are a strong plus in considering gardening submissions."

$ $ WINE SPECTATOR, M. Shanken Communications, Inc., 387 Park Ave. S., New York NY 10016. (212)684-4224. Fax: (212)684-5424. Website: http://www.winespectator.com. **Contact**: Jim Gordon, managing editor. **20% freelance written.** Prefers to work with published/established writers. Biweekly consumer newsmagazine. Estab. 1976. Circ. 200,000. Pays within 30 days of publication. Publishes ms an average of 2 months after acceptance. Byline given. Buys all rights and makes work-for-hire assignments. Submit seasonal material 4 months in advance. Reports in 3 months. Sample copy for $5. Writer's guidelines free.

Nonfiction: General interest (news about wine or wine events); interview/profile (of wine, vintners, wineries); opinion; travel, dining and other lifestyle pieces; photo feature. No "winery promotional pieces or articles by writers who lack sufficient knowledge to write below just surface data." Query. Length: 100-2,000 words average. **Pays $50-500.**

Photos: Send photos with ms. Pays $75 minimum for color transparencies. Captions, model releases, identification of subjects required. Buys all rights.

Tips: "A solid knowledge of wine is a must. Query letters essential, detailing the story idea. New, refreshing ideas which have not been covered before stand a good chance of acceptance. *Wine Spectator* is a consumer-oriented *news magazine*, but we are interested in some trade stories; brevity is essential."

GAMES & PUZZLES

These publications are written by and for game enthusiasts interested in both traditional games and word puzzles and newer role-playing adventure, computer and video games. Other puzzle markets may be found in the Juvenile section.

N ★ $ ACTION PURSUIT GAMES, CFW Enterprises, Inc., 4201 Van Owen Place, Burbank CA 91505. (818)845-2656. Fax: (818)845-7761. **Contact:** Daniel Reeves, editor. **60% freelance written.** Monthly magazine covering paintball. Estab. 1987. Circ. 85,000. Pays on publication. Publishes ms an average of 2 months after acceptance. Byline given. Buys first North American serial rights. Editorial lead time 3 months. Submit seasonal material 6 months in advance. Reports in 1 month. Sample copy for 9×12 SAE and 4 first-class stamps. Writer's guidelines free.

Nonfiction: Essays, exposé, general interest, historical/nostalgic, how-to, humor, interview/profile, new product, opinion, personal experience. No sexually oriented material or foul language. **Buys 70 mss/year.** Send complete ms. Length: 500-1,500 words. **Pays $100.** Sometimes pays expenses of writers on assignment.

Photos: Send photos with submission. Reviews transparencies and prints. Negotiates payment individually. Captions, model releases and identification of subjects required. Buys all rights.

Columns/Departments: Guest Editorial, 400 words; Professor Paintball (Q&A) 50 words; TNT (tournament news), 500-800 words. **Buys 24 mss/year.** Send complete ms. **Pays $100.**

Fiction: Adventure, historical. Must be paintball-related. **Buys 1-2 mss/year.** Send complete ms. Length: 500 words. **Pays $100.**

Poetry: Avant-garde, free verse, haiku, light verse, traditional. Must be paintball-related. **Buys 1-2 poems/year.** Submit 1 poem maximum. Length: 20 lines. **Pays $100.**

Fillers: Anecdotes, gags to be illustrated by cartoonist. **Buys 2-4/year.** Length: 20-50 words. **Pays $25.**

Tips: "Good graphic support is critical. Read the magazine for a couple of months before submitting."

$ $ CHESS LIFE, United States Chess Federation, 3054 NYS Route 9W, New Windsor NY 12553-7698. (914)562-8350. Fax: (914)561-2437 or (914)236-4852. E-mail: chesslife-uscf@juno.com. Website: http://www.uschess.org. **Contact:** Glenn Petersen, editor. **15% freelance written.** Works with a small number of new/unpublished writers each year. Monthly. "*Chess Life* is the official publication of the United States Chess Federation, covering news of most major chess events, both here and abroad, with special emphasis on the triumphs and exploits of American players." Estab. 1939. Circ. 70,000. Publishes ms an average of 8 months after acceptance. Byline given. Offers 50% kill fee. Buys first or negotiable rights. Submit seasonal material 8 months in advance. Accepts simultaneous submissions. Reports in 3 months. Sample copy and writer's guidelines for 9×11 SAE with 5 first-class stamps.

Nonfiction: General interest, historical, interview/profile, technical—all must have some relation to chess. No "stories about personal experiences with chess." **Buys 30-40 mss/year.** Query with samples "if new to publication." Length: 3,000 words maximum. **Pays $100/page (per 800-1,000 words).** Sometimes pays expenses of writers on assignment.

Reprints: Send tearsheet or photocopy of article or short story or typed ms with rights for sale noted and information about when and where the article or story previously appeared.
Photos: Reviews b&w contact sheets and prints, and color prints and slides. Captions, model releases and identification of subjects required. Buys all or negotiable rights. Pays $25-35 inside; $100-300 for covers.
Columns/Departments: Chess Review (brief articles on unknown chess personalities and "Chess in Everyday Life."
Fiction: Short stories and novel excerpts. "Chess-related, high quality." **Buys 2-3 mss/year.** Pays variable fee.
Fillers: Cartoons, poems, puzzles. Submit with samples and clips. Buys first or negotiable rights. **Pays $25 upon acceptance.**
Tips: "Articles must be written from an informed point of view—not from view of the curious amateur. Most of our writers are specialized in that they have sound credentials as chessplayers. Freelancers in major population areas (except New York and Los Angeles, which we already have covered) who are interested in short personality profiles and perhaps news reporting have the best opportunities. We're looking for more personality pieces on chessplayers around the country; not just the stars, but local masters, talented youths, and dedicated volunteers. Freelancers interested in such pieces might let us know of their interest and their range. Could be we know of an interesting story in their territory that needs covering. Examples of published articles include a locally produced chess television program, a meeting of chess set collectors from around the world, chess in our prisons, and chess in the works of several famous writers."

$ $ DRAGON MAGAZINE, TSR, Inc., P.O. Box 707, Renton WA 98057-0707. (425)226-6500. Fax: (425)204-5928. E-mail: dmail@wizards.com. Website: http://tsrinc.com. Editor: Dave Gross. **Contact**: Jesse Decker, editorial assistant. Monthly magazine of fantasy and science-fiction role-playing games. **90% freelance written.** Eager to work with published/established writers as well as new/unpublished writers. Estab. 1976. Circ. 100,000, primarily across the US, Canada and Great Britain. Byline given. Offers kill fee. Submit seasonal material 8 months in advance. **Pays on acceptance** for articles to which all rights are purchased; **pays on acceptance** for articles to which first/worldwide rights in English are purchased. Publishing dates of mss vary from 1-24 months after acceptance. Reports in 3 months. Sample copy $5.50. Writer's guidelines for #10 SASE.
Nonfiction: Articles on the hobby of science fiction and fantasy role-playing. No general articles on gaming hobby. "Our article needs are *very* specialized. Writers should be experienced in gaming hobby and role-playing. No strong sexual overtones or graphic depictions of violence." **Buys 120 mss/year.** Query. Length: 1,000-8,000 words. **Pays $50-500 for assigned articles; $5-400 for unsolicited articles.**
Fiction: Jesse Decker, fiction editor. Fantasy only. "No strong sexual overtones or graphic depictions of violence." **Buys 6-12 mss/year.** Send complete ms. Length: 2,000-8,000 words. **Pays 6-8¢/word.** Publishes novel excerpts.
Columns/Departments: Appear at irregular intervals. Arcane Lore (original magical or technological items for use in TSR's role-playing games); Bazaar of the Bizarre (original magical or technological items for use in *TSR*'s role playing games); The Dragon's Bestiary (new monsters, beasts, and aliens that characters might encounter); use standard Monstrous Compendium® format for AD&D game monsters; The Ecology . . . (highly detailed looks at standard fantasy-game creatures); Campaign Classics (material written for particular AD&D campaign settings that are not currently produced).
Tips: "*Dragon Magazine* is *not* a periodical that the 'average reader' appreciates or understands. A writer must *be* a reader and must share the serious interest in gaming our readers possess."

$ $ GAMEPRO, IDG Games Media Group, 951 Mariner's Island Blvd. Suite 700, San Mateo CA 94404. (415)349-4300. Fax:(650)349-8347. Website: http://www.gamepro.com. Publisher: John Rousseau. **Contact**: Kathy Skaggs, managing editor. Monthly magazine. "*GamePro* is a multi-platform interactive gaming magazine covering the electronic game market. It is edited for the avid online, video and PC game enthusiast. The editorial includes a mix of news, reviews, strategy and specific topical sections such as Fighter's Edge, Role Player's Realm and the Sports Pages." Estab.1988. Circ. 3,932. Query before submitting.

$ $ $ $ GAMES MAGAZINE, Games Publications, Inc., 7002 W. Butler Pike, Suite 210, Ambler PA 19002. (215)643-6385. Fax: (215)628-3571. E-mail: gamespub@itw.com. **Contact:** R. Wayne Schmittberger, editor-in-chief. **50% freelance written.** Bimonthly magazine covering puzzles and games. "*Games* is a magazine of puzzles, contests, and features pertaining to games and ingenuity. It is aimed primarily at adults and has an emphasis on pop culture." Estab. 1977. Circ. 225,000. Pays on publication. Publishes ms an average of 4 months after acceptance. Byline given. Offers 25% kill fee. Buys first North American serial rights, first rights, one-time rights, second serial (reprint) rights, all rights or makes work-for-hire assignments. Editorial lead time 3 months. Submit seasonal material 6 months in advance. Accepts simultaneous submissions. Reports in 6 weeks on queries; 3 months on mss. Sample copy for $5. Writer's guidelines for #10 SASE.
Nonfiction: Photo features, puzzles, games. **Buys 3 mss/year; 100 puzzles/year.** Query. Length: 1,500-2,500 words. **Pays $1,000-1,750.** Sometimes pays expenses of writers on assignment.
Reprints: Accepts previously published submissions.
Photos: State availability of photos with submission. Reviews contact sheets, negatives, transparencies, prints. Negotiates payment individually. Captions, model releases, identification of subjects required. Buys one-time rights.
Columns/Departments: Gamebits (game/puzzle news), 250 words; Games & Books (product reviews), 350 words; Wild Cards (short text puzzles), 100 words. **Buys 50 mss/year.** Query. **Pays $25-250.**
Fiction: Interactive adventure and mystery stories. **Buys 1-2 mss/year.** Query. Length: 1,500-2,500 words. **Pays $1,000-1,750.**

Tips: "Look for real-life people, places, or things that might in some way be the basis for a puzzle."

$ GIANT CROSSWORDS, Scrambl-Gram, Inc., Puzzle Buffs International, 41 Park Dr., Port Clinton OH 43452. (216)923-2397. **Contact:** C.R. Elum, editor. Submissions Editor: S. Bowers. **40% freelance written.** Eager to work with new/unpublished writers. Quarterly crossword puzzle and word game magazine. Estab. 1970. **Pays on acceptance.** Publishes ms an average of 1 month after acceptance. No byline given. Buys all rights. Reports in 1 month. "We offer constructors' kits, master grids, clue sheets and a 'how-to-make-crosswords' book for $37.50 postpaid." Send #10 SASE for details.
Nonfiction: Crosswords and word games only. Query. Pays according to size of puzzle and/or clues.
Reprints: Send information about when and where material previously appeared.
Tips: "We are expanding our syndication of original crosswords and our publishing schedule to include new titles and extra issues of current puzzle books."

☆ $ $ INQUEST, 151 Wells Ave., Congers NY 10920-2036. (914)268-2000. **Contact:** Tom Slizewski, managing editor. Monthly magazine covering all of adventure gaming, particularly collectible card games (i.e., Magic) but also roleplaying and fantasy, sci fi and board games. Pays on publication. Publishes ms an average of 2 months after acceptance. Byline given. Buys one-time and all rights. Reports in 6 weeks. Sample copy for $5. Writer's guidelines for #10 SASE.
Nonfiction: Interview/profile (Q&As with big-name personalities in sci-fi and fantasy field, special access stories like set visits to popular TV shows or films). No advertorials or stories on older, non-current games. **Buys 60 mss/year.** Query with published clips. Length: 2,000-4,000 words. **Pays $350-1,000.**
Columns/Departments: On Deck (mini game reviews), technical columns on how to play currently popular games. **Buys 100 mss/year.** Query with published clips. **Pays $50-250.**
Tips: "*InQuest* is always looking for good freelance news and feature writers who are interested in card, roleplaying or electronic games. A love of fantasy or science fiction books, movics, or art is desirable. Experience is preferred; sense of humor a plus; a flair for writing mandatory. Above all you must be able to find interesting new angles to a story, work hard and meet deadlines."

$ $ $ SCHOOL MATES, United States Chess Federation, 186 Route 9W, New Windsor NY 12553-5794. (914)562-8350 ext. 152. Fax: (914)561-CHES (2437). E-mail: beatchess@aol.com. Website: http://www.uschess.org. Publication Director: Jay Hastings. **Contact:** Beatriz Marinello, editor. **10% freelance written.** Bimonthly magazine of chess for the beginning (some intermediate) player. Includes instruction, player profiles, chess tournament coverage, listings. Estab. 1987. Circ. 30,000. Pays on publication. Publishes ms an average of 6 months after acceptance. Byline given. Publication copyrighted "but not filed with Library of Congress." Buys first rights. Editorial lead time 2 months. Submit seasonal material 3 months in advance. Accepts simultaneous submissions. Reports in 6 months. Sample copy and writer's guidelines free.
Nonfiction: How-to, humor, personal experience (chess, but not "my first tournament"), photo feature, technical, travel and any other chess related item. **Buys 10-20 mss/year.** Query. Length: 250-1,000 words. **Pays $50/1,000 words, $20 minimum).** "We are not-for-profit; we try to make up for low $ rate with complimentary copies." Sometimes pays expenses of writers on assignment.
Reprints: Send tearsheet, photocopy of article or typed ms with rights for sale noted and information about when and where the article previously appeared. Pays 100% of amount paid for an original article.
Photos: Send photos with submission. Reviews prints. Offers $25/photo for first time rights. Captions, identification of subjects required. Buys one-time rights, pays $15 for subsequent use.
Columns/Departments: Test Your Tactics/Winning Chess Tactics (explanation, with diagrams, of chess tactics; 8 diagrammed chess problems, e.g., "white to play and win in 2 moves"); Basic Chess (chess instruction for beginners). Query with published clips. **Pays $50/1,000 words ($20 minimum).**
Tips: "Know your subject; chess is a technical subject, and you can't fake it. Human interest stories on famous chess players or young chess players can be 'softer,' but always remember you are writing for children, and make it lively. We use the Frye readability scale (3rd-6th grade reading level), and items written on the appropriate reading level do stand out immediately! We are most open to human interest stories, puzzles, cartoons, photos. We are always looking for an unusual angle, e.g., (wild example) a kid who plays chess while surfing, or (more likely) a blind kid and how she plays chess with her specially-made chess pieces and board, etc."

$ $ $ VIDEOGAMES FOR VIRGINS, Com Ent Media Group, Inc., 3932 Wilshire Blvd., #212, Los Angeles CA 90010. Fax: (213)383-1093. Website: http://www.allmediadist.com. **Contact**: Sean Perkin, editor. **80% freelance written.** Biannual publication. "Designed as not only a reference guide on technological change, *VideoGames For Virgins* explores the impact and implications of technology on all of us. The CDZeene also includes a special section on cyberculture as well as a promotional CD-ROM containing game demos, interviews and product profiles. From the very best CD-ROM adventures to the latest in hardware, Internet information, and emerging techno trends, *VideoGames For Virgins* is the comprehensive guide to understanding the technological world." Estab. 1992. Circ. 25,000. Pays within 2 weeks after publication. Publishes ms an average of 1 month after acceptance. Byline given. Buys one-time rights, makes work-for-hire assignments. Editorial lead time 3 months. Submit seasonal material 4 months in advance. Accepts simultaneous submissions. Sample copy for $12.50. Writer's guidelines provided upon hiring.
Nonfiction: Exposé, interview/profile, new product, travel.

Reprints: Send photocopy of article and information about when and where the article previously appeared. Payment varies.

GAY & LESBIAN INTEREST

The magazines listed here cover a wide range of politics, culture, news, art, literature and issues of general interest to gay and lesbian communities. Magazines of a strictly sexual content are listed in the Sex section.

$ $ THE ADVOCATE, Liberation Publications, Inc., 6922 Hollywood Blvd., 10th Floor, Suite 1000, Los Angeles CA 90028-6148. (213)871-1225. Fax: (213)467-6805. E-mail: newsroom@advocate.com. **Contact**: Judy Wieder, editor-in-chief. Biweekly magazine covering national news events with a gay and lesbian perspective on the issues. Estab. 1967. Circ. 80,000. Pays on publication. Byline given. Buys first North American serial rights. Responds in 1 month. Sample copy for $3.95. Writer's guidelines for #10 SASE.
Nonfiction: Essays, exposé, interview/profile, personal experience. "Here are elements we look for in all articles: *Angling*: An angle is the one editorial tool we have to attract a reader's attention. An *Advocate* editor won't make an assignment unless he or she has worked out a very specific angle with you. Once you've worked out the angle with an editor, don't deviate from it without letting the editor know. Some of the elements we look for in angles are: a news hook; an open question or controversy; a 'why' or 'how' element or novel twist; national appeal; and tight focus. *Content*: Lesbian and gay news stories in all areas of life: arts, sciences, financial, medical, cyberspace, etc. *Tone*: Tone is the element that makes an emotional connection. Some characteristics we look for: toughness; edginess; fairness and evenhandedness; multiple perspectives." Special issues: gays on campus, coming out interviews with celebrities, HIV and health. Query. Length: 1,200 words. **Pays $550.**
Columns/Departments: Arts & Media (news and profiles of well-known gay or lesbians in entertainment) is most open to freelancers. Query. Length: 750 words. **Pays $100-500.**
Fiction: Publishes novel excerpts.
Tips: "*The Advocate* is a unique newsmagazine. While we report on gay and lesbian issues and are published by one of the country's oldest and most established gay-owned companies, we also play by the rules of mainstream-not gay-community-journalism."

N $ $ ARROW MAGAZINE, For the Rest of Us, High Road Publishing, 930 Westborne Dr., Suite 318, West Hollywood CA 90069. (310)360-8022. Fax: (310)360-8023. E-mail: editor@arrowmag.com. Website: http://arrowmag.com. Editor: Sam Francis. **Contact:** Paul Horne, executive editor. **90% freelance written**. Monthly magazine covering pro-commitment magazine for gay men. Estab. 1996. Circ. 20,000. Pays on publication. Publishes ms an average of 2 months after acceptance. Byline given. Buys one-time rights. Editorial lead time 2 months. Submit seasonal material 4 months in advance. Reports in 1 month on queries. Sample copy for $5.95. Writer's guidelines free.
Nonfiction: Book excerpts, essays, exposé, general interest, how-to, humor inspirational, interview/profile, opinion, personal experience, photo feature, technical, travel. "*Arrow* selects articles which challenge and broaden the current depiction of gay men in the media. Therefore, erotic material and overtly sexual submissions will likely be overlooked." Query with published clips. **Buys 30 mss/year**. Length: 300-4,000 words. **Pays 25-50¢/word** for print publication only, not for online publication.
Reprints: Accepts previously published submissions.
Photos: Send photos with submission. Reviews contact sheets. Offers no additional payment for photos accepted with ms. Model releases required. Buys one time rights.
Columns/Departments: Notebook (positive book reviews), 300-1,000 words; Cool Kids (profile of kids making a difference), Boy Toys (technology, high-tech gadgets), all 500-1,000 words. **Buys 20 mss/year**. Query with published clips. **Pays 25-50¢/word**.
Tips: "*Arrow* is not the typical 'gay' lifestyle magazine. We are the first and only national magazine for gay men that features commitment, romance, monogamy and a balanced approach to life. Successful freelances will research our online website and get a feel for our audience and vision before querying. Fresh looks at modern gay life are most welcome."

$ BAY WINDOWS, New England's Largest Gay and Lesbian Newspaper, Bay Windows, Inc., 631 Tremont St., Boston MA 02118-2034. (617)266-6670. Fax: (617)266-5973. E-mail: news@baywindows.com. Editor: Jeff Epperly. Arts Editor: Rudy Kikel. **Contact**: Loren King, assistant editor. **30-40% freelance written.** Weekly newspaper of gay news and concerns. "*Bay Windows* covers predominantly news of New England, but will print non-local news and features depending on the newsworthiness of the story. We feature hard news, opinion, news analysis, arts reviews

ALWAYS CHECK the most recent copy of a magazine for the address and editor's name before you send in a query or manuscript.

and interviews." Estab. 1983. Publishes ms within 2 months of acceptance, pays within 2 months of publication. Byline given. Offers 50% kill fee. Rights obtained varies, usually first serial rights. Simultaneous submissions accepted if other submissions are outside of New England. Submit seasonal material 3 months in advance. Reports in 3 months. Sample copy for $5. Writer's guidelines for #10 SASE.

Nonfiction: Hard news, general interest with a gay slant, interview/profile, opinion, photo features. **Publishes 200 mss/year.** Query with published clips or send complete ms. Length: 500-1,500 words. **Pay varies: $25-100 news; $25-100 arts.**

Reprints: Send tearsheet or photocopy of article and information about when and where the article previously appeared. Pays 75% of amount paid for an original article.

Photos: Pays $25/published photo. Model releases and identification of subjects required.

Columns/Departments: Film, music, dance, books, art. Length: 500-1,500 words. **Buys 200 mss/year. Pays $25-100.** Letters, opinion to Jeff Epperly, editor; news, features to Loren King, assistant editor; arts, reviews to Rudy Kikel, arts editor.

Poetry: All varieties. **Publishes 50 poems/year.** Length: 10-30 lines. No payment.

Tips: "Too much gay-oriented writing is laden with the clichés and catch phrases of the movement. Writers must have intimate knowledge of gay community; however, this doesn't mean that standard English usage isn't required. We look for writers with new, even controversial perspectives on the lives of gay men and lesbians. While we assume gay is good, we'll print stories which examine problems within the community and movement. No pornography or erotica."

$ $ CURVE MAGAZINE, Outspoken Enterprises, Inc., 1 Haight St., #B, San Francisco CA 94102. Fax: (415)863-1609. E-mail: curvemag@aol.com. Editor-in-chief: Frances Stevens. **Contact:** Gretchen Lee, managing editor. **40% freelance written.** Bimonthly magazine covering lesbian general interest categories. "We want dynamic and provocative articles written by, about and for lesbians." Estab. 1991. Circ. 68,000. Pays on publication. Byline given. Offers 25% kill fee. Buys first North American serial rights. Editorial lead time 3 months. Submit seasonal material 3 months in advance. Sample copy for $3.95 with $2 postage. Writer's guidelines free.

Nonfiction: Book excerpts, essays, exposé, general interest, how-to, humor, interview/profile, opinion, photo feature, travel. Special issues: Pride issue (June/July); Music issue (August/September). No fiction or poetry. **Buys 25 mss/year.** Query by mail, fax or e-mail. Length: 200-2,500 words. **Pays $40-300.** Sometimes pays expenses of writers on assignment.

Photos: Send photos with submission. Offers $50-100/photo; negotiates payment individually. Captions, model releases, identification of subjects required. Buys one-time rights.

Columns/Departments: Buys 72 mss/year. Query. **Pays $75-300.**

$ EVERGREEN CHRONICLES, A Journal of Gay, Lesbian, Bisexual, and Transgender Arts and Cultures, P.O. Box 8939, Minneapolis MN 55408. (612)823-6638. E-mail: cynatecoff@aol.com. **Contact:** Cynthia Fogard, managing editor. **75% freelance written.** Triannual magazine covering gay, lesbian, bisexual, and transgender literary and visual art. "We are interested in work that examines, challenges and values the unique sensibility of the GLBT experience." Estab. 1984. Circ. 2,000. Pays on publication. Byline given. Does not return submissions. Deadline: January 1 and July 1. Buys first rights. Reports in 2 months after submission deadline. Sample copy for $9. Writer's guidelines for #10 SASE.

Submissions: "We encourage submissions that explore the diversity of GLBT culture through poetry, short fiction, creative nonfiction, experimental writing, one-act plays, performance art, b&w visual art, b&w photography, or other genres. Send 4 copies of complete ms with cover letter, bio and Mac-readable disk of submission (Microsoft Word preferred). *Evergreen* holds an annual novella contest with a September 30 deadline. Send SASE for guidelines. **Pays $50.**

$ $ $ GENRE, Genre Publishing, 7080 Hollywood Blvd., #1104, Hollywood CA 90028. (213)896-9778. Fax: (213)467-8365. E-mail: genre@aol.com. Website: http://www.genremagazine.com. Editor: Peter McQuaid. **Contact:** Mark Olmstead, senior editor and Robert Ellsworth, arts editor. **60% freelance written.** Magazine published 10 times/year. "*Genre*, America's best-selling gay men's lifestyle magazine, covers entertainment, fashion, travel and relationships in a hip, upbeat, upscale voice. The award-winning publication's mission is best summarized by its tagline—'How We Live.' " Estab. 1991. Circ. 50,000. Pays on publication. Publishes ms an average of 3 months after acceptance. Byline given. Offers 25% kill fee. Buys first North American serial rights and all rights. Editorial lead time 3 months. Submit seasonal material 3 months in advance. Sample copy for $7.95 ($5 plus $2.95 postage). Guidelines for #10 SASE.

Nonfiction: Book excerpts, exposé, general interest, interview/profile, photo feature, travel, relationships, fashion. Query with published clips. Length: 1,500-3,500 words. **Pays 10-50¢/word.** Pays writer with contributor copies or other premiums rather than a cash payment if so negotiated.

Photos: State availability of photos with submission. Negotiates payment individually. Model releases and identification of subjects required.

Fiction: Adventure, experimental, horror, humorous, mainstream, mystery, novel excerpts, religious, romance, science fiction, slice-of-life vignettes, suspense. **Buys 10 mss/year.** Send complete ms. Length: 2,000-4,000 words.

GIRLFRIENDS MAGAZINE, America's fastest-growing lesbian magazine, 3415 Cesar Chavez, Suite 101, San Francisco CA 94110. (415)648-9464. Fax: (415)648-4705. E-mail: staff@gfriends.com. Website: http://www.gfriends.c

om. Editorial Director: Heather Findlay. **Contact**: Diane Anderson, executive editor. Monthly lesbian magazine. "*Girlfriends* provides its readers with intelligent, entertaining and visually-pleasing coverage of culture, politics and entertainment—all from an informed and critical lesbian perspective." Estab. 1994. Circ. 75,000. Pays on publication. Publishes ms an average of 6 months after acceptance. Byline given. Offers 25% kill fee. Buys first rights, use for advertising/promoting *Girlfriends*. Editorial lead time 3 months. Submit seasonal material 6 months in advance. Accepts simultaneous submissions. Reports in 3 weeks on queries; 2 months on mss. Sample copy for $4.95 plus $1.50 shipping and handling. Writer's guidelines for #10 SASE.

Nonfiction: Investigative features, celebrity profiles, exposé, humor, interviews, photo feature, travel. Special features: lesbians related to famous historical figures; best lesbian restaurants in the US; best places to live. Special issues: sex issue, gay pride issue, breast cancer issue. **Buys 20-25 mss/year.** Query with published clips. Length: 1,000-3,500 words. **Pays 10¢/word.**

Reprints: Send photocopy of article or short story or typed ms with rights for sale noted and information about when and where the article previously appeared. Negotiable payment.

Photos: Send photos with submissions. Reviews contact sheets, 4×5 or 2¼×2¼ transparencies, prints. Offers $30-250/photo. Captions, model releases, identification of subjects required. Buys one-time rights, use for advertising/promoting *GF*.

Columns/Departments: Lesbian Parenting, 600 words; Sports, 800 words; Travel, 900 words; Health, 600 words; Spirituality, 600 words. **Buys 50 mss/year.** Query with published clips. **Pays 10¢/word.**

Fiction: Ethnic, experimental, fantasy, historical, humorous, mystery, novel concepts, science fiction. **Buys 6-10 mss/year.** Query with complete ms. Length: 800-2,500 words. **Pays 10¢/word.**

Poetry: Avant-garde, free verse, Haiku, light verse, traditional. **Buys 3-5 poems/year.** Submit maximum 5 poems. Length: 3-75 lines. **Pays $50.**

Fillers: Gags to be illustrated by cartoonist, short humor. Buys 3-5/year. Length: 500-800 words. Pays $50.

Tips: "Be unafraid of controversy—articles should focus on problems and debates raised around lesbian culture, politics, and sexuality. Fiction should be innovative and eyebrow-raising. Avoid being 'politically correct.' Photographers should aim for the suggestive, not the explicit. We don't want just to know what's happening in the lesbian world, we want to know how what's happening in the world affects lesbians."

$ $ THE GUIDE, To Gay Travel, Entertainment, Politics and Sex, Fidelity Publishing, P.O. Box 990593, Boston MA 02199-0593. (617)266-8557. Fax: (617)266-1125. E-mail: theguide@guidemag.com. Website: http://www.guidemag.com. **Contact**: French Wall, editor. **25% freelance written.** Monthly magazine on the gay and lesbian community. Estab. 1981. Circ. 31,000. **Pays on acceptance.** Publishes ms an average of 2 months after acceptance. Kill fee negotiable. Buys first-time rights. Submit seasonal material 2 months in advance. Accepts simultaneous submissions. Reports in 3 months. Sample copy for 9×12 SAE with 8 first-class stamps. Writer's guidelines for #10 SASE.

Nonfiction: Book excerpts (if yet unpublished), essays, exposé, general interest, historical/nostalgic, humor, interview/profile, opinion, personal experience, photo feature, religious. **Buys 24 mss/year.** Query with or without published clips or send complete ms. Length: 500-5,000 words. **Pays $75-220.**

Reprints: Occasionally buys previously published submissions. Pays 100% of amount paid for an original article.

Photos: Send photos with submission. Reviews contact sheets. Offers no additional payment for photos accepted with ms (although sometimes negotiable). Captions, model releases, identification of subjects preferred; releases required sometimes. Buys one-time rights.

Tips: "Brevity, humor and militancy appreciated. Writing on sex, political analysis and humor are particularly appreciated. We purchase very few freelance travel pieces; those that we do buy are usually on less commercial destinations."

$ $ HX MAGAZINE, Two Queens, Inc., 230 W. 17th St., Eighth Floor, New York NY 10011. (212)352-3535. Fax: (212)352-3596. E-mail: editor@hx.com. Website: http://www.hx.com. **Contact**: Joseph Manghise, editor. **25% freelance written.** Weekly magazine covering gay New York City nightlife and entertainment. "We publish a magazine for gay men who are interested in New York City nightlife and entertainment." Estab. 1991. Circ. 39,000. Pays on publication. Publishes ms an average of 1 month after acceptance. Byline given. Buys first North American serial, second serial (reprint) and electronic reprint rights. Editorial lead time 2 months. Submit seasonal material 2 months in advance. "We must be exclusive East Coast publisher to accept." Only responds if interested.

Nonfiction: General interest, arts and entertainment, celebrity profiles, reviews. **Buys 50 mss/year.** Query with published clips. Length: 500-2,000 words. **Pays $50-150 for assigned articles; $25-100 for unsolicited articles.**

Reprints: Send tearsheet or photocopy of article or typed ms with rights for sale noted and information about when and where the article previously appeared. Pays 50% of amount paid for an original article.

Photos: State availability of photos with submission. Reviews contact sheets, negatives, 8×10 prints. Negotiates payment individually. Captions, model releases, identification of subjects required. Buys one-time, reprint and electronic reprint rights.

Columns/Departments: Buys 200 mss/year. Query with published clips. **Pays $25-125.**

N $ $ IN THE FAMILY, The Magazine for Lesbians, Gays, Bisexuals and Their Relations, Family Magazine, Inc., P.O. Box 5387, Takoma Park MD 20913. (301)270-4771. Fax: (301)270-4660. E-mail: lmarkowitz@aol.com. Website: http://www.inthefamily.com. **Contact:** Laura Markowitz, editor. **10% freelance written.** Quarterly magazine covering lesbian, gay and bisexual family relationships. "Using the lens of psychotherapy, our magazine looks at the complexities of L/G/B family relationships as well as professional issues for L/G/B therapists." Estab. 1995. Circ.

2,000. Pays on publication. Byline given. Buys first rights. Editorial lead time 4 months. Submit seasonal material 4 months in advance. Reports in 3 weeks on queries; 4 months on mss. Sample copy for $5.50. Writer's guidelines free on request.

Nonfiction: Essays, exposé, humor, opinion, personal experience, photo feature. "No autobiography." Send complete ms. Length: 2,000-4,000 words. **Pays up to $250, depending on length.** Sometimes pays expenses of writers on assignment.

Photos: State availability of photos with submission. Reviews contact sheets. Offers no additional payment for photos accepted with ms. Captions, model releases, identification of subjects required. Buys one-time rights.

Columns/Departments: Wayne Scott, book review editor. Book Reviews (therapy), 2,000 words. Query. **Pays $25-50.**

Fiction: Helena Lipstadt, fiction editor. Ethnic, humorous, slice-of-life vignettes, anything about therapy. "No erotica." **Buys 3 mss/year.** Send complete ms. Length: 2,000-3,000 words. **Pays $25-60.**

Poetry: Helena Lipstadt, fiction editor. Free verse, haiku, light verse, traditional. **Buys 4 poems/year.** Submit maximum 4 poems. Length: 15-30 lines. **Pays $25-50.**

$ LAMBDA BOOK REPORT, A Review of Contemporary Gay and Lesbian Literature, Lambda Rising, Inc., P.O. Box 73910, Washington DC 20056-3910. (202)462-7924. Fax: (202)462-5264. E-mail: lbreditor@aol.com. **Contact:** Kanani Kauka, senior editor. **90% freelance written.** Monthly magazine that covers gay/lesbian literature. "*Lambda Book Report* devotes its entire contents to the discussion of gay and lesbian books and authors. Any other submissions would be inappropriate." Estab. 1987. Circ. 11,000. Pays 30 days after publication. Byline given. Buys first rights. Reports in 2 months. Sample copy for $4.95 and 9×12 SAE with 5 first-class stamps. Guidelines free.

- This editor sees an increasing need for writers familiar with economic and science/medical-related topics.

Nonfiction: Book excerpts, essays (on gay literature), interview/profile (of authors), book reviews. "No historical essays, fiction or poetry." Query with published clips. Length: 200-2,000 words. **Pays $15-125 for assigned articles; $5-25 for unsolicited articles.**

Photos: Send photos with submission. Reviews contact sheets. Offers $10-25/photo. Model releases required. Buys one-time rights.

Tips: "Assignments go to writers who query with 2-3 published book reviews and/or interviews. It is helpful if the writer is familiar with gay and lesbian literature and can write intelligently and objectively on the field. Review section is most open. Clips should demonstrate writers' knowledge, ability and interest in reviewing gay books."

$ MOM GUESS WHAT NEWSPAPER, 1725 L St., Sacramento CA 95814. (916)441-6397. Fax: (916)441-6422. E-mail: info@mgwnew.com. Website: http://www.mgwnews.com. **Contact:** Linda Birner, editor. **80% freelance written.** Works with small number of new/unpublished writers each year. Biweekly tabloid covering gay rights and gay lifestyles. A newspaper for gay men, lesbians and their straight friends in the State Capitol and the Sacramento Valley area. First and oldest gay newspaper in Sacramento. Estab. 1977. Circ. 21,000. Publishes ms an average of 3 months after acceptance. Byline given. Buys all rights. Submit seasonal material 3 months in advance. Reports in 2 months. Sample copy for $1. Writer's guidelines for 10×13 SAE with 4 first-class stamps.

Nonfiction: Interview/profile and photo feature of international, national or local scope. **Buys 8 mss/year.** Query. Length: 200-1,500 words. Payment depends on article. Pays expenses of writers on special assignment.

Reprints: Send tearsheet or photocopy and information about when and where it previously appeared. Pay varies.

Photos: Send photos with submission. Reviews 5×7 prints. Offers no additional payment for photos accepted with ms. Captions and identification of subjects required. Buys one-time rights.

Columns/Departments: News, Restaurants, Political, Health, Film, Video, Book Reviews. **Buys 12 mss/year.** Query. Payment depends on article.

Tips: "*MGW* is published primarily from volunteers. With some freelancers payment is made. Put requirements in your cover letter. Byline appears with each published article; photos credited. Editors reserve right to edit, crop, touch up, revise, or otherwise alter manuscripts, and photos, but not to change theme or intent of the work. Enclose SASE postcard for acceptance or rejection. We will not assume responsibility for returning unsolicited material lacking sufficient return postage or lost in the mail."

$ $ $ OUT, 110 Greene St., Suite 600, New York NY 10012. (212)334-9119. Editor: James Collard. **Contact:** department editor. **80% freelance written.** Monthly national gay and lesbian general-interest magazine. "Our subjects range from current affairs to culture, from fitness to finance." Estab. 1992. Circ. 120,000. Pays on publication. Publishes ms an average of 3 months after acceptance. Byline given. Offers 25% kill fee. Buys first North American serial rights, second serial (reprint) rights for anthologies (additional fee paid) and 30-day reprint rights (additional fee paid if applicable). Editorial lead time 3 months. Submit seasonal material 5 months in advance. Accepts simultaneous submissions. Reports in 6 weeks on queries; 2 months on mss. Sample copy for $6. Writer's guidelines for #10 SASE.

Nonfiction: Book excerpts, essays, exposé, general interest, historical/nostalgic, humor, interview/profile, new product, opinion, personal experience, photo feature, travel, fashion/lifestyle. **Buys 200 mss/year.** Query with published clips and SASE. Length: 50-1,500 words. Pay varies. Sometimes pays expenses of writers on assignment.

Photos: State availability of photos with submission. Reviews contact sheets, transparencies, prints. Negotiates payment individually. Captions, model releases, identification of subjects required. Buys one-time rights.

Tips: "*Out's* contributors include editors and writers from the country's top consumer titles: skilled reporters, columnists, and writers with distinctive voices and specific expertise in the fields they cover. But while published clips and relevant experience are a must, the magazine also seeks out fresh, young voices. The best guide to the kind of stories we publish is to review our recent issues—is there a place for the story you have in mind? Be aware of our long lead time. No phone queries, please."

$ OUTSMART, Up & Out Communications, 3406 Audubon Place, Houston TX 77006. (713)520-7237. Fax: (713)522-3275. E-mail: outsmartmagazine.com. Website: http://outsmartmagazine.com. **Contact**: Greg Jeu, publisher. **70% freelance written.** Monthly magazine covering gay and lesbian issues. "*OutSmart* provides positive information to gay men, lesbians and their associates to enhance and improve the quality of our lives." Estab. 1994. Circ. 15,000. Pays on publication. Publishes ms an average of 2 months after acceptance. Byline given. Buys one-time rights and simultaneous rights. Editorial lead time 2 months. Submit seasonal material 2 months in advance. Accepts simultaneous submissions. Reports in 6 weeks on queries; 2 months on mss. Sample copy and writer's guidelines for SASE.
Nonfiction: Historical/nostalgic, interview/profile, opinion, personal experience, photo feature, travel, health/wellness, local/national news. **Buys 10 mss/year.** Send complete ms. Length: 700-2,000 words. **Pays $20-60.**
Reprints: Send photocopy of article.
Photos: State availability of photos with submission. Reviews 4×6 prints. Negotiates payment individually. Identification of subjects required. Buys one-time rights.
Tips: "Outsmart is a mainstream publication that covers culture, politics, personalities, entertainment and health/wellness as well as local and national news and events. It is our goal to address the diversity of the lesbian and gay community, fostering understanding among all Houston's citizens."

$ $ Q SAN FRANCISCO, Q Communications Inc., 584 Castro St., Suite 521, San Francisco CA 94114. (415)764-0324. Fax: (415)626-5744. E-mail: qsf1@aol.com. Website: http://www.qsanfrancisco.com. Editor: Robert Adams. **Contact**: Steve Cirrone, associate editor. **50% freelance written.** Bimonthly magazine covering gay and lesbian travel and entertainment with "positive images of gay men, lesbians, bisexuals and transgenders." Estab. 1994. Circ. 47,000. Pays on publication. Publishes ms an average of 1 month after acceptance. Buys first North American serial rights and second serial (reprint) rights. Editorial lead time 2 months. Submit seasonal material 2 months in advance. Accepts simultaneous submissions. Reports in 2 months. Writer's guidelines for #10 SASE.
Nonfiction: Book excerpts, essays, exposé, general interest, humor, inspirational, interview/profile, photo feature, travel. **Buys 6 mss/year.** Query with published clips. Length: 500-3,000 words. **Pays $50-200.** Sometimes pays expenses of writers on assignment.
Photos: State availability of photos with submission. Reviews contact sheets and transparencies. Negotiates payment individually. Model releases required. Negotiable rights are purchased on photos.
Columns/Departments: Music (contemporary/gay and lesbian), 900 words; Wellness (holistic medicine), 900 words. **Buys 6 mss/year.** Query with published clips. **Pays $50-100.**
Fiction: Adventure, fantasy, historical, humorous, mystery, romance, science fiction, slice-of-life vignette, suspense. **Buys 4 mss/year.** Query with published clips. Length: 700-2,000 words. **Pays $75-125.**
Poetry: Avant-garde, free verse, haiku, light verse, traditional. **Buys 4 poems/year.** Submit maximum 6 poems. Length: 5-50 lines. **Pays $25-100.**
Tips: "Perseverance is the key; send a follow-up letter after two weeks, and e-mail or fax after 3 weeks. Commitment to gay and lesbian civil rights is important."

GENERAL INTEREST

General interest magazines need writers who can appeal to a broad audience—teens and senior citizens, wealthy readers and the unemployed. Each magazine still has a personality that suits its audience—one that a writer should study before sending material to an editor. Other markets for general interest material are in these Consumer categories: Contemporary Culture, Ethnic/Minority, Inflight, Men's, Regional and Women's.

$ $ THE AMERICAN LEGION MAGAZINE, P.O. Box 1055, Indianapolis IN 46206-1055. (317)630-1200. Fax: (317)630-1280. Website: http://www.legion.org. Editorial Administrator: Joan L. Berzins. **Contact**: Joe Stuteville, editor. **70% freelance written.** Monthly magazine. "Working through 15,000 community-level posts, the honorably discharged wartime veterans of The American Legion dedicate themselves to God, country and traditional American values. They believe in a strong defense; adequate and compassionate care for veterans and their families; community service; and the wholesome development of our nation's youth. We publish articles that reflect these values. We inform our readers and their families of significant trends and issues affecting our nation, the world and the way we live. Our major features focus on national security, foreign affairs, business trends, social issues, health, education, ethics and the arts. We also publish selected general feature articles, articles of special interest to veterans, and question-and-answer interviews with prominent national and world figures." Prefers to work with published/established writers, but works with a small number of new/unpublished writers each year. Estab. 1919. Circ. 2,850,000. Buys first North American serial rights. Reports in 6 weeks on submissions. **Pays on acceptance.** Publishes ms an average of 6 months after acceptance. Byline given. Reports in 2 months. Sample copy for $3.50 and 9×12 SAE with 6 first-class stamps. Writer's guidelines for #10 SASE.

Nonfiction: Query with SASE first, will only consider unsolicited mss that are humorous or are from veterans concerning their wartime experiences. Query should explain the subject or issue, article's angle and organization, writer's qualifications and experts to be interviewed. Well-reported articles or expert commentaries cover issues/trends in world/national affairs, contemporary problems, general interest, sharply-focused feature subjects. Monthly Q&A with national figures/experts. Few personality profiles. No regional topics or promotion of partisan political agendas. **Buys 50-60 mss/year.** Length: 1,000-2,000 words. **Pays 30¢/word and up.** Pays phone expenses of writers on assignment.
Photos: On assignment.
Tips: "Queries by new writers should include clips/background/expertise; no longer than 1½ pages. Submit suitable material showing you have read several issues. *The American Legion Magazine* considers itself '*the* magazine for a strong America.' Reflect this theme (which includes economy, educational system, moral fiber, social issues, infrastructure, technology and national defense/security). We are a general interest, national magazine, not a strictly military magazine. We are widely read by members of the Washington establishment and other policy makers. No unsolicited jokes. No phone queries."

$ $ THE AMERICAN SCHOLAR, The Phi Beta Kappa Society, 1811 Q Street NW, Washington DC 20009-9974. (202)265-3808. Fax: (202)986-1601. E-mail: scholar@pbk.org. Editor: Anne Fadiman. **Contact:** Jean Stipicevic, managing editor. **100% freelance written.** Intellectual quarterly. "Our writers are specialists writing for the college-educated public." Estab. 1932. Circ. 25,000. Pays after author has seen edited piece in galleys. Byline given. Offers 50% kill fee. Buys first rights. Submit seasonal material 6 months in advance. Reports in 2 weeks on queries; 2 months on ms. Sample copy for $6.95. Writer's guidelines for #10 SASE.
Nonfiction: Book excerpts (prior to publication only), essays, historical/nostalgic, humor. **Buys 40 mss/year.** Query. Length: 3,000-5,000 words. **Pays $500.**
Columns/Departments: Buys 16 mss/year. Query. Length: 3,000-5,000 words. **Pays $500.**
Poetry: Rob Farnsworth, poetry editor. **Buys 20/year.** Submit maximum 3 poems. Length: 34-75 lines. **Pays $50.** "Write for guidelines."
Tips: "The section most open to freelancers is the book review section. Query and send samples of reviews written. No phone queries."

$ $ $ $ THE ATLANTIC MONTHLY, 77 N. Washington St., Boston MA 02114. Editor: William Whitworth. Managing Editor: Cullen Murphy. **Contact**: Michael Curtis, senior editor. Monthly magazine of arts and public affairs. "Seeks fiction that is clear, tightly written with strong sense of 'story' and well-defined characters." Circ. 500,000. Pays on acceptance. Byline given. Buys first North American serial rights. Simultaneous submissions discouraged. Reporting time varies. All unsolicited mss must be accompanied by SASE.

- Writers should be aware that this is not a market for beginner's work (nonfiction and fiction), nor is it truly for intermediate work. Study this magazine before sending only your best, most professional work.

Nonfiction: Book excerpts, essays, general interest, humor, personal experience, religious, travel. Query with or without published clips or send complete ms with SASE. Length: 1,000-6,000 words. Payment varies. Sometimes pays expenses of writers on assignment.
Fiction: Literary and contemporary fiction. **Buys 12-15 mss/year.** Send complete ms. Length: 2,000-6,000 words preferred. **Pays $2,500.**

- Ranked as one of the best markets for fiction writers in *Writer's Digest* magazine's "Fiction 50," June 1998.

Poetry: Peter Davison, poetry editor. **Buys 40-60 poems/year.**
Tips: When making first contact, "cover letters are sometimes helpful, particularly if they cite prior publications or involvement in writing programs. Common mistakes: melodrama, inconclusiveness, lack of development, unpersuasive characters and/or dialogue."

$ $ CAPPER'S, Ogden Publications, Inc., 1503 SW 42nd St., Topeka KS 66609-1265. (913)274-4346. Fax: (913)274-4305. E-mail: npeavler@kspress.com. Website: http://www.cappers.com. **Contact**: Nancy Peavler, editor. Associate Editors: Cheryl Ptacek, Ann Crahan, Rosemary Rebek. **25% freelance written.** Works with a small number of new/unpublished writers each year. Biweekly tabloid emphasizing home and family for readers who live in small towns and on farms. Estab. 1879. Circ. 250,000. **Pays for poetry and fiction on acceptance;** articles on publication. Publishes ms an average of 3-6 months after acceptance. Buys one-time serial rights only. Submit seasonal material at least 3 months in advance. Reports in 4 months; 10 months for serialized novels. Sample copy for $1.50. Writer's guidelines for #10 SASE.
Nonfiction: Historical (local museums, etc.), inspirational, nostalgia, budget travel (Midwest slants), people stories (accomplishments, collections, etc.). **Buys 50 mss/year.** Submit complete ms. Length: 700 words maximum. **Pays $2.50/inch. Pays additional $10 if used on website.**
Reprints: Send typed ms with rights for sale noted and information about when and where the article previously appeared. Pays 75% of amount paid for original article.
Photos: Purchased with accompanying ms. Submit prints. Pays $5-15 for 8×10 or 5×7 b&w glossy prints. Purchase price for ms includes payment for photos. Limited market for color photos (35mm color slides); pays $30 for color photos, $40 for covers. Additional payment of $10 if used on website.
Columns/Departments: Heart of the Home (homemakers' letters, recipes, hints); Community Heartbeat (volunteerism). Submit complete ms. Length: 300 words maximum. **Pays $1 gift certificate-$20.**
Fiction: "We buy very few fiction pieces—longer than short stories, shorter than novels." Adventure and romance

mss. No explicit sex, violence or profanity. **Buys 4-5 mss/year.** Query. **Pays $75-400 for 7,500-40,000 words.**
Poetry: Free verse, haiku, light verse, traditional, nature, inspiration. "The poems that appear in *Capper's* are not too difficult to read. They're easy to grasp. We're looking for everyday events and down-to-earth themes." **Buys 5-6/issue.** Limit submissions to batches of 5-6. Length: 4-16 lines. **Pays $10-15.**
Tips: "Study a few issues of our publication. Most rejections are for material that is too long, unsuitable or out of character for our magazine (too sexy, too much profanity, wrong kind of topic, etc.). On occasion, we must cut material to fit column space."

$ $ THE CHRISTIAN SCIENCE MONITOR, 1 Norway St., Boston MA 02115. (617)450-2000. Website: http://www.csmonitor.com. **Contact:** Amelia Newcomb (Learning); Jim Bencivenga (Ideas); Jennifer Wolcott (Arts & Leisure); David Scott (Home Front). International newspaper issued daily except Saturdays, Sundays and holidays in North America; weekly international edition. Estab. 1908. Circ. 95,000. Buys all newspaper rights worldwide for 3 months following publication. Buys limited number of mss, "top quality only." Publishes original (exclusive) material only. Pays on publication. Reports in 1 month. Writer's guidelines for #10 SASE.
Nonfiction: In-depth features and essays. The magazine is divided into 4 sections: Learning (education and life-long learning); Arts & Leisure; Ideas (religion, ethics, science and technology, environment, book reviews); and Home Front (home and community issues). Query to the appropriate section editor. **Pays $200.** Home Forum page buys essays of 400-900 words. Pays $150 average.
Poetry: Traditional, blank and free verse. Seeks non-religious poetry of high quality and of all lengths up to 75 lines. Pays $35-75 average.
Tips: "Style should be bright but not cute, concise but thoroughly researched. Try to humanize news or feature writing so reader identifies with it. Avoid sensationalism, crime and disaster. Accent constructive, solution-oriented treatment of subjects."

$ $ $ $ CIVILIZATION, Capital Publications, 575 Lexington Ave., New York NY 10022. (212)223-3100. Fax: (212)832-4883. Publisher: Quentin Walz. **Contact:** Sara Sklaroff, senior features editor. Bimonthly magazine. "*Civilization* is the membership magazine of the Library of Congress covering contemporary culture. Well-known writers contribute articles on the arts, travel, government, history, education, biography and social issues." Estab. 1994. Circ. 200,000. Pays ⅓ on acceptance, ⅔ on publication, for exclusive 90-day rights to features.
Nonfiction: *Civilization*'s departments and columns are staff written, but virtually all features come from freelancers. **Pays up to $5,000.** (Pay depends on subject matter, quality and the amount of time a writer has put into a piece.)
Tips: "*Civilization* is not a history magazine. We are a magazine of American culture. The key thing for us is that when we do look into the past, we connect it to the present." The magazine is now giving more emphasis to contemporary subjects. We take relatively few over-the-transom pieces. But we do look at everything that comes in, and sometimes we pick up something that looks really impressive. We put an enormous stress on good writing. Subject is important, but unless a writer can show us a sheaf of clips, we won't get started with them. There is a *Civilization* sensibility that we try to maintain. If you don't know the magazine well, you won't really understand what we're trying to do." To break in, look to contemporary subjects and the arts—including fine arts, the lively arts and book reviews.

$ $ $ $ EQUINOX: Canada's Magazine of Discovery, Malcolm Publishing, 11450 Albert-Hudon Blvd., Montreal North, Quebec H1G 3J9 Canada. (514)327-4464. Fax: (514)327-0514. E-mail: equinox@kos.net. **Contact**: Alan Morantz, editor. Bimonthly magazine "encompassing the worlds of human cultures and communities, the natural world and science and technology. *Equinox* is Canada's world-class magazine of discovery. It serves a large readership of intelligent Canadians who share a desire to learn more about themselves, their country, and the world around them. Its editorial range is eclectic, with a special emphasis on biology, ecology, wildlife, the earth sciences, astronomy, medicine, geography, natural history, the arts, travel and adventure. Throughout the theme is that of discovery and, in many cases, rediscovery. While exploring the unfamiliar, *Equinox* also provides fresh insights into the familiar." Estab. 1982. Circ. 120,000. **Pays on acceptance.** Byline given. Offers 50% kill fee. Buys first North American serial rights only. Submit seasonal queries 1 year in advance. Reports in 2 months. Sample copy for $5 and SAE with Canadian postage or IRCs. Writer's guidelines for #10 SASE (U.S. writers must send IRCs, not American stamps).
Nonfiction: Book excerpts (occasionally). No travel articles. Should have Canadian focus. Query with SAE including Canadian postage or IRCs. Length: 1,500-5,000 words. **Pays $1,500-3,500 negotiated.**
Reprints: Accepts previously published submissions. Send tearsheet of article and information about when and where the article previously appeared. Pays 30% of amount paid for an original article.
Photos: Send photos with ms. Reviews color transparencies—must be of professional quality; no prints or negatives. Captions and identification of subjects required. Pays $110-350. Pays $500 for covers. Sometimes pays package fees.
Columns/Departments: You Are Here (quirky back page that casts readers in another role—for example, you are a cellular phone), 700 words. **Pays $500.** Nexus (current science that isn't covered by daily media); Pursuits (service section for active living). Query with clips of published work. Length: 200-1,000 words. **Pays $250-500.**
Tips: "Submit ideas for short photo essays as well as longer features. We welcome queries by mail and e-mail."

$ $ $ FRIENDLY EXCHANGE, The Aegis Group: Publishers, Friendly Exchange Business Office, P.O. Box 2120, Warren MI 48090-2120. Publication Office: (810)558-7026. **Contact**: Dan Grantham, editor. **80% freelance written.** Works with a small number of new/unpublished writers each year. Quarterly magazine for policyholders of Farmers Insurance Group of Companies exploring travel, lifestyle and leisure topics of interest to active families. "These are traditional families (median adult age 39) who live primarily in the area bounded by Ohio on the east and the Pacific Ocean on the west, along with Tennessee, Alabama, and Virginia." Estab. 1981. Circ. 5,700,000. **Pays on acceptance.** Publishes ms an average of 5 months after acceptance. Offers 25% kill fee. Buys all rights. Submit seasonal material 1 year in advance. Accepts simultaneous queries. Reports in 2 months. Sample copy for 9×12 SAE with 5 first-class stamps. Writer's guidelines for #10 SASE.

Nonfiction: "We provide readers with 'news they can use' through articles that help them make smart choices about lifestyle issues. We focus on home, auto, health, personal finance, travel and other lifestyle/consumer issues of interest to today's families. Readers should get a sense of the issues involved, and information that could help them make those decisions. Style is warm and colorful, making liberal use of anecdotes and quotes." **Buys 8 mss/issue.** Query. Length: 200-1,200 words. **Pays $500-$1,000/article including expenses.**

Photos: Art director. Pays $150-250 for 35mm color transparencies; $50 for b&w prints. Cover photo payment negotiable. Pays on publication.

Columns/Departments: Consumer issues, health and leisure are topics of regular columns.

Tips: "We concentrate on providing readers information relating to current trends. Don't focus on destination-based travel, but on travel trends. We prefer tightly targeted stories that provide new information to help readers make decisions about their lives."

☆ $ $ **GRIT: American Life and Traditions**, Ogden Publications, 1503 SW 42nd St., Topeka KS 66609-1265. (913)274-4300. Fax: (785)274-4305. E-mail: grit@kspress.com. Website: http://www.grit.com. **Contact:** Donna Doyle, editor-in-chief. **80% freelance written.** Open to new writers. "*Grit* is Good News. As a wholesome, family-oriented magazine published for more than a century and distributed nationally, *Grit* features articles about family lifestyles, traditions, values and pastimes. *Grit* accents the best of American life and traditions—past and present. Our readers cherish family values and appreciate practical and innovative ideas. Many of them live in small towns and rural areas across the country; others live in cities but share many of the values typical of small-town America." Estab. 1882. Circ. 200,000. Pays on publication. Byline given. Buys all and first rights. Submit seasonal material 3 months in advance. Sample copy and writer's guidelines for $4 and 11×14 SAE with 4 first-class stamps.

Nonfiction: Need features (timely, newsworthy, touching but with a *Grit* angle), profiles, humor, readers' true stories, outdoor hobbies, collectibles. Also articles on gardening, crafts, hobbies, leisure pastimes. The best way to sell work is by reading each issue cover to cover. Special issues: Gardening (January-October); Health (twice a year). **Pays 15-22¢/word for articles plus $25-200 each for photos depending on finality and placement.** Main features run 1,200 to 1,500 words. Department features average 800-1,000 words.

Fiction: Short stories, 1,500-2,000 words; may also purchase accompanying art if of high quality and appropriate. Need serials (romance, westerns, mysteries) of at least 3,500 words. Send ms with SASE to Fiction Dept.

Photos: Professional quality photos (b&w prints or color slides) increase acceptability of articles. Photos: $25-200 each according to quality, placement and color/b&w.

Tips: "Articles should be directed to a national audience. Sources identified fully. Our readers are warm and loving. They want to read about others with heart. Send us something that will make us cry with joy."

$ $ $ $ **HARPER'S MAGAZINE**, 666 Broadway, 11th Floor, New York NY 10012. (212)614-6500. Fax: (212)228-5889. Editor: Lewis H. Lapham. **Contact:** Ann Gollin, editor's assistant. **90% freelance written.** Monthly magazine for well-educated, socially concerned, widely read men and women who value ideas and good writing. "*Harper's Magazine* encourages national discussion on current and significant issues in a format that offers arresting facts and intelligent opinions. By means of its several shorter journalistic forms—Harper's Index, Readings, Forum, and Annotation—as well as with its acclaimed essays, fiction, and reporting, *Harper's* continues the tradition begun with its first issue in 1850: to inform readers across the whole spectrum of political, literary, cultural, and scientific affairs." Estab. 1850. Circ. 216,000. Rights purchased vary with author and material. Pays negotiable kill fee. **Pays on acceptance.** Reports in 2 weeks. Publishes ms an average of 3 months after acceptance. Sample copy for $3.95.

Nonfiction: "For writers working with agents or who will query first only, our requirements are: public affairs, literary, international and local reporting and humor." No interviews; no profiles. Complete ms and query must include SASE. No unsolicited poems will be accepted. Publishes one major report per issue. Length: 4,000-6,000 words. Publishes one major essay/issue. Length: 4,000-6,000 words. "These should be construed as topical essays on all manner of subjects (politics, the arts, crime, business, etc.) to which the author can bring the force of passionate and informed statement."

- *Harper's Magazine* is the first national magazine to announce a policy of splitting past and future revenues from new-media and online sources with the material's original writers.

Reprints: Accepts previously published material for its "Readings" section. Send typed ms with rights for sale noted and information about when and where the article previously appeared.

Fiction: Publishes 1 short story/month. Generally pays 50¢-$1/word.

Photos: Contact: Angela Riechers, art director. Occasionally purchased with mss; others by assignment. Pays $50-500.

Tips: "Some readers expect their magazines to clothe them with opinions in the way that Bloomingdale's dresses them for the opera. The readers of *Harper's Magazine* belong to a different crowd. They strike me as the kind of people who would rather think in their own voices and come to their own conclusions."

☆ $ $ $ $ **HOPE MAGAZINE, People Making A Difference**, Hope Publishing, Inc., P.O. Box 160, Brooklin ME 04616. (207)359-4651. Fax: (207)359-8920. E-mail: editor@hopemag.com. Website: http://www.hopemag.com. Editor-in-Chief/Publisher: Jon Wilson. Editor: Kimberly Ridley. Associate Editor: Frances Lefkowitz. **Contact:**

Adrienne Bassler, editorial assistant. **90% freelance written.** Bimonthly magazine covering humanity at its best and worst. "We strive to evoke empathy among readers." Estab. 1996. Circ. 50,000. Pays on publication. Publishes ms an average of 6 months after acceptance. Byline given. Offers 20% kill fee. Buys first, one-time or second serial (reprint) rights. Editorial lead time 4 months. Submit seasonal material 6 months in advance. Accepts simultaneous submissions. Reports in 6 months. Sample copy for $5. Writer's guidelines for #10 SASE.

Nonfiction: Book excerpts, essays, general interest, interview/profile, personal experience, photo feature. Nothing explicitly religious, political or New Age. **Buys 50-75 mss/year.** Query with published clips or writing samples and SASE. Length: 250-4,000 words. **Pays $50-2,000.** Sometimes pays expenses of writers on assignment.

Photos: State availability of or send photos with submission. Reviews contact sheets and 5×7 prints. Negotiates payment individually. Captions and identification of subjects required. Buys one-time rights.

Columns/Departments: Contact Departments Editor. Signs of Hope (inspiring dispatches/news) 250-500 words. **Buys 50-60 mss/year.** Query with published clips or send complete ms and SASE. **Pays $50-150.**

Tips: "Write very personally, and very deeply. We're not looking for shallow 'feel-good' pieces. Approach uncommon subjects. Cover the ordinary in extraordinary ways. Go to the heart. Surprise us. Many stories we receive are too 'soft.' Absolutely no phone queries."

$ $ IDEALS MAGAZINE, Ideals Publications Inc., P.O. Box 305300, Nashville TN 37230. (615)333-0478. Publisher: Patricia Pingry. **Contact:** Lisa Ragan, editor. **95% freelance written.** Seasonal magazine. "Our readers are generally conservative, educated women over 50. The magazine is mainly light poetry and short articles with a nostalgic theme. Issues are seasonally oriented and thematic." Circ. 180,000. Pays on publication. Byline given. Buys one-time, worldwide serial and subsidiary rights. Submit seasonal material 8 months in advance. Accepts simultaneous submissions. Reports in 3 months. Sample copy for $4. Writer's and photographer's guidelines for #10 SASE.

Nonfiction: Essays, historical/nostalgic, humor, inspirational, personal experience. "No depressing articles." **Buys 20 mss/year.** Send complete ms. Length: 800-1,000 words. **Pays 10¢/word.**

Reprints: Send tearsheet or photocopy of article or short story and information about when and where the article previously appeared. Pays 10¢/word.

Photos: Guidelines for SASE. Reviews tearsheets. Offers no additional payment for photos accepted with ms. Captions, model releases, identification of subjects required. Buys one-time rights. Payment varies.

Fiction: Slice-of-life vignettes. **Buys 10 mss/year.** Length: 800-1,000 words. **Pays 10¢/word.**

Poetry: Light verse, traditional. "No erotica or depressing poetry." **Buys 250 poems/year.** Submit maximum 15 poems, 20-30 lines. **Pays $10/poem.**

Tips: "Poetry is the area of our publication most open to freelancers. It must be oriented around a season or theme. Nostalgia is an underlying theme of every issue. Poetry must be optimistic. We prefer that you submit complete ms instead of a query. No phone queries, please."

N $ IMPLOSION, A Journal of the Bizarre and Eccentric, Implosion Publishing, P.O. Box 533653, Orlando FL 32853. (407)645-3924. E-mail: info@implosion-mag.com. **Contact**: Cynthia Conlin, editor. **75% freelance written.** Quarterly magazine covering anything bizarre. "As the title implies, *Implosion* is a publication devoted to the bizarre. Everything we publish falls into this realm." Estab. 1995. Circ. 18,000. Pays on publication. Publishes ms an average of 6 months after acceptance. Byline given. Offers 100% kill fee. Buys first North American serial rights or one-time rights. Editorial lead time 6 months. Accepts simultaneous submissions. Reports in 1 month on queries; 4 months on mss. Sample copy for $5. Writer's guidelines for #10 SASE.

Nonfiction: Exposé, interview/profile, photo feature, travel, strange. **Buys 30 mss/year.** Send complete ms. Length: 1,000-8,000 words. **Pays $20-100 for assigned articles; $15-50 for unsolicited articles.** Sometimes pays expenses of writers on assignment.

Photos: Send photos with submission. Reviews contact sheets, 4×5 transparencies, 4×6 prints. Negotiates payment individually. Captions, model releases and identification of subjects required. Buys one-time rights.

Columns/Departments: Book reviews (must be unusual and bizarre), 250-500 words; CD reviews (must be unusual and bizarre), 250-500 words. **Buys 50 mss/year.** Send complete ms. **Pays $10.**

Fiction: Experimental, horror, science fiction. "The volume of unsolicited fiction is astronomical. Read the magazine to understand the format." **Buys 15 mss/year.** Send complete ms. Length: 200-8,000 words. **Pays $10-25.**

Tips: "We are especially interested in reviewing interviews with odd and eccentric musicians, filmmakers, artists, etc. Also, we have an on-going need for book reviews. We've got more fiction manuscripts than we know what to do with."

$ LEFTHANDER MAGAZINE, Lefthander International, P.O. Box 8249, Topeka KS 66608-0249. (913)234-2177. **Contact:** Kim Kipers, managing editor. **80% freelance written.** Eager to work with new/unpublished writers. Bimonthly magazine for "lefthanded people of all ages and interests in 50 US states and 12 foreign countries. The one thing they have in common is an interest in lefthandedness." Estab. 1975. Circ. 26,000. Pays on publication. Publishes ms an average of 4 months after acceptance. Byline usually given. Offers 25% kill fee. Rights negotiable. Reports on queries in 2 months. Sample copy for $2 and 9×12 SAE. Writer's guidelines for #10 SASE.

Nonfiction: Interviews with famous lefthanders; features about lefthanders with interesting talents and occupations; how-to features (sports, crafts, hobbies for lefties); research on handedness and brain dominance; exposé on discrimination against lefthanders in the work world; features on occupations and careers attracting lefties; education features relating to ambidextrous right brain teaching methods. **Buys 50-60 mss/year.** Length: 1,500-2,000 words for features.

Pays $100-150. Buys 6 personal experience shorts/year. Pays $35. Pays expenses of writer on assignment. Query with SASE.
Photos: State availability of photos for features. Pays $10-15 for good contrast color glossies, slides, transparencies. Rights negotiable.
Tips: "All material must have a lefthanded hook. We prefer practical, self-help and self-awareness types of editorial content of general interest."

$ $ $ $ LIFE, Time & Life Bldg., Rockefeller Center, New York NY 10020. (212)522-1212. **Contact**: Isolde Motley, managing editor. **10% freelance written.** Prefers to work with published/established writers; rarely works with new/unpublished writers. Monthly general interest picture magazine for people of all ages, backgrounds and interests. "*Life* shows the world through the power of pictures. It explores domestic and international news, business, the arts, lifestyle and human interest stories." Estab. 1936. Circ. 1,500,000. **Pays on acceptance.** Publishes ms an average of 3 months after acceptance. Byline given. Buys first North American serial rights. Submit seasonal material 4 months in advance. Accepts simultaneous submissions. Reports in 2 months.
Nonfiction: "We've done articles on anything in the world of interest to the general reader and on people of importance. It's extremely difficult to break in since we buy so few articles. Most of the magazine is pictures. We're looking for very high quality writing. We select writers whom we think match the subject they are writing about." Query with clips of previously published work. Length: 1,000-4,000 words.

N $ LIVING, For the Whole Family, Shalom Publishers, Route 2, Box 656, Grottoes VA 24441. E-mail: tgether @aol.com. **Contact**: Melodie M. Davis, editor. Managing Editor: Eugene Souder. **90% freelance written.** "*Living* is a quarterly 'good news' paper published to encourage and strengthen family life at all stages, directed to the general newspaper-reading public." Estab. 1992. Circ. 250,000. Pays on publication. Publishes ms an average of 9 months after acceptance. Byline given. Buys one-time or second serial (reprint) rights. Editorial lead time 6 months. Submit seasonal material 6 months in advance. Accepts simultaneous submissions. Reports in 2 months on queries; 6 months on mss. Sample copy for 9×12 SAE with 4 first-class stamps. Writer's guidelines for #10 SASE or by e-mail.
Nonfiction: General interest, humor, inspirational, personal experience. **Buys 40-50 mss/year.** Send complete ms. Length: 300-1,000 words. **Pays $35-50.**
Reprints: Accepts previously published submissions.
Photos: State availability of photos with submission or send photos with submission. Reviews 3×5 or larger prints. Offers $25/photo. Identification of subjects required. Buys one-time rights.
Fiction: Slice-of-life vignettes, emotionally grabbing stories of interest to all. No dog stories. **Buys 4 mss/year.** Send complete ms. Length: 500-1,000 words. **Pays $50.**
Tips: "This paper is for a general audience in the community, but written from a Christian-value perspective. It seems to be difficult for some writers to understand our niche—*Living* is not a 'religious' periodical but handles an array of general interest family topics and mentioning Christian values or truths as appropriate. Writing is extremely competitive and we attempt to publish only high quality writing."

$ $ $ $ NATIONAL GEOGRAPHIC MAGAZINE, 1145 17th St. NW, Washington DC 20036. (202)857-7000. Fax: (202)828-6667. Website: http://www.nationalgeographic.com. Editor: William Allen. **Contact**: Robert M. Poole, associate editor. **60% freelance written.** Prefers to work with published/established writers. Monthly magazine for members of the National Geographic Society. "Timely articles written in a compelling, 'eyewitness' style. Arresting photographs that speak to us of the beauty, mystery, and harsh realities of life on earth. Maps of unprecedented detail and accuracy. These are the hallmarks of *National Geographic* magazine. Since 1888, the *Geographic* has been educating readers about the world. Circ. 9,200,000.
Nonfiction: *National Geographic* publishes general interest, illustrated articles on science, natural history, exploration, cultures and geographical regions. Of the freelance writers assigned, a few are experts in their fields; the remainder are established professionals. Fewer than 1% of unsolicited queries result in assignments. Query (500 words with clips of published magazine articles) to Associate Editor Robert Poole. Do not send mss. Before querying, study recent issues and check a *Geographic Index* at a library since the magazine seldom returns to regions or subjects covered within the past 10 years. Length: 2,000-8,000 words. Pays expenses of writers on assignment.
Photos: Photographers should query in care of the Photographic Division.
Tips: "State the theme(s) clearly, let the narrative flow, and build the story around strong characters and a vivid sense of place. Give us rounded episodes, logically arranged."

$ $ $ THE NEW YORK TIMES, 229 W. 43rd St., New York NY 10036. (212)556-1234. Fax: (212)556-3830. *The New York Times Magazine* appears in *The New York Times* on Sunday. The *Arts and Leisure* section appears during the week. The *Op Ed* page appears daily.
Nonfiction: *Lives*: "Most articles are assigned but some unsolicited material is published, especially in the "Lives" column, a weekly personal-essay feature. Views should be fresh, lively and provocative on national and international news developments, science, education, family life, social trends and problems, arts and entertainment, personalties, sports and the changing American scene." Length: 900 words. **Pays $1,000.** Address unsolicited essays with SASE to the "Lives" Editor. *Arts and Leisure*: Wants "to encourage imaginativeness in terms of form and approach—stressing ideas, issues, trends, investigations, symbolic reporting and stories delving deeply into the creative achievements and processes of artists and entertainers—and seeks to break away from old-fashioned gushy, fan magazine stuff." Length:

1,500-2,000 words. **Pays $100-350**, depending on length. Address unsolicited articles with SASE to the Arts and Leisure Articles Editor. *Op Ed page*: "The Op Ed page is always looking for new material and publishes many people who have never been published before. We want material of universal relevance which people can talk about in a personal way. Wehn writing for the Op Ed page, there is no formula, but the writing itself should have some polish. Don't make the mistake of pontificating on the news. We're not looking for more political columnists." Length: 750 words. **Pays $150.**

$ $ $ $ THE NEW YORKER, 20 W. 43rd St., New York NY 10036-7441. (212)536-5400. Fax: (212)536-5735. Editor: David Remnick. Weekly. Estab. 1925. Circ. 750,000. "*The New Yorker* is a national magazine edited to address current issues, ideas and events. The magazine blends domestic and international news analysis with in-depth features, critiques and humorous observations on politics and business, culture and the arts, education, style, science, sports and literature." *The New Yorker* is one of today's premier markets for top-notch nonfiction, fiction and poetry. To submit material, please direct your ms to the appropriate editor, (i.e., fact, fiction or poetry) and enclose SASE. The editors deal with a tremendous number of submissions every week; writers hoping to crack this market should be prepared to wait at least 2 or 3 months for a reply. **Pays on acceptance.**
Tips: "We are always happy to welcome new contributors to our pages, but our editors generally find it impossible to make judgments on the basis of descriptions of or excerpts from stories; they prefer to read the stories themselves. If you plan to submit a long Fact piece, however, you may send a query letter, with a detailed proposal, to the Fact Editors. We have no guidelines as such. If you feel that your work might be right for us, please send your submission (prose typed double-spaced; poetry single-spaced, and no more than six poems at a time) to the appropriate editors—Fact, Fiction, Talk of the Town, or Poetry. Please include SASE with any submission."

$ $ $ NEWSWEEK, 251 W. 57th St., New York NY 10019. (212)445-4000. Circ. 3,180,000. Contact: Owen Clark. "*Newsweek* is edited to report the week's developments on the newsfront of the world and the nation through news, commentary and analysis." Accepts unsolicited mss for My Turn, a column of personal opinion. The 1,000- to 1,100-word essays for the column must be original, not published elsewhere and contain verifiable facts. **Payment is $1,000, on publication.** Buys non-exclusive world-wide rights. Reports in 2 months only on submissions with SASE.

THE OXFORD AMERICAN, The Southern Magazine of Good Writing, The Oxford American, Inc., P.O. Drawer 1156, Oxford MS 38655. Editor: Marc Smirnoff. **Contact:** Kelly Caudle, assistant editor. **30-50% freelance written.** Bimonthly magazine covering the South. "*The Oxford American* is a general-interest literary magazine about the South." Estab. 1992. Circ. 30,000. Pays 30 days after publication. Publishes ms an average of 6 months after acceptance. Byline given. Offers 25% kill fee. Buys first North American serial rights and one-time rights. Editorial lead time 2 months. Submit seasonal material 4 months in advance. Reports in 3 weeks on queries; 3 months on mss. Sample copy for $6.50. Writer's guidelines for #10 SASE.
Nonfiction: Essays, general interest, humor, personal experience, reporting, profiles, memoirs concerning the South. **Buys 6 mss/year.** Query with published clips or send complete ms. Pay varies. Sometimes pays expenses of writers on assignment.
Reprints: Send tearsheet, photocopy or typed ms with info about when and where the article previously appeared.
Photos: Negotiates payment individually. Captions required. Buys one-time rights.
Columns/Departments: Send complete ms. Pay varies.
Fiction: Publishes novel excerpts. **Buys 10 mss/year.** Send complete ms. Pay varies.
Tips: "Like other editors, I stress the importance of being familiar with the magazine. Those submitters who know the magazine always send in better work because they know what we're looking for. To those who don't bother to at least flip through the magazine, let me point out we only publish articles with some sort of Southern connection."

$ $ $ $ PARADE, Parade Publications, Inc., 711 Third Ave., New York NY 10017. (212)450-7000. Fax: (212)450-7284. Editor: Walter Anderson. **Contact:** Dakila D. Divina, Articles Editor. Weekly magazine for a general interest audience. 90% freelance written. Circ. 37,000,000. **Pays on acceptance.** Publishes ms an average of 3 months after acceptance. Kill fee varies in amount. Buys first North American serial rights. Reports in 6 weeks on queries. Writer's guidelines for #10 SASE.
Nonfiction: General interest (on health, trends, social issues or anything of interest to a broad general audience); interview/profile (of news figures, celebrities and people of national significance); and "provocative topical pieces of news value." Spot news events are not accepted, as *Parade* has a 6-week lead time. No fiction, fashion, travel, poetry, cartoons, nostalgia, regular columns, quizzes or fillers. Unsolicited queries concerning celebrities, politicians, sports figures, or technical are rarely assigned. Address single-page queries to Articles Editor; include SASE. Length of published articles: 800-1,500 words. **Pays $2,500 minimum.** Pays expenses of writers on assignment.
Tips: "Send a well-researched, well-written paragraph query targeted to our national market. No phone or fax queries. Keep subject tightly focused—you should be able to state the point or theme in three or four sentences."

$ $ $ $ READER'S DIGEST, Reader's Digest Rd., Pleasantville NY 10570-7000. E-mail: readersdigest@notes.compuserve.com. Website: http://www.readersdigest.com. **Contact:** Editorial Correspondence. Monthly general interest magazine. "We are looking for contemporary stories of lasting interest that give the magazine variety, freshness and originality." Estab. 1922. Circ. 15,000,000. **Pays on acceptance.** Byline given. Buys exclusive world periodical rights, electronic rights, among others. Editorial lead time 3 months. Submit seasonal material 6 months in advance. Address article queries and tearsheets of published articles to the editors.

- Ranked as one of the best markets for freelance writers in *Writer's Yearbook* magazine's annual "Top 100 Markets," January 1998.

Nonfiction: Book excerpts, essays, exposé, general interest, historical/nostalgic, humor, inspirational, interview/profile, opinion, personal experience. **Buys 100 mss/year.** Query with published clips. Does not read or return unsolicited mss. Length: 2,500-4,000 words. **Original article rates generally begin at $5,000.**

Reprints: Send tearsheet or photocopy with rights for sale noted and information about where and when the article appeared. Pays $1,200/*Reader's Digest* page for World Digest rights (usually split 50/50 between original publisher and writer).

Columns/Departments: "Original contributions become the property of *Reader's Digest* upon acceptance and payment. Life-in-These-United States contributions must be true, unpublished stories from one's own experience, revealing adult human nature, and providing appealing or humorous sidelights on the American scene." Length: 300 words maximum. **Pays $400 on publication.** True, unpublished stories are also solicited for Humor in Uniform, Campus Comedy, Tales Out of School and All in a Day's Work. Length: 300 words maximum. **Pays $400 on publication.** Towards More Picturesque Speech—the first contributor of each item used in this department is paid $50 for original material, $35 for reprints. For items used in Laughter, the Best Medicine, Personal Glimpses, Quotable Quotes, Notes From All Over, Points to Ponder and elsewhere in the magazine payment is as follows; to the *first* contributor of each from a published source, $35. For original material, $30/*Reader's Digest* two-column line. Previously published material must have source's name, date and page number. Contributions cannot be acknowledged or returned. Send complete anecdotes to *Reader's Digest*, Box LL, Pleasantville NY 10570, or fax to (914)238-6390. CompuServe address is notes:readersdigest or use readersdigest@notes.compuserve.com from other online services and the Internet."

"Roughly half the 30-odd articles we publish every month are reprinted from magazines, newspapers, books and other sources. The remaining 15 or so articles are original—most of them assigned, some submitted on speculation. While many of these are written by regular contributors—on salary or on contract—we're always looking for new talent and for offbeat subjects that help give our magazine variety, freshness and originality. Above all, in the writing we publish, *The Digest* demands accuracy—down to the smallest detail. Our worldwide team of 60 researchers scrutinizes every line of type, checking every fact and examining every opinion. For an average issue, they will check some 3500 facts with 1300 sources. So watch your accuracy. There's nothing worse than having an article fall apart in our research checking because an author was a little careless with his reporting. We make this commitment routinely, as it guarantees that the millions of readers who believe something simply because they saw it in *Reader's Digest* have not misplaced their trust."

READERS REVIEW, The National Research Bureau, Inc., 320 Valley St., Burlington IA 52601. (319)752-5415. Fax: (319)752-3421. **Contact**: Nancy Heinzel, editor. **75% freelance written.** Works with a small number of new/unpublished writers each year, and is eager to work with new/unpublished writers. Quarterly magazine. Estab. 1948. Pays on publication. Publishes ms an average of 1 year after acceptance. Buys all rights. Submit seasonal material 7 months in advance of issue date. Sample copy and writers guidelines for #10 SAE with 2 first-class stamps.

Nonfiction: General interest (steps to better health, attitudes on the job); how-to (perform better on the job, do home repairs, car maintenance); travel. **Buys 10-12 mss/year.** Query with outline or submit complete ms. Length: 500-700 words. **Pays 4¢/word.**

Tips: "Writers have a better chance of breaking in at our publication with short articles."

$ $ REAL PEOPLE, The Magazine of Celebrities and Interesting People, Main Street Publishing Co., Inc., 450 Seventh Ave., Suite 1701, New York NY 10123. (212)244-2351. Fax: (212)244-2367. E-mail: mrs-2@idt.net. **Contact**: Alex Polner, editor. **75% freelance written.** Bimonthly magazine for ages 30 and up focusing on celebs and show business, but also interesting people who might appeal to a national audience. Estab. 1988. Circ. 100,000. Pays on publication. Byline given. Pays 33% kill fee. Buys all rights. Submit seasonal material 6 months in advance. Reports on queries in 6 weeks. Sample copy for $4 and 8×11 SAE with 3 first-class stamps. Guidelines for #10 SASE.

Nonfiction: Interview/profile. Q&A formats are not encouraged. "We do a fall preview of TV and film in September. Material must be in by June. Other seasonal stories are 3-6 months in advance." **Buys 80 mss/year.** Query with published clips and SASE. Length: 200-1,500 words. **Pays $200-500 for assigned articles; $100-250 for unsolicited articles.**

Columns/Departments: Contact: Brad Hamilton. Newsworthy shorts—up to 200 words. "We are doing more shorter (75-250 word) pieces for our 'Real Shorts' column." Psst (gossip), 100 words; Follow-up (humor), 100 words. **Pays $25-50.**

Photos: State availability of photos with submissions. Reviews 5×7 prints and/or slides. Offers no additional payment for photos accepted with ms. Captions, model releases and identification of subjects required. Buys one-time rights.

Tips: "We are mainly interested in articles/interviews with celebrities of national prominence (Hollywood, music, authors, politicians, businesspeople in the media). Profiles must be based on personal interviews. As a rule, profiles should be tough, revealing, exciting and entertaining."

$ REUNIONS MAGAZINE, P.O. Box 11727, Milwaukee WI 53211-0727. (414)263-4567. Fax: (414)263-6331. E-mail: reunions@execpc.com. Website: www.reunionsmag.com. **Contact**: Edith Wagner, editor. **75% freelance written.** Quarterly magazine covering reunions—all aspects, all types. "*Reunions Magazine* is primarily for people actively involved with family, class, military and other reunions. We want easy, practical ideas about organizing, planning, researching/searching, attending or promoting reunions." Estab. 1990. Circ. 18,000. Pays on publication. Publishes ms an average of 1 year after acceptance. Byline given. Buys one-time rights. Editorial lead time minimum 6 months. Submit seasonal material 1 year in advance. Appreciates e-mail submissions. Reports in 9 months on queries. Sample copy free. Writer's guidelines for #10 SASE.

Nonfiction: Historical/nostalgic, how-to, humor, interview/profile, new product, personal experience, reunion recipes with reunion anecdote, photo feature, travel—all must be reunion-related. Needs reviewers for books, videos, software (include your requirements). Special issues: Ethnic/African-American family reunions (Winter); Food and Kids features (Summer); Golf and Travel features (Autumn); reunions in various sections of the US. **Buys 25 mss/year.** Query with published clips. Length: 500-3,000 words. **Pays $25.** Often rewards with generous copies.

Reprints: Send tearsheet or photocopy of article or typed ms with rights for sale noted and information about when and where the article previously appeared. Usually pays $10.

Photos: State availability of photos with submission. Reviews contact sheets, negatives, 35mm transparencies and prints. Offers no additional payment for photos accepted with ms. Captions, model releases and identification of individuals or small groups required. Buys one-time rights. Always looking for vertical cover photos.

Fillers: Anecdotes, facts, news, short humor—must be reunion-related. **Buys 20/year.** Length: 50-250 words. **Pays $5.**

Tips: "Write a lively account of an interesting or unusual reunion, either upcoming or soon afterward while it's hot. Tell readers why reunion is special, what went into planning it and how attendees reacted. Our *Masterplan* section is a great place for a freelancer to start. Send us how-tos or tips on any aspect of reunion organizing. Open your minds to different types of reunions—they're all around!"

$ $ $ $ ROBB REPORT, The Magazine for the Luxury Lifestyle, 1 Acton Place, Acton MA 01720. (978)263-7749. Fax: (978)263-0722. E-mail: robb@robbreport.com. Website: http://www.robbreport.com. **Contact:** Steven Castle, editor. **60% freelance written.** Monthly magazine. "We are a lifestyle magazine geared toward active, affluent readers. Addresses upscale autos, luxury travel, boating, technology, lifestyles, watches, fashion, sports, investments, collectibles." Estab. 1976. Circ. 100,000. Pays on publication. Byline given. Offers 50% kill fee. Buys all rights or first North American serial rights. Submit seasonal material 5 months in advance. Reports in 2 months on queries; 1 month on mss. Sample copy for $10.95 plus shipping and handling. Writer's guidelines for #10 SASE.

Nonfiction: General interest (autos, lifestyle, etc.), interview/profile (business owners/entrepreneurs), new product (autos, boats, consumer electronics), travel (international and domestic). No essays, bargain travel. Special issues: Home issue (September); Watch issue (November). Buys 60 mss/year. Query with published clips if available. Length: 500-3,500 words. **Pays $150-1,500.** Sometimes pays expenses of writers on assignment.

Photos: State availability of photos with submission. Payment depends on article. Buys one-time rights.

Tips: "We want to put the reader there, whether the article is about test driving a car, fishing for marlin, touring a luxury home or profiling a celebrity. The best articles will be those that tell stories, with all the details about products or whatever else you may be writing about placed in that context. Anecdotes should be used liberally, especially for leads, and the fun should show up in your writing."

$ $ THE SATURDAY EVENING POST, The Saturday Evening Post Society, 1100 Waterway Blvd., Indianapolis IN 46202. (317)636-8881. Editor: Cory SerVaas, M.D. Managing Editor: Ted Kreiter. Travel Editor: Holly Miller. **30% freelance written.** Bimonthly general interest, family-oriented magazine focusing on physical fitness, preventive medicine. "Ask almost any American if he or she has heard of *The Saturday Evening Post*, and you will find that many have fond recollections of the magazine from their childhood days. Many readers recall sitting with their families on Saturdays awaiting delivery of their *Post* subscription in the mail. *The Saturday Evening Post* has forged a tradition of 'forefront journalism.' *The Saturday Evening Post* continues to stand at the journalistic forefront with its coverage of health, nutrition, and preventive medicine." Estab. 1728. Circ. 500,000. Pays on publication. Publishes ms an average of 3 months after acceptance. Byline given. Buys second serial (reprint) and all rights. Submit seasonal material 4 months in advance. Accepts simultaneous submissions. Reports in 1 month on queries; 6 weeks on mss. Writer's guidelines for #10 SASE.

Nonfiction: Book excerpts, general interest, how-to (gardening, home improvement), humor, interview/profile, travel. "No political articles or articles containing sexual innuendo or hypersophistication." **Buys 50 mss/year.** Query with or without published clips, or send complete ms. Length: 750-2,500 words. **Pays $200 minimum**, negotiable maximum for assigned articles. Sometimes pays expenses of writers on assignment.

Photos: State availability of photos with submission. Reviews negatives and transparencies. Offers $50 minimum, negotiable maxmium per photo. Model release, identification required. Buys one-time or all rights.

Columns/Departments: Travel (destinations); Post Scripts (well-known humorists); Post People (activities of celebrities). **Buys 16 mss/year.** Query with published clips or send complete ms. Length: 750-1,500 words. **Pays $200 minimum,** negotiable maximum.

Fiction: Jack Gramling, fiction editor. Historical, humorous, mainstream, mystery, science fiction, western. "No sexual innuendo or profane expletives." Send complete ms. Length: 1,000-2,500 words. **Pays $150 min., negotiable max.**

Poetry: Light verse.

Fillers: Post Scripts Editor: Steve Pettinga. Anecdotes, short humor. **Buys 200/year.** Length: 300 words. **Pays $15.**

Tips: "Areas most open to freelancers are Health, Post Scripts and Travel. For travel we like text-photo packages, pragmatic tips, side bars and safe rather than exotic destinations. Query by mail, not phone. Send clips."

$ $ $ $ **SATURDAY NIGHT**, Saturday Night Magazine Ltd., 184 Front St. E, Suite 400, Toronto, Ontario M5A 4N3 Canada. Phone: (416)368-7237. Fax: (416)368-5112. E-mail: editorial@saturdaynight.ca. Editor: Kenneth Whyte. **Contact:** Liza Cooperman, assistant to the editor. **95% freelance written.** Monthly magazine. Readership is urban concentrated. Well-educated, with a high disposable income. Average age is 43. Estab. 1887. Circ. 410,000. Pays on receipt of a publishable ms. Byline sometimes given. Offer 50% kill fee. Buys first North American serial rights. Editorial lead time 4 months. Submit seasonal material 4 months in advance. Accepts simultaneous submissions. Sample copy for $3.50. Writer's guidelines free.

Nonfiction: Book excerpts, essays, general interest, interview/profile, opinion, personal experience, photo feature. **Buys 100 mss/year.** Query. Length: 200-5,000 words. **Pays $1/word.**

Photos: State availability of photos with submission. Negotiates payment individually. Model releases and identification of subjects required. Buys one-time rights.

Columns/Departments: Findings (short, interesting stories), Flavor of the Month, both 200-500 words. Query. **Pays $1/word.**

Fiction: Publishes novel excerpts.

$ $ $ $ **SMITHSONIAN MAGAZINE**, 900 Jefferson Dr., Washington DC 20560. E-mail: siarticles@aol.com. Website: http://www.smithsonianmag.si.edu. **Contact:** Marlane A. Liddell, articles editor. **90% freelance written.** Prefers to work with published/established writers. Monthly magazine for associate members of the Smithsonian Institution; 85% with college education. "*Smithsonian Magazine*'s mission is to inspire fascination with all the world has to offer by featuring unexpected and entertaining editorial that explores different lifestyles, cultures and peoples, the arts, the wonders of nature and technology, and much more. The highly educated, innovative readers of *Smithsonian* share a unique desire to celebrate life, seeking out the timely as well as the timeless, the artistic as well as the academic and the thought-provoking as well as the humorous." Circ. 2,300,000. Buys first North American serial rights. "Payment for each article to be negotiated depending on our needs and the article's length and excellence." **Pays on acceptance.** Publishes ms an average of 2-6 months after acceptance. Submit seasonal material 3 months in advance. Reports in 2 months. Sample copy for $5, % Judy Smith. Writer's guidelines for #10 SASE.

- Ranked as one of the best markets for freelance writers in *Writer's Yearbook* magazine's annual "Top 100 Markets," January 1998.

Nonfiction: "Our mandate from the Smithsonian Institution says we are to be interested in the same things which now interest or should interest the Institution: cultural and fine arts, history, natural sciences, hard sciences, etc." Query. Back Page humor: 1,000 words; full length article 3,500-4,500 words. Pays various rates per feature, **$1,000 per department article,** and various rates per short piece. Pays expenses of writers on assignment.

Photos: Purchased with or without ms and on assignment. Captions required. Pays $400/full color page.

Tips: "We prefer a written proposal of one or two pages as a preliminary query. The proposal should convince us that we should cover the subject, offer descriptive information on how you, the writer, would treat the subject and offer us an opportunity to judge your writing ability. Background information and writing credentials and samples are helpful. All unsolicited proposals are sent to us on speculation and you should receive a reply within eight weeks. Please include a self-addressed stamped envelope. We also accept proposals via electronic mail at siarticles@aol.com. If we decide to commission an article, the writer receives full payment on acceptance of the manuscript. If the article is found unsuitable, one-third of the payment serves as a kill fee."

"We consider focused subjects that fall within the general range of Smithsonian Institution interests, such as: culturall history, physical science, art and natural history. We are always looking for offbeat subjects and profiles. We do not consider fiction, poetry, travel features, political and news events, or previously published articles. We have a two-month lead time. Illustrations are not the responsibility of authors, but if you do have photographs or illustration materials, please include a selection of them with your submission. In general, 35mm color transparencies or black-and-white prints are perfectly acceptable. Photographs published in the magazine are usually obtained through assignments, stock agencies or specialized sources. No photo library is maintained and photographs should be submitted only to accompany a specific article proposal. We publish only 12 issues a year, so it is difficult to place an article in *Smithsonian*, but please be assured that all proposals are considered."

$ $ **THE STAR**, 660 White Plains Rd., Tarrytown NY 10591. (914)332-5000. Fax: (914)332-5043. **Contact:** Phil Bunton, editor-in-chief. Executive Editor: Steve LeGrice. **40% freelance written.** Prefers to work with published/established writers. Weekly magazine features celebrity news and upbeat human interest stories. Estab. 1974. Circ. 2,277,263. Pays on publication. Publishes ms an average of 1 month after acceptance. Buys first North American serial, occasionally second serial book rights. Reports in 2 months. Pays expenses of writers on assignment.

Nonfiction: Exposé (government waste, consumer, education, anything affecting family); general interest (human interest, consumerism, informational, family and women's interest); how-to (psychological, practical on all subjects affecting readers); interview (celebrity or human interest); new product; photo feature; profile (celebrity or national figure); health; medical; diet. No first-person articles. Query or submit complete ms. Length: 500-1,000 words. **Pays $100-400.**

Photos: Contact: Alistair Duncan, photo director. State availability of photos with query or ms. Pays $25-100 for 8×10 b&w glossy prints, contact sheets or negatives; $150-1,000 for 35mm color transparencies. Captions required. Buys one-time or all rights.

$ $ THE SUN, A Magazine of Ideas, The Sun Publishing Company, 107 N. Roberson St., Chapel Hill NC 27516. (919)942-5282. **Contact:** Sy Safransky, editor. **90% freelance written.** Monthly general interest magazine. "We are open to all kinds of writing, though we favor work of a personal nature." Estab. 1974. Circ. 31,000. Pays on publication. Publishes ms an average of 6 months after acceptance. Byline given. Buys first or one-time rights. Reports in 1 month on queries; 3 months on mss. Sample copy for $5. Send SASE for writer's guidelines.

Nonfiction: Book excerpts, essays, general interest, interview, opinion, personal experience, spiritual. **Buys 36 mss/year.** Send complete ms. Length: 7,000 words maximum. **Pays $300-750.** "Complimentary subscription is given in addition to payment (applies to payment for *all* works, not just nonfiction)."

Reprints: Send photocopy of article or short story and information about when and where the article or story previously appeared. Pays 50% of amount paid for an original article or story.

Photos: Send b&w photos with submission. Offers $50-200/photo. Model releases preferred. Buys one-time rights.

Fiction: Experimental, literary. "We avoid stereotypical genre pieces like sci-fi, romance, western and horror. Read an issue before submitting." **Buys 30 mss/year.** Send complete ms. Length: 7,000 words maximum. **Pays $300-500 for original fiction.**

- Ranked as one of the best markets for fiction writers in *Writer's Digest* magazine's "Fiction 50," June 1998.

Poetry: Free verse, prose poems, short and long poems. **Buys 24 poems/year.** Submit 6 poems max. **Pays $50-200.**

TIME, Time Inc. Magazine, Time & Life Bldg., 1271 Avenue of the Americas, New York NY 10020. (212)522-1212. Fax: (212)522-0536. **Contact**: Walter Isaacson, managing editor. Weekly magazine. "*Time* covers the full range of information that is important to people today—breaking news, national and world afairs, business news, societal and lifestyle issues, culture and entertainment news and reviews." Estab. 1923. Circ. 4,096,000. This magazine did not respond to our request for information. Query before submitting.

$ $ $ $ TOWN & COUNTRY, The Hearst Corp., 1700 Broadway, New York NY 10019. (212)903-5000. Fax: (212)765-8308. **Contact**: John Cantrell, deputy editor. **40% freelance written.** Monthly lifestyle magazine. "*Town & Country* is a lifestyle magazine for the affluent market. Features focus on fashion, beauty, travel, interior design, and the arts as well as individuals' accomplishments and contributions to society." Estab. 1846. Circ. 488,000. **Pays on acceptance.** Offers 25% kill fee. Buys first North American serial and electronic rights. Reports in 1 month on queries.

- Ranked as one of the best markets for freelance writers in *Writer's Yearbook* magazine's annual "Top 100 Markets," January 1998.

Nonfiction: "We're looking for engaging service articles for a high income, well-educated audience, in numerous categories: travel, personalities, interior design, fashion, beauty, jewelry, health, city news, country life news, the arts, philanthropy." Length: column items, 100-300 words; feature stories, 800-2,000 words. Special issues: Annual home issue (October 1998); Annual weddings issue (February 1999); Annual travel issue (April 1999). **Pays $1.50/word.** Query with clips before submitting.

Tips: "We have served the affluent market for over 150 years, and our writers need to be expert in the needs and interests of that market."

$ $ $ TROIKA, Wit, Wisdom & Wherewithal, Lone Tout Publications, Inc., 125 Main St., Suite 360, Westport CT 06880. (203)227-5377. E-mail: troikamag@aol.com. **Contact**: Celia Meadow, editor. **80% freelance written.** Quarterly magazine covering general interest, lifestyle. "A magazine for men and women seeking a balanced, three-dimensional lifestyle: personal achievement, family commitment, community involvement. Readers are upscale, educated, 30-50 age bracket. The *Troika* generation is a mix of what is called the X generation and the baby boomers. We are that generation. We grew up with sex, drugs and rock 'n roll, but now it really is our turn to make a difference, if we so choose." Estab. 1993. Circ. 100,000. Pays on publication. Publishes ms an average of 6 months after acceptance. Byline given. Buys first North American serial rights. Editorial lead time 3 months. Submit seasonal material 6 months in advance. Accepts simultaneous submissions. Reports in 2 months. Sample copy for $5. Guidelines for #10 SASE.

Nonfiction: Essays, exposé, general interest, historical/nostalgic, how-to (leisure activities, pro bono, finance), humor, inspirational, interview/profile (non-celebrity), opinion, personal experience. No celebrity profiles. **Buys 60-80 mss/year.** Query or send complete ms. Length:1,800-3,000 words. **Pays $250-1,000 for assigned articles; $250-400 for first appearance of unsolicited articles.**

Reprints: Send photocopy with information about when and where the article or story previously appeared.

Photos: State availability of photos with submission. Reviews negatives, transparencies. Offers no additional payment for photos accepted with ms. Captions, model releases, identification of subjects required.

Columns/Departments: Literati; Pub Performances (literary, theater, arts, culture); Blueprints (architecture, interior design, fashion); Body of Facts (science); Hippocratic Horizons (health); Home Technology; Capital Commitments (personal finance); all 750-1,200 words. **Buys 40-60 mss/year.** Query or send complete ms. **Pays $250 maximum.**

Fiction: Adventure, confession, experimental, fantasy, historical, mainstream, mystery, novel excerpts, slice-of-life vignettes, suspense. **Buys 4-8 mss/year.** Send complete ms. Length: 3,000 words maximum. **Pays $250 maximum.**

VANITY FAIR, Condé Nast Publications, Inc., 350 Madison Ave., New York NY 10017. (212)880-8800. Publisher: Mitchell B. Fox. Monthly. "*Vanity Fair* presents the issues, events and people that define our times. This chronicle of contemporary culture features art, entertainment, politics, business, and the media." This magazine did not respond to our request for information. Query before submitting.

$ $ THE WORLD & I, The Magazine for Serious Readers, News World Communications, Inc., 3600 New York Ave. NE, Washington DC 20002. (202)635-4000. Fax: (202)269-9353. E-mail: theworldandi@mcimail.com. Website: http://www.worldandi.com. Editor: Morton A. Kaplan. Executive Editor: Michael Marshall. **Contact**: Gary Rowe, editorial office coordinator. **90% freelance written.** Monthly magazine. "A broad interest magazine for the thinking, educated person. Estab. 1986. Circ. 30,000. Pays on publication. Publishes ms an average of 6 months after acceptance. Byline given. Offers 20% kill fee. Buys all rights. Submit seasonal material 5 months in advance. Reports in 6 weeks on queries; 10 weeks on mss. Sample copy for $5 and 9×12 SASE. Guidelines for #10 SASE.

Nonfiction: "Description of Sections: Current Issues: Politics, economics and strategic trends covered in a variety of approaches, including special report, analysis, commentary and photo essay. The Arts: International coverage of music, dance, theater, film, television, craft, design, architecture, photography, poetry, painting and sculpture—through reviews, features, essays, opinion pieces and a 6-page Gallery of full-color reproductions. Life: Surveys all aspects of life in 22 rotating subsections which include: Travel and Adventure (first person reflections, preference given to authors who provide photographic images), Profile (people or organizations that are "making a difference"), Food and Garden (must be accompanied by photos), Education, Humor, Hobby, Family, Consumer, Trends, and Health. Send SASE for complete list of subsections. Natural Science: Covers the latest in science and technology, relating it to the social and historical context, under these headings: At the Edge, Impacts, Nature Walk, Science and Spirit, Science and Values, Scientists: Past and Present, Crucibles of Science and Science Essay. Book World: Excerpts from important, timely books (followed by commentaries) and 10-12 scholarly reviews of significant new books each month, including untranslated works from abroad. Covers current affairs, intellectual issues, contemporary fiction, history, moral/religious issues and the social sciences. Currents in Modern Thought: Examines scholarly research and theoretical debate across the wide range of disciplines in the humanities and social sciences. Featured themes are explored by several contributors. Investigates theoretical issues raised by certain current events, and offers contemporary reflection on issues drawn from the whole history of human thought. Culture: Surveys the world's people in these subsections: Peoples (their unique characteristics and cultural symbols), Crossroads (changes brought by the meeting of cultures), Patterns (photo essay depicting the daily life of a distinct culture), Folk Wisdom (folklore and practical wisdom and their present forms), and Heritage (multicultural backgrounds of the American people and how they are bound to the world). Photo Essay: Patterns, a 6- or 8-page photo essay, appears monthly in the Culture section. Emphasis is placed on comprehensive photographic coverage of a people or group, their private or public lifestyle, in a given situation or context. Accompanying word count: 300-500 words. Photos must be from existing stock, no travel subsidy. Life & Ideals, a 6- or 8-page photo essay, occasionally appears in the Life section. First priority is given to those focused on individuals or organizations that are "making a difference." Accompanying word count: 700-1,000 words. 'No *National Enquirer*-type articles.' " **Buys 1,200 mss/year.** Query with published clips and SASE. Length: 1,000-5,000 words. Pays on a per-article basis that varies according to the length of the article, the complexity of special research required, and the experience of the author. Seldom pays expenses of writers on assignment.

Reprints: Send typed ms with rights for sale noted and information about when and where the article previously appeared.

Fiction: Publishes novel excerpts.

Poetry: Contact: Arts Editor. Avant-garde, free verse, haiku, light verse, traditional. **Buys 4-6 poems/year.** Query with maximum 5 poems. **Pays $30-75.**

Photos: State availability of photos with submission. Reviews contact sheets, transparencies and prints. Payment negotiable. Model releases and identification of subjects required. Buys one-time rights.

Tips: "We accept articles from journalists, but also place special emphasis on scholarly contributions. It is our hope that the magazine will enable the best of contemporary thought, presented in accessible language, to reach a wider audience than would normally be possible through the academic journals appropriate to any given discipline."

HEALTH & FITNESS

The magazines listed here specialize in covering health and fitness topics for a general audience. Health and fitness magazines have experienced a real boom lately. Most emphasize developing healthy lifestyle choices in exercise, nutrition and general fitness. Many magazines offer alternative healing and therapies that are becoming more mainstream, such as medicinal herbs, health foods and a holistic mind/body approach to well-being. As wellness is a concern to all demographic groups, publishers have developed editorial geared to specific audiences: African-American women, older readers, men, women. Also see the Sports/Miscellaneous section where publications dealing with health and particular sports may be listed. For magazines that cover healthy eating, refer to the Food and Drink section. Many general interest publications are also potential markets for health or fitness articles. Magazines covering health topics from a medical perspective are listed in the Medical category of Trade.

$ $ AMERICAN FITNESS, 15250 Ventura Blvd., Suite 200, Sherman Oaks CA 91403. (818)905-0040. Fax: (818)990-5468. **Contact:** Peg Jordan, R.N., editor-at-large. Managing Editor: Rhonda J. Wilson. **75% freelance written.**

Eager to work with new/unpublished writers. Bimonthly magazine covering exercise and fitness, health and nutrition. "We need timely, in-depth, informative articles on health, fitness, aerobic exercise, sports nutrition, age-specific fitness and outdoor activity." Circ. 36,000. Pays 6 weeks after publication. Publishes ms an average of 6 months after acceptance. Byline given. Buys all rights. Submit seasonal material 4 months in advance. Accepts simultaneous submissions. Reports in 6 weeks. Sample copy for $3 and SAE with 6 first-class stamps. Writer's guidelines for SAE.

Nonfiction: Health and fitness, including women's issues (pregnancy, family, pre- and post-natal, menopause and eating disorders); aerobic exercise; sports nutrition; sports medicine; innovations and trends in aerobic sports; tips on teaching exercise and humorous accounts of fitness motivation; physiology; exposé (on nutritional gimmickry); historical/nostalgic (history of various athletic events); inspirational (sports leader's motivational pieces); interview/profile (fitness figures); new product (plus equipment review); personal experience (successful fitness story); photo feature (on exercise, fitness, new sport); youth and senior fitness; travel (activity adventures). No articles on unsound nutritional practices, popular trends or unsafe exercise gimmicks. **Buys 18-25 mss/year.** Query with published clips or send complete ms. Length: 800-1,200 words. **Pays $140-180.** Sometimes pays expenses of writers on assignment.

Reprints: Accepts previously published submissions.

Photos: Sports, action, fitness, aquatic aerobics, aerobics competitions and exercise classes. "We are especially interested in photos of high-adrenalin sports like rock climbing and mountain biking." Pays $15 for b&w prints; $50 for transparencies. Captions, model release and identification of subjects required. Usually buys all rights; other rights purchased depend on use of photo.

Columns/Departments: Alternative paths (non-mainstream approaches to health, wellness and fitness); strength (latest breakthroughs in weight training); research (latest exercise and fitness findings); clubscene (profiles and highlights of fitness club industry); Adventure (treks, trails and global challenges); Food (low-fat/non-fat, high-flavor dishes); Homescene (home workout alternatives); Clip 'n' Post (concise exercise research to post in health clubs, offices or on refrigerators). Query with published clips or send complete ms. Length: 800-1,000 words. **Pays $100-140.**

Tips: "Cover a unique aerobics or fitness angle, provide accurate and interesting findings, and write in a lively, intelligent manner. We are looking for new health and fitness reporters and writers. *AF* is a good place for first-time authors or regularly published authors who want to sell spin-offs or reprints."

$ $ AMERICAN HEALTH FOR WOMEN, Reader's Digest Corp., 28 W. 23rd St., New York NY 10010. (212)366-8900. Fax: (212)627-3833. **Contact:** Miriam Arond. **70% freelance written.** Women's health magazine published 10 times/year covering both scientific and "lifestyle" aspects of women's health at mid-life, including medicine, fitness, nutrition and psychology. Estab. 1982. Circ. 1,000,000. **Pays on acceptance.** Publishes ms an average of 6 months after acceptance. Byline or tagline given. Offers 25% kill fee. Buys first North American serial rights. Sample copy for $3. Writer's guidelines for #10 SASE.

- Ranked as one of the best markets for freelance writers in *Writer's Yearbook* magazine's annual "Top 100 Markets," January 1998.

Features: Mail to Editorial. News-based articles usually with a service angle; well-written pieces with an investigative or unusual slant; profiles (health, fitness or celebrity related). No mechanical research reports, unproven treatments. "Stories should be written clearly, without jargon. Information should be new, authoritative and helpful to readers." **Buys 60-70 mss/year.** Query with 2 clips of published work. Length: 800-2,000 words. Payment varies. Pays expenses of writers on assignment.

Reprints: Send information about when and where the article previously appeared.

Columns/Departments: Mail to Editorial: Medicine, Alternative Medicine, Fitness, Diet/Nutrition, Medical Mystery, Lifestyle, Mental Health, Healthscope, Family, Dental. Other news sections included from time to time. **Buys about 300 mss/year.** Query with clips of published work. **Pays on acceptance**.

Tips: "*American Health For Women* has no full-time staff writers; we rely on outside contributors for most of our articles. The magazine needs good ideas and good articles from experienced journalists and writers. Feature queries should be short (no longer than a page) and to the point. Give us a good angle and a paragraph of background. Queries only. We are not responsible for material not accompanied by a SASE."

$ $ BETTER HEALTH, Better Health Press, 1450 Chapel St., New Haven CT 06511-4440. (203)789-3972. Fax: (203)789-4053. **Contact:** Director: Magaly Olivero, executive editor. **90% freelance written.** Prefers to work with published/established writers; will consider new/unpublished writers. Bimonthly magazine devoted to health, wellness and medical issues. Estab. 1979. Circ. 450,000. **Pays on acceptance.** Byline given. Offers $75 kill fee. Buys first rights. Query first; do not send article. Sample copy for $2.50. Writer's guidelines for #10 SASE.

Nonfiction: Wellness/prevention issues are of prime interest. New medical techniques or nonmainstream practices are not considered. No fillers, poems, quizzes, seasonal, heavy humor, inspirational or personal experience. Length: 2,500-3,000 words. **Pays $500.**

$ $ BETTER NUTRITION, Intertec/Primedia, 5 Penn Plaza, 13th Floor, New York NY 10001. (212)613-9757. Fax: (212)563-3028. E-mail: james_gormley@intertec.com. **Contact**: James J. Gormley, editor. **57% freelance written.** Monthly magazine covering nutritional news and approaches to optimal health. "Since 1938, *Better Nutrition*'s mission has been to inform our readers about the latest breakthroughs in nutritional (and lifestyle) approaches to optimal health and ongoing research into supplementation with vitamins, botanicals, minerals and other natural products." Estab. 1938. Circ. 475,000. Pays on publication. Publishes ms an average of 2 months after acceptance. Byline given. Offers 100% kill fee. Rights purchased vary. Editorial lead time 3 months. Sample copy free.

Nonfiction: Clinical research crystallized into accessible articles on nutrition, health, alternative medicine, disease prevention, FDA exposés. Each issue has a featured article (e.g., February, Healthy Heart; April, Allergies). **Buys 120-180 mss/year.** Query. Length: 700-2,000 words. **Pays $150-300.** Sometimes pays expenses of writers on assignment.
Photos: State availability of photos with query. Reviews 4×5 transparencies and 3×5 prints. Negotiates payment individually. Captions, model releases, identification of subjects required if applicable. Buys one-time rights or non-exclusive reprint rights.
Columns/Departments: Nutrition Hotline, Health Watch, Nutrition News, Women's Health, Veggie Corner, Lifestyles, Supplement Update, Natural Energy, Children's Health, Sports Nutrition, Earth Watch, Homeopathy, Botanical Medicine, Meatless Meals, Trim Time, Liquid Nutrition, Healthier Pets, Ayurvedic Medicine, Chinese Herbs, Longevity, Healing Herbs, Natural Beauty, Tea Time, Healthbites, Frontiers of Science.
Fillers: Anecdotes, facts and newsbreaks. All related to nutrition and alternative medicine.
Tips: "Be on top of what's newsbreaking in nutrition and alternative medicine. Be responsibly pro-supplementation-oriented. Be available for one-week-assignment/in-our-hands turnarounds. Fact-check, fact-check, fact-check. Find out what distinguishes us from other consumer-directed industry publications. Send in a résumé (including Social Security/IRS number) a couple of clips and a list of article possibilities."

$ $ COUNTRY LIVING'S HEALTHY LIVING, Hearst Magazines, 224 W. 57th St., New York NY 10019. Fax: (212)586-5430. Executive Editor: Diane DiCostanzo. Editor: Rachel Newman. **Contact:** Alyssa Shaffer, managing editor. **80% freelance written.** Bimonthly magazine. "*Country Living's Healthy Living* covers alternative health for a mainstream audience. Subjects include nutrition, fitness, beauty, profiles, news, recipes. Most readers are baby boomer women." Estab. 1996. Circ. 350,000. **Pays on acceptance.** Byline given. Offers 15% kill fee. Editorial lead time 3 months. Submit seasonal material 6 months in advance. Accepts simultaneous submissions. Reports in 3 months.
Nonfiction: Book excerpts, essays, general interest, humor, inspirational, interview/profile, new product, opinion, personal experience, photo feature, travel. **Buys 60 mss/year.** Query with published clips or send complete ms on spec. Length: 200-1,500 words. **Pays $75-1,000 for assigned articles; $75-500 for unsolicited articles.** Sometimes pays expenses of writers on assignment.
Reprints: Accepts previously published submissions.
Photos: State availability of photos with submission. Reviews transparencies. Negotiates payment individually. Identification of subjects required. Buys all rights.
Columns/Departments: "Our columnists are already chosen, and departments make up most of the magazine. See the nonfiction list of topics." **Pays $75-800.**
Tips: "Have some knowledge of the world of alternative health. We love it if a writer is reading the journals and attending the conferences, so the ideas are timely."

$ $ DELICIOUS!, Your Magazine of Natural Living, New Hope Communications, 1301 Spruce St., Boulder CO 80302. E-mail: delicious@newhope.com. Website: http://www.deliciousonline.com. Editor: Kathryn Arnold. **Contact:** Heather Prouty, senior editor. 85% freelance written. Monthly magazine covering natural products, nutrition, alternative medicines, herbal medicines. "*Delicious!* magazine empowers natural foods store shoppers to make health-conscious choices in their lives. Our goal is to improve consumers' perception of the value of natural methods in achieving health. To do this, we educate consumers on nutrition, disease prevention, botanical medicines and natural personal care products." Estab. 1985. Circ. 420,000. **Pays on acceptance**. Publishes ms an average of 6 months after acceptance. Byline given. Offers 20% kill fee. Editorial lead time 4 months. Submit seasonal material 6-8 months in advance. Accepts simultaneous submissions. Reports in 3 months. Sample copy and writer's guidelines free.
Nonfiction: Book excerpts, how-to, personal experience (regarding natural or alternative health), health nutrition, herbal medicines, alternative medicine. **Buys 150 mss/year.** Query with published clips. Length: 500-2,000 words. **Pays $100-700 for assigned articles; $50-300 for unsolicited articles.**
Photos: State availability of photos with submission. Reviews 3×5 prints. Offers no additional payment for photos accepted with ms. Identification of subjects required. Buys one-time rights.
Columns/Departments: Herbal Kingdom (scientific evidence supporting herbal medicines) 1,500 words; Nutrition (new research on diet for good health) 1,200 words; Dietary Supplements (new research on vitamins/minerals, etc.) 1,200 words. Query with published clips. **Pays $100-500.**
Tips: "Highlight any previous health/nutrition/medical writing experience. Demonstrate a knowledge of natural medicine, nutrition, or natural products. Health practitioners who demonstrate writing ability are ideal freelancers."

$ $ ENERGY TIMES, Enhancing Your Life Through Proper Nutrition, 548 Broadhollow Rd., Melville NY 11747. (516)777-7773. Fax: (516)755-1064. E-mail: kristine@natplus.com. Editor: Gerard McIntee. **Contact**: Kristine Garland, associate editor. **70% freelance written.** Magazine published 10 times/year covering nutrition, health and beauty aids, complementary medicinal, herbs (medicinal and culinary), natural foods. "*Energy Times* is an informative magazine read by consumers who frequent health food stores. Our editorial material is designed to help readers make informed choices as they take responsibility for their own health. All editorial material must be based on verifiable scientific research, not opinions, and should be compatible with the healthy-lifestyle philosophy of the health food industry." Estab. 1991. Circ. 650,000. Pays on publication. Publishes ms an average of 2 months after acceptance. Byline given. Offers 10% kill fee. Buys all rights. Editorial lead time 2 months. Submit seasonal material 6 months in advance. Reports in 1 month on queries, 2 months on mss. Sample copy for $2.50. Writer's guidelines for #10 SASE.
Nonfiction: Book excerpts, how-to (recipes, natural beauty aids), interview/profile, new product, photo feature, techni-

cal (science related to nutrition and complementary medicines), travel. Special issue: Book excerpts, July/August. **Buys 36 mss/year.** Query. Length: 1,500-2,500 words. **Pays $300.**

Photos: State availability of photos with submissions. Reviews negatives, transparencies, prints. Negotiates payment individually. Model releases, identification of subjects required. Buys one-time rights.

Columns/Departments: Nutritional news (current information on nutrition foods/supplements/vitamins), 850 words; university update (current research on nutrition, health related topics, herbs, vitamins), 850 words; Medicine Chest (natural remedies), 850 words; Longevity (improve quality of life through natural methods. Recent topics include stress reduction and t'ai chi). Send complete ms. **Pays $50.**

Tips: "Although we hire lay freelancers and professional journalists, we prefer to maintain an active group of professional medical/healthcare practitioners with accredited degrees. Because our editorial calendar is prepared a year in advance, send résumé and clips in addition to your query. We may not need the article you suggest, but we may want to contact you about article assignment. No calls, please. Assiduously avoid references to specific manufacturers, products or formulations. *All information must be generic.*"

$ $ $ FDA CONSUMER, 5600 Fishers Lane, Rockville MD 20857. (301)443-3220. Fax: (301)443-9057. Website: http://www.fda.gov. **Contact:** FDA Consumer Editor. **10% freelance written.** Prefers to work with experienced health and medical writers. Bimonthly magazine for general public interested in health issues. A federal government publication (Food and Drug Administration). Circ. 20,000. Pays after acceptance. Publishes ms an average of 3 months after acceptance. Byline given. Not copyrighted. Pays 50% kill fee. "All rights must be assigned to the USA so that the articles may be reprinted without permission. This includes electronic rights." Query with résumé and clips only. Buys 5-10 freelance mss/year. "We cannot be responsible for any work by writer not agreed upon by prior contract."

Nonfiction: "Upbeat feature articles of an educational nature about FDA regulated products and specific FDA programs and actions to protect the consumer's health and pocketbook. Articles based on health topics connected to food, drugs, medical devices, and other products regulated by FDA. All articles subject to clearance by the appropriate FDA experts as well as acceptance by the editor. All articles based on prior arrangement by contract." Length: 2,000-2,500 words. **Pays $800-950** for "first-timers;" **$1,200** for those who have previously published in *FDA Consumer*. Pays phone and mailing expenses.

Photos: Black and white photos are purchased on assignment only.

Tips: "Besides reading the feature articles in *FDA Consumer*, a writer can best determine whether his/her style and expertise suit our needs by submitting a résumé and clips; story suggestions are unnecessary as most are internally generated. No phone queries please."

$ $ FIT, Goodman Media Group, Inc., 1700 Broadway, 34th Floor, New York NY 10019. (212)541-7100. Fax: (212)246-0820. Editor: Lisa Klugman. Managing Editor: Sandra Kosherick. **Contact:** Megan McMorris, senior editor. **50% freelance written.** Works with a small number of new/unpublished writers each year. Bimonthly magazine covering fitness and health for active, young women. Circ. 125,000. **Pays on acceptance.** Publishes ms an average of 5 months after acceptance. Byline given. Offers 20% kill fee. Buys all rights. Submit seasonal material 6 months in advance. Reports in 1 month if rejecting ms, longer if considering for publication.

Nonfiction: Health, fitness, sports, beauty, psychology, relationships, athletes and nutrition. **Buys 20 mss/year.** Query with published clips. No phone queries. Length: 1,000-1,500 words. **Pays 50¢/word.**

Photos: Reviews contact sheets, transparencies, prints. Model releases, identification of subjects required. Buys all rights.

Columns/Departments: Finally Fit Contest. Readers can submit "before and after" success stories along with color slides or photos. **Pays $100.**

Tips: "We strive to provide the latest health and fitness news in an entertaining way—that means coverage of real people (athletes, regular women, etc.) and/or events (fitness shows, marathons, etc.), combined with factual information. First-person is okay. Looking for stories that are fun to read, revealing, motivational and informative."

$ $ $ $ FITNESS MAGAZINE, 375 Lexington Ave., New York NY 10017-5514. (212)499-2000. Fax: (212)499-1568. **Contact**: Jennifer Cook, executive editor. Published 10 times/year for women in their twenties and thirties who are interested in fitness and living a healthy life. **Pays on acceptance**. Byline given. Offers 20% kill fee. Buys first North American serial rights. Reports in 2 months on queries. Writer's guidelines for #10 SASE.

Nonfiction: "We need timely, well-written nonfiction articles on exercise and fitness, beauty, health, diet/nutrition, and psychology. We always include boxes and sidebars in our stories." **Buys 40 mss/year.** Query. Length: 1,500-2,500 words. **Pays $1,500-2,500.** Pays expenses of writers on assignment.

Reprints: Accepts previously published submissions. Send photocopy of article. Negotiates fee.

Columns/Departments: Buys 60 mss/year. Query. Length: 600-1,200 words. **Pays $600-1,200.**

Tips: "Our pieces must get inside the mind of the reader and address her needs, hopes, fears and desires. *Fitness* acknowledges that getting and staying fit is difficult in an era when we are all time-pressured."

N **FITNESSLINK, 'All the News That's Fit'**, FitnessLink, 113 Circle Dr. S., Lambertville NJ 08530. Fax: (609)397-7347. E-mail: editor@fitnesslink.com. Website: http://www.fitnesslink.com. **Contact:** Shannon Entin, editor. **90% freelance written**. Daily consumer website covering fitness, exercise and nutrition. "*FitnessLink* is an on-line fitness information provider. We publish articles and tips on a variety of topics, as well as provide a storehouse of information on associations and continuing education in the health and fitness industry." Estab. 1996. Circ. 500,000.

Pays on publication. Publishes ms an average of 2 months after acceptance. Byline given. Buys first electronic rights. Editorial lead time 1 month. Submit seasonal material 1 month in advance. Accepts simultaneous submissions. Reports in 1 month. Sample copy and writer's guidelines free on request.
Nonfiction: How-to (exercise, nutrition), interview/profile, new product, travel. No personal experience. **Buys 30 mss/year**. Length: 300-1,200 words. **Pays $10-150.**
Reprints: Accepts previously published submissions.
Photos: State availability of photos with submission. Reviews prints. Offers no additional payment for photos accepted with ms. Identification of subject required.
Tips: "Since our publication is online, we archive all of our articles. It's important for writers to be aware of what we have already published and not duplicate the idea."

$ $ $ $ HEALTH, Time, Inc., Two Embarcadero Center, Suite 600, San Francisco CA 94111. (415)248-2700. Editor-in-Chief: Barbara Paulsen. **Contact**: Kristin Kloberdanz, editorial assistant. Magazine published 8 times/year on health, fitness and nutrition. "Our readers are predominantly college-educated women in their 30s and 40s. Edited to focus not on illness, but on events, ideas and people." Estab. 1987. Circ. 1,050,000. **Pays on acceptance**. Byline given. Offers 25% kill fee. Buys first North American serial rights. Accepts simultaneous submissions. Reports in 2 months on queries. Sample copy for $5 to "Back Issues." Writer's guidelines for #10 SASE. "No phone calls, please."

- *Health* stresses that writers must send for guidelines before sending a query, and that only queries that closely follow the guidelines get passed on to editors.

Nonfiction: Buys 25 mss/year. No unsolicited mss. Query with published clips and SASE. Length: 1,200 words. **Pays $1,800.** Pays the expenses of writers on assignment.
Columns/Departments: Food, Mind, Healthy books, Fitness.
Tips: "We look for well-articulated ideas with a narrow focus and broad appeal. A query that starts with an unusual local event and hooks it legitimately to some national trend or concern is bound to get our attention. Use quotes, examples and statistics to show why the topic is important and why the approach is workable. We need to see clear evidence of credible research findings pointing to meaningful options for our readers. Stories should offer practical advice and give clear explanations."

N $ $ HEALTH FOR WOMEN, Woman's Day Special Interest Publications, Hachette-Filipacchi Magazines, 1633 Broadway, New York NY 10019. Fax: (212)767-5612. E-mail: wdspecials@aol.com. **Contact:** Janice Wright, managing editor. Editor: Carolyn Gatto. Semiannual consumer magazine covering women, health, fitness. "This magazine aims at helping the reader take care of herself and live a healthy lifestyle. Topics include weight control and reduction, exercise, food, emotions, and broader health issues. Exercise must be from a qualified professional in the field. The largest group of readers is in the 18 to 34 age group. Research guidelines will be supplied upon assignment." **Pays on acceptance**. Publishes ms an average of 3 months after acceptance. Byline given. Offers up to 25% kill fee. Buys first North American serial or second serial (printing) rights. Editorial lead time 6 months. Submit seasonal material 10 months in advance. Reports in 2 months. Sample copy not available; writer's guidelines for #10 SASE.
Nonfiction: How-to (diet, fitness), new product, service for women's health issues. **Buys 40 mss/year**. Query with published clips. Length: 250-1,000 words. Payment varies based on length, writer, importance. Sometimes pays expenses of writers on assignment.
Reprints: Accepts previously published submissions.
Photos: State availability of photos with submission. Model releases required. Buys one-time rights.
Columns/Departments: Skin Deep (causes & cures for common problems, with a health/medical angle); Pain Patrol (causes & cures for common aches & pains); Alternative Medicine (a look at the pros & cons of acupuncture, homeopathy, etc.); all 500-800 words. **Buys 6 mss/year**. Query with published clips. Payment varies based on length, writer, and level/amount of research required.
Tips: "Send a brief, clear query letter with relevant clips, and be patient."

✪ $ $ HEALTH, MONEY & TRAVEL, A Guide to Good Living, Grass Roots Publishing, 450 Seventh Ave., Suite 1701, New York NY 10123. **Contact**: Marcia McCluer, editor. **90% freelance written.** Bimonthly magazine covering health, money and travel. "We are a national consumer magazine for men and women ages 25 and up. We cover health topics that are mainstream such as 'Is Your Multi-Vitamin Right For You?,' etc." Estab. 1997. Circ. 50,000. Pays on publication. Publishes ms an average of 6 months after acceptance. Byline given. Buys all rights. Editorial lead time 8 months. Submit seasonal material 8 months in advance. Accepts simultaneous submissions occasionally. Reports in 2 months. Sample copy for $5. Writer's guidelines for #10 SASE.
Nonfiction: Celebrity health profiles, book excerpts, how-to, inspirational, interview/profile, travel, health, personal finance. No essays, editorials, memoirs, fiction. **Buys 60 mss/year.** Query with published clips or send complete ms. Length: 1,000-2,000 words. **Pays $250 minimum.**
Photos: State availability of photos with submissions. Offers $25/photo maximum.

$ $ LET'S LIVE MAGAZINE, Franklin Publications, Inc., 320 N. Larchmont Blvd., P.O. Box 74908, Los Angeles CA 90004-3030. (213)469-3901. Fax: (213)469-9597. E-mail: letslive@earthlink.net. Editor-in-Chief: Beth Salmon. **Contact:** Elizabeth Coombs, managing editor. Monthly magazine emphasizing health and preventive medicine. "Our editorial mission at *Let's Live* is to encourage readers to manage and promote their own health and well-being by providing well-researched, authoritative and practical information on preventive and complementary medicine, natural health products and the importance of an active lifestyle." **75% freelance written.** Works with a small number of new/unpublished writers each year; expertise in health field helpful. Estab. 1933. Circ. 1,700,000. Pays on publication. Publishes ms an average of 4 months after acceptance. Buys all rights. Byline given. Submit seasonal material 6 months in advance. Reports in 2 months on queries; 3 months on mss. Sample copy for $5 and 10×13 SAE with 6 first-class stamps. Writer's guidelines for #10 SASE.

- The editors are looking for more cutting-edge, well-researched natural health information that is substantiated by experts and well-respected scientific research literature.

Nonfiction: General interest (effects of vitamins, minerals and nutrients in improvement of health or afflictions); historical (documentation of experiments or treatment establishing value of nutrients as boon to health); how-to (enhance natural beauty, exercise/bodybuilding, acquire strength and vitality, improve health of adults and/or children and prepare tasty, healthy meals); interview (benefits of research in establishing prevention as key to good health); personal opinion (views of orthomolecular doctors or their patients on value of health foods toward maintaining good health); profile (background and/or medical history of preventive medicine, M.D.s or Ph.D.s, in advancement of nutrition). Manuscripts must be well-researched, reliably documented and written in a clear, readable style. **Buys 2-4 mss/issue.** Query with published clips and SASE. Length: 1,200-1,400 words. **Pays $650 for features.**

Columns/Departments: Smart Food, Sports Nutrition (Expert Column, Your Personal Trainer), Natural Medicine Chest, Herbs for Health, Homeopathic Healing. Query with published clips and SASE. Length: 1,200-1,400 words. **Pays $500.**

Photos: Send photos. Pays $50 for 8×10 color prints, 35mm transparencies. Captions, model releases required.

Tips: "We want writers with experience in researching nonsurgical medical subjects and interviewing experts with the ability to simplify technical and clinical information for the layman. A captivating lead and structural flow are essential. The most frequent mistakes made by writers are in writing articles that are too technical; in poor style; written for the wrong audience (publication not thoroughly studied), or have unreliable documentation or overzealous faith in the topic reflected by flimsy research and inappropriate tone."

N ✪ $ $ $ LIFE EXTENSION MAGAZINE, Life Extension Foundation, 1881 N.E. 26th St., #221, Fort Lauderdale FL 33305. (954)561-7909. Fax: (954)561-8335. E-mail: lemagazine@compuserve.com. Website: http://www.Lef.org. **Contact**: Christopher Hosford, editor. **80% freelance written.** Monthly magazine covering "health care, anti-aging, gerontology research, medical, alternative medicines. *Life Extension* covers all aspects of health and longevity, with particular emphasis on alternative therapies, dietary supplements, and anti-aging research. Rigorous medical/science articles are complemented by articles on healthy people." Estab. 1994. Circ. 101,000. **Pays on acceptance**. Publishes ms an average of 2 months after acceptance. Byline given. Buys first North American serial rights. Editorial lead time 3 months. Accepts simultaneous submissions. Reports in 1 month. Sample copy and writer's guidelines free.

Nonfiction: Book excerpts, general interest, interview/profile, opinion, personal experience, company profiles, case histories. **Buys 60 mss/year.** Query or query with published clips. Length: 2,000-4,000 words. **Pays 50¢-$1/word.** Pays expenses of writers on assignment.

Reprints: Send typed ms with rights for sale noted and information about when and where the article appeared.

Photos: State availability of photos with submission. Reviews transparencies. Negotiates payment individually. Identification of subjects required. Buys all rights.

Columns/Departments: Point of view (opinion of aspects of the gerontological/medical/health care world), 1,500-2,000 words. **Buys 12 mss/year.** Query with published clips. **Pays 50¢-$1/word.**

Tips: "A phone call to the editor to discuss story idea may help refine query. Written follow-up query then required. A working knowledge of how to access medical research/abstracts essential (online or otherwise). Important to understand how, latest anti-aging research affects real people with therapies they can use now."

N $ $ $ MAMM MAGAZINE, Courage, Respect & Survival, Poz Publishing L.L.C., 349 W. 12th St., New York NY 10014. (212)242-2163. Fax: (212)675-8505. E-mail: ninacoz.com. Website: http://www.poz.com. **Contact:** Gwen Darien, editor. Managing Editor: Jennifer Hsu. **100% freelance written**. Bimonthly consumer women's magazine focusing on cancer prevention, treatment and survival. "*MAMM* gives its readers the essential tools and emotional support they need before, during and after diagnosis of breast, ovarian and other female reproductive cancers. We offer a mix of survivor profiles, conventional and alternative treatment information, investigative features, essays and cutting-edge news." Estab. 1997. Circ. 70,000. Pays within 45 days of acceptance. Publishes ms an average of 5 months after acceptance. Byline given. Offers 20% kill fee. Buys exclusive rights up to 90 days after publishing, first rights after that. Editorial lead time 4 months. Submit seasonal material 4 months in advance. Accepts simultaneous submissions. Sample copy and writers guidelines free on request.

Nonfiction: Book excerpts, essays, exposé, historical/nostalgic, how-to, humor, inspirational, interview/profile, opinion, personal experience, photo features. **Buys 90 mss/year**. Query with published clips. Length: 200-3,000 words. **Pays $50-1,000.** Sometimes pays expenses of writers on assignment.

Photos: Send photos with submission. Reviews contact sheets and negatives. Negotiates payment individually. Identification of subjects required. Buys first rights.

Columns/Departments: Cancer Girl (humor/experience); Opinion (cultural/political); International Dispatch (experience); all 600 words. **Buys 30 mss/year**. Query with published clips. **Pays $200-250.**

Fiction: Adventure, confession, historical, humorous, mainstream, novel excerpts, romance, science fiction, slice-of-life vignettes, must relate to women's health issues. **Buys 6 mss/year**. Query with published clips. Please inquire for word length and payment.

Poetry: Avant-garde, free verse, haiku, light verse, traditional. **Buys 6 poems/year**. Submit maximum 3 poems. Length: 10-40 lines. **Pays $100-150.**

Fillers: Anecdotes, facts, gags to be illustrated, newsbreaks. **Buys 30/year**. Length: 50-150 words. **Pays $50-75.**

$ $ MASSAGE MAGAZINE, Keeping Those Who Touch—In Touch, 200 Seventh Ave. #240, Santa Cruz CA 95062. (408)477-1176. Fax: (408)477-2918. E-mail: edit@massagemag.com. Website: http://www.massagemag.com. **Contact:** Karen Menehan, managing editor. **60% freelance written.** Prefers to work with published/established writers, but works with a number of new/unpublished writers each year. Bimonthly magazine on massage-bodywork and related healing arts. Estab. 1985. Circ. 35,000. Pays 30 days after publication. Publishes ms an average of 1 year after acceptance. Byline given. Buys first North American rights. Reports in 1 month on queries; 2 months on mss. Sample copy and writer's guidelines free.

Nonfiction: General interest, historical/nostalgic, how-to, experiential, inspirational, interview/profile, new product, photo feature, technical, travel. Length: 600-2,000 words. **Pays $25-250 for articles.**

Reprints: Send tearsheet of article and typed ms with rights for sale noted and information about when and where the article previously appeared. Pays 50-75% of amount paid for an original article.

Photos: Send photos with submission. Offers $10-25/photo. Identification of subjects and photographer required. Buys one-time rights.

Columns/Departments: Touching Tales (experiential); Profiles, Insurance; Table Talk (news briefs); Practice Building (business); In Touch with Associations (convention highlights); In Review/On Video (product, book, and video reviews); Technique; Body/mind. Length: 800-1,200 words. **Pays $60-150** for most of these columns.

Fillers: Facts, news briefs. Length: 100-800 words. **Pays $125 maximum.**

Tips: "In-depth profiles of innovative and exceptional bodywork professionals are a high priority."

$ $ $ MEN'S FITNESS, Men's Fitness, Inc., 21100 Erwin St., Woodland Hills CA 91367-3712. (818)884-6800. Fax: (818)704-5734. **Contact:** Dean Brierly, managing editor. **95% freelance written.** Works with small number of new/unpublished writers each year. Monthly magazine for health-conscious men ages 18-45. Provides reliable, entertaining guidance for the active male in all areas of lifestyle. Estab. 1984. Circ. 315,000. Pays 1 month after acceptance. Publishes ms an average of 4 months after acceptance. Offers 33% kill fee. Buys all rights. Submit seasonal material 4 months in advance. Reports in 2 months. Writer's guidelines for 9×12 SAE. Query before sending ms.

Nonfiction: Service, informative, inspirational and scientific studies written for men. Few interviews or regional news unless extraordinary. Query with published clips. Length: 1,200-1,800 words. **Pays $500-1,000.**

Columns/Departments: Nutrition, Mind, Appearance, Sexuality, Health. Length: 1,200-1,500 words. **Pays $400-500.**

$ $ $ MEN'S HEALTH, Rodale Press, Inc., 33 E. Minor St., Emmaus PA18098. (610)967-5171. Fax: (610)967-8963. Editor: Michael Lafavore. **Contact:** Peter Moore, managing editor. **10% freelance written.** Prefers to work with established/published writers. Magazine published 10 times/year covering men's health and fitness. "*Men's Health* is a lifestyle magazine showing men the practical and positive actions that make their lives better, with articles covering fitness, nutrition, relationships, travel, careers, grooming and health issues." Estab. 1986. Circ. 1,511,000. Buys all rights. Responds in 1 week. Writer's guidelines for SASE.

Nonfiction: Freelancers have the best chance with the front-of-the-book piece, Malegram. Query with published clips and SASE. Pay negotiable.

Tips: "We have a wide definition of health. We believe that being successful in every area of your life is being healthy. The magazine focuses on all aspects of health, from stress issues to nutrition to exercise to sex. It is mostly staff written, but about 10% of the final product comes from freelancers. The best way to break in is not by covering a particular subject, but by covering it within the magazine's style. There is a very particular tone and voice to the magazine. A writer has to be a good humor writer as well as a good service writer. Prefers mail queries. No phone calls, please."

$ $ $ MUSCLE & FITNESS, The Science of Living Super-Fit, Weider Health & Fitness, 21100 Erwin St., Woodland Hills, CA 91367. (818)884-6800. Fax: (818)595-0463. Website: http://www.muscle-fitness.com. Editor: Bill Geiger. **Contact:** Vincent Scalisi, editor. **50% freelance written.** Monthly magazine covering fitness, health, injury prevention and treatment, bodybuilding, nutrition. Estab. 1950. Circ. 500,000. **Pays on acceptance.** Publishes ms an average of 2 months after acceptance. Offers 25-40% kill fee. Buys all rights and second serial (reprint) rights. Editorial lead time 5 months. Submit seasonal material 5 months in advance. Accepts simultaneous submissions. Reports in 2 weeks on queries.

- Ranked as one of the best markets for freelance writers in *Writer's Yearbook* magazine's annual "Top 100 Markets," January 1998.

Nonfiction: Bill Geiger. Book excerpts, how-to (training), humor, interview/profile, photo feature. **Buys 120 mss/year.** "All features and departments are written on assignment." Query with published clips. Length: 800-1,800 words. **Pays $250-800.** Pays expenses of writers on assignment.

Reprints: Send photocopy of article or typed ms with rights for sale noted and information about when and where the article previously appeared. Payment varies.

Photos: State availability of photos with submission.

Tips: "Have a knowledge of weight-training (especially in gyms); know the 'culture'; know applied-nutrition."

$ $ $ $ NATURAL HEALTH, Boston Common Press, 17 Station St., P.O. Box 1200, Brookline Village MA 02147. Fax: (617)232-1572. Editor: Bill Thomson. **Contact:** Cheryl Spiller, editorial assistant. **50% freelance written.** Bimonthly magazine covering alternative health and natural living. "We are an authoritative guide to the best in mind, body and spirit self-care." Estab. 1971. Circ. 350,000. **Pays on acceptance**. Publishes ms an average of 3 months after acceptance. Byline given. Offers 25% kill fee. Buys first rights and reprint rights. Editorial lead time 8 months. Submit seasonal material 8 months in advance. Accepts simultaneous submissions. Reports in 4 months on queries.

Nonfiction: Book excerpts, exposé, how-to, inspirational, personal experience. No fiction, reprints from other publications or event/personality coverage. **Buys 15 mss/year.** Query with published clips. Length: 150-3,000 words. **Pays $75-2,000.** Sometimes pays the expenses of writers on assignment.

Photos: State availability of photos with submission. Buys one-time rights.

Columns/Departments: My Story (personal account of illness or condition treated naturally), 1,500 words. **Buys 6 mss/year.** Query. **Pays $100-200.**

Tips: "Read the magazine. The recipes are always vegan. The products are non-chemical. Read books written by the columnists: Andrew Weil, James Gordon, Joseph Pizzorno, Jennifer Jacobs, etc.)"

$ $ $ $ NEW CHOICES, Living Even Better After 50, Reader's Digest Publications, Inc., 28 W. 23rd St., New York NY 10010. (212)366-8600. Fax: (212)366-8786. E-mail: newchoices@readersdigest.com. Website: http://www.seniornews.com/new-choices/. **Contact:** JoAnn Tomback, editorial administrative assistant. Magazine published 10 times/year covering retirement lifestyle. "*New Choices* is a lifestyle and service magazine for adults 50 and over. Editorial focuses on travel, health, fitness, investments, food and home." Estab. 1960. Circ. 604,000.

Nonfiction: Planning for retirement, personal health and fitness, financial strategies, housing options, travel, profiles/interviews (celebrities and newsmakers), relationships, leisure pursuits, various lifestyle/service subjects. **Buys 60 mss/year.** Length: 750-2,000 words. **Pays $1/word**, negotiable. Query with 2-3 published clips and SASE.

Columns/Departments: Personal essays, online bargains, taxes, cooking, travel, style. **Buys 84 mss/year.** Pay varies. Query with 2-3 published clips. No phone calls.

$ $ $ OXYGEN!, Serious Fitness for Serious Women, Muscle Mag International, 6465 Airport Rd., Mississauga, Ontario L4V 1E4 Canada. (905)678-7311. Fax: (905)678-9236. **Contact:** Pamela Cottrell, editor. **70% freelance written.** Bimonthly magazine covering women's health and fitness. "*Oxygen* encourages various exercise, good nutrition to shape and condition the body." Estab. 1997. Circ. 180,000. **Pays on acceptance**. Publishes ms an average of 4 months after acceptance. Byline given. Offers 25% kill fee. Buys all rights. Editorial lead time 3 months. Submit seasonal material 6 months in advance. Reports in 5 weeks on queries; 2 months on mss. Sample copy for $5.

Nonfiction: Exposé, how-to (training and nutrition), humor, inspirational, interview/profile, new product, personal experience, photo feature. No "poorly researched articles that do not genuinely help the readers towards physical fitness, health and physique." **Buys 100 mss/year.** Send complete ms. Length: 1,400-1,800 words. **Pays $250-1,000.** Sometimes pays expenses of writers on assignment.

Reprints: Send tearsheet, photocopy or typed manuscript with rights for sale noted and information about when and where the article previously appeared. Pay varies.

Photos: State availability of or send photos with submission. Reviews contact sheets, 35mm transparencies, prints. Offers $35-500. Identification of subjects required. Buys all rights.

Columns/Departments: Nutrition (low fat recipes), 1,700 words; Weight Training (routines and techniques), 1,800 words; Aerobics (how-tos), 1,700 words. **Buys 50 mss/year.** Send complete ms. **Pays $150-500.**

Tips: "Every editor of every magazine is looking, waiting, hoping and praying for the magic article. The beauty of the writing has to spring from the page; the edge imparted has to excite the reader because of its unbelievable information."

N $ $ $ POZ, Poz Publishing L.L.C., 349 W 12th St., New York NY 10014. (212)242-2163. Fax: (212)675-8505. E-mail: ninacoz.com. Website: http://www.poz.com. **Contact:** Walter Armstrong, editor. Managing Editor: Jennifer Hsu. **100% freelance written**. Monthly national magazine for people impacted by HIV and AIDS. "*POZ* is a trusted source of conventional and alternative treatment information, investigative features, survivor profiles, essays and cutting-edge news for people living with AIDS and their caregivers. *POZ* is a lifestyle magazine with both health and cultural content." Estab. 1994. Circ. 91,000. Pays 45 days after acceptance. Publishes ms an average of 3 months after acceptance. Byline given. Offers 20% kill fee. Buys first rights. Editorial lead time 4 months. Submit seasonal material 4 months in advance. Accepts simultaneous submissions. Sample copy and writers guidelines free.

Nonfiction: Book excerpts, essays, expose, historical/nostalgic, how-to, humor, inspirational, interview/profile, opinion, personal experience, photo features. **Buys 180 mss/year**. Query with published clips. Length: 200-3,000 words. **Pays $50-1,000.** We take unsolicited mss on speculation only. Sometimes pays expenses of writers on assignment.

Photos: Send photos with submission. Reviews contact sheets and negatives. Negotiates payment individually. Identification of subjects required. Buys first rights.

Columns/Departments: Life (personal experience); Back Page (humor); Data Dish (opinion/experience/information), all 600 words. **Buys 120 mss/year**. Query with published clips. **Pays $200-3,000.**

Fiction: Buys 10 mss/year. Send complete ms. Length: 700-2,000 words. Payment negotiable.

Poetry: Avant-garde, free verse, haiku, light verse, traditional. **Buys 12 poems/year**. Submit maximum 3 poems. Length: 10-40 lines. Pay negotiable.

Fillers: Anecdotes, facts, gags to be illustrated by cartoonist, newsbreaks, short humor. **Buys 90/year**. Length: 50-150 words. **Pays $50-75.**

PREVENTION, Rodale Press, Inc., 33 E. Minor St., Emmaus, PA 18098. (610)967-5171. Fax: (610)967-7654. Editor: Anne Alexander. **Contact:** Denise Foley, features editor. Monthly magazine covering health and fitness. "*Prevention* is for readers who take an active role in achieving and maintaining good health and fitness for themselves and their families. Stressing health promotion and disease prevention, *Prevention* features practical guidance on nutrition, diet and food preparation, medical care, alternative medicine, fitness, weight control, skin care and personal psychology with a mind-body component." Estab. 1950. Circ. 3,519,000.

Tips: *Prevention*, "America's Leading Health Magazine," is a market only for the most experienced freelancers. "We are not a good market for somebody who's interested in breaking into the health market. The monthly aims to inform readers about current developments in health. Because this information is medically and scientifically specialized, expertise and research are primary requirements. Only experienced health writers should query the magazine. No phone queries, please."

$ $ $ PRIME HEALTH & FITNESS, Weider Publication, Inc., 21100 Erwin St., Woodland Hills CA 91367. (818)595-0442. Fax: (818)595-0463. E-mail: primefit1@aol.com. Website: http://www.getbig.com/magazine/prime/prime.htm?. **Contact:** Bill Bush, editor. **75% freelance written.** Bi-monthly magazine covering health & fitness for the baby boomer or over-40 male. "*Prime Health & Fitness* is for the man who refuses to grow old as he grows up. We offer straight talk on parenthood, careers, diseases, stress and success with cutting-edge information for men of experience who know what they like and are confident enough to try something new." Estab. 1995. Circ. 200,000. **Pays on acceptance.** Publishes ms an average of 2 months after acceptance. Byline given. Offers 30% kill fee. Buys all rights. Editorial lead time 2-4 months. Submit seasonal material 5 months in advance. Reports in 2 months. Sample copy and writer's guidelines free.

Nonfiction: General interest, how-to, humor, inspirational, interview/profile, new product, technical, travel, health, fitness, disease, boomer lifestyle. No women's issues or under-40 male interests. **Buys 40 mss/year.** Query with published clips. Length: 800-2,000 words plus sidebars. **Pays 60-80¢/word for assigned articles; 60-70¢/word for unsolicited articles.** Sometimes pays expenses of writers on assignment.

Photos: State availability of photos with submission. Reviews transparencies. Offers no additional payment for photos accepted with ms or negotiates payment individually. Captions, model releases, identification of subjects required. Buys all rights or offers negotiable rights.

Columns/Departments: Research & Development (new products, health & fitness oriented), 150-200 words; Success Stories (before and after with pictures), Antiaging/Longevity, Nutrition, Work-outs, Sex, 400-800 words. **Buys 60 mss/year.** Query with published clips. **Pays 60-80¢/word.**

Tips: "We write to the over-40 male audience in guy language so twist your topics accordingly. Back your research with references. Be accurate on word count. We prefer a written proposal of 250-300 words as a preliminary query. Familiarize yourself with our style, readers and editorial message. Don't query without having read our magazine."

$ $ $ $ ℞EMEDY MAGAZINE, Prescriptions for a Healthy Life, ℞emedy, Inc., 120 Post Rd. W., Westport CT 06880. Editor-in-chief: Valorie G. Weaver. **Contact:** Shari Miller Sims, consulting editor. **95% freelance written.** Bimonthly magazine covering health for people age 50 and over. "*℞EMEDY* covers everything that affects and improves the health of people 50 and up—nutrition and exercise, medicine and medications, mainstream and alternative approaches, hormones and hair loss, you name it—and does it in an in-depth but reader-friendly way." Estab. 1992. Circ. 2,200,000 households. **Pays on acceptance**. Publishes ms an average of 4 months after acceptance. Byline given. Offers 20% kill fee. Buys first North American serial rights. Editorial lead time 3 months. Submit seasonal material 6 months in advance. Accepts simultaneous submissions. Reports in 6 weeks on queries; 2 months on mss. Samples for $3 and SAE with 4 first-class stamps. Writer's guidelines free.

- Ranked as one of the best markets for freelance writers in *Writer's Yearbook* magazine's annual "Top 100 Markets," January 1998.

Nonfiction: Book excerpts, exposé (medical), how-to (exercise and nutrition for people age 50 and over), interview/profile (health); medical journalism/reporting for lay readers. **Buys 30 mss/year.** Query with published clips. Length: 600-2,500 words. **Pays $1-1.25/word for assigned articles; 75¢-$1.25/word for unsolicited articles.** Pays pre-approved expenses of writers on assignment.

Photos: State availability of photos with submission. Negotiates payment individually. Model releases, identification of subjects required. Buys one-time rights.

Columns/Departments: The Nutrition Prescription (how-to research), The Fitness Prescription (how-to research), Housecall (interviews with top specialists), Mediview (overviews of topical subjects, e.g., "endless" menopause, see-better surgery), all 600-900 words. **Buys 15 mss/year.** Query. **Pays $1-1.25/word.**

Tips: "Query should include specific doctors/practitioners likely to be interviewed for piece, and at least one clip showing writing/reporting familiarity with topic of query. Also, an ability to write in a casual, friendly way about often complex material is essential."

N $ $ RHYTHM OF THE DRUM, Our Wholistic Magazine, P.O. Box 470379, Los Angeles CA 90047-0379. (800)324-DRUM. Fax: (310)323-0634. **Contact:** Jacquetta Parhams, publisher. **20% freelance written.** Quarterly magazine covering wholistic health (health and fitness). "*Rhythm of the Drum* deals with all aspects of our health—the physical, mental, emotional, spiritual, financial, political, etc., health. *The Drum* covers issues and solutions facing Africans all over the globe with respect to the whole health of individuals, the family and the community." Estab. 1994. Circ. 17,000. Pays on publication. Publishes ms an average 6 months after acceptance. Byline given. Offers 15% kill fee. Buys one-time and second serial (reprint) rights. Editorial lead time 4 months. Submit seasonal material 6 months in advance. Accepts simultaneous submissions. Reports in 6 weeks on queries. Please request guidelines before querying. Sample copy for $2.50 and 9×12 SASE and 4 first-class stamps. Writer's guidelines for #10 SASE.

Nonfiction: Book excerpts, essays, exposé, historical/nostalgic, how-to, inspirational, interview/profile, new product, opinion, personal experience, photo feature, religious, technical, travel, cartoons, puzzles, political. Special issue: Black History Month/Anniversary Issue (February). Query with published clips if available. Length: 25-2,000 words. **Pays $10-500 for assigned articles; $3-240 for unsolicited articles.**

Reprints: Send tearsheet or photocopy of article with rights for sale noted and information about when and where it previously appeared.

Photos: Send photos. Reviews 8½×11 transparencies and 3×5 or larger prints. Offers no additional payment for photos accepted with ms. Negotiates payment individually. Model releases and identification of subjects required.

Columns/Departments: The Political Skinny (political); Tree of Life (physical health); Ourstory (our history); Safety First (being careful in- and outdoors); The Dollars & $ense of It (economics and finance); Spiritually Speaking (spiritual health and growth); Sci-Non-Fi (the sciences).

Poetry: Avant-garde, free verse, haiku, light verse, traditional. **Buys 20 poems/year.** Submit maximum 2 poems. Length: 1-50 lines. **Pays $5-100.**

Fillers: Anecdotes, facts, newsbreaks. **Buys 8/year.** Length: 5-50 words. **Pays 50¢-$5.**

Tips: "*Rhythm of the Drum* is an uplifting magazine of enlightenment. We do not need to tear down others to build ourselves up. Photos and other photo-ready artwork are encouraged but not required; many articles are published without photos."

SHAPE MAGAZINE, Weider Health & Fitness, 21100 Erwin St., Woodland Hills CA 91367. (818)595-0593. Fax: (818)992-6895. Website: http://www.shapemag.com. Editor-in-Chief: Barbara Harris. **Contact:** Peg Moline, editorial director. **70% freelance written.** Prefers to work with published/established writers. Monthly magazine covering women's health and fitness. "*Shape* reaches women who are committed to the healthful, active lifestyles. Our readers are participating in a variety of sports and fitness related activities, in the gym, at home and outdoors, and they are also proactive about their health and are nutrition conscious." Estab. 1981. Circ. 900,000. **Pays on acceptance**. Offers 33% kill fee. Buys all rights and reprint rights. Submit seasonal material 8 months in advance. Reports in 2 months. Sample copy for 9×12 SAE and 4 first-class stamps.

- Weider Health & Fitness also publishes *Living Fit*, covering women's health and fitness for women over 35.

Nonfiction: Book excerpts; exposé (health, fitness, nutrition related); how-to (get fit); interview/profile (of fit women); health/fitness, recipes. "We use some health and fitness articles written by professionals in their specific fields. No articles that haven't been queried first." Special issues: every September is an anniversary issue. Query with clips of published work. Length: 500-2,000 words. Pays negotiable fee.

Photos: Submit slides or photos with photographer's name or institution to be credited. Provide necessary captions and all model releases.

Tips: "Review a recent issue of the magazine. Provide source verification materials and sources for items readers may buy, including 800 numbers. Not responsible for unsolicited material. We reserve the right to edit any article."

$ $ VIBRANT LIFE, A Magazine for Healthful Living, Review and Herald Publishing Assn., 55 W. Oak Ridge Dr., Hagerstown MD 21740-7390. (301)791-7000. Fax: (301)790-9734. E-mail: vleditor@rhpa.org. Website: http://www.vibrantlife.com. **Contact:** Larry Becker, editor. **80% freelance written.** Enjoys working with published/established writers; works with a small number of new/unpublished writers each year. Bimonthly magazine covering health articles (especially from a prevention angle and with a Christian slant). Estab. 1845. Circ. 50,000. **Pays on acceptance.** "The average length of time between acceptance of a freelance-written manuscript and publication of the material depends upon the topics: some immediately used; others up to 2 years." Byline always given. Buys first serial, first world serial, or sometimes second serial (reprint) rights. Submit seasonal material 9 months in advance. Reports in 2 months. Sample copy for $1. Writer's guidelines for #10 SASE.

- Ranked as one of the best markets for freelance writers in *Writer's Yearbook* magazine's annual "Top 100 Markets," January 1998.

Nonfiction: Interview/profile (with personalities on health). "We seek practical articles promoting better health and a more fulfilled life. We especially like features on breakthroughs in medicine, and most aspects of health. We need articles on how to integrate a person's spiritual life with their health. We'd like more in the areas of exercise, nutrition, water, avoiding addictions of all types and rest—all done from a wellness perspective." **Buys 50-60 mss/year.** Send complete ms. Length: 500-1,500 words. **Pays $75-250.**

Reprints: Send tearsheet of article and information about when and where the article previously appeared. Pays 50% of amount paid for an original article.

Photos: Send photos with ms. Needs 35mm transparencies. Not interested in b&w photos.

Tips: "*Vibrant Life* is published for baby boomers, particularly young professionals, age 35-50. Articles must be written in an interesting, easy-to-read style. Information must be reliable; no faddism. We are more conservative than other magazines in our field. Request a sample copy, and study the magazine and writer's guidelines."

$ $ VIM & VIGOR, America's Family Health Magazine, 1010 E. Missouri Ave., Phoenix AZ 85014-2601. (602)395-5850. Fax: (602)395-5853. E-mail: jennw@mcpub.com. **Contact:** Jennifer Daack Woolson, associate publisher/editor. **75% freelance written.** Quarterly magazine covering health and healthcare. Estab. 1985. Circ. 900,000.

Pays on acceptance. Publishes ms an average of 3 months after acceptance. Byline given. Buys all rights. Sample copy for 9×12 SAE with 8 first-class stamps. Writer's guidelines for #10 SASE.

Nonfiction: Health, diseases, medical breakthroughs, exercise/fitness trends, wellness, and healthcare. "Absolutely no complete manuscripts will be accepted. All articles are assigned to freelance writers. Send samples of your style. Any queries regarding story ideas will be placed on the following year's conference agenda and will be addressed on a topic-by-topic basis. Consideration for actual article assignment will be given to those individuals who have submitted story ideas; however, the magazine welcomes anyone with feature- or news-writing ability to submit qualifications for assignment." **Buys 12 mss/year.** Query with published clips. Length: 2,000 words. **Pays $500.** Pays expenses of writers on assignment.

Photos: Send photos with submission. Reviews contact sheets and any size transparencies. Offers no additional payment for photos accepted with ms. Captions, model releases, identification of subjects required. Buys one-time rights.

N $ $ VITALITY MAGAZINE, Toronto's Monthly Wellness Journal, 356 Dupont St., Toronto, Ontario M5R 1V9 Canada. **Contact:** Julia Woodford, editor. **50% freelance written.** Monthly magazine covering holistic health, nutritional medicine. "We give top priority to well-researched articles on nutritional medicine, healing properties of foods and herbs, environmental health issues, natural lifestyles, alternative healing for cancer, arthritis, heart disease, etc. Organic foods and issues. Estab. 1989. Circ. 41,000. Pays on publication. Publishes ms 3 months after acceptance. Byline given. Buys first rights, one-time rights or second serial (reprint) rights. Editorial lead time 3 months. Submit seasonal material 3 months in advance. Accepts simultaneous submissions. Reports "when we have time." Sample copy for $2 (cash only).

Nonfiction: Book excerpts, exposé, how-to (on self-health care), inspirational, personal experience. "Nothing endorsing drugs, surgery, pharmaceuticals. No submissions from public relations firms." **Buys 8-12 mss/year.** Send complete ms. Length 1,000-1,800 words. **Pays 10¢/word (Canadian).**

Reprints: Send photocopy of article or typed ms with rights for sale noted and information about when and where the article previously appeared. Pays 10¢/word (Canadian) for reprints.

Photos: Send photos with submission. Offers $25-30 (Canadian)/photo. Identification of subjects required. Buys one-time rights.

Fillers: Facts, newsbreaks.

Tips: "Must have a good working knowledge of subject area and be patient if not responded to immediately. Features are most open to freelancers. Write well, give me the facts, but do it in layman's terms. A sense of humor doesn't hurt. All material must be relevant to our *Canadian* readership audience. If you're doing a critical piece on products in the marketplace, give me brand names."

$ $ $ $ THE WALKING MAGAZINE, Walking Inc., 9-11 Harcourt St., Boston MA 02116. (617)266-3322. Fax: (617)266-7373. **Contact:** Seth Bauer, editor. **60% freelance written.** Bimonthly magazine covering health and fitness. "*The Walking Magazine* is written for healthy, active adults who are committed to fitness walking as an integral part of their lifestyle. Each issue offers advice on exercise techniques, diet, nutrition, personal care and contemporary health issues. It also covers information on gear and equipment, competition and travel, including foreign and domestic destinations for walkers." Estab. 1986. Circ. 650,000. **Pays on acceptance.** Offers 25% kill fee. Editorial lead time 3 months. Accepts simultaneous submissions. Responds in 2 months. Sample copy for $3.95. Writer's guidelines for SASE.

Nonfiction: Walks for travel and adventure, fitness, health, nutrition, fashion, equipment, famous walkers, and other walking-related topics. **Buys 35-42 mss/year.** Query with published clips (no more than 3). Length: 1,500-2,500 words. **Pays $750-2,500.**

Columns/Departments: Walking Shorts, Your Self, Health, Nutrition, Active Beauty, Walk It Off, Events, Walking Gear (gear and equipment), Ramblings (back page essay), 300-1,200 words. Query with clips. **Pays $150-600.**

☆ $ $ $ WEIGHT WATCHERS MAGAZINE, Healthy Living, Inc., P.O. Box 12847, Birmingham AL 35202-2847. (205)877-6000. Fax: (205)877-5790. E-mail: wwmag@mindspring.com. Editor-in-Chief: Kate Greer. Editorial Coordinator: Chris O'Connell. Beauty Editor: Barbara Silver. **Contact:** Melissa Chessher Aspell, executive editor. Food Editor: Alyson Haynes. Fitness Editor: Mary Martin Niepold. **Approximately 80% freelance written.** Monthly magazine mostly for women interested in healthy lifestyle/behavior information/advice, including news on health, nutrition, fitness, beauty, fashion, psychology and food/recipes. Success and before-and-after stories also welcome. Estab. 1968. Circ. 1,000,000. **Pays on acceptance**. Buys first North American rights. Editorial lead time 3-12 months. Sample copy and writer's guidelines $1.95 for 9×12 SASE.

- Ranked as one of the best markets for freelance writers in *Writer's Yearbook* magazine's annual "Top 100 Markets," January 1998.

Nonfiction: Covers fitness, nutrition, psychology, health clubs, spas, beauty, fashion, style, travel and products for both the kitchen and an active lifestyle. "We are interested in general health, nutrition and behavorial/psychological articles (stories with a strong weight loss angle always a plus). Some fitness—everything from beginner to advanced ideas—freelanced out. Personal triumph/success stories of individuals who lost weight also of interest. Back page a humorous look at some aspect of getting/staying in shape or achieving better health. Our articles have an authoritative yet friendly tone. How-to and service information crucial for all stories. To expedite fact-checking, we require a second, annotated manuscript including names, phone numbers, journal/newsletter citations of sources." Send detailed queries with published clips and SASE. Average article length: 700-1,200 words. **Pays: $350-800.**

Reprints: Pays 33% of amount paid for an original article.

Tips: "Well developed, tightly written queries always a plus, as are ideas that have a strong news peg. Trend pieces welcome and we're always on the lookout for a fresh angle on an old topic. Sources must be reputable; we prefer subjects to be medical professionals with university affiliations who are published in their field of expertise. Lead times require stories to be seasonal, long-range and forward-looking. Keep in mind that a trend today may be old news in six months. We're looking for fresh, innovative stories that yield worthwhile information for our readers—the latest exercise alternatives, a suggestion of how they can reduce stress, nutritional information that may not be common knowledge, suggestions from experts on skin care, reassurance about their lifestyle or health concerns, etc."

$ $ $ THE YOGA JOURNAL, California Yoga Teachers Association, 2054 University Ave., Berkeley CA 94704. (510)841-9200. Website: http://www.yogajournal.com. **Contact:** Rick Fields, editor-in chief; Todd James, assistant editor. **75% freelance written.** Bimonthly magazine covering yoga, holistic health, conscious living, spiritual practices, ecology and nutrition. Estab. 1975. Circ. 108,000. Publishes mss an average of 10 months after acceptance. Byline given. Offers kill fee on assigned articles. Buys first North American serial rights. Submit seasonal material minimum 4 months in advance. Reports in approx. 3 months. Sample copy $3.50. Writer's guidelines free.

Nonfiction: Book excerpts; how-to (yoga, exercise, massage, etc.); inspirational (yoga or related); profile/interview; opinion; photo feature; yoga-related travel. "Yoga is a main concern, but we also highlight other conscious living/New Age personalities and endeavors (nothing too "woo-woo"). **Buys 50-60 mss/year.** Query with SASE. Length: 2,500-6,000 words. **Pays $1,000-3,000.**

Reprints: Submit tearsheet or photocopy of article with information about when and where the article previously appeared and rights for sale noted.

Columns/Departments: Open Forum (opinion; first person); Health (self-care; well-being); Body-Mind (hatha Yoga; other body-mind modalities; meditation; yoga philosophy; Western mysticism); Community (service; profiles; organizations; events). Length: 1,500-2,000 words. **Pays $600-800.** Living (books; video; food; arts; music), 800 words. **Pays $250-300.** World of Yoga Spectrum (brief yoga and healthy living news/events/fillers), 150-600 words. **Pays $50-150.**

Tips: "Please read out writer's guidelines before submission. We are very open to freelance material and encourage writers to submit their ideas. Do not e-mail or fax unsolicited manuscripts."

$ $ YOUR HEALTH, Globe Communications Corp., 5401 NW Broken Sound Blvd., Boca Raton FL 33487. (561)997-7733. Fax: (561)997-9210. E-mail: yhealth@aol.com. Website: http://www.yourhealthmag.com. **Contact:** Susan Gregg, editor. Associate Editor: Lisa Rappa. **80% freelance written.** Monthly magazine on health and fitness. "*Your Health* is dedicated to presenting timely health and medical information to consumers. Our audience is healthy, middle-class + concerned about improving and maintaining highest levels of physical, emotional and spiritual health. Emphasis on self-care and prevention (through sound nutrition, exercise, and behavioral and spiritual health) as opposed to treatment of disease. We give readers information that will help them take charge of their health and become a health parnter with—rather than patient of—their doctors." Estab. 1962. Circ. 50,000. Pays on publication. Byline given. Buys first North American serial and second serial (reprint) rights. Submit seasonal material 3 months in advance. Reports in 1 month on queries; 6 weeks on mss. Sample copy and writer's guidelines free.

Nonfiction: Book excerpts, general interest, how-to (on general health and fitness topics), inspirational, interview/profile, medical breakthroughs, natural healing and alternative medicine, new products, celebrities. "Give us something new and different." **Buys 75-100 mss/year.** Query with published clips or send complete ms. Length: 800-1,500 words. **Pays $25-200.**

Reprints: Send tearsheet of article and information about when and where the article previously appeared. Pays 75% of amount paid for original article.

Photos: Send photos with submission. Reviews contact sheets, negatives, transparencies, prints. Offers $50-100/photo. Captions, model releases, identification of subjects required. Buys one-time rights.

Columns/Departments: Nutrition (general nutrition and healthful eating, supplements). Weight Loss (sensible advice from experts on how to achieve permanent weight loss without "dieting"; evaluation of new diet fads, books or trends). Cooking (recipes and low-fat cooking tips). Fitness (cardiovascular conditioning, strength training, stretching, exercise for weight loss, sports activities, movement therapies such as yoga, tai chi, Pilates). Behavior (mind/body emotional and spiritual health, stress management, relationships). Successful Aging (health and fitness after 50; profiles of successful agers). Alternative Medicine (our approach: alternative and natural remedies or therapies should be used as an adjunct to, not replacement for, traditional treatments and prevention strategies. Sources and experts for these stories should be reputable, responsible advocates). Women (preventive health issues; skin care and beauty). Men (preventive health issues). Sexual Health. Parenting. Remedies (sensible advice for common ailments such as headaches, back pain, allergies, colds, everyday aches and pains, etc.). Healthy Getaways (fitness/adventure travel; wellness vacations). Length: 600-800 words. **Pays $25-200.**

Tips: "Freelancers can best break in by offering us stories of national interest that we won't find through other channels, such as wire services. Well-written self-help articles, especially ones that focus on natural prevention and cures are always welcome. We're looking for more natural health and alternative therapy stories."

$ $ YOUR HEALTH & FITNESS, General Learning Communications, 900 Skokie Blvd., Northbrook IL 60062-1574. (847)205-3000. Fax: (847)564-8197. **Contact:** Carol Lezak, executive editor. **90-95% freelance written.** Prefers to work with published/established writers. Quarterly magazine covering health and fitness. Needs "general, educational material on health, fitness and safety that can be read and understood easily by the layman." Estab. 1969. Circ. 1,000,000.

Pays after publication. Publishes ms an average of 6 months after acceptance. No byline given (contributing editor status given in masthead). Offers 50% kill fee. Buys all rights.
Nonfiction: Health-related general interest. No alternative medicine. "All article topics assigned. No queries; if you're interested in writing for the magazine, send a cover letter, résumé, curriculum vitae and writing samples. All topics are determined a year in advance of publication by editors. No unsolicited manuscripts." **Buys approximately 65 mss/year.** Length: 350-850 words. Pay varies, commensurate with experience and quality of ms.
Tips: "Write to a general audience with only a surface knowledge of health and fitness topics. Possible subjects include exercise and fitness, psychology, nutrition, safety, disease, drug data, and health concerns. No phone queries."

HISTORY

Listed here are magazines and other periodicals written for historical collectors, genealogy enthusiasts, historic preservationists and researchers. Editors of history magazines look for fresh accounts of past events in a readable style. Some publications cover an era, such as the Civil War, while others may cover a region or subject area, such as aviation history.

AMERICAN HERITAGE, 60 Fifth Ave., New York NY 10011. (212)206-5500. Fax: (212)620-2332. E-mail: mail@americanheritage.com. Website: http://www.americanheritage.com. **Contact:** Richard Snow, editor. **70% freelance written.** Magazine published 8 times/year. "*American Heritage* writes from a historical point of view on politics, business, art, current and international affairs, and our changing lifestyles. The articles are written with the intent to enrich the reader's appreciation of the sometimes nostalgic, sometimes funny, always stirring panorama of the American experience." Circ. 300,000. Usually buys first North American rights or all rights. Byline given. **Pays on acceptance.** Publishes ms an average of 6-12 months after acceptance. Before submitting material, "check our index to see whether we have already treated the subject." Submit seasonal material 1 year in advance. Reports in 2 months. Writer's guidelines for #10 SASE.
Nonfiction: Wants "historical articles by scholars or journalists intended for intelligent lay readers rather than for professional historians." Emphasis is on authenticity, accuracy and verve. "Interesting documents, photographs and drawings are always welcome. Query. Style should stress readability and accuracy." **Buys 30 unsolicited mss/year.** Length: 1,500-6,000 words. Pay varies. Sometimes pays the expenses of writers on assignment.
Tips: "We have over the years published quite a few 'firsts' from young writers whose historical knowledge, research methods and writing skills met our standards. The scope and ambition of a new writer tell us a lot about his or her future usefulness to us. A major article gives us a better idea of the writer's value. Everything depends on the quality of the material. We don't really care whether the author is 20 and unknown, or 80 and famous, or vice versa. No phone calls, please."

$ $ $ AMERICAN HISTORY, P.O. Box 8200, Harrisburg PA 17112. (717)657-9555. Website: http://www.thehistorynet.com. **Contact:** Christine Technke, managing editor. **60% freelance written.** Bimonthly magazine of cultural, social, military and political history published for a general audience. Estab. 1966. Circ. 120,000. **Pays on acceptance.** Byline given. Buys all rights. Reports in 10 weeks on queries. Writer's guidelines for #10 SASE. Sample copy and guidelines for $5 (includes 3rd class postage) or $4 and 9×12 SAE with 4 first-class stamps.
Nonfiction: Features biographies of noteworthy historical figures and accounts of important events in American history. Also includes pictorial features on artists, photographers and graphic subjects. "Material is presented on a popular rather than a scholarly level." Query with published clips and SASE. "Query letters should be limited to a concise 1 page proposal defining your article with an emphasis on its unique qualities." **Buys 20 mss/year.** Length: 2,000-4,000 words depending on type of article. **Pays $200-1,000.**
Photos: Welcomes suggestions for illustrations.
Tips: "Key prerequisites for publication are thorough research and accurate presentation, precise English usage and sound organization, a lively style, and a high level of human interest. Submissions received without return postage will not be considered or returned. Inappropriate materials include: fiction, book reviews, travelogues, personal/family narratives not of national significance, articles about collectibles/antiques, living artists, local/individual historic buildings/landmarks and articles of a current editorial nature. Currently seeking articles on significant Civil War subjects. No phone, fax or e-mail queries, please."

$ $ AMERICA'S CIVIL WAR, Cowles History Group, 741 Miller Dr., SE, Suite D-2, Leesburg VA 20175-8920. (703)771-9400. Fax: (703)779-8345. E-mail: cheryls@cowles.com. Website: http://www.thehistorynet.com. **Contact:** Roy Morris, Jr., editor. Managing Editor: Carl Von Wodtke. **95% freelance written.** Bimonthly magazine of "popular history and straight historical narrative for both the general reader and the Civil War buff covering strategy, tactics, personalities, arms and equipment." Estab. 1988. Circ. 125,000. Pays on publication. Publishes ms up to 2 years after acceptance. Byline given. Buys all rights. Reports in 3 months on queries; 6 months on mss. Sample copy for $5. Writer's guidelines for #10 SASE.
Nonfiction: Book excerpts, historical, travel. No fiction or poetry. **Buys 24 mss/year.** Query. Length: 3,500-4,000 words and should include a 500-word sidebar. **Pays $300 maximum.**
Photos: Send photos with submission or cite sources. "We'll order." Captions and identification of subjects required.

Columns/Departments: Personality (probes); Ordnance (about weapons used); Commands (about units); Eyewitness to War (about appropriate historical sites). **Buys 24 mss/year.** Query. Length: 2,000 words. **Pays up to $150.**

Tips: "Include suggested readings in a standard format at the end of your piece. Manuscript must be typed, double-spaced on one side of standard white 8½×11, 16 to 30 pound paper—no onion skin paper or dot matrix printouts. All submissions are on speculation. Prefer subjects to be on disk. Choose stories with strong art possibilities."

$ $ AVIATION HISTORY, Cowles History Group, 741 Miller Dr., SE, Suite D-2, Leesburg VA 20175-8920. (703)771-9400. Fax: (703)779-8345. E-mail: cheryls@cowles.com. Website: http://www.thehistorynet.com. **Contact:** Arthur Sanfelici, editor. Managing Editor: Carl von Wodtke. **95% freelance written.** Bimonthly magazine covering military and civilian aviation from first flight to the jet age. It aims to make aeronautical history not only factually accurate and complete, but also enjoyable to varied subscriber and newsstand audience. Estab. 1990. Circ. 80,000. Pays on publication. Publishes ms up to 2 years after acceptance. Byline given. Buys all rights. Editorial lead time 6 months. Submit seasonal material 1 year in advance. Accepts simultaneous submissions. Reports in 3 months on queries; 6 months on mss. Sample copy for $5. Writers guidelines for #10 SASE.

Nonfiction: Book excerpts, historical/nostalgic, interview/profile, personal experience, travel. **Buys 24 mss/year.** Query. Length: Feature articles should be 3,500-4,000 words, each with a 500-word sidebar, author's biography and book suggestions for further reading. **Pays $300.**

Photos: State availability of art and photos with submission, cite sources. "We'll order." Reviews contact sheets, negatives, transparencies. Identification of subjects required. Buys one-time rights.

Columns/Departments: People and Planes, Enduring Heritage, Aerial Oddities, Art of Flight; all 2,000 words. **Pays $150.** Book reviews, 300-750 words; payment by the word.

Tips: "Choose stories with strong art possibilities."

$ $ CHICAGO HISTORY, The Magazine of the Chicago Historical Society, Chicago Historical Society, Clark St. at North Ave., Chicago IL 60614-6099. (312)642-4600. Fax: (312)277-2066. E-mail: adams@chicagohistory.org. Website: http://www.chicagohistory.org. **Contact:** Rosemary Adams, editor-in-chief. **100% freelance written.** Works with a small number of new/unpublished writers each year. Quarterly magazine covering Chicago history: cultural, political, economic, social and architectural. Estab. 1945. Circ. 9,500. Pays on publication. Publishes ms an average of 1 year after acceptance. Byline given. Buys all rights. Submit seasonal material 9 months in advance. Reports in 4 months. Sample copy for $3.50 and 9×12 SAE with 3 first-class stamps. Writer's guidelines free.

- Writer's guidelines for *Chicago History* are also available on its website.

Nonfiction: Book excerpts, essays, historical, photo feature. Articles should be "analytical, informative, and directed at a popular audience with a special interest in history." No "cute" articles, no biographies. **Buys 8-12 mss/year.** Query or send complete ms. Length: approximately 4,500 words. **Pays $150-250.**

Photos: Send photocopies with submission. No originals. Offers no additional payment for photos accepted with ms. Identification of subjects required.

Tips: "A freelancer can best break in by 1) calling to discuss an article idea with editor; and 2) submitting a detailed outline of proposed article. All sections of *Chicago History* are open to freelancers, but we suggest that authors do not undertake to write articles for the magazine unless they have considerable knowledge of the subject and are willing to research it in some detail. We require a footnoted manuscript, although we do not publish the notes."

N ☆ $ $ CIVIL WAR TIMES ILLUSTRATED, 6405 Flank Dr., Harrisburg PA 17112. (717)657-9555. Fax: (717)657-9552. E-mail: cwt@cowles.com. Website: http://www.thehistorynet.com. Editor: Jim Kushlan. 90% freelance written. Works with a small number of new/unpublished writers each year. Bimonthly magazine. Estab. 1961. Circ. 189,505. **Pays on acceptance.** Publishes ms an average of 18 months after acceptance. Buys all rights. Submit seasonal material 1 year in advance. Reports in 8 months on mss. Sample copy for $5.50. Writer's guidelines for SASE.

Nonfiction: Profile, photo feature, Civil War historical material. "Positively no fiction or poetry." **Buys 20 freelance mss/year.** Length: 2,500-3,000 words. **Pays $75-600.**

Photos: Renée Myers, art director.

Tips: "We're very open to new submissions. Send submissions after examining writer's guidelines and several recent issues. Include photocopies of photos that could feasibly accompany the article."

N ☆ $ $ COMMAND, Military History, Strategy & Analysis, XTR Corp., P.O. Box 4017, San Luis Obispo CA 93403. (805)546-9596. Fax: (805)546-0570. Managing Editor: Christopher Perello. **Contact:** Ty Bomba, editor-in-chief. **95% freelance written.** Bimonthly magazine. "*Command* is a magazine of popular—not scholarly—analytic military history." Estab. 1989. Circ. 35,000. Pays on publication. Publishes ms 1 year after acceptance. Byline given. Buys first rights or all rights. Editorial lead time 2 months. Submit seasonal material 4 months in advance. Reports in 2 weeks on queries; 2 months on mss. Sample copy for $4.95. Writer's guidelines for #10 SASE.

Nonfiction: Book excerpts, essays, opinion, personal experience, photo feature, analytical-historical current military affairs. **Buys 36-48 mss/year.** Query. Length: 700-10,000 words. **Pays $35-500.**

Photos: Send photos with submission. Negotiates payment individually. Captions required. Buys one-time or all rights.

Tips: "Read guidelines and do what they say. Be broadly knowledgeable in military history, current affairs, etc."

$ $ GATEWAY HERITAGE, Missouri Historical Society, P.O. Box 11940, St. Louis MO 63112-0040. (314)746-4557. Fax: (314)746-4548. **Contact:** Tim Fox, editor. **75% freelance written.** Quarterly magazine covering Missouri history. "*Gateway Heritage* is a popular history magazine which is sent to members of the Missouri Historical Society. Thus, we have a general audience with an interest in history." Estab. 1980. Circ. 6,200. Pays on publication. Publishes ms an average of 6 months after acceptance. Byline given. Offers $75 kill fee. Buys first North American serial rights. Editorial lead time 6 months. Submit seasonal material 1 year in advance. Reports in 2 weeks on queries; 2 months on mss. Sample copy for 9×12 SAE with 7 first-class stamps. Writer's guidelines for #10 SASE.

Nonfiction: Book excerpts, historical/nostalgic, interview/profile, personal experience, photo feature. No genealogies. **Buys 12-15 mss/year.** Query with published clips. Length: 3,500-5,000 words. **Pays $200.**

Photos: State availability of photos with submission.

Columns/Departments: Literary Landmarks (biographical sketches and interviews of famous Missouri literary figures) 1,500-2,500 words; Missouri Biographies (biographical sketches of famous and interesting Missourians) 1,500-2,500 words; Gateway Album (excerpts from diaries and journals) 1,500-2,500 words. **Buys 6-8 mss/year.** Query with published clips. **Pays $100.**

Tips: "Ideas for our departments are a good way to break into *Gateway Heritage*."

$ GOOD OLD DAYS, America's Premier Nostalgia Magazine, House of White Birches, 306 E. Parr Rd., Berne IN 46711. (219)589-8741. **Contact:** Ken Tate, editor. **75% freelance written.** Monthly magazine of first person nostalgia, 1900-1955. "We look for strong narratives showing life as it was in the first half of this century. Our readership is comprised of nostalgia buffs, history enthusiasts and the people who actually lived and grew up in this era." Pays within 45 days of signed contract. Publishes ms an average of 8 months after acceptance. Byline given. Buys all, first North American serial or one-time rights. Submit seasonal material 10 months in advance. Reports in 2 months. Sample copy for $2. Writer's guidelines for #10 SASE.

Nonfiction: Historical/nostalgic, humor, interview/profile, personal experience, favorite food/recipes and photo features, year-round seasonal material, biography, memorable events, fads, fashion, sports, music, literature, entertainment. Regular features: Good Old Days on Wheels (transportation auto, plane, horse-drawn, tram, bicycle, trolley, etc.); Good Old Days In the Kitchen (favorite foods, appliances, ways of cooking, recipes); Home Remedies (herbs and poultices, hometown doctors, harrowing kitchen table operations). **Buys 350 mss/year.** Query or send complete ms. Preferred. length: 500-1,200 words. **Pays $15-75, depending on quality and photos.** No fiction accepted.

Photos: Send photos or photocopies of photos alone or with submission. Offers $5/photo. Identification of subjects required. Buys one-time or all rights.

Tips: "Most of our writers are not professionals. We prefer the author's individual voice, warmth, humor and honesty over technical ability."

$ $ MILITARY HISTORY, Cowles History Group, 741 Miller Dr., SE, Suite D-2, Leesburg VA 20175-8920. (703)771-9400. Fax: (703)779-8345. E-mail: cheryls@cowles.com. Website: http://www.thehistorynet.com. **Contact:** Jon Guttman, editor. Managing Editor: Carl Von Wodtke. **95% freelance written.** Circ. 150,000. "We'll work with anyone, established or not, who can provide the goods and convince us as to its accuracy." Bimonthly magazine covering all military history of the world. "We strive to give the general reader accurate, highly readable, often narrative popular history, richly accompanied by period art." Pays on publication. Publishes ms 2 years after acceptance. Byline given. Buys all rights. Submit anniversary material at least 1 year in advance. Reports in 3 months on queries; 6 months on mss. Sample copy for $5. Writer's guidelines for #10 SASE.

Nonfiction: Historical; interview (military figures of commanding interest); personal experience (only occasionally). **Buys 18 mss, plus 6 interviews/year.** Query with published clips. "Submit a short, self-explanatory query summarizing the story proposed, its highlights and/or significance. State also your own expertise, access to sources or proposed means of developing the pertinent information." Length: 4,000 words with a 500-word sidebar. **Pays $400.**

Columns/Departments: Intrigue, Weaponry, Perspectives, Personality and review of books, video, CD-ROMs, software—all relating to military history. **Buys 24 mss/year.** Query with published clips. Length: 2,000 words. **Pays $200.**

Tips: "We would like journalistically 'pure' submissions that adhere to basics, such as full name at first reference, same with rank, and definition of prior or related events, issues cited as context or obscure military 'hardware.' Read the magazine, discover our style, and avoid subjects already covered. Pick stories with strong art possibilities (*real* art and photos), send photocopies, tell us where to order the art. Avoid historical overview; focus upon an event with appropriate and accurate context. Provide bibliography. Tell the story in popular but elegant style."

$ $ PERSIMMON HILL, National Cowboy Hall of Fame and Western Heritage Center, 1700 NE 63rd St., Oklahoma City OK 73111. Fax: (405)478-4714. E-mail: nchf@aol.com. Website: http://www.cowboyhalloffame.org. **Contact:** M.J. Van Deventer, editor. **70% freelance written.** Prefers to work with published/established writers; works with a small number of new/unpublished writers each year. Quarterly magazine for an audience interested in Western art, Western history, ranching and rodeo, including historians, artists, ranchers, art galleries, schools, and libraries. Estab. 1970. Circ. 15,000. Buys first rights. Byline given. Pays on publication. Publishes ms an average of 6-24 months after acceptance. Reports in 3 months. Sample copy for $9 and 12 first-class stamps. Writer's guidelines for #10 SASE.

Nonfiction: Historical and contemporary articles on famous Western figures connected with pioneering the American West, Western art, rodeo, cowboys, etc. (or biographies of such people), stories of Western flora and animal life and environmental subjects. "We want thoroughly researched and historically authentic material written in a popular style. May have a humorous approach to subject. No broad, sweeping, superficial pieces; i.e., the California Gold Rush or rehashed pieces on Billy the Kid, etc." Length: 1,500 words. Special issues: Women of the West (Autumn 1998); Transportation in the West (Spring 1999). **Buys 35-50 mss/year.** Query with clips. **Pays $150-250.**

Photos: Glossy b&w prints or color transparencies purchased with ms, or on assignment. Pays according to quality and importance for b&w and color photos. Suggested captions required.
Tips: "Send us a story that captures the spirit of adventure and individualism that typifies the Old West or reveals a facet of the Western lifestyle in contemporary society. Excellent illustrations for articles are essential!"

N **PRESERVATION MAGAZINE**, National Trust for Historic Preservation, 1785 Massachusetts Ave. NW, Washington DC 20036. (202)673-4075. **Contact:** Robert Wilson, editor. **75% freelance written.** Prefers to work with published/established writers. Bimonthly tabloid covering preservation of historic buildings in the US. "We cover subjects related in some way to place. Most entries are features, department or opinion pieces." Circ. 250,000. Pays on publication. Publishes ms an average of 1 month after acceptance. Byline given. Offers variable kill fee. Buys one-time rights. Reports in 2 months on queries. No writer's guidelines.
Nonfiction: Features, news, profiles, opinion, photo feature, travel. **Buys 30 mss/year.** Query with published clips. Length: 500-3,500 words. Sometimes pays expenses of writers on assignment, but not long-distance travel.
Tips: "Do not send or propose histories of buildings, descriptive accounts of cities or towns or long-winded treatises."

$ $ $ TIMELINE, Ohio Historical Society, 1982 Velma Ave., Columbus OH 43211-2497. (614)297-2360. Fax: (614)297-2367. E-mail: cduckworth@ee.net. **Contact:** Christopher S. Duckworth, editor. **90% freelance written.** Works with a small number of new/unpublished writers each year. Bimonthly magazine covering history, prehistory and the natural sciences, directed toward readers in the Midwest. Estab. 1885. Circ. 19,000. **Pays on acceptance.** Publishes ms an average of 1 year after acceptance. Byline given. Offers $75 minimum kill fee. Buys first North American serial or all rights. Submit seasonal material 6 months in advance. Reports in 3 weeks on queries; 6 weeks on mss. Sample copy for $6 and 9×12 SAE. Writer's guidelines for #10 SASE.
Nonfiction: Book excerpts, essays, historical, profile (of individuals), photo feature. Topics include the traditional fields of political, economic, military, and social history; biography; the history of science and technology; archaeology and anthropology; architecture; the fine and decorative arts; and the natural sciences including botany, geology, zoology, ecology, and paleontology. **Buys 22 mss/year.** Query. Length: 1,500-6,000 words. Also vignettes of 500-1,000 words. **Pays $100-900.**
Photos: Send photos with submission. Submissions must include ideas for illustration. Reviews contact sheets, transparencies, 8×10 prints. Captions, model releases, identification of subjects required. Buys one-time rights.
Tips: "We want crisply written, authoritative narratives for the intelligent lay reader. An Ohio slant may strengthen a submission, but it is not indispensable. Contributors must know enough about their subject to explain it clearly and in an interesting fashion. We use high-quality illustration with all features. If appropriate illustration is unavailable, we can't use the feature. The writer who sends illustration ideas with a manuscript has an advantage, but an often-published illustration won't attract us."

$ $ TRACES OF INDIANA AND MIDWESTERN HISTORY, Indiana Historical Society, 315 W. Ohio St., Indianapolis IN 46202-3299. (317)233-6073. Fax: (317)233-3109. E-mail: mmckee@statelib.lib.in.us. Website: http://www.ihs1830.org/traces.htm. Executive Editor: Thomas A. Mason. Managing Editor: J. Kent Calder. **Contact:** Megan McKee, editor. **80% freelance written.** Quarterly magazine on Indiana and Midwestern history. "Conceived as a vehicle to bring to the public good narrative and analytical history about Indiana in its broader contexts of region and nation, *Traces* explores the lives of artists, writers, performers, soldiers, politicians, entrepreneurs, homemakers, reformers, and naturalists. It has traced the impact of Hoosiers on the nation and the world. In this vein, the editors seek nonfiction articles that are solidly researched, attractively written, and amenable to illustration, and they encourage scholars, journalists, and freelance writers to contribute to the magazine." Estab. 1989. Circ. 11,000. **Pays on acceptance.** Publishes ms an average of 6 months after acceptance. Byline given. Buys one-time rights. Submit seasonal material 1 year in advance. Reports in 3 months on mss. Sample copy for $5 and 9×12 SAE with 6 first-class stamps. Writer's guidelines for #10 SASE.
Nonfiction: Book excerpts, historical essays, historical photographic features on topics of biography, literature, folklore, music, visual arts, politics, economics, industry, transportation and sports. **Buys 20 mss/year.** Send complete ms. Length: 2,000-4,000 words. **Pays $100-500.**
Photos: Send photos with submission. Reviews contact sheets, photocopies, transparencies and prints. Pays "reasonable photographic expenses." Captions, permissions and identification of subjects required. Buys one-time rights.
Tips: "Freelancers should be aware of prerequisites for writing history for a broad audience. Should have some awareness of this magazine and other magazines of this type published by midwestern and western historical societies. Preference is given to subjects with an Indiana connection and authors who are familiar with *Traces*. Quality of potential illustration is also important."

$ TRUE WEST and OLD WEST, Western Periodicals, Inc., P.O. Box 2107, Stillwater OK 74076-2107. (405)743-3370. Fax: (405)743-3374. E-mail: western@cowboy.net. Website: http://www.cowboy.net/western. **Contact:**

Marcus Huff, editor. **100% freelance written.** Works with a small number of new/unpublished writers each year. *True West* (monthly), and *Old West* (quarterly) are magazines on Western American history from prehistory to 1930. "We want reliable research on significant historical topics written in lively prose for an informed general audience. More recent topics may be used if they have a historical angle or retain the Old West flavor of trail dust and saddle leather." Estab. 1953. Circ. 40,000. **Pays on acceptance.** Sends galleys. Publishes ms an average of 4 months after acceptance. Byline given. Buys first North American serial rights. Editorial lead time 3 months. Submit seasonal material 6 months in advance. Accepts simultaneous submissions. Reports in 1 month on queries; 2 months on mss. Sample copy for $2 and 9×12 SAE. Writer's guidelines for #10 SASE.

Nonfiction: Historical/nostalgic, how-to, humor, photo feature, travel, Native Americans, trappers, miners, cowboys, ranchers, pioneers, military ghost towns, lost mines, women and minorities. "We do not want rehashes of worn-out stories, historical fiction or history written in a fictional style." Special issue: ghost stories published every October (deadline June 5.) **Buys 150 mss/year.** Query. Ideal length: 2,000 words, maximum length 4,000 words; shorter pieces, especially humor, 300-1,500 words. **Pays 3-6¢/word.**

Photos: "We usually need from four to eight photos for each story, and we rely on writers to provide them." Send photos with accompanying query or ms. "Appropriate maps enhance our articles, and we appreciate receiving sketches for our artists to work from." Pays $10 for b&w prints. Identification of subjects required. Buys one-time rights.

Columns/Departments: Western Roundup—200-300-word short articles on historically oriented places to go and things to do in the West. Should include one b&w print. **Buys 24 mss/year.** Send complete ms. **Pays $25-75.**

Fillers: Short humor. **Buys 12/year.** Length: 500-1,000 words. **Pays 3-6¢/word.**

Tips: "Do original research on fresh topics. Stay away from controversial subjects unless you are truly knowledgable in the field. Read our magazines and follow our guidelines. A freelancer is most likely to break in with us by submitting thoroughly researched, lively prose on relatively obscure topics. First person accounts rarely fill our needs. Historical accuracy and strict adherence to the facts are essential. We much prefer material based on primary sources (archives, court records, documents, contemporary newspapers and first person accounts) to those that rely mainly on secondary sources (published books, magazines, and journals). Note: We are currently trying to take *True West* and *Old West* back to their 'roots' by publishing shorter pieces. Ideal length is between 1,500-3,000 words."

$ $ VIETNAM, Cowles History Group, 741 Miller Dr. SE, #D-2, Leesburg VA 20175-8920. (703)771-9400. Fax: (703)779-8345. E-mail: cheryls@cowles.com. Website: http://www.thehistorynet.com. **Contact:** Colonel Harry G. Summers, Jr., editor. Managing Editor: Carl Von Wodtke. **80-90% freelance written.** Bimonthly magazine that "provides in-depth and authoritative accounts of the many complexities that made the war in Vietnam unique, including the people, battles, strategies, perspectives, analysis and weaponry." Estab. 1988. Circ. 115,000. Pays on publication. Publishes ms up to 2 years after acceptance. Byline given. Buys all rights. Reports in 3 months on queries; 6 months on mss. Sample copy for $5. Writer's guidelines for #10 SASE.

Nonfiction: Book excerpts (if original), historical, interview, personal/experience, military history. "Absolutely no fiction or poetry; we want straight history, as much personal narrative as possible, but not the gung-ho, shoot-em-up variety, either." **Buys 24 mss/year.** Query. Length: 4,000 words maximum. **Pays $300 for features, sidebar 500 words.**

Photos: Send photos with submission or state availability and cite sources. Identification of subjects required.

Columns/Departments: Arsenal (about weapons used, all sides); Personality (profiles of the players, all sides); Fighting Forces (various units or types of units: air, sea, rescue); Perspectives. Query. Length: 2,000 words. **Pays $150.**

Tips: "Choose stories with strong art possibilities."

$ $ WILD WEST, Cowles History Group, 741 Miller Dr., SE, Suite D-2, Leesburg VA 20175-8920. (703)771-9400. Fax: (703)779-8345. E-mail: cheryls@cowles.com. Website: http://www.thehistorynet.com. **Contact:** Gregory Lalire, editor. Managing Editor: Carl Von Wodtke. **100% freelance written.** Bimonthly magazine on history of the American frontier, from its eastern beginnings to its western terminus. "*Wild West* covers the popular (narrative) history of the American West—events, trends, personalities, anything of general interest." Estab. 1988. Circ. 200,000. Pays on publication. Publishes ms an average of 2 years after acceptance. Byline given. Buys all rights. Editorial lead time 6 months. Submit seasonal material 1 year in advance. Accepts simultaneous submissions. Reports in 3 months on queries; 6 months on mss. Sample copy for $5. Writer's guidelines for #10 SASE.

Nonfiction: Book excerpts, historical/nostalgic, humor, personal experience, travel. No fiction or poetry—nothing current. **Buys 36 mss/year.** Query. Length: 4,000 words with a 500-word sidebar. **Pays $300.**

Photos: State availability of photos with submission; cite sources. Reviews negatives, transparencies. Offers no additional payment for photos accepted with ms. Captions, identification of subjects required. Buys one-time rights.

Columns/Departments: Travel; Gun Fighters & Lawmen, 2,000 words; Personalities; Warriors & Chiefs, 2,000 words; Artist West, 2,000 words; Books Reviews, 500 words. **Buys 36 mss/year.** Query. **Pays $150 for departments, book reviews by the word, minimum $30.**

Tips: "Always query the editor with your story idea. Successful queries include a description of sources of information and suggestions for color and black-and-white photography or artwork. The best way to break into our magazine is to write an entertaining, informative and unusual story that grabs the reader's attention and holds it. We favor carefully researched, third-person articles or firsthand accounts that give the reader a sense of experiencing historical events."

$ $ WORLD WAR II, Cowles History Group, 741 Miller Dr., SE, Suite D-2, Leesburg VA 20175-8920. (703)771-9400. Fax: (703)779-8345. E-mail: cheryls@cowles.com. Website: http://www.thehistorynet.com. **Contact:** Michael Haskew, editor. Managing Editor: Carl Von Wodtke. **95% freelance written.** Prefers to work with published/established writers. Bimonthly magazine covering "military operations in World War II—events, personalities, strategy, national policy, etc." Estab. 1986. Circ. 200,000. Pays on publication. Publishes ms an average of 2 years after acceptance. Byline given. Buys all rights. Submit anniversary-related material 1 year in advance. Reports in 3 months on queries; 6 months or more on mss. Sample copy for $4. Writer's guidelines for #10 SASE.

Nonfiction: World War II military history. No fiction. **Buys 24 mss/year.** Query. Length: 4,000 words with a 500-word sidebar. **Pays $200.**

Photos: State availability of art and photos with submission. For photos and other art, send photocopies and cite sources. "We'll order." Captions and identification of subjects required.

Columns/Departments: Undercover (espionage, resistance, sabotage, intelligence gathering, behind the lines, etc.); Personalities (WW II personalities of interest); Armaments (weapons, their use and development), all 2,000 words. **Pays $100.** Book reviews, 300-750 words. **Buys 18 mss/year (plus book reviews).** Query with SASE.

Tips: "List your sources and suggest further readings in standard format at the end of your piece—as a bibliography for our files in case of factual challenge or dispute. All submissions are on speculation."

HOBBY & CRAFT

Magazines in this category range from home video to cross-stitch. Craftspeople and hobbyists who read these magazines want new ideas while collectors need to know what is most valuable and why. Collectors, do-it-yourselfers and craftspeople look to these magazines for inspiration and information. Publications covering antiques and miniatures are also listed here. Publications covering the business side of antiques and collectibles are listed in the Trade Art, Design and Collectibles section.

$ $ AMERICAN WOODWORKER, Rodale Press, Inc., 33 E. Minor St., Emmaus PA 18098-0099. (610)967-5171. Fax: (610)967-7692. Fax: (610)967-9287. E-mail: awletters@aol.com. Website: http://www.americanwoodworker.com. Editor/Publisher: David Sloan. **Contact:** Tim Snyder, executive editor. **70% freelance written.** Magazine published 7 times/year. "*American Woodworker* is a how-to magazine edited for the woodworking enthusiast who wants to improve his/her skills. We strive to motivate, challenge and entertain." Estab. 1988. Circ. 380,000. Pays on publication. Publishes ms an average of 6 months after acceptance. Byline given. Buys one-time and second serial (reprint) rights. Submit seasonal material 8 months in advance. Reports in 1 month. Sample copy and writer's guidelines free.

Nonfiction: Essays, historical/nostalgic, how-to (woodworking projects and techniques), humor, inspirational, interview/profile, new product, personal experience, photo feature, technical. ("All articles must have woodworking theme.") **Buys 30 mss/year.** Query. Length: up to 2,500 words. **Pays new authors base rate of $150/published page.** Sometimes pays expenses of writers on assignment.

Reprints: Send photocopy of article or typed ms with rights for sale noted. Payment varies.

Photos: Send photos with submission. Reviews 35mm or larger transparencies. Model releases required. Buys one-time rights.

Columns/Departments: Offcuts (woodworking news and nonsense, 1,000 word maximum). **Buys 10 mss/year.** Send complete ms. **Pays $100-300.**

Tips: "Reading the publication is the only real way to get a feel for the niche market of *American Woodworker* and the needs and interests of our readers. Feature stories and articles most accessible for freelancers. Articles should be technically accurate, well organized." Captions, model releases, identification of subjects required. Buys one-time rights.

☆ $ $ ANTIQUE REVIEW, P.O. Box 538, Worthington OH 43085-0538. **Contact:** Charles Muller, editor. (614)885-9757. Fax: (614)885-9762. **60% freelance written.** Eager to work with new/unpublished writers. Monthly tabloid for an antique-oriented readership, "generally well-educated, interested in Early American furniture and decorative arts, as well as folk art." Estab. 1975. Circ. 10,000. Pays on publication date assigned at time of purchase. Publishes ms an average of 2 months after acceptance. Buys first North American serial and second (reprint) rights to material originally published in dissimilar publications. Byline given. Reports in 3 months. Free sample copy and writer's guidelines for #10 SASE.

- In 1998 *Antique Review* is adding a new section focusing on trends and collectibles.

Nonfiction: "The articles we desire concern history and production of furniture, pottery, china, and other quality Americana. In some cases, contemporary folk art items are acceptable. We are also interested in reporting on antiques shows and auctions with statements on conditions and prices." **Buys 5-8 mss/issue.** Query with clips of published work. Query should show "author's familiarity with antiques, an interest in the historical development of artifacts relating to early America and an awareness of antiques market." Phone queries OK. Length: 200-2,000 words. **Pays $100-200.** Sometimes pays expenses of writers on assignment.

Reprints: Accepts previously published submissions if not first printed in competitive publications. Send tearsheet or photocopy of article or typed ms with rights for sale noted and information about when and where the article previously appeared. Pays 100% of amount paid for an original article.

Photos: Send photos with query. Payment included in ms price. Uses 3×5 or larger glossy b&w or color prints. Captions required. Articles with photographs receive preference.

Tips: "Give us a call and let us know of specific interests. We are more concerned with the background in antiques than in writing abilities. The writing can be edited, but the knowledge imparted is of primary interest. A frequent mistake is being too general, not becoming deeply involved in the topic and its research. We are interested in primary research into America's historic material culture."

$ $ THE ANTIQUE TRADER WEEKLY, P.O. Box 1050, Dubuque IA 52004-1050. (319)588-2073, ext. 121. Fax: (800)531-0880. E-mail: traderpubs@aol.com. **Contact:** Kyle Husfloen, editor. **50% freelance written.** Works with a small number of new/unpublished writers each year. Weekly newspaper for collectors and dealers in antiques and collectibles. Estab. 1957. Circ. 60,000. Publishes ms an average of 1 year after acceptance. Buys all rights. Payment at beginning of month following publication. Submit seasonal material 4 months in advance. Sample copy for $1 and #10 SASE. Writer's guidelines free.

Nonfiction: "We invite authoritative and well-researched articles on all types of antiques and collectors' items and in-depth stories on specific types of antiques and collectibles. No human interest stories. We do not pay for brief information on new shops opening or other material printed as a service to the antiques hobby." **Buys 60 mss/year.** Query or submit complete ms. Length: 1,000-2,000 words. **Pays $50-150 for features $150-250 for cover stories.**

Photos: Submit a liberal number of good color photos to accompany article. Uses 35mm slides for cover. Offers no additional payment for photos accompanying mss.

Tips: "Send concise, polite letter stating the topic to be covered in the story and the writer's qualifications. No 'cute' letters rambling on about some 'imaginative' story idea. Writers who have a concise yet readable style and know their topic are always appreciated. I am most interested in those who have personal collecting experience or can put together a knowledgable and informative feature after interviewing a serious collector/authority."

$ AUTOGRAPH COLLECTOR, Odyssey Publications, 510-A South Corona Mall, Corona CA 91719. (909)734-9636. Fax: (909)371-7139. E-mail: DBTOGI@aol.com. Website: http://www.AutographCollector.com. **Contact:** Ev Phillips, editor. **80% freelance written.** Monthly magazine covering the autograph collecting hobby. "The focus of *Autograph Collector* is on documents, photographs or any collectible item that has been signed by a famous person, whether a current celebrity or historical figure. Articles stress how and where to locate celebrities and autograph material, authenticity of signatures and what they are worth." Byline given. Negotiable kill fee. Buys all rights. Editorial lead time 2 months. Submit seasonal material 3 months in advance. Reports in 2 weeks on queries; 1 month on mss. Sample copy and writer's guidelines free.

Nonfiction: Historical/nostalgic, how-to, interview/profile, personal experience. "Articles must address subjects that appeal to autograph collectors and should answer six basic questions: Who is this celebrity/famous person? How do I go about collecting this person's autograph? Where can I find it? How scarce or available is it? How can I tell if it's real? What is it worth?" **Buys 25-35 mss/year.** Query. Length: 1,750-2,250 words. **Pays 5¢/word.** Sometimes pays expenses of writers on assignment.

Photos: State availability of photos with submission. Reviews transparencies, prints. Offers $3/photo. Captions, identification of subjects required. Buys one-time rights.

Columns/Departments: "*Autograph Collector* buys 8-10 columns per month written by regular contributors. Send query for more information." **Buys 90-100 mss/year.** Query. **Pays $50 or as determined on a per case basis.**

Fillers: Anecdotes, facts. **Buys 20-25/year.** Length: 200-300 words. **Pays $15.**

Tips: "Ideally writers should be autograph collectors themselves and know their topics thoroughly. Articles must be well-researched and clearly written. Writers should remember that *Autograph Collector* is a celebrity-driven magazine and name recognition of the subject is important."

$ $ BECKETT BASEBALL CARD MONTHLY, Statabase, Inc., 15850 Dallas Pkwy., Dallas TX 75248. (972)991-6657. Fax: (972)233-6488. Website: http://www.beckett.com. Editorial Director: Rudy Klanchik. **Contact:** Jim Thompson, editor. **85% freelance written.** Monthly magazine on baseball card and sports memorabilia collecting. "Our readers expect our publication to be entertaining and informative. Our slant is that hobbies are fun and rewarding. Especially wanted are how-to-collect articles." Estab. 1984. **Pays on acceptance.** Publishes ms an average of 4 months after acceptance. Byline given. Pays $50 kill fee. Buys all rights. Submit seasonal material 6 months in advance. Reports in 1 month. Sample copy for $3.95. Writer's guidelines free.

Nonfiction: Book excerpts, historical/nostalgic, how-to, humor, interview/profile, new product, opinion, personal experience, photo feature, technical. Special issues: Spring training (February); season preview (April); All-Star game (July); World Series (October). No articles that emphasize speculative prices and investments. **Buys 145 mss/year.** Send complete ms. Length: 300-1,500 words. **Pays $100-400 for assigned articles; $50-200 for unsolicited articles.** Sometimes pays expenses of writers on assignment.

Photos: Send photos with submission. Reviews 35mm transparencies, 5×7 or larger prints. Offers $10-300/photo. Captions, model releases and identification of subjects required. Buys one-time rights.

Fiction: Humorous only.

Tips: "A writer for *Beckett Baseball Card Monthly* should be an avid sports fan and/or a collector with an enthusiasm for sharing his/her interests with others. Articles must be factual, but not overly statistic-laden. First person (not research) articles presenting the writer's personal experiences told with wit and humor, and emphasizing the stars of the game, are *always* wanted. Acceptable articles must be of interest to our two basic reader segments: teenaged boys and their middle-aged fathers who are re-experiencing a nostalgic renaissance of their own childhoods. Prospective writers should write down to neither group!"

$ $ BECKETT BASKETBALL MONTHLY, Statabase, Inc., 15850 Dallas Pkwy., Dallas TX 75248. (972)991-6657. Fax: (972)991-8930. Website: http://www.beckett.com. Publisher: Dr. James Beckett. Editorial Director: Rudy Klanchik. **Contact:** Mike McAllister, managing editor. **60% freelance written.** Monthly magazine on basketball card and sports memorabilia collecting. "Our readers expect our publication to be entertaining and informative. Our slant is that hobbies are fun and rewarding. Especially wanted are articles dealing directly with the hobby of basketball card and memorabilia collecting." Estab. 1990. Circ. 300,000. **Pays on acceptance.** Publishes ms an average of 4 months after acceptance. Byline given. Pays $50 kill fee. Buys first North American serial rights. Submit seasonal material 6 months in advance. Reports in 1 month. Sample copy for $2.95. Writer's guidelines free.

Nonfiction: Book excerpts, historical/nostalgic, how-to, humor, interview/profile, new product, opinion, personal experience, photo feature, technical. No articles that emphasize speculative prices and investments. **Buys 145 mss/year.** Send complete ms. Length: 300-1,500 words. **Pays $100-400 for assigned articles; $100-200 for unsolicited articles.** Sometimes pays expenses of writers on assignment.

Photos: Send photos with submission. Reviews 35mm transparencies, 5×7 or larger prints. Offers $10-300/photo. Captions, model releases and identification of subjects required. Buys one-time rights.

Tips: "A writer for *Beckett Basketball Monthly* should be an avid sports fan and/or a collector with an enthusiasm for sharing his/her interests with others. Articles must be factual, but not overly statistic-laden."

$ $ BECKETT FOOTBALL CARD MONTHLY, Statabase, Inc., 15850 Dallas Pkwy., Dallas TX 75248. (214)991-6657. Fax: (972)233-6488. Website: http://www.beckett.com. Editorial Director: Rudy Klanchik. **Contact:** Tracy Hackler, features editor. **85% freelance written.** Monthly magazine on football card and sports memorabilia collecting. "Our readers expect our publication to be entertaining and informative. Our slant is that hobbies are fun and rewarding. Especially wanted are how-to-collect articles." Estab. 1989. **Pays on acceptance.** Publishes ms an average of 4 months after acceptance. Byline given. Pays $50 kill fee. Buys all rights. Submit seasonal material 6 months in advance. Reports in 1 month. Sample copy for $3.95. Writer's guidelines free.

Nonfiction: Book excerpts, historical/nostalgic, how-to, humor, interview/profile, new product, opinion, personal experience, photo feature, technical. Special issues: Super Bowl (January); Pro Bowl (February); NFL draft (April); preview (September). No articles that emphasize speculative prices and investments. Buys 145 mss/year. Send complete ms. Length: 300-1,500 words. Pays $100-400 for assigned articles; $50-200 for unsolicited articles. Sometimes pays expenses of writers on assignment.

Photos: Send photos with submission. Reviews 35mm transparencies, 5×7 or larger prints. Offers $10-300/photo. Captions, model releases, identification of subjects required. Buys one-time rights.

Fiction: Humorous only.

Tips: "A writer for *Beckett Football Card Monthly* should be an avid sports fan and/or a collector with an enthusiasm for sharing his/her interests with others. Articles must be factual, but not overly statistic-laden. Acceptable articles must be of interest to our two basic reader segments: teenaged boys and their middle-aged fathers who are re-experiencing a nostalgic renaissance of their own childhoods. Prospective writers should write down to neither group!"

$ $ BECKETT HOCKEY MONTHLY, Statabase, Inc., 15850 Dallas Pkwy., Dallas TX 75248. (972)991-6657. Fax: (972)233-6488. Website: http://www.beckett.com. Associate Editor: Al Muin. **Contact:** Tracy Hackler, feature editor. **85% freelance written.** Monthly magazine on hockey, hockey card and memorabilia collecting. "Our readers expect our publication to be entertaining and informative. Our slant is that hobbies are for fun and rewarding. Especially wanted are how-to-collect articles." Estab. 1990. **Pays on acceptance.** Publishes ms an average of 3 months after acceptance. Byline given. Pays $50 kill fee. Buys all rights. Submit seasonal material 6 months in advance. Reports in 1 month. Sample copy for $3.95. Writer's guidelines free.

Nonfiction: Book excerpts, historical/nostalgic, how-to, humor, interview/profile, new product, opinion, personal experience, photo feature, technical. Special issues: All-Star game (February); Stanley Cup preview (April); draft (June); season preview (October). No articles that emphasize speculative prices and investments. Buys 145 mss/year. Send complete ms. Length: 300-1,500 words. Pays $100-400 for assigned articles; $50-200 for unsolicited articles. Sometimes pays expenses of writers on assignment.

Photos: Send photos with submission. Reviews 35mm transparencies, 5×7 or larger prints. Offers $10-300/photo. Captions, model releases and identification of subjects required. Buys one-time rights.

Fiction: Humorous only.

Tips: "A writer for *Beckett Hockey Monthly* should be an avid sports fan and/or a collector with an enthusiasm for sharing his/her interests with others. Articles must be factual, but not overly statistic-laden. Acceptable articles must be of interest to our two basic reader segments: teenaged boys and their middle-aged fathers who are re-experiencing a nostalgic renaissance of their own childhoods. Prospective writers should write down to neither group!"

$ $ BECKETT RACING MONTHLY, Statabase, Inc., 15850 Dallas Pkwy., Dallas TX 75248. (972)991-6657. Fax: (972)991-8930. E-mail: markzeske@beckett.com. Website: http://www.beckett.com. Editor: Dr. James Beckett. Editorial Director: Pepper Hastings. **Contact:** Mark Zeske, senior editor. **85% freelance written.** Monthly magazine on racing card, die cast and sports memorabilia collecting. "Our readers expect our publication to be entertaining and informative. Our slant is that hobbies are fun and rewarding. Especially wanted are articles dealing directly with the hobby of card collecting." Estab. 1994. Circ. 100,000 **Pays on acceptance**. Publishes ms an average of 4 months after acceptance. Byline given. Pays $50 kill fee. Buys all rights. Submit seasonal material 6 months in advance. Reports in 1 month. Sample copy for $3.95. Writer's guidelines free.

Nonfiction: Book excerpts, historical/nostalgic, how-to, humor, interview/profile, new product, opinion, personal experience, photo feature, technical. No articles that emphasize speculative prices and investments. Send complete ms. Length: 300-1,500 words. **Pays $100-400 for assigned articles; $100-200 for unsolicited articles.** Sometimes pays expenses of writer on assignment.
Photos: Send photos with submission. Reviews 35mm transparencies, 5×7 or larger prints. Offers $10-300/photo. Captions, model releases and identification of subjects required. Buys one-time rights.
Fiction: Humorous only.
Tips: "A writer for *Beckett Racing Monthly* should be an avid sports fan and/or a collector with an enthusiasm for sharing his/her interests with others. Articles must be factual, but not overly statistic-laden. First person (not research) articles presenting the writer's personal experiences told with wit and humor, and emphasizing the stars of the sport, are always wanted."

$ $ BECKETT SPORTS COLLECTIBLES AND AUTOGRAPHS, (formerly *Beckett Focus on Future Stars and Sports Collectibles*), Statbase, Inc., 15850 Dallas Pkwy., Dallas TX 75248. (972)991-6657. Fax: (972)991-8930. E-mail: mpagel@beckett.com. Website: http://www.beckett.com. Editor: Dr. James Beckett. Editorial Director: Pepper Hastings. **Contact:** Mike Pagel, associate editor. **85% freelance written.** Monthly magazine offering coverage of sports, collectibles and autographs from stars of all sports. "Our readers expect our publication to be entertaining and informative. Our slant is that hobbies are fun and rewarding. Especially wanted are how-to-collect articles." Estab. 1991. Circ. 73,128. **Pays on acceptance.** Publishes ms an average of 4 months after acceptance. Byline given. Pays $50 kill fee. Buys all rights. Submit seasonal material 8 months in advance. Reports in 1 month. Sample copy for $2.95. Writer's guidelines free.
Nonfiction: Book excerpts, historical/nostalgic, how-to, humor, interview/profile, new product, opinion, personal experience, photo feature, technical. Special issues: card sets in review (January); stay in school (February); draft special (June). No articles that emphasize speculative prices and investments on cards. **Buys 145 mss/year.** Send complete ms. Length: 300-1,500 words. **Pays $100-400 for assigned articles; $50-200 for unsolicited articles.** Sometimes pays expenses of writers on assignment.
Photos: Send photos with submission. Reviews 35mm transparencies, 5×7 or larger prints. Offers $25-300/photo. Captions, model releases and identification of subjects required. Buys one-time rights.
Tips: "A writer for *Beckett Sports Collectibles and Autographs* should be an avid sports fan and/or a collector with an enthusiasm for sharing his/her interests with others. Articles must be factual, but not overly statistic-laden. First person (not research) articles presenting the writer's personal experiences told with wit and humor, and emphasizing the stars of the game, are *always* wanted. Acceptable articles must be of interest to our two basic reader segments: teenaged boys and their middle-aged fathers who are re-experiencing a nostalgic renaissance of their own childhoods. Prospective writers should write down to neither group!"

★ $ $ THE BLADE MAGAZINE, Krause Publications, 700 E. State St., Iola WI 54945. (715)445-2214. Fax: (423)479-3586. E-mail: shacklefords@aol.com or stumpy479@aol.com. Website: http://www.krause.com. **Contact:** Steve Shackleford, editor. **75% freelance written.** Monthly magazine for knife enthusiasts who want to know as much as possible about quality knives and edged tools. Estab. 1973. Circ. 70,000. Pays on publication. Publishes ms an average of 6 months after acceptance. Buys all rights. Submit seasonal material 6 months in advance. Reports in 2 months. Sample copy for $3.25. Writer's guidelines for #10 SASE.

- *Blade Magazine* is putting more emphasis on new products, knife accessories, knife steels, knife handles, knives and celebrities, knives in the movies.

Nonfiction: How-to; historical (on knives); adventure on a knife theme; celebrities who own knives; knives featured in movies with shots from the movie, etc.; new product; nostalgia; personal experience; photo feature; technical. "We would also like to receive articles on knives in adventuresome life-saving situations." No poetry. **Buys 75 unsolicited mss/year.** "We evaluate complete manuscripts and make our decision on that basis." Length: 500-1,000 words, longer if content warrants it. **Pays $200/story minimum;** more for "better" writers. "We will pay top dollar in the knife market." Sometimes pays the expenses of writers on assignment.
Reprints: Accepts previously published submissions if not run in other knife publications. Send photocopy of article or typed ms with rights for sale noted and information about when and where the article previously appeared. Pays 90% of the amount paid for an original article.
Photos: Send photos with ms. Offers no additional payment for photos accepted with ms. Captions required. "Photos are critical for story acceptance."
Fiction: Publishes novel excerpts.
Tips: "We are always willing to read submissions from anyone who has read a few copies and studied the market. The ideal article for us is a piece bringing out the romance, legend, and love of man's oldest tool—the knife. We like articles that place knives in peoples' hands—in life saving situations, adventure modes, etc. (Nothing gory or with the knife as the villain.) People and knives are good copy. We are getting more and better written articles from writers who are reading the publication beforehand. That makes for a harder sell for the quickie writer not willing to do his homework."

N ★ $ BREW YOUR OWN, The How-to Homebrew Beer Magazine, (formerly *Brew*), 216 F. Street, Suite 160, Davis CA 95616. (530)758-4596. Fax: (530)758-7477. E-mail: edit@byo.com. Website: http://www.byo.com. **Contact:** Craig Bystrynski, editor. Managing Editor: Gailen Jacobs. **85% freelance written.** Monthly magazine covering home brewing. "Our mission is to provide practical information in an entertaining format. We try to capture the spirit

and challenge of brewing while helping our readers brew the best beer they can." Estab. 1995. Circ. 38,000. Pays on publication. Publishes ms 2-4 months after acceptance. Byline given. Offers 25% kill fee. Buys all rights. Editorial lead time 3 months. Submit seasonal material 3 months in advance. Reports in 2 months. Writer's guidelines for #10 SASE.
Nonfiction: How-to (home brewing), informational pieces on equipment, ingredients and brewing methods. Length: 1,500-3,000 words. Humor (related to home brewing), interview/profile, personal experience, historical, trends. Length: 800-2,000 words. **Buys 75 mss/year.** Query with published clips and SASE. **Pays $50-150 depending on length, complexity of article and experience of writer.** Sometimes pays expenses of writers on assignment.
Photos: State availability of photos with submission. Reviews contact sheets, transparencies, 5×7 prints. Negotiates payment individually. Captions required. Buys all rights.
Columns/Departments: News (humorous, unusual news about homebrewing), 50-250 words; Last Call (humorous stories about homebrewing), 700 words. **Buys 12 mss/year.** Query with or without published clips. **Pays $50.**
Tips: "*Brew Your Own* is for anyone who is interested in brewing beer, from beginners to advanced all-grain brewers. We seek articles that are straightforward and factual, not full of esoteric theories or complex calculations. Our readers tend to be intelligent, upscale, and literate."

$ $ CAR MODELER, Kalmbach Publishing Co., 21027 Crossroads Circle, P.O. Box 1612, Waukesha WI 53187-1612. (414)796-8776. Fax: (414)796-1383. E-mail: editor@carmodeler.com. Website: http://www.Kalmbach.com/carmodeler/carmodeler.html. **Contact:** Kirk Bell, senior editor. Managing Editor: Mark Thompson. **50% freelance written.** Bimonthly magazine covering model car building indepth. "Freelancers should have a strong knowledge of how to build models, with lots of experience." Estab. 1990, Circ. 50,000. Pays on publication. Publishes ms an average of 6 months after acceptance. Byline given. Buys all rights. Editorial lead time 4 months. Submit seasonal material 3 months in advance. Reports in 1 month on queries; 3 months on mss. Sample copy and writer's guidelines free.
Nonfiction: Book excerpts, historical/nostalgic, how-to, interview/profile, personal experience, photo feature, technical. Query or send complete ms. Length: 200-4,000 words. **Pays $75-100/published page.**
Photos: Send photos and negatives with submission. Prefers b&w glossy prints and 35mm color transparencies. When writing how-to article be sure to take photos *during* project. Negotiates payment individually. Captions, model releases, identification of subjects required. Buys all rights.
Columns/Departments: Buys 30-40 mss/year. Query. **Pays $75-100/published page.**
Fillers: Gags to be illustrated by cartoonist. **Buys 5/year. Pays percentage of $75/page rate.**
Tips: "Ask for writer's guidelines; then send queries or call with ideas. We are always interested in seeing material from new writers. Although we do not 'assign' or commission articles, we do review those sent to us and, if suitable, they are eventually used in either *Car Modeler* or *Scale Auto Enthusiast* magazine. We don't expect our writers to be Pulitzer Prize-winning journalists. We are looking for model builders, collectors, and enthusiasts who feel their models and/or modeling techniques and experiences would be of interest and benefit to our readership. When we evaluate articles we look at the quality of accompanying photos and illustrations (diagrams, drawings, etc.), content of the how-to material, and finally, the writing style. If the photos and content are good, the article can be worked on by our staff, if necessary, to improve its readability. Send us more photos than you would ever possibly imagine we could use. This permits us to pick and choose the best of the bunch."

N $ CERAMICS MONTHLY, American Ceramic Society, P.O. Box 6102, Westerville OH 43086. (614)523-1660. Fax: (614)891-8960. E-mail: editorial@ceramicmonthly.org. **Contact:** Ruth C. Butler, editor. **50% freelance written.** Monthly magazine, except July and August, covering the ceramic art and craft field. "Technical and business information for potters and ceramic artists." Estab. 1953. Circ. 39,000. Pays on publication. Byline given. Editorial lead time 3 months. Submit seasonal material 6 months in advance. Reports in 6 weeks on queries; 2 months on mss. Sample copy for cost plus $2 shipping & handling. Writer's guidelines free.
Nonfiction: Essays, how-to, interview/profile, opinion, personal experience, technical. **Buys 100 mss/year**. Send complete ms. Length: 500-3,000 words. **Pays 7¢/word.**
Photos: Send photos with submission. Reviews transparencies (2 ¼×2¼ or 4×5). Offers $15 for black and white; $25 for color photos. Captions required.
Columns/Departments: Up Front (workshop/exhibition review), 500-1,000 words. **Buys 20 mss/year**. Send complete ms. **Pays 7¢/word.**

$ $ CLASSIC TOY TRAINS, Kalmbach Publishing Co., 21027 Crossroads Circle, Waukesha WI 53187. (414)796-8776. Fax: (414)796-1142. E-mail: editor@classtrain.com. Website: http://www.kalmbach.com/ctt/toytrains.html. **Contact:** Neil Besougloff, editor. **75-80% freelance written.** Magazine published 8 times/year covering collectible toy trains (O, S, Standard, G scale, etc.) like Lionel, American Flyer, Marx, Dorfan, etc. "For the collector and operator of toy trains, *CTT* offers full-color photos of layouts and collections of toy trains, restoration tips, operating information, new product reviews and information, and insights into the history of toy trains." Estab. 1987. Circ. 72,000. **Pays on acceptance**. Publishes ms an average of 1 year after acceptance. Byline given. Buys all rights. Editorial lead time 3 months. Submit seasonal material 6 months in advance. Reports in 3 weeks on queries; 3 months on mss. Sample copy for $4.50 plus s&h. Writer's guidelines for #10 SASE.
Nonfiction: General interest, historical/nostalgic, how-to (restore toy trains; design a layout; build accessories; fix broken toy trains), interview/profile, personal experience, photo feature, technical. **Buys 90 mss/year.** Query. Length: 500-5,000 words. **Pays $75-500.** Sometimes pays expenses of writers on assignment.
Photos: Send photos with submission. Reviews 4×5 transparencies; 5×7 prints preferred. Offers no additional payment

for photos accepted with ms or $15-75/photo. Captions required. Buys all rights.
Fillers: Uses cartoons. **Buys 6 fillers/year. Pays $30.**
Tips: "It's important to have a thorough understanding of the toy train hobby; most of our freelancers are hobbyists themselves. One-half to two-thirds of *CTT*'s editorial space is devoted to photographs; superior photography is critical."

$ $ COLLECTOR EDITIONS, Collector Communications Corp., 170 Fifth Ave., New York NY 10010-5911. (212)989-8700. Fax: (212)645-8976. **Contact:** Joan M. Pursley, editor. **40% freelance written.** Works with a small number of new/unpublished writers each year. Published 7 times/year, it covers porcelain and glass collectibles and limited-edition prints. "We specialize in contemporary (post-war ceramic and glass) collectibles, including reproductions, but also publish articles about antiques, if they are being reproduced today and are generally available." Estab. 1973. Circ. 96,000. Buys first North American serial rights. "First assignments are always done on a speculative basis." Pays within 30 days of acceptance. Publishes ms an average of 6 months after acceptance. Reports in 2 months. Sample copy for $2. Writer's guidelines for #10 SASE.
Nonfiction: "Short features about collecting, written in tight, newsy style. We specialize in contemporary (postwar) collectibles. Values for pieces being written about should be included." Informational, interview, profile, exposé, nostalgia. Special issues: Christmas Collectibles (December). **Buys 15-20 mss/year.** Query with sample photos. Length: 800-1,500 words. **Pays $250-400.** Sometimes pays expenses of writers on assignment.
Photos: B&w and color photos purchased with accompanying ms with no additional payment. Captions are required. "We want clear, distinct, full-frame images that say something."
Columns/Departments: Staff written; not interested in freelance columns.
Tips: "Unfamiliarity with the field is the most frequent mistake made by writers in completing an article for us."

$ $ COLLECTOR'S MART, Contemporary Collectibles, Limited Edition Art & Gifts, Krause Publications, 700 E. State St., Iola WI 54990. (715)445-2214. Fax: (715)445-4087. Website: http://www.krause.com. **Contact:** Mary L. Sieber, editor. **50% freelance written.** Bimonthly magazine covering contemporary collectibles, for collectors of all types. Estab. 1976. Circ. 150,000. Pays on publication. Publishes ms an average of 6 months after acceptance. Byline given. Buys perpetual but non-exclusive rights. Editorial lead time 2 months. Submit seasonal material 4 months in advance. Reports in 1 month on mss. Writer's guidelines not available.
Nonfiction: Buys 35-50 mss/year. Send complete ms. Length: 1,000-2,000 words. **Pays $50-300.**
Photos: Send only color photos with submission. Reviews transparencies, prints. Offers no additional payment for photos accepted with ms. Captions required. Buys one-time rights.

N $ $ CQ VHF, Ham Radio Above 50 MHz, CQ Communications, Inc., 76 N. Broadway, Hicksville NY 11801. (516)681-2922. Fax: (516)681-2926. E-mail: cqvhf@aol.com. **Contact**: Richard Moseson, editor. Managing Editor: Edith Lennon. **90% freelance written.** Monthly magazine covering amateur (ham) radio. "All of our articles must be related to amateur (ham) radio and its usage on frequencies above 50 MHz. Since many of our readers are either new to ham radio or new to specific aspects of the hobby, we require that all technical terminology and on-air abbreviations be explained, either within the main text or in a sidebar. Don't assume prior knowledge of your topic, but do assume that the reader is an intelligent person who will understand a well-written and clearly-explained article. Writing style is friendly and informal, but not 'cute.' " Estab. 1996. Circ. 30,000. Pays 2 months after publication. Publishes ms an average of 6 months after acceptance. Byline given. Buys first North American serial rights and second serial (reprint) rights. Editorial lead time 3 months. Submit seasonal material 4 months in advance. Reports in 3 weeks on queries; 2 months on mss. Sample copy and writer's guidelines free via e-mail, on website or for #10 SASE.
Nonfiction: How-to, interview/profile, new product (reviews), opinion (Op-Ed pays in 1-year subscription only), personal experience, photo feature, technical. "All articles must be related to VHF ham radio. No 'How My 5-Year-Old Got Her Ham License' or any article that is not related to VHF ham radio." **Buys 60-70 mss/year.** Query. Length: 2,000-3,500 words. **Pays $40/page.** "Some writers prefer to be paid in a subscription or some of our books."
Reprints: Accepts previously published submissions, if so noted.
Photos: Send photos with submissions. Reviews 3½×5 or 4×6 prints. Offers no additional payment for photos accepted with ms. Captions, identification of subjects required. Buys one-time rights.
Tips: "You must be familiar with ham radio and/or ham radio operators. If you are writing about a related topic, you must be able to show how it ties in with ham radio above 50 MHz. If you're not a ham, try to find a ham radio club in your area. Find out what they're up to that might be interesting to write about, and be a reporter—ask if you can tag along; take notes, conduct interviews, take pictures. And don't be afraid to ask the hams to translate 'hamspeak' into English for you. You can't explain what you don't understand. E-mail queries will get the quickest reply."

$ $ CRAFTS MAGAZINE, 2 News Plaza, Peoria IL 61656. Fax: (309)679-5454. E-mail: craftsmag@aol.com. **Contact:** Miriam Olson, editor. Monthly magazine covering crafts and needlecrafts, mostly how-to projects using products found in a craft, needlework or fabric store. **Pays on acceptance**. Byline given. Buys all rights. Editorial lead time 5 months. Reports in 1 month on queries. Writer's guidelines for #10 SASE.
Nonfiction: All how-to articles. "We are tentatively planning three scrapbooking (memory-album-making) issues." **Buys 400 mss/year.** Query with photo or sketch of how-to project. **Pays $150-400.**
Tips: "Project should use readily-available supplies. Project needs to be easily duplicated by reader. Most projects are made for gifts, home decorating accents, wearables and holidays, especially Christmas. Must know likes, dislikes and

needs of today's crafter and have in-depth knowledge of craft products. *Crafts* is a mix of traditional techniques plus all the latest trends and fads."

$ $ CRAFTS 'N' THINGS, Clapper Communications Companies, 2400 Deven, Suite 375, Des Plaines IL 60018-4618. (847)635-5800. Fax: (847)635-6311. **Contact:** Nona Piorkowski, associate editor. **80% freelance written.** How-to and craft project magazine published 10 times/year. "We publish instruction for craft projects for beginners to intermediate level hobbyists." Estab. 1975. Circ. 300,000. Publishes ms an average of 4 months after acceptance. Byline given. Buys all rights. Submit seasonal material 6 months in advance.

Nonfiction: How-to craft projects: include time it takes to complete, cost of supplies used, and skill level; new product (for product review column). Send SASE for list of issue themes and writer's guidelines. **Buys 240 mss/year.** Send complete ms with photos, instructions and SASE. **Pays $50-400.** Offers listing exchange as a product source instead of payment in some cases.

Reprints: Send photocopy of article and information about when and where the article previously appeared.

Columns/Departments: Bright Ideas (original ideas for working better with crafts—hints and tips). **Buys 30 mss/year.** Send complete ms. Length: 25-50 words. **Pays $20.**

Tips: "Query for guidelines and list of themes and deadlines. How-to articles are the best bet for freelancers. A how-to project will have a good chance for acceptance if it is quick, easy, and has broad appeal; supplies are limited and easy to find; cost is $10 or less; takes less than 5 hours to complete and can be done with children or groups."

$ $ CROCHET WORLD, House of White Birches, P.O. Box 776, Henniker NH 03242. Fax: (219)589-8093. E-mail: www.whitebirches.com. Website: http://www.whitebirches.com. **Contact:** Susan Hankins, editor. **100% freelance written.** Bimonthly magazine covering crochet patterns. "*Crochet World* is a pattern magazine devoted to the art of crochet. We also feature a Q&A column, letters (swap shop) column and occasionally non-pattern manuscripts, but it must be devoted to crochet." Estab. 1978. Circ. 75,000. Pays on publication. Byline given. Buys all rights. Editorial lead time 4 months. Submit seasonal material 6 months in advance. Reports in 1 month. Sample copy for $2. Writer's guidelines free.

Nonfiction: How-to (crochet). **Buys 0-2 mss/year.** Send complete ms. Length: 500-1,500 words. **Pays $50.**

Columns/Departments: Touch of Style (crocheted clothing); It's a Snap! (quick one-night simple patterns); Pattern of the Month, first and second prize each issue. **Buys dozens of mss/year.** Send complete pattern. **Pays $40-300.**

Poetry: Strictly crochet-related. **Buys 0-10 poems/year.** Submit maximum 2 poems. Length: 6-20 lines. **Pays $10-20.**

Fillers: Anecdotes, facts, gags to be illustrated by cartoonist, short humor. **Buys 0-10/year.** Length: 25-200 words. **Pays $5-30.**

Tips: "Be aware that this is a pattern generated magazine for crochet designs. I prefer the actual item sent along with complete directions/graphs etc., over queries. In some cases a photo submission or good sketch will do. Crocheted designs must be well-made and original and directions must be complete. Write for Designer's Guidelines which detail how to submit designs. Non-crochet items, such as fillers, poetry *must* be crochet-related, not knit, not sewing, etc."

$ $ DECORATIVE ARTIST'S WORKBOOK, F&W Publications, Inc., 1507 Dana Ave., Cincinnati OH 45207-1005. (513)531-2690, ext. 461. Fax: (513)531-2902. E-mail: dawedit@aol.com. **Contact:** Anne Hevener, editor. Estab. 1987. **75% freelance written.** Bimonthly magazine covering decorative painting projects and products of all sorts. Offers "straightforward, personal instruction in the techniques of decorative painting." Circ. 90,000. **Pays on acceptance.** Byline given. Offers 25% kill fee. Buys first North American serial rights. Submit seasonal material 8 months in advance. Reports in 1 month. Sample copy for $4.65 and 9×12 SAE with 5 first-class stamps.

Nonfiction: How-to (related to decorative painting projects), new products, techniques, artist profiles. **Buys 30 mss/year.** Query with slides or photos. Length: 1,200-1,800 words. **Pays 15-25¢/word.**

Photos: Send photos with submission. Reviews 35mm, 4×5 transparencies and quality photos. Offers no additional payment for photos accepted with ms. Captions required. Buys one-time rights.

Tips: "The more you know—and can prove you know—about decorative painting the better your chances. I'm looking for experts in the field who, through their own experience, can artfully describe the techniques involved. How-to articles are most open to freelancers. Be sure to query with photo/slides, and show that you understand the extensive graphic requirements for these pieces and can provide painted progressives—slides or illustrations that show works in progress."

$ DOLL COLLECTOR'S PRICE GUIDE, House of White Birches, 306 E. Parr Rd., Berne IN 46711. (219)589-8741. **Contact:** Cary Raesner, editor. Quarterly magazine covering doll collecting. Audience is interested in informative articles about collecting and investing in dolls, museum exhibits, doll history, etc. Estab. 1991. Circ. 43,985. Pays pre-publication. Byline given. Buys all rights. Editorial lead time 6 months. Accepts previously published submissions. Reports in 3 months. Writer's guidelines for #10 SASE.

Nonfiction: Historical/nostalgic. Special issues: How to keep your dolls (Summer 1999, deadline December 5, 1998); Resources for collectors (Autumn 1999, deadline March 12, 1999); New dolls, Christmas dolls (Winter 1999, deadline June 21, 1999). **Buys 20 mss/year.** Send complete ms. **Pays $50 and up.**

Photos: Send top-quality photos with submission. Captions and identification of subjects required.

Reprints: Send photocopy of article or typed ms with rights for sale noted.

$ DOLL WORLD The Magazine for Doll Lovers, House of White Birches, 306 E. Parr Rd., Berne IN 46711. (219)589-8741. Fax: (219)589-8093. **Contact:** Cary Raesner, editor. **90% freelance written.** Bimonthly magazine covering doll collecting, restoration. "Interested in informative articles about doll history and costumes, interviews with doll artists and collectors, and how-to articles." Estab. 1978. Circ. 54,000. Pays pre-publication. Byline given. Buys all rights. Submit seasonal material 6 months in advance. Reports in 2 months on queries; 4 months on mss. Writer's guidelines for SASE.

Nonfiction: How-to, interview/profile. Special issues: Primitives (June 1999, deadline November 1, 1998); Ethnic dolls (August 1999, deadline January 1, 1999); Talking dolls (October 1999, deadline March 15, 1999); Christmas stories, new products, favorite dolls, a look back, doll collections (December 1999, deadline May 15, 1999). **Buys 100 mss/year.** Send complete ms. **Pays $50 and up.**

Reprints: Send photocopy of article or typed ms with rights for sale noted.

Photos: Send top-quality photos. Captions and identification of subjects required. Buys one-time or all rights.

Tips: "Choose a specific manufacturer and talk about his dolls or a specific doll—modern or antique—and explore its history and styles made."

$ $ DOLLHOUSE MINIATURES, (formerly *Nutshell News*), Kalmbach Publishing Co., 21027 Crossroads Circle, Waukesha WI 53187-9951. (414)798-6618. Fax: (414)796-1383. E-mail: kayolson@dhminiatures.com. Website: http://www.dhminiatures.com. Editor: Kay Melchiasedech Olson. **Contact:** Christine Paul, managing editor. **50% freelance written.** Monthly magazine covering dollhouse scale miniatures. "*Dollhouse Miniatures* is aimed at passionate miniatures hobbyists. Our readers take their miniatures seriously and do not regard them as toys. We avoid 'cutesiness' and treat our subject as a serious art form and/or an engaging leisure interest." Estab. 1971. Circ. 47,000. **Pays on acceptance.** Byline given. Buys all rights but will revert rights by agreement. Submit seasonal material 1 year in advance. Reports in 3 weeks on queries; 2 months on mss. Sample copy for $3.95. Writer's guidelines for #10 SASE.

Nonfiction: How-to miniature projects in 1″, ½″, ¼″ scales, interview/profile (artisans or collectors), photo feature (dollhouses, collections, museums). No articles on miniature shops or essays. **Buys 120 mss/year.** Query with few sample photos. Length: 1,000-1,500 words for features, how-to's may be longer. **"Payment varies, but averages $150."**

Photos: Send photos with submission. Requires 35mm slides and larger, 3×5 prints. "Photos are paid for with manuscript. Seldom buy individual photos." Captions preferred; identification of subjects required. Buys all rights.

Tips: "It is essential that writers for *Dollhouse Miniatures* be active miniaturists, or at least very knowledgeable about the hobby. Our readership is intensely interested in miniatures and will discern lack of knowledge or enthusiasm on the part of an author. A writer can best break in to magazine by sending photos of work, credentials and a story outline. Photographs must be sharp and properly exposed to reveal details. Photos showing scale are especially appreciated. For articles about subjects in the Chicago/Milwaukee area, we can usually send our staff photographer."

✪ $ $ $ ELECTRONICS NOW, Gernsback Publications, Inc., 500 Bi-County Blvd., Farmingdale NY 11735. (516)293-3000. Fax: (516)293-3115. Website: http://www.gernsback.com. **Contact:** Carl Laron, editor. **75% freelance written.** Monthly magazine on electronics technology and electronics construction, such as communications, computers, test equipment, components, video and audio. Estab. 1929. Circ. 104,000. **Pays on acceptance.** Publishes ms an average of 6 months after acceptance. Byline given. Buys all rights. Submit seasonal material 5-6 months in advance. Reports in 2 months on queries; 4 months on mss. Sample copy and writer's guidelines free.

Nonfiction: How-to (electronic project construction), humor (cartoons), new product. **Buys 150-200 mss/year.** Send complete ms. Length: 1,000-10,000 words. **Pays $200-800 for assigned articles; $100-800 for unsolicited articles.**

Photos: Send photos with submission. Offers no additional payment for photos accepted with ms. Captions, model releases and identification of subjects required. Buys all rights.

$ $ FIBERARTS, The Magazine of Textiles, Altamont Press, 50 College St., Asheville NC 28801. (704)253-0467. Fax: (704)253-7952. E-mail: fiberarts@larkbooks.com/fiberarts.html. Website: http://www.larkbooks.com. **Contact:** Ann Batchelder, editor. **100% freelance written.** Eager to work with new writers. Magazine published 5 times/year covering textiles as art and craft (contemporary trends in fiber sculpture, weaving, quilting, surface design, stitchery, papermaking, basketry, felting, wearable art, knitting, fashion, crochet, mixed textile techniques, ethnic dying, fashion, eccentric tidbits, etc.) for textile artists, craftspeople, hobbyists, teachers, museum and gallery staffs, collectors and enthusiasts. Estab. 1975. Circ. 25,250. Pays 30 days after publication. Publishes ms an average of 4 months after acceptance. Byline given. Buys first rights. Editorial guidelines and style sheet available. Sample copy for $5 and 10×12 SAE with 2 first-class stamps. Writer's guidelines for #10 SAE with 2 first-class stamps.

Nonfiction: Historical, artist interview/profile, opinion, photo feature, technical, education, trends, exhibition reviews, textile news. Query with brief outline prose synopsis and SASE. No phone queries. "Please be very specific about your proposal. Also an important consideration in accepting an article is the kind of photos—35mm slides and/or b&w glossies—that you can provide as illustration. We like to see photos in advance." Length: 250-2,000 words plus 4-5 photos. **Pays $100-400,** depending on article. Rarely pays the expenses of writers on assignment or for photos.

Photos: Visuals must accompany every article. The more photos to choose from, the better. Full photo captions are essential. Please include a separate, number-keyed caption sheet. The names and addresses of those mentioned in the article or to whom the visuals are to be returned are necessary.

Columns/Departments: Swatches (new ideas for fiber, unusual or offbeat subjects, work spaces, resources and marketing, techniques, materials, equipment, design and trends), 300-400 words. **Pays $80-100**. Profile (focuses on one artist), 400 words and one photo. **Pays $100.** Reviews (exhibits and shows; summarize quality, significance, focus and atmosphere, then evaluate selected pieces for aesthetic quality, content and technique—because we have an international readership, brief biographical notes or quotes might be pertinent for locally or regionally known artists), 400 words and

3-5 photos. **Pays $100.** (Do not cite works for which visuals are unavailable; you are not eligible to review a show in which you have participated as an artist, organizer, curator or juror.)

Tips: "Our writers are very familiar with the textile field, and this is what we look for in a new writer. Familiarity with textile techniques, history or events determines clarity of an article more than a particular style of writing. The writer should also be familiar with *Fiberarts*, the magazine. While the professional is essential to the editorial depth of *Fiberarts*, and must find timely information in the pages of the magazine, this is not our greatest audience. Our editorial philosophy is that the magazine must provide the non-professional textile enthusiast with the inspiration, support, useful information, and direction to keep him or her excited, interested, and committed. No phone queries."

$ $ FINE TOOL JOURNAL, Antique & Collectible Tools, Inc., 27 Fickett Rd., Pownal ME 04069. (207)688-4962. Fax: (207)688-4152. E-mail: ftjceb@aol.com. Website: http://www.wowpages.com/FTJ/. **Contact:** Clarence Blanchard, editor. **90% freelance written.** Quarterly magazine covering user and antique hand tools. "The *Fine Tool Journal* is a quarterly magazine specializing in older or antique hand tools from all traditional trades. Readers are primarily interested in woodworking tools, but some subscribers have interests in such areas as leatherworking, wrenches, kitchen tools and machinist tools. Readers range from beginners just getting into the hobby to advanced collectors and organizations." Estab. 1970. Circ. 2,000. Pays on publication. Publishes ms an average of 6 months after acceptance. Byline given. Offers $50 kill fee. Buys first and second serial (reprint) rights. Editorial lead time 3-9 months. Submit seasonal material 6 months in advance. Reports in 2 months on queries; 3 months on mss. Sample copy for $5. Guidelines for SASE.

Nonfiction: General interest, historical/nostalgic, how-to (make, use, fix and tune tools), interview/profile, personal experience, photo feature, technical. "We're looking for articles about tools from all trades. Interests include collecting, preservation, history, values and price trends, traditional methods and uses, interviews with collectors/users/makers, etc. Most articles published will deal with vintage, pre-1950, hand tools. Also seeking articles on how to use specific tools or how a specific trade was carried out. However, how-to articles must be detailed and not just of general interest. We do on occasion run articles on modern toolmakers who produce traditional hand tools." **Buys 24 mss/year.** Send complete ms. Length: 400-2,000 words. **Pays $50-200.** Sometimes pays expenses of writers on assignment.

Reprints: Accepts previously published submissions.

Photos: Send photos with submisison. Reviews 4×5 prints. Negotiates payment individually. Model releases, identification of subjects required. Buys all rights.

Columns/Departments: Stanley Tools (new finds and odd types), 300-400 words; Tips of the Trade (how to use tools), 100-200 words. **Buys 12 mss/year.** Send complete ms. **Pays $30-60.**

Tips: "The easiest way to get published in the *Journal* is to have personal experience or know someone who can supply the detailed information. We are seeking articles that go deeper than general interest and that knowledge requires experience and/or research. Short of personal experience find a subject that fits our needs and that interests you. Spend some time learning the ins and outs of the subject and with hard work and a little luck you will earn the right to write about it."

$ $ FINE WOODWORKING, The Taunton Press, P.O. Box 5506, Newtown CT 06470-5506. (203)426-8171. Fax: (203)270-6751. E-mail: jkolle@taunton.com. Website: http://www.taunton.com. **Contact:** Tim Schreiner, editor. Bimonthly magazine on woodworking in the small shop. "All writers are also skilled woodworkers. It's more important that a contributor be a woodworker than a writer. Our editors (also woodworkers) will fix the words." Estab. 1975. Circ. 270,000. **Pays on acceptance.** Byline given. Kill fee varies; "editorial discretion." Buys first rights and rights to republish in anthologies and use in promo pieces. Submit seasonal material 6 months in advance. Accepts simultaneous submissions. Reports in 2 months. Writer's guidelines free.

Nonfiction: How-to (woodworking). **Buys 120 mss/year.** Query with proposal letter. "No specs—our editors would rather see more than less." **Pays $150/magazine page.** Sometimes pays expenses of writers on assignment.

Photos: Send photos with submission. Reviews contact sheets, negatives, transparencies, prints. Captions, model releases, identification of subjects required. Buys one-time rights.

Columns/Departments: Notes & Comment (topics of interest to woodworkers); Question & Answer (woodworking Q & A); Methods of Work (shop tips); Tools & Materials (short reviews of new tools). **Buys 400 items/year.** Length varies. **Pays $10-150/published page.**

Tips: "Send for authors guidelines and follow them. Stories about woodworking reported by non-woodworkers are *not* used. Our magazine is essentially reader-written by woodworkers."

"We're looking for good articles on almost all aspects of woodworking from the basics of tool use, stock preparation and joinery to specialized techniques and finishing. We're especially keen on articles about shop-built tools, jigs and fixtures or any stage of design, construction, finishing and installation of cabinetry and furniture. Whether the subject involves fundamental methods or advanced techniques, we look for high-quality workmanship, thoughtful designs, safe and proper procedures."

$ $ FINESCALE MODELER, Kalmbach Publishing Co., 21027 Crossroads Circle, P.O. Box 1612, Waukesha WI 53187. (414)796-8776. Fax: (414)796-1383. E-mail: rmcnally@finescale.com. Website: http://www.finescale.html. Editor: Bob Hayden. **Contact:** Dick McNally, managing editor. **80% freelance written.** Eager to work with new/unpublished writers. Magazine published 10 times/year "devoted to how-to-do-it modeling information for scale model builders who build non-operating aircraft, tanks, boats, automobiles, figures, dioramas, and science fiction and fantasy models." Circ. 80,000. **Pays on acceptance.** Publishes ms an average of 14 months after acceptance. Byline given.

Buys all rights. Reports in 6 weeks on queries; 3 months on mss. Sample copy for 9×12 SAE with 3 first-class stamps. Writer's guidelines free.

Nonfiction: How-to (build scale models); technical (research information for building models). Query or send complete ms. Length: 750-3,000 words. **Pays $45/published page minimum.**

• *Finescale Modeler* is especially looking for how-to articles for car modelers.

Photos: Send color photos with ms. Pays $7.50 minimum for transparencies and $5 minimum for color prints. Captions and identification of subjects required. Buys one-time rights.

Columns/Departments: *FSM* Showcase (photos plus description of model); *FSM* Tips and Techniques (model building hints and tips). **Buys 25-50 Tips and Techniques/year.** Query or send complete ms. Length: 100-1,000 words. **Pays $10-20.**

Tips: "A freelancer can best break in first through hints and tips, then through feature articles. Most people who write for *FSM* are modelers first, writers second. This is a specialty magazine for a special, quite expert audience. Essentially, 99% of our writers will come from that audience."

N $ $ GENEALOGICAL COMPUTING, Ancestry Inc., 266 W. Center St., Orem UT 84057. (801)426-3500. Fax: (801)426-3501. E-mail: gceditor@ancestry.com. Website: http://www.ancestry.com. **Contact**: Dick Eastman, editor. **85% freelance written.** Quarterly magazine covering genealogy and computers. Estab. 1980. Circ. 8,000. Pays on publication. Publishes ms an average of 4 months after acceptance. Byline given. Buys all rights. Editorial lead time 4 months. Submit seasonal material 4 months in advance.

Nonfiction: How-to, interview/profile, new product, technical. **Buys 40 mss/year.** Query. Length: 1,500-2,500 words. **Pays $40-200.**

Reprints: Accepts previously published submissions. Pays 75% of amount paid for an original article.

$ $ THE HOME SHOP MACHINIST, 2779 Aero Park Dr., P.O. Box 1810, Traverse City MI 49685. (616)946-3712. Fax: (616)946-3289. E-mail: vpshop@aol.com. Website: http://members.aol.com/vpshop/hsm.htm. **Contact:** Joe D. Rice, editor. **95% freelance written.** Bimonthly magazine covering machining and metalworking for the hobbyist. Circ. 29,400. Pays on publication. Publishes ms an average of 2 years after acceptance. Byline given. Buys first North American serial rights only. Reports in 2 months. Free sample copy and writer's guidelines for 9×12 SASE.

Nonfiction: How-to (projects designed to upgrade present shop equipment or hobby model projects that require machining), technical (should pertain to metalworking, machining, drafting, layout, welding or foundry work for the hobbyist). No fiction or "people" features. **Buys 40 mss/year.** Query or send complete ms. Length: open—"whatever it takes to do a thorough job." **Pays $40/published page, plus $9/published photo.**

Photos: Send photos with ms. Pays $9-40 for 5×7 b&w prints; $70/page for camera-ready art; $40 for b&w cover photo. Captions and identification of subjects required.

Columns/Departments: Book Reviews; New Product Reviews; Micro-Machining; Foundry. "Become familiar with our magazine before submitting." Query first. **Buys 25-30 mss/year.** Length: 600-1,500 words. **Pays $40-70/page.**

Fillers: Machining tips/shortcuts. No news clippings. **Buys 12-15/year.** Length: 100-300 words. **Pays $30-48.**

Tips: "The writer should be experienced in the area of metalworking and machining; should be extremely thorough in explanations of methods, processes—always with an eye to safety; and should provide good quality b&w photos and/or clear dimensioned drawings to aid in description. Visuals are of increasing importance to our readers. Carefully planned photos, drawings and charts will carry a submission to our magazine much farther along the path to publication."

N $ $ HOT TOYS, Beckett Publications, 15850 Dallas Pkwy., Dallas TX 75248. (972)991-6657. Fax: (972)233-6488. E-mail: dkale@beckett.com. Website: http://www.beckett.com. **Contact:** Doug Kale, editor. Managing Editor: Mike Payne. **80% freelance written.** Monthly magazine covering toys ranging from action figures to yo-yo's. "We're reaching the consumer of toys, toy enthusiasts, as well as collectors." Estab. 1998. Circ. 120,000. **Pays on acceptance.** Byline given. Buys all rights. Editorial lead time 3 months. Submit seasonal material 3 months in advance. Accepts simultaneous submissions. Sample copy for $4.95, writer's guidelines for #10 SASE.

Nonfiction: General interest, historical/nostalgic, how-to, humor, interview/profile, new product, personal experience, photo feature. "We're also looking for authors for book publishing." **Pays $100-250.**

Photos: State availability of photos with submission. Reviews contact sheets, negatives, transparencies and prints. Negotiates payment individually. Buys all rights.

$ $ KITPLANES, For designers, builders and pilots of experimental aircraft, A Primedia Publication, 8745 Arrow Dr., Suite 105, San Diego CA 92123. (619)694-0491. Fax: (619)694-8147. E-mail: dave@kitplanes.com. Website: http://www.kitplanes.com. Managing Editor: Keith Beveridge. **Contact:** Dave Martin, editor. **70% freelance written.** Eager to work with new/unpublished writers. Monthly magazine covering self-construction of private aircraft for pilots and builders. Estab. 1972. Circ. 85,000. Pays on publication. Publishes ms an average of 3 months after acceptance. Byline given. Offers negotiable kill fee. Buys first North American serial rights. Submit seasonal material 6 months in advance. Reports in 2 weeks on queries; 6 weeks on mss. Sample copy for $3. Writer's guidelines free.

Nonfiction: How-to, interview/profile, new product, personal experience, photo feature, technical, general interest. "We are looking for articles on specific construction techniques, the use of tools, both hand and power, in aircraft building, the relative merits of various materials, conversions of engines from automobiles for aviation use, installation of instruments and electronics." No general-interest aviation articles, or "My First Solo" type of articles. **Buys 80 mss/year.** Query. Length: 500-5,000 words. **Pays $100-400,** including story photos.

Photos: State availability of or send photos with query or ms. Pays $250 for cover photos. Captions and identification of subjects required. Buys one-time rights.
Tips: "*Kitplanes* contains very specific information—a writer must be extremely knowledgeable in the field. Major features are entrusted only to known writers. I cannot emphasize enough that articles must be directed at the individual aircraft builder. We need more 'how-to' photo features in all areas of homebuilt aircraft."

$ $ KNIVES ILLUSTRATED, The Premier Cutlery Magazine, 265 S. Anita Dr., Suite 120, Orange CA 92868-3310. (714)939-9991. Fax: (714)939-9909. E-mail: budlang@pacbell.net. **Contact:** Bud Lang, editor. **40-50% freelance written.** Bimonthly magazine covering high-quality factory and custom knives. "We publish articles on different types of factory and custom knives, how-to make knives, technical articles, shop tours, articles on knife makers and artists. Must have knowledge about knives and the people who use and make them. We feature the full range of custom and high tech production knives, from miniatures to swords, leaving nothing untouched. We're also known for our outstanding how-to articles and technical features on equipment, materials and knife making supplies. We do not feature knife maker profiles as such, although we do spotlight some makers by featuring a variety of their knives and insight into their background and philosophy." Estab. 1987. Circ. 35,000. Pays on publication. Byline given. Editorial lead time 3 months. Reports in 2 weeks on queries. Sample copy available. Writer's guidelines for #10 SASE.
Nonfiction: How-to, interview/profile, photo features, technical. **Buys 35-40 mss/year.** Query first. Length: 400-2,000 words. **Pays $100-500 minimum.** Sometimes pays expenses of writers on assignment.
Photos: Send photos with submission. Reviews 35mm, 2¼×2¼, 4×5 transparencies, 5×7 prints. Negotiates payment individually. Captions, model releases, identification of subjects required.
Tips: "Most of our contributors are involved with knives, either as collectors, makers, engravers, etc. To write about this subject requires knowledge. A 'good' writer can do OK if they study some recent issues. If you are interested in submitting work to *Knives Illustrated* magazine, it is suggested you analyze at least two or three different editions to get a feel for the magazine. It is also recommended that you call or mail in your query to determine if we are interested in the topic you have in mind. While verbal or written approval may be given, all articles are still received on a speculation basis. We cannot approve any article until we have it in hand, whereupon we will make a final decision as to its suitability for our use. Bear in mind we do not suggest you go to the trouble to write an article if there is doubt we can use it promptly. Fax queries OK."

$ $ LAPIDARY JOURNAL, 60 Chestnut Ave., Suite 201, Devon PA 19333-1312. (610)293-1112. Fax: (610)293-1717. E-mail: ljeditor@aol.com. Website: http://www.lapidaryjournal.com. Editor: Merle White. **Contact:** Hazel Wheaton, managing editor. **70% freelance written.** Monthly magazine covering gem, bead and jewelry arts. "Our audience is hobbyists who usually have some knowledge of and proficiency in the subject before they start reading. Our style is conversational and informative. There are how-to projects and profiles of artists and materials." Estab. 1947. Circ. 59,800. **Pays on acceptance.** Publishes ms an average of 4 months after acceptance. Byline given. Buys one-time and worldwide rights. Editorial lead time 3 months.
Nonfiction: How-to jewelry/craft, interview/profile, new product, personal experience, technical, travel. Special issues: Bead Annual, Gemstone Annual, Design issue. **Buys 100 mss/year.** Query. Sometimes pays expenses of writers on assignment.
Reprints: Send photocopy of article. **Pays up to $500.**

$ $ THE LEATHER CRAFTERS & SADDLERS JOURNAL, 331 Annette Court, Rhinelander WI 54501-2902. (715)362-5393. Fax: (715)362-5391. **Contact:** William R. Reis, editor-in-chief. Managing Editor: Dorothea Reis. **100% freelance written.** Bimonthly magazine. "A leather-working publication with how-to, step-by-step instructional articles using full-size patterns for leathercraft, leather art, custom saddle, boot and harness making, etc. A complete resource for leather, tools, machinery and allied materials plus leather industry news." Estab. 1990. Circ. 8,000. Pays on publication. Publishes ms an average of 2 months after acceptance. Byline given. Buys first North American serial and second serial (reprint) rights. Submit seasonal material 6 months in advance. Accepts simultaneous submissions. Reports in 1 month. Sample copy for $5. Writer's guidelines for #10 SASE.
Nonfiction: How-to (crafts and arts and any other projects using leather). "I want only articles that include hands-on, step-by-step, how-to information." **Buys 75 mss/year.** Send complete ms. Length: 500-2,500 words. **Pays $20-250 for assigned articles; $20-150 for unsolicited articles.**
Reprints: Send tearsheet or photocopy of article. Pays 50% of amount paid for an original article.
Columns/Departments: Beginners, Intermediate, Artists, Western Design, Saddlemakers, International Design and Letters (the open exchange of information between all peoples). Length: 500-2,500 words on all. **Buys 75 mss/year.** Send complete ms. **Pays 5¢/word.**
Photos: Send good contrast color print photos and full-size patterns and/or full-size photo-carve patterns with submission. Lack of these reduces payment amount. Captions required.
Fillers: Anecdotes, facts, gags illustrated by cartoonist, newsbreaks. Length: 25-200 words. **Pays $5-20.**
Tips: "We want to work with people who understand and know leathercraft and are interested in passing on their knowledge to others. We would prefer to interview people who have achieved a high level in leathercraft skill."

$ LINN'S STAMP NEWS, Amos Press, 911 Vandemark Rd., P.O. Box 29, Sidney OH 45365. (937)498-0801. Fax: (800)340-9501. E-mail: linns@linns.com. Website: http://www.linns.com. Editor: Michael Laurence. **Contact:** Elaine Boughner, managing editor. **50% freelance written.** Weekly tabloid on the stamp collecting hobby. "All articles must be about philatelic collectibles. Our goal at *Linn's* is to create a weekly publication that is indispensable to stamp collectors." Estab. 1928. Circ. 70,000. Pays within one month of publication. Publishes ms an average of 1 month after acceptance. Byline given. Buys first North American serial rights. Submit seasonal material 2 months in advance. Reports in 2 weeks on mss. Free sample copy. Writer's guidelines for #10 SAE with 2 first-class stamps.

Nonfiction: General interest, historical/nostalgic, how-to, interview/profile, technical, club and show news, current issues, auction realization and recent discoveries. "No articles merely giving information on background of stamp subject. Must have philatelic information included." **Buys 300 mss/year.** Send complete ms. Length: 500 words maximum. **Pays $20-50.** Rarely pays expenses of writers on assignment.

Photos: Good illustrations a must. Send photos with submission. Provide captions on separate sheet of paper. Prefers crisp, sharp focus, high-contrast glossy b&w prints. Offers no additional payment for photos accepted with ms. Captions required. Buys all rights.

Tips: "Check and double check all facts. Footnotes and bibliographies are not appropriate to our newspaper style. Work citation into the text. Even though your subject might be specialized, write understandably. Explain terms. *Linn's* features are aimed at a broad audience of relatively novice collectors. Keep this audience in mind. Do not write down to the reader but provide information in such a way to make stamp collecting more interesting to more people. Embrace readers without condescending to them."

N $ $ MILITARY TRADER, Antique Trader Publications, P.O. Box 1050, Dubuque IA 52004. (319)588-2073. Fax: (319)588-0888. E-mail: atpzines@aol.com. **Contact:** Juli Kernall, editor. **98% freelance written.** Monthly tabloid covering militaria/collecting. Estab. 1994. Circ. 7,000. Pays on publication. Publishes ms an average of 5 months after acceptance. Byline given. Offers 20% kill fee. Buys first rights. Editorial lead time 6 weeks. Submit seasonal material 6 weeks in advance. Sample copy and writer's guidelines free.

Nonfiction: Interview/profile, new product, opinion, photo feature, technical. **Buys 125 mss/year.** Query. Length: 800-3,000 words. **Pays $50-250**, depending on the length and quality of writing and photos. "Longer, more in-depth articles with good, sharp photos, are worth more to us."

Photos: Send photos with submission. Reviews 3×5 prints. Offers no additional payment for photos accepted with ms. Captions and identification of subjects required. Buys one-time rights.

Columns/Departments: Book reviews **pay from $50 to $75** and require a photostat or color copy of cover.

Fillers: Anecdotes, facts, gags to be illustrated by cartoonist, newsbreaks, short humor. **Buys 25/year.** Length: 200-500 words. **Pays $15-50.**

Tips: "We're looking for authoritative and well-researched articles on all types of military antiques and collectibles. Send 4-12 photos (color photos, slides or b&w) with cutlines for each. Each article should be double-spaced and typed. In addition to the hardcopy, you may also submit the article on a computer disk, ASCII, either Mac or IBM. We pay anywhere from $50 to $250 for feature articles.

$ MINIATURE QUILTS, Chitra Publications, 2 Public Ave., Montrose PA 18801. (717)278-1984. Fax: (717)278-2223. E-mail: chitra@epix.net. Website: http://www.quilttownusa.com. **Contact:** Editorial Team. **40% freelance written.** Bimonthly magazine on miniature quilts. "We seek articles of an instructional nature (all techniques), profiles of talented quiltmakers and informational articles on all aspects of miniature quilts. Article should be written by quilters or quilting professionals. Miniature is defined as quilts made up of blocks smaller than five inches." Estab. 1990. Circ. 70,000. Pays on publication. Publishes ms an average of 6 months after acceptance. Byline given. Buys second serial (reprint) rights. Submit seasonal material 8 months in advance. Reports in 2 months on queries and mss. Writer's guidelines for SASE.

Nonfiction: How-to; profile articles about quilters who make small quilts, photo features about noteworthy miniature quilts or exhibits. "Publication hinges on good photo quality. Query with ideas; send samples of prior work." Length: 1,500 words maximum. **Pays $75/published page of text.**

Photos: Send photos with submission. Reviews 35mm slides and larger transparencies. Offers $20/photo. Captions, model releases and identification of subjects required. Buys all rights, unless rented from a museum.

$ $ MODEL RAILROADER, P.O. Box 1612, Waukesha WI 53187. Fax: (414)796-1142. E-mail: mrmag@mrmag.com. Website: http://www.modelrailroader.com/. **Contact:** Andy Sperandeo, editor. Monthly for hobbyists interested in scale model railroading. "We publish articles on all aspects of model-railroading and on prototype (real) railroading as a subject for modeling." Buys exclusive rights. Reports on submissions within 60 days.

Nonfiction: Wants construction articles on specific model railroad projects (structures, cars, locomotives, scenery, benchwork, etc.). Also photo stories showing model railroads. Query. "Study publication before submitting material." First-hand knowledge of subject almost always necessary for acceptable slant. **Pays base rate of $90/page.**

Photos: Buys photos with detailed descriptive captions only. Pays $10 and up, depending on size and use. Pays double b&w rate for color; full color cover earns $200.

Tips: "Before you prepare and submit any article, you should write us a short letter of inquiry describing what you want to do. We can then tell you if it fits our needs and save you from working on something we don't want."

$ $ MONITORING TIMES, Grove Enterprises Inc., P.O. Box 98, Brasstown NC 28902-0098. (704)837-9200. Fax: (704)837-2216. E-mail: mteditor@grove.net. Website: http://www.grove.net/hmpgmt.html. **Contact:** Rachel Baughn, managing editor. Publisher: Robert Grove. **20% freelance written.** Monthly magazine for radio hobbyists. Estab. 1982. Circ. 30,000. Pays on publication. Publishes ms an average of 4 months after acceptance. Byline given. Buys first North

American serial rights and limited reprint rights. Submit seasonal material 4 months in advance. Reports in 1 month. Sample copy and writer's guidelines for 9×12 SAE and 9 first-class stamps.

Nonfiction: General interest, how-to, humor, interview/profile, personal experience, photo feature, technical. **Buys 72 mss/year.** Query. Length: 1,000-2,500 words. **Pays $50/published page average.**

Reprints: Send photocopy of article and information about when and where the article previously appeared. Pays 25% of amount paid for an original article.

Photos: Send photos with submission. Captions required. Buys one-time rights.

Columns/Departments: "Query managing editor."

Tips: "Need articles on radio communications systems and shortwave broadcasters. We are accepting more technical projects."

THE NUMISMATIST, American Numismatic Association, 818 N. Cascade Ave., Colorado Springs CO 80903-3279. (719)632-2646. Fax: (719)634-4085. E-mail: anaedi@money.org. **Contact:** Barbara Gregory, editor/publisher. Monthly magazine covering numismatics (study of coins, tokens, medals and paper money). Estab. 1888. Circ. 28,000. Pays on publication. Publishes ms 6-12 months after acceptance. Byline given. Buys first North American serial rights. Editorial lead time 2 months. Sample copy free.

Nonfiction: Book excerpts, essays, historical/nostalgic, opinion, technical. "Submitted material should present new information and/or constitute a contribution to numismatic education for the experienced collector and beginner alike." Special issues: First Strike, a supplement for young or new collectors, is published twice yearly, in December and June. **Buys 60 mss/year.** Query or send complete ms. Length: 3,500 words maximum. **Pays $2.75/column inch.** Sometimes pays expenses of writers on assignment.

Photos: Send photos with submission. Negotiates payment individually. Captions and identification of subjects required.

Columns/Departments: Send complete ms. **Pays $25-100.**

PACK-O-FUN, Projects For Kids & Families, Clapper Communications, 2400 Devon Ave., Des Plaines IL 60018-4618. (847)635-5800. Fax: (847)635-6311. E-mail: 72567.1066@compuserve.com. Editor: Billie Ciancio. Contact: Georgianne Detzner, assistant editor. **85% freelance written.** Bimonthly magazine covering crafts and activities for kids and those working with kids. Estab. 1951. Circ. 102,000. Pays 30 days after signed contract. Byline given. Buys all rights. Editorial lead time 8 months. Submit seasonal material 8 months in advance. Accepts simultaneous submissions. Reports in 1 month. Sample copy for $2.95.

Nonfiction: "We request quick and easy, inexpensive crafts and activities. Projects must be original, and complete instructions are required upon acceptance." Pay is negotiable.

Reprints: Send tearsheet of article and information about when and where the article previously appeared.

Photos: Photos of project may be submitted in place of project at query stage.

Fillers: Facts, gags to be illustrated by cartoonist. **Buys 20/year.** Length: 25-50 words.

Tips: "*Pack-O-Fun* is looking for original how-to projects for kids and those working with kids. We're looking for recyclable ideas for throwaways. It would be helpful to check out our magazine before submitting."

$ POP CULTURE COLLECTING, Odyssey Publications, Inc., 510-A South Corona Mall, Corona CA 91719. (909)734-9636. Fax: (909)371-7139. E-mail: DBTOGI@aol.com. **Contact:** Ev Phillips, editor. **80% freelance written.** Monthly magazine for people interested in collecting celebrity or pop culture-related memorabilia. "Focus is on movie and TV props, costumes, movie posters, rock 'n' roll memorabilia, animation art, space or sports memorabilia, even vintage comic books, newspapers and magazines. Any collectible item that has a celebrity or pop culture connection and evokes memories. *Pop Culture Collecting* likes to profile people or institutions with interesting and unusual collections and tell why they are meaningful or memorable. Articles stress how to find and collect memorabilia, how to preserve and display it, and determine what it is worth." Estab. 1995. Circ. 15,000. Pays on publication. Publishes ms 3 months after acceptance. Byline given. Offers negotiable kill fee. Buys all rights. Editorial lead time 2 months. Submit seasonal material 3 months in advance. Reports in 2 weeks on queries; 1 month on mss. Sample copy and writer's guidelines free.

Nonfiction: Historical/nostalgic, how-to, interview/profile, personal experience, description of celebrity memorabilia collections. "No material not related to celebrity memorabilia, such as antiques. Articles must address subjects that appeal to collectors of celebrity or pop culture memorabilia and answer the following: What are these items? How do I go about collecting them? Where can I find them? How scarce or available are they? How can I tell if they're real? What are they worth?" **Buys 25-35 mss/year.** Query. Length: 1,500-2,000 words. **Pays 5¢/word.** Sometimes pays expenses of writers on assignment.

Photos: State availability of photos with submission. Reviews transparencies and prints. Offers $3/photo. Captions and identification of subjects required. Buys one-time rights.

Columns/Departments: "We print 8-10 columns a month written by regular contributors." Send query for more information. **Buys 90-100 mss/year. Pays $50 or as determined on a per case basis.**

Tips: "Writers ideally should be collectors of celebrity or pop culture memorabilia and know their topics thoroughly. Feature articles must be well-researched and clearly written. Writers should remember that *Pop Culture Collecting* is a celebrity/pop culture/nostalgia magazine. For this reason topics dealing with antiques or other non-related items are not suitable for publication."

$ POPULAR COMMUNICATIONS, CQ Communications, Inc., 25 Newbridge Rd., Hicksville NY 11801. (516)681-2922. Fax: (516)681-2926. E-mail: popularcom.@aol.com. Website: http://www.popcomm.com. **Contact:** Harold Ort, editor. **25% freelance written.** Monthly magazine covering the radio communications hobby. Estab. 1982. Circ. 65,000. Pays on publication. Publishes ms an average of 6 months after acceptance. Buys first North American serial rights. Editorial lead time 3 months. Submit seasonal material 6 months in advance. Reports in 1 month on queries; 2 months on mss. Sample copy free. Writer's guidelines for #10 SASE.

Nonfiction: General interest, how-to, new product, photo feature, technical. **Buys 6-10 mss/year.** Query. Length: 1,800-3,000 words. **Pays $35/printed page.**

Photos: State availability of photos with submission. Negotiates payment individually. Captions, model releases, identification of subjects required.

Tips: "Be a radio enthusiast with a keen interest in ham, shortwave, amateur, scanning or CB radio."

$ $ POPULAR ELECTRONICS, Gernsback Publications, Inc., 500 Bi-County Blvd., Farmingdale NY 11735-3931. (516)293-3000. Fax: (516)293-3115. E-mail: peeditor@gernsback.com. Website: http://www.gernsback.com. **Contact:** Edward A. Whitman, managing editor. **80% freelance written.** Monthly magazine covering hobby electronics—"features, projects, ideas related to audio, radio, experimenting, test equipment, computers, antique radio, communications, amateur radio, consumer electronics, state-of-the-art, etc." Circ. 78,000. **Pays on acceptance.** Byline given. Buys all rights. Submit seasonal material 9 months in advance. Reports in 1 month. Free sample copy, "include mailing label." Writer's guidelines for #10 SASE.

Nonfiction: General interest, how-to, photo feature, technical. **Buys 200 mss/year.** Query or send complete ms. Length: 1,000-3,500 words. **Pays $100-500.**

Photos: Send photos with submission. Wants b&w glossy photos. Offers no additional payment for photos accepted with ms. Captions required. Buys all rights.

Tips: "All areas are open to freelancers. Project-type articles and other 'how-to' articles have best success."

$ $ $ $ POPULAR MECHANICS, Hearst Corp., 224 W. 57th St., 3rd Floor, New York NY 10019. (212)649-2000. Fax: (212)586-5562. E-mail: popularmechanics@hearst.com. Website: http://www.popularmechanics.com. **Contact:** Joe Oldham, editor-in-chief. Managing Editor: Sarah Deem. **10% freelance written.** Monthly magazine on automotive, home improvement, science, boating, outdoors, electronics. "We are a men's service magazine that tries to address the diverse interests of today's male, providing him with information to improve the way he lives. We cover stories from do-it-yourself projects to technological advances in aerospace, military, automotive and so on." Estab. 1902. Circ. 1,400,000. **Pays on acceptance**. Publishes ms an average of 6 months after acceptance. Byline given. Offers 25% kill fee. Buys all rights. Submit seasonal material 6 months in advance. Reports in 3 weeks on queries; 1 month on mss. Writer's guidelines for SASE.

Nonfiction: General interest, how-to (shop projects, car fix-its), new product, technical. Special issues: Boating Guide (February); Home Improvement Guide (April); Consumer Electronics Guide (May); New Cars Guide (October); Woodworking Guide (November). No historical, editorial or critique pieces. **Buys 2 mss/year.** Query with or without published clips or send complete ms. Length: 500-1,500 words. **Pays $500-1,500 for assigned articles; $300-1,000 for unsolicited articles.** Sometimes pays expenses of writers on assignment.

Photos: Send photos with submission. Reviews slides and prints. Offers no additional payment for photos accepted with ms. Captions, model releases and identification of subjects required. Buys all rights.

Columns/Departments: New Cars (latest and hottest cars out of Detroit and Europe), Car Care (Maintenance basics, How It Works, Fix-Its and New products: send to Don Chaikin. Electronics, Audio, Home Video, Computers, Photography: send to Toby Grumet. Boating (new equipment, how-tos, fishing tips), Outdoors (gear, vehicles, outdoor adventures): send to James Gorant. Home & Shop Journal: send to Steve Willson. Science (latest developments), Tech Update (breakthroughs) and Aviation (sport aviation, homebuilt aircraft, new commercial aircraft, civil aeronautics): send to Jim Wilson. All columns are about 800 words.

$ $ POPULAR WOODWORKING, F&W Publications, 1507 Dana Ave., Cincinnati OH 45207. (513)531-2690, ext 407. Fax: (513)531-7107. E-mail: popwood@earthlink.net. Editor: Steve Shanesy. **Contact:** Christopher Schwarz, managing editor. **10% freelance written.** "*Popular Woodworking* is a bimonthly magazine that invites woodworkers of all levels into a community of experts who share their hard-won shop experience through in-depth projects and technique articles, which helps the readers hone their existing skills and develop new ones. Related stories increase the readers' understanding and enjoyment of their craft. Any project submitted must be aesthetically pleasing, of sound construction and offer a challenge to readers. On the average, we use two features per issue. Our primary needs are 'how-to' articles on woodworking projects. Our secondary need is for articles that will inspire discussion concerning woodworking. Tone of articles should be conversational and informal, as if the writer is speaking directly to the reader. Our readers are the woodworking hobbyist and small woodshop owner. Writers should have a knowledge of woodworking, or be able to communicate information gained from woodworkers." Estab. 1981. Circ. 284,000. **Pays on acceptance**. Publishes ms an average of 10 months after acceptance. Byline given. Buys first North American serial rights. Submit seasonal material 6 months in advance. Reports in 2 months. Sample copy and writer's guidelines for $4.50 and 9×12 SAE with 6 first-class stamps.

Nonfiction: How-to (on woodworking projects, with plans); humor (woodworking anecdotes); technical (woodworking techniques). Special issues: Shop issue, Outdoor Projects issue, Tool issue, Holiday Projects issue. **Buys 10 mss/year.** Query with or without published clips or send complete ms. **Pays up to $125/published page.** "The project must be

well designed, well constructed, well built and well finished. Technique pieces must have practical application."
Reprints: Send photocopy of article or typed ms with rights for sale noted and information about when and where the article previously appeared. Pays 25% of amount paid for an original article.
Photos: Send photos with submission. Reviews color only, slides and transparencies, 3×5 glossies acceptable. Offers no additional payment for photos accepted with ms. Photographic quality may affect acceptance. Need sharp close-up color photos of step-by-step construction process. Captions and identification of subjects required.
Columns/Departments: Tricks of the Trade (helpful techniques), Out of the Woodwook (thoughts on woodworking as a profession or hobby, can be humorous or serious), 500-1,500 words. **Buys 6 mss/year.** Query.
Fillers: Anecdotes, facts, short humor, shop tips. **Buys 15/year.** Length: 50-500 words.
Tips: "Submissions should include materials list, complete diagrams (blueprints not necessary), and discussion of the step-by-step process. We have become more selective on accepting only practical, attractive projects with quality construction. We are also looking for more original topics for our other articles."

N ★ $ POSTCARD COLLECTOR, Antique Trader Publications, P.O. Box 1050, Dubuque IA 52004. (319)588-2073. Fax: (319)588-0888. E-mail: atpzines@aol.com. **Contact**: Juli Kernall, editor. **98% freelance written.** Monthly magazine covering postcards, paper/ephemera. Estab. 1983. Circ. 4,700. Pays on publication. Byline given. Offers 20% kill fee. Buys first rights. Editorial lead time 2 months. Submit seasonal material 2 months in advance. Sample copy and writer's guidelines free.
Nonfiction: Historical/nostalgic, interview/profile, new product, opinion, photo feature, technical. **Buys 125 mss/year.** Query. No phone calls. Length: 550-2,000 words. **Pays $50-125.**
Reprints: Accepts previously published submissions.
Photos: Send photos. Reviews prints. Captions and identification of subjects required. Buys one-time rights.
Fillers: Facts, gags to be illustrated by cartoonist, newsbreaks. **Buys 3-5/year.** Length: 10-200 words. **Pays $10-50.**

$ $ QST, American Radio Relay League, Inc., 225 Main St., Newington CT 06111-1494. (869)594-0200. Fax: (860)594-0259. E-mail: qst@arrl.org. Website: http://www.arrl.org. Editor: Mark Wilson. **Contact:** Steve Ford, managing editor. **40% freelance written.** Monthly magazine covering amateur radio interests and technology. "Ours are topics of interest to radio amateurs and persons in the electronics and communications fields." Estab. 1914. Circ. 175,000. Pays on publication. Publishes ms an average of 4 months after acceptance. Byline given. Usually buys all rights. Submit seasonal material 5 months in advance. Reports in 3 weeks on queries. Sample copy and writer's guidelines for 10×13 SAE with 5 first-class stamps.
Nonfiction: General interest, how-to, humor, new products, personal experience, photo feature, technical (anything to do with amateur radio). **Buys 50 mss/year.** Query with or without published clips, or send complete ms. Length: open. **Pays $65/published page.** Sometimes pays expenses of writers on assignment.
Photos: Send photos with submission. Sometimes offers additional payment for photos accepted with ms or for cover. Captions, model releases and identification of subjects required. Usually buys all rights.
Columns/Departments: Hints and Kinks (hints/time saving procedures/circuits/associated with amateur radio), 50-200 words. **Buys 100 mss/year.** Send complete ms. **Pays $20.**
Tips: "Write with an idea, ask for sample copy and writer's guide. Technical and general interest to amateur operators, communications and electronics are most open."

$ QUILT WORLD, House of White Birches, 306 E. Parr Rd., Berne IN 46711. (219)589-8741. Fax: (207)794-3290. E-mail: hatch@agate.net. **Contact:** Sandra L. Hatch, editor. **100% freelance written.** Works with a small number of new/unpublished writers each year. Bimonthly magazine covering quilting. "We publish articles on quilting techniques, profiles of quilters and coverage of quilt shows. Reader is 30-70 years old, midwestern." Circ. 130,000. Pays 45 days after acceptance. Byline given. Buys all, first and one-time rights. Submit seasonal material 10 months in advance. Reports in 2-3 months. Writer's guidelines for #10 SASE.
Nonfiction: How-to, interview/profile (quilters), technical, new product (quilt products), photo feature. **Buys 18-24 mss/year.** Query or send complete ms. Length: open. **Pays $50-100.**
Reprints: Send photocopy of article and information about when and where it previously appeared.
Photos: Send photos with submission. Reviews transparencies and prints. Offers $15/photo (except covers). Identification of subjects required. Buys all or one-time rights.
Tips: "Read several recent issues for style and content."

★ $ $ QUILTING TODAY MAGAZINE, Chitra Publications, 2 Public Ave., Montrose PA 18801. (717)278-1984. Fax: (717)278-2223. E-mail: chitra@epix.net. Website: http://www.quilttownusa.com. **Contact:** Editorial Team. **80% freelance written.** Bimonthly magazine on quilting, traditional and contemporary. "We seek articles that will cover one or two full pages (800 words each); informative to the general quilting public, present new ideas, interviews, instructional, etc." Estab. 1986. Circ. 70,000. Pays on publication. Publishes ms an average of 6 months after acceptance. Byline given. Buys second serial (reprint) rights. Submit seasonal material 8 months in advance. Reports in 1 month on queries; 2 months on mss. Writer's guidelines for SASE.

- *Quilting Today Magazine* has a department appearing occasionally—"History Lessons," featuring a particular historical style or period in quiltmaking history.

Nonfiction: Book excerpts, essays, how-to (for various quilting techniques), humor, interview/profile, new product,

opinion, personal experience, photo feature. "No articles about family history related to a quilt or quilts unless the quilt is a masterpiece of color and design, impeccable workmanship." **Buys 20-30 mss/year.** Query with or without published clips, or send complete ms. Length: 800-1,600 words. **Pays $75/full page of published text.**
Reprints: Occasionally accepts previously published submissions. Send photocopy of article or typed ms with rights for sale noted and information about when and where the article previously appeared. Pays $75/published page.
Photos: Send photos with submission. Reviews 35mm slides and larger transparencies. Offers $20/photo. Captions, identification of subjects required. Buys all rights unless rented from a museum.
Columns/Departments: Quilters Lesson Book (instructional), 800-1,600 words. **Buys 10-12 mss/year.** Send complete ms. **Pays up to $75/column.**
Tips: "Query with ideas; send samples of prior work so that we can assess and suggest assignment. Our publications appeal to traditional quilters (generally middle-aged) who use the patterns in each issue. Must have excellent photos."

N $ $ $ RAILMODEL JOURNAL, Golden Bell Press, 2403 Champa St., Denver CO 80205. **Contact**: Robert Schleicher, editor. 80% freelance written. "Monthly magazine for advanced model railroaders. **100% photo journalism.** We use step-by-step how-to articles with photos of realistic and authentic models." Estab. 1989. Circ. 16,000. Pays on publication. Byline given. Offers 100% kill fee. Buys first and second serial (reprint) rights. Editorial lead time 6 months. Submit seasonal material 6 months in advance. Reports in 4 months on queries; 8 months on mss. Sample copy for $3.50. Writer's guidelines free.
Nonfiction: Historical/nostalgic, how-to, photo feature, technical. "No beginner articles or anything that could even be mistaken for a toy train." **Buys 70-100 mss/year.** Query. Length: 200-5,000 words. **Pays $60-800.** Sometimes pays expenses of writers on assignment.
Photos: Send photos with submission. Reviews contact sheets, 35mm transparencies and 5×7 prints. Captions, model releases and identification of subjects required. Buys one-time and reprint rights.
Tips: "Writers must understand dedicated model railroaders who recreate 100% of their model cars, locomotives, buildings and scenes from specific real-life prototypes. Close-up photos a must."

N $ RENAISSANCE MAGAZINE, Phantom Press, 13 Appleton Rd., Nantucket MA 02554. Fax: (508)325-5992. E-mail: renzine@compuserve.com. **Contact**: Kim Guarnaccia, managing editor. **90% freelance written.** Quarterly magazine covering the history of the Middle Ages and the Renaissance. "Our readers include historians, reenactors, roleplayers, medievalists and Renaissance Faire enthusiasts." Estab. 1996. Circ. 14,000. Pays on publication. Publishes ms an average of 1 year after acceptance. Byline given. Buys North American serial rights. Editorial lead time 6 months. Submit seasonal material 4 months in advance. Reports in 3 weeks on queries; 2 months on mss. Sample copy for $6. Writer's guidelines for #10 SASE.
Nonfiction: Essays, exposé, historical/nostalgic, how-to, interview/profile, new product, opinion, photo feature, religious, travel. No fiction. **Buys 25 mss/year.** Query or send ms with SASE. Length: 1,000-5,000 words. **Pays 4¢/word.** Pays writers with 2 contributor copies or other premiums upon request.
Reprints: Accepts previously published submissions.
Photos: State availability of photos with submission. Reviews contact sheets, any size negatives, transparencies and prints. Offers no additional payment for photos accepted with ms or negotiates payment individually. Captions, model releases and identification of subjects required. Buys all rights.
Columns/Departments: Book reviews, 500 words. Include original or good copy of book cover. **Pays 4¢/word.**
Tips: "Send in all articles in the standard manuscript format with photos/slides or illustrations for suggested use. Writers *must* be open to critique and all historical articles should also include a recommended reading list. An SASE must be included to receive a response to any submission."

$ $ RUG HOOKING MAGAZINE, Stackpole Magazines, 500 Vaughn St., Harrisburg PA 17110-2220. Fax: (717)234-1359. E-mail: rughook@paonline.com. Website: http://www.rughookingonline.com. Editor: Patrice Crowley. **Contact:** Brenda Wilt, editorial assistant. **75% freelance written.** Magazine published 5 times/year covering the craft of rug hooking. "This is the only magazine in the world devoted exclusively to rug hooking. Our readers are both novices and experts. They seek how-to pieces, features on fellow artisans and stories on beautiful rugs new and old." Estab. 1989. Circ. 10,000. **Pays on acceptance**. Publishes ms an average of 1 year after acceptance. Byline given. Buys all rights. Editorial lead time 6 months. Submit seasonal material 6 months in advance. Reports in 2 months. Sample copy for $5.
Nonfiction: How-to (hook a rug or a specific aspect of hooking), personal experience. **Buys 30 mss/year.** Query with published clips. Length: 825-2,475 words. **Pays $74.25-222.75.** Sometimes pays expenses of writers on assignment.
Reprints: Send photocopy of article and information about when and where the article previously appeared.
Photos: Send photos with submission. Reviews 2×2 transparencies, 3×5 prints. Negotiates payment individually. Identification of subjects required. Buys all rights.

$ $ SCALE AUTO ENTHUSIAST, Kalmbach Publishing Co., 21027 Crossroads Circle, P.O. Box 1612, Waukesha WI 53187-1612. (414)796-8776. Fax: (414)796-1383. E-mail: editor@scaleautomag.com. Website: http://www.kalmbach.com/scaleauto/scaleauto.html. **Contact:** Kirk Bell, senior editor. Managing editor: Mark Thompson. **70% freelance written.** Bimonthly magazine covering model car building. "We are looking for model builders, collectors and enthusiasts who feel their models and/or modeling techniques and experiences would be of interest and benefit to our readership." Estab. 1979. Circ. 75,000. Pays on publication. Publishes ms an average of 6 months after acceptance.

Byline given. Buys all rights. Editorial lead time 4 months. Submit seasonal material 3 months in advance. Reports in 1 month on queries; 3 months on mss. Sample copy and writer's guidelines free.

Nonfiction: Book excerpts, historical/nostalgic, how-to (build models, do different techniques), interview/profile, personal experience, photo feature, technical. Query or send complete ms. Length: 750-3,000 words. **Pays $75-100/published page.**

Photos: Send photos and negatives with submission. Prefers b&w glossy prints and 35mm color transparencies. When writing how-to articles be sure to take photos *during* project. Negotiates payment individually. Captions, model releases, identification of subjects required. Buys all rights.

Columns/Departments: Buys 50 mss/year. Query. **Pays $75-100/published page.**

Fillers: Gags to be illustrated by cartoonist. **Buys 5/year.** Pays percentage of **$75/published page rate.**

Tips: "First and foremost, our readers like how-to material: how-to paint, how-to scratchbuild, how-to chop a roof, etc. Basically, our readers want to know how to make their own models better. Therefore, any help or advice you can offer is what modelers want to read. Also, the more photos you send, taken from a variety of views, the better choice we have in putting together an outstanding article layout. Send us more photos than you would ever possibly imagine we could use. This permits us to pick and choose the best of the bunch."

$ $ SEW NEWS, The Fashion Magazine for People Who Sew, Primedia Special Interest Publications, News Plaza, P.O. Box 1790, Peoria IL 61656. (309)682-6626. Fax: (309)682-5454. E-mail: sewnews@aol.com. Website: http://www.sewnews.com. **Contact:** Linda Turner Griepentrog, editor. **90% freelance written.** Works with a small number of new/unpublished writers each year. 12 issues/year covering fashion-sewing. "Our magazine is for the beginning home sewer to the professional dressmaker. It expresses the fun, creativity and excitement of sewing." Estab. 1980. Circ. 261,000. **Pays on acceptance.** Publishes ms an average of 6 months after acceptance. Byline given. Buys all rights. Submit seasonal material 6 months in advance. Reports in 2 months. Sample copy for $4.95. Writer's guidelines for #10 SAE with 2 first-class stamps.

- All stories submitted to *Sew News* must be on disk.

Nonfiction: How-to (sewing techniques), interview/profile (interesting personalities in home-sewing field). **Buys 200-240 ms/year.** Query with published clips if available. Length: 500-2,000 words. **Pays $25-500.**

Photos: Send photos. Prefers color photographs or slides. Payment included in ms price. Identification of subjects required. Buys all rights.

Tips: "Query first with writing sample and outline of proposed story. Areas most open to freelancers are how-to and sewing techniques; give explicit, step-by-step instructions plus rough art. We're using more home decorating editorial content."

N $ SHUTTLE SPINDLE & DYEPOT, Handweavers Guild of America, Inc., 3327 Duluth Highway, Two Executive Concourse, Suite 201, Duluth GA 30096. (770)495-7702. Fax: (770)495-7703. E-mail: 73744.202@compuserve.com. Website: http://www.weavespindye.org. **Contact**: Sandra Bowles, editor-in-chief. Publications Manager: Pat King. Editorial Assistant: Emily Herman. **60% freelance written.** "Quarterly membership publication of the Handweavers Guild of America, Inc., *Shuttle Spindle & Dyepot* magazine seeks to encourage excellence in contemporary fiber arts and to support the preservation of techniques and traditions in fiber arts. It also provides inspiration for fiber artists of all levels and develops public awareness and appreciation of the fiber arts. *Shuttle Spindle & Dyepot* appeals to a highly educated, creative and very knowledgeable audience of fiber artists and craftsmen—weavers, spinners, dyers and basket makers." Estab. 1969. Circ. 30,000. Pays on publication. Publishes ms 6 months after acceptance. Byline given. Buys first North American serial, reprint and electronic rights. Editorial lead time 8 months. Submit seasonal material 8 months in advance. Sample copy for $7.50 plus shipping. Writer's guidelines free on website.

Nonfiction: Inspirational, interview/profile, new product, personal experience, photo feature, technical, travel. "No self-promotional and no articles from those without knowledge of area/art/artists." **Buys 40 mss/year.** Query with published clips. Length: 1,000-2,000 words. **Pays $75-150.**

Photos: State availability of photos with query. Offers no additional payment for photos accepted with ms. Captions, model releases and identification of subjects required.

Columns/Departments: Books and Videos, News and Information, Calendar and Conference, Travel and Workshop, Guildview (all fiber/art related). **Buys 8 mss/year.** Query with published clips. **Pays $50-75.**

Tips: "Become knowledgeable about the fiber arts and artists. Query by telephone (once familiar with publication) by appointment helps editor and writer.

$ SPORTS COLLECTORS DIGEST, Krause Publications, 700 E. State St., Iola WI 54990. (715)445-2214. Fax: (715)445-4087. E-mail: kpsports@aol.com. **Contact:** Tom Mortenson, editor. Estab. 1952. **50% freelance written.** Works with a small number of new/unpublished writers each year. Weekly sports memorabilia magazine. "We serve collectors of sports memorabilia—baseball cards, yearbooks, programs, autographs, jerseys, bats, balls, books, magazines, ticket stubs, etc." Circ. 52,000. Pays after publication. Publishes ms an average of 3 months after acceptance. Byline given. Buys first North American serial rights only. Submit seasonal material 3 months in advance. Reports in 5 weeks on queries; 2 months on mss. Free sample copy. Writer's guidelines for #10 SASE.

Nonfiction: General interest (new card issues, research on older sets); historical/nostalgic (old stadiums, old collectibles, etc.); how-to (buy cards, sell cards and other collectibles, display collectibles, ways to get autographs, jerseys and other memorabilia); interview/profile (well-known collectors, ball players—but must focus on collectibles); new product (new card sets); personal experience ("what I collect and why"-type stories). No sports stories. "We are not competing with

The Sporting News, *Sports Illustrated* or your daily paper. Sports collectibles only." **Buys 100-200 mss/year.** Query. Length: 300-3,000 words; prefers 1,000 words. **Pays $50-125.**

Reprints: Send tearsheet of article. Pays 100% of amount paid for an original article.

Photos: Unusual collectibles. Send photos. Pays $5-15 for b&w prints. Identification of subjects required. Buys all rights.

Columns/Departments: "We have all the columnists we need but welcome ideas for new columns." **Buys 100-150 mss/year.** Query. Length: 600-3,000 words. **Pays $90-125.**

Tips: "If you are a collector, you know what collectors are interested in. Write about it. No shallow, puff pieces; our readers are too smart for that. Only well-researched articles about sports memorabilia and collecting. Some sports nostalgia pieces are OK. Write only about the areas you know about."

$ SUNSHINE ARTIST, America's Premier Show & Festival Publication, Palm House Publishing Inc., 2600 Temple Dr., Winter Park FL 32789. (407)539-1399. Fax: (407)539-1499. E-mail: sunart@magicnet.net. Website: http://www.sunshineartist.com. Publisher: Christi Ashby. **Contact:** Amy Detwiler, editor. Monthly magazine covering art shows in the United States. "We are the premier-marketing/reference magazine for artists and crafts professionals who earn their living through art shows nationwide. We list more than 2,000 shows monthly, critique many of them and publish articles on marketing, selling and other issues of concern to professional show circuit artists." Estab. 1972. Circ. 12,000. Pays on publication. Publishes ms an average of 3 months after acceptance. Byline given. Buys first North American serial rights. Reports within 2 months. Sample copy for $5.

Nonfiction: "We publish articles of interest to artists and crafts professionals who travel the art show circuit. Current topics include marketing, computers and RV living." No how-to. **Buys 5-10 freelance mss/year.** Query or ms. Length: 1,000-2,000 words. **Pays $50-150 for accepted articles.**

Reprints: Send photocopy of article and information about when and where the article previously appeared.

Photos: Send photos with submission. Offers no additional payment for photos accepted with ms. Captions, model releases and identification of subjects required.

☆ $ $ TEDDY BEAR REVIEW, Collector Communications Corp., 170 Fifth Ave., New York NY 10010. (212)989-8700. **Contact:** Stephen L. Cronk, editor. **75% freelance written.** Works with a small number of new/unpublished writers each year. Bimonthly magazine on teddy bears for collectors, enthusiasts and bearmakers. Estab. 1985. Pays 30 days after acceptance. Byline given. Buys first North American serial rights. Submit seasonal material 6 months in advance. Sample copy and writer's guidelines for $2 and 9×12 SAE.

Nonfiction: Book excerpts, historical, how-to, interview/profile. No nostalgia on childhood teddy bears. **Buys 30-40 mss/year.** Query with photos and published clips. Length: 900-1,800 words. **Pays $100-350.** Sometimes pays the expenses of writers on assignment "if approved ahead of time."

Photos: Send photos with submission. Reviews transparencies and b&w prints. Offers no additional payment for photos accepted with ms. Captions required. Buys one-time rights.

Tips: "We are interested in good, professional writers around the country with a strong knowledge of teddy bears. Historical profile of bear companies, profiles of contemporary artists and knowledgeable reports on museum collections are of interest."

N $ $ THREADS, Taunton Press, 63 S. Main St., P.O. Box 5506, Newtown CT 06470. (203)426-8171. **Contact:** Chris Timmons, editor. Bimonthly magazine covering sewing, garment construction, and related fabric crafts (quilting and embroidery). "We're seeking proposals from hands-on authors who first and foremost have a skill. Being an experienced writer is of secondary consideration." Estab. 1985. Circ. 176,000. Pays $150/page. Byline given. Offers $150 kill fee. Buys one-time rights or reprint rights in article collections. Editorial lead time 4 months minimum. Query for electronic submissions. Reports in 1-2 months. Writer's guidelines free.

Nonfiction: "We prefer first-person experience."

Columns/Departments: Notes (current events, new products, opinions); Book reviews; Tips; Yarns (stories of a humorous nature). Query. **Pays $150/page.**

Tips: "Send us a proposal (outline) with photos of your own work (garments, samplers, etc.)."

$ $ TODAY'S COLLECTOR, The Nation's Antiques and Collectibles Marketplace, Krause Publications, 700 E. State St., Iola WI 54990. (715)445-2214. Fax: (715)445-4087. E-mail: ellingboes@krause.com. Website: http://www.krause.com. **Contact:** Steve Ellingboe, editor. **50% freelance written.** Monthly magazine covering antiques and collectibles. "*Today's Collector* is for serious collectors of all types of antiques and collectibles." Estab. 1993. Circ. 85,000. Pays on publication. Publishes ms an average of 6 months after acceptance. Byline given. Offers $25-50 kill fee. Buys perpetual but non-exclusive rights. Editorial lead time 2 months. Submit seasonal material 4 months in advance. Accepts simultaneous submissions. Reports in 1 month on mss. Sample copy free.

Nonfiction: How-to (antiques and collectibles). No articles that are too general—specific collecting areas only. **Buys 60-75 mss/year.** Send complete ms. Length: 500-3,000 words. **Pays $50-200.**

Reprints: Send typed ms with rights for sale noted and information about when and where the article previously appeared. Pays 50% of amount paid for an original article.

Photos: Send photos with submission. Reviews transparencies, prints. Offers no additional payment for photos accepted with ms. Captions required. Buys one-time rights.

Tips: "I want detailed articles about specific collecting areas—nothing too broad or general. I need lots of information about pricing and values, along with brief history and background."

$ $ $ TODAY'S WOODWORKER, Rockler Companies, Inc., 4365 Willow Dr., Medina MN 55340. (612)478-8255. Fax: (612)478-8396. E-mail: editor@todayswoodworker.com. **Contact:** Rob Johnstone, editor. **50% freelance written.** Bimonthly magazine on woodworking. "Projects, tips and techniques for the beginner and the serious woodworking hobbyist." Estab. 1989. Circ. 130,000. **Pays on acceptance.** Publishes ms 1 year after acceptance. Byline given. Buys first North American serial rights. Editorial lead time 1 year. Submit seasonal material 1 year in advance.
Nonfiction: How-to (woodworking). **Buys 12 mss/year.** Query. Length: 200-2,000 words. **Pays $40-1,500.**
Photos: State availability of photos with submission. Reviews transparencies. Negotiates payment individually. Identification of subjects required. Buys one-time rights.
Columns/Departments: Techniques; Today's Shop (operating specific tools); Finishing Thoughts (applying specific finishes) 500 words. **Buys 6 mss/year.** Query. **Pays $100-500.**

$ TOY FARMER, Toy Farmer Publications, 7496-106 A Ave. SE, LaMoune ND 58458. (701)883-5206. Fax: (701)883-5209. Editor: Claire D. Scheibe. Contact: Cathy Scheibe, assistant editor. **65% freelance written.** Monthly magazine covering farm toys. Must slant toward youth involvement. Estab. 1978. Circ. 27,000. Pays on publication. Publishes ms an average of 1 month after acceptance. Byline given. Buys first North American serial rights. Editorial lead time 3 months. Submit seasonal material 3 months in advance. Accepts previously published submissions. Reports in 1 month on queries; 2 months on mss. Sample copy for $4. Writer's guidelines free.
Nonfiction: General interest, historical/nostalgic, humor, new product, technical. **Buys 100 mss/year.** Query with published clips. 800-1,500 words. **Pays $50-150.** Sometimes pays expenses of writers on assignment.
Photos: State availability of photos with submission. Reviews transparencies. Offers no additional payment for photos accepted with ms. Buys one-time rights.
Columns/Departments: Buys 36 mss/year. Query with published clips. **Pays $50-150.**

☆ $ $ TOY SHOP, Krause Publications, 700 E. State St., Iola WI 54990. (715)445-2214. Fax: (715)445-4087. E-mail: korbecks@kraus.com. Website: http://www.krause.com. **Contact:** Sharon Korbeck, editor. **95% freelance written.** Biweekly tabloid covering toy collecting. "We cover primarily vintage collectible toys from the 1930s-present. Stories focus on historical toy companies, the collectibility of toys and features on prominent collections." Estab. 1986. Circ. 70,000. Pays on publication. Publishes ms an average of 4-8 months after acceptance. Byline given. Buys "perpetual, nonexclusive rights." Editorial lead time 6 months. Accepts simultaneous submissions. Reports in 1 month. Sample copy for $1. Writer's guidelines free.
Nonfiction: Essays, general interest, historical/nostalgic (toys, toy companies), interview/profile (toy collectors), new product (toys), personal experience, photo feature (toys), features on old toys. No opinion, broad topics or poorly researched pieces. **Buys 100 mss/year.** Query. Length: 1,000-3,000 words. **Pays $50-200.** Contributor's copies included with payment. Sometimes pays expenses of writers on assignment.
Reprints: Send photocopy of article and information about when and where the article previously appeared.
Photos: State availability of or send photos with submission. Reviews negatives, transparencies, 3×5 prints. Negotiates payment individually. Captions, model releases, identification of subjects required. Rights purchased with ms rights.
Columns/Departments: Collector Profile (profile of toy collectors), 1,000 words; Toy I Loved (essay on favorite toys), 250-500 words. **Buys 25 mss/year.** Query. **Pays $50-150.**
Tips: "Articles must be specific. Include historical info, quotes, photos with story. Talk with toy dealers and get to know how big the market is."

N $ $ TOY TRUCKER & CONTRACTOR, Toy Farmer Limited, 7496 106th Ave. SE, LaMoure ND 58458-9404. (701)883-5206. Fax: (701)883-5209. E-mail: zekesez@aol.com. Website: http://www.toyfarmer.com. **Contact:** Colleen Keller, editorial assistant. Editor: Claire Scheibe. Managing Editor: Cathy Scheibe. **75% freelance written.** Monthly consumer magazine covering collectible toys. "We are a magazine on hobby and collectible toy trucks and construction pieces." Estab. 1990. Circ. 6,500. Pays on publication. Publishes ms an average of 3 months after acceptance. Byline given. Buys first North American serial rights. Editorial lead time 3 months. Submit seasonal material 3 months in advance. Reports in 1 month on queries; 2 months on mss. Sample copy for $4. Writer's guidelines free on request.
Nonfiction: Historical/nostalgic, interview/profile, new product, technical. **Buys 35 mss/year**. Query. Length: 800-2,400. **Pays 10¢/word. Sometimes pays expenses of writers on assignment.**
Reprints: Accepts previously published submissions.
Photos: Send photos with submission. Offers no additional payment for photos accepted with ms. Captions, model releases and identification of subjects required.

N ☆ $ $ TOYFARE, The Toy Magazine, Wizard Entertainment Group, 151 Wells Ave., Congers NY 10920. (914)268-2000. Fax: (914)268-0053. E-mail: toyfare@aol.com. **Contact:** Scott Beatty, editor. Managing Editor: Joe Yanarella. **70% freelance written.** Monthly magazine covering action figures and collectible toys. Estab. 1997. Pays on publication. Byline given. Offers 50% kill fee. Buys all rights. Editorial lead time 4 months. Submit seasonal material 4 months in advance. Sample copy and writer's guidelines free.
Nonfiction: Historical/nostalgic, how-to, humor, interview/profile, new product, personal experience, photo feature,

technical. No column or opinion pieces. **Buys 75-100 mss/year.** Query with published clips. Length: 250-4,000 words. **Pays 15¢/word.**

Photos: State availability of photos with submission. Negotiates payment individually. Identification of subjects required. Buys all rights.

Columns/Departments: Toy Story (profile of past toy line), Sneak Peek (profile of new action figure), both 750-900 words. Query with published clips. **Pays $75-100.**

$ $ TRADITIONAL QUILTER, The Leading Teaching Magazine for Creative Quilters, All American Crafts, Inc., 243 Newton-Sparta Rd., Newton NJ 07860. (973)383-8080. Fax: (973)383-8133. E-mail: craftpub@aol.com. **Contact:** Phyllis Barbieri, editor. **45% freelance written.** Bimonthly magazine on quilting. Estab. 1988. Pays on publication. Byline given. Buys first or all rights. Submit seasonal material 6 months in advance. Reports in 2 months. Sample copy for 9×12 SAE with 4 first-class stamps. Writer's guidelines for #10 SASE.

Nonfiction: Quilts and quilt patterns with instructions, quilt-related projects, guild news, interview/profile, photo feature—all quilt related. Query with published clips. Length: 350-1,000 words. **Pays 10¢/word.**

Photos: Send photos with submission. Reviews all size transparencies and prints. Offers $10-15/photo. Captions and identification of subjects required. Buys one-time or all rights.

Columns/Departments: Feature Teacher (qualified quilt teachers with teaching involved—with slides); Profile (award-winning and interesting quilters); The Guilded Newsletter (reports on quilting guild activities, shows, workshops, and retreats). Length: 1,000 words maximum. **Pays 10¢/word, $15/photo.**

$ $ $ TRADITIONAL QUILTWORKS, The Pattern Magazine for Traditional Quilters, Chitra Publications, 2 Public Ave., Montrose PA 18801. (717)278-1984. Fax: (717)278-2223. E-mail: chitra@epix.net. Website: http://www.quilttownusa.com. **Contact:** Editorial Team. **50% freelance written.** Bimonthly magazine on quilting. "We seek articles of an instructional nature, profiles of talented teachers, articles on the history of specific areas of quiltmaking (patterns, fiber, regional, etc.)." Estab. 1988. Circ. 70,000. Pays on publication. Publishes ms an average of 6 months after acceptance. Byline given. Buys second serial (reprint) rights. Submit seasonal material 8 months in advance. Reports in 2 months. Writer's guidelines for SASE.

Nonfiction: Historical, instructional, quilting education. "No light-hearted entertainment." **Buys 12-18 mss/year.** Query with photos, with or without published clips, or send complete ms. "Publication hinges on photo quality." Length: 1,500 words maximum. **Pays $75/published page of text.**

Reprints: Send photcopy of article and information about when and where the article previously appeared. Payment varies depending on amount of material used.

Photos: Send photos with submission. Reviews 35mm slides and larger transparencies (color). Offers $20/photo. Captions, model releases and identification of subjects required. Buys all rights.

Tips: "Our publications appeal to traditional quilters, generally middle-aged and mostly who use the patterns in the magazine. Publication hinges on good photo quality."

$ $ VIDEOMAKER, Camcorders, Computers, Tools & Techniques for Creating Video, York Publishing, P.O. Box 4591, Chico CA 95927. (530)891-8410. Fax: (530)891-8443. E-mail: editor@videomaker.com. Website: http://www.videomaker.com. Editor: Matt York. **Contact:** Chuck Peters, managing editor. **75% freelance written.** Monthly magazine on video production. "Our audience encompasses video camera users ranging from broadcast and cable TV producers to special-event videographers to video hobbyists . . . labeled professional, industrial, 'prosumer' and consumer. Editorial emphasis is on video*making* (production and exposure), *not* reviews of commercial videos. Personal video phenomenon is a young 'movement'; readership is encouraged to participate—get in on the act, join the fun." Estab. 1986. Circ. 90,000. Pays on publication. Publishes ms an average of 6 months after acceptance. Byline given. Buys all rights. Submit seasonal material 6 months in advance. Accepts simultaneous submissions. Reports in 3 months. Sample copy for 9×12 SAE with 9 first-class stamps. Writer's guidelines free.

Nonfiction: How-to (tools, tips, techniques for better videomaking); interview/profile (notable videomakers); product probe (review of latest and greatest or innovative); personal experience (lessons to benefit other videomakers); technical (state-of-the-art audio/video). Articles with comprehensive coverage of product line or aspect of videomaking preferred. **Buys 70 mss/year.** Query with or without published clips, or send complete ms. Length: open. **Pays 10¢/word.**

Reprints: Send tearsheet and information about when and where the article previously appeared. Payment negotiable.

Photos: Send photos and/or other artwork with submissions. Reviews contact sheets, transparencies and prints. Captions required. Payment for photos accepted with ms included as package compensation. Buys one-time rights.

Columns/Departments: Sound Track (audio information); Getting Started (beginner's column); Quick Focus (brief reviews of current works pertaining to video production); Profitmaker (money-making opportunities); Edit Points (tools and techniques for successful video editions). **Buys 40 mss/year. Pays 10¢/word.**

Tips: "Comprehensiveness a must. Article on shooting tips covers *all* angles. Buyer's guide to special-effect generators cites *all* models available. Magazine strives for an 'all-or-none' approach. Most topics covered once (twice tops) per year, so we must be thorough. Manuscript/photo package submissions helpful. *Videomaker* wants videomaking to be fulfilling and fun."

$ $ VOGUE KNITTING, Butterick Company, 161 Sixth Ave., New York NY 10013-1205. Fax: (212)620-2731. Editor: Trisha Malcolm. Managing Editor: Daryl Brower. Quarterly magazine that covers knitting. "High fashion magazine with projects for knitters of all levels. In-depth features on techniques, knitting around the world, interviews, bios and other articles of interest to well-informed readers." Estab. 1982. Circ. 200,000. **Pays on acceptance**. Publishes ms an average of 4 months after acceptance. Buys all rights. Editorial lead time 6 months. Submit seasonal material 6 months in advance. Accepts simultaneous submissions. Writer's guidelines free.

Nonfiction: Essays, general interest, historical/nostalgic, how-to, interview/profile, personal experience, photo feature, technical, travel. **Buys 25 mss/year.** Query. Length: 600-1,200 words. **Pays $250 minimum.**

Photos: Send photos with submission. Reviews 3×5 transparencies. Negotiates payment individually. Captions, model releases and identification of subjects required. Buys all rights.

N $ $ WEEKEND WOODCRAFTS, EGW Publishing Inc., 1041 Shary Circle, Concord CA 94518. (925)671-9852. Fax: (925)671-0692. E-mail: rjoseph@egw.com. Website: http://www.weekendwoodcrafts.com. **Contact:** Robert Joseph, editor. Bimonthly consumer magazine covering woodworking/crafts. "Projects that can be completed in one weekend." Estab. 1992. Circ. 91,000. **Pays half on acceptance and half on publication**. Publishes ms an average of 3 months after acceptance. Byline given. Buys first rights. Editorial lead time 2 months. Submit seasonal material 2 months in advance. Accepts simultaneous submissions. Reports in 2 months. Sample copy and writer's guidelines free.

Nonfiction: How-to (tips and tech), woodworking projects. **Buys 10 mss/year**. Send complete ms. Length: 400-1,500 words. **Pays $100-500.**

Photos: Send photos with submission. Reviews contact sheets and print (4×6). Offers no additional payment for photos accepted with ms. Buys all rights.

Tips: "Build simply and easy weekend projects, build one to two hour projects."

$ $ WOODSHOP NEWS, Soundings Publications Inc., 35 Pratt St., Essex CT 06426-1185. (860)767-8227. Fax: (860)767-1048. E-mail: woodshop@ix.netcom.net. Website: http://www.woodshopnews.com. Editor: Ian C. Bowen. **Contact:** Thomas Clark, senior editor. **20% freelance written.** Monthly tabloid "covering woodworking for professionals and hobbyists. Solid business news and features about woodworking companies. Feature stories about interesting amateur woodworkers. Some how-to articles." Estab. 1986. Circ. 100,000. Pays on publication. Publishes ms an average of 3 months after acceptance. Byline given. Offers 25% kill fee. Buys first North American serial rights. Submit seasonal material 4 months in advance. Reports in 1 month. Sample copy and writer's guidelines free.

- *Woodshop News* needs writers in major cities in all regions except the Northeast. Also looking for more editorial opinion pieces.

Nonfiction: How-to (query first), interview/profile, new product, opinion, personal experience, photo feature. Key word is "newsworthy." No general interest profiles of "folksy" woodworkers. **Buys 50-75 mss/year.** Query with published clips or submit ms. Length: 100-1,200 words. **Pays $50-400 for assigned articles; $40-250 for unsolicited articles; $40-100 for workshop tips.** Pays expenses of writers on assignment.

Photos: Send photos with submission. Reviews contact sheets and prints. Offers $20-35/b&w photo; $250/4-color cover, usually with story. Captions and identification of subjects required. Buys one-time rights.

Columns/Departments: Pro Shop (business advice, marketing, employee relations, taxes etc. for the professional written by an established professional in the field); 1,200-1,500 words. **Buys 12 mss/year.** Query. **Pays $250-350.**

Fillers: Small filler items, briefs, or news tips that are followed up by staff reporters. **Pays $10.**

Tips: "The best way to start is a profile of a business or hobbyist woodworker in your area. Find a unique angle about the person or business and stress this as the theme of your article. Avoid a broad, general-interest theme that would be more appropriate to a daily newspaper. Our readers are woodworkers who want more depth and more specifics than would a general readership. If you are profiling a business, we need standard business information such as gross annual earnings/sales, customer base, product line and prices, marketing strategy, etc. Black and white 35 mm photos are a must. We need more freelance writers from the Mid-Atlantic, Midwest and West Coast."

$ $ WOODWORK, A Magazine For All Woodworkers, Ross Periodicals, P.O. Box 1529, Ross CA 94957-1529. (415)382-0580. Fax: (415)382-0587. E-mail: woodwrkmag@aol.com. **Contact:** John Lavine, editor. Publisher: Tom Toldrian. **90% freelance written.** Bimonthly magazine covering woodworking. "We are aiming at a broad audience of woodworkers, from the home enthusiast/hobbyist to professional. Articles run the range from the simple to the complex. We cover such subjects as carving, turning, veneering, tools old and new, design, innovations, projects and more. Personality and show coverage are kept to a minimum, with the emphasis being always on communicating woodworking methods, practices, theories and techniques. Suggestions for articles are always welcome." Estab. 1986. Circ. 80,000. Pays on publication. Byline given. Buys first North American serial and second serial (reprint) rights. Sample copy for $3 and 9×12 SAE with 6 first-class stamps. Writer's guidelines for #10 SASE.

Nonfiction: How-to (simple or complex, making attractive furniture), interview/profile (of established woodworkers that make attractive furniture), photo feature (of interest to woodworkers), technical (tools, techniques). "Do not send a how-to unless you are a woodworker." Query first. Length: 1,500-2,000 words. **Pays $150/published page.**

Photos: Send photos with submission. Reviews 35mm slides. Pays higher page rate for photos accepted with ms. Captions and identification of subjects required. Buys one-time rights. Photo guidelines available on request.

Columns/Departments: Tips and Techniques column **pays $35-75.** Interview/profiles of established woodworkers. Bring out woodworker's philosophy about the craft, opinions about what is happening currently. Good photos of attractive furniture a must. Section on how-to desirable. Query with published clips. **Pays $150/published page.**

Tips: "Our main requirement is that each article must directly concern woodworking. If you are not a woodworker, the interview/profile is your best, really only chance. Good writing is essential as are good photos. The interview must be entertaining, but informative and pertinent to woodworkers' interests. Include sidebar written by the profile subject."

HOME & GARDEN

The baby boomers' turn inward, or "cocooning," has caused an explosion of publications in this category. Gardening magazines in particular have blossomed, as more people are developing leisure interests at home. Some magazines here concentrate on gardens; others on the how-to of interior design. Still others focus on homes and gardens in specific regions of the country. Be sure to read the publication to determine its focus before submitting a manuscript or query.

N $ $ $ ADDITIONS & DECKS, Woman's Day Special Interest Publications, Hachette-Filipacchi Magazines, 1633 Broadway, New York NY 10019. Fax: (212)767-5612. E-mail: wdspecials@aol.com. **Contact:** Janice Wright, managing editor. Editor: Carolyn Gatto. Semiannual consumer magazine covering information and ideas for homeowners about adding space, indoors or out. "This magazine is for anyone who's thinking of or is engaged in the process of adding on to their home, indoors or out. It showcases design ideas and includes planning strategies for increasing living space. Legal and financial issues and tips on working with professionals are included." **Pays on acceptance**. Publishes ms an average of 3 months after acceptance. Byline given. Offers up to 25% kill fee. Buys first North American serial or second serial (printing) rights. Editorial lead time 6 months. Submit seasonal material 10 months in advance. Reports in 2 months. Sample copy not available; writer's guidelines for #10 SASE.

Nonfiction: How-to (do-it-yourself information, hire and work with professionals), new products, photo feature (homes with dramatic expansions or beautiful decks), technical (info about materials, procedures that a homeowner should know). **Buys 20 mss/year**. Query with published clips. Length: 250-1,000 words. Payment varies based on length, writer, importance. Sometimes pays expenses of writers on assignment.

Reprints: Accepts previously published submissions.

Photos: Send before & after photos with query. Model releases required. Buys one-time rights.

Columns/Departments: Weekend Projects (how-to instructions for 1 or 2 relevant projects that can be completed in a day or two), 400-800 words; Legal Issues (relevant legal issues: awareness and what to do), 400-800 words; Money Matters (relevant financial issues: awareness and what to do). **Buys 6 mss/year**. Query with published clips. Payment varies based on length, writer, and level/amount of research required.

Tips: "Send a brief, clear query letter with relevant clips, and be patient. Before and after photos are very helpful, as are floor plans. Photo(s) of weekend project ideas are also helpful."

$ THE ALMANAC FOR FARMERS & CITY FOLK, Greentree Publishing, Inc., 850 S. Rancho, #2319, Las Vegas NV 89106. (702)387-6777. Editor: Lucas McFadden. **Contact:** Thomas Alexander, managing editor. **40% freelance written.** Annual almanac of "down-home, folksy material pertaining to farming, gardening, animals, etc." Estab. 1983. Circ. 800,000. Pays on publication. Publishes ms 6 months after acceptance. Byline given. Buys first North American serial rights. Deadline: January 31. Sample copy for $3.95.

Nonfiction: Essays, general interest, how-to, humor. No fiction or controversial topics. "Please, no first-person pieces!" **Buys 30 mss/year.** Send complete ms. No queries please. Length: 350-1,400 words. **Pays $45/page.**

Poetry: Buys 1-4 poems/year. Pays $45 for full pages, otherwise proportionate share thereof.

Fillers: Anecdotes, facts, short humor, gardening hints. **Buys 60/year.** Length 125 words maximum. **Pays $10-45.**

Tips: "Typed submissions essential as we scan in manuscript. Short, succinct material is preferred. Material should appeal to a wide range of people and should be on the 'folksy' side, preferably with a thread of humor woven in."

$ $ THE AMERICAN GARDENER, Publication of the American Horticultural Society, 7931 E. Boulevard. Dr., Alexandria VA 22308-1300. (703)768-5700. Fax: (703)768-7533. E-mail: editorahs@aol.com. Website: http://www.ahs.org. **Contact**: David J. Ellis, editor. Managing Editor: Mary Yee. **90% freelance written.** Bimonthly magazine covering gardening and horticulture. "*The American Gardener* is the official publication of the American Horticultural Society (AHS), a national, nonprofit, membership organization for gardeners founded in 1922. AHS is dedicated to educating and inspiring people of all ages to become successful, environmentally responsible gardeners by advancing the art and science of horticulture. Readers of *The American Gardener* are sophisticated amateur gardeners; about 22% are professionals. Most prefer not to use chemicals." Estab. 1922. Circ. 25,000. Pays on publication. Publishes ms an average of 6 months after acceptance. Offers 25% kill fee. Byline given. Buys first North American serial rights; negotiates electronic rights separately. Editorial lead time 14 weeks. Submit seasonal material 1 year in advance. Reports in 3 months on queries if SASE included. Sample copy for $5. Writer's guidelines for #10 SASE.

Nonfiction: Book excerpts, essays, historical, how-to (landscaping, environmental gardening), inspirational, interview/profile, personal experience, technical (explain science of horticulture to lay audience), children and nature, plants and health, city gardening, humor. **Buys 30 mss/year.** Query with published clips. Length: 750-2,000 words. **Pays $100-400** depending on article's length, complexity, author's horticultural background, and publishing experience. Pays with contributor copies or other premiums when other horticultural organizations contribute articles.

Reprints: Send photocopy of article with information about when and where the article previously appeared. Pay varies.

Photos: State availability of photos with submission. Reviews transparencies, prints. Pays $50-200/photo. Identification of subjects required. Buys one-time rights. Sometimes pays expenses of writers on assignment.

Columns/Departments: Offshoots (humorous, sentimental or expresses an unusual viewpoint), 1,200 words; Conservationist's Notebook (articles about individuals or organizations attempting to save endangered species or protect natural areas), 750 words; Natural Connections (explains a natural phenonmenon—plant and pollinator relationships, plant and fungus relationships, parasites—that may be observed in nature or in the garden), 750 words; Urban Gardener (looks at a successful small space garden—indoor, patio, less than a quarter-acre; a program that successfully brings plants to city streets or public spaces; or a problem of particular concern to city dwellers), 750-1,500 words; Planting the Future (children and youth gardening programs), 750 words; Plants and Your Health (all aspects of gardening and health, from sunburn, poison ivy and strained backs to herbal medicines), 750 words; Regional Happenings (events that directly affect gardeners only in 1 area, but are of interest to others: an expansion of a botanical garden, a serious new garden pest, the launching of a regional flower show, a hot new gardening trend), 250-500 words. **Buys 20 mss/year.** Query with published clips. **Pays $100-150.**

Tips: "We run very few how-to articles. Our readers are advanced, sophisticated amateur gardeners; about 20 percent are horticultural professionals. Our articles are intended to bring this knowledgeable group new information, ranging from the latest scientific findings that affect plants, to the history of gardening and gardens in America."

$ $ $ $ AMERICAN HOMESTYLE & GARDENING MAGAZINE, Gruner & Jahr USA Publishing, 375 Lexington Ave., New York NY 10017. (212)499-2000. Fax: (212)499-1536. Editor-in-Chief: Douglas Turshen. **Contact:** Lea Rosch. Bimonthly magazine. "*American Homestyle & Gardening* is a guide to complete home design. It is edited for buyers of decorating, building and remodeling products. It focuses on an actionable approach to home design." Estab. 1986. Circ. 1,000,000. **Pays on acceptance.** Byline given. Offers 25% kill fee. Buys first North American serial rights. Reports in 1 month on queries. Sample copy and writer's guidelines for #10 SASE.

Nonfiction: Writers with expertise in design, decorating, building or gardening. "Because stories begin with visual elements, queries without scouting photos rarely lead to assignments." Length: 750-2,000 words. **Pays $750-2,500.** Pays expenses of writers on assignment.

Tips: "Writers must have knowledge of interior design, remodeling or gardening."

$ $ ATLANTA HOMES AND LIFESTYLES, 1100 Johnson Ferry Rd., Suite 595, Atlanta GA 30342. (404)252-6670. Fax: (404)252-6673. E-mail: atlhomes@aol.com. Website: http://www.atlantahandl.com. **Contact:** Barbara S. Tapp, editor. **65% freelance written.** Magazine published 10 times/year. "*Atlanta Homes and Lifestyles* is designed for the action-oriented, well-educated reader who enjoys his/her shelter, its design and construction, its environment, and living and entertaining in it." Estab. 1983. Circ. 33,091. Pays on publication. Byline given. Publishes ms an average of 6 months after acceptance. Pays 25% kill fee. Buys all rights. Reports in 3 months. Sample copy for $3.95.

Nonfiction: Historical, interview/profile, new products, well-designed homes, antiques (Q&A), photo features, gardens, local art, remodeling, food, preservation, entertaining. "We do not want articles outside respective market area, not written for magazine format, or that are excessively controversial, investigative or that cannot be appropriately illustrated with attractive photography." **Buys 35 mss/year.** Query with published clips. Length: 500-750 words. **Pays $350 for features.** Sometimes pays expenses of writers on assignment "if agreed upon in advance of assignment."

Reprints: Send tearsheet or photocopy of article and information about where and when it previously appeared. Pays 50% of amount paid for an original article.

Photos: Send photos with submission; most photography is assigned. Reviews transparencies. Offers $40-50/photo. Captions, model releases and identification of subjects required. Buys one-time rights.

Columns/Departments: Short Takes (newsy items on home and garden topics); Quick Fix (simple remodeling ideas); Cheap Chic (stylish decorating that is easy on the wallet); Digging In (outdoor solutions from Atlanta's gardeners); Big Fix (more extensive remodeling projects); Real Estate News; Interior Elements (hot new furnishings on the market); Weekender (long or short weekend getaway subjects). Query with published clips. **Buys 25-30 mss/year.** Length: 350-500 words. **Pays $50-200.**

N $ $ $ BEST IDEAS FOR CHRISTMAS, Woman's Day Special Interest Publications, Hachette-Filipacchi Magazines, 1633 Broadway, New York NY 10019. Fax: (212)767-5612. E-mail: wdspecials@aol.com. **Contact:** Janice Wright, managing editor. Editor: Carolyn Gatto. Annual consumer magazine covering crafts, holiday, lifestyle. "This magazine offers ideas and how-to information for all the fun aspects of the holidays—cooking, entertaining, decorating the home and making, wrapping and giving gifts." **Pays on acceptance**. Publishes ms an average of 3 months after acceptance. Byline given. Offers up to 25% kill fee. Buys first North American serial or second serial (printing) rights. Editorial lead time 6 months. Submit seasonal material 10 months in advance. Reports in 2 months. Sample copy not available; writer's guidelines for #10 SASE.

Nonfiction: Historical/nostalgic (where various traditions come from); how-to (crafts); interview/profile (notable people with holiday connections); new product; photo feature (homes decorated for the holidays); designs for ornaments and other Christmas decorations. **Buys 5 mss/year**. Query with published clips. Length: 250-1,000 words. Payment varies based on length, writer, importance. Sometimes pays expenses of writers on assignment.

Reprints: Accepts previously published submissions.

Photos: Send photos of craft with query. Model releases required. Buys one-time rights.

Columns/Departments: Query with published clips. Payment varies based on length, writer, and level/amount of research required.

Tips: "Send a brief, clear query letter with relevant clips, and be patient."

BETTER HOMES AND GARDENS, 1716 Locust St., Des Moines IA 50309-3023. Fax: (515)284-3684. Website: http://www.bhglive.com. Editor-in-Chief: Jean LemMon. Editor (Building): Joan McCloskey. Editor (Food & Nutrition): Nancy Byal. Editor (Garden/Outdoor Living): Mark Kane. Editor (Health): Martha Miller. Editor (Education & Parenting): Richard Sowienski. Editor (Money Management, Automotive, Electronics): Lamont Olson. Editor (Features & Travel): Nina Elder. Editor (Interior Design): Sandy Soria. **10-15% freelance written.** "*Better Homes and Gardens* provides home service information for people who have a serious interest in their homes." Estab. 1922. Circ. 7,605,000. **Pays on acceptance.** Buys all rights. "We read all freelance articles, but much prefer to see a letter of query rather than a finished manuscript."

Nonfiction: Travel, education, gardening, health, cars, money management, home entertainment. "We do not deal with political subjects or with areas not connected with the home, community, and family." Pays rates "based on estimate of length, quality and importance." No poetry.

- Most stories published by this magazine go through a lengthy process of development involving both editor and writer. Some editors will consider *only* query letters, not unsolicited manuscripts.

Tips: Direct queries to the department that best suits your story line.

$ $ BIRDS & BLOOMS, Reiman Publications, 5925 Country Lane, Greendale WI 53129. Editor: Tom Curl. **Contact:** Jeff Nowak, managing editor. **15% freelance written.** Bimonthly magazine focusing on the "beauty in your own backyard. *Birds & Blooms* is a sharing magazine that lets backyard enthusiasts chat with each other by exchanging personal experiences. This makes *Birds & Blooms* more like a conversation than a magazine, as readers share tips and tricks on producing beautiful blooms and attracting feathered friends to their backyards." Estab. 1995. Circ. 1,500,000. Pays on publication. Publishes ms an average of 7 months after acceptance. Byline given. Buys all rights. Editorial lead time 2 months. Submit seasonal material 4 months in advance. Accepts simultaneous submissions. Reports in 1 month on queries; 2 months on mss. Sample copy for $2, 9×12 SAE and $1.95 postage. Writer's guidelines free.

Nonfiction: Essays, how-to, humor, inspirational, personal experience, photo feature, natural crafting and "plan" items for building backyard accents. No bird rescue or captive bird pieces. **Buys 12-20 mss/year.** Send complete ms. Length: 250-1,000 words. **Pays $100-400.**

Photos: Trudi Bellin, photo coordinator. Send photos with submission. Reviews transparencies and prints. Identification of subjects required. Buys one-time rights.

Columns/Departments: Backyard Banter (odds, ends and unique things); Bird Tales (backyard bird stories); Local Lookouts (community backyard happenings); all 200 words. **Buys 12-20 mss/year.** Send complete ms. **Pays $50-75.**

Fillers: Anecdotes, facts, gags to be illustrated by cartoonist. **Buys 25/year.** Length: 10-250 words. **Pays $10-75.**

Tips: "Focus on conversational writing—like you're chatting with a neighbor over your fence. Manuscripts full of tips and ideas that people can use in backyards across the country have the best chance of being used. Photos that illustrate these points also increase chances of being used."

$ $ CANADIAN GARDENING, Camar Communications, 340 Ferrier St., Suite 210, Markham, Ontario L3R 2Z5 Canada. (905)475-8440. Fax: (905)475-9560. Editor: Liz Primeau. **Contact:** Rebecca Fox, editor. **99% freelance written.** Magazine published 7 times/year covering home gardening. "We cover garden design, growing, projects for the garden, products, regional information (pests, growing, etc.) for the Canadian gardener. Fundamental plants are the focus, but each issue contains at least one vegetable piece, usually with recipes." Estab. 1990. Circ. 130,000. **Pays on acceptance.** Publishes ms 1 year after acceptance. Byline given. Offers 25-50% kill fee. Buys first North American serial rights. Editorial lead time 3 months. Submit seasonal material 5 months in advance. Reports in 3 months on queries. Sample copy and writer's guidelines free.

Nonfiction: Book excerpts, how-to (gardening, garden projects, pruning, pest control, etc.). No US gardens or growing; no *public* gardens. **Buys 50 mss/year.** Query by mail or e-mail with published clips and SASE with IRCs. Length: 300-2,000 words. **Pays $50-700.** Sometimes pays expenses of writers on assignment.

Photos: State availability of photos with submission. Offers $50-250/photo. Identification of subjects required. Buys one-time rights. "We rarely buy photos from writers. We *are* interested in stockphotos of plants."

Tips: "Short outlines that are already well focused receive the most attention. Most of our freelancers are Canadian."

$ $ $ CANADIAN WORKSHOP, The Do-It-Yourself Magazine, Camar Publications (1984) Inc., 340 Ferrier St., Suite 210, Markham, Ontario L3R 2Z5 Canada. (416)475-8440. Fax: (905)475-4856. E-mail: letters@canadianworkshop.ca. Website: http://www.canadianworkshop.ca. **Contact:** Doug Bennet, editor. **90% freelance written;** half of these are assigned. Monthly magazine covering the "do-it-yourself" market including woodworking projects, renovation, restoration and maintenance. Circ. 100,000. Payment in two installments: half when received, half the month following. Byline given. Offers 50% kill fee. Rights are negotiated with the author. Submit seasonal material 6 months in advance. Reports in 4-6 weeks. Sample copy for 9×12 SASE. Writer's guidelines for #10 SASE.

Nonfiction: How-to (home maintenance, renovation and woodworking projects and features). **Buys 40-60 mss/year.** Query with published clips. Length: 1,500-2,500 words. **Pays $800-1,200.** Pays expenses of writers on assignment.

Photos: Send photos with ms. Payment for photos, transparencies negotiated with the author. Captions, model releases, identification of subjects required.

Tips: "Freelancers must be aware of our magazine format. Products used in how-to articles must be readily available across Canada. Deadlines for articles are four months in advance of cover date. How-tos should be detailed enough for the amateur but appealing to the experienced. Articles must have Canadian content: sources, locations, etc."

N $ $ $ COASTAL LIVING, Southern Progress Corp., 2100 Lakeshore Dr., Birmingham AL 35209. (205)877-6000. Fax: (205)877-6990. E-mail: lynn_carter@spc.com. Website: http://www.coastllivingmag.com. **Contact:** Lynn Carter, managing editor. Bimonthly magazine "for those who live or vacation along our nation's coasts. The magazine emphasizes home design and travel, but also covers a wide variety of other lifestyle topics and coastal concerns." Estab. 1997. Circ. 350,000. Reports in 2 months.

Nonfiction: The magazine is roughly divided into 5 areas, with regular features, columns and departments for each area. **Currents** offers short, newsy features of 30-75 words on *New Products and Ideas* (fun accessories to upscale furnishings), *Happenings* (interesting events), and *Coastal Curiosities* (facts and statistics about the shore). **Travel** contains not only longer travel features but also shorter pieces treating *Active Vacations*, *Nature Vacations*, *Heritage and Historical Vacations* and *Our Favorite Places* (can't miss places). 40% of editorial will be home-oriented stories. **Homes** places the accent on casual living, with "warm, welcoming houses and rooms designed for living. Sections include *Building and Remodeling*, *Good Decisions* (featuring a particular construction component of building or remodeling, with installation or maintenance techniques), *New Communities* (profiles of environmentally sensitive coastal developments); and *Decorating*. **Food** is divided into *Entertaining* (recipes and tips), *Seafood Primer* (basics of buying and preparing seafood), and *Chef's Catch* (coastal chefs and their secrets). The **Lifestyle Service** section is a catch all of subjects to help readers live better and more comfortably: *The Good Life* (profiles of people who have moved to the coast), *Coastal Home* (original plans for the perfect coastal home), *Upkeep* (tips for maintaining a beach house), *Planning & Dreaming* (getting finances in shape for shore living), *So You Want to Live In...* (profiles of coastal communities), and *Shelling Out* (financial and real estate advice and comparisons). Query with SASE.

Photos: State availability of photos with submission.

⊘ **COLONIAL HOMES** does not accept freelance submissions.

$ $ COLORADO HOMES & LIFESTYLES, Wiesner Publishing, LLC, 7009 S. Potomac St., Englewood CO 80112-4029. (303)397-7600. Fax: (303)397-7619. E-mail: emcgraw@winc.usa.com. Website: http://www.coloradohandl.com. **Contact**: Evalyn McGraw, editor. Associate Editor: Jenna Samelson. **70% freelance written.** "Bimonthly upscale shelter magazine—glossy, 4-color—containing beautiful homes, gardens, travel articles, art and artists, food and wine, architecture, calendar, antiques, etc. All of Colorado is included. Geared toward home-related and lifestyle areas, personality profiles, etc." Estab. 1981. Circ. 35,000. **Pays on acceptance.** Publishes ms an average of 6 months after acceptance. Byline given. Offers 15% kill fee. Buys first North American serial rights. Editorial lead time 3 months. Submit seasonal material 1 year in advance. Sometimes accepts simultaneous submissions. Reports in 1 month. Sample copy and writer's guidelines free.

- The editor reports that *Colorado Homes & Lifestyles* is doing many more lifestyle articles and needs more unusual and interesting worldwide travel and upbeat health stories.

Nonfiction: Fine homes and furnishings, regional interior design trends, interesting personalities and lifestyles, gardening and plants—all with a Colorado slant. Book excerpts, general interest, historical/nostalgic, new product, photo feature, travel. No personal essays, religious, humor, technical. Special issues: Mountain Homes and Lifestyles (people, etc.) (January/February); Great Bathrooms (March/April); Home of the Year Contest (July/August); Great Kitchens (September/October). **Buys 40-50 mss/year.** Query with published clips. Length: 1,000-1,500 words. **Pays $125-300 for assigned articles; $125-200 for unsolicited articles.** Sometimes pays the expenses of writers on assignment. Provide sources with phone numbers.

Columns/Departments: Gardening (informative); Artisans (profile of Colorado artisans/craftspeople and work); Travel (worldwide, personal experience preferred); Architecture (Colorado), Health, all 1,100-1,300 words. **Buys 60-75 mss/year.** Query with published clips. **Pays $125-200.**

Reprints: Send photocopy of article or typed ms with rights for sale noted and information about when and where the article previously appeared. Pays 35-50% of amount paid for an original article.

Photos: Send photos with ms. Reviews 35mm, 4×5 and 2¼ color transparencies and b&w glossy prints. Identification of subjects required. Title and caption suggestions appreciated. Please include photographic credits.

Fiction: Occasionally publishes novel excerpts.

Tips: "Send query, lead paragraph, clips (published and unpublished, if possible). Send ideas for story or stories. Include some photos, if applicable. The more interesting and unique the subject the better. A frequent mistake made by writers is failure to provide material with a style and slant appropriate for the magazine, due to poor understanding of the focus of the magazine."

$ $ $ $ COTTAGE LIFE, Quarto Communications, 111 Queen St. E., Suite 408, Toronto, Ontario M5C 1S2 Canada. (416)360-6880. Fax: (416)360-6814. E-mail: dzimmer@cottagelife.com. **Contact:** David Zimmer, editor. Managing Editor: Penny Caldwell. **80% freelance written.** Bimonthly magazine. "*Cottage Life* is written and designed for the people who own and spend time at waterfront cottages throughout Canada and bordering U.S. states. The magazine has a strong service slant, combining useful "how-to" journalism with coverage of the people, trends, and issues in cottage country. Regular columns are devoted to boating, fishing, watersports, projects, real estate, cooking, nature, personal cottage experience, and environmental, political, and financial issues of concern to cottagers." Estab. 1988. Circ. 70,000. **Pays on acceptance.** Publishes ms an average of 2 months after acceptance. Byline given. Offers 50-100% kill fee. Buys first North American serial rights.

Nonfiction: Book excerpts, exposé, historical/nostalgic, how-to, humor, interview/profile, personal experience, photo feature, technical. **Buys 90 mss/year.** Query with published clips and SAE with Canadian postage or IRCs. Length: 1,500-3,500 words. **Pays $100-2,200 for assigned articles; $50-1,000 for unsolicited articles.** Sometimes pays expenses of writers on assignment. Query first.

Columns/Departments: On the Waterfront (front department featuring short news, humor, human interest, and service

items), 400 words. **Pays $100.** Cooking, Real Estate, Fishing, Nature, Watersports, Personal Experience and Issues. Length: 150-1,200 words. Query with published clips and SAE with Canadian postage or IRCs. **Pays $100-750.**
Tips: "If you have not previously written for the magazine, the 'On the Waterfront' section is an excellent place to break in."

$ $ COUNTRY FOLK ART MAGAZINE, Long Publications, 8393 E. Holly Rd., Holly MI 48442. Fax: (248)634-0301. E-mail: longpub@tir.com. Website: http://www.countryfolkart. Editor: Cheryl Anderson. **Contact:** Managing Editor. Bimonthly magazine "catering to those who have an interest in country decorating, how-to crafts, gardening, recipes, artist profiles." Estab. 1988. Circ. 173,000. **Pays on acceptance**; photography paid on publication. Publishes ms 1 year after acceptance. Byline given. Buys first North American serial rights. Editorial lead time 6 months. Submit seasonal material 1 year in advance. Reports in 2 months. Sample copy and writer's guidelines for 9×12 SASE.
Nonfiction: Historical/nostalgic, how-to craft, interview/profile, photo feature, home decorating. **Buys 50-75 mss/year.** Query with published clips. Length: 1,200 words. **Pays $250.** Pays expenses of writers on assignment.
Photos: State availability of photos or send photos with submission. Reviews (2¼×2¼, 4×5, 35mm) transparencies. Offer $25/photo. Captions, identification of subjects required. Buys one-time rights.
Tips: "Solid writing background is preferred. Be prepared to work with editor for clean, concise copy."

$ $ $ COUNTRY JOURNAL, Cowles Enthusiast Media, 4 High Ridge Park, Stamford CT 06905. (203) 321-1778. Fax: (203) 322-1966. E-mail: cntryjrnl@aol.com. **Contact:** Carole Nicksin, assistant editor. Bimonthly magazine. "*Country Journal* covers homes, tools, and projects, emphasizing craftsmanship, quality, value and usefuness." Estab. 1974. Circ. 154,344.
Nonfiction: Features cover gardening, food, health, the natural world, small-scale farming, land conservation, the environment, energy and other issues affecting country life. Length: 2,500 words. Query with published clips, a list of sources and details as to why you are an authority on the subject, as well as your qualifications for writing the piece.
Reprints: Send photocopy of article with information about when it previously appeared.
Photos: Photographs and/or drawings are critical for the acceptance of any article. Original color transparencies, 35mm or larger—no dupes; also accepts b&w prints 5×7 or larger with white borders; no negatives.
Columns/Departments: Sentinel: brief ideas, information and resources for country life. This department is a good way for new writers to break into the magazine (300-600 words). Cook's Tour: Recipes with a short narrative (1,000-1,500 words). Housesmith: Projects, procedures, tools and other subjects dealing with home and grounds maintenance and improvement (1,000-1,500 words). Making Do: Simple, inexpensive ways of fixing, building and improvising (up to 1,000 words).
Tips: "We are looking for short (1,000 words or less), first-person accounts of living in or moving to the country."

$ $ $ COUNTRY LIVING, The Hearst Corp., 224 W. 57th St., New York NY 10019. (212)649-3509. **Contact:** Marjorie Gage, features editor. Monthly magazine covering home design and interior decorating with an emphasis on "country" style. "A lifestyle magazine for readers who appreciate the warmth and traditions associated with American home and family life. Each monthly issue embraces American country decorating and includes features on furniture, antiques, gardening, home building, real estate, cooking, entertaining and travel." Estab. 1978. Circ. 1,816,000.
Nonfiction: Most open to freelancers: antiques articles from authorities, personal essay. **Buys 20-30 mss/year.** Pay varies. Send complete ms and SASE.
Columns/Departments: Most open to freelancers: Readers Corner. Pay varies. Send complete ms and SASE.

N $ $ $ DECORATING IDEAS, Woman's Day Special Interest Publications, Hachette-Filipacchi Magazines, 1633 Broadway, New York NY 10019. Fax: (212)767-5612. E-mail: wdspecials@aol.com. **Contact:** Janice Wright, managing editor. Editor: Carolyn Gatto. Consumer magazine published 3 times a year covering home decorating. "This magazine aims to inspire and teach readers how to create a beautiful home." **Pays on acceptance**. Publishes ms an average of 3 months after acceptance. Byline given. Offers up to 25% kill fee. Buys first North American serial or second serial (printing) rights. Editorial lead time 6 months. Submit seasonal material 10 months in advance. Reports in 2 months. Sample copy not available; writer's guidelines for #10 SASE.
Nonfiction: How-to (home decor projects for beginner/intermediate skill levels—sewing, woodworking, painting, etc.), new product, photo feature, technical, collectibles, hard to find services, unique stores. **Buys 30 mss/year**. Query with published clips. Length: 250-1,000 words. Payment varies based on length, writer, importance. Sometimes pays expenses of writers on assignment.
Reprints: Accepts previously published submissions.
Photos: Send representative photos with query. Model releases required. Buys one-time rights.
Columns/Departments: Weekend Projects (how-to instructions for 1 or 2 relevant projects that can be completed in a day or two), 400-800 words. **Buys 3 mss/year**. Query with published clips. Payment varies based on length, writer, and level/amount of research required.
Tips: "Send a brief, clear query letter with relevant clips, and be patient. Before and after photos are very helpful, as are photos of ideas for Weekend Projects column. In addition to specific ideas and projects (for which how-to information is provided), we look at decorating trends, provide advice on how to get the most design for your money (with and without help from a professional), and highlight noteworthy new products and services."

$ $ EARLY AMERICAN HOMES, Primedia, 6405 Flank Dr., Harrisburg PA 17112. Fax: (717)657-9552. **Contact:** Mimi Handler, editor. **20% freelance written.** Bimonthly magazine for "people who are interested in capturing the warmth and beauty of the 1600 to 1840 period and using it in their homes and lives today. They are interested in antiques, traditional crafts, architecture, restoration and collecting." Estab. 1970. Circ. 130,000. Buys worldwide rights. **Pays on acceptance.** Publishes ms an average of 1 year after acceptance. Reports in 3 months. Sample copy and writer's guidelines for 9×12 SAE with 4 first-class stamps. Query or submit complete ms with SASE.

• The editor of this publication is looking for more on architecture, gardens and antiques.

Nonfiction: "Social history (the story of the people, not epic heroes and battles), travel to historic sites, antiques and reproductions, restoration, architecture and decorating. We try to entertain as we inform. We're always on the lookout for good pieces on any of our subjects. Would like to see more on how real people did something great to their homes." **Buys 40 mss/year.** Query or submit complete ms. Length: 750-3,000 words. **Pays $100-600.** Pays expenses of writers on assignment.

Tips: "Our readers are eager for ideas on how to bring early America into their lives. Conceive a new approach to satisfy their related interests in arts, crafts, travel to historic sites, and especially in houses decorated in the early American style. Write to entertain and inform at the same time. Be prepared to help us with sources for illustrations."

$ $ $ FINE GARDENING, Taunton Press, 63 S. Main St., P.O. Box 5506, Newtown CT 06470-5506. (203)426-8171. Fax: (203)426-3434. E-mail: fg@taunton.com. Website: http://www.finegardening.com. **Contact:** LeeAnne White, editor. Bimonthly "high-value magazine on landscape and ornamental gardening. Articles written by avid gardeners—first person, hands-on gardening experiences." Estab. 1988. Circ. 200,000. **Pays on acceptance**. Publishes ms an average of 6 months after acceptance. Byline given. Buys all rights. Editorial lead time 1 year. Submit seasonal material 1 year in advance. Writer's guidelines free.

Nonfiction: Book review, how-to, personal experience, photo feature. **Buys 60 mss/year.** Query. Length: 1,000-3,000 words. **Pays $300-1,200.** Sometimes pays expenses of writers on assignment.

Photos: Send photos with submission. Reviews 35mm transparencies. Buys serial rights.

Columns/Department: Book, video and software reviews (on gardening); Last Word (essays/serious, humorous, fact or fiction). Length: 250-500 words. Query. **Buys 30 mss/year. Pays $50-200.**

Tips: "It's most important to have solid first-hand experience as a gardener. Tell us what you've done with your own landscape and plants."

$ $ FINE HOMEBUILDING, The Taunton Press, 63 S. Main St., P.O. Box 5506, Newtown CT 06470-5506. (800) 283-7252. Fax: (203) 270-6751. E-mail: fh@taunton.com. Website: http://www.taunton.com. **Contact:** Kevin Ireton, editor. "*Fine Homebuilding* is a bimonthly magazine for builders, architects, contractors, owner/builders and others who are seriously involved in building new houses or reviving old ones." Estab. 1981. Circ. 247,712. Pays half on acceptance, half on publication. Publishes ms 1 year after acceptance. Byline given. Offers on acceptance payment as kill fee. Buys first and reprint rights. Reports in 1 month. Writer's guidelines for SASE.

Nonfiction: "We're interested in almost all aspects of home building, from laying out foundations to capping cupolas." Query with outline, description, photographs, sketches and SASE. **Pays $150/published page** with "a possible bonus on publication for an unusually good manuscript."

Photos: "Take lots of work-in-progress photos. Color print film, ASA 400, from either Kodak or Fuji works best. If you prefer to use slide film, use ASA 100. Keep track of the negatives; we will need them for publication. If you're not sure what to use or how to go about it, feel free to call for advice."

Columns/Departments: Tools & Materials, Reviews, Questions & Answers, Tips & Techniques, Cross Section, What's the Difference?, Finishing Touches, Great Moments. Query with outline, description, photographs, sketches and SASE. **Pays $150/published page.**

Tips: "Our chief contributors are home builders, architects and other professionals. We're more interested in your point of view and technical expertise than your prose style. Adopt an easy, conversational style and define any obscure terms for non-specialists. We try to visit all our contributors and rarely publish building projects we haven't seen, or authors we haven't met."

$ $ FLOWER AND GARDEN MAGAZINE, 700 W. 47th St., Suite 810, Kansas City MO 64112. (816)531-5730. Fax: (816)531-3873. **Contact:** Doug Hall, editor. **80% freelance written.** Works with a small number of new/unpublished writers each year. Bimonthly picture magazine. "*Flower & Garden* focuses on ideas that can be applied to the home garden and outdoor environs, primarily how-to, but also historical and background articles are considered if a specific adaptation can be obviously related to home gardening." Estab. 1957. Circ. 525,000. Buys first-time nonexclusive reprint rights. Byline given. **Pays on acceptance.** Publishes ms an average of 1 year after acceptance. Reports in 2 months. Sample copy for $4.50. Writer's guidelines for #10 SASE.

• The editor tells us good quality photos accompanying articles are more important than ever.

Nonfiction: Interested in illustrated articles on how to do certain types of gardening and descriptive articles about individual plants. Flower arranging, landscape design, house plants and patio gardening are other aspects covered. "The approach we stress is practical (how-to-do-it, what-to-do-it-with). We emphasize plain talk, clarity and economy of words. An article should be tailored for a national audience." **Buys 20-30 mss/year.** Query. Length: 500-1,000 words. Rates vary depending on quality and kind of material and author's credentials, **$200-500.**

Reprints: Sometimes accepts previously published articles. Send typed ms with rights for sale noted, including information about when and where the article previously appeared.

Photos: Color slides and transparencies preferred, 35mm and larger but 35mm slides or prints not suitable for cover. Submit cover photos as 2¼×2¼ or larger transparencies. An accurate packing list with appropriately labeled photographs and numbered slides with description sheet (including Latin botanical and common names) must accompany submissions. In plant or flower shots, indicate which end is up on each photo. Photos are paid for on publication, $100-200 inside, $300-500 for covers.
Tips: "The prospective author needs good grounding in gardening practice and literature. Offer well-researched and well-written material appropriate to the experience level of our audience. Photographs help sell the story. Describe special qualifications for writing the particular proposed subject."

$ $ $ GARDEN DESIGN, 100 Avenue of the Americas, New York NY 10013. (212)334-1212. Fax: (212)334-1260. E-mail: gardendesign@meigher.com. Editor: Douglas Brenner. **Contact:** Sarah Gray Miller, senior associate editor. Magazine published 8 times/year devoted to the fine art of garden design. Circ. 325,000. Pays 2 months after acceptance. Byline given. Buys first North American rights. Submit seasonal material 6 months in advance. Sample copy for $5. Writer's guidelines for #10 SASE.
Nonfiction: "We look for literate writing on a wide variety of garden-related topics—history, architecture, the environment, furniture, decorating, travel, personalities." Query with outline, published clips and SASE. Length: 200-1,200 words. Sometimes pays expenses of writer or photographer on assignment.
Photos: Submit scouting photos when proposing article on a specific garden.
Tips: "Our greatest need is for extraordinary private gardens. Scouting locations is a valuable service freelancers can perform, by contacting designers and garden clubs in the area, visiting gardens and taking snapshots for our review. All departments of the magazine are open to freelancers. Familiarize yourself with our departments and pitch stories accordingly. Writing should be as stylish as the gardens we feature."

N $ $ $ GARDENING & OUTDOOR LIVING IDEAS, Woman's Day Special Interest Publications, Hachette-Filipacchi Magazines, 1633 Broadway, New York NY 10019. Fax: (212)767-5612. E-mail: wdspecials@aol.com. **Contact:** Janice Wright, managing editor. Editor: Carolyn Gatto. Annual consumer magazine covering gardening, home outdoor space (decks, lawn, patios). "This magazine, which appears in the spring, aims to give readers inspiration, practical advice, and how-to's." **Pays on acceptance**. Publishes ms an average of 3 months after acceptance. Byline given. Offers up to 25% kill fee. Buys first North American serial or second serial (printing) rights. Editorial lead time 6 months. Submit seasonal material 10 months in advance. Reports in 2 months. Sample copy not available; writer's guidelines for #10 SASE.
Nonfiction: How-to, new product (gardens or outdoor home spaces), photo features (beautiful gardens; inviting outdoor home settings), technical (care for), travel (gardens around US). **Buys 50 mss/year**. Query with published clips. Length: 250-1,000 words. Payment varies. Sometimes pays expenses of writers on assignment.
Reprints: Accepts previously published submissions.
Photos: State availability of or send representative photos with query. Model releases required. Buys one-time rights.
Columns/Departments: Weekend Projects (how-to instructions for 1 or 2 relevant projects that can be completed in a day or two), 400-800 words. **Buys 2 mss/year**. Query with published clips. Payment varies based on length, writer, and level/amount of research required.
Tips: "Send a brief, clear query letter with relevant clips, and be patient."

$ $ THE HERB COMPANION, Interweave Press, 201 E. Fourth St., Loveland CO 80537-5655. (970)669-7672. Fax: (970)667-8317. E-mail: hc@iwp.ccmail.compuserve.com. **Contact:** Kathleen Halloran, editor. **80% freelance written.** Bimonthly magazine about herbs: culture, history, culinary, crafts and some medicinal use for both experienced and novice herb enthusiasts. Circ. 110,000. Pays on publication. Byline given. Buys first North American serial rights. Editorial lead time 4 months. Reports in 2 months. Query in writing. Sample copy for $4. Guidelines for #10 SASE.
Nonfiction: Practical horticultural, original recipes, historical, how-to, herbal crafts, profiles, helpful hints and book reviews. Submit detailed query or ms. Length: 4 pages or 1,000 words. **Pays $125/published page.**
Photos: Send photos with submission. Transparencies preferred. Returns photos and artwork.
Tips: "New approaches to familiar topics are especially welcome. If you aren't already familiar with the content, style and tone of the magazine, we suggest you read a few issues. Technical accuracy is essential. Please use scientific as well as popular names for plants and cover the subject in depth while avoiding overly academic presentation. Information should be made accessible to the reader, and we find this is best accomplished by writing from direct personal experience where possible and always in an informal style."

$ $ HERB QUARTERLY, P.O. Box 689, San Anselmo CA 94960-0689. Fax: (415)455-9541. E-mail: herbquart@aol.com. Publisher: James Keough. **Contact:** Associate Editor. **80% freelance written.** Quarterly magazine for herb enthusiasts. Estab. 1979. Circ. 35,000. Pays on publication. Publishes ms an average of 6 months after acceptance. Buys first North American serial and second (reprint) rights. Query letters recommended. Reports in 2 months. Sample copy for $5 and 9×12 SASE. Writer's guidelines for #10 SASE.
Nonfiction: Gardening (landscaping, herb garden design, propagation, harvesting); medicinal and cosmetic use of herbs; crafts; cooking; historical (folklore, focused piece on particular period—*not* general survey); interview of a famous person involved with herbs or folksy herbalist; personal experience; photo essay ("cover quality" 8×10 b&w or color prints). "We are particularly interested in herb garden design, contemporary or historical." No fiction. Query. Length: 1,000-3,500 words. **Pays $75-250.**

Tips: "Our best submissions are narrowly focused on herbs with much practical information on cultivation and use for the experienced gardener."

N $ $ HOME DIGEST, The Homeowner's Family Resource Guide, Home Digest International Inc., 268 Lakeshore Rd. E, Unit 604, Oakville, Ontario L6J 7S4 Canada. Fax: (905)849-4618. **Contact:** William Roebuck, editor. **40% freelance written**. Quarterly magazine covering house, home and life management for families in stand-alone houses. "*Home Digest* has a strong service slant, combining useful how-to journalism with coverage of the trends and issues of home ownership and family life. In essence, our focus is on the concerns of families living in their own homes in the greater Toronto region." Estab. 1995. Circ. 606,000. Pays on publication. Publishes ms an average of 3 months after acceptance. Byline given. Buys first North American serial rights. Editorial lead time 3 months. Submit seasonal material 3 months in advance. Accepts simultaneous submissions. Reports in 1 month. Sample copy for 9×6 SASE and 2 Canadian stamps. Writer's guidelines for #10 SASE.
Nonfiction: Expose, general interest, how-to (household hints, basic home renovation, decorating), humor (living in Toronto), inspirational. No travel, opinion, puff pieces. **Buys 12 mss/year**. Query. Length: 350-1,000 words. **Pays $50-150** (Canadian).
Reprints: Accepts previously published submission.
Photos: Send photos with submission. Reviews transparencies and prints. Offers $10-20 per photo. Captions, model releases, and identification of subjects required. Buys one-time rights.
Columns/Departments: Household Hints (tested tips that work); Healthy Living (significant health/body/fitness news); all 300-350 words. **Buys 8 mss/year**. Query. **Pays $40-75** (Canadian).
Fillers: Anecdotes, facts. **Buys 25/year**. Length: 10-30 words. **Pays $2.50-5** (Canadian).
Tips: "Base your ideas on practical experiences. We're looking for 'uncommon' advice that works."

N $ $ $ HOME REMODELING, Woman's Day Special Interest Publications, Hachette-Filipacchi Magazines, 1633 Broadway, New York NY 10019. Fax: (212)767-5612. E-mail: wdspecials@aol.com. **Contact:** Janice Wright, managing editor. Editor: Carolyn Gatto. Quarterly consumer magazine covering home improvement, upgrades, repairs. "This guide is for anyone who is thinking about remodeling all or part of their home features design ideas, new products and materials, along with detailed service information about how to save time, money and energy on large and small projects." **Pays on acceptance**. Publishes ms an average of 3 months after acceptance. Byline given. Offers up to 25% kill fee. Buys first North American serial or second serial (printing) rights. Editorial lead time 6 months. Submit seasonal material 10 months in advance. Reports in 2 months. Sample copy not available; writer's guidelines for #10 SASE.
Nonfiction: How-to (planning & construction), new product, photo features (dramatic successfully remodeled homes), technical (information about materials procedures that a homeowner should know), healthy home issues. **Buys 60 mss/year**. Query with published clips. Length: 250-1,000 words. Payment varies based on length, writer, importance. Sometimes pays expenses of writers on assignment.
Reprints: Accepts previously published submissions.
Photos: Send representative photos with query. Model releases required. Buys one-time rights.
Columns/Departments: Weekend Projects (how-to instructions for one or two relevant projects that can be completed in a day or two), 400-800 words; Legal Issues (relevant legal issues: awareness and what-to-do), 400-800 words; Money Matters (relevant financial issues: awareness and what-to-do). **Buys 12 mss/year**. Query with published clips. Payment varies based on length, writer, and level/amount of research required.
Tips: "Send a brief, clear query letter with relevant clips, and be patient. Before and after photos are very helpful, as are floor plans. Photos for Weekend Projects also helpful."

$ $ HOMES & COTTAGES, The In-Home Show Ltd., 6557 Mississauga Rd., Suite D, Mississauga, Ontario L5N 1A6 Canada. (905)567-1440. Fax: (905)567-1442. E-mail: jimhc@pathcom.com. Website: http://www.homesandcottages.com. Editor: Janice Naisby. **Contact:** Jim Adair, editor-in-chief. 50% freelance written. Magazine published 8 times/year covering building and renovating; "technically comprehensive articles." Estab. 1987. Circ. 64,000. Pays on publication. Publishes mss average of 2 months after acceptance. Byline given. Offers 10% kill fee. Buys first North American serial rights. Editorial lead time 3 months. Submit seasonal material 3 months in advance. Sample copy for SAE. Writer's guidelines free.
Nonfiction: Humor (building and renovation related), new product, technical. **Buys 32 mss/year.** Query. Length: 1,000-2,000 words. **Pays $300-750.** Sometimes pays expenses of writers on assignment.
Photos: Send photos with submission. Reviews transparencies and prints. Negotiates payment individually. Captions and identification of subjects required. Buys one-time rights.

$ $ $ HORTICULTURE, The Magazine of American Gardening, 98 N. Washington St., Boston MA 02114. (617) 742-5600. Fax: (617) 367-6364. **Contact:** Thomas Fischer, executive editor. Magazine published 10 times/year. "*Horticulture*, the country's oldest gardening magazine, is designed for active amateur gardeners. Our goal is to offer a blend of text, photographs and illustrations that will both instruct and inspire readers." Circ. 300,000. Byline given. Offers kill fee. Buys one-time or first North American serial rights. Submit seasonal material 10 months in advance. Reports in 3 months. Writer's guidelines for SASE.
Nonfiction: "We look for an encouraging personal experience, anecdote and opinion. At the same time, a thorough article should to some degree place its subject in the broader context of horticulture." **Buys 15 mss/year.** Query with

published clips, subject background material and SASE. Include disk where possible. Length: 1,500-2,500 words. **Pays $600-1,500.** Pays expenses of writers on assignment if previously arranged with editor.

Columns/Departments: Query with published clips, subject background material and SASE. Include disk where possible. Length: 1,000-1,500 words. **Pays $50-600.**

Tips: "We believe every article must offer ideas or illustrate principles that our readers might apply on their own gardens. No matter what the subject, we want our readers to become better, more creative gardeners."

N $ $ $ **KITCHEN & BATHS, Woman's Day Special Interest Publications**, Hachette-Filipacchi Magazines, 1633 Broadway, New York NY 10019. Fax: (212)767-5612. E-mail: wdspecials@aol.com. **Contact:** Janice Wright, managing editor. Editor: Carolyn Gatto. Quarterly consumer magazine covering information, ideas for home kitchen and bathrooms. "This magazine showcases hundreds of the newest, brightest, and boldest ideas for these two important rooms in the home." **Pays on acceptance.** Publishes ms an average of 3 months after acceptance. Byline given. Offers up to 25% kill fee. Buys first North American serial or second serial (printing) rights. Editorial lead time 6 months. Submit seasonal material 10 months in advance. Reports in 2 months. Sample copy not available; writer's guidelines for #10 SASE.

Nonfiction: How-to (design tips, problem solving), new product, photo features (homes with beautiful kitchens & baths), technical (information about plumbing, hardware, materials relevant to a consumer). **Buys 50 mss/year.** Query with published clips. Length: 250-1,000 words. Payment varies based on length, writer, importance. Sometimes pays expenses of writers on assignment.

Reprints: Accepts previously published submissions.

Photos: Send photos with query. Model releases required. Buys one-time rights.

Columns/Departments: Weekend Projects (how-to instructions for one or two relevant projects that can be completed in a day or two), 400-800 words; Legal Issues (relevant legal issues: awareness and what-to-do), 400-800 words; Money Matters (relevant financial issues: awareness and what-to-do). **Buys 12 mss/year.** Query with published clips. Payment varies based on length, writer, and level/amount of research required.

Tips: "Send a brief, clear query letter with relevant clips, and be patient. Before and after photos are very helpful, as are floor plans. Whether readers are planning a new home, remodeling or even just redecorating, here they'll find designs and products that are innovative, efficient, and environmentally sound. Advice about trends and storage and safety issues, and tips for solving problems, are included."

$ $ $ **KITCHEN GARDEN: Growing and Cooking Great Food**, The Taunton Press, 63 S. Main St., P.O. Box 5506, Newtown CT 06470. (203)426-8171. Fax: (203)426-3434. E-mail: kg@taunton.com. Website: http://www.taunton.com. **Contact:** Mary Morgan, editor. **90% freelance written.** Bimonthly magazine covering vegetable gardening for both expert and novice home gardeners and cooks. Estab. 1996. Circ. 100,000. **Pays on acceptance.** Publishes ms an average of 6 months after acceptance. Byline given. Kill fee negotiated. Buys all rights. Editorial lead time 1 year. Submit seasonal material 1 year in advance. Reports in 1 month. Writer's guidelines free.

Nonfiction: How-to. Regular features include Plant Profiles (in-depth coverage of vegetable, fruit or herb); Kitchen Talk (1-3 sidebar recipes featuring profiled plant); Garden Profiles (tours of beautiful, striking or unusual kitchen gardens); basic and advanced Techniques; Design; Projects (things to build and do); and Cooking (as distinct from Kitchen Talk, focuses entirely on cooking). **Buys 60 mss/year.** Query by letter, phone or e-mail. Length: 1,000-3,000 words. **Pays $300-1,000.** Sometimes pays expenses of writer on assignment.

Photos: Send photos with submission. Reviews contact sheets, negatives, transparencies, prints. Negotiates payment individually. Identification of subjects required. Buys all rights.

Columns/Departments: Reviews (books, software), 500 words. **Buys 30 mss/year.** Query with published clips. **Pays $50-200.**

Tips: "Our articles are written in the first-person by people with first-hand experience who have something of substance to say. While we are happy to find accomplished writers who also have significant gardening or cooking expertise, the expertise is more important than the writing skills. Our editors work very closely with authors throughout the process of generating a story, and they are very good at working with words, as well as with gardeners, so first-time authors should not be deterred."

"In most cases, an editor visits the author before an article is definitely assigned. This is so scouting photographs can be taken and the editor can get to know the author, which facilitates developing an outline and then the story. It is important that our authors grow the plants about which they write, and that their gardens be suitable for photographing for the magazine."

$ $ **LOG HOME LIVING**, Home Buyer Publications Inc., 4200-T Lafayette Center Dr., Chantilly VA 20151. (703)222-9411. Fax: (703)222-3209. E-mail: jbrewster@homebuyerpubs.com. Website: http://www.loghomeliving.com. **Contact:** Janice Brewster, editor. **50% freelance written.** Monthly magazine for enthusiasts who are dreaming of, planning for, or actively building a log home. Estab. 1989. Circ. 132,000. **Pays on acceptance.** Publishes ms an average of 6 months after acceptance. Byline given. Offers $100 kill fee. Buys first or second serial (reprint) rights. Editorial lead time 6 months. Submit seasonal material 6 months in advance. Reports in 6 weeks. Sample copy for $4. Writer's guidelines for #10 SASE.

Nonfiction: Book excerpts, how-to (build or maintain log home), interview/profile (log home owners), personal experience, photo feature (log homes), technical (design/decor topics), travel. "We do not want historical/nostalgic material." **Buys 6 mss/year.** Query. Length: 1,000-2,000 words. **Pays $250-500.** Pays expenses of writers on assignment.

Reprints: Send tearsheet or photocopy of article and information about when and where the article previously appeared. Pays 50% of amount paid for an original article.
Photos: State availability of photos with submission. Reviews contact sheets, 4×5 transparencies and 4×6 prints. Negotiates payment individually. Buys one-time rights.

N $ $ **LOG HOMES ILLUSTRATED**, Goodman Media Group, Inc., 1700 Broadway, New York NY 10019. (212)541-7100. Fax: (212)245-1241. Editor: Roland Sweet. **Contact:** Stacy M. Durr, managing editor. **30-40% freelance written.** Bimonthly magazine. "*Log Homes Illustrated* presents full-color photo features and inspirational stories of people who have fulfilled their dream of living in a log home. We show readers how they can make it happen too." Estab. 1994. Circ. 126,000. Pays on publication. Publishes ms 6 months after acceptance. Byline given. Buys first rights or second serial (reprint) rights. Editorial lead time 4 months. Submit seasonal material 6 months in advance. Accepts simultaneous submissions. Sample copy for $3.99.
Nonfiction: Book excerpts, how-to (gardening, building), profile (architects), new product, personal experience, photo feature, technical, travel. Special issues: Annual Buyer's Guide; PLANS issue. "We tend to stay away from articles that focus on just one craftsman, promotional pieces." **Buys 20-25 mss/year.** Query with published clips or send complete ms. Length: 1,200-3,000 words. **Pays $300-600.** Pays expenses of writers on assignment with limit agreed upon in advance.
Reprints: Accepts previously published submissions.
Photos: Send photos with submission. Reviews 4×5 transparencies, slides or prints. Negotiates payment individually. Captions required. Buys one-time rights.
Columns/Departments: Diary (personal glimpses of log experience), 1,200-2,000 words; Going Places (visiting a log B&B, lodge, etc.), 1,200-2,000 words; Worth a Look (log churches, landmarks, etc.), 1,200-2,000 words; Gardening (rock gardens, water gardens, etc.), 2,000-3,000 words. **Buys 15 mss/year.** Query with published clips or send complete ms. **Pays $300-600.**
Tips: "It is always best to include photos with your submission. Present a clear idea of how and where your story will fit into our magazine."

$ $ $ $ **METROPOLITAN HOME**, Hachette Filipacchi Inc., 1633 Broadway, New York NY 10019. (212)767-5522. Fax: (212)767-5636. E-mail: meteditl@aol.com. **Contact:** Michael Lassell, articles director. Bimonthly magazine covering "home design, home furnishings, fashion, food, wines and spirits, entertaining and electronics with an editorial focus on the art of living well. It is edited for quality-conscious adults and contains news and guidance toward achieving personal style." Estab. 1969. Circ. 632,000. **Pays on acceptance.** Byline given. Offers 25% kill fee. Buy first North American serial rights. Reports in 1-2 months on queries.

- Ranked as one of the best markets for freelance writers in *Writer's Yearbook*'s annual "Top 100 Markets," January 1998.

Nonfiction: Needs home-related lifestyle stories for sophisticated audience; full of accessible ideas; written from expert view. No how-to stories. **Buys 8-12 mss/year.** Query with published clips. Length: 1,000-2,000 words. **Pays $1,000-2,000. Pays expenses of writers on assignment.**
Columns/Departments: 800-1,500 words. **Buys 10-20 mss/year.** Query with published clips. **Pays $750-1,800.**
Tips: "We use only experienced writers or experts who know their subject—interior design and home style. We're on the cutting edge of home style."

$ $ **MOUNTAIN LIVING**, Wiesner Publishing, 7009 S. Potomac St., Englewood CO 80112. (303)397-7600. Fax: (303)397-7619. E-mail: rgriggs@winc.usa.com. Website: http://www.mtnliving.com. **Contact:** Robyn Griggs, editor. **90% freelance written.** Bimonthly magazine covering "shelter and lifestyle issues for people who live in, visit or hope to live in the mountains." Estab. 1994. Circ. 35,000. **Pays on acceptance.** Publishes ms an average of 4 months after acceptance. Byline given. Offers 15% kill fee. Buys first North American serial rights. Editorial lead time 6 months. Submit seasonal material 6 months in advance. Accepts simultaneous submissions. Reports in 6 weeks on queries; 2 months on mss. Sample copy for $5. Writer's guidelines for #10 SASE.
Nonfiction: Book excerpts, essays, historical/nostalgic, interview/profile, personal experience, photo feature, travel, home features. **Buys 30 mss/year.** Query with published clips. Length: 1,200-2,000 words. **Pays $50-400.** Sometimes pays expenses of writers on assignment.
Reprints: Send photocopy of article or typed ms with rights for sale noted. Payment varies.
Photos: State availability of photos with submission. Negotiates payment individually. Buys one-time rights.
Columns/Departments: Architecture, Art, Gardening, Sporting Life, Travel (often international), Off the Beaten Path (out-of-the-way mountain areas in U.S.), History, Health, Cuisine, Environment, Destinations (an art-driven department featuring a beautiful mountain destination in U.S.—must be accompanied by quality photograph), Trail's End (mountain-related essays). **Buys 35 mss/year.** Query with published clips. Length: 300-1,500 words. **Pays $50-300.**
Tips: "A deep understanding of and respect for the mountain environment is essential. Think out of the box. We love to be surprised. And always send clips."

★ $ $ **NATIONAL GARDENING**, National Gardening Association, 180 Flynn Ave., Burlington VT 05401. (802)863-1308. Fax: (802)863-5962. E-mail: eileenm@garden.org. Website: http://www.garden.org. Editor: Michael MacCaskey. **Contact:** Eileen Murray, managing editor. **80% freelance written.** Bimonthly magazine covering all aspects of food gardening and ornamentals. "We publish not only how-to garden techniques, but also news that affects home gardeners, like breeding advancements and new variety releases. Detailed, experienced-based articles with carefully worked-out techniques for planting, growing, harvesting and using garden fruits and vegetables are sought as well as profiles of expert gardeners in this country's many growing regions. Our material is for both experienced and beginning gardeners." Estab. 1979. Circ. 250,000. Pays on publication. Publishes ms an average of 9 months after acceptance. Byline given. Buys first serial and occasionally second (reprint) rights. Sample copy for $3. Writer's guidelines for #10 SASE.

Nonfiction: How-to, humor, interview/profile, pest profiles, personal experience, recipes. **Buys 50-60 mss/year.** Query first. Length: 500-2,500 words. Sometimes pays expenses of writers on assignment with prior approval.

Photos: Linda Provost, art director. Send photos with ms. Pays $20-40 for b&w photos; $50 for color slides. Captions, model releases and accurate botanical identification of subjects required.

Tips: "Take the time to study the style and format of the magazine—focus on the format of features and the various departments. Keep in mind that you'll be addressing a national audience."

N $ $ $ $ OLD-HOUSE INTERIORS, Gloucester Publishers, 2 Main St., Gloucester MA 01930. (978)283-3200. Fax: (978)283-4629. **Contact:** Regina Cole, senior editor. **55% freelance written.** Bimonthly magazine for "furnishing residential period houses with a knowledge of historic house styles." Estab. 1994. Circ. 160,000. **Pays on acceptance.** Publishes ms 6 months after acceptance. Byline given. Offers 25% kill fee. Buys first North American serial rights. Editorial lead time 9 months. Submit seasonal material 1 year in advance. Reports in 1 month on queries; 2 months on mss. Sample copy and writer's guidelines free.

Nonfiction: Historical, decorator's how-to, interview/profile, opinion, photo feature, technical, travel, historic house tours. No nostalgia. **Buys 25 mss/year.** Query. Length: 300-1,500 words. **Pays $25-1,500.** Sometimes pays expenses of writers on assignment.

Photos: State availability of photos with submission or send photos with submission. Negotiates payment individually. Captions and identification of subjects required. Buys one-time rights.

Columns/Departments: History of Furniture (academic), 1,200 words; Open House (friendly, informational), 400 words; Period Accents (informative), 750 words. Query. **Pays $25-1,500.**

Tips: "Writers should know that we are not a decorating magazine, but rather a beautifully photographed, intelligently written guide on finishing and furnishing period homes of every era."

$ $ $ $ ORGANIC GARDENING, Rodale Press, 33 E. Minor, Emmaus PA 18098. (610)967-5171. **Contact:** Vicki Mattern, managing editor. **75% freelance written.** Magazine published 8 times/year. "*Organic Gardening* is for gardeners who garden, who enjoy gardening as an integral part of a healthy lifestyle. Editorial shows readers how to grow anything they choose without chemicals. Editorial details how to grow flowers, edibles and herbs, as well as information on ecological landscaping. Also organic topics including soil building and pest control." Circ. 700,000. Pays between acceptance and publication. Buys all rights. Reports in 2 months on queries; 1 month on mss.

Nonfiction: "The natural approach to the whole home landscape." Query with published clips and outline. **Pay varies, up to $1/word for experienced writers.**

$ $ PLANT & GARDEN, Canada's Practical Gardening Magazine, Helpard Publishing, Inc., 1200 Markham Rd., Suite 300, Scarborough, Ontario M1H 3C3 Canada. (416)438-7777. Fax: (416)438-5333. **Contact:** Lorraine Hunter. **85% freelance written.** Bimothly magazine covering gardening in Canada. "*Plant & Garden* is a *practical* gardening magazine focusing on how-to, step-by-step type articles on all aspects of garden and houseplant care. Readers are both novice and experienced Canadian gardeners." Estab. 1988. Pays on publication. Byline given. Buys first North American serial rights. Editorial lead time 4 months. Submit seasonal material 4 months in advance. Accepts simultaneous submissions. Reports in 2 months. Sample copy for $4 and 9×12 SAE. Writer's guidelines for SAE and IRC or, preferably, SAE with sufficient Canadian postage affixed.

Nonfiction: How-to, interview/profile, new product—garden-related topics only. **Buys 60 mss/year.** Query with published clips by mail, e-mail or fax. Length: 600-1,800 words. **Pays 20¢/word.** Sometimes pays expenses of writers on assignment.

Photos: Send photos with submission. Reviews negatives and 4×5 transparencies. Offers no additional payment for photos accepted with ms. Captions required. Buys one-time rights. Illustrations are usually commissioned.

Columns/Departments: Profile (profiles of gardens and/or gardeners); Hydroponics (how-to for home gardener); Environment. Length: 600-800 words. Query with published clips. **Pays 20¢/word.**

Tips: "Please be knowledgeable about gardening—not just a freelance writer. Be accurate and focus on plants/techniques that are appropriate to Canada. Be as down to earth as possible. We want good quality writing and interesting subject matter. We are especially looking for garden profiles from outside Ontario and Quebec. All submitted materials must be accompanied by a SAE with sufficient Canadian postage affixed to ensure return."

$ $ SAN DIEGO HOME/GARDEN LIFESTYLES, Mckinnon Enterprises, Box 719001, San Diego CA 92171-9001. (619)571-1818. Fax: (619)571-1889. E-mail: sdhg@adnc.com. Senior Editor: Phyllis Van Doren. **Contact:** Wayne Carlson, editor. **50% freelance written.** Monthly magazine covering homes, gardens, food, intriguing people, real estate, art, culture, and local travel for residents of San Diego city and county. Estab. 1979. Circ. 50,000. Pays on publication. Publishes ms an average of 3 months after acceptance. Byline given. Buys first North American serial rights only. Submit seasonal material 3 months in advance. Reports in 3 months. Sample copy for $4.

Nonfiction: Residential architecture and interior design (San Diego-area homes only); remodeling (must be well-designed—little do-it-yourself); residential landscape design; furniture; other features oriented towards upscale readers interested in living the cultured good life in San Diego. Articles must have local angle. Query with published clips. Length: 700-2,000 words. **Pays $50-350.**

Tips: "No out-of-town, out-of-state subject material. Most freelance work is accepted from local writers. Gear stories to the unique quality of San Diego. We try to offer only information unique to San Diego—people, places, shops, resources, etc. We plan more food and entertaining-at-home articles and more articles on garden products. We also need more in-depth reports on major architecture, environmental, and social aspects of life in San Diego and the border area."

$ $ $ $ SOUTHERN ACCENTS, Southern Progress Corp., 2100 Lakeshore Dr., Birmingham AL 35209. (205) 877-6000. Fax: (205)877-6990. E-mail: lynn_carter@spc.com. **Contact:** Lynn Carter, managing editor. "*Southern Accents* celebrates the best of the South." Estab. 1977. Circ. 318,657. Reports in 2 months.

Nonfiction: "Each issue features the finest homes and gardens along with a balance of features that reflect the affluent lifestyles of its readers, including architecture, antiques, entertaining, collecting and travel." Query with SASE, clips and photos.

N $ $ $ STYLE AT HOME, Telemedia Communications, Inc., 25 Sheppard Ave. W., Suite 100, Toronto, Ontario M2N 6S7 Canada. (416)733-7600. Fax: (416)218-3632. E-mail: letters@styleathome.com. **Contact:** Gail Johnston Hass, editor. Managing Editor: Laurie Grass. **90% freelance written.** Home decor magazine published 8 times/year. "The number one magazine choice of Canadian women aged 25 to 54 who own a home and have a serious interest in decorating. Provides an authoritative, stylish collection of inspiring and accessible interiors, decor projects; reports on style design trends and provides great take-away value." Estab. 1997. Circ. 204,000. **Pays on acceptance.** Publishes ms 3 months after acceptance. Byline given. Offers 50% kill fee. Buys first and second serial (reprint) rights. Editorial lead time 3 months. Submit seasonal material 4 months in advance. Reports in 1 months on queries, 1 week on mss. Sample copy for $1.75 plus tax. Writer's guidlines free.

Nonfiction: Humor, interview, new product. "No how-to; these are planned in-house." **Buys 100 mss/year.** Query with published clips. Length: 100-800 words. **Pays $100-1,000.** Sometimes pays expenses of writers on assignment.

Photos: State availability of photos with submission. Reviews transparencies. Negotiates payment individually. Captions required. Buys one-time rights.

Columns/Departments: Query with published clips. **Pays $100-500.**

$ $ TEXAS GARDENER, The Magazine for Texas Gardeners, by Texas Gardeners, Suntex Communications, Inc., P.O. Box 9005, Waco TX 76714-9005. (254)772-1270. E-mail: suntex@calpha.com. Editor: Chris S. Corby. **Contact:** Vivian Whatley, managing editor. **80% freelance written.** Works with a small number of new/unpublished writers each year. Bimonthly magazine covering vegetable and fruit production, ornamentals and home landscape information for home gardeners in Texas. Estab. 1981. Circ. 30,000. Pays on publication. Publishes ms an average of 4 months after acceptance. Byline given. Buys first North American serial and all rights. Submit seasonal material 6 months in advance. Reports in 2 months. Sample copy for $2.75 and SAE with 5 first-class stamps. Writer's guidelines for #10 SASE.

Nonfiction: How-to, humor, interview/profile, photo feature. "We use feature articles that relate to Texas gardeners. We also like personality profiles on hobby gardeners and professional horticulturists who are doing something unique." **Buys 50-100 mss/year.** Query with clips of published work. Length: 800-2,400 words. **Pays $50-200.**

Photos: "We prefer superb color and b&w photos; 90% of photos used are color." Send photos. Pays negotiable rates for 2¼ or 35mm color transparencies and 8×10 b&w prints and contact sheets. Model release and identification of subjects required.

Columns/Departments: Between Neighbors. **Pays $25.**

Tips: "First, be a Texan. Then come up with a good idea of interest to home gardeners in this state. Be specific. Stick to feature topics like 'How Alley Gardening Became a Texas Tradition.' Leave topics like 'How to Control Fire Blight' to the experts. High quality photos could make the difference. We would like to add several writers to our group of regular contributors and would make assignments on a regular basis. Fillers are easy to come up with in-house. We want good writers who can produce accurate and interesting copy. Frequent mistakes made by writers in completing an article assignment for us are that articles are not slanted toward Texas gardening, show inaccurate or too little gardening information or lack good writing style. We will be doing more 'people' features and articles on ornamentals."

N $ $ TIMBER HOMES ILLUSTRATED, Goodman Media Group, Inc., 1700 Broadway, New York NY 10019. (212)541-7100. Fax: (212)245-1241. Editor: Roland Sweet. **Contact:** Stacy M. Durr, managing editor. **30% freelance written.** Quarterly. "*Timber Homes Illustrated* presents full-color photo features and stories about timber-frame, log, post-and-beam and other classic wood homes. We feature stories of homeowners who've achieved their dream and encouragement for those who dream of owning a timber home." Estab. 1996. Circ. 75,000. Pays on publication. Byline given. Buys first North American serial rights or second serial (reprint) rights. Editorial lead time 4 months. Submit seasonal material 6 months in advance. Accepts simultaneous submissions. Sample copy for $3.99.

Nonfiction: Book excerpts, historical/nostalgic, how-to (building), interview/profile (architects), personal experience, photo feature, travel. Special issue: Annual Buyer's Directory. No self-promotion pieces about furniture designers, etc. **Buys 15 mss/year.** Query with published clips or send complete ms. Length: 1,200-3,000 words. **Pays $300-600.** Pays expenses of writers on assignment with limit agreed upon in advance.

Reprints: Accepts previously published submissions.

Photos: Send photos with submission. Reviews 4×5 transparencies, slides or prints. Negotiates payment individually. Captions required. Buys one-time rights.

Columns/Departments: Traditions (history of timber-framing), 1,200-3,000 words; Interior Motives (decorating timber homes), 1,200-2,200 words; Space & Place (decor ideas, timber-frame components), 1,200-2,000 words. **Buys 10 mss/year.** Query with published clips or send complete ms. **Pays $300-600.**

Tips: "We suggest including photos with your submission. Present a clear idea of where and how your story will fit into our magazine."

$ $ $ TODAY'S HOMEOWNER, 2 Park Ave., New York NY 10016. (212)779-5000. Fax: (212)725-3281. Website: http://www.homideas.com. Editor: Michael Chotiner. **Contact:** Alan Kearney. **50% freelance written.** Prefers to work with published/established writers. "If it's good, and it fits the type of material we're currently publishing, we're interested, whether writer is new or experienced." Magazine published 10 times/year for the active home and car owner. "Articles emphasize an active, home-oriented lifestyle. Includes information useful for maintenance, repair and renovation to the home and family car. Information on how to buy, how to select products useful to homeowners/car owners. Emphasis in home-oriented articles is on good design, inventive solutions to styling and space problems, useful home-workshop projects." Estab. 1928. Circ. 1,000,000. **Pays on acceptance.** Publishes ms an average of 6 months after acceptance. Byline given. Buys first North American serial rights. Reports in 3 months. Query.

Nonfiction: Feature articles relating to homeowner/car owner, 1,500-2,500 words. "This may include personal home-renovation projects, professional advice on interior design, reports on different or unusual construction methods, energy-related subjects, outdoor/backyard projects, etc. No high-tech subjects such as aerospace, electronics, photography or military hardware. Most of our automotive features are written by experts in the field, but fillers, tips, how-to repair, or modification articles on the family car are welcome. Articles on construction, tool use, refinishing techniques, etc., are also sought. **Pays $300 minimum for features**; fees based on number of printed pages, photos accompanying mss., etc." Query only; *no unsolicited mss*. Pays expenses of writers on assignment.

Photos: Photos should accompany mss. Pays $600 and up for transparencies for cover. Inside color: $300/1 page, $500/2, $700/3, etc. Captions and model releases required.

Tips: "The most frequent mistake made by writers in completing an article assignment for *Home Mechanix* is not taking the time to understand its editorial focus and special needs."

N $ $ $ WALLS, WINDOWS & FLOORS, Woman's Day Special Interest Publications, Hachette-Filipacchi Magazines, 1633 Broadway, New York NY 10019. Fax: (212)767-5612. E-mail: wdspecials@aol.com. **Contact:** Janice Wright, managing editor. Editor: Carolyn Gatto. Consumer magazine published 3 times a year covering home decorating ideas focused on walls, windows, and floors. **Pays on acceptance**. Publishes ms an average of 3 months after acceptance. Byline given. Offers up to 25% kill fee. Buys first North American serial or second serial (printing) rights. Editorial lead time 6 months. Submit seasonal material 10 months in advance. Reports in 2 months. Sample copy not available; writer's guidelines for #10 SASE.

Nonfiction: How-to (floor, walls and window treatments), interview/profile (designers), new product, photo features, technical (information about paint, wallpaper, floor coverings). **Buys 40 mss/year**. Query with published clips. Length: 250-1,000 words. Payment varies. Sometimes pays expenses of writers on assignment.

Reprints: Accepts previously published submissions.

Photos: Send photos with query. Model releases required. Buys one-time rights.

Columns/Departments: Query with published clips. Payment varies based on length, writer, and level/amount of research required.

Tips: "Tips from professionals, how-to's and timesaving techniques make this a hands-on magazine that deals with all sorts of ways to color, cover, and decorate these surfaces of the home. Many ideas are presented in a problem/solving format so readers can easily achieve the looks that express their own personal style. Product and trend information keep readers current. Send a brief, clear query letter with relevant clips, and be patient. Before and after photos are very helpful."

HUMOR

Publications listed here specialize in gaglines or prose humor, some for readers and others for performers or speakers. Other publications that use humor can be found in nearly every category in this book. Some have special needs for major humor pieces; some use humor as fillers; many others are interested in material that meets their ordinary fiction or nonfiction requirements but also has a humorous slant. The majority of humor articles must be submitted as complete manuscripts on speculation because editors usually can't know from a query whether or not the piece will be right for them.

$ FUNNY TIMES, A Monthly Humor Review, Funny Times, Inc., P.O. Box 18530, Cleveland Heights OH 44118. (216)371-8600. Fax: (216)371-8696. E-mail: ft@funnytimes.com. Website: http://www.funnytimes.com. **Contact:** Raymond Lesser, Susan Wolpert, editors. **10% freelance written.** Monthly tabloid for humor. "*Funny Times* is a monthly

review of America's funniest cartoonists and writers. We are the *Reader's Digest* of modern American humor with a progressive/peace-oriented/environmental/politically activist slant." Estab. 1985. Circ. 50,000. Pays on publication. Publishes ms an average of 3 months after acceptance. Byline given. Buys one-time or second serial (reprint) rights. Editorial lead time 2 months. Accepts simultaneous submissions. Reports in 3 months on mss. Sample copy for $3 or 9×12 SAE with 4 first-class stamps. Writer's guidelines for #10 SASE.
Nonfiction: Essays (funny), humor, interview/profile, opinion (humorous), personal experience (absolutely funny). "We only publish humor or interviews with funny people (comedians, comic actors, cartoonists, etc.). Everything we publish is very funny. If your piece isn't extremely funny then don't bother to send it. Don't send us anything that's not outrageously funny. Don't send anything that other people haven't already read and told you they laughed so hard they peed their pants." **Buys 36 mss/year.** Send complete ms. Length: 1,000 words. **Pays $50 minimum for unsolicited articles.**
Reprints: Accepts previously published submissions.
Fiction: Humorous. **Buys 6 mss/year.** Query with published clips. Length: 500 words. **Pays $50-150.**
Fillers: Short humor. **Buys 6/year. Pays $20.**
Tips: "Send us a small packet (1-3 items) of only your very funniest stuff. If this makes us laugh we'll be glad to ask for more. We particularly welcome previously published material that has been well-received elsewhere."

$ LATEST JOKES, P.O. Box 23304, Brooklyn NY 11202-0066. (718)855-5057. **Contact:** Robert Makinson, editor. Estab. 1974. **20% freelance written.** Bimonthly newsletter of humor for TV and radio personalities, comedians and professional speakers. **Pays on acceptance.** Byline given. Buys all rights. Reports in 2 months. Sample copy for $3 and SASE.

- The editor says jokes for public speakers are most needed.

Nonfiction: Humor (short jokes). "No way-out, vulgar humor. Jokes about human tragedy also unwelcome." Send up to 20 jokes with SASE. **Pays $1-3/joke.**
Tips: "No famous personality jokes. Clever statements are not enough. Be original and surprising. Our emphasis is on jokes for professional speakers."

$ $ NEW HUMOR MAGAZINE, New Communications, Inc. Publishers, P.O. Box 216, Lafayette Hill PA 19444. Fax: (215)487-2670. E-mail: Newhumor@aol.com. **Contact:** Edward Savaria Jr., editor-in-chief. Managing Editor: Suzanne Savaria. **90% freelance written.** Quarterly magazine covering humor. "Tasteful, intelligent and funny. Looking for clean humor in a sense that funny stories, jokes, poems and cartoons do not have to sink to sexist, bathroom or ethnic subjects to be humorous." Estab. 1994. Circ. 9,500. Pays on publication. Publishes ms an average of 4 months after acceptance. Byline given. Buys first North American serial, second serial (reprint) or simultaneous rights. Editorial lead time 4 months. Submit seasonal material 4 months in advance. Accepts simultaneous submissions. Reports in 1 month on queries. Sample copy for $3.50. Writer's guidelines for #10 SASE.
Nonfiction: Book excerpts, essays, humor, interview/profile, new product (humorous), travel. **Buys 12 mss/year.** Send complete ms. Length: 250-1,000 words. **Pays $25-85.**
Reprints: Send photocopy of article or short story or typed ms with rights for sale noted. Pays same amount paid for an original article or story.
Columns/Departments: Open to Column Ideas, 250-750 words. **Pays $25-85.**
Fiction: Humorous, novel excerpts. **Buys 40 mss/year.** Send complete ms. Length: 25-1,500 words. **Pays $25-85.**
Poetry: Avant-garde, free verse, haiku, light verse. **Buys 30 poems/year.** Submit maximum 10 poems. Length: 1-50 lines. **Pays $7-30.**
Fillers: Anecdotes, short humor. **Buys 20/year.** Length: 25-300 words. **Pays $15-50.**
Tips: "If you think it's funny—it might be. Test stories on friends, see if they laugh. Don't be afraid to send odd humor—something completely different."

INFLIGHT

Most major inflight magazines cater to business travelers and vacationers who will be reading, during the flight, about the airline's destinations and other items of general interest.

$ ABOARD MAGAZINE, 100 Almeria Ave., Suite 220, Coral Gables FL 33134. Fax: (305)441-9739. Associate Editor: Reynaldo Alés. **Contact:** Vanessa Otero, editorial assistant. **40% freelance written.** Bimonthly bilingual inflight magazine designed to reach travelers to and from Latin America, carried on 11 major Latin-American airlines. Estab. 1976. Circ. 180,000. Pays on publication. Byline given. Buys one-time or simultaneous rights. Accepts simultaneous submissions. Reports in 2 months.
Nonfiction: General interest, new product, business, science, art, fashion, photo feature, technical, travel. "No controversial or political material." Query with SASE. **Buys 50 mss/year.** Length: 1,200-1,500 words. **Pays $100-150.**
Reprints: Send photocopy of article or typed ms with rights for sale noted and information about when and where the article previously appeared. Pays 0-50% of amount paid for an original article.
Photos: Send photos with submission. Reviews 35mm slides or transparencies only. Offers no additional payment for photos accepted with ms. Offers $20/photo minimum. Identification of subjects required. Buys one-time rights.
Fillers: Facts. **Buys 6/year.** Length: 800-1,200 words. **Pays $100.**

Tips: "Send article with photos. We need lots of travel material on Chile, Ecuador, Bolivia, El Salvador, Honduras, Guatemala, Uruguay, Nicaragua, Paraguay, Brazil."

$ $ ABOVE & BEYOND, The Magazine of the North, Above & Beyond Ltd., Box 2348, Yellowknife, Northwest Territory X1A 2P7 Canada. (867)873-2299. Fax: (867)873-2295. E-mail: abeyond@internorth.com. **Contact:** Annelies Pool, editor. **100% freelance written.** Quarterly inflight magazine for First Air, Canada's 3rd largest airline serving Northern Canada. Estab. 1988. Circ. 30,000. Pays on publication. Publishes ms an average of 4 months after acceptance. Byline given. Offers 50% kill fee. Buys first North American serial rights. Editorial lead time 8 months. Submit seasonal material 1 year in advance. Sample copy and writer's guidelines free.
Nonfiction: "We are interested in feature articles pertaining to: political, social and economic activities from a northern perspective; outdoor and recreational activities; profile pieces on northern individuals, communities and destinations; wildlife, fishing and hunting; travel features. We don't want articles about new products being used in the North or any articles that don't concern the North." **Buys 20 mss/year.** Send complete ms via mail (include SASE) or e-mail. Length: 1,000-1,500 words. **Pays 25¢/word.** Sometimes pays expenses of writers on assignment.
Reprints: Send tearsheet of article with information about when and where the article previously appeared. Pay varies.
Photos: Send photos with submission. Reviews color transparencies and prints. No b&w. Pays $25/photo. Captions, identification of subjects required. Buys one-time rights.
Tips: "Submit clean, insightful articles about life in the North that are within our length requirements. A large part of our readership is in Northern Canada so we don't want any 'Gee, whiz, aren't things different in the North' type of articles. We're looking for stories that paint a picture. Excellent photographs are essential, yes, but don't rely on these to provide your visual images. Your words should do this so that the photos and text work harmonize."

⊘ **AMERICA WEST AIRLINES MAGAZINE** does not accept freelance submissions at this time.

$ $ $ AMERICAN WAY, P.O. Box 619640, Mail Drop 5598, Dallas/Fort Worth Airport TX 75261-9640. (817)967-1804. Fax: (817)967-1571. **Contact:** John H. Ostdick, editor-in-chief. Managing Editor: Elaine Srnka. **98% freelance written.** Works exclusively with published/established writers. Biweekly inflight magazine for passengers flying with American Airlines. Estab. 1966. **Pays on acceptance.** Publishes ms an average of 4 months after acceptance. Buys first serial rights. Reports in 5 months.
Fiction: Nancy Stevens, associate editor. Length: 2,500 words maximum. **Pays $1,100.**

$ THE AUSTRALIAN WAY, Qantas Inflight Magazine, BRW Media, G.P.O. Box 55A, Melbourne, Victoria 3001 Australia. Fax: (03)96420852. E-mail: tbrentnall@brw.fairfax.com.au. **Contact:** Tom Brentnall, editor. **80% freelance written.** Monthly magazine catering to Qantas Airways passengers travelling on both internal Australian routes and overseas. It provides articles on international events, travel, the arts, science and technology, sport, natural history and humor. The focus is on elegant writing and high-quality photography. There is a heavy emphasis on Austrialian personalities, culture and lifestyle." Estab. 1993. Circ. 1,600,000. Pays on publication. Publishes ms an average of 2 months after acceptance. Byline given. Buys first rights. Editorial lead time 2 months. Submit seasonal material 3 months in advance.
Nonfiction: General interest, historical/nostalgic, interview/profile, photo feature, travel. Query with published clips. **Buys 50 mss/year.** Length: 800-1,500 words. **Pays $500 (Australian)/1,000 words.**
Fiction: Publishes novel excerpts (Australian authors only).
Photos: State availability of photos with submission. Reviews transparencies and prints. Negotiates payment individually. Captions, identification of subjects required. Buys all rights if commissioned; one-time rights if unsolicited.
Tips: "Guidelines for writers available on request. Writers should entertain as well as inform both an Australian and international readership. Features can be of general interest, about personalities, or on cultural, business or sporting interests. The magazine tends to avoid travel 'destination' pieces *per se*, though it carries appropriate stories that use these locations as backdrops."

$ $ $ $ CONTINENTAL, The Magazine of Continental Airlines, Cadmus Custom Publishing, 101 Huntington Ave., 13th Floor, Boston MA 02199. (617)424-7700. Fax: (617)437-7714. E-mail: beaulieuk@cadmus.com. Website: http://www.cadmuscustom.com. Editor: Anne Studabaker. Managing Editor: Heather Sargent. **Contact:** Ken Beaulieu, executive editor. 80% freelance written. Monthly inflight magazine "for a business traveler audience. We look for the person behind the company." Estab. 1986. Circ. 400,000. Pays 30 days from invoice. Publishes ms 3 months after acceptance. Byline given. Offers 25% kill fee. Buys first rights. Editorial lead time 4-6 months. Submit seasonal material 6 months in advance. Reports in 1 month on queries. Sample copy and writer's guidelines free.
Nonfiction: Business executives, destinations, entertainers and athletes, luxuries, social and political leaders. **Buys 45 mss/year.** Query with published clips and SASE. Length: 100-1,500 words. **Pays $1/word,** but occasionally varies. Pays expenses of writers on assignment.
Reprints: Send photocopy of article and information about when and where the article previously appeared. Pays 25% of amount paid for an original article.
Photos: State availability of photos with submission. Reviews transparencies. Negotiates payment individually.
Columns/Departments: Gusto (food and culture); Time Out (outdoor sports); Room Service (hotel reviews); Executive Edge (products and services for the frequent traveler); City Focus (development issues in Continental destinations); Personal Finance; Mind of the Manager (issues); Reviews in Brief (books, software and websites); Fun (crosswords,

games and cartoons). **Buys 60 mss/year.** Length: 100-1,500 words. Query with SASE.
Tips: "Consult a recent issue of the magazine for content and style. We look for timely hooks."

$ $ $ HEMISPHERES, Pace Communications for United Airlines, 1301 Carolina St., Greensboro NC 27401. (336)378-6065. **Contact:** Randy Johnson, editor. **95% freelance written.** Monthly magazine for the educated, sophisticated business and recreational frequent traveler on an airline that spans the globe. Estab. 1992. Circ. 500,000. **Pays on acceptance**. Publishes ms 3 months after acceptance. Byline given. Offers 20% kill fee. Usually buys first, worldwide rights. Editorial lead time 8 months. Submit seasonal material 8 months in advance. Reports in 10 weeks on queries; 4 months on mss. Sample copy for $5. Writer's guidelines for #10 SASE.

- Ranked as one of the best markets for freelance writers in *Writer's Yearbook* magazine's annual "Top 100 Markets," January 1998.

Nonfiction: General interest, humor, personal experience. "Keeping 'global' in mind, we look for topics that reflect a modern appreciation of the world's cultures and environment. No 'What I did (or am going to do) on a trip to.' . . ." Query with published clips. Length: 500-3,000 words. **Pays 50¢/word and up.**
Photo: State availability of photos with submission. Reviews transparencies "only when we request them." Negotiates payment individually. Captions, model releases, identification of subjects required. Buys one-time rights.
Columns/Departments: Making a Difference (Q&A format interview with world leaders, movers, and shakers. A 500-600 word introduction anchors the interview. We want to profile an international mix of men and women representing a variety of topics or issues, but all must truly be making a difference. No puffy celebrity profiles.); On Location (A snappy selection of one or two sentences, "25 Fascinating Facts" that are obscure, intriguing, or travel-service-oriented items that the reader never knew about a city, state, country or destination.); Executive Secrets (Things that top executives know); Case Study (Business strategies of international companies or organizations. No lionizations of CEOs. Strategies should be the emphasis. "We want international candidates."); Weekend Breakway (Takes us just outside a major city after a week of business for a physically active, action-packed weekend. This isn't a sedentary "getaway" at a "property."); Roving Gourmet (Insider's guide to interesting eating in major city, resort area, or region. The slant can be anything from ethnic to expensive; not just "best." The four featured eateries span a spectrum from "hole in the wall," to "expense account lunch" and on to "big deal dining."); Collecting (Photo with lengthy caption or occasional 800-word story on collections and collecting that can emphasize travel); Eye on Sports (Global look at anything of interest in sports); Vintage Traveler (Options for mature, experienced travelers); Savvy Shopper (Insider's tour of best places in the world to shop. *Savvy Shopper* steps beyond all those stories that just mention the great shopping at a particular destination. A shop-by-shop, gallery-by-gallery tour of the best places in the world."); Science and Technology alternates with Computers (Substantive, insightful story. Not just another column on audio components or software. No gift guides!"); Aviation Journal (For those fascinated with aviation. *Aviation Journal* is an opportunity to enthrall all of those fliers who are fascinated with aviation. Topics range widely. A fall 1998 redesign of the magazine ushered in a reader-service-oriented "Great Airports" guide series, the classic DC-3, airport identifiers, Of Grape And Grain (Wine and spirits with emphasis on education, not one-upmanship); Show Business (Films, music and entertainment); Musings (Humor or just curious musings); Quick Quiz (Tests to amuse and educate); Travel News (Brief, practical, invaluable, trend-oriented tips); Book Beat (Tackles topics like the Wodehouse Society, the birth of a book, the competition between local bookshops and national chains. Please, no review proposals. Slant—what the world's reading—residents explore how current best sellers tell us what their country is thinking.). Length: 1,400 words. Query with published clips. **Pays 50¢/word and up.**
Fiction: Adventure, humorous, mainstream, slice-of-life vignettes. **Buys 4 mss/year.** Query. Length: 500-2,000 words. **Pays 50¢/word and up.**
Tips: "We increasingly require writers of 'destination' pieces or departments to 'live whereof they write.' Increasingly want to hear from U.S., U.K. or other English speaking/writing journalists (business & travel) who reside outside the U.S. in Europe, South America, Central America and the Pacific Rim—all areas that United flies."

"We're not looking for writers who aim at the inflight market. *Hemispheres* broke the fluffy mold of that tired domestic genre. Our monthly readers are a global mix on the cutting edge of the global economy and culture. They don't need to have the world filtered by US writers. We want a Hong Kong restaurant writer to speak for that city's eateries, so we need English speaking writers around the globe. That's the 'insider' story our reader's respect. We use resident writers for departments such as Roving Gourmet, Savvy Shopper, On Location, 3 Perfect Days (which became a cable TV program in September 1998) and Weekend Breakaway, but authoritative writers can roam in features. Sure we cover the US, but with a global view: No 'in this country' phraseology. 'Too American' is a frequent complaint for queries. We use UK English spellings in articles that speak from that tradition and we specify costs in local currency first before US dollars. Basically, all of above serves the realization that today, 'global' begins with respect for 'local.' That approach permits a wealth of ways to present culture, travel and business for a wide readership. We anchor that with a reader service mission that grounds everything in 'how to do it.' "

N MIDWEST EXPRESS MAGAZINE, Paradigm Communications Group, 2701 First Ave., Suite 250, Seattle WA 98121. **Contact:** Mike Olson, editor. **90% freelance written.** Bimonthly magazine for Midwest Express Airlines. "Positive depiction of the changing economy and culture of the US, plus travel and leisure features." Estab. 1993. Circ. 32,000. Pays on publication. Byline given. Buys first North American serial rights. Editorial lead time 9 months. Reports in 6 weeks on queries. Do not phone or fax. Sample copy for 9×12 SASE. Writer's guidelines free.

- *Midwest Express* continues to look for *sophisticated* travel and golf writing.

INSIDER REPORT

Hemispheres: "an American magazine that lets the world speak for itself"

Randy Johnson

You could accuse Randy Johnson of having his head in the clouds, and he wouldn't deny it. But the editor of United Airlines inflight magazine *Hemispheres* has his feet firmly planted on the ground. The magazine publishes 500,000 copies a month, and has an estimated 2 million readers every month. Johnson's success is reflected in a host of awards for graphic design and travel writing, and in the growing respectability the magazine has brought to the genre.

"When *Hemispheres* was launched, 'inflight' magazine was a derisive term," Johnson says. "People saw it as a company newsletter . . . something that just served the ends of the airline and advertisers." Johnson challenged that idea from the very first issue in 1992, with sophisticated graphic design, a focus on art and culture, and a new editorial approach.

"Rather than look at inflight as a genre of editorial, we view it as a method of delivery," he says. The first step was to look at the audience and focus on how to serve their interests. Johnson says in many respects, the audience is an editor's dream. Primarily business people and regular travelers, Johnson says they are "educated, affluent, often the upper echelon of their profession; a sophisticated audience." And most importantly, it is a global audience. Johnson says inflight magazines have the potential, if they accept the challenge, to be on the cutting edge of global media.

"Globalization is a popular term these days" he notes. "Globalization of business; globalization of culture." But Johnson says that doesn't mean simply sharing an American perspective. Because United is an international airline, Johnson's goal is to provide material that's just as relevant to a French reader as an American business traveler. He wants *Hemispheres* to be "an American magazine that lets the world speak for itself."

Johnson says that global perspective is difficult for American writers, who often assume that because American culture is so widespread, the American perspective is equally dominant. That "global perspective" means the magazine probably wouldn't cover some American-only topics, like NASCAR racing, but takes a different tack on subjects with a wider audience. Johnson says women's basketball is a perfect illustration of the mental shift required to "write globally."

"Other American magazines might cover the new women's basketball leagues in terms of men's basketball in the U.S." he says. "But *Hemispheres* would cast the recent success of the ABL and WNBA against the global success of women's professional basketball elsewhere around the world."

Johnson says many of the magazine's best writers are foreign nationals writing about their own countries. *Hemispheres*'s most popular series, "Three Perfect Days," provides

INSIDER REPORT, *Johnson*

a detailed look at the culture and history of a city like Dublin, along with adetailed, three-day itinerary of sights. While the idea has been copied by other magazines, Johnson says *Hemispheres*'s insistence on using local writers gives the articles a verisimilitude the others lack.

"It's how a local would put together a tour of their hometown," he explains, "so when you're finished, you've not only seen the major attractions, but the behind-the-scenes and most current things as well, the kind of things that haven't made the tourist guides yet." He says he receives thousands of reprint requests every month for the "Three Perfect Days" series, precisely because it gives readers a big picture perspective, almost a lifestyle appreciation for a new city. "It's not as if we're reporting on the oddities of some other place for an American audience" he says. "It's very much a dialogue between cultures." The idea has proved so popular the magazine plans to release bound volumes of the series, and a video version for cable TV is in the works.

Johnson says the magazine has received high praise for its range of topics and the quality of writing. He says a London newspaper recently evaluated the world's inflight magazines; *Hemispheres* was the only American publication included. While the review praised the high caliber of writing, he was most pleased with a throwaway comment at the end of the review. "They said, 'this is a rare thing; a magazine you can take from the seat back, spend more than an hour with, and find ample to interest you.' "

The magazine also has an emphasis on art. The cover of each issue is uncluttered poster art, and every month features a different artist's portfolio. Articles tend to focus on business and travel topics, but Johnson is open to anything of interest to the business and frequent flyer. He says the magazine has a hard time getting appropriate queries and reminds would-be freelancers to remember the basics; be familiar with the topic and the magazine's orientation before you submit article ideas.

"You always hear 'be familiar with the magazine before you submit,' " he says. "And when you're working hard, trying to make a living, sitting down for several hours with several issues seems like a waste of time. Believe me, it's not." Johnson says he welcomes American writers, but they need to know their subject matter. Because of the magazine's global emphasis, he says he's unlikely to consider a proposal from a Milwaukee writer about Hong Kong. Johnson says the magazine doesn't discourage American freelancers, but says, "write about what you know."

Johnson also stresses that writers should be familiar enough with the magazine and its departments to know where their article would fit in, and to include that in a query letter. He says a freelancer who has obviously done his homework is more likely to get published than one who simply says, "I have a great idea; you tell me where it fits in." Johnson, who worked as a freelance writer for years, says writers would do well to take a "customer service" approach to queries. "Essentially, [the editor] is the customer," he notes. "You need to sell us on an idea, and convince us that it will work, before you can expect us to buy a story."

—Alison Holm

Nonfiction: Business, travel, sports and leisure. No humor or how-to. "Need good ideas for golf articles in spring." **Buys 20-25 mss/year.** Query with published clips and résumé. Length: 250-3,000 words. **Pays $100 minimum.** Sometimes pays expenses of writers on assignment.
Columns/Department: Preview (arts and events), 200-400 words; Portfolio (business), 200-500 words. **Buys 12-15 mss/year.** Query with published clips. **Pays $100-150.**
Tips: "Article ideas *must* encompass areas within the airline's route system. We buy quality writing from reliable writers. Editorial philosophy emphasizes innovation and positive outlook. Do not send manuscripts unless you have no clips."

$ $ $ $ SKY, Pace Communications for Delta Air Lines, 1301 Carolina St., Greensboro NC 27401. E-mail: skymag@aol.com. **Contact:** Mickey McLean, managing editor. Published monthly for business and leisure travelers aboard Delta Air Lines. **Pays on acceptance.** Byline given. Offers 25% kill fee. Buys first worldwide serial rights. Reports in 2-4 months on queries. Sample copy for $7.50.
Nonfiction: "Needs timely, interesting and informative articles on business, technology, travel, sports and humor." **Buys 48 mss/year.** Query with published clips. Length: 1,500-3,000 words. **Pays $1,500-3,000.** Pays the expenses of writers on assignment.
Columns/Departments: Buys 180 mss/year. Query with published clips. **Pays $1,000-1,500.** Length: 1,000-1,500 words.
Fillers: Length: 100-400 words. **Pays $75-300.**
Tips: "*USA Today* said *Sky* is 'redefining inflight magazines.' We don't want run-of-the-mill inflight articles; we want fresh—sometimes humorous—takes on business, technology, travel and sports."

$ $ $ $ SOUTHWEST AIRLINES SPIRIT, 4333 Amon Carter Blvd., Fort Worth TX 76155-9616. (817)967-1804. Fax: (817)967-1571. E-mail: 102615.376@compuserve.com. Website: http://www.spiritmag.com. **Contact:** John Clark, editor. Monthly magazine for passengers on Southwest Airlines. Estab. 1992. Circ. 280,000. **Pays on acceptance**. Byline given. Buys first North American serial and electronic rights. Reports in 1 month on queries.
Nonfiction: "Seeking accessible, entertaining, relevant and timely glimpses of people, places, products and trends in the regions Southwest Airlines serves. Newsworthy/noteworthy topics; well-researched and multiple source only. Experienced magazine professionals only. Business, travel, technology, sports and lifestyle (food, fitness and culture) are some of the topics covered in *Spirit*." Special issues: Destination: Little Rock, Restaurants: Steakhouses, Estate Planning, Nutrition: Weight Food (September 1998); Destination: Undertermined, Restaurants: French, Financial Advisers, Fitness: Quickies (October 1998); Destination: San Diego, Hotel Dining, Housing Affordability, Nutrition: Organic (November 1998); *Spirit's* Annual Holiday Feature, Destination: Las Vegas, Restaurants: Middle Eastern, College Loans, Fitness: Sick Workouts (December 1998). **Buys 48 mss/year.** Query with published clips. Length: 2,500 words. **Pays $2,000.** Pays expenses of writers on assignment.
Columns/Departments: Buys 21 mss/year. Query with published clips. Length: 1,200-2,200 words. Pay varies.
Fillers: Buys 12/year. Length: 250 words. Pay varies.

N $ $ SPIRIT OF ALOHA, The Inflight Magazine of Aloha Airlines and Island Air, Honolulu Publishing Co. Ltd., 36 Merchant St., Honolulu HI 96701. (808)524-7400. Fax: (808)531-2306. E-mail: honpub@aloha.net. **Contact:** Janice Otaguro, editor. **50% freelance written**. Monthly magazine covering visitor activities/destinations and Hawaii culture and history. "Although we are an inflight magazine for an international airline, we try to keep our editorial as fresh and lively residents as much as for visitors." Estab. 1978. Circ. 60,000. **Pays on acceptance**. Publishes ms an average of 2 months after acceptance. Byline given. Buys first (one-time) rights. Editorial lead time 2 months. Submit seasonal material 2 months in advance. Reports in 2 months. Sample copy and writer's guidelines free.
Nonfiction: Book excerpts, general interest, historical/nostalgic, interview/profile, photo feature, travel. All must related to Hawaii. No poetry, "How I spent my vacation in Hawaii" type pieces. **Buys 24 mss/year**. Query with published clips. Length: 1,500-2,500 words. **Pays $400**. Sometimes pay expenses of writers on assignment.
Photos: State availability of photos with submission. Reviews transparencies. Negotiates payment individually. Captions, model releases and identification of subjects required. Buys one-time rights.

$ $ $ $ TWA AMBASSADOR, 4636 E. Elwood St., Suite 5, Phoenix AZ 85040-1963. **Contact:** Ellen Alperstein, consulting editor. Monthly magazine for foreign and domestic TWA passengers. Estab. 1968. Circ. 223,000. **Pays on acceptance**. Byline given. Offers 25% kill fee. Buys first rights. Reports in 6 weeks on queries. Sample copy for 9×12 SASE plus $2.02 postage. Writer's guidelines for #10 SASE.
Nonfiction: "We need solid journalism stylishly rendered. We look for first-rate reporting by professionals with a track record. Also, essays and commentaries, the first one usually on spec. Stories cover a range of general interest topics—business, sports, entertainment, food, media, money, family and more. No traditional travel stories." **Buys 40-45 mss/year.** Query with published clips. Length: 700-2,500 words. **Pays 75¢-$1/word.** Pays expenses of writers on assignment.
Columns/Departments: Buys 45-50 mss/year. Query with published clips. **Pays 75¢-$1/word.** Length: 500-1,200 words.
Fiction: "We accept fiction but buy very little."
Tips: "We have a small staff and a huge volume of mail—please query with SASE."

$ $ $ $ U.S. AIRWAYS ATTACHÉ, Pace Communications, 1301 Carolina St., Greensboro NC 27401. Fax: (336)378-8278. E-mail: AttacheAir@aol.com. **Contact:** Lance Elko, managing editor. Editor: Jay Heinrichs. Editorial Assistant: Kendra Gemma. **90% freelance written.** Monthly magazine for travelers on U.S. Airways. Estab. 1997. Circ. 441,000. **Pays on acceptance**. Publishes ms an average of 4 months after acceptance. Byline given. Offers 25% kill fee. Buys first global serial rights for most articles. Editorial lead time 3 months. No simultaneous submissions. Reports in 1 month on queries. Sample copy for $5. Writer's guidelines for #10 SASE.

Nonfiction: Essays, food, general interest, lifestyle, sports, travel. "A 1,500-word feature called *The Insider's Guide to the World* anchors the main editorial well. This image-heavy piece appeals to the business traveler who wants to find the lesser-known restaurants, shops, and attractions in a different major business city each month. The writer should be a resident of or live close to the featured city. Other features are also highly visual, focusing on some unusual or unique angle of travel, food, business, or other topic approved by an *Attaché* editor." **Buys 120-150 mss/year.** Query with published clips. Length: 350-2,500 words. Pay varies with freelancers' degree of experience and expertise. Sometimes pays expenses of writers on assignment.

Photos: State availability of photos with submission. Reviews contact sheets, negatives, transparencies. Negotiates payment individually. Model releases, identification of subjects required. Buys one-time rights.

Columns/Departments: *Passions* includes several topics such as "Vices," "Food," "Golf," "Sporting," "Shelf Life," and "Things That Go"; *Paragons* features short lists of the best in a particular field or category, as well as 400-word pieces describing the best of something—for example, the best home tool, the best ice cream in Paris, and the best reading library. Each piece should lend itself to highly visual art; *Informed Sources* are departments of expertise and first-person accounts. They include "How It Works," "Keys to the City," "Home Front," "Improvement," "To Market," and "Genius at Work." **Buys 50-75 mss/year.** Query with published clips. Pay varies with freelancers' degree of experience and expertise.

Tips: "We look for cleverly written, entertaining articles with a unique angle, particularly pieces that focus on 'the best of' something. Study the magazine for content, style and tone. Queries for story ideas should be to the point and presented clearly. Any correspondence should include SASE."

$ $ $ WASHINGTON FLYER MAGAZINE, #111, 1707 L St., NW, Washington DC 20036. Fax: (202)331-7311. **Contact:** Melanie McLeod, associate editor. **80% freelance written.** Bimonthly inflight magazine for business and pleasure travelers at Washington National and Washington Dulles International airports INSI. "Primarily affluent, well-educated audience that flies frequently in and out of Washington, DC." Estab. 1989. Circ. 180,000. **Pays on acceptance.** Byline given. Buys first North American rights. Submit seasonal material 4 months in advance. Reports in approximately 10 weeks. Sample copy and writer's guidelines for 9×12 SAE with $2 postage.

Nonfiction: General interest, interview/profile, travel, business. One international destination feature per issue, determined 6 months in advance. One feature per issue on aspect of life in Washington. **Buys 20-30 mss/year.** Query with published clips and SASE. Length: 800-1,200 words. **Pays $500-900.**

Photos: State availability of photos. Reviews negatives and transparencies (almost always color). Considers additional payment for top-quality photos accepted with ms. Identification of subjects required. Buys one-time rights.

Columns/Departments: Business, Real Estate, Travel, Hospitality, Airports and Airlines, Restaurants, Shopping. Query with SASE. Length: 800-1,200 words. **Pays $500-900.**

Tips: "Know the Washington market and issues relating to frequent business/pleasure travelers as we move toward a global economy. With a bimonthly publiclation schedule it's important that stories remain viable as possible during the magazine's two-month 'shelf life.' No telephone calls, please."

JUVENILE

Just as children change and grow, so do juvenile magazines. Children's magazine editors stress that writers must read recent issues. A wide variety of issues are addressed in the numerous magazines for the baby boom echo. Respecting nature, developing girls' self-esteem and establishing good healthy habits all find an editorial niche. This section lists publications for children up to age 12. Magazines for young people 13-19 appear in the Teen and Young Adult category. Many of the following publications are produced by religious groups and, where possible, the specific denomination is given. A directory for juvenile markets, *Children's Writer's and Illustrator's Market*, is available from Writer's Digest Books.

$ $ AMERICAN GIRL, Pleasant Company Publications, 8400 Fairway Place, Middleton WI 53562. E-mail: readermail@ag.pleasantco.com. Website: http://www.americangirl.com. Editor: Sarah Jane Brian. Managing Editor: Julie Finlay. **Contact:** Magazine Department Assistant. **5% freelance written.** Bimonthly 4-color magazine covering hobbies, crafts, profiles and history of interest to girls ages 8-12. Estab. 1992. Circ. 750,000. **Pays on acceptance**. Byline given for larger features, not departments. Offers 50% kill fee. Buys all rights, occasionally first North American serial rights. Editorial lead time 6 months. Submit seasonal material 6 months in advance. Accepts simultaneous submissions. Reports in 3 months on queries. Sample copy for 9×12 SAE with $1.93 postage. Writer's guidelines for #10 SASE.

• Mattel Inc., manufacturer of Barbie, bought Pleasant Company. Best opportunity for freelancers is the Girls Express section.

Nonfiction: General contemporary interest, how-to. No historical profiles about obvious female heroines—Annie Oakley, Amelia Earhart; no romance or dating. **Buys 3-10 mss/year.** Query with published clips. Length: 100-800 words, depending on whether its a feature or for a specific department. **Pays $300 minimum for feature articles.** Pays expenses of writers on assignment.

Reprints: Accepts reprints of previously published fiction.

Photos: State availability of photos with submission. "We prefer to shoot." Buys all rights.

Fiction: Adventure, condensed novels, ethnic, historical, humorous, slice-of-life vignettes. No romance, science fiction, fantasy. **Buys 6 mss/year.** Query with published clips. Length: 2,300 words maximum. **Pays $500 minimum.**

Columns/Departments: Girls Express (short profiles of girls with unusual and interesting hobbies that other girls want to read about), 175 words, query; Giggle Gang (puzzles, games, etc—especially looking for seasonal).

$ BABYBUG, Carus Corporation, P.O. Box 300, Peru IL 61354. (815)224-6656. Editor-in-Chief: Marianne Carus. **Contact:** Paula Morrow, editor. **50% freelance written.** Board-book magazine published every 6 weeks. "*Babybug* is 'the listening and looking magazine for infants and toddlers,' intended to be read aloud by a loving adult to foster a love of books and reading in young children ages 6 months-2 years." Estab. 1994. Circ. 45,000. Pays on publication. Publishes ms an average of 18 months after acceptance. Byline given. Buys first, second serial (reprint) or all rights. Editorial lead time 8-10 months. Submit seasonal material 1 year in advance. Accepts simultaneous submissions, if so noted. Sample copy for $5. Writer's guidelines for #10 SASE.

Nonfiction: General interest and "World Around You" for infants and toddlers. **Buys 5-10 mss/year.** Send complete ms. Length: 1-10 words. **Pays $25.**

Fiction: Adventure, humorous and anything for infants and toddlers. **Buys 5-10 mss/year.** Send complete ms. Length: 2-8 short sentences. **Pays $25.**

Poetry: Buys 8-10 poems/year. Submit maximum 5 poems. Length: 2-8 lines. **Pays $25.**

Tips: "Imagine having to read your story or poem—out loud—fifty times or more! That's what parents will have to do. Babies and toddlers demand, 'Read it again!' Your material must hold up under repetition."

$ $ BOYS' LIFE, Boy Scouts of America, P.O. Box 152079, Irving TX 75015-2079. **Contact:** W.E. Butterworth IV, managing editor. 75% freelance written. Prefers to work with published/established writers; works with small number of new/unpublished writers each year. Monthly magazine covering activities of interest to all boys ages 8-18. Most readers are Scouts or Cub Scouts. Estab. 1911. Circ. 1,300,000. **Pays on acceptance.** Publishes ms an average of 1 year after acceptance. Buys one-time rights. Reports in 2 months. Sample copy for $3 and 9×12 SAE. Writer's guidelines for #10 SASE.

• Ranked as one of the best markets for freelance writers in *Writer's Yearbook* magazine's annual "Top 100 Markets," January 1998.

Nonfiction: Subject matter is broad, everything from professional sports to American history to how to pack a canoe. Look at a current list of the BSAs more than 100 merit badge pamphlets for an idea of the wide range of subjects possible. Major articles run 500-1,500 words; preferred length is about 1,000 words including sidebars and boxes. **Pays $400-1,500.** Uses strong photo features with about 500 words of text. Separate payment or assignment for photos. **Buys 60 major articles/year.** Also needs how-to features and hobby and crafts ideas. Query in writing with SASE. No phone queries. Pays expenses of writers on assignment.

Columns: Rachel Buchholz, special features editor. "Science, nature, earth, health, sports, space and aviation, cars, computers, entertainment, pets, history, music are some of the columns for which we use 300-750 words of text. This is a good place to show us what you can do." Query first in writing. **Buys 75-80 columns/year. Pays $250-300.**

Fiction: Shannon Lowry, associate editor. Humor, mystery, science fiction and adventure. Short stories 1,000-1,500 words; rarely longer. **Buys 12-15 short stories/year.** Send complete ms with SASE. **Pays $750 minimum.**

• Ranked as one of the best markets for fiction writers by *Writer's Digest* magazine's "Fiction 50," June 1998.

Fillers: Also buys freelance comics pages and scripts.

Tips: "We strongly recommend reading at least 12 issues of the magazine before you submit queries. We are a good market for any writer willing to do the necessary homework."

$ $ CALLIOPE: The World History Magazine for Young People, Cobblestone Publishing, Inc., 30 Grove St., Peterborough NH 03458-1454. (603)924-7209. Fax: (603)924-7380. E-mail: editorial@cobblestone.mv.com. Website: http://www.cobblestonepub.com. Editors: Rosalie and Charles Baker. **Contact:** Rosalie F. Baker. **50% freelance written.** Prefers to work with published/established writers. Magazine published 9 times/year covering world history (East and West) through 1800 AD for 8- to 14-year-olds. Articles must relate to the issue's theme. Pays on publication. Byline given. Buys all rights. Prefers not to accept simultaneous submissions. Sample copy for $4.50 and 7½×10½ SASE with 4 first-class stamps. Writer's guidelines for SASE.

Nonfiction: Essays, general interest, historical/nostalgic, how-to (activities), recipes, humor, interview/profile, personal experience, photo feature, technical, travel. Articles must relate to the theme. No religious, pornographic, biased or sophisticated submissions. **Buys 30-40 mss/year.** Query with published clips. Length: feature articles 700-800 words. Supplemental nonfiction 300-600 words. **Pays 20-25¢/printed word.**

Photos: State availability of photos with submission. Reviews contact sheets, color slides and b&w prints. Buys one-time rights. Pays $15-100 (color cover negotiated).

Fiction: All fiction must be theme-related. **Buys 10 mss/year.** Query with published clips. Length: up to 800 words. **Pays 20-25¢/printed word.**

Columns/Departments: Activities (crafts, recipes, projects); up to 700 words. Pays on an individual basis.

Fillers: Puzzles and Games (no word finds). Crossword and other word puzzles using the vocabulary of the issue's theme. Mazes and picture puzzles that relate to the theme. Pays on an individual basis.

Tips: "A query must consist of all of the following to be considered (please use non-erasable paper): a brief cover letter stating the subject and word length of the proposed article; a detailed one-page outline explaining the information to be presented in the article; an extensive bibliography of materials the author intends to use in preparing the article; a self-addressed stamped envelope. (Authors are urged to use primary resources and up-to-date scholarly resources in their bibliography.) Writers new to *Calliope* should send a writing sample with the query. If you would like to know if your query has been received, please also include a stamped postcard that requests acknowledgement of receipt. In all correspondence, please include your complete address as well as a telephone number where you can be reached."

$ $ CHICKADEE MAGAZINE, Discover a World of Fun, The Owl Group, Bayard Press Canada, 179 John St., Suite 500, Toronto, Ontario M5T 3G5 Canada. (416)340-2700. Fax: (416)340-9769. E-mail: chickadeenet@owl.on.ca. Website: http://www.owl.on.ca. **Contact:** Kat Mototsune, editor. **25% freelance written.** Magazine published 9 times/year for 6- to 9-year-olds. "We aim to interest children in the world around them in an entertaining and lively way." Estab. 1979. Circ. 110,000 Canada and US. Pays on publication. Byline given. Buys all rights. Reports in 3 months. Sample copy for $4 and SAE ($2 money order or IRCs). Writer's guidelines for SAE ($2 money order or IRCs).

Nonfiction: How-to (easy and unusual arts and crafts); personal experience (real children in real situations). No articles for older children; no religious or moralistic features.

Photos: Send photos with ms. Reviews 35mm transparencies. Identification of subjects required.

Fiction: Adventure (relating to the 6-9-year-old), humor. No talking animal stories or religious articles. Send complete ms with $2 money order or IRCs for handling and return postage. **Pays $200** (US).

Tips: "A frequent mistake made by writers is trying to teach too much—not enough entertainment and fun."

⊘ **CHILD LIFE** does not accept freelance submissions.

N ☆ **$ $ CHILDREN'S DIGEST**, Children's Better Health Institute, P.O. Box 567, Indianapolis IN 46206-0567. (317)636-8881. Fax: (317)684-8094. **Contact:** Daniel Lee, editor. **85% freelance written.** Works with a small number of new/unpublished writers each year. Magazine published 8 times/year covering children's health for preteen children. Estab. 1950. Pays on publication. Publishes ms an average of 1 year after acceptance. Byline given. Buys all rights. Submit seasonal material 8 months in advance. Submit *only* complete mss. "No queries, please." Reports in 2 months. Sample copy for $1.25. Writer's guidelines for #10 SASE.

- *Children's Digest* would like to see more photo stories about current events and topical matters and more nonfiction in general.

Nonfiction: Historical, craft ideas, health, nutrition, fitness and sports. "We're especially interested in factual features that teach readers about fitness and sports or encourage them to develop better health habits. We are *not* interested in material that is simply rewritten from encyclopedias. We try to present our health material in a way that instructs *and* entertains the reader." **Buys 15-20 mss/year.** Send complete ms. Length: 500-1,000 words. **Pays up to 12¢/word.**

Photos: State availability of full color or b&w photos. Payment varies. Model releases and identification of subjects required. Buys one-time rights.

Fiction: Adventure, humorous, mainstream, mystery. Stories should appeal to both boys and girls. "We need some stories that incorporate a health theme. However, we don't want stories that preach, preferring instead stories with implied morals. We like a light or humorous approach." **Buys 15-20 mss/year.** Length: 500-1,500 words. **Pays up to 12¢/word.**

Poetry: Pays $20 minimum.

☆ **$ $ CHILDREN'S PLAYMATE**, Children's Better Health Institute, P.O. Box 567, Indianapolis IN 46206-0567. (317)636-8881. Fax: (317)684-8094. **Contact:** (Ms.) Terry Harshman, editor. **75% freelance written.** Eager to work with new/unpublished writers. Magazine published 8 times/year for children ages 6-8. "We are looking for articles, stories, poems, and activities with a health, sports, fitness or nutritionally oriented theme. We also publish general interest fiction and nonfiction. We try to present our material in a positive light, and we try to incorporate humor and a light approach wherever possible without minimizing the seriousness of what we are saying." Estab. 1929. Buys all rights. Byline given. Pays on publication. Submit seasonal material 8 months in advance. Reports in 3 months; sometimes may hold mss for up to 1 year, with author's permission. Sample copy for $1.25. Writer's guidelines for #10 SASE.

Nonfiction: "A feature may be an interesting presentation on good health, exercise, proper nutrition and safety." Include word count. Length: 500 words maximum. **Buys 40 mss/year.** "We would very much like to see more nonfiction features on nature and gardening. Material will not be returned unless accompanied by a SASE." Submit complete ms; no queries. **Pays up to 17¢/word.**

Fiction: Short stories for beginning readers, not over 700 words. Seasonal stories with holiday themes. Humorous stories, unusual plots. "We are interested in stories about children in different cultures and stories about lesser-known holidays (not just Christmas, Thanksgiving, Halloween, Hanukkah)." Vocabulary suitable for ages 6-8. Submit complete ms. Include word count with stories. **Pays up to 17¢/word.**

Fillers: Recipes, crafts, puzzles, dot-to-dots, color-ins, hidden pictures, mazes. **Buys 30 fillers/year.** Payment varies.

Prefers camera-ready activities. Activity guidelines for #10 SASE.
Tips: "We're especially interested in features, stories, poems and articles about health, nutrition, fitness, and fun."

$ $ CLUBHOUSE MAGAZINE, Focus on the Family, 8605 Explorer Dr., Colorado Springs CO 80920. Website: http://www.fotf.org. Editor: Jesse Florea. **Contact:** Annette Bourland, associate editor. **40% freelance written.** Monthly magazine geared for Christian kids ages 8-12. Estab. 1987. Circ. 100,000. **Pays on acceptance.** Byline given. Offers negotiable kill fee. Buys first rights. Editorial lead time 5 months. Submit seasonal material 5 months in advance. Reports in 2 months on mss. Sample copy for $1.50. Writer's guidelines for #10 SASE.
Nonfiction: General interest, historical/nostalgic, how-to, humor, inspirational, interview/profile, religious. **Buys 20 mss/year.** Send complete ms. Length: 400-2,000 words. **Pays 10-25¢/word.** Sometimes pays expenses of writers on assignment.
Photos: State availability of photos with submission. Reviews contact sheets. Negotiates payment individually. Captions, model releases, identification of subjects required. Buys negotiable rights.
Fiction: Adventure, ethnic, fantasy, holiday, humor, historical, religious (Christian), mystery, western, children's literature (Christian), novel excerpts. **Buys 40 mss/year.** Send complete ms. Length: 400-2,000 words. **Pays $75-500.**

$ $ COBBLESTONE: American History for Kids, Cobblestone Publishing, 30 Grove St., Suite C, Peterborough NH 03458-1457. (603)924-7209. Fax: (603)924-7380. **Contact:** Meg Chorlian, editor. **100% freelance written** (except letters and departments); approximately 1 issue/year is by assignment only. Prefers to work with published/established writers. Monthly magazine (September-May) covering American history for children ages 8-14. "Each issue presents a particular theme, making it exciting as well as informative. Half of all subscriptions are for schools." Circ. 36,000. Pays on publication. Publishes ms an average of 4 months after acceptance. Byline given. Offers 50% kill fee if assigned. Buys all rights. All material must relate to monthly theme. Editorial lead time 8 months. Accepts simultaneous submissions. Reports in 4 months. Sample copy for $4.50 and 7½×10½ SAE with 4 first-class stamps. Writer's guidelines and query deadlines for SASE.
Nonfiction: Historical, interview, plays, biography, recipes, activities, personal experience. "Request a copy of the writer's guidelines to find out specific issue themes in upcoming months." No material that editorializes rather than reports. **Buys 80 mss/year.** Query with published clips, outline and bibliography. Length: Feature articles 600-800 words. Supplemental nonfiction 300-500 words. **Pays 20-25¢/printed word.**
Photos: State availability of photos with submission. Reviews contact sheets, transparencies, prints. Offers $15-50 for non-professional quality, $100 for professional quality. Captions, identification of subjects required. Buys one-time rights. Photos must relate to theme.
Fiction: Adventure, ethnic, historical, biographical fiction, relating to theme. "Has to be very strong and accurate." **Buys 5 mss/year.** Length: 500-800 words. Query with published clips. **Pays 20-25¢/printed word.**
Poetry: Free verse, light verse, traditional. **Buys 5 poems/year.** Length: up to 50 lines. Pays on an individual basis. Must relate to theme.
Columns/Departments: Puzzles and Games (no word finds); crossword and other word puzzles using the vocabulary of the issue's theme.
Tips: "All material is considered on the basis of merit and appropriateness to theme. Query should state idea for material simply, with rationale for why material is applicable to theme. Request writer's guidelines (includes themes and query deadlines) before submitting a query. Include SASE. In general, please keep in mind that we are a magazine for children ages 8-14. We want the subject to be interesting and historically accurate, but not condescending to our readers. We are looking for articles from social science teachers and educators in the middle school grades. Queries should include a detailed outline and a bibliography."

$ COUNSELOR, Scripture Press Publications, 4050 Lee Vance View, Colorado Springs CO 80918. (719)536-0100. Fax: (719)536-3243. E-mail: SPEditorl@aol.com. **Contact:** Janice K. Burton, editor. **60% freelance written.** Quarterly Sunday School take-home paper with 13 weekly parts. "Our readers are 8-11 years old. All materials attempt to show God's working in the lives of children. Must have a true Christian slant, not just a moral implication." **Pays on acceptance.** Publishes ms an average of 1-2 years after acceptance. Byline given. Buys all or one-time rights with permission to reprint. Editorial lead time 1 year. Submit seasonal material 1 year in advance. Reports in 1-2 months on mss. Sample copy and writer's guidelines for #10 SASE.
Nonfiction: Inspirational (stories), interview/profile, personal experience, religious. All stories must have a spiritual perspective. Show God at work in a child's life. **Buys 10-20 mss/year.** Send complete ms with SASE. Length: 900-1,000 words. **Pays 10¢/word.**
Reprints: Send typed ms with rights for sale noted and information about when and where the article previously appeared. **Pays 7¢/word.**
Columns/Departments: God's Wonders (seeing God through creation and the wonders of science), Kids in Action (kids doing unusual activities to benefit others), World Series (missions stories from child's perspective), all 300-500 words. Send complete ms. **Pays 10¢/word.**
Fiction: Adventure, ethnic, religious. **Buys 10-15 mss/year.** Send complete ms. Length: 900-1,000 words. **Pays 10¢/word.**
Fillers: Buys 8-12 puzzles, games, fun activities/year. Length: 150 words maximum. **Pays 10¢/word.**
Tips: "Show a real feel for the age level. Know your readers and what is age appropriate in terms of concepts and

vocabulary. Submit only best quality manuscripts. If submitting nonfiction, you must include permission from story's subject."

$ CRAYOLA KIDS MAGAZINE, Co-published by Meredith Corporation and Binney & Smith Properties, Inc., 1716 Locust St., Des Moines IA 50309-3023. (515)284-2390. Fax: (515)284-2064. E-mail: bpalar@mdp.com. **Contact:** Barbara Hall Palar, editor. **25% freelance written.** Bimonthly magazine covering children (ages 3-8). "Our mission is to excite families with young children about the magic of reading and the wonder of creativity. We do that by reprinting a children's trade book (in its entirety) and by presenting open-ended crafts and fun puzzles and activities related to a particular theme." Estab. 1994. Circ. 500,000 subscribers plus newsstand. **Pays on acceptance**. Publishes ms an average of 4 months after acceptance. Byline sometimes given. Buys second serial (reprint) and all rights, makes work-for-hire assignments. Editorial lead time 8 months. Submit seasonal material anytime. Accepts simultaneous submissions, if so noted. Reports in 3 weeks on queries; 4 months on mss. Sample copy for $2.95 and writer's guidelines for #10 SASE.
Nonfiction: How-to/kids' crafts—seasonal and theme-related, puzzles. **Buys 30-40 mss/year.** Themes: "Let's Put on a Show" and "Creatures and Critters." Query. Length: 250 words maximum. **Pays $50-300 for assigned articles; $30-150 for unsolicited articles.**
Fillers: "For fillers we want ideas for visual puzzles that are fresh and fun. Do not send art except as a rough indicator of how the puzzle works."
Tips: "We're looking for crafts and family activities involving children ages four to ten. Send a sample with crafts—they should be made from easy-to-find materials, be fun to make and then play with and should be kid-tested. Send for list of themes before submitting crafts or puzzles or activities that are not seasonal."

$ $ CRICKET, Carus Publishing Co., P.O. Box 300, Peru IL 61354-0300. (815)224-6656. **Contact:** Marianne Carus, editor-in-chief. Monthly general interest literary magazine for children ages 9-14. Estab. 1973. Circ. 74,000. Pays on publication. Byline given. Buys first publication rights in the English language. Submit seasonal material 1 year in advance. Reports in 3 months. Sample copy and writer's guidelines for $4 and 9×12 SAE. Writer's guidelines only for #10 SASE.

- *Cricket* is looking for more fiction and nonfiction for the older end of its 9-14 age range. It also seeks humorous stories.

Nonfiction: Adventure, biography, foreign culture, geography, history, natural science, science, social science, sports, technology, travel. (A short bibliography is required for *all* nonfiction articles.) Send complete ms. Length: 200-1,500 words. **Pays up to 25¢/word.**
Reprints: Send typed ms with rights for sale noted and information about when and where the article previously appeared. Pays 50% of amount paid for an original article.
Fiction: Adventure, ethnic, fairy tales, fantasy, historical, humorous, mystery, novel excerpts, science fiction, suspense, western. No didactic, sex, religious or horror stories. **Buys 75-100 mss/year.** Send complete ms. Length: 200-2,000 words. **Pays up to 25¢/word.**

- Ranked as one of the best markets for fiction writers in *Writer's Digest* magazine's "Fiction 50," June 1998.

Poetry: Buys 20-30 poems/year. Length: 50 lines maximum. **Pays up to $3/line.**

$ CRUSADER MAGAZINE, P.O. Box 7259, Grand Rapids MI 49510-7259. Fax: (616)241-5558. E-mail: cadets@aol.com. Website: http://www.gospelcom.net/cadets/. **Contact:** G. Richard Broene, editor. **40% freelance written.** Works with a small number of new/unpublished writers each year. Magazine published 7 times/year. "*Crusader Magazine* shows boys 9-14 how God is at work in their lives and in the world around them." Estab. 1958. Circ. 13,000. **Pays on acceptance.** Byline given. Publishes ms an average of 8 months after acceptance. Rights purchased vary with author and material; buys first serial, one-time, second serial (reprint) and simultaneous rights. Accepts simultaneous submissions. Reports in 2 months. Sample copy and writer's guidelines for 9×12 SAE with $1.01 in postage.
Nonfiction: Articles about young boys' interests: sports, outdoor activities, bike riding, science, crafts, etc., and problems. Emphasis is on a Christian multi-racial perspective, but no simplistic moralisms. Informational, how-to, personal experience, interview, profile, inspirational, humor. Special issues: Let Your Light Shine (September/October); Responsibility (November); Christmas (December); Courage (January); Integrity (February); Richard Poor (March); and Friends (input from subscribers only—April/May). **Buys 20-25 mss/year.** Submit complete ms. Length: 500-1,500 words. **Pays 2-5¢/word.**
Reprints: Send typed ms with rights for sale noted. Pay varies.
Photos: Pays $4-25 for b&w photos purchased with mss.
Columns/Departments: Project Page—uses simple projects boys 9-14 can do on their own.
Fiction: "Considerable fiction is used. Fast-moving stories that appeal to a boy's sense of adventure or sense of humor are welcome. Avoid preachiness. Avoid simplistic answers to complicated problems. Avoid long dialogue and little action." Length: 900-1,500 words. **Pays 2¢/word minimum.**
Fillers: Uses short humor and any type of puzzles as fillers.

$ $ CURIOCITY FOR KIDS, Thomson Newspapers, 730 N. Franklin, Suite 706, Chicago IL 60610. Fax: (312)573-3810. E-mail: dscott@ttmedia.com. Website: http://www.freezone.com. **Contact:** Andrew Scott, editor. 10% freelance written. Monthly magazine. "*Curiocity* is a kid-driven magazine that uses humor and a light-hearted, inquisitive approach to inform and entertain kids 7-12 about people, places and things around the country and around the town." Estab. 1994. Circ. 250,000. Pays on publication. Publishes ms an average of 2 months after acceptance. Offers 50%

kill fee. Buys all rights. Editorial lead time 2 months. Submit seasonal material 5 months in advance. Reports in 1 month. Sample copy $5.

Nonfiction: Interested mostly in profiles of outstanding and unusual kids; new angles and how-tos for sports stories; and fun takes on educational topics. Length: 300-600 words. **Pays: $100-200.**

Photos: State availability of photos with submission. Offers no additional payment for photos accepted with ms. Identification of subjects required.

Tips: "We publish only a small percentage of freelance stories, so we prefer queries to be right on target for our needs. No fiction, please. Just query us in our range of needs; please include clips of other published works."

$ $ CURRENT HEALTH I, The Beginning Guide to Health Education, General Learning Communications, 900 Skokie Blvd., Suite 200, Northbrook IL 60062-4028. (847)205-3000. Fax: (847)564-8197. E-mail: ruben@glcomm.com. **Contact:** Carole Rubenstein, senior editor. **95% freelance written.** An educational health periodical published monthly, September-May. "Our audience is 4th-7th grade health education students. Articles should be written at a 5th grade reading level. As a curriculum supplementary publication, info should be accurate, timely, accessible and highly readable." Estab. 1976. Circ. 152,000. Pays on publication. Publishes ms an average of 9 months after acceptance. Buys all rights.

Nonfiction: Health curriculum. **Buys 70 mss/year.** Query with introductory letter, résumé and clips. *No unsolicited mss. Articles are on assignment only.* Length: 800-2,000 words. **Pays $100-400.**

Tips: "We are looking for good writers with preferably an education and/or health background, who can write for the age group in a scientifically accurate way. Ideally, the writer should be an expert in the area in which he or she is writing. All topics are open to freelancers: disease, drugs, fitness and exercise, psychology, nutrition, first aid and safety, environment, and personal health."

N $ DISCOVERIES, Word Action Publishing Co., 6401 The Paseo, Kansas City MO 64131. Fax: (816)333-4439. **Contact**: Kathleen M. Johnson, assistant editor. Editor: Rebecca S. Raleigh. **75% freelance written.** Weekly Sunday school take-home paper. "Our audience is third and fourth graders. We require that the stories relate to the Sunday school lesson for that week." Circ. 5,000. Pays on publication. Publishes ms an average of 1 year after acceptance. Byline given. Buys second serial (reprint) rights or multi-use rights. Accepts simultaneous submissions. Reports in 6 weeks on queries; 2 months on mss. Sample copy and writer's guidelines for #10 SASE.

Reprints: Send typed ms with rights for sale noted and information about when and where the article previously appeared.

Fiction: Religious. Must relate to our theme list. **Buys 45 mss/year.** Send complete ms. Length: 400-500 words. **Pays $20-25.**

Fillers: Gags to be illustrated by cartoonist, puzzles, Bible trivia (need bibliography documentation). **Buys 100/year.** Length: 50-200 words. **Pays $15.**

Tips: "Follow our theme list, read the Bible verses that relate to the theme. September 1999 begins our new curriculum."

☆ $ $ FACES, People, Places and Cultures, Cobblestone Publishing, 30 Grove St., Peterborough NH 03458. (603)924-7209. E-mail: faces@cobblestonepub.com. Website: http://www.cobblestonepub.com. **Contact:** Elizabeth Crooker, editor. **90-100% freelance written.** Monthly magazine published during school year. "*Faces* stands apart from other children's magazines by offering a solid look at one subject and stressing strong editorial content, color photographs throughout and original illustrations. *Faces* offers an equal balance of feature articles and activities, as well as folktales and legends." Estab. 1984. Circ. 15,000. Pays on publication. Publishes ms an average of 4 months after acceptance. Byline given. Offers 50% kill fee. Buys all rights. Editorial lead time 1 year. Accepts simultaneous submissions. Sample copy for $4.95 and 7½×10½ SAE with 4 first-class stamps. Writer's guidelines for #10 SASE.

Nonfiction: Historical/nostalgic, humor, interview/profile, personal experience, photo feature, travel, recipes, activities (puzzles, mazes). All must relate to theme. **Buys 45-50 mss/year.** Query with published clips. Length: 300-1,000. **Pays 20-25¢/word.**

Reprints: Send tearsheet of article or short story. Pay is negotiable.

Photos: State availability of photos with submission or send copies of related images for photo researcher. Reviews contact sheets, transparencies, prints. Offers $15-100 (for professional). Negotiates payment individually (for non-professional). Captions, model releases, identification of subjects required. Buys one-time rights.

Fiction: Ethnic, historical, retold legends or folktales. Depends on theme. Query with published clips. Length: 500-1,000 words. **Pays 20-25¢/word.**

Poetry: Avant-garde, free verse, haiku, light verse, traditional. Length: 100 words maximum. Pays on individual basis.

Tips: "Freelancers should send for a sample copy of magazine and a list of upcoming themes and writer's guidelines. The magazine is based on a monthly theme (upcoming themes include the Koreas, The Dominican Republic, Bosnia. We appreciate professional queries that follow our detailed writer's guidelines."

☆ $ THE FRIEND, 50 E. North Temple, Salt Lake City UT 84150. Fax: (801)240-5997. **Contact:** Vivian Paulsen, managing editor. **50% freelance written.** Eager to work with new/unpublished writers as well as established writers. Monthly publication of The Church of Jesus Christ of Latter-Day Saints for children ages 3-11. Circ. 350,000. **Pays on acceptance.** Buys all rights. Submit seasonal material 8 months in advance. Sample copy and writer's guidelines for $1.50 and 9×12 SAE with 4 first-class stamps.

Nonfiction: Subjects of current interest, science, nature, pets, sports, foreign countries, things to make and do. Special issues: Christmas, Easter. "Submit only complete manuscript—no queries, please." Length: 1,000 words maximum. **Pays 9¢/word minimum.**

Fiction: Seasonal and holiday stories, stories about other countries and their children. Wholesome and optimistic; high motive, plot and action. Character-building stories preferred. Length: 1,200 words maximum. Stories for younger children should not exceed 250 words. Submit complete ms. **Pays 9¢/word minimum.**

Poetry: Serious, humorous, holiday. Any form with child appeal. **Pays $25 minimum.**

Tips: "Do you remember how it feels to be a child? Can you write stories that appeal to children ages 3-11 in today's world? We're interested in stories with an international flavor and those that focus on present-day problems. Send material of high literary quality slanted to our editorial requirements. Let the child solve the problem—not some helpful, all-wise adult. No overt moralizing. Nonfiction should be creatively presented—not an array of facts strung together. Beware of being cutesy."

$ $ $ GIRL'S LIFE, Monarch Publishing, 4517 Harford Rd., Baltimore MD 21214. Fax: (410)254-0991. Website: http://www.girlslife.com. Editor: Karen Bokram. **Contact:** Kelly A. White, senior editor. Bimonthly magazine covering girls ages 7-14. Estab. 1994. Circ. 980,000. Pays on publication. Publishes ms an average of 3 months after acceptance. Byline given. Buys first North American serial rights. Editorial lead time 5 months. Submit seasonal material 6 months in advance. Reports in 3 months. Sample copy for $5. Writer's guidelines for #10 SASE.

Nonfiction: Book excerpts, essays, general interest, how-to, humor, inspirational, interview/profile, new product, personal experience, travel. Special issues: Back to School (August/September); Fall, Halloween (October/November); Holidays, Winter (December/January); Valentine's Day, Crushes (February/March); Spring, Mother's Day (April/May); and Summer, Father's Day (June/July). **Buys 20 mss/year.** Query with published clips. Submit complete mss on spec only. Length: 700-2,000 words. **Pays $150-800.**

Photos: State availability of photos with submission. Reviews contact sheets, negatives, transparencies. Negotiates payment individually. Captions, model releases, identification of subjects required.

Columns/Departments: Outta Here! (travel information); Sports (interesting); It Happened to Me (personal accounts); Huh? (explain something like Watergate or Woodstock, at anniversary of an event); Try It! (new stuff to try); all 1,200 words. **Buys 12 mss/year.** Query with published clips. **Pays $150-450.**

Fiction: Publishes novel excerpts.

Fillers: Gags to be illustrated by cartoonist, short humor. **Buys 12/year. Pays $25-100.**

Tips: Send queries with published writing samples and detailed résumé.

★ $ GUIDE®, Stories Pointing to Jesus, Review and Herald Publishing Association, 55 W. Oak Ridge Dr., Hagerstown MD 21740. (301)791-7000. Fax: (301)790-9734. E-mail: guide@rhpa.org. Website: http://www.rhpa.org/guide. **Contact**: Tim Lale, editor. Associate Editor: Randy Fishell. **90% freelance written.** Weekly magazine featuring all-true stories showing God's involvement in 10-14-year-olds' lives. Estab. 1953. Circ. 33,000. **Pays on acceptance**. Publishes ms an average of 6 months after acceptance. Byline given. Offers 25% kill fee. Buys first North American serial rights. Editorial lead time 8 months. Submit seasonal material 8 months in advance. Reports in 1 month. Sample copy for SAE with 2 first-class stamps. Writer's guidelines for #10 SASE.

Nonfiction: Religious. "No fiction. Non-fiction should set forth a clearly-evident spiritual application." **Buys 300 mss/year.** Send complete ms. Length: 750-1,500 words. **Pays $25-125.**

Reprints: Send photocopy of article. **Pays $50.**

Fillers: Games, puzzles, religious. **Buys 75/year. Pays $25-40.**

Tips: "The majority of 'misses' are due to the lack of a clearly-evident (not 'preachy') spiritual application."

$ $ GUIDEPOSTS FOR KIDS, P.O. Box 638, Chesterton IN 46304. Fax: (219)926-3839. Website: http://www.guideposts.org. **Contact:** Mary Lou Carney, editor. **30% freelance written.** Bimonthly magazine for kids. "*Guideposts for Kids* is a value-centered, fun-to-read kids magazine for 7-12-year-olds (with an emphasis on the upper end of this age bracket). Issue-oriented, thought-provoking. No preachy stories." *Guideposts For Kids* is very interested in seasonal stories, especially Thanksgiving and Christmas. Estab. 1990. Circ. 200,000. **Pays on acceptance.** Byline given. Offers 25% kill fee. Buys all rights. Editorial lead time 6 months. Submit seasonal material 6 months in advance. Reports in 6 weeks. Sample copy for $3.25. Writer's guidelines for #10 SASE.

Nonfiction: Issue-oriented, thought-provoking features, general interest, humor, inspirational, interview/profile, photo essays, technical (technology). No articles with adult voice/frame of reference or Sunday-School-type articles. **Buys 20 mss/year.** Query with SASE. Length: 700-1,500 words. **Pays $250-350.** Sometimes pays expenses of writers on assignment.

Photos: State availability of or send photos with submission. Negotiates payment individually. Identification of subjects required. Buys one-time rights.

Columns/Departments: Tips from the Top (Christian celebrities), 650 words; Featuring Kids (profiles of interesting kids), 200-500 words. **Buys 15 mss/year.** Query or send complete ms with SASE. **Pays $250-350.**

Fiction: Adventure, fantasy, historical, humorous, mystery, suspense, western. **Buys 8 mss/year.** Send complete ms and SASE. Length: 500-1,300 words. **Pays $175-350.**

Fillers: Facts, newsbreaks, short humor, puzzles, mazes, jokes. **Buys 8-10/year.** Length: 300 words maximum. **Pays $25-175.**

Tips: "Before you submit to one of our departments, study the magazine. In most of our pieces, we look for a strong kid voice/viewpoint. We do not want preachy or overtly religious material. Looking for value-driven stories and profiles.

In the fiction arena, we are very interested in historical and mysteries. In nonfiction, we welcome tough themes and current issues. This is not a beginner's market."

$ HIGHLIGHTS FOR CHILDREN, 803 Church St., Honesdale PA 18431-1824. Managing Editor: Christine French Clark. **Contact:** Beth Troop, manuscript coordinator. **80% freelance written.** Monthly magazine for children ages 2-12. Estab. 1946. Circ. 3,000,000. **Pays on acceptance.** Buys all rights. Reports in about 2 months. Sample copy free. Writer's guidelines for #10 SASE.

Nonfiction: "We need articles on science, technology and nature written by persons with strong backgrounds in those fields. Contributions always welcomed from new writers, especially engineers, scientists, historians, teachers, etc., who can make useful, interesting facts accessible to children. Also writers who have lived abroad and can interpret the ways of life, especially of children, in other countries in ways that will foster world brotherhood. Sports material, biographies and articles of general interest to children. Direct, original approach, simple style, interesting content, not rewritten from encyclopedias. State background and qualifications for writing factual articles submitted. Include references or sources of information." Length: 900 words maximum. **Pays $100 minimum.** Articles geared toward our younger readers (3-7) especially welcome, up to 400 words. Also buys original party plans for children ages 4-12, clearly described in 300-600 words, including drawings or samples of items to be illustrated. Also, novel but tested ideas in crafts, with clear directions and made-up models. Projects must require only free or inexpensive, easy-to-obtain materials. Especially desirable if easy enough for early primary grades. Also, fingerplays with lots of action, easy for very young children to grasp and to dramatize. Avoid wordiness. We need creative-thinking puzzles that can be illustrated, optical illusions, brain teasers, games of physical agility and other 'fun' activities." **Pays minimum $50 for party plans; $25 for crafts ideas; $25 for fingerplays.**

- Ranked as one of the best markets for freelance writers in *Writer's Yearbook* magazine's annual "Top 100 Markets," January 1998.

Photos: Color 35mm slides, photos or art reference materials are helpful and sometimes crucial in evaluating mss.

Fiction: Unusual, meaningful stories appealing to both girls and boys, ages 2-12. "Vivid, full of action. Engaging plot, strong characterization, lively language." Prefers stories in which a child protagonist solves a dilemma through his or her own resources. Seeks stories that the child ages 8-12 will eagerly read, and the child ages 2-7 will begin to read and/or will like to hear when read aloud (400-900 words). "We publish stories in the suspense/adventure/mystery, fantasy and humor category, all requiring interesting plot and a number of illustration possiblities. Also need rebuses (picture stories 125 words or under), stories with urban settings, stories for beginning readers (100-400 words), sports and horse stories and retold folk tales. We also would like to see more material of 1-page length (300-500 words), both fiction and factual. War, crime and violence are taboo." **Pays $120 minimum.**

- Ranked as one of the best markets for fiction writers in *Writer's Digest* magazine's "Fiction 50," June, 1998.

Tips: "We are pleased that many authors of children's literature report that their first published work was in the pages of *Highlights*. It is not our policy to consider fiction on the strength of the reputation of the author. We judge each submission on its own merits. With factual material, however, we do prefer that writers be authorities in their field or people with first-hand experience. In this manner we can avoid the encyclopedic article that merely restates information readily available elsewhere. We don't make assignments. Query with simple letter to establish whether the nonfiction subject is likely to be of interest. A beginning writer should first become familiar with the type of material that *Highlights* publishes. Include special qualifications, if any, of author. Write for the child, not the editor."

$ HOPSCOTCH, The Magazine for Girls, Bluffton News Publishing & Printing Co., P.O. Box 164, Bluffton OH 45817-0164. (419)358-4610. Editor: Marilyn B. Edwards. **Contact:** Becky Jackman, editorial assistant. **90% freelance written.** Bimonthly magazine on basic subjects of interest to young girls. "*Hopscotch* is a digest-size magazine with a four-color cover and two-color format inside. It is designed for girls ages 6-12, with youngsters 8, 9 and 10 the specific target age; it features pets, crafts, hobbies, games, science, fiction, history, puzzles, careers, etc." Estab. 1989. Pays on publication. Byline given. Buys first or second rights. Submit seasonal material 8 months in advance. Accepts simultaneous submissions. Reports in 3 weeks on queries; 2 months on mss. Sample copy for $3. Writer's guidelines, current theme list and needs for #10 SASE.

- *Hopscotch* has a sibling magazine, *Boys' Quest*, for ages 6-13, with the same old-fashioned principles that *Hopscotch* has and is a good market for freelance writers.

Nonfiction: General interest, historical/nostalgic, how-to (crafts), humor, inspirational, interview/profile, personal experience, pets, games, fiction, careers, sports, cooking. "No fashion, hairstyles, sex or dating articles." **Buys 60 mss/year.** Send complete ms. Length: 400-1,000 words. **Pays 5¢/word.**

Reprints: Send tearsheet or photocopy of article or typed ms with rights for sale noted. **Pays 5¢/word.**

Photos: Send photos with submission. Prefers b&w photos, but color photos accepted. Offers $5-10/photo. Captions, model releases and identification of subjects required. Buys one-time rights.

Columns/Departments: Science—nature, crafts, pets, cooking (basic), 400-700 words. Send complete ms. **Pays $10-35/column.**

Fiction: Adventure, historical, humorous, mainstream, mystery, suspense. **Buys 15 mss/year.** Send complete ms. Length: 600-900 words. **Pays 5¢/word.**

Poetry: Free and light verse, traditional. "No experimental or obscure poetry." Send 6 poems max. **Pays $10-30.**

Tips: "Almost all sections are open to freelancers. Freelancers should remember that *Hopscotch* is a bit old-fashioned, appealing to *young* girls (6-12). We cherish nonfiction pieces that have a young girl or young girls directly involved in unusual and/or worthwhile activities. Any piece accompanied by decent photos stands an even better chance of being accepted."

$ $ HUMPTY DUMPTY'S MAGAZINE, Children's Better Health Institute, P.O. Box 567, Indianapolis IN 46206-0567. (317)636-8881. **Contact**: Nancy S. Axelrad, editor. **75% freelance written.** Magazine published 8 times/year covering health, nutrition, hygiene, fitness and safety for children ages 4-6. "Our publication is designed to entertain and to educate young readers in healthy lifestyle habits. Fiction, poetry, pencil activities should have an element of good nutrition or fitness." Estab. 1948. Circ. 350,000. Pays on publication. Publishes ms 8 months after acceptance. Byline given. Buys all rights. Editorial lead time 8 months. Submit seasonal material 10 months in advance. Accepts simultaneous submissions. Reports in 2 months. Sample copy for $1.25. Writer's guidelines for #10 SASE.

Nonfiction: "We are open to nonfiction on almost any age-appropriate subject, but we especially need material with a health theme—nutrition, safety, exercise, hygiene. We're looking for articles that encourage readers to develop better health habits without preaching. Very simple factual articles that creatively teach readers about their bodies. We use simple crafts, some with holiday themes. We also use several puzzles and activities in each issue—dot-to-dot, hidden pictures and other activities that promote following instructions, developing finger dexterity and working with numbers and letters." **Buys 3-4 mss/year.** Submit complete ms with word count. Length: 500 words maximum. **Pays 22¢/word.**

Photos: Send photos with submission. Offers no additional payment for photos accepted with ms. Buys all rights.

Columns/Departments: Mix & Fix (no-cook recipes), 100 words. **Buys 8 mss/year.** Send complete ms. Pay varies.

Fiction: Humorous, mainstream, folktales retold. "We use some stories in rhyme and a few easy-to-read stories for the beginning reader. All stories should work well as read-alouds. Currently we need sports/fitness stories and seasonal stories with holiday themes. We use contemporary stories and fantasy, most employing a health theme. We try to present our health material in a positive light, incorporating humor and a light approach wherever possible. Avoid stereotyping. Characters in contemporary stories should be realistic and up-to-date and reflect good, wholesome values." **Buys 4-6 mss/year.** Submit complete ms with word count. Length: 500 words maximum. **Pays 22¢/word.**

Poetry: Free verse, light verse, traditional. Short, simple poems. **Buys 6-8 poems/year.** Submit 2-3 poems at one time. **Pays $20 minimum.**

Tips: "We strive for at least 50% art per page (in stories and articles), so space for text is limited, and text should work well with visual imagery. We are always looking for cute, funny content with a health or fitness theme. This should be primary or secondary and written from a healthy lifestyle perspective."

$ $ JACK AND JILL, Children's Better Health Institute, P.O. Box 567, Indianapolis IN 46206-0567. (317)636-8881. Fax: (317)684-8094. **Contact:** Daniel Lee, editor. **50% freelance written.** Magazine published 8 times/year for children ages 7-10. Pays on publication. Publishes ms an average of 8 months after acceptance. Buys all rights. Byline given. Submit seasonal material 8 months in advance. Reports in 10 weeks. May hold material being seriously considered for up to 1 year. "Material will not be returned unless accompanied by SASE with sufficient postage." Sample copy for $1.25. Writer's guidelines for #10 SASE.

Nonfiction: "Because we want to encourage youngsters to read for pleasure and for information, we are interested in material that will challenge a young child's intelligence *and* be enjoyable reading. Our emphasis is on good health, and we are in particular need of articles, stories, and activities with health, safety, exercise and nutrition themes. We try to present our health material in a positive light—incorporating humor and a light approach wherever possible without minimizing the seriousness of what we are saying." Straight factual articles are OK if they are short and interestingly written. "We would rather see, however, more creative alternatives to the straight factual article. Items with a news hook will get extra attention. We'd like to see articles about interesting kids involved in out-of-the-ordinary activities. We're also interested in articles about people with unusual hobbies for our Hobby Shop department." **Buys 10-15 nonfiction mss/year.** Length: 500-800 words. **Pays 17¢/word minimum.**

Photos: When appropriate, photos should accompany ms. Reviews sharp, contrasting b&w glossy prints. Sometimes uses color slides, transparencies or good color prints. Pays $15 for photos. Buys one-time rights.

Fiction: May include, but is not limited to, realistic stories, fantasy adventure—set in past, present or future. "All stories need a well-developed plot, action and incident. Humor is highly desirable. Stories that deal with a health theme need not have health as the primary subject." **Buys 20-25 mss/year.** Length: 500-800 words (short stories). **Pays 15¢/word minimum.**

Fillers: Puzzles (including various kinds of word and crossword puzzles), poems, games, science projects, and creative craft projects. We get a lot of these. To be selected, an item needs a little extra spark and originality. Instructions for activities should be clearly and simply written and accompanied by models or diagram sketches. "We also have a need for recipes. Ingredients should be healthful; avoid sugar, salt, chocolate, red meat and fats as much as possible. In all material, avoid references to eating sugary foods, such as candy, cakes, cookies and soft drinks."

Tips: "We are constantly looking for new writers who can tell good stories with interesting slants—stories that are not full of out-dated and time-worn expressions. We like to see stories about kids who are smart and capable, but not sarcastic or smug. Problem-solving skills, personal responsibility and integrity are good topics for us. Obtain *current* issues of the magazine and *study* them to determine our present needs and editorial style."

N $ JUNIOR TRAILS, Gospel Publishing House, 1445 Boonville Ave., Springfield MO 65802-1894. (417)862-2781. **Contact**: Sinda S. Zinn, editor. **98% freelance written.** Weekly 8-page Sunday school take-home paper. *Junior Trails* is written for boys and girls 10-12 (slanted toward older group). Fiction, adventure and mystery stories showing children applying Christian principles in everyday living are used in the paper. **Pays on acceptance**. Publishes ms an average of 12-18 months after acceptance. Byline given. Buys one-time, second serial (reprint) and simultaneous rights. Editorial lead time 12-18 months. Submit seasonal material 18 months in advance. Accepts simultaneous submissions. Reports in 1 month. Sample copy and writer's guidelines for #10 SASE.

Nonfiction: Humor, religious. Wants articles with reader appeal, emphasizing some phase of Christian living and historical, scientific or natural material with a spiritual lesson. **Buys 15-20 mss/year.** Send complete ms. Length: 1,000 words maximum. **Pays 4-7¢/word.**

Reprints: Send typed ms with rights for sale noted and information about when and where the article previously appeared. Pays 50% of amount paid for an original article.

Photos: Offers no additional payment for photos accepted with ms.

Fiction: Adventure, historical, humorous, mystery. No Bible fiction, "Halloween" or "Santa Claus" stories. Wants fiction that presents realistic characters working out their problems according to Bible principles, presenting Christianity in action without being preachy. Serial stories acceptable. **Buys 80-90 mss/year.** Send complete ms. Length: 1,000-1,500 words (except for serial stories). **Pays 4-7¢/word.**

Poetry: Light verse, traditional. **Buys 10-12 poems/year.** Submit maximum 2-3 poems. **Pays $5-15.**

Tips: "Follow the guidelines, remember the story should be interesting—carried by dialogue and action rather than narration—and appropriate for a Sunday school take-home paper. Don't send groups of stories in one submission."

$ LADYBUG, the Magazine for Young Children, Carus Publishing Co., P.O. Box 300, Peru IL 61354-0300. (815)224-6656. Editor-in-Chief: Marianne Carus. **Contact:** Paula Morrow, editor. Monthly general interest magazine for children ages 2-6. "We look for quality writing—quality literature, no matter the subject." Estab. 1990. Circ. 134,000. Pays on publication. Byline given. Buys first publication rights in the English language. Submit seasonal material 1 year in advance. Reports in 3 months. Sample copy and guidelines for $4 and 9×12 SAE. Guidelines only for #10 SASE.

- *Ladybug* needs even more activities based on concepts (size, color, sequence, comparison, etc.) and interesting, appropriate nonfiction. Also needs articles and parent-child activities for its parents' section. See sample issues.

Nonfiction: Can You Do This?, 1-2 pages; The World Around You, 2-4 pages; activities based on concepts (size, color, sequence, comparison, etc.), 1-2 pages. **Buys 35 mss/year.** Send complete ms; no queries. "Most *Ladybug* nonfiction is in the form of illustration. We'd like more simple science, how-things-work and behind-the-scenes on a preschool level." Length: 250-300 words maximum. **Pays up to 25¢/word.**

Fiction: Adventure, ethnic, fantasy, folklore, humorous, mainstream, mystery. **Buys 30 mss/year.** Send complete ms. Length: 850 words maximum. **Pays up to 25¢/word.**

Poetry: Light verse, traditional, humorous. **Buys 20 poems/year.** Submit *maximum* 5 poems. Length: 20 lines maximum. **Pays up to $3/line.**

Fillers: Anecdotes, facts, short humor. **Buys 10/year.** Length: 250 words maximum. **Pays up to 25¢/word.** "We welcome interactive activities: rebuses, up to 100 words; *original* fingerplays and action rhymes (up to 8 lines)."

Tips: "Reread manuscript *before* sending in. Keep within specified word limits. Study back issues before submitting to learn about the types of material we're looking for. Writing style is paramount. We look for rich, evocative language and a sense of joy or wonder. Remember that you're writing for preschoolers—be age-appropriate but not condescending. A story must hold enjoyment for both parent and child through repeated read-aloud sessions. Remember that we live in a multicultural world. People come in all colors, sizes, physical conditions and have special needs. Be inclusive!"

N ★ $ LIVE, A Weekly Journal of Practical Christian Living, Gospel Publishing House, 1445 Boonville Ave., Springfield MO 65802-1894. (417)862-2781. Fax: (417)862-6059. **Contact**: Paul W. Smith, adult curriculum editor. **100% freelance written.** Quarterly magazine for weekly distribution covering practical Christian living. "*LIVE* is a take-home paper distributed weekly in young adult and adult Sunday school classes. We seek to encourage Christians in living for God through fiction and true stories which apply biblical principles to everyday problems." Estab. 1928. Circ. 125,000. **Pays on acceptance**. Publishes ms an average of 18 months after acceptance. Byline given. Buys first rights or second serial (reprint) rights. Editorial lead time 8-12 months. Submit seasonal material 12-18 months in advance. Accepts simultaneous submissions. Reports in 2 weeks on queries; 2 months on mss. Sample copy and writer's guidelines for #10 SASE.

Nonfiction: Inspirational, religious. No preachy articles or stories that refer to religious myths (e.g. Santa Claus, Easter bunny, etc.) **Buys 50-100 mss/year.** Send complete ms. Length: 400-1,500 words. **Pays 7-10¢/word.**

Reprints: Send tearsheet, photocopy or typed ms with rights for sale noted and information about when and where the article previously appeared. Pays 70% of amount paid for an original article.

Photos: Send photos with submission. Reviews 35mm transparencies and 3×4 prints or larger. Offers $35-60/photo. Identification of subjects required. Buys one-time rights.

Columns/Departments: Reflections (collection of quotations on a single topic relating to Christianity), 600-800 words. **Buys 12 mss/year.** Query. **Pays $75.**

Fiction: Religious, inspirational. No preachy fiction, fiction about Bible characters or stories that refer to religious myths (e.g. Santa Claus, Easter bunny, etc.). No science or Bible fiction. **Buys 50-100 mss/year.** Send complete ms. Length: 800-1,600 words. **Pays 7-10¢/word.**

Poetry: Free verse, haiku, light verse, traditional. **Buys 36-48 poems/year.** Submit maximum 3 poems. Length: 12-25 lines. **Pays $35-60.**

Fillers: Anecdotes, short humor. **Buys 12-36/year.** Length: 300-600 words. **Pays 7-10¢/word.**

Tips: "Be very clear in character development and development of plot. Don't moralize or be preachy. Allow the events to flow naturally to a clear conclusion that demonstrates a Christian living principle."

$ $ $ MUSE, Carus Publishing, 332 S. Michigan, #2000, Chicago IL 60604. (312)939-1500. Fax: (312)939-8150. E-mail: muse@caruspub.com. Website: http://www.musemag.com. Editor: Diane Lutz. Associate Editor: Laurence Schorsch. **Contact:** Submissions Editor, the Cricket Magazine Group, P.O. Box 300, Peru IL 61354. **100% freelance written.** Bimonthly nonfiction magazine for children. Estab. 1996. Pays 60 days after acceptance or upon acceptance. Offers 50% kill fee. Buys all rights. Reports in 3 months on queries. Sample copy for $5. Writer's guidelines for #10 SASE.

Nonfiction: Children's. "The goal of *Muse* is to give as many children as possible access to the most important ideas and concepts underlying the principle areas of human knowledge. It will take children seriously as developing intellects by assuming that, if explained clearly, the ideas and concepts of an article will be of interest to them. Articles should meet the highest possible standard of clarity and transparency aided, wherever possible, by a tone of skepticism, humor and irreverence." Please send SASE for writer's guidelines first. Query with published clips, résumé and possible topics. Length: 1,000-2,500 words. **Pays 50¢/word for assigned articles; 25¢/word for unsolicited articles;** plus 3 free copies of issue in which article appears.

Tips: "Unsolicited manuscripts should be sent to Submissions Editor, The Cricket Magazine Group, P.O. Box 300, Peru IL 61354."

$ MY FRIEND, The Catholic Magazine for Kids, Pauline Books & Media/Daughters of St. Paul, 50 St. Paul's Ave., Jamaica Plain, Boston MA 02130-3491. (617)522-8911. Fax: (617)504-9801. E-mail: myfriendsk@aol.com. Website: http://www.pauline.org. (click on Kidstuff). Editor-in-Chief: Sister Rose Pacatte, fsp. **Contact:** Sister Kathryn James Hermes, fsp, managing editor. **40% freelance written.** Magazine published 10 times/year for children ages 6-12. Circ. 12,000. "*My Friend* is a 32-page monthly Catholic magazine for boys and girls. Its goal is to celebrate the Catholic Faith—as it is lived by today's children and as it has been lived for centuries." Pays on editorial completion of the issue (five months ahead of publication date). Buys serial rights. Reports in 2 months. Sample copy for $2.95. Writer's guidelines for #10 SASE. No theme lists.

Nonfiction: How-to, religious, technical, media-related articles, real-life features. "This year we are emphasizing cultural and ecumenical themes. We prefer authors who have a rich background and mastery in these areas. We are looking for fresh perspectives into a child's world that are imaginative, unique, challenging, informative, current and fun. We prefer articles that are visual, not necessarily text-based—articles written in 'windows' style with multiple points of entry." Send complete ms. Length: 150-800 words. **Pays $35-100.** Pays in contributor copies by prior agreement with an author "who wishes to write as a form of sharing our ministry."

Photos: Send photos with submission.

- *My Friend* needs "fun fiction with a message relevant to a child's life."

Fiction: "We are looking for stories that immediately grab the imagination of the reader. Good dialogue, realistic character development, current lingo are necessary. A child protagonist must resolve a dilemma through his or her own resources. We prefer seeing a sample or submission of a story. Often we may not be able to use a particular story but the author will be asked to write another for a specific issue based on his or her experience, writing ability, etc. At this time we are especially analyzing submissions for the following: intercultural relations, periodic appearance of a child living with a disability or a sibling of a child or adult with a disability, realistic and current issues kids face today and computer literacy."

Fillers: Puzzles and jokes. "We need new creative ideas, small-size puzzles, picture puzzles, clean jokes." **Jokes pay $7. Puzzles pay $10-15.**

Tips: "We have a strong commitment to working with our authors to produce material that is factual, contemporary and inspiring. We prefer those authors who write well and are able to work as a team with us."

$ NEW MOON: THE MAGAZINE FOR GIRLS & THEIR DREAMS, New Moon Publishing, Inc., P.O. Box 3620, Duluth MN 55803-3620. (218)728-5507. Fax: (218)728-0314. E-mail: newmoon@computerpro.com. Website: http://www.newmoon.org. **Contact**: Barbara Stretchberry, managing editor. **25% freelance written.** Bimonthly magazine covering girls ages 8-14, edited by girls aged 8-14. "In general, all material should be pro-girl and feature girls and women as the primary focus. *New Moon* is for every girl who wants her voice heard and her dreams taken seriously. *New Moon* celebrates girls, explores the passage from girl to woman and builds healthy resistance to gender inequities. The New Moon girl is true to herself and *New Moon* helps her as she pursues her unique path in life, moving confidently into the world." Estab. 1992. Circ. 35,000. Pays on publication. Publishes ms 6-12 months after acceptance. Byline given. Offers 50% kill fee. Buys one-time or all rights. Editorial lead time 5 months. Submit seasonal material 8 months in advance. Accepts simultaneous submissions. Reports in 8 months. Sample copy for $6.50. Guidelines for SASE.

Nonfiction: Essays, general interest, humor, inspirational, interview/profile, opinion, personal experience, photo feature, religious, technical, travel, multicultural/girls from other countries. Special issues: Business, Power and Money (March/April 1999, deadline September 1, 1998); Writers and Writing (May/June 1999, deadline November 1, 1998); Humor and Happiness (July/August 1999, deadline January 1, 1999); Families (September/October 1999, deadline March 1, 1999); Preserving the Past and Foreseeing the Future (November/December 1999, deadline May 1, 1999). No fashion, beauty or dating. **Buys 20 mss/year.** Query or send complete ms. Length: 300-1,000 words. **Pays 8-10¢/word for assigned articles; 5-10¢/word for unsolicited articles.**

Reprints: Send typed ms with rights for sale noted and information about when and where the article previously appeared. Negotiates fee.

Photos: State availability of photos with submission. Reviews contact sheets, transparencies, 4×5 prints. Negotiates payment individually. Captions and identification of subjects required. Buys one-time rights.
Columns/Departments: Global Village (girl's life in a non-North American country, usually but not always written by a girl), 900 words; Women's Work (profile of a woman and her job(s)), 600-1,200 words; She Did It (real girls doing real things), 300-600 words; Herstory (historical woman relating to theme), 600-1,200 words. **Buys 10 mss/year.** Query. **Pays 8-10¢/word.**
Fiction: Adventure, fantasy, historical, humorous, slice-of-life vignettes, all girl-centered. **Buys 6 mss/year.** Query or send complete ms. Length: 300-1,200 words. **Pays 8-12¢/word.**
Poetry: No poetry by adults.
Tips: "Please read *New Moon* before submitting to get a sense of our style. Writers and artists who comprehend our goals have the best chance of publication. We love creative articles—both nonfiction and fiction—that are not condescending to our readers. Keep articles to suggested word lengths; avoid stereotypes. Refer to our guidelines and upcoming themes."

$ ON THE LINE, Mennonite Publishing House, 616 Walnut Ave., Scottdale PA 15683-1999. (724)887-8500. Fax: (724)887-3111. E-mail: mary@mph.org. **Contact:** Mary Clemens Meyer, editor. **90% freelance written.** Works with a small number of new/unpublished writers each year. Monthly Christian magazine for children ages 9-14. "*On the Line* helps upper elementary and junior high children understand and appreciate God, the created world, themselves and others." Estab. 1908. Circ. 6,000. **Pays on acceptance.** Publishes ms an average of 1 year after acceptance. Byline given. Buys one-time rights. Submit seasonal material 6 months in advance. Accepts simultaneous submissions. Reports in 1 month. Sample copy for 9×12 SAE with 2 first-class stamps.
Nonfiction: How-to (things to make with easy-to-get materials including food recipes); informational (300-500 word articles on wonders of nature, people who have made outstanding contributions). **Buys 95 unsolicited mss/year.** Send complete ms. **Pays $10-30.**
Reprints: Send typed ms with rights for sale noted and information about when and where the article previously appeared. Pays 65% of amount paid for an original article.
Photos: Limited number of photos purchased with or without ms. Pays $25-50 for 8×10 b&w photos. Total purchase price for ms includes payment for photos.
Fiction: Adventure, humorous, religious. **Buys 50 mss/year.** Send complete ms. Length: 1,000 1,500 words. **Pays 2-5¢/word.**
Poetry: Light verse, religious. Length: 3-12 lines. **Pays $5-15.**
Fillers: Appropriate puzzles, cartoons, quizzes.
Tips: "Study the publication first. We need short well-written how-to and craft articles. Don't send query; we prefer to see the complete manuscript."

$ $ OWL MAGAZINE, The Discovery Magazine for Children, Owl Communications, 179 John St., Suite 500, Toronto, Ontario M5T 3G5 Canada. (416)340-2700. Fax: (416)340-9769. E-mail: owl@owlkids.com. Website: http://www.owl.on.ca. Editor: Nyla Ahmad. **Contact:** Keltie Thomas, editor. **25% freelance written.** Works with small number of new writers each year. Magazine published 9 times/year (no June, July or August issues) covering science and nature. Aims to interest children in their environment through accurate, factual information about the world presented in an easy, lively style. Estab. 1976. Circ. 75,000. Pays on publication. Publishes ms an average of 3 months after acceptance. Byline given. Buys all rights. Submit seasonal material 1 year in advance. Reports in 10 weeks. Sample copy for $4.28. Writer's guidelines for SAE (large envelope if requesting sample copy) and money order for $1 postage (no stamps please).
Nonfiction: Personal experience (real life children in real situations); photo feature (natural science, international wildlife, and outdoor features); science and environmental features. No problem stories with drugs, sex or moralistic views, or talking animal stories. **Buys 2 mss/year.** Query with clips of published work. Length: 500-1,500 words. **Pays $200-500** (Canadian).
Photos: State availability of photos. Reviews 35mm transparencies. Identification of subjects required. Send for photo package before submitting material.
Tips: "Write for editorial guidelines first. Review back issues of the magazine for content and style. Know your topic and approach it from an unusual perspective. Our magazine never talks down to children. We would like to see more articles about science and technology that aren't too academic."

$ $ POCKETS, The Upper Room, P.O. Box 189, Nashville TN 37202-0189. (615)340-7333. Fax: (615)340-7006. E-mail: pockets@upperroom.org. Website: http://www.upperroom.org. Editor: Janet R. Knight. **Contact:** Lynn Gilliam, associate editor. **60% freelance written.** Eager to work with new/unpublished writers. Monthly magazine (except January/February) covering children's and families' spiritual formation. "We are a Christian, inter-denominational publication for children 6-11 years of age." Estab. 1981. Circ. 99,000. **Pays on acceptance.** Byline given. Offers 4¢/word kill fee. Buys first North American serial rights. Submit seasonal material 1 year in advance. Reports in 10 weeks on mss. Sample copy for 7½×10½ SAE with 4 first-class stamps. Writer's guidelines and themes for #10 SASE.

- *Pockets* has expanded to 48 pages and needs more fiction and poetry, as well as short, short stories (500-750 words) for children 4-7. They publish one of these stories per issue.

Nonfiction: Interview/profile, religious (retold scripture stories), personal experience. Each issue is built around a specific theme; list of themes for special issues available with SASE. No violence or romance. **Buys 5 mss/year.** Send complete ms. Length: 400-1,000 words. **Pays 12¢/word.**

Reprints: Accepts one-time previously published submissions. Send typed ms with rights for sale noted and information about when and where the article previously appeared. Pays 100% of amount paid for an original article.
Photos: Send photos with submission. Prefer no photos unless they accompany an article. Reviews contact sheets, transparencies and prints. Offers $25-50/photo. Buys one-time rights.
Columns/Departments: Refrigerator Door (poetry and prayer related to themes), 25 lines; Pocketsful of Love (family communications activities), 300 words; Activities/Games ($25 and up); Peacemakers at Work (profiles of people, particularly children, working for peace, justice and ecological concerns), 300-800 words. **Buys 20 mss/year.** Send complete ms. **Pays 12¢/word; recipes $25.**
Fiction: Adventure, ethnic, slice-of-life. "Stories should reflect the child's everyday experiences through a Christian approach, but not be preachy or heavy-handed." **Buys 44 mss/year.** Send complete ms. Length: 600-1,500 words. **Pays 12¢/word and up.**

• Ranked as one of the best markets for fiction writers in *Writer's Digest* magazine's "Fiction 50," June 1998.

Poetry: Buys 22 poems/year. Length: 4-24 lines. **Pays $2/line. Pays $25 minimum.**
Tips: "Theme stories, role models and retold scripture stories are most open to freelancers. We are also looking for nonfiction stories about children involved in peace/justic/ecology efforts. Poetry is also open. It's very helpful if writers send for our themes. These are *not* the same as writer's guidelines. We also have an annual $1,000 Fiction Writing Contest. Guidelines available with SASE. Writer's guidelines and themes are also available on our website."

$ POWER AND LIGHT, 6401 The Paseo, Kansas City MO 64131. Fax: (816)333-4439. E-mail: mhammer@nazarene.org. **Contact:** Beula Postlewait, editor. Associate Editor: Melissa Hammer. **Mostly freelance written.** Weekly magazine for boys and girls ages 11-12 using WordAction Sunday School curriculum. Estab. 1992. Publishes ms an average of 1 year after acceptance. Buys multiple use rights. Reports in 3 months. "Minimal comments on pre-printed form are made on rejected material." Sample copy and guidelines for SASE.
Fiction: Stories with Christian emphasis on high ideals, wholesome social relationships and activities and right choices. Informal style. Submit complete ms. Length: 500-700 words. **Pays 5¢/word.**
Tips: "All themes and outcomes should conform to the theology and practices of the Church of the Nazarene."

R-A-D-A-R, 8121 Hamilton Ave., Cincinnati OH 45231. (513)931-4050. Fax: (513)931-0950. **Contact:** Gary Thacker, editor. **75% freelance written.** Weekly for children in grades 3 and 4 in Christian Sunday schools. Estab. 1866 (publishing house). Rights purchased vary with material; prefers buying first serial rights, but will buy second (reprint) rights. Occasionally overstocked. **Pays on acceptance.** Publishes ms an average of 1 year after acceptance. Reports in 2-3 months. Sample copy and writer's guidelines and theme list for #10 SASE.

• R-A-D-A-R is undergoing a format change. New guidelines will be available beginning June 1998.

$ $ RANGER RICK, National Wildlife Federation, 8925 Leesburg Pike, Vienna VA 22184. (703)790-4274. **Contact:** Gerald Bishop, editor. **40% freelance written.** Works with a small number of new/unpublished writers each year. Monthly magazine for children from ages 7-12, with the greatest concentration in the 7-10 age bracket. Buys all world rights unless other arrangements made. Byline given "but occasionally, for very brief pieces, we will identify author by name at the end. Contributions to regular columns usually are not bylined." Estab. 1967. **Pays on acceptance.** Publishes ms an average of 18 months after acceptance. Reports in 6 weeks. "Anything written with a specific month in mind should be in our hands at least 10 months before that issue date." Sample copy for $2.15 and 9×12 SASE. Writer's guidelines for #10 SASE.
Nonfiction: "Articles may be written on anything related to nature, conservation, the outdoors, environmental problems or natural science. Please avoid articles about animal rehabilitation, unless the species are endangered." **Buys 25-35 unsolicited mss/year.** Query with SASE. **Pays up to $575,** depending on length, quality and content (maximum length, 900 words). Unless you are an expert in the field or are writing from direct personal experience, all factual information must be footnoted and backed up with current, reliable references.
Photos: "Photographs, when used, are paid for separately. It is not necessary that illustrations accompany material."
Fiction: "Fantasy, mystery, fables, straightforward fiction, plays, and science fiction." Particularly interested in stories with minority or multicultural characters and stories that don't take place in the suburbs. Present-day stories need to be about today's kids (with working and/or single parents, day care, etc.). Stories must treat children respectfully (no wise old grandfather teaches dumb kid, please). All nature and environmental subjects OK, but no anthropomorphizing of wildlife. Length: 900 words maximum. **Buys 4 mss/year.**
Fillers: Not buying riddles, word searches, dot-to-dot or crossword puzzles, but would like to see more nature-related, challenging, original freelance puzzles, something an 8-10 year old can finish without help. Buys 1-2/year, but would like to buy more.
Tips: "In your query letter, include details of what the manuscript will cover; sample lead; evidence that you can write playfully and with great enthusiasm, conviction and excitement (formal, serious, dull queries indicate otherwise). Think of an exciting subject we haven't done recently, sell it effectively with query, and produce a manuscript of highest quality. Read past issues to learn successful styles and unique approaches to subjects. No phone or fax queries."

$ $ SHOFAR MAGAZINE, 43 Northcote Dr., Melville NY 11747-3924. (516)643-4598. Fax: (516)643-4598. **Contact:** Gerald H. Grayson, managing editor. **80-90% freelance written.** Children's magazine on Jewish subjects published monthly from October to May, double issues December/January and April/May. Estab. 1984. Circ. 17,000. Pays on publication. Byline given. Buys First North American or first serial rights. Submit seasonal material 6 months

in advance. Accepts simultaneous submissions. Reports in 2 months. Sample copy and writer's guidelines for 9×12 SAE and $1.01 postage.
Nonfiction: Historical/nostalgic, humor, inspirational, interview/profile, personal experience, photo feature, religious, travel. **Buys 15 mss/year.** Send complete ms. Length: 600-1,000 words. **Pays 10¢/word** and 5 copies of publication. Sometimes pays the expenses of writers on assignment.
Photos: State availability of or send photos with submission. Offers $10-50/photo. Identification of subjects required. Buys one-time rights.
Fiction: Adventure, historical, humorous, religious. **Buys 15 mss/year.** Send complete ms. Length: 600-1,000 words. **Pays 10¢/word** and 5 copies of publication.
Poetry: Free verse, light verse, traditional. **Buys 4-5 poems/year.** Length: 8-50 words. **Pays 7-10¢/word.**
Tips: "Submissions *must* be on a Jewish theme and should be geared to readers who are 9- to 13-years-old."

$ $ SPIDER, The Magazine for Children, The Cricket Magazine Group, P.O. Box 300, Peru IL 61354. (815)224-6656. Fax: (815)224-6615. Editor-in-Chief: Marianne Carus. Editor: Laura Tillotson. **Contact:** Submissions Editor. **80% freelance written.** Monthly magazine covering literary, general interest. "*Spider* introduces 6- to 9-year-old children to the highest quality stories, poems, illustrations, articles and activities. It was created to foster in beginning readers a love of reading and discovery that will last a lifetime. We're looking for writers who respect children's intelligence." Estab. 1994. Circ. 87,000. Pays on publication. Publishes ms an average of 1 year after acceptance. Byline given. Buys first North American serial rights (for stories, poems, articles), second serial (reprint) rights or all rights (for crafts, recipes, puzzles). Editorial lead time 9 months. Submit seasonal material 1 year in advance. Accepts simultaneous submissions. Reports in 4 months on mss. Sample copy for $4. Writer's guidelines for #10 SASE.
Nonfiction: Adventure, biography, geography, history, science, social science, sports, technology, travel. A bibliography is required with all nonfiction submissions. **Buys 12-15 mss/year.** Send complete ms. Length: 300-800 words. **Pays 25¢/word.**
Reprints: Note rights for sale and information about when and where article previously appeared.
Photos: Send photos with submission (prints or slide dupes OK). Reviews contact sheets, 35mm to 4×4 transparencies, 8×10 maximum prints. Offers $50-200/photo. Captions, model releases, identification of subjects required. Buys one-time rights.
Fiction: Adventure, ethnic, fantasy, historical, humorous, mystery, science fiction, suspense, realistic fiction, folk tales, fairy tales. No romance, horror, religious. **Buys 30-40 mss/year.** Send complete ms. Length: 300-1,000 words. **Pays 25¢/word.**

- Ranked as one of the best magazines for fiction writers in *Writer's Digest* magazine's "Fiction 50," June 1998.

Poetry: Free verse, traditional, nonsense, humorous, serious. No forced rhymes, didactic. **Buys 20-30 poems/year.** Submit maximum 5 poems. Length: 20 lines maximum. **Pays $3/line maximum.**
Fillers: Puzzles, mazes, hidden pictures, games, brainteasers, math and word activities. **Buys 15-20/year.** Payment depends on type of filler.
Tips: "Most importantly, do not write down to children. We'd like to see more of the following: multicultural fiction and nonfiction, strong female protagonists, stories about people who are physically or mentally challenged, fantasy, science fiction, environmental articles, hard science (e.g., physics, chemistry, cosmology, microbiology, science biography and history)."

$ $ $ SPORTS ILLUSTRATED FOR KIDS, Time-Warner, Time & Life Building, 1271 Sixth Ave., New York NY 10020. (212)522-5437. Fax: (212)522-0120. Managing Editor: Neil Cohen. **Contact:** Erin Egan, senior editor. **20% freelance written.** Monthly magazine on sports for children 8 years old and up. Content is divided 20/80 between sports as played by kids, and sports as played by professionals. Estab. 1989. **Pays on acceptance.** Publishes ms an average of 3 months after acceptance. Byline given. Offers 25% kill fee. Buys all rights. For sample copy call (800)992-0196. Writer's guidelines for #10 SASE.
Nonfiction: Games, general interest, how-to, humor, inspirational, interview/profile, photo feature, puzzles. **Buys 15 mss/year.** Query with published clips. Length: 100-1,500 words. **Pays $75-1,000 for assigned articles; $75-800 for unsolicited articles.** Pays expenses of writers on assignment.
Photos: State availability of photos with submission. Buys one-time rights.
Columns/Departments: The Worst Day I Ever Had (tells about day in pro athlete's life when all seemed hopeless), 500-600 words; Sports Shorts (short, fresh news about kids doing things on and off the field), 100-250 words. **Buys 10-15 mss/year.** Query with published clips. **Pays $75-600.**

$ STONE SOUP, The Magazine by Young Writers and Artists, Children's Art Foundation, P.O. Box 83, Santa Cruz CA 95063-0083. (408)426-5557. Fax: (408)426-1161. E-mail: editor@stonesoup.com. Website: http://www.stonesoup.com. **Contact:** Ms. Gerry Mandel, editor. **100% freelance written.** Bimonthly magazine of writing and art by children, including fiction, poetry, book reviews, and art by children through age 13. Estab. 1973. Audience is children, teachers, parents, writers, artists. "We have a preference for writing and art based on real-life experiences; no formula stories or poems." Pays on publication. Publishes ms an average of 3 months after acceptance. Buys all rights. Submit seasonal material 6 months in advance. Reports in 1 month. Sample copy for $4. Writer's guidelines with SASE.
Nonfiction: Book reviews. **Buys 12 mss/year.** Query with SASE. **Pays $15.**
Reprints: Send photocopy of article or story and information about when and where the article or story previously appeared. Pays 100% of amount paid for an original article or story.

Fiction: Adventure, ethnic, experimental, fantasy, historical, humorous, mystery, science fiction, slice-of-life vignettes, suspense. "We do not like assignments or formula stories of any kind." **Accepts 60 mss/year.** Send complete ms nd SASE. **Pays $10 for stories.** Authors also receive 2 copies and discounts on additional copies and on subscriptions.
Poetry: Avant-garde, free verse. **Accepts 20 poems/year.** Pays $10/poem. (Same discounts apply.)
Tips: "All writing we publish is by young people ages 13 and under. We do not publish any writing by adults. We can't emphasize enough how important it is to read a couple of issues of the magazine. We have a strong preference for writing on subjects that mean a lot to the author. If you feel strongly about something that happened to you or something you observed, use that feeling as the basis for your story or poem. Stories should have good descriptions, realistic dialogue and a point to make. In a poem, each word must be chosen carefully. Your poem should present a view of your subject and a way of using words that are special and all your own."

$ STORY FRIENDS, Mennonite Publishing House, 616 Walnut Ave., Scottdale PA 15683-1999. (412)887-8500. Fax: (412)887-3111. **Contact:** Rose Mary Stutzman, editor. **80% freelance written.** Monthly magazine for children ages 4-9. "*Story Friends* is planned to provide wholesome Christian reading for the 4-9-year-old. Practical life stories are included to teach moral values and remind the children that God is at work today. Activities introduce children to the Bible and its message for them." Estab. 1905. Circ. 7,000. **Pays on acceptance.** Publishes ms an average of 1 year after acceptance. Byline given. Publication not copyrighted. Buys one-time and second serial (reprint) rights. Submit seasonal material 6 months in advance. Accepts simultaneous submissions. Reports in 2 months. Sample copy for 9×12 SAE with 2 first-class stamps. Writer's guidelines for #10 SASE.
Nonfiction: How-to (craft ideas for young children), photo feature. **Buys 20 mss/year.** Send complete ms. Length: 300-500 words. **Pays 3-5¢/word.**
Reprints: Send photocopy or typed ms with rights for sale noted and information about when and where the article previously appeared. Pays 100% of amount paid for an original article.
Photos: Send photos with submission. Reviews 8½×11 b&w prints. Offers $20-25/photo. Model releases required. Buys one-time rights.
Fiction: See writer's guidelines for *Story Friends*. **Buys 50 mss/year.** Send complete ms. Length: 300-800 words. **Pays 3-5¢/word.**
Poetry: Traditional. **Buys 20 poems/year.** Length: 4-16 lines. **Pays $10/poem.**
Tips: "Send stories that children from a variety of ethnic backgrounds can relate to; stories that deal with experiences similar to all children. For example, all children have fears but their fears may vary depending on where they live. Send stories with a humorous twist."

$ $ TURTLE MAGAZINE FOR PRESCHOOL KIDS, Children's Better Health Institute, P.O. Box 567, Indianapolis IN 46206-0567. (317)636-8881. Fax: (317)684-8094. **Contact:** Terry Harshman, editor. **90% freelance written.** Bimonthly magazine (monthly March, June, September, December). General interest, interactive magazine with the purpose of helping preschoolers develop healthy minds and bodies. Circ. 300,000. Pays on publication. May hold mss for up to 1 year before acceptance/publication. Byline given. Buys all rights. Submit seasonal material 8 months in advance. Reports in 3 months. Sample copy for $1.25. Writer's guidelines for #10 SASE.
Nonfiction: "Uses very simple science experiments. These should be pretested. Also publish simple, healthful recipes." **Buys 24 mss/year.** Length: 150-300 words. **Pays up to 22¢/word.**
Fiction: All should have single-focus story lines and work well as read-alouds. "Most of the stories we use have a character-building bent, but are not preachy or overly moralistic. We are in constant need of stories to help a preschooler appreciate his/her body and what it can do; stories encouraging active, vigorous play; stories about good health. We no longer buy stories about 'generic' turtles because we now have PokeyToes, our own trade-marked turtle character. All should 'move along' and lend themselves well to illustration. Writing should be energetic, enthusiastic and creative—like preschoolers themselves." **Buys 50 mss/year.** Length: 150-300 words. **Pays up to 22¢/word.**
Poetry: "We're especially looking for action rhymes to foster creative movement in preschoolers. We also use short verse on our back cover."
Tips: "We are trying to include more material for our youngest readers. Stories must be age-appropriate for two- to five-year-olds, entertaining and written from a healthy lifestyle perspective. We are especially interested in material concerning sports and fitness, including profiles of famous amateur and professional athletes; 'average' athletes (especially children) who have overcome obstacles to excel in their areas; and new or unusual sports, particularly those in which children can participate."

$ $ U.S. KIDS, A Weekly Reader Magazine, Children's Better Health Institute, P.O. Box 567, Indianapolis IN 46206-0567. (317)636-8881. **Contact:** Jeff Ayers, editor. **50% freelance written.** Published 8 times/year featuring "kids doing extraordinary things, especially activities related to heatlh, sports, the arts, interesting hobbies, the environment, computers, etc." Reading level appropriate for 2nd/4th grade readers. Estab. 1987. Circ. 230,000. Pays on publication. Publishes ms an average of 4 months after acceptance. Byline given. Buys all rights. Editorial lead time 6 months. Submit seasonal material 6 months in advance. Reports in 2 months on mss. Sample copy for $2.95. Writer's guidelines for #10 SASE.
Nonfiction: Especially interested in articles with a health/fitness angle. Also general interest, how-to, interview/profile, science, kids using computers, multicultural. **Buys 16-24 mss/year.** Send complete ms. Length: 400-800 words. **Pays up to 20¢/word.**
Photos: State availability of photos with submission. Reviews contact sheets or color photocopies, negatives, transparen-

cies, prints. Negotiates payment individually. Captions, model releases, identification of subjects required. Buys one-time rights.

Columns/Departments: Real Kids (kids doing interesting things); Fit Kids (sports, healthy activities); Computer Zone. Length: 300-400 words. Send complete ms. **Pays up to 20¢/word.**

Fiction: Adventure, rebus, historical, humorous, mainstream, suspense. No anthropomorphized animals or objects. **Buys 8 mss/year.** Send complete ms. Length: 400-800 words. **Pays up to 20¢/word.**

Poetry: Light verse, traditional, kid's humorous, health/fitness angle. **Buys 6-8 poems/year.** Submit maximum 6 poems. Length: 8-24 lines. **Pays $25-50.**

Fillers: Facts, newsbreaks (related to kids, especially kids' health), short humor, puzzles, games, activities. Length: 200-500 words. **Pays 20¢/word.**

Tips: "Looking for fun and informative articles on activities, hobbies, accomplishments of real kids, especially those related to fitness, sports and health. Should appeal to readers in a broad age range. Availability of good photos a plus."

$ WONDER TIME, 6401 The Paseo Blvd., Kansas City MO 64131-1213. (816)333-7000. Fax: (816)333-4439. E-mail: dfillmore@nazarene.org. or tforrest@nazarene.org. **Contact:** Donna Fillmore, editor. **75% freelance written.** "Willing to read and consider appropriate freelance submissions." Published weekly by WordAction for children ages 6-8. Correlates to the Bible Truth in the weekly Sunday School lesson. Pays on publication. Publishes ms an average of 1 year after acceptance. Byline given. Buys rights to reuse and all rights for curriculum assignments. Reports in 1 month. Sample copy and writer's guidelines for 9×12 SAE with 2 first-class stamps.

Fiction: Buys stories portraying Christian attitudes without being preachy. Uses true-to-life stories teaching honesty, truthfulness, kindness, helpfulness or other important spiritual truths, and avoiding symbolism. Also, stories about real life problems children face today. "God should be spoken of as our Father who loves and cares for us; Jesus, as our Lord and Savior." **Buys 52 mss/year.** Length: 250-350 words. **Pays $25 on publication.**

Tips: "Any stories that allude to church doctrine must be in keeping with Wesleyan beliefs. Avoid fantasy, precocious children or personification of animals. Write on a first to second grade readability level."

LITERARY & "LITTLE"

Fiction, poetry, essays, book reviews and scholarly criticism comprise the content of the magazines listed in this section. Some are published by colleges and universities, and many are regional in focus.

Everything about "little" literary magazines is different than other consumer magazines. Most carry few or no ads, and many do not seek them. Circulations under 1,000 are common. And sales often come more from the purchase of sample copies than from the newsstand.

The magazines listed in this section cannot compete with the pay rates and exposure of the high-circulation general interest magazines also publishing fiction and poetry. But most "little" literary magazines don't try. They are more apt to specialize in publishing certain kinds of fiction or poetry: traditional, experimental, works with a regional sensibility, or the fiction and poetry of new and younger writers. For that reason, and because fiction and poetry vary so widely in style, writers should *always* invest in the most recent copies of the magazines they aspire to publish in.

Many "little" literary magazines pay contributors only in copies of the issues in which their works appear. *Writer's Market* lists only those that pay their contributors in cash. However, *Novel & Short Story Writer's Market* includes nonpaying fiction markets, and has in-depth information about fiction techniques and markets. The same is true of *Poet's Market* for nonpaying poetry markets (both books are published by Writer's Digest Books). Many literary agents and book editors regularly read these magazines in search of literary voices not found in mainstream writing. There are also more literary opportunities listed in the Contests and Awards section.

$ AGNI, Dept. WM, Boston University, 236 Bay State Rd., Boston, MA 02215. (617)353-5389. Fax: (617)353-7136. E-mail: agni@bu.edu. Website: http://www.webdelsol.com/AGNI. **Contact:** Askold Melnyczuk, editor; Valerie Duff, managing editor. Biannual literary magazine. "*AGNI* publishes poetry, fiction and essays. Also regularly publishes translations and is committed to featuring the work of emerging writers. We have published Derek Walcott, Joyce Carol Oates, Sharon Olds, John Updike, and many others. Estab. 1972. Circ. 2,000. Pays on publication. Publishes ms an average of 6 months after acceptance. Byline given. Buys first North American serial rights and rights to reprint in *AGNI* anthology (with author's consent). Editorial lead time 6 months. Accepts simultaneous submissions. Reports in 2 weeks on queries; 6 months on mss. Sample copy for $9. Writer's guidelines for #10 SASE.

Fiction: Short stories. **Buys 6-12 mss/year.** Send complete ms with SASE. **Pays $20-150.**
Poetry: Buys more than 140/year. Submit maximum 5 poems with SASE. **Pays $20-150.**
Tips: "It is important to look at a copy of *AGNI* before submimtting, to see if your work might be compatible. We received a tremendous amount of mail in the fall of 1997 and had to shorten our reading period due to the backlog. We will begin reading again in Fall 1998. Please write for guidelines or a sample."

$ $ ALASKA QUARTERLY REVIEW, ESB 208, University of Alaska-Anchorage, 3211 Providence Dr., Anchorage AK 99508. (907)786-6916. **Contact:** Ronald Spatz, executive editor. **95% freelance written.** Prefers to work with published/established writers; eager to work with new/unpublished writers. Semiannual magazine publishing fiction, poetry, literary nonfiction and short plays in traditional and experimental styles. Estab. 1982. Circ. 2,200. Pays honorariums on publication when funding permits. Publishes ms an average of 6 months after acceptance. Byline given. Buys first North American serial rights. Upon request, rights will be transferred back to author after publication. Reports in 4 months. Sample copy for $5. Writer's guidelines for SASE.

• *Alaska Quarterly* reports they are always looking for freelance material and new writers.

Nonfiction: Literary nonfiction: essays and memoirs. **Buys 0-5 mss/year.** Query. Length: 1,000-20,000 words. **Pays $50-200** subject to funding; pays in copies and subscriptions when funding is limited.
Reprints: Accepts previously published submissions under special circumstances (special anthologies or translations). Send photocopy of article or short story or typed ms with rights for sale noted and information about when and where the article previously appeared.
Fiction: Experimental and traditional literary forms. No romance, children's or inspirational/religious. Publishes novel excerpts. **Buys 20-30 mss/year.** Send complete ms. Length: Up to 20,000 words. **Pays $50-200** subject to funding; pays in contributor's copies and subscriptions when funding is limited.
Drama: Experimental and traditional one-act plays. **Buys 0-2 mss/year.** Query. Length: Up to 20,000 words but prefers short plays. **Pays $50-200** subject to funding; contributor's copies and subscriptions when funding is limited.
Poetry: Avant-garde, free verse, traditional. No light verse. Buys 20-65 poems/year. Submit maximum 10 poems. Pays $10-50 subject to availability of funds; pays in contributor's copies and subscriptions when funding is limited.
Tips: "All sections are open to freelancers. We rely almost exclusively on unsolicited manuscripts. *AQR* is a nonprofit literary magazine and does not always have funds to pay authors."

$ AMELIA MAGAZINE, Amelia Press, 329 E St., Bakersfield CA 93304. (805)323-4064. E-mail: amelia@lightspeed.net. **Contact:** Frederick A. Raborg, Jr., editor. Estab. 1983. 100% freelance written. Eager to work with new/unpublished writers. "*Amelia* is a quarterly international magazine publishing the finest poetry and fiction available, along with expert criticism and reviews intended for all interested in contemporary literature. *Amelia* also publishes two separate magazines each year: *Cicada* and *SPSM&H*." Circ. 1,750. **Pays on acceptance.** Publishes ms an average of 6 months after acceptance. Byline given. Offers 50% kill fee. Buys first North American serial rights. Submit seasonal material 2 months in advance. Reports in 2 weeks-3 months on mss. Sample copy for $9.95 (includes postage). Writer's guidelines for #10 SASE.

• An eclectic magazine, open to greater variety of styles—especially genre and mainstream stories unsuitable for other literary magazines. Receptive to new writers.

Nonfiction: Historical/nostalgic (in the form of belles lettres); humor (in fiction or belles lettres); interview/profile (poets and fiction writers); opinion (on poetry and fiction only); personal experience (as it pertains to poetry or fiction in the form of belles lettres); travel (in the form of belles lettres only); criticism and book reviews of poetry and small press fiction titles. "Nothing overtly slick in approach. Criticism pieces must have depth; belles lettres must offer important insights into the human scene." Buys 8 mss/year. Send complete ms and SASE. Length: 1,000-2,000 words. Pays $25 or by arrangement. Sometimes pays the expenses of writers on assignment.
Fiction: Adventure, book excerpts (original novel excerpts only), erotica (of a quality seen in Anais Nin or Henry Miller only), ethnic, experimental, fantasy, historical, horror, humorous, mainstream, mystery, novel excerpts, science fiction, suspense, western. "We would consider slick fiction of the quality seen in *Esquire* or *Vanity Fair* and more excellent submissions in the genres—science fiction, wit, Gothic horror, traditional romance, stories with complex *raisons d'être*; avant-garde ought to be truly avant-garde." No pornography ("good erotica is not the same thing"). **Buys 24-36 mss/year.** Send complete ms. Length: 1,000-5,000 words, sometimes longer. "Longer stories really have to sparkle." **Pays $35** or by arrangement for exceptional work.

• Ranked as one of the best markets for fiction writers in *Writer's Digest* magazine's "Fiction 50," June 1998.

Poetry: Avant-garde, free verse, haiku, light verse, traditional. "No patently religious or stereotypical newspaper poetry." **Buys 100-240 poems**/year depending on lengths. Prefers submission of at least 3 poems. Length: 3-100 lines. "Shorter poems stand the best chance." **Pays $2-25.**
Tips: "*Have something to say* and say it well. If you insist on waving flags or pushing your religion, then do it with

ALWAYS SUBMIT unsolicited manuscripts or queries with a self-addressed, stamped envelope (SASE) within your country or a self-addressed envelope with International Reply Coupons (IRC) purchased from the post office for other countries.

subtlety and class. We enjoy a good cry from time to time, too, but sentimentality does not mean we want to see mush. Read our fiction carefully for depth of plot and characterization, then try very hard to improve on it. With the growth of quality in short fiction, we expect to find stories of lasting merit. I also hope to begin seeing more critical essays which, without sacrificing research, demonstrate a more entertaining obliqueness to the style sheets, more 'new journalism' than MLA. In poetry, we also often look for a good 'storyline' so to speak. Above all we want to feel a sense of honesty and value in every piece. No e-mail manuscript submissions."

$ $ THE ANTIGONISH REVIEW, St. Francis Xavier University, P.O. Box 5000, Antigonish, Nova Scotia B2G 2W5 Canada. (902)867-3962. Fax: (902)867-2389. E-mail: tar@stfx.ca. Website: http://www.stfx.ca/publications/TAR. Managing Editor: Gertrude Sanderson. **Contact:** George Sanderson, editor. **100% freelance written.** Quarterly literary magazine. Estab. 1970. Circ. 850. Pays on publication. Publishes ms an average of 2-4 months after acceptance. Byline given. Offers variable kill fee. Rights retained by author. Editorial lead time 4 months. Submit seasonal material 4 months in advance. Reports in 4 months on mss; 1 month on queries. Sample copy for $4. Writer's guidelines free.
Nonfiction: Essays, interview/profile, book reviews/articles. No academic pieces. **Buys 15-20 mss/year.** Query. Length: 1,500-5,000 words. **Pays $50-200.**
Fiction: Literary. No erotica. **Buys 35-40 mss/year.** Send complete ms. Length: 500-5,000 words. **Pays in copies.**
Poetry: Buys 100-125 poems/year. Submit maximum 5 poems. **Pays in copies.**
Tips: "Send for guidelines and/or sample copy. Send ms with cover letter and SASE with submission."

$ ANTIOCH REVIEW, P.O. Box 148, Yellow Springs OH 45387-0148. **Contact:** Robert S. Fogarty, editor. Quarterly magazine for general, literary and academic audience. Estab. 1941. Rights reverts to author upon publication. Byline given. Pays on publication. Publishes ms an average of 10 months after acceptance. Reports in 2 months. Sample copy for $6. Writer's guidelines for #10 SASE.
Nonfiction: "Contemporary articles in the humanities and social sciences, politics, economics, literature and all areas of broad intellectual concern. Somewhat scholarly, but never pedantic in style, eschewing all professional jargon. Lively, distinctive prose insisted upon." Length: 2,000-8,000 words. **Pays $10/published page.**
Fiction: "Quality fiction only, distinctive in style with fresh insights into the human condition." No science fiction, fantasy or confessions. **Pays $10/published page.**
Poetry: No light or inspirational verse. "We do not read poetry May 1-September 1."

$ ARC, Canada's National Poetry Magazine, Arc Poetry Society, Box 7368, Ottawa, Ontario K1L 8E4 Canada. **Contact:** John Barton, Rita Donovan, co-editors. Semiannual literary magazine featuring poetry, poetry-related articles and criticism. "Our focus is poetry, and Canadian poetry in general, although we do publish writers from elsewhere. We are looking for the best poetry from new and established writers. We often have special issues. SASE for upcoming special issues and contests." Estab. 1978. Circ. 750. Pays on publication. Publishes ms an average of 6 months after acceptance. Byline given. Buys one-time rights. Reports in 4 months. Sample copy for $4 with 10 first-class stamps.
Nonfiction: Essays, interview/profile, photo feature. Query. Length: 1,000 words. **Pays $25** plus 2 copies.
Photos: Query with samples. Pays $25/photo. Buys one-time rights.
Poetry: Avant-garde, free verse, haiku. Buys 40/year. Submit maximum 6 poems. **Pays $25/printed page** (Canadian).
Tips: "SASE for guidelines. Please include brief biographical note."

B&A: NEW FICTION, P.O. Box 702, Station P, Toronto, Ontario M5S 2Y4 Canada. (416)822-8708. E-mail: fiction@interlog.com. **Contact:** Michelle Alfano, fiction editor. **100% freelance written.** Quarterly magazine of literary fiction, essays, scripts and reviews. Estab. 1990. Circ. 2,000. Pays on publication. Publishes ms an average of 6 months after acceptance. Byline given. Buys first North American serial rights, electronic and anthology rights. Editorial lead time 2 months. Accepts simultaneous submissions. Reports in 1 month on queries; 2 months on mss. Sample for $6 (US). Writer's guidelines for #10 SASE with IRCs.
Nonfiction: Essays, book reviews. Query or send complete ms with SASE. **Pays $35/printed page.**
Fiction: Experimental, novel excerpts. No mystery, sci-fi, poetry. **Buys 20-30 mss/year.** Send complete ms. Length: 500-7,000 words. **Pays $35/printed page.**
Tips: See *B&A: New Fiction*'s annual fiction contest in Contest and Awards section.

$ BLACK WARRIOR REVIEW, P.O. Box 862936, Tuscaloosa AL 35486-0027. (205)348-4518. Website: http://www.sa.ua.edu/osm/bwr. **Contact:** Christopher Chambers, editor. **90% freelance written.** Semiannual magazine of fiction, poetry, essays and reviews. Estab. 1974. Circ. 2,000. Pays on publication. Publishes ms an average of 6 months after acceptance. Byline given. Buys first rights. Reports in 2 weeks on queries; 3 months on mss. Sample copy for $8. Writer's guidelines for #10 SASE.

- Consistently excellent magazine. Placed stories and poems in recent *Best American Short Stories*, *Best American Poetry* and *Pushcart Prize* anthologies.

Nonfiction: Interview/profile, book reviews and literary/personal essays. **Buys 5 mss/year.** Query or send complete ms. No limit on length. **Pays up to $100** and 2 contributor's copies.
Photos: State availability of photos with submission. Offers no additional payment for photos accepted with ms. Identification of subjects required. Buys one-time rights.
Fiction: Matt McDonald, fiction editor. **Buys 10 mss/year.** Publishes novel excerpts if under contract to be published. One story/chapter per envelope, please. **Pays up to $100** and 2 contributor's copies.

INSIDER REPORT

B&A: New Fiction—break-in market for talented new writers

Michelle Alfano knows what it feels like to be an unpublished writer trying to break in. Her big break came in 1991 when *B&A: New Fiction* was the first to publish one of her stories. Later Alfano became an associate editor at *B&A* and, in 1997, was named fiction editor.

Now in a position to give other writers their first break, Alfano says, "We tend to focus on publishing new, emerging writers." And many writers published in *B&A* go on to publish with major publishing houses: Larry Hill with HarperCollins, Dennis Bock with Doubleday and Ken Sparling and Oakland Ross with Knopf, to name a few.

Alfano, 15 volunteers and 3 associate editors all work from their homes or their full-time work places. "We have no formal office," says Alfano, "unless you call the publisher's home an office." She and the associate editors share the task of reviewing 200-300 fiction submissions for each quarterly edition of *B&A*. "I ask them to forward the best submissions to me, and I in turn ask the other associates to read the work put forward." Alfano also asks her editors to do a preliminary edit or synopsis of why a story works. Then she decides if a story will be one of the six or seven included in the upcoming issue. When a story is finally selected for publication, she corresponds with the writer and does the final edits of one to three drafts of the proposed piece. She also secures the permission forms, bios and disk, and forwards them to the designer who puts the issue together.

Although unsolicited submissions of fiction are the norm at *B&A*, other features in the magazine are usually assigned. For the interviews with writers and book reviews that appear in each issue, Alfano says, "Our Interviews editors stake out readings and approach writers for interviews, and the Reviews editor will corral two or three writers to review mostly Canadian literary fiction and nonfiction."

The things that attract Alfano to an unsolicited fiction submission package may seem small and superficial, but, she says, "they are the things which tell me that the writer cares about the work." She wants a clean, legible manuscript, double-spaced ("a single-spaced manuscript is a nightmare to get through when you have 20-30 submissions in front of you!") and a brief cover letter with the appropriate return postage if you've included a SASE ("Canadian stamps if you're in the U.S.—hey, we're a separate country, guys!"). Alfano also likes some indication that writers submitting stories have read *B&A*. "Don't for instance, send us vampire Gothic fiction; we never publish work of that type."

The things that compel Alfano to publish a story are "honesty, the moral ambiguity of complex characters, freshness, originality, poetic sensibility and sensuality." She advises writers to avoid clichés and to write with passion and honesty, "even if what comes out is disturbing or politically incorrect." She does, however, have "a problem with juvenile fixation on bodily functions and emissions. Generally speaking, if the character is throwing

INSIDER REPORT, *Alfano*

up, urinating or defecating on the first page, I feel like the writer is trying to shock me into being interested in the piece. And I am decidedly not interested in this sort of presentation."

Other topics Alfano suggests writers avoid include "drunken nights in the college dorm; instead, give me a reason to care about your character." Alfano also advises that sexual and physical abuse as a plot device is starting to be a turnoff for her, "because it's now common in so many stories. That's not to say I would discount the story, but it does give me pause because it's become almost a cliché."

The most common mistake Alfano sees among new writers is their over-reliance on personal anecdote and memories for source material. "It's true that we are encouraged to write what we know, but I feel there should be an underlying theme or message that would pertain universally. How does a fight with your father when you were 14 pertain to the reader? Is it about the struggle for independence against an oppressive force? Is it about the loss of innocence as a child? Is it the classical Oedipal struggle of the son's need to overpower and dominate the father? We can and should think about the larger issues or themes at hand."

At a time when many lament the difficulty of getting published, especially for the first time, Alfano identifies one advantage for today's writers: "Virtually every topic is open territory for the new writers. There are few taboos. You are free to explore areas that one generation ago writers were forbidden to talk about."

However, when not handled skillfully, this advantage can prove detrimental to writers. "Today, there is less attempt at subtlety, at creating a subtext," says Alfano. "Much of the new writing I receive is explicit, in your face, nothing held back. It's wide open: incest, child abuse, fetishist sex, necrophilia. Unfortunately, most of us are unable to broach these topics with subtlety and confidence. We plunge ahead with all the lurid details thinking that shocking information can or should pass for art."

Alfano also notes that *B&A*'s new publisher has opted for theme issues. "I am divided about this. On the one hand, it discourages good stories that don't fit into a category. On the other hand, it's interesting finding broad interpretations of stories that do fit our themes."

As for the perception by some that *B&A* only publishes or gives preference to Canadian writers, Alfano says, "We don't discount writers who are non-Canadian. Some former staff members have objected to publishing American writers. Sometimes the publisher who is trying to access federal and provincial grants to fund a magazine may encounter opposition to public funds going to American writers. But I personally don't care about the country of origin."

Alfano stresses again that at *B&A* it does not matter if a writer has been published previously. "I only care about the originality of the piece. I think excellence in writing should rule."

—*Barbara Kuroff*

Poetry: Matt Doherty, poetry editor. Submit 3-6 poems. **Buys 50 poems/year. Pays $35-40** and 2 copies.
Tips: "Read the *BWR* before submitting; editors change each year. Send us your best work. Submissions of photos and/or artwork is encouraged. We sometimes choose unsolicited photos/artwork for the cover. Address all submissions to the appropriate genre editor."

$ $ BOMB MAGAZINE, 594 Broadway, #905, New York NY 10012. (212) 431-3943. **Contact:** Jennifer Berman, senior editor. Quarterly literary magazine covering art, literature, film, theater and music. Estab. 1981. Circ. 12,000. Pays on publication. Publishes ms an average of 6 months after acceptance. Byline given. Buys one-time rights. Reports in 4 months. Sample copy for $4.50 and 10 first-class stamps.
Nonfiction: Book excerpts. "Literature only." Query. Length: 250-5,000 words. **Pays $100 minimum.**
Photos: Pays $100 minimum. Captions required. Buys one-time rights.
Fiction: Experimental, novel excerpts. "No commercial fiction." **Buys 28 mss/year.** Send complete ms. Length: 250-5,000 words. **Pays $100 minimum.**
Poetry: Avant-garde. **Buys 10/year.** Submit maximum 5 poems. **Pays $50.**

☆ $ $ BOULEVARD, Opojaz, Inc., 4579 Laclede Ave., #332, St. Louis MO 63108-2103. **Contact:** Richard Burgin, editor. **100% freelance written.** Triannual literary magazine covering fiction, poetry and essays. "*Boulevard* is a diverse literary magazine presenting original creative work by well-known authors, as well as by writers of exciting promise." Estab. 1985. Circ. 3,500. Pays on publication. Publishes ms an average of 9 months after acceptance. Byline given. No kill fee. Buys first North American serial rights. Accepts simultaneous submissions. Reports in 2 weeks on queries; 2 months on mss. Sample copy for $7. Writer's guidelines for #10 SASE.
Nonfiction: Book excerpts, essays, interview/profile. "No pornography, science fiction, children's stories or westerns." **Buys 8 mss/year.** Send complete ms. Length: 8,000 words maximum. **Pays $50-250** (sometimes higher).
Fiction: Confession, experimental, mainstream, novel excerpts. "We do not want erotica, science fiction, romance, western or children's stories." **Buys 20 mss/year.** Send complete ms. Length: 8,000 words maximum. **Pays $50-250** (sometimes higher). Publishes novel excerpts.

- Ranked as one of the best markets for fiction writers in *Writer's Digest* magazine's "Fiction 50," June 1998.

Poetry: Avant-garde, free verse, haiku, traditional. "Do not send us light verse." **Buys 80 poems/year.** Submit maximum 5 poems. Length: up to 200 lines. **Pays $25-250** (sometimes higher).
Tips: "Read the magazine first. The work *Boulevard* publishes is generally recognized as among the finest in the country. We continue to seek more good literary or cultural essays. Send only your best work."

$ $ THE CAPILANO REVIEW, The Capilano Press Society, 2055 Purcell Way, North Vancouver, British Columbia V7J 3H5 Canada. Fax: (604)983-7520. E-mail: bsherrin@capcollege.bc.ca. Website: http://www.capcollege.bc.ca/dept/TCR/tcr./html. **Contact:** Robert Sherrin, editor. **100% freelance written.** "Triannual visual and literary arts magazine that publishes only what the editors consider to be the very best fiction, poetry, or visual art being produced. *TCR* editors are interested in fresh, original work that stimulates and challenges readers. Over the years, the magazine has developed a reputation for pushing beyond the boundaries of traditional art and writing. We are interested in work that is new in concept and in execution." Estab. 1972. Circ. 1,000. Pays on publication. Publishes ms 3 months after acceptance. Byline given. Buys first North American serial rights. Reports in 1 month on queries; 5 months on mss. Sample copy for $9. Writer's guidelines for #10 SASE with IRC or Canadian stamps.

- *The Capilano Review* is seeking more stories focusing on experiences in British Columbia or other areas of Canada, and more stories that reflect multiculturalism.

Nonfiction: Essays, interview/profile, personal experience, creative nonfiction. **Buys 1-2 mss/year.** Length: 6,000 words maximum. Query. **Pays $50-200,** plus 2 copies and 1 year subscription. "Most nonfiction is assigned to writers we have worked with before. If we know you, you may send a query. If we don't, send complete ms with SASE and Canadian postage or IRCs."
Fiction: Literary. **Buys 10-15 mss/year.** Length: 6,000 words maximum. Send complete ms with SASE and Canadian postage or IRCs. **Pays $50-200.** Publishes novel excerpts.
Poetry: Avant-garde, free verse. **Buys 40 poems/year.** Submit 5-10 poems with SASE. **Pays $50-200.**

$ THE CHARITON REVIEW, Truman State University, Kirksville MO 63501-9915. (816)785-4499. Fax: (816)785-7486. **Contact:** Jim Barnes, editor. **100% freelance written.** Semiannual (fall and spring) magazine covering contemporary fiction, poetry, translation and book reviews. Circ. 600. Pays on publication. Publishes ms an average of 6 months after acceptance. Byline given. Buys first North American serial rights. Reports in 1 week on queries; 1 month on mss. Sample copy for $5 and 7×10 SAE with 4 first-class stamps.
Nonfiction: Essays, essay reviews of books. **Buys 2-5 mss/year.** Send complete ms. Length: 1,000-5,000. Pays $15.
Fiction: Ethnic, experimental, mainstream, novel excerpts, traditional. Publishes novel excerpts if they can stand alone. "We are not interested in slick or sick material." **Buys 6-10 mss/year.** Send complete ms. Length: 1,000-6,000 words. **Pays $5/page.**
Poetry: Avant-garde, traditional. **Buys 50-55 poems/year.** Submit maximum 5 poems. Length: open. **Pays $5/page.**
Tips: "Read *Chariton*. Know the difference between good literature and bad. Know what magazine might be interested in your work. We are not a trendy magazine. We publish only the best. All sections are open to freelancers. Know your market or you are wasting your time—and mine. Do *not* write for guidelines; the only guideline is excellence."

$ CHELSEA, Chelsea Associates, P.O. Box 773, Cooper Station, New York NY 10276. **Contact:** Richard Foerster, editor. **70% freelance written.** Semiannual literary magazine. "We stress style, variety, originality. No special biases or requirements. Flexible attitudes, eclectic material. We take an active interest, as always, in cross-cultural exchanges, superior translations, and are leaning toward cosmopolitan, interdisciplinary techniques, but maintain no strictures against traditional modes." Estab. 1958. Circ. 1,800. Pays on publication. Publishes ms an average of 6 months after acceptance. Byline given. Buys first North American serial rights. Reports in 3 months on mss. Include SASE. Sample copy for $6.

• *Chelsea* also sponsors fiction and poetry contests. Send SASE for guidelines.

Nonfiction: Essays, book reviews (query first with sample). **Buys 6 mss/year.** Send complete ms. Length: 6,000 words. **Pays $15/page.**

Fiction: Mainstream, literary, novel excerpts. **Buys 12 mss/year.** Send complete ms. Length: 5-6,000 words. **Pays $15/page.** Publishes novel excerpts.

Poetry: Avant-garde, free verse, traditional. **Buys 60-75 poems/year. Pays $15/page.**

Tips: "We only accept written queries. We are looking for more super translations, first-rate fiction and work by writers of color. We suggest writers look at a recent issue of *Chelsea*."

$ CICADA, *Amelia Magazine*, 329 E St., Bakersfield CA 93304. (805)323-4064. **Contact:** Frederick A. Raborg, Jr., editor. **100% freelance written.** Quarterly magazine covering Oriental fiction and poetry (haiku, etc.). "Our readers expect the best haiku and related poetry forms we can find. Our readers circle the globe and know their subjects. We include fiction, book reviews and articles related to the forms or to the Orient." Estab. 1984. Circ. 600. Pays on publication. Publishes ms an average of 6 months after acceptance. Byline given. Offers 50% kill fee. Buys first North American serial rights. Editorial lead time 2 months. Submit seasonal material 3 months in advance. Accepts simultaneous submissions. Reports in 2 weeks on queries, 3 months on mss. Sample copy for $4.95. Guidelines for #10 SASE.

Nonfiction: Essays, general interest, historical/nostalgic, humor, interview/profile, opinion, personal experience, travel. **Buys 1-3 mss/year.** Send complete ms. Length: 500-2,500 words. **Pays $10.**

Photos: Send photos with submission. Reviews 5×7 or 8×10 b/w prints. Offers $10-25/photo. Model releases required. Buys one-time rights.

Fiction: Adventure, erotica, ethnic, experimental, fantasy, historical, horror, humorous, mainstream, mystery, romance, science fiction, slice-of-life vignettes, suspense. **Buys 4 mss/year.** Send complete ms. Length: 500-2,500 words. **Pays $10-20.**

Poetry: Buys 400 poems/year. Submit maximum 12 poems. Length: 1-50 lines. Pays 3 "best of issue" poets $10.

Fillers: Anecdotes, short humor. Buys 1-4/year. Length: 25-500 words. No payment for fillers.

Tips: "Writers should understand the limitations of contemporary Japanese forms particularly. We also use poetry based on other Asian ethnicities and on the South Seas ethnicities. Don't be afraid to experiment within the forms. Be professional in approach and presentation."

$ CIMARRON REVIEW, Oklahoma State University, 205 Morrill Hall, OSU, Stillwater OK 74078-0135. (405)744-9476. **Contact:** E.P. Walkiewicz, editor. **85% freelance written.** Quarterly literary magazine. "We publish short fiction, poetry, and essays of serious literary quality by writers often published, seldom published and previously unpublished. We have no bias with respect to subject matter, form (traditional or experimental) or theme. Though we appeal to a general audience, many of our readers are writers themselves or members of a university community." Estab. 1967. Circ. 500. Pays on publication. Published ms an average of 1 year after acceptance. Byline given. Buys all rights (reprint permission freely granted on request). Reports in 1 week on queries; 3 months on mss. Sample copy for $3 and 7×10 SASE. Writer's guidelines for #10 SASE.

Nonfiction: Essays, general interest, historical, interview/profile, opinion, personal experience, travel, literature and arts. "We are not interested in highly subjective personal reminiscences, obscure or arcane articles, or short, light 'human interest' pieces." Special issues: flash fiction; Native American writers; Irish writers. **Buys 9-12 mss/year.** Send complete ms. Length: 1,000-7,500 words. **Pays $50** plus 1 year's subscription.

Fiction: Mainstream, literary, novel excerpts. No juvenile or genre fiction. **Buys 12-17 mss/year.** Send complete ms. Length: 1,250-7,000 words. **Pays $50.**

Poetry: Free verse, traditional. No haiku, light verse or experimental poems. **Buys 55-70 poems/year.** Submit maximum 6 poems. **Pays $15/poem.**

Tips: "For prose, submit legible, double-spaced typescript with name and address on manuscript. Enclose SASE and brief cover letter. For poetry, same standards apply, but single-spaced is conventional. Be familiar with high quality, contemporary mainstream writing. Evaluate your own work carefully."

$ CLOCKWATCH REVIEW, (a journal of the arts), Dept. of English, Illinois Wesleyan University, Bloomington IL 61702-2900. (309)556-3352. Fax: (309)556-3411. E-mail: jplath@titan.iwu.edu. Website: http://titan.iwu.edu/~jplath/clockwatch.html. **Contact:** James Plath, Zarina Mullan Plath, editors. **85% freelance written.** Semiannual literary magazine. Estab. 1983. Circ. 1,500. **Pays on acceptance.** Byline given. Buys first North American serial rights. Submit seasonal material 6 months in advance. Reports in 6 months. Sample copy for $4. Writer's guidelines for #10 SASE.

Nonfiction: Literary essays, criticism (MLA style), interviews with writers, musicians, artists. Special issue: Sex and Gender in American Culture. **Buys 4-8 mss/year.** Query by mail, e-mail. Length: 1,500-4,000 words. **Pays up to $25.** Pays in copies for criticism.

Photos: State availability of photos with submission. Reviews contact sheets, negatives, transparencies. Offers no additional payment for photos accepted with ms. Buys one-time rights.

Fiction: Experimental, humorous, mainstream, novel excerpts. "Also literary quality genre stories that break the mold. No straight mystery, fantasy, science fiction, romance or western." **Buys 8-10 mss/year.** Send complete ms. Length: 1,500-4,000 words. **Pays up to $25.** Pays in copies for criticism.

• Ranked as one of the best markets for fiction writers in *Writer's Digest* magazine's "Fiction 50," June 1998.

Poetry: Avant-garde, free verse, light verse, traditional. **Buys 30-40 poems/year.** Submit maximum 6 poems. Length: 32 lines maximum. **Pays $5.**

Tips: "E-mail queries are okay, but no electronic submissions accepted."

$ $ CONFRONTATION, A Literary Journal, Long Island University, Brookville NY 11548. (516)299-2391. Fax: (516)299-2735. **Contact:** Martin Tucker, editor-in-chief. Assistant to Editor: Michael Hartnett. **75% freelance written.** Semiannual literary magazine. "We are eclectic in our taste. Excellence of style is our dominant concern." Estab. 1968. Circ. 2,000. Pays on publication. Publishes ms an average of 1 year after acceptance. Byline given. "Rarely offers kill fee." Buys first North American serial, first, one-time or all rights. Accepts simultaneous submissions. Reports in 3 weeks on queries; 2 months on mss. Sample copy for $3.

Nonfiction: Essays, personal experience. **Buys 15 mss/year.** Send complete ms. Length: 1,500-5,000 words. **Pays $100-300 for assigned articles; $15-300 for unsolicited articles.**

Photos: State availability of photos with submission. Offers no additional payment for photos accepted with ms. Buys one-time rights.

Fiction: Jonna Semeiks. Experimental, mainstream, slice-of-life vignettes, novel excerpts (if they are self-contained stories). "We judge on quality, so genre is open." **Buys 60-75 mss/year.** Send complete ms. Length 6,000 words maximum. **Pays $25-250.**

Poetry: Katherine Hill-Miller. Avant-garde, free verse, haiku, light verse, traditional. **Buys 60-75 poems/year.** Submit maximum 6 poems. Length open. **Pays $10-100.**

Tips: "Most open to fiction and poetry."

$ DANDELION, Dandelion Magazine Society, 922 Ninth Ave. SE, Calgary, Alberta T2G 0S4 Canada. (403)265-0524. **Contact:** Richard Jogodzinski, managing editor. **90% freelance written.** Semiannual magazine. "*Dandelion* is a literary and visual arts journal with an international audience. There is no restriction on subject matter or form, be it poetry, fiction, visual art or review." Reviews Canadian book authors—showcases Canadian visual artists. Estab. 1975. Circ. 1,000. Pays on publication. Publishes ms an average of 3 months after acceptance. Byline given. Buys one-time rights. Editorial lead time 3 months. Reports in 3 weeks on queries; 4 months on mss. Sample copy for $7. Writer's guidelines for #10 SAE and IRC.

Nonfiction: Reviews Editor. **Buys 4-6 mss/year.** Query with published clips. Length: 750 words.

Photos: Alice Simmons. Send photos with submission. Reviews contact sheets. Negotiates payment individually. Captions required. Buys one-time rights.

Fiction: Elizabeth Haynes and Adele Megann, fiction editors. Adventure, ethnic, experimental, historical, humorous, mainstream, novel excerpts. **Buys 6-8 mss/year.** Send complete ms. Length: approx. 3,500 words maximum. **Pays $150.**

Poetry: Gordon Pengilly, poetry editor. Avant-garde, free verse, haiku, traditional, long poem. **Buys 50 poems/year.** Submit maximum 10 poems. **Pays $20/page** or more depending on length.

Tips: "The mandate is so large and general, only a familiarity with literary journals and reviews will help. Almost all our material comes unsolicited; thus, find out what we publish and you'll have a means of 'breaking in.' "

$ DESCANT, Descant Arts & Letters Foundation, P.O. Box 314, Station P, Toronto, Ontario M5S 2S8. (416)593-2557. Editor: Karen Mulhallen. Managing Editor: Mary Myers. Quarterly literary journal. Estab. 1970. Circ. 1,200. Pays on publication. Publishes ms 16 months after acceptance. Editorial lead time 4 months. Submit seasonal material 4 months in advance. Sample copy for $8. Writer's guidelines for SASE.

Nonfiction: Book excerpts, essays, historical/nostalgic, interview/profile, personal experience, photo feature, travel. Query or send complete ms. **Pays $100** honorarium plus 1 year's subscription.

Photos: State availability of photos with submission. Reviews contact sheets and prints. Offers no additional payment for photos accepted with ms. Buys one-time rights.

Fiction: Send complete ms. **Pays $100.**

Poetry: Free verse, light verse, traditional. Submit maximum 10 poems. **Pays $100.**

Tips: "Familiarize yourself with our magazine before submitting."

$ DOGWOOD TALES MAGAZINE, P.O. Box 172068, Memphis TN 38187. E-mail: write2me@aol.com or dogwoodmag@bellsouth.net. Website: http://www.sftwarestuff.com/dogwood. **Contact:** P. Carman, fiction editor. **Pays on acceptance.** Buys first and reprint rights. Submit seasonal material at least 6 months in advance. Accepts simultaneous submissions. Reports in 1 month on mss. Sample copy for $3.50. Writer's guidelines for #10 SASE.

Fiction: Any genre suitable for a family environment. No religious, pornography, nonfiction, poorly developed plots, cardboard characters or weak endings. Each issue will include a special feature story with a southern theme, person or place from any genre. **Buys 48-60 mss/year.** Send complete ms with cover letter. Length: 3,000 words. **Pays ¼-½¢/word** plus contributor copy.

Reprints: Send typed ms with rights for sale noted and information about when and where the article previously appeared. Pays 100% of amount paid for an original story.

$ $ $ DOUBLE TAKE, 1317 W. Pettigrew St., Durham NC 27705. **Contact:** Fiction Editor. **Pays on acceptance.** Byline given. Buys first North American serial rights. Accepts simultaneous submissions. Reports in 3 months on mss. Sample copy for $12. Writer's guidelines for #10 SASE.

Fiction: "We accept realistic fiction in all of its variety; its very unlikely we'd ever publish science fiction or gothic horror, for example." **Buys 12 mss/year.** Send complete ms with cover letter. Length: 3,000-8,000 words. **Pays competitively.**

Tips: "Use a strong, developed narrative voice. Don't attempt too much or be overly melodramatic, lacking in subtlety, nuance and insight."

$ DREAMS OF DECADENCE, P.O. Box 13, Greenfield MA 01302-0013. (413)772-0725. **Contact:** Angela Kessler, editor. Quarterly literary magazine featuring vampire fiction and poetry. Pays on publication. Publishes ms an average of 6 months after acceptance. Buys first North American serial rights. Accepts simultaneous submissions. Reports in 1 month. Sample copy for $5. Writer's guidelines for #10 SASE.

Fiction: "I like elegant prose with a Gothic feel. The emphasis is on dark fantasy rather than horror. No vampire feeds, vampire has sex, someone becomes a vampire pieces." **Buys 30-40 mss/year.** Send complete ms. Length: 1,000-5,000 words. **Pays 1-5¢/word.**

Poetry: "Looking for all forms; however, the less horrific and the more explicitly vampiric a poem is, the more likely it is to be accepted." Pays in copies.

Tips: "We look for atmospheric, well-written stories with original ideas, not rehashes."

$ $ EVENT, Douglas College, P.O. Box 2503, New Westminster, British Columbia V3L 5B2 Canada. (604)527-5293. Fax: (604)527-5095. Editor: Calvin Wharton. **Contact:** Bonnie Bauder, assistant editor. **100% freelance written.** Triannual magazine containing fiction, poetry and reviews. "We are eclectic and always open to content that invites involvement. Generally, we like strong narrative." Estab. 1971. Circ. 1,000. Pays on publication. Publishes ms an average of 8 months after acceptance. Byline given. Buys first North American serial rights. Accepts simultaneous submissions. Reports in 1 month on queries; 4 months on mss. Sample copy for $5. Guidelines for #10 SASE.

- *Event* does not read manuscripts in July.

Fiction: Christine Dewar, fiction editor. "We look for readability, style and writing that invites involvement." **Buys 20-25 mss/year.** Send complete ms. Length: 5,000 words. Submit maximum 2 stories. **Pays $22/page to $500.**

Poetry: Gillian Garding-Russell, poetry editor. Free verse and prose poems. No light verse. "In poetry, we tend to appreciate the narrative and sometimes the confessional modes." **Buys 30-40 poems/year.** Submit maximum 10 poems. **Pays $25-500.**

$ FIELD MAGAZINE, Contemporary Poetry & Poetics, Rice Hall, Oberlin College, Oberlin OH 44074-1095. (440)775-8407/8. Fax: (440)775-8124. E-mail: ocpress@oberlin.edu. Website: http://www.oberlin.edu/~ocpress. **Contact:** David Young, David Walker, Alberta Turner, editors. Business Manager: Heather Smith. **60% freelance written.** Semiannual magazine of poetry, poetry in translation, and essays on contemporary poetry by poets. Estab. 1969. Circ. 2,300. Pays on publication. Byline given. Buys first rights. Editorial lead time 4 months. Reports in 1 month on mss. Sample copy for $7.

Poetry: Buys 100 poems/year. Submit maximum 10 poems. **Pays $15-25/page.**

$ FIRST WORD BULLETIN, Amick Associates Magazines, Calle Domingo Fernandez 5, Box 500, 28036 Madrid Spain. (34)1-359-64-18. Fax: (34)1-320-8961. E-mail: gw83@correo.interlink.es. Website: http://www.interlink.es/peraso/first. **Contact:** G.W. Amick, editor. **60-80% freelance written.** Quarterly magazine printed in Madrid, Spain, with worldwide distribution to the English-speaking community. "Our audience is the general public, but the magazine is specifically aimed at writers who wish to get published for credits. We welcome unpublished writers; since our audience is mainly writers we expect high-quality work. We like writers who have enough self-confidence to be willing to pay the postage to get to us. They should write for guidelines first and then follow them to the letter." Estab. 1995. Pays on publication. Publishes ms an average of 6 months after acceptance. Byline given. Offers 10% kill fee or $5. Buys first world or second serial (reprint) rights. Editorial lead time 3 months. Submit seasonal material 5 months in advance. Accepts simultaneous submissions. Reports in 3 weeks on queries; 2 months on mss. Sample copy for $3.50 and SAE with $3.50 postage or 4 IRCs. Writer's guidelines free for SAE with $2 postage or 2 IRCs.

Nonfiction: General interest, how-to, humor, personal experience, environment, self-help, preventive medicine, literary, experimental. **Buys 40 mss/year.** Send complete ms. Length: 500-4,000 words. **Pays 2½¢/word up to $50.** Pays in contributor copies for fillers, bullets, pieces less than 50 words.

Reprints: Send tearsheet or photocopy of article or short story and information about when and where the article previously appeared. **Pays 2½¢/word up to $50.**

ALWAYS SUBMIT unsolicited manuscripts or queries with a self-addressed, stamped envelope (SASE) within your country or a self-addressed envelope with International Reply Coupons (IRC) purchased from the post office for other countries.

Fiction: Adventure, environment, experiment, humorous, mainstream, self-help. No smut, pornography, science fiction, romance/love stories or horror. **Buys 10-30 mss/year.** Send complete ms. Length: 500-4,000 words. **Pays 2½¢/word up to $50.**
Poetry: Free verse, light verse. "We are not interested in poetry per se, but will accept poetry as a sidebar or filler." **Buys 4-8 poems/year.** Submit maximum 1 poem. Length: 14 lines for filler; 24 lines for sidebar. **Pays 2½¢/word up to $50.**
Fillers: Anecdotes, facts, gags to be illustrated by cartoonist, short humor. **Buys 32/year.** Length: 10-80 words. **Pays 2½¢/word up to $50.**
Tips: "Write for guidelines. Pay close attention to the market study. Follow directions to the letter. Get the editor's name correct. Don't request return of manuscript, ask for the first page only to save postage. If you submit a self-help article, don't let God do all the work. For an environmental article, study the subject carefully and get your facts correct. Use positive thinking at all times. I still feel strong about ecology, but I would like to see something on alternative medicine, homeopathy, perhaps some exotic stories on medicines from herbs in Brazil and Venezuela. I need crossword puzzles also. We now have an office in the United States for accepting submissions from the U.S., Canada and all American possessions. Also accepting submissions from Jamaica. The U.S. office address: The First Word Bulletin, PDS Margaret H. Swain, 2046 Lothbury Dr., Fayetteville NC 28304-5666 USA."

$ FRANK, An International Journal of Contemporary Writing & Art, Association Frank, 32 rue Edouard Vaillant, Montreuil France. Phone: (33)(1)48596658. Fax: (31)(1)48596668. E-mail: david@paris-anglo.com. Website: http://www.paris-anglo.com/frank. **Contact:** David Applefield, editor. **80% freelance written.** Bilingual magazine covering contemporary writing of all genres. "Writing that takes risks and isn't ethnocentric is looked upon favorably." Estab. 1983. Circ. 4,000. Pays on publication. Publishes ms an average of 1 year after acceptance. Byline given. Buys one-time rights. Editorial lead time 6 months. Reports in 1 month on queries; 2 months on mss. Sample copy for $10. Writer's guidelines free.
Nonfiction: Interview/profile, travel. **Buys 2 mss/year.** Query. **Pays $100.** Pays in contributor copies by agreement.
Photos: State availability of photos with submission. Negotiates payment individually. Buys one-time rights.
Fiction: Experimental, international, novel excerpts. **Buys 8 mss/year.** Send complete ms. Length: 1-3,000 words. **Pays $10/printed page.**
Poetry: Avant-garde, translations. **Buys 20 poems/year.** Submit maximum 10 poems. **Pays $20.**
Tips: "Suggest what you do or know best. Avoid query form letters—we won't read the ms. Looking for excellent literary/cultural interviews with leading American writers or cultural figures."

$ THE GETTYSBURG REVIEW, Gettysburg College, Gettysburg PA 17325. (717)337-6770. **Contact:** Peter Stitt, editor. Emily Ruark Clarke, managing editor. Quarterly literary magazine. "Our concern is quality. Manuscripts submitted here should be extremely well-written." Estab. 1988. Circ. 4,000. Pays on publication. Byline given. Buys first North American serial rights. Editorial lead time 1 year. Submit seasonal material 9 months in advance. Reports in 1 month on queries; 3 months on mss. Sample copy for $7. Writer's guidelines for #10 SASE. Reading period September-May. No simultaneous submissions.
Nonfiction: Essays. **Buys 20/year.** Send complete ms. Length: 3,000-7,000. **Pays $25/page.**
Fiction: High quality, literary. Publishes novel excerpts. **Buys 20 ms/year.** Send complete ms. Length: 2,000-7,000, **Pays $25/page.**
Poetry: Buys 50 poems/year. Submit maximum 3 poems. **Pays $2/line.**

$ $ GLIMMER TRAIN STORIES, Glimmer Train Press, Inc., 710 SW Madison St., #504, Portland OR 97205. (503)221-0836. Fax: (503)221-0837. Website: http://www.GlimmerTrain.com. Contact: Linda Burmeister Davies, co-editor. Co-editor: Susan Burmeister-Brown. **90% freelance written.** Quarterly magazine covering short fiction. "We are interested in well-written, emotionally-moving short stories published by unknown, as well as known, writers." Estab. 1991. Circ. 16,000. **Pays on acceptance.** Byline given. Buys first rights. Accepts simultaneous submissions. Reports in 3 months on mss. Sample copy for $9.95. Writer's guidelines for #10 SASE.
Fiction: "We are not restricted to any types." Publishes novel excerpts. **Buys 32 mss/year.** Send complete ms. Length: 1,200-7,500 words. **Pays $500.**

- Ranked as one of the best markets for fiction writers in *Writer's Digest* magazine's "Fiction 50," June 1998.

Tips: "Manuscripts should be sent to us in the months of January, April, July and October. Be sure to include a sufficiently-stamped SASE. We are particularly interested in receiving work from new writers." See *Glimmer Train*'s Short Story Award for New Writers listing in Contest and Awards section.

$ GRAIN LITERARY MAGAZINE, Saskatchewan Writers Guild, P.O. Box 1154, Regina, Saskatchewan S4P 3B4 Canada. Fax: (306)244-0255. E-mail: grain.mag@sk.sympatico.ca. Website: http://www.skwriter.com. **Contact:** J. Jill Robinson, editor. Business Manager: Steven Smith. **100% freelance written.** Quarterly literary magazine covering poetry, fiction, creative nonfiction, drama. "*Grain* publishes writing of the highest quality, both traditional and nontraditional in nature. *The Grain* editors' aim: To publish work that challenges readers; to encourage promising new writers; and to produce a well-designed, visually interesting magazine." Estab. 1973. Circ. 1,500. Pays on publication. Publishes ms an average of 11 months after acceptance. Byline given. Buys first, Canadian, serial rights. Editorial lead time 6 months. Reports in 1 month on queries; 4 months on mss. Sample copy for $7. Writer's guidelines free.
Nonfiction: Interested in creative nonfiction.

Photos: Review transparencies and prints. Submit 12-20 slides and b&w prints, short statement (200 words) and brief resume. Pays $100 for front cover art, $30/photo.
Fiction: Literary fiction of all types. "No romance, confession, science fiction, vignettes, mystery." **Buys 40 mss/year.** Query or send 2 stories maximum or 30 pages of novel-in-progress and SAE with postage or IRCs. Does not accept e-mail submissions, but will respond by e-mail—save on stamps. **Pays $30-100.**
Poetry: Avant-garde, free verse, haiku, traditional. "High quality, imaginative, well-crafted poetry. No sentimental, end-line rhyme, mundane." **Buys 78 poems/year.** Submit maximum 10 poems and SASE with postage or IRCs. **Pays $30-100.**

- Ranked as one of the best markets for fiction writers in *Writer's Digest* magazine's "Fiction 50," June 1998.

$ HAPPY, 240 E. 35th St., Suite 11A, New York NY 10016. E-mail: bayardy@aol.com. **Contact:** Bayard, editor. Pays on publication. Byline given. Buys one-time rights. Accepts simultaneous and previously published submissions. Reports in 1 month on mss. Sample copy for $9. Writer's guidelines for #10 SASE.
Fiction: Novel excerpts, short stories. "We accept anything that's beautifully written. Genre isn't important. It just has to be incredible writing." **Buys 100-130 mss/year.** Send complete ms with cover letter. Length: 250-5,000 words. **Pays $5/1,000 words.**
Reprints: Send typed ms with rights for sale noted with information about when and where the article previously appeared. Pays $5/1,000 words.

- Ranked as one of the best markets for fiction writers in *Writer's Digest* magazine's "Fiction 50," June 1998.

Tips: "If you imagine yourself Ernest Hemingway, you and your work have been dead for 30 years and are of no interest to us."

$ HIGH PLAINS LITERARY REVIEW, 180 Adams St., Suite 250, Denver CO 80206. (303)320-6828. Fax: (303)320-0463. **Contact:** Robert O. Greer, Jr., editor-in-chief. Managing Editor: Phyllis A. Harwell. **80% freelance written.** Triannual literary magazine. "The *High Plains Literary Review* publishes short stories, essays, poetry, reviews and interviews, bridging the gap between commercial quarterlies and academic reviews." Estab. 1986. Circ. 1,200. Pays on publication. Byline given. Buys first North American serial rights. Accepts simultaneous submissions. Reports in 3 months. Sample copy for $4. Writer's guidelines for #10 SASE.

- Its unique editorial format—between commercial and academic—makes for lively reading. Could be good market for that "in between" story.

Nonfiction: Essays, reviews. **Buys 20 mss/year.** Send complete ms. Length: 10,000 words maximum. **Pays $5/page.**
Fiction: Ethnic, historical, humorous, mainstream. **Buys 12 mss/year.** Send complete ms. Length: 10,000 words maximum. **Pays $5/page.**
Poetry: Buys 45 poems/year. Pays $10/page.

$ $ INDIANA REVIEW, Indiana University, 465 Ballantine Hall, Bloomington IN 47405. (812)855-3439. Website: http://www.indiana.edu/~inreview/. **Contact:** Laura McCoid, editor. Associate Editor: Brian Leung. **100% freelance written.** Semiannual magazine. "*Indiana Review*, a non-profit organization run by IU graduate students, is a journal of previously unpublished poetry and fiction. Literary interviews and essays also considered. We publish innovative fiction and poetry. We're interested in energy, originality and careful attention to craft. While we publish many well-known writers, we also welcome new and emerging poets and fiction writers." Estab. 1982. **Pays on acceptance.** Byline given. Buys first North American serial rights. Reports within 4 months. Sample copy for $7. Writer's guidelines free.
Nonfiction: Essays. No strictly academic articles dealing with the traditional canon. **Buys 8 mss/year.** Query with author bio, previous publications and SASE. Length: 7,500 maximum. **Pays $25-200.**
Fiction: Experimental, mainstream, novel excerpts. "We look for daring stories which integrate theme, language, character and form. We like polished writing, humor and fiction which has consequence beyond the world of its narrator." **Buys 18 mss/year.** Send complete ms. Length: 250-15,000. **Pays $5/page.**

- Ranked as one of the best markets for fiction writers in *Writer's Digest* magazine's "Fiction 50," June 1998.

Poetry: Avant-garde, free verse. Looks for inventive and skillful writing. **Buys 80 mss/year.** Submit up to 5 poems at one time only. Length: 5 lines minimum. **Pays $5/page.**
Tips: "Read us before you submit. Often reading is slower in summer months."

N $ INDIGENOUS FICTION, I.F. Publishing, P.O. Box 2078, Redmond WA 98073-2078. Fax: (425)836-4298. E-mail: deckr@earthlink.net. **Contact:** Sherry Decker, editor. **98% freelance written.** Semiannual magazine covering short fiction, poetry and art. "We want literary—fantasy, dark fantasy, science fiction, horror, mystery and mainstream. We enjoy elements of the supernatural or the unexplained, odd, intriguing characters and beautiful writing. Most accepted stories will be between 2,500-8,000 words in length." Estab. 1998. Circ. 250. Pays on publication. Publishes ms an average of 6 months after acceptance. Byline given. Buys first North American serial and second serial (reprint) rights. Editorial lead time 6 months. Submit seasonal material 6 months in advance. Accepts simultaneous submissions. Reports in 2 weeks on queries; 1 month on mss. Sample copy not available. Writer's guidelines free.
Reprints: Accepts previously published submissions.
Fiction: Adventure, erotica, experimental, fantasy, dark fantasy, horror, humorous, mainstream, mystery, science fiction, suspense, odd, bizarre, supernatural and the unexplained. "No porn, abuse of children, gore; no it was all a dream, evil cat, unicorn or sweet nostalgic tales. No vignettes or slice-of-life (without beginning, middle and end)." **Buys 30 mss/year.** Send complete ms, cover letter and credits. Length: 500-8,000 words. **Pays $5-20.**

Poetry: Free verse, haiku, light verse, traditional. No poetry that neither tells a story nor evokes an image. **Buys 20 poems/year**. Submit maximum 5 poems. Length: 3-30 lines. **Pays $5.**
Fillers: Short humor. **Buys 6/year**. Length: 100-500 words. **Pays $5.**
Tips: "Proper manuscript format; no e-mail or fax submissions. No disks unless asked. We like beautiful, literary writing where something happens in the story. By literary we don't mean a long, rambling piece of beautiful writing for the sake of beauty—we mean characters and situations, fully developed, beautifully. Ghosts, time travel, parallel words, 'the bizarre'—fine! Vampires? Well, okay, but no clichés or media tie-ins. Vampire tales should be bone-chillingly dark, beautiful, erotic or humorous. Everything else has been done. Writers we admire: Joyce Carol Oates, Ray Bradbury, Pat Conroy, Carol Emshwiller, Holly Wade Matter, Tanith Lee."

$ THE IOWA REVIEW, 369 EPB, The University of Iowa, Iowa City IA 52242. (319)335-0462. Fax: (319)335-2535. E-mail: iareview@blue.weeg.uiowa.edu. Website: http://www.uiowa.edu/~english/iareview.html. Editor: David Hamilton. **Contact:** Mary Hussmann, editor. Triannual magazine. Estab. 1970. Buys first North American and non-exclusive anthology, classroom and online serial rights. Reports in 3 months. Sample copy for $6.
Nonfiction, Fiction and Poetry: "We publish essays, reviews, novel excerpts, stories and poems and would like for our essays not always to be works of academic criticism. We have no set guidelines as to content or length." **Buys 65-85 unsolicited mss/year.** Submit complete ms with SASE. **Pays $1/line for verse; $10/page for prose.**

- This magazine uses the help of colleagues and graduate assistants. Its reading period is September-April.

$ JAPANOPHILE PRESS, P.O. Box 7977, 415 N. Main St., Ann Arbor MI 48107. E-mail: susanlapp@aol.com. Website: http://www.japanophile.com. **Contact:** Susan Lapp, editor. **80% freelance written.** Works with a small number of new/unpublished writers each year. Quarterly magazine for literate people interested in Japanese culture anywhere in the world. Estab. 1974. Pays on publication. Publishes ms an average of 3 months after acceptance. Buys first North American serial rights. Reports in 3 months. Sample copy for $4, postpaid. Writer's guidelines for #10 SASE.

- *Japanophile* has changed hands, moved and has a new editor. It continues to offer an annual contest; see the Contest & Awards section.

Nonfiction: "We want material on Japanese culture in *North America or anywhere in the world*, even Japan. We want articles, preferably with pictures, about persons engaged in arts of Japanese origin: a Virginia naturalist who is a haiku poet, a potter who learned raku in Japan, a vivid 'I was there' account of a Go tournament in California. We would like to hear more about what it's like to be a Japanese in the U.S. Our particular slant is a certain kind of culture wherever it is in the world: Canada, the U.S., Europe, Japan. The culture includes flower arranging, haiku, sports, religion, travel, art, photography, fiction, etc. It is important to study the magazine." **Buys 8 mss/issue.** Query preferred but not required. Length: 1,800 words maximum. **Pays $8-20.**
Reprints: Send information about when and where the article was previously published. Pays up to 100% of amount paid for original article.
Photos: Pays $10-20 for glossy prints. "We prefer b&w people pictures."
Columns/Departments: Regular columns and features are Tokyo Topics and Japan in North America. "We also need columns about Japanese culture in various American cities." Query. Length: 1,000 words. **Pays $120.**
Fiction: Experimental, mainstream, mystery, adventure, humorous, romance, historical. Themes should relate to Japan or Japanese culture. Length: 1,000-4,000 words. Annual contest pays $100 to best short story (contest reading fee $5). Should include 1 or more Japanese and non-Japanese characters in each story.
Poetry: Traditional, avant-garde and light verse related to Japanese culture or any subject in a Japanese form such as haiku. Length: 3-50 lines. **Pays $1-20.**
Fillers: Newsbreaks, clippings and short humor of up to 200 words. **Pays $1-5.**
Tips: "We want to see more articles about Japanese culture in the U.S., Canada and Europe. Lack of convincing fact and detail is a frequent mistake."

$ THE JOURNAL, Ohio State University, 421 Denney Hall, 164 W. 17th Ave., Columbus OH 43210. (614)292-4076. Fax: (614)292-7816. E-mail: thejournal05@postbox.acs.ohio-state.edu. Website: http://www.cohums.ohio-state.edu/english/journals/the_journal/homepage.htm. **Contact:** Kathy Fagan, Michelle Herman, editors. **100% freelance written.** Semiannual literary magazine. "We're open to all forms; we tend to favor work that gives evidence of a mature and sophisticated sense of the language." Estab. 1972. Circ. 1,500. Pays on publication. Byline given. Buys first North American serial rights. Reports in 2 weeks on queries; 2 months on mss. Sample copy for $7. Writer's guidelines for #10 SASE.
Nonfiction: Essays, interview/profile. **Buys 2 mss/year.** Query. Length: 2,000-4,000 words. **Pays $25 maximum.**
Columns/Departments: Reviews of contemporary poetry, 2,000-4,000 words. **Buys 2 mss/year.** Query. **Pays $25.**
Fiction: Novel excerpts, literary short stories. **Pays $25 minimum.**
Poetry: Avant-garde, free verse, traditional. **Buys 100 poems/year.** Submit maximum 5 poems/year. **Pays $25.**

$ KALLIOPE, a journal of women's art, Florida Community College at Jacksonville, 3939 Roosevelt Blvd., Jacksonville FL 32205. (904)381-3511. **Contact:** Mary Sue Koeppel, editor. **100% freelance written.** Triannual magazine. "*Kalliope* publishes poetry, short fiction, reviews, and b&w art, usually by women artists. We look for artistic excellence." Estab. 1978. Circ. 1,600. Pays on publication. Publishes ms an average of 3 months after acceptance. Buys first rights. Reports in 1 week on queries. Sample copy for $7 (recent issue) or $4 (back copy). Writer's guidelines for #10 SASE. Reading period: September through May.

Nonfiction: Interview/profile, reviews of new works of poetry and fiction. **Buys 6 mss/year.** Send complete ms. Length: 500-2,000 words. **Pays $10 honorarium.** Special issue: Short shorts and prose poetry. Deadline: March 1, 1999.
Fiction: Ethnic, experimental, fantasy, humorous, mainstream, slice-of-life vignettes, suspense, novel excerpts. **Buys 12 mss/year.** Send complete ms. Length: 100-2,000 words. **Pays $10.**
Poetry: Avant-garde, free verse, haiku, light verse, traditional. **Buys 75 poems/year.** Submit 3-5 poems. Length: 2-120 lines. **Pays $10.**
Tips: "We publish the best of the material submitted to us each issue. (We don't build a huge backlog and then publish from that backlog for years.) Although we look for new writers and usually publish several with each issue alongside already established writers, we love it when established writers send us their work. We've recently published Tess Gallagher, Enid Shomer and works of Colette published in English for the first time. Send a bio with all submissions."

$ THE KENYON REVIEW, Kenyon College, Gambier OH 43022. (740)427-5208. Fax: (740)427-5417. E-mail: kenyonreview@kenyon.edu. Website: http://www.kenyonreview.com. **Contact:** Doris Jean Dilts, operations coordinator; David H. Lynn, editor. **100% freelance written.** Triannual magazine covering contemporary literature and criticism. "An international journal of literature, culture and the arts dedicated to an inclusive representation of the best in new writing, interviews and criticism from established and emerging writers." Estab. 1939. Circ. 4,500. Pays on publication. Publishes ms 1 year after acceptance. Byline given. Buys first, one-time rights. Editorial lead time 1 year. Submit seasonal material 1 year in advance. Reports in 2 weeks on queries; 3 months on mss. Sample copy for $8. Writer's guidelines for 4×9 SASE.

- *The Kenyon Review* does not read unsolicited submissions during April through August.

Nonfiction: Book excerpts (before publication), essays, interview/profile (query first), translations. **Buys 12 mss/year.** Query. Length: 7,500 words maximum. **Pays $10/published page.**
Fiction: Experimental, humorous, mainstream, novel excerpts (before publication), science fiction, slice-of-life vignettes, translations. **Buys 30 mss/year.** Send complete ms. Length: 7,500 words maximum. **Pays $10/published page.**
Poetry: Avant-garde, free verse, haiku, light verse, traditional; translations. **Buys 60 poems/year.** Submit maximum 6 poems. **Pays $15/published page.**

$ LEGIONS OF LIGHT, Box 874, Margaretville, NY 12455. Phone/fax: (914)586-2759. E-mail: beth@stepahead.net. Website: http://www.stepahead.net/~lol/legions.htm. **Contact:** Elizabeth Mami, editor. **100% freelance written.** Bimonthly magazine. "*Legions of Light* accepts all material except graphic violence or sex. All ages read the magazine, all subjects welcomed." Estab. 1990. Circ. 2,000. Pays on publication. Publishes ms an average of 1 year after acceptance. Byline sometimes given. Buys one-time rights. Editorial lead time 4 months. Submit seasonal material 6 months in advance. Accepts simultaneous submissions. Reports in 6 weeks on queries. Sample copy for $3. Writer's guidelines free.
Nonfiction: Historical/nostalgic, humor, inspirational, humor/profile, personal experience, religious. No graphic violence or adult material. **Buys 10-20 mss/year.** Send complete ms. Length: 500-1,500 words. **Pays $5-10.**
Reprints: Accepts previously published submissions. Send photocopy of article or short story. Publishes novel excerpts.
Photos: State availability of photos with submission. Reviews 3×5 prints. Offers no additional payment for photos accepted with ms. Identification of subjects required. Buys one-time rights.
Fiction: Adventure, ethnic, experimental, fantasy, historical, horror, humorous, mainstream, mystery, religious, romance, science fiction, slice-of-life vignettes, suspense, western. No adult or graphic violence. **Buys 20-30 mss/year.** Query or send complete ms. Length: 1,500 words maximum. **Pays $5-10.**
Poetry: Avant-garde, free verse, haiku, light verse, traditional. No erotica. **Buys 15-20 poems/year.** Pays $5-10.
Fillers: Anecdotes, facts, newsbreaks, short humor. Buys 5-15/year. **Pays $5-10.**
Tips: "*Legions of Light* caters to unpublished talent, especially children. Subscribers are used first, but subscribing is *not* a requirement to be accepted for publication."

$ LIBIDO, The Journal of Sex & Sensibility, Libido, Inc., 5318 N. Paulina St., Chicago IL 60640. (773)275-0842. Fax: (773)275-0752. E-mail: rune@mcs.com. Website: www.sensualsource.com. Co-editors: Marianna Beck and Jack Hafferkamp. **Contact**: J.L. Beck, submissions editor. **50% freelance written.** Quarterly magazine covering literate erotica. "*Libido* is about sexuality. Orientation is not an issue, writing ability is. The aim is to enlighten as often as it is to arouse. Humor—sharp and smart—is important, so are safer sex contexts." Estab. 1988. Circ. 10,000. Pays on publication. Byline given. Kill fee "rare, but negotiable." Buys one-time or second serial (reprint) rights. Editorial lead time 3 months. Submit seasonal material 4 months in advance. Payment negotiable. Reports in 6 months. Sample copy for $8. Writer's guidelines for #10 SASE.
Nonfiction: Book excerpts, essays, historical/nostalgic, humor, photo feature, travel. "No violence, sexism or misty memoirs." Buys 10-20 mss/year. Send complete ms. Length: 300-2,500 words. **Pays $50 minimum for assigned articles; $15 minimum for unsolicited articles.** Pays contributor copies "when money isn't an issue and copies or other considerations have equal or higher value." Sometimes pays expenses of writers on assignment.
Reprints: Send photocopy of article or short story or typed ms with rights for sale noted and information about when and where the material previously appeared. Pays 100% of amount paid for an original article.
Photos: Reviews contact sheets and 5×7 and 8×10 prints. Negotiates payment individually. Model releases required. Buys one-time rights.
Fiction: Erotica, short novel excerpts. **Buys 20 mss/year.** Send complete ms. Length: 800-2,500 words. **Pays $20-50.**

Poetry: Uses humorous short erotic poetry. No limericks. **Buys 10 poems/year.** Submit maximum 3 poems. **Pays $15.**
Tips: "*Libido*'s guidelines are purposely simple and loose. All sexial orientations are appreciated. The only taboos are exploitative and violent sex. Send us a manuscript—make it short, sharp and with a lead that makes us want to read. If we're not hooked by paragraph three, we reject the manuscript."

$ $ THE MALAHAT REVIEW, The University of Victoria, P.O. Box 1700, STN G5C, Victoria, British Columbia V8W 2Y2 Canada. E-mail: malahat@uvic.ca. **Contact:** Derk Wynand, editor. **100% freelance written.** Eager to work with new/unpublished writers. Quarterly covering poetry, fiction, drama and reviews. Estab. 1967. Circ. 1,700. **Pays on acceptance.** Publishes ms up to 1 year after acceptance. Byline given. Offers 100% kill fee. Buys first serial rights. Reports in 2 weeks on queries; 3 months on mss. Sample copy for $8.
Nonfiction: "Query first about review articles, critical essays, interviews and visual art which we generally solicit. Include SASE with Canadian postage or IRCs. **Pays $25/magazine page.**
Photos: Pays $25 for b&w prints. Captions required. Pays $100 for color print used as cover.
Fiction: Buys 20 mss/year. Send complete ms up to 20 pages. **Pays $25/magazine page.**

- Ranked as one of the best markets for fiction writers in *Writer's Digest* magazine's "Fiction 50," 1998.

Poetry: Avant-garde, free verse, traditional. Length: 5-10 pages. **Buys 100/year. Pays $25/magazine page.**
Tips: "Please do not send more than one manuscript (the one you consider your best) at a time. See the *Malahat Review's* long poem and novella contests in Contest & Awards section."

$ $ MANOA, A Pacific Journal of International Writing, University of Hawaii Press, 1733 Donaghho Rd., Honolulu HI 96822. (808)956-3070. Fax: (808)956-7808. E-mail: fstewart@hawaii.edu. Website: http://www2.hawaii.edu/mjournal. **Contact:** Frank Stewart, editor. Charlene Gilmore, associate editor; Patricia Matsueda, managing editor. Semiannual literary magazine. "High quality literary fiction, poetry, essays, personal narrative, reviews. About half of each issue devoted to U.S. writing, and half new work from Pacific and Asian nations. Our audience is primarily in the U.S., although expanding in Pacific countries. U.S. writing need not be confined to Pacific settings or subjects." Estab. 1989. Circ. 2,500. Pays on publication. Byline given. Buys first North American serial or non-exclusive, one-time reprint rights. Editorial lead time 6 months. Submit seasonal material 8 months in advance. Reports in 3 weeks on queries; 2 months on poetry mss, 4 months on fiction. Sample copy for $10. Writer's guidelines free with SASE.
Nonfiction: Frank Stewart, editor. Book excerpts, essays, interview/profile, creative nonfiction or personal narrative related to literature or nature. Charlene Gilmore, reviews editor. Book reviews on recent books in arts, humanities and natural sciences, usually related to Asia, the Pacific or Hawaii or published in these places. No Pacific exotica. **Buys 3-4 mss/year,** excluding reviews. Query or send complete ms. Length: 1,000-5,000 words. **Pays $25/printed page.**
Fiction: Ian MacMillan, fiction editor. "We're potentially open to anything of literary quality, though usually not genre fiction as such." Publishes novel excerpts. No Pacific exotica. **Buys 12-18 mss/year** in the US (excluding translation). Send complete ms. Length: 1,000-7,500. **Pays $100-500** normally ($25/printed page).
Poetry: Frank Stewart, editor. No light verse. **Buys 40-50 poems/year.** Send 5-6 poems minimum. **Pays $25.**
Tips: "Although we are a Pacific journal, we are a general interest U.S. literary journal, not limited to Pacific settings or subjects."

$ THE MASSACHUSETTS REVIEW, Memorial Hall, University of Massachusetts, Amherst MA 01003-9934. (413)545-2689. Editors: Mary Heath, Jules Chametzky, Paul Jenkins. Quarterly magazine. Estab. 1959. Pays on publication. Publishes ms 6-18 months after acceptance. Buys first North American serial rights. Reports in 3 months. Does not return mss without SASE. Sample copy for $7 with 3 first-class stamps.
Nonfiction: Articles on literary criticism, women, public affairs, art, philosophy, music and dance. No reviews of single books. Send complete ms or query with SASE. Length: 6,500 words average. **Pays $50.**
Fiction: Publishes one short story per issue. Length: 25-30 pages maximum. **Pays $50.**
Poetry: Submit 6 poems maximum. **Pays 35¢/line** to **$10 minimum.**
Tips: "No manuscripts are considered June-October. No fax or e-mail submissions."

$ MICHIGAN QUARTERLY REVIEW, 3032 Rackham Bldg., University of Michigan, Ann Arbor MI 48109-1070. E-mail: dorisk@umich.edu. Website: http://www.umich.edu/~mqr. **Contact:** Laurence Goldstein, editor. **75% freelance written.** Prefers to work with published/established writers. Quarterly. Estab. 1962. Circ. 1,500. Publishes ms an average of 1 year after acceptance. Pays on publication. Buys first serial rights. Reports in 2 months. Sample copy for $2.50 with 2 first-class stamps.

- The Lawrence Foundation Prize is a $1,000 annual award to the best short story published in the *Michigan Quarterly Review* during the previous year.

Nonfiction: "*MQR* is open to general articles directed at an intellectual audience. Essays ought to have a personal voice and engage a significant subject. Scholarship must be present as a foundation, but we are not interested in specialized essays directed only at professionals in the field. We prefer ruminative essays, written in a fresh style and which reach interesting conclusions. We also like memoirs and interviews with significant historical or cultural resonance." Length: 2,000-5,000 words. **Pays $100-150.**
Fiction and Poetry: No restrictions on subject matter or language. **Buys 10 mss/year.** "We are very selective. We like stories which are unusual in tone and structure, and innovative in language." Send complete ms. **Pays $10/published page.**

Tips: "Read the journal and assess the range of contents and the level of writing. We have no guidelines to offer or set expectations; every manuscript is judged on its unique qualities. On essays—query with a very thorough description of the argument and a copy of the first page. Watch for announcements of special issues which are usually expanded issues and draw upon a lot of freelance writing. Be aware that this is a university quarterly that publishes a limited amount of fiction and poetry; that it is directed at an educated audience, one that has done a great deal of reading in all types of literature."

$ MID-AMERICAN REVIEW, Dept. of English, Bowling Green State University, Bowling Green OH 43403. (419)372-2725. **Contact:** George Looney, editor-in-chief. Willing to work with new/unpublished writers. Semiannual literary magazine of "the highest quality fiction, poetry and translations of contemporary poetry and fiction." Also publishes critical articles and book reviews of contemporary literature. Estab. 1972. Pays on publication. Publishes ms less than 6 months after acceptance. Byline given. Buys one-time rights. Reports in 4 months. Sample copy for $7 (current issue), $5 (back issue); rare back issues $10.

• *Mid-American Review* reads manuscripts September through May.

Nonfiction: Essays and articles focusing on contemporary authors and topics of current literary interest. Length: 15-20 pages; also short (500-1,000 words) book reviews. **Pays $10/page up to $50,** pending funding.
Fiction: Michael Czyzniejewski, fiction editor. Character-oriented, literary. Buys 12 mss/year. Send complete ms; do not query. **Pays $10/page up to $50,** pending funding.
Poetry: David Hawkins, poetry editor. Strong imagery and sense of vision. **Buys 60 poems/year. Pays $10/page up to $50,** pending funding.
Tips: "We are seeking translations of contemporary authors from all languages into English; submissions must include the original."

$ $ THE MISSOURI REVIEW, 1507 Hillcrest Hall, University of Missouri, Columbia MO 65211. (573)882-4474. Fax: (573)884-7839. E-mail: moreview@showme.missouri.edu. Website: http://www.missouri.edu/~moreview. Editor: Speer Morgan. Managing Editor: Greg Michalson. **Contact:** Evelyn Somers, associate editor. **100% freelance written.** Triannual literary magazine. "We publish contemporary fiction, poetry, interviews, personal essays, cartoons, special features—such as 'History as Literature' series and 'Found Text' series—for the literary and the general reader interested in a wide range of subjects." Estab. 1978. Circ. 6,500. Pays on signed contract. Byline given. Buys first rights or one-time rights. Editorial lead time 6 months. Reports in 2 weeks on queries; 3 months on mss. Sample copy for $7. Writer's guidelines for #10 SASE.
Nonfiction: Evelyn Somers, associate editor. Book excerpts, essays. No literary criticism. **Buys 10 mss/year.** Send complete ms. **Pays $15-20/printed page up to $750.**
Fiction: Mainstream, literary, novel excerpts. **Buys 25 mss/year.** Send complete ms. **Pays $15-20/printed page up to $750.**

• Ranked as one of the best markets for fiction writers in *Writer's Digest* magazine's "Fiction 50," June 1998.

Poetry: Greg Michalson, poetry editor. Publishes 3-5 poetry features of 6-12 pages each per issue. "Please familiarize yourself with the magazine before submitting poetry." **Buys 50 poems/year. Pays $125-250.**

$ NEW ENGLAND REVIEW, Middlebury College, Middlebury VT 05753. (802)443-5075. E-mail: nereview@middlebury.edu. Website: http://www.middlebury.edu/~nereview/nereview.html. Editor: Stephen Donadio. Managing Editor: Jodee Stanley Rubins. Contact on envelope: Poetry, Fiction, or Nonfiction Editor; on letter: Stephen Donadio. Literary quarterly magazine. Serious literary only. Estab. 1978. Circ. 2,000. Pays on publication. Publishes ms an average of 6 months after acceptance. Byline given. Buys first North American serial rights. Accepts simultaneous submissions. Reads September 31 to May 31 (postmark dates). Reports in 2 weeks on queries; 3 months on mss. Sample copy for $7. Writer's guidelines for #10 SASE.
Nonfiction: Serious literary only. **Buys 20-25 mss/year.** Send complete ms. Length: 7,500 words maximum, though exceptions may be made. **Pays $10/page, $20 minimum** plus 2 copies.
Reprints: Rarely accepts previously published submissions, (if out of print or previously published abroad only.)
Fiction: Serious literary only, novel excerpts. **Buys 25 mss/year.** Send complete ms. Send 1 story at a time. **Pays $10/page, minimum $20,** plus 2 copies.
Poetry: Serious literary only. **Buys 75-90 poems/year.** Submit 6 poems max. **Pays $10/page or $20** and 2 copies.
Tips: "We consider short fiction, including shorts, short-shorts, novellas, and self-contained extracts from novels. We consider a variety of general and literary, but not narrowly scholarly, nonfiction: long and short poems; speculative, interpretive, and personal essays; book reviews; screenplays; graphics; translations; critical reassessments; statements by artists working in various media; interviews; testimonies; and letters from abroad. We are committed to exploration of all forms of contemporary cultural expression in the United States and abroad. With few exceptions, we print only work not published previously elsewhere."

$ NEW LETTERS, University of Missouri-Kansas City, University House, 5101 Rockhill Rd., Kansas City MO 64110-2499. (816)235-1168. Fax: (816)235-2611. **Contact:** James McKinley, editor. Managing Editor: Robert Stewart. **100% freelance written.** Quarterly magazine. "*New Letters* is intended for the general literate reader. We publish literary fiction, nonfiction, essays, poetry. We also publish art." Estab. 1934. Circ. 1,800. Pays on publication. Publishes ms an average of 5 months after acceptance. Byline given. Buys first North American serial rights. Editorial lead time

6 months. Submit seasonal material 6 months in advance. Accepts simultaneous submissions. Reports in 1 month on queries; 3 months on mss. Sample copy for $2.50. Writer's guidelines free.
Nonfiction: Essays. No self-help, how-to or non-literary work. **Buys 6-8 mss/year.** Send complete ms. Length: 5,000 words maximum. **Pays $40-100.**
Photos: Send photos with submission. Reviews contact sheets, 2×4 transparencies, prints. Offers $10-40/photo. Buys one-time rights.
Fiction: No genre fiction. **Buys 12 mss/year.** Send complete ms. Length: 5,000 words maximum. **Pays $30-75.**
Poetry: Avant-garde, free verse, haiku, traditional. No light verse. **Buys 40 poems/year.** Submit maximum 3 poems. Length: open. **Pays $10-25.**

$ NEW THOUGHT JOURNAL, the beat of a thousand drummers, 2520 Evelyn Dr., Dayton OH 45409. (937)293-9717. Fax: (937)293-9717. E-mail: ntjmag@aol.com. **Contact:** Jeffrey M. Ohl, editor. **100% freelance written.** Quarterly literary magazine covering "psychology, philosophy, ecology, spirituality, art, literature, poetry and music. *New Thought Journal* reflects the creative and inspirational intent of authors, artists, musicians, poets and philosophers as they mirror a quiet, intuitive consensus that is building naturally in our world." Estab. 1994. Circ. 5,000. Pays on publication. Publishes ms an average of 3 months after acceptance. Byline given. Buys one-time rights. Editorial lead time 6 months. Submit seasonal material 6 months in advance. Accepts simultaneous and previously published submission. Reports in 3 months on queries; 6 months on mss. Sample copy for $6. Writer's guidelines for #10 SASE.
Nonfiction: Book excerpts, inspirational, interview/profile, opinion, personal experience, photo feature. **Buys 20-30 mss/year.** Send complete ms. Length: 250-2,500 words. **Pays up to $20/printed page** and contributor copies.
Reprints: Send photocopy of article or short story and information about when and where the article previously appeared. Publishes novel excerpts.
Photos: State availability of photos with submission or send photos with submission. Reviews contact sheets, transparencies and prints. Negotiates payment individually. Buys one-time rights.
Columns/Departments: Reviews, 100-500 words. Buys 18 mss/year. Send complete ms.
Fiction: Experimental, fantasy, novel excerpts, slice-of-life vignettes, spiritual, tranformational. **Buys 18 mss/year.** Send complete ms. **Pays up to $20/printed page** and contributor copies.
Poetry: Avant-garde, free verse, haiku, light verse, traditional. **Buys 40-50 poems/year.** Submit maximum 5 poems.

N $ THE NORTH AMERICAN REVIEW, University of Northern Iowa, Cedar Falls IA 50614-0516. (319)273-6455. **Contact:** Robley Wilson, editor. **50% freelance written.** Bimonthly. Circ. 4,000. Buys first rights. Pays on publication. Publishes ms an average of 9 months after acceptance. Reports in 10 weeks. Sample copy for $4.

- This is one of the oldest and most prestigious literary magazines in the country. Also one of the most entertaining—and a tough market for the young writer.

Nonfiction: No restrictions, but most nonfiction is commissioned. Query. Rate of payment arranged.
Fiction: No restrictions; highest quality only. Length: open. **Pays $15/published page minimum.** Fiction department closed (no mss read) from April 1-December 31.
Poetry: Peter Cooley. No restrictions; highest quality only. Length: open. **Pays 50¢/line; $20 minimum.**

$ $ NORTH CAROLINA LITERARY REVIEW: A Magazine of Literature, Culture, and History, English Dept., East Carolina University, Greenville NC 27858-4353. (919)328-1537. Fax: (919)328-4889. E-mail: bauerm@mail.ecu.edu. **Contact:** Margaret Bauer, editor. **80% freelance written.** Annual literary magazine published in spring covering North Carolina/Southern writers, literature, culture, history. "Articles should have North Carolina/Southern slant; essays by writers associated with North Carolina may address any subject. First consideration is always for quality of work. Although we treat academic and scholarly subjects, we do not wish to see jargon-laden prose; our readers, we hope, are found as often in bookstores and libraries as in academia. We seek to combine best elements of magazine for serious readers with best of scholarly journal." Estab. 1992. Circ. 1,500. Pays on publication. Publishes ms 9 months after acceptance. Byline given. Offers 25% kill fee. Buys first North American serial rights. Rights returned to writer on request. Editorial lead time 6 months. Reports in 10 weeks on queries, 2 months on mss, 8 months on unsolicited mss. Sample copy for $10. Writer's guidelines free with SASE or via e-mail.
Nonfiction: Book excerpts, essays, exposé, general interest, historical/nostalgic, humor, interview/profile, opinion, personal experience, photo feature, travel, reviews, short narratives; surveys of archives. "No reviews that treat single books by contemporary authors or jargon-laden academic articles." Special issues: The Civil War in North Carolina, fictional and non-fictional subjects, (Issue #8, 1999, deadline for completed papers, Setpember 15,1998); New Voices and Other Genres, this topic to be broadly defined, (Issue #9, 2000, deadline for completed papers, September 15, 1999). **Buys 25-35 mss/year.** Query with published clips. Length: 500-5,000 words. **Pays $50 minimum** (usually $100-300.)
Photos: State availability of photos with query. Reviews 5×7 or 8×10 prints; snapshot size or photocopy OK. Negotiates payment individually. Captions and identification of subjects required, releases when appropriate. Buys one-time rights.
Columns/Departments: Archives (survey of North Carolina-writer archives), 500-1,500 words; Thomas Wolfe (Wolfe-related articles/essays), 1,000-2,000 words; Readers/Writers Places (bookstores or libraries, or other places readers and writers gather), 500-1,500; Black Mountain College, 1,000-2,000 words; Reviews (essay reviews of North Carolina-related literature (fiction, creative nonfiction, poetry). **Buys 10 mss/year.** Send complete ms. **Pays $50-150.**
Fiction: No unsolicited mss; fiction and poetry are published in thematic sections or by invitation. Adventure, ethnic, experimental, fantasy, historical, horror, humorous, mainstream, mystery, novel excerpts, romance, science fiction, slice-

of-life vignettes, suspense, western. **Buys 3-4 mss/year.** Query. Length: 5,000 words maximum. **Pays $100-300.**
Poetry: Buys 8-10 poems/year. Length: 30-150 lines. **Pays $30-150.**
Fillers: Buys 2-10/year. Length: 50-300 words. **Pays $10-25.**
Tips: "By far the easiest way to break in is with departments; we are especially interested in reports on conferences, readings, meetings that involve North Carolina writers, and personal essays or short narratives with strong sense of place to use in loosely defined Readers/Writers Places department. We are more interested in essays that use creative nonfiction approaches than in straight articles of informational nature. See back issues for other departments. These are the only areas in which we encourage unsolicited manuscripts; but we welcome queries and proposals for all others. Interviews are probably the other easiest place to break in; no discussions of poetics/theory, etc., except in reader-friendly (accessible) language; interviews should be personal, more like conversations, that explore connections between a writer's life and his/her work."

$ NOSTALGIA, A Sentimental State of Mind, Nostalgia Publications, P.O. Box 2224, Orangeburg SC 29116. **Contact:** Connie L. Martin, editor. 100% freelance written. Semiannual magazine for "true, personal experiences that relate faith, struggle, hope, success, failure and rising above problems common to all." Estab. 1986. Circ. 1,000. Pays on publication. Publishes ms an average of 1 year after acceptance. Byline given. Buys one-time rights. Submit seasonal material 6 months in advance. Reports in 6 weeks on queries. Sample copy for $5. Writer's guidelines for #10 SASE.
Nonfiction: General interest, historical/nostalgic, humor, inspirational, opinion, personal experience, photo feature, religious and travel. Does not want to see anything with profanity or sexual references. **Buys 20 mss/year.** Send complete ms. Length: 1,500 words. **Pays $25 minimum.** Pays contributor copies if preferred. Short Story Award $300 annually.
Reprints: Send tearsheet, typed ms or photocopy of article or short story and information about when and where the article previously appeared. Payment varies.
Photos: State availability of photos with submission. Offers no additional payment for photos with ms.
Poetry: Free verse, haiku, light verse, traditional and modern prose. "No ballads; no profanity; no sexual references." Submit 3 poems maximum. Length: no longer than 45-50 lines preferably. Poetry Awards $300 annually.
Tips: Write for guidelines before entering contests. Short Story Award (deadlines March 31 and August 31); Poetry Award (deadlines June 30 and December 31). Entry fees reserve future edition.

$ THE OHIO REVIEW, 209C Ellis Hall, Ohio University, Athens OH 45701-2979. (740)593-1900. Editor: Wayne Dodd. **Contact:** Robert Kinsley, assistant editor. **40% freelance written.** Semiannual magazine. "A balanced, informed engagement of contemporary American letters, with special emphasis on poetics." Circ. 3,500. Publishes ms an average of 8 months after acceptance. Rights acquired vary with author and material; usually buys first serial or first North American serial rights. Unsolicited material will be read September-May only. Reports in 10 weeks.
Nonfiction, Fiction and Poetry: Buys essays of general intellectual and special literary appeal. Not interested in narrowly focused scholarly articles. Seeks writing that is marked by clarity, liveliness and perspective. Interested in the best fiction and poetry. Submit complete ms. **Buys 75 unsolicited mss/year. Pays $5/page minimum,** plus copies.
Tips: "Make your query very brief, not gabby—one that describes some publishing history, but no extensive bibliographies. We publish mostly poetry—essays, short fiction, some book reviews."

$ $ THE PARIS REVIEW, 45-39 171st Place, Flushing NY 11358. Submit mss to 541 E. 72nd St., New York NY 10021. (212)861-0016. Fax: (212)861-4504. **Contact:** George A. Plimpton, editor. Quarterly magazine. Buys all rights. Pays on publication. Reporting time varies. Address submissions to proper department. Sample copy for $11. Writer's guidelines for #10 SASE (from Flushing Office). Reporting time often 6 months or longer.
Fiction: Study the publication. No length limit. **Pays up to $600.** Annual Aga Khan Fiction Contest award of $1,000.
Poetry: Richard Howard, poetry editor. Study the publication. **Pays $35 minimum** varies according to length. Awards $1,000 in Bernard F. Conners Poetry Prize contest.

$ $ PARNASSUS, Poetry in Review, Poetry in Review Foundation, 205 W. 89th St., #8-F, New York NY 10024. (212)362-3492. Fax: (212)875-0148. E--mail: parnew@aol.com. Managing Editor: Ben Downing. **Contact:** Herbert Leibowitz, editor. Semiannual trade paperback-size magazine covering poetry and criticism. Estab. 1972. Circ. 1,500. Pays on publication. Publishes ms an average of 5 months after acceptance. Byline given. Buys one-time rights. Sample copy for $15.
Nonfiction: Essays. **Buys 30 mss/year.** Query with published clips. Length: 1,500-7,500 words. **Pays $50-300.** Sometimes pays writers in contributor copies or other premiums rather than a cash payment upon request.
Poetry: Accepts most types of poetry including avant-garde, free verse, traditional. **Buys 3-4 unsolicited poems/year.**

N $ $ $ $ PLAY THE ODDS, The Big Dog Press, 11614 Ashwood, Little Rock AZ 72211. (501)224-9452. **Contact:** Tom Raley, editor. Monthly consumer magazine covering gambling. "We cover gambling activities all across the country. We offer tips, reviews, instructions and advice. We also cover cruise lines since most have casinos on board." Estab. 1997. **Pays on acceptance**. Publishes ms an average of 4 months after acceptance. Buys one-time rights. Accepts simultaneous submissions. Reports in 2 weeks on queries; 2 months on mss. Sample copy for $2. Writer's guidelines for #10 SASE.
Nonfiction: Primarily dealing with casino gaming, *Play the Odds* also covers horse racing, dog racing, sports wagering and online casinos. Also features service articles on entertainment, lodging, and dining facilities located in or near gaming resorts. **Buys 85-145 mss/year**. Length: 800 words. **Pays $500-1,750.**

Fiction: Adventure, fantasy (science fantasy), horror, mystery/suspense (cozy, private eye/hardboiled, romantic suspense), science fiction (soft sociological), senior citizen/retirement, sports, westerns (traditional). **Buys 12-20 mss/year.** Length: 600-800 words. **Pays $1,500-3,000.**

Columns/Departments: Reviews (shows, games, hotels, casinos, books), up to 300 words; humorous fillers, up to 80 words. **Buys 24-36 reviews/year; 36-60 fillers/year. Pays $50-350.**

Tips: In nonfiction, the editor advises that a writer present an aspect or area of gaming which is out of the mainstream. In fiction, "we look for fast-paced stories with real characters. The stories should be fun, enjoyable and the main character doesn't need to be trying to save the world. Few, if any of us, do that. We do, however, get in bad situations. You must write what you enjoy writing about. If you don't want to write a story about gambling or a gambler, it will show in your work. If it is something you want, that will also show in your work and we will notice."

$ PLEIADES, Pleiades Press, Dept. of English & Philosophy, Central Missouri State University, Warrensburg MO 64093. (816)543-4425. Fax: (816)543-8544. **Contact:** R.M. Kinder, editor. Kevin Prufer, co-editor. **100% freelance written.** Semiannual journal (5½×8½ perfect bound). "We publish contemporary fiction, poetry, interviews, literary essays, special-interest personal essays, reviews. We're especially interested in cross genre pieces and ethnic explorations. General and literary audience." Estab. 1991. Circ. 600. Pays on publication. Publishes ms an average of 9 months after acceptance. Byline given. Buys first North American and second serial (reprint) rights (occasionally requests rights for WordBeat, TV, radio reading, website). Editorial lead time 9 months. Submit seasonal material 9 months in advance. Accepts simultaneous submissions. Reports in 2 months. Sample copy for $5 (back issue), $6 (current issue). Writer's guidelines for #10 SASE.

Nonfiction: Book excerpts, essays, interview/profile, reviews. "Nothing pedantic, slick or shallow." **Buys 4-6 mss/year.** Send complete ms. Length: 2,000-4,000 words. **Pays $10.**

Fiction: Ethnic, experimental, humorous, mainstream, novel excerpts, magic realism. No science fiction, fantasy, confession, erotica. **Buys 16-20 mss/year.** Send complete ms. Length: 2,000-6,000 words. **Pays $10.**

Poetry: Kevin Prufer, co-editor. Avant-garde, free verse, haiku, light verse, traditional. "Nothing didactic, pretentious, or overly sentimental." **Buys 40-50 poems/year.** Submit maximum 6 poems. **Pays $3/poem.**

Tips: "Show care for your material and your readers—submit quality work in a professional format. Include cover letter with brief bio and list of publications. Include SASE."

$ $ PLOUGHSHARES, Emerson College, Dept. M, 100 Beacon St., Boston MA 02116. Website: http://www.emerson.edu/ploughshares/. **Contact:** Don Lee, editor. Triquarterly magazine for "readers of serious contemporary literature." Circ. 6,000. Pays on publication. Publishes ms an average of 6 months after acceptance. Buys first North American serial rights. Accepts simultaneous submissions if so noted. Reports in 5 months. Sample copy for $8 (back issue). Writer's guidelines for SASE. Reading period: August 1-March 31.

- A competitive and highly prestigious market. Rotating and guest editors make cracking the line-up even tougher, since it's difficult to know what is appropriate to send.

Nonfiction: Personal and literary essays (accepted only occasionally). Length: 5,000 words maximum. **Pays $25/printed page, $50-$250.** Reviews (assigned). Length: 500 words maximum. **Pays $30.**

Fiction: Literary, mainstream. **Buys 25-35 mss/year.** Length: 300-6,000 words. **Pays $25/printed page, $50-250.**

- Ranked as one of the best markets for fiction writers in *Writer's Digest* magazine's "Fiction 50," June 1998.

Poetry: Traditional forms, blank verse, free verse and avant-garde. Length: open. **Pays $25/printed page, $50-$250.**

Tips: "We no longer structure issues around preconceived themes. If you believe your work is in keeping with our general standards of literary quality and value, submit at any time during our reading period."

$ THE PRAIRIE JOURNAL of Canadian Literature, P.O. Box 61203, Brentwood Postal Services, 217K-3630 Brentwood Rd. NW, Calgary, Alberta T2L 2K6 Canada. E-mail: cmpainfo@cmpa.ca. Website: http://www.ampa.ab.ca or http://wwwcmpa.ca//. **Contact:** A. Burke, editor. **100% freelance written.** Semiannual magazine of Canadian literature. Estab. 1983. Circ. 600. Pays on publication; "honorarium depends on grant." Byline given. Buys first North American serial rights. Reports 6 months. Sample copy for $6 and IRC (Canadian stamps) or 50¢ payment for postage.

Nonfiction: Interview/profile, scholarly, literary. **Buys 5 mss/year.** Query first. Include IRCs. **Pays $25-100.**

Photos: Send photocopies of photos with submission. Offers additional payment for photos accepted with ms. Identification of subjects required. Buys first North American rights.

Fiction: Literary. **Buys 10 mss/year.** Send complete ms. Pays contributor copies or honoraria for literary work.

Poetry: Avant-garde, free verse. **Buys 10 poems/year.** Submit maximum 6-10 poems.

Tips: "Commercial writers are advised to submit elsewhere. Art needed, black and white pen and ink drawings or good-quality photocopy. Do not send originals. We are strictly small press editors interested in highly talented, serious artists. We are oversupplied with fiction but seek more high-quality poetry, especially the contemporary long poem or sequences from longer works. We welcome freelancers."

N $ PRESS, Daniel Roberts, Inc., 125 W. 72nd St., Suite 3-M, New York NY 10023. E-mail: pressltd@aol.com. **Contact**: Sean Anthony, managing editor. Editor: Daniel Roberts. **100% freelance written.** Quarterly literary magazine containing poetry and fiction with "clarity, memorable lines, captivating plots and excellence." Estab. 1995. Circ. 15,000. **Pays on acceptance**. Publishes ms an average of 3 months after acceptance. Byline given. Buys first rights. Editorial lead time 3 months. Reports in 2 months on queries; 1 year on mss. Sample copy for $9.24. Guidelines free.

Fiction: "While almost all forms are acceptable, prose poems and more experimental writing (stories that don't actually

tell a story) are discouraged." **Buys 40 mss/year.** Send complete ms. Length: up to 25 typed pages. **Pays $100.**
Poetry: Avant-garde, free verse, haiku, light verse, traditional. "All poems must make sense. That is all complicated rhythms and fanciful word choices, all emotional and psychological gestures must have a public value as well as a personal value." No careless, seasonal, immature poetry. **Buys 120 poems/year.** Submit maximum 3 poems. **Pays $50.**

$ PRISM INTERNATIONAL, Department of Creative Writing, Buch E462, 1866 Main Mall, University of British Columbia, Vancouver, British Columbia V6T 1Z1 Canada. (604)822-2211. Fax: (604)822-3616. E-mail: prism@unixg.ubc.ca. Website: http://www.arts/ubc.ca/crwr/prism/prism.html. **Contact:** Melanie Little or Sioux Browning, editors. Executive Editor: Shannon McFerran. **100% freelance written.** Eager to work with new/unpublished writers. Quarterly magazine emphasizing contemporary literature, including translations, for university and public libraries, and private subscribers. Estab. 1959. Circ. 1,200. Pays on publication. Publishes ms an average of 4 months after acceptance. Buys first North American serial rights. Reports in 3 months. Sample copy for $5. Writer's guidelines for #10 SAE with 1 first-class Canadian stamp (Canadian entries) or 1 IRC (US entries).
Nonfiction: "*Creative* nonfiction that reads like fiction." No reviews, tracts or scholarly essays.
Fiction: Rick Maddocks, fiction editor. Experimental, traditional, novel excerpts. **Buys 3-5 mss/issue.** Send complete ms. Length: 5,000 words maximum. **Pays $20/printed page** and 1-year subscription. Publishes novel excerpts, maximum length: 25 double-spaced pages.
Poetry: Regina Weaver, poetry editor. Avant-garde, traditional. **Buys 20 poems/issue.** Submit maximum 6 poems. **Pays $20/printed page** and 1-year subscription.
Drama: One-acts preferred. **Pays $20/printed page** and 1-year subscription.
Tips: "We are looking for new and exciting fiction. Excellence is still our number one criterion. As well as poetry, imaginative nonfiction and fiction, we are especially open to translations of all kinds, very short fiction pieces and drama which work well on the page. Translations must come with a copy of the original language work. Work may be submitted through e-mail or our website. We pay an additional $10/printed page to selected authors whose work we place on our on-line version of *Prism*."

$ $ QUARTERLY WEST, University of Utah, 200 S. Central Campus Dr., Rm. 317, Salt Lake City UT 84112-9109. (801)581-3938. **Contact:** Margot Schilpp, editor. Semiannual magazine. "We publish fiction, poetry, and nonfiction in long and short formats, and will consider experimental as well as traditional works." Estab. 1976. Circ. 1,900. Pays on publication. Publishes ms an average of 6 months after acceptance. Buys first North American serial and all rights. Accepts simultaneous submissions, if so noted. Reports in 6 months on mss. Sample copy for $7.50. Writer's guidelines for #10 SASE.
Nonfiction: Essays, interview/profile, book reviews. **Buys 4-5 mss/year.** Send complete ms with SASE. Length: 10,000 words maximum. **Pays $25.**
Fiction: Charlotte Freeman. Ethnic, experimental, humorous, mainstream, novel excerpts, short shorts, slice-of-life vignettes, translations. **Buys 20-30 mss/year.** Send complete ms with SASE. Pays $25-500. No preferred lengths; interested in longer, fuller short stories, as well as short shorts. Biennial novella competition deadline December 31, 1998. Length: 50-125 pages. **Pays $500.**
Poetry: Contact: Danielle Dubrasky and Melanie Figg. Avant-garde, free verse, traditional. **Buys 30-50 poems/year.** Submit 5 poems maximum. **Pays $15-100.**
Tips: "We publish a special section or short shorts every issue, and we also sponsor a biennial novella contest. We are open to experimental work—potential contributors should read the magazine! We solicit quite frequently, but tend more toward the surprises—unsolicited. Don't send more than one story per submission, but submit as often as you like. Biennial novella competition guidelines available upon request with SASE."

$ $ QUEEN'S QUARTERLY, A Canadian Review, Queen's University, Kingston, Ontario K7L 3N6 Canada. (613)545-2667. Fax: (613)545-6822. E-mail: qquartly@post.queensu.ca. Website: http://info.queensu.ca/quarterly. **Contact:** Boris Castel, editor. Estab. 1893. Quarterly magazine covering a wide variety of subjects, including science, humanities, arts and letters, politics and history for the educated reader. **15% freelance written.** Circ. 3,000. Pays on publication. Publishes ms an average of 3 months after acceptance. Byline given. Buys first North American serial rights. Requires 1 double-spaced hard copy and 1 copy on disk in WordPerfect. Reports in 1 month on mss. *Writer's Market* recommends allowing 2 months for reply. Sample copy $6.50.
Fiction: Historical, humorous, mainstream and science fiction. No fantasy. Publishes novel excerpts. **Buys 8-12 mss/year.** Send complete ms. Length: 4,000 words maximum. **Pays $150-250.**
Poetry: Avant-garde, free verse, haiku, light verse, traditional. No "sentimental, religious, or first efforts by unpublished writers." **Buys 25/year.** Submit maximum 6 poems. Length: open. **Pays $100-200.**
Tips: "Poetry and fiction are most open to freelancers. Don't send less than the best. No multiple submissions. No more than six poems or two stories per submission. We buy very few freelance submissions."

$ RARITAN A Quarterly Review, 31 Mine St., New Brunswick NJ 08903. (732)932-7887. Fax: (732)932-7855. Editor: Richard Poirier. **Contact:** Suzanne Katz Hyman, managing editor. Quarterly magazine covering literature, general culture. Estab. 1981. Circ. 3,500. Pays on publication. Publishes ms 1 year after acceptance. Byline given. Buys first North American serial rights. Editorial lead time 5 months. Accepts simultaneous submissions.
Nonfiction: Book excerpts, essays. **Buys 50 mss/year.** Send complete ms. Length 15-30 pages. **Pays $100.**
Reprints: Accepts previously published submissions.

$ $ ROSEBUD, The Magazine For People Who Enjoy Good Writing, Rosebud, Inc., P.O. Box 459, Cambridge WI 53523. (608)423-9609. Website: http://www.itis.com/rosebud. **Contact:** Rod Clark, editor. **100% freelance written.** Quarterly magazine "for people who love to read and write. Our readers like good storytelling, real emotion, a sense of place and authentic voice." Estab. 1993. Circ. 9,000. Pays on publication. Publishes ms an average of 2 months after acceptance. Byline given. Buys one-time or second serial (reprint) rights. Editorial lead time 3 months. Submit seasonal material 3 months in advance. Accepts simultaneous submissions. Sends acknowledgment postcard upon receipt of submission and reports in 1-5 months. Sample copy for $5.95. Writer's guidelines for SASE.

Nonfiction: Book excerpt, essays, general interest, historical/nostalgic, humor, interview/profile, personal experience, travel. "No editorializing." **Buys 6 mss/year.** Send complete ms and SASE. Length: 1,200-1,800 words. **Pays $45-195.**

Reprints: Send tearsheet, photocopy or typed ms with rights for sale noted. Pays 100% of amount paid for an original article.

Photos: State availability of photos with submission. Offers no additional payment for photos accepted with ms. Captions, model releases and identification of subjects required. Buys one-time rights.

Fiction: Ethnic, experimental, historical, humorous, mainstream, novel excerpts, slice-of-life vignettes, suspense. "No formula pieces." **Buys 80 mss/year.** Send complete ms and SASE. Length: 1,200-1,800 words. **Pays $45-195.**

- Ranked as one of the best markets for fiction writers in *Writer's Digest* magazine's "Fiction 50," June 1998.

Poetry: Avant-garde, free verse, traditional. No inspirational poetry. **Buys 36 poems/year.** Submit maximum 5 poems. Length: open. **Pays $45-195** and 3 contributor's copies.

Tips: "Something has to 'happen' in the pieces we choose, but what happens inside characters is much more interesting to us than plot manipulation. We prefer to respond with an individualized letter (send SASE for this) and recycle submitted manuscripts. We will return your manuscript only if you send sufficient postage. We can only give detailed editorial feedback on pieces we are going to buy."

$ SHORT STUFF, for Grown-ups, Bowman Publications, P.O. Box 7057, Loveland CO 80537. (970)669-9139. **Contact:** Donna Bowman, editor. 98% freelance written. Bimonthly magazine. "We are perhaps an enigma in that we publish only clean stories in any genre. We'll tackle any subject, but don't allow obscene language or pornographic description. Our magazine is for grown-ups, *not* X-rated 'adult' fare." Estab. 1989. Circ. 5,400. Payment and contract on publication. Byline given. Buys first North American serial rights. Editorial lead time 3 months. Submit seasonal material 3 months in advance. Reports in 6 months on mss. Sample copy for $1.50 and 9×12 SAE with 5 first-class stamps. Writer's guidelines for #10 SASE.

Nonfiction: Humor. Special issues: "We are holiday oriented and each issue reflects the appropriate holidays." **Buys 20 mss/year.** Most nonfiction is staff written. Send complete ms. Length: 500-1,600 words. **Pays $10-50.**

Reprints: Send typed ms with rights for sale noted.

Photos: Send photos with submission. Offers no additional payment for photos accepted with ms. Identification of subjects required. Buys one-time rights.

Fiction: Adventure, historical, humorous, mainstream, mystery, romance, science fiction (seldom), suspense, western. **Buys 144 mss/year.** Send complete ms. Length: 500-1,600 words. **Pays $10-50.**

Fillers: Anecdotes, short humor. **Buys 200/year.** Length: 20-500 words. **Pays $1-5.**

Tips: "Don't send floppy disks or cartridges. Do include cover letter about the author, not a synopsis of the story. We are holiday oriented; mark on *outside* of envelope if story is for Easter, Mother's Day, etc. We receive 500 manuscripts each month. This is up about 200%. Because of this, I implore writers to send one manuscript at a time. I would not use stories from the same author more than once an issue and this means I might keep the others too long."

$ THE SOUTHERN REVIEW, 43 Allen Hall, Louisiana State University, Baton Rouge LA 70803-5001. (504)388-5108. Fax: (504)388-5098. E-mail: bmacon@unix1.sncc.lsu.edu. **Contact:** James Olney and Dave Smith, editors. **100% freelance written.** Works with a moderate number of new/unpublished writers each year. Quarterly magazine "with emphasis on contemporary literature in the United States and abroad, and with special interest in Southern culture and history." Estab. 1935. Circ. 3,100. Buys first serial rights only. Byline given. Pays on publication. Publishes ms an average of 6 months after acceptance. No queries. Reports in 2 months. Sample copy for $6. Writer's guidelines for #10 SASE. Reading period: September through May.

Nonfiction: Essays with careful attention to craftsmanship, technique and seriousness of subject matter. "Willing to publish experimental writing if it has a valid artistic purpose. Avoid extremism and sensationalism. Essays should exhibit thoughtful and sometimes severe awareness of the necessity of literary standards in our time." Emphasis on contemporary literature, especially southern culture and history. No footnotes. **Buys 25 mss/year.** Length: 4,000-10,000 words. **Pays $12/page.**

Fiction and Poetry: Short stories of lasting literary merit, with emphasis on style and technique, also novel excerpts. Length: 4,000-8,000 words. **Pays $12/page.**

Poetry: Length: 1-4 pages. **Pays $20/page.**

$ SPARROW, Sparrow Press, 103 Waldron St., West Lafayette IN 47906. **Contact:** Felix Stefanile, editor. 60% freelance written. Annual magazine covering poetry, the sonnet, articles on craft, criticism. "Writers who admire and are loyal to the lyric tradition of the English language enjoy our magazine. We are not affiliated with any group or ideology and encourage poetry that uses meter, rhyme and structured verse, mainly the sonnet. We are not a 'school of resentment' publication." Estab. 1954. Circ. 1,000. Pays on publication. Publishes ms 8 months after acceptance. Byline given. Offers 100% kill fee. Buys first North American serial rights and second serial (reprint) rights. Editorial lead time up to 6 months. Reports in 6 weeks. Sample copy for $5, back issue; $6, current issue. Guidelines for #10 SASE.

• 1998 will be a year of reorganization for *Sparrow*, and they will not be reading until 1999. The next issue of the yearbook will be in 1999.

Reprints: By invitation. "90% of our work is original."

N $ SPORTS LITERATE, Honest Reflections on Life's Leisurely Diversions, Pint Size Publications, P.O. Box 577166, Chicago IL 60657-7166. Fax: (773)929-0818. E-mail: sportlit@aol.com. Website: http://www.avalon.net/librarian/sportliterate/. **Contact:** William Meiners, editor. Managing Editor: Jotham Burrello. **95% freelance written.** Quarterly literary journal covering leisure/sport . . .life outside the daily grind of making a living. "*Sport Literate* publishes the highest quality nonfiction and poets on themes of leisure and sport. Our writers use a leisure activity to explore a larger theme. The writing is allegoric. We serve a broad audience." Estab. 1985. Circ. 1,500. Pays on publication. Publishes ms an average of 3 months after acceptance. Byline given. Buys first North American serial rights. Editorial lead time 3 months. Submit seasonal material 4 months in advance. Reports in 3 weeks on queries; 2 months on mss. Sample copy for $5.75. Writer's guidelines for #10 SASE.

Nonfiction: Essays, historical/nostalgic, humor, interview/profile, personal experience, travel, creative nonfiction. "Planning Chicago issues for early 1999. Writers with connection to the city should send essays." No book reviews or straight reporting on sports. **Buys 28 mss/year**. Send complete ms. Length: 250-10,000 words. **Pays up to $20.**

Poetry: Contact: Jennifer Richter, poetry editor. Avant-garde, free verse, haiku, light verse, traditional. **Buys 25 poems/year**. Submit maximum 5 poems. Length: 10 lines. **Pays up to $20.**

Tips: "Explore our website. It has back issues, guidelines, etc . . . Keep trying us, we have published writers on their second or third attempt. Remember, *Sport* has 14 definitions and we explore all of them."

$ SPSM&H, *Amelia Magazine*, 329 E St., Bakersfield CA 93304. (805)323-4064. **Contact:** Frederick A. Raborg, Jr., editor. **100% freelance written.** Quarterly magazine featuring fiction and poetry with Romantic or Gothic theme. "*SPSM&H* (Shakespeare, Petrarch, Sidney, Milton and Hopkins) uses one short story in each issue and 20-36 sonnets, plus reviews of books and anthologies containing the sonnet form and occasional articles about the sonnet form or about some romantic or Gothic figure or movement. We look for contemporary aspects of the sonnet form." Estab. 1984. Circ. 600. Pays on publication. Publishes ms an average of 6 months after acceptance. Byline given. Offers 50% kill fee. Buys first North American serial rights. Editorial lead time 2 months. Submit seasonal material 3 months in advance. Accepts simultaneous submissions. Reports in 2 weeks on queries; 3 months on mss. Sample copy for $4.95. Writer's guidelines for #10 SASE.

Nonfiction: Essays, general interest, historical/nostalgic, humor, interview/profile, opinion and anything related to sonnets or to romance. **Buys 1-4 mss/year.** Send complete ms. Length: 500-2,000 words. **Pays $10.**

Photos: Send photos with submission. Reviews 8×10 or 5×7 b&w prints. Offers $10-25/photo. Model releases required. Buys one-time rights.

Fiction: Confession, erotica, experimental, fantasy, historical, humor, humorous, mainstream, mystery, romance, slice-of-life vignettes. **Buys 4 mss/year.** Send complete ms. Length: 500-2,500 words. **Pays $10-20.**

Poetry: Sonnets, sonnet sequences. **Buys 140 poems/year.** Submit maximum 10 poems. Length: 14 lines. Two "best of issue" poets each receive $14.

Fillers: Anecdotes, short humor. Buys 2-4/year. Length: 25-500 words. No payment for fillers.

Tips: "Read a copy certainly. Understand the limitations of the sonnet form and, in the case of fiction, the requirements of the romantic or Gothic genres. Be professional in presentation, and realize that neatness does count. Be contemporary and avoid Victorian verse forms and techniques. Avoid convolution and forced rhyme. Idiomatics ought to be contemporary. Don't be afraid to experiment. We consider John Updike's 'Love Sonnet' to be the extreme to which poets may experiment."

$ STAND MAGAZINE, 179 Wingrove Rd., Newcastle Upon Tyne NE4 9DA United Kingdom. Phone/fax: (0191)273-3280. E-mail: dlatane@vcu.edu. Website: http://saturn.vcu.edu/~dlatane/stand.html. Editors: Lorna Tracy, Rodney Pybus, Peter Bennet. Managing Editor: Philip Bomford. **Contact:** David Latané, U.S. editor, Dept. of English, VCU, Richmond VA 23284-2005. **99% freelance written.** Quarterly magazine covering short fiction, poetry, criticism and reviews. "*Stand Magazine* was given this name because it was begun as a stand against apathy towards new writing and in social relations." Estab. 1952. Circ. 4,500 worldwide. Pays on publication. Publishes ms an average of 2 years after acceptance. Byline given. Buys first world rights. Editorial lead time 2 months. Reports in 1 week on queries, 2 months on mss. Sample copy for $7. Writer's guidelines for sufficient number of IRCs.

Nonfiction: Reviews of poetry/fiction. "Reviews are commissioned from known freelancers." **Buys 8 mss/year.** Query. Length: 200-5,000 words. **Pays $30/1,000 words.**

Fiction: "No genre fiction." **Buys 8-10 mss/year.** Send complete ms. Length: 8,000 words maximum. **Pays $37.50/**

MARKETS THAT WERE listed in the 1998 edition of *Writer's Market* but do not appear this year are listed in the General Index with a notation explaining why they were omitted.

1,000 words.
Poetry: Avant-garde, free verse, traditional. **Buys 30-40 poems/year.** Submit maximum 6 poems. **Pays $37.50/poem.**
Tips: "Poetry/fiction areas are most open to freelancers. Buy a sample copy first (suggestion)." Submissions to England should be accompanied by U.K. SAE or sufficient IRCs.

$ $ $ STORY, F&W Publications, Inc., 1507 Dana Ave., Cincinnati OH 45207-1005. (513)531-2960. Fax: (513)531-1843. **Contact:** Lois Rosenthal, editor. **100% freelance written.** Quarterly literary magazine of short fiction. "We want short stories and self-inclusive novel excerpts that are extremely well written. Our audience is sophisticated and accustomed to the finest imaginative writing by new and established authors." Estab. 1931. Circ. 40,000. **Pays on acceptance.** Byline given. Buys first North American serial rights. Reports in 1 month. Sample copy for $6.95 and 7½×10½ SAE with 5 first-class stamps. Writer's guidelines for #10 SASE.

- STORY won the National Magazine Award for Fiction in 1992 and 1995, was nominated in 1994, 1996 and 1997. The magazine sponsors two annual contests, the STORY Short Short Competition and STORY's Carson McCullers Prize for the Short Story. See the listings in the Contests & Awards section.

Fiction: No genre fiction. **Buys 50-60 mss/year.** Send complete ms with word count on first page. No faxed submissions. Length: up to 8,000 words. **Pays $1,000 for short stories and $750 for short shorts.** No replies without SASE.

N $ THE STRAND MAGAZINE, P.O. Box 1418, Birmingham MI 48012-1418. Fax: (248)874-1046. E-mail: strandmag@worldnet.att.net. **Contact:** A.F. Gulli, managing editor. Quarterly magazine covering mysteries, short stories, essays, book reviews and poetry. "Mysteries and short stories written in the classic tradition of this century's great authors." Estab. 1998. **Pays on acceptance**. Publishes ms 4 months after acceptance. Byline given. Buys first North American serial rights. Reports in 1 month on queries; 4 months on mss. Sample copy and guidelines for #10 SASE.
Fiction: Horror, humorous, mystery, suspense. Send complete ms. Length: 2,000-6,000 words. **Pays $10-40.**
Poetry: Free verse, light verse, traditional. Length: 33 lines. Pays honorarium.

$ $ THEATER MAGAZINE, Yale School of Drama, Yale University, 222 York St., New Haven CT 06511. (203)432-8336. E-mail: theater.magazine@yale.edu. Website: http://www.yale.edu/drama/publications/theater. Editor: Erika Munk. **Contact:** Editoral Staff. University journal published 3 times/year covering theater—US and abroad. Estab. 1968. Circ. 3,000. Pays on publication. Publishes ms an average of 4 months after acceptance. Byline given. Editorial lead time 4 months. Writer's guidelines free.
Nonfiction: Essays, general interest, interview/profile, reviews. **Buys 3 mss/year.** Query. **Pays $75-200.** Sometimes pays expenses of writers on assignment.
Photos: Send photos with submission. Negotiates payment. Captions required. Photographer retains rights.
Columns/Departments: Book Reviews, Performance Reviews, Symposia. **Buys 3 mss/year.** Query.
Fiction: Buys 2 mss/year. Query. **Pays $150 minimum.**
Tips: "We want critical writing and polemics on modern and contemporary theater in the U.S. and abroad; new plays, translations, adaptations; book and production reviews."

$ THEMA, Box 74109, Metairie LA 70033-4109. (504)887-1263. E-mail: bothomos@juno.com. Website: http://www.litline.org/html/THEMA.html. **Contact:** Virginia Howard, editor. **100% freelance written.** Triannual literary magazine covering a different theme for each issue. "*Thema* is designed to stimulate creative thinking by challenging writers with unusual themes, such as 'laughter on the steps' and 'jogging on ice.' Appeals to writers, teachers of creative writing and general reading audience." Estab. 1988. Circ. 350. **Pays on acceptance.** Byline given. Buys one-time rights. Reports in 5 months on mss (after deadline for particular issue). Sample copy for $8. Writer's guidelines for #10 SASE. Query with SASE for upcoming themes.
Fiction: Adventure, ethnic, experimental, fantasy, historical, humorous, mainstream, mystery, religious, science fiction, slice-of-life vignettes, suspense, western, novel excerpts. "No alternate lifestyle or erotica." Special issues: A postcard not received (November 1, 1998); On the road to the villa (March 1, 1999); The wrong cart (July 1, 1999). **Buys 30 mss/year.** Send complete ms and *specify theme* for which it is intended. **Pays $10-25.**

- Ranked as one of the best markets for fiction writers in *Writer's Digest* magazine's "Fiction 50," June 1998.

Reprints: Send typed ms with rights for sale noted and information about when and where the article previously appeared. Pays same amount paid for original story or poem.
Poetry: Avant-garde, free verse, haiku, light verse, traditional. No erotica. **Buys 27 poems/year.** Submit maximum 3 poems. Length: 4-50 lines. **Pays $10.**
Tips: "Be familiar with the themes. *Don't submit* unless you have an upcoming theme in mind. Specify the target theme on the first page of your manuscript or in a cover letter. Put your name on *first* page of manuscript only. (All submissions are judged in blind review after the deadline for a specified issue.) Most open to fiction and poetry. Don't be hasty when you consider a theme—mull it over and let it ferment in your mind. We appreciate interpretations that are carefully constructed, clever, subtle, well thought out."

$ $ THE THREEPENNY REVIEW, P.O. Box 9131, Berkeley CA 94709. (510)849-4545. **Contact:** Wendy Lesser, editor. **100% freelance written.** Works with small number of new/unpublished writers each year. Quarterly literary tabloid. "We are a general interest, national literary magazine with coverage of politics, the visual arts and the performing arts as well." Estab. 1980. Circ. 9,000. **Pays on acceptance.** Publishes ms an average of 1 year after acceptance. Byline given. Buys first North American serial rights. Reports in 1 month on queries; 2 months on mss.

Does *not* read mss in summer months. Sample copy for $7 and 10×13 SAE with 5 first-class stamps. Writer's guidelines for SASE.

Nonfiction: Essays, exposé, historical, personal experience, book, film, theater, dance, music and art reviews. **Buys 40 mss/year.** Query with or without published clips, or send complete ms. Length: 1,500-4,000 words. **Pays $200.**

Fiction: No fragmentary, sentimental fiction. **Buys 10 mss/year.** Send complete ms. Length: 800-4,000 words. **Pays $200.**

- Ranked as one of the best markets for fiction writers in *Writer's Digest* magazine's "Fiction 50," June 1998.

Poetry: Free verse, traditional. No poems "without capital letters or poems without a discernible subject." **Buys 30 poems/year.** Submit 5 poems maximum. **Pays $100.**

Tips: "Nonfiction (political articles, memoirs, reviews) is most open to freelancers."

THE TRICKSTER REVIEW: ART, LITERATURE, POLITICS AND COMMUNICATIONS, The International Citizen's Corps., 122 E. Texas Ave. #1016, Baytown TX 77520. E-mail: intlccorps@aol.com. **Contact:** Yvonne McCall, editor. Semiannual literary magazine. Publishes ms an average of 1 year after acceptance. Buys first North American serial rights. Accepts simultaneous submissions. Reports in 2 months on queries; 6 months on mss. Sample copy for $7. Writer's guidelines for #10 SASE and $1.

Nonfiction: Book excerpts, essays, exposé, general interest, historical/nostalgic, humor, interview/profile, opinion, personal experience, photo feature, politics, art, literature, communication. Send complete ms. **Pays $10** plus 3 copies.

Fiction: Larry Jacob, fiction editor. Ethnic, experimental, fantasy, historical, humorous, mainstream, novel excerpts, literary, suspense, censorship issues." **Buys 10-15 mss/year.** Send complete ms. Length: approximately 2,000 words.

Poetry: Richard Wayne, poetry editor. Avant-garde, free verse, traditional. **Buys 10/year.** Submit maximum 5 poems.

Tips: "Our readers have read extensively. Many are writers themselves. We are open to new and established writers. We publish lucid writers representing the best of the material submitted each issue. We are interested in translations into English of contemporary authors."

$ TRIQUARTERLY, 2020 Ridge Ave., Northwestern University, Evanston IL 60208-4302. (847)491-3490. Fax: (847)467-2096. Website: http://triquarterly.nwu.edu. **Contact:** Susan Firestone Hahn, editor. **70% freelance written.** Eager to work with new/unpublished writers. Triannual magazine of fiction, poetry and essays, as well as artwork. Estab. 1964. Pays on publication. Publishes ms an average of 1 year after acceptance. Buys first serial and nonexclusive reprint rights. Reports in 3 months. Study magazine before submitting. Sample copy for $5. Writer's guidelines for #10 SASE.

- *TriQuarterly* has had several stories published in the *O. Henry Prize* anthology and *Best American Short Stories* as well as poetry in *Best American Poetry.*

Nonfiction: Query before sending essays (no scholarly or critical essays except in special issues).

Fiction and Poetry: No prejudice against style or length of work; only seriousness and excellence are required. Publishes novel excerpts. **Buys 20-50 unsolicited mss/year.** Payment varies depending on grant support. Does not read mss between April 1 and September 30.

$ VIRGINIA QUARTERLY REVIEW, University of Virginia, One West Range, Charlottesville VA 22903. (804)924-3124. Fax: (804)924-1397. E-mail: jco7e@virginia.edu. **Contact:** Staige D. Blackford, editor. Quarterly magazine. "A national journal of literature and thought." Estab. 1925. Circ. 4,000. Pays on publication. Publishes ms an average of 1 year after acceptance. Byline given. Buys first rights. Editorial lead time 6 months. Submit seasonal material 6 months in advance. Reports in 2 weeks on queries; 2 months on mss. Sample copy $5. Guidelines for #10 SASE.

Nonfiction: Book excerpts, essays, general interest, historical/nostalgic, humor, inspirational, personal experience, travel. Send complete ms. Length: 2,000-4,000 words. **Pays $10/page maximum.**

Fiction: Adventure, ethnic, historical, humorous, mainstream, mystery, novel excerpts, romance. Send complete ms. Length: 2,000-4,000 words. **Pays $10/page maximum.**

Poetry: Gregory Orr, poetry editor. All types. Submit maximum 5 poems. Pays $1/line.

WASCANA REVIEW OF CONTEMPORARY POETRY AND SHORT FICTION, University of Regina, Department of English, Regina, Saskatchewan S4T 0A2 Canada. Fax: (306)585-4827. E-mail: Kathleen.wall@uregina.ca **Contact:** Kathleen Wall, editor. **100% freelance written.** Semiannual magazine covering contemporary poetry and short fiction. "We seek poetry and short fiction that combines craft with risks, pressure with grace. Critical articles should articulate a theoretical approach and also explore either poetry or short fiction. While we frequently publish established writers, we also welcome—and seek to foster—new voices." Estab. 1966. Circ. 200. Pays on publication. Publishes ms an average of 4 months after acceptance. Buys first North American rights. Editorial lead time 4 months. Reports in 1 week on queries; 2 months on mss. Writer's guidelines free.

Columns/Departments: Reviews of contemporary poetry and short fiction (ask for guidelines), 1,000-1,500 words. **Buys 8 mss/year.** Query. **Pays $3/printed page.**

Fiction: No genre-bound fiction, or stories with sentimental or predictable endings. **Buys 8-10 mss/year.** Send complete ms. **Pays $3/printed page** plus 2 contributor's copies.

Poetry: Troni Grande. Avant-garde, free verse. No sentimental, fee-good verse, no predictable rhyme and meter. **Buys 40 poems/year.** Submit maximum 5 poems. **Pays $10/printed page** plus contributor's copies.

Tips: "The best advice I can give is to read back issues."

$ WEST COAST LINE, A Journal of Contemporary Writing & Criticism, West Coast Review Publishing Society, 2027 EAA. Simon Fraser University, Burnaby, British Columbia V5A 1S6 Canada. (604)291-4287. Fax: (604)291-5737. E-mail: jlarson@sfu.ca. Website: http://www.sfu.ca/west-coast-line/WCL.html. **Contact:** Jacqueline Larson, managing editor. Triannual magazine of contemporary literature and criticism. Estab. 1990. Circ. 500. Pays on publication. Buys one-time rights. Editorial lead time 4 months. Submit seasonal material 4 months in advance. Reports in 2 weeks on queries; 3 months on mss. Sample copy for $10. Writer's guidelines for SASE (US must include IRC).
Nonfiction: Essays (literary/scholarly), experimental prose. "No journalistic articles or articles dealing with nonliterary material." **Buys 8-10 mss/year.** Send complete ms. Length: 1,000-5,000 words. **Pays $8/page,** 2 contributor's copies, and a year's free subscription.
Fiction: Experimental, novel excerpts. **Buys 3-6 mss/year.** Send complete ms. Length: 1,000-7,000 words. **Pays $8/page.**
Poetry: Avant-garde. "No light verse, traditional." **Buys 10-15/year.** Length: 5-6 pages max. **Pays $8/page.**
Tips: "Submissions must be either scholarly or formally innovative. Contributors should be familiar with current literary trends in Canada and the U.S. Scholars should be aware of current schools of theory. All submissions should be accompanied by a brief cover letter; essays should be formatted according to the MLA guide. The publication is not divided into departments. We accept innovative poetry, fiction, experimental prose and scholarly essays."

$ WESTERN HUMANITIES REVIEW, University of Utah, Salt Lake City UT 84112-1107. (801)581-6070. Fax: (801)585-5167. E-mail: whr.lists@m.cc.utah.edu. **Contact:** Dawn Corrigan, managing editor. Quarterly magazine for educated readers. Estab. 1947. Circ. 1,200. **Pays on acceptance.** Publishes ms an average of 3-12 months after acceptance. Buys all rights. Accepts simultaneous submissions. Reports in 5 months.
Nonfiction: Barry Weller, editor-in-chief. Authoritative, readable articles on literature, art, philosophy, current events, history, religion and anything in the humanities. Interdisciplinary articles encouraged. Departments on film and books. **Buys 4-5 unsolicited mss/year. Pays $50-100.**
Fiction: David Kranes, fiction editor. Any type, including experimental. **Buys 8-12 mss/year.** Send complete ms. **Pays $100** on average.
Poetry: Richard Howard, poetry editor.
Tips: "Because of changes in our editorial staff, we urge familiarity with *recent* issues of the magazine. Inappropriate material will be returned without comment. We do not publish writer's guidelines because we think that the magazine itself conveys an accurate picture of our requirements."

$ WITNESS, Oakland Community College, 27055 Orchard Lake Rd., Farmington Hills MI 48334. (313)471-7740. E-mail: stinepj@umich.edu. **Contact:** Peter Stine, editor. **100% freelance written.** Semiannual literary magazine. "*Witness* highlights the role of writer as witness." Estab. 1987. Circ. 2,800. Pays on publication. Publishes ms an average of 1 year after acceptance. Byline given. Buys first North American serial rights. Editorial lead time 6 months. Accepts simultaneous submissions. Reports in 3 months. Sample copy for $7. Writer's guidelines for #10 SASE.

- A rising and energetic magazine. *Witness* alternates general issues with issues focused upon a special subject of wide social/political concern.

Nonfiction: Essays, interview/profile. **Buys 10 mss/year.** Send complete ms. Length: 1,000-10,000 words. **Pays $6/page.**
Fiction: Ethnic, experimental, mainstream, literary. **Buys 20 mss/year.** Send complete ms. Length: 1,000-6,000 words. **Pays $6/page.**
Poetry: Avant-garde, free verse, traditional. **Buys 20 poems/year.** Submit maximum 4 poems. **Pays $10/page.**
Tips: Send SASE for information on special issues. "One story or essay per submission at a time, please."

$ YELLOW SILK: Journal of Erotic Arts, verygraphics, Box 6374, Albany CA 94706. (510)644-4188. **Contact:** Lily Pond, editor. **90% freelance written.** Prefers to work with published/established writers. Annual international journal of erotic literature and visual arts. "Editorial policy: All persuasions; no brutality. Our publication is artistic and literary, not pornographic or pandering. Humans are involved: heads, hearts and bodies—not just bodies alone; and the quality of the literature is as important as the erotic content though erotic content is important too." Pays on publication. Byline given. Buys all publication rights for 1 year following publication, at which time they revert to author, non-active and reprint electronic and anthology rights for duration of copyright.
Nonfiction: Book excerpts, essays, humor, reviews. "We often have theme issues, but non-regularly and usually not announced in advance. No pornography, romance-novel type writing, sex fantasies. No first-person accounts or blow-by-blow descriptions. No articles. No novels." **Buys 5-10 mss/year.** Send complete ms. All submissions should be typed, double-spaced, with name, address and phone number on each page; always enclose SASE. No specified length requirements.
Reprints: Send tearsheet of article or short story and information about when and where the article previously appeared.
Fiction: Erotic literature, including ethnic, experimental, fantasy, humorous, mainstream, novel excerpts, science fiction. See "Nonfiction." Buys 12-16 mss/year. Send complete ms.
Poetry: Avant-garde, free verse, haiku, light verse, traditional. "No greeting-card poetry." Buys 40-60 poems/year. No limit on number of poems submitted, "but don't send book-length manuscripts."
Tips: "The best way to get into *Yellow Silk* is produce excellent, well-crafted work that includes eros freshly, with strength of voice, beauty of language, and insight into character. I'll tell you what I'm sick of and have, unfortunately,

been seeing more of lately: the products of 'How to Write Erotica' classes. This is not brilliant fiction; it is poorly written fantasy and not what I'm looking for."

$ $ $ $ ZOETROPE: ALL STORY, AZX Publications, 260 Fifth Ave. #1200, New York NY 10001-6408. (212)696-5720. Fax: (212)696-5845. **Contact:** Adrienne Brodeur, editor-in-chief. A triannual literary magazine specializing in high caliber short fiction. "*Zoetrope: All Story* seeks to provide a new forum for short fiction and to make short fiction more accessible to the public at large." Open to outstanding work by beginning and established writers. Estab. 1997. Circ. 40,000. Publishes ms 6 months after acceptance. Byline given. Buys first serial rights. Accepts simultaneous submissions. Reports in 5 months. Guidelines for SASE. The magazine will not accept submissions from June 1 through August 31.

Fiction: Literary, mainstream/contemporary, one act plays. 7,000 words maximum. No short shorts or reprints. Receives 6,000 submissions/year. **Buys 32-40 ms/year.** Query with SASE and complete ms (1 story maximum).

• Ranked as one of the best markets for fiction writers in *Writer's Digest* magazine's "Fiction 50," June 1998.

Tips: "*Zoetrope* considers unsolicited submissions of short stories no longer than 7,000 words. Excerpts from larger works, screenplays, treatments and poetry will be returned unread. We regret we are unable to respond to submissions without SASE."

$ $ ZYZZYVA, The Last Word: West Coast Writers & Artists, 41 Sutter St., Suite 1400, San Francisco CA 94104-4987. (415)752-4393. Fax: (415)752-4391. E-mail: zyzzyvainc@aol.com. Website: http://www.webdelsol.com/ZYZZYVA. **Contact:** Howard Junker, editor. **100% freelance written.** Works with a small number of new/unpublished writers each year. "We feature work by West Coast writers only. We are essentially a literary magazine, but of wide-ranging interests and a strong commitment to nonfiction." Estab. 1985. Circ. 3,500. **Pays on acceptance.** Publishes ms an average of 3 months after acceptance. Byline given. Buys first North American serial rights and one-time anthology rights. Reports in 1 week on queries; 1 month on mss. Sample copy for $5.

Nonfiction: Book excerpts, general interest, historical/nostalgic, humor, personal experience. **Buys 15 mss/year.** Query by mail or e-mail. Length: open. **Pays $50.**

Photos: Copies or slides only.

Fiction: Ethnic, experimental, humorous, mainstream. **Buys 20 mss/year.** Send complete ms. Length: open. **Pays $50.**

• Ranked as one of the best markets for fiction writers in *Writer's Digest* magazine's "Fiction 50," June 1998.

Poetry: Buys 20 poems/year. Submit maximum 5 poems. Length: 3-200 lines. **Pays $50.**

Tips: "West Coast writers means those currently living in California, Alaska, Washington, Oregon or Hawaii."

MEN'S

Magazines in this section offer features on topics of general interest primarily to men. Magazines that also use material slanted toward men can be found in Business and Finance, Child Care and Parental Guidance, Ethnic/Minority, Gay & Lesbian Interest, General Interest, Health and Fitness, Military, Relationships and Sports sections. Magazines featuring pictorial layouts with stories and articles of a sexual nature, both gay and straight, appear in the Sex section.

$ $ $ $ DETAILS, Condé Nast Publications, Inc., 632 Broadway, New York NY 10012. Editor-in-chief: Michael Caruso. **Contact:** Mary Gail Pezzimenti. Monthly magazine for men ages 18-34 interested in style, sex, pop cultures, new and sports. "*Details* is edited as a lifestyle magazine for today's generation of young adults who are rapidly assuming their places as leaders in American society. Articles are written from the standpoint of a peer—in contemporary language that readers can relate to, within an intelligent, sophisticated perspective on the world. From culture to sports to entertaining to relationships—fashion, careers, music, clubs and technology, *Details* covers the various aspects of its readers' lives." Estab. 1982. Circ. 473,000. **Pays on acceptance**. Byline given. Offers 25-50% kill fee. Accepts simultaneous submissions. Reports in 2 months on queries.

Nonfiction: News stories of interest to young men; personal essays and service features on lifestyle topics from shops to booze, sports, travel, relationships, courtship, automotive. **Buys 60 mss/year.** Query with published clips. Length: 3,000-5,000 words. **Pays 75¢-$1/word.**

Columns/Departments: 800-1,500 words. **Buys 120 mss/year.** Query with published clips. **Pays 75-$1/word.**

Fillers: Buys 60/year. Length: 500-800 words. **Pays 75¢-$1/word.**

Tips: "Topical news stories that affect or interest men in their 20s. Timely subject, stylishly written that makes people laugh and cry. *Details* maintains a high standard of modern journalism and encourages a creative, stylish, confessional, personal emotional writing style. We include all kinds of people with all kinds of interest and beliefs. We speak to our readers in a contemporary manner, with a unique tone that touches the heart and mind and tickles that funny bone."

$ $ $ $ ESQUIRE, 250 W. 55th St., New York NY 10019. (212)649-4020. Editor-in-Chief: David Granger. Features Editor: Mark Warne. Monthly magazine for smart, well-off men. Estab. 1933. General readership is college educated and sophisticated, between ages 30 and 45. Written mostly by contributing editors on contract. Rarely accepts unsolicited mss. **Pays on acceptance**. Offers 20% kill fee. Publishes ms an average of 2 months after acceptance. Retains first worldwide periodical publication rights for 90 days from cover date.

● Ranked as one of the best markets for freelance writers in *Writer's Yearbook* magazine's annual "Top 100 Markets," January 1997.

Nonfiction: Columns average 1,500 words; features average 5,000 words; short front-of-book pieces average 200-400 words. Focus is on the ever-changing trends in American culture. Topics include current events and politics, social criticism, sports, celebrity profiles, the media, art and music, men's fashion. Queries must be sent by letter. **Buys 4 features and 12 short pieces. Pays $1/word.**

Photos: Marianne Butler, photo editor. Uses mostly commissioned photography. Payment depends on size and number of photos.

Fiction: Contact: literary editor. "Literary excellence is our only criterion." Accepts work chiefly from literary agencies. Publishes short stories, some poetry, and excerpts from novels, memoirs and plays.

Tips: "A writer has the best chance of breaking in at *Esquire* by querying with a specific idea that requires special contacts and expertise. Ideas must be timely and national in scope."

$ $ $ $ GENTLEMEN'S QUARTERLY, Condé Nast, 350 Madison Ave., New York NY 10017. (212)880-8800. Editor-in-Chief: Arthur Cooper. **Contact:** Martin Beiser, managing editor. Prefers to work with established/published writers. **60% freelance written.** Circ. 650,000. Monthly magazine emphasizing fashion, general interest and service features for men ages 25-45 with a large discretionary income. **Pays on acceptance.** Byline given. Pays 25% kill fee. Submit seasonal material 6 months in advance. Reports in 1 month.

Nonfiction: Politics, personality profiles, lifestyles, trends, grooming, nutrition, health/fitness, sports, travel, money, investment and business matters. **Buys 4-6 mss/issue.** Query with published clips. Length: 1,500-4,000 words. Pay varies.

Columns/Departments: Query with published clips. Length: 1,000-2,500 words. Pay varies.

Tips: "Major features are usually assigned to well-established, known writers. Pieces are almost always solicited. The best way to break in is through the columns, especially Contraria, Enthusiasms or First Person."

$ $ $ HEARTLAND USA, UST Publishing, 1 Sound Shore Dr., Greenwich CT 06830-7251. (203)622-3456. Fax: (203)863-5393. E-mail: husaedit@aol.com. **Contact:** Brad Pearson, editor. **10% freelance written.** Bimonthly magazine for working men. "*Heartland USA* is a general interest, lifestyle magazine for working men 18 to 55. It covers spectator sports (primarily motor sports, football, baseball and basketball), hunting, fishing, how-to, travel, music, gardening, human interest, etc." Estab. 1991. Circ. 850,000. **Pays on acceptance**. Byline given. Offers 20% kill fee. Buys first North American serial and second serial (reprint) rights. Submit seasonal material 1 year in advance. Accepts simultaneous submissions. Reports in 1 month on queries. Sample copy on request. Writer's guidelines free.

Nonfiction: Book excerpts, general interest, historical/nostalgic, how-to, humor, inspirational, interview/profile, new product, personal experience, photo feature, technical, travel. "No fiction or dry expository pieces." **Buys 6 mss/year.** Query with or without published clips or send complete ms. Length: 350-1,200 words. **Pays 50-80¢/word** for assigned articles; 25-80¢/word for unsolicited articles. Sometimes pays expenses of writers on assignment.

Reprints: Send photocopy of article and information about when and where the article previously appeared. Pays 25% of amount paid for an original article.

Photos: Send photos with submission. Reviews transparencies. Identification of subjects required. Buys one-time rights.

Tips: "Features with the possibility of strong photographic support are open to freelancers, as are our shorter departments. We look for a relaxed, jocular, easy-to-read style, and look favorably on the liberal use of anecdote or interesting quotations. Our average reader sees himself as hardworking, traditional, rugged, confident, uncompromising and daring."

$ $ $ $ ICON Thoughtstyle Magazine for Men, 595 Broadway, 4th Floor, New York NY 10012. (212)219-2654. Fax: (212)219-4045. E-mail: rtdolch@iconmag.com. **Contact:** Robin Dolch, senior editor. Bimonthly magazine covering general interest issues for young men, ages 18-34. "*Icon*'s mission is to confront the concept of success carefully and objectively and to explore its many meanings and manifestations boundlessly, so that young men are better able to define the concept for themselves. Editorial focuses on comprehensive profile/interviews of men who have achieved large-scale successes in their respective fields. *Icon* will aim to educate and civilize, to inspire and encourage." Estab. 1997. Circ. 150,000. Pays within 30 days after acceptance. Byline given. Buys all rights. Reports in 2 weeks. Writer's guidelines for #10 SASE.

Nonfiction: Interview/profile. "*Icon* Profiles examine the world's most successful, interesting men, providing blueprints for success. These pieces could cover a CEO, a physicist or a choreographer. We hold no preconceived definitions of what exactly *success* is. Our role is to find people who are working to fulfill their own vision of it and then report on their efforts." Feature articles also focus on organizations, places, ideas, etc. "Whereas the *Icon* Profiles start with an individual and work inward, features start with one or more people and work outward, looking at their lives' work, the effort in which they are presently or were previously involved. The stories are personality based, with a heavy stress on reporting, observation and interviews. Recurrent themes are business ventures, failures and comebacks, off-the-beaten path characters and families, and generally provocative characters." Query with published clips. Length: 5,000 words. **Pays $1/word.**

Columns/Departments: Iconography: "Two articles examining the everyday symbols we take for granted, i.e. the bar code, the middle finger, The *Happy Days* living room, 750 words; Thoughstyles: Entry-point gallery of 5 personalities, entrepreneurs and professionals from a broad range of pursuits, 750 words; Iconnoisseur, (mini-mag of 5 departments within *Icon* that 'examines the tools and rituals of a man's life): Clothing (the 3-piece suit, the white shirt, the motorcycle jacket), Tools (the roller-ball pen, the diamond engagement ring, the condom), Elixirs (bitters, tap water, opium), Ego (caffeine, the yawn, red meat), Form and Function (chemical warfare, the sound barrier, smart highways), and Bonus (processed cheese, the insult, the breast), 2000 words; Re: Views (3 departments covering the realm of artistic expression): Vision (examining the artist), Creation (dealing with the artistic process) and Effect (reactions or responses elicited by the artist and his or her work), 2,000 words." **Pays $1/word.**

N $ $ $ $ THE INTERNATIONAL, The Magazine of Adventure and Pleasure for Men, Tomorrow Enterprises, 2228 E. 20th St., Oakland CA 94606. (510)532-6501. Fax: (510)536-5886. E-mail: tonyattomr@aol.com. **Contact:** The International (Submissions). **70% freelance written.** Monthly magazine covering "bush and seaplane flying, seafaring, pleasure touring, etc. with adventure stories from all men who travel on sexual tours to Asia, Latin America, The Caribbean and the Pacific." Estab. 1997. Circ. 5,000. Pays on publication. Publishes ms 2 months after acceptance. Buys first rights. Editorial lead time 2 months. Submit seasonal material 3 months in advance. Accepts simultaneous submissions. Reports in 2 weeks on queries; 2 months on mss. Writer's guidelines free.

Nonfiction: Exposé, general interest, historical/nostalgic, humor, interview/profile, opinion, personal experience, photo feature, travel. Seafaring stories of all types published with photos. Military and veteran stories also sought, as well as ex-pats living abroad. Especially interested in airplane flying stories with photos. No pornography, no family or "honeymoon" type travel. **Buys 40-50 mss/year.** Query or send complete ms. Length: 700 words max. **Pays $100-2,000 for assigned articles, $25-1,000 for unsolicited articles.** Sometimes pays expenses of writers on assignment.

Photos: Send photos with submission. Reviews negatives and 5×6 prints. Offers no additional payment for photos accepted with ms. Identification of subjects required. Buys one-time rights or all rights.

Columns/Departments: Asia/Pacific Beat; Latin America/Caribbean Beat (Nightlife, Adventure, Air & Sea), 450 words; Lifestyles Abroad (Expatriate Men's Doings Overseas), 600-1,000 words. **Buys 25 mss/year.** Query or send complete ms. **Pays $25-1,000.**

Fillers: Anecdotes, facts, gags to be illustrated by cartoonist, newsbreaks, short humor. **Buys 25/year.** Length: 200-600 words. **Pays $25-100.**

Tips: "If a single male lives in those parts of the world covered, and is either a pleasure tourist, pilot or seafarer, we are interested in his submissions. He can visit our upcoming website or contact us directly. Stories from female escorts or party girls are also welcomed."

N $ $ $ $ MAXIM, The Best Thing to Happen to Men Since Woman, 1040 Sixth Ave., 23rd Floor, New York City NY 10018. Fax: (212)302-2635. E-mail: editors@maximmag.com. **Contact:** Keith Blanchard, editor. **50% freelance written.** Monthly magazine. "*Maxim* covers every aspect of real men's real lives, from sports and sex to health and fitness to fashion and beer with irreverence, edge and humor." Estab. 1996. Circ. 350,000. **Pays on acceptance.** Publishes ms an average of 1 month after acceptance. Byline sometimes given. Offers 20% kill fee. Buys all rights. Editorial lead time 3 months. Submit seasonal material 6 months in advance. Accepts simultaneous submissions. Reports in 6 weeks on queries; 6 months on mss. Writer's guidelines for #10 SASE.

Nonfiction: Book excerpts, humorous essays, expose, general interest, how-to, humor, new product, personal experience, photo features. **Buys hundreds of mss/year.** Query by mail or e-mail. Length: 300-3,000 words. **Pays $1/word minimum for assigned articles; 50¢/ward minimum for unsolicited articles.** Pays expenses of writers on assignment.

Reprints: Accepts previously published submissions.

Photos: State availability of photos with submission. Negotiates payment individually. Identification of subjects required. Buys all rights.

Columns/Departments: How-to (service with irreverance), Out There (weird news items), all 300 words. Query. **Pays $1/word.**

$ $ $ MEN'S JOURNAL, Wenner Media Inc., 1290 Avenue of the Americas, New York NY 10104-0298. (212)484-1616. Fax: (212)767-8204. **Contact:** Terry MacDonnell, editor. Magazine published 10 times/year covering general lifestyle for men, ages 25-49. "*Men's Journal* is for active men with an interest in participatory sports, travel, fitness and adventure. It provides practical, informative articles on how to spend quality leisure time." Estab. 1992. Circ. 550,000.

Nonfiction: Features and profiles. 2,000-7,000 words; shorter features of 400-1,200 words; equipment and fitness stories 400-1,800 words. Query with SASE. "No phone queries, please. Fax queries OK." Pay varies.

$ $ $ P.O.V. , BYOB Ventures/Freedom Communications, 56 W. 22nd St., 3rd Floor, New York NY 10010. (212)367-7600. Website: http://www.povmag.com. Editor: Randall Lane. **Contact:** Michael Callahan, managing editor. **80% freelance written.** Published 10 times/year. "Our motto is cash, careers and living large. Our audience is up-and-coming guys in their twenties and early thirties. If it's not of interest to them, it's not of interest to us." Estab. 1995. Circ. 225,000. Pays 30 days after acceptance. Publishes ms an average of 3 months after acceptance. Byline given. Offers 20% kill fee. Buys first North American serial and electronic rights. Editorial lead time 4 months. Submit seasonal material 6 months in advance. Reports in 2 months on queries. Sample copy for $3 plus postage.

Nonfiction: Book excerpts, essays, how-to (business), interview, travel, personal finance, in-depth investigative feature stories. "No 'memory' essays or personal experience (unless it relates specifically to our audience)." **Buys 150 mss/year.** Query with published clips. Length: 400-3,000 words. **Pays 50¢/word.** Sometimes pays expenses of writers on assignment.

Photos: State availability of photos with submission. Negotiates payment individually. Captions, identification of subjects required. Buys one-time rights.

Tips: "Numerous story ideas that show a strong familiarity with the editorial content of the magazine are critical. Solid writing experience for national magazines is preferred."

N $ $ $ VERGE, Essential Gear for Real Life, Times Mirror Magazines, 2 Park Ave., 9th Floor, New York NY 10016. (212)779-5000. Fax: (212)481-8062. E-mail: letters@verge.com. Website: http://www.verge.com. **Contact:** Jeffrey J. Csatari, editor. Managing editor: William G. Phillips. Bimonthly magazine covering "essential gear and gadgets for an active man's lifestyle. Each issue features the latest new products, including computer hardware and software, automobiles, home entertainment equipment and sports gear. In addition, there are regular features on fitness, adventure, travel, business tips, celebrities and scientific breakthroughs." Estab. 1996. Circ. 150,000. **Pays on acceptance**. Publishes ms an average of 1 month after acceptance. Byline given. Offers 25% kill fee. Buys all rights. Editorial lead time 3 months. Submit seasonal material at least 3 months in advance. Accepts simultaneous submissions. Writer's guidelines for #10 SASE.

Nonfiction New product, men's issues, technology. Query. Pay varies. Sometimes pays expenses of writers on assignment.

Photos: State availability of photos with submission. Negotiates payment individually. Buys all rights.

Fiction: Adventure, humorous, mainstream, slice-of-life vignettes. Query with or without published clips. Pay varies.

MILITARY

These publications emphasize military or paramilitary subjects or other aspects of military life. Technical and semitechnical publications for military commanders, personnel and planners, as well as those for military families and civilians interested in Armed Forces activities are listed here. Publications covering military history can be found in the History section.

$ $ AMERICAN SURVIVAL GUIDE, Y-Visionary Publishing, 265 S. Anita Dr., Suite 120, Orange CA 92868-3310. Fax: (714)939-9909. E-mail: jim4asg@aol.com. **Contact:** Jim Benson, editor. Scott Stoddard, managing editor. **50% freelance written.** Monthly magazine covering "self-reliance, defense, meeting day-to-day and possible future threats—survivalism for survivalists." Circ. 60,000. Pays on publication. Publishes ms up to 1 year after acceptance. Byline given. Submit seasonal material 5 months in advance. Sample copy for $6. Writer's guidelines for SASE.

- *American Survival Guide* is always looking for more good material with quality artwork (photos). They want articles on recent events and new techniques, etc. giving the latest available information to their readers.

Nonfiction: Exposé (political); how-to; interview/profile; personal experience (how I survived); photo feature (equipment and techniques related to survival in all possible situations); emergency medical; health and fitness; communications; transportation; food preservation; water purification; self-defense; terrorism; nuclear dangers; nutrition; tools; shelter; etc. "No general articles about how to survive. We want specifics and single subjects." **Buys 60-100 mss/year.** Query or send complete ms. Length: 1,500-2,000 words. **Pays $160-400.** Sometimes pays some expenses of writers on assignment.

Photos: Send photos with ms. "One of the most frequent mistakes made by writers in completing an article assignment for us is sending photo submissions that are inadequate." Captions, model releases and identification of subjects mandatory. Buys exclusive one-time rights.

Tips: "We need hard copy with computer disk and photos or other artwork. Prepare material of value to individuals who wish to sustain human life no matter what the circumstance. This magazine is a text and reference."

$ $ ARMY MAGAZINE, Box 1560, Arlington VA 22210. (703)841-4300. Fax: (703)841-3505. E-mail: armymag@ausa.org.com. Website: http://www.ausa.org/armyzine/. **Contact:** Mary Blake French, editor. **70% freelance written.** Prefers to work with published/established writers. Monthly magazine emphasizing military interests. Estab. 1904. Circ. 100,000. Pays on publication. Publishes ms an average of 5 months after acceptance. Buys all rights. Byline given except for back-up research. Submit seasonal material 3 months in advance. Sample copy and writer's guidelines for 9×12 SAE with $1 postage.

- *Army Magazine* looks for shorter articles.

Nonfiction: Historical (military and original); humor (military feature-length articles and anecdotes); interview; new product; nostalgia; personal experience dealing especially with the most recent conflicts in which the US Army has been involved (Desert Storm, Panama, Grenada); photo feature; profile; technical. No rehashed history. "We would like to see more pieces about little-known episodes involving interesting military personalities. We especially want material lending itself to heavy, contributor-supplied photographic treatment. The first thing a contributor should recognize is that our readership is very savvy militarily. 'Gee-whiz' personal reminiscences get short shrift, unless they hold their own in a company in which long military service, heroism and unusual experiences are commonplace. At the same time, Army readers like a well-written story with a fresh slant, whether it is about an experience in a foxhole or the fortunes of a corps in battle." **Buys 8 mss/issue.** Submit complete ms. Length: 1,500 words, but shorter items, especially in 1,000 to 1,500 range, often have better chance of getting published. **Pays 12-18¢/word.** No unsolicited book reviews.

Photos: Submit photo material with accompanying ms. Pays $25-50 for 8×10 b&w glossy prints; $50-350 for 8×10 color glossy prints or 2¼×2¼ transparencies; will also accept 35mm. Captions preferred. Buys all rights. Pays $35-50 for cartoon with strong military slant.

Columns/Departments: Military news, books, comment (*New Yorker*-type "Talk of the Town" items). **Buys 8/issue.** Submit complete ms. Length: 1,000 words. **Pays $40-150.**

$ $ FAMILY MAGAZINE, The Magazine for Military Wives, PABCO, 51 Atlantic Ave., Suite 200, New York NY 11011. E-mail: soleprop@aol.com. **Contact:** Don Hirst, Editor. Monthly. "*Family* contains features on military family life: relocating, decorating, cooking, travel, education, children, careers, marriage and family health." Estab. 1973. Circ. 500,000. Pays on publication. Byline given. Buys one-time rights. Editorial lead time varies. Submit seasonal material 6 months in advance. Accepts simultaneous submissions if notified. Reports in 2 months on queries only if interested. Sample copy for $1.25. Writer's guidelines for #10 SASE.
Nonfiction: Military-related; must pertain to family life. **Buys fewer than 20 mss/year from outside contributors.** Query. **Pays $100-200.**
Photos: State availability of photos with query. Offers $25-50/photo. Buys one-time rights.
Tips: "No unsolicited manuscripts or phone queries. E-mail queries OK. Include your phone number with e-mail queries. Inquiries are welcome, but right now regular contributors provide much of the content."

N $ $ NAVAL HISTORY, US Naval Institute, 118 Maryland Ave., Annapolis MD 21402-5035. (410)268-6110. Fax: (410)269-7940. E-mail: fschultz@usni.org. Website: http://www.usni.org. **Contact:** Fred L. Schultz, editor-in-chief. Kimberly Couranz, associate editor. **90% freelance written.** Bimonthly magazine covering naval and maritime history, worldwide. "We are committed, as a publication of the 125-year-old US Naval Institute, to presenting the best and most accurate short works in international naval and maritime history. We do find a place for academicians, but they should be advised that a good story generally wins against a dull topic, no matter how well researched." Estab. 1988. Circ. 40,000. **Pays on acceptance**. Publishes ms an average of 2 years after acceptance. Byline given. Buys first North American serial rights; occasionally allows rights to revert to authors. Editorial lead time 6 months. Submit seasonal material 6 months in advance. Reports in 1 month on queries; 2 months on mss. Sample copy for $3.50 and SASE. Writer's guidelines free.
Nonfiction: Book excerpts, essays, historical/nostalgic, humor, inspirational, interview/profile, personal experience, photo feature, technical. **Buys 80-100 mss/year.** Query. Length: 1,000-3,000 words. **Pays $300-500 for assigned articles; $75-400 for unsolicited articles.**
Photos: State availability of photos with submission. Reviews contact sheets, transparencies, 4×6 or larger prints. Offers $10 minimum. Captions, model releases, identification of subjects required. Buys one-time rights.
Fillers: Anecdotes, news breaks (naval-related), short humor. **Buys 40-50/year.** Length: 50-1,000 words. **Pays $10-50.**
Tips: "A good way to break in is to write a good, concise, exciting story supported by primary sources and substantial illustrations. Naval history-related news items (ship decommissionings, underwater archaeology, etc.) are also welcome. Because our story bank is substantial, competition is severe. Tying a topic to an anniversry many times is an advantage. We are in need of Korean and Vietnam War-era material."

$ $ NAVY TIMES, 6883 Commercial Dr., Springfield VA 22159. (703)750-8636. Fax: (703)750-8622. E-mail: navydesk@aol.com. Website: http://www.navytimes.com. Editor: Tobias Naegele. **Contact:** Jean Reid Norman, managing editor. Weekly newspaper covering sea services. News and features of men and women in the Navy, Coast Guard and Marine Corps. Estab. 1950. Circ. 90,000. **Pays on acceptance.** Byline given. Buys first North American serial or second serial (reprint) rights. Submit seasonal material 2 months in advance. Reports in 2 months. Guidelines free.
Nonfiction: Historical/nostalgic, opinion. No poetry. **Buys 100 mss/year.** Query. Length: 500-1,000 words. **Pays $50-500.** Sometimes pays expenses of writers on assignment.
Reprints: Send tearsheet of article or short story.
Photos: Send photos with submission. Offers $20-100/photo. Captions and identification of subjects required. Buys one-time rights.

$ $ OFF DUTY MAGAZINE, 3505 Cadillac Ave., Suite O-105, Costa Mesa CA 92626-1500. (714)549-7172. Fax: (714)549-4222. E-mail: odutyedit@aol.com. Website: http://www.offduty.com. **Contact:** Tom Graves, managing editor. **30% freelance written.** Bimonthly magazine covering the leisure-time activities and interests of the military community. "Our audience is solely military members and their families; many of our articles could appear in other consumer magazines, but we always slant them toward the military; i.e. where to get a military discount when traveling." Estab. 1970. Circ. 507,000. **Pays on acceptance.** Publishes ms an average of 3 months after acceptance. Byline given. Buys one-time rights. Submit seasonal material at least 4 months in advance. Accepts simultaneous submissions. Reports in 2 months on queries. Sample copy for 9×12 SAE with 6 first class stamps. Writer's guidelines for SASE.
Nonfiction: Travel, finance, lifestyle (with a military angle), interview/profile (music and entertainment). "Must be familiar with *Off Duty* and its needs." **Buys 30-40 mss/year.** Query. Length: 800-1,800 words. **Pays $150-500.**

- Editor is not interested in seeing war reminiscences. He reports they are buying fewer articles due to slimmer issues and fewer magazines per year.

Reprints: Send tearsheet or photocopy of article and information about when and where the article previously appeared. Pays 50% of amount paid for an original article.
Photos: State availability of photos with submission. Reviews contact sheets, websites or sample prints/slides. Offers $50-300/photo (cover). Captions and identification of subjects required. Buys one-time rights. Unsolicited photos not returned without SASE.
Columns/Departments: Dialogue—A Forum for Women (active-duty, spouse or dependent, subjects related to both

off-duty and on-duty life). Length: 1,200 words. Address them to "Dialogue." **Pays $150.**
Tips: "Get to know the military community and its interests beyond the stereotypes. Query with the idea of getting on our next year's editorial calendar. We choose our primary topics at least six months in advance."

$ PARAMETERS: U.S. Army War College Quarterly, US Army War College, Carlisle Barracks PA 17013-5050. (717)245-4943. E-mail: awca-parameters@carlisle-emh2.army.mil. Website: http://carlisle-www.army.mil/usawc/Parameters/. **Contact:** Col. John J. Madigan, US Army Retired, editor. **100% freelance written.** Prefers to work with published/established writers or experts in the field. Readership consists of senior leadership of US defense establishment, both uniformed and civilian, plus members of the media, government, industry and academia interested in national and international security affairs, military strategy, military leadership and management, art and science of warfare, and military history (provided it has contemporary relevance). Estab. 1971. Circ. 13,500. Not copyrighted; unless copyrighted by author, articles may be reprinted with appropriate credits. Buys first serial rights. Byline given. Pays on publication. Publishes ms an average of 6 months after acceptance. Reports in 6 weeks. Sample copy and writer's guidelines free.
Nonfiction: Articles are preferred that deal with current security issues, employ critical analysis and provide solutions or recommendations. Liveliness and verve, consistent with scholarly integrity, appreciated. Theses, studies and academic course papers should be adapted to article form prior to submission. Documentation in complete endnotes. Submit complete ms. Length: 4,500 words average, preferably less. **Pays $150** average (including visuals).
Tips: "Make it short; keep it interesting; get criticism and revise accordingly. Tackle a subject only if you are an authority. No fax submissions."

N $ $ PROCEEDINGS, U.S. Naval Institute, 118 Maryland Ave., Annapolis MD 21402-5035. (410)268-6110. Fax: (410)269-7940. Website: http://www.usni.org. Editor: Fred H. Rainbow. **Contact:** John G. Miller, managing editor. **80% freelance written.** Monthly magazine covering Navy, Marine Corps, Coast Guard. Estab. 1873. Circ. 100,000. **Pays on acceptance.** Publishes ms an average of 3-9 months after acceptance. Byline given. Buys all rights. Editorial lead time 3 months. Reports in 2 months on submissions. Sample copy for $3.95. Writer's guidelines free.
Nonfiction: Essays, historical/nostalgic, interview/profile, photo feature, technical. **Buys 100-125 mss/year.** Query or send complete ms. Length: 3,000 words. **Pays $60-150/printed page** for unsolicited articles.
Photos: State availability of or send photos with submission. Reviews transparencies and prints. Offers $25/photo maximum. Buys one-time rights.
Columns/Departments: Comment & Discussion (letters to editor), 7,500 words; Commentary (opinion), 1,000 words; Nobody Asked Me, But . . . (opinion), less than 1,000 words. **Buys 150-200 mss/year.** Query or send complete ms. **Pays $32-150.**
Fillers: Anecdotes. **Buys 20/year.** Length: 100 words. **Pays $25.**

$ $ $ THE RETIRED OFFICER MAGAZINE, 201 N. Washington St., Alexandria VA 22314-2539. (800)245-8762. Fax: (703)838-8179. E-mail: heatherl@troa.org. Website: http://www.troa.org. Editor: Col. Warren S. Lacy, USA-Ret. Managing Editor: Joanne Hodges. **Contact:** Heather Lyons, senior editor. **60% freelance written.** Prefers to work with published/established writers. Monthly magazine for officers of the 7 uniformed services and their families. "*The Retired Officer Magazine* covers topics such as current military/political affairs; recent military history, especially Vietnam and Korea; travel; money; hobbies; health and fitness; second career job opportunities; and military family and retirement lifestyles." Estab. 1945. Circ. 395,000. **Pays on acceptance.** Publishes ms an average of 1 year after acceptance. Byline given. Buys first serial rights. Submit seasonal material (holiday stories with a military theme) at least 12 months in advance. Reports on material accepted for publication within 2 months. Sample copy and writer's guidelines for 9×12 SAE with 6 first-class stamps or on website.

- Ranked as one of the best markets for freelance writers in *Writer's Yearbook* magazine's annual "Top 100 Markets," January 1998.

Nonfiction: Current military/political affairs, health and wellness, recent military history, travel, second-career job opportunities, military family lifestyle. Emphasis now on current military and defense issues. "We rarely accept unsolicited manuscripts. We look for detailed query letters with résumé, sample clips and SASE attached. We do not publish poetry or fillers." **Buys 48 mss/year.** Length: 800-2,000 words. **Pays up to $1,200.**
Photos: Query with list of stock photo subjects. Pays $20 for each 8×10 b&w photo (normal halftone) used. Original slides or transparencies must be suitable for color separation. Pays $75-200 for inside color; $300 for cover.

$ $ $ $ SOLDIER OF FORTUNE, The Journal of Professional Adventurers, Omega Group, Ltd., P.O. Box 693, Boulder CO 80306-0693. (303)449-3750. Fax: (303)444-5617. E-mail: editor@sofmag.com. Website: http://wwwsofmag.com. Managing Editor: Dwight Swift. Deputy Editor: Tom Reisinger. **Contact:** Marty Kufus, assistant editor. **50% freelance written.** Monthly magazine covering military, paramilitary, police, combat subjects and action/adventure. "We are an action-oriented magazine; we cover combat hot spots around the world. We also provide timely features on state-of-the-art weapons and equipment; elite military and police units; and historical military operations. Readership is primarily active-duty military, veterans and law enforcement." Estab. 1975. Circ. 175,000. Byline given. Offers 25% kill fee. Buys all rights; will negotiate. Submit seasonal material 5 months in advance. Reports in 3 weeks on queries; 1 month on mss. Sample copy for $5. Writer's guidelines for #10 SASE.
Nonfiction: Exposé; general interest; historical/nostalgic; how-to (on weapons and their skilled use); humor; profile; new product; personal experience; novel excerpts; photo feature ("number one on our list"); technical; travel; combat reports; military unit reports and solid Vietnam and Operation Desert Storm articles. "No 'How I won the war' pieces;

no op-ed pieces *unless* they are fully and factually backgrounded; no knife articles (staff assignments only). *All* submitted articles should have good art; art will sell us on an article." **Buys 75 mss/year.** Query with or without published clips or send complete ms. Send mss to articles editor; queries to managing editor. Length: 2,000-3,000 words. **Pays $150-250/page.** Sometimes pays the expenses of writers on assignment.

Reprints: Send disk copy and photocopy of article and information about when and where the article previously appeared. Pays 25% of amount paid for an original article.

Photos: Send photos with submission (copies only, no originals). Reviews contact sheets and transparencies. Offers no additional payment for photos accepted with ms. Pays $500 for cover photo. Captions, identification of subjects required. Buys one-time rights.

Columns/Departments: Combat craft (how-to military and police survival skills); I Was There (first-person accounts of the arcane or unusual based in a combat or law-enforcement environment), both 600-800 words. **Buys 16 mss/year.** Send complete ms. Length: 600-800 words. **Pays $150.**

Fillers: Bulletin Board editor. Newsbreaks; military/paramilitary related, "*has* to be documented." Length: 100-250 words. **Pays $50.**

Tips: "Submit a professionally prepared, complete package. All artwork with cutlines, double-spaced typed manuscript with 5.25 or 3.5 IBM-compatible disc, if available, cover letter including synopsis of article, supporting documentation where applicable, etc. Manuscript must be factual; writers have to do their homework and get all their facts straight. One error means rejection. We will work with authors over the phone or by letter, tell them if their ideas have merit for an acceptable article, and help them fine-tune their work. I Was There is a good place for freelancers to start. Vietnam features, if carefully researched and art heavy, will always get a careful look. Combat reports, again, with good art, are number one in our book and stand the best chance of being accepted. Military unit reports from around the world are well received as are law-enforcement articles (units, police in action). If you write for us, be complete and factual; pros read *Soldier of Fortune*, and are *very* quick to let us know if we (and the author) err. Read a current issue to see where we're taking the magazine in the 1990s."

$ $ TIMES NEWS SERVICE, Army Times Publishing Co., 6883 Springfield Dr., Springfield VA 22159-0200. (703)750-8125. Fax: (703)750-8781. E-mail: mconews@aol.com. Website: http://www.armytimes.com. Special Sections Editor: Cindi Florit. **Contact:** Features Editor. **15% freelance written.** Willing to work with new/unpublished writers. Manages weekly lifestyle section of Army, Navy and Air Force Times covering current lifestyles and problems of career military families around the world. Circ. 300,000. **Pays on acceptance.** Publishes ms an average of 2 months after acceptance. Byline given. Buys first worldwide rights. Submit seasonal material 3 months in advance. Reports in about 1 month. Writer's guidelines for #10 SASE.

- *Times News Service* accepts few exposé-type articles from freelancers but it is always interested in seeing queries. If you have news, they will accept it from a freelancer, but staff writers generally get the news before any freelancers can.

Nonfiction: Exposé (current military); interview/profile (military); personal experience (military only); travel (of military interest). **Buys 200 mss/year.** Query with published clips. Length: 500-2,000 words. **Pays $75-300.** Sometimes pays the expenses of writers on assignment.

Photos: Send photos or send photos with ms. Reviews 35mm color contact sheets and prints. Captions, model releases and identification of subjects required.

Tips: "In your query write a detailed description of story and how it will be told. A tentative lead is nice. A military angle is crucial. Just one good story 'breaks in' a freelancer. Follow the outline you propose in your query letter and humanize articles with quotes and examples."

MUSIC

Music fans follow the latest industry news in these publications that range from opera to hip hop. Types of music and musicians or specific instruments are the sole focus of some magazines. Publications geared to the music industry and professionals can be found in the Trade Music section. Additional music and dance markets are found in the Contemporary Culture and Entertainment section.

$ AMERICAN SONGWRITER, 121 17th Ave. S., Nashville TN 37203-2707. (615)244-6065. Fax: (615)256-6858. E-mail: asongmag@aol.com. Website: http://www.nol.com/~nol/asongmag.html. **Contact:** Vernell Hackett, editor. **30% freelance written.** Bimonthly magazine about songwriters and the craft of songwriting for many types of music, including pop, country, rock, metal, jazz, gospel, and r&b. Estab. 1984. Circ. 5,000. Pays on publication. Publishes ms an average of 2 months after acceptance. Offers 25% kill fee. Buys first North American serial rights. Reports in 2 months. Sample copy for $3. Writer's guidelines for SASE.

Nonfiction: General interest, interview/profile, new product, technical, home demo studios, movie and TV scores, performance rights organizations. No fiction. **Buys 20 mss/year.** Query with published clips. Length: 300-1,200 words. **Pays $25-60.**

Reprints: Send tearsheet or photocopy of article and information about when and where the article previously appeared. Pays same amount as paid for an original article.

Photos: Send photos with submission. Reviews 3×5 prints. Offers no additional payment for photos accepted with ms. Identification of subjects required. Buys one-time rights.
Tips: "*American Songwriter* strives to present articles which can be read a year or two after they were written and still be pertinent to the songwriter reading them."

N $ $ $ $ AUDIO, The Equipment Authority, Hachette Filipacchi Magazines, Inc., 1633 Broadway, New York NY 10019. Fax: (212)767-5633. Managing Editor: Kay Blummenthal. **Contact**: Alan Lofft, senior editor. **90% freelance written.** Monthly magazine covering high-performance audio and audio/video equipment. Estab. 1947. Circ. 110,000. Pays on publication. Publishes ms an average of 2 months after acceptance. Byline given. Buys first North American serial rights and electronic rights. Editorial lead time 3 months. Accepts simultaneous submissions. Sample copy for $6.95. Writer's guidelines not available.
Nonfiction: Essays, how-to, interview/profile, new product, technical. **Buys 20 mss/year.** Query. Length: 1,500-5,000 words. **Pays $100-2,500.** Sometimes pays the expenses of writers on assignment.
Photos: State availability of photos with submission. Negotiates payment individually. Buys one-time and electronic rights.
Columns/Departments: Ivan Berger, technical editor. Playback (short equipment reviews), 250 words; Spectrum (news), 600 words; Music reviews, 250 words. **Buys 130 mss/year.** Query. **Pays $100-500.**

$ $ $ BBC MUSIC MAGAZINE, Complete Guide to Classical Music, BBC Magazines, 80 Wood Lane, London W12 0TT England. Phone: (181)576-3283. Fax: (181)576-3292. E-mail: music.magazine@bbc.co.ok. Website: http://www.bbcworldwide.com/musicmagazine. **Contact:** Graeme Kay, editor. Managing Editor: Jessica Gibson. **90% freelance written.** Monthly magazine covering all aspects of classical music, including CDs, composers etc., for all levels of interest and knowledge. Estab. 1992. Circ. 120,000. Pays on publication. Publishes ms 3-4 months after acceptance. Byline given. Buys all rights. Editorial lead time 3 months. Submit seasonal material 1 year in advance.
Nonfiction: Essays, exposé, how-to (understand aspects of music better), interview/profile, opinion. **Buys 300 mss/year.** Query. Length: 500-2,500 words. **Pays $150-1,500.** Sometimes pays expenses of writers on assignments.
Photos: State availability of photos with submissions. Negotiates payment individually.
Fillers: Newsbreaks. **Buys 100/year.** Length: 100-200 words. **Pays $50.**
Tips: Send brief letter outlining idea(s) to editor.

$ $ BLUEGRASS UNLIMITED, Bluegrass Unlimited, Inc., P.O. Box 111, Broad Run VA 20137-0111. (540)349-8181 or (800)BLU-GRAS. Fax: (540)341-0011. E-mail: editor@blugrassmusic.com. Editor: Peter V. Kuykendall. **Contact:** Sharon Watts, managing editor. **80% freelance written.** Prefers to work with published/established writers. Monthly magazine on bluegrass and old-time country music. Estab. 1966. Circ. 27,000. Pays on publication. Publishes ms an average of 4 months after acceptance. Byline given. Kill fee negotiated. Buys first North American serial, one-time, all rights and second serial (reprint) rights. Submit seasonal material 4 months in advance. Reports in 2 weeks on queries; 2 months on mss. Sample copy free. Writer's guidelines for #10 SASE.
Nonfiction: General interest, historical/nostalgic, how-to, interview/profile, personal experience, photo feature, travel. No "fan"-style articles. **Buys 75-80 mss/year.** Query with or without published clips. Length: open. **Pays 8-10¢/word.**
Reprints: Send photocopy or typed ms with rights for sale noted and information about when and where the article previously appeared. Payment is negotiable.
Photos: State availability of or send photos with query. Reviews 35mm transparencies and 3×5, 5×7 and 8×10 b&w and color prints. Pays $50-150 for transparencies; $25-50 for b&w prints; $50-250 for color prints. Identification of subjects required. Buys one-time and all rights.
Fiction: Ethnic, humorous. **Buys 3-5 mss/year.** Query. Length: negotiable. **Pays 8-10¢/word.**
Tips: "We would prefer that articles be informational, based on personal experience or an interview with lots of quotes from subject, profile, humor, etc."

$ $ CHAMBER MUSIC, Chamber Music America, 305 Seventh Ave., New York NY 10001-6008. (212)242-2022. Fax: (212)242-7955. Website: http://www.chamber-music.org. **Contact:** Johanna B. Keller, editor. Bimonthly magazine covering chamber music. Estab. 1977. Circ. 13,000. Pays on publication. Publishes ms an average of 8 months after acceptance. Byline given. Offers kill fee. Buys all rights. Editorial lead time 4 months.
Nonfiction: Issue-oriented stories of relevance to the chamber music field. **Buys 50 mss/year.** Query with clips by mail only. Length: 2,500-3,500 words. **Pays $500 minimum.** Sometimes pays expenses of writers on assignment.
Photos: State availability of photos with submission. Offers no additional payment for photos accepted with ms.

$ $ GUITAR PLAYER MAGAZINE, Miller Freeman, Inc., 411 Borel Ave., Suite 100, San Mateo CA 94402. (650)358-9500. Fax: (650)358-9216. E-mail: guitplyr@mfi.com. Website: http://www.guitarplayer.com. **Contact:** Michael Molenda, editor-in-chief. **70% freelance written.** Monthly magazine for persons "interested in guitars, guitarists, manufacturers, guitar builders, equipment, careers, etc." Circ. 140,000. Buys first serial and all reprint rights. **Pays on acceptance.** Publishes ms an average of 3 months after acceptance. Byline given. Reports in 6 weeks. Writer's guidelines for #10 SASE.
Nonfiction: Publishes "wide variety of articles pertaining to guitars and guitarists: interviews, guitar craftsmen profiles, how-to features—anything amateur and professional guitarists would find fascinating and/or helpful. In interviews with 'name' performers, be as technical as possible regarding strings, guitars, techniques, etc. We're not a pop culture

magazine, but a magazine for musicians. The essential question: What can the reader take away from a story to become a better player?" **Buys 30-40 mss/year.** Query. Length: open. **Pays $250-450.** Sometimes pays expenses of writers on assignment.
Photos: Reviews b&w glossy prints. Buys 35mm color transparencies. Payment varies. Buys one time rights.

$ HIT PARADER, 210 Route 4 E., Suite 401, Paramus NJ 07652. (201)843-4004. Editor: Andy Secher. Managing Editor: Mary Anne Cassata. **2% freelance written.** Monthly magazine covering heavy metal music. "We look for writers who have access to the biggest names in hard rock/heavy metal music." Estab. 1943. Circ. 200,000. Pays on publication. Publishes ms an average of 4 months after acceptance. Byline given. Buys all rights. Submit seasonal material 5 months in advance. Sample copy for 9×12 SAE with 6 first-class stamps.
Nonfiction: General interest, interview/profile. **Buys 3-5 mss/year.** Query with published clips. Length: 600-800 words. **Pays $75-140.** Lifestyle-oriented and hardball pieces. "Study and really know the bands to get new angles on story ideas."
Photos: Reviews transparencies, 5×7 and 8×10 b&w prints, Kodachrome 64 slides. Offers $25-200/photo. Buys one-time rights. "We don't work with new photographers."
Tips: "Interview big names in hard rock/metal, get published in other publications. We don't take chances on new writers."

$ $ MODERN DRUMMER, 12 Old Bridge Rd., Cedar Grove NJ 07009. (201)239-4140. Fax: (201)239-7139. Features Editor: William F. Miller. Managing Editor: Rick Van Horn. **Contact:** Ronald Spagnardi, editor-in-chief. Monthly magazine for "student, semi-pro and professional drummers at all ages and levels of playing ability, with varied specialized interests within the field." **60% freelance written.** Circ. 98,000. Pays on publication. Publishes ms an average of 3 months after acceptance. Buys all rights. Reports in 2 weeks. Sample copy for $4.95. Guidelines free.
Nonfiction: How-to, informational, interview, new product, personal experience, technical. "All submissions must appeal to the specialized interests of drummers." **Buys 20-30 mss/year.** Query or submit complete ms. Length: 5,000-8,000 words. **Pays $200-500.**
Reprints: Accepts previously published submissions.
Photos: Purchased with accompanying ms. Reviews 8×10 b&w prints and color transparencies.
Columns/Departments: Music columns: Jazz Drummers Workshop, Rock Perspectives, Rock 'N' Jazz Clinic, Driver's Seat (Big Band), In The Studio, Show Drummers Seminar, Teachers Forum, Drum Soloist, The Jobbing Drummer, Strictly Technique, Shop Talk, Latin symposium. Profile columns: Portraits, Up & Coming, From the Past. Book Reviews, Record Reviews, Video Reviews. "Technical knowledge of area required for most columns." **Buys 40-50 mss/year.** Query or submit complete ms. Length: 500-1,000 words. **Pays $50-150.**
Tips: "*MD* is looking for music journalists rather than music critics. Our aim is to provide information, not to make value judgments. Therefore, keep all articles as objective as possible. We are interested in how and why a drummer plays a certain way; the readers can make their own decisions about whether or not they like it."

N $ THE MUSIC PAPER, MC2 International, P.O. Box 5167, Bay Shore NY 11706. (516)666-4892. Fax: (516)666-7445. **Contact:** V. Layla Ferrante, editor. **75% freelance written**. Monthly magazine covering "all aspects of music industry—from artist interviews, CD reviews and instructional/technical columns. Editorial slanted to reach musicians of all ages, genres and professional (beginners to working) levels." Estab. 1979. Circ. 75,000. Pays on publication. Publishes ms an average of 2 months after acceptance. Byline given. Buys all rights. Editorial lead time 4 months. Submit seasonal material 3 months in advance. Accepts simultaneous submissions. Sample copy for $2.
Nonfiction: How-to (play an instrument, write songs, record music), interview/profile (music industry people), new music products, technical (music-related). No fiction, personal experience, editorials, opinions. **Buys 120 mss/year**. Query with résumé and published clips. Length: 200-1,500 words. **Pays $15-50**. Sometimes pays expenses of writers on assignment.
Photos: Send photos with submission. Reviews prints of all sizes. Negotiates payment individually. Identification of subjects required. Buys one time rights.
Columns/Departments: Features (artist interviews), 800 words; Workshops (instructional music info), 400 words; Reviews (books, CDs, music videos), 100 words. "All should be slanted towards 'musicians' angle." **Buys 120 mss/year**. Query with published clips. **Pays $15-50**.
Tips: "Let me know if you have your own industry contacts for features/reviews or work/life experience/training for technical columns. Would like to see one unpublished sample of writing (raw text not edited by pro editor)."

$ $ $ OPERA NEWS, Metropolitan Opera Guild, Inc., 70 Lincoln Center Plaza, New York NY 10023-6593. (212)769-7080. Fax: (212)769-7007. Editor: Patrick J. Smith. Managing Editor: Brian Kellow. **Contact:** Kitty March. **75% freelance written.** Monthly magazine (May-November) and biweekly (December-April), for people interested in opera; the opera professional as well as the opera audience. Estab. 1936. Circ. 120,000. Pays on publication. Publishes ms an average of 4 months after acceptance. Byline given. Buys first serial rights only. Sample copy for $4.
Nonfiction: Most articles are commissioned in advance. Monthly issues feature articles on various aspects of opera worldwide; biweekly issues contain articles related to the broadcasts from the Metropolitan Opera. Emphasis is on high quality writing and an intellectual interest to the opera-oriented public. Informational, personal experience, interview, profile, historical, think pieces, personal opinion, opera reviews. "Also willing to consider quality fiction and poetry

on opera-related themes though acceptance is rare." Query by mail. Length: 1,500-2,800 words. **Pays $450-1,000.** Sometimes pays expenses of writers on assignment.
Photos: State availability of photos with submission. Buys one-time rights.
Columns/Departments: Buys 24 mss/year.

$ $ RAP SHEET, James Communications, Inc., 2270 Centinela Ave., Box B-40, Los Angeles CA 90064. Fax: (310)670-6236. E-mail: sheetrap@aol.com. Editor: Darryl James. **Contact:** Billy Johnson, Jr., managing editor. Monthly newspaper covering hip hop artists, music and culture. Estab. 1992. Circ. 100,000. Pays on publication. Byline given. Editorial lead time 2 months.
Nonfiction: Exposé, general interest, historical/nostalgic, interview/profile, photo feature, technical. Query with published clips. Length: 500-3,500. **Pays $50-300.** Sometimes pays expenses of writers on assignment.
Photos: Send photos with submission. Negotiates payment individually.
Columns/Departments: Check the Wax, Trax (album and single reviews), albums (200-300 words) singles (100 words); Back in the Day (profile on old school hip hop artist) 500-800 words; On the set (hip hop related film news) 1,000 words. **Buys 50 mss/year.** Query with published clips. **Pays $50-300.**
Tips: "Submit writing samples consistent with our style and format. Explain specifically how you would like to contribute and offer ideas. Articles must be well organized, containing a powerful lead, thesis statement, body and conclusion. Writing the traditional, biography-styled profile is discouraged. The biography only works with extremely interesting life stories, which are rare. Instead, we prefer the writer to familiarize his/herself with the artist's background through research, finding the most intriguing things about the artist. Then, the story should be shaped around that information. Again, the articles must be tightly focused, avoiding rambling, and drifting off to unrelated subjects."

N $ RELEASE INK MAGAZINE, Vox Publishing, 2525-C Lebanon Pike, Box 6, Nashville TN 37214. (615)872-8080. Fax: (615)872-9786. E-mail: stacie@releasemagazine.com. Editor: Chris Well. **Contact**: Stacie Kish, managing editor. **70% freelance written.** Bimonthly magazine covering Christian books, music, art and more. "*Release Ink* is the only magazine of its kind, covering the spectrum of Christian products from books and music to children's resources and gifts. It reaches the core Christian retail customer—females between the ages of 21 and 50." Estab. 1994. Circ. 95,000. Pays within 30 days after publication. Publishes ms an average of 2 months after acceptance. Byline sometimes given. Buys first North American serial rights and electronic rights. Editorial lead time 6 months. Submit seasonal material 4 months in advance. Sample copy for $5.
Nonfiction: Artist interview/profile. No essays, inspirational pieces. **Buys 20-30 mss/year.** Query with published clips. Length: 500-2,500 words. **Pays 6-10¢/word.** Sometimes pays expenses of writers on assignment.
Photos: State availability of photos with submission. Offers no additional payment for photos accepted with ms. Identification of subjects required. Buys one-time rights.
Columns/Departments: Noteworthy (brief profiles of Christian music artists), 400-600 words; Between the lines (brief profiles of people writing/making books), 400-600 words; Showcase (reviews of Christian books and music), 250 words. **Buys 30 mss/year.** Query with published clips. **Pays 6-10¢/word.**
Tips: "We're looking for people who can exhibit working knowledge of the authors, books and artists we cover. We also want to be convinced that they've read our magazine."

N $ RELEASE MAGAZINE, Christian Music Covered in Style, Vox Publishing, 2525-C Lebanon Pike, Box 6, Nashville TN 37214. (615)872-8080. Fax: (615)872-9786. E-mail: stacie@releasemagazine.com. Editor: Chris Well. **Contact**: Stacie Kish, managing editor. **50% freelance written.** Bimonthly magazine covering Christian pop music/artists. "*Release* is the most widely-circulated magazine in the Christian music industry, reaching its fans through retail stores and individual subscriptions. Its core audience is the 12- to 30-year-old pop or mainstream music fan." Estab. 1991. Circ. 110,000. Pays within 30 days after publication. Publishes ms an average of 2 months after acceptance. Byline given. Buys first North American serial rights and electronic rights. Editorial lead time 6 months. Submit seasonal material 4 months in advance. Sample copy for $5.
Nonfiction: Artist interview/profile, new product reviews. "We have an annual 'year in review' issue that features the newsmakers of the year and the winners of the Readers' Choice poll." No essays, non-Christian music-related articles. **Buys 45 mss/year.** Query with published clips. Length: 500-2,500 words. **Pays 6-10¢/word.**
Columns/Departments: Word on the Street (Christian artist news), 500-700 words; Views On the New (new music/product reviews), 200-300 words; Faces (brief artist profiles), 600-800 words. **Buys 10-15 mss/year.** Query with published clips. **Pays 6-10¢/word.**
Tips: "We're looking for people who can exhibit working knowledge of the music and artists we cover, and can convince us that they've read our magazine."

$ RELIX MAGAZINE, Music for the Mind, P.O. Box 94, Brooklyn NY 11229. E-mail: relixedit@aol.com. Website: http://www.relix.com. **Contact:** Toni A. Brown, editor. **60% freelance written.** Eager to work with new/unpublished writers. Bimonthly magazine covering classic rock 'n' roll music and specializing in Grateful Dead and other San Francisco and 60s-related groups, but also offering new music alternatives, such as "Roots Rock" and "Jam Bands." Estab. 1974. Circ. 70,000. Pays on publication. Publishes ms an average of 6 months after acceptance. Byline given. Buys all rights. Reports in 1 year. Sample copy for $5.
Nonfiction: Historical/nostalgic, interview/profile, new product, personal experience, photo feature, technical. Feature topics include blues, bluegrass, rock, jazz and world music; also deals with environmental and cultural issues. Special

issue: year-end special. Query with published clips if available or send complete ms. Length: 1,200-3,000 words. **Pays $1.75/column inch.**

Reprints: Send photocopy of article and information about when and where the article previously appeared.

Photos: "Whenever possible, submit promotional photos with articles."

Fiction: Publishes novel excerpts.

Columns/Departments: Query with published clips, if available, or send complete ms. Pays variable rates.

Tips: "The most rewarding aspects of working with freelance writers are fresh writing and new outlooks."

$ $ RHYTHM MUSIC, Global Sounds and Ideas, World Marketing Corporation, 928 Broadway, Suite 1206, New York NY 10010. E-mail: rhymusedit@aol.com. Publisher: Alecia J. Cohen. **Contact:** Larry Birnbaum, editor-in-chief. **80% freelance written.** Monthly magazine covering world music and culture. "We want vivid writing and informed substance dealing with music interacting with and/or reflecting greater culture from anywhere in the world. Our audience is literate and broad in age and interests." Estab. 1992. Pays on publication. Publishes ms an average of 2 months after acceptance. Byline given. Offers 15% kill fee. Buys first North American serial and second serial (reprint) rights. Editorial lead time 3 months. Submit seasonal material 4 months in advance. Accepts simultaneous submissions. Reports 1 month on queries; 2 months on mss. Sample copy for 9×12 SASE. Writer's guidelines free.

Nonfiction: Book excerpts, essays, exposé, general interest, historical/nostalgic, how-to, humor, interview/profile, new product, opinion, photo feature, travel. No "My First Trip to Where Everyone Else Has Been" articles. **Buys 30 mss/year.** Query with published clips. Length: 200-4,000 words. **Pays $50-350.** Sometimes pays expenses of writers on assignment.

Reprints: Accepts previously published submissions.

Photos: State availability of photos with submission. Negotiates payment individually. Captions required. Buys one-time rights.

Columns/Departments: Mark Schwartz, reviews editor. Talk of the Globe (news items), 200-500 words; Live Reviews (world music performance), 300-750 words; Endnote (oddities, lifestyle, world music; informative essay with a critical slant), 500-800 words; Theater, Film, Art, Fashion reviews, all 500-1,000 words. **Buys 30 mss/year.** Query with published clips. **Pays $50-150.**

Tips: "Give us a call or e-mail with specific ideas, but know us and your subject."

N ☆ $ 7BALL MAGAZINE, modern rock on cue, Vox Publishing, 2525-C Lebanon Pike, Box 6, Nashville TN 37214. (615)872-8080. Fax: (615)872-9786. E-mail: chris7b@7ball.com. Editor: Chris Well. **Contact**: Stacie Kish, managing editor. **70% freelance written.** Bimonthly magazine covering Christian modern rock/alternative music. "*7ball*—the fastest growing magazine in Christian music—captivates the teenage and young adult music lover whose tastes include modern rock, alternative, hip-hop and other styles of music with an edge." Estab. 1995. Circ. 52,000. Pays within 30 days after publication. Publishes ms an average of 2 months after acceptance. Byline given. Buys first North American serial rights and electronic rights. Editorial lead time 6 months. Submit seasonal material 4 months in advance. Sample copy for $5.

Nonfiction: Artist interview/profile, media that is of interest to rock fans (extreme sports, video, etc.). **Buys 20 mss/year.** Query with published clips. Length: 500-2,500 words. **Pays 6-10¢/word.** Sometimes pays expenses of writers on assignment.

Photos: State availability of photos with submission. Offers no additional payment for photos accepted with ms. Identification of subjects required. Buys one-time rights.

Columns/Departments: Bankshots (brief artist profiles), 400-800 words; Reviews (new music/product reviews), 200-300 words. **Buys 80 mss/year.** Query with published clips. **Pays 6-10¢/word.**

Tips: "We're looking for people who can exhibit working knowledge of the music and artists we cover and can convince us that they've read our magazine."

$ $ $ STEREO REVIEW, Hachette Filipacchi Magazines, Inc., 1633 Broadway, New York NY 10019. (212)767-6000. E-mail: bfenton@aol.com. Editor-in-Chief: Bob Ankosko. **Contact:** Brian Fenton, executive editor. Classical Music Editor: Robert Ripps. Popular Music Editor: Ken Richardson. **65% freelance written,** almost entirely by established contributing editors, and on assignment. Monthly magazine. Estab. 1958. Circ. 400,000. **Pays on acceptance.** Publishes ms an average of 5 months after acceptance. Byline given. Buys first North American serial or all rights. Reports in 5 months. Sample copy for 9×12 SAE with 11 first-class stamps.

Nonfiction: Stereo and home theater equipment and music reviews, how-to-buy, how-to-use, stereo, interview/profile. **Buys 25 mss/year.** Query with published clips. Length: 1,500-3,000 words. **Pays $800-1,000.**

Tips: "Send proposals or outlines, rather than completed articles, along with published clips to establish writing ability. Publisher assumes no responsibility for return or safety of unsolicited art, photos or manuscripts."

$ $ $ XSeSS MUSIC, ComEnt Media Group, Inc., 3932 Wilshire Blvd., #212, Los Angeles CA 90010. Fax: (213)383-1093. E-mail: xsesscdzne@aol.com. Website: http://www.allmediadist.com. **Contact:** Sean Perkin, editor. **80% freelance written.** Quarterly publication covering music and entertainment. "Focusing on both the national and international music scenes, every issue explores the relationship of music and its influence on pop culture, fashion, art, politics and sex. It is also one of the first music basic products that examines the ever changing music universe with editorial, photography and a full length music CD sampler." Estab. 1992. Circ. 25,000. Pays within 2 weeks after publication. Publishes ms an average of 1 month after acceptance. Byline given. Buys one-time rights, makes work-

for-hire assignments. Editorial lead time 3 months. Submit seasonal material 4 months in advance. Accepts simultaneous submissions. Sample copy for $12.50. Writer's guidelines provided only upon assignment.
Nonfiction: Exposé, interview/profile, new product, travel. **Pays $50-800.**
Reprints: Send photocopy and information about when and where the article previously appeared. Pay varies.

MYSTERY

These magazines buy fictional accounts of crime, detective work, mystery and suspense. Skim through other sections to identify markets for fiction; some will consider mysteries. Markets for true crime accounts are listed under Detective and Crime. Also see the second edition of *Mystery Writer's Sourcebook* (Writer's Digest Books).

$ HARDBOILED, Gryphon Publications, P.O. Box 209, Brooklyn NY 11228. **Contact:** Gary Lovisi, editor. **100% freelance written.** Quarterly magazine covering crime/mystery fiction and nonfiction. "Hard-hitting crime fiction and columns/articles and reviews on hardboiled crime writing and private-eye stories—the newest and most cutting-edge work and classic reprints." Estab. 1988. Circ. 1,000. Pays on publication. Publishes ms an average of 6-18 months after acceptance. Byline given. Offers 100% kill fee. Buys one-time rights. Editorial lead time 2 months. Submit seasonal material 6 months in advance. Reports in 2 weeks on queries; 1 month on mss. Sample copy for $7. Writer's guidelines for #10 SASE.
Nonfiction: Book excerpts, essays, exposé. Query first. **Buys 4-6 mss/year.** Length: 500-3,000 words. Pays 1 copy.
Reprints: Query first.
Photos: State availability of photos with submission.
Columns/Departments: Various review columns/articles on hardboiled writers. Query first. **Buys 2-4 mss/year.**
Fiction: Mystery, hardboiled crime and private-eye stories *all* on the cutting-edge. **Buys 40 mss/year.** Send complete ms. Length: 500-3,000 words. **Pays $5-50,** depending on length and quality.

$ ALFRED HITCHCOCK'S MYSTERY MAGAZINE, Dell Magazines Fiction Group, 1270 Avenue of the Americas, New York NY 10020. Editor: Cathleen Jordan. **100% freelance written.** Monthly magazine featuring new mystery short stories. Circ. 215,000 paid; 615,000 readers. **Pays on acceptance.** Byline given. Buys first and foreign rights. Submit seasonal material 7 months in advance. Reports in 2 months. Sample issue for $4. Writer's guidelines for SASE.
Fiction: Original and well-written mystery and crime fiction. "Because this is a mystery magazine, the stories we buy must fall into that genre in some sense or another. We are interested in nearly every kind of mystery, however: stories of detection of the classic kind, police procedurals, private eye tales, suspense, courtroom dramas, stories of espionage, and so on. We ask only that the story be about crime (or the threat or fear of one). We sometimes accept ghost stories or supernatural tales, but those also should involve a crime." Length: up to 14,000 words. Send complete ms with SASE. **Pays 8¢/word.**
Tips: "No simultaneous submissions, please. Submissions sent to *Alfred Hitchcock's Mystery Magazine* are not considered for or read by *Ellery Queen's Mystery Magazine*, and vice versa."

$ MURDEROUS INTENT, Mystery Magazine, Madison Publishing Co., P.O. Box 5947, Vancouver WA 98668-5947. Fax: (360)693-3354. E-mail: madison@teleport.com. Website: http://www.teleport.com/~madison. **Contact:** Margo Power, editor. **90% freelance written.** Quarterly magazine covering mystery. "Everything in *Murderous Intent* is mystery/suspense related. We bring you quality nonfiction articles, columns, interviews and 10-12 (or more) pieces of short mystery fiction per issue. You'll find stories and interviews by Carolyn Hart, Ed Gorman, Barbara Paul, Jerimiah Healy and many more excellent authors." Estab. 1994. Circ. 5,000. **Pays on acceptance**. Publishes ms an average of 12-18 months after acceptance. Byline given. Offers 100% kill fee or $10. Buys first North American serial rights. Submit seasonal material 6 months in advance. Accepts simultaneous submissions, if so noted. Reports in 1 month on queries; 4 months on mss. Sample copy for $5.95, 9×12 SAE and 4 first-class stamps. Writer's guidelines for #10 SASE.
Nonfiction: Humor (mystery), interview/profile (mystery authors), mystery-related nonfiction. **Buys 8-12 mss/year.** Query with published clips. Length: 2,000-4,000 words. **Pays $10.** Sometimes pays expenses of writers on assignment.
Photos: State availability of photos and artwork with submission. Offers no additional payment for photos accepted with ms or negotiates payment individually. Captions, model releases, identification of subjects required. Buys one-time rights.
Fiction: Humorous (mystery), mystery. "Please don't send anything that is not mystery/suspense-related in some way." **Buys 48-52 mss/year.** Send complete ms. Length: 200-5,000 words. **Pays $10.**

• Ranked as one of the best markets for fiction writers in *Writer's Digest* magazine's "Fiction 50," June 1998.

Poetry Free verse, haiku, light verse, traditional. Nothing that is not mystery/suspense-related. **Buys 12-36 poems/year.** Length: 4-16 lines. **Pays $2-5.**
Fillers: Anecdotes, facts. All fillers must be mystery related. Length: 25-200 words. **Pays $2-5.**
Tips: "Mail all submissions flat in 9×12 envelopes. Follow the guidelines. Submit only one story or article at a time. Do include a typed cover letter. Be prepared to submit accepted material on 3½" floppy. We don't publish material that

is not on disk. We also seek permission to include select stories and articles on the website. There is no additional payment at this time."

$ THE MYSTERY REVIEW, A Quarterly Publication for Mystery Readers, C. von Hessert & Associates, P.O. Box 233, Colborne, Ontario K0K 1S0 Canada. (613)475-4440. Fax: (613)475-3400. E-mail: 71554.551@compuserve.com. Website: http://www.inline-online.com/mystery/. **Contact:** Barbara Davey, editor. **80% freelance written.** Quarterly magazine covering mystery and suspense. "Our readers are interested in mystery and suspense books, films. All topics related to mystery—including real life unsolved mysteries." Estab. 1992. Circ. 5,000 (80% of distribution is in US). Pays on publication. Publishes ms an average of 6 months after acceptance. Byline given. Buys first North American serial rights. Editorial lead time 6 months. Submit seasonal material 6 months in advance. Reports in 6 weeks on queries; 1 month on mss. Does not assume responsibility for unsolicited manuscripts. Sample copy for $5. Writer's guidelines free.

Nonfiction: Interview/profile. Query. Length: 2,000-5,000 words. **Pays $30 maximum.**

Photos: Send photos with submission. Reviews 5×7 b&w prints. Offers no additional payment for photos accepted with ms. Model releases, identification of subjects required. Buys all rights.

Columns/Departments: Book reviews (mystery/suspense titles only), 500 words; Truly Mysterious ("unsolved," less-generally-known, historical or contemporary cases), 2,000-5,000 words; Book Shop Beat (bookstore profiles), 500 words. **Buys 50 mss/year.** Query with published clips. **Pays $10-30.**

Poetry: Only poems with a mystery theme. **Buys 3 poems/year.** Submit maximum 2 poems. **Pays $10-20.**

Fillers: Puzzles (particularly crosswords), trivia, shorts (items related to mystery/suspense). **Buys 4/year.** Length: 100-500 words. **Pays $10-20.**

$ $ NEW MYSTERY, The World's Best Mystery, Crime and Suspense Stories, 175 Fifth Ave., 2001 The Flatiron Bldg., New York NY 10010. E-mail: newmyste@frols.com. Website: http://www.NewMystery.com. Editor: Charles Raisch III. **Contact:** Editorial Committee. **100% freelance written.** Quarterly magazine featuring mystery short stories and book reviews. Estab. 1989. Circ. 120,000. **Pays on acceptance.** Publishes ms an average of 6 months after acceptance. Byline given. Does not return mss. Buys first North American serial or all rights. Editorial lead time 6 months. Submit seasonal material 1 year in advance. Reports in 2 months on mss. Not responsible for unsolicited mss. Sample copy for $7 and 9×12 SAE with 4 first-class stamps.

- *Find Miriam*, a short story by Stuart M. Kaminsky appearing on *NewMystery.com*, has been nominated for the Edgar Allen Poe Award for '98 Best Mystery Short Story.

Nonfiction: New product, short book reviews. **Buys 40 mss/year.** Send complete ms. Length: 250-2,000 words. **Pays $20-50.**

Fiction: Mystery, crime, noire, police procedural, hardboiled, child-in-jeopardy, suspense. **Buys 50 mss/year.** Send complete ms. Length: 2,000-6,000 words. **Pays $50-500.**

Fillers: Acrostic or crossword puzzles. **Pays $25-50.**

$ ELLERY QUEEN'S MYSTERY MAGAZINE, Dell Magazine Fiction Group, 1270 Avenue of the Americas, New York NY 10020. (212)698-1313. Fax: (212)698-1198. **Contact:** Janet Hutchings, editor. **100% freelance written.** Magazine published 11 times/year featuring mystery fiction. Estab. 1941. Circ. 500,000 readers. **Pays on acceptance.** Publishes ms an average of 6 months after acceptance. Byline given. Buys first serial or second serial (reprint) rights. Accepts simultaneous submissions. Reports in 3 months. Writer's guidelines for #10 SASE.

Fiction: Special consideration given to "anything timely and original. We publish every type of mystery: the suspense story, the psychological study, the private-eye story, the deductive puzzle—the gamut of crime and detection from the realistic (including stories of police procedure) to the more imaginative (including 'locked rooms' and impossible crimes). We always need detective stories. No sex, sadism or sensationalism-for-the-sake-of-sensationalism, no gore or horror. Seldom publishes parodies or pastiches. **Buys up to 13 mss/issue.** Length: 10,000 words maximum; occasionally higher but not often. Also buys 2-3 short novels/year of up to 20,000 words, by established authors and minute mysteries of 250 words. Short shorts of 1,500 words welcome. **Pays 3-8¢/word,** occasionally higher for established authors. Send complete ms with SASE.

Poetry: Short mystery verses, limericks. Length: 1 page, double-spaced maximum.

Tips: "We have a Department of First Stories to encourage writers whose fiction has never before been in print. We publish an average of 11 first stories every year."

NATURE, CONSERVATION & ECOLOGY

These publications promote reader awareness of the natural environment, wildlife, nature preserves and ecosystems. Many of these "green magazines" also concentrate on recycling and related issues, and a few focus on environmentally-conscious sustainable living. They do not publish recreation or travel articles except as they relate to conservation or nature. Other markets for this kind of material can be found in the Regional; Sports (Hiking and Backpacking in particular); and Travel, Camping and Trailer categories, although magazines listed there require that nature or conservation articles be slanted to their specialized subject matter and audience. Some publications listed in Juvenile and Teen, such as *Ranger Rick* or *Owl*, focus on nature-related material for young audiences, while others occasionally purchase such material. For more information on recycling publications, turn to the Resources and Waste Reduction section in Trade, Technical and Professional Journals.

$ $ AMC OUTDOORS, The Magazine of the Appalachian Mountain Club, Appalachian Mountain Club, 5 Joy St., Boston MA 02108. (617)523-0655 ext. 312. Fax: (617)523-0722. E-mail: amcoutdoors@mcimail.com. **Contact:** Catherine K. Buni, editor/publisher. **90% freelance written.** Monthly magazine covering outdoor recreation and conservation issues in the Northeast. Estab. 1907. Circ. 66,000. Pays on publication. Publishes ms an average of 3 months after acceptance. Byline given. Offers 25% kill fee. Buys all rights. Editorial lead time 3 months. Submit seasonal material 4 months in advance. Reports in 1 month on queries; 2 months on mss. Sample copy for 9×12 SASE. Writer's guidelines free.

Nonfiction: Book excerpts, essays, exposé, general interest, historical/nostalgic, how-to, interview/profile, opinion, personal experience, photo feature, technical, travel. Special issues: Northern Forest Report (April) featuring the northern areas of New York, New Hampshire, Vermont, and Maine, and protection efforts for these areas. **Buys 10 mss/year.** Query with or without published clips. Length: 500-3,000 words. Sometimes pays expenses of writers on assignment.

Photos: State availability of photos with submission. Reviews contact sheets, transparencies and prints. Model releases and identification of subjects required.

Columns/Departments: Jane Bambery. News (environmental/outdoor recreation coverage of Northeast), 1,300 words. **Buys 20 mss/year.** Query. **Pays $50-500.**

$ $ $ AMERICAN FORESTS, American Forests, P.O. Box 2000, Washington DC 20013. (202)955-4500. Fax: (202)887-1075. E-mail: mrobbins@amfor.org. Website: http://www.amfor.org. **Contact:** Michelle Robbins, editor. **75% freelance written** (mostly assigned). Quarterly magazine "of trees and forests, published by a nonprofit citizens' organization for the advancement of intelligent management and use of our forests, soil, water, wildlife and all other natural resources necessary for an environment of high quality." Estab. 1895. Circ. 21,000. **Pays on acceptance.** Publishes ms an average of 8 months after acceptance. Byline given. Buys one-time rights. Submit seasonal material 5 months in advance. Reports in 2 months. Sample copy for $2. Writer's guidelines for SASE.

- This magazine is looking for more urban and suburban-oriented pieces.

Nonfiction: General interest, historical, how-to, humor, inspirational. All articles should emphasize trees, forests, forestry and related issues. **Buys 2-3 mss/issue.** Written queries. Send résumé and clips to be considered for assignment. Length: 1,200-2,000 words. **Pays $250-800.**

Reprints: Send tearsheet of article or typed ms with rights for sale noted and information about when and where the article previously appeared. Pays 50% of amount paid for an original article.

Photos: Send photos. Offers no additional payment for photos accompanying ms. Uses 8×10 b&w glossy prints; 35mm or larger transparencies, originals only. Captions required. Buys one-time rights.

Tips: "Query should have honesty and information on photo support. We *do not* accept fiction or poetry at this time."

$ $ $ THE AMICUS JOURNAL, 40 W. 20th St., New York NY 10011. (212)727-2700. Fax: (212)727-1773. E-mail: amicus@nrdc.org. Website: http:///www.nrdc.org/eamicus/index.html. **Contact:** Kathrin Day Lassila, editor. **80% freelance written.** Quarterly magazine covering national and international environmental issues. "*The Amicus Journal* is intended to provide the general public with a journal of thought and opinion on environmental affairs, particularly those relating to policies of national and international significance." Estab. 1979. Circ. 175,000. Pays on publication. Publishes ms an average of 6 months after acceptance. Offers 25% kill fee. Buys first North American serial rights (and print/electronic reprint rights). Submit seasonal material 6 months in advance. Reports in 3 months on queries. Sample copy for $4 with 9×12 SAE. Writer's guidelines for SASE.

- This publication is now accepting occasional literary (personal) essays on environmental issues or with environmental themes. The editor stresses that submissions must be of the highest quality only and must be grounded in thorough knowledge of subject.

Nonfiction: Exposé, interview/profile, essays, reviews. Query with published clips. Length: 200-3,500 words. Pay negotiable. Sometimes pays expenses of writers on assignment. **Buys 35 mss/year.**

Photos: State availability of photos with submission. Reviews contact sheets, color transparencies, 8×10 b&w prints. Negotiates payment individually. Captions, model releases, identification of subjects required. Buys one-time rights.

Columns/Departments: News & Comment (summary reporting of environmental issues, tied to topical items), 700-2,000 words; International Notebook (new or unusual international environmental stories), 700-2,000 words; People, 2,000 words; Reviews (in-depth reporting on issues and personalities, well-informed essays on books of general interest to environmentalists interested in policy and history), 500-1,000 words. Query with published clips. Pay negotiable.

Poetry: Brian Swann. Avant-garde, free verse, haiku, others. All poetry should be rooted in nature. Must submit with SASE. **Buys 16 poems/year.** Length: 1 ms page. **Pays $50** plus a year's subscription.

Tips: "Please stay up to date on environmental issues, and review *The Amicus Journal* before submitting queries. Except for editorials all departments are open to freelance writers. Queries should precede manuscripts, and manuscripts should conform to the Chicago Manual of Style."

$ $ APPALACHIAN TRAILWAY NEWS, Appalachian Trail Conference, P.O. Box 807, Harpers Ferry WV 25425-0807. (304)535-6331. Fax: (304)876-6918. E-mail: bking@atconf.org. Editor: Judith Jenner. **Contact:** Brian King. **50% freelance written.** Bimonthly magazine. Estab. 1925. Circ. 26,000. **Pays on acceptance.** Byline given. Buys first North American serial or second serial (reprint) rights. Reports in 2 months. Sample copy, guidelines for $2.50. Writer's guidelines only for SASE.

- Articles must relate to Appalachian Trail.

Nonfiction: Essays, general interest, historical/nostalgic, how-to, humor, inspirational, interview/profile, photo feature, technical, travel. No poetry or religious materials. **Buys 15-20 mss/year.** Query with or without published clips, or send complete ms. Length: 250-3,000 words. **Pays $25-300.** Pays expenses of writers on assignment. Publishes, but does not pay for "hiking reflections."

Reprints: Send photocopy of article or typed ms with rights for sale noted and information about when and where the article previously appeared.

Photos: State availability of photos with submission. Reviews contact sheets, negatives, 5×7 prints. Offers $25-125/photo. Identification of subjects required. Negotiates future use by Appalachian Trail Conference.

Tips: "Contributors should display a knowledge of or interest in the Appalachian Trail. Those who live in the vicinity of the Trail may opt for an assigned story and should present credentials and subject of interest to the editor."

N $ $ THE ATLANTIC SALMON JOURNAL, The Atlantic Salmon Federation, P.O. Box 429, St. Andrews, New Brunswick E0G 2X0 Canada. Fax: (506)529-4985. E-mail: asfpub@nbnet.nb.ca. Website: http://www.asf.ca. **Contact:** Jim Gourlay, editor. **50-68% freelance written.** Quarterly magazine covering conservation efforts for the Atlantic salmon, catering to "affluent and responsive audience—the dedicated angler and conservationist." Circ. 10,000. Pays on publication. Publishes ms an average of 6 months after acceptance. Byline given. Buys first serial rights to articles and one-time rights to photos. Submit seasonal material 3 months in advance. Accepts simultaneous submissions. Reports in 2 months. Sample copy for 9×12 SAE with $1 (Canadian), or IRC. Writer's guidelines free.

Nonfiction: Exposé, historical/nostalgic, how-to, humor, interview/profile, new product, opinion, personal experience, photo feature, technical, travel, conservation, science, research and management. "We are seeking articles that are pertinent to the focus and purpose of our magazine, which is to inform and entertain our membership on all aspects of the Atlantic salmon and its environment, preservation and conservation." **Buys 15-20 mss/year.** Query with published clips and state availability of photos. Length: 1,500-2,500 words. **Pays $200-400.** Sometimes pays the expenses of writers on assignment.

Columns/Departments: Conservation issues and salmon research; the design, construction and success of specific flies (*Fit To Be Tied*); interesting characters in the sport; opinion pieces by knowledgeable writers, 900 words, **pays $150-250;** *Casting Around* (short, informative, entertaining reports, book reviews and quotes from the world of Atlantic salmon angling and conservation), **pays $50.** Query.

Photos: Send photos with query. Pays $50 for 3×5 or 5×7 b&w prints; $50-100 for 2¼×3¼ or 35mm color slides. Captions and identification of subjects required.

Tips: "Articles must reflect informed and up-to-date knowledge of Atlantic salmon. Writers need not be authorities, but research must be impeccable. Clear, concise writing is essential, and submissions must be typed. The odds are that a writer without a background in outdoor writing and wildlife reporting will not have the 'informed' angle I'm looking for. Our readership is well read and critical of simplification and generalization."

$ $ $ $ AUDUBON, The Magazine of the National Audubon Society, National Audubon Society, 700 Broadway, New York NY 10003-9501. Fax: (212)477-9069. Website: http://magazine.audubon.org. Lisa Gusselin, editor. **Contact:** Editorial Office. **85% freelance written.** Bimonthly magazine "reflecting nature with joy and reverence and reporting the issues that affect and endanger the delicate balance and life on this planet." Estab. 1887. Circ. 430,000. **Pays on acceptance.** Byline given. Buys first North American serial rights, second serial (reprint) rights on occasion. Reports in 3 months. Sample copy for $4 and 9×12 SAE with 10 first-class stamps or $5 for magazine and postage. Writer's guidelines for #10 SASE.

- Ranked as one of the best markets for freelance writers in *Writer's Yearbook* magazine's annual "Top 100 Markets," January 1998.

Nonfiction: Essays, investigative, historical, humor, interview/profile, opinion, photo feature, book excerpts (well in advance of publication). Query before submission. "No fax or e-mail queries, please." Length: 150-3,000 words. **Pays $250-4,000.** Pays expenses of writers on assignment.

Photos: Query with photographic idea before submitting slides. Reviews 35mm transparencies. Offers page rates per photo on publication. Captions and identification of subjects required. Write for photo guidelines.

"*Audubon* articles deal with the natural and human environment. They cover the remote as well as the familiar. What they all have in common, however, is that they have a story to tell, one that will not only interest *Audubon* readers, but that will interest everyone with a concern for the affairs of humans and nature. We want good solid journalism. We want stories of people and places, good news and bad: humans and nature in conflict, humans and nature working together, humans attempting to comprehend, restore and renew the natural world. We are looking for new voices and fresh ideas. Among the types of stories we seek: profiles of individuals whose life and work illuminate some issues relating to natural history, the environment, conservation, etc.; balanced reporting on environmental issues and events here in North America and abroad; analyses of events, policies, and issues from fresh points of view. We do not publish fiction or poetry. We're not seeking first person meditations on 'nature,' accounts of wild animals rescue or taming, or birdwatching articles."

N ★ $ THE BEAR ESSENTIAL MAGAZINE, Orlo, P.O. Box 10342, Portland OR 97296. (503)242-1047. E-mail: orlo@teleport.com. Managing Editor: Matt Buckingham. **Contact:** Thomas L. Webb, editor. **80% freelance written.** Quarterly magazine. "*The Bear Essential Magazine* provides a fresh voice amid often strident and polarized environmental discourse. Street level, solution-oriented and non-dogmatic, *The Bear Essential* presents lively creative discussion to a diverse readership." Estab. 1993. Circ. 15,000. Pays on publication. Publishes ms 2 months after acceptance. Byline given. Offers 25% kill fee. Buys first rights. Editorial lead time 3 months. Submit seasonal material 4 months in advance. Accepts simultaneous and previously published submissions. Reports in 1 month on queries; 2 months on mss. Sample copy for $3. Writer's guidelines for #10 SASE.

Nonfiction: Book excerpts, essays, exposé, general interest, humor, interview/profile, new product, opinion, personal experience, photo feature, travel, artist profiles. Publishes 1 theme/year. Send #10 SASE for theme. **Buys 40 mss/year.** Query with published clips. Length: 250-4,500 words. **Pays 5¢/word.** Sometimes pays expenses of writers on assignment.

Photos: State availability of photos with submission. Reviews contact sheets, transparencies and 8×10 prints. Offers $15-30/photo. Model releases and identification of subjects required. Buys one-time rights.

Columns/Departments: Reviews (almost anything), 300 words; Hands-On (individuals or groups working on eco-issues, getting their hands dirty), 1,200 words; Talking Heads (creative first person), 500 words; News Bites (quirk of eco-news), 300 words; Portrait of an Artist (artist profiles), 1,200 words. **Buys 16 mss/year.** Query with published clips. **Pays 5¢/word.**

Fiction: Adventure, condensed novels, historical, horror, humorous, mystery, novel excerpts, science fiction, western. "Stories must have some environmental context." **Buys 8 mss/year.** Send complete ms. Length: 750-4,500 words. **Pays 5¢/word.**

Poetry: Avant-garde, free verse, Haiku, light verse, traditional. **Buys 16-20 poems/year.** Submit 5 poems maximum. Length: 50 lines maximum. **Pays $10.**

Fillers: Facts, newsbreaks, short humor. **Buys 10/year.** Length: 100-750 words. **Pays 5¢/word.**

Tips: "Offer to be stringer for future ideas. Get a sample copy. Be as specific as possible in queries."

$ $ BIRD WATCHER'S DIGEST, Pardson Corp., P.O. Box 110, Marietta OH 45750. Editor: William H. Thompson III. **60% freelance written.** Works with a small number of new/unpublished writers each year. Bimonthly magazine covering natural history—birds and bird watching. "*BWD* is a nontechnical magazine interpreting ornithological material for amateur observers, including the knowledgeable birder, the serious novice and the backyard bird watcher; we strive to provide good reading and good ornithology." Estab. 1978. Circ. 90,000. Pays on publication. Publishes ms 1-2 years after acceptance. Byline given. Buys one-time, first serial and second serial (reprint) rights. Submit seasonal material 6 months in advance. Reports in 2 months. Sample copy for $3.50. Writer's guidelines for #10 SASE.

Nonfiction: Book excerpts, how-to (relating to birds, feeding and attracting, etc.), humor, personal experience, travel (limited—we get many). "We are especially interested in fresh, lively accounts of closely observed bird behavior and displays and of bird-watching experiences and expeditions. We often need material on less common species or on unusual or previously unreported behavior of common species." No articles on pet or caged birds; none on raising a baby bird. **Buys 75-90 mss/year.** Send complete ms. All submissions must be accompanied by SASE. Length: 600-3,500 words. **Pays from $50.**

Reprints: Accepts previously published submissions.

Photos: Send photos. Pays $10 min for b&w prints; $50 min for transparencies. Buys one-time rights.

Tips: "We are aimed at an audience ranging from the backyard bird watcher to the very knowledgeable birder; we include in each issue material that will appeal at various levels. We always strive for a good geographical spread, with material from every section of the country. We leave very technical matters to others, but we want facts and accuracy, depth and quality, directed at the veteran bird watcher and at the enthusiastic novice. We stress the joys and pleasures of bird watching, its environmental contribution, and its value for the individual and society."

$ $ $ CALIFORNIA WILD, Natural Science for Thinking Animals, (formerly *Pacific Discovery*), California Academy of Sciences, Golden Gate Park, San Francisco CA 94118. (415)750-7116. Fax: (415)221-4853. Website: http://www.calacademy.org/calwild. **Contact**: Keith Howell, editor. **75% freelance written.** Quarterly magazine covering natural sciences and the environment. "Our readers' interests range widely from ecology to geology, from endangered species to anthropology, from field identification of plants and birds to armchair understanding of complex scientific issues." Estab. 1948. Circ. 32,000. Pays prior to publication. Publishes ms an average of 3 months after acceptance. Byline given. Offers 50% kill fee. Buys first North American serial or one-time rights. Editorial lead time 3 months. Submit seasonal material 6 months in advance. Reports in 6 weeks on queries; 6 months on mss. Sample copy for 9×12 SASE. Writer's guidelines free.

Nonfiction: Personal experience, photo feature, biological and earth sciences. No travel pieces. Mostly California stories, but also from Pacific Ocean countries. **Buys 20 mss/year.** Query with published clips. Length: 1,000-3,000 words. **Pays $250-1,000 for assigned articles; $200-800 for unsolicited articles.** Sometimes pays expenses of writers on assignment.

Photos: State availability of photos with submission. Reviews transparencies. Offers $75-150/photo. Model releases and identification of subjects required. Buys one-time rights.

Columns/Departments: Trail Less Traveled (unusual places); Wild Lives (description of unusual plant or animal); Science Track (innovative student, teacher, young scientist), all 1,000-1,500 words; Skywatcher (research in astronomy), 2,000-3,000 words. **Buys 12 mss/year.** Query with published clips. **Pays $200-400.**

Fillers: Facts. **Pays $25-50.**

Tips: "We are looking for unusual and/or timely stories about California environment or ecosystem."

$ $ E THE ENVIRONMENTAL MAGAZINE, Earth Action Network, P.O. Box 5098, Westport CT 06881-5098. (203)854-5559. Fax: (203)866-0602. E-mail: emagazine@prodigy.net. Website: http://www.emagazine.com. Editor: Jim Motavalli. **Contact:** Tracey C. Rembert, managing editor. **80% freelance written.** Bimonthly magazine. "*E Magazine* was formed for the purpose of acting as a clearinghouse of information, news and commentary on environmental issues." Estab. 1990. Circ. 50,000. Pays on publication. Byline given. Buys first North American serial rights. Editorial lead time 3 months. Submit seasonal material 6 months in advance. Accepts simultaneous submissions. Query for all submissions. Sample copy for $5. Writer's guidelines for #10 SASE.

Nonfiction: Exposé (environmental), how-to (the "Green Living" section), interview/profile, new product. No fiction or poetry. **Buys 100 mss/year.** Query with published clips. Length: 100-5,000 words. **Pays 20¢/word.** On spec or free contributions welcome.

Photos: State availability of photos. Reviews printed samples, e.g., magazine tearsheet, postcards, etc. to be kept on file. Negotiates payment individually. Identification of subjects required. Buys one-time rights.

Columns/Departments: In Brief/Currents (environmental news stories/trends), 400-1,000 words; Interviews (environmental leaders), 2,000 words; Green Living; Your Health; Going Green (travel); Eco-home; Green Business; Consumer News; New & Different Products (each 700-1,200 words). Query with published clips. **Pays 20¢/word.** On spec or free contributions welcome.

Tips: "Contact us to obtain writer's guidelines and back issues of our magazine. Tailor your query according to the department/section you feel it would be best suited for. Articles must be lively, well-researched, and relevant to a mainstream, national readership."

N **$ $ $ $ EARTH, The Science of Our Planet**, Kalmbach Publishing Co., 21027 Crossroads Circle, Waukesha WI 53186-4055. (414)796-8776. E-mail: mail@earthmag.com. Website: http://www.earthmag.com. **Contact:** Diane Pinkalla, editorial assistant. Editor: Joshua Fischman. **75% written freelance**. Bimonthly consumer magazine covering science (earth science). Estab. 1992. Circ. 90,000. **Pays on acceptance**. Publishes ms an average of 4-12 months after acceptance. Byline given. Offers 15% kill fee. Buys first rights. Editorial lead time 4 months. Sample copy and writer's guidelines for #10 SASE or see website.

Nonfiction: Earth science: Geology, oceans, atmosphere, climate, paleontology, evolution, minerals. No environmental cause pieces. **Buys 60 mss/year**. Query with published clips. Length: 500-3,500 words. **Pays $4,000**. Sometimes pays expenses of writers on assignment.

Photos: Reviews contact sheets, 35mm to 4×5 transparencies or 3×5 to 8×10 prints . Offers no additional payment for photos accepted with ms. Sometimes package deal. Negotiates payment individually, especially if photos are not property of writer. Captions, model releases, identification of subjects required. Buys one-time rights.

Columns/Departments: Expeditions (personal journey, great photos), 1,000 words; Elemental (focus on a mineral), 500 words; Reviews (books, software, videos, etc.), 500 words; Reports (new findings and events in earth science), 800-1,000 words. Query with published clips. **Pays $75-500.**

$ $ ENVIRONMENT, Heldref Publications, 1319 18th St. NW, Washington DC 20036-1802. **Contact:** Barbara T. Richman, managing editor. **2% freelance written.** Magazine published 10 times/year for high school and college students and teachers, scientists, business and government executives, citizens interested in environment or effects of technology and science in public affairs. Estab. 1958. Circ. 12,500. Buys all rights. Byline given. Pays on publication to professional writers. Publishes ms an average of 4 months after acceptance. Reports in 3 months. Sample copy $7.

Nonfiction: Scientific and environmental material, effects of science on policymaking and vice versa. Preferred length: 2,500-4,000 words for full-length article. **Pays $100-300.** Query or submit 3 double-spaced copies of complete ms. "All full-length articles must offer readers authoritative analyses of key environmental problems. Articles must be annotated (referenced), and all conclusions must follow logically from the facts and arguments presented." Prefers articles centering around policy-oriented, public decision-making, scientific and technological issues.

Photos: Send photos with submission. Include captions and credits.

Columns/Departments: Focus: (education, energy, economics, public opinion, elucidating small portion of a larger problem), 1,000-1,700/words; Report on Reports (reviews of institutions and government reports), 1,500-2,000 words; Commentary, 750 words; Books of Note, 100-150. **Pays $100-300.**

$ $ HIGH COUNTRY NEWS, High Country Foundation, P.O. Box 1090, Paonia CO 81428-1090. (303)527-4898. E-mail: bestym@HCN.org. Website: http://www.hcn.org. **Contact:** Betsy Marston, editor. **80% freelance written.** Works with a small number of new/unpublished writers each year. Biweekly tabloid covering Rocky Mountain West, the Great Basin and Pacific Northwest environment, rural communities and natural resource issues in 10 western states for environmentalists, politicians, companies, college classes, government agencies, grass roots activists, public land managers, etc. Estab. 1970. Circ. 19,000. Pays on publication. Publishes ms an average of 2 months after acceptance. Byline given. Buys one-time rights. Reports in 1 month. Sample copy and writer's guidelines free.

Nonfiction: Reporting (local issues with regional importance); exposé (government, corporate); interview/profile; personal experience; centerspread photo feature. Length: up to 3,000 words. **Buys 100 mss/year.** Query. **Pays 20¢/word minimum.** Sometimes pays expenses of writers on assignment for lead stories.

Reprints: Send tearsheet of article and info about when and where the article previously appeared. Pays 15¢/word.

Photos: Send photos with ms. Prefers b&w prints. Captions and identification of subjects required.
Columns/Departments: Roundups (topical stories), 800 words; opinion pieces, 1,500 words.
Tips: "We use a lot of freelance material, though very little from outside the Rockies. Familiarity with the newspaper is a must. Start by writing a query letter. We define 'resources' broadly to include people, culture and aesthetic values, not just coal, oil and timber."

$ $ $ $ INTERNATIONAL WILDLIFE, National Wildlife Federation, 8925 Leesburg Pike, Vienna VA 22184-0001. (703)790-4510. Fax: (703)827-2585. E-mail: pubs@nwf.org. Website: http://www.nwf.org/nwf. **Contact:** Jonathan Fisher, editor. **85% freelance written.** Prefers to work with published/established writers. Bimonthly magazine for persons interested in natural history and the environment in countries outside the US. Estab. 1971. Circ. 300,000. **Pays on acceptance.** Publishes ms an average of 4 months after acceptance. Usually buys all rights. "We are now assigning most articles but will consider detailed proposals for quality feature material of interest to a broad audience." Reports in 6 weeks. Writer's guidelines for #10 SASE.

- Ranked as one of the best markets for freelance writers in *Writer's Yearbook* magazine's annual "Top 100 Markets," January 1998.

Nonfiction: Focuses on world wildlife, environmental problems and peoples' relationship to the natural world as reflected in such issues as population control, pollution, resource utilization, food production, etc. Stories deal with non-US subjects. Especially interested in articles on animal behavior and other natural history, first-person experiences by scientists in the field, well-reported coverage of wildlife-status case studies which also raise broader themes about international conservation and timely issues. Query. Length: 2,000 words. Examine past issues for style and subject matter. **Pays $2,000** minimum for long features. Sometimes pays expenses of writers on assignment.
Photos: Purchases top-quality color photos; prefers packages of related photos and text, but single shots of exceptional interest and sequences also considered. Prefers Kodachrome or Fujichrome transparencies. Buys one-time rights.
Tips: "*International Wildlife* readers include conservationists, biologists, wildlife managers and other wildlife professionals, but the majority are not wildlife professionals. In fact, *International Wildlife* caters to the unconverted—those people who may have only a passing interest in wildlife. Consequently, our writers should avoid a common pitfall: talking only to an 'in group.' *International Wildlife* is in competition with television and hundreds of other periodicals for the limited time and attention of busy people. So our functions include attracting readers with engaging subjects, pictures and layouts; then holding them with interesting and entertaining, as well as instructional, text."

$ $ $ $ NATURAL HISTORY, Natural History Magazine, Central Park W. at 79th St., New York NY 10024. (212)769-5500. Fax: (212)769-5511. E-mail: nhmag@amnh.org. **Contact:** Bruce Stutz, editor-in-chief. **15% freelance written.** Monthly magazine for well-educated, ecologically aware audience: professional people, scientists and scholars. Circ. 500,000. Pays on publication. Publishes ms an average of 3 months after acceptance. Byline given. Buys first serial rights and becomes agent for second serial (reprint) rights. Submit seasonal material at least 6 months in advance.

- Ranked as one of the best markets for freelance writers in *Writer's Yearbook* magazine's annual "Top 100 Markets," January 1998.

Nonfiction: Uses all types of scientific articles except chemistry and physics—emphasis is on the biological sciences and anthropology. "We always want to see new research findings in almost all branches of the natural sciences—anthropology, archeology, zoology and ornithology. We find it is particularly difficult to get something new in herpetology (amphibians and reptiles) or entomology (insects), and would like to see material in those fields." **Buys 60 mss/year.** Query or submit complete ms. Length: 1,500-3,000 words. **Pays $500-2,500,** additional payment for photos used.
Photos: Rarely uses 8×10 b&w glossy prints; pays $125/page maximum. Much color is used; pays $300 for inside and up to $600 for cover. Buys one-time rights.
Columns/Departments: Journal (reporting from the field); Findings (summary of new or ongoing research); Naturalist At Large; The Living Museum (relates to the American Museum of Natural History); Discovery (natural or cultural history of a specific place).
Tips: "We expect high standards of writing and research. We favor an ecological slant in most of our pieces, but do not generally lobby for causes, environmental or other. The writer should have a deep knowledge of his subject, then submit original ideas either in query or by manuscript. Acceptance is more likely if article is accompanied by high-quality photographs."

$ $ NATURAL LIFE, The Alternate Press, RR1, St. George, Ontario N0E 1N0 Canada. Fax: (519)448-4411. E-mail: natural@life.ca. Website: http://www.life.ca. **Contact:** Wendy Priesnitz, editor. **10% freelance written.** Bimonthly tabloid covering "news about self-reliance and sustainability. How-to and inspiration for people living an environmentally aware lifestyle. Includes gardening, natural foods, health, home business, renewal energy." Estb. 1976. Circ. 100,000. Pays on publication. Publishes ms an average of 3 months after acceptance. Byline given. Offers 50% kill fee. Buys first North American serial and electronic rights. Editorial lead time 4 months. Submit seasonal material 4 months in advance. Reports in 3 weeks on queries. Sample copy for $4. Guidelines for #10 SASE (Canadian stamps please).
Nonfiction: How-to articles based on personal experience, profiles of environmentally conscious people. **Buys 10 mss/year.** Query with published clips and SASE with Canadian postage or IRCs. Length: 800-1,000 words. **Pays 10¢/word to $100** maximum.
Photos: State availability of photos with query. Reviews prints. Offers no additional payment for photos accepted with ms. Captions, identification of subjects required. Buys all rights.

$ NATURE CANADA, Canadian Nature Federation, 1 Nicholas St., Suite 606, Ottawa, Ontario KIN 7B7 Canada. Fax: (613)562-3371. E-mail: cnf@cnf.ca. Website: http://www.magna.ca/~cnfgen. **Contact:** Barbara Stevenson, editor. Quarterly membership magazine covering conservation, natural history and environmental/naturalist community. "*Nature Canada* is written for an audience interested in nature. Its content supports the Canadian Nature Federation's philosophy that all species have a right to exist regardless of their usefulness to humans. We promote the awareness, understanding and enjoyment of nature." Estab. 1971. Circ. 18,000. Pays on publication. Publishes ms an average of 3 months after acceptance. Byline given. Offers $100 kill fee. Buys one-time rights. Editorial lead time 3 months. Submit seasonal material 6 months in advance. Reports in 3 months on mss. Sample copy for $5. Writer's guidelines free.

Nonfiction: Canadian environmental issues and natural history. **Buys 20 mss/year.** Query with published clips. Length: 2,000-4,000 words. **Pays 25¢/word** (Canadian).

Photos: State availability of photos with submission. Offers $40-100/photo (Canadian). Identification of subjects required. Buys one-time rights.

Columns/Departments: The Green Gardener (naturalizing your backyard), 1,200 words; Small Wonder (on less well-known species such as invertebrates, nonvascular plants, etc.), 800-1,500 words; Connections (Canadians making a difference for the environment), 1,000-1,500 words; Weatherwise (weather phenomena). **Buys 16 mss/year.** Query with published clips. **Pays 25¢/word** (Canadian).

Tips: "Our readers are knowledgeable about nature and the environment so contributors should have a good understanding of the subject. We also deal exclusively with Canadian issues and species."

$ $ $ SEASONS, Ontario's Nature and Environment Magazine, Federation of Ontario Naturalists, 355 Lesmill Rd., Don Mills, Ontario M3B 2W8 Canada. (416)444-8419. E-mail: seasons@ontarionature.org. Website: http://www.ontarionature.org. **Contact:** Nancy Clark, editor. **75% freelance written.** Quarterly magazine. "*Seasons* focuses on Ontario natural history, parks and environmental issues, with appeal for general readers as well as naturalists." Estab. 1963 (published as *Ontario Naturalist* 1963-1980). Circ. 16,000. Pays on publication. Publishes ms an average of 6 months after acceptance. Byline given. Offers 50% kill fee. Buys first Canadian serial rights. Editorial lead time 6 months. Submit seasonal material 1 year in advance. Reports in 2-3 months. Sample copy for $7.20. Writer's guidelines for #10 SASE.

Nonfiction: Essays, general interest, how-to (identify species, be a better birder, etc.), opinion, personal experience, photo feature, travel. No cute articles about cute animals or biology articles cribbed from reference books. **Buys 16-20 mss/year.** Query with published clips. Length: 1,500-3,000 words. **Pays $350-1,000.** Sometimes pays expenses of writers on assignment.

Photos: State availability of photos with submission. Reviews 35mm transparencies. Negotiates payment individually. Model releases, identification of subjects required. Buys one-time rights.

Columns/Departments: Naturalist's Notebook (tips on birding, improving naturalist's skills), 700 words. **Buys 4 mss/year.** Query with published clips. **Pays $200-400.**

$ $ $ $ SIERRA, 85 Second St., 2nd Floor, San Francisco CA 94105-3441. (415)977-5656. Fax: (415)977-5794. E-mail: sierra.letters@sierraclub.org. Website: http://www.sierraclub.org. Editor-in-Chief: Joan Hamilton. Senior Editors: Reed McManus, Paul Rauber. **Contact:** Robert Schildgen, managing editor. Works with a small number of new/unpublished writers each year. Bimonthly magazine emphasizing conservation and environmental politics for people who are well educated, activist, outdoor-oriented and politically well informed with a dedication to conservation. Estab. 1893. Circ. 550,000. **Pays on acceptance.** Publishes ms an average of 4 months after acceptance. Byline given. Kill fees negotiable when a story is assigned. Buys first North American serial rights. Reports in 2 months. Sample copy for $3 and SASE.

- Ranked as one of the best markets for freelance writers in *Writer's Yearbook* magazine's annual "Top 100 Markets," January 1998.

Nonfiction: Exposé (well-documented articles on environmental issues of national importance such as energy, wilderness, forests, etc.); general interest (well-researched nontechnical pieces on areas of particular environmental concern); photo feature (photo essays on threatened or scenic areas); journalistic treatments of semi-technical topics (energy sources, wildlife management, land use, waste management, etc.). No "My trip to . . ." or "why we must save wildlife/nature" articles; no poetry or general superficial essays on environmentalism; no reporting on purely local environmental issues. Special issues: Children, Religion and Environment (September/October 1998); Travel (March/April 1999). **Buys 5-6 mss/issue.** Query with published clips. Length: 800-3,000 words. **Pays $450-2,000.** Pays limited expenses of writers on assignment.

Reprints: Send photocopy of article or typed ms with rights for sale noted and information about when and where the article previously appeared. Pay negotiable.

Photos: Larissa Zimberoff, art and production manager. Send photos. Pays $300 maximum for transparencies; more for cover photos. Buys one-time rights.

Columns/Departments: Food for Thought (food's connection to environment—include a recipe); Good Going (adventure journey); Hearth & Home (advice for environmentally sound living); Way to Go (wilderness trips), 750 words. **Pays $500**. Lay of the Land (national/international concerns), 500-700 words. Pay varies. Natural Resources (book reviews), 200-300 words. **Pays $50.**

Tips: "Queries should include an outline of how the topic would be covered and a mention of the political appropriateness and timeliness of the article. Statements of the writer's qualifications should be included."

$ $ WATERFOWL & WETLANDS, South Carolina Waterfowl Association, 434 King St., Charleston SC 29403. (803)452-6001. **Contact:** Doug Gardner, editor. **35% freelance written.** Quarterly company publication of South Carolina Waterfowl Association covering waterfowl and wetland issues. "We are a 5,000+ member nonprofit association. Our quarterly magazine includes feature articles on waterfowl and current issues affecting duck and goose populations, hunting and behavior." Estab. 1987. Circ. 6,500. **Pays on acceptance**. Publishes ms an average of 6 months after acceptance. Byline given. Not copyrighted. Buys one-time or second serial (reprint) rights. Editorial lead time 4 months. Submit seasonal material 4 months in advance. Accepts simultaneous and previously published submissions. Reports in 3 weeks on queries. Sample copy and writer's guidelines free.

Nonfiction: Book excerpts, general interest, historical/nostalgic, how-to, humor, interview/profile, new product, opinion, personal experience, photo feature, travel. **Buys 6 mss/year.** Query. Length: 1,000-3,000 words. **Pays $75-300.**

Photos: State availability of photos with submission. Reviews 3×5 prints. Pays $50-125. Captions, identification of subjects required. Buys one-time rights.

Columns/Departments: Going Places (hunting/fishing trips) 1,200 words. **Buys 2 mss/year.** Query. **Pays $50-200.**

Poetry: Avant-garde, free verse, traditional.

Tips: "We are interested in national waterfowl issues and also articles which address the waterfowler and waterfowling tradition. A query letter to the editor will be responded to in a timely fashion."

N ✪ $ WHOLE EARTH REVIEW, Point Foundation, 1408 Mission Ave., San Rafael CA 94901. (415)256-2800. Fax: (415)256-2808. E-mail: wer@well.com. Editor: Peter Warshall. Managing Editor: Michael Stone. **Contact**: Elizabeth Thompson, assistant editor. **80% freelance written.** "Quarterly periodical supplement, continuation of the Whole Earth catalog. Evaluates tools, ideas and practices to sow the seeds for a long-term, viable planet." Estab. 1971. Circ. 30,000. Pays on publication. Publishes ms an average of 6 months after acceptance. Byline given. Buys one-time rights. Editorial lead time 3 months. Accepts simultaneous submissions. Reports in 1 month on queries (no promises). Writer's guidelines free.

Nonfiction: Book excerpts, essays, exposé, general interest, historical/nostalgic, how-to, humor, interview/profile, new product, personal experience, photo feature, religious, travel. "No dull repeats of old ideas or material." Query or send complete ms. Length: 500-3,000 words. Pay negotiable. Pays writers with contributor copies or other premiums by agreement, usually for reviews. Sometimes pays expenses of writers on assignment.

Reprints: Accepts previously published submissions.

Photos: State availability of photos with submission. Offers $50 maximum/photo or negotiates payment individually. Buys one-time rights.

Fiction: Adventure, erotica, ethnic, experimental, humorous, novel excerpts, science fiction, slice-of-life vignettes. **Buys 2-4 mss/year.** Query or send complete ms. Length: 500-3,000 words. Pay negotiable.

Poetry: Peter Warshall, editor. Avant-garde, free verse, haiku, light verse, traditional. No long works. **Buys 1-4 poems/year.** Length: 100 lines maximum. Pay negotiable.

Tips: "Submit. Don't take rejection personally. Submit again."

$ $ $ WILDLIFE CONSERVATION MAGAZINE, Wildlife Conservation Society, 185th St. and Southern Blvd., Bronx NY 10460-1068. (212)220-5121. Fax: (718)584-2625. E-mail: 2014358@mcimail.com. Website: (Wildlife Conservation Society) http://www.wcs.org/news. **Contact:** Joan Downs, editor. **50% freelance written.** Bimonthly magazine. "*Wildlife Conservation* is edited for the reader interested in conservation through first-hand accounts by wildlife researchers." Estab. 1895. Circ. 150,000. **Pays on acceptance.** Publishes ms an average of 1 year or more after acceptance. Byline given. Buys first North American serial rights. Submit seasonal material 1 year in advance. Accepts simultaneous submissions. Reports in 2 months on queries; 3 months on mss. Sample copy for $3.95 and 9×12 SAE with 7 first-class stamps. Writer's guidelines for SASE.

- Ranked as one of the best markets for freelance writers in *Writer's Yearbook* magazine's annual "Top 100 Markets," January 1998.

Nonfiction: Nancy Simmons, senior editor. Essays, personal experience, wildlife articles. No pet or domestic animal stories. Special issues: Fantastic Frogs (Papua New Guinea), Turtle Trade (Asia), The Making of a National Park (Madagascar), Flying Squirrels (Pakistan), The Saga of the Saiga (Russian Steppes), At the Zoo (Lufkin, Texas), September/October 1998; Ghosts of the Gobi (Mongolia's wild camels), Animal Magnetism (whales, turtles and other critters), Flight of the Condor (California condor), The Death of Monogamy, The "Trouble" With Crocs (Belize), At the Zoo (Honolulu), November/December 1998. **Buys 12 mss/year.** Query. Length: 1,500 words. **Pays $500-1,500 for assigned articles; $500-750 for unsolicited articles.**

Photos: Send photos with submission. Reviews transparencies. Buys one-time rights.

Tips: "Articles for *Wildlife Conservation* should be lively and entertaining, as well as informative. We feature articles from an author's own research and experience. We like them to be first-person, but we don't want the author to intrude. Avoid textbookish or encyclopedic articles. Pin the article to an underlying theme, point or reason and weave in atmosphere—sights, smells, sounds, colors, weather. Let the reader see through your eyes and help them become involved."

PERSONAL COMPUTERS

Personal computer magazines continue to evolve. The most successful have a strong focus on a particular family of computers or widely-used applications and carefully target a specific type of computer use, although as technology evolves, some computers and applications fall by the wayside. Be sure you see the most recent issue of a magazine before submitting material.

N $ $ $ COMPUTER BUYER'S GUIDE & HANDBOOK, Bedford Communications, 150 Fifth Ave., Suite 714, New York NY 10011. Fax: (212)807-0589. E-mail: daf521@aol.com. Editor: David A. Finck. **Contact**: Leigh Friedman, managing editor. **50% freelance written.** Monthly magazine covering computer hardware, software and peripherals; industry trends. "Publication is geared toward the computer buyer, with an emphasis on the small office." Estab. 1982. Pays on publication. Publishes ms an average of 3 months after acceptance. Byline given. Offers 25% kill fee. Buys all rights. Editorial lead time 3 months. Submit seasonal material 3 months in advance. Reports in 3-4 weeks on queries; 2 months on mss. Sample copy and writer's guidelines not available.
Nonfiction: How-to (e.g., how to install a CD-ROM drive), technical, hands-on reviews. **Buys 80-100 mss/year.** Query with published clips. "Will not accept unsolicited articles or manuscripts." Length: 3,500-5,000 words. **Pays $750-1,250 for assigned articles.** Sometimes pays expenses of writers on assignment.
Tips: "Send résumé with clips to editorial offices. Unsolicited manuscripts are not accepted or returned."

N $ COMPUTER CREDIBLE MAGAZINE, Assimilations, Inc., 1249 W. Jordan River Dr., South Jordan UT 84095-8250. (801)254-5432. Fax: (801)253-1040. E-mail: computer@credible.com. Website: http://www.credible.com. Editor: Rick Simi. **Contact:** Kerry Simi, managing editor. **100% freelance written.** Bimonthly consumer magazine covering computers. Estab. 1995. Circ. 35,000. **Pays on acceptance**. Publishes ms an average of 1 month after acceptance. Byline given. Buys first North American serial rights and second serial (reprint) rights. Sample copy free. Writer's guidelines for #10 SASE.
Nonfiction: General interest, how-to, humor, interview/profile, new product, opinion, technical. **Buys 40 mss/year.** Length: 650-1,500 words. **Pays 5-10¢/word.**
Reprints: Accepts previously published submissions.
Photos: State availability of photos with submission.
Columns/Departments: Buys 40 mss/year. Send complete ms. **Pays 5-10¢/word.**
Fiction: Humorous. **Buys 6 mss/year.** Send complete ms. Length: 650-1,000 words. **Pays 5-10¢/word.**
Fillers: Facts, short humor. Length: 250-650 words. **Pays 5-10¢/word.**

$ $ $ COMPUTER CURRENTS, Real World Solutions for Business Computing, Computer Currents Publishing, 1250 Ninth St., Berkeley CA 94710. (510)527-0333. Fax: (510)527-4106. E-mail: editorial@compcurr.com. Website: http://www.currents.net. **Contact:** Robert Luhn, editor-in-chief. **90% freelance written.** Biweekly magazine "for fairly experienced PC and Mac business users. We provide where to buy, how to buy and how to use information. That includes buyers guides, reviews, tutorials and more." Estab. 1983. Circ. 700,000. **Pays on acceptance**. Byline given. Offers 20% kill fee. Buys all rights. Editorial lead time 2 months. Submit seasonal material 2 months in advance. Reports in 2 weeks on queries; 2 months on mss. Sample copy for 10×12 SAE with $5 postage. Writer's guidelines for #10 SASE.
Nonfiction: Book excerpts, exposé, how-to (using PC or Mac products), new product, opinion, technical. Special issues: CD-ROM Buyers Guide (October); Holiday Gift Guide (November). "No fiction, poetry or 'I just discovered PCs' essays." **Buys 40 mss/year.** Query with published clips and SASE. Length: 1,000-2,500 words. **Pays $700-2,000.** Sometimes pays expenses of writers on assignment.
Reprints: Send tearsheet or typed ms with rights for sale noted and information about when and where the article previously appeared. Pays 10-40% of amount paid for an original article.
Photos: State availability of photos with submission. Reviews 35mm transparencies, 8×10 prints. Offers no additional payment for photos accepted with ms. Buys first North American and nonexclusive reprint rights.
Columns/Departments: Melissa Riofrio, senior editor. "Previews & Reviews" of new and beta hardware, software and services, 300-600 words; Features (PC, Mac, hardware, software, investigative pieces), 1,000-2,500 words. **Buys 60 mss/year.** Query with published clips and SASE. **Pays $50-500.**
Tips: "Writers must know PC or Mac technology and major software and peripherals. Know how to write, evaluate products critically, and make a case for or against a product under review. *Computer Currents* is the magazine for the rest of us. We don't torture test 500 printers or devote space to industry chit-chat. Instead, we provide PC and Mac users with real-world editorial they can use every day when determining what to buy, where to buy it, and how to use it. Along with supplying this kind of nitty-gritty advice to both small and large business users alike, we also demystify the latest technologies and act as a consumer advocate. We're also not afraid to poke fun at the industry, as our annual 'Editor's Choice' issue and biweekly 'Gigglebytes' column demonstrate."

$ COMPUTOREDGE, San Diego's Computer Magazine, The Byte Buyer, Inc., P.O. Box 83086, San Diego CA 92138. (619)573-0315. Fax: (619)573-0205. E-mail: patricia@computoredge.com. Website: http://www.comp

FOR INFORMATION on setting your freelance fees, see How Much Should I Charge?

utoredge.com. Executive Editor: Leah Steward. Senior Editor: Patricia Smith. **Contract:** John San Filippo, editor. **90% freelance written.** "We are the nation's largest regional computer weekly, providing San Diego County with non-technical, entertaining articles on all aspects of computers. We cater to the novice/beginner/first-time computer buyer. Humor is welcome." Estab. 1983. Circ. 80,000. Pays on publication. Net 30 day payment after publication. Byline given. Offers $15 kill fee. Buys first North American serial rights. Submit seasonal material 2 months in advance. Reports in 2 months. Writer's guidelines and editorial calendar for #10 SASE or download writer's guidelines and editorial calendar from website. Read sample issue online." Sample issue for SAE with 7 first-class stamps.

• *ComputorEdge* has added another regional publication in the Denver area.

Nonfiction: General interest (computer), how-to, humor, personal experience. **Buys 80 mss/year.** Send complete ms. Length: 900-1,200 words. **Pays $100-150.**

Columns/Departments: Beyond Personal Computing (a reader's personal experience). **Buys 80 mss/year.** Send complete ms. Length: 500-1,000 words. **Pays $50-75.**

Fiction: Confession, fantasy, slice-of-life vignettes. No poetry. **Buys 20 mss/year.** Send complete ms. Length: 900-1,200 words. **Pays $100-150.**

Tips: "Be relentless. Convey technical information in an understandable, interesting way. We like light material, but not fluff. Write as if you're speaking with a friend. Avoid the typical 'Love at First Byte' and the 'How My Grandmother Loves Her New Computer' article. We do not accept poetry. Avoid sexual innuendoes/metaphors. Reading a sample issue is advised."

$ EQUIP MAGAZINE, (formerly *Computer Life*), Ziff-Davis Publishing, 135 Main St., 14th Floor, San Francisco CA 94105. (415)357-5200. Fax: (415)357-5201 and (415)357-5266. E-mail: computerlife_edit_sf@zd.com. Website: http://www.equip.com. **Contact:** Adam Meyerson, editor-in-chief; Michael Penwarden, executive editor. **80% freelance written.** Monthly magazine covering personal computers, home audio, home theater and digital consumer electronics. "*Equip Magazine* presents products, ideas and techniques that enable enthusiasts to further enrich their personal computing experience and better fulfill their aspirations. *Equip Magazine* is aimed at computer enthusiasts who are looking for new and interesting ways to use PCs in their personal (nonwork) lives." Estab. 1994. Circ. 450,000. **Pays on acceptance**. Publishes ms an average of 3 months after acceptance. Byline given. Offers 25% kill fee. Buys all rights. Editorial lead time 3 months. Submit seasonal material 5 months in advance. Reports in 6 weeks on queries. Writer's guidelines free.

Nonfiction: "*Equip Magazine* contains features, reviews and step-by-step visual guides to help readers use their computers in new and exciting ways." How-to, new product, technical. **Buys 50-100 mss/year.** Query with published clips. Length: 500-1,300 words. **Pays $100 minimum.** Sometimes pays expenses of writers on assignment.

Photos: State availability of photos with submissions. Negotiates payment individually. Captions, model releases, identification of subjects required. Buys one-time rights.

$$$$ MACADDICT, Imagine Media, 150 North Hill Dr., Suite 40, Brisbane CA 94005. (415)468-4684. Fax: (415)468-4686. E-mail: cengland@macaddict.com. Managing Editor: Ruth Hennich. **Contact:** David Reynolds, editor. **25% freelance written.** Monthly magazine covering Macintosh computers. "*MacAddict* is a magazine for Macintosh computer enthusiasts of all levels. Writers must know, love and own Macintosh computers." Estab. 1996. Circ. 154,000. Pays on publication. Publishes ms an average of 3 months after acceptance. Byline given. Buys all rights. Editorial lead time 3 months. Submit seasonal material 5 months in advance. Accepts simultaneous submissions. Reports in 1 month.

Nonfiction: General interest, how-to, new product, photo feature, technical. No humor, case studies, personal experiences, essays. **Buys 30 mss/year.** Query with or without published clips and SASE. Length: 750-5,000 words. **Pays $50-2,500.** Sometimes pays expenses of writers on asssignment.

Photos: State availability of photos with submission. Negotiates payment individually. Captions, model releases, identification of subjects required. Buys one-time rights.

Columns/Departments: Reviews (always assigned), 300-750 words; How-to's (detailed, step-by-step), 500-4,000 words; features, 1,000-4,000 words. **Buys 30 mss/year.** Query with or without published clips. **Pays $50-2,500.**

Fillers: Kathy Tafel, senior editor. Get Info. **Buys 20/year.** Length: 50-500 words. **Pays $25-200.**

Tips: "Send us an idea for a short one to two page how-to and/or send us a letter outlining your publishing experience and areas of Mac expertise so we can assign a review to you (reviews editor is Robert Capps). Your submission should have great practical hands-on benefit to a reader, be fun to read in the author's natural voice, and include lots of screenshot graphics. We require electronic submissions."

N $$$ MACHOME JOURNAL, 703 Market St., Suite 535, San Francisco CA 94103. Fax: (415)882-9502. E-mail: editor@machome.com. Managing Editor: Carrie Shepherd. **Contact**: Ed Prasek, editor. **10% freelance written.** Monthly magazine covering Macintosh computers. "Our philosophy is 'no jargon.' We write for a nontechnical consumer audience; everything must be easily understandable to a layperson." Estab. 1992. Circ. 100,000. Pays on publication. Publishes ms an average of 3 months after acceptance. Byline given. Buys all rights. Editorial lead time 4 months. Submit seasonal material 4 months in advance. Accepts simultaneous submissions. Reports in 1 week on queries; 1 month on mss.

Nonfiction: Exposé, general interest (industry), how-to (use Macs efficiently), new product reviews, technical. No Mac or Apple bashing. **Buys 6 mss/year.** Query with published clips. Length: 250-5,000 words. **Pays $100-800.** Pays writers with contributor copies or other premiums if negotiated with editor. Sometimes pays expenses of writers on assignment.

Photos: Send photos with submission. Reviews transparencies, prints. Offers no additional payment for photos accepted with ms. Captions required. Buys all rights.
Columns/Departments: Software review (kids'/games/family/hardware/utility), 250-400 words; Education/Your Office/Entertainment articles, all 1,500-3,000 words. **Buys 200 mss/year.** Query with published clips. **Pays $50-800.**
Tips: "Have specific article ideas and be ultra-knowledgeable of the Mac industry and marketplace. Be in tune with our audience: non-technical home and small-office users. Don't ask for outrageous fees—we can't afford them."

N MACPOWER MAGAZINE, The Magazine for the Macintosh PowerBook and Newton, Hollow Earth Publishing, P.O. Box 1355, Boston MA 02205-1355. E-mail: hep2@aol.com. **Contact:** Heilan Yvette Grimes, editor. **95% freelance written.** Monthly magazine covering PowerBooks and Newton. "We offer helpful information about the PowerBook and Newton." Estab. 1994. Circ. 35,000. **Pays on acceptance**. Byline given. Buys all rights or makes work-for-hire assignments. Editorial lead time 2 months. Reports in 2 weeks on queries; 1 months on mss. Sample copy for 9×12 SAE with 3 first-class stamps. Writer's guidelines for #10 SASE.
Nonfiction: Book excerpts, general interest, historical/nostalgic, how-to, humor, interview/profile, new product, personal experience, technical. E-mail queries only. Length: 300 or more words. Pays per page, negotiated. Sometimes pays expenses of writers on assignment.
Photos: Send photos with submission. Reviews transparencies. (Prefers electronic PICT of TIFF files.) Negotiates payment individually. Captions, model releases and identification of subjects required. Buys all rights.
Columns/Departments: "We are interested in Help columns on individual topics. Check the magazine for an idea of what we publish." **Buys 60 mss/year.** Query with published clips.
Fillers: Anecdotes, facts, gags to be illustrated by cartoonist, newsbreaks, short humor. Length: 20-50 words.
Tips: "Know your subject and have something interesting to say. Reviews and new ideas are most open to freelancers."

$ $ $ $ MACWEEK, Mac Publishing LLC, 301 Howard St., 15th Floor, San Francisco CA 94105. (415)243-3500. Fax: (415)243-3535. E-mail: catherine_lacroix@macweek.com. Website: http://www.macweek.com. **Contact:** Catherine LaCroix, executive editor/features. **35% freelance written.** Weekly tabloid "reaching sophisticated buyers of Macintosh-related products for large organizations." Estab. 1986. Circ. 85,000. **Pays on acceptance.** Publishes ms an average of 1 month after acceptance. Byline given. Offers 25% kill fee. Buys all worldwide rights. Editorial lead time: news, 10 days; reviews, 2 months; features, 1 month. Reports in 1 month on mss. Writer's guidelines free.

- Ranked as one of the best markets for freelance writers in *Writer's Yearbook* magazine's "Top 100 Markets," January 1998.

Columns/Departments: David Morgenstern and Joanna Pearlstein (news); Missy Roback (reviews); Catherine LaCroix (features and special reports). Reviews (new product testing), 500-1,200 words; Solutions (case histories), 1,600 words. **Buys 30 mss/year.** Query with published clips. **Pays 65¢-$1/word.** *No unsolicited mss.*
Tips: "We do not accept unsolicited material. If a writer would like to pitch a story to me by e-mail. I'm open to that. Knowledge of the Macintosh market is essential. Know which section you would like to write for and submit to the appropriate editor."

$ $ $ PC PORTABLES MAGAZINE, LFP, Inc., 8484 Wilshire Blvd., Beverly Hills CA 90211. (213)651-5400. E-mail: tnozick@lfp.com. Editor-in-Chief: Mark Kellner. **Contact:** Theresa Barry Nozick, managing editor. **40% freelance written.** "We are a monthly, comprehensive, reader-friendly portable computer magazine with a focus on portable computer users in the workplace and mobile situations." Estab. 1989. Circ. 60,000. **Pays on acceptance**. Publishes ms an average of 3 months after acceptance. Byline given. Offers 20% kill fee. Buys all rights and makes work for hire assignments. Editorial lead time 4 months. Sample copy for $5. Writer's guidelines for #10 SASE.
Nonfiction: New product reviews, technical. Query with published clips. Length: 300-1,500 words. **Pays $400-1,500** (negotiable). *No accept unsolicited articles.* Sometimes pays the expenses of writers on assignment.
Photos: State availability of photos with submission. Reviews contact sheets, negatives, transparencies and prints. Negotiates payment individually. Captions, model releases, identification of subjects required. Buys all rights.
Tips: "This is a portable computer and mobile technology magazine targeting the portable and hand held computer user. Focus is on hardware and software that applies to portable computing and mobile situations. *PC Portables* is a 'reader friendly' publication for mobile computing professionals, and small business and home users. All information is presented in a clear, concise format, and technical information should be defined in easy to understand terms."

PUBLISH, The Magazine for Electronic Publishing Professionals, 501 Second St., San Francisco CA 94107. (415)243-0600. Fax: (415)975-2613. E-mail: mnaman@publish.com. Website: http://www.publish.com. Editor-in-Chief: Jake Widman. **Contact:** M. Naman. **50% freelance written.** Monthly magazine for electronic publishers and corporate communicators on desktop publishing and presentations. Estab. 1986. Circ. 97,000. Pays on publication. Publishes ms an average of 4-5 months after acceptance. Byline given. Buys first international rights. Guidelines for #10 SASE.
Nonfiction: Product reviews, how-to (publishing topics), news, technical tips. **Buys 120 mss/year.** Query with published clips. Length: 400-2,300 words. *No unsolicited mss.*
Photos: Send photos with submission. Reviews contact sheets. Captions and identification of subjects required.
Tips: "Newcomers can best break in with a review or technology primer. Unsolicited manuscripts will not be returned."

N $ $ $ SMART COMPUTING, Sandhills Publishing, 120 W. Harvest Dr., Lincoln NE 68521. (800)544-1264. Fax: (402)479-2104. E-mail: editor@smartcomputing.com. Website: http://www.smartcomputing.com. **Contact:**

Ron Kobler, editor. Managing Editor: Trevor Meers. **45% freelance written.** Monthly. "We focus on plain-English computing articles with an emphasis on tutorials that improve productivity without the purchse of new hardware." Estab. 1990. Circ. 300,000. **Pays on acceptance.** Publishes ms 2 months after acceptance. Byline given. Offers 25% kill fee. Buys all rights. Editorial lead time 4 months. Submit seasonal material 4 months in advance. Accepts simultaneous submissions. Reports in 1 month. Sample copy for $7.99. Writer's guidelines free.

Nonfiction: How-to, new product, technical. No humor, opinion, personal experience. **Buys 250 mss/year.** Query with published clips. Length: 800-3,200 words. **Pays $240-960.** Pays the expenses of writers on assignment up to $75.

Photos: Send photos with submission. Offers no additional payment for photos accepted with ms. Captions required. Buys all rights.

Tips: "Focus on practical, how-to computing articles. Our readers are intensely productivity-driven. Carefully review recent issues. We receive many ideas for stories printed in the last six months."

$ $ $ $ WINDOWS MAGAZINE, CMP Media Inc., 1 Jericho Plaza, Jericho NY 11753. (516)733-8300. Fax: (516)733-8390. Website: http://www.winmag.com. Senior Managing Editor: Donna Tapellini. Monthly magazine for business users of Windows hardware and software. "*Windows* contains information on how to evaluate, select, acquire, implement, use, and master Windows-related software and hardware." Estab. 1990. Circ. 800,000. **Pays on acceptance**. Byline given. Offers 25% kill fee. Reports in 1-2 months on queries. Sample copy and writer's guidelines available.

- Ranked as one of the best markets for freelance writers in *Writer's Yearbook* magazine's annual "Top 100 Markets," January 1996.

Nonfiction: How-to, technical. **Buys 30 mss/year.** Query with published clips. Length: 1,500-4,000 words. **Pays $1,200-3,000.**

Tips: Needs "clear, entertaining, technical features on Windows hardware and software." Wants to see "how-to and how-to-buy articles, and insider's look at new products." Should be well-written, entertaining and technically accurate. "We concentrate on hands-on tips and how-to information."

☆ $ $ $ WIRED MAGAZINE, 520 Third St., 4th Floor, San Francisco CA 94107-1815. (415)276-5000. Fax: (415)276-5150. E-mail: submit@wired.com. Website: http://www.wired.com. Editor/Publisher: Louis Rossetto. **Contact:** Patricia Reilly, editorial assistant. **95% freelance written.** Monthly magazine covering technology and digital culture. "We cover the digital revolution and related advances in computers, communications and lifestyles." Estab. 1993. Circ. 350,000. **Pays on acceptance.** Publishes ms an average of 3 months after acceptance. Byline given. Offers 25% kill fee. Buys first North American serial rights, global rights with 25% payment. Editorial lead time 3 months. Reports in 3 weeks on queries. Sample copy for $4.95. Guidelines for #10 SASE or e-mail to guidelines@wired.com.

Nonfiction: Essays, interview/profile, opinion. "No poetry or trade articles." **Buys 85 features, 130 short pieces, 200 reviews, 36 essays and 50 other mss/year.** Query. Pays expenses of writers on assignment.

$ $ $ WORDPERFECT SUITE MAGAZINE, (formerly *Wordperfect for Windows Magazine*), Ivy International Communications, 270 W. Center St., Orem UT 84057-4683. (801)226-5555. Fax: (801)226-8804. E-mail: editor@ivypub.com. Website: http://www.wpmag.com. **Contact:** Ana Nelson Shaw, editor-in-chief. **80% freelance written.** Monthly magazine of "how-to" articles for users of Corel WordPerfect Suites and compatible software. Estab. 1991. Circ. 100,000. **Pays on acceptance**. Publishes ms an average of 4 months after acceptance. Byline given. Pays negotiable kill fee. Buys all world rights. Submit seasonal material 8 months in advance. Reports in 2 months. Sample copy for 9×12 SAE with 7 first-class stamps. Free writers guidelines.

Nonfiction: How-to, step-by-step applications (with keystrokes and screenshots in TIF format), new product, technical. "Easy-to-understand articles written with *minimum* jargon. Articles should provide readers good, useful information about word processing and other computer functions." **Buys 120-160 mss/year.** Query with published clips. Length: 800-1,800 words. **Pays $600-800.**

Columns/Departments: Desktop Publishing; Printing; Basics (tips for beginners); Macros, Troubleshooting, all 1,200-1,600 words. **Buys 90-120 mss/year.** Query with published clips. **Pays $400-800.**

Tips: "Studying our publication provides the best information. We're looking for writers who can both inform *and* entertain our specialized group of readers."

PHOTOGRAPHY

Readers of these magazines use their cameras as a hobby and for weekend assignments. To write for these publications, you should have expertise in photography. Magazines geared to the professional photographer can be found in the Professional Photography section.

$ NATURE PHOTOGRAPHER, Nature Photographer Publishing Co., Inc., P.O. Box 2019, Quincy MA 02269. (617)847-0095. Fax: (617)847-0952. E-mail: mjsquincy@pipeline.com. Editor: Evamarie Mathaey. **Contact:** Helen Longest-Slaughter, photo editor. **65% freelance written.** Bimonthly magazine "emphasizing nature photography that uses low-impact and local less-known locations, techniques and ethics. Articles include how-to, travel to world-wide wilderness locations, and how nature photography can be used to benefit the environment and environmental education of the public." Estab. 1990. Circ. 24,000. Pays on publication. Buys one-time rights. Submit seasonal material 8 months in advance. Accepts simultaneous submissions. Reports in 2 months. Sample copy for 9×12 SAE with 6 first-class stamps. Writer's guidelines for #10 SASE.

Nonfiction: How-to (underwater, exposure, creative techniques, techniques to make photography easier, low-impact techniques, macro photography, large-format, wildlife), photo feature, technical, travel. No articles about photographing in zoos or on game farms. **Buys 12-18 mss/year.** Query with published clips or writing samples. Length: 750-2,500 words. **Pays $75-150.**

Reprints: Send photocopy of article and information about when and where the article previously appeared. Pays 75% of amount *Nature Photographer* pays for an original article.

Photos: Send photos upon request. Do not send with submission. Reviews 35mm, 2¼×2¼ and 4×5 transparencies. Offers no additional payment for photos accepted with ms. Identification of subjects required. Buys one-time rights.

Tips: "Query with original, well-thought-out ideas and good writing samples. Make sure you send SASE. Areas most open to freelancers are travel, how-to and conservation. Must have good, solid research and knowledge of subject. Be sure to obtain guidelines by sending SASE with request before submitting query. If you have not requested guidelines within the last year, request an updated version of guidelines."

$ $ $ PHOTO TECHNIQUES, Preston Publications, Inc., 6600 W. Touhy Ave., Niles IL 60714. (847)647-2900. Fax: (847)647-1155. E-mail: 70007.3477@compuserve.com. Publisher: S. Tinsley Preston III. Managing Editor: Bert Stern. **Contact:** Mike Johnston, editor. **50% freelance written.** Bimonthly publication covering photochemistry, lighting, optics, processing and printing, Zone System, special effects, sensitometry, etc. Aimed at advanced workers. Prefers to work with experienced photographer-writers; happy to work with excellent photographers whose writing skills are lacking. "Article conclusions often require experimental support." Estab. 1979. Circ. 35,000. Pays within 2 weeks of publication. Publishes ms an average of 8 months after acceptance. Byline given. Buys one-time rights. Sample copy for $5. Writer's guidelines with #10 SASE.

Nonfiction: Special interest articles within above listed topics; how-to, technical product reviews, photo features. Query or send complete ms. Length open, but most features run approximately 2,500 words or 3-4 magazine pages. **Pays $200-1,000** for well-researched technical articles.

Photos: Photographers have a much better chance of having their photos published if the photos accompany a written article. Manuscript payment includes payment for photos. Prefers 8×10 b&w and color prints. Captions, technical information required. Buys one-time rights.

Tips: "Study the magazine! Virtually all writers we publish are readers of the magazine. We are now more receptive than ever to articles about photographers, history, aesthetics and informative backgrounders about specific areas of the photo industry or specific techniques. Successful writers for our magazine are doing what they write about."

⊘ **POPULAR PHOTOGRAPHY** does not accept freelance submissions.

POLITICS AND WORLD AFFAIRS

These publications cover politics for the reader interested in current events. Other publications that will consider articles about politics and world affairs are listed under Business and Finance, Contemporary Culture, Regional and General Interest. For listings of publications geared toward the professional, see Government and Public Service in the Trade section.

$ $ $ AMERICAN SPECTATOR, 2020 N. 14th St., #750, Arlington VA 22201. (703)243-3733. Fax: (703)243-6814. Editor-in-Chief: R. Emmett Tyrell. Monthly magazine. "For many years, one ideological viewpoint dominated American print and broadcast journalism. Today, that viewpoint still controls the entertainment and news divisions of the television networks, the mass-circulation news magazines, and the daily newspapers. *American Spectator* has attempted to balance the Left's domination of the media by debunking its perceived wisdom and advancing alternative ideas through spirited writing, insightful essays, humor and, most recently, through well-researched investigative articles that have themselves become news." Estab. 1967. Circ. 200,011. Send queries and mss to Attn: Manuscripts.

Nonfiction: "Topics include politics, the press, foreign relations, the economy, culture. Stories most suited for publication are timely articles on previously unreported topics with national appeal. Articles should be thoroughly researched with a heavy emphasis on interviewing and reporting, and the facts of the article should be verifiable. We prefer articles in which the facts speak for themselves and shy away from editorial and first person commentary. No unsolicited poetry, fiction, satire or crossword puzzles." Query with resume, clips and SASE.

Columns/Departments: The Continuing Crisis and Current Wisdom (humor); On the Prowl ("Washington insider news"). Query with resume, clips and SASE.

$ $ $ CALIFORNIA JOURNAL, 2101 K St., Sacramento CA 95816. (916)444-2840. Fax: (916)444-2339. E-mail: agb@statenet.com. **Contact:** Steve Scott, managing editor. **20% freelance written.** Prefers to work with published/established writers. Monthly magazine "with non-partisan coverage aimed at a literate, well-informed, well-educated readership with strong involvement in issues, politics or government." Estab. 1970. Circ. 17,000. Pays on publication. Publishes ms an average of 3 months after acceptance. Byline given. Buys all rights. Reports in 2 weeks on queries, 2 months on mss. Writer's guidelines and sample copy for #10 SASE.

Nonfiction: Profiles of state and local government officials and political analysis. No outright advocacy pieces, fiction, poetry, product pieces. **Buys 25 unsolicited mss/year.** Query. Length: 900-3,000 words. **Pays $300-1,000.** Sometimes pays the expenses of writers on assignment.
Photos: State availability of photos with submission. Reviews contact sheets. Negotiates payment individually. Identification of subjects required. Buys all rights.
Columns/Departments: Soapbox (opinion on current affairs), 800 words. Does not pay.
Tips: "Be well versed in political and environmental affairs as they relate to California."

$ $ CHURCH & STATE, Americans United for Separation of Church and State, 1816 Jefferson Place, NW, Washington DC 20036. (202)466-3234. Fax: (202)466-2587. Website: http://www.au.org. **Contact:** Joseph Conn, editor. **10% freelance written.** Prefers to work with published/established writers. Monthly magazine emphasizing religious liberty and church/state relations matters. Strongly advocates separation of church and state. Readership is well-educated. Estab. 1947. Circ. 33,000. **Pays on acceptance.** Publishes ms an average of 2 months after acceptance. Buys all rights. Accepts simultaneous submissions. Reports in 2 months. Sample copy and writer's guidelines for 9×12 SAE with 3 first-class stamps.
Nonfiction: Exposé, general interest, historical, interview. **Buys 11 mss/year.** Query. Length: 800-1,600 words. **Pays $150-300.** Sometimes pays expenses of writers on assignment.
Reprints: Send tearsheet of article, photocopy of article or typed ms with rights for sale noted and information about when and where the article previously appeared.
Photos: Send photos with query. Pays negotiable fee for b&w prints. Captions preferred. Buys one-time rights.
Tips: "We're looking for feature articles on underreported local church-state controversies. We also consider 'viewpoint' essays that offer a unique or personal take on church-state issues."

$ COMMONWEAL, A Review of Public Affairs, Religion, Literature and the Arts, Commonweal Foundation, 475 Riverside Dr., Room 405, New York NY 10115. (212)662-4200. Fax: (212)662-4183. E-mail: commonweal@msn.com. Website: http://www.commonwealmagazine.org. Editor: Margaret O'Brien Steinfels. **Contact:** Patrick Jordan, managing editor. Biweekly journal of opinion edited by Catholic lay people, dealing with topical issues of the day on public affairs, religion, literature and the arts. Estab. 1924. Circ. 19,000. **Pays on acceptance** or publication. Byline given. Buys all rights. Submit seasonal material 2 months in advance. Reports in 2 months. Free sample copy.
Nonfiction: Essays, general interest, interview/profile, personal experience, religious. **Buys 20 mss/year.** Query with published clips. Length: 1,200-3,000 words. **Pays $75-100.**
Columns/Departments: Upfronts (brief, newsy reportorials, giving facts, information, and some interpretation behind the headlines of the day), 750-1,000 words; Last Word (usually of a personal nature, on some aspect of the human condition: spiritual, individual, political or social), 150 words.
Poetry: Rosemary Deen, poetry editor. Free verse, traditional. **Buys 25-30 poems/year. Pays 75¢/line.**
Tips: "Articles should be written for a general but well-educated audience. While religious articles are always topical, we are less interested in devotional and churchy pieces than in articles which examine the links between 'worldly' concerns and religious beliefs."

$ COUNTRY CONNECTIONS, Seeking the Good Life—For the Common Good, Earth Alert, Inc., 14431 Ventura Blvd., #407, Sherman Oaks CA 91423. (818)501-1896. Fax: (818)501-1897. E-mail: countryink@countryink.com. Website: http://countryink.com. Editor: Catherine Roberts Leach. **Contact:** Britt Leach, co-editor/publisher. **25% freelance written.** Bimonthly magazine with "outspoken, literate and from-the-heart essays and articles on progressive politics, social activism, ecological protection, ethics, animal rights, civil liberties and economic democracy." Estab. 1995. Circ. 2,000. Pays on publication. Publishes ms an average of 4 months after acceptance. Byline given. Offers 100% kill fee. Buys first North American serial rights. Editorial lead time 2 months. Submit seasonal material 4 months in advance. Accepts simultaneous submissions. Reports in 2 months. Sample copy for $4. Guidelines for #10 SASE.
Nonfiction: Essays, humor/satire, interview/profile, opinion, political, environmental. "We have a specific audience. Read the magazine first." **Buys 30 mss/year.** Send complete ms. Length: 1,000-2,500 words. **Pays $25-50.** Sometimes pays the expenses of writers on assignment.
Columns/Departments: Guest Room (opinion), 900-1,200 words; Book Reviews, 1,000 words. **Buys 6 mss/year.** Query with published clips for book reviews. Send complete ms for column. **Pays $50.**
Fiction: "No erotica, horror, mystery, religious, romance, western. Read the magazine first." **Buys 3 mss/year.** Send complete ms. Length: 900-2,500 words. **Pays $25-50.**
Poetry: "Send anything but very long poems." **Buys 12 poems/year.** Submit maximum 4 poems. **Pays $15.**
Tips: "Please include address and phone number. Cover letter not required; we read work and decide on that rather than what the writer has published in the past. Our title is deceptive. We are not a country magazine, but rather an alternative/progressive journal for those reconsidering the status quo. Clear, honest writing is appreciated, also satire and humor."

$ $ EMPIRE STATE REPORT, The Magazine of Politics and Public Policy in New York State, 33 Century Hill Dr., Latham NY 12210. Fax: (518)783-0005. **Contact:** Victor Schaffner, editor. **75% freelance written.** Monthly magazine providing "timely political and public policy features for local and statewide public officials in New York State. Anything that would be of interest to them is of interest to us." Estab. 1983. Circ. 10,000. Pays 2 months after publication. Byline given. Buys first North American serial rights. Reports in 1 month on queries; 2 months on mss. Sample copy for $4.50 with 9×12 SASE.

Nonfiction: Essays, exposé, interview/profile and opinion. "Writers should send for our editorial calendar." **Buys 48 mss/year.** Query with published clips. Length: 500-4,500 words. **Pays $50-600.** Sometimes pays expenses of writers on assignment.

Photos: Send photos with submission. Reviews any size prints. Offers $50-100/photo. Identification of subjects required. Buys one-time rights.

Columns/Departments: ESR Notebook (short news stories about state politics), 300-900 words; Perspective (opinion pieces), 900-950 words. Perspectives do not carry remuneration.

Tips: "Send us a query. If we are not already working on the idea, and if the query is well written, we might work something out with the writer."

$ $ THE FREEMAN, 30 S. Broadway, Irvington-on-Hudson NY 10533. (914)591-7230. Fax: (914)591-8910. E-mail: slr@erols.com. Website: http://www.fee.org. **Contact:** Sheldon Richman, editor. **85% freelance written.** Eager to work with new/unpublished writers. Monthly publication for "the layman and fairly advanced students of liberty." Buys all rights, including reprint rights. Estab. 1946. Pays on publication. Byline given. Publishes ms an average of 5 months after acceptance. Sample copy for 7½×10½ SASE with 4 first-class stamps.

Nonfiction: "We want nonfiction clearly analyzing and explaining various aspects of the free market, private property, limited-government philosophy. Though a necessary part of the literature of freedom is the exposure of collectivistic cliches and fallacies, our aim is to emphasize and explain the positive case for individual responsibility and choice in a free economy. We avoid name-calling and personality clashes. Ours is an intelligent analysis of the principles underlying a free-market economy. No political strategy or tactics." **Buys 100 mss/year.** Query with SASE. Length: 3,500 words maximum. **Pays 10¢/word.** Sometimes pays expenses of writers on assignment.

Tips: "It's most rewarding to find freelancers with new insights, fresh points of view. Facts, figures and quotations cited should be fully documented, to their original source, if possible."

GEORGE, Hachette Filippacchi Magazines, 1633 Broadway, 41st Floor, New York NY 10019. (212)767-6100. Publisher: Elinor Carmody. **Contact:** Matthew Cowen, editorial assistant. "*George* is edited to spotlight the personalities who shape public issues: from elected officials to media moguls to Hollywood stars. It contains insightful reporting, commentary, cartoons, photos and charts. It covers the points where politics and popular culture converge. *George* demystifies the political process and shows readers how to get the most from their government while staying abreast of the issues." Estab. 1995. This magazine did not respond to our request for information. Query before submitting.

Nonfiction: "We are primarily a political magazine publishing profiles, process stories, reviews, news items and interviews." Query with published clips and SASE. "The rate of payment depends upon the importance and quality of the feature, and our presentation of it."

$ $ THE NATION, 72 Fifth Ave., New York NY 10011-8046. (212)242-8400. Fax: (212)463-9712. Editor: Katrina Vanden Heuvel. **Contact:** Peggy Suttle, assistant to editor. **75% freelance written.** Estab. 1865. Works with a small number of new/unpublished writers each year. Weekly magazine "firmly committed to reporting on the issues of labor, national politics, business, consumer affairs, environmental politics, civil liberties, foreign affairs and the role and future of the Democratic Party." Buys first serial rights. Free sample copy and writer's guidelines for 6×9 SASE.

Nonfiction: "We welcome all articles dealing with the social scene, from an independent perspective." Queries encouraged. **Buys 100 mss/year.** Length: 2,000 words maximum. **Pays $225-300.** Sometimes pays expenses of writers on assignment.

Columns/Departments: Editorial, 500-700 words. **Pays $75.**

Poetry: Contact: Grace Schulman, poetry editor. Send poems with SASE. *The Nation* publishes poetry of outstanding aesthetic quality. **Pays $1/poem.**

$ $ $ NATIONAL REVIEW, 215 Lexington Ave., New York NY 10016. E-mail: articles@nationalreview.com. Website: http://www.nationalreview.com. Articles Editor: Andrew Oliver. Biweekly magazine featuring political commentary from a conservative viewpoint. Pays on publication. Byline given. Kill fee varies. Buys all rights. Reports in 2 months.

Nonfiction: Send complete ms. Length: 800-2,000 words. **Pays $250/printed page.** Sometimes pays expenses of writers on assignment.

Columns/Departments: Length: 900 words. **Pays $250/printed page.**

Fillers: Length: 1,000 words. **Pays $250/printed page.**

N $ $ THE NEIGHBORHOOD WORKS, Building Alternative Visions for the City, Center for Neighborhood Technology, 2125 W. North Ave., Chicago, IL 60647. (773)278-4800 ext. 113. Fax: (773)278-3840. E-mail: tnwedit@cnt.org. Website: http://www.cnt.org/tnw. Editor: Christine McConville. **Contact:** Ed Finkel, associate editor. **50% freelance written.** Bimonthly magazine covering community organizing, urban environmentalism. "We write to, for and about community organizers in low- and middle-income neighborhoods specifically areas of environmentalism, energy, transportation, housing and economic development." Estab. 1978. Circ. 2,000. Pays on publication. Publishes ms an average of 4 months after acceptance. Byline given. Kill fee negotiable. Buys all rights. Editorial lead time 2 months. Submit seasonal material 4 months in advance. Accepts simultaneous submissions. Reports in 2 months. Sample copy for 8½×11 SAE with 4 first-class stamps. Writer's guidelines free.

Nonfiction: Exposé, general interest, how-to (related to organizing and technical assistance to urban communities), interview/profile. **Buys 10-20 mss/year.** Query with published clips. Length: 800-2,000 words. **Pays $250-500 for assigned articles; $150-300 for unsolicited articles.** "We don't pay students and policy people for writing articles, but will give them a subscription." Sometimes pays expenses of writers on assignment.

Reprints: Accepts previously published submissions.

Photos: State availability of photos with submission. Reviews contact sheets, 5×7 prints. Negotiates payment individually. Identification of subjects required. Buys one-time rights.

Columns/Departments: Reproducible feature (how-to), 1,400 words. **Buys 4 mss/year.** Query with published clips. Pay varies.

Tips: "We plan our editorial calendar at least two or three issues in advance, and organize our issues around themes more often than not. Contact us for our upcoming themes."

$ $ $ THE NEW REPUBLIC, 1220 19th St. NW, Washington DC 20036. (202)331-7494. Fax: (202)331-0275. Editor-in-Chief: Martin Peretz. "*The New Republic* is a weekly journal of opinion with an emphasis on politics and domestic and international affairs. It carries feature articles by staff and contributing editors. The second half of each issue is devoted to books and the arts." This magazine did not respond to our request for information. Query.

$ $ POLICY REVIEW: The Journal of American Citizenship, The Heritage Foundation, 214 Massachusetts Ave. NE, Washington DC 20002. (202)546-4400. Editor: Adam Meyerson. **Contact:** D.W. Miller, managing editor; Joe Loconte, deputy editor. Bimonthly magazine. "We have been described as 'the most thoughtful, the most influential and the most provocative publication of the intellectual right.' *Policy Review* illuminates the families, communities, voluntary associations, churches and other religious organizations, business enterprises, public and private schools, and local governments that are solving problems more effectively than large, centralized, bureaucratic government." Estab. 1977. Circ. 30,000. Pays on publication. Byline given.

Nonfiction: "We are looking especially for articles on private and local institutions that are putting the family back together, cutting crime, improving education and repairing the bankruptcy of government." **Buys 4 mss/year.** Send complete ms. Length: 2,000-6,000 words. **Pays average $500.**

$ POLITICALLY CORRECT MAGAZINE, Turquoise Butterfly Press, P.O. Box 750, Athens OH 45701-0750. (614)664-3030. E-mail: tuqbutfy@bright.net. **Contact:** Terri J. Andrews, editor. **50% freelance written.** Quarterly alternative teen magazine. "*Politically Correct* is an alternative, 'underground' black and white small press magazine that allows teens to speak out and up—about the issues, laws, politics and people that pertain to them." Estab. 1997. Pays on publication. Publishes ms an average of 4 months after acceptance. Byline given. Offers 50% kill fee. Buys one-time rights. Editorial lead time 3 months. Submit seasonal material 4 months in advance. Reports in 6 weeks. Sample copy for $5. Writer's guidelines for #10 SASE.

Nonfiction: Book excerpts, essays, exposé, general interest, historical/nostalgic, how-to, humor, inspirational, interview/profile, opinion, personal experience. **Buys 12 mss/year.** Query or send complete ms. Length: 100-3,000 words. **Pays 1¢/word.** Sometimes pays writers with contributor copies or other premiums when writer agrees.

Reprints: Send photocopy of article or ms with rights for sale noted and information about when and where the article previously appeared. Negotiates fee.

Photos: Send photos alone or with submission. Reviews contact sheets. Negotiates payment individually. Captions, model releases, identification of subjects required. Buys one-time rights.

Fillers: Anecdotes, facts, gags to be illustrated by cartoonist, newsbreaks, poetry, short humor. **Buys 24/year.** Length: 20-200 words. **Pays 1¢/word.**

Tips: "Teens and college age students have the best chance of getting published in *P.C.* The shorter the piece, the better! We are interested in any topic that would pertain to young adults—from teen pregnancy and alcohol advertising to women in history and today's political systems. If young people are talking about it, we want to publish it!"

$ $ THE PROGRESSIVE, 409 E. Main St., Madison WI 53703-2899. (608)257-4626. Fax: (608)257-3373. E-mail: progressive@peacenet.org. Website: http://www.progressive.org. **Contact:** Matthew Rothschild, editor. **75% freelance written.** Monthly. Estab. 1909. Pays on publication. Publishes ms an average of 6 weeks after acceptance. Byline given. Buys all rights. Reports in 1 month. Sample copy for 9×12 SAE with 4 first-class stamps. Guidelines for #10 SASE.

Nonfiction: Primarily interested in articles which interpret, from a progressive point of view, domestic and world affairs. Occasional lighter features. "*The Progressive* is a *political* publication. General-interest material is inappropriate." Query. Length: 500-4,000 words maximum. **Pays $100-500.**

Tips: "*The Progressive* is always looking for writers who can describe and explain political, social and economic developments in a way that will interest non-specialists. We like articles that recount specific experiences of real people to illustrate larger points. We're looking for writing that is thoughtful, clear and graceful, conversational and non-academic. Display some familiarity with our magazine, its interests and concerns, its format and style. We want query letters that fully describe the proposed article without attempting to sell it—and that give an indication of the writer's competence to deal with the subject."

N $ $ $ REASON, Free Minds and Free Markets, Reason Foundation, 3415 S. Sepulveda Blvd., Suite 400, Los Angeles CA 90034. (310)391-2245. Fax: (310)391-4395. E-mail: editor@reason.com. Editor: Virginia Postrel. Managing Editor: Rick Henderson. **Contact**: Brian Doherty, assistant editor. **50% freelance written.** Monthly magazine covering politics, current events, culture, ideas. "*Reason* covers politics, culture and ideas from a dynamic libertarian perspective. It features reported works, opinion pieces, and book reviews." Estab. 1968. Circ. 55,000. **Pays on acceptance**. Byline given. Offers 33% kill fee. Buys first North American serial rights, first rights or all rights. Editorial lead time 2 months. Submit seasonal material 3 months in advance. Reports in 6 weeks on queries; 2 months on mss. Sample copy for $4. Writer's guidelines free.

Nonfiction: Book excerpts, essays, exposé, general interest, humor, interview/profile, opinion. No products, personal experience, how-to, travel. **Buys 50-60 mss/year.** Query with published clips. Length: 1,000-5,000 words. **Pays $250-1,000.** Sometimes pays expenses of writers on assignment.

Tips: "We prefer queries of no more than one or two pages with specifically developed ideas about a given topic rather than more general areas of interest. Enclosing a few published clips also helps."

$ $ TOWARD FREEDOM, A progressive perspective on world events, Toward Freedom Inc., P.O. Box 468, Burlington VT 05422-0468. (802)658-2523. Fax: (802)658-3738. E-mail: tfmag@aol.com. Website: http://www.towardfreedom.com. Editor: Greg Guma. **75% freelance written.** Political magazine published 8 times/year covering politics/culture, focus on Third World, Europe and global trends. "*Toward Freedom* is an internationalist journal with a progressive perspective on political, cultural, human rights and environmental issues around the world. Also covers the United Nations, the post-nationalist movements and U.S. foreign policy." Estab. 1952. Byline given. Circ. 3,500. Pays on publication. Kill fee "rare–negotiable." Buys first North American serial and one-time rights. Editorial lead time 1 month. Reports in 1-3 months on queries and mss. Sample copy for $3. Writer's guidelines free.

Nonfiction: Features, essays, book reviews, interview/profile, opinion, personal experience, travel, foreign, political analysis. Special issues: Women's Visions (March); Global Media (December/January). No how-to, fiction. **Buys 80-100 mss/year.** Query. Length: 700-2,500 words. **Pays up to 10¢/word.**

Photos: Send photos with submission, if available. Reviews any prints. Offers $35 maximum/photo. Identification of subjects required. Buys one-time rights.

Columns/Departments: *TF* Reports (from foreign correspondents), UN, Population, Art and Book Reviews, 800-1,200 words. **Buys 20-30 mss/year.** Query. **Pays up to 10¢/word.** Last Word (creative commentary), 900 words. **Buys 8/year.** Query. **Pays $100.**

Tips: "Except for book or other reviews, writers should have first-hand knowledge of country, political situation, foreign policy, etc., on which they are writing. Occasional cultural 'travelogues' accepted, especially those that would enlighten our readers about a different way of life. Writing must be professional."

PSYCHOLOGY AND SELF-IMPROVEMENT

These publications focus on psychological topics, how and why readers can improve their own outlooks, and how to understand people in general. Many General Interest, Men's and Women's publications also publish articles in these areas. Magazines treating spiritual development appear in the Astrology, Metaphysical and New Age section, as well as in Religion, while markets for holistic mind/body healing strategies are listed in Health and Fitness.

$ THE HEALING WOMAN, The Monthly Newsletter for Women Survivors of Childhood Sexual Abuse, P.O. Box 28040, San Jose CA 95159. (408)246-1788. Fax: (408)247-4309. E-mail: healingw@healingwoman.com. Website: http://www.healingwoman.org. Publisher/Editorial Director: Anita Montero. **Contact:** Molly Fisk, editor. **70% freelance written.** Bimonthly newsletter covering recovery from childhood sexual abuse. "Submissions accepted only from writers with personal or professional experience with childhood sexual abuse. We are looking for intelligent, honest and compassionate articles on topics of interest to survivors. We also publish first-person stories, poetry, interviews and book reviews." Estab. 1992. Circ. 11,000. **Pays on acceptance**. Publishes ms an average of 3 months after acceptance. Byline given. Offers 50% kill fee. Buys first North American serial rights and one-time electronic rights. Submit seasonal material 4 months in advance. Submit no more than 3 pieces at a time. Reports in 1 month on queries. Writer's guidelines for #10 SASE. "No fax or e-mail submissions please."

Nonfiction: Book excerpts, essays, general interest, interview/profile, opinion, personal experience. "No articles on topics with which the writer has not had first-hand experience. If you've been there, you can write about it for us. If not, don't write about it." **Buys 30 mss/year.** Query with published clips. Length: 300-2,500 words. **Pays $25-50.** "Pays in copies for poems, short first-person pieces."

Reprints: Send photocopy of article or typed ms with rights for sale noted and information about when and where the article previously appeared. Pay negotiable.

Photos: Send photos with submission. Negotiates payment for photos individually. Identification of subjects required. Buys one-time rights.

Columns/Departments: Book Reviews (books or accounts of incest survivors, therapy for incest survivors), 500-600 words; and Survivors Speak Out (first-person stories of recovery), 200-400 words.

Poetry: No poems preoccupied with painful aspects of sexual abuse. 40 line limit. Buys 25 poems/year. Pays copies.

Tips: "Although our subject matter is painful, *The Healing Woman* is not about suffering—it's about healing. Our department called 'Survivors Speak Out' features short, honest, insightful first-person essays with a conversational tone. We are happy to work with unpublished writers in this department. Articles should be more storytelling than lecture. In other words, articles should include your own—or your clients'—first-hand experiences in struggling and coping with the issues you are writing about. Specific examples should be used to illustrate your points, and the more the better. This is extremely important to us."

$ $ $ $ PSYCHOLOGY TODAY, Sussex Publishers, Inc., 49 E. 21st St., 11th Floor, New York NY 10010. (212)260-7210, ext. 134. Fax: (212)260-7445. **Contact:** Peter Doskoch, executive editor. Bimonthly magazine. "*Psychology Today* explores every aspect of human behavior, from the cultural trends that shape the way we think and feel to the intricacies of modern neuroscience. We're sort of a hybrid of a science magazine, a health magazine and a self-help magazine. While we're read by many psychologists, therapists and social workers, most of our readers are simply intelligent and curious people interested in the psyche and the self." Estab. 1967. Circ. 331,400. Pays on publication. Publishes ms an average of 3 months after acceptance. Byline given. Buys first North American serial rights. Editorial lead time 5 months. Reports in 1 month. Sample copy for $3.50. Writer's guidelines for #10 SASE.

Nonfiction: "Nearly any subject related to psychology is fair game. We value originality, insight and good reporting; we're not intereted in stories or topics that have already been covered *ad nauseum* by other magazines unles you can provide a fresh new twist and much more depth. We're not interested in simple-minded 'pop psychology.' " No fiction, poetry or first-person essays on "How I Conquered Mental Disorder X." **Buys 20-25 mss/year.** Query with published clips. Length: 1,500-5,000 words. **Pays $1,000-2,500.**

Columns/Departments: Contact: News Editor. News & Trends (short pieces, mostly written by staff, occasionally by freelancers), 150-300 words; Style (looks at trends in style from a psychological point of view), 600 words. Query with published clips to news editor. **Pays $150-500.**

$ SCIENCE OF MIND MAGAZINE, 3251 W. Sixth St., P.O. Box 75127, Los Angeles CA 90075-0127. (213)388-2181. Fax: (213)388-1926. E-mail: edit@scienceofmind.com. Website: http://www.scienceofmind.com. Editor: Elaine Sonne. **Contact:** Jim Shea, assistant editor. **30% freelance written.** Monthly magazine that features articles on spirituality, self-help and inspiration. "Our publication centers on oneness of all life and spiritual empowerment through the application of Science of Mind principles." Pays on publication. Publishes ms an average of 5 months after acceptance. Byline given. Buys first North American serial rights. Submit seasonal material 6 months in advance. Reports in 6 weeks on queries; 3 months on mss. Writer's guidelines free.

Nonfiction: Book excerpts, inspirational, personal experience of Science of Mind, spiritual. **Buys 35-45 mss/year.** Query only. Length: 750-2,000 words. **Pays $25/printed page.** Pays in copies for some features written by readers.

Photos: Reviews 35mm transparencies and 5×7 or 8×10 b&w prints. Buys one-time rights.

Poetry: Inspirational and Science of Mind oriented. "We are not interested in poetry not related to Science of Mind principles." **Buys 10-15 poems/year.** Length: 7-25 lines. **Pays $25.**

Tips: "We are interested in first person experiences of a spiritual nature having to do with the Science of Mind."

REGIONAL

Many regional publications rely on staff-written material, but others accept work from freelance writers who live in or know the region. The best regional publication to target with your submissions is usually the one in your hometown, whether it's a city or state magazine or a Sunday supplement in a newspaper. Since you are familiar with the region, it is easier to propose suitable story ideas.

Listed first are general interest magazines slanted toward residents of and visitors to a particular region. Next, regional publications are categorized alphabetically by state, followed by Canada. Publications that report on the business climate of a region are grouped in the regional division of the Business and Finance category. Recreation and travel publications specific to a geographical area are listed in the Travel, Camping and Trailer section. Keep in mind also that many regional publications specialize in specific areas, and are listed according to those sections. Regional publications are not listed if they only accept material from a select group of freelancers in their area or if they did not want to receive the number of queries and manuscripts a national listing would attract. If you know of a regional magazine that is not listed, approach it by asking for writer's guidelines before you send unsolicited material.

General

☆ $ $ BLUE RIDGE COUNTRY, Leisure Publishing, P.O. Box 21535, Roanoke VA 24018-9900. (703)989-6138. Fax: (703)989-7603. E-mail: leisure@roanoke.infi.net. **Contact**: Kurt Rheinheimer, editor-in-chief. **75% freelance written.** Bimonthly magazine. "The magazine is designed to celebrate the history, heritage and beauty of the Blue Ridge region. It is aimed at the adult, upscale readers who enjoy living or traveling in the mountain regions of Virginia, North Carolina, West Virginia, Maryland, Kentucky, Tennessee, South Carolina and Georgia." Estab. 1988. Circ. 75,000. Pays on publication. Publishes ms an average of 8 months after acceptance. Byline given. Offers $50 kill fee for commissioned pieces only. Buys first and second serial (reprint) rights. Submit seasonal material 6 months in advance. Reports in 2 months. Sample copy for 9×12 SAE with 6 first-class stamps. Writer's guidelines for #10 SASE.
Nonfiction: General interest, historical/nostalgic, personal experience, photo feature, travel, history. "Looking for more backroads travel, history and legend/lore pieces." **Buys 25-30 mss/year.** Query with or without published clips or send complete ms. Length: 500-1,800 words. **Pays $50-250 for assigned articles; $25-250 for unsolicited articles.**
Photos: Send photos with submission. Prefers transparencies. Offers $10-25/photo and $100 for cover photo. Identification of subjects required. Buys all rights.
Columns/Departments: Country Roads (shorts on people, events, travel, ecology, history, antiques, books). **Buys 12-24 mss/year.** Query. **Pays $10-40.**
Tips: "Freelancers needed for regional departmental shorts and 'macro' issues affecting whole region. Need field reporters from all areas of Blue Ridge region. Also, we need updates on the Blue Ridge Parkway, Appalachian Trail, national forests, ecological issues, preservation movements."

$ $ NORTHWEST TRAVEL, Northwest Regional Magazines, 1525 12th St., P.O. Box 18000, Florence OR 97439. (541)997-8401. (800)348-8401. Fax: (541)997-1124. Contact: Judy Fleagle,co-editor. Co-editor: Jim Forst. **60% freelance written.** Bimonthly magazine. "We like energetic writing about popular activities and destinations in the Pacific Northwest. *Northwest Travel* aims to give readers practical ideas on where to go in the region. Magazine covers Oregon, Washington, Idaho and British Columbia; occasionally Alaska and Western Montana." Estab. 1991. Circ. 50,000. Pays after publication. Publishes ms an average of 8 months after acceptance. Buys first North American serial rights. Submit seasonal material 6 months in advance. Reports in 1 month on queries; 3 months on mss. Sample copy for $4.50. Writer's guidelines for #10 SASE.

- *Northwest Travel* now emphasizes day trips or loop drives in the Pacific Northwest area.

Nonfiction: Book excerpts, general interest, historical/nostalgic, interview/profile (rarely), photo feature, travel (only in Northwest region). "No cliché-ridden pieces on places that everyone covers." **Buys 40 mss/year.** Query with or without published clips. Length: 1,250-2,000 words. **Pays $100-350** for feature articles and 2-5 contributor copies.
Reprints: Rarely accepts reprints of previously published submissions. Send photocopy of article or short story and information about when and where the article appeared. Pays 60% of amount paid for an original article.
Photos: State availability of photos with submission. Reviews transparencies (prefers dupes) and prints ("for good color we need reproduction negatives with prints"). Captions, model releases (cover photos), credits and identification of subjects required. Buys one-time rights.
Columns/Departments: Restaurant Features, 1,000 words. Pays $125. Worth a Stop (brief items describing places "worth a stop"), 300-500 words. **Buys 25-30 mss/year.** Send complete ms. **Pays $50.** Back Page (photo and text package on a specific activity, season or festival with some technical photo info), 80-100 words and 1 photo. **Pays $75.**
Tips: "Write fresh, lively copy (avoid clichés) and cover exciting travel topics in the region that haven't been covered in other magazines. A story with stunning photos will get serious consideration. Areas most open to freelancers are Worth a Stop and the Restaurant Feature. Take us to fascinating and interesting places we might not otherwise discover."

$ $ NOW AND THEN, The Appalachian Magazine, Center for Appalachian Studies and Services, P.O. Box 70556-ETSU, Johnson City TN 37614-0556. (423)439-6173. Fax: (423)439-6340. E-mail: woodsidj@etsu-tn.edu. Website: http://cass.etsu.edu/n+t/guidelin.html. Managing Editor: Nancy Fischman. **Contact**: Jane Harris Woodside, editor. **80% freelance written.** Magazine published 3 times/year covering Appalachian region from Southern New York to Northern Mississippi. "*Now & Then* accepts a variety of writing genres: fiction, poetry, nonfiction, essays, interviews, memoirs and book reviews. All submissions must relate to Appalachia and to the issue's specific theme. Our readership is educated and interested in the region." Estab. 1984. Circ. 1,000. Pays on publication. Publishes ms an average of 4 months after acceptance. Byline given. Buys all rights. Editorial lead time 5 months. Accepts simultaneous submissions. Reports in 5 months. Sample copy for $5. Writer's guidelines for #10 SASE or on website.
Nonfiction: Book excerpts, essays, general interest, historical/nostalgic, humor, interview/profile, opinion, personal experience, photo feature, book reviews of books from and about Appalachia. "No articles which have nothing to do with Appalachia; articles which blindly accept and employ regional stereotypes (dumb hillbillies, poor and downtrodden hillfolk and miners)." Special issues: Appalachian Architecture (November 1 deadline); Appalachian Biographies and Autobiographies (March 1 deadline); Appalachian Health Care (July 1 deadline). Query with published clips. Length: 1,000-2,500 words. **Pays $15-250 for assigned articles; $15-100 for unsolicited articles.** Sometimes pays expenses of writers on assignment.
Reprints: Send typed ms with rights for sale noted and information about when and where the article previously appeared. Pays 100% of amount paid for an original article. Typically $15-60.
Photos: State availability of photos with submission. Offers no additional payment for photos accepted with ms.

Captions and identification of subjects required. Buys one-time rights.

Fiction: Adventure, ethnic, experimental, fantasy, historical, humorous, mainstream, slice-of-life vignettes. "Fiction has to relate to Appalachia and to the issue's theme in some way." **Buys 3-4 mss/year.** Send complete ms. Length: 750-2,500 words. **Pays $15-100.**

Poetry: Free verse, haiku, light verse, traditional. "No stereotypical work about the region. I want to be surprised and embraced by the language, the ideas, even the form." **Buys 25-30 poems/year.** Submit 5 poems maximum. **Pays $10.**

Tips: "Get the Writers' Guidelines and read them carefully. Show in your cover letter that you know what the theme of the upcoming issue is and how your submission fits the theme."

⊘ **SOUTHERN LIVING** does not accept freelance submissions.

$ $ $ $ SUNSET MAGAZINE, Sunset Publishing Corp., 80 Willow Rd., Menlo Park CA 94025-3691. (650)321-3600. Fax: (650)327-7537. Website: http://www.sunsetmagazine.com. Editor-in-Chief: Rosalie Muller Wright. **Contact:** Editorial Services. Monthly magazine covering the lifestyle of the Western states. "*Sunset* is a Western lifestyle publication for educated, active consumers. Editorial provides localized information on gardening and travel, food and entertainment, home building and remodeling." Freelance articles should be timely and only about the 13 Western states. Pays on acceptance. Byline given. Guidelines for freelance travel items for #10 SASE addressed to Editorial Services.

Nonfiction: "Travel items account for the vast majority of *Sunset*'s freelance assignments, although we also contract out some short garden items. However, *Sunset* is largely staff-written." Travel in the West. **Buys 50-75 mss/year.** Length: 550-750 words. **Pays $1/word.** Query before submitting.

Columns/Departments: Departments open to freelancers are: Building & Crafts, Food, Garden, Travel. *Travel Guide* length: 300-350 words. Direct queries to the specific editorial department.

Tips: "Here are some subjects regularly treated in *Sunset*'s stories and Travel Guide items: outdoor recreation (i.e., bike tours, bird-watching spots, walking or driving tours of historic districts); indoor adventures (i.e., new museums and displays, hands-on science programs at aquariums or planetariums, specialty shopping); special events (i.e., festivals that celebrate a region's unique social, cultural, or agricultural heritage). Also looking for great weekend getaways, backroad drives, urban adventures and culinary discoveries such as ethnic dining enclaves. Planning and assigning begins a year before publication date."

$ $ $ $ YANKEE, Yankee Publishing Inc., P.O. Box 520, Dublin NH 03444-0520. (603)563-8111. Fax: (603)563-8252. E-mail: queries@yankeepub.com. Website: http://www.newengland.com. Editor: Judson D. Hale, Sr. Managing Editor: Tim Clark. **Contact**: Jeanne Wheaton, editorial assistant. **50% freelance written.** Monthly magazine that features articles on New England. "Our mission is to express and perhaps, indirectly, preserve the New England culture—and to do so in an entertaining way. Our audience is national and has one thing in common—they love New England." Estab. 1935. Circ. 700,000. Pays within 30 days of acceptance. Byline given. Offers 33% kill fee. Buys first rights. Submit seasonal material 6 months in advance. Accepts simultaneous submissions. Reports in 2 months on queries. Writer's guidelines for #10 SASE.

Nonfiction: Essays, general interest, historical/nostalgic, humor, interview/profile, personal experience. "No 'good old days' pieces, no dialect humor and nothing outside New England!" **Buys 30 mss/year.** Query with published clips and SASE. Length: 250-2,500 words. **Pays $800.** Pays expenses of writers on assignment.

- Ranked as one of the best market for freelance writers in *Writers Yearbook* magazine's annual "Top 100 Markets," January 1998.

Photos: Send photos with submission. Reviews contact sheets and transparencies. Offers $50-150/photo. Identification of subjects required. Buys one-time rights.

Columns/Departments: New England Sampler (short bits on interesting people, anecdotes, historical oddities), 100-400 words, **pays $50-200.** Great New England Cooks (profile recipes), 500 words, **pays $800.** Recipe with a History (family favorites that have a story behind them), 100-200 words plus recipe, **pays $50.** I Remember (nostalgia focused on specific incidents), 400-500 words, **pays $200.** Travel, 25-200 words, query first, **pays $25-250.** Last Page (personal or humorous essay that evokes New England place or time of year), 500-600 words, **pays $400. Buys 80 mss/year.** Query with published clips and SASE.

Fiction: Edie Clark, fiction editor. "We publish high-quality literary fiction that explores human issues and concerns in a specific place—New England." Publishes novel excerpts. **Buys 6 mss/year.** Send complete ms. Length: 500-2,500 words. **Pays $1,000.**

- Ranked as one of the best markets for fiction writers in *Writer's Digest* magazine's "Fiction 50," June 1998.

Poetry: Jean Burden, poetry editor. "We don't choose poetry by type. We look for the best. No inspirational, holiday-oriented, epic, limericks, etc." **Buys 40 poems/year.** Submit maximum 3 poems. Length: 2-20 lines. **Pays $50.**

Tips: "Submit lots of ideas. Don't censor yourself—let *us* decide whether an idea is good or bad. We might surprise you. Remember we've been publishing for 60 years, so chances are we've already done every 'classic' New England subject. Try to surprise us—it isn't easy. These departments are most open to freelancers: New England Sampler; I Remember; Recipe with a History. Study the ones we publish—the format should be apparent. It is to your advantage to read several issues of the magazine before sending us a query or a manuscript."

Alabama

$ $ ALABAMA HERITAGE, University of Alabama, Box 870342, Tuscaloosa AL 35487-0342. (205)348-7467. Fax: (205)348-7434. **Contact**: Suzanne Wolfe, editor. **50% freelance written.** "*Alabama Heritage* is a nonprofit historical quarterly published by the University of Alabama and the University of Alabama at Birmingham for the intelligent lay reader. We are interested in lively, well-written and thoroughly researched articles on Alabama/Southern history and culture. Readability and accuracy are essential." Estab. 1986. Pays on publication. Byline given. Buys first rights and second serial (reprint) rights. Reports in 1 month. Sample copy for $5. Writer's guidelines for #10 SASE.

Nonfiction: Historical. "We do not want fiction, poetry, book reviews, articles on current events or living artists and personal/family reminiscences." **Buys 10 mss/year.** Query. Length: 1,500-5,000 words. **Pays $100 minimum.** Also sends 10 copies to each author plus 1-year subscription.

Photos: Reviews contact sheets. Identification of subjects required. Buys one-time rights.

Tips: "Authors need to remember that we regard history as a fascinating subject, not as a dry recounting of dates and facts. Articles that are lively and engaging, in addition to being well researched, will find interested readers among our editors. No term papers, please. All areas are open to freelance writers. Best approach is a written query."

$ $ ALABAMA LIVING, Alabama Rural Electric Assn., P.O. Box 244014, Montgomery AL 36124. (334)215-2732. Fax: (334)215-2733. E-mail: area@mindspring.com. Website: http://www.areapower.com. **Contact**: Darryl Gates, editor. **10% freelance written.** Monthly magazine covering rural electric consumers. "Our magazine is an editorially balanced, informational and educational service to members of rural electric cooperatives. Our mix regularly includes Alabama history, nostalgia, gardening, outdoor and consumer pieces." Estab. 1948. Circ. 330,000. Pays on publication. Publishes ms an average of 3 months after acceptance. Byline given. Publication is not copyrighted. Buys second serial (reprint) rights. Editorial lead time 3 months. Submit seasonal material 4 months in advance. Accepts simultaneous submissions. Reports in 1 month on queries. Sample copy free.

Nonfiction: Historical/nostalgic, rural-oriented. Special issues: Gardening (November); Holiday Recipes (December). **Buys 6 mss/year.** Send complete ms (copy). Length: 300-750 words. **Pays $100 minimum for assigned articles; $40 minimum for unsolicited articles.**

Reprints: Send typed ms with rights for sale noted. **Pays $40.**

Tips: "The best way to break into *Alabama Living* is to give us a bit of history or nostalgia about Alabama or the Southeast."

N $ $ BIRMINGHAM WEEKLY, Birmingham Weekly Publishing Co., Inc., 2101 Magnolia Ave. S., Birmingham AL 35205. (205)322-2426. Fax: (205)322-0040. E-mail: editor@bhamweekly.com. **Contact**: Shawn Ryan, executive editor. **40% freelance written.** "We are an alternative newsweekly; alternative in the sense that we're an alternative to daily papers and TV news. We are edgy, hip, well written but based in solid journalism. Our audience is 18-54, educated with disposable income and an irreverant but intelligent point of view." Estab. 1997. Circ. 30,000. Pays on publication. Publishes ms an average of 2 weeks after acceptance. Byline given. Editorial lead time 3 weeks. Submit seasonal material 2 months in advance. Accepts simultaneous submissions. Reports in 2 weeks on queries. Sample copy free.

Nonfiction: Essays, exposé, general interest, historical/nostalgic, humor, interview/profile. "No opinion columns, i.e., op-ed stuff. We are strictly interested in stories that have a Birmingham connection, except in reviews, where the requirement is for readers to be able to buy the CD or book or see the film in Birmingham." Query with or without published clips. Length: 100-1,000 words. **Pays 10¢/word.** Sometimes pays expenses of writers on assignment.

Columns/Departments: Sound Advice (CD reviews), 100 words; Between the Covers (book reviews), 300 words. Query with or without published clips. **Pays 10¢/word.**

$ $ MOBILE BAY MONTHLY, PMT Publishing, P.O. Box 66200, Mobile AL 36660. (334)473-6269. Fax: (334)479-8822. **Contact:** Michelle Roberts, editor. **50% freelance written.** "*Mobile Bay Monthly* is a monthly lifestyle magazine for the South Alabama/Gulf Coast region focusing on the people, ideas, issues, arts, homes, food, culture and businesses that make Mobile an interesting place." Estab. 1990. Circ. 10,000. Pays on publication. Publishes ms an average of 4 months after acceptance. Byline given. Buys first rights. Editorial lead time 4 months. Submit seasonal material 6 months in advance. Sample copy for $2.

Nonfiction: Historical/nostalgic, interview/profile, personal experience, photo feature, travel. **Buys 10 mss/year.** Query with published clips. Length: 1,200-3,000 words. **Pays $100-300.**

Photos: State availability of photos with submission. Negotiates payment individually. Identification of subjects required. Buys one-time rights.

Tips: "We use mostly local writers. Strong familiarity with the Mobile area is a must. No phone calls; please send query letters with writing samples."

Alaska

★ $ $ $ ALASKA, The Magazine of Life on the Last Frontier, 4220 B St., Suite 210, Anchorage AK 99503. (907)561-4772. Fax: (907)561-5669. General Manager: David C. Foster. **Contact**: Bruce Woods, editor; Donna

Rae Thompson, editorial assistant. **80% freelance written.** Eager to work with new/unpublished writers. Monthly magazine covering topics "uniquely Alaskan." Estab. 1935. Circ. 205,000. Pays on publication. Publishes ms an average of 6 months after acceptance. Byline given. Buys first or one-time rights. Submit seasonal material 1 year in advance. Reports in 2 months. Sample copy for $3 and 9×12 SAE with 7 first-class stamps. Writer's guidelines for #10 SASE.

Nonfiction: Historical/nostalgic, adventure, how-to (on anything Alaskan), outdoor recreation (including hunting, fishing), humor, interview/profile, personal experience, photo feature. Also travel articles and Alaska destination stories. No fiction or poetry. **Buys 60 mss/year.** Query. Length: 100-2,500 words. **Pays $100-1,250.** Pays expenses of writers on assignment.

Photos: Send photos. Reviews 35mm or larger transparencies. Captions and identification of subjects required.

Tips: "We're looking for top-notch writing—original, well-researched, lively. Subjects must be distinctly Alaskan. A story on a mall in Alaska, for example, won't work for us; every state has malls. If you've got a story about a Juneau mall run by someone who is also a bush pilot and part-time trapper, maybe we'd be interested. The point is *Alaska* stories need to be vivid, focused and unique. Alaska is like nowhere else—we need our stories to be the same way."

Arizona

$ $ ARIZONA HIGHWAYS, 2039 W. Lewis Ave., Phoenix AZ 85009-9988. (602)271-5900. Fax: (602)254-4505. Website: http://www.arizonahighways.com. **Contact:** Rebecca Mong, managing editor. **90% freelance written.** Prefers to work with published/established writers. State-owned magazine designed to help attract tourists into and through Arizona. Estab. 1925. Circ. 425,000. **Pays on acceptance.** Buys first serial rights. Reports in up to 3 months. Writer's guidelines for SASE.

- Ranked as one of the best markets for freelance writers in *Writer's Yearbook* magazine's annual "Top 100 Markets," January 1998.

Nonfiction: Feature subjects include narratives and exposition dealing with history, anthropology, nature, wildlife, armchair travel, out of the way places, small towns, Old West history, Indian arts and crafts, travel, etc. Travel articles are experience-based. All must be oriented toward Arizona. **Buys 6 mss/issue.** Query with a lead paragraph and brief outline of story. "We deal with professionals only, so include list of current credits." Length: 600-2,000 words. **Pays 35-55¢/word.** Pays expenses of writers on assignment.

Photos: "We will use transparencies of 2¼×2¼, 4×5 or larger, and 35mm when they display exceptional quality or content. We prefer 35mm Kodachrome. Each transparency *must* be accompanied by information attached to each photograph: where, when, what. No photography will be reviewed by the editors unless the photographer's name appears on *each* and *every* transparency." Pays $80-350 for "selected" transparencies. Buys one-time rights.

Columns/Departments: Departments include Focus on Nature, Along the Way, Back-Road Adventure, Legends of the Lost, Hike of the Month and Arizona Humor. "Back Road and Hikes also must be experience-based."

Tips: "Writing must be of professional quality, warm, sincere, in-depth, well-peopled and accurate. Avoid themes that describe first trips to Arizona, the Grand Canyon, the desert, Colorado River running, etc. Emphasis is to be on Arizona adventure and romance as well as flora and fauna, when appropriate, and themes that can be photographed. Double check your manuscript for accuracy. Our typical reader is a 50-something person with the time, the inclination and the means to travel."

$ $ TUCSON LIFESTYLE, Citizen Publishing Company of Wisconsin, Inc., dba Old Pueblo Press, Suite 12, 7000 E. Tanque Verde Rd., Tucson AZ 85715-5318. (520)721-2929. Fax: (520)721-8665. E-mail: tucsonlife@aol.com. **Contact**: Scott Barker, executive editor. **90% freelance written.** Prefers to work with published/established writers. Monthly magazine covering Tucson-related events and topics. Estab. 1982. Circ. 27,000. **Pays on acceptance.** Publishes ms an average of 6 months after acceptance. Byline given. Buys first rights and second serial (reprint) rights. Submit seasonal material 1 year in advance. Reports in 2 months on queries; 3 months on mss. Sample copy for $2.50 plus $3 postage. Writer's guidelines free.

Nonfiction: All stories need a Tucson angle. Historical/nostalgic, humor, interview/profile, personal experience, travel, local stories. Special issues: Remodeling & Redecorating (October); In Health (November); New Homes (December). "We do not accept *anything* that does not pertain to Tucson or Arizona." **Buys 20 mss/year.** Query by mail or fax. **Pays $50-500.** Sometimes pays expenses of writers on assignment.

Photos: Reviews contact sheets, 2¼×2¼ transparencies and 5×7 prints. Offers $25-100/photo. Identification of subjects required. Buys one-time rights.

Columns/Departments: In Business (articles on Tucson businesses and business people); Lifestylers (profiles of interesting Tucsonans); Travel (Southwest, Baja and Mexico). Query. **Pays $100-200.**

Tips: Features are most open to freelancers. "Style is not of paramount importance; good, clean copy with interesting lead is a must."

California

N $ $ **BRNTWD MAGAZINE**, PTL Productions, 2118 Wilshire Blvd., #1060, Santa Monica CA 90403. (310)390-0251. Fax: (310)390-0261. E-mail: brntwdmag@aol.com. **Contact**: Dylan Nugent, editor. **100% freelance written.** Quarterly magazine covering entertainment, business, lifestyles, reviews. "Wanting in-depth interviews with top entertainers, politicians and similar individuals. Also travel, sports, adventure." Estab. 1995. Circ. 53,000. Pays on publication. Byline given. Editorial lead time 2-3 months. Submit seasonal material 3 months in advance. Accepts simultaneous submissions. Sample copy for $2. Writer's guidelines not available.
Nonfiction: Book excerpts, exposé, general interest, historical/nostalgic, humor, interview/profile, new product, opinion, personal experience, photo feature, travel. **Buys 80 mss/year.** Query with published clips. Length: 1,000-2,500 words. **Pays 10-15¢/word.**
Photos: State availability of photos with submission. Reviews contact sheets, negatives, transparencies, prints. Offers no additional payment for photos accepted with ms. Captions and identification of subjects required.
Columns/Departments: Reviews (film/books/theater/museum), 100-500 words; Sports (Southern California angle), 200-600 words. **Buys 20 mss/year.** Query with published clips or send complete ms. **Pays 10-15¢/word.**
Tips: "Los Angeles-based writers preferred for most articles."

$ $ $ $ **LOS ANGELES MAGAZINE**, ABC, 11100 Santa Monica Blvd., 7th Floor, Los Angeles CA 90025. (310)312-2200. Fax: (310)312-2285. **Contact:** Spencer Beck, editor-in-chief. **60% freelance written.** Monthly magazine about southern California. "Our editorial mission is to provide an authentic, compelling voice that engages and entertains one of the most media-savvy audiences in the world. Showcasing the diversity and vitality of the city, *Los Angeles*' quest is to deliver a timely, vibrant, must-read magazine that is witty, funny, sophisticated and skeptical but not cynical—a book that has regional resonance and national import." Estab. 1963. Circ. 174,000. Pays on publication. Publishes ms an average of 4 months after acceptance. Byline given. Offers 30% kill fee. Buys first North American serial rights. Submit seasonal material 6 months in advance. Reports in 3 months. Sample copy for $5. Writer's guidelines for #10 SASE.

- *Los Angeles Magazine* continues to do stories with local angles, but it is expanding its coverage to include topics of interest on a national level.

Nonfiction: "Coverage includes both high and low culture—people, places, politics, the Industry and lifestyle trends." Book excerpts (about L.A. or by famous L.A. author); exposé (any local issue); general interest; historical/nostalgic (about L.A. or Hollywood); interview/profile (about L.A. person). **Buys 100 mss/year.** Query with published clips. Length: 250-3,500 words. **Pays $50-2,000.** Sometimes pays expenses of writers on assignment.
Photos: Lisa Thackaberry, photo editor. Send photos.
Columns/Departments: Buys 170 mss/year. Query with published clips. Length: 250-1,200 words. **Pays $50-600.**
Tips: "*Los Angeles* magazine seeks a stimulating mix of timely journalism, eye-catching design and useful service pieces that will appeal to the broadest possible audience."

LOS ANGELES TIMES MAGAZINE, *Los Angeles Times*, Times Mirror Sq., Los Angeles CA 90053. (213)237-7000. Fax: (213)237-7386. **Contact:** Alice Short, editor. **50% freelance written.** Weekly magazine of regional general interest. Circ. 1,164,388. Payment schedule varies. Publishes ms an average of 2 months after acceptance. Byline given. Buys first North American serial rights. Submit seasonal material 3 months in advance. Accepts simultaneous submissions. Reports in 2 months. Sample copy and writer's guidelines free.
Nonfiction: General interest, investigative and narrative journalism, interview/profiles and reported essays. Covers California, the West, the nation and the world. Query with published clips only. Length: 2,500-4,500 words. Payment agreed upon expenses.
Photos: Query first; prefers to assign photos. Reviews color transparencies and b&w prints. Payment varies. Captions, model releases and identification of subjects required. Buys one-time rights.
Tips: "Prospective contributors should know their subject well and be able to explain why a story merits publication. Previous national magazine writing experience preferred."

$ $ **METRO**, Metro Newspapers, 550 S. 1st St., San Jose CA 95113-2806. (408)298-8000. Website: http://www.metroactive.com. Editor: Dan Pulcrano. Managing Editor: Corinne Asturias. **20-30% freelance written.** Weekly alternative newspaper. "*Metro* is for a sophisticated urban audience—stories must be more in-depth with an unusual slant not covered in daily newspapers. Subjects with local, Silicon Valley preferred." Estab. 1985. Circ. 212,000. Pays on publication from one week to two months. Publishes ms after acceptance. Byline given. Offers kill fee only with assignment memorandum signed by editor. Buys first North American serial and second serial (reprint) rights—non-exclusive. Submit seasonal material 3 months in advance. Reports in 2 months on queries; 4 months on mss. Sample copy for $4. Writer's guidelines for #10 SASE.
Nonfiction: Book excerpt, exposé and interview/profile (particularly entertainment oriented), personal essay. Some sort of local angle needed. **Buys 75 mss/year.** Query with published clips. Length: 500-4,000 words. **Pays $50-500.** Sometimes pays expenses of writers on assignment.
Reprints: Send photocopy of article including information about when and where it previously appeared. **Pays $25-200.**
Photos: Send photos with submission. Reviews contact sheets, negatives, any size transparencies and prints. Offers

$25-50/photo, more if used on cover. Captions, model releases, identification of subjects required. Buys one-time rights.
Columns/Departments: MetroMenu (food, dining out), 500-1,000 words; MetroGuide (entertainment features, interviews), 500-1,500 words. **Buys 75 mss/year.** Query with published clips. **Pays $25-200.**
Tips: "Seasonal features are most likely to be published, but we take only the best stuff. Local stories or national news events with a local angle will also be considered. Preferred submission format is Macintosh disk with printout. We are enthusiastic about receiving freelance inquiries. What impresses us most is newsworthy writing, compellingly presented. We define news broadly and consider it to include new information about old subjects as well as a new interpretation of old information. We like stories which illustrate broad trends by focusing in detail on specific examples."

$ $ METRO SANTA CRUZ, Metro Newspapers, 111 Union St., Santa Cruz CA 95060. (408)457-9000. Fax: (408)457-5829. E-mail: buz@metcruz.com. Website: http://www.metroactive.com. **Contact**: Buz Bezore, editor. **20-30% freelance written.** Weekly alternative newspaper. "*Metro* is for a sophisticated coastal university town audience—stories must be more in-depth with an unusual slant not covered in daily newspapers." Estab. 1994. Circ. 50,000. Pays on publication from 2-3 weeks. Publishes ms after acceptance. Byline given. Offers kill fee only with assignment memorandum signed by editor. Buys first North American serial and second serial (reprint) rights—nonexclusive. Submit seasonal material 3 months in advance. Reports in 2 months on queries; 4 months on mss.
Nonfiction: Features include a cover story of 3,000-3,500 words and a hometown story of 1,000-1,200 words about an interesting character. Book excerpt, exposé and interview/profile (particularly entertainment oriented), personal essay. Some local angle needed. **Buys 75 mss/year.** Query with published clips. Length: 500-4,000 words. **Pays $50-500.**
Reprints: Send photocopy of article including information about when and where it previously appeared. **Pays $25-200.**
Photos: Send photos with submission. Reviews contact sheets, negatives, any size transparencies and prints. Offers $25-50/photo, more if used on cover. Captions, model releases, identification of subjects required. Buys one-time rights.
Columns/Departments: MetroMenu (food, dining out), 500-1,000 words; MetroGuide (entertainment features, interviews), 500-3,000 words; Taste (quarterly), 3,000 words. **Buys 75 mss/year.** Query with published clips. **Pays $25-200.**
Tips: "Seasonal features are most likely to be published, but we take only the best stuff. Local stories or national news events with a local angle will also be considered. Preferred submission format is Macintosh disk with printout. We are enthusiastic about receiving freelance inquiries. What impresses us most is newsworthy writing, compellingly presented. We define news broadly and consider it to include new information about old subjects as well as a new interpretation of old information. We like stories which illustrate broad trends by focusing in detail on specific examples."

$ $ $ ORANGE COAST MAGAZINE, The Magazine of Orange County, Orange Coast Kommunications Inc., 3701 Birch St., Suite 100, Newport Beach CA 92660-2618. (714)862-1133. Fax: (714)862-0133. E-mail: ocmag@aol.com. Website: http://www.orangecoast.com. Managing Editor: Sharon Chan. **Contact**: Patrick Mott, editor. **95% freelance written.** Monthly magazine "designed to inform and enlighten the educated, upscale residents of Orange County, California; highly graphic and well researched." Estab. 1974. Circ. 40,000. **Pays on acceptance.** Publishes ms an average of 4 months after acceptance. Byline given. Buys one-time rights. Submit seasonal material at least 6 months in advance. Accepts simultaneous submissions. Reports in 2 months. Sample copy for $2.95 and 10×12 SAE with 8 first-class stamps. Writer's guidelines for SASE.
Nonfiction: Exposé (Orange County government, politics, business, crime), general interest (with Orange County focus); historical/nostalgic, guides to activities and services, interview/profile (prominent Orange County citizens), local sports, travel. Special issues: Health and Fitness (January); Dining and Entertainment (March); Home and Garden (June); Resort Guide (November); Holiday (December). **Buys 100 mss/year.** Query or send complete ms. Absolutely no phone queries. Length: 2,000-3,000 words. **Pays $400-800.**
Reprints: Send tearsheet or photocopy of article or typed ms with rights for sale noted and information about when and where the article previously appeared.
Columns/Departments: Most departments are not open to freelancers. **Buys 200 mss/year.** Query or send complete ms. Length: 1,000-2,000 words. **Pays $200 maximum.**
Fiction: Buys only under rare circumstances. Send complete ms. Length: 1,000-5,000 words. **Pays $250.**
Tips: "Most features are assigned to writers we've worked with before. Don't try to sell us 'generic' journalism. *Orange Coast* prefers articles with specific and unusual angles focused on Orange County. A lot of freelance writers ignore our Orange County focus. We get far too many generalized manuscripts."

N ☆ $ $ ORANGE COUNTY WOMAN, Orange Coast Publishing, 3701 Birch, Suite 100, Newport Beach CA 92660. (714)862-1133. Fax: (714)862-0133. E-mail: ocmag@aol.com. Website: http://www.orangecoast.com. **Contact**: Janine Robinson, editor. **90% freelance written.** "*Orange County Woman* is published monthly for the educated and affluent woman of Orange County, California." Estab. 1997. Present distribution: 65,000. **Pays on acceptance**. Publishes ms an average of 2 months after acceptance. Byline given. Offers 20% kill fee. Buys first North American serial and electronic rights. Editorial lead time 2 months. Submit seasonal material 4 months in advance. Accepts simultaneous submissions. Sample copy and writer's guidelines free.
Nonfiction: Essays, exposé, general interest, historical/nostalgic, how-to, humor, inspirational, interview/profile, new product, personal experience, photo feature, travel. Query with published clips or send complete ms and SASE. Length: 1,000-1,500 words. **Pays $50-200.**
Reprints: Send information about when and where the article previously appeared.
Photos: State availability of photos with submission or send photos with submission. Reviews contact sheets, negatives,

transparencies, prints. Negotiates payment individually. Captions, model releases and identification of subjects required. Buys one-time rights.

Columns/Departments: Seen & Heard (off-beat items/trends with strong local hook), 250 words. **Buys 20 mss/year.** Query with published clips or send complete ms. **Pays $75-500.**

Tips: "We are looking for profiles or trends related to women in Orange County—both for mothers and professionals. Read previous issues to gauge the range of story ideas and how they were handled. Write about real women in real situations; let their stories crystallize the broader issues. Remember that you are writing for an audience that generally is literate, wealthy and sophisticated, but avoid dry intellectual discourse. Our readers are busy women."

$ $ PALM SPRINGS LIFE, The Town & Club Magazine, Desert Publications, Inc., 303 N. Indian Canyon, Palm Springs CA 92262. (760)325-2333. Fax: (760)325-7008. Editor: Stewart Weiner. Contact: Sarah Hagerty, executive editor. **75% freelance written.** Monthly magazine covering "affluent resort/southern California/Palm Springs desert resorts. *Palm Springs Life* is a luxurious magazine aimed at the affluent market." Estab. 1958. Circ. 20,000. Pays on publication. Publishes ms an average of 3 months after acceptance. Byline given. Offers 25% kill fee. Buys all rights (negotiable). Submit seasonal material 6 months in advance. Reports in 3 weeks on queries. Sample copy for $3.95.

Nonfiction: Book excerpts, essays, interview/profile. Query with published clips. Length: 500-2,500 words. **Pays $50-750 for assigned articles; $25-500 for unsolicited articles.**

- Increased focus on desert region and business writing opportunities.

Photos: State availability of photos with submissions. Reviews contact sheets. Offers $5-125/photo. Captions, model releases, identification of subjects required. Buys all rights.

Columns/Departments: Around Town (local news), 50-250 words. **Buys 12 mss/year.** Query with or without published clips. **Pays $5-200.**

$ $ SACRAMENTO MAGAZINE, 4471 D St., Sacramento CA 95819. Fax: (916)452-6061. Managing Editor: Darlena Belushin McKay. **Contact**: Krista Minard, editor. **100% freelance written.** Works with a small number of new/unpublished writers each year. Monthly magazine with a strong local angle on politics, local issues, human interest and consumer items for readers in the middle to high income brackets. Estab. 1975. Circ. 19,610. Pays on publication. Publishes ms 3 months after acceptance. Rights vary; generally buys first North American serial rights, rarely second serial (reprint) rights. Reports in 2 months. Sample copy for $4.50. Writer's guidelines for #10 SASE.

Nonfiction: Local issues vital to Sacramento quality of life. **Buys 5 unsolicited feature mss/year.** Query first in writing. Length: 1,500-3,000 words, depending on author, subject matter and treatment. **Pays minimum $250.** Sometimes pays expenses of writers on assignment.

Photos: Send photos. Payment varies depending on photographer, subject matter and treatment. Captions (including IDs, location and date) required. Buys one-time rights.

Columns/Departments: Business, home and garden, media, parenting, first person essays, regional travel, gourmet, profile, sports, city arts (1,000-1,800 words); City Lights (250-400 words). **Pays $50-400.**

N $ $ SAN DIEGO MAGAZINE, San Diego Magazine Publishing Co., 401 W. A St., Suite 250, San Diego CA 92101. (619)230-9292. Fax: (619)230-9220. E-mail: rdonoho@sandiego-online.com. Editor: Tom Blair. **Contact:** Ron Donoho, managing editor. **30% freelance written.** Monthly magazine. "We produce informative and entertaining features about politics, community and neighborhood issues, sports, design and other facets of life in San Diego." Estab. 1948. Circ. 55,000. Pays on publication. Publishes ms an average of 2 months after acceptance. Byline given. Offers 25% kill fee. Buys first North American serial rights and second serial (reprint) rights. Editorial lead time 2 months. Submit seasonal material 4 months in advance. Accepts simultaneous submissions. Sample copy and writer's guidelines not available.

Nonfiction: Exposé, general interest, historical/nostalgic, how-to, humor, interview/profile, travel. **Buys 12-24 mss/year.** Query with published clips or send complete ms. Length: 1,000-3,000 words. **Pays $250-750.** Sometimes pays expenses of writers on assignment.

Photos: State availability of photos with submission. Offers no additional payment for photos accepted with ms. Buys one-time rights.

$ $ $ $ SAN FRANCISCO, Focus on the Bay Area, 243 Vallejo St., San Francisco CA 94111. (415)398-2800. Fax: (415)398-6777. E-mail: melanie@sanfran.com. Website: http://www.sanfran.com. **Contact**: Melanie Haiken, managing editor. **80% freelance written.** Prefers to work with published/established writers. Monthly city/regional magazine. Estab. 1968. Circ. 180,000. Pays on publication. Publishes ms an average of 2 months after acceptance. Byline given. Offers 25% kill fee. Submit seasonal material 5 months in advance. Reports in 2 months. Sample copy for $2.50. Writer's guidelines for SASE.

Nonfiction: Exposé, interview/profile, the arts, politics, public issues, sports, consumer affairs and travel. All stories should relate in some way to the San Francisco Bay Area (travel excepted). Query with published clips. Length: 750-4,000 words. **Pays $75-2,000** plus some expenses.

SAN FRANCISCO BAY GUARDIAN, 520 Hampshire St., San Francisco CA 94110-1417. (415)255-3100. Fax: (415)255-8762. E-mail: mandy@sfbg.com. Website: http://www.sfbg.com. Editor/Publisher: Bruce Brugmann. Contact: Mandy Weltman, editorial coordinator. **40% freelance written.** Works with a small number of new/unpublished writers each year. Weekly news magazine specializing in investigative, consumer and lifestyle reporting for a sophisticated, urban audience. Estab. 1966. Circ. 153,000. Pays 2 weeks after publication. Publishes ms an average of 1 month after acceptance. Byline given. **Buys 200 mss/year.** Buys first rights. Reports in 2 months.

Nonfiction: Gabriel Ruth, news editor; J.H. Tompkins, arts & entertainment editor; Miriam Wolf, features editor. Publishes "incisive local news stories, investigative reports, features, analysis and interpretation, how-to, consumer and entertainment reviews. Most stories have a Bay Area angle." Freelance material should have a "public interest advocacy journalism approach." Query with 3 clips. Sometimes pays the expenses of writers on assignment.

Reprints: Send tearsheet or photocopy of article and information about when and where the article previously appeared. Payment varies.

Photos: Elyse Hochstadt, art director. Purchased with or without mss.

Tips: "Work with our intern projects in investigative, political and consumer reporting. We teach the techniques and send interns out to do investigative research."

$ VENTURA COUNTY & COAST REPORTER, VCR Inc., 1567 Spinnaker Dr., Suite 202, Ventura CA 93001. (805)658-2244. Fax: (805)658-7803. E-mail: vcreporter@aol.com. **Contact:** Nancy Cloutier, editor. **12% freelance written.** Works with a small number of new/unpublished writers each year. Weekly tabloid covering local news. Circ. 35,000. Pays on publication. Publishes ms an average of 2 weeks after acceptance. Byline given. Buys first North American serial rights. Reports in 3 weeks.

Nonfiction: General interest (local slant), humor, interview/profile, travel (local—within 500 miles). Ventura County slant predominates. Length: 2-5 double-spaced typewritten pages. **Pays $10-25.**

Photos: Send photos with ms. Reviews b&w contact sheet.

Columns/Departments: Entertainment, Sports, Dining News, Real Estate, Boating Experience (Southern California). Send complete ms. **Pays $10-25.**

Tips: "As long as topics are up-beat with local slant, we'll consider them."

Colorado

$ $ STEAMBOAT MAGAZINE, Mac Media LLC, 2955 Village Dr., P.O. Box 4328, Steamboat Springs CO 80477. (303)879-5250 ext. 13. Fax: (970)879-4650. E-mail: dolsen@mtnmags.com. Website: http://www.steamboatweb.com. **Contact**: Deborah Olsen, editor. **80% freelance written.** Semiannual magazine "showcases the history, people, lifestyles and interests of Northwest Colorado. Our readers are generally well-educated, well-traveled, active people visiting our region to ski in winter and recreate in summer. They come from all 50 states and many foreign countries. Writing should be fresh, entertaining and informative." Estab. 1978. Circ. 20,000. Pays on publication. Publishes ms an average of 6 months after acceptance. Byline given. Buys one-time and electronic reprint rights. Editorial lead time 1 year. Submit seasonal material 1 year in advance. Accepts simultaneous submissions. Reports in 1 month on queries; 2 months on mss. Sample copy for $5.95 and SAE with 10 first-class stamps. Writer's guidelines free.

Nonfiction: Essays, general interest, historical/nostalgic, humor, interview/profile, personal experience, photo feature. **Buys 10-15 mss/year.** Query with published clips. Length: 500-3,000 words. **Pays $100-500 for assigned articles; $50-300 for unsolicited articles.** Sometimes pays expenses of writers on assignment.

Reprints: Send typed ms with rights for sale noted and information about when and where the article previously appeared. Payment negotiable.

Photos: State availability of photos with submission. Reviews transparencies. Offers $50-250/photo. Captions, model releases, identification of subjects required. Buys one-time rights.

Tips: "Western lifestyles, regional history, nature (including environmental subjects), sports and recreation are very popular topics for our readers. Please query first with ideas to make sure subjects are fresh and appropriate. We try to make subjects and treatments 'timeless' in nature because our magazine is a 'keeper' with a multi-year shelf life."

$ $ VAIL/BEAVER CREEK MAGAZINE, P.O. Box 1414, Vail CO 81658. (970)476-6600. Fax: (970)949-9176. E-mail: bergerd@vail.net. **Contact:** Don Berger, editor. **80% freelance written.** Semiannual magazine "showcases the lifestyles and history of the Vail Valley. We are particularly interested in personality profiles, home and design features, the arts, winter and summer recreation and adventure stories, and environmental articles." Estab. 1975. Circ. 30,000. Pays on publication. Publishes ms an average of 6 months after acceptance. Byline given. Offers 100% kill fee. Buys one-time rights. Editorial lead time 1 year. Submit seasonal material 1 year in advance. Accepts simultaneous submissions. Reports in 1 month on queries; 2 months on mss. Sample copy for $5.95 and SAE with 10 first-class stamps. Writer's guidelines free.

Nonfiction: Essays, general interest, historical/nostalgic, humor, interview/profile, personal experience, photo feature. **Buys 20-25 mss/year.** Query with published clips. Length: 500-3,000 words. **Pays 15-20¢/word.** Sometimes pays expenses of writers on assignment.

Reprints: Send typed ms with rights for sale noted and information about when and where it previously appeared.

Photos: State availability of photos with submission. Reviews transparencies. Offers $50-250/photo. Captions, model releases and identification of subjects required. Buys one-time rights.

Tips: "Be familiar with the Vail Valley and its 'personality.' Approach a story that will be relevant for several years to come. We produce a magazine that is a 'keeper.' "

Connecticut

$ $ $ CONNECTICUT MAGAZINE, Communications International, 35 Nutmeg Dr., Trumbull CT 06611. Fax: (203)380-6612. E-mail: ctmaga@pcnet.com. Website: http://www.connecticutmag.com. Editor: Charles Monagan. **Contact:** Dale Salm, managing editor. **80% freelance written.** Prefers to work with published/established writers who know the state and live/have lived here. Monthly magazine "for an affluent, sophisticated, suburban audience. We want only articles that pertain to living in Connecticut." Estab. 1971. Circ. 93,000. Pays on publication. Publishes ms an average of 4 months after acceptance. Byline given. Offers 20% kill fee. Buys first North American serial rights. Submit seasonal material 4 months in advance. Reports in 6 weeks on queries. Writer's guidelines for #10 SASE.

Nonfiction: Book excerpts, exposé, general interest, interview/profile, other topics of service to Connecticut readers. No personal essays. **Buys 50 mss/year.** Query with published clips. Length: 3,000 words maximum. **Pays $600-1,200.** Sometimes pays the expenses of writers on assignment.

Photos: Send photos with submission. Reviews contact sheets and transparencies. Offers $50 minimum/photo. Model releases and identification of subjects required. Buys one-time rights.

Columns/Departments: Business, Health, Politics, Connecticut Guide, Arts, Gardening, Environment, Education, People, Sports, Media. **Buys 50 mss/year.** Query with published clips. Length: 1,500-2,500 words. **Pays $400-700.**

Fillers: Short pieces about Connecticut trends, curiosities, interesting short subjects, etc. **Buys 50/year.** Length: 150-400 words. **Pays $75.**

Tips: "Make certain your idea has not been covered to death by the local press and can withstand a time lag of a few months. Freelancers can best break in with Around and About; find a story that is offbeat and write it in a lighthearted, interesting manner. Again, we don't want something that has already received a lot of press."

$ $ $ $ NORTHEAST MAGAZINE, *The Hartford Courant*, 285 Broad St., Hartford CT 06115-2510. (860)241-3700. Fax: (860)241-3853. E-mail: northeast@courant.com. Website: http://www.courant.com. **Contact**: Jane Bronfman, editorial assistant. Editor: Lary Bloom. **5% freelance written.** Eager to work with new/unpublished writers. Weekly Sunday magazine for a Connecticut audience. Estab. 1982. Circ. 316,000. **Pays on acceptance.** Publishes ms an average of 5 months after acceptance. Byline given. Buys one-time rights. Reports in 3 months.

Nonfiction: "We are primarily interested in hard-hitting nonfiction articles spun off the news and compelling personal stories, as well as humor, fashion, style and home. We have a strong emphasis on Connecticut subject matter." General interest (has to have strong Connecticut tie-in); in-depth investigation of stories behind news (has to have strong Connecticut tie-in); historical/nostalgic; personal essays (humorous or anecdotal). No poetry. **Buys 10 mss/year.** Length: 750-2,500 words. **Pays $200-1,500.**

Photos: Most assigned; state availability of photos. "Do not send originals."

Fiction: Well-written, original short stories and (rarely) novel excerpts. Length: 750-1,500 words.

Tips: "Less space available for all types of writing means our standards for acceptance will be much higher. We can only print three to four short stories a year recently confined to a yearly fiction issue. It is to your advantage to read several issues of the magazine before submitting a manuscript or query. Virtually all our pieces are solicited and assigned by us, with about two percent of what we publish coming in 'over the transom' (four pieces of about 150 in 1997)."

Delaware

N $ $ DELAWARE TODAY, 3301 Lancaster Pike, Suite 5C, Wilmington DE 19805. (302)656-1809. Fax: (302)656-5843. E-mail: editors@delawaretoday.com. Website: http://www.delawaretoday.com. **Contact:** Ted Spiker, editor. **40% freelance written.** "Monthly regional magazine geared toward Delaware people, places and issues. "All stories must have Delaware slant. No pitches such as Delawareans will be interested in a national topic." Estab. 1962. Circ. 25,000. Pays on publication. Publishes ms an average of 4 months after acceptance. Byline given. Offers 50% kill fee. Buys all rights for 1 year. Editorial lead time 3 months. Submit seasonal material 6 months in advance. Reports in 2 months on queries. Sample copy for $2.95.

Nonfiction: Historical/nostalgic, interview/profile, photo feature, lifestyles, issues. Special issue: Newcomer's Guide to Delaware. **Buys 40 mss/year.** Query with published clips. Length: 100-3,000 words. **Pays $50-750.** Sometimes pays expenses of writers on assignment.

Photos: State availability of photos with submission. Negotiates payment individually. Identification of subjects required. Buys one-time rights.

Columns/Departments: Business, Health, History, People, all 1,500 words. **Buys 24 mss/year.** Query with published clips. **Pays $150-250.**

Fillers: Anecdotes, newsbreaks, short humor. **Buys 10/year.** Length: 100-200 words. **Pays $50-75.**

Tips: "No story ideas that we would know about, i.e., a profile of the governor. Best bets are profiles of quirky/unique Delawareans that we'd never know about or think of."

District of Columbia

N $ $ $ THE WASHINGTONIAN, 1828 L St. NW, #200, Washington DC 20036. (202)296-3600. **Contact**: Landis Neal, communications director. Editor: Jack Limpert. **20-25% freelance written.** Monthly magazine. "Writers should keep in mind that we are a general interest city-and-regional magazine. Nearly all our articles have a hard Washington connection. And, please, no political satire." Estab. 1965. Circ. 160,000. Pays on publication. Publishes ms an average of 3 months after acceptance. Byline given. Buys first North American serial rights, limited, non-exclusive electronic rights. Editorial lead time 6 weeks. Writer's guidelines for #10 SASE.

Nonfiction: Book excerpts, general interest, historical/nostalgic (with specific Washington, DC focus), interview/profile, personal experience, photo feature, travel. **Buys 15-30 mss/year.** Query with published clips. **Pays 50¢/word.** Sometimes pays expenses of writers on assignment.

Columns/Departments: Howard Means, senior editor. First Person (personal experience that somehow illuminates life in Washington area), 650-700 words. **Buys 9-12 mss/year.** Query. **Pays $325.**

Tips: "The types of articles we publish include service pieces; profiles of people; investigative articles; rating pieces; institutional profiles; first-person articles; stories that cut across the grain of conventional thinking; articles that tell the reader how Washington got to be the way it is; light or satirical pieces (send the complete manuscript, not the idea, because in this case execution is everything); and fiction that tells readers how a part of Washington works or reveals something about the character or mood or people of Washington. Subjects of articles include the federal government, local government, dining out, sports, business, education, medicine, fashion, environment, how to make money, how to spend money, real estate, performing arts, visual arts, travel, health, nightlife, home and garden, self-improvement, places to go, things to do, and more. Again, we are interested in almost anything as long as it relates to the Washington area. We don't like puff pieces or what we call 'isn't-it-interesting' pieces. In general, we try to help our readers understand Washington better, to help our readers live better, and to make Washington a better place to live.

A magazine article is different from a newspaper story. Newspaper stories start with the most important facts, are written in short paragraphs with a lot of transitions, and usually can be cut from the bottom up. A magazine article usually is divided into sections that are like 400-word chapters of a very short book. The introductory section is very important—it captures the reader's interest and sets the tone for the article. Scenes or anecdotes often are used to draw the reader into the subject matter. The next section then might foreshadow what the article is about without trying to summarize it—you want to make the reader curious. Each succeeding section develops the subject. Any evaluations or conclusions come in the closing section."

Florida

$ $ BOCA RATON MAGAZINE, JES Publishing, 6413 Congress Ave., Suite 100, Boca Raton FL 33487. (561)997-8683. Fax: (561)997-8909. E-mail: bocamag@aol.com. Website: http://www.bocamag.com. **Contact**: Marie Speed, editor. Associate Editor: Gail Friedman. **70% freelance written.** Bimonthly lifestyle magazine "devoted to the residents of South Florida, featuring fashion, interior design, food, people, places and issues that shape the affluent South Florida market." Estab. 1981. Circ. 20,000. **Pays on acceptance.** Publishes ms an average of 3 months after acceptance. Byline given. Buys second serial (reprint) rights. Submit seasonal material 7 months in advance. Accepts simultaneous submissions. Reports in 1 month. Sample copy for $4.95 for 10×13 SAE with 10 first-class stamps. Writer's guidelines for #10 SASE.

Nonfiction: General interest, historical/nostalgic, humor, interview/profile, photo feature, travel. Special issues: Interior Design (September-October); Beauty (January-February); Health (July-August). Query with published clips, or send complete ms. Length: 800-2,500 words. **Pays $50-600 for assigned articles; $50-300 for unsolicited articles.**

Reprints: Send tearsheet of article. Payment varies.

Photos: Send photos with submission.

Columns/Departments: Body & Soul (health, fitness and beauty column, general interest), 1,000 words; Hitting Home (family and social interactions), 1,000 words. Query with published clips or send complete ms. **Pays $50-250.**

Tips: "We prefer shorter manuscripts, highly localized articles, excellent art/photography."

N $ $ FLORIDA LIVING MAGAZINE, Florida Media, Inc., 102 NE Tenth Ave., Suite 6, Gainesville FL 32601-2322. Fax: (352)372-3453. E-mail: flliving@earthlink.net. Website: http://www.floridaliving.org. Editor: E. Douglas Cifers. **Contact**: Kristen Crane, managing editor. Monthly lifestyle magazine covering Florida travel, food and dining, heritage, homes and gardens and all aspects of Florida lifestyle. Full calendar of events each month. Estab. 1981. Circ. 156,080. Publishes ms an average of 6 months after acceptance. Byline given. No kill fee. Buys first rights only. Submit seasonal material 1 year in advance. Reports in 2 months. Writer's guidelines sent on request with SASE.

Nonfiction: General Florida interest, historical/nostalgic, interview/profile, personal experience, travel, out-of-the-way Florida places, dining, attractions, festivals, shopping, resorts, bed & breakfast reviews, retirement real estate, business, finance, health, recreation and sports. **Buys 50-60 mss/year.** Query or submit ms with SASE. Length: 500-1,500 words. **Pays $25-200 for assigned articles; $25-100 for unsolicited articles.**

Photos: Send photos with submission. Reviews 3×5 color prints and slides. Offers $2-6/photo. Captions required.

Fiction: Historical. **Buys 2-3 mss/year.** Send complete ms. Length: 1,000-3,000 words. Publishes novel excerpts. **Pays $50-200.**

$ $ $ GULFSHORE LIFE, 2975 S. Horseshoe Dr., Suite 100, Naples FL 34104. (941)643-3933. Fax: (941)643-5017. E-mail: gsleditor@aol.com. **Contact**: Amy Bennett, editor. **75% freelance written.** Magazine published 11 times/year for "southwest Florida, the workings of its natural systems, its history, personalities, culture and lifestyle." Estab. 1970. Circ. 26,000. Pays on publication. Publishes ms an average of 4 months after acceptance. Byline given. Offers 25% kill fee. Buys first North American serial rights. Submit seasonal material 8 months in advance. Accepts simultaneous submissions. Sample copy for 9×12 SAE with 10 first-class stamps.

Nonfiction: Historical/nostalgic, interview/profile, issue/trend. All articles must be related to southwest Florida. **Buys 100 mss/year.** Query with published clips. Length: 500-3,000 words. **Pays $100-1,000.**

Photos: Send photos with submission, if available. Reviews 35mm transparencies and 5×7 prints. Pays $25-50. Model releases and identification of subjects required. Buys one-time rights.

Tips: "We buy superbly written stories that illuminate southwest Florida personalities, places and issues. Surprise us!"

N $ ISLAND LIFE, The Enchanting Barrier Islands of Florida's Southwest Gulf Coast, Island Life Publications, P.O. Box 929, Sanibel FL 33957. **Contact:** Joan Hooper, editor. **40% freelance written.** Prefers to work with published/established writers, but works with a small number of new/unpublished writers each year. Quarterly magazine of the Barrier Islands Sanibel, Captiva, Marco, for upper-income residents and vacationers of Florida's Gulf Coast area. Estab. 1980. Circ. 20,000. Pays on publication. Publishes ms 1 year after acceptance. Byline given. Buys first serial and second serial (reprint) rights. Accepts simultaneous submissions. Reports in 1 month on queries; 3 months on mss.

Nonfiction: General interest, historical. "Travel and interview/profile done by staff. Our past use of freelance work has been heavily on Florida wildlife (plant and animal) and sports, Florida cuisine, and Florida parks and conservancies. We are a regional magazine. No fiction or first-person experiences. No poetry. Our editorial emphasis is on the history, culture, wildlife, art, scenic, sports, social and leisure activities of the area." **Buys 10-20 mss/year.** Query with ms, photos and SASE. Length: 500-1,500 words. **Pays 3-8¢/word.**

Reprints: Send typed ms with rights for sale noted and information about when and where it previously appeared.

Photos: Send photos (color only) with ms. No additional payment. Captions, model releases, identification of subjects required.

Tips: "Submissions are rejected, most often, when writer sends other than SW Florida focus."

$ $ JACKSONVILLE, White Publishing Co., 1032 Hendricks Ave., Jacksonville FL 32207. (904)396-8666. Fax: (904)396-0926. Contact: Joseph White, managing editor. **80% freelance written.** Monthly magazine covering life and business in northeast Florida "for upwardly mobile residents of Jacksonville and the Beaches, Orange Park, St. Augustine and Amelia Island, Florida." Estab. 1985. Circ. 25,000. Pays on publication. Byline given. Offers 25-33% kill fee to writers on assignment. Buys first North American serial rights or second serial (reprint) rights. Editorial lead time 3 months. Submit seasonal 4 months in advance. Reports in 6 weeks on queries; 1 month on mss. Sample copy for $5 (includes postage). Writer's guidelines free.

Nonfiction: Book excerpts, exposé, general interest, historical, how-to (service articles), humor, interview/profile, personal experience, commentary, photo feature, travel, local business successes, trends, personalities, community issues, how institutions work. All articles *must* have relevance to Jacksonville and Florida's First Coast (Duval, Clay, St. Johns, Nassau, Baker counties). **Buys 50 mss/year.** Query with published clips. Length: 1,200-3,000 words. **Pays $50-500 for feature-length pieces.** Sometimes pays expenses of writers on assignment.

Reprints: Accepts reprints of previously published submissions. Send photocopy of article. Pay varies.

Photos: State availability of photos with submission. Reviews contact sheets, transparencies. Negotiates payment individually. Captions, model releases required. Buys one-time rights.

Columns/Departments: Business (trends, success stories, personalities), 1,000-1,200 words; Health (trends, emphasis on people, hopeful outlooks), 1,000-1,200 words; Smart Money (practical personal financial/advice using local people, anecdotes and examples), 1,000-1,200 words; Real Estate/Home (service, trends, home photo features), 1,000-1,200 words; Technology (local people and trends concerning electronics and computers), 1,000-1,200 words; Travel (weekends; daytrips; excursions locally and regionally, 1,000-1,200 words; occasional departments and columns covering local history, sports, family issues, etc. **Buys 40 mss/year. Pays $150-250.**

Tips: "We are a writer's magazine and demand writing that tells a story with flair."

$ $ MIAMI METRO MAGAZINE, (formerly *South Florida*), Florida Media Affiliates, 800 Douglas Rd., Suite 500, Coral Gables FL 33134. (305)445-4500. Fax: (305)445-4600. **Contact:** Felicia Levine, executive editor. **50% freelance written.** Monthly general interest magazine for Miami, Fort Lauderdale, the Florida Keys and Palm Beach County. Estab. 1975. Circ. 70,000. Pays 30-45 days after acceptance. Publishes ms an average of 3 months after acceptance. Byline given. Buys all North American serial rights. Submit seasonal material 4 months in advance. Reports in 2 months on queries. Sample copy for $3 plus 5 first-class stamps. Florida residents add 6% sales tax. Writer's guidelines for #10 SASE.

- *Miami Metro* has a new editorial focus—more topical, newsy, harder edged; fewer soft articles.

Nonfiction: Exposé, general interest, interview/profile, lifestyle. **Buys 60 mss/year.** Query with published clips. Length: 3,500 words maximum. **Pays $100-750.** Sometimes pays expenses of writers on assignment.

Photos: Send photos with submission. Identification of subjects required. Buys one-time rights.

Fiction: Publishes novel excerpts.

N $ $ ORLANDO WEEKLY, Alternative Media Inc., 807 S. Orlando, Suite R, Winter Park FL 32789. (407)645-5888. Fax: (407)645-2547. E-mail: orlandoweekly@aminc.com. Website: http://www.orlandoweekly.com. Managing Editor: Lawrence Budd. **Contact**: Jeff Truesdell, editor. 50% freelance written. Alternative weekly tabloid. "The *Orlando Weekly* covers news, entertainment, providing an alternative perspective to that provided by mainstream media. Our audience is 18-54, educated. We circulate 40,000 papers in Metropolitan Orlando." Estab. 1995. Circ. 42,000. **Pays on acceptance**. Byline given.

Nonfiction: Essays, exposé, general interest, interview/profile. Query. Length: 300-3,000 words. **Pays $50-250.** Sometimes pays expenses of writers on assignment.

$ SENIOR VOICE OF FLORIDA, Florida's Leading Newspaper for Active Mature Adults, Suncoast Publishing Group, 18860 US Hwy. 19N, Suite 151, Clearwater FL 33764-3168. Publisher: LoRee Russell. **Contact**: Nancy Yost, editor. **25% freelance written.** Prefers to work with published/established writers. Monthly newspaper serving the needs of mature adults 50 years of age and over on the Florida Gulf Coast. Estab. 1981. Circ. 70,000. Pays on publication. Publishes ms an average of 3 months after acceptance. Byline given. Buys one-time rights. Submit seasonal material 6 months in advance. Accepts simultaneous submissions. Reports in 2 months. Sample copy for $1 and 10×13 SAE with 6 first-class stamps. Writer's guidelines for SAE with 1 first-class stamp.

Nonfiction: General interest, historical, how-to, humor, inspirational, interview/profile, opinion, photo feature, travel, health, finance, all slanted to a senior audience. **Buys 10 mss/year.** Send complete ms. Length: 300-600 words. **Pays $5-15.**

Reprints: Send typed ms with rights for sale noted and information about when and where the article previously appeared. Pays 50% of amount paid for an original article. Pays flat fee.

Photos: Send photos with submission. Reviews 4×6 color and 5×7 b&w prints. Identification of subjects required.

Columns/Departments: Travel (senior slant) and V.I.P. Profiles (mature adults). **Buys 3 mss/year.** Send complete ms. Length: 300-600 words. **Pays $5-15.**

Fillers: Anecdotes, facts, cartoons, short humor. **Buys 3/year.** Length: 150-250 words. **Pays $5.**

Tips: "Our service area is the Florida Gulf Coast, an area with a high population of resident retirees and repeat visitors who are 50 plus. In writing for that readership, keep their interests in mind; what they are interested in, we are interested in. We like a clean, concise writing style. Photos are important."

$ $ $ SUNSHINE: THE MAGAZINE OF SOUTH FLORIDA, The Sun-Sentinel Co., 200 E. Las Olas Blvd., Fort Lauderdale FL 33301-2293. (305)356-4685. **60% freelance written.** Prefers to work with published/established writers, but works with a small number of new/unpublished writers each year. General interest Sunday magazine for the *Sun-Sentinel*'s 800,000 readers in south Florida. Pays within 1 month of acceptance. Publishes ms an average of 2 months after acceptance. Byline given. Offers 25% kill fee for assigned material. Buys first serial rights or one-time rights in the state of Florida. Submit seasonal material 2 months in advance. Accepts simultaneous submissions. Reports in 1 month on queries; 2 months on mss. Sample copy and writer's guidelines free.

Nonfiction: General interest, interview/profile, travel. "Articles must be relevant to the interests of adults living in south Florida." **Buys 150 mss/year.** Query with published clips. Length: 1,000-3,000 words; preferred length 2,000-2,500 words. **Pays 30-35¢/word to $1,200 maximum.**

Reprints: Send tearsheet or photocopy of article or typed ms with rights for sale noted and information about when and where the article previously appeared.

Photos: Send photos. Pays negotiable rate for 35mm and 2¼×2¼ color slides. Captions and identification of subjects required; model releases required for sensitive material. Buys one-time rights for the state of Florida.

Tips: "Do not phone, but do include your phone number on query letter. Keep your writing tight and concise—south Florida readers don't have the time to wade through masses of prose. We are always in the market for first-rate profiles, human-interest stories, travel stories and contributions to our regular 1,000-word features, 'First Person,' 'Weekenders' and 'Unsolved Mysteries.' "

N $ $ TALLAHASSEE MAGAZINE, 1932 Miccosokee Rd., P.O. Box 1837, Tallahassee FL 32308. (850)878-0554. Fax: (850)656-1871. Website: http://www.talmag.talstar.com. **Contact:** Kathleen M. Grobe, managing editor. **65% freelance written.** Bimonthly magazine covering Tallahassee area—North Florida and South Georgia. *Tallahassee Magazine* is dedicated to reflecting the changing needs of a capital city challenged by growth and increasing economic, political and social diversity. Estab. 1979. Circ. 17,300. **Pays on acceptance.** Publishes ms an average of 3 months after acceptance. Byline given. Buys one-time rights. Editorial lead time 6 months. Submit seasonal material 6 months in advance. Reports in 1 month. Sample copy for $2.95 and 8½×11 SASE. Writer's guidelines free.

Nonfiction: General interest, historical/nostalgic, humor, interview/profile, personal experience, photo feature, technical, travel. **Buys 10-12 mss/year.** Query or submit ms with SASE. Length: 800-3,500 words. **Pays $100-350.**

Reprints: Send typed ms with rights for sale noted and information about when and where the article previously appeared. **Pays $100-350.**

Photos: State availability of photos with submission. Reviews 35mm transparencies, 3×5 prints. Offers no additional payment for photos accepted with ms. Model releases and identification of subjects required. Buys one-time rights.

Columns/Departments: Humor, 800 words or less; College News (FSU/family TCC), 800 words or less; Cooking, 800 words or less. **Buys 12-18 mss/year.** Query. **Pays $100.**

Tips: "Know the area we cover. This area is unusual in terms of the geography and the people. We are a Southern city, not a Florida city, in many ways."

$ $ $ TROPIC MAGAZINE, Sunday Magazine of the Miami Herald, Knight Ridder, 1 Herald Plaza, Miami FL 33132-1693. (305)376-3432. Fax: (305)376-8930. E-mail: brose@herald.com. **Contact**: Bill Rose, editor. Executive Editor: Tom Shroder. **20% freelance written.** Works with small number of new/unpublished writers each year. Weekly magazine covering general interest, locally oriented topics for south Florida readers. Circ. 500,000. Pays on publication. Publishes ms an average of 2 months after acceptance. Byline given. Buys first serial rights. Submit seasonal material 2 months in advance. Reports in 3 months. Sample copy for 11×14 SAE.

Nonfiction: General interest, interview/profile (first person), personal experience. No poetry. **Buys 20 mss/year.** Query with published clips or send complete ms with SASE. Length: 1,500-3,000 words. **Pays $200-1,000/article.**

Reprints: Send photocopy of article or short story or typed ms with rights for sale noted and information about when and where the article or story previously appeared. Pays 50% of amount paid for an original article.

Photos: Janet Santelices, art director. Do not send original photos.

Fiction: Short fiction, novel excerpts (needs a strong local tie). Length: up to 900 words. Query with SASE.

Columns/Departments: Relationships. Length: 900 words. Query with SASE.

$ WATERFRONT NEWS, Ziegler Publishing Co., Inc., 1523 S. Andrews Ave., Ft. Lauderdale FL 33316-2507. (954)524-9450. Fax: (954)524-9464. E-mail: h2onews@aol.com. Website: http://hobbyline.com/public/waterfront.htm. **Contact**: Jennifer Heit, editor. **40% freelance written.** Monthly tabloid covering marine and boating topics for the Greater Ft. Lauderdale waterfront community. Estab. 1984. Circ. 36,000. Pays on publication. Publishes ms an average of 2 months after acceptance. Byline given. Buys first serial, second serial (reprint) rights or simultaneous rights in certain circumstances. Submit seasonal material 3 months in advance. Reports in 1 month on queries. Sample copy for 9×12 SAE with 4 first-class stamps.

- Travel pieces with a boaters slant are always welcome. Include photos, prints or digital.

Nonfiction: Regional articles on south Florida's waterfront issues; marine communities; profiles on people important in boating, i.e., racers, boat builders, designers, etc. from south Florida); trends in boating and waterfront lifestyle; some how-to (how-to find a good marina, boat mechanic, teach kids about sailing); humor with an eye toward boating topics. **Buys 50 mss/year.** Query with published clips. Length: 500-1,000 words. **Pays $50-125 for assigned articles; $25-150 for unsolicited articles.**

Photos: Send photos or send photos with submission. Reviews contact sheets and 3×5 or larger prints. Offers $15/photo. Buys one-time rights. Photos may be submitted digitally.

Tips: "Nonfiction marine, nautical or south Florida stories only. No fiction or poetry. Keep it under 1,000 words. Photos or illustrations help. Send for a sample copy of *Waterfront News* so you can acquaint yourself with our publication and our unique audience. Although we're not necessarily looking for technical articles, it helps if the writer has sailing or powerboating experience. Writers should be familiar with the region and be specific when dealing with local topics."

Georgia

$ $ $ $ ATLANTA, 1360 Peachtree St., Suite 1800, Atlanta GA 30309. **Contact**: Emma Edwards, executive editor. Monthly magazine devoted to Atlanta. It explores government, education, the arts, urban affairs, politics, regional happenings, restaurants, shopping, etc. for a general adult audience. "*Atlanta* magazine articulates the special nature of Atlanta and appeals to an audience that wants to understand and celebrate the uniqueness of the region. The magazine's mission is to serve as a tastemaker by virtue of in-depth information and authoritative, provocative explorations of issues, personalities and lifestyles." Circ. 51,142. **Pays on acceptance.** Byline given. Offers 20% kill fee. Buys first North American serial rights. Reports in 1 month on queries.

Nonfiction: Buys 36-40 mss/year. Query with published clips. Length: 1,500-5,000 words. **Pays $300-2,000.** Pays expenses of writer on assignment.

Columns/Departments: Buys 48 mss/year. Query with published clips. **Pays $500.** Length: 1,000-1,500 words.

Fiction: Publishes novel excerpts.

Fillers: Buys 120/year. Length: 75-175 words. **Pays $50-100.**

Tips: "Writers must know what makes their piece a story rather than just a subject."

N ★ $ FLAGPOLE MAGAZINE, Flagpole, P.O. Box 1027, Athens GA 30603. Fax: (706)548-8981. E-mail: editor@flagpole.com. Website: http://www.flagpole.com. **Contact**: Richard Fausset, editor. **75% freelance written.** Local "alternative" weekly with a special emphasis on popular (& unpopular) music. "Will consider stories on national, international musicians, authors, politicians, etc., even if they don't have a local or regional news peg. However, those stories should be original, irreverent enough to justify inclusion. Of course, local/Southern news/feature stories are best. We like reporting, storytelling more than opinion pieces." Estab. 1987. Circ. 16,000. Pays on publication. Publishes ms an average of 1 month after acceptance. Byline given. Makes work-for-hire assignments. Editorial lead time 1-2 months. Submit seasonal material 2 months in advance. Reports in 2 weeks on queries; 1 month on mss. Sample copy on Internet (flagpole@negia.net). Writer's guidelines not available.

Nonfiction: Book excerpts, essays, exposé, interview/profile, new product, personal experience. **Buys 200 mss/year.** Query with published clips. Length: 600-3,500 words. **Pays $10-100.** Sometimes pays expenses of writers on assignment.

Reprints: Send tearsheet, photocopy or typed ms with rights for sale noted and information about when and where the article previously appeared.

Photos: State availability of photos with submission. Reviews prints. Negotiates payment individually. Captions required. Buys all rights.

Columns/Departments: Lit. (book reviews), 800 words. **Buys 30 mss/year.** Send complete ms. **Pays $10.**

Tips: "Read our publication online before querying, but don't feel limited by what you see. We can't afford to pay much, so we're open to young/inexperienced writer-journalists looking for clips. Fresh, funny/insightful voices make us happiest, as does reportage over opinion. If you've ever succumbed to the temptation to call a pop record 'ethereal,' we probably won't bother with your music journalism. No faxed submissions, please."

$ $ GEORGIA JOURNAL, The Indispensable Atlanta Co., Inc., P.O. Box 1604, Decatur GA 30031-1604. (404)377-4275. Fax: (404)377-1820. E-mail: georgiajournal@compuserve.com. Website: http://www.georgiajournal.com. **Contact:** David R. Osier, editor. **90% freelance written.** Works with a small number of new/unpublished writers each year. Bimonthly magazine primarily interested in "*authoritative* nonfiction articles with a *well-defined point of view* on any aspect of Georgia's human and natural history." Estab. 1980. Circ. 40,000. Please query first. Pays on publication. Publishes ms an average of 1 year after acceptance. Byline given. Buys first serial rights. Submit seasonal material 6 months in advance. Reports in 6 months. Sample copy for $5. Writer's guidelines for #10 SASE.

Nonfiction: "*Georgia Journal* has published articles on the roles historic personalities played in shaping our state, important yet sometimes overlooked historical/political events, archaeological discoveries, unsolved mysteries (natural and human), flora and fauna, and historic preservation. Sidebars are encouraged, such as interesting marginalia and bibliographies. We also are looking for adventures that explore the Georgia landscape from weekend antique hunting, camping, walking tours, arts & crafts festivals, and auto trips to more strenuous activities such as biking, boating, rafting, back-packing, rock climbing and caving. Adventures should also have a well-defined point of view, and be told through the author's personal experience. Articles should be accompanied by detailed map data and other pertinent location information, such as tips on access, lodging and camping. *Georgia Journal* has a place for authoritative topical articles as well—Georgia's environment, mysteries and trends in living or profiles of Georgia authors, adventurers, artisans, artists, sports figures and other personalities." SASE for editorial calendar. **Buys 30-40 mss/year.** Query. Length: 200-5,000 words. **Pays 10¢/word.**

Reprints: Accepts previously published submissions. Send photocopy or typed ms of article or short story with rights for sale noted and information about when and where the article previously appeared. Pays 10% of amount paid for an original article.

Columns/Departments: Books and writers; interesting or historic houses/buildings; Commentary section; Pure Georgia—uses shorter pieces; Calendar of events; reviews of restaurants, B&Bs and historic inns.

Fiction: See submission guidelines. *Georgia Journal* publishes a limited amount of fiction, but while it encourages promising new writers, it is not looking for first-time or unpublished authors. Publishes novel excerpts. Optimum length is 4,000 words. Stories must have a Georgia theme or setting. Payment varies, depending on publishing history. Unless mss are submitted with a return envelope with sufficient postage, they will not be returned. Publishes novel excerpts.

Poetry: Contact: Janice Moore. Free verse, haiku, light verse, traditional. Uses poetry from or dealing with Georgia suitable for a general audience. Uses 20 poems/year. Submit maximum 4 poems. Length: 25 lines. Pays in copies.

$ $ GEORGIA MAGAZINE, Georgia Electric Membership Corp., P.O. Box 1707, Tucker GA 30085. (770)270-6950. Fax: (770)270-6995. E-mail: ann.orowski@georgiaemc.com. Website: http://www.Georgiamag.com. **Contact**: Ann Oronowski, editor. **50% freelance written.** "We are a monthly magazine for and about Georgians, with a friendly, conversational tone and human interest topics." Estab. 1945. Circ. 260,000. Pays on publication. Publishes ms an average of 4 months after acceptance. Byline given. Buys first North American serial rights and website rights. Editorial lead time 2 months. Submit seasonal material 6 months in advance. Accepts simultaneous submissions. Reports in 1 month on subjects of interest. Sample copy for $2 each. Writer's guidelines free.

Nonfiction: General interest, historical/nostalgic, how-to (in the home and garden), humor, inspirational, interview/profile, photo feature, travel. **Buys 8 mss/year.** Query with published clips. Length: 800-1,000 words; 500 words for smaller features and departments. **Pays $50-300.** Pays contributor copies upon negotiation. Sometimes pays expenses of writers on assignment.

Photos: State availability of photos with submission. Reviews contact sheets, transparencies, prints. Negotiates payment individually. Model releases, identification of subjects required. Buy one-time rights.

$ $ NORTH GEORGIA JOURNAL, Legacy Communications, Inc., P.O. Box 127, Roswell GA 30077. Fax: (770)642-1415. E-mail: sumail@mindspring.com. Website: http://mindspring.com/~north.ga.travel. **Contact:** Olin Jackson, editor. **70% freelance written.** Quarterly magazine "for readers interested in travel, history, and mountain lifestyles of north Georgia." Estab. 1984. Circ. 18,450. Pays on publication. Publishes ms an average of 5 months after acceptance. Byline given. Offers 25% kill fee. Buys first and all rights. Editorial lead time 6 months. Submit seasonal material 6 months in advance. Sample copy for 9×12 SAE and 8 first-class stamps. Writer's guidelines for #10 SASE.

Nonfiction: Historical/nostalgic, how-to (survival techniques; mountain living; do-it-yourself home construction and repairs, etc.), interview/profile (celebrity), personal experience (anything unique or unusual pertaining to north Georgia mountains), photo feature (any subject of a historic nature which can be photographed in a seasonal context, i.e.—old mill with brilliant yellow jonquils in foreground), travel (subjects highlighting travel opportunities in North Georgia). Query with published clips. **Pays $75-350.**

Photos: Send photos with submission. Reviews contact sheets, transparencies. Negotiates payment individually. Captions, model releases, identification of subjects required. Buys all rights.

Fiction: Publishes novel excerpts.
Tips: "Good photography is crucial to acceptance of all articles. Send written queries then *wait* for a response. *No telephone calls please.* The most useful material involves a first person experience of an individual who has explored a historic site or scenic locale and *interviewed* a person or persons who were involved with or have first-hand knowledge of a historic site/event. Interviews and quotations are crucial. Articles should be told in writer's own words."

Hawaii

$ $ ALOHA, THE MAGAZINE OF HAWAII AND THE PACIFIC, Davick Publications, P.O. Box 3260, Honolulu HI 96801. (808)593-1191. Fax: (808)593-1327. E-mail: alohamag@aol.com. **Contact:** Lance Tominaga, editorial director. **50% freelance written.** Bimonthly regional magazine of international interest. "Most of our readers do not live in Hawaii, although most readers have been to the Islands at least once. The magazine is directed primarily to residents of Hawaii in the belief that presenting material to an immediate critical audience will result in a true and accurate presentation that can be appreciated by everyone. Travelers to Hawaii will find *Aloha* shares vignettes of the real Hawaii." Estab. 1977. Circ. 95,000. Pays on publication. Publishes ms an average of 6 months after acceptance; unsolicited mss can take a year or more. Byline given. Offers variable kill fee. Buys first rights. Submit seasonal material 1 year in advance. Reports in 2 months. Sample copy for $2.95, SAE and 10 first-class stamps. Writer's guidelines free.
Nonfiction: Book excerpts, historical/nostalgic (historical articles must be researched with bibliography), interview/profile, photo features. Subjects include the arts, business, flora and fauna, people, sports, destinations, food, interiors, history of Hawaii. "We don't want stories of a tourist's experiences in Waikiki or odes to beautiful scenery." **Buys 24 mss/year.** Query with published clips. Length: 2,000-3,000 words average. **Pays $150-400.** Sometimes pays expenses of writers on assignment.
Photos: Send photos with query. Pays $25 for b&w prints; prefers negatives and contact sheets. Pays $75 for 35mm (minimum size) color transparencies used inside; $100 for full page; $125 for double-page bleeds; $250 for color transparencies used as cover art. "*ALOHA* features Beautiful Hawaii, a collection of photographs illustrating that theme, in every issue. A second photo essay by a sole photographer on a theme of his/her own choosing is also published occasionally. Queries are essential for the sole photographer essay." Model releases, identification of subjects are required. Buys one-time rights.
Fiction: Ethnic, historical. "Fiction depicting a tourist's adventures in Waikiki is not what we're looking for. As a general statement, we welcome material reflecting the true Hawaiian experience." **Buys 2 mss/year.** Send complete ms. Length: 1,000-2,500 words. **Pays $300.**
Poetry: Haiku, light verse, traditional. No seasonal poetry or poetry related to other areas of the world. **Buys 6 poems/year.** Submit maximum 6 poems. Prefers "shorter poetry"—20 lines or less. **Pays $30.**
Tips: "Read *Aloha*. Research meticulously and have good illustrative material to accompany your text."

$ $ HAWAII MAGAZINE, Fancy Publications, Inc., 1400 Kapiolani Blvd., A-25, Honolulu HI 96814. (808)942-2556. Fax: (808)947-0924. E-mail: hawaii@fancypubs.com. **Contact:** John Hollon, editorial director. **60% freelance written.** Bimonthly magazine "written for residents and frequent visitors who enjoy the culture, people and places of the Hawaiian Islands." Estab. 1984. Circ. 71,000. Pays on publication. Byline given. Buys first North American serial rights. Submit seasonal material 6 months in advance. Reports in 1 month on queries; 6 weeks on mss. Sample copy for $3.95. Writer's guidelines free.
Nonfiction: General interest, historical/nostalgic, how-to, interview/profile, personal experience, photo feature, travel. "No articles on the following: first trip to Hawaii, how I discovered the Islands, the Hula, Poi, or Luaus." **Buys 66 mss/year.** Query with or without published clips, or send complete ms. Length: 4,000 words maximum. **Pays $100-500.**
Photos: Send photos with submission. Reviews contact sheets and transparencies. Prefers color transparencies. Offers $35/photo. Identification of subjects preferred. Buys one-time rights.
Columns/Departments: Backdoor Hawaii (a light or nostalgic look at culture or history), 800-1,200 words; Hopping the Islands (news, general interest items), 100-200 words. **Buys 6-12 mss/year.** Query. Length: 800-1,500 words. **Pays $100-200.** New department, WeatherWatch, focuses on Hawaii weather phenomena (450 words). **Pays $50.**
Fiction: Publishes novel excerpts.
Tips: "Freelancers must be knowledgeable about Island subjects, virtual authorities on them. We see far too many first-person, wonderful-experience types of gushing articles. We buy articles only from people who are thoroughly grounded in the subject on which they are writing."

$ $ HONOLULU, Honolulu Publishing Co., Ltd., 36 Merchant St., Honolulu HI 96813. (808)524-7400. Fax: (808)531-2306. E-mail: honmag@pixi.com. Publisher: John Alves. **Contact**: John Heckathorn, editor. **50% freelance written.** Prefers to work with published/established writers. Monthly magazine covering general interest topics relating to Hawaii residents. Estab. 1888. Circ. 30,000. **Pays on acceptance.** Publishes ms an average of 4 months after acceptance. Byline given. Buys first-time rights. Submit seasonal material 5 months in advance. Accepts simultaneous submissions. Reports in 2 months. Sample copy for $2 and 9×12 SAE with 8 first-class stamps. Writer's guidelines free.
Nonfiction: Exposé, general interest, historical/nostalgic, photo feature—all Hawaii-related. "We write for Hawaii residents, so travel articles about Hawaii are not appropriate." **Buys 30 mss/year.** Query with published clips if available.

Length: 2,000-3,000 words. **Pays $100-700.** Sometimes pays expenses of writers on assignment.
Photos: Teresa Black, art director. Send photos. Pays $75-175 for single image inside; $500 maximum for cover. Captions and identification of subjects required as well as model release. Buys one-time rights.
Columns/Departments: Calabash ("newsy," timely, humorous department on any Hawaii-related subject). **Buys 15 mss/year.** Query with published clips or send complete ms. Length: 50-750 words. **Pays $35-100.** First Person (personal experience or humor). **Buys 10 mss/year.** Length: 1,500 words. **Pays $200-300.**

Idaho

N ☆ $ $ BOISE MAGAZINE, Earls Communications, P.O. Box 1457, 102 S. 17th St., Suite 100, Boise ID 83701. Fax: (208)338-0006. E-mail: boisemag@micron.net. **Contact**: Alan Minskoff, editor. **90% freelance written.** "*Boise Magazine* is a city/regional quarterly devoted to Idaho's capital and its environs. We publish profiles, articles, reviews and features on business, sports, the arts, politics, community development and have regular departments that cover travel, design, books, food and wine as well as a calendar of events and a section entitled Valley." Estab. 1997. Circ. 10,000. Pays on publication. Byline given. Buys first rights. Editorial lead time 3 months. Submit seasonal material 6 months in advance. Reports in 6 weeks on queries; 3 months on mss. Sample copy for $3.50. Writer's guidelines for #10 SASE.
Nonfiction: Book excerpts, essays, general interest, humor, photo feature, travel. **Buys 12 mss/year.** Query with published clip. Length: 500-3,500 words. **Pays 18-20¢/word.** Sometimes pays expenses of writers on assignment.
Photos: State availability of photos with submission. Negotiates payment individually. Model releases and identification of subjects required. Buys one-time rights.
Columns/Departments: Valley (short pieces on life around Boise), 500-1,250 words. **Buys 30 mss/year.** Query with published clips. **Pays 18-20¢/word.**
Fiction: Mainstream, novel excerpts, slice-of-life vignettes. No romance, science fiction, western, erotica, adventure, religious. **Buys 2-3 mss/year.** Query. Length: 1,000-2,500 words. **Pays 20¢/word.**
Tips: "The Valley and Book Reviews are the best entry-levels for freelance writers. Profiles and other departments are not as easy, and features are virtually all done by local writers."

$ $ SUN VALLEY MAGAZINE, Wood River Publishing, Drawer 697, Hailey ID 83333. (208)788-0770. Fax: (208)788-3881. E-mail: sumag@micron.net. **Contact**: Colleen Daly, editor. **95% freelance written.** Triannual magazine covering lifestyle of Sun Valley area (recreation, history, profiles). Estab. 1973. Circ. 15,000. Pays on publication. Publishes ms an average of 4 months after acceptance. Byline given. Buys first North American serial rights. Editorial lead time 1 year. Submit seasonal material 14 months in advance. Accepts simultaneous submissions. Reports in 1 month on queries; 6 weeks on mss. Sample copy for $3.95 and $3 postage.
Nonfiction: All articles are focused specifically on Sun Valley, the Wood River Valley and immediate surrounding areas. Special issues: Sun Valley Home Design (fall). Query with published clips. Length varies. **Pays $40-450.** Sometimes pays expenses of writers on assignment.
Reprints: Occasionally accepts previously published submissions.
Photos: State availability of photos with submission. Reviews transparencies. Offers $60-250/photo. Model releases, identification of subjects required. Buys one-time rights.
Columns/Departments: Conservation issues, winter/summer sports, mountain-related activities and subjects, home (interior design), garden. All must have local slant. Query with published clips. **Pays $40-250.**
Fiction: We use local writers exclusively.
Tips: "Most of our writers are locally based. Also, we rarely take submissions that are not specifically assigned, with the exception of fiction. However, we always appreciate queries."

Illinois

$ $ $ $ CHICAGO READER, Chicago's Free Weekly, Chicago Reader, Inc., 11 E. Illinois, Chicago IL 60611. (312)828-0350. Fax: (312)828-9926. E-mail: mail@chireader.com. Website: http://www.chireader.com. Editor: Alison True. **Contact**: Patrick Arden, managing editor. **50% freelance written.** Alternative weekly tabloid for Chicago. Estab. 1971. Circ. 136,000. Pays on publication. Publishes ms an average of 3 months after acceptance. Byline given. No kill fee. Buys one-time rights. Editorial lead time up to 6 months. Accepts simultaneous submissions. Responds if interested. Sample copy and writer's guidelines free.
Nonfiction: Book excerpts, essays, exposé, general interest, historical/nostalgic, humor, interview/profile, opinion, personal experience, photo feature. No celebrity interviews, national news or issues. **Buys 500 mss/year.** Send complete ms. Length: 4,000-50,000 words. **Pays $100-2,000.** Sometimes pays expenses of writers on assignment.
Reprints: Accepts previously published submissions.
Columns/Departments: Reading, First Person, Cityscape, Neighborhood News, all 1,500-2,500 words; arts and entertainment reviews, up to 1,200 words; calendar items, 400-1,000 words. **Pays $100-2,000.**
Tips: "Our greatest need is for full-length magazine-style feature stories on Chicago topics. We're *not* looking for:

hard news (What the Mayor Said About the Schools Yesterday); commentary and opinion (What I Think About What the Mayor Said About the Schools Yesterday); fiction; poetry. We are not particularly interested in stories of national (as opposed to local) scope, or in celebrity for celebrity's sake (a la *Rolling Stone*, *Interview*, etc.). More than half the articles published in the *Reader* each week come from freelancers, and once or twice a month we publish one that's come in 'over the transom'—from a writer we've never heard of and may never hear from again. We think that keeping the *Reader* open to the greatest possible number of contributors makes a fresher, less predictable, more interesting paper. We not only publish unsolicited freelance writing, we depend on it."

N $ $ CHICAGO SOCIAL, Chicago's Monthly Social Magazine, Prairie City Media, 727 N. Hudson Ave., #001, Chicago IL 60610. (312)787-4600. Fax: (312)787-4628. Editor: Michael Blaise Kong. Managing Editor: Royaa G. Silver. **Contact**: Katherine C. Raff, senior editor. **50% freelance written.** Monthly luxury lifestyle magazine. "We cover the good things in life—fashion, fine dining, the arts, etc.—from a sophisticated, cosmopolitan, well-to-do perspective." Circ. 75,000. Pays on publication. Byline given. Offers 50% kill fee. Buys first rights and all rights in this market. Editorial lead time 6 months. Submit seasonal material 6 months in advance. Reports in 1 month. Sample copy for $3 for current issue; $8 for back issue. Writer's guidelines free.
Nonfiction: General interest, historical/nostalgic (local), how-to (gardening, culinary, home design), interview/profile, photo feature (occasional), travel. *No fiction; no unsolicited mss.* Query with published clips only. Length: 500-4,500 words. **Pays $50-350.** Pays writers with contributor copies. Pays expenses of writers on assignment.
Photos: State availability of photos with submission. Reviews transparencies and prints. "We pay for film and processing only." Captions, model releases and identification of subjects required. Buys one-time rights.
Columns/Departments: Few Minutes With (Q&A), 800 words; Sporting Life (feature), 2,000 words. Query with published clips only. **Pays $0-150.**
Tips: "Send résumé, clips and story ideas. Mention interest and expertise in cover letter. We need writers who are knowledgeable about home design, architecture, art, culinary arts, entertainment, fashion and retail."

$ $ $ THE CHICAGO TRIBUNE MAGAZINE, Chicago Tribune Newspaper, 435 N. Michigan Ave., Chicago IL 60611. (312)222-3573. Website: http://www.trib mag@aol.com. Editor: Elizabeth Taylor. Managing Editor: Douglas Balz. **50% freelance written.** Weekly Sunday magazine. "We look for unique, compelling, all-researched, elequently written articles on subjects of general interest." Circ. 1,300,000. Pays on publication. Publishes ms an average of 2 months after acceptance. Offers $250 kill fee. Buys one-time rights. Submit seasonal material 6 months in advance. Reports in 1 month on queries; 6 weeks on mss.
Nonfiction: Book excerpts, exposé, general interest, interview/profile, photo feature, technical, travel. **Buys 35 mss/year.** Query or send complete ms. Length: 2,500-5,000 words. **Pays $750-1,000.** Sometimes pays the expenses of writers on assignment.
Reprints: Send typed ms and information on when and where the article previously appeared. Pay negotiable.
Photos: Send photos with submission. Payment varies for photos. Captions and identification of subjects required. Buys one-time rights.
Columns/Departments: First Person (Chicago area subjects only, talking about their occupations), 1,000 words; Chicago Voices (present or former high-profile Chicago area residents with their observations on or reminiscences of the city of Chicago), 1,000 words. **Buys 52 mss/year.** Query. **Pays $250.**
Fiction: Length: 1,500-2,000 words. **Pays $750-1,000.**

$ ILLINOIS ENTERTAINER, Chicago's Music Monthly, Roberts Publishing, Inc., 124 W. Polk, #103, Chicago IL 60605. (312)922-9333. E-mail: ieeditors@aol.com. Contact: Michael C. Harris, editor. **80% freelance written.** Free monthly magazine covering "popular and alternative music, as well as other entertainment: film, theater, media. We're more interested in new, unknown artists than the usual Madonna/Prince fare. Also, we cover lots of Chicago-area artists." Estab. 1974. Circ. 75,000. Pays on publication. Publishes ms an average of 2 months after acceptance. Byline given. Offers 50% kill fee. Buys first North American serial rights. Editorial lead time 2 months. Submit seasonal material 2 months in advance. Accepts simultaneous submissions. Reports in 2 months. Sample copy for $5.
Nonfiction: Exposé, how-to, humor, interview/profile, new product, reviews. No personal, confessional, inspirational articles. **Buys 75 mss/year.** Query with published clips. Length: 600-2,600 words. **Pays $10-125.** Sometimes pays expenses of writers on assignment.
Reprints: Send typed ms with rights for sale noted and information about when and where the article previously appeared. Pays 100% of amount paid for an original article.
Photos: Send photos with submission. Reviews contact sheets, transparencies and 5×7 prints. Offers $20-200/photo. Captions, model releases, identification of subjects required. Buys one-time rights.
Columns/Departments: Spins (LP reviews), 250-300 words. **Buys 200-300 mss/year.** Query with published clips. **Pays $10-20.**
Tips: "Send clips, résumé, etc. and be patient. Also, sending queries that show you've seen our magazine and have a feel for it greatly increases your publication chances."

$ $ NEW CITY, Chicago's News and Arts Weekly, New City Communications, Inc., 770 N. Halsted, Suite 208, Chicago IL 60622. (312)243-8786. Fax: (312)243-8802. E-mail: frank@newcitynet.com. Website: http://www.newcitynet.com. Editor: Brian Hieggelke. **Contact:** Frank Sennett, managing editor. **50% freelance written.** Weekly magazine. Estab. 1986. Circ. 65,000. Pays 30 days after publication. Publishes ms an average of 1 month after acceptance.

Byline given. Offers 20% kill fee in certain cases. Buys first rights and non-exclusive electronic rights. Editorial lead time 2 months. Submit seasonal material 2 months in advance. Reports in 1 month. Sample copy for $3. Writer's guidelines for #10 SASE.

Nonfiction: Essays, exposé, general interest, interview/profile, personal experience, service. **Buys 100 mss/year.** Query via e-mail, if possible. Length: 100-4,000 words. **Pays $15-450.** Rarely pays expenses of writers on assignment.

Photos: State availability of photos with submissions. Reviews contact sheets. Captions, model releases, identification of subjects required. Buys one-time rights.

Columns/Departments: Lit (literary supplement), 300-2,000 words; Music, Film, Arts (arts criticism), 150-800 words; Chow (food writing), 300-2,000 words. **Buys 50 mss/year.** Query via e-mail, if possible. **Pays $15-300.**

$ $ $ NORTH SHORE, The Magazine of Chicago's North and Northwest Suburbs, PB Communications, 874 Green Bay Rd., Winnetka IL 60093. Phone/fax: (847)441-7892. Publisher: Pioneer Press. **Contact**: Tom McNamee, executive editor. Senior Editor: Barry Hochfelder. **75% freelance written.** Monthly magazine. "Our readers are diverse, from middle-class communities to some of the country's wealthiest zip codes. But they all have one thing in common—proximity to Chicago." Circ. 57,092. Pays on publication. Publishes ms an average of 1-3 months after acceptance. Byline given. Offers 50% kill fee. Buys first North American serial rights. Submit seasonal material 5 months in advance. Reports in 3 months.

Nonfiction: Book excerpts, exposé, general interest, how-to, interview/profile, photo feature, travel. Special issues: Weddings (January, July); Fitness (February); Homes/Gardens (March, June, September, December); Weekend Travel (May); Nursing/Retirement Homes (August); Dining and Nightlife (October). **Buys 50 mss/year.** Query with published clips. Length: 500-4,000 words. **Pays $100-800.** Sometimes pays expenses of writers on assignment.

Reprints: Send photocopy of article and information about when and where the article previously appeared.

Photos: Send photos with submission. Reviews contact sheets, negatives, transparencies, prints. Identification of subjects required. Buys one-time rights.

Fiction: Publishes novel excerpts.

Columns/Departments: "Prelude" (shorter items of local interest), 250 words. **Buys 12 mss/year.** Query with published clips. **Pays $50.**

Tips: "We're always looking for something of local interest that's fresh and hasn't been reported elsewhere. Look for local angle. Offer us a story that's exclusive in the crowded Chicago-area media marketplace. Well-written feature stories have the best chance of being published. We cover all of Chicago's north and northwest suburbs together with some Chicago material, not just the North Shore."

N $ $ WHERE CHICAGO MAGAZINE, Miller Publishing, 1165 N. Clark St., Suite 302, Chicago IL 60610. (312)642-1896. Fax: (312)642-5467. E-mail: wherechicago@insnet.com. Website: http://www.wheremags.com/world. **Contact**: Margaret Doyle, editor. **10% freelance written.** Monthly magazine covering Chicago tourism market. "Where Chicago is geared to the leisure and business traveler visiting Chicago. We are the premier source for shopping, dining, culture, nightlife and entertainment in the city and suburbs." Estab. 1985. Circ. 101,000. **Pays on acceptance**. Publishes ms an average of 2 months after acceptance. Byline given. Buys all rights. Editorial lead time 2 months. Submit seasonal material 4 months in advance. Accepts simultaneous submissions. Reports immediately. Sample copy free. Writer's guidelines not available.

Nonfiction: General interest, historical/nostalgic, interview/profile, photo feature, travel. No "personal experiences or anything not related to Chicago." Special issue: November/December (holiday supplement that focuses on shopping, dining, family entertainment and cultural events in Chicago, primarily in the magnificent mile area). **Buys 4 mss/year.** Query with published clips. Length varies. **Pays $100-500.**

Photos: State availability of photos with submission. Reviews 4×5 transparencies, 10×12 prints. Negotiates payment individually. Captions, model releases and identification of subjects required. Buys one-time rights.

Tips: "Don't call us—we'll call you. Best to simply send a query and writing samples. Pitch an idea, if you've got one."

$ WINDY CITY SPORTS MAGAZINE, Chicago Sports Resources, 1450 W. Randolph, Chicago IL 60607. (312)421-1551. Fax: (312)421-2060. E-mail: wcpublish@aol.com. **Contact:** Jeff Banowetz, editor. **75% freelance written.** "*Windy City Sports Magazine* is a 70-130 page monthly magazine covering amateur, participatory, endurance sports in the Chicago metropolitan area. We cover running, cycling, in-line skating, outdoor sports; we do not cover professional football, basketball, etc." Estab. 1987. Circ. 100,000. Pays on publication. Byline given. Offers 25% kill fee. Buys one-time rights. Editorial lead time 2 months. Submit seasonal material at least 2 months in advance. Accepts simultaneous submissions. Reports in 1 month. Sample copy for $2 or SAE (manila) with $2 postage. Writer's guidelines free.

Nonfiction: Book excerpts, essays, general interest, historical/nostalgic, how-to, humor, inspirational, interview/profile, new product, opinion, personal experience, technical, travel. "No articles on professional sports." Query with published clips. Length: 700-1,200 words. **Pays $75-150.** Sometimes pays expenses of writers on assignment.

Reprints: Send photocopy of article or typed ms with rights for sale noted and information about when and where the article previously appeared. Payment varies.

Photos: Freelancers should state availability of photos with submission. Send photos with submission. Reviews b&w photos. Negotiates payment individually. Captions, identification of subject required. Buys one-time rights.

Columns/Departments: Running, women's, nutrition, cycling, road trip, sports medicine, fitness centers. 800-1,000

words for all columns. **Buys 70 mss/year.** Query with published clips. Send complete ms. **Pays $75-125.**
Poetry: Anything. "Must be sports related."
Fillers: Anecdotes, facts, cartoons, short humor. **Buys 25/year.** Length: 50-250 words. **Pays $25-100.**
Tips: "It helps to be active in the sport you choose to write about. Being a runner when writing a running article gives extra credentials. The columns/departments are most open to freelancers. I must fill these columns every month, 11 times per year. Also, be aware of the season when pitching ideas."

Indiana

$ $ INDIANAPOLIS MONTHLY, Emmis Publishing Corp., 950 N. Meridian St., Suite 1200, Indianapolis IN 46204. (317)237-9288. Fax: (317)237-9496. E-mail: im-input@iquest.net. Website: http://www.iquest.net/indymonthly. **Contact**: Sam Stall, editor. Editor-in-Chief: Deborah Paul. **50% freelance written.** Prefers to work with published/established writers. Monthly. "*Indianapolis Monthly* attracts and enlightens its upscale, well-educated readership with bright, lively editorial on subjects ranging from personalities to social issues, fashion to food. Its diverse content and attention to service make it the ultimate source by which the Indianapolis area lives." Estab. 1977. Circ. 45,000. Pays on publication. Publishes ms an average of 2 months after acceptance. Byline given. Offers negotiable kill fee. Buys first North American serial rights or one-time rights. Editorial lead time 3 months. Submit seasonal material 3 months in advance. Accepts simultaneous submissions. Reports in 3 weeks. Sample copy for $6.10. Writers' guidelines for #10 SASE.

- This magazine is using more first-person essays, but they must have a strong Indianapolis or Indiana tie. It will consider nonfiction book excerpts of material relevant to its readers.

Nonfiction: Book excerpts (by Indiana authors or with strong Indiana ties), essays, exposé, general interest, interview/profile, photo feature. Must have a strong Indianapolis or Indiana angle. No poetry, fiction or domestic humor; no "How Indy Has Changed Since I Left Town," "An Outsider's View of the 500," or generic material with no or little tie to Indianapolis/Indiana stories. **Buys 50 mss/year.** Query with published clips by mail or e-mail, or send complete ms. Length: 200-3,000 words. **Pays $50-600.**
Reprints: Accepts reprints only from non-competing markets. Send typed ms with rights for sale noted and information about when and where the article previously appeared. Pays 100% of the amount paid for an original article.
Photos: State availability of photos with submission. Reviews upon request. Negotiates payment individually. Captions, model releases and identification of subjects required. Buys one-time rights.
Columns/Departments: Sport; Health; First Person; Hoosiers at Large (essays by Indiana natives); Business; Religion; Books, all 2,000-2,500 words. **Buys 35 mss/year. Pays $300.**

"Our standards are simultaneously broad and narrow: broad in that we're a general interest magazine spanning a wide spectrum of topics, narrow in that we buy only stories with a heavy emphasis on Indianapolis (and, to a lesser extent, Indiana). Simply inserting an Indy-oriented paragraph into a generic national article won't get it: all stories must pertain primarily to things Hoosier. Once you've cleared that hurdle, however, it's a wide-open field. We've done features on national celebrities—Indiana Pacers coach Larry Bird and *Mir* astronaut David Wolf of Indianapolis, to name two—and we've published two-paragraph items on such quirky topics as an Indiana gardening supply house that sells insects by mail. We also like local pieces on national celebs: one of our most popular cover stories was titled 'Oprah's Indiana Home.' Probably the easiest place to break in is our newly redesigned front-of-the-book section, IndyScene, a collection of short takes on trendy topics (including Homegrown, spotlighting Hoosiers making it big elsewhere). Query with clips showing lively writing and solid reporting. E-mail queries are OK, and snail mail queries should include SASE. No phone queries please."

Kansas

$ $ KANSAS!, Kansas Department of Commerce and Housing, 700 SW Harrison, Suite 1300, Topeka KS 66603-3957. (785)296-3479. Fax: (785)296-6988. **Contact**: Andrea Glenn, editor. **90% freelance written.** Quarterly magazine emphasizing Kansas travel attractions and events. Estab. 1945. Circ. 52,000. **Pays on acceptance.** Publishes ms an average of 1 year after acceptance. Byline given. Buys one-time rights. Submit seasonal material 8 months in advance. Reports in 2 months. Sample copy and writer's guidelines available.
Nonfiction: General interest, photo feature, travel. "Material must be Kansas-oriented and have good potential for color photographs. The focus is on travel with articles about places and events that can be enjoyed by the general public. In other words, events must be open to the public, places also. Query letter should clearly outline story. I'm especially interested in Kansas freelancers who can supply their own quality photos." Length: 750-1,250 words. **Pays $200-300.**
Photos: "We are a full-color photo/manuscript publication." Send photos (original transparencies only) with query. Pays $50-75 (generally included in ms rate) for 35mm or larger format transparencies. Captions required.
Tips: "History and nostalgia stories do not fit into our format because they can't be illustrated well with color photos."

Kentucky

$ BACK HOME IN KENTUCKY, Greysmith Publishing Inc., P.O. Box 681629, Franklin TN 37068-1629. (615)794-4338. Fax: (615)790-6188. **Contact**: Nanci P. Gregg, managing editor. **50% freelance written.** "Bimonthly magazine covering Kentucky heritage, people, places, events. We reach Kentuckians and 'displaced' Kentuckians living outside the state." Estab. 1977. Circ. 8,163. Pays on publication. Publishes ms an average of 6 months after acceptance. Byline given. Buys first North American serial rights. Submit seasonal material 8 months in advance. Reports in 2 months. Sample copy for $3 and 9×12 SAE with 5 first-class stamps. Writer's guidelines for #10 SASE.

- This magazine is increasing its emphasis on the "Back Home." It is interested in profiles of Kentucky gardeners, Kentucky cooks, Kentucky craftspeople.

Nonfiction: Historical (Kentucky-related eras or profiles), profiles (Kentucky cooks, gardeners and craftspersons), memories (Kentucky related), photo feature (Kentucky places and events), travel (unusual/little known Kentucky places). No inspirational or religion. **Buys 25 mss/year.** Query with or without published clips, or send complete ms. Length: 500-2,000 words. **Pays $50-150 for assigned articles; $15-75 for unsolicited articles.** "In addition to normal payment, writers receive 4 copies of issue containing their article." Sometimes pays expenses of writers on assignment.
Reprints: Occasionally accepts previously published submissions. Send tearsheet of article and information about when and where the article previously appeared. Pays 50% of amount paid for an original article.
Photos: Send photos with submission. Reviews transparencies and 4×6 prints. Offers no additional payment for photos accepted with ms. Model releases and identification of subjects required. Rights purchased depends on situation. Also looking for color transparencies for covers. Vertical format. Pays $50-150.
Columns/Departments: Kentucky travel, Kentucky crafts, Kentucky gardeners. **Buys 10-12 mss/year.** Query with published clips. Length: 500-750 words. **Pays $15-40.**
Tips: "We work mostly with unpublished writers who have a feel for Kentucky's people, places and events. Areas most open are little known places in Kentucky, unusual history and profiles of interesting, unusual Kentuckians."

N $ $ KENTUCKY LIVING, P.O. Box 32170, Louisville KY 40232-0170. (502)451-2430. Fax: (502)459-1611. **Contact**: Paul Wesslund, editor. Mostly freelance written. Prefers to work with published/established writers. Monthly feature magazine primarily for Kentucky residents. Estab. 1948. Circ. 440,000. **Pays on acceptance.** Publishes ms on average of 4-12 months after acceptance. Byline given. Buys first serial rights for Kentucky. Submit seasonal material at least 6 months in advance. Will consider previously published and simultaneous submissions (if previously published and/or submitted outside Kentucky). Reports in 1 month. Sample copy for 9×12 SAE with 4 first-class stamps.
Nonfiction: Kentucky-related profiles (people, places or events), recreation, travel, leisure, lifestyle articles, book excerpts. **Buys 18-24 mss/year.** Query or send complete ms. **Pays $75-125** for "short" features (600-800 words) used in section known as "Commonwealths." For major articles (800-2,000 words) **pays $150-350.** Sometimes pays the expenses of writers on assignment.
Photos: State availability of or send photos with submission or advise as to availability. Reviews color slides and b&w prints. Identification of subjects required. Payment for photos included in payment for ms.
Tips: "The quality of writing and reporting (factual, objective, thorough) is considered in setting payment price. We prefer general interest pieces filled with quotes and anecdotes. Avoid boosterism. Well-researched, well-written feature articles are preferred. All articles must have a strong Kentucky connection."

$ $ LOUISVILLE MAGAZINE, 137 W. Muhammad Ali Blvd., Louisville KY 40202-1438. (502)625-0100. Fax: (502)625-0109. E-mail: lanas@louisville.com. Website: http://www.louisville.com. **Contact**: Larry Anas, editor. **67% freelance written.** Monthly magazine "for and generally about people of the Louisville Metro area. Routinely covers arts, entertainment, business, sports, dining and fashion. Features range from news analysis/exposé to silly/funny commentary. We like lean, clean prose, crisp leads." Estab. 1950. Circ. 20,000. Publishes ms an average of 2-3 months after acceptance. Byline given. Offers 50% kill fee. Buys first North American serial rights. Editorial lead time 6 weeks. Submit seasonal material 6 months in advance. Reports in 3 months. Sample copy for $2.
Nonfiction: Book excerpts, essays, exposé, general interest, historical, interview/profile, photo feature. Special issues: City Guide (January); Kentucky Derby (May). **Buys 75 mss/year.** Query. Length: 500-3,500 words. **Pays $100-500 for assigned articles; $100-400 for unsolicited articles.**
Photos: State availability of photos with submissions. Reviews transparencies. Offers $25-50/photo. Identification of subjects required. Buys one-time rights.
Columns/Departments: End Insight (essays), 850 words. **Buys 10 mss/year.** Send complete ms. **Pays $100-150.**

Louisiana

$ $ SUNDAY ADVOCATE MAGAZINE, P.O. Box 588, Baton Rouge LA 70821-0588. (504)383-1111, ext. 350. Fax: (504)388-0351. E-mail: fyarbrough@theadvocate.com. Website: http://www.TheAdvocate.com. **Contact**: Freda Yarbrough, news/features editor. **5% freelance written.** Byline given. "Freelance features are put on our website." Estab. 1925. Pays on publication. Publishes ms up to 3 months after acceptance.
Nonfiction and Photos: Well-illustrated, short articles; must have local, area or Louisiana angle, in that order of preference. Also interested in travel pieces. Photos purchased with mss. **Pays $100-200,** $30/published photo.

Reprints: Send tearsheet or typed ms with rights for sale noted and information about when and where the article previously appeared. **Pays $100-200.**
Tips: "Style and subject matter vary. Local interest is most important. No more than four to five typed, double-spaced pages."

Maine

$ ISLESBORO ISLAND NEWS, 814 Billy Shore Dr., Islesboro ME 04848. (207)734-6745. Fax: (207)734-6519. **Contact:** Agatha Cabaniss, publisher. **10% freelance written.** Monthly tabloid on island of Islesboro and people. Estab. 1985. **Pays on acceptance.** Byline given. Buys one-time rights. Sample copy for $4. Writer's guidelines for #10 SASE.
Nonfiction: Articles about contemporary issues on Islesboro, historical pieces, personality profiles, arts, lifestyles and businesses on Islesboro. Any story must have a definite Maine island connection. No travel pieces. Query or send complete ms. **Pays $20-50.**
Reprints: Accepts previously published submissions or short stories. Send typed ms with rights for sale noted. Payment varies.
Photos: Send photos with submission.
Tips: "Writers must know the Penobscot Bay Islands. We are not interested in pieces of a generic island nature. We want things about Islesboro."

Maryland

$ $ $ $ BALTIMORE MAGAZINE, Inner Harbor East, 1000 Lancaster St., Suite 1000, Baltimore MD 21202. (410)752-4200. Fax: (410)625-0280. E-mail: bmag@abs.net. Website: http://www.baltimoremag.com. Editor: Ramsey Flynn. **Contact:** Ken Iglehart, managing editor. **10-20% freelance written.** Monthly magazine. "Pieces must address an educated, active, affluent reader and must have a very strong Baltimore angle." Estab. 1907. Circ. 57,000. Pays within 60 days of acceptance. Byline given. Offers 30% kill fee. Buys first rights. Submit seasonal material 4 months in advance. Reports in 2 months on queries; 2 weeks on assigned mss; 3 months on unsolicited mss. Sample copy for $2.95 and 9×12 SAE with 10 first-class stamps. Writer's guidelines for #10 SASE.
Nonfiction: Book excerpt (Baltimore subject or author), essays, exposé, humor, interview/profile (w/Baltimorean), personal experience, photo feature, travel (local and regional to Maryland *only*). "Nothing that lacks a strong Baltimore focus or angle." Special issues: Education (October); Top Doctors (November); Holiday Events (December). Query with published clips or send complete ms. Length: 2,000-4,500 words. **Pays $25-2,500 for assigned articles; $25-500 for unsolicited articles.** Sometimes pays expenses of writers on assignment.
Columns/Departments: Hot Shot, Body & Soul. Length: 1,000-1,500 words. Query with published clips. "These shorter pieces are the best places to break into the magazine."
Tips: "Writers who live in the Baltimore area can send résumé and published clips to be considered for first assignment. Must show an understanding of writing that is suitable to an educated magazine reader and show ability to write with authority, describe scenes, help reader experience the subject. Too many writers send us newspaper-style articles. We are seeking: 1) *Human interest features*—strong, even dramatic profiles of Baltimoreans of interest to our readers. 2) *First-person accounts* of experience in Baltimore, or experiences of a Baltimore resident. 3) *Consumer*—according to our editorial needs, and with Baltimore sources. Writers new to us have most success with small humorous stories and 1,000-word personal essays that exhibit risky, original thought."

Massachusetts

BOSTON GLOBE MAGAZINE, *Boston Globe*, P.O. Box 2378, Boston MA 02107. (617)929-2955. Website: http://www.globe.com/globe/magazine. **Contact**: Evelynne Kramer, editor-in-chief. Assistant Editors: Bennie Dinardo, Jan Freeman. **50% freelance written.** Weekly magazine. Circ. 805,099. **Pays on acceptance**. Publishes ms an average of 2 months after acceptance. Buys first serial rights. Editorial lead time 2 months. Submit seasonal material 3 months in advance. Reports in 2 months. Sample copy for 9×12 SAE with 2 first-class stamps.
Nonfiction: Exposé (variety of issues including political, economic, scientific, medical and the arts), interview (not Q&A), profile, book excerpts (first serial rights only). No travelogs or poetry. **Buys up to 100 mss/year.** Query; SASE must be included with ms or queries for return. Length: 2,500-5,000 words. Payment negotiable.
Photos: Purchased with accompanying ms or on assignment. Reviews contact sheets. Pays standard rates according to size used. Captions required.

$ $ $ $ BOSTON MAGAZINE, Metrocorp, 300 Massachusetts Ave., Boston MA 02115. (617)262-9700. Fax: (617)267-1774. E-mail: bosmag@aol.com. Website: http://www.bostonmagazine.com. **Contact:** Amy Traverso. Editor: Craig Unger. **15% freelance written.** Monthly magazine covering the city of Boston. Estab. 1972. Circ. 114,476. Pays on publication. Publishes ms an average of 3 months after acceptance. Byline given. Offers 20% kill fee. Buys first

North American serial rights. Editorial lead time 2 months. Submit seasonal material 4 months in advance. Reports in 2 weeks on queries; 1 month on mss. Writer's guidelines free with SASE.
Nonfiction: Book excerpts, exposé, general interest, how-to, interview/profile, new product. **Buys 20 mss/year.** Query. Length: 1,200-5,000 words. **Pays $400-5,000.** *No unsolicited mss.* Sometimes pays expenses of writers on assignment.
Photos: State availability of photos with submissions. Negotiates payment individually. Buys one-time rights.
Columns/Departments: Sports, Dining, Finance, City Life, Personal Style, Politics. Query. **Pays $400-1,200.**

$ $ CAPE COD LIFE, Including Martha's Vineyard and Nantucket, Cape Cod Life, Inc., P.O. Box 1385, Pocasset MA 02559-1385. (508)564-4466. Fax: (508)564-4470. E-mail: capelife@capecodlife.com. Website: http://www.capecodlife.com. Editor: Brian F. Shortsleeve. **Contact:** Nancy Berry, managing editor. **80% freelance written.** Bimonthly magazine focusing on "area lifestyle, history and culture, people and places, business and industry, and issues and answers for year-round and summer residents of Cape Cod, Nantucket and Martha's Vineyard as well as non-residents who spend their leisure time here." Circ. 39,500. Pays 30 days after publication. Byline given. Offers 20% kill fee. Buys first North American serial rights or makes work-for-hire assignments. Submit seasonal material 6 months in advance. Reports in 6 months on queries and ms. Sample copy for $5. Writer's guidelines for #10 SASE.
Nonfiction: General interest, historical, gardening, interview/profile, photo feature, travel, marine, nautical, nature, arts, antiques. **Buys 20 mss/year.** Query with or without published clips. Length: 1,000-3,000 words. **Pays $100-400.**
Photos: Pays $25-225 for photos. Captions and identification of subjects required. Buys first rights with right to reprint. Photo guidelines for #10 SASE.
Tips: "Freelancers submitting *quality* spec articles with a Cape Cod and Islands angle have a good chance at publication. We like to see a wide selection of writer's clips before giving assignments. We accept more spec work written about Cape and Islands history than any other subject. We also publish *Cape Cod Home*: *Living and Gardening on the Cape and Islands* covering architecture, landscape design and interior design with a Cape and Islands focus."

$ $ PROVINCETOWN ARTS, Provincetown Arts, Inc., 650 Commercial St., Provincetown MA 02657. (508)487-3167. Fax: (508)487-8634. Website: http://www.capecodaccess.com. **Contact**: Christopher Busa, editor. **90% freelance written.** Annual magazine for contemporary art and writing. "*Provincetown Arts* focuses broadly on the artists and writers who inhabit or visit the Lower Cape, and seeks to stimulate creative activity and enhance public awareness of the cultural life of the nation's oldest continuous art colony. Drawing upon a 75-year tradition rich in visual art, literature and theater, *Provincetown Arts* offers a unique blend of interviews, fiction, visual features, reviews, reporting and poetry." Estab. 1985. Circ. 8,000. Pays on publication. Publishes ms an average of 4 months after acceptance. Offers 50% kill fee. Buys one-time and second serial (reprint) rights. Editorial lead time 6 months. Submit seasonal material 6 months in advance. Reports in 3 weeks on queries; 2 months on mss. Sample copy for $10. Writer's guidelines for #10 SASE.
Nonfiction: Book excerpts, essays, humor, interview/profile. **Buys 40 mss/year.** Send complete ms. Length: 1,500-4,000 words. **Pays $150 minimum for assigned articles; $125 minimum for unsolicited articles.** Sometimes pays expenses of writers on assignment.
Photos: Send photos with submission. Reviews 8×10 prints. Offers $20-100/photo. Identification of subjects required. Buys one-time rights.
Fiction: Mainstream. Also publishes novel excerpts. **Buys 7 mss/year.** Send complete ms. Length: 500-5,000 words. **Pays $75-300.**
Poetry: Buys 25 poems/year. Submit maximum 3 poems. **Pays $25-150.**

$ $ WORCESTER MAGAZINE, 172 Shrewsbury St., Worcester MA 01604-4636. (508)755-8004. Fax: (508)755-4734. E-mail: 75662.1176@compuserve.com. **Contact**: Martha M. Akstin, managing editor. **10% freelance written.** Weekly tabloid emphasizing the central Massachusetts region. Estab. 1976. Circ. 40,000. Pays on publication. Publishes ms an average of 3 weeks after acceptance. Byline given. Buys all rights. Submit seasonal material 2 months in advance. Does not report on unsolicited material.
Nonfiction: Exposé (area government, corporate), how-to (concerning the area, homes, vacations), interview (local), personal experience, opinion (local), photo feature. "We are interested in any piece with a local angle." **Buys 75 mss/year.** Length: 500-1,500 words. **Pays $35-250.**

Michigan

$ ABOVE THE BRIDGE MAGAZINE, P.O. Box 41, Marquette MI 49855. E-mail: classen@mail.portup.com. Website: http://www.portup.com/above. Contact: Mikel B. Classen, editor. **75% freelance written.** Bimonthly magazine. "All material, including fiction, has an Upper Peninsula of Michigan slant. Our readership is past and present UP residents." Circ. 3,500. Pays on publication. Publishes ms an average of 1 year after acceptance. Byline given. Buys one-time rights. Submit seasonal material 6 months in advance. Reports in 1 year. Sample copy for $4.50. Writer's guidelines for #10 SASE.
Nonfiction: Book excerpts (books on Upper Peninsula or UP writer), essays, historical/nostalgic (UP), interview/profile (UP personality or business), personal experience, photo feature (UP). Travel by assignment only. "This is a

family magazine. No material in poor taste." **Buys 90 mss/year.** Send complete ms. Length: 500-2,000 words. **Pays 2¢/word.**

Reprints: Send photocopy of article or short story with rights for sale noted and information about when and where the article previously appeared.

Photos: Send photos with submission. Reviews prints (5×7 or larger). Offers $5. Captions, model releases, identification of subjects required. Buys one-time rights.

Fiction: Ethnic (UP heritage), humorous, mainstream, mystery. No horror or erotica. "Material set in UP is required for publication." **Buys 18 mss/year.** Send complete ms. Length: 1,000-2,000 words. **Pays 2¢/word.**

Poetry: Free verse, haiku, light verse, traditional. No erotica. **Buys 30 poems/year.** Shorter poetry preferred. **Pays $5.**

Fillers: Anecdotes, short humor. **Buys 25/year.** Length: 100-500 words. **Pays 2¢/word maximum.**

Tips: "Material on the shorter end of our requirements has a better chance for publication. We're very well-stocked at the moment. We can't use material by out-of-state writers with content not tied to Upper Peninsula of Michigan. Know the area and people, read the magazine. Most material received is too long or not UP related. Stick to our guidelines. We love to publish well written material by previously unpublished writers."

$ $ $ ANN ARBOR OBSERVER, Ann Arbor Observer Company, 201 E. Catherine, Ann Arbor MI 48104. Fax: (734)769-3375. E-mail: hilton@aaobserver.com. Website: http://www.arborweb.com. Editor: John Hilton. **50% freelance written.** Works with a small number of new/unpublished writers each year. Monthly magazine featuring the people and events in Ann Arbor. "We depend heavily on freelancers and we're always glad to talk to new ones. We look for the intelligence and judgment to fully explore complex people and situations, and the ability to convey what makes them interesting. We've found that professional writing experience is not a good predictor of success in writing for the *Observer*. So don't let lack of experience deter you. Writing for the *Observer* is, however, a demanding job. Our readers range from U-M faculty members to hourly workers at GT Products. That means articles have to be both accurate and accessible." Estab. 1976. Circ. 60,000. Pays on publication. Publishes ms an average of 2 months after acceptance. Byline given. Reports in 3 weeks on queries; several months on mss. Sample copy for 12½×15 SAE with $3 postage. Writer's guidelines free.

Nonfiction: Historical, investigative features, profiles, brief vignettes. Must pertain to Ann Arbor. **Buys 75 mss/year.** Length: 100-7,000 words. **Pays up to $1,000/article.** Sometimes pays expenses of writers on assignment.

Columns/Departments: Inside Ann Arbor (short, interesting tidbits), 200-500 words. **Pays $75.** Around Town (unusual, compelling ancedotes), 750-1,500 words. **Pays $150-200.**

Tips: "If you have an idea for a story, write a 100-200-word description telling us why the story is interesting. We are open most to intelligent, insightful features of up to 5,000 words about interesting aspects of life in Ann Arbor."

N $ GRAND RAPIDS MAGAZINE, Gemini Corp., 549 Ottawa NW, Grand Rapids MI 49503. (616)549-4545. Fax: (616)459-4800. **Contact**: Carole Valade, editor. "*Grand Rapids* is a general interest magazine designed for those who live in the Grand Rapids metropolitan area or desire to maintain contact with the community." Estab. 1964. Pays on publication. Byline given. Editorial lead time 2 months. Submit seasonal material 2 months in advance. Sample copy for $2 and a SASE with $1.50 postage. Writer's guidelines for #10 SASE.

Nonfiction: "*Grand Rapids Magazine* is approximately 60 percent service articles—dining guide, calendar, travel, personal finance, humor and reader service sections—and 40 percent topical and issue-oriented editorial that centers on people, politics, problems and trends in the region." Query. **Pays $25-100.** Pays some expenses of writers on assignment.

N $ HOUR DETROIT, Hour Media LLC, 117 W. Third St., Royal Oak MI 48067. (248)691-1800. Fax: (248)691-4531. **Contact:** Ric Bohy, editor. Assistant Editors: George Bulanda/Brenna Sanchez. **75% freelance written.** Monthly "general interest/lifestyle magazine aimed at a middle- to upper-income readership aged 17-70." Estab. 1996. Circ. 40,000. **Pays on acceptance**. Publishes ms an average of 2 months after acceptance. Byline given. Offers 30% kill fee. Buys first North American serial rights. Editorial lead time 1½ months. Submit seasonal material 12 months in advance. Sample copy for $6.

Nonfiction: Book excerpts, exposé, general interest, historical/nostalgic, interview/profile, new product, photo feature, technical, travel. **Buys 150 mss/year**. Query with published clips. Length: 300-2,500 words. Sometimes pays expenses of writers on assignment.

Photos: State availability of photos with submission.

N $ LANSING CITY LIMITS, CityLimits Magazine, Inc., 325-B N. Clippert, Lansing MI 48912. **Contact**: Steve Lange, managing editor. Editor: Marcia Cipriani. **75% freelance written.** Monthly magazine covering the Lansing area. "All material must have a strong Lansing-area slant." Estab. 1994. Circ. 10,000. Pays on publication. Publishes ms an average of 3 months after acceptance. Byline given. Offers 25% kill fee. Buys first North American serial rights or one-time rights. Editorial lead time 2 months. Submit seasonal material 5 months in advance. Accepts simultaneous submissions. Reports in 1 month. Sample copy for 10×12 SASE and $5. Writer's guidelines for #10 SASE.

Nonfiction: Exposé, general interest, historical/nostalgic, humor, interview/profile, personal experience, travel. **Buys 30 mss/year.** Query with published clips. Length: 200-1,800 words. **Pays $50-250.** Sometimes pays expenses of writers on assignment.
Photos: State availability of photos with submission. Reviews transparencies. Negotiates payment individually. Model releases and identification of subjects required. Buys one-time rights.
Columns/Departments: Where Are They Now? (profiles of Lansing-ites), 800 words. Query with published clips. **Pays $50-150.**

$ $ TRAVERSE, Northern Michigan's Magazine, Prism Publications, Inc., 148 E. Front St., Traverse City MI 49684. (616)941-8174. Fax: (616)941-8391. E-mail: traverse@freshwater.com. **Contact:** Jeff Smith, managing editor. Editor: Deborah W. Fellows. **40% freelance written.** Monthly magazine covering "the lifestyle, natural beauty and current events, including scenic and environmental points of interest, history, culture, art, homes, dining, shopping, activities and the people and places of Northern Michigan." Estab. 1981. Circ. 15,000. Pays on publication. Publishes ms an average of 6 months after acceptance. Offers 25% kill fee. Buys first North American serial rights. Editorial lead time 6 months. Submit seasonal material 1 year in advance. Accepts simultaneous submissions. Reports in 3 weeks on queries; 1 month on mss. Sample copy for $3.50 and SAE. Writer's guidelines for #10 SASE.
Nonfiction: Book excerpts, essays, exposé, general interest, historical/nostalgic, how-to, humor, interview/profile, personal experience. **Buys 25-35 mss/year.** Query with published clips or send complete ms. Length: 700-2,500 words. **Pays $75-500 for assigned articles; $50-400 for unsolicited articles.** Sometimes pays expenses of writers on assignment.
Reprints: Send tearsheet of article or short story and information about when and where the article previously appeared.
Columns/Departments: Up in Michigan (profiles or first person accounts of elements of life in Northern Michigan), 750 words; Your Environment (what *you* can do to help the Northern environment—i.e., from land use to nature preservation, etc. Also, detail a hike or other natural experience as a destination.), 750 words. **Buys 9-12 mss/year.** Query with published clips or send complete ms. **Pays $50-175.** Great Northern Discovery (off-the-beaten-path short features—i.e., a shop, restaurant, hike, product, place to stay unique to Northern Michigan), 500-700 words. **Buys 4-6 mss/year. Pays $50-100.**
Fiction: Publishes very little fiction and only that which is rooted in or about Northern Michigan. Query with published clips or send complete ms. Length: 1,000-3,500 words. **Pays $150-350.**
Tips: "We're very writer-friendly! We encourage submissions on spec. We will review and accept, or return with comments/suggestions where applicable."

Minnesota

$ $ LAKE SUPERIOR MAGAZINE, Lake Superior Port Cities, Inc., P.O. Box 16417, Duluth MN 55816-0417. (218)722-5002. Fax: (218)722-4096. E-mail: edit@lakesuperior.com. Website: http://www.lakesuperior.com. Editor: Paul L. Hayden. **Contact**: Hugh Bishop, managing editor. **60% freelance written.** Works with a small number of new/unpublished writers each year. Bimonthly regional magazine covering contemporary and historic people, places and current events around Lake Superior. Estab. 1979. Circ. 20,000. Pays on publication. Publishes ms an average of 10 months after acceptance. Byline given. Offers $25 kill fee. Buys first North American serial and some second rights. Submit seasonal material 1 year in advance. Reports in 2 months. Sample copy for $3.95 and 5 first-class stamps. Writer's guidelines for #10 SASE.
Nonfiction: Book excerpts, general interest, historic/nostalgic, humor, interview/profile (local), personal experience, photo feature (local), travel (local), city profiles, regional business, some investigative. **Buys 45 mss/year.** Query with published clips. Length 300-2,200 words. **Pays $80-600.** Sometimes pays the expenses of writers on assignment.
Photos: Quality photography is our hallmark. Send photos with submission. Reviews contact sheets, 2×2 and larger transparencies, 4×5 prints. Offers $20 for b&w and $40 for color; $75 for covers. Captions, model releases, identification of subjects required.
Columns/Departments: Current events and things to do (for Events Calendar section), less than 300 words; Around The Circle (media reviews; short pieces on Lake Superior; Great Lakes environmental issues; themes, letters and short pieces on events and highlights of the Lake Superior Region); I Remember (nostalgic lake-specific pieces), up to 1,100 words; Life Lines (single personality profile with photography), up to 900 words. Other headings include Destinations, Nature, Wilderness Living, Heritage, Shipwreck, Chronicle, Lake Superior's Own, House for Sale. **Buys 20 mss/year.** Query with published clips. **Pays $90.**
Fiction: Ethnic, historic, humorous, mainstream, novel excerpts, slice-of-life vignettes, ghost stories. Must be targeted regionally. **Buys only 2-3 mss/year.** Query with published clips. Length: 300-2,500 words. **Pays $1-125.**
Tips: "Well-researched queries are attended to. We actively seek queries from writers in Lake Superior communities.

ALWAYS ENCLOSE a self-addressed, stamped envelope (SASE) with all your queries and correspondence.

We prefer manuscripts to queries. Provide enough information on why the subject is important to the region and our readers, or why and how something is unique. We want details. The writer must have a thorough knowledge of the subject and how it relates to our region. We prefer a fresh, unused approach to the subject which provides the reader with an emotional involvement. Almost all of our articles feature quality photography, color or black and white. It is a prerequisite of all nonfiction. All submissions should include a *short* biography of author/photographer; mug shot sometimes used. Blanket submissions need not apply."

$ $ MINNESOTA MONTHLY, 10 S. Fifth St., Suite 1000, Minneapolis MN 55402. Fax: (612)371-5801. E-mail: dmahoney@mnmo.com. Website: http://www.mnmo.com. **Contact**: David Mahoney, editor. **50% freelance written.** "*Minnesota Monthly* is a regional lifestyle publication written for a sophisticated, well-educated audience living primarily in the Twin Cities area." Estab. 1967. Circ. 80,000. **Pays on acceptance.** Writer's guidelines for SASE.
Nonfiction: Regional news and events, issues, services, places, people. "We are looking for fresh ideas and concise, compelling, well-crafted writing." Query with résumé, published clips and SASE. Length: 1,000-4,000 words. Pay negotiable.
Columns/Departments: Insider (Minnesota news and slice-of-life stories), fewer than 400 words; Portrait (photo-driven profile), 360 words; People (three short profiles), 250 words each; Just Asking (interview), 900 words; Arts & Entertainment, 450 words; Midwest Traveler, 950-2,000 words; History; Back Page (essay), 500-600 words. Query with résumé, published clips and SASE. Pay negotiable.
Tips: "Our readers like to travel, eat out, attend arts events and read. With that in mind, our goal is to provide readers with the information they need to enrich their active lives."

Mississippi

$ COAST MAGAZINE, Ship Island Holding Co., P.O. Box 1209, Gulfport MS 39502. (228)594-0004. Fax: (228)594-0074. **Contact**: Carla Arsaga, editor. **30% freelance written.** Bimonthly magazine. "We describe ourselves as a lifestyle magazine." Estab. 1993. Circ. 15,000. Pays on publication. Publishes ms an average of 4 months after acceptance. Byline given. Offers $25 kill fee. Buys first North American serial rights. Editorial lead time 6 months. Writer's guidelines for #10 SASE.
Nonfiction: General interest, historical/nostalgic, interview/profile, photo feature, travel. All content is related to the Mississippi gulf coast. **Buys 6 mss/year.** Query with published clips. **Pays $25-150.**
Photos: Transparencies preferred. Negotiates payment individually. Captions, model releases, identification of subjects required. Buys all rights. Does not return unsolicited material.
Columns/Departments: Shelly Powers, assistant editor. Hot Shots (interesting people), 400 words; Art Scene (local artists), 750 words; Reflections (historical), 1,200 words. **Buys 6 mss/year.** Query with published clips. **Pays $25-75.**
Tips: "Being familiar with *Coast Magazine* and its readership is a must. Freelancers should send the editor a cover letter that is indicative of his or her writing style along with strong writing samples."

Missouri

N $ $ FOCUS/KANSAS CITY, Communications Publishing Group, 3100 Broadway, #660, Kansas City MO 64111. (816)960-1988. Fax: (816)960-1989. **Contact:** Neoshia M. Paige, editor. **80% freelance written.** Quarterly consumer magazine covering professional and business development. "Positive how-to, motivational profiles." Estab. 1994. Circ. 30,000. Pays on publication. Publishes ms an average of 6 months after acceptance. Byline given. Buys first rights. Accepts simultaneous submissions. Reports in 2 months. Sample copy for $3. Writer's guidelines for #10 SASE.
Nonfiction: Book excerpts, general interest, historical/nostalgic, how-to, humor, inspirational, interview/profile, personal experience, photo feature, technical, travel. **Buys 15 mss/year**. Length: 750-2,000 words. **Pays $150-400 for assigned articles; 12¢/word for unsolicited articles**. Sometimes pays expenses of writers on assignment.
Photos: State availability of photos with submission. Reviews transparencies. Offers $20-25 per photo. Captions, model releases and identification of subjects required. Buys all rights.
Columns/Departments: Profiles of Achievement (regional Kansas Citians), 500-1,500 words. **Buys 30 mss/year. Pays 10¢/word.**
Fiction: Adventure, ethnic, historical, humorous, mainstream, slice-of-life vignettes. **Buys 3 mss/year**. Length: 25-250 words. **Pays $25-100.**
Fillers: Anecdotes, facts, gags to be illustrated by cartoonist, newsbreaks, short humor. **Buys 10/year**. Length: 25-250 words. **Pays $25-100.**
Tips: "For new writers—Send complete manuscript, double-spaced; clean copy only. If available, send clips of previously published work and résumé. Should state when available to write. Include on first page of manuscript: name, address, phone, social security number, word count and include SASE."

$ $ $ KANSAS CITY MAGAZINE, 118 Southwest Blvd., 3rd Floor, Kansas City MO. (816)421-4111. Fax: (816)936-0509. **Contact:** Zim Loy, editorial director. **75% freelance written.** Bimonthly magazine. "Our mission is to celebrate living in Kansas City. We are a consumer lifestyle/general interest magazine focused on Kansas City, its people and places." Estab. 1994. Circ. 31,000. **Pays on acceptance**. Publishes ms an average of 3 months after acceptance. Byline given. Offers 10% kill fee. Buys first North American serial rights. Editorial lead time 4 months. Submit seasonal material 6 months in advance. Accepts simultaneous submissions. Sample copy for #10 SASE.
Nonfiction: Exposé, general interest, interview/profile, photo feature. **Buys 30-50 mss/year.** Query with published clips. Length: 250-2,500 words. **Pays 50¢/word minimum.** Sometimes pays expenses of writers on assignment.
Photos: Negotiates payment individually. Buys one-time rights.
Columns/Departments: Entertainment (Kansas City only), 1,000 words; Food (Kansas City food and restaurants only), 1,000 words. **Buys 10 mss/year.** Query with published clips. **Pays $200-500.**

$ $ PITCHWEEKLY, Pitch Publishing, Inc., 3535 Broadway, Suite 400, Kansas City MO 64111-2826. (816)561-6061. Fax: (816)756-0502. E-mail: brodgers@pitch.com. Website: http://www.pitch.com. **Contact**: Bruce Rodgers, editor. **75% freelance written.** Weekly alternative newspaper that covers arts, entertainment, politics and social and cultural awareness in the Kansas City metro region. Estab. 1980. Circ. 90,000. Pays 1 month from publication. Buys first or one-time rights or makes work-for-hire assignments. Editorial lead time 1 month. Submit seasonal material 2 months in advance. *Query first!* Reports in 2 months on queries.
Nonfiction: Exposé, humor, interview/profile, opinion, news, photo feature. Special issues: all holidays; Best of Music; Best of Film; Education Guide. **Buys 40-50 mss/year.** Query with published clips. Length: 500-5,000 words. **Pays $25-300.** Sometimes pays expenses of writers on assignment. Prefers nonfiction with local hook.
Reprints: Send tearsheet or photocopy of article or short story or typed ms with rights for sale noted and information about when and where the article previously appeared. Pays 50% of amount paid for an original article.
Photos: Send photos with submission. Reviews contact sheets. Pays for photos with ms: $25-75. Captions and identification of subjects required. Buys one-time rights.
Fiction: Holiday-theme fiction published on Christmas, Thanksgiving, Valentine's Day, Halloween, April Fool's (humor/satire). "Must be slightly off-beat and good." Length: 1,500-2,500 words. **Pays $75-125.**
Tips: "Approach us with unusual angles on current political/social topics. Send well-written, clear, concise query with identifiable direction of proposed piece and SASE for reply or return. Previous publication in AAN paper a plus. We're looking for features and secondary features: current events in visual and performing arts (include new trends, etc.); social issues (OK to have an opinion as long as facts are well documented); liberal politics."

$ RIVER HILLS TRAVELER, Todd Publishing, Route 4, Box 4396, Piedmont MO 63957. (314)223-7143. **Contact**: Bob Todd, editor. **60% freelance written.** Monthly consumer tabloid covering "outdoor sports and nature in the southeast quarter of Missouri, the east and central Ozarks. Topics like those in *Field & Stream* and *National Geographic*." Estab. 1973. Circ. 7,500. Pays on publication. Publishes ms an average of 2 months after acceptance. Byline given. Buys one-time rights. Editorial lead time 2 months. Submit seasonal material 1 year in advance. Accepts simultaneous submissions. Reports in 1-2 months. Sample copy and writer's guidelines free.
Nonfiction: Historical/nostalgic, how-to, humor, opinion, personal experience ("Me and Joe"), photo feature, technical, travel. "No stories about other geographic areas." **Buys 80 mss/year.** Query with writing samples. Length: 1,500 maximum words. **Pays $15-50.** Sometimes pays expenses of writers on assignment.
Reprints: Send typed ms with rights for sale noted and information about when and where the article previously appeared.
Photos: Send photos with submission. Negotiates payment individually. Pays $25 for covers. Buys one-time rights.
Tips: "We are a 'poor man's' *Field & Stream* and *National Geographic*—about the eastern Missouri Ozarks. We prefer stories that relate an adventure that causes a reader to relive an adventure of his own or consider embarking on a similar adventure. Think of an adventure in camping or cooking, not just fishing and hunting. How-to is great, but not simple instructions. We encourage good first-person reporting."

$ $ SPRINGFIELD! MAGAZINE, Springfield Communications Inc., P.O. Box 4749, Springfield MO 65808-4749. (417)882-4917. **Contact**: Robert C. Glazier, editor. **85% freelance written.** Eager to work with a small number of new/unpublished writers each year. "This is an extremely local and provincial monthly magazine. No *general* interest articles." Estab. 1979. Circ. 10,000. Pays on publication. Publishes ms from 3 months to 3 years after acceptance. Byline given. Buys first serial rights. Submit seasonal material 1 year in advance. Reports in 3 months on queries; 2 weeks on queries with Springfield hook; 6 months on mss. Sample copy for $5.30 and 9½×12½ SAE.
Nonfiction: Book excerpts (Springfield authors only), exposé (local topics only), historical/nostalgic (top priority but must be local history), how-to, humor, interview/profile (needs more on females than males), personal experience, photo feature, travel (1 page/month). Local interest *only*; no material that could appeal to other magazine elsewhere. **Buys 150 mss/year.** Query with published clips or send complete ms with SASE. Length: 500-5,000 words. **Pays $35-250.**
Photos: Send photos or send photos with query or ms. Reviews b&w and color contact sheets, 4×5 color transparencies, 5×7 b&w prints. Pays $5-35 for b&w, $10-50 for color. Captions, model releases, identification of subjects required. Buys one-time rights.

- "Needs more photo features of a nostalgic bent."

Columns/Departments: **Buys 250 mss/year.** Query or send complete ms. Length varies, usually 500-2,500 words.
Tips: "We prefer writers read eight or ten copies of our magazine prior to submitting any material for our consideration.

The magazine's greatest need is for features which comment on these times in Springfield. We are overstocked with nostalgic pieces right now. We also need profiles about young women and men of distinction."

Montana

N $ **MONTANA JOURNAL**, IMM Publishing, P.O. Box 4087, Missoula MT 59806. (406)728-5520. **Contact:** M. Haser, editor. **100% freelance written.** Bimonthly newspaper, tabloid covering Montana history—human interest news and historical stories about the people, places, and events that helped build Montana. Estab. 1989. Circ. 2,500. Byline given. Offers 100% kill fee. Buys first North American serial rights. Editorial lead time 3 months. Submit seasonal material 1 year in advance. Reports in 3 months. Sample copy free. Writer's guidelines for #10 SASE.
Nonfiction: Historical/nostalgic, personal experience. Send complete ms. Length: 1,000 words maximum. **Pays 2¢/word.** Sometimes pays expenses of writers on assignment.
Photos: State availability of or send photos with submission. Reviews 5×7 prints. Negotiates payment individually. Captions, identification of subjects required. Buys one-time rights.
Reprints: Accepts previously published submissions.

$ $ **MONTANA MAGAZINE**, Lee Enterprises, P.O. Box 5630, Helena MT 59604-5630. (406)443-2842. Fax: (406)443-5480. Website: http://www.montanamagazine.com. **Contact:** Beverly R. Magley, editor. **90% freelance written.** Bimonthly "strictly Montana-oriented magazine that features community and personality profiles, contemporary issues, travel pieces." Estab. 1970. Circ. 40,000. Publishes ms an average of 1 year after acceptance. Byline given. Offers $50-100 kill fee on assigned stories only. Buys one-time rights. Submit seasonal material at least 6 months in advance. Accepts simultaneous submissions. Reports in 3 months. Sample copy for $5. Writer's guidelines for #10 SASE.
Nonfiction: Essays, general interest, interview/profile, photo feature, travel. Special features on summer and winter destination points. Query by September for summer material; March for winter material. No 'me and Joe' hiking and hunting tales; no blood-and-guts hunting stories; no poetry; no fiction; no sentimental essays. **Buys 30 mss/year.** Query with samples and SASE. Length: 300-3,000 words. **Pays 15¢/word for articles.** Sometimes pays the expenses of writers on assignment.
Reprints: Send information about when and where the article previously appeared. Pays 50% of amount paid for an original article.
Photos: Send photos with submission. Reviews contact sheets, 35mm or larger format transparencies, 5×7 prints. Offers additional payment for photos accepted with ms. Captions, model releases, identification of subjects required. Buys one-time rights.
Columns/Departments: Memories (reminisces of early-day Montana life), 800-1,000 words; Small Towns (profiles of communities), 1,500-2,000 words; Made in MT (successful cottage industries), 700-1,000 words plus b&w or color photo. Humor, 800-1,000 words. Query with samples and SASE.
Tips: "We avoid commonly-known topics so Montanans won't ho-hum through more of what they already know. If it's time to revisit a topic, we look for a unique slant."

Nevada

$ $ **NEVADA MAGAZINE**, 1800 E. Hwy. 50, Carson City NV 89710-0005. (702)687-5416. Fax: (702)687-6159. E-mail: nevmag@aol.com. Website: http://www.travelnevada.com. Editor: David Moore. **Contact:** Carolyn Graham, associate editor. **50% freelance written.** Works with a small number of new/unpublished writers each year. Bimonthly magazine published by the state of Nevada to promote tourism. Estab. 1936. Circ. 90,000. Pays on publication. Publishes ms an average of 6 months after acceptance. Byline given. Buys first North American serial rights. Submit seasonal material at least 6 months in advance. Reports in 1 month. Sample copy for $1. Writer's guidelines free.
Nonfiction: Nevada topics only. Historical, nostalgia, photo feature, people profile, recreational, travel, think pieces. "We welcome stories and photos on speculation." Publishes nonfiction book excerpts. **Buys 40 unsolicited mss/year.** Submit complete ms or query. Accepts phone queries. Length: 500-1,800 words. **Pays $50-500.**
Photos: Denise Barr, art director. Send photo material with accompanying ms. Pays $20-100 for color transparencies and glossy prints. Name, address and caption should appear on each photo or slide. Buys one-time rights.
Tips: "Keep in mind the magazine's purpose is to promote Nevada tourism. Keys to higher payments are quality and editing effort (more than length). Send cover letter; no photocopies. We look for a light, enthusiastic tone of voice without being too cute; articles bolstered by facts and thorough research; and unique angles on Nevada subjects."

New Hampshire

$ $ **NEW HAMPSHIRE EDITIONS**, Network Publications, Inc., 100 Main St., Nashua NH 03060. Fax: (603)889-5557. E-mail: editor@nh.com. Website: http://www.nheditions.nh.com. **Contact:** Rick Broussard, editor. **50%**

freelance written. Monthly magazine devoted to New Hampshire people, issues, places, business. "We want stories written for, by and about the people of New Hampshire with emphasis on qualities that set us apart from other states. We promote business and economic development." Estab. 1986. Circ. 24,000. Pays on publication. Byline given. Offers 50% kill fee. Buys all rights. Editorial lead time 3 months. Submit seasonal material 3 months in advance. Accepts simultaneous submissions. Reports in 2 months on queries; 3 months on mss.

Nonfiction: Essays, general interest, historical/nostalgic, photo feature, travel, business. **Buys 30 mss/year.** Query with published clips. Length: 800-2,000 words. **Pays $25-175.** "We sometimes barter with advertisers and offer their products and services to writers." Sometimes pays expenses of writers on assignment.

Photos: State availability of photos with submission. Offers no additional payment for photos accepted with ms. Captions, model releases, identification of subjects required. Right purchased vary.

Tips: Network Publications publishes 1 monthly magazine entitled *New Hampshire Editions* and 4 "specialty" publications, *Destination New Hampshire*, *The World Trader*, *New Hampshire Legacy* and *New Hampshire Guide to the Internet*, each relating to aspects of the economic development, commerce, and diverse culture of New Hampshire. "In general, our articles deal with the people of New Hampshire—their lifestyles and interests. We also present localized stories about national and international issues, ideas and trends. We will only use stories that show our readers how these issues have an impact on their daily lives. We cover a wide range of topics, including relationships, politics, law, real-life dramas, regional history, medical issues, business, careers, environmental issues, the arts, the outdoors, education, food, travel, recration, etc. Many of our readers are what we call 'The New Traditionalists'—aging Baby Boomers who have embraced solid American values and contemporary New Hampshire lifestyles."

New Jersey

$ $ ATLANTIC CITY MAGAZINE, P.O. Box 2100, Pleasantville NJ 08232-1924. (609)272-7900. Fax: (609)272-7910. E-mail: epifanio@earthlink.net. **Contact:** Mike Epifanio, editor. **80% freelance written.** Works with small number of new/unpublished writers each year. Monthly regional magazine covering issues pertinent to the Jersey Shore area. Estab. 1978. Circ. 50,000. Pays on publication. Publishes ms an average of 4 months after acceptance. Byline given. Buys one-time rights. Offers variable kill fee. Submit seasonal material 6 months in advance. Reports in 6 weeks. Sample copy for $3 and 9×12 SAE with 6 first-class stamps. Writer's guidelines for SASE.

Nonfiction: Entertainment, general interest, recreation, history, lifestyle, interview/profile, photo feature, trends. "No hard news or investigative pieces. No travel pieces or any article without a south Jersey shore area/Atlantic City slant." Query. Length: 100-3,000 words. **Pays $50-500 for assigned articles; $50-350 for unsolicited articles.** Sometimes pays the expenses of writers on assignment.

Photos: Send photos. Reviews contact sheets, negatives, 2¼×2¼ transparencies, 8×10 prints. Pay varies. Captions, model releases, identification of subjects required. Buys one-time rights.

Columns/Departments: Art, Gambling, Entertainment, Sports, Dining, History, Style, Real Estate. Query with published clips. Length: 500-2,000 words. **Pays $150-400.**

Tips: "Our readers are a broad base of local residents and visiting tourists. We need stories that will appeal to both audiences."

$ $ NEW JERSEY MONTHLY, P.O. Box 920, Morristown NJ 07963-0920. (973)539-8230. Contact: Jenny De Monte, editor. **50% freelance written.** Monthly magazine covering "almost anything that's New Jersey-related." Estab. 1976. Circ. 94,000. Pays on completion of fact-checking. Byline given. Offers 10-30% kill fee. Buys first rights. Submit seasonal material 6 months in advance. Reports in 3 months. Sample copy for $5.95 (% Back Issue Dept.); writer's guidelines for #10 SASE.

- This magazine continues to look for strong investigative reporters with novelistic style and solid knowledge of New Jersey issues.

Nonfiction: Book excerpts, essays, exposé, general interest, historical, humor, interview/profile, opinion, personal experience, travel. Special issues: Dining Out (February, August); Real Estate (March); Home & Garden (April); Great Weekends (May); Shore Guide (June); Fall Getaways (October); Holiday Shopping & Entertaining (November). "No experience pieces from people who used to live in New Jersey or general pieces that have no New Jersey angle." **Buys 96 mss/year.** Query with published magazine clips and SASE. Length: 200-3,000 words. **Pays 30¢/word and up.** Pays reasonable expenses of writers on assignment with prior approval.

- Ranked as one of the best markets for freelance writers in *Writer's Yearbook* magazine's annual "Top 100 Markets," January 1996.

Photos: Send photos with submission. Payment negotiated. Identification of subjects and return postage required. "Submit dupes only. To drop off portfolio contact the art director. The magazine accepts no responsibility for unsolicited photography, artwork or cartoons." Buys exclusive first serial or one-time rights.

Columns/Departments: Business (company profile, trends, individual profiles); Health & Fitness (trends, personal experience, service); Home & Garden (homes, gardens, trends, profiles, etc.); Travel (in state). **Buys 36 mss/year.** Query with published clips. Length: 750-1,500 words. **Pays 30¢ and up/word.**

Tips: "To break in, we suggest contributing briefs to our front-of-the-book section, 'Garden Variety' (light, off-beat items, trends, people, things; short service items, such as the 10 best NJ-made ice creams; short issue-oriented items; gossip; media notes). We pay a flat fee, from $50-150."

$ $ NEW JERSEY OUTDOORS, New Jersey Department of Environmental Protection, CN 402, Trenton NJ 08625. (609)777-4182. Fax: (609)984-0583. E-mail: njo@dep.state.nj.us. Website: http://www.state.nj.us/dep/njo. **Contact:** Denise Damiano Mikics, editor. **75% freelance written.** Quarterly magazine highlighting New Jersey's natural and historic resources and activities related to them. Estab. 1950. Circ. 15,000. Pays on publication. Byline given. Buys one-time rights. Editorial lead time 1 year. Submit seasonal material 1 year in advance. Reports in 3 months on queries. Sample copy for $4.25. Writer's guidelines for #10 SASE.

Nonfiction: How-to, personal experience and general interest articles and photo features about the conservation and enjoyment of natural and historic resources (e.g., fishing, hunting, hiking, camping, skiing, boating, gardening, trips to/activities in specific New Jersey locations). "*New Jersey Outdoors* is not interested in articles showing disregard for the environment or in items demonstrating unskilled people taking extraordinary risks." **Buys 30-40 mss/year.** Query with published clips. Length: 600-2,000 words. **Pays $100-500.** Sometimes pays expenses of writers on assignment.

Reprints: Rarely accepts previously published submissions. Send typed ms with rights for sale noted and information about when and where the article previously appeared. Pays up to 100% of amount paid for the original article.

Photos: State availability of photos with submission. Reviews duplicate transparencies and prints. Offers $20-125/photo. Buys one-time rights.

Tips: "*New Jersey Outdoors* generally publishes season-specific articles, planned a year in advance. Topics should be fresh, and stories should be accompanied by *great* photography. Articles and photos *must* relate to New Jersey."

$ $ THE SANDPAPER, Newsmagazine of the Jersey Shore, The SandPaper, Inc., 1816 Long Beach Blvd., Surf City NJ 08008-5461. (609)494-2034. Fax: (609)494-1437. E-mail: lbinews@hotmail.com. **Contact:** Jay Mann, managing editor. **10% freelance written.** Weekly tabloid covering subjects of interest to Jersey shore residents and visitors. "*The SandPaper* publishes two editions covering many of the Jersey Shore's finest resort communities including Long Beach Island and Ocean City, New Jersey. Each issue includes a mix of news, human interest features, opinion columns and entertainment/calendar listings." Estab. 1976. Circ. 60,000. Pays on publication. Publishes ms an average of 1 month after acceptance. Byline given. Offers 100% kill fee. Buys first or all rights. Submit seasonal material 3 months in advance. Accepts simultaneous submissions. Reports in 1 month. Sample copy for 9×12 SAE with 8 first-class stamps.

Nonfiction: Essays, general interest, historical/nostalgic, humor, opinion, environmental submissions relating to the ocean, wetlands and pinelands. Must pertain to New Jersey shore locale. Also, arts, entertainment news, reviews if they have a Jersey Shore angle. **Buys 10 mss/year.** Send complete ms. Length: 200-2,000 words. **Pays $25-200.** Sometimes pays the expenses of writers on assignment.

Reprints: Send photocopy of article and information about when and where the article previously appeared. Pays 25-50% of amount paid for an original article.

Photos: Send photos with submission. Offers $8-25/photo. Buys one-time or all rights.

Columns/Departments: SpeakEasy (opinion and slice-of-life, often humorous); Commentary (forum for social science perspectives); both 1,000-1,500 words, preferably with local or Jersey Shore angle. **Buys 50 mss/year.** Send complete ms. **Pays $30.**

Tips: "Anything of interest to sun worshippers, beach walkers, nature watchers and water sports lovers is of potential interest to us. There is an increasing coverage of environmental issues. The opinion page and columns are most open to freelancers. We are steadily increasing the amount of entertainment-related material in our publication. Articles on history of the shore area are always in demand."

New York

$ $ ADIRONDACK LIFE, P.O. Box 410, Jay NY 12941-0410. Fax: (518)946-7461. E-mail: aledit@westelcom.com. **Contact:** Elizabeth Folwell, editor. **70% freelance written.** Prefers to work with published/established writers. Emphasizes the Adirondack region and the North Country of New York State in articles concerning outdoor activities, history and natural history directly related to the Adirondacks. Publishes 8 issues/year, including special Annual Outdoor Guide. Estab. 1970. Circ. 50,000. Pays 45 days after acceptance. Publishes ms an average of 6 months after acceptance. Buys first North American serial rights. Byline given. Submit seasonal material 1 year in advance. Reports in 1 month. Sample copy for $3 and 9×12 SAE. Writer's guidelines for #10 SASE.

Nonfiction: "*Adirondack Life* attempts to capture the unique flavor and ethos of the Adirondack mountains and North Country region through feature articles directly pertaining to the qualities of the area and through department articles examining specific aspects. Example: Barkeater (personal essay); Special Places (unique spots in the Adirondack Park); Working (careers in the Adirondacks); Wilderness (environmental issues); personal experiences." Special issues: Outdoors (May); Adirondack Photography (September). **Buys 20-25 unsolicited mss/year.** Query. Length: for features,

ALWAYS CHECK the most recent copy of a magazine for the address and editor's name before you send in a query or manuscript.

2,500-5,000 words; for departments, 1,200-2,400 words. **Pays 25¢/word.** Sometimes pays expenses of writers on assignment.

Photos: All photos must have been taken in the Adirondacks. Each issue contains a photo feature. Purchased with or without ms or on assignment. All photos must be individually identified as to subject or locale and must bear photographer's name. Submit color transparencies or b&w prints. Pays $100 for full page, b&w or color; $300 for cover (color only, vertical in format). Credit line given.

Columns/Departments: Special Places; Watercraft; Barkeater (personal to political); Wilderness; Working; Home; Yesteryears; Kitchen; Profile; Historic Preservation; Sporting Scene.

Fiction: Considers first-serial novel excerpts in its subject matter and region.

Tips: "We are looking for clear, concise, well-organized manuscripts that are strictly Adirondack in subject. Check back issues to be sure we haven't already covered your topic."

N $ $ $ **BROOKLYN BRIDGE MAGAZINE**, 388 Atlantic Ave., Brooklyn NY 11217-1703. (719)596-7400. E-mail: bkbridge@iac.net. Editor: Melissa Ennen. **Contact:** Joe Fodor, senior editor. **50% freelance written.** Monthly magazine covering Brooklyn. Estab. 1995. Circ. 40,000. Pays on publication. Byline given. Offers 25% kill fee. Buys first North American serial rights. Editorial lead time 2 months. Submit seasonal material 3 months in advance. Reports in 1 week on queries; 1 month on mss. Sample copy for 9×11 and $2.39 postage.

Nonfiction Essays, expose, general interest, historical/nostalgic, interview/profile, personal experience, photo feature, Brooklyn's health, home and education. Must be related to Brooklyn. **Buys 100 mss/year.** Query with published clips. Length: 200-3,000 words. **Pays $100-1,000.** Sometimes pays expenses of writers on assignment.

Photos: Offers no additional payment for photos accepted with ms. Identification of subjects required. Acquires one-time rights.

Columns/Departments: Family, 1,250 words; Last Exit, 850 words; Street 1,100 words. **Buys 24 mss/year.** Query with published clips or send complete ms. **Pays $250-500.**

Tips: "'Original ideas are not those you have read somewhere else and pitch to us."

$ **BUFFALO SPREE MAGAZINE**, Spree Publishing Co., Inc., 3993 Harlem Rd., Buffalo NY 14226-4707. (716)634-0820. Fax: (716)634-4659. Editor: Johanna Hall Van De Mark. **Contact:** Kerry Maguire, associate editor. **90% freelance written.** Quarterly literary, consumer-oriented, city magazine. Estab. 1967. Circ. 21,000. Pays on publication. Publishes ms an average of 6-12 months after acceptance. Byline given. Buys first North American serial rights. Submit seasonal material 1 year in advance. Reports in 6 months on mss. Sample copy for $2 and 9×12 SAE with 9 first-class stamps.

Nonfiction: Essays, interview/profile, historical/nostalgic, humor, personal experience, regional, travel. **Buys 50 mss/year.** Send complete ms. Length: 1,000-2,000 words. **Pays $100-150 for unsolicited articles.**

Fiction: Original pieces with a strong sense of story. Literary humorous, mainstream and occasionally experimental. No pornographic or religious mss. **Buys 60 mss/year.** Send complete ms. Ideal length: 2,000 words. **Pays $100-150.**

Poetry: Janet Goldenberg, poetry editor. **Buys 24 poems/year.** Submit maximum 4 poems. Length: 50 lines maximum. **Pays $25.**

$ $ $ $ **NEW YORK MAGAZINE**, Primedia Magazines, 440 Madison Ave., New York NY 10022. (212)880-0700. Editor: Caroline Miller. Managing Editor: Sarah Jewler. **Contact:** Nick Meyer, editorial assistant. **25% freelance written.** Weekly magazine focusing on current events in the New York metropolitan area. Circ. 433,813. **Pays on acceptance.** Offers 25% kill fee. Buys first world serial and electronic rights. Submit seasonal material 2 months in advance. Reports in 1 month. Sample copy for $3.50. Writer's guidelines for SASE.

Nonfiction: Exposé, general interest, profile, new product, personal experience, travel. Query. **Pays $1/word.** Pays expenses of writers on assignment.

Tips: "Submit a detailed query to Sarah Jewler, *New York*'s managing editor. If there is sufficient interest in the proposed piece, the article will be assigned."

$ $ **NEWSDAY**, Melville NY 11747-4250. Website: http://www.newsday.com. **Contact:** Noel Rubinton, viewpoints editor. Opinion section of daily newspaper. Byline given. Estab. 1940. Circ. 555,203.

Nonfiction: Seeks "opinion on current events, trends, issues—whether national or local, government or lifestyle. Must be timely, pertinent, articulate and opinionated. Preference for authors within the circulation area including New York City." Length: 700-800 words. **Pays $150-200.**

Tips: "It helps for prospective authors to be familiar with our paper and section."

$ $ **SPOTLIGHT MAGAZINE**, Meadow Publications Inc., 126 Library Lane, Mamaroneck NY 10543. (914)381-4740. Fax: (914)381-4641. E-mail: meadowpub@aol.com. **Contact:** Dana B. Asher, editor-in-chief. **50% freelance written.** Monthly lifestyle magazine for the "upscale, educated, adult audience in the New York-New Jersey-Connecticut tri-state area. We try to appeal to a broad audience throughout our publication area." Estab. 1977. Circ. 75,000. **Pays on acceptance.** Byline given. Editorial lead time 3 months. Submit seasonal material 5 months in advance. Reports in 1 month. Sample copy for $2.

- *Spotlight* is looking for human interest articles and issue-related features woven around New York, New Jersey and Connecticut.

Nonfiction: Book excerpts, essays, exposé, general human interest, how-to, humor, interview/profile, new product,

photo feature, travel, illustrations. Annual special-interest guides: Wedding (February, June, September); Dining (December); Home Design (March, April, October); Health (July, January); Education (January, August); Holiday Gifts (November); Corporate (March). No fiction or poetry. **Buys 40 mss/year.** Query. **Pays $150 minimum.**
Photos: State availability of or send photos with submission. Reviews transparencies and prints. Negotiates payment individually. Captions, model releases, identification of subjects required (when appropriate). Buys one-time rights.

$ $ TIME OUT NEW YORK, Time Out New York Partners, LP, 627 Broadway, 7th Floor, New York NY 10012. (212)539-4444. Fax: (212)673-8382. President/Editor-in-Chief: Cyndi Stivers. **Contact:** Nicole Keeter, editorial assistant. **20% freelance written.** Weekly magazine covering entertainment in New York City. "Those who want to contribute to *Time Out New York* must be intimate with New York City and its environs." Estab. 1995. Circ. 55,000. **Pays on acceptance.** Publishes ms an average of 1 month after acceptance. Byline sometimes given. Offers 25% kill fee. Makes work-for-hire assignments. Reports in 2 months.
Nonfiction: General interest, interview/profile, travel (primarily within NYC area), reviews of various entertainment topics. No essays, articles about trends, unpegged articles. Query with published clips. Length: 250-1,500. **Pays 20¢/word for b&w features and $300/page for color features.**
Tips: "We're always looking for quirky, less-known news about what's going on in New York City."

North Carolina

N ✫ $ $ OUR STATE, Down Home in North Carolina, Mann Media, P.O. Box 4552, Greensboro NC 27404. Fax: (336)286-0100. **Contact**: Mary Ellis, editor. **95% freelance written.** Monthly magazine covering North Carolina. "*Our State* is dedicated to providing editorial about the history, destinations, out-of-the-way places and culture of North Carolina." Estab. 1933. Circ. 35,000. Pays on publication. Publishes ms an average of 6-12 months after acceptance. Byline given. Buys first North American serial rights. Editorial lead time 4 months. Submit seasonal material 4 months in advance. Reports in 6 weeks on queries; 2 months on mss. Sample copy for $2.95. Writer's guidelines for #10 SASE.
Nonfiction: Historical/nostalgic, humor, personal experience, photo feature, travel. **Buys 60 mss/year.** Send complete ms. Length: 1,000-1,500 words. **Pays $125-250 for assigned articles; $50-125 for unsolicited articles.** Sometimes pays expenses of writers on assignment.
Photos: State availability of photos with submission. Reviews 35mm or 4×5 transparencies. Negotiates payment individually. Identification of subjects required. Buys one-time rights.
Columns/Departments: Tar Heel Memories (remembering something specific about NC), 1,200 words; Tar Heel Profile (profile of interesting North Carolinian), 1,500 words; Tar Heel Literature (review of books by NC writers and about NC), 300 words. **Buys 40 mss/year.** Send complete ms. **Pays $75-150.**
Tips: "We are developing a style for travel stories that is distinctly *Our State*. That style starts with outstanding photographs, which not only depict an area, but interpret it and thus become an integral part of the presentation. Our stories need not dwell on listings of what can be seen. Concentrate instead on the experience of being there, whether the destination is a hiking trail, a bed and breakfast, a forest or an urban area. What thoughts and feelings did the experience evoke? What was happening? What were the mood and comportment of the people? What were the sounds and smells? What was the feel of the area? Did bugs get in the sleeping bag? Were the crows curious about the intruders? Could you see the bottom of the lake, and if so, what was there? We want to know why you went there, what you experienced, and what impressions you came away with. With at least one travel story an issue, we run a short sidebar called *Our State* Travel Guide. It explains how to get to the destination; rates or admission costs if there are any; a schedule of when the attraction is open or list of relevant dates; and an address and phone number for readers to write or call for more information. This sidebar eliminates the need for general-service information in the story."

North Dakota

$ $ N.D. REC/RTC MAGAZINE, N.D. Association of RECs, P.O. Box 727, Mandan ND 58554-0727. (701)663-6501. Fax: (701)663-3745. **Contact:** Kent Brick, editor. **10% freelance written.** Prefers to work with published/established writers. Monthly. "Our magazine goes to the 75,000 North Dakota families who get their electricity from rural electric cooperatives. We cover lifestyle, energy use, farm and family matters, and other features of importance to this state. Of course, we represent the views of our statewide association." Estab. 1954. Circ. 78,000. Pays on publication; **pays on acceptance for assigned features.** Publishes ms an average of 6 months after acceptance. Byline given. Buys first North American serial rights. Submit seasonal material 6 months in advance. Reports in 2 months. Sample copy for 9×12 SAE with 6 first-class stamps.

- *N.D. REC/RTC* reports a need for articles with greater emphasis on matters pertaining to equipment for the home and family issues related to money, parenting, personal health, small business and telecommunications.

Nonfiction: Exposé (subjects of ND interest dealing with rural electric, rural enterprises, rural lifestyle); historical/nostalgic (ND events or people only); how-to (save energy, weatherize homes, etc.); interview/profile (on great leaders

of the rural electric program, rural and small town America); opinion. **Buys 10-12 mss/year. Pays $100-500.** Pays expenses of writers on assignment.
Reprints: Send photocopy of article or short story or typed ms with rights for sale noted. Pays 25% of amount paid for an original article.
Photos: "Good quality photos accompanying ms improve chances for sale."
Fiction: Historical. "No fiction that does not relate to our editorial goals." **Buys 2-3 mss/year.** Length: 400-1,200 words. **Pays $100-300.** Reprints novel excerpts.
Tips: "Write about a North Dakotan—one of our rural residents who has done something notable in the ag/energy/rural electric/rural lifestyle areas."

Ohio

N ☆ $ BEND OF THE RIVER MAGAZINE, P.O. Box 859, Maumee OH 43537. (419)893-0022. **Contact:** R. Lee Raizk, publisher. **90% freelance written.** Eager to work with new/unpublished writers. "We buy material that we like whether it is by an experienced writer or not." Monthly magazine for readers interested in northwestern Ohio history, antiques, etc. Estab. 1972. Circ. 5,000. Pays on publication. Publishes ms an average of 6 months after acceptance. Byline given. Buys one-time rights. Accepts previously published submissions. Send tearsheet of article and information about when and where the article previously appeared. For reprints, pays 100% of the amount paid for an original article. Submit seasonal material 2 months in advance; deadline for holiday issue is November 1. Reports in up to 6 months. Sample copy for $1.50.
Nonfiction: "We deal heavily in Northwestern Ohio history and nostalgia. We are looking for old snapshots of the Toledo area to accompany articles, personal reflection, etc. **Buys 75 unsolicited mss/year.** Submit complete ms or send query. Length: 1,500 words. **Pays $10-75.**
Photos: Purchases b&w or color photos with accompanying mss. Pays $1 minimum. Captions required.
Tips: "Any Toledo area, well-researched nostalgia, local history will be put on top of the heap. If you send a picture with manuscript, it gets an A+! We pay a small amount but usually use our writers often and through the years. We're loyal."

N ☆ $ $ CINCINNATI WOMAN MAGAZINE, Niche Publishing and Media L.L.C., 542 Northland Blvd., Cincinnati OH 45240. (513)851-8916. Fax: (513)851-8575. E-mail: alicia@cincinnatiwoman.com. **Contact**: Alicia Wiehe, co-publisher. Managing Editor: Jill Salamone. **80% freelance written.** Monthly consumer publication magazine covering women's issues. Estab. 1998. Circ. 30,000. Pays on publication. Byline given. Buys one-time, second serial (reprint) rights and makes work-for-hire assignments. Editorial lead time 2 months. Submit seasonal material 3 months in advance. Accepts simultaneous submissions. Reports in 2 weeks on queries. Sample copy free. Writer's guidelines for #10 SASE.
Nonfiction: Book excerpts, essays, general interest, humor, inspirational, interview/profile, new product, opinion, personal experience, photo feature, religious, travel. **Buys 36 mss/year.** Query with published clips. Length: 450-2,500 words. **Pays $100-250.** Sometimes pays expenses of writers on assignment.
Reprints: Send photocopy of article or typed ms with rights for sale noted and information about when and where the article previously appeared.
Photos: Reviews transparencies, 4×6 prints. Negotiates payment individually. Captions and identification of subjects required. Buys one-time rights.
Columns/Departments: Jill Salamone, co-publisher. Garden (varying monthly topics), 500 words; *CWM* Cooks (timely recipes), 300 words plus photos; Style (women's fashion), 500 words. **Buys 20 mss/year.** Send complete ms. **Pays $50-250.**
Fiction: Publishes novel excerpts.
Poetry: Karen Fye, calendar editor. Avant-garde, free verse, light verse, traditional. **Buys 4 poems/year.** Submit maximum 10 poems. Length: 5-60 lines. **Pays $25-100.**
Fillers: Anecdotes, facts, newsbreaks, short humor. **Buys 30/year.** Length: 50-150 words. **Pays $10-45.**

$ $ $ CLEVELAND MAGAZINE, City Magazines, Inc., 1422 Euclid Ave., #730Q, Cleveland OH 44115. **Contact:** Liz Ludlow, editor. **70% freelance written,** mostly by assignment. Monthly magazine with a strong Cleveland/northeast Ohio angle. Estab. 1972. Circ. 45,000. Pays on publication. Publishes ms an average of 3 months after acceptance. Byline given. Offers 50% kill fee. Buys first rights and second serial (reprint) rights. Editorial lead time 6 months. Submit seasonal material 8 months in advance. Accepts simultaneous submissions. Reports in 2 months.
Nonfiction: Book excerpts, general interest, historical/nostalgic, humor, interview/profile. **Buys 1 ms/year.** Query with published clips. Length: 800-5,000 words. **Pays $200-800.** Sometimes pays expenses of writers on assignment.
Columns/Departments: City Life (Cleveland trivia/humor/info briefs), 200 words. **Buys 2 mss/year.** Query with published clips. **Pays $50.**

THE LIVING MAGAZINES, Community Publications, Inc., 179 Fairfield Ave., Bellevue KY 41073. (606)291-1412. Fax: (606)291-1417. E-mail: livingreat@aol.com. **Contact:** Linda R. Krummel, editor-in-chief (*Hyde Park Living, Indian Hill Living, Wyoming Living*); Linda Johnson, editor (*Fort Thomas Living, Fort Mitchell Living*); Paul Krummel, editor (*Blue Ash Living*); Mary Sikora, editor (*Oakwood Living*). **50% freelance written.** Group of monthly neighborhood magazines covering the people, places and events of Hyde Park, Oakwood, Wyoming, Orange Village, Moreland Hills, Pepper Pike, Indian Hill, and Blue Ash, Ohio; and Fort Mitchell and Fort Thomas, Kentucky. "We will not even entertain submissions without a direct tie to one of our communities." Circ. 1,100-5,500/magazine. Pays on publication. Publishes ms an average of 6 months after acceptance. Byline given, except for press releases. Buys one-time rights. Editorial lead time 3 months. Sample copy for $2 plus postage.

Nonfiction: General interest, historical/nostalgic, humor, interview/profile, photo feature. Query with published clips. Length: 100-1,000 words. **Pays $50 maximum.** Does not pay for unsolicited articles. Sometimes pays the expenses of writers on assignment.

Photos: Send photos with submission. Negotiates payment individually. Identification of subjects required. Buys one-time rights. Payment negotiated.

Fiction: No unsolicited fiction. Query with published clips.

Tips: "Write feature stories specific to one of our covered communities, and find undiscovered stories among our readers. Keep the stories positive, but can be poignant and/or investigative. Be courteous and friendly when researching the story."

$ $ NORTHERN OHIO LIVE, LIVE Publishing Co., 11320 Juniper Rd., Cleveland OH 44106. (216)721-1800. Fax: (216)721-2525. E-mail: tmudd@livepub.com. **Contact:** Tom Mudd, editor. Managing Editor: Kate Maloney. **70% freelance written.** Monthly magazine covering Northern Ohio news, politics, business, arts, entertainment, education and dining. "Reader demographic is mid-30s to 50s, though we're working to bring in the late 20s. Our readers are well educated, many with advanced degrees. They're interested in Northern Ohio's cultural scene and support it." Estab. 1980. Circ. 32,000. Pays 20th of publication month. Publishes ms an average of 1 month after acceptance. Byline given. Offers 50% kill fee. Buys first North American serial rights. Editorial lead time 3 months. Submit seasonal material 4 months in advance. Reports in 3 weeks on queries; 2 months on mss. Sample copy for $3.

Nonfiction: Essays, exposé, general interest, humor, interview/profile, photo feature, travel. All should have a Northern Ohio slant. Special issues: Gourmet Guide (restaurants) (May). "No business/corporate articles." **Buys 100 mss/year.** Query with published clips. Length: 1,000-3,500 words. **Pays $100-1,000.** Sometimes pays expenses of writers on assignment.

Reprints: Send photocopy of article and information about when and where the article previously appeared.

Photos: State availability of photos with submission. Reviews contact sheets, 4×5 transparencies and 3×5 prints. Negotiates payment individually. Identification of subjects required. Buys one-time rights.

Columns/Departments: News & Reviews (arts previews, personality profiles, general interest), 800-1,800 words. **Buys 60-70 mss/year.** Query with published clips. **Pays $100-150.** Place (essay), 400-450 words. **Pays $100.**

Fiction: Publishes novel excerpts.

$ $ $ OHIO MAGAZINE, Ohio Magazine, Inc., Subsidiary of Dispatch Printing Co., 62 E. Broad St., Columbus OH 43215-3522. (614)461-5083. Fax: (614)461-5506. E-mail: editorial@ohiomagazine.com. Website: http://www.ohiomagazine.com. **Contact:** Shannon Jackson, editor. **70% freelance written.** Works with a small number of new/unpublished writers/year. Magazine published 10 times/year emphasizing Ohio-based travel, news and feature material that highlights what's special and unique about the state. Estab. 1978. Circ. 75,000. **Pays on acceptance.** Publishes ms an average of 6 months after acceptance. Buys all, second serial (reprint), one-time, first North American serial or first serial rights. Byline given except on short articles appearing in sections. Submit seasonal material minimum 6 months in advance. Reports in 3 months. Sample copy for $3 and 9×12 SAE. Writer's guidelines for #10 SASE.

Nonfiction: Features: 1,500-3,000 words. **Pays $800-1,800.** Sometimes pays expenses of writers on assignment.

Columns/Departments: Buys minimum 10 unsolicited mss/year. Length: 500-1,500 words. **Pays $50-500.**

Reprints: Accepts previously published submissions. Send tearsheet or photocopy of article and information about when and where the article previously appeared. Pays 50% of amount paid for an original article.

Photos: Brooke Wenstrup, art director. Rate negotiable.

Tips: "Freelancers should send all queries in writing, not by telephone or fax. Successful queries demonstrate an intimate knowledge of the publication. The magazine has undergone a reformatting recently, placing an emphasis on Ohio travel and people that will appeal to a wide audience. We are looking to increase our circle of writers who can write about the state in an informative and upbeat style."

$ $ OVER THE BACK FENCE, Southern and Northern Ohio's Own Magazine, Back Fence Publishing, Inc., P.O. Box 756, Chillicothe OH 45601. (740)772-2165. Fax: (740)773-9273. E-mail: backfencpb@aol.com. Website: http://www.backfence.com. Editor-in-Chief: Ann Zalek. **Contact:** Sarah Williamson, managing editor. Quarterly magazine. "We are a regional magazine serving 18 counties in Southern Ohio and 7 counties in Northern Ohio. *Over The Back Fence* has a wholesome, neighborly style. It appeals to readers from young adults to seniors, often encouraging reader participation through replies." Estab. 1994. Circ. 15,000. Pays on publication. Byline given. Buys one-time North American print publication rights, making some work-for-hire assignments. Editorial lead time 6-12 months. Submit seasonal material 6-12 months in advance. Accepts simultaneous submissions, if so noted. Reports in 3 months. Sample copy for $4. Writer's guidelines for #10 SASE.

Nonfiction: General interest, historical/nostalgic, humor, inspirational, interview/profile, personal exprience, photo feature, travel. **Buys 9-12 mss/year.** Query with or without published clips or send complete ms. Length: 750-2,000 words. **Pays 10¢/word minimum,** negotiable depending on experience.

Reprints: Send photocopy of article or short story and typed ms with rights for sale noted and information about when and where the article previously appeared. Pay negotiable.
Photos: State availability of photos or send photos with submission. Reviews color transparencies (35mm or larger), 3⅕×5 prints. Offers $25-100/photo. Captions, model releases and identification of subjects required. Buys one-time usage rights. "If photos are sent as part of a text/photo package, please request our photo guidelines and submit color transparencies."
Columns/Departments: The Arts, 750-2,000 words; History (relevant to a designated county), 750-2,000 words; Inspirational (poetry or short story), minimum for poetry 4 lines, short story 600-850 words; Recipes, 750-2,000 words; Profiles From Our Past, 300-600 words; Sport & Hobby, 750-2,000 words; Our Neighbors (i.e., people helping others), 750-2,000 words. All must be relevant to Southern or Northern Ohio. **Buys 24 mss/year.** Query with or without published clips or send complete ms. **Pays 10¢/word minimum,** negotiable depending on experience.
Fiction: Humorous. **Buys 4 mss/year.** Query with published clips. Length: 300-850 words. **Pays 10¢/word minimum,** negotiable depending on experience.
Poetry: Wholesome, traditional free verse, light verse and rhyming. **Buys 4 poems/year.** Submit maximum 4 poems. Length: 4-32 lines preferred. **Pays 10¢/word or $25 minimum.**
Fillers: Anecdotes, short humor. Buys 0-8/year. Length: 100 words maximum. Pays 10¢/word or $25 minimum.
Tips: "Our approach can be equated to a friendly and informative conversation with a neighbor about interesting people, places and events in Southern Ohio (counties: Adams, Athens, Clinton, Fayette, Fairfield, Gallia, Greene, Highland, Hocking, Jackson, Lawrence, Meigs, Pickaway, Pike, Ross, Scioto, Vinton and Washington) and Northern Ohio (counties: Erie, Western Cuyahoga, Huron, Lorain, Medina, Ottawa and Sandusky)."

Oklahoma

$ $ OKLAHOMA TODAY, P.O. Box 53384, Oklahoma City OK 73152-9971. Fax: (405)522-4588. E-mail: oktededitor@mail.otrd.state.ok.us. Website: http://www.oklahomatoday.com. **Contact:** Louisa McCune, editor. **80% freelance written.** Works with a small number of new/unpublished writers each year. Bimonthly magazine covering people, places and things Oklahoman. "We are interested in showing off the best Oklahoma has to offer; we're pretty serious about our travel slant but regularly run history, nature and personality profiles." Estab. 1956. Circ. 50,000. **Pays on final acceptance.** Publishes ms an average of 6 months after acceptance. Byline given. Buys first serial rights. Submit seasonal material 1 year in advance "depending on photographic requirements." Reports in 4 months. Sample copy for $2.50 and 9×12 SASE. Writer's guidelines for #10 SASE.

• *Oklahoma Today* has won Magazine of the Year, awarded by the International Regional Magazine Association, four out of the last seven years.

Nonfiction: Book excerpts (on Oklahoma topics); photo feature and travel (in Oklahoma). Special issues: Music issue (summer 1999). **Buys 40-60 mss/year.** Query with published clips; no phone queries. Length: 1,000-3,000 words. **Pays $25-750.**
Reprints: Send photocopy of article and information about when and where the article previously appeared. Pay varies.
Photos: High-quality transparencies, b&w prints. "We are especially interested in developing contacts with photographers who live in Oklahoma or have shot here. Send samples and price range." Photo guidelines for SASE. Pays $50-100 for b&w and $50-750 for color; reviews 2¼ and 35mm color transparencies. Model releases, identification of subjects, other information for captions required. Buys one-time rights plus right to use photos for promotional purposes.
Fiction: Publishes novel excerpts.
Tips: "The best way to become a regular contributor to *Oklahoma Today* is to query us with one or more story ideas, each developed to give us an idea of your proposed slant. We're looking for *lively*, concise, well-researched and reported stories, stories that don't need to be heavily edited and are not newspaper style. We have a two full-time person editorial staff, and freelancers who can write and have done their homework get called again and again."

Oregon

$ CASCADES EAST, P.O. Box 5784, Bend OR 97708-5784. (541)382-0127. Fax: (541)382-7057. E-mail: sunpub@sun-pub.com. Website: http://www.sunpub.com. Publisher: Geoff Hill. **Contact:** Kim Hogue, associate publisher/editor: **90% freelance written.** Prefers to work with published/established writers. Quarterly magazine for "all ages as long as they are interested in outdoor recreation, history, people and arts and entertainment in central Oregon: fishing, hunting, sight-seeing, golf, tennis, hiking, bicycling, mountain climbing, backpacking, rockhounding, skiing, snowmobiling, etc." Estab. 1972. Circ. 10,000 (distributed throughout area resorts and motels and to subscribers). Pays on publication. Publishes ms an average of 6 months after acceptance. Buys all rights. Byline given. Submit seasonal material at least 6 months in advance. Reports in 3 months. Sample copy and writer's guidelines for $5 and 9×12 SAE.

• *Cascades East* now accepts and prefers manuscripts along with a 3.5 disk. They can translate most word processing programs. You can also send electronic submissions.

Nonfiction: General interest (first person experiences in outdoor central Oregon—with photos, can be dramatic, humorous or factual), historical (for feature, "Little Known Tales from Oregon History," with b&w photos), personal experience (needed on outdoor subjects: dramatic, humorous or factual). Art feature (on recognized Central Oregon artists of any medium, with color photos/transparencies and b&w photos). Homes & Living (unique custom/"dream" homes, architectural styles, alternative energy designs, interior designs, building locations, etc. in central Oregon); 1,000-2,500 words with color photos/transparencies. "No articles that are too general, sight-seeing articles that come from a travel folder, or outdoor articles without the first-person approach." **Buys 20-30 unsolicited mss/year.** Query. Length: 1,000-2,000 words. **Pays 5-15¢/word.**

Reprints: Send photocopy of article and information about when and where the article previously appeared.

Photos: "Old photos will greatly enhance chances of selling a historical feature. First-person articles need b&w photos also." Pays $10-25 for b&w; $15-100 for transparencies. Captions preferred. Buys one-time rights.

Columns/Departments: Short features on a successful Central Oregon businessperson making an impact on the community or excelling in the business market: local, national, or worldwide, with color/b&w photo. Length: 1,000-1,500 words. Query preferred.

Tips: "Submit stories a year or so in advance of publication. We are seasonal and must plan editorials for summer '99 in the spring of '98, etc., in case seasonal photos are needed."

$ $ OREGON COAST, P.O. Box 18000, 1525 12st St., Florence OR 97439-0130. (541)997-8401 or (800)348-8401. Fax: (541)997-1124. Website: http://www.ohwy.com. Judy Fleagle and Jim Forst, editors. **65% freelance written.** Bimonthly regional magazine covering the Oregon Coast. Estab. 1982. Circ. 70,000. Pays after publication. Publishes ms an average of 1 year after acceptance. Byline given. Offers 33% kill fee. Buys first North American serial rights. Submit seasonal material 6 months in advance. Reports in 1 month on queries; 3 months on mss. Sample copy for $4.50. Writer's guidelines for #10 SASE.

- This company also publishes *Northwest Travel* and *Oregon Outside*.

Nonfiction: "A true regional with general interest, historical/nostalgic, humor, interview/profile, personal experience, photo feature, travel and nature as pertains to Oregon Coast." **Buys 55 mss/year.** Query with published clips. Length: 500-2,000 words. **Pays $75-350** plus 2-5 contributor copies.

Reprints: Sometimes accepts previously published submissions. Enclose clips. Send tearsheet or photocopy of article and information about when and where the article previously appeared. Pays an average of 75% of the amount paid for an original article.

Photos: Send photos with submission. Reviews 35mm or larger transparencies. Photo submissions with no ms or stand alone or cover photos. Captions, model releases (for covers), photo credits, identification of subjects required. Buys one-time rights.

Fillers: Newsbreaks (no-fee basis).

Tips: "Slant article for readers who do not live at the Oregon Coast. At least one historical article is used in each issue. Manuscript/photo packages are preferred over mss with no photos. List photo credits and captions for each print or slide. Check all facts, proper names and numbers carefully in photo/ms packages. Need stories with great color photos—could be photo essays. Must pertain to Oregon Coast somehow."

$ $ OREGON OUTSIDE, Educational Publications Foundation, P.O. Box 18000, 1525 12th St., Suite C, Florence OR 97439-0130. (800)348-8401. Fax: (541)997-1124. Website: http://www.ohwy.com. **Contact:** Judy Fleagle, editor. **70% freelance written.** Quarterly magazine covering "outdoor activities for experts as well as for families and older folks, from easy hikes to extreme skiing. We like first person, lively accounts with quotes, anecdotes, compelling leads and satisfying endings. Nitty-gritty info can be in sidebars. Send a rough map if needed." Estab. 1993. Circ. 20,000. Publishes ms an average of 1 year after acceptance. Byline given. Offers 33% kill fee. Buys first North American serial (stories and story/photo packages) and one-time rights (stand alone photos, covers and calendars). Editorial lead time 4 months. Submit seasonal material 6 months in advance. Reports in 2 months on queries; 3 months on mss. Sample copy for $4.50. Writer's guidelines for #10 SASE.

Nonfiction: Book excerpts, how-to, interview/profile, new product, personal experience, photo feature. "Nothing overdone. We like understatement." Query with published clips. Length: 800-1,750 words. **Pays $100-350.**

Reprints: Send photocopy of article and information about when and where the story previously appeared. Pays 60% of amount paid for an original article.

Photos: Send photos with submission. "We need more photos showing human involvement in the outdoors." Reviews 35mm up to 4×5 transparencies and prints (color with negatives). Offers $25-75 with story, $350/cover photo, $75/stand alone, $100/calendar. Captions, model releases, identification of subjects required for cover consideration. Buys one-time rights.

Columns/Departments: Back Page (unusual outdoor photo with technical information), 80-100 words. Contact: Judy Fleagle. Query with photo. **Pays $75.** Product Roundup, 800-1,000 words. Contact: Jim Forst. Query with published clips. **Pays $100-150. Buys 12 mss/year.**

Fillers: Newsbreaks, events. **Uses 10/year.** Length: 200-400 words. Does not pay for fillers.

Tips: "A short piece with a couple super photos for a 1- or 2-page article" is a freelancer's best chance for publication.

$ $ WILLAMETTE WEEK, Portland's Newsweekly, City of Roses Co., 822 SW Tenth Ave., Portland OR 97205. (503)243-2122. Fax: (503)243-1115. E-mail: jschrag@wweek.com. Website: http://www.wweek.com. Editor: Mark Zusman. **50% freelance written.** Weekly alternative newsweekly focusing on local news. Estab. 1974. Circ. 80,000. Pays on publication. Byline given. Offers 25% kill fee. Buys first North American serial rights. Editorial lead time 2 months. Submit seasonal material 2 months in advance. Accepts simultaneous submissions. Reports in 1 month. Sample copy and writer's guidelines for #10 SASE.

Nonfiction: Exposé, interview/profile. Special issues: Summer Guide, Best of Portland, Fall Arts, 21st Anniversary. **Buys 30 mss/year.** Query. Length: 400-3,000 words. **Pays 10-30¢/word.** Sometimes pays expenses of writers on assignment.

Reprints: Accepts previously published submissions. Pay negotiable.

Photos: State availability of photos with submission. Reviews contact sheets. Negotiates payment individually. Model releases, identification of subjects required. Buys one-time rights.

Fiction: Rarely accepts novel excerpts.

Pennsylvania

N $ $ CENTRAL PA, WITF, Inc., P.O. Box 2954, Harrisburg PA 17105-2954. (717)236-6000. Fax: (717)236-4628. E-mail: cenpa@witf.org. Editor: Howard Lalli. **Contact:** Steve Kennedy, deputy editor. **90% freelance written.** Monthly magazine covering life in Central Pennsylvania. Estab. 1982. Circ. 42,000. Pays on publication. Publishes ms 4 months after acceptance. Offers 20% kill fee. Buys first North American serial rights. Editorial lead time 3 months. Submit seasonal material 6 months in advance. Accepts simultaneous submissions. Reports in 6 weeks on queries and mss. Sample copy for $3.50 and SASE. Writer's guidelines free.

Nonfiction: Essays, general interest, historical/nostalgic, how-to, humor, interview/profile, opinion, personal experience, photo feature, travel. Special issues: Dining/Food (January); Regional Insider's Guide (July). **Buys 50 mss/year.** Query with published clips or send complete ms. Length: 1,000-3,000 words. **Pays $200-750 for assigned articles; $50-500 for unsolicited articles.** Sometimes pays expenses of writers on assignment.

Photos: State availability of photos with submission. Reviews contact sheets, transparencies, prints. Negotiates payment individually. Identification of subjects required. Buys one-time rights.

Columns/Departments: Central Stories (quirkly, newsy, regional), 500 words; Thinking Aloud (essay), 1,300 words; Cameo (interview), 800 words. **Buys 90 mss/year.** Query with published clips or send complete ms. **Pays $50-200.**

Tips: "Wow us with something you wrote, either a clip or a manuscript on spec. If it's off target but shows you can write well and know the region, we'll ask for more. We're looking for creative nonfiction, with an emphasis on conveying valuable information through near literary-quality narrative."

$ $ PENNSYLVANIA, Pennsylvania Magazine Co., P.O. Box 576, Camp Hill PA 17001-0576. (717)697-4660. Publisher: Albert E. Holliday. **Contact:** Matt Holliday, editor. **90% freelance written.** Bimonthly magazine covering people, places, events and history in Pennsylvania. Estab. 1981. Circ. 40,000. **Pays on acceptance** except for articles (by authors unknown to us) sent on speculation. Publishes ms an average of 1 year after acceptance. Byline given. Offers 25% kill fee for assigned articles. Buys first North American serial or one-time rights. Submit seasonal queries 6-9 months in advance. Reports in 1 month. Sample copy for $2.95. Writer's guidelines for #10 SASE.

Nonfiction: Features include general interest, historical/nostalgic, photo feature, vacations and travel, people/family success stories, consumer-related inventions, serious statewide issues—all dealing with or related to Pennsylvania. Nothing on Amish topics, hunting or skiing. **Buys 75-120 mss/year.** Query with SASE. Length: 750-2,500 words. **Pays 10-15¢/word.** *Will not consider without illustrations*; send photocopies of possible illustrations with query or mss.

Reprints: Send photocopy of article, typed ms with rights for sale noted and information about when and where the article previously appeared. Pays 5¢/word.

Photos: Reviews 35mm and 2¼ color transparencies (no originals) and 5×7 to 8×10 color and b&w prints. Do not send original slides. Americana Photo Journal includes 1-4 interesting photos and a 250 word caption; Photography Essay highlights annual photo contest entries. Pays $15-25 for inside photos; up to $100 for covers. Captions required. Buys one-time rights.

Columns/Departments: Panorama (short items about people, unusual events, family and individually owned consumer-related businesses), 250-900 words; Almanac (short historical items), 1,000-2,500 words; Museums, 400-500 words. All must be illustrated. Query with SASE. **Pays 10-15¢/word.**

Tips: "Our publication depends upon freelance work—send queries."

$ $ $ PITTSBURGH MAGAZINE, WQED Pittsburgh, 4802 5th Ave., Pittsburgh PA 15213. (412)622-1360. Fax: (412)622-7066. Website: http://www.wqed.org/. **Contact:** Michelle Pilecki, managing editor. "*Pittsburgh* presents issues, analyzes problems and strives to encourage a better understanding of the community." **60% freelance written.** Prefers to work with published/established writers. The monthly magazine is purchased on newsstands and by subscription, and is given to those who contribute $40 or more/year to public TV in western Pennsylvania. Estab. 1970. Circ. 75,000. Pays on publication. Publishes ms an average of 2 months after acceptance. Buys first North American serial rights and second serial (reprint) rights. Offers kill fee. Byline given. Submit seasonal material 6 months in advance. Reports in 2 months. Sample copy for $2 (old back issues).

- Editor reports a need for more hard news and stories targeting readers in their 30s and 40s, especially those with young families.

Nonfiction: "Without exception—whether the topic is business, travel, the arts or lifestyle—each story is clearly oriented to Pittsburghers or the greater Pittsburgh region of today. We have minimal interest in historical articles and do not publish fiction, poetry, advocacy or personal reminiscence pieces." Exposé, lifestyle, sports, informational, service, business, medical, profile. Must have greater Pittsburgh angle. Query in writing with outline and clips. No fax queries. Length: 3,500 words or less. **Pays $100-1,200.**

Columns/Departments: Upfront, Destination and Interface. Length: 300 words. **Pays $35-100.**

Photos: Query for photos. Model releases required. Pays pre-negotiated expenses of writers on assignment.

Tips: "Less need for soft stories, e.g. feature profiles and historical pieces. Expanded need for service pieces geared to our region. More hard news."

$ $ WHERE & WHEN, Pennsylvania Travel Group, The Barash Group, 403 S. Allen St., State College PA 16801. (800)326-9584. Fax: (814)238-3415. E-mail: tdoom@barashgroup.com. **Contact:** Tracey Dooms, editor. **75% freelance written.** Bimonthly magazine covering travel and tourism in Pennsylvania. "*Where & When* presents things to see and do in Pennsylvania." Circ. 100,000. Pays on publication. Byline given. Offers 50% kill fee. Buys first North American serial rights. Editorial lead time 6 months in advance. Submit seasonal material 6 months in advance. Reports in 1 month. Sample copy and writer's guidelines free.

Nonfiction: Travel. **Buys 20-30 mss/year.** Query. Length: 800-2,500 words. **Pays $150-400.**

Photos: State availability of photos with submission. Reviews transparencies, slides and prints. Negotiates payment individually. Captions, identification of subjects required. Buys one-time rights.

Columns/Departments: Bring the Kids (children's attractions); Heritage Traveler (state heritage parks); Small Town PA (villages and hamlets in Pennsylvania); On the Road Again (attractions along a particular road); all 800-1,200 words. **Buys 10 mss/year.** Query. **Pays $100-250.**

South Carolina

$ $ CHARLESTON MAGAZINE, P.O. Box 1794, Mt. Pleasant SC 29465-1794. (803)971-9811. Fax: (803)971-0121. E-mail: ldettman@awod.com. **Contact:** Louise Chase Dettman, editor. Associate Editors: Dawn Chipman. **80% freelance written.** Quarterly magazine covering current issues, events, arts and culture, leisure pursuits, personalities as they pertain to the city of Charleston. "Each issue reflects an essential element of Charleston life and Lowcountry living." Estab. 1986. Circ. 20,000. Pays 30 days after publication. Publishes ms an average of 3 months after acceptance. Byline given. Buys one-time rights. Submit seasonal material 4 months in advance. Reports in 1 month. Sample copies for 9×12 SAE with 5 first-class stamps. Writer's guidelines free.

Nonfiction: General interest, humor, food, architecture, sports, interview/profile, opinion, photo feature, travel, current events/issues, art. "Not interested in 'Southern nostalgia' articles or gratuitous history pieces. Must pertain to the Charleston area and its present culture." **Buys 50 mss/year.** Query with published clips with SASE. Length: 150-1,500 words. **Pays 15¢/published word.** Sometimes pays expenses of writers on assignment.

Reprints: Send photocopy of article and information about when and where the article previously appeared. Pay negotiable.

Photos: Send photos with submission if available. Reviews contact sheets, transparencies, slides. Offers $35/photo maximum. Identification of subjects required. Buys one-time rights.

Columns/Departments: Channel Markers (general local interest), 200-400 words; Spotlight (profile of local interest), 300-400 words; The Home Front (interiors, renovations and gardens), 1,000 words; Sporting Life (humorous, adventurous tales of life outdoors), 1,000-1,200 words; Dining (restaurants and culinary trends in the city), 1,000-1,200 words; On the Road (travel opportunities near Charleston), 1,000-1,200 words.

Tips: "Charleston, although a city with a 300-year history, is a vibrant, modern community with a tremendous dedication to the arts and no shortage of newsworthy subjects. Don't bother submitting coffee-table magazine-style pieces. Areas most open to freelancers are Columns/Departments and features. Should be of local interest. We're looking for the freshest stories about Charleston—and those don't always come from insiders, but outsiders who are keenly observant."

$ $ SANDLAPPER, The Magazine of South Carolina, The Sandlapper Society, Inc., P.O. Box 1108, Lexington SC 29071-1108. (803)359-9954. Fax: (803)359-0629. E-mail: sandlap@alltel.net. Website: http://www.sandlapper.org. Executive Director: Dolly Patton. Editor: Robert P. Wilkins. **Contact:** Aida Rogers, assistant editor. **35% freelance written.** Quarterly feature magazine focusing on the positive aspects of South Carolina. "*Sandlapper* is intended to be read at those times when people want to relax with an attractive, high-quality magazine that entertains and informs them about their state." Estab. 1989. Circ. 10,000. Pays during the dateline period. Publishes ms an average of 4 months after acceptance. Byline given. Buys first North American serial rights and the right to reprint. Submit seasonal material 6 months in advance. Writer's guidelines free.

Nonfiction: Feature articles and photo essays about South Carolina's interesting people, places, cuisine, things to do. Occasional history articles. Query with clips and SASE. Length: 800-4,000 words. **Pays $50-500.** Sometimes pays the expenses of writers on assignment.

Photos: "*Sandlapper* buys black-and-white prints, color transparencies and art. Photographers should submit working cutlines for each photograph." Pays $25-75, $100 for cover or centerspread photo.

Tips: "We're not interested in articles about topical issues, politics, crime or commercial ventures. Avoid first-person nostalgia and remembrances of places that no longer exist. We look for top-quality literature. Humor is encouraged. Good taste is a standard. Unique angles are critical for acceptance. Dare to be bold, but not too bold."

South Dakota

$ DAKOTA OUTDOORS, South Dakota, Hipple Publishing Co., P.O. Box 669, 333 W. Dakota Ave., Pierre SD 57501-0669. (605)224-7301. Fax: (605)224-9210. E-mail: dakdoor@aol.com. Website: http://www.capjournal.com\dakotaoutdoors. **Contact:** Rachel Engbrecht, managing editor. Editor: Kevin Hipple. **85% freelance written.** Monthly magazine on Dakota outdoor life, focusing on hunting and fishing. Estab. 1974. Circ. 7,000. Pays on publication. Publishes ms an average of 2 months after acceptance. Byline given. Submit seasonal material 3 months in advance. Accepts simultaneous submissions. Reports in 3 months. Sample copy for 9×12 SAE with 3 first-class stamps.

Nonfiction: General interest, how-to, humor, interview/profile, personal experience, technical (all on outdoor topics—prefer in Dakotas). "Topics should center on fishing and hunting experiences and advice. Other topics, such as boating, camping, hiking, environmental concerns and general nature, will be considered as well." **Buys 120 mss/year.** Send complete ms. Length: 500-2,000 words. **Pays $5-50.** Sometimes pays in contributor copies or other premiums (inquire).

Reprints: Send typed ms with rights for sale noted and information about when and where the article previously appeared. Pays 50% of amount paid for an original article.

Photos: Send photos with submission. Reviews 3×5 or 5×7 prints. Offers no additional payment for photos accepted with ms or negotiates payment individually. Identification of subjects preferred. Buys one-time rights.

Columns/Departments: Kids Korner outdoors column addressing kids from 12 to 16 years of age. Length: 50-500 words. **Pays $5-15.**

Fiction: Adventure, humorous. **Buys 15 mss/year.** Send complete ms.

Fillers: Anecdotes, facts, gags to be illustrated by cartoonist, newsbreaks, short humor. **Buys 10/year.** Also publishes line drawings of fish and game. Prefers 5×7 prints.

Tips: "Submit samples of manuscript or previous works for consideration; photos or illustrations with manuscript are helpful."

Texas

N $ $ $ HOUSTON PRESS, New Times, Inc., 2000 W. Loop S, Suite 1900, Houston TX 77027. (713)624-1400. Fax: (713)624-1496. Website: http://www.houstonpress.com. **Contact:** Kirsten Bubier, editorial assistant. Editor: Margaret Downing. Managing Editor: Lisa Gray. **40% freelance written**. Alternative weekly tabloid covering "news and arts stories of interest to a Houston audience. If the same story could run in Seattle, then it's not for us." Estab. 1989. Pays on publication. Publishes ms an average of 2 weeks after acceptance. Byline given. Buys first North American serial and website rights. Editorial lead time 2 months. Submit seasonal material 3 months in advance. Sample copy for $2.

Nonfiction: Contact Lisa Gray, managing editor. Expose, general interest, interview/profile, arts reviews, music. Query with published clips. Length: 300-4,500 words. **Pays $10-1,000**. Sometimes pays expenses of writers on assignment.

Photos: State availability of photos with submission. Negotiates payment individually. Identification of subjects required. Buys all rights.

N $ THE 104 ZONE, KRBE's Lifestyle Magazine, 104 KRBE (104.1 FM), 9801 Westheimer, #700, Houston TX 77057. (713)266-1000. Fax: (713)954-2344. Website: http://krbe.com. **Contact:** Charlotee Crawford, editor. **75% freelance written**. Monthly entertainment/lifestyle magazine covering music, local attractions and entertainment, consumer issues. "Our audience is 18-44. Stories should be entertaining, interesting, informative and well written." Circ. 90,000. Byline given. Makes work-for-hire assignments. Editorial lead time 6 weeks. Submit seasonal material 2 months in advance. Sample copy free.

Nonfiction: General interest, how-to (buy/invest a home), humor, interview/profile. "We do not accept pre-written stories. We assign topics but will accept inquiries about being on writer list. We do not accept or pay for blind submissions." Length: 850-1,500 words. **Pays $75-150**. Sometimes pays expenses of writers on assignment.

Photos: State availability of photos with submission. Reviews 4×6 prints. Negotiates payment individually. Captions, model releases, identification of subjects required. Returns photos; gives credit to photographer.

Tips: "Contact the editor, provide writing samples. Prefer Houston-based writers but will consider out-of-towners."

N $ $ SPECIAL OCCASIONS SOURCEBOOK, A Resource Guide to Parties, Abarta Metro Publishing, 4809 Cole Ave., Suite 205, Dallas TX 75205. (214)522-0050. Fax: (214)522-0504. E-mail: j1where@airmail.net. **Contact:** Jenny Burg, editor. **70% freelance written.** "Semiannual reader-service guide to planning events ranging from rehearsal dinners to debutante balls." Estab. 1997. Circ. 15,000. Pays on publication. Publishes ms 6 months after acceptance. Byline given. Buys all rights. Editorial lead time 10 months. Submit seasonal material 10 months in advance. Accepts simultaneous submissions. Writer's guidelines for $3.95.

Nonfiction: How-to, photo feature. Does not want to see material not specific to the Dallas/Fort Worth area. **Buys 4 mss/year.** Query with published clips. Length: 1,000-2,500 words. **Pays $300-400 for assigned articles.** Sometimes pays expenses of writers on assignment.

Photos: Send photos with submission. Reviews transparencies. Negotiates payment individually. Captions, model releases and identification of subjects required. Buys one-time rights, all rights for cover photos.

Tips: Editor prefers e-mail queries rather than phone queries.

$ $ $ TEXAS HIGHWAYS, The Travel Magazine of Texas, Box 141009, Austin TX 78714-1009. (512)483-3675. Fax: (512)483-3672. E-mail: editors@texashighways.com. Website: http://www.texashighways.com. **Contact:** Jack Lowry, editor. **80% freelance written.** Monthly magazine "encourages travel within the state and tells the Texas story to readers around the world." Estab. 1974. Circ. 325,000. Publishes ms 1 year after acceptance. Buys first North American serial and electronic rights. Reports in 2 months. Writer's guidelines for SASE.
Nonfiction: "Subjects should focus on things to do or places to see in Texas. Include historical, cultural and geographic aspects if appropriate. Text should be meticulously researched. Include anecdotes, historical references, quotations and, where relevant, geologic, botanical and zoological information." Query with description, published clips, additional background materials (charts, maps, etc.) and SASE. Include disk copy if available. Length: 1,200-2,000 words. **Pays 40-50¢/word.** Send for copy of writer's guidelines.
Columns/Departments: Contact: Ann Gallaway. Speaking of Texas (history, folklore, facts), 50-200 words. **Prints 3-5 items/month.** Send complete ms with reference sources. **Pays 40¢/word.**
Tips: "We like strong leads that draw in the reader immediately and clear, concise writing. Specify and avoid superlatives. Avoid overused words. Don't forget the basics—who, what, where, why and how."

$ $ $ TEXAS MONTHLY, P.O. Box 1569, Austin TX 78767-1569. Website: http://www.texasmonthly.com. **Contact:** Gregory Curtis, editor. Monthly magazine appealing to an educated, urban Texas audience. Estab. 1973. Circ. 307,663. **Pays on acceptance.** Byline given. Reports in 2 months. Writer's guidelines for SASE.
Nonfiction: Texas politics, sports, business, culture, lifestyles, reviews, entertainment. "We like solidly researched reporting that uncovers issues of public concern, reveals offbeat and previously unreported topics or uses a novel approach to familiar topics. No fiction, poetry or cartoons." Query with outline and a description of the direction of the article and SASE. Length: 2,000-5,000 words. Pay negotiable.
Columns/Departments: Query with SASE. Length: 750-1,000 words. Pay negotiable.

$ $ $ TEXAS PARKS & WILDLIFE, 3000 South I.H. 35, Suite 120, Austin TX 78704. (512)912-7000. Fax: (512)707-1913. E-mail: susan.ebert@tpwd.state.tx.us. Website: http://www.tpwd.state.tx.us. Managing Editor: Mary-Love Bigony. **Contact:** Susan C. Ebert, senior editor. **80% freelance written.** Monthly magazine featuring articles about Texas hunting, fishing, outdoor recreation, game and nongame wildlife, state parks, environmental issues. All articles must be about Texas. Estab. 1942. Circ. 141,000. **Pays on acceptance.** Publishes ms an average of 6 months after acceptance. Byline given. Kill fee determined by editor, usually $200-250. Buys first rights. Submit seasonal material 6 months in advance. Reports in 1 month on queries; 3 months on mss. Sample copy and writer's guidelines free.

- *Texas Parks & Wildlife* needs more hunting and fishing material.

Nonfiction: General interest (Texas only), how-to (outdoor activities), photo feature, travel (state parks). **Buys 60 mss/year.** Query with published clips. Length: 500-1,500 words. **Pays $600 maximum.**
Photos: Send photos with submission. Reviews transparencies. Offers $65-350/photo. Captions and identification of subjects required. Buys one-time rights.
Tips: "Read outdoor pages of statewide newspapers to keep abreast of news items that can lead to story ideas. Feel free to include more than one story idea in one query letter. All areas are open to freelancers. All articles must have a Texas focus."

N $ UPTOWN HEALTH AND SPIRIT, Up & Out Communications, 3406 Audubon Place, Houston TX 77006. (713)520-7237. Fax: (713)522-3275. Website: http://www.uptownerpress.com. **Contact:** Mari Chow, managing editor. **70% freelance written.** Bimonthly magazine covering holistic community. "In addition to a strong belief in natural and holistic based medicines and alternative therapies, *Uptown Health and Spirit* provides proven techniques in managing stress; inspiring insight for spiritual growth; news about the environment; and the latest information for individuals and juveniles who place a priority on creating healthy bodies, minds, and spirits." Estab. 1985. Circ. 32,000. Pays on publication. Publishes ms an average of 2 months after acceptance. Byline given. Buys one-time rights and simultaneous rights. Editorial lead time 2 months. Submit seasonal material 2 months in advance. Accepts simultaneous submissions. Reports in 6 weeks on queries, 2 months on mss. Sample copy and writer's guidelines for SASE.

- This company also publishes *Out Smart*, a monthly gay and lesbian magazine. Website: http://www.outsmartmagazine.com.

Nonfiction: Book excerpts, inspirational, interview/profile, new product. **Buys 10 mss/year.** Send complete ms. Length: 700-4,000 words. **Pays $20-200.**
Reprints: Send photocopy of article. Pay negotiable.
Photos: State availability of photos with submission. Reviews 4×6 prints. Negotiates payment individually. Identification of subjects required. Buys one-time rights.

N $ $ WHERE DALLAS MAGAZINE, Abarta Metro Publishing, 4809 Cole Ave., Suite 205, Dallas TX 75205. (214)522-0050. Fax: (214)522-0504. E-mail: j1where@airmail.net. **Contact**: Jenny Burg, editor. **30% freelance written.** Monthly visitor's magazine. "*WHERE Dallas* is part of the *WHERE Magazine International* network, the world's largest publisher of travel magazines. Published in more than 40 cities around the world, travelers trust *WHERE* to guide them to the best in shopping, dining, nightlife and entertainment." Estab. 1996. Circ. 40,000. Pays on publication. Publishes ms an average of 2 months after acceptance. Byline given. Buys all rights. Editorial lead time 2 months. Submit seasonal material 2 months in advance. Accepts simultaneous submissions. Sample copy for $3.

Nonfiction: General interest, historical/nostalgic, photo feature, travel, special events. **Buys 30 mss/year.** Query with published clips, preferably by e-mail. Length: 150-1,200 words. **Pays $100-350.** Sometimes pays expenses of writers on assignment.
Photos: Send photos with submission. Reviews transparencies. Negotiates payment individually. Captions, model releases and identification of subjects required. Buys one-time rights, all rights on cover photos.
Columns/Departments: Pays $100-350.

Utah

$ $ SALT LAKE CITY, 1270 West 2320 S., Suite A, Salt Lake City UT 84119-1449. (801)975-1927. Fax: (801)975-1982. E-mail: slmagazine@aol.com. Website: http://www.slcmag.com. **Contact:** Barry Scholl, editor. Art Director: Scott Perry. **60% freelance written.** Bimonthly publication that caters to educated, affluent, and active citizens of the intermountain West. "Generally, our features profile people around the state, outdoor activities and attractions, and historical aspects of Utah." Estab. 1989. Circ. 18,000. Pays on publication. Publishes ms an average of 6 months after acceptance. Byline given. Offers $25 kill fee. Buys first North American serial rights. Submit seasonal material 6 months in advance. Accepts simultaneous submissions. Reports in 6-8 weeks. Writer's guidelines free.
Nonfiction: Essays (health, family matters, financial), general interest, historical/nostalgic (pertaining to Utah and Intermountain West), humor, interview/profile (famous or powerful people associated with Utah business, politics, media), personal experience, photo feature, travel. "No movie reviews or current news subjects, please. Even essays need a tight local angle." **Buys 5 mss/year.** Query with 3 published clips or send complete ms and SASE. Follows Chicago style. Length: 1,000-5,000 words. **Pays $75-400 for assigned articles; $75-250 for unsolicited articles.** "Payment for a major feature is negotiable."
Photos: Send photos with submission. Reviews transparencies (size not important). Captions, model releases, identification of subjects required. Payment and rights negotiable. Don't send original negs/transparencies unless requested.
Columns/Departments: Up Close (standard personality profile), 1,200-1,500 words; Q & A of famous person, 1,200-1,500 words; Executive Signature (profile, business slant of major Utah entrepeneur); and Food (recipes must be included), 1,000-1,500 words. **Buys 5-10 mss/year.** Query with published clips or send complete ms. **Pays $75-250.**

- No longer accepting fiction and poetry. Also, more articles are being produced in-house. They are overstocked on general travel pieces and are focusing on travel pieces on the intermountain West.

Tips: "We are looking for well-written, well-researched, complete manuscripts. Writers are advised to refer to a sample issue before submitting work. *Salt Lake City* magazine is most interested in unique, people-oriented profiles, historical pieces and stories of local interest. For instance, the magazine has covered local recreation, child abuse, education, air pollution, health care issues, wilderness, militias and local personalities. The majority of our stories are focused on Utah and the West. Please write for a free sample issue if you have never read our magazine."

Vermont

$ $ VERMONT LIFE MAGAZINE, 6 Baldwin St., Montpelier VT 05602-2109. (802)828-3241. E-mail: vtlife@lif.state.vt.us. Website: http://www.state.vt.us/vtlife. **Contact:** Thomas K. Slayton, editor-in-chief. **90% freelance written.** Prefers to work with published/established writers. Quarterly magazine. "*Vermont Life* is interested in any article, query, story idea, photograph or photo essay that has to do with Vermont. As the state magazine, we are most favorably impressed with pieces that present positive aspects of life within the state's borders." Estab. 1946. Circ. 90,000. Publishes ms an average of 9 months after acceptance. Byline given. Offers kill fee. Buys first serial rights. Submit seasonal material 1 year in advance. Reports in 1 month. Writer's guidelines for #10 SASE.
Nonfiction: Wants articles on today's Vermont, those which portray a typical or, if possible, unique aspect of the state or its people. Style should be literate, clear and concise. Subtle humor favored. No "Vermont clichés"—maple syrup, town meetings or stereotyped natives. **Buys 60 mss/year.** Query by letter essential. Length: 1,500 words average. **Pays 20¢/word.** Seldom pays expenses of writers on assignment.
Photos: Buys photographs with mss; buys seasonal photographs alone. Prefers b&w contact sheets to look at first on assigned material. Color submissions must be 4×5 or 35mm transparencies. Pays $75-250 inside color; $500 for cover. Gives assignments but only with experienced photographers. Query in writing. Captions, model releases, identification of subjects required. Buys one-time rights, but often negotiates for re-use rights.
Fiction: Publishes novel excerpts.
Tips: "Writers who read our magazine are given more consideration because they understand that we want authentic articles about Vermont. If a writer has a genuine working knowledge of Vermont, his or her work usually shows it. Vermont is changing and there is much concern here about what this state will be like in years ahead. It is a beautiful, environmentally sound place now and the vast majority of residents want to keep it so. Articles reflecting such concerns in an intelligent, authoritative, non-hysterical way will be given very careful consideration. The growth of tourism makes us interested in intelligent articles about specific places in Vermont, their history and attractions to the traveling public."

Virginia

☆ $ $ **THE ROANOKER**, Leisure Publishing Co., 3424 Brambleton Ave., P.O. Box 21535, Roanoke VA 24018-9900. (540)989-6138. Fax: (540)989-7603. E-mail: leisure@roanoke.infi.net. **Contact:** Kurt Rheinheimer, editor. **75% freelance written.** Works with a small number of new/unpublished writers each year. Magazine published 6 times/year. "*The Roanoker* is a general interest city magazine for the people of Roanoke, Virginia and the surrounding area. Our readers are primarily upper-income, well-educated professionals between the ages of 35 and 60. Coverage ranges from hard news and consumer information to restaurant reviews and local history." Estab. 1974. Circ. 14,000. Pays on publication. Publishes ms an average of 4 months after acceptance. Byline given. Buys all rights; makes work-for-hire assignments. Submit seasonal material 4 months in advance. Reports in 2 months. Sample copy for $2 and 9×12 SAE with 5 first-class stamps.

Nonfiction: Exposé, historical/nostalgic, how-to (live better in western Virginia), interview/profile (of well-known area personalities), photo feature, travel (Virginia and surrounding states). "Were looking for more photo feature stories based in western Virginia. We place special emphasis on investigative and exposé articles." Periodic special sections on fashion, real estate, media, banking, investing. **Buys 30 mss/year.** Query with published clips or send complete ms. Length: 1,400 words maximum. **Pays $35-200.**

Reprints: Occasionally accepts previously published submissions. Send tearsheet of article. Pays 50% of amount paid for an original article.

Photos: Send photos with ms. Reviews color transparencies. Pays $5-10 for 5×7 or 8×10 b&w prints; $10-50 for color transparencies. Captions and model releases required. Rights purchased vary.

Tips: "It helps if freelancer lives in the area. The most frequent mistake made by writers in completing an article for us is not having enough Roanoke-area focus: use of area experts, sources, slants, etc."

N $ $ **VIRGINIA DYNAMICS IN HIGHER EDUCATION**, The Reflective Publishers, Inc., P.O. Box 798, 113 E. Main St., Berryville VA 22611. (540)955-1298. Fax: (540)955-3447. E-mail: schulte@shentel.net. **Contact**: Mark Schulte, managing editor. Editor: Garrison Ellis. **80% freelance written.** Bimonthly magazine offering "reflective coverage of issues in higher education in Virginia." Estab. 1997. Pays on publication. Publishes ms an average of 4 months after acceptance. Byline given. Accepts simultaneous submissions. Writer's guidelines free.

Nonfiction: Essays, exposé, general interest, historical/nostalgic, humor, inspirational, interview/profile, new product, opinion, personal experience, religious, travel. **Buys 12 mss/year.** Query or send complete ms. Length: 50-2,000 words. **Pays $250.** Sometimes pays expenses of writers on assignment.

Reprints: Accepts previously published submissions.

Columns/Departments: Sports, Humor, Opinion, all on Virginia higher education. **Pays $250.**

Fillers: Anecdotes, facts, gags to be illustrated by cartoonist, short humor.

Tips: "Call us."

Washington

$ $ $ **SEATTLE WEEKLY**, Quickfish Media, 1008 Western Ave., Suite 300, Seattle WA 98104. (206)623-0500. Fax: (206)467-4377. E-mail: kberger@seattleweekly.com. **Contact:** Skip Berger, editor-in-chief. **20% freelance written.** Eager to work with writers in the region. Weekly tabloid covering arts, politics, food, business and books with local and regional emphasis. Estab. 1976. Circ. 70,000. Pays 1 week after publication. Publishes ms an average of 1 month after acceptance. Byline given. Offers variable kill fee. Buys first North American serial rights. Submit seasonal material minimum 2 months in advance. Reports in 1 month. *Writer's Market* recommends allowing 2 months for reply. Sample copy for $3. Writer's guidelines for #10 SASE.

Nonfiction: Book excerpts, exposé, general interest, historical/nostalgic (Northwest), humor, interview/profile, opinion, arts-related essays. **Buys 6-8 cover stories/year.** Query with résumé, published clips and SASE. Length: 700-4,000 words. **Pays $75-800.** Sometimes pays the expenses of writers on assignment.

Reprints: Send tearsheet of article. Pay varies.

Tips: "The *Seattle Weekly* publishes stories on Northwest politics and art, usually written by regional and local writers, for a mostly upscale, urban audience; writing is high-quality magazine style."

Wisconsin

$ $ $ **MILWAUKEE MAGAZINE**, 312 E. Buffalo St., Milwaukee WI 53202. (414)273-1101. Fax: (414)273-0016. E-mail: jfennell@qgraph.com. **Contact:** John Fennell, editor. **40% freelance written.** Monthly magazine. "We publish stories about Milwaukee, of service to Milwaukee-area residents and exploring the area's changing lifestyle, business, arts, politics and dining." Circ. 42,000. Pays on publication. Publishes ms an average of 2 months after acceptance. Byline given. Offers 20% kill fee. Buys first rights. Submit seasonal material 6 months in advance. Reports in 6 weeks on queries. Sample copy for $4.

Nonfiction: Essays, exposé, general interest, historical, interview/profile, photo feature, travel, food and dining and

other services. "No articles without a strong Milwaukee or Wisconsin angle." **Buys 30-50 mss/year.** Query with published clips and SASE. Full-length features: 2,500-6,000 words. **Pays $400-1,000.** Two-page "breaker" features (short on copy, long on visuals), 1,800 words. Query. **Pays $150-400.** Sometimes pays expenses of writers on assignment.
Photos: Send photos with submission. Reviews contact sheets, negatives, any transparencies and any prints. Offers no set rate per photo. Identification of subjects required. Buys one-time rights.
Columns/Departments: Steve Filmanowicz, departments editor. Insider (inside information on Milwaukee, exposé, slice-of-life, unconventional angles on current scene), up to 500 words; Mini reviews for Insider, 125 words; Endgame column (commentary), 850 words. **Buys 60 mss/year.** Query with published clips. **Pays $25-125.**
Tips: "Pitch something for the Insider, or suggest a compelling profile we haven't already done. Submit clips that prove you can do the job. The department most open is Insider. Think short, lively, offbeat, fresh, people-oriented. We are actively seeking freelance writers who can deliver lively, readable copy that helps our readers make the most out of the Milwaukee area. Because we're only human, we'd like writers who can deliver copy on deadline that fits the specifications of our assignment. If you fit this description, we'd love to work with you."

$ $ WISCONSIN OUTDOOR JOURNAL, Krause Publications, 700 E. State St., Iola WI 54990-0001. (715)445-2214. Fax: (715)445-4087. Website: http://www.krause.com/outdoors. **Contact:** Brian Lovett, editor. **95% freelance written.** Magazine published 8 times/year. "*Wisconsin Outdoor Journal* is more than a straight hook-and-bullet magazine. Though *WOJ* carries how-to and where-to information, it also prints narratives, nature features and state history pieces to give our readers a better appreciation of Wisconsin's outdoors." Estab. 1987. Circ. 48,000. **Pays on acceptance.** Byline given. Buys first North American serial rights. Submit seasonal material 1 year in advance. Reports in 6 weeks. *Writer's Market* recommends allowing 2 months for reply. Sample copy for 9×12 SAE with 7 first-class stamps. Writer's guidelines for #10 SASE.
Nonfiction: Book excerpts, essays, historical/nostalgic, how-to, humor, interview/profile, personal experience, photo feature. No articles outside of the geographic boundaries of Wisconsin. **Buys 80 mss/year.** Query. Send complete ms. "Established writers may query, send the complete ms." Length: 1,500-2,000 words. **Pays $100-250.**
Photos: Send photos with submission. Reviews 35mm transparencies. Offers no additional payment. Captions required. Buys one-time rights. Photos without mss pay from $10-150. Credit line given.
Fiction: Adventure, historical, humorous, novel excerpts. "No eulogies of a good hunting dog." **Buys 10 mss/year.** Send complete ms. Length: 1,500-2,000 words. **Pays $100-250.**
Tips: "Writers need to know Wisconsin intimately—stories that appear as regionals in other magazines probably won't be printed within *WOJ*'s pages."

$ $ WISCONSIN TRAILS, P.O. Box 5650, Madison WI 53705-1056. (608)231-2444. Fax: (608)231-1557. E-mail: klb@wistrails.com. **Contact:** Kate Bast, managing editor. **40% freelance written.** Prefers to work with published/established writers. Bimonthly magazine for readers interested in Wisconsin and its contemporary issues, personalities, recreation, history, natural beauty and arts. Estab. 1959. Circ. 55,000. Buys first serial rights, one-time rights occasionally. Pays on publication. Submit seasonal material at least 1 year in advance. Publishes ms an average of 6 months after acceptance. Byline given. Reports in 3 months. Sample copy for 9×12 SAE with 10 first-class stamps. Writer's guidelines for #10 SASE.
Nonfiction: "Our articles focus on some aspect of Wisconsin life: an interesting town or event, a person or industry, history or the arts, and especially outdoor recreation. We do not use first-person essays or biographies about people who were born in Wisconsin but made their fortunes elsewhere. No poetry. No articles that are too local for our regional audience, or articles about obvious places to visit in Wisconsin. We need more articles about the new and little-known." **Buys 3 unsolicited mss/year.** Query or send outline. "Queries accepted only in written form." Length: 1,000-3,000 words. **Pays $150-500 (negotiable),** depending on assignment length and quality. Sometimes pays expenses of writers on assignment.
Reprints: Rarely accepts reprints. Send photocopy of article or typed ms with rights for sale noted and information about when and where the article previously appeared.
Photos: Purchased with or without mss or on assignment. Uses 35mm transparencies; larger format OK. Color photos usually illustrate an activity, event, region or striking scenery. Prefer photos with people in scenery. Black and white photos usually illustrate a given article. Pays $50 each for b&w on publication. Pays $50-75 for inside color; $100-200 for covers. Caption information required.
Tips: "We're looking for active articles about people, places, events and outdoor adventures in Wisconsin. We want to publish one in-depth article of state-wide interest or concern per issue, and several short (600-1,500 words) articles about short trips, recreational opportunities, personalities, restaurants, inns and cultural activities. We're looking for more articles about out-of-the-way Wisconsin places that are exceptional in some way."

Wyoming

$ WYOMING RURAL ELECTRIC NEWS, P.O. Box 380, Casper WY 82602-0380. (307)234-6152. Fax: (307)234-4115. E-mail: wrea@trib.com. Editor: Kris Wendtland. **10% freelance written.** Monthly magazine for audience of small town residents, vacation-home owners, farmers and ranchers. Estab. 1955. Circ. 32,400. Byline given. Pays on publication. Publishes ms an average of 1 month after acceptance. Buys one-time rights. Submit seasonal material 2 months in advance. Reports in 3 months. Sample copy for SAE with 3 first-class stamps.

Nonfiction: We print science, ag, how-to and human interest but not fiction. Topics of interest in general include: hunting, cooking, gardening, commodities, sugar beets, wheat, oil, coal, hard rock mining, beef cattle, electric technologies such as lawn mowers, car heaters, air cleaners and assorted gadgets, surge protectors, pesticators, etc. Wants science articles with question/answer quiz at end—test your knowledge. Buys electrical appliance articles. No nostalgia. No sad stories. Articles welcome that put present and/or future in positive light. Submit complete ms. **Buys 4-10 mss/year.** Length: 500-800 words. **Pays $25-45.**

Reprints: Sometimes buys reprints from noncompeting markets. Send tearsheet or photocopy of article or short story and information about when and where the article previously appeared. Pays 100% of amount paid for an original article.

Photos: Pays up to $40 for cover photos. Color only.

Tips: "Study an issue or two of the magazine to become familiar with our focus and the type of freelance material we're using. We're always looking for positive humor. Always looking for fresh, new writers, original perspectives. Submit entire manuscript. Don't submit a regionally set story from some other part of the country. Photos and illustrations (if appropriate) are always welcomed."

Canada/International

$ ATLANTIC BOOKS TODAY, Atlantic Provinces Book Review Society, 1657 Barrington St., #502, Halifax, Nova Scotia B3J 2A1 Canada. (902)429-4454. E-mail: booksatl@istar.ca Website: http://www.atlanticonline.nsca/index. **Contact:** Elizabeth Eve, managing editor. **50% freelance written.** Quarterly tabloid covering books and writers in Atlantic Canada. "We only accept written inquiries for stories pertaining to promoting interest in the culture of the Atlantic region." Estab. 1992. Circ. 20,000. Pays on publication. Byline given. Offers $25 kill fee. Buys one-time rights. Editorial lead time 6 months. Submit seasonal material 3 months in advance. Accepts simultaneous submissions. Reports in 1 month on queries. Sample copy and writer's guidelines free.

Nonfiction: Book excerpts, general interest. Query with published clips. Length: 1,000 words maximum. **Pays $120 maximum.** Sometimes pays expenses of writers on assignment.

$ BRAZZIL, Brazzil, P.O. Box 42536, Los Angeles CA 90050. (213)255-8062. Fax: (213)257-3487. E-mail: brazzil@brazzil.com. Website: http://www.brazzil.com. **Contact:** Rodney Mello, editor. **60% freelance written.** Monthly magazine covering Brazilian culture. Estab. 1989. Circ. 12,000. Pays on publication. Publishes ms an average of 2 months after acceptance. Byline given. Offers 10% kill fee. Buys one-time rights. Editorial lead time 2 months. Submit seasonal material 2 months in advance. Accepts simultaneous submissions. Reports in 2 weeks on queries. Sample copy free.

Nonfiction: Book excerpts, essays, exposé, general interest, historical/nostalgic, interview/profile, personal experience, travel. "All subjects have to deal in some way with Brazil and its culture. We assume our readers know very little or nothing about Brazil, so we explain everything." **Buys 15 mss/year.** Query. Length: 800-5,000 words. **Pays $20-50.** Pays writers with contributor copies or other premiums by mutual agreement.

Reprints: Accepts reprints of previously published submissions. Include information about when and where the article previously appeared. Pays 50% of amount paid for an original article.

Photos: State availability of photos with submission. Reviews prints. Offers no additional payment for photos accepted with ms. Identification of subjects required. Buys one-time rights.

Tips: "We are interested in anything related to Brazil: politics, economy, music, behavior, profiles. Please document material with interviews and statistical data if applicable. Controversial pieces are welcome."

N $ $ BRITISH COLUMBIA REPORT, BC Report Magazine Ltd., 305-535 Thurlow St., Vancouver, British Columbia V6E 3L2 Canada. (604)682-8202. Fax: (604)682-0963. E-mail: bcreport@axionet.com. Editor: Terry O'Neill. **Contact:** Kevin Michael Grace, managing editor. **20% freelance written.** Weekly magazine covering British Columbia. Estab. 1989. Circ. 22,000. Pays on publication. Publishes ms 2 months after acceptance. Byline given. Offers 50% kill fee. Buys all rights. Editorial lead time 2 weeks. Sample copy for SASE.

Nonfiction: News from British Columbia. **Buys 250 mss/year.** Query. Length: 250-1,250 words. **Pays $50-250 for assigned articles.** Pays expenses of writers on assignment.

Photos: State availability of photos with submission. Negotiates payment individually. Captions required. Rights purchased negotiable.

$ $ $ CANADIAN GEOGRAPHIC, 39 McArthur Ave., Ottawa, Ontario K1L 8L7 Canada. (613)745-4629. Fax: (613)744-0947. E-mail: editorial@cangeo.ca. Website: http://www.cangeo.ca/. Contact: Rick Boychuk, editor. Managing Editor: Eric Harris. **90% freelance written.** Works with a small number of new/unpublished writers each year. Estab. 1930. Circ. 240,000. Bimonthly magazine. "*Canadian Geographic*'s colorful portraits of our ever-changing population show readers just how important the relationship between the people and the land really is." **Pays on acceptance.** Publishes ms an average of 3 months after acceptance. Buys first Canadian rights; interested only in first-time publication. Reports in 1 month. Sample copy for $4.25 (Canada.) and 9×12 SAE.

Nonfiction: Buys authoritative geographical articles, in the broad geographical sense, written for the average person, not for a scientific audience. Predominantly Canadian subjects by Canadian authors. **Buys 30-45 mss/year.** *Always* *query first in writing and enclose SASE.* Cannot reply personally to all unsolicited proposals. Length: 1,500-3,000 words. **Pays 80¢/word minimum. Usual payment for articles ranges between $1,000-3,000.** Higher fees reserved for commissioned articles. Sometimes pays the expenses of writers on assignment.

• *Canadian Geographic* reports a need for more articles on earth sciences.

Photos: Pays $75-400 for color photos, depending on published size.

$ $ OUTDOOR CANADA MAGAZINE, 703 Evans Ave., Suite 202, Toronto, Ontario M9C 5E9 Canada. (416)695-0311. Fax: (416)695-0381. Epmail: ocanada@istar.ca. **Contact:** James Little, editor-in-chief. **90% freelance written.** Works with a small number of new/unpublished writers each year. Magazine published 8 times/year emphasizing noncompetitive outdoor recreation in Canada *only.* Estab. 1972. Circ. 95,000. Pays on publication. Publishes ms an average of 8 months after acceptance. Buys first rights. Submit seasonal material 1 year in advance of issue date. Byline given. *Enclose SASE or IRCs or material will not be returned.* Reports in 1 month. *Writer's Market* recommends allowing 2 months for reply. Mention *Writer's Market* in request for editorial guidelines.

Nonfiction: Fishing, hiking, canoeing, hunting, adventure, outdoor issues, exploring, outdoor destinations in Canada, some how-to. **Buys 35-40 mss/year, usually with photos.** Length: 2,500 words. **Pays $500 and up.**

Reprints: Send information about when and where the article previously appeared. Pay varies. Publishes book excerpts.

Photos: Emphasize people in the outdoors. Pays $100-250 for 35mm transparencies; and $400/cover. Captions and model releases required.

Fillers: Short news pieces. **Buys 70-80/year.** Length: 200-500 words. **Pays $100 and up.**

$ $ $ TORONTO LIFE, 59 Front St. E., Toronto, Ontario M5E 1B3 Canada. (416)364-3333. Fax: (416)861-1169. E-mail: editorial@torontolife.com. Website: http://www.tor-lifeline.com. **Contact:** John Macfarlane, editor. **95% freelance written.** Prefers to work with published/established writers. Monthly magazine emphasizing local issues and social trends, short humor/satire, and service features for upper income, well-educated and, for the most part, young Torontonians. Circ. 97,624. **Pays on acceptance.** Publishes ms an average of 4 months after acceptance. Byline given. Buys first North American serial rights. Pays 50% kill fee for commissioned articles only. Reports in 3 weeks. Sample copy for $3.50 with SAE and IRCs.

Nonfiction: Uses most types of articles. Buys 17 mss/issue. Query with published clips and SASE. Phone queries OK. **Buys about 40 unsolicited mss/year.** Length: 1,000-6,000 words. **Pays $800-5,000.**

Photos: Send photos with query. Uses good color transparencies and clear, crisp b&w prints. Seldom uses submitted photos. Captions and model release required.

Columns/Departments: "We run about five columns an issue. They are all freelanced, though most are from regular contributors. They are mostly local in concern and cover politics, money, fine art, performing arts, movies and sports." Length: 1,800 words. **Pays $1,500.** Query with SASE.

Tips: "Submissions should have strong Toronto orientation."

$ $ UP HERE, Exploring the True North, (formerly *Up Here, Life in Canada's North*), OUTCROP: The Northern Publishers, Box 1350, Yellowknife, Northwest Territories X1A 2N9 Canada. (403)920-4652. Fax: (403)873-2844. E-mail: uphere@outcrop.com. **Contact:** Cooper Langfore, editor. **70% freelance written.** Bimonthly magazine covering general interest about Canada's North. "We publish features, columns and shorts about people, wildlife, native cultures, travel and adventure in Northern Canada, with an occasional swing into Alaska. Be informative, but entertaining." Estab. 1984. Circ. 35,000. Pays on publication. Publishes ms an average of 6 months after acceptance. Byline given. Offers 50% kill fee. Buys first North American serial rights. Editorial lead time 6 months. Submit seasonal material 1 year in advance. Reports in 4 months. Sample copy for $3.50 (Canadian) and 9×12 SASE with $1.45 Canadian postage. Writer's guidelines for legal-sized SASE and 45¢ Canadian postage.

• This publication was a finalist for Best Editorial Package, National Magazine Awards.

Nonfiction: Book excerpts, essays, general interest, historical/nostalgic, how-to, humor, interview/profile, new product, personal experience, photo feature, technical, travel. No poetry or fiction. **Buys 30 mss/year.** Query. Length: 1,500-3,000 words. **Pays $250-750 or 15-25¢/word.** Pays with advertising space where appropriate.

Photos: Send photos with submission. Reviews transparencies and prints. Offers $25-350/photo (Canadian). Captions and identification of subjects required. Buys one-time rights.

Columns/Departments: Natural North (natural oddities of Northern landscape, animals, vegetation, etc.), 750-1,200 words; How We Live (northern lifestyle), 750-1,500 words; Arctic Traveller (travelling in the North), 750-1,200 words. **Buys 20 mss/year.** Query with published clips. **Pays $150-250 or 15-25¢/word.**

Tips: "You must have lived in or visited Canada's North (the Northwest Territories, Yukon, the extreme north of British Columbia, Alberta, etc.). We like well-researched, concrete adventure pieces, insights about Northern people and lifestyles, readable natural history. Features are most open to freelancers—travel, adventure and so on. Outer Edge (a shorter, newsy, gee-whiz section) is a good place to break in with a 50-500 word piece. We don't want a comprehensive 'How I spent my summer vacation' hour-by-hour account. We want stories with angles, articles that look at the North through a different set of glasses. Photos are very important, and you will increase your chances greatly with top-notch images."

$ $ WESTERN PEOPLE, Supplement to the Western Producer, Western Producer Publications, Box 2500, Saskatoon, Saskatchewan S7K 2C4 Canada. (306)665-3500. E-mail: people@producer.com. Website: http://www.producer.com. **Contact:** Michael Gillgannon, managing editor. Weekly farm newspaper supplement "reflecting the life and people of rural Western Canada both in the present and historically." Estab. 1978. Circ. 100,000. **Pays on acceptance.** Publishes ms an average of 6 months after acceptance. Byline given. Buys first rights. Submit seasonal material 3 months in advance. Reports in 3 weeks. Sample copy for 9×12 SAE and 3 IRCs. Writer's guidelines for #10 SAE and 2 IRCs.

Nonfiction: General interest, historical/nostalgic, humor, interview/profile, personal experience, photo feature. **Buys 225 mss/year.** Send complete ms. Length: 500-1,800 words. **Pays $100-275.**

Photos: Send photos with submission. Reviews transparencies and prints. Captions and identification of subjects required. No stand-alone photos.

Fiction: Adventure, historical, humorous, mainstream, mystery, romance, suspense, western stories reflecting life in rural Western Canada. **Buys 25 mss/year.** Send complete ms. Length: 1,000-2,000 words. **Pays $100-200.**

Poetry: Free verse, traditional, haiku, light verse. **Buys 75 poems/year.** Submit maximum 3 poems. Length: 4-50 lines. **Pays $15-50.**

Tips: "Western Canada is geographically very large. The approach for writing about an interesting individual is to introduce that person *neighbor-to-neighbor* to our readers."

$ $ $ WESTWORLD MAGAZINE, Canada Wide Magazines and Communications, 4180 Lougheed Hwy., 4th floor, Burnaby, British Columbia V5C 6A7 Canada. Fax: (604)299-9188. E-mail: pprice@canadawide.com. **Contact:** Pat Price, editor. **30% freelance written.** Quarterly association "magazine distributed to members of The Canadian Automobile Association, so we require automotive and travel-related topics of interest to members." Estab. 1983. Circ. 500,000. Pays on publication. Byline given. Offers 50% kill fee. Buys first North American serial rights; second serial (reprint) rights at reduced rate. Editorial lead time 6 months. Submit seasonal material 1 year in advance. Accepts simultaneous submissions. Reports in 1 month on queries; 4 months on mss. Writer's guidelines for #10 SASE.

Nonfiction: Automotive, travel (domestic and foreign). "No purple prose." **Buys 6 mss/year.** Query with published clips. Length: 1,000-1,500 words. **Pays 35-50¢/word.**

Reprints: Submit photocopy of article and information about when and where the article previously appeared. Pays 50% of amount paid for an original article.

Photos: State availability of photos with submission. Reviews transparencies and prints. Offers $35-75/photo. Captions, model releases and identification of subjects required. Buys one-time rights.

Columns/Departments: Buys 6 mss/year. Query with published clips. **Pays 35-50¢/word.**

Tips: "Don't send gushy, travelogue articles. We prefer stories that are informative with practical, useful tips that are well written and researched. Approach an old topic/destination in a fresh/original way."

RELATIONSHIPS

These publications focus on lifestyles and relationships of single adults. Other markets for this type of material can be found in the Women's category. Magazines of a primarily sexual nature, gay or straight, are listed under the Sex category. Gay and Lesbian Interest contains general interest editorial targeted to that audience.

CHRISTIAN SINGLE, Baptist Sunday School Board, 127 9th Ave. N., Nashville TN 37234-0140. (615)251-5721. Fax: (615)251-5008. E-mail: christiansingle@bssb.com. Website: http://www.christiansingle.com. **Contact:** Wendi Gibson, copy editor. **30% freelance written.** Prefers to work with published/established writers. Monthly "current events magazine that addresses day-to-day issues from a Christian perspective. Seeks to be constructive and creative in approach." Estab. 1979. Circ. 63,000. **Pays on acceptance.** Byline given. Buys first rights or makes work-for-hire assignments. Submit seasonal material 6 months in advance. Reports in 2 months. Sample copy and writer's guidelines for 9×12 SAE with 4 first-class stamps.

• *Christian Single* reports they want more humor and articles dealing with current news events.

Nonfiction: Humor (good, clean humor that applies to Christian singles), how-to (specific subjects which apply to singles), inspirational (of the personal experience type), high adventure personal experience (of single adults), photo feature (on outstanding Christian singles), financial articles targeted to single adults. **Buys 60-75 unsolicited mss/year.** Query with published clips. Length: 600-1,200 words. Payment negotiable.

Reprints: Send photocopy of article and typed ms and disk with rights for sale noted and information about when and where article previously appeared. Pays 75% of amount paid for an original article.

Fiction: "We are also looking for fiction suitable for our target audience." Publishes novel excerpts.

Tips: "We are looking for people who experience single living from a positive, Christian perspective."

N $ $ DIVORCE MAGAZINE, Segue Esprit Inc., 45 Front St., Toronto, Ontario M5A 1E3 Canada. Fax: (416)368-4978. E-mail: editors@divorcemag.com. Website: http://www.divorcemag.com. **Contact**: Meg Mathur, managing editor. Editor: Diana Shepherd. **20% freelance written.** Quarterly magazine covering separation and divorce. "We have four quarterly editions: New York/New Jersey, Chicago, Southern California and Toronto. "*Divorce Magazine* is designed to help people cope with the difficult transition of separation and divorce. We provide a unique, friendly resource of vital information and timely advice to help our readers survive—even thrive—during their divorce." Estab. 1996. Circ. 80,000. Pays on publication. Publishes ms an average of 6 months after acceptance. Byline given. Offers

25% kill fee. Buys all rights. Editorial lead time 2-3 months. Submit seasonal material 6 months in advance. Accepts simultaneous submissions. Reports in 6 months on queries. Sample copy for $3.95 with SASE (note to Americans: Must use International postage not US postage). Writer's guidelines free.

Nonfiction: Book excerpts, how-to (see our website for previous examples), humor, family law. No first-person narrative stories (except for the humor column), poetry, fiction, celebrity gossip, "The Divorce from Hell" stories. **Buys 10-15 mss/year.** Query with published clips. Length: 1,000-3,000 words. **Pays 10¢/word.**

Reprints: Accepts previously published submissions.

Columns/Departments: Expert Advice (questions and answers about divorce), 500-600 words; Last Word (humor), 750-900 words. **Buys 20 mss/year.** Query with published clips. **Pays 10¢/word.**

Tips: "We accept submissions in writing only. To get an idea of the types of articles we publish, visit our website."

N $ $ LOVING MORE MAGAZINE, PEP, P.O. Box 4358, Boulder CO 80306. Phone/fax: (303)543-7540. E-mail: brett@lovemore.com. Website: http://www.lovemore.com. **Contacts**: Ryam Nearing/Brett Hill, editors. **80% freelance written.** "*Loving More* is a quarterly publication whose mission is to support, explore and enhance the many beautiful forms which families and loving relationships can take. We affirm that loving more than one can be a natural expression of health, exuberance, joy and intimacy. We view the shift from enforced monogamy and isolated families to polyamory and intentional families or tribes in the context of a larger shift toward a more balanced, peaceful and sustainable way of life." Estab. 1984. Circ. 3,000. Pays on publication. Publishes ms 6 months after acceptance. Byline given. Buys one-time rights or all rights. Editorial lead time 3 months. Submit seasonal material 6 months in advance. Reports in 1 month on queries. Sample copy $6. Guidelines for #10 SASE or via e-mail at writers@lovemore.com.

Nonfiction: Book excerpts, essays, exposé, how-to, humor, interview/profile, opinion, personal experience, photo feature. "No swinging sex, hardcore." **Buys 12-20 mss/year.** Query with published clips. Length: 750-3,000 words. **Pays $25-200.**

Reprints: Send information about when and where the article previously appeared. Pays 50% of amount paid for an original article.

Photos: Send photos with submission. Negotiates payment individually. Model releases required. Buys one-time rights.

Poetry: "We publish select poetry relevant to our theme."

$ ON THE SCENE MAGAZINE, 3507 Wyoming NE, Albuquerque NM 87111-4427. (505)299-4401. Website: http://www.onthescene-alb.com. **Contact:** Gail Skinner, editor. **60% freelance written.** Eager to work with new/unpublished writers. Monthly magazine covering lifestyles for all ages. Estab. 1979. Circ. 30,000. Pays on publication. Publishes ms within 1 year after acceptance. Byline given. Submit seasonal material 3 months in advance. Reports in 3 months. Sample copy for $3 postage or send 9×12 SAE with $1.01 postage. Writer's guidelines for #10 SASE.

Nonfiction: General interest, how-to, humor, inspirational, opinion, personal experience, relationships, consumer guide, travel, finance, real estate, parenting, astrology. No suggestive or pornographic material. **Buys 60 mss/year.** Send complete ms. Mss returned only if adequate SASE included. Length: 600-1,200 words. **Pays $5-35.**

Reprints: Send typed ms with rights for sale noted. Pays 100% of amount paid for original article.

Photos: Send photos with ms. Captions, model releases, identification of subjects required. Photo returned only if adequate SASE is included.

Tips: "We are looking for articles that deal with every aspect of living—whether on a local or national level. Our readers are of above-average intelligence, income and education. The majority of our articles are relationships, humor and seasonal submissions. Also publishes some fiction."

N $ THE ROMANTIC, Hundreds of Tips to Enrich Your Relationship, Sterling Publications, 750 SE Maynard Rd., Suite 108, Cary NC 27511. (919)462-0900. Fax: (919)461-8333. E-mail: romantc@aol.com. Website: http://www.TheRomantic.com. **Contact:** Michael Webb. **20% freelance written**. Bimonthly newsletter covering the art of romance. "*The RoMANtic* aims to inspire its readers to continually improve their relationships by providing them with creative ideas, practical advice and lots of fun suggestions." Estab. 1996. Circ. 10,000. Pays on publication. Publishes ms 4 months after acceptance. Byline given. Buys first North American serial rights or second serial (reprint) rights. Editorial lead time 3 months. Submit seasonal material 4 months in advance. Accepts simultaneous submissions. Reports in 3 months on mss. Sample copy for $3.

Nonfiction: Inspirational, personal experience. No sex, erotica or romance novels. Send complete ms. Length: 500 words. **Pays 2¢/word**.

Tips: "Read one or more back issues to see the types of romantic ideas and stories that are printed."

$ SINGLES LIFESTYLE & ENTERTAINMENT MAGAZINE, Single Lifestyle Publishing Group, 7611 S. Orange Blossom Trail, #190, Orlando FL 32809. **Contact:** Michael Orlando, editor. **50% freelance written.** Bimonthly tabloid "for single, divorced and widowed persons ages 25-50." Estab. 1997. Circ. 25,000. **Pays on acceptance**. Publishes ms 1 month after acceptance. Byline given. Offers 100% kill fee. Buys one-time rights. Editorial lead time 2 months. Submit seasonal material 2 months in advance. Reports in 3 weeks on queries. Sample copy and writer's guidelines free.

Nonfiction: General interest, humor, interview/profile, travel, single life, lifestyles, relationships, single parenting, trends, health, fitness. **Buys 20 mss/year.** Query with published clips. Length: 500-1,500 words. **Pays 10¢/word.** Sometimes pays expenses of writers on assignment (limit agreed upon in advance).

Photos: State availability of photos with submission. Reviews contact sheets. Negotiates payment individually. Model releases required. Buys one-time rights.

Columns/Departments: Single Lifestyles; Single Parenting; Coping with Divorce. Length: 250-1,000 words. **Buys 25 mss/year.** Query with published clips. **Pays 10¢/word.**

Fiction: Humor, romance. **Buys 12 mss/year.** Query with published clips. Length: 1,000-2,000 words. **Pays 10¢/word.**

Reprints: Send tearsheet or photocopy of article and informtion about when and where the article previously appeared. Payment negotiable.

Fillers: Anecdotes, facts, gags to be illustrated by cartoonist, newsbreaks, short humor. **Buys 50/year.** Length: 50-150 words. **Pays 10¢/word.**

Tips: "Freelance writers must review our writer's guidelines in depth, plus thoroughly read our issues for a true feel for what we look for in articles and features. Query first with past published clips (any subject). Be creative in your query. Think Single Lifestyle!"

RELIGIOUS

Religious magazines focus on a variety of subjects, styles and beliefs. Most are sectarian, but a number approach topics such as public policy, international affairs and contemporary society from a non-denominational perspective. Fewer religious publications are considering poems and personal experience articles, but many emphasize special ministries to singles, seniors or other special interest groups. Such diversity makes reading each magazine essential for the writer hoping to break in. Educational and inspirational material of interest to church members, workers and leaders within a denomination or religion is needed by the publications in this category. Religious magazines for children and teenagers can be found in the Juvenile and Teen and Young Adult classifications. Other religious publications can be found in the Contemporary Culture and Ethnic/Minority sections as well. Spiritual topics are also addressed in Astrology, Metaphysical and New Age as well as Health and Fitness. Publications intended to assist professional religious workers in teaching and managing church affairs are classified in Church Administration and Ministry in the Trade section.

$ AMERICA, 106 W. 56th St., New York NY 10019. (212)581-4640. **Contact:** Rev. George W. Hunt, editor. Published weekly for adult, educated, largely Roman Catholic audience. Estab. 1909. **Pays on acceptance.** Byline given. Usually buys all rights. Reports in 3 weeks. Free writer's guidelines.

Nonfiction: "We publish a wide variety of material on politics, economics, ecology and so forth. We are not a parochial publication, but almost all pieces make some moral or religious point. We are not interested in purely informational pieces or personal narratives which are self-contained and have no larger moral interest." Articles on literature, current political, social events. Length: 1,500-2,000 words. **Pays $50-200.**

Poetry: Patrick Samway, S.J., poetry editor. Length: 15-30 lines.

N ✪ $ $ ANGELS ON EARTH, Guideposts, Inc., 16 E. 34th St., New York NY 10016. (212)251-8100. E-mail: angelsedtr@guideposts.org. Editor: Fulton Oursler, Jr. **Contact:** Colleen Hughes, managing editor. **90% freelance written.** Bimonthly. "*Angels on Earth* publishes true stories about God's messengers at work in today's world. We are interested in stories of heavenly angels and stories involving humans who have played angelic roles in daily life." Estab. 1995. Circ. 800,000. Pays on publication. Byline given. Buys all rights. Editorial lead time 6 months. Submit seasonal material 6 months in advance. Reports in 3 months. Sample copy for 6½×9½ SAE with $1.01 postage. Writer's guidelines for SASE.

Nonfiction: True, inspirational, personal experience, religious (most stories are first-person experiences but can be ghost-written). Nothing that directly preaches, no how-to's. **Buys 80-100 mss/year.** Send complete ms. Length: 100-2,000 words. **Pays $25-400.**

Photos: State availability of photos or send photos with submission. Offers no additional payment for photos accepted with ms. Buys one-time rights.

Columns/Departments: Earning Their Wings (unusual stories of good deeds worth imitating); Only Human? (Is the angelic character a human being? The narrator is pleasantly unsure and so is the reader), both 500 words. **Buys 25 mss/year.** Send complete ms. **Pays $50-100.**

Fillers: Allison Sample, assistant editor. Short angel incidents, attributed quotes about angels. **Buys 20-30/year.**

$ THE ANNALS OF SAINT ANNE DE BEAUPRÉ, Redemptorist Fathers, P.O. Box 1000, St. Anne De Beaupré, Quebec, Quebec G0A 3C0 Canada. (418)827-4538. Fax: (418)827-4530. Editor: Father Bernard Mercier, CSs.R. **Contact:** Father Roch Archard, managing editor. **80% freelance written.** Monthly religious magazine. "Our mission statement includes a dedication to Christian family values and a devotion to St. Anne." Estab. 1885. Circ. 45,000. **Pays on acceptance.** Buys first North American rights. Editorial lead time 6 months. Submit seasonal material 4 months in advance. Reports in 3 weeks. Sample copy and writer's guidelines for 8½×11 SAE and IRCs.

Nonfiction: Inspirational, religious. **Buys 250 mss/year.** Send complete ms. Length: 500-1,500 words. **Pays 3-4/word,** plus 3 copies.
Photos: Send photos with submission. Negotiates payment individually. Identification of subjects required. Buys one-time rights.
Fiction: Religious, inspirational. "No senseless, mockery." **Buys 200 mss/year.** Send complete ms. Length: 500-1,500 words. **Pays 3-4¢/word.**
Tips: "Write something inspirational with spiritual thrust. Reporting rather than analysis is simply not remarkable. Each article must have a spiritual theme. Please only submit first North American rights mss with the rights clearly stated. We maintain an article bank and pick from it for each month's needs which loosely follow the religious themes for each month. Right now, our needs lean towards nonfiction of approximately 1,100 words."

$ THE ASSOCIATE REFORMED PRESBYTERIAN, Associate Reformed Presbyterian General Synod, 1 Cleveland St., Suite 110, Greenville SC 29601-3696. (803)232-8297. Fax: (864)271-3729. E-mail: aprmaged@sprynet.com. Website: http://www.arpsynod.org. **Contact:** Ben Johnston, editor. **5% freelance written.** Works with a small number of new/unpublished writers each year. Christian magazine serving a conservative, evangelical and Reformed denomination. Estab. 1976. Circ. 6,000. **Pays on acceptance.** Publishes ms an average of 4 months after acceptance. Byline given. Not copyrighted. Buys first, one-time or second serial (reprint) rights. Submit seasonal material 4 months in advance. Accepts simultaneous submissions. Reports in 1 month. Sample copy for $1.50. Guidelines for #10 SASE.
Nonfiction: Book excerpts, essays, inspirational, opinion, personal experience, religious. **Buys 10-15 mss/year.** Query. Length: 400-2,000 words. **Pays $70 maximum.**
Reprints: Send information about when and where the article previously appeared. Pays 100% of amount paid for an original article.
Photos: State availability of photos with submission. Offers $25 maximum/photo. Captions and identification of subjects required. Buys one-time rights.
Fiction: Religious and children's. **Pays $50 maximum.**
Tips: "Feature articles are the area of our publication most open to freelancers. Focus on a contemporary problem and offer Bible-based solutions to it. Provide information that would help a Christian struggling in his daily walk. Writers should understand that we are denominational, conservative, evangelical, Reformed and Presbyterian. A writer who appreciates these nuances would stand a much better chance of being published here than one who does not."

N $ BAPTIST LEADER, P.O. Box 851, Valley Forge PA 19482-0851. (610)768-2143. Fax: (610)768-2056. E-mail: don_ng@ecunet.org. **Contact:** Don Ng, editor. For pastors, teachers lay leaders and Christian education staff in churches. **5% freelance written.** Works with several new/unpublished writers each year. Quarterly magazine. Estab. 1939. Pays on publication. Publishes ms an average of 8 months after acceptance. Editorial lead time 8 months. Accepts previously published submissions. Send typed ms with rights for sale noted and information about when and where the article previously appeared. For reprints, pays 100% of amount paid for an original article. Sample copy for $1.50. Writer's guidelines for #10 SASE.
Nonfiction: Educational topics. How-to articles and programs for local church teachers and leaders. Length: 1,500-2,000 words. **Pays $25-75.**
Reprints: Send tearsheet or photocopy of article or typed ms with rights for sale noted and information about when and where the article previously appeared. **Pays $25-75.**
Tips: "Emphasis on Christian education administration and planning and articles for all church leaders. We will be looking for articles focusing on ministry with young adults, also ministry with senior adults. Share ideas that worked in your church."

$ BIBLE ADVOCATE, Bible Advocate Press, Church of God (Seventh Day), P.O. Box 33677, Denver CO 80233. (303)452-7973. E-mail: cofgsd@denver.net. Editor: Calvin Burrell. **Contact**: Sherri Langton, associate editor. **25% freelance written.** Religious magazine published 10 times/year. "Our purpose is to advocate the Bible and represent the Church of God (Seventh Day) to a Christian audience." Estab. 1863. Circ. 13,500. Pays on publication. Publishes ms an average of 9 months after acceptance. Byline given. Offers 50% kill fee. Buys first and second serial (reprint) rights, plus electronic rights. Editorial lead time 6 months. Submit seasonal material 6 months in advance. Accepts simultaneous submissions. Reports in 6 weeks. Sample copy for 9×12 SASE with 4 first-class stamps. Writer's guidelines for #10 SASE.
Nonfiction: Inspirational, interview/profile, opinion, personal experience, religious, biblical studies. No articles on Christmas or Easter. **Buys 20-25 mss/year.** Send complete ms and SASE. Length: 1,500-2,000 words long. Longer articles may be serialized. **Pays $10-35.**
Reprints: Send typed ms with rights for sale noted.
Photos: Send photos with submission. Reviews prints. Offers no additional payment for photos accepted with ms. Identification of subjects required. Buys one-time rights.
Columns/Departments: Viewpoint (opinion), 500-700 words. **Buys 6 mss/year.** Send complete ms and SASE. No payment for opinion pieces.
Poetry: Free verse, traditional. No avant-garde. **Buys 10-12 poems/year.** Submit maximum 5 poems. Length: 5-25 lines. **Pays $10.**
Fillers: Anecdotes, facts. **Buys 5/year.** Length: 50-100 words. **Pays $5-10.**
Tips: "Be fresh, not preachy! We're trying to reach a younger audience now, so think how you can cover contemporary

and biblical topics with this audience in mind. Articles must be in keeping with the doctrinal understanding of the Church of God (Seventh Day). Therefore, the writer should become familiar with what the Church generally accepts as truth as set forth in their doctrinal beliefs. We reserve the right to edit manuscripts to fit our space requirements, doctrinal stands and church terminology. Significant changes are referred to writers for approval. No fax or handwritten submissions, please."

BIBLE ADVOCATE ONLINE, Bible Advocate Press/Church of God (Seventh Day), P.O. Box 33677, Denver CO 80233. (303)452-7973. E-mail: cofgsd@denver.net. Website: http://www.denver.net/~baonline. Editor: Calvin Burrell. **Contact**: Sherri Langton, associate editor. **75% freelance written.** "Online religious publication covering social and religious topics; more inclusive of non-Christians." Estab. 1996. Pays on publication. Publishes ms an average of 6 months after acceptance. Byline given. Offers 50% kill fee. Buys first rights and second serial (reprint) rights. Editorial lead time 6 months. Submit seasonal material 6 months in advance. Accepts simultaneous submissions. Reports in 6 weeks on queries. Sample copy for 9×12 SAE and 3 first-class stamps. Writer's guidelines for #10 SASE.

Nonfiction: Inspirational, personal experience, religious. No Christmas or Easter pieces. **Buys 20-25 mss/year.** Send complete ms and SASE. Length: 1,500-2,000 words. **Pays $15-35.**

Reprints: Accepts previously published submissions. Send typed ms with rights for sale noted and information about when and where the article previously appeared. **Pays $15-35.**

Photos: Send photos with submission. Reviews prints. Offers no additional payment for photos accepted with ms. Identification of subjects required. Buys one-time rights.

Fillers: Anecdotes, facts. **Buys 6-10/year.** Length: 50-250 words. **Pays $5-10.**

Tips: "Be vulnerable in your personal experiences. Show, don't tell! Delete Christian jargon and write from perspective of a non-Christian. Articles must be in keeping with the doctrinal understanding of the Church of God (Seventh Day). Therefore, the writer should become familiar with what the Church generally accepts as truth as set forth in their doctrinal beliefs. We reserve the right to edit manuscripts to fit our space requirements, doctrinal stands and church terminology. Significant changes are referred to writers for approval. No fax or handwritten submissions, please."

$ BRIGADE LEADER, Christian Service Brigade, P.O. Box 150, Wheaton IL 60189. (630)665-0630. Fax: (630)665-0372. E-mail: brigadecsb@aol.com. Website: http://CSBministries.org. **Contact:** Deborah Christensen, editor. Quarterly magazine covering leadership issues for Christian Service Brigade leaders. "*Brigade Leader* is distributed to leaders with Christian Service Brigade across North America. CSB is a nonprofit, nondenominational agency dedicated to winning and training boys to serve Jesus Christ. Hundreds of churches throughout the U.S. and Canada make use of our wide range of services." Estab. 1960. Circ. 6,000. Pays on publication. Publishes ms an average of 3 months after acceptance. Byline given. Offers $35 kill fee. Buys first rights or second serial (reprint) rights. Editorial lead time 3 months. Reports in 1 week on queries. Sample copy for $1.50 and 10×13 SAE with 4 first-class stamps. Writer's guidelines for #10 SASE.

Nonfiction: Religious leadership. **Buys 8 mss/year.** Query only. Length: 500-1,500 words. **Pays 5-10¢/word.** Sometimes pays expenses of writers on assignment.

Reprints: Send typed ms with rights for sale noted. Pays 50% of amount paid for an original article.

Photos: State availability of photos with submission. Reviews prints. Negotiates payment. Buys one-time rights.

Tips: "We're looking for male writers who are familiar with Christian Service Brigade and can address leadership issues. Know *Brigade* and be able to offer practical and creative ideas for men to be better leaders."

$ $ CATHOLIC DIGEST, University of St. Thomas, P.O. Box 64090, St. Paul MN 55164. (612)962-6739. Fax: (612)962-6755. E-mail: cdigest@stthomas.edu. Website: http://www.CatholicDigest.org. Editor: Richard J. Reece, **Contact:** Kathleen Stauffer, managing editor. **15% freelance written.** Monthly magazine "publishes features and advice on topics ranging from health, psychology, humor, adventure and family, to ethics, spirituality and Catholics, from modern-day heroes to saints through the ages. Helpful and relevant reading culled from secular and religious periodicals." Estab. 1936. Circ. 509,385. **Pays on acceptance** for articles. Publishes ms an average of 4 months after acceptance. Byline given. Buys first rights, one-time rights or second serial (reprint) rights. Editorial lead time 4 months. Submit seasonal material 5 months in advance. Reports in 2 months on mss. Sample copy and writer's guidelines free.

Nonfiction: Book excerpts, essays, general interest, historical/nostalgic, how-to, humor, inspirational, interview/profile, personal experience, religious, travel. **Buys 60 mss/year.** Send complete ms. Length: 1.000-5,000 words. **Pays $200-400.**

Reprints: "Most articles we use are reprinted." Send tearsheet of article or typed ms with rights for sale noted and information about when and where the article previously appeared. Pays $100.

Photos: State availability of photos with submission. Reviews contact sheets, transparencies, prints. Negotiates payment individually. Captions, model releases, identification of subjects required.

Columns/Departments: Buys 75 mss/year. Send complete ms. **Pays $4-50.**

Fillers: Contact: Filler Editor. Anecdotes, short humor. **Buys 200/year.** Length: 1 line minimum, 500 words maximum. **Pays $2/per published line upon publication.**

Tips: "We're a lot more aggressive with inspirational/pop psychology/how-to articles these days. Spiritual and all other wellness self-help is a good bet for us."

$ $ CATHOLIC HERITAGE, Our Sunday Visitor, Inc., 200 Noll Plaza, Huntington IN 46750. (219)356-8400. Fax: (219)359-9117. E-mail: 76440.3571@compuserve.com. **Contact:** Bill Dodds, editor. **75% freelance written.**

Bimonthly magazine "explores the history and heritage of the Catholic faith with special emphasis on its impact on culture." Estab. 1991. Circ. 25,000. **Pays on acceptance.** Publishes ms an average of 1 year after acceptance. Byline given. Buys first North American serial rights. Editorial lead time 8-12 months. Submit seasonal material 6 months in advance. Reports in 3 weeks on queries; 1 month on mss. Send SASE for guidelines.

Nonfiction: Feature topics include scripture, US heritage, saints and personalities, religious art and culture, catechtics and apologetics, liturgy, universal Church heritage, seasonal celebrations and the history of prayers and devotions. Also book excerpts, general interest, interview/profile, photo feature, travel. "No nostalgia pieces about what it was like growing up Catholic or about life in the Church prior to Vatican II." **Buys 30 mss/year.** Query with SASE. Length: 1,200-1,300 words. **Pays $100-200.**

Columns/Departments: Book, tape and software reviews related to the above feature topics. Length: 200-250 words. **Pays $25.** Query with SASE.

Photos: State availability of photos with submission. Reviews prints. Negotiates payment individually. Captions required. Buys one-time rights.

Tips: "Write solid queries that take an aspect of the Catholic heritage and apply it to developments today. Show a good knowledge of the Church and a flair for historical writing. General features are most open to freelancers. Use a non-academic style and remember our readers are: Catholics who enjoy articles about the Church; recent converts who want to learn more about the Church; and 30-somethings who want to supplement their Church education. No fiction, fillers, poetry or reprints. Suggestions that have a news or time 'peg' stand a better chance of being accepted. (For example, a Vatican art exhibit scheduled to be coming to the United States. Or the 500th anniversary of a saint's death. It can take a while for a freelancer to 'break into' *Catholic Heritage* but we frequently assign articles to writers in our freelance 'pool.' Almost all our articles are written by freelancers."

$ $ CATHOLIC NEAR EAST MAGAZINE, Catholic Near East Welfare Association, 1011 First Ave., New York NY 10022-4195. (212)826-1480. Fax: (212)826-8979. **Contact:** Michael La Civitä, executive editor. **50% freelance written.** Bimonthly magazine for a Catholic audience with interest in the Near East, particularly its current religious, cultural and political aspects. Estab. 1974. Circ. 100,000. Pays on publication. Publishes ms an average of 6 months after acceptance. Byline given. Buys all rights. Reports in 2 months. Sample copy and writer's guidelines for 7½×10½ SAE with 2 first-class stamps.

Nonfiction: "Cultural, devotional, political, historical material on the Near East, with an emphasis on the Eastern Christian churches. Style should be simple, factual, concise. Articles must stem from personal acquaintance with subject matter, or thorough up-to-date research." Length: 1,200-1,800 words. **Pays 20¢/edited word.**

Photos: "Photographs to accompany manuscript are welcome; they should illustrate the people, places, ceremonies, etc. which are described in the article. We prefer color transparencies but occasionally use b&w. Pay varies depending on use—scale from $50-300."

Tips: "We are interested in current events in the regions listed above as they affect the cultural, political and religious lives of the people."

N $ CATHOLIC SENTINEL, Oregon Catholic Press, P.O. Box 18030, Portland OR 97218. (503)281-1191. Fax: (503)282-3486. E-mail: casentinel@aol.com. **Contact**: Bob Pfohman, editor. **10% freelance written.** "Catholic diocesan newspaper about and for the Catholic community in Oregon. All articles must have Catholic and Oregon connections." Estab. 1870. Circ. 17,000. Pays on publication. Publishes ms an average of 1 month after acceptance. Byline given. Offers 100% kill fee. "We reserve the right to rewrite (and cut fee) to fit our publication." Not copyrighted. Buys first rights. Editorial lead time 1 month. Submit seasonal material 2 months in advance. Reports in 6 weeks. Sample copy for 75¢ and SAE with 3 first-class stamps.

Nonfiction: Bob Pfohman, editor. Historical/nostalgic (Oregon Catholic history), interview/profile (Oregon Catholics), opinion (no payment), personal experience, travel (no payment). **Buys 5-10 mss/year.** Query for features and personal experiences. Send complete ms for opinion pieces. Length: 750-1,500 words. **Pays $25-150 for assigned articles; $10-50 for unsolicited articles.** Sometimes pays expenses of writers on assignment.

Reprints: Accepts previously published submissions.

Photos: State availability of photos with submission. Reviews prints. Negotiates payment individually. Captions and identification of subjects required. Buys one-time rights.

Columns/Departments: Buys 10-15 mss/year. Query or send complete ms. **Pays $0-25.**

$ $ THE CHRISTIAN CENTURY, Christian Century Foundation, 407 S. Dearborn St., Suite 1405, Chicago IL 60605-1150. (312)427-5380. Fax: (312)427-1302. Website: http://www.christiancentury.org. Editor: James M. Wall. Senior Editors: Martin E. Marty and Dean Peerman. Managing Editor: David Heim. **Contact**: Attn: Manuscripts. **90% freelance written.** Eager to work with new/unpublished writers. Weekly magazine for ecumenically-minded, progressive Protestant church people, both clergy and lay. "Authors must have a critical and analytical perspective on the church and be familiar with contemporary theological discussion." Estab. 1884. Circ. 30,000. Pays on publication. Publishes ms an average of 3 months after acceptance. Buys all rights. Editorial lead time 1 month. Submit seasonal material 4 months in advance. Accepts simultaneous submissions. Reports in 1 week on queries; 2 months on mss. Sample copy available for $3.

Nonfiction: Essays, humor, interview/profile, opinion, religious. "We use articles dealing with social problems, ethical dilemmas, political issues, international affairs and the arts, as well as with theological and ecclesiastical matters. We focus on concerns that arise at the juncture between church and society, or church and culture." No inspirational. **Buys**

150 mss/year. Send complete ms; query appreciated, but not essential. All queries, mss should be accompanied by 9×12 SASE. Length: 1,000-3,000 words. **Pays $75-200 for assigned articles; $75-150 for unsolicited articles.**
Photos: State availability of photos. Reviews any size prints. Offers $25-100/photo. Buys one-time rights.
Fiction: Humorous, religious, slice-of-life vignettes. No moralistic, unrealistic fiction. **Buys 4 mss/year.** Send complete ms. Length: 1,000-3,000. **Pays $75-200.**
Poetry: Jill Peláez Baumgaertner, poetry editor. Avant-garde, free verse, haiku, traditional. No sentimental or didactic poetry. **Buys 50 poems/year.** Length: 20 lines. **Pays $50.**
Tips: "We seek manuscripts that articulate the public meaning of faith, bringing the resources of religious tradition to bear on such topics as poverty, human rights, economic justice, international relations, national priorities and popular culture. We are also interested in articles that examine or critique the theology and ethos of individual religious communities. We welcome articles that find fresh meaning in old traditions and which adapt or apply religious traditions to new circumstances. Authors should assume that readers are familiar with main themes in Christian history and theology; are unthreatened by the historical-critical study of the Bible; and are already engaged in relating faith to social and political issues. Many of our readers are ministers or teachers of religion at the college level."

$ CHRISTIAN COURIER, Calvinist Contact Publishing, 4-261 Martindale Rd., St. Catharines, Ontario L2W 1A1 Canada. (905)682-8311. Fax: (905)682-8313. E-mail: cceditor@aol.com. **Contact:** Bert Witvoet, editor. **20% freelance written.** Weekly newspaper covering news of importance to Christians, comments and features. "We assume a Christian perspective which acknowledges that this world belongs to God and that human beings are invited to serve God in every area of society." Estab. 1945. Circ. 5,000. Pays 30 days after publication. Publishes ms an average of 2 months after acceptance. Byline given. Offers 50% kill fee. Editorial lead time 1 month. Submit seasonal material 6 months in advance. Accepts simultaneous submissions. Reports back only if material accepted.
Nonfiction: Interview/profile, opinion. **Buys 40 mss/year.** Send complete ms. Length: 500-1,200 words. **Pays $35-60 for assigned articles; $25-50 for unsolicited articles.** Sometimes pays expenses of writers on assignment.
Reprints: Accepts previously published submissions.
Photos: State availability of photos with submission.

$ CHRISTIAN EDUCATION COUNSELOR, General Council of the Assemblies of God, 1445 Boonville, Springfield MO 65802-1894. (417)862-2781. Fax: (417)862-0503. E-mail: ceeditor@ag.org. Website: http://www.we-build-people.org. Editor: Sylvia Lee. **20% freelance written.** Works with small number of new/unpublished writers each year. Bimonthly magazine on religious education in the local church—the official Sunday school voice of the Assemblies of God channeling programs and help to local, primarily lay, leadership. Estab. 1939. Circ. 20,000. **Pays on acceptance.** Publishes ms an average of 9 months after acceptance. Byline given. Offers variable kill fee. Buys first North American serial, one-time, all, simultaneous, first serial or second serial (reprint) rights or makes work-for-hire assignments. Submit seasonal material 7 months in advance. Accepts simultaneous submissions. Reports in 1 month. Sample copy and writer's guidelines for SASE.
Nonfiction: How-to, inspirational, interview/profile, personal experience, photo feature. All related to religious education in the local church. **Buys 100 mss/year.** Send complete ms. Length: 300-700 words. **Pays $25-150.**
Reprints: Send tearsheet of article or typed ms with rights for sale noted and information about when and where the article previously appeared. Pays 50% of amount paid for an original article.
Photos: Send photos with ms. Reviews b&w and color prints. Model releases and identification of subjects required. Buys one-time rights.

- Looking for more photo-illustrated mss.

$ $ CHRISTIAN HOME & SCHOOL, Christian Schools International, 3350 East Paris Ave. SE, Grand Rapids MI 49512. (616)957-1070, ext. 234. Fax: (616)957-5022. E-mail: chrschint@aol.com. Website: http://www.ChristianSchoolsInt.com. Executive Editor: Gordon L. Bordewyk. **Contact:** Roger Schmurr, senior editor. **30% freelance written.** Circ. 62,000. Works with a small number of new/unpublished writers each year. Bimonthly magazine covering family life and Christian education. "*Christian Home & School* is designed for parents in the United States and Canada who send their children to Christian schools and are concerned about the challenges facing Christian families today. These readers expect a mature, biblical perspective in the articles, not just a bible verse tacked onto the end." Estab. 1922. Pays on publication. Publishes ms an average of 4 months after acceptance. Byline given. Buys first North American serial rights. Submit seasonal material 4 months in advance. Reports in 1 month. Sample copy and writer's guidelines for 9×12 SAE with 4 first-class stamps. Writer's guidelines only for #10 SASE.
Nonfiction: Book excerpts, interview/profile, opinion, personal experience, articles on parenting and school life. "We publish features on issues that affect the home and school and profiles on interesting individuals, providing that the profile appeals to our readers and is not a tribute or eulogy of that person." **Buys 40 mss/year.** Send complete ms. Length: 750-2,000 words. **Pays $125-200.** Sometimes pays the expenses of writers on assignment.
Photos: "If you have any color photos appropriate for your article, send them along."
Tips: "Features are the area most open to freelancers. We are publishing articles that deal with contemporary issues that affect parents. Use an informal easy-to-read style rather than a philosophical, academic tone. Try to incorporate vivid imagery and concrete, practical examples from real life."

$ $ CHRISTIAN READER, Stories of Faith, Hope and God's Love, Christianity Today, 465 Gundersen Dr., Carol Stream IL 60188. (630)260-6200. Fax: (630)260-0114. E-mail: creditoria@aol.com. Website: http://www.Christian

reader.net. Contact: Bonne Steffen, editor. **35% freelance written.** Bimonthly magazine for adult evangelical Christian audience. Estab. 1963. Circ. 225,000. **Pays on acceptance for first rights**; on publication for reprints. Byline given. Editorial lead time 6 months. Submit seasonal material 9 months in advance. Reports in 3 weeks. Sample copy for 5×8 SAE with 4 first-class stamps. Writer's guidelines for #10 SASE.
Nonfiction: Humor, inspirational, personal experience, religious. **Buys 50 mss/year.** Query or article on spec. Length: 500-1,200 words. **Pays $100-250** depending on length. Pays expenses of writers on assignment.
Reprints: Send tearsheet or photocopy of article or typed manuscript with rights for sale noted and information about when and where the article previously appeared. Pays 35-50% of amount paid for original article on publication.
Photos: State availability of photos with submission. Negotiates payment individually. Buys one-time rights.
Columns/Departments: Contact: Cynthia Thomas, editorial coordinator. Lite Fare (adult church humor), 50-200 words; Kids of the Kingdom (kids say and do funny things), 50-200 words; Rolling Down the Aisle (humorous wedding tales), 50-200 words. **Buys 150 mss/year.** Send complete ms. **Pays $25-35.**
Fillers: End-of-article vignettes, 100-250 words. Send complete ms.
Tips: "Most of our articles are reprints or staff-written. Freelance competition is keen, so tailor submissions to meet our needs by observing the following: *The Christian Reader* audience is truly a general interest one, including men and women, urban professionals and rural homemakers, adults of every age and marital status, and Christians of every church affiliation. We seek to publish a magazine that people from the variety of ethnic groups in North America will find interesting and relevant."

$ CHRISTIAN SOCIAL ACTION, 100 Maryland Ave. NE, Washington DC 20002. (202)488-5621. Fax: (202)488-1617. E-mail: lranck@igc.org. **Contact:** Lee Ranck, editor. **2% freelance written.** Works with a small number of new/unpublished writers each year. Monthly for "United Methodist clergy and lay people interested in in-depth analysis of social issues, with emphasis on the church's role or involvement in these issues." Circ. 2,500. May buy all rights. Pays on publication. Publishes ms an average of 2 months after acceptance. Rights purchased vary with author and material. Returns rejected material in 5 weeks. Reports on material accepted for publication in a month. Sample copy and writer's guidelines for #10 SASE.
Nonfiction: "This is the social action publication of The United Methodist Church published by the denomination's General Board of Church and Society. Our publication tries to relate social issues to the church—what the church can do, is doing; why the church should be involved. We only accept articles relating to social issues, e.g., war, draft, peace, race relations, welfare, police/community relations, labor, population problems, drug and alcohol problems. No devotional, 'religious,' superficial material, highly technical articles, personal experiences or poetry." **Buys 25-30 mss/year.** "Query to show that writer has expertise on a particular social issue, give credentials, and reflect a readable writing style." Length: 2,000 words maximum. **Pays $75-125.** Sometimes pays the expenses of writers on assignment.
Reprints: Send tearsheet of article and information about where and when the article previously appeared. Payment negotiable.
Tips: "Write on social issues, but not superficially; we're more interested in finding an expert who can write (e.g., on human rights, alcohol problems, peace issues) than a writer who attempts to research a complex issue."

$ $ CHRISTIANITY TODAY, 465 Gundersen Dr., Carol Stream IL 60188-2498. Fax: (630)260-0114. E-mail: carolthi@aol.com or ctedit@aol.com. Website: http://www.christianitytoday.net. **Contact:** Carol Thiessen, administrative editor. **80% freelance written.** Works with a small number of new/unpublished writers each year. Semimonthly magazine emphasizing orthodox, evangelical religion "covers Christian doctrine, issues, trends and current events and news from a Christian perspective. It provides a forum for the expression of evangelical conviction in theology, evangelism, church life, cultural life, and society. Special features include issues of the day, books, films, missions, schools, music and services available to the Christian market." Estab. 1956. Circ. 187,000. Publishes ms an average of 6 months after acceptance. Usually buys first serial rights. Submit seasonal material at least 8 months in advance. Reports in 3 months. Sample copy and writer's guidelines for 9×12 SAE with 3 first-class stamps.
Nonfiction: Theological, ethical, historical, informational (not merely inspirational). **Buys 4 mss/issue.** *Query only.* Unsolicited mss not accepted and not returned. Length: 1,000-4,000 words. Pays negotiable rates. Sometimes pays the expenses of writers on assignment.
Reprints: Pays 25% of amount paid for an original article.
Columns/Departments: Church in Action (profiles of not-so-well-known Christians involved in significant or offbeat services). **Buys 7 mss/year.** Query only. Length: 900-1,000 words.
Tips: "We are developing more of our own manuscripts and requiring a much more professional quality from others. Queries without SASE will not be answered and manuscripts not containing SASE will not be returned."

$ $ CHRYSALIS READER, P.O. Box 549, West Chester PA 19381-0549. Fax: (804)983-1074. E-mail: lawson@aba.org. Send inquiries and mss directly to the editorial office: Route 1, Box 184, Dillwyn VA 23936-9616. **Contact:** Carol S. Lawson, editor. Managing Editor: Susanna van Rensselaer. **60% freelance written.** Biannual literary magazine on spiritually related topics. "*It is very important to send for writer's guidelines and sample copies before submitting.* Content of fiction, articles, reviews, poetry, etc., should be directly focused on that issue's theme and directed to the educated, intellectually curious reader." Estab. 1985. Circ. 3,000. Pays at page-proof stage. Publishes ms an average of 9 months after acceptance. Byline given. Buys first rights and makes work-for-hire assignments. Reports in 1 month on queries; 3 months on mss. Sample copy for $10 and 9×12 SAE. Writer's guidelines and copy deadlines for SASE.
Nonfiction: Essays and interview/profile. Upcoming themes: Symbols (Autumn 1998); Choices (Spring 1999); Ages

(Autumn 1999). Education (Spring 2000). **Buys 30 mss/year.** Query. Length: 2,500-3,500 words. **Pays $50-250 for assigned articles; $50-150 for unsolicited articles.**

Photos and Illustrations: Send suggestions for illustrations with submission. Offers no additional payment for photos accepted with ms. Captions and identification of subjects required. Buys original artwork for cover and inside copy; b&w illustrations related to theme; pays $25-150. Buys one-time rights.

Fiction: Patte Levan, fiction editor. Adventure, experimental, historical, mainstream, mystery, science fiction, related to theme of issue. **Buys 6 mss/year.** Query. Length: 2,500-3,500 words. Short fiction more likely to be published. **Pays $50-150.**

Poetry: Rob Lawson, senior editor. Avant-garde and traditional *but not religious.* **Buys 15 poems/year.** Submit maximum 6. **Pays $25.**

$ $ COLUMBIA, 1 Columbus Plaza, New Haven CT 06510. (203)772-2130. Fax: (203)777-0114. **Contact:** Richard McMunn, editor. Monthly magazine for Catholic families. Caters particularly to members of the Knights of Columbus. Estab. 1921. Circ. 1,500,000. **Pays on acceptance.** Buys first serial rights. Free sample copy and writer's guidelines.

Nonfiction and Photos: Fact articles directed to the Catholic layman and his family dealing with current events, social problems, Catholic apostolic activities, education, ecumenism, rearing a family, literature, science, arts, sports and leisure. Color glossy prints, transparencies or contact prints with negatives are required for illustration. Articles without ample illustrative material are not given consideration. **Pays $250-500, including photos.** Query with SASE. Length: 1,000-1,500 words. **Buys 20 mss/year.**

Tips: "Few unsolicited manuscripts are accepted."

$ CONSCIENCE, A Newsjournal of Prochoice Catholic Opinion, Catholics for a Free Choice, 1436 U St. NW, Suite 301, Washington DC 20009-3997. (202)986-6093. E-mail: cffc@igc.apc.org. **Contact:** Editor. **80% freelance written.** Sometimes works with new/unpublished writers. Quarterly newsjournal covering reproductive health and rights, including but not limited to abortion rights in the church, and church-state issues in US and worldwide. "A feminist, pro-choice perspective is a must, and knowledge of Christianity and specifically Catholicism is helpful." Estab. 1980. Circ. 12,000. Pays on publication. Publishes ms an average of 4 months after acceptance. Byline given. Buys first North American serial rights or makes work-for-hire assignments. Reports in 4 months. Sample copy for 9×12 SAE with 4 first-class stamps. Writer's guidelines for #10 SASE.

Nonfiction: Book excerpts, interview/profile, opinion, issue anaylsis, a small amount of personal experience. Especially needs material that recognizes the complexity of reproductive issues and decisions, and offers original, honest insight. **Buys 8-12 mss/year.** Query with published clips or send complete ms. Length: 1,000-3,500 words. **Pays $25-150.** "Writers should be aware that we are a nonprofit organization."

Reprints: Sometimes accepts previously published submissions. Send typed ms with rights for sale noted and information about when and where the article previously appeared. Pays 20-30% of amount paid for an original article.

Photos: State availability of photos with query or ms. Prefers b&w prints. Identification of subjects required.

Columns/Departments: Book reviews. **Buys 6-10 mss/year.** Length: 600-1,200 words. **Pays $25-50.**

Tips: "Say something new on the issue of abortion, or sexuality, or the role of religion or the Catholic church, or women's status in the church. Thoughtful, well-researched and well-argued articles needed. The most frequent mistakes made by writers in submitting an article to us are lack of originality and wordiness."

$ $ CORNERSTONE, Cornerstone Communications, Inc., 939 W. Wilson, Chicago IL 60640-5718. (773)561-2450, ext. 2080. Fax: (773)989-2076. Editor: Jon Trott. **Contact:** Joyce Paskewich, submissions editor. **10% freelance written.** Eager to work with new/unpublished writers. Quarterly magazine covering contemporary issues in the light of Evangelical Christianity. Estab. 1972. Pays after publication. Byline given. Buys first serial rights. Submit seasonal material 6 months in advance. Accepts simultaneous submissions. Does not return mss. "We will contact you *only* if your work is accepted for possible publication. We *encourage* simultaneous submissions because we take so long to get back to people! We prefer actual manuscripts to queries." Sample copy and writer's guidelines for 8½×11 envelope with 5 first-class stamps.

Nonfiction: Essays, personal experience, religious. **Buys 1-2 mss/year.** Query with SASE or send complete ms. Length: 2,700 words maximum. **Pays 8-10¢/word.** Sometimes pays expenses of writers on assignment.

Reprints: Accepts previously published submissions. Send typed ms with rights for sale noted and information about when and where the article previously appeared. Pays 8-10¢/word.

Columns/Departments: Music (interview with artists, mainly rock, focusing on artist's world view and value system as expressed in his/her music), Current Events, Personalities, Film and Book Reviews (focuses on meaning as compared and contrasted to biblical values). **Buys 1-4 mss/year.** Query. Length: 100-2,500 words (negotiable). **Pays 8-10¢/word.**

Fiction: "Articles may express Christian world view but should not be unrealistic or 'syrupy.' Other than porn, the sky's the limit. We want fiction as creative as the Creator." **Buys 1-4 mss/year.** Send complete ms. Length: 250-2,500 words (negotiable). **Pays negotiable rate, 8-10¢/word.**

Poetry: Tammy Perlmutter, poetry editor. Avant-garde, free verse, haiku, light verse, traditional. No limits *except* for epic poetry ("We've not the room!"). **Buys 10-50 poems/year.** Submit maximum 5 poems. **Payment negotiated. 1-15 lines: $10. Over 15 lines: $25.**

Tips: "A display of creativity which expresses a biblical world view without clichés or cheap shots at non-Christians is the ideal. We are known as one of the most avant-garde magazines in the Christian market, yet attempt to express orthodox beliefs in language of the '90s. *Any* writer who does this may well be published by *Cornerstone*. Creative fiction is begging for more Christian participation. We anticipate such contributions gladly. Interviews where well-known personalities respond to the gospel are also strong publication possibilities."

$ $ DECISION, Billy Graham Evangelistic Association, 1300 Harmon Place, Minneapolis MN 55403-1988. (612)338-0500. Fax: (612)335-1299. E-mail: submissions@graham-assn.org. Website: http://www.graham-assn.org/decision. Interim Editor: Kersten Beckstrom. **Contact**: Bob Paulson, associate editor. **25-40% freelance written.** Works each year with small number of new/unpublished writers, as well as a solid stable of experienced writers. Monthly magazine with a mission "to set forth to every reader the Good News of salvation in Jesus Christ with such vividness and clarity that he or she will be drawn to make a commitment to Christ; to encourage, teach and strengthen Christians." Estab. 1960. Circ. 1,700,000. Pays on publication. Byline given. Buys first rights and assigns work-for-hire manuscripts, articles, projects. Include telephone number with submission. Submit seasonal material 10 months in advance; other mss published up to 18 months after acceptance. Reports in 3 months on mss. Sample copy for 9×12 SAE with 4 first-class stamps. Writer's guidelines for #10 SASE.

Nonfiction: How-to, motivational, personal experience and religious. "No personality-centered articles or articles that are issue-oriented or critical of denominations." **Buys approximately 75 mss/year.** Send complete ms. Length: 400-1,500 words. **Pays $30-250.** Pays expenses of writers on assignment.

Photos: State availability of photos with submission. Reviews prints. Captions, model releases and identification of subjects required. Buys one-time rights.

Poetry: Accepting submissions. No queries.

Tips: "We are seeking personal conversion testimonies and personal experience articles that show how God intervened in a person's daily life and the way in which Scripture was applied to the experience in helping to solve the problem. The conversion testimonies describe in first person what author's life was like before he/she became a Christian, how he/she committed his/her life to Christ and what difference He has made since that decision. We also are looking for vignettes on various aspects of personal evangelism. SASE required with submissions."

$ $ DISCIPLESHIP JOURNAL, NavPress, a division of The Navigators, P.O. Box 35004, Colorado Springs CO 80935-0004. (719)531-3529. Fax: (719)598-7128. E-mail: susan_nikaido@navigators.org. Website: http://www.navigators.org/djhome.html. **Contact:** Susan Nikaido, editor. **90% freelance written.** Works with a small number of new/unpublished writers each year. Bimonthly magazine. "The mission of *Discipleship Journal* is to help believers develop a deeper relationship with Jesus Christ, and to provide practical help in understanding the scriptures and applying them to daily life and ministry. We prefer those who have not written for us before begin with nontheme articles about almost any aspect of Christian living. We'd like more articles that explain a Bible passage and show how to apply it to everyday life, as well as articles about developing a relationship with Jesus; reaching the world; or specific issues related to leadership and helping other believers grow." Estab. 1981. Circ. 110,000. **Pays on acceptance.** Publishes ms an average of 6 months after acceptance. Byline given. Buys first North American serial rights and second serial (reprint) rights. Submit seasonal material 6 months in advance. Reports in 6 weeks. Sample copy and writer's guidelines for $2.24 and 9×12 SAE.

Nonfiction: Book excerpts (rarely); how-to (grow in Christian faith and disciplines; help others grow as Christians; serve people in need; understand and apply the Bible); inspirational; interview/profile (focusing on one aspect of discipleship); and interpretation/application of the Bible. No personal testimony; humor; anything not directly related to Christian life and faith; politically partisan articles. **Buys 80 mss/year.** Query with published clips and SASE only. Length: 500-3,000 words. **Pays 20¢/word for first rights.** Sometimes pays the expenses of writers on assignment.

Reprints: Send tearsheet of article and information about when and where the article previously appeared. Pays 25% of amount paid for an original article.

Tips: "Our articles are meaty, not fluffy. Study writer's guidelines and back issues and try to use similar approaches. Don't preach. Polish before submitting. About half of the articles in each issue are related to one theme. Freelancers should write to request theme list. We are looking for more practical articles on ministering to others and more articles dealing with world missions. Be vulnerable. Show the reader that you have wrestled with the subject matter in your own life. We can no longer accept unsolicited manuscripts. Query first."

N $ DOVETAIL, A Journal By and For Jewish/Christian Families, Dovetail Publishing, Inc., P.O. Box 19945, Kalamazoo MI 49019. Fax: (616)342-1012. E-mail: dovetail@mich.com. **Contact**: Joan C. Hawxhurst, editor. **75% freelance written.** Bimonthly newsletter for interfaith families. "All articles must pertain to life in an interfaith (Jewish/Christian) family. We accept all kinds of opinions related to this topic." Estab. 1992. Circ. 1,500. Pays on publication. Publishes ms an average of 9 months after acceptance. Byline given. Buys first, one-time or second serial (reprint) rights. Editorial lead time 6 months. Submit seasonal material 6 months in advance. Accepts simultaneous submissions. Reports in 3 months. Sample copy for 9×12 SAE with 3 first-class stamps. Writer's guidelines free.

Nonfiction: Interview/profile, opinion, personal experience. No fiction. **Buys 5-8 mss/year.** Send complete ms. Length: 800-1,000 words. **Pays $20** plus 2 copies.

Reprints: Accepts previously published submissions.

Photos: Send photos with submission. Reviews 5×7 prints. Offers no additional payment for photos accepted with ms. Model releases and identification of subjects required. Buys one-time rights.

Fillers: Anecdotes, short humor. **Buys 1-2/year.** Length: 25-100 words. **Pays $10.**

Tips: "Successful freelancers are part of an interfaith family themselves, or have done solid research/interviews with members of interfaith families. We look for honest, reflective personal experience."

$ EMPHASIS ON FAITH & LIVING, Missionary Church, Inc., P.O. Box 9127, Fort Wayne IN 46899. (219)747-2027. Fax: (219)747-5331. E-mail: rlransom@aol.com. Website: http://www.mcusa.org. **Contact**: Robert Ransom, managing editor. Editor: Vernon Petersen. **5% freelance written.** "Bimonthly denominational magazine targeted at the constituents of the missionary church focusing on Christian articles and news." Estab. 1969. Circ. 14,000. Pays on publication. Publishes ms an average of 4 months after acceptance. Byline given. Buys one-time rights. Editorial lead time 8 months. Submit seasonal material 6 months in advance. Accepts simultaneous submissions. Reports in 1 month on queries; 4 months on mss. Sample copy for 9×12 SAE and 2 first-class stamps. Writer's guidelines for #10 SASE.
Nonfiction: Inspirational, personal experience, religious. **Buys 3 mss/year.** Query. Length: 250-1,500 words. **Pays $15-50.**
Reprints: Send photocopy of article or short story or typed ms with rights for sale noted and information about when and where the article or story previously appeared. Negotiates payment.
Photos: State availability of photos with submission. Negotiates payment individually. Buys one-time rights.
Fiction: Religious. **Buys 1-2 mss/year.** Query. Length: 250-1,500 words. **Pays $15-50.**

$ EVANGEL, Free Methodist Publishing House, P.O. Box 535002, Indianapolis IN 46253-5002. (317)244-3660. **Contact:** Julie Innes, editor. **100% freelance written.** Weekly take-home paper for adults. Estab. 1897. Circ. 22,000. Pays on publication. Publishes ms an average of 1 year after acceptance. Buys simultaneous, second serial (reprint) or one-time rights. Submit seasonal material 9 months in advance. Reports in 1 month. Sample copy and writer's guidelines for #10 SASE.
Nonfiction: Interview (with ordinary person who is doing something extraordinary in his community, in service to others), profile (of missionary or one from similar service profession who is contributing significantly to society), personal experience (finding a solution to a problem common to young adults; coping with handicapped child, for instance, or with a neighborhood problem. Story of how God-given strength or insight saved a situation). **Buys 100 mss/year.** Submit complete ms. Length: 300-1,000 words. **Pays 4¢/word.**
Reprints: Send typed ms with rights for sale noted and information about when and where the article previously appeared.
Photos: Purchased with accompanying ms. Captions required.
Fiction: Religious themes dealing with contemporary issues dealt with from a Christian frame of reference. Story must "go somewhere." **Buys 50 mss/year.** Submit complete ms.
Poetry: Free verse, light verse, traditional, religious. **Buys 20 poems/year.** Submit maximum 5 poems. Length: 4-24 lines. **Pays $10.**
Tips: "Seasonal material will get a second look. Write an attention-grabbing lead followed by an article that says something worthwhile. Relate the lead to some of the universal needs of the reader—promise in that lead to help the reader in some way. Lack of SASE brands author as a nonprofessional; I seldom even bother to read the script."

$ $ FAITH TODAY, Informing Canadian Evangelicals On Thoughts, Trends, Issues and Events, Evangelical Fellowship of Canada, MIP Box 3745, Markham, Ontario L3R 0Y4 Canada. (905)479-5885. Fax: (905)479-4742. E-mail: ft@efc-canada.com. Website: http://www.efc-canada.com. **Contact:** Marianne Meed Ward, managing editor. "*FT* is a bimonthly interdenominational, evangelical news/feature magazine that informs Canadian Christians on issues facing church and society, and on events within the church community. It focuses on corporate faith interacting with society rather than on personal spiritual life. Writers should have a thorough understanding of the *Canadian evangelical* community." Estab. 1983. Circ. 18,000. Pays on publication. Publishes ms an average of 6 months after acceptance. Byline given. Offers 30-50% kill fee. Buys first rights. Editorial lead time 4 months. Reports in 6 weeks. Sample copy and writer's guidelines free.
Nonfiction: Religious, news feature. **Buys 75 mss/year.** Query. Length: 400-2,000 words. **Pays $100-500 Canadian,** more for cover topic material. Sometimes pays expenses of writers on assignment.
Reprints: Send photocopy of article. Pays 50% of amount paid for an original article.
Photos: State availability of photos with submission. Reviews contact sheets, prints. Identification of subjects required. Buys one-time rights.
Tips: "Query should include brief outline and names of the sources you plan to interview in your research. Use Canadian postage on SASE."

$ $ GUIDEPOSTS MAGAZINE, 16 E. 34th St., New York NY 10016-4397. Website: http://www.guideposts.org. **Contact:** Fulton Oursler, Jr., editor. **30% freelance written.** Works with a small number of new/unpublished writers each year. "*Guideposts* is an inspirational monthly magazine for people of all faiths, in which men and women from all walks of life tell in first-person narrative how they overcame obstacles, rose above failures, handled sorrow, learned to master themselves and became more effective people through faith in God." Estab. 1945. Publishes ms an "indefinite" number of months after acceptance. Pays 25% kill fee for assigned articles. "Most of our stories are ghosted articles, so the writer would not get a byline unless it was his/her own story." Buys all rights and second serial (reprint) rights. Reports in 2 months.
Nonfiction and Fillers: Articles and features should be written in simple, anecdotal style with an emphasis on human interest. Short mss of approximately 250-750 words **(pays $100-250)** considered for such features as "Angels Among Us," "The Divine Touch" and general one-page stories. Address short items to Celeste McCauley. For full-length mss, 750-1,500 words, **pays $250-500.** All mss should be typed, double-spaced and accompanied by SASE. Annually awards

scholarships to high school juniors and seniors in writing contest. **Buys 40-60 unsolicited mss/year.** Pays expenses of writers on assignment.

Tips: "Study the magazine before you try to write for it. Each story must make a single spiritual point. The freelancer would have the best chance of breaking in by aiming for a one- or two-page article. Sensitively written anecdotes are extremely useful. And it is much easier to just sit down and write them than to have to go through the process of preparing a query. They should be warm, well written, intelligent and upbeat. We like personal narratives that are true and have some universal relevance, but the religious element does not have to be driven home with a sledge hammer. A writer succeeds with us if he or she can write a true article in short-story form with scenes, drama, tension and a resolution of the problem presented. We are especially in need of stories in which faith in God helps people succeed in business or with other life challenges."

N $ LIGHT AND LIFE MAGAZINE, Free Methodist Church of North America, P.O. Box 535002, Indianapolis IN 46253-5002. Fax: (317)244-1247. E-mail: llmeditor@aol.com. **Contact:** Doug Newton, editor. Works with a small number of new/unpublished writers each year. Bimonthly magazine emphasizing evangelical Christianity with Wesleyan slant for a cross section of adults. Also includes discipleship guidebook and national/international and denominational religion news. Estab. 1868. Circ. 21,000. Pays on publication. Byline given. Prefers first serial rights. Sample copy and guidelines for $4. Writer's guidelines for SASE.

Nonfiction: Submit complete ms. **Pays 4¢/word, 5¢/word if submitted on disk.** Varying word lengths.

Photos: Purchased without accompanying ms. Send prints or slides. Pays $35 and higher for color or b&w photos.

$ $ LIGUORIAN, Liguori MO 63057-9999. Fax: (314)464-8449. E-mail: 104626.1547@compuserve.com. Website: http://www.liguori.org. Managing Editor: Cheryl Plass. **Contact:** Rev. Allan Weinert, editor-in-chief. **25% freelance written.** Prefers to work with published/established writers. General interest monthly magazine for Catholics. "Our purpose is to lead our readers to a fuller Christian life by helping them better understand the teachings of the gospel and the church and by illustrating how these teachings apply to life and the problems confronting them as members of families, the church and society." Estab. 1913. Circ. 275,000. **Pays on acceptance.** Buys all rights but will reassign rights to author *after* publication upon written request. Submit seasonal material 8 months in advance. Reports in 3-6 months. Sample copy and writer's guidelines for 6×9 SAE with 3 first-class stamps.

Nonfiction: "Pastoral, practical and personal approach to the problems and challenges of people today. No travelogue approach or unresearched ventures into controversial areas. Also, no material found in secular publications—fad subjects that already get enough press, pop psychology, negative or put-down articles." **Buys 60 unsolicited mss/year. Buys 12 fiction mss/year.** Length: 400-2,000 words. **Pays 10-12¢/word.** Sometimes pays expenses of writers on assignment.

Photos: Photographs on assignment only unless submitted with and specific to article.

$ THE LIVING CHURCH, Living Church Foundation, 816 E. Juneau Ave., P.O. Box 92936, Milwaukee WI 53202. (414)276-5420. Fax: (414)276-7483. E-mail: livngchrch@aol.com. Managing Editor: John Schuessler. **Contact:** David Kalvelage, editor. **50% freelance written.** Weekly religious magazine on the Episcopal church. News or articles of interest to members of the Episcopal church. Estab. 1878. Circ. 9,000. Does not pay unless article is requested. Publishes ms an average of 3 months after acceptance. Byline given. Buys one-time rights. Editorial lead time 3 weeks. Submit seasonal material 1 month in advance. Reports in 2 weeks on queries; 1 month on mss. Sample copy free on request.

Nonfiction: Opinion, personal experience, photo feature, religious. **Buys 10 mss/year.** Send complete ms. Length: 1,000 words. **Pays $25-100.** Sometimes pays expenses of writers on assignment.

Photos: Send photos with submission. Reviews any size prints. Offers $15-50/photo. Buys one-time rights.

Columns/Departments: Benediction (devotional) 250 words; Viewpoint (opinion) under 1,000 words. Send complete ms. **Pays $50 maximum.**

Poetry: Light verse, traditional.

$ LIVING LIGHT NEWS, Living Light Ministries, 5304 89 St., #200, Edmonton, Alberta T6E 5P9 Canada. (403)468-6397. Fax: (403)468-6872. E-mail: livinglight@enabel.ab.ca. Website: http://www.livinglightnews.org. **Contact**: Jeff Caporale, editor. **75% freelance written.** Bimonthly tabloid covering Christianity. "We are an evangelical Christian newspaper slanted towards proclaiming the gospel and encouraging Christians." Estab. 1995. Circ. 10,000. Pays on publication. Publishes ms an average of 4 months after acceptance. Byline sometimes given. Offers 100% kill fee. Buys first North American serial rights, first rights, one-time rights, second serial (reprint) rights and makes work-for-hire assignments. Editorial lead time 3 months. Submit seasonal material 3 months in advance. Accepts simultaneous submissions. Sample copy for 9×12 SAE with 2 IRCs. Writer's guidelines free.

Nonfiction: General interest, humor, inspirational, interview/profile, religious. "We have a special Christmas issue focused on the traditional meaning of Christmas." No issue-oriented, controversial stories. **Buys 5-10 mss/year.** Query. Length: 300-1,200 words. **Pays $20-125 for assigned articles; $10-70 for unsolicited articles.** Sometimes pays expenses of writers on assignment.

Reprints: Send photocopy of article or short story or typed ms with rights for sale noted and information about when and where it previously appeared. Pays 5¢/word.

Photos: State availability of photos with submission. Reviews 3×5 prints. Offers $10-50/photo. Identification of subjects required. Buys one-time rights.

Columns/Departments: Marriage (Christian perspective), 500 words; Seniors Living (Christian perspective), 500

words; Book, music, video reviews (Christian perspective), 250-350 words. **Buys 5-10 mss/year.** Query with published clips. **Pays $15-40.**
Fiction: Christmas. "We only want to see Christmas-related fiction." **Buys 2-3 mss/year.** Query with published clips. Length: 500-2,000 words. **Pays $20-100.**
Tips: "It is very helpful if the person is a Bible believing Christian interested in proclaiming the gospel through positive, uplifting and timely stories of interest to Christians and non-Christians."

$ $ THE LOOKOUT, 8121 Hamilton Ave., Cincinnati OH 45231-9981. (513)931-4050. Fax: (513)931-0950. **Contact:** Patricia McCarty, assistant editor. **40-50% freelance written.** Weekly magazine for Christian adults, with emphasis on spiritual growth, family life, and topical issues. Audience is mainly conservative Christians. Estab. 1894. **Pays on acceptance.** Publishes ms an average of 6 months after acceptance. Byline given. Buys first serial, one-time, second serial (reprint) or simultaneous rights. Accepts simultaneous submissions. Reports in 4 months, sometimes longer. Sample copy and writer's guidelines for 75¢. "We now work from a theme list, which is available on request with our guidelines." Guidelines only for #10 SASE.
Nonfiction: "Seeks stories about real people; items that are helpful in practical Christian living (how-to's) or shed Biblical light on matters of contemporary controversy; and items that motivate, that lead the reader to ask, 'Why shouldn't I try that?' Articles should tell how real people are involved for Christ. In choosing topics, *The Lookout* considers timeliness, the church and national calendar, and the ability of the material to fit the above guidelines. Aim at laymen." Submit complete ms. Length: 400-1,800 words. **Pays 5-12¢/word.** We also use inspirational short pieces. "About 400-700 words is a good length for these. Relate an incident that illustrates a point without preaching."
Reprints: Send typed ms with rights for sale noted and information about when and where the article previously appeared. Pays 60% of amount paid for an original article.
Tips: "We have tightened the focus of *The Lookout*, to concentrate on three areas: (1) personal Christian growth; (2) home and family life; (3) social issues from a Christian perspective."

$ $ $ THE LUTHERAN, Magazine of the Evangelical Lutheran Church in America, 8765 W. Higgins Rd., Chicago IL 60631-4183. (773)380-2540. Fax: (773)380-2751. E-mail: lutheran@elca.org. Editor: Edgar R. Trexler. Managing Editor: Roger R. Kahle. **30% freelance written.** Monthly magazine for "lay people in church. News and activities of the Evangelical Lutheran Church in America, news of the world of religion, ethical reflections on issues in society, personal Christian experience." Estab. 1988. Circ. 650,000. **Pays on acceptance.** Publishes ms an average of 3 months after acceptance. Byline given. Offers 50% kill fee. Buys first rights. Submit seasonal material 4 months in advance. Reports in 3 weeks. Free sample copy and writer's guidelines.
Nonfiction: David L. Miller. Inspirational, interview/profile, personal experience, photo feature, religious. "No articles unrelated to the world of religion." **Buys 40 mss/year.** Query with published clips. Length: 1,000-1,500 words. **Pays $400-1,000 for assigned articles; $100-500 for unsolicited articles.** Pays expenses of writers on assignment.
Photos: Send photos with submission. Reviews contact sheets, transparencies, prints. Offers $50-175/photo. Captions and identification of subjects required. Buys one-time rights.
Columns/Departments: Lite Side (humor—church, religious), In Focus, Living the Faith, Values & Society, In Our Churches, Our Church at Work, 25-100 words. Send complete ms. **Pays $10.**
Tips: "Writers have the best chance selling us feature articles."

$ THE LUTHERAN JOURNAL, 7317 Cahill Rd., Suite 201, Minneapolis MN 55439-2081. Publisher: Michael L. Beard. Editor: Rev. Armin U. Deye. **Contact:** Stephani Karges, editorial assistant. Published 3 times/year. Family magazine for Lutheran Church members, middle age and older. Estab. 1938. Circ. 130,000. Pays on publication. Byline given. Buys one-time rights. Accepts simultaneous submissions. Reports in 4 months. Sample copy for 9×12 SAE with 78¢ postage.
Nonfiction: Inspirational, religious, human interest, historical articles. Interesting or unusual church projects. Informational, how-to, personal experience, interview, humor, think articles. **Buys 25-30 mss/year.** Submit complete ms. Length: 1,500 words maximum; occasionally 2,000 words. **Pays 1-4¢/word.**
Reprints: Send tearsheet or photocopy of article or typed ms with rights for sale noted and information about when and where the article previously appeared. Pays up to 50% of amount paid for an original article.
Photos: Send photocopies of b&w and color photos with accompanying ms. Please do not send original photos.
Poetry: Publishes 2-3 poems/issue, as space allows. **Pays $5-30.**
Tips: "Send submissions with SASE so we may respond."

$ MENNONITE BRETHREN HERALD, 3-169 Riverton Ave., Winnipeg, Manitoba R2L 2E5 Canada. (204)669-6575. Fax: (204)654-1865. E-mail: mbherald@cdnmbconf.ca. Website: http://www.cdnmbconf.ca/mb/mbherald.htm. **Contact:** Jim Coggins, editor or Susan Brandt, managing editor. **25% freelance written.** Biweekly family publication "read mainly by people of the Mennonite faith, reaching a wide cross section of professional and occupational groups, including many homemakers. Readership includes people from both urban and rural communities. It is intended to inform members of events in the church and the world, serve personal and corporate spiritual needs, serve as a vehicle of communication within the church, serve conference agencies and reflect the history and theology of the Mennonite Brethren Church." Estab. 1962. Circ. 15,500. Pays on publication. Publishes ms 6 months after acceptance. Not copyrighted. Byline given. Buys one-time rights. Sample copy for $1 and 9×12 SAE with 2 IRCs. Reports in 6 months.
Nonfiction: Articles with a Christian family orientation; youth directed, Christian faith and life, and current issues.

Wants articles critiquing the values of a secular society, attempting to relate Christian living to the practical situations of daily living; showing how people have related their faith to their vocations. Send complete ms. "Articles and manuscripts not accepted for publication will be returned if a SASE (Canadian stamps or IRCs) is provided by the writer." Length: 250-1,500 words. **Pays $30-40.** Pays the expenses of writers on assignment.
Reprints: Send tearsheet or photocopy of article or typed ms with rights for sale noted and information about when and where the article previously appeared. Pays 70% of amount paid for an original article.
Photos: Photos purchased with ms.
Columns/Departments: Viewpoint (Christian opinion on current topics), 850 words. Crosscurrent (Christian opinion on music, books, art, TV, movies), 350 words.
Poetry: Length: 25 lines maximum.
Tips: "We like simple style, contemporary language and fresh ideas. Writers should take care to avoid religious clichés."

$ $ MESSAGE MAGAZINE, Review and Herald Publishing, 55 West Oak Ridge Dr., Hagerstown MD 21740. (301)791-7000 ext. 2565. Fax: (301)714-1753. E-mail: 74617.3047@compuserve.com. Editor: Stephen P. Ruff. Assistant Editor: Dwain Esmond. **Contact:** Editorial Secretary. **10-20% freelance written.** Bimonthly magazine. "*Message* is the oldest religious journal addressing ethnic issues in the country. Our audience is predominantly black and Seventh-day Adventist; however, *Message* is an outreach magazine geared to the unchurched." Estab. 1898. Circ. 120,000. **Pays on acceptance**. Publishes ms an average of 6-12 months after acceptance. Byline given. Buys first North American serial rights; "the exception to this rule is for supplemental issues, for which we usually purchase all rights." Editorial lead time 6 months. Submit seasonal material 6 months in advance. Send complete ms. Reports in 6-9 months. Sample copy and writer's guidelines free.
Nonfiction: General interest to a Christian audience, how-to (overcome depression; overcome defeat; get closer to God; learn from failure, etc.), inspirational, interview/profile (profiles of famous African-Americans), personal experience (testimonies), religious. **Buys 10 mss/year.** Send complete ms. Length: 800-1,300 words. **Pays $50-300.**
Photos: State availability of photos with submission. Identification of subjects preferred. Buys one-time rights.
Columns/Departments: Voices in the Wind (community involvement/service/events/health info); Message, Jr. (stories for children with a moral, explain a biblical or moral principle); Recipes (no meat or dairy products—12-15 recipes and an intro); Healthspan (health issues); all 500 words. **Buys 12-15 mss/year.** Send complete ms for Message, Jr. and Healthspan. Query assistant editor with published clips for Voices in the Wind and Recipes. **Pays $50-300.**
Fiction: "We do not generally accept fiction, but when we do it's for Message, Jr. and/or has a religious theme. We buy about 3 (if that many) fictional manuscripts a year." Send complete ms. Length: 500-700 words. **Pays $50-125.**
Fillers: Anecdotes, facts, newsbreaks. **Buys 1-5 fillers/year.** Length: 200-500 words. **Pays $50-125.**
Tips: "Please look at the magazine before submitting manuscripts. *Message* publishes a variety of writing styles as long as the writing style is easy to read and flows—please avoid highly technical writing styles."

$ THE MESSENGER OF THE SACRED HEART, Apostleship of Prayer, 661 Greenwood Ave., Toronto, Ontario M4J 4B3 Canada. (416)466-1195. **Contact:** Rev. F.J. Power, S.J., editor. Monthly magazine for "Canadian and U.S. Catholics interested in developing a life of prayer and spirituality; stresses the great value of our ordinary actions and lives." **20% freelance written.** Estab. 1891. Circ. 15,000. Buys first rights only. Byline given. **Pays on acceptance.** Submit seasonal material 5 months in advance. Reports in 1 month. Sample copy for $1, 7½×10½ SAE. Writer's guidelines for SASE.
Fiction: Religious/inspirational. Stories about people, adventure, heroism, humor, drama. **Buys 12 mss/year.** Send complete ms with SAE and IRCs. Does not return mss without SASE. Length: 750-1,500 words. **Pays 4¢/word.**
Tips: "Develop a story that sustains interest to the end. Do not preach, but use plot and characters to convey the message or theme. Aim to move the heart as well as the mind. Before sending, cut out unnecessary or unrelated words or sentences. If you can, add a light touch or a sense of humor to the story. Your ending should have impact, leaving a moral or faith message for the reader."

N $ $ MINNESOTA CHRISTIAN CHRONICLE, Beard Communications, 7317 Cahill Rd., Suite 201, Minneapolis MN 55439. Fax: (612)941-3010. E-mail: chronicle@myhometown.net. **Contact**: Doug Trouten, editor. **10% freelance written.** Biweekly newspaper covering Christian community in Minnesota. "Our readers tend to be conservative evangelicals with orthodox Christian beliefs and conservative social and political views." Estab. 1978. Circ. 8,000. Pays 1 month following publication. Publishes ms an average of 2 months after acceptance. Byline given. Buys one-time rights. Editorial lead time 1 month. Submit seasonal material 2 months in advance. Accepts simultaneous submissions. Reports in 1 month. Sample copy for $2. Writer's guidelines for #10 SASE.
Nonfiction: Exposé, general interest, historical/nostalgic, how-to, humor, inspirational, interview/profile, new product, photo feature, religious. Special issues: Higher education guide, Christmas section, Christian school directory. **Buys 36 mss/year.** Query. Length: 500-2,000 words. **Pays $20-200.** Sometimes pays expenses of writers on assignment.
Reprints: Send typed ms with rights for sale noted. Pays 50% of amount paid for an original article.
Photos: State availability of photos with submission. Reviews contact sheets. Negotiates payment individually. Captions preferred. Buys one-time rights.
Columns/Departments: Lis Trouten, associate editor. Family Gatherings (home and family), 200-500 words. **Buys 6 mss/year.** Query. **Pays $10-50.**
Tips: "Stories for the Minnesota Christian Chronicle must have a strong Minnesota connection and a clear hook for

the Christian community. We do not publish general nonreligious stories or devotionals. We rarely buy from writers who are not in Minnesota."

$ THE MIRACULOUS MEDAL, 475 E. Chelten Ave., Philadelphia PA 19144-5785. (215)848-1010. Fax: (215)848-1014. Editorial Director: Rev. William J. O'Brien, C.M. **Contact:** Mr. Charles Kelly, office manager. **40% freelance written.** Quarterly. Estab. 1915. **Pays on acceptance.** Publishes ms an average of 2 years after acceptance. Buys first North American serial rights. Buys articles only on special assignment. Reports in 3 months. Sample copy for 6×9 SAE with 2 first-class stamps.

Fiction: Should not be pious or sermon-like. Wants good general fiction—not necessarily religious, but if religion is basic to the story, the writer should be sure of his facts. Only restriction is that subject matter and treatment must not conflict with Catholic teaching and practice. Can use seasonal material, Christmas stories. Length: 2,000 words maximum. Occasionally uses short-shorts from 1,000-1,250 words. **Pays 2¢/word minimum.**

Poetry: Maximum of 20 lines, preferably about the Virgin Mary or at least with religious slant. **Pays 50¢/line minimum.**

$ THE MONTANA CATHOLIC, Diocese of Helena, P.O. Box 1729, Helena MT 59624. (406)442-5820. Fax: (406)442-5191. **Contact:** Gerald M. Korson, editor. **5% freelance written.** Tabloid published every 3 weeks. "We publish news and features from a Catholic perspective, particularly as they pertain to the church in western Montana." Estab. 1932. Circ. 9,200. **Pays on acceptance**. Publishes ms an average of 6 months after acceptance. Byline given. Offers 25% kill fee. Buys first, one-time, second serial (reprint) or simultaneous rights. Editorial lead time 1 month. Submit seasonal material 3 months in advance. Accepts simultaneous submissions. Reports in 1 month. Sample copy for $2. Writer's guidelines for #10 SASE.

Nonfiction: Special issues: Vocations (January); Easter; Lent; Christmas; Advent. **Buys 5 mss/year.** Send complete ms with SASE for reply and/or return of mss. Length: 400-1,200 words. **Pays 10¢/word for assigned articles; 5¢/word for unsolicited articles.**

Reprints: Send tearsheet, photocopy or typed ms with rights for sale noted and information about when and where article previously appeared.

Photos: Reviews contact sheets, prints. Offers $5-20/photo. Identification of subjects required. Buys one time rights.

Tips: "Best bets are seasonal pieces, topics related to our special supplements and features with a tie-in to western Montana—always with a Catholic angle. No poetry, please. Avoid preachiness including excessive quotation of scripture. Maintain positive, uplifting tone but avoid Pollyanism."

$ $ MOODY MAGAZINE, Moody Bible Institute, 820 N. LaSalle Blvd., Chicago IL 60610. (312)329-2164. Fax: (312)329-2149. E-mail: moodyedit@aol.com. Website: http://www.moody.edu. **Contact:** Andrew Scheer, managing editor. **62% freelance written.** Bimonthly magazine for evangelical Christianity (6 issues/year). "Our readers are conservative, evangelical Christians highly active in their churches and concerned about applying their faith in daily living." Estab. 1900. Circ. 112,000. **Pays on acceptance.** Publishes ms an average of 9 months after acceptance. Byline given. Buys first North American serial rights. Submit seasonal material 9 months in advance. Query first for all submissions but not by phone. Unsolicited mss will be returned unread. Reports in 2 months. Sample copy for 9×12 SAE with $2 first-class postage. Writer's guidelines for #10 SASE.

- Ranked as one of the best markets for freelance writers in *Writer's Yearbook* magazine's annual "Top 100 Markets," January 1998.

Nonfiction: Personal narratives (on living the Christian life), a few reporting articles. **Buys 55 mss/year.** "No biographies, historical articles, or studies of Bible figures." Query. Length: 1,200-2,200 words. **Pays 15¢/word for queried articles; 20¢/word for assigned articles.** Sometimes pays the expenses of writers on assignment.

Columns/Departments: First Person (the only article written for non-Christians; a personal conversion testimony written by the author [will accept "as told to's"]; the objective is to tell a person's testimony in such a way that the reader will understand the gospel and want to receive Christ as Savior), 800-900 words; News Focus (in-depth, researched account of current news or trend), 1,000-1,400 words. **Buys 12 mss/year.** May query by fax or e-mail for News Focus only. **Pays 15¢/word.**

Fiction: Will consider well-written contemporary stories that are directed toward scriptural application. Avoid clichéd salvation accounts, biblical fiction, parables, and allegories. Length: 1,200-2,000 words. **Pays 15¢/word.**

Tips: "We have moved to bimonthly publication, with a larger editorial well in each issue. We want articles that cover a broad range of topics, but with one common goal: to foster application by a broad readership of specific biblical principles. By publishing accounts of people's spiritual struggles, growth and discipleship, our aim is to encourage readers in their own obedience to Christ. While *Moody* continues to look for many authors to use a personal narrative style, we're also looking for some pieces that use an anecdotal reporting approach."

$ $ NEW WORLD OUTLOOK, The Mission Magazine of The United Methodist Church, General Board of Global Ministries, 475 Riverside Dr., Room 1470, New York NY 10115. (212)870-3600. Fax: (212)870-3940. E-mail: nwo@gbgm-umc.org. Website: http://www.gbgm-umc.org. Editor: Alma Graham. **Contact:** Christie R. House. **20% freelance written.** Bimonthly magazine covering United Methodist mission programs, projects, and personnel. "As the mission magazine of The United Methodist Church, we publish articles on or related to the mission programs, projects, institutions, and personnel of the General Board of Global Ministries, both in the United States and around the world." Estab. 1911. Circ. 30,000. Pays on publication. Publishes ms an average of 4 months after acceptance. Byline given.

Offers 50% kill fee or $100. Buys all rights. Editorial lead time 4 months. Submit seasonal material 4 months in advance. No simultaneous or previously published submissions. Sample copy for $2.50.

Nonfiction: Photo features, mission reports, mission studies. Special issues: Indonesia; Refugees and Global Migration. **Buys 24 mss/year.** Query. Length: 500-2,000 words. **Pays $50-300.** Sometimes pays expenses of writers on assignment.

Photos: State availability of photos with submission. Reviews transparencies, prints. Offers $25-150/photo. Captions, identification of subjects required.

Tips: "Write for a list of United Methodist mission institutions, projects, or personnel in the writer's geographic area or in an area of the country or the world to which the writer plans to travel (at writer's own expense). Photojournalists have a decided advantage."

$ OBLATES, Missionary Association of Mary Immaculate, 9480 N. De Mazenod Dr., Belleville IL 62223-1160. (618)398-4848. Fax: (618)398-8788. Managing Editor: Christine Portell. **Contact:** Mary Mohrman, manuscripts editor. **30-50% freelance written.** Prefers to work with published writers. Bimonthly inspirational magazine for Christians; audience mainly older Catholic adults. Circ. 500,000. **Pays on acceptance.** Usually publishes ms within 2 years after acceptance. Byline given. Buys first North American serial rights. Submit seasonal material 6 months in advance. Reports in 2 months. Sample copy and writer's guidelines for 6×9 or larger SAE with 2 first-class stamps.

Nonfiction: Inspirational and personal experience with positive spiritual insights. No preachy, theological or research articles. Avoid current events and controversial topics. Send complete ms; 500-600 words. "No queries." **Pays $80.**

Poetry: Light verse—reverent, well written, perceptive, with traditional rhythm and rhyme. "Emphasis should be on inspiration, insight and relationship with God." Submit maximum 2 poems. Length: 8-16 lines. **Pays $30.**

Tips: "Our readership is made up mostly of mature Americans who are looking for comfort, encouragement, and a positive sense of applicable Christian direction to their lives. Focus on sharing of personal insight to problem (i.e. death or change), but must be positive, uplifting. We have well-defined needs for an established market but are always on the lookout for exceptional work."

$ $ OUR FAMILY, Oblate Fathers of St. Mary's Province, P.O. Box 249, Battleford, Saskatchewan S0M 0E0 Canada. (306)937-7771. Fax: (306)937-7644. **Contact:** Nestor Gregoire, editor. **60% freelance written.** Prefers to work with published/established writers. Monthly magazine for average family men and women with high school and early college education. Estab. 1949. Circ. 8,000. **Pays on acceptance.** Publishes ms an average of 6 months after acceptance. Byline given. Offers 100% kill fee. Generally purchases first North American serial rights; also buys all, simultaneous, second serial (reprint) or one-time rights. Submit seasonal material 4 months in advance. Accepts simultaneous submissions. Reports in 1 month. *Writer's Market* recommends allowing 2 months for reply. Sample copy for 9×12 SAE with $2.50 postage. Only Canadian postage or IRC useful in Canada. Writer's guidelines.

Nonfiction: Humor (related to family life or husband/wife relations), inspirational (anything that depicts people responding to adverse conditions with courage, hope and love), personal experience (with religious dimensions), photo feature (particularly in search of photo essays on human/religious themes and on persons whose lives are an inspiration to others). Special issues: How to Make the Sunday Eucharist Work (October 1998); Will Our Children Have Steady Long-term Work (November 1998); the Forgotten Parts of Christmas (December 1998). Accepts phone queries. **Buys 72-88 unsolicited mss/year.** Length: 1,000-3,000 words. **Pays 7-12¢/word.** Pays expenses of writers on assignment.

Reprints: Send tearsheet or photocopy of article or typed ms with rights for sale noted and information about when and where the article previously appeared.

Photos: Photos purchased with or without accompanying ms. Pays $35 for 5×7 or larger b&w glossy prints and color photos (which are converted into b&w). Offers additional payment for photos accepted with ms (payment for these photos varies according to their quality). Free photo spec sheet for SASE.

Poetry: Avant-garde, free verse, haiku, light verse, traditional. **Buys 4-10 poems/issue.** Length: 3-30 lines. **Pays 75¢-$1/line.** Must have a religious dimension.

Fillers: Jokes, gags, anecdotes, short humor. **Buys 2-10/issue.**

Tips: "Writers should ask themselves whether this is the kind of an article, poem, etc. that a busy housewife would pick up and read when she has a few moments of leisure. We are particularly looking for articles on the spirituality of marriage. We will be concentrating more on recent movements and developments in the church to help make people aware of the new church of which they are a part."

$ PENTECOSTAL EVANGEL, The General Council of the Assemblies of God, 1445 Boonville, Springfield MO 65802-1894. (417)862-2781. Fax: (417)862-0416. E-mail: pevangel@ag.org. Website: http://www.ag.org/evangel. Editor: Hal Donaldson. **Contact:** Ann Floyd, associate editor. **10% freelance written.** Works with a small number of new/unpublished writers each year. Weekly magazine emphasizing news of the Assemblies of God for members of the Assemblies and other Pentecostal and charismatic Christians. Estab. 1913. Circ. 245,000. **Pays on acceptance.** Publishes ms an average of 6 months after acceptance. Byline given. Buys first serial rights, electronic rights and a few second serial (reprint) or one-time rights. Submit seasonal material 6 months in advance. Reports in 3 months. Sample copy and writer's guidelines available for $1.

Nonfiction: Informational (articles on homelife that convey Christian teachings), inspirational, personal experience, news, human interest, evangelical, current issues, seasonal. **Buys 3 mss/issue.** Send complete ms. Length: 500-1,200 words. **Pays $25-100.** Pays expenses of writers on assignment.

Reprints: Send typed ms with rights for sale noted and information about when and where the article previously appeared. Pays 30% of amount paid for original article.

Photos: Photos purchased without accompanying ms. Pays $30 for 8×10 b&w glossy prints; $50 for 35mm or larger color transparencies. Total purchase price for ms includes payment for photos.
Tips: "We publish first-person articles concerning spiritual experiences; that is, answers to prayer for help in a particular situation, of unusual conversions or healings through faith in Christ. All articles submitted to us should be related to religious life. We are Protestant, evangelical, Pentecostal, and any doctrines or practices portrayed should be in harmony with the official position of our denomination (Assemblies of God)."

N $ THE PENTECOSTAL MESSENGER, Messenger Publishing House, P.O. Box 850, Joplin MO 64802-0850. (417)624-7050. Fax: (417)624-7102. E-mail: awilson@pcg.org. Website: http://www.pcg.ord. **Contact:** Aaron M. Wilson, editor. **10% or less freelance written.** Works with small number of new/unpublished writers each year. Monthly magazine covering Pentecostal Christianity. "*The Pentecostal Messenger* is the official organ of the Pentecostal Church of God. It goes to ministers and church members." Estab. 1919. Circ. 12,000. Pays on publication. Publishes ms an average of 6 months after acceptance. Byline given. Buys second serial (reprint) or simultaneous rights. Submit seasonal material 4 months in advance. Accepts simultaneous submissions. Reports in 2 months. Sample copy for 6×9 SAE with 2 first-class stamps. Writer's guidelines free.
Nonfiction: Spiritual solutions to life's problems, preferably through human experience; testimony; family-strengthening ideas; financial advice; inspirational, religious. Send complete ms. Length: 400-1,200 words. **Pays 2¢/word.**
Reprints: Send tearsheet or photocopy of article or typed ms with rights for sale noted and information about when and where the article previously appeared. Pays 100% of amount paid for an original article.
Tips: "Articles need to be inspirational, informative, written from a positive viewpoint, and not extremely controversial. No blatant use of theology or sermonizing. *Spirit* is designed to be read by laymen and features testimonies, healing reports, solutions to problems, learning experiences and other inspirational material. Format is similar to *Guideposts*. Each issue focuses on the work of the Holy Spirit in the lives of today's believers."

N $ $ PFI WORLD REPORT, Prison Fellowship International, P.O. Box 17434, Washington DC 20041. (703)481-0000. Fax: (703)481-0003. E-mail: cnicholson@pfi.org. **Contact**: Christopher P. Nicholson, editor. **10% freelance written.** Bimonthly newsletter covering the people and programs of Prison Fellowship in 80+ countries. Estab. 1981. Circ. 6,000. **Pays on acceptance of final draft**. Publishes ms an average of 2 months after acceptance. Byline given. Buys all rights. Editorial lead time 4 months. Submit seasonal material 4 months in advance. Accepts simultaneous submissions. Reports in 2 weeks on queries. Sample copy for #10 SASE.
Nonfiction: How-to, inspirational, interview/profile, religious. No fiction or USA topics. **Buys 4 mss/year.** Query. Length: 500-750 words. **Pays $100-350.** Sometimes pays expenses of writers on assignment.
Reprints: Accepts previously published submissions.
Photos: State availability of photos with submission. Offers no additional payment for photos accepted with ms. Captions required. Buys one-time rights.
Tips: "Our audience is narrowly targetted and passionate about prison ministry. It's important to work with the affiliate P.F. ministry in whatever country you're writing about. Vague personal testimonies are not what we're looking for. Tangible examples of how God is changing lives in foreign prisons are what we're looking for."

$ $ PIME WORLD, P.I.M.E. Missionaries, 17330 Quincy St., Detroit MI 48221-2765. (313)342-4066. Fax: (313)342-6816. E-mail: pimemiss@flash.net. Website: http://www.rc.net/pime/. **Contact**: Paul W. Witte, managing editor. **15% freelance written.** Monthly (except July and August) magazine emphasizing foreign missionary activities of the Roman Catholic Church in Burma, India, Bangladesh, the Philippines, Hong Kong, Africa, etc., for an adult audience interested in current issues in the missions. Audience is largely high school educated, conservative in both religion and politics." Estab. 1954. Circ. 26,000. Pays on publication. Publishes ms an average of 5 months after acceptance. Byline given. Buys one-time rights. Editorial lead time 2 months. Submit seasonal material 2 months in advance. Accepts simultaneous submissions. Reports in 2 weeks on queries; 2 months on mss. Sample copy free. Writer's guidelines for #10 SASE.
Nonfiction: Essays, inspirational, personal experience, photo feature, religious. Informational and inspirational foreign missionary activities of the Catholic Church, Christian social commentary. **Buys 10 mss/year.** Query or send complete ms. Length: 800-1,200 words. **Pays $50-200.**
Reprints: Accepts previously published submissions.
Photos: State availability of or send photos with submission. Pays $10/color photo. Identification of subjects required. Buys one-time rights.
Tips: "Submit articles produced from a faith standpoint, dealing with current issues of social justice, evangelization and pastoral work in Third World countries. Interviews of missionaries accepted. Good quality color photos greatly appreciated."

N ✪ $ $ THE PLAIN TRUTH, Renewing faith & values, Plain Truth Ministries, 300 W. Green St., Pasadena CA 91129. Fax: (626)795-0107. E-mail: susan_stewart@ptm.org. Website: http://www.ptm.org. Editor: Greg Albrecht. **Contact**: Susan Stewart, managing editor. **75-100% freelance written.** Bimonthly religious magazine. "We seek to reignite the flame of hope and faith in a world of shattered lives by illustrating the joy of a new life in Christ." Estab. 1935. Circ. 137,000. Pays on publication. Publishes ms an average of 8 months after acceptance. Byline given. Offers $50 kill fee. Buys all-language, world, first and reprint rights. Editorial lead time 6 months. Submit seasonal material 6 months in advance. Query first. Will not accept unsolicited mss. Accepts simultaneous submissions. Sample copy for 9×12 SAE with 4 first-class stamps. Writer's guidelines for #10 SASE.

Nonfiction: Inspirational, interview/profile, personal experience, religious. **Buys 48-50 mss/year.** Query with published clips and SASE. Length: 750-2,500 words. **Pays 25¢/word.** Sometimes pays expenses of writers on assignment.

Reprints: Send tearsheet or photocopy of article or typed ms with rights for sale noted with information about when and where the article previously appeared. Pays 15¢/word.

Photos: State availability of photos with submission. Reviews transparencies, prints. Negotiates payment individually. Captions required. Buys one-time rights.

Columns/Departments: Christian People (interviews with Christian leaders), 1,500 words. **Buys 6-12 mss/year.** Send complete ms. **Pays 15-25¢/word.**

Fillers: Anecdotes. **Buys 0-20/year.** Length: 25-200 words. **Pays 15-25¢/word.**

Tips: "Material should offer biblical solutions to real life problems. Both first person and third person illustrations are encouraged. Articles should take a unique twist on a subject. Material must be insightful and practical for the Christain reader. All articles must be well researched and biblically accurate without becoming overly scholastic. Use convincing arguments to support your Christian platform. Use vivid word pictures, simple and compelling language, and avoid stuffy academic jargon. Captivating anecdotes are vital."

$ PRAIRIE MESSENGER, Catholic Journal, Benedictine Monks of St. Peter's Abbey, P.O. Box 190, Muenster, Saskatchewan S0K 2Y0 Canada. (306)682-1772. Fax: (306)682-5285. E-mail: pmessenger@sk.sympatico.ca. Editor: Rev. Andrew Britz, OSB. **Contact:** Marian Noll, associate editor. **10% freelance written.** Weekly Catholic journal with strong emphasis on social justice, Third World and ecumenism. Estab. 1904. Circ. 7,300. Pays on publication. Publishes ms an average of 4 months after acceptance. Byline given. Not copyrighted. Buys first North American serial, first, one-time, second serial (reprint) or simultaneous rights. Submit seasonal material 3 months in advance. Reports in 2 months. Sample copy and writers guidelines for 9×12 SAE with $1 Canadian postage or IRCs.

Nonfiction: Interview/profile, opinion, religious. "No articles on abortion or homosexuality." **Buys 15 mss/year.** Send complete ms. Length: 250-600 words. **Pays $40-60.** Sometimes pays expenses of writers on assignment.

Photos: Send photos with submission. Reviews 3×5 prints. Offers $15/photo. Captions required. Buys all rights.

$ PRESBYTERIAN RECORD, 50 Wynford Dr., North York, Ontario M3C 1J7 Canada. (416)444-1111. Fax: (416) 441-2825. E-mail: pcrecord@presbyterian.ca. Website: http://www.presbycan.ca/. **Contact:** Rev. John Congram, editor. **50% freelance written.** Eager to work with new/unpublished writers. Monthly magazine for a church-oriented, family audience. Circ. 55,000. Pays on publication. Publishes ms an average of 4 months after acceptance. Buys first serial, one-time or simultaneous rights. Submit seasonal material 3 months in advance. Reports on accepted ms in 2 months; returns rejected material in 3 months. Sample copy and writer's guidelines for 9×12 SAE with $1 Canadian postage or IRCs.

Nonfiction: Material on religious themes. Check a copy of the magazine for style. Also personal experience, interview, inspirational material. No material solely or mainly American in context. No sermons, accounts of ordinations, inductions, baptisms, receptions, church anniversaries or term papers. When possible, photos should accompany manuscript; e.g., current events, historical events and biographies. Special upcoming themes: small groups in the church; conflict in the church; lay leadership. **Buys 15-20 unsolicited mss/year.** Query. Length: 600-1,500 words. **Pays $50 (Canadian).** Sometimes pays expenses of writers on assignment.

Reprints: Send tearsheet, photocopy of article or typed ms with rights for sale noted and information about when and where the article previously appeared.

Photos: Pays $15-20 for glossy photos. Uses positive transparencies for cover. Pays $50 plus. Captions required.

Columns/Departments: Vox Populi (items of contemporary and often controversial nature), 700 words; Mission Knocks (new ideas for congregational mission and service), 700 words.

Tips: "There is a trend away from maudlin, first-person pieces redolent with tragedy and dripping with simplistic, pietistic conclusions. Writers often leave out those parts which would likely attract readers, such as anecdotes and direct quotes. Using active rather than passive verbs also helps most manuscripts."

N PRESBYTERIANS TODAY, Presbyterian Church (U.S.A.), 100 Witherspoon St., Louisville KY 40202-1396. (502)569-5637. Fax: (502)569-8073. E-mail: survey@pcusa.org. Managing Editor: Catherine Cottingham. **Contact:** Eva Stimson, associate editor. Estab. 1867. **65% freelance written.** Prefers to work with published/established writers. Denominational magazine published 10 times/year covering religion, denominational activities and public issues for members of the Presbyterian Church (U.S.A.). "The magazine's puspose is to increase understanding and appreciation of what the church and its members are doing to live out their Christian faith." Estab. 1862. Circ. 82,000. **Pays on acceptance.** Publishes ms an average of 6 months after acceptance. Byline given. Offers kill fee, $100-200 average. Buys first North American serial rights. Editorial lead time 3 months. Submit seasonal material 3 months in advance. Reports in 2 weeks on queries; 1 month on mss. Sample copy and writer's guidelines free.

Nonfiction: How-to (everyday Christian living), inspirational, Presbyterian programs, issues, peoples. **Buys 25 mss/year.** Send complete ms. Length: 1,000-1,800 words. **Pays $300 maximum for assigned articles; $75-200 for unsolicited articles.**

Photos: State availability of photos. Reviews contact sheets, transparencies, b&w prints. Negotiates payment individually. Identification of subjects required. Buys one-time rights.

N $ PRESERVING CHRISTIAN HOMES, General Youth Division, 8855 Dunn Rd., Hazelwood MO 63042. Fax: (314)837-4503. E-mail: gyouth8855@aol.com. **Contact**: Scott Graham, editor and general youth secretary. **40% freelance written.** Bimonthly magazine covering Christian home and family. "All submissions must conform to Christian perspective." Estab. 1970. Circ. 4,500. Pays on publication. Publishes ms an average of 9 months after acceptance. Byline sometimes given. Buys one-time or simultaneous rights. Editorial lead time 6 months. Submit seasonal material 6 months in advance. Accepts simultaneous submissions. Reports in 2 weeks on queries; 2 months on mss. Sample copy for 10×13 SAE with 2 first-class stamps.

Nonfiction: General interest, humor, inspirational, personal experience, religious. Special issues: Mothers Day/Fathers Day. No "editorial or political." **Buys 15 mss/year.** Send complete ms. Length: 500-1,500 words. **Pays $30-40.**

Photos: State availability of photos with submission. Negotiates payment individually. Buys all rights.

Fiction: Humorous, religious, slice-of-life vignettes. **Buys 6 mss/year.** Send complete ms. Length: 500-1,500 words. **Pays $30-40.**

Poetry: Free verse, light verse, traditional. **Buys 3 poems/year.** Submit maximum 5 poems. Length: 10-40 lines. **Pays $20-25.**

Fillers: Anecdotes, facts, short humor. **Buys 2/year.** Length: 50-200 words. **Pays $10-20.**

Tips: "Be relevant to today's Christian families!"

☆ $ PURPOSE, 616 Walnut Ave., Scottdale PA 15683-1999. (412)887-8500. E-mail: horsch%mph@mcimail.com. **Contact:** James E. Horsch, editor. **95% freelance written.** Weekly magazine "for adults, young and old, general audience with varied interests. My readership is interested in seeing how Christianity works in difficult situations." Estab. 1968. Circ. 13,000. **Pays on acceptance.** Publishes ms an average of 8 months after acceptance. Byline given, including city, state/province. Buys one-time rights. Submit seasonal material 6 months in advance. Accepts simultaneous submissions. Reports in 3 months. Sample copy and writer's guidelines for 6×9 SAE with 2 first-class stamps.

Nonfiction: Inspirational stories from a Christian perspective. "I want upbeat stories that deal with issues faced by believers in family, business, politics, religion, gender and any other areas—and show how the Christian faith resolves them. *Purpose* conveys truth through quality fiction or true life stories. Our magazine accents Christian discipleship. Christianity affects all of life, and we expect our material to demonstrate this. I would like story-type articles about individuals, groups and organizations who are intelligently and effectively working at such problems as hunger, poverty, international understanding, peace, justice, etc., because of their faith." **Buys 130 mss/year.** Submit complete ms. Length: 750 words maximum. **Pays 5¢/word maximum.** Buys one-time rights only.

Reprints: Send tearsheet or photocopy of article or short story, or typed ms with rights for sale noted and information about when and where the material previously appeared.

Photos: Photos purchased with ms. Pays $5-15 for b&w (less for color), depending on quality. Must be sharp enough for reproduction; requires prints in all cases. Captions desired.

Fiction: Humorous, religious, historical fiction related to discipleship theme. "Produce the story with specificity so that it appears to take place somewhere and with real people. Essays and how-to-do-it pieces must include a lot of anecdotal, life exposure examples."

Poetry: Traditional poetry, blank verse, free verse, light verse. **Buys 130 poems/year.** Length: 12 lines maximum. **Pays $7.50-20/poem** depending on length and quality. Buys one-time rights only.

Fillers: Anecdotal items up to 599 words. Pays 4¢/word maximum.

Tips: "We are looking for articles which show the Christian faith working at issues where people hurt; stories need to be told and presented professionally. Good photographs help place material with us."

$ QUEEN OF ALL HEARTS, Montfort Missionaries, 26 S. Saxon Ave., Bay Shore NY 11706-8993. (516)665-0726. Fax: (516)665-4349. **Contact:** Roger Charest, S.M.M., managing editor. **50% freelance written.** Bimonthly magazine. "Subject: Mary, Mother of Jesus, as seen in the sacred scriptures, tradition, history of the church, the early Christian writers, lives of the saints, poetry, art, music, spiritual writers, apparitions, shrines, ecumenism, etc." Estab. 1950. Circ. 3,000. **Pays on acceptance.** Publishes ms an average of 6 months after acceptance. Byline given. Not copyrighted. Submit seasonal material 6 months in advance. Reports in 2 months. Sample copy for $2.50.

Nonfiction: Essays, inspirational, personal experience, religious. **Buys 25 ms/year.** Send complete ms. Length: 750-2,500 words. **Pays $40-60.** Sometimes pays writers in contributor copies or other premiums "by mutual agreement."

Photos: Send photos with submission. Reviews transparencies, prints. Pay varies. Buys one-time rights.

Fiction: Religious. **Buys 6 mss/year.** Send complete ms. Length: 1,500-2,500 words. **Pays $40-60.**

Poetry: Joseph Tusiani, poetry editor. Free verse. **Buys approximately 10 poems/year.** Submit maximum of 2 poems at one time. Pays in contributor copies.

$ $ REFORM JUDAISM, Union of American Hebrew Congregations, 838 5th Ave., New York NY 10021. (212)650-4240. Website: http://www.uahc.org/rjmag/. Editor: Aron Hirt-Manheimer. **Contact:** Joy Weinberg, managing editor. **30% freelance written.** Quarterly magazine of Reform Jewish issues. "*Reform Judaism* is the official voice of the Union of American Hebrew Congregations, linking the institutions and affiliates of Reform Judaism with every Reform Jew. RJ covers developments within the Movement while interpreting events and Jewish tradition from a Reform perspective." Pays on publication. Publishes ms an average of 3 months after acceptance. Byline given. Offers kill fee for commissioned articles. Buys first North American serial rights. Submit seasonal material 6 months in advance. Deadlines: Spring 1999: November 1998; Summer 1999: January 1999; Fall 1999: April 1999; Winter 1999: July 1999. Reports in 2 months on queries and mss. Writer's guidelines for SASE. Sample copy for $3.50.

Nonfiction: Book excerpts, exposé, general interest, historical/nostalgic, inspirational, interview/profile, opinion, personal experience, photo feature, travel. **Buys 30 mss/year.** Submit complete ms with SASE. Length: cover stories: 2,500-3,500 words; major feature: 1,800-2,500 words; secondary feature: 1,200-1,500 words; department (e.g., Travel): 1,200 words; letters: 200 words maximum; opinion: 630 words maximum. **Pays 30¢/word.** Sometimes pays expenses of writers on assignment.
Reprints: Send tearsheet or photocopy of article or short story or typed ms with rights for sale noted and information about when and where the material previously appeared. Usually does not publish reprints.
Photos: Send photos with ms. Prefers 8×10/color or slides and b&w prints. Pays $25-75. Identification of subjects required. Buys one-time rights.
Fiction: Sophisticated, cutting-edge, superb writing. **Buys 4 mss/year.** Send complete ms. Length: 600-2,500 words. **Pays 30¢/word.** Publishes novel excerpts.
Tips: "We prefer a stamped postcard including the following information/checklist: _yes we are interested in publishing; _no, unfortunately the submission doesn't meet our needs; _maybe, we'd like to hold on to the article for now. Submissions sent this way will receive a faster response."

$ $ THE REPORTER, Women's American ORT, Inc., 315 Park Ave. S., New York NY 10010. (212)505-7700. Fax: (212)674-3057. **Contact:** Aviva Patz, editor. **85% freelance written.** Quarterly nonprofit journal published by Jewish women's organization covering "Jewish topics, social issues, education, Mideast and women." Estab. 1966. Circ. 80,000. Payment time varies. Publishes ms ASAP after acceptance. Byline given. Buys first North American serial rights. Submit seasonal material 6 months in advance. Reports in 3 months. Free sample copy for 9×12 SAE with 3 first-class stamps. Writer's guidelines for SASE.
Nonfiction: Book excerpts, general interest. Cover feature profiles a dynamic Jewish woman making a difference in Judaism, women's issues, education, profiles, business, journalism, sports or the arts. Send complete ms. Length varies. No more than 1,800 words. **Pays $425 and up.**
Photos: Send photos with submission. Identification of subjects required.
Columns/Departments: Education Update (trends in teaching methods, standards, censorship, etc.); Q&A (one-page interview); Last Impression (personal essay). Length: 800 words; **pays $150-300**. Up Front (short news item from Jewish world), 50-200 words; **pays $50 each**. ORT Matters, (length and pay varies). **Buys 4-6 mss/year.** Send complete ms.
Fiction: Publishes novel excerpts and short stories as past of "Last Impressions." **Buys 4 ms/year.** Length: 800 words. Pays $150-300.
Tips: "Simply send manuscript or query; do not call. Looking for well-written, well-researched and lively stories on relevant topics that evoke a response from the reader."

$ REVIEW FOR RELIGIOUS, 3601 Lindell Blvd., Room 428, St. Louis MO 63108-3393. (314)977-7363. Fax: (314)977-7362. E-mail: foppema@slu.edu. **Contact:** David L. Fleming, S.J., editor. **100% freelance written.** Bimonthly magazine for Roman Catholic priests, brothers and sisters. Estab. 1942. Pays on publication. Publishes ms an average of 9 months after acceptance. Byline given. Buys first North American serial rights; rarely buys second serial (reprint) rights. Reports in 2 months.
Nonfiction: Articles on spiritual, liturgical, canonical matters only; not for general audience. Length: 1,500-5,000 words. **Pays $6/page.**
Tips: "The writer must know about religious life in the Catholic Church and be familiar with prayer, vows, community life and ministry."

$ $ ST. ANTHONY MESSENGER, 1615 Republic St., Cincinnati OH 45210-1298. Fax: (513)241-0399. E-mail: stanthony@americancatholic.org. Website: http://www.AmericanCatholic.org. **Contact:** Norman Perry, editor. **55% freelance written.** "Willing to work with new/unpublished writers if their writing is of a professional caliber." Monthly general interest magazine for a national readership of Catholic families, most of which have children or grandchildren in grade school, high school or college. Circ. 350,000. **Pays on acceptance.** Publishes ms an average of 9 months after acceptance. Byline given. Buys first worldwide serial and all electronic rights. Submit seasonal material 6 months in advance. Reports in 2 months. Sample copy and writer's guidelines for 9×12 SAE with 4 first-class stamps.
Nonfiction: How-to (on psychological and spiritual growth, problems of parenting/better parenting, marriage problems/marriage enrichment), humor, informational, inspirational, interview, personal experience (if pertinent to our purpose), social issues, personal opinion (limited use; writer must have special qualifications for topic), profile. **Buys 35-50 mss/year.** Length: 1,500-3,000 words. **Pays 15¢/word.** Sometimes pays the expenses of writers on assignment.
Fiction: Mainstream, religious. **Buys 12 mss/year.** Submit complete ms. Length: 2,500-3,000 words. **Pays 15¢/word.**
Poetry: "*Our poetry needs are very limited.*" Submit 4-5 poems maximum. Up to 20-25 lines, "the shorter, the better." **Pays $2/line.**
Tips: "The freelancer should ask why his or her proposed article would be appropriate for us, rather than for *Redbook* or *Saturday Review.* We treat human problems of all kinds, but from a religious perspective. Articles should reflect Catholic theology, spirituality and employ a Catholic terminology and vocabulary. We need more articles on prayer, scripture, Catholic worship. Get authoritative information (not merely library research); we want interviews with experts. Write in popular style; use lots of examples, stories and personal quotes. Word length is an important consideration."

$ ST. JOSEPH'S MESSENGER & ADVOCATE OF THE BLIND, Sisters of St. Joseph of Peace, St. Joseph's Home, P.O. Box 288, Jersey City NJ 07303-0288. **Contact:** Sister Mary Kuiken, CSJP, editor. **30% freelance written.** Eager to work with new/unpublished writers. Semi annual magazine. Estab. 1898. Circ. 15,500. **Pays on acceptance.** Publishes ms an average of 3 months after acceptance. Buys first serial and second serial (reprint) rights; reassigns rights back to author after publication in return for credit line in next publication. Submit seasonal material 3 months in advance (no Christmas issue). Accepts simultaneous submissions. Reports in 1 month. Sample copy and writer's guidelines for 9×12 SAE with 2 first-class stamps.

Nonfiction: Humor, inspirational, nostalgia, personal opinion, personal experience. **Buys 24 mss/year.** Submit complete ms. Length: 800-1,500 words. **Pays $3-15.**

Reprints: Send typed ms with rights for sale noted and information about when and where the article previously appeared. Pays 100% of amount paid for an original article.

Fiction: Romance, suspense, contemporary, mainstream, religious. **Buys 30 mss/year.** Submit complete ms. Length: 800-1,500 words. **Pays $6-25.**

Poetry: Light verse, traditional. **Buys 25 poems/year.** Submit 10 poems max. Length: 50-300 words. **Pays $5-20.**

Tips: "It's rewarding to know that someone is waiting to see freelancers' efforts rewarded by 'print'. It's annoying, however, to receive poor copy, shallow material or inane submissions. Human interest fiction, touching on current happenings, is what is most needed. We look for social issues woven into story form. We also seek non-preaching articles that carry a message that is positive."

SCP JOURNAL and SCP NEWSLETTER, Spiritual Counterfeits Project, P.O. Box 4308, Berkeley CA 94704-4308. (510)540-0300. Fax: (510)540-1107. E-mail: scp@dnai.com. Website: http://www.scp-inc.org/. **Contact:** Tal Brooke, editor. Co-editor: Brooks Alexander. **5-10% freelance written.** Prefers to work with published/established writers. "The *SCP Journal* and *SCP Newsletter* are quarterly publications geared to reach demanding non-believers while giving Christians authentic insight into the very latest spiritual and cultural trends." Their targeted audience is the educated lay reader. Estab. 1975. Circ. 18,000. Pays on publication. Publishes ms an average of 6 months after acceptance. Byline given. Rights negotiable. Accepts simultaneous submissions. Reports in 3 months. Sample copy for $8.75. Writer's guidelines for SASE.

Nonfiction: Book excerpts, essays, exposé, interview/profile, opinion, personal experience, religious. Query by telephone. Length: 2,500-3,500 words. Pay negotiated by phone.

- Less emphasis on book reviews and more focus on specialized "single issue" topics.

Reprints: Call for telephone inquiry first. Send photocopy of article and ms on disk with rights for sale noted and information about when and where the article previously appeared. Payment is negotiated.

Photos: State available photos. Reviews contact sheets and prints or slides. Offers no additional payment for photos accepted with ms. Captions, model releases, identification of subjects required. Buys one-time rights.

Tips: "The area of our publication most open to freelancers is specialized topics covered by *SCP*. Do not send unsolicited samples of your work until you have checked with us by phone to see it it fits *SCP*'s area of interest and publication schedule. The usual profile of contributors is that they are published within the field, have advanced degrees from top ranked universities, as well as experience that makes their work uniquely credible."

N $ SCROLL, Deerhaven Press, 8992 Preston Rd., Suite 110-120, Frisco TX 75034-3964. (972)335-3201. Fax: (972)377-9705. E-mail: mnsurratt@aol.com. **Contact**: Marshall N. Surratt, editor-in-chief. **50% freelance written.** "We offer readers help in better using computers in their ministries, churches and families. We are committed to quality reviews of faith-related software and in-depth discussion on issues relating to faith and technology." Estab. 1984. Circ. 10,000. Pays on publication. Publishes ms an average of 2 months after acceptance. Byline given. Buys first, second serial (reprint) or simultaneous rights. "Some of our articles might be published in denominational or preaching journals. These would be noncompeting. Otherwise, we ask for first rights." Editorial lead time 3 months. Submit seasonal material 3 months in advance. Accepts simultaneous submissions. Reports in 1 week on queries; 3 weeks on mss. Sample copy for 9×12 SAE with 5 first-class stamps. Writer's guidelines for #10 SASE.

Nonfiction: Book excerpts, essays, how-to (how to use computers in a church or ministry), interview/profile, new product, opinion, religious, technical. **Buys 15-20 mss/year.** Query with SASE. Length: 1,000-2,000 words. **Pays $50.**

Reprints: Accepts previously published submissions.

Photos: State availability of photos with submission. Reviews negatives, 35mm transparencies and 3×5 or larger prints. Offers no additional payment for photos accepted with ms. Identification of subjects required. Buys one-time rights.

$ SEEK, Standard Publishing, 8121 Hamilton Ave., Cincinnati OH 45231. (513)931-4050, ext. 365. Fax: (513)931-0950. **Contact:** Eileen H. Wilmoth, editor. **98% freelance written.** Prefers to work with published/established writers. Quarterly Sunday school paper, in weekly issues for young and middle-aged adults who attend church and Bible classes. Circ. 45,000. **Pays on acceptance.** Publishes ms an average of 1 year after acceptance. Byline given. Buys first serial and second serial (reprint) rights. Submit seasonal material 1 year in advance. Accepts previously published submissions. Send tearsheet of article or typed ms with rights for sale noted. For reprints, pays 50% of amount paid for an original article. Reports in 3 months. Sample copy and writer's guidelines for 6×9 SAE with 2 first-class stamps.

Nonfiction: "We look for articles that are warm, inspirational, devotional, of personal or human interest; that deal with controversial matters, timely issues of religious, ethical or moral nature, or first-person testimonies, true-to-life happenings, vignettes, emotional situations or problems; communication problems and examples of answered prayers.

Article must deliver its point in a convincing manner but not be patronizing or preachy. It must appeal to either men or women, must be alive, vibrant, sparkling and have a title that demands the article be read. We always need stories about families, marriages, problems on campus and life testimonies." **Buys 150-200 mss/year.** Submit complete ms. Length: 400-1,200 words. **Pays 5¢/word.**

Reprints: Accepts previously published submissions. Send tearsheet or photocopy of article or typed ms with rights for sale noted and information about when and where the article previously appeared. Pays 50% of amount paid for an original article.

Photos: B&w photos purchased with or without mss. Pays $20 minimum for good 8×10 glossy prints.

Fiction: Religious fiction and religiously slanted historical and humorous fiction. No poetry. Length: 400-1,200 words. **Pays 5¢/word.**

• Ranked as one of the best markets for fiction writers in *Writer's Digest* magazine's "Fiction 50," June 1998.

Tips: "Submit manuscripts which tell of faith in action or victorious Christian living as central theme. We select manuscripts as far as one year in advance of publication. Complimentary copies are sent to our published writers immediately following printing."

N $ $ SHAMBHALA SUN, Creating Enlightened Society, 1345 Spruce St., Boulder CO 80302-4886. (902)422-8404. Fax: (902)423-2701. E-mail: magazine@shambhalasun.com. Website: http://www.shambhalasun.com. Molly DeShong, managing editor. **Contact:** Melvin McLeod, editor. **95% freelance written.** Bimonthly magazine covering Buddhism, contemplative spiritual life, western/eastern thought, arts, lifestyles. "A contemplative arts and philosophy magazine covering Buddhism, and spiritual issues of the Western world. Audience: spiritual seekers, artists, those interested in health/well-being issues; no special slant required." Estab. 1978. Circ. 20,000. Pays on publication. Publishes ms an average of 2 months after acceptance. Byline given. Buys first North American serial, first, second serial and simultaneous rights or makes work-for-hire assignments. Editorial lead time 2 months. Submit seasonal material 2 months in advance. Accepts simultaneous and previously published submissions. Reports in 1 week on queries; 1 month on mss.

Nonfiction: Book excerpts, essays, exposé, general interest, historical/nostalgic, how-to (meditation, disciplines of arts, science, cooking, etc.), humor, inspirational, interview/profile, new product, opinion, personal experience, photo feature, religious, technical, travel. **Buys 4-5 mss/year.** Query. Length: 600-4,000 words. **Pays $400.** Pays expenses of writers in assignment.

Reprints: Send tearsheet of article.

Photos: State availability of photos with submissions. Reviews 3×4 prints. Negotiates payment individually. Identification of subjects required.

Columns/Departments: Cooking, 3,000 words; Travel, book and film reviews, 1,000 words; political/philosophical (spirituality, world issues, community issues), 1-3,000 words. **Buys 4-5 mss/year.** Query. **Pays $40-400.**

Fiction: Adventure, condensed novels, confession, erotica, ethnic, experimental, fantasy, historical, horror, humorous, mainstream, mystery, novel excerpts, religious, science fiction, slice-of-life vignettes, suspense. **Buys 2-3 mss/year.** Query. Length: 600-3,000 words. **Pays $0-400.**

Poetry: Avant-garde, free verse, haiku, light verse, traditional. **Buys 1-2 poems/year.** Submit maximum 5 poems. **Pays $0-100.**

Fillers: Anecdotes, facts, gags to be illustrated by cartoonist, newsbreaks, short humor. **Buys 1-2/year.** Length: 0-1,000 words. **Pays $0-400.**

$ $ SHARING THE VICTORY, Fellowship of Christian Athletes, 8701 Leeds Rd., Kansas City MO 64129. (816)921-0909. Fax: (816)921-8755. E-mail: stu@fca.org. Website: http://www.fca/org. **Contact:** John Dodderidge, managing editor. Assistant Editor: Robyne Baker. **50% freelance written.** Prefers to work with published/established writers, but works with a growing number of new/unpublished writers each year. Monthly (September-May) magazine. "We seek to encourage and enable athletes and coaches at all levels to take their faith seriously on and off the 'field'." Estab. 1959. Circ. 60,000. Pays on publication. Publishes ms an average of 4 months after acceptance. Byline given. Buys first rights. Submit seasonal material 3 months in advance. Reports in 3 months on queries; 3 months on mss. *Writer's Market* recommends allowing 2 months for reply. Sample copy for $1 and 9×12 SAE with 3 first-class stamps. Free writer's guidelines for #10 SASE.

Nonfiction: Humor, inspirational, interview/profile (with "name" athletes and coaches solid in their faith), personal experience, photo feature. No "sappy articles on 'I became a Christian and now I'm a winner.' " **Buys 5-20 mss/year.** Query. Length: 500-1,000 words. **Pays $100-200** for unsolicited articles, more for the exceptional profile.

Reprints: Send typed ms with rights for sale noted. Pays 50% of amount paid for an original article.

Photos: State availability of photos with submission. Reviews contact sheets. Pay depends on quality of photo but usually a minimum $50. Model releases required for "name" individuals. Buys one-time rights.

Poetry: Free verse. Buys 9 poems/year. Pays $25.

Tips: "Profiles and interviews of particular interest to coed athlete, primarily high school and college age. Our graphics and editorial content appeal to youth. The area most open to freelancers is profiles on or interviews with well-known athletes or coaches (male, female, minorities) and offbeat but interscholastic team sports."

$ $ SIGNS OF THE TIMES, Pacific Press Publishing Association, P.O. Box 5353, Nampa ID 83653-5353. (208)465-2579. Fax: (208)465-2531. E-mail: mmoore@pacificpress.com. **Contact**: Marvin Moore, editor. **40% freelance written.** Works with a small number of new/unpublished writers each year. "We are a monthly Seventh-day

Adventist magazine encouraging the general public to practice the principles of the Bible." Estab. 1874. Circ. 225,000. **Pays on acceptance**. Publishes ms an average of 6 months after acceptance. Byline given. Offers kill fee. Buys first North American serial rights, one-time rights, or second serial reprint rights. Editorial lead time 1 year. Submit seasonal material 1 year in advance. "Gospel articles deal with salvation and how to experience it. While most of our gospel articles are assigned or picked up from reprints, we do occasionally accept unsolicited manuscripts in this area. Gospel articles should be 1,000 to 1,200 words. Christian lifestyle articles deal with the practical problems of everyday life from a biblical and Christian perspective. These are typically 1,000 to 1,200 words. We request that authors include sidebars that give additional information on the topic wherever possible. First-person stories must illuminate a spiritual or moral truth that the individual in the story learned. We especially like stories that hold the reader in suspense or that have an unusual twist at the end. First-person stories are typically 600 to 1,000 words long." Reports in 1 month on queries; 2 months on mss. Sample copy and writer's guidelines for 9×12 SAE with 3 first-class stamps.

Nonfiction: General interest, how-to, humor, inspirational, interview/profile, personal experience, religious. "We want writers with a desire to share the good news of reconciliation with God. Articles should be people-oriented, well-researched and should have a sharp focus." **Buys 75 mss/year.** Query with or without published clips or send complete ms. Length: 500-1,500 words. **Pays 10-20¢/word.** Sometimes pays the expenses of writers on assignment.

Reprints: Send tearsheet or photocopy of article or typed ms with rights for sale noted and information about when and where the article previously appeared. Pays 50% of amount paid for an original article.

Photos: Merwin Stewart, photo editor. Reviews b&w contact sheets, 35mm color transparencies, 5×7 or 8×10 b&w prints. Pays $35-300 for transparencies; $20-50 for prints. Model releases and identification of subjects required (captions helpful). Buys one-time rights.

Columns/Departments: Send complete ms. **Pays $25-150.**

Fillers: "Short fillers can be inspirational/devotional, Christian lifestyle, stories, comments that illuminate a biblical text—in short, anything that might fit in a general Christian magazine. Fillers should be 500 to 600 words."

Tips: The audience for *Signs of the Times* includes both Christians and nonChristians of all ages. However, we recommend that our authors write with the nonChristian in mind, since most Christians can easily relate to articles that are written from a nonChristian perspective, whereas many nonChristians will have no interest in an article that is written from a Christian perspective. While *Signs* is published by Seventh-day Adventists, we mention even our own denominational name in the magazine rather infrequently. The purpose is not to hide who we are but to make the magazine as attractive to nonChristian readers as possible.We are especially interested in articles that respond to the questions of everyday life that people are asking and the problems they are facing. Since these questions and problems nearly always have a spiritual component, articles that provide a biblical and spiritual response are especially welcome. Any time you can provide us with one or more sidebars that add information to the topic of your article, you enhance your change of getting our attention. Two kinds of sidebars seem to be especially popular with readers: Those that give information in lists, with each item in the list consisting of only a few words or at the most a sentence or two; and technical information or long explanations that in the main article might get the reader too bogged down in detail. Whatever their length, sidebars need to be part of the total word count of the article. We like the articles in *Signs of the Times* to have interest-grabbing introductions. One of the best ways to do this is with anecdotes, particularly those that have a bit of suspense or conflict.

$ SISTERS TODAY, The Liturgical Press, St. John's Abbey, Collegeville MN 56321-2099. Fax: (320)363-7130. E-mail: mwagner@csbsju.edu. Website: http://www.csbsju/osb.sisters/public.html. **Contact:** Sister Mary Anthony Wagner, O.S.B., editor-in-chief. **80% freelance written.** Prefers to work with published/established writers. Bimonthly magazine exploring the role of women and the Church, primarily. Circ. 3,500. Pays on publication. Publishes ms several months after acceptance probably. Byline given. Buys first rights. Submit seasonal material 4 months in advance. Sample copy for $4.50.

Nonfiction: How-to (pray, live in a religious community, exercise faith, hope, charity etc.), informational, inspirational. Also articles concerning religious renewal, community life, worship, the role of women in the Church and in the world today. **Buys 50-60 unsolicited mss/year.** Query. Length: 500-2,500 words. **Pays $5/printed page.** Send book reviews to Sister Stephanie Weisgram, O.S.B.

Poetry: Sister Mary Virginia Micka, C.S.J. Free verse, haiku, light verse, traditional. Buys 5-6 poems/issue. Submit maximum 4 poems. Pays $10.

Tips: "Some of the freelance material evidences the lack of familiarity with *Sisters Today.* We would prefer submitted articles not to exceed eight or nine pages."

$ SOCIAL JUSTICE REVIEW, 3835 Westminster Place, St. Louis MO 63108-3472. (314)371-1653. **Contact:** Rev. John H. Miller, C.S.C., editor. **25% freelance written.** Works with a small number of new/unpublished writers each year. Bimonthly. Estab. 1908. Publishes ms an average of 1 year after acceptance. Not copyrighted; "however special articles within the magazine may be copyrighted, or an occasional special issue has been copyrighted due to author's request." Buys first serial rights. Sample copy for 9×12 SAE with 3 first-class stamps.

Nonfiction: Scholarly articles on society's economic, religious, social, intellectual, political problems with the aim of bringing Catholic social thinking to bear upon these problems. Query with SASE. Length: 2,500-3,000 words. **Pays about 2¢/word.**

Reprints: Send typed ms with rights for sale noted and information about when and where the article previously appeared. Pays about 2¢/word.

☆ $ SPIRITUAL LIFE, 2131 Lincoln Rd. NE, Washington DC 20002-1199. (202)832-8489. Fax: (202)832-8967. E-mail: edodonnell@aol.com. Website: http://www.Spiritual-Life.org. **Contact:** Br. Edward O'Donnell, O.C.D., editor. **80% freelance written.** Prefers to work with published/established writers. Quarterly magazine for "largely Catholic, well-educated, serious readers. A few are non-Catholic or non-Christian." Circ. 12,000. **Pays on acceptance.** Publishes ms an average of 1 year after acceptance. Buys first North American serial rights. Reports in 2 months. Sample copy and writer's guidelines for 7×10 or larger SASE with 5 first-class stamps.

Nonfiction: Serious articles of contemporary spirituality and its pastoral application to everyday life. High quality articles about our encounter with God in the present day world. Language of articles should be college level. Technical terminology, if used, should be clearly explained. Material should be presented in a positive manner. Sentimental articles or those dealing with specific devotional practices not accepted. Buys inspirational and think pieces. "Brief autobiographical information (present occupation, past occupations, books and articles published, etc.) should accompany article." No fiction or poetry. **Buys 20 mss/year.** Length: 3,000-5,000 words. **Pays $50 minimum** and 2 contributor's copies. Book reviews should be sent to Br. Edward O'Donnell, O.C.D.

$ STANDARD, Nazarene International Headquarters, 6401 The Paseo, Kansas City MO 64131. (816)333-7000. **Contact:** Everett Leadingham, editor. **100% freelance written.** Works with a small number of new/unpublished writers each year. Weekly inspirational paper with Christian reading for adults. Estab. 1936. Circ. 160,000. **Pays on acceptance.** Publishes ms an average of 15-18 months after acceptance. Byline given. Buys one-time rights and second serial (reprint) rights. Submit seasonal material 6 months in advance. Reports in 10 weeks. Free sample copy. Writer's guidelines for SAE with 2 first-class stamps.

Reprints: Send tearsheet of short story.

Fiction: Prefers fiction-type stories *showing* Christianity in action. Send complete ms; no queries. Length: 500-1,500 words. **Pays 3½¢/word for first rights; 2¢/word for reprint rights.**

- Ranked as one of the best markets for fiction writers in *Writer's Digest* magazine's "Fiction 50," June 1998.

Poetry: Free verse, haiku, light verse, traditional. Buys 50 poems/year. Submit maximum 5 poems. Length: 50 lines maximum. **Pays 25¢/line.**

Tips: "Stories should express Christian principles without being preachy. Setting, plot and characterization must be realistic."

$ TEACHERS INTERACTION, Concordia Publishing House, 3558 S. Jefferson Ave., St. Louis MO 63118-3968. Fax: (314)268-1329. E-mail: NummelaTA@cphnet.org. Editorial Associate: Jean Muser, editorial associate. **Contact:** Tom Nummela, editor. **20% freelance written.** Quarterly magazine of practical, inspirational, theological articles for volunteer church school teachers. Material must be true to the doctrines of the Lutheran Church—Missouri Synod. Estab. 1960. Circ. 16,000. Pays on publication. Publishes ms an average of 1 year after acceptance. Byline given. Buys all rights. Submit seasonal material 1 year in advance. Reports in 3 months on mss. Sample copy for $2.75. Writer's guidelines for #10 SASE.

Nonfiction: How-to (practical help/ideas used successfully in own classroom), inspirational (to the church school worker—must be in accordance with LCMS doctrine), personal experience (of a Sunday school classroom nature—growth). No theological articles. **Buys 6 mss/year.** Send complete ms. Length: 750-1,500 words. **Pays up to $100.**

Fillers: "*Teachers Interaction* buys short Interchange items—activities and ideas planned and used successfully in a church school classroom." **Buys 48/year.** Length: 200 words maximum. **Pays $20.**

Tips: "Practical or 'it happened to me' experiences articles would have the best chance. Also short items—ideas used in classrooms; seasonal and in conjunction with our Sunday school material, Our Life in Christ. Our format includes *all* volunteer church school teachers, Sunday school teachers, Vacation Bible School, and midweek teachers, as well as teachers of adult Bible studies."

N $ THESE DAYS, Presbyterian Publishing Corp., 100 Witherspoon St., Louisville KY 40202-1396. Fax: (502)569-5453. **Contact:** Kay Snodgrass, editor. **95% freelance written**. Bimonthly consumer magazine covering religious devotionals. "*These Days* is published especially for the Cumberland Presbyterian Church, The Presbyterian Church in Canada, The Presbyterian Church (U.S.A.), The United Churches of Canada, and The United Church of Christ as a personal, family and group devotional guide." Estab. 1970. Circ. 200,000. **Pays on acceptance**. Publishes ms an average of 8 months after acceptance. Byline given. Buys all rights and makes work-for-hire assignments. Editorial lead time 10 months. Submit seasonal material 12 months in advance. Reports in 1 month on queries; 6 months on mss. Sample copy for 6×9 SASE and 2 first-class stamps. Writer's guidelines for #10 SASE.

Nonfiction: Devotionals in our format. "Use freelance in all issues. Only devotional material will be accepted. Send for issue themes and scripture references. Enclose #10 SASE." **Buys 365 mss/year**. Query or query with published clips. Length: 200-250 words. **Pays $10.**

Poetry: Buys 2-6 poems/year. Submit maximum 5 poems. Length: 3-20 lines. **Pays $10.**

Tips: "The best way is to send a one-page query that includes your religious affiliation and your religious, writing-related experience plus a sample devotional in our format and/or published clips of similar material."

☆ $ $ THIS PEOPLE MAGAZINE, Exploring LDS issues and personalities, Utah Alliance Publishing Co., P.O. Box 50748, Provo UT 84605-0748. (801)375-1700 ext 19. Fax: (801)375-1703. **Contact:** Editor. **75% freelance written.** Quarterly magazine "aimed at Mormon readers and examines Mormon issues and people in an upbeat, problem-solving way." Estab. 1979. Circ. 20,000. Pays on publication. Publishes ms an average of 6 months after

acceptance. Byline given. Offers 15% kill fee. Buys first rights. Submit seasonal material 6 months in advance. Reports in 2 months. Sample copy for 9×12 SAE with 4 first-class stamps. Writer's guidelines for #10 SASE.
Nonfiction: Essays, historical/nostalgic, humor, inspirational, interview/profile, personal experience, photo feature, travel—all Mormon oriented. No poetry, cartoons, fiction. **Buys 15-20 mss/year.** Query with or without published clips, or send complete ms. Length: 1,000-3,500 words. **Pays $150-400 for assigned articles; $100-400 for unsolicited articles.** Sometimes pays expenses of writers on assignment.
Reprints: Send tearsheet or photocopy of article.
Photos: State availability of photos. Model releases and identification of subjects required. Buys all rights.
Fiction: Publishes novel excerpts.
Tips: "I prefer query letters that include the first 6-8 paragraphs of an article plus an outline of the article. Clips and credits of previous publications are helpful."

N $ TOGETHER, Shalom Publishers, Box 656, Route 2, Grottoes VA 24441. E-mail: tgether@aol.com. Managing Editor: Eugene Souder. **Contact**: Melodie M. Davis, editor. **95% freelance written.** "*Together* is used quarterly by churches as an outreach paper to encourage readers to faith in Christ and God and participation in a local church. In addition to testimonies of spiritual conversion or journey, we publish general inspirational or family-related articles." Estab. 1987. Circ. 150,000. Pays on publication. Publishes ms an average of 9 months after acceptance. Byline given. Buys one-time or second serial (reprint) rights. Editorial lead time 6 months. Submit seasonal material 9 months in advance. Accepts simultaneous submissions. Reports in 2 months on queries; 6 months on mss. Sample copy for 9×12 SAE and 4 first-class stamps. Writer's guidelines for #10 SASE or e-mail.
Nonfiction: Inspirational, personal experience/testimony, religious. **Buys 22-24 mss/year.** Send complete ms. Length: 300-1,000 words. **Pays $35-50.**
Reprints: Accepts previously published submissions.
Photos: State availability of photos with submission. Reviews 3×5 prints. Offers $25/photo. Identification of subjects required. Buys one-time rights.
Tips: "We can use good contemporary conversion stories (to Christian faith) including as-told-to's. Read other stuff that is being published and then ask if your writing up to the level of what is being published today."

THE UNITED CHURCH OBSERVER, 478 Huron St., Toronto, Ontario M5R 2R3 Canada. (416)960-8500. Fax: (416)960-8477. E-mail: general@ucobserver.org. Website: http://www.ucobserver.org. **Contact:** Muriel Duncan, editor. **20% freelance written.** Prefers to work with published/established writers. Monthly newsmagazine for people associated with The United Church of Canada. Deals primarily with events, trends and policies having religious significance. Most coverage is Canadian, but reports on international or world concerns will be considered. Pays on publication. Publishes ms an average of 4 months after acceptance. Byline usually given. Buys first serial rights and occasionally all rights.
Nonfiction: Occasional opinion features only. Extended coverage of major issues usually assigned to known writers. No opinion pieces or poetry. Submissions should be written as news, no more than 1,200 words length, accurate and well-researched. Queries preferred. Rates depend on subject, author and work involved. Pays expenses of writers on assignment "as negotiated."
Reprints: Send tearsheet or photocopy of article with information about when and where the article previously appeared. Payment negotiated.
Photos: Buys photographs with mss. B&w should be 5×7 minimum; color 35mm or larger format. Payment varies.
Tips: "The writer has a better chance of breaking in at our publication with short articles; this also allows us to try more freelancers. Include samples of previous *news* writing with query. Indicate ability and willingness to do research, and to evaluate that research. The most frequent mistakes made by writers in completing an article for us are organizational problems, lack of polished style, short on research, and a lack of inclusive language."

$ THE UPPER ROOM, Daily Devotional Guide, P.O. Box 189, Nashville TN 37202-0189. (615)340-7252. Fax: (615)340-7006. E-mail: jstafford@upperroom.org. Website: http://www.upperroom.org. Editor and Publisher: Stephen D. Bryant. **Contact**: Jim Stafford, associate editor. **95% freelance written.** Eager to work with new/unpublished writers. Bimonthly magazine "offering a daily inspirational message which includes a Bible reading, text, prayer, 'Thought for the Day,' and suggestion for further prayer. Each day's meditation is written by a different person and is usually a personal witness about discovering meaning and power for Christian living through scripture study which illuminates daily life." Circ. 2.2 million (US); 385,000 outside US Pays on publication. Publishes ms an average of 1 year after acceptance. Byline given. Buys first North American serial rights and translation rights. Submit seasonal material 14 months in advance. "Manuscripts are not returned. If writers include a stamped, self addressed postcard, we will notify them that their writing has reached us. This does not imply acceptance or interest in purchase. Does not respond unless material is accepted for publication." Sample copy and writer's guidelines with a 4× SAE and 2 first-class stamps. For guidelines only send #10 envelope with stamp.
Nonfiction: Inspirational, personal experience, Bible-study insights. No poetry, lengthy "spiritual journey" stories. Special issues: Lent and Easter 2000; Advent 1999. **Buys 365 unsolicited mss/year.** Send complete ms. Length: 250 words maximum. **Pays $20.**
Tips: "The best way to break into our magazine is to send a well-written manuscript that looks at the Christian faith in a fresh way. Standard stories and sermon illustrations are immediately rejected. We very much want to find new writers and welcome good material. We are particularly interested in meditations based on Old Testament characters

and stories. Good repeat meditations can lead to work on longer assignments for our other publications, which pay more. A writer who can deal concretely with everyday situations, relate them to the Bible and spiritual truths, and write clear, direct prose should be able to write for *The Upper Room.* We want material that provides for more interaction on the part of the reader—meditation suggestions, journaling suggestions, space to reflect and link personal experience with the meditation for the day. Meditations that are personal, authentic, exploratory and full of sensory detail make good devotional writing."

$ $ VIRTUE, Helping women build Christ-like character, 4050 Lee Vance View, Colorado Springs CO 80918-7102. (719)531-7776. Fax: (719)535-0172. E-mail: virtuemag@aol.com. Editor-at-Large: Nancie Carmichael. **Contact**: Laura J. Barker, editor. **75% freelance written.** Works with small number of new/unpublished writers each year. Bimonthly magazine that "shows through features and columns the depth and variety of expression that can be given to women and faith." Estab. 1978. Circ. 111,000. Pays on acceptance or publication. Publishes ms an average of 4 months after acceptance. Byline given. Buys first North American serial rights. Submit seasonal material 9 months in advance. Reports in 2 months. Sample copy for 9×12 SAE with 7 first-class stamps. Guidelines for #10 SASE.
Nonfiction: Book excerpts, health, how-to, humor, inspirational, interview/profile, opinion, personal experience, enhancing relationships, religious. **Buys 60 mss/year.** Query. Length: 1,000-1,300 words. **Pays 15-25¢/word.**
Reprints: Accepts previously published submissions from a non-competing market. Send typed ms with rights for sale noted and information about when and where the article previously appeared.
Photos: State availability of photos with submission.
Columns/Departments: Virtue in Action (Christianity in our culture and time); One Woman's Journal (personal experience); Family Matters (practical ideas and advice for baby-boomer women). **Buys 25 mss/year.** Query. Length: 200-500 words. **Pays 15-25¢/word.**
Fiction: Humorous, religious. **Buys 4-6 mss/year.** Send complete ms. Length: 1,500-1,800 words. **Pays 15-25¢/word.**
Poetry: Free verse, traditional. **Buys 2-3 poems/year.** Submit maximum 3 poems. Length: 3-30 lines. **Pays $15-50.**

$ $ THE WAR CRY, The Salvation Army, 615 Slaters Lane, Alexandria VA 22313. Fax: (703)684-5539. E-mail: warcry@usn.salvationarmy.org. Website: http://publications.salvationarmyusa.org. Managing Editor: Jeff McDonald. **Contact:** Lt. Colonel Marlene Chase, editor. **10% freelance written.** Biweekly magazine covering army news and Christian devotional writing. Estab. 1881. Circ. 500,000. **Pays on acceptance.** Publishes ms an average of 3-12 months after acceptance. Byline given. Buys one-time rights. Editorial lead time 6 weeks. Submit seasonal material 1 year in advance. Reports in 1 month. Sample copy and writer's guidelines free.
Nonfiction: Humor, inspirational, interview/profile, personal experience, religious. No missionary stories, confessions. **Buys 40 mss/year.** Send complete ms. **Pays up to 20¢/word for assigned articles; 10-20¢/word for unsolicited articles.** Sometimes pays expenses of writers on assignment.
Reprints: Send typed ms with rights for sale noted and information about when and where the article previously appeared. Pays 15¢/word.
Photos: Offers $35-200/photo. Identification of subjects required. Buys one-time rights.
Fiction: Religious. **Buys 2-4 mss/year.** Send complete ms. Length: 1,200-1,500 words maximum. **Pays 20¢/word.**
Poetry: Free verse. Inspirational only. **Buys 10-20 poems/year.** Submit maximum 5 poems. Length: 16 lines maximum. **Pays $20-50.**
Fillers: Anecdotes (inspirational). **Buys 10-20/year.** Length: 200-500 words. **Pays 15-20¢/word.**
Tips: "We are soliciting more short fiction, inspirational articles and poetry, interviews with Christian athletes, evangelical leaders and celebrities, and theme-focused articles."

$ $ WEAVINGS, A Journal of the Christian Spiritual Life, The Upper Room, 1908 Grand Ave., P.O. Box 189, Nashville TN 37202-0189. (615)340-7254. Fax: (615)340-7006. E-mail: weavings@upperroom.org. Website: http://www.upperroom.org. **Contact**: Kathleen Stephens, associate editor. Editor: John S. Mogabgab. **75% freelance written.** Bimonthly magazine covering Christian spirituality. "*Weavings* invites participation in the spiritual life, seeking to provide a forum in which our life in the world and the spiritual resources of the Christian heritage can encounter and illumine one another. The journal is for clergy, lay leaders and all thoughtful seekers who want to understand how God's life and human lives are being woven together in the world." Circ. 40,000. Pays on publication. Publishes ms an average of 11 months after acceptance. Byline given. Offers $100 kill fee. Buys first, one-time, second serial (reprint) or all rights. Editorial lead time 11 months. Submit seasonal material 11 months in advance. Reports in 2 months. Sample copy for 6½×10 SAE with 4 first-class stamps. Writer's guidelines for #10 SASE.
Nonfiction: Book excerpts, essays, inspirational, religious. Special issue: "Hope in God" (November/December). **Buys 25 mss/year.** Send complete ms. Length: 1,250-2,500 words. **Pays 12¢/word and up.**
Reprints: Accepts previously published submissions.
Columns/Departments: Sermons and meditations on scripture (examine the rich variety of insights and incentives to action when we begin to see the connections between the biblical story of God's love and our own life story), 500-2,000 words; book reviews, 750 words. Send complete ms. **Pays 12¢/word and up.**
Fiction: Religious. **Buys 4 mss/year.** Send complete ms. Length: 2,000 words. **Pays 12¢/word and up.**
Poetry: Free verse, haiku, light verse, traditional. **Buys 2 poems/year. Pays $75 and up.**
Tips: Check upcoming issue themes and make sure your submission closely fits one of the themes.

$ THE WESLEYAN ADVOCATE, The Wesleyan Publishing House, P.O. Box 50434, Indianapolis IN 46250-0434. (317)576-8156. Fax: (317)842-1649. E-mail: communications@wesleyan.org. Executive Editor: Dr. Norman G. Wilson. **Contact**: Jerry Brecheisen, managing editor. **50% freelance written.** Monthly magazine of The Wesleyan Church. Estab. 1842. Circ. 20,000. Pays on publication. Byline given. Buys first rights or simultaneous rights (prefers first rights). Submit seasonal material 6 months in advance. Accepts simultaneous submissions. Reports in 2 weeks. Sample copy for $2. Writer's guidelines for #10 SASE.

Nonfiction: Humor, inspirational, religious. Send complete ms. Length: 500-700 words. **Pays $10-40 for assigned articles; $5-25 for unsolicited articles.**

Reprints: Send photocopy of article and typed ms with rights for sale noted and information about when and where the article previously appeared.

Photos: Send photos with submission. Buys one-time rights.

Poetry: Accepts some seasonal poetry. Length: 10-15 lines. **Pays $5-10.**

Tips: "Write for a guide."

$ THE WESLEYAN WOMAN, Wesleyan Publishing House, P.O. Box 50434, Indianapolis IN 46250. (317)570-5164. Fax: (317)570-5254. E-mail: wwi@wesleyan.org. Editor: Nancy Heer. **Contact**: Martha Blackburn, managing editor. **60-70% freelance written.** "Quarterly instruction and inspiration magazine for women 20-80. It is read by believers mainly." Estab. 1980. Circ. 4,000. Pays on publication. Byline given. Buys one-time and second serial (reprint) rights. Editorial lead time 3 months. Submit seasonal material 6 months in advance. Accepts simultaneous submissions. Sample copy and writer's guidelines free.

Nonfiction: General interest, how-to (ideas for service and ministry), humor, inspirational, personal experience, religious. "No 'preaching' articles that tell others what to do." **Buys 60 mss/year.** Send complete ms. Length: 200-700 words. **Pays 2-4¢/word.**

Reprints: Send photocopy of article or typed ms with rights for sale noted and information about when and where the article previously appeared. Pays 50-75% of amount paid for an original article.

Photos: Send photos with submission. Offers $30/photo. Captions and identification of subjects required. Buys one-time rights.

Fillers: Anecdotes, facts, newsbreaks, short humor. **Buys 20/year.** Length: 150-350 words. **Pays 2-4¢/word.**

Tips: "Send a complete article after seeing our guidelines. Articles that are of your personal journey are welcomed. We seldom publish sermons and Bible studies. Our denomination has other magazines which do these."

$ $ THE WITNESS, Episcopal Church Publishing Co., 1249 Washington Blvd., #3115, Detroit MI 48226. (313)962-2650. Fax: (313)841-1967. E-mail: marianne@thewitness.org. Website: http://www.thewitness.org/. Co-editors: Jeanie Wylie-Kellermann and Julie A. Wortman. **Contact:** Marianne Arbogast, assistant editor. **20% freelance written.** Monthly magazine covering religion and politics from a left perspective. "Our readers are people of faith who are interested in wrestling with scripture and current events with the goal of serving God and effecting change that diminishes the privilege of the rich." Estab. 1917. Circ. 4,000. Pays on publication. Publishes ms an average of 3 months after acceptance. Byline given. Offers 50% kill fee. Buys first rights. Editorial lead time 6 weeks. Submit seasonal material 3 months in advance. Responds only to material accepted for publication. Manuscripts not returned. Sample copy and writer's guidelines free.

Nonfiction: Exposé, general interest, historical/nostalgic, humor, interview/profile, personal experience, photo feature, religious. **Buys 10 mss/year.** Query with or without published clips, or send complete ms. Length: 250-1,800 words. **Pays $50-250 for assigned articles; $50-100 for unsolicited articles;** and 1-year subscription. Sometimes pays expenses of writers on assignment.

Photos: State availability of photos with submissions. Reviews prints. Offers $0-30/photo. Captions, identification of subjects required. Buys one-time rights.

Poetry: Buys 10 poems/year. Submit maximum 5 poems. **Pays $0-30.**

Tips: "We're eager for *short* news pieces that relate to racial-, gender- and eco-justice. Our issues are thematic which makes queries advisable. We don't publish material written in a dry academic style. We like stories that allow marginalized people to speak in their own words."

$ WOMAN'S TOUCH, Assemblies of God Women's Ministries Department (GPH), 1445 Boonville Ave., Springfield MO 65802-1894. (417)862-2781. Fax: (417)862-0503. E-mail: womanstouch@ag.org. **Contact:** Peggy Musgrove, editor. Managing Editor: Aleda Swartzendruber. **50% freelance written.** Willing to work with new/unpublished writers. Bimonthly inspirational magazine for women. "Articles and contents of the magazine should be compatible with Christian teachings as well as human interests. The audience is women, both homemakers and those who are career-oriented." Estab. 1977. Circ. 21,000. Pays on publication. Byline given. Buys one-time rights. Submit seasonal material 8 months in advance. Reports in 3 months. Sample copy for 9½×11 SAE with 3 first-class stamps. Writer's guidelines for #10 SASE.

Nonfiction: General interest, how-to, inspirational, personal experience, religious, health. **Buys 30 mss/year.** Send complete ms. Length: 500-800 words. **Pays $10-35 for unsolicited articles.**

Reprints: Send photocopy of article and information about when and where the article previously appeared. Pays 50-75% of amount paid for an original article.

Photos: State availability of photos with submission. Reviews negatives, transparencies, 4×6 prints. Offers no additional payment for photos accepted with ms. Identification of subjects required. Buys one-time rights.

Columns/Departments: A Final Touch for short human interest articles—home and family or career-oriented," length: 80-500 words, **pays $20-35;** A Better You (health, wellness, beauty), length: 200-500 words; **pays $15-25;** A Lighter Touch (true, unpublished anecdotes), length: 100 words, **pays $10.**
Fillers: Facts. **Buys 5/year.** Length: 50-200. **Pays $5-15.**

$ $ THE WORLD, Unitarian Universalist Association, 25 Beacon St., Boston MA 02108-2800. (617)742-2100. Fax: (617)742-7025. E-mail: ahoffman@uua.org. Website: http://www.uva.org. Editor-in-Chief: Tom Stites. **Contact**: Amy Hoffman. **50% freelance written.** Bimonthly magazine "to promote and inspire denominational self-reflection; to inform readers about the wide range of Unitarian Universalist values, purposes, activities, aesthetics, and spiritual attitudes, and to educate readers about the history, personalities, and congregations that comprise UUism; to enhance its dual role of leadership and service to member congregations." Estab. 1987. Circ. 115,000. **Pays on acceptance.** Publishes ms an average of 1 year after acceptance. Byline given. Buys one-time rights. Editorial lead time 3 months. Submit seasonal material 3 months in advance. Pay varies. Reports in 2 months on queries; 3 months on mss. Sample copy and writer's guidelines for 9×12 SASE.
Nonfiction: All articles must have a clear UU angle. Essays, historical/nostalgic (Unitarian or Universalist focus), inspirational, interview/profile (with UU individual or congregation), commentary, photo feature (of UU congregation or project), religious. "We are planning issues on family, spirituality and welfare reform." No unsolicited poetry or fiction. **Buys 5 mss/year.** Query with published clips. Length: 1,500-3,500 words. **Pays $400 minimum for assigned feature articles.** Sometimes pays expenses of writers on assignment.
Photos: State availability of photos with submission. Reviews contact sheets. Offers no additional payment for photos accepted with ms. Captions, model releases and identification of subjects required. Buys one-time rights.
Columns/Departments: Focus On (profiles); Community Projects (social service project profiles); Book Reviews (liberal religion, social issues, politics), 600-800 words. Query (profiles, book reviews). **Pays $75-250 for assigned articles and book reviews.**

RETIREMENT

January 1, 1996 the first baby boomer turned 50. With peak earning power and increased leisure time, this generation is able to pursue varied interests while maintaining active lives. More people are retiring in their 50s, while others are starting a business or traveling and pursuing hobbies. These publications give readers specialized information on health and fitness, medical research, finances and other topics of interest, as well as general articles on travel destinations and recreational activities.

$ $ $ ACTIVETIMES MAGAZINE, 417 Main St., Carbondale CO 81623. Fax: (970)963-8271. **Contact**: Chris Kelly, editor. **80% freelance written.** Quarterly magazine covering over 50 market. "We target active, adults over 50. We emphasize the positive, enjoyable aspects of aging." Estab. 1992. Circ. 7,000,000. Pays on publication. Publishes ms an average of 4 months after acceptance. Byline given. Offers 50% kill fee. Buys first North American serial and electronic rights. Editorial lead time 3 months. Submit seasonal material 9 months in advance. Reports in 2 months. Sample copy and guidelines for 9×12 SAE with 3 first-class stamps. Writer's guidelines only for #10 SASE.
Nonfiction: General interest, how-to, interview/profile, travel round-ups (not destination stories), outdoor, business, careers, education, housing, entertainment, books, celebrities, food, nutrition, health, products, relationships, sex, volunteerism, community service, sports/recreation. No personal essays, first person narratives or nostalgia. **Buys 40 mss/year.** Query with published clips and SASE or postcard. No SASE, no reply. Length: 400-1,200 words. **Pays $75-500 for assigned articles; $50-250 for unsolicited articles.**
Photos: State availability of photos with submission. Reviews contact sheets, 35mm transparencies, prints. Negotiates payment individually. Identification of subjects required.
Columns/Departments: Profile (interesting over-50), 500-600 words. **Buys 4 mss/year.** Query with published clips. **Pays $75-250.** Never-Evers (over-50 doing something never, ever did including b&w photo), 150 words. Send complete ms. **Pays $35.**
Tips: "Write a detailed query, with substantiating clips. Show how story will appeal to active over-50 reader. Not interested in pain, death, suffering, loss, illness and other similarly depressing subjects."

$ ALIVE! A Magazine for Christian Senior Adults, Christian Seniors Fellowship, P.O. Box 46464, Cincinnati OH 45246-0464. (513)825-3681. Fax: (513)825-3301. Editor: J. David Lang. **Contact**: A. June Lang, office editor. **60% freelance written.** Bimonthly magazine for senior adults ages 50 and older. "We need timely articles about Christian seniors in vital, productive lifestyles, travels or ministries." Estab. 1988. Pays on publication. Byline given. Buys first or second serial (reprint) rights. Submit seasonal material 6 months in advance. Reports in 2 months. Membership $15/year. Sample copy for 9×12 SAE with 3 first-class stamps. Writer's guidelines for #10 SASE.
Nonfiction: General interest, humor, inspirational, interview/profile, photo feature, religious, travel. **Buys 25-50 mss/year.** Send complete ms and SASE. Length: 600-1,200 words. **Pays $18-75.** Organization membership may be deducted from payment at writer's request.

Reprints: Send tearsheet, photocopy of article or typed ms with rights for sale noted and information about when and where the article previously appeared. Pays 60-75% of amount paid for an original article.
Photos: State availability of photos with submission. Offers $10-25. Model releases and identification of subjects required. Buys one-time rights.
Columns/Departments: Heart Medicine (humorous personal anecdotes; prefer grandparent/grandchild stories or anecdotes re: over-55 persons), 10-100 words; Games n' Stuff (word games, puzzles, word search), 200-500 words. **Buys 50 mss/year.** Send complete ms and SASE. **Pays $2-25.**
Fiction: Adventure, humorous, religious, romance (if it fits age group), slice-of-life vignettes, motivational/inspirational. **Buys 12 mss/year.** Send complete ms. Length: 600-1,500 words. **Pays $20-60.**
Fillers: Anecdotes, facts, gags to be illustrated by cartoonist, short humor. **Buys 15/year.** Length: 50-500 words. **Pays $2-15.**
Tips: "Include SASE and whether manuscript is to be returned or tossed."

$ $ FIFTY-FIVE PLUS, Promoting An Active Mature Lifestyle, Valley Publishers Inc., 95 Abbeyhill Dr., Kanata, Ontario K2L 2M8 Canada. (613)592-3578. Fax: (613)592-9033. **Contact:** Pat den Boer, editor. **95% freelance written.** Bimonthly magazine. "We focus on the health, financial, nutrition and travel interests of active retirees." Circ. 40,000. Pays on publication. Publishes ms an average of 1 year after acceptance. Byline given. Offers 50% kill fee. Buys first North American serial rights. Editorial lead time 3 months. Submit seasonal material 6 months in advance. Sample copy for 9×12 SAE and 3 first-class stamps. Writer's guidelines for #10 SASE.
Nonfiction: How-to, inspirational, travel. **Buys 70 mss/year.** Send complete ms. Length: 500-1,000 words. **Pays $60-300.** Pays writers with contributor copies or other premiums for travel promotional pieces. Sometimes pays expenses of writer on assignment.
Photos: Send photos with submission. Reviews 2×3 and 4×5 transparencies. Offers no additional payment for photos accepted with ms or negotiates payment individually. Buys one-time rights.
Columns/Departments: Health; Backyard Heroes (people giving back to community); Personal Finance; Nutrition; Great Mature Getaways. Length: 600 words. **Buys 6 mss/year.** Send complete ms. **Pays $60.**

$ GET UP & GO, (formerly *Senior Highlights*), 26081 Merit Circle, Suite 101, Laguna Hills CA 92653. (714)367-0776. Fax: (714)367-1006. **Contact**: Eve Lash, editor. **30% freelance written.** "*Get Up & Go!* is a monthly magazine designed to enrich the lifestyle for persons 50 and older. It features interesting and inspiring stories relative to this age group. Our objective is 'Making Your Next Years Your Best Years.' *Get Up & Go!* informs readers throughout Central and Southern California. Five separate editions reach Greater Los Angeles, Orange and San Diego counties as well as the Inland Empire (Riverside and San Bernardino counties) and the San Fernando Valley (including Ventura county)." Estab. 1983. Circ. 444,000. Pays on publication. Publishes ms an average of 3 months after acceptance. Byline given. Buys first, second serial (reprint) rights and simultaneous rights. Editorial lead time 2 months. Submit seasonal material 3 months in advance. Accepts simultaneous submissions. Reports in 3 months. Sample copy for $3 and 9×12 SAE with 4 first-class stamps. Writer's guidelines for #10 SASE.

- Age Wave Communications publishes a number of regional magazines for older adults, all under the name of *Get Up & Go!*

Nonfiction: General interest, historical/nostalgic, humor, inspirational, interview/profile, opinion/commentary, personal experience, travel (domestic and international), breakthroughs in science and medicine, health, exercise and nutrition, arts and entertainment (film, stage, art, music, literature, restaurants), hobbies, gardening and sports, retirement living/housing, personal finance, consumer protection & information. Special issues: editorial calendar available. "Do not send articles that discuss how to 'cure' old age. Do not send articles that talk 'about' seniors rather than 'to' seniors. Recognize who you are talking to: active, talented and intelligent older people." **Buys 60 mss/year.** Query or send complete ms. Length: 300-800 words. **Pays $0-100 for assigned articles; $0-25 for unsolicited articles.**
Reprints: Send information about when and where the article previously appeared. Does not pay for reprints.
Photos: State availability of or send photos with submission. Reviews color slides or transparencies, b&w prints. Offers no additional payment for photos accepted with ms. Captions are required.
Columns/Departments: Celebrity Feature (high profile, easily recognizable celebrities that are still actively involved), 800 words; Letters to the Editor (publish one per month; must be clearly written), 300 words; Health (nutrition/fitness; medical breakthroughs), 800 words; Lifestyles (housing, food/recipes, restaurants, gardening, hobbies, sports and legislation), 800 words; Moneywise (consumer issues, personal finance and investing), 800 words; Travel (domestic and international), 800 words; Who's to Say (outstanding, extraordinary seniors), 800 words. **Buys 120 mss/year.** Query or send complete ms. **Pays $0-50.**
Tips: "We are looking for articles that tie in to our editorial calendar topics in exciting and innovative ways. We have a special need for upbeat health articles that avoid stereotyping our readers as sickly and emphasize prevention. Talk directly to our readers and stick with subjects that directly impact their lives. Keep in mind our readers' needs and interests differ dramatically from 50 to over 100 years old. No telephone queries. Unorganized thoughts and materials are tossed."

$ GET UP & GO!, A monthly newsmagazine for maturing adults, (formerly *Mature Lifestyles*), Age Wave Communications, Inc., 4575 Via Royale, Suite 102, Fort Myers FL 33919. Fax: (941)931-9195. E-mail: maturelifestyles @worldnet.att.com. **Contact**: Linda Heffley, managing editor. **30% freelance written.** Monthly magazine covers "all types of features that appeal to the 50-plus reader, preferably with a Florida connection." Estab. 1986. Circ. 200,000.

Pays on publication. Publishes ms an average of 6-12 months after acceptance. Byline given. Buys one-time or second serial (reprint) rights. Editorial lead time 2 months. Submit seasonal material 4 months in advance. Accepts simultaneous submissions. Reports in 6 weeks weeks on queries; 2 months on mss. Sample copy and writer's guidelines free.

• Age Wave Communications publishes a number of regional magazines for older adults, all under the name of *Get Up & Go!*

Nonfiction: Historical/nostalgic, opinion, holiday tie-in. Query for special issues. **Buys 30-50 mss/year.** Send complete ms. Length: 500-1,000 words. **Pays $35-75 for unsolicited articles.** Sometimes pays expenses of writers on assignment.

Photos: State availability of photos with submission. Offers no additional payment for photos accepted with ms. Identification of subjects required. Buys one-time rights.

Columns/Departments: Pays $35-75.

$ $ $ MATURE OUTLOOK, Meredith Corp., 1716 Locust St., Des Moines IA 50309-3023. E-mail: outlook@mdp.com. **Contact**: Peggy Person, editor. **80% freelance written.** Bimonthly magazine on travel, health, nutrition, money and people for over-50 audience. "*Mature Outlook* is for the 50+ reader who is discovering new possibilities for a new time of life. It provides information for establishing a secure base of health and financial well-being, as well as stories of travel, hobbies, volunteerism and more. They may or may *not* be retired." Circ. 725,000. **Pays on acceptance.** Publishes ms an average 7 months after acceptance. Byline given. Offers 25% kill fee. Buys all rights or makes work-for-hire assignments. Submit all material 9 months in advance. Reports in 2 weeks. Sample copy for $1 and 9×12 SAE. Writer's guidelines for #10 SASE.

Nonfiction: How-to, travel, health, fitness, financial, people profiles. No poetry, celebrities or reprints. **Buys 50-60 mss/year.** Query with published clips. Length: 75-1,500 words. **Pays $50-1,250.** Pays telephone expenses of writers on assignment.

Photos: State availability of photos with submission. Pays for photos on publication.

Tips: "Please query. Please don't call. Reviews manuscripts for short articles or department briefs of 500 words or less. Travel briefs with the greatest chance of acceptance will alert readers to a little-known regional opportunity within the U.S.—a festival, museum, exhibition, scenic hiking trail, boat ride, etc."

$ MATURE YEARS, The United Methodist Publishing House, 201 Eighth Ave. S., Nashville TN 37202-0801. Fax: (615)749-6512. E-mail: mcropsey@umpublishing.org. **Contact**: Marvin W. Cropsey, editor. **50% freelance written.** Prefers to work with published/established writers. Quarterly magazine "designed to help persons in and nearing the retirement years understand and appropriate the resources of the Christian faith in dealing with specific problems and opportunities related to aging. Estab. 1954. Circ. 70,000. **Pays on acceptance.** Publishes ms an average of 1 year after acceptance. Buys one-time North American serial rights. Submit seasonal material 14 months in advance. Reports in 2 weeks on queries; 2 months for mss. Sample copy for $5 and 9×12 SAE. Writer's guidelines for #10 SASE.

Nonfiction: How-to (hobbies), inspirational, religious, travel (special guidelines), older adult health, finance issues. Especially important are opportunities for older adults to read about service, adventure, fulfillment and fun. **Buys 75-80 mss/year.** Send complete ms. Length: 900-2,000 words. **Pays $45-125.** Sometimes pays expenses of writers on assignments.

Reprints: Send photocopy or typed ms with rights for sale noted and information about when and where the article previously appeared. Pays 100% of amount paid for an original article.

Photos: Send photos with submission. Negotiates payment individually. Captions, model releases required. Buys one-time rights.

Columns/Departments: Health Hints (retirement, health), 900-1,500 words; Going Places (travel, pilgrimmage), 1,000-1,500 words; Fragments of Life (personal inspiration), 250-600 words; Modern Revelations (religious/inspirational), 900-1,500 words; Money Matters (personal finance), 1,200-1,800 words; Merry-Go-Round (cartoons, jokes, 4-6 line humorous verse); Puzzle Time (religious puzzles, crosswords). **Buys 4 mss/year each.** Send complete ms. **Pays $25-45.**

Fiction: Religious, slice-of-life vignettes, retirement years. **Buys 4 mss/year.** Send complete ms. Length: 1,000-2,000 words. **Pays $60-125.**

Poetry: Free verse, haiku, light verse, traditional. **Buys 24 poems/year.** Submit 6 poems maximum. Length: 3-16 lines. **Pays $5-20.**

$ $ $ $ MODERN MATURITY, American Association of Retired Persons, 601 E St., NW, Washington DC 20049. (202)434-6880. **Contact:** J. Henry Fenwick, editor. **50% freelance written.** Prefers to work with published/established writers. Bimonthly magazine. "*Modern Maturity* is devoted to the varied needs and active life interests of AARP members, age 50 and over, covering such topics as financial planning, travel, health, careers, retirement, relationships and social and cultural change. Its editorial content serves the mission of AARP seeking through education, advocacy and service to enhance the quality of life for all by promoting independence, dignity and purpose." Circ. 20,500,000. **Pays on acceptance.** Publishes ms an average of 6 months after acceptance. Byline given. Buys first North American serial rights. Submit seasonal material 6 months in advance. Reports in 3 months. Free sample copy and writer's guidelines.

Nonfiction: Careers, workplace, practical information in living, financial and legal matters, personal relationships, consumerism. Query first. *No unsolicited mss*. Length: up to 2,000 words. **Pays up to $3,000.** Sometimes pays expenses of writers on assignment.

Photos: Photos purchased with or without accompanying ms. Pays $250 and up for color; $150 and up for b&w.

Fiction: Very occasional short fiction.
Tips: "The most frequent mistake made by writers in completing an article for us is poor follow-through with basic research. The outline is often more interesting than the finished piece. We do not accept unsolicited manuscripts."

$ $ PRIME TIMES, Grote Publishing, 634 W. Main St., Suite 207, Madison WI 53703-2634. **Contact:** Barbara Walsh, managing editor. **75% freelance written.** Bimonthly membership magazine for the National Association for Retired Credit Union People (NARCUP). "*Prime Times* is a topical magazine of broad appeal to a general adult audience, emphasizing issues relevant to people over age 50. It offers timely articles on health, fitness, finance, travel, outdoor sports, consumer issues, lifestyle, home arts and family relationships. Estab. 1979. Circ. 76,000. May share a core of editorial material with sister magazine *American Times* (est. 1993), sent to financial institutions' older adult customers. Pays on publication. Publishes ms an average of 6 months after acceptance. Byline given. Buys first North American serial rights, one-time rights and second serial (reprint) rights. Editorial lead time 7 months. Submit seasonal material 8 months in advance. Reports in 6 weeks on queries; 2 months on mss. Sample copy for $3.75 and 9×12 SAE with 4 first-class stamps. Writer's guidelines for #10 SASE.
Nonfiction: Book excerpts, general interest, health/fitness, travel, historical, humor, recipes, photo features. "No nostalgia pieces, medical or financial pieces based solely on personal anecdotes, personal opinion essays, fiction or poetry." **Buys 8-12 mss/year.** Prefers to see complete ms. Length: 1,000-2,000 words. **Pays $250 minimum for full-length assigned articles; $100 minimum for unsolicited full-length articles.**
Reprints: Buys 8-16 reprints/year. Send photocopy of article or typed ms with rights for sale noted and information about when and where the article previously appeared. **Pays $50-125,** depending on length, quality and number of times published.
Photos: Needs professional-quality photos. State availability of or send photos with submission. Welcomes text-photo packages. Reviews contact sheets, transparencies and prints. Negotiates payment individually. Model releases and identification of subjects required. Buys one-time rights.
Tips: "Articles that contain useful, well-documented, up-to-date information have the best chance of publication. Don't send personal essays, or articles that repeat information readily available in mainstream media. Articles on health and medical issues *must* be founded in sound scientific method and include current data. Quotes from experts add to an article's validity. You must be able to document your research. Make it easy for us to make a decision on your submission. If the article is written, submit the entire thing—manuscript with professional-quality photos. If you query, be specific. Write part of it in the style in which you would write the article. Be sure to enclose clips. With every article we publish, something about the story must lend itself to strong graphic representation."

N $ SENIOR LIVING NEWSPAPERS, Smith III Publications, Inc., 318 E. Pershing, Springfield MO 65806. Fax: (417)862-9079. Website: http://www.seniorlivingnewspaper.com. Editor: Robert Smith. **Contact**: Joyce O'Neal, managing editor. **10% freelance written.** Monthly newspaper covering active seniors in retirement. "For people 55+. Positive and upbeat attitude on aging, prime of life times. Slant is directed to mid-life and retirement lifestyles. Readers are primarily well-educated and affluent retirees, homemakers and career professional. *Senior Living* informs; health, fitness-entertains; essays, nostalgia, humor, etc." Estab. 1988. Circ. 57,000. Pays 30 days after publication. Publishes ms an average of 2 months after acceptance. Byline given. Offers 25% kill fee. Buys first and second serial (reprint) rights. Editorial lead time 3 months. Submit seasonal material 3 months in advance. Reports in 2 weeks on queries; 1 month on mss. Sample copy for 9×12 SAE with 5 first-class stamps. Writer's guidelines for #10 SASE.
Nonfiction: Essays, general interest, historical/nostalgic, humor, inspirational, personal experience, photo feature, health-related. No youth oriented, preachy, sugar coated, technical articles. **Buys 30-40 mss/year.** Send complete ms. Length: 300-800 words. **Pays $35-50 for assigned articles; $5-35 for unsolicited articles.** Pays expenses of writers on assignment.
Reprints: Accepts previously published submissions.
Photos: Send photos with submission. Offers $1-5/photo. Captions, model releases and identification of subjects required. Buys one-time rights.
Poetry: Free verse, haiku, light verse, traditional. **Buys 12 poems/year.** Submit maximum 3 poems. Length: 2-14 lines. **Pays $1-5.**
Fillers: Anecdotes, facts, short humor. **Buys 15/year.** Length: 150-250 words. **Pays $1-5.**
Tips: "Beginning writers who are in need of byline clips stand a good chance if they indicate that they do not require payment for article."

$ SENIOR MAGAZINE, 3565 S. Higuera St., San Luis Obispo CA 93401. (805)544-8711. Fax: (805)544-4450. Editor/Publisher: Gary D. Suggs. **Contact**: George Brand, managing editor. **90% freelance written.** Monthly magazine covering seniors to inform and entertain the "over-50" but young-at-heart audience. Estab. 1981. Circ. 240,000. Pays on publication. Byline given. Publishes ms an average of 1 month after acceptance. Not copyrighted. Buys first or second rights. Accepts simultaneous submissions. Submit seasonal material 2 months in advance. Reports in 2 weeks. Sample copy for 9×12 SAE with $1.50 postage. Writer's guidelines for SASE.
Nonfiction: Health, historical/nostalgic, humor, inspirational, personal experience, unique hobbies, second careers, book reviews, personality profiles of unusual or notable people (actors, sports figures, writers, travel). Special issues: Second Careers; Going Back to School; Christmas (December); Travel (October, March). **Buys 30-75 mss/year.** Query with SASE. Length: 900-1,200 words. **Pays $1.50/inch.**
Reprints: Send typed ms with rights for sale noted and information about when and where the article previously

appeared. Pays 100% of amount paid for an original article.
Photos: Send photos with submission. Reviews 8×10 b&w prints only. Offers $10-15/photo. Captions and identification of subjects required. Buys one-time rights. Uses mostly well known personalities.
Columns/Departments: Finance (investment), Taxes, Auto, Health. Length: 300-900 words. **Pays $1.50/inch.**

ROMANCE AND CONFESSION

Listed here are publications that need stories of romance ranging from ethnic and adventure to romantic intrigue and confession. Each magazine has a particular slant; some are written for young adults, others to family-oriented women. Some magazines also are interested in general interest nonfiction on related subjects.

$ AFFAIRE DE COEUR,, 3976 Oak Hill Rd., Oakland CA 94605. Fax: (510)632-8868. E-mail: sseven@msn.com. Website: http://www.affairdecoeur.com. **Contact:** Louise Snead, publisher. 56% freelance written. Monthly magazine of book reviews, articles and information on publishing for romance readers and writers. Circ. 115,000. Pays on publication. Publishes ms an average of 1 year after acceptance. Byline given. Buys one-time rights. Submit seasonal material 3 months in advance. Accepts simultaneous submissions. Reports in 4 months. Sample copy for $5.
Nonfiction: Book excerpts, essays, general interest, historical/nostalgic, how-to, interview/profile, personal experience, photo feature. **Buys 2 mss/year.** Query. Length: 500-2,200 words. **Pays $25-35.** Sometimes pays writers with copies.
Reprints: Accepts previously published submissions.
Photos: State availability of photos with submission. Review prints. Identification of subjects required. Buys one-time rights.
Columns/Departments: Reviews (book reviews), bios, articles, 2,000 word or less.
Fiction: Historical, mainstream, romance. Only accepts fiction for short story contest. **Pays $25.**
Fillers: Newsbreaks. **Buys 2/year.** Length: 50-100 words. Does not pay.
Tips: "Please send clean copy. Do not send material without SASE. Do not expect a return for 2-3 months. Type all information. Send some sample of your work."

$ BLACK SECRETS, Sterling/McFadden Partnership, 233 Park Ave. S., 7th Floor, New York NY 10003. (212)780-3500. Fax: (212)979-7342. **Contact:** Marcia Mahan, editor. See *Intimacy/Black Romance*.
Fiction: "This is our most romantic magazine of the five. We use one longer story between 20-24 pages for this book, and sometimes we feature it on the cover. Save your harsh, sleazy stories for another magazine. Give us your softest, dreamiest, most imaginative, most amorous story with a male love interest we can't help but fall in love with. Make sure your story has body and not just bodies. Our readers love romance, but also require substance." **Pays $100-125.**
Tips: "Please request a sample and guidelines before submitting. Enclose a 9×12 SASE with 5 first-class stamps."

$ INTIMACY/BLACK ROMANCE, Sterling/McFadden Partnership, 233 Park Ave. S., 7th Floor, New York NY 10003. (212)780-3500. Fax: (212)979-7342. **Contact:** Marcia Mahan, editor. **100% freelance written.** Eager to work with new/unpublished writers. Bimonthly magazine of romance and love. Estab. 1982. Circ. 100,000. Pays on publication. Publishes ms an average of 2 months after acceptance. Byline given on articles only. Buys all rights. Submit seasonal material 6 months in advance. Reports in 2 months. Sample copy for 9×12 SAE with 5 first-class stamps. Writer's guidelines for #10 SASE.
Nonfiction: How-to (relating to romance and love) and feature articles on any aspect of relationships. **Buys 100 mss/year.** Query with published clips or send complete ms. Length: 3-5 pages. **Pays $100-125.**
Photos: Send photos with submission. Reviews contact sheets, negatives, transparencies.
Fiction: Confession and romance. "Stories that are too graphic in content and lack romance are unacceptable." **Buys 300 mss/year.** Accepts stories which are a bit more romantic than those written for *Jive*, *Black Confessions* or *Bronze Thrills*. Send complete ms (4,000-5,000 words). **Pays $100-125.**
Tips: "I still get excited when I read a manuscript by an unpublished writer whose use of language is magical and fresh. I'm always looking for that diamond in the fire. Send us your *best* shot. Writers who are careless, sloppy and ungrammatical are an immediate turn-off for me. Please do your homework first. Is it the type of story we buy? Is it written in ms format? Does it make one want to read it?"

$ INTIMACY/BRONZE THRILLS, Sterling/McFadden Partnership, 233 Park Ave. S., 5th Floor, New York NY 10003. (212)780-3500. Fax: (212)979-7342. **Contact:** Marcia Mahan, editor. Estab. 1982. See *Intimacy/Black Romance*.
Fiction: "Stories can be a bit more extraordinary and uninhibited than in the other magazines but still they have to be romantic. For example, we might buy a story about a woman who finds out her husband is a transsexual in *Bronze Thrills*, but not for *Jive* (our younger magazine). The stories for this magazine tend to have a harder, more adult edge of reality than the others."

$ JIVE, Sterling/McFadden Partnership, 233 Park Ave. S., 7th Floor, New York NY 10003. (212)780-3500. Fax: (212)979-7342. **Contact:** Marcia Mahan, editor. 100% freelance written. Eager to work with new/unpublished writers. Bimonthly magazine of romance and love. Estab. 1982. Circ. 100,000. Pays on publication. Publishes ms an average of 2 months after acceptance. Byline given on articles only. Buys all rights. Submit seasonal material 6 months in advance. Reports in 2 months on queries; 6 months on mss. Sample copy for 9×12 SASE with 5 first-class stamps. Free writer's guidelines.

Nonfiction: How-to (relating to romance and love) and feature articles on any aspect of relationships. "We like our articles to have a down-to-earth flavor. They should be written in the spirit of sisterhood, fun and creativity. Come up with an original idea our readers may not have thought of but will be dying to try out." **Buys 100 mss/year.** Query with published clips or send complete ms. Length: 3-5 typed pages. **Pays $100-125.**

Fiction: Confession and romance. "Stories that are too graphic and lack romance are unacceptable. However, all stories must contain one or two love scenes. Love scenes should allude to sex—romantic, not lewd." **Buys 300 mss/year.** Send complete ms (4,000-5,000 words). **Pays $100-125.**

Tips: "We are leaning toward more romantic writing styles as opposed to the more graphic stories of the past. Our audience is largely black teenagers. The stories should reinforce Black pride and should be geared toward teenage issues. Our philosophy is to show our experiences in as positive a light as possible without promoting any of the common stereotypes that are associated with Black men, lovemaking prowess, penile size, etc. Stereotypes of any kind are totally unacceptable. The fiction section which accepts romance stories and confession stories is most open to freelancers. Also, our special features section is very open. We would also like to see stories that are set outside the US (perhaps they could be set in the Caribbean, Europe, Africa, etc.) and themes that are reflective of things happening around us in the 90s—abortion, AIDS, alienation, surrogate mothers, etc. But we also like to see stories that transcend our contemporary problems and can give us a moment of pleasure, warmth, joy and relief. The characters should be anywhere from teenage to 30s but not the typical 'country bumpkin girl who was turned out by a big city pimp' type story. Please, writers who are not Black, research your story to be sure that it depicts Black people in a positive manner. Do not make a Black character a caricature of a non-Black character. Read contemporary Black fiction to ensure that your dialogue and speech idioms are natural to the Black vernacular."

$ MODERN ROMANCES, Sterling/Macfadden Partnership, 233 Park Ave. S., New York NY 10003. (212)979-4800. Fax: (212)979-7342. Editor: Colleen M. Dorsey. **100% freelance written.** Monthly magazine for family-oriented working women, ages 18-65 years old. Circ. 200,000. Pays the last week of the month of issue. Buys all rights. Submit seasonal material at least 6 months in advance. Reports in 11 months. Writer's guidelines for #10 SASE.

- This editor is especially in need of short, well-written stories (approximately 3,000-7,000 words).

Nonfiction: Confession stories with reader identification and a strong emotional tone; a strong emphasis on characterization and well-defined plots. Should be realistic and compelling. No third-person material. Timely holiday stories (e.g., Christmas themes) should be submitted at least 6 months in advance (by July). **Buys 10 mss/issue.** No query letters; submit complete ms. Length: 2,500-10,000 words. **Pays 5¢/word.** Buys all rights.

Poetry: Light, romantic poetry and seasonal subjects. Length: 24 lines maximum. **Pays $2/line.** Look at poetry published in previous issues before submitting.

$ TRUE CONFESSIONS, Macfadden Women's Group, 233 Park Ave. S., New York NY 10003. (212)979-4800. Fax: (212)979-7342. **Contact:** Pat Byrdsong, editor. **100% freelance written.** Eager to work with new/unpublished writers. Monthly magazine for high-school-educated, working class women, teens through maturity. Circ. 200,000. Buys all rights. Byline given on featured columns. Pays during the last week of month of issue. Publishes ms an average of 4 months after acceptance. Submit seasonal material 8 months in advance. Reports in 1 year.

Nonfiction: Timely, exciting, true emotional first-person stories on the problems that face today's women. The narrators should be sympathetic, and the situations they find themselves in should be intriguing, yet realistic. Many stories may have a strong romantic interest and a high moral tone; however, personal accounts or "confessions," no matter how controversial the topic, are encouraged and accepted. Careful study of a current issue is suggested. Length: 4,000-7,000 words and mini stories 1,000-1,500 words; also book lengths of 8,000-9,000 words. **Pays 5¢/word.** Submit complete ms. No simultaneous submissions. SASE required. Buys all rights.

- Asian-, Latina-, Native- and African-American stories are encouraged.

Columns/Departments: Family Zoo (pet feature), 50 words or less, **pays $50 for pet photo and story.** All other features are 200-300 words: My Moment With God (a short prayer); Incredible But True (an incredible/mystical/spiritual experience); My Man (a man who has been special in your life); Woman to Woman (a point of view about a contemporary subject matter or a woman overcoming odds). Send complete ms and SASE.

Poetry: Poetry should rhyme. Length: 4-20 lines. **Pays $10 minimum.**

Tips: "Our magazine is almost 100% freelance. We purchase all stories that appear in our magazine. Read 3-4 issues before sending submissions. Do not talk down to our readers. We prefer manuscripts on disk as well as hard copy."

$ TRUE ROMANCE, Sterling/Macfadden Partnership, 233 Park Ave. S., New York NY 10003. (212)979-4800. Fax: (212)979-7342. **Contact:** Pat Vitucci, editor. **100% freelance written.** Monthly magazine for women, teens through retired, offering compelling confession stories based on true happenings, with reader identification and strong emotional tone. No third-person material. Estab. 1923. Circ. 225,000. Pays 1 month after publication. Buys all rights. Submit seasonal material at least 6 months in advance. Reports within 8 months.

Nonfiction: Confessions, true love stories; mini-adventures: problems and solutions; dating and marital and child-rearing difficulties. Realistic yet unique stories dealing with current problems, everyday events; strong emotional appeal. **Buys 12 stories/issue.** Submit complete ms. Length: 3,000-8,000 words. **Pays 3¢/word;** slightly higher rates for short-shorts.

Columns/Departments: That's My Child (photo and 50 words); Loving Pets (photo and 50 words), **both pay $50;** Cupid's Corner (photo and 500 words about you and spouse), **pays $100;** That Precious Moment (1,000 words about a unique experience), **pays $50.**
Poetry: Light romantic poetry. Length: 24 lines maximum. **Pays $10-30.**
Tips: "A timely, well-written story that is told by a sympathetic narrator who sees the central problem through to a satisfying resolution is *all* important to break into *True Romance*. We are always looking for interesting, emotional, identifiable stories."

$ TRUE STORY, Sterling/Macfadden Partnership, 233 Park Ave. S., New York NY 10003. (212)979-4800. Fax: (212)979-7342. **Contact**: Tina Pappalardo, editor. **80% freelance written.** Monthly magazine for young married, blue-collar women, 20-35; high school education; increasingly broad interests; home-oriented, but looking beyond the home for personal fulfillment. Circ. 1,000,000. Buys all rights. Byline given "on articles only." Pays 1 month after publication. Submit seasonal material 1 year in advance. Reports in 1 year.
Nonfiction: "First-person stories covering all aspects of women's interests: love, marriage, family life, careers, social problems, etc. The best direction a new writer can be given is to carefully study several issues of the magazine; then submit a fresh, exciting, well-written true story. We have no taboos. It's the handling and believability that make the difference between a rejection and an acceptance." **Buys about 125 full-length mss/year.** Submit only complete mss for stories. Length: 1,500-10,000 words. **Pays 5¢/word; $150 minimum.** Pays a flat rate for columns or departments, as announced in the magazine. Query for fact articles.

RURAL

These publications draw readers interested in rural lifestyles. Surprisingly, many readers are from urban centers who dream of or plan to build a house in the country. Magazines featuring design, construction, log homes and "country" style interior decorating appear in Home and Garden.

$ $ THE COUNTRY CONNECTION, The Magazine for Country Folk, Pinecone Publishing, P.O. Box 100, Boulter, Ontario K0L 1G0 Canada. Fax: (613)332-5183. E-mail: pinecone@northcom.net. Website: http://www.cyberus.ca/~queenswood/pinecone/. **Contact**: Gus Zylstra, editor. **75% freelance written.** Semiannual magazine covering country life and tourism. "*The Country Connection* is a magazine for true nature lovers and the rural adventurer. Building on our commitment to heritage, cultural, artistic, and outdoor themes, we continually add new topics to illuminate the country experience of people living within nature. Our goal is to chronicle rural life in its many aspects, giving 'voice' to the countryside." Estab. 1989. Circ. 15,000. Pays on publication. Publishes ms an average of 6 months after acceptance. Byline given. Buys first rights. Editorial lead time 4 months. Submit seasonal material 4 months in advance. Sample copy $4.55. For writer's guidelines send #10 SAE (in Canada) or IRC (in US).
Nonfiction: General interest, historical/nostalgic, humor, personal experience, photo feature, lifestyle, leisure, art and culture, travel, vegetarian recipes only. No hunting, fishing, animal husbandry or pet articles. **Buys 20 mss/year.** Send complete ms. Length: 500-2,000 words. **Pays 7-10¢/word.** Sometimes pays expenses of writers on assignment.
Photos: Send photos with submission. Reviews transparencies and prints. Offers $10-50/photo. Captions required. Buys one-time rights.
Columns/Departments: Pays 7-10¢/word.
Fiction: Adventure, fantasy, historical, humorous, slice-of-life vignettes, country living. **Buys 4 mss/year.** Send complete ms. Length: 500-1,500 words. **Pays 7-10¢/word.**
Tips: "Send (original content) manuscript with appropriate support material such as photos, illustrations, maps, etc. Do not send American stamps. They have no value in Canada!"

N $ COUNTRY FOLK, Salaki Publishing & Design, HC77, Box 608, Pittsburg MO 65724. Phone/fax: (417)993-5944. **Contact**: Susan Salaki, editor. **100% freelance written.** Quarterly magazine. "*Country Folk* publishes true stories of the Ozarks." Estab. 1994. Circ. 2,500. Pays on publication. Publishes ms an average of 3 months after acceptance. Byline given. Buys first rights. Editorial lead time 2 months. Submit seasonal material 3 months in advance. Reports in 1 month on queries; 2 months on mss. Sample copy for $4. Writer's guidelines for #10 SASE.
Nonfiction: Historical/nostalgic, how-to, humor, inspirational, personal experience, photo feature, true ghost stories of the Ozarks. **Buys 10 mss/year.** Send complete ms and SASE. Length: 750-1,000 words. **Pays $5-20.** Pays writers with contributor copies or other premiums if we must do considerable editing to the work.
Photos: Send photos with submission. Buys one-time rights.
Fiction: Historical, humorous, mystery, novel excerpts. **Buys 10 mss/year.** Send complete ms. Length: 750-800 words. **Pays $5-50.**
Poetry: Haiku, light verse, traditional. **Buys 25 poems/year.** Submit maximum 3 poems. **Pays $1-5.**
Fillers: Anecdotes, facts, gags to be illustrated by cartoonist, newsbreaks, short humor. **Buys 25/year. Pays $1-5.**
Tips: "We want material from people who are born and raised in the country, especially the Ozark region. We accept submissions in any form, handwritten or typed. Many of the writers and poets whose work we publish are first time

submissions. Most of the work we publish is written by older men and women who have heard stories from their parents and grandparents about how the Ozark region was settled in the 1800s."

N $ COUNTRY ROAD CHRONICLES, Meadow Ridge Graphics, RR2, Box 132, Dingmans Ferry PA 18328. Fax: (717)828-7959. E-mail: cherokee@pikeonline.net. **Contact**: Elaine B. Van Raper, editor/publisher. **50% freelance written.** "Bimonthly tabloid dedicated to nature (environment), animals, people, with a country-oriented view of the environment, wildlife, pets, horses, hunting, fishing, Native American culture." Estab. 1993. Circ. 6,400. Pays on publication. Publishes ms an average of 4 months after acceptance. Byline given. Buys first North American serial rights and makes work-for-hire assignments. Editorial lead time 2 months. Submit seasonal material 3 months in advance. Accepts simultaneous submissions. Sample copy for $3. Writer's guidelines for #10 SASE.
Nonfiction: General interest, historical/nostalgic, humor, inspirational (Native American), interview/profile, personal experience, photo feature, travel. All must be country-oriented relative to environment, animals, people, Native American culture. **Buys 145 mss/year.** Send complete ms. Length: 1,000-1,500 words. **Pays $20-30.** "Will swap articles for free advertising space—submit with manuscript and state that in cover letter."
Reprints: Send typed ms with rights for sale noted and information about when and where the article previously appeared.
Photos: Send photos with submission. Reviews 3×5 or 4×6 prints. Offers $5/photo. Captions and identification of subjects required. Buys one-time or all rights.

$ $ FARM & RANCH LIVING, Reiman Publications, 5925 Country Lane, Greendale WI 53129. (414)423-0100. Fax: (414)423-8463. E-mail: 76150.162@compuserve.com. **Contact**: Nick Pabst, editor. **30% freelance written.** Eager to work with new/unpublished writers. Bimonthly lifestyle magazine aimed at families that farm or ranch full time. "*F&RL* is *not* a 'how-to' magazine—it focuses on people rather than products and profits." Estab. 1968. Circ. 380,000. Pays on publication. Publishes ms an average of 6 months after acceptance. Byline given. Buys first serial rights and one-time rights. Submit seasonal material 6 months in advance. Reports in 6 weeks. Sample copy for $2 and 9×12 SAE with $1.93 postage. Writer's guidelines for #10 SASE.
Nonfiction: Interview/profile, photo feature, nostalgia, humor, inspirational, personal experience, "Prettiest Place in the Country" (photo/text tour of ranch or farm). No how-to articles or stories about "hobby farmers" (doctors or lawyers with weekend farms); no issue-oriented stories (pollution, animal rights, etc.). **Buys 30 mss/year.** Query or send ms. Length: 600-1,200 words. **Pays $200 for text/photos package.** Payment for "Prettiest Place" negotiable.
Reprints: Send photocopy of article with rights for sale noted. Payment negotiable.
Photos: Scenic. State availability of photos with query. Pays $75-200 for 35mm color slides. Buys one-time rights.
Fillers: Jokes, anecdotes, short humor with farm or ranch slant. **Buys 50/year.** Length: 50-150 words. **Pays $20.**
Tips: "Our readers enjoy stories and features that are upbeat and positive. A freelancer must see *F&RL* to fully appreciate how different it is from other farm publications—ordering a sample is strongly advised (not available on newsstands). Photo features (about interesting farm or ranch families) and personality profiles are most open to freelancers. We can make separate arrangements for photography if writer is unable to provide photos."

$ $ FARM FAMILY AMERICA, Fieldhagen Publishing, Inc., 190 Fifth St. E., Suite 121, St. Paul MN 55101. (612)292-1747. **Contact:** George Ashfield, editor. **75% freelance written.** Five issues per year. Published by American Cyanamid and written to the non-farm related lifestyle, activities and travel interests of American farm families. Circ. 300,000. **Pays on acceptance.** Publishes ms an average of 2 months after acceptance. Byline given. Offers 25% kill fee. Buys first rights or second serial (reprint) rights. Submit seasonal material 6 months in advance. Accepts simultaneous submissions. Reports in 6 weeks. Writer's guidelines for #10 SASE.
Nonfiction: General interest and travel. "Articles are generally not farm-related and are geared to activities and travel destinations that can be enjoyed independent of farming and farm management practices." **Buys 30 mss/year.** Query with published clips. Length: 1,000-1,800 words. **Pays $400-650.**
Photos: State availability of photos with submission. Reviews 35mm transparencies and prints. Offers $160-700/photo. Model releases and identification of subjects required. Buys one-time rights.

$ FARM TIMES, 504 Sixth St., Rupert ID 83350. (208)436-1111. Fax: (208)436-9455. E-mail: farmtimes@safelink.net. Website: http://www.farmtimes.com. **Contact**: Robin Maxfield, managing editor. **50% freelance written.** Monthly regional tabloid for agriculture-farming/ranching. "*Farm Times* is dedicated to rural living in the Intermountain and Pacific Northwest. Stories related to farming and ranching in the states of Idaho, Montana, Nevada, Oregon, Utah, Washington and Wyoming are our mainstay, but farmers and ranchers do more than just work. Human interest articles that appeal to rural readers are used on occasion." Estab. 1987. Pays on publication. Byline given. Editorial lead time 1 month. Submit seasonal material 3 months in advance. Reports in 2 months on queries. Writer's guidelines free with SASE. Send $2.50 for sample copy.
Nonfiction: Farm or ranch issues, exposé, general interest, how-to, interview/profile, new product (few), opinion, late breaking ag news. Always runs one feature article of interest to women. No humor, essay, first person, personal experience or book excerpts. Special issues: Irrigation, Chemical/Fertilizer, Potato Production. **Buys 200 mss/year.** Query with published clips. Send complete ms. Length: 500-800 words. **Pays $1.50/column inch.**
Reprints: Send typed ms with rights for sale noted and information about when and where the article previously appeared. Pays 100% of amount paid for an original article.
Photos: Send photocopy of article and photos with submission. Reviews contact sheets with negatives, 35mm or larger

transparencies and 3×5 or larger prints. Offers $7/b&w inside, $35/color front page cover. Captions, model releases, identification of subjects required. Buys one-time rights.

Column/Departments: Horse (horse care/technical), 500-600 words; Rural Religion (interesting churches/missions/ religious activities) 600-800 words; Dairy (articles of interest to dairy farmers) 600-800 words. **Buys 12 mss/year.** Query. Send complete ms. **Pays $1.50/column inch.**

Tips: "Query with a well-thought-out idea that will appeal to rural readers. Of special interest is how environmental issues, public opinions and world affairs will affect farmers/ranchers, Endangered Species Act, EPA, etc. We are always looking for well-written articles on subjects that affect western farmers and ranchers."

$ $ MOTHER EARTH NEWS, Sussex Publishers, 49 E. 21st St., 11th Floor, New York NY 10010. (212)260-7210. Fax: (212)260-7445. E-mail: mearthnews@aol.com. Editor: Matthew Scanlon. Managing Editor: Lisa Degliantoni. **Contact**: Molly Miller, senior editor. Mostly freelance written. Bimonthly magazine emphasizing "country living and country skills, for both long-time and would-be ruralites. *Mother Earth News* is dedicated to presenting information which will help readers become more self-sufficient, financially independent, and environmentally aware." Circ. 450,000. Pays on publication. Byline given. Submit seasonal material 5 months in advance. No handwritten mss. Reports within 3 months. Publishes ms an average of 6 months after acceptance. Sample copy for $5. Writer's guidelines for #10 SASE with 2 first-class stamps.

Nonfiction: How-to, home business, alternative energy systems, home building, home retrofit and home maintenance, energy-efficient structures, seasonal cooking, gardening, crafts. **Buys 100-150 mss/year.** Query. "A short, to-the-point paragraph is often enough. If it's a subject we don't need at all, we can answer immediately. If it tickles our imagination, we'll ask to take a look at the whole piece. No phone queries, please." Length: 300-3,000 words. Payment negotiated. Publishes nonfiction book excerpts.

Photos: Purchased with accompanying ms. Send prints or transparencies. Uses 8×10 b&w glossies or any size color transparencies. Include type of film, speed and lighting used. Total purchase price for ms includes payment for photos. Captions and credits required.

Columns/Departments: Country Lore (down-home solutions to everyday problems); Bits & Pieces (snippets of news, events and silly happenings); Herbs & Remedies (home healing, natural medicine); Energy Tips (ways to conserve energy while saving money).

Tips: "Probably the best way to break in is to study our magazine, digest our writer's guidelines, and send us a concise article illustrated with color transparencies that we can't resist. When folks query and we give a go-ahead on speculation, we often offer some suggestions. Failure to follow those suggestions can lose the sale for the author. We want articles that tell what real people are doing to take charge of their own lives. Articles should be well-documented and tightly written treatments of topics we haven't already covered. The critical thing is length, and our payment is by space, not word count. *No phone queries.*"

$ RURAL HERITAGE, 281 Dean Ridge Lane, Gainesboro TN 38562-5039. (931)268-0655. E-mail: editor@ruralheritage.com. Website: http://www.ruralheritage.com. Publisher: Allan Damerow. **Contact**: Gail Damerow, editor. **98% freelance written.** Willing to work with a small number of new/unpublished writers. Bimonthly magazine devoted to preserving a way of life such as the training and care of draft animals, and other traditional country skills. Estab. 1976. Circ. 3,000. Pays on publication. Publishes ms an average of 6 months after acceptance. Byline given. Buys first English language rights. Submit seasonal material 6 months in advance. Reports in 3 months. Sample copy for $6. Writer's guidelines #10 SASE or on website.

Nonfiction: How-to (crafting and farming); interview/profile (people using draft animals); photo feature. No articles on *mechanized* farming. **Buys 100 mss/year.** Query or send complete ms. Length: 1,200-1,500 words. **Pays 5¢/word.**

Reprints: Accepts previously published submissions, but only if previous publication had limited or regional circulation. Send tearsheet or photocopy of article, typed ms with rights for sale noted and information about when and where the article previously appeared. Pays 100% of amount paid for an original article.

Photos: Send photos with ms. Pays $10. Captions and identification of subjects required. Buys one-time rights. Six covers/year (color transparency or 5×7 horizontal print), animals in harness $75. Photo guidelines for #10 SASE.

Columns/Departments: Self-sufficiency (modern people preserving traditional American lifestyle), 750-1,500 words; Drafter's Features (draft animals used for farming, shows and pulls—their care), 750-1,500 words; Crafting (horse-drawn implement designs and patterns), 750-1,500 words; Humor, 750-900 words. **Pays 5¢/word.**

Poetry: Traditional. **Pays $5-25.**

Tips: "Always welcome are: 1) Detailed descriptions and photos of horse-drawn implements 2) Prices and other details of draft animal and implement auctions and sales."

$ $ RURALITE, P.O. Box 558, Forest Grove OR 97116-0558. (503)357-2105. Fax: (503)357-8615. E-mail: ruralite@europa.com. Website: www.europa.com/~ruralite/. **Contact**: Curtis Condon, editor-in-chief. **80% freelance written.** Works with new, unpublished writers "who have mastered the basics of good writing." Monthly magazine aimed at members of consumer-owned electric utilities throughout 9 western states, including Alaska. Publishes 48 regional editions. Estab. 1954. Circ. 273,000. Buys first rights, sometimes reprint rights. Byline given. **Pays on acceptance**. Query first; unsolicited manuscripts submitted without request rarely read by editors. Reports in 1 month. Sample copy and writer's guidelines for 10×13 SAE with 4 first-class stamps.

Nonfiction: Looking for well-written nonfiction, dealing primarily with human interest topics. Must have strong Northwest perspective and be sensitive to Northwest issues and attitudes. Wide range of topics possible, from energy-related subjects to little-known travel destinations to unusual businesses located in areas served by consumer-owned electric utilities. "About half of our readers are rural and small town residents; others are urban and suburban. Topics with an obvious 'big-city' focus not accepted. Family-related issues, Northwest history (no encyclopedia rewrites), people and events, unusual tidbits that tell the Northwest experience are best chances for a sale. Special issues: Home Improvement (September 1998 and 1999); Gardening (February 1999). **Buys 50-60 mss/yr.** Length 300-2,000 words. **Pays $75-400.**

Reprints: Send typed ms with rights for sale noted and information about when and where the article previously appeared. For reprints, pays 50% of "*our* regular freelance rates."

Photos: "Illustrated stories are the key to a sale. Stories without art rarely make it, with the exception of humor pieces. Black and white prints, color slides, all formats, accepted with 'razor-sharp' focus."

Tips: "Study recent issues. Follow directions when given an assignment. Be able to deliver a complete package (story and photos). We're looking for regular contributors to whom we can assign topics from our story list after they've proven their ability to deliver quality mss."

SCIENCE

These publications are published for laymen interested in technical and scientific developments and discoveries, applied science and technical or scientific hobbies. Publications of interest to the personal computer owner/user are listed in the Personal Computers section. Journals for scientists and engineers are listed in Trade in various sections.

$ $ AD ASTRA, The Magazine of the National Space Society, 600 Pennsylvania Ave. SE, Suite 201, Washington DC 20003-4316. (202)543-1900. Fax: (202)546-4189. E-mail: adastraed@aol.com. Website: http://www.nss.org/adastra. Editor-in-Chief: Pat Dasch. **Contact**: Johanna McKinzey, managing editor. **80% freelance written.** Bimonthly magazine covering the space program. "We publish non-technical, lively articles about all aspects of international space programs, from shuttle missions to planetary probes to plans for the future." Estab. 1989. Circ. 25,000. Pays on publication. Byline given. Buys first North American serial rights. Reports on queries when interested. Sample copy for 9×12 SASE. Writer's guidelines for #10 SASE.

Nonfiction: Book excerpts, essays, expose, general interest, interview/profile, opinion, photo feature, technical. No science fiction or UFO stories. Query with published clips. Length: 1,500-3,000 words. **Pays $150-250 for features.**

Photos: State availability of photos with submission. Reviews 35mm slides, 3×5 color transparencies and b&w prints. Negotiates payment. Identification of subjects required. Buys one-time rights.

Columns/Departments: Touchdown (opinion pieces). Reviews, editorials, education. Length: 750 words. Query. **Pays $75.**

Tips: "Require manuscripts to be accompanied by ASCII or Word or Word Perfect 6.0 floppy disk."

$ $ ARCHAEOLOGY, Archaeological Institute of America, 135 William St., New York NY 10038. (212)732-5154. Fax: (212)732-5707. E-mail: editl@archaeology.org. Website: www.archaeology.org. **Contact**: Peter A. Young, editor-in-chief. **5% freelance written.** "*Archaeology* combines worldwide archaeological findings with photography, specially rendered maps, drawings, and charts. Articles cover current excavations, recent discoveries, and special studies of ancient cultures. Regular features: Timelines, Newsbriefs, film and book reviews, current museum exhibits, The Forum. Two annual Travel Guides give trip planning information. We generally commission articles from professional archaeologists. The only magazine of its kind to bring worldwide archaeology to the attention of the general public." Estab. 1948. Circ. 200,000. Pays on publication. Byline given. Offers 25% kill fee. Buys first North American serial rights. Submit seasonal material 6 months in advance. Accepts simultaneous submissions. Query preferred. Free sample copy and writer's guidelines.

Nonfiction: Essays, general interest. **Buys 6 mss/year.** Length: 1,000-3,000 words. **Pays $750 maximum.** Sometimes pays expenses of writers on assignment.

Photos: Send photos with submission. Reviews 35mm color slides or 4×5 color transparencies. Identification of subjects and credits required.

Tips: "We reach nonspecialist readers interested in art, science, history, and culture. Our reports, regional commentaries, and feature-length articles introduce readers to recent developments in archaeology worldwide."

$ $ ASTRONOMY, Kalmbach Publishing, P.O. Box 1612, Waukesha WI 53187-1612. (414)796-8776. Fax: (414)798-6468. E-mail: astro@astronomy.com. Managing Editor: David Eicher. **Contact**: Bonnie Gordon, editor. **75% freelance written.** Monthly magazine covering astronomy—the science and hobby of. "Half of our magazine is for hobbyists (who may have little interest in the heavens in a scientific way); the other half is directed toward armchair astronomers who may be intrigued by the science." Estab. 1973. Circ. 170,000. **Pays on acceptance.** "We are governed by what is happening in the space program and the heavens. It can be up to a year before we publish a manuscript." Byline given. Buys first North American serial, one-time and all rights. Query for electronic submissions. Reports in 1 month on queries; 2 months on mss. Writer's guidelines for SASE.

Nonfiction: Book excerpts, space and astronomy, how-to for astro hobbyists, humor (in the viewpoints column and about astro), new product, photo feature, technical. **Buys 100-200 mss/year.** Query. Length: 500-4,500 words. **Pays $50-500.**

Photos: Send photos with submission. Reviews transparencies and prints. Pays $25/photo. Captions, model releases and identification of subjects required.

Tips: "Submitting to *Astronomy* could be tough. (Take a look at how technical astronomy is.) But if someone is a physics teacher (or math or astronomy), he or she might want to study the magazine for a year to see the sorts of subjects and approaches we use and then submit a proposal."

⊘ **DISCOVER** does not accept freelance submissions.

$ $ THE ELECTRON, CIE Publishing, 1776 E. 17th St., Cleveland OH 44114-3679. (216)781-9400. Fax: (216)781-0331. Website: http://www.cie.wc.edu. Managing Editor: Michael Manning. **Contact**: Ted Sheroke, advertising manager. **80% freelance written.** Bimonthly tabloid on development and trends electronics and high technology. Estab. 1934. Circ. 25,000. Pays on publication. Publishes ms an average of 2 months after acceptance. Byline given. Buys all rights. Reports as soon as possible. Sample copy and writer's guidelines for 8½×11 SASE.

Nonfiction: Technical (tutorial and how-to), technology news and feature, photo feature, career/educational. All submissions must be electronics/technology-related. Special issue: Electronics into the Year 2001 (October, November, December). Query with letter/proposal and published clips. Length: 800 words. **Pays $50-500.**

Reprints: Send photocopy of article or short story or typed ms with rights for sale noted and information about when and where the article previously appeared. Does not pay for reprints.

Photos: State availability of photos. Reviews 8×10 and 5×7 b&w prints. Captions and identification of subjects required.

Tips: "We would like to receive educational electronics/technical articles. They must be written in a manner understandable to the beginning-intermediate electronics student. We are also seeking news/feature-type articles covering timely developments in high technology."

$ $ FINAL FRONTIER, 1017 S. Mountain Ave., Monrovia CA 91016. Fax: (818)932-1036. **Contact:** Dave Cravotta, editor. Bimonthly magazine covering space exploration. "*Final Frontier* is about space technology, commerce and exploration. The missions and machines. People and politics. The pure adventures of space travel and astronomical discovery. Plus behind-the-scenes coverage of the international arena of space, commerce and exploration." Estab. 1988. Circ. 175,200. **Pays on acceptance**. Byline given. Buys first North American serial rights. Offers 30% kill fee. Reports in 2 months on queries. Sample copy free for SASE.

- Ranked as one of the best markets for freelance writers in *Writer's Yearbook*'s annual "Top 100 Markets," January 1998.

Nonfiction: Interview/profile, human interest, international space program, profiles of scientists, new spacecraft design and commercial space ventures. **Buys 20 mss/year.** Query with published clips and SASE. Length:1,240-2,400 words. **Pays 40¢/word.** Sometimes pays expenses of writers on assignment.

Reprints: Accepts previously published submissions from non-competing markets. Pays 30¢/word.

Columns/Departments: Buys 90 mss/year. "Notes from Earth" (news stories, mission updates, inventions, discoveries), 150-400 words; "Down to Earth" (stories about space missions, technologies and experiments with applications that directly benefit people on Earth, 450-600 words. **Pays 40 cents/word.** Query with published clips and SASE.

Reprints: Accepts previously published submissions from non-competing markets. Pays 30 cents/word.

Tips: Needs "strong reporting on all aspects of space. 'Notes from Earth' is the best place for new writers to break in. When querying, mention the availability of photographs or artist's conceptions. Our readers are technically savvy, but you must clearly explain the science and technology in your story, without oversimplifying. Avoid NASA jargon and acronyms. Write in a lively, engaging style—we want stories, not dry, technical reports. We do not run stories about UFOs or *Star Trek.* We no longer purchase science fiction."

POPULAR SCIENCE, 2 Park Ave., New York NY 10016. (212)779-5000. Fax: (212)481-8062. Website: http://www.popsci.com. Editor-in-Chief: Fred Abatemarco. **Contact:** Cecelia Wessner, editor. **50% freelance written.** Prefers to work with published/established writers. Monthly magazine for the well-educated adult, interested in science, technology, new products. "*Popular Science* is devoted to exploring (and explaining) to a nontechnical but knowledgeable readership the technical world around us. We cover all of the sciences, engineering and technology, and above all, products. We are largely a 'thing'-oriented publication: things that fly or travel down a turnpike, or go on or under the sea, or cut wood, or reproduce music, or build buildings, or make pictures. We are especially focused on the new, the ingenious and the useful. Contributors should be as alert to the possibility of selling us pictures and short features as they are to major articles. Freelancers should study the magazine to see what we want and avoid irrelevant submissions." Estab. 1872. Circ. 1.55 million. **Pays on acceptance.** Publishes ms an average of 4 months after acceptance. Byline given. Buys first North American serial rights only. Pays negotiable kill fee. Reports in 4 weeks. Query. Writer's guidelines for #10 SASE.

Nonfiction: Buys several hundred mss/year. Query. Uses only color photos. Pays expenses of writers on assignment.

Tips: "Probably the easiest way to break in here is by covering a news story in science and technology that we haven't heard about yet. We need people to be acting as scouts for us out there and we are willing to give the most leeway on these performances. We are interested in good, sharply focused ideas in all areas we cover. We prefer a vivid, journalistic style of writing, with the writer taking the reader along with him, showing the reader what he saw, through words."

$ $ SCIENCE SPECTRA, The Intl. Magazine of Contemporary Scientific Thought, G&B Magazines Unlimited, P.O. Box 26430, Collegeville PA 19426. Editor: Gerhart Friedlander. **Contact**: Heather Wagner, managing editor. **25% freelance written.** Quarterly magazine covering science. "Our magazine's audience is composed primarily of scientists and the 'scientifically literate.' Writers must have experience writing for a scientific audience." Estab. 1995. Circ. 10,000. Pays on publication. Byline given. Buys all rights. Editorial lead time 3 months. Reports in 1 month on queries. Writer's guidelines for SAE and 1 first-class stamp.
Nonfiction: Interview/profile, science and technology. **Buys 10-15 mss/year.** Length: approximately 2,000 words. **Pays 25¢/word for assigned articles.**
Photos: Offers no additional payment for photos accepted with ms. Captions required. Buys all time rights.
Columns/Departments: From the Front Lines (cutting edge research/technology) 2,000 words; Portrait (profile of leading scientific figure) 2,000 words; Controversy Corner (presents both sides of current scientific debate) 2,000 words. **Buys 5-10 mss/year.** Query with published clips. **Pays 25¢/word.**
Tips: "Writers should include clips that demonstrate their knowledge of and/or experience in the scientific area about which they are writing. Do not send complete manuscripts; query letter with clips only."

N $ $ $ SKY & TELESCOPE, The Essential Magazine of Astronomy, Sky Publishing Corp., P.O. Box 9111, Belmont MA 02178. (617)864-7360. Fax: (617)576-0336. E-mail: skytel@skypub.com. Website: http://www.skypub.com. **Contact:** Timothy Lyster, managing editor. Editor: Leif J. Robinson. **15% freelance written**. Monthly magazine covering astronomy. "*Sky & Telescope* is the magazine of record for astronomy. We cover amateur activities, research news, equipment, book and software reviews. Our audience is the amateur astronomer who wants to learn more about the night sky." Estab. 1941. Circ. 120,000. Pays on publication. Publishes ms an average of 6 months after acceptance. Byline given. Buys first rights. Editorial lead time 4 months. Submit seasonal material 6-12 months in advance. Reports in 3 weeks on queries; 1 month on mss. Sample copy for $3.99. Guidelines free by e-mail request or for #10 SASE.
Nonfiction: Essays, historical/nostalgic, how-to, opinion, personal experience, photo feature, technical. No poetry, crosswords, new age or alternative cosmologies. **Buys 10 mss/year**. Query. Length: 1,500-4,000 words. **Pays $1,000**. Sometimes pays expenses for writers on assignment.
Photos: Send photos with submission. Reviews contact sheets. Negotiates payment individually. Identification of subjects required. Buys one-time rights.
Columns/Departments: Focal Point (opinion), 1,000 words; Books & Beyond (reviews), 800 words; Amateur Astronomers (profiles), 1,500 words. **Buys 20 mss/year**. Query. **Pays 15¢/word**.
Tips: "Good artwork is key. Keep the text lively and provide captions."

☆ $ $ WEATHERWISE, The Magazine About the Weather, Heldref Publications, 1319 18th St. NW, Washington DC 20036. (202)296-6267. Fax: (202)296-5149. E-mail: ww@heldref.org. Website: http://www.heldref.org/ww/ww.html. Associate Editor: Kimbra Cutlip. **Contact**: Doyle Rice, managing editor. **75% freelance written.** Bimonthly magazine covering weather and meteorology. "*Weatherwise* is America's only magazine about the weather. Our readers range from professional weathercasters and scientists to basement-bound hobbyists, but all share a common craving for information about weather as it relates to technology, history, culture, society, art, etc." Estab. 1948. Circ. 21,000. Pays on publication. Publishes ms an average of 6 months after acceptance. Byline given. Offers 25% kill fee. Buys all rights or first North American serial or second (reprint) serial rights. Editorial lead time 6 months. Submit seasonal material 6 months in advance. Reports in 2 months on queries. Sample copy for $4 and a 9×12 SAE with 10 first-class stamps. Writer's guidelines for #10 SASE.
Nonfiction: Book excerpts, essays, general interest, historical/nostalgic, how-to, humor, interview/profile, new product, opinion, personal experience, photo feature, technical, travel. Special issue: Photo Contest (September/October deadline June 1). Special issue: 1998 Weather in Review (March/April 99). "No blow-by-blow accounts of the biggest storm to ever hit your backyard." **Buys 15-18 mss/year.** Query with published clips. Length: 1,500-2,500 words. **Pays $200-500 for assigned articles; $0-300 for unsolicited articles.** Sometimes pays expenses of writers on assignment.
Reprints: Send photocopy of article and information about when and where the article previously appeared. Pays 25% of amount paid for an original article. Publishes book excerpts.
Photos: State availability of or send photos with submission. Reviews contact sheets, negatives, transparencies, prints. Negotiates payment individually. Captions, identification of subjects required. Buys one-time rights.
Columns/Departments: Front & Center (news, trends, opinion), 300-400 words; Weather Talk (folklore and humor), 1,000 words; The Lee Word (humorous first-person accounts of adventures with weather), 1,000 words. **Buys 12-15 mss/year.** Query with published clips. **Pays $0-200.**
Tips: "Don't query us wanting to write about broad types like the Greenhouse Effect, the Ozone Hole, El Niño, etc. If it's capitalized, you can bet you won't be able to cover it all in 2,000 words. With these topics and all others, find the story within the story. And whether you're writing about a historical storm or new technology, be sure to focus on the human element—the struggles, triumphs, and other anecdotes of individuals."

SCIENCE FICTION, FANTASY AND HORROR

These publications often publish experimental fiction and many are open to new writers. More information on these markets can be found in the Contests & Awards section under the Fiction heading.

$ ABERRATIONS, Sirius Fiction, P.O. Box 460430, San Francisco CA 94146-0430. (415)648-3908. **Contact**: Richard Blair, editor. Monthly magazine of science fiction, fantasy, and horror. "We're looking for speculative stories that run the gamut from the pulp-era SF/F/H of the 30s and 40s to the experimental and literary work of today." Estab. 1991. Circ. 1,500. Pays on publication. Publishes ms an average of 1 year after acceptance. Byline given. Buys first English language serial and one-time rights. Submit seasonal material 8 months in advance. Reports in 4 months. Sample copy for $4.50 postpaid. Writer's guidelines for #10 SASE.

Nonfiction: Anything with a SF/F/H tie-in. "However, please keep in mind that we're not interested in the paranormal, UFOs, nor are we looking for 'how to write science fiction' pieces." Send complete ms. Length: 3,000 words (query for longer). **Pays ½¢/word.**

Fiction: Science fiction, fantasy, and horror. "We use a variety of 'types' of stories within the speculative genres. Whether it's humorous horror or cerebral sci-fi, we want character-driven, plot-intensive storylines. From sword-&-sorcery to space opera to psychological horror, however and whatever your muse is trying to beat out of you send it our way." **Buys 120 mss/year.** Send complete ms. Length: 8,000 words max. **Pays ½¢/word.**

Tips: "While there are still no restrictions on language and subject matter, we're seeking to expand the scope of stories within the magazine, and are therefore no longer looking exclusively for shock or splatter SF/F/H fiction. Stories that do possess graphically violent/sexual scenes should have these aspects be crucial to the plot. Under *no* circumstances are we interested in stories dealing with the violent/sexual abuse of children. All that said, we're very open to stories that take chances (whether this be through characterization, plotting, or structuring) as well as those that take more traditional approaches to science fiction, fantasy and horror. Both fiction and nonfiction are wide open."

$ ABSOLUTE MAGNITUDE, Science Fiction Adventures, DNA Publications, P.O. Box 13, Greenfield MA 01302. E-mail: absmag@shaysnet.com. **Contact:** Warren Lapine, editor-in-chief. 95% freelance written. Quarterly science fiction magazine covering science fiction short stories. "We specialize in action/adventure science fiction with an emphasis on hard science. Interested in tightly-plotted, character-driven stories." Estab. 1993. Circ. 6,000. Pays on publication. Publishes ms an average of 6 months after acceptance. Byline given. Buys first English language serial rights, first rights and second serial (reprint) rights. Editorial lead time 6 months. Accepts simultaneous submissions. Reports in 2 weeks on queries; 1 month on mss. Sample copy for $5. Writer's guidelines for #10 SASE.

- This editor is still looking for tightly plotted stories that are character driven. He is now purchasing more short stories than before.

Reprints: Send typed ms with rights for sale noted and information about when and where the article previously appeared. Pays 33% of amount paid for an original article.

Fiction: Science fiction. **Buys 40 mss/year.** Send complete ms. Length: 1,000-25,000 words. **Pays 1-5¢/word.**

- Ranked as one of the best markets for fiction writers in *Writer's Digest* magazine's "Fiction 50," June 1998.

Poetry: Any form. **Buys 4 poems/issue.** Submit maximum 5 poems. Length: up to 25,000 words. **Pays 10¢/line.** Best chance with light verse.

Tips: "We are very interested in working with new writers but we are not interested in 'drawer-cleaning' exercises. There is no point in sending less than your best effort if you are interested in a career in writing. We do not use fantasy, horror, satire, or funny science fiction. We're looking for character-driven action/adventure based Technical Science Fiction. We want tightly plotted stories with memorable characters. Characters should be the driving force behind the action of the story; they should not be thrown in as an afterthought. We need to see both plot development and character growth. Stories which are resolved without action on the protagonist's part do not work for us; characters should not be spectators in situations completely beyond their control or immune to their influence. Some of our favorite writers are Roger Zelazny, Frank Herbert, Robert Silverberg, and Fred Saberhagen."

$ ADVENTURES OF SWORD & SORCERY, Box 285, Xenia OH 45385. **Contact**: Randy Dannenfelser, editor. **Pays on acceptance.** Byline given. Buys first North American serial rights. Reports in 2 months on mss. Sample copy for $6. Writer's guidelines for #10 SASE.

Fiction: Fantasy. **Buys 40 mss/year.** Send complete ms with cover letter. Length: 1,000-20,000 words. **Pays 3-6¢/word.**

- Ranked as one of the best markets for fiction writers in *Writer's Digest* magazine's "Fiction 50," June 1998.

Tips: "We want sword-and-sorcery, high fantasy and heroic fantasy that entertains and involves the reader with an emphasis on action and adventure, but still cognizant of the struggles within as they play against the struggles without. As examples, think of the fiction of J.R.R. Tolkien, Fritz Leiber, and Katherine Kurtz, but with 90s sensibilities for a 90s audience. Include sexual content only as required by the story. Some problems I see often are story beginnings just aren't enough to pull readers into the story. Also, endings are either obvious or inappropriate. A great ending is a surprise, but at the same time such a natural extension of the story that readers can't imagine a better way that it could have ended."

N $ AGONY IN BLACK, Chanting Monks Studios, Inc., 360-A W. Merrick Rd., Suite 350, Valley Stream NY 11580. E-mail: chntngmnks@aol.com. Publisher: Joseph M. Monks. **Contact**: Pamela Hazelton, editor. "*Agony In Black* is looking for fiction that stretches the boundaries and pushes the envelope." Writer's guidelines for #10 SASE.

Fiction: "The movie *Seven* is a very good example of work that we seek to publish. Work that strikes a chord or a nerve, in essence, work that some might read and ask rhetorically, 'Why on Earth would somebody write this?' " No poetry. No science fiction masked as horror. No fantasy or humor. Length: 500-7,500 words. Send complete ms with SASE. Query with SASE for material longer than 7,500 words.
Tips: "If you believe you have successfully transcended genres, there are probably other magazines far more receptive to those stories than *Agony In Black*."

N ✪ $ **AMAZING STORIES**, Wizards of the Coast, Inc., 1801 Lind Ave. SW, Renton WA 98055. Fax: (425)204-5928. E-mail: tommygyn@wizards.com. Website: http://www.wizards.com. Executive Editor: Pierce Watters. **Contact**: Mr. Kim Mohan, editor. **100% freelance written.** Quarterly magazine featuring quality science fiction short stories. Estab. 1926 (relaunched July 1998). Circ. 40,000. **Pays on acceptance.** Publishes ms an average of 6 months after acceptance. Byline given. Offers 33% kill fee. Buys first North American serial or all rights. Editorial lead time 6 months. Submit seasonal material 1 year in advance. Reports in 2 months on queries; 3 months on mss. Writer's guidelines free with SASE or available online.
Nonfiction: Opinion, reviews. **Buys 2 mss/year.** Query with published clips. Length: 1,000-2,500 words. **Pays 6-8¢/word.**
Columns/Departments: Query.
Fiction: Science fiction. **Buys 40 mss/year.** Query. Length: 1,000-8,000 words. **Pays 6-8¢/word.**
Tips: "Read writer's guidelines. Write a good, short query letter. Your manuscript should look professional. We are not likely to publish sword-and-sorcery fantasy; ethnic fantasy that is a rehash or an interpretation of a myth or legend; and horror that relies on gratuitous vulgarity or excessive gore to make the story work."

$ $ **ANALOG SCIENCE FICTION & FACT**, Dell Magazine Fiction Group, 1270 Avenue of the Americas, New York NY 10020. (212)698-1313. Fax: (212)698-1198. E-mail: 71154.662@compuserve.com. Website: http://www.sfsite.com/analog. **Contact**: Dr. Stanley Schmidt, editor. **100% freelance written.** Eager to work with new/unpublished writers. For general future-minded audience. Monthly. Estab. 1930. Buys first North American serial and nonexclusive foreign serial rights. **Pays on acceptance.** Publishes ms an average of 10 months after acceptance. Byline given. Reports in 1 month. Sample copy for $3 and 6×9 SASE with 5 first-class stamps. Writer's guidelines for #10 SASE.
Nonfiction: Illustrated technical articles dealing with subjects of not only current but future interest, i.e., topics at the present frontiers of research whose likely future developments have implications of wide interest. **Buys about 12 mss/year.** Query; no e-mail queries or submissions. Length: 5,000 words. **Pays 6¢/word.**
Fiction: "Basically, we publish science fiction stories. That is, stories in which some aspect of future science or technology is so integral to the plot that, if that aspect were removed, the story would collapse. The science can be physical, sociological or psychological. The technology can be anything from electronic engineering to biogenetic engineering. But the stories must be strong and realistic, with believable people doing believable things—no matter how fantastic the background might be." Publishes novel excerpts only if they can stand alone as independent stories. **Buys 60-100 unsolicited mss/year.** Send complete ms of short fiction; query about serials. Length: 2,000-80,000 words. **Pays 4¢/word for novels; 5-6¢/word for novelettes; 6-8¢/word for shorts under 7,500 words; $450-600 for intermediate lengths.**

• Ranked as one of the best markets for fiction writers in *Writer's Digest* magazine's "Fiction 50," June 1998.

Tips: "In query give clear indication of central ideas and themes and general nature of story line—and what is distinctive or unusual about it. We have no hard-and-fast editorial guidelines, because science fiction is such a broad field that I don't want to inhibit a new writer's thinking by imposing 'Thou Shalt Not's.' Besides, a really good story can make an editor swallow his preconceived taboos. I want the best work I can get, regardless of who wrote it—and I need new writers. So I work closely with new writers who show definite promise, but of course it's impossible to do this with *every* new writer. No occult or fantasy."

$ **ASIMOV'S SCIENCE FICTION**, Dell Magazine Fiction Group, 1270 Avenue of the Americas, New York NY 10020. (212)698-1313. Fax: (212)698-1198 (for correspondence only, no submissions). E-mail: 71154.662@compuserve.com. Website: http://www.asimovs.com. Executive Editor: Sheila Williams. **Contact**: Gardner Dozois, editor. **98% freelance written.** Works with a small number of new/unpublished writers each year. Published 11 times a year, including 1 double issue. Estab. 1977. Circ. 50,000. **Pays on acceptance.** Buys first North American serial and nonexclusive foreign serial rights; reprint rights occasionally. No simultaneous submissions. Reports in 2 months. Sample copy for $5 and 6½×9½ SAE. Writer's guidelines for #10 SASE.
Reprints: Send typed ms with rights for sale noted and information about when and where the article previously appeared.
Fiction: Science fiction primarily. Some fantasy and humor but no "Sword and Sorcery." No explicit sex or violence. Publishes novel excerpts; doesn't serialize novels. "It's best to read a great deal of material in the genre to avoid the use of some *very* old ideas." **Buys 10 mss/issue.** Submit complete ms and SASE with *all* submissions. Length: 750-15,000 words. **Pays 5-8¢/word.**
Poetry: Length should not exceed 40 lines; **pays $1/line.**

• Ranked as one of the best markets for fiction writers in *Writer's Digest* magazine's "Fiction 50," June 1998.

Tips: "In general, we're looking for 'character-oriented' stories, those in which the characters, rather than the science, provide the main focus for the reader's interest. Serious, thoughtful, yet accessible fiction will constitute the majority of our purchases, but there's always room for the humorous as well. Borderline fantasy is fine, but no Sword & Sorcery, please. Neither are we interested in explicit sex or violence. A good overview would be to consider that all fiction is written to examine or illuminate some aspect of human existence, but that in science fiction the backdrop you work against is the size of the Universe. Please do not send us submissions on disk. We've bought some of our best stories from people who have never sold a story before."

$ MARION ZIMMER BRADLEY'S FANTASY MAGAZINE, P.O. Box 249, Berkeley CA 94701-0249. Fax: (510)644-9222. Website: http://www.mzbfm.com. **Contact**: Mrs. Marion Z. Bradley, editor. **100% freelance written.** Quarterly magazine of fantasy fiction. Estab. 1988. **Pays on acceptance.** Publishes ms 1 year after acceptance. Byline given. Buys first North American serial rights. Reports in 3 months. Sample copy for $4 and 9″×12″ SAE.

Fiction: Fantasy. No science fiction, no horror. **Buys 55-60 mss/year.** Send complete ms. Length: 300-5,500 words; short shorts, 1,000 words maximum. **Pays 3-10¢/word.**

Tips: "Do not submit without first reading guidelines."

"We buy original fantasy (*not* sex fantasies) with no particular objection to modern settings, but we do want action and adventure. The primary purpose of your story should should be to entertain the reader; and although any good story has a central point behind the plot, the reader should be able to deduce it rather than having it thrust upon him. Fantasy content should start on the first page and must appear within the first three pages. We prefer strong female characters, and we will reject stories in which we find objectionable sexism. We also reject stories with bad grammar or spelling. We do not favor strong language because, although we ARE NOT a magazine aimed at children or young adults, we do have many young readers. Non-fiction should be queried; it is done on commission only. *Please read a few issues before submitting so that you can see the kind of thing we do buy.* Please *do not* submit: Poetry, serials, novel excerpts, children's stories, shared world stories, science fiction, hard technology, occult, horror, re-written fairy tales, radical feminism, romances (in which love, romance and marriage are the main motivations), surrealism, or avant-garde stories, stories written in the present tense, or stories about God, the Devil, or hearth-witches. Beware of: 'dime-a-dozen' subjects such as dragons, elves, unicorns, wizards, vampires, writers, sea creatures, brute warriors, ghosts, adventuring sorcerers/sorceresses, thieves/assassins, or final exams for wizards. We get dozens of these kings of stories every week, and we reject all but the *truly* unusual and well-written ones."

$ $ THE CRYSTAL BALL, The Starwind Press, P.O. Box 98, Ripley OH 45167. **Contact**: Marlena Powell, editor. **90% freelance written.** Quarterly magazine covering science fiction and fantasy for young adult readers. "We are especially targeting readers of middle school age." Estab. 1997. **Pays on acceptance**. Publishes ms an average of 6 months after acceptance. Byline given. Offers 100% kill fee. Buys first or second serial (reprint) rights. Editorial lead time 4 months. Sample copy for 9×12 SASE and $3. Writer's guidelines for #10 SASE.

Nonfiction: How-to (science), interview/profile, personal experience, book reviews, science information. **Buys 4-6 mss/year.** Query. Length: 900-3,000 words. **Pays ¼¢/word.**

Reprints: Send typed ms with rights for sale noted and information and when and where the article previously appeared. Pays 100% of amount paid for an original article.

Photos: Send photos with submission. Negotiates payment individually. Captions and identification of subjects required.

Columns/Departments: Book reviews (science fiction and fantasy), 100-200 words or less; museum reviews (science & technology, museums & centers, children's museums), 900 words. **Buys 10-15 mss/year.** Query. **Pays ¼¢/word.**

Fiction: Fantasy, science fiction. **Buys 10-12 mss/year.** Send complete ms. Length: 1,000-5,000 words. **Pays ¼¢/word.**

Tips: "Have a good feel for writing for kids. Don't 'write down' to your audience because they're kids. We look for articles of scientific and technological interest."

N $ $ INTERZONE, Science Fiction and Fantasy, 217 Preston Drove, Brighton England BN1 6FL United Kingdom. 01273-504710. E-mail: interzone@cix. compulink.co.uk. Editor: David Pringle. Mostly freelance written. Monthly magazine covering science fiction and fantasy. Estab. 1982. Circ. 10,000. Pays on publication. Publishes ms an average of 3 months after acceptance. Byline given. Buys first or one-time rights. Editorial lead time 3 months. Reports in 3 months on mss. Sample copy for $5.50. Writer's guidelines free on request.

Nonfiction: Essays, interview/profile, opinion. Send complete ms. Length: 1,000-5,000 words. Pays by agreement.

Photos: State availability of photos with submissions. Offers no additional payment for photos accepted with ms.

Fiction: Science fiction and fantasy. **Buys 75mss/year.** Send complete ms. Length: 2,000-6,000 words. **Pays £30/1,000 words.**

★ $ THE MAGAZINE OF FANTASY & SCIENCE FICTION, Mercury Press, P.O. Box 1806, Madison Square Station, New York NY 10159-1806. Fax: (212)982-2676. E-mail: gordonfsf@aol.com. Website: http://www.fsfmag.com. **Contact**: Gordon Van Gelder, editor. **100% freelance written.** Monthly fantasy fiction and science fiction magazine. "*The Magazine of Fantasy and Science Fiction* publishes various types of science fiction and fantasy short stories and novellas, making up about 80% of each issue. The balance of each issue is devoted to articles about science fiction, a science column, book and film reviews, cartoons and competitions." Estab. 1949. Circ. 80,000. **Pays on acceptance.** Byline given. Buys first North American and foreign serial rights. Submit seasonal material 8 months in advance. Reports in 2 months. Sample copy for $5. Writer's guidelines for #10 SASE.

Fiction: Fantasy, horror, science fiction. Prefers character-oriented stories. Send complete ms. No electronic submissions. Length: 2,000-20,000 words. **Pays 5-8¢/word.**

- Ranked as one of the best markets for fiction writers in *Writer's Digest* magazine's "Fiction 50," June 1998.

Tips: "We need more hard science fiction and humor."

$ NIGHTCRY, Illustrated Magazine of Horror, Chanting Monks Studios, 360-A W. Merrick Rd., Suite 350, Valley Stream NY 11580. E-mail: chntngmnks@aol.com. Website: http://www.loginet.com/cfd. Managing Editor and Publisher: Joseph M. Monks. **Contact**: Pamela Hazelton, editor. **100% freelance written.** Illustrated magazine of horror. "Our readers like twisted, horrific stories. No 'things that go bump in the night.' Psychological horror also is enjoyed." Estab. 1994. Circ. 15,000. Pays one month after publication. Publishes ms an average of 8 months after acceptance. Byline given. Buys first North American serial rights. Editorial lead time 4 months. Accepts simultaneous submissions. Reports in 2 months. Copy for $3.50. Writer's guidelines for #10 SASE.

Fiction: Horror, mystery, science fiction. Publishes novel excerpts. **Buys 10-30 mss/year.** Send complete ms, comic script and/or panel to panel art. **Pays $20-100.**

Reprints: Send typed ms with information about when and where the article previously appeared (no "buying of second rights").

Tips: "Follow comic script format guidelines—they are different from standard scripts. Many writers adapt their short stories to comics fairly well."

$ ON SPEC, The Copper Pig Writers Society, P.O. Box 4727, Edmonton, Alberta T6E 5G6 Canada. Fax: (403)413-0215. E-mail: onspec@earthling.net. Website: http://www.icomm.ca/onspec/. Editorial Collective: Barry Hammond, Susan MacGregor, Hazel Sangster, Jena Snyder, Diane L. Walton. **95% freelance written.** Quarterly literary magazine covering Canadian science fiction, fantasy and horror. "*On Spec* is Canada's premier speculative fiction magazine. Strong preference given to Canadian writers." Estab. 1989. Circ. 2,000. **Pays on acceptance**. Publishes ms an average of 1 year after acceptance. Byline given. Buys first North American serial rights. Editorial lead time 6 months. Reports in 3 months after deadline on mss. Reports in 3 weeks on queries. Sample copy for $6. Writer's guidelines for #10 SASE with Canadian stamp or IRC.

Nonfiction: Commissioned only. Yearly theme issue. 1999 theme is "Earth, Air, Fire and Water"; all stories should contain reference to the four elements. "Each year we offer $100 prize to best story by a young and upcoming author published in *On Spec* in the past year."

Fiction: Science fiction, fantasy, horror, magic realism. No media tie-in or shaggy-alien stories. **Buys 40 mss/year.** Send complete ms only. Length: 6,000 words maximum. **Pays $40-180 (Canadian) 3¢/word.**

Poetry: Barry Hammond, poetry editor. Avant-garde, free verse. "We rarely buy rhyming or religious material." **Buys 6 poems/year.** Submit maximum 6 poems. Length: 4-100 lines. **Pays $20.**

Tips: "Send for guidelines! We have specific (i.e. competition) format requirements. Absolutely no e-mailed submissions. Strong preference given to submissions by Canadians."

N $ OUTSIDE, Clocktower Fiction's Spectulative and Dark Fiction Magazine, C&C Clocktower Fiction, Box 260, 6549 Mission Gorge Rd., San Diego CA 92120. E-mail: outside@clocktowerfiction.com. Website: http://www.clocktowerfiction.com. **Contact:** Editorial. Editors: Brian Callohan and John Cullen. **100% freelance written**. Online magazine offering science fiction and dark imaginative and horror. "*Outside* is a paying professional magazine of science fiction and dark imaginative fiction, aimed at people who love to read well-plotted character-driven genre fiction." Estab. 1998. **Pays on acceptance**. Publishes ms an average of 6 months after acceptance. Byline given. Buys first North American serial and first North American electronic serial rights. Editorial lead time 6 months. Submit seasonal material 6 months in advance. Reports in 3 months on mss. Sample copy and writer's guidelines on website.

Fiction: Horror, science fiction. "We seek well-written, character-driven fiction that is tightly plotted. Professionally executed, with attention to basics—grammar, punctuation, usage. No sword and sorcery, shared worlds, porno of any kind, excessive violence or goes beyond the legitimate needs of a story, no vulgarity unless it furthers the story (sparingly at that). No derivative works emulating TV shows or movies (e.g., Star Trek)." **Buys 12 mss/year**. Send complete ms. Length: 1,500-4,000 words. **Pays 3¢/word.**

Tips: "Please read the tips and guidelines on the magazine's website for further and up-to-the-moment details. *Submissions by mail only.* Traditional format, #10 SASE minimum for reply. E-mail submissions will be deleted unread."

N $ $ SCI-FI INVASION!, The Science Fiction Magazine, Wizard Entertainment, 151 Wells Ave., Congers NY 10920. Fax: (914)268-0053. E-mail: sfimail@aol.com. Website: http://www.wizardpress.com. Editor: Douglas Goldstein. **Contact:** Matthew Saunders, associate editor. **80% freelance written.** Quarterly magazine focused exclusively on science fiction (movies, TV shows, books, toys, comics, new media). No fantasy or horror. It strives to be both informative and entertaining for a young, teenage audience." Estab. 1997. Circ. 100,000. Pays on publication. Publishes ms 3 months after acceptance. Byline given. Offers 50% kill. Buys all rights. Editorial lead time 3 months. Submit seasonal material 4 months in advance. Reports in 6 weeks. Sample copy free. Guidelines for #10 SASE.

Nonfiction: General interest (related to science fiction), humor, interview/profile, new product (previews of films and TV shows), photo feature. "No personal experience, reviews, opinion pieces, articles on gaming, retrospectives of old TV shows, films or sci-fi personalities." **Buys 30 mss/year.** Query with published clips. Length: 1,300-3,500 words. **Pays 15¢/word.** Sometimes pays expenses of writers on assignment.

Photos: State availability of photos with submission. Reviews negatives, 4×5 transparencies, 8½×11 prints. Negotiates payment individually. Identification of subjects required. Buys one-time rights.

Columns/Departments: Reference/Episode Guides (topics must be current), 3,500 words; Road Trip (topics must be current), 600 words; News, 200-500 words. **Buys 30 mss/year.** Query with published clips. **Pays 15¢/word.**

Tips: "It's an old line, but become familiar with our style and content. Remember, we are devoted exclusively to current sci-fi topics, and are aimed at a young, teenage audience. Always query first, with published clips that showcase your ability to write for the sci-fi and entertainment genres. And start small, with news, departments or sidebars—we continue using writers who have proven their talent and reliability and this often leads to bigger assignments. No unsolicited manuscripts."

N $ SHIVER MAGAZINE, The Magazine for Active Minds Bent on Twisting Others, Shiver Publications, P.O. Box 178, Surrey, British Columbia V3T 4W8 Canada. E-mail: shiver@clubtek.com. Website: http://www.clubtek.com/shiver. **Contact:** T.L. Craigen, editor. Managing Editor: L.K. Mason. **90% freelance written**. Semiannual consumer magazine. "*Shiver* is a shared-world magazine. Writers should SASE for guidelines or visit our website for more information. We publish fantasy, horror and science fiction and our intended audience is 17 and up." Estab. 1995. Circ. 1,200. **Pays on acceptance**. Publishes ms an average of 6 months after acceptance. Byline given. Buys first North American serial or second serial (reprint) rights. Reports in 2 months. Sample copy for $5 (US) or $4.50 (CD). Writer's guidelines for #10 SASE.
Nonfiction: Contact: Ken Hurrell, staff writer. How-to (aspects of writing), interview/profile. **Buys 4 mss/year**. Send complete ms. Length: 1,000-3,000 words. **Pays $10-30.**
Reprints: Accepts previously published submissions.
Columns/Departments: Contact: Ken Hurrell, staff writer. Horror Homework (advice for writers), 1,500 words. **Buys 2 mss/year**. Query. **Pays $10-30.**
Fiction: Contact: L.K. Mason, managing editor. Fantasy, horror, science fiction. No gratuitous sex or profanity. **Buys 12 mss/year**. Send complete ms. Length: 1,000-10,000 words. **Pays $10-100.**
Poetry: Contact: L.K. Mason, managing editor. Avant-garde, free verse, traditional. **Buys 2 poems/year**. Submit maximum 5 poems. Length: 3-100 lines. **Pays $5-15.**
Tips: "Check out our website. Writers have a greater chance of being published if they participate in our shared-world theme."

$ THE SILVER WEB, A Magazine of the Surreal, Buzzcity Press, P.O. Box 38190, Tallahassee FL 32315. (850)385-8948. Fax: (850)385-4063. E-mail: annk19@mail.idt.net. **Contact**: Ann Kennedy, publisher/editor. **100% freelance written.** Semiannual literary magazine. "*The Silver Web* is a semi-annual publication featuring science fiction, dark fantasy and horror, fiction, poetry, art, and thought-provoking articles. The editor is looking for works ranging from speculative fiction to dark tales and all weirdness in between; specifically works of the surreal." Estab. 1988. Circ. 2,000. **Pays on acceptance.** Byline given. Offers 100% kill fee. Buys first North American serial, one-time or second serial (reprint) rights. Editorial lead time 2 months. Accepts simultaneous submissions. Reports in 1 week on queries; 2 months on mss. Sample copy for $7.20; subscription: $12. Writer's guidelines for #10 SASE or via e-mail.
Nonfiction: Book excerpts, essays, interview/profile, opinion. **Buys 6 mss/year.** Query. Length: 500-8,000 words. **Pays $20-250.**
Reprints: Send information before submitting ms about when and where material previously appeared. Pays 100% of amount paid for an original article.
Photos: State availability of photos with submission. Reviews prints. Negotiates payment individually. Identification of subjects required. Buys one-time rights.
Columns/Departments: Book Reviews, Movie Reviews, TV Reviews, all 3,000 words. **Buys 6 mss/year.** Send complete ms. **Pays $20-250.**
Fiction: Experimental, horror, science fiction, dark fantasy, surreal. "We do not want to see typical storylines, endings or predictable revenge stories." **Buys 20-25 mss/year.** Send complete ms. Length: 500-8,000 words. **Pays $10-320.** Publishes novel excerpts but query first. Open to submissions January 1 to September 30.

- Ranked as one of the best markets for fiction writers in *Writer's Digest* magazine's "Fiction 50," June 1998.

Poetry: Avant-garde, free verse, haiku, light verse, traditional. **Buys 18-30/year.** Submit maximum 5 poems. **Pays $10-50.**
Fillers: Art fillers. **Buys 10/year. Pays $5-10.**
Tips: "Give us an unusual unpredictable story with strong, believable characters we care about. Surprise us with something unique. We do look for interviews with people in the field (writers, artists, filmmakers)."

$ SPACE AND TIME, 138 W. 70th St., 4B, New York NY 10023-4468. Website: http://www.bway.net/~cburns/space&time.html. Editor-in-Chief: Gordon Linzner. **Contacts**: Tom Piccirilli, fiction editor; Lawrence Greenberg, poetry editor. **99% freelance written.** Semiannual magazine of science fiction and fantasy. "We feature a mix of fiction and poetry in all aspects of the fantasy genre—science fiction, supernatural horror, sword & sorcery, mixed genre, unclassifiable. Its variety makes it stand out from more narrowly focused magazines. Our readers enjoy quality material that surprises and provokes." Estab. 1966. Circ. 1,200. **Pays on acceptance.** Publishes ms an average of 9 months after acceptance. Byline given. Buys first North American serial rights. Editorial lead time 1 year. Reports in 3 months on mss. Sample copy $1.50. Writer's guidelines for #10 SASE.
Nonfiction: Essays on fantasy, science fiction, science, etc. "No so-called 'true' paranormal." **Buys 1-2 mss/year.** Send complete ms. Length: 1,000 words maximum. **Pays 1¢/word plus 2 contributor copies.**
Photos/Artwork: Charles Burns, art director. Artwork (could include photos). Send nonreturnable photocopies. Reviews prints. Pays $10 for interior illustration, $25 for cover, plus 2 contributor copies. Model releases required. Buys one-time rights.

Fiction: Tom Piccirilli, fiction editor. Fantasy, horror, science fiction, mixed genre (i.e., science-fiction-mystery, western-horror, etc.) and unclassifiable; "Do not want anything that falls outside of fantasy/science fiction (but that leaves a lot). No fiction set in a franchised universe, i.e., Star Trek." **Buys 20-24 mss/year.** Send complete ms. Length: 10,000 words maximum. **Pays 1¢/word plus 2 contributor copies, $5 minimum.**

Poetry: Lawrence Greenberg, poetry editor. Avant-garde, free verse, haiku, light verse, traditional. "Do not send poetry without a solid connection to the genres we publish. Imaginative metaphors alone do not make it fantasy." **Buys 20 poems/year.** Submit maximum 5 poems. Length: no limits. **Pays 1¢/word ($5 minimum) plus 2 contributor copies.**

Tips: "Avoid clichés and standard plots unless you have something new to add."

$ $ STARLOG MAGAZINE, The Science Fiction Universe, Starlog Group, 475 Park Ave. S., 8th Floor, New York NY 10016-1689. Fax: (212)889-7933. E-mail: communications@starloggroup.com. **Contact**: David McDonnell, editor. **90% freelance written.** We are hesitant to work with unpublished writers. Monthly magazine covering "the science fiction-fantasy genre: its films, TV, books, art and personalities." Estab. 1976. "We concentrate on interviews with actors, directors, writers, producers, special effects technicians and others. Be aware that 'sci-fi' and 'Trekkie' are seen as derogatory terms by our readers and by us." Pays on publication. Publishes ms an average of 4 months after acceptance. Byline given. Offers kill fee "only to manuscripts *written* or interviews *done for us*." Buys all rights. No simultaneous submissions. Reports in 6 weeks or less. "We provide an assignment sheet to *all* writers with deadline and other info, authorizing a queried piece. No such sheets provided for already completed stories sent in on speculation. Manuscripts *must* be submitted on computer disk or by e-mail. Printouts helpful." Sample copy for $5. Writer's guidelines for #10 SASE.

Nonfiction: Interview/profile (actors, directors, screenwriters who've made science fiction films and science fiction novelists); coverage of science fiction fandom, etc. "We also sometimes cover science fiction/fantasy animation and comics." No personal opinion think pieces/essays. *No* first person. Avoids articles on horror films/creators. "We prefer article format as opposed to Q&A interviews." **Buys 175 mss/year.** Query first with published clips. "We accept queries by mail *only*, by fax if there's a critical time factor. No phone calls. Ever! Unsolicited phone calls *cannot* be returned." Length: 500-3,000 words. **Pays $35 (500-word or less items); $50-75 (sidebars); $150-275 (1,000-4,000 word pieces).**

Reprints: Pays $50 for *each* reprint in online magazine version, foreign edition or such.

Photos: State availability of photos. Pays $10-25 for color slide transparencies depending on quality. "No separate payment for photos provided by film studios." Captions, model releases, identification of subjects and credit line on photos required. Photo credit given. Buys all rights.

Columns/Departments: Loglines (mini interviews or stray quotes from celebrities, 25-200 words each, **$25-35**); Booklog (book reviews, **$15 each,** by assignment only). Buys 150 reviews/year. Query with published clips. Book review, 125 words maximum. No kill fee.

Tips: "Absolutely *no fiction*. We do *not* publish it and we throw away fiction manuscripts from writers who *can't* be bothered to include SASE. Nonfiction only please! A writer can best break into *Starlog* by getting an unusual interview or by *out-thinking* us and coming up with something *new* on a current film or TV series. We are always looking for *fresh* angles on the various *Star Trek* shows, *The X-Files*, and *Star Wars*. Know your subject before you try us. Most full-length major assignments go to freelancers with whom we're already dealing. But if we like your clips and ideas, it's possible we'll give *you* a chance. No phone calls for *any* reason please—we *mean* that!"

$ STARSHIP EARTH, Black Moon Publishing, P.O. Box 484, Bellaire OH 43906. Phone/fax: (740)671-3253. E-mail: shadowhorse@aol.com. Managing Editor: Kirin Lee. **Contact**: Silver Shadowhorse, fiction editor. **30% freelance nonfiction; 100% freelance fiction written.** Bimonthly magazine featuring science fiction. "*Starship Earth* is geared toward science fiction fans of all ages. We do mostly nonfiction, but do print short stories. Our nonfiction focus: profiles of actors and industry people, conventions, behind the scenes articles on films and TV shows. We do cover action/adventure films and TV as well. Heavy Star Trek focus. We cover classic science fiction, too." Estab. 1996. Pays on publication. Publishes ms an average of 1 year after acceptance. Byline sometimes given. Buys first or one-time rights. Editorial lead time 9-12 months. Submit seasonal material 6 months in advance. Reports in 3 weeks on queries; 2 months on mss. Writer's guidelines for #10 SASE.

- *Starship Earth* is planning an anthology of short stories of up to 4,000 words. Stories submitted to *Starship Earth* will automatically be considered.

Nonfiction: General interest, how-to (relating to science fiction, writing, model building, crafts, etc.), humor (cartoons), interview/profile, new product (relating to science of science fiction), nostalgia, personal experience, photo feature, travel (relating to attending conventions), behind the scenes of film/TV science fiction, book reviews. **Buys variable number of mss/year.** Query. Length: up to 3,000 words. Please query for longer pieces. **Pays ½-3¢/word.** Pays in copies for book or film reviews. Sometimes pays expenses of writers on assignment.

Photos: State availability of photos with submission. Reviews transparencies, prints. Negotiates payment individually. Captions, model releases, identification of subjects required. Buys one-time rights.

Columns/Departments: Jenna Dawson, assistant editor. Costumes, conventions/events, science fiction music, upcoming book, film, TV releases, film reviews, book reviews, new products; all up to 700 words. **Buys variable number of mss/year.** Query. **Pays ½-3¢/word.**

Fiction: Silver Shadowhorse, editor. Fantasy, historical (with a science fiction twist), science fiction. No erotic content, horror, "Sword & Sorcery" violence, explicit language or religious material. **Buys variable number of mss/year, 12 short stories/year.** Query. Length: 500-3,000 words. **Pays ½-3¢/word.**

Fillers: Contact: Jenna Dawson, assistant editor. Anecdotes, facts, newsbreaks, short humor. **Buys variable number**

of mss/year. Length: 50-250 words. **Pays ½-3¢/word.**

Tips: "We are willing to work with new and unpublished writers in most areas. All manuscripts must be in standard format. We are always looking for new or unusual angles on old science fiction shows/films, conventions, costumes, fx and people in the business. Articles from interviews must have sparkle and be interesting to a variety of readers. Absolutely no gossip or fluff. Anyone sending a disposable manuscript can simply include their e-mail address instead of a SASE for reply."

$ THE URBANITE, Surreal & Lively & Bizarre, Urban Legend Press, P.O. Box 4737, Davenport IA 52808. **Contact:** Mark McLaughlin, editor. **95% freelance written.** Triannual magazine covering surreal fiction and poetry. "We look for quality fiction in an urban setting with a surrealistic tone. . . We prefer character-driven storylines. Our audience is urbane, culture-oriented, and hard to please!" Estab. 1991. Circ. 600. **Pays on acceptance.** Contributors to recent issues include Thomas Ligotti, Basil Copper, Hugh B. Cave, Hertzan Chimera and Pamela Briggs. Fiction from the magazine has been reprinted in *The Year's Best Fantasy and Horror* and England's *Best New Horror,* and is forthcoming in *The Year's Best Fantastic Fiction*. Publishes ms an average of 6 months after acceptance. Byline given. Buys first North American serial rights or second serial (reprint) rights and non-exclusive rights for public readings. "We hold readings of the magazine at various venues—like libraries." Editorial leadtime 6 months. Reports in 1 month on queries; 2 months on mss. Sample copy for $5. Writer's guidelines for #10 SASE.

Nonfiction: Essays, humor, interview/profile. "After September 1998, we will be reading for issue No. 12 The Zodiac. Each issue has a theme. We don't publish recipes, fishing tips or music/CD reviews." **Buys up to 6 mss/year.** Query. Length: 500-3,000 words. **Pays $15-90 for assigned articles; $10-60 for unsolicited articles.**

Reprints: Accepts previously published submissions (but query first). Send typed ms with rights for sale noted and information about when and where the article previously appeared. Pays 100% of amount paid for an original article.

Columns/Departments: "We haven't run any columns, but would like to. Unfortunately, we haven't seen any queries that really thrill us." **Pays $15-90.**

Fiction: Experimental, fantasy (contemporary), horror, humorous, science fiction (but not "high-tech"), slipstream/cross genre, surrealism of all sorts. Upcoming theme: No. 12: The Zodiac. **Buys 54 mss/year.** Send complete ms. Length: 500-3,000 words. **Pays $10-90 (2-3¢/word).** Publishes novel excerpts. Each issue has a Featured Writer, who receives 3¢/word, 6 contributor copies, and a lifetime subscription to the magazine.

- Ranked as one of the best markets for fiction writers in *Writer's Digest* magazine's "Fiction 50," June 1998.

Poetry: Avant-garde, free verse, traditional, narrative poetry. No haiku or light verse. **Buys 18 poems/year.** Submit maximum 3 poems. Length: up to 2 ms pages. **Pays $10/poem.**

Tips: "Writers should familiarize themselves with surrealism in literature: too often, we receive stories filled with genre clichés. Also: we prefer character-driven stories.We're looking to add nonfiction (at the same pay rate—2-3¢/word—as fiction). Reviews, articles, cultural commentary . . . the more unusual, the better. Don't just write because you want to see your name in print. Write because you have something to say."

N $ WICKED MYSTIC MAGAZINE, FTWS Press, 532 La Guardia Place, #371, New York NY 10012. (718)638-1533. E-mail: wickedmyst@aol.com. Website: http://www.wickedmystic.com. **Contact**: Andre Scheluchin, editor. **90% freelance written.** Quarterly literary magazine featuring extreme, cutting-edge horror fiction and nonfiction. Estab. 1990. Circ. 10,000. Pays on publication. Publishes ms an average of 6 months after acceptance. Byline given. Buys first North American serial rights. Editorial lead time 2 months. Submit seasonal material 2 months in advance. Reports in 2 weeks on queries; 4 months on mss. Sample copy for $5.95. Writer's guidelines for #10 SASE.

Nonfiction: Book excerpts, essays, general interest, how-to, humor, inspirational, interview/profile, new product, opinion, personal experience, photo feature. **Buys 10 mss/year.** Send complete ms. Length: 500-4,000 words. **Pays 1¼¢/word.** Sometimes pays expenses of writers on assignment.

Photos: Send photos with submission. Reviews prints. Negotiates payment individually. Buys one-time rights.

Columns/Departments: Horror-related book, music, event reviews, all 2,000 words. **Buys 4 mss/year.** Send complete ms. **Pays 1¼¢/word.**

Fiction: Adventure, erotica, experimental, fantasy, horror, science fiction, suspense, novel excerpts. No mainstream fiction. **Buys 35 mss/year.** Send complete ms. Length: 500-4,000 words. **Pays 1¼¢/word.**

Poetry: Avant-garde, free verse, haiku, light verse, traditional. No rhyming poetry. **Buys 40 poems/year.** Submit maximum 5 poems. Length: 4-40 lines. **Pays $5-20.**

Fillers: Anecdotes, facts, gags to be illustrated by cartoonist, newsbreaks, short humor. **Buys 10/year.** Length: 1-75 words. **Pays $5-20.**

Tips: "We're not mainstream, not traditional. We need shock, twists and extremes."

SEX

Magazines featuring pictorial layouts accompanied by stories and articles of a sexual nature, both gay and straight, are listed in this section. Dating and single lifestyle magazines appear in the Relationships section. Other markets for articles relating to sex can be found in the Men's and Women's sections.

BOUDOIR NOIR, P.O. Box 5, Station F, Toronto, Ontario M4Y 2L4 Canada. Fax: (416)591-1572. E-mail: boudoir@boudoir~noir.com. Website: http://www.boudoir-noir.com. **Contact**: Diane Wilputte, editor. **70% freelance written.** Quarterly magazine covering the S&M and fetish lifestyles in North America. "We publish only nonfiction articles that seek to explain S&M sexuality to our readers." Estab. 1992. Circ. 7,000. Publishes ms an average of 3 months after acceptance. Byline given. Buys second serial (reprint) rights. Submit seasonal material 3 months in advance. Reports in 2 weeks on queries; 1 month on mss. Sample copy for $10. Writer's guidelines free.

Nonfiction: Reviews, feature articles. Length: 500-1,000 words. Query first. No simultaneous submissions please.

Tips: "We like to get stories by e-mail or on disk, but we accept typed mss from a few writers (one writer in Russia sends handwritten copy). We like to know if someone has a particular fetish or area of expertise which gives them extra credentials to write a particular story. We prefer stories that focus on people, rather than abstract fetishes or issues. No fiction or poetry."

$ $ EXOTIC MAGAZINE, X Publishing, 625 SW 10th Ave. #324, Portland OR 97205. Fax: (503)241-7239. E-mail: xmag@teleport.com. **Contact**: Editor. Monthly magazine covering adult entertainment, sexuality. "*Exotic* is pro-sex, informative, amusing, mature, intelligent. Our readers rent and/or buy adult videos, visit strip clubs and are interested in topics related to the adult entertainment industry and sexuality/culture. Don't talk down to them or fire too far over their heads. Many readers are computer literate and well-traveled. We're also interested in insightful fetish material. We are not a 'hard core' publication." Estab. 1993. Circ. 40,000. Pays 30 days after publication. Publishes ms an average of 6 months after acceptance. Byline given. Buys first North American serial rights; and on-line rights; may negotiate second serial (reprint) rights. Accepts simultaneous submissions. Reports in 2 weeks on queries; 2 months on mss. Sample copy for 9×12 SASE and 5 first-class stamps. Writer's guidelines for #10 SASE.

Nonfiction: Exposé, general interest, historical/nostalgic, how-to, humor, interview/profile, travel, news. No "men writing as women, articles about being a horny guy, opinion pieces pretending to be fact pieces." **Buys 36 mss/year.** Send complete ms. Length: 1,000-1,800 words. **Pays 10¢/word up to $150.**

Reprints: Send typed ms with rights for sale noted and information about when and where the article previously appeared. Pays 100% of amount paid for an original article.

Photos: Rarely buys photos. Most provided by staff. Reviews prints. Negotiates payment individually. Model releases required.

Fiction: We are currently overwhelmed with fiction submissions. Please only send fiction if it's really amazing. Erotica, slice-of-life vignettes. (Must present either erotic element or some "vice" of modern culture, such as gambling, music, dancing). Send complete ms. Length: 1,000-1,800 words. **Pays 10¢/word up to $150.**

Tips: "Read adult publications, spend time in the clubs doing more than just tipping and drinking. Look for new insights in adult topics. For the industry to continue to improve, those who cover it must also be educated consumers and affiliates. Please type, spell-check and be realistic about how much time the editor can take 'fixing' your manuscript."

$ ✪ FIRST HAND, Experiences For Loving Men, Firsthand, Ltd., 310 Cedar Lane, Teaneck NJ 07666. (201)836-9177. Fax: (201)836-5055. E-mail: firsthand3@aol.com. Publisher: Jackie Lewis. **Contact:** Bob Harris, editor. **75% freelance written.** Eager to work with new/unpublished writers. Magazine of homosexual erotica published 16 times/year. Estab. 1980. Circ. 70,000. Pays on publication. Publishes ms an average of 8 months after acceptance. Byline given. Buys all rights (exceptions made) and second serial (reprint) rights. Submit seasonal material 10 months in advance. Reports in 4 months. Sample copy for $5. Writer's guidelines for #10 SASE.

Reprints: Send photocopy of previously published article. Pays 50% of amount paid for original articles.

Columns/Departments: Survival Kit (short nonfiction articles, up to 1,000 words, featuring practical information on safe sex practices, health, travel, psychology, law, fashion, and other advice/consumer/lifestyle topics of interest to gay or single men). "For this section, we sometimes also buy reprint rights to appropriate articles previously published in local gay newspapers around the country." Infotainment (short reviews up to 1,000 words on books, film, TV, video, theater, performance art, museums, etc.). Reviews must have a gay slant. Query. **Pays $35-70,** depending on length.

Fiction: Erotic fiction up to 5,000 words, average 2,000-3,000 words. "We prefer fiction in the first person which is believable—stories based on the writer's actual experience have the best chance. We're not interested in stories which involve underage characters in sexual situations. Other taboos include bestiality, rape—except in prison stories, as rape is an unavoidable reality in prison—and heavy drug use. Writers with questions about what we can and cannot depict should write for our guidelines, which go into this in more detail. We print mostly self-contained stories; we will look at novel excerpts, but only if they stand on their own."

Tips: "*First Hand* is a very reader-oriented publication for gay men. Half of each issue is made up of letters from our readers describing their personal experiences, fantasies and feelings. Our readers are from all walks of life, all races and ethnic backgrounds, all classes, all religious and political affiliations, and so on. They are very diverse, and many live in far-flung rural areas or small towns; for some of them, our magazines are the primary source of contact with gay life, in some cases the only support for their gay identity. Our readers are very loyal and save every issue. We return that loyalty by trying to reflect their interests—for instance, by striving to avoid the exclusively big-city bias so common to national gay publications. So bear in mind the diversity of the audience when you write."

$ $ $ $ FOX MAGAZINE, Montcalm Publishing, 401 Park Ave. S., New York NY 10016-8802. (212)779-8900. Fax: (212)725-7215. Website: http://www.gallerymagazine.com. Editorial Director: Chip Maloney. Managing Editor: Rich Friedman. **50% freelance written.** Prefers to work with published/established writers. Monthly magazine "focusing on features of interest to the young American man." Estab. 1972. Circ. 500,000. Pays on publication. Byline given. Offers 25% kill fee. Buys first North American serial rights or makes work-for-hire assignments. Submit seasonal material 6 months in advance. Reports in 1 month on queries; 2 months on mss. Sample copy for $8.95 (add $2 for Canadian and foreign orders). Writers' guidelines for #10 SASE.

Nonfiction: Investigative pieces, general interest, how-to, humor, interview, new products, profile. **Buys 4-5 mss/year.** Query or send complete ms. Length: 1,500-5,000 words. **Pays $300-1,500.** "Special prices negotiated." Sometimes pays expenses of writers on assignment.

Reprints: Send tearsheet or photocopy of article or short story or typed ms with rights for sale noted and information about when and where the article previously appeared. Pays 25% of amount paid for an original article.

Photos: Send photos with accompanying ms. Pay varies. Reviews b&w or color contact sheets and negatives. Buys one-time rights. Captions preferred; model releases and photo IDs required.

Fiction: Adventure, erotica (special guidelines available), experimental, humorous, mainstream, mystery, suspense. **Buys 1 ms/issue.** Send complete ms. Length: 1,000-3,000 words. **Pays $350-500.**

$ $ $ GALLERY MAGAZINE, Montcalm Publishing Corp., 401 Park Ave. S., New York NY 10016-8802. (212)779-8900. Fax: (212)725-7215. Managing Editor: Rich Friedman. **Contact:** Chip Maloney, editorial director. **50% freelance written.** Prefers to work with published/established writers. Monthly magazine "focusing on features of interest to the young American man. *Gallery* is a magazine aimed at entertaining and educating the contemporary man. *Gallery* covers political, cultural, and social trends on a national and global level through serious and provocative investigative reports, candid interviews, human-interest features, service-oriented articles, fiction, humor and photographic portfolios of beautiful women. Each issue of *Gallery* contains our 'Heroes' feature, a first-person account of the effects of the Vietnam War, 'Toys for Men' service feature; and columns dealing with travel, entertainment news, automotives, men's fashion, health and fitness, and outdoor leisure activities." Estab. 1972. Circ. 500,000. Pays on publication. Byline given. Pays 25% kill fee. Buys first North American serial rights or makes work-for-hire assignments. Submit seasonal material 6 months in advance. Reports in 1 month on queries; 2 months on mss. Sample copy for $7.95 (add $2 for Canadian and foreign orders). Writer's guidelines for SASE.

• *Gallery* works on Macintosh, so it accepts material on Mac or compatible disks if accompanied by hard copy.

Nonfiction: Investigative pieces, general interest, how-to, humor, interview, new products, profile. **Buys 4-5 mss/issue.** Query or send complete mss. Length: 1,500-3,500 words. **Pays $1,500-3,000.** "Special prices negotiated." Sometimes pays expenses of writers on assignment.

Reprints: Send tearsheet, photocopy or typed ms of article or story with rights for sale noted and information about when and where the article previously appeared. Pays 25% of amount paid for an original article.

Photos: Send photos with accompanying mss. Pay varies for b&w or color contact sheets and negatives. Buys one-time rights. Captions preferred; model release, photo ID required.

Fiction: Adventure, erotica (special guidelines available), experimental, humorous, mainstream, mystery, suspense. **Buys 1 ms/issue.** Send complete ms. Length: 1,000-3,000 words. **Pays $350-500.**

N $ $ GENESIS, Magna Publications, 210 Route 4 E., Suite 401, Paramus NJ 07652. (201)843-4004. Fax: (201)843-4636. E-mail: genesismag@aol.com. Website: www.genesismagazine.com. Editor: Paul Gambino. **Contact:** Dan Davis, managing editor. **85% freelance written.** "Monthly men's sophisticate with celebrity interviews, erotic and non-erotic fiction, exposé, product and media reviews, lifestyle pieces." Estab. 1974. Circ. 450,000. Pays on publication. Publishes ms an average of 3 months after acceptance. Byline given. Offers 50% kill fee. Buys first or second serial (reprint) rights. Editorial lead time 2 months. Submit seasonal material 6 months in advance. Accepts simultaneous submissions. Reports in 1 month on queries; 2 months on mss. Sample copy for $6.99. Writer's guidelines for #10 SASE.

Nonfiction: Book excerpts, exposé, general interest, how-to, humor, interview/profile, new product, personal experience, photo feature, film, music, book, etc., reviews, lifestyle pieces. "No investigative articles not backed up by facts." **Buys 24 mss/yr.** Send complete ms. Length: 150-2,500 words. **Pays 22¢/word.** Sometimes pays expenses of writers on assignment.

Reprints: Send tearsheet, photocopy of article or typed ms with rights for sale noted with information about when and where the article previously appeared. Pays 50% of amount paid for an original article.

Photos: State availability of photos with submission. Reviews 4×5 transparencies, 8×10 prints, slides. Negotiates payment individually. Captions, model releases and identification of subjects required. Buys first/exclusive rights.

Columns/Departments: Film/video/B movies (interviews, sidebars), music, books, all 150-500 words. **Buys 30 mss/year.** Query with published clips or send complete ms. Length: 2,500-3,500. **Pays 22¢/word.**

Fiction: Adventure, confession, erotica, fantasy, horror, humorous, mainstream, mystery, romance, science fiction, slice of life vignettes, suspense. Publishes novel excerpts. **Buys 36 mss/year.** Query or send complete ms. Length: 2,500-3,500 words. **Pays $500.**

Fillers: Anecdotes, facts, newsbreaks, short humor. **Buys 24/year.** Length: 25-500 words. **Pays 22¢/word ($50 minimum).**

Tips: "Be patient, original and detail-oriented."

★ $ $ GENT, "Home of the D-Cups," Firestone Publishing, Inc., 14411 Commerce Way, Suite 420, Miami Lakes FL 33016. Fax: (305)557-6005. E-mail: nye@dugent.com. Website: http://www.sexmags.com. Managing Editor: Nye Willden. **80% freelance written.** Monthly men's sophisticate magazine with emphasis on big breasts. Estab. 1960. Circ. 150,000. Pays on publication. Byline given. Buys first North American serial or second serial (reprint) rights.

Editorial lead time 4 months. Submit seasonal material 6 months in advance. Reports in 2 weeks on queries; 3 months on mss. Sample copy for $7. Writer's guidelines for #10 SASE.
Nonfiction: How-to ("anything sexually related"), personal experience ("any and all sexually related matters"). **Buys 13-26 mss/year.** Query. Length: 2,000-3,500 words. **Pays $300.**
Reprints: Send typed ms with rights for sale noted and information about when and where the article previously appeared. Pays 33% of amount paid for an original article.
Photos: Send photos with submission. Reviews 35mm transparencies. Negotiates payment individually. Model releases and identification of subjects required. Buys first North American with reprint rights.
Fiction: Erotica, fantasy. **Buys 26 mss/year.** Send complete ms. Length: 2,000-3,000 words. **Pays $200-250.**

$ $ GUYS, First Hand Ltd., P.O. Box 1314, Teaneck NJ 07666-3441. (201)836-9177. Fax: (201)836-5055. E-mail: firsthand3@aol.com. **Contact**: William Spencer, editor. **80% freelance written.** Bimonthly magazine of erotica for gay men. "A positive, romantic approach to gay sex." Estab. 1988. Circ. 100,000. Pays on publication. Publishes ms an average of 1 year after acceptance. Byline given. Buys first North American serial or all rights. Reports in 6 months. Sample copy for $5.50. Writer's guidelines for #10 SASE.
Fiction: Erotica. **Buys 72 mss/year.** Send complete ms. Length: 1,000-10,000 words. **Pays $75-250.**

$ $ $ $ HUSTLER, HG Inc., 8484 Wilshire Blvd., Suite 900, Beverly Hills CA 90211. Fax: (213)651-2741. Editor: Allan MacDonell. E-mail: ahaberman@lfp.com. Website: http://www.hustler.com. **Contact**: Aaron Haberman, associate editor. **60% freelance written.** Magazine published 13 times/year. "*Hustler* is the no-nonsense men's magazine. Our audience does not need to be told whether to wear their trousers cuffed or plain. The *Hustler* reader expects honest, unflinching looks at hard topics—sexual, social, political, personality profile, true crime." Estab. 1974. Circ. 750,000. Pays as boards ship to printer. Publishes ms an average of 3 months after acceptance. Byline given. Offers 20% kill fee. Buys all rights. Editorial lead time 4 months. Submit seasonal material 6 months in advance. Reports in 2 weeks on queries; 1 month on mss. Writer's guidelines for #10 SASE.

- *Hustler* is most interested in profiles of dynamic ground-breaking, indomitable individuals who don't mind "flipping a bird" at the world in general.

Nonfiction: Book excerpts, exposé, general interest, how-to, interview/profile, personal experience, trends. **Buys 30 mss/year.** Query. Length: 3,500-4,000 words. **Pays $1,500.** Sometimes pays expenses of writers on assignment.
Columns/Departments: Sex Play (some aspect of sex that can be encapsulated in a limited space), 2,500 words. **Buys 13 mss/year.** Send complete ms. **Pays $750.**
Fiction: "Difficult fiction market. Must have two sex scenes; yet not be rote or boring." Publishes novel excerpts. **Buys 2 mss/year.** Send complete ms. Length: 3,000-3,500. **Pays $1,000.**
Fillers: Pays $50-100. Jokes and "Graffilthy," bathroom-wall humor.
Tips: "Don't try and mimic the *Hustler* style. If a writer needs to be molded into our voice, we'll do a better job of it than he or she will."

N $ HUSTLER BUSTY BEAUTIES, America's Breast Magazine, HG Publications, Inc., 8484 Wilshire Blvd., Suite 900, Beverly Hills CA 90211. (213)651-5400. Fax: (213)651-2741. E-mail: busty@lfp.com. Website: http://www.hustler.com. **Contact:**N. Morgen Hagen, associate publisher. **40% freelance written.** Men's monthly sophisticate magazine. "*Hustler Busty Beauties* is an adult title that showcases attractive large-breasted women with accompanying erotic fiction, reader letters, humor." Estab. 1974. Circ. 180,000. Pays on publication. Publishes ms an average of 6 months after acceptance. Byline given. Buys all rights. Reports in 1 month. Sample copy for $6 and 9×12 SAE. Free writer's guidelines.
Columns/Departments: LewDDD Letters (erotic experiences involving large-breasted women from first-person point-of-view), 500-1,000 words. **Buys 24-36 mss year.** Send complete ms. **Pays $50-75.**
Fiction: Adventure, erotica, fantasy, humorous, mystery, science fiction, suspense. "No violent stories or stories without a bosomy female character." **Buys 12 mss year.** Send complete ms. Length: 750-2,500 words. **Pays $250-500.**
Jokes: Appropriate for audience. **Pays $10-25.**

$ IN TOUCH/INDULGE FOR MEN, In Touch International, Inc., 13122 Saticoy St., North Hollywood CA 91605-3402. (818)764-2288. Fax: (818)764-2307. E-mail: alan@intouchformen.com. Website: http://www.intouchformen.com. **Contact**: Alan W. Mills, editor. **80% freelance written.** Works with a small number of new/unpublished writers each year. Monthly magazine covering the gay male lifestyle, gay male humor and erotica. Estab. 1973. Circ. 70,000. Pays on publication. Byline given, pseudonym OK. Buys one-time rights. Accepts simultaneous submissions. Reports in 2 months. Sample copy for $6.95. Writer's guidelines for #10 SASE.
Nonfiction: Rarely buys nonfiction. Send complete ms. Length: 3,000-3,500 words. **Pays $25-75.**
Photos: Send photos with submission. Reviews contact sheets, transparencies, prints. Offers $25/photo. Captions, model releases, identification of subjects required. Buys one-time rights.
Fiction: Gay male erotica. **Buys 82 mss/year.** Send complete ms. Length: 3,000-3,500 words. **Pays $75 maximum.**
Fillers: Short humor. **Buys 12/year.** Length: 1,500-2,500 words. **Pays $25-50.**
Tips: "Our publications feature male nude photos plus three fiction pieces, several articles, cartoons, humorous comments on items from the media, photo features. We try to present positive aspects of the gay lifestyle, with an emphasis on humor. Humorous pieces may be erotic in nature. We are open to all submissions that fit our gay male format; the

emphasis, however, is on humor and the upbeat. We receive many fiction manuscripts but not nearly enough unique, innovative, or even experimental material."

$ $ NUGGET, Firestone Publishing Corp., 14411 Commerce Way, Suite 420, Miami Lakes FL 33016-1598. Fax: (305)557-6005. E-mail: editor-nugget@dugent.com. Website: http://www.dugent.com/nug/. Managing Editor: Nye Willden. **Contact:** Christopher James, editor-in-chief. **100% freelance written.** Monthly magazine covering fetish and kink. "*Nugget* is a one-of-a-kind publication which appeals to daring, open-minded adults who enjoy all forms of both kinky, alternative sex (catfighting, transvestism, fetishism, bi-sexuality, etc.) and conventional sex." Estab. 1960. Circ. 100,000. Pays on publication. Publishes ms an average of 1 year after acceptance. Byline given. Buys first North American serial rights. Editorial lead time 5 months. Submit seasonal material 1 year in advance. Accepts simultaneous submissions. Reports in 2 weeks on queries; 2 months on mss. Sample copy for $5. Writer's guidelines free.
Nonfiction: Interview/profile, sexual matters/trends (fetish and kink angle). **Buys 8 mss/year.** Query. Length: 2,000-3,000 words. **Pays $200 minimum.**
Photos: Send photos with submission. Reviews transparencies. Offers no additional payment for photos accepted with ms. Model releases required. Buys one-time second rights.
Fiction: Erotica, fantasy. **Buys 20 mss/year.** Send complete ms. Length: 2,000-3,000 words. **Pays $200-250.**
Tips: Most open to fiction submissions. (Follow guidelines for suitable topics.)

$ OPTIONS, AJA Publishing, P.O. Box 170, Irvington NY 10533. E-mail: dianaeditr@aol.com. Editor: Don Stone. **Contact**: Diana Sheridan, associate editor. Mostly freelance written. Sexually explicit magazine for and about bisexuals and to a lesser extent homosexuals, published 10 times/year. "Articles, stories and letters about bisexuality. Positive approach. Safe-sex encounters unless the story clearly pre-dates the AIDS situation." Estab. 1977. Circ. 100,000. Pays on publication. Publishes mss an average of 10 months after acceptance. Byline given, usually pseudonymous. Buys all rights. Buys almost no seasonal material. Reports in 3 weeks. Sample copy for $2.95 and 6×9 SAE with 5 first-class stamps. Writer's guidelines for SASE.
Nonfiction: Essays (occasional), how-to, humor, interview/profile, opinion, personal experience (especially). All must be bisexually or gay related. Does not want "anything not bisexually/gay related, anything negative, anything opposed to safe sex, anything dry/boring/ponderous/pedantic. Write even serious topics informally if not lightly." **Buys 10 nonfiction mss/year.** Send complete ms. Length: 2,000-3,000. **Pays $100.**
Photos: Reviews transparencies and prints. Pays $20 for b&w photos; $200 for full color. Color or b&w sets $150. Previously published photos acceptable.
Fiction: "We don't usually get enough true first-person stories and need to buy some from writers. They must be bisexual, usually man/man, hot and believable. They must not read like fiction." **Buys 70 fiction mss/year.** Send complete ms. Length: 2,000-3,000. **Pays $100.**
Tips: "We use many more male/male pieces than female/female. Use only one serious article per issue. A serious/humorous approach is good here, but only if it's natural to you; don't make an effort for it. No longer buying 'letters'. We get enough real ones."

$ $ $ $ PENTHOUSE, General Media, 277 Park Ave., 4th Floor, New York NY 10172-0033. (212)702-6000. Fax: (212)702-6279. Website: http://www.penthousemag.com. Editor: Peter Bloch. Monthly magazine. "*Penthouse* is for the sophisticated male. Its editorial scope ranges from outspoken contemporary comment to photography essays of beautiful women. *Penthouse* features interviews with personalities, sociological studies, humor, travel, food and wines, and fashion and grooming for men." Estab. 1969. Circ. 1,100,000. **Pays 2 months after acceptance.** Byline given. Offers 25% kill fee. Buys all rights. Editorial lead time 3 months. Accepts simultaneous submissions. Guidelines for #10 SASE.
Nonfiction: Exposé, general interest (to men), interview/profile. **Buys 50 mss/year.** Query with published clips or send complete ms. Length: 4,000-6,000. **Pays $3,000.**
Columns/Departments: Length: 1,000 words. **Buys 25 mss/year.** Query or send complete ms. **Pays $500.**
Fiction: L. Nahon, fiction editor. Erotica (written by women only).
Fillers: Buys 25/year. Length: 1,000. **Pays $500.**
Tips: "Because of our long lead time, writers should think at least 6 months ahead. We take chances. Go against the grain; we like writers who look under rocks and see what hides there."

$ $ $ $ PLAYBOY, 680 N. Lakeshore Dr., Chicago, IL 60611. Website: http://www.playboy.com. **Contact:** Articles Editor or Fiction Editor. Monthly. "As the world's largest general-interest lifestyle magazine for men, *Playboy* spans the spectrum of contemporary men's passions. From hard-hitting investigative journalism to light-hearted humor, the latest in fashion and personal technology to the cutting edge of the popular culture, *Playboy* is and always has been both guidebook and dream book for generations of American men. In addition, *Playboy*'s 'Interview' and '20 Questions' present profiles of politicians, athletes and today's hottest personalities." Estab. 1953. Circ. 3,283,000. Buys first North American serial rights. Editorial lead time 6 months. Reports in 1 month. Writer's guidelines for SASE. Query with SASE.
Nonfiction: "*Playboy* regularly publishes nonfiction articles on a wide range of topics—sports, politics, music, topical humor, personality profiles, business and finance, science and technology—and other topics that have a bearing on our readers' lifestyles." Length 4,000-5,000 words. **Pays $3,000 minimum.**
Tips: "*Playboy* is not a venue where beginning writers should expect to be published. Nearly all of our writers have

long publication histories. Aspiring writers should gain experience and an extensive file of by-lined features before approaching *Playboy*."

☆ $ $ **SWANK**, Swank Publications, 210 Route 4 E., Suite 401, Paramus NJ 07652. (201)843-4004. Fax: (201)843-8636. Website: www.swank.com. Editor: Paul Gambino. **Contact**: Peter Lauria, associate editor. **75% freelance written.** Works with new/unpublished writers. Monthly magazine on "sex and sensationalism, lurid. High quality adult erotic entertainment." Audience of men ages 18-38, high school and some college education, medium income, skilled blue-collar professionals, union men, some white-collar. Estab. 1954. Circ. 400,000. Pays on publication. Publishes ms an average of 4 months after acceptance. Byline given, pseudonym if wanted. Buys first North American serial rights. Submit seasonal material 6 months in advance. Reports in 3 weeks on queries; 1 month on mss. Sample copy for $6.95. Writer's guidelines for SASE.

• *Swank* reports a need for more nonfiction, non-sex-related articles.

Nonfiction: Exposé (researched), adventure must be accompanied by color photographs. "We buy articles on sex-related topics, which don't need to be accompanied by photos." Interested in unusual lifestyle pieces. How-to, interviews with entertainment, sports and sex industry celebrities. Buys photo pieces on autos, action, adventure. **Buys 34 mss/year.** Query with or without published clips. **Pays $350-500.** Sometimes pays the expenses of writers on assignment. "It is strongly recommended that a sample copy is reviewed before submitting material."

Reprints: Send photocopy or article or short story or typed ms with rights for sale noted and information and when and where the article previously appeared. Pays 50% of amount paid for an original article.

Photos: Bruce Perez, photo editor. Send photos. "If you have good photographs of an interesting adventure/lifestyle subject, the writing that accompanies is bought almost automatically." Model releases required.

Fiction: Publishes novel excerpts. "We will consider stories that are not strictly sexual in theme (humor, adventure, detective stories, etc.) However, these types of stories are much more likely to be considered if they portray some sexual element, or scene, within their context."

SPORTS

A variety of sports magazines, from general interest to sports medicine, are covered in this section. For the convenience of writers who specialize in one or two areas of sport and outdoor writing, the publications are subcategorized by the sport or subject matter they emphasize. Publications in related categories (for example, Hunting and Fishing; Archery and Bowhunting) often buy similar material. Writers should read through this entire section to become familiar with the subcategories. Publications on horse breeding and hunting dogs are classified in the Animal section, while horse racing is listed here. Publications dealing with automobile or motorcycle racing can be found in the Automotive and Motorcycle category. Markets interested in articles on exercise and fitness are listed in the Health and Fitness section. Outdoor publications that promote the preservation of nature, placing only secondary emphasis on nature as a setting for sport, are in the Nature, Conservation and Ecology category. Regional magazines are frequently interested in sports material with a local angle. Camping publications are classified in the Travel, Camping and Trailer category.

Archery and Bowhunting

$ $ **BOWHUNTER, The Number One Bowhunting Magazine**, Cowles Enthusiast Media, 6405 Flank Dr., Harrisburg PA 17112-8200. (717)657-9555. Fax: (717)657-9552. E-mail: bowhunter@cowles.com. Website: http://www.bowhunter.com. Founder/Editor-in-Chief: M.R. James. **Contact:** Richard Cochran, associate publisher/editorial director. **50% freelance written.** Bimonthly magazine (with three special issues) on hunting big and small game with bow and arrow. "We are a special interest publication, produced by bowhunters for bowhunters, covering all aspects of the sport. Material included in each issue is designed to entertain and inform readers, making them better bowhunters." Estab. 1971. Circ. 180,000. **Pays on acceptance.** Publishes ms an average of 1 year after acceptance. Byline given. Kill fee varies. Buys first North American serial and one-time rights. Submit seasonal material 8 months in advance. Reports in 1 month on queries; 5 weeks on mss. Sample copy for $2. Free writer's guidelines.

Nonfiction: General interest, how-to, interview/profile, opinion, personal experience, photo feature. "We publish a special 'Big Game' issue each Fall (September) but need all material by mid-March. Another annual publication, *Whitetail Bowhunter*, is staff written or by assignment only. Our latest special issue is the *Gear Guide*, which highlights the latest in equipment. We don't want articles that graphically deal with an animal's death. And, please, no articles written from the animal's viewpoint." **Buys 60 plus mss/year.** Query. Length: 250-2,000 words. **Pays $500 maximum for assigned articles; $100-400 for unsolicited articles.** Sometimes pays expenses of writers on assignment.

Photos: Send photos with submission. Reviews 35mm and $2\frac{1}{4} \times 2\frac{1}{4}$ transparencies and 5×7 and 8×10 prints. Offers

$75-250/photo. Captions required. Buys one-time rights.
Tips: "A writer must know bowhunting and be willing to share that knowledge. Writers should anticipate *all* questions a reader might ask, then answer them in the article itself or in an appropriate sidebar. Articles should be written with the reader foremost in mind; we won't be impressed by writers seeking to prove how good they are—either as writers or bowhunters. We care about the reader and don't need writers with 'I' trouble. Features are a good bet because most of our material comes from freelancers. The best advice is: Be yourself. Tell your story the same as if sharing the experience around a campfire. Don't try to write like you think a writer writes."

$ $ BOWHUNTING WORLD, Ehlert Publishing Group, Suite 600, 601 Lakeshore Parkway, Minnetonka MN 55305-5215. (612)476-2200. Fax: (612)476-8065. Contact: Mike Strandlund, editor. **70% freelance written.** Monthly magazine for bowhunting and archery enthusiasts who participate in the sport year-round. Estab. 1951. Circ. 130,000. **Pays on acceptance**. Publishes ms an average of 5 months after acceptance. Byline given. Buys first rights and reprint rights. Reports in 3 weeks on queries, 6 weeks on mss. Sample copy for $3 and 9×12 SAE with 10 first-class stamps. Writer's and photographers guidelines for SASE.
Nonfiction: How-to articles with creative slants on knowledgeable selection and use of bowhunting equipment and bowhunting methods. Articles must emphasize knowledgeable use of archery or hunting equipment, and/or specific bowhunting techniques. Straight hunting adventure narratives and other types of articles now appear only in special issues. Equipment-oriented articles must demonstrate wise and insightful selection and use of archery equipment and other gear related to the archery sports. Some product-review, field-test, equipment how-to and technical pieces will be purchased. We are not interested in articles whose equipment focuses on random mentioning of brands. Technique-oriented articles most sought are those that briefly cover fundamentals and delve into leading-edge bowhunting or recreational archery methods. Primarily focusing on retail archery and tournament coverage." **Buys 60 mss/year**. Query or send complete ms. Length: 1,500-3,000 words. **Pays $350 to over $500.**
Photos: "We are seeking cover photos that depict specific behavioral traits of the more common big game animals (scraping whitetails, bugling elk, etc.) and well-equipped bowhunters in action. Must include return postage."
Tips: "Writers are strongly advised to adhere to guidelines and become familiar with our format, as our needs are very specific. Writers are urged to query before sending packages. We prefer detailed outlines of six or so article ideas per query. Assignments are made for the next 18 months."

$ $ PETERSEN'S BOWHUNTING, Petersen Publishing Company, L.L.C., 6420 Wilshire Blvd., Los Angeles CA 90048-5515. (213)782-2179. Fax: (213)782-2477. Editor: Jay Michael Strangis. **Contact:** Joe Bell, associate editor. **70% freelance written.** Magazine published 8 times/year covering bowhunting. "Very equipment oriented. Our readers are 'superenthusiasts,' therefore our writers must have an advanced knowledge of hunting archery." Circ. 155,000. **Pays on acceptance.** Byline given. Buys all rights. Editorial lead time 6 months. Submit seasonal material 6 months in advance. Reports in 1 month. Sample copy for #10 SASE. Writer's guidelines free on request.
Nonfiction: How-to, humor, interview/profile, new product, opinion, personal experience, photo feature. **Buys 40 mss/year.** Send complete ms. Length: 2,000 words. **Pays $300.**
Photos: Send photos with submission. Reviews contact sheets, 35mm transparencies, 5×7 prints. Offers $35-250/photo. Captions and model releases required. Buys one-time rights.
Columns/Departments: Query. **Pays $200-300.**
Fillers: Facts, newsbreaks. Buys 12/year. Length: 150-400 words. Pays $25-75.
Tips: Feature articles must be supplied in either 5.25 IBM (or compatible) or 3.50 Mac floppy disks.

Baseball

N **$ $ BASEBALL AMERICA**, Baseball America Inc., P.O. Box 2089, Durham NC 27702. (919)682-9635. Fax: (919)682-2880. E-mail: ba@interpath.com. **Contact**: Steve Borelli, assistant editor. Editor: Allan Simpson. Managing Editor: Will Lingo. **10% freelance written.** Biweekly tabloid covering baseball. "*Baseball America* is read by industry insiders and passionate, knowledgeable fans. Writing should go beyond routine baseball stories to include more depth or a unique angle." Estab. 1981. Circ. 80,000. Pays on publication. Publishes ms an average of 2 months after acceptance. Byline given. Buys one-time rights. Editorial lead time 1 month. Submit seasonal material 2 months in advance. Accepts simultaneous submissions. Sample copy for $2.95.
Nonfiction: Historical/nostalgic, interview/profile, theme or issue-oriented baseball features. "No major league player features that don't cover new ground; superficial treatments of baseball subjects." **Buys 10 mss/year.** Send complete ms. Length: 100-2,000 words. **Pays $10-500 for assigned articles; $10-250 for unsolicited articles.**
Reprints: Accepts previously published submissions.
Photos: State availability of photos with submission. Negotiates payment individually. Identification of subjects required. Buys one-time rights.
Tips: "We use little freelance material, in part because we have a large roster of excellent correspondents and because much of what we receive is too basic or superficial for our readership. Sometimes writers stray too far the other way and get too arcane. But we're always interested in great stories that baseball fans haven't heard yet."

N $ $ JUNIOR LEAGUE BASEBALL, America's Youth Baseball Magazine, 2D Publishing, P.O. Box 9099, Canoga Park CA 91309. (818)710-1234. E-mail: editor@jlbmag.com. Website: http://www.jblmag.com. **Contact**: Dave Destler, editor. **25% freelance written.** Bimonthly magazine covering youth baseball. "Focused on youth baseball players ages 7 through 17 (including high school) and their parents/coaches. Edited to various reading levels, depending upon age/skill level of feature." Estab. 1996. Circ. 60,000. Pays on publication. Publishes ms an average of 4 months after acceptance. Byline given. Buys all rights. Editorial lead time 3 months. Submit seasonal material 3 months in advance. Accepts simultaneous submissions. Reports in 2 weeks on queries; 1 month on mss. Sample copy for $5 (also online). Writer's guidelines for #10 SASE.

Nonfiction: How-to (skills, tips, features, how to play better baseball, etc.), interview/profile (with major league players; only on assignment), personal experience (from coaches' or parents' perspective).When I Was a Kid (a current Major League Baseball player profile); Leagues, Tournaments (spotlighting a particular youth baseball league, organization, event, tournament); Industry (featuring businesses involved in baseball, e.g., how bats are made); Parents Feature (topics of interest to parents of youth ball players), all 1,000-1,500 words. In the Spotlight (news, events, new products), 50-100 words; League Notebook (news, events, new ideas or tips geared to the parent or league volunteer, adult level), 250-500 words; Hot Prospect (written for the 14-and older competitive player. High school baseball is included, and the focus is on improving the finer points of the game to make the high school team, earn a college scholarship, or attract scouts, written to an adult level), 500-1,000 words. **Buys 6 mss/year.** Query. **Pays $50-100.** "No trite first-person articles about your kid." **Buys 8-12 mss/year.** Query. Length: 500-1,500 words. **Pays 10-20¢/word.**

Photos: State availability of or send photos with submission. Reviews 35mm transparencies, 3×5 prints. Offers $10-100/photo; negotiates payment individually. Captions and identification of subjects required.

Tips: "Must be well-versed in baseball! Having a child who is very involved in the sport, or being a coach or manager, etc. Must know your stuff. This magazine is read by experts."

Basketball

N ☆ $ $ $ SLAM, Harris Publications, 1115 Broadway, 8th Floor, New York NY 10010. E-mail: annag@harris-pub.com. Website: http://www.slamonline.com. **Contact**: Anna Gebbie, managing editor. Editor: Tony Gerrino. **80% freelance written.** Published 8 times/year covering basketball, sports journalism with a hip-hop sensibility targeting ages 13-24. Estab. 1994. Circ. 200,000. Pays on publication. Publishes ms an average of 10 weeks after acceptance. Byline given. Offers 25% kill fee. Buys all rights. Writer's guidelines free.

Nonfiction: Interview/profile, team story. **Buys 150 mss/year.** Query with published clips. Length: 250-2,500 words. **Pays $100-1,000.** Sometimes pays expenses of writers on assignment.

Photos: State availability of photos with submission. Reviews transparencies. Negotiates payment individually. Buys all rights.

Tips: "Pitch profiles of unknown players; send queries not manuscripts; do not try to fake a hip-hop sensibility. *Never* contact the editor-in-chief. Story meetings are held every 6-7 weeks at which all submissions are considered."

Bicycling

☆ ADVENTURE CYCLIST, Adventure Cycling Assn., Box 8308, Missoula MT 59807. (406)721-1776. Fax: (406)721-8754. E-mail: acaeditor@aol.com. Website: http://www.adv-cycling.org. **Contact:** Daniel D'Ambrosio, editor. **75% freelance written.** Bicycle touring magazine for Adventure Cycling Association members published 9 times/year. Circ. 30,000. Pays on publication. Byline given. Buys first serial rights. Submit seasonal material 3 months in advance. Sample copy and guidelines for 9×12 SAE with 4 first-class stamps.

Nonfiction: Features include: U.S. or foreign tour accounts; special focus (on tour experience); how-to; humor; interview/profile; photo feature; technical; travel. **Buys 20-25 mss/year.** Query with published clips or send complete ms; include short bio with ms. Length: 800-2,500 words. Pay negotiable.

Reprints: Send photocopy of article.

Photos: Color transparencies should accompany tour accounts and profiles. Bicycle, scenery, portraits. State availability of photos. Model releases, identification of subjects required.

$ $ $ BICYCLING, Rodale Press, Inc., 33 E. Minor St., Emmaus PA 18098. (610)967-5171. Fax: (610)967-8960. E-mail: bicmag@aol.com. Website: http://www.bicyclingmagazine.com. Publisher: Mike Greehan. **Contact:** Stan Zukowski, managing editor. **20-25% freelance written.** Prefers to work with published/established writers. Magazine published 11 times/year. "*Bicycling* features articles about fitness, training, nutrition, touring, racing, equipment, clothing, maintenance, new technology, industry developments, and other topics of interest to committed bicycle riders. Editorially, we advocate for the sport, industry, and the cycling consumer." Estab. 1961. Circ. 280,000. **Pays on acceptance**. Byline given. Buys all rights. Submit seasonal material 6 months in advance. Reports in 2 months. Sample copy for $2.99. Writer's guidelines for #10 SASE.

Nonfiction: How-to (on all phases of bicycle touring, repair, maintenance, commuting, new products, clothing, riding technique, nutrition for cyclists, conditioning); fitness is more important than ever; also travel (bicycling must be central here); photo feature (on cycling events of national significance); and technical (component review—query). "We are strictly a bicycling magazine. We seek readable, clear, well-informed pieces. We sometimes run articles that are pure humor or inspiration and some of each might flavor even our most technical pieces. No poetry or fiction." **Buys 1-2 unsolicited mss/issue.** Send complete ms. Length: 1,500 words average. **Pays $25-1,200.** Sometimes pays expenses of writers on assignment.

Reprints: Occasionally accepts previously published submissions. Send photocopy or typed ms with information about when and where the article previously appeared.

Photos: State availability of photos with query letter or send photo material with ms. Pays $15-50 for b&w prints and $35-250 for transparencies. Captions preferred; model release required.

Fillers: Anecdotes and news items for Shorts section.

Tips: "We're alway seeking interesting accounts of cycling as a lifestyle."

N $ $ **BIKE MAGAZINE**, Surfer Publications, 33046 Calle Aviador, San Juan Capistrano CA 92675. (714)496-5922. Fax: (714)496-7849. **Contact**: Steve Casimiro, editor. **35% freelance written.** Magazine published 10 times/year covering mountain biking. Estab. 1993. Circ. 85,000. **Pays on acceptance**. Publishes ms an average of 2 months after acceptance. Byline given. Offers 25% kill fee. Buys first North American serial rights. Editorial lead time 4 months. Submit seasonal material 6 months in advance. Reports in 2 months. Sample copy for $8. Guidelines for #10 SASE.

Nonfiction: Humor, interview/profile, new product, personal experience, photo feature, technical, travel. No fiction. **Buys 20 mss/year.** Send complete ms. Length: 1,000-2,500 words. **Pays 40¢/word.** Sometimes pays expenses of writers on assignment.

Photos: Send photos with submission. Negotiates payment individually. Captions and identification of subjects required. Buys one-time rights.

Columns/Departments: Splatter (news), 600 words. **Buys 10 mss/year.** Send complete ms. **Pays 40¢/word.**

Tips: "Remember that we focus on hard core mountain biking, not beginners. We're looking for ideas that deliver the excitement and passion of the sport in ways that aren't common or predictable. Ideas should be vivid, unbiased, irreverent, probing, fun, humorous, funky, quirky, smart, good. Great feature ideas are always welcome, especially features on cultural matters or issues in the sport. However, you're much more likely to get published in *Bike* if you send us great ideas for short articles. In particular we need stories for our Splatter, a front-of-the-book section devoted to news, funny anecdotes, quotes, and odds and ends. These stories range from 50 to 700 words. We also need personality profiles of 600 words or so for our People Who Ride section. Racers are OK but we're more interested in grassroots people with interesting personalities—it doesn't matter if they're Mother Theresas or scumbags, so long as they make mountain biking a little more interesting. Short descriptions of great rides are very welcome for our travel column; the length should be from 700 to 900 words."

$ $ **BIKE RACING NATION**, (formerly *Cycling USA*), One Olympic Plaza, Colorado Springs CO 80909. (719)578-4581. Fax: (719)578-4596. E-mail: usacycling@aol.com. Website: http://www.usacycling.org. **Contact:** Kip Mikler and Frank Stanley, co-editors. **25% freelance written.** Monthly magazine covering reportage and commentary on American bicycle racing, personalities and sports physiology, for USCF licensed cyclists. Circ. 35,000. Pays on publication. Publishes ms an average of 2 months after acceptance. Byline given. Reports in 2 weeks. Sample copy for 10×12 SAE with 2 first-class stamps.

- *Bike Racing Nation* is looking for longer, more in-depth features (1,000-1,500 words).

Nonfiction: How-to (train, prepare for a bike race), interview/profile, opinion, personal experience, photo feature, technical and race commentary on major cycling events. No comparative product evaluations. **Buys 15 mss/year.** Query with published clips. Length: 800-1,200 words. **Pays 10¢/word.**

Reprints: Send photocopy of article. Pays 100% of amount paid for an original article.

Photos: State availability of photos. Pays $15-50 for 5×7 b&w prints; $100 for transparencies used as cover. Captions required. Buys one-time rights.

Tips: "A background in bicycle racing is important because the sport is somewhat insular, technical and complex. Most major articles are generated inhouse. Race reports are most open to freelancers. Be concise, informative and anecdotal. Our format is more compatible with 800-1,200 word articles than longer features."

$ **CRANKMAIL, Cycling in Northeastern Ohio**, P.O. Box 45346, Cleveland OH 44145-0346. Fax: (216)281-9933. E-mail: editor@crankmail.com. Website: http://www.crankmail.com. **Contact:** James Guilford, editor. Monthly magazine covering bicycling in all aspects. "Our publication serves the interests of bicycle enthusiasts . . . established, accomplished adult cyclists. These individuals are interested in reading about the sport of cycling, bicycles as transportation, ecological tie-ins, sports nutrition, the history and future of bicycles and bicycling." Estab. 1977. Circ. 1,000. Pays on publication. Byline given. Not copyrighted. Buys one-time or second serial (reprint) rights. Editorial lead time 1 month. Submit seasonal material 3 months in advance. Sample copy for $1. Writer's guidelines for #10 SASE.

Nonfiction: Essays, historical/nostalgic, how-to, humor, interview/profile, personal experience, technical. "No articles encouraging folks to start or get involved in bicycling—our readers are already cyclists." Send complete ms; no queries. Length: 600-1,800 words. **Pays $10 minimum for unsolicited articles.**

Reprints: Send typed ms with rights for sale noted and info about when and where it previously appeared.

Fiction: Publishes very short novel excerpts.

Fillers: Cartoons. **Pays $5-10.**

N $ $ CYCLE CALIFORNIA!, Advanced Project Management, P.O. Box 283, Mountain View CA 94042. (650)961-2663. Fax: (650)968-9030. E-mail: cycleca@cyclecalifornia.com. **Contact:** Tracy Corral, editor. **60% freelance written.** Magazine published 11 times/year "covering Northern California bicycling events, races, people. Issues (topics) covered include bicycle commuting, bicycle politics, touring, racing, nostalgia, history, anything at all to do with riding a bike." Estab. 1995. Circ. 25,500. Pays on publication. Publishes ms 3 months after acceptance. Byline given. Buys first North American serial rights. Editorial lead time 6 weeks. Submit seasonal material 6 weeks in advance. Accepts simultaneous submissions. Reports in 1 month. Sample copy for 10×13 SAE with 3 first-class stamps. Writer's guidelines for #10 SASE.

Nonfiction: Historical/nostalgic, interview/profile, opinion, personal experience, technical, travel. Special issues: Bicycle Tour & Travel (January/February). No articles about any sport that doesn't relate to bicycling, no product reviews. **Buys 36 mss/year.** Query with or without published clips. Length: 500-1,500 words. **Pays 3-10¢/word.** Sometimes pays expenses of writers on assignment.

Photos: Send photos with submission. Reviews 3×5 prints. Negotiates payment individually. Identification of subjects required. Buys one-time rights.

Columns/Departments: Buys 2-3 mss/year. Query with published clips. **Pays 3-10¢/word.**

Tips: "E-mail or call editor with good ideas. While we don't exclude writers from other parts of the country, articles really should reflect a Northern California slant, or be of general interest to bicyclists. We prefer stories written by people who like and use their bikes."

☆ $ DIRT RAG, A.K.A. Productions, 181 Saxonburg Rd., Pittsburgh PA 15238. (412)767-9910. Fax: (412)767-9920. E-mail: dirtrag@dirtragmag.com. Website: http://www.dirtragmag.com. Publisher: Maurice Tierney. **Contact:** Elaine Tierney, editor. **75% freelance written.** Mountain biking magazine published 7 times/year. "*Dirt Rag*'s style is much looser, fun and down to earth than mainstream (glossy) magazines on the same subject. We appeal to hard-core (serious) mountain bikers, and these people make our finest contributions. Avant-garde, humorous, off-beat, alternative." Estab. 1989. Circ. 30,000. Pays on publication. Byline given. No kill fee. Buys one-time rights. Accepts simultaneous submissions. Sample copy for 5 first-class stamps. Writer's guidelines for SASE.

Nonfiction: Book excerpts, essays, exposé, general interest, historical/nostalgic, how-to (bike maintenance, bike technique), humor, interview/profile, opinion, personal experience, photo feature, technical, travel (places to ride). Anything with mountain biking. **Buys 24 mss/year.** Query. **Pays $25-200.**

Reprints: Send typed ms with rights for sale noted and info about when and where it previously appeared.

Photos: Send art or photos with or without submission. Reviews contact sheets and/or prints. Offers additional payment for photos accepted with ms. $300 for color cover. $25 inside. Captions preferred. Buys one-time rights. Always looking for good photography and art regardless of subject.

Columns/Departments: Buys 14 mss/year. Query. **Pays $10-50.**

Fiction: Adventure, fantasy, historical, humorous, mainstream, slice-of-life vignettes. **Buys 1-10 mss/year.** Query. **Pays $25-100.**

Poetry: Avant-garde, free verse, light verse, traditional. **Pays $20-100.**

Fillers: Anecdotes, facts, gags, newsbreaks, short humor. **Buys 20/year. Pays $0-50.**

$ $ VELONEWS, The Journal of Competitive Cycling, 1830 55th St., Boulder CO 80301-2700. (303)440-0601. Fax: (303)444-6788. E-mail: vnedit@7dogs.com. Website: http://www.VeloNews.com/VeloNews. **Contact:** John Rezell, senior editor. **60% freelance written.** Monthly tabloid September-February, biweekly March-August covering bicycle racing. Estab. 1972. Circ. 48,000. Pays on publication. Publishes ms an average of 1 month after acceptance. Byline given. Buys one-time rights. Accepts simultaneous submissions. Reports in 3 weeks. Sample copy for 9×12 SAE with 7 first-class stamps.

Nonfiction: Freelance opportunities include race coverage, reviews (book and videos), health-and-fitness departments. **Buys 100 mss/year.** Query. Length: 300-1,200 words.

Reprints: Send typed ms with rights for sale noted and info about when and where it previously appeared.

Photos: State availability of photos. Pays $16.50-50 for b&w prints. Pays $200 for color used on cover. Captions and identification of subjects required. Buys one-time rights.

Boating

N $ $ BASS & WALLEYE BOATS, The Magazine of Performance Fishing Boats, Poole Publications, Inc., 20700 Belshaw Ave., Carson CA 90746. (310)537-6322. Fax: (310)537-8735. E-mail: bassboats@aol.com. **Contact:** Mike Blake, managing editor. Editor: Bruce Smith. **50% freelance written.** "*Bass & Walleye Boats* is published 8 times/year for the bass and walleye fisherman/boater. Directed to give priority to the boats, the tech, the how-to, the after-market add-ons and the devices that help anglers enjoy their boating experience." Estab. 1994. Circ. 70,000. **Pays on acceptance.** Publishes ms 3 months after acceptance. Byline given. Offers 25% kill fee. Buys all rights. Editorial lead time 2 months. Submit seasonal material 2 months in advance. Reports "A.S.A.P." Sample copy for $3.95 and 9×12 SAE with 7 first-class stamps. Writer's guidelines free.

Nonfiction: General interest, how-to, interview/profile, new product, personal experience, photo feature, technical,

travel. Special issues: Annual towing guide and new boats. No fiction. **Buys 120 mss/year.** Query. Length: 1,000-3,000 words. **Pays $300-700.** Sometimes pays expenses of writers on assignment.
Photos: State availability of photos with submission. Reviews 2¼×2¼ transparencies and 35mm slides. Negotiates payment individually. Captions and identification of subjects required. Buys one-time rights.
Columns/Departments: Product review (consumer report), Quick-fix (how-to), both 750 words, plus photos. **Buys 15/year.** Query. Pay varies.
Tips: "Write from and for the bass and walleye boaters' perspective."

N $ $ **BOATING FOR WOMEN**, K-111 Magazines, 249 W. 17th St., New York NY 10011. (212)462-3600. Fax: (212)367-8331. **Contact**: Amy Rapaport, editor-in-chief. **65% freelance written.** Quarterly "how-to, informational magazine on the sport of boating. Lifestyle and product." Estab. 1996. Circ. 180,000. **Pays on acceptance**. Publishes ms an average of 8 months after acceptance. Byline sometimes given. Offers 33% kill fee. Buys first North American serial rights, second serial (reprint) rights and electronic rights. Editorial lead time 6 months. Submit seasonal material 8 months in advance. Accepts simultaneous submissions. Sample copy free. Guidelines for #10 SASE.
Nonfiction: Humor, interview/profile, travel. **Buys 1 ms/year.** Query with published clips. Length: 800-1,200 words. **Pays $200-750 for assigned articles; $100-500 for unsolicited articles.** Sometimes pays expenses of writers on assignment.
Photos: Send photos with submission. Reviews transparencies, prints. Offers no additional payment for photos accepted with ms. Captions and identification of subjects required. Buys one-time rights.
Columns/Departments: Buys 10 mss/year. Query with published clips. **Pays $200-500.**

N $ $ **BOATING LIFE**, World Publications Inc., 330 W. Canton Ave., Winter Park FL 32789. (407)628-4802. Fax: (407)628-7061. E-mail: BB2@worldzine.com. **Contact**: Brett Becker, managing editor. Editor: Pierce Hoover. **30-40% freelance written.** Bimonthly. "Unlike the majority of boating publications, we are an entry-level, lifestyle title. As such, we focus on people, fun and basic boating skills rather than technical subjects or product reviews. We also demand a higher caliber of writing than has been the norm in the boating industry. In other words, we try not to use established 'boating writers,' and instead prefer qualified generalists who can bring color and excitement to the water." Estab. 1997. Circ. 110,000. **Pays on acceptance**. Publishes ms an average of 4 months after acceptance. Byline given. Offers 50% kill fee. Editorial lead time 4 months. Submit seasonal material 6 months in advance. Accepts simultaneous submissions. Reports in 1 month. Sample copy and writer's guidelines free.
Nonfiction: How-to, interview/profile, personal experience, photo feature, technical, travel. **Buys 24-30 mss/year.** Query with published clips. Length: 800-2,900 words. **Pays $300-750 for assigned articles; $100-500 for unsolicited articles.**
Photos: State availability of photos with submission. Reviews transparencies. Offers $50-500/photo. Captions, model releases and identification of subjects required.
Columns/Departments: Boat Maintenance, Boat Handling, Boating-related lifestyle (power boat only). **Buys 12 mss/year.** Query with published clips. **Pays $100-500.**
Fillers: Anecdotes. **Buys 6/year.** Length: 200-450 words. **Pays $200.**
Tips: "Our focus is 90 percent fresh water, 10 percent coastal. We avoid straight travelogues and instead favor activity or personality-based stories. The general tone is light and conversational, but all articles should in some way help the reader through the boat buying or owning process, and/or promote some aspect of the "boating lifestyle."

N ✪ $ $ **CANOE & KAYAK MAGAZINE**, Canoe America Associates, 10526 NE 68th St., Kirkland WA 98034. (425)827-6363. Fax: (425)827-1893. E-mail: bryan@canoekayak.com. Website: http://www.canoekayak.com. **Contact:** Michelle Funk, associate editor. Editor: Bryan Chitwood. Editor-in-Chief: Jan Nesset. **75% freelance written.** Bimonthly magazine. "*Canoe & Kayak Magazine* is North America's #1 paddlesports resource. Our readers include flatwater and whitewater canoeists and kayakers of all skill levels. We provide comprehensive information on destinations, technique and equipment. Beyond that, we cover canoe and kayak camping, safety, the environment, and the history of boats and sport." Estab. 1972. Circ. 90,000. Pays on publication. Publishes ms an average of 6 months after acceptance. Byline given. Offers 50% kill fee. Buys first North American serial rights or one-time rights. Editorial lead time 4 months. Submit seasonal material 6 months in advance. Reports in 2 months. Sample copy and writer's guidelines for 9×12 SAE with 7 first-class stamps.
Nonfiction: Historical/nostalgic, how-to (canoe, kayak camp; load boats; paddle whitewater, etc.), personal experience, photo feature, technical, travel. Annuals: Whitewater Paddling; Beginner's Guide; Kayak Touring; Canoe Journal. "No cartoons, stories in which bad judgment is portrayed or 'Me and Molly' articles." **Buys 20 mss/year.** Query with or without published clips or send complete ms. Length: 400-2,500 words. **Pays $25-800 for assigned articles; $25-450 for unsolicited articles.** Sometimes pays the expenses of writers on assignment.
Photos: State availability of or send photos with submission. "Good photos help sell a story." Reviews 35mm transparencies and 4×6 prints. "Some activities we cover are canoeing, kayaking, canoe fishing, camping, canoe sailing or poling, backpacking (when compatible with the main activity) and occasionally inflatable boats. We are not interested in groups of people in rafts, photos showing disregard for the environment, gasoline-powered, multi-horsepower engines unless appropriate to the discussion, or unskilled persons taking extraordinary risks." Offers $25-350/photo. Captions, model releases and identification of subjects required. Buys one-time rights.
Columns/Departments: Put In (environment, conservation, events), 650 words; Destinations (canoe and kayak desti-

nations in US, Canada), 1,500 words; Traditions (essays: traditional paddling), 750 words. **Buys 40 mss/year.** Query with or without published clips or send complete ms. **Pays $175-350.**

Fillers: Anecdotes, facts, newsbreaks. **Buys 20/year.** Length: 500-1,000 words. **Pays $5/column inch.**

Tips: "Start with Put-In articles (short featurettes), book reviews, or short, unique equipment reviews. Or give us the best, most exciting article we've ever seen—with great photos. Short Strokes is also a good entry forum focusing on short trips on good waterways accessible to lots of people. Focusing more on technique and how-to articles."

N $ $ $ CHESAPEAKE BAY MAGAZINE, Boating at Its Best, Chesapeake Bay Communications, 1819 Bay Ridge Ave., Annapolis MD 24403. Fax: (410)267-6924. E-mail: cbmeditor@aol.com. **Contact:** Tim Sayles, editor. Managing Editor: Jim Duffy. **40% freelance written.** Monthly magazine covering boating and the Chesapeake Bay. "Our readers are boaters. Our writers should know boats and boating. Read the magazine before submitting." Estab. 1972. Circ. 60,000. **Pays on acceptance.** Publishes ms 4 months after acceptance. Byline given. Buys first North American serial rights. Editorial lead time 1 year. Submit seasonal material 1 year in advance. Accepts simultaneous submissions. Reports in 2 months on queries; 3 months on mss. Sample copy for $5.19 prepaid.

Nonfiction: Essays, historical/nostalgic, how-to, new product, personal experience, travel. **Buys 20 mss/year.** Query with published clips. Length: 500-2,000 words. **Pays $250-1,000.** Pays expenses of writers on assignment.

Photos: Offers $45-150/photo. Captions, model releases and identification of subjects required. Buys one-time rights.

$ $ $ CRUISING WORLD, Cruising World Publications, Inc., Box 3400, Newport RI 02840-0992. (401)847-1588. **Contact:** Bernadette Bernon, editorial director. **70% freelance written.** Monthly magazine for all those who cruise under sail. Circ. 146,000. **Pays on acceptance.** Publishes ms an average of 8 months after acceptance. Offers variable kill fee, $50-150. Buys first North American periodical rights or first world periodical rights. Reports in about 2 months. Writer's guidelines free.

Nonfiction: Book excerpts, how-to, humor, inspirational, opinion, personal experience. "We are interested in seeing informative articles on the technical and enjoyable aspects of cruising under sail, especially seamanship, navigation and how-to." **Buys 135-140 unsolicited mss/year.** Submit complete ms. Length: 500-3,500 words. **Pays $150-800.**

Photos: 35mm slides purchased with accompanying ms. Captions and identification of subjects required. Buys one-time rights.

Columns/Departments: People & Food (recipes for preparation aboard sailboats); Shoreline (sailing news, vignettes); Workbench (projects for upgrading your boat). Send complete ms. Length: 150-500 words. **Pays $25-150.**

Tips: "Cruising stories should be first-person narratives. In general, authors must be sailors who read the magazine. Color slides always improve a ms's chances of acceptance. Technical articles should be well-illustrated."

$ CURRENTS, Voice of the National Organization for Rivers, 212 W. Cheyenne Mountain Blvd., Colorado Springs CO 80906. (719)579-8759. Fax: (719)576-6238. E-mail: nors@rmi.net. Website: http://www.nors.org. **Contact:** Greg Moore, Eric Leaper, editors. 25% freelance written. Quarterly magazine covering river running (kayaking, rafting, river canoeing). Estab. 1979. Circ. 5,000. Pays on publication. Publishes ms an average of 6 months after acceptance. Byline given. Offers 25% kill fee. Buys first North American serial, first and one-time rights. Submit seasonal material 4 months in advance. Reports in 2 weeks on queries; 1 month on mss. Sample copy for $1 and 9×12 SAE with 3 first-class stamps. Writer's guidelines for #10 SASE.

Nonfiction: How-to (run rivers and fix equipment), in-depth reporting on river conservation and access issues and problems, humor (related to rivers), interview/profile (any interesting river runner), opinion, personal experience, technical, travel (rivers in other countries). "We tell river runners about river conservation, river access, river equipment, how to do it, when, where, etc." No trip accounts without originality; no stories about "my first river trip." **Buys 20 mss/year.** Query with or without clips. Length: 500-2,500 words. **Pays $35-150.**

Reprints: Accepts previously published submissions, if so noted.

Photos: State availability of photos. Pays $35-50. Reviews color prints or photos on disk. Captions and identification of subjects (if racing) required. Buys one-time rights. Captions must include names of the river and rapid.

Columns/Departments: Book and film reviews (river-related). **Buys 5 mss/year.** Query with or without clips, or send complete ms. Length: 100-500 words. **Pays $25.**

Fiction: Adventure (river). Buys 2 mss/year. Query. Length: 1,000-2,500 words. Pays $35-75. "Must be well-written, on well-known river and beyond the realm of possibility."

Fillers: Clippings, jokes, gags, anecdotes, short humor, newsbreaks. Must be related to river running. **Buys 5/year.** Length: 25-100 words. **Pays $5-10.**

Tips: "We need more material on river news—proposed dams, wild and scenic river studies, accidents, etc. If you can provide brief (300-500 words) on these subjects, you will have a good chance of being published. Material must be on rivers. Go to a famous river and investigate it; find out something we don't know—especially about rivers that are *not* in Colorado or adjacent states—we already know about those."

$ $ GO BOATING MAGAZINE, Fun for the Whole Family, Duncan McIntosh Co., 17782 Cowan, Suite C, Irvine CA 92614. (714)660-6150. Fax: (714)660-6172. Website: goboatingmag.com.. **Contact:** Erin McNiff, managing editor. **60% freelance written.** Published 6 times/year covering family power boating. Typical reader "owns a power boat between 14-25 feet long and has for 3-9 years. Boat reports that appear in *GO Boating* are designed to give readers a quick look at a new model. They must be lively, entertaining and interesting to our savvy boat-owning readership." Estab. 1997. Circ. 100,000. Pays on publication. Publishes ms an average of 3-6 months after acceptance. Byline given.

Buys first North American serial rights. Editorial lead time 3 months. Submit seasonal material 4 months in advance. Accepts simultaneous submissions. Reports in 3 months. Sample copy free. Writer's guidelines for #10 SASE.
Nonfiction: General interest, how-to, humor, new product, personal experience, travel. **Buys 10-15 mss/year.** Query. Length: 1,000-1,200 words. **Pays $150-400.** Sometimes pays expenses of writers on assignment.
Photos: State availability of photos with submission. Reviews transparencies and prints. Offers $50-250/photo. Model releases and identification of subjects required. Buys one-time rights.
Columns/Departments: Buys 10 mss/year. Query. **Pays $150-350.**
Fillers: Anecdotes, facts and newsbreaks. **Buys 10/year.** Length: 250-500 words. **Pays $50-100.**
Tips: "Every vessel has something about it that makes it stand apart from all the others. Tell us what makes this boat different from all the rest on the market today. Include specifications and builder's address and phone number. See past issues for format."

HEARTLAND BOATING, The Waterways Journal, Inc., 319 N. Fourth St., Suite 650, St. Louis MO 63102. (314)241-4310. Fax: (314)241-7354. E-mail: hlboating@aol.com. **Contact:** Carol-Faye McDonald, editor. Estab. 1988. **50% freelance written.** Magazine published 7 times/year during boating season. "*Heartland Boating*'s content is both informative and humorous—describing boating life as the heartland boater knows it. We are boating and enjoying the outdoor, water-oriented way of life. The content reflects the challenge, joy and excitement of our way of life afloat. We are devoted to both power and sail boating enthusiasts throughout middle America; houseboats are included. The focus is on the freshwater inland rivers and lakes of the Heartland, primarily the Tennessee, Cumberland, Ohio, Missouri and Mississippi rivers and the Tennessee-Tombigbee Waterway." Circ. 15,000. Pays on publication. Publishes ms an average of 3 months after acceptance. Byline given. Buys first North American serial and sometimes second serial (reprint) rights. Submit seasonal material 6 months in advance. Accepts simultaneous submissions. Reports in 4 months. Sample copy for $5. Free writer's guidelines.
Nonfiction: General interest, historical/nostalgic, how-to, humor, interview/profile, new product, personal experience, photo feature, technical, travel. Special issue: Houseboats (May). **Buys 20-40 mss/year.** Query with or without published clips. Length: 800-2,000 words. Negotiates payment.
Reprints: Send photocopy of article or typed ms and information about where and when it previously appeared. Pays 50% of amount paid for an original article.
Photos: Send photos with query. Reviews contact sheets, transparencies. Buys one-time rights.
Columns/Departments: Buys 50 mss/year. Query. Negotiates payment.

$ $ HOT BOAT, LFP Publishing, 8484 Wilshire Blvd., Suite 900, Beverly Hills CA 90211. (213)651-5400. Fax: (213)651-1201. **Contact:** Brett Bayne, executive editor. **50% freelance written.** Monthly magazine on performance boating (16-35 feet), water skiing and water sports in general. "We're looking for concise, technically oriented 'how-to' articles on performance modifications; personality features on interesting boating-oriented personalities, and occasional event coverage." Circ. 90,000. Pays upon publication. Publishes ms an average of 2 months after acceptance. Byline given. Offers 40% kill fee. Buys all rights; also reprint rights occasionally. Submit seasonal material 3 months in advance. Reports in 3 weeks on queries; 1 month on mss. Sample copy for $3 and 9×12 SAE with $1.35 postage.
Nonfiction: How-to (increase horsepower, perform simple boat related maintenance), humor, interview/profile (racers and manufacturers), new product, personal experience, photo feature, technical. "Absolutely no sailing—we deal strictly in powerboating." **Buys 30 mss/year.** Query with published clips. Length: 500-2,000 words. **Pays $75-450.** Sometimes pays expenses of writers on assignment.
Reprints: Pays $150-200/printed page.
Photos: Send photos with submission. Reviews transparencies. Captions, model releases, identification of subjects required. Buys all rights.
Tips: "We're always open to new writers. If you query with published clips and we like your writing, we can keep you on file even if we reject the particular query. It may be more important to simply establish contact. Once we work together there will be much more work to follow."

$ $ LAKELAND BOATING, The Magazine for Great Lakes Boaters, O'Meara-Brown Publications, 500 Davis St., Suite 1000, Evanston IL 60201-4802. (847)869-5400. Fax: (847)869-5989. E-mail: lbonline@aol.com. Associate Editor: Chad Schegel. **Contact:** Randy Hess, editor. **50% freelance written.** Monthly magazine covering Great Lakes boating. Estab. 1946. Circ. 60,000. Pays on publication. Byline given. Buys first North American serial rights. Reports in 4 months. Sample copy for $5.50 and 9×12 SAE with 6 first-class stamps. Guidelines for #10 SASE.
Nonfiction: Book excerpts, historical/nostalgic, how-to, interview/profile, personal experience, photo feature, technical, travel. No inspirational, religious, expose or poetry. Must relate to boating in Great Lakes. **Buys 20-30 mss/year.** Query. Length: 800-3,500 words. **Pays $100-600.**
Photos: State availability of photos. Reviews transparencies; prefers 35mm. Captions required. Buys one-time rights.
Columns/Departments: Bosun's Locker (technical or how-to pieces on boating), 100-1,000 words. **Buys 40 mss/year.** Query. **Pays $30-100.**

N $ NORTHERN BREEZES, SAILING MAGAZINE, Northern Breezes, Inc., 245 Brunswick Ave. S., Golden Valley MN 55416. (612)542-9707. Fax: (612)542-8998. E-mail: thomnbreez@aol.com. **Contact:** Gloria Peck, editor. Managing Editor: Thom Burns. **70% freelance written.** Regional monthly sailing magazine for the Upper Midwest. Estab. 1989. Circ. 22,300. Pays on publication. Byline given. Buys first North American serial rights. Editorial lead time 1 month. Submit seasonal material 3 months in advance. Reports in 1 month on queries; 2 months on mss. Sample copy and writer's guidelines free.

Nonfiction: Book excerpts, how-to (sailing topics), humor, inspirational, interview/profile, new product, personal experience, photo feature, technical, travel. No boat reviews. **Buys 24 mss/year.** Query with published clips. Length: 300-2,000 words. **Pays $25-100.**

Reprints: Accepts previously published submissions.

Photos: Send photos with submission. Reviews negatives, 35mm slides, 3×5 or 4×6 prints. Offers no additional payment for photos accepted with ms or negotiates payment individually. Captions required. Buys one-time rights.

Columns/Departments: This Old Boat (sailboat), 500-1,000 words; Surveyor's Notebook, 500-800 words. **Buys 8 mss/year.** Query with published clips. **Pays $25-100.**

Tips: "Query with a regional connection already in mind."

$ NOR'WESTING, Nor'westing Publications, Inc., P.O. Box 70608, Seattle WA 98107. (206)783-8939. Fax: (206)783-9011. **Contact:** Peter Worthington, editor. **75% freelance written.** Monthly magazine. "We want to pack our pages with cruising articles, special Northwest destinations, local boating personalities, practical boat maintenance tips." Estab. 1965. Circ. 9,000. Pays 1 month after publication. Publishes timely ms an average of 2 months after acceptance. Byline given. Buys first North American serial rights. Editorial lead time 3 months. Submit seasonal material 3 months in advance. Accepts simultaneous submissions; note where else it's being submitted. Reports in 2 months. Sample copy and writer's guidelines for large SASE.

Nonfiction: History, how-to (boat outfitting, electronics, fish, galley), interview/profile (boater personalities), new product, personal experience (cruising), photo feature, technical, travel (local destinations). **Buys 35-40 mss/year.** Send complete ms or query. Length: 1,500-3,000 words. **Pays $100-150.**

Reprints: Accepts previously published submissions if "reworked, timely and pertain to our cruising area." Send tearsheet of article with rights for sale noted and information about when and where the article previously appeared. Payment varies.

Photos: Send photos with submission. Reviews transparencies, 3×5 prints. Negotiates payment individually. Identification of subjects required. Normally buys one-time rights.

Columns/Departments: Trailerboating (small craft boating—tech/destination), 700-900 words; Galley Ideas (cooking afloat—recipes/ideas), 700-900 words; Hardwired (Boating Electronics), 1,000 words; Cruising Fisherman (Fishing tips, destinations), 700-900 words. **Buys 36-40 mss/year.** Query with published clips. **Pays $50-75.**

Fiction: Publishes novel excerpts.

Tips: "Include specifics of destinations—how many moorage buoys, cost for showers, best time to visit. Any hazards to watch for while approaching? Why bother going if excitement for area/boating doesn't shine through?"

$ $ OFFSHORE, Northeast Boating at its Best, Offshore Communications, Inc., 220-9 Reservoir St., Needham MA 02194. (781)449-6204. Fax: (781)449-9702. E-mail: offeditor@aol.com. **Contact:** Betsy Haggerty, editor. Estab. 1976. **80% freelance written.** Monthly magazine covering power and sail boating and the coast from Maine to New Jersey. Circ. 35,000. Publishes ms an average of 3-5 months after acceptance. Byline given. Offers negotiable kill fee. Buys first North American serial rights. Submit seasonal material 6 months in advance. Accepts simultaneous submissions. Reports in 2 weeks. *Writer's Market* recommends allowing 2 months for reply. Sample copy for 10×13 SAE with 8 first-class stamps. Writer's guidelines for #10 SASE.

Nonfiction: Articles on boats, boating, New York, New Jersey and New England coastal places and people, northeast coastal history. Thumbnail and/or outline of topic will elicit immediate response. **Buys 90 mss/year.** Query with writing sample or send complete ms. Length: 1,800-2,500 words. **Pays approximately $400 for features depending on length.**

Reprints: Send photocopy of article or short story, or typed ms with rights for sale noted and information about when and where the article previously appeared. Pay negotiable.

Fiction: Boat-related fiction.

Photos: Reviews 35mm slides only. For covers, pays $300. Pays $125-150 for last-page photos—humorous or whimsical nautical subjects. Identification of subjects required. Buys one-time rights.

Tips: "Demonstrate familiarity with boats or region and ability to recognize subjects of interest to regional boat owners. Those subjects need not be boats. *Offshore* is serious but does not take itself as seriously as most national boating magazines. We are always open to new people, the best of whom may gradually work their way into regular writing assignments. Important to ask for (and follow) our writer's guidelines if you're not familiar with our magazine."

$ $ PACIFIC YACHTING, Western Canada's Premier Boating Magazine, OP Publishing Ltd., 780 Beatty St., Suite 300, Vancouver, British Columbia V6B 2M1 Canada. (604)606-4644. Fax: (604)687-1925. E-mail: oppubl@istar.ca. **Contact:** Duart Snow, editor. **90% freelance written.** Monthly magazine covering all aspects of recreational boating on British Columbia coast. "The bulk of our writers and photographers not only come from the local boating community, many of them were long-time PY readers before coming aboard as a contributor. The PY reader buys the magazine to read about new destinations or changes to old haunts on the B.C. coast and to learn the latest about boats and gear." Circ. 14,598. Pays on publication. Publishes ms an average of 6 months after acceptance. Byline given. Buys first North American serial and simultaneous rights. Editorial lead time 4 months. Submit seasonal material 6 months in advance. "We prefer electronic submissions by disk or modem." Sample copy for $2 plus postage charged to VISA credit card. Writer's guidelines free.

Nonfiction: Historical/nostalgic, how-to, humor, interview/profile, personal experience, travel, cruising and destina-

tions on the B.C. coast. "No articles from writers who are obviously not boaters!" Length: 2,000 words. Query with SAE and IRCs or by e-mail or phone. **Pays $150-500.** Pays expenses of writers on assignment if arranged in advance.
Photos: Send sample photos with query. Reviews transparencies, 4×6 prints and slides. Offers no additional payment for photos accepted with ms and $25-300/photo not accepted with ms. Identification of subjects required. Buys one-time rights. Covers: (transparencies): $300.
Columns/Departments: Currents (current events, coast guard and other government updates, trade and people news, boat gatherings and festivities), 50-250 words. Query Tonnae Hennigan, editorial assistant. Other departments, 800-1,000 words. Query. Pay varies.
Tips: "We strongly encourage queries before submission (written with SAE and IRCs, or by phone or e-mail). While precise nautical information is important, colorful anecdotes bring your cruise to life. Both are important. In other words, our reader wants you to balance important navigation details with first-person observations, blending the practical with the romantic. Write tight, write short, write with the reader in mind, write to inform, write to entertain. Be specific, accurate and historic."

N $ $ PONTOON & DECK BOAT, Harris Publishing, Inc., 520 Park Ave., Idaho Falls ID 83402. (208)524-7000. Fax: (208)522-5241. E-mail: steve@houseboating.net. Website: http://www.houseboating.net. **Contact:** Steve Smede, editor. **15% freelance written**. "We are a bimonthly boating niche publication geared towards the pontoon and deck boating lifestyle and consumer market. Our audience is comprised of people who utilize these boats for varied family activities and fishing. Our magazine is promotional of the PDB industry and its major players. We seek to give the reader a twofold reason to read our publication. To celebrate the lifestyle and to do it aboard a first-class craft." Estab. 1995. Circ. 82,000. Pays on publication. Byline given. Buys one-time rights. Editorial lead time 2 months. Submit seasonal material 3 months in advance. Accepts simultaneous submissions. Reports in 6 weeks on queries; 3 months on mss. Sample copy and writer's guidelines free.
Nonfiction: How-to, personal experience, technical, remodeling, rebuilding. "We are saturated with travel pieces, no general boating, no humor, no fiction, poetry." **Buys 15 mss/year**. Query or send complete ms. Length: 600-2,000 words. **Pays $50-300**. Sometimes pays expenses of writers on assignment.
Photos: State availability of photos. Reviews transparencies. Captions, model releases required. Rights negotiable.
Columns/Departments: Miracle Makeover (do it yourself innovations); Family At Large (family experiences); Better Boater (how-to). **Buys 6-12 mss/year**. Query with published clips. **Pays $50-150**.
Tips: "Be specific to pontoon and deck boats. Any general boating material goes to the slush pile. The more you can tie together the lifestyle, attitudes and the PDB industry, the more interest we'll take in what you send us."

$ $ POWER BOATING CANADA, 2585 Skymark Ave., Unit 306, Mississauga, Ontario L4W 4L5 Canada. (905)624-8218. Fax: (905)624-6764. **Contact:** Peter Tasler, editor. **70% freelance written.** Bimonthly magazine covering recreational power boating. "*Power Boating Canada* offers boating destinations, how-to features, boat tests (usually staff written), lifestyle pieces—with a Canadian slant—and appeal to recreational power boaters across the country." Estab. 1984. Circ. 50,000. Pays on publication. Publishes ms an average of 3 months after acceptance. Byline given. Buys first North American serial rights. Editorial lead time 2 months. Submit seasonal material 3 months in advance. Reports in 1 month on queries, 2 months on mss. Sample copy free.
Nonfiction: "Any articles related to the sport of power boating, especially boat tests." Historical/nostalgic, how-to, interview/profile, personal experience, travel (boating destinations). No general boating articles or personal anecdotes. **Buys 40-50 mss/year.** Query. Length: 1,200-2,500 words. **Pays $150-300.** Sometimes pays expenses of writers on assignment.
Reprints: Send photocopy of article or typed ms with rights for sale noted and information about when and where the article previously appeared.
Photos: Send photos with submission. Reviews contact sheets, negatives, transparencies, prints. No additional payment for photos accepted with ms. Captions, identification of subjects required. Buys one-time rights. Pay varies.

$ $ $ SAIL, 84 State St., Boston MA 02109-2262. (617)720-8600. Fax: (617)723-0912. E-mail: sailmail@channel1.com. Editor: Patience Wales. **Contact:** Amy Ullrich, managing editor. **50% freelance written.** Works with a small number of new/unpublished writers each year. Monthly magazine "written and edited for everyone who sails—aboard a coastal or bluewater cruiser, trailerable, one-design or offshore racer, or daysailer. How-to and technical articles concentrate on techniques of sailing and aspects of design and construction, boat systems, and gear; the feature section emphasizes the fun and rewards of sailing in a practical and instructive way." Estab. 1970. Circ. 180,000. **Pays on acceptance.** Publishes ms an average of 10 months after acceptance. Buys first North American rights. Submit seasonal or special material at least 6 months in advance. Reports in 10 weeks. Writer's guidelines for SASE.
Nonfiction: Technical, techniques, how-to, personal experience, distance cruising, destinations. "Generally emphasize the excitement of sail and the human, personal aspect. No logs." Length: 1,500-3,000 words. Examples of shorter features are: vignettes of day sailing, cruising and racing life (at home or abroad, straight or humorous); maritime history; astronomy; marine life; cooking; nautical love; fishing; boat owning, boat building and outfitting; regatta reports. Length: 1,000-1,500 words. Special issues: "Cruising, chartering, fitting-out, special race (e.g., America's Cup), boat show." **Buys 100 mss/year** (freelance and commissioned). Query with SASE. **Pays $200-800.** Sometimes pays the expenses of writers on assignment.
Reprints: Send photocopy of article or typed ms with rights for sale noted and information about when and where the article previously appeared. Pays 33-50% of amount paid for an original article.

Photos: Offers additional payment for photos. Uses 50-100 ASA transparencies. Identification of subjects, captions and credits required. Pay varies, on publication. Pays $600 if photo is used on the cover.
Columns/Departments: Sailing Memories (short essay); Sailing News (cruising, racing, legal, political, environmental). Query.
Tips: "Request an articles specification sheet."

"We look for unique ways of viewing sailing. Skim old issues of *Sail* for ideas about the types of articles we publish. Always remember that *Sail* is a sailing magazine. Stay away from gloomy articles detailing all the things that went wrong on your boat. Think constructively and write about how to avoid certain problems. You should focus on a theme or choose some aspect of sailing and discuss a personal attitude or new philosophical approach to the subject. Notice that we have certain issues devoted to special themes—for example, chartering, electronics, commissioning, and the like. Stay away from pieces that chronicle your journey in the day-by-day style of a logbook. These are generally dull and uninteresting. Select specific actions or events (preferably sailing events, not shorebound activities), and build your articles around them. Emphasize the sailing."

$ $ SAILING MAGAZINE, 125 E. Main St., Port Washington WI 53074-0249. (414)284-3494. Fax: (414)284-7764. E-mail: 75553.3666@compuserv.com. Website: http://www.sailnet.com/sailing. **Contact:** Micca Leffingwell Hutchins, editor. Publisher: William F. Schanen, III. Monthly magazine for the experienced sailor. Estab. 1966. Circ. 52,000. Pays on publication. Buys one-time rights. Reports in 2 months.
Nonfiction: "Experiences of sailing—cruising, racing or learning, including recent (within one year) cruising article with photos; boat profiles (full pictorial essays of particular outstanding yachts, historical or otherwise); regattas (all current types, but only if there really is a story to the event). No pictures of award ceremonies, please." Must be written to AP Stylebook. **Buys 8 mss/year.** Length: 750-1,500 words. Must be accompanied by photos, and maps if applicable. **Pays $75-300.**
Photos: Color photos (transparencies) purchased with or without accompanying text. Captions required. Pays $50-100.
Tips: Prefers text in Word on disk for Mac or to e-mail address.

$ $ SAILING WORLD, N.Y. Times Magazine Group, 5 John Clarke Rd., Box 3400, Newport RI 02840-0992. Fax: (401)848-5048. E-mail: editor@sailingworld.com. Website: http://www.sailingworld.com. Editor: John Burnham. **Contact:** Kristan McClintock, managing editor. **40% freelance written.** Monthly magazine emphasizing performance sailing. Estab. 1962. Circ. 62,678. Pays on publication. Publishes ms an average of 4 months after acceptance. Buys first North American and world serial rights. Byline given. Reports in 3 months. Sample copy for $5.
Nonfiction: How-to for racing and performance-oriented sailors, photo feature, profile, regatta reports and charter. No travelogs. **Buys 5-10 unsolicited mss/year.** Query. Length: 500-1,500 words. **Pays $400 for up to 2,000 words.**
Tips: "Send query with outline and include your experience. The writer may have a better chance of breaking in with short articles and fillers such as regatta news reports from his or her own area. Prospective contributors should study recent issues of the magazine to determine appropriate subject matter. The emphasis here is on performance sailing: keep in mind that the *Sailing World* readership is relatively educated about the sport. Unless you are dealing with a totally new aspect of sailing, you can and should discuss ideas on an advanced technical level. 'Gee-whiz' impressions from beginning sailors are generally not accepted."

$ $ SEA KAYAKER, Sea Kayaker, Inc., P.O. Box 17170, Seattle WA 98107-0870. (206)789-1326. Fax: (206)781-1141. E-mail: mail@seakayakermag.com. Website: http://eskimo.com/~seakayak. **Contact**: Leslie Forsberg, executive editor. Editor: Christopher Cunningham. **95% freelance written.** Works frequently with new/unpublished writers each year. "*Sea Kayaker* is a bimonthly publication with a worldwide readership that covers all aspects of kayak touring. It is well-known as an important source of continuing education by the most experienced paddlers." Estab. 1984. Circ. 24,000. Pays on publication. Publishes ms an average of 6 months after acceptance. Byline given. Offers 10% kill fee. Buys first North American serial or second serial (reprint) rights. Editorial lead time 4 months. Submit seasonal material 4 months in advance. Reports in 2 months. Sample copy for $5.30. Writer's guidelines for SASE.
Nonfiction: Essays, historical, how-to (on making equipment), humor, new product, profile, opinion, personal experience, technical, travel. **Buys 18 mss/year.** Query or send complete ms. Length: 1,500-5,000 words. **Pays 20¢/word for assigned articles; 12¢/word for unassigned articles.**
Photos: Send photos with submission. Reviews transparencies and prints. Offers $15-400. Captions and identification of subjects required. Buys one-time rights.
Columns/Departments: Technique, Equipment, Do-It-Yourself, Food, Safety, Health, Environment, Book Reviews. Length: 1,000-2,500 words. **Buys 40-45 mss/year.** Query. **Pays 20¢/word for assigned articles; 12¢/word for unassigned articles.**
Tips: "We consider unsolicited manuscripts that include a SASE, but we give greater priority to brief descriptions (several paragraphs) of proposed articles accompanied by at least two samples—published or unpublished—of your writing. Enclose a statement as to why you're qualified to write the piece and indicate whether photographs or illustrations are available to accompany the piece."

N $ $ SOUTHERN BOATING MAGAZINE, The South's Largest Boating Magazine, Southern Boating & Yachting Inc., 1766 Bay Rd., Miami Beach FL 33139. (305)538-0700. Fax: (305)532-8657. E-mail: sboating@icanect.net. **Contact**: David Strickland, managing editor. Editor: Skip Allen. Executive Editor: Rick Eyerdam. **50% freelance written.** "Upscale monthly yachting magazine focusing on SE U.S., Bahamas, Caribbean and Gulf of Mexico." Estab.

1972. Circ. 35,000. Pays on publication. Publishes ms an average of 2 months after acceptance. Byline given. Buys one-time rights. Editorial lead time 6 weeks. Submit seasonal material 2 months in advance. Sample copy free.
Nonfiction: How-to (boat maintenance), travel (boating related and destination pieces). **Buys 100 mss/year.** Query. Length: 600-3,000 words. **Pays $200.**
Reprints: Accepts previously published submissions.
Photos: State availability of or send photos. Reviews transparencies, prints. Offers $50/photo maximum; negotiates payment individually. Captions, model releases and identification of subjects required. Buys one-time rights.
Columns/Departments: Weekend Workshop (how to/maintenance), 600 words; What's New in Electronics (electronics), 1,000 words; Engine Room (new developments), 1,000 words. **Buys 24 mss/year.** Query. **Pays $150.**
Tips: "Query. Send clips."

$ $ TRAILER BOATS MAGAZINE, Poole Publications, Inc., 20700 Belshaw Ave., Carson CA 90746-3510. (310)537-6322. Fax: (310)537-8735. E-mail: tbmeditors@aol.com. **Contact:** Jim Henricks, editor. Managing Editor: Mike Blake. **50% freelance written.** Works with a small number of new/unpublished writers each year. Monthly magazine (November/December issue combined) covering legally trailerable power boats under 28 feet long and related powerboating activities. Estab. 1971. Circ. 85,000. **Pays on acceptance.** Publishes ms 3 months after acceptance. Byline given. Buys all rights. Editorial lead time 4 months. Submit seasonal material 5 months in advance. Reports in 1 month. Sample copy for 9×12 SAE with 7 first-class stamps. Writer's guidelines for #10 SASE.
Nonfiction: General interest (trailer boating activities); historical (places, events, boats); how-to (repair boats, installation, etc.); humor (almost any power boating-related subject); nostalgia (same as historical); personal experience; photo feature; profile; technical; and travel (boating travel on water or highways), product evaluations. Annual new boat review. No "How I Spent My Summer Vacation" stories, or stories not even remotely connected to trailerable boats and related activities. **Buys 70-80 unsolicited mss/year.** Query. Length: 1,000-3,500 words. **Pays $150-1,000.** Sometimes pays expenses of writers on assignment.
Photos: Send photos with ms. Reviews transparencies (2¼×2¼) and 35mm slides. Negotiates payment individually. Captions, model releases and identification of subjects required. Buys one-time rights.
Columns/Departments: Boaters Bookshelf (boating book reviews); Over the Transom (funny or strange boating photos). Watersports (boat-related); Seamanship (experienced boaters' tips on navigation, survival, safety etc.); Marine Electronics (what and how to use); Back to Basics (elementary boating tips), all 1,000-1,500 words. **Buys 60-70/year.** Query. **Pays $250-450.** Open to suggestions for new columns/departments.
Tips: "Query should contain short general outline of the intended material; what kind of photos; how the photos illustrate the piece. Write with authority, covering the subject like an expert. Frequent mistakes are not knowing the subject matter or the audience. Use basic information rather than prose, particularly in travel stories. The writer may have a better chance of breaking in at our publication with short articles and fillers if they are typically hard-to-find articles. We do most major features inhouse, but try how-to stories dealing with smaller boats, installation and towing tips, boat trailer repair. Good color photos will win our hearts every time."

$ $ $ $ WATERWAY GUIDE, Intertec Publishing Corp., a K-III Media Co., 6151 Powers Ferry Rd. NW, Atlanta GA 30339-2941. (770)618-0313. Fax: (770)618-0349. Associate Publisher: Judith Powers. **90% freelance written.** Quarterly magazine on intracoastal waterway travel for recreational boats. "Writer must be knowledgeable about navigation and the areas covered by the guide." Estab. 1947. Circ. 45,000. Pays on publication. Publishes ms an average of 3 months after acceptance. Byline given sometimes. Kill fee varies. Buys all rights. Reports in 3 months on queries; 4 months on mss. Sample copy for $36.95 with $3 postage.
Nonfiction: Historical/nostalgic, how-to, photo feature, technical, travel. "No personal boating experiences." **Buys 25 mss/year.** Query with or without published clips, or send complete ms. Length: 200 words minimum. **Pays $50-3,000.** Pays in contributor copies or other premiums for helpful tips and useful information.
Photos: Send photos with submission. Reviews 3×5 prints. Offers $50/color photo, $600/color photos used on the cover. Identification of subjects required. Buys all rights.
Fillers: Facts. **Buys 6/year.** Length: 250-1,000 words. **Pays $50-150.**
Tips: "Must have on-the-water experience and be able to provide new and accurate information on geographic areas covered by *Waterway Guide*."

$ $ WOODENBOAT MAGAZINE, The Magazine for Wooden Boat Owners, Builders, and Designers, WoodenBoat Publications, Inc., P.O. Box 78, Brooklin ME 04616. (207)359-4651. Fax: (207)359-8920. E-mail: wbeditor@woodenboat.com. Website: http://www.media4.hypernet.com/~WOODENBOAT/wb.htm. Editor-in-Chief: Jonathan A. Wilson. Senior Editor: Mike O'Brien. Associate Editor: Tom Jackson. **Contact:** Matthew P. Murphy, editor. **50% freelance written.** Works with a small number of new/unpublished writers each year. Bimonthly magazine for wooden boat owners, builders and designers. "We are devoted exclusively to the design, building, care, preservation, and use of wooden boats, both commercial and pleasure, old and new, sail and power. We work to convey quality, integrity and involvement in the creation and care of these craft, to entertain, inform, inspire, and to provide our varied readers with access to individuals who are deeply experienced in the world of wooden boats." Estab. 1974. Circ. 106,000. Pays on publication. Publishes ms an average of 1 year after acceptance. Byline given. Offers variable kill fee. Buys first North American serial rights. Accepts simultaneous submissions. Reports in 3 weeks on queries; 2 months on mss. Sample copy for $4.50. Writer's guidelines for SASE.
Nonfiction: Technical (repair, restoration, maintenance, use, design and building wooden boats). No poetry, fiction.

Buys 50 mss/year. Query with published clips. Length: 1,500-5,000 words. **Pays $150-200/1,000 words.** Sometimes pays expenses of writers on assignment.

Reprints: Send tearsheet or photocopy of article or typed ms with rights for sale noted with information about when and where the article previously appeared.

Photos: Send photos with query. Negatives must be available. Pays $15-75 for b&w; $25-350 for color. Identification of subjects required. Buys one-time rights.

Columns/Departments: On the Waterfront pays for information on wooden boat-related events, projects, boatshop activities, etc. **Buys 25/year.** "We use the same columnists for each issue." Send complete information. Length: 250-1,000 words. **Pays $5-50 for information.**

Tips: "We appreciate a detailed, articulate query letter, accompanied by photos, that will give us a clear idea of what the author is proposing. We appreciate samples of previously published work. It is important for a prospective author to become familiar with our magazine first. It is extremely rare for us to make an assignment with a writer with whom we have not worked before. Most work is submitted on speculation. The most common failure is not exploring the subject material in enough depth."

Gambling

N $ $ $ $ PLAY THE ODDS, The Big Dog Press, 11614 Ashwood, Little Rock AZ 72211. (501)224-9452. **Contact:** Tom Raley, editor. Monthly consumer magazine covering gambling. "We cover gambling activities all across the country. We offer tips, reviews, instructions and advice on gaming. We also cover cruise lines since most have casinos on board." Estab. 1997. **Pays on acceptance**. Publishes ms an average of 4 months after acceptance. Buys one-time rights. Accepts simultaneous submissions. Reports in 2 weeks on queries; 2 months on mss. Sample copy for $2. Writer's guidelines for #10 SASE.

Nonfiction: Primarily dealing with casino gaming, *Play the Odds* also covers horse racing, dog racing, sports wagering and online casinos. Also features service articles on entertianment, lodging, and dining facilities located in or near gameing resorts. **Buys 85-145 mss/year**. Length: 800 words. **Pays $500-1,750**.

Fiction: Adventure, fantasy (science fantasy), horror, mystery/suspense (cozy, private eye/hardboiled, romantic suspense), science fiction (soft sociological), senior citizen/retirement, sports, westerns (traditional). **Buys 12-20 mss/year**. Length: 600-800 words. **Pays $1,500-3,000.**

Columns/Departments: Reviews (shows, games, hotels, casinos, books), up to 300 words; humorous fillers, up to 80 words. **Buys 24-36 reviews/year; 36-60 fillers/year. Pays 50-350.**

Tips: In nonfiction, the editor advises that a writer present an aspect or area of gaming which is out of the mainstream. In fiction, "we look for fast paced stories with real characters. The stories should be fun, enjoyable and the main character doesn't need to be trying to save the world. Few, if any of us, do that. We do however get in bad situations. You must write what you enjoy writing about. If you don't want to write a story about gambling or a gambler, it will show in your work. If it is something you want, that will also show in your work and we will notice."

General Interest

$ ALL-STATER SPORTS, America's High School Sports Almanac, All-Stater Publishing, LLC, 1500 W. Third Ave., Suite 222, Columbus OH 43212. (614)487-1280. Fax: (614)487-1283. E-mail: contact@allstatersports.com. Website: http://www.all-statersports.com. **Contact:** Stephanie Strong, associate editor. **80% freelance written.** Quarterly tabloid. "The mission of *All-Stater Sports* is to inform, inspire and recognize today's high school student-athlete. Our audience consists of student-athletes, coaches and athletic directors, but our intention is to speak primarily to student-athletes." Estab. 1995. Circ. 55,000. Pays on publication. Publishes ms an average of 1 month after acceptance. Byline given. Editorial lead time 2 months. Submit seasonal material 1 month in advance. Accepts simultaneous submissions. Reports in 1 month. Sample copy $5 for writers only.

Nonfiction: How-to (training, cross-training, strength building, etc.), humor inspirational, interview/profile, new product, opinion, personal experience, photo feature, technical (sports issues, skill building). **Pays $50-100.** "Profiles writers in our contributor's column, provides extra copies of issue, plugs product, institution, company, etc. Sometimes pays expenses of writers on assignment.

Reprints: Send typed ms with rights for sale noted and information about when and where the article previously appeared.

Photos: State availability of photos with submission. Reviews 5×7 minimum prints. Negotiates payment individually. Model release (if deemed necessary) and identification of subjects required. Buys one-time rights.

Columns-Departments: Getting The Edge (sports training/skill building), 1,200 words; Next Step articles about sports in (college sports), 1,200 words; Winning with Heart (overcoming odds to play sports), 1,000 words; In Recognition of Sportsmanship (specific act of sportsmanship in high school sports—real incidents), 1,000 words. **Buys 10-15 mss/year.** Query. **Pays $50-100.**

Fillers: Anecdotes, facts, gags to be illustrated, newsbreaks, short humor. Length: 50-300 words. **Pays $15-30.**

Tips: "We are happy to consider any material that would be of interest to high school athletes—even something that is not already included in our issues printed to date. We profile outstanding achievers, but would also like to have human interest stories of accomplishment, satisfaction, team bonding, unusually fine coaches, etc., from non-blue chipper's perspective as well."

$ $ $ INSIDE SPORTS, Century Publishing Co., 990 Grove St., Evanston IL 60201. (847)491-6440. Fax: (847)491-0867. E-mail: edit@insidesports.com. Website: http://www.insidesports.com. **Contact:** Ken Leiker, editor. **50% freelance written.** Monthly magazine. "*Inside Sports*' contributors John Feinstein, Doc Rivers, Randy Cross,Terry Bradshaw, Billy Packer, Stedman Graham, Bob Trumpy and others provide sports enthusiasts of all kinds with previews and predictions, profiles, and insights that go beyond scores and statistics. The publication focuses primarily on football, basketball, baseball, hockey, motor sports, and boxing." Circ. 850,000. Pays on publication. Publishes ms an average of 1 month after acceptance. Byline given. Offers 50% kill fee. Rights are negotiated individually. Reports on queries and mss in 1 month.

Nonfiction: Query with or without published clips, or send complete ms. Length of article and payment vary with each article and writer. Most run 2,000-3,500 words. **Pays 10¢-$1/word.** "Please include a SASE with query/article."

Columns/Departments: The Insider, Media, Inside Interview, Numbers, The Fan. All 300-1,500 words.

Tips: "Please do not query us on obvious ideas; please limit submissions and queries to exclusive (not mass-mailed to other publications) and unique ideas."

N $ MARYLAND SPORTS, HEALTH & FITNESS NEWS, Frontline Communications Group, Inc., P.O. Box 32684, Baltimore MD 21282-2684. Fax: (410)922-8115. E-mail: MSH&FN@frontlinegroup.com. **Contact**: Dr. Gladson Nwanna, executive editor. Editor: Edith Adjaye. **100% freelance written.** "Bimonthly magazine covering sports, fitness, health, related lifestyles and activities of Marylanders." Estab. 1996. Circ. 50,000. Pays on publication. Publishes ms an average of 4 months after acceptance. Byline given. Buys all rights. Submit seasonal material 5 months in advance. Accepts simultaneous submissions. Reports in 3 weeks on queries; 6 weeks on mss. Sample copy for 9×12 SAE with 4 first-class stamps. Writer's guidelines for #10 SASE.

Nonfiction: Book excerpts, essays, exposé, historical/nostalgic, how-to (expert tips, advice, instructions on various sports, fitness), humor, inspirational, interview/profile, new product/service, opinion, personal experience, photo feature, medical news, fitness news. "No articles on unsound nutritional practices or unsafe exercise gimmicks." **Buys 150 mss/year.** Send complete ms and SASE. Length: 800-2,000 words. **Pays $15-30.** Sometimes pays expenses of writers on assignment.

Reprints: Send photocopy of article or typed ms with rights for sale noted and information about when and where the article previously appeared. Pays 50% of amount paid for an original article.

Photos: Send photos with submission. Captions, model releases and identification of subjects required. Buys all rights.

Columns/Departments: Spotlight (new product/service information, including equipment reviews); In the News (news about the people, places and events in our Maryland sporting community); Club News (what's happening at local fitness centers and sports organizations); Health Today (information from the medical community addressing current health care concerns, community medical news and breakthroughs); Wholistic Living (information on alternative medicine, therapies and treatments); Food and Nutrition (the latest information on how to fuel your body for peak performance, including natural foods); Sports Medicine (sports and medicine experts discuss prevention and treatment of common sports injuries); Fitness Matters (general information on fitness, all facets, including exercises); Fitness Panorama (a pictorial look at Marylanders enjoying fitness and sports); Kids Fitness (information to keep our children fit and healthy); Photo-Finish (photos and results from Maryland's top sporting events); Calendar of Events (a calendar of forthcoming (mostly), amateur sports events, clubs and ongoing training in Maryland); How-to (expert tips, instructions, advice on various sports); Inside in-Line (in-line skating products, news, events, profiles and training tips); Adventure (outdoor sports experiences); S&F Profile (amateur and professional athletes from the Maryland area). **Pays $15-30.**

Tips: "Submit list of articles, including a few complete articles. Familiarize yourself with our departments/columns. Try to submit 'evergreen' stories, meaning they can be used anytime throughout the year. That way, whenever we have a 'hole' in the magazine, we can drop in your story. Submit initial sets of articles free-of-charge."

N $ $ METRO SPORTS MAGAZINE, Hebdo Sports Inc., 27 W. 24th St., New York NY 10010. (212)627-7040. Fax: (212)627-7446. E-mail: metrosport@aol.com. Website: http://www.metrosports.com. **Contact:** Angela Garber, assistant editor. **30% freelance written.** Monthly tabloid covering participation sports. "We write about active sports for young professionals: running, cycling, in-line, tennis, skiing, outdoor. The message is 'get out and play.' And here is how, where, when." Estab. 1987. Circ. 160,000. Pays on publication. Publishes ms an average of 2 months after acceptance. Byline given. Buys first North American serial rights. Editorial lead time 3 months. Submit seasonal material 3 months in advance. Accepts simultaneous submissions. Sample copy for $4. Writer's guidelines free.

Nonfiction: Book excerpts, exposé, general interest, how-to, humor, inspirational, interview/profile, new product, opinion, personal experience, travel. Special issues: Back to Cool (September 1998); Running (October 1998); Skiing (November 1998); Holiday and Winter Sports (December 1998). **Buys 20 mss/year.** Query. Length: 300-1,200 words. **Pays $50-500 for assigned articles. Pays $50-200 for unsolicited articles.**

Reprints: Send tearsheet or photocopy of article.

Photos: State availability of photos with submission. Reviews transparencies and prints. Offers no additional payment for photos accepted with ms. Buys one-time rights.

Columns/Departments: Running (how to, events); Sports Medicine; Equipment (innovations). All 700 words. Query.

Tips: "Be aware of active (not TV) sports with East Coast focus."

$ $ ROCKY MOUNTAIN SPORTS MAGAZINE, Rocky Mountain Sports, Inc., 428 E. 11th Ave, Suite 104, Denver CO 80203. (303)861-9229. Fax: (303)861-9209. E-mail: Rockedit@aol.com. Website: http://www.diveindenver.com. Publisher: Mary Thorne. **Contact:** Kellee Van Keuren, editor. **50% freelance written.** Monthly magazine of sports in the Rocky Mountain States and Canada. "*Rocky* is a magazine for sports-related lifestyles and activities. Our mission is to reflect and inspire the active lifestyle of Rocky Mountain residents." Estab. 1986. Circ. 60,000. Pays on publication. Publishes ms an average of 2 months after acceptance. Byline given. Offers 25% kill fee. Buys second serial (reprint) rights. Editorial lead time 1½ months. Submit seasonal material 2 months in advance. Reports in 3 weeks on queries; 2 months on mss. Sample copy and writer's guidelines for #10 SASE.

- The editor of this publication says she wants to see mountain outdoor sports writing **only**. No ball sports, no hunting, no fishing.

Nonfiction: Book excerpts, essays, exposé, how-to: (no specific sports, trips, adventures), humor, inspirational, interview/profile, new product, opinion, personal experience, photo feature, travel. Special issues: Snowboarding (December); Alpine and Nordic (January and February); Running (March); Mountain Biking (April). No articles on football, baseball, basketball or other sports covered in-depth by newspapers. **Buys 24 mss/year.** Query with published clips. Length: 2,500 words maximum. **Pays $150 minimum.** Also publishes short articles on active outdoor sports, catch-all topics that are seasonably targeted. Query with idea first by mail or e-mail. **Pays 10-15¢/word.** Sometimes pays expenses of writers on assignment.

Reprints: Send photocopy of article and information about when and where the article previously appeared. Pays 20-25% of amount paid for an original article.

Photos: State availability of photos with submission. Reviews transparencies and prints. Offers $25-250/photo. Captions and identification of subjects required. Buys one-time rights.

Columns/Departments: Short Shorts (short newsy items), 50-800 words; High Altitude (essay on quirky topics related to Rockies). **Buys 20 mss/year.** Query. **Pays $25-200.**

Tips: "Submit stories for the Short Shorts section first."

$ SILENT SPORTS, Waupaca Publishing Co., P.O. Box 152, Waupaca WI 54981-9990. (715)258-5546. Fax: (715)258-8162. **Contact:** Greg Marr, editor. **75% freelance written.** Eager to work with new/unpublished writers. Monthly magazine on running, cycling, cross-country skiing, canoeing, kayaking, snowshoeing, in-line skating, camping, backpacking and hiking aimed at people in Wisconsin, Minnesota, northern Illinois and portions of Michigan and Iowa. "Not a coffee table magazine. Our readers are participants from rank amateur weekend athletes to highly competitive racers." Estab. 1984. Circ. 10,000. Pays on publication. Publishes ms an average of 3 months after acceptance. Byline given. Offers 20% kill fee. Buys one-time rights. Submit seasonal material 4 months in advance. Reports in 3 months. Sample copy and writer's guidelines for 10×13 SAE with 6 first-class stamps.

- The editor needs local angles on in-line skating, recreation bicycling and snowshoeing.

Nonfiction: General interest, how-to, interview/profile, opinion, technical, travel. All stories/articles must focus on the Upper Midwest. First-person articles discouraged. **Buys 25 mss/year.** Query. Length: 2,500 words maximum. **Pays $15-100.** Sometimes pays expenses of writers on assignment.

Reprints: Send typed ms with rights for sale noted and information about when and where the article previously appeared. Pays 50% of amount paid for an original article.

Photos: State availability of photos with submission. Reviews transparencies. Pays $5-15 for b&w story photos; $50 for color covers. Buys one-time rights.

Tips: "Where-to-go and personality profiles are areas most open to freelancers. Writers should keep in mind that this is a regional, Midwest-based publication. We want only stories/articles with a focus on our region."

N $ $ $ SPIKE, The Magazine from Finish Line, Emmis Publishing, 950 N. Meridian St., Suite 1200, Indianapolis IN 46204. **Contact:** John Thomas, special projects editor. **100% freelance written.** Quarterly. "*Spike* goes to customers of Finish Line, a chain of more than 300 athletic shoe and apparel stores. Most readers are young males with an interest in sports and pop culture. Writing should be bright, hip and tight." Estab. 1997. Circ. 650,000. Pays on publication. Publishes ms 3 months after acceptance. Byline given. Buys first North American serial rights and one-time rights. Editorial lead time 4 months. Submit seasonal material 6 months in advance. Sample copy for 9×12 SAE and 5 first-class stamps.

Nonfiction: General interest, how-to (fitness), interview/profile, new product. *No unsolicited mss.* No first-person essays. **Buys 12-15 mss/year.** Query with published clips. Length: 750-2,000 words. **Pays $250-1,000.** Sometimes pays expenses of writers on assignment.

Columns/Departments: Fitness (for ages 15-20); Music (hot new groups); High Tech (games, web pages, etc. that are sports related), all 500-750 words. **Buys 12 mss/year.** Query with published clips. **Pays $50-500.**

Tips: "Demonstrated access to and ability to work with top athletes and pop-culture figures is a plus."

✪ $ $ $ SPORT, Petersen Publishing Co., 6420 Wilshire Blvd., Los Angeles CA 90048-5515. (213)782-2828. Fax: (213)782-2835. E-mail: sport@petersonpub.com. **Contact:** Cam Benty, editor. **80% freelance written.** Monthly magazine "for the active adult sports fan. *Sport* offers profiles of the players and the people behind the scenes in the world of sports. *Sport* magazine is the oldest, largest, monthly sports feature publication reaching over 4.3 million young, active, sports-minded enthusiasts each issue. Not a recap of what happened last week, but previews and predictions of what will happen this month, next month, next year. In-depth profiles, investigative reporting, lively features about the action on and off the field! *Sport* magazine is the complete sports magazine written and edited for the ultimate

sports fan!" Estab. 1946. Circ. 792,000. **Pays on acceptance**. Publishes ms an average of 3 months after acceptance. Offers 25% kill fee. Buys first North American serial or all rights. Reports in 2 months.
Nonfiction: "Prefers to see articles on professional, big-time sports: basketball, football, baseball, some boxing. Articles must be contemporary pieces, not a history of sports or a particular sport." Query with published clips. Length: News briefs, 200-300 words; Departments, 1,400 words; Features, 1,500-3,000 words. **Averages 50¢/word for articles.**

SPORTS ILLUSTRATED, Time Inc. Magazine Co., Time & Life Bldg., Rockefeller Center, New York NY 10020. (212)522-1212. **Contact:** Myra Gelband. Weekly. "*Sports Illustrated* reports and interprets the world of sport, recreation and active leisure. It previews, analyzes and comments upon major games and events, as well as those noteworthy for character and spirit alone. It features individuals connected to sport and evaluates trends concerning the part sport plays in contemporary life. In addition, the magazine has articles on such subjects as fashion, physical fitness and conservation. Special departments deal with sports equipment, books and statistics." Estab. 1954. Circ. 3,339,000. Query only by mail before submitting.

$ $ SPORTS SPECTRUM, Discovery House Publishers, P.O. Box 3566, Grand Rapids MI 49501-3566. (616)974-2711. Fax: (616)957-5741. E-mail: ssmag@sport.org. Website: http://www.sport.org/. **Contact:** Dave Branon, managing editor. "*Sports Spectrum* is produced 10 times/year as a way of presenting the Christian faith through the lives of Christian athletes. Writers should share our love for sports and our interest in telling readers about Jesus Christ." Estab. 1987. Circ. 50,000. **Pays on acceptance.** Publishes ms an average of 2 months after acceptance. Byline given. Offers 40% kill fee. Not copyrighted. Buys first North American print rights. Editorial lead time 4 months. Reports in 1 month on queries. Sample copy for 8½×11 SAE and 4 first-class stamps. Writer's guidelines free.
Nonfiction: Interview/profile. No poems, reprints, fiction, profiles of sports ministries or unsolicited mss. **Buys 60 mss/year.** Query with published clips. Length: 225-2,000 words. **Pays $40-360.** Sometimes pays expenses of writers on assignment.
Photos: State availability of photos. Reviews transparencies and prints. Negotiates payment individually.
Columns/Departments: Leaderboard (athletes in service to others), 725 words; Front Row (sports scene), 800 words; Champions (stories of lesser-known athletes), 225 words. **Buys 15 mss/year.** Query with published clips. **Pays $40-145.**
Tips: "Make sure you understand our unique purpose and can write articles that contribute to the purpose. Send a query letter and clips. Tell why your story idea fits and how you propose to research the article."

$ $ WINDY CITY SPORTS MAGAZINE, Windy City Publishing, 1450 W. Randolph, Chicago IL 60607. (312)421-1551. Fax: (312)421-2060. E-mail: wcpublish@aol.com. **Contact:** Jeff Banowetz, editor. **75% freelance written.** Monthly magazine covering amateur, participatory sports. Estab. 1987. Circ. 100,000 (Chicago and suburbs). Pays on publication. Offers 25% kill fee. Buys one-time rights. Editorial lead time 2 months. Submit seasonal material 2-12 months in advance. Accepts simultaneous submissions. Reports in 1-2 months on queries. Sample copy for $3 or 11½×14 SAE with $2 in postage. Writer's guidelines free.
Nonfiction: Essays (re: sports controversial issues), how-to (do sports), inspirational (profiles of accomplished athletes), interview/profile, new product, opinion, personal experience, photo feature (in Chicago), travel. No articles on professional sports. Special issues: Chicago Marathon (October); Skiing and Snowboarding (November); Winter Sports (December). **Buys 120 mss/year.** Query with clips. Length: 500-1,200 words. **Pays 10¢/word.** Sometimes pays expenses of writers on assignment.
Reprints: Send information about when and where the article previously appeared.
Photos: State availability or send photos with submission. Reviews contact sheets and prints. Negotiates payment individually. Captions and identification of subjects required. Buys one-time rights.
Columns/Departments: "We run the following columns every month: running, cycling, fitness centers, nutrition, sports medicine, women's, road trip (adventure travel) and in-line skating, all 1,000-1,200 words." **Buys 70 mss/year.** Query with published clips. **Pays $125.**
Fillers: Anecdotes, facts, gags to be illustrated by cartoonist, short humor. **Buys 10/year.** Length: 20-500 words. **Pays $25-100.**
Tips: "Best way to get assignment: ask for writer's guidelines, editor's schedule and sample copy ($3). *Read magazine!* Query me with story ideas for a column or query on features using editorial schedule. Always try to target Chicago looking Midwest."

WOMEN'S SPORTS & FITNESS, (formerly known as *Condé Nast Sports for Women*), Condé Nast Publications, Inc., 342 Madison Ave., 21st Floor, New York NY 10017. (212)880-8800. Fax: (212)880-4656. **Contact:** Carol Plum, managing editor. Bimonthly magazine covering sports and fitness from a women's perspective. "A magazine all about participatory sports and spectator sports, we focus on women's involvement and roles in these ever-changing fields." Estab. 1997. Circ. 350,000. **Pays on acceptance.** Byline given. Buys first North American serial and nonexclusive syndication rights. Reports in 2 months.
Nonfiction: "We're interested in emerging sport trends, athletes and attitudes, as well as breaking health and nutrition news." **Buys 90 mss/year.** Query with published clips. Length: 1,000-3,000 words. **Pays $1/word.**
Columns/Departments: Active File (fitness, health and nutrition, 300-700 words). **Pays $1/word.** Other departments written by regular columnists.
Tips: "The best way to break in is to know something we don't: what's the new sport, the new hybrid sport, the new

face in emerging sport trends."

Golf

N $ $ CHICAGO DISTRICT GOLFER, TPG Sports Inc., 1710 Douglas Dr. N., #201, Golden Valley MN 59422. (612)595-0808. Fax: (612)595-0016. E-mail: bob pgsports.com or rdoyle@cdga.org. Website: http://www.tpgsports.com or http://www.cdga.org. Managing Editor: Bob Fallen. **Contact:** Ryan Doyle, editor [(630)954-2180]. **90% freelance written.** Bimonthly magazine covering golf in Illinois, the official publication of the Chicago District Golf Association and Golf Association of Illinois. Estab. 1922. Circ. 65,000. Pays on acceptance or publication. Byline given. Buys all rights. Editorial lead time 2 months. Submit seasonal material 3 months in advance. Accepts simultaneous submissions. Sample copy and writer's guidelines free.

Nonfiction: Book excerpts, general interest, historical/nostalgic, how-to (golf), humor, interview/profile, new product, opinion, personal experience, photo feature, technical, travel. **Buys 25-35 mss/year.** Query with or without published clips. Length: 500-5,000 words. **Pays $50-500.** Sometimes pays expenses of writers on assignment.

Reprints: Accepts previously published submissions.

Photos: State availability of photos with submission. Reviews contact sheets. Negotiates payment individually. Captions, identification of subjects required.

$ $ $ $ GOLF ILLUSTRATED, NatCom Inc., 5300 Cityplex Tower, 2448 E. 81st, Tulsa OK 74137. (918)491-6100. Fax: (918)491-9424. Editor-in-Chief: Mark Chesnut. **Contact:** Jason Sowards, managing editor. **80% freelance written.** Bimonthly golf magazine. "We cover everything and anything to do with golf, but we're not into the *politics* of the game. Instruction is the primary focus." Estab. 1914. Circ. 300,000. Pays 30 days after acceptance. Publishes ms an average of 3 months after acceptance. Byline given. Offers 20% kill fee. Buys first North American serial rights. Editorial lead time 10 weeks. Submit seasonal material 6 months in advance. Reports in 2 months. Writer's guidelines free.

Nonfiction: Historical/nostalgic, how-to (golf instruction), humor, interview/profile (golf figures), technical, travel (focus on golf) and golf equipment. "No opinion or politics." **Buys 50 mss/year.** Query. Length: 1,200-1,500 words. **Pays $1/word minimum.** Sometimes pays expenses of writers on assignment.

Photos: Negotiates payment individually. Identification of subjects required. Buys one-time rights.

Columns/Departments: Gallery Shots (short pieces), 200-400 words. **Buys 20 mss/year.** Query. **Pays $50-400.**

Tips: "Offer a unique perspective; short, sweet queries with SASE are appreciated. *Don't* call every two weeks to find out when your story will be published. Be patient, we get lots of submissions and try our best to respond promptly."

$ $ $ GOLF TIPS, The Game's Most In-Depth Instruction & Equipment Magazine, Werner Publishing Corp., 12121 Wilshire Blvd., Suite 1200, Los Angeles CA 90025. (310)826-1500. Fax: (310)826-5008. Website: http://www.golftipsmag.com. Senior Editor: Mike Chwasky. Editor at Large: Tom Ferrell. **Contact:** David DeNunzio, managing editor. **95% freelance written.** Magazine published 9 times/year covering golf instruction and equipment. "We provide mostly concise, very clear golf instruction pieces for the serious golfer." Estab. 1986. Pays on publication. Publishes ms an average of 2 months after acceptance. Byline given. Offers 33% kill fee. Buys first rights and second serial (reprint) rights. Editorial lead time 3 months. Submit seasonal material 4 months in advance. Accepts previously published submissions. Reports in 1 month. Sample copy and writer's guidelines free.

Nonfiction: Book excerpts, how-to, interview/profile, new product, photo feature, technical, travel: all golf related. "General golf essays rarely make it." **Buys 125 mss/year.** Send complete ms. Length: 250-2,000 words. **Pays $300-750 for assigned articles; $300-800 unsolicited articles.** Occasionally negotiates other forms of payment. Sometimes pays expenses of writers on assignment.

Photos: State availability of photos with submission. Reviews 2×2 transparencies. Negotiates payment individually. Captions and identification of subjects required. Buys all rights.

Columns/Departments: Stroke Saver (very clear, concise instruction), 350 words; Lesson Library (book excerpts—usually in a series), 1,000 words; Travel Tips (formated golf travel), 2,500 words. **Buys 40 mss/year.** Query with published clips or send complete ms. **Pays $300-850.**

Tips: "Contact a respected PGA Professional and find out if they're interested in being published. A good writer can turn an interview into a decent instruction piece."

$ $ GOLF TRAVELER, Official Publication of Golf Card International, Affinity Group, Inc., 2575 Vista del Mar, Ventura CA 93001. Fax: (805)667-4217. E-mail: vlaw@affinity.com. Website: http://www.tl.com. **Contact:** Valerie Law, editor. **90% freelance written.** Bimonthly magazine "is the membership magazine for the Golf Card an organization that offers its members reduced or waived greens fees at 3,000 affiliated golf courses in North America." Estab. 1976. Circ. 130,000. **Pays on acceptance.** Byline given. Offers 33% kill fee. Buys first North American serial rights. Editorial lead time 4 months. Submit seasonal material 4 months in advance. Accepts simultaneous and previously published submissions. Reports in 1 month. Sample copy for $2.50. Writer's guidelines free with SASE.

Nonfiction: Book excerpts, essays, how-to, interview/profile, new product, personal experience, photo feature, technical. PGA Orlando Merchandise Show (January-February). No poetry or cartoons. **Buys 25 mss/year.** Query with published clips or send complete ms. Length: 500-2,500 words. **Pays $75-500.** Sometimes pays expenses of writers on assignment.

Photos: Send photos with submission. Reviews transparencies. Negotiates payment individually. Model releases and identification of subjects required. Buys one-time rights.

Tips: "We're always looking for golf writers who can put together destination features revolving around our affiliated golf courses."

$ $ GULF COAST GOLFER, Golfer Magazines, Inc., 9182 Old Katy Rd., Houston TX 77055. (713)464-0308. Fax: (713)464-0129. Editor: Bob Gray. **Contact:** David Widener, managing editor. **30% freelance written.** Monthly tabloid covering golf in Texas. Estab. 1984. Circ. 35,000. Pays on publication. Publishes ms an average of 2 months after acceptance. Byline given. Buys first, one-time or second serial (reprint) rights. Editorial lead time 2 months. Submit seasonal material 3 months in advance. Reports in 2 weeks on queries; 1 month on mss. Sample copy free. Prefers direct phone discussion for writer's guidelines.

Nonfiction: Book excerpts, humor, personal experience all golf-related. No stories about golf outside of Texas. **Buys 40 mss/year.** Query. **Pays $50-425.**

Photos: State availability of photos. Reviews contact sheets and prints. No additional payment for photos accepted with ms, but pays $125 for cover photo. Captions and identification of subjects required. Buys one-time rights.

Tips: Most of the our purchases are in how-to area, so writers must know golf quite well and play the game."

N MICHIGAN LINKS, TPG Sports Inc., 1710 Douglas Dr. N., #201, Golden Valley MN 59422. (612)595-0808. Fax: (612)595-0016. E-mail: bob@tpgsports.com or rdoyle@cdga.org. Website: http://www.tpgsports.com or http://www.gam.org. Managing Editor: Bob Fallen. **Contact:** Tonia Branch, editor [(245)553-4200]. **80% freelance written.** Bimonthly magazine covering golf in Michigan, the official publication of the Golf Association of Michigan. Estab. 1997. Circ. 40,000. Pays on acceptance or publication. Byline sometimes given. Buys all rights. Editorial lead time 3 months. Submit seasonal material 3 months in advance. Accepts simultaneous submissions. Sample copy and writer's guidelines free.

Nonfiction: Book excerpts, essays, historical/nostalgic, how-to (golf), humor, inspirational, interview/profile, new product, opinion, personal experience, photo feature. **Buys 20-30 mss/year**. Query with or without published clips. Length: 500-5,000 words. **Pays $50-500**. Sometimes pays expenses of writers on assignment.

Reprints: Accepts previously published submissions.

Photos: State availability of photos with submission. Reviews contact sheets. Negotiates payment individually. Captions, identification of subjects required. Negotiates payment individually. Rights purchased varies.

N MINNESOTA GOLFER, TPG Sports Inc., 1710 Douglas Dr. N., #201, Golden Valley MN 59422. (612)595-0808. Fax: (612)595-0016. E-mail: bob@tpgsports.com or rdoyle@cdga.org. Website: http://www.tpgsports.com or http://www.mga.org. Managing Editor: Bob Fallen. **Contact:** Chris Geer, editor [(612)927-4643]. **80% freelance written**. Bimonthly magazine covering golf in Minnesota, the official publication of the Minnesota Golf Association. Estab. 1975. Circ. 72,000. Pays on acceptance or publication. Byline given. Buys all rights. Editorial lead time 3 months. Submit seasonal material 3 months in advance. Accepts simultaneous submissions. Sample copy and guidelines free.

Nonfiction: Book excerpts, essays, historical/nostalgic, how-to (golf), humor, inspirational, interview/profile, new product, opinion, personal experience, photo feature. **Buys 20-30 mss/year**. Query with or without published clips. Length: 500-5,000 words. **Pays $50-500**. Sometimes pays expenses of writers on assignment.

Reprints: Accepts previously published submissions.

Photos: State availability of photos with submission. Reviews contact sheets. Negotiates payment individually. Captions, identification of subjects required. Negotiates payment individually. Rights purchased varies.

$ $ NORTH TEXAS GOLFER, Golfer Magazines, Inc., 9182 Old Katy Rd., Houston TX 77055. (713)464-0308. Fax: (713)464-0129. Editor: Bob Gray. **Contact:** David Widener, managing editor. **30% freelance written.** Monthly tabloid covering golf in Texas. Estab. 1984. Circ. 31,000. Pays on publication. Publishes ms an average of 2 months after acceptance. Byline given. Buys first rights or second serial (reprint) rights. Editorial lead time 2 months. Submit seasonal material 3 months in advance. Reports in 2 weeks on queries; 1 month on mss. Sample copy free. Prefers direct phone discussion for writer's guidelines.

Nonfiction: Book excerpts, humor, personal experience, all golf related. **Buys 40 mss/year.** Query. **Pays $50-425.**

Photos: State availability of photos with submission. Reviews contact sheets and prints. Offers no additional payment for photos accepted with ms, but offers $125 for cover photo. Captions and identification of subjects required. Buys one-time rights.

Tips: "Most of our purchases are in how-to area, so writers must know golf quite well and play the game."

N $ $ $ PACIFIC GOLF, Canada Wide Magazines & Communications Ltd., 4180 Lougheed Hwy., 4th Floor, Burnaby, British Columbia V5C 6A7 Canada. (604)299-7311. Fax: (604)299-9188. E-mail: pgolf@canadawide.com. **Contact:** Ross Sullivan, editor. **80% freelance written.** Magazine published 7 times/year. "*Pacific Golf* appeals to B.C.'s golfers and reflects the west coast golf experience. We concentrate on the new, the influential, Canadian golfers and subject matter based in British Columbia. No American golfer profiles, we want a B.C. perspective." Circ. 20,000. Pays on publication. Publishes ms an average of 2 months after acceptance. Byline given. Kill fee varies. Buys first Canadian rights. Editorial lead time 4 months. Submit seasonal material 4 months in advance. Reports in 6 weeks.

Nonfiction: Query with published clips. Length: 500-1,800 words. **Pays 30-40¢/word.** Sometimes pays expenses of writers on assignment.
Photos: State availability of photos with submission.

$ $ $ $ SENIOR GOLFER MAGAZINE, Weider Publications, One Park Ave., 10th Floor, New York NY 10016. (212)545-4800. Fax: (212)646-5356. Editor-in-Chief: David Chmiel. Executive Editor: Chris Millard. **Contact:** Kevin Morris, managing editor (features) or Steve Donahue, managing editor (news). **33% freelance written.** Magazine published 10 times/year covering golf in the 50+ market (Senior PGA Tour, travel, instruction, equipment). "We appeal to a market of those who are close to 50, have turned 50 and some who are well past 50. It's a market that knows and loves golf—from instruction to the Senior PGA Tour to travel and finances. It's an upscale market catering to players of all skill levels who have the time and disposable income to chase and—hopefully—capture their golf dreams." Estab. 1993. Circ. 275,000. **Pays on acceptance**. Publishes ms an average of 6 months after acceptance. Byline given. Buys all rights. Editorial lead time 2 months. Submit seasonal material 4 months in advance. Sample copy free.
Nonfiction: Book excerpts, exposé, general interest, historical/nostalgic, humor, interview/profile, new product, opinion, photo feature, travel. "No cliched rehashes of players who've been in the spotlight for more than 30 years; stories with no regard for our demographic." Query with published clips or send complete ms. **Pays approximately $1/word.** Sometimes pays expenses of writers on assignment.
Photos: Art Director: Melissa Antler. State availability of photos with submission. Reviews contact sheets and transparencies. Negotiates payment individually. Captions and identification of subjects required.
Columns/Departments: Up & Down (interesting events in golf), 150-200 words; Inside Information (news from the Senior PGA Tour). Query with published clips or send complete manuscript.
Fillers: Anecdotes, facts, newsbreaks, short humor.
Tips: "To get your works printed in *Senior Golfer*, it's imperative that you exhibit your knowledge, understanding and love of the game. Our readers are a sophisticated and fickle lot and know if someone's pretending to be golf literate."

N $ $ VIRGINIA GOLFER, TPG Sports Inc., 1710 Douglas Dr. N., #201, Golden Valley MN 59422. (612)595-0808. Fax: (612)595-0016. E-mail: bob pgsports.com or rdoyle@cdga.org. Website: http://www.tpgsports.com or http://www.vsga.org. Managing Editor: Bob Fallen. **Contact:** Harold Pearson, editor [(804)378-2300]. **80% freelance written.** Bimonthly magazine covering golf in Virginia, the official publication of the Virginia Golf Association. Estab. 1997. Circ. 40,000. Pays on publication. Byline given. Buys all rights. Editorial lead time 2 months. Submit seasonal material 3 months in advance. Accepts simultaneous submissions. Sample copy and writer's guidelines free.
Nonfiction: Book excerpts, essays, historical/nostalgic, how-to (golf), humor, inspirational, interview/profile, new product, opinion, personal experience, photo feature, technical (golf equipment). **Buys 30-40 mss/year**. Query with or without published clips or send complete ms. Length: 500-5,000 words. **Pays $50-500**. Sometimes pays expenses of writers on assignment.
Reprints: Accepts previously published submissions.
Photos: State availability of photos with submission. Reviews contact sheets. Negotiates payment individually. Captions, identification of subjects required. Negotiates payment individually. Rights purchased varies.
Columns/Departments: Golf Travel (where to play), Golf Business (what's happening?). Query.

Guns

$ $ AMERICAN RIFLEMAN, National Rifle Association of America, 11250 Waples Mill Rd., Fairfax VA 22030. (703)267-1336. Fax: (703)267-3971. Editor: E.G. Bell, Jr. **Contact**: Mark A. Keefe, IV, managing editor. **25% freelance written.** Monthly magazine covering firearms and related topics for members of the NRA. "We are a member magazine devoted to the history, use, manufacturing, development and care of all types of portable small arms. We have a relatively sophisticated audience and international readership in this subject area." Estab. 1871. Circ. 1.4 million. **Pays on acceptance.** Publishes ms an average of 3-5 months after acceptance. Byline given. No kill fee. Buys first North American serial rights. Submit seasonal material 3 months in advance. Accepts simultaneous submissions. Reports in 1 week on queries; 1 month on mss. Sample copy and writer's guidelines free on request.
Nonfiction: Historical/nostalgic (firearms), how-to (firearms making/repair), technical (firearms related). "No fiction, poetry, essays, pure hunting tales or anything unrelated to firearms." **Buys 30-35 mss/year.** Query or submit ms with SASE. Length: 1,500-2,000 words maximum. **Pays $300-$600.** Sometimes pays expenses of writers on assignment.
Photos: Send photos with submission. Offers no additional payment for photos accepted with ms. Captions and identification of subjects required. Buys one-time rights.
Columns/Departments: From The Bench (articles on reloading ammunition or how-to firearms-related pieces), 800-1,200 words. **Buys 12 mss/year.** Query. **Pays $250-400 maximum.**
Tips: "For starters, it is unlikely that any of our potential authors are unfamiliar with this magazine. Well illustrated, high-quality gunsmithing articles are needed, as well as innovative material on reloading, any of the shooting sports, historical topics, etc. We have an abundance of scholarly material on the gun control issue, but we have bought the occasional thoughtful piece. Aside from our 'From The Bench' column we purchase only feature articles. We do accept unpaid submissions called 'In My Experience' that might introduce authors to us, but most are from long-time readers."

$ $ GUN DIGEST, DBI Books, Inc., Division of Krause Communications, 700 E. State St., Iola WI 54990. (800)767-6310. Fax: (715)445-4087. **Contact:** Ken Warner, editor-in-chief. **50% freelance written.** Prefers to work with published/established writers but works with a small number of new/unpublished writers each year. Annual journal covering guns and shooting. Estab. 1944. **Pays on acceptance.** Publishes ms an average of 20 months after acceptance. Byline given. Buys all rights. Reports in 1 month.

Nonfiction: Buys 50 mss/issue. Query. Length: 500-5,000 words. **Pays $100-600** for text/art package.

Photos: State availability of photos with query letter. Reviews 8×10 b&w prints. Payment for photos included in payment for ms. Captions required.

Tips: Award of $1,000 to author of best article (juried) in each issue.

$ $ GUNGAMES MAGAZINE, Wallyworld Publishing Incorporated, P.O. Box 516, Moreno Valley CA 92556. (909)485-7986. Fax: (909)485-6628. E-mail: ggamesed@aol.com. Website: http://www.gungames.com. **Contact:** Roni Toldanes, editor. **80% freelance written.** Bimonthly magazine covering shooting sports. "This is the only gun magazine that doesn't talk about what type of bullet you should use to kill Bambi or what's the best gun to defend yourself in a dark alley. It talks only about the fun side of guns. All of its writers are World Champions in various shooting disciplines." Estab. 1995. Circ. 300,000. Pays on publication. Publishes ms an average of 2 months after acceptance. Byline given. Buys all rights. Editorial lead time 3 months. Submit seasonal material 3 months in advance. Accepts simultaneous submissions. Reports in 2 weeks on queries. Sample copy for $3.50.

Nonfiction: General interest, historical/nostalgic, how-to, humor, interview/profile, new product, personal experience, technical. Special issues: Shot Show (February-March) and Christmas issues. No articles on hunting or self-defense. **Buys 24 mss/year.** Send complete ms. Length: 1,200-2,000 words. **Pays $150-350.** Pays expenses or writers on assignment.

Reprints: Send tearsheet of article or short story and information about when and where the article previously appeared. Pays 50% of amount paid for an original article.

Photos: Send photos with submission. Reviews negatives, transparencies and prints. Negotiates payment individually. Captions and identification of subjects required. Buys one-time rights.

Columns/Departments: Shooting/Action Shooting (the fun side); 1,500 words. **Buys 24 mss/year.** Send complete ms. **Pays $150-300.**

Fiction: Fantasy, humorous. "Not too serious or too boring." Buys 24 mss/year. Send complete ms. Length: 1,200-1,500 words. Pays $150-300.

Tips: "*Gun Games* is a shooting sports magazine. It covers all the major shooting disciplines from handguns to rifles to shotguns. And its readers are mainly gun owners who do not necessarily understand every aspect of every shooting tournament. How-to articles are our mainstay: how to shoot better, improve scores, speed reloads, sight-in electronic sights . . . and more. We cover every championship match of major shooting disciplines, including Cowboy Action Shooting, IPSC, Bull's-eye, Bianchi Cup, Silhouette, Trap, Sporting Clays, High-Power rifle, Skeet."

$ $ GUNS & AMMO, Petersen Publishing Co., 6420 Wilshire Blvd., Los Angeles CA 90048. (213)782-2160. Fax: (213)782-2477. E-mail: JamesG@PetersenPub.com. Editor: Garry James. **Contact:** Wendy Camacho, editorial assistant. **10% freelance written.** Monthly magazine covering firearms. "*Guns & Ammo* is written for the firearms enthusiast. It contains articles about the history of guns, their application in hunting and target shooting, and the ammunition used by them, plus field tests of selected examples. Rifles, shotguns, handguns, black powder arms, and airguns are covered. Tables of ballistic characteristics of commercial ammunition are also included. Contains articles on other outdoor-related subjects such as knives, leather goods, vehicles, reloading equipment, and personality profiles." Circ. 575,000. **Pays on acceptance.** Publishes ms 6 months after acceptance. Byline given. Buys all rights. Submit seasonal material 6 months in advance. Writer's guidelines for #10 SASE.

Nonfiction: Opinion. **Buys 24 mss/year.** Send complete ms and SASE. Length: 800-2,500 words. **Pays $125-500.**

Reprints: Send typed ms with rights for sale noted along with info about when and where it previously appeared.

Photos: Send photos with submissions. Review 7×9 prints. Offers no additional payment for photos accepted with ms. Captions, model releases, identification of subjects required. Buys all rights.

Columns/Departments: RKBA (opinion column on right to keep and bear arms). Send complete ms. Length: 800-1,200 words. **Pays $300.**

Tips: "No 'hunting' stories, although evaluating an applicable firearm, load or product 'in the field' is acceptable."

$ $ GUNS MAGAZINE, Suite 200, 591 Camino de la Reina, San Diego CA 92108. (619)297-5352. Fax: (619)297-5353. **Contact:** Scott Ferrell, editor. Managing Editor: Lisa Parsons. **100% freelance written.** Monthly magazine for firearms enthusiasts covering firearms, reviews, tactics and related products. Circ. 200,000. Pays on publication. Publishes manuscripts 4-6 months after acceptance. Buys all world rights. Offers $50 kill fee. Reports in 2 weeks. Writer's guidelines for SASE.

Nonfiction: Test reports on new firearms; round-up articles on firearms types; guns for specific purposes (hunting, target shooting, self-defense); custom gunmakers; and history of modern guns. **Buys approximately 10 ms/year.** Query. Length: 1,000-2,500 words. **Pays $300-500.**

Photos: Major emphasis on quality photography. Additional payment of $50-200 for color, 4×5 or 2¼×2¼ preferred.

Columns/Departments: Buys 5-10 columns. Query. Length: 1,000 words. **Pays $400.**

$ $ HANDGUNS, Petersen Publishing Co., 6420 Wilshire Blvd., Los Angeles CA 90048. (213)782-2153. Fax: (213)782-2477. **Contact:** (Mr.) Jan M. Libourel, editor. **60% freelance written.** Monthly magazine covering handguns and handgun accessories. Estab. 1986. Circ. 150,000. **Pays on acceptance.** Byline given. No kill fee. Buys all rights. Reporting time varies. Free sample copy and writer's guidelines.

Nonfiction: General interest, historical, how-to, profile, new product and technical. "No articles not germane to established topics of magazine." **Buys 50 mss/year.** Send complete ms. **Pays $300-500.**

Photos: Send photos with submission. Reviews contact sheets, color transparencies, 5×7 prints. No additional payment for photos. Captions, model releases and identification of subjects required. Buys all rights.

Tips: "Send manuscript after querying editor by telephone and establishing acceptability. We are most open to feature stories. Be guided by published examples appearing in the magazine."

N $ $ MUZZLE BLASTS, National Muzzle Loading Rifle Association, P.O. Box 67, Friendship IN 47021. (812)667-5131. Fax: (812)667-5137. E-mail: nmlra@nmlra.org. Website: http://www.nmlra.org. Editor: Eric A. Bye. **Contact:** Terri Trowbridge, director of publications. **65% freelance written.** Monthly association magazine. "Articles must relate to muzzleloading or the muzzleloading era of American history." Estab. 1939. Circ. 25,000. Pays on publication. Publishes ms an average of 6 months after acceptance. Byline given. Offers $50 kill fee. Buys first North American serial rights, one-time rights and second serial (reprint) rights. Editorial lead time 4 months. Submit seasonal material 6 months in advance. Reports in 1 month on mss. Sample copy and writer's guidelines free.

- *Muzzle Blasts* now accepts manuscripts on 5.25 or 3.5 DOS diskettes in most major word processing programs; they prefer any of the Word Perfect™ formats.

Nonfiction: Book excerpts, general interest, historical/nostalgic, how-to, humor, interview/profile, new product, personal experience, photo feature, technical, travel. "No subjects that do not pertain to muzzleloading." **Buys 80 mss/year.** Query. Length: 2,500 words. **Pays $300 minimum for assigned articles; $50 minimum for unsolicited articles.**

Photos: Send photos with submission. Reviews 5×7 prints. Negotiates payment individually. Captions and model releases required. Buys one-time rights.

Columns/Departments: Buys 96 mss/year. Query. **Pays $50-200.**

Fiction: Adventure, historical, humorous. Must pertain to muzzleloading. **Buys 6 mss/year.** Query. Length: 2,500 words. **Pays $50-300.**

Fillers: Facts. **Pays $50.**

Tips: The National Muzzle Loading Rifle Association also publishes *Muzzle Blasts Online* on the World Wide Web. This electronic magazine is focused primarily for a nonmember audience. Writers and photographers are free to accept or reject this use of their work, and statements regarding this issue can be enclosed with your submission. (No additional payment will be made for use on *Muzzle Blasts Online*. The only time payment will be made for electronic use is when your article is used exclusively on the Web and has not been printed on the paper version of the magazine.) Please contact the NMLRA for writer's guidelines.

N ★ $ $ SHOTGUN NEWS, Primedia, Box 1790, Peoria IL 61656. (309)679-5408. Fax: (309)679-5476. E-mail: sgnews@aol.com. Website: http://www.shotgunnews.com. **Contact:** Robert W. Hunnicutt, general manager/editor. **95% freelance written.** Tabloid published every 10 days covering firearms, accessories, ammunition and militaria. "The nation's oldest and largest gun sales publication. Provides up-to-date market information for gun trade and consumers." Estab. 1946. Circ. 100,000. **Pays on acceptance.** Publishes ms 3 months after acceptance. Byline given. Buys first North American serial rights. Editorial lead time 1 month. Submit seasonal material 3 months in advance. Reports in 1 month on queries. Sample copy free.

Nonfiction: How-to, technical, historical. No political pieces, fiction or poetry. **Buys 50 mss/year.** Query. Length: 1,000-3,000 words. **Pays $200-500 for assigned articles.** Sometimes pays expenses of writers on assignment.

Photos: Send photos with submission. Reviews prints. Offers no additional payment for photos accepted with ms. Captions required. Buys one-time rights.

Hiking/Backpacking

$ $ $ $ BACKPACKER, Rodale Press, Inc., 33 E. Minor St., Emmaus PA 18098-0099. (610)967-8296. Fax: (610)967-8181. E-mail: mailbp@aol.com. Executive Editor: Thom Hogan. Managing Editor: Tom Shealey. **Contact:** Jim Gorman, Michele Morris, senior editors. **50% freelance written.** Magazine published 9 times/year covering wilderness travel for backpackers. Estab. 1973. Circ. 265,000. **Pays on acceptance.** Byline given. Buys one-time rights or all rights. Reports in 2 months. Writer's guidelines for #10 SASE.

Nonfiction: Essays, exposé, historical/nostalgic, how-to (expedition planner), humor, inspirational, interview/profile, new product, opinion, personal experience, technical, travel. No step-by-step accounts of what you did on your summer vacation—stories that chronicle every rest stop and gulp of water. Query with published clips and SASE. Length: 750-3,000 words. **Pays $400-2,000.** Sometimes pays (pre-determined) expenses of writers on assignment. "What we want are features that let us and the readers 'feel' the place, and experience your wonderment, excitement, disappointment or other emotions encountered 'out there.' If we feel like we've been there after reading your story, you've succeeded."

Photos: State availability of photos with submission. Pay varies. Buys one-time rights.

Columns/Departments: Signpost, "News From All Over" (adventure, environment, wildlife, trails, techniques, organizations, special interests—well-written, entertaining, short, newsy item), 50-500 words; Body Language (in-the-field column), 750-1,200 words; Moveable Feast (food-related aspects of wilderness: nutrition, cooking techniques, recipes, products and gear), 500-750 words; Weekend Wilderness (brief but detailed guides to wilderness areas, providing thorough trip-planning information, only enough anecdote to give a hint, then the where/when/hows), 500-750 words; Technique (ranging from beginner to expert focus, written by people with solid expertise, details ways to improve performance, how-to-do-it instructions, information on equipment manufacturers and places readers can go), 750-1,500 words; and Backcountry (personal perspectives, quirky and idiosyncratic, humorous critiques, manifestos and misadventures, interesting angle, lesson, revelation or moral), 750-1,200 words. **Buys 50-75 mss/year.** Query with published clips. **Pays $200-600.** No phone calls regarding story ideas. Written queries only.

Tips: "Our best advice is to read the publication—most freelancers don't know the magazine at all. The best way to break in is with an article for the Backcountry, Weekend Wilderness or Signpost Department."

$ $ $ $ OUTSIDE, Mariah Media Inc., Outside Plaza, 400 Market St., Santa Fe NM 87501. (505)989-7100. Editor: Mark Bryant. **Contact:** Hal Espen, features editor. **90% freelance written.** "*Outside* is a monthly national magazine for active, educated, upscale adults who love the outdoors and are concerned about its preservation." Estab. 1977. Circ. 500,000. **Pays on acceptance.** Publishes ms an average of 3 months after acceptance. Byline given. Offers 25% kill fee. Buys first North American serial rights. Submit seasonal material 4-5 months in advance. Electronic submission OK for solicited materials; not for unsolicited. Reports in 6 weeks on queries; 2 months on mss. Sample copy for $5 and 9×12 SAE with 9 first-class stamps. Writer's guidelines for SASE.

Nonfiction: Book excerpts; essays; reports on the environment; outdoor sports and expeditions; general interest; how-to; humor; inspirational; interview/profile (major figures associated with sports, travel, environment, outdoor); opinion; personal experience (expeditions; trying out new sports); photo feature (outdoor photography); technical (reviews of equipment, how-to); travel (adventure, sports-oriented travel). All should pertain to the outdoors: Bike section; Downhill Skiing; Cross-country Skiing; Adventure Travel. Do not want to see articles about sports that we don't cover (basketball, tennis, golf, etc.). **Buys 40 mss/year.** Query with published clips and SASE. Length: 1,500-4,000 words. **Pays $1/word.** Pays expenses of writers on assignment.

Photos: "Do not send photos; if we decide to use a story, we may ask to see the writer's photos." Reviews transparencies. Offers $180/photo minimum. Captions, identification of subjects required. Buys one-time rights.

Columns/Departments: Dispatches, contact Adam Horowitz (news, events, short profiles relevant to outdoors), 200-1,000 words; Destinations, contact Stephanie Gregory (places to explore, news, and tips for adventure travelers), 250-400 words; Review, contact Eric Hagerman (evaluations of products), 200-1,500 words. **Buys 180 mss/year.** Query with published clips. Length: 200-2,000 words. **Pays $1/word.**

Tips: "Prospective writers should study the magazine before querying. Look at the magazine for our style, subject matter and standards." The departments are the best areas for freelancers to break in.

Hockey

N $ $ AMERICAN HOCKEY, Official Publication of USA Hockey, 1710 Douglas Dr. N., #201, Golden Valley MN 55422. (612)595-0808. Fax: (612)595-0016. E-mail: bob pgsports.com. Website: http://www.tpgsports.com or http://www.usahockey.org. Editor: Darryl Seibel. **Contact:** Chuck Menke, managing editor. **85% freelance written.** Monthly magazine covering amateur hockey in the US. "The world's largest hockey magazine, *AHM* is the official magazine of USA Hockey, Inc., the national governing body of hockey." Estab. 1980. Circ. 400,000. Pays on acceptance or publication. Byline given. Buys all rights. Editorial lead time 3 months. Submit seasonal material 3 months in advance. Accepts simultaneous submissions. Sample copy and writer's guidelines free.

Nonfiction: Essays, general interest, historical/nostalgic, how-to (play hockey), humor, inspirational, interview/profile, new product, opinion, personal experience, photo feature, travel. No hockey camps, NCAA Championships, Olympics, etc. **Buys 20-30 mss/year**. Query. Length: 500-5,000 words. **Pays $50-300**. Sometimes pays expenses of writers on assignment.

Reprints: Accepts previously published submissions.

Photos: State availability of writers on assignment. Reviews contact sheets. Negotiates payment individually. Captions, identification of subjects required. Rights purchased varies.

Columns/Departments: Officials Crease (officiating), American Star (US-born stars). **Pays $50-300.**

Fiction: Adventure, humorous, slice-of-life vignettes. **Buys 10-20 mss/year. Pays $50.**

Fillers: Anecdotes, facts, gags to be illustrated by cartoonist, newsbreaks, short humor. **Buys 20-30/year**. Length: 10-100 words. **Pays $25-250.**

Tips: Writers must have a general knowledge and enthusiasm for hockey, including, ice, inline, street and other. The primary audience is youth players in the US.

$ $ ROLLER HOCKEY MAGAZINE, Straight Line Communications, 12327 Santa Monica Blvd. #202, Los Angeles CA 90025. (310)442-6660. Fax: (310)442-6663. E-mail: rhm@artnet.net. **Contact:** Amber Vasques, associate editor. **70% freelance written.** Monthly. "We cover everything from the beginning/recreational roller hockey player to the pros, offering instruction, new product information and anything else of interest to this audience." Estab. 1992. Circ. 35,000. Pays on publication. Publishes ms an average of 2 months after acceptance. Byline given. Buys first North American serial rights. Editorial lead time 2 months. Submit seasonal material 3 months in advance. Reports in 1 month.

Nonfiction: General interest, how-to, interview/profile, new product, personal experience, photo feature, technical.

Buys 24 mss/year. Query with published clips. Length: 1,000-1,500 words. **Pays 10-20¢/word for assigned articles.** Sometimes pays expenses of writers on assignment.

Photos: State availability of photos with submission. Negotiates payment individually.

Columns/Departments: Pays $150-200.

Horse Racing

$ $ THE BACKSTRETCH, United Thoroughbred Trainers of America, Inc., P.O. Box 7065, Louisville KY 40257-0065. (502)893-0025. Fax: (502)893-0026. E-mail: macagain@aol.com. Website: http://www.thebackstretch.com. **Contact:** Melissa McIntosh, production manager. **90% freelance written.** Estab. 1962. Circ. 10,000. Uses mostly established turf writers, but works with a few less experienced writers each year. Bimonthly magazine directed chiefly to Thoroughbred trainers but also to owners, fans and others working in or involved with the racing industry. Pays on publication. Publishes ms 3 months after acceptance, often longer. Sample copy on request.

Nonfiction: Profiles of trainers, owners, jockeys, horses and other personalities who make up the world of racing; analysis of industry issues; articles on particular tracks or races, veterinary topics; information on legal or business aspects of owning, training or racing horses; and historical perspectives. Opinions should be informed by expertise on the subject treated. Non-commissioned articles are accepted on a speculation basis. Pays on publication. If not suitable, articles are returned only if a SASE is included. Length: 1,500-2,500 words. **Pays $150-450.**

Reprints: Occasionally accepts previously published material, especially if it has appeared only in a regional or specialized publication. Send typed ms with rights for sale noted and information about when and where the article previously appeared. Payment negotiable.

Photos: It is advisable to include photo illustrations when possible, or these can be arranged for separately.

Tips: "If an article is a simultaneous submission, this must be stated and we must be advised if it is accepted elsewhere. Articles should be double spaced and may be submitted by mail, fax or e-mail on 3½-inch disk saved in text or in program compatible with PageMaker 5.0 for Macintosh."

$ $ HOOF BEATS, United States Trotting Association, 750 Michigan Ave., Columbus OH 43215. (614)224-2291. Fax: (614)228-1385. **Contact:** Dean A. Hoffman, editor. **25% freelance written.** Works with a small number of new/unpublished writers each year. Monthly magazine covering harness racing for the participants of the sport of harness racing. "We cover all aspects of the sport—racing, breeding, selling, etc." Estab. 1933. Circ. 15,000. Pays on publication. Publishes ms an average of 3 months after acceptance. Byline given. Buys negotiable rights. Submit seasonal material 4 months in advance. Reports in 1 month. Free sample copy, postpaid.

Nonfiction: General interest, historical/nostalgic, humor, inspirational, interview/profile, new product, personal experience, photo feature. **Buys 15-20 mss/year.** Query. Length: open. **Pays $100-400.**

Reprints: Send photocopy of article or short story. Pay is negotiable.

Photos: State availability of photos. Pays variable rates for 35mm transparencies and prints. Identification of subjects required. Buys one-time rights.

Fiction: Historical, humorous, novel excerpts, interesting fiction with a harness racing theme. **Buys 2-3 mss/year.** Query. Length: open. **Pays $100-400.**

$ $ THE QUARTER RACING JOURNAL, American Quarter Horse Association, P.O. Box 32470, Amarillo TX 79120. (806)376-4888. Fax: (806)349-6400. E-mail: aowens@aqha.org. Website: http://www.aqha.com. **Contact:** Amy Owens, editor. Executive Editor: Jim Jennings. **10% freelance written.** Monthly magazine. "The official racing voice of the American Quarter Horse Association. We promote quarter horse racing. Articles include training, breeding, nutrition, sports medicine, health, history, etc." Estab. 1988. Circ. 10,000. **Pays on acceptance.** Publishes ms an average of 3 months after acceptance. Buys first North American serial rights. Submit seasonal material 3 months in advance. Reports in 1 month on queries. Free sample copy and writer's guidelines.

Nonfiction: Historical (must be on quarter horses or people associated with them), how-to (training), nutrition, health, breeding and opinion. "We welcome submissions year-round." Special issues: Stallion and Broodmare Care (January-March 1998). Query. Length: 700-2,500 words. Pays $150-300.

Reprints: Send photocopy of article and information about when and where the article previously appeared.

Photos: Send photos with submission. Additional payment for photos accepted with ms might be offered. Captions and identification of subjects required.

Fiction: Publishes novel excerpts.

Tips: "Query first—must be familiar with quarter horse racing and be knowledgeable of the sport. The *Journal* directs its articles to those who own, train and breed racing quarter horses, as well as fans and handicappers. Most open to features covering training, nutrition, health care. Use a knowledgeable source with credentials."

Hunting and Fishing

$ $ ALABAMA GAME & FISH, Game & Fish Publications, Inc., P.O. Box 741, Marietta GA 30061. **Contact:** Jimmy Jacobs, editor. See *Game & Fish Publications*.

☆ $ $ AMERICAN ANGLER, the Magazine of Fly Fishing & Fly Tying, Abenaki Publishers, Inc., 160 Benmont Ave., Bennington VT 05201. Fax: (802)447-2471. **Contact:** Gary Soucie, editor. **95% freelance written.** Bimonthly magazine covering fly fishing. "*American Angler* is dedicated to giving fly fishers information they can use—wherever they fish, whatever they fish for. The *practical* dimension looms large." Estab. 1976. Circ. 50,000. Pays on publication. Publishes ms an average of 6 months after acceptance. Byline given. Buys first North American serial rights (articles) or one-time rights (photos). Editorial lead time over 3 months. Submit seasonal material 5 months in advance. Reluctantly accepts simultaneous submissions, if so noted. Reports in 6 weeks on queries; 2 months on mss. Sample copy for $6. Writer's guidelines for SASE.

Nonfiction: Book excerpts (well in advance of publication), essays (a few), how-to (most important), humor, opinion (query first), personal experience ("but tired of the 'me 'n' Joe' stories"), photo feature (seldom), technical. No promotional flack to pay back free trips or freebies, no superficial, broad-brush coverage of subjects. **Buys 45-60 mss/year.** Query with published clips and SASE. Length: 800-2,200 words. **Pays $200-400.**

Reprints: Send information about when and where the article previously appeared. Pay negotiable.

Photos: Send photos with submission. Reviews contact sheets, transparencies. Offers no additional payment for photos accepted with ms. Captions, identification of subjects required. Acquires one-time rights. "Photographs are important. Some articles can stand on the strength of the writing, but most need to be illustrated. Naturally, anecdotal and place-oriented stories must be illustrated with scenics, fishing shots, and other pictures that help flesh out the story and paint the local color. Technical pieces—those that deal with casting, rigging, fly tying and the like—must be accompanied by appropriate photography or rough sketches for our illustrator. A fly-tying submission should always include samples of flies to send to our staff photographer, even if photos of the flies are included."

Columns/Departments: "Safe & Sound" (health and safety issues), 700-1,500 words. One-page shorts (problem solvers), 350-750 words. **Buys 4-6 mss/year.** Query with published clips. **Pays $100-300.**

Fiction: Humorous, mainstream, slice-of-life vignettes. No stories unrelated to fly fishing or aimed at novice fly fishers. **Buys 1-2 mss/year.** Send complete ms. Writing must be top-drawer. Length: 500-2,000 words. **Pays $200-350.**

Fillers: Anecdotes, facts, short humor. Length: 25-150 words. **Pays $10-25.**

Tips: "If you are new to this editor, please submit complete queries. They needn't be long, but they should give what I need to decide to give you a go-ahead. Besides briefly outlining the subject, tell me *how* you will treat the material. As straightforward how-to? As first-person experiential narrative? As third-person piece of journalistic reporting? As writerly essay? Does the subject have seasonal or other *timeliness*? Some stories need to be run in a certain season; others can be run any time. Keep in mind that we work four months ahead of the issue date on the cover. *How few or many words will you need*? Most of our articles run 1,500 to 2,000 words. Some are too long or too short at that length. Write too long, and I'll reject or cut the article. Write too short, and I'll reject it or ask for a rewrite. We need some articles that are under 1,500 words and a few that are longer than 2,000. What are the *sidebar opportunities*? (Sources of further info, area contacts, tackle and pattern suggestions, fishing techniques in more detail than you can gracefully include in the article. Anything else about the subject that you found and think the reader will find interesting)? What sorts of *photos*, and how many of them, do you plan to submit? What *other sorts of illustrations* may be necessary or possible? Maps, Process drawings? Historical photos or art? Your rough sketches for our artist to finish? Do you plan to submit *patterns or dressings for flies*? (If so, we'd appreicate receiving a photo or photos, and a sample fly—in case we decide to use artwork or a specific setup photo instead of your snap.) Very important: Plan and write your query as carefully as you plan to write the article you are suggesting. I can only judge your ability by the organization and the writing in the query. Don't think I will believe you can write better than you've done in your query; I won't."

$ $ AMERICAN HUNTER, 11250 Waples Mill Rd., Fairfax VA 22030-9400. Fax: (703)267-3971. Editor: John Zent. **Contact:** Bill Rooney, managing editor. For hunters who are members of the National Rifle Association. "*The American Hunter* contains articles dealing with various sport hunting and related activities both at home and abroad. With the encouragment of the sport as a prime game management tool, emphasis is on technique, sportsmanship and safety. In each issue hunting equipment and firearms are evaluated, legislative happenings affecting the sport are reported, lore and legend are retold and the business of the Association is recorded in the Official Journal section." Circ. 1,300,000. **Pays on acceptance** for articles and on publication for photos. Buys first North American serial rights and subsequent reprint rights for NRA publications. Byline given. Reports in 1 month. Writer's guidelines for #10 SASE.

Nonfiction: Factual material on all phases of hunting: expository how-to, where-to, and general interest pieces; humor: personal narratives; and semi-technical articles on firearms, wildlife management or hunting. "Subject matter for feature articles falls into five general categories that run in each issue: deer, upland birds, waterfowl, big game and varmints/small game. Special issues: pheasants, whitetail tactics, black bear feed areas, mule deer, duck hunters' transport by land and sea, tech topics to be decided (October 1998); rut strategies, muzzleloader moose and elk, fall turkeys, staying warm, goose talk, long-range muzzleloading (November/December 1998). Not interested in material on fishing, camping or firearms legislation." Prefers queries. Length: 1,800-2,000 words. **Pays $250-500.**

Reprints: Send typed ms with rights for sale noted and information about when and where the article previously appeared.

Photos: No additional payment made for photos used with mss. Pays $25 for b&w photos purchased without accompa-

nying mss. Pays $50-175 for color.
Columns/Departments: Hunting Guns, Hunting Loads and Public Hunting Grounds. Study back issues for appropriate subject matter and style. Length: 1,200-1,500 words. **Pays $300-350.**
Tips: "Although unsolicited manuscripts are welcomed, detailed query letters outlining the proposed topic and approach are appreciated and will save both writers and editors a considerable amount of time. If we like your story idea, you will be contacted by mail or phone and given direction on how we'd like the topic covered. NRA Publications accept all manuscripts and photographs for consideration on a specualtion basis only. Story angles should be narrow, but coverage must have depth. How-to articles are popular with readers and might range from methods for hunting to techniques on making gear used on successful hunts. Where-to articles should contain contacts and information needed to arrange a similar hunt. All submissions are judged on three criteria: story angle (it should be fresh, interesting, and informative); quality of writing (clear and lively—capable of holding the readers' attention throughout); and quality and quantity of accompanying photos (sharpness, reproduceability, and connection to text are most important.)"

$ $ ARKANSAS SPORTSMAN, Game & Fish Publications, Inc., P.O. Box 741, Marietta GA 30061. (770)953-9222. **Contact:** Chuck Smock, editor. See *Game & Fish Publications.*

N $ BAIT FISHERMAN, Beaver Pond Publishing, P.O. Box 224, Greenville PA 16125. (724)588-3492. Fax: (724)588-2486. **Contact:** Rich Faler, editor. **80% freelance written.** Bimonthly magazine covering natural bait fishing, fresh and saltwater. "We are slanted exclusively toward bait fishing of all species of fresh and saltwater fish." Estab. 1995. Circ. 5,000. Pays on publication. Publishes ms an average of 6 months after acceptance. Byline given. Buys first rights, one-time rights or second serial (reprint) rights. Editorial lead time 4 months. Submit seasonal material 4-6 months in advance. Accepts simultaneous submissions. Accepts electronic submissions by disk but hard copy preferred. Reports in 2 months on queries; 3 months on mss. Writer's guidelines free.
Nonfiction: General interest, how-to (bait collection, presentation, maintenance, etc.), interview/profile, personal experience (with bait fishing-specific slant), travel ("hot spot" locations). **Buys 30-40 mss/year.** Query. Length: 1,000-2,000 words. **Pays $30-100** plus 3 copies.
Reprints: Send ms and information about when and where the article previously appeared. Pays 50-70% of amount paid for an original article.
Photos: Send photos with submission. Reviews contact sheets, negatives, 35mm transparencies, 5×7 prints (preferred). No additional payment for photos accepted with ms. Captions, identification of subjects required. Buys one-time rights.
Fillers: Anecdotes, facts, newsbreaks, bait-specific legislation pieces, how-tos and hints. **Buys 10-20/year.** Length: 50-500 words. **Pays $10-30.**
Tips: "Query with detailed description of what you can provide our readers. State availability of photos, graphics and sidebars. We want detailed how-to, where-to and natural history pieces regarding all facets of bait fishing."

$ $ BASSMASTER MAGAZINE, B.A.S.S. Publications, 5845 Carmichael Pkwy., Montgomery AL 36117. (334)272-9530. Fax: (334)279-7148. E-mail: bassmag@mindspring.com. Website: http://www.bassmaster.com. **Contact**: Johnna Pitts, assistant editor. Editor: Dave Precht. **80% freelance written.** Prefers to work with published/established writers. Magazine published 10 issues/year about largemouth, smallmouth and spotted bass, offering "how-to" articles for dedicated beginning and advanced bass fishermen, including destinations and new product reviews. Estab. 1968. Circ. 600,000. **Pays on acceptance.** Publishes ms an average of 6-12 months after acceptance. Byline given. Buys all rights. Editorial lead time 2 months. Submit seasonal material 6 months in advance. Reports in 2 months. Sample copy for $2. Writer's guidelines for #10 SASE.
Nonfiction: Historical, how-to (patterns, lures, etc.), interview (of knowledgeable people in the sport), profile (outstanding fishermen), travel (where to go to fish for bass), how-to (catch bass and enjoy the outdoors), new product (reels, rods and bass boats), conservation related to bass fishing. "No first person, personal experience 'Me and Joe go fishing' type articles." **Buys 100 mss/year.** Query. Length: 500-2,500 words. **Pays $100-500.**
• Needs destination stories (how to fish a certain area) for the Northwest and Northeast.
Photos: Send photos with submission. Reviews transparencies. Offers no additional payment for photos accepted with ms. Pays $600 for color cover transparencies. Captions required; model releases preferred. Buys all rights.
Columns/Departments: Short Cast/News & Views (upfront regular feature covering news-related events such as new state bass records, unusual bass fishing happenings, conservation, new products and editorial viewpoints); 250-400 words. **Pays $100-3,000.**
Fillers: Anecdotes, newsbreaks. **Buys 4-5 mss/issue.** Length: 250-500 words. **Pays $50-100.**
Tips: "Editorial direction continues in the short, more direct how-to article. Compact, easy-to-read information is our objective. Shorter articles with good graphics, such as how-to diagrams, step-by-step instruction, etc., will enhance a writer's articles submitted to *Bassmaster Magazine*. The most frequent mistakes made by writers in completing an article for us are poor grammar, poor writing, poor organization and superficial research. Send in detailed queries outlining specific objectives of article, obtain writer's guidelines. Be as concise as possible."

$ $ BC OUTDOORS, OP Publishing, 780 Beatty St., Suite 300, Vancouver, British Columbia V6B 2M1 Canada. (604)606-4644. Fax: (604)687-1925. E-mail: oppubl@istar.ca. Acting Editor: Roegan Lloydd. **80% freelance written.** Works with a small number of new/unpublished writers each year in BC. Magazine published 8 times/year covering fishing, camping, hunting and the environment of outdoor recreation. Estab. 1945. Circ. 42,000. Pays on publication. Publishes ms an average of 3 months after acceptance. Byline given. Offers negotiable kill fee. Buys first

North American serial rights. Reports in 1 month (approximately). Sample copy and writer's guidelines for 8×10 SAE with 7 Canadian first-class stamps or International equivalent.

Nonfiction: How-to (new or innovative articles on fishing/hunting subjects), personal experience (outdoor adventure), outdoor topics specific to British Columbia. "We would like to receive how-to, where-to features dealing with hunting and fishing in British Columbia." **Buys 80-90 mss/year.** Query. Length: 1,500-2,000 words. **Pays $300-500.** Sometimes pays the expenses of writers on assignment.

- Wants in-depth, informative, professional writing only.

Photos: State availability of photos with query. Pays $25-75 on publication for 5×7 b&w prints; $35-150 for color contact sheets and 35mm transparencies. Captions and identification of subjects required. Buys one-time rights.

Tips: "Emphasis on environmental issues. Those pieces with a conservation component have a better chance of being published. Subject must be specific to British Columbia. We receive many manuscripts written by people who obviously do not know the magazine or market. The writer has a better chance of breaking in with short, lesser-paying articles and fillers, because we have a stable of regular writers who produce most main features."

$ $ BUGLE, Journal of Elk and the Hunt, Rocky Mountain Elk Foundation, 2291 W. Broadway, Missoula MT 59802. (406)523-4568. Fax: (406)523-4550. E-mail: lcromrich@rmef.org. Website: http://www.rmef.org. Editor: Dan Crockett. **Contact:** Lee Cromrich, editorial assistant; David Stalling, conservation editor; Don Burgess, hunting editor. **50% freelance written.** Bimonthly magazine covering conservation and hunting. "*Bugle* is the membership publication of the Rocky Mountain Elk Foundation, a nonprofit wildlife conservation group; it also sells on newsstands. Our readers are predominantly hunters, many of them naturalists who care deeply about protecting wildlife habitat. Hunting stories and essays should celebrate the hunting experience, demonstrating respect for wildlife, the land and the hunt. Articles on elk behavior or elk habitat should include personal observations and entertain as well as educate." Estab. 1984. Circ. 195,000. **Pays on acceptance**. Publishes ms 3-9 months after acceptance. Byline given. Offers variable kill fee. Buys one-time rights. Editorial lead time 6 months. Submit seasonal material 6 months in advance. Reports in 1 month on queries; 2 months on mss. Sample copy $5. Writer's guidelines for #10 SASE.

Nonfiction: Book excerpts, essays, general interest (elk related), historical/nostalgic, humor, opinion, personal experience, photo feature. No how-to, where-to. Buys 20 mss/year. Query with or without published clips, or send complete ms. Length: 1,500-4,500 words. **Pays 20¢/word** and 3 contributor copies; more issues at cost.

Reprints: Send typed ms with information about when and where the article previously appeared and rights for sale noted. Pays 75% of amount paid for an original article.

Columns/Departments: Situation Ethics, 1,000-2,000 words; Thoughts & Theories, 1,500-4,000 words; Women in the Outdoors, 1,000-2,500 words. Bows & Arrows, 1,500-2,000 words. **Buys 12 mss/year.** Query with or without published clips or send complete ms. **Pays 20¢/word.**

Fiction: Adventure, historical, humorous, slice-of-life vignettes, western, novel excerpts. No fiction that doesn't pertain to elk or elk hunting. **Buys 4 mss/year.** Query with or without published clips or send complete ms. Length: 1,500-4,500 words. **Pays 20¢/word.**

Poetry: Free verse, haiku, light verse, traditional. **Buys 6 poems/year.** Submit maximum 6 poems.

Tips: "Creative queries (250-500 words) that showcase your concept and your style remain the most effective approach. We're hungry for submissions for four specific columns: Situation Ethics, Thoughts & Theories, Bows & Arrows and Women in the Outdoors. Send a SASE for guidelines. We also welcome strong, well-reasoned opinion pieces on topics pertinent to hunting and wildlife conservation, and humorous pieces about elk behavior or encounters with elk (hunting or otherwise)."

$ $ CALIFORNIA GAME & FISH, Game & Fish Publications, Inc., Box 741, Marietta GA 30061. **Contact:** Burt Carey, editor. See *Game & Fish Publications*.

$ $ CANADIAN SPORTFISHING MAGAZINE, Canada's Fishing Authority, Canadian Sportfishing Productions, 937 Centre Rd., Dept. 2020, Waterdown, Ontario L0R 2H0 Canada. **Contact:** Matt Nichols, editor. **70% freelance written.** Bimonthly magazine covering sport fishing. Estab. 1988. Circ. 30,000. Pays on publication. Publishes ms an average of 3 months after acceptance. Byline given. Offers 50% kill fee. Buys all rights. Editorial lead time 6 months. Submit seasonal material 8 months in advance. Reports in 2 months on queries; 6 months on mss. Sample copy for $4. Writer's guidelines for #10 SASE.

Nonfiction: How-to, humor, new product. **Buys 40 mss/year.** Query. Length: 1,500-4,000 words. **Pays 15¢/word minimum (Canadian funds).** Sometimes pays expenses of writers on assignment.

Photos: Send photos with submission. Reviews contact sheets, transparencies and prints. Offers no additional payment for photos accepted with ms. Captions, model releases and identification of subjects required. Buys all rights.

☆ $ $ DEER & DEER HUNTING, Krause Publications, 700 E. State St., Iola WI 54990-0001. Fax: (715)445-4087. Editor: Patrick Durkin. Website: http://www.krause.com. **Contact:** Dan Schmidt, associate editor. **95% freelance written.** Published 8 times/year covering white-tailed deer and deer hunting. "Readers include a cross section of the deer hunting population—individuals who hunt with bow, gun or camera. The editorial content of the magazine focuses on white-tailed deer biology and behavior, management principle and practices, habitat requirements, natural history of deer, hunting techniques, and hunting ethics. We also publish a wide range of 'how-to' articles designed to help hunters locate and get close to deer at all times of the year. The majority of our readership consists of two-season hunters (bow and gun) and approximately one-third camera hunt." Estab. 1977. Circ. 140,000. **Pays on acceptance**. Byline given.

Editorial lead time 6 months. Submit seasonal material 6 months in advance. Reports in 3 months. Sample copy for 9×12 SASE. Writer's guidelines free.
Nonfiction: General interest, how-to, inspirational, photo feature. No "Me and Joe" articles. Buys 30-50 mss/year. Query. Length: 750-3,000 words. **Pays $150-525 for assigned articles; $150-325 for unsolicited articles.** Sometimes pays expenses of writers on assignment.
Photos: Send photos with submission. Reviews transparencies. Negotiates payment individually. Captions, model releases and identification of subjects required.
Fiction: "Mood" deer hunting pieces. **Buys 8 mss/year.** Send complete ms.
Fillers: Facts, newsbreaks. **Buys 40-50/year.** Length: 100-500 words. **Pays $15-150.**
Tips: "Feature articles dealing with deer biology or behavior should be documented by scientific research (the author or that of others) as opposed to a limited number of personal observations."

$ $ DISCOVERING AND EXPLORING NEW JERSEY'S FISHING STREAMS AND THE DELAWARE RIVER, New Jersey Sportsmen's Guides, P.O. Box 100, Somerdale NJ 08083. Fax: (609)665-8656. **Contact:** Steve Perrone, editor. **60-70% freelance written.** Annual magazine covering freshwater stream and river fishing. Estab. 1993. Circ. 4,500. **Pays on acceptance**. Publishes ms an average of 6 months after acceptance. Byline given. Buys first rights and makes work-for-hire assignments. Editorial lead time 6 months. Sample copy for $12.50 postage paid.
Nonfiction: How-to fishing and freshwater fishing. **Buys 6-8 mss/year.** Query with published clips. Length: 500-2,000 words. **Pays $75-250.**
Photos: State availability of photos with submission. Reviews 4×5 transparencies and prints. Negotiates payment individually. Captions, model releases, identification of subjects required. Buys one-time rights.
Tips: "We want queries with published clips of articles describing fishing experiences on New Jersey streams and the Delaware River."

$ $ $ $ FIELD & STREAM, 2 Park Ave., New York NY 10016-5695. Editor: Duncan Barnes. **Contact:** David E. Petzal, executive editor. **50% freelance written.** Eager to work with new/unpublished writers. Monthly. "Broad-based service magazine for the hunter and fisherman. Editorial content ranges from very basic how-to stories detailing a useful technique or a device that sportsmen can make, to articles of penetrating depth about national hunting, fishing, and related activities. Also humor and personal essays, nostalgia and 'mood pieces' on the hunting or fishing experience and profiles on outdoor people." Estab. 1895. Circ. 1,790,400. **Pays on acceptance.** Buys first rights. Byline given. Reports in 2 months. Query. Writer's guidelines for #10 SASE.

- Ranked as one of the best markets for freelance writers in *Writer's Yearbook* magazine's annual "Top 100 Markets," January 1998.

Nonfiction: Length: 1,000 words for features. Payment varies depending on the quality of work, importance of the article. **Pays $800 and up to $1,000 and more on a sliding scale for major features.** *Field & Stream* also publishes regional sections with feature articles on hunting and fishing in specific areas of the country. The sections are geographically divided into East, Midwest, West and South, and appear 12 months/year. Regional articles and ideas should be addressed to John Merwin, regionals editor.
Photos: Prefers color slides to b&w. Query first with photos. When photos purchased separately, pays $450 minimum for color. Buys first rights to photos.
Columns/Departments: Personal essays suitable for the "Finally . . . " department. Length: 750-800 words.
Fillers: Buys short "how it's done" fillers, 75 to 150 words, on unusual or helpful subjects. Also buys short (up to 500 words) pieces on tactics or techniques for specific hunting or fishing situations; short "Field Guide" pieces on natural phenomena as related to hunting and fishing; "Myths and Misconceptions," short pieces debunking a commonly held belief about hunting and fishing; short "Outdoor Basics" and "Sportsman's Projects" articles; and short pieces for the "Up Front" section that run the gamut from natural history to conservation news, anecdotal humor, short tips, and carefully crafted opinion pieces (word length: 25-400).
Tips: "Writers are encouraged to submit queries on article ideas. These should be no more than a paragraph or two, and should include a summary of the idea, including the angle you will hang the story on, and a sense of what makes this piece different from all others on the same or a similar subject. Many queries are turned down because we have no idea what the writer is getting at. Be sure that your letter is absolutely clear. We've found that if you can't sum up the point of the article in a sentence or two, the article doesn't have a point. Pieces that depend on writing style, such as humor, mood, and nostalgia or essays often can't be queried and may be submitted in manuscript form. The same is true of short tips. All submissions to *Field & Stream* are on an on-spec basis. Before submitting anything, however, we encourage you to *study*, not simply read, the magazine. Many pieces are rejected because they do not fit the tone or style of the magazine, or fail to match the subject of the article with the overall subject matter of *Field & Stream*. Above all, study the magazine before submitting anything."

$ $ THE FISHERMAN, LIF Publishing Corp., 14 Ramsey Rd., Shirley NY 11967-4704. (516)345-5200. Fax: (516)345-5304. Publisher: Fred Golofaro. Associate Publisher: Pete Barrett. Senior Editor: Tim Coleman. 4 regional editions: *Long Island*, *Metropolitan New York*, Tom Melton, editor; *New England*, Tim Coleman, editor; *New Jersey*, Pete Barrett, editor; *Delaware-Maryland-Virginia*, Keith Kaufman, editor. 75% freelance written. A weekly magazine covering fishing with an emphasis on saltwater. Combined circ. 100,000. Pays on publication. Byline given. Offers variable kill fee. Buys all rights. Articles may be run in one or more regional editions by choice of the editors. Submit seasonal material 2 months in advance. Reports in 4-6 weeks. Free sample copy and writer's guidelines.

Nonfiction: Send submission to regional editor. General interest, historical/nostalgic, how-to, interview/profile, personal experience, photo feature, technical, travel. Special issues: Boat & Motor Buyer's Guide and Winter Workbench (January); Tackle, Trout (March); Inshore Fishing (April); Saltwater Fly, Party Boat, Black Bass (May); Offshore Fishing (June); Surf Fishing (August); Striped Bass (October); Travel (December). "No 'me and Joe' tales. We stress how, where, when, why." **Buys 300 mss/year, each edition.** Length: 1,000-1,500 words. **Pays $110-150.**
Photos: Send photos with submission; also buys single color photos for cover use (pays $50-$100). Offers no additional payment for photos accepted with ms. Identification of subjects required.
Tips: "Focus on specific how-to and where-to subjects within each region."

$ $ FLORIDA GAME & FISH, Game & Fish Publications, Inc., Box 741, Marietta GA 30061. (770)953-9222. **Contact:** Jimmy Jacobs, editor. See *Game & Fish Publications*.

$ $ FLORIDA SPORTSMAN, Wickstrom Publishers Inc., 5901 SW 74 St., Miami FL 33143. (305)661-4222. Fax: (305)284-0277. E-mail: fseditor@aol.com. Website: http://www.floridasportsman.com. Editor: Glenn Law. **70% freelance written.** Works with new/unpublished writers. Monthly magazine covering fishing, boating and related sports—Florida and Caribbean only. "*Florida Sportsman* is edited for the boatowner and offshore, coastal and fresh water fisherman. It provides a how, when and where approach in its articles, which also include occasional camping, diving and hunting stories—plus ecology; in-depth articles and editorials attempting to protect Florida's wilderness, wetlands and natural beauty." Circ. 115,000. **Pays on acceptance**. Publishes ms an average of 6 months after acceptance. Byline given. Offers 50% kill fee. Buys first North American serial rights. Submit seasonal material 6 months in advance. Reports in 2 months on queries; 1 month on mss. Sample copy free. Writer's guidelines for #10 SASE.
Nonfiction: Essays (environment or nature), how-to (fishing, hunting, boating), humor (outdoors angle), personal experience (in fishing, etc.), technical (boats, tackle, etc., as particularly suitable for Florida specialties). "We use reader service pieces almost entirely—how-to, where-to, etc. One or two environmental pieces per issue as well. Writers *must* be Florida based, or have lengthy experience in Florida outdoors. All articles must have strong Florida emphasis. We do not want to see general how-to-fish-or-boat pieces which might well appear in a national or wide-regional magazine." **Buys 40-60 mss/year.** Query; no e-mail queries. Length: 2,000-3,000 words. **Pays $400.** Sometimes pays expenses of writers on assignment.
Photos: Send photos with submission. Reviews 35mm transparencies and 4×5 and larger prints. Offers no additional payment for photos accepted with ms. Pays up to $1,000 for cover photos. Buys one-time rights.
Tips: "Feature articles are most open to freelancers; however there is little chance of acceptance unless contributor is an accomplished and avid outdoorsman *and* a competent writer-photographer with considerable experience in Florida."

$ $ FLY FISHING IN SALT WATERS, Hook and Release Publications, Inc., 2001 Western Ave., Suite 210, Seattle WA 98121. (206)443-3273. Fax: (206)443-3293. E-mail: flyfishinsalt@flyfishers.com. Website: http://www.flyfishinsalt.com/ffsw. **Contact:** R.P. Van Gytenbeek, managing editor. **90% freelance written.** Bimonthly magazine covering fly fishing in salt waters anywhere in the world. Estab. 1994. Circ. 44,000. Pays on publication. Publishes ms an average of 1 year after acceptance. Byline given. Buys first North American serial rights and electronic rights. Editorial lead time 3 months. Submit seasonal material at least 2 months in advance. Reports in 1 month on queries; 2 months on mss. Sample copy for $6. Writer's guidelines for #10 SASE.
Nonfiction: Book excerpts, essays, historical/nostalgic, how-to, interview/profile, new product, personal experience, photo feature, technical, travel, resource issues (conservation); all on flyfishing. **Buys 40-50 mss/year.** Query with or without published clips. Length: 1,500-2,500 words. **Pays $400-500.**
Photos: Send photos with submission. Reviews transparencies (35mm color only). Negotiates payment individually: offers no additional payment for photos accepted with ms; pays $80-300/photo if purchased separately. Captions, identification of subjects required. Buys one-time rights.
Columns/Departments: Legends/Reminiscences (history-profiles-nostalgia), 2,000-2,500 words; Resource (conservation issues), 1,000-1,500 words; Fly Tier's Bench (how to tie saltwater flies), 1,000-1,200 words, photos critical; Tackle & Technique (technical how-to), 1,000-1,500 words, photos or illustrations critical; Boating (technical how-to), 2,000-2,500 words. (Other departments are mostly staff written or by assignment only.) **Buys 25-30 mss/year.** Query. **Pays $400-500.**
Fiction: Adventure, humorous, mainstream; all dealing with flyfishing. **Buys 2-3 mss/year.** Send complete ms. Length: 2,000-3,000 words. **Pays $500.**
Fillers: Most fillers are staff-written.
Tips: "Follow up on your inquiry with a phone call."

$ FUR-FISH-GAME, 2878 E. Main, Columbus OH 43209-9947. **Contact:** Mitch Cox, editor. **65% freelance written.** Works with a small number of new/unpublished writers each year. Monthly magazine for outdoorsmen of all ages who are interested in hunting, fishing, trapping, dogs, camping, conservation and related topics. Estab. 1900. Circ. 108,000. **Pays on acceptance.** Publishes ms an average of 7 months after acceptance. Byline given. Buys first serial rights or all rights. Reports in 2 months. Sample copy for $1 and 9×12 SAE. Writer's guidelines for #10 SASE.
Nonfiction: "We are looking for informative, down-to-earth stories about hunting, fishing, trapping, dogs, camping, boating, conservation and related subjects. Nostalgic articles are also used. Many of our stories are 'how-to' and should appeal to small-town and rural readers who are true outdoorsmen. Some recent articles have told how to train a gun dog, catch big-water catfish, outfit a bowhunter and trap late-season muskrat. We also use personal experience stories

and an occasional profile, such as an article about an old-time trapper. 'Where-to' stories are used occasionally if they have broad appeal." Query with SASE. Length: 500-3,000 words. **Pays $150 or more** for features depending upon quality, photo support, and importance to magazine. **Short filler stories pay $75-125.**
Photos: Send photos with ms. Photos are part of ms package and receive no additional payment. Prefers color prints or transparencies. Prints can be 5×7 or 8×10. Pays $25 for separate freelance photos. Captions and credits required.
Tips: "We are always looking for quality how-to articles about fish, game animals or birds that are popular with everyday outdoorsmen but often overlooked in other publications, such as catfish, bluegill, crappie, squirrel, rabbit, crows, etc. We also use articles on standard seasonal subjects such as deer and pheasant, but like to see a fresh approach or new technique. Instructional trapping articles are useful all year. Articles on gun dogs, ginseng and do-it-yourself projects are also popular with our readers. An assortment of photos and/or sketches greatly enhances any manuscript, and sidebars, where applicable, can also help. No phone queries, please."

$ $ GAME & FISH PUBLICATIONS, INC., 2250 Newmarket Pkwy., Suite 110, Marietta GA 30067. (770)953-9222. Fax: (770)933-9510. **Contact:** Ken Dunwoody, editorial director. Publishes 30 different monthly outdoor magazines, each one covering the fishing and hunting opportunities in a particular state or region (see individual titles and editors). **90% freelance written.** Estab. 1975. Circ. 550,000. Pays 75 days prior to cover date of issue. Publishes ms an average of 7 months after acceptance. Byline given. Offers negotiable kill fee. Buys first North American serial rights. Submit seasonal material at least 8 months in advance. Editors prefer to hold queries until that season's material is assigned. Reports in 3 months on mss. Sample copy for $2.50 and 9×12 SASE. Writer's guidelines for #10 SASE.
Nonfiction: Prefer queries over unsolicited ms. Article lengths either 1,500 or 2,500 words. Pays separately for articles and accompanying photos. **Manuscripts pay $125-300,** cover photos $250, inside color $75 and b&w $25. Reviews transparencies and b&w prints. Prefers captions and identification of species/subjects. Buys one-time rights to photos.
Fiction: Buys some humor and nostalgia pertaining to hunting and fishing. **Pays $125-250.** Length 1,500-2,500 words.
Tips: "Our readers are experienced anglers and hunters, and we try to provide them with useful, entertaining articles about where, when and how to enjoy the best hunting and fishing in their state or region. We also cover topics concerning game and fish management. Most articles should be aimed at outdoorsmen in one particular state. After familiarizing themselves with our magazine(s), writers should query the appropriate state editor (see individual listings) or send to Ken Dunwoody."

$ $ GEORGIA SPORTSMAN, Game & Fish Publications, Box 741, Marietta GA 30061. (770)953-9222. **Contact:** Jimmy Jacobs, editor. See *Game & Fish Publications.*

$ $ GREAT PLAINS GAME & FISH, Game & Fish Publications, Box 741, Marietta GA 30061. (770)953-9222. **Contact:** Nick Gilmore, editor. See *Game & Fish Publications.*

$ $ GULF COAST FISHERMAN, Harold Wells Gulf Coast Fisherman, Inc., P.O. Drawer P, 401 W. Main St., Port Lavaca TX 77979. Fax: (512)552-8864. **Contact:** David Widener, managing editor. **95% freelance written.** Quarterly magazine. "All editorial material is designed to expand the knowledge of the Gulf Coast angler and promote saltwater fishing in general." Estab. 1979. Circ 15,000. Pays on publication. Publishes ms an average of 2 months after acceptance. Byline given. Buys first North American serial rights. Submit seasonal queries 5 months in advance. Reports in 1 month. Sample copy and writer's guidelines for 9×12 SAE with 5 first-class stamps.
Nonfiction: How-to (any aspect relating to saltwater fishing that provides the reader specifics on use of tackle, boats, finding fish, etc.), interview/profile, new product, personal experience, technical. **Buys 25 mss/year.** Query with or without published clips or send complete ms. Length: 1,200-1,800 words. **Pays $150-225.**
Photos: State availability of photos with submission. Prefers b&w prints. Offers no additional payment for photos accepted with ms. Captions and identification of subjects required. Pays $125 for cover photos. Buys one-time rights.
Tips: "Features are the area of our publication most open to freelancers. Subject matter should concern some aspect of or be in relation to saltwater fishing in coastal bays or offshore. Prefers electronic submissions—3.5 Mac-compatible, 3.5 Mac or PC. Articles may be as broad as a review of the different technique used in pursuing redfish or trout by Gulf fishermen, to one on a particular bay, person or fish. From offshore to pier fishing, the reader should know enough about the subject after reading the article to repeat the writer's experience."

$ $ ILLINOIS GAME & FISH, Game & Fish Publications, Inc., Box 741, Marietta GA 30061. (770)953-9222. **Contact:** Bill Hartlage, editor. See *Game & Fish Publications.*

$ $ INDIANA GAME & FISH, Game & Fish Publications, Inc., Box 741, Marietta GA 30061. (770)953-9222. **Contact:** Ken Freel, editor. See *Game & Fish Publications.*

$ $ IOWA GAME & FISH, Game & Fish Publications, Inc., Box 741, Marietta GA 30061. (770)953-9222. **Contact:** Bill Hartlage, editor. See *Game & Fish Publications.*

$ $ KENTUCKY GAME & FISH, Game & Fish Publications, Inc., Box 741, Marietta GA 30061. (770)953-9222. **Contact:** Bill Hartlage, editor. See *Game & Fish Publications.*

$ $ LOUISIANA GAME & FISH, Game & Fish Publications, Inc., Box 741, Marietta GA 30061. (770)953-9222. **Contact:** Chuck Smock, editor. See *Game & Fish Publications*.

☆ $ $ THE MAINE SPORTSMAN, P.O. Box 365, Augusta ME 04330. **Contact:** Harry Vanderweide, editor. **80% freelance written.** "Eager to work with new/unpublished writers, but because we run over 30 regular columns, it's hard to get into *The Maine Sportsman* as a beginner." Monthly tabloid. Estab. 1972. Circ. 30,000. Pays during month of publication. Buys first rights. Publishes ms 3 months after acceptance. Byline given. Reports in 2 weeks.
Nonfiction: "We publish only articles about Maine hunting and fishing activities. Any well-written, researched, knowledgeable article about that subject area is likely to be accepted by us." **Buys 25-40 mss/issue.** Submit complete ms. Length: 200-2,000 words. **Pays $20-300.** Sometimes pays the expenses of writers on assignment.
Reprints: Send typed ms with rights for sale. Pays 100% of amount paid for an original article.
Photos: "We can have illustrations drawn, but prefer 1-3 b&w photos." Submit photos with accompanying ms. Pays $5-50 for b&w print.
Tips: "It's rewarding finding a writer who has a fresh way of looking at ordinary events. Specific where-to-go about Maine is needed."

☆ $ $ MARLIN, The International Sportfishing Magazine, Marlin Magazine, a division of World Publications, Inc., P.O. Box 2456, Winter Park FL 32790. (407)628-4802. Fax: (407)628-7061. E-mail: marlin@worldzine.com. **Contact:** David Ritchie, editor. **90% freelance written.** Bimonthly magazine on big game fishing. "*Marlin* covers the sport of big game fishing (billfish, tuna, dorado and wahoo). Our readers are sophisticated, affluent and serious about their sport—they expect a high-class, well-written magazine that provides information and practical advice." Estab. 1982. Circ. 40,000. **Pays on acceptance for text**, on publication for photos. Publishes ms an average of 3 months after acceptance. Byline given. Buys first North American serial rights. Submit seasonal material 2-3 months in advance. Query for electronic submissions. Sample copy and writer's guidelines for $3.20 and SAE.
Nonfiction: General interest, how-to (bait-rigging, tackle maintenance, etc.), new product, personal experience, photo feature, technical, travel. "No freshwater fishing stories. No 'me & Joe went fishing' stories." **Buys 30-50 mss/year.** Query with published clips. Length: 800-3,000 words. **Pays $250-500.**
Photos: State availability of photos with submission. Original slides, please. Offers $25-300/photo. $750 for a cover. Buys one-time rights.
Columns/Departments: Tournament Reports (reports on winners of major big game fishing tournaments), 200-400 words; Blue Water Currents (news features), 100-400 words. **Buys 25 mss/year.** Query. **Pays $75-250.**
Reprints: Accepts previously published articles in news section only. Send photocopy of article, including information about when and where the article previously appeared. Pays 50-75% of the amount paid for an original article.
Tips: "Tournament reports are a good way to break in to *Marlin*. Make them short but accurate, and provide photos of fishing action or winners' award shots (*not* dead fish hanging up at the docks!). We always need how-tos and news items. Our destination pieces (travel stories) emphasize where and when to fish, but include information on where to stay also. For features: crisp, high action stories with emphasis on exotic nature, adventure, personality, etc.—nothing flowery or academic. Technical/how-to: concise and informational—specific details. News: Again, concise with good details—watch for legislation affecting big game fishing, outstanding catches, new clubs and organizations, new trends and conservation issues."

$ MICHIGAN OUT-OF-DOORS, P.O. Box 30235, Lansing MI 48909. (517)371-1041. Fax: (517)371-1505. E-mail: mucc@mucc.org. Website: http://www.mucc.org. **Contact:** Dennis C. Knickerbocker, editor. **50% freelance written.** Works with a small number of new/unpublished writers each year. Monthly magazine emphasizing Michigan outdoor recreation, especially hunting and fishing, conservation, nature and environmental affairs. Estab. 1947. Circ. 120,000. **Pays on acceptance.** Publishes ms an average of 6 months after acceptance. Byline given. Buys first North American serial rights. Phone queries OK. Submit seasonal material 6 months in advance. Reports in 1 month. Sample copy for $2.50. Free writer's guidelines.
Nonfiction: Exposé, historical, how-to, informational, interview, nostalgia, personal experience, personal opinion, photo feature, profile. No humor or poetry. "Stories *must* have a Michigan slant unless they treat a subject of universal interest to our readers." Special issues: Archery Deer Hunting (October); Firearm Deer Hunting (November); Cross-country Skiing and Early-ice Lake Fishing (December). **Buys 8 mss/issue.** Send complete ms. Length: 1,000-2,000 words. **Pays $90 minimum for feature stories.** Pays expenses of writers on assignment.
Photos: Purchased with or without accompanying ms. Pays $20 minimum for any size b&w glossy prints; $175 maximum for color (for cover). Offers no additional payment for photos accepted with accompanying ms. Buys one-time rights. Captions preferred.
Tips: "Top priority is placed on true accounts of personal adventures in the out-of-doors—well-written tales of very unusual incidents encountered while hunting, fishing, camping, hiking, etc. The most rewarding aspect of working with freelancers is realizing we had a part in their development. But it's annoying to respond to queries that never produce a manuscript."

$ $ MICHIGAN SPORTSMAN, Game & Fish Publications, Inc., Box 741, Marietta GA 30061. (770)953-9222. **Contact:** Dennis Schmidt, editor. See *Game & Fish Publications*.

☆ $ MID WEST OUTDOORS, Mid West Outdoors, Ltd., 111 Shore Drive, Hinsdale (Burr Ridge) IL 60521-5885. (630)887-7722. Fax: (630)887-1958. E-mail: mwdmagtv30@aol.com. **Contact:** Gene Laulunen, editor. Monthly tabloid emphasizing fishing, hunting, camping and boating. **100% freelance written.** Estab. 1967. Circ. 50,000. Pays on publication. Buys simultaneous rights. Byline given. Submit seasonal material 2 months in advance. Accepts simultaneous submissions. Reports in 3 weeks. Publishes ms an average of 3 months after acceptance. Sample copy for $1. Writer's guidelines for #10 SASE.

Nonfiction: How-to (fishing, hunting, camping in the Midwest) and where-to-go (fishing, hunting, camping within 500 miles of Chicago). "We do not want to see any articles on 'my first fishing, hunting or camping experiences,' 'cleaning my tackle box,' 'tackle tune-up,' or 'catch and release.' " **Buys 1,800 unsolicited mss/year.** Send complete ms and 1 or 2 photos on 3.5 diskette with ms included. Length: 1,000-1,500 words. **Pays $15-30.**

Reprints: Send tearsheet of article.

Photos: Offers no additional payment for photos accompanying ms unless used as covers; uses slides and b&w prints. Buys all rights. Captions required.

Columns/Departments: Fishing, Hunting. Open to column/department suggestions. Send complete ms. **Pays $25.**

Tips: "Break in with a great unknown fishing hole or new technique within 500 miles of Chicago. Where, how, when and why. Know the type of publication you are sending material to."

$ $ MID-ATLANTIC GAME & FISH, Game & Fish Publications, Inc., Box 741, Marietta GA 30061. (770)953-9222. **Contact:** Ken Freel, editor. See *Game & Fish Publications*.

$ $ MINNESOTA SPORTSMAN, Game & Fish Publications, Inc., Box 741, Marietta GA 30061. (770)953-9222. **Contact:** Dennis Schmidt, editor. See *Game & Fish Publications*.

$ $ MISSISSIPPI GAME & FISH, Game & Fish Publications, Inc., Box 741, Marietta GA 30061. (770)953-9222. **Contact:** Chuck Smock, editor. See *Game & Fish Publications*.

$ $ MISSOURI GAME & FISH, Game & Fish Publications, Inc., Box 741, Marietta GA 30061. (770)953-9222. **Contact:** Chuck Smock, editor. See *Game & Fish Publications*.

$ $ NEW ENGLAND GAME & FISH, Game & Fish Publications, Inc., Box 741, Marietta GA 30061. (770)953-9222. **Contact:** Steve Carpenteri, editor. See *Game & Fish Publications*.

$ $ NEW JERSEY LAKE SURVEY FISHING MAPS GUIDE, New Jersey Sportsmen's Guides, P.O. Box 100, Somerdale NJ 08083. (609)783-1271. (609)665-8350. Fax: (609)665-8656. **Contact:** Steve Perrone, editor. **30-40% freelance written.** Annual magazine covering freshwater lake fishing. "*New Jersey Survey Fishing Maps Guide* is edited for freshwater fishing for trout, bass, perch, catfish and other species. It contains 132 pages and approximately 100 full-page maps of the surveyed lakes that illustrate contours, depths, bottom characteristics, shorelines and vegetation present at each location. The guide includes a 10-page chart which describes over 250 fishing lakes in New Jersey. It also covers trout stocked lakes, fishing tips and 'Bass'n Notes.' " Estab. 1989. Circ. 4,500. **Pays on acceptance**. Publishes ms an average of 6 months after acceptance. Byline given. Buys first rights and makes work-for-hire assignments. Editorial lead time 6 months. Sample copy for $12.50 postage paid.

Nonfiction: How-to fishing, freshwater fishing. Length: 500-2,000 words. **Pays $75-250.**

Photos: State availability of photos with submission. Reviews transparencies 4×5 slides or 4×6 prints. Captions, model releases, identification of subjects required. Buys one-time rights.

Tips: "We want queries with published clips of articles describing fishing experiences on New Jersey lakes and ponds."

$ $ NEW YORK GAME & FISH, Game & Fish Publications, Inc., Box 741, Marietta GA 30061. (770)953-9222. **Contact:** Steve Carpenteri, editor. See *Game & Fish Publications*.

$ $ NORTH AMERICAN WHITETAIL, The Magazine Devoted to the Serious Trophy Deer Hunter, Game & Fish Publications, Inc., 2250 Newmarket Pkwy., Suite 110, Marietta GA 30067. (770)953-9222. Fax: (770)933-9510. **Contact:** Gordon Whittington, editor. **70% freelance written.** Magazine published 8 times/year about hunting trophy-class white-tailed deer in North America, primarily the US. "We provide the serious hunter with highly sophisticated information about trophy-class whitetails and how, when and where to hunt them. We are not a general hunting magazine or a magazine for the very occasional deer hunter." Estab. 1982. Circ. 170,000. Pays 75 days prior to cover date of issue. Publishes ms an average of 6 months after acceptance. Byline given. Offers negotiable kill fee. Buys first North American serial rights. Submit seasonal material 10 months in advance. Reports in 3 months on mss. Editor prefers to keep queries on file, without notification, until the article can be assigned or author informs of prior sale. Sample copy for $3 and 9×12 SAE with 7 first-class stamps. Writer's guidelines for #10 SASE.

Nonfiction: How-to, interview/profile. **Buys 50 mss/year.** Query. Length: 1,000-3,000 words. **Pays $150-400.**

Photos: Send photos with submission. Reviews 2×2 transparencies and 8×10 prints. Offers no additional payment for photos accepted with ms. Captions and identification of subjects required. Buys one-time rights.

Columns/Departments: Trails and Tails (nostalgic, humorous or other entertaining styles of deer-hunting material, fictional or nonfictional), 1,400 words. **Buys 8 mss/year.** Send complete ms. **Pays $150.**

Tips: "Our articles are written by persons who are deer hunters first, writers second. Our hard-core hunting audience can see through material produced by non-hunters or those with only marginal deer-hunting expertise. We have a continual need for expert profiles/interviews. Study the magazine to see what type of hunting expert it takes to qualify for our use, and look at how those articles have been directed by the writers. Good photography of the interviewee and his hunting results must accompany such pieces."

$ $ NORTH CAROLINA GAME & FISH, Game & Fish Publications Inc., Box 741, Marietta GA 30061. (770)953-9222. Fax: (770)933-9510. **Contact:** Steve Walburn, editor. See *Game & Fish Publications.*

$ $ OHIO GAME & FISH, Game & Fish Publications, Inc., Box 741, Marietta GA 30061. (770)953-9222. **Contact:** Steve Carpenteri, editor. See *Game & Fish Publications.*

$ $ OKLAHOMA GAME & FISH, Game & Fish Publications, Box 741, Marietta GA 30061. (770)953-9222. Fax: (770)933-9510. **Contact:** Nick Gilmore, editor. See *Game & Fish Publications.*

✪ $ $ ONTARIO OUT OF DOORS, Maclean Hunter Publishing Ltd., 777 Bay St., 6th Floor, Toronto, Ontario M5W 1A7 Canada. (416)596-5908. Fax: (416)596-2517. E-mail: 102677.1125@compuserv.com. Website: http://www.fishontario.com. **Contact:** Burt Myers, editor. Managing Editor: John Kerr. **90% freelance written.** Magazine published 10 times/year covering the outdoors (hunting, fishing, camping). Estab. 1968. **Pays on acceptance**. Circ. 88,967. Publishes ms an average of 6 months after acceptance. Byline given. Offers 100% kill fee. Buys first and electronic rights. Editorial lead time 6 months. Submit seasonal material 6 months in advance. Reports in 3 months on queries. Sample copy and writer's guidelines free.

- Editor notes that *Ontario Out of Doors* needs more articles on camping, boating, recreational vehicles, photography, target shooting and archery as they relate to angling and hunting.

Nonfiction: Book excerpts, essays, exposé, how-to and where-to (fishing and hunting), humor, inspirational, interview/profile, new product, opinion, personal experience, photo feature, technical, travel, wildlife management and environmental concerns. "No Me and Joe features or articles written from a women's point of view on how to catch a bass." Special issues: Travel (March); Trout (April). **Buys 100 mss/year.** Query with SASE. Length: 500-2,500 words maximum. **Pays $750 maximum for assigned articles; $700 maximum for unsolicited articles.** Sometimes pays expenses of writers on assignment.

Photos: Send photos with submission. Reviews transparencies. Offers no additonal payment for photos accepted with ms except for cover and contents use. Pays $450-750 for covers. Captions required. Buys one-time rights.

Columns/Departments: Trips & Tips (travel pieces), 50-150 words; Short News, 50-500 words. **Buys 30-40 mss/year.** Query. **Pays $50-250.**

Fiction: Humorous. **Buys 6 mss/year.** Send complete ms. Length: 1,000 words maximum. **Pays $500 maximum.** Occasionally publishers novel excerpts.

Fillers: Facts, newsbreaks. **Buys 40/year.** Length: 25-100 words. **Pays $15-50.**

Tips: "With the exception of short news stories, it is suggested that writers query prior to submission."

$ $ $ $ OUTDOOR LIFE, Times Mirror Magazines, Inc., 2 Park Ave., New York NY 10016. (212)779-5000. Fax: (212)686-6877. E-mail: olmagazine@aol.com. Editor: Todd W. Smith. Executive Editor: Bob Brown. **Contact:** Ed Scheff, senior editor. **95% freelance written.** Monthly. "*Outdoor Life* is an information source for the active outdoor enthusiast. The editorial provides the fishing and hunting enthusiast (and his family) with the 'how to', 'where-to-go' and what to bring on an outdoor adventure. It covers national and regional interests with wide range of subjects including: conservation, sportsmen's issues, photography, cooking, travel and nostalgia/history." Estab. 1898. Circ. 1,350,000. **Pays on acceptance.** Publishes ms an average of 1 year after acceptance. Byline given. Buys first North American serial rights. Submit seasonal material 1 year in advance. Reports in 1 month on queries; 2 months on mss. Writer's guidelines for #10 SASE.

Nonfiction: Book excerpts, essays, how-to (must cover hunting, fishing or related outdoor activities), interview/profile, new product, personal experience, photo feature, technical, travel. No articles that are too general in scope—need to write specifically. **Buys 200 mss/year.** "E-mail queries preferred." Length: 800-3,000 words. **Pays $500-750** for 1,000-word features, national or regional; **$1,200-2,000** for 1,500-word or longer features.

Photos: Send photos with submission. Do not send photos with queries. Pays $250 for ¼ page color to $850 for 2-page spread in color; $1,000 for covers. All requested photos must be stamped with name and address.

Fillers: National and International newsbreaks (500 words maximum). Do-it-yourself for hunters and fishermen. Length: 1,000 words maximum. Payment varies.

Tips: "It is best for freelancers to break in by writing features for one of the regional sections—East, Midwest, South, West. One-page queries recommended."

✪ $ $ PENNSYLVANIA ANGLER & BOATER, Pennsylvania Fish and Boat Commission, P.O. Box 67000, Harrisburg PA 17106-7000. (717)657-4520. E-mail: amichaels@fish.state.pa.us. Website: http://www.fish.state.pa.us. **Contact:** Art Michaels, editor. **80% freelance written.** Prefers to work with published/established writers but works with a few unpublished writers every year. Bimonthly magazine covering fishing, boating and related conservation topics in Pennsylvania. Circ. 40,000. Pays 2 months after acceptance. Publishes ms an average of 8 months after acceptance. Byline given. Rights purchased vary. Submit seasonal material 8 months in advance. Reports in 1 month on queries; 2 months on mss. Sample copy for 9×12 SAE with 9 first-class stamps. Guidelines for #10 SASE.

Nonfiction: How-to, where-to, technical. No saltwater or hunting material. **Buys 100 mss/year.** Query. Length: 500-3,500 words. **Pays $25-300.**

Photos: Send photos with submission. Reviews 35mm and larger transparencies and 8×10 b&w prints. Offers no additional payment for photos accepted with ms. Captions, model releases and identification of subjects required. Also reviews photos separately. Rights purchased and rates vary.

Tips: "Our mainstays are how-tos, where-tos and conservation pieces. Articles are occasionally aimed at novice anglers and boaters, and some material is directed toward the most skilled fishermen and boaters. Most articles cater to people between these extremes."

$ $ PENNSYLVANIA GAME & FISH, Game & Fish Publications, Inc., Box 741, Marietta GA 30061. (770)953-9222. **Contact:** Steve Carpenteri, editor. See *Game & Fish Publications*.

$ $ PETERSEN'S HUNTING, Petersen Publishing Co., 6420 Wilshire Blvd., Los Angeles CA 90048. (213)782-2184. Fax: (213)782-2477. Editor: Greg Tinsley. Managing Editor: Duke Anderson. **40% freelance written.** Works with a small number of new/unpublished writers each year. Monthly magazine covering sport hunting. "We are a 'how-to' magazine devoted to all facets of sport hunting, with the intent to make our readers more knowledgeable, more successful and safer hunters." Circ. 325,000. **Pays on acceptance.** Publishes ms an average of 9 months after acceptance. Byline given. Offers $50 kill fee. Buys all rights. Submit seasonal queries 9 months in advance. Reports in 2 weeks. Free sample copy and writer's guidelines covering format, sidebars and computer disks available on request.

Nonfiction: General interest, historical/nostalgic, how-to (on hunting techniques), travel. Special issues: Hunting Annual (August). **Buys 30 mss/year.** Query. Length: 2,000 words. **Pays $350 minimum.**

Photos: Send photos with submission. Reviews 35mm transparencies and 8×10 b&w prints. Offers no additional payment for b&w photos accepted with ms; offers $50-250/color photo. Captions, model releases, identification of subjects required. Buys one-time rights.

$ $ ROCKY MOUNTAIN GAME & FISH, Game & Fish Publications, Inc., Box 741, Marietta GA 30061. Fax: (770)933-9510. **Contact:** Burt Carey, editor. See *Game & Fish Publications*.

$ $ SAFARI MAGAZINE, The Journal of Big Game Hunting, Safari Club International, 4800 W. Gates Pass Rd., Tucson AZ 85745. (520)620-1220. Fax: (520)617-0233. Director of Publications/Editor: William R. Quimby. **Contact:** Merrik Bush-Pirkle, manuscripts editor. **90% freelance written.** Bimonthly club journal covering international big game hunting and wildlife conservation. Circ. 30,000. Pays on publication. Publishes ms an average of 18 months after acceptance. Byline given. Offers $100 kill fee. Buys all rights on story; first rights on photos. Submit seasonal material 1 year in advance. Reports in 2 weeks on queries; 6 weeks on mss. Sample copy for $4. Guidelines for SASE.

Nonfiction: Photo feature (wildlife), technical (firearms, hunting techniques, etc.). **Buys 72 mss/year.** Query or send complete ms. Length: 2,000-2,500 words. **Pays $200 for professional writers, lower rates if not professional.**

Photos: State availability of photos with query; or send photos with ms. Payment depends on size in magazine. Pays $45 for b&w; $100 color. Captions, model releases, identification of subjects required. Buys first rights.

Tips: "Study the magazine. Send complete manuscript and photo package. Make it appeal to knowledgeable, world-traveled big game hunters. Features on conservation contributions from big game hunters around the world are open to freelancers. We have enough stories on first-time African safaris and North American hunting. We need South American and Asian hunting stories, plus stories dealing with hunting and conservation, especially as it applies to our organization and members."

$ $ SALT WATER SPORTSMAN MAGAZINE, 77 Franklin St., Boston MA 02110. (617)338-2300. Fax: (617)338-2309. E-mail: swsfish@ultranet.com. Website: http://www.saltwatersportsman.com. **Contact:** Barry Gibson, editor. **85% freelance written.** Works with a small number of new/unpublished writers each year. Monthly magazine. "*Salt Water Sportsman* is edited for serious marine sport fishermen whose lifestyle includes the pursuit of game fish in US waters and around the world. It provides information on fishing trends, techniques and destinations, both local and international. Each issue reviews offshore and inshore fishing boats, high-tech electronics, innovative tackle, engines, vehicles and other new products. Coverage also focuses on sound fisheries management and conservation." Circ. 150,000. **Pays on acceptance.** Publishes ms an average of 5 months after acceptance. Byline given. Buys first North American serial rights. Offers 100% kill fee. Submit seasonal material 8 months in advance. Reports in 1 month. Sample copy and writer's guidelines for 9×12 SAE with 10 first-class stamps.

- Ranked as one of the best markets for freelance writers in *Writer's Yearbook*'s annual "Top 100 Markets," January 1998.

Nonfiction: How-to, personal experience, technical, travel (to fishing areas). "Readers want solid how-to, where-to information written in an enjoyable, easy-to-read style. Personal anecdotes help the reader identify with the writer." Prefers new slants and specific information. Query. "It is helpful if the writer states experience in salt water fishing and any previous related articles. We want one, possibly two well-explained ideas per query letter—not merely a listing. Good pictures with query often help sell the idea." **Buys 100 mss/year.** Length: 1,200-1,500 words. **Pays $350 and up.** Sometimes pays the expenses of writers on assignment. Also seeking short feature articles (500-1,000 words) on regional hot spots, species, special rigs, fishing methods, etc. **Pays $200-500,** depending on the quality of writing and accompanying photos. Query.

Reprints: Occasionally accepts reprints of previously published submissions. Send tearsheet of article. Pays up to 50%

of amount paid for an original article.

Photos: Purchased with or without accompanying ms. Captions required. Uses color slides. Pays $1,000 minimum for 35mm, 2¼×2¼ or 8×10 transparencies for cover. Offers additional payment for photos accepted with accompanying ms.

Columns/Departments: Sportsman's Workbench (short, how-to tips and techniques on salt water fishing, emphasis is on building, repairing, or reconditioning specific items or gear). Send ms. Length: 100-300 words.

Tips: "There are a lot of knowledgeable fishermen/budding writers out there who could be valuable to us with a little coaching. Many don't think they can write a story for us, but they'd be surprised. We work with writers. Shorter articles that get to the point which are accompanied by good, sharp photos are hard for us to turn down. Having to delete unnecessary wordage—conversation, clichés, etc.—that writers feel is mandatory is annoying. Often they don't devote enough attention to specific fishing information."

$ $ SOUTH CAROLINA GAME & FISH, Game & Fish Publications, Inc., Box 741, Marietta GA 30061. (770)953-9222. **Contact:** Steve Walburn, editor. See *Game & Fish Publications*.

$ $ SOUTH CAROLINA WILDLIFE, P.O. Box 167, Rembert Dennis Bldg., Columbia SC 29202-0167. (803)734-3972. E-mail: scwmed@scdnr.state.sc.us. Editor: John Davis. **Contact:** Linda Renshaw, managing editor. Bimonthly magazine for South Carolinians interested in wildlife and outdoor activities. **75% freelance written.** Estab. 1954. Circ. 60,000. Byline given. **Pays on acceptance.** Publishes ms an average of 6 months after acceptance. Buys first rights. Free sample copy. Reports in 2 months.

Nonfiction: Articles on outdoor South Carolina with an emphasis on preserving and protecting our natural resources. "Realize that the topic must be of interest to South Carolinians and that we must be able to justify using it in a publication published by the state department of natural resources—so if it isn't directly about outdoor recreation, a certain plant or animal, it must be somehow related to the environment and conservation. Readers prefer a broad mix of outdoor related topics (articles that illustrate the beauty of South Carolina's outdoors and those that help the reader get more for his/her time, effort, and money spent in outdoor recreation). These two general areas are the ones we most need. Subjects vary a great deal in topic, area and style, but must all have a common ground in the outdoor resources and heritage of South Carolina. Review back issues and query with a one-page outline citing sources, giving ideas for photographs, explaining justification and giving an example of the first two paragraphs." Does not need any column material. Generally does not seek photographs. The publisher assumes no responsibility for unsolicited material. **Buys 25-30 mss/year.** Length: 1,000-3,000 words. **Pays an average of $200-400/article** depending upon length and subject matter.

Tips: "We need more writers in the outdoor field who take pride in the craft of writing and put a real effort toward originality and preciseness in their work. Query on a topic we haven't recently done. Frequent mistakes made by writers in completing an article are failure to check details and go in-depth on a subject."

$ $ SPORT FISHING, The Magazine of Saltwater Fishing, 330 W. Canton Ave., Winter Park FL 32789-7061. (407)628-4802. Fax: (407)628-7061. Email: do1@worldzine.com. **Contact:** Doug Olander, editor-in-chief. Managing Editor: Dave Ferrell. **60% freelance written.** Magazine covering offshore sport fishing. Estab. 1986. Circ. 150,000. Pays within 6 weeks of acceptance. Byline given. Offers $100 kill fee. Buys first North American serial or one-time rights. Submit seasonal material 4-5 months in advance. Accepts simultaneous submission. Reports in 2 weeks. Sample copy and writer's guidelines for SASE.

Nonfiction: How-to (rigging & techniques tips), technical, conservation, travel and where-to (all on sport fishing). **Buys 32-40 mss/year.** Query with or without clips, e-mail preferred; fax, letter acceptable. Length: 1,500-2,500 words. **Pays $150-600.**

Photos: Send photos with submission. Reviews transparencies and returns within 1 week. Pays $50-300 inside; $1,000 cover. Identification of subjects required. Buys one-time rights.

Columns/Departments: Fish Tales (humorous sport fishing anecdotes); Rigging (how-to rigging for sport fishing); Technique (how-to technique for sport fishing). Length: 800-1,200 words. **Buys 8-24 mss/year.** Send complete ms. **Pays $150 for Fish Tales, $200 for other departments.**

Tips: "Don't query unless you are familiar with the magazine; note—*salt water only.* Find a fresh idea or angle to an old idea. We welcome the chance to work with new/unestablished writers who know their stuff—and how to say it."

$ SPORTING CLAYS MAGAZINE, Patch Communications, 5211 S. Washington Ave., Titusville FL 32780. (407)268-5010. Fax: (407)267-1894. E-mail: dsage@megabits.net. Website: http://www.sportingclays.net. Editor: George Conrad. **Contact:** Dan Sage, managing editor. Monthly magazine. "*Sporting Clays* reports on shooting activities with instructional columns, equipment reviews and range listings, and is the official publication of the National Sporting Clays Association." Estab. 1987. Circ. 30,000. Pays on publication. Publishes ms an average of 6 months after acceptance. Byline given. Buys first North American serial rights. Editorial lead time 4 months. Submit seasonal material 6 months in advance. Reports in 1 month.

Nonfiction: Historical/nostalgic, how-to (technique), interview/profile, new product, personal experience, photo feature, technical, travel. Query with published clips and SASE. Length: 700-1,000 words.

Photos: Send photos with submission. Reviews transparencies, prints. Negotiates payment individually. Captions, identification of subjects required. Buys one-time rights.

$ $ $ SPORTS AFIELD, Hearst Magazines, 250 W. 55th St., New York NY 10019-5201. (212)649-4000. Fax: (212)581-3923. E-mail: saletter@hearst.com. Website: http://www.sportsafield.com. Editor-in-Chief: John Atwood. Executive Editor: Fred Kesting. **20% freelance written.** Magazine for the outdoor enthusiast with special interest in wilderness sports. Covers a wide range of outdoor interests such as: hiking, kayaking, mountain biking, camping, canoeing, fishing, hunting, boating, off-road, archery, survival, conservation, tackle, new gear, shooting sports, camping. Published 10 times/year. Estab. 1887. Circ. 450,000. Buys first North American serial rights for features. **Pays on acceptance.** Publishes ms an average of 6 months after acceptance. Byline given. "Our magazine is seasonal and material submitted should be in accordance. Fishing in spring and summer; hunting in the fall." Submit seasonal material 9 months in advance. Reports in 2 months. SASE for reply or writer's guidelines.

Nonfiction: "Informative how-to articles with emphasis on product and service and personal experiences with good photos on wilderness sports, camping, conservation, and environmental issues (limited where-to-go) related to hunting and fishing. We want first-class writing and reporting." **Buys 15-17 unsolicited mss/year.** Length: 500-2,000 words. Query or submit complete ms.

Columns/Departments: Almanac (outdoor tips specifically for hunters, fishermen and campers, unusual, how-to and nature items), 200-300 words. Query or submit complete ms.

Photos: "For photos without ms, duplicates of 35mm color transparencies preferred."

Fiction: Adventure, humor, nostalgia (if related to wilderness sports). Query or submit complete ms.

Tips: "Read a recent copy so you know the market you're writing for. Manuscript *must* be available on disk."

"We are interested in where-to-go and how-to articles. Features based on outdoor products are welcome if they have a fresh slant. We also publish fiction, humor and cartoons, but no poetry. We prefer detailed queries first. This saves time and effort on your part as well as ours. If you are sending a finished manuscript, it should be double-spaced and a computer disk should be available if the story is accepted. If you are submitting photos, send only duplicates because there is always the chance that originals could be lost. Should we want original photos for publication, we will contact the photographer. *Sports Afield* is not responsible for any unsolicited photos or manuscripts."

$ $ TENNESSEE SPORTSMAN, Game & Fish Publications, Box 741, Marietta GA 30061. (770)953-9222. **Contact:** Steve Walburn, editor. See *Game & Fish Publications*.

$ $ TEXAS SPORTSMAN, Game & Fish Publications, Inc., Box 741, Marietta GA 30061. (770)953-9222. **Contact:** Nick Gilmore, editor. See *Game & Fish Publications*.

$ $ TIDE MAGAZINE, Coastal Conservation Association, 220W, 4801 Woodway, Houston TX 77056. (713)626-4222. Fax: (713)961-3801. E-mail: ccatide@pdq.net. **Contact:** Doug Pike, editor. Bimonthly magazine on saltwater fishing and conservation of marine resources. Estab. 1977. Circ. 60,000. Pays on publication. Byline given. Buys one-time rights. Submit seasonal material 6 months in advance. Reports in 1 month.

Nonfiction: Essays, exposé, general interest, historical/nostalgic, humor, opinion, personal experience and travel, related to saltwater fishing and Gulf/Atlantic coastal habits. **Buys 30 mss/year.** Query with published clips. Length: 1,200-1,500 words. **Pays $300 for ms/photo package.**

Photos: Reviews 35mm transparencies and 8×10 b&w prints. Offers no additional payment for photos accepted with ms. Captions required. Buys one-time rights. Pays $25 for b&w, $50 for color inside.

$ $ TRAPPER & PREDATOR CALLER, Krause Publications Inc., 700 E. State St., Iola WI 54990. (715)445-2214. Fax: (715)445-4087. E-mail: gkrahn@add-inc.com. Website: http://www.krause.com. **Contact:** Gordy Krahn, editor. **90% freelance written.** Monthly tabloid covers trapping, predator calling and muzzleloading. "Our editorial goal is to entertain and educate our readers with national and regional articles that promote trapping." Estab. 1975. Circ. 35,000. Pays on publication. Offers $50 kill fee. Buys first North American serial rights. Submit seasonal material 6 months in advance. Reports in 2 weeks. Free sample copy and writer's guidelines.

Nonfiction: How-to, humor, interview/profile, new product, opinion and personal experience. **Buys 60 mss/year.** Query with or without published clips, or send complete ms. Length: 1,200-2,500 words. **Pays $80-250 for assigned articles; $40-200 for unsolicited articles.**

Photos: Send photos with submission. Reviews prints. Offers no additional payment for photos accepted with ms. Captions and identification of subjects required. Buys one-time rights.

Fillers: Facts, gags to be illustrated, newsbreaks, short humor. **Buys 60/year.** Length: 200-800 words. **Pays $25-80.**

Tips: "We are always looking for new ideas and fresh material on trapping, predator calling and black powder hunting."

$ $ TURKEY & TURKEY HUNTING, Krause Publications, 700 E. State St., Iola WI 54990-0001. (715)445-2214, ext. 484. Fax: (715)445-4087. E-mail: lovettb@krause.com. Website: http://www.krause.com/outdoors. **Contact:** Brian Lovett, editor. **90% freelance written.** Magazine published 6 times/year (4 spring, 1 fall, 1 winter) covering turkey hunting and turkey biology. "*Turkey & Turkey Hunting* is for serious, experienced turkey hunters." Estab. 1983. Circ. 28,000. **Pays on acceptance.** Publishes ms an average of 1 year after acceptance. Byline given. Offers 50% kill fee. Buys first North American serial rights. Editorial lead time 1 year. Submit seasonal material 1 year in advance. Reports in 2 months. Sample copy and writer's guidelines free.

Nonfiction: How-to, personal experience. **Buys 45 mss/year.** Query with published clips. Length: 2,000 words. **Pays $275-300.** Sometimes pays expenses of writers on assignment.

Photos: Send photos with submission. Reviews transparencies. Offers $75-300/photo, depending on size. Pays on publication for photos. Buys one-time rights.

Tips: "Have a thorough knowledge of turkey hunting and the hunting industry. Send fresh, informative queries, and indicate topics you'd feel comfortable covering on assignment."

$ $ TURKEY CALL, Wild Turkey Center, P.O. Box 530, Edgefield SC 29824-0530. (803)637-3106. Fax: (803)637-0034. E-mail: nwtf@gab.net. Editor: Jay Langston. **Contact:** Mary Busbee, publishing assistant. **50-60% freelance written.** Eager to work with new/unpublished writers and photographers. Bimonthly educational magazine for members of the National Wild Turkey Federation. Estab. 1973. Circ. 120,000. Buys one-time rights. Byline given. **Pays on acceptance.** Publishes ms an average of 6 months after acceptance. Reports in 1 month. Queries required. Submit complete package. Wants original mss only. Sample copy for $3 and 9×12 SAE. Writer's guidelines for #10 SASE.

Nonfiction: Feature articles dealing with the hunting and management of the American wild turkey. Must be accurate information and must appeal to national readership of turkey hunters and wildlife management experts. No poetry or first-person accounts of unremarkable hunting trips. May use some fiction that educates or entertains in a special way. Length: up 2,500 words. **Pays $100 for short fillers of 600-700 words, $200-500 for illustrated features.**

Reprints: Send photocopy of article and information about when and where the article previously appeared. Pays 50% of amount paid for an original article.

Photos: "We want quality photos submitted with features." Art illustrations also acceptable. "We are using more and more inside color illustrations." For b&w, prefer 8×10 glossies, but accepts 5×7. Transparencies of any size are acceptable. No typical hunter-holding-dead-turkey photos or setups using mounted birds or domestic turkeys. Photos with how-to stories must make the techniques clear (example: how to make a turkey call; how to sculpt or carve a bird in wood). Pays $35 minimum for one-time rights on b&w photos and simple art illustrations; up to $100 for inside color, reproduced any size; $200-400 for covers.

Tips: "The writer should simply keep in mind that the audience is 'expert' on wild turkey management, hunting, life history and restoration/conservation history. He/she *must know the subject*. We are buying more third-person, more fiction, more humor—in an attempt to avoid the 'predictability trap' of a single subject magazine."

$ $ VIRGINIA GAME & FISH, Game & Fish Publications, Inc., Box 741, Marietta GA 30061. (770)953-9222. **Contact:** Steve Walburn, editor. See *Game & Fish Publications*.

$ $ WARMWATER FLY FISHING, Abenaki Publishers, Inc., 160 Benmont Ave., P.O. Box 4100, Bennington VT 05201. (802)447-1518. **Contact:** John M. Likakis, editor. **95% freelance written.** Bimonthly magazine covering fly fishing for bass, panfish, and other warmwater fish. "*Warmwater Fly Fishing* specializes in how-to, where-to, and when-to stories about fly fishing for warmwater species of fish. The emphasis is on nuts-and-bolts articles that tell the reader about specific techniques, places, equipment, etc." Estab. 1997. Pays on publication. Publishes ms an average of 6 months after acceptance. Byline given. Buys first North American and one-time rights. Editorial lead time 6 months. Submit seasonal material 6 months in advance. Reports in 6 weeks on queries; 3 months on mss. Sample copy for $4.99. Writer's guidelines for $3 and #10 SASE.

Nonfiction: Historical/nostalgic, how-to, technical. No 'Me and Joe' fishing stories, exotic destinations, product reviews or puff pieces. **Buys 70 mss/year.** Query. Length: 1,000-2,500 words. **Pays $250-350.**

Photos: Send photos with submission. Reviews transparencies. Offers no additional payment for photos accepted with ms. "Unless otherwise specified, photos are considered part of the submission." Captions, model releases, identification of subjects required. Buys one-time rights.

Columns/Departments: Tech Tackle (innovative rigging); The Deep (fly fishing in deep water); Conservation, Boating, Roots (nostalgia, classic flies); Basic Techniques, Musings (essay); The Tier (tying warmwater flies); all 1,500 words. **Buys 54 mss/year.** Query. **Pays $250-350.**

Tips: "Brief but complete query letters detailing what the article intends to cover. Neatness counts! Check your letter carefully for typos, misspellings, proper address and so forth."

$ $ WASHINGTON-OREGON GAME & FISH, Game & Fish Publications, Inc., Box 741, Marietta GA 30061. **Contact:** Burt Carey, editor. See *Game & Fish Publications*.

$ $ WEST VIRGINIA GAME & FISH, Game & Fish Publications, Inc., Box 741, Marietta GA 30061. (770)953-9222. **Contact:** Ken Freel, editor. See *Game & Fish Publications*.

$ $ WESTERN OUTDOORS, 3197-E Airport Loop, Costa Mesa CA 92626. (714)546-4370. Fax: (714)662-3486. E-mail: woutdoors@aol.com. **Contact:** Jack Brown, editor. **60% freelance written.** Works with a small number of new/unpublished writers each year. Emphasizes fishing, boating for California, Oregon, Washington, Baja California, and Alaska. "We are the West's leading authority on fishing techniques, tackle and destinations, and all reports present the latest and most reliable information." Publishes 9 issues/year. Estab. 1961. Circ. 100,000. **Pays on acceptance.** Publishes ms an average of 6 months after acceptance. Buys first North American serial rights. Submit seasonal material 6 months in advance. Reports in 2 weeks. Sample copy for $2, OWAA members, $1. Writer's guidelines for #10 SASE.

- *Western Outdoors* now emphasizes freshwater and saltwater fishing and boating exclusively. Area of coverage is limited to far west states and Baja California.

Nonfiction: Where-to (catch more fish, improve equipment, etc.), how-to informational, photo feature. "We do not

accept fiction, poetry." **Buys 45-55 assigned mss/year.** Query with SASE. Length: 1,200-2,000 words. **Pays $300-400.**
Photos: Purchased with accompanying ms. Captions required. Prefers professional quality 35mm slides. Offers no additional payment for photos accepted with accompanying ms. Pays $250 for covers.
Tips: "Provide a complete package of photos, map, trip facts and manuscript written according to our news feature format. Excellence of color photo selections make a sale more likely. Include sketches of fishing patterns and techniques to guide our illustrators. Graphics are important. The most frequent mistake made by writers in completing an article for us is that they don't follow our style. Our guidelines are quite clear. One query at a time via mail or e-mail. No faxes or phone calls. You can become a regular *Western Outdoors* byliner by submitting professional quality packages of fine writing accompanied by excellent photography. Pros anticipate what is needed, and immediately provide whatever else we request. Furthermore, they meet deadlines!"

$ $ WESTERN SPORTSMAN, 140 Avenue F North, Saskatoon, Saskatchewan S7L 1V8 Canada. (306)665-6302. Fax: (306)244-8859. E-mail: copi@sk.sympatico.ca. **Contact:** George Gruenefeld, editor. **90% freelance written.** Bimonthly magazine for fishermen, hunters, campers and others interested in outdoor recreation. "Note that our coverage area is Alberta, Saskatchewan and Manitoba." Estab. 1968. Circ. 29,000. Rights purchased vary with author and material. Usually buys first North American serial or second serial (reprint) rights. Byline given. Pays on publication. "We try to include as much information as possible on all subjects in each edition. Therefore, we often publish fishing articles in our winter issues along with a variety of winter stories." Reports in 1 month. Sample copy for $4 and 9×12 SAE with 4 IRCs (US). Free writer's guidelines with SAE and IRC (US).

- *Western Sportsman* now accepts articles and news items relating to British Columbia, Yukon and Northwest Territories hunting and fishing.

Nonfiction: "It is necessary that all articles can identify with our coverage area. We are interested in manuscripts from writers who have had an interesting fishing or hunting experience. We also publish other informational pieces as long as they relate to our coverage area. We are more interested in articles which tell about the average guy living on beans, guiding his own boat, stalking his game and generally doing his own thing in our part of Western Canada than a story describing a well-to-do outdoorsman traveling by motorhome, staying at an expensive lodge with guides doing everything for him except catching the fish or shooting the big game animal. The articles that are submitted to us need to be prepared in a knowledgeable way and include more information than the actual fish catch or animal or bird kill. Discuss the terrain, the people involved on the trip, the water or weather conditions, the costs, the planning that went into the trip, the equipment and other data closely associated with the particular event. We're always looking for new writers." **Buys 60 mss/year.** Submit complete ms and SASE or IRCs. Length: 1,500-2,000 words. Payment negotiable.
Reprints: Send typed ms with rights for sale noted and information about when and where the article previously appeared.
Photos: Photos purchased with ms with no additional payment. Also purchased without ms. Pays $150 for 35mm or larger transparency for front cover.

$ $ WISCONSIN OUTDOOR JOURNAL, Krause Publications, 700 E. State St., Iola WI 54990. (715)445-2214, ext. 484. Fax: (715)445-4087. E-mail: lovettb@krause.com. Website: http://www.krause.com/outdoors. **Contact:** Brian Lovett, editor. **90% freelance written.** Magazine published 8 times/year covering Wisconsin hunting, fishing, trapping, wildlife and related issues. "*Wisconsin Outdoor Journal* is for people interested in state-specific hunting, fishing, trapping and wildlife. We mix how-to features with area profiles and state outdoor issues." Estab. 1987. Circ. 26,000. **Pays on acceptance.** Publishes ms an average of 8-12 months after acceptance. Byline given. Offers 50% kill fee. Buys first North American serial rights. Editorial lead time 1 year. Submit seasonal material 1 year in advance. Reports in 2 months. Sample copy and writer's guidelines for SASE.
Nonfiction: General interest, historical/nostalgic, how-to. No stories focusing on out-of-state topics; no general recreation (hiking, biking, skiing) features. **Buys 65 mss/year.** Query with published clips. Length: 1,600-2,000 words. **Pays $150-250.** Sometimes pays expenses of writers on assignment.
Photos: Send photos with submission. Reviews transparencies. Offers $75-275/photo. Buys one-time rights.
Columns/Departments: Wisconsin Field Notes (anecdotes, outdoor news items not extensively covered by newspapers, interesting outdoor occurrences, all relevant to Wisconsin; may include photos), 50-750 words. **Pays $5-75 on publication.** "Include SASE with photos only. Submissions other than photos for Field Notes will not be returned.
Tips: "Don't submit personal hunting and fishing stories. Seek fresh, new topics, such as an analysis of long-term outdoor issues."

$ $ WISCONSIN SPORTSMAN, Game & Fish Publications, Inc., Box 741, Marietta GA 30061. (770)953-9222. **Contact:** Dennis Schmidt, editor. See *Game & Fish Publications*.

Martial Arts

$ $ BLACK BELT, Rainbow Publications, Inc., 24715 Ave. Rockefeller, Valencia CA 91355. (805)257-4066. Fax: (805)257-3028. E-mail: rainbow@cygnus.rsabbs.com. Website: http://www.blackbeltmag.com. **Contact:** Robert Young, executive editor. **80-90% freelance written.** Works with a small number of new/unpublished writers each year. Monthly magazine emphasizing martial arts for both experienced practitioner and layman. Estab. 1961. Circ. 100,000.

Pays on publication. Publishes ms an average of 6-8 months after acceptance. Buys all rights, retains right to republish. Submit seasonal material 6 months in advance. Accepts simultaneous submissions if notified. Reports in 3 weeks.
Nonfiction: Exposé, how-to, informational, health/fitness, interview, new product, personal experience, technical, training, travel. "We never use personality profiles." **Buys 8-9 mss/issue.** Query with outline. Length: 1,200 words minimum. **Pays $100-300.**
Photos: Very seldom buys photos without accompanying mss. Captions required. Total purchase price for ms includes payment for photos. Model releases required.
Tips: "We also publish an annual yearbook and special issues periodically. The yearbook includes our annual 'Black Belt Hall of Fame' inductees."

$ $ INSIDE KUNG-FU, The Ultimate In Martial Arts Coverage!, CFW Enterprises, 4201 Vanowen Place, Burbank CA 91505. (818)845-2656. Fax: (818)845-7761. **Contact:** Dave Cater, editor. **90% freelance written.** Monthly magazine for those with "traditional, modern, athletic and intellectual tastes. The magazine slants toward little-known martial arts, and little-known aspects of established martial arts." Estab. 1973. Circ. 125,000. Pays on publication date on magazine cover. Publishes ms an average of 6 months after acceptance. Byline given. Offers 20% kill fee. Buys first North American serial rights. Editorial lead time 6 months. Submit seasonal material 6 months in advance. Accepts simultaneous submissions. Reports in 1 month on queries; 2 months on mss. Sample copy for $2.95 and 9×12 SAE with 5 first-class stamps. Writer's guidelines for #10 SASE.
Nonfiction: Book excerpts, essays, exposé (topics relating to the martial arts), general interest, historical/nostalgic, how-to (primarily technical materials), cultural/philosophical, inspirational, interview/profile, new product, personal experience, photo feature, technical, travel. "Articles must be technically or historically accurate." *Inside Kung-Fu* is looking for external-type articles (fighting, weapons, multiple hackers). No "sports coverage, first-person articles or articles which constitute personal aggrandizement." **Buys 120 mss/year.** Query or send complete ms. Length: 1,500-3,000 words (8-10 pages, typewritten and double-spaced). **Pays $125-175.**
Reprints: Send tearsheet of article or short story or typed ms with rights for sale noted and information about when and where the article previously appeared. No payment.
Photos: State availability or send photos with ms. Reviews contact sheets, negatives, 5×7 or 8×10 color prints. No additional payment for photos. Captions, model release and identification of subjects required. Buys all rights.
Fiction: Adventure, historical, humorous, mystery, novel excerpts, suspense. "Fiction must be short (1,000-2,000 words) and relate to the martial arts. We buy very few fiction pieces." Publishes novel excerpts. **Buys 2-3 mss/year.**
Tips: "See what interests the writer. May have a better chance of breaking in at our publication with short articles and fillers since smaller pieces allow us to gauge individual ability, but we're flexible—quality writers get published, period. The most frequent mistakes made by writers in completing an article for us are ignoring photo requirements and model releases (always number one—and who knows why? All requirements are spelled out in writer's guidelines)."

$ $ JOURNAL OF ASIAN MARTIAL ARTS, Via Media Publishing Co., 821 W. 24th St., Erie PA 16502-2523. (814)455-9517. Fax: (814)838-7811. E-mail: viamedia@ncinter.net. Website: http://www.ncinter.net/~viamedia. Contact: Michael A. DeMarco, editor. **90% freelance written.** Quarterly magazine covering "all historical and cultural aspects related to Asian martial arts, offering a mature, well-rounded view of this uniquely fascinating subject. Although the journal treats the subject with academic accuracy (references at end), writing need not lose the reader!" Estab. 1991. Pays on publication. Publishes ms an average of 1 year after acceptance. Byline given. Buys first world rights and second serial (reprint) rights. Submit seasonal material 6 months in advance. Reports in 1 month on queries; 2 months on mss. Sample copy for $10. Writer's guidelines for #10 SASE.
Nonfiction: Essays, exposé, historical/nostalgic, how-to (martial art techniques and materials, e.g., weapons, symbols), interview/profile, personal experience, photo feature (place or person), religious, technical, travel. "All articles should be backed with solid, reliable reference material. No articles overburdened with technical/foreign/scholarly vocabulary, or material slanted as indirect advertising or for personal aggrandizement." **Buys 30 mss/year.** Query with short background and martial arts experience. Length: 2,000-10,000 words. **Pays $150-500 for unsolicited articles.**
Reprints: Send information about when and where the article previously appeared. Pays 50% of amount paid for an original article.
Photos: State availability of photos with submission. Reviews contact sheets, negatives, transparencies, prints. Offers no additional payment for photos accepted with ms. Model releases and identification of subjects required. Buys one-time and reprint rights.
Columns/Departments: Location (city, area, specific site, Asian or Non-Asian, showing value for martial arts, researchers, history); Media Review (film, book, video, museum for aspects of academic and artistic interest). **Buys 16 mss/year.** Query. Length: 1,000-2,500 words. **Pays $50-200.**
Fiction: Adventure, historical, humorous, slice-of-life vignettes, translation. No material that does not focus on martial arts culture. **Buys 1 mss/year.** Query. Length: 1,000-10,000 words. **Pays $50-500 or copies.**
Poetry: Avant-garde, free verse, haiku, light verse, traditional, translation. "No poetry that does not focus on martial art culture." **Buys 2 poems/year.** Submit maximum 10 poems. Pays **$10-100 or copies.**
Fillers: Anecdotes, facts, gags to be illustrated by cartoonist, newsbreaks, short humor. **Buys 2/year.** Length: 25-500 words. **Pays $1-50 or copies.**
Tips: "Always query before sending a manuscript. We are open to varied types of articles; most however require a strong academic grasp of Asian culture. For those not having this background, we suggest trying a museum review, or interview, where authorities can be questioned, quoted and provide supportive illustrations. We especially desire articles/

reports from Asia, with photo illustrations, particularly of a martial art style, so readers can visually understand the unique attributes of that style, its applications, evolution, etc. 'Location' and media reports are special areas that writers may consider, especially if they live in a location of martial art significance."

$ KARATE/KUNG FU ILLUSTRATED, Rainbow Publications, Inc., P.O. Box 918, Santa Clarita CA 91380. (805)257-4066. Fax: (805)257-3028. E-mail: rainbow@rsabbs.com. Website: http://www.blackbeltmag.com. **Contact:** Douglas Jeffrey, executive editor. **70% freelance written.** Bimonthly. "KKI presents factual historical accounts of the development of the martial arts, along with technical pieces on self-defense. We use only material from which readers can learn." Estab. 1969. Circ. 35,000. Pays on publication. Publishes ms an average of 8 months after acceptance. Byline given. Buys all rights. Editorial lead time 3 months. Submit seasonal material 4 months in advance. Accepts simultaneous submissions. Reports in 2 weeks on queries; 1 month on mss. Sample copy for 9×12 SAE and 5 first-class stamps. Writer's guidelines free.

- *Karate/Kung Fu Illustrated* now publishes "Black Belt for Kids," a separate section currently attached to the main magazine. Query with article ideas for young martial artists.

Nonfiction: Book excerpts, general interest (martial arts), historical/nostalgic (martial arts development), how-to (technical articles on specific kicks, punches, etc.), interview/profile (only with *major* martial artist), new products (for annual product review), travel (to Asian countries for martial arts training/research), comparisons of various styles and techniques. "No self-promotional pieces." **Buys 30 mss/year.** Query. Length: 1,000-3,000 words. **Pays $100-200.**
Reprints: Send tearsheet, photocopy or typed ms with rights for sale noted and information about when and wher the article previously appeared. Pays 75-100% of amount paid for an original article.
Photos: Freelancers should send photos with submission. Reviews contact sheets, negatives and 5×7 prints. Offers no additional payment for photos accepted with ms. Captions, model releases and identification of subjects required.
Columns/Departments: Bushido (essays explaining martial arts philosophy), 1,000-1,500 words; Counterkicks (letters to the editor). **Buys 12 mss/year.** Query. **Pays $0-100.**
Fiction: Publishes novel excerpts.
Tips: "You need not be an expert in a specific martial art to write about it. But if you are not an expert, find one and use his knowledge to support your statements. Also, references to well-known books can help lend credence to the work of unknown writers. Inexperienced writers should begin by writing about a subject they know well. For example, if you study karate, start by writing about karate. Don't study karate for one year, then try to break in to a martial arts magazine by writing about Kung fu, because we already have Kung fu practitioners who write about that."

☆ $ $ MARTIAL ARTS TRAINING, Rainbow Publications, P.O. Box 918, Santa Clarita CA 91380-9018. (805)257-4066. Fax: (805)257-3028. E-mail: rainbow@rsabbs.com. Website: http://www.blackbeltmag.com. **Contact:** Douglas Jeffrey, executive editor. **75% freelance written.** Works with many new/unpublished writers each year. Bimonthly magazine about martial arts training. Estab. 1973. Circ. 35,000. Pays on publication. Publishes ms an average of 6 months after acceptance. Buys all rights. Submit seasonal material 4 months in advance. Reports in 1 month. Writer's guidelines for #10 SASE.
Nonfiction: How-to (training related features). **Buys 30-40 unsolicited mss/year.** Query. Length: 1,500-2,500 words. **Pays $125-200.**
Reprints: Send tearsheet, photocopy or typed ms of article with rights for sale noted and information about when and where the article previously appeared. Pays 75-100% of amount paid for an original article.
Photos: "We prefer color prints. Please include the negatives." Model releases required. Buys all rights.
Fiction: Publishes novel excerpts.
Tips: "I'm looking for how-to, nuts-and-bolts training stories that are martial arts related. Weight training, plyometrics, speed drills, cardiovascular workouts, agility drills, etc. Our magazine covers fitness and conditioning, not the martial arts techniques themselves."

☆ $ $ T'AI CHI, Leading International Magazine of T'ai Chi Ch'uan, Wayfarer Publications, P.O. Box 26156, Los Angeles CA 90026. (213)665-7773. Fax: (213)665-1627. E-mail: taichi@tai-chi.com. Website: http://www.tai-chi.com. **Contact:** Marvin Smalheiser, editor. **90% freelance written.** Bimonthly consumer magazine covering T'ai Chi Ch'uan as a martial art and for health and fitness. "Covers T'ai Chi Ch'uan and other internal martial arts, plus qigong and Chinese health, nutrition and philosophical disciplines. Readers are practitioners or laymen interested in developing skills and insight for self-defense, health and self-improvement." Estab. 1977. Circ. 30,000. Pays on publication. Publishes ms an average of 3 months after acceptance. Byline given. Buys first North American serial rights. Editorial lead time 3 months. Submit seasonal material 6 months in advance. Reports in 3 weeks on queries; 3 months on mss. Sample copy for $3.50. Writer's guidelines for #10 SASE.
Nonfiction: Book excerpts, essays, how-to (on T'ai Chi Ch'uan, qigong and related Chinese disciplines), interview, personal experience. "Do not want articles promoting an individual, system or school." **Buys 50-60 mss/year.** Query or send complete ms. Length: 1,200-4,500 words. **Pays $75-500.** Sometimes pays expenses of writers on assignment.
Photos: Send photos with submission. Reviews color transparencies and color or b&w 4×6 or 5×7 prints. Offers no additional payment for photos accepted with mss but overall payment takes into consideration the number and quality of photos. Captions, model releases and identification of subjects required. Buys one-time and reprint rights.
Poetry: Free verse, light verse, traditional. "No poetry unrelated to our content." **Buys 6 poems/year.** Submit maximum 3 poems. Length: 12-30 lines. **Pays $25-50.**
Tips: "Think and write for practitioners and laymen who want information and insight and who are trying to work

through problems to improve skills and their health. No promotional material."

Miscellaneous

N $ $ AMERICAN CHEERLEADER, Lifestyle Ventures, 250 W. 57th St., Suite 1701, New York NY 10107. (212)265-8890. E-mail: editors@americancheerleader.com. Website: http://www.americancheerleader.com. Editor: Julie Davis. Managing Editor: Susie Eley. **Contact:** Nayda Rondon, senior editor. **50% freelance written.** Bimonthly magazine covering high school and college cheerleading. Estab. 1995. Circ. 200,000. Pays on publication. Publishes ms 2 months after acceptance. Byline given. Buys all rights. Editorial lead time 4 months. Submit seasonal material 4 months in advance. Reports in 3 weeks on queries; 2 months on mss. Writer's guidelines for #10 SASE.
Nonfiction: How-to (cheering techniques, routines, pep songs, etc.), interview/profile (sports personalities), new product, personal experience. **Buys 20 mss/year.** Query with published clips. Length: 750-2,000 words. **Pays $75-200.** Sometimes pays expenses of writers on assignment.
Photos: State availability of photos with submission. Reviews transparencies and 5×7 prints. Offers no additional payment for photos accepted with ms. Captions, model releases and identification of subjects required. Buys all rights.

$ CANADIAN RODEO NEWS, Canadian Rodeo News, Ltd., #223, 2116 27th Ave. NE, Calgary, Alberta T2E 7A6 Canada. (403)250-7292. Fax: (403)250-6926. E-mail: rodeonews@iul-ccs.com. Website: http://www.rodeocanada.com. **Contact:** Vicki Mowat, editor. **60% freelance written.** Monthly tabloid covering "Canada's professional rodeo (CPRA) personalities and livestock. Read by rodeo participants and fans." Estab. 1964. Circ. 48,000. Pays on publication. Publishes ms an average of 1 month after acceptance. Byline given. Buys first and second serial (reprint) rights. Editorial lead time 1 month. Submit seasonal material 1 month in advance. Accepts simultaneous submissions. Reports in 1 month on queries; 2 months on mss. Sample copy and writer's guidelines free.
Nonfiction: General interest, historical/nostalgic, interview/profile. **Buys 70-80 mss/year.** Query. Length: 500-1,200 words. **Pays $30-60.**
Reprints: Send photocopy of article or typed ms with rights for sale noted, and information about when and where the article previously appeared. Pays 100% of amount paid for an original article.
Photos: Send photos with submission. Reviews 4×6 prints. Offers $15-25/cover photo. Buys one-time rights.
Tips: "Best to call first with the story idea to inquire if it is suitable for publication. Readers are very knowledgeable of the sport, so writers need to be as well."

N $ $ $ INLINE MAGAZINE, Sports & Fitness Publishing, 2025 Pearl St., Boulder CO 80302. (303)440-5111. Fax: (303)440-3313. E-mail: rebroida@aol.com. Website: http://www.inlinemagazine.com. **Contact**: Rebecca Broida, editor. **70% freelance written.** Published 8 times/year. "*InLine Magazine* speaks to the whole community of skaters by focusing on the essential elements of skating: a love of performance, of product, of street, and of style." Estab. 1991. Circ. 100,000. **Pays on acceptance**. Publishes ms an average of 3 months after acceptance. Byline given. Offers 25% kill fee. Buys first North American serial rights. Editorial lead time 2 months. Submit seasonal material 3 months in advance. Accepts simultaneous submissions. Reports in 1 month. Sample copy and guidelines free.
Nonfiction: Essays, general interest, historical/nostalgic, how-to (skating methods), interview/profile, opinion, personal experience, photo feature, technical, travel. Special issues: Buyer's Guide (March), Photo Annual (December). **Buys 40-50 mss/year.** Query. Length: 500-2,000 words. **Pays $200-1,500.** Sometimes pays expenses of writers on assignment.
Photos: State availability of photos with submission. Reviews contact sheets, negatives, transparencies, prints. Negotiates payment individually. Identification of subjects required. Buys one-time rights.
Columns/Departments: Out There (travel and skating), 800 words; Voice (opinion piece), 600 words; Who? (profile on a skater), 500-800 words. Query. **Pays $200-1,500.**
Tips: "Send queries, clips and a cover letter and we'll go from there!"

N $ $ LEFTY SPORTS, Lefthanders International, P.O. Box 8249, Topeka KS 66608. (785)234-2177. **Contact:** Kim Kipers, editor. **75% freelance written.** Quarterly magazine covering lefthanders involved in any variety of sports or sports information. Subject matter must have a very definite lefthanded slant. Estab. 1998. Pays on publication. Publishes ms 4 months after acceptance. Byline given. Offers 25% kill fee. Buys all rights unless otherwise agreed. Editorial lead time 10 weeks. Submit seasonal material 3 months in advance. Accepts simultaneous submissions. Reports in 3 weeks on queries; 3 months on mss. Writer's guidelines for #10 SASE.
Nonfiction: General interest, historical/nostalgic, how-to (specific sport instructions for lefties), interview/profile, new product. No fiction, articles not specifically related to lefthandedness, lefthanders and sports. Query. Length: 1,500-2,200 words. **Pays $85-200 for assigned articles; $80-150 for unsolicited articles.** Sometimes pays expenses of writers on assignment.
Photos: Send photos with submission. Offers no additional payment for photos accepted with ms. Buys one-time rights.
Columns/Departments: Feature Interview (lefthanded sports figure), 1,800 words; Sports World (sports lefties excel in and why), 1,500 words; Historical (not on regular basis, nostalgic lefty athletes from past), 1,800 words. Query. **Pays $85-200.**
Fillers: Facts, newsbreaks. Length: 150-800 words. **Pays $50-85.**

Tips: "Always query with the specifics of the intended article, stating whether photos are available. Send stories that have a definite lefthanded bent—facts, thoughts, how the interviewee feels about being a lefty. Too many submissions contain nothing about lefthandedness."

$ $ POLO PLAYERS' EDITION, (formerly *Polo*), Rizzo Management Corp., 3500 Fairlane Farms Rd., Suite 9, Wellington FL 33414. (561)793-9524. Fax: (561)793-9576. E-mail: polomag@magg.net. **Contact:** Gwen Rizzo, editor. Monthly magazine on polo—the sport and lifestyle. "Our readers are affluent, well-educated, well-read and highly sophisticated." Circ. 6,500. **Pays on acceptance.** Publishes ms an average of 2 months after acceptance. Kill fee varies. Buys first North American serial rights and makes work-for-hire assignments. Submit seasonal material 3 months in advance. Accepts simultaneous submissions. Reports in 3 months. Writer's guidelines for #10 SAE with 2 stamps.

Nonfiction: Historical/nostalgic, interview/profile, personal experience, photo feature, technical, travel. Special issues: Annual Art Issue/Gift Buying Guide (November 1998, deadline September 20); Winter Preview/Florida Supplement (December 1998, deadline October 20). **Buys 20 mss/year.** Query with published clips or send complete ms. Length: 800-3,000 words. **Pays $150-400 for assigned articles; $100-300 for unsolicited articles.** Sometimes pays expenses of writers on assignment.

Reprints: Send tearsheet of article or typed ms with rights for sale noted and information about when and where the article previously appeared. Pays 50% of amount paid for an original article.

Fiction: Publishes novel excerpts.

Photos: State availability of photos or send photos with submission. Reviews contact sheets, transparencies, prints. Offers $20-150/photo. Captions required. Buys one-time rights.

Columns/Departments: Yesteryears (historical pieces), 500 words; Profiles (clubs and players), 800-1,000 words. **Buys 15 mss/year.** Query with published clips. **Pays $100-300.**

Tips: "Query us on a personality or club profile or historic piece or, if you know the game, state availability to cover a tournament. Keep in mind that ours is a sophisticated, well-educated audience."

N $ PRIME TIME SPORTS & FITNESS, GND Prime Time Publishing, P.O. Box 6097, Evanston IL 60204. Fax: (847)784-8126. E-mail: rallyeguyden@aol.com. **Contact:** Dennis A. Dorner, editor. Managing Editor: Steven Ury. **80% freelance written.** Eager to work with new/unpublished writers. Monthly magazine covering seasonal pro sports and racquet and health club sports and fitness. Estab. 1974. Circ. 35,000. Pays on publication. Publishes ms an average of 6 months after acceptance. Byline given. Buys all rights; will assign back to author in 85% of cases. Submit seasonal material 6 months in advance. Accepts simultaneous submissions. Reports in 6 months. Sample copy on request.

Nonfiction: Book excerpts (fitness and health), exposé (in tennis, fitness, racquetball, health clubs, diets), adult (slightly risqué and racy fitness), how-to (expert instructional pieces on any area of coverage), humor (large market for funny pieces on health clubs and fitness), inspirational (on how diet and exercise combine to bring you a better body, self), interview/profile, new product, opinion (only from recognized sources who know what they are talking about), personal experience (definitely—humor), photo feature (on related subjects); technical (on exercise and sport), travel (related to fitness, tennis camps, etc.), news reports (on racquetball, handball, tennis, running events). Special issues: Swimwear (March); Baseball Preview (April); Summer Fashion (July); Pro Football Preview (August); Aerobic Wear (September); Fall Fashion (October); Ski Issue (November); Workout and Diet Routines (December/January). "We love short articles that get to the point. Nationally oriented big events and national championships. No articles on local only tennis and racquetball tournaments without national appeal." **Buys 150 mss/year.** Length: 2,000 words maximum. **Pays $20-150.** Sometimes pays the expenses of writers on assignment.

Reprints: Send tearsheet or photocopy of article or short story or typed ms with rights for sale noted and information about when and where the article or story previously appeared. Pays 20% of amount paid for an original article or story.

Photos: Nancy Thomas, photo editor. Specifically looking for fashion photo features. Send photos with ms. Pays $5-75 for b&w prints. Captions, model releases, identification of subjects required. Buys all rights, "but returns 75% of photos to submitter."

Columns/Departments: George Thomas, column/department editor. New Products; Fitness Newsletter; Handball Newsletter; Racquetball Newsletter; Tennis Newsletter; News & Capsule Summaries; Fashion Spot (photos of new fitness and bathing suits and ski equipment); related subjects. **Buys 100 mss/year.** Send complete ms. Length: 50-250 words ("more if author has good handle to cover complete columns"). "We want more articles with photos and we are searching for one woman columnist, Diet and Nutrition." **Pays $5-25.**

Fiction: Judy Johnson, fiction editor. Erotica (if related to fitness club), fantasy (related to subjects), humorous, religious ("no God-is-my shepherd, but Body-is-God's-temple"), romance (related subjects), novel excerpts. "Upbeat stories are needed." **Buys 20 mss/year.** Send complete ms. Length: 500-2,500 words maximum. **Pays $20-150.**

Poetry: Free verse, haiku, light verse, traditional on related subjects. Length: up to 150 words. **Pays $10-25.**

Tips: "Send us articles dealing with court club sports, exercise and nutrition that exemplify an upbeat 'you can do it' attitude. Pro sports previews 3-4 months ahead of their seasons are also needed. Good short fiction or humorous articles can break in. Expert knowledge of any related subject can bring assignments; any area is open. We consider everything as a potential article, but are turned off by credits, past work and degrees. We have a constant demand for well-written articles on instruction, health and trends in both. Other articles needed are professional sports training techniques, fad diets, tennis and fitness resorts, photo features with aerobic routines. A frequent mistake made by writers is in length—articles are too long. When we assign an article, we want it newsy if it's news and opinion if opinion."

N **$ PRORODEO SPORTS NEWS**, Professional Rodeo Cowboys Association, 101 ProRodeo Dr., Colorado Springs CO 80919. (719)593-8840. Fax: (719)548-4889. E-mail: pasay@prorodeo.com. Website: http://www.prorodeo.com. **Contact**: Paul Asay, editor. **10% freelance written.** Newspaper published weekly in the summer (biweekly otherwise) covering professional rodeo. "Our readers are extremely knowledgeable about the sport of rodeo, and anyone who writes for us should have that same, in-depth knowledge." Estab. 1952. Circ. 40,000. Pays on publication. Publishes ms an average of 1 month after acceptance. Byline given. Buys first, one-time rights and makes work-for-hire assignments. Editorial lead time 2 months. Submit seasonal material 2 months in advance. Reports in 2 weeks on queries. Sample copy for #10 SASE. Writer's guidelines free.

Nonfiction: Historical/nostalgic, how-to, humor, interview/profile, photo feature, technical. **Buys 20 mss/year.** Query with published clips. Length: 300-1,000 words. **Pays $50-100.** Sometimes pays expenses of writers on assignment.

Photos: State availability of photos with submission. Reviews 8×10 prints. Offers $15-85/photo. Identification of subjects required. Buys one-time rights.

$ REFEREE, Referee Enterprises, Inc., P.O. Box 161, Franksville WI 53126-9987. (414)632-8855. Fax: (414)632-5460. E-mail: refmag@execpc.com. Website: http://www.refmag.com. Editor: Barry Mano. **Contact:** Jim Arehart, associate editor. **50-60% freelance written.** Works with a number of new/unpublished writers each year. Monthly magazine for well-educated, mostly 26- to 50-year-old male sports officials of all levels and all sports. Estab. 1975. Circ. 35,000. **Pays on acceptance** of completed ms. Publishes ms an average of 4 months after acceptance. Rights purchased vary. Submit seasonal material 6 months in advance. Reports in 2 weeks. Sample copy for 10×13 SAE with 7 first-class stamps. Writer's guidelines for #10 SASE.

Nonfiction: How-to, informational, humor, interview, profile, personal experience, photo feature, technical. **Buys 54 mss/year.** Query. Length: 500-3,000 words. **Pays 10¢/word.** "No general sports articles."

Reprints: Send photocopy of article and information about when and where it previously appeared. Pays 50% of amount paid for an original article.

Photos: Purchased with or without accompanying ms or on assignment. Captions preferred. Send contact sheet, prints, negatives or transparencies. Pays $20/b&w; $35/color; $100/color cover; $75/b&w cover.

Columns/Departments: Law (legal aspects). **Buys 24 mss/year.** Query. Length: 200-700 words. **Pays 5¢/word up to $100.**

Tips: "Queries with a specific idea appeal most to readers. Generally, we are looking more for feature writers, as we usually do our own shorter/filler-type material. It is helpful to obtain suitable photos to augment a story. Don't send fluff—we need hard-hitting, incisive material tailored just for our audience. Anything smacking of public relations is a no sale. Don't gloss over the material too lightly or fail to go in-depth looking for a quick sale (taking the avenue of least resistance). Always keep in mind you're a referee talking to a bunch of referees. Keep it simple. No one wants to read "$10 words" when a nickel word works just fine. We write very concisely; get your five-word sentences down to three. You'll be amazed at how often it improves the message. We do not want a lot of first-person material. Using humor is fine, but be careful. It's very difficult to do without offending somebody. Write from a position of authority. We welcome early submissions. We like to work ahead."

$ RUGBY MAGAZINE, Rugby Press Limited, 2350 Broadway, New York NY 10024. (212)787-1160. Fax: (212)595-0934. E-mail: rugby@inch.com or rugbymag@aol.com. Website: http://www.inch.com/~rugby. Editor: Ed Hagerty. **Contact:** Christian Averill, managing editor. **75% freelance written.** Monthly tabloid. "*Rugby Magazine* is the journal of record for the sport of rugby in the U.S. Our demographics are among the best in the country." Estab. 1975. Circ. 10,000. Pays on publication. Publishes ms 2 months after acceptance. Byline given. Buys all rights. Editorial lead time 1 month. Submit seasonal material 2 months in advance. Accepts simultaneous submissions. Reports in 2 weeks on queries; 1 months on mss. Sample copy for $3. Writer's guidelines free.

Nonfiction: Book excerpts, essays, general interest, historical/nostalgic, how-to, humor, interview/profile, new product, opinion, personal experience, photo feature, technical, travel. **Buys 15 mss/year.** Send complete ms. Length: 600-2,000 words. **Pays $50 minimum.** Pays expenses of writers on assignment.

Reprints: Send tearsheet of article or short story or typed ms with rights for sale noted and information about when and where the article or story previously appeared. Pay varies.

Photos: Send photos with submission. Reviews negatives, transparencies and prints. Offers no additional payment for photos accepted with ms. Buys all rights.

Columns/Departments: Nutrition, athletic nutrition, 900 words; Referees' Corner, 1,200 words; The Zen Rugger (Rugby as Zen), 650 words. **Buys 2-3 mss/year.** Query with published clips. **Pays $50 maximum.**

Fiction: Condensed novels, humorous, novel excerpts, slice-of-life vignettes. **Buys 1-3 mss/year.** Query with published clips. Length: 1,000-2,500 words. **Pays $50.**

Tips: "Give us a call. Send along your stories or photos; we're happy to take a look. Tournament stories are a good way to get yourself published in *Rugby Magazine*."

$ SKYDIVING, 1725 N. Lexington Ave., DeLand FL 32724. (904)736-4793. Fax: (904)736-9786. E-mail: skydiving@interserv.com. **Contact:** Michael Truffer, editor. **25% freelance written.** Works with a small number of new/unpublished writers each year. Monthly tabloid featuring skydiving for sport parachutists, worldwide dealers and equipment manufacturers. "*Skydiving* is a news magazine. Its purpose is to deliver timely, useful and interesting information about the equipment, techniques, events, people and places of parachuting. Our scope is national. *Skydiving*'s audience spans the entire spectrum of jumpers, from first-jump students to veterans with thousands of skydives. Some readers are riggers with a keen interest in the technical aspects of parachutes, while others are weekend 'fun' jumpers who want information to help them make travel plans and equipment purchases." Circ. 14,200. Average issue includes 3 feature articles and 3 columns of technical information. Pays on publication. Publishes ms an average of 3 months after acceptance. Byline given. Buys one-time rights. Accepts simultaneous submissions, if so noted. Reports in 1 month. Sample copy for $2. Writer's guidelines for 9×12 SAE with 4 first-class stamps.

Nonfiction: "Send us news and information on how-to, where-to, equipment, techniques, events and outstanding personalities who skydive. We want articles written by people who have a solid knowledge of parachuting." No personal experience or human-interest articles. Query. Length: 500-1,000 words. **Pays $25-100.** Sometimes pays the expenses of writers on assignment.

Reprints: Accepts previously published submissions.

Photos: State availability of photos. Reviews 5×7 and larger b&w glossy prints. Offers no additional payment for photos accepted with ms. Captions required.

Fillers: Newsbreaks. Length: 100-200 words. **Pays $25 minimum.**

Tips: "The most frequent mistake made by writers in completing articles for us is that the writer isn't knowledgeable about the sport of parachuting. Articles about events are especially time-sensitive so yours must be submitted quickly. We welcome contributions about equipment. Even short, 'quick look' articles about new products are appropriate for *Skydiving*. If you know of a drop zone or other place that jumpers would like to visit, write an article describing its features and tell them why you liked it and what they can expect to find if they visit it. Avoid first person articles."

Motor Sports

N $ $ AUTO RACING DIGEST, Century Publishing, 990 Grove St., Evanston IL 60207-4370. (847)491-6440. Fax: (847)491-0867. **Contact:** Jamie Trecker, editor. Editor: Ken Leiker. Managing Editor: James O'Connor. **100% freelance written.** "Bimonthly digest focusing on American stock-car racing. Occasionally features F1, Indy car style." Estab. 1974. Circ. 50,000. Pays on publication. Publishes ms an average of 1 months after acceptance. Byline given. Offers 50% kill fee. Buys all rights. Editorial lead time 6 weeks. Submit seasonal material 6 weeks in advance. Accepts simultaneous submission. Reports in 1 month. Sample copy for $5.

Nonfiction: Essays, exposé, general interest, opinion, technical. No "remember when" pieces. No personal experience unless extraordinary. **Buys 70 mss/year.** Query. Length: 1,200-2,000 words. **Pays $50-200.** Sometimes pays the expenses of writers on assignment.

Photos: State availability of photos with submission. Reviews negatives, 35mm, 4×6 transparencies, 8×10 prints. Offers $10-30 per photo, $100 for cover. Identification of subjects required. Buys one-time rights.

Columns/Departments: Circuit No Circuit (racing roundup), 1,000 words; Biz (business), 500-1,000 words; Notes & Quotes (racing filler), 1,000 words. **Buys 25 mss/year.** Query. **Pays $50-150.**

Tips: "Query by mail. Clips should reflect subject matter you're trying to sell me."

$ $ BRACKET RACING USA, McMullen/Argus publishing, 774 S. Placentia Ave., Placentia CA 92870. (770)442-0376. Fax: (770)410-9253. Website: http://www.cskpub.com. Managing Editor: Debra Wentz. **Contact:** Dale Wilson, editor. Magazine published 8 times/year covering bracket cars and bracket racing. Estab. 1989. Circ. 45,000. Pays on publication. Publishes ms 6 months after acceptance. Byline given. Buys first North American serial rights. Sample copy for $3 and 9×12 SAE with 5 first-class stamps.

Nonfiction: Automotive how-to and technical. **Buys 35 mss/year.** Query by mail only. Length: 500-4,000 words. **Pays $150/page.** Sometimes pays expenses of writers on assignment.

Photos: Send photos with submission.

N $ $ SAND SPORTS MAGAZINE, Wright Publishing Co. Inc., P.O. Box 2260, Costa Mesa CA 92628. (714)979-2560 ext. 107. Fax: (714)979-3998. **Contact:** Michael Sommer, editor. **20% freelance written.** Bimonthly magazine covering vehicles for off-road and sand dunes. Estab. 1995. Circ. 25,000. Pays on publication. Byline given. Buys first rights and one-time rights. Editorial lead time 3 months. Submit seasonal material 6 months in advance. Sample copy and writer's guidelines free.

Nonfiction: How-to technical-mechanical, photo feature, technical. **Buys 20 mss/year.** Query. Length: 1,500 words minimum. **Pays $125-175/page.** Sometimes pays expenses of writers on assignment.

Photos: Send photos with submission. Reviews contact sheets, transparencies, 5×7 prints. Negotiates payment individually. Captions, model releases, identification of subjects required. Buys one-time rights.

☆ $ $ STOCK CAR RACING MAGAZINE, General Media, 65 Parker St., #2, Newburyport MA 01950. (508)463-3789. Fax: (508)463-3250. **Contact:** Dick Berggren, editor. **80% freelance written.** Eager to work with new/unpublished writers. Monthly magazine for stock car racing fans and competitors. Circ. 400,000. Pays on publication. Publishes ms 3 months after acceptance. Buys all rights. Byline given. Reports in 6 weeks. Guidelines free.

Nonfiction: General interest, historical/nostalgic, how-to, humor, interviews, new product, photo features, technical. "Uses nonfiction on stock car drivers, cars and races. We are interested in the story behind the story in stock car racing. We want interesting profiles and colorful, nationally interesting features. We are looking for more technical articles, particularly in the area of street stocks and limited sportsman." Query with or without published clips or submit complete ms. **Buys 50-200 mss/year.** Length: 100-6,000 words. **Pays up to $450.**

Photos: State availability of photos. Pays $20 for 8×10 b&w photos; up to $250 for 35mm or larger transparencies. Captions required.

Fillers: Anecdotes, short humor. Buys 100 each year. Pays $35.

Tips: "We get more queries than stories. We just don't get as much material as we want to buy. We have more room for stories than ever before. We are an excellent market with 12 issues per year. Virtually all our features are submitted without assignment. An author knows much better what's going on in his backyard than we do. We ask that you write to us before beginning a story theme. If nobody is working on the theme you wish to pursue, we'd be glad to assign it to you if it fits our needs and you are the best person for the job. Judging of material is always a combination of a review of the story and its support illustration. Photography should accompany manuscript on first submission."

Olympic Sports

N $ INTERNATIONAL GYMNAST, Paul Ziert & Associates, P.O. Box 721020, Norman OK 73070. **Contact:** Dwight Normile, editor. **10% freelance written.** Specialty magazine for the gymnastics community published 10 times/year. "Contributing writers must know and understand gymnastics. Most accepted freelance work is fiction." Estab. 1956. Circ. 26,000. Pays on publication. Publishes ms an average of 4 months after acceptance. Byline given. Buys one-time rights. Submit seasonal material 4 months in advance. Reports in 2 weeks on queries; 4 months on mss. Sample copy for $4. Writer's guidelines free.

Nonfiction: Humor, interview/profile, opinion, personal experience. **Buys 3 mss/year.** Query with published clips. Length: 1,000-2,500 words. **Pays $15-50 for assigned articles; $15-25 for unsolicited articles.** Pays writers with contributor copies or other premums at writer's request. Sometimes pays expenses of writers on assignment.

Photos: State availability of photos with submission. Reviews negatives, transparencies. Offers $5-50/photo. Captions and identification of subjects required. Buys one-time rights.

Columns/Departments: Stretching Out (opinion), 600-1,000 words. **Buys 3 mss/year.** Query with published clips. **Pays $15-25.**

Fiction: Humorous, slice-of-life vignettes. **Buys 3 mss/year.** Send complete ms. Length: 1,000-1,500 words. **Pays $15-25.**

Tips: "Please be polite, professional and patient. We use few freelancers, so the chances of being published are slim."

$ $ OLYMPIAN MAGAZINE, US Olympic Committee, One Olympic Plaza, Colorado Springs CO 80909. (719)578-4529. Fax: (719)578-4677. **Contact:** Managing Editor. **50% freelance written.** Bimonthly magazine covering olympic sports and athletes. Estab. 1974. Circ. 120,000. Pays on publication. Byline given. Offers 100% kill fee. Free writer's guidelines.

Nonfiction: Photo feature, feature/profiles of athletes in Olympic sports. Query by mail or fax. Length: 1,200-2,000 words. **Pays $300.**

Reprints: Send photocopy of article. Pay 50% of amount paid for an original article.

Photos: State availability of photos with submission. Reviews transparencies and prints. Offers $50-250/photo. Captions, model releases and identification of subjects required. Buys one-time rights.

USA GYMNASTICS, 201 S. Capitol Ave., Suite 300, Pan American Plaza, Indianapolis IN 46225. (317)237-5050. Fax: (317)237-5069. E-mail: lpeszek@usa-gymnastics.org. Website: http://www.usa-gymnastics.org. **Contact:** Luan Peszek, editor. **20% freelance written.** Bimonthly magazine covering gymnastics—national and international competitions. Designed to educate readers on fitness, health, safety, technique, current topics, trends and personalities related to the gymnastics/fitness field. Readers are ages 7-18, parents and coaches. Estab. 1981. Circ. 63,000. Pays on publication. Publishes ms an average of 4 months after acceptance. Byline given. Buys all rights. Submit seasonal material 4 months in advance. Accepts simultaneous submissions. Reports in 2 months. Sample copy for $5.

Nonfiction: General interest, how-to (related to fitness, health, gymnastics), inspirational, interview/profile, opinion (Open Floor section), photo feature. **Buys 3 mss/year.** Query. Length: 1,500 words maximum. Payment negotiated.

Reprints: Accepts previously published submissions. Send photocopy of article.

Photos: Send photos with submission. Offers no additional payment for photos accepted with ms. Identification of subjects required. Buys all rights.

Tips: "Any articles of interest to gymnasts (men, women and rhythmic gymnastics) coaches, judges and parents, are what we're looking for. This includes nutrition, toning, health, safety, trends, techniques, timing, etc."

Running

$ INSIDE TEXAS RUNNING, 9514 Bristlebrook Dr., Houston TX 77083. (281)498-3208. Fax: (281)879-9980. E-mail: insidetxrunning@prodigy.net. Website: http://www.RunningNetwork.com/TexasRunning. **Contact:** Joanne Schmidt, editor. **70% freelance written.** Monthly (except June and August) tabloid covering running and running-

related events. "Our audience is made up of Texas runners who may also be interested in cross training." Estab. 1977. Circ. 10,000. **Pays on acceptance.** Publishes ms an average of 1-2 months after acceptance. Byline given. Buys first rights, one-time rights, second serial (reprint) rights, exclusive Texas and all rights. Submit seasonal material 2 months in advance. Reports in 1 month on mss. Sample copy for $1.50. Writer's guidelines for #10 SASE.
Nonfiction: Various topics of interest to runners. No personal experience such as "Why I Love to Run," "How I Ran My First Marathon." Special issues: Fall Race Review (September); Marathon Focus (October); El Paso-Juarez International 15K results, Championship 20K results (November); Christmas gifts for runners, complete San Antonio Marathon results (December). **Buys 20 mss/year.** Send complete ms. Length: 500-1,500 words. **Pays $100 maximum for assigned articles; $50 maximum for unsolicited articles.**
Reprints: Send tearsheet, photocopy or e-mail or typed ms with rights for sale noted and information about when and where the article previously appeared. Pays 100% of amount paid for an original article.
Photos: Send photos with submission. Offers $25 maximum/photo. Captions required. Buys one-time rights.
Tips: "Writers should be familiar with the sport and the publication. The best way to break in to our publication is to submit brief (2 or 3 paragraphs) fillers for our 'Texas Roundup' section."

$ $ NEW YORK RUNNER, (formerly *New York Running News*), New York Road Runners Club, 9 E. 89th St., New York NY 10128. (212)860-2280. Fax: (212)860-9754. E-mail: newyorkrun@nyrrc.org. Website: http://www.nyrrc.org. **Contact:** Rob Hustick or Nancy Rowe, co-editors. Assistant Editor: Roger Rebber. Bimonthly regional sports magazine covering running, racewalking, nutrition and fitness. Material should be of interest to members of the New York Road Runners Club. Estab. 1958. Circ. 45,000. Pays on publication. Time to publication varies. Byline given. Offers 33% kill fee. Buys first North American serial rights. Submit seasonal material 4 months in advance. Accepts simultaneous submissions. Reports in 2 months. Sample copy for $3. Writer's guidelines for #10 SASE.
Nonfiction: Running and marathon articles. Special issues: N.Y.C. Marathon (submissions in by August 1). No non-running stories. **Buys 25 mss/year.** Query. Length: 750-1,000 words. **Pays $50-250.**
Reprints: Send photocopy of article with information about when and where it previously appeared. Pays 25-50% of amount paid for an original article.
Photos: Send photos with submission. Reviews 8×10 b&w prints. Offers $35-300/photo. Captions, model releases, identification of subjects required. Buys one-time rights.
Tips: "Be knowledgeable about the sport of running. Write like a runner."

Skiing and Snow Sports

$ AMERICAN SKATING WORLD, Independent Newsmonthly of American Ice Skating, American Skating World Inc., 1816 Brownsville Rd., Pittsburgh PA 15210-3908. (412)885-7600. Fax: (412)885-7617. E-mail: editorial@americansk8world.com. Website: americansk8world.com. Editor: Robert A. Mock. **Contact:** H. Kermit Jackson, executive editor. **70% freelance written.** Eager to work with new/unpublished writers. Monthly magtab on figure skating. Estab. 1979. Circ. 15,000. Pays following publication. Publishes ms an average of 3 months after acceptance. Byline given. Buys first North American serial rights and occasionally second serial (reprint) rights. Submit seasonal material 3 months in advance. Reports in 3 months. Sample copy and writer's guidelines for $3.50.

- The increased activity and interest in figure skating have increased demands on *American Skating World*'s contributor network. New writers from nontraditional areas (i.e., outside of East Coast, Upper Midwest, California) are particularly welcome.

Nonfiction: Competition coverage (both technical and human interest), exposé, historical/nostalgic, how-to (technique in figure skating), humor, inspirational, interview/profile and overview (leading current or past individuals in the field, whether they are skaters, coaches, choreographers, arrangers or parents), new product, opinion, performance coverage (review or human interest), personal experience, photo feature, technical, travel. Also interested in amateur recreational skating (overseen by the Ice Skating Institute); "eligible" competitive skating (overseen by the USFSA, the CFSA and other bodies associated with the Olympics) and professional skating (overseen by the Professional Skaters Association [formerly PSGA]). Rarely accepts fiction. "AP Style Guidelines are the basic style source, but we are not bound by that convention. Short, snappy paragraphs desired." **Buys 150 mss/year.** Send complete ms. "Include phone number; response time longer without it." Length: 600-1,000 words. **Pays $25-100.**
Reprints: Occasionally accepts previously published submissions. Send tearsheet of article or typed ms with rights for sale noted and information about when and where the article previously appeared. Pays 50% of amount paid for an original article.
Photos: Send photos with query or ms. Reviews transparencies and b&w prints. Pays $5 for b&w; $10 for color. Identification of subjects required. Buys all rights for b&w; one-time rights for color.
Columns/Departments: Buys 30 mss/year. Send complete ms. Length: 500-750 words. **Pays $25-50.**
Fillers: Clippings, anecdotes. No payment for fillers.
Tips: "Event coverage is most open to freelancers; confirm with executive editor to ensure event has not been assigned. We are drawing more extensively from non-U.S. based writers. Questions are welcome; call executive editor EST, 10-4, Monday-Friday."

$ $ AMERICAN SNOWMOBILER, The Enthusiast Magazine, Recreation Publications, Inc., 7582 Currell Blvd., #212, St. Paul MN 55125. (612)738-1953. Fax: (612)738-2302. E-mail: editor@amsnow.com. Website: http://www.amsnow.com. **Contact:** Amy Joynson, assistant editor. **30% freelance written.** Magazine published 6 times seasonally covering snowmobiling. Estab. 1985. Circ. 80,000. **Pays on acceptance.** Publishes ms an average of 4 months after acceptance. Byline given. Offers 15% kill fee. Buys all rights including electronic. Editorial lead time 4 months. Submit seasonal material 6 months in advance. Reports in 1 month on queries; 2 months on mss. Guidelines for #10 SASE.

Nonfiction: General interest, historical/nostalgic, how-to, interview/profile, new product, personal experience, photo feature, travel. **Buys 10 mss/year.** Query with published clips. Length: 1,000-2,000 words. Pay varies for assigned articles; **$100 minimum for unsolicited articles.**

Photos: State availability of photos with submission. Offers no additional payment for photos accepted with ms. Captions, model releases and identification of subjects required. Buys all rights.

$ $ $ SKI MAGAZINE, Times Mirror Magazines, 929 Pearl St., Suite 200, Boulder CO 80302. (303)440-3636. Website: http://www.skinet.com. Editor-in-Chief: Andy Bigford. **Contact:** Natalie Kurylko, managing editor. **15% freelance written.** Monthly. "*Ski* is a ski-lifestyle publication written and edited for recreational skiers. Its content is intended to help them ski better (technique), buy better (equipment and skiwear), and introduce them to new experiences, people and adventures." Estab. 1936. Circ. 430,000. **Pays on acceptance.** Publishes ms 3 months after acceptance. Byline given. Offers 15% kill fee. Buys first North American serial rights. Submit seasonal material 8 months in advance. Reports in 1 month. Sample copy for 9×12 SAE with 5 first-class stamps.

Nonfiction: Essays, historical/nostalgic, how-to, humor, interview/profile and personal experience. **Buys 5-10 mss/year.** Send complete ms. Length: 1,000-3,500 words. **Pays $500-1,000 for assigned articles; $300-700 for unsolicited articles.** Pays the expenses of writers on assignment.

Photos: Send photos with submission. Offers $75-300/photo. Captions, model releases and identification of subjects required. Buys one-time rights.

Columns/Departments: Ski Life (interesting people, events, oddities in skiing), 150-300 words; Going Places (items on new or unique places, deals or services available to skiers); and Take It From Us (special products or services available to skiers that are real values or out of the ordinary), 25-50 words.

Fillers: Facts and short humor. **Buys 10/year.** Length: 60-75 words. **Pays $50-75.**

Tips: "Writers must have an extensive familiarity with the sport and know what concerns, interests and amuses skiers. Columns are most open to freelancers."

$ $ $ $ SKIING, Times Mirror Magazines, Inc., 929 Pearl St., Suite 200, Boulder CO 80302. (303)448-7600. Fax: (303)448-7676. E-mail: rkahljr@aol.com. Website: http://www.skinet.com. Editor-in-Chief: Rick Kahl. **Contact:** Bill Grout, senior executive editor. Magazine published 7 times/year for skiers who deeply love winter, who live for travel, adventure, instruction, gear, and news. "*Skiing*, is the user's guide to winter adventure. It is equal parts jaw-dropping inspiration and practical information, action and utility, attitude and advice. It relates the lifestyles of dedicated skiers and captures their spirit of daring and exploration. Dramatic photography transports readers to spine-tingling mountains with breathtaking immediacy. Reading *Skiing* is almost as much fun as being there." Estab. 1948. Circ. 400,000. Byline given. Offers 40% kill fee. Query. No previously published articles or poetry.

Nonfiction: Buys 10-15 features (1,500-2,000 words) and **12-24 short pieces** (100-700 words). **Pays $1,000-2,500/feature; $175-500/short piece.**

Columns/Departments: Buys 2-3 articles/year. Length: 1,000-1,500 words. **Pays $700-1,200.**

Tips: "Consider less obvious subjects: smaller ski areas, specific local ski cultures, unknown aspects of popular resorts. Be expressive, not merely descriptive! We want readers to feel the adventure in your writing—to tingle with the excitement of skiing steep powder, of meeting intriguing people, of reaching new goals or achieving dramatic new insights. We want readers to have fun, to see the humor in and the lighter side of skiing and their fellow skiers."

$ $ $ SNOW COUNTRY, The Year-Round Magazine of Mountain Sports & Living, Miller Sports Group, 5520 Park Ave., Trumbull CT 06611. (203)323-7038. Fax: (203)373-7111. E-mail: editor@snowcountry.com. Website: http://www.snowcountry.com. Editor: Perkins Miller. **Contact:** Lynn Prowitt-Smith, associate editor. **85% freelance written.** Monthly (September-February) and Spring/Summer issue. Focuses on mountain lifestyle and recreation at and around ski resorts. "Because we publish year-round, we cover a broader range of subjects than ski-only publications. Besides skiing, topics include scenic drives, mountain biking, hiking, ski town news, real estate, etc." Estab. 1988. Circ. 465,000. **Pays on acceptance.** Publishes ms an average of 6 months after acceptance. Byline given. Kill fee varies. Buys all world periodical rights and foreign affiliates. Submit seasonal material 6 months in advance. Reports in 1 month. Free writer's guidelines.

Nonfiction: General interest, historical/nostalgic, how-to, humor, interview/profile, new product, photo feature, technical and travel. **Buys 45 mss/year.** Query with published clips. Length: 250-1,200 words. **Pays $200-1,000.** Pays expenses of writers on assignment.

Photos: State availability of photos. Reviews transparencies. Identification of subjects required. Buys one-time rights.

Tips: "We're always looking for short articles on unique people, events and news in snow country that we may not already know about."

$ $ SNOWEST MAGAZINE, Harris Publishing, 520 Park Ave., Idaho Falls ID 83402. (208)524-7000. Fax: (208)522-5241. E-mail: lindstrm@snowest.com. **Contact**: Lane Lindstrom. editor. Managing Editor: Steve Janes. **10-25% freelance written.** Magazine published 5 times/year. "*SnoWest* covers the sport of snowmobiling, products and personalities in the western states. This includes mountain riding, deep powder and trail riding as well as destination pieces, tech tips and new model reviews." Estab. 1972. Circ. 172,000. Pays on publication. Publishes ms an average of 2 months after acceptance. Byline given. Buys first North American serial rights. Editorial lead time 6 months. Submit seasonal material 3 months in advance. Sample copy and writer's guidelines free.
Nonfiction: How-to (fix a snowmobile, make it high performance), new product, technical, travel. **Buys 3-5 mss/year.** Query with published clips. Length: 500-1,500 words. **Pays $150-300.**
Photos: Send photos with submission. Negotiates payment individually. Captions and identification of subjects required. Buys one-time rights.

Soccer

N $ $ SOCCER DIGEST, Century Publishing, 990 Grove St., Evanston IL 60207-4370. (847)491-6440. Fax: (847)491-0867. **Contact**: Jamie Trecker, editor. Editor: Ken Leiker. Managing Editor: James O'Connor. **80% freelance written.** "Bimonthly digest featuring investigative reportage on national and international soccer. Writers must be well-established and previously published." Estab. 1977. Circ. 40,000. Pays on publication. Publishes ms 1 month after acceptance. Byline given. Offers 50% kill fee. Buys all rights. Editorial lead time 6 weeks. Submit seasonal material 2 months in advance. Accepts simultaneous submissions. Reports in 1 month. Sample copy for $5. Guidelines free.
Nonfiction: Essays, exposé, general interest, interview/profile, opinion. No how-to, nostalgic, humor, personal experience. **Buys 60 mss/year.** Query. Length: 1,200-2,000 words. **Pays $75-500 for assigned articles; $75-200 for unsolicited articles.** Sometimes pays expenses of writers on assignment.
Photos: State availability of photos with submission. Reviews negatives, 35mm transparencies, 8×10 prints. Offers $10-30/photo, $100 for cover. Captions required. Buys one-time rights.
Columns/Departments: Touch Line (opinion), 1,000-1,200 words; Biz (business-related), 500-1,000 words. Buys 12 mss/year. Query. Pays $75-200.
Tips: "Send query by mail. Include related clips—do not deluge us with cooking clips (for example) if you're trying to sell me a sports story!"

SOCCER MAGAZINE, Patch Communications, 5211 S. Washington Ave., Titusville FL 32780. (407)268-5010. Fax: (407)267-1894. E-mail: dsage@megabits.net. Editor: Michael Lewis. **Contact:** Dan Sage, managing editor. Magazine published 6 times/year covering "the sport at every level for players, coaches, referees and parents, offering tournament and league coverage as well as player profiles and coaching, nutrition, youth/women's game and training tips columns." Estab. 1993. Circ. 20,000. Pays on publication. Publishes ms an average of 6 months after acceptance. Byline given. Buys first North American serial rights. Editorial lead time 4 months. Submit seasonal material 6 months in advance. Reports in 1 month on queries. Writer's guidelines for #10 SASE.
Nonfiction: How-to (coaching), interview/profile, new product, personal experience, photo feature, technical (nutrition). **Buys 6 mss/year.** Query with published clips and SASE. Length: 600-1,200 words.
Photos: Send photos with submission. Reviews transparencies, prints. Negotiates payment individually. Captions, identification of subjects required. Buys one-time rights.
Fiction: Publishes novel excerpts.

Water Sports

$ $ DIVER, Seagraphic Publications, Ltd., 11780 Hammersmith Way, Suite 230, Richmond, British Columbia V7A 5E3 Canada. (604)274-4333. Fax: (604)274-4366. E-mail: divermag@axionet.com. Website: http://medianetcom.com/divermag/. Editor/Publisher: Peter Vassilopoulos. **Contact:** Stephanie Bold, editor. Magazine published 9 times/year emphasizing scuba diving, ocean science and technology (commercial and military diving) for a well-educated, outdoor-oriented readership. Circ. 17,500. Payment "follows publication." Buys first North American serial rights. Byline given. Submit seasonal material July-September for consideration for following year. Send SAE with IRCs. Reports in up to 3 months. Publishes ms up to 1 year after acceptance. "Articles are subject to being accepted for use in supplement issues on tabloid."
Nonfiction: How-to (underwater activities such as photography, etc.), general interest (underwater oriented), humor, historical (shipwrecks, treasure artifacts, archeological), interview (underwater personalities in all spheres—military, sports, scientific or commercial), personal experience (related to diving), photo feature (marine life), technical (related to oceanography, commercial/military diving, etc.), travel (dive resorts). No subjective product reports. **Buys 25 mss/year.** Travel features considered only in September/October for use following year. **Buys 6 freelance travel items/year.** Submit complete ms. Length: 800-1,000 words. **Pays $2.50/column inch.**
Photos: "Features are mostly those describing dive sites, experiences, etc. Photo features are reserved more as specials, while almost all articles must be well illustrated with color or b&w prints supplemented by color transparencies."

Submit original photo material with accompanying ms. Pays $15 minimum for 5×7 or 8×10 b&w glossy prints; $20 minimum for 35mm color transparencies. Captions and model releases required. Buys one-time rights.
Columns/Departments: Book reviews. Submit complete ms. Length: 200 words maximum. No payment.
Fillers: Anecdotes, newsbreaks, short humor. **Buys 8-10/year.** Length: 50-150 words. No payment for news items.
Tips: "No phone calls about status of manuscript. Write if no response within reasonable time. Only brief, to-the-point correspondence will be answered. Lengthy communications will probably result in return of work unused. Publisher assumes no liability to use material even after lengthy waiting period. Acceptances subject to final and actual use."

$ THE DIVER, P.O. Box 28, Saint Petersburg FL 33731-0028. (813)866-9856. Fax: (813)866-9740. **Contact:** Bob Taylor, publisher/editor. **50% freelance written.** Magazine published 6 times/year for divers, coaches and officials. Estab. 1978. Circ. 1,500. Pays on publication. Byline given. Submit material at least 2 months in advance. Accepts simultaneous submissions. Reports in 2 weeks on queries; 1 month on mss. Sample copy for 9×12 SAE with 3 first-class stamps.
Nonfiction: Interview/profile (of divers, coaches, officials), results, tournament coverage, any stories connected with platform and springboard diving, photo features, technical. **Buys 35 mss/year.** Query. Length: 500-2,500 words. **Pays $25-50.**
Reprints: Send tearsheet of article. Pays 50% of amount paid for an original article.
Photos: Pays $5-10 for b&w prints. Captions and identification of subjects required. Buys one-time rights.
Tips: "We're very receptive to new writers."

$ $ HOT WATER, Taylor Publishing Group, 2585 Skymark Ave., Unit 306, Mississauga, Ontario L4W 4L5 Canada. (905)624-8218. Fax: (905)624-6764. **Contact:** Yvan Marston , editor. **50% freelance written.** Quarterly magazine covering personal watercraft market (jet skis, sea-doo's). "Focused on fun-loving watersports enthusiasts, *Hot Water* contains features on new personal watercraft and accessories, places to ride, racing, and profiles on people in the industry. Technical and handling tips are also included." Estab. 1993. Circ. 18,000. Pays on publication. Publishes ms an average of 2 months after acceptance. Byline given. Buys first North American serial rights. Editorial lead time 2 months. Submit seasonal material 3 months in advance. Sample copy and writer's guidelines free.
Nonfiction: Historical/nostalgic, how-to (anything technical or handling etc.), humor, interview/profile, personal experience, photo feature, technical, travel. Send complete ms. Length: 1,000-3,000 words. **Pays $300 maximum.** Sometimes pays expenses of writers on assignment.
Reprints: Send photocopy of article or typed ms with rights for sale noted and information about when and where the article previously appeared. Pay negotiable.
Photos: Send photos with submission. Reviews transparencies, 4×6 prints. Offers no additional payment for photos accepted with ms. Captions, model releases, identification of subjects required.
Columns/Departments: Klipboard (a racer's viewpoint); Workbench (technical tips); Hot Waterways (riding adventures); all 1,000 words. Buys 6 mss/year. Send complete ms. **Pays $200 maximum.**
Fillers: Facts, newsbreaks. Length: 500-1,000 words. **Pays $150 maximum.**
Tips: "If you have a story idea you feel is appropriate, feel free to contact the editor to discuss. Or, if you're familiar with watercraft but need some direction, call the editor who will gladly assign a feature."

$ $ SALT, (formerly *Surfwriter's Quarterly*), Pacific Trades, 283 N. Brent St., Ventura CA 93003. (805)652-0973. **Contact:** Philip S. Wikel, editor. **90% freelance written.** Quarterly magazine covering all subjects related to the ocean. "*Salt* is a publication for the passionate ocean enthusiast." Estab. 1998. Circ. 10,000. Byline sometimes given. Buys one-time rights. Editorial lead time 3 months. Submit seasonal material 3 months in advance. Accepts simultaneous submissions. Reports in 2 months. Sample copy for $3.50. Writer's guidelines for #10 SASE.
Nonfiction: Book excerpts, essays, exposé, general interest, historical/nostalgic, how-to, humor, inspirational, interview/profile, new product, opinion, personal experience, photo feature, technical, travel. No melodrama or pornography. **Buys 15 mss/year.** Query with published clips. Length: 1,000-4,000 words. **Pays $50-400.** Sometimes pays expenses of writers on assignment.
Reprints: Send photocopy or typed ms with rights for sale noted, and information about when and where the article or story previously appeared. Pays 50% of amount paid for an original article.
Photos: Send photos with submission. Reviews transparencies. Captions and identification of subjects required. Buys one-time rights.
Columns/Departments: Travel, 1,500-4,000 words; related to surfing, sailing or ocean sports. **Buys 40 mss/year.** Send complete ms. **Pays $50-1,500.**
Fiction: Adventure, ethnic, historical, humorous, mainstream, novel excerpts, slice-of-life vignettes. All related to surfing, sailing or ocean sports. No melodrama, science fiction or pornography. **Buys 16 mss/year.** Send complete ms. Length: 1,000-4,000 words. **Pays $50-400.**
Poetry: Avant-garde, free verse, haiku, traditional. All related to surfing, sailing or ocean sports. No melodrama. **Buys 16 poems/year.** Submit maximum 4 poems. Length: 75 line maximum. **Pays $20-100.**
Fillers: Anecdotes, facts, newsbreaks. **Buys 8/year.** Length: 50-300 words. **Pays $25-100.**
Tips: "Please be sure to know your subject matter as thoroughly as possible."

$ $ SPLASH MAGAZINE, The Complete Personal Watercraft Magazine, McMullen/Argus Publishing, 774 S. Placentia Ave., Placentia CA 92870. (714)572-2255. Fax: (714)572-4265. E-mail: splashmagazine@mcmullenarg us.com. **Contact:** Rob Halstrom, editor. Associate Editor: Erin Molholland (freelance development coordinator). **20% freelance written.** "From month to month, *Splash Magazine* provides extensive coverage of personal watercraft, equipment, accessories and personalities. Stunning color photography highlights all makes and models and showcases the best in custom craft, watersport events and races." Estab. 1987. Circ. 55,000. Pays on publication. Byline given. Buys first North American serial rights. Editorial lead time 3 months. Submit seasonal material 5 months in advance. Reports in 1 month. Sample copy free. Writer's guidelines for #10 SASE.

Nonfiction: General interest, how-to, humor, inspirational, interview/profile, new product, opinion, photo feature, technical, travel, race and new product test features. **Buys 15-20 mss/year.** Query with published clips. Length varies. **Pays $100-150/page.** Sometimes pays expenses of writers on assignment.

Photos: Send photos with submission. Reviews 35mm transparencies. Negotiates payment individually. Captions, model releases, identification of subjects required.

Tips: "Submit query or completed text/photos with cover letter. Text must be submitted on disk in Windows '95 supported Microsoft Word 97. Photos must be captioned and numbered. Be knowledgeable of the sport."

$ $ SPORT DIVER, World Publications, 330 W. Canton Ave., Winter Park FL 32789. (407)628-4802. Fax: (407)628-7061. E-mail: GJ1@worldzine.com. Editor: Pierce Hoover. **Contact:** Gary P. Joyce, managing editor. **75% freelance written.** Bimonthly magazine covering scuba diving. "We portray the adventure and fun of diving—the reasons we all started diving in the first place." Estab. 1993. Circ. 120,000. Pays on publication, sometimes on acceptance. Byline given. Offers 50% kill fee. Buys first North American serial rights. Editorial lead time 3 months. Submit seasonal material 4 months in advance. Accepts simultaneous submissions. Reports in 2 weeks on queries; 3 months on mss. Writer's guidelines for #10 SASE.

Nonfiction: Personal experience, travel, diving. No non-diving related articles. **Buys 150 mss/year.** Query with SASE. Length: 800-2,000 words. **Pays $300-500.**

Photos: State availability of photos with submission. Reviews transparencies. Offers $50-200/photo. Offers $500 for covers. Captions required. Buys one-time rights.

Columns/Departments: Photo Op (underwater photography), 1,000 words; Dive Briefs (shorts), 150-450 words; Destinations (travel), 600-1,000 words. Instructional columns, 1,000-2,000 words. **Buys 90-100 mss/year.** Query. **Pays $50-250.**

Tips: "Know diving, and even more importantly, know how to write. Destinations is probably the best place to break in with a new look at any of the traditional tropical dive islands."

$ $ SURFER, Surfer Publications, P.O. Box 1028, Dana Point CA 92629. (949)496-5922. Fax: (949)496-7849. E-mail: surferedit@aol.com. Website: http://www.surfermag.com. Editor: Steve Hawk. Assistant Editor: Lisa Eilertson. **Contact:** Evan Slater, managing editor. **75% freelance written.** Monthly magazine "aimed at experts and beginners with strong emphasis on action surf photography." Estab. 1960. Circ. 110,000. Pays on publication. Byline given. Buys first North American serial rights. Submit seasonal material 6 months in advance. Accepts simultaneous submissions. Reports in 2 months. Sample copy for $3.99 with 9×12 SASE. Writer's guidelines for #10 SASE.

Nonfiction: How-to (technique in surfing), humor, inspirational, interview/profile, opinion, personal experience (all surf-related), photo feature (action surf and surf travel), technical (surfboard design), travel (surf exploration and discovery—photos required). **Buys 30-50 mss/year.** Query with or without published clips, or send complete ms. Length: 500-2,500 words. **Pays 25-30¢/word.** Sometimes pays the expenses of writers on assignment.

Reprints: Send typed ms with rights for sale noted and information about when and where the article previously appeared. Pays 100% of amount paid for an original article.

Photos: Send photos with submission. Reviews 35mm transparencies. Buys 12-24 illustrations/year. Prices vary. Used for columns: Environment, Surf Docs and sometimes features. Send samples with SASE to Art Director. Offers $45-300/photo. Identification of subjects required. Buys one-time and reprint rights.

Columns/Departments: Environment (environmental concerns to surfers), 1,000-1,500 words; Surf Stories (personal experiences of surfing), 1,000-1,500 words; Reviews (surf-related movies, books), 500-1,000 words; Sections (humorous surf-related items with b&w photos), 100-500 words. **Buys 25-50 mss/year.** Send complete ms. **Pays 25-30¢/word.**

Fiction: Surf-related adventure, fantasy, horror, humorous, science fiction. **Buys 10 mss/year.** Send complete ms. Length: 750-2,000 words. **Pays 25-30¢/word.**

Tips: "All sections are open to freelancers but interview/profiles are usually assigned. 'People Who Surf' is a good way to get a foot in the door. Stories must be authoritative, oriented to the hard-core surfer."

$ $ SWIM MAGAZINE, The Official Magazine of U.S. Masters Swimming, Sports Publications, Inc., 90 Bell Rock Plaza, Suite 200, Sedona AZ 86351. (520)284-4005. Fax: (520)284-2477. E-mail: swimworld@aol.com. Website: http://www.swimworld.com **Contact:** Dr. Phillip Whitten, editor. **50% freelance written.** Prefers to work with published/selected writers. Bimonthly magazine for adults interested in swimming for fun, fitness and competition. Readers are fitness-oriented adults from varied social and professional backgrounds who share swimming as part of their lifestyle. Readers are well-educated, affluent and range in age from 20-100 with most in the 30-49 age group; about 50% female, 50% male." Estab. 1984. Circ. 46,000. Pays 1 month after publication. Publishes ms an average of 3 months after acceptance. Byline given. Buys all rights. Editorial lead time 3 months. Submit seasonal material 3 months in advance. Accepts simultaneous submissions. Reports in 1 month on queries; 4 months on mss. Sample copy for $5 (prepaid) and 9×12 SAE with 4 first-class stamps. Writer's guidelines for #10 SASE.

Nonfiction: Book excerpts, essays, exposé, general health, general interest, historical, how-to (training plans and techniques), humor, inspirational, interview/profile (people associated with fitness and competitive swimming), new product (articles describing new products for fitness and competitive training), personal experience, photo feature, technical, travel. "Articles need to be informative as well as interesting. In addition to fitness and health articles, we are interested in exploring fascinating topics dealing with swimming for the adult reader." **Buys 12-18 mss/year.** Query with or without published clips. Length: 250-2,500 words. **Pays 12¢/word minimum.**

Photos: Send photos with ms. Negotiates payment individually. Captions, model releases, identification of subjects required.

Tips: "*Always* query first. Writers should be familiar with or an expert in adult fitness and/or adult swimming. Our how-to and profile articles best typify *Swim Magazine*'s style for fitness and competitive swimmers. *Swim Magazine* accepts medical guidelines and exercise physiology articles primarily by M.D.s and Ph.Ds."

N $ $ SWIMMING WORLD, Sports Publications, Inc., 90 Bell Rock Plaza, Suite 200, Sedona AZ 86351. (520)284-4005. Fax: (520)284-2477. E-mail: swimworld@aol.com. **Contact**: Dr. Phillip Whitten, editor-in-chief. Managing Editor: Bob Ingram. **25-50% freelance written.** Monthly magazine. "*Swimming World* is recognized as the authoritative source in the sport of swimming. It publishes articles about all aspects of competitive swimming." Estab. 1959. Circ. 30,000. Pays on publication. Byline given. Kill fee negotiated. Buys all rights. Editorial lead time 2 months. Submit seasonal material 3 months in advance. Accepts simultaneous submissions. Reports in 1 month. Sample copy for $5 and SAE with 4 first-class stamps. Writer's guidelines free.

Nonfiction: Book excerpts, essays, exposé, general interest, historical/nostalgic, how-to, humor, inspirational, interview/profile, new product, opinion, personal experience, photo feature, technical, travel. **Buys 30 mss/year.** Query. Length: 300-3,000 words. **Pays $75-400.** Sometimes pays expenses of writers on assignment.

Photos: State availability of photos with submission. Reviews prints. Negotiates payment individually. Captions, model releases and identification of subjects required. Buys negotiable rights.

Columns/Departments: Buys 18 mss/year. Query with published clips. **Pays $75-200.**

$ $ WAHINE MAGAZINE, Wahine, Inc., 191 Argonne Ave., Suite 3, Long Beach CA 90803. Fax: (562)434-1966. E-mail: wahinemag@aol.com. Website: http://www.wahinemagazine.com. **Contact:** Elizabeth A. Glazner, editor. **50% freelance written.** Quarterly magazine covering water sports and beach culture for women. "*Wahine* is for athletic, intelligent, adventurous women who pursue all the beach lifestyle has to offer, including surfing, bodyboarding, windsurfing, sailing, swimming, diving, kayaking, canoeing, or just standing in appreciation of the water's edge. *Wahine* offers insightful travel, challenging tutorials, contemplative profiles, wearable fashions, enlightening environmental notes and informative food and fitness for both body and mind. Our readers are primarily female from 18-45." Byline given. Buys first rights. Editorial lead time 3 months. Submit seasonal material 6 months in advance. Reports in 2 months. Sample copy for 9×12 SAE and $5 check or money order.

Nonfiction: Book excerpts (relevant to water sports), essays, historical/nostalgic (old surf lifestyle), how-to (water sports technique), inspirational (personal stories of overcoming obstacles), interview/profile (athletes, filmmakers, other females of interest to wahines), new product, personal experience, photo feature, technical (board buyer's guides, other equipment, repair etc.), travel (water destinations). Holiday shopping guide (November), wetsuits (July), swimsuits (April). "We receive numerous manuscripts intent on bemoaning sexism in surfing. Please, no more. We're pro-female—not anti-male!" Query with published clips or send complete ms. Length: 500-3,000 words. **Pays 20¢/word.** Pays previously unpublished writers with contributor copies or other premiums.

Reprints: Send tearsheet of article and information about when and where the article previously appeared. Pays 25% of amount paid for an original article.

Photos: Send photos with submission if possible. Reviews transparencies. Negotiates payment individually. Captions, model releases and identification of subjects required.

Columns/Departments: Offshore (beach culture), 50-500 words; Body (fitness), 800-1,200 words; Soul (personal stories relating to mind/spirit), 800-1,200 words; Food (whole foods explored in all their glory), 800-1,200 words; Planet (environmental success stories), 800-1,200 words. **Buys 20 mss/year.** Send complete ms. **Pays 20¢/word.**

Tips: "We appreciate positive, fresh, well-focused ideas. A good way to break in is by sending ideas for our Offshore section, along with good art. If you write well and understand the tone of *Wahine*, we'll encourage more. Also, we will read unsolicited manuscripts, but must SASE for return."

$ THE WATER SKIER, American Water Ski Association, 799 Overlook Dr., Winter Haven FL 33884. (941)324-4341. Fax: (914)325-8259. E-mail: usawaterski@worldnet.att.net. Website: usawaterski.org. Publisher and Editor: Greg Nixon. **Contact:** Scott Atkinson, associate editor. **10-20% freelance written.** Magazine published 7 times/year. "*The Water Skier* is the official publication of the American Water Ski Association (AWSA), the national governing body for organized water skiing in the United States. The magazine has a controlled circulation and is available only to AWSA's membership, which is made up of 20,000 active competitive water skiers and 10,000 members who are supporting the sport. These supporting members may participate in the sport but they don't compete. The editorial content of the magazine features distinctive and informative writing about the sport of water skiing only." Estab. 1951. Circ. 30,000. Byline given. Offers 30% kill fee. Buys all rights (no exceptions). Editorial lead time 4 months. Submit seasonal material 6 months in advance. Reports in 2 weeks. Sample copy for $1.25. Writer's guidelines for #10 SASE.

Nonfiction: Historical/nostalgic (has to pertain to water skiing), interview/profile (call for assignment), new product (boating and water ski equipment), travel (water ski vacation destinations). **Buys 10-15 mss/year.** Query. Length: 1,500-3,000 words. **Pays $100-150 for assigned feature articles.**

Reprints: Send photocopy of article. Pay negotiable.
Photos: State availability of photos with submission. Reviews contact sheets. Negotiates payment individually. Captions and identification of subjects required. Buys all rights.
Columns/Departments: The Water Skier News (small news items about people and events in the sport), 400-500 words. Other topics include safety, training (3-event, barefoot, disabled, show ski, ski race, kneeboard and wakeboard); champions on their way; new products. Query. **Pays $50-100.** Pay for columns negotiated individually with each writer.
Tips: "Contact the associate editor through a query letter (please no phone calls) with an idea. Avoid instruction, these articles are written by professionals. Concentrate on articles about the people of the sport. We are always looking for the interesting stories about people in the sport. Also, short news features which will make a reader say to himself, 'Hey, I didn't know that.' Keep in mind that the publication is highly specialized about the sport of water skiing." Most open to material for: feature articles (query editor with your idea).

$ $ WATERSKI MAGAZINE, The World's Leading Water Skiing Magazine, World Publications, 330 W. Canton Ave., Winter Park FL 32789. (407)628-4802. Fax: (407)628-7061. E-mail: waterski@worldzine.com. Managing Editor: Sue Whitney. **Contact:** Pierce Hoover, editor. **25% freelance written.** Magazine published 9 times/year for water skiing and related watersports. "*WaterSki* instructs, advises, enlightens, informs *and* creates an open forum for skiers around the world. It provides definitive information on instruction, products, people and travel destinations." Estab. 1978. Circ. 105,000. **Pays on acceptance**. Publishes ms an average of 4 months after acceptance. Offers 25% kill fee. Buys first North American serial and second serial (reprint) rights. Editorial lead time 2 months. Submit seasonal material 2 months in advance. Query for electronic submissions. Reports in 1 month on queries; 2 months on mss. Sample copy for 8½×11 SAE with 4 first-class stamps. Writer's guidelines for #10 SASE.
Nonfiction: General interest, historical/nostalgic, how-to (water ski instruction boating-related), interview/profile, new product, photo feature, technical, travel. Nothing unrelated to water skiing. **Buys 10 mss/year.** Query with published clips. Length: 800-2,000 words. Pay negotiable. Sometimes pays expenses of writers on assignment.
Photos: Send photos with submission. Reviews 2¼×2¼ transparencies, all slides. Negotiates payment individually. Identification of subjects required. Buys one-time rights on color, all rights on b&w.
Columns/Departments: Shortline (interesting news of the sport), 300 words. **Buys 10 mss/year.** Query with published clips. **Pays $75-125.**
Fillers: Anecdotes, facts, gags to be illustrated by cartoonist, newsbreaks, short humor. **Buys 15/year.** Length: 200-500 words. **Pays $75-125.**
Tips: "I recommend a query call to see if there are any immediate openings in the calendar. Follow-up with a published submission (if applicable). Writers should have some interest in the sport, and understand its people, products and lifestyle. The features sections offer the most opportunity for freelancers. One requirement: It must have a positive, strong water skiing slant, whether it be personality, human interest, or travel."

Wrestling

$ WRESTLING WORLD, Sterling/MacFadden, 233 Park Ave. S., New York NY 10003. (212)780-3500. Fax: (212)780-3555. **Contact:** Stephen Ciacciarelli, editor. **100% freelance written.** Bimonthly magazine for professional wrestling fans. We run profiles of top wrestlers and managers and articles on current topics of interest on the mat scene." Circ. 100,000. **Pays on acceptance.** Byline given. Buys first North American serial rights. Reports in 2 weeks. Sample copy for $3 and SAE with 3 first-class stamps.
Nonfiction: Interview/profile and photo feature. "No general think pieces." **Buys 100 mss/year.** Query with or without published clips or send complete ms. Length: 1,500-2,500 words. **Pays $75-125.**
Photos: State availability of photos with submission. Reviews 35mm transparencies and prints. Offers $25-50/photo package. Pays $50-150 for transparencies. Identification of subjects required. Buys one-time rights.
Tips: "Anything topical has the best chance of acceptance. Articles on those hard-to-reach wrestlers stand an excellent chance of acceptance."

TEEN AND YOUNG ADULT

Publications in this category are for teens (13-19). Publications for college students are in Career, College and Alumni. Those for younger children are in Juvenile.

N $ $ ALL ABOUT YOU, Petersen Publishing Company, 6420 Wilshire Blvd., 15th Floor, Los Angeles CA 90048-5515. E-mail: allaboutyou@petersenpub.com. **Contact:** Beth Mayall, editor. **50% freelance written.** Monthly magazine covering fashion/beauty/lifestyle for junior high girls. "We strive to promote self-esteem in our girls. We look for fun quizzes, self-help pieces and articles on dating and friends that are geared toward the younger segment of the teen market." Estab. 1994. Circ. 325,000. **Pays on acceptance**. Publishes ms 4 months after acceptance. Byline given. Offers 10% kill fee. Buys all rights. Editorial lead time 4 months. Submit seasonal material 5 months in advance. Accepts simultaneous submissions. Reports in 1 month. Sample copy for a fee. Call 800-482-0957. Guidelines for SASE.

Nonfiction: How-to (examples: throw a party, talk to your crush, overcome shyness), inspirational, personal experience. "No fiction, profiles on teens or businesspeopl; no articles that are preachy, stiff or sexual." **Buys 100-140 mss/year.** Query with published clips or send complete ms. Length: 700-4,000 words. **Pays $150-700.**
Photos: "We buy paparazzi/celeb photos only." Send photos with submission. Negotiates payment individually. Model releases and identification of subjects required. Buys one-time rights.
Tips: "Submit a list of quiz ideas and we'll select one for you to write on spec. Have fun with the writing, but don't force the teen lingo."

$ $ CAMPUS LIFE, Christianity Today, Inc., 465 Gundersen Dr., Carol Stream IL 60188. (630)260-6200. Fax: (630)260-0114. E-mail: cledit@aol.com. Website: http://www.campuslife.net. **Contact:** Christopher Lutes, editor. **35% freelance written.** Magazine published 9 times/year for the Christian life as it relates to today's teen. "*Campus Life* is a magazine for high-school and early college-age teenagers. Our editorial slant is not overtly religious. The indirect style is intended to create a safety zone with our readers and to reflect our philosophy that God is interested in all of life. Therefore, we publish 'message stories' side by side with general interest, humor, etc." Estab. 1942. Circ. 100,000. **Pays on acceptance.** Publishes ms an average of 5 months after acceptance. Byline given. Offers 50% kill fee. Buys first and one-time rights. Editorial lead time 4 months. Accepts simultaneous submissions. Reports in 5 weeks on queries; 2 months on mss. Sample copy for $3 and 8×10 SAE with 3 first-class stamps. Guidelines for #10 SASE.
Nonfiction: Humor, personal experience, photo feature. **Buys 5-10 mss/year.** Query with published clips. Length: 750-1,500 words. **Pays 15-20¢/word minimum.**
Reprints: Send tearsheet or photocopy of article or short story or typed ms with rights for sale noted and information about when and where the article or story previously appeared. Pays $50.
Photos: State availability of photos with submission. Reviews contact sheets, transparencies, 5×7 prints. Negotiates payment individually. Model release required. Buys one-time rights.
Fiction: Buys 1-5 mss/year. Query. Length: 1,000-2,000 words. **Pays 15-20¢/word.**
Tips: "The best way to break in to *Campus Life* is through writing first-person or as-told-to first-person stories. We want stories that capture a teen's everyday 'life lesson' experience. A first-person story must be highly descriptive and incorporate fictional technique. While avoiding simplistic religious answers, the story should demonstrate that Christian values or beliefs brought about a change in the young person's life. But query first with theme information telling the way this story would work for our audience."

$ CHALLENGE, North American Mission Board, 4200 North Point Parkway., Alpharetta GA 30022. (770)410-6000. Fax: (770)410-6018. E-mail: jconway@namb.net. Website: http://www.student2.com. **Contact:** Joe Conway, editor. **5% freelance written.** Monthly magazine for "boys age 12-18 who are members of a missions organization in Southern Baptist churches." Circ. 24,500. Byline given. Pays on publication. Publishes ms an average of 8 months after acceptance. Buys simultaneous rights. Submit seasonal material 8 months in advance. Accepts simultaneous submissions. Reports in 1 month. Sample copy and guidelines for 9×12 SAE with 3 first-class stamps. Guidelines only for #10 SASE.
Nonfiction: How-to (crafts, hobbies), informational (youth), inspirational (sports/entertainment personalities); photo feature (sports, teen subjects). No "preachy" articles, fiction or excessive dialogue. Submit complete ms. Length: 500-800 words. **Pays $20-100.**
Reprints: Send typed manuscript with rights for sale noted. Pays 90% of the amount paid for an original article.
Photos: Purchased with accompanying ms or on assignment. Captions required. Query. Pays $10 for 8×10 b&w glossy prints.
Tips: "Anything relevant to a young man 16 years old is acceptable. Say like, music, fashion, technology, family, dating, money, school, fun, communication, history, death, AIDS, suicide, peer pressure and parent-esse. We cover spirit, soul, mind and body. Sorry, we don't use, 'When I was your age' or soap-box, down talk."

$ $ EDGE, The High Performance Magazine for Students, Journalistic Inc., 4905 Pine Cone Dr., Suite 2, Durham NC 27707. Fax: (919)489-4767. E-mail: gsanders@jayi.com. Website: http://www.jayi.com/so/Edge. **Contact:** Greg M. Sanders, editor. **60% freelance written.** Bimonthly online magazine covering the teen market. "*Edge*'s readers are bright, sophisticated teenagers. In *Edge* we show them what's going on in the world around them, with the idea that they can learn from that. Think of it as 'industry coverage' for teenagers." Estab. 1993. Circ. 5,000. Pays within 30 days of acceptance. Publishes ms an average of 2 months after acceptance. Byline given. Offers 25% kill fee. Buys all rights. Editorial lead time 3 months. Submit seasonal material 6 months in advance. Reports in 6 weeks on queries; 2 months on mss. Sample copy and writer's guidelines free online.
Nonfiction: Book excerpts, expose, general interest, how-to, personal experience (teenagers only), travel, literary nonfiction. "We'll consider any topic that's relevant to our readers. Examples include travel, summer programs, cars and driving, summer jobs, sports, college admissions, and technology. No 'Good Grades Aren't Enough' or 'How to Succeed in College'—these topics are way too general." **Buys 15 mss/year.** Query with published clips. Length: 1,200-2,000 words. **Pays $300-500 for assigned articles, $200-275 for unsolicited articles.**
Reprints: Send information about when and where the article previously appeared. Pays 50% of amount paid for an original article.
Photos: Send photos with submission. Reviews transparencies, prints. Negotiates payment individually. Identification of subjects required. Rights purchased negotiable.
Columns/Departments: Performance (fine-tuning body and mind), 700-800 words; News to Use (what's up with teenagers around the world), 400-650 words; What's Hot Now (new products), 200-400 words; Mindstuff (reviews of

vintage books), 400-600 words. **Buys 30 mss/year.** Query with published clips or send complete ms. **Pays $25-300.**
Fiction: Publishes novel excerpts.
Tips: "For our features we're keen on story—that is, a structure of complication, development and resolution. If you can do that well, you'll endear yourself to us forever. (I'd love to require all our writers to read Jon Franklin's excellent book, *Writing for Story.*) For shorter pieces, a firm grasp of the material and its relevance to teenagers is key."

$ FLORIDA LEADER (for high school students), Oxendine Publishing, Inc., P.O. Box 14081, Gainesville FL 32604-2081. (352)373-6907. Fax: (352)373-8120. E-mail: oxendine@compuserve.com. Editor: W.H. "Butch" Oxendine Jr. Managing Editor: Kay Quinn. **Contact:** Teresa Beard, assistant editor. Tri-annual magazine covering high school and pre-college youth. Estab. 1983. Circ. 50,000. Pays on publication. Publishes ms an average of 3 months after acceptance. Buys all rights. Submit seasonal material 4 months in advance. Accepts simultaneous submissions. Reports in 2 months on queries. Sample copy for $3.50 and 8×11 SAE, with 3 first-class stamps. For query response and/or writer's guidelines send #10 SASE.
Nonfiction: How-to, humor, new product, opinion. "No lengthy individual profiles or articles without primary and secondary sources of attribution." Length: 250-1,000 words. Payment varies. Pays students or first-time writers with contributor's copies.
Photos: Send photos with submission. Reviews contact sheets, negatives, transparencies. Offers $50/photo maximum. Captions, model releases, identification of subjects required. Buys all rights.
Columns/Departments: College Living (various aspects of college life, general short humor oriented to high school or college students), 250-1,000 words. **Buys 10 mss/year.** Query. **Pays $35 maximum.**
Fillers: Facts, newsbreaks, tips, book reviews. **Buys 2/year.** Length: 100-300 words. No payment.
Tips: "Read other high school and college publications for current issues, interests. Send manuscripts or outlines for review. All sections open to freelance work. Always looking for lighter, humorous articles as well as features on Florida colleges and universities, careers, jobs. Multi-sourced (5-10) articles are best."

$ INSIGHT, A Spiritual Lift for Teens, The Review and Herald Publishing Association, 55 W. Oak Ridge Dr., Hagerstown MD 21740. (301)791-7000. Fax: (301)790-9734. E-mail: lpeckham@rhpa.org or insight@rhpa.org. Website: http://www.rhpa.org. **Contact:** Lori Peckham, editor. **80% freelance written.** Weekly magazine covering spiritual life of teenagers. "*Insight* publishes true dramatic stories, interviews, and community and mission service features that relate directly to the lives of Christian teenagers, particularly those with a Seventh-day Adventist background." Estab. 1970. Circ. 20,000. Pays on publication. Publishes ms an average of 4 months after acceptance. Byline given. Offers 50% kill fee. Buys first rights and second serial (reprint) rights. Editorial lead time 3 months. Submit seasonal material 6 months in advance. Reports in 1 month. Sample copy for $2 and #10 SASE. Guidelines free.
Nonfiction: How-to (teen relationships and experiences), humor, interview/profile, personal experience, photo feature, religious. **Buys 120 mss/year.** Send complete ms. Length: 500-2,000 words. **Pays $25-150 for assigned articles; $25-125 for unsolicited articles.**
Reprints: Send typed ms with rights for sale noted and information about when and where the article previously appeared. Pays $50.
Photos: State availability of photos with submission. Reviews contact sheets, negatives, transparencies, prints. Negotiates payment individually. Model releases required. Buys one-time rights.
Columns/Departments: Big Deal (topic of importance to teens) 1,200-1,700 words; Interviews (Christian culture figures, esp. musicians), 2,000 words; Service With a Smile (teens contributing to community or church), 1,000 words; On the Edge (dramatic true stories about Christians), 2,000 words. Accepting reviews of contemporary Christian music and Christian books for teens. **Buys 80 mss/year.** Send complete ms. **Pays $40-125.**

- "Big Deal" is a new column that appears in *Insight* every other week, each covering a topic of importance to teens. Each feature contains: an opening story involving real teens (can be written in first-person), "Scripture Picture" (a sidebar that discusses what the Bible says about the topic) and another sidebar (optional) that adds more perspective and help.

Tips: "Skim two months of *Insight*. Write about your teen experiences. Use informed, contemporary style and vocabulary. Become a Christian if you haven't already."

N $ $ $ JUMP, For Girls Who Dare to be Real, Weider, 21100 Erwin St., Woodland Hills CA 91367. Fax: (818)594-0972. E-mail: letters@jumponline.com. Website: http://www.jumponline.com. **Contact:** Elizabeth Sosa, editorial assistant. Editor: Lori Berger. Managing Editor: Maureen Meyers. **50% freelance written.** Monthly magazine for a female teen market. Estab. 1997. Circ. 300,000. Pays on publication. Publishes ms 4 months after acceptance. Byline given. Offers 33% kill fee. Buys all rights. Editorial lead time 4 months. Submit seasonal material 5 months in advance. Accepts simultaneous submissions. Reports in 1 month.
Nonfiction: General interest, how-to, interview/profile, new product, personal experience. Query with published clips. Length: 1,500-2,000 words. **Pays 50¢-$1/word.**
Columns/Departments: Busted! (quirky, bizarre and outrageous trends, news, quotes), 6 items, 50 words each; The Dish (food and nutrition for teens), 1,500 words; Jump On . . . In, Music, Sports, Body & Soul (small news and trend items on sports, health, music, etc.), 6 items per page, 75 words each. Query with published clips. Pays 50¢-$1/word.
Tips: "Writers must read magazine before submitting queries. Will turn away queries that clearly show the writer is not familiar with the content of the magazine."

N $ $ **KEYNOTER**, Key Club International, 3636 Woodview Trace, Indianapolis IN 46268-3196. **Contact:** Julie A. Carson, executive editor. **65% freelance written.** Works with a small number of new writers each year, but is eager to work with new/unpublished writers willing to adjust their writing styles. Monthly youth magazine (December/January combined issue), distributed to members of Key Club International, a high school service organization for young men and women. Estab. 1946. Circ. 171,000. **Pays on acceptance.** Publishes ms an average of 5 months after acceptance. Byline given. Buys first North American serial rights. Submit seasonal material 7 months in advance. Accepts simultaneous submissions. Reports in 2 months. Sample copy for 65¢ and 8½×11 SAE. Guidelines for SASE.

Nonfiction: Book excerpts (included in articles), general interest (for intelligent teen audience), academic, self-help, historical/nostalgic (generally not accepted), how-to (advice on how teens can enhance the quality of lives or communities), humor (accepted if adds to story), interview/profile (rarely purchased, "would have to be on/with an irresistible subject"), new product (affecting teens), photo feature (if subject is right), technical (understandable and interesting to teen audience), travel (must apply to club travel schedule), subjects that entertain and inform teens on topics that relate directly to their lives. "We would also like to receive self-help and school-related nonfiction on leadership, community service, and teen issues. *Please, no first-person confessions, fiction or articles that are written down to our teen readers. No filler, or book, movie or music reviews.*" **Buys 10-15 mss/year.** Query with SASE. Length: 1,200-1,500 words. **Pays $150-350.** Sometimes pays the expenses of writers on assignment.

Reprints: Send tearsheet or photocopy of article and information about when and where the article previously appeared.

Photos: State availability of photos. Reviews color contact sheets and negatives. Identification of subjects required. Buys one-time rights. Payment for photos included in payment for ms.

Tips: "We want to see articles written with attention to style and detail that will enrich the world of teens. Articles must be thoroughly researched and must draw on interviews with nationally and internationally respected sources. Our readers are 13-18, mature and dedicated to community service. We are very committed to working with good writers, and if we see something we like in a well-written query, we'll try to work it through to publication."

★ $ **LISTEN MAGAZINE**, Review & Herald Publishing Association, 55 W. Oak Ridge Dr., Hagerstown MD 21740. (301)745-3888. Fax: (301)790-9734. E-mail: 74617.3102@compuserve.com. **Contact:** Lincoln Steed, editor. Editorial Assistant: Anita Jacobs. **75% freelance written.** Works with a small number of new/unpublished writers each year. Monthly magazine specializing in drug and alcohol prevention, presenting positive alternatives to various drug and alcohol dependencies. "*Listen* is used in many high school classes and by professionals: medical personnel, counselors, law enforcement officers, educators, youth workers, etc." Circ. 65,000. Buys first rights for use in *Listen*, reprints and associated material. Byline given. **Pays on acceptance.** Publishes ms 6 months after acceptance. Accepts simultaneous submissions if notified. Reports in 2 months. Sample copy for $1 and 9×12 SASE. Guidelines for SASE.

Nonfiction: Seeks articles that deal with causes of drug use such as poor self-concept, family relations, social skills or peer pressure. Especially interested in youth-slanted articles or personality interviews encouraging non-alcoholic and non-drug ways of life and showing positive alternatives. Teenage point of view is essential. Popularized medical, legal and educational articles. Also seeks narratives which portray teens dealing with youth conflicts, especially those related to the use of or temptation to use harmful substances. Growth of the main character should be shown. "We don't want typical alcoholic story/skid-row bum, AA stories. We are also being inundated with drunk-driving accident stories. Unless yours is unique, consider another topic." **Buys 30-50 unsolicited mss/year.** Query. Length: 1,000-1,200 words. **Pays 5-10¢/word.** Sometimes pays the expenses of writers on assignment.

Reprints: Send photocopy of article or typed ms with rights for sale noted and information about when and where it previously appeared. Pays their regular rates.

Photos: Purchased with accompanying ms. Captions required. Color photos preferred, but b&w acceptable.

Fillers: Word square/general puzzles are also considered. Pays $15.

Tips: "True stories are good, especially if they have a unique angle. Other authoritative articles need a fresh approach. In query, briefly summarize article idea and logic of why you feel it's good. Make sure you've read the magazine to understand our approach."

$ $ **THE NEW ERA**, 50 E. North Temple, Salt Lake City UT 84150. (801)240-2951. Fax: (801)240-5997. **Contact:** Richard M. Romney, managing editor. **60% freelance written.** "We work with both established writers and newcomers." Monthly magazine for young people (ages 12-18) of the Church of Jesus Christ of Latter-day Saints (Mormon), their church leaders and teachers. Estab. 1971. Circ. 230,000. **Pays on acceptance.** Publishes ms an average of 1 year after acceptance. Byline given. Buys all rights. Rights reassigned upon written request. Submit seasonal material 1 year in advance. Reports in 2 months. Sample copy for $1.50 and 9×12 SAE with 2 first-class stamps. Guidelines for SASE.

Nonfiction: Material that shows how the Church of Jesus Christ of Latter-day Saints is relevant in the lives of young people today. Must capture the excitement of being a young Latter-day Saint. Special interest in the experiences of young Mormons in other countries. No general library research or formula pieces without the *New Era* slant and feel. Uses informational, how-to, personal experience, interview, profile, inspirational, humor, historical, think pieces, travel, spot news. Query preferred. Length: 150-2,000 words. **Pays 3-12¢/word.** Pays expenses of writers on assignment.

Photos: Uses b&w photos and transparencies with mss. Payment depends on use, $10-125 per photo. Individual photos used for *Photo of the Month*.

Columns/Departments: For Your Information (news of young Mormons around the world); How I Know; Scripture Lifeline. **Pays 3-12¢/word.**

Fiction: Adventure, science fiction, humorous. Must relate to young Mormon audience. **Pays minimum 3¢/word.**

Poetry: Traditional forms, blank verse, free verse, light verse, all other forms. Must relate to editorial viewpoint. **Pays**

25¢/line minimum.

Tips: "The writer must be able to write from a Mormon point of view. We're especially looking for stories about successful family relationships. We anticipate using more staff-produced material. This means freelance quality will have to improve. Try breaking in with a department piece for 'How I Know' or 'Scripture Lifeline.' Well-written, personal expereinces are always in demand."

$ $ $ REACT, The Magazine That Raises Voices, Parade Publications, 711 Third Ave., New York NY 10017. (212)450-0900. E-mail: srgarvey@react.com. Website: http://www.react.com. Editor: Lee Kravitz. **Contact:** Susan Garvey, managing editor. **98% freelance written.** "*React* is a weekly news, sports and entertainment magazine for teens." Estab. 1995. Circ. 3.3 million. **Pays on acceptance.** Publishes ms an average of 2 months after acceptance. Editorial lead time 2 months. Submit seasonal material 4 months in advance. Sample copy for 10½×12 SAE and 80¢ postage. Writer's guidelines for #10 SASE.

Nonfiction: No fiction or articles written for adults from adult points of view. Query with published clips. **Pays $50-1,500.** Pays expenses of writers on assignment.

Photos: All photos by assignment only; others purchased from stock houses. Model releases and identification of subjects required. Buys all rights.

Columns/Departments: Query with published clips.

Fiction: Considers novel excerpts.

Tips: "We are interested in established writers with experience in writing for and about teenagers."

$ REAL, The magazine for growing minds, Elbert/Alan Publishing Co., Inc., 3811 East 75th Terrace., Kansas City MO 64110. (816)363-8336. Fax: (816)333-8262. E-mail: aengage@aol.com. **Contact:** Susan Campbell, editor. 20% freelance written. Bimonthly magazine covering teen issues and lifestyle. "Features should cover social issues faced by teens in a hip and positive way. Partnerships between adult freelancers and teen writers are encouraged. Departments cover lifestyle subjects, including but not limited to fashion, music, movies, sports, technology, advice, editorials, events and holidays." Estab. 1995. Circ. 100,000. Pays on publication. Publishes ms an average of 6 months after acceptance. Byline sometimes given. Editorial lead time 4 months. Submit seasonal material 4 months in advance. Accepts simultaneous submissions. Reports in 1 month on queries; 2 months on mss. Sample copy for $2.95 and SAE with 6 first-class stamps. Writer's guidelines free.

Nonfiction: Book excerpts, humor, interview/profile, new product, personal experience. **Buys 6 mss/year.** Query with published clips. Length: 1,000-4,000 words. **Pays $20-100.** Sometimes pays teen writers with contributor copies or other premiums rathern than a cash payment.

Reprints: Accepts previously published submissions.

Photos: State availability of photos with submission. Reviews prints. Negotiates payment individually. Model releases and identification of subjects required.

Columns/Departments: Advice (answers teen questions), 600 words. **Buys 6 mss/year.** Query. **Pays $50.**

Fiction: Humorous, slice-of-life vignettes. Nothing that's not applicable to teen-oriented issues. Query. Length: 600-2,000 words. **Pays $20-100.**

Fillers: Quirky facts. **Buys 10/year.** Length: 10-50 words. **Pays $5.**

$ $ $ SEVENTEEN, 850 Third Ave., New York NY 10022. Fax: (212)407-9899. Editor-in-Chief: Meredith Berlin. Contact: Robert Rorke, features editor. **80% freelance written.** Works with a small number of new/unpublished writers each year. Monthly. "*Seventeen* is a young women's first fashion and beauty magazine. Tailored for young women in their teens and early twenties, *Seventeen* covers fashion, beauty, health, fitness, food, cars, college, careers, talent, entertainment, fiction, plus crucial personal and global issues." Circ. 2,500,000. Buys one-time rights for nonfiction and fiction by adult writers and work by teenagers. Pays 25% kill fee. **Pays on acceptance.** Publishes ms an average of 6 months after acceptance. Byline given. Reports in up to 3 months.

- *Seventeen* broke new ground last year with stories on international issues like Filipino child labor camps and body image.

Nonfiction: Articles and features of general interest to young women who are concerned with intimate relationships and how to realize their potential in the world; strong emphasis on topicality and service. Send brief outline and query, including a typical lead paragraph, summing up basic idea of article with clips of previously published works. Length: 1,200-3,000 words. Articles are commissioned after outlines are submitted and approved. Sometimes pays the expenses of writers on assignment. **Pays $1/word, occasionally more.**

Photos: Margaret Kemp, art director. Photos usually by assignment only.

Fiction: Ben Schrank, fiction editor. Thoughtful, well-written stories on subjects of interest to young women between the ages of 13 and 21. Avoid formula stories—"My sainted Granny," "My crush on Brad," etc.—no heavy moralizing or condescension of any sort. Length: 1,000-3,000 words. Pays $500-1,500.

- Ranked as one of the best markets for fiction writers in *Writer's Digest* magazine's "Fiction 50," June 1998.

Tips: "Writers have to ask themselves whether or not they feel they can find the right tone for a *Seventeen* article—a tone which is empathetic yet never patronizing; lively yet not superficial. Not all writers feel comfortable with, understand or like teenagers. If you don't like them, *Seventeen* is the wrong market for you. An excellent way to break in to the magazine is by contributing ideas for quizzes or the Voice (personal essay) column."

$ $ SPIRIT, Lectionary-based Weekly for Catholic Teens, Good Ground Press, 1884 Randolph Ave., St. Paul MN 55105-1700. (612)690-7005. Fax: (612)690-7039. E-mail: jmcsj9@mail.idt.net. **Contact:** Joan Mitchell, CSJ, editor. Managing Editor: Therese Sherlock, CSJ. **50% freelance written.** Weekly newsletter for religious education of Catholic high schoolers. "We want realistic fiction and nonfiction that raises current ethical and religious questions and that deals with conflicts that teens face in multi-racial contexts. The fact we are a religious publication does *not* mean we want pious, moralistic fiction." Estab. 1981. Circ. 26,000. Pays on publication. Publishes ms an average of 3 months after acceptance. Byline given. Buys all rights. Editorial lead time 6 months. Submit seasonal material 6 months in advance. Accepts simultaneous submissions. Reports in 1 month on queries; 6 months on mss. Sample copy and writer's guidelines free.

Nonfiction: Interview/profile, personal experience, photo feature (homelessness, illiteracy), religious, Roman Catholic leaders, human interest features, social justice leaders, projects, humanitarians. "No Christian confessional, born-again pieces." Buys 4 mss/year. Query with published clips or send complete ms. Length: 1,000-1,200 words. **Pays $150-250 for assigned articles; $150 for unsolicited articles.**

Photos: State availability of photos with submission. Reviews 8×10 prints. Offers $40-80/photo. Identification of subjects required. Buys one-time rights.

Fiction: Conflict vignettes. "We want realistic pieces for and about teens—non-pedantic, non-pious. We need good Christmas stories that show spirit of the season, and stories about teen relationship conflicts (boy/girl, parent/teen)." **Buys 10 mss/year.** Query with published clips, or send complete ms. Length: 1,000-1,200 words. **Pays $150-200.**

Tips: "Writers must be able to write from and for teen point of view rather than adult or moralistic point of view. In nonfiction, interviewed teens must speak for themselves." Query to receive call for stories, spec sheet, sample issues."

$ STRAIGHT, Standard Publishing Co., 8121 Hamilton Ave., Cincinnati OH 45231-2323. (513)931-4050. Fax: (513)931-0950. **Contact:** Heather E. Wallace, editor. **90% freelance written.** Estab. 1950. Weekly magazine (published quarterly) for "teens, age 13-19, from Christian backgrounds who generally receive this publication in their Sunday School classes or through subscriptions." **Pays on acceptance.** Publishes ms an average of 1 year after acceptance. Buys first rights and second serial (reprint) rights. Byline given. Submit seasonal material 9-12 months in advance. Reports in 2 months. Sample copy and writer's guidelines for #10 SAE with 2 first-class stamps. "We use freelance material in every issue. Our theme list is available on a quarterly basis. Writers need only give us their name and address in order to be added to our mailing list."

Nonfiction: Religious-oriented topics, teen interest (school, church, family, dating, sports, part-time jobs), humor, inspirational, personal experience. "We want articles that promote Christian values and ideals." No puzzles. Query or submit complete ms. Include Social Security number on ms. "We're buying more short pieces these days; 12 pages fill up much too quickly." Length: 800-1,500 words. **Pays 3-7¢/word.**

Reprints: Send tearsheet of article or story or typed ms with rights for sale noted. Pays 5¢/word.

Fiction: Adventure, humorous, religious, suspense. "All fiction should have some message for the modern Christian teen. Fiction should deal with all subjects in a forthright manner, without being preachy and without talking down to teens. No tasteless manuscripts that promote anything adverse to the Bible's teachings." Submit complete ms. Length: 1,000-1,500 words. **Pays 5-7¢/word.**

- Ranked as one of the best markets for fiction writers in *Writer's Digest* magazine's "Fiction 50," June 1998.

Photos: Submit photos with ms. Pays $75-125 for color slides. Model releases should be available. Buys one-time rights.

Tips: "Don't be trite. Use unusual settings or problems. Use a lot of illustrations, a good balance of conversation, narration, and action. Style must be clear, fresh—no sermonettes or sickly-sweet fiction. Take a realistic approach to problems. Be willing to submit to editorial policies on doctrine; knowledge of the *Bible* a must. Also, be aware of teens today, and what they do. Language, clothing, and activities included in manuscripts should be contemporary. We are also looking for articles for a monthly feature entitled 'Straight Spotlight,' which is about real teens who are making a difference in their school, community or church. Articles for this feature should be approx. 900 words in length. We would also like a picture of the teen or group of teens to run with the article."

$ $ 'TEEN, Petersen Publishing Co., 6420 Wilshire Blvd., Los Angeles CA 90048. (213)782-2950. Fax: (213)782-2660. **Contact:** Roxanne Camron, editor. **40% freelance written.** Monthly magazine covering teenage girls ages 12-19. " *'Teen* is edited for high school girls. We include all topics that are of interest to females aged 12-19. Our readers want articles on heavy hitting subjects like drugs, sex, teen pregnancy, etc., and we also devote a significant number of pages each month to health, beauty and fashion." Estab. 1957. Circ. 2,000,000. **Pays on acceptance.** Byline sometimes given. Buys all rights. Editorial lead time 4 months. Submit seasonal material 6 months in advance. Accepts simultaneous submissions. Reports in 10 weeks. Sample copy for $2.50. Writer's guidelines for #10 SASE.

Nonfiction: General interest, inspirational, personal experience. **Buys 35 mss/year.** Query with or without published clips. Length: 750-1,500 words. Payment varies depending on length of research required.

Fiction: Adventure, condensed novels, fantasy, horror, mainstream, mystery, romance. **Buys 12 mss/year.** Send complete ms. Length: 2,500-3,500 words. **Pays $450-500.**

$ TEEN LIFE, Gospel Publishing House, 1445 Boonville Ave., Springfield MO 65802-1894. (417)862-2781, ext. 4370. Fax: (417)862-6059. E-mail: youthcurr@ag.org. **Contact:** Tammy Bicket, editor. Quarterly magazine of Assemblies of God denomination of Christian fiction and articles for church-oriented teenagers, ages 12-17. Circ. 50,000. **Pays on acceptance.** Publishes ms an average of 15 months after acceptance. Byline given. Buys first North American serial, one-time, simultaneous and second serial (reprint) rights. Submit seasonal material 18 months in advance. Accepts simultaneous and previously published submissions. Send tearsheet or photocopy of article or typed ms with rights for sale noted and information about when and where the article previously appeared. Response time varies. Sample copy for 9×12 SAE with 2 first-class stamps.

- *Teen Life* is currently inundated with manuscripts and not accepting freelance until January 1, 1999.

Nonfiction: Interviews with Christian athletes, musicians, missionaries, authors, or others with notable and helpful Christian testimonies or helpful experiences; transcriptions of discussion sessions where a group of teens talk about a particular issue; information on a topic or issue of interest gathered from experts in those fields (i.e., a doctor talks about teens' sexuality, a psychologist talks about dysfunctional families, a police officer talks about the dangers of gangs, etc.). Book excerpts, church history, general interest, how-to (deal with various life problems), humor, inspirational, personal experience, world issues, apologetics, prayer, devotional life, the occult, angels, church. **Buys 25-50 mss/year.** Send complete ms. Length: 500-1,200 words. **Pays 5-8¢/word.**

Reprints: Send tearsheet or photocopy of article and information about when and where the article previously appeared. Pays 50% of amount paid for an original article.

Photos: Photos purchased with accompanying ms. Pays $35 for 8×10 b&w glossy print; $50 for 35mm slide.

Fiction: Adventure, humorous, mystery, romance, suspense. **Buys 25-50 mss/year.** Send complete ms. Length: 500-1,200 words. **Pays 3-5¢/word.**

Tips: "We need more male-oriented stories or articles and more about life in the city and about people of diverse races. Avoid stereotypes. Avoid clichéd or trite situations with pat Christian answers and easy solutions. Avoid stories or articles without a Christian slant or emphasis, or those with a moral just tacked on at the end."

N $ $ TIGER BEAT, TV & Movie Screen, Sterling/Macfadden, 233 Park Ave., New York NY 10003. Fax: (212)780-3555. E-mail: tigerbmail@aol.com. Website: http://www.nextlevel.com/tigerbeat. **Contact:** Louise Barile, editor. **10% freelance written.** Teenage entertainment magazine published 10 times/year. "*Tiger Beat* is a fun, lively magazine for teen and preteen girls interested in young celebrities in music, movies and on TV." Estab. 1965. Circ. 200,000. Pays on publication. Publishes ms 3 months after acceptance. Byline sometimes given. Offers $25 kill fee. Buys first North American serial or second serial (reprint) rights. Editorial lead time 3 months. Submit seasonal material 3 months in advance. Accepts simultaneous submissions. Reports in 1 month on queries; 2 months on mss.

Nonfiction: Book excerpts, exposé, interview/profile, new product, personal experience, travel. No service, inspirational or how-to articles. **Buys 30 mss/year.** Query with SASE. Length: 500 words minimum. **Pays $25-300.**

Reprints: Accepts previously published submissions.

Photos: State availability of photos with submission. Reviews contact sheets, negatives, transparencies and prints. Negotiates payment individually. Identification of subjects required. Buys one-time rights.

Tips: "We want fact-filled celebrity features with quotes and personal details our readers can't find anywhere else."

N $ $ $ $ TWIST, Bauer Publishing, 270 Sylvan Ave., Englewood Cliffs NJ 07632. Fax: (201)569-4458. E-mail: twistmail@aol.com. **Contact**: Jeannie Kim or Jena Hofstedt, senior editors. Editor: Lisa Lombardi. Managing Editor: Christine Summer. **20% freelance written.** "Monthly magazine targeting 14-19 year old girls, with an emphasis on using the words, viewpoints and faces of real teenagers. Estab. 1997. Circ. 700,000. **Pays on acceptance**. Publishes ms an average of 3 months after acceptance. Byline given. Offers 20% kill fee. Buys first North American serial rights. Editorial lead time 3 months. Submit seasonal material 4 months in advance. Accepts simultaneous submissions. Reports in 1 month on queries. Writer's guidelines for #10 SASE.

Nonfiction: Essays (preferably by teenagers), interview/profile, personal experience (real teens' experiences, preferably in first person), relationships, health, sex, celebrities, quizzes, Internet. "No articles written from an adult point of view about teens—i.e., a mother's or teacher's personal account." **Buys 60 mss/year.** Query with published clips. Length: 100-1,800 words. **Pays minimum $50 for short item; up to $1/word for longer pieces.** Pays expenses of writers on assignment.

Photos: State availability of photos with submission. "We generally prefer to provide/shoot our own art." Negotiates payment individually. Model releases and identification of subjects required.

Columns/Departments: College Scene (news/fun items about college); Pop Life (reviews, short celebrity/media items); Body Buzz (health news/tips), all 75-200 words. **Buys 15 mss/year.** Query with published clips. **Pays minimum $50 for short item; up to $1/word for longer pieces.**

Tips: "*Tone* must be conversational, neither condescending to teens nor trying to be too slangy. If possible, send clips that show an ability to write for the teen market. We are in search of real life stories, and writers who can find teens with compelling real-life experiences (who are willing to use their full names and be photographed for the magazine). Please refer to a current issue to see examples of tone and content. No e-mail queries or submissions, please."

$ $ WHAT! A MAGAZINE, What! Publishers Inc., 108-93 Lombard Ave., Winnipeg, Manitoba R3B 3B1 Canada. (204)985-8173. Fax: (204)943-8991. E-mail: what@fox.nstn.ca. **Contact:** Stu Slayen, editor. **60% freelance written.** Magazine covering teen issues published 5 times during the school year. "*What! A Magazine* is distributed to high school students across Canada. We produce a mag that is empowering, interactive and entertaining. We respect the reader—today's teens are smart and creative (and critical)." Estab. 1987. Circ. 200,000. Pays 30 days after publication. Publishes ms an average of 3 months after acceptance. Byline given. Offers negotiable kill fee. Buys first North American serial rights. Editorial lead time 5 months. Submit seasonal material 5 months in advance. Reports in 2 months on queries; 1 month on mss. Sample copy for 9×12 SAE with Canadian postage. Writer's guidelines for #10 SAE with Canadian postage.

Nonfiction: General interest, humor, interview/profile, issue-oriented features. No cliché teen material. **Buys 6-10 mss/year.** Query with published clips. Length: 700-1,900 words. **Pays $100-500 (Canadian).** Sometimes pays expenses of writers on assignment.

Photos: Send photos with submission. Reviews transparencies, 4×6 prints. Negotiates payment individually. Identification of subjects required.

Tips: "Because *What! A Magazine* is distributed through schools (with the consent of school officials), it's important that each issue find the delicate balance between very cool and very responsible. We target very motivated young women and men. Pitches should stray from cliché and stories should challenge readers with depth, insight and color. All stories must be meaningful to a Canadian readership."

YM, Gruner & Jahr, 375 Lexington Ave, 8th Floor, New York NY 10017-5514. (212)499-2000. Editor: Lesley Seymour. **Contact:** Christina Boyle, senior editor. **25% freelance written.** Magazine covering teenage girls/dating. "We are a national magazine for young women ages 15-24. They're bright, enthusiastic and inquisitive. Our goal is to guide them—in effect, to be a 'best friend' and help them through the many exciting, yet often challenging, experiences of young adulthood." Estab. 1940s. Circ. 2,000,000. **Pays on acceptance.** Byline given. Offers 25% kill fee. Buys all rights. Editorial lead time 4 months. Submit seasonal material 5 months in advance. Accepts simultaneous submissions. Reports in 1 month. Sample copy for $2.50. Writer's guidelines free.

Nonfiction: How-to, interview/profile, personal experience, first-person stories. "*YM* publishes four special issues a year, including a self-discovery issue and a love issue filled with articles on relationships." Query with published clips (mark "Query" on the envelope). Length: 2,000 words maximum. Pays expenses of writers on assignment.

Tips: "Our relationship articles are loaded with advice from psychologists and real teenagers. Areas most open to freelancers are: 2,000 word first-person stories covering a personal triumph over adversity—incorporating a topical social/political problem; 2,000 word relationship stories; 1,200 word relationship articles. All articles should be lively and informative, but not academic in tone, and any 'expert' opinions (psychologists, authors and teachers) should be included as a supplement to the feelings and experiences of young women."

$ $ YOUNG SALVATIONIST, The Salvation Army, P.O. Box 269, Alexandria VA 22313-0269. (703)684-5500. Fax: (703)684-5539. E-mail: ys@usn.salvationarmy.org. Website: http://www.publications.salvationarmyusa.org. **Contact:** Lesa Davis, production manager. **80% freelance written.** Works with a small number of new/unpublished writers each year. Monthly magazine for high school teens. "Only material with a definite Christian emphasis or from a Christian perspective will be considered." Circ. 48,000. **Pays on acceptance.** Publishes ms an average of 10 months after acceptance. Byline given. Buys first North American serial, first, one-time or second serial (reprint) rights. Submit seasonal material 6 months in advance. Reports in 2 months. Sample copy for 9×12 SAE with 3 first-class stamps. Writer's guidelines and theme list for #10 SASE.

Nonfiction: Inspirational, how-to, humor, interview/profile, personal experience, photo feature, religious. "Articles should deal with issues of relevance to teens (high school students) today; avoid 'preachiness' or moralizing." **Buys 60 mss/year.** Send complete ms. Length: 1,000-1,500 words. **Pays 15¢/word for first rights.**

Reprints: Send tearsheet, photocopy of article or typed ms with rights for sale noted and information about when and where the article previously appeared. Pays 10¢/word for reprints.

Fiction: Adventure, fantasy, humorous, religious, romance, science fiction—all from a Christian perspective. Length: 500-1,200 words. **Pays 15¢/word.**

Tips: "Study magazine, familiarize yourself with the unique 'Salvationist' perspective of *Young Salvationist*; learn a little about the Salvation Army; media, sports, sex and dating are strongest appeal."

$ $ YOUTH UPDATE, St. Anthony Messenger Press, 1615 Republic St., Cincinnati OH 45210-1298. (513)241-5615. Fax: (513)241-0399. E-mail: CarolAnn@americancatholic.org. Website: http://www.AmericanCatholic.org. **Contact:** Carol Ann Morrow, editor. **90% freelance written.** Monthly 4-page newsletter of faith life for teenagers, "designed to attract, instruct, guide and challenge Catholics of high school age by applying the Gospel to modern problems/situations." Circ. 20,000. **Pays on acceptance.** Publishes ms an average of 6 months after acceptance. Byline given. Reports in 3 months. Sample copy and writer's guidelines for #10 SASE.

Nonfiction: Inspirational, practical self-help, spiritual. "Adults who pay for teen subs want more church-related and curriculum-related topics." **Buys 12 mss/year.** Query or send outline. Length: 2,200-2,300 words. **Pays $350-400.** Sometimes pays expenses of writers on assignment.

Tips: "Write for a 15-year-old with a C+ average."

TRAVEL, CAMPING AND TRAILER

Travel magazines give travelers indepth information about destinations, detailing the best places to go, attractions in the area and sites to see—but they also keep them up-to-date about potential negative aspects of these destinations. Publications in this category tell tourists and campers the where-tos and how-tos of travel. This category is extremely competitive, demanding quality writing, background information and professional photography. Each has its own slant. *Eco Traveler,* for example, covers "adventure travel with an environmental conscience," while *Trailer Life* presents articles on the recreational vehicle lifestyle. Sample copies should be studied carefully before sending submissions.

N $ **AAA GOING PLACES, Magazine for Today's Traveler**, AAA Auto Club South, 1515 N. Westshore Blvd., Tampa FL 33607. (813)289-5923. **Contact:** Phyllis Zeno, editor. **50% freelance written.** Bimonthly magazine on auto news, driving trips, cruise travel, tours. Estab. 1982. Circ. 2,000,000. Pays on publication. Publishes ms an average of 6 months after acceptance. Byline given. Buys one-time rights. Submit seasonal material 9 months in advance. Accepts simultaneous submissions. Reports in 2 months. Sample copy for 8×10 SAE and 4 first-class stamps. Free writer's guidelines.

Nonfiction: Historical/nostalgic, how-to, humor, interview/profile, personal experience, photo feature, travel. Travel stories feature domestic and international destinations with practical information and where to stay, dine and shop, as well as personal anecdotes and historical background; they generally relate to tours currently offered by AAA Travel Agency. Special issues include Cruise Guide and Europe Issue. **Buys 15 mss/year.** Send complete ms. Length: 500-1,500 words. **Pays $15/printed page.**

Photos: State availability of photos with submission. Reviews 2×2 transparencies. Offers no additional payment for photos accepted with ms. Captions required.

Columns/Departments: AAAway We Go (local attractions in Florida, Georgia or Tennessee).

Tips: "We prefer lively, upbeat stories that appeal to a well-traveled, sophisticated audience, bearing in mind that AAA is a conservative company."

N $ $ **AAA TODAY**, Pro Publishing Service, 378 Whooping Loop, Suite 1272, Altamonte Springs FL 32701. (407)834-6777. Fax: (407)834-3535. E-mail: margcavanaugh@sprintmail.com. **Contact:** Margaret Cavanaugh, managing editor. **50% freelance written**. Bimonthly AAA Club publication magazine covering travel destinations. Estab. 1960. Circ. 600,000. Pays on publication. Publishes ms an average of 6 months after acceptance. Byline given. Offers 25% kill fee. Buys first North American serial rights. Editorial lead time 12 months. Submit seasonal material 1 year in advance. Reports in 2 months. Sample copy and writer's guidelines free.

Nonfiction: Travel. **Buys 18 mss/year**. Query with published clips. Length: 500-1,000 words. **Pays $250-400**. Sometimes pays expenses of writers on assignment.

Photos: State availability or send photos with submission. Offers $50-200/photo. Captions required. Buys one-time rights.

N $ $ **ADVENTURE JOURNAL, The Adventure Travel Magazine**, Travel Publishing Group, Inc., 50 Oak St., Suite 301, San Francisco CA 94102. (415)431-9640. Fax: (415)431-5273. E-mail: ecotrav@aol.com. **Contact:** Lisa Tabb, editor. Bimonthly consumer magazine covering adventure travel. Estab. 1990. Circ. 160,000. Pays on publication. Byline given. Buys first or one-time rights. Editorial lead time 6 months. Submit seasonal material 6 months in advance. Accepts simultaneous submissions. Reports in 2 months. Sample copy for $5. Writer's guidelines for #10 SASE.

Nonfiction: Book excerpts, essays, historical/nostalgic, how-to, inspirational, interview/profile, personal experience, photo feature, travel. Special section in each issue on Ecotourism. No non-adventure travel related stories or service pieces. Sometimes pays expenses of writers on assignment.

Photos: State availability of photos with submission. Reviews contact sheets. Offers $125-350/photo; negotiates payment individually. Captions, identification of subjects required. Buys one-time rights.

Columns/Departments: Global Village (travel tech), 750 words; Compass Pointers (travel tips), 750 words; In Gear (gera reviews), 400 words;Media Messages (brief books, CD, and website reviews), 300 words; Profiles (famous & worthy adventure travel professionals, expeditioners and environmental activists), 300-1,200 words; Services Pieces (how-to pieces on useful topics from health on the road to travel tips), 100-800 words. **Buys 30 mss/year**. Query with published clips. **Pays $200-400**.

Fillers: Anecdotes, facts, newsbreaks, short humor. **Buys 100/year**. Length: 50-150 words. **Pays $50-150**.

$ $ $ $ **AQUA, The Padi (Professional Assocation of Diving Instructors) Diving Society Magazine**, Islands Publishing Co., P.O. Box 4728, Santa Barbara CA 93140-4728. Fax: (805)569-0349. E-mail: aqua@aquamag.com. Managing Editor: Angela Tripp. **Contact:** Bob Morris, executive editor. **90% freelance written with established writers.** Bimonthly magazine covering international travel for scuba diving, snorkeling, kayaking and other water sports enthusiasts. "*Aqua* puts its highest premium on lively storytelling. We avoid the 'been there, done that' treatment by

sending our favorite writers to places they've never before visited. We want our readers to discover new destinations and share in waterborne adventures with a sense of awe and wonder that can only be conveyed by facile writers who craft stylish reportage." Estab. 1997. Circ. 125,000. **Pays on acceptance.** Publishes ms an average of 6 months after acceptance. Byline given. Offers 25% kill fee. Buys all rights. Editorial lead time 6 months. Submit seasonal material 6 months in advance. Reports in 2 months. Sample copy for $6. Writer's guidelines for #10 SASE.
Nonfiction: General interest, historical/nostalgic, humor, interview/profile, photo feature, travel. No technical articles or gear reviews; no 'my family dive vacation' articles. **Buys 30 feature mss/year.** Query with published clips; feature articles are commissioned. Length: 500-4,000 words. **Pays $250-4,000.** Pays expenses of writers on assignment.
Photos: Feature articles are commissioned. Reviews high-quality dupes in 4×5 or 35mm transparency format. Offers $75-350/photo. Model releases, identification of subjects required. Buys one-time rights.
Columns/Departments: Local Dive (humorous profile of seedy or colorful watering hole or restaurant on the water), 500 words; Amphibian at Large (short feature piece on a water-related destination), 1,200-1,500 words; Aqua Culture (an aspect of the water enthusiast lifestyle, i.e., 'The Evolution of Aquaman,' a glimpse at the history and development of the DC Comics superhero), 1,200 words; Get-Wet-Aways (service pieces on diving, snorkeling, kayaking, whitewater rafting, etc., destinations in the U.S., Mexico, Canada and the Caribbean; basic nuts and bolts information on places that are good for day trips), 500 words. **Buys 50 mss/year.** Query with published clips. **Pays $250-1,500.**
Tips: "*Aqua* places a premium on stylish writing. We look for writers with uncommonly good storytelling skills and avoid articles that are overly technical or laden with gear-head jargon. In each issue there are usually four or five feature articles, ranging from 2,000 to 4,000 words. We aim for a lively mix of topics: destination, adventure, and profiles. Most features are staff-generated ideas assigned to a core group of freelance writers, but we welcome proposals with a well-defined focus and point of view.

All first-time queries should include recent writing samples and a SASE. Allow at least two months for a response. You may send queries or articles on speculation via E-mail to aqua@aquamag.com (writing samples should follow via regular mail). All telephone queries will be politely indulged and told: "Please put it in writing." Writers hoping to break in with *Aqua* might consider submissions to one of the following departments: *Flotsam & Jetsam*—Short (100-500 words), newsy pieces collected from all over the world. *Amphibian at Large*—A singular water adventure or experience, typically from some far-flung or exotic location, approximately 1,200 words. *Local Dive*—A dossier-type report on a funky bar/restaurant favored by water sports lovers. It can be anywhere in the world, just as long as it's on or near the water and is open to the public.

$ **ARRIVING MAGAZINE, The Ultimate in Transportation**, M.A.K. Publishing, 3249 Cherry Ave., Long Beach CA 90807. (562)492-9394. Fax: (562)492-1345. Website: http://www.arriving.com. **Contact:** James G. Redfern, editor. **75% freelance written.** Monthly magazine offering a superlative collection of full-color articles devoted specifically to the big-ticket items in today's transportation marketplace. Estab. 1995. Circulation 20,000. Pays on publication. Buys first North American serial rights. Guidelines for #10 SASE. Accepts unsolicited mss; encourages first time writers.
Nonfiction: "The central focus of Arriving is $800,000+ buses/Rvs; however, we also publish articles profiling custom jets, high-end yachts, unique automobiles and other speciality vehicles, as well as reviews of luxury RV resorts, pertinent industry pieces, and a few travel/destination pieces." Query with SASE. **Pays $50-100.**
Reprints: Send typed ms with rights for sale noted and information about when and where the article previously appeared.
Photos: Include color photos (glossy) or slides with submission. Photos/slides not returned unless other arrangements are made.
Columns/Departments: Industry Update; Products of Interest; The Road Less Traveled (focuses on extreme destinations/ultimate travel); The Travel Wonders of the World (past topics have profiled the Concorde and the Shinkansen; future topics include the Chunnel and the Panama Canal); The Ultimate Traveler..
Tips: "We are always in need of clean, accurate and intriguing stories profiling celebrity buses."

$ $ **ARUBA NIGHTS**, Nights Publications, 1831 Rene Levesque Blvd. W., Montreal, Quebec H3H 1R4 Canada. Fax: (514)931-6273. E-mail: editor@nightspublications.com. Website: www.nightspublications.com. Managing Editor: Zelly Zuskin. **Contact:** Stephen Trotter, editor. **90% freelance written.** Annual magazine covering the Aruban vacation lifestyle experience with an upscale, upbeat touch. Estab. 1988. Circ. 225,000. **Pays on acceptance.** Publishes ms an average of 9 months after acceptance. Byline given. Buys first North American serial and first Caribbean rights. Editorial lead time 1 month. Reports in 2 weeks on queries; 1 month on mss. Sample copy for $5 (make checks payable to "Nights Publications Inc."). Writer's guidelines free.
Nonfiction: General interest, historical/nostalgic, how-to features relative to Aruba vacationers, humor, inspirational, interview/profile, eco-tourism, opinion, personal experience, photo feature, travel, Aruban culture, art, activities, entertainment, topics relative to vacationers in Aruba. "No negative pieces or stale rewrites." **Buys 5-10 mss/year.** Submit ms and SASE with Canadian postage or IRC. Length: 250-750 words. **Pays $100-250.**
Photos: State availability with submission. Offers $50/photo. Captions, model releases, identification of subjects required. Buys one-time rights.
Tips: "Demonstrate your voice in your query letter. Be descriptive, employ vivid metaphors. Focus on individual aspects of the Aruban lifestyle and vacation experience (e.g., art, gambling tips, windsurfing, a colorful local character, a personal experience, etc.), rather than generalized overviews. Provide an angle that will be entertaining to vacationers who are already there. E-mail submissions OK."

$ $ ASU TRAVEL GUIDE, ASU Travel Guide, Inc., 1525 Francisco Blvd. E., San Rafael CA 94901. (415)459-0300. Fax: (415)459-0494. E-mail: chris@asuguide.com. Website: http://www.ASUguide.com. **Contact:** Christopher Gil, managing editor. **80% freelance written.** Quarterly guidebook covering international travel features and travel discounts for well-traveled airline employees. Estab. 1970. Circ. 60,000. Publishes ms an average of 4 months after acceptance. Byline given. Buys first North American serial rights, first and second rights to the same material, and second serial (reprint) rights to material originally published elsewhere; also makes work-for-hire assignments. Submit seasonal material 6 months in advance. Accepts simultaneous submissions. Reports in 1 year. Sample copy available for 6×9 SAE with 5 first-class stamps. Writer's guidelines for #10 SASE.

Nonfiction: International travel articles "similar to those run in consumer magazines. Not interested in amateur efforts from inexperienced travelers or personal experience articles that don't give useful information to other travelers." **Buys 16 ms/year.** Destination pieces only; no "Tips On Luggage" articles. Unsolicited mss or queries without SASE will not be acknowledged. No telephone queries. Length: 1,800 words. **Pays $200.**

Reprints: Send tearsheet of article with information about when and where the article previously appeared. Pays 100% of amount paid for an original article.

Photos: "Interested in clear, high-contrast photos." Reviews 5×7 and 8×10 b&w or color prints. "Payment for photos is included in article price; photos from tourist offices are acceptable."

Tips: "Query with samples of travel writing and a list of places you've recently visited. We appreciate clean and simple style. Keep verbs in the active tense and involve the reader in what you write. Avoid 'cute' writing, coined words and stale clichés. The most frequent mistakes made by writers in completing an article for us are: 1) Lazy writing—using words to describe a place that could describe any destination such as 'there is so much to do in (fill in destination) that whole guidebooks have been written about it'; 2) Including fare and tour package information—our readers make arrangements through their own airline."

$ BIG WORLD, Big World Publishing, P.O. Box 8743-G, Lancaster PA 17604. E-mail: jim@bigworld.com. Website: www.bigworld.com. **Contact:** Jim Fortney, editor. **85% freelance written.** Quarterly magazine covering independent travel. "Big World is a magazine for people who like their travel on the cheap and down-to-earth. And not necessarily because they have to—but because they want to. It's for people who prefer to spend their travelling time responsibly discovering, exploring, and learning, in touch with local people and their traditions, and in harmony with the environment. We're looking for casual, first-person narratives that take into account the cultural/sociological/political side of travel." Estab. 1995. Circ. 5,000. Pays on publication. Publishes ms an average of 3 months after acceptance. Byline given. Buys one-time rights. Editorial lead time 2 months. Submit seasonal material 4 months in advance. Reports in 1 months on queries; 2 months on mss. Sample copy for $3. Writer's guidelines for #10 SASE.

Nonfiction: New product, opinion, personal experience, photo feature, travel, how-to, tips on transportation bargains and adventuring, overseas work study advice. **Buys 20 mss/year.** Length: 500-4,000 words. Query. Pay varies. Sometimes pays with subscriptions.

Reprints: Send photocopy of article. Pays 50% of amount paid for original article.

Photos: Reviews prints. Negotiates payment individually. Captions required. Buys one-time rights.

Columns/Departments: Readers Writes (book reviews by subscribers), 400-500 words; Dispatches (slice of life pieces), 200-800 words; Hostel Intentions, My Town, Bike World, Better Adventuring. Pay varies.

Tips: "Take a look at the glossy, fluffy travel mags in the bookstore. They're *not* what we're about. We're *not* looking for romantic getaway pieces or lap-of-luxury bits. Our readers are decidedly downbeat and are looking for similarly-minded on-the-cheap and down-to-earth, first-person articles. Be breezy. Be yourself. First-time writers especially encouraged. You can submit your story to us on paper, 3.5 and Windows-readable disc, or via e-mail."

$ $ BONAIRE NIGHTS, Nights Publications, 1831 René Lévesque Blvd. W., Montreal, Quebec H3H 1R4 Canada. Fax: (514)931-6273. E-mail: editor@nightspublications.com. **Contact:** Stephen Trotter, editor. **90% freelance written.** Annual magazine covering Bonaire vacation experience. "Upbeat entertaining lifestyle articles: colorful profiles of locals, eco-tourism; lively features on culture, activities (particularly scuba and snorkeling), special events, historical attractions, how-to features. Audience is North American tourist." Estab. 1993. Circ. 60,000. **Pays on acceptance.** Publishes ms an average of 9 months after acceptance. Byline given. Buys first North American serial rights and first Caribbean rights. Editorial lead time 1 month. Reports in 2 weeks on queries; 1 month on mss. Sample copy for $5 (make check payable to "Nights Publications, Inc). Writer's guidelines for #10 SAE.

Nonfiction: Lifestyle, general interest, historical/nostalgic, how-to, humor, inspirational, interview/profile, opinion, personal experience, photo feature, travel, local culture, art, activities, especially scuba diving, snorkeling, eco-tourism. **Buys 6-9 mss/year.** Length: 250-750 words. Query or submit ms and SASE with Canadian postage or IRC. **Pays $100-250.**

Photos: State availability of photos with submission. Reviews transparencies. Offers $50/slide. Captions, model releases, identification of subjects required. Buys one-time or first rights.

Tips: "Demonstrate your voice in your query letter. Focus on the Bonaire lifestyle, what sets it apart from other islands. We want personal experience, not generalized overviews. Be positive and provide an angle that will appeal to vacationers who are already there. Our style is upbeat, friendly, fluid and descriptive."

$ CAMPERS MONTHLY, Northeast Edition–Maine to New York; Mid Atlantic Edition—New York to Virginia, P.O. Box 260, Quakertown PA 18951. (215)536-6420. Fax: (215)536-6509. E-mail: werv2@aol.com. Website: http://www.RVGuide.com/campers. **Contact:** Paula Finkbeiner, editor. **50% freelance written.** Monthly (except December) tabloid. "With the above emphasis, we want to encourage our readers to explore all forms of outdoor recreation using a tent or recreational vehicle as a 'home away from home.' Travel—places to go, things to do and see." Estab. 1991 (Mid-Atlantic), 1993 (Northeast). Circ. 35,000 (Mid-Atlantic), 25,000 (Northeast). Pays on publication. Publishes ms an average of 2 months after acceptance. Byline given. Buys simultaneous rights. Editorial lead time 2 months. Submit seasonal material 4 months in advance. Accepts simultaneous submissions. Reports in 2 months. Sample copy and writer's guidelines for 10×13 SASE.

Nonfiction: Historical/nostalgic (tied into a camping trip), how-to (selection, care, maintenance of RV's, tents, accessories, etc.) humor, personal experience, travel (camping in the Mid-Atlantic or Northeast region). Special issue: Snowbird Issue (October)—geared towards campers heading South; Christmas Gift Ideas (November). "This is generally the only time we accept articles on areas outside our coverage area." **Buys 20-40 mss/year.** Send complete ms. Length: 800-2,000 words. **Pays $90-150 for assigned articles; $50 or more for unsolicited articles.** Sometimes pays expenses of writers on assignment.

Reprints: Send photocopy of article or typed ms with rights for sale noted and information about when and where the article previously appeared. Pays 50% of amount paid for an original article.

Photos: Send photos with submission. Reviews 5×7 or 8×10 glossy b&w and color prints. Offers $3-5/photo. Don't send snapshots or polaroids.

Columns/Departments: Campground Cook (ideas for cooking in RV's, tents and over campfires; include recipes), 500-1,000 words; Tales From The Road (humorous stories of "on-the-road" travel), 350-800 words; Tech Tips (technical pieces on maintenance and enhanced usage of RV-related equipment), 350-1,800 words. **Buys 15 mss/year.** Send complete ms. **Pays $40-60.** Cybersite (websites of interest to RVer's), 500-1,000 words. **Buys 10 mss/year.**

Fiction: Humorous, slice-of-life vignettes. **Buys 10 mss/year.** Query. Length: 300-1,000 words. **Pays $60-75.**

Fillers: Facts, short humor (must be RV-oriented). **Buys 8/year.** Length: 30-350. **Pays $20-35.**

Tips: Most open to freelancers are "destination pieces focusing on a single attraction or activity or closely clustered attractions are always needed. General interest material, technical or safety ideas (for RVs) is an area we're always looking for pieces on. Off-the-beaten track destinations always get priority. We're always looking for submissions for destination pieces for our Mid-Atlantic edition."

$ $ CAMPING CANADA'S RV LIFESTYLES, 2585 Skymark Ave., Unit 306, Mississauga, Ontario L4W 4L5 Canada. (905)624-8218. Fax: (905)624-6764. Editor: Howard Elmer. **Contact:** Peter Tasler, editorial director. **50% freelance written.** Magazine published 7 times/year (monthly January-June and November). "*Camping Canada's RV Lifestyles* is geared to readers who enjoy travel/camping. Upbeat pieces only. Readers vary from owners of towable campers or motorhomes to young families and entry-level campers (RV only)." Estab. 1971. Circ. 45,000. Pays on publication. Byline given. Buys first North American serial rights. Editorial lead time 2 months. Reports in 1 month on queries; 2 months on mss. Sample copy free.

Nonfiction: How-to, personal experience, travel. No inexperienced, unresearched or too general pieces. **Buys 20-30 mss/year.** Query. Length: 1,200-2,000 words. Pay varies. Sometimes pays expenses of writers on assignment.

Reprints: Occasionally accepts previously published submissions, if so noted.

Photos: Send photos with submission. Offers no additional payment for photos accepted with ms. Buys one-time rights.

Tips: "Pieces should be slanted toward RV living. All articles must have an RV slant."

$ CAMPING TODAY, Official Publication of the Family Campers & RVers, 126 Hermitage Rd., Butler PA 16001-8509. (412)283-7401. **Contact:** DeWayne Johnston and June Johnston, editors. **30% freelance written.** Prefers to work with published/established writers. Monthly official membership publication of the FCRV, "the largest nonprofit family camping and RV organization in the United States and Canada. Members are heavily oriented toward RV travel, both weekend and extended vacations. Concentration is on member activities in chapters. Group is also interested in conservation and wildlife. The majority of members are retired." Estab. 1983. Circ. 25,000. Pays on publication. Publishes ms an average of 6 months after acceptance. Byline given. Buys one-time rights. Submit seasonal material 3 months in advance. Accepts simultaneous submissions. Reports in 2 months. Sample copy and guidelines for 4 first-class stamps. Writer's guidelines only for #10 SASE.

Nonfiction: Travel (interesting places to visit by RV, camping), humor (camping or travel related, please, no "our first campout stories"), interview/profile (interesting campers), new products, technical (RVs related). **Buys 10-15 mss/year.** Send complete ms with photos. Length: 750-2,000 words. **Pays $50-150.**

Reprints: Send typed ms with rights for sale noted and information about when and where the article previously appeared. Pays 35-50% of amount paid for an original article.

Photos: Send photos with ms. Need b&w or sharp color prints inside (we can make prints from slides) and vertical transparencies for cover. Captions required.

Tips: "Freelance material on RV travel, RV maintenance/safety, and items of general camping interest throughout the United States and Canada will receive special attention."

$ $ CARIBBEAN TRAVEL AND LIFE, 33 W. Canton Ave., Winter Park FL 32789. (407)628-4802. Fax: (407)628-7061. E-mail: jb2@worldzine.com. Editor-in-Chief: Steve Blount. **Contact:** James Bartlett, managing editor. **90% freelance written.** Prefers to work with published/established writers. Magazine covering travel to the Caribbean, Bahamas and Bermuda for sophisticated upscale audience, published 8 times/year. Estab. 1985. Circ. 130,000. **Pays on acceptance.** Publishes ms an average of 3 months after acceptance. Byline given. Offers 25% kill fee. Buys first North

American serial rights. Submit seasonal material 6 months in advance. Reports in 2 months. Sample copy for 9×12 SAE with 9 first-class stamps. Writer's guidelines for #10 SASE.

- Ranked as one of the best markets for freelance writers in *Writer's Yearbook* magazine's annual "Top 100 Markets," January 1998.

Nonfiction: General interest, how-to, interview/profile, culture, personal experience, travel. No guidebook rehashing, superficial destination pieces or critical exposes. **Buys 30 mss/year.** Query with published clips and SASE. Length: 1,000-2,500 words. **Pays $550.**

Photos: Send photos with submission. Reviews 35mm transparencies. Offers $100-600/photo. Captions and identification of subjects required. Buys one-time rights.

Columns/Departments: Gazette (new, humor); Travel Desk (hotels, cruises, airlines); Day Trip (island excursions); Active Traveler (active, sports-oriented activites); Caribbean Life (people, arts, culture, music); Caribbean Kitchen (restaurants, chefs, food); Passages (books excerpts—fiction and non-fiction by and about the Caribbean). Query with published clips and SASE. Length: 500-1,250 words. **Pays $75-300.**

Tips: "Our only requirements are that the writing be superb, the subject be something unique and interesting, and the writer must know his/her subject. We are NOT interested in stories about the well-known, over-publicized and commonly visited places of the Caribbean. Our readers have likely already 'been there, done that.' We want to guide them to the new, the unusual and the interesting. Please do not call and do not send a complete manuscript unless requested by an editor. E-mail queries OK."

$ $ CHICAGO TRIBUNE, Travel Section, 435 N. Michigan Ave., Chicago IL 60611. (312)222-3999. **Travel Contact:** Randy Curwen, editor. Weekly Sunday newspaper leisure travel section averaging 22 pages aimed at vacation travelers. Circ. 1,100,000. Pays on publication. Publishes ms an average of 6 weeks after acceptance. Byline given. Buys one-time rights (which includes microfilm, online and CD/ROM usage). Submit seasonal material 2 months in advance. Accepts simultaneous submissions. Reports in 1 month. Sample copy for large SAE with $1.50 postage. Writer's guidelines for #10 SASE.

Nonfiction: Essays, general interest, historical/nostalgic, how-to (travel, pack), humor, opinion, personal experience, photo feature, travel. "There will be 16 special issues in the next 18 months." **Buys 150 mss/year.** Send complete ms. Length: 500-2,000 words. **Pays $50-500.**

Photos: State availability of photos with submission. Reviews 35mm transparencies, 8×10 or 5×7 prints. Offers $100/color photo; $25/b&w; $100 for cover. Captions required. Buys one-time rights.

Tips: "Be professional. Use a word processor. Make the reader want to go to the area being written about. Only 1% of manuscripts make it."

$ $ CHRISTIAN CAMP & CONFERENCE JOURNAL, (formerly *Journal of Christian Camping*), Christian Camping International U.S.A., P.O. Box 62189, Colorado Springs CO 80962-2189. (719)260-9400. Fax: (719)260-6398. E-mail: editor@cciusa.org. Website: http://www.cciusa.org. **Contact:** Dean Ridings, editor. **75% freelance written.** Prefers to work with published/established writers. Bimonthly magazine emphasizing the broad scope of organized camping with emphasis on Christian camping. "All who work in youth camps and adult conferences read our magazine for inspiration and to get practical help in ways to serve in their operations." Estab. 1963. Circ. 7,500. Pays on publication. Publishes ms an average of 4 months after acceptance. Rights negotiable. Byline given. Reports in 1 month. Sample copy for $2.25 plus 9×12 SASE. Writer's guidelines for #10 SASE.

Nonfiction: General interest (trends in organized camping in general, Christian camping in particular); how-to (anything involved with organized camping from motivating staff, to programming, to record keeping, to camper follow-up); inspirational (interested in profiles and practical applications of Scriptural principles to everyday situations in camping); interview (with movers and shakers in Christian camping; submit a list of basic questions first); and opinion (letter to the editor). **Buys 20-30 mss/year.** Query required. Length: 600-1,200 words. **Pays 12¢/word.**

Reprints: Send photocopy of article and information about when and where the article previously appeared. Pays 50% of amount paid for an original article.

Photos: Send photos with ms. Pays $25-200 for 5×7 b&w contact sheet or print; price negotiable for 35mm color transparencies. Rights negotiable.

Poetry: Considers free verse.

Tips: "The most frequent mistake made by writers is that they send articles unrelated to our readers. Ask for our publication guidelines first. Profiles/interviews are the best bet for freelancers."

☆ $ $ COAST TO COAST MAGAZINE, Affinity Group, Inc., 2575 Vista Del Mar Dr., Ventura CA 93001-3920. Fax: (805)667-4217. E-mail: wlaw@affinity.com. Website: http://www.tl.com. **Contact:** Valerie Law, editor. **80% freelance written.** Club magazine published 8 times/year for members of Coast to Coast Resorts. "*Coast to Coast* focuses on travel, recreation and good times, with some stories targeted to recreational vehicle owners." Estab. 1982. Circ. 300,000. **Pays on acceptance.** Publishes ms an average of 5 months after acceptance. Byline given. Offers 33% kill fee. Buys first North American serial and electronic rights. Submit seasonal material 5 months in advance. Reports in 1 month on queries; 2 months on mss. Sample copy for $2 and 9×12 SASE.

Nonfiction: Book excerpts, essays, general interest, historical/nostalgic, how-to, humor, inspirational, interview/profile, new product, opinion, personal experience, photo feature, technical, travel. No poetry, cartoons. **Buys 50 mss/year.** Query with published clips. Length: 500-2,500 words. **Pays $75-600.**

Reprints: Send photocopy of article, information about when and where the article previously appeared. Pays approximately 50% of the amount paid for an original article.

Photos: Send photos with submission. Reviews transparencies. Offers $50-600/photo. Identification of subjects required. Buys one-time rights.

Tips: "Send published clips with queries, or story ideas will not be considered."

$ $ $ $ CONDÉ NAST TRAVELER, The Condé Nast Publications, 360 Madison Ave., New York NY 10017. (212)880-8800. Fax: (212)880-2190. Website: www.epicurious.com. Editor: Thomas J. Wallace. **Contact:** Dee Aldrich, managing editor. 75% freelance written. Monthly. "Our motto, Truth in Travel, sums up our editorial philosophy: to present travel destinations, news and features in a candid, journalistic style. Our writers do not accept complimentary tickets, hotel rooms, gifts, or the like. While our departments present service information in a tipsheet or newsletter manner, our destination stories are literary in tone. Our readers are affluent, well-educated, and sophisticated about travel." Estab. 1987. Circ. 850,000. "Please keep in mind that we very rarely assign stories based on unsolicited queries because (1) our inventory of unused stories (features and departments) is very large, and (2) most story ideas are generated inhouse by the editors, as it is very difficult for outsiders to anticipate the needs of our inventory. To submit story ideas, send a brief (one paragraph) description of the idea(s) to the appropriate editor. Please do not send clips, résumés, photographs, itineraries, or abridged or full-length manuscripts. Due to our editorial policy, we *do not* purchase completed manuscripts. Telephone calls are not accepted."

- *Conde Nast Traveler* tells us that they are no longer accepting unsolicited submissions. Research this market carefully before submitting your best work.

$ $ CRUISE TRAVEL MAGAZINE, World Publishing Co., 990 Grove St., Evanston IL 60201-4370. (708)491-6440. Editor: Robert Meyers. **Contact:** Charles Doherty, managing editor. **95% freelance written.** Bimonthly magazine. "This is a consumer-oriented travel publication covering the world of pleasure cruising on large cruise ships (with some coverage of smaller ships), including ports, travel tips, roundups." Estab. 1979. **Pays on acceptance.** Publishes ms an average of 6 months after acceptance. Byline given. Offers 50% kill fee. Buys first North American serial, one-time or second serial (reprint) rights. Accepts simultaneous submissions. Reports in 1 month. Sample copy for $5 postpaid. Writer's guidelines for #10 SASE.

Nonfiction: General interest, historical/nostalgic, interview/profile, personal experience, photo feature, travel. "No daily cruise 'diary', My First Cruise, etc." **Buys 72 mss/year.** Query with or without published clips, or send complete ms. Length: 500-1,500 words. **Pays $100-400.**

Reprints: Send tearsheet or photocopy of article and typed ms with rights for sale noted.

Photos: Send photos with submission. Reviews transparencies and prints. "Must be color, 35m preferred (other format OK); color prints second choice." Offers no additional payment for photos accepted with ms "but pay more for well-illustrated ms." Captions and identification of subjects required. Buys one-time rights.

Fillers: Anecdotes, facts. **Buys 3 mss/year.** Length: 300-700 words. **Pays $75-200.**

Tips: "Do your homework. Know what we do and what sorts of things we publish. Know the cruise industry—we can't use novices. Good, sharp, bright color photography opens the door fast. We still need good pictures—we are not interested in developing any new contributors who cannot provide color support to manuscripts."

$ $ CURAÇAO NIGHTS, Nights Publications, 1831 Rene Levesque Blvd. West, Montreal, Quebec H3H 1R4 Canada. (514)931-1987. Fax: (514)931-6273. E-mail: editor@nightspublications.com. **Contact:** Stephen Trotter, editor. Managing Editor: Zelly Zuskin. **90% freelance written.** Annual magazine covering the Curaçao vacation experience. "We are seeking upbeat, entertaining lifestyle articles; colorful profiles of locals; lively features on culture, activities, night life, eco-tourism, special events, gambling; how-to features; humor. Our audience is the North American vacationer." Estab. 1989. Circ. 155,000. **Pays on acceptance.** Publishes ms 9 months after acceptance. Byline given. Buys first North American serial and first Caribbean rights. Editorial lead time 1 month. Reports in 2 weeks on queries; 1 month on mss. Sample copy for $5 (check payable to Nights Publications Inc.). Guidelines free.

Nonfiction: General interest, historical/nostalgic, how-to help a vacationer get the most from their vacation, eco-tourism, humor, inspirational, interview/profile, lifestyle, opinion, personal experience, photo feature, travel, local culture, art, activities, night life, topics relative to vacationers in Curaçao. "No negative pieces, generic copy or stale rewrites." **Buys 5-10 mss/year.** Query with published clips and SASE that includes Canadian postage or IRC. Length: 250-750 words. **Pays $100-$250.**

Photos: State availability of photos with submission. Reviews transparencies. Offers $50/photo. Captions, model releases, identification of subjects required. Buys one-time rights.

Tips: "Demonstrate your voice in your query letter. Focus on individual aspects of the island lifestyle and vacation experience (e.g., art, gambling tips, windsurfing, a colorful local character, a personal experience, etc.), rather than generalized overviews. Provide an angle that will be entertaining to vacationers who are already on island. Our style is upbeat, friendly, fluid and descriptive."

$ $ $ EXPLORE! The Port Magazine of Royal Caribbean Cruise Line (formerly *Crown and Anchor*), Onboard Media Inc., 960 Alton Rd., Miami Beach FL 33137. (305)673-0400. Fax: (305)674-9396. **Contact:** Lynn Santa Lucia, managing editor. **95% freelance written.** "This annual publication reaches cruise vacationers on board RCCL ships on 3-11 night Caribbean, Bahamas, Mexican Riviera, Alaska and Far East itineraries. Culture, art, architecutre, natural wonders, food, folklore, legends, lingo/idioms, festivals, literature, eco-systems, local wares of these regions. Current themes such as celebrity retreats, hit recordings and hot artists and writers are welcomed." Estab. 1992. Circ.

792,184. Pays half on execution of agreement, **half on acceptance** of material. Publishes ms 4 months after acceptance. Offers 50% kill fee. Buys first or second serial (reprint) rights. Byline and bionote given. Editorial lead time 6 months. Reports in 1 month. Sample copy for 11×14 SAE with 10 first-class stamps. Writer's guidelines for #10 SASE.

Nonfiction: Book excerpts, essays, general interest, humor, interview/profile, new product, photo feature, travel. Does not want politics, sex, religion, general history, shopping information or advertorials, no personal experience. **Buys 25 features/year,** plus assigned editorial covering ports-of-call and numerous fillers. Query with published clips. Length: 800-2,000 words. **Pays $400-1,000** and copies. Sometimes pays expenses of writers on assignment.

Reprints: Accepts previously published submissions, if so noted.

Photos: State availability of photos with submission. Negotiates payment individually. Captions, model releases, identification of subjects required. Buys one-time and seasonal reprint rights.

Fillers: Anecdotes, facts, newsbreaks, short humor. **Buys 50/year.** Length: 50-200 words. **Pays $25-100** or copies.

Tips: "Know the port destinations we cover. Know our magazine. Demonstrate your voice in your query letter. Send a selection of published writing samples that reveals your range. The three essential things we look for are: 1) an authoritative voice; 2) intimate knowledge of the subject matter; and 3) original material. Having a clear-cut article in mind is a must. Do not query 'with an idea for an article on San Juan.' Outline your proposal and indicate your angle."

$ $ FAMILY MOTOR COACHING, Official Publication of the Family Motor Coach Association, 8291 Clough Pike, Cincinnati OH 45244-2796. (513)474-3622. Fax: (513)388-5286. E-mail: rgould@mfca.com Website: http://www.fmca.com. Publishing Director: Pamela Wisby Kay. **Contact:** Robbin Gould, editor. **80% freelance written.** "We prefer that writers be experienced RVers." Monthly magazine emphasizing travel by motorhome, motorhome mechanics, maintenance and other technical information. "*Family Motor Coaching* magazine is edited for the members and prospective members of the Family Motor Coach Association who own or about to purchase recreational vehicles of the motor coach style and use them exclusively for pleasure. Featured are articles on travel and recreations, association news; meetings, activities, and conventions plus articles on new products. Approximately ⅓ of editorial content is devoted to travel and entertainment, ⅓ to Association news, and ⅓ to new products and industry news." Estab. 1963. Circ. 110,000. **Pays on acceptance.** Publishes ms an average of 8 months after acceptance. Buys first North American serial rights. Byline given. Submit seasonal material 4 months in advance. Reports in 2 months. Sample copy for $2.50. Writer's guidelines for #10 SASE.

Nonfiction: Motorhome travel (various areas of country accessible by motor coach), how-to (do it yourself motor home projects and modifications), bus conversions, humor, interview/profile, new product, technical, nostalgia. **Buys 8-10 mss/issue.** Query with published clips . Length: 1,000-2,000 words. **Pays $100-500.**

Photos: State availability of photos with query. Offers no additional payment for b&w contact sheets, 35mm or 2¼×2¼ color transparencies. Captions, model releases required. Prefers first North American serial rights but will consider one-time rights on photos only.

Tips: "The greatest number of contributions we receive are travel; therefore, that area is the most competitive. However, it also represents the easiest way to break in to our publication. Articles should be written for those traveling by self-contained motor home. The destinations must be accessible to motor home travelers and any peculiar road conditions should be mentioned."

$ $ GO MAGAZINE, AAA Carolinas, P.O. Box 29600, Charlotte NC 28229-9600. (704)569-7733. Fax: (704)532-4346. Website: www.aaacarolinas.com. **Contact:** Tom Crosby, editor. **10% freelance written.** Bimonthly newspaper covering travel, automotive, safety (traffic) and insurance."Consumer oriented membership publication providing information on complex or expensive subjects—car buying, vacations, traffic safety problems, etc." Estab. 1928. Circ. 565,000. **Pays on acceptance.** Publishes ms an average of 2 months after acceptance. Buys second serial (reprint) rights, simultaneous rights or makes work-for-hire assignments. Editorial lead time 6 weeks. Submit seasonal material 6 weeks in advance. Reports in 2 weeks on queries; 2 months on mss. Sample copy for SAE with 4 first-class stamps. Writer's guidelines for #10 SASE.

Nonfiction: How-to (fix auto, travel safety, etc.), travel, automotive insurance, traffic safety. Special issues: Canadian Rockies, Alaska, Amelia Island, Pinehurst 1998 Open, Hawaii (November-December 1998); European Tours, Tennessee Places to Visit, North Carolina Skiing, Disney—What's New in 1999, Alaska Cruises, Alaska Vacation Packages (January 1999); Alaska Vacation Packages, Georgia Places to Visit, Cruises in General, Mexico, European Destinations, Caribbean Islands, (February 1999); Disney, Spring Festivals in the Carolinas, Caribbean Islands and Cruises, Spring/European Cruises, European Destinations, (March-April 1999). **Buys 12-14 mss/year.** Query with published clips. Length: 600-900 words. **Pays 15¢/published word.**

Photos: Send photos with submission. Offers no additional payment for photos accepted with ms. Buys one-time rights.

$ $ $ $ GOLF & TRAVEL, Turnstile Publishing Co., 49 W. 45th St., 6th Floor, New York NY 10036. E-mail: golfntravl@aol.com. **Contact:** Mary Arendt, managing editor. **50% freelance written.** Bi-monthly magazine. *Golf & Travel* wants "solid travel writing with a critical eye. No fluff. No common tourist stops unless you've got a unique angle. Destination stories with golf as one of the elements, but not the only element." Estab. 1997. Circ. 150,000. **Pays on acceptance**. Publishes ms an average of 3 months after acceptance. Byline given. Buys first rights or all rights. Editorial lead time 6 months. Submit seasonal material 18 months in advance. "We only reply to queries we're interested in. Too small a staff to answer every letter. Sorry." Sample copy for $3.95 plus postage; (800)678-9717. Writer's guidelines for #10 SASE.

Nonfiction: Interview/profile, travel. "No articles about golf courses only; no articles on common golf destinations;

no articles written in 'fluff' language." **Buys 30 mss/year.** Query with published clips. Length: 100-3,000 words. **Pays $50-2,500.** Sometimes pays expenses of writers on assignment.
Columns/Departments: Starter (golf packages, golf events, golf destination news), 100-150 words; Road & Driver (great road trips with golf along the way), 1,500-2,000 words; Urban Outings (places to play golf within city limits), 1,000-1,500 words; Fairway Living (destination stories about places to live that offer good golf environment), 1,200-1,500 words; Suite Spot (lesser known golf resort), 250-750 words. Query with published clips. **Pays $50-1,500.**
Fiction: Publishes novel excerpts.
Tips: "Must be established travel writers with great destination stories in their clips file. Clips must demonstrate unusual angles—off the beaten path. Knowledge of golf extremely helpful. Straight golf writers are not encouraged to query. We do not cover golf instruction, golf equipment or golf teaching aids. We are interested in writers who can combine the two subjects of golf and travel with a third element that is not easily named but has to do with a sophisticated tone, an intelligent attitude, a sensitive eye and, where appropriate, a sense of humor or irony. Magazines whose editorial voice we like include *Town & Country, Men's Journal, Departures, Saveur* and *Smart Money.*"

N ★ $ HEALING RETREATS & SPAS, 24 E. Cota St., Suite 101, Santa Barbara CA 93101. Fax: (805)962-1337. E-mail: walters@grayphics.com. Editor: Anthony Carroccio. **Contact:** E.M. Kennedy, assistant editor. **90% freelance written.** Bimonthly magazine covering retreats, spas, health and lifestyle issues. "We try to present healing and nurturing *alternatives* for the global community, and provide a bridge between travel, health, and New Age magazine material." Estab. 1996. Circ. 45,000. Pays on publication. Publishes ms 3 months after acceptance. Byline given. Buys one-time rights. Editorial lead time 2 months. Submit seasonal material 3 months in advance. Reports in 1 month on queries; 2 months on mss. Sample copy for $6.95. Writer's guidelines for #10 SASE.
Nonfiction: Book excerpts, general interest, how-to (at-home therapies), inspirational, interview/profile, new product, personal experience, photo feature, travel (spas and retreats only), health alternatives. **Buys 50 mss/year.** Query with published clips. Length: 700-3,000 words. **Pays $25-75.** Pays writers with contributor copies or other premiums if they want 20 or more copies for self-promotion.
Photos: Send photos with submission. Reviews transparencies. Offers no additional payment for photos accepted with ms. Captions required. Buys one-time rights.
Columns/Departments: Buys 40 mss/year. Send complete ms. **Pays $25-50.**
Tips: "Writers can break in with well-written, first-hand knowledge of an alternative health issue or therapy. Even our travel pieces require this type of knowledge. Once a writer proves capable, other assignments can follow."

$ $ HIGHWAYS, The Official Publication of the Good Sam Club, TL Enterprises Inc., 2575 Vista Del Mar, Ventura CA 93001. (805)667-4100. Fax: (805)667-4454. E-mail: repstein@tl.com. Website: http://www.goodsamclub/highways/. **Contact:** Ronald H. Epstein, editor. **40% freelance written.** Monthly magazine (November/December issues combined) covering recreational vehicle lifestyle. "All of our readers—since we're a membership publication—own or have a motorhome, trailer, camper or van conversion. Thus, our stories include road-travel conditions and terms and information about campgrounds and locations. Estab. 1966. Circ. 912,214. **Pays on acceptance**. Publishes ms an average of 6 months after acceptance. Byline given. Offers 50% kill fee. Buys first North American serial and electronic rights. Editorial lead time 15 weeks. Submit seasonal material 5 months in advance. Accepts simultaneous submissions. Reports in 3 weeks on queries; 1 month on mss. Sample copy and writer's guidelines free.
Nonfiction: How-to (repair/replace something on an RV); humor; technical; travel; (all RV related). **Buys 15-25 mss/year.** Query or send complete ms. Length: 1,500-2,500 words. **Pays $150-500 for unsolicited articles.**
Photos: Send photos with submission. Reviews contact sheets, negatives, transparencies, prints. No additional payment for photos accepted with ms. Captions, model releases, identification of subjects required. Buys one-time rights.
Columns/Departments: Beginners (people buying an RV for the first time), 1,200 words; View Points (issue-related, 750 words. Query. **Pays $200-250.**
Tips: "Understand RVs and RVing. It's a unique lifestyle and different than typical traveling. Aside from that, we welcome good writers!"

$ $ $ HISTORIC TRAVELER, The Guide to Great Historic Destinations, Cowles Magazines, Inc. 6405 Flank Dr., Harrisburg PA 17112. (717)657-9555. E-mail: ht@cowles.com. **Contact:** Tom Huntington, editor. **80% freelance written.** Bimonthly magazine covering "historic destinations for upscale readers with a strong interest in history and historic sites." Estab. 1994. Circ. 130,000. **Pays on acceptance.** Publishes ms an average of 4 months after acceptance. Byline given. Offers 25% kill fee. Buys first North American serial rights or all rights. Editorial lead time 6 months. Submit seasonal material 6 months in advance. Reports in 2 months. Sample copy for $5. Writer's guidelines for #10 SASE.
Nonfiction: Historical, travel. "Nothing without a strong historic destination(s) as the focus." **Buys 42 mss/year.** Query with published clips and SASE. Length: 1,500-3,000 words. **Pays $300-1,000.**
Photos: State availability of photos with submission. Negotiates payment individually. Identification of subjects required. Buys one-time rights.
Columns/Departments: All-American Towns (small towns); Museum Watch (unusual museums); Grand Tour (early travel experiences); all 1,500 words. **Buys 20 mss/year.** Query with published clips and SASE. **Pays $300-500.**
Tips: "A good query is always a strong start. Don't offer to write about something unless it interests you personally."

$ $ INTERNATIONAL LIVING, Agora, Inc., 105 W. Monument St., Baltimore MD 21201. Fax: (410)223-2696. E-mail: 103114.2472@compuserve.com. Editorial Director: Siri Lise Doub. **Contact:** Kerstin A. Czarra, assistant editor. **50% freelance written.** Monthly newsletter covering retirement, travel, investment and real estate overseas. "We do not want descriptions of how beautiful places are. We want specifics, recommendations, contacts, prices, names, addresses, phone numbers, etc. We want offbeat locations and off-the-beaten-track spots." Estab. 1981. Circ. 110,000. Pays on publication. Publishes ms an average of 3 months after acceptance. Byline given. Offers 25-50% kill fee. Buys all rights. Editorial lead time 2 months. Submit seasonal material 3 months in advance. Accepts simultaneous submissions. Reports in 2 months. Sample copy for #10 SASE. Writer's guidelines free.

Nonfiction: How-to (get a job, buy real estate, get cheap airfares overseas, start a business, etc.), interview/profile (entrepreneur abroad), new product (travel), personal experience, travel, shopping, cruises, etc. No descriptive, run-of-the-mill travel articles. "We produce special issues each year focusing on Asia, Eastern Europe and Latin America." **Buys 100 mss/year.** Send complete ms. Length: 500-2,000 words. **Pays $200-500 for assigned articles; $100-400 for unsolicited articles.**

Photos: State availability of photos with submission. Reviews contact sheets, negatives, transparencies or prints. Offers $50/photo. Identification of subjects required. Buys all rights.

Fillers: Facts. **Buys 20/year.** Length: 50-250 words. **Pays $25-100.**

Tips: "Make recommendations in your articles. We want first-hand accounts. Tell us how to do things: how to catch a cab, order a meal, buy a souvenir, buy property, start a business, etc. *International Living*'s philosophy is that the world is full of opportunities to do whatever you want, whenever you want. We will show you how."

$ THE INTERNATIONAL RAILWAY TRAVELER, Hardy Publishing Co., Inc., Editorial offices: P.O. Box 3747, San Diego CA 92163. (619)260-1332. Fax: (619)296-4220. E-mail: irt.trs@worldnet.att.net. **Contact:** Gena Holle, editor. **100% freelance written.** Monthly newsletter covering rail travel. Estab. 1983. Circ. 3,500. Pays within 3 months of publication date. Byline given. Offers 25% kill fee. Buys first North American serial rights and all electronic rights. Editorial lead time 4 months. Submit seasonal material 6 months in advance. Query for electronic submissions. Reports in 1 month on queries; 2 months on mss. Sample copy for $6. Writer's guidelines for #10 SASE.

Nonfiction: Book reviews, general interest, how-to, interview/profile, new product, opinion, personal experience, travel. **Buys 24-30 mss/year.** Query with published clips or send complete ms. Include SASE for return of ms. Length: 800-1,200 words. **Pays 3¢/word.**

Photos: Send photos with submission. Include SASE for return of photos. Reviews contact sheets, negatives, transparencies, prints (8×10 preferred; will accept 5×7). Offers $10 b&w; $20 cover photo. Costs of converting slides and negatives to prints are deducted from payment. Captions and identification of subjects required. Buys one-time rights.

Tips: "We want factual articles concerning world rail travel which would not appear in the mass-market travel magazines. IRT readers and editors love stories and photos on off-beat train trips as well as more conventional train trips covered in unconventional ways. With IRT, the focus is on the train travel experience, not a blow-by-blow description of the view from the train window. Be sure to include details (prices, passes, schedule info, etc.) for readers who might want to take the trip."

☒ $ $ $ $ ISLANDS, An International Magazine, Islands Publishing Company, 3886 State St., Santa Barbara CA 93105-3112. Fax: (805)569-0349. E-mail: diest@islandsmag.com. Website: http://www.islandsmag.com. Editor: Joan Tapper. **Contact:** Denise Iest, copy/production editor. **95% freelance written.** Works with established writers. Bimonthly magazine covering "accessible and once-in-a-lifetime islands from many different perspectives: travel, culture, lifestyle. We ask our authors to give us the essence of the island and do it with literary flair." Estab. 1981. Circ. 200,000. **Pays on acceptance.** Publishes ms an average of 8 months after acceptance. Byline given. Buys all rights. Reports in 2 months on queries; 6 weeks on ms. Sample copy for $6. Writer's guidelines for #10 SASE.

- Ranked as one of the best markets for freelance writers in *Writer's Yearbook* magazine's annual "Top 100 Markets," January 1998.

Nonfiction: General interest, personal experience, photo feature, any island-related material. No service stories. "Each issue contains 5-6 feature articles and 6-7 departments. Any authors who wish to be commissioned should send a detailed proposal for an article, an estimate of costs (if applicable) and samples of previously published work." **Buys 25 feature mss/year.** "The majority of our feature manuscripts are commissioned." Query with published clips or send complete ms. Feature length: 2,000-4,000 words. **Pays $1,000-4,000.** Pays expenses of writers on assignment.

Photos: State availability of or send photos with query or ms. Pays $75-300 for 35mm transparencies. "Fine color photography is a special attraction of *Islands*, and we look for superb composition, technical quality and editorial applicability." Label slides with name and address, include captions, and submit in protective plastic sleeves. Identification of subjects required. Buys one-time rights.

Columns/Departments: Arts, Profiles, Nature, Sports, Lifestyle, Encounters, Island Hopping featurettes—all island related, 750-1,500 words; Brief Logbook highly focused-item on some specific aspect of islands, 500 words." **Buys 50 mss/year.** Query with published clips. **Pays $100-700.**

Tips: "A freelancer can best break in to our publication with short (500-1,000 word) departments or Logbooks that are highly focused on some aspect of island life, history, people, etc. Stay away from general, sweeping articles. We are always looking for topics for our Islanders and Logbook pieces. We will be using big name writers for major features; will continue to use newcomers and regulars for columns and departments."

$ $ LEISURE WORLD, Ontario Motorist Publishing Company, 1253 Ouellette Ave., Box 580, Windsor, Ontario N8X 1J3 Canada. (519)971-3208. Fax: (519)977-1197. E-mail: ompc@mns.net. **Contact:** Douglas O'Neil, editor. **20% freelance written.** Bimonthly magazine distributed to members of the Canadian Automobile Association in southwestern and midwestern Ontario, the Niagara Peninsula and the maritime provinces. Editorial content is focused on travel, entertainment and leisure time pursuits of interest to CAA members." Estab. 1988. Circ. 345,000. Pays on publication. Publishes ms an average of 2 months after acceptance. Buys first rights only. Submit seasonal material 4 months in advance. Reports in 2 months. Sample copy for $2. Free writer's guidelines with SASE.

Nonfiction: Lifestyle, humor, travel. **Buys 20 mss/year.** Send complete ms. Length: 800-1,200 words. **Pays $50-200.**

Photos: Reviews slides only. Offers $60/photo. Captions, model releases required. Buys one-time rights.

Tips: "We are most interested in travel destination articles that offer a personal, subjective and positive point of view on international (including U.S.) destinations. Good quality color slides are a must."

$ $ LEISUREWAYS, Canada Wide Magazines & Communications, Ltd., 2 Carlton St., Suite 801, Toronto, Ontario M5B 1J3 Canada. Fax: (416)924-6308. **Contact:** Deborah Milton, editor. **80% freelance written.** Bimonthly magazine. "*Leisureways* is the publication of two Canadian Automobile Association clubs offering readers superior local and international travel stories and information. *Leisureways* also features automotive columns as well as club information and detailed stories on products and services available to CAA members." Circ. 685,000. **Pays on acceptance.** Publishes ms an average of 2 months after acceptance. Byline given. Offers 50% kill fee. Buys first North American serial rights. Editorial lead time 6 months. Submit seasonal material 1 year in advance. Reports in 2 months on queries; 6 months on mss. Writer's guidelines free.

Nonfiction: Travel. **Buys 20 mss/year.** Query with published clips or send complete ms. Length: 800-1,500 words. **Pays $400-750 (Canadian funds).**

Photos: State availability of photos with submission. Reviews transparencies. Offers no additional payment for photos accepted with ms or negotiates payment individually if photos are offered without mss. Buys one-time rights.

Columns/Departments: Travel (Canada/international), 1,500 words. Query with published clips. **Pays $400-750.**

Tips: "All manuscripts and queries receive consideration. We do not usually buy from U.S. writers since our needs can easily be met in Canada."

$ THE MATURE TRAVELER, Travel Bonanzas for 49ers-Plus, GEM Publishing Group, Box 50400, Reno NV 89513-0400. (702)786-7419. **Contact:** Gene E. Malott, editor. **20% freelance written.** Monthly newsletter on senior citizen travel. Estab. 1984. Circ. 2,500. **Pays on acceptance.** Publishes ms an average of 3 months after acceptance. Byline given. Offers 25% kill fee. Buys one-time rights. Submit seasonal material 3 months in advance. Accepts simultaneous submissions. Reports in 1 month. Sample copy and guidelines for $1 and #10 SAE with 2 first-class stamps. Writer's guidelines only for #10 SASE.

Nonfiction: Travel for seniors. "General travel and destination pieces should be senior-specific, aimed at 49ers and older." Query. Length: 900-1,200 words. **Pays $80-100.**

Reprints: Send tearsheet or photocopy of article and information about when and where the article previously appeared. Pays 50% of amount paid for an original article.

Photos: State availability of photos with submission. Reviews contact sheets and only prints. Pays $10/photo. Captions required. Buys one-time rights.

Columns/Departments: Deals for 49ers-Plus, Trips for 49ers-Plus, Cruise News, Other Bargains, Places. Length 50-250 words. Query. **Pays $5-10.**

Tips: "Read the guidelines and write stories to our readers' needs—not to the general public. Most articles we reject are not senior-specific. Most articles we buy could not appear in 99% of other travel publications. Your query should indicate how the article meets the travel needs or interests of seniors."

$ $ MICHIGAN LIVING, AAA Michigan, 1 Auto Club Dr., Dearborn MI 48126-2963. (313)336-1506. Fax: (313)336-1344. E-mail: michliving@aol.com **Contact:** Ron Garbinski, editor. **50% freelance written.** Monthly magazine. "*Michigan Living* is edited for the residents of Michigan and contains information about travel and lifestyle activities in Michigan, the U.S. and around the world. Articles also cover automotive developments, highway safety. Regular features include a car care column, a calendar of coming events, restaurant and overnight accomodations reviews and news of special interest to Auto Club members." Estab. 1922. Circ. 1,099,000. Pays on publication. Publishes ms an average of 6 months after acceptance. Buys first North American serial rights. Offers 20% kill fee. Byline given. Submit seasonal material 6-9 months in advance. Reports in 6 weeks. Free sample copy and writer's guidelines.

Nonfiction: Travel articles on US and Canadian topics. **Buys few unsolicited mss/year.** Query. Length: 200-1,000 words. **Pays $75-600.**

Photos: Photos purchased with accompanying ms. Captions required. Pays $400 for cover photos; $50-400 for color transparencies.

Tips: "In addition to descriptions of things to see and do, articles should contain accurate, current information on costs the traveler would encounter on his trip. Items such as lodging, meal and entertainment expenses should be included, not in the form of a balance sheet but as an integral part of the piece. We want the sounds, sights, tastes, smells of a place or experience so one will feel he has been there and knows if he wants to go back. Prefers most travel-related queries via e-mail rather than mail."

$ $ THE MIDWEST MOTORIST, AAA Auto Club of Missouri, 12901 N. 40 Dr., St. Louis MO 63141. (314)523-7350. Fax: (314)523-6982. E-mail: acmdmk@ibm.net. Editor: Michael J. Right. **Contact:** Deborah M. Klein, managing editor. **80% freelance written.** Bimonthly magazine. "We feature articles on regional and world travel, area history, auto safety, highway and transportation news." Estab. 1971. Circ. 430,000. **Pays on acceptance.** Byline given. Not copyrighted. Buys first North American print serial rights, second serial (reprint) rights. Accepts simultaneous submissions. Reports in 1 month with SASE enclosed. Sample copy or media kit for 12½×9½ SAE with 3 first-class stamps. Writer's guidelines for #10 SASE.
Nonfiction: Buys 40 mss/year. Query. Length: 2,000 words maximum. **Pays $350 (maximum).**
Reprints: Send typed ms with rights for sale noted and information about when and where the article previously appeared. Pays $150-250.
Photos: State availability of photos with submission. Reviews transparencies. Offers no additional payment for photos accepted with ms. Captions required. Buys one-time rights.
Tips: "Editorial schedule set 18 months in advance. Request a copy. Serious writers ask for media kit to help them target their piece. Some stories available throughout the year. Travel destinations and tips are most open to freelancers; auto-related topics handled by staff. Make the story bright and quick to read. We see too many 'Here's a recount of our family vacation' manuscripts. Go easy on first-person accounts."

$ $ MOTORHOME, TL Enterprises, 2575 Vista Del Mar Dr., Ventura CA 93001. (805)667-4100. Fax: (805)667-4484. E-mail: http://motorhome.tl.com. Editor: Barbara Leonard. **Contact**: Sherry McBride, senior managing editor. **60% freelance written.** Monthly. "*MotorHome* is a magazine for owners and prospective buyers of self-propelled recreational vehicles who are active outdoorsmen and wide-ranging travelers. We cover all aspects of the RV lifestyle; editorial material is both technical and non-technical in nature. Regular features include tests and descriptions of various models of motorhomes and mini-motorhomes, travel adventures and hobbies pursued in such vehicles, objective analysis of equipment and supplies for such vehicles and do-it-yourself articles. Guides within the magazine provide listings of manufacturers, rentals and other sources of equipment and accessories of interest to enthusiasts. Articles must have an RV slant and excellent transparencies accompanying text." Estab. 1968. Circ. 140,000. **Pays on acceptance.** Publishes ms 6 months after acceptance. Byline given. Offers 33% kill fee. Buys first North American serial and electronic rights. Editorial lead time 4 months. Submit seasonal material 6 months in advance. Reports in 3 weeks on queries; 2 months on mss. Sample copy free. Guidelines for #10 SASE.
Nonfiction: How-to, humor, new product, personal experience, photo feature, technical, travel, profiles, recreation, lifestyle, legislation, all RV related. No diaries of RV trips or negative RV experiences. **Buys 120 mss/year.** Query with or without published clips. Length: 250-2,500 words. **Pays $300-600.**
Photos: Send photos with submission. Offers no additional payment for photos accepted with ms. Pays $400-600 for covers. Captions, model releases and identification of subjects required. Buys one-time rights.
Columns/Departments: Crossroads (offbeat briefs of people, places of interest to travelers), 100-200 words; Keepers (tips, recipes). Query or send complete ms. **Pays $100-200.**
Tips: "If a freelancer has an idea for a good article, it's best to send a query and include possible photo locations to illustrate the article. We prefer to assign articles and work with the author in developing a piece suitable to our audience. We are in a specialized field with very enthusiastic readers who appreciate articles by authors who actually enjoy motorhomes. The following areas are most open: Travel—places to go with a motorhome, where to stay, what to see, etc.; we prefer not to use travel articles where the motorhome is secondary; and How-to—personal projects on author's motorhomes to make travel easier, etc., unique projects, accessories. Also articles on unique personalities, motorhomes, humorous experiences. Be sure to submit appropriate photography (35mm slides) with at least one good motorhome shot to illustrate travel articles. No phone queries, please."

NATIONAL GEOGRAPHIC TRAVELER, National Geographic Society, 17th & M Sts. NW, Washington DC 20036. (202)775-6700. Website: http://nationalgeographic.com/media/traveler. Bimonthly magazine. "*National Geographic Traveler* is filled with practical information and detailed maps designed to encourage readers to explore and travel. Features domestic and foreign destinations, photography, the economics of travel, scenic drives, and weekend getaways help readers plan a variety of excursions." This magazine did not respond to our request for information. Query first.

$ $ NEW YORK DAILY NEWS, Travel Section, 450 W. 33rd St., New York NY 10001. (212)210-1699. Fax: (212)210-2203. **Contact:** Linda Perney, travel editor. **30% freelance written.** Prefers to work with published/established writers. Weekly tabloid. Circ. 1.8 million. "We are the largest circulating newspaper travel section in the country and take all types of articles ranging from experiences to service oriented pieces that tell readers how to make a certain trip." Pays on publication. Publishes ms an average of 3 months after acceptance. Byline given. Submit seasonal material 4 months in advance. Reports "as soon as possible."
Nonfiction: General interest, historical/nostalgic, travel. "Most of our articles involve practical trips that the average family can afford—even if it's one you can't afford every year. We rarely run stories for the Armchair Traveler, an exotic and usually expensive trip. We are looking for professional quality work from professional writers who know what they are doing. The pieces have to give information and be entertaining at the same time. No 'How I Spent My Summer Vacation' type articles. No PR hype." **Buys 60 mss/year.** Query with SASE. Length: 1,000 words maximum. **Pays $75-200.**
Photos: "Good pictures always help sell good stories." State availability of photos with ms. Reviews contact sheets and negatives. Captions and identification of subjects required. Buys all rights.

$ $ NEWSDAY, 235 Pinelawn Rd., Melville NY 11747. (516)843-2980. Fax: (516)843-2065. E-mail: travel@newsday.com. Travel Editor: Marjorie Robins. **Contact:** Francine Brown, editorial assistant. **30% freelance written.** General readership of Sunday newspaper travel section. Estab. 1940. Circ. 650,000. Buys all rights for New York area only. Pays on publication. Simultaneous submissions considered if outside the New York area.

Nonfiction: No assignments to freelancers. No query letters. Complete typewritten mss only accepted on spec. All trips must be paid for in full by writer; proof required. Service stories preferred. Destination pieces must be for the current year. **Buys 75 mss/year.** Length: 1,200 words maximum. **Pays $75-350.**

Photos: Color slides and b&w photos accepted: pays $50-250, depending on size of photo used.

N ☆ $ $ NORTHWEST TRAVEL, Northwest Regional Magazines, 1525 12th St., P.O. Box 18000, Florence OR 97439-0130. (800)348-8401. Editor: Dave Peden. **Contact:** Judy Fleagle, managing editor. **75% freelance written.** Bimonthly magazine of Northwest living. Estab. 1991. Circ. 50,000. Pays after publication. Publishes ms an average of 6-12 months after acceptance. Byline given. Offers 33% kill fee. Buys first North American serial rights. Submit seasonal material 6 months in advance. Reports in 1 month on queries; 3 months on mss. Sample copy for $4.50. Writer's guidelines for #10 SASE.

- This magazine is using fewer freelancers due to more inhouse writing.

Nonfiction: Travel as pertains to Pacific Northwest. "Any article not related to the Pacific Northwest will be returned." Query with published clips. Length: 500-2,000 words. **Pays $50-350** and 2-5 copies.

Reprints: Send tearsheet or photocopy of article or typed ms with rights for sale noted and information about when and where the article previously appeared. Pays approximately 65% of the amount paid for an original article.

Photos: Send photos with submission. Prefers slides and transparencies. Captions and identification of subjects required as well as who to credit. Buys one-time rights.

Fillers: Newsbreaks (no-fee basis), short articles. **Buys 30/year.** Byline given. Length: 300-500 words. **Pays $35-65.**

Tips: "Slant article for readers who do not live in the Pacific Northwest. We try to use at least one historical article and at least two travel articles in each issue. City and town profiles, special out-of-the-way places to visit, will also be used in each issue. An occasional restaurant feature will be used. Short articles with photos (transparencies preferred) will be easiest to fit in. Query first. After go-ahead, send cover letter with manuscript/photo package. Photos often make the difference in deciding which article gets published."

N $ PATHFINDERS, Travel Information for People of Color, 6424 N. 13th St., Philadelphia PA 19126. (215)927-9950. Fax: (215)927-3359. E-mail: blaktravel@aol.com. Website: http://www.Pathfinderstravel.com. **Contact:** Pamela Thomas, editor-in-chief. **99% freelance written**. Quarterly magazine covering travel for minorities, primarily African-Americans. "We look for lively, original, well-written stories that provide a good sense of place, with useful information and fresh ideas about travel and the travel industry. Our main audience is African-Americans, though we do look for articles relating to other persons of color: Native Americans, Hispanics and Asians." Estab. 1997. Circ. 50,000. Pays on publication. Byline given. Buys first North American serial rights and electronic rights. Reports in 2 months. Sample copy at bookstores (Barnes & Noble, Borders, Waldenbooks) or by e-mail request. Writer's guidelines on website.

Nonfiction: Essays, historical/nostalgic, how-to, personal experience, photo feature, travel, all vacation travel oriented. **Buys 16-20 mss/year**. Send complete ms. Length: 1,200-1,400 words for cover stories, 1,000-1,200 words features. **Pays $100**.

Photos: State availability of photos with submission.

Columns/Departments: Chef's Table, Post Cards from Home, 500-600 words. Send complete ms. **Pays $50**.

Tips: "We prefer seeing finished articles rather than queries. All articles are submitted on spec. Articles should be saved in either WordPerfect of Microsoft Word, double-spaced and saved as a text-only file. Include a hard copy. E-mail articles are accepted only by request of the editor."

☆ $ $ PORTHOLE MAGAZINE, A View of the Sea and Beyond, Panoff Publishing, 7100 W. Commercial Blvd., Suite 106, Ft. Lauderdale FL 33319. (954)746-5554. Fax: (954)746-5244. E-mail: cruiseed@aol.com. Website: www.porthole.com. **Contact**: Lesley Abravanel, managing editor. **90% freelance written.** Bimonthly magazine. "*Porthole* is a first-of-its-kind, internationally distributed glossy consumer cruise and travel magazine, distributed by Time Warner." Estab. 1994. Circ. 65,000. Pays on publication. Publishes ms an average of 6 months after acceptance. Byline given. Offers 35% kill fee. Buys first international serial rights and second serial (reprint) rights and makes work-for-hire assignments. Editorial lead time 3 months. Submit seasonal material 4 months in advance. Accepts simultaneous submissions. Reports in 1 month. Sample copy for 8×11 SAE with $3 postage. Writer's guidelines for #10 SASE.

Nonfiction: Essays (your cruise experience), general interest (cruise-related), historical/nostalgic, how-to (i.e., pick a cruise, not get seasick, travel tips), humor, interview/profile (crew on board or industry executives), new product, personal experience, photo features, travel (off-the-beaten path, adventure, ports, destinations, cruises), onboard fashion, spa articles, duty-free shopping, port shopping, ship reviews. No articles on destinations that can't be reached by ship. "Please don't write asking for a cruise so that you can do an article! You must be an experienced cruise writer to do a ship review." **Buys 75 mss/year.** Query with published clips or send letter with complete ms. Length: 400-2,000 words, average 1,100. **Pays 25¢/word average.** Sometimes pays expenses of writers on assignment

Reprints: Send photocopy of article or typed ms with rights for sale noted and information about when and where the article previously appeared. Negotiates payment.

Photos: Linda Douthat, creative director. State availability of photos with submission. Reviews transparencies. Negoti-

ates payment individually. Captions, model releases, identification of subjects required. Buys one-time rights.
Columns/Departments: "My" Port City (personal accounts of experiences in certain destination), 1,200 words; Beautiful Thing (spa service on board), 700 words; Brass Tacks (travel tips, short bits); Personality Plus (intriguing travel-oriented profiles), 400 words; Fashion File (onboard fashion), 400 words. Also humor, cruise cuisine, shopping, photo essays. **Buys 50 mss/year.** Query with published clips or send letter with complete ms. **Pays 25¢/word.**
Fillers: Facts, gags to be illustrated by cartoonist, newsbreaks, short humor. **Buys 30/year.** Length: 25-200 words. **Pays 25¢/word.**
Tips: "We prefer to be queried via e-mail. Clips are not necessary. Offbeat, original travel stories are preferred. Tie-ins to celebrity culture, pop culture, arts/entertainment, politics, cuisine, architecture, are highly regarded."

$ $ ST. MAARTEN NIGHTS, Nights Publications Inc., 1831 Rene Levesque Blvd. West, Montreal, Quebec H3H 1R4 Canada. Fax: (514)931-6273. E-mail: editor@nightspublications.com. Website: http://www.nightspublications.com. Managing Editor: Zelly Zuskin. **Contact**: Stephen Trotter, editor. **90% freelance written.** Annual magazine covering the St. Maarten/St. Martin vacation experience seeking "upbeat entertaining lifestyle articles. Our audience is the North American vacationer." Estab. 1981. Circ. 225,000. **Pays on acceptance.** Publishes ms an average of 9 months after acceptance. Byline given. Buys first North American serial and first Caribbean rights. Editorial lead time 1 month. Reports in 2 weeks on queries; 1 month on mss. Sample copy for $5 (make check payable to Nights Publications Inc.). Writer's guidelines free.
Nonfiction: Lifestyle with a lively, upscale touch. General interest, colorful profiles of islanders, historical/nostalgia, how-to (gamble), sailing, humor, inspirational, interview/profile, opinion, ecological (eco-tourism), personal experience, photo feature, travel, local culture, art, activities, entertainment, night life, special events, topics relative to vacationers in St. Maarten/St. Martin. "No negative pieces or stale rewrites or cliché copy." **Buys 8-10 mss/year.** Query with published clips and SASE with Canadian postage or IRC. Length: 250-750 words. **Pays $100-250.**
Photos: State availability of photos with submission. Reviews transparencies. Offers $50/photo. Captions, model releases, identification of subjects required. Buys one-time rights.
Tips: "Our style is upbeat, friendly, fluid and descriptive. Our magazines cater to tourists who are already at the destination, so ensure your story is of interest to this particular audience. We welcome stories that offer fresh angles to familiar tourist-related topics."

$ $ SCOTTISH LIFE, 36 Highland Ave., Hull MA 02045. (781)925-2100. Fax: (781)925-1439. **Contact**: Neill Kennedy Ray, editor. **80% freelance written.** Quarterly magazine. "*Scottish Life* covers the whole spectrum of Scottish experiences: Scotland's treasures and traditions, special events and public celebrations, tours of great houses and interesting places, historic sites, lore and legends. Stories should go beyond a step-by-step recounting of 'we did this and then did that.' They should be evocative, allowing readers to *experience* as they read, to feel like they are there." Estab. 1996. Circ. 10,000. **Pays on acceptance.** Publishes ms an average of 6 months after acceptance. Byline given. Buys first North American serial rights or second serial (reprint) rights. Editorial lead time 6 months. Submit seasonal material 6 months in advance. Accepts simultaneous submissions. Reports in 2 months on queries; 3 months on mss. Sample copy for $6. Writer's guidelines for #10 SASE.
Nonfiction: Historical/nostalgic, interview/profile, personal experience, photo feature, travel. Buys 30-50 mss/year. Query with published clips. Length: 1,200-1,800 words. **Pays $350-500 for assigned articles; $250-300 for unsolicited articles.**
Reprints: Accepts previously published submissions.
Photos: State availability of photos with submission. Reviews transparencies, prints. Negotiates payment individually. Identification of subjects required. Buys one-time rights.
Fillers: Facts, newsbreaks. **Buys 30/year.** Length: 50-100 words. **Pays $25.**

N $ $ THE SOUTHERN TRAVELER, AAA Auto Club of Missouri, 12901 N. Forty Dr., St. Louis MO 63141. (314)523-7350. Fax: (314)523-6982. Editor: Michael J. Right. **Contact:** Deborah Klein, managing editor. **80% freelance written.** Bimonthly magazine. Estab. 1997. Circ. 130,000. **Pays on acceptance**. Byline given. Not copyrighted. Buys first North American print serial, second serial (reprint) rights. Accepts simultaneous submissions. Reports in 1 month with SASE enclosed. Sample copy for 12½×9½ SAE with 3 first-class stamps. Guidelines for SASE.
Nonfiction: "We feature articles on regional and world travel, area history, auto safety, highway and transportation news." Buys 30 mss/year. Query, with best chance for good reception January-March for inclusion in following year's editorial calendar. Length: 2,000 words maximum. **Pays $250 (maximum).**
Reprints: Send typed ms with rights for sale noted and information about when and where the article previously appeared. Pays $125-150.
Photos: State availability of photos with submission. Reviews transparencies. Offers no additional payment for photos accepted with ms. Captions required. Buys one-time photo reprint rights.
Tips: "Editorial schedule is set 18 months in advance. Request a copy. Serious writers ask for media kit to help them target their story. Some stories available throughout the year, but most as assigned early. Travel destinations and tips are most open to freelancers; auto-related topics handled by staff. Make story bright and quick to read. We see too many 'Here's what I did on my vacation' manuscripts. Go easy on first-person accounts."

$ $ $ $ SPA, Travel, Well-Being and Renewal, Waterfront Press Co., 5305 Shilshole Ave. NW, #200, Seattle WA 98107. (206)789-6506. Fax: (206)789-9193. E-mail: editor@spamagazine.com. Website: http://www.spamagazine.c

om. **Contact**: Janet Thomas, editor. Quarterly magazine covering spa resorts, retreats, lifestyle issues, well-being and travel. "Our readership is sophisticated, well-educated and discerning. We want reporting of real substance and writing that is clear and bright. We also want to encourage a variety of voices. Our philosophy is simple: As the unrelenting pace of contemporary life takes its toll, *Spa* is an opportunity for our readers to experience a touch of well-being and renewal through thoughtful, informative and inspired writing as well as a practical guide to available spa facilities—from local day spas to international destination spas." Estab. 1996. Circ. 75,000. **Pays on acceptance**. Publishes ms an average of 3 months after acceptance. Byline sometimes given. Buys first North American serial, one-time, second serial (reprint) rights and makes work-for-hire assignments. Editorial lead time 6 months. Reports in 1 month on queries. Sample copy for 9×12 and 8 first-class stamps. Writer's guidelines for #10 SASE.

- Ranked as one of the best markets for freelance writers in *Writer's Yearbook* magazine's annual "Top 100 Markets," January 1998.

Nonfiction: Essays, how-to (healing, rest and relaxation techniques), interview/profile, personal experience, photo feature, travel, health, fitness and nutrition, horticulture (medicinal herbs, flowers, plants), psychology insights, spiritual renewal, connection to community, outdoor adventure. **Buys 30 mss/year.** Query with published clips and SASE. Length: 1,500-3,000 words. **Pays $300-2,500.**

Reprints: Send tearsheet or photocopy of article or typed ms with rights for sale noted and information about where and when an article previously appeared. Payment negotiable.

Photos: State availability of photos with submission. Reviews transparencies (any format). Negotiates payment individually. Captions, identification of subjects required. Buys one-time rights.

Columns/Departments: Vital Signs (short news pieces on health and science; trends, discoveries, insights, profiles), 75-300 words or 500-700 words; **pays $100-500.** Life At Large (short news on psychology, education, culture, government, philosophy, theology, spirituality, travel, arts), 75-300 words or 500-700 words; **pays $100-500.** Day to Day (insights that enrich and inform daily life at home, work or play), 750-1,000 words; **pays $600-1,000.** Round Table (panel of experts on subject of significance), 1,000-2,000 words; **pays $800-1,500.** The Arts (photo essays, poetry, profiles of artists/writers on themes of serenity), **pays $1,000-2,000.** Personal Essay, 800-1,200 words, **pays $100-400.** Books Reviews, 500-700 words; **pays $300-500.** Reflection (back page contribution to mindful, meditative musing), 700-800 words; **pays $500.** Destinations (short travel pieces involving resort spas and day spas) 400-800 words; **pays $100-500.** Cuisine (spa food) 600-1,000 words; Personal Space (add a spa touch at home), 800-1,000 words; Wild At Heart (a celebration of the adventurous spirit, portraits of people who take risks), 1,000-2,000 words; **pays $800-1,500. Buys 20 mss/year.** Query with published clips and SASE.

Fiction: Unpublished work preferred. Short (800-1,200 words). **Pays $600-800.**

Poetry: Some. Pay varies.

$ $ TIMES OF THE ISLANDS, The International Magazine of the Turks & Caicos Islands, Times Publications Ltd., P.O. Box 234, Caribbean Place, Providenciales Turks & Caicos Islands, British West Indies. (649)946-4788. Fax: (649)946-4703. E-mail: timespub@caribsurf.com. Website: http://www.turkscai.com. **Contact**: Kathy Borsuk, editor. **80% freelance written.** Quarterly magazine covering The Turks & Caicos Islands. "*Times of the Islands* is used by the public and private sector to attract visitors and potential investors/developers to the Islands. It strives to portray the advantages of the Islands and their friendly people. It is also used by tourists, once on-island, to learn about services, activities and accommodations available." Estab. 1988. Circ. 5,500-8,000. Pays on publication. Publishes ms an average of 6 months after acceptance. Byline given. Buys second serial (reprint) rights and publication rights for 6 months with respect to other publications distributed in Caribbean. Editorial lead time 4 months. Submit seasonal material 4 months in advance. Accepts simultaneous submissions. Reports in 6 weeks on queries; 2 months on mss. "Keep in mind, mail to Islands is SLOW. Faxing can speed response time." Sample copy for $4 and postage between Miami and your destination. Writer's guidelines for #10 SASE.

Nonfiction: Book excerpts or reviews, essays, general interest (Caribbean art, culture, cooking, crafts), historical/nostalgic, humor, interview/profile (locals), personal experience (trips to the Islands), photo feature, technical (island businesses), travel, nature, ecology, business (offshore finance), watersports. **Buys 30 mss/year.** Query. Length: 500-3,000 words. **Pays $200-600.**

Reprints: Send photocopy of article along with information about when and where it previously appeared. Send information about when and where the article previously appeared. Pay varies.

Photos: Send photos with submission. Reviews 3×5 slides or prints. Offers no additional payment for photos accepted with ms. Pays $15-100/photo. Identification of subjects required.

Columns/Departments: Profiles from Abroad (profiles of T&C Islanders who are doing something outstanding internationally), 500 words. **Buys 4 mss/year.** Query. **Pays $100-200.** On Holiday (unique experiences of visitors to Turks & Caicos), 500-1,500 words. **Buys 4 mss/year.** Query. **Pays $200-300.**

Fiction: Adventure (sailing, diving), ethnic (Caribbean), historical (Caribbean), humorous (travel-related), mystery, novel excerpts. **Buys 1 ms/year.** "Would buy 3-4 if available." Query. Length: 1,000-2,000 words. **Pays $250-400.**

Tips: "Make sure that the query/article specifically relates to the Turks and Caicos Islands. The theme can be general (ecotourism, for instance), but the manuscript should contain specific and current references to the Islands. We're a high-quality magazine, with a small budget and staff and are very open-minded to ideas (and manuscripts). Writers who have visited the Islands at least once would probably have a better perspective from which to write."

$ $ TRAILER LIFE, RVing At Its Best, Affinity Group, Inc., 2575 Vista Del Mar Dr., Ventura CA 93001. (805)667-4100. Fax: (805)667-4184. Website: http://www.tl.com. Managing Editor: Jim Brightly. **Contact**: Barbara

Leonard, editorial director. **60% freelance written.** Monthly magazine. "*Trailer Life* magazine is written specifically for active people whose overall lifestyle is based on travel and recreation in their RV. Every issue includes product tests, travel articles, and other features—ranging from lifestyle to vehicle maintenance." Estab. 1941. Circ. 290,000. **Pays on acceptance**. Publishes ms an average of 6 months after acceptance. Byline given. Offers 33% kill fee for assigned articles that are not acceptable. Buys first North American rights and non-exclusive rights for other media. Editorial lead time 4 months. Submit seasonal material 6 months in advance. Reports in 2 months. Sample copy free. Writer's guidelines for #10 SASE.

Nonfiction: Historical/nostalgic, how-to (technical), new product, opinion, humor, personal experience, travel. No vehicle tests, product evaluations or road tests; tech material is strictly assigned. No diaries or trip logs, no non-RV trips; nothing without an RV-hook. **Buys 75 mss/year.** Query with or without published clips. Length: 250-2,500 words. **Pays $150-600.** Sometimes pays expenses of writers on assignment.

Photos: Send photos with submission. Reviews b&w contact sheets, transparencies (which should be labeled). Offers no additional payment for photos accepted with ms. Model releases, identification of subjects required. Buys one-time and occasionally electronic rights.

Columns/Departments: Campground Spotlight (report with 1 photo of campground recommended for RVers) 250 words; Bulletin Board (news, trends of interest to RVers) 100 words; Etcetera (useful tips and information affecting RVers), 240 words. **Buys 70 mss/year.** Query or send complete ms. **Pays $75-250.**

Tips: "Prerequisite: must have RV focus. Photos must be magazine quality. These are the two biggest reasons why manuscripts are rejected. Our readers are travel enthusiasts who own all types of RVs (travel trailers, truck campers, van conversions, motorhomes, tent trailers, fifth-wheels) in which they explore North America and beyond, embrace the great outdoors in national, state and private parks as well as scenic roads, city sights, etc. They're very active and very adventurous."

$ TRANSITIONS ABROAD, P.O. Box 1300, Amherst MA 01004-1300. E-mail: trabroad@aol.com. Website: http://www.transabroad.com. Editor/Publisher: Clay Hubbs. **Contact**: David Cline, managing editor. **80-90% freelance written.** Eager to work with new/unpublished writers. Magazine resource for low-budget international travel, often with an educational or work component. Focus is on the alternatives to mass tourism. Estab. 1977. Circ. 29,000. Pays on publication. Buys first rights and second (reprint) rights. Byline given. Written or e-mail queries only. Reports in 1 month. Sample copy for $6.25. Writer's guidelines and topics schedule for #10 SASE or by e-mail.

Nonfiction: Lead articles (up to 1,500 words) provide first-hand practical information on independent travel to featured country or region (see topics schedule). Pays $75-150. Also, how to find educational and specialty travel opportunities, practical information (evaluation of courses, special interest and study tours, economy travel), travel (new learning and cultural travel ideas). Foreign travel only. Few destination ("tourist") pieces. *Transitions Abroad* is a resource magazine for independent, educated, and adventurous travelers, not for armchair travelers or those addicted to packaged tours or cruises. Emphasis on information—which must be usable by readers—and on interaction with people in host country. **Buys 20 unsolicited mss/issue.** Query with credentials and SASE. Length: 500-1,500 words. **Pays $25-150.** Include author's bio with submissions.

Photos: Send photos with ms. Pays $10-45 for prints (color acceptable, b&w preferred), $125 for covers (b&w only). Photos increase likelihood of acceptance. Buys one-time rights. Captions and ID on photos required.

Columns/Departments: Worldwide Travel Bargains (destinations, activities and accomodations for budget travelers—featured in every issue); Tour and Program Notes (new courses or travel programs); Travel Resources (new information and ideas for independent travel); Working Traveler (how to find jobs and what to expect); Activity Vacations (travel opportunities that involve action and learning, usually by direct involvement in host culture); Responsible Travel (information on community-organized tours). **Buys 10/issue.** Send complete ms. Length: 1,000 words maximum. **Pays $20-50.**

Fillers: Info Exchange (information, preferably first-hand—having to do with travel, particularly offbeat educational travel and work or study abroad). **Buys 10/issue.** Length: 750 words maximum. **Pays $20.**

Tips: "We like nuts and bolts stuff, practical information, especially on how to work, live and cut costs abroad. Our readers want usable information on planning a travel itinerary. Be specific: names, addresses, current costs. We are very interested in educational and long-stay travel and study abroad for adults and senior citizens. *Overseas Travel Planner* published each year in July provides best information sources on work, study, and independent travel abroad. Each bimonthly issue contains a worldwide directory of educational and specialty travel programs."

$ $ TRAVEL AMERICA, The U.S. Vacation Magazine, World Publishing Co., 990 Grove St., Evanston IL 60201-4370. (847)491-6440. Editor-in-Chief/Associate Publisher: Bob Meyers. **Contact**: Randy Mink, managing editor. **80% freelance written.** Estab. 1985. Bimonthly magazine covering US vacation travel. Circ. 400,000. Byline given. Buys first North American serial rights. Submit seasonal material 6 months in advance. Reports in 1 month on queries; 6 weeks on ms. Sample copy for $5 and 9×12 SASE with 6 first-class stamps.

Nonfiction: Primarily destination-oriented travel articles and resort/hotel profiles and roundups, but will consider essays, how-to, humor, nostalgia, Americana. "It is best to study current contents and query first." **Buys 60 mss/year.** Average length: 1,000 words. **Pays $125-300.**

Reprints: Send typed ms with rights for sale noted. Pay varies.

Photos: Top-quality original color slides preferred. Captions required. Buys one-time rights. Prefers photo feature package (ms plus slides), but will purchase slides only to support a work in progress.

Tips: "Because we are heavily photo-oriented, superb slides are our foremost concern. The most successful approach is to send 2-3 sheets of slides with the query or complete ms. Include a list of other subjects you can provide as a photo feature package."

$ $ $ $ TRAVEL & LEISURE, American Express Publishing Corp., 1120 Avenue of the Americas, New York NY 10036. (212)382-5600. E-mail: tlquery@amexpub.com. Website: http://www.travelandleisure.com. Editor-in-Chief: Nancy Novogrod. Executive Editor: Barbara Peck. Managing Editor: Mark Orwoll. **80% freelance written.** "*Travel & Leisure* is a monthly magazine edited for affluent travelers. It explores the latest resorts, hotels, fashions, foods and drinks." Circ. 960,000. **Pays on acceptance.** Byline given. Offers 25% kill fee. Buys first world rights. Reports in 6 weeks. Sample copy for $5 from (800)888-8728 or P.O. Box 2094, Harlan IA 51537-4094. Writer's guidelines for #10 SASE.

- There is no single editorial contact for *Travel & Leisure*. It is best to find the name of the editor of each section, as appropriate for your submission.

Nonfiction: Travel. **Buys 40-50 features** (3,000-5,000 words) **and 200 short pieces** (125-500 words). Query by e-mail preferred. **Pays $4,000-6,000/feature; $100-500/short piece.** Pays the expenses of writers on assignment.

- Ranked as one of the best markets for freelance writers in *Writer's Yearbook* magazine's annual "Top 100 Markets," January 1998.

Columns/Departments: Buys 125-150 mss. Length: 1,200-2,500 words. **Pays $1,000-2,500.**
Photos: Discourages submission of unsolicited transparencies. Payment varies. Captions required. Buys one-time rights.
Tips: "Read the magazine. There are 2 regional editions: East and West. Short-takes sections (e.g., "T&L Reports" and "Strategies") are best places to start."

TRAVEL HOLIDAY does not accept freelance submissions.

$ TRAVELER PUBLICATIONS, Publishers of *Sea Mass Traveler*, *Mystic Traveler* and *Newport Traveler*, 174 Bellevue Ave., Suite 207, Newport RI 02840. (401)847-0226. Fax: (401)847-5267. Editor: Joe Albano (*Mystic Traveler*). **Contact:** John Pantalone, editor. **40% freelance written.** Monthly regional tabloid covering places of interest in southern Massachusetts, southern Connecticut and all of Rhode Island. "Stories that get the reader to do, see, or act upon." Estab. 1992. Circ. 120,000 winter 240,000 summer. Pays on publication. Byline given. Buys all rights. Editorial lead time 2 months. Submit seasonal material at least 2 months in advance. Accepts simultaneous submissions. Reports in 2 months on mss. Sample copy and writer's guidelines free with 9×12 SASE and 5 first-class stamps.

- Three magazines (above) are published by one editorial office. Send only one manuscript and it will be circulated among magazines.

Nonfiction: Essays, general interest, historical/nostalgic, photo feature (travel). All must be related to southern New England. **Buys 30 mss/year.** Send complete ms or query. Length: 500-800 words. **Pays 7¢/word.** Sometimes pays expenses of writers on assignment.
Reprints: Send photocopy of article or typed ms with rights for sale noted and information about when and where the article previously appeared. Pays 100% of amount paid for an original article.
Photos: Send photos with submission. Reviews prints. Negotiates payment individually. Buys one-time rights.
Columns/Departments: Dining reviews, Kids' Page, Galleries, Outdoors, Where to Stay in New England, Club Review, Vineyards, Antiques.
Fillers: Facts. **Buys 30/year.** Length: 50-200 words. **Pays 5¢/word.**
Tips: "We are very interested in tours that cover an entire area. It could be a tour of wineries, a certain kind of shop, golf courses, etc. Always include address, phone, hours, admissions prices."

N $ $ trips, a travel journal, 8 Bernice St., #207, San Francisco CA 94103. (415)431-5133. Fax: (415)431-9074. E-mail: office@tripsmag.com. Website: http://www.tripsmag.com. **Contact**: Tony Stucker, editor. **90% freelance written.** Quarterly magazine. "*trips magazine* is the travel journal for younger, active travelers, looking for travel information in an unusual, offbeat, irreverent voice. We are looking for travel articles that would not, or could not, appear anywhere else. We want the exotic, unusual destinations, but we are also looking for traditional sites viewed in unconventional ways. All editorial should be as interesting and entertaining to someone whether they're planning on visiting a destination, have just returned from the destination, or never plan on going there. It should educate and inform, but also entertain. Travel is fun—travel writing should be as well." Estab. 1997. Circ. 40,000. Pays on publication. Publishes ms 3 months after acceptance. Byline given. Buys first North American serial rights. Editorial lead time 6 months. Submit seasonal material 6 months in advance. Accepts simultaneous submissions. Reports in 6 weeks on queries; 3 months on mss. Sample copy for 10×13 SAE with 6 first-class stamps. Writer's guidelines for #10 SASE.
Nonfiction: Book excerpts, essays, exposé, general interest, how-to, humor, interview/profile, new product, personal experience, photo feature, travel. No "run-of-the-mill travel stories that would appear in Sunday travel sections." **Buys 40 mss/year.** Query with published clips. Length: 450-6,000 words. **Pays $100-1,500.** Sometimes pays expenses of writers on assignment.
Reprints: Send photocopy of article and information about when and where the article previously appeared.
Photos: State availability of photos with submission. Reviews contact sheets, negatives. Negotiates payment individually. Identification of subjects required. Buys one-time rights.
Columns/Departments: "Lessons In . . ." (travel reader service); "Vice" (unusual vices from around the world); "A Travel Journal" (first person essays), all 800-1,000 words. **Buys 30 mss/year.** Query. **Pays $100-500.**
Tips: "We want to develop relationships with writers arond the world. If you don't have a piece that works now, perhaps

a future trip will yield something that's right. E-mail queries OK."

$ $ VIA, California State Automobile Assn., 150 Van Ness Ave., San Francisco CA 94102. (415)565-2451. **Contact**: Lynn Ferrin, editor. **20% freelance written.** Bimonthly magazine specializing in northern California and the West, with occasional stories on world-wide travel and cruises. Also, traffic safety and motorists' consumer issues. "Our magazine goes to members of the AAA in northern California, Nevada and Utah. Our surveys show they are an upscale audience, well-educated, adventurous and widely traveled. We like our travel stories to be finely crafted, evocative and personal, but we also include nitty gritty details to help readers arrange their own travel to the destinations covered." Estab. 1917. Circ. 2,400,000. **Pays on acceptance.** Byline usually given. Offers 25% kill fee. Buys first rights; occasional work-for-hire assignments. Editorial lead time 2 months. Submit seasonal material 6 months in advance. Usually reports in 1 month on queries. Writer's guidelines for #10 SASE.
Nonfiction: Travel. **Buys 15-20 mss/year.** Prefers to see finished mss with SASE from writers new to them. Length: 500-2,000 words. **Pays $150-700.** Sometimes pays expenses of writers on assignment, but assignments are rare except to writers we've already worked with.
Photos: State availability of photos with submission. Reviews 35mm and 4×5 transparencies. Offers $50-400/photo. Model releases, identification of subjects required. Buys first-time rights. Not responsible for unsolicited photographs.
Tips: "We do not like to receive queries via fax or e-mail unless the writer does not expect a reply. We are looking for beautifully written pieces that evoke a destination. We purchase less than 1% of the material submitted. Send SASE with all queries and mss."

$ $ $ VOYAGEUR, The Magazine of Carlson Hospitality Worldwide, Pace Communications, 1301 Carolina St., Greensboro NC 27401. **Contact:** Jaci H. Ponzoni, editor. 90% freelance written. In room magazine for Radisson hotels and affiliates. "*Voyageur* is an international magazine published quarterly for Carlson Hospitality Worldwide and distributed in the rooms of Radisson Hotels worldwide, Radisson SAS Hotels, Carlson Cruises Worldwide, and Country Inns & Suites By Carlson throughout North and South America, Europe, Australia, Asia and the Middle East. All travel related stories must be in destinations where Radisson or Country Inns & Suites have hotels." Estab. 1992. Circ. 210,000. **Pays on acceptance**. Publishes ms an average of 2 months after acceptance. Offers 25% kill fee. Buys first North American serial rights. Editorial lead time 4 months. Submit seasonal material 6 months in advance. Reports in 2 months. Sample for $5. Writer's guidelines for #10 SASE.
Nonfiction: Travel. The *Cover Story* is an authoritative yet personal profile of a destination where Radisson has a major presence, featuring a mix of standard and off-the-beaten path activities and sites including sightseeing, recreation, restaurants, shopping and cultural attractions. Length: 1,000 words including one sidebar, plus At a Glance, a roundup of useful and intriguing facts for travelers. *Our World* brings to life the spectrum of a country's or region's arts and culture, including performing, culinary, visual and folk arts. The successful article combines a timely sample of cultural activities for travelers with a sense of the destination's unique spirit or personality as reflected in the arts. Must be a region where Radisson has a major presence. Length: 1,000 words plus one 200-word sidebar. Query with published clips. **Pays $800-1,000.** Sometimes pays expenses of writers on assignment.
Photos: State availability of photos with submission. Reviews contact sheets, transparencies, prints. Negotiates payment individually. Model releases and identification of subjects required. Buys one-time rights.
Columns/Departments: In The Bag (place-specific shopping story with cultural context and upscale attitude), 600-800 words and 50-word mini-sidebar; Good Sport (action-oriented, first person focusing on travel involving sports such as biking, kayaking, scuba diving, hiking or sailing), 600-800 words plus 50-word mini-sidebar; Business Wise (insights into conducting business and traveling for business internationally) 350-400 words with 50-word mini-sidebar. **Buys 24 mss/year.** Query with published clips. **Pays $300-500.**
Tips: "We look for authoritative, energetic and vivid writing to inform and entertain business and leisure travelers, and we are actively seeking writers with an authentic European, Asian, Latin American or Australian perspective. Travel stories should be authoritative yet personal."

$ WESTERN RV NEWS, 42070 SE Locksmith Lane, Sandy OR 97055. (503)668-5660. Fax: (503)668-6387. E-mail: editor@westernrvnews.com. Website: http://www.westernrvnews.com. **Contact**: Terie Snyder, editor. **75% freelance written.** Monthly magazine for owners of recreational vehicles and those interested in the RV lifestyle. Estab. 1966. Pays on publication. Publishes ms an average of 6 months after acceptance. Byline given. Buys first rights and second serial (reprint) rights. Accepts simultaneous submissions. Reports in 1 month. Sample copy and writer's guidelines for 9×12 SAE with 5 first-class stamps. Guidelines for #10 SASE.
Nonfiction: How-to (RV oriented, purchasing considerations, maintenance), humor (RV experiences), new product (with ancillary interest to RV lifestyle), personal experiences (varying or unique RV lifestyles) technical (RV systems or hardware), travel. "No articles without an RV slant." **Buys 100 mss/year.** Submit complete ms. Length: 250-1,200 words. **Pays $15-100.**
Reprints: Send photocopy of article or typed ms with rights for sale noted and information about when and where the article previously appeared. Pays 60% of *Western RV News* first rights.
Photos: Send photos with submission. Accepts b&w or color slides or photos. Can submit on 3.5" IBM-compatible disk in TIF format. Offers $5/photo. Captions, model releases, identification of subjects required. Buys one-time rights.
Fillers: Encourage anecdotes, related tips and short humor. Length: 50-250 words. **Pays $5-25.**
Tips: "Highlight the RV lifestyle! Western travel articles should include information about the availability of RV sites, dump stations, RV parking and accessibility. Thorough research and a pleasant, informative writing style are paramount.

Technical, how-to, and new product writing is also of great interest. Photos enhance the possibility of article acceptance."

$ $ $ $ WESTWAYS, The Magazine for Southern California, A327-206, P.O. Box 25222, Santa Ana CA 92799. Fax: (714)885-2335. Editor-in-Chief: Susan LaTempa. **Contact:** Richard Stayton. **80% freelance written.** "*Westways* is a bimonthly magazine for Southern Californians. It publishes travel, automobile-related, lifestyle, culture and history features by writers from a variety of disciplines and includes destinations in the U.S. and internationally." Estab. 1909. Circ. 300,000. **Pays on acceptance.** Byline given. Offers 25-50% kill fee. Submit seasonal material 18 months in advance. Reports in 3 months on queries; 2 weeks on assigned mss.

- *Avenues* will be merging with *Westways* as of January 1, 1999.

Nonfiction: Annual great drives, travel and art, family travel and cruising themes issues. Destination stories based on a writer's single trip to the place described. **Buys 50 mss/year.** Query with published clips. *No unsolicited mss.* Length: 600-2,500 words. **Pays 50¢-$1/word.** Pays the expenses of writers on assignment.
Photos: "Freelancers should not concern themselves with photography. We assign professional photographers."
Columns/Departments: Weekender (weekend travel in Southern California), 1,500 words; Good Sports (outdoor recreation), 1,700 words; Food Souvenirs (memoir and recipe from Western travel), 400 words plus recipe. Buys 30 mss/year. Query with published clips. **Pays 50¢/word.**
Tips: "We are most interested in writers with a special expertise to bring to the travel experience, i.e., architecture, theater, snowboarding, etc."

WOMEN'S

Women have an incredible variety of publications available to them. A number of titles in this area have been redesigned to compete in the crowded marketplace. Many have stopped publishing fiction and are focusing more on short, human interest nonfiction articles. Magazines that also use material slanted to women's interests can be found in the following categories: Business and Finance; Child Care and Parental Guidance; Contemporary Culture; Food and Drink; Gay and Lesbian Interest; Health and Fitness; Hobby and Craft; Home and Garden; Relationships; Religious; Romance and Confession; and Sports.

$ $ $ AMERICAN WOMAN, Goodman Publishing, 1700 Broadway, 34th Floor, New York NY 10019-5905. (212)541-7100. Fax: (212)245-1241. Managing Editor: Sandy Kosherick. **50% freelance written.** Magazine published 7 times/year for "women in their 20s, 30s, 40s, single and married, dealing with relationships and self-help." Estab. 1990. Circ. 138,000. Pays on publication. Publishes ms an average of 2 months after acceptance. Byline given. Offers 25% kill fee. Buys one-time and second serial (reprint) rights. Submit seasonal material 5 months in advance. Accepts simultaneous submissions. Reports in 2 months. Sample copy for $2.99. Writer's guidelines for #10 SASE.
Nonfiction: Book excerpts, self-help, inspirational, interview/profile, personal experience, true life drama. "No poetry, recipes or fiction." **Buys 40 mss/year.** Query with published clips. Length: 750-1,900 words. **Pays $300-900 for assigned articles; $200-500 for unsolicited articles.** Pays for phone, mailings, faxes, transportation costs of writers on assignment.
Reprints: Send photocopy of article and information about when and where the article previously appeared. Pays $200-400.
Photos: State availability of photos with submission. Reviews contact sheets, transparencies, prints. Offers $100-175/photo. Captions, model releases, identification of subjects required. Buys one-time rights.
Tips: "We are always interested in true-life stories and stories of inspiration—women who have overcome obstacles in their lives, trends (new ideas in dating, relationships, places to go, new ways to meet men), articles about health, beauty, diet, self-esteem, fun careers, and money-saving articles (on clothes, beauty, vacations, mail order, entertainment)."

$ $ $ BRIDAL GUIDE, Globe Communications Corp., 3 E. 54th St., 15th Floor, New York NY 10022. (212)838-7733. Fax: (212)308-7165. Editor-in-Chief: Diane Forden. Travel Editor: Laurie Bain Wilson. **Contact:** Denise Schipani, senior editor. **50% freelance written.** Prefers to work with experienced/published writers. A bimonthly magazine covering relationships, sexuality, fitness, wedding planning, psychology, finance, travel. "Please do not send queries concerning beauty and fashion, since we produce them in-house. We do not accept personal wedding essays, fiction, or poetry. Address travel queries to travel editor." **Pays on acceptance.** Reports in 3 months. Sample copy for $4.95 and SASE with 4 first-class stamps. Writer's guidelines available.

- Ranked as one of the best markets for freelance writers in *Writer's Yearbook* magazine's annual "Top 100 Markets," January 1998.

Nonfiction: Queries only, accompanied by published clips. All correspondence accompanied by an SASE will be answered (response time is within 8 weeks). Length: 1,500-3,000 words. **Pays 50¢/word. Buys 100 mss/year.**
Photos: Lisa del Altomare, art director; Catherine Diaz, associate art director. Photography and illustration submissions should be sent to the art department.
Columns/Departments: The only columns written by freelancers cover finance finance and wedding-planning issues. Welcome queries from men who are engaged or married for Groom with a View essay.

$ $ BRIDE AGAIN, The Only Magazine Designed for Second Time Brides, 1240 N. Jefferson Ave., Suite G, Anaheim CA 92807. (714)632-7000. Fax: (714)632-5405. Website: www.brideagain.com. **Contact:** Beth Reed Ramirez, editor. Quarterly magazine for the second time bride. "*Bride Again* is targeted primarily to women ages 35-45 and secondarily to those 45 and over. They have been married at least once before, and most likely have children from a previous marriage or will be marrying someone with children. They have a career and income of over $45,000 per year, and are more mature and sophisticated than the 26-year-old first-time bride." Estab. 1997. Circ. 125,000. Pays on publication. Byline given. Buys all rights. Writer's guidelines for #10 SASE.

Nonfiction: Essays, how-to, humor, inspirational, interview/profile, personal experience. "Topics can be on, but not limited to: remarriage, blending families, becoming a stepmother, combining households, dealing with children in the wedding party, children—his, mine and ours; joint custody, dealing with difficult ex-spouses, real dresses for real women, legal aspects of remarriage, pre- and post-nuptial agreements, alternatives to the wedding veil, unusual wedding and/or honeymoon locations." Special issues: Honeymoon locations: Egypt, Greece, the Seychelles, Mauritius; Remarriage as a widow; Interfaith marriages; Handling extended step families; Having another child together. Send complete ms. *No queries, please.* Length: 1,500-2,000 words. **Pays 35¢/word.**

Photos: Send photos with submission. Reviews transparencies. Will return photos only if accompanied with SASE. Negotiates payment individually. Buys all rights.

Columns/Departments: Finances, Blending Families, Religion, Wedding Plans: Problems & Solutions, Real Life Weddings, Groom's Viewpoint, Unusual Honeymoon Locations, Beauty for Ages 30+/40+/50+, Remarriage, Fashion; all 800-1,000 words. Book reviews (on the feature topics listed above), 250 words. Send complete ms. **Pays 35¢/word.**

Fiction: Publishes novel excerpts.

Tips: "Personal experience, first person and 'as told to' stories are preferred."

$ $ $ $ CHATELAINE, 777 Bay St., #800, Toronto, Ontario M5W 1A7 Canada. Fax: (416)596-5516. E-mail: editors@chatelaine.com. Website: http://www.chatelaine.com. **Contact:** Senior Editor, Articles. Monthly magazine. "*Chatelaine* is edited for Canadian women ages 25-55, their changing attitudes and lifestyles. Emphasis is on food, fashion, beauty and home decoration. Other key editorial ingredients include parenting, health, finance, crafts, social issues and trends, high profile personalities, politics and original fiction. Regular departments include Mind & Body, Parents & Kids, Free For The Asking, advice columns, Laugh Lines, How-to. **Pays on acceptance.** Byline given. Offers 25-100% kill fee. Buys first and electronic rights. Reports in 2 months on queries. Writer's guidelines for #10 SASE with IRCs.

- Ranked as one of the best markets for freelance writers in *Writer's Yearbook* magazine's annual "Top 100 Markets," January 1998.

Nonfiction: Seeks "agenda-setting reports on national issues and trends as well as pieces on health, careers, personal finance and other facts of Canadian life." **Buys 50 mss/year.** Query or query with published clips. Length: 1,000-2,500 words. **Pays $1,000-2,500.** Pays expenses of writers on assignment.

Columns/Departments: Length: 500-1,000 words. Query with published clips. **Pays $500-750.**

Fiction: Trish Snyder. Send ms with SASE.

Fillers: Buys 30/year. Length: 200-500 words. **Pays $250-350.**

N CHICKEN SOUP FOR THE SINGLE SOUL, FOR THE MOTHER'S SOUL 2 and FOR THE WOMAN'S SOUL 3, P.O. Box 1959, Dept. AD, Fairfield IA 52556. Fax: (515)472-7288. E-mail: chickensoup@lisco.com. Co-editors: Jennifer Read Hawthorne and Marci Shimoff. **Contact:** Address submissions to the appropriate book title. **100% freelance written.** Pays on publication. Byline given. Buys one-time rights. Deadlines: December 31, 1998 for *Single Soul;* June 30, 1999 for *Mother's Soul 2;* December 31, 1999 for *Woman's Soul 3.*

- The editors are looking for stories for three upcoming books, one with stories for mothers; one for single, divorced or widowed people; and one for women. Stories should be written with one of these audiences in mind. See the interview with Jack Canfield for more on the *Chicken Soup for the Soul* series.

Nonfiction: "Submissions should be true stories or anecdotes that will uplift, inspire or entertain. We're looking for stories that will make a single person, mother or a woman laugh, cry or sigh." Editors recommend reading previous *Chicken Soup for the Soul* books for examples of desirable stories. **Buys 101 mss/edition.** Length: under 1,100 words. **Pays $300** for first-time authors, negotiates fee for previously published authors.

$ $ COMPLETE WOMAN, For All The Women You Are, Associated Publications, Inc., 875 N. Michigan Ave., Suite 3434, Chicago IL 60611-1901. (312)266-8680. Editor: Bonnie L. Krueger. **Contact**: Lora Wintz, associate editor. **90% freelance written.** Bimonthly. "Manuscripts should be written for today's busy women, in a concise, clear format with useful information. Our readers want to know about the important things: sex, love, relationships, career and self-discovery. Examples of true-life anecdotes, incorporated into articles work well for our readers, who are always interested in how other women are dealing with life's ups and downs." Estab. 1980. Circ. 350,000. Pays on publication. Publishes ms an average of 6 months after acceptance. Byline given. Buys first North American serial, second serial (reprint) or simultaneous rights. Editorial lead time 6 months. Submit seasonal material 5 months in advance. Accepts simultaneous submissions. Reports in 2 months. Writer's guidelines for #10 SASE.

- The editor reports a need for more relationship stories.

Nonfiction: Book excerpts, exposé (of interest to women), general interest, how-to (beauty/diet-related), humor, inspirational, interview/profile (celebrities), new product, personal experience, photo feature, sex, love and relationship advice. "We want self-help articles written for today's woman. Articles that address dating, romance, sexuality and relationships are an integral part of our editorial mix, as well as inspirational and motivational pieces." **Buys 60-100 mss/year.** Query with published clips, or send complete ms. Length: 800-2,000 words. **Pays $80-400.** Sometimes pays expenses of writers on assignment.

Reprints: Send tearsheet or photocopy of article or short story or send typed ms with rights for sale noted and information about when and where the article previously appeared.

Photos: Photo features with little or no copy should be sent to Juli McMeekin. Send photos with submission. Reviews 2¼ or 35mm transparencies and 5×7 prints. Offers $35-75/photo. Captions, model releases, identification of subjects required. Buys one-time rights.

Poetry: Josephine Sharif, assistant editor. Free verse, light verse, traditional. **Buys 15-20 poems/year.** Submit maximum 3 poems. Length: 3-10 lines. Pays in contributor's copies.

Tips: "Freelance writers should review publication, review writer's guidelines, then submit their articles for review. We're looking for new ways to explore the usual topics, written in a format that will be easy for our readers to understand. We also like sidebar information that readers can review quickly before or after reading the article. Our focus is relationship-driven, with an editorial blend of beauty, health and career."

$ $ $ $ CONDÉ NAST BRIDE'S, Condé Nast, 140 E. 45th St., 39th Floor, New York NY 10017. (212)880-2518. Managing Editor: Sally Kilbridge. Editor-in-Chief: Millie Martini-Bratten. **Contact:** Features or travel editors. Bimonthly magazine for the first- and second-time bride, the groom and their families and friends. Circ. 400,000. **Pays on acceptance.** Byline given. Offers 25% kill fee. Buys all rights. Editorial lead time 8 months. Accepts simultaneous submissions. Reports in 2 months on queries. Writer's guidelines for #10 SASE.

Nonfiction: Topic (1) Personal essays on wedding planning, aspects of weddings or marriage. Length: 800 words. Written by brides, grooms, attendants, family members, friends in the first person. The writer's unique experience qualifies them to tell this story. (2)Articles on specific relationship and lifestyle issues. Length: 800 words. Select a specialized topic in the areas of relationships, religion, in-laws, second marriage, finances, careers, health, fitness, nutrition, sex, decorating, or entertaining. Written either by experts (attorneys, doctors, financial planners, marriage counselors, etc) or freelancers who interview and quote experts and real couples. (3) In-depth explorations of relationship and lifestyle issues. Length: 2,000-3,000 words. Well-researched articles on finances, health, sex, wedding and marriage trends. Should include statistics, quotes from experts and real couples, a resolution of the issues raised by each couple. **Buys 100 mss/year.** Query with published clips. Length: 2,000 words. **Pays 50¢-$1/word.** Pays expenses of writers on assignment.

Columns/Departments: Length: 750 words. **Buys 100 mss/year.** Query with published clips. **Pays 50¢-$1/word.**

Tips: "We look for good, helpful relationship pieces that will help a newlywed couple adjust to marriage. Wedding planning articles are usually written by experts or depend on a lot of interviews with experts. Writers must have a good idea of what we would and would not do: Read the 3 or 4 most current issues. What separates us from the competition is quality—writing, photographs, amount of information."

$ $ $ $ COSMOPOLITAN, The Hearst Corp., 224 W. 57th St., New York NY 10019. (212)649-2000. **Contact:** Stephen Perrine, executive editor. **90% freelance written.** Monthly magazine for 18- to 35-year-old single, married, divorced women—all working. "*Cosmopolitan* is edited for young women for whom beauty, fashion, fitness, career, relationships and personal growth are top priorities. Nutrition, personal finance, home/lifestyle and celebrities are other interests reflected in the editorial lineup." Estab. 1886. Circ. 2,300,100. **Pays on acceptance.** Byline given. Offers 10-15% kill fee. Buys all magazine rights and occasionally negotiates first North American rights. Submit seasonal material 6 months in advance. Reports in 1 week on queries; 3 weeks on mss. Sample copy for $2.95. Writer's guidelines for #10 SASE.

- Ranked as one of the best markets for freelance writers in *Writer's Yearbook* magazine's annual "Top 100 Markets," January 1998.

Nonfiction: Book excerpts, how-to, humor, opinion, personal experience and anything of interest to young women. **Buys 350 mss/year.** Query with published clips or send complete ms. Length: 500-3,500 words. **Pays $2,000-3,500 for features; $1,000-1,500 for short pieces.** Pays expenses of writers on assignment.

Columns/Departments: Buys 45 mss/year. Length: 750 words. **Pays $650-1,300.**

Reprints: Accepts previously published submissions appearing in minor publications. Send tearsheet of article, typed ms with rights for sale noted and information about when and where the article previously appeared. Pays 100% of amount paid for an original article.

Fiction: Betty Kelly. Condensed novels, humorous, novel excerpts, romance. **Buys 18 mss/year.** Query. Length: 750-3,000 words.

- *Cosmopolitan* no longer accepts short stories or poetry.

Fillers: Irene Copeland. Facts. **Buys 240/year.** Length: 300-1,000 words.

Tips: "Combine information with entertainment value, humor and relatability." Needs "information- and emotion- and fun-packed relationship and sex service stories; first-person stories that deal with women's issues; essays from both men and women on topics that most women either relate to or are curious about." This editorial team headed American *Marie Claire* until September 1996.

$ COUNTRY WOMAN, Reiman Publications, P.O. Box 643, Milwaukee WI 53201. (414)423-0100. **Contact:** Kathy Pohl, managing editor. **75-85% written by readers.** Willing to work with new/unpublished writers. Bimonthly magazine. "*Country Woman* is for contemporary rural women of all ages and backgrounds and from all over the U.S.

and Canada. It includes a sampling of the diversity that makes up rural women's lives—love of home, family, farm, ranch, community, hobbies, enduring values, humor, attaining new skills and appreciating present, past and future all within the context of the lifestyle that surrounds country living." Estab. 1970. **Pays on acceptance.** Byline given. Buys first North American serial, one-time and second serial (reprint) rights. Submit seasonal material 5 months in advance. Reports in 2 months on queries; 3 months on mss. Sample copy for $2. Writer's guidelines for #10 SASE.

Nonfiction: General interest, historical/nostalgic, how-to (crafts, community projects, decorative, antiquing, etc.), humor, inspirational, interview/profile, personal experience, photo/feature packages profiling interesting country women—all pertaining to a rural woman's interest. Articles must be written in a positive, light and entertaining manner. Query. Length: 1,000 words maximum. **Pays $35-150.**

Reprints: Send typed ms with rights for sale noted and information about when and where the material previously appeared. Payment varies.

Photos: Send color photos with query or ms. Reviews 35mm or 2¼ transparencies or excellent-quality color prints. Uses only excellent quality color photos. No b&w. "We pay for photo/feature packages." Captions, model releases and identification of subjects required. Buys one-time rights.

Columns/Departments: Why Farm Wives Age Fast (humor), I Remember When (nostalgia) and Country Decorating. **Buys 10-12 mss/year** (maximum). Query or send complete ms. Length: 500-1,000 words. **Pays $50-125.**

Fiction: Main character *must* be a country woman. All fiction must have a country setting. Fiction must have a positive, upbeat message. Includes fiction in every issue. Would buy more fiction if stories suitable for our audience were sent our way. Send complete ms. Length: 750-1,000 words. **Pays $90-125.**

Poetry: Traditional, light verse. "Poetry must have rhythm and rhyme! It must be country-related, positive and upbeat. Always looking for seasonal poetry." **Buys 6-12/year.** Submit 6 poems max. Length: 5-24 lines. **Pays $10-25.**

Tips: "We have broadened our focus to include 'country' women, not just women on farms and ranches but also women who live in a small town or country home and/or simply have an interest in country-oriented topics. This allows freelancers a wider scope in material. Write as clearly and with as much zest and enthusiasm as possible. We love good quotes, supporting materials (names, places, etc.) and strong leads and closings. Readers relate strongly to where they live and the lifestyle they've chosen. They want to be informed and entertained, and that's just exactly why they subscribe. Readers are busy—not too busy to read—but when they do sit down, they want good writing, reliable information and something that feels like a reward. How-to, humor, personal experience and nostalgia are areas most open to freelancers. Profiles, to a certain degree, are also open. Be accurate and fresh in approach."

$ $ ESSENCE, 1500 Broadway, New York NY 10036. (212)642-0600. Editor-in-Chief: Susan L. Taylor. **Contact:** Monique Greenwood, executive editor. Monthly. "*Essence* is the magazine for today's Black women. Edited for career-minded, sophisticated and independent achievers, *Essence*'s editorial is dedicated to helping its readers attain their maximum potential in various lifestyles and roles. The editorial content includes career and educational opportunities; fashion and beauty; investing and money management; health and fitness; parenting; information on home decorating and food; travel; cultural reviews; fiction; and profiles of achievers and celebrities." Estab. 1970. Circ. 1 million. **Pays on acceptance.** Makes assignments on one-time serial rights basis. 3 month lead time. Pays 25% kill fee. Byline given. Submit seasonal material 6 months in advance. Reports in 2 months. Sample copy for $3.25. Guidelines free.

- Ranked as one of the best markets for freelance writers in *Writer's Yearbook*'s annual "Top 100 Markets," January 1998.

Nonfiction: Buys 200 mss/year. Query only; word length will be given upon assignment. **Pays $500 minimum.** Also publishes novel and nonfiction book excerpts.

Reprints: Send tearsheet of article, information about when and where the article previously appeared. Pays 50% of the amount paid for an original article.

Photos: Marcia Minter, creative director. State availability of photos with query. Pays $100 for b&w page; $300 for color page. Captions and model release required. "We particularly would like to see photographs for our travel section that feature Black travelers."

Columns/Departments: Query department editors: Lifestyle (food, lifestyle, travel, consumer information): Jay Cain; Entertainment: Yvette Russell; Health & Fitness: Ziba Kashef. Query only, word length will be given upon assignment. **Pays $100 minimum.**

Fiction: Martha Southgate, editor. Publishes novel excerpts.

Tips: "Please note that *Essence* no longer accepts unsolicited mss for fiction, poetry or nonfiction, except for the Brothers, Windows, Back Talk and Interiors columns. So please only send query letters for nonfiction story ideas."

$ $ $ $ FAMILY CIRCLE MAGAZINE, Gruner & Jahr, 375 Lexington Ave., New York NY 10017-5514. (212)499-2000. Fax: (212)499-1987. Website: www.familycircle.com. Editor-in-Chief: Susan Ungaro. **Contact**: Nancy Clark, deputy editor. Managing Editor: Wallace Kunukau. **80% freelance written.** Magazine published every 3 weeks. "We are a national women's service magazine which covers many stages of a woman's life, along with her everyday concerns about social, family and health issues. Query should stress the unique aspects of an article and expert sources; we want articles that will help our readers or make a difference in how they live." Estab. 1932. Circ. 5,000,000. Byline given. Offers 20% kill fee. Buys first North American serial rights or all rights. Editorial lead time 4 months. Submit seasonal material 4 months in advance. Reports in 2 months. Writer's guidelines for #10 SASE.

- Ranked as one of the best markets for freelance writers in *Writer's Yearbook* magazine's annual "Top 100 Markets," January 1998.

Nonfiction: Essays, humor, opinion, personal experience. Women's interest subjects such as family and personal

relationships, children, physical and mental health, nutrition and self-improvement. "We look for well-written, well-reported stories told through interesting anecdotes and insightful writing. We want well-researched service journalism on all subjects." Special issues: Computers Made Easy (3 times/year). No fiction or poetry. **Buys 200 mss/year.** Query with SASE. Length: 1,000-2,500 words. **Pays $1/word.** Pays expenses of writers on assignment.
Columns/Departments: Women Who Make a Difference (profiles of volunteers who have made a significant impact on their community), 1,500 words; Profiles in Courage/Love (dramatic narratives about women and families overcoming adversity), 2,000 words; Full Circle (opinion/point of view on current issue/topic of general interest to our readers), 750 words; Humor, 750 words. **Buys 200 mss/year.** Query with published clips and SASE. **Pays $1/word.**
Tips: "Query letters should be concise and to the point. Also, writers should keep close tabs on *Family Circle* and other women's magazines to avoid submitting recently run subject matter."

$ $ $ FIRST FOR WOMEN, Bauer Publishing Co., P.O. Box 1648, 270 Sylvan Ave., Englewood Cliffs NJ 07632. (201)569-6699. Fax: (201)569-6264. E-mail: firstfw@aol.com. Magazine published 18 times/year. **Contact:** Teresa Hagen, executive editor. "*First for Women* speaks directly to a woman about her real-life needs, concerns and interests. *First* provides an equal combination of service editorial (family, kids, health, food and home) with personal lifestyle and general interest topics (personal health, fitness, nutrition, beauty, fashion and contemporary issues) for the '30-something' woman." Estab. 1989. Circ. 1,282,600. **Pays on acceptance.** Byline given. Offers 20% kill fee.

- Ranked as one of the best markets for freelance writers in *Writer's Yearbook* magazine's annual "Top 100 Markets," January 1998.

Non-fiction: Buys 300 articles (1,200-word features and 550- to 750-word short pieces). Send ms or query with SASE. No e-mail queries. Feature sections more open to freelancers. Pay is negotiable, from **$200-1,200.**
Reprints: Send photocopy of article and information about when and where the article previously appeared. Payment negotiable, but less than amount paid for an original article. Buys first North American serial rights.

☆ $ $ $ GLAMOUR, Condé Nast, 350 Madison Ave., New York NY 10017. (212)880-8800. Fax: (212)880-6922. E-mail: glamourmag@aol.com. **Contact:** Ruth Whitney, editor-in-chief. **75% freelance written.** Works with a small number of new/unpublished writers each year. Monthly magazine for college-educated women, 18-35 years old. "*Glamour* is edited for the contemporary American woman, it informs her of the trends, recommends how she can adapt them to her needs, and motivates her to take action. Over half of *Glamour*'s editorial content focuses on fashion, beauty and health, as well as coverage of personal relationships, career, travel, food and entertainment." Estab. 1939. Circ. 2,300,000. **Pays on acceptance.** Offers 25% kill fee. Publishes ms an average of 1 year after acceptance. Buys first North American serial rights. Byline given. Reports in 3 months. Writer's guidelines for #10 SASE.

- Ranked as one of the best markets for freelance writers in *Writer's Yearbook* magazine's annual "Top 100 Markets," January 1998.

Nonfiction: Mary Hickey, articles editor. "Editorial approach is 'how-to' with articles that are relevant in the areas of careers, current events, health, psychology, interpersonal relationships, etc. We look for queries that are fresh and include a contemporary, timely angle. Fashion, beauty, travel, food and entertainment are all staff-written. We use 1,000-word opinion essays for our Viewpoint section. Our His/Hers column features generally stylish essays on relationships or comments on current mores by male and female writers in alternate months." The Bridges column accepts thoughtful essays on life outside of the mainstream. **Pays $1,000 for His/Hers and Bridges mss; $1,000 for Viewpoint mss. Buys 10-12 mss/issue.** Query "with letter that is detailed, well-focused, well-organized, and documented with surveys, statistics and research; personal essays excepted." Short articles and essays (1,500-2,000 words) **pays $1,000 and up;** longer mss (2,500-3,000 words) **pays $1,500 minimum.** Sometimes pays the expenses of writers on assignment.
Reprints: Send information about when and where the article previously appeared. Payment varies.
Tips: "We're looking for sharply focused ideas by strong writers and are constantly raising our standards. We are interested in getting new writers, and we are approachable, mainly because our range of topics is so broad. We've increased our focus on male-female relationships."

$ $ $ $ GOOD HOUSEKEEPING, Hearst Corp., 959 Eighth Ave., New York NY 10019. (212)649-2000. Editor-in-Chief: Ellen Levine. Executive Editor: Diane Salvatore. Prefers to work with published/established writers. Monthly magazine. "*Good Housekeeping* is edited for the 'New Traditionalist.' Articles which focus on food, fitness, beauty, and child care draw upon the resources of the Good Housekeeping Institute. Editorial includes human interest stories, articles that focus on social issues, money management, health news, travel, and 'The Better Way,' an 8-page hard-fact guide to better living." Circ. 5,000,000. **Pays on acceptance.** Buys first North American serial rights. Pays 25% kill fee. Byline given. Submit seasonal material 6 months in advance. Reports in 2 months. For sample copy, call (800)925-0485. Writer's guidelines for #10 SASE.

- Ranked as one of the best markets for freelance writers in *Writer's Yearbook* magazine's annual "Top 100 Markets," January 1998.

Nonfiction: Diane Salvatore, executive editor. Deborah Pike, health editor. Consumer, social issues, dramatic narrative, nutrition, work, relationships, psychology, trends. **Buys 4-6 mss/issue.** Query. Length: 1,500-2,500 words. **Pays $1,500**+ on acceptance for full articles from new writers. **Pays $250-350** for local interest and travel pieces of 2,000 words. Pays expenses of writers on assignment.
Photos: Scott Yardley, art director. Maya MacMillan, photo editor. Photos purchased on assignment mostly. Pays $100-350 for b&w; $200-400 for color photos. Query. Model releases required.
Columns/Departments: The Better Way, editor: Kristin Godsey (consumer advice, how-to, shopping strategies,

money savers, health). Profiles editor: Diane Baroni (inspirational, activist or heroic women), 300-600 words. My Problem and How I Solved It, My Problem editor (as told-to format), 2,000 words. Query. **Pays $1/word** for items 300-600 words.

Fiction: Lee Quarfoot, fiction editor. Uses original short fiction and condensations of novels that can appear in one issue. Looks for reader identification. "We get 1,500 unsolicited mss/month. A freelancer's odds are overwhelming, but we do look at all submissions." Send complete mss. Manuscripts will not be returned. Responds only on acceptance. Length: 1,500 words (short-shorts); novel according to merit of material; average 5,000-word short stories. **Pays $1,000** minimum for fiction from new writers.

• Ranked as one of the best markets for fiction writers in *Writer's Digest* magazine's "Fiction 50, June 1998."

Tips: "Always send a SASE and clips. We prefer to see a query first. Do not send material on subjects already covered in-house by the Good Housekeeping Institute—these include food, beauty, needlework and crafts."

$ $ $ $ HARPER'S BAZAAR, The Hearst Corp., 1700 Broadway, New York, NY 10019. (212)903-5300. Publisher: Jeannette Chang. **Contact:** Liz Tilberis, features director. "*Harper's Bazaar* is a monthly specialist magazine for women who love fashion and beauty. It is edited for sophisticated women with exceptional taste. *Bazaar* offers ideas in fashion and beauty, and reports on issues and interests relevant to the lives of modern women." Estab. 1867. Circ. 711,000. Pays on publication. Byline given. Offers 25% kill fee. Buys worldwide rights. Reports in 2 months on queries.

Nonfiction: Buys 36 mss/year. Query with published clips. Length: 2,000-3,000 words. Payment negotiable.

Columns/Departments: Length: 500-700 words. Payment negotiable.

$ $ $ $ LADIES' HOME JOURNAL, Meredith Corporation, 125 Park Ave., 20th Floor, New York NY 10017-5516. (212)557-6600. Publishing Director/Editor-in-Chief: Myrna Blyth. **50% freelance written.** Monthly magazine focusing on issues of concern to women 30-45. They cover a broader range of news and political issues than many other women's magazines. "*Ladies' Home Journal* is for active, empowered women who are evolving in new directions. It addresses informational needs with highly focused features and articles on a variety of topics including beauty and fashion, food and nutrition, health and medicine, home decorating and design, parenting and self-help, personalities and current events." Circ. 5,000,000. **Pays on acceptance.** Offers 25% kill fee. Rights bought vary with submission. Reports on queries within 3 months with SASE. Writer's guidelines for #10 SASE, Attention: Writer's Guidelines on envelope.

Nonfiction: Submissions on the following subjects should be directed to the editor listed for each: investigative reports, news-related features, psychology/relationships/sex (Pam O'Brien, features editor); medical/health (Elena Rover, health editor); celebrities/entertainment (Melina Gerosa, entertainment editor); travel stories (Karyn Dabaghian, associate editor). Query with published clips. Length: 2,000-3,000 words. **Pays $2,000-4,000.** Pays expenses of writers on assignment.

Photos: State availability of photos with submission. Offers variable payment for photos accepted with ms. Captions, model releases and identification of subjects required. Rights bought vary with submission. (*LHJ* arranges for its own photography almost all the time.)

Columns/Departments: Query the following editor or box for column ideas. A Woman Today (Box WT); Woman to Woman (Box WW); Parents' Journal (Mary Mohler, senior editor); Pet News (Shana Aborn, News & Human Interest editor). **Pays $750-2,000.**

Fiction: Mary Mohler, editor, books and fiction. Only short stories and novels submitted by an agent or publisher will be considered. Buys 12 mss/year. No poetry of any kind.

N $ THE LINK & VISITOR, Baptist Women's Missionary Society of Ontario and Quebec, 30 Arlington Ave., Toronto, Ontario M6G 3K8 Canada. (416)651-7192. Fax: (416)651-0438. **Contact:** Esther Barnes, editor. **50% freelance written.** "Magazine published 9 times/year designed to help Baptist women grow their world, faith, relationship, creativity, and mission vision-evangelical, egalitarian, Canadian." Estab. 1878. Circ. 4,300. Pays on publication. Publishes ms 2 months after acceptance. Byline given. Buys one-time, second serial (reprint) or simultaneous rights or makes work-for-hire assignments. Editorial lead time 2 months. Submit seasonal material 3 months in advance. Accepts simultaneous submissions. Sample copy for 9×12 SAE with 2 first-class Canadian stamps or IRCs. Writer's guidelines free.

Nonfiction: Inspirational, interview/profile, religious. "Articles must be Biblically literate. No easy answers, American mindset or U.S. focus, retelling of Bible stories, sermons." **Buys 30-35 mss/year.** Send complete ms. Length: 750-2,000 words. **Pays 5¢/word (Canadian).** Sometimes pays expenses of writers on assignment.

Photos: State availability of photos with submission. Reviews any prints. Offers no additional payment for photos accepted with ms. Captions required. Buys one-time rights.

Tips: "Canadian women writers preferred. Don't send little stories with a moral attached. Show some thought, research, depth of insight. We're looking for material on joy."

$ $ MADEMOISELLE, Condé Nast, 350 Madison Ave., New York NY 10017. (212)880-8800. **Contact:** Faye Haun, managing editor. **95% freelance written.** Prefers to work with published/established writers. Columns are written by columnists; "sometimes we give new writers a 'chance' on shorter, less complex assignments." Monthly magazine for women age 18-31. "*Mademoiselle* is edited for a woman in her twenties. It focuses on the decade when she is starting out in life as an independent adult and experiencing being on her own for the first time. Editorial offers advice on fashion, beauty, relationships, work and self-discovery." Circ. 1,200,000. Buys first North American serial rights. **Pays on acceptance**; rates vary.

Nonfiction: Particular concentration on articles of interest to the intelligent young woman 18-31, including personal relationships, health, careers, trends, and current social problems. Send entertainment queries to Jeanie Pyun. Query with published clips and SASE. Length: 1,000-2,000 words. Rates vary.

Photos: Cindy Searight, creative director. Commissioned work assigned according to needs. Photos of fashion, beauty, travel. Payment ranges from no-charge to an agreed rate of payment per shot, job series or page rate. Buys all rights. Pays on publication for photos.

Tips: "We are looking for timely, well-researched manuscripts."

$ $ $ $ MARIE CLAIRE, Hearst Corp., 1790 Broadway, 3rd Floor, New York NY 10019. Fax: (212)649-5050. E-mail: marieclaire@hearst.com. Editor-in-chief: Glenda Bailey. Executive Editor: Jenny Barnett. **Contact:** Brett Mirsky, senior editor. Michele Lavery, deputy editor. "*Marie Claire* is a monthly lifestyle magazine with a focus on beauty and fashion. It covers a broad range of topics such as world issues, entertaining, celebrity profiles and decorating." American *Marie Claire* was launched in September, 1994. There are currently 22 other international editions. The magazine aims to provide a great read on everything from world issues to intimate advice, fashion, beauty and service." Estab. 1994. Circ. 500,000. **Pays on acceptance**. Publishes ms an average of 5 months after acceptance. Byline given. Offers 25% kill fee. Makes work-for-hire assignments. Editorial lead time 3 months. Submit seasonal material 6 months in advance. Accepts simultaneous submissions. Reports in 3 weeks. Sample copy for $5. Guidelines free.

- Ranked as one of the best markets for freelance writers in *Writer's Yearbook* magazine's annual "Top 100 Market," January 1998.

Nonfiction: Book excerpts, exposé, general interest, humor, personal experience. Does not want to see fiction, personal essays. **Buys 50 mss/year.** Query with published clips. Length: 500-3,000 words. **Pays $1-1.50/word.** Sometimes pays expenses of writers on assignment.

Photos: State availability of photos with submission. Reviews contact sheets, negatives, prints. Negotiates payment individually. Model releases, identification of subjects required.

Columns/Departments: Women of the world (the lead feature in every edition, an issue addressing women of another country or culture, but somehow relatable to an American woman as well); first person (personal and dramatic stories, always written from the female subject's point of view); true lives (may be written in first or third person, male or female, discussing a non-traditional lifestyle or unusual experience); emotional issues (relationship/sex related stories, provocative and newsy); working (career issues women face at work, at home, or in relationships); love life (any facet of love, sex, marriage and dating); review (movies, music, books, celebrities, TV, etc.).

$ $ $ $ McCALL'S, Gruner & Jahr, 375 Lexington Ave., New York NY 10017-5514. (212)499-2000. Fax: (212)499-1778. Editor: Sally Koslow. **Contact:** Cathy Cavender, executive editor. **90% freelance written.** Monthly. "Our constantly evolving publication carefully and conscientiously serves the needs of the woman reader—concentrating on matters that directly affect her life and offering information and understanding on subjects of personal importance to her." Circ. 4.2 million. **Pays on acceptance.** Publishes ms an average of 6 months after acceptance. Offers 20% kill fee. Byline given. Buys exclusive or First North American rights. Reports in 2 months. Guidelines for SASE.

- Ranked as one of the best markets for freelance writers in *Writer's Yearbook* magazine's annual "Top 100 Markets," January 1998.

Nonfiction: The editors are seeking meaningful stories of personal experience, fresh slants for self-help and relationship pieces, and well-researched action-oriented articles and narratives dealing with social problems concerning readers. Topics must have broad appeal, but they must be approached in a fresh, new, you-haven't-read-this-elsewhere way. **Buys 200-300 mss/year,** many in the 1,500-2,000-word length. **Pays $1/word.** These are on subjects of interest to women: health, personal narratives, celebrity biographies and autobiographies, etc. Almost all features on food, fashion, beauty and decorating are staff-written." Sometimes pays expenses of writers on assignment.

Columns/Departments: Real Life (stories of women who have lived through or accomplished something extraordinary), 1,800 words; Inspirations (first person stories of women who have changed their lives or accomplished a goal or dream—not stories about overcoming odds), 600 words; Couples (how to make marriages work better), 1,200 words; Consumer Watch (how to spend and save wisely, avoid scams and shop smarter), 600 words; Health Alert, 600 words; Medical Report, 2,000 words; Mind and Body, 1,800 words; Staying Fit, 1,200 words; Prime Time (articles on health, finance and self-help for readers over 50), 800-1,000 words. Query. **Pays $1/word.**

Tips: "Query first. Articles about food, fashion, beauty, home decorating and travel are staff-written. Read our writer's guidelines and know the type of women we are looking to profile. Use the tone and format of our most recent issues as your guide. Address submissions to executive editor unless otherwise specified. We do make outside assignments for our department categories."

$ $ $ MODERN BRIDE, Primedia, 249 W. 17th St., New York NY 10011. (212)337-7096. Fax: (212)367-8342. Website: http://www.modernbride.com. Editor: Stacy Morrison. **Contact:** Lisa Milbrand. "*Modern Bride* is designed as the bride-to-be's guide to planning her wedding, honeymoon, and first home or apartment. Issues cover: (1) bridal fashion (including attendants and mother-of-the-bride), travel trousseau and lingerie; (2) home furnishings (tableware, furniture, linens, appliances, housewares, coverings, accessories, etc.); (3) honeymoon travel (covering the United States, Canada, Mexico, the Bahamas, the Caribbean, Europe and Asia). Additional regular features include personal and beauty care, wedding gifts, etiquette, marital relations, financial advice, and shopping information." **Pays on acceptance.** Offers 25% kill fee. Buys first periodical rights. Reports in 6 weeks.

- Ranked as one of the best markets for freelance writers in *Writer's Yearbook* magazine's annual "Top 100 Markets," January 1998.

Nonfiction: Book excerpts, general interest, how-to, personal experience. **Buys 60 mss/year.** Query with published clips. Length: 500-2,000 words. **Pays $600-1,200.**
Reprints: Send tearsheet of article or short story. Pays 50% of amount paid for an original article.
Columns/Departments: Geri Bain, editor. Travel.

N ☆ $ $ MORE MAGAZINE, Meredith Corp. (Ladies Home Journal), 125 Park Ave., New York NY 10017. Fax: (212)455-1433. **Contact:** Ila Stanger, managing editor. Editor-in-Chief: Myrna Blyth. **90% freelance written.** Bimonthly consumer magazine covering smart, sophisticated 45+ women. Estab. 1998. Circ. 400,000. **Pays on acceptance.** Publishes ms an average of 3 months after acceptance. Byline given. Offers 25% kill fee. Buys first North American serial, first, all rights. Editorial lead time 4 months. Submit seasonal material 6 months in advance. Accepts simultaneous submissions. Reports in 3 months. Writer's guidelines for #10 SASE.
Nonfiction: Contact: Debra Birnbaum, senior editor. Essays, exposé, general interest, interview/profile, personal experience, travel. **Buys 50 mss/year.** Query with published clips. Length: 300-3,000 words. Payment depending on writer/story length. Pays expenses of writers on assignment.
Photos: State availability of photos with submission. Negotiates payment individually. Captions, model releases and identification of subjects required. Buys all rights.
Columns/Departments: Contact: Debra Birnbaum, senior editor. **Buys 20 mss/year.** Query with published clips. **Pays $300.**

☆ $ $ $ $ MS. MAGAZINE, MacDonald Communications, Inc., 135 W. 50th St., 16th Floor, New York NY 10020. (212)445-6162. Fax: (212)586-7441. E-mail: ms@echonyc.com. Editor-in-Chief: Marcia Gillespie. Executive Editors: Barbara Findlen, Gloria Jacobs. **Contact:** Manuscript Editor. **85% freelance written.** Bimonthly magazine on women's issues and news. Estab. 1972. Circ. 200,000. Byline given. Offers 20% kill fee. Buys first North American serial rights. Reports in 1-2 months. Sample copy for $9. Writer's guidelines for #10 SASE.
Nonfiction: International and national (US) news, the arts, books, popular culture, feminist theory and scholarship, ecofeminism, women's health, spirituality, political and economic affairs. Photo essays. **Buys 4-5 features** (3,000 words) and **4-5 short pieces** (500 words)/year. **Pays $1/word.** Query with published clips. Length: 300-3,000 words. Pays expenses of writers on assignment.
Reprints: Send tearsheets of article or typed ms with rights for sale noted and information about when and where the article previously appeared. Pays 50% of amount paid for an original article.
Photos: State availability of photos with submission. Model releases and identification of subjects required. Buys one-time rights.
Columns/Departments: Buys 4-5 mss/year. Length: up to 3,000 words. **Pays $1/word.**
Tips: Needs "international and national women's news, investigative reporting, personal narratives, humor, world-class fiction and poetry, and prize-winning journalists and feminist thinkers."

☆ $ $ $ PLAYGIRL, 801 Second Ave., New York NY 10017. (212)661-7878. Fax: (212)697-6343. E-mail: ckeel@crespub.com. Website: http://www.playgirlmag.com. Editor-in-Chief: Judy Cole. **Contact:** Charlene Keel Razack, managing editor. **75% freelance written.** Prefers to work with published/established writers. Monthly magazine. "*Playgirl* addresses the needs, interests and desires of women 18 years of age and older. We provide something no other American women's magazine can: an uninhibited approach to exploring sexuality and fantasy that empowers, enlightens and entertains. We publish features articles of all sorts: interviews with top celebrities; essays and humor pieces on sexually related topics; first-person accounts of sensual adventures; articles on the latest trends in sex, love, romance and dating; and how-to stories that give readers sexy news they can use. We also publish erotic fiction—from a women's perspective or from an empathic, sex-positive male point of view—and reader fantasies. The common thread—besides, of course, good, lively writing and scrupulous research—is a fresh, open-minded, inquisitive attitude." Circ. 500,000. Pays within 6 weeks of acceptance. Publishes ms an average of 3 months after acceptance. Byline given. Offers 20% kill fee. Buys all rights. Submit seasonal material 6 months in advance. Accepts simultaneous submissions, if so noted. Reports in 1 month on queries; 3 months on mss. Writer's guidelines for #10 SASE.
Nonfiction: Humor for the modern woman/man, exposés (related to women's issues), interview (Q&A format with major show business celebrities), articles on sexuality, medical breakthroughs, relationships, coping, careers, insightful, lively articles on current issues, investigative pieces particularly geared to *Playgirl*. Average issue: 3 articles; 1 celebrity interview. **Buys 6 mss/issue.** Query with published clips. Length: 1,000-2,500 words. **Pays $300-1,000.** Sometimes pays expenses of writers on assignment.
Fiction: Publishes novel excerpts.
Tips: "Best bet for first-time writers: Fantasy Forum. No phone calls please."

☆ $ RADIANCE, The Magazine for Large Women, Box 30246, Oakland CA 94604. (510)482-0680. E-mail: radmag2@aol.com. Website: http://www.radiancemagazine.com. Editor: Alice Ansfield. **95% freelance written.** Quarterly magazine "that encourages and supports *all* sizes of large to live fully now, to stop putting their lives on hold until they lose weight." Estab. 1984. Circ. 15,000. Pays on publication. Publishes ms an average of 12-20 months after acceptance. Byline given. Offers $25 kill fee. Buys one-time and second serial (reprint) rights. Submit seasonal material at least 1 year in advance. Accepts previously published submissions. Reports in 4 months. Sample copy for $3.50. Writer's guidelines for #10 SASE.

- *Radiance* welcomes participation in their new Kids Project! They've expanded to include essays from girls and boys about *their* lives, specifically on issues of body size, self-esteem, self-acceptance, and will provide information for those who work with (or parent) kids on how to raise children to feel seen, loved, and valued for the person they are.

Nonfiction: Book excerpts (related to large women), essays, exposé, general interest, historical/nostalgic, how-to (on health/well-being/fashion/fitness, etc.), humor, inspirational, interview/profile, opinion, personal experience, photo feature, travel. "No diet successes or articles condemning people for being fat." Query with published clips. Length: 1,000-2,500 words. **Pays $35-100** and contributor copy.

Photos: State availability of photos with submission. Offers $15-50/photo. Captions and identification of subjects preferred. Buys one-time rights.

Columns/Departments: Up Front and Personal (personal profiles of women from all areas of life); Health and Well-Being (physical/emotional well-being, self care, research); Expressions (features on artists who celebrate the full female figure); Images (designer interviews, color/style/fashion, features); Inner Journeys (spirituality, personal experiences, interviews); Perspectives (cultural and political aspects of being in a larger body); On the Move (women active in all kinds of sports, physical activities); Young Activists (bringing size awareness and esteem to the younger generation); Getaways (vacation spots and world travel, with tips specifically for people of size); Women and Mid-Life, Aging (articles on all important passages in a woman's life); Book reviews (nonfiction and fiction, related to size issue). **Buys 60 mss/year.** Query with published clips. Length: 1,000-3,500 words. **Pays $50-100; book reviews $35-75.**

Fiction: Condensed novels, ethnic, fantasy, historical, humorous, mainstream, novel excerpts, romance, science fiction, serialized novels, slice-of-life vignettes relating somehow to large women. "No woman-hates-self-till-meets-man-type fiction!" **Buys 15 mss/year.** Query with published clips. Length: 800-2,500 words. **Pays $35-100.**

Poetry: Reflective, empowering, experiential. Related to women's feelings and experience, re: their bodies, self-esteem, acceptance. "We want well-crafted poems; prefer unrhymed; not preachy poetry." **Buys 30 poems/year.** Length: 4-45 lines. **Pays $10-15.**

Tips: "We welcome talented, sensitive, responsible, open-minded writers. We profile women from all walks of life who are all sizes of large, of all ages and from all ethnic groups and lifestyles. We welcome writers' ideas on interesting large women from across the US and abroad. We're an open, size-positive magazine that documents and celebrates body acceptance. *Radiance* is one of the major forces working for size acceptance. We want articles to address all areas of vital importance in women's lives. Please read a copy of *Radiance* before writing for us."

$ $ $ REDBOOK MAGAZINE, 224 W. 57th St., New York NY 10019. Senior Editors: Pamela Lister and Susan Gifford. Deputy Editor: Toni Gerber Hope. Health Editor: Andrea Bauman. Fiction Editor: Dawn Raffel. **Contact:** Any of editorial assistants listed on masthead. **90% freelance written.** Monthly magazine. "*Redbook* addresses young married women between the ages of 25 and 44. Most of our readers are married with children 12 and under; over 60 percent work outside the home. The articles entertain, educate and inspire our readers to confront challenging issues. Each article must be timely and relevant to *Redbook* readers' lives." Estab. 1903. Circ. 3,200,000. **Pays on acceptance.** Publishes ms an average of 6 months after acceptance. Rights purchased vary with author and material. Reports in 3 months. Writer's guidelines for #10 SASE.

Nonfiction: Contact: Articles Department. Subjects of interest: social issues, parenting, sex, marriage, news profiles, true crime, dramatic narratives, money, psychology, health. Query with published clips. Length: articles, 2,500-3,000 words; short articles, 1,000-1,500 words. "Please review at least the past six issues of *Redbook* to better understand subject matter and treatment." Enclose SASE for response.

Fiction: Contact: Fiction Department. "Of the 20,000 unsolicited manuscripts that we receive annually, **we buy less than five.** We also find many more stories that are not necessarily suited to our needs but are good enough to warrant our encouraging the author to send others. *Redbook* looks for fresh, well-crafted stories that reflect some aspect of the experiences and interests of our readers; it's a good idea to read several issues to get a feel for what we buy. No unsolicited novels or novellas, please." **Payment begins at $1,000 for short stories.** Please include SASE with all stories.

- Ranked as one of the best markets for fiction writers in *Writer's Digest* magazine's "Fiction 50," June 1998.

Tips: "Most *Redbook* articles require solid research, well-developed anecdotes from on-the-record sources, and fresh, insightful quotes from established experts in a field that pass our 'reality check' test."

$ $ $ $ SELF, 350 Madison Ave., 23rd Floor, New York NY 10017. **Contact:** Judith Daniels, executive editor. Monthly magazine for women ages 22-45. "*Self* is a magazine about total well-being. It is edited for active, professional women who are interested in improving the quality of their lives and the world they live in. The magazine provides a balanced approach to attain individual satisfaction with information on beauty, health, fitness, psychology, food, fashion, culture, career, politics and the environment." **Pays on acceptance**. Byline given. Buys one-time rights. Accepts simultaneous submissions. Reports in 1 month on queries. Sample copy free. Writer's guidelines for #10 SASE.

- Ranked as one of the best markets for freelance writers in *Writer's Yearbook* magazine's annual "Top 100 Markets," January 1998.

Nonfiction: Considers proposals for major pieces on health, nutrition, psychology, fitness, family relationships and sociological issues. **Buys 40 mss/year.** Query with published clips. Length: 1,500-5,000 words. **Pays $1-2/word.**

Columns/Departments: Uses short, news-driven items on health, nutrition, money, jobs, love/sex, mind/body, fitness, travel. Length: 300-1,000 words. **Buys 50 mss/year.** Query with published clips. **Pays $1-2/word.**

Tips: "Our articles contain a lot of factual information—and related anecdotes; most rely on the advice and opinion of experts. Our readers seek very focused and useful information about their interests."

$ $ TODAY'S BRIDE, Family Communications, 37 Hanna Ave., Suite #1, Toronto, Ontario M6K 1W9 Canada. (416)537-2604. Fax: (416)538-1794. Editor: Bettie Bradley. **Contact:** Tracy Hitchcock, assistant editor. **Less than 10% freelance written.** Semiannual magazine "geared to engaged couples looking for bridal fashion and wedding planning tips. All standard planning pieces and travel are written in-house; freelance articles we purchase look at something unique or different." Estab. 1980. Circ. 108,000. **Pays on acceptance**. Byline given. Buys all rights. Editorial lead time 6 months. Accepts simultaneous submissions. Reports in 1 month on queries. Writer's guidelines free.
Nonfiction: Humor, opinion, personal experience. No travel and standard planning pieces (i.e. choosing flowers, music, etc.). Query with or without published clips or send complete ms. Length: 800-1,400 words. **Pays $250-300.**
Reprints: Send tearsheet or photocopy of article or typed ms with rights for sale noted and information about where and when the article previously appeared. Pays $250-300.
Photos: Send photos with submission. Reviews transparencies, prints. Negotiates payment individually. Identification of subjects required. Rights purchased negotiated on individual basis.

$ $ TODAY'S CHRISTIAN WOMAN, 465 Gundersen Dr., Carol Stream IL 60188-2498. (630)260-6200. Fax: (630)260-0114. E-mail: tcwedit@aol.com. Editor: Ramona Cramer Tucker. Managing Editor: Linda Piepenbrink. Senior Associate Editor: Jane Johnson Struck. Associate Editor: Camerin Courtney. **25% freelance written.** Works with a small number of new/unpublished writers each year. Bimonthly magazine for Christian women of all ages, single and married, homemakers and career women. Estab. 1979. Circ. 310,000. **Pays on acceptance.** Publishes ms an average of 6 months after acceptance. Byline given. Buys first rights only. Submit seasonal material 9 months in advance. Reports in 2 months. Sample copy for $5. Writer's guidelines for #10 SASE.
Nonfiction: How-to, narrative, inspirational. Query only; no unsolicited mss. "The query should include article summary, purpose and reader value, author's qualifications, suggested length and date to send." **Pays 15¢/word.**
Tips: "Articles focus on the following relationships: marriage, parenting, self, spiritual life, single life, work, family, issues, health and friendship. All articles should be highly anecdotal, personal in tone, and universal in appeal."

⊘ **VICTORIA** does not accept freelance submissions.

$ $ $ $ VOGUE, Condé Nast, 350 Madison Ave., New York NY 10017. (212)880-8800. E-mail: voguemail@aol.com. **Contact:** Laurie Jones, managing editor. Monthly magazine. "*Vogue* mirrors the changing roles and concerns of women, covering not only evolutions in fashion, beauty and style, but the important issues and ideas of the arts, health care, politics and world affairs." Estab. 1892. Circ. 1,136,000. **Pays on acceptance**. Byline sometimes given. Offers 25% kill fee. Reports in 3 months on queries. Writer's guidelines for #10 SASE.
Nonfiction: "Needs fresh voices on unexpected topics." **Buys 5 unsolicited mss/year.** Query with published clips. Length: 2,500 words maximum. **Pays $1-2/word.**
Tips: "Sophisticated, surprising and compelling writing a must." Please note: *Vogue* accepts *very* few unsolicited manuscripts. Most stories are generated in-house and are written by staff.

$ $ $ $ WOMAN'S DAY, 1633 Broadway, New York NY 10019. (212)767-6000. Deputy Editor: Maureen McFadden. 75% or more of articles freelance written. "*Woman's Day* is written and edited for the contemporary woman. *Woman's Day* editorial package covers the various issues that are important to women today. Editorial features are devoted to information on Food & Nutrition, Health & Fitness, Beauty & Fashion, as well as the traditional values of Home, Family and Children. The changing needs of women are also addressed with articles that focus on Money Management, Law, and Relationships." 17 issues/year. Circ. 6,000,000. Pays 25% kill fee. Byline given. **Pays on acceptance.** Reports in 1 month or less on queries. Submit detailed queries.

- Ranked as one of the best markets for freelance writers in *Writer's Yearbook* magazine's annual "Top 100 Markets," January 1998.

Nonfiction: Uses articles on all subjects of interest to women—family life, childrearing, education, homemaking, money management, careers, family health, work and leisure activities. Also interested in fresh, dramatic narratives of women's lives and concerns. "These must be lively to read with a high emotional content." Length: 500-1,500 words, depending on material. Payment varies depending on length, type, writer, and whether it's for regional or national use, but rates are high. Pays a bonus fee in addition to regular rate for articles based on writer's idea (as opposed to assigned story.) Bonus fee is an additional 20% of fee (up to $500). Pays the expenses of writers on confirmed assignment. "We no longer accept unsolicited manuscripts except for backtalk essays of 750 words—and cannot return or be responsible for those that are sent to us."
Columns/Departments: "We welcome short (750 words), thought-provoking spirited essays on controversial topics for Back Talk page. We prefer to cover significant issues that concern a large number of women and families rather than the slight or trivial or those that affect only a few. Essays are usually based on personal experience and always written in the first person, but they must have reader identification." Submit completed essays only, no queries, with SASE. **Pays $2,000.**
Fillers: Neighbors columns also **pay $75/each** for brief practical suggestions on homemaking, childrearing and relationships. Address to the editor of the section.
Tips: "Our primary need is for ideas with broad appeal that can be featured on the cover. These include diet stories, organizing tips and money saving information. We're buying more short pieces. Submissions must be double spaced and must include a SASE. Faxes and e-mails will *not* be read."

$ $ WOMAN'S LIFE, A Publication of Woman's Life Insurance Society, 1338 Military St., P.O. Box 5020, Port Huron MI 48061-5020. (313)985-5191, ext. 29. Fax: (810)985-6881. Editor: Janice U. Whipple. **Contact:** Patricia J. Samar, director of communications. **30% freelance written.** Works only with published/established writers. Quarterly magazine published for a primarily female-membership to help them care for themselves and their families. Estab. 1892. Circ. 32,000. Pays on publication. Publishes ms an average of 1 year after acceptance. Byline given. Not copyrighted. Buys one-time, simultaneous and second serial (reprint) rights. Submit seasonal material 6 months in advance. Accepts simultaneous submissions. Reports in 1 year (usually less). Sample copy for 9×12 SASE with 4 first-class stamps. Writer's guidelines for #10 SASE.

Nonfiction: Looking primarily for general interest stories for women aged 25-44 regarding physical, mental and emotional health and fitness; and financial/fiscal health and fitness. "We would like to see more creative financial pieces that are directed at women. Also interested in creative interesting stories about marketing life insurance and annuities to the women's market." **Buys 4-10 mss/year.** Send complete ms. Length: 1,000-2,000 words. **Pays $150-500/ms.**

Reprints: Send tearsheet or photocopy of article or send typed ms with rights for sale noted and information about when and where ms previously appeared. Pays 15% of amount paid for an original article.

Photos: Only interested in photos included with ms. Model release and identification of subjects required.

Tips: "We have begun more clearly defining the focus of our magazine. We receive far too many stories from people who clearly ignore the information in this listing and/or our writer's guidelines. No more stories about Tippy the Spotted Pig, please!"

N $ $ WOMAN'S OWN, Harris Publications, Inc., 1115 Broadway, 8th Floor, New York NY 10010. (212)807-7100. Fax: (212)627-4678. E-mail: womansown@aol.com. Website: http://woman'sown.com. **Contact:** Lynn Varacalli, editor-in-chief. **30% freelance written**. Consumer magazine published 8 times a year. "Woman's Own is a self-improvement/lifestyles magazine for women 25-45. It is a service publication which offers advice, inspiration and tips on relationships, self esteem, beauty, health and jobs." Estab. 1993. Circ. 200,000. Pays on publication. Publishes ms an average of 2 months after acceptance. Bylines given. Offers 25% kill fee. Buys first North American serial rights, one-time rights, and second serial (reprint) rights. Editorial lead time 4 months. Submit seasonal material 5 months in advance. Accepts simultaneous submissions. Reports in 3 weeks on queries; 1 month on mss. Sample copy for cost $2.95. Writer's guidelines for #10 SASE.

Nonfiction: Book excerpts, inspirational, interview/profile, personal experience, travel. No fiction, poetry, recipes or humor. **Buys 30 mss/year**. Query with published clips or send complete ms. Length: 900-2,000 words. **Pays $350 minimum for assigned articles; $250 for unsolicited articles**. Pays expenses of writers on assignment.

Reprints: Accepts previously published submissions.

Photos: State availability of or send photo with submission. Reviews transparencies and prints. Negotiates payment individually. Captions, model releases required. Buys one-time rights.

Columns/Departments: Women Making a Difference (real women entrepreneurs or women who overcome obstacles to find success), 100-250 words; Money Matters (saving money, ideas, best ideas), 900-1,200 words. **Buys 10 mss/year**. Query with published clips or send complete ms. **Pays $100-300**.

Tips: "Be very specific, very narrowly focused about what you want to write about. Keep queries concise. Do not try to oversell an idea. If it's good, it'll sell itself."

N $ WOMEN ALIVE, Encouraging Excellence in Holy Living, Women Alive Inc., P.O. Box 4683, Overland Park KS 66204. Phone/fax: (913)649-8583. Website: http://www.womenalivemagazine.org. Managing Editor: Jeanette Littleton. **Contact**: Aletha Hinthorn, editor. **50% freelance written.** Bimonthly magazine covering Christian living. "*Women Alive* encourages and equips women to live holy lives through teaching them to live out Scripture." Estab. 1984. Circ. 3,500. Pays on publication. Publishes ms an average of 6 months after acceptance. Byline given. Buys first North American serial, first, one-time, second serial (reprint) or simultaneous rights. Editorial lead time 4 months. Submit seasonal material 6 months in advance. Accepts simultaneous submissions. Reports in 4-6 weeks on mss. Sample copy for 9×12 SAE with 4 first-class stamps. Writer's guidelines for #10 SASE.

Nonfiction: Book excerpts, how-to, inspirational, opinion, personal experience, religious. **Buys 20 mss/year.** Send complete ms. Length: 900-1,800 words. **Pays $15-50.**

Reprints: Send typed ms with rights for sale noted and information about when and where the article previously appeared.

Photos: State availability of photos with submission. Offers no additional payment for photos accepted with ms.

MARKETS THAT WERE listed in the 1998 edition of *Writer's Market* but do not appear this year are listed in the General Index with a notation explaining why they were omitted.

Trade, Technical and Professional Journals

Many writers who pick up a *Writer's Market* for the first time do so with the hope of selling an article or story to one of the popular, high-profile consumer magazines found on newsstands and in bookstores. Many of those writers are surprised to find an entire world of magazine publishing that exists outside the realm of commercial magazines and that they may have never known about—trade journals. Writers who *have* discovered trade journals have found a market that offers the chance to publish regularly in subject areas they find interesting, editors who are typically more accessible than their commercial counterparts and pay rates that rival those of the big-name magazines.

Trade journal is the general term for any publication focusing on a particular occupation or industry. Other terms used to describe the different types of trade publications are business, technical and professional journals. They are read by truck drivers, brick layers, farmers, fishermen, heart surgeons—let's not forget butchers, bakers, and candlestick makers—and just about everyone else working in a trade or profession. Trade periodicals are sharply angled to the specifics of the professions they report on. They offer business-related news, features and service articles that will foster their readers' professional development. A beautician reads *American Salon* to keep up with developments in hair care and cosmetics as well as business management. Readers of *Wine Business Monthly* find the latest news and information about viticulture.

Trade magazine editors tell us their readers are a knowledgeable and highly interested audience. Writers for trade magazines have to either possess knowledge about the field in question or be able to report it accurately from interviews with those who do. Writers who have or can develop a good grasp of a specialized body of knowledge will find trade magazine editors who are eager to hear from them. And since good writers with specialized knowledge are a somewhat rare commodity, trade editors tend, more than typical consumer magazine editors, to cultivate ongoing relationships with writers. If you can prove yourself as a writer who "delivers," you will be paid back with frequent assignments and regular paychecks.

An ideal way to begin your foray into trade journals is to write for those that report on your present profession. Whether you've been teaching dance, farming or working as a paralegal, begin by familiarizing yourself with the magazines that serve your occupation. After you've read enough issues to have a feel for the kinds of pieces they run, approach the editors with your own article ideas. If you don't have experience in a profession but can demonstrate an ability to understand (and write about) the intricacies and issues of a particular trade that interests you, editors will still be willing to hear from you.

Photographs help increase the value of most stories for trade journals. If you can provide photos, mention that in your query or send copies. Since selling photos with a story usually means a bigger paycheck, it is worth any freelancer's time to develop basic camera skills.

Query a trade journal as you would a consumer magazine. Most trade editors like to discuss an article with a writer first and will sometimes offer names of helpful sources. Mention any direct experience you may have in the industry in your cover letter. Send a resume and clips if they show you have some background or related experience in the subject area. Read each listing carefully for additional submission guidelines.

To stay abreast of new trade magazines starting up, watch for news in *Folio* and *Advertising Age* magazines. Another source for information about trade publications is the *Business Publica-*

tion Advertising Source, published by Standard Rate and Data Service (SRDS) and available in most libraries. Designed primarily for people who buy ad space, the volume provides names and addresses of thousands of trade journals, listed by subject matter.

Information on trade publications listed in the previous edition of *Writer's Market* but not included in this edition can be found in the General Index.

ADVERTISING, MARKETING AND PR

Trade journals for advertising executives, copywriters and marketing and public relations professionals are listed in this category. Those whose main focus is the advertising and marketing of specific products, such as home furnishings, are classified under individual product categories. Journals for sales personnel and general merchandisers can be found in the Selling and Merchandising category.

N $ $ $ **BRAND PACKAGING**, Independent Publishing Co., 210 S. Fifth St., St. Charles IL 60174. (630)377-0100. Fax: (630)377-1688. E-mail: editor@brandpackaging.com. Website: http://www.brandpackaging.com. **Contact:** James W. Peters, editor. **15% freelance written.** "Bimonthly magazine about how packaging can be a marketing tool." Estab. 1997. Circ. 35,000. **Pays on acceptance.** Publishes ms an average of 2 months after acceptance. Byline sometimes given. Buys all rights. Editorial lead time 6 months. Sample copy and writer's guidelines free.
Nonfiction: How-to, interview/profile, new product. **Buys 4 mss/year.** Query. Length: 1,200-2,500 words. **Pays $350-1,250.** Pays expenses of writers on assignment.
Photos: State availability of photos with submission. Reviews 35mm transparencies and 4×5 prints. Negotiates payment individually. Captions required. Buys all rights.
Tips: "Be knowledgeable on marketing techniques and be able to grasp packaging techniques."

$ **DECA DIMENSIONS**, 1908 Association Dr., Reston VA 20191. (703)860-5000. Fax: (703)860-4013. E-mail: carol_lund@deca.org. Website: http://www.DECA.org. **Contact:** Carol Lund, editor. **30% freelance written.** Bimonthly magazine covering professional development, business, vocational training. "*Deca Dimensions* is the membership magazine for the Association of Marketing Students—primarily ages 16-20 in all 50 states and Canada. The magazine is delivered through the classroom. Students are interested in developing professional, leadership and career skills." Estab. 1947. Circ. 145,000. Pays on publication. Byline given. Buys first rights and second serial (reprint) rights. Editorial lead time 3 months. Submit seasonal material 4 months in advance. Accepts simultaneous submissions. Sample copy free.
Nonfiction: Essays, general interest, how-to (get jobs, start business, plan for college, etc.), interview/profile (business leads), personal experience (working). **Buys 4 mss/year.** Send complete ms. Length: 800-1,000 words. **Pays $125 for assigned articles; $100 for unsolicited articles.**
Reprints: Send photocopy of article and information about when and where the article previously appeared. Pays 85% of amount paid for an original article.
Photos: State availability of photos with submission. Reviews negatives, transparencies, prints. Offers $15-25/photo. Captions required. Buys one-time rights.
Columns/Departments: Professional Development leadership. **Buys 4 mss/year.** Send complete ms. **Pays $75-100.** Length: 200-500 words.
Fillers: Anecdotes, facts, short humor. Length: 400-600 words. **Pays $25-50.**

$ $ **MARKETING TOOLS, Information-based Tactics and Techniques**, American Demographics, 127 W. State St., Ithaca NY 14850. Fax: (607)273-3196. E-mail: claudia_montague@marketingtools.com. Website: http://www.marketingtools.com. **Contact:** Claudia Montague, editor. **85% freelance written.** Magazine published 10 times/year. "*Marketing Tools* is a magazine for professionals who deal with customer information—consumer and business-to-business. Our focus is on the technology used to gather, analyze, and act on customer data, as opposed to the data itself." Estab. 1994. Circ. 25,000. **Pays on acceptance.** Publishes ms an average of 2 months after acceptance. Byline given. Offers 50% kill fee. Rights shared with author. Editorial lead time 5 months. Submit seasonal material 1 year in advance. Sample copy for 9×12 SAE. Writer's guidelines for #10 SASE.
Nonfiction: Book excerpts, essays, how-to, interview/profile, new product, technical. **Buys 100 mss/year.** Query with published clips. Length: 750-4,000 words. **Pays $200-800.** Sometimes pays expenses of writers on assignment.
Reprints: Send tearsheet or typed ms with rights for sale noted and information about when and where the article previously appeared. Pay varies.
Photos: State availability of photos with submission. Reviews prints. Negotiates payment individually. Captions, model releases, identification of subjects required. Buys one-time rights.
Columns/Departments: Marketing Research (collecting, analyzing data); Database/Direct Marketing (collecting,

managing, using data); Business-to-business (special concerns of B2B companies); all 1,500 words. **Buys 50 mss/year.** Query. **Pays $350-400.**

Tips: "Well-written queries from writers with some knowledge/experience in database or direct marketing are always welcome. Do NOT telephone to pitch a story idea. We stipulate in our writer's agreement that we reserve the right to reproduce work electronically—i.e., to upload it to our website."

MEDIA INC., Pacific Northwest Media, Marketing and Creative Services News, P.O. Box 24365, Seattle WA 98124-0365. (206)382-9220. Fax: (206)382-9437. E-mail: media@media-inc.com. Website: http://www.media-inc.com. Publisher: Richard K. Woltjer. **Contact:** Beth Taylor, editor. **20% freelance written.** Monthly tabloid covering Northwest US media, advertising, marketing and creative-service industries. Audience is Northwest ad agencies, marketing professionals, media and creative-service professionals. Estab. 1987. Circ. 10,000. Byline given. Reports in 1 month. Sample copy for 9×12 SAE with 6 first-class stamps.

Tips: "It is best if writers live in the Pacific Northwest and can report on local news and events in Media Inc.'s areas of business coverage."

$ $ RESPONSE TV, The Information Leader for the Electronic Merchandising Industry, Advanstar Communications, 201 E. Sandpointe, Suite 600, Santa Ana CA 92707. (800)854-3112. Fax: (714)513-8482. E-mail: dnagel@advanstar.com. Website: http://www.responsetv.com. **Contact:** David Nagel, editor. **25% freelance written.** "*Response TV* is a monthly trade journal for advertising agencies, their clients and marketers who use television to sell products and services or who use television as a means of generating ideas. We look for business writers with experience in advertising, marketing, direct marketing, telemarketing, TV production, cable TV industry and home shopping." Estab. 1992. Circ. 21,000. **Pays on acceptance.** Byline given. Offers 50% kill fee. Buys all rights. Editorial lead time 1 month. Submit seasonal material 3 months in advance. Reports in 2 weeks on queries, 1 month on mss. Sample copy free. Writer's guidelines free from website.

Nonfiction: How-to (market products via direct response TV, save money, produce infomercials); interview/profile (ad agency executives). **Buys 20 mss/year.** Query with published clips. Length: 2,000-4,000 words. **Pays 25-30¢/word.** Pays writers with contributor copies or other premiums when the article comes from an industry contributor.

Photos: State availability of photos with submission. Reviews contact sheets, negatives, transparencies. Negotiates payment individually. Model releases, identification of subjects required. Buys one-time rights.

Tips: "Familiarity with topics such as home shopping, direct response TV, internet commerce and infomercials. General interest in advertising and marketing. Send a résumé and 3-5 outstanding clips. Obey our style rules and submit a clean finished product, and we'll use you again."

$ $ SIGNCRAFT, The Magazine for the Commercial Sign Shop, SignCraft Publishing Co., Inc., P.O. Box 60031, Fort Myers FL 33906. (941)939-4644. **Contact:** Tom McIltrot, editor. **10% freelance written.** Bimonthly magazine of the sign industry. "Like any trade magazine, we need material of direct benefit to our readers. We can't afford space for material of marginal interest." Estab. 1980. Circ. 19,500. Pays on publication. Publishes ms an average of 6 months after acceptance. Byline given. Offers negotiable kill fee. Buys first North American serial or all rights. Reports in 1 month. Sample copy and writer's guidelines for $3.

Nonfiction: Interviews, profiles. "All articles should be directly related to quality commercial signs. If you are familiar with the sign trade, we'd like to hear from you." **Buys 20 mss/year.** Query with or without published clips. Length: 500-2,000 words. **Pays up to $350.**

Reprints: Accepts previously published submissions.

$ SIGNS OF THE TIMES, The Industry Journal Since 1906, ST Publications, Dept. WM, 407 Gilbert Ave., Cincinnati OH 45202-2285. (513)421-2050. Fax: (513)421-5144. E-mail: zhyder@stpubs.com. Website: http://www.signweb.com. **Contact:** Zakia Hyder, managing editor. **15-30% freelance written.** "We are willing to use more freelancers." Monthly magazine special buyer's guide between November and December issues. Estab. 1906. Circ. 16,000. Pays on publication. Publishes ms an average of 3 months after acceptance. Byline given. Buys variable rights. Accepts simultaneous and previously published submissions. Reports in 3 months. Free sample copy and writer's guidelines for 9×12 SAE with 10 first-class stamps.

Nonfiction: Historical/nostalgic (regarding the sign industry); how-to (carved signs, goldleaf, etc.); interview/profile (focusing on either a signshop or a specific project); photo feature (query first); and technical (sign engineering, etc.). This publication is looking for more business-related articles and short profiles. Nothing "nonspecific on signs, an example being a photo essay on 'signs I've seen.' We are a trade journal with specific audience interests." **Buys 15-20 mss/year.** Query with clips. **Pays $150-500.** Sometimes pays the expenses of writers on assignment.

Reprints: Send tearsheet of article or typed ms with rights for sale noted and information about when and where the article previously appeared. Payment is negotiated.

Photos: Send photos with ms. "Sign industry-related photos only. We sometimes accept photos with funny twists or misspellings."

Fillers: Open to queries; request rates.

N $ SUBSCRIBE, Ideas & Marketing Tips for Newsletter Publishers, Page One, P.O. Box 156, Spring City PA 19475. (610) 948-6031. Fax: (610)948-6081. E-mail: foodwriter@aol.com. Website: http://www.food-journalist.net. **Contact:** Lynn Kerrigan, editor. **25% freelance written.** Bimonthly trade newsletter covering newsletter marketing, editing and publishing. Estab. 1997. Circ. 1,500. Pays on publication. Publishes ms an average of 3 months after acceptance. Byline given. Buys first North American serial rights, first rights, one-time rights, or second serial (reprint) rights. Editorial lead time 3 months. Accepts simultaneous submissions. Reports in 1 month on queries; 2 months on mss. Sample copy for $7; writer's guidelines free.

Nonfiction: Book excerpts, essays, how-to, interview/profile, new product. **Buys 6 mss/year.** Send complete ms. Length: 200-1,000 words. **Pays $25.**

Reprints: Accepts previously published submissions.

ART, DESIGN AND COLLECTIBLES

The businesses of art, art administration, architecture, environmental/package design and antiques/collectibles are covered in these listings. Art-related topics for the general public are located in the Consumer Art and Architecture category. Antiques and collectibles magazines for enthusiasts are listed in Consumer Hobby and Craft. (Listings of markets looking for freelance artists to do artwork can be found in *Artist's and Graphic Designer's Market*, Writer's Digest Books.)

$ $ $ ADOBE MAGAZINE, Adobe Systems Inc., 411 First Ave. S., Seattle WA 98104-2871. Fax: (206)470-7106. E-mail: magazine.editor@adobe.com. Editor-in-Chief: Christine Yarrow. **Contact:** Tamis Nordling, editor. **60% freelance written.** Quarterly magazine covering graphic design, publishing, Adobe software. "Mission: To help users of Adobe products get their work done better and faster, and to entertain, educate, and inspire along the way." Estab. 1989. Circ. 600,000. **Pays on acceptance.** Publishes ms an average of 3 months after acceptance. Byline given. Offers 25% kill fee. Buys all rights. Editorial lead time 5 months. Sample copy free on request.

Nonfiction: How-to, humor, interview/profile, technical. **Buys 30-40 mss/year.** Query with published clips. *No unsolicited mss.* Length: 500-2,500 words. **Pays $300-1,500.**

Columns/Departments: How-to (technical guide to problem solving), 1,500-3,000 words. Pay varies.

$ THE APPRAISERS STANDARD, New England Appraisers Association, 5 Gill Terrace, Ludlow VT 05149-1003. (802)228-7444. E-mail: llt44@ludl.tds.net. **Contact:** Linda L. Tucker, publisher/editor. **50% freelance written.** Works with a small number of new/unpublished writers each year. Bimonthly publication on the appraisals of antiques, art, collectibles, jewelry, coins, stamps and real estate. "The writer should be extremely knowledgeable on the subject, and the article should be written with appraisers in mind, with prices quoted for objects, good pictures and descriptions of articles being written about." Estab. 1980. Circ. 1,300. Pays on publication. Publishes ms an average of 1 year after acceptance. Short bio and byline given. Buys first and simultaneous rights. Submit seasonal material 2 months in advance. Accepts simultaneous submissions. Reports in 1 month on queries, 2 months on mss. Sample copy for 9×12 SAE with 78¢ postage. Writer's guidelines for #10 SASE.

Nonfiction: Interview/profile, personal experience, technical, travel. "All geared toward professional appraisers." Query with or without published clips, or send complete ms. Length: 700 words. **Pays $50.**

Reprints: Send typed ms with rights for sale noted and information about when and where the article previously appeared. Pays 75% of amount paid for an original article.

Photos: Send photos with submission. Reviews negatives and prints. Offers no additional payment for photos accepted with ms. Identification of subjects required. Buys one-time rights.

Tips: "Interviewing members of the association for articles, reviewing, shows and large auctions are all ways for writers who are not in the field to write articles for us."

N $ $ ART MATERIALS RETAILER, Fahy-Williams Publishing, 171 Reed St., P.O. Box 1080, Geneva NY 14456-8080. (315)489-0458. Fax: (315)781-6820. E-mail: fahwill@epix.net. **Contact:** Tina Manzer, editor. **50% freelance written.** Quarterly trade magazine. Estab. 1998. Pays on publication. Byline given. Buys one-time rights. Editorial lead time 2 months. Submit seasonal material 3 months in advance. Accepts simultaneous submissions. Reports in 3 weeks on queries; 3 months on mss. Sample copy and writer's guidelines free.

Nonfiction: Book excerpts, how-to, interview/profile, personal experience. **Buys 10 mss/year.** Send complete ms. Length: 1,500-3,000. **Pays $50-250.** Sometimes pays expenses of writers on assignment.

Photos: State availability of photos with submission. Reviews transparencies. Offers no additional payment for photos accepted with ms. Identification of subjects required. Buys one time rights.

Fillers: Anecdotes, facts, newsbreaks. **Buys 5/year.** Length: 500-1,500 words. **Pays $50-125.**

Tips: "We like to review mss rather than queries. Artwork (photos, drawings, etc.) is real plus. We enjoy (our readers enjoy) practical, nuts and bolts, news-you-can-use articles."

N ART PLUS, Reproducible Resource for Christian Communicators, Mission Media, Inc., P.O. Box 4710, Sarasota FL 34230-4710. (941)955-2950. Fax: (941)955-5723. E-mail: mail@mmi-art.com. **Contact:** Wayne Hepburn, editor. **100% freelance written.** Quarterly magazine and computer disk for churches, schools and ministries. "Our readers are reproducing our content in their bulletins and newsletters to church members." Estab. 1983. Circ. 3,000.

Pays on acceptance. Publishes ms an average of 6 months after acceptance. Byline sometimes given. Buys all rights. Accepts simultaneous submissions. Reports in 3 months. Sample copy for 9×12 SAE and 4 first-class stamps. Writer's guidelines for #10 SASE.

Nonfiction: Humor, inspirational. **Buys 20 mss/year.** Send complete ms. Length: 100 words. **Pays $5-25.**

Poetry: Traditional, rhyming poetry only. Buys 12-20 poems/year. Submit maximum 10 poems. Length: 4-24 lines. Pays $10-25.

Fillers: Anecdotes, short humor. **Buys 50/year.** Length: 1-25 words. **Pays $5-10.**

$ $ CONTEMPORARY STONE DESIGN, Business News Publishing Co., 299 Market St., Suite 320, Saddle Brook NJ 07663. (201)291-9001. Fax: (201)291-9002. E-mail: stoneworld@aol.com. Website: http://www.stoneworld.com. Publisher: Alex Bachrach. **Contact:** Michael Reis, editor or Jennifer Adams, managing editor. Quarterly magazine covering the full range of stone design and architecture—from classic and historic spaces to current projects. Estab. 1995. Circ. 14,000. Pays on publication. Publishes ms an average of 3 months after acceptance. Byline given. Buys first rights only. Submit seasonal material 6 months in advance. Reports in 3 weeks. Sample copy for $10.

Nonfiction: Overall features on a certain aspect of stone design or specific articles on individual architectural projects. Interview/profile of a prominent architect/designer or firm. Photo feature, technical, architectural design. **Buys 8 mss/year.** Query with published clips. Length: 1,500-3,000 words. **Pays $6/column inch.** Pays expenses of writers on assignment.

Photos: State availability of photos with submission. Reviews transparencies and prints. Pays $10/photo accepted with ms. Captions and identification of subjects required. Buys one-time rights.

Columns/Departments: Upcoming Events (for the architecture and design community); Stone Classics (featuring historic architecture); question and answer session with a prominent architect or designer. 1,500-2,000 words. **Pays $6/inch.**

Tips: "The visual aspect of the magazine is key, so architectural photography is a must for any story. Cover the entire project, but focus on the stonework and how it relates to the rest of the space. Architects are very helpful in describing their work and often provide excellent quotes. As a relatively new magazine, we are looking for freelance submissions and are open to new feature topics. This is a narrow subject, however, so it's a good idea to speak with an editor before submitting anything."

N $ $ $ DESIGN CONCEPTS, An Interior Design Magazine from Pier 1 Imports, Imagination Publishing, 820 W. Jackson, Suite 450, Chicago IL 60657. (312)627-1020. Fax: (312)627-1105. E-mail: imagepub@aol.com. **Contact:** Rebecca Rolfes, editor. **50% freelance written.** Semiannual magazine covering residential interior design. "Our readers form one of largest data bases of professional interior designers. Writing must be at a level of expertise acceptable to the audience. Availability of high-quality color photography very important." Estab. 1996. Circ. 30,000. Pays on publication. Publishes ms an average of 4 months after acceptance. Byline given. Offers 33% kill fee. Buys first North American serial rights. Editorial lead time 4 months. Submit seasonal material 6 months in advance. Reports in 6 weeks on queries; 1 month on mss. Sample copy for $1.70

Nonfiction: Book excerpts, interview/profile. **Buys 6-8 mss/year.** Query. Length: 800-1,200 words. **Pays $300-1,000.** Pays expenses of writers on assignment.

Photos: State availability of photos with submission. Buys one-time rights.

N DESIGN JOURNAL, Design Publications, 1431 7th St., #205, Santa Monica CA 90401. Fax: (310)394-0966. **Contact:** John Moses, editor. **100% freelance written.** Monthly trade magazine covering architecture & design. Estab. 1988. Circ. 30,000. Pays net 30 days after final. Byline given. Buys one-time rights. Editorial lead time 2 months. Submit seasonal material 2 months in advance. Accepts simultaneous submissions. Sample copy and writer guidelines free.

Nonfiction: Sometimes pays expenses of writers on assignment.

Reprints: Accepts previously published submissions.

Photos: Send photos with submission. Negotiates payment individually. Captions, model releases and identification of subjects required. Buys all rights.

$ $ HOW, The Bottomline Design Magazine, F&W Publications, Inc., 1507 Dana Ave., Cincinnati OH 45207-1005. (513)531-2222. Fax: (513)531-2902. E-mail: editorial@howdesign.com. Website: http://www.howdesign.com. Contact: Kathleen Reinmann, editor. **75% freelance written.** Bimonthly graphic design and illustration business journal. "*HOW* gives a behind-the-scenes look at not only *how* the world's best graphic designers and illustrators conceive and create their work, but *why* they did it that way. We also focus on the *business* side of design—how to run a profitable studio." Estab. 1985. Circ. 38,000. **Pays on acceptance.** Byline given. Buys first North American serial rights. Reports in 6 weeks. Sample copy for cover price plus $1.50 (cover price varies per issue). Writer's guidelines for #10 SASE.

Nonfiction: Features: interview/profile, business tips, new products, environmental graphics, digital design, hot design markets. Special issues: Self-Promotion Annual (September/October); Business Annual (November/December); International Annual of Design (March/April); Creativity/Paper/Stock Photography (May/June); Digital Design Annual (July/August). No how-to articles for beginning artists or fine-art-oriented articles. **Buys 40 mss/year.** Query with published clips and samples of subject's work (artwork or design). Length: 1,500-2,000 words. **Pays $400-700.** Sometimes pays expenses of writers on assignment.

Photos: State availability of artwork with submission. Reviews 35mm or larger transparencies (dupes only) or digital files. Captions are required. Buys one-time rights.

Columns/Departments: Marketplace (focuses on lucrative fields for designers/illustrators); Production (ins, outs and tips on production); Interactivity (behind the scenes of electronically produced design projects); Software Review and Workspace (takes an inside look at the design of creatives' studios). Other columns include Web Workshop (examines the web-design process) and Bottomline (business issues that impact design studios). **Buys 35 mss/year.** Query with published clips. Length: 1,200-1,500 words. **Pays $250-400.**

Tips: "We look for writers who can recognize graphic designers on the cutting-edge of their industry, both creatively and business-wise. Writers must have an eye for detail, and be able to relay *HOW*'s step-by-step approach in an interesting, concise manner—without omitting any details. Showing you've done your homework on a subject—and that you can go beyond asking 'those same old questions'—will give you a big advantage."

$ $ LETTER ARTS REVIEW, 1624 24th Ave. SW, Norman OK 73072. (405)364-8794. Fax: (405)364-8914. E-mail: letterarts@netplus.net. Website: http://www.letterarts.com. Contact: Karyn L. Gilman, publisher/editor. **98% freelance written.** Eager to work with new/unpublished writers with calligraphic expertise and language skills. Quarterly magazine on lettering and related book arts, both historical and contemporary in nature. Estab. 1982. Circ. 5,500. Pays on publication. Publishes ms an average of 9 months after acceptance. Byline given. Offers 20% kill fee. Buys first rights. Reports in 3 months. Sample copy for 9×12 SAE with 7 first-class stamps. Free writer's guidelines.

Nonfiction: Interview/profile, opinion, contemporary, historical. **Buys 50 mss/year.** Query with or without published clips, or send complete ms. Length: 1,000-2,000 words. **Pays $50-250 for assigned articles; $25-200 for unsolicited articles.** Sometimes pays the expenses of writers on assignment.

Photos: State availability of photos with submission. Reviews contact sheets, negatives, transparencies and prints. Pays agreed upon cost. Captions and identification of subjects required. Buys one-time rights.

Columns/Departments: Book Reviews, Viewpoint (critical), 500-1,500 words; Ms. (discussion of manuscripts in collections), 1,000-2,000 words; Profile (contemporary calligraphic figure), 1,000-2,000 words; exhibition reviews; font reviews. Query. **Pays $50-200.**

Tips: "*Letter Arts Review*'s primary objective is to encourage the exchange of ideas on calligraphy and the lettering arts—its past and present as well as trends for the future. Historical research, typography, graphic design, fine press and artists' books, and other related aspects of the lettering arts are welcomed. Third person is preferred, however first person will be considered if appropriate. Writer should realize that this is a specialized audience."

$ THE MIDATLANTIC ANTIQUES MAGAZINE, Monthly Guide to Antiques, Art, Auctions & Collectibles, Henderson Newspapers, Inc., P.O. Box 908, Henderson NC 27536-0908. (919)492-4001. Fax: (919)430-0125. **Contact:** Lydia Stainback, editor. **65% freelance written.** Monthly tabloid covering antiques, art, auctions and collectibles. "The *MidAtlantic* reaches dealers, collectors, antique shows and auction houses primarily on the East Coast, but circulation includes 48 states and Europe." Estab. 1984. Circ. 14,000. Pays on publication. Byline given. Buys first rights. Submit seasonal material 6 months in advance. Reports in 1 month on queries; 2 months on mss. Sample copy and writer's guidelines for 10×13 SAE with 10 first-class stamps.

Nonfiction: Book excerpts, historical/nostalgic, how-to (choose an antique; collect; sell your collection; identify market trends), interview/profile, personal experience, photo feature, technical. **Buys 20-30 mss/year.** Query. Length: 800-2,000 words. **Pays $50-125.** Trades for advertising space. Rarely pays expenses of writers on assignment.

Photos: Send color photos with submission. Offers no additional payment for photos accepted with ms. Identification of subjects required. Buys one-time rights.

Tips: "Please contact by mail first, but a writer may call with specific ideas after initial contact. Looking for writers who have extensive knowledge in specific areas of antiques. Articles should be educational in nature. We are also interested in how-to articles, i.e., how to choose antiques to collect; how to sell your collection and get the most for it; looking for articles that focus on future market trends. We want writers who are active in the antiques business and can predict good investments. (Articles with photographs are given preference.) We are looking for people who are not only knowledgeable, but can write well."

N $ $ SIGN BUILDER ILLUSTRATED, America's How-To Sign Magazine, Journalistic Inc., 4905 Pine Cone Dr., Suite 2, Durham NC 27707. (919)489-1416. Fax: (919)489-4707. E-mail: jhyatt@jayi.com. Website: http://www.signshop.com. **Contact:** James Hyatt, editor. **40% freelance written.** Bimonthly trade magazine covering sign and graphic industry. "We provide how-to articles and information on all aspects of sign-making." Estab. 1987. Circ. 14,000. **Pays on acceptance.** Publishes ms an average of 3 months after acceptance. Byline given. Offers 25% kill fee. Buys all rights. Editorial lead time 4 months. Submit seasonal material 5 months in advance. Sample copy for 9×12 SASE and $1.25 postage; writer's guidelines free.

Nonfiction: Essays, how-to, interview/profile, new product, personal experience, photo feature, technical. **Buys 3-6 mss/year.** Query with published clips. Length: 1,000-3,000 words. **Pays $300-600.**

Reprints: Accepts previously published submissions.

Photos: Send photos with submission. Reviews contact sheets, negatives, transparencies. Negotiates payment individually. Captions and identification of subjects required. Buys one time rights.

Columns and Departments: All-American Sign Shop (profiles of sign shops), 1,500-2,500 words; Signs Over . . . (geographic samples of signage), 1,000 words. **Buys 3-9 mss/year.** Query with published clips. **Pays $300-600.**

N $ $ TEXAS ARCHITECT, Texas Society of Architects, 816 Congress Ave., Suite 970, Austin TX 78701. (512)478-7386. Fax: (512)478-0528. E-mail: txarch@txarch.com. Website: http://www.txarch.com. Executive Editor: Susan Williamson. **Contact:** Kelly Roberson, managing editor. Publisher: Canan Yetmen. **30% freelance written** by unpaid members of the professional society. Bimonthly trade journal of architecture and architects of Texas. "*Texas Architect* is a highly visually-oriented look at Texas architecture, design and urban planning. Articles cover varied subtopics within architecture. Readers are mostly architects and related building professionals." Estab. 1951. Circ. 12,000. Pays on publication. Publishes ms an average of 3 months after acceptance. Byline given. Buys one-time rights, all rights or makes work-for-hire assignments. Submit seasonal material 4 months in advance. Reports in 6 weeks. Sample copy and writer's guidelines free.

Nonfiction: Book reviews, interview/profile, photo feature, technical. Query with published clips. Length: 100-2,000 words. **Pays $50-500 for assigned articles.**

Photos: Send photos with submission. Reviews contact sheets, 35mm or 4×5 transparencies and 4×5 prints. Offers no additional payment for photos accepted with ms. Identification of subjects required. Buys one-time rights.

Columns/Departments: News (timely reports on architectural issues, projects and people); 100-500 words. **Buys 10 mss/year.** Query with published clips. **Pays $50-100.**

AUTO AND TRUCK

These publications are geared to automobile, motorcycle and truck dealers; professional truck drivers; service department personnel; or fleet operators. Publications for highway planners and traffic control experts are listed in the Government and Public Service category.

N $ ARKANSAS TRUCKING REPORT, Official Journal of the Arkansas Motor Carriers Association, Belmont Publishing Corporation, P.O. Box 3413, Little Rock AR 72203-3413. (501)666-0500. E-mail: roadnews@aristotle.net. **Contact:** Emily Roberts, managing editor. **20% freelance written.** "Bimonthly magazine covering issues related to trucking industry, particularly in Arkansas. News-focused, with analytical emphasis. Audience primarily trucking and related industry managers." Estab. 1996. Circ. 1,300. Pays on publication. Publishes ms an average of 1 month after acceptance. Byline given. Negotiates kill fee. Makes work-for-hire assignments. Editorial lead time 2 months. Accepts simultaneous submissions. Reports in 1 week on phone or e-mail queries. Sample copy for 9×12 SAE and $1.24.

Nonfiction: How-to (business and trucking management), interview/profile, news; government/regulatory analysis. Query only; no mss. **Buys 6 mss/year.** Query (no mss). Length: 450-1,300 words. **Pays $25-150.** Sometimes pays expenses of writers on assignment.

Photos: State availability of photos with query. Reviews 4×6 prints. Negotiates payment individually. Captions and identification of subjects required. Buys all rights.

Tips: "We seek queries for timely news stories about issues in the trucking industry, specifically as such news relates to Arkansas trucking companies. Telephone or e-mail queries strongly preferred."

$ AUTO GLASS JOURNAL, Grawin Publications, Inc., 303 Harvard E., Suite 101, P.O. Box 12099, Seattle WA 98102-0099. (206)322-5120. **Contact:** Jeff Martin, editor. **10% freelance written.** Prefers to work with published/established writers. Monthly magazine for the auto glass replacement industry. Includes step-by-step glass replacement procedures for current model cars and business management, industry news and trends. Estab. 1953. Circ. 5,700. **Pays on acceptance.** Publishes ms an average of 5 months after acceptance. No byline given. Buys all rights. Reports in 5 months. Sample copy for 6×9 SAE with 3 first-class stamps. Writer's guidelines for #10 SASE.

Nonfiction: Articles relating to auto glass and general business management. **Buys 12-20 mss/year.** Query with published clips. Length: 1,000-1,500 words. **Pays $50-200**, with photos.

Photos: State availability of photos. Reviews b&w contact sheets and negatives. Payment included with ms. Captions required. Buys all rights.

N $ $ INSIDE AUTOMOTIVES, Ancar Publications, Inc., 21700 Northwestern Hwy., Suite 565, Southfield MI 48075-4906. Fax: (248)557-2431. E-mail: carlak@ancarpub.com. Website: http://www.insideautomotives.com. **Contact:** Carla Kalogeridis, publisher. **25% freelance written.** Bimonthly magazine covering automotive interiors. "Our readers are OEM designers and engineers as well as material and component suppliers." Estab. 1994. Circ. 11,200. Pays on publication. Publishes ms an average of 4 months after acceptance. Byline given. Buys one-time rights. Editorial lead time 2 months. Submit seasonal material 6 months in advance. Reports in 2 weeks on queries; 1 month on mss. Sample copy and writer's guidelines free.

Nonfiction: Interview/profile, new product, technical. **Buys 10-12 mss/year.** Query. Length: 1,500 words minimum. **Pays $75-300/page.** Sometimes pays expenses of writers on assignment.

Photos: Send photos with submission. Reviews negatives, 3×5 transparencies and prints. Offers no additional payment for photos accepted with ms. Captions, identification of subjects required. Buys one-time rights.

Columns/Departments: Issue Spotlight (industry specific issue), 1,500-2,500 words; Material/Components Spotlight (current material), 1,500-2,500 words; Supplier Spotlight (tier one suppliers), 3,000 words. **Buys 5-6 mss/year.** Query. **Pays $75-300/page.**

Tips: "We are always looking for articles specific to automotive interiors. It's best to contact editorial department to check on current trends and issues. Fax queries work best. Contact publication for editorial calendar."

N NORTHWEST MOTOR, Journal for the Automotive Industry, Northwest Automotive Publishing Co., P.O. Box 46937, Seattle WA 98146-0937. (206)935-3336. Fax: (206)937-9732. E-mail: nwautopub@galaxy-7.net. **Contact:** J.B. Smith, editor. **5% freelance written.** Monthly magazine covering the automotive industry. Estab. 1909. Circ. 6,000. Pays on publication. Byline sometimes given. Offers 10% kill fee. Buys all rights. Editorial lead time 1 month. Submit seasonal material 2 months in advance. Accepts simultaneous submissions. Sample copy for $2. Writer's guidelines for #10 SASE.

Nonfiction: Book excerpts, general interest, how-to, new product, photo feature, technical. **Buys 6 mss/year.** Query. Length: 250-1,200 words. Pay varies. Sometimes pays expenses of writers on assignment.

Photos: Send photos with submission. Reviews 3×5 prints. Negotiates payment individually. Buys all rights.

Columns/Departments: Buys 4-6 mss/year. Query. Pay varies.

Fillers: Anecdotes, facts. Buys 4-9/year. Length: 15-100 words. Pay varies.

O&A MARKETING NEWS, KAL Publications Inc., 532 El Dorado St., Suite 200, Pasadena CA 91101. Fax: (626)683-0969. **Contact:** Kathy Laderman, editor. **10% freelance written.** Bimonthly tabloid. "*O&A Marketing News* is editorially directed to people engaged in the distribution, merchandising, installation and servicing of gasoline, oil, TBA, quick lube, carwash, convenience store, alternative fuel and automotive aftermarket products in the 13 Western states." Estab. 1966. Circ. 8,000. Pays on publication. Publishes ms an average of 3 months after acceptance. Byline sometimes given. Not copyrighted. Buys one-time rights. Editorial lead time 1 month. Accepts simultaneous submissions. Reports in 1 month on mss. Sample copy for $3.

Nonfiction: Exposé, interview/profile, photo feature, industry news. **Buys 20 mss/year.** Send complete ms. Length: 100-10,000 words. Pays per column-inch typeset.

Photos: State availability of photos with submission. Reviews contact sheets, prints (5×7 preferred). Offers $5/photo. Identification of subjects required. Buys one-time rights.

Fillers: Gags to be illustrated by cartoonist, short humor. **Buys 7 mss/year.** Length: 1-200 words. Pays per column-inch.

Tips: "Seeking Western industry news. We're always seeking more stories covering the more remote states such as Montana, Idaho, and Hawaii—but any timely, topical *news*-oriented stories will be considered."

$ OLD CARS, Krause Publications, 700 E. State St., Iola WI 54990. (715)445-2214. Fax: (715)445-4087. E-mail: jgunnell@www.krause.com. Website: http://www.krause.com. **Contact:** John A. Gunnell, editorial director; Chad Elmore, news director. **60% freelance written.** Weekly tabloid covering old cars. Estab. 1971. Circ. 100,000. Pays in the month after publication date. Buys perpetual but non-exclusive rights. For sample copy call circulation department. Writer's guidelines for #10 SASE.

Nonfiction: How-to, technical, auction prices realized lists. **Buys 1,000-1,200 mss/year.** Send complete ms. Length: 400-1,000 words. **Pays 3¢/word.**

Photos: Pays $5/photo. Offers no additional payment for photos accepted with ms.

Tips: "Ninety percent of our material is done by a small group of regular contributors. Many new writers break in here, but we are *usually overstocked* with material and *never* seek nostalgic or historical pieces from new authors. Our big need is for well-written items that fit odd pieces in a tabloid page layout. Budding authors should try some short, catchy items that help us fill odd-ball 'news holes' with interesting writing. Authors with good skills can work up to longer stories. A weekly keeps us too busy to answer mail and phone calls. The best queries are 'checklists' where we can quickly mark a 'yes' or 'no' to article ideas."

$ $ OVERDRIVE, The Magazine for the American Trucker, Randall Publishing Co./Overdrive, Inc., P.O. Box 3187, Tuscaloosa AL 35403-3187. (205)349-2990. Fax: (205)750-8070. E-mail: longton@overdriveonline.com. Website: http://www.overdriveonline.com. Editorial Director: Linda Longton. **Contact:** Deborah Lockridge, senior editor. **15% freelance written.** Monthly magazine for independent truckers. Estab. 1961. Circ. 115,800. Pays on publication. Publishes ms an average of 2 months after acceptance. Byline given. 10% kill fee. Buys all North American rights, including electronic rights. Reports in 2 months. Sample copy and writers' guidelines for 9×12 SASE.

Nonfiction: Essays, exposé, how-to (truck maintenance and operation), interview/profile (successful independent truckers), personal experience, photo feature, technical. All must be related to independent trucker interest. Query with or without published clips, or send complete ms. Length: 500-2,000 words. **Pays $100-600 for assigned articles; $50-500 for unsolicited articles.**

Photos: Send photos with submission. Reviews transparencies and 5×7 prints. Offers $25-50/photo. Identification of subjects required. Buys all rights.

Tips: "Talk to independent truckers. Develop a good knowledge of their concerns as small-business owners, truck drivers and individuals. We prefer articles that quote experts, people in the industry and truckers to first-person expositions on a subject. Get straight facts. Look for good material on truck safety, on effects of government regulations, and on rates and business relationships between independent truckers, brokers, carriers and shippers."

N $ PML, The Market Letter for Porsche Automobiles, PML Consulting, P.O. Box 6010, Oceanside CA 92058. (760)940-9170. Fax: (760)940-9170. E-mail: pmletter@aol.com. Website: http://www.pmletter.com. **Contact:** Phil Van Buskirk, publisher/editor. **100% freelance written.** Monthly magazine covering technical tips, personality

profiles and race coverage of Porsche automobiles. Estab. 1981. Circ. 1,500. Pays on publication. Publishes ms an average of 2 months after acceptance. Byline given. Buys one-time rights. Editorial lead time 2 months. Submit seasonal material 2 months in advance. Accepts simultaneous and previously published submissions. Reports in 2 weeks on queries; 1 month on mss. Sample copy for $5. Writer's guidelines for #10 SASE.
Nonfiction: General interest, historical/nostalgic, how-to, humor, interview/profile, new product, personal experience, photo feature, technical, travel, race results. **Buys 30-40 mss/year.** Query with published clips. Length: 500-2,000 words. **Pays $30-50 and up**, depending on length and topic. Sometimes pays expenses of writers on assignment.
Reprints: Accepts previously published submissions.
Photos: Send photos with submission. Reviews 8×10 b&w prints. Negotiates payment individually. Captions, model releases and identification of subjects required. Buys one-time rights.
Fillers: Anecdotes, facts, gags to be illustrated by cartoonist, newsbreaks, short humor. Pay negotiable.
Tips: "Check any auto-related magazine for types, styles of articles. We are looking for people doing anything unusual or interesting in the Porsche world."

$ $ ROAD KING MAGAZINE, For the Professional Driver, Hammock Publishing, Inc., 3322 West End Ave. #700, Nashville TN 37203. (615)385-9745. Fax: (615)386-9349. E-mail: roadking@hammock.com. Website: http://www.roadking.com. Editor: Tom Berg. **Contact:** Bill Hudgins, editorial director. **80% freelance written.** "*Road King* is published bimonthly for long-haul truckers. It celebrates the lifestyle and work and profiles interesting and/or successful drivers. It also reports on subjects of interest to our audience, including outdoors, vehicles, music and trade issues." Estab. 1963. Circ. 229,900. **Pays on acceptance.** Publishes ms an average of 4 months after acceptance. Byline given. Offers 50% kill fee. Buys first North American serial rights or electronic rights. Editorial lead time 3 months. Submit seasonal material 4 months in advance. Reports in 2 months on queries. Sample copy for 9×12 SAE and 5 first-class stamps. Writer's guidelines for #10 SASE.
Nonfiction: How-to (trucking-related), humor, interview/profile, new product, photo feature, technical, travel. Road-Runner Tools (the latest tools, techniques and industry developments to help them run a smarter, more efficient trucking business; Haul of Fame (salutes drivers whose work or type of rig makes them unique); At Home on the Road ("creature comfort" products, services and information for the road life, including what's new, useful, interesting or fun for cyber-trucking drivers); Fleet Focus (asks fleet management about what their companies offer, and drivers about why they like it there); Weekend Wheels (from Harleys to Hondas, most drivers have a passion for their "other" set of wheels. This section looks at this aspect of drivers' lives)."No fiction, poetry." **Buys 20 mss/year.** Query with published clips. Length: 850-2,000 words. Pay is negotiable. Sometimes pays expenses of writers on assignment.
Photos: State availability of photos with submission. Reviews contact sheets. Negotiates payment individually. Model releases and identification of subjects required. Buys negotiable rights.
Columns/Departments: Lead Driver (profile of outstanding trucker), 500-700 words; **Buys 6-10 mss/year.** Query. Pay is negotiable. Roadrunner (new products, services suited to the business of trucking or to truckers' lifestyles).
Fillers: Anecdotes, facts, gags to be illustrated by cartoonist, short humor. Length: 100-250 words. **Pays $50.**

N $ $ RV TRADE DIGEST, The Marketplace of the RV Industry, Continental Communications, Inc., 58025 C.R. 9, Elkhart IN 46517. (219)295-1962. Fax: (219)295-7574. **Contact:** Lee C. Keyser, editor. **25% freelance written.** "Controlled-circulation monthly magazine for manufacturers, suppliers, dealers, campground and other service providers to the recreational vehicle industry. Company and industry news, dealer profiles, manufacturer profiles, sales and marketing articles, technical articles." Estab. 1980. Circ. 17,000. Pays 30 days after acceptance. Publishes ms an average of 3 months after acceptance. Byline given. Buys first North American serial rights. Editorial lead time 3 months. Submit seasonal material 4 months in advance. Accepts simultaneous submissions. Reports in 2 months. Sample copy and writer's guidelines free.
Nonfiction: How-to (install, service parts, accessories), interview/profile, new product, technical, business subjects, mobile electronics. No sales and marketing subjects. **Buys 30-36 mss/year.** Query. Length: 1,000-2,000 words. **Pays $100-500.**
Photos: Send photos with submission. Reviews transparencies and prints. Negotiates payment individually. Model releases required. Buys one-time rights.
Tips: "Send query with or without completed manuscript but background/experience and published clips are a must."

N $ $ SPORTS TRUCK ACCESSORY DIGEST, Covering the Light Truck-Van-SUV Aftermarket, Continental Communications, Inc., 58025 C.R. 9, Elkhart IN 46517. (219)295-1962. Fax: (219)295-7574. **Contact:** Lee C. Keyser, editor. **25% freelance written.** "Published bimonthly for manufacturers and retailers of accessories ranging from caps and bedliners and towing equipment for pickup trucks, vans and sport utility vehicles, controlled circulation. Balanced between news, how-to, trade shows, product trends, etc." Estab. 1996. Circ. 15,000. Pays 30 days after acceptance. Publishes ms an average of 6 months after acceptance. Byline given. Buys first North American serial rights. Editorial lead time 6 months. Submit seasonal material 6 months in advance. Accepts simultaneous submissions. Reports in 2 months. Sample copy and writer's guidelines free.
Nonfiction: General interest, how-to (installation, service), interview/profile, new product, technical; would consider cartoons. No travel, sales and marketing advice. **Buys 12-18 mss/year.** Query. Length: 1,000-2,000 words. **Pays $100-500.**
Photos: Send photos with submission. Reviews transparencies and prints. Negotiates payment individually. Model releases required. Buys one-time rights.

Tips: "Send query with or without completed manuscripts. Background/experience and published clips are required."

$ TOW-AGE, P.O. Box M, Franklin MA 02038-0822. **Contact:** J. Kruza, editor. For readers who run their own towing service business. **5% freelance written.** Prefers to work with published/established writers. Published every 6 weeks. Estab. 1960. Circ. 18,000. Buys all rights; usually reassigns rights. **Pays on acceptance.** Accepts simultaneous submissions. Reports in 1 month. Sample copy for $5. Writer's guidelines for #10 SASE.

Nonfiction: Articles on business, legal and technical information for the towing industry. "Light reading material; short, with punch." Informational, how-to, personal, interview, profile. **Buys about 18 mss/year.** Query or submit complete ms. Length: 600-800 words. **Pays $50-150.** Spot news and successful business operations. Length: 300-800 words. Technical articles. Length: 400-1,000 words. Pays expenses of writers on assignment.

Photos: Black and white 8×10 photos purchased with or without mss, or on assignment. Pays $25 for first photo; $10 for each additional photo in series. Captions required.

N $ TOWING & RECOVERY PHOOTNOTES, Phootnote Publishing Co., 11520 N Princeville Jubilee Rd., Princeville IL 61559-9360. (309)243-7900. Fax: (309)243-7801. E-mail: pnotes@ix.netcom.com. **Contact:** Jon Lehman, editor. **100% freelance written.** Monthly trade newspaper, tabloid covering towing. "Business management." Estab. 1991. Circ. 46,000. Pays on publication. Publishes ms an average of 2 months after acceptance. Byline given. Buys industry rights. Editorial lead time 1 month. Submit seasonal material 2 months in advance. Sample copy free.

Nonfiction: Technical, business management. Query. Length: 25,000 words. **Pays $50.**

Reprints: Accepts previously published submissions not in same industry.

Columns and Departments: Business Management, 1,500-2,500 words. **Buys 12-18 mss/year.** Query. **Pays $50.**

N $ THE TRUCKER, America's Trucking Newspaper, Belmont Publishing Corporation, P.O. Box 3413, Little Rock AR 72203-3413. (501)666-0500. E-mail: roadnews@aristotle.net. **Contact:** Emily Roberts, managing editor. **10% freelance written.** "Biweekly national newspaper for the truckload freight industry. Content must be written to appeal to and inform audience that includes over-the-road drivers as well as CEOs." Estab. 1987. Circ. 75,000. Pays on publication. Publishes ms an average of 1 month after acceptance. Byline given. Offers negotiable kill fee. Makes work-for-hire assignments. Editorial lead time 3 weeks. Query for seasonal material. Reports in 2 weeks on queries; 24 hours on phone queries. Sample copy for 10×13 SAE and $1.47 postage. Writer's guidelines free (call).

Nonfiction: How-to (trucking technology and management), interview/profile, new product, technical, spot news. Send for current issue focus list. "Timely industry news only. No unsolicited manuscripts, please." **Buys 10-15 mss/year.** Query by phone. Length: 300-1,200 words. **Pays $25-150 for assigned articles, $25 for unsolicited articles.** ("We have a 'stringer' option available for writers in the trucking industry; call for information.") Sometimes pays expenses of writers on assignment.

Reprints: Accepts previously published submissions.

Photos: State availability of photos with query. Reviews 4×6 prints. Negotiates payment individually. Captions and identification of subjects required. Buys all rights.

Tips: "We strongly prefer telephone or e-mail queries for stories based solidly on the news. Unsolicited manuscripts will not be acknowledged. Because of our quick turnaround, a written query may be stale before we see it. Our need is for breaking news significant to the trucking industry."

$ $ WESTERN CANADA HIGHWAY NEWS, Craig Kelman & Associates, 3C-2020 Portage Ave., Winnipeg, Manitoba R3J 0K4 Canada. (204)885-7798. Fax: (204)889-3576. E-mail: kelman@escape.com. **Contact:** Terry Ross, managing editor. **30% freelance written.** Quarterly magazine covering trucking. "The official magazine of the Alberta, Saskatchewan and Manitoba trucking associations." Estab. 1995 (formerly *Manitoba Highway News*). Circ. 4,000. Pays on publication. Publishes ms an average of 2 months after acceptance. Byline given. Buys one-time rights. Editorial lead time 3 months. Submit seasonal material 3 months in advance. Accepts simultaneous submissions. Reports in 2 months on queries; 4 months on mss. Sample copy for 10×13 SAE with 1 IRC. Writer's guidelines free.

Nonfiction: Essays, general interest, how-to (run a trucking business), interview/profile, new product, opinion, personal experience, photo feature, technical, profiles in excellence (bios of trucking or associate firms enjoying success). **Buys 10-12 mss/year.** Query. Length: 500-3,000 words. **Pays 18-25¢/word.** Sometimes pays expenses of writers on assignment.

Reprints: Send photocopy of article or short story and information about when and where the article previously appeared. Pays 60% of amount paid for an original article.

Photos: State availability of photos with submission. Reviews 4×6 prints. Identification of subjects required. Buys one-time rights.

Columns/Departments: Safety (new safety innovation/products), 500 words; Trade Talk (new products), 300 words. Query. **Pays 18-25¢/word.**

Tips: "Our publication is fairly time-sensitive re: issues affecting the trucking industry in Western Canada. Current 'hot' topics are international trucking (NAFTA-induced changes), deregulation, driver fatigue, health and safety, alcohol and drug testing legislation/programs and national/international highway systems."

AVIATION AND SPACE

In this section are journals for aviation business executives, airport operators and aviation technicians. Publications for professional and private pilots are in the Consumer Aviation section.

$ $ $ AIR CARGO WORLD, Journal of Commerce/Economist Group, 1230 National Press Bldg., Washington DC 20045. (202)783-1148. Fax: (202)783-2550. **Contact:** Paul Page, editor. **70% freelance written.** Monthly magazine covering air cargo industry, including airline-related and logistics issues. "We are an international monthly aimed at top executives in the air cargo and related industries. We strive for independent, sophisticated business journalism." Estab. 1948. Circ. 25,000. Pays on publication. Publishes ms an average of 2 months after acceptance. Byline given. Buys first and second serial (reprint) rights. Editorial lead time 2 months. Submit seasonal material 3 months in advance. Reports in 1 month on mss. Sample copy and writer's guidelines free.

Nonfiction: Book excerpts, exposé, how-to (shipping), interview/profile, new product, opinion, technical. **Buys 28 mss/year.** Query with published clips. Length: 900-3,000 words. **Pays $400-800.** Sometimes pays expenses of writers on assignment.

Tips: "Show a sophisticated knowledge of business concerns. Be topical and show the implications of contemporary events on long-term decision making."

$ $ GSE TODAY, P.O. Box 480, Hatch NM 87937. Fax: (505)267-1920. **Contact:** Dixie Binning, managing editor. **50% freelance written.** Magazine published 8 times/year. "Our readers are those aviation professionals who are involved in ground support—the equipment manufacturers, the suppliers, the ramp operators, ground handlers, airport and airline managers. We cover issues of interest to this community—deicing, ramp safety, equipment technology, pollution, etc." Estab. 1993. Circ. 15,000. Pays on publication. Publishes ms an average of 2 months after acceptance. Buys all rights. Editorial lead time 2 months. Accepts unsolicited mss. Reports in 3 weeks on queries; 3 months on mss. Sample copy for 9×11 SAE with 5 first-class stamps.

Nonfiction: How-to (use or maintain certain equipment), interview/profile, new products, personal experience (from ramp operators), technical aspects of ground support equipment and issues, industry events, meetings, new rules and regulations. **Buys 12-20 mss/year.** Send complete ms. Length: 400-3,000 words. **Pays 25¢/published word.**

Reprints: Send photocopy or typed ms with rights for sale noted and information about when and where the article previously appeared. Pays 50% of the amount paid for an original article.

Photos: Send photos with submissions. Reviews 5×7 prints. Offers no additional payment for photos accepted with ms. Identification of subjects required. Buys all rights.

Tips: "Write about subjects that relate to ground services. Write in clear and simple terms—personal experience is always welcome. If you have an aviation background or ground support experience, let us know."

N $ $ MILITARY SPACE, Pasha Publications, 1600 Wilson Blvd., 6th Floor, Arlington VA 22209. Fax: (703)528-4926. E-mail: military@pasha.com. Website: http://www.pasha.com. **Contact:** Frank Sietzen, editor. Managing Editor: Len Famlisentti. **10% freelance written.** Biweekly newsletter covering space technology with military applications. "Assume your typical reader knows more about the subject than you do—write tight, technical pieces for the space community." Estab. 1983. Pays on publication. Publishes ms an average of 1 month after acceptance. Byline sometimes given. Buys all rights or makes work-for-hire assignments. Editorial lead time 1 month. Reports in 2 weeks on queries. Sample copy free.

Nonfiction: Technical. All assignments are made for specific needs only. **Buys 10-20 mss/year.** Query with published clips. Length: 300-500 words. **Pays $150-250.** Sometimes pays expenses of writers on assignment.

Tips: "We are the second-oldest periodical covering space today. Our audience is the primary builders and system integrators in space, plus the top analysts and policymakers in the field. To write for us, you *must* know the industry."

$ MOUNTAIN PILOT, 7009 S. Potomac St., Englewood CO 80112-4209. (303)397-7600. Fax: (303)397-7619. E-mail: ehuber@winc.usa.com. Website: http://www.mountainpilot.com. **Contact:** Edward D. Huber, publisher/editor. **50% freelance written.** Bimonthly magazine. Considers anything on mountain flying or destination, also camping at mountain airstrips. Estab. 1985. Circ. 15,000. Pays on publication. Publishes ms an average of 6 months after acceptance. Byline given. Offers $25 kill fee. Buys all rights. Submit seasonal/holiday material 6 months in advance. Sample copy available. Writing and photographic guidelines available.

Nonfiction: Editorial material focuses on mountain performance—flying, safety and education. Regular features include: aviation experiences, technology, high-altitude maintenance and flying, cold-weather tips and pilot techniques. **Buys 18-35 mss/year.** Send cover letter with copy of ms, Mac or DOS file saved as text only, unformed ASCII, or in QuarkXPress (Mac) on 3½-inch floppy diskette (telephonic submissions (303)397-6987), author's bio and photo. Length: 800-2,000 words. **Pay starts at $50/published page** (includes text and photos).

Reprints: Send tearsheet or photocopy of article or short story and information about when and where the article previously appeared.

Photos: Send photos with submission (copies acceptable for evaluation). Credit line given.

Columns/Departments: Mountain airports, lodging, survival, mountain flying, travel, product news and reviews, industry news. *Mountain Pilot* purchases first serial rights. May consider second serial reprint rights; query.

BEAUTY AND SALON

$ $ AMERICAN SALON, Advanstar, 270 Madison Ave., New York NY 10016. (212)951-6600. Fax: (212)481-6562. Website: http://www.hairnet.com. Editor: Lorraine Korman. **Contact:** Amanda Hathaway, managing editor. **5% freelance written.** Monthly magazine covering "business stories of interest to salon owners and stylists, distributors and manufacturers of professional beauty products." Estab. 1878. Circ. 132,000. **Pays on acceptance.** Publishes ms an average of 3 months after acceptance. Byline given. Buys first and second North American serial rights. Editorial lead time 3 months. Sample copy and writer's guidelines free.

$ $ COSMETICS, Canada's Business Magazine for the Cosmetics, Fragrance, Toiletry and Personal Care Industry, Maclean Hunter Publishing Ltd., 777 Bay St., 5th Floor, Toronto, Ontario M5W 1A7 Canada. (416)596-5817. Fax: (416)596-5179. E-mail: rawood@mhpublishing.com. Website: http://www.mhbizlink.com.cosmetics. **Contact:** Ronald A. Wood, editor. **35% freelance written**; "99.9% of freelance articles are assigned by the editor to writers whose work he is familiar with and who have a broad knowledge of this industry as well as contacts, etc." Bimonthly magazine. "Our main reader segment is the retail trade—department stores, drugstores, salons, estheticians—owners and cosmeticians/beauty advisors; plus manufacturers, distributors, agents and suppliers to the industry." Estab. 1972. Circ. 13,000. **Pays on acceptance.** Publishes ms an average of 3 months after acceptance. Byline given. Offers 50% kill fee. Buys all rights. Editorial lead time 4 months. Submit seasonal material 4 months in advance. Reports in 1 month. Sample copy for $6 (Canadian) and 8% GST.

Nonfiction: General interest, interview/profile, photo feature. **Buys 60 mss/year.** Query. Length: 250-1,200 words. **Pays 25¢/word.** Sometimes pays expenses of writers on assignment.

Photos: Send photos with submission. Reviews transparencies (2½ up to 8×10) and prints (4×6 up to 8×10). Offers no additional payment for photos accepted with ms. Captions, model releases and identification of subjects required. Buys all rights.

Columns/Departments: Behind the Scenes (brief profile of person not directly involved with major industry firms), 300 words and portrait photo. **Buys 28 mss/year**, "all assigned on a regular basis from correspondents and columnists that we know personally from the industry." **Pays 25¢/word.**

Tips: "Must have broad knowledge of the Canadian cosmetics, fragrance and toiletries industry and retail business."

N $ $ DAYSPA, For the Salon of the Future, Creative Age Publications, 7628 Densmore Ave., Van Nuys CA 91406. (818)782-7328. Fax: (818)782-7450. E-mail: dayspamag@aol.com. **Contact:** Linda Lewis, editor. Managing Editor: Amy Hamaker. **60% freelance written.** "Bimonthly magazine covering the business of day spas, skincare salons, wellness centers. "*Dayspa* includes only well targeted business articles directed at the owners and managers of high-end, multi-service salons, day spas, resort spas and destination spas." Estab. 1996. Circ. 31,000. **Pays on acceptance.** Publishes ms an average of 4 months after acceptance. Byline given. Buys first or one-time rights. Editorial lead time 4 months. Submit seasonal material 4 months in advance. Reports in 2 months. Sample copy for $5.

Nonfiction: Book excerpts, how-to, interview/profile, photo feature. **Buys 40 mss/year.** Query. Length: 1,200-3,000 words. **Pays $150-500.**

Photos: Send photos with submission. Negotiates payment individually. Model releases and identification of subjects required. Buys one-time rights.

Columns/Departments: Legal Pad (legal issues affecting salons/spas); Money Matters (financial issues), all 1,200-1,500 words. Buys 20 mss/year. Query. Pays $150-300.

$ $ NAILPRO, The Magazine for Nail Professionals, Creative Age Publications, 7628 Densmore Ave., Van Nuys CA 91406. Fax: (818)782-7450. E-mail: nailpro@aol.com. Website: http://nailpro.com. **Contact:** Linda Lewis, editor. **75% freelance written.** Monthly magazine "written for manicurists and nail technicians working in full-service salons or nails-only salons. It covers technical and business aspects of working in and operating a nail-care service, as well as the nail-care industry in general." Estab. 1989. Circ. 52,000. **Pays on acceptance.** Publishes ms 6 months after acceptance. Byline given. Offers 50% kill fee. Buys one-time, second serial (reprint), simultaneous or all rights. Editorial lead time 3 months. Submit seasonal material 3 months in advance. Accepts simultaneous submissions. Reports in 6 weeks. Sample copy for $2 and 8½×11 SASE.

Nonfiction: Book excerpts, how-to, humor, inspirational, interview/profile, personal experience, photo feature, technical. No general interest articles or business articles not geared to the nail-care industry. **Buys 50 mss/year.** Query. Length: 1,000-3,000 words. **Pays $150-450.**

Reprints: Send typed ms with rights for sale noted and information about when and where the article previously appeared. Pays 50-75% of amount paid for an original article.

Photos: Send photos with submission. Reviews transparencies and prints. Negotiates payment individually. Model releases and identification of subjects required. Buys one-time rights.

Columns/Departments: Building Business (articles on marketing nail services/products), 1,500-3,000 words; Shop Talk (aspects of operating a nail salon), 1,500-3,000 words; Hollywood File (nails in the news, movies or TV), 1,000-1,500 words. **Buys 50 mss/year.** Query. **Pays $200-300.**

$ $ SKIN INC. MAGAZINE, The Complete Business Guide for Face & Body Care, Allured Publishing Corp., 362 S. Schmale Rd., Carol Stream IL 60188. (630)653-2155. Fax: (630)653-2192. E-mail: taschetta-millane@allur ed.com. Publisher/Editor: Marian Raney. **Contact:** Melinda Taschetta-Millane, editor. **30% freelance written.** Magazine published 8 times/year. "Manuscripts considered for publication that contain original and new information in the general fields of skin care and makeup, dermatological and esthetician-assisted surgical techniques. The subject may cover the science of skin, the business of skin care and makeup, and plastic surgeons on healthy (i.e. non-diseased) skin. Subjects may also deal with raw materials, formulations and regulations concerning claims for products and equipment." Estab. 1988. Circ. 15,000. Pays on publication. Publishes ms an average of 6 months after acceptance. Byline given. No kill fee. Buys all rights. Editorial lead time 6 months. Submit seasonal material 1 year in advance. Reports in 1 week on queries; 1 month on mss. Sample copy and writer's guidelines free.

Nonfiction: General interest, how-to, interview/profile, personal experience, technical. **Buys 6 mss/year.** Query with published clips. Length: 2,000 words. **Pays $100-300 for assigned articles; $50-200 for unsolicited articles.**

Photos: State availability of photos with submission. Reviews 3×5 prints. Offers no additional payment for photos accepted with ms. Captions, model releases, identification of subjects required. Buys one-time rights.

Columns/Departments: Finance (tips and solutions for managing money), 2,000-2,500 words; Personnel (managing personnel), 2,000-2,500 words; Marketing (marketing tips for salon owners), 2,000-2,500 words; Retail (retailing products and services in the salon environment), 2,000-2,500 words. Query with published clips. **Pays $50-200.**

Fillers: Facts, newsbreaks. **Buys 6 mss/year.** Length: 250-500 words. **Pays $50-100.**

Tips: Have an understanding of the skin care industry.

BEVERAGES AND BOTTLING

Manufacturers, distributors and retailers of soft drinks and alcoholic beverages read these publications. Publications for bar and tavern operators and managers of restaurants are classified in the Hotels, Motels, Clubs, Resorts and Restaurants category.

$ $ AMERICAN BREWER, The Business of Beer, Box 510, Hayward CA 94543-0510. (415)538-9500. Fax: (510)538-7644. Website: http://www.ambrew.com. **Contact:** Bill Owens, publisher. **100% freelance written.** Magazine published 5 times/year covering micro-breweries. Estab. 1986. Circ. 20,000. Pays on publication. Publishes ms an average of 4 months after acceptance. Byline given. Buys one-time rights. Reports in 2 weeks on queries. Sample copy for $5.

Nonfiction: Business humor, opinion, travel. Query. Length: 1,500-2,500 words. **Pays $50-250 for assigned articles.**

Reprints: Send tearsheet or photocopy of article.

N $ $ BEBI DAS, Global Beverage Publishers, P.O. Box 16116, Cleveland OH 44116. (440)331-9100. Fax: (440)331-9020. **Contact:** W.R. Dolan, president. 40% freelance written. Bimonthly magazine covering beverages, soft drinks, beer, juice, wine, but not spirits. "*Bebi Das* is for Latin American beverage producers and distributors. Focus is on marketing, distribution and technology. 100% in Spanish. We translate." Estab. 1942. Circ. 10,000. Pays on publication. Publishes ms an average of 3 months after acceptance. Byline sometimes given. Buys all rights. Editorial lead time 3 months. Sample copy and writer's guidelines free.

Nonfiction: New product, technical. **Buys 20-25 mss/year.** Query. Length: 1,500-2,500 words. **Pays $300-500.** Sometimes pays expenses of writers on assignment.

Photos: State availability of photos with submission. Negotiates payment individually. Indentification of subjects required. Buys all rights.

N $ $ BREWPUB, Successful Brewpub Management Strategies, 216 F St., Davis CA 95616. (530)758-4596. Fax: (530)758-7477. E-mail: bp@brewpubmag.com. **Contact:** Craig Bystrynski, editor. Managing Editor: Gailen Jacobs. **100% freelance written.** "Monthly trade magazine aimed at Brewpub general managers, restaurant managers, brewers, and other personnel." Estab. 1996. Circ. 5,000. Pays on publication. Publishes ms an average of 4 months after acceptance. Byline given. Offers 25% kill fee. Buys all rights. Editorial lead time 3 months. Submit seasonal material 3 months in advance. Reports in 2 months. Writer's guidelines for #10 SASE.

Nonfiction: General interest (Brewpub business), how-to (market and brew beer, manage restaurants, run a brewpub business). No general interest features on brewpubs. **Buys 80 mss/year.** Query with published clips. Length: 1,200-3,000 words. **Pays $50-200.**

Photos: State availability of photos with submission. Negotiates payment individually.

Columns/Departments: Marketing; Startups (brewpub startup issues); Craft Brewer (beer brewing tips); After Hours (funny business stories), all 750-1,500 words. **Buys 48 mss/year.** Query with or without published clips. **Pays $50-150.**

$ $ MASSACHUSETTS BEVERAGE BUSINESS, New Beverage Publications Inc., 55 Clarendon St., Boston MA 02116. (617)423-7200. Fax: (617)482-7163. E-mail: beverage@tiac.net. Website: http://www.beveragebusiness.com. **Contact:** P.J. Stone, executive editor. **100% freelance written.** Monthly magazine covering beverage alcohol industry. Estab. 1934. Circ. 7,800. Pays on publication. Publishes ms an average of 2 months after acceptance. Byline given. Offers $250-350 kill fee. Buys one-time rights or makes work-for-hire assignments. Editorial lead time 2 months. Submit seasonal material 3 months in advance. Accepts simultaneous submissions.

Nonfiction: General interest, new product, technical, travel. *Massachusetts Beverage Business* is expanding its editorial

coverage to include cigars, store design, ancillary products, etc. **Buys 96 mss/year.** Send complete ms. Length: 1,200-3,000 words. **Pays $200-300.** Sometimes pays expenses of writers on assignment.
Reprints: Send typed ms with rights for sale noted and information about when and where the article previously appeared. Pays 20% of amount paid for an original article.
Photos: Send photos with submission. Reviews negatives, transparencies. Offers no additional payment for photos accepted with ms. Buys one-time rights.

N $ $ THE OBSERVER MAGAZINE, 531 E. Front St., Berwick PA 18603. (717)752-0711. Fax: (717)752-0722. E-mail: paobs@aol.com. **Contact:** Julie Crispis, editor. Managing Editor: Sean Curran. Monthly magazine. "*The Observer* is Pennsylvania's oldest and largest journal of the state's alcohol beverage industry. Our readers are bar and restaurant owners, beer distributors and liquor wholesalers." Estab. 1934. Circ. 5,500. Pays on publication. Publishes ms an average of 2 months after acceptance. Byline given. Offers 30% kill fee. Buys first or one-time rights. Editorial lead time 2 months. Submit seasonal material 2 months in advance. Accepts simultaneous submissions. Reports in 2 weeks on queries; 2 months on mss. Sample copy for $1.50.
Nonfiction: Interview/profile (restaurant/alcohol industry); alcohol/restaurant-related articles. No restaurant/bar reviews. **Buys 15-30 mss/year.** Query with published clips or send complete ms. Length: 500-1,500 words. **Pays $75-200 for assigned articles; $50-125 for unsolicited articles.** Pays writers with free ad for related service/product. Sometimes pays the expenses of writers on assignment.
Photos: Send photos with submission. Offers no additional payment for photos accepted with ms. Identification of subjects required. Buys one-time rights.
Columns/Departments: Wine, beer or industry-related, 750 words. **Buys 15-30 mss/year.** Query with published clips or send complete ms. **Pays $50-125.**
Fillers: Anecdotes, facts. **Buys 15/year.** Length: 35-150 words. **Pays $15-35.**
Tips: "Feel free to call with any questions."

$ $ VINEYARD & WINERY MANAGEMENT, P.O. Box 231, Watkins Glen NY 14891-0231. (607)535-7133. Fax: (607)535-2998. E-mail: vandwm@aol.com. Website: http://www.wines.com/vwm-online. **Contact:** J. William Moffett, editor. **80% freelance written.** Bimonthly trade magazine of professional importance to grape growers, winemakers and winery sales and business people. Estab. 1975. Circ. 4,500. Pays on publication. Byline given. Buys first North American serial rights and occasionally simultaneous rights. Reports in 3 weeks on queries; 1 month on mss. Sample copy free. Writer's guidelines for #10 SASE.
Nonfiction: How-to, interview/profile, technical. Subjects are technical in nature and explore the various methods people in these career paths use to succeed, and also the equipment and techniques they use successfully. Business articles and management topics are also featured. The audience is national with western dominance. **Buys 30 mss/year.** Query. Length: 300-5,000 words. **Pays $30-1,000.** Pays some expenses of writers on some assignments.
Photos: State availability of photos with submission. Reviews contact sheets, negatives and transparencies. Identification of subjects required. Black and white often purchased for $20 each to accompany story material; 35mm and/or 4×5 transparencies for $50 and up; 6/year of vineyard and/or winery scene related to story. Query.
Tips: "We're looking for long-term relationships with authors who know the business and write well. Electronic submissions preferred; query for formats."

N $ $ WINE BUSINESS MONTHLY, New World Wine Communications, 867 W. Napa St., Sonoma CA 95476. E-mail: wbm@smartwine.com. Editor: Greg Walter. **Contact:** Abby Sawyer, managing editor. **70% freelance written.** Monthly trade magazine. Estab. 1994. Circ. 8,300. Pays on publication. Publishes ms an average of 2-3 months after acceptance. Byline given. Offers 50% kill fee. Buys all rights. Editorial lead time 2 months. Submit seasonal material 2 months in advance. Reports in 6 weeks on queries. Sample copy and writer's guidelines free.
Nonfiction: Special interest articles on the wine trade by query and assignment only. **Buys 60 mss/year**. Query with published clips. Length: varies. **Pays $150-500**. Sometimes pays expenses of writers on assignment.
Photos: Graphic/art supporting story to be agreed upon at time of assignment.
Tips: "Experienced writers with knowledge of various aspects of the wine industry are sought. Please see guidelines. Note most articles consist of at least 40% quotes. Good interviewing skills are essential."

BOOK AND BOOKSTORE

Publications for book trade professionals from publishers to bookstore operators are found in this section. Journals for professional writers are classified in the Journalism and Writing category.

$ THE HORN BOOK MAGAZINE, The Horn Book, Inc., 11 Beacon St., Suite 1000, Boston MA 02108. (617)227-1555. (800)325-1170. Fax: (617)523-0299. E-mail: magazine@hbook.com. Website: http://www.hbook.com. **Contact:** Roger Sutton, editor-in-chief. **10% freelance written.** Prefers to work with published/established writers. Bimonthly magazine covering children's literature for librarians, booksellers, professors, teachers and students of children's literature. Estab. 1924. Circ. 21,500. Pays on publication. Publishes ms an average of 4 months after acceptance. Byline given. Submit seasonal material 6 months in advance. Accepts simultaneous submissions. Reports in 2 months. Writer's guidelines available upon request.

Nonfiction: Interview/profile (children's book authors and illustrators); topics of interest to the children's bookworld. Writers should be familiar with the magazine and its contents. **Buys 20 mss/year.** Query or send complete ms. Length: 1,000-2,800 words. Honorarium paid upon publication.
Tips: "Writers have a better chance of breaking in to our publication with a query letter on a specific article they want to write."

$ $ INDEPENDENT PUBLISHER, (formerly *Small Press Magazine*), The Jenkins Group, 121 E. Front St., Traverse City MI 49684. (616)933-0445. Fax: (616)933-0448. E-mail: editorial@smallpress.com. **Contact:** Mardi Link, executive editor. Reviews Editor: Phil Murphy. **25% freelance written.** "*Independent Publisher* is a bimonthly trade journal for small and independent publishing companies. We focus on marketing, promoting and producing books and how independent publishers can compete in this competitive industry. We also run profiles of successful publishers, an awards section and book reviews." Estab. 1983. Circ. 10,000. Pays on publication. Publishes ms an average of 2 months after acceptance. Byline given. Offers 10% kill fee. Buys first North American serial rights or all rights. Editorial lead time 2 months. Submit seasonal material 4 months in advance. Accepts simultaneous submissions. Reports in 3 weeks on queries; 1 month on mss. Sample guidelines and writer's guidelines free.
Nonfiction: Book excerpts, essays, exposé, how-to, interview/profile, opinion, travel. "No consumer-oriented stories. We are a trade magazine for publishers." **Buys 12 mss/year.** Query with published clips. Length: 1,000-4,000 words. **Pays $60-400 for assigned articles, $50-250 for unsolicited articles.** Sometimes pays expenses of writers on assignment.
Photos: State availability of photos with submission. Reviews transparencies and prints. Offers no additional payment for photos accepted with ms. Identification of subjects required. Buys one-time rights.
Columns/Departments: Sell More Rights (intellectual rights, sales advice); Passageways to Profit (distribution strategies), all 1,200-1,600 words. **Buys 6 mss/year.** Query with published clips. **Pays $100-200.**

$ $ $ QUILL & QUIRE, Canada's Magazine of Book News & Reviews, Key Publishers, 70 The Esplanade, Suite 210, Toronto, Ontario M5E 1R2 Canada. (416)360-0044. Fax: (416)955-0794. E-mail: quill@idirect.com. **Contact:** Scott Anderson, editor. Monthly tabloid covering Canadian book industry. "Our readers are primarily booksellers, librarians, publishers and writers." Estab. 1935. Circ. 7,000. **Pays on acceptance.** Publishes ms an average of 1 month after acceptance. Offers 50% kill fee. Buys all rights. Editorial lead time 2 months. Submit seasonal material 2 months in advance. Reports in 1 month on queries; 2 months on mss. Sample copy for $4.75 (Canadian).
Nonfiction: Essays, interview/profile, opinion, technical, business, book reviews. **Buys hundreds of mss/year.** Query. Length: 250-3,000 words. **Pays $50-1,000 (Canadian).** Sometimes pays writers with contributor copies or other premiums. Pays expenses of writers on assignment.
Reprints: Pays 50% of amount paid for an original article.
Photos: State availability of photos with submission. Reviews contact sheets. Offers $100-300/photo.
Columns/Departments: Carol Toller, news editor. Writers' Bloc (issues of interest to writers); Terms of Trade (issues relating to book trade in Canada); Circulating (issues relating to librarianship in Canada); all 850-1,000 words. **Buys 36 mss/year.** Query. **Pays $100 (Canadian) minimum.**

$ $ THE WOMEN'S REVIEW OF BOOKS, The Women's Review, Inc., Wellesley College, Wellesley MA 02181-8259. (781)283-2555. Website: http://www.wellesley.edu/WCW/CRW/WROB/welcome.html. **Contact:** Linda Gardiner, editor. Monthly newspaper. "Feminist review of recent trade and academic titles by and about women. Reviews recent nonfiction books, primarily." Estab. 1983. Circ. 16,000. Pays on publication. Publishes ms an average of 2 months after acceptance. Byline given. Offers $50 kill fee. Buys first North American serial rights. Editorial lead time 2 months. Reports in 2 months. Sample copy free.
Nonfiction: Book reviews only. No articles considered. Query. No unsolicited mss. **Buys 200 mss/year.** Query with published clips. **Pays 12¢/word.** Sometimes pays expenses of writers on assignment.
Tips: "Only experienced reviewers for national media are considered. Reviewers must have expertise in subject of book under review. Never send unsolicited manuscripts."

BRICK, GLASS AND CERAMICS

These publications are read by manufacturers, dealers and managers of brick, glass and ceramic retail businesses. Other publications related to glass and ceramics are listed in the Consumer Art and Architecture and Consumer Hobby and Craft sections.

$ $ GLASS MAGAZINE®, For the Architectural Glass Industry, National Glass Association, Suite 302, 8200 Greensboro Dr., McLean VA 22102-3881. (703)442-4890. Fax: (703)442-0630. **Contact:** Sean McKenna, managing editor. **25% freelance written.** Prefers to work with published/established writers. Monthly magazine covering the architectural glass industry. Circ. 16,500. **Pays on acceptance.** Publishes ms an average of 6 months after acceptance. Byline given. Kill fee varies. Buys first rights only. Reports in 2 months. Sample copy for $5 and 9×12 SAE with 10 first-class stamps. Writer's guidelines free.
Nonfiction: Interview/profile (of various glass businesses; profiles of industry people or glass business owners); and

technical (about glazing processes). **Buys 15 mss/year.** Query with published clips. Length: 1,000 words minimum. **Pays $150-300.**
Photos: State availability of photos.
Tips: *Glass Magazine* is doing more inhouse writing; freelance cut by half. "Do *not* send in general glass use stories. Research the industry first, then query."

$ STAINED GLASS, Stained Glass Association of America, 6 S.W. Second St., #7, Lee's Summit MO 64063. Fax: (816)524-9405. E-mail: sgmagaz@kcnet.com. Website: http://www.stainedglass.org. **Contact:** Richard Gross, editor. **70% freelance written.** Quarterly magazine. "Since 1906, *Stained Glass* has been the official voice of the Stained Glass Association of America. As the oldest, most respected stained glass publication in North America, *Stained Glass* preserves the techniques of the past as well as illustrates the trends of the future. This vital information, of significant value to the professional stained glass studio, is also of interest to those for whom stained glass is an avocation or hobby." Estab. 1906. Circ. 5,000. Pays on publication. Publishes ms an average of 6 months after acceptance. Byline given. Buys one-time rights. Editorial lead time 3 months. Submit seasonal material 6 months in advance. No longer accepts simultaneous submissions. Reports in 3 months. Sample copy and writer's guidelines free.
Nonfiction: How-to, humor, interview/profile, new product, opinion, photo feature, technical. Strong need for technical and how to create architectural type stained glass. Glass etching, use of etched glass in stained glass compositions, framing. **Buys 9 mss/year.** Query or send complete ms but must include photos or slides—very heavy on photos. **Pays $25/page.**
Reprints: Accepts previously published submissions from non-stained glass publications only. Send tearsheet of article. Pay negotiable.
Photos: Send slides with submission. Reviews 4×5 transparencies. Pays $75 for non-illustrated. Pays $125 plus 3 copies for line art or photography. Identification of subjects required. Buys one-time rights.
Columns/Departments: Teknixs (technical, how-to, stained and glass art), word length varies by subject. **Buys 4 mss/year.** Query or send complete ms, but must be illustrated.
Tips: "Writers should be extremely well versed in the glass arts. Photographs are extremely important and must be of very high quality. Very sight-oriented magazine. Submissions without photographs or illustrations are seldom considered unless something special and writer states that photos are available. However, prefer to see with submission."

$ $ US GLASS, METAL & GLAZING, Key Communications Inc., P.O. Box 569, Garrisonville VA 22463. (540)720-5584. Fax: (540)720-5687. E-mail: usglass@aol.com. Website: http://www.usglassmag.com. **Contact:** Regina Johnson, editor. **25% freelance written.** Monthly magazine for companies involved in the auto glass and flat glass trades. Estab. 1966. Circ. 23,000. Pays on publication. Publishes ms an average of 3 months after acceptance. Byline given. Buys all rights. Editorial lead time 3 months. Submit seasonal material 2 months in advance. Accepts simultaneous submissions. Reports in 1 month on queries; 2 months on mss. Sample copy and writer's guidelines for $10.
Nonfiction: Contact: Helen Price. How-to, new product, technical. **Buys 12 mss/year.** Query with published clips. **Pays $300-600 for assigned articles.** Sometimes pays expenses of writers on assignment.
Photos: State availability of photos with submission. Reviews contact sheets. Offers no additional payment for photos accepted with ms. Captions, identification of subjects required. Buys first North American rights.

BUILDING INTERIORS

Owners, managers and sales personnel of floor covering, wall covering and remodeling businesses read the journals listed in this category. Interior design and architecture publications may be found in the Consumer Art, Design and Collectibles category. For journals aimed at other construction trades see the Construction and Contracting section.

$ $ PWC, Painting & Wallcovering Contractor, Finan Publishing Co. Inc., 8730 Big Bend Blvd., St. Louis MO 63119-3730. (314)961-6644. Fax: (314)961-4809. E-mail: jbeckner@finan.com. Website: http://www.paintstore.com. **Contact:** Jeffery Beckner, editor. **90% freelance written.** Bimonthly magazine "*PWC* provides news you can use: information helpful to the painting and wallcovering contractor in the here and now." Estab. 1928. Circ. 30,000. Pays 30 days after acceptance. Publishes ms an average of 1 month after acceptance. Byline given. Kill fee determined on individual basis. Buys first North American serial rights. Editorial lead time 2 months. Submit seasonal material 2 months in advance. Accepts simultaneous submissions. Reports in 2 weeks. Sample copy free.
Nonfiction: Essays, exposé, how-to (painting and wallcovering), interview/profile, new product, opinion personal experience. **Buys 40 mss/year.** Query with published clips. Length: 1,500-2,500 words. **Pays $300 minimum.** Pays expenses of writers on assignment.
Reprints: Send photocopy of article and information about when and where the article previously appeared. Negotiates payment.
Photos: State availability of or send photos with submission. Reviews contact sheets, negatives, transparencies and digital prints. Offers no additional payment for photos accepted with ms. Identification of subjects required. Buys one-time and all rights.
Columns/Departments: Anything of interest to the small businessman, 1,250 words. Buys 2 mss/year. Query with

published clips. **Pays $50-100.**
Tips: "We almost always buy on an assignment basis. The way to break in is to send good clips, and I'll try and give you work."

BUSINESS MANAGEMENT

These publications cover trends, general theory and management practices for business owners and top-level business executives. Publications that use similar material but have a less technical slant are listed in the Consumer Business and Finance section. Journals for middle management, including supervisors and office managers, appear in the Management and Supervision section. Those for industrial plant managers are listed under Industrial Operations and under sections for specific industries, such as Machinery and Metal. Publications for office supply store operators are included in the Office Environment and Equipment section.

$ $ ACCOUNTING TODAY, Faulkner & Gray, 11 Penn Plaza, New York NY 10001. (212)967-7000. **Contact:** Rick Telberg, editor. Biweekly newspaper. "*Accounting Today* is the newspaper of record for the accounting industry." Estab. 1987. Circ. 35,000. Pays on publication. Publishes ms an average of 1 month after acceptance. Byline given. Buys all rights. Editorial lead time 2 weeks. Reports in 1 month. Sample copy for $5.
Nonfiction: Book excerpts, essays, exposé, how-to, interview/profile, new product, technical. **Buys 35 mss/year.** Query with published clips. Length: 500-1,500 words. **Pays 25-50¢/word for assigned articles.** Pays expenses of writers on assignment.
Photos: State availability of photos with submission. Negotiates payment individually.

$ $ $ ACROSS THE BOARD, The Conference Board Magazine, The Conference Board, 845 Third Ave., New York NY 10022. (212)339-0450. Fax: (212)980-7014. E-mail: atb@conference-board.org. **Contact:** A.J. Vogl, editor. Managing Editor: Matthew Budman. **60% freelance written.** Monthly magazine covering business issues of interest to senior executives of Fortune 500 companies. "For leaders in business, government, and other organizations. It is published by The Conference Board, America's preeminent business research and forecasting organization, and most of its readers are top-level managers in the United States and abroad—many of them CEOs." Estab. 1979. Circ. 26,000. Pays on publication. Publishes ms an average of 6 months after acceptance. Byline given. Offers 33% kill fee. Buys first North American serial rights. Editorial lead time 3 months. Accepts simultaneous submissions. Reports in 3 weeks. Sample copy and writer's guidelines for #10 SASE.
Nonfiction: Book excerpts, essays, interview/profile, opinion, personal experience. Business perspectives on timely issues, including management practices, foreign policy, social issues, and science and technology. We aren't interested in highly technical articles about business strategy. We don't publish oversimple "how-to" articles. **Buys 75-100 mss/year.** Query with published clips, or send complete ms. Length: 2,500-3,500 words. **Pays $500-1,000.** Sometimes pays expenses of writers on assignment.
Reprints: Send tearsheet, photocopy or typed ms of article or short story with rights for sale noted and information about when and where the article previously appeared.
Photos: State availability of photos with submission.
Columns/Departments: Soundings (strong opinions on subjects of pertinence to our readers), 400-800 words. **Buys 75 mss/year.** Query. **Pays $200-400.**
Tips: "We let *Forbes*, *Fortune*, and *Business Week* do most of the straight reporting, while we do some of the critical thinking; that is, we let writers explore the implications of the news in depth. *Across the Board* tries to provide different angles on important topics, and to bring to its readers' attention issues that they might otherwise not devote much thought to. A few examples from past issues: Ethics overseas; how and why a company should set up shop on the Internet; and business lessons learned from the art world. We emphasize the human side of organizational life at all levels. We're as concerned with helping managers who are 'lonely at the top' as with motivating workers and enhancing job satisfaction."

N $ $ CBA MARKETPLACE, CBA Service Corporation, P.O. Box 200, Colorado Springs CO 80901. (719)576-7880. E-mail: publications@cba-intl.org. **Contact:** Sue Grise, editor. Managing Editor: Debby Weaver. **20% freelance written.** Monthly magazine covering the Christian retail industry. "Writers must have knowledge of and direct experience in the Christian retail industry. Subject matter must specifically pertain to the Christian retail audience." Estab. 1968. Pays on publication. Publishes ms an average of 3 months after acceptance. Byline given. Offers 15¢/word kill fee. Buys all rights in all media. Editorial lead time 5 months. Submit seasonal material 9 months in advance. Reports in 2 months. Sample copy for $7.50.
Nonfiction: Christian retail. **Buys 24 mss/year.** Query. Length: 750-1,500 words. **Pays 15-25¢/word.**
Fillers: Contact: Graphic designer. Cartoons. **Buys 12/year. Pays $150.**
Tips: "Only experts on Christian retail industry, completely familiar with retail audience and their needs and consideration, who can address our specific audience should submit a query. Do not submit articles unless requested."

$ $ COMMUNICATION BRIEFINGS, Capitol Publications Inc., Dept. WM, 1101 King St., Suite 110, Alexandria VA 22314. (703)548-3800. Fax: (703)684-2136. E-mail: ibrudersmith@combriefings.com. Website: http://www.combriefings.com. Editor: Jack Gillespie. **Contact:** Isabelle Broder Smith, managing editor. **15% freelance written.** Prefers to work with published/established writers. Monthly newsletter covering business communication and business management. "Most readers are in middle and upper management. They are public relations professionals, editors of company publications, marketing and advertising managers, fund raisers, directors of associations and foundations, school and college administrators, human resources professionals, and other middle managers who want to communicate better on the job." Estab. 1980. Circ. 60,000. **Pays on acceptance.** Publishes ms an average of 3 months after acceptance. Byline given sometimes on Bonus Items and on other items if idea originates with the writer. Buys one-time rights. Submit seasonal material 3 months in advance. Reports in 1 month. Sample copy and writer's guidelines for #10 SAE and 2 first-class stamps.

Nonfiction: "Most articles we buy are 'how-to,' consisting of practical ideas, techniques and advice that readers can use to improve business communication and management. Areas covered: writing, speaking, listening, employee communication, human relations, public relations, interpersonal communication, persuasion, conducting meetings, advertising, marketing, fund raising, telephone techniques, teleconferencing, selling, improving publications, handling conflicts, negotiating, etc. Articles that appeal to both profit and nonprofit organizations are given priority." *Short Items:* Articles with one or two brief tips that can stand alone. Length: 40-70 words. *Articles:* A collection of tips or ideas that offer a solution to a communication or management problem or that show a better way to communicate or manage. Examples: "How to produce slogans that work," "The wrong way to criticize employees," "Mistakes to avoid when leading a group discussion," and "5 ways to overcome writer's block." Length: 125-150 words. *Bonus Items:* In-depth pieces that probe one area of communication or management and cover it thoroughly. Examples: "Producing successful special events," "How to evaluate your newsletter," and "How to write to be understood." Length: 1,300 words. **Buys 30-50 mss/year. Pays $20-50** for 40- to 150-word pieces; Bonus Items, **$300.** Pays expenses of writers on assignment.

Reprints: Previously published submissions "must be rewritten to conform to our style."

Tips: "Our readers are looking for specific, practical ideas and tips that will help them communicate better both within their organizations and with outside publics. Most ideas are rejected because they are too general or too elementary for our audience. Our style is down-to-earth and terse. We pack a lot of useful information into short articles. Our readers are busy executives and managers who want information dispatched quickly and without embroidery. We omit anecdotes, lengthy quotes and long-winded exposition. The writer has a better chance of breaking in at our publication with short articles and fillers since we buy only six major features (bonus items) a year. We require queries on longer items and bonus items. Writers may submit short tips (40-70 words) without querying. The most frequent mistakes made by writers completing an article for us are failure to master the style of our publication and to understand our readers' needs."

N $ $ CONSUMER GOODS MANUFACTURER, Partnering with Retail through Technology, Edgell Communications, 10 W. Hanover Ave., Suite 107, Randolph NJ 07869. **Contact:** Mark Frantz, editor. **60% freelance written.** Bimonthly tabloid covering suppliers to retailers. "Readers are the functional managers/executives in all types of retail and consumer goods firms. They are making major improvements in company operations and in alliances with customers/suppliers." Estab. 1991. Circ. 26,000. Pays on publication. Byline sometimes given. Buys first rights and second serial (reprint) rights. Editorial lead time 3 months. Submit seasonal material 3 months in advance. Sample copy for 11×15 SAE with 6 first-class stamps. Writer's guidelines for #10 SASE.

Nonfiction: How-to, interview/profile, technical. **Buys 100 mss/year.** Query with published clips. Length: 1,200-2,400 words. **Pays $500 maximum for assigned articles.** Sometimes pays contributor copies as negotiated. Sometimes pays expenses of writers on assignment.

Photos: Send photos with submission. Reviews contact sheets, negatives, transparencies and prints. Offers no additional payment for photos accepted with ms. Identification of subjects required. Buys one-time rights plus reprint, if applicable.

Tips: "Case histories about companies achieving substantial results using advanced management practices and/or advanced technology are best intro."

$ CONVENTION SOUTH, Covey Communications Corp., 2001 W. First St., P.O. Box 2267, Gulf Shores AL 36547-2267. (334)968-5300. Fax: (334)968-4532. E-mail: info@conventionsouth.com. Website: http://www.conventionsouth.com. **Contact:** Kristen McIntosh, executive editor. Editor: J. Talty O'Connor. **50% freelance written.** Monthly tabloid for meeting planners who plan events in the South. Topics relate to the meetings industry—how-to articles, industry news, destination spotlights. Estab. 1983. Circ. 11,800. Pays on publication. Publishes ms an average of 2 months after acceptance. Byline given. Buys first rights or second serial (reprint) rights. Editorial lead time 3 months. Submit seasonal/holiday material 3 months in advance. Accepts simultaneous submissions. Reports in 2 months on queries. Sample copy free. Writer's guidelines for #10 SASE.

Nonfiction: How-to (relative to meeting planning/travel), interview/profile, photo feature, technical, travel. **Buys 50 mss/year.** Query. Length: 1,250-3,000 words. **Pays $75-150.** Pays in contributor copies or other premiums if arranged in advance. Sometimes pays expenses of writers on assignment.

Reprints: Accepts previously published submissions. Send photocopy of article and information about when and where the article previously appeared. Pay negotiable.

Photos: Send photos with submission. Reviews 5×7 prints. Offers no additional payment for photos accepted with ms. Captions and identification of subjects required. Buys one-time rights.

Columns/Departments: How-tos (related to meetings), 700 words. **Buys 12 mss/year.** Query with published clips. Payment negotiable.

Tips: "Know who our audience is and make sure articles are appropriate for them."

$ $ CREDIT UNION EXECUTIVE JOURNAL, CUNA & Affiliates' Management Journal, Credit Union National Association, Inc., P.O. Box 431, Madison WI 53701-0431. (608)231-4081. Fax: (608)231-4370. E-mail: lgregg-@cuna.com. Website: http://www.cuna.org. **Contact:** Leigh Gregg, editor. Managing Editor: Kathryn Kuehn. Associate Editor: Mary Mink. **50% freelance written.** Bimonthly trade journal "directed toward CEO's and senior management of large, sophisticated, leading-edge credit unions. It features articles on management, human resources, lending, marketing, technology and finance, written in a business-like, no-nonsense tone." Estab. 1963. Circ. 3,300. **Pays on acceptance.** Publishes ms 4 months after acceptance. Byline given. Makes work-for-hire assignments so CUNA has all rights. Editorial lead time 5 months. Reports in 1 month. Sample copy and writer's guidelines free.

Nonfiction: How to manage operations and functions of credit unions, issues of importance to credit unions and financial industry. No first-person, humor, product promotions. Case studies are OK. **Buys 12-15 mss/year.** Query with published clips. Length: 650 words for smaller articles, 1,800-2,000 for major features. **Pays $500-600 for assigned articles.** "We don't pay technical experts or vendors who are seeking wider exposure of their ideas to CU's. They get contributor's copies." Sometimes pays expenses of writers on assignment (usually phone expenses for interviews).

Tips: "Learn about credit unions before you call. Phone queries are OK. We use a lot of how-to articles geared to people running credit unions, not to the consumer or members of credit unions.

N $ $ EXECUTIVE UPDATE, Greater Washington Society of Association Executives, 1426 21st St. NW, Washington DC 20036. Fax: (202)429-0553. E-mail: jschultz@gwsae.org. Website: http://www.executiveupdate.com. **Contact:** Jane Schultz, executive editor. **60% freelance written.** "Monthly magazine exploring a broad range of association management issues and for introducing and discussing management and leadership philosophies. It is written for individuals at all levels of association management, with emphasis on senior staff and CEOs." Estab. 1979. Circ. 14,000. **Pays on acceptance.** Publishes ms an average of 6 months after acceptance. Byline given. Offers 20% kill fee. Buys first rights. Editorial lead time 3 months. Submit seasonal material 6 months in advance. Accepts simultaneous submissions. Reports in 2 weeks on queries; 2 months on mss. Sample copy and writer's guidelines free.

Nonfiction: How-to, humor, interview/profile, opinion, personal experience, travel, workplace issues. **Buys 24-36 mss/year.** Query with published clips. Length: 2,500-3,500 words. **Pays $500-700.** Pays expenses of writers on assignment.

Reprints: Accepts previously published submissions.

Columns/Departments: Intelligence (new ways to tackle day-to-day issues), 500-700 words; Off the Cuff (guest column for association executives). Query. **Pays $100-200.**

N $ $ IN TENTS, The Magazine for the Tent Rental and Special-Event Industries, Industrial Fabrics Association International, 1801 County Rd. B W., Roseville MN 55113-4061. (612)225-6988. Fax: (612)225-6966. E-mail: intents@ifai.com. Website: http://www.ifai.com. **Contact:** Chris Mikko, editor. Managing Editor: Andrew Bacskai. **50% freelance written.** Quarterly magazine covering tent-rental and special-event industries. Estab. 1994. Circ. 15,000. **Pays on acceptance.** Publishes ms an average of 2 months after acceptance. Byline given. Buys all rights. Editorial lead time 3 months. Sample copy and writer's guidelines free.

Nonfiction: How-to, interview/profile, new product, photo feature, technical. **Buys 10-12 mss/year.** Query. Length: 1,500-4,000 words. **Pays $100-400.** Sometimes pays expenses of writers on assignment.

Photos: State availability of photos with submission. Reviews contact sheets, negatives, transparencies and prints. Negotiates payment individually. Captions, model releases and identification of subjects required. Buys one-time rights.

Tips: "We look for lively, intelligent writing that makes technical subjects come alive."

$ $ $ $ JOURNAL OF ACCOUNTANCY, American Institution of CPAs, 201 Plaza 3, Harborside Financial Center, Jersey City NJ 07311. (201)938-3292. Fax: (201)938-3741. E-mail: scobb@aicpa.org. Publisher/Editor-in-Chief: Colleen Katz. Managing Editor: Elizabeth Uva. **Contact:** Sarah Cobb, manuscript editor. **20% freelance written.** Monthly magazine covering financial reporting and all subjects of concern to CPAs. "The Journal is published as a teaching tool for CPAs in public practice and in business and industry. Any business problem encountered by them is a good subject for the J of A as long as it is clearly stated and the solution given. Actual case studies are desired." Estab. 1897. Circ. 370,000. **Pays on acceptance.** Publishes ms an average of 3 months after acceptance. Byline given. Offers 25% kill fee. Buys all rights. Editorial lead time 4 months. Reports in 2 weeks on queries; 2 months on mss. Sample copy and writer's guidelines free.

Nonfiction: How-to, technical, business solutions. No non-business or non-CPA-related pieces. **Buys 24-40 mss/year.** Query with published clips and final ms. Length: 1,000-2,000 words. **Pays $1,000-2,200.**

Photos: State availability of photos with submission. Reviews transparencies. Negotiates payment individually. Identification of subjects required. Buys one-time rights.

Tips: "We want practical, how-to, implementation articles, based on CPAs' experience in solving companies' problems in areas such as financial reporting, mgt. accounting, cost management, benefits/compensation, technology, human resources, that is, teaching models."

N $ $ MEETINGS IN THE WEST, Stamats Communications, 550 Montgomery St., #750, San Francisco CA 94111. Fax: (415)788-0301. E-mail: 74117.432@compuserve.com. Website: http://www.meetingsweb.com. **Contact:** Jeanne Ricci, editor. Associate Editor: Sandi Garza. **50% freelance written.** Monthly tabloid covering meeting, event and conference planning. Estab. 1986. Circ. 30,000. Pays 1 month after acceptance. Publishes ms an average of 1 month after acceptance. Byline given. Offers 50% kill fee. Buys first North American serial rights and electronic rights. Editorial lead time 3 months. Submit seasonal material 3 months in advance. Reports in 3 weeks. Sample copy for 9×13 SAE and 5 first-class stamps. Writer's guidelines for #10 SASE.

Nonfiction: How-to (save money, theme party ideas, plan interesting meetings, etc.), travel (as it pertains to meetings and conventions, what to do after the convention, etc.). "No first-person fluff. We are a business magazine." **Buys 30 mss/year.** Query with published clips. Length: 1,200-2,400 words. **Pays 14¢/word.** Sometimes pays expenses of writers on assignment.

Photos: State availability of photos with submission. Offers no additional payment for photos accepted with ms. Identification of subjects required. Buys one-time rights.

$ $ MINI-STORAGE MESSENGER, MiniCo., Inc., 2531 W. Dunlap Ave., Phoenix AZ 85021. (602)870-1711. Fax: (602)861-1094. E-mail: messenger@minico.com. Website: http://www.minico.com. **Contact:** Bill Marks, managing editor. **90% freelance written.** Monthly magazine. "The *Mini-Storage Messenger* is written for owners and managers of self-storage facilities to help them run their business on a day-to-day basis. Topics include marketing, management, legal and operations." Estab. 1979. Circ. 6,000. **Pays on acceptance.** Publishes ms an average of 3 months after acceptance. Byline given. Offers 25% kill fee. Buys first rights and second serial (reprint) rights. Editorial lead time 4 months. Submit seasonal material 4 months in advance. Sample copy and writer's guidelines free.

Nonfiction: Business how-to (anything related to self-storage, e.g., how to market your facility); interview/profile. **Buys 72 mss/year.** Query. Length: 2,000-2,500 words. **Pays $200-350 for assigned articles; $50-350 for unsolicited articles.**

Columns/Departments: Finance, Legal, Management, Marketing, Operations. Length: 800-1,000 words. **Buys 48 mss/year.** Query. **Pays $50-350.**

Tips: "The *Mini-Storage Messenger* is very how-to oriented. Our intention is to help managers/owners run all aspects of their business. Step-by-step approaches, 10 tips, etc. are succinct and very appropriate articles. Articles should be specific to self-storage with real-life examples."

$ $ MINORITY BUSINESS ENTREPRENEUR (MBE), 3528 Torrance Blvd., Suite 101, Torrance CA 90503. (310)540-9398. Fax: (310)792-8263. E-mail: mbewbe@ix.netcom.com. Website: http://www.mbemag.com. **Contact:** Jeanie M. Barnett, editor-in-chief. Managing Editor: Lauren L. Bechen. **50% freelance written.** Bimonthly magazine covering minority and women business ownership and development. "*MBE* magazine examines programs in the public and private sectors designed to develop minority and women owned businesses into viable enterprises. *MBE* magazine covers a broad range of industries, from construction and banking to telecommunications and high tech." Estab. 1984. Circ. 50,000. Pays on publication. Byline given. Buys first North American serial rights. Editorial lead time 3 months. Reports in 3 weeks on queries. Sample copy for 9½×12½ SASE and 7 first-class stamps. Writer's guidelines free.

Nonfiction: Interview/profile. Nothing unrelated to minority or women's business. **Buys 4-6 mss/year.** Query with published clips. Length: 750-1,000 words. **Pays $0-300.** Sometimes pays expenses of writers on assignment.

Tips: Every issue features a Cover Story (spotlighting the achievements of an individual entrepreneur); Corporate View (highlighting corporate minority and women supplier programs); and Different Drummers (profiling innovators, risk takers, visionaries).

NORTHEAST EXPORT, A Magazine for New England Companies Exporting to the World, Laurentian Business Publishing, 404 Chestnut St., Suite 201, Manchester NH 03101-1831. (603)626-6354. Fax: (603)626-6359. E-mail: neexport@aol.com. **Contact:** Anita Becker, editor. **80% freelance written.** Bimonthly business-to-business magazine. "*Northeast Export* is the only publication directly targeted at New England's $21 billion export business community. All stories relate to issues affecting New England exporters and feature only New England-based exporters as profiles and examples. No unsolicited material." Estab. 1997. Circ. 13,500. Pays on publication. Byline given. Offers 10% kill fee. Buys all rights. Editorial lead time 2 months. Sample copy free.

Nonfiction: Interview/profile, new product, industry trends/analysis. "We will not take unsolicited articles. Query first with clips." **Buys 18-20 mss/year.** Query with published clips and SASE. Length: 800-2,000 words. Pay varies.

Photos: State availability of photos with submission or send photos with submission. Reviews 2¼ transparencies and 5×7 prints. Negotiates payment individually. Captions, model releases and identification of subjects required. Buys one-time rights.

Tips: "We're interested in freelancers with business writing and magazine experience, especially those with contacts in the New England manufacturing/exporting community."

$ $ $ $ PROFESSIONAL COLLECTOR, Cadmus Custom Publishing, 101 Huntington Ave., 13th Floor, Boston MA 02199-7603. (617)424-7700. Fax: (617)437-7714. E-mail: procollector@cadmuscustom.com. Editor: Michael Buller. **Contact:** Leeann Boyer, managing editor. **90% freelance written.** Quarterly magazine published for Western Union's Financial Services Inc.'s Quick Collect Service, covering debt collection business/lifestyle issues. "We gear our articles directly to the debt collectors, not their managers. Each issue offers features covering the trends and players, the latest technology, legislation and other issues affecting the collections industry. It's all designed to help collectors be more productive and improve their performance." Estab. 1993. Circ. 161,000. Pays on publication. Byline given. Buys first North American serial rights. Editorial lead time 6 months. Submit seasonal material 6 months in advance. Sample copy and writer's guidelines free.

Nonfiction: Book excerpts, general interest, how-to (tips on good collecting), humor, interview/profile, new product, legal issues for collectors/FDCPA, business/industry issues dealing with debt collectors. **Buys 10-15 mss/year.** Query with published clips. Length: 400-2,000 words. Pay negotiable for assigned articles. Sometimes pays expenses of writers on assignment.

Photos: State availability of photos with submission. Reviews contact sheets and 3×5 prints. Negotiates payment individually. Captions, model releases and identification of subjects required. Buys one-time rights.

Columns/Departments: Collectors & the Courts (collections legal issues), 250 words; Industry Roundup (issues within industry), 500-1,000 words; Tips, 750-1,000 words; Q&A (questions & answers for collectors), 1,500 words. **Buys 15-20 mss/year.** Query with published clips. Pay negotiable.

Tips: "Writers should be aware that *Professional Collector* is a promotional publication, and that its content must support the overall marketing goals of Western Union. It helps to have extensive insider knowledge about the debt collection industry."

$ $ RECORDS MANAGEMENT QUARTERLY, Association of Records Managers and Administrators, Inc., 310 Appomattox Dr., Brentwood TN 37027. E-mail: rmqeditor@aol.com. **Contact:** Ira A. Penn, editor. **10% freelance written.** Eager to work with new/unpublished writers. Quarterly professional journal covering records and information management. Estab. 1967. Circ. 12,000. Pays on publication. Publishes ms an average of 6 months after acceptance. Byline given. Buys all rights. Accepts simultaneous submissions. Reports in 1 month on mss. Sample copy $16. Free writer's guidelines.

Nonfiction: Professional articles covering theory, case studies, surveys, etc., on any aspect of records and information management. **Buys 20-24 mss/year.** Send complete ms and SASE. Mss must include 50- 75-word abstract, brief bio sketch and b&w photo of author. Length: 2,500 words minimum. **Pays $100-300 "stipend" and 2 copies of publication.** No contract.

Photos: Send photos with ms. Offers no additional payment for photos accepted with ms. Prefers b&w prints. Captions required.

Tips: "A writer *must* know our magazine. Most work is written by practitioners in the field. We use very little freelance writing, but we have had some and it's been good. A writer must have detailed knowledge of the subject he/she is writing about. Superficiality is not acceptable. No e-mail submissions!"

$ $ RENTAL MANAGEMENT, American Rental Association, 1900 19th St., Moline IL 61265. Fax: (309)764-1533. E-mail: brian.alm@ararental.org. Website: http://www.ararental.org. Editor: Brian R. Alm. Managing Editor: Tamera Dawson. 30% freelance written. Monthly business magazine for the equipment rental industry worldwide (*not* property, real estate, appliances, furniture or cars), emphasizing management topics in particular but also marketing, merchandising, technology, etc. Estab. 1970. Circ. 16,500. **Pays on acceptance.** Publishes ms an average of 3 months after acceptance. Byline sometimes given. Buys first North American serial rights. Editorial lead time 2 months. Submit seasonal material 3 months in advance. Does not report on unsolicited work unless being considered for publication. Sample copy for 9×12 SAE and 6 first-class stamps.

Nonfiction: Small-business management and marketing. **Buys 12-15 mss/year.** Query with published clips. Length: 600-1,500 words. Pay is negotiated. Sometimes pays expenses of writers on assignment.

Reprints: Sometimes accepts previously published submissions. Send tearsheet or typed ms with rights for sale noted and information about when and where the article previously appeared.

Photos: State availability of photos with submission. Reviews contact sheets, negatives, 35mm or 2¼ transparencies and any size prints. Negotiates payment individually. Identification of subjects required. Buys one-time rights.

Columns/Departments: "We are adequately served by existing columnists and have a long waiting list of others to use pending need." **Buys 20 mss/year.** Query with published clips. Pay is negotiated.

Tips: "Show me you can write maturely, cogently and fluently on management matters of direct and compelling interest to the small-business owner or manager in a larger operation; no sloppiness, no unexamined thoughts, no stiffness or affectation—genuine, direct and worthwhile English."

$ $ RETAIL INFO SYSTEMS NEWS, Where Retail Management Shops for Technology, Edgell Communications, 10 W. Hanover Ave., Suite 107, Randolph NJ 07869. **Contact:** Mark Frantz, editor. **60% freelance written.** Monthly magazine. "Readers are functional managers/executives in all types of retail and consumer goods firms. They are making major improvements in company operations and in alliances with customers/suppliers." Estab. 1988. Circ. 18,500. Pays on publication. Byline sometimes given. Buys first rights and second serial (reprint) rights. Editorial lead time 2-3 months. Submit seasonal material 3 months in advance. Sample copy for 11×15 SAE with 6 first-class stamps. Writer's guidelines for #10 SAE.

Nonfiction: How-to, interview/profile, technical. **Buys 100 mss/year.** Length: 1,200-2,400 words. **Pays $500 maximum for assigned articles.** Sometimes pays in contributor copies as negotiated. Sometimes pays expenses of writers on assignment.

Photos: Send photos with submission. Reviews contact sheets, negatives, transparencies and prints. Offers no additional payment for photos accepted with ms. Identification of subjects required. Buys one-time rights plus reprint, if applicable.

Tips: "Case histories about companies achieving substantial results using advanced management practices and/or advanced technology are best intro."

N $ $ $ SCRAP, Institute of Scrap Recycling Industries, 1325 G St. NW, Suite 1000, Washington DC 20005-3104. (202)662-8547. Fax: (202)626-0947. E-mail: kentkiser@compuserve.com. **Contact:** Kent Kiser, editor. Managing

Editor: Robert L. Reid. **15% freelance written.** Bimonthly magazine for the scrap recycling industry. "The magazine caters to processors, brokers and consumers of metallic and nonmetallic scrap commodities. Knowledge of recycling and the commodity market is helpful." Estab. 1987. Circ. 7,090. **Pays on acceptance.** Publishes ms an average of 2 months after acceptance. Byline given. Offers 50-75% kill fee. Buys all rights. Editorial lead time 3 months. Submit seasonal material 4 months in advance. Reports in 2 weeks on queries; 3 weeks on mss. Sample copy for $7.50.

Nonfiction: General interest, historical/nostalgic, how-to, interview/profile, new product, technical, multi-sourced features on a specific topic. "We use one to three freelancers per issue. Our six issues are themed as follows: Market Forecast (January/February); Convention (March/April); International (May/June); Operations and Equipment (July/August); Management (September/October); Commodities (November/December)." **Buys 6-10 mss/year.** "Query or call the editor." Length: 2,400-3,000 words. **Pays $600-1,000.** Pays expenses of writers on assignment.

Photos: State availability of photos with submission. Reviews contact sheets, transparencies and prints. Negotiates payment individually. Captions and identification of subjects required. Buys one-time rights.

Columns/Departments: Word to the Wise (business advice), 1,000 words; Over the Scale (operations/plant advice), 1,000 words. **Buys 4-6 mss/year.** Query. **Pays $50-300.**

Tips: "Call the editor to get a feel for the magazine and the industry."

$ $ SECURITY DEALER, PTN Publishing Co., 445 Broad Hollow Rd., Melville NY 11747. (516)845-2700. Fax: (516)845-7109. **Contact:** Susan A. Brady, editor. **25% freelance written.** Monthly magazine for electronic alarm dealers, burglary and fire installers, with technical, business, sales and marketing information. Circ. 25,000. Pays 3 weeks after publication. Publishes ms an average of 4 months after acceptance. Byline sometimes given. Buys first North American serial rights. Accepts simultaneous submissions.

Nonfiction: How-to, interview/profile, technical. No consumer pieces. Query or send complete ms. Length: 1,000-3,000 words. **Pays $300 for assigned articles; $100-200 for unsolicited articles.** Sometimes pays the expenses of writers on assignment.

Photos: State availability of photos with submission. Reviews contact sheets and transparencies. Offers $25 additional payment for photos accepted with ms. Captions and identification of subjects required.

Columns/Departments: Closed Circuit TV, Access Control (both on application, installation, new products), 500-1,000 words. **Buys 25 mss/year.** Query. **Pays $100-150.**

Tips: "The areas of our publication most open to freelancers are technical innovations, trends in the alarm industry and crime patterns as related to the business as well as business finance and management pieces."

$ $ SMALL BUSINESS NEWS, Philadelphia/South Jersey edition, Small Business News, 325 Chestnut St., Suite #1116, Philadelphia PA 19106. (215)923-6395. Fax: (215)923-5059. Website: http://www.sbnpub.com. **Contact:** Darrell L. Browning, editor. **10% freelance written.** Monthly magazine covering regional businesses with 500 employees or less. "We publish business articles showing, *by example*, how smaller businesses grow, avoid mistakes, turn their companies around, use innovation and creativity or engage in new trends to meet business objectives." Estab. 1988. Circ. 27,000. Pays on publication. Byline given. Offers 10% kill fee. Buys all rights. Editorial lead time 2 months. Submit seasonal material 2 months in advance. Sample copy for $2. Writer's guidelines for #10 SASE.

Nonfiction: How-to (save on employee turnover, avoid telephone fraud, etc.), opinion (industry trends). No fiction or book reviews. Query with 3 published clips. Length: 350-1,500 words. **Pays $150-500.**

Tips: "We publish *regional* business news combined with practical advice for owning and operating enterprises having 500 or less employees."

$ $ SMALL BUSINESS NEWS, Pittsburgh edition, Small Business News, Inc. 800 Vinial St., Suite B-208, Pittsburgh PA 15212. (412)321-6050. Fax: (412)321-6058. E-mail: sbnpubpi@interramp.com. Website: http://www.sbnpub.com. **Contact:** Daniel Bates, editor. **5% freelance written.** Monthly regional tabloid. "We provide information and insight designed to help companies grow. Our focus is on local companies and their successful business strategies, with the ultimate goal of educating entrepreneurs. Our target audience is business owners and other top executives." Estab. 1994. Circ. 23,000. Pays on publication. Publishes ms an average of 3 months after acceptance. Byline given. Buys all rights and makes work-for-hire assignments. Editorial lead time 2 months. Submit seasonal material 4 months in advance. Reports in 1 month on queries. Sample copy for $3. Writer's guidelines free.

Nonfiction: Book excerpts, how-to, interview/profile, opinion. Annual Golf, Energy and Telecommunication supplements, among others. "No basic profiles about 'interesting' companies or stories about companies with no ties to Pittsburgh." Query with published clips. Length: 250-1,000 words. **Pays $150-300 for assigned articles.**

Reprints: Accepts reprints of previously published submissions (mainly columns from business professionals). Send photocopy of article or short story and information about when and where the article previously appeared. Payment negotiable.

Photos: State availability of photos with submission. Reviews negatives and transparencies. Negotiates payment individually. Identification of subjects required. Buys one-time rights or all rights.

Tips: "Call the editor and set up a meeting for submission guidelines."

$ THE STATE JOURNAL, The State Journal Corp., 904 Virginia St. E., Charleston WV 25301. (304)344-1630. Fax: (304)345-2721. E-mail: sjeditor@aol.com. **Contact:** Jack Bailey, editor. **30% freelance written.** "We are a bi-weekly journal dedicated to providing stories of interest to the business community in West Virginia." Estab. 1984. Circ. 12,000. Pays on publication. Publishes ms an average of 2 months after acceptance. Byline given. Buys first rights.

Editorial lead time 2 months. Submit seasonal material 4 months in advance. Reports in 3 weeks on queries; 2 months on mss. Sample copy and writer's guidelines for #10 SASE.
Nonfiction: General interest, interview/profile, new product, opinion, all business related. **Buys 150 mss/year.** Query. Length: 250-1,500 words. **Pays $50.** Sometimes pays expenses of writers on assignment.
Photos: State availability of photos with submission. Reviews contact sheets. Offers $15/photo. Captions required. Buys one-time rights.
Columns/Departments: Business related, especially slanted toward West Virginia. **Buys 25 mss/year.** Query. **Pays $50.**

N $ TOWING AND RECOVERY PHOOTNOTES, Phootnote Publishing, 11520 N. Princeville Jubilee Rd., Princeville IL 61559. (309)243-7900. Fax: (309)243-7801. E-mail: pnotes@ix.netcom.com. **Contact:** Jon Lehman, editor. **99% freelance written.** Monthly business management tabloid for towing operators. Estab. 1990. Circ. 46,000. Pays on publication. Publishes ms an average of 3 months after acceptance. Byline given. Buys North American serial rights. Editorial lead time 1 month. Sample copy and writer's guidelines free.
Nonfiction: How-to, technical, business management. **Buys 60 mss/year.** Query with published clips. Length: 1,000-2,500 words. **Pays $50-100.**

N $ $ VIDEO BUSINESS, 245 W. 17th St., New York NY 10011-5300. Fax: (212)463-6710. E-mail: bapar@chilton.net. Website: http://www.chilton.com. **Contact:** Bruce Apar, executive editor. **10% freelance written.** Weekly magazine. "*Video Business* covers trends in marketing and videocassette programming for 50,000 retailers of all sizes. All articles should be written with the intent of providing information that a retailer can apply to his/her business immediately." Estab. 1981. Byline given. Buys first rights. Submit seasonal/holiday material 2 months in advance. Reports in 2 weeks. Free sample copy.
Nonfiction: Interview/profile, new product, technical. Query with published clips. **Pays 20-35¢/word.** Sometimes pays the expenses of writers on assignment.
Photos: State availability of photos with submission. Reviews negatives. Offers additional payment for photos accepted with ms. Buys one-time rights.

CHURCH ADMINISTRATION AND MINISTRY

Publications in this section are written for clergy members, church leaders and teachers. Magazines for lay members and the general public are listed in the Consumer Religious section.

N $ CE CONNECTION COMMUNIQUE, Creative Christian Ministries, P.O. Box 12624, Roanoke VA 24027. Fax: (540)342-7511. E-mail: ccmbbr@juno.com. **Contact:** Betty Robertson, editor. **50% freelance written.** Bimonthly newsletter, "a vehicle of communication for pastors, local church Christian education leaders and volunteer teachers." Estab. 1995. **Pays on acceptance.** Publishes ms an average of 6 months after acceptance. Byline given. Buys one-time rights. Editorial lead time 6 months. Submit seasonal material 6 months in advance. Accepts simultaneous submissions. Reports in 6 months. Sample copy for $3. Writer's guidelines for #10 SASE.
Nonfiction: How-to, new product. **Buys 12 mss/year.** Send complete ms. Length: 100-600 words. **Pays $5-10.**
Reprints: Accepts previously published submissions.

N $ THE CHRISTIAN MINISTRY, The Christian Century Foundation, 407 S. Dearborn St., Suite 1405, Chicago IL 60605. Fax: (312)427-1302. **Contact:** Victoria A. Rebeck, managing editor. Editor: James M. Wall. **80% freelance written.** Bimonthly magazine covering "practical concerns of Protestant clergy. Our readers are mainline (Presbyterian, Methodist, Episcopal, Lutheran, etc.) ministers who are comfortable with scholarly research and free inquiry." Estab. 1969. Circ. 6,000. Pays on publication. Publishes ms an average of 9 months after acceptance. Byline given. Offers 50% kill fee. Buys all rights. Editorial lead time 4 months. Submit seasonal material 9 months in advance. Reports in 1 month on queries; 2 months on mss. Sample copy for 9×11 SAE and $3. Writer's guidelines for #10 SASE.
Nonfiction: Essays, how-to, humor, interview/profile, personal experience, religious. "Articles must reflect our readers' theological sophistication." **Buys 50 mss/year.** Query. Length: 1,500-1,800 words. **Pays $65-100.** Pays writers with contributor copies or other premiums for book reviews. Sometimes pays expenses of writers on assignment.
Photos: Send photos with submission. Reviews 8×10 prints. Offers $35/photo. Captions required. Buys first rights.
Columns/Departments: Tricks of the Trade (short solutions to parish needs), 500 words; Reflection on Ministry (personal experiences of pastors), 1,800 words; Ministers' Workshop (practical approaches), 1,800 words. **Buys 24 mss/year.** Send complete ms. **Pays $75-100.**
Fiction: Religious. "Nothing unrelated to congregational life." **Buys 1 ms/year.** Send complete ms. Length: 1,500-1,800 words. **Pays $65-75.**
Tips: "Present manuscript neatly typed or printed out (double-spaced). Begin manuscript with an anecdote or narrative that represents the concern that the manuscript addresses. Keep aware of current trends in theological scholarship."

$ CREATOR MAGAZINE, Bimonthly Magazine of Balanced Music Ministries, 735 Industrial, San Carlos CA 94070. (650)598-0785. Fax: (650)593-0423. E-mail: creatormag@aol.com. **Contact:** Rod Ellis, editor. **35% freelance written.** Bimonthly magazine. "All readers are church music choir directors. Content focuses on the spectrum of worship styles from praise and worship to traditional to liturgical. All denominations subscribe. Articles on worship, choir rehearsal, handbells, children's/youth choirs, technique, relationships, etc." Estab. 1978. Circ. 6,000. Pays on publication. Publishes ms an average of 3 months after acceptance. Byline given. Buys first rights, one-time rights or second serial (reprint) rights; occasionally buys no rights. Editorial lead time 3 months. Submit seasonal material 4 months in advance. Accepts simultaneous submissions, if so noted. Sample copy for 9 × 12 SAE with 5 first-class stamps. Writer's guidelines free.

Nonfiction: Essays, how-to (be a better church musician, choir director, rehearsal technician, etc.), humor (short personal perspectives), inspirational, interview/profile (call first), new product (call first), opinion, personal experience, photo feature, religious, technical (choral technique). Special issues: July/August is directed toward adult choir members, rather than directors. **Buys 20 mss/year.** Query or send complete ms. Length: 1,000-10,000 words. **Pays $30-75 for assigned articles; $30-60 for unsolicited articles.** Pays expenses of writers on assignment.

Reprints: Accepts previously published submissions.

Photos: State availability of or send photos with submission. Reviews negatives, 8 × 10 prints. Offers no additional payment for photos accepted with ms. Captions appreciated. Buys one-time rights.

Columns/Departments: Hints & Humor (music ministry short ideas, anecdotes [cute] ministry experience), 75-250 words; Inspiration (motivational ministry stories), 200-500 words; Children/Youth (articles about specific choirs), 1,000-5,000 words. **Buys 15 mss/year.** Query or send complete ms. **Pays $20-60.**

Tips: "Request article guidelines and stick to them. If theme is relevant and guidelines are followed, we will probably publish."

$ THE JOURNAL OF ADVENTIST EDUCATION, General Conference of SDA, 12501 Old Columbia Pike, Silver Spring MD 20904-6600. (301)680-5075. Fax: (301)622-9627. E-mail: 74617.1231@compuserve.com. **Contact:** Beverly J. Rumble, editor. Bimonthly (except skips issue in summer) professional journal covering teachers and administrators in Seventh Day Adventist school systems. Estab. 1939. Circ. 7,500. Pays on publication. Publishes ms 1 year after acceptance. Byline given. Buys first rights. Editorial lead time 3 months. Reports in 6 weeks on queries; 4 months on mss. Sample copy for 10 × 12 SAE with 5 first-class stamps. Writer's guidelines free.

Nonfiction: Book excerpts, essays, how-to, personal experience, photo feature, religious, education. Theme issues have assigned authors. "No brief first-person stories about Sunday Schools." Query. Length: 1,000-1,500 words. **Pays $25-100.**

Reprints: Send tearsheet or photocopy of article and information about when and where the article previously appeared.

Photos: State availability of photos or send photos with submission. Uses mostly b&w. Reviews prints. Negotiates payment individually. Captions required. Buys one-time rights.

Tips: "Articles may deal with educational theory or practice, although the *Journal* seeks to emphasize the practical. Articles dealing with the creative and effective use of methods to enhance teaching skills or learning in the classroom are especially welcome. Whether theoretical or practical, such essays should demonstrate the skillful integration of Seventh-day Adventist faith/values and learning."

N $ KIDS' MINISTRY IDEAS, Review and Herald Publishing Association, 55 W. Oak Ridge Dr., Hagerstown MD 21740. (301)791-7000. Fax: (301)790-9734. E-mail: kidsmin@rhpa.org. **Contact:** Patricia Fritz, editor. Assistant Editor: Dwain Esmond. **95% freelance written.** "A quarterly resource for those leading children to Jesus, *Kids' Ministry Ideas* provides affirmation, pertinent and informative articles, program ideas, resource suggestions, and answers to questions from a Seventh-day Adventist Christian perspective." Estab. 1991. Circ. 5,000. **Pays on acceptance.** Publishes ms an average of 3 months after acceptance. Byline given. Kill fee varies. Buys first North American serial and electronic rights. Editorial lead time 3 months. Submit seasonal material 3 months in advance. Reports in 3 weeks on queries; 3 months on mss. Sample copy and writer's guidelines free.

Nonfiction: Inspirational, new product (related to children's ministry), articles fitting the mission of *Kids' Ministry Ideas.* **Buys 40-60 mss/year.** Send complete ms. Length: 500-1,500 words. **Pays $120 for assigned articles; $80 for unsolicited articles.**

Photos: State availability of photos with submission. Captions required. Buys one-time rights.

Columns/Departments: Buys 20-30 mss/year. Query. **Pays $60-120.**

Tips: "Request writers' guidelines and a sample issue."

$ $ LEADERSHIP, A Practical Journal for Church Leaders, Christianity Today, Inc., 465 Gundersen Dr., Carol Stream IL 60188. (630)260-6200. Fax: (630)260-0114. E-mail: leaderj@aol.com. Website: http://www.LeadershipJournal.net. Editor: Kevin A. Miller. **Contact:** Ginger MacFarland, editorial coordinator. **75% freelance written.** Works with a small number of new/unpublished writers each year. Quarterly magazine. Writers must have a "knowledge of and sympathy for the unique expectations placed on pastors and local church leaders. Each article must support points by illustrating from real life experiences in local churches." Estab. 1980. Circ. 70,000. **Pays on acceptance.** Publishes ms an average of 6 months after acceptance. Byline given. Buys first North American serial rights. Submit seasonal material 6 months in advance. Reports in 6 weeks on queries; 2 months on mss. Sample copy for $5. Free writer's guidelines.

Nonfiction: How-to, humor, personal experience. "No articles from writers who have never read our journal." **Buys 50 mss/year.** Send complete ms. Length: 100-5,000 words. **Pays $75-375.** Sometimes pays expenses of writers on assignment.

Photos: State availability of photos with submission. Offers no additional payment for photos accepted with ms.

Identification of subjects required. Buys one-time rights.
Columns/Departments: To Illustrate (short stories or analogies that illustrate a biblical principle), 100 words. **Buys 25 mss/year.** Send complete ms. **Pays $25-50.** To Quip (clean, funny humor that makes a point), 100 words. **Buys 12 mss/year.** Send complete ms. **Pays $25-35.**

N $ MOMENTUM, Official Journal of the National Catholic Educational Association, National Catholic Educational Association, 1077 30th St. NW, Suite 100, Washington DC 20007-3852. (202)337-6232. Fax: (202)333-6706. E-mail: momentum@ncea.org. Website: http://www.ncea.org. **Contact:** Patricia Feistritzer, editor. **25% freelance written.** Quarterly educational journal covering educational issues in Catholic schools, parishes and private schools. "*Momentum* is a membership journal of the National Catholic Educational Association. The audience is educators and administrators in Catholic and private schools K-12, and parish programs." Estab. 1970. Circ. 24,000. Pays on publication. Publishes ms an average of 3 months after acceptance. Byline given. Buys first rights. Sample copy for $5 SASE and 8 first-class stamps; writer's guidelines free.
Nonfiction: Educational trends, issues, research. "Do not want to see articles unrelated to educational and catechesis issues." **Buys 25-30 mss/year.** Query and send complete ms. Length: 1,500 words. **Pays $75 maximum.**
Photos: State availability of photos with submission. Reviews prints. Offers no additional payment for photos accepted with ms. Captions and identification of subjects required.
Columns and Departments: From the Field (practical application in classroom), 500 words; Justice and Peace Education (examples); DRE Direction (parish catechesis), all 900 words. **Buys 12-18 mss/year.** Query and send complete ms. **Pays $35 for From the Field; $50 for Justice and Peace & DRE Directions.**

$ PASTORAL LIFE, Society of St. Paul, P.O. Box 595, Canfield OH 44406-0595. Fax: (216)533-1076. **Contact:** Anthony Chenevey, SSP, editor. **66% freelance written.** Works with new/unpublished writers. "Monthly magazine designed to focus on the current problems, needs, issues and all important activities related to all phases of pastoral work and life." Estab. 1953. Circ. 2,000. Buys first rights only. Byline given. Pays on publication. Publishes ms an average of 4 months after acceptance. Reports in 1 month. Sample copy and writer's guidelines for 6×9 SAE with 4 first-class stamps.
Nonfiction: "*Pastoral Life* is a professional review, principally designed to focus attention on current problems, needs, issues and important activities related to all phases of pastoral work and life." Query with outline before submitting ms. "New contributors are expected to include, in addition, a few lines of personal data that indicate academic and professional background." **Buys 30 unsolicited mss/year.** Length: 2,000-3,000 words. **Pays 4¢/word minimum.**

$ PREACHING, Preaching Resources, Inc., P.O. Box 369, Jackson TN 38302. (901)668-9948. Fax: (901)668-9633. E-mail: 74114.275@compuserve.com. Website: http://www.preaching.com. Editor: Dr. Michael Duduit. **Contact:** Dr. Mark A. Johnson, managing editor. **75% freelance written.** Bimonthly magazine written by and for vocational ministers; articles by non-ministers are not accepted. Estab. 1985. Circ. 10,000. Pays on publication. Publishes ms an average of 1 year after acceptance. Byline given. Buys first rights. Submit seasonal material 1 year in advance. Reports in 4 months. Sample copy for $3.50. Writer's guidelines for SASE.
Nonfiction: How-to (preparation and delivery of sermon, worship leadership). "All articles must deal with preaching. Most articles used offer practical assistance in preparation and delivery of sermons, generally from an evangelical stance." Special issues: Personal Computing in Preaching (September-October); materials/resources to assist in preparation of seasonal preaching (November-December, March-April). **Buys 18-24 mss/year.** Query. Length: 1,000-2,000 words. **Pays $35-50.**
Photos: Send photos with submission. Reviews prints. Offers no additional payment for photos accepted with ms. Captions, model releases and identification of subjects required. Buys one-time rights.
Fillers: Buys 10-15/year. "Buys only completed cartoons." Art must be related to preaching. **Pays $25.**
Tips: "Most desirable are practical, 'how-to' articles on preparation and delivery of sermons."

$ $ THE PRIEST, Our Sunday Visitor, Inc., 200 Noll Plaza, Huntington IN 46750-4304. (219)356-8400. Fax: (219)359-9117. Editor: Father Owen F. Campion. **Contact:** George P. Foster, associate editor. **80% freelance written.** Monthly magazine. "We run articles that will aid priests in their day-to-day ministry. Includes items on spirituality, counseling, administration, theology, personalities, the saints, etc." **Pays on acceptance.** Byline given. Not copyrighted. Buys first North American serial rights. Editorial lead time 3 months. Submit seasonal material at least 4 months in advance. Reports in 2 weeks on queries; 6 weeks on mss. Sample copy and writer's guidelines free.
Nonfiction: Essays, historical/nostalgic, humor, inspirational, interview/profile, opinion, personal experience, photo feature, religious. **Buys 96 mss/year.** Send complete ms. Length: 1,500-5,000 words. **Pays $200 minimum for assigned articles; $50 minimum for unsolicited articles.**
Photos: Send photos with submission. Reviews transparencies and prints. Negotiates payment individually. Captions and identification of subjects required. Buys one-time rights.
Columns/Departments: Viewpoint (whatever applies to priests and the Church), 1,000 words. **Buys 36 mss/year.** Send complete ms. **Pays $50-100.**
Tips: "Say what you have to say in an interesting and informative manner and stop. Freelancers are most often published in 'Viewpoints.' Please do not stray from the magisterium of the Catholic Church."

N $ VISION NEWSLETTER, Christian Educators Association International, P.O. Box 41300, Pasadena CA 91114. (626)798-1124. Fax: (626)798-2346. E-mail: ceaieduca@aol.com. Website: http://www.ceai.com. **Contact:** Denise Jones, managing editor. Editor: Forrest Turpen. Newsletter published 9 times/year. "*Vision* is the official publication of CEAI, focusing on education issues pertinent to the Christian educator in public education. Topics include prayer in public schools, union activities, religious expression and activity in public schools and legal rights of Christian educators." Estab. 1953. Circ. 7,000. Pays on publication. Publishes ms an average of 6 months after acceptance. Byline given. Buys first rights. Editorial lead time 4 months. Submit seasonal material 6 months in advance. Accepts simultaneous submissions. Reports in 6 weeks on queries; 3 months on mss. Sample copy for 9×12 SAE and 4 first-class stamps. Writer's guidelines free.

Nonfiction: Humor, inspirational, interview/profile, opinion, personal experience, religious, book review, curriculum review. **Buys 1-2 mss/year.** Query. Length: 300-1,000 words. **Pays $30-40.** Pays in contributor copies for non-main features (book reviews, etc.).

Reprints: Accepts previously published submissions. Send information about when and where the article previously appeared. Pays our standard rate.

Photos: Send photos with submission. Offers no additional payment for photos accepted with ms. Identification of subjects required. Buys one-time rights.

Columns/Departments: Bible Study (for public school educators), 200-250 words.

Fiction: Ethnic, historical, humorous, religious. **Buys 2-6 mss/year.** Send complete ms. Length: 600-1,200 words. **Pays $30-40.**

Poetry: Avant-garde, free verse, haiku, light verse, traditional. Buys 1-4 poems/year. Submit maximum 1-2 poems. Pays in copies.

Fillers: Anecdotes, facts, newsbreaks, book reviews of interest to educators. Buys 1-5/year. Pays in copies..

N $ $ WORSHIP LEADER MAGAZINE, CCM Communications, 107 Kenner Ave., Nashville TN 37205. Fax: (615)385-4112. **Contact:** Melissa Riddle, managing editor. Editor: Chuck Fromm. **80% freelance written.** Bimonthly magazine covering all aspects of Christian worship. "*Worship Leader Magazine* exists to challenge, serve, equip and train the worship team of the 21st century church. The intended readership is the worship team (all those who plan and lead) of the local church." Estab. 1992. Circ. 45,000. Pays on publication. Byline given. Offers 50% kill fee. Buys first North American serial or all rights. Editorial lead time 3 months. Submit seasonal material 6 months in advance. Reports in 6 weeks on queries; 3 months on mss. Sample copy for $5. Writer's guidelines for #10 SASE.

Nonfiction: General interest, how-to (related to purpose/audience), inspirational, interview/profile, opinion. **Buys 15-30 mss/year.** Query with published clips. Length: 1,200-2,000 words. **Pays $200-800 for assigned articles; $200-500 for unsolicited articles.** Sometimes pays expenses of writers on assignment.

Photos: State availability of photos with submission. Negotiates payment individually. Identification of subjects required. Buys one-time rights.

Tips: "Our goal has been and is to provide the tools and information pastors, worship leaders, and ministers of music, youth, and the arts need to facilitate and enhance worship in their churches. In achieving this goal, we strive to maintain high journalistic standards, Biblical soundness, and theological neutrality. Our intent is to present the philosophical, scholarly insight on worship, as well as the day-to-day, 'putting it all together' side of worship, while celebrating our unity and diversity."

$ $ YOUR CHURCH, Helping You With the Business of Ministry, Christianity Today, Inc., 465 Gundersen Dr., Carol Stream IL 60188. (630)260-6200. Fax: (630)260-0114. E-mail: yceditor@aol.com. Website: http://www.christianity.net/yc. **Contact:** Phyllis Ten Elshof, editor. **70% freelance written.** Bimonthly magazine. "Articles pertain to the business aspects of ministry pastors are called upon to perform: administration, purchasing, management, technology, building, etc." Estab. 1955. Circ. 150,000. **Pays on acceptance.** Publishes ms an average of 4 months after acceptance. Byline given. Buys one-time rights. Submit seasonal material 5 months in advance. Accepts simultaneous submissions. Reports in 1 month on queries; 2 months on mss. Sample copy and writer's guidelines for 9×12 SAE with 5 first-class stamps.

Nonfiction: How-to, new product, technical. Special issues: Church Management, Construction. **Buys 25 mss/year.** Send complete ms. Length: 900-1,500 words. **Pays about 12½¢/word.**

Reprints: Send photocopy of article and information about when and where the article previously appeared. Pays 30% of the amount paid for an original article.

Photos: State availability of photos with submission. Reviews 4×5 transparencies and 5×7 or 8×10 prints. Offers no additional payment for photos accepted with ms. Captions, model releases and identification of subjects required. Buys one-time rights.

Tips: "The editorial is generally geared toward brief and helpful articles dealing with some form of church business. Concise, bulleted points from experts in the field are typical for our articles."

ALWAYS CHECK the most recent copy of a magazine for the address and editor's name before you send in a query or manuscript.

CLOTHING

$ $ APPAREL INDUSTRY MAGAZINE, The Industry's Voice Since 1946, Shore-Varrone, Inc., 6255 Barfield Rd., Suite 200, Atlanta GA 30328-4300. (404)252-8831. Fax: (404)252-4436. E-mail: aconrad@aimagazine.com. Website: http://www.aimagazine.com. **Contact:** Andrée Conrad, editor. Senior Editor: Faye Musselman. **50% freelance written.** Monthly magazine covering apparel manufacturing (not fashion) and management topics for apparel industry. "*Apparel Industry* just completed its 50th year of existence. It is one of the most respected business-to-business trade publications in the country, having won Neal Awards and many other prestigious prizes. Estab. 1946. Circ. 18,600. Pays on publication. Publishes ms an average of 3 months after acceptance. Byline given. Offers 50% kill fee. Buys first North American serial and second serial (reprint) rights. Editorial lead time 3 months. Submit seasonal material 3 months in advance. Sample copy for $5.

Nonfiction: Technical. "Articles are always assigned. We are looking for first-rate business writers all over the country who have the skills and the interest to write about high-tech apparel manufacturing today. Please send clips showing ability to write for trade publications." Query with ample published clips and SASE. *No unsolicited mss.* Sometimes pays expenses of writers on assignment.

Photos: Negotiates payment individually. Captions and identification of subjects required.

Tips: "Absolutely no unsolicited mss. will be considered. The magazine has too specific a focus for the editors to hope that freelancers could hit upon an article idea without editorial guidance. Writers who live in a town where apparel is manufactured may have a strike against them, having witnessed the ups and downs of the manufacturer in a period when much apparel manufacturing has moved offshore. Also, adverse publicity has tended to cloud perception of an industry which is actually very high-tech and continues to provide rewarding, interesting careers to highly creative individuals both here and abroad."

$ $ ATI, America's Textiles International, Billian Publishing Co., 2100 Powers Ferry Rd., Atlanta GA 30339. (770)955-5656. Fax: (770)952-0669. Website: http://www.billian.com/textile. **Contact:** Christopher Delporte, managing editor. **10% freelance written.** Monthly magazine covering "the business of textile, apparel and fiber industries with considerable technical focus on products and processes. No puff pieces pushing a particular product." Estab. 1887. Pays on publication. Byline given. Buys first North American serial rights.

Nonfiction: Technical, business. "No PR, just straight technical reports." **Buys 10 mss/year.** Query. Length: 500 words minimum. **Pays $200/published page.** Sometimes pays expenses of writers on assignment.

Photos: Send photos with submission. Reviews prints. Offers no additional payment for photos accepted with ms. Captions required. Buys one-time rights.

$ $ EMB-EMBROIDERY/MONOGRAM BUSINESS, Miller Freeman Inc., 13760 Noel Rd., #500, Dallas TX 75240. (972)239-3060. Fax: (972)419-7825. E-mail: lhowle@mfi.com. Website: http://www.embmag.com. **Contact:** LoLa Howle, editor. **30% freelance written.** Monthly magazine covering computerized embroidery and digitizing design. "Readable, practical business and/or technical articles that show our readers how to succeed in their profession." Estab. 1994. Circ. 20,100. **Pays on acceptance.** Publishes ms an average of 3 months after accceptance. Byline given. Buys one-time rights or all rights. Editorial lead time 2 months. Submit seasonal material 4 months in advance. Accepts simultaneous submissions. Reports in 6 weeks on queries; 2 months on mss. Sample copy for $7. Writer's guidelines not available.

Nonfiction: How to (embroidery, sales, marketing, design, general business info), new product, photo feature, technical (computerized embroidery). No PR fluff on a manufacturer. **Buys 4-6 mss/year.** Query. Length: 800-2,000 words. **Pays $200 and up for assigned articles.**

Photos: Send photos with submission. Reviews transparencies, prints. Negotiates payment individually. Buys one-time or all rights.

N $ FASHION MARKET MAGAZINE, Fashion Market Directory Group, 330 W. 38th St., 15th Floor, New York NY 10018. (212)760-5100. Fax: (212)760-5112. **Contact:** Jessica Goodman, editor. **85% freelance written.** Tabloid published 8 times/year. "The magazine is for buyers (fashion-women's apparel) when they come into town during market weeks. Manufacturers feature their clothes in the editorial, and the buyers see the clothing listed with the manufacturer's address and phone." Estab. 1985. Circ. 24,000. Pays on publication. Publishes ms an average of 1 month after acceptance. Byline given. Offers 100% kill fee. Buys all rights. Editorial lead time 1 month. Submit seasonal material 1 month in advance. Sample copy and writer's guidelines for 11×15 SASE.

Nonfiction: General interest, new product, photo feature, trend stories, general news in industry. No opinion pieces. **Buys 200 mss/year.** Query with published clips. Length: 100-250 words. **Pays 4¢/word; $25/column.** Sometimes pays expenses of writers on assignment.

Columns/Departments: News from the market (new people/products/changes), 200 words; Columns (trends with buyer's quotes), 200 words; Features (word and photo essays), 250 words. **Buys 100 mss/year.** Query with published clips. **Pays 4¢/word; $25/column.**

Tips: "We are looking for straightforward, journalistic news on the New York fashion market. Through news, trends supported by quotes from industry insiders. We want to tell what will sell."

$ $ MR MAGAZINE, The Magazine of Menswear Retailing, Business Journals, Inc., 185 Madison Ave., New York NY 10016. (212)686-4412. Fax: (212)686-6821. Editor: Karen Alberg Grossman. **Contact:** Hollee Actman, managing editor. **20% freelance written.** Magazine published 8 times/year covering "up-to-the-minute coverage of menswear industry and retailers." Estab. 1990. Circ. 30,000. Pays on publication. Publishes ms an average of 2 months after acceptance. Byline given. Buys all rights. Editorial lead time 2 months. Submit seasonal material 2 months in advance. Reports in 1 month. Sample copy for $3.50 (if available). Writer's guidelines free.

Nonfiction: Humor, interview/profile, new product, opinion, personal experience (all dealing with men and menswear). Editorial calendar available. **Buys 25-30 mss/year.** Query with published clips or send complete ms. Length: 500-2,000 words. **Pays $150-750.** Sometimes pays expenses of writers on assignment.

Reprints: Send tearsheet of article or typed ms with rights for sale noted and information about when and where the article previously appeared. Pays 100% of amount paid for an original article.

Photos: Send photos with submission. Reviews transparencies or prints. Offers no additional payment for photos accepted with ms. Identification of subjects required. Buys all rights.

CONFECTIONERY AND SNACK FOODS

These publications focus on the bakery, snack and candy industries. Journals for grocers, wholesalers and other food industry personnel are listed in Groceries and Food Products.

$ $ CONFECTIONER, APC, American Publishing Corp., 3108 Sowell Dr., Plano TX 75093. (972)758-0522. Fax: (972)758-0523. E-mail: treats@onramp.net. Website: http://www.confectioner.com. **Contact:** Lisbeth Echeandia, editor. **80% freelance written.** Bimonthly magazine covering the confectionery and snack food retailing and distribution industries. Estab. 1916. Circ. 13,571. Pays on publication. Byline given. Buys all rights. Editorial lead time 1 month. Submit seasonal material 2 months in advance. Accepts simultaneous submissions. Sample copy and writer's guidelines free.

Nonfiction: How-to, interview/profile, new product, opinion, technical. **Buys 15 mss/year.** Send complete ms. Length: 1,000-2,000 words. **Pays 30-35¢/word.** Sometimes pays expenses of writers on assignment.

Photos: State availability of photos with submission. Offers no additional payment for photos accepted with ms. Captions required. Buys all rights.

Tips: "Call the editor and ask for editorial calendar; discuss potential work; send samples."

$ $ PACIFIC BAKERS NEWS, 180 Mendell St., San Francisco CA 94124-1740. (415)826-2664. **Contact:** C.W. Soward, publisher. **30% freelance written.** Eager to work with new/unpublished writers. Monthly business newsletter for commercial bakeries in the western states. Estab. 1961. Pays on publication. No byline given; uses only 1-paragraph news items.

Nonfiction: Uses bakery business reports and news about bakers. Buys only brief "boiled-down news items about bakers and bakeries operating only in Alaska, Hawaii, Pacific Coast and Rocky Mountain states. We welcome clippings. We need monthly news reports and clippings about the baking industry and the donut business. No pictures, jokes, poetry or cartoons." Length: 10-200 words. **Pays 10¢/word for news and 6¢ for clips (words used).**

N $ $ PROFESSIONAL CANDY BUYER, The Business Magazine for Retail & Wholesale Decision Makers, Adams Business Media, 10225 Berea Rd. #C, Cleveland OH 44102-2501. Fax: (216)631-8210. E-mail: candybuyer@aol.com. Website: http://www.candybuyer.com. **Contact:** Teresa Tarantino, editor-in-chief. **20% freelance written.** "Bimonthly magazine covering retail and wholesale candy and snack buying and merchandising. All editorial *must* be written and directed to increasing retail and wholesale sales/profits of candy and snack items. Market trends in retailing only as they directly relate to candy and snacks and candy and snack segment trends are included." Estab. 1993. Circ. 12,500. Pays on publication. Publishes ms an average of 4 months after acceptance. Byline sometimes given. Offers 25% or $100 kill fee. Buys all rights. Editorial lead time 2 months. Submit seasonal material 10 months in advance. Reports in 6 weeks. Sample copy for 9×12 SASE.

Nonfiction: Interview/profile, new product. "No articles unrelated to candy/snack. No general business, general interest, retailing or distributing articles." **Buys 8-10 mss/year.** Query. Length: 1,800-3,000 words. **Pays $250-400.** Sometimes pays expenses of writers on assignment.

Photos: State availability of photos with submission. Reviews 2¼×2¼ or 4×5 prints. Negotiates payment individually. Captions and identification of subjects required. Buys all rights.

Tips: "Make sure to be well-versed in retail lingo. (FSIs, Wings, End Caps)."

CONSTRUCTION AND CONTRACTING

Builders, architects and contractors learn the latest industry news in these publications. Journals targeted to architects are also included in the Consumer Art and Architecture category. Those for specialists in the interior aspects of construction are listed under Building Interiors.

$ $ ABERDEEN'S CONCRETE CONSTRUCTION, The Aberdeen Group, 426 S. Westgate St., Addison IL 60101. (630)543-0870. Fax: (630)543-5399. E-mail: cceditor@wocnet.com. Website: http://www.supernetwork.net. Managing **Contact:** Anne Balogh, managing editor. Editor: Ward Malisch. **20% freelance written.** Monthly how-to magazine for concrete contractors, engineers, architects, specifiers and others who design and build residential, commercial, industrial and public works, cast-in-place concrete structures. It also covers job stories and new equipment in the industry. Estab. 1956. Circ. 80,000. **Pays on acceptance.** Publishes ms an average of 4 months after acceptance. Byline given. Editorial lead time 4 months. Submit seasonal material 4 months in advance. Reports in 2 weeks on queries; 1 month on mss. Sample copy and writer's guidelines free.
Nonfiction: How-to, new product, personal experience, photo feature, technical, job stories. Buys 7-10 mss/year. Query with published clips. Length: 2,000 words maximum. **Pays $250 or more for assigned articles; $200 minimum for unsolicited articles.** Pays expenses of writers on assignment.
Photos: Send photos with submission. Reviews contact sheets, negatives, transparencies, prints. Offers no additional payment for photos accepted with ms. Captions required. Buys one-time rights.
Tips: "Must have a good understanding of the concrete construction industry. How-to stories only accepted from industry experts. Job stories must cover the procedures, materials, and equipment used as well as the scope of the project."

N $ $ $ $ ARCHITECTURE MAGAZINE, BPI Communications, 1515 Broadway, 11th Floor, New York NY 10036. (212)536-6221. Fax: (212)382-6016. E-mail: info@architecturemag.com. Website: http://www.architecturemag.com. Editor: Reed Kroloff. **Contact:** Sam Barry, managing editor. **50% freelance written.** Monthly trade magazine covering architecture. "*Architecture* is edited for the architects, specifiers, and design professionals responsible for designing and specifying today's new building construction, existing rehabilitation, and remodeling projects." Estab. 1912. Circ. 80,000. **Pays on acceptance.** Publishes ms an average of 1 month after acceptance. Byline given. Offers 25% kill fee. Buys all rights. Editorial lead time 4 months. Writer's guidelines free.
Nonfiction: Architecture (related design, practice, and technology articles). Do not want to see product endorsements. **Buys 60 mss/year.** Query with published clips. Length: 300-2,000 words. **Pays $200-1,500 for assigned articles.** Sometimes pays expenses of writers on assignment.
Photos: State availability of photos with submission. Reviews 4×5 transparencies. Negotiates payment individually. Buys one time rights.
Columns and Departments: Pays $75-300.

$ $ AUTOMATED BUILDER, CMN Associates, Inc., 1445 Donlon St., Suite 16, Ventura CA 93003. (805)642-9735. Fax: (805)642-8820. E-mail: abmag@autbldrmag.com. Website: http://www.autbldrmag.com. Editor-in-Chief: Don Carlson. **15% freelance written.** Monthly magazine specializing in management for industrialized (manufactured) housing and volume home builders. Estab. 1964. Circ. 25,000. **Pays on acceptance.** Publishes ms an average of 3 months after acceptance. Buys first North American serial rights. Reports in 2 weeks. Sample copy and writer's guidelines free.
Nonfiction: Case history articles on successful home building companies which may be 1) production (big volume) home builders; 2) mobile home manufacturers; 3) modular home manufacturers; 4) prefabricated (panelized) home manufacturers; 5) house component manufacturers; or 6) special unit (in-plant commercial building) manufacturers. Also uses interviews, photo features and technical articles. "No architect or plan 'dreams'. Housing projects must be built or under construction." **Buys 15 mss/year.** Query. Phone queries OK. Length: 500-1,000 words maximum. **Pays $300 minimum.**
Photos: Purchased with accompanying ms. Query. No additional payment. Wants 4×5, 5×7 or 8×10 glossies or 35mm or larger color transparencies (35mm preferred). Captions required.
Tips: "Stories often are too long, too loose; we prefer 500 to 750 words. We prefer a phone query on feature articles. If accepted on query, article usually will not be rejected later."

$ $ CAM MAGAZINE, Construction Association of Michigan, 1625 S. Woodward, Bloomfield Hills MI 48302-3204. (248)972-1000. Fax: (248)972-1001. **Contact:** Phyllis L. Brooks, editor. **5% freelance written.** Monthly magazine covering all facets of the construction industry. "*CAM Magazine* is devoted to the growth and progress of individuals and companies serving and servicing the industry. It provides a forum on new construction-related technology, products and services, plus publishes information on industry personnel changes and advancements." Estab. 1978. Circ. 5,000. Pays on publication. Byline given. Buys all rights. Editorial lead time 2 months. Submit seasonal material 3 months in advance. Sample copy and editorial subject calendar with query and SASE.
Nonfiction: Construction-related only. **Buys 3 mss/year.** Query with published clips. Length: features: 1,000-2,000 words; will also review short pieces. **Pays $250-500.**
Photos: Send photos with submission. Reviews contact sheets, negatives, transparencies and color or b&w prints. Offers no additional payment for photos accepted with mss. Buys one-time rights.
Tips: "Anyone having *current* knowledge or expertise on trends and innovations related to construction is welcome to submit articles. Our readers are construction experts."

N $ $ CONSTRUCTION DIMENSIONS, Association of the Wall and Ceiling Industries-International, 307 E. Annandale Rd., Suite 200, Falls Church VA 22042. (703)534-8300. Fax: (703)534-8307. E-mail: editorcd@ix.netcom.com. Website: http://www.awci.org. **Contact:** L.M. Porinchak, editor. **25% freelance written.** Monthly magazine "written and edited for acoustical, ceiling, drywall, EIFS, fireproofing, insulation, plaster, steel framing and stucco contractors, suppliers and distributors, manufacturers and those in allied trades. Editorial coverage focuses on general management and human resources, construction systems how-to applications, new products and techniques available to the industry, and information to help contractors increase business an operate profitably." Estab. 1972. Circ. 23,000. **Pays on acceptance.** Publishes ms an average of 2 months after acceptance. Byline given. Buys first North American serial, second serial (reprint) rights and makes work-for-hire assignments. Editorial lead time 2 months. Reports in 6 months. Sample copy for $3 plus postage and handling prepaid.

Nonfiction: How-to, humor, interview/profile, new product, opinion, personal experience, photo feature, technical. No advertorials. **Buys 20 mss/year.** Send complete ms. Length: 800-1,200 words. Pay negotiated; no set rates. Pays 3 copies in addition to payment.

Photos: State availability of photos with submission. Negotiates payment individually. Captions required. Rights purchased are negotiable.

Columns/Departments: Time Out for Safety (construction safety advice), 500 words. **Buys 3 mss/year** ("would publish more if we got them"). Query. **Pays $50-150.**

Fiction: Humorous, slice-of-life vignettes. **Buys 3 mss/year.** Query. Length: 500-1,200 words. Pays $50.

Tips: "The best approach—a phone call. The editor will gladly speak to freelancers about potential work."

$ CONSTRUCTION EQUIPMENT GUIDE, 470 Maryland Ave., Ft. Washington PA 19034. (800)523-2200. Fax: (215)885-2910. E-mail: ceggltd@erols.com. **Contact:** Beth Baker, editor. **25% freelance written.** Biweekly newspaper. "We are looked at as the primary source of information in the construction industry by equipment manufacturers, sellers and users. We cover the Midwest, Northeast and Southeast states with our 3 editions published biweekly. We give the latest news on current construction projects, legislative actions, political issues, mergers and acquisitions, new unique applications of equipment and in-depth features." Estab. 1957. Circ. 80,000. Pays on publication. Publishes ms an average of 1 month after acceptance. Byline given. Offers 100% kill fee. Buys all rights. Editorial lead time varies. Accepts simultaneous submissions. Sample copy and writer's guidelines free.

Nonfiction: General interest, historical/nostalgic, how-to (winterizing construction equipment, new methods of construction applications), interview/profile, new product, personal experience, photo feature, technical. **Buys 150 mss/year.** Query with published clips. Length: 150-600 words. Negotiates payment individually. Pays expenses of writers on assignment.

Photos: Send photos with submission. Negotiates payment individually. Captions, identification of subjects required.

Columns/Departments: Equipment Auctions (photo coverage only with captions). Query. Pays $60 and expenses.

Tips: "Keep an eye out for commercial construction in your area. Take note of the name of the contractors on site. Then give us a call to see if you should follow up with a full story and photos. Pay attention to large and small jobs right around you. Read articles in *Construction Equipment Guide* to learn what information is important to our readers, who are mostly equipment users, sellers and makers."

$ $ CONSTRUCTION MARKETING TODAY, The Aberdeen Group, 426 S. Westgate St., Addison IL 60101. (708)543-0870. Fax: (708)543-3112. E-mail: rbrown@wocnet.com. Website: http://www.cmarket.net. **Contact:** Ross Brown, managing editor. **25% freelance written.** Monthly tabloid. "Our readers are manufacturers of construction equipment and building materials. Specifically, our readers are marketing people and top execs at those companies. The magazine carries business news, marketing case studies and marketing how-to articles. The magazine does not have heavily technical content, so writers need not be knowledgeable of the industry. Business writing and company profile writing experience are a plus." Estab. 1990. Circ. 4,000. Pays on publication. Byline given. Buys first rights and simultaneous rights. Editorial lead time 2 months. Pay varies. Reports in 5 weeks on queries; 2 months on mss. Sample copy free.

Nonfiction: Exposé, how-to (marketing), interview/profile, opinion, personal experience, business news, marketing trends. "No stories aimed at contractors or stories that show no relevancy to the industry." **Buys 7 mss/year.** Query with published clips. Length: 800-3,000 words. **Pays $300.** Pays in contributor's copies if "author is an industry consultant or has a service he is trying to sell to our readers, or he works for a manufacturing company." Sometimes pays expenses of writers on assignment.

Reprints: Occasionally accepts previously published submissions. Send photocopy of article and information about when and where the article previously appeared.

Photos: State availability of photos with submission. Reviews contact sheets. Negotiates payment individually. Captions and identification of subjects required. Buys all rights.

Tips: "Show that you have a grasp of what the magazine is about. We are not a technical how-to magazine geared to contractors, as most construction publications are. We have a unique niche. We are targeted to manufacturers marketing to contractors. We are looking for stories that have a fresh and intriguing look, that are entertaining to read, that are relevant to our readers, that are informative and that show an attention to detail in the reporting. Page one news, inside features, company profiles, industry marketing trends and marketing how-to stories are most open to freelancers. Stories should be tailored to our industry."

N $ $ CUSTOM BUILDER, Miller Freeman, Inc., 1 Penn Plaza, New York NY 10119. (212)615-2841. Fax: (212)279-3963. **Contact:** Marie Stock, managing editor. Editor: Matthew Power. **40% freelance written.** "*Custom Builder* is the bimonthly business magazine for builders of premier homes. The magazine spotlights the work of outstanding custom builders, provides in-depth coverage of products and technical info." Estab. 1987. Circ. 30,000. **Pays on**

acceptance. Publishes ms an average of 2 months after acceptance. Byline given. Buys all rights. Editorial lead time 4 months.

Nonfiction: How-to, interview/profile, new product, technical. Special issues: electronics (September-October); high-end kitchens and baths (July-August). **Buys 12-18 mss/year.** Query with published clips. Length: 1,000-1,200 words. **Pays $250-650.** Sometimes pays expenses of writers on assignment.

Photos: Send photos with submission. Reviews contact sheets, transparencies and prints. Negotiates payment individually. Captions and identification of subjects required. Buys all rights.

Columns/Departments: Query with published clips. **Pays $250-650.**

Tips: "It's best for freelancers to query first and provide photos (if possible) of an outstanding single-family custom home. We aim to provide custom builders with new information regarding homebuilding innovations, techniques, news, etc."

$ $ $ HARD HAT NEWS, Lee Publications, Inc., 6113 State Highway 5, Palatine Bridge NY 13428. (518)673-3237. Fax: (518)673-2381. **Contact:** Mary Hilton, editor. **25% freelance written.** Biweekly tabloid covering heavy construction, equipment, road and bridge work. "Our readers are contractors and heavy construction workers involved in excavation, highways, bridges, utility construction and underground construction." Estab. 1980. Circ. 24,000. Byline given. Not copyrighted. Editorial lead time 2 weeks. Submit seasonal material 2 weeks in advance. Accepts simultaneous submissions. Sample copy and writer's guidelines free.

Nonfiction: Interview/profile, new product, opinion, photo feature, technical. "No finished projects—we only look at job sites in progress." Send complete ms. Length: 50-1,400 words. **Pays $2.50/inch.** Sometimes pays expenses of writers on assignment.

Reprints: Accepts previously published submissions. Send tearsheet, photocopy or typed ms with rights for sale noted and information about when and where the article previously appeared. Pays 50% of amount paid for an original article.

Photos: Send photos with submission. Reviews 5×7 prints. Offers $5/photo. Captions and identification of subjects required.

Columns/Departments: New Products (user benefits); Open Houses (who was there); Association Meetings (coverage of national issues); all columns 50-600 words.

Fillers: Cartoons. **Pays $10/cartoon.**

Tips: "Visit the job site! Talk to the person in charge. Take photos of equipment—get manufacturer's name and model number and operator's name. Look for new techniques, procedures and products. We are especially interested in roads, bridges, excavation and demolition. When interviewing, find a problem/solution aspect of the job."

$ $ JOINERS' QUARTERLY, Journal of Timber Framing & Traditional Joinery, Fox Maple Press, Inc., P.O. Box 249, Brownfield ME 04010. (207)935-3720. Fax: (207)935-4575. E-mail: foxmaple@nxi.com. Website: http://www.nxi.com/WWW/joinersquarterly/Welcome.html. Managing Editor: Laurie LaMountain. **Contact:** Steve K. Chappell, editor. **75% freelance written.** Quarterly magazine covering traditional building, timber framing, natural and sustainable construction. Estab. 1982. Circ. 10,000. Pays on publication. Publishes ms an average of 9 months after acceptance. Byline given. Buys all rights. Editorial lead time 9 months. Submit seasonal material 6 months in advance. Accepts simultaneous submissions. Reports in 1 month on queries; 2 months on mss. Sample copy for $4.50. Writer's guidelines for #10 SASE.

Nonfiction: Historical/nostalgic (building techniques), how-to (timber frame, log build, sustainable materials, straw building), inspirational (craftsmanship), new product, technical (alternative building techniques). **Buys 12 mss/year.** Query. Length: 500-2,500 words. **Pays $50/published page.** Sometimes pays expenses of writers on assignment.

Reprints: Send photocopy of article or short story and information about when and where the article previously appeared. Pays 50-100% of amount paid for an original article.

Photos: Send photos with submission. Reviews transparencies and prints. Offers no additional payment for photos accepted with ms. Identification of subjects required. Buys all rights.

Tips: "We're looking for articles on sustainable construction, especially from a timber framing aspect. Architects, builders and owner/builders are our primary readers and writers. We also like to feature natural and historical home building techniques such as straw/clay, roof thatching, sod home, etc."

$ $ PERMANENT BUILDINGS & FOUNDATIONS (PBF), R.W. Nielsen Co., P.O. Box 11067, 5245 N. Kensington, Kansas City MO 64119. (816)453-0590. Fax: (816)453-0591. E-mail: rnielsen@pbf.org. Website: http://www.pbf.org. Managing Editor: Carolyn R. Nielsen. **Contact:** Roger W. Nielsen, editor. **35% freelance written.** Magazine published 7 times/year. "*PBF* readers are contractors who build residential, commercial and industrial buildings. Editorial focus is on materials that last: concrete and steel and new technologies to build solid, energy efficient structures, insulated concrete and tilt-up, waterproofing, underpinning, roofing and the business of contracting and construction." Estab. 1989. Circ. 35,000. Pays on publication. Byline given. Buys first North American serial rights. Editorial lead time 1 month. Submit seasonal material 2 months in advance. Reports in 2 weeks on queries; 2 months on mss. Sample copy for 9×12 SASE. Writer's guidelines free.

Nonfiction: How-to (construction methods, management techniques), humor, interview/profile, new product, technical, book reviews, tool reviews. Special issues: Steel framing supplement (November); Insulated Concrete Forming supplement (April). **Buys 25 mss/year.** Query. Length: 500-1,500 words. **Pays $150-750 for assigned articles; $50-500 for unsolicited articles.** Sometimes pays expenses of writers on assignment.

Photos: State availability of photos with submission. Reviews contact sheets. Offers no additional payment for photos

accepted with ms. Captions and identification of subjects required. Buys one-time rights.
Columns/Departments: Marketing Tips, 250-500 words; Q&A (solutions to contractor problems), 200-500 words. Query. **Pays $50-500.**

N $ $ **ST. LOUIS CONSTRUCTION NEWS & REVIEW**, Finan Publishing Co., 8730 Big Bend Blvd., St. Louis MO 63119. (314)961-6644. Fax: (314)961-4809. E-mail: mjolds@finan.com. Website: http://www.stlconstruction.com. **Contact:** Michael J. Olds, editor. **75% freelance written.** Monthly regional magazine covering projects, products, processes that affect the local industry. Estab. 1969. Circ. 6,500. Pays 30 days after acceptance. Byline given. Buys first North American serial rights or makes work-for-hire assignment. Editorial lead time 2 months. Submit seasonal material 3 months in advance. Sample copy free.
Nonfiction: Business, insurance, finance, hazard, computers as they relate to local construction. Query with published clips. Length: 1,600-2,000 words. **Pays $100-350.** Pays in contributor copies for business-related or sidebar-type articles published for byline only. Sometimes pays expenses of writers on assignment.
Reprints: Accepts previously published submissions. Send photocopy or typed ms with rights for sale noted and information about when and where the article previously appeared. Pay is negotiable.
Photos: State availability of photos with submission. Reviews contact sheets. Negotiates payment individually. Identification of subjects required. Negotiates rights purchased.
Columns/Departments: Business, Finance, Insurance (all construction-related), 800 words. Buys very few mss/year. Query with published clips. **Pays $50-300.**
Tips: "Anyone interested in freelance writing on an assigned basis may inquire regarding feature-length stories. All others interested in submitting business-related material which may be utilized in conjunction with a previously scheduled feature topic may do so. *CNR* also considers news stories."

$ $ **SHOPPING CENTER WORLD**, Intertec Publishing Corp., 6151 Powers Ferry Rd., Atlanta GA 30339-2941. (404)955-2500. Fax: (404)955-0400. E-mail: tdefranks@mindspring.com. Website: http://www.InternetReview.com. **Contact:** Teresa DeFranks, editor. **75% freelance written.** Prefers to work with published/established writers. Monthly magazine. "Material is written with the shopping center developer, owner, manager and shopping center tenant in mind." Estab. 1972. Pays on publication. Publishes ms an average of 3 months after acceptance. Byline given. Buys all rights. Reports in 2 months. Sample copy for $10.
Nonfiction: Interview/profile, new product, opinion, photo feature, technical. **Buys 50 mss/year.** Query with published clips or send complete ms. Length: 750-3,000 words. **Pays $75-500.** Sometimes pays expenses of writers on assignment.
Photos: State availability of photos with submission. Reviews 4×5 transparencies and 35mm slides. Offers no additional payment for photos accepted with ms. Model releases and identification of subjects required. Buys one-time rights.
Tips: "We are always looking for talented writers to work on assignment. Writers with real estate writing and business backgrounds have a better chance. Industry trends and state reviews are all freelance written on an assignment basis. Most assignments are made to those writers who are familiar with the magazine's subject matter and have already reviewed our editorial calendar of future topics."

DENTAL

$ $ **PROOFS, The Magazine of Dental Sales and Marketing**, PennWell Publishing Co., P.O. Box 3408, Tulsa OK 74101-3400. (800)633-1681. Fax: (918)831-9804. E-mail: markh@pennwell.com. Assistant Editor: Julie Harris. **Contact:** Mark Hartley, group editorial director. **5% freelance written.** Magazine published 10 times/year. "*Proofs* is the only publication of the dental trade, for dental dealers, sales forces and key marketing personnel of manufacturers. It publishes news of the industry (not the profession), personnel changes and articles on how to sell dental equipment and merchandise and services that can be provided to the dentist-customer." Estab. 1917. Circ. 7,000. Pays on publication. Byline given. Buys first North American serial rights. Editorial lead time 1 month. Reports in 2 weeks on queries. Sample copy and writer's guidelines free.
Nonfiction: General interest, historical/nostalgic, how-to, interview/profile, opinion, personal experience. "No articles written for dentist-readers." **Buys 15 mss/year.** Query or send complete ms. Length: 400-1,250. **Pays $100-200.**
Photos: Either state availability of photos with submission or send photos with submission. Reviews minimum size 3½×5 prints. Now uses color photographs. Offers no additional payment for photos accepted with ms. Identification of subjects required. Buys one-time rights.
Tips: "Learn something about the dental industry and how it operates. We do not want information on products and how they work, but will take news items on manufacturers' promotions involving products. Most interested in stories on how to sell *in the dental industry*; industry personnel feel they are 'unique' and not like other industries. In many cases, this is true, but not entirely. We are most open to feature articles on selling, supply-house operations, providing service."

DRUGS, HEALTH CARE AND MEDICAL PRODUCTS

N $ $ $ EYE NET MAGAZINE, Resources and Perspective for Eye Care, American Academy of Ophthalmology, 655 Beach St., San Francisco CA 94109. (415)561-8500. Fax: (415)561-8567. E-mail: eyenet@aao.org. Website: http://www.eyenet.org. **Contact:** Leslie Roberts, executive editor. Senior Editor: Melissa Hurley. **80% freelance written.** Monthly tabloid covering ophthalmology. "We circulate to medical eye doctors in the U.S. and abroad. We offer our readers coverage of clinical, socioeconomic and practice management issues that affect their lives." Circ. 18,000. **Pays on acceptance.** Publishes ms an average of 3 months after acceptance. Byline given. Offers $200 kill fee. Buys first North American serial rights. Editorial lead time 6 months. Submit seasonal material 6 months in advance. Reports in 1 month on queries; 2 months on mss. Sample copy for SAE and 5 first-class stamps. Writer's guidelines free.

Nonfiction: How-to, interview/profile, opinion, technical, clinical science relating to medical eye care. Does not want essays or historic. **Buys 120 mss/year.** Query with published clips. Length: 350-2,000 words. **Pays 50¢-$1/word.** Sometimes pays expenses of writers on assignment.

Reprints: Accepts previously published submissions.

Photos: State availability of photos with submission. Reviews transparencies and prints. Buys one-time rights.

$ $ OPTICAL PRISM, Canada's Optical Business Magazine, Vezcom, Inc., 31 Hastings Dr., Unionville, Ontario L3R 4Y5 Canada. (905)475-9343. Fax: (905)477-2821. E-mail: prism@istar.ca. **Contact:** Allan Vezina, editor. **90% freelance written.** Trade journal published 9 times/year covering the Canadian optical industry for "optometrists, opticians, ophthalmologists and optical suppliers and their sales staffs. Material covers clinical papers, practice management, contact lenses (clinical and practical), marketing, selling, motivation and merchandising." Estab. 1983. Circ. 7,800. **Pays on acceptance.** Publishes ms an average of 4 months after acceptance. Byline given. Not copyrighted. Buys one-time rights or second serial (reprint) rights. Editorial lead time 2 months. Submit seasonal material 3 months in advance. Accepts previously published submissions "with permission of original publisher in writing." Reports in 2 weeks. Sample copy and writer's guidelines free.

- *Optical Prism* offers detailed writer's guidelines that include a long list of possible topics for future freelance articles.

Nonfiction: How-to, inspirational, interview/profile, new product (article), technical (article). "No U.S.-specific material. We try to concentrate on the Canadian market." **Buys 35-40 mss/year.** Query. Length: 500-10,000 words. **Pays $100-700 (20¢/word)(Canadian).**

Reprints: Accepts previously published submissions. Send tearsheet, photocopy or typed ms with rights for sale noted and information about when and where the article previously appeared. Pays 3¢/word.

Photos: Send photos with submission. Reviews transparencies and prints. Offers no additional payment for photos accepted with ms. Captions, model releases and indentification of subjects required. Buys one-time rights.

Tips: "Send query with reasonably detailed outline of the article to be written along with the 'slant' to be taken, if any."

N $ $ OPTICAL TECHNOLOGY 21ST CENTURY, Frames Data, 16269 Laguna Canyon Rd., Irvine CA 92618. (714)788-0150. Fax: (714)788-0130. Website: http://www.framesdata.com. **Contact:** Christie Costanzo, editor. **20% freelance written.** Quarterly magazine for the eye wear industry. "*Optical Technology 21st Century* features articles for information-aware professionals who are looking for the newest and best means to improve their practices and increase profits through technology." Estab. 1970. Circ. 19,000. Pays on publication. Publishes ms an average of 3 months after acceptance. Byline given. Buys first North American serial rights. Editorial lead time 3 months. Submit seasonal material 3 months in advance. Accepts simultaneous submissions. Reports in 2 weeks on queries; 1 month on mss. Sample copy for 8×10 SAE with 2 first-class stamps. Writer's guidelines free.

Nonfiction: How-to, new product. **Buys 10 mss/year.** Query with published clips. Length: 800-1,600 words. **Pays $300-500.** Sometimes pays expenses of writers on assignment.

Reprints: Accepts previously published submissions.

Photos: Send photos with submission. Offers no additional payment for photos accepted with ms. Captions and identification of subjects required. Buys one-time rights.

$ OPTI-COURIER, Opti-Courier, Ltd., 158 Fisher Rd., Huntington Valley PA 19006. (215)938-1739. Fax: (215)947-5549. E-mail: eyetrain@aol.com. **Contact:** Linda Herman, editor. **65% freelance written.** Monthly magazine. "*Opti-Courier* is a zany publication that addresses the needs of optical practitioners and salespeople. Serious subjects such as technical articles and business suggestions are addressed, but always kept on the wild and crazy side." Estab. 1994. Circ. 36,000. Pays on publication. Publishes ms an average of 2 months after acceptance. Byline given. Buys all rights and makes work-for-hire assignments. Editorial lead time 3 months. Submit seasonal material 4 months in advance. Reports in 6 weeks on queries; 2 months on mss. Sample copy free.

Nonfiction: General interest, how-to (optical), humor, interview/profile, new product, personal experience, photo feature, technical, business. **Buys 100 mss/year.** Query. Length: 800-1,000 words. **Pays $50-100.** Sometimes pays expenses of writers on assignment.

Reprints: Accepts previously published submissions. Send tearsheet or photocopy of article.

Photos: Send photos with submission. Reviews b&w prints. Negotiates payment individually. Identification of subjects

required. Buys one-time rights.
Columns/Departments: Various optically-related columns. **Buys 15 mss/year.** Query. **Pays $50-100.**
Fillers: Facts, gags to be illustrated by cartoonist, short humor, cartoons, crossword puzzles, recipes. **Buys 100 mss/year.**
Tips: "Be familiar with the optical, or at least the business world. Offer the small-business person tips in a crazy, fun way. Do not send over-photocopied, fly-specked submissions that have clearly made the rounds. Clear copy is greatly appreciated. If you don't know anything about optical, go out and talk to someone in the business before writing anything. *You must know the differences among the 3 O's.*"

N $ $ SUN & SPORT EYEWEAR, Frames Data, 16269 Laguna Canyon Rd., Irvine CA 92618. (714)788-0150. Fax: (714)788-0130. Website: http://www.framesdata.com. **Contact:** Christie Costanzo, editor. **20% freelance written.** Quarterly magazine for the eye wear industry. "*Sun & Sport Eyewear* brings readers current information on all the latest designs and innovations available in the field of fashion and sports sunwear." Estab. 1970. Circ. 19,000. Pays on publication. Publishes ms an average of 3 months after acceptance. Byline given. Buys first North American serial rights. Editorial lead time 3 months. Submit seasonal material 3 months in advance. Accepts simultaneous submissions. Reports in 2 weeks on queries; 1 month on mss. Sample copy for 8×10 SAE with 2 first-class stamps. Writer's guidelines free.
Nonfiction: How-to, new product. **Buys 10 mss/year.** Query with published clips. Length: 800-1,600 words. **Pays $300-500.** Sometimes pays expenses of writers on assignment.
Reprints: Accepts previously published submissions.
Photos: Send photos with submission. Offers no additional payment for photos accepted with ms. Captions and identification of subjects required. Buys one-time rights.

EDUCATION AND COUNSELING

Professional educators, teachers, coaches and counselors—as well as other people involved in training and education—read the journals classified here. Many journals for educators are non-profit forums for professional advancement; writers contribute articles in return for a byline and contributor's copies. *Writer's Market* includes only educational journals that pay freelancers for articles. Education-related publications for students are included in the Consumer Career, College and Alumni; and Teen and Young Adult sections. Listings in the Childcare and Parental Guidance and Psychology and Self-Improvement sections of Consumer Magazines may also be of interest.

$ THE ATA MAGAZINE, The Alberta Teachers' Association, 11010 142nd St., Edmonton, Alberta T5N 2R1 Canada. (403)447-9400. Fax: (403)455-6481. E-mail: postmaster@teachers.ab.ca. Website: http://www.teachers.ab.ca. Editor: Tim Johnston. **Contact:** Raymond Gariepy, managing editor. **50% freelance written.** Quarterly magazine covering education. Estab. 1920. Circ. 39,500. Pays on publication. Publishes ms an average of 2 months after acceptance. Byline given. Offers kill fee of $75. Buys one-time rights. Editorial lead time 2 months. Submit seasonal material 2 months in advance. Accepts simultaneous submissions. Reports in 2 months. Sample copy and writer's guidelines free on request.
Nonfiction: Education-related topics. Length: 750-1,250 words. **Pays $75** (Canadian).
Photos: Send photos with submission. Reviews 4×6 prints. Negotiates payment individually. Captions required. Negotiates rights.

N THE CHRISTIAN CLASSROOM, Great River Publishing Company, Inc., 2026 Exeter Rd., Suite 2, Germantown TN 38138. (901)624-5911. Fax: (901)624-5910. **Contact:** Sherry Campbell, editor. **25% freelance written.** "*The Christian Classroom* is the only national magazine devoted exclusively to the interests and issues of concern to teachers in Christian schools." Estab. 1997. Circ. 20,000. Pays on publication. Publishes ms an average of 6 months after acceptance. Byline given. Offers negotiable kill fee. Buys all rights. Editorial lead time 3 months. Submit seasonal material 3 months in advance. Reports in 2 weeks on queries; 3 months on mss. Sample copy and writer's guidelines free.
Nonfiction: How-to, personal experience. "No articles that preach rather than give practical advice." **Buys 20 mss/year.** Query. Length: 300-1,500 words. Pay is negotiable.
Photos: State availability of photos with submission. Reviews prints (up to 8×10). Offers no additional payment for photos accepted with ms. Model releases required. Buys one-time rights.

N THE CHRISTIAN SCHOOL ADMINISTRATOR, Great River Publishing Company, Inc., 2026 Exeter Rd., Suite 2, Germantown TN 38138. (901)624-5911. Fax: (901)624-5910. **Contact:** Sherry Campbell, editor. **35% freelance written.** Bimonthly. "*The Christian School Administrator* provides Christian school administrators with news and information on such topics as legal issues, school financial management, parent and school relations, curriculum and educational materials, student recruitment, new technologies and school improvements. These administrators all face the same issues of budgeting, setting tuition rates, attracting new students, buying new equipment, fund raising and setting strong academic standards in a Christian environment." Estab. 1993. Circ. 13,000. Pays on publication. Publishes ms an average of 6 months after acceptance. Byline given. Offers negotiable kill fee. Buys all rights. Editorial lead time 3 months. Submit seasonal material 3 months in advance. Reports in 2 weeks on queries; 3 months on mss. Sample copy and writer's guidelines free.

Nonfiction: How-to, personal experience. "No articles that preach rather than give advice or relate experiences." **Buys 20-30 mss/year.** Query. Length: 300-1,500 words. Pay is negotiable.

Photos: State availability of photos with submission. Reviews prints (up to 8×10). Offers no additional payment for photos accepted with ms. Model releases required. Buys one-time rights.

Tips: "Writers should be familiar with private Christian schools, their practices, problems and issues of interest and concern to them."

$ CLASS ACT, Class Act, Inc., P.O. Box 802, Henderson KY 42419. E-mail: classact@henderson.net. **Contact:** Susan Thurman, editor. **65% freelance written.** Educational newsletter published 9 times/year covering English/language arts education. "Our writers must know English as a classroom subject and should be familiar with writing for teens. If you can't make your manuscript interesting to teenagers, we're not interested." Estab. 1993. Circ. 300. **Pays on acceptance.** Publishes ms an average of 6 months after acceptance. Byline given. Offers 100% kill fee. Buys all rights. Editorial lead time 2 months. Submit seasonal material 3 months in advance. Accepts simultaneous submissions. Reports in 1 month. Sample copy for $3. Writer's guidelines for #10 SASE.

Nonfiction: How-to (games, puzzles, assignments relating to English education). "NO Masters theses; no esoteric articles; no poetry; no educational theory or jargon." **Buys 15 mss/year.** Send complete ms. Length: 100-2,000 words. **Pays $10-40.**

Columns/Departments: Writing assignments (innovative, thought-provoking for teens), 500 words; puzzles, games (English education oriented), 200 words; teacher tips (bulletin boards, time-saving devices), 100 words. Send complete ms. **Pays $10-40.**

Fillers: Teacher tips. **Pays $10.**

Tips: "Please know the kind of language used by junior/senior high students. Don't speak above them. Also, it helps to know what these students *don't* know, in order to explain or emphasize the concepts. Clip art is sometimes used but is not paid extra for. We like material that's slightly humorous while still being educational. Especially open to innovative writing assignments, educational puzzles and games, and instructions on basics. Again, be familiar with this age group."

$ $ DANCE TEACHER NOW, The Practical Magazine of Dance, SMW Communications, Inc., 3101 Poplarwood Court, #310, Raleigh NC 27604-1010. Fax: (919)872-6888. E-mail: danceditor@aol.com. Website: http://www.dance-teacher.com. **Contact:** Neil Offen, editor. **80% freelance written.** Magazine published 10 times/year. "Our readers are professional dance educators, business persons and related professionals in all forms of dance. Estab. 1979. Circ. 8,000. Pays on publication. Publishes ms an average of 3 months after acceptance. Byline given. Negotiates rights and permission to reprint on request. Submit seasonal/holiday material 6 months in advance. Reports in 3 months. Sample copy for 9×12 SAE with 6 first-class stamps. Free writer's guidelines by mail or on website.

Nonfiction: How-tos (teach, business), interview/profile, new product, personal experience, photo feature. Special issues: Auditions (January); Summer Programs (February); Music & More (July/August); Costumes and Production Preview (November); College/Training Schools (December). No PR or puff pieces. All articles must be well researched. **Buys at least 50 mss/year.** Query first. Length: 1,500-3,500 words. **Pays $100-400.**

Reprints: Rarely buys previously published submissions. Send typed ms with rights for sale noted and information about when and where the article previously appeared.

Photos: Send photos with submission. Reviews contact sheets, negatives, transparencies and prints. Limited photo budget.

Columns/Departments: Practical Tips (how-tos or updates), 100-350 words. **Pays $25/published tip.** Free Calendar Listings (auditions/competitions/workshops), 50 words.

Tips: "Read several issues—particularly seasonal. Stay within writer's guidelines."

$ $ EARLY CHILDHOOD NEWS, The Journal of Professional Development, Peter Li, Inc., 330 Progress Rd., Dayton OH 45449. Fax: (937)847-5910. Website: http://www.earlychildhoodnews.com. **Contact:** Megan Shaw, editor. **95% freelance written.** Bimonthly magazine. "All articles must promote the professional development of those who work with children in child care settings." Estab. 1988. Circ. 24,000. Pays on publication. Publishes ms an average of 2 months after acceptance. Byline given. Buys first and second serial (reprint) rights. Editorial lead time 2 months. Submit seasonal material 4 months in advance. Accepts simultaneous and previously published submissions. Sample copy for $3. Writer's guidelines for #10 SASE.

Nonfiction: How-to (working with children), opinion, professional research-based development articles. No non-research-based activity articles. **Buys 40 mss/year.** Send complete ms. Length: 600-3,000 words. **Pays $75-200.**

Reprints: Accepts previously published submissions. Send photocopy of article or short story and information about when and where the article previously appeared. Pays 100% of amount paid for an original article.

Photos: Send photos with submission. Reviews 3×5 prints. Offers no additional payment for photos accepted with ms. Model releases and identification of subjects required. Buys one-time rights.

Columns/Departments: Parent Handout (reproducible newsletter for parents); Back Page ("warm and fuzzy" editorial). Length: 600 words. **Buys 12 mss/year.** Send complete ms. **Pays $75-100.**

Tips: "Have experience working with children in child care settings or have an advanced degree in early childhood education."

$ $ INSTRUCTOR MAGAZINE, Scholastic, Inc., 555 Broadway, New York NY 10012-3199. Website: http://www.scholastic.com/Instructor. **Contact:** Lauren Leon, managing editor. Publishing Coordinator: Joan Tashman. Eager to work with new/unpublished writers, especially teachers. Monthly magazine emphasizing elementary education. Estab. 1891. Circ. 275,000. **Pays on acceptance.** Publishes ms an average of 1 year after acceptance. Byline given. Buys all rights. Submit seasonal material 6 months in advance. Reports in 1 month on queries; 2 months on mss. Sample copy for $3. Writer's guidelines for SASE; mention *Writer's Market.*
Nonfiction: How-to articles on elementary classroom practice—practical suggestions and project reports. Occasionally publishes first-person accounts of classroom experiences. **Buys 100 mss/year.** Query. Length: 400-2,000 words. **Pays $25-75 for short items; $125-400 for articles and features.** Send all queries Attention: manuscripts editor.
Photos: Send photos with submission. Reviews 4×5 transparencies and prints. Offers no additional payment for photos accepted with ms. Model releases, identification of subjects required. Buys all rights.
Columns/Departments: Idea Notebook (quick teacher tips and ideas, seasonal activities, bulletin boards and crafts). Buys 100 mss/year. Query with SASE. Length: 50-1,000 words. Pays $20-100.
Tips: "How-to articles should be kept practical, with concrete examples whenever possible. Writers should keep in mind that our audience is elementary teachers."

$ THE MAILBOX TEACHER™, (formerly *Learning*), 3515 W. Market St., Greensboro NC 27403. E-mail: mteacher@theeducationcenter.com. Website: http://www.themailbox.com. **Contact:** Irv Crump, senior editor. **100% freelance written** by teachers and former teachers. Quarterly magazine covering educational topics for teachers in grades K-6. **Pays on acceptance.** Buys all rights. Submit seasonal material 9 months in advance. Reports in 9 months. Sample copy for $5.95. Writer's guidelines for SASE.
Nonfiction: "We publish manuscripts that describe innovative, practical teaching strategies." How-to and personal experience with unusual, innovative, and creative teaching techniques. Strong interest in articles that deal with discipline, working with parents, ways to save time and money, hints for helping different types of children, tips for dealing with everyday classroom challenges. **Buys 250 mss/year.** Query. Length: 100-500 words. **Pays $15-100.** Also pays with gift certificates for educational products.
Tips: "We are looking for innovative teaching ideas and practices as well as brief, first-hand personal accounts of funny or heartwarming teaching moments. No theoretical or academic papers. Noncurriculum topics. We are also interested in examples of especially creative classrooms and teachers. Emphasis is on top teachers telling what they do best and how."

$ SCHOOL ARTS MAGAZINE, 50 Portland St., Worcester MA 01608-9959. Fax: (610)683-8229. E-mail: katter@kutztown.edu. Website: http://www.Davis-art.com. **Contact:** Eldon Katter, editor. 85% freelance written. Monthly magazine (September-May), serving arts and craft education profession, K-12, higher education and museum education programs written by and for art teachers. Estab. 1901. Pays on publication. Publishes ms an average of 3 months "if timely; if less pressing, can be 1 year or more" after acceptance. Buys all rights. Reports in 3 months. Free sample copy and writer's guidelines.
Nonfiction: Articles on art and craft activities in schools. Should include description and photos of activity in progress, as well as examples of finished artwork. Query or send complete ms and SASE. Length: 600-1,400 words. **Pays $30-150.**
Tips: "We prefer articles on actual art projects or techniques done by students in actual classroom situations. Philosophical and theoretical aspects of art and art education are usually handled by our contributing editors. Our articles are reviewed and accepted on merit and each is tailored to meet our needs. Keep in mind that art teachers want practical tips, above all—more hands-on information than academic theory. Write your article with the accompanying photographs in hand." The most frequent mistakes made by writers are "bad visual material (photographs, drawings) submitted with articles, or a lack of complete descriptions of art processes; and no rationale behind programs or activities. Familiarity with the field of art education is essential. Review recent issues of *School Arts*."

N $ $ TEACHING THEATRE, Educational Theatre Association, 3368 Central Pkwy., Cincinnati OH 45225. (513)559-1996. **Contact:** James Palmarini, editor. **65% freelance written.** Membership benefit of the Educational Theatre Association. Quarterly magazine covering education theater K-12, primary emphasis on secondary level education. "*Teaching Theatre* emphasizes the teaching, theory, philosophy issues that are of concern to teachers at the elementary, secondary, and—as they relate to teaching K-12 theater—college levels. We publish work that explains specific approaches to teaching (directing, acting, curriculum development and management, etc.); advocates curriculum reform; or offers theories of theater education." Estab. 1989. Circ. 3,000. **Pays on acceptance.** Publishes ms an average of 1-3 months after acceptance. Byline given. Buys one-time rights. Editorial lead time 2 months. Submit seasonal material 3 months in advance. Accepts simultaneous and previously published submissions. Reports in 1 month on queries; 3 months on mss. Sample copy for $2. Writer's guidelines for #10 SASE.
Nonfiction: Book excerpts, essays, how-to, interview/profile, opinion, technical theater. "*Teaching Theatre*'s audience is well-educated and most have considerable experience in their field; *generalist* articles are discouraged; readers already *possess* basic skills." **Buys 20 mss/year.** Query. **Pays $100-300 for published articles.** "We generally pay cash and 5 copies of issue."

Reprints: Accepts previously published submissions.
Photos: State availability of photos with submission. Reviews contact sheets, 5×7 and 8×10 transparencies and prints. Offers no additional payment for photos accepted with ms.

$ $ $ $ TEACHING TOLERANCE, The Southern Poverty Law Center, 400 Washington Ave., Montgomery AL 36104. (205)264-0286. Fax: (205)264-3121. Website: http://www.splcenter.org. **Contact:** Jim Carnes, editor. **50% freelance written.** Semiannual magazine. "*Teaching Tolerance* is dedicated to helping K-12 teachers promote tolerance and understanding between widely diverse groups of students. Includes articles, teaching ideas, and reviews of other resources available to educators." Estab. 1991. Circ. 600,000. **Pays on acceptance.** Byline given. Buys all rights. Editorial lead time 6 months. Submit seasonal material 6 months in advance. Sample copy and writer's guidelines free.
Nonfiction: Features, essays, how-to (classroom techniques), personal classroom experiences, photo features. "No jargon, rhetoric or academic analysis. No theoretical discussions on the pros/cons of multicultural education." **Buys 6-8 mss/year.** Query with published clips. Length: 1,000-3,000 words. **Pays $500-3,000.** Sometimes pays expenses of writers on assignment.
Photos: State availability of photos with submission. Reviews contact sheets and transparencies. Offers no additional payment for photos accepted with ms. Captions and identification of subjects required. Buys one-time rights.
Columns/Departments: Essays (personal reflection, how-to, school program), 400-800 words; Idea Exchange (special projects, successful anti-bias activities), 400 words; Between the Lines, (using literature to teach tolerance), 1,200 words; Student Writings (Short essays dealing with diversity, tolerance & justice), 300-500 words. **Buys 8-12 mss/year. Pays $100-1,000.** Query with published clips.
Tips: "We want lively, simple, concise writing. The writing style should be descriptive and reflective, showing the strength of programs dealing successfully with diversity by employing clear descriptions of real scenes and interactions, and by using quotes from teachers and students. We ask that prospective writers study previous issues of the magazine and writer's guidelines before sending a query with ideas. Most open to articles that have a strong classroom focus. We are interested in approaches to teaching tolerance and promoting understanding that really work—approaches we might not have heard of. We want to inform our readers; we also want to inspire and encourage them. We know what's happening nationally; we want to know what's happening in your neighborhood classroom."

$ TEACHING K-8, The Professional Ideabook for Teachers, Early Years, Inc., 40 Richards Ave., 7th Floor, Norwalk CT 06854-2319. E-mail: teachingk8@aol.com. Website: http://www.teachingK-8.com. **Contact:** Patricia Broderick, editorial director. **75% freelance written.** Monthly magazine published September through May. "*Teaching K-8* is a professional journal for teachers of kindergarten through 8th grade. Features focus on successful teaching strategies, projects or programs based on classroom-tested ideas. Read several issues and thoroughly familiarize yourself with the types of articles we use." Estab. 1972. Circ. 120,000. Pays on publication. Publishes ms an average of 9 months after acceptance. Byline given. Buys all rights. Editorial lead time 2-12 months. Submit seasonal material 6 months in advance. Reports in 4-6 weeks. Sample copy for $4.50 and 9×12 SAE with 10 first-class stamps. Writer's guidelines for #10 SASE.
Nonfiction: Classroom curriculum material. No fiction, essays/memoirs, tributes. **Buys 40-50 mss/year.** "Shorter articles may appear in our Letters department." Send complete ms and SASE. "We welcome mss submitted on 3.5-inch Macintosh disk—WordPerfect or Word preferred. Do not fax or e-mail queries or mss." Length: 1,200 words. **Pays $50 maximum.**
Tips: "We do not accept queries, only complete manuscripts. Manuscripts should be specifically oriented to a successful teaching strategy, idea, project or program. Broad overviews of programs or general theory manuscripts are not usually the type of material we select for publication. Because of the definitive learning level we cover (preschool through grade eight), we try to avoid presenting general groups of unstructured ideas. We prefer classroom-tested ideas and techniques. Our market is classroom teachers. Read several issues to understand why they read *Teaching K-8*; this will give you the best idea of the material we publish."

N $ TECH DIRECTIONS, Prakken Publications, Inc., P.O. Box 8623, Ann Arbor MI 48107-8623. (734)975-2800. Fax: (734)975-2787. **Contact:** Tom Bowden, managing editor. **100% freelance written.** Eager to work with new/unpublished writers. Monthly magazine (except June and July) covering issues, trends and activities of interest to industrial, vocational, technical and technology educators at the secondary and postsecondary school levels. Estab. 1934. Circ. 45,000. Buys all rights. Pays on publication. Publishes ms an average of 8-12 months after acceptance. Byline given. No simultaneous submissions. Reports in 1 month. Sample copy $5. Writer's guidelines for #10 SASE.
Nonfiction: Uses articles pertinent to the various teaching areas in industrial and technology education (woodwork, electronics, drafting, machine shop, graphic arts, computer training, etc.). Prefers authors who have direct connection with the field of industrial and/or technical education. "The outlook should be on innovation in educational programs, processes or projects that directly apply to the industrial/technical education area." Buys general interest, how-to, opinion, personal experience, technical and think pieces, interviews and coverage of new products. **Buys 135 unsolicited mss/year.** Length: 1,000-2,000 words. **Pays $50-150.**
Photos: Send photos with accompanying query or ms. Reviews color prints. Payment for photos included in payment for ms.
Columns/Departments: Tech-Niques (brief items which describe short-cuts or special procedures relevant to the technology or vocational education). **Buys 30 mss/year.** Send complete ms. Length: 20-100 words. **Pays $25 minimum.**
Tips: "We are most interested in articles written by industrial, vocational and technical educators about their class

projects and their ideas about the field. We need more and more technology-related articles, especially written for the community college level."

$ $ $ TECHniques, Making Educational and Career Connections, American Vocational Associations, 1410 King St., Alexandria VA 22314. Fax: (703)683-7424. E-mail: marlene@avaonline.org. Website: http://www.avaonline.org. Editor: Ann Dykman. **Contact:** Marlene Lozada, associate editor. **10% freelance written.** Magazine published 8 times/year covering education with an emphasis on career preparation. "*TECHniques* has no 'slant.' We aim for an objective, journalistic treatment of issues. Readers are high school and community college teachers, administrators and counselors and also state education department or labor department employees." Estab. 1926. Circ. 40,000. Pays on publication. Publishes ms an average of 3 months after acceptance. Byline given. Offers 25% kill fee. Buys first North American serial rights and second serial (reprint) rights. Editorial lead time 3 months. Submit seasonal material 2 months in advance. Reports in 1 week on queries; 3 months on mss. Sample copy for $4.50. Writer's guidelines for #10 SASE.
Nonfiction: Book excerpts, general interest, how-to (teach, manage, setup a new school, implement educational reform), humor, interview/profile, opinion, personal experience, photo feature. No scholarly or technical articles. **Buys 8-10 mss/year.** Query with published clips or send complete ms. Length: 750-3,500 words. **Pays $200-1,000.** Sometimes pays expenses of writers on assignment.
Reprints: Send photocopy of article. Pay varies.
Photos: State availability of photos with submission. Reviews contact sheets, 2¼×2¼ transparencies, 4×6 prints. Negotiates payment individually. Model releases, identification of subjects required. Buys one-time rights.
Columns/Departments: Forum (opinion on issues), 750 words; Book reviews (subjects should relate to education or labor trends), 500-1,000 words. Query with published clips. **Pays $50-150.**
Tips: "Suggest story ideas, don't be cute, don't use exclamation points anywhere. Be enthusiastic, be professional—expect a 'round 2' of questions and requests for additional info."

$ $ TECHNOLOGY & LEARNING, 600 Harrison St., San Francisco CA 94107. Fax: (415)908-6604. E-mail: editors@techlearning.com. Website: http://www.techlearning.com. Editor-in-Chief: Judy Salpeter. **50% freelance written.** Works with a small number of new/unpublished writers each year. Monthly magazine published during school year emphasizing elementary through high school educational technology topics. Estab. 1980. Circ. 80,000. Pays on publication. Publishes ms an average of 8 months after acceptance. Buys all rights. Submit seasonal material 6 months in advance. Reports in 3-5 months. Sample copy for 8×10 SAE with $3 postage. Writer's guidelines for #10 SASE and online.
Nonfiction: "We publish manuscripts that describe innovative ways of using technology in the classroom as well as articles that discuss controversial issues in computer education." Interviews, brief technology-related activity ideas and longer featurettes describing fully developed and tested classroom ideas. **Buys 20 mss/year.** Query. Length: 800 words for software reviews; 1,500-2,500 words for major articles. **Pays $150 or more for reviews; $400 or more for articles.** Educational software reviews are assigned through editorial offices. "If interested, send a letter telling us of your areas of interest and expertise as well as the computer(s) and other equipment you have available to you." Pays expenses of writers on assignment.
Photos: State availability of photos with query.
Tips: "The talent that goes into writing our shorter hands-on pieces is different from that required for features (e.g., interviews, issues pieces, etc.). Write whatever taps your talent best. A frequent mistake is taking too 'novice' or too 'expert' an approach. You need to know our audience well and to understand how much they know about computers. Also, too many manuscripts lack a definite point of view or focus or opinion. We like pieces with clear, strong, well thought-out opinions."

$ $ TODAY'S CATHOLIC TEACHER, 330 Progress Rd., Dayton OH 45449-2386. (937)847-5900. Fax: (937)847-5910. **Contact:** Mary C. Noschang, editor. **40% freelance written.** Works with a small number of new/unpublished writers each year. For administrators and teachers concerned with Catholic schools and education in general. Estab. 1967. Circ. 50,000. Pays after publication. Publishes ms an average of 3 months after acceptance. Byline given. Buys all rights. Phone queries OK. Submit seasonal material 3 months in advance. Reports in 4 months. Sample copy for $3. Writer's guidelines for #10 SASE; mention *Writer's Market* in request.
Nonfiction: How-to (based on experience, particularly for teachers to use in the classroom to supplement curriculum, philosophy with practical applications); interview (of practicing educators, educational leaders); personal experience (classroom happenings other educators can learn from); a few profiles (of educational leaders). **Buys 40-50 mss/year.** Submit complete ms. Length: 800-2,000 words. **Pays $150-250.**
Reprints: Send typed ms with rights for sale noted and information about when and where the article previously appeared.
Photos: State availability of photos with ms. Possible additional payment for color or b&w glossy prints or transparencies. Buys one-time rights. Captions preferred; model releases required.
Tips: "We prefer articles that are of interest or practical help to educators—educational trends, teaching ideas, curriculum-related material, administration suggestions; articles teachers can use in classrooms to teach current topics, etc."

$ $ $ UNIVERSITY AFFAIRS, Association of Universities and Colleges of Canada, 600-350 Albert St., Ottawa, Ontario K1R 1B1 Canada. (613)563-1236. Fax: (613)563-9745. E-mail: pberkowi@aucc.ca. Website: http://www.aucc.ca. Publisher: Christine Tausig Ford. **Contact:** Peggy Berkowitz, managing editor. **25% freelance written.** Tabloid published 10 times/year "for university faculty and administrators across Canada, *University Affairs* contains news, issues and commentary about higher education and research." Estab. 1959. Circ. 24,000. **Pays on acceptance.** Byline given for features. Buys first or all rights. Editorial lead time 3 months. Reports in 2 weeks on queries; 1 month on mss. Sample copy free.

- *University Affairs* is looking for greater analysis and more issues-oriented articles related to "hot" topics in higher education.

Nonfiction: Essays, general interest, interview/profile, opinion, photo feature. **Buys 25 mss/year.** Query with published clips. Length: 1,000-1,800 words. **Pays $400-1,000 (Canadian).**

Photos: State availability of photos with submission. Reviews contact sheets, negatives, transparencies, prints. Negotiates payment individually. Captions, model releases, identification of subjects required. Buys one-time rights.

Columns/Departments: Around the Universities (short articles about research or teaching achievements or "firsts"), 200 words. Query with published clips. **Pay $50-75 (Canadian).**

Tips: "Read the publication before contacting me. Have a solid understanding of both my needs and the subject matter involved. Be accurate, check facts, and make sure your writing is high quality. Most articles and ideas we accept are focused specifically on Canadian universities."

N $ VISION, Christian Educators Association, P.O. Box 41300, Pasadena CA 91114. E-mail: ceaieduca@aol.com. **Contact:** Judy Turpen, contributing editor. Editor: Forrest L. Turpen. Managing Editor: Denise Jones. **30% freelance written.** Newsletter published 9 times/year for Christian teachers in public education. Estab. 1953. Circ. 10,000. Pays on publication. Publishes ms an average of 6 months after acceptance. Byline given. Buys first North American serial or second serial (reprint) rights. Editorial lead time 6 months. Submit seasonal material 4 months in advance. Accepts simultaneous submissions. Reports in 1 month on queries; 6 months on mss. Sample copy for 9×12 SAE and 4 first-class stamps. Writer's guidelines for #10 SASE.

Nonfiction: How-to, inspirational, interview/profile, personal experience, religious. "Nothing preachy." **Buys 15-20 mss/year.** Query or send complete ms if 2,000 words or less. Length: 600-2,500 words. **Pays $30-40.** Pays for poetry and book reviews.

Reprints: Accepts previously published submissions.

Photos: State availability of photos with submission. Offers no additional payment for photos accepted with ms. Buys one-time and reprint rights.

Columns/Departments: Query. **Pays $30-40.**

Poetry: Free verse, traditional. **Buys 2-4 poems/year.** Submit maximum 3 poems. Length: 6-40 lines. **Pays $20-30.**

Fillers: Anecdotes, facts. Buys 2-4/year.

$ WONDERFUL IDEAS, P.O. Box 64691, Burlington VT 05406-4691. 1-(800)92-IDEAS. Fax: (973)376-9382. E-mail: nancy@wonderful.com. **Contact:** Nancy Segal Janes, publisher. **40% freelance written.** Newsletter published 5 times/year. "*Wonderful Ideas* provides elementary and middle school teachers with creative and thought-provoking math activities, games, and lessons, with a focus on manipulatives and problem solving. Teacher-written and classroom-tested, these activities are designed to challenge students, while drawing strong connections between mathematical concepts and concrete problems. Book reviews and relationships of activities to NCTM Standards are also included." Estab. 1989. Circ. 1,700. Pays on publication. Publishes ms an average of 6 months after acceptance. Byline given. Buys all rights. Editorial lead time 3 months. Submit seasonal material 3 months in advance. Accepts simultaneous submissions. Reports in 1 month on queries; 3 months on mss. Sample copy and writer's guidelines free.

Nonfiction: Ideas for teaching elementary and middle school mathematics. **Buys 10-15 mss/year.** Query or send ms with SASE. Length: 900 words. **Pays $20-60.**

Reprints: Photocopy of article or short story and information about when and where the article previously appeared. **Pays $20-60.**

Columns/Departments: Wonderful Materials (review of new math materials and books), 700 words. **Buys 3 mss/year.** Puzzlers (double-sided problem-solving cards), **buys 30 mss/year;** Make-It Math (article featuring puzzle or activity); Wonderful Ideas. Query or send ms with SASE. **Pays $20-60.**

ELECTRONICS AND COMMUNICATION

These publications are edited for broadcast and telecommunications technicians and engineers, electrical engineers and electrical contractors. Included are journals for electronic equipment designers and operators who maintain electronic and telecommunication systems. Publications for appliance dealers can be found in Home Furnishings and Household Goods.

N $ THE ACUTA JOURNAL OF TELECOMMUNICATION IN HIGHER EDUCATION, ACUTA, 152 W. Zandale Dr., Suite 200, Lexington KY 40503-2486. (606)278-3338. Fax: (606)278-3268. E-mail: pscott@acuta.org. Website: http://www.acuta.org. **Contact:** Patricia Scott, editor. **20% freelance written.** Quarterly professional association journal covering telecommunications in higher education. "Our audience includes, primarily, middle to upper management in the telecommunications department on college/university campuses. They are highly skilled, technology-oriented professionals who provide data, voice and video communications services for residential and academic purposes." Estab. 1997. Circ. 2,200. Pays on publication. Publishes ms an average of 6 months after acceptance. Byline given. Buys first rights. Editorial lead time 5-6 months. Reports in 2-4 weeks on queries; 1-2 months on mss. Sample copy for 9×12 SASE and 6 first-class stamps; writer's guidelines free.

Nonfiction: How-to (telecom), technical (telecom), case study (college/university application of technology). "Each issue has a focus. Available with writer's guidelines. We are only interested in articles described in article types." **Buys 6-8 mss/year.** Query. Length: 1,200-4,000 words. **Pays 8-10¢/word.** Sometimes pays expenses of writers on assignment.

Photos: State availability of photos with submission. Reviews prints. Offers no additional payment for photos accepted with ms. Captions and model releases required.

Tips: "Our audience expects every article to be relevant to telecommunications on the college/university campus, whether it is related to technology, facilities, or management. Writers must read back issues to understand this focus and the level of technicality we expect."

$ $ AMERICA'S NETWORK, Advanstar Communications, 201 Sandpointe Ave., Suite 600, Santa Ana CA 92707. (714)513-8400. Fax: (714)513-8634. Website: http://www.americasnetwork.com. **Contact:** Mary Slepicka, executive editor. Managing Editor: David Kopf. **25% freelance written.** Published twice monthly covering the public telecommunications network. "*America's Network* evaluates emerging technologies from a business-case perspective for those who conceive, design and run America's public network." Estab. 1909. Circ. 57,000. Pays on publication. Byline given. Offers $100 kill fee. Buys all rights. Editorial lead time 2 months. Submit seasonal material 2 months in advance. Reports in 1 month on queries; 2 weeks on mss. Sample copy for $4.95 (call (800)346-0085, ext 477). Writer's guidelines free (call (714)513-8422).

Nonfiction: Technical, market research. No news or business pieces. **Buys 35 mss/year.** Query with published clips. Length: 1,500-3,000 words. **Pays 50¢/word for "high-tech" and 35¢/word for "low-tech" articles.**

Photos: State availability of photos with query or send photos with submission. Reviews transparencies and prints. Offers no additional payment for photos accepted with ms. Captions, model releases and identification of subjects required. Buys one-time rights or all rights.

Tips: "Send your full résumé with technical writing/engineering experience highlighted. We keep a file of potential writers."

N $ $ $ COMMUNICATION SYSTEMS DESIGN, Miller Freeman, Inc., 525 Market St., Suite 500, San Francisco CA 94105. (415)278-5255. Fax: (415)278-5340. Website: http://www.csdmag.com. **Contact:** Nicole Westmoreland, editor-in-chief. **75% freelance written.** Monthly magazine covering communication electronics design. "Our readers are electronic engineers who design communication products, like cellular phones, networking gear and satellite equipment, etc. The editorial coverage focuses on 'how to' design specific applications at the chip, board and box/system level." Estab. 1995. Circ. 35,000. Pays on publication. Publishes ms an average of 2 months after acceptance. Byline given. Buys all rights. Editorial lead time 4 months. Reports in 2 weeks on queries; 1 month on mss. Sample copy and writer's guidelines free.

Nonfiction: Technical, engineering. No market trend or product pitches. **Buys 48-52 mss/year.** Query. Length: 2,400-3,000 words. **Pays $500-950.** Sometimes pays expenses of writers on assignment.

Columns/Departments: Top 10 (10 short issues on communication technologies), 1,100 words; CSD 2018 (back page opinion piece), 750 words. **Buys 24-26 mss/year. Pays $350-500.**

$ $ $ COMMUNICATIONS NEWS, Nelson Publishing, 2504 N. Tamiami Trail, Nokomis FL 34275. (941)966-9521. Fax: (941)966-2590. E-mail: nelpub@ix.netcom.com. Website: http://www.comnews.com. Editor: Ripley Hotch. **Contact:** Features Editor. **40% freelance written.** Monthly magazine covering communications networks with "controlled circulation for data and voice communications, specifically network managers. Solutions-oriented for end users of networking software and equipment at medium-sized to large organizations." Estab. 1966. Circ. 80,000. **Pays on acceptance.** Publishes ms an average of 2 months after acceptance. Byline given. Offers 25% kill fee. Buys first rights. Editorial lead time 3 months. Reports in 2 weeks on queries.

Nonfiction: Interview/profile, new product, networking solutions. **Buys 30 mss/year.** Query with published clips. Length: 200-1,400 words. **Pays $100-1,200.** Pays expenses of writers on assignment.

Photos: Send photos with submission. Reviews transparencies. Negotiates payment individually. Identification of subjects required. Buys one-time rights.

Tips: "All submissions and initial contacts should be written. We advise checking our website for latest editorial calendar and guidelines."

$ COMMUNICATIONS QUARTERLY, P.O. Box 465, Barrington NH 03825-0465. Phone/Fax: (603)664-2515. E-mail: ka1stc@aol.com or commquart@aol.com. Publisher: Richard Ross. **Contact:** Terry Littlefield, editor. **80% freelance written.** Quarterly publication on theoretical and technical aspects of amateur radio and RF communication industry technology. Estab. 1990. Circ. 10,000. Pays on publication. Publishes ms an average of 6 months after acceptance. Byline given. Buys first rights. Reports in 1 month. Writer's guidelines for #10 SASE.

Nonfiction: "Interested in technical and theory pieces on all aspects of amateur radio and the RF communications industry. State-of-the-art developments are of particular interest to our readers. No human interest stories or articles related to the cable TV or broadcast industries." Query or send complete ms. **Pays $40/published page.**

Reprints: Sometimes accepts previously published submissions. Send photocopy of article and information about when and where the article previously appeared. Pays 100% of amount paid for an original article.

Photos: Send photos with submission. Reviews 5×7 prints. Offers no additional payment for photos accepted with ms. Captions and identification of subjects required. Buys one-time rights.
Tips: "We are looking for writers with knowledge of the technical or theoretical aspects of the amateur radio and communication industries. Our readers are interested in state-of-the-art developments, high-tech construction projects and the theory behind the latest technologies."

N $ $ CUSTOM HOME ELECTRONICS, Bobit Publishing, 21061 South Western Ave., Torrance CA 90501. (310)533-2400. Fax: (310)533-2504. E-mail: che@bobit.com. **Contact:** Amanda Finch, editor. **75% freelance written.** Monthly magazine covering custom home installation and design. "We are trade only. We speak directly to the custom installing dealer, not to the consumer. If you have a technical expertise, we would love to hear from you." Estab. 1995. Circ. 10,000. Pays on publication. Publishes ms an average of 2 months after acceptance. Byline given. Buys first North American serial rights. Editorial lead time 4 months. Submit seasonal material 6 months in advance. Accepts simultaneous submissions. Reports in 3 weeks on queries; 2 months on mss. Sample copy and writer's guidelines free.
Nonfiction: How-to, interview/profile, new product, photo feature, technical, installation features. No reviews. **Buys 30 mss/year.** Query with published clips. Length: 1,500-5,000 words. **Pays $100/printed page.** Sometimes pays expenses of writers on assignment.
Photos: Send photos with submission. Reviews transparencies and prints. Negotiates payment individually. Captions, model releases and identification of subjects required. Buys one-time rights.
Tips: "If you are an expert in an area of custom installation and design, your submissions are welcome. Our publication is *very* technical and not aimed at the consumer market. Study the publication and then query with clips."

$ $ RADIO WORLD NEWSPAPER, IMAS Publishing, Suite 310, 5827 Columbia Pike, Falls Church VA 22041. (703)998-7600. E-mail: 74103.2435@compuserve.com. Editor-in-Chief: Lucia Cobo. **Contact:** Paul J. McLane, managing editor. News Editor: Matt Spangler. **Contact:** Al Peterson, technical editor. **75% freelance written.** Biweekly newspaper on radio station technology and ownership concerns. "Articles should be geared toward radio station engineers, producers, technical people and managers. The approach should be more how-to than theoretical, although emerging technology may be approached in a more abstract way." Estab. 1977. Circ. 18,000. Pays on publication. Publishes ms an average of 2 months after acceptance. Byline given. Buys first rights. Submit seasonal material 2 months in advance. Reports in 2 months. Sample copy and writer's guidelines free.
Nonfiction: Book excerpts, exposé, historical/nostalgic, how-to (radio equipment maintenance and repair), humor, interview/profile, new product, opinion, personal experience, photo feature, technical. **Buys 500 mss/year.** Length: 500-1,000 words. Query with published clips. **Pays $75-250.** Pays in contributor copies or other premiums "if they request it, and for one special feature called Workbench." Sometimes pays expenses of writers on assignment.
Reprints: Send tearsheet or typed ms with rights for sale noted and information about when and where the article previously appeared. Pay varies.
Photos: Send photos with submission. Reviews 3×5 or larger prints. Negotiates payment individually. Identification of subjects required. Buys one-time rights.
Columns/Departments: Chris Joaquim, Buyers Guide editor. Buyers Guide User Reports (field reports from engineers on specific pieces of radio station equipment). Query. Length: 750-1,250 words.
Fillers: Newsbreaks, short humor. **Buys 6/year.** Length: 500-1,000 words. **Pays $25-75.**
Tips: "I frequently assign articles by phone. Sometimes just a spark of an idea can lead to a story assignment or publication. The best way is to have some radio station experience and try to think of articles other readers would benefit from reading."

N $ $ $ $ SOUND & VIDEO CONTRACTOR, Intertec Publishing, 9800 Metcalf Ave., Overland Park KS 66212-2286. (913)967-1755. Fax: (913)967-1905. E-mail: nat_hecht@intertec.com. **Contact:** Nathaniel Hecht, editor. **60% freelance written.** Monthly magazine covering "professional audio, video, security, acoustical design, sales and marketing." Estab. 1983. Circ. 24,000. **Pays on acceptance.** Publishes ms an average of 3 months after acceptance. Byline given. Buys one-time or all rights. Editorial lead time 3 months. Accepts simultaneous submissions. Reports ASAP on mss and queries. Sample copy and writer's guidelines free.
Nonfiction: Historical, how-to, photo feature, technical, professional audio/video applications, installations. No product reviews, opinion pieces, advertorial, interview/profile, exposé/gossip. **Buys 60 mss/year.** Query. Length: 1,000-2,500 words. **Pays $200-3,500 for assigned articles; $200-650 for unsolicited articles.**
Reprints: Accepts previously published submissions "if not previously or simultaneously published in our market segment."
Photos: Send photos with submission. Reviews transparencies and prints. Offers no additional payment for photos accepted with ms. Identification of subjects required.
Columns/Departments: Security Technology Review (technical install information); Sales & Marketing (sales and marketing techniques for installation industry); Video Happenings (Pro video/projection/storage technical info), all 1,500 words. **Buys 30 mss/year.** Query. **Pays $200-350.**
Tips: "We want materials and subject matter that would be of interest to audio/video/security/low-voltage product installers/contractors/designers professionals. If the piece allows our readers to save time, money and/or increases their revenues, then we have reached our goals. Highly technical is desirable."

ENERGY AND UTILITIES

People who supply power to homes, businesses and industry read the publications in this section. This category includes journals covering the electric power, natural gas, petroleum, solar and alternative energy industries.

$ $ ELECTRICAL APPARATUS, The Magazine of Electromechanical & Electronic Application & Maintenance, Barks Publications, Inc., 400 N. Michigan Ave., Chicago IL 60611-4198. (312)321-9440. **Contact:** Elsie Dickson, editorial director. Senior Editor: Kevin N. Jones. Monthly magazine for persons working in electrical and electronic maintenance, chiefly in industrial plants, who install and service electrical motors, transformers, generators, controls and related equipment. Estab. 1967. Circ. 17,000. **Pays on acceptance.** Publishes ms an average of 3 months after acceptance. Byline given. Buys all rights unless other arrangements made. Reports in 1 week on queries; 1 month on mss. Sample copy for $4.

Nonfiction: Technical. Length: 1,500-2,500. **Pays $250-500 for assigned articles. Pays authorized expenses.**

Tips: "All feature articles are assigned to staff and contributing editors and correspondents. Professionals interested in appointments as contributing editors and correspondents should submit résumé and article outlines, including illustration suggestions. Writers should be competent with a camera, which should be described in résumé. Technical expertise is absolutely necessary, preferably an E.E. degree, or practical experience. We are also book publishers and some of the material in *EA* is now in book form, bringing the authors royalties. Also publishes an annual directory, subtitled *ElectroMechanical Bench Reference.*"

$ $ HOME ENERGY, Energy Auditor and Retrofitter, Inc., 2124 Kittredge St., Berkeley CA 94704. (510)486-6048. Fax: (510)486-4673. E-mail: homeenergy@anl.gov. Website: http://www.homeenergy.org. **Contact:** Steven Bodzin, managing editor. **40% freelance written.** Bimonthly magazine. "We provide practical information for professionals in residential energy conservation and home energy auditing." Estab. 1984. Circ. 3,500 (readership 12,000). Pays on publication. Publishes ms an average of 2 months after acceptance. Byline given. Buys one-time rights and electronic rights. Editorial lead time 2 months after acceptance. Submit seasonal material 4 months in advance. Accepts simultaneous submissions. Reports in 3 weeks on queries; 1 month on mss. Sample copy for 9×12 SAE with 4 first-class stamps. Writer's guidelines for #10 SASE or fax number.

Nonfiction: How-to (install, repair, or maintain HVAC, analyze energy use, implement conservation measures), new product (HVAC, insulation). No articles that promote products rather than offering a critical view. **Buys 10-15 mss/year.** Query. Length: 1,000-3,500 words. **Pays 20¢/word to $300.** Sometimes pays expenses of writers on assignment.

Reprints: Accepts previously published submissions.

Photos: State availability of photos with submission. Reviews contact sheets, transparencies, prints. Offers no additional payment for photos accepted with ms. Captions required. Buys one-time rights.

Columns/Departments: Trends (developments and other short reports about residential energy use), 1,000 words. **Buys 15-20 mss/year.** Send complete ms. **Pays 20¢/word.**

Tips: "Know the technology you are covering and make the article interesting and readable for an informed consumer."

$ $ PUBLIC POWER, Dept. WM, 2301 M St. NW, Washington DC 20037-1484. (202)467-2948. Fax: (202)467-2910. **Contact:** Jeanne Wickline LaBella, editor/publisher. **60% freelance written.** Prefers to work with published/established writers. Bimonthly. Estab. 1942. **Pays on acceptance.** Publishes ms an average of 3 months after acceptance. Byline given. Reports in 6 months. Sample copy and writer's guidelines free.

Nonfiction: Features on municipal and other local publicly owned electric utilities. **Pays $400 and up.**

Photos: Reviews transparencies, slides and prints.

N $ $ $ PUBLIC UTILITIES FORTNIGHTLY, Public Utilities Reports, 8229 Boone Blvd., Suite 401, Vienna VA 22182. Fax: (703)847-0683. Website: http://www.pur.com. **Contact:** Joseph F. Schuler, Jr., senior associate editor. Editor: Bruce Radford. Managing Editor: Elizabeth Striano. **65% freelance written.** Biweekly (monthly during August and December) magazine covering the electric, natural gas and telecommunications markets. "We are rooted in regulation. That is our history. However, to be competitive we need to anticipate issues 6-12 months out. Writing for our readers requires 'forward thinking.' " Estab. 1928. Circ. 6,627. **Pays on acceptance.** Publishes ms an average of 3 months after acceptance. Byline given. Offers $250 kill fee. Buys all rights. Editorial lead time 2 months. Accepts simultaneous submissions. Reports in 1 month on queries; 2 months on mss. Sample copy for 10×13 SAE with 5 first-class stamps. Writer's guidelines for #10 SASE.

Nonfiction: Technical, features. No interview/profiles, essays, opinion pieces, nuts-and-bolts articles. **Buys 12 mss/year,** also contracts for 24 others that pay only in reprints. Query with published clips. Length: 2,500-3,000 words. **Pays $1,250 for assigned articles; $1,000 for unsolicited articles.** "Our freelance budget is new this year. We are shifting from 'free' experts to journalists to boost editorial quality." Pays writers with contributor copies or other premiums for assigned pieces by experts in the field. Sometimes pays expenses of writers on assignment.

Photos: State availability of photos with submission. Reviews transparencies. Negotiates payment individually. Captions, model releases and identification of subjects required. Buys one-time rights.

Tips: "Know the business. Know the publication, and that's hard, as we're a $119/year subscription-based publication. Libraries and university libraries subscribe, and our website is somewhat informative. We are a trade publication, but we like stories that quote sources around all sides of an issue. We like issues that spring from regulation but that haven't yet blipped on the radar. We're looking for well-rounded features, proposed in queries that surprise us."

$ RELAY MAGAZINE, Florida Municipal Electric Association, P.O. Box 10114, Tallahassee FL 32302-2114. (904)224-3314. **Contact:** Stephanie Wolanski, editor. **5% freelance written.** Monthly magazine. "Must be electric utility-oriented, or must address legislative issues of interest to us." Estab. 1942. Circ. 2,100. Pays on publication. Byline given. Not copyrighted. Buys first North American serial, one-time and second serial (reprint) rights. Accepts simultaneous submissions. Reports in 3 months.
Nonfiction: Interview/profile, technical and electric innovations. Query first; no unsolicited mss. Length: 3-6 pages double-spaced. **Pays $50, minimum.**
Reprints: Accepts previously published submissions. Query first. Send photocopy of article or typed ms with rights for sale noted and information about when and where article previously appeared.
Photos: State availability of photos with submission. Pay and rights purchased vary. Captions and identification of subjects required.

N $ UTILITY AND TELEPHONE FLEETS, Practical Communications, Inc., 321 Cary Point Dr., P.O. Box 183, Cary IL 60013-0183. (847)639-2200. Fax: (847)639-9542. E-mail: utfmag@utfmag.com. Website: http://www.utfmag.com. **Contact:** Alan Richter, editor/publisher. **10% freelance written.** Magazine published 8 times/year for fleet managers and maintenance supervisors for electric gas and water utilities, telephone, interconnect and cable TV companies, public works departments and related contractors. "Case history/application features are also welcome." Estab. 1987. Circ. 18,000. Pays on publication. Publishes ms an average of 1 month after acceptance. Byline given. Offers 20% kill fee. Buys all rights. Submit seasonal material 2 months in advance. Reports in 2 months. Free sample copy and writer's guidelines.
Nonfiction: How-to (ways for performing fleet maintenance/improving management skills/vehicle tutorials), technical, case history/application features. No advertorials in which specific product or company is promoted. **Buys 2-3 mss/year.** Query with published clips. Length: 1,000-2,800 words. **Pays $55/page.**
Photos: Send photos with submission. Reviews contact sheets, negatives, 3×5 transparencies and prints. Offers no additional payment for photos accepted with ms. Captions required. Buys one-time rights.
Tips: "Working with a utility or telephone company and gathering information about a construction, safety or fleet project is the best approach for a freelancer."

ENGINEERING AND TECHNOLOGY

Engineers and professionals with various specialties read the publications in this section. Publications for electrical, electronics and telecommunications engineers are classified separately under Electronics and Communication. Magazines for computer professionals are in the Information Systems section.

$ $ CANADIAN CONSULTING ENGINEER, Southam Magazine Group Ltd., 1450 Don Mills Rd., Don Mills, Ontario M3B 2X7 Canada. (416)445-6641. E-mail: skneisel@southam.ca. **Contact:** Sophie Kneisel, editor. **20% freelance written.** Bimonthly magazine covering consulting engineering in private practice. Estab. 1958. Circ. 8,900. Pays on publication. Publishes ms an average of 2 months after acceptance. Byline given depending on length of story. Offers 50% kill fee; $100 minimum. Buys first North American serial rights. Editorial lead time 6 months. Reports in 3 months on queries. Sample copy free.
Nonfiction: Historical, new product, technical. **Buys 8-10 mss/year.** Query with published clips. Length: 300-1,500 words. **Pays $200-500 for assigned articles; $100-400 for unsolicited articles.** Sometimes pays expenses of writers on assignment.
Photos: State availability of photos with submission. Negotiates payment individually. Buys one-time rights.
Columns/Departments: Export (selling consulting engineering services abroad); Management (managing consulting engineering businesses); On-Line (trends in AEC systems). Length: 800 words. **Buys 4 mss/year.** Query with published clips. **Pays $250-400.**

N $ $ $ GRADUATING ENGINEER & COMPUTER CAREERS, Peterson's, 202 Carnegie Center, P.O. Box 2123, Princeton NJ 08543-2123. Fax: (609)243-8928. E-mail: paulal@petersons.com. Website: http://www.careertech.com. **Contact:** Paula Lipp, editor-in-chief. Managing Editor: Terry Deal. **30% freelance written.** "Recruitment publication for engineering/computer science students published 7 times/year. Our readers are college technical students—they're smart, savvy and hip. The writing must be, too." Circ. 70,000. **Pays on acceptance.** Publishes ms an average of 2 months after acceptance. Byline given. Offers $50 kill fee. Buys all rights. Editorial lead time 2 months. Submit seasonal material 6 months in advance. Accepts simultaneous submissions. Reports in 2 weeks on queries; 3 months on mss. Sample copy and writer's guidelines free.
Nonfiction: Book excerpts, exposé, interview/profile, personal experience. Special issues: Minorities (February and October); Women (March). **Buys 40 mss/year.** Send complete ms. Length: 1,500-3,000 words. **Pays $200-800 for assigned articles; $50-300 for unsolicited articles.** Sometimes pays expenses of writers on assignment.
Photos: Send photos with submission. Reviews 3×5 prints. Offers no additional payment for photos accepted with

ms. Identification of subjects required. Buys one-time rights.

Columns/Departments: Industry Focus (analysis of hiring market within particular industry), 1,500 words. **Buys 25 mss/year.** Query. **Pays $200-300.**

Tips: ("Know the hiring market for entry-level tech professionals and be able to communicate to college students at their level."

N $ $ LIGHTING DESIGN & APPLICATION, Illuminating Engineering Society of North America, 120 Wall St., 17th Floor, New York NY 10005-4001. (212)248-5000. Fax: (212)248-5018. E-mail: ldanewman@aol.com. **Contact:** Mark A. Newman, editor. **40% freelance written.** Monthly magazine. "*LD&A* is geared to professionals in lighting design and the lighting field in architecture, retail, entertainment, etc. From designers to educators to sales reps, *LD&A* has a very unique, dedicated and well-educated audience." Estab. 1971. Circ. 10,000. **Pays on acceptance.** Publishes ms an average of 4 months after acceptance. Byline given. Buys first rights. Editorial lead time 4 months. Submit seasonal material 6 months in advance. Accepts simultaneous submissions. Reports in 2 weeks. Sample copy free.

Nonfiction: Historical/nostalgic, how-to, opinion, personal experience, photo feature, technical. "Every year we have entertainment, outdoor, retail and arts and exhibits issues. No articles blatantly promoting a product, company or individual." **Buys 6-10 mss/year.** Query. Length: 1,500-2,200 words. **Pays $300-400 for assigned articles.** Pays writers with contributor copies or other premiums if writer is a member of IESNA or article promotes his/her own interest.

Photos: Send photos with submission. Reviews 4×5 transparencies. Offers no additional payment for photos accepted with ms. Captions required.

Columns/Departments: Essay by Invitation (industry trends), 1,200 words. Query. Does not pay.

Tips: "Most of our features detail the ins and outs of a specific lighting project. From the musical *Rent* to the Getty Museum, *LD&A* gives its readers an in-depth look at how the designer(s) reached their goals."

$ $ $ MECHANICAL ENGINEERING, American Society of Mechanical Engineers, Dept. WM, 345 E. 47th St., New York NY 10017. (212)705-7782. Fax: (212)705-7841. E-mail: memag@asme.org. Website: http://www.memagazine.org. **Contact:** Dan Dietz, executive editor. **20% freelance written.** Monthly magazine on mechanical process and design. "We publish general interest articles for mechanical engineers on high-tech topics." Circ. 135,000. **Pays on acceptance.** Byline sometimes given. Kill fee varies. Buys first rights. Submit seasonal material 4 months in advance. Reports in 6 weeks. Writer's guidelines for SASE.

Nonfiction: Historical, interview/profile, new product, photo feature, technical. **Buys 25 mss/year.** Query with or without published clips or send complete ms. Length: 1,500-3,500 words. **Pays $500-1,500.**

Photos: Send photos with submission. Reviews transparencies and prints. Offers no additional payment for photos accepted with ms. Captions and identification of subjects required. Buys one-time rights.

N $ $ MICROSTATION MANAGER, Bentley Systems, Inc., 690 Pennsylvania Dr., Exton PA 19341. (610)458-2801. Fax: (610)458-6284. E-mail: randall.newton@bentley.com. Website: http://www.mmicorp.com/msmanager/. **Contact:** Randall Newton, editor. Managing Editor: Rachael Dalton. **75% freelance written.** Monthly magazine covering engineering and architecture using MicroStation. "Almost all our freelance writers use MicroStation and other related CAD/CAM/CAE products on a daily basis. We have a small need for case studies of companies using MicroStation-based products from non-technical writers." Estab. 1992. Circ. 75,000. Pays on publication. Publishes ms an average of 3 months after acceptance. Byline given. Offers 50% kill fee. Makes work-for-hire assignments. Editorial lead time 3 months. Submit seasonal material 4 months in advance. Reports in 1 week on queries; 1 month on mss. Sample copy free.

Nonfiction: Technical. Special issue: A/E/C Systems (June). "No AutoCAD or other CAD companies/products." **Buys 25 mss/year.** Query. Length: 250-2,500 words. **Pays $250-750.** Pays expenses of writers on assignment.

Photos: State availability of photos with submission. Reviews transparencies. Negotiates payment individually. Captions, model releases and identification of subjects required. Buys all rights.

Tips: "We are always interested in 'tips and tricks' using MicroStation and related products."

$ $ $ MILITARY & AEROSPACE ELECTRONICS, The Newspaper for Decision Makers in the Changing Worldwide Military/Aerospace Industry, Penn Well Publishing, 10 Tara Blvd., 5th Floor, Nashva NH 03062. (603)891-9117. Fax: (603)891-9146. E-mail: jkeller@pennwell.com. **Contact:** John Keller, editor. **20% freelance written.** Monthly tabloid covering "design issues and enabling technologies for the military and aerospace electronic design engineers and engineering managers, with an emphasis on open-system standards and commercial off-the-shelf components." Estab. 1990. Circ. 40,000. Pays on publication. Publishes ms an average of 2 months after acceptance. Byline given. Offers 50% kill fee. Buys all rights. Editorial lead time 2 months. Submit seasonal material 3 months in advance. Reports in 1 month on queries, 3 months on mss. Sample copy free.

Nonfiction: Exposé, how-to, technical. **Buys 24 mss/year.** Query. Length: 500-3,000 words. **Pays 50¢/word.** Sometimes pays expenses of writers on assignment.

Photos: Send photos with submission. Reviews transparencies and prints. Offers no additional payment for photos accepted with ms. Captions required. Buys all rights.

Columns/Departments: Special Report (in-depth applications), 3,000 words; Technology Focus (indepth technologies), 3,000 words; Analysis (varied slants), 1,500 words. **Buys 20 mss/year.** Query. **Pays 50¢/word.**

Tips: "It's easy: get me on the phone and we'll talk. Lead with a COTS angle and include customer testimony on design trends."

N $ $ $ MINNESOTA TECHNOLOGY, Inside Technology and Manufacturing Business, Minnesota Technology, Inc., 111 Third Ave. S., Minneapolis MN 55401. (612)672-3412. Fax: (612)339-5214. E-mail: tsmith@mail.mntech.org. **Contact:** Terri Peterson Smith, editor. **75% freelance written.** "*Minnesota Technology* is read bimonthly by owners and top management of Minnesota's technology and manufacturing companies. The magazine covers technology trends and issues, global trade, management techniques and finance. We profile new and growing companies, new products and the innovators and entrepreneurs of Minnesota's technology sector." Estab. 1991. Circ. 20,000. **Pays on acceptance.** Publishes ms an average of 5 months after acceptance. Byline given. Offers 25% kill fee. Buys first North American serial rights. Editorial lead time 6 months. Submit seasonal material 1 year in advance. Reports in 1 month. Sample copy for 9×12 SAE and 5 first-class stamps. Writer's guidelines for #10 SASE.

Nonfiction: General interest, how-to, interview/profile. **Buys 60 mss/year.** Query with published clips. Length: 500-2,000 words. **Pays $175-800.** Pays expenses of writers on assignment.

Reprints: Accepts previously published submissions.

Columns/Departments: Viewpoint (Q&A format, provocative ideas from business and industry leaders), 700 words; Tech Watch (cutting edge, gee whiz technology), 250-500 words. **Buys 10 mss/year.** Query with published clips. **Pays $150-300.**

$ $ MINORITY ENGINEER, An Equal Opportunity Career Publication for Professional and Graduating Minority Engineers, Equal Opportunity Publications, Inc., 1160 E. Jericho Turnpike, Suite 200, Huntington NY 11743. (516)421-9421. Fax: (516)421-0359. E-mail: info@aol.com. Website: http://www.esp.com. **Contact:** James Schneider, editor. **60% freelance written.** Prefers to work with published/established writers. Triannual magazine covering career guidance for minority engineering students and minority professional engineers. Estab. 1969. Circ. 15,000. Pays on publication. Publishes ms an average of 6 months after acceptance. Byline given. Buys first rights. Accepts simultaneous submissions. Sample copy and writer's guidelines for 9×12 SAE with 5 first-class stamps.

Nonfiction: Book excerpts; articles (on job search techniques, role models); general interest (on specific minority engineering concerns); how-to (land a job, keep a job, etc.); interview/profile (minority engineer role models); new product (new career opportunities); opinion (problems of ethnic minorities); personal experience (student and career experiences); technical (on career fields offering opportunities for minority engineers). "We're interested in articles dealing with career guidance and job opportunities for minority engineers." No career-guidance strategies or role-model profiles. Query. Length: 1,000-2,000 words. Sometimes pays expenses of writers on assignment. **Pays 10¢/word.**

Reprints: Send typed ms with rights for sale noted and information about when and where the article previously appeared. Pays 100% of amount paid for an original article.

Photos: State availability of photos with submission. Reviews transparencies and prints. Captions required. Buys all rights. Pays $15.

Tips: "Articles should focus on career guidance, role model and industry prospects for minority engineers. Prefer articles related to careers, not politically or socially sensitive."

$ $ PROGRESSIVE ENGINEER, Buck Mountain Publishing Co., P.O. Box 20305, Roanoke VA 24018. (540)772-2225. Fax: (540)776-0871. **Contact:** Tom Gibson, editor. **75% freelance written.** Bimonthly magazine. "*Progressive Engineer* is written for all disciplines of engineers in the Mid-Atlantic region (VA, NC, MD, WV, DC). We take a less technical slant than most engineering magazines and cover the engineers behind the technology as well as the technology itself. Promotes the profession of engineering by writing about engineers, projects and related activities." Estab. 1997. Circ. 20,000. Pays on publication. Publishes ms an average of 4 months after acceptance. Byline given. Offers $25 kill fee. Buys first North American serial rights and second serial (reprint) rights. Editorial lead time 6 months. Accepts simultaneous submissions. Reports in 3 weeks on queries; 1 month on mss. Sample copy and writer's guidelines free.

Nonfiction: Book excerpts, expose, general interest, historical/nostalgic, how-to, interview/profile, new product, technical, travel. **Buys 50 mss/year.** Query with published clips. Length: 750-2,500 words. **Pays $150-350.** Sometimes pays expenses of writers on assignment.

Reprints: Accepts previously published submissions. Send photocopy or typed ms with rights for sale noted and information about when and where the article previously appeared. Pays 50% of amount paid for original article.

Photos: State availability of photos with submission. Reviews contact sheets, transparencies, prints. Offers $25-100. Captions, identification of subjects required. Buys one-time rights.

Columns/Departments: Profiles (individual engineers), 800 words; Issues (affecting engineers), 1,500 words; Travel, Places to Visit (see technology in action), 1,000 words. Query with published clips. **Pays $150-225.**

Tips: "If you know of an engineer doing something interesting or unique in your area, we'd like to hear about it."

$ $ $ SENSORS, The Journal of Applied Sensor Technology, Helmers Publishing, Inc., 174 Concord St., Peterborough NH 03458. (603)924-9631. Fax: (603)924-2076. Website: http://www.sensorsmag.com. Editor: Dorothy Rosa. **3% freelance written.** Monthly magazine. "*Sensors* is edited for design, production and manufacturing engineers involved in the detection, control and measurement of specific physical properties and conditions. Editorial content focuses on using sensing devices to increase efficiency, economy and productivity in applications ranging from manufacturing systems to process control, from aircraft to consumer products. Emphasis is placed on new developments in sensor technology and on innovative applications of existing sensing methods." Estab. 1984. Circ. 75,000. Pays on publication. Publishes ms an average of 4 months after acceptance. Byline given. Buys first North American serial rights or makes work-for-hire assignments. Editorial lead time 3 months. Reports in 1 week on queries; 2 weeks on mss. Sample copy and writer's guidelines free.

Nonfiction: Technical, book reviews. "No pop fluff. Most of our writers work in the sensor industry. We consider publicity for their company to be payment. We also send complimentary copies." **Buys 15 mss/year.** Query. Length: 900-2,500 words. **Pays $700-1,200.** Sometimes pays expenses of writers on assignment.

Photos: Send photos with submission. Reviews transparencies and prints. Negotiates payment individually. Caption, model releases and identification of subjects required. Buys one-time rights.

Columns/Departments: DA Systems (data acquisition), 1,500 words. **Buys 10 mss/year.** Query. **Pays $750-1,200.**

Tips: "*Think* like a mechanical or electrical engineer, but don't *write* like one."

$ $ WOMAN ENGINEER, An Equal Opportunity Career Publication for Graduating Women and Experienced Professionals, Equal Opportunity Publications, Inc., 1160 E. Jericho Turnpike, Suite 200, Huntington NY 11743. (516)421-9478. Fax: (516)421-0359. **Contact:** Anne Kelly, editor. **60% freelance written.** Works with a small number of new/unpublished writers each year. Triannual magazine covering career guidance for women engineering students and professional women engineers. Estab. 1968. Circ. 16,000. Pays on publication. Publishes ms an average of 3-12 months after acceptance. Byline given. Buys First North American serial rights. Reports in 3 months. Free sample copy and writer's guidelines.

Nonfiction: "Interested in articles dealing with career guidance and job opportunities for women engineers. Looking for manuscripts showing how to land an engineering position and advance professionally. We want features on job-search techniques, engineering disciplines offering career opportunities to women; companies with career advancement opportunities for women; problems facing women engineers and how to cope with such problems; and role-model profiles of successful women engineers, especially in major U.S. corporations." Query. Length: 1,000-2,500 words. **Pays 10¢/word.**

Photos: Prefers color slides but will accept b&w. Captions and identification of subjects required. Buys all rights. Pays $15.

Tips: "We will be looking for shorter manuscripts (800-1,000 words) on job-search techniques and first-person 'As I See It.' "

ENTERTAINMENT AND THE ARTS

The business of the entertainment/amusement industry in arts, film, dance, theater, etc. is covered by these publications. Journals that focus on the people and equipment of various music specialties are listed in the Music section, while art and design business publications can be found in Art, Design and Collectibles. Entertainment publications for the general public can be found in the Consumer Entertainment section.

$ AMUSEMENT BUSINESS, Billboard Publications, Inc., P.O. Box 24970, Nashville TN 37202. (615)321-4250. Fax: (615)327-1575. **Contact:** Linda Deckard, managing editor. **15% freelance written.** Works with a small number of new/unpublished writers each year. Weekly tabloid emphasizing hard news of the amusement park, sports arena, concert and fair industries for top management. Circ. 15,000. Pays on publication. Publishes ms an average of 3 weeks after acceptance. Byline sometimes given; "it depends on the quality of the individual piece." Buys all rights. Submit seasonal/holiday material 3 weeks in advance. Sample copy for 11 × 14 SAE with 5 first-class stamps.

- *Amusement Business* is placing an increased emphasis on international developments and looking for shorter news stories.

Nonfiction: How-to (case history of successful advertising campaigns and promotions); interviews (with leaders in the areas we cover highlighting appropriate problems and issues of today, i.e., insurance, alcohol control, etc.). Likes lots of financial support data: grosses, profits, operating budgets and per-cap spending. Also needs lots of quotes. No personality pieces or interviews with stage stars. **Buys 50-100 mss/year.** Query. Phone queries OK. Length: 400-700 words.

Photos: State availability of photos with query. Captions and model release required. Buys all rights.

Columns/Departments: Auditorium Arenas; Fairs; Parks & Attractions; Food Concessions; Merchandise; Promotion; Carnivals; Talent & Touring; Management Changes; Sports; Profile; Eye On Legislation; Commentary and International News.

Tips: "There will be more and more emphasis on financial reporting of areas covered. Submission must contain the whys and whos, etc., and be strong enough that others in the same field will learn from it and not find it naive. We will be increasing story count while decreasing story length."

$ $ BOXOFFICE MAGAZINE, RLD Publishing Co., 6640 Sunset Blvd., Suite 100, Hollywood CA 90028-7159. (213)465-1186. Fax: (213)465-5049. E-mail: boxoffice@earthlink.net. Website: http://www.boxoffice.com. **Contact:** Kim Williamson, editor-in-chief. **15% freelance written.** Monthly business magazine about the motion picture industry for members of the film industry: theater owners, film producers, directors, financiers and allied industries. Estab. 1920. Circ. 8,000. Pays on publication. Publishes ms an average of 4 months after acceptance. Byline given. Buys all rights, including electronic publishing. Submit seasonal material 4 months in advance. Sample copy for $5.50.

Nonfiction: Investigative, interview, profile, new product, photo feature, technical. "We are a general news magazine about the motion picture industry and are looking for stories about trends, developments, problems or opportunities facing the industry. Almost any story will be considered, including corporate profiles, but we don't want gossip or celebrity coverage." Query with published clips. Length: 800-2,500 words. **Pays 10¢/word or set price.**
Photos: State availability of photos. Pays $10 maximum for 8×10 b&w prints. Captions required.
Tips: "Request a sample copy, indicating you read about *Boxoffice* in *Writer's Market.* Write a clear, comprehensive outline of the proposed story and enclose a résumé and clip samples."

N $ FILM QUARTERLY, University of California Press, 2120 Berkeley Way, Berkeley CA 94720. **Contact:** Ann Martin, editor. **100% freelance written.** "Academic quarterly covering film theory, analysis, criticism, history and book reviews." Estab. 1958. Circ. 7,500. Pays on publication. Publishes ms an average of 1 year after acceptance. Byline given. Buys all rights. Reports in 3 months on mss. Writer's guidelines free.
Nonfiction: Essays. No humor, personal, star profile. **Buys 12 mss/year.** Send complete ms. Length: 4,000-7,000 words. **Pays $15-150.**
Photos: State availability of photos with submission. Offers no additional payment for photos accepted with ms. Identification of subjects required.
Tips: "In preparing material for submission to *Film Quarterly*, keep in mind that while many of our contributors are academics, only a fraction of our readers are. Since its inception in 1958, *Film Quarterly*'s mission has been to bring intelligent film thought to as large a readership as possible."

$ $ FUNWORLD, International Association of Amusement Parks, 1448 Duke St., Alexandria VA 22314. (703)836-4800. Fax: (703)836-4801. E-mail: mmoron@iaapa.org. Website: http://www.iaapa.org. **Contact:** Michael Moran, managing editor. **80% freelance written.** Monthly magazine covering the amusement industry for park owners and operators. Circ. approximately 8,000. Pays on publication. Publishes ms an average of 3 months after acceptance. Byline given. Buys all rights. Editorial lead time 2 months. Submit seasonal material 2 months in advance. Accepts simultaneous and previously published submissions. Sample copy and writer's guidelines free.
Nonfiction: How-to (training programs, etc.), interview/profile. **Buys 65 mss/year.** Query with published clips. Length: 1,500-3,500 words. **Pays 20-30¢/word.** Sometimes pays expenses of writers on assignment.
Photos: State availability of photos with submission. Reviews transparencies and prints. Offers no additional payment for photos accepted with ms. Identification of subjects required. Buys all rights.
Columns/Departments: Query with published clips. **Pays 20-30¢/word.**

N $ $ POINT OF VIEW, Producers Guild of America, Empire Productions and Publishing, 1600 Castleview Court, Westlake Village CA 91361. (805)495-4551. Fax: (805)495-2384. E-mail: wrobison@producersguild.com Website: http://www.producersguild.com. **Contact:** Diane Robison, editor-in-chief. Managing Editor: William Robison. **95% freelance written.** Quarterly magazine covering film and television production, including sound and multimedia. Estab. 1990. Circ. 11,000. Pays on publication. Publishes ms an average of 3 months after acceptance. Byline given. Buys one-time rights. Editorial lead time 3 months. Submit seasonal material 3 months in advance. Accepts simultaneous submissions. Sample copy and writer's guidelines free.
Nonfiction: Book excerpts, essays, how-to, new product, personal experience, photo feature, technical, travel (related to production). **Buys 60 mss/year.** Query. Length: 2,000 words and up. **Pays 25¢/word.**
Reprints: Accepts previously published submissions.
Photos: State availability of photos with submission. Reviews transparencies. Offers no additional payment for photos accepted with ms. Model releases and identification of subjects required. Buys one-time rights.

N $ $ RELEASE PRINT, The Magazine of Film Arts Foundation, Film Arts Foundation, 346 9th St., 2nd Floor, San Francisco CA 94103. (415)552-8760. Fax: (415)552-0882. E-mail: filmarts@best.com. Website: http://www.filmarts.org. **Contact:** Thomas J Powers, editor. **80% freelance written.** Monthly trade magazine covering US independent filmmaking. "We have a knowledgable readership of film and videomakers. They are interested in the financing, production, exhibition and distribution of independent films and videos. They are interested in practical and technical issues and, to a lesser extent, aesthetic ones." Estab. 1977. Circ. 4,500. Pays on publication. Publishes ms an average of 1-3 months after acceptance. Byline given. All rights for commissioned works. For works submitted on spec, buys first rights and requests acknowledgement of release print in any subsequent publication. Editorial lead time 2 months. Reports in 2-3 weeks on queries; 2 months on mss. Writer's guidelines for 9×12 SASE with $1.47 postage.
Nonfiction: Interview/profile, personal experience, technical, book reviews. Do not want to see film criticism or reviews. **Buys 30-35 mss/year.** Query. Length: 300-2,000 words. **Pays 10¢/word.** Sometimes pays expenses of writers on assignment.
Photos: Send photos with submission. Reviews prints. Offers no additional payment for photos accepted with ms. Identification of subjects required. Buys one time rights.
Columns and Departments: Book Reviews (independent film & video), 800-1,000 words. **Buys 4 mss/year.** Query. **Pays 10¢/word.**

$ $ STAGE DIRECTIONS, The Practical Magazine of Theater, *SMW* Communications, Inc., 3101 Poplarwood, Suite 310, Raleigh NC 27604. Fax: (919)872-6888. E-mail: stagedir@aol.com. Website: http://www.stage-directions.com. **Contact:** Neil Offen, editor. **50% freelance written.** Magazine published 10 times/year covering theater:

community, regional and academic. "*Stage Directions* covers a full range of theater—productions, design, management and marketing. Articles are based on problem-solving." Estab. 1988. Circ. 4,500. Pays on publication. Publishes ms an average of 3 months after acceptance. Byline given. Buys all rights. Editorial lead time 6 months. Submit seasonal material 6 months in advance. Reports in 3 weeks on queries. Sample copy for 9×12 SAE with 2 first-class stamps. Writer's guidelines free.

Nonfiction: How-to, new product, personal experience, photo feature, technical. **Buys 30 mss/year.** Special issues: Sets and Scenery (September); Costumes (February); Summer Learning (January); Season Planner (November); Light, Sound, Special Effects (March). Query. Length: 350-1,000 words. **Pays 10¢/word.** Sometimes pays expenses of writers on assignment.

Reprints: Send typed ms with rights for sale noted and information about when and where the article previously appeared. Pays 50% of the amount paid for an original article.

Photos: State availability of photos with submission and describe. Reviews contact sheets, 2×2 transparencies and 5×7 prints. Offers $25/photo. Captions, model releases and identification of subjects required. Buys one-time rights.

Tips: "We are very receptive to new writers, but they must give evidence of quality writing and ability to follow through. Keep story focused and upbeat as you describe a theatrical problem-solving experience or situation. Use quotes from participants/experts."

FARM

The successful farm writer focuses on the business side of farming. For technical articles, editors feel writers should have a farm background or agricultural training, but there are opportunities for the general freelancer too. The following farm publications are divided into seven categories, each specializing in a different aspect of farming: equipment; crops and soil management; dairy farming; livestock; management; miscellaneous; and regional.

Agricultural Equipment

$ $ DEALER @ APPLICATOR, Vance Publishing Corp., 5050 Poplar Ave., Suite 2000, Memphis TN 38157. (901)767-4020. Fax: (901)767-4026. **Contact:** Rob Wiley, editor. **50% freelance written.** Works with a small number of new/unpublished writers each year. Magazine for firms that sell and custom apply agricultural fertilizer and chemicals. Estab. 1957. Circ. 18,500. **Pays on acceptance.** Publishes ms an average of 2 months after acceptance. Buys all rights. Free sample copy and writer's guidelines.

Nonfiction: "We need articles on spray/dry chemical delivery technology related to the agriculture industry. We are seeing an incredible jump in computer-related technology and software packages for farm and custom application management that need reviewing. And we always need business management stories, interviews of actual dealers & applicators." Length: 750-1,200 words. Must have color photos. **Pays 20¢/word.**

Reprints: Send typed ms with rights for sale noted and information about when and where the article previously appeared. Payment negotiable.

Photos: Accepts b&w glossy prints, prefers color. Color slides accepted for cover photos. Pays extra for cover shots.

Tips: "Our audience doesn't need to decipher 'computerese' or 'tech lingo' so make it readable; for a general audience. Conciseness sells here. A story without photos will not be published, so plan that into your work. Our readers are looking for methods to increase efficiency and stay abreast of new government regulations, so accuracy is important."

N $ $ IMPLEMENT & TRACTOR, Freiberg Publishing, 2302 W. First St., Cedar Falls IA 50613. (319)277-3599. Fax: (319)277-3783. E-mail: mshepherd@cfu-cybernet.net. Website: http://www.ag-implements.com. **Contact:** Mary Shepherd, editor. **5% freelance written.** Bimonthly magazine covering farming equipment, light construction, commercial turf and lawn and garden equipment. "*Implement & Tractor* offers technical and business news for equipment dealers, manufacturers, consultants and others involved as suppliers to the industry. Writers must know machinery and the industry trends." Estab. 1895. Circ. 10,000. **Pays on acceptance.** Publishes ms an average of 6 months after acceptance. Byline given. Buys all rights. Editorial lead time 4 months. Submit seasonal material 4 months in advance. Accepts simultaneous submissions. Reports in 2 months on queries. Sample copy for $6.

Nonfiction: Interview/profile, new product, photo feature, technical. No lightweight technical articles, general farm machinery articles, "Isn't farm life great!" articles. Query with published clips. Length: 200-600 words. **Pays $100-250.** Sometimes pays expenses of writers on assignment.

Photos: State availability of photos with submission. Reviews contact sheets. Offers no additional payment for photos accepted with ms. Captions and identification of subjects required. Buys one-time rights.

Tips: "Know the equipment industry, have an engineer's outlook for analyzing machinery and a writer's skills to communicate that information. Technical background is helpful, as is mechanical aptitude. We'd like to see a maintenance/repair column about farm equipment—something a professional in the business could relate to."

Crops and Soil Management

$ $ CITRUS & VEGETABLE MAGAZINE, 7402 N. 56th St., Suite 560, Tampa FL 33617-7737. (813)980-6386. Fax: (813)980-2871. **Contact:** Scott Emerson, editor. Monthly magazine on the citrus and vegetable industries. Estab. 1938. Circ. 12,000. BPA pays on publication. Publishes ms an average of 1 month after acceptance. Byline given. Kill fee varies. Buys exclusive first rights. Query first. Reports in 2 months on queries. Free sample copy and writer's guidelines.

Nonfiction: Book excerpts (if pertinent to relevant agricultural issues); how-to (grower interest—cultivation practices, etc.); new product (of interest to Florida citrus or vegetable growers); personal experience; photo feature. **Buys 20 mss/year.** Query with published clips or send complete ms. Length: approximately 1,200 words. **Pays about $200.**

Photos: Send photos with submission. Reviews 5×7 prints. Prefers color slides. Offers $15 minimum/photo. Captions and identification of subjects required. Buys first rights.

Columns/Departments: Citrus Summary (news to citrus industry in Florida: market trends, new product lines), Vegetable Vignettes (new cultivars, anything on trends or developments within vegetable industry of Florida). Send complete ms.

Tips: "Show initiative—don't be afraid to call whomever you need to get your information for story together—accurately and with style. Submit ideas and/or completed manuscript well in advance. Focus on areas that have not been widely written about elsewhere in the press. Looking for fresh copy. Have something to sell and be convinced of its value. Become familiar with the key issues, key players in the citrus industry in Florida. Have a specific idea in mind for a news or feature story and try to submit manuscript at least one month in advance of publication."

$ GRAIN JOURNAL, Grain Publications, Inc., 2490 N. Water St., Decatur IL 62526. (217)877-8660. Fax: (217)877-6647. E-mail: ed@grainnet.com. Website: http://www.grainnet.com. **Contact:** Ed Zdrojewski, editor. **10% freelance written.** Bimonthly magazine covering grain handling and merchandising. "*Grain Journal* serves the North American grain industry, from the smallest country grain elevators and feed mills to major export terminals." Estab. 1972. Circ. 12,000. Pays on publication. Publishes ms an average of 2 months after acceptance. Byline sometimes given. Buys first rights. Editorial lead time 2 months. Submit seasonal material 2 months in advance. Accepts simultaneous submissions. Sample copy free.

Nonfiction: How-to, interview/profile, new product, technical. Query. Length: 750 words maximum. **Pays $100.**

Photos: Send photos with submission. Reviews contact sheets, negatives, transparencies, 3×5 prints. Offers $50-100/photo. Captions and identification of subjects required. Buys one-time rights.

Tips: "Call with your idea. We'll let you know if it is suitable for our publication."

$ ONION WORLD, Columbia Publishing, P.O. Box 9036, Yakima WA 98909-0036. (509)248-2452. Fax: (509)248-4056. **Contact:** D. Brent Clement, editor. **50% freelance written.** Monthly magazine covering the world of onion production and marketing for onion growers and shippers. Estab. 1985. Circ. 5,500. Pays on publication. Publishes ms an average of 1 month after acceptance. Byline given. Not copyrighted. Buys first North American serial rights. Submit seasonal material 1 month in advance. Accepts simultaneous submissions. Reports in 1 month. Sample copy for 9×12 SAE with 5 first-class stamps.

- Columbia Publishing also produces *Fresh Cut*, *Packer/Shipper*, *The Tomato Magazine*, *Potato Country* and *Carrot Country*.

Nonfiction: General interest, historical/nostalgic, interview/profile. **Buys 60 mss/year.** Query. Length: 1,200-1,500 words. **Pays 5¢/word for assigned articles.**

Reprints: Send photocopy of article and information about when and where the article previously appeared. Pays 50% of amount paid for an original article.

Photos: Send photos with submission. Offers no additional payment for photos accepted with ms unless it's a cover shot. Captions, identification of subjects required. Buys all rights.

Tips: "Writers should be familiar with growing and marketing onions. We use a lot of feature stories on growers, shippers and others in the onion trade—what they are doing, their problems, solutions, marketing plans, etc."

Dairy Farming

N $ $ DAIRY FIELD, Stognito Communications, an MWC Company, 1935 Shermer Rd., Suite 100, Northbrook IL 60062. (847)205-5660. Fax: (847)205-5680. Managing Editor: Cathy Behrendt. **Contact:** Tom Judge, editor. Monthly trade tabloid covering dairy processing. "The how-to magazine for dairy processor growth. Dairy processors start with raw milk and make bottled milk, ice cream, yogurt, cheese, etc. . . ." Estab. 1905. Circ. 22,500. Pays on publication. Publishes ms an average of 1 month after acceptance. Byline sometimes given. Makes work-for-hire assignments. Editorial lead time 2 months. Submit seasonal material 3 months in advance. Reports in 1 week on queries; 1 month on mss. Sample copy for 9×12 SASE and 10 first-class stamps.

Nonfiction: Technical. "We do not serve the dairy farmer market." **Buys 10 mss/year.** Query. Length: 1,000-2,000 words. **Pays $300-600.** Sometimes pays expenses of writers on assignment.

Photos: State availability of photos with submission. Reviews contact sheets. Negotiates payment individually. Captions, model releases and identification of subjects required. Buys one time rights.

Tips: "Needs credentials in dairy processing and/or allied fields such as packaging, marketing, etc. . . ."

$ DAIRY GOAT JOURNAL, P.O. Box 10, 128 E. Lake St., Lake Mills WI 53551. (920)648-8285. Fax: (920)648-3770. **Contact:** Dave Thompson, editor. **50% freelance written.** Monthly. "We are looking for clear and accurate articles about dairy goat owners, their herds, cheesemaking, and other ways of marketing products. Some readers own two goats; others own 1,500 and are large commercial operations." Estab. 1917. Circ. 8,000, including copies to more than 70 foreign countries. Pays on publication.
Nonfiction: Information on personalities and on public issues affecting dairy goats and their owners. How-to articles with plenty of practical information. Health and husbandry articles should be written with appropriate experience or academic credentials. **Buys 100 mss/year.** Query with published clips. Makes assignments. Length: 750-2,500 words. **Pays $50-150.** Pays expenses of writers on assignment.
Photos: Color or b&w. Vertical or horizontal for cover. Goats and/or people. Pays $100 maximum for 35mm slides for covers; $20 to $70 for inside use or for b&w. Accurate identification of all subjects required.
Tips: "We love good articles about dairy goats and will work with beginners, if you are cooperative."

$ $ THE WESTERN DAIRYMAN, Dept. WM, P.O. Box 819, Corona CA 91718-0819. (909)735-2730. Fax: (909)735-2460. E-mail: westdairy2@aol.com. **Contact:** Dennis Halladay, editor. **10% freelance written.** Prefers to work with published/established writers. Monthly magazine dealing with large herd commercial dairy industry. *Rarely* publishes information about non-Western producers or dairy groups and events. Estab. 1922. Circ. 19,000. Pays on acceptance or publication. Publishes ms an average of 3 months after acceptance. Byline given. Buys first North American serial rights. Submit seasonal material 3 months in advance. Reports in 1 month. Sample copy for 9×12 SAE with 4 first-class stamps.
Nonfiction: Interview/profile, new product, opinion, industry analysis. Special issues: A.I. & breeding (September); Milking equipment and facilities (November); and 1999 Outlook (December). "No religion, nostalgia, politics or 'mom and pop' dairies." Query or send complete ms. Length: 300-5,000 words. **Pays $100-300.**
Reprints: Seldom accepts previously published submissions. Send information about when and where the article previously appeared. Pays 50% of amount paid for an original article.
Photos: "Photos are now a more critical part of story packages." Send photos with query or ms. Reviews b&w contact sheets, 35mm or 2¼×2¼ transparencies. Pays $25 for b&w; $50-100 for color. Captions and identification of subjects required. Buys one-time rights.
Tips: "Pretend you're an editor for a moment; would you want to buy a story without any artwork? Neither would I. Writers often don't know modern commercial dairying and they forget they're writing for an audience of *dairymen.* Publications are becoming more and more specialized. You've really got to know who you're writing for and why they're different."

Livestock

$ CANADIAN GUERNSEY JOURNAL, Canadian Guernsey Association, 368 Woolwich St., Guelph, Ontario N1H 3W6 Canada. (519)836-2141. Fax: (519)824-9250. **Contact:** Vivianne Macdonald, editor. **10% freelance written.** Bimonthly magazine covering diary farming and especially Guernsey cattle. Estab. 1905. Circ. 400. Pays on publication. Publishes ms an average of 3 months after acceptance. Byline given. Buys one-time rights. Editorial lead time 2 months. Sample copy for $5.
Nonfiction: How-to, humor, new product, personal experience, technical. **Buys 2-4 mss/year.** Query. Length: 400-2,000 words. **Pays $25-150.**
Reprints: Send tearsheet, photocopy or typed ms with rights for sale noted and information about when and where the article previously appeared. Payment negotiable.
Photos: Send photos with submission. Negotiates payment individually. Buys one-time rights.
Columns/Departments: Buys 2 mss/year. Pays $25-150.

$ $ LLAMAS MAGAZINE, The International Camelid Journal, Clay Press, Inc., P.O. Box 250, Jackson CA 95642. (209)223-0469. Fax: (209)223-0466. E-mail: claypress@aol.com. **Contact:** Cheryl Dal Porto, editor. Magazine published 5 times/year covering llamas, alpacas, camels, vicunas and guanacos. Estab. 1979. Circ. 6,000. Pays on publication. Publishes ms an average of 4 months after acceptance. Byline given. Buys first rights, second serial (reprint) rights and makes work-for-hire assignments. Submit seasonal material 6 months in advance. Reports in 1 month. Free sample copy. Writer's guidelines for 8½×11 SAE with $2.90 postage.
Nonfiction: How-to (on anything related to raising llamas), humor, interview/profile, opinion, personal experience, photo feature, travel (to countries where there are camelids). "All articles must have a tie-in to one of the camelid species." **Buys 30 mss/year.** Query with published clips. Length: 1,000-5,000 words. **Pays $50-300 for assigned articles; $50-250 for unsolicited articles.** May pay new writers with contributor copies. Sometimes pays expenses of writers on assignment.
Reprints: Send tearsheet of article and information about when and where the article previously appeared. Pays 50% of amount paid for an original article.
Photos: State availability of or send duplicate photos with submission. Reviews transparencies, 5×7 prints. Offers

$25-100/photo. Captions, model releases and identification of subjects required. Buys one-time rights.
Fillers: Anecdotes, gags, short humor. **Buys 25/year.** Length: 100-500 words. **Pays $25-50.**
Tips: "Get to know the llama folk in your area and query us with an idea. We are open to any and all ideas involving llamas, alpacas and the rest of the camelids. We are always looking for good photos. You must know about camelids to write for us."

$ SHEEP! MAGAZINE, P.O. Box 10, 128 E. Lake St., Lake Mills WI 53551. (920)648-8285. Fax: (920)648-3770. **Contact:** Dave Thompson, editor. **50% freelance written.** Prefers to work with published/established writers. Monthly magazine. "We're looking for clear, concise, useful information for sheep raisers who have a few sheep to a 1,000 ewe flock." Estab. 1980. Circ. 15,000. Pays on publication. Byline given. Offers $30 kill fee. Buys all rights. Makes work-for-hire assignments. Submit seasonal material 3 months in advance. Free sample copy and writer's guidelines.
Nonfiction: Book excerpts; information (on personalities and/or political, legal or environmental issues affecting the sheep industry); how-to (on innovative lamb and wool marketing and promotion techniques, efficient record-keeping systems or specific aspects of health and husbandry). Health and husbandry articles should be written by someone with extensive experience or appropriate credentials (i.e., a veterinarian or animal scientist); profiles (on experienced sheep producers who detail the economics and management of their operation); features (on small businesses that promote wool products and stories about local and regional sheep producers' groups and their activities); new products (of value to sheep producers; should be written by someone who has used them); technical (on genetics, health and nutrition); first-person narratives. **Buys 80 mss/year.** Query with published clips or send complete ms. Length: 750-2,500 words. **Pays $45-150.** Pays expenses of writers on assignment.
Reprints: Send tearsheet or photocopy of article. Pays 40% of amount paid for an original article.
Photos: Color—vertical compositions of sheep and/or people—for cover. Use only b&w inside magazine. Black and white, 35mm photos or other visuals improve chances of a sale. Pays $100 maximum for 35mm color transparencies; $20-50 for 5×7 b&w prints. Identification of subjects required. Buys all rights.
Tips: "Send us your best ideas and photos! We love good writing!"

Management

$ $ FARM & COUNTRY, Ontario's Commercial Farmer Trade Journal, Agricultural Publishing Co., 1 Yonge St., Suite 1504, Toronto, Ontario M5E 1E5 Canada. (416)364-5324. Fax: (416)364-5857. E-mail: agpub@inforam p.net. Website: http://www.agpub.on.ca. **Contact:** Richard Charteris, editor. **25% freelance written.** Tabloid published 24 times/year covering business-oriented topics in agriculture of interest to commercial farmers in Ontario. Estab. 1935. Circ. 40,000. Pays on publication. Publishes ms an average of 1 month after acceptance. Not copyrighted. Buys first rights and one-time rights. Editorial lead time 2 weeks. Submit seasonal material 1 month in advance. Reports in 1 month. Sample copy and writer's guidelines free.
Nonfiction: Book excerpts, essays, exposé, general interest, historical/nostalgic, how-to, humor, interview/profile, new product, opinion, personal experience, photo feature, technical, travel. **Buys 200 mss/year.** Query with published clips. Length: 500-1,000 words. **Pays $100-400 (Canadian).**
Reprints: Send tearsheet, photocopy or typed ms with rights for sale noted and information about when and where the article previously appeared. Pays 100% of amount paid for an original article.
Photos: Send photos with submission. Reviews 2¼×2¼ transparencies and 4×5 prints. Offers $10-300 (Canadian)/photo. Captions, identification of subjects required. Buys one-time rights.
Columns/Departments: Opinion, humour, how-to (all dealing with agriculture), 700 words. **Buys 75 mss/year.** Query with published clips. **Pays $100-200 (Canadian).**
Tips: "Remember: We are not a newspaper. Stories should be bright and punchy. More emphasis on narrative than most newspaper styles would permit. If you're stuck for a lead, take the money angle since it's what our readers find most interesting. Lead should pique the reader's interest, and 'trick' them into reading on. Avoid hard news style, with the five Ws in the lead. In every story, keep in mind the 'give a darn' factor—why should a farmer care? Will this article help them improve their farm businesses? Avoid verbiage. Say it in three words, not 30."

N $ $ FARM JOURNAL, Centre Square West, 1500 Market St., Philadelphia PA 19102-2181. (215)557-8900. Fax: (215)568-3989. Website: http://www.farmjournal.com. Editor: Sonja Hillgreen. **Contact:** Karen Freiberg, managing editor. Magazine published 13 times/year with many regional editions. Material bought for one or more editions depending upon where it fits. Buys all rights. Byline given "except when article is too short or too heavily rewritten to justify one." **Pays on acceptance.** Payment is the same regardless of editions in which the piece is used.
Nonfiction: Timeliness and seasonableness are very important. Material must be highly practical and should be helpful to as many farmers as possible. Farmers' experiences should apply to one or more of these 8 basic commodities: corn, wheat, milo, soybeans, cotton, dairy, beef and hogs. Technical material must be accurate. No farm nostalgia. Query to describe a new idea that farmers can use. Length: 500-1,500 words. **Pays 10-30¢/published word.**
Photos: Much in demand as illustrations for articles. Warm human-interest-pix for covers—activities on modern farms. For inside use, shots of homemade and handy ideas to get work done easier and faster, farm news photos, and pictures of farm people with interesting sidelines. In b&w, 8×10 glossies are preferred; color submissions should be 35mm. Pays $50 and up for b&w shot; $75 and up for color.

Tips: "*Farm Journal* now publishes in hundreds of editions reflecting geographic, demographic and economic sectors of the farm market."

$ SMALL FARM TODAY, The How-to Magazine of Alternative and Traditional Crops, Livestock, and Direct Marketing, Missouri Farm Publishing, Inc., Ridge Top Ranch, 3903 W. Ridge Trail Rd., Clark MO 65243-9525. (573)687-3525. Fax: (573)687-3148. E-mail: smallfarm@socket.net. Editor: Ron Macher. **Contact:** Paul Berg, managing editor. Bimonthly magazine "for small farmers and small-acreage landowners interested in diversification, direct marketing, alternative crops, horses, draft animals, small livestock, exotic and minor breeds, home-based businesses, gardening, vegetable and small fruit crops." Estab. 1984 as *Missouri Farm Magazine.* Circ. 12,000. Pays 60 days after publication. Publishes ms an average of 6 months after acceptance. Byline given. Buys first serial and nonexclusive reprint rights (right to reprint article in an anthology). Submit seasonal/holiday material 4 months in advance. Reports in 3 months. Sample copy for $3. Writer's guidelines available.
Nonfiction: Practical and how-to (small farming, gardening, alternative crops/livestock). Special issues: Wool & Fiber (February); Equipment (April). Query letters recommended. Length: 1,200-2,600 words. **Pays 3½¢/word.**
Reprints: Send photocopy or typed ms with rights for sale noted and information about when and where the article previously appeared. Pays 57% of amount paid for an original article.
Photos: Send photos with submission. Offers $6 for inside photos and $10 for cover photos. Captions required. Pays $4 for negatives or slides. Buys one-time rights and nonexclusive reprint rights (for anthologies).
Tips: "Topic must apply to the small farm or acreage. It helps to provide more practical and helpful information without the fluff. We need 'how-to' articles (how to grow, raise, market, build, etc.), as well as articles about small farmers who are experiencing success through diversification, specialty/alternative crops and livestock, and direct marketing."

Miscellaneous

N $ $ FOREST LANDOWNER, Forest Landowners Association, Inc., P.O. Box 95385, Atlanta GA 30347. (404)325-2954. Fax: (404)325-2954. E-mail: snewton100@aol.com. Website: http://www.forestland.org. **Contact**: Steve Newton, editor. Bimonthly magazine covering southern forestry management, such as timber production, tax issues, alternative enterprises, wildlife management and legislative issues. Estab. 1941. Circ. 8,000. Pays on publication. Publishes ms an average of 4 months after acceptance. Not copyrighted. Buys all rights or makes work-for-hire assignments. Editorial lead time 4 months. Submit seasonal material 2 months in advance. Accepts simultaneous submissions. Reports in months on queries. Sample copy for $5. Writer's guidelines free.
Nonfiction: Book excerpts, exposé, general interest, humor, inspirational, technical. **Buys 4 mss/year.** Query. Length: 2,000-3,000 words. **Pays $500 for assigned articles; $250 for unsolicited articles.**
Photos: State availability of photos with submissions. Reviews 5×7 prints. Offers no additional payment for photos accepted with ms. Buys one-time rights.
Tips: Best approach to break in would be "articles about how forest landowners can generate more timber or wildlife on their property and how U.S. congressional actions affect the value or management of private property."

Regional

$ FARMWEEK, Mayhill Publications, Inc., P.O. Box 90, Knightstown IN 46148-1242. (317)345-5133. Fax: (800)318-1055. E-mail: farmwk@aol.com. Editor: Nancy Searfoss. **Contact:** Amy McKenzie, associate editor. **5% freelance written.** Weekly newspaper that covers agriculture in Indiana, Ohio and Kentucky. Estab. 1955. Circ. 35,000. Pays on publication. Byline given. Buys first rights. Submit seasonal material 1 month in advance. Reporting time varies; up to 1 year. Free sample copy and writer's guidelines.
Nonfiction: General interest (agriculture), interview/profile (ag leaders), new product, photo feature (Indiana, Ohio, Kentucky agriculture). "We don't want first-person accounts or articles from states outside Indiana, Kentucky, Ohio (unless of general interest to all farmers and agribusiness)." Query with published clips. Length: 500-1,500 words. **Pays $50 maximum.** Sometimes pays expenses of writers on assignment.
Photos: State availability of photos with submission. Reviews contact sheets and 4×5 and 5×7 prints. Offers $10 maximum/photo. Identification of subjects required. Buys one-time rights.
Tips: "We want feature stories about farmers and agribusiness operators in Indiana, Ohio and Kentucky. How do they operate their business? Keys to success? etc. Best thing to do is call us first with idea, or write. Could also be a story about some pressing issue in agriculture nationally that affects farmers everywhere."

$ THE LAND, Minnesota's Ag Publication, Free Press Co., P.O. Box 3169, Mankato MN 56002-3169. E-mail: kschulz@the-land.com. **Contact:** Kevin Schulz, editor. **50% freelance written.** Weekly tabloid "covering farming in Minnesota. Although we're not tightly focused on any one type of farming, our articles must be of interest to farmers. In other words, will your article topic have an impact on people who live and work in rural areas?" Estab. 1976. Circ. 40,000. **Pays on acceptance.** Publishes ms an average of 3 months after acceptance. Byline given. Buys first North American serial rights. Editorial lead time 1 month. Submit seasonal material 2 months in advance. Reports in 3 weeks on queries; 2 months on mss. Prefer to work with Minnesota writers. Writer's guidelines for #10 SASE.

Nonfiction: General interest (ag), how-to, interview/profile, personal experience, technical. **Buys 15-40 mss/year.** Query. Length: 500-1,500 words. **Pays $30 minimum for assigned articles.**

Photos: State availability of photos with submission. Reviews contact sheets. Negotiates payment individually. Buys one-time rights.

Tips: "Be enthused about rural Minnesota life and agriculture and be willing to work with our editors. We try to stress relevance." Most open to feature articles.

$ MAINE ORGANIC FARMER & GARDENER, Maine Organic Farmers & Gardeners Association, RR 2, Box 594, Lincolnville ME 04849. (207)763-3043. **Contact:** Jean English, editor. **40% freelance written.** Prefers to work with published/established local writers. Quarterly magazine. "*MOF&G* promotes and encourages sustainable agriculture and environmentally sound living. Our primary focus is organic farming, gardening and forestry, but we also deal with local, national and international agriculture, food and environmental issues." Estab. 1976. Circ. 10,000. Pays on publication. Publishes ms an average of 8 months after acceptance. Byline and bio given. Buys first North American serial, one-time, first serial or second serial (reprint) rights. Submit seasonal material 1 year in advance. Accepts simultaneous submissions. Reports in 2 months. Sample copy for $2 and SAE with 7 first-class stamps. Writer's guidelines free.

Nonfiction: Book reviews; how-to based on personal experience, research reports, interviews. Profiles of farmers, gardeners, plants. Information on renewable energy, recycling, nutrition, health, non-toxic pest control, organic farm management and marketing. "We use profiles of New England organic farmers and gardeners and news reports (500-1,000 words) dealing with US/international sustainable ag research and development, rural development, recycling projects, environmental and agricultural problems and solutions, organic farms with broad impact, cooperatives and community projects." **Buys 30 mss/year.** Query with published clips or send complete ms. Length: 1,000-3,000 words. **Pays $20-150.**

Reprints: Send typed ms with rights for sale noted and information about when and where the article previously appeared. Pays 50% of amount paid for an original article.

Photos: State availability of b&w photos with query; send 3×5 b&w photos with ms. Captions, model releases, identification of subjects required. Buys one-time rights.

Tips: "We are a nonprofit organization. Our publication's primary mission is to inform and educate, but we also want readers to enjoy the articles."

FINANCE

These magazines deal with banking, investment and financial management. Publications that use similar material but have a less technical slant are listed under the Consumer Business and Finance section.

N $ $ BANK DIRECTOR, Board Member, Inc., P.O. Box 3468, Brentwood TN 37220. (615)371-0406. Fax: (615)371-0899. E-mail: bankdir@edge.net. **Contact:** Kimberly Crowe, associate editor. Editor: Deborah Scally. **75% freelance written.** "*Bank Director* is the only magazine written for directors of financial companies. Each quarterly issue focuses on the information directors need, from mergers and acquisitions to retail strategies, compensation and technology." Estab. 1990. Circ. 42,000. Pays on publication. Publishes ms an average of 2 months after acceptance. Byline given. Offers negotiable (20% average) kill fee. Buys all rights. Editorial lead time 3 months. Submit seasonal material 3 months in advance. Reports in 3 weeks on queries; 2 months on mss. Sample copy free.

Nonfiction: Financial/banking. **Buys 16-20 mss/year.** Query with published clips. Length: 2,000-5,000 words. **Pays 30-75¢/word.** Sometimes pays expenses of writers on assignment.

Photos: State availability of photos with submission. Negotiates payment individually. Identification of subjects required. Buys one-time rights.

Columns/Departments: For You Review, 250-500 words; Boardroom Basics, 2,000-3,000 words; Perspective (opinion), 2,000-3,000 words. **Buys 10 mss/year.** Query with published clips. **Pays 30-50¢/word.**

Tips: "Call or write with a story idea relevant to our audience—bank directors."

N $ $ $ CONTINGENCIES, American Academy of Actuaries, 1100 17th St. NW, 7th Floor, Washington DC 20036. (202)223-8196. Fax: (202)872-1948. E-mail: sullivan@actuary.org. **Contact:** Steven Sullivan, editor. **15% freelance written.** Bimonthly. "Though our membership is primarily actuaries, we are a magazine designed to be read by an outside audience. We look for nontechnical articles about what actuaries do and how it affects public policy." Estab. 1988. Circ. 18,000. Pays on publication. Publishes ms an average of 3 months after acceptance. Byline given. Buys first North American serial and second serial rights. Editorial lead time 2 months. Reports in 2 weeks on queries; 1 month on mss. Sample copy and writer's guidelines free.

Nonfiction: Humor, interview/profile, opinion, personal experience. "*Contingencies* is not an academic journal or newsletter. Features should be written for, and accessible to, the educated laymen, while technical pieces are directed principally to actuaries. Even those articles, however, should not be so burdened by equations and tables that they're prohibitively uninviting to the general reader." **Buys 6 mss/year.** Query with published clips. Length: 2,000 words.

Pays $800-1,000. Pays writers with contributor copies or other premiums. Sometimes pays expenses of writers on assignment.
Tips: "I'm always looking for good ideas, and I'm willing to listen to any ideas relating to insurance, risk management, actuaries' involvement in public policy."

N $ $ $ $ DOW JONES INVESTMENT ADVISOR, Dow Jones Financial Publishing, 170 Avenue at the Common, Shrewsbury NJ 07702. (732)389-8700. Fax: (732)389-8701. E-mail: rclark7000@aol.com. Website: http://www.djfpc.com. **Contact:** Robert Clark, editor-in-chief. Editor: David Bumke. Managing Editor: Janet Eldon. **100% freelance written.** "Monthly magazine providing the information and insight professional financial advisors need to fully serve their clients." Estab. 1975. Circ. 75,000. Pays on publication. Publishes ms an average of 1 month after acceptance. Byline given. Offers 25% kill fee. Buys first North American serial rights. Editorial lead time 2 months. Submit seasonal material 3 months in advance. Accepts simultaneous submissions. Reports in 1 month on queries; 4 months on mss. Sample copy and writer's guidelines free.
Nonfiction: Book excerpts, essays, exposé, historical/nostalgic, how-to, interview/profile, new product, opinion, technical. "We publish a 13th 'technology' issue in December. No consumer personal finance articles or company profiles." **Buys 150 mss/year.** Query with published clips. **Pays $1,000-4,000.** Pays expenses of writers on assignment.
Columns/Departments: Buys 80 mss/year. Query. **Pays $500-2,000.**
Tips: "Exhibit knowledge of a specific area of finance."

$ $ $ THE FEDERAL CREDIT UNION, National Association of Federal Credit Unions, P.O. Box 3769, Washington DC 20007-0269. (703)522-4770. Fax: (703)524-1082. (Do not query by fax.) E-mail: tfcu@nafcunet.org. Website: http://www.nafcunet.org. Executive Editor: Patrick M. Keefe. **Contact:** Robin Johnston, publisher/managing editor. **25% freelance written.** "Looking for writers with financial, banking or credit union experience, but will work with inexperienced (unpublished) writers based on writing skill. Published bimonthly, *The Federal Credit Union* is the official publication of the National Association of Federal Credit Unions. The magazine has a unique focus among credit union publications, one which is well-suited to the large institutions that make up its primary reader base. Its editorial concentrates on Washington, D.C., and the rapidly changing regulatory and legislative environment affecting credit unions. More importantly, it covers how this environment will affect credit union strategy, operations, management, technology, and human resources." Estab. 1967. Circ. 11,136. Pays on publication. Publishes ms an average of 3 months after acceptance. Byline given. Buys first North American serial rights. Submit seasonal material 5 months in advance. Accepts simultaneous submissions. Reports in 2 months. Sample copy for 10×13 SAE with 5 first-class stamps. Writer's guidelines for #10 SASE.
Nonfiction: Query with published clips and SASE. Length: 1,200-2,000 words. Query. **Pays $200-800.**
Photos: Send photos with submission. Reviews 35mm transparencies and 5×7 prints. Offers no additional payment for photos accepted with ms. Model releases and identification of subjects required. Buys all rights.
Tips: "Provide résumé or listing of experience pertinent to subject. Looking only for articles that focus on events in Congress, regulatory agencies or technological developments applicable to financial institutions."

N INVESTMENT NEWS, Crain Communications, 220 E. 42nd St., New York NY 10017. (212) 210-0298. Fax: (212) 210-0444. E-mail: mstar@crain.com. Website: http://www.investmentnews.com. Editor: Glenn Coleman. **Contact:** Marlene Star, managing editor. **10% freelance written.** Weekly trade magazine, newsletter, tabloid covering financial planning and investing. "It covers the business of personal finance to keep its audience of planners, brokers and other tax investment professionals informed of the latest news about their industry." Estab. 1997. Circ. 60,000. Pays on publication. Publishes ms an average of 1 month after acceptance. Byline given. Negotiate kill fee. Buys all rights or makes work-for-hire assignments. Editorial lead time 1-2 weeks. Submit seasonal material 1 month in advance. Sample copy and writer's guidelines free.
Tips: "Come to us with a specific pitch-preferably based on a news tip. We prefer to be contacted by fax or e-mail."

N $ $ INVESTOR RELATIONS BUSINESS, News and Strategies for Financial Communications Professionals, Securities Data Publishing, 1260 Sixth Ave., 36th Floor, New York NY 10104. (212)765-5311. Fax: (212)957-0420. E-mail: Greco@tfn.com. **Contact:** Matthew Greco, editor. **25% freelance written.** Biweekly newsletter covering financial communications. Estab. 1996. Circ. 1,000. Pays on publication. Publishes ms an average of 1 month after acceptance. Byline given. Offers 25% kill fee. Buys all rights. Editorial lead time 1 month. Reports in 2 weeks.
Nonfiction: Interview/profile, new product, news. **Buys 10 mss/year.** Query. Length: 250-1,000 words. **Pays $250-500.** Pays expenses of writers on assignment.
Photos: State availability of photos with submission. Offers no additional payment for photos accepted with ms or negotiates payment individually. Buys all rights.
Columns/Departments: Book Reviews (finance related), 500-1,000 words. Query. **Pays $250-500.**

N MORTGAGE BANKING, The Magazine of Real Estate Finance, Mortgage Bankers Association of America, 1125 15th St., NW, Washington DC 20005. (202)861-1930. Fax: (202)861-0736. **Contact:** Janet Reilley Hewitt, editor. **40% freelance written.** Monthly trade magazine covering the mortgage banking industry. "Timely examination of major news and trends in the business of mortgage lending for both commercial and residential real estate. Well written articles targeted at sophisticated business audience involved in financial services industry." Estab. 1939. Circ. 10,000. Pays on publication. Publishes ms an average of 2 months after acceptance. Bylines given. Negotiates kill fee. Buys

other rights, specified with author. Editorial lead time 2 months. Sample copy and writer's guidelines free.
Nonfiction: Essays, interview/profile, opinion. **Buys 36 mss/year.** Query. Length: 2,800-4,000 words. Pay negotiated. Pays expenses of writers on assignment.
Photos: State availability of photos with submission. Captions, model releases and identification required.
Columns and Departments: Book reviews (objective), 1,000 words. Query. Pay negotiated.
Tips: "Read several issues over period of time. (i.e. January-December)"

N $ $ $ **TRADERS MAGAZINE**, Securities Data Publishing, 40 West 57th St., New York NY 10019. (212)333-9246. Fax: (212)956-0112. E-mail: byrnej@tfn.com. **Contact:** John A.C. Byrne, editor. **35% freelance written.** Monthly plus 2 specials trade magazine covering equity trading and technology. "Understanding of how retail and institutional trades are done on NASDAQ and The New York Stock Exchange and appreciation of trading as a unique and demanding job." Circ. Controlled at 6,000. Pays on publication. Publishes ms an average of 2 months after acceptance. Byline given. Buys all rights. Editorial lead time 2 months. Submit seasonal material 3 months in advance. Sample copy free for writer assigned a story.
Nonfictions: Essays, expose, general interest, historical/nostalgic, how-to, humor, interview/profile, new product, opinion, personal experience, religious, technical. Special issues: Correspondent clearing (every market) and market making survey of broker deadlines. No stories that are related to fixed income and other non-equity topics. **Buys 12-20 mss/year.** Query with published clips or send complete ms. Length: 750-2,800 words. **Pays 50¢-$1/word.**
Columns and Departments: Special Features (market regulation & human interest), 1,600 words; Trading & Technology (technology), 1,600 words; Washington Watch (market regulation), 750 words. Query with published clips. **Pays 50¢-$1.**
Fiction: Ethnic (Irish & Italian American), historical, humorous, mystery, science fiction, slice-of-life vignettes. No erotica. **Buys 1 mss/year.** Query with or without published clips or send complete ms. Length: 2,100-2,800 words. **Pays 50¢-$2/word.**
Tips: "Know how to explain in plain English how an equity trade is entered and executed by Wall Street traders."

FISHING

$ $ **NORTHERN AQUACULTURE**, Capemara Communications, 4611 William Head Rd., Victoria, British Columbia V9C 3Y7 Canada. (604)478-3973. Fax: (604)478-1184. **Contact:** Peter Chettleburgh, west coast editor. **50% freelance written.** Works with a small number of new/unpublished writers each year. Monthly trade paper covering aquaculture in Canada and northern US. Estab. 1985. Circ. 4,000. Pays on publication. Publishes ms an average of 3 months after acceptance. Byline given. Buys first North American serial rights. Submit seasonal material 5 months in advance. Reports in 3 weeks. Sample copy for 9×12 SAE with $2 IRCs. Writer's guidelines free.
Nonfiction: How-to, interview/profile, new product, opinion, photo feature. **Buys 20-24 mss/year.** Query. Length: 200-1,500 words. **Pays 15¢/word for articles.** May pay writers with contributor copies if writer requests. Sometimes pays the expenses of writers on assignment.
Photos: Send photos with submission. Reviews 5×7 prints. Captions required. Buys one-time rights.

$ $ **PACIFIC FISHING**, Salmon Bay Communications, 1515 NW 51st St., Seattle WA 98107. (206)789-5333. Fax: (206)784-5545. **Contact:** Brad Warren, editor. **75% freelance written.** Works with some new/unpublished writers. Monthly business magazine for commercial fishermen and others in the West Coast commercial fishing industry. "*Pacific Fishing* views the fisherman as a small businessman and covers all aspects of the industry, including harvesting, processing and marketing." Estab. 1979. Circ. 11,000. Pays on publication. Publishes ms an average of 2 months after acceptance. Byline given. Offers 10-15% kill fee on assigned articles deemed unsuitable. Buys one-time rights. Reports in 3 weeks. Sample copy and writer's guidelines for 9×12 SAE with 10 first-class stamps.
Nonfiction: Interview/profile, technical (usually with a business hook or slant). "Articles must be concerned specifically with *commercial* fishing. We view fishermen as small businessmen and professionals who are innovative and success-oriented. To appeal to this reader, *Pacific Fishing* offers 4 basic features: technical, how-to articles that give fishermen hands-on tips that will make their operation more efficient and profitable; practical, well-researched business articles discussing the dollars and cents of fishing, processing and marketing; profiles of a fisherman, processor or company with emphasis on practical business and technical areas; and in-depth analysis of political, social, fisheries management and resource issues that have a direct bearing on West Coast commercial fishermen." Editors here are

FOR EXPLANATIONS OF THESE SYMBOLS,
SEE THE INSIDE FRONT AND BACK COVERS OF THIS BOOK

putting more focus on local and international seafood marketing, technical coverage of gear and vessels. **Buys 20 mss/year.** Query noting whether photos are available, and enclosing samples of previous work and SASE. Length varies. One-paragraph news items to 3,000-word features. Payment varies. Sometimes pays the expenses of writers on assignment.
Reprints: Send photocopy of article and information about when and where the article previously appeared. Pays 100% of the amount paid for an original article.
Photos: "We need good, high-quality photography, especially color, of West Coast commercial fishing. We prefer 35mm color slides. Our rates are $200 for cover; $50-100 for inside color; $25-50 for b&w and $10 for table of contents."
Tips: "Because of the specialized nature of our audience, the editor strongly recommends that freelance writers query the magazine in writing with a proposal. We enjoy finding a writer who understands our editorial needs and satisfies those needs, a writer willing to work with an editor to make the article just right. Most of our shorter items are staff written. Our freelance budget is such that we get the most benefit by using it for feature material."

$ $ WESTCOAST FISHERMAN, Westcoast Publishing Ltd., 1496 West 72nd Ave., Vancouver, British Columbia V6P 3C8 Canada. (604)266-8611. Fax: (604)266-6437. E-mail: wcoast@west-coast.com. Website: http://www.west-coast.com. **Contact:** Kevin MacDonell, managing editor. **25% freelance written.** Monthly trade journal covering commercial fishing in British Columbia. "We're a non-aligned magazine dedicated to the people in the B.C. commercial fishing industry. Our publication reflects and celebrates the individuals and communities that collectively constitute B.C. fishermen." Estab. 1986. Pays on publication. Publishes ms an average of 3 months after acceptance. Byline given. Buys first and one-time rights. Reports in 2 months.
Nonfiction: Interview/profile, photo feature, technical. **Buys 30-40 mss/year.** Query with or without published clips or send complete ms. Length: 250-2,500 words. **Pays $25-450.**
Reprints: Send photocopy of article or typed ms with rights for sale noted and information about when and where the article previously appeared. Pays 100% of amount paid for an original article.
Photos: Send photos with submission. Reviews contact sheets, negatives, transparencies and 5×7 prints. Offers $5-100/photo. Identification of subjects required. Buys one-time rights.
Poetry: Avant-garde, free verse, haiku, light verse, traditional. "We use poetry written by or for West Coast fishermen." **Buys 6 poems/year.** Length: 1 page. **Pays $25.**

FLORISTS, NURSERIES AND LANDSCAPERS

Readers of these publications are involved in growing, selling or caring for plants, flowers and trees. Magazines geared to consumers interested in gardening are listed in the Consumer Home and Garden section.

$ $ FLORIST, The FTD Association, 33031 Schoolcraft Rd., Livonia MI 48150-1618. (800)383-4383. Fax: (734)466-8978. E-mail: flormag@ix.netcom.com. Editor-in-Chief: William P. Golden. **Contact:** Sallyann Moore, managing editor. **5% freelance written.** Monthly magazine for retail flower shop owners, managers and floral designers. Other readers include floriculture growers, wholesalers, researchers and teachers. Circ. 22,000. **Pays on acceptance.** Publishes ms an average of 2 months after acceptance. Buys one-time rights. Pays 10-25% kill fee. Reports in 1 month.
Nonfiction: Articles should pertain to marketing, merchandising, financial management or personnel management in a retail flower shop. Also, giftware, floral and interior design trends. No general interest, fiction or personal experience. **Buys 5 unsolicited mss/year.** Query with published clips. Length: 1,200-1,500 words. **Pays $200-400.**
Photos: State availability of photos with query. Pays $10-25 for 5×7 b&w photos or color transparencies. Buys one-time rights.
Tips: "Business management articles must deal specifically with retail flower shops and their unique merchandise and concerns. Send samples of published work with query. Suggest several ideas in query letter."

N $ $ FLOWERS, The Beautiful Magazine About the Business of Flowers, Teleflora, 11444 W. Olympic, Los Angeles CA 90064. Editor: Joanne Jaffe. **Contact:** Bruce Wright. **20% freelance written.** Monthly magazine. "We are primarily a small business publication, aimed at flower shop owners and managers." Estab. 1980. Circ. 30,000. **Pays on acceptance.** Publishes ms an average of 3 months after acceptance. Byline given. Offers 20% kill fee. Buys one-time rights. Editorial lead time 2 months. Submit seasonal material 4 months in advance. Accepts simultaneous and previously published submissions. Reports in 1 month. Sample copy for 8½×11 SAE with 4 first-class stamps.
Nonfiction: Tailored business articles, interview/profile. **Buys 12-15 mss/year.** Query with published clips. Length: 500-1,000 words. **Pays $200-500 for assigned articles.**
Photos: State availability of photos with submission. Reviews 2¼ or 3×5 transparencies. Negotiates payment individually. Identification of subjects required. Buys one-time rights.
Tips: "Talk to local florists about types of articles they would like to read. That will give you insight into the issues in retail floristry. We are open to any aspect of small business operations, from creating a newsletter for customers to dealing with the IRS."

$ GROWERTALKS, Ball Publishing, 335 N. River St., P.O. Box 9, Batavia IL 60510. (630)208-9080. Fax: (630)208-9350. E-mail: stalks@xnet.com. Website: http://www.growertalks.com. **Contact:** Chris Beytes, editor. **50% freelance written.** Monthly magazine. "*GrowerTalks* serves the commercial greenhouse grower. Editorial emphasis is on floricultural crops: bedding plants, potted floral crops, foliage and fresh cut flowers. Our readers are growers, managers and owners. We're looking for writers who've had experience in the greenhouse industry." Estab. 1937. Circ. 10,500. Pays on publication. Publishes ms an average of 6 months after acceptance. Byline given. Buys first North American serial rights. Editorial lead time 4 months. Submit seasonal material 6 months in advance. Reports in 1 month. Sample copy and writer's guidelines free.

Nonfiction: How-to (time- or money-saving projects for professional flower/plant growers); interview/profile (ornamental horticulture growers); personal experience (of a grower); technical (about growing process in greenhouse setting). "No articles that promote only one product." **Buys 36 mss/year.** Query. Length: 1,200-1,600 words. **Pays $125 minimum for assigned articles; $75 minimum for unsolicited articles.** Sometimes pays in other premiums or contributor copies.

Photos: State availability of photos with submission. Reviews 2½×2½ slides and 3×5 prints. Negotiates payment individually. Captions, model releases and identification of subjects required. Buys one-time rights.

Tips: "Discuss magazine with ornamental horticulture growers to find out what topics that have or haven't appeared in the magazine interest them."

$ $ THE GROWING EDGE, New Moon Publishing Inc., 341 SW Second, Suite 201, P.O. Box 1027, Corvallis OR 97339-1027. (541)757-2511. Fax: (541)757-0028. E-mail: aknutson@peak.org. Website: http://www.growingedge.com. Editor: Amy Knutson. **85% freelance written.** Bimonthly magazine signature covering indoor and outdoor high-tech gardening techniques and tips. Estab. 1980. Circ. 20,000. Pays on publication. Publishes ms an average of 3 months after acceptance. Byline given. Buys first serial and reprint rights. Submit seasonal material at least 6 months in advance. Reports in 3 months. Sample copy for $7. Writer's guidelines for #10 SASE.

Nonfiction: Book excerpts and reviews relating to high-tech gardening, general interest, how-to, interview/profile, personal experience, technical. Query first. Length: 500-2,500 words. **Pays 20¢/published word.**

Reprints: Send tearsheet, photocopy or typed ms with rights for sale noted and information about when and where the article previously appeared. Payment negotiable.

Photos: Pays $175/color cover photos; $25-50/inside photo. Pays on publication. Credit line given. Buys first and reprint rights.

Tips: Looking for more hydroponics articles and information which will give the reader/gardener/farmer the "growing edge" in high-tech gardening and farming on topics such as high intensity grow lights, water conservation, drip irrigation, advanced organic fertilizers, new seed varieties and greenhouse cultivation.

$ $ LINK MAGAZINE, Wholesale Florists and Florist Suppliers of America, P.O. Box 639, Vienna VA 22183. (703)242-7000. Fax: (703)319-1647. E-mail: lgough@wffsa.org. **Contact:** Lisa Gough, editor. **1% freelance written.** Monthly magazine. "*LINK Magazine* covers floral and business issues that help WF & FSA members run their companies more effectively." Estab. 1978. Circ. 2,300. Pays on publication. Publishes ms an average of 2 months after acceptance. Byline given. Buys first North American serial rights. Editorial lead time 2 months. Submit seasonal material 4 months in advance. Accepts simultaneous submissions. Reports in 1 month. Sample copy for 8½×11 SAE with 7 first-class stamps.

Nonfiction: General interest (business, economics), technical (floriculture). **Buys 5-10 mss/year.** Query. Length: 1,500-2,500 words. **Pays $250 minimum.**

Reprints: Send typed ms with rights for sale noted and information about when and where the article previously appeared. Payment negotiable.

Photos: State availability of photos with submission. Offers no additional payment for photos accepted with ms. Captions, model releases and identification of subjects required. Buys one-time rights.

Tips: Looking for "business articles centering on new laws, new management or marketing techniques, new technology or analysis of industry trends are most desirable. Learn something about *Link*'s audience. Articles that are too broad or basic aren't accepted."

$ $ ORNAMENTAL OUTLOOK, Your Connection To The South's Horticulture Industry, Meister Publishing Co., 1555 Howell Branch Rd., Suite C204, Winter Park FL 32789. (407)539-6552. Fax: (407)539-6544. **Contact:** Kris Sweet, editor. **50% freelance written.** Monthly magazine. "*Ornamental Outlook* is written for commercial growers of ornamental plants in Florida. Our goal is to provide interesting and informative articles on such topics as production, legislation, safety, technology, pest control, water management and new varieties as they apply to Florida growers." Estab. 1991. Circ. 12,500. Pays 30 days after publication. Publishes ms an average of 4 months after acceptance. Byline given. Buys all rights. Editorial lead time 2 months. Submit seasonal material 3 months in advance. Reports in 1-3 months. Sample copy for 9×12 SAE with 5 first-class stamps. Writer's guidelines free.

Nonfiction: Interview/profile, photo feature, technical. "No first-person articles. No word-for-word meeting transcripts or all-quote articles." Query with published clips. Length: 750-1,000 words. **Pays $250/article including photos.**

Photos: Send photos with submission. Reviews contact sheets, transparencies and prints. Offers $50-100/photo. Captions and identification of subjects required. Buys one-time rights.

Tips: "I am most impressed by written queries that address specific subjects of interest to our audience, which is the *Florida* grower of *commercial* horticulture. Our biggest demand is for features, about 1,000 words, that follow subjects listed on our editorial calendar (which is sent with guidelines). Please do not send articles of national or consumer interest."

$ $ TREE CARE INDUSTRY MAGAZINE, National Arborist Association, P.O. Box 1094, Amherst NH 03031-1094. (800)733-2622. (603)673-3311. E-mail: 76142.462@compuserve.com. Website: http://www.natlarb.com. **Contact:** Mark Garvin, editor. **50% freelance written.** Monthly magazine covering tree care and landscape maintenance. Estab. 1990. Circ. 28,500. Pays within 30 days of publication. Publishes ms an average of 3 months after acceptance. Byline given. Buys first North American serial rights. Editorial lead time 10 weeks. Submit seasonal material 3 months in advance. Reports in 2 weeks on queries; 2 months on mss. Sample copy for 9×12 SAE with 6 first-class stamps. Writer's guidelines free.

Nonfiction: Book excerpts, general interest, historical/nostalgic, humor, interview/profile, new product, personal experience, technical. **Buys 40 mss/year.** Query with published clips Length: 900-3,500 words. Payment negotiable. Sometimes pays expenses of writers on assignment.

Photos: Send photos with submission. Reviews prints. Negotiates payment individually. Captions, identification of subjects required. Buys one-time rights.

Columns/Departments: Management Exchange (business management-related), 1,200-1,800 words; Industry Innovations (inventions), 1,200 words; From The Field (OP/ED from practitioners), 1,200 words. **Buys 40 mss/year.** Send complete ms. **Pays $100 and up.**

Tips: "Preference is given to writers with background and knowledge of the tree care industry; our focus is relatively narrow. Preference is also given to photojournalists willing to work on speculation."

GOVERNMENT AND PUBLIC SERVICE

Listed here are journals for people who provide governmental services at the local, state or federal level or for those who work in franchised utilities. Journals for city managers, politicians, bureaucratic decision makers, civil servants, firefighters, police officers, public administrators, urban transit managers and utilities managers are listed in this section.

$ THE CALIFORNIA HIGHWAY PATROLMAN, California Association of Highway Patrolmen, 2030 V Street, Sacramento CA 95818-1730. Fax: (916)457-3398. E-mail: cperni@chpmagazine.com. Website: http://www.chpmagazine.com. **Contact:** Carol Perri, editor. **60% freelance written.** Monthly magazine covering CHP info, California history, history of vehicles and/or transportation. "Our readers are either uniformed officers or pro-law enforcement." Estab. 1937. Circ. 20,000. Pays on publication. Publishes ms an average of 9 months after acceptance. Byline given. Buys one-time rights. Submit seasonal material 6 months in advance. Accepts simultaneous submissions. Reports in 1 month on queries, up to 3 months on mss. Sample copy for 9×12 SAE with 5 first-class stamps. Writer's guidelines for #10 SASE.

Nonfiction: General interest, historical/nostalgic, humor, interview/profile, photo feature, technical, travel. "No 'how you felt when you received a ticket (or survived an accident)!' No fiction." **Buys 80-100 mss/year.** Query with or without published clips, or send complete ms. *No telephone queries.* Length: 750-3,000 words. **Pays 5¢/word or $50 minimum.**

Reprints: Send tearsheet or photocopy of article telling when and where the article previously appeared.

Photos: Articles with accompanying photos receive preference. State availability of photos with submission. Send photos (or photocopies of available photos) with submission. Reviews prints. Offers $5/photo. Captions and identification of subjects required. Returns all photos. Buys one-time rights.

N $ $ CORRECTIONS TECHNOLOGY & MANAGEMENT, Hendon Publishing, Inc., 1000 Skokie Blvd, Suite 500, Wilmette IL 60091. (847)256-8555. Fax: (847)256-8574. E-mail: timburke@flash.net. **Contact:** Tim Burke, editor-in-chief. **50% freelance written.** Monthly trade magazine covering correctional facility management. "We focus on positive stories of corrections professionals doing their job. For stories . . . lots of quotes, dramatic photos. Make it real. Make it useful." Estab. 1997. Circ. 18,000. Pays on publication. Publishes ms an average of 2 months after acceptance. Byline given. Buys first North American serial rights. Editorial lead time 4 months. Submit seasonal material 6 months in advance. Accepts simultaneous submissions. Reports 1 month on mss. Sample copy for 9×12 SAE and 6 first-class stamps.

Nonfiction: How-to (design a facility, training), interview/profile, photo features. "Nothing 'general market.' Must be corrections-specific." **Buys 60 mss/year.** Query with published clips. Length: 2,000-3,000 words.

Photos: Send photos with submission. Reviews transparencies and prints 8×10. Negotiates payment individually. Captions, model releases and identification of subjects required. Buys all rights.

Columns and Departments: Corrections Profile (spotlight on one facility), 2,000 words; Tactical Profile (products in corr. tactics), 1,000 words. **Buys 10 mss/year.** Query with published clips. **Pays 10-25¢/word.**

N $ $ COUNTY, Texas Association of Counties, P.O. Box 2131, Austin TX 78768. (512)478-8753. Fax: (512)477-1324. E-mail: jiml@county.org. Website: http://www.county.org. **Contact:** Jim Lewis, editor. **15% freelance written.** Bimonthly magazine covering county and state government in Texas. "We provide elected and appointed

county officials with insights and information that helps them do their jobs and enhances communications among the independent office-holders in the courthouse." Estab. 1988. Circ. 5,500. **Pays on acceptance.** Publishes ms an average of 2 months after acceptance. Byline given. Makes work-for-hire assignments. Editorial lead time 2 months. Submit seasonal material 4 months in advance. Reports in 2 weeks on queries; 1 month on mss. Sample copy and writer's guidelines for 8×10 SAE with 3 first-class stamps.
Nonfiction: Historical/nostalgic, photo feature, government innovations. **Buys 5 mss/year.** Query with published clips. Length: 1,000-3,000 words. **Pays $300-500.** Sometimes pays expenses of writers on assignment.
Reprints: Accepts previously published submissions.
Photos: State availability of photos with submission. Negotiates payment individually. Captions, model releases and identification of subjects required. Buys all rights.
Columns/Departments: Safety, Human Resources, Risk Management (all directed toward education of Texas county officials), maximum length 1,000 words. **Buys 2 mss/year.** Query with published clips. **Pays $300.**
Tips: "Identify innovative practices or developing trends that affect Texas county officials and have the basic journalism skills to write a multi-sourced, informative feature."

$ $ FIREHOUSE MAGAZINE, Cygnus Publishing, 445 Broad Hollow Rd., Suite 21, Melville NY 11747. (516)845-2700. Fax: (516)845-7109. Editor-in-Chief: Harvey Eisner. Contact: Jeff Barrington, executive editor. **85% freelance written.** Works with a small number of new/unpublished writers each year. Monthly magazine. "*Firehouse* covers major fires nationwide, controversial issues and trends in the fire service, the latest firefighting equipment and methods of firefighting, historical fires, firefighting history and memorabilia. Fire-related books, fire safety education, hazardous materials incidents and the emergency medical services are also covered." Estab. 1976. Circ. 127,000. Pays on publication. Byline given. Exclusive submissions only. Sample copy for 9×12 SAE with 7 first-class stamps. Writer's guidelines free.
Nonfiction: Book excerpts (of recent books on fire, EMS and hazardous materials); historical/nostalgic (great fires in history, fire collectibles, the fire service of yesteryear); how-to (fight certain kinds of fires, buy and maintain equipment, run a fire department); technical (on almost any phase of firefighting, techniques, equipment, training, administration); trends (controversies in the fire service). No profiles of people or departments that are not unusual or innovative, reports of nonmajor fires, articles not slanted toward firefighters' interests. No poetry. **Buys 100 mss/year.** Query with or without published clips, or send complete ms. Length: 500-3,000 words. **Pays $50-400 for assigned articles; $50-300 for unsolicited articles.** Sometimes pays expenses of writers on assignment.
Photos: Send photos with query or ms. Pays $15-45 for b&w prints; $20-200 for transparencies and color prints. Cannot accept negatives. Captions and identification of subjects required.
Columns/Departments: Training (effective methods); Book Reviews; Fire Safety (how departments teach fire safety to the public); Communicating (PR, dispatching); Arson (efforts to combat it). **Buys 50 mss/year.** Query or send complete ms. Length: 750-1,000 words. **Pays $100-300.**
Tips: "Read the magazine to get a full understanding of the subject matter, the writing style and the readers before sending a query or manuscript. Send photos with manuscript or indicate sources for photos. Be sure to focus articles on firefighters."

$ FOREIGN SERVICE JOURNAL, Dept. WM, 2101 E St. NW, Washington DC 20037-2990. (202)944-5511. Fax: (202)338-8244. E-mail: guldin@afsa.org. Website: http://www.afsa.org. **Contact:** Bob Guldin, editor. **75% freelance written.** Monthly magazine for Foreign Service personnel and others interested in foreign affairs and related subjects. Estab. 1924. Pays on publication. Publishes ms an average of 3 months after acceptance. Byline given. Buys first North American serial rights. Reports in 1 month. Sample copy for $3.50 and 10×12 SAE with 6 first-class stamps. Writer's guidelines for SASE.
Nonfiction: Uses articles on "diplomacy, professional concerns of the State Department and Foreign Service, diplomatic history and articles on Foreign Service experiences. Much of our material is contributed by those working in the profession. Informed outside contributions are welcomed, however." Query. **Buys 15-20 unsolicited mss/year.** Length: 1,000-4,000 words. Offers honoraria.
Fiction: Publishes short stories about foreign service life in the annual August fiction issue.
Tips: "We're more likely to want your article if it has something to do with diplomacy or U.S. foreign policy."

$ $ HEADWAY, 13555 Bammel N. Houston, Suite 227, Houston TX 77066. (281)444-4265. Fax: (281)583-9534. E-mail: grichardson@ghgcorp.com. Website: http://www.headwaymag.com. **Contact:** Gwen Daye Richardson, editor. **10-15% freelance written.** Monthly award-winning opinion and news magazine taking a moderate to conservative political approach. Estab. 1988. Circ. 15,000. Pays on publication. Publishes ms an average of 1 month after acceptance. Byline given. Buys one-time rights. Editorial lead time 2 months. Submit seasonal material 2 months in advance. Accepts simultaneous submissions. Reports in 1 month on queries. Sample copy and writer's guidelines for $2.
Nonfiction: Exposé, interview/profile, commentary and features on national political topics. "These topics can be, but are not limited to, those considered traditionally 'minority' concerns, but prefer a broad view or analysis of national or regional political elections, trends, issues, and economic issues as well." **Buys approximately 24 mss/year.** Query with published clips. Length: 750-1,000 words. **Pays $150-250 for assigned articles; $100 for unsolicited mss.**
Columns/Departments: The Nation (commentaries on national issues), 750-1,000 words; features, 1,000-1,500 words; Speaking Out, (personal commentary), 750-1,000 words.
Fillers: Political cartoons. **Pays $25.**

Tips: "Submissions must be well-written, timely, have depth and take an angle not generally available in national newspapers and magazines. Since our magazine takes a moderate to conservative approach, we prefer not to receive commentaries which do not fall in either of these categories."

$ $ THE JOURNAL OF SAFE MANAGEMENT OF DISRUPTIVE AND ASSAULTIVE BEHAVIOR, Crisis Prevention Institute, Inc., 3315-K N. 124th St., Brookfield WI 53005. Fax: (414)783-5906. E-mail: cpi@execpc.com. **Contact:** Diana B. Kohn, editor. **20% freelance written.** Quarterly journal covering safe management of disruptive and assaultive behavior. "Our audience is human service and business professionals concerned about workplace violence issues. *CPI* is the world leader in violence prevention training." Estab. 1992. Circ. 8,000. Pays on publication. Publishes ms an average of 6 months after acceptance. Byline given. Offers 50% kill fee. Buys one-time and second serial (reprint) rights. Editorial lead time 6 months. Submit seasonal material 3 months in advance. Reports in 1 month on queries. Sample copy and writer's guidelines free.

Nonfiction: Interview/profile, new product, opinion, personal experience, research. Inquire for editorial calendar. **Buys 30-40 mss/year.** Query. Length: 1,500-3,000 words. **Pays $50-300 for assigned articles; $50-100 for unsolicited mss.**

Reprints: Accepts previously published submissions.

Tips: "Writers can inquire more about what our company does and how our resources fit in the marketplace. We can provide them with a good background on CPI if they write or e-mail us."

$ LAW AND ORDER, Hendon Co., 1000 Skokie Blvd., Wilmette IL 60091. (847)256-8555. Fax: (847)256-8574. E-mail: 71171.1344@compuserve.com. **Contact:** Bruce W. Cameron, editor. **90% freelance written.** Prefers to work with published/established writers. Monthly magazine covering the administration and operation of law enforcement agencies, directed to police chiefs and supervisors. Estab. 1952. Circ. 38,000. Pays on publication. Publishes ms an average of 6 months after acceptance. Byline given. Buys first North American serial rights. Submit seasonal material 3 months in advance. Reports in 1 month. Sample copy for 9×12 SAE. Free writer's guidelines.

Nonfiction: General police interest; how-to (do specific police assignments); new product (how applied in police operation); technical (specific police operation). Special issues: Buyers Guide (January); Communications (February); International (March); Community Relations (April); Administration (May); Science & Technology (June); Mobile Patrol (July); Uniforms & Equipment (August); Weapons (September); Investigations (November); Training (December). No articles dealing with courts (legal field) or convicted prisoners. No nostalgic, financial, travel or recreational material. **Buys 150 mss/year.** Length: 2,000-3,000 words. Query; no simultaneous queries. **Pays 15¢/word for professional writers; 10¢/word for others.**

Photos: Send photos with ms. Reviews transparencies and prints. Identification of subjects required. Buys all rights.

Tips: "*L&O* is a respected magazine that provides up-to-date information that police chiefs can use. Writers must know their subject as it applies to this field. Case histories are well received. We are upgrading editorial quality—stories *must* show some understanding of the law enforcement field. A frequent mistake is not getting photographs to accompany article."

N $ $ NATIONAL FIRE & RESCUE, SpecComm International, Inc., 3000 Highwoods Blvd., Suite 300, Raleigh NC 27604. (919)872-5040. Fax: (919)876-6531. E-mail: editor@nfrmag.com. Website: http://www.nfrmag.com. **Contact:** Pat C. West, managing editor. **80% freelance written.** "*National Fire & Rescue* is a bimonthly magazine devoted to informing the nation's fire and rescue services, with special emphasis on fire departments serving communities of less than 25,000. It is the *Popular Science* for fire and rescue with easy-to-understand information on science, technology and training." Estab. 1980. Circ. 35,000. Pays on publication. Publishes ms an average of 5 months after acceptance. Byline given. Offers 50% kill fee. Buys first North American serial rights. Editorial lead time 2 months. Submit seasonal material 3 months in advance. Accepts simultaneous submissions. Reports in 1 month. Sample copy for $6. Call for writer's guidelines.

Nonfiction: Book excerpts, how-to, humor, inspirational, interview/profile, new product, personal experience, photo feature. No pieces marketing specific products or services. **Buys 40 mss/year.** Query with published clips. Length: 600-2,000 words. **Pays $100-350 for assigned articles; $100-200 for unsolicited articles.** Pays expenses of writers on assignment.

Photos: State availability of photos with submission. Offers $35-150/photo. Identification of subjects required. Buys one-time rights.

Columns/Departments: Leadership (management); Training; Special Operations, all 800 words. **Buys 16 mss/year.** Send complete ms. **Pays $100-150.**

Tips: "Discuss your story ideas with the editor."

N $ $ 9-1-1 MAGAZINE, Official Publications, Inc., 18201 Weston Place, Tustin CA 92680-2251. (714)544-7776. Fax: (714)838-9233. E-mail: publisher@9-1-1magazine.com. **Contact:** Randall Larson, editor. **85% freelance written.** Bimonthly magazine for knowledgeable public safety communications personnel and those associated with this respected profession. "*9-1-1 Magazine* is published to provide information valuable to all those interested in this exciting and rewarding profession." Estab. 1947. Circ. 13,000. Pays on publication. Publishes ms an average of 2 months after acceptance. Byline given. Offers 20% kill fee. Buys one-time and second serial (reprint) rights. Submit seasonal material well in advance. Accepts simultaneous submissions. Reports in 2 months on queries; 3 months on mss. Sample copy for 9×12 SAE with 5 first-class stamps. Writer's guidelines for #10 SASE.

Nonfiction: Incident report, new product, photo feature, technical. **Buys 20-30 mss/year.** Query with SASE. "We prefer

queries, but will look at manuscripts on speculation. Most positive responses to queries are considered on spec, but occasionally we will make assignments." Length: 1,000-2,500 words. **Pays $100-300 for unsolicited articles.**
Photos: Send photos with submission. Reviews color transparencies and prints. Offers $25-300/photo. Captions and identification of subjects required. Buys one-time rights.
Fillers: Cartoons. **Buys 10/year. Pays $25-50.**
Tips: "What we don't need are 'my first call' articles, or photography of a less-than-excellent quality. We seldom use poetry or fiction. *9-1-1 Magazine* is published for a knowledgeable, upscale professional. Our primary considerations in selecting material are: quality, appropriateness of material, brevity, knowledge of our readership, accuracy, accompanying photography, originality, wit and humor, a clear direction and vision, and proper use of the language."

$ $ $ PLANNING, American Planning Association, 122 S. Michigan Ave., Suite 1600, Chicago IL 60603. (312)431-9100. Fax: (312)431-9985. E-mail: slewis@planning.org. Website: http://www.planning.org. **Contact:** Sylvia Lewis, editor. **25% freelance written.** Monthly magazine emphasizing urban planning for adult, college-educated readers who are regional and urban planners in city, state or federal agencies or in private business or university faculty or students. Estab. 1972. Circ. 30,000. Pays on publication. Publishes ms an average of 3 months after acceptance. Buys all rights. Byline given. Reports in 2 months. Sample copy and writer's guidelines for 9×12 SAE with 5 first-class stamps.
Nonfiction: Exposé (on government or business, but topics related to planning, housing, land use, zoning); general interest (trend stories on cities, land use, government); how-to (successful government or citizen efforts in planning, innovations, concepts that have been applied); technical (detailed articles on the nitty-gritty of planning, zoning, transportation but no footnotes or mathematical models). Also needs news stories up to 400 words. "It's best to query with a fairly detailed, one-page letter. We'll consider any article that's well written and relevant to our audience. Articles have a better chance if they are timely and related to planning and land use and if they appeal to a national audience. All articles should be written in magazine feature style." **Buys 2 features and 1 news story/issue.** Length: 500-2,000 words. **Pays $100-900.** "We pay freelance writers and photographers only, not planners."
Photos: "We prefer that authors supply their own photos, but we sometimes take our own or arrange for them in other ways." State availability of photos. Pays $25 minimum for 8×10 matte or glossy prints and $200 for 4-color cover photos. Captions required. Buys one-time rights.

$ $ POLICE AND SECURITY NEWS, DAYS Communications, Inc., 15 Thatcher Rd., Quakertown PA 18951-2503. (215)538-1240. Fax: (215)538-1208. E-mail: P&SN@netcarrier.com. **Contact:** James Devery, editor. **40% freelance written.** Bimonthly tabloid on public law enforcement and private security. "Our publication is designed to provide educational and entertaining information directed toward management level. Technical information written for the expert in a manner that the non-expert can understand." Estab. 1985. Circ. 20,964. Pays on publication. Publishes ms an average of 2 months after acceptance. Byline given. Buys first North American serial rights. Accepts simultaneous submissions. Sample copy and writer's guidelines for 9×12 SAE with $1.93 postage.
Nonfiction: Al Menear, articles editor. Exposé, historical/nostalgic, how-to, humor, interview/profile, opinion, personal experience, photo feature, technical. **Buys 12 mss/year.** Query. Length: 200-4,000 words. **Pays 10¢/word.** Sometimes pays in trade-out of services.
Reprints: Accepts previously published submissions. Send photocopy of article or short story or typed ms with rights for sale noted and information about when and where the article previously appeared.
Photos: State availability of photos with submission. Reviews 3×5 prints. Offers $10-50/photo. Buys one-time rights.
Fillers: Facts, newsbreaks, short humor. **Buys 6 mss/year.** Length: 200-2,000 words. **Pays 10¢/word.**

$ POLICE TIMES, American Federation of Police & Concerned Citizens, Inc., 3801 Biscayne Blvd., Miami FL 33137. (305)573-0070. Fax: (305)573-9819. **Contact:** Jim Gordon, executive editor. **80% freelance written.** Eager to work with new/unpublished writers. Quarterly magazine covering "law enforcement (general topics) for men and women engaged in law enforcement and private security, and citizens who are law and order concerned." Circ. 55,000. **Pays on acceptance.** Publishes ms an average of 6 months after acceptance. Byline given. Buys second serial (reprint) rights. Submit seasonal material 4 months in advance. Accepts simultaneous submissions. Sample copy for $2.50 and 9×12 SAE with 3 first-class stamps. Writer's guidelines for #10 SASE.
Nonfiction: Book excerpts; essays (on police science); exposé (police corruption); general interest; historical/nostalgic; how-to; humor; interview/profile; new product; personal experience (with police); photo feature; technical—all police-related. "We produce a special edition on police killed in the line of duty. It is mailed May 15 so copy must arrive six months in advance. Photos required." No anti-police materials. **Buys 50 mss/year.** Send complete ms. Length: 200-4,000 words. **Pays $5-50 for assigned articles; $5-25 for unsolicited articles.** Payment includes right to publish on organization's website.
Reprints: Accepts previously published submissions.
Photos: Send photos with submission. Reviews 5×6 prints. Offers $5-25/photo. Identification of subjects required. Buys all rights.
Columns/Departments: Legal Cases (lawsuits involving police actions); New Products (new items related to police services); Awards (police heroism acts). Buys variable number of mss/year. Send complete ms. Length: 200-1,000 words. **Pays $5-25.**
Fillers: Anecdotes, facts, newsbreaks, cartoons, short humor. **Buys 100 mss/year.** Length: 50-100 words. **Pays $5-10.**

Fillers are usually humorous stories about police officer and citizen situations. Special stories on police cases, public corruptions, etc., are most open to freelancers.

TRANSACTION/SOCIETY, Bldg. 4051, Rutgers University, New Brunswick NJ 08903. (908)445-2280 ext. 83. Fax: (908)445-3138. E-mail: horowitz@transaction.pub. Website: www/transactionpub.com. **Contact:** Irving Louis Horowitz, editor. Publisher: Mary E. Curtis. **10% freelance written.** Prefers to work with published/established writers. Bimonthly magazine for social scientists (policymakers with training in sociology, political issues and economics). Estab. 1962. Circ. 45,000. Buys all rights. Byline given. Pays on publication. Publishes ms an average of 6 months after acceptance. Reports in 3 months. Sample copy and writer's guidelines for 9×12 SAE with 5 first-class stamps.
Nonfiction: Andrew McIntosh, managing editor. "Articles of wide interest in areas of specific interest to the social science community. Must have an awareness of problems and issues in education, population and urbanization that are not widely reported. Articles on overpopulation, terrorism, international organizations. No general think pieces." Query. Payment for assigned articles only; *no payment for unsolicited articles.*
Photos: Douglas Harper, photo editor. Pays $200 for photographic essays done on assignment or upon publication.
Tips: "Submit an article on a thoroughly unique subject, written with good literary quality. Present new ideas and research findings in a readable and useful manner. A frequent mistake is writing to satisfy a journal, rather than the intrinsic requirements of the story itself. Avoid posturing and editorializing."

N **WOMEN POLICE**, International Assoc. of Women Police, RR#1, Box 149, Deer Isle ME 04627. (207)348-6976. Fax: (207)348-6171. E-mail: jeanet6877@aol.com. Website: http://www.iawp.org. **Contact:** Jeanette Taylor, editor. **15% freelance written.** Quarterly trade magazine covering women and men in law enforcement. Estab. 1958. Circ. 6,000. Publishes ms an average of 3 months after acceptance. Byline given. Buys first rights. Accepts simultaneous submissions. Editorial lead time 3 months. Submit seasonal material 6 months in advance. Sample copy and writer's guidelines free.
Nonfiction: Book excerpts, how-to (training), humor, interview/profile, new product, personal experience. Query with published clips. Length: 1,500-2,500 words.
Reprints: Accepts previously published submissions.
Photos: State availability of or send photos with submission. Reviews contact sheets. Offers no additional payment for photos accepted with ms. Buys one time rights.
Columns and Departments: Internet Alert (websites), 1,500 words.
Poetry: Light verse, traditional. Submit maximum 4 poems. Length: 20-30 words.
Fillers: Anecdotes, short humor.
Tips: "Writing anything pertaining to law enforcement, training articles or women in policing.

$ $ YOUR VIRGINIA STATE TROOPER MAGAZINE, Virginia State Police Association, 6944 Forest Hill Ave., Richmond VA 23225. **Contact:** Rebecca V. Jackson, editor. **30% freelance written.** Triannual magazine covering police topics for troopers and special agents (state police), non-sworn members of the department and legislators. Estab. 1974. Circ. 5,000. **Pays on acceptance.** Publishes ms an average of 3 months after acceptance. Byline given. Buys first North American serial, one-time rights and all rights on assignments. Submit seasonal material 4 months in advance. Accepts simultaneous submissions. Reports in 2 months.
Nonfiction: Exposé (consumer or police-related); general interest; fitness/health; tourist (VA sites); historical/nostalgic; how-to; book excerpts/reports (law enforcement related); humor, interview/profile (notable police figures); technical (radar); other (recreation). **Buys 55-60 mss/year.** Query with clips or send complete ms. Length: 2,500 words. **Pays $250 maximum/article (10¢/word).** Sometimes pays expenses of writers on assignment.
Reprints: Send typed ms with rights for sale noted and information about when and where the article previously appeared.
Photos: Send photos with ms. Pays $50 maximum for several 5×7 or 8×10 b&w glossy prints to accompany ms. Cutlines and model releases required. Buys one-time rights.
Cartoons: Send copies. Buys 20 cartoons/year. Pays $20. Buys one-time rights.

GROCERIES AND FOOD PRODUCTS

In this section are publications for grocers, food wholesalers, processors, warehouse owners, caterers, institutional managers and suppliers of grocery store equipment. See the section on Confectionery and Snack Foods for bakery and candy industry magazines.

$ $ CANADIAN GROCER, Maclean-Hunter Ltd., Maclean Hunter Building, 777 Bay St., Toronto, Ontario M5W 1A7 Canada. (416)596-5772. Fax: (416)593-3162. E-mail: gcondon@mhpublishing.com. Website: http://www.mhbizlink.com/grocer. Managing Editor: Julie Cooper. **Contact:** George H. Condon, editor. **20% freelance written.** Prefers to work with published/established writers. Monthly magazine about supermarketing and food retailing for Canadian chain and independent food store managers, owners, buyers, executives, food brokers, food processors and manufacturers. Estab. 1886. Circ. 19,500. **Pays on acceptance.** Publishes an average of 2 months after acceptance. Byline given. Buys first Canadian rights. Submit seasonal material 2 months in advance. Reports in 2 months. Sample copy for $6.
Nonfiction: Interview (Canadian trendsetters in marketing, finance or food distribution); technical (store operations,

equipment and finance); news features on supermarkets. "Freelancers should be well versed on the supermarket industry. We don't want unsolicited material. Writers with business and/or finance expertise are preferred. Know the retail food industry and be able to write concisely and accurately on subjects relevant to our readers: food store managers, senior corporate executives, etc. A good example of an article would be 'How a dairy case realignment increased profits while reducing prices, inventory and stock-outs.' " Query with published clips. Phone queries OK. **Pays 32¢/word.** Pays expenses of writers on assignment.
Reprints: Send typed ms with rights for sale noted and information about when and where the article previously appeared. Pays 50% of amount paid for an original article.
Photos: State availability of photos. Pays $10-25 for prints or slides. Captions preferred. Buys one-time rights.
Tips: "Suitable writers will be familiar with sales per square foot, merchandising mixes and efficient consumer response."

N $ $ DAIRY FIELD, Stagnito Communications, 1935 Shermer Rd., Suite 100, Northbrook IL 60062. (847)205-5660. Fax: (847)205-5680. **Contact:** Tom Judge, editor. Managing Editor: Cathy Behrendt. **5% freelance written.** Monthly tabloid covering dairy processing. "We serve those who bottle milk, make cheese, make ice cream, etc. We do not serve dairy farmers." Estab. 1910. Circ. 22,000. Pays on publication. Publishes ms an average of 2 months after acceptance. Byline given. Buys all rights. Editorial lead time 2 months. Submit seasonal material 3 months in advance. Reports in 1 week on queries; 1 month on mss.
Nonfiction: Photo feature, technical. No dairy producer (farmer) articles. **Buys 15 mss/year.** Query. Length: 1,000-3,000 words. **Pays $350-700.** Sometimes pays expenses of writers on assignment.
Reprints: Accepts previously published submissions.
Photos: State availability of photos with submission. Reviews contact sheets. Negotiates payment individually. Identification of subjects required. Buys one-time rights.
Columns/Departments: Category Review (focus on product/market, e.g., ice cream, fluid milk, cottage cheese, etc.), 1,200 words. **Buys 12 mss/year.** Query. **Pays $350-700.**
Tips: "Writers need credentials in the dairy processing industry."

$ $ $ DISTRIBUTION CHANNELS, AWMA's Magazine for Candy, Tobacco, Grocery and General Merchandise Marketers, American Wholesale Marketers Association, 1128 16th St. NW, Washington DC 20036. (202)463-2124. Fax: (202)467-0559. E-mail: jillk@awmanet.org. Website: http://www.awmanet.org. **Contact:** Jill Kosko, managing editor. **75% freelance written.** Magazine published 10 times/year. "We cover trends in candy, tobacco, groceries, beverages, snacks and other product categories found in convenience stores, grocery stores and drugstores, plus distribution topics. Contributors should have prior experience writing for the food industry. Editorial includes a mix of columns, departments and features (2-6 pages). We also cover AWMA programs." Estab. 1948. Circ. 10,000. **Pays on acceptance.** Publishes ms an average of 2 months after acceptance. Byline given. Editorial lead time 4 months.
Nonfiction: How-to, interview/profile, technical, industry trends; also technical and profiles of distribution firms or manufacturers. No comics, jokes, poems or other fillers. **Buys 80 mss/year.** Query with published clips. Feature length: 1,200-3,600 words. **Pays $200-800.** Sometimes pays industry members who author articles. Pays expenses of writers on assignment.
Photos: Authors must provide artwork (with captions) with articles.
Tips: "We're looking for reliable, accurate freelancers with whom we can establish a long-term working relationship. We need writers who understand this industry. We accept very few articles on speculation. Most are assigned."

$ $ FOOD & SERVICE, Texas Restaurant Association, P.O. Box 1429, Austin TX 78767-1429. (512)472-3666. Fax: (512)472-2777. **Contact:** Olivia Carmichael Solis, editor. **40% freelance written.** Bimonthly magazine. "As the official publication of the Texas Restaurant Association, Food & Service targets restaurateurs and foodservice professionals. The magazine's focus is on informing readers of profitable industry practices, trends, legislative issues and actions, employee concerns and new products." Estab. 1941. Circ. 6,000. Pays on publication. Publishes ms an average of 2 months after acceptance. Byline given. Buys first rights. Editorial lead time 2 months. Submit seasonal material 3 months in advance. Reports in 3 weeks on queries; 1 month on mss. Writer's guidelines free.
Nonfiction: Interview/profile, new product, technical. No human interest, restaurant reviews, recipe stories or wine articles. **Buys 12 mss/year.** Query with published clips. Length: 1,000-2,000 words. **Pays $250-500.** Sometimes pays expenses of writers on assignment.
Reprints: Send photocopy of article and information about when and where the article previously appeared. Pays 50% of amount paid for an original article.
Columns/Departments: Creative Marketing (creative restaurant marketing ideas), 1,000 words. **Buys 6 mss/year.** Query with published clips. **Pays $200-300.**
Tips: "Sources must be members of the Texas Restaurant Association. Write informally, but don't use jargon, trendy 90s cant, journalese, legalese or computerese. If a sidebar seems natural for a feature, write it. Think in terms of tips, numbers, do's and don'ts, lists, testimonials, how-to's."

N FOOD PEOPLE, Olson Publications, Inc., P.O. Box 1208, Woodstock GA 30188. (800)647-3724. Fax: (770)974-1911. E-mail: johnnie@foodpeople.com. Website: http://www.foodpeople.com. **Contact:** Johnnie Nelson, associate publisher. Editor: Wayne Bryan. **50% freelance written.** Monthly tabloid. "*Food People* features articles covering the food processing, wholesaling and retailing industry. *FP* is edited for top executives and decision makers who directly affect purchasing. Each month includes special emphasis as well as regular sections on general merchandise/HBA, groceries, perishables, operations and new products." Estab. 1981. Circ. 47,000. Pays on publication. Publishes ms an average of 2 months after acceptance. Byline given. Makes work-for-hire assignments. Editorial lead time 2 months. Sample copy free.

Nonfiction: "Articles include: interviews with food industry executives; detailed analysis of the latest trends in marketing and promotions, home meal replacement, category management, technology and logistics; the latest new product information and news concerning the supermarket, convenience stores and food service industries." No articles that do not pertain to the retail food industry. **Buys 20 mss/year.** Query with published clips. Length: 500-750 words. Pays per published column inch. Pays expenses of writers on assignment.

Photos: State availability of photos with submission. Negotiates payment individually. Captions required. Buys one-time rights.

Columns/Departments: "We assign all articles with a varied slant each time pertinent to the feature each month." **Buys 20 mss/year.** Query with published clips. Pays per published column inch.

Tips: "Send samples of work, and call and ask to speak with Johnnie Nelson. We are glad to hear from any writer who is interested enough to call and make inquiries about the types of articles we are looking for at any time."

N $ $ $ $ FOOD PRODUCT DESIGN MAGAZINE, Weeks Publishing, 3400 Dundee Rd., Suite 100, Northbrook IL 60062. Fax: (847)559-0389. E-mail: weeksfpd@aol.com. **Contact:** Lynn Kuntz, editor. **50% freelance written.** Monthly trade magazine covering food processing industry. "The magazine written for food technologies by food technologists. No food service/restaurant, consumer or recipe development." Estab. 1991. Circ. 25,000. Pays on publication. Publishes ms an average of 2 months after acceptance. Byline given. Offers 50% kill fee. Buys one-time rights, all rights or makes work-for-hire assignments. Editorial lead time 4 months. No queries all feature assignments. Sample copy for 9×12 SASE and 5 first-class stamps.

Nonfiction: Technical. **Buys 30 mss/year.** Query with published clips. Length: 1,500-7,000 words. **Pays $100-1,500.** Sometimes pays expenses of writers on assignments.

Reprints: Accepts previously published submissions depending on where it was published.

Photos: State availability of photos with submission. Reviews transparencies and prints. Offers no additional payment for photos accepted with ms. Captions required. Buys rights depending on photo.

Columns and Departments: Pays $100-150.

Tips: "If you haven't worked in the food industry in Research & Development, or QC/QA, don't bother to call us. If you can't communicate technical information in a way that is clear, easy-to-understand and well organized, don't bother to call us. While perfect grammar is not expected, good grammar and organization is."

N $ FOOD WRITER, Page One, P.O. Box 156, Spring City PA 19475. (610) 948-6031. Fax: (610)948-6081. E-mail: foodwriter@aol.com. Website: http://www.food-journalist.net. **Contact:** Lynn Kerrigan, editor. **50% freelance written.** Bimonthly trade newsletter covering food industry news, food trends, freelance markets for food writers, cookbook marketing. "Subscribers are professional food writers, editors, cookbook authors and publishers seeking high quality how-to material, marketing tips, etc . . ." Estab. 1997. Circ. 1,500. Pays on publication. Publishes ms an average of 3 months after acceptance. Byline given. Buys first North American serial rights, first rights, one-time rights, or second serial (reprint) rights. Editorial lead time 6 months. Submit seasonal material 6 months in advance. Accepts simultaneous submissions. Reports in 1 month. Sample copy for $5; writer's guidelines free.

Nonfiction: Book excerpts, essays, how-to, interview/profile, new product, personal experience. **Buys 10 mss/year.** Send complete ms. Length: 200-1,000 words. **Pays $25.**

Reprints: Accepts previously published submissions.

$ $ FRESH CUT MAGAZINE, The Magazine for Value-added Produce, Columbia Publishing, P.O. Box 9036, Yakima WA 98909-0036. (509)248-2452. Fax: (509)248-4056. E-mail: ken@freshcut.com. **Contact:** Ken Hodge, editor. **40% freelance written.** Monthly magazine covering minimally processed fresh fruits and vegetables, packaged salads, etc. "We want informative articles about processing produce. We also want stories about how these products are sold at retail, in restaurants, etc." Estab. 1993. Circ. 9,500. Pays on publication. Publishes ms an average of 2 months after acceptance. Byline given. Buys all rights. Editorial lead time 2 months. Submit seasonal material 3 months in advance. Reports in 1 month on queries; 2 months on mss. Sample copy for 9×12 SASE. Writer's guidelines for #10 SASE.

Nonfiction: Historical/nostalgic, new product, opinion, technical. **Buys 2-4 mss/year.** Query with published clips. Special issues: Retail (May 99); Foodservice (February 99); Packaging Technology (December). **Pays $5/column inch for assigned articles; $75-125 for unsolicited articles.**

Reprints: Send tearsheet of article with rights for sale noted and information about when and where the article previously appeared. Pays 50% of aount paid for an original article.

Photos: Send photos with submission. Reviews transparencies. Offers no additional payment for photos accepted with ms. Identification of subjects required. Buys one-time rights.

Columns/Departments: Packaging; Food Safety; Processing/engineering. **Buys 20 mss/year.** Query. **Pays $125-200.**

Fillers: Facts. Length: 300 words maximum. **Pays $25-50.**

N $ $ GROCERY DISTRIBUTION MAGAZINE, The Magazine for Physical Distribution and Plant Development for the Food Industry, Trend Publishing, Inc., 625 N. Michigan Ave., #2500, Chicago IL 60611. Fax: (312)654-2323. E-mail: rachelemay@aol.com. **Contact:** Amy Hardgrove, editor. **35% freelance written.** Bimonthly magazine covering food distribution, "edited for executives responsible for food warehousing/transportation functions." Estab. 1975. Circ. 15,000. **Pays on acceptance.** Publishes ms an average of 2 months after acceptance. No byline. Offers 100% kill fee. Buys all rights. Editorial lead time 1 month. Reports in 2 weeks on queries. Writer's guidelines free.

Nonfiction: How-to (emphasize case history articles detailing use of systems or equipment by food distributors). **Buys 4-5 mss/year.** Query with published clips. Length: 1,500-3,000. **Pays $150-400** (more if photos submitted by writer). Sometimes pays expenses of writers on assignment (if overnight travel required).

Photos: State availability of photos with submissions. Reviews contact sheets, negatives, 3×5 transparencies or prints. "All forms acceptable, usually make agreement beforehand." Negotiates payment individually. Captions, identification of subjects required. Buys all rights.

Tips: "Write advising us of availability to do articles. If indicated, we send form for freelancer to complete and return to us (gives us information on territory covered, experience, payment expected, photographic abilities, etc."

$ HEALTH FOODS BUSINESS, PTN Publishing Co., 2 University Plaza, Suite 204, Hackensack NJ 07601. (201)487-7800. Fax: (201)487-1061. E-mail: ptnpubz@idt.net. **Contact:** Gina Geslewitz, editor. **70% freelance written.** Monthly magazine covering health foods. "The business magazine for natural products retailers." Estab. 1953. Circ. 12,600. Pays on publication. Publishes ms an average of 3 months after acceptance. Byline given. Buys first North American serial rights. Editorial lead time 4 months. Submit seasonal material 3 months in advance. Reports in 1 month on queries. Sample copy for $3. Writer's guidelines free.

Nonfiction: Store profile. Query. **Pays $150-200.**

Photos: State availability of photos with submissions.

Tips: "We are always looking for well-written store profiles with lots of detailed information, but new writers should always query first to receive writer's guidelines and other directions."

N $ THE PACKER, Vance Publishing, 10901 W. 84th Terrace, Lenexa KS 66214. (913)438-8700. Fax: (913)438-0691. E-mail: thepacker@compuserve.com. Website: http://www.thepacker.com. **Contact:** Ben Wood, managing editor. Editor: Gordon Billingsley. **15% freelance written.** "We're the weekly business newspaper of the fresh produce industry. We focus on buyers." Estab. 1893. Circ. 15,000. Pays on publication. Buys all rights. Accepts simultaneous submissions. Sample copy free.

Nonfiction: Interview/profile, new product, produce news. Query with published clips. **Pays $5/inch.** Pays expenses of writers on assignment.

Photos: Send photos with submission. Reviews negatives. Offers $5/inch. Captions required. Buys all rights.

$ $ PRODUCE MERCHANDISING, Vance Publishing Corp., 10901 W. 84th Terrace, Lenexa KS 66214. (913)438-8700. Fax: (913)438-0691. E-mail: producemerchandising@compuserve.com. Website: http://www.producemerchandising.com. Editor: Elaine Symanski. **Contact:** Janice L. McCall, managing editor. **33% freelance written.** Monthly. "The magazine's editorial purpose is to provide information about promotions, merchandising and operations in the form of ideas and examples. *Produce Merchandising* is the only monthly journal on the market that is dedicated solely to produce merchandising information for retailers." Circ. 12,000. **Pays on acceptance.** Publishes ms an average of 3 months after acceptance. Byline given. Buys all rights. Editorial lead time 2-3 months. Reports in 2 weeks on queries. Sample copy free. Writer's guidelines for #10 SASE.

Nonfiction: How-to, interview/profile, new product, photo feature, technical (contact the managing editor for a specific assignment). **Buys 48 mss/year.** Query with published clips. Length: 1,000-1,500 words. **Pays $200-600.** Pays expenses of writers on assignment.

Photos: State availability of photos with submission or send photos with submission. Reviews color slides and 3×5 or larger prints. Offers no additional payment for photos accepted with ms. Captions, model releases and identification of subjects required. Buys all rights.

Columns/Departments: Contact managing editor for a specific assignment. **Buys 30 mss/year.** Query with published clips. **Pays $200-450.**

Tips: "Send in clips and contact the managing editor with specific story ideas. Story topics are typically outlined up to a year in advance."

$ $ PRODUCE NEWS, 2185 Lemoine Ave., Fort Lee NJ 07024-6003. Fax: (201)592-0809. E-mail: prod2185@aol.com. **Contact:** John Groh, managing editor. Editor: Gordon Hochberg. **10% freelance written.** Works with a small number of new/unpublished writers each year. Weekly magazine for commercial growers and shippers, receivers and distributors of fresh fruits and vegetables, including chain store produce buyers and merchandisers. Estab. 1897. Pays on publication. Publishes ms an average of 2 weeks after acceptance. Deadline is 2 weeks before Thursday press day. Reports in 1 month. Sample copy and writer's guidelines for 10×13 SAE with 4 first-class stamps.

Nonfiction: News stories (about the produce industry). Buys profiles, spot news, coverage of successful business operations and articles on merchandising techniques. Query. **Pays $1/column inch minimum.** Sometimes pays expenses of writers on assignment.

Photos: Black and white glossies. Pays $8-10/photo.

Tips: "Stories should be trade-oriented, not consumer-oriented. As our circulation grows in the next year, we are interested in stories and news articles from all fresh-fruit-growing areas of the country."

$ QUICK FROZEN FOODS INTERNATIONAL, E.W. Williams Publishing Co., Suite 305, 2125 Center Ave., Fort Lee NJ 07024-5898. (201)592-7007. Fax: (201)592-7171. **Contact:** John M. Saulnier, editor-in-chief. **20% freelance written.** Works with a small number of new writers each year. Quarterly magazine covering "every phase of frozen food manufacture, retailing, food service, brokerage, transport, warehousing, merchandising. Especially interested in stories from Europe, Asia and emerging nations." Circ. 13,700. Pays on publication. Publishes ms an average of 3 months after acceptance. Byline given. Offers kill fee; "if satisfactory, we will pay promised amount. If bungled, half." Buys all rights, but will relinquish any rights requested. Submit seasonal material 6 months in advance. Sample copy for $10.

Nonfiction: Book excerpts, general interest, interview/profile, new products (from overseas), personal experience, photo feature, technical, travel. No articles peripheral to frozen food industry such as taxes, insurance, government regulation, safety, etc. **Buys 20-30 mss/year.** Query or send complete ms. Length: 500-4,000 words. **Pays 7¢/word or by arrangement.** "We will reimburse postage on articles ordered from overseas."

Photos: "We prefer photos with all articles." State availability of photos or send photos with accompanying ms. Pays $10 for 5×7 color or b&w prints (contact sheet if many shots) that are used. Captions and identification of subject required. Buys all rights. Release on request.

Columns/Departments: News or analysis of frozen foods abroad. **Buys 20 columns/year.** Query. Length: 500-1,500 words. Pays by arrangement.

Fillers: Newsbreaks. Length: 100-500 words. **Pays $5-20.**

Tips: "We are primarily interested in feature materials (1,000-3,000 words with pictures). We are now devoting more space to frozen food company developments in Pacific Rim and East European countries. Stories on frozen food merchandising and retailing in foreign supermarket chains in Europe, South America, Japan, China, Korea and Australia/New Zealand are welcome. National frozen food production profiles are also in demand worldwide. A frequent mistake is submitting general interest material instead of specific industry-related stories."

$ $ $ SCHOOL FOODSERVICE & NUTRITION, American School Food Service Association, 1600 Duke St., 7th Floor, Alexandria VA 22314. Fax: (703)739-3915. E-mail: sf&n@asfsa.org. Editor: Patricia L. Fitzgerald. **25% freelance written.** Magazine published 11 times/year covering school foodservice, child nutrition and noncommercial foodservice. "Members/readers range from district directors who manage multi-million-dollar budgets to part-time line workers. Magazine presents information on how-to-do jobs, innovative practices and trends, strategies for improving participation and the bottom line. Has a very business-like, how-to approach, but with a lively, active voice and tone." Estab. 1946. Circ. 63,000. Publishes ms an average of 6 months after acceptance. Byline given. Makes work-for-hire assignments. Editorial lead time 3 months. Submit seasonal material 6 months in advance. Reports in 3 months on queries; 4 months on mss. Sample copy and writer's guidelines free.

Nonfiction: How-to, interview/profile, technical. **Assigns 11-15 mss/year.** Query with published clips. Length: 1,500-2,500 words. **Pays $400-800.**

Photos: State availability of photos with submission. Offers no additional payment for photos accepted with ms. Captions and identification of subjects required. Buys one-time rights.

Columns/Departments: At Your Service, Playing It Safe, Marketing Notebook, Cafeteria Classroom, It's Your Business, Partners for Progress, Ideas At Work, Tools of the Trade, 700-1,500 words.

Tips: "Know the market and audience. *Always* query first. Request a copy of editorial calendar and base ideas on upcoming topics. We're a small shop and reviews and phone call returns can be slow. *Don't* hound!"

TODAY'S GROCER, F.G. Publications, Inc., P.O. Box 430760, South Miami FL 33243-0760. (305)441-1138. Fax: (305)661-6720. **Contact:** Dennis Kane, editor. **3% freelance written.** "*Today's Grocer* is a monthly trade newspaper, serving members of the food industry in Alabama, Florida, Georgia, Louisiana, Mississippi, North Carolina and South Carolina. Our publication is edited for chain and independent food store owners and operators as well as members of allied industries." Estab. 1956. Circ. 19,500. **Pays on acceptance.** Byline given. Buys all rights. Submit seasonal material 3 months in advance. Reports in 2 months. Sample copy for 10×14 SAE with 10 first-class stamps.

Nonfiction: Book excerpts, exposé, general interest, humor, features on supermarkets and their owners, new product, new equipment, photo feature, video. Buys variable number of mss/year. Query with or without published clips or send complete ms. Payment varies.

Photos: State availability of photos with submission. Terms for payment on photos "included in terms of payment for assignment."

Tips: "We prefer feature articles on new stores (grand openings, etc.), store owners, operators; food manufacturers, brokers, wholesalers, distributors, etc. We also publish a section in Spanish and also welcome the above types of materials in Spanish (Cuban)."

N WHOLE FOODS, Informing and Educating Natural Product Retailers, WFC, Inc., 3000 Hadley Rd., South Plainfield NJ 07080-1117. Fax: (908)769-1171. E-mail: user886276@aol.com. Website: http://www.wfcinc.com. **Contact:** Alan Richman, editor. Assistant Editor: Caroline Krastek. Monthly magazine covering the natural products industry. "Virtually all stories should in some way enable retailers of natural products (i.e., health foods, vitamins, herbs, etc.) to do their work more easily or more effectively." Estab. 1978. Circ. 14,000. Pays on publication. Publishes ms an average of 9 months after acceptance. Byline given. Buys all rights. Editorial lead time 3 months. Submit seasonal material 6-12 months in advance. Reports in 3 weeks on queries; 2 months on mss. Sample copy for $10.

Nonfiction: Book excerpts, essays, how-to, interview/profile. All must relate to natural products industry. **Buys 2-5 mss/year.** Query with published clips. Length: 1,000-3,000 words. Pay is negotiable. "Some stories are published and payment is in the form of an author's box."

Photos: State availability of photos with submission. Offers no additional payment for photos accepted with ms. Captions, model releases and identification of subjects required. Photo credits are available when requested. Buys all rights.

HARDWARE

Journals for general and specialized hardware wholesalers and retailers are listed in this section. Journals specializing in hardware for a certain trade, such as plumbing or automotive supplies, are classified with other publications for that trade.

N $ $ $ **FASTENING**, McGuire Fasteners, Inc., 293 Hopewell Dr., Powell OH 43065-9350. (614)848-3232. Fax: (614)848-5045. E-mail: mmcguire@mail.fastening.com. Website: http://www.fastening.com. **Contact:** Mike McGuire, editor/publisher. **50% freelance written.** "Quarterly magazine seeking to advance fastener design and application engineering. Readership is made up of OEM design/application engineers and PAS." Estab. 1995. Circ. 28,000. Pays 30 days after publication. Publishes ms an average of 1 month after acceptance. Byline given. Buys all rights. Editorial lead time 2 months. Submit seasonal material 2 months in advance. Accepts simultaneous submissions. Sample copy and writer's guidelines free.

Nonfiction: How-to (fastening), new product. "No company profiles that are ads." **Buys 10-12 mss/year.** Query with published clips. Length: 500-2,000 words. **Pays $200-800.** Pays expenses of writers on assignment.

Photos: Send photos with submission. Reviews negatives. Offers no additional payment for photos accepted with ms. Captions, model releases and identification of subjects required. Buys all rights.

Columns/Departments: Case Study (history of applications), 800-1,000 words; Company Profile, 1,800-2,000 words with photos. **Buys 8-10 mss/year.** Query with published clips. **Pays $200-800.**

Fillers: Anecdotes. **Buys 2-3/year.** Length: 200-600 words. **Pays $50-100.**

Tips: *Fastening* seeks technical articles in regards to fasteners and applications.

N $ $ **SPRINGS, The Magazine of Spring Technology**, Spring Manufacturers Institute, 2001 Midwest Rd., Suite 106, Oak Brook IL 60523-1335. (630)495-8588. Fax: (630)495-8595. E-mail: smieditor@aol.com. **Contact:** Rita Schauer, editor. **10% freelance written.** "Quarterly magazine covering precision mechanical spring manufacture. Articles should be aimed at spring manufacturers." Estab. 1962. Circ. 8,900. Pays on publication. Publishes ms an average of 6 months after acceptance. Byline given. Buys first rights. Editorial lead time 4 months. Accepts simultaneous submissions. Sample copy and writer's guidelines free.

Nonfiction: General interest, how-to, interview/profile, opinion, personal experience, technical. **Buys 4-6 mss/year.** Query or send complete ms. Length: 2,000-10,000 words. **Pays $100-600 for assigned articles; $50-300 for unsolicited articles.**

Photos: State availability of photos with submission. Reviews transparencies and prints. Offers no additional payment for photos accepted with ms. Captions required. Buys one-time rights.

Fillers: Facts, newsbreaks. **Buys 4/year.** Length: 200-1,000 words. **Pays $25-50.**

Tips: "Call the editor. Contact springmakers and spring industry suppliers and ask about what interests them. Include interviews/quotes from people in the spring industry in the article. The editor can supply contacts."

HOME FURNISHINGS AND HOUSEHOLD GOODS

Readers rely on these publications to learn more about new products and trends in the home furnishings and appliance trade. Magazines for consumers interested in home furnishings are listed in the Consumer Home and Garden section.

$ $ $ **HOME FURNISHINGS EXECUTIVE**, National Home Furnishings Association, P.O. Box 2396, High Point NC 27261. (910)883-1650. Fax: (910)883-1195. E-mail: hfe@hpe.infi.net. **Contact:** Trisha L. McBride, editor. **75% freelance written.** Monthly magazine covering the home furnishings industry. "We hope that home furnishings retailers view our magazine as a profitability tool. We want each issue to help them make money or save money." Estab. 1927. Circ. 12,000. **Pays on acceptance.** Publishes ms an average of 6 weeks after acceptance. Byline given. Buys first North American serial rights. Editorial lead time 3 months. Reports in 1 month on queries; 6 weeks on mss. Writer's guidelines for #10 SASE.

Nonfiction: Book excerpts, interview/profile, new product. **Buys 55 mss/year.** Query with published clips. Length: 300-2,000 words. **Pays $50-750.** Sometimes pays expenses of writers on assignment.

Photos: State availability of photos with submission. Reviews transparencies. Negotiates payment individually. Identification of subjects required. Buys one-time rights.

Columns/Departments: Executive Tipsheet (short "in box" items of interest—trend analysis, etc.), 250-300 words; On Managing Well (point-by-point articles on how retailers can manage their people better), 1,500 words; Advertising (how small retailers can create effective, low-cost advertising), 1,500 words. Query. **Pays $50-500.**

Fillers: Anecdotes, facts, newsbreaks, short humor. Buys about 15/year. Length: 50-200 words. Pays $10-25.

Tips: "Our readership includes owners of small 'ma and pa' furniture stores, executives of medium-sized chains (two to ten stores), and the executives of big chains (e.g., Heilig-Meyers), which have hundreds of stores."

$ HOME LIGHTING & ACCESSORIES, P.O. Box 2147, Clifton NJ 07015. (973)779-1600. Fax: (973)779-3242. Website: http://www.homelighting.com. **Contact:** Linda Longo, editor. **25% freelance written.** Prefers to work with published/established writers. Monthly magazine for lighting showrooms/department stores. Estab. 1923. Circ. 10,000. Pays on publication. Publishes ms an average of 6 months after acceptance. Buys first rights. Submit seasonal material 6 months in advance. Reports in 2 months. Sample copy for 9×12 SAE with 4 first-class stamps.

Nonfiction: Interview (with lighting retailers); personal experience (as a businessperson involved with lighting); profile (of a successful lighting retailer/lamp buyer); technical (concerning lighting or lighting design). Special issues: Outdoor (March); tribute to Tiffany's (August). **Buys less than 6 mss/year.** Query. **Pays $60/published page.** Sometimes pays the expenses of writers on assignment.

Reprints: Send tearsheet of article and information about when and where the article previously appeared.

Photos: State availability of photos with query. Offers no additional payment for 5×7 or 8×10 b&w glossy prints. Pays additional $90 for color transparencies used on cover. Captions required.

Tips: "We don't need fillers—only features. Deadline for all editorial is two months prior to publication."

HOSPITALS, NURSING AND NURSING HOMES

In this section are journals for medical and nonmedical nursing home personnel, clinical and hospital staffs and medical laboratory technicians and managers. Journals publishing technical material on medical research and information for physicians in private practice are listed in the Medical category.

$ JOURNAL OF CHRISTIAN NURSING, Nurses Christian Fellowship, a division of InterVarsity Christian Fellowship, 430 E. Plaza Dr., Westmont IL 60559. (630)887-2500. Fax: (630)887-2520. E-mail: jcn@ivpress.com. Editor: Judith Allen Shelly. **Contact:** Melodee Yohe, Managing Editor. **30% freelance written.** Quarterly professional journal/magazine covering spiritual care, ethics, crosscultural issues, etc. "Our target audience is Christian nurses in the U.S. and is nondenominational in character. We are prolife in position. We strive to help Christian nurses view nursing practice through the eyes of faith. Articles must be relevant to Christian nursing and consistent with our statement of faith." Estab. 1984. Circ. 10,000. Pays on publication. Publishes ms 1-2 years after acceptance. Byline given unless subject matter requires pseudonym. Offers 50% kill fee. Not copyrighted. Buys first rights; second serial (reprint) rights, rarely; all rights, only multiple-authored case studies. Editorial lead time up to 2 years. Submit seasonal material 1 year in advance. Reports in 1 month on queries; 2 months on mss. Sample copy for $5 and SAE with 4 first-class stamps. Writers guidelines for #10 SASE.

Nonfiction: How-to, humor, inspirational, interview/profile, opinion, personal experience, photo feature, religious. All must be appropriate for Christian nurses. Poetry not accepted. No purely academic articles, subjects not appropriate for Christian nurses, devotionals, Bible study. **Buys 20-30 mss/year.** Send complete ms. Length: 6-12 pages (typed, double spaced). **Pays $25-80** and up to 8 complimentary copies.

Reprints: Occasionally accepts previously published submissions. Send tearsheet or photocopy of article and information about when and where the article previously appeared.

Photos: State availability of photos or send photos with submission. Offers no additional payment for photos accepted with ms. Model releases and identification of subjects required. No rights purchased; all photos returned.

Columns/Departments: Book Reviews (Resources). No payment for Book Reviews.

Tips: "Unless an author is a nurse, it will be unlikely that he/she will have an article accepted—unless they write a very interesting story about a nurse who is involved in creative ministry with a strong faith dimension."

$ JOURNAL OF NURSING JOCULARITY, The Humor Magazine for Nurses, JNJ Publishing, Inc., P.O. Box 40416, Mesa AZ 85274. (602)835-6165. E-mail: candace@jocularity.com. Website: http://www.jocularity.com. **Contact:** Fran London, RN, MS, editor. **75% freelance written.** Quarterly magazine covering nursing and medical humor. "*Journal of Nursing Jocularity* is read by health care professionals. Published manuscripts pertain to the lighter side of health care, from the perspective of the health care provider." Estab. 1990. Circ. 20,000. Pays on publication. Publishes ms an average of 1 year after acceptance. Buys one-time rights. Editorial lead time 1 year. Submit seasonal material 1 year in advance. Accepts simultaneous submissions. Reports in 2 months on queries; 3 months on mss. Sample copy for $2. Writer's guidelines for 9×10 SAE with 2 first-class stamps.

Nonfiction: Essays, historical/nostalgic, humor, interview/profile, opinion, personal experience, *current* research on therapeutic use of humor. "Our readers are primarily active nurses. Our focus is *insider humor.*" **Buys 4-8 mss/year.** Length: 500-1,500 words. **Pays $5 and up.** Sometimes pays expenses of writers on assignment.

Reprints: Send typed ms with rights for sale noted and information about when and where the article previously appeared.
Photos: State availability of photos with submission. Model releases required. Buys one-time rights.
Columns/Departments: Stories from the Floor (anecdotes—true nursing experiences), 16-200 words; Call Lites (health care jokes with insider edge), 16-200 words; Student Nurse Cut-Ups (anecdotes—true student nurse experiences), 16-150 words; Liven Up (anecdotes using humor therapeutically at work), 50-200 words. Pays *JNJ* T-shirt.
Fiction: Humorous, slice-of-life vignettes. **Buys 30 mss/year.** Query or send complete ms. Length: 500-1,500 words. **Pays $5 and up.**
Poetry: Avant-garde, free verse, haiku, light verse, traditional, songs and cheers. **Buys 4-6 poems/year.** Submit maximum 3 poems. **Pays $5.**
Fillers: Anecdotes, gags to be illustrated by cartoonist, short humor. Length: 16-200 words. Pays *JNJ* T-shirt.
Tips: "Our readers are primarily working nurses. *JNJ*'s focus is insider humor—the kind only a health care provider understands. *Very few* non-health care providers have been able to submit material that rings true. We do not publish material written from a patient's point of view."

$ $ $ LONG TERM CARE, The Ontario Nursing Home Assoc., 345 Renfrew Dr., Suite 102-202, Markham, Ontario L3R 9S9 Canada. (905)470-8995. Fax: (905)470-9595. E-mail: heather_runtz@sympatico.ca. Assistant Editor: Tracey Ann Schofield. **Contact:** Heather Lang-Runtz, editor. Quarterly magazine covering "practical articles of interest to staff working in a long term care setting (nursing home, retirement home); professional issues; information must be applicable to a Canadian setting; focus should be on staff and for resident well-being." Estab. 1990. Circ. 4,600. Pays on publication. Publishes ms an average of 4 months after acceptance. Byline given. Buys one-time rights. Editorial lead time 3 months. Submit seasonal material 5 months in advance. Reports in 3 months. Sample copy and writer's guidelines free.
Nonfiction: General interest, how-to (practical, of use to long term care practitioners), inspirational, interview/profile. No product-oriented articles. Query with published clips. Length: 800-1,500 words. **Pays up to $1,000.**
Reprints: Send photocopy of article or short story and information about when and where the article previously appeared. Pays 50% of amount paid for an original article.
Photos: Send photos with submission. Reviews contact sheets, 5×5 prints. Offers no additional payment for photos accepted with ms. Captions, model releases required. Buys one-time rights.
Columns/Departments: Resident Health (nursing, rehabilitation, food services); Resident Life (activities, volunteers, spiritual and pastoral care); Environment (housekeeping, laundry, maintenance, safety, landscape and architecture, staff health and well being); all 800 words. Query with published clips. **Pays up to $1,000.**
Tips: "Articles must be positive, upbeat, and contain helpful information that staff and managers working in the long term care field can use. Focus should be on staff and resident well being. Articles that highlight new ways of doing things are particularly useful. Please call the editor to discuss ideas. Must be applicable to Canadian settings."

$ $ NURSEWEEK, NurseWeek Publishing Inc., 1156-C Aster Ave., Sunnyvale CA 94086. (408)249-5877. Fax: (408)249-3756. E-mail: editor@nurseweek.com. Website: http://www.nurseweek.com. **Contact:** Whitney Wood, managing editor. **75% freelance written.** Biweekly nursing newspaper for greater L.A., Orange County and S.F. areas with 6 additional statewide issues throughout year. Estab. 1989. Circ. 125,000 metro; 225,000+ statewide. Pays on publication. Byline given. Offers kill fee, which may vary. Buys all rights. Sample copy and writer's guidelines for 9×12 SAE with 4 first class stamps.
Nonfiction: News, workplace, socio-economic, interview/profile, technical (continuing education articles written by nurses) and travel, all nursing related. **Buys 120 mss/year.** Query with published clips. Length: 300-2,500 words. **Pays $100-500.** Pays expenses of writers on assignment.
Photos: State availability of photos with submission. Reviews transparencies and prints. Captions, model releases and identification of subjects required; no exceptions. Buys one-time rights.
Columns/Departments: Newsmaker (profile of a distinguished nurse or health care leader), 1,000-1,400 words. Query with published clips. **Pays $100-500.**
Tips: "We prefer queries to submissions. Keep the audience in mind; we are more focused and professionally oriented than consumer health publications. Strongly urge writers to read several issues before inquiring. We generally work on assignment; you'll do best to let us know of your availability."

$ $ NURSING99, Springhouse Corporation, 1111 Bethlehem Pike, P.O. Box 908, Springhouse PA 19477-0908. (215)646-8700. Fax: (215)653-0826. E-mail: nursing@springnet.com. Website: http://www.springnet.com. **Contact:** Pat Wolf, Editorial Dept. Administrator. Executive Director: Patricia Nornhold. Managing Editor: Jane Benner. **100% freelance written by nurses.** Monthly magazine "written by nurses for nurses; we look for practical advice for the direct caregiver that reflects the author's experience." Estab. 1971. Circ. over 300,000. Pays on publication. Publishes ms an average of 18 months after acceptance. Byline given. Offers 50% kill fee. Buys all rights. Submit seasonal material 8 months in advance. "Any form acceptable, but focus must be nursing." Reports in 2 weeks on queries; 3 months on mss. Sample copy for $4. Call 800-617-1717, ext. 300 for free writers' guidelines. Guidelines also available on our website.
Nonfiction: Book excerpts, exposé, how-to (specifically as applies to nursing field), inspirational, new product, opinion, personal experience, photo feature. No articles from patients' point of view, humor articles, poetry, etc. **Buys 100 mss/year.** Query. Length: 100 words minimum. **Pays $50-400 for feature articles.**

Reprints: Send photocopy of article and information about when and where the article previously appeared. Pays 50% of amount paid for an original article.
Photos: State availability of photos with submission. Offers no additional payment for photos accepted with ms. Model releases required. Buys all rights.
Tips: "Basically, *Nursing99* is a how-to journal, full of hands-on, practical articles. We look for the voice of experience from authors and for articles that help our readers deal with problems they face. We're always interested in taking a look at manuscripts that fall into the following categories: clinical articles, drug articles, charting/documentation, emotional problems, legal problems, ethical dilemnas, difficult ot challenging cases."

HOTELS, MOTELS, CLUBS, RESORTS AND RESTAURANTS

These publications offer trade tips and advice to hotel, club, resort and restaurant managers, owners and operators. Journals for manufacturers and distributors of bar and beverage supplies are listed in the Beverages and Bottling section.

$ $ BARTENDER MAGAZINE, Foley Publishing, P.O. Box 158, Liberty Corner NJ 07938. (908)766-6006. Fax: (908)766-6607. E-mail: barmag@aol.com. Website: http://www.bartender.com. Editor: Jaclyn M. Wilson. **Contact:** Jackie Foley, publisher. Quarterly magazine emphasizing liquor and bartending for bartenders, tavern owners and owners of restaurants with full-service liquor licenses. **100% freelance written.** Prefers to work with published/established writers; eager to work with new/unpublished writers. Circ. 147,000. Pays on publication. Publishes ms an average of 3 months after acceptance. Buys first serial, first North American serial, one-time, second serial (reprint), all or simultaneous US rights. Byline given. Submit seasonal material 3 months in advance. Accepts simultaneous submissions. Reports in 2 months. Sample copies for 9×12 SAE with 4 first-class stamps.
Nonfiction: General interest, historical, how-to, humor, interview (with famous bartenders or ex-bartenders), new products, nostalgia, personal experience, unique bars, opinion, new techniques, new drinking trends, photo feature, profile, travel, bar sports or bar magic tricks. Special issue: 1999 Calendar and Daily Cocktail Recipe Guide. Send complete ms and SASE. Length: 100-1,000 words.
Reprints: Send tearsheet of article and information about when and where the article previously appeared. Pays 25% of amount paid for an original article.
Photos: Send photos with ms. Pays $7.50-50 for 8×10 b&w glossy prints; $10-75 for 8×10 color glossy prints. Caption preferred and model release required.
Columns/Departments: Bar of the Month; Bartender of the Month; Drink of the Month; Creative Cocktails; Bar Sports; Quiz; Bar Art; Wine Cellar; Tips from the Top (from prominent figures in the liquor industry); One For The Road (travel); Collectors (bar or liquor-related items); Photo Essays. Query with SASE. Length: 200-1,000 words. **Pays $50-200.**
Fillers: Clippings, jokes, gags, anecdotes, short humor, newsbreaks, anything relating to bartending and the liquor industry. Length: 25-100 words. **Pays $5-25.**
Tips: "To break in, absolutely make sure that your work will be of interest to all bartenders across the country. Your style of writing should reflect the audience you are addressing. The most frequent mistake made by writers in completing an article for us is using the wrong subject."

$ $ BED & BREAKFAST, The Business of Innkeeping, Virgo Publishing Inc., Box 5400, Scottsdale AZ 85261. (602)990-1101. Fax: (602)675-8109. E-mail: cecileb@vpico.com. Website: http://www.vpico.com. **Contact:** Cecile Blaine, managing editor. **20% freelance written.** Magazine published 10 times/year covering the bed-and-breakfast and innkeeping industries with regard to innkeepers. "Articles must be thoroughly researched, and we prefer that the author have some experience or expertise in the industry." Estab. 1994. Circ. 15,000. Pays on publication. Publishes ms 4 months after acceptance. Byline given. Buys first North American serial rights. Editorial lead time 4 months. Submit seasonal material 6 months in advance. Reports in 2 weeks on queries; 1 month on mss. Sample copy for 9×12 SASE.
Nonfiction: Book excerpts, interview/profile, new product, personal experience, technical. **Buys 12 mss/year.** Query with or without published clips. Length: 800-3,500 words. **Pays $200 maximum for assigned articles.** Pays expenses of writers on assignment.
Reprints: Send photocopy of article or short story and information about when and where the article previously appeared.
Photos: Send photos, slides or transparencies with submission. Negotiates payment individually. Model releases and identification of subjects required. Buys one-time rights.
Columns/Departments: Buys 6 mss/year. Pays $200 maximum.

$ $ CAMP MANAGEMENT, Camp Resources, Inc., 94 Station St., Hingham MA 02043. Fax: (781)740-0888. E-mail: campmngt@camp1.com. Website: http://www.camp1.com. **Contact:** Jenny Beeh, Elisa Kronish, editors. **25% freelance written.** Bimonthly magazine covering children's summer camps. "As a magazine for camp professionals, *Camp Management* is designed to be a valuable resource, offering practical tips and solutions, news from the field and profiles of successful programs. We aim to be a forum for the camp community." Estab. 1994. Circ. 8,000. Pays on publication. Publishes ms an average of 3 months after acceptance. Byline given. Buys first rights, one-time rights or makes work-for-hire assignments. Editorial lead time 2 months. Submit seasonal material 4 months in advance. Accepts simultaneous submissions. Reports in 3 weeks on queries; 1 month on mss. Sample copy and writer's guidelines free.

Nonfiction: Essays, how-to, humor, inspirational, interview/profile, new product, personal experience, photo feature, technical, any issues affecting camp programs (i.e., education, safety, child development, staff, legal, financial, etc.). "We look for articles that offer practical, in-the-field information and hands-on ideas. We do not publish scholarly or academic theory pieces on the summer camp industry." **Buys 12 mss/year.** Query with published clips. Length: 500-3,000 words. **Pays $100-500.** Sometimes pays expenses of writers on assignment.

Reprints: Send tearsheet or photocopy of article or short story, typed ms with rights for sale noted and information about when and where the article previously appeared.

Photos: State availability of photos with submission. Reviews contact sheets, transparencies, prints. Negotiates payment individually. Captions, model releases, identification of subjects required. Buys one-time rights.

Columns/Departments: Jenny Beeh, editor. Kidology (practical insights into child development issues); Earth Etiquette (environmental issues); Safe & Sound (camp health issues); all 1,500 words. **Buys 12 mss/year.** Query with published clips. **Pays $25-300.**

Fiction: Elisa Kronish, editor. Adventure, ethnic, historical, humorous, mainstream, slice-of-life vignettes. "Longer pieces of fiction that are not camp related are not accepted. We run very little fiction—only occasional short, relevant, entertaining pieces on camp or camp life." **Buys 1 mss/year.** Send complete ms. Length: 100-1,500 words. **Pays $100-500.**

Tips: "We are interested in any submissions that summer camp directors (our readers) would find helpful, interesting or entertaining in their pursuit of providing quality camp programs for children. Please send queries, clips or manuscripts: we are open to a wide range of topics and offer a quick turnaround on ideas. Remember: Camp is a *fun* business."

$ $ CULINARY TRENDS, Dedicated to the World of Culinary Arts, Culinary Publications, Inc., 6285 E. Spring St., Long Beach CA 90808. (714)826-9188. Fax: (714)826-0333. Editor: Fred Mensinga. **Contact:** Linda Mensinga, art director. **50% freelance written.** Quarterly magazine. "Our primary audience is chefs, restaurant owners, caterers, hotel managers, and anyone interested in cooking and food!" Pays on publication. Publishes ms an average of 4 months after acceptance. Byline given. Buys first or one-time rights. Editorial lead time 4 months. Sample copy for $7.

Nonfiction: How-to (cooking techniques), humor, interview/profile, opinion, photo feature, articles on restaurants must include photos and recipes. **Buys 12 mss/year.** Query with published clips. Length: 700-3,000 words. **Pays $100-300.**

Photos: Send photos with submission. Reviews transparencies, prints. Offers no additional payment for photos accepted with ms. Captions required. Buys one-time rights.

Columns/Departments: Wine (selling wine), 700 words. **Buys 4 mss/year.** Query with published clips. **Pays $0-100.**

Tips: "We like to get stories about restaurants with the focus on the chef and the food. Quality color or transparencies or slides are essential along with recipes."

$ $ FLORIDA HOTEL & MOTEL JOURNAL, The Official Publication of the Florida Hotel & Motel Association, Accommodations, Inc., P.O. Box 1529, Tallahassee FL 32302-1529. (850)224-2888. Fax: (850)222-FHMA. Editor: Mrs. Jayleen Woods. **Contact:** Janet Litherland, associate editor. **10% freelance written.** Prefers to work with published/established writers. Magazine published 10 times/year for managers in every licensed hotel, motel and resort in Florida. Estab. 1978. Circ. 7,000. Pays on publication. Publishes ms an average of 2 months after acceptance. Byline given. Offers $50 kill fee. Buys all rights and makes work-for-hire assignments. Submit seasonal material 2 months in advance. Reports in 6 weeks. Sample copy and writer's guidelines for 9×12 SAE with 4 first-class stamps.

Nonfiction: General interest (business, finance, taxes); historical/nostalgic (old Florida hotel reminiscences); how-to (improve management, housekeeping procedures, guest services, security and coping with common hotel problems); humor (hotel-related anecdotes); inspirational (succeeding where others have failed); interview/profile (of unusual hotel personalities); new product (industry-related and non-brand preferential); photo feature (queries only); technical (emerging patterns of hotel accounting, telephone systems, etc.); travel (transportation and tourism trends only—no scenics or site visits); property renovations and maintenance techniques. "We would like to run more humorous anecdotes on hotel happenings than we're presently receiving." **Buys 10-12 mss/year.** Query with proposed topic and clips of published work. Length: 750-2,500 words. **Pays $75-250** "depending on type of article and amount of research." Sometimes pays expenses of writers on assignment.

Reprints: Send tearsheet of article and information about when and where the article previously appeared. Pays flat fee of $55.

Photos: Send photos with ms. Pays $10-15 for 5×7 b&w prints and color slides. Captions, model release and identification of subjects required.

Tips: "We prefer feature stories on properties or personalities holding current membership in the Florida Hotel and Motel Association. We're open to articles showing how hotel management copes with energy systems, repairs, renovations, new guest needs and expectations. The writer may have a better chance of breaking in at our publication with short articles and fillers because the better a writer is at the art of condensation, the better his/her feature articles are likely to be."

FOOD & SERVICE, Texas Restaurant Association, P.O. Box 1429, Austin TX 78767-1429. (512)472-3666 (in Texas, 1-800-395-2872). Fax: (512)472-2777. E-mail: osolis@tramail.org. Website: http://www.txrestaurant.org. **Contact:** Olivia Carmichael Solis, editor. **40% freelance written.** Magazine published 7 times/year providing business solutions to Texas restaurant owners and operators. Estab. 1941. Circ. 6,000. Pays on publication. Reports in 1 month. Byline given. Buys first rights. Pay varies. Sample copy and editorial calendar for 11×14 SAE with 6 first-class stamps. Writer's guidelines free.

Nonfiction: Features must provide business solutions to problems in the restaurant and food service industries. Topics vary but always have business slant; usually particular to Texas. No restaurant critiques, human interest stories or seasonal copy. Quote members of the Texas Restaurant Association; substantiate with facts and examples. Query in writing. Length: 1,500-2,500 words, features; shorter articles sometimes used; product releases, 300-word maximum. Payment rates vary.

Reprints: Send tearsheet or photocopy of article and information about when and where the article previously appeared. Pays 50% of amount paid for an original article.

Photos: State availability of photos, but photos usually assigned.

$ $ FOODSERVICE AND HOSPITALITY, Kostuch Publications, 23 Lesmill Rd., Don Mills, Ontario M3B 3P6 Canada. (416)447-0888. Fax: (416)447-5333. E-mail: rcaira@foodservice.ca. Website: http://www.foodserviceworld.com. **Contact:** Rosanna Caira, editor. Associate Editor: Carolyn Cooper. **40% freelance written.** Monthly magazine covering restaurant and hotel trade. Estab. 1968. Circ. 25,000. Pays on publication. Byline given. Buys first North American serial rights. Editorial lead time 3 months. Submit seasonal material 2 months in advance. Sample copy and writer's guidelines free.

Nonfiction: How-to, new product. No case studies. **Buys 30-50 mss/year.** Query with or without published clips. Length: 700-1,500 words. **Pays 30-35¢ for assigned articles.** Sometimes pays expenses of writers on assignment.

Photos: Send photos with submission. Offers $30-75/photo.

N $ $ THE INN TIMES, Interbriefs, 2101 Crystal Plaza Arcade #246, Arlington VA 22202-4600. (202)363-9305. Fax: (202)686-3966. **Contact:** Jeanine Meiers, editor-in-chief. **80% freelance written.** Monthly newspaper covering bed and breakfast inns—business and feature articles. "Business-related articles are usually best. The audience is established innkeepers and aspiring innkeepers." Estab. 1990. Circ. 7,000. Pays on publication. Publishes ms an average of 3 months after acceptance. Byline given. Buys first North American serial rights. Editorial lead time 3 months. Submit seasonal material 2 months in advance. Sample copy and writer's guidelines free.

Nonfiction: Book excerpts, general interest, historical/nostalgic, how-to (working with computers, preservation, starting an inn), humor, interview/profile, new product, personal experience, photo feature, technical, travel. No religious or exposé. Query with published clips. Length: 1,700-2,300 words. **Pays 12-15¢/word for assigned articles; 10¢/word for unsolicited articles.** Sometimes pays expenses of writers on assignment.

Photos: Captions and identification of subjects required.

Columns/Departments: The columns we have are assigned to specific writers. We are always looking for ideas, though, and are willing to think about adding new columns.

Fillers: Anecdotes, facts, newsbreaks, short humor. Length: 300-500 words. **Pays 10¢/word.**

Tips: "It is helpful if writers are familiar with the bed and breakfast industry. It is also helpful if writers have ideas and/or sources they are familiar with, though this is by no means necessary or required."

$ $ PIZZA TODAY, The Monthly Professional Guide To Pizza Profits, ProTech Publishing and Communications, Inc., P.O. Box 1347, New Albany IN 47151. (812)949-0909. Fax: (812)941-9711. E-mail: PizEditor@aol.com. Website: http://PizzaToday.com. **Contact:** Bruce Allar, editor. **75% freelance written.** Prefers to work with published/established writers. Monthly magazine for the pizza industry, covering trends, features of successful pizza operators, business and management advice, etc. Estab. 1983. Circ. 40,000. Pays on publication. Publishes ms an average of 2 months after acceptance. Byline given. Offers 10-30% kill fee. Buys all and negotiable rights. Submit seasonal/holiday material 3 months in advance. "All articles must be supplied on a 3½-inch disk and accompanied by a hard copy. Most major word processor formats accepted; else submit in ASCII format." Reports in 2 months on queries; 3 weeks on mss. Sample copy and writer's guidelines for 10×13 SAE with 6 first-class stamps. No phone calls, please.

Nonfiction: Interview/profile, new product, entrepreneurial slants, time management, pizza delivery, employee training. No fillers, fiction, humor or poetry. **Buys 40-60 mss/year.** Query with published clips. Length: 750-2,500 words. **Pays $50-125/page.** Sometimes pays expenses of writers on assignment.

Photos: Send photos with submission. Reviews contact sheets, negatives, 4×5 transparencies, color slides and 5×7 prints. Offers $5-25/photo. Captions required.

Tips: "We would like to receive nutritional information for low-cal, low-salt, low-fat, etc., pizza. Writers must have strong pizza business and foodservice background."

$ $ QSR, The Magazine of Quick Service Restaurant Success, Journalistic, Inc., 4905 Pine Cone Dr., Suite 2, Durham NC 27707. Fax: (919)489-4767. E-mail: lea@jayi.com. **Contact:** Lea Davis Paul, editor. **90% freelance written.** Bimonthly magazine covering the quick-service segment of the restaurant industry. Estab. 1997. **Pays on acceptance.** Publishes ms an average of 6 weeks after acceptance. Byline given. Offers 25% kill fee. Buys all rights and makes work-for-hire assignments. Editorial lead time 2 months. Reports in 3 weeks on queries; 1 month on mss. Sample copy and writer's guidelines free.

Nonfiction: Book excerpts, exposé, interview/profile, new product, industry reports, industry news analysis. No religious, essays, humor, inspirational or travel. **Buys 120 mss/year.** Query with résumé and published clips. Length: 1,800-2,500 words. **Pays $50-500.** Sometimes pays expenses of writers on assignment.
Photos: Send photos with submission. Reviews prints. Offers no additional payment for photos accepted with ms. Captions, identification of subjects required. Buys one-time rights.
Columns/Departments: Management (news analysis, industry reporting, profiles, interviews, book reviews), 800-1,100 words; Service in America (customer service), 800-1,100 words; Short Order (brief news analysis), 400-600 words. **Buys 75 mss/year.** Query with published clips. **Pays $75-250.**
Tips: "The most successful writers for *QSR* will (1) be familiar with the quick service restaurant industry and able to report on it with minimal direction, and (2) be able to apply literary journalism techniques to their writing."

N $ $ VACATION INDUSTRY REVIEW, Interval International, P.O. Box 431920, South Miami FL 33243-1920. (305)666-1861, ext. 7022. Fax: (305)668-3408. E-mail: gleposky@interval-intl.com. **Contact:** George Leposky, editor. **30% freelance written.** Prefers to work with published/established writers. Bimonthly magazine covering leisure lodgings (timeshare resorts, fractionals, and other types of vacation-ownership properties). Estab. 1982. Circ. 15,000. Pays on publication. Publishes ms an average of 6 months after acceptance. Byline given. Buys all rights and makes work-for-hire assignments. Submit seasonal material at least 6 months in advance. Reports in 1 month. Writer's guidelines for #10 SASE.
Nonfiction: How-to, interview/profile, new product, opinion, personal experience, technical, travel. No consumer travel or non-vacation real-estate material. **Buys 10-12 mss/year.** Query with published clips. Length: 1,000-1,500 words. **Pays 30¢/word.** Pays expenses of writers on assignment, if previously arranged.
Photos: Send photos with submission. Reviews contact sheets, 35mm transparencies, 5×7 or larger prints. Offers no additional payment for photos accepted with ms. Captions and identification of subjects required. Buys one-time rights.
Tips: "We want articles about the business aspects of the vacation ownership industry: entrepreneurship, project financing, design and construction, sales and marketing, operations, management—anything that will help our readers plan, build, sell and run a quality vacation ownership property that satisfies the owners/guests and earns a profit for developer and marketer. Our destination pieces are trade-oriented, reporting the status of tourism and the development of various kinds of vacation-ownership facilities in a city, region, or country. You can discuss things to see and do in the context of a resort located near an attraction, but that shouldn't be the main focus or reason for the article. We're also interested in owner associations at vacation-ownership resorts (not residential condos). Prefers electronic submissions. Query for details."

INDUSTRIAL OPERATIONS

Industrial plant managers, executives, distributors and buyers read these journals. Some industrial management journals are also listed under the names of specific industries. Publications for industrial supervisors are listed in Management and Supervision.

N $ $ CANADIAN PLASTICS, Southam Publishing Magazine Group, 1450 Don Mills Rd, Don Mills Ontario M1E 1E8, Canada. (416)442-2290. Fax: (416)442-2213. E-mail: mlegault@southam.ca. **Contact:** Michael LeGault, editor. Associate Editor: Cindy Macdonald. **20% freelance written.** Monthly trade magazine, tabloid covering plastics. "*Canadian Plastics Magazine* reports on and interprets development in plastics markets and technologies for plastics processors and end-users based in Canada." Estab. 1942. Circ. 11,000. **Pays on acceptance.** Publishes ms an average of 3 months after acceptance. Byline sometimes given. Offers 25% kill fee. Editorial lead time 2 months. Submit seasonal material 4 months in advance. Reports in 2 weeks on queries; 1 month on mss. Sample copy and writer's guidelines free.
Nonfiction: Technical, industry news (Canada only). **Buys 6 mss/year.** Query with published clips. Length: 400-1600 words. **Pays $120-350.** Sometimes pays expenses of writers on assignment.
Reprints: Accepts previously published submissions.
Photos: State availability of photos with submission.
Columns and Departments: Pays $100-300.
Tips: "Give the editor a call."

COMPRESSED AIR, 253 E. Washington Ave., Washington NJ 07882-2495. Fax: (908)689-3095. E-mail: camag@ingersoll-rand.com. Website: http://www.ingersoll-rand.com/compair. **Contact:** Tom McAloon, editor/publications manager. **75% freelance written.** Magazine published 8 times/year emphasizing applied technology and industrial management subjects for engineers and managers. "*Compressed Air* is looking for articles that inform our readers of technological innovations in the workplace and at home, enhance our readers' ability to manage their professional lives, and increase our readers' awareness of their surroundings and history. Potential authors should be guided by the fact that we prefer articles that tell our readers 'why,' instead of 'how-to.' " Estab. 1896. Circ. 145,000. Buys all rights. Publishes ms an average of 6 months after acceptance. Reports in 2 months. Free sample copy; mention *Writer's Market* in request.
Nonfiction: "Articles must be reviewed by experts in the field." **Buys 56 mss/year.** Query with published clips. Pays negotiable fee. Sometimes pays expenses of writers on assignment.

Photos: State availability of photos in query. Payment for slides, transparencies and glossy prints is included in total purchase price. Captions required. Buys all rights.

Tips: "First, I like a good strong lead that grabs the reader's attention. Start off with a great quote, an interesting example, something, anything that will make the reader *want* to read your story. I also want experts in the field to tell me facts, not the writer. Use quotes or attribute facts to their source. I'm suspicious of articles where I only hear the writer's voice. And when you mention a company or organization, please give the city and state where it is located. Use headings and subheadings in your story. Headings/subheadings make life easier for the reader *and* help writers to stay organized and focused on the topic. Be sure to include good transitions between sections, too. Stay focused on the topic and avoid the temptation to dump every fact into the story. Last, I want endings! Wrap up your story with observations about what the future holds, strong quotes on the impact of the technology, etc. I hate stories that suddenly end, like in a newspaper. We are presently looking for freelancers with a track record in industrial/technology/management writing. Editorial schedule is developed in the summer before the publication year and relies heavily on article ideas from contributors. Résumé and samples help. Writers with access to authorities preferred; we prefer interviews over library research. The magazine's name doesn't reflect its contents. We suggest writers request sample copies."

N **INDUSTRIAL FABRIC PRODUCTS REVIEW**, Industrial Fabrics Association International, 1801 County Rd. B W, Roseville MN 55113-4052. (612)222-2508. Fax: (612)225-6966. E-mail: chmikko@ifai.com. Website: http://www.ifai.com. **Contact:** Chris Mikko, managing editor. **75% staff- and industry-written.** Monthly magazine covering industrial textiles and products made from them for company owners, salespeople and researchers in a variety of industrial textile areas. Estab. 1915. Circ. 11,000. Pays on publication. Publishes ms an average of 2 months after acceptance. Byline given. Buys all rights. Reports in 1 month.

Nonfiction: Technical, marketing and other topics related to any aspect of industrial fabric industry from fiber to finished fabric product. Special issues: new products, new fabrics and equipment. No historical or apparel-oriented articles. Buys 8-10 mss/year. Query with phone number. Length: 1,200-3,000 words.

Tips: "We encourage freelancers to learn our industry and make regular, solicited contributions to the magazine. We do not buy photography."

N $ $ **INTERNATIONAL FIBER JOURNAL**, International Media Group, Inc., 1515 Mockingbird Lane, Suite 210, Charlotte NC 28209. Fax: (704)565-5177. E-mail: ifj@bluenet.net. Website: http://www.fiberjournal.com. **Contact:** Charles Heschmeyer, editor. **60% freelance written.** Bimonthly magazine covering fiber technology, polyester, nylon, etc." Estab. 1985. Circ. 10,000. **Pays on acceptance.** Byline given. Offers $50 kill fee. Buys first rights. Editorial lead time 1 month. Submit seasonal material 6 months in advance. Reports in 2 weeks. Sample copy for $6 plus postage.

Nonfiction: Book excerpts, new product, technical. Seeking "technical and business articles, company and company executive profiles, news, trends and analysis of manmade fiber industry." Query. Length: 750-2,000 words. **Pays $150-300 for assigned articles; $50-100 for unsolicited articles.** Sometimes pays expenses of writers on assignment.

Photos: State availability of photos with submission. Reviews 3×5 or 5×7 prints. Offers no additional payment for photos accepted with ms. Captions and identification of subjects required. Buys one-time rights.

Columns/Departments: Books (reviews); new products. **Buys 6 mss/year.** Query. **Pays $50-100.**

N $ $ **LUBRICANTS WORLD**, Hart Publications, Inc., 4545 Post Oak Place, Suite 210, Houston TX 77027. (713)993-9320. **Contact:** Tim Cornitius, editor. **35% freelance written.** Monthly magazine covering lubricants and their markets. "Every month we cover: additives, automotive lubricants, lubricating grease, industrial lubricants, lubricant manufacturing and marketing, metalworking fluids, packaging, quick lube operations, testing and analysis, and used oil and recycling." Estab. 1991. Circ. 13,000. Pays on publication. Publishes ms an average of 1 month after acceptance. Byline given. Buys all rights unless otherwise agreed. Editorial lead time 1-2 months. Submit seasonal material 1-2 months in advance. Query for electronic submissions. Sample copy and writer's guidelines free on request.

Nonfiction: Historical/nostalgic, new product, opinion, photo feature, technical, business. Query. Length: 1,000 words maximum. **Pays $400 maximum for assigned articles; $200 maximum for unsolicited articles.** Sometimes pays expenses of writers on assignment.

Photos: State availability of photos with submissions. Reviews prints. Offers $5-200/photo. Identification of subjects required. Buys one-time rights.

Tips: "Get a copy of magazine. Read it. Then contact us with story ideas."

N $ $ **NEW STEEL MAGAZINE, Mini & Integrated Mill Management & Technologies**, Cahners Business Information, 191 S. Gary Ave., Carol Stream IL 60188. Fax: (630)462-2862. Website: http://www.newsteel.com. Managing Editor: Michael Greissel. **Contact:** Adam Ritt, editor. **15% freelance written.** Monthly trade magazine covering steel industry. "*Iron Age/New Steel* serves the ferrous and non-ferrous metal producing industries. Also included are others allied to the field including engineering and architectural services, as well as miscellaneous business services. Qualified recipients are corporate management, operating management, maintenance, engineering, metallurgical and chemical, purchasing, and research and development, managers and engineers in the above industries." Estab. 1855. Circ. 19,000. **Pays on acceptance.** Publishes ms an average of 1 month after acceptance. Byline given. Buys first rights and all rights. Editorial lead time 1 month. Reports in 2 weeks on queries. Do not send ms without prior approval. Sample copy free.

Non-fiction: Does not want to see applications at work or any public-relations copy. Query with published clips.

Length: 750-10,000 words. **Pays $150/page. Does not publish unsolicited articles. Pay expenses of writers on assignment.**

Photos: Send photos with submission. Reviews contact sheets and transparencies. Negotiates payment individually. Captions and identification of subjects required. Buys all rights.

N $ $ $ PHOTONICS SPECTRA, Laurin Publishing Co., Inc., 2 South St., Pittsfield MA 01201. (413)499-0514. Fax: (413)442-3180. E-mail: photonics@laurin.com. Website: http://www.laurin.com. **Contact:** Stephanie A. Weiss, executive editor. **10% freelance written.** Monthly magazine covering photonics: optics, lasers, fiber optics and imaging. "*Photonics Spectra* covers the application of photonic technologies to solving real-world problems. Its audience includes developers, manufacturers and users of these technologies and its mission to provide a dialogue among those groups to enable the proliferation of light-based technologies." Estab. 1960. Circ. 98,000. Pays on publication. Publishes ms an average of 1 month after acceptance. Byline given. Buys all rights. Editorial lead time 2 months. Reports in 1 week on queries; 1 month on mss. Sample copy for $1. Writer's guidelines for #10 SASE.

Nonfiction: Opinion, technical. Technical journal-type articles with footnotes and lots of technical jargon and acronyms. Query with published clips. Length: 200-2,000 words. **Pays 50¢/word.** Sometimes pays expenses of writers on assignment.

Photos: Send photos with submission. Offers no additional payment for photos accepted with ms. Captions required. Buys negotiable rights.

Columns/Departments: Technology World (trends in photonics technology), 700-1,000 words; Business World (trends in photonics business/marketing), 700-1,000 words; Accent on Applications (case studies of how specific companies used photonics to solve a problem), 400 words. **Buys 12-30 mss/year.** Query with published clips. **Pays 50¢/word.**

Fillers: Newsbreaks, short humor. Must be related to photonics technology, preferably "newsy." **Buys 12-30/year.** Length: 200 words. **Pays 50¢/word.**

Tips: "Reading the magazine is the key! Every *Photonics Spectra* article must answer four questions: 1. What problem does this technology solve? 2. How is it better than previous solutions? 3. What are some other potential commercial applications? 4. Where does the technology go from here? Articles must be written in *English,* not in engineering-ese. We also prefer regular over occasional contributors."

$ $ QUALITY DIGEST, 40 Declaration Dr., Suite 100, Chico CA 95973. (530)893-4095. Fax: (530)893-0395. E-mail: editorial@qualitydigest.com. Website: http://www.qualitydigest.com. **Contact:** Scott M. Paton, editor. **75% freelance written.** Monthly trade magazine covering quality improvement. Estab. 1981. Circ. 65,000. **Pays on acceptance.** Byline given. Buys all rights. Submit seasonal material 4 months in advance. Accepts simultaneous submissions. Reports in 3 months. Free sample copy and writer's guidelines.

Nonfiction: Book excerpts, how-to implement quality programs and solve problems for benefits, etc., interview/profile, opinion, personal experience, technical. **Buys 25 mss/year.** Query with or without published clips or send complete ms. Length: 800-3,000 words. **Pays $200-600.** Pays in contributor copies for unsolicited mss. Sometimes pays expenses of writers on assignment.

Reprints: Send tearsheet of article and information about when and where the article previously appeared. Pays 25% of amount paid for original article.

Photos: Send photos with submission. Reviews any size prints. Offers no additional payment for photos accepted with ms. Captions, model releases and identification of subjects required. Buys one-time rights.

Tips: "Please be specific in your articles. Explain what the problem was, how it was solved and what the benefits are. Tell the reader how the technique described will benefit him or her. We now feature shorter, tighter, more focused articles than in the past. This means we have more articles in each issue. We're striving to present our readers with concise, how-to, easy-to-read information that makes their job easier."

N $ $ WAREHOUSING MANAGEMENT, Reed Elsevier Business Information, 201 King of Prussia Rd., Radnor PA 19089. Fax: (610)964-4381. E-mail: mlearoli@chilton.net. Website: http://www.chilton.net/warehouse. **Contact:** Michael Lear-Olimpi, chief editor. **80% freelance written.** Controlled-circulation business/trade magazine published 10 times/year covering warehousing, distribution centers, inventory. "*Warehousing Management* is a 10 times-a-year glossy national magazine read by managers of warehouses and distribution centers. We focus on lively, well-written articles telling our readers how they can achieve maximum facility productivity and efficiency. Heavy software and management components." Estab. 1994. Circ. 50,000. **Pays on acceptance.** Publishes ms an average of 1 month after acceptance. Byline given. Offers 20% or $100 kill fee. Editorial lead time 3 months. Sample copy and writer's guidelines free.

Nonfiction: How-to, new product, technical. Special issues: State-of-the-Industry Report, Peak Performer, Salary and Wage survey, Warehouse of the Year. Doesn't want to see anything that doesn't deal with our topic—warehousing. Articles must be on-point, how-to pieces for managers. No general-interest profiles or interviews. **Buys 50 mss/year.** Query with published clips. **Pays $500.**

Photos: State availability of photos with submission. Reviews negatives, transparencies or prints. Offers no additional payment for photos accepted with ms. Captions and identification of subjects required. Buys all rights.

Columns/Departments: Buys 15 mss/year. Query with published clips. **Pays $200-750.**

Tips: "We typically don't accept specific article queries, but welcome introductory letters from journalists to whom we can assign articles. But authors are welcome to request an editorial calendar and develop article queries from it."

$ $ WEIGHING & MEASUREMENT, Key Markets Publishing Co., P.O. Box 5867, Rockford IL 61125. (815)636-7739. Fax: (815)636-7741. E-mail: dwam34@inwave.com. Website: http://www.weighingandmeasurement.com. **Contact:** David M. Mathieu, editor. Bimonthly magazine for users of industrial scales. Estab. 1914. Circ. 12,000. **Pays on acceptance.** Buys all rights. Offers 20% kill fee. Byline given. Reports in 2 weeks. Sample copy for $2.
Nonfiction: Interview (with presidents of companies); personal opinion (guest editorials on government involvement in business, etc.); profile (about users of weighing and measurement equipment); product reviews; technical. **Buys 25 mss/year.** Query on technical articles; submit complete ms for general interest material. Length: 1,000-2,500 words. **Pays $175-300.**

INFORMATION SYSTEMS

These publications give computer professionals more data about their field. Consumer computer publications are listed under Personal Computers.

$ $ AS/400 SYSTEMS MANAGEMENT, Adams Business Media, 2101 S. Arlington Heights Rd., Suite 150, Arlington Heights IL 60005. (847)427-2027. Fax: (847)427-2006. E-mail: 73222.3344@compuserve.com. Website: http://www.hotlink400.com. **Contact:** Sue Garrison, managing editor. Editor: Wayne Rhodes. **10% freelance written.** Works with a small number of new/unpublished writers. Monthly magazine covering applications of IBM AS/400 systems in business. Estab. 1973. Circ. 45,000. Pays on publication. Publishes ms an average of 3 months after acceptance. Byline given. Buys all rights. Submit seasonal material 4 months in advance. Reports in 3 months on queries. Sample copy for 9×12 SAE with 4 first-class stamps. Writer's guidelines sent via fax or e-mail.
Nonfiction: How-to (use the computer in business), technical (organization of a data base or file system). "A writer who submits material to us should be well versed in computer applications and in writing for business publications. No material on large-scale computer equipment." No poetry. **Buys 8 mss/year.** Query. Length: 1,500 words.
Tips: "Frequent mistakes are not understanding the audience and not having read past issues of the magazine."

N AUTOMATIC I.D. NEWS, Advanstar Communications, 7500 Old Oak Blvd., Cleveland OH 44130. Fax: (216)891-2733. E-mail: autoid@en.com. **Contact:** Doris Kilbane, managing editor. Editor: Mark David. **33% freelance written.** "World's leading monthly magazine covering automatic capture technologies and communications. Provides info on new products, systems and applications to 75,000+ subscribers in US and Canada and 20,000 in Latin America and Asia/Pacific regions. The editorial is written to help readers best define their system requirements and choose the right technology." Estab. 1982. Circ. 100,000. **Pays on acceptance.** Publishes ms an average of 5 months after acceptance. Byline given. Buys first and second serial (reprint) rights. Editorial lead time 4 months. Submit seasonal material 5 months in advance. Sample copy and writer's guidelines free.
Nonfiction: How-to (use and select automatic data capture technology and products), new product, opinion, technical. "No profiles of automatic data capture manufacturers, the people or the companies." **Buys 12 mss/year.** Send complete ms. Length: 1,200-2,000 words. Pay varies. Sometimes pays expenses of writers on assignment.
Photos: Send photos with submission. Reviews transparencies and prints. Model releases required. Buys all rights.
Fillers: Gags to be illustrated by cartoonist. **Buys 4 cartoons/year.**
Tips: "Submit a case study about a specific company's success with automatic data capture technology that clearly explains what problem was solved and also follows our guidelines."

$ $ COMPUTER GRAPHICS WORLD, PennWell Publishing Company, 10 Tara Blvd., 5th Floor, Nashua NH 03062-2801. (603)891-9160. Fax: (603)891-0539. E-mail: phill@pennwell.com. Website: www.cgw.com. **Contact:** Phil Lo Piccolo, editor. **50% freelance written.** Monthly magazine. "*Computer Graphics World* specializes in covering computer-aided 3D modeling, animation, and visualization and their uses in engineering, science, and entertainment applications." Estab. 1978. Circ. 70,000. **Pays on acceptance.** Publishes ms an average of 4 months after acceptance. Byline given. Offers 20% kill fee. Buys all rights. Editorial lead time 4 months. Submit seasonal material 3 months in advance. Sample copy free.
Nonfiction: General interest, how-to (how-to create quality models and animations), interview/profile, new product, opinion, technical, user application stories. "We do not want to run articles that are geared to computer programmers. Our focus as a magazine is on users involved in specific applications." **Buys 40 mss/year.** Query with published clips. Length: 1,200-3,000 words. **Pays $500 minimum.** Sometimes pays expenses of writers on assignment.
Columns/Departments: Technology stories (describes innovation and its implication for computer graphics users), 750-1,000 words; Reviews (offers hands-on review of important new products), 750 words; and Application Stories (highlights unique use of the technology by a single user), 800 words. **Buys 36-40 mss/year.** Query with published clips. **Pays $300-500.**
Tips: "Freelance writers will be most successful if they have some familiarity with computers and know how to write from a user's perspective. They do not need to be computer experts, but they do have to understand how to explain the impact of the technology and the applications in which a user is involved. Our technology stories, feature section, and our application story section are quite open to freelancers. The trick to winning acceptance for your story is to have a well-developed idea that highlights a fascinating new trend or development in computer graphics technology or profiles a unique and fascinating use of the technology by a single user or a specific class of users."

N $ $ $ $ CONTRACT PROFESSIONAL, The Magazine for IT Contractors and Consultants, Skinner-James, 125 Walnut St., Watertown MA 02172. (617)926-7077. E-mail: conpro@shore.net. **Contact:** Tony Bogar, editor-in-chief. **90% freelance written.** "Bimonthly magazine geared toward high-tech contractors, from software writers to top-level project managers. Writers must understand contract workstyle and/or IT issues." Estab. 1996. Circ. 55,000. **Pays on acceptance.** Publishes ms an average of 3 months after acceptance. Byline given. Offers 10% kill fee. Buys all rights. Editorial lead time 4 months. Reports in 1 month. Sample copy for $5. Writer's guidelines free.
Nonfiction: Book excerpts, how-to, interview/profile, new product, personal experience, technical. **Buys 30 mss/year.** Query with published clips. Length: 700-2,000 words. **Pays $1/word.** Sometimes pays expenses of writers on assignment.
Columns/Departments: Your Turn (first-person IT issue), 800 words. **Buys 20 mss/year.** Query with published clips. **Pays 50¢-$1/word.**

$ $ $ DBMS, Miller Freeman, Dept. WM, 411 Borel Ave., San Mateo CA 94402-32522. (650)358-9500. Fax: (650)358-9855. E-mail: cparkes@mfi.com. Website: http://www.dbmsmag.com. **Contact:** Clara Parkes, executive editor. **60% freelance written.** Monthly magazine covering client/server, internet/intranet, database application development. "Our readers are database developers, consultants, VARs, programmers in MIS/DP departments and serious users." Estab. 1988. Circ. 90,000. **Pays on acceptance.** Publishes ms 3 months after acceptance. Byline given. Offers 33% kill fee. Buys all rights. Reports in 6 weeks on queries. Sample copy for 9×12 SAE with 8 first-class stamps.

• *DBMS* offers extensive guidelines on its website.

Nonfiction: Technical. **Buys 40-50 mss/year.** Query with published clips. Length: 750-4,000 words. **Pays $300-1,000.**
Photos: Publishes screen shots.
Tips: "New writers should submit clear, concise queries of specific article subjects and ideas. *Read the magazine* to get a feel for the kind of articles we publish. This magazine is written for a highly technical computer database developer, consultant and user readership. We need technical and strategic features that inform this audience of new trends, software and techniques."

$ $ $ DESKTOP ENGINEERING, Complete Computer Resource for Engineers, Helmers Publishing, 174 Concord St., Peterborough NH 03458. (603)924-9631. Fax: (603)924-4004. E-mail: de-editors@helmers.com. Website: http://www.deskeng.com. **Contact:** Anthony J. Lockwood, editor. Managing Editor: Vinoy Laughner. **90% freelance written.** Monthly magazine covering microcomputer hardware/software for engineers. Estab. 1995. Circ. 55,000. Pays on publication. Publishes ms an average of 4 months after acceptance. Byline given. Buys all rights. Editorial lead time 3 months. Reports in 6 weeks on queries; 6 months on mss. Sample copy and writer's guidelines free; editorial calendar on website.
Nonfiction: How-to, new product, technical, reviews. "No fluff." **Buys 120 mss/year.** Query. Length: 750-3,000 words. **Pays 60¢/word for assigned articles.** Negotiates fee for unsolicited articles. Sometimes pays expenses of writers on assignment.
Photos: Send photos with submission. Negotiates payment and rights purchased individually. Captions required.
Columns/Departments: Product Briefs (new products), 50-100 words; Reviews (software, hardware, books), 500-1,500 words. **Buys 30 mss/year.** Query. Pay varies.
Tips: "Call the editor or e-mail him for submission tips."

DESKTOP PUBLISHERS JOURNAL, Business Media Group, 462 Boston St., Topsfield MA 01983. (978)887-7900. Fax: (978)887-6117. E-mail: edit@dtpjournal.com. Website: http://www.dtpjournal.com. Editor-in-Chief: Barry Harrigan. **Contact:** Heather Surface. **80% freelance written.** "Monthly magazine that serves as a forum for the examination of information, ideas and issues important to professionals involved in content development, collaboration and management. We concentrate on the areas of prepress, wide-format printing, digital photography, Internet publishing and multimedia design." Estab. 1987. Circ. 100,000. Pays 45 days after acceptance. Publishes ms an average of 3 months after acceptance. Byline given. Kill fee. Buys all rights. Editorial lead time 4 months. Reports in 1 month on queries. Sample copy for $6. Writer's guidelines for #10 SASE.
Nonfiction: "We run several types of articles: stories on technology which may provide tips on how to apply it; roundups that introduce readers to new or updated products; user stories that highlight how 'real' people are using technologies; and trend pieces that look to the future." **Buys 60 mss/year.** Query with published clips. Length: 750-3,000 words. Rates negotiated based on article length and complexity of topic.
Columns/Departments: Book Reviews, Business, Color, Design, Digital Imaging, Emerging Technology, Internet Issues, On the Desktop, Paper, Prepress & Printing, Product Reviews, Profile, Special Report, Type, Web watch, Wide-format (all helping readers to understand and apply existing and emerging technologies in their work as desktop publishers), 750-1,500 words. **Buys 100 mss/year.** Query with published clips. Rates negotiated based on topic and complexity.
Tips: "*DPJ* welcomes queries from writers who are experienced in writing on the desktop publishing industry and/or are experts in certain areas of electronic publishing, including any of our topic areas. Departments are the easiest way to break in, although we're always looking for new writers for feature-length articles."

N $ $ $ GAME DEVELOPER, Miller Freeman Inc., 600 Harrison St., San Francisco CA 94107. (415)905-2200. Fax: (415)905-4962. E-mail: gdmag@mfi.com. **Contact:** Wesley Hall, editorial assistant. Editor: Alex Donne. Managing Editor: Tor Berg. **95% freelance written.** Monthly magazine covering computer game development. Estab. 1994. Circ. 30,000. Pays on publication. Publishes ms an average of 3 months after acceptance. Byline given. Buys first North American serial, first, all, and electronic rights. Editorial lead time 3 months. Submit seasonal material 4 months in advance. Sample copy and writer's guidelines free.

Nonfiction: How-to, personal experience, technical. **Buys 50 mss/year.** Query. Length: 3,000-5,000 words. **Pays $150-200/page.**

Photos: State availability of photos with submission.

N $ $ $ **GIS WORLD**, GIS World, Inc., 400 N. College Ave., Suite 100, Fort Collins CO 80524. (970)221-0037. Fax: (970)221-5150. E-mail: info@gisworld.com. **Contact:** John R. Hughes, editor. Managing Editor: Todd Danielson. **20% freelance written.** Monthly magazine covering "geographic information systems and related technologies, including remote sensing, computer-aided design and the global positioning system. *GIS World* is the primary source of GIS news to and from industry and government readers worldwide. Every month, *GIS World* responds to the main concerns of the GIS novice and professional alike by covering new products; company news; GIS applications; federal, state and local government; associations; and GIS uses inaucillary industries such as remote sensing, the global positioning system, surveying, computer-aided design, and aerial photography." Estab. 1988. Circ. 21,575. Pays on publication. Publishes ms an average of 4 months after acceptance. Byline given. Buys first North American serial rights. Editorial lead time 4 months. Accepts simultaneous submissions. Reports in 1 month. Sample copy and writer's guidelines free.

Nonfiction: General interest (to GIS users), how-to, new product, opinion, technical. **Buys 12 mss/year.** Query. Length: 1,500-2,500 words. **Pays $300-1,500.** Sometimes pays expenses of writers on assignment.

Photos: Send photos with submission. Offers no additional payment for photos accepted with ms. Captions required. Buys one-time rights.

GOVERNMENT COMPUTER NEWS, 8601 Georgia Ave., Suite 300, Silver Spring MD 20910. Fax: (301)650-2111. E-mail: editor@gen.com. Website: http://www.gcn.com. **Contact:** Thomas Temin, editorial director. Published biweekly for government information technology managers. **Pays on acceptance.** Byline given. Kill fee varies. Buys all rights. Reports in 1 month. Sample copy free. Writer's guidelines for #10 SASE.

Nonfiction: Buys 30 mss/year. Query. Length: 700-1,200 words. **Pays $800-2,000.** Pays expenses of writers on assignment.

Columns/Departments: Length: 400-600 words. **Buys 75 mss/year.** Query. **Pays $250-400.**

Fillers: Buys 10 mss/year. Length: 300-500 words. **Pays $250-450.**

Tips: Needs "technical case histories of applications of computers to governmental missions and trends in information technology."

$ $ **ID SYSTEMS, The Source for Automatic Identification & Data Capture**, Helmers Publishing, Inc., 174 Concord St., Peterborough NH 03458. (603)924-9631. Fax: (603)924-7408. E-mail: editors@idsystems.com. Website: http://www.idsystems.com. **Contact:** Roberta Bell, editor. Managing Editor: Mark E. Reynolds. **50% freelance written.** Monthly. "*ID Systems* is targeted to purchasers and users of automated data collection technology, including bar code labeling and equipment, radio-frequency ID and data collection systems, smart cards, and biometrics." Estab. 1981. Circ. 75,000. **Pays on acceptance.** Publishes ms an average of 4 months after acceptance. Byline given. Buys worldwide serial and electronic rights. Editorial lead time 3 months. Reports in 2 months on queries. Writer's guidelines free.

Nonfiction: Case studies, guest columns, technology updates. "Freelancers would primarily write technology tutorials and application stories, and those should include specific technical details as to how a system works and what products are involved. However, avoid writing an advertorial." We have no interest in any material not related to the automated data collection industry (bar codes, RFID, warehouse management, etc.)." **Buys 36-40 mss/year.** Query with published clips. Length: 1,200-2,000 words. **Pays $300.**

Photos: Send photos with submission. Reviews contact sheets, transparencies (35mm) and prints. Offers no additional payment for photos accepted with ms. Captions and identification of subjects required. Rights vary article to article.

Columns/Departments: Bar Code Basics (beginner into on basic aspect of ADC technology); Guest Column (opinion on a particular aspect of ADC industry), both 500 words.

Tips: "Writers must be able to describe specific ADC implementations—the problems it solved, the benefits it brought—so that even non-technical readers can understand it. They must include specific technical details, including the type of bar code used, the other ADC equipment and how all equipment communicates. We don't want fluff or hype. We want to know exactly how each ADC system works."

N $ $ **INFORMATION TODAY**, Information Today, Inc., 143 Old Marlton Pike, Medford NJ 08055-8750. (609)654-6266. Fax: (609)654-4309. Publisher: Thomas H. Hogan. **Contact:** David Hoffman, editor. **30% freelance written.** Tabloid published 11 times/year for the users and producers of electronic information services. Estab. 1979. Circ. 10,000. Pays on publication. Publishes ms an average of 1-3 months after acceptance. Byline given. Buys first North American serial rights. Submit seasonal material 2 months in advance. Reports in 2 weeks. Sample copy and writer's guidelines for 9×12 SAE with 6 first-class stamps.

Nonfiction: Book reviews; interview/profile and new product; technical (dealing with computerized information services); articles on library technology, artificial intelligence, online databases and services, and integrated online library systems. Also covers software and optical publishing (CD-ROM and multimedia). **Buys approximately 25 mss/year.** Query with published clips or send complete ms on speculation. Length: 500-1,500 words. **Pays $90-220.**

Photos: State availability of photos with submission.

Tips: "We look for clearly-written, informative articles dealing with the electronic delivery of information. Writing style should not be jargon-laden or heavily technical."

INFORMATION WEEK, 600 Community Dr., Manhasset NY 11030. (516)562-5000. Fax: (516)562-5036. E-mail: pkrass@cmp.com. Website: http://www.informationweek.com. Editor-in-Chief: Bob Evans. **Contact:** Peter Krass, senior managing editor. **20% freelance written.** Weekly magazine for information systems managers. Estab. 1985. Circ. 375,000. **Pays on acceptance.** Publishes ms an average of 1 month after acceptance. Byline given. Offers 25% kill fee. Buys first and non-exclusive serial rights. Accepts simultaneous submissions, if noted. Reports in 1 month. Sample copy free. Writer's guidelines for #10 SASE.

Nonfiction: Book excerpts, how-to, interview/profile, new product, technical, news analysis, company profiles. **Buys 30 mss/year.** Query with published clips. Length: 1,500-4,000 words. **Pays $1.10/word minimum.** Pays expenses of writers on assignment.

Reprints: Considers previously published submissions.

Tips: Needs "feature articles on technology trends—all with a business angle. We look at implementations by users, new products, management issues, intranets, the Internet, web, networks, PCs, objects, workstations, sewers, etc. Our competitors are tabloids—we're better written, more selective, and more analytical."

N $ $ $ JAVA™ REPORT, Independent Source for Java Development, SIGS Publication, 71 W. 23rd St., New York NY 10010. (212)242-7447. Fax: (212)242-7578. **Contact:** Dwight Deugo (dwight@objectpeople.com), editor-in-chief. Managing Editor: Kathleen M. Major (kmajor@sigs.com). **100% freelance written.** Monthly magazine covering technical writing for Java development. Article must satisfy the need to the Java community. Estab. 1996. Circ. 32,000. Pays on publication. Byline given. Offers 50% kill fee. Buys all rights. Editorial lead time 3 months. Submit seasonal material 4 months in advance. Accepts simultaneous submissions. Reports in 3-6 weeks on queries; 3-6 months on mss. Sample copy and writer's guidelines free.

Nonfiction: How-to, interview/profile, new product, technical, case study. Query. Length: 2,500-5,000 words. **Pays $250-1,000.**

Photos: Send photos with submission. Reviews transparencies. Offers no additional payment for photos accepted with ms. Identification of subjects required. Buys one-time rights.

Columns/Departments: Kathleen Major (kmajor@sigs.com), managing editor. Pooh Review; Product Review; interviews, case study, all 2,500 words. **Buys 12 mss/year.** Query. **Pays $50-750.**

Fillers: Facts, newsbreaks. **Buys 12 mss/year.** Length: 350-500 words. **Pays $50.**

Tips: "Send abstracts to editor; articles are published on need basis."

$ JOURNAL OF INFORMATION ETHICS, McFarland & Co., Inc., Publishers, Box 611, Jefferson NC 28640. (336)246-4460. Fax: (336)246-5018. **Contact:** Robert Hauptman, LRS, editor, 720 Fourth Ave. S., St. Cloud State University, St. Cloud MN 56301. (320)255-4822. Fax: (320)255-4778. **90% freelance written.** Semiannual scholarly journal. "Addresses ethical issues in all of the information sciences with a deliberately interdisciplinary approach. Topics range from electronic mail monitoring to library acquisition of controversial material. The journal's aim is to present thoughtful considerations of ethical dilemmas that arise in a rapidly evolving system of information exchange and dissemination." Estab. 1992. Circ. 500. Pays on publication. Publishes ms an average of 9 months after acceptance. Byline given. Buys all rights. Submit seasonal material 8 months in advance. Sample copy for $21. Writer's guidelines free.

Nonfiction: Essays, opinion, book reviews. **Buys 10 mss/year.** Send complete ms. Length: 500-3,500 words. **Pays $25.**

Tips: "Familiarize yourself with the many areas subsumed under the rubric of information ethics, e.g., privacy, scholarly communication, errors, peer review, confidentiality, e-mail, etc."

$ $ $ $ NETWORK WORLD, Network World Publishing, 161 Worcester Rd., Framingham MA 01701. (508)875-6400. Fax: (508)820-1103. E-mail: pdesmond@nww.com. Website: http://www.nwfusion.com. Editor-in-Chief: John Gallant. **Contact:** Paul Desmond, features editor. **25% freelance written.** Weekly tabloid covering data, voice and video communications networks (including news and features on communications management, hardware and software, services, education, technology and industry trends) for senior technical managers at large companies. Estab. 1986. Circ. 157,500. Pays on publication. Byline given. Offers negotiable kill fee. Buys all rights. Submit all material 2 months in advance. Free sample copy and writer's guidelines.

Nonfiction: Exposé, general interest, how-to (build a strong communications staff, evaluate vendors, choose a value-added network service), opinion, technical. Editorial calendar available. "Our readers are users: avoid vendor-oriented material." **Buys 100-150 mss/year.** Query with published clips. Length: 500-2,500 words. **Pays $250 minimum for columns, $1,800 for features.**

Photos: Send photos with submission. Reviews 35mm, 2¼ and 4×5 transparencies and b&w prints (prefers 8×10 but can use 5×7). Captions, model releases and identification of subjects required. Buys one-time rights.

Tips: "We look for accessible treatments of technological, managerial or regulatory trends. It's OK to dig into technical issues as long as the article doesn't read like an engineering document. Feature section is most open to freelancers. Be informative, stimulating, controversial and technically accurate. Take a stand."

$ $ WINDOWS NT MAGAZINE, Duke Communications International, Inc., 221 E. 29th St., Loveland CO 80539-0447. (970)663-4700. Website: http://www.winntmag.com. Editor: Mark Smith. Managing Editor: Janet Robbins. **Contact:** Dina Ralston, article acquisitions coordinator. **90% freelance written.** Monthly magazine "giving NT professionals explanations, techniques, insights and ideas that help them do their job." Estab. 1995. Circ. 100,000. Pays on publication. Publishes ms an average of 3 months after acceptance. Byline given. Offers $100 kill fee. Buys all rights. Editorial lead time 3 months. Submit seasonal material 3 months in advance. Sample copy and writer's guidelines free.
Nonfiction: How-to (use a technology to solve a problem). No articles related to a product promoted by the writer. **Buys 300 mss/year.** Query or send complete ms. Length: 1,500-3,000 words. **Pays 25¢/word.** Sometimes pays expenses of writers on assignment.
Reprints: Accepts previously published submissions. Send typed ms with rights for sale noted—electronic copy of article and information about when and where the article previously appeared.
Photos: State availability of photos with submission. Identification of subjects required.
Tips: *Windows NT Magazine* is looking for articles about Windows NT and related fields from qualified authors. We accept contributions in four areas: "How To" Feature Articles: Give NT professionals explanations, techniques, and ideas that help them do their job, how to use a technology to solve a problem, and suggestions for making the most of NT-related products. Articles up to 2,000 words, plus figures, charts, graphs, screen shots, photos, listings, etc. These articles cover a technology, a way to solve a problem, how to use NT and related products, comparative product reviews, specific applications, etc. "Strategic" Focus Articles: Focus articles examine a specific issue and technology affecting NT managers. These articles center on one theme and investigate products, situations, case studies, and companies to give a well-rounded view of how NT works in the real world. Length: 1,000 words or less. Case Studies: These should focus on an enterprise solving a very specific technological problem using Windows N.T. Length: 1,400 words.

INSURANCE

$ $ $ BUSINESS & HEALTH, Solutions in Managed Care, Medical Economics Publishing Co., 5 Paragon Dr., Montvale NJ 07645-1742. (201)358-7276. Fax: (201)772-2676. E-mail: b&h@medec.com. Website: http://www.medec.com. Editor: Richard Service. **Contact:** Helen Lippman, executive editor. **90% freelance written.** Monthly magazine. "*B&H* carries articles about how employers can cut their health care costs and improve the quality of care they provide to workers. We also write about health care policy at the federal, state and local levels." Estab. 1983. Circ. 52,000. **Pays on acceptance.** Publishes ms an average of 2 months after acceptance. Byline given. Offers 20% kill fee. Buys all rights. Editorial lead time 2 months. Submit seasonal material 4 months in advance. Reports in 3 months. Sample copy for 9×12 SAE with 6 first-class stamps. Writer's guidelines for #10 SASE.
Nonfiction: How-to (cut health care benefits costs, provide better care); case studies (of successful employer-led efforts); trend piece on broad issues such as 24-hour coverage or benefits for retirees. **Buys approx. 50 mss/year.** Query with published clips and SASE. Length: 2,000-3,500 words. **Pays $1,000-1,700 for features.** Pays expenses of writers on assignment.
Columns/Departments: Primarily staff-written but will consider queries.
Tips: "Please be familiar with *B&H* and follow writer's guidelines. Articles should combine a business angle with a human interest approach and address both cost-containment and quality of care. Include cost-benefit analysis data and material for charts or graphs whenever possible."

JEWELRY

N $ $ AMERICAN JEWELRY MANUFACTURER, Manufacturing Jewelers and Silversmiths of America, One State St., 6th Floor, Providence RI 02908. (401)274-3840. Fax: (401)274-0265. E-mail: ajmmagazine@compuserve.com. Website: http://mjsa.polygon.net. **Contact:** Suzanne Wade, editor/associate publisher. Managing Editor: Rich Youmans. **90% freelance written.** "*AJM* is a monthly magazine providing technical, marketing and business information for finished jewelry manufacturers and supporting industries." Estab. 1956. Circ. 5,000. **Pays on acceptance.** Publishes ms an average of 6 months after acceptance. Byline given. Offers 25% kill fee. Buys all rights for limited period of 18 months. Editorial lead time 1 year. Submit seasonal material 6 months in advance. Reports in 2 months. Sample copy and writer's guidelines free.
Nonfiction: How-to, interview/profile, new product, technical. All articles should focus on jewelry manufacturing techniques, especially how-to and technical articles. "No generic articles for a wide variety of industries, articles for hobbyists, or articles written for a consumer audience or for retailers. Our focus is professional jewelry manufacturers and designers, and articles for *AJM* should be carefully targeted for this audience." **Buys 40 mss/year.** Query. Length: 1,800-3,000 words. **Pays $500-600 for assigned articles; $400-500 for unsolicited articles.** Sometimes pays expenses of writers on assignment.
Reprints: Accepts previously published submissions.
Photos: State availability of photos with submission. Negotiates payment individually. Captions required. Buys one-time rights.
Columns/Departments: Making Contact (Q&A interviews), 1,200 words; Gem News (short gemstone-related news

briefs), 500-750 words; Street Style (news briefs on street-level fashions/humorous), 500-750 words. **Buys 12-18 mss/year.** Query. **Pays $50-400.**

Tips: "Because our editorial content is highly focused and specific, we assign most article topics rather than relying on outside queries. We are, as a result, always seeking new writers comfortable with business and technical topics who will work with us long term and whom we can develop into 'experts' in jewelry manufacturing. We invite writers to send an introductory letter and clips highlighting business and technical writing skills if they would like to be considered for a specific assignment."

$ THE DIAMOND REGISTRY BULLETIN, 580 Fifth Ave., #806, New York NY 10036. (212)575-0444. Fax: (212)575-0722. E-mail: diamond58@aol.com. Website: http://www.diamondregistry.com. **Contact:** Joseph Schlussel, editor-in-chief. **50% freelance written.** Monthly newsletter. Estab. 1969. Pays on publication. Buys all rights. Submit seasonal material 1 month in advance. Accepts simultaneous submissions. Reports in 3 weeks. Sample copy for $5.

Nonfiction: Prevention advice (on crimes against jewelers); how-to (ways to increase sales in diamonds, improve security, etc.); interview (of interest to diamond dealers or jewelers). Submit complete ms. Length: 50-500 words. **Pays $75-150.**

Reprints: Accepts previously published submissions.

Tips: "We seek ideas to increase sales of diamonds. We also have interest in diamond mining."

$ $ THE ENGRAVERS JOURNAL, 26 Summit St., P.O. Box 318, Brighton MI 48116. (810)229-5725. Fax: (810)229-8320. E-mail: editor@engraversjournal.com. Website: http://www.engraversjournal.com. Co-Publisher: Michael J. Davis. Managing Editor: Rosemary Farrell. **Contact:** Jackie Zack, senior editor. **15% freelance written.** "We are eager to work with published/established writers as well as new/unpublished writers." Monthly magazine covering the recognition and identification industry (engraving, marking devices, awards, jewelry, and signage.) "We provide practical information for the education and advancement of our readers, mainly retail business owners." Estab. 1975. **Pays on acceptance.** Publishes ms an average of 1 year after acceptance. Byline given "only if writer is recognized authority." Buys one-time rights and makes work-for-hire assignments. Reports in 2 weeks. Writer's guidelines free. Sample copy to "those who send writing samples with inquiry."

Nonfiction: General interest (industry-related); how-to (small business subjects, increase sales, develop new markets, use new sales techniques, etc.); technical. No general overviews of the industry. Query with writing samples "published or not, or send samples and résumé to be considered for assignments on speculation." Length: 1,000-5,000 words. **Pays $100-500 for assigned articles; $50 for unsolicited articles.**

Reprints: Accepts previously published submissions. Send photocopy of article or typed ms with rights for sale noted and information about when and where the article previously appeared. Pays 50-100% of amount paid for original article.

Photos: Send photos with query. Pays variable rate. Captions, model release, identification of subjects required.

Tips: "Articles should always be down to earth, practical and thoroughly cover the subject with authority. We do not want the 'textbook' writing approach, vagueness, or theory—our readers look to us for sound practical information. We use an educational slant, publishing both trade-oriented articles and general business topics of interest to a small retail-oriented readership."

N $ $ LUSTRE, The Jeweler's Magazine on Design & Style, Cygnus Publishing Company, 445 Broad Hollow Rd., Melville NY 11747. (516)845-2700. Fax: (516)845-7109. Managing Editor: Matthew Kramer. **Contact:** Lorraine DePasque. Bimonthly trade magazine covering fine jewelry and related accessories. "*LUSTRE* is deducted to helping the retail jeweler stock, merchandise, sell and profit from upscale, high-quality brand name and designer jewelry. Many stories are how-to. We also offer sophisticated graphics to showcase new products." Estab. 1997. Circ. 20,000. Pays on publication. Publishes ms an average of 4 months after acceptance. Byline given. Offers 50% kill fee. Buys all rights. Editorial lead time 4 months. Submit seasonal material four months in advance. Reports in 4 weeks on queries; 2 months on mss. Sample copy free.

Nonfiction: How-to, new product. **Buys 24 mss/year.** Query with published clips. Length: 1,000-2,500 words. **Pays $500-700.** Sometimes pays expenses of writers on assignment.

Photos: State availability of photos with submission. Offers no additional payment for photos accepted with ms. Captions and identification of subjects required. Buys one time rights plus usage for one year after publication date (but not exclusive usage).

Columns and Departments: Celebrity Link (tie in designer jewelry with celebrity), 500 words; Details (news about designer jewelry), 200-500 words. **Buys 8 mss/year.** Query. **Pays $200-500.**

Fillers: Facts, newsbreaks. **Buys 4 mss/year.** Length: 200-300 words. **Pays $200.**

Tips: "Step 1: Request an issue sent to them; call (212) 921-1091; ask for assistant. Step 2: Write a letter to Connie DePasque with clips. Step 3: Connie will call back."

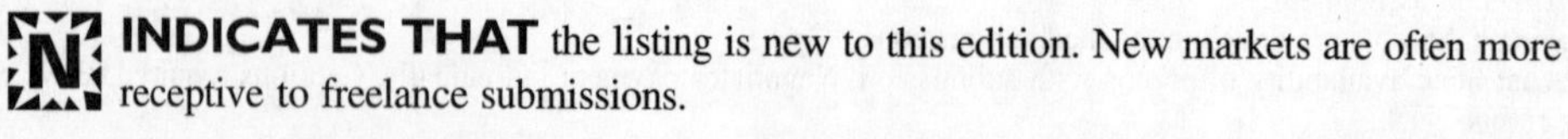

INDICATES THAT the listing is new to this edition. New markets are often more receptive to freelance submissions.

JOURNALISM AND WRITING

Journalism and writing magazines cover both the business and creative sides of writing. Writing publications offer inspiration and support for professional and beginning writers. Although there are many valuable writing publications that do not pay, we list those that pay for articles.

N $ $ **AMERICAN WRITERS REVIEW**, Blue Dolphin Institute, 526 Boston Post Rd., Wayland MA 01778. (508)358-7373. Fax: (508)358-5795. E-mail: rlieblich@luedolphin.org. Editor-At-Large: Don Nicholas. **Contact:** Rebecca Lieblich, editor. **90% freelance written.** Bimonthly newsletter covering tips from successful authors with current books. "We interview writers who have published books or writings. We then present the story in their own words." Estab. 1996. Pays on publication. Publishes ms an average of 2 months after acceptance. Byline given. Offers 25% kill fee. Buys all rights. Editorial lead time 3 months. Submit seasonal material 6 months in advance. Reports in 4 weeks on queries; 2 months on mss. Sample copy free.

Nonfiction: Interview/profile. **Buys 36 mss/year.** Query with published clips. Length: 1,500-2,000 words. **Pays $100-200.** Sometimes pays expenses of writers on assignment.

Tips: "Find an author you want to interview within these topics, fiction, nonfiction, poetry, scriptwriting, skills, inspirational and business."

$ **BOOK DEALERS WORLD**, North American Bookdealers Exchange, P.O. Box 606, Cottage Grove OR 97424. Phone/fax: (541)942-7455. Editorial Director: Al Galasso. **50% freelance written.** Quarterly magazine covering writing, self-publishing and marketing books by mail. Circ. 20,000. Pays on publication. Publishes ms an average of 3 months after acceptance. Byline given. Buys first serial and second serial (reprint) rights. Accepts simultaneous submissions. Reports in 1 month. Sample copy for $3.

Nonfiction: Book excerpts (writing, mail order, direct mail, publishing); how-to (home business by mail, advertising); interview/profile (of successful self-publishers). Positive articles on self-publishing, new writing angles, marketing, etc. **Buys 10 mss/year.** Send complete ms. Length: 1,000-1,500 words. **Pays $25-50.**

Reprints: Send typed ms with rights for sale noted and information about when and where the article previously appeared. Pays 80% of amount paid for an original article.

Columns/Departments: Print Perspective (about new magazines and newsletters); Self-Publisher Profile (on successful self-publishers and their marketing strategy). **Buys 20 mss/year.** Send complete ms. Length: 250-1,000 words. **Pays $5-20.**

Fillers: Fillers concerning writing, publishing or books. **Buys 6/year.** Length: 100-250 words. **Pays $3-10.**

Tips: "Query first. Get a sample copy of the magazine."

$ **BYLINE**, P.O. Box 130596, Edmond OK 73013-0001. (405)348-5591. Website: http://www.bylinemag.com. **Contact:** Kathryn Fanning, managing editor. Editor/Publisher: Marcia Preston. **80% freelance written.** Eager to work with new/unpublished writers. Magazine published 11 times/year for writers and poets. "We stress encouragement of beginning writers." Estab. 1981. **Pays on acceptance.** Publishes ms an average of 3 months after acceptance. Byline given. Buys first North American serial rights. Editorial lead time 3 months. Submit seasonal material 6 months in advance. Accepts simultaneous submissions. Reports in 2 months or less. Sample copy for $4 postpaid. Writer's guidelines for #10 SASE.

Nonfiction: Essays, how-to, humor, inspirational, personal experience, interview, *all* connected with writing and selling. No profiles of writers. **Buys approximately 100 mss/year.** Prefers queries; will read complete mss. Send SASE. Length: 1,500-1,800 words for features. **Pays $50.**

Columns/Departments: End Piece (humorous, philosophical or motivational personal essay related to writing), 700-750 words, **pays $35;** First Sale (account of a writer's first sale), 300 words, **pays $20;** Only When I Laugh (writing-related humor), 100-600 words, **pays $15-35. Buys 30 mss/year.** Send complete ms.

Fiction: Adventure, humorous, mainstream, mystery, romance, suspense, western. Open to genre, mainstream and literary. No science fiction, erotica or extreme violence. **Buys 11 mss/year.** Send complete ms: 2,000-4,000 words preferred. **Pays $100.**

Poetry: Free verse, haiku, light verse, traditional. "All poetry should connect in some way with the theme of writing or writers." **Buys 100 poems/year.** Submit 3 poems max. Preferred length: 4-30 lines. **Pays $5-10** plus free issue.

Tips: "Pay attention to word length in various sections, and don't forget your SASE."

$ **CANADIAN AUTHOR**, Canadian Authors Association, 776 Colborne St., London, Ontario N6A 3Z9 Canada. (519)438-2011. E-mail: dougbale@netcom.ca. Website: http://www.canauthors.org/cauthor.html. **Contact:** Doug Bale, editor. **100% freelance written.** Quarterly. "*Canadian Author* is Canada's oldest literary magazine, by and for writers of all genres, and both journalistic and literary writers." Estab. 1919. Circ. 3,000. Pays on publication. Publishes ms an average of 6 months after acceptance. Byline given. Buys first North American rights, second serial (reprint) rights or one-time rights. Editorial lead time 6 months. Submit seasonal material 6 months in advance. Accepts simultaneous submissions and previously published submissions. Reports in 3 weeks on queries, 1 month on manuscripts. Sample copy for $4.75. Writer's guidelines for #10 SAE and IRC.

Nonfiction: Essays, expose, how-to (on writing, selling; the specifics of the different genres—what they are and how to write them); humor, inspirational; informational (the writing scene—who's who and what's what); interview (with Canadian writers, mainly leading ones, but also those with a story that can help others write and sell more often); new product, opinion, personal experience, technical. "Nothing boring." **Buys 40-60 mss/year.** Query with published clips and submit complete ms. Length: 800-3,500 words. **Pays $20-60,** plus copy. Sometimes pays the expenses of writers on assignment.

Photos: State availability of photos with query. Reviews prints (5×7 minimum). Negotiates payment individually for cover photos, offers no additional payment for other photos. Captions, model releases, identification of subjects required. Buys one-time rights.

Columns/Departments: Legal Issues; Usage, The Internet, all 800 words. Send complete ms. **Pays $20-60,** plus copy.

Fiction: W.D. Valgardson, fiction editor. Adventure, condensed novels, confession, erotica, ethnic, experimental, fantasy, historical, horror, humorous, mainstream, mystery, romance, science fiction, slice-of-life vignettes, suspense, western. "Nothing boring, didactic or proselytizing." **Buys 4 mss/year.** Send complete ms. Length: 2,000-3,000 words. **Pays $125.**

Poetry: High quality. Avant garde, free verse, haiku, light verse, traditional. "Nothing boring or incompetent." **Buys 20-60 poems/year.** Submit 12 poems max. Length: 3-60 lines max. **Pays $20-60.**

Fillers: Anecdotes, facts, short humor. **Buys 5-20 mss/year.** Length: 200-800 words. **Pays $20.**

N $ $ THE EDITORIAL EYE, Focusing on Publications Standards and Practices, EEI, 66 Canal Center Plaza, Suite 200, Alexandria VA 22314-5507. (703)683-0683. Fax: (703)683-4915. E-mail: eye@eeicom.com. Website: http://www.eeicom.com/eye/. **Contact:** Linda B. Jorgensen, editor. **25% range freelance written.** Prefers to work with published, established and working professional editors and writers. Monthly professional newsletter on editorial subjects: writing, editing, graphic design, production, quality control and language usage. "Our readers are professional publications people. Use journalistic style but avoid overly general topics and facile prescriptions. Our review process is vigorous." Circ. 2,600. **Pays within 30 days of acceptance.** Publishes ms an average of 6 months after acceptance. Byline usually given. Pays 40% kill fee on solicited articles. Buys first North American serial rights. "We retain the right to use articles in our training division and in an anthology of collected articles, and we request permission to use in our website sampler for a limited time." Reports in 3 months. Sample copy for #10 SAE with 2 first-class stamps. Guidelines tailored to the article following a proposal or outline.

Nonfiction: Editorial and production problems, issues, standards, practices and techniques; publication management; publishing technology; writing, style, grammar and usage, and neologisms. Needs articles on electronic and workgroup publishing, online editing and changing usage. No word games, vocabulary building, language puzzles or poetry. **Buys 30 mss/year.** "Would buy more if quality were higher. *Must* look at sample issue." Query. Length: 500-1,500. **Pays $50-200 and 6 copies.**

Tips: "We seek mostly lead articles written by people in the publications field about the practice of editing or writing. Our style is journalistic with a light touch (not cute). We are interested in submissions on the craft of editing, levels of editing, writing and editing aided by computer, publications management, lexicography, usages, quality control, resources, and interviews with nonfiction writers and editors. Our website sampler provides a good idea of the kinds of articles we run. Do not send articles without inquiring first and looking at a sample. Do not expect an extensive critique. Do not send a vilification of editors and expect me to print it. Welcome repeat work from a roster of writers I'm developing, and always looking for new voices. We now produce four-page special reports, so longer articles that lend themselves to overview-plus-examples of about 2,500 words, are solicited. Send ideas by e-mail for quick response."

N $ EXCHANGE, A Newsletter for Writers Who Are Christian, Exchange Publishing, 15 Torrance Rd., #104, Scarborough, Ontario M1J 3K2 Canada. (416)439-4320. Fax: (416)439-5089. E-mail: exchange@ica.net. **Contact:** Audrey Dorsch, editor. **70% freelance written.** Quarterly newsletter on the craft of writing. "A vehicle for Christian writers to exchange information and ideas, and receive professional development." Estab. 1991. Circ. 300. Pays on publication. Byline given. Offers 30-50% kill fee. Not copyrighted. Buys one-time rights. Editorial lead time 2 months. Reports in 1 month.

Nonfiction: How-to, humor, opinion, personal experience. All must be related to writing. **Buys 20 mss/year.** Send complete ms. Length: 300-500 words. **Pays 8¢/word.** Sometimes pays copies or other premiums to foreign contributors who cannot exchange Canadian currency.

Reprints: Include information about when and where the article previously appeared. Pays 100% of amount paid for an original article.

Tips: "Think about what writing help you would have liked. Now that you are past that hurdle, write about it to help other writers."

N FACTSHEET FIVE, The Definitive Guide to the Zine Revolution, P.O. Box 170099, San Francisco CA 94117-0099. Fax: (415)668-1781. E-mail: seth@factsheet5.com. Website: http://www.factsheet5.com. Editor: R. Seth Friedman. **Contact:** Miriam Wolf. Magazine published 5 times/year covering 'zines. "*Factsheet Five* reviews more than 1,000 small press publications each issue. We also run features of interest to the 'zine community." Circ. 13,000. Pays on publication. Byline given. Not copyrighted. Buys first North American serial rights. Editorial lead time 2 months. Submit seasonal material 3 months in advance. Accepts simultaneous submissions. Sample copy for $6. Writer's guidelines for #10 SASE.

Nonfiction: Book excerpts, essays, exposé, general interest, historical/nostalgic, how-to, interview/profile, opinion, personal experience. **Buys 10 mss/year.** Send complete ms. Length: 500-3,000 words. **Pays $25-100.** Sometimes pays expenses of writers on assignment.

Photos: State availability of photos with submission. Negotiates payment individually. Identification of subjects required.

$ FICTION WRITER'S GUIDELINE, The Newsletter of Fiction Writer's Connection (FWC), P.O. Box 4065, Deerfield Beach FL 33442-4065. (954)426-4705. E-mail: bcamenson@aol.com. Website: http://www.fictionwriters.com. **Contact:** Blythe Camenson, editor. **50% freelance written.** Monthly newsletter covering how-to for fiction writers. "*Fiction Writer's Guideline* takes an upbeat approach to encourage writers, but doesn't shy away from the sometimes harsh realities of the publishing industry." Estab. 1993. Circ. 1,000. Pays on publication. Publishes ms an average of 6 months after acceptance. Byline given. Buys first, one-time or second serial (reprint) rights. Editorial lead time 2 months. Submit seasonal material 3 months in advance. Accepts simultaneous submissions. Reports in 2 weeks on queries; 1 month on mss. Sample copy for SASE with 55¢ postage. Writer's guidelines for #10 SASE.
Nonfiction: General interest, how-to (the business and craft of writing fiction), interview/profile (of agents, editors, and authors), new product, short book reviews (how-to books for writers). **Buys 12 mss/year.** Length: 200-1,200 words. **Pays $1-25.** Sometimes pays expenses of writers on assignment. Send complete ms.
Reprints: Send typed ms with rights for sale noted and information about when and where the article previously appeared. Pay varies.
Columns/Departments: Advice From An Agent/Editor (how to approach, what they're looking for, advice to fiction writers), 1,500 words; "Writing Tips" (specific advice on style and structure), 400 words. **Buys 12 mss/year.** Query. **Pays $1-25.**
Fillers: Anecdotes, facts, newsbreaks; all to do with the business or craft of writing fiction. **Buys 50/year.** Length: 20-100 words. **Pays $1-10.**
Tips: Looking for "interviews with agents or editors. Our guidelines include specific questions to ask. Query or call first to make sure your choice hasn't already been interviewed. We also need a monthly cover article on some aspect of writing fiction, from specific tips for different categories/genres, to handling viewpoint, characterization, dialogue, etc. Also fillers. Request sample copy to see the format."

N $ $ FREELANCE WRITER'S REPORT, CNW Publishing, Inc., Main St., P.O. Box A, North Stratford NH 03590-0167. (603)922-8338. Fax: (603)922-8339. E-mail: danakcnw@ncia.net. **Contact:** Dana K. Cassell, editor. **25% freelance written.** Monthly. "*FWR* covers the marketing and business/office management aspects of running a freelance writing business. Articles must be of value to the established freelancer; nothing basic." Estab. 1982. Pays on publication. Publishes ms an average of 6 months after acceptance. Byline given. Buys one-time rights. Editorial lead time 2 months. Submit seasonal material 2 months in advance. Accepts simultaneous submissions. Reports in 1 week on queries; 1 month on mss. Sample copy for 6×9 SAE with 2 first-class stamps (for back copy); $4 for current copy.
Nonfiction: Book excerpts, how-to (market, increase income or profits). No articles about the basics of freelancing. **Buys 50 mss/year.** Send complete ms. Length: 500 words. **Pays 10¢/word.**
Reprints: Accepts previously published submissions.
Tips: "Write in a terse, newsletter style."

N $ GOTTA WRITE NETWORK LITMAG, Maren Publications, 515 E. Thacker, Hoffman Estates IL 60194. Fax: (847)882-8054. E-mail: netera@aol.com. **Contact:** Denise Fleischer, editor. **80% freelance written.** Semiannual literary magazine covering writer's techniques, markets. "Any article should be presented as if openly speaking to the reader. It should inform from the first paragraph to the last." Estab. 1988. Circ. 200. Pays after publication. Publishes ms an average of 6 months after acceptance. Byline given. Buys first North American serial rights or makes work-for-hire assignments. Editorial lead time 6 months. Reports in 3 months. Sample copy for $5. Writer's guidelines for #10 SASE.
Nonfiction: Articles (on writing), how-to (on writing techniques), interview/profile (for Behind the Scenes section), new product (books, software, computers), photo feature (on poets/writers/editors big and small press). "Don't want to see 'My First Sale,' 'When I Can't Write,' 'Dealing With Rejection,' 'Writer's Block,' a speech from a writers convention, an article published 10 times by other editors." **Buys 25 mss/year.** Query with published clips or send complete ms. Accepts e-mail queries and submissions. Length: 3-5 pages. **Pays $5** and contributor's copy.
Photos: State availability of photos with submission. Offers $10 (more for cover art). Captions, model releases and identification of subjects required. Buys one-time rights.
Columns/Departments: In Print (writing books—reviews), 2 pages. **Buys 50 mss/year. Pays $5.**
Fiction: Adventure, ethnic, experimental, fantasy, historical, horror, humorous, mainstream, mystery, romance, science fiction, slice-of-life vignettes, suspense, western. No dark fantasy. **Buys 15 and up mss/year.** Query with published clips. Send complete ms. Page length: 5-10. **Pays $10 maximum.**
Poetry: Avant-garde, free verse, haiku, beat—experimental. No poetry no one can understand or that has no meaning.
Fillers: Anecdotes, facts, newsbreaks, tips. Buys 100/year. Length: 100-250 words. Pays in contributor's copies. Open to editor's releases, feature ideas and product information from the manufacturer.

N $ INKLINGS, Inkspot's Newsletter for Writers, Inkspot, 55 McCaul St., Box 123, Toronto, Ontario M5J 2S9 Canada. E-mail: editor@inkspot.com. Website: http://www.inkspot.com. **Contact:** submissions@inkspot.com. Editor: Debbie Ridpath Ohi. **75% freelance written.** Biweekly electronic newsletter for writers of all levels of experience. Estab. 1995. Circ. 12,000. Pays on publication. Publishes ms an average of 3 months after acceptance. Byline given. Inkspot retains the non-exclusive right to archive the article online. Accepts simultaneous submissions. Submissions by

modem preferred. Reports in 2 weeks on queries; 1 month on mss. For free subscription, send e-mail to subscribe@inkspo t.com or see website for back issues. For writer's guidelines send any e-mail to guidelines@inkspot.com.
Nonfiction: How-to (focus on writing, selling and promoting), interview/profile. No inspirational first-person essays, fiction, poetry. **Buys 50-60 mss/year.** Query. Length: 500-2,000 words. **Pays 3¢/word, $50 maximum.**
Reprints: Accepts previously published submissions if informed.
Tips: "Focus should be heavily 'how to' with examples. Query with article idea/slant, publishing credits (if any), sample of writing style. E-mail submissions strongly preferred."

$ NEW WRITER'S MAGAZINE, Sarasota Bay Publishing, P.O. Box 5976, Sarasota FL 34277-5976. (941)953-7903. E-mail: newriters@aol.com. Website: http://www.newriters.com. **Contact:** George J. Haborak, Editor. **95% freelance written.** Bimonthly magazine. "*New Writer's Magazine* believes that *all* writers are *new* writers in that each of us can learn from one another. So, we reach pro and non-pro alike." Estab. 1986. Circ. 5,000. Pays on publication. Byline given. Buys first rights. Reports in 3 weeks on queries; 1 month on mss. *Writer's Market* recommends allowing 2 months for reply. Sample copy for $3. Writer's guidelines for #10 SASE.
Nonfiction: General interest, how-to (for new writers), humor, interview/profile, opinion, personal experience (with pro writer). **Buys 50 mss/year.** Send complete ms. Length: 700-1,000 words. **Pays $10-50.**
Photos: Send photos with submission. Reviews 5×7 prints. Offers no additional payment for photos accepted with ms. Captions required.
Fiction: Experimental, historical, humorous, mainstream, slice-of-life vignettes. "Again, we do *not* want anything that does not have a tie-in with the writing life or writers in general." **Buys 2-6 mss/year.** "We offer a special fiction contest held each year with cash prizes." Send complete ms. Length: 700-800 words. **Pays $20-40.**
Poetry: Free verse, light verse, traditional. Does not want anything *not* for writers. **Buys 10-20 poems/year.** Submit maximum 3 poems. Length: 8-20 lines. **Pays $5 maximum.**
Fillers: Anecdotes, facts, newsbreaks, short humor. **Buys 5-15 mss/year.** Length: 20-100 words. **Pays $5 maximum.** Cartoons, writing lifestyle slant. Buys 20-30/year. Pays $10 maximum.
Tips: "Any article *with photos* has a good chance, especially an *up close and personal* interview with an established professional writer offering advice, etc."

$ OHIO WRITER, Poets League of Greater Cleveland, P.O. Box 91801, Cleveland OH 44101. **Contact:** Ron Antonucci, editor. **75% freelance written.** Bimonthly magazine covering writing and Ohio writers. Estab. 1987. Pays on publication. Publishes ms an average of 4 months after acceptance. Byline given. Buys one-time rights and second serial (reprint) rights. Editorial lead time 4 months. Submit seasonal material 4 months in advance. Reports in 6 weeks. Sample copy for $2.50. Writer's guidelines for SASE.
Nonfiction: Essays, how-to, humor, inspirational, interview/profile, opinion, personal experience—"all must relate to the writing life or Ohio writers, or Ohio publishing scene." **Buys 24 mss/year.** Send complete ms and SASE. Length: 2,000-2,500 words. **Pays $25 minimum, up to $50 for lead article;** other payment under arrangement with writer.
Reprints: Send typed ms with rights for sale noted and information about when and where the article previously appeared. Pays 50% of amount paid for an original article.
Columns/Departments: Subjectively Yours (opinions, controversial stance on writing life), 1,500 words; Reviews (Ohio writers, publishers or publishing), 400-600 words; Focus On (Ohio publishing scene, how to write/publish certain kind of writing, e.g., travel), 1,500 words. **Buys 6 mss/year.** Send complete ms. **Pays $25-50; $5/book review.**
Tips: "Profiles and interviews of writers who live in Ohio are always needed. *Ohio Writer* is read by both beginning and experienced writers and hopes to create a sense of community among writers of different genres, abilities and backgrounds. We want to hear a personal voice, one that engages the reader. We're looking for intelligent, literate prose that isn't stuffy."

$ $ POETS & WRITERS, 72 Spring St., 3rd Floor, New York NY 10012. Fax: (212)226-3963. E-mail: editor@pw.org. Website: http://www.pw.org. **Contact:** Therese Eiben, editor. **100% freelance written.** Bimonthly professional trade journal for poets and fiction writers. No poetry or fiction. Estab. 1973. Circ. 58,000. **Pays on acceptance** of finished draft. Publishes ms an average of 4 months after acceptance. Byline given. Offers 20% kill fee. Buys first North American serial and first rights or makes work-for-hire assignments. Submit seasonal material at least 4 months in advance. Reports in 6 weeks on mss. Sample copy for $3.95 to Circulation Dept. Writer's guidelines for #10 SASE.
Nonfiction: Personal essays about literature, how-to (craft of poetry or fiction writing), profiles with poets or fiction writers (no Q&A), regional reports of literary activity, reports on small presses, service pieces about publishing trends. **Buys 35 mss/year.** Query with published clips or send complete ms. "We do *not* accept submissions by fax or e-mail." Length: 500-3,600 words (depending on topic).
Photos: State availability of photos with submission. Reviews b&w prints. Offers no additional payment for photos accepted with ms.
Columns/Departments: Literary and publishing news, 500-600 words; profiles of emerging and established poets and fiction writers, 2,400-3,600 words; regional reports (literary activity in US), 1,800-3,600 words. Query with published clips, or send complete ms. **Pays $100-300.**

N $ $ PUBLISHING ENTREPRENEUR, Profit Strategies for the Information Industry, The Jenkins Group, 121 E. Front St., Traverse City MI 49684. (616)933-0445. Fax: (616)933-0448. E-mail: editorial@smallpress.com. **Contact:** March Link, executive editor. Managing Editor: Phil Murphy. **60% freelance written.** Bimonthly maga-

zine covering publishing and self-publishing. Estab. 1995. Circ. 6,000. Pays on publication. Byline given. Offers 10% kill fee. Buys first North American serial or all rights. Editorial lead time 4 months. Submit seasonal material 4 months in advance. Accepts simultaneous submissions. Reports in 3 weeks on queries; 1 month on mss. Sample copy and writer's guidelines free.
Nonfiction: Book excerpts, essays, exposé, historical/nostalgic, how-to, interview/profile, opinion, personal experience, technical. All publishing related. **Buys 10 mss/year.** Query with published clips. Length: 1,000-4,000 words. **Pays $60-400 for assigned articles; $50-250 for unsolicited articles.** Pays writers with contributor copies or other premiums for ad trade. Sometimes pays expenses of writers on assignment.
Photos: State availability of photos with submission. Offers no additional payment for photos accepted with ms. Identification of subjects required. Buys one-time rights.
Columns/Departments: The Legal Corner (laws for publishers); Trend Watch (trends in publishing), all 1,200 words. **Buys 6 mss/year.** Query with published clips. **Pays $100-200.**

$ SCAVENGER'S NEWSLETTER, 519 Ellinwood, Osage City KS 66523-1329. (913)528-3538. E-mail: foxscav1@jc.net. Website: http://www.cza.com/scav/index.html. **Contact:** Janet Fox, editor. **15% freelance written.** Eager to work with new/unpublished writers. Monthly newsletter covering markets for science fiction/fantasy/horror/mystery materials especially with regard to the small press. Estab. 1984. Circ. 850. **Pays on acceptance.** Publishes ms an average of 8 months after acceptance. Byline given. Not copyrighted. Buys one-time rights. Accepts simultaneous submissions. Reports in 1 month if SASE included. Sample copy for $2.50. Writer's guidelines for #10 SASE. Now accepting e-mail submissions for everything except art.
Nonfiction: Essays, general interest, how-to (write, sell, publish science fiction/fantasy/horror/mystery), humor, interview/profile (writers, artists in the field), opinion. **Buys 12-15 mss/year.** Send complete ms. Length: 1,000 words maximum. **Pays $4.**
Reprints: Send information about when and where the article previously appeared. Pays 100% of amount paid for an original article.
Fiction: "Seeking a few (4-6) outstanding pieces of flash fiction to 1,200 words in the genre of SF/fantasy/horror/mystery. Looking for work that uses poetry techniques to make a short piece seem like a complete story." **Pays $4.**
Poetry: Avant-garde, free verse, haiku, traditional. All related to science fiction/fantasy/horror/mystery genres. **Buys 24 poems/year.** Submit maximum 3 poems. Length: 10 lines maximum. **Pays $2.**
Tips: "Because this is a small publication, it has occasional overstocks. We're especially looking for science fiction/flash fiction/fantasy/horror/mystery."

SMALL PRESS REVIEW, P.O. Box 100, Paradise CA 95967. **Contact:** Len Fulton, editor. Monthly for "people interested in small presses and magazines, current trends and data; many libraries." Circ. 3,500. Byline given. Reports in 2 months. Free sample copy.
Nonfiction: News, short reviews. Uses spot news, historical, think pieces. **Accepts 50-200 mss/year.** Length: 100-200 words. "Query if you're unsure."

THE WRITER, 120 Boylston St., Boston MA 02116-4615. Website: http://www.channel1.com/thewriter/. Editor-in-Chief/Publisher: Sylvia K. Burack. **20% freelance written.** Prefers to buy work of published/established writers. Monthly. Estab. 1887. **Pays on acceptance.** Publishes ms an average of 8 months after acceptance. Buys first serial rights. Sample copy for $3.50.
Nonfiction: Practical articles for writers on how to write for publication, and how and where to market manuscripts in various fields. Considers all submissions promptly. No assignments. Length: 2,000 words maximum.
Reprints: Occasionally buys previously published submissions from the *New York Times* and *Washington Post* book review sections. Send tearsheet or photocopy of article and information about when and where the article previously appeared.
Tips: "New types of publications and our continually updated market listings in all fields will determine changes of focus and fact."

N $ $ WRITER & EDITOR, The Newsletter for Professional Feature Writers and Editors, Blue Dolphin Institute, 526 Boston Post Rd., Wayland MA 01778. (508)358-7373. Fax: (508)358-5795. E-mail: rlieblich@bluedolphin.org. **Contact:** Rebecca Lieblich, managing editor. **90% freelance written.** Bimonthly trade newsletter covering feature writing and editing. "We offer how-to advice to professional and aspiring writers and editors. It's like earning a masters degree in journalism." Estab. 1996. Pays on publication. Publishes ms an average of 2 months after acceptance. Byline given. Offers 25% kill fee. Buys first North American serial, one-time, or all rights. Editorial lead time 3 months. Submit seasonal material 6 months in advance. Reports in 2 weeks on queries; 1 month on mss. Sample copy free; writer's guidelines for #10 SASE.
Nonfiction: Essays, how-to, inspirational, interview/profile, personal experience. No poetry, fiction or reviews. **Buys 36 mss/year.** Query with published clips. Length: 1,400-2,500 words. **Pays $100-200.** Sometimes pays expenses of writers on assignment.
Reprints: Occasionally accepts previously published submissions.
Columns and Departments: The Writer's Craft (language & style); Hitting Your Market (Freelancer's, Inc.), 1,400-2,000 words; Reporting & Research.

$ $ WRITER'S DIGEST, 1507 Dana Ave., Cincinnati OH 45207. (513)531-2222. Fax: (513)531-1843. E-mail: writersdig@fwpubs.com. Website: http://www.writersdigest.com. **Contact:** Dawn Simonds Ramirez, submissions editor. **90% freelance written.** Monthly magazine about writing and publishing. "Our readers write fiction, poetry, nonfiction, plays and all kinds of creative writing. They're interested in improving their writing skills, improving their ability to sell their work and finding new outlets for their talents." Estab. 1920. Circ. 225,000. **Pays on acceptance.** Publishes ms an average of 1 year after acceptance. Buys first North American serial rights for one-time editorial use, possible electronic posting, microfilm/microfiche use and magazine promotional use. Pays 20% kill fee. Byline given. Submit seasonal material 8 months in advance. Reports in 2 months. Sample copy for $4. Writer's guidelines for #10 SASE.

- Ranked as one of the best markets for freelance writers in *Writer's Yearbook* magazine's annual "Top 100 Markets," January 1998.

Nonfiction: "Our mainstay is the how-to article—that is, an article exploring some technique of how to write or sell more of what you write. For instance, how to write compelling leads and conclusions, how to improve your character descriptions, how to become more efficient and productive. We like plenty of examples, anecdotes and $$$ in our articles—so other writers can actually see what's been done successfully by the author of a particular piece. We like our articles to speak directly to the reader through the use of the first-person voice. Don't submit an article on what five book editors say about writing mysteries. Instead, submit an article on how you cracked the mystery market and how our readers can do the same. But don't limit the article to your experiences; include the opinions of those five editors to give your article increased depth and authority." General interest (about writing); how-to (writing and marketing techniques that work); inspirational; interview and profile (query first); new product; personal experience (marketing and freelancing experiences). "We can always use articles on fiction and nonfiction technique, and solid articles on poetry or scriptwriting are always welcome. No articles titled 'So You Want to Be a Writer,' and no first-person pieces that ramble without giving a lesson or something readers can learn from in the sharing of the story." **Buys 90-100 mss/year.** Queries are preferred. Length: 500-3,000 words. **Pays 15-40¢/word.** Sometimes pays expenses of writers on assignment.

Reprints: Accepts previously published submissions from noncompeting markets. Send tearsheet or photocopy of article, noting rights for sale and when and where the article previously appeared.

Photos: Used only with interviews and profiles. State availability of photos or send contact sheet with ms. Captions required.

Columns/Departments: Chronicle (first-person narratives about the writing life; length: 1,200-1,500 words); The Writing Life (length: 50-500 words); and Tip Sheet (short items that offer solutions to writing and freelance business-related problems that writers commonly face). "Chronicle is an area of continuing need, and we welcome all styles of personal essays here. Humor is much in demand, but we also look for the heartfelt and the life-affirming. Chronicles are articles we expect will linger in the memory of readers." Humor is welcome for Writing Life. **Buys approximately 150 articles/year** for Writing Life and Tip Sheet sections. Send complete ms.

Poetry: Light verse about "the writing life"—joys and frustrations of writing. "We are also considering poetry other than short light verse—but still related to writing, publishing, other poets and authors, etc." **Buys an average of 1 an issue.** Submit poems in batches of 1-5. Length: 2-20 lines. **Pays $10-50/poem.**

Fillers: Anecdotes and short humor, primarily for use in The Writing Life column. **Uses up to 4/issue.** Length: 50-250 words.

$ WRITER'S FORUM, Writer's Digest School, 1507 Dana Ave., Cincinnati OH 45207. (513)531-2222. Website: http://www.writersmarket.com. Editor: Amanda Boyd. **100% freelance written.** Quarterly newsletter covering writing techniques, marketing and inspiration for students enrolled in fiction and nonfiction writing courses offered by Writer's Digest School. Estab. 1970. Circ. 13,000. **Pays on acceptance.** Publishes ms an average of 6 months after acceptance. Byline given. Buys first serial or second serial (reprint) rights. Submit seasonal/holiday material 4 months in advance. Accepts simultaneous submissions. Reports in 6 weeks. Free sample copy.

Nonfiction: How-to (write or market short stories, or articles, novels and nonfiction books); articles that will motivate beginning writers. **Buys 12 mss/year.** Prefers complete mss to queries. "If you prefer to query, please do so by mail, not phone." Length: 500-1,000 words. **Pays $10-25.**

Reprints: Accepts previously published submissions.

$ WRITER'S YEARBOOK, 1507 Dana Ave., Cincinnati OH 45207. (513)531-2222. Fax: (513)531-1843. E-mail: writersdig@fwpubs.com. Website: http://www.writersdigest.com. **Contact:** Dawn Simonds Ramirez, submissions editor. **90% freelance written.** Newsstand annual for freelance writers, journalists and teachers of creative writing. "Please note that the *Yearbook* is a 'best of' format. That is, we are reprinting the best writing about writing published in the last year: articles, fiction and book excerpts. The *Yearbook* uses little original material, so do not submit queries or original manuscripts. We will, however, consider already-published material from high-quality sources for possible inclusion." Estab. 1929. **Pays on acceptance.** Publishes ms an average of 6 months after acceptance. Offers 20% kill fee. Byline given. Buys reprint rights. "If you don't want your manuscript returned, indicate that on the first page of the manuscript or in a cover letter."

Reprints: "In reprints, we want articles that reflect the current state of writing in America: trends, inside information, and money-saving and money-making ideas for the freelance writer. We try to touch on the various facets of writing in each issue of the *Yearbook*—from fiction to poetry to playwriting, and any other endeavor a writer can pursue. How-to articles—that is, articles that explain in detail how to do something—are very important to us. For example, you could explain how to establish mood in fiction, how to improve interviewing techniques, how to write for and sell to specialty magazines, or how to construct and market a good poem. We are also interested in the writer's spare time—what she/he does to retreat occasionally from the writing wars, where and how to refuel and replenish the writing spirit. Articles that delve into the philosophy of writing or that examine in-depth some issue of concern to writers are of interest, but the authors should have a base of experience from which to make his or her observations. We also want interviews or profiles of well-known bestselling authors, always with good pictures. Articles on writing techniques that are effective today are always welcome. We provide how-to features and information to help our readers become more skilled at writing and successful at selling their writing." **Buys 15-20 mss/year.** Send tearsheet or photocopy of article, noting rights for sale and when and where the article previously appeared. Note: It is very rare that we purchase articles that originally appeared in our direct competitors or local-level writing publications. Length: 750-4,500 words. **Pays 10¢/word minimum.**

Photos: Interviews and profiles must be accompanied by high-quality photos. Reviews b&w photos only, depending on use. Captions required.

Fillers: Interested in funny, weird, wacky or otherwise offbeat incidents for our annual "Year in Revue" roundup. Send us the clip reporting the incident, indicate date and source. Pays $20 finder's fee.

N $ WRITING FOR MONEY, Where to Sell What You Write, Blue Dolphin Institute, 526 Boston Post Rd., Wayland MA 01778. (508)358-7373. Fax: (508)358-5795. E-mail: rlieblich@bluedolphin.org. **Contact:** Rebecca Lieblich, managing editor. **50% freelance written.** Trade newsletter published every three weeks covering freelance writing. "It's all about how to make money as a writer." Estab. 1994. Circ. 3,600. Pays on publication plus 30 days. Publishes ms an average of 2 months after acceptance. Byline given. Offers 25% kill fee. Buys all rights. Editorial lead time 2 months. Submit seasonal material 6 months in advance. Reports in 3 weeks on queries; 2 months on mss. Sample copy free.

Nonfiction: Essays, how-to. **Buys 34 mss/year.** Query with published clips. Length: 900-1,200 words. **Pays $100.** Sometimes pays expenses of writers on assignment.

Reprints: Occasionally accepts previously published submissions.

$ $ $ WRITTEN BY, The Journal of the Writers Guild of America, west, 7000 W. Third St., Los Angeles CA 90048. (213)782-4522. Fax: (213)782-4802. E-mail: writtenby@wga.org. **Contact:** Lisa Chambers, editor. **25% freelance written.** "*Written By* is the premier monthly magazine written by and for America's screen and TV writers. We focus on the craft of screenwriting and cover all aspects of the entertainment industry from the perspective of the writer. We are read by all screenwriters and most entertainment executives." Estab. 1987. Circ. 12,500. **Pays on acceptance.** Publishes ms an average of 2 months after acceptance. Byline given. Offers 25% kill fee. Buys first rights and electronic rights. Editorial lead time 2 months. Submit seasonal material 4 months in advance. Accepts simultaneous submissions. Reports in 2 months. Sample copy for $5. Writer's guidelines free.

Nonfiction: Essays, historical/nostalgic, humor, technical. No "how to break into Hollywood," "how to write scripts"-type beginner pieces. **Buys 5-8 mss/year.** Query with published clips. Length: 500-2,500 words. **Pays $500-1,500 for assigned articles; $100-800 for unsolicited articles.** Sometimes pays expenses of writers on assignment.

Reprints: Accepts previously published submissions.

Photos: State availability of photos with assignment. Reviews contact sheets. Negotiates payment individually. Captions, model releases, identification of subjects required. Buys one-time rights.

Tips: "The writer must *always* keep in mind that our audience is made up primarily of working writers who are inside the business, therefore all articles need to have an 'insider' feel and not be written for those who are still trying to break in to Hollywood. We prefer submissions on diskette."

LAW

While all of these publications deal with topics of interest to attorneys, each has a particular slant. Be sure that your subject is geared to a specific market—lawyers in a single region, law students, paralegals, etc. Publications for law enforcement personnel are listed under Government and Public Service.

N $ $ $ $ ABA JOURNAL, The Lawyer's Magazine, American Bar Association, 750 N. Lake Shore Dr., Chicago IL 60611. (312)988-6018. Fax: (312)988-6014. E-mail: abajournal@abanet.org. Website: http://www.abanet.org/journal/home.html. **Contact:** Kerry Klumpe, managing editor. **10% freelance written.** Monthly trade magazine covering law. Estab. 1914. Circ. 390,000. **Pays on acceptance.** Publishes ms an average of 1 month after acceptance. Byline given. Offers 20% kill fee. Buys all rights and makes work-for-hire assignments. Editorial lead time 2 months. Submit seasonal material 4 months in advance. Accepts simultaneous submissions. Reports in 1 week on queries; 1 month on mss. Sample copy for $7. Writer's guidelines free.

Nonfiction: How-to on law topics. "No local interest topics without national significance." **Buys 40 mss/year.** Send complete ms. Length: 250-3,000 words. **Pays $300-2,000.** Sometimes pays expenses of writers on assignment.

Photos: State availability of photos with submission. Reviews contact sheets. Negotiates payment individually. Identification of subjects required. Buys all rights.

Tips: "We require sophisticated treatment of current legal, political and social issues."

$ THE ALTMAN WEIL REPORT TO LEGAL MANAGEMENT, Altman Weil Publications, Inc., 8555 W. Forest Home Ave., Milwaukee WI 53228. (414)427-5400. Fax: (414)427-5300. E-mail: jameswilber@counsel.com. Website: http://www.altmanweil.com. **Contact:** James Wilber, editor. **15% freelance written.** Works with a small number of new/unpublished writers each year. Monthly newsletter covering law office management, purchases (equipment, insurance services, space, etc.) and technology. Estab. 1974. Circ. 2,200. Pays on publication. Publishes ms an average of 6 months after acceptance. Byline given. Buys all rights; sometimes second serial (reprint) rights. Reports in 1 month on queries; 3 months on mss. Sample copy for #10 SASE.

Nonfiction: How-to (buy, use, repair), interview/profile, new product. "Looking especially for practical, "how-to" articles on law office management and technology." **Buys 12 mss/year.** Query. Submit a sample of previous writing. Length: 500-2,500 words. **Pays $125/published page.**

Reprints: Send photocopy of article or typed ms with rights for sale noted plus diskette, and information about when and where the article previously appeared. Pays 50% of amount paid for an original article.

$ $ $ BENCH & BAR OF MINNESOTA, Minnesota State Bar Association, 514 Nicollet Ave., Suite 300, Minneapolis MN 55402-1021. (612)333-1183. Fax: (612)333-4927. **Contact:** Judson Haverkamp, editor. **10% freelance written.** Magazine published 11 times/year. "Audience is mostly Minnesota lawyers. *Bench & Bar* seeks reportage, analysis, and commentary on trends and issues in the law and the legal profession, especially in Minnesota. Preference to items of practical/human interest to professionals in law." Estab. 1931. Circ. 16,000. **Pays on acceptance.** Publishes ms an average of 3 months after acceptance. Byline given. Buys first North American serial rights and makes work-for-hire assignments. Reports in 1 month. Sample copy for 9×12 SAE with 4 first-class stamps. Writer's guidelines free.

Nonfiction: General interest, historical/nostalgic, how-to (how to handle particular types of legal, ethical problems in office management, representation, etc.), humor, interview/profile, technical/legal. "We do not want one-sided opinion pieces or advertorial." **Buys 4-5 mss/year.** Query with published clips or send complete ms. Length: 1,500-3,000 words. **Pays $300-800.** Sometimes pays expenses of writers on assignment.

Photos: State availability of photos with submission. Reviews 5×7 or larger prints. Offers $25-100/photo upon publication. Model releases and identification of subjects required. Buys one-time rights.

Tips: "Articles should open with an interesting, 'catchy' lead, followed by a 'thesis paragraph' that tersely states the gist of the article. The exposition of the topic should then follow with a summary as the conclusion. Don't overwrite. If it only takes 8 pages to cover your subject, don't write a 12-page article."

$ $ $ $ CALIFORNIA LAWYER, Suite 1210 Fox Plaza, 1390 Market St., San Francisco CA 94102. (415)252-0500. Fax: (415)252-0288. E-mail: tema_goodwin@dailyjournal.com. Editor: Peter Allen. **Contact:** Tema Goodwin, managing editor. **80% freelance written.** Monthly magazine of law-related articles and general-interest subjects of appeal to lawyers and judges. Estab. 1928. Circ. 135,000. **Pays on acceptance.** Publishes ms an average of 3 months after acceptance. Byline given. Buys first rights; publishes only original material. Accepts simultaneous submissions. Reports in 2 weeks on queries; 3 weeks on mss. *Writer's Market* recommends allowing 2 months for reply. Sample copy and writer's guidelines with SASE.

Nonfiction: Book excerpts, general interest, news and feature articles on law-related topics. "We are interested in concise, well-written and well-researched articles on issues of current concern, as well as well-told feature narratives with a legal focus. We would like to see a description or outline of your proposed idea, including a list of possible sources." **Buys 36 mss/year.** Query with published clips if available. Length: 400-3,500 words. **Pays $200-1,800.**

Photos: Louise Kollenbaum, art director. State availability of photos with query letter or ms. Reviews prints. Identification of subjects and releases required.

Columns/Departments: Legal Technology, Short News, Sole Practitioner, Strategies, Expert Advice, Books. Query with published clips if available. Length: 750-1,500 words. **Pays $200-600.**

$ $ $ $ CORPORATE LEGAL TIMES, 3 E. Huron St., Chicago IL 60611. (312)654-3500. E-mail: jking@gsteps.com. **Contact:** Jennifer E. King, editor. **50% freelance written.** Monthly tabloid. "*Corporate Legal Times* is a monthly national magazine that gives general counsel and inhouse attorneys information on legal and business issues to help them better manage corporate law departments. It routinely addresses changes and trends in law departments, litigation management, legal technology, corporate governance and in-house careers. Law areas covered monthly include: environmental, intellectual property, international, and labor and employment. All stories need to be geared toward the inhouse attorney's perspective." Estab. 1991. Circ. 40,000. Pays on publication. Publishes ms an average of 3 months after acceptance. Byline given. Buys all rights. Editorial lead time 3 months. Submit seasonal material 6 months in advance. Reports in 3 weeks on queries. Sample copy for $17. Writer's guidelines for #10 SASE.

Nonfiction: Interview/profile, technical, news about legal aspects of business issues and events. **Buys 12-25 mss/year.** Query with published clips. Length: 500-3,000 words. **Pays $500-2,000.** Freelancers should state availability of photos with submission.

Photos: Reviews color transparencies, b&w prints. Offers $25-150/photo. Identification of subjects required. Buys all rights.

Tips: "Our publication targets general counsel and inhouse lawyers. All stories need to speak to them—not to the general attorney population. Query with clips and a list of potential inhouse sources. Non-paid, contributed articles from law firm attorneys are accepted only if there is an inhouse attorney co-author."

N $ $ $ LAW OFFICE COMPUTING, James Publishing, 3505 Cadillac Ave., Suite H, Costa Mesa CA 92626. (714)755-5468. Fax: (714)751-5508. E-mail: editorloc@jamespublishing.com. **Contact:** Paul S. Amos, managing editor. Editor: Daryl Techima. **90% freelance written.** Bimonthly magazine covering legal technology industry. "*Law Office Computing* is a magazine written for attorneys and other legal professionals. It covers the legal technology field and features software reviews, profiles of prominent figures in the industry and 'how to' type articles." Estab. 1991. Circ. 8,000. Pays on publication. Publishes ms an average of 2 months after acceptance. Byline given. Kill fee varies. Buys first North American serial rights. Editorial lead time 2 months. Submit seasonal material 2 months in advance. Sample copy and writer's guidelines free.

Nonfiction: How-to, humor, interview/profile, new product, technical. **Buys 30 mss/year.** Query. Length: 2,000-4,000 words. **Pays $500-1,000.** Sometimes pays expenses of writers on assignment.

Photos: State availability of photos with submission.

Columns/Departments: Tech profile (profile firm using technology), 1,200 words; Software reviews: Short reviews (a single product), 400-500 words; Software Shootouts (two or three products going head-to-head), 1,000-1,500 words; Round-Ups/Buyer's Guides (8 to 15 products), 300-500 words per product. Each type of software review article has its own specific guidelines. Request the appropriate guidelines from your editor. **Buys 6 mss/year.** Query. **Pays $300-500.**

Tips: We seek authors who have an understanding of the legal technology field, who often (although not always) are attorneys working with technology and who have the expertise necessary to write authoritatively on this niche subject.

$ $ LAW PRACTICE MANAGEMENT—The Magazine of the Law Practice Management Section of the American Bar Association, P.O. Box 11418, Columbia SC 29211-1418. Managing Editor/Art Director: Delmar L. Roberts. **Contact:** Mark A. Robertson, articles editor, Robertson & Williams, 3033 N.W. 63rd St., Suite 160, Oklahoma City OK 73116-3607. **10% freelance written.** Magazine published 8 times/year for the practicing lawyer and law practice administrator. Estab. 1975. Circ. 20,288 (BPA). Rights purchased vary with author and material. Usually buys all rights. Byline given. Pays on publication. Publishes ms an average of 8 months after acceptance. Query. Sample copy for $8 plus $2 postage/handling (make check payable to American Bar Association). Free writer's guidelines. Returns rejected material in 3 months, if requested.

Nonfiction: "We assist the practicing lawyer in operating and managing his or her office by providing relevant articles and departments written in a readable and informative style. Editorial content is intended to aid the lawyer by conveying management methods that will allow him or her to provide legal services to clients in a prompt and efficient manner at reasonable cost. Typical topics of articles include fees and billing; client/lawyer relations; computer hardware/software; mergers; retirement/disability; marketing; compensation of partners and associates; legal data base research; and use of paralegals." No elementary articles on a whole field of technology, such as, "why you need computers in the law office." **Typical articles pay $300-500.**

Photos: Pays $50-60 for b&w photos purchased with mss; $50-100 for color; $350-450 for cover transparencies.

Tips: "We have a theme for each issue with two to three articles relating to the theme. We also publish thematic issues occasionally in which an entire issue is devoted to a single topic. The March and November/December issues each year are devoted to law practice technology."

N $ $ THE LEGAL INTELLIGENCER, Legal Communications Ltd., 1617 JFK Blvd., Suite 960, Philadelphia PA 19103. (215)557-2300. **Contact:** Zan Hale, editor. **5% freelance written.** Law newspaper published daily with a weekly suburban edition. "*The Legal Intelligencer* covers the Philadelphia courts and legal community. We are a daily newspaper, not a legal journal, and articles should be written accordingly." Estab. 1843. Circ. 10,000. Pays on publication. Byline given. Buys all rights. Editorial lead time 2 months. Reports in 2 weeks. Sample copy for $5. Writer's guidelines for #10 SASE.

Nonfiction: Interview/profile, technical (law). Business of law, business law, real estate, litigation, special sections (see editorial calendar). Query. Length: 800-2,000 words. **Pays $60-250.** Vendors and attorneys write for the marketing value.

Photos: State availability of photos with submission. Offers no additional payment for photos accepted with ms.

$ $ THE PENNSYLVANIA LAWYER, Pennsylvania Bar Association, P.O. Box 186, 100 South St., Harrisburg PA 17108-0186. **Contact:** Donald C. Sarvey, editorial director. Executive Editor: Marcy Carey Mallory. Managing Editor: Sherri Kimmel. **25% freelance written.** Prefers to work with published/established writers. Bimonthly magazine published as a service to the legal profession and the members of the Pennsylvania Bar Association. Estab. 1979. Circ. 30,000. **Pays on acceptance.** Publishes ms an average of 6 months after acceptance. Byline given. Buys generally first rights or one-time rights. Submit seasonal material 6 months in advance. Reports in 2 months. Sample copy for $2. Writer's guidelines for #10 SASE.

Nonfiction: General interest, how-to, interview/profile, new product, law-practice management, personal experience. All features *must* relate in some way to Pennsylvania lawyers or the practice of law in Pennsylvania. **Buys 8-10 mss/year.** Query. Length: 600-1,500 words. **Pays $75-400 for assigned articles, $150 for unsolicited articles.** Sometimes pays expenses of writers on assignment.

Photos: State availability of photos with submission. Reviews contact sheets. Negotiates payment individually. Identification of subjects required. Buys one-time rights.

$ $ $ STUDENT LAWYER, The Magazine of the Law Student Division, American Bar Association, 750 N. Lake Shore Dr., Chicago IL 60611. (312)988-6048. Fax: (312)988-6081. E-mail: abastulawyer@abanet.org. Website:

http://www.abanet.org/lsd. **Contact:** Stephanie Johnston, editor. **85% freelance written.** Works with a small number of new writers each year. Monthly magazine (September-May). "*Student Lawyer* is not a legal journal. It is a legal-affairs features magazine that competes for a share of law students' limited spare time, so the articles we publish must be informative, lively, well-researched good reads." Estab. 1972. Circ. 35,000. **Pays on acceptance.** Buys first rights. Byline given. Editorial lead time 5 months. Submit seasonal material 6 months in advance. Publishes ms an average of 3 months after acceptance. Sample copy for $8. Free writer's guidelines.

Nonfiction: Features cover legal education and careers and social/legal subjects. Also profiles (prominent persons in law-related fields); opinion (on matters of current legal interest); essays (on legal affairs); interviews. Query with published clips. **Buys 25 mss/year.** Length: 2,500-4,000 words. **Pays $450-800 for features.** Covers some writer's expenses. *No* fiction, please!

Columns/Departments: Esq. (profiles out-of-the-ordinary lawyers), 800 words; Coping (dealing with law school), 1,500 words; Online (Internet and the law), 1,500 words; Legal-ease (language and legal writing), 1,500 words; From the Associate's Desk (first hand look at large firm life), 1,500 words; Jobs (marketing to legal employers), 1,500 words; Opinion (opinion on legal issue), 800 words. **Buys 45 mss/year.** Query with published clips. **Pays $200-350.**

Tips: "*Student Lawyer* actively seeks good new reporters and writers eager to prove themselves. Legal training definitely not essential; writing talent is. The writer should not think we are a law review; we are a features magazine with the law (in the broadest sense) as the common denominator. Find issues of national scope and interest to write about; be aware of subjects the magazine—and other media—have already covered and propose something new. Write clearly and well. Expect to work with editor to polish manuscripts to perfection. We do not make assignments to writers with whose work we are not familiar. If you're interested in writing for us, send a detailed, thought-out query with three previously published clips. We are always willing to look at material on spec. Sorry, we don't return manuscripts."

LUMBER

$ $ SOUTHERN LUMBERMAN, Greysmith Publishing, Inc., P.O. Box 681629, Franklin TN 37068-1629. (615)791-1961. Fax: (615)790-6188. E-mail: grey@edge.net. **Contact:** Nanci P. Gregg, editor. **20% freelance written.** Works with a small number of new/unpublished writers each year. Monthly trade journal for the sawmill industry. Estab. 1881. Circ. 13,000. Pays on publication. Publishes ms an average of 3 months after acceptance. Byline given. Buys first North American rights. Submit seasonal material 6 months in advance. Reports in 1 month on queries; 2 months on mss. Sample copy for $3 and 9×12 SAE with 5 first-class stamps. Writer's guidelines for #10 SASE.

Nonfiction: How-to (sawmill better), interview/profile, equipment analysis, technical. Sawmill features. **Buys 10-15 mss/year.** Query with or without published clips, or send complete ms. Length: 500-2,000 words. **Pays $150-350 for assigned articles; $100-250 for unsolicited articles.** Sometimes pays expenses of writers on assignment.

Reprints: Send tearsheet or photocopy of article and information about when and where the article previously appeared. Pays 25-50% of amount paid for an original article.

Photos: Send photos with submission. Reviews transparencies, 4×5 color prints. Offers $10-25/photo. Captions and identification of subjects required. Always looking for news feature types of photos featuring forest products, industry materials or people.

Tips: "Like most, we appreciate a clearly-worded query listing merits of suggested story—what it will tell our readers they need/want to know. We want quotes, we want opinions to make others discuss the article. Best hint? Find an interesting sawmill operation owner and start asking questions—I bet a story idea develops. We need color photos too. Find a sawmill operator and ask questions—what's he doing bigger, better, different. We're interested in new facilities, better marketing, improved production."

MACHINERY AND METAL

N $ ANVIL MAGAZINE, Voice of the Farrier & Blacksmith, P.O. Box 1810, 2770 Sourdough Flat, Georgetown CA 95634. (530)333-2142. Fax: (530)333-2906. E-mail: anvil@anvilmag.com. Website: http://www.anvilmag.com. **Contact:** Rob Edwards, publisher. **40% freelance written.** Monthly magazine featuring "how-to articles on hoof care and horseshoeing and blacksmithing, tips on running your own farrier or blacksmith business and general articles on those subjects." Estab. 1978. Circ. 4,000. Pays on publication. Publishes ms an average of 1 year after acceptance. Byline sometimes given. Buys first North American serial rights. Editorial lead time 3 months. Submit seasonal material 6 months in advance. Accepts simultaneous submissions. Sample copy for $6. Writer's guidelines free.

Nonfiction: General interest, how-to, humor, new product, photo feature, technical, book reviews of farrier/blacksmithing publications. Material has to be specific to the subjects of horseshoeing, hoof care, farrier interests, blacksmithing interests. **Buys 8-10 mss/year.** Send complete ms. Length: 1,200-1,600 words. **Pays $25-100.** Sometimes pays expenses of writers on assignment.

Reprints: Accepts previously published submissions.

Photos: Send photos with submission. Reviews transparencies and prints. Offers no additional payment for photos accepted with ms. Negotiates payment individually if photos only, such as for a how-to article. Identification of subjects required. Buys one-time rights.

Poetry: Traditional on blacksmithing and farriery subjects only. No cowboy poetry. **Buys 5-6 poems/year.** Submit maximum 1-2 poems. Length: 20-40 lines. **Pays $25.**

MODERN MACHINE SHOP, Gardner Publications, Inc., 6915 Valley Ave., Cincinnati OH 45244-3029. (513)527-8800. Fax: (513)527-8801. E-mail: malbert@gardnerweb.com. Website: http://www.mmsonline.com. **Contact:** Mark Albert, executive editor. **5% freelance written.** Monthly. Estab. 1928. Pays 1 month following acceptance. Publishes ms an average of 6 months after acceptance. Byline given. Reports in 1 month. Call for sample copy. Writer's guidelines for #10 SASE.

Nonfiction: Uses only articles dealing with all phases of metalworking, manufacturing and machine shop work, with photos. "Ours is an industrial publication, and contributing authors should have a working knowledge of the metalworking industry. We regularly use contributions from machine shop owners, engineers, other technical experts, and suppliers to the metalworking industry. Almost all of these contributors pursue these projects to promote their own commercial interests." **Buys 5 or fewer unsolicited mss/year.** Query. Length: 1,000-3,500 words. Pays current market rate.

Tips: "Articles that review basic metalworking/machining processes, especially if they include a rethinking or re-evaluation of these processes in light of today's technical trends, are always welcome."

$ $ ORNAMENTAL AND MISCELLANEOUS METAL FABRICATOR, National Ornamental And Miscellaneous Metals Association, 804 Main St., Suite E, Forest Park GA 30297. Fax: (404)363-2857. E-mail: nomma2@aol.com. **Contact:** Todd Daniel, editor. **20% freelance written.** Bimonthly trade magazine "to inform, educate and inspire members of the ornamental and miscellaneous metalworking industry." Estab. 1959. Circ. 11,000. Pays when article actually received. Byline given. Buys one-time rights. Editorial lead time 2 months. Submit seasonal material 2 months in advance. Reports in 1 month on queries. Sample copy for 9×12 SAE and 6 first-class stamps. Writer's guidelines for $1.

Nonfiction: Book excerpts, essays, exposé, general interest, historical/nostalgic, how-to, humor, inspirational, interview/profile, new product, opinion, personal experience, photo feature, technical. **Buys 5-7 mss/year.** Query. Length: 1,200-2,000 words. **Pays $200 for assigned articles; $50 minimum for unsolicited articles.** Sometimes pays expenses of writers on assignment.

Reprints: Send photocopy of article, typed ms with rights for sale noted and information about when and where the article previously appeared. Pays 100% of amount paid for an original article.

Photos: State availability of photos with submission. Reviews contact sheets, negatives, transparencies, prints. May offer additional payment for photos accepted with ms. Model releases required.

Tips: "Make article relevant to our industry. Don't write in passive voice."

N $ $ WIRE ROPE NEWS & SLING TECHNOLOGY, VS Enterprises, P.O. Box 871, Clark NJ 07066. Fax: (732)396-4215. **Contact:** Edward J. Bluvias, publisher. Editor: Barbara McGrath. Managing Editor: Conrad Miller. **100% freelance written.** Bimonthly magazine "published for manufacturers and distributors of wire rope, chain, cordage, related hardware, and sling fabricators. Content includes technical articles, news and reports describing the manufacturing and use of wire rope and related products in marine, construction, mining, aircraft and offshore drilling operations." Estab. 1979. Circ. 3,400. **Pays on acceptance.** Publishes ms an average of 6 months after acceptance. Byline sometimes given. Buys all rights. Editorial lead time 2 months. Submit seasonal material 2 months in advance. Accepts simultaneous submissions.

Nonfiction: General interest, historical/nostalgic, interview/profile, photo feature, technical. **Buys 30 mss/year.** Send complete ms. Length: 2,500-5,000 words. **Pays $300-500.**

Reprints: Accepts previously published submissions.

Photos: Send photos with submission. Reviews contact sheets, 3×5 transparencies, 5×7 prints. Offers no additional payment for photos accepted with ms. Identification of subjects required. Buys all rights.

MAINTENANCE AND SAFETY

N $ $ AMERICAN WINDOW CLEANER MAGAZINE, Voice of the Professional Window Cleaner, 27 Oak Creek Rd., El Sobrante CA 94803. (510)222-7080. Fax: (510)223-7080. E-mail: awcmag@aol.com. Website: http://www.awcmag.com. **Contact:** Richard Fabry, editor. **20% freelance written.** Bimonthly trade magazine covering window cleaning. "Articles to help window cleaners become more profitable, safe, professional and feel good about what they do." Estab. 1986. Circ. 9,000. **Pays on acceptance.** Publishes ms an average of 4 months after acceptance. Byline given. Offers 33% kill fee. Buys first rights. Editorial lead time 2 months. Submit seasonal material 3 months in advance. Reports in 2 weeks on queries; 1 month on mss. Sample copy and writer's guidelines free.

Nonfiction: How-to, humor, inspirational, interview/profile, personal experience, photo feature, technical, add-on businesses. Special issues: Covering a window cleaner, convention in February 3-6, 1999 in Nashville, Tennessee. "Do not want PR-driven pieces. Want to educate not push a particular product." **Buys 12 mss/year.** Query. Length: 500-5,000 words. **Pays $50-250.** Sometimes pays expenses of writers on assignment.

Reprints: Accepts previously published submissions.

Photos: State availability of photos with submission. Reviews contact sheets, transparencies and 4×6 prints. Offers $10-50 per photo. Captions required. Buys one time rights.

Columns/Department: Window Cleaning Tips (tricks of the trade), 1,000-2,000 words; Humor-anecdotes-feel good-abouts (window cleaning industry); Computer High-tech (tips on new technology), all 1,000 words. **Buys 12 mss/year.** Query. **Pays $50-70.**

Tips: "One way to get quotes from window cleaners is to subscribe to a window cleaners chat e-mail group (it is free) and ask questions to the group as a whole. If they are interested, they will e-mail you back. To subscribe to this group, go to this site: http://window-cleaning-net.com If you have access to the web, look at our subject index at our website: http://www.awcmag.com. Make your articles down-to-earth and usable. If you make a general statement, follow it up with specific examples, quotes, techniques, etc. . . . If there are references to particular products, get the manufacturer's name, address, contacts, etc. . . . Sidebars are good. They simplify, make it easy for those who want a quick read or tips. Subheadings make article easy to follow. I encourage their use. Do not evaluate products unless it is a generally positive observation. We don't have the budget for a lab to do a complete and objective report, so the only place opinions can go is in the center 'Forum' section."

$ $ $ BRUSHWARE, Centaur, Inc., 5515 Dundee Rd., Huddleston VA 24104. (540)297-1517. **Contact:** Leslie W. Neff, editor. Publisher: Carl H. Wurzer. **100% freelance written.** Bimonthly magazine covering brush, applicator, mop industry. "General management articles are what we look for. Writers who can do plant profiles of our industry." Estab. 1898. Circ. 1,800. **Pays on acceptance.** Publishes ms an average of 4 months after acceptance. Byline given. Offers 100% kill fee. Buys second serial (reprint) rights or makes work-for-hire assignments. Editorial lead time 4 months. Accepts simultaneous submissions.

Nonfiction: General interest, plant profiles with photos. **Buys 20 mss/year.** Query with or without published clips. Length: 800-2,000 words. **Pays $500-1,000 for assigned articles; $25-100 for unsolicited articles.** Pays expenses of writers on assignment.

Reprints: Accepts previously published submissions.

Photos: State availability of photos with submissions. Reviews 4×6 prints. Negotiates payment individually. Captions, identification of subjects required. Buys one-time rights.

$ $ $ CANADIAN OCCUPATIONAL SAFETY, Clifford/Elliot Ltd., 3228 S. Service Rd., Suite 202, Burlington, Ontario L7N 3H8 Canada. (905)634-2100. Fax: (905)634-2238. E-mail: mg@industrialsourcebook.com. Website: http://www.industrialsourcebook.com. **Contact:** Matt Green, managing editor. **40% freelance written.** Bimonthly magazine. "We want informative articles dealing with issues that relate to occupational health and safety." Estab. 1989. Circ. 12,000. Pays on publication. Publishes ms an average of 3 months after acceptance. Byline given. Buys one-time rights. Editorial lead time 4 months. Submit seasonal material 4 months in advance. Accepts simultaneous and previously published submissions. Reports in 3 weeks on queries; 1 month on mss. Sample copy and writer's guidelines free.

Nonfiction: How-to, interview/profile. **Buys 6-8 mss/year.** Query with published clips. Length: 750-3,500 words. **Pays $400-1,000 (Canadian).** Sometimes pays expenses of writers on assignment.

Photos: State availability of photos with submission. Reviews transparencies. Negotiates payment individually. Captions required. Buys one-time rights.

N $ $ EXECUTIVE HOUSEKEEPING TODAY, The International Executive Housekeepers Association, 1001 Eastwind Dr., Suite 301, Westerville OH 43081. (614)895-7166. Fax: (614)895-1248. E-mail: excel@ieha.org. Website: http://www.ieha.org. **Contact:** Joanne Cooper, editor. **95% freelance written.** Monthly magazine for "nearly 8,000 decision makers responsible for housekeeping management (cleaning, grounds maintenance, laundry, linen, pest control, waste management, regulatory compliance, training) for a variety of institutions: hospitality, healthcare, education, retail, government." Estab. 1936. Circ. 5,500. **Pays on acceptance.** Publishes ms an average of 6 months after acceptance. Byline given. Buys first North American serial rights. Editorial lead time 2 months. Submit seasonal material 3 months in advance. Sample copy and writer's guidelines free.

Nonfiction: General interest, interview/profile, new product, personal experience, technical. **Buys 30 mss/year.** Query with published clips. Length: 500-1,500 words. **Pays $250-300.**

Photos: State availability of photos with submission. Reviews negatives. Offers no additional payment for photos accepted with ms. Identification of subjects required. Buys one-time rights.

Columns/Departments: Federal Report (OSHA/EPA requirements), 1,000 words; Industry News; Management Perspectives (industry specific), 500-1,500 words. Query with published clips. **Pays $250-300.**

Tips: "Have a background in the industry or personal experience with any aspect of it."

$ $ INTERACTIVE TECHNOLOGIES, INC., 2266 N. Second St., North St. Paul MN 55109. (612)773-4696. Fax: (612)779-4879. E-mail: jmoses@securitypro.com. Website: http://www.securitypro.com. **Contact:** Joe Moses, senior editor. Monthly magazines covering "applications of wireless security systems; written for dealers and installers." **Pays on acceptance.** Publishes ms an average of 4 months after acceptance. Byline sometimes given. Buys first rights or makes work-for-hire assignments. Editorial lead time varies. Submit seasonal material 6 months in advance. Writer's guidelines for #10 SASE.

- This listing differs from others. Interactive Technologies, Inc., is a wireless security company seeking articles on their products which they then place in appropriate trade journals. "We pay for the article ($300-400), and we worry about getting it published."

Nonfiction: How-to, interview/profile, new product, photo feature, technical. No unsolicited mss. No non-wireless

installations. **Buys 8-12 mss/year.** Query with published clips. Length: 1,200-2,500 words. **Pays $300-400.** Sometimes pays expenses of writers on assignment.
Photos: State availability of photos with submission. Reviews 4×6 prints. Negotiates payment individually. Model releases, identification of subjects required. Buys one-time rights.
Tips: "We're looking for technical articles and profiles of dealers who install our wireless security products. Go through the Yellow Pages and find an ITI security dealer and tell him/her you want to write a story on a noteworthy wireless installation they've done. Then call us."

$ $ $ SAFETY & HEALTH, National Safety Council, 1121 Spring Lake Dr., Itasca IL 60143. Fax: (630)775-2285. Website: http:www.nsc.org/pubs/sh.htm. **Contact:** Carrie Fearn, editor. **90% freelance written.** Monthly association magazine. "Our audience is safety and health professionals. *Safety & Health* is the flagship publication of the National Safety Council, reporting on safety, health and environmental issues that affect the workplace." Circ. 40,000. Pays on publication. Publishes ms an average of 3 months after acceptance. Byline given. Offers 25% kill fee. Buys second serial (reprint) rights. Editorial lead time 3 months.
Nonfiction: How-to, interview/profile, technical. **Buys 72 mss/year.** Query with published clips. Length: 1,500-2,000 words. **Pays $600-1,200 for features.**
Columns/Departments: Query with published clips. Payment varies.

$ SECURITY SALES, Management Resource for the Professional Installing Dealer, Bobit Publishing, 21061 South Western, Torrance CA 90501. (310)533-2400. Fax: (310)533-2504. E-mail: bobitpub@aol.com. Website: http://www.securitysales.com. Publisher: Jason Knott. Managing Editor: Vi Pangelinan. **Contact:** Amy Jones, executive editor. Dave Stepner, assistant editor. **5% freelance written.** Monthly magazine "covers technology, management and marketing designed to help installing security dealers improve their businesses. Closed-circuit TV, burglary and fire equipment, integrated systems and access control systems are main topics." Estab. 1979. Circ. 25,000. Pays on publication. Publishes ms an average of 6 months after acceptance. Byline sometimes given. Buys all rights or one-time rights. Editorial lead time 2 months. Submit seasonal material 4 months in advance. Accepts simultaneous submissions. Sample copy free.
Nonfiction: How-to, technical. "No generic business operations articles. Submissions must be specific to security and contain interviews with installing dealers." **Buys 6-10 mss/year.** Send complete ms. Length: 800-1,500 words. **Pays $50 minimum.**
Reprints: Send typed ms with rights for sale noted and information about when and where the article previously appeared.
Photos: Send photos with submission. Reviews prints. Offers no additional payment for photos accepted with ms. Captions, model releases, identification of subjects required.
Tips: "Case studies of specific security installations with photos and diagrams are needed. Interview dealers who installed system and ask how they solved specific problems, why they chose certain equipment, cost of job, etc."

MANAGEMENT AND SUPERVISION

This category includes trade journals for middle management business and industrial managers, including supervisors and office managers. Journals for business executives and owners are classified under Business Management. Those for industrial plant managers are listed in Industrial Operations.

$ $ HR MAGAZINE, On Human Resource Management, Society for Human Resource Management, 1800 Duke St., Alexandria VA 22314-3497. (703)548-9140. Fax: (703)836-0367. E-mail: hrmag@shrm.org. Website: http://www.shrm.org. **Contact:** Patrick Mirza, managing editor. Editor: Leon Rubis. **50% freelance written.** Monthly magazine covering human resource management professions with special focus on business news that affects the workplace including compensation and benefits, recruiting, training and development, management trends, court decisions, legislative actions and government regulations. Estab. 1948. Circ. 100,000. **Pays on acceptance.** Publishes ms an average of 2 months after acceptance. Byline given. Buys first or all rights. Editorial lead time 4 months. Reports in 2 weeks on queries, 3 months on manuscripts. Sample copy free. Writer's guidelines for #10 SASE.
Nonfiction: Interview/profile, expert advice and analysis, news features, technical. **Buys 50 mss/year.** Query. Length: 1,500-2,200 words. Pays expenses of writers on assignment.
Photos: State availability of photos with submission. Model releases and identification of subjects required. Buys one-time rights.
Tips: "Readers are members of the Society for Human Resource Management (SHRM), mostly HR managers in private employers."

$ $ $ HUMAN RESOURCE EXECUTIVE, LRP Publications Magazine Group, 747 Dresher Rd., P.O. Box 980, Dept. 500, Dresher PA 19044. (215)784-0910. Fax: (215)784-0870. E-mail: dshadovitz@lrp.com. Website: http://www.workindex.com. **Contact:** David Shadovitz, editor. **30% freelance written.** "Monthly magazine serving the information needs of chief human resource professionals/executives in companies, government agencies and nonprofit institutions with 500 or more employees." Estab. 1987. Circ. 45,000. **Pays on acceptance.** Publishes ms an average of 2 months after acceptance. Byline given. Offers 50% kill fee on assigned stories. Buys first and all rights including reprint rights. Reports in 1 month. Sample copy for 10×13 SAE with 2 first-class stamps. Writer's guidelines for #10 SAE with 1 first-class stamp.

Nonfiction: Book excerpts, interview/profile. **Buys 16 mss/year.** Query with published clips. Length: 1,700-2,000 words. **Pays $200-900.** Sometimes pays expenses of writers on assignment.

Photos: State availability of photos with submission. Reviews contact sheets. Offers no additional payment for photos accepted with ms. Identification of subjects required. Buys first and repeat rights.

$ $ $ $ INCENTIVE, Managing & Marketing Through Motivation, Bill Communications, 355 Park Ave. S., New York NY 10010. (212)592-6458. Fax: (212)592-6459. E-mail: jjincent@aol.com. Editor: Jennifer Juergens. **Contact:** Joan Steinauer, managing editor. **20% freelance written.** Monthly magazine concerning "motivating through the use of merchandise and travel, managing employees and motivating workers." Estab. 1891. Circ. 40,000. Pays on publication. Publishes ms an average of 3 months after acceptance. Byline given. Buys one-time rights. Editorial lead time 3 months. Submit seasonal material 3 months in advance. Accepts simultaneous submissions. Reports in 1 month. Sample copy free.

Nonfiction: Book excerpts, how-to (motivate), inspirational, interview/profile, new product, travel. **Buys 15 mss/year.** Query with published clips. Length: 500-1,500 words. **Pays $400-2,000.** Sometimes pays the expenses of writers on assignment.

Photos: State availability of photos with submission.

Columns/Departments: Query. **Pays $100-500.**

$ MANAGE, 2210 Arbor Blvd., Dayton OH 45439. (937)294-0421. Fax: (937)294-2374. E-mail: doug@nma.org. Website: http://www.nma1.org. **Contact:** Douglas E. Shaw, editor-in-chief. **60% freelance written.** Works with a small number of new/unpublished writers each year. Quarterly magazine for first-line and middle management and scientific/technical managers. Estab. 1925. Circ. 40,000. **Pays on acceptance.** Publishes ms an average of 6 months after acceptance. Buys North American magazine rights with reprint privileges; book rights remain with the author. Reports in 3 months. Sample copy and writer's guidelines for 9×12 SAE with 3 first-class stamps.

Nonfiction: "All material published by *Manage* is in some way management-oriented. Most articles concern one or more of the following categories: communications, executive abilities, human relations, job status, leadership, motivation and productivity and professionalism. Articles should be specific and tell the manager how to apply the information to his job immediately. Be sure to include pertinent examples, and back up statements with facts. *Manage* does not want essays or academic reports, but interesting, well-written and practical articles for and about management." **Buys 6 mss/issue.** Phone queries OK. Submit complete ms. Length: 600-1,000 words. **Pays 5¢/word.**

Reprints: Accepts previously published submissions. Send photocopy of article or short story. Pays 100% of amount paid for an original article.

Tips: "Keep current on management subjects; submit timely work. Include word count on first page of manuscript."

$ $ MANAGEMENT REVIEW, The American Management Association Magazine, American Management Association, 1601 Broadway, New York NY 10019-7420. Fax: (212)903-8083. E-mail: mgmtreview@amanet.org. Website: http://www.amanet.org. **Contact:** Martha H. Peak, editor. Monthly magazine covering "Hands On" management issues for top/middle managers. "*Management Review* is the global membership magazine of the American Management Association, dedicated to broadening managers' know-how through insightful reporting of management trends and tips on how to manage more effectively." Estab. 1923. Circ. 75,000. Pays on publication. Publishes ms an average of 5 months after acceptance. Byline given. Buys first worldwide rights. Editorial lead time 3-4 months. Submit seasonal material 3-4 months in advance. Reports in 4-5 weeks on queries. Sample copy for $5. Writer's guidelines free.

Nonfiction: Business stories only. **Buys 24 mss/year.** Query. Length: 1,200-2,000 words.

Photos: State availability of photos with submission. Captions and identification of subjects required.

Tips: "Submissions in writing ONLY. No fax. No cold calls."

$ $ $ MOBILITY, Employee Relocation Council, 1720 N St., NW, Washington DC 20036. (202)857-0857. Fax: (202)659-8631. E-mail: mobility@erc.org. Website: http://www.erc.org. Editor: Jerry Holloman. **Contact:** Christine M. Wilson, managing editor. **10% freelance written.** Monthly magazine covering corporate employee relocation, human resources, real estate, technology. "*Mobility* is published by an association of corporations that transfer their own employees and anyone providing services to those moving families or administrators. Diverse industry groups include corporate representatives, brokers, appraisers, household goods companies, etc." Estab. 1980. Circ. 12,000. **Pays on acceptance.** Publishes ms an average of 2 months after acceptance. Byline given. Offers 25% kill fee. Buys first North American serial rights. Editorial lead time 2 months. Submit seasonal material 3 months in advance. Reports as soon as possible. Sample copy for $5. Writer's guidelines free.

Nonfiction: Interview/profile, relocation, human resources, real estate, technology. Special issues: Human Resources (March); Technology (June). **Buys 4-6 mss/year.** Query with published clips. Length: 2,000-3,000 words. **Pays $1,000.** Sometimes pays expenses of writers on assignment.

Reprints: Send photocopy of article or short story and information about when and where the article previously appeared.

Photos: Send photos with submission. Reviews transparencies. Identification of subjects required. Buys one-time rights.
Tips: "You may already have an idea what you would like to write about, but if you do not, you may wish to review *Mobility*'s 'Articles in Search of Authors' list. This list is the result of brainstorming by *Mobility*'s Editorial Advisory Committee and represents that group's opinions about what topics are currently of interest to our readers. The list is intended as food for thought, and you may choose your topic from it, or it may spark another idea. If you are unsure whether your idea would be appropriate, please feel free to contact the editorial staff to discuss it. Writers may wish to view website http://www.erc.org. Be familiar with related topic areas."

$ $ SECURITY MANAGEMENT BULLETIN: Protecting People, Property & Assets, Bureau of Business Practice, 24 Rope Ferry Rd., Waterford CT 06386. Fax: (860)437-3150. E-mail: alex_vaughn@prenhall.com. Website: http://www.bbpnews.com. **Contact:** Alex Vaughn, editor. **75% freelance written.** Eager to work with new/unpublished writers. Biweekly newsletter "slanted toward security directors, primarily industrial, retail and service businesses, but others as well." Circ. 3,000. Pays when article assigned to future issue. Buys all rights. Sample copy and writer's guidelines free.
Nonfiction: Interview (with security professionals only). "Articles should be tight and specific. They should deal with new security techniques or new twists on old ones." **Buys 2-5 mss/issue.** Query; phone queries OK. Length: 750-1,000 words. **Pays 15¢/word and up.**

$ $ STRATEGIC SALES MANAGEMENT, (formerly *Sales Manager's Bulletin*), The Bureau of Business Practice, 24 Rope Ferry Rd., Waterford CT 06386-0001. (860)442-4365. Fax: (860)437-1593. E-mail: karen_barretta@prenhall.com. Website: http://www.bbpnews.com. **Contact:** Karen Barretta, editor. **33% freelance written.** Prefers to work with published/established writers. Monthly newsletter for sales managers. Estab. 1917. **Pays on acceptance.** Publishes ms an average of 6 months after acceptance. Submit seasonal material 6 months in advance. Original interview-based material only. No byline. Buys all rights. Sample copy and writer's guidelines for #10 SAE with 2 first-class stamps.
Nonfiction: How-to (hire, train, motivate, and manage a sales force and get results); interview (with working sales managers who use innovative techniques). "Break into this publication by reading the guidelines and sample issue. Follow the directions closely and chances for acceptance go up dramatically. One easy way to start is with an interview article ('Here's what sales executives have to say about . . .'). Query is vital to acceptance. Send a simple note explaining briefly the subject matter, the interviewees, slant, length, and date of expected completion, accompanied by a SASE." No unsolicited mss. Length: 800-1,000 words. **Pays 18-20¢/word.**
Tips: "Freelancers should always request samples and writer's guidelines, accompanied by SASE. Requests without SASE are discarded immediately. Examine the sample, and don't try to improve on our style. Write as we write. Don't 'jump around' from point to point and don't submit articles that are too chatty and with not enough real information. The more time a writer can save the editors, the greater his or her chance of a sale and repeated sales, when queries may no longer be necessary."

$ SUPERVISION, 320 Valley, Burlington IA 52601-5513. Fax: (319)752-3421. Publisher: Michael S. Darnall. **Contact:** Teresa Levinson, editor. **95% freelance written.** Monthly magazine for first-line foremen, supervisors and office managers. "*Supervision*'s objective is to provide informative articles which develop the attitudes, skills, personal and professional qualities of supervisory staff, enabling them to use more of their potential to maximize productivity, minimize costs, and achieve company and personal goals." Estab. 1939. Circ. 2,620. Pays on publication. Publishes ms an average of 6 months after acceptance. Buys all rights. Reports in 1 month. Sample copy and writer's guidelines for 9×12 SAE with 4 first-class stamps; mention *Writer's Market* in request.
Nonfiction: How-to (cope with supervisory problems, discipline, absenteeism, safety, productivity, goal setting, etc.); personal experience (unusual success story of foreman or supervisor). No sexist material written from only a male viewpoint. Include biography and/or byline with ms submissions. Author photos requested. **Buys 12 mss/issue.** Query. Length: 1,500-1,800 words. **Pays 4¢/word.**
Tips: "Following AP stylebook would be helpful." Uses no advertising. Send correspondence to Editor.

$ $ TRAINING MAGAZINE, The Human Side of Business, Lakewood Publications, 50 S. Ninth St., Minneapolis MN 55402. (612)333-0471. Fax: (612)333-6526. E-mail: edit@trainingmag.com. Website: http://www.trainingsupersite.com. Editor: Jack Gordon. **Contact:** Chris Lee, managing editor. **10% freelance written.** Monthly magazine. "Our core readers are managers and professionals who specialize in employee training and development (e.g., corporate training directors, VP-human resource development, etc.). We have a large secondary readership among managers of all sorts who are concerned with improving human performance in their organizations. We take a businesslike approach to training and employee education." Estab. 1964. Circ. 60,000. **Pays on acceptance.** Publishes ms an average of 3 months after acceptance. Byline given. Buys first North American serial and second serial (reprint) rights. Reports in 2 weeks on queries; 2 months on mss. Sample copy for 10×13 SAE with 4 first-class stamps. Writer's guidelines for #10 SASE.
Nonfiction: Essays; how-to (on training, management, sales, productivity improvement, etc.); humor; interview/profile; new product; opinion; photo feature; technical (use of audiovisual aids, computers, etc.). "No puff, no 'testimonials' or disguised ads in any form." **Buys 15 mss/year.** Query. Length: 200-3,000 words. **Pays $150-1,200.**
Photos: State availability of photos with submission. Reviews transparencies, prints. Negotiates payment individually. Identification of subjects required. Buys first rights and limited reprint rights.
Columns/Departments: Training Today (news briefs, how-to tips, reports on pertinent research, trend analysis, etc.),

400 words. **Buys 12 mss/year.** Query. **Pays $50-125.**

Tips: "Send an intriguing query that demonstrates writing ability, as well as some insight into the topic you propose to cover. Then be willing to submit the piece on spec. We accept and publish only a small fraction of the manuscripts we receive. How can you improve the chances that your submission will be accepted? Remember two things: 1. *Training* exists for its readers, not its authors. 2. *Training* is, as the name suggests, a magazine; it is not an academic or professional 'journal.' What do those statements mean? The first means that while authors may have many reasons for submitting articles to *Training*, we do not publish articles in order to publicize authors or to promote or help sell their products or services. Regardless of its form—testimonial, case history or whatever—a manuscript that trumpets the benefits of some product, program or technique without explaining how the reader can achieve those benefits (other than by hiring the author or buying the author's products) will not be accepted. 'Tell 'em what you're going to do for them but don't give 'em the recipe' is a legitimate formula for an advertisement or a client proposal, but not for an article submitted to *Training*. The second statement means that we want manuscripts written in the style of magazine articles, not formal 'papers.' Do not begin with phrases such as 'The purpose of this paper is to. . . .' Do not use footnotes; quote sources directly, as newspapers do. Your writing should be clear, crisp, simple, informal and direct."

N $$$$ WORKFORCE, ACC Communications, 245 Fischer Ave., Suite B-2, Costa Mesa CA 92626. Fax: (714)751-4106. E-mail: ddekirkn@workforcemag.com. Website: http://www.workforceonline.com. **Contact:** Dawn Anfuso, managing editor. Editor: Allan Holcrow. **25% freelance written.** Monthly human resources magazine. "We look at the human resources function as a strategic business partner—it's not the 'soft' issues, but bottom-line impact issues we address." Estab. 1922. Circ. 32,000. **Pays on acceptance.** Publishes ms an average of 6 months after acceptance. Byline given. Offers 50% kill fee. Buys all rights. Editorial lead time 3 months. Submit seasonal material 6 months in advance. Reports in 1 month on queries; 2 months on mss. Sample copy for #10 SAE and $2.50 postage. Writer's guidelines free.

Nonfiction: Book excerpts, trends. No viewpoints or product/service/book reviews. **Buys 24 mss/year.** Query with published clips. Length: 1,500-2,500 words. **Pays $1,200-2,500.** Sometimes pays expenses of writers on assignment.

Photos: State availability of photos with submission. Reviews contact sheets, negatives, transparencies and prints. Offers no additional payment for photos accepted with ms. Model releases and identification of subjects required. Buys one-time rights.

Tips: "Learn the subject matter. Understand the human resources function's role in business."

MARINE AND MARITIME INDUSTRIES

N $$ MARINE BUSINESS JOURNAL, The Voice of the Marine Industries Nationwide, 1766 Bay Rd., Miami Beach FL 33139. (305)538-0700. Fax: (305)532-8657. E-mail: sboating@icanect.net. Executive Editor: Rick Eyerdam. **Contact:** Barbara Pace. **25% freelance written.** Bimonthly magazine that covers the recreational boating industry. "*The Marine Business Journal* is aimed at boating dealers, distributors and manufacturers, naval architects, yacht brokers, marina owners and builders, marine electronics dealers, distributors and manufacturers, and anyone involved in the US marine industry. Articles cover news, new product technology and public affairs affecting the industry." Estab. 1986. Circ. 26,000. Pays on publication. Publishes ms an average of 1 month after acceptance. Byline given. Buys first North American serial, one-time or second serial (reprint rights). Reports in 2 weeks on queries. Sample copy for $2.50 and 9×12 SAE with 7 first-class stamps. Writer's guidelines for #10 SASE.

Nonfiction: Buys 20 mss/year. Query with published clips. Length: 500-2,000 words. **Pays $100-200 for assigned articles.** Sometimes pays expenses of writers on assignment.

Photos: State availability of photos with submission. Reviews 35mm or larger transparencies, 5×7 prints. Offers $25-50/photo. Captions, model releases, identification of subjects required. Buys one-time rights.

Tips: "Query with clips. It's a highly specialized field, written for professionals by professionals, almost all on assignment or by staff."

$$ PROFESSIONAL MARINER, Journal of the Maritime Industry, Navigator Publishing, 18 Danforth St., Portland ME 04101. (207)772-2466. Fax: (207)772-2879. E-mail: navigatorpublishing@compuserve.com. **Contact:** Evan True, editor. **50% freelance written.** Bimonthly magazine covering professional seamanship and maritime industry news. Estab. 1993. Circ. 22,000. Pays on publication. Byline given. Buys all rights. Editorial lead time 3 months. Accepts simultaneous submissions. Sample copy and writer's guidelines free.

Nonfiction: For professional mariners on vessels and ashore. Seeks submissions on industry regulations, towing, piloting, technology, engineering, business maritime casualties and feature stories about the maritime industry. Does accept "sea stories" and personal professional experiences as correspondence pieces. **Buys 15 mss/year.** Query. Length varies: short clips to long profiles/features. **Pays 15¢/word.** Sometimes pays expenses of writers on assignment.

Reprints: Accepts previously published submissions. Pays 100% of amount paid for original article.

Photos: Send photos and photo captions with submission. Reviews slides and prints. Negotiates payment individually. Identification of subjects required. Buys one-time rights.

MEDICAL

Through these journals physicians, therapists and mental health professionals learn how other professionals help their patients and manage their medical practices. Publications for nurses, laboratory technicians and other medical personnel are listed in the Hospitals, Nursing and Nursing Home section. Publications for drug store managers and drug wholesalers and retailers, as well as hospital equipment suppliers, are listed with Drugs, Health Care and Medical Products. Publications for consumers that report trends in the medical field are found in the Consumer Health and Fitness categories.

N **AMERICAN MEDICAL NEWS**, American Medical Association, 515 N. State St., Chicago IL 60610. (312)464-4429. **Contact:** Kathryn Trombatore. "*American Medical News* is the nation's most widely circulated newspaper focusing on socioeconomic issues in medicine." Circ. 375,000. Pays on publication. Buys first rights. Reports in 1 month. Writer's guidelines for #10 SASE.

Nonfiction: Health, business. Needs "market driven features reporting developments that affect the structure of the health care industry." **Buys 20-25 mss/year.** Query with SASE. Length: 1,500-2,000 words. Pay varies.

HEALTHPLAN, American Association of Health Plans, 1129 20th St. NW, Suite 600, Washington DC 20036. (202)778-3250. Fax: (202)331-7487. E-mail: dmadden@aahp.org. Website: http://www.aahp.org. Editor: Susan Pisano. **Contact:** Diana Madden, managing editor. **75% freelance written.** Bimonthly magazine. "*Healthplan* is geared toward senior administrative and medical managers in HMOs, PPOs, and similar health plans. Articles must ask 'why' and 'how' and answer with examples. Articles should inform and generate interest and discussion about topics on anything from patient care to regulatory issues." Estab. 1990. Circ. 7,000. Pays within 30 days of acceptance of article in final form. Publishes ms an average of 2 months after acceptance. Byline given. Offers 30% kill fee. Buys all rights. Editorial lead time 2 months. Submit seasonal material 4 months in advance. Accepts simultaneous submissions. Reports in 1 month on queries. Sample copy and writer's guidelines free.

Nonfiction: How-to (how industry professionals can better operate their health plans), opinion. "We do not accept stories that promote products." **Buys 20 mss/year.** Query or send complete ms and SASE. Length: 1,800-2,500 words. **Pays 50¢/word minimum.** Pays phone expenses of writers on assignment.

Photos: State availability of photos with submission. Reviews contact sheets. Offers no additional payment for photos accepted with ms. Buys all rights.

Columns/Departments: Information Technology (case study or how-to), 1,800 words; Chronic Care (case studies), 1,800 words; Preventive Care (case study or discussion of public health), 1,800 words; The Market (market niches for HMOs—with examples), 1,800 words. **Buys 6 mss/year.** Query with published clips or send complete ms and SASE. **Pays 50¢/word minimum.**

Tips: "Follow the current health care debate. Look for health plan success stories in your community; we like to include case studies on everything from patient care to provider relations to regulatory issues so that our readers can learn from their colleagues. Our readers are members of our trade association and look for advice and news. Topics relating to the quality of health plans are the ones most frequently assigned to writers, whether a feature or department. We also welcome story ideas. Just send us a letter with the details."

$ $ JEMS, The Journal of Emergency Medical Services, Jems Communications, 1947 Camino Vida Roble, Suite 200, Carlsbad CA 92008-2789. (760)431-9797. Fax: (760)930-9567. Website: http://www.jems.com. **Contact:** A.J. Heightman, editor. **95% freelance written.** Monthly magazine directed to personnel who serve the pre-hospital emergency medicine industry: paramedics, EMTs, emergency physicians and nurses, administrators, EMS consultants, etc. Estab. 1980. Circ. 45,000. Pays on publication. Publishes ms an average of 6 months after acceptance. Byline given. Buys all North American serial rights. Submit seasonal material 6 months in advance. Reports in 6 weeks on queries. Sample copy and writer's guidelines free.

Nonfiction: Essays, exposé, general interest, how-to, continuing education, humor, interview/profile, new product, opinion, personal experience, photo feature, technical. **Buys 50 mss/year.** Query. Length: 1,500-2,500 words. **Pays $300-450.**

Photos: State availability of photos with submission. Reviews 4×6 prints. Offers $25 minimum per photo. Model releases and identification of subjects required. Buys one-time rights.

Columns/Departments: "Columns and departments are staff-written with the exception of commentary on EMS issues and practices." Length: 1,000 words maximum. Query with or without published clips. **Pays $125-175.**

Tips: "We are trying to build a cadre of EMS providers nationwide to submit news tips and write news stories. Fee is $10-50. It's a good way to attract the editors' attention."

$ $ $ $ MANAGED CARE, A Guide for Physicians, Stezzi Communications, Inc., 301 Oxford Valley Rd., Suite 1105A, Yardley PA 19067. (215)321-5480. Fax: (215)321-6670. E-mail: editors@managedcaremag.com. Website: http://www.managedcaremag.com. **Contact:** John Marcille, editor. **75% freelance written.** Monthly magazine. "We emphasize practical, usable information that helps the physician or HMO administrator cope with the ever-more complex array of options, challenges and hazards that accompanies the rapidly changing health care industry. Our regular readers understand that 'health care reform' isn't a piece of legislation; it's an evolutionary process that's already well under way. But we hope to help our readers also keep the faith that led them to medicine in the first place." Estab. 1992. Circ. 80,000. **Pays on acceptance.** Publishes ms an average of 1 month after acceptance. Byline given. Offers 20% kill fee. Buys all rights. Editorial lead time 3 months. Submit seasonal material 4 months in advance. Reports in 3 weeks on queries; 2 months on mss. Sample copy free.

Nonfiction: Book excerpts, general interest, how-to (deal with requisites of managed care, such as contracts with health plans, affiliation arrangements, relationships with staffers, computer needs, etc.), technical. Also considered occasionally are personal experience, opinion, interview/profile and humor pieces, *but these must have a strong managed care angle and draw upon the insights of* (if they are not written by) *a knowledgeable MD or other managed care professional.* Don't waste those stamps on "A Humorous View of My Recent Gall Bladder Operation." **Buys 40 mss/year.** Query with clips. Length: 1,000-3,000 words. **Pays $1,000-1,500 for assigned articles; $100-1,000 for unsolicited articles.** Pays expenses of writers on assignment.

Photos: State availability of photos with submissions. Reviews contact sheets, negatives, transparencies, prints. Negotiates payment individually. Buys one-time rights.

Columns/Departments: Michael Dalzell, senior editor. News/Commentary (usually staff-written, but factual anecdotes involving managed care's effect on providers are welcome. 100-300 words. **Pays $50-100.** Employer Update focuses on practical advice for purchasers of healthcare. 800-1,000 words. **Pays $100-300.**

Tips: "We're looking for reliable freelancers who can write for our audience with our approach, so 'breaking in' may yield assignments. Do this by writing impeccably and with flair, and try to reflect the interests and perspective of the practicing physician or the active managed care executive. (Cardinal rule: The reader is busy, with many things vying for his/her reading time. Be sprightly, but don't waste our readers' time.)"

$ $ $ $ MEDICAL ECONOMICS, 5 Paragon Dr., Montvale NJ 07645. (201)358-7500. Fax: (201)722-2688. E-mail: helen_mckenna@medec.com. Website: http://www.medec.com. **Contact:** Helen A. McKenna, outside copy editor. **2% freelance written.** Biweekly magazine. Circ. 192,000. **Pays on acceptance.** Byline given. Offers 25% kill fee. Buys first world publication rights. Reports in 1 month on queries. Sample copy free.

Nonfiction: Articles about private physicians in innovative, pioneering and/or controversial situations affecting medical care delivery, patient relations or malpractice prevention/litigation; personal finance topics. **Buys 40-50 mss/year.** Query with published clips. Length: 1,500-3,000 words. **Pays $1,200-2,500 for assigned articles.** Pays expenses of writers on assignment; expenses over $100 must be approved in advance—receipts required.

Tips: "We look for articles about physicians who run high-quality, innovative practices suited to the age of managed care. We also look for how-to service articles—on practice-management and personal-finance topics—which must contain anecdotal examples to support the advice."

N $ $ MODERN PHYSICIAN, Essential Business News for the Executive Physician, Crain Communications, 740 N. Rush St., Chicago IL 60611-2590. (312)649-5324. Fax: (312)649-5393. Website: http://www.modernhealthcare.com. **Contact:** Karen Petitte, editor. **40% freelance written.** Monthly magazine covering business and management news for doctors. "*Modern Physician* offers timely topical news features with lots of business information—revenues, earnings, financial data." Estab. 1997. Circ. 31,000. **Pays on acceptance.** Publishes ms an average of 2 months after acceptance. Byline given. Buys all rights. Editorial lead time 2 months. Reports in 6 weeks on queries. Sample copy free. Writer's guidelines sent after query.

Nonfiction: Length: 1,000-2,000 words. **Pays 40-50¢/word.**

$ $ THE NEW PHYSICIAN, 1902 Association Dr., Reston VA 20191. **Contact:** Amy Myers-Payne, editor. 40% freelance written. Magazine published 9 times/year for medical students, interns, residents and educators. Circ. 25,000. **Pays on acceptance.** Publishes an average of 3 months after acceptance. Accepts simultaneous submissions. Reports in 2 months. Sample copy for 10×13 SAE with 5 first-class stamps. Writer's guidelines for SASE.

Nonfiction: Articles on social, political, economic issues in medical education/health care. **Buys 12 features/year.** Query or send complete ms. Length: 800-3,000 words. **Pays 25-50¢/word; higher fees for selected pieces.** Pays some expenses of writers on assignment.

Reprints: Send photocopy of article and information about when and where the article previously appeared. Pay varies.

Tips: "Although we are published by an association (the American Medical Student Association), we are not a 'house organ.' We are a professional magazine for readers with a progressive view on health care issues and a particular interest in improving medical education and the health care system. Our readers demand sophistication on the issues we cover. Freelancers should be willing to look deeply into the issues in question and not be satisfied with a cursory review of those issues."

N $ $ PHYSICIAN, Focus on the Family, 8605 Explorer Dr., Colorado Springs CO 80920. (719)531-3400. Fax: (719)531-3499. **Contact:** Melissa Cox, editor. Managing Editor: Charles Johnson. **20% freelance written.** Bimonthly. "The goal of our magazine is to encourage physicians in their faith, family and medical practice. Writers should understand the medical lifestyle." Estab. 1989. Circ. 69,000. Pays on publication. Publishes ms an average of 6 months after acceptance. Byline given. Offers 50% or $100 kill fee. Buys first North American serial rights. Editorial lead time 1 year. Reports in 2 months. Sample copy free.

Nonfiction: Book excerpts, general interest, interview/profile, personal experience, religious, technical. "No patient's opinions of their doctor." **Buys 20-30 mss/year.** Query. Length: 900-2,400 words. **Pays $100-500.** Sometimes pays expenses of writers on assignment.

Reprints: Accepts previously published submissions.

Photos: State availability of photos with submission. Reviews transparencies. Negotiates payment individually. Buys one-time rights.

Tips: "Most writers are M.D.'s."

N $ $ $ THE PHYSICIAN AND SPORTSMEDICINE, McGraw-Hill, 4530 W. 77th St., Edina MN 55435. (612)835-3222. **Contact:** Susan Hawthorne, executive editor. **15% freelance written.** Prefers to work with published/established writers. Monthly magazine covering medical aspects of sports and exercise. "We publish articles that are of practical, clinical interest to our physician audience." Estab. 1973. Circ. 115,000. **Pays on acceptance.** Publishes ms an average of 4 months after acceptance. Byline given. Generally buys all rights. Reports in 2 months. Sample copy for $8. Writer's guidelines for #10 SASE.

- This publication is relying more heavily on the clinical component of the journal, meaning review articles written by physicians who have expertise in a specific specialty.

Nonfiction: New developments and issues in sports medicine. Query. Length: 250-2,500 words. **Pays $150-1,200.**

Photos: Grace Voss, photo editor. State availability of photos. Buys one-time rights.

PHYSICIAN'S MANAGEMENT, Advanstar Communications, 7500 Old Oak Blvd., Cleveland OH 44130. (440)243-8100. Fax: (440)891-2683. E-mail: advedhc@en.com; Subject: "Physician's Management." Website: http://www.modernmedicine.com. **Contact:** Larry Frederick, editor-in-chief. Prefers to work with published/established writers. Monthly magazine emphasizing finances, investments, malpractice, socioeconomic issues, estate and retirement planning, office administration, practice management, computers and taxes for primary care physicians in private practice. Estab. 1960. Circ. 133,000. **Pays on acceptance.** Sample copy for $10. Writer's guidelines for #10 SASE.

Nonfiction: "*Physician's Management* is a practice management/economic publication, not a clinical one." Publishes how-to articles (limited to medical practice management); informational (when relevant to audience); personal experience articles (if written by a physician). No fiction, clinical material, or soap opera articles. Length: 2,000-2,500 words. Query with SASE. Use of charts, tables, graphs, sidebars and photos strongly encouraged. Sometimes pays expenses of writers on assignment. Buys all rights to articles and graphics.

Tips: "Talk to doctors first about their practices, financial interests, and day-to-day nonclinical problems and then query us. Also, the ability to write a concise, well-structured and well-researched magazine article is essential."

$ $ PODIATRY MANAGEMENT, Kane Communications, Inc., P.O. Box 750129, Forest Hills NY 11375. (718)897-9700. Fax: (718)896-5747. E-mail: kanecominc@aol.com. Website: http://www.podiatryMGT.com. **Contact:** Martin Kruth, managing editor. Publisher: Scott C. Borowsky. Editor: Barry Block, DPM, J.D. Magazine published 9 times/year for practicing podiatrists. "Aims to help the doctor of podiatric medicine to build a bigger, more successful practice, to conserve and invest his money, to keep him posted on the economic, legal and sociological changes that affect him." Estab. 1982. Circ. 13,000. Pays on publication. Byline given. Buys first North American serial and second serial (reprint) rights. Submit seasonal material 4 months in advance. Accepts simultaneous submissions. Reports in 2 weeks. Sample copy for $3 and 9×12 SAE. Writer's guidelines for #10 SASE.

Nonfiction: General interest (taxes, investments, estate planning, recreation, hobbies); how-to (establish and collect fees, practice management, organize office routines, supervise office assistants, handle patient relations); interview/profile about interesting or well-known podiatrists; and personal experience. "These subjects are the mainstay of the magazine, but offbeat articles and humor are always welcome." Send tax and financial articles to Martin Kruth, 5 Wagon Hill Lane, Avon CT 06001. **Buys 25 mss/year.** Query. Length: 1,000-2,500 words. **Pays $150-600.**

Reprints: Send photocopy of article. Pays 33% of amount paid for an original article.

Photos: State availability of photos. Pays $15 for b&w contact sheet. Buys one-time rights.

N $ $ PRACTICE STRATEGIES, American Optometric Association, 243 N. Lindbergh Blvd., St. Louis MO 63141. (314)991-4100. Fax: (314)991-4101. E-mail: OptoEcon@aol.com. **Contact:** Gene Mitchell, senior editor. **90% freelance written.** Monthly section of the AOA News, tabloid newspaper, covering practice management for optometrists. Estab. 1991. Circ. 29,000. **Pays on acceptance.** Publishes ms an average of 3 months after acceptance. Buys first, second serial (reprint) and all rights, or makes work-for-hire assignments. Editorial lead time 3 months. Submit seasonal material 5 months in advance. Reports in 2 weeks on queries; 1 month on mss. Sample copy for $5. Writer's guidelines for #10 SASE.

Nonfiction: "Feature articles with strong 'how-to' slant that cover nuts and bolts of specific issues: business/financial management, marketing, staff management, dispensing, patient communication, managed care, comanagement of refractive surgery, insurance payor issues, computers, computerized equipment and other technology, office management, office design, etc. Articles should offer practical resources/information. Style is conversational, not stuffy or overly clinical. Stories that promote products not accepted." How-to (practice/business management), opinion, photo feature, technical. **Buys 30 mss/year.** Query with published clips. Length: 1,200-3,000 words. **Pays $200-600 for asssigned articles; $80-250 for unsolicited articles.** Sometimes pays expenses of writers on assignment.

Photos: State availability of photos with submissions. Reviews contact sheets, transparencies, prints. Captions, model releases, identification of subjects required. Buys one-time or all rights.

Columns/Departments: Computing (software and computerized ophthalmic equipment), 500-1,200 words. Query with published clips. **Pays $100-250.**

Fillers: Anecdotes, facts, gags to be illustrated by cartoonist, short humor. **Buys 3/year.** Length: 10-50 words. **Pays $0-25.**

Tips: "Our readers are practicing professionals who need in-depth exploration of specific practice management topics. Avoid overly general or elementary articles, e.g., "Top Ten Ways to Market your Practice." We usually avoid 'generalist' freelancers in favor of writers who've specialized in a given area or areas. Submit letter of inquiry and/or article outline. Show that you've read the magazine and have made an effort to understand readers' needs and the profession of optometry."

$ $ STITCHES, The Journal of Medical Humour, 16787 Warden Ave., R.R. #3, Newmarket, Ontario L3Y 4W1 Canada. (905)853-1884. Fax: (905)853-6565. **Contact:** Simon Hally, editor. **90% freelance written.** Magazine published 11 times/year covering humor for physicians. "*Stitches* is read primarily by physicians in Canada. Stories with a medical slant are particularly welcome, but we also run a lot of non-medical material. It must be funny and, of course, brevity is the soul of wit." Estab. 1990. Circ. 43,000. Pays on publication. Publishes ms 6 months after acceptance. Byline given. Offers 50% kill fee. Buys first North American serial rights and first electronic rights. Editorial lead time 2 months. Submit seasonal material 3 months in advance. Reports in 6 weeks on queries; 2 months on mss. Sample copy free.

Nonfiction: Humor, personal experience. **Buys 20 mss/year.** Send complete ms. Length: 100-2,000 words. **Pays $35-750 (Canadian).**

Fiction: Humorous. **Buys 30 mss/year.** Send complete ms. Length: 100-2,000 words. **Pays $35-750 (Canadian).**

Poetry: Humorous. **Buys 5 poems/year.** Submit maximum 5 poems. Length: 2-20 lines. **Pays $20-100.**

Fillers: Gags to be illustrated by cartoonist, short humor. Pay negotiable.

Tips: "Due to the nature of humorous writing, we have to see a completed manuscript, rather than a query, to determine if it is suitable for us. Along with a short cover letter, that's all we require."

$ $ STRATEGIC HEALTH CARE MARKETING, Health Care Communications, 11 Heritage Lane, P.O. Box 594, Rye NY 10580. (914)967-6741. E-mail: healthcomm@aol.com. **Contact:** Michele von Dambrowski, editor. **90% freelance written.** Works with published/established writers only. Monthly newsletter covering health care marketing and management in a wide range of settings including hospitals and medical group practices, home health services and managed care organizations. Emphasis is on strategies and techniques employed within the health care field and relevant applications from other service industries. Estab. 1984. Pays on publication. Publishes ms an average of 2 months after acceptance. Byline given. Offers 25% kill fee. Buys first North American serial rights. Reports in 1 month. Sample copy for 9×12 SAE with 3 first-class stamps. Guidelines sent with sample copy only.

- *Strategic Health Care Marketing* is specifically seeking writers with expertise/contacts in managed care, integrated delivery systems and demand management.

Nonfiction: How-to, interview/profile, new product, technical. "Preferred format for feature articles is the case history approach to solving marketing problems. Crisp, almost telegraphic style." **Buys 50 mss/year.** Query with published clips. No unsolicited mss. Length: 700-3,000 words. **Pays $100-500.** Sometimes pays expenses of writers on assignment with prior authorization.

Photos: State availability of photos with submissions. (Photos, unless necessary for subject explanation, are rarely used.) Reviews contact sheets. Offers $10-30/photo. Captions and model releases required. Buys one-time rights.

Tips: "Writers with prior experience on business beat for newspaper or newsletter will do well. We require a sophisticated, indepth knowledge of health care reform issues and impact. This is not a consumer publication—the writer with knowledge of both health care and marketing will excel. Interviews or profiles are most open to freelancers. Absolutely no unsolicited manuscripts; any received will be returned or discarded unread."

$ $ $ $ UNIQUE OPPORTUNITIES, The Physician's Resource, U O Inc., Suite 1236, 455 S. Fourth Ave., Louisville KY 40202. Fax: (502)587-0848. E-mail: bettuo@aol.com. **Contact:** Bett Coffman, associate editor. Editor: Mollie Vento Hudson. **45% freelance written.** Bimonthly magazine covering physician relocation and career development. "Published for physicians interested in a new career opportunity. It offers physicians useful information and first-hand experiences to guide them in making informed decisions concerning their first or next career opportunity. It provides regular features and columns about specific aspects of the search process." Estab. 1991. Circ. 80,000 physicians. **Pays on acceptance.** Publishes ms an average of 2 months after acceptance. Byline given. Offers 33% kill fee. Buys first North American serial rights. Editorial lead time 3 months. Submit seasonal material 6 months in advance. Reports in 2 months on queries. Sample copy for 9×12 SAE with 6 first-class stamps. Writer's guidelines for #10 SASE.

Nonfiction: Opinion (on issues relating to physician recruitment), practice options and information of interest to physicians in career transition. **Buys 12 mss/year.** Query with published clips. Length: 1,500-3,500 words. **Pays $750-2,000.** Sometimes pays expenses of writers on assignment.

Photos: State availability of photos with submission. Negotiates payment individually. Model releases and identification of subjects required. Buys one-time rights.

Columns/Departments: Remarks (opinion from physicians and industry experts on physician career issues), 500-1,000 words; Physician Profiles (doctors with unusual or interesting careers), 500 words. **Buys up to 6 mss/year.** Query with published clips. **Pays $250-500.**

Tips: "Submit queries via letter with ideas for articles that directly pertain to physician career issues, such as specific or unusual practice opportunities, relocation or practice establishment subjects, etc. Feature articles are most open to freelancers. Physician sources are most important, with tips and advice from both the physicians and business experts. Physicians like to know what other physicians think and do and appreciate suggestions from other business people."

MUSIC

Publications for musicians and for the recording industry are listed in this section. Other professional performing arts publications are classified under Entertainment and the Arts. Magazines featuring music industry news for the general public are listed in the Consumer Entertainment and Music sections. (Markets for songwriters can be found in *Songwriter's Market*, Writer's Digest Books.)

N **CLAVIER MAGAZINE**, The Instrumentalist Publishing Co., 200 Northfield Rd., Northfield IL 60093. Fax: (847)446-6263. **Contact:** Judy Nelson, editor. **1% freelance written.** "Published 10 times/year featuring practical information on teaching subjects that are of value to studio piano teachers and interviews with major artists." Estab. 1937. Circ. 16,000. Pays on publication. Publishes ms an average of 18 months after acceptance. Byline given. Buys all rights. Submit seasonal material 6 months in advance. Reports in 6 weeks. Sample copy and writer's guidelines free.
Nonfiction: "Articles should be of interest and direct practical value to concert pianists, harpsichordists and organists who are teachers of piano, organ, harpsichord and electronic keyboards. Topics may include pedagogy, technique, performance, ensemble playing and accompanying." Length: 10-12 double-spaced pages. Pays "a small honorarium."
Reprints: "Occasionally we will reprint a chapter in a book."
Photos: Send photos with submission. Reviews negatives, 2¼×2¼ transparencies and 3×5 prints. Offers no additional payment for photos accepted with ms. Identification of subjects required. Buys all rights.

N $ **INTERNATIONAL BLUEGRASS**, International Bluegrass Music Association, 207 E. Second St., Owensboro KY 42303. (502)684-9025. **Contact:** Dan Hays and Nancy Cardwell, editors. **10% freelance written.** Bimonthly newsletter. "We are the business publication for the bluegrass music industry. IBMA believes that our music has growth potential. We are interested in hard news and features concerning how to reach that potential and how to conduct business more effectively." Estab. 1985. Circ. 4,500. Pays on publication. Publishes ms an average of 2 months after acceptance. Byline given. Not copyrighted. Buys one-time rights. Submit seasonal/holiday material 4 months in advance. Accepts simultaneous submissions. Reports in 1 month on queries. Sample copy for 6×9 SAE with 2 first-class stamps.
Nonfiction: Book excerpts, essays, how-to (conduct business effectively within bluegrass music), new product and opinion. No interview/profiles of performers (rare exceptions) or fans. **Buys 6 mss/year.** Query with or without published clips. Length: 300-1,200 words. Unsolicited mss are not accepted, but unsolicited news about the industry is accepted. **Pays up to $150/article for assigned pieces.** Buys 1-2 mss/issue.
Reprints: Send photocopy of article and information about when and where the article previously appeared. Does not pay for reprints.
Photos: Send photos with submission. Reviews 5×8 prints. Offers no additional payment for photos accepted with ms. Captions and identification of subjects required. Buys one-time rights.
Columns/Departments: Staff written.
Fillers: Anecdotes, facts, newsbreaks.
Tips: "The easiest break-in is to submit an article about an organizational member of IBMA—such as a bluegrass associate, instrument manufacturer or dealer, or performing venue. We're interested in a slant strongly toward the business end of bluegrass music. We're especially looking for material dealing with audience development and how to book bluegrass bands outside of the existing market."

N **MUSIC CONNECTION, The West Coast Music Trade Magazine**, Music Connection, Inc., 4731 Laurel Canyon Blvd., North Hollywood CA 91607. (818)755-0101. Fax: (818)755-0102. E-mail: muscon@earthlink.net. Website: http://www.musicconnection.com. **Contact:** Jeremy M. Helfgot, associate editor. Senior Editor: Steven P. Wheeler. **50% freelance written.** "Biweekly magazine geared toward working musicians and/or other industry professionals, including producers/engineers/studio staff, managers, agents, publicists, music publishers, record company staff, concert promoters/bookers, etc." Estab. 1977. Circ. 70,000. Pays on publication. Publishes ms an average of 2 months after acceptance. Byline given. Kill fee varies. Buys all rights. Editorial lead time 2 months. Submit seasonal material 2 months in advance. Sample copy for $5. Writer's guidelines free.
Nonfiction: How-to (music industry related), interview/profile, new product, technical. Query with published clips. Length: 1,000-5,000 words. Pay varies. Sometimes pays expenses of writers on assignment.
Photos: State availability of photos with submission or send photos with submission. Reviews transparencies and prints. Negotiates payment individually. Identification of subjects required. Buys one-time rights.
Tips: "Articles must be informative music/music industry-related pieces, geared toward a trade-reading audience comprised mainly of musicians."

N **THE NEW YORK OPERA NEWSLETTER, The Classical Singer's Magazine**, P.O. Box 278, Maplewood NJ 07040. (973)348-9549. Fax: (973)378-2372. **Contact:** Ms. C.J. Williamson, editor. Monthly trade magazine covering classical singers. Estab. 1988. Circ. 4,000. Pays on publication. Publishes ms an average of 3 months after acceptance. Byline given. Offers 35% kill fee. Not copyrighted. Buys one-time rights or second serial (reprint) rights. Editorial lead time 3 months. Submit seasonal material 3 months in advance. Reports in 4 weeks on queries. Sample copy and writer's guidelines free.

Nonfiction: Book excerpts, expose (carefully done), how-to, humor, interview/profile, new product, personal experience, photo feature, religious, technical, travel. Editorial calendar available on request. "No reviews of performances until website goes up. No advertorial, agenda-tainted, complaints." Query with published clips. Length: 1,000-2,500 words. **Pays $50-100.** Sometimes pays expenses of writers on assignment.

Reprints: Accepts previously published submissions.

Photos: Send photos with submission. Negotiates payment individually. Captions required. Buys one time rights.

Tips: "*TNYON, The Classical Singer's Magazine*, is a 36+ page monthly magazine for singers, about singers and generally, by singers. Our purpose is to increase respect for the profession and to connect the classical singer to opportunities, information, and support. Non-singers are welcome to submit queries but will need singers as their source. We are not interested in fan-type interviews, but rather sideways interview with singers who are willing to share information with their peers."

N $ $ SONGWRITER MAGAZINE, P.O. Box 25044, Colorado Springs CO 80936-5044. (719)591-5866. **Contact:** Roberta Redford, editor. **75% freelance written.** Monthly trade magazine covering songwriting. "The purpose of *Songwriter Magazine* is to educate readers on the business and craft of songwriting. I'm looking for writers who can share their expertise on all aspects of songwriting from the first seeds of an idea, through the publishing and recording of the song. Most of our readers are at the beginning on intermediate stages of their careers and look to us for answers to all their questions. We're here to serve." Estab. 1998. Circ. 5,000. **Pays on acceptance.** Publishes ms an average of 3 months after acceptance. Byline given. Offers 20% kill fee. Buys first North American serial rights. Editorial lead time 4 months. Submit seasonal material 8 months in advance. Accepts simultaneous submissions. Reports in 2-3 weeks on queries; 2 months on mss. Sample copy for $2.50; writer's guidelines for #10 SASE.

Nonfiction: Essays, how-to (contacts, record demo, etc . . .), humor, interview/profile (songwriters), new product (relating to songwriting/recording), opinion, personal experience. **Buys 80 mss/year.** Query with published clips. Length: 50-2,500 words. **Pays $200-500 for assigned articles; $25-350 for unsolicited articles.** Sometimes pays expenses for writers on assignment.

Photos: State availability of photos with submission. Reviews contact sheets. Negotiates payment individually. Identification of subjects required. Buys one time rights.

Columns and Departments: Book Report (books for songwriters), New Product Review (as relate to songwriting), all 250 words; Ad Lib (personal experience as a songwriter), 1,200-1,500 words. **Buys 36 mss/year.** Query for reviews or send complete ms for Ad Lib. **Pays $25-200.**

Fillers: Anecdotes, facts, gags to be illustrated by cartoonist, newsbreaks, short humor. **Buys 60/year.** Length: 50-250 words. **Pays $5-25.**

Tips: "Writers should have some experience in the music business. Our readers come to us for answers to all kinds of questions. Anticipate these and answer them clearly & concisely. We're always open to fresh ideas and new slants on old ideas. Good writing always has a place here."

$ SONGWRITER'S MONTHLY, The Stories Behind Today's Songs, 332 Eastwood Ave., Feasterville PA 19053. Phone/fax: (215)953-0952. E-mail: a1foster@aol.com. **Contact:** Allen Foster, editor. **20% freelance written.** Monthly magazine covering songwriting. Estab. 1992. Circ. 2,500. **Pays on acceptance.** Publishes ms an average of 6 months after aceptance. Byline given. Offers 100% kill fee. Buys first rights or one-time rights. Editorial lead time 3 months. Submit seasonal material 6 months in advance. Reports in 2 weeks on queries, 1 month on mss. Sample copy free. Writer's guidelines for #10 SASE.

Nonfiction: How-to (write better songs, get a deal, etc.), technical. No interviews or reviews. **Buys 36 mss/year.** Query. Length: 300-800 words. **Pays $15.**

Reprints: Send information about when and where the article previously appeared. Pays approximately 60% of amount paid for an original article.

Photos: State availability of photos with submission. Reviews prints. Offers no additional payment for photos accepted with ms. Identification of subjects required.

Fillers: Anecdotes, facts, newsbreaks, short humor. **Buys 60/year.** Length: 25-300 words. **Pays $0-5.**

Tips: "Currently *Songwriter's Monthly* is interested in 500-800 'How-To' articles which deal with some aspect of songwriting or the music business. Be friendly. Be knowledgeable. Keep the focus of the article tight. I will take a fresh idea that is poorly written over a brilliantly written piece that rehashes old territory every time. There is a lot of false information floating around, it's easy to see if you don't know your topic, so please write from honest experience or research. Again, I will publish raw writing from a songwriter before I publish pristine writing from someone with no 'hands on' experience."

OFFICE ENVIRONMENT AND EQUIPMENT

OFFICEPRO®, (formerly The Secretary®), Stratton Publishing & Marketing, Inc., 2800 Shirlington Rd., Suite 706, Arlington VA 22206. Fax: (703)379-4561. E-mail: officepromag@strattonpub.com. Website: http://www.psi.org. Pub-

lisher: Debra J. Stratton. **Contact:** Angela Hickman Brady, managing editor. **90% freelance written unpaid.** Magazine published 9 times/year covering the administrative support profession. Estab. 1946. Circ. 40,000. Publishes ms an average of 6-18 months after acceptance. Byline given. Buys first rights. Editorial lead time 3 months. Submit seasonal material 5 months in advance. Accepts simultaneous submissions. For electronic (IBM) PC-compatible, Word Perfect or ASCII on disk. Reports in 2-3 months. Sample copy $3 through (816)891-6600 ext. 235. Writer's guidelines free.
Nonfiction: Book excerpts, general interest, how-to (buy and use office equipment, advance career, etc.), interview/profile, new product, personal experience. Query. Length: 2,000 words. **Pays $50 or more for assigned articles; $0 minimum for unsolicited articles.** Pays expenses of writers on assignment.
Reprints: Send typed ms with rights for sale noted (on disk, preferred) and information about when and where the article previously appeared.
Photos: Send photos with submission. Reviews transparencies and prints. Negotiable payment for photos accepted with ms. Identification of subjects required. Buys one-time rights.
Columns/Departments: Product News (new office products, non promotional), 500 words maximum; On The Run (general interest—career, woman's, workplace issues), 500 words maximum; Virtual Office, 800 words; Office Entrepreneur, 800 words; Electronic Office Suite, 800 words. Send complete ms.
Tips: "We're in search of articles addressing travel; meeting and event-planning; office recycling programs; computer hardware and software; workplace issues; international business topics. Must be appropriate to office professionals."

PAPER

$ $ THE PAPER STOCK REPORT, News and Trends of the Paper Recycling Markets, McEntee Media Corp., 13727 Holland Rd., Cleveland OH 44142. (216)362-7979. E-mail: mcenteemedia@compuserve.com. Website: http://ourworld.compuserve.com/homepages/mcenteemedia. **Contact:** Ken McEntee, editor. Biweekly newsletter covering "market trends, news in the paper recycling industry. Audience is interested in new innovative markets, applications for recovered scrap paper as well as new laws and regulations impacting recycling." Estab. 1990. Circ. 2,000. Pays on publication. Publishes ms an average of 1 month after acceptance. Byline given. Buys first or all rights. Editorial lead time 2 months. Submit seasonal material 2 months in advance. Accepts simultaneous submissions. Reports in 1 month on queries. Sample copy for #10 SAE with 55¢ postage.
Nonfiction: Book excerpts, essays, exposé, general interest, historical/nostalgic, interview/profile, new product, opinion, technical, all related to paper recycling. **Buys 0-13 mss/year.** Send complete ms. Length: 250-1,000 words. **Pays $50-250 for assigned articles; $25-250 for unsolicited articles.** Pays expenses of writers on assignment.
Reprints: Accepts previously published submissions.
Photos: State availability of photos with submissions. Reviews contact sheets. Negotiates payment individually. Identification of subjects required.
Tips: "Article must be valuable to readers in terms of presenting new market opportunities or cost-saving measures."

N $ $ PULP & PAPER CANADA, Southam Inc., Suite 410, 3300 Côte Vertu, St. Laurent, Quebec H4R 2B7 Canada. (514)339-1399. Fax: (514)339-1396. Publisher: Mark Yerbary. **Contact:** Graeme Rodden, editor. **5% freelance written.** Prefers to work with published/established writers. Monthly magazine. Estab. 1903. Circ. 10,361. Pays on publication. Publishes ms "as soon as possible" after acceptance. Byline given. Negotiates kill fee. Buys first North American serial rights. Reports in 1 month. Free sample copy.
Nonfiction: How-to (related to processes and procedures in the industry); interview/profile (of Canadian leaders in pulp and paper industry); technical (relevant to modern pulp and/or paper industry). No fillers, short industry news items, or product news items. **Buys 5 mss/year.** Query first with published clips or send complete ms. Articles with photographs (b&w glossy) or other good quality illustrations will get priority review. Length: 1,200 words maximum (with photos). **Pays $160 (Canadian)/published page including photos, graphics, charts, etc.**
Tips: "Any return postage must be in either Canadian stamps or International Reply Coupons *only*."

$ $ RECYCLED PAPER NEWS, Independent Coverage of Environmental Issues in the Paper Industry, McEntee Media Corporation, 13727 Holland Rd., Brook Park OH 44142. (216)362-7979. Fax: (216)362-6553. E-mail: mcenteemedia@compuserve.com. Website: http://ourworld.compuserve.com/homepages/mcenteemedia. **Contact:** Ken McEntee, editor. **10% freelance written.** Monthly newsletter. "We are interested in any news impacting the paper recycling industry as well as other environmental issues in the paper industry, i.e., water/air pollution, chlorine-free paper, forest conservation, etc., with special emphasis on new laws and regulations." Estab. 1990. Pays on publication. Publishes ms an average of 2 months after acceptance. Buys first or all rights. Editorial lead time 1 month. Submit seasonal material 1 month in advance. Accepts simultaneous submissions. Reports in 2 months. Sample copy for 9×12 SAE and 55¢ postage. Writer's guidelines for #10 SASE.
Nonfiction: Book excerpts, essays, interview/profile, new product, opinion, personal experience, technical, new business, legislation, regulation, business expansion. **Buys 0-5 mss/year.** Query with published clips. Length: 100-5,000 words. **Pays $10-500.** Pays writers with contributor copies or other premiums by prior agreement.
Reprints: Accepts previously published submissions.
Columns/Departments: Query with published clips. **Pays $10-500.**
Tips: "We appreciate leads on local news regarding recycling or composting, i.e., new facilities or businesses, new

laws and regulations, unique programs, situations that impact supply and demand for recyclables, etc. International developments are also of interest."

PLUMBING, HEATING, AIR CONDITIONING AND REFRIGERATION

N $ INDOOR COMFORT NEWS, Institute of Heating & Air Conditioning Industries, Inc., 454 W. Broadway, Glendale CA 91204. (818)551-1555. Fax: (818)551-1115. **Contact:** Chris Callard, editor. **10% freelance written.** Monthly tabloid. "We cover the heating, cooling, ventilating and refrigeration industries in Washington, Oregon, California, Nevada, Arizona and Texas. Our audience is made up of contractors, engineers and service technicians." Estab. 1955. Circ. 20,000. Pays on publication. Publishes ms an average of 3 months after acceptance. Byline given. Buys one-time rights. Editorial lead time 1 month. Submit seasonal material 3 months in advance. Reports in 2 weeks on queries; 1 month on mss. Sample copy for 8×10 SAE and $1.25 postage.
Nonfiction: Book excerpts, how-to (equipment, sales, etc.), interview/profile, new product, technical. **Buys 25-30 mss/year.** Query with published clips. Length: 700-1,500 words. **Pays $75-150.** Sometimes pays expenses of writers on assignment.
Photos: Send photos with submission. Reviews 3×5 prints. Offers no additional payment for photos accepted with ms. Captions and identification of subjects required. Buys one-time rights.
Tips: "We're looking for specific coverage of industry events and people in the geographic areas we cover. Know the industry. Send a query rather than making original contact via phone."

N $ $ REFRIGERATION SERVICE & CONTRACTING MAGAZINE, Business News Publishing, 999 Plaza Dr., Suite 675, Schaumburg IL 60173. (847)413-1323. Fax: (847)413-9030. E-mail: 103145.3653@compuserve.com. **Contact:** Peter Powell, editor. Managing Editor: Kelly Lindsey. **80% freelance written.** Monthly magazine featuring "technical, hands-on knowledge of heating, air conditioning and refrigeration service." Estab. 1933. Circ. 25,000. Pays on publication. Byline given. Editorial lead time 2 months. Submit seasonal material 4 months in advance. Accepts simultaneous submissions.
Nonfiction: How-to, new product, personal experience, technical. **Buys 4-5 mss/year.** Query. Length: 1,500-2,000 words. **Pays approximately 10¢/word.**
Reprints: Accepts previously published submissions.
Photos: State availability of photos with submission. Reviews contact sheets, negatives, transparencies and prints. Offers no additional payment for photos accepted with ms. Identification of subjects required.

PRINTING

$ $ $ AMERICAN INK MAKER, PTN Publishing, 445 Broad Hollow Rd., Melville NY 11747. (516)845-2700. **Contact:** Linda M. Casatelli, editor-in-chief. Associate Editor: Mary Waters. **80% freelance written.** Monthly magazine covering printing ink. Estab. 1922. Circ. 6,000. Pays on publication. Publishes ms an average of 2 months after acceptance. Byline given. Buys first rights. Editorial lead time 3 months. Accepts simultaneous submissions. Reports in 2 weeks on queries; 1 month on mss. Sample copy and writer's guidelines free.
Nonfiction: Interview/profile, technical. "No P.R./puff pieces." **Buys 30 mss/year.** Query. Length: 2,000-3,500 words. **Pays $400-800 for assigned articles; $300-500 for unsolicited articles.** Pays writers with contributor copies or other premiums for consultants wanting ads. Sometimes pays expenses of writers on assignment.
Photos: State availability of photos with submission. Reviews contact sheets, negatives, transparencies or prints. Offers no additional payment for photos accepted with ms. Captions and identification of subjects required. Buys one-time rights.
Columns/Departments: International News (segment of market), 1,500 words. **Buys 12-18 mss/year.** Query. **Pays $350-600.**
Fillers: Management. **Buys 4/year.** Length: 1,500-2,500 words. **Pays $300-500.**
Tips: "Offer to do an assigned piece as a trial."

N $ $ CANADIAN PRINTER, Maclean Hunter Ltd., 777 Bay St., Toronto, Ontario M5W 1A7 Canada. (416)596-2639. Fax: (416)596-5965. Editor: Catherine Wilson. **Contact:** Vincent Hempsall, associate editor. **20% freelance written.** Monthly magazine for printing and the allied industries. "*Canadian Printer* wants technical matter on graphic arts, printing, binding, typesetting, specialty production and trends in technology." Circ. 13,000. **Pays on acceptance.** Publishes ms an average of 1-3 months after acceptance. Byline given. Buys first North American serial rights. Reports in 6 months. Sample copy for 9×12 SAE with 2 IRCs.
Nonfiction: Technical. "We do not want U.S. plant articles—this is a Canadian magazine." **Buys 5-10 mss/year.** Query or send complete ms. Length: 400-1,600 words. **Pays 30¢/word (Canadian).** Pays expenses of writers on assignment "on prior arrangement."
Photos: Send photos with submission. Reviews 4×5 prints. Offers $50 (Canadian)/photo. Captions and identification

of subjects required. Buys one-time rights.

N $ $ IN-PLANT GRAPHICS, North American Publishing Co., 401 N. Broad St., Philadelphia PA 19108. Fax: (215)574-3321. E-mail: editor.ipg@napco.com. Website: http://www.ipgonline.com. **Contact:** Bob Neubauer, editor. **10% freelance written.** Monthly. "*In-Plant Graphics* features articles designed to help in-house printing departments increase productivity, save money and stay competitive. *IPG* features advances in graphic arts technology and shows in-plants how to put this technology to use. Our audience consists of print shop managers working for (non-print related) corporations (i.e., hospitals, insurance companies, publishers, non-profits), universities and government departments. They often oversee graphic design, prepress, printing, bindery and mailing departments." Estab. 1951. Circ. 34,600. Pays on publication. Publishes ms an average of 5 months after acceptance. Byline given. Buys first North American serial rights. Editorial lead time 2 months. Submit seasonal material 3 months in advance.

Nonfiction: New product (graphic arts), technical (graphic arts/printing/prepress). "Stories include: profiles of successful in-house printing operations (not commercial or quick printers); updates on graphic arts technology (new features, uses); reviews of major graphic arts and printing conferences (seminar and new equipment reviews)." No articles on desktop publishing software or design software. No Internet publishing articles. **Buys 5 mss/year.** Query with published clips. Length: 800-1,500 words. **Pays $150-250.** Pays writers with contributor copies or other premiums for consultants who agree to write just for exposure.

Photos: State availability of photos with submission. Reviews transparencies and prints. Negotiates payment individually. Captions and identification of subjects required. Buys one-time rights.

Tips: "To get published in *IPG*, writers must contact the editor with an idea in the form of a query letter that includes published writing samples. Writers who have covered the graphic arts in the past may be assigned stories for an agreed-upon fee. We don't want stories that tout only one vendor's products and serve as glorified commercials. All profiles must be well-balanced, covering a variety of issues. If you can tell us about an in-house printing operation that is doing innovative things, we will be interested."

PERSPECTIVES, International Publishing Management Association (IPMA), 1205 W. College St., Liberty MO 64068-3733. (816)781-1111. Fax: (816)781-2790. E-mail: laaron@ipma.org. Website: http://www.ipma.org. **Contact:** Beth Norman, editor. **40% freelance written.** Monthly trade newsletter covering "corporate print and mail departments are faced with competition from commercial printers and facilities management companies. Writers must be pro-insourcing and reflect that this industry is a profitable profession." Estab. 1986. Circ. 2,300; twice a year it reaches 5,000. Pays on publication. Publishes ms an average of 2 months after acceptance. Byline given. Buys all rights. Editorial lead time 2 months. Reports in 1 month. Sample copy for 9×12 SAE.

Nonfiction: Interview/profile, new product, technical, general management. Payment negotiated individually. Sometimes pays expenses of writers on assignment.

Reprints: Send photocopy of article and information about when and where the article previously appeared.

Photos: State availability of photos with submission. Reviews contact sheets, 5×7 prints. Offers no additional payment for photos accepted with ms. Captions required. Buys one-time rights.

Columns/Departments: Executive Insight (management, personnel how-tos, employment law), 650-1,500 words. **Buys 12 mss/year.** Query with published clips.

Tips: "A knowledge of the printing industry is helpful. Articles with concrete examples or company/individual profiles work best."

$ $ PRINT & GRAPHICS/PRINTING JOURNAL, 30 E. Padonia Rd., Suite 504, Timonium MD 21093. (410)628-7826. Fax: (410)628-7829. E-mail: spencecom1@aol.com. Publisher: Kaj Spencer. **Contact:** Henry Mortimer, editor. **10% freelance written.** Eager to work with new/unpublished writers. Monthly tabloid of the commercial printing industry for owners and executives of graphic arts firms. Estab. 1980. Circ. 20,000. **Pays on acceptance.** Publishes ms an average of 2 months after acceptance. Byline given. Buys one-time rights. Accepts simultaneous submissions. Reports in 2 months. Sample copy for $2.

Nonfiction: Book excerpts, historical/nostalgic, how-to, interview/profile, new product, opinion, personal experience, photo feature, technical. "All articles should relate to graphic arts management or production." **Buys 20 mss/year.** Query with published clips. Length: 750-2,000 words. **Pays $100-250.**

Reprints: Send photocopy of article and information about when and where the article previously appeared. Pays $150 flat fee. Publishes trade book excerpts.

Photos: State availability of photos. Pays $25-75 for 5×7 b&w prints. Captions, identification of subjects required.

$ $ QUICK PRINTING, PTN Publishing, 445 Broadhollow Rd., Melville NY 11747. (516)845-2700. Fax: (516)249-5774. E-mail: ptngrafnet@aol.com. Publisher: William Lewis. Managing Editor: Liz Fedorowicz. **Contact:** Gerald Walsh, editor. **5% freelance written.** Monthly magazine covering the quick printing industry. "Our articles tell quick printers how they can be more profitable. We want art or photography to illustrate points made." Estab. 1977. Circ. 62,000. Pays on publication. Publishes ms an average of 4 months after acceptance. Byline given. Buys first North American serial or all rights. Submit seasonal material 6 months in advance. Reports in 3 months. Sample copy for $5 and 9×12 SAE with 7 first-class stamps. Writer's guidelines for #10 SASE.

Nonfiction: How-to (on marketing products better or accomplishing more with equipment); new product; opinion (on the quick printing industry); personal experience (from which others can learn); technical (on printing). *No generic* *business articles*, or articles on larger printing applications. **Buys 5-10 mss/year.** Send complete ms. Length: 1,250-2,000 words. **Pays $150 and up.**

Photos: State availability of photos with submission. Reviews transparencies, prints. Offers no additional payment for photos accepted with ms. Captions and identification of subjects required.

Tips: "The use of digital publishing systems by quick printers is of increasing interest. Show a knowledge of the industry. Try visiting your local quick printer for an afternoon to get to know about us. When your articles make a point, back it up with examples, statistics, and dollar figures. We need good material in all areas, including equipment/software user profiles. Technical articles are most needed, but they must be accurate. No promotional pieces for a certain industry supplier."

$ $ SERIF, THE MAGAZINE OF TYPE & TYPOGRAPHY, Quixote Digital Typography, 1105 W. Chicago Ave., Suite 156, Oak Park IL 60302. (312)803-0698. Fax: (312)953-3679. E-mail: serif@quixote.com. **Contact:** D.A. Hosek, editor. **80-100% freelance written.** Quarterly magazine "covering the full spectrum of type and typography from classical to radical." Estab. 1994. Circ. 2,000. Pays on publication. Byline given. Buys first North American serial rights and the option to reprint in book form. Editorial lead time 6 months. Accepts simultaneous and previously published submissions. Sample copy for 9×12 SASE and 6 first-class stamps. Writer's guidelines for #10 SASE.

Nonfiction: Book excerpts, essays, exposé, general interest, historical/nostalgic, how-to, humor, interview/profile, new product, opinion, personal experience, photo feature, technical. **Buys 12 mss/year.** Send complete ms. Length: 500-5,000 words. **Pays 10¢/word.**

Photos: Send photos with submission. Reviews negatives and transparencies. Offers no additional payment for photos accepted with ms. Captions required. Buys one-time rights.

Tips: "Just because we haven't published something similar is no indication of disinterest."

PROFESSIONAL PHOTOGRAPHY

Journals for professional photographers are listed in this section. Magazines for the general public interested in photography techniques are in the Consumer Photography section. (For listings of markets for freelance photography use *Photographer's Market*, Writer's Digest Books.)

$ THE PHOTO REVIEW, 301 Hill Ave., Langhorne PA 19047-2819. (215)757-8921. Fax: (215)757-6421. E-mail: photorev@libertynet.org. **Contact:** Stephen Perloff, editor. **50% freelance written.** Quarterly magazine on photography with reviews, interviews and articles on art photography. Estab. 1976. Circ. 2,500. Pays on publication. Publishes ms an average of 3 months after acceptance. Byline given. Buys one-time rights. Accepts simultaneous submissions. Reports in 1 month on queries; 2 months on mss. Sample copy for 9×12 SAE with 6 first-class stamps. Writer's guidelines for #10 SASE.

Nonfiction: Essays, historical/nostalgic, interview/profile, opinion. No how-to articles. **Buys 10-15 mss/year.** Query. **Pays $25-200.**

Reprints: Send tearsheet, photocopy or typed ms with rights for sale noted and information about when and where the article previously appeared. Payment varies.

Photos: Send photos with submission. Reviews 8×10 prints. Offers no additional payment for photos accepted with ms. Captions and identification of subjects required. Buys one-time rights.

$ $ PHOTOGRAPHIC PROCESSING, Cygnus Publishing, 445 Broad Hollow Rd., Melville NY 11747. (516)845-2700. Fax: (516)845-2797. E-mail: photoprocessing@erols.com. Website: http://www.labsonline.com. **Contact:** Bill Schiffner, editor. **30% freelance written.** Monthly magazine covering photographic (commercial/minilab) and electronic processing markets. Estab. 1965. Circ. 23,000. Pays on publication. Publishes ms an average of 4 months after acceptance. Byline given. Offers $75 kill fee. Editorial lead time 3 months. Submit seasonal material 3 months in advance. Accepts simultaneous submissions. Sample copy and writer's guidelines free.

Nonfiction: How-to, interview/profile, new product, photo processing/digital imaging features. **Buys 30-40 mss/year.** Query with published clips. Length: 1,500-2,200 words. **Pays $250-350 for assigned articles; $200-300 for unsolicited articles.**

Photos: Send photos with submission. Reviews 4×5 transparencies, 4×6 prints. Offers no additional payment for photos accepted with ms. Captions required. Buys one-time rights. Looking for digitally manipulated covers.

Columns/Departments: Surviving in the 90s (business articles offering tips to labs on how make their businesses run better), 1,500-1,800 words; Business Side (getting more productivity out of your lab). **Buys 10 mss/year.** Query with published clips. **Pays $150-250.**

N $ $ PHOTOMEDIA MAGAZINE, For Serious Creators and Users of Photography, The Photomedia Group, Inc., 19019 Corliss Ave. N, Seattle WA 98133. (206)364-7068. Fax: (206)364-7931. Website: http://www.photomediagroup.com. **Contact:** Editor. **80% freelance written.** Quarterly trade magazine, excluding summer quarter, covering photography, digital imaging. "The only regional publication of its sort in the country. *Photomedia* is a 4-color gloss, 10×13 magazine targeting serious creators and users of photography with news and features about photography and

photographers. Northwest & west coast emphasis." Estab. 1988. Circ. 21,000. Pays 30 days after publication. Publishes ms an average of 2 months after acceptance. Byline given. Buys first rights. Editorial lead time 2 months. Submit seasonal material 2 months in advance. Accepts simultaneous submissions. Reports in 1 month on queries and mss. Sample copy for 9×12 SASE and 7 first-class stamps; writer's guidelines for #10 SASE.
Nonfiction: General interest, how-to, humor, inspirational, interview/profile, new product, photo features, technical, travel. All with photography emphasis. **Buys 25 mss/year.** Query with published clips. Length: 700-2,500 words. **Pays $100-350 for assigned articles only.** Sometimes pays expenses of writers on assignment.
Photos: State availability of photos with submission. Reviews transparencies (35mm) and prints (5×7). Offers no additional payment for photos accepted with ms. Captions required. Buys one-time rights.
Columns and Departments: Destinations (locations of photography interest), 1,500 words; Market (technical product solutions), 1,000 words. **Buys 9 mss/year.** Query with published clips. **Pays $100-250.**
Tips: Write for guidelines with SASE. Follow query guidelines. "Do not e-mail or fax requests (or call)."

N $ $ TODAY'S PHOTOGRAPHER INTERNATIONAL, American Image Press Inc., P.O. Box 777, Lewisville NC 27023. (336)945-9867. Fax: (336)945-3711. Website: http://www.aipress.com. **Contact:** Vonda H. Blackburn, editor. **100% freelance written.** Bimonthly; "The make money with your camera magazine." Estab. 1984. Circ. 93,000. Pays on publication. Publishes ms an average of 4 months after acceptance. Byline given. Buys simultaneous rights. Editorial lead time 4 months. Submit seasonal material 8 months in advance. Accepts simultaneous submissions. Reports in 1 month on queries; 2 months on mss. Sample copy for $3. Writer's guidelines free.
Nonfiction: How freelance photographers make money. How-to (make money with your camera). Nothing outside making money with a camera. Query. Length: 800-2,000 words. **Pays $50-200.**
Reprints: Accepts previously published submissions.
Photos: State availability of photos with submission. Reviews contact sheets, transparencies and prints. Offers no additional payment for photos accepted with ms. Captions, model releases and identification of subjects required. Buys one-time rights.
Columns/Departments: Query with published clips.

REAL ESTATE

$ $ AFFORDABLE HOUSING FINANCE, Business Communication Services, 657 Mission St., Suite 502, San Francisco CA 94105. (415)546-7255. Fax: (415)546-0954. E-mail: ahf@housingfinance.com. Website: http://www.housingfinance.com. Editor: Andre Shashaty. **Contact:** Robert Freedman, associate editor. **20% freelance written.** Monthly magazine. "We are a nuts-and-bolts magazine written for developers of affordable housing." Estab. 1992. Circ. 9,000. **Pays on acceptance.** Publishes ms an average of 1 month after acceptance. Byline given. Offers 50% kill fee. Buys all rights including electronic rights. Accepts simultaneous submissions. Reports in 1 month. Sample copy for 9×12 SAE with $2.16 postage. Writer's guidelines free.
Nonfiction: How-to, interview/profile (developer or financier), new product (new financing services), case studies of innovative affordable housing projects. Special issues: Rehab, Renovation and Repositioning, seniors housing, and tax exempt bond financing. "We have a very knowledgeable reader base in terms of housing finance—articles need to have hard news angle and skip the basics. Not generally interested in articles aimed at realtors or home buyers." **Buys 10-20 mss/year.** Query with published clips. Length: 500-2,000. **Pays 25-50¢/word.** Pays expenses of writers on assignment.
Reprints: Accepts previously published submissions. Payment varies.
Photos: State availability of photos with submission. Reviews prints. Offers additional payment for photos accepted with ms. Captions required. Buys all rights.
Tips: "Best to see sample copy before submitting. Writers with a strong background in business writing are welcome to query."

$ $ AREA DEVELOPMENT MAGAZINE, Sites and Facility Planning, Halcyon Business Publications, Inc., 400 Post Ave., Westbury NY 11590. (516)338-0900. Fax: (516)338-0100. E-mail: Gerriarea@aol.com. Website: www.area-development.com. Managing Editor: Pam Karr. **Contact:** Geraldine Gambale, editor. **80% freelance written.** Prefers to work with published/established writers. Monthly magazine covering corporate facility planning and site selection for industrial chief executives worldwide. Estab. 1965. Circ. 42,000. Pays on publication. Publishes ms an average of 2 months after acceptance. Byline given. Buys all rights. Reports in 3 months. Free sample copy. Writer's guidelines for #10 SASE.

Nonfiction: How-to (experiences in site selection and all other aspects of corporate facility planning); historical (if it deals with corporate facility planning); interview (corporate executives and industrial developers); and related areas of site selection and facility planning such as taxes, labor, government, energy, architecture and finance. **Buys 60 mss/year.** Query. Length: 800-1,200 words. **Pays 25¢/word.** Sometimes pays expenses of writers on assignment.
Photos: State availability of photos with query. Reviews transparencies. Captions, identification preferred. Negotiates payment individually.

$ $ CANADIAN REALTOR NEWS, The Canadian Real Estate Association, 344 Slater St., 1600 Canada Building, Ottawa, Ontario K1R 7Y3 Canada. (613)237-7111. Fax: (613)234-2567. E-mail: jmccarthy@crea.ca. **Contact:** James McCarthy, editor. **10-30% freelance written.** Monthly tabloid (10 times a year) for licensed real estate professionals. Estab. 1955. Circ. 72,000. Pays on publication. Publishes ms an average of 1 month after acceptance. Byline given. Buys one-time rights and electronic rights for website. Editorial lead time 1 month. Sample copy for SAE.
Nonfiction: How-to (sell/manage real estate sales), interview/profile. Query. Length: 400-1,000 words. **Pays $200-500.** Sometimes pays expenses of writers on assignment.
Reprints: Accepts previously published submissions (except from competitors).
Photos: Negotiates payment individually. Identification of subjects required. Buys one-time rights. Reproduction with credit (not for profit).
Tips: "Call with suggested topics."

$ $ $ $ COMMERCIAL INVESTMENT REAL ESTATE JOURNAL, Commercial Investment Real Estate Institute, 430 N. Michigan Ave., Suite 800, Chicago IL 60611-4092. (312)321-4460. Fax: (312)321-4530. E-mail: csimpson@cirei.com. Website: http://www.ccim.com. **Contact:** Catherine Simpson, editor/publisher. **10% freelance written.** Bimonthly magazine. "*CIERJ* offers practical articles on current trends and business development ideas for commercial investment real estate practitioners." Estab. 1982. Circ. 11,000. **Pays on acceptance.** Publishes ms an average of 4 months after acceptance. Byline given. Offers 25% kill fee. Buys all rights. Editorial lead time 4 months. Submit seasonal material 4 months in advance. Reports in 2 weeks on queries; 1 month on mss. Sample copy for 9×12 SAE with 5 first-class stamps. Writer's guidelines for #10 SASE.
Nonfiction: Book excerpts, how-to, personal experience, technical. **Buys 6-8 mss/year.** Query with published clips. Length: 2,000-3,500 words. **Pays $1,000-2,000.** Sometimes pays expenses of writers on assignment.
Photos: Send photos with submission. Reviews prints. Offers no additional payment for photos accepted with ms. Buys all rights.
Tips: "Always query first with a detailed outline and published clips. Authors should have a background in writing on real estate or business subjects."

$ $ THE COOPERATOR, The Co-op and Condo Monthly, Manhattan Cooperator Publications, Inc., 301 E. 45th St., 17E, New York NY 10017. (212)697-1318. Fax: (212)682-7369. E-mail: diana@cooperator.com. **Contact:** Diana Mosher, managing editor. Executive Editor: Victoria Chesler. **20% freelance written.** Monthly tabloid covering real estate. "*The Cooperator* covers condominium and cooperative issues in New York and beyond. It is read by unit owners and shareholders, board members and managing agents. We have just become a national publication and are interested in receiving articles from states outside of New York." Estab. 1980. Circ 60,000. Pays on publication. Publishes ms an average of 3 months after acceptance. Byline given. Buys all rights and makes work-for-hire assignments. Submit seasonal material 3 months in advance. Reports in 2 weeks on queries. Sample copy free. Writer's guidelines not available.
Nonfiction: Interview/profile, new product, personal experience; all related to co-op and condo ownership. No submissions without queries. **Buys 20 mss/year.** Query with published clips. Length: 1,000-2,000 words. **Pays $150-250.** Sometimes pays expenses of writers on assignment.
Photos: State availability of photos with submission. Reviews contact sheets, negatives, transparencies and prints. Negotiates payment individually. Captions and identification of subjects required. Rights purchased vary.
Columns/Departments: Management profile (profile of prominent management company); Building finance (investment and financing issues); Buying and selling (market issues, etc.), all 1,500 words. Buys 20 mss/year. Query with published clips. Pays $150-250.
Tips: "You must have experience doing journalistic reporting, especially real estate, business, legal or financial. Must have published clips to send in with résumé and query."

THE DEALMAKER, TKO, P.O. Box 2630, Mercerville NJ 08690. (609)587-6200. Fax: (609)587-3511. E-mail: deal.makers@property.com. **Contact:** Ann O'Neal, editor. Managing Editor: Chris Gel. **10% freelance written.** Weekly newsletter covering "commercial real estate brokers, developers, management companies and investors." Estab. 1979. Circ. 6,100. Pays on publication. Publishes ms an average of 2 months after acceptance. Byline given. Offers 25% kill fee. Buys first North American serial rights. Editorial lead time 2 months. Accepts simultaneous submissions. Reports in 2 months on queries. Sample copy and writer's guidelines free.
Nonfiction: Interview/profile. **Buys 8 mss/year.** Query. Length: 2,000 words minimum. Pay varies.
Photos: State availability of photos with submission. Offers no additional payment for photos accepted with ms. Captions and identification of subjects required. Buys all rights.

N $ $ FINANCIAL FREEDOM REPORT QUARTERLY, 4505 S. Wasatch Blvd., Salt Lake City UT 84124. (801)273-2335. Fax: (801)273-2399. E-mail: carolyn@homebusiness.com. Chairman of the Board: Mark O. Haroldsen. **Contact:** Carolyn Tice, managing editor. **25% freelance written.** Eager to work with new/unpublished writers. Quarterly magazine for "professional and nonprofessional investors and would-be investors in real estate—real estate brokers, insurance companies, investment planners, truck drivers, housewives, doctors, architects, contractors, etc. The magazine's content is presently expanding to interest and inform the readers about other ways to put their money to work for them." Estab. 1976. Pays on publication. Publishes ms an average of 3 months after acceptance. Buys all rights. Accepts simultaneous submissions. Reports in 3 months. Sample copy for $5.

Nonfiction: How-to (find real estate bargains, finance property, use of leverage, managing property, developing market trends, goal setting, motivational); interviews (success stories of those who have relied on own initiative and determination in real estate market or related fields). **Buys 10 unsolicited mss/year.** Query with clips of published work or submit complete ms. Phone queries OK. Length: 1,500-3,000 words. **Pays 5-10¢/word.** Sometimes pays the expenses of writers on assignment.

Reprints: Send typed manuscript with rights for sale noted and information about when and where the article previously appeared.

Photos: Send photos with ms. Uses 8×10 b&w or color matte prints. Captions required.

Tips: "We would like to find several specialized writers in our field of real estate investments. A writer must have had some hands-on experience in the real estate field."

N $ $ GULF COAST CONDO OWNER, Covey Communications Corporation, P.O. Box 2267, Gulf Shores AL 36547-2267. (334)968-5300. Fax: (334)968-4532. **Contact:** Abby Farris, managing editor. Editor: Kristen McIntosh. **90% freelance written.** "Quarterly tabloid covering the business of owning a condominium on the Gulf Coast." Estab. 1997. Circ. 7,000. Pays on publication. Publishes ms an average of 2 months after acceptance. Byline given. Buys first or one-time rights. Editorial lead time 3 months. Submit seasonal material 5 months in advance. Accepts simultaneous submissions. Reports in 2 weeks on queries; 2 months on mss. Sample copy and writer's guidelines free.

- *Gulf Coast Condo Owner* publishes Alabama/Perdido Bay and Fort Walton Beach/Destin editions. Submissions should be specific for a particular region/edition.

Nonfiction: Essays, historical/nostalgic (area specific), how-to (related to condominium ownership), humor, interview/profile, new product, personal experience, photo feature. "No articles related to tourism or directed toward tourists." **Buys 16-20 mss/year.** Query. Length: 500-4,000 words. **Pays $50-400.** Pays writers with contributor copies or other premiums (when agreed upon in advance). Sometimes pays expenses of writers on assignment.

Photos: Send photos with submission. Reviews prints. Negotiates payment individually. Model releases and identification of subjects required. Buys one-time rights.

Columns/Departments: Investing (owning condos as investment properties), 2,500 words; Association Matters (living/working with a condo association), 2,000 words; Dollars & Sense (financing, investment and rental income issues), 2,000 words. Buys 4-8 mss/year. Query. Pays $50-400.

$ $ JOURNAL OF PROPERTY MANAGEMENT, Institute of Real Estate Management, P.O. Box 109025, Chicago IL 60610-9025. (312)329-6058. Fax: (312)661-0217. E-mail: mevans@irem.org. Website: http://www.irem.org. **Contact:** Mariwyn Evans, executive editor. **30% freelance written.** Bimonthly magazine covering real estate management. "The *Journal* has a feature/information slant designed to educate readers in the application of new techniques and to keep them abreast of current industry trends." Circ. 23,000. **Pays on acceptance.** Publishes ms an average of 3 months after acceptance. Byline given. Buys all rights. Reports in 6 weeks on queries; 1 month on mss. Sample copy and writer's guidelines free.

Nonfiction: How-to, interview, technical (building systems/computers), demographic shifts in business employment and buying patterns, marketing. "No non-real estate subjects, personality or company, humor." **Buys 8-12 mss/year.** Query with published clips. Length: 1,200-1,500 words. Sometimes pays the expenses of writers on assignment.

Reprints: Send photocopy of article or short story. Pays 35% of amount paid for an original article.

Photos: State availability of photos with submission. Reviews contact sheets. May offer additional payment for photos accepted with ms. Model releases, identification of subjects required. Buys one-time rights.

Columns/Departments: Jennifer Towne, associate editor. Insurance Insights, Tax Issues, Investment and Finance Insights, Legal Issues. **Buys 6-8 mss/year.** Query. Length: 500-750 words.

$ $ MANAGERS REPORT: The Only National Trade Journal Serving Condominiums and Property Management, Ivor Thomas and Associates, 1700 Southern Blvd., West Palm Beach FL 33406. (407)687-4700. Fax: (407)687-9654. E-mail: mgrreport@aol.com. Editor: Ivor Thomas. Managing Editor: Marcia Thomas. **Contact:** Lisa Pinder, executive editor. **40% freelance written.** Monthly magazine covering condominiums and property management. Estab. 1987. Circ. 20,000. **Pays on acceptance.** Buys second serial (reprint) rights. Editorial lead time 3 months. Submit seasonal material 4 months in advance. Accepts simultaneous submissions. Sample copy and writers guidelines free.

Nonfiction: How-to, interview/profile, new product, opinion, personal experience, photo feature, technical. **Buys 120 mss/year.** Query. Length: 50-3,000 words. **Pays $25** (200-400 words); **$75** (400-1,000 words); **$150** (1,000-2,000 words).

Reprints: Accepts previously published submissions. Send typed ms with rights for sale noted.

Photos: Send photos with submission. Reviews contact sheets, negatives, prints. Offers $5-50/photo. Identification of subjects required. Buys all rights.

Poetry: Light verse, humorous relating to condominiums. **Buys 12 poems/year.** Submit maximum 12 poems at one time. **Pays $10-50.**

Fillers: Anecdotes, facts, gags to be illustrated by cartoonist, newsbreaks, short humor. **Buys 60/year.** Length: 6-50 words. **Pays $10-50.**

Tips: "We want to get more technical information. We need a layman's description of: e.g., how an air conditioner really cools air. We would like maintenance remedies: e.g., what is the best thing to be done for cracked pavement in a parking lot. Consult the reader response in the magazine for maintenance categories. We ask that our advertisers be used exclusively for research. Our readers are extrememly interested in knowing such things as the difference between latex and acrylic paint and when you use one or the other. We find that the more specific and technical the better. This also applies to interviews. Interviews are to gather good technical information. Legal, administrative maintenance. See our guidelines for primer questions. We would like interviews with pictures of individuals and/or associations. 95% of our interviews are done by phone. We would like to have regular correspondents in different areas of the country."

N $ $ **MIDWEST REAL ESTATE NEWS**, Intertec Publishing, 35 E. Wacker Dr., Suite 700, Chicago IL 60601. (312)726-7277. **Contact:** Matt Valley, editor. **70% freelance written.** Monthly tabloid covering all aspects of commercial real estate including office, industrial, retail, hotel and multifamily in Ohio, Michigan, Indiana, Illinois, Wisconsin, Montana, Missouri, Nebraska, Kansas and Iowa." Estab. 1987. Circ. 18,000. Pays on publication. Publishes ms an average of 4 months after acceptance. Byline given. Buys all rights. Editorial lead time 3 months. Submit seasonal material 3 months in advance. Accepts simultaneous submissions. Sample copy and writer's guidelines free.

Nonfiction: Essays, general interest, how-to (perform and succeed in commercial real estate), area real estate reports, interview/profile, personal experience, technical. "We do a special pull-out section in September and October on Detroit and Chicago." **Buys 50 mss/year.** Query. Length: 2,000-4,000 words. **Pays $300-500.**

Reprints: Accepts previously published submissions.

Photos: Send photos with submission. Offers no additional payment for photos accepted with ms. Captions required. Buys one-time rights.

Tips: "Freelancers should call me and get a copy of our editorial calendar. Determine what topics are of interest and then call me to discuss how to go about writing the article."

N $ $ $ **OFFICE BUILDINGS MAGAZINE**, Yale Robbins, Inc., 31 E. 28th St., New York NY 10016. (212)683-5700. **Contact:** Peg Rivard, managing editor. **15% freelance written.** "Annual magazine covering market statistics, trends and thinking of area professionals on the current and future state of the real estate market." Estab. 1987. Circ. 10,500. Pays half on acceptance and half on publication. Byline sometimes given. Offers 25% kill fee. Buys all rights. Editorial lead time 2 months. Sample copy and writer's guidelines free.

Nonfiction: Survey of specific markets. **Buys 15-20 mss/year.** Query with published clips. Length: 1,200-2,000 words. **Pays $500-1,200.** Sometimes pays expenses of writers on assignment.

N **RETIREMENT COMMUNITY BUSINESS**, Great River Publishing Company, Inc., 2026 Exeter Rd., Suite 2, Germantown TN 38138. (901)624-5911. Fax: (901)624-5910. **Contact:** Sherry Campbell, editor. **25% freelance written.** Quarterly magazine covering management of retirement and assisted living communities. Estab. 1992. Circ. 13,000. Pays on publication. Publishes ms an average of 6 months after acceptance. Byline given. Offers negotiable kill fee. Buys all rights. Editorial lead time 3 months. Submit seasonal material 3 months in advance. Reports in 2 weeks on queries; 3 months on mss. Sample copy and writer's guidelines free.

Nonfiction: How-to (management and operational issues of seniors housing), personal experience. Only articles specific to industry. **Buys 20-30 mss/year.** Query with published clips. Length: 300-1,500 words. Pay is negotiated.

Photos: State availability of photos with submission. Offers no additional payment for photos accepted with ms. Model releases required. Buys one-time rights.

Tips: "Writers should have basic knowledge of the industry sufficient to understand some management issues. Writer should understand what a retirement or assisted living community is and isn't."

N $ $ $ **TITLE TECHNOLOGY, The Technology Magazine for the Land Title Services Industry**, Condell & Co., P.O. Box 7768, Hilton Head Island SC 29938. (843)686-6636. Fax: (843)686-6515. E-mail: timag@condell.com. Website: http://www.condell.com. **Contact:** Mike Thompson, editor. **50% freelance written.** Monthly magazine covering technology use within the title and settlement services industry. "We consider the magazine to be a training tool for managers and owners of title insurance agencies. Most of these people have little or no opportunity to learn about technology that exists or is being developed that can be used by them." Estab. 1993. Circ. 5,000. Pays on publication. Publishes ms an average of 2 months after acceptance. Byline given. Buys one-time rights. Editorial lead time 4 months. Accepts simultaneous submissions. Reports in 2 weeks on queries; 2 months on mss. Sample copy and writer's guidelines free.

Nonfiction: How-to, interview/profile, new product, personal experience, technical. Special issues: Electronic Commerce Review (January 1999). No thinly veiled commercials for a specific product or service—or worse, a blatant commercial for a product or service. **Buys 24 mss/year.** Query with published clips. Length: 1,000-4,000 words. **Pays $250-800 for assigned articles; $175-750 for unsolicited articles.**

Photos: Send photos with submission. Reviews prints smaller than 8×10. Offers no additional payment for photos accepted with ms. Captions, model releases and identification of subjects required.

Columns/Departments: Image Technology (use of imaging systems in title ops), 750-1,250 words; Electronic Com-

merce (news, tips, guidelines, breakthroughs in e-commerce), 1,000 words; Hardware (news, reviews, how-to, trends in small office automation), 1,000 words. **Buys 24 mss/year.** Query with published clips. **Pays $150-400.**
Tips: "Avoid trying to cover too much ground. An article that focuses on a single point or principle, elaborates on that point, and uses several examples and illustrations of the point, makes excellent reading. Use pictures, charts, and graphics whenever possible and as many as you like. *Title Technology* can handle graphic files containing .tif or .cgm file extensions."

RESOURCES AND WASTE REDUCTION

$ $ THE AMERICAN OIL & GAS REPORTER, National Publisher's Group, P.O. Box 343, Derby KS 67037-0343. Editor: Bill Campbell. **Contact:** Tim Beims, special sections editor. **20% freelance written.** Monthly magazine covering "cutting-edge technologies used in oil and gas exploration and production, with an emphasis on independent E&P companies. We also report on legislative and regulatory issues of importance to independent oilmen. Articles must be written to the industry, and about the industry." Estab. 1958. Circ. 13,540. Pays on publication. Publishes ms an average of 2 months after acceptance. Byline given. Offers 50% kill fee. Buys first rights. Editorial lead time 4 months. Submit seasonal material 4 months in advance. Accepts simultaneous submissions. Reports in 6 weeks on queries; 4 months on mss. Sample copy and writer's guidelines free.
Nonfiction: Interview/profile, technical. No blatantly promotional pieces, opinion, historical. **Buys 24 mss/year.** Query with published clips. Length: 1,500-2,300 words. **Pays $200-750.** Pays expenses of writers on assignment.
Tips: "Please send a *brief* abstract proposing a technical topic. Particularly interested in advanced technologies (geophysics, computer applications, 3- and 4-D seismic, subsea/offshore development, horizontal/multi-lateral drilling, etc.) with good case study applications."

N $ AMERICAN WASTE DIGEST, 226 King St., Pottstown PA 19464. (610)326-9480. Fax: (610)326-9752. E-mail: awd610@aol.com. **Contact:** Charles G. Moody, editor. **90% freelance written.** Monthly magazine covering solid waste and recycling. "Articles should pertain to active waste and recycling ideas and issues or self-help to the small independent business." Estab. 1989. Circ. 17,500. Pays on publication. Publishes ms an average of 3 months after acceptance. Byline given. Buys second serial (reprint) rights. Editorial lead time 3 months. Submit seasonal material 3 months in advance. Reports in 2 weeks on queries; 1 month on mss. Sample copy and writer's guidelines free.
Nonfiction: How-to (buy computers, insurance, motivate), technical, general business. No fiction, poetry. **Buys 32 mss/year.** Query with published clips. Length: 750-2,000 words. **Pays $75-150.**
Reprints: Accepts previously published submissions.
Photos: State availability of photos with submission. Reviews prints. Offers no additional payment for photos accepted with ms. Captions required.
Columns/Departments: Along The Way (self help for the independent businessman); Something To Think About, both 1,500 words. **Buys 18 mss/year.** Query with published clips. **Pays $75-150.**
Fillers: Facts, newsbreaks. **Buys 9/year.** Length: 200-1,000 words. **Pays $25-75.**
Tips: "Article should contain information for the small business person: how to buy insurance, health insurance, motivate employees, computer related articles on Internet, electronic billing, updating computers, time management, accounts receivable, business plans."

$ $ COMPOSTING NEWS, The Latest News in Composting and Scrap Wood Management, McEntee Media Corporation, 13727 Holland Rd., Brook Park OH 44142. (216)362-7979. Fax: (216)362-6553. E-mail: mcenteemedia@compuserve.com. **Contact:** Ken McEntee, editor. **5% freelance written.** Monthly newsletter. "We are interested in any news impacting the composting industry including new laws, regulations, new facilities/programs, end-uses, research, etc." Estab. 1992. Circ. 1,000. Pays on publication. Publishes ms an average of 1 month after acceptance. Buys first or all rights. Editorial lead time 1 month. Submit seasonal material 1 month in advance. Accepts simultaneous and previously published submissions. Reports in 2 months. Sample copy for 9×12 SAE and 55¢ postage. Writer's guidelines for #10 SASE.
Nonfiction: Book excerpts, essays, interview/profile, new product, opinion, personal experience, technical, new business, legislation, regulation, business expansion. **Buys 0-5 mss/year.** Query with published clips. Length: 100-5,000 words. **Pays $10-500.** Pays writers with contributor copies or other premiums by prior agreement.
Columns/Departments: Query with published clips. **Pays $10-500.**
Tips: "We appreciate leads on local news regarding composting, i.e., new facilities or business, new laws and regulations, unique programs, situations that impact supply and demand for composting. International developments are also of interest."

$ $ EROSION CONTROL, The Journal for Erosion and Sediment Control Professionals, Forester Communications, Inc., 5638 Hollister Ave., Suite 301, Santa Barbara CA 93117. (805)681-1300. Fax: (805)681-1312. E-mail: erosion@ix.netcom.com. **Contact:** John Trotti, editor. **60% freelance written.** Bimonthly magazine covering all aspects of erosion prevention and sediment control. "*Erosion Control* is a practical, hands-on, 'how-to' professional journal. Our readers are civil engineers, landscape architects, builders, developers, public works officials, road and highway construction officials and engineers, soils specialists, farmers, landscape contractors and others involved with any activity that disturbs significant areas of surface vegetation." Estab. 1994. Circ. 17,000. Pays on publication. Publishes ms an average of 3 months after acceptance. Byline given. Buys all rights. Editorial lead time 4 months. Submit seasonal material 3 months in advance. Reports in 2 weeks. Accepts simultaneous submissions. Sample copy and writer's guidelines free.

Nonfiction: Photo feature, technical. **Buys 15 mss/year.** Query with published clips. Length: 3,000-4,000 words. **Pays $350-650.** Sometimes pays expenses of writers on assignment.

Photos: Send photos with submission. Reviews transparencies, prints. Offers no additional payment for photos accepted with ms. Captions, model releases, identification of subjects required. Buys all rights.

Tips: "Writers should have a good grasp of technology involved, good writing and communication skills, unbounded curiosity and no hidden agenda. Think like your audience. Put yourself in an erosion control professional's boots. What makes this subject important enough that you would take time out from your busy schedule to stop and read the article? Where's the hook? How best to bait it, cast it, troll it and sink it? When you've satisfied yourself on those scores, you're ready to write. Engage your reader. Leave no doubt in anyone's mind who your audience is and why what you have to say is important. Rivet your full attention on your readers and drag them into the middle of your subject; address them directly and personally. For instance, instead of saying, 'Sediment can be kept out of the watercourse in a number of ways,' you might say, 'If you want to keep sediment out of the streambed, here are some things you can do.' "

N $ **PUMPER**, COLE Publishing Inc., P.O. Box 220, Three Lakes WI 54562-0220. (715)546-3347. Fax: (715)546-3786. E-mail: cole@pumper.com. Website: http://www.pumper.com. President: Tom Rulseh. **Contact:** Ken Lowther, editor. **50% freelance written.** Eager to work with new/unpublished writers. Monthly tabloid covering the liquid waste hauling industry (portable toilet renters, septic tank pumpers, industrial waste haulers, chemical waste haulers, oil field haulers, and hazardous waste haulers). "Our publication is read by companies that handle liquid waste and manufacturers of equipment." Estab. 1979. Circ. 20,000. Pays on publication. Publishes ms an average of 1 month after acceptance. Byline given. Buys first serial rights. Free sample copy and writer's guidelines.

Nonfiction: Exposé (government regulations, industry problems, trends, public attitudes, etc.); general interest (state association meetings, conventions, etc.); how-to (related to industry, e.g., how to incorporate septage or municipal waste into farm fields, how to process waste, etc.); humor (related to industry, especially septic tank pumpers or portable toilet renters); interview/profile (including descriptions of business statistics, type of equipment, etc.); new product; personal experience; photo feature; technical (especially reports on research projects related to disposal). "We are looking for quality articles that will be of interest to our readers; length is not important. We publish trade journals. We need articles that deal with the trade. Studies on land application of sanitary waste are of great interest." Query or send complete ms. **Pays 7½¢/word.**

Photos: Send photos with query or ms. Pays $15 for b&w and color prints that are used. No negatives. "We need good contrast." Captions, model release required. Buys one-time rights.

Tips: "Material must pertain to liquid waste-related industries listed above. We hope to expand the editorial content of our monthly publications. We also have a publication for sewer and drain cleaners with the same format as *Pumper*; however, *Cleaner* has a circulation of 22,000. We are looking for the same type of articles and pay is the same."

N $ $ **RECYCLING TODAY**, GIE, Inc., Publishers, 4012 Bridge Ave., Cleveland OH 44113. (216)961-4130. Fax: (216)961-0364. E-mail: bfeigenbaum@gie.net. **Contact:** Robert A. Feigenbaum, editor. Managing Editor: Brian Taylor. **10-25% freelance written.** "*Recycling Today* circulates monthly to business professionals in the recycling industry. The magazine covers issues pertaining to the scrap industry, secondary commodity markets and municipal recycling." Estab. 1963. Circ. 20,000. **Pays on acceptance.** Publishes ms an average of 3 months after acceptance. Byline given. Buys all rights. Editorial lead time 3 months. Submit seasonal material 3 months in advance. Reports in 3 weeks on queries. Sample copy for $5.

Nonfiction: Interview/profile, technical. "No articles on hazardous or radioactive waste. No articles on consumer recycling." **Buys 12-18 mss/year.** Query with published clips. Length: 2,000-2,500 words. **Pays $400.** Sometimes pays expenses of writers on assignment.

Photos: State availability of photos with submission. Negotiates payment individually. Captions, model releases and identification of subjects required. Buys all rights.

Tips: "Query with SASE. Remember, we circulate to professionals in the scrap and recycling industries, not to home-owners who recycle."

$ $ **WORLD WASTES MAGAZINE, The Business Magazine For Waste Management Professionals**, Intertec Publishing, 6151 Powers Ferry Rd. NW, Atlanta GA 30339-2941. (770)618-0197. Fax: (770)618-0349. E-mail: patti_verbanas@intertec.com. Editor: Bill Wolpin. **Contact:** Patti Verbanas, managing editor. **90% freelance written.** Monthly magazine. "*World Wastes* reaches individuals and firms engaged in the removal and disposal of solid/hazardous wastes. This includes: refuse contractors; landfill operators; municipal, county and other government officials; recyclers and handlers of secondary materials; major generators of waste, such as plants and chain stores; engineers, architects and consultants; manufactures and distributors of equipment; universities, libraries and associations; and legal, insurance and financial firms allied to the field. Readers include: owners, presidents, vice-presidents, directors, superintendents, engineers, managers, supervisors, consultants, purchasing agents and commissioners." Estab. 1958. Circ. 38,000. Pays on publication. Publishes ms an average of 4 months after acceptance. Byline given. Buys all rights. Editorial lead time 2 months. Reports in 1 week on queries; 1 month on mss. Sample copy and writer's guidelines free.

Nonfiction: How-to (practical information on improving solid waste management, i.e., how to rehabilitate a transfer

station, how to improve recyclable collection, how to manage a landfill, etc.), interview/profile (of prominent persons in the solid waste industry). "No feel-good 'green' articles about recycling. Remember our readers are not the citizens but the governments and private contractors. No 'why you should recycle' articles." **Buys over 50 mss/year.** Query. Length: 700-2,500 words. **Pays $75 flat rate to $175/printed page.** Will pay for expenses of writers on assignment.
Photos: Send photos with submission. Reviews contact sheets, negatives, transparencies, prints. Negotiates payment individually. Identification of subjects required.
Tips: "Read the magazine and understand our audience. Write useful articles with sidebars that the readers can apply to their jobs. Use the Associated Press style book. Freelancers can send in queries or manuscripts or can fax a letter of interest (including qualifications/resume) in possible assignments. Writers must be deadline-oriented."

SELLING AND MERCHANDISING

Sales personnel and merchandisers interested in how to sell and market products successfully consult these journals. Publications in nearly every category of Trade also buy sales-related materials if they are slanted to the product or industry with which they deal.

$ $ THE AMERICAN SALESMAN, 320 Valley, Burlington IA 52601-5513. Fax: (319)752-3421. Publisher: Michael S. Darnall. **Contact:** Teresa Levinson, editor. Monthly magazine for distribution through company sales representatives. Estab. 1955. Circ. 1,500. Publishes ms an average of 4 months after acceptance. Sample copy and writer's guidelines for 6×9 SAE with 3 first-class stamps; mention *Writer's Market* in request.
Nonfiction: Sales seminars, customer service and follow-up, closing sales, sales presentations, handling objections, competition, telephone usage and correspondence, managing territory, new innovative sales concepts. No sexist material. Written from a salesperson's viewpoint. Public relations articles or case histories reviewed. Length: 900-1,200 words. Uses no advertising. Follow AP Stylebook. Include biography and/or byline with ms submissions. Author photos used. Send correspondence to Editor.

$ $ BALLOONS AND PARTIES MAGAZINE, Festivities Publications, 815 Haines St., Jacksonville FL 32206. (904)634-1902. Fax: (904)633-8764. **Contact:** Debra Paulk, publisher/editor. **10% freelance written.** Monthly international trade journal for professional party decorators and for gift delivery businesses. Estab. 1986. Circ. 7,000. Pays on publication. Publishes ms an average of 3 months after acceptance. Byline given. Buys all rights. Submit seasonal material 6 months in advance. Reports in 6 weeks. Sample copy for 9×12 SAE.
Nonfiction: Interview/profile, photo feature, technical, craft. **Buys 12 mss/year.** Query with or without published clips, or send complete ms. Length: 500-1,500 words. **Pays $100-300 for assigned articles; $50-200 for unsolicited articles.** Sometimes pays expenses of writers on assignment.
Reprints: Send typed ms with rights for sale noted and information about when and where the article previously appeared. Length: up to 2,500 words. Pays 10¢/word.
Photos: Send photos with submission. Reviews 2×2 transparencies, 3×5 prints. Captions, model releases, identification of subjects required. Buys all rights.
Columns/Departments: Great Ideas (craft projects using balloons, large scale decorations), 200-500 words. Send complete ms with photos.
Tips: "Show unusual, lavish, and outstanding examples of balloon sculpture, design and decorating and other craft projects. Offer specific how-to information. Be positive and motivational in style."

$ $ CARD TRADE, Krause Publications, 700 E. State St., Iola WI 54990. (715)445-2214. Fax: (715)445-4087. E-mail: cardtrade@krause.com. Website: http://www.krause.com. Editor: Kevin Isaacson. **Contact:** Scott Kelnhofer, managing editor. **20% freelance written.** Monthly magazine covering the sports collectible industry. "We're looking for experts in small business retailing and related sales." Estab. 1994. Circ. 9,000. Pays on publication. Buys perpetual but non-exclusive rights. Editorial lead time 1 month.
Nonfiction: How-to (retail advice), new product. **Buys 6-10 mss/year.** Query. Length: 1,000-2,500 words. **Pays $125-300.**
Reprints: Send photocopy of article and information about when and where the article previously appeared. Pays 50% of amount paid for an original article.
Columns/Departments: Buys 30 mss/year. Query. **Pays $125-200.**

N $ $ $ CBA FRONTLINE, CBA Service Corp., P.O. Box 200, Colorado Springs CO 80901. Fax: (719)576-0795. E-mail: publications@cba-intl.org. Website: http://www.cbaonline.org. Managing Editor: Debby Weaver. **Contact:** Sue Grise/Steve Parolini, editors. **100% freelance written.** Monthly trade magazine covering Christian retail, product and staff issues. "Knowledge of Christian retail, Christian products and audience, interviews of relevant experts, issues related to retail business." Estab. 1997. Circ. 7,000. **Pays on assignment completion.** Byline given. Offers 100% kill fee. Buys all rights. Editorial lead time 5 months. Submit seasonal material 8 months in advance. Accepts simultaneous submissions. Reports in 3 months. Sample copy for $5.
Nonfiction: How-to (Christian retail), interviews/profile (well-known Christian authors, artists, etc . . .), personal experience (success in Christian retail), technical, consumer audience profiles. **Buys 33 mss/year.** Query only; no mss.

Length: 750-2,000 words. **Pays 16-50¢/word.** Sometimes pays expenses for writers on assignment.
Reprints: Rarely uses previously published submissions.
Photos: Offers no additional payment for photos accepted with ms. Captions required. Buys all rights.
Fillers: Contact: Mark Ford, art director. Gags to be illustrated by cartoonist, cartoons about Christian retail. **Buys 10/ year. Pays $25-150.**
Tips: "Experience working in Christian retail, direct experience with our audience which is Christian retail, broad knowledge of retail business and of Christian products."

N $ $ $ CBA MARKETPLACE, CBA Service Corp., P.O. Box 200, Colorado Springs CO 80901. Fax: (719)576-0795. E-mail: publications@cba-intl.org. Website: http://www.cbaonline.org. Managing Editor: Debby Weaver. **Contact:** Sue Grise/Steve Parolini, editors. **20% freelance written.** Monthly trade magazine covering Christian retail, product and staff issues. "Knowledge of Christian retail, Christian products and audience, interviews of relevant experts, issues related to retail business." Estab. 1968. Circ. 9,000. **Pays on assignment completion.** Byline given. Offers 100% kill fee. Buys all rights. Editorial lead time 5 months. Submit seasonal material 8 months in advance. Accepts simultaneous submissions. Reports in 3 months. Sample copy for $7.50.
Nonfiction: How-to (Christian retail), interviews/profile (well-known Christian authors, artists, etc . . .), personal experience (success in Christian retail), technical, consumer audience profiles. **Buys 36 mss/year.** Query only; no mss. Length: 750-2,000 words. **Pays 16-50¢/word.** Sometimes pays expenses for writers on assignment.
Reprints: Rarely uses previously published submissions.
Photos: Offers no additional payment for photos accepted with ms. Captions required. Buys all rights.
Fillers: Contact: Mark Ford, art director. Gags to be illustrated by cartoonist, cartoons about Christian retail. **Buys 12/ year. Pays $25-150.**
Tips: "Experience working in Christian retail, direct experience with our audience which is Christian retail, broad knowledge of retail business and of Christian products."

N $ $ CONVENIENCE STORE DECISIONS, Donohue-Meehan Publishing, Two Greenwood Square, Suite 410, Bensalem PA 19020. (215)245-4555. Fax: (215)245-4060. E-mail: donmee@aol.com. **Contact:** Jay Gordon, editor. Managing Editor: Bill McKee. **40% freelance written.** Monthly magazine. "*CSD* is read by executives of convenience store companies and seeks to be the 'idea store' by reporting on all facets of these specialized retail businesses, such as the marketing and merchandising of gasoline, food and merchandise." Estab. 1990. Circ. 42,000. Pays on publication. Byline given. Makes work-for-hire assignments. Editorial lead time 2 months. Submit seasonal material 4 months in advance. Sample copy free.
Nonfiction: How-to, interview/profile, new product, technical. **Buys 24 mss/year.** Query with published clips. Length: 500-2,500 words. **Pays $600.** Pays expenses of writers on assignment.
Photos: State availability of photos with submission. Negotiates payment individually.
Columns/Departments: Query. **Pays $350-500.**
Tips: "Writers with strong retail/business writing experience should write or call Jay Gordon, editor. We will work to find an acceptable 'trial' assignment (for pay) to assess the writer's abilities."

N $ $ GIFT BASKET REVIEW, Festivities Publications, 1205 W. Forsyth St., Jacksonville FL 32204. (904)634-1902. Fax: (904)633-8764. E-mail: readermail@festivities-pub.com. Website: http://www.festivities-pub.com. Publisher: Debra Paulk. **Contact:** Kathy Horak, editor. **25% freelance written.** Monthly magazine for gourmet food and gift basket retailers. "Our readers are creative small business entrepreneurs. Many are women who start their business out of their homes and eventually branch into retail." Estab. 1990. Circ. 15,000. Pays on publication. Publishes ms an average of 3 months after acceptance. Byline given. Buys all rights. Submit seasonal material 9 months in advance. Accepts simultaneous submissions. Reports in 2 months.
Nonfiction: How-to (how to give a corporate presentation, negotiate a lease, etc.), photo feature, technical. "No personal profiles or general experience." **Buys 6-8 mss/year.** Send complete ms. Length: 500-2,000 words. **Pays 10¢/ word.** Sometimes pays expenses of writers on assignment.
Reprints: Accepts previously published submissions. Send photocopy or typed ms with rights for sale noted and information about when and where the article previously appeared.
Photos: Send photos with submission. Reviews contact sheets, negatives, 2×2 transparencies, 3×5 prints. Model releases, identification of subjects required. Buys all rights.
Columns/Departments: Corporate Talk (deals with obtaining corporate clients), 1,500 words; In the Storefront (emphasis on small business owners with a retail storefront), 1,500 words; On the Homefront (specifically for home-based entrepreneurs), 1,500 words. **Buys 12 mss/year.** Send complete ms. **Pays 10¢/word.**
Fillers: Anecdotes, facts, newsbreaks, short humor. Length: 300 words maximum. **Pays 10¢/word.**

$ $ GIFTWARE NEWS, Talcott Corp., 112 Adrossan, P.O. Box 5398, Deptford NJ 08096. (609)227-0798. Fax: (609)227-6511. **Contact:** Anthony DeMasi, editor. **55% freelance written.** Monthly magazine covering gifts, collectibles, and tabletops for giftware retailers. Estab. 1976. Circ. 45,000. Pays on publication. Publishes ms an average of 2 months after acceptance. Byline given. Buys all rights. Submit seasonal/holiday material 4 months in advance. Reports in 2 months on mss. Sample copy for $5.
Nonfiction: How-to (sell, display), new product. Buys 50 mss/year. Send complete ms. Length: 1,500-2,500 words. **Pays $150-250 for assigned articles; $75-100 for unsolicited articles.**

Photos: Send photos with submission. Reviews 4×5 transparencies and 5×7 prints. Offers no additional payment for photos accepted with ms. Identification of subjects required.
Columns/Departments: Stationery, giftbaskets, collectibles, holiday merchandise, tabletop, wedding market and display—all for the gift retailer. **Buys 36 mss/year.** Send complete ms. Length: 1,500-2,500 words. **Pays $100-250.**
Tips: "We are not looking so much for general journalists but rather experts in particular fields who can also write."

N $ $ INCENTIVE, Bill Communications, Dept. WM, 355 Park Ave., New York NY 10010. (212)986-4800. Fax: (212)867-4395. E-mail: jjuergens@billcom.com. Website: http://www.incentivemag.com. **Contact:** Jennifer Juergens, editor. Executive Editor: Vincent Alonzo. Monthly magazine covering sales promotion and employee motivation: managing and marketing through motivation. Estab. 1905. Circ. 41,000. **Pays on acceptance.** Publishes ms an average of 3 months after acceptance. Byline always given. Buys all rights. Reports in 1 month on queries; 2 months on mss. Sample copy for 9×12 SAE.

- *Incentive* won the *Folio* Award of Excellence in 1994, 1995, 1996, as well as the Jesse H. Neal Award.

Nonfiction: General interest (motivation, demographics), how-to (types of sales promotion, buying product categories, using destinations), interview/profile (sales promotion executives); corporate case studies; travel (incentive-oriented). **Buys up to 48 mss/year.** Query with 2 published clips. Length: 1,000-2,000 words. **Pays $250-700 for assigned articles; does not pay for unsolicited articles.** Pays expenses of writers on assignment.
Reprints: Send information about when and where article previously appeared. Send tearsheet and information about when and where the article previously appeared. Pays 50% of the amount paid for an original article.
Photos: Send photos with submission. Reviews contact sheets and transparencies. Offers no additional payment for photos accepted with ms. Identification of subjects required.
Tips: "Read the publication, then query."

N THE INSIDER, The Trade Journal for Cosmic-Minded Industry, Destiny Productions, 5536 W. Viking Rd., Las Vegas NV 89103. (800)457-0654. Fax: (702)648-3898. E-mail: destinymag@aol.com. Website: http://www.bosewell.com/insider/. **Contact:** Jody Williams, editor. **20% freelance written.** Quarterly trade journal dedicated to the professional and economic development of the New Age and alternative health field. Estab. 1996. Circ. 250,000. Pays on publication. Byline given. Makes work-for-hire assignments. Editorial lead time 2 months. Submit seasonal material 4 months in advance. Accepts simultaneous submissions. Reports in 3 weeks. Writer's guidelines free.
Nonfiction: Book excerpts, essays, how-to, humor, inspirational, interview/profile, new product, personal experience, technical, travel, events. "No more articles about beliefs—our journal is about the business practices of these fields." Query. Pay varies. Pays writers with contributor copies or other premiums. Sometimes pays expenses of writers on assignment.
Reprints: Accepts previously published submissions.
Photos: Send photos with submission. Reviews contact sheets and prints (5×7 or larger). Negotiates payment individually. Model releases and identification of subjects required. Buys all rights.
Columns/Departments: News Updates; Events; Profiles in Business.
Fillers: Anecdotes, facts, newsbreaks. Length and pay vary.
Tips: "We want stories from successful people and companies in our industry. Please, no stories on how to market books from someone who has sold three copies. Each story receives individual consideration."

N $ NICHE, The Magazine For Progressive Retailers, The Rosen Group, 3000 Chestnut Ave., Suite 300, Baltimore MD 21211. (410)889-3093. **Contact:** Hope Daniels, editor. **10% freelance written.** Quarterly magazine covering contemporary art and craft retailers. "*NICHE* centers on creative answers to the various problems and dilemmas retailers face daily. Minimal coverage of product. Audience is 80% independent retailers of contemporary craft and unique products designed and made in the US, other 20% are professional craftspeople." Estab. 1988. Circ. 20,000. Pays on publication. Publishes ms an average of 4 months after acceptance. Byline given. Buys second serial (reprint) or all rights. Editorial lead time 2 months. Submit seasonal material 6 months in advance. Reports in 1 month on queries; 6 weeks on mss. Sample copy for $3. Writer's guidelines for #10 SASE.
Nonfiction: Interview/profile, opinion, photo feature, and articles targeted to independent retailers and small business owners. *Niche* is looking for in-depth articles on store security, innovative merchandising/display or marketing and promotion. Stories of interest to independent retailers, such as gallery owners, may be submitted. **Buys 6-10 mss/year.** Query with published clips. Length: 500-700 words. **Pays $100.** Sometimes pays expenses of writers on assignment.
Reprints: Accepts previously published submissions.
Photos: Send photos with submission. Reviews 4×5 transparencies or slides. Negotiates payment individually. Identification of subjects required. Buys all rights.
Columns/Departments: Retail Details (general retail information); Artist Profiles (biographies of American Craft Artists); Resources (book/video/seminar reviews pertaining to retailers). Length: 200 words minimum. **Buys 6 mss/year.** Query with published clips. **Pays $40-300.**

$ $ PARTY & PAPER RETAILER, 4Ward Corp, 70 New Canaan Ave., Norwalk CT 06850. (203)845-8020. Fax: (203)845-8022. E-mail: party@partypaper.com. Website: http://www.partypaper.com. **Contact:** Trisha McMahon Drain, editor-in-chief. **90% freelance written.** Monthly magazine for "every aspect of how to do business better for owners of party and fine stationery shops. Tips and how-tos on display, marketing, success stories, merchandising, operating costs, etc." Estab. 1986. Circ. 25,000. Pays on publication. Offers 15% kill fee. Buys first North American serial rights.

Editorial lead time 6 months. Submit seasonal material 6 months in advance. Reports in 2 months. Sample copy for $6.
Nonfiction: Book excerpts, how-to (retailing related), new product. No articles written in the first person. Buys 100 mss/year. Query with published clips. Length: 800-1,800 words. Pay "depends on topic, word count expertise, deadline." Pays telephone expenses of writers on assignment.
Reprints: Send tearsheet or photocopy of article and information about when and where the article previously appeared.
Photos: State availability of photos with submission. Reviews transparencies. Negotiates payment individually. Captions, identification of subjects required. Buys one-time rights.
Columns/Departments: Shop Talk (successful party/stationery store profile), 1,800 words; Storekeeping (selling, employees, market, running store), 800 words; Cash Flow (anything finance related), 800 words; On Display (display ideas and how-to). Buys 30 mss/year. Query with published clips. Pay varies.

$ $ PROFESSIONAL SELLING, The Bureau of Business Practice, 24 Rope Ferry Rd., Waterford CT 06386-0001. (860)442-4365. Fax: (860)437-1593. E-mail: karen_barretta@prenhall.com. Website: http://www.bbpnews.com. **Contact:** Karen Barretta, editor. **33% freelance written.** Prefers to work with published/established writers. Twice monthly newsletter. "*Professional Selling* offers skill and career building ideas for field sales professionals, particularly in the industrial, wholesale, pharmaceutical, high-tech and financial services fields." Estab. 1917. **Pays on acceptance.** Publishes ms an average of 3 months after acceptance. No byline given. Buys all rights. Submit seasonal material 6 months in advance. Sample copy and writer's guidelines for #10 SAE with 2 first-class stamps.
Nonfiction: How-to (successful sales techniques and the results of using them); interview/profile (interview-based articles). "We buy only interview-based material." **Buys 12-15 mss/year.** Written queries only; no unsolicited mss. Length: 800-1,000 words. **Pays 12-20¢/word.**
Tips: "Freelancers may occasionally interview sales managers, but the slant must be toward field sales, *not* management."

$ $ $ $ PROSALES, Hanley-Wood, Inc., One Thomas Circle, Suite 600, Washington DC 20005. (202)452-0800. Fax: (202)785-1974. E-mail: hkanter@hanley-wood.com. Website: http://www.hanley-wood.com. Editor: Greg Brooks. **Contact:** Hilary Kanter, managing editor. **30% freelance written.** Monthly magazine covering construction supply dealers. Estab. 1989. Circ. 40,000. **Pays on acceptance.** Publishes ms an average of 4 months after acceptance. Byline given. Offers 25% kill fee. Buys all rights. Editorial lead time 6 months. Submit seasonal material 6 months in advance. Reports in 2 months on queries; 3 months on mss. Sample copy free.
Nonfiction: Interview/profile, new product, personal experience, technical. **Buys 35 mss/year.** Query with published clips. Length: 500-2,000 words. **Pays $350-1,800. Sometimes pays expenses of writers on assignment.**
Photos: State availability of photos with submission. Offers no additional payment for photos accepted with ms. Identification of subjects required. Buys all rights.

$ $ SALES AND MARKETING STRATEGIES & NEWS, Hughes Communications, 211 W. State St., Rockford IL 61101. Fax: (815)963-7773. **Contact:** Paul Greenland, associate editor. Executive Editor: Mike Bacidore. Tabloid published 8 times/year covering brand marketing, promotion, incentives, sales automation, sales training, integrated marketing, meetings, p.o.p., trade show marketing. Estab. 1991. Circ. 65,000. Pays on publication. Publishes ms 3 months after acceptance. Byline given. Offers 15% kill fee. Buys first North American serial rights. Editorial lead time 4 months. Sample copy and writer's guidelines free.
Nonfiction: How-to, technical. **Buys 120 mss/year.** Query. Length: 500-900 words. **Pays $150-300 for assigned articles.** Expert writers are given a bio at end of story. Sometimes pays expenses of writers on assignment.
Photos: Send photos with submission. Reviews transparencies and prints. Offers no additional payment for photos accepted with ms. Identification of subjects required.

$ $ VIDEO STORE MAGAZINE, Advanstar Communications, 201 E. Sandpointe Ave. #600, Santa Ana CA 92707. (714)513-8465. Fax: (714)513-8403. E-mail: vstore@aol.com. Editor: Thomas K. Arnold. **Contact:** Marion Flanagan, executive editor. **35% freelance written.** "We are a weekly business magazine for the home video industry. Our primary readers are the nation's video retailers. We focus on industry news and retailing trends." Estab. 1979. Circ. 45,000. Pays on publication. Publishes ms an average of 1 month after acceptance. Byline given. Offers 50% kill fee. Buys first North American serial rights. Submit seasonal material 1 month in advance. Reports in 2 weeks on queries; 1 month on mss. Sample copy for 11×14 SAE and 3 first-class stamps.
Nonfiction: How-to (features on retailing, merchandising and management). **Buys 30 mss/year.** Query or query with published clips. Length: 1,600-2,400 words. **Pays $400.** Pays expenses of writers on assignment.
Photos: State availability of photos with submission. Reviews contact sheets. Offers $50/photo. Captions, model releases and identification of subjects required. Buys one-time rights.
Tips: "Be familiar with video stores and with the video business. Read our magazine and talk to video retailers about their concerns and needs. We need more management-type features; product stories are best handled by staff."

SPORT TRADE

Retailers and wholesalers of sports equipment and operators of recreation programs read these journals. Magazines about general and specific sports are classified in the Consumer Sports section.

N $ $ AQUATICS INTERNATIONAL, Leisure Publications Inc., 4160 Wilshire Blvd., Los Angeles CA 90010. Website: http://www.aquaticsintl@earthlink.com. **Contact:** Mark Edelstein, editor. Bimonthly trade magazine covering swimming pools, spas, hot tubs (commercial). Estab. 1961. Circ. 16,300. Pays on publication. Publishes ms an average of 1-2 months after acceptance. Byline given. Offers $50. Buys first North American serial rights, second serial (reprint) rights and makes work-for-hire assignments. Editorial lead time 1 month. Submit seasonal material 2 months in advance. Reports in 1 month on queries. Sample copy for $10.50.

Nonfiction: How-to, interview/profile, technical. **Buys 6 mss/year.** Query with published clips. Length: 1,500-4,500 words. **Pays $200 minimum for assigned articles; $150 minimum for unsolicited articles.** Sometimes pays expenses of writers on assignment.

Columns and Departments: Pays $150.

Tips: "Query letter with samples."

$ $ BICYCLE RETAILER & INDUSTRY NEWS, Miller Freeman Publishing, 502 W. Cordova, Santa Fe NM 87501. (505)988-5099. Fax: (505)988-7224. E-mail: mgamstetter@mfi.com. **Contact:** Michael Gamstetter, editor. **10% freelance written.** Tabloid published 18 times/year covering bicycle industry. "*Bicycle Retailer & Industry News* provides timely, in-depth coverage of issues confronting the bicycle industry. Typical articles include breaking industry news, new product development, new companies, marketing strategy, and international news. While long range planning for key articles is important, most stories fall into the "breaking news" category." Very news-oriented. Estab. 1991. Circ. 14,500. **Pays on acceptance.** Publishes ms an average of 2 weeks after acceptance. Byline given. Buys all rights. Accepts simultaneous submissions. Reports in 3 days on queries. Sample copy and writer's guidelines free.

Nonfiction: Interview/profile, new product, technical. No travel, nostalgia, essays, humor. **Buys 50-60 mss/year.** Query. Length: 1,200 words. **Pays up to $600 for assigned articles; 20¢/word for unsolicited articles.**

Reprints: Accepts previously published submissions.

Photos: Offers $50/photo. Negotiates payment individually. Identification of subjects required. Buys one-time rights.

N $ $ BOATING INDUSTRY, The Management Magazine for the Recreational Marine Industry, National Trade Publications, 13 Century Hill Dr., Latham NY 12110. (518)783-1281. Fax: (518)783-1386. E-mail: adantz@boatbiz.com. **Contact:** Anne Dantz, managing editor. **60% freelance written.** Monthly magazine covering recreational marine industry management. Estab. 1929. Circ. 34,000. Pays on publication. Publishes ms an average of 3 months after acceptance. Byline given. Offers 50% kill fee. Buys all rights. Editorial lead time 3 months. Submit seasonal material 3 months in advance. Reports in 1 month. Sample copy and writer's guidelines free.

Nonfiction: Essays, exposé, general interest, how-to, humor, interview/profile, new product, opinion, personal experience, technical, travel, marine-related sales management. **Buys 140 mss/year.** Query with published clips. Length: 250-2,500 words. **Pays $50-650.** Pays writers with contributor copies or other premiums, if there is a contract with editor. Sometimes pays expenses of writers on assignment.

Photos: Send photos with submission. Reviews contact sheets, negatives, transparencies and prints. Negotiates payment individually. Captions, model releases and identification of subjects required. Buys one-time rights.

$ $ $ FITNESS MANAGEMENT, Issues and Solutions in Fitness Services, Leisure Publications, Inc., 215 S. Highway 101, Suite 110, P.O. Box 1198, Solana Beach CA 92075-0910. (619)481-4155. Fax: (619)481-4228. E-mail: fmedit@fitnessworld.com. Website: http://www.fitnessworld.com. Co-Publisher: Edward H. Pitts. **Contact:** Ronale Tucker, editor. **50% freelance written.** Monthly magazine. "Readers are owners, managers and program directors of physical fitness facilities. *FM* helps them run their enterprises safely, efficiently and profitably. Ethical and professional positions in health, nutrition, sports medicine, management, etc., are consistent with those of established national bodies." Estab. 1985. Circ. 26,000. Pays on publication. Publishes ms an average of 5 months after acceptance. Byline given. Pays 50% kill fee. Buys all rights (all articles published in *FM* are also published and archived on its website). Submit seasonal material 6 months in advance. Reports in 3 months. Sample copy for $5. Writer's guidelines for #10 SASE.

Nonfiction: Book excerpts (prepublication); how-to (manage fitness center and program); new product (no pay); photo feature (facilities/programs); technical; other (news of fitness research and major happenings in fitness industry). No exercise instructions or general ideas without examples of fitness businesses that have used them successfully. **Buys 50 mss/year.** Query. Length: 750-2,000 words. **Pays $60-300 for assigned articles.** Pays expenses of writers on assignment.

Photos: Send photos with submission. Reviews contact sheets, 2×2 and 4×5 transparencies; prefers glossy prints, 5×7 to 8×10. Captions, model releases required.

Tips: "We seek writers who are expert in a business or science field related to the fitness-service industry or who are experienced in the industry. Be current with the state of the art/science in business and fitness and communicate it in human terms (avoid intimidating academic language; tell the story of how this was learned and/or cite examples or quotes of people who have applied the knowledge successfully)."

N $ $ GOLF BUSINESS MAGAZINE, Waterfront Publishing, Inc., 960 Morrison Dr., Suite 200, Charleston SC 29403. (803)722-6400. Fax: (803)722-7022. Website: http://www.ngcoa.com. **Contact:** Jack Bacot, executive editor. **80% freelance written.** "Monthly magazine covering business issues (legal, personal, finance, etc.) and general business topics to assist golf operators with running their businesses." Estab. 1995. Circ. 17,000. Pays 30 days after publication. Byline given. Offers 20% kill fee. Buys one-time rights. Editorial lead time 2 months. Submit seasonal material 2 months in advance. Accepts simultaneous submissions. Reports in 3 weeks on queries; 2 months on mss. Sample copy for SAE and $3 postage. Writer's guidelines for #10 SASE.

Nonfiction: How-to (business), interview/profile, new product, technical. Query with published clips. Length: 800-2,000 words. **Pays $200.** Sometimes pays expenses of writers on assignment.

Reprints: Accepts previously published submissions.

Photos: State availability of photos with submission. Reviews transparencies. Negotiates payment individually. Captions and identification of subjects required. Buys one-time rights.

N $ $ GOLF COURSE MANAGEMENT, Golf Course Superintendents Association of America, 1421 Research Park Dr., Lawrence KS 66049. (785)841-2240. Fax: (785)932-3665. E-mail: ehiscock@gcsaa.org. Website: http://www.gcsan.org. Managing Editor: Christine Slape. **Contact:** Ed Hiscock, editor. **85% freelance written.** Monthly trade magazine covering the golf course superintendent. "*GFC* helps the golf course superintendent become more efficient in all aspects of their job." Estab. 1924. Circ. 40,000. **Pays on acceptance.** Publishes ms an average of 6 months after acceptance. Byline given. Buys first North American serial rights, web rights, and makes work-for-hire assignments. Editorial lead time 6 months. Submit seasonal material 6 months in advance. Accepts simultaneous submissions. Reports in 3 weeks on queries; 1 month on mss. Sample copy and writer's guidelines free.

Nonfiction: How-to, interview/profile. No articles about playing golf. **Buys 40 mss/year.** Query. Length: 1,500-2,500 words. **Pays $300-450.** Sometimes pays expenses of writers on assignment.

Reprints: Accepts previously printed submissions.

Photos: Send photos with submission. Offers no additional payment for photos accepted with ms. Identification of subjects required. Buys all rights.

$ $ INLINE RETAILER & INDUSTRY NEWS, Sports & Fitness Publishing, 2025 Pearl St., Boulder CO 80302. (303)440-5111. Fax: (303)440-3313. E-mail: hlbernard@aol.com. Website: http://www.s2.com/inline. **Contact:** Heather L. Bernard, editor. **15% freelance written.** Monthly tabloid covering the in-line skating industry. "*InLine Retailer* is a business magazine dedicated to spotting new trends, products and procedures that will help in-line retailers and manufacturers keep a competitive edge." Estab. 1992. Circ. 8,000. Pays on publication. Publishes ms an average of 1 month after acceptance. Byline given. Offers 30% kill fee. Buys first North American serial rights. Editorial lead time 2 months. Submit seasonal material 4 months in advance. Reports in 2 weeks on queries. Sample copy for $5.

- *Inline Retailer* reports that it is looking for more writers with a background in business, particularly sporting goods, to help write news pieces providing insight or analysis into the in-line industry.

Nonfiction: How-to, interview/profile, new product, technical. **Buys 30 mss/year.** Query with published clips. Length: 500-2,000 words. **Pays 15¢/word minimum for assigned articles; 10¢/word for unsolicited articles.** Sometimes pays expenses of writers on assignment.

Columns/Departments: Retailer Corner (tips for running an in-line retail store), 1,000-1,200 words; First Person (insights from high-level industry figures), 1,200-1,500 words. **Buys 20 mss/year.** Query with published clips or send complete ms. **Pays 15-20¢/word.**

Tips: "It's best to write us and explain your background in either the sporting goods business or in-line skating. Mail several clips and also send some ideas that you think would be suitable for our readers. The features and Retailer Corner sections are the ones we typically assign to freelancers. Writers should have solid reporting skills, particularly when it comes to getting subjects to disclose technology, news or tips that they may be unwilling to do without some prodding."

$ $ NSGA RETAIL FOCUS, National Sporting Goods Association, 1699 Wall St., Suite 700, Mt. Prospect IL 60056-5780. (847)439-4000. Fax: (847)439-0111. E-mail: nsga1699@aol.com. **Contact:** Larry N. Weindruch, editor/publisher. **75% freelance written.** Works with a small number of new/unpublished writers each year. "*NSGA Retail Focus* serves as a monthly trade journal for presidents, CEOs and owners of more than 22,000 retail sporting goods firms." Estab. 1948. Circ. 8,500. Pays on publication. Publishes ms an average of 1 month after acceptance. Byline given. Offers 50% kill fee. Buys first rights and second serial (reprint) rights. Submit seasonal material 3 months in advance. Sample copy for 9×12 SAE with 5 first-class stamps.

Nonfiction: Interview/profile, photo feature. "No articles written without sporting goods retail businesspeople in mind as the audience. In other words, no generic articles sent to several industries." **Buys 25 mss/year.** Query with published clips. **Pays $75-500.** Sometimes pays the expenses of writers on assignment.

Photos: State availability of photos with submission. Reviews contact sheets, negatives, transparencies and 5×7 prints. Payment negotiable. Buys one-time rights.

Columns/Departments: Personnel Management (succinct tips on hiring, motivating, firing, etc.); Tax Advisor (simplified explanation of how tax laws affect retailer); Sales Management (in-depth tips to improve sales force performance); Retail Management (detailed explanation of merchandising/inventory control); Advertising (case histories of successful ad campaigns/ad critiques); Legal Advisor; Computers; Store Design; Visual Merchandising; all 1,500 words. **Buys 50 mss/year.** Query. Length: 1,000-1,500 words. **Pays $75-300.**

$ $ POOL & SPA NEWS, Leisure Publications, 4160 Wilshire Blvd., Los Angeles CA 90010. (213)385-3926. Fax: (213)383-1152. E-mail: psn@poolspanews.com. Website: http://poolspaworld.com. **Contact:** Anne Blakey, editor-in-chief. **15% freelance written.** Semimonthly magazine emphasizing news of the swimming pool and spa industry for builders, retail stores and service firms. Estab. 1960. Circ. 16,300. Pays on publication. Publishes ms an average of 2 months after acceptance. Buys all rights. Reports in 2 weeks. Sample copy for $5 and 9×12 SAE with 10 first-class stamps.

Nonfiction: Interview, profile, technical. Length: 500-2,000 words. **Pays 5-14¢/word.** Pays expenses of writers on assignment. Query with published clips.

Reprints: Send typed ms with rights for sale noted and information about when and where the article previously appeared. Pay varies.

Photos: Pays $10/b&w photo used.

Columns/Departments: Pays $150.

N $ $ REFEREE, Referee Enterprises, Inc., P.O. Box 161, Franksville WI 53126. Fax: (414)632-4560. E-mail: refmag@execpc.com. Website: http://www.refmag.com. **Contact:** Jim Arehart, associate editor. Editor: Barry Mano. **75% freelance written.** Monthly trade magazine covering sports officiating. "*Referee* is a magazine for and read by sports officials of all kinds with a focus on baseball, basketball, football, softball and soccer officiating. Estab. 1976. Circ. 40,000. **Pays on acceptance.** Publishes ms an average of 6 months after acceptance. Byline given. Kill fee negotiable. Buys all rights. Editorial lead time 6 months. Reports in 2 weeks on queries; 1 month on mss. Sample copy for #10 SASE; writer's guidelines free.

Nonfiction: Book excerpts, essays, historical/nostalgic, how-to (sports officiating related), humor, interview/profile, opinion, photo feature, technical (as it relates to sports officiating). "We don't want to see articles with themes not relating to sport officiating. General sports articles, although of interest to us, will not be published." **Buys 40 mss/year.** Query with published clips. Length: 500-2,500 words. **Pays $100-400.** Sometimes pays expenses of writers on assignment.

Reprints: Accepts previously published submissions.

Photos: State availability of photos with submission. Reviews contact sheets, negatives, transparencies and prints. Offers $35-40 per photo. Identification of subjects required. Purchase of rights negotiable.

Tips: "Query first and be persistent. We may not like your idea but that doesn't mean we won't like your next one. Professionalism pays off."

N $ $ SPORTING GOODS DEALER, PTN Publishing Company, 445 Broad Hollow Rd., Melville NY 11747. (516)845-2700. Fax: (516)845-7109. **Contact:** Susan Stegemann, managing editor. Editor: Mike Reynolds. **35% freelance written.** "Monthly magazine covering sporting goods for the retailer—not the consumer. What is it the *retailer* can benefit from?" Estab. 1902. Circ. 33,000. Pays on publication. Publishes ms an average of 6 months after acceptance. Byline given. Buys first rights. Editorial lead time 3 months. Submit seasonal material 4 months in advance. Accepts simultaneous submissions. Sample copy free.

Nonfiction: General interest, interview/profile, technical. Special issue: Skate Retailer (February and July). **Buys 30 mss/year.** Query. Length: 1,200-2,500 words. **Pays $250-600 for assigned articles; $250-400 for unsolicited articles.** Sometimes pays expenses of writers on assignment.

Photos: Send photos with submission. Reviews transparencies and prints. Negotiates payment individually. Captions required. Buys one-time rights.

Columns/Departments: Buys 24 mss/year. Query. **Pays $250-600.**

$ $ WHITETAIL BUSINESS, Krause Publications, Inc., 700 E. State St., Iola WI 54990. (715)445-2214, ext. 425. Fax: (715)445-4087. Website: http://www.krause.com. **Contact:** Pat Durkin, editor. Associate editor: Kathy Dugan. Bimonthly magazine. "*Whitetail Business* targets the hunting industry's driving force, the white-tailed deerhunting market. Archery, modern firearm and muzzleloader retail dealers make their largest profit from whitetail hunters, and *Whitetail Business* devotes itself to this largest profit category." Estab. 1997. Circ. 11,000. **Pays on acceptance.** Byline given. Offers $50 kill fee. Buys first North American serial rights. Editorial lead time up to 1 year. Submit seasonal material up to 1 year in advance. Sample copy and writer's guidelines free.

Nonfiction: Retail management, personal experience, technical. Muzzleloading/camouflage (December); Bow-hunting (August); Firearms (October); Accessories/treestands (June). No humor. Query with or without published clips. Length: 400-1,500 words. **Pays $200-350.**

Photos: State availability of photos with submission. Reviews transparencies. Offers $25-300/photo. Identification of subjects required. Buys one-time rights.

Columns/Departments: Archery, Firearms/Muzzleloaders, Marketing (all dealing with white-tailed deer hunting); all 400 words. **Buys 25 mss/year.** Query with published clips. **Pays $250 maximum.**

Fillers: Anecdotes. Length: 100 words maximum. **Pays $25 maximum.**

Tips: "Keep it short."

STONE, QUARRY AND MINING

$ COAL PEOPLE MAGAZINE, Al Skinner Inc., Dept. WM, 629 Virginia St. W., P.O. Box 6247, Charleston WV 25362. (304)342-4129. Fax: (304)343-3124. Editor/Publisher: Al Skinner. **Contact:** Christina Karawan, president. **50% freelance written.** Monthly magazine. "Most stories are about people or historical—either narrative or biographical on all levels of coal people, past and present—from coal execs down to grass roots miners. Most stories are upbeat—showing warmth of family or success from underground up!" Estab. 1976. Circ. 11,000. Pays on publication. Publishes ms an average of 3 months after acceptance. Byline given. Buys first rights, second serial (reprint) rights and makes work-for-hire assignments. Submit seasonal material 2 months in advance. Reports in 3 months. Sample copy for 9×12 SAE with 10 first-class stamps.

Nonfiction: Book excerpts (and film if related to coal), historical/nostalgic (coal towns, people, lifestyles), humor (including anecdotes and cartoons), interview/profile (for coal personalities), personal experience (as relates to coal mining), photo feature (on old coal towns, people, past and present). Special issues: calendar issue for more than 300 annual coal shows, association meetings, etc. (January); surface mining/reclamation award (July); Christmas in Coal Country (December). No poetry, fiction or environmental attacks on the coal industry. **Buys 32 mss/year.** Query with published clips. Length: 5,000 words. **Pays $75.**

Reprints: Send tearsheet of article and information about when and where the article previously appeared. Pays 50% of amount paid for an original article.

Photos: Send photos with submission. Reviews contact sheets, transparencies, 5×7 prints. Captions, identification of subjects required. Buys one-time reprint rights.

Columns/Departments: Editorials—anything to do with current coal issues (non-paid); Mine'ing Our Business (bull pen column—gossip—humorous anecdotes), Coal Show Coverage (freelance photojournalist coverage of any coal function across the US). **Buys 10 mss/year.** Query. Length: 300-500 words. **Pays $15.**

Fillers: Anecdotes. **Buys 10/year.** Length: 300 words. **Pays $15.**

Tips: "We are looking for good feature articles on coal people, towns, companies—past and present, color slides (for possible cover use) and b&w photos to complement stories. Could also use a few news writers to take photos and do journalistic coverage on coal events across the country. Slant stories more toward people and less on historical. More faces and names than old town, company store photos. Include more quotes from people who lived these moments!" The following geographical areas are covered: Eastern Canada; Mexico; Europe; China; Russia; Poland; Australia; as well as U.S. states: Alabama, Tennessee, Virginia, Washington, Oregon, North and South Dakota, Arizona, Colorado, Alaska and Wyoming.

N $ $ $ MINING VOICE, National Mining Association, 1130 17th St., NW, Washington DC 20036-4677. (202)463-2625. Fax: (202)857-0135. E-mail: jchircop@pr.nma.org. Website: http://www.nma.org. **Contact:** Jeanne Chircop, editor. **60% freelance written.** Bimonthly. "*Mining Voice* magazine is intended to serve as the 'voice' of America's hardrock and coal mining industries, informing and educating readers about business issues impacting mining companies. Stories should be written to appeal to those both inside and outside the industry." Estab. 1995. Circ. 10,000. Pays on publication. Publishes ms an average of 3 months after acceptance. Byline given. Offers $50 kill fee. Buys all rights. Editorial lead time 3 months. Submit seasonal material 3 months in advance. Reports in 1-2 months. Sample copy and writer's guidelines free.

Nonfiction: General interest, interview/profile, business interest. No promotional articles, satire, anti-mining, religious, technical. **Buys 50 mss/year.** Query with published clips. Length: 250-3,000 words. **Pays $50-1,200.** Sometimes pays expenses of writers on assignment.

Photos: State availability of photos with submission. Reviews prints. Negotiates payment individually. Identification of subjects required. Buys one-time rights.

Columns/Departments: Mineral Focus (the use of minerals in everyday life), 750 words; Personalities (mining industry employees with interesting outside accomplishments), 750 words; Briefings (soft news items pertaining to mining), 250-350 words. **Buys 20 mss/year.** Query with published clips. **Pays $50-300.**

Tips: "Writers should familiarize themselves with business, political and social trends affecting American business in general and mining in particular. Each issue is theme-based, so obtain a copy of our editorial calendar and guidelines before querying."

$ $ PIT & QUARRY, Advanstar Communications, 7500 Old Oak Blvd., Cleveland OH 44130. (440)891-2607. Fax: (440)891-2675. E-mail: pitquar@en.com. **Contact:** Mark S. Kuhar, editor. Managing Editor: Darren Constantino. 20-**30% freelance written.** Monthly magazine covering nonmetallic minerals, mining and crushed stone. Audience has "knowledge of construction-related markets, mining, minerals processing, etc." Estab. 1918. Circ. 25,000. **Pays on acceptance.** Publishes ms an average of 6 months after acceptance. Byline given. Buys first North American serial rights. Editorial lead time 6 months. Accepts simultaneous submissions. Reports in 1 month on queries; 4 months on mss. Sample copy for 9×12 SAE and 4 first-class stamps. Writer's guidelines free.

Nonfiction: How-to, interview/profile, new product, technical. No humor or inspirational articles. **Buys 12-15 mss/year.** Query. Length: 1,200-2,500 words. **Pays $250-700 for assigned articles; $250-500 for unsolicited articles.** Pays writers with contributor copies or other premiums for simple news items, etc. Sometimes pays expenses of writers on assignment.

Photos: State availability of photos with submission or send photos with submission. Offers no additional payment for photos accepted with ms. Model releases and identification of subjects required. Buys one-time rights.

Columns/Departments: Environmental, economics. Length: 700 words. Buys 5-10 mss/year. Query. Pays $250-300.

Tips: "Be familiar with quarry operations (crushed stone or sand and gravel), not coal or metallic minerals mining. Know construction markets. We need more West Coast-focused stories."

$ $ STONE WORLD, Business News Publishing Company, 299 Market St., Third Floor, Saddle Brook NJ 07663. (201)291-9001. Fax: (201)291-9002. E-mail: stoneworld@aol.com. Website: http://www.stoneworld.com. Publisher: Alex Bachrach. **Contact:** Michael Reis, editor, or Jennifer Adams, managing editor. Monthly magazine on natural building stone for producers and users of granite, marble, limestone, slate, sandstone, onyx and other natural stone products. Estab. 1984. Circ. 18,000. Pays on publication. Publishes ms an average of 6 months after acceptance. Byline given. Buys first rights or second serial (reprint) rights. Submit seasonal material 6 months in advance. Reports in 2 months. Sample copy for $10.

Nonfiction: How-to (fabricate and/or install natural building stone), interview/profile, photo feature, technical, architectural design, artistic stone uses, statistics, factory profile, equipment profile, trade show review. Publishes technical book excerpts. **Buys 10 mss/year.** Query with or without published clips, or send complete ms. Length: 600-3,000 words. **Pays $6/column inch.** Pays expenses of writers on assignment.

Reprints: Send photocopy of article or typed ms with rights for sale noted and information about when and where the article previously appeared. Pays 50% of amount paid for an original article.

Photos: State availability of photos with submission. Reviews transparencies, prints. Pays $10/photo accepted with ms. Captions, identification of subjects required. Buys one-time rights.

Columns/Departments: News (pertaining to stone or design community); New Literature (brochures, catalogs, books, videos, etc., about stone); New Products (stone products); New Equipment (equipment and machinery for working with stone); Calendar (dates and locations of events in stone and design communities). Query or send complete ms. Length: 300-600 words. **Pays $4/inch.**

Tips: "Articles about architectural stone design accompanied by professional color photographs and quotes from designing firms are often published, especially when one unique aspect of the stone selection or installation is highlighted. We are also interested in articles about new techniques of quarrying and/or fabricating natural building stone."

TOY, NOVELTY AND HOBBY

Publications focusing on the toy and hobby industry are listed in this section. For magazines for hobbyists see the Consumer Hobby and Craft section.

N $ $ EDPLAY MAGAZINE, Magazine for the Specialty Toy Retailer, Fahy-Williams Publishing, 171 Reed St., P.O. Box 1080, Geneva NY 14456-8080. (315)489-0458. Fax: (315)781-6820. E-mail: fahwill@epix.net. **Contact:** Tina Manzer, editor. **50% freelance written.** Quarterly trade magazine covering specialty toy industry. "*Edplay Magazine* is geared toward buyers of specialty toys, which include gift stores, specialty toy stores, science and nature stores, educational stores and museum stores. Different from mass market toy retailers such as Target, Wal-Mart, and Toys 'R' Us, specialty toy retailers carry products that are more unique, educational and classic. The trade association for this group is The American Specialty Toy Retailing Association, which has a convention once a year. Most people in this industry attend The American International Toy Fair in New York each February." Estab. 1996. Circ. 8,877. Pays on publication. Publishes ms an average of 4 months after acceptance. Byline given. Buys one-time rights. Editorial lead time 2 months. Submit seasonal material 3 months in advance. Accepts simultaneous submissions. Reports in 3 weeks on queries; 3 months on mss. Sample copy and writer's guidelines free.

Nonfiction: Book excerpts, how-to, interview/profile, personal experience. Special issues: Holiday issue deadline, August 1; Toy Fair issue deadline, December 1. **Buys 10 mss/year.** Send complete ms. Length: 1,500-3,000. **Pays $50-250.** Sometime pays expenses of writers on assignment.

Reprints: Accepts previously published submissions.

Photos: State availability of photos with submission. Reviews transparencies. Offers no additional payment for photos accepted with ms. Identification of subjects required. Buys one time rights.

Fillers: Anecdotes, facts, newsbreaks. **Buys 5/year.** Length: 500-1,500 words. **Pays $50-125.**

Tips: "We like to review mss rather than queries. Artwork (photos, drawings, etc.) is real plus. We enjoy (our readers enjoy) practical, nuts and bolts, news-you-can-use articles."

N $ $ MODEL RETAILER, Resources for Successful Hobby Retailing, Kalmbach Publishing Co., 21027 Crossroads Circle, Waukesha WI 53187-1612. (414)796-8776. Fax: (414)796-1383. E-mail: jslocum@modelretailer.com. Website: http://www.modelretailer.com. **Contact:** Micheal Kuchta, managing editor. Editor: James Slocum. **15% freelance written.** Monthly trade magazine. "*Model Retailer* covers the business of hobbies, from financial and shop management issues to industry trends and the latest product releases. Our goal is to provide hobby shop entrepreneurs with the tools and information they need to be successful retailers." Estab. 1987. Circ. 6,600 (controlled circulation). **Pays on acceptance.** Publishes ms an average of 3 months after acceptance. Byline given. Buys first rights. Editorial lead time 3 months. Submit seasonal material 6 months in advance. Sample copy and writers guidelines free.

Nonfiction: How-to (business), new product. "No articles that do not have a strong hobby or small retail component." **Buys 6-12 mss/year.** Query with published clips. Length: 750-2,000 words. **Pays $200-500 for assigned articles; $100-250 for unsolicited articles.** Sometimes pays expenses for writers on assignment.

Photos: State availability of photos with submission. Reviews prints (4×6). Negotiates payment individually. Captions and identification of subjects required. Buys one-time rights.

Columns and Departments: Contact: James Slocum, editor. Shop Management, Sales Marketing, Technology Advice, 500-750 words; Industry Trends. **Buys 35 mss/year.** Query with published clips. **Pays $100-200.**

TRANSPORTATION

These publications are for professional movers and people involved in transportation of goods. For magazines focusing on trucking see also Auto and Truck.

N $ BUS CONVERSIONS, The First and Foremost Bus Converters Magazine, MAK Publishing, 3431 Cherry Ave., Long Beach CA 90807. (562)492-9394. Fax: (562)492-1345. Website: http://www.busconversions.com. **Contact:** James G. Redfern, editor. Monthly magazine covering the history and industry of buses and bus systems. **95% freelance written.** Estab. 1992. Circ. 20,000. Pays on publication. Buys first North American serial rights. Guidelines sent on request. Encourages first-time writers.

Nonfiction: How-to articles on the electrical, plumbing, mechanical, decorative and structural aspects of bus conversions (buses that are converted into RVs). Each month, *Bus Conversions* publishes a minimum of two coach reviews, usually anecdotal stories told by those who have completed their own bus conversion. Publishes some travel/destination stories (all of which are related to bus/RV travel). Accepts unsolicited mss. **Pays $25-75.**

Photos: Include color photos (glossy) or slides with submission. Photos/slides not returned unless other arrangements are made.

Columns/Departments: Industry Update; Products of Interest; Electrical Shorts; Building a Balanced Energy System; Ask the Experts; One For the Road.

Tips: "Most of our writers are our readers. Knowledge of bus conversions and the associate lifestyle is a prerequisite."

N $ BUS WORLD, Magazine of Buses and Bus Systems, MAK Publishing, 3431 Cherry Ave., Long Beach CA 90807. Website: http://www.busworld.com. **Contact:** James G. Redfern, editor. Monthly magazine covering the history and industry of buses and bus systems. **25% freelance written.** Estab. 1976. Circ. 20,000. Pays on publication. Payment varies ($50-100). Buys first North American serial rights. Guidelines sent on request. Accepts unsolicited manuscripts. Encourages first-time writers.

Nonfiction: *Bus World* caters to those in the transit, intercity and tour industries as well as the individual bus enthusiast. Articles, profiles, interviews relating to the history of the bus and busing, the developments in the industry, and buses themselves. Query. Length: 1,200-3,500 words; 1,800 words average. **Pays $50-125.**

Photos: Include color photos (glossy) or slides with submission. Photos/slides not returned unless other arrangements are made.

Columns/Departments: Industry Update; Products of Interest; Bus Shots (4-page pictorial).

Tips: The history of buses draws in many areas, such as legal history, economics, political developments, and technology. Tap into your knowledge of these areas and relate it to buses. The industry's current trends are the development of alternative-fueled buses and consolidation.

$ $ ITS WORLD, Technology and applications for intelligent transportation systems, Advanstar Communication, Inc., 859 Willamette St., Eugene OR 97401-6806. Fax: (541)344-3514. E-mail: its@itsworld.com. **Contact:** Nancy Johnson, editor. **20% freelance written.** Bimonthly tabloid covering intelligent transporation systems (the application of communications and computer technologies to surface transportation). Estab. 1996. Circ. 18,000. **Pays on acceptance.** Publishes ms an average of 3 months after acceptance. Byline given. Buys first rights or all rights. Editorial lead time 4-6 months. Reports in 6 weeks on queries; 1 month on mss. Sample copy and writer's guidelines free.

Nonfiction: How-to (applications of technology), interview/profile, technical. Query with published clips. Length: 1,500-3,000 words. **Pays $500-650.** Sometimes pays expenses of writers on assignment.

Photos: Send photos with submission. Reviews 2×2 transparencies, prints. Negotiates payment individually. Captions, identification of subjects required. Buys one-time or all rights.

Columns/Departments: World Watch (trends, activities and market opportunities in intelligent transportation systems in a country or region outside the U.S.); Point A/Point B (opinion, insight and advice about varied aspects of ITS), 1,250 words. Query with published clips. **Pays $500-650.**

Tips: "Expertise in surface transportation and/or the application of advanced technologies (telecommunications, computers, etc.) to surface transportation is a must. Writers who demonstrate this through published works and other background information will be given highest consideration."

N $ $ SCHOOL BUS FLEET, Bobit Publishing Co., 21061 S. Western Ave., Torrance CA 90501. (310)533-2400. Fax: (310)533-2503. E-mail: sbf@bobit.com. Website: http://www.schoolbusfleet.com. **Contact:** Steve Hirano, executive editor. Senior Editor: Dale MacDiarmid. **10% freelance written.** Magazine published 9 times/year covering school transportation for K-12 population. "Most of our readers are school bus operators, public and private." Estab. 1965. Circ. 22,000. **Pays on acceptance.** Publishes ms an average of 3 months after acceptance. Byline given. Offers 25% kill fee or $50. Buys first North American serial rights. Editorial lead time 3 months. Submit seasonal material 3 months in advance. Reports in 1 month. Sample copy and writer's guidelines free.

Nonfiction: Interview/profile, new product, technical. **Buys 6 mss/year.** Query with published clips. Length: 600-1,800 words. **Pays 20-25¢/word.** Sometimes pays expenses of writers on assignment.

Photos: State availability of photos with submission. Reviews transparencies and 4×6 prints. Negotiates payment individually. Captions and identification of subjects required. Buys one-time rights.

Columns/Departments: Shop Talk (maintenance information for school bus mechanics), 650 words. **Buys 2 mss/year.** Query with published clips. **Pays $100-150.**

Tips: "Freelancers should submit ideas pertaining to innovative ideas dealing with school bus safety and operations."

$ $ TAXI NEWS, Chedmount Investments Ltd., 38 Fairmount Crescent, Toronto, Ontario M4L 2H4 Canada. (416)466-2328. Fax: (416)466-4220. E-mail: taxinews@the-wine.com. **Contact:** Bill M'Ouat, editor. **100% freelance written.** Monthly tabloid covering the taxicab industry for owners, drivers and regulators primarily in the Toronto area. "We don't care about your biases/philosophy, but they must be clear to the reader. You must know what you are writing about and be able to back up opinions with facts. We are an independent newspaper covering news and views of a specific industry so you will be writing for a knowledgeable audience, while we also require stories, news items to be understandable to a wider, general audience." Estab. 1984. Circ. 10,300. Pays on publication. Publishes ms an average of 2 months after acceptance. Byline given. Offers 50% kill fee or $50 (Canadian). Buys all rights. Editorial lead time 2 months. Submit seasonal material 3 months in advance. Accepts simultaneous submissions. Reports in 3 weeks on queries; 1 month on mss. Sample copy for #10 SASE and Canadian stamp.

Nonfiction: Essays, exposé, general interest, historical/nostalgic, how-to, humor, interview/profile, opinion, personal experience, photo feature. **Buys 20-30 mss/year.** Query or send complete ms. Length: 50-1,000 words. **Pays $25-200 (Canadian).** Sometimes pays the expenses of writers on assignment.

Photos: Send photos with submission. Reviews 3×5 prints. Offers $10-25/photo (Canadian). Captions, identification of subjects required. Buys all rights.

Columns/Departments: Dining Alone; Racetrack Hack; Street Fare. **Buys 36/year.** Query. **Pays $50-100 (Cdn.).**

Fillers: Anecdotes, facts, gags to be illustrated, short humor. **Buys 3-4/year.** Length: 75 words. **Pays $28.**

Tips: "We cover Toronto very well. Occasionally we'll use out-of-town material if it is A) well-written and/or B) of direct applicability to our readers' working lives, e.g., tips (new) on avoiding robberies/violence—how to save money, new regulatory approaches, cab drivers helping people (gratuitous kindness...), etc. Don't get us sued."

TRAVEL

Travel professionals read these publications to keep up with trends, tours and changes in transportation. Magazines about vacations and travel for the general public are listed in the Consumer Travel section.

$ $ $ CORPORATE MEETINGS & INCENTIVES, Adams Business Media, 60 Main St., Maynard MA 01754. (508)448-8211. E-mail: bscofidio@mail.aip.com. Website: http://www.meetingsnet.com. **Contact:** Barbara Scofidio, editor. **75% freelance written.** Monthly magazine covering meetings and incentive travel. "Our cover stories focus on issues of interest to senior execs—from customer service to encouraging innovation—and the integral role meetings play in achieving these goals." Circ. 36,000. Pays 30 days after acceptance. Offers kill fee. Buys all rights. Editorial lead time 3 months. Submit seasonal material 4 months in advance. Sample copy for SAE with $1.50 postage. Writer's guidelines for #10 SASE.

Nonfiction: Interview/profile, travel with a meetings angle. Special issue: Golf (April). **Buys 50 mss/year.** Query with published clips. Length: 1,000-2,500 words. **Pays 50¢/word.** Sometimes pays expenses of writers on assignment.

Photos: State availability of photos with submissions. Reviews contact sheets, transparencies, prints. Negotiates payment individually. Identification of subjects required. Buys one-time rights.

Columns/Departments: Buys 50 mss/year. Query. **Pays $250-500.**

Tips: "Looking for strong business writers with experience writing about employee motivation, incentive programs—ways that companies improve productivity. Best to send relevant clips with a letter after taking a look at the magazine."

N $ $ THE GROUP TRAVEL LEADER, The National Newspaper for Senior Group Travel, The Group Travel Leader, Inc., 401 W. Main St., Suite 222, Lexington KY 40507. Fax: (606)253-0499. E-mail: gtl@mis.net. Website: http://www.grouptravelleader.com. **Contact:** Herb Sparrow, editor. **15% freelance written.** Monthly tabloid. "Topics must be of interest to those who plan travel for senior groups including church groups, bank senior programs or senior citizens groups." Estab. 1991. Circ. 35,000. Pays on publication. Publishes ms an average of 6 months after acceptance. Byline given. Buys all rights. Editorial lead time 2 months. Submit seasonal material 9 months in advance. Sample copy for $3.

Nonfiction: Travel. **Buys 4-6 mss/year.** Query with published clips. Length: 1,800-2,000 words. **Pays $200-300.** Pays expenses of writers on assignment.

Photos: State availability of photos with submission. Reviews transparencies. Offers no additional payment for photos accepted with ms. Captions required.

Columns/Departments: Destination Discovery, 2,000 words; Worth A Trip, 1,100 words. Pays $200-300.

Tips: "We usually hire freelancers to write destination articles when staff writers cannot make the trip themselves. Letting us know your location and availability is more important than suggesting story ideas. We are not looking for ideas for our editorial calendar."

$ $ $ RV BUSINESS, Affinity Group, Inc., 2575 Vista del Mar Dr., Ventura CA 93001. (800)765-1912. Fax: (805)667-4484. E-mail: rvb@tl.com. **Contact:** Sherman Goldenberg, associate publisher. Editor: John Sullaway. **50% freelance written.** Monthly magazine. "*RV Business* caters to a specific audience of people who manufacture, sell,

market, insure, finance, service and supply, components for recreational vehicles." Estab. 1972. Circ. 15,000. **Pays on acceptance.** Publishes ms an average of 2 months after acceptance. Byline given. Offers kill fee. Buys first North American serial rights. Editorial lead time 3 months. Reports in 2 months. Sample copy and writer's guidelines free.
Nonfiction: New product, photo feature, industry news and features. "No general articles without specific application to our market." **Buys 300 mss/year.** Query with published clips. Length: 125-2,200 words. **Pays $35-800.** Sometimes pays expenses of writers on assignment.
Photos: Send photos with submission. Reviews 35mm transparencies. Offers $25-50/photo. Captions, identification of subjects required. Buys one-time rights.
Columns/Departments: Top of the News (RV industry news), 75-400 words; Retailers (RV dealer news), 75-400 words; Features (indepth industry features), 800-2,000 words. **Buys 300 mss/year.** Query. **Pays $25-800.**
Tips: "Query. Send one or several ideas and a few lines letting us know how you plan to treat it/them. We are always looking for good authors knowledgeable in the RV industry or related industries. We need more articles that are brief, factual, hard hitting and business oriented. Review other publications in the field, including enthusiast magazines."

$ $ SPECIALTY TRAVEL INDEX, Alpine Hansen, 305 San Anselmo Ave., #313, San Anselmo CA 94960. (415)455-1643. Fax: (415)459-4974. E-mail: spectrav@ix.netcom.com. Website: http://www.specialtytravel.com. Editor: C. Steen Hansen. **Contact:** Susan Kostrzewa, managing editor. **90% freelance written.** Semiannual magazine covering adventure and special interest travel. Estab. 1980. Circ. 45,000. Pays on publication. Byline given. Buys one-time rights. Editorial lead time 3 months. Submit seasonal material 3 months in advance. Writer's guidelines on request.
Nonfiction: How-to, new product, personal experience, photo feature, travel. **Buys 15 mss/year.** Query. Length: 1,250 words. **Pays $200 minimum.**
Reprints: Send tearsheet of article. Pays 100% of amount paid for an original article.
Photos: State availability of photos with submission. Reviews 35mm transparencies, 5×7 prints. Negotiates payment individually. Captions, identification of subjects required.

N $ $ VACATION INDUSTRY REVIEW, Interval International, 6262 Sunset Dr., Penthouse One, Miami FL 33143. (305)666-1861, ext. 7022. E-mail: gleposky@interval-intl.com. **Contact:** George Leposky, editor. **30% freelance written.** Bimonthly magazine covering the vacation ownership/timeshare industry. Estab. 1982. Circ. 15,000. **Pays on acceptance.** Publishes ms an average of 6 months after acceptance. Byline given. Buys all rights. Editorial lead time 2 months. Submit seasonal material 6 months in advance. Reports in 1 month. Sample copy for 9×12 SAE and 3 first-class stamps. Writer's guidelines for #10 SASE.
Nonfiction: Essays, interview/profile, new product, opinion, photo feature, technical, travel. No consumer travel or hotel material. **Buys 10-12 mss/year.** Query with published clips. Length: 1,000-1,500 words. **Pays 30¢/word.** Sometimes pays expenses of writers on assignment.
Photos: Send photos with submission. Reviews 35mm or larger transparencies and 5×7 or larger prints. Negotiates payment individually. Captions and identification of subjects required. Buys one-time rights.
Tips: "The readership of *VIR* consists of people who develop, finance, market, sell and manage timeshare resorts and mixed-use projects such as hotels, resorts and second-home communities with a vacation-ownership component; and suppliers of products and services to the vacation-ownership industry."

MARKETS THAT WERE listed in the 1998 edition of *Writer's Market* but do not appear this year are listed in the General Index with a notation explaining why they were omitted.

Scriptwriting

Everyone has a story to tell, something to say. In telling that story as a play, movie, TV show or educational video you have selected that form over other possibilities. Scriptwriting makes some particular demands, but one thing remains the same for authors of novels, nonfiction books and scripts: you'll learn to write by rewriting. Draft after draft your skills improve until, hopefully, someone likes your work enough to hire you.

Whether you are writing a video to train doctors in a new surgical technique, alternative theater for an Off-Broadway company or you want to see you name on the credits of the next Harrison Ford movie, you must perfect both writing and marketing skills. A successful scriptwriter is a talented artist and a savvy business person. But marketing must always be secondary to writing. A mediocre pitch for a great script will still get you farther than a brilliant pitch for a mediocre script. The art and craft of scriptwriting lies in successfully executing inspiration.

Writing a script is a private act. Polishing it may involve more people as you ask friends and fellow writers to take a look at it. Marketing takes your script public in an effort to find the person willing to give the most of what you want, whether it's money, exposure or control, in return for your work.

There are accepted ground rules to presenting and marketing scripts. Following those guidelines will maximize your chances of getting your work before an audience.

Presenting your script professionally earns a serious consideration of its content. Certain types of scripts have a definite format and structure. An educational video written in a one-column format, a feature film much longer than 120 pages or an hour-long TV show that peaks during the first 20 minutes indicates an amateur writer. There are several sources for correct formats, including *The Complete Guide to Script Formats*, by Cole and Haig.

Submission guidelines are similar to those for other types of writing. The initial contact is a one-page query letter, with a brief synopsis and a few lines as to your credits or experience relevant to the subject of your script. Never send a complete manuscript until it is requested. Almost every script sent to a producer, studio, or agent must be accompanied by a release form. Ask the producer or agent for his form when invited to submit the complete script. Always include a self-addressed stamped envelope if you want your work returned; a self-addressed stamped postcard will do for acknowledgement or reply if you do not need your script returned.

Most writers break in with spec scripts, written "for free," which serve as calling cards to show what they can do. These scripts plant the seeds of your professional reputation by making the rounds of influential people looking to hire writers, from advertising executives to movie moguls. Good writing is more important than a specific plot. Make sure you are sending out your best work; a first draft is not a finished product. Have several spec scripts completed, as a producer will often decide that a story is not right for him, or a similar work is already in production, but want to know what else you have. Be ready for that invitation.

Writing a script is a matter of learning how to refine your writing so that the work reads as a journey, not a technical manual. The best scripts have concise, visceral scenes that demand to be presented in a specific order and accomplish definite goals.

Educational videos have a message that must be expressed economically and directly, engaging the audience in an entertaining way while maintaining interest in the topic. Theatrical plays are driven by character and dialogue that expose a thematic core and engender enthusiasm or involvement in the conflict. Cinematic screenplays, while more visually-oriented, are a series of discontinuous scenes stacked to illuminate the characters, the obstacles confronting them and the resolution they reach.

A script is a difficult medium—written words that sound natural when spoken, characters that are original yet resonate with the audience, believable conflicts and obstacles in tune with the end result. One theater added to their listing the following tip: "Don't write plays. Write novels, short stories, anything but plays. But if you *must* write plays. . . ." If you are compelled to present your story visually, be aware of the intense competition. Hone it, refine it, keep working on it until it can be no better, then look for the best home you can find. That's success.

BUSINESS & EDUCATIONAL WRITING

"It's no longer the plankton of the filmmaking food chain," says Kirby Timmons, creative director of the video production company CRM Films. Scripts for corporate training, business management and education videos have become as sophisticated as those designed for TV and film, and they carry the additional requirement of conveying specific content. With an audience that is increasingly media literate, anything that looks and feels like a "training film" will be dead in the water. The trick is to produce a script that engages, compels *and* informs about the topic, whether it's customer relations, listening skills or effective employee management, while staying on a tight budget.

This can create its own challenges, but is an excellent way to increase your skills and exercise your craft. Good scriptwriters are in demand in this field. There is a strong emphasis on producing a polished complete script before filming begins, and a writer's involvement doesn't end until the film is "in the can."

A remarkably diverse industry, educational and corporate video is a $18-25 billion business, compared to theatrical films and TV, estimated at $5 billion. And there is the added advantage that opportunities are widespread, from large local corporations to small video production houses in your area. Larger companies often have inhouse video production companies, but others rely on freelance writers. Your best bet would be to find work with companies that specialize in making educational and corporate video while at the same time making yourself known to the creative directors of inhouse video staffs in large corporations. Advertising agencies are also a good source of work, as they often are asked by their clients for help in creating films and use freelance writers and producers.

Business and educational video is a market-driven industry, with material created either in response to a general need or a specific demand. The production company usually identifies a subject and finds the writer. As such, there is a perception that a spec script will not work in this media. While it is true that, as in TV and theatrical films, a writer's spec script is rarely produced, it is a good résumé of qualifications and sample of skills. It can get you other work even though it isn't produced. Your spec script should demonstrate a knowledge of this industry's specific format. For the most part video scripts are written in two-columns, video on the left, audio on the right. A variety of references cover the basics of video script format. Computer software is available to format the action and dialogue.

Aside from the original script, another opportunity for the writer is the user's guide that often accompanies a video. If you are hired to create the auxiliary material you'll receive a copy of the finished video and write a concurrent text for the teacher or implementor to use.

Networking is very important. There is no substitute for calling companies and finding out what is in your area. Contact local training and development companies and find out who they serve and what they need. It pays to join professional organizations such as the Association of Visual Communicators and the Association for Training and Development, which offer seminars and conventions. Making the rounds at a business convention of video producers with your business card could earn you a few calls and invitations to submit writing samples.

Budgets are tighter for educational or corporate videos than for theatrical films. You'll want to work closely with the producer to make sure your ideas can be realized within the budget. Your fee will vary with each job, but generally a script written for a production house in a subject area with broad marketability will pay $5,000-7,000. A custom-produced video for a specific company will usually pay less. The pay does not increase exponentially with your experience; large increases come if you choose to direct and produce as well as write.

With the expansion of cable TV-based home shopping opportunities, direct response TV (informercials) is an area with increasing need for writers to create the scripts that sell the products. Production companies are located across the country, and more are popping up as the business grows. Pay can range from $5,000-18,000, depending on the type, length and success of the program.

The future of business and educational video lies in interactive media or multimedia. Interactive media combines computer and video technology to create a product that doesn't have to progress along a linear path. Videos that offer the viewer the opportunity to direct the course of events hold exciting possibilities for corporate training and educational applications. Writers will be in high demand as stories offer dozens of choices in storylines. Interactive video will literally eat up pages of script as quickly as a good writer produces them. A training session may last only 20 minutes, but the potential untapped story lines could add up to hours worth of script that must be written, realized and made available. From training salespeople to doctors, or teaching traffic rules to issues in urbanization, corporate and educational video is about to undergo a tremendous revolution.

Information on business and educational script markets listed in the previous edition of *Writer's Market* but not included in this edition can be found in the General Index.

N **ABS ENTERPRISES**, P.O. Box 5127, Evanston IL 60204-5127. (847)982-1414. Fax: (847)982-1418. President: Alan Soell. "We produce material for all levels of corporate, medical, cable and educational institutions for the purposes of training and development, marketing and meeting presentations. We also are developing programming for the broadcast areas." 75% freelance written. "We work with a core of three to five freelance writers from development to final drafts." All scripts published are unagented submissions. Buys all rights. Accepts previously produced material. Reports in 2 weeks on queries.
Needs: Videotape, multimedia, realia, slides, tapes and cassettes, television shows/series. Currently interested in "sports instructional series that could be produced for the consumer market on tennis, gymnastics, bowling, golf, aerobics, health and fitness, cross-country skiing and cycling. Also motivational and self-improvement type videos and film ideas to be produced. These could cover all ages '6-60' and from professional to blue collar jobs. These two areas should be 30 minutes and be timeless in approach for long shelf life. Sports audience, age 25-45; home improvement, 25-65. Cable TV needs include the two groups of programming detailed here. We are also looking for documentary work on current issues, nuclear power, solar power, urban development, senior citizens—but with a new approach." Query or submit synopsis/outline and résumé. Pays by contractual agreement.
Tips: "I am looking for innovative approaches to old problems that just don't go away. The approach should be simple and direct so there is immediate audience identification with the presentation. I also like to see a sense of humor used. Trends in the audiovisual field include interactive video with disk—for training purposes."

A/V CONCEPTS CORP., 30 Montauk Blvd., Oakdale NY 11769-1399. (516)567-7227. Fax: (516)567-8745. Contact: P. Solimene or L. Solimene. Produces supplementary materials for elementary-high school students, either on grade level or in remedial situations. Estab. 1971. 100% freelance written. Buys 25 scripts/year from unpublished/unproduced writers. Employs video, book and personal computer media. Reports in 1 month on outline, 6 weeks on final scripts. Buys all rights. Sample copy for 9×12 SAE with 5 first-class stamps.
Needs: Interested in original educational computer (disk-based) software programs for Apple II family, IBM, Macintosh. Main concentration in language arts, mathematics and reading. "Manuscripts must be written using our lists of vocabulary words and meet our readability formula requirements. Specific guidelines are devised for each level. Student activities required. Length of manuscript and subjects will vary according to grade level for which material is prepared. Basically, we want material that will motivate people to read." Pays $300 and up.
Tips: "Writers must be highly creative and disciplined. We are interested in high interest/low readability materials."

N **SAM BLATE ASSOCIATES**, 10331 Watkins Mill Dr., Montgomery Village MD 20886-3950. (301)840-2248. Fax: (301)990-0707. E-mail: samblate@bellatlantic.net. President: Sam Blate. Produces educational and audiovisual material for business, education, institutions, state and federal governments. "We work with 2 *local* writers per year on a per project basis—it varies as to business conditions and demand." Buys first rights when possible. Reports in 1 month. SASE for return.

Needs: Scripts on technical, business and outdoor subjects. Query with samples and SASE for return. Payment "depends on type of contract with principal client." Pays some expenses of writers on assignment.

Tips: "Writers must have a strong track record of technical and aesthetic excellence. Clarity and accuracy are not next to divinity—they are above it."

N **CAMBRIDGE EDUCATIONAL**, 90 MacCorkle Ave. SW, South Charleston WV 25303. Production Staff: Charlotte Angel. Estab. 1983. Audience is junior high/high schools, vocational schools, libraries, guidance centers. Buys 18-24 video scripts/year. Works with 12-18 writers/year. Buys all rights. "Samples are kept for file reference." Reports only if interested. Free catalog. Query with synopsis, résumé or writing sample ("excerpt from a previous script, preferably"). Makes outright purchase of $2,000-4,000. Will only respond if interested.

Needs: Videotapes. Educational programming suitable for junior high and high school age groups (classroom viewing and library reference). "Programs range from 20-35-minutes in length. Each should have a fresh approach for how-tos, awareness, and introductions to various subject matters. Subjects range from guidance, home economics, parenting, health, and vocational to social studies, science and business."

Tips: "We are looking for a new slant on standard educational topics, as well as contemporary issues. Currently focusing on science and social studies. We also produce CD-ROMs and may need script developers for these projects."

N **CLEARVUE/EAV, INC.**, Dept. WM, 6465 N. Avondale Ave., Chicago IL 60631-1909. (773)775-9433. Fax: (773)775-9855. E-mail: mary@clearvue.com. Website: http://www.clearvue.com. President: Mark Ventling. Contact: Mary Watanabe. Produces material for educational market—grades K-12. 75% freelance written. Prefers to work with published/established writers. Buys 5 scripts/year, also some teaching materials. Buys all rights. Accepts previously produced material. Reports in 2 weeks on queries; 3 weeks on submissions.

Needs: Videos, multimedia kits, CD-ROM. "Our videos are 8-30 minutes for all curriculum areas." Query. Makes outright purchase, $500-1,000. Sometimes pays the expenses of writers on assignment.

Tips: "Our interests are in video and CD-ROM for the elementary and high school markets on all subjects."

N **CONTINENTAL FILM PRODUCTIONS CORPORATION**, P.O. Box 5126, 4315 North Creek Rd., Chattanooga TN 37406. (423)622-1193. Fax: (423)629-0853. President: James L. Webster. Estab. 1951. Produces "AV and video presentations for businesses and nonprofit organizations for sales, training, public relations, documentation, motivation, etc." Works with many writers annually. Buys all rights. Reports in 1 week.

Needs: "We do need new writers of various types." Produces multi-media presentations, interactive programs and videos. Query with samples and résumé. Unsolicited submissions not returned.

Tips: Looks for writers whose work shows technical understanding, humor, common sense, practicality, simplicity, creativity, etc. Important for writers to adapt script to available production budget.

CRM FILMS, 1801 Avenue of the Stars, #715, Los Angeles CA 90067-5802. Fax: (310)789-5392. E-mail: kirby@crmfilms.com. Website: http://www.crmfilms.com. Creative Director: Kirby Timmons. Estab. 1960. Material for business and organizational training departments. Buys 2-4 scripts/year. Works with 6-8 writers/year. Buys all rights and interactive training rights. No previously produced material. Reports in 1 month. Catalog for 10×13 SAE with 4 first-class stamps. Query with résumé and script sample of writer's work in informational or training media. Makes outright purchase of $4,000-7,000, or in accordance with Writers Guild standard. "We accept WGA standard one-page informational/interactive agreement which stipulates *no* minimum but qualifies writer for pension and health coverage."

Needs: Videotapes, multimedia kits. "CRM is looking for short (10- 20-minute) scripts on management topics such as communication, decision making, team building and customer service. No 'talking heads,' prefer drama-based, 'how to' approach as opposed to awareness style, but will on occasion produce either. 'Attitude and Positivity' training will be bigger this year; 'change' is always a hot topic."

Tips: "Know the *specific* training need which your idea or script fulfills! Recent successes relate real-life events as basis for organizational or team learning—The Challenger incident to illustrate how groupthink can negatively impact team decisions, for example. Other titles document the challenges of retaining skilled employees in an active job market and compliance with ADA and other laws in hiring and evaluation."

THE FILM HOUSE INC., 602 Main, Cincinnati OH 45202-2545. (513)381-2211. President: Ken Williamson. Estab. 1973. Audience is corporate communications and television commercials. Buys 5 scripts/year. Works with 3 writers/year. Buys all rights. No previously published material. Reoprts in 1 month on queries. Query with résumé.

Needs: Films, videotapes. Corporate, training and new product video. Writing assignments on a project basis only.

Tips: "We hire only seasonal, experienced writers on a freelance, per project basis. If interested send only a résumé."

HAYES SCHOOL PUBLISHING CO., INC., 321 Pennwood Ave., Wilkinsburg PA 15221-3398. (412)371-2373. Fax: (412)371-6408. Contact: Clair N. Hayes III, president. Estab. 1940. Produces material for school teachers and principals, elementary through high school. Also produces charts, workbooks, teacher's handbooks, posters, bulletin board material and reproducible blackline masters (grades K-12). 25% freelance written. Prefers to work with published/established writers. Buys 5-10 scripts/year from unpublished/unproduced writers. 100% of scripts produced are un-

agented submissions. Buys all rights. Reports in 3 months. Catalog for SAE with 3 first-class stamps. Writer's guidelines for #10 SAE with 2 first-class stamps.
Needs: Educational material only. Particularly interested in foreign language material and educational material for elementary school level. Query. Pays $25 minimum.

JIST WORKS, INC., 720 N. Park Ave., Indianapolis IN 46202. (317)264-3767. Fax: (317)264-3763. E-mail: jistworks @aol.com. Website: http://www.jistworks.com. Video Production Manager: Kelli Lawrence. Estab. 1981. Produces career counseling, motivational materials (youth to adult) that encourage good planning and decision making for a successful future. Buys 3-5 scripts/year. Works with 2-3 writers/year. Buys all rights. Accepts previously produced material. Reports in 2 months. Catalog free. Query with synopsis. Makes outright purchase of $500 minimum.
Needs: Videotapes, multimedia kits. 15-30 minute video VHS tapes on job search materials and related markets.
Tips: "We need writers for long formats, such as scripts and instructor's guides, as well as short formats for catalogs, press releases, etc. We pay a royalty on finished video productions. We repackage, market, duplicate and take care of all other expenses when we acquire existing programs. Average sell price is $139. Producer gets a percentage of this and is not charged for any costs. Contact us, in writing, for details."

N **PAUL S. KARR PRODUCTIONS**, 2925 W. Indian School Rd., Box 11711, Phoenix AZ 85017. Phone/fax: (602)266-4198. Utah Division: 1024 N. 250 E., Box 1254, Orem UT 84057. (801)226-8209. Produces films and videos for industry, business, education, TV spots and entertainment. Works on co-production ventures that have been funded.
Needs: Produces 16mm films and videos. Query. "*Do not submit material unless requested.*" Payment varies.
Tips: "One of the best ways for a writer to become a screenwriter is to come up with a client that requires a film or video. He can take the project to a production company, such as we are, assume the position of an associate producer, work with an experienced professional producer in putting the production into being, and in that way learn about video and filmmaking, chalk up some meaningful credits, and share in the profits. Direct consumer TV spots (that is, 800-number sales spots) have become a big business in the Phoenix market the last few years. Our company is set up to handle all facets of this area of television marketing."

MOTIVATION MEDIA INC., 1245 Milwaukee Ave., Glenview IL 60025-2499. (847)297-4740. Fax: (847)297-6829. E-mail: frank.stedronsky@motivationmedia.com. Website: http://www.motivationmedia.com. CEO: Frank Stedronsky. Produces customized meeting, training and marketing material for presentation to salespeople, customers, shareholders, corporate/industrial employees and distributors. 90% freelance written. Buys 50 scripts/year. Prefers to work with published/established writers. 100% unagented submissions. Buys all rights. Reports in 1 month.
Needs: Material for all audiovisual media—particularly marketing-oriented (sales training, sales promotional, sales motivational) material. Produces sales meeting programs, training videotapes, print collateral, audio programs and interactive multimedia. Software should be AV oriented. Query with samples and résumé. Pay is commensurate with scope of assignment and writer's qualifications and experience. Pays expenses of writers on assignment.

PALARDO PRODUCTIONS, 1807 Taft Ave., Suite 4, Hollywood CA 90028. Phone/fax: (213)469-8991. Website: http://www.palardo.com. Director: Paul Ardolino. Estab. 1971. Produces material for youth ages 13-35. Buys 3-4 scripts/year. Buys all rights. Reports in 2 weeks on queries; 1 month on scripts.
Needs: Multimedia kits, tapes and cassettes, videotapes. "We are seeking comedy feature scripts involving technology and coming of age; techno-shortform projects." Submit synopsis/outline and résumé. Pays in accordance with Writers Guild standards.
Tips: "Do not send a complete script—only synopsis of four pages or less *first.*"

N **PHOTO COMMUNICATION SERVICES, INC.**, 6055 Robert Dr., Traverse City MI 49684. (616)943-5050. President: M'Lynn Hartwell. Produces commercial, industrial, sales, training material etc. 95% freelance written. No scripts from unpublished/unproduced writers. 100% of scripts produced are unagented submissions. Buys all rights and first serial rights. Reports in 1 month.
Needs: Multimedia kits, tapes and cassettes, video presentations. Query with samples or submit completed script and résumé. Pays by agreement.

CHARLES RAPP ENTERPRISES, INC., 1650 Broadway, New York NY 10019. (212)247-6646. President: Howard Rapp. Estab. 1954. Produces materials for firms and buyers. Works with 5 writers/year. "Work as personal manager/agent in sales." Accepts previously produced material. Reports in 1 month on queries; 2 months on submissions. Submit résumé or sample of writing. Pays in accordance with Writers Guild standards.
Needs: Videotapes, treatments, scripts.

N **PETER SCHLEGER COMPANY**, 200 Central Park S., 27-B, New York NY 10019-1415. Phone/fax: (212)245-4973. Contact: Peter R. Schleger, president. Produces material primarily for employee populations in corporations and non-profit organizations. Buys all rights, "most work is for a one-time use, and that piece may have no life beyond one project." Accepts previously produced material. Reports in 1 month. "Typical programs are customized workshops or specific individual programs from subjects such as listening and presentation skills to medical benefits communication. No program is longer than 10 minutes. If they need to be, they become shorter modules."
Needs: Produces sound filmstrips, video and printed manuals and leader's guides. Send completed script and résumé.

Makes outright purchase; payment "depends on script length."
Tips: "We are looking to receive and keep on file a résumé and short, completed script sample of a program not longer than 10 minutes. The shorter the better to get a sense of writing style and the ability to structure a piece. We would also like to know the fees the writer expects for his/her work. Either per-diem, by project budget or by finished script page. We want communicators with a training background or who have written training programs, modules and the like. We want to know of people who have written print material, as well. We do not want to see scripts that have been written and are looking for a producer/director. We will look at queries for possible workshops or new approaches for training, but these must be submitted as longshots only; it is not our primary business. As we also produce video and audio media, we will work with writers who have clients needing these services."

SPENCER PRODUCTIONS, INC., 736 West End Ave., New York NY 10025. (212)865-8829. General Manager: Bruce Spencer. Executive Producer: Alan Abel. Produces material for high school students, college students and adults. Occasionally uses freelance writers with considerable talent. Reports in 1 month.
Needs: Prerecorded tapes and cassettes. Satirical material only. Query. Pay is negotiable.
Tips: "For a comprehensive view of our humor requirements, we suggest viewing our feature film production, *Is There Sex After Death* (Rated R), starring Buck Henry. It is available at video stores."

TALCO PRODUCTIONS, 279 E. 44th St., New York NY 10017-4354. (212)697-4015. President: Alan Lawrence. Vice President: Marty Holberton. Estab. 1968. Produces variety of material for TV, radio, business, trade associations, nonprofit organizations, public relations (chiefly political and current events), etc. Audiences range from young children to senior citizens. 20-40% freelance written. Buys scripts from published/produced writers only. Buys all rights. No previously published material. Reports in 3 weeks on queries.

- Talco reports that it is doing more public relations-oriented work: print, videotape and radio.

Needs: Films (16, 35mm), slides, radio tapes and cassettes, videotape. "We maintain a file of writers and call on those with experience in the same general category as the project in production. We do not accept unsolicited manuscripts. We prefer to receive a writer's résumé listing credits. If his/her background merits, we will be in touch when a project seems right." Makes outright purchase/project and in accordance with Writers Guild standards (when appropriate). Sometimes pays expenses of writers on assignment.
Tips: "Concentration is now in TV productions. Production budgets will be tighter."

TEL-AIR INTERESTS, INC., 1755 NE 149th St., Miami FL 33181. (305)944-3268. Fax: (305)944-1143. E-mail: telair@aol.com. Contact: Grant H. Gravitt, president. Produces material for groups and theatrical and TV audiences. Buys all rights. Submit résumé.
Needs: Documentary films on education, travel and sports. Produces films and videotape. Makes outright purchase.

ULTITECH, INC., Foot of Broad St., Stratford CT 06497. (203)375-7300. Fax/BBS: (203)375-6699. E-mail: utilitech @meds.com. Website: http://www.meds.com. Contact: William J. Comcowich, president. Estab. 1993. Designs, develops and produces online services and interactive communications programs including video, multimedia, expert systems, software tools, computer-based training and audience response meetings. Specializes in medicine, science and technology. Prefers to work with published/established writers with video, multimedia and medical experience. 90% freelance written. Buys writing for approximately 15-20 programs/year. Electronic submissions onto BBS or via ftp or e-mail attachment. Buys all rights. Reports in 1 month.
Needs: Currently producing about 10 interactive programs for medical audiences. Submit résumé and complete script. Makes outright purchase. Pays expenses of writers on assignment.
Tips: "Interactive media for learning and entertainment is a growing outlet for writers—acquiring skills for interactive design and development will pay back in assignments."

VISUAL HORIZONS, 180 Metro Park, Rochester NY 14623. (716)424-5300. Fax: (716)424-5313. E-mail: slides1@aol.com. or info@horizons.com. Website: http://www.visualhorizons.com. President: Stanley Feingold. Produces material for general audiences. Buys 5 programs/year. Reports in 5 months. Free catalog.
Needs: Business, medical and general subjects. Produces silent and sound filmstrips, multimedia kits, slide sets, videotapes. Query with samples. Payment negotiable.
Tips: "We offer materials to help our audience make powerful presentations, train staff or customers, sell products or services and inspire audiences."

PLAYWRITING

TV and movies are visual media where the words are often less important than the images. Writing plays uses different muscles, different techniques. Plays are built on character and dialogue—words put together to explore and examine characters.

The written word is respected in the theater by producer, cast, director and even audience, to a degree unparalleled in other formats. While any work involving so many people to reach its final form is in essence a collaboration, it is presided over by the playwright and changes can be made only with her approval, a power many screenwriters can only envy. If a play is worth producing, it will be produced "as is."

Counterbalancing the greater freedom of expression are the physical limitations inherent in live performance: a single stage, smaller cast, limited sets and lighting and, most importantly, a strict, smaller budget. These conditions affect not only what but also how you write.

Start writing your play by reading. Your local library has play anthologies. Check the listings in this section for play publishers such as Baker's Plays and Samuel French. Reading gives you a feel for how characters are built, layer by layer, word by word, how each interaction presents another facet of a character. Exposition must mean something to the character, and the story must be worth telling for a play to be successful.

There are plenty of books, seminars and workshops to help you with the writing of your play. The development of character, setting, dialogue and plot are skills that will improve with each draft. The specific play format is demonstrated in *The Complete Book of Script Formats*, by Cole and Haig and *The Writer's Digest Book of Manuscript Formats*, by Buchman and Groves.

Once your play is finished you begin marketing it, which can take as long (or longer) than writing it. Before you begin you must have your script bound (three brads and a cover are fine) and copyrighted at the Copyright Office of the Library of Congress or registered with the Writers Guild of America. Write either agency and ask for information and an application.

Your first goal will be to get at least a reading of your play. You might be lucky and get a small production. Community theaters or smaller regional houses are good places to start. Volunteer at a local theater. As prop mistress or spotlight operator you will get a sense of how a theater operates, the various elements of presenting a play and what can and cannot be done, physically as well as dramatically. Personal contacts are important. Get to know the literary manager or artistic director of local theaters, which is the best way to get your script considered for production. Find out about any playwrights' groups in your area through local theaters or the drama departments of nearby colleges and universities. Use your creativity to connect with people that might be able to push your work higher.

Contests can be a good way to get noticed. Many playwriting contests offer as a prize at least a staged reading and often a full production. Once you've had a reading or workshop production, set your sights on a small production. Use this as a learning experience. Seeing your play on stage can help you view it more objectively and give you the chance to correct any flaws or inconsistencies. Incorporate any comments and ideas from the actors, director or even audience that you feel are on the mark into revisions of your script.

Use a small production also as a marketing tool. Keep track of all the press reviews, any interviews with you, members of the cast or production and put together a "press kit" for your play that can make the rounds with the script.

After you've been produced you have several directions to take your play. You can aim for a larger commercial production; you can try to get it published; you can seek artistic grants. After you have successfully pursued at least one of those avenues you can look for an agent. Choosing one direction does not rule out pursuing others at the same time. *The Dramatists Sourcebook*, published annually by Theatre Communications Group (355 Lexington Ave., New York NY 10017) lists opportunities in all these areas. The Dramatists Guild (234 W. 45th St., New York NY 10036) has three helpful publications: a bimonthly newsletter with articles, news and up-to-date information and opportunities; a quarterly journal; and an annual directory, a resource book for playwrights listing theaters, agents, workshops, grants, contests, etc.

Good reviews in a smaller production can get you noticed by larger theaters paying higher royalties and doing more ambitious productions. To submit your play to larger theaters you'll put together a submission package. This will include a one-page query letter to the literary manager or dramaturg briefly describing the play. Mention any reviews and give the number of cast members and sets. You will also send a two- to three-page synopsis, a ten-page sample of the most interesting section of your play, your résumé and the press kit you've assembled. Do not send your complete manuscript until it is requested.

You can also explore publishing your play. *Writer's Market* lists many play publishers. When your script is published your play will make money while someone else does the marketing. You'll be listed in a catalog that is sent out to hundreds or thousands of potential performance spaces—high schools, experimental companies, regional and community theaters—for possible production. You'll receive royalty checks for both performance fees and book sales. In contacting publishers you'll want to send your query letter with the synopsis and reviews.

There are several sources for grants. Some are federal or state, but don't overlook sources closer to home. The category "Arts Councils and Foundations" in Contests and Awards in this book lists a number of sources. On the national level contact the NEA Theater Program Fellowship for Playwrights (1100 Pennsylvania Ave. NW, Washington DC 20506). State arts commissions are another possible source, and also offer opportunities for involvement in programs where you can meet fellow playwrights. Some cities have arts and cultural commissions that offer grants for local artists. PEN publishes a comprehensive annual book, *Grants and Awards Available to American Writers* that also includes a section for Canadian writers. The latest edition is available from the PEN American Center (568 Broadway, New York NY 10012).

Once you have been produced on a commercial level, your play has been published or you have won an important grant, you can start pursuing an agent. This is not always easy. Fewer agents represent playwrights alone—there's more money in movies and TV. No agent will represent an unknown playwright. Having an agent does *not* mean you can sit back and enjoy the ride. You will still need to get out and network, establishing ties with theaters, directors, literary managers, other writers, producers, state art agencies and publishers, trying to get your work noticed. You will have some help, though. A good agent will have personal contacts that can place your work for consideration at a higher level than your efforts alone might.

There is always the possibility of moving from plays to TV and movies. There is a certain cachet in Hollywood surrounding successful playwrights. The writing style will be different—more visually oriented, less dependent on your words. The money is better, but you will have less command over the work once you've sold that copyright. It seems to be easier for a playwright to cross over to movies than for a screenwriter to cross over to plays.

Writing can make you feel isolated, even when your characters are so real to you they seem to be in the room as you write. Sometimes the experience and companionship of other playwrights is what you need to get you over a particular hurdle in your play. Membership and service organizations such as The Dramatists Guild, The International Women's Writing Guild and local groups such as the Playwright's Center in Minneapolis and the Northwest Playwright's Guild in Seattle can help you feel still a part of this world as you are off creating your own.

Information on playwriting markets listed in the previous edition of *Writer's Market* but not included in this edition can be found in the General Index.

[N] ACTORS & PLAYWRIGHTS' INITIATIVE, P.O. Box 50051, Kalamazoo MI 49005-0051. (616)343-8310. Contact: Robert C. Walker, producing artistic director. Estab. 1989. Produces 9 full lengths plus 'Late Night' 1 acts/year. Produces professional, regional material for an academic audience age 25-45. Query with synopsis. Reports in 2 months. Pays 5-6% royalty.

Needs: Character driven, social/political provocative and adaptations—primarily non-musical. "Our theater is a small, 60-seat black box thrust stage; absolute minimum tech—sets, props, etc." Limit cast to 10.

Tips: "Study the greats—from Sophocles to Mamet."

[N] ACTORS' STOCK COMPANY, 3884 Van Ness Lane, Dallas TX 75220. (214)353-9916. Contact: Keith Oncale, artistic director. Estab. 1988. Produces 3-4 plays/year. "We stage semi-professional productions to a young adult to middle-aged general audience." Query with synopsis. Reports in 3 months. Purchases reading privileges. Pays royalty.

- Actors Stock Company reports that two scripts by *Writer's Market* readers have received staged readings, one of which also had a full production.

Needs: Two- and three-act plays, covering a wide variety of styles, but with fewer than 12 cast members. Average

staging facilities are 100-seat houses or smaller.
Tips: "Trends today reflect a return to comic realism that comments on our society without commenting on the play itself."

ALLEYWAY THEATRE, 1 Curtain Up Alley, Buffalo NY 14202-1911. Fax: (716)852-2266. E-mail: alleywayth.com. Dramaturg: Kevin Stevens. Estab. 1980, competition 1990. Produces 4 full-length, 10-15 short plays/year. Submit complete ms. "Musicals must be accompanied by audio tape." Reports in 6 months. Buys first production, credit rights. Pays 7% royalty plus travel and accommodations for opening.

- Alleyway Theatre also sponsors the Maxim Mazumdar New Play Competition. See the Contest & Awards section for more information.

Needs: "Theatrical" work as opposed to mainstream TV.
Tips: Sees a trend toward social issue-oriented works. Also interested in "non-traditional" children's pieces.

[N] **ALLIANCE THEATRE COMPANY**, 1280 Peachtree St. NE, Atlanta GA 30309. (404)733-4650. Fax: (404)733-4625. Website: http://www.alliancetheatre.org. Contact: Kathy McKee, artistic director. Estab. 1969. Produces 10 plays/year. Professional production for local audience. Query with synopsis or submit through agent. Reports in 6 months.
Needs: Full-length scripts and scripts for young audiences (max. length 60 minutes).

AMELIA MAGAZINE, 329 "E" St., Bakersfield CA 93304. (805)323-4064. Editor: Frederick A. Raborg, Jr. Estab. 1983. Publishes 1 play/year. Submit complete ms. Reports in 2 months. Buys first North American serial rights only. Pays $150 plus publication as winner of annual Frank McClure One-Act Play Award (for the contest, deadline is May 15 annually with an entry fee of $15). No fee for normal submissions and consideration. Guidelines for SASE.
Needs: "Plays with virtually any theme or concept. We look for excellence within the one-act, 45-minute running time format. We welcome the avant-garde and experimental. We do not object to the erotic, though not pornographic. Fewer plays are being produced on Broadway, but the regionals seem to be picking up the slack. That means fewer equity stages and more equity waivers."

AMERICAN MUSIC FESTIVAL, 123 S. Broad St., Suite 1820, Philadelphia PA 19109. (215)893-1570. Fax: (215)893-1233. E-mail: amtf@philly.infi.net. Website: http://members.aol.com/loud82/amtfpage.html. Contact: Ben Levit, artistic director. Estab. 1983. Produces 4 musicals/year. Professional productions. Synopsis, treatment of 2 scenes w/lyrics, and sample audio tape with no more than 4 songs. Reports in 6 months. Pays royalty.
Needs: Music-driven music theater/opera pieces, varied musical styles. Seven in orchestra, 10-14 cast, 28×40 stage.
Tips: Innovative topics and use of media, music, technology a plus. Sees trends of arts in technology (interactive theater, virtual reality, sound design); works are shorter in length (1-1½ hours with no intermissions or two hours with intermission).

[N] **AMERICAN RENEGADE THEATRE CO.**, 11136 Magnolia Blvd., North Hollywood CA 91601. (818)763-4430. Fax: (818)763-8082. Artistic Director: David A. Cox. Estab. 1991. Produces 8-10 plays/year. Query with synopsis or submit complete. Reports in 8-10 weeks. Pays 6% royalty after 6 week run.
Needs: Mostly original dramas and comedies.
Tips: "We prefer plays that have already been work shopped."

[N] [A] **AMERICAN REPERTORY THEATRE; ART NEWSTAGES**, 64 Brattle St., Cambridge MA. (617)495-2668. Artistic Director: Robert Brustein. Estab. 1980. Produces 8 plays/year. Loebe Stage, which is a professional regional theatre, intended for the Boston, MA and nearby New England play-goers. LORT B and D contracts. Query with synopsis or agented submissions only. Rights negotiable.
Needs: "We produce both classic works and world premieres; comedies, dramas and musicals; usually full-length productions. We prefer plays that show a good grasp of the theatrical medium, poetic or imaginative dialog, and which possess strong thematic messages."
Tips: No plays that could easily be sold as screenplays or novels; plays that lack theatricality or a uniqueness. "Works submitted should not only be well written, they should look professional: they should be properly formatted, and have a well-conceived cover letter. Copies of reviews, if applicable, and a resume are also appreciated."

AN CLAIDHEAMH SOLUIS/CELTIC ARTS CENTER, P.O. Box 861778, Los Angeles CA 90086-1778. (213)462-6844. Artistic Director: Sean Walsh. Estab. 1985. Produces 6 plays/year. Equity 99-seat plan. Query with synopsis. Reports in 6 months. Rights acquired vary. Pays $25-50.
Needs: Scripts of Celtic interest (Scottish, Welsh, Irish, Cornish, Manx, Breton). "This can apply to writer's background or subject matter. We are particularly concerned with works that relate to the survival of ethnic cultures and traditions, especially those in danger of extinction."

ARDEN THEATRE COMPANY, 40 N. 2nd St., Philadelphia PA 19106. (215)922-8900. Fax: (215)922-1122. E-mail: Ardenthco@aol.com. Website: http://www.libertynet.org/~arden. Contact: Aaron Posner, resident director. Estab. 1988. Produces 5 plays/year. Query with synopsis. Reports in 6 months. Pays 5% royalty.
Needs: Full-length, adaptations and musicals. Flexible in terms of cast size.

N **ARENA STAGE**, 1101 Sixth St. NW, Washington DC 20024. (202)554-9066. Fax: (202)488-4056. Artistic Director: Molly Smith. Estab. 1950. Produces 8 plays/year. This is a professional theater. The Kreeger Theater seats 514. The Fichandler Stage seats 827. The Old Vat Room seats 110. Query and synopsis. Reports in 12 months. Buys license from owner. Pays 5% royalty.

Needs: Full lengths comedy, drama, satire, musicals, plays by writers of color. We are beginning to consider one-person shows. We prefer cast sizes under 10, unless the play is a musical.

Tips: One-acts, 10-minute plays, 'first plays'. "Since our theater does not currently focus on new play development, our process for considering plays for possible production is extremely competitve. In a season of reading over 300 plays, one or two non-agent represented scripts might be seriously considered for some type of production. Best for writer if he/she is agent-represented."

ARTISTS REPERTORY THEATRE, 1516 S.W. Alder St., Portland OR 97205. (503)241-9807. Fax: (503)241-8268. E-mail: allen@artistsrep.org. Website: http://www.europa.com/artistsrep/. Contact: Allen Nause, artistic director. Estab. 1982. Produces 6 plays/year. Plays performed in professional theater. With a subscriber-based audience. Reports in 6 months. Pays royalty. Send synopsis, sample and résumé. No unsolicited mss accepted.

Needs: "Full-length, hard-hitting, emotional, intimate, actor-oriented shows with small casts (rarely exceeds 10-13, usually 2-7). Language and subject matter are not a problem."

Tips: "No one-acts or children's scripts."

N **ASIAN AMERICAN THEATER COMPANY**, 1840 Sutter St., Suite 207, San Francisco CA 94115-3220. (415)440-5545. Fax: (415)440-5597. Contact: Pamela A. Wu, producing director. Estab. 1973. Produces 2 plays/year. Produces amateur (emerging artists) and professional productions for API audiences. Submit complete ms. Reports in 1 month. Payment varies.

Needs: Anything by, for and about an API audience. No limitations in cast, props or staging.

Tips: Looking for plays by, for and about Asian Pacific Islander Americans. Scripts from Asian Pacific Islander American women and under-represented Asian Pacific Islander ethnic groups are especially welcome.

ASOLO THEATRE COMPANY, 5555 N. Tamiami Trail, Sarasota FL 34234. (941)351-9010. Fax: (941)351-5796. Website: http://www.sarasota-online.com/asolo. Contact: Bruce E. Rodgers, associate artistic director. Estab. 1960. Produces 7-8 plays/year. 10% freelance written. A LORT theater with 2 intimate performing spaces. No unsolicited scripts. Send a letter with 1-page synopsis, 1 page of dialogue and SAE. Reports in 8 months. Negotiates rights and payment.

Needs: Play must be *full length*. "We operate with a resident company in rotating repertory. We have a special interest in adaptations of great literary works."

N **THE B STREET THEATRE**, 2711 B St., Sacramento CA 95816. (916)443-5391. Contact: Buck Busfield, producing director. Estab. 1992. Produces 8 plays/year. Small professional theatre operating year-round for urban audience in capital region of California. Query with synopsis and SASE. Reports in 1 month on query; 3-6 months on script. Obtains production rights at this theatre for previously produced plays; possibility of some subsidiary rights for world premiere. Pays negotiable royalty.

Needs: Contemporary comedies, romances and dramas with an edge. "The majority of our work is drama from recent off-Broadway and larger regional theatre premieres. Full-length only. No restrictions as to topic or style, but we lean toward work which is entertaining without being fluff, and thought-provoking without being assaultive." Limit cast to 6. "Theatre is 150-seat black box with limited backstage and no fly space, so multiple sets and complex tech is impossible."

Tips: "No musicals, one-act plays, children's plays, 'TV writing.' Intelligence, humor and theatricality are of interest but highly experimental or avant-garde works are not. Earn audience involvement through craft rather than insisting on it via cleverness."

BAILIWICK REPERTORY, 1229 W. Belmont Ave., Chicago IL 60657-3205. (773)883-1090. Fax: (773)525-3245. E-mail: Bailiwickr@aol.com. Contact: Literary Department. Artistic Director: David Zak. Estab. 1982. Produces 5 mainstage plays (classic and newly commissioned) each year; 5 new full-length in New Directions series; 50 1-acts in annual Directors Festival; pride performance series (gay and lesbian plays, poetry), includes one acts, poetry, workshops, and staged adaptations of prose. Submit year-round. "Our audience is a typical Chicago market. Our plays are highly theatrical and politically aware." One acts should be submitted *before* April 1. (One-act play fest runs July-August). Reports in 9 months for full-length only. Pays 6% royalty.

Needs: "We need daring scripts that break the mold. Large cast or musicals are OK. Creative staging solutions are a must."

Tips: "Know the rules, then break them creatively and *boldly*! Please send SASE for manuscript submission guidelines before you submit."

BAKER'S PLAYS PUBLISHING CO., Dept. WM, 100 Chauncy St., Boston MA 02111-1783. (617)482-1280. Fax: (617)482-7613. Contact: Ray Pape, associate editor. Estab. 1845. 80% freelance written. Plays performed by amateur groups, high schools, children's theater, churches and community theater groups. 75% of scripts unagented submissions. Works with 2-3 unpublished/unproduced writers annually. Submit complete script with news clippings, résumé. Submit

complete cassette of music with musical submissions. Publishes 18-25 straight plays and musicals. Pay varies; negotiated royalty split of production fees; 10% book royalty. Reports in 2-6 months.
Needs: "We are finding strong support in our new division—plays from young authors featuring contemporary pieces for high school production."
Tips: "We are particularly interested in adaptation of lesser-known folk tales from around the world. Also of interest are plays which feature a multicultural cast and theme. Collections of one-act plays for children and young adults tend to do very well. Also, high school students: Write for guidelines for our High School Playwriting Contest."

MARY BALDWIN COLLEGE THEATRE, Mary Baldwin College, Staunton VA 24401. (703)887-7192. Website: http://www.mbc.edu. Contact: Virginia R. Francisco. Estab. 1842. Produces 5 plays/year. 10% freelance written. 75% of scripts are unagented submissions. Works with 0-1 unpublished/unproduced writer annually. An undergraduate women's college theater with an audience of students, faculty, staff and local community (adult, conservative). Query with synopsis. Reports in 1 year. Buys performance rights only. Pays $10-50/performance.
Needs: Full-length and short comedies, tragedies, musical plays, particularly for young women actresses, dealing with women's issues both contemporary and historical. Experimental/studio theater not suitable for heavy sets. Cast should emphasize women. No heavy sex; minimal explicit language.
Tips: "A perfect play for us has several roles for young women, few male roles, minimal production demands, a concentration on issues relevant to contemporary society, and elegant writing and structure."

BARTER THEATRE, P.O. Box 867, Abingdon VA 24212-0867. (540)628-2281. Fax: (540)628-4551. E-mail: Barter@naxs.com. Website: http://www.BarterTheatre.com. Contact: Richard Rose, artistic director. Estab. 1933. Produces 14 plays/year. Play performed in residency at 2 facilities, a 500-seat proscenium theater and a smaller 150-seat flexible theater. "Our plays are intended for diversified audiences of all ages." Submit synopsis and dialogue sample only with SASE. Reports in 9 months. Royalty negotiable.

- Barter Theatre has premiered fifteen new works over the past three years. One of the premieres was optioned for Broadway for the 1995-96 season. In 1997 Barter will take one of its productions off-Broadway.

Needs: "We are looking for good plays, comedies and dramas, that entertain and are relevant; plays that comment on the times and mankind; plays that are universal. We prefer casts of 4-12, single or unit set. Hard language can be a factor."

N **BILINGUAL FOUNDATION OF THE ARTS**, 421 North Ave., #19, Los Angeles CA 90031. (213)225-4044. Fax: (213)225-1250. Artistic Director: Margarita Galban. Dramaturg/Literary Manager: Agustin Coppola. Estab. 1973. Produces 3-5 plays plus 9-10 staged readings/year. "Productions are presented at home theater in Los Angeles, California. Our audiences are largely Hispanic and all productions are performed in English and Spanish. The Bilingual Foundation of the Arts produces plays in order to promote the rich heritage of Hispanic history and culture. Though our plays must be Hispanic in theme, we reach out to the entire community." Submit complete script. Reports in 6 months. Rights negotiable. Pays royalty.
Needs: "Plays must be Hispanic in theme. Comedy, drama, light musical, children's theater, etc., are accepted for consideration. More plays in Spanish are needed. Theater is 99-seater, no flies."

BOARSHEAD THEATER, 425 S. Grand Ave., Lansing MI 48933. (517)484-7800. Contact: John Peakes, artistic director. Estab. 1966. Produces 8 plays/year (6 mainstage, 2 Young People's Theater productions inhouse), 4 or 5 staged readings. Mainstage Actors' Equity Association company; also Youth Theater—touring to schools by our intern company. Query with one-page synopsis, cast list (with descriptions), 5-10 pages of representative dialogue, *with sufficient postage*. Reports on query and synopsis in 1 month. Full scripts (when requested) in 3-8 months. Pays royalty for mainstage productions, transport/per diem for staged readings.
Needs: Thrust stage. Cast usually 8 or less; ocassionally up to 12-14. Prefer staging which depends on theatricality rather than multiple sets. Send plays to Young People's Theater % Education Director. No musicals considered. One-acts only for Young People's Theater.

BRISTOL RIVERSIDE THEATRE, P.O. Box 1250, Bristol PA 19007. (215)785-6664. Fax: (215)785-2762. Producing Artistic Director: Susan D. Atkinson. Contact: David Abers, assistant to the artistic director. Estab. 1986. "Due to a backlog of submitted scripts, we will not be accepting any new scripts until summer, 1998."

CALIFORNIA THEATER CENTER, P.O. Box 2007, Sunnyvale CA 94087. (408)245-2978. Fax: (408)245-0235. E-mail: whudd@ix.netcom.com. Contact: Will Huddleston, literary manager/resident director. Estab. 1976. Produces 15 plays/year. "Plays are for young audiences in both our home theater and for tour." Query with synopsis. Reports in 6 months. Negotiates set fee.
Needs: All plays must be suitable for young audiences, must be around 1 hour in length. Cast sizes vary. Many shows require touring sets.
Tips: "Almost all new plays we do are for young audiences, one-acts with fairly broad appeal, not over an hour in length, with mixed casts of two to eight adult, professional actors. We read plays for all ages, though plays for kindergarten through fourth grade have the best chance of being chosen. Plays with memorable music are especially looked for, as well as plays based upon literary works or historical material young people know from school. Serious plays written in the style of psychological realism must be especially well written. Satires and parodies are difficult for our audiences

unless they are based upon material familiar to children. Anything "cute" should be avoided. In the summer we seek large cast plays that can be performed entirely by children in our Summer Conservatory programs. We particularly look for plays that can do well in difficult venues, such as high school gymnasiums, multi-purpose rooms, etc."

CENTER THEATER ENSEMBLE, (formerly Center Theater), 1346 W. Devon Ave., Chicago IL 60660. (773)508-0200. Contact: Dale Calandra, artistic director: Estab. 1984. Produces approximately 4 plays/year. "We run professional productions in our Chicago 'off-Loop' theaters for a diverse audience. We also hold an international play contest annually. For more info send SASE to Dale Calandra." *Agented submissions only.* Reports in 3 months.

- This theater has recently established a playwright-in-residence program and professional seminars in playwriting and screenwriting.

CENTRE STAGE—SOUTH CAROLINA!, P.O. Box 8451, Greenville SC 29604-8451. (864)233-6733. Fax: (864)233-3901. Executive Artistic Director: Douglas P. McCoy. Estab. 1983. Produces 10 plays/year. "We are a TCG professional theater. Our youth theater targets ages 10-18, and our mainstage targets all ages." Query with synopsis or submit complete manuscript. Reports in 2 months; written acknowlegement sent on receipt. Pays negotiable royalty.
Needs: "Our productions include all types-musicals, comedies, dramas. We produce for entertainment, educational and issue themes." Cast size 1-25. Staging-single set or revolve. Props-some limitation, particularly with extra large prop requirements. No restrictions on material. Sees a "shift in what attracts today's audiences, and what competes for their time. The more entertainment value a productions has, the larger the audience that is attracted to it."

THE CHANGING SCENE THEATER, 1527½ Champa St., Denver CO 80202. Director: Alfred Brooks. Contact: Maxine Munt, literary manager. Year-round productions in theater space. Cast may be made up of both professional and amateur actors. For public audience; age varies, but mostly youthful and interested in taking a chance on new and/or experimental works. No limit to subject matter or story themes. Emphasis is on the innovative. "Also, we require that the playwright be present for at least one performance of his work, if not for the entire rehearsal period. We have a small stage area, but are able to convert to round, semi-round or environmental. Prefer to do plays with limited sets and props." Two and three acts only.
Needs: Produces 8-10 nonmusicals a year; all are originals. 90% freelance written. 65% of scripts produced are unagented submissions. Works with 3-4 unpublished/unproduced writers annually. "We do not pay royalties or sign contracts with playwrights. We function on a performance-share basis of payment. Our theater seats 76; the first 50 seats go to the theater; the balance is divided among the participants in the production. The performance-share process is based on the entire production run and not determined by individual performances. We do not copyright our plays." Send complete script. Reporting time varies; usually several months.
Recent Production: *Under Construction*, by Lenore Blumenfeld.
Tips: "We are experimental: open to young artists who want to test their talents and open to experienced artists who want to test new ideas/explore new techniques. Dare to write 'strange and wonderful' well-thought-out scripts. We want upbeat ones. Consider that we have a small performance area (24′×31′) when submitting."

CHARLOTTE REPERTORY THEATRE, 201 S. College St., Suite 2040, Charlotte NC 28244. (704)333-8587. Fax: (704)333-0224. Literary Manager: Claudia Carter Covington. Literary Associate: Carol Bellamy. Estab. 1976. "We are a not-for-profit regional theater." Submit complete script with SASE. Reports in 3 months. Writers receive free plane fare and housing for festival, stipend.
Needs: Need full-length scripts not previously produced professionally. No limitations in cast, props, staging, etc.

CHILDREN'S STORY SCRIPTS, Baymax Productions, 2219 W. Olive Ave., Suite 130, Burbank CA 91506-2648. (818)563-6105. Fax: (818)563-2968. E-mail: baymax@earthlink.net. Website: Website: http://home.earthlink.net/~baymax. Contact: Deedra Bébout, editor. Estab. 1990. "Our audience consists of children, grades K-8 (5-13-year-olds)." Send complete script with SASE. Reports in 1 month. Licenses all rights to story; author retains copyright. Pays graduated royalty based on sales.
Needs: "We add new titles as we find appropriate stories. We look for stories which are fun for kids to read, involve a number of readers throughout, and dovetail with school subjects. This is a must! Not life lessons . . . school subjects."
Tips: "The scripts are not like theatrical scripts. They combine dialogue and prose narration, à la Readers Theatre. If a writer shows promise, we'll work with him. Our most important goal is to benefit children. We want stories that bring alive subjects studied in classrooms. Facts must be worked unobtrusively into the story—the story has to be fun for the kids to read. Send #10 SASE for guidelines with samples. We do not respond to submissions without SASE."

CHILDSPLAY, INC., P.O. Box 517, Tempe AZ 85280. (602)350-8101. Fax: (602)350-8584. Contact: David P. Saar, artistic director. Estab. 1978. Produces 5-6 plays/year. "Professional: Touring and in-house productions for youth and family audiences." Submit synopsis, character descriptions and 7- 10-page dialogue sample. Reports in 6 months. "On commissioned work we hold a small percentage of royalties for 3-5 years." Pays royalty of $20-35/performance (touring) or pays $3,000-8,000 commission.
Needs: Seeking *theatrical* plays on a wide range of contemporary topics. Touring shows: 5-6 actors; van-size. Inhouse: 6-10 actors; no technical limitations.
Tips: No traditionally-handled fairy tales. "Theater for young people is growing up and is able to speak to youth and

adults. The material *must* respect the artistry of the theater and the intelligence of our audience. Our most important goal is to benefit children. If you wish your materials returned send SASE."

CIRCUIT PLAYHOUSE/PLAYHOUSE ON THE SQUARE, 51 S. Cooper, Memphis TN 38104. (901)725-0776. Artistic Director: Jackie Nichols. Produces 16 plays/year. 100% freelance written. Professional plays performed for the Memphis/Mid-South area. Member of the Theatre Communications Group. 100% of scripts unagented submissions. Works with 1 unpublished/unproduced writer/year. Contest held each fall. Submit complete script. Reports in 6 months. Buys percentage of royalty rights for 2 years. Pays $500.
Needs: All types; limited to single or unit sets. Cast of 20 or fewer.
Tips: "Each play is read by three readers through the extended length of time a script is kept. Preference is given to scripts for the southeastern region of the U.S."

I.E. CLARK PUBLICATIONS, P.O. Box 246, Schulenburg TX 78956-0246. (409)743-3232. Contact: Donna Cozzaglio, editorial manager. Estab. 1956. Publishes 15 plays/year for educational theater, children's theater, religious theater, regional professional theater and amateur community theater. 20% freelance written. Publishes 3-4 scripts/year, unagented submissions. Submit complete script, 1 at a time with SASE. Reports in 6 months. Buys all available rights; "We serve as an agency as well as a publisher." Pays standard book and performance royalty, amount and percentages dependent upon type and marketability of play. Catalog for $3. Writer's guidelines for #10 SASE.
Needs: "We are interested in plays of all types—short or long. Audiotapes of music or videotapes of a performance are requested with submissions of musicals. We require that a play has been produced (directed by someone other than the author); photos, videos, and reviews of the production are helpful. No limitations in cast, props, staging, etc. Plays with only one or two characters are difficult to sell. We insist on literary quality. We like plays that give new interpretations and understanding of human nature. Correct spelling, punctuation and grammar (befitting the characters, of course) impress our editors."

- "One of our specialties is "Young Adult Awareness Drama"—plays for ages 13 to 25 dealing with sex, drugs, popularity, juvenile, crime, and other problems of young adults. We also need plays for children's theatre, especially dramatizations of children's classic literature."

Tips: Publishes plays only. "Entertainment value and a sense of moral responsibility seem to be returning as essential qualities of a good play script. The era of glorifying the negative elements of society seems to be fading rapidly. Literary quality, entertainment value and good craftsmanship rank in that order as the characteristics of a good script in our opinion. 'Literary quality' means that the play must—in beautiful, distinctive, and un-trite language—say something; preferably something new and important concerning man's relations with his fellow man or God; and these 'lessons in living' must be presented in an intelligent, believable and creative manner. Plays for children's theater are tending more toward realism and childhood problems, but fantasy and dramatization of fairy tales are also needed."

N **CLEVELAND PUBLIC THEATRE**, 6415 Detroit Ave., Cleveland OH 44102. (216)631-2727. Fax: (216)631-2575. E-mail: cpt@en.com. Website: http://www.en.com/cpt. Contact: James A. Levin, artistic director. Estab. 1982. Produces 6 (full production) plays/year. Also sponsors Festival of New Plays. 150-seat alternative performance space. "Our audience believes that art touches your heart and your nerve endings." Query with synopsis for full season. Rights negotiable. Pays $15-100/performance.
Needs: Poetic, experimental, avant-garde, political, multicultural works that need a stage (not a camera); interdisciplinary cutting-edge work (dance/performance art/music/visual); works that stretch the imagination and conventional boundaries. "We are a black box with no fly space. We are low-budget—imagination must substitute for dollars."
Tips: "No conventional comedies, musicals, adaptations, children's plays—if you think Samuel French would love it, we probably won't. No TV sitcoms or soaps masquerading as theater. Theater is *not* TV or films. Learn the impact of what live bodies do to an audience in the same room. We are particularly interested in artists from our region who can grow with us on a longterm basis."

COAST TO COAST THEATER COMPANY, P.O. Box 3855, Hollywood CA 90078. (818)782-1212. Fax: (818)782-1931. Artistic Director: Bryan W. Simon. Contact: Douglas Coler. Estab. 1989. Produces 2-3 plays/year. Equity and equity waiver theater. Query with synopsis. Responds if interested. Buys West Coast, Midwest or East Coast rights, depending on location of production. Pays 5% royalty, makes outright purchase of $100-250, or pays per performance.
Needs: Full-length off-beat comedies or dramas with small casts, simple sets.

N **COLONY STUDIO THEATRE**, 1944 Riverside Dr., Los Angeles CA 90039. Website: http://www.colonytheatre.org. Contact: Judith Goldstein, new play selection committee. Produces 3 mainstage productions, 3 second stage productions/year. Professional 99-seat theater with thrust stage. Casts from resident company of professional actors. No unsolicited scripts. Submission guidelines for SASE. Reports only if interested. Negotiated rights. Pays royalties for each performance.
Needs: Full length (90-120 minutes) with a cast of 4-12. No musicals or experimental works.
Tips: "A polished script is the mark of a skilled writer. Submissions should be in professional (centered) format."

CONTEMPORARY DRAMA SERVICE, Meriwether Publishing Ltd., P.O. Box 7710, Colorado Springs CO 80933. (303)594-4422. Editor-in-Chief: Arthur Zapel. Associate Editors: Theodore Zapel, Rhonda Wray. Estab. 1969. Publishes 50-60 plays/year. "We publish for the secondary school market and colleges. We also publish for mainline liturgical churches—drama activities for church holidays, youth activities and fundraising entertainments. These may be plays, musicals or drama-related books." Query with synopsis or submit complete script. Reports in 6 weeks. Obtains either amateur or all rights. Pays 10% royalty or negotiates purchase.

- Contemporary Drama Service is now looking for play or musical adaptations of classic children's stories, for example: *Wizard of Oz*, *The Secret Garden*, *Huckleberry Finn*.

Needs: "Most of the plays we publish are one acts, 15-45 minutes in length. We also publish full-length two-act musicals or three-act plays. We prefer comedies. Musical plays must have name appeal either by prestige author, prestige title adaptation. Comedy sketches, monologues and 2-character plays are welcomed. We prefer simple staging appropriate to high school, college or church performance. We like playwrights who see the world positively and with a sense of humor. Offbeat themes and treatments are accepted if the playwright can sustain a light touch and not take himself or herself too seriously. In documentary or religious plays we look for good research and authenticity. We are publishing many scenebooks for actors (which can be anthologies of great works excerpts), scenebooks on special themes and speech and theatrical arts textbooks. We are especially interested in authority-books on a variety of theater-related subjects."

Tips: Contemporary Drama Service is looking for creative books on: comedy writing, staging amateur theatricals and Christian youth activities.

THE COTERIE, 2450 Grand Ave., Kansas City MO 64108-2520. (816)474-6785. Fax: (816)474-7112. Contact: Jeff Church, artistic director. Estab. 1979. Produces 7-8 plays/year. "Plays produced at Hallmark's Crown Center in downtown Kansas City in the Coterie's resident theater (capacity 240). A typical performance run is one month in length." Query with synopsis, résumé, sample scene; submit complete script only if an established playwright in youth theater field. Reports in 6 months. "We retain some rights on commissioned plays." Pays royalty per performance and flat fee.

Needs: "We produce plays which are universal in appeal; they may be original or adaptations of classic or contemporary literature. Typically, not more than 12 in a cast—prefer 5-9 in size. No fly space or wing space."

Tips: "No couch plays. Prefer plays by seasoned writers who have established reputations. Groundbreaking and exciting scripts from the youth theater field welcome. It's perfectly fine if your play is a little off-center." Trends in the field that writers should be mindful of: "Make certain your submitted play to us is *very* theatrical and not cinematic. Writers need to see how far the field of youth and family theater has come—the interesting new areas we're going—before sending us your query or manuscript."

CREATIVE PRODUCTIONS, INC., 2 Beaver Place, Aberdeen NJ 07747. (732)566-6985. Contact: Walter L. Born, artistic director. Produces 2 musicals/year. Non-equity, professional, nonprofit company with year-round productions. "We use musicals where performers are an integrated company of traditional and non-traditional individuals for the broad spectrum of viewers." Query with synopsis. Reports in 1 month. Buys rights to perform play for specified number of performances. Fee negotiable.

Needs: Musicals only. Original musicals with upbeat themes adaptable to integrated company of traditional and non-traditional performers. Maximum cast of 12, sets can't fly, facilities are schools, no mammoth sets or multiple scene changes, 90 minutes maximum run time.

Tips: No "blue" material, pornographic, obscene language. Submit info on any performances. Demo tape (musicals), vocal/piano score, plus list of references on users of their material to confirm bio info.

N **DALLAS CHILDREN'S THEATER**, 2215 Cedar Springs, Dallas TX 75201. (214)978-0110. Fax: (214)978-0118. Executive Director: Robyn Flatt. Estab. 1984. Produces 12 plays/year. Professional theater for family and student audiences. Query with synopsis. Report in 6-8 months. Rights negotiable. Pays negotiable.

Needs: Substantive material appropriate for youth and family audiences. Most consideration given to full-length, non-musical works, especially classic & contemporary adaptions of literature. Also interested in social, topical issue-oriented material. Very interested in scripts which enlighten diverse cultural experiences, particularly Hispanic and African-American experiences. Prefer scripts with no more than 15 cast members. 6-12 is ideal.

Tips: No adult experience material. "We are a family theater." Not interested in material intended for performance by children or in a classroom. Productions are performed by professional adults. Children are cast in child-appropriate roles. We receive far too much light musical material that plays down to children and totally lack any substance. "Be patient. We receive an enormous amount of submissions. Most of the material we have historically produced has had previous production. We are not against perusing non-produced material, but it has rarely gone into our season unless we have been involved in its development."

N **TIPPEN DAVIDSON**, Seaside Music Theater, P.O. Box 2835, Daytona Beach FL 32120. (904)252-3394. Fax: (904)252-8991. General Manager: Lester Malizia. Estab. 1977. Produce 9-10 plays/year. SMT produces a summer repertory season consisting of 5 mainstage productions, at least 4 of which are full scale musicals, operas, or operettas, plus 3-4 production winter season, all professional. Query and synopsis with cassette tape of score or sample songs. Reports in 2-3 months. Rights individually negotiated. Pays individually negotiated.

Needs: Musicals only, both full-scale and "chamber." Summer musicals are played in rep, so set must be easily changeable.

Tips: Do not want non-musicals. Avoid the megamusical.

N DENVER CENTER THEATRE COMPANY, 1050 13th St., Denver CO 80204. (303)446-4856. Fax: (303)825-2117. Associate Artistic Director: Bruce K. Sevy. Estab. 1979. Produce 12 plays/year. Professional productions. The complex has four theatres. Primarily subscription audience. Write for quidelines. Send SASE. Reports in 4-6 months. Pays royalty.
Needs: "We are looking for full-length plays that have not been produced and are unencumbered. We do not accept one-act plays, one-character plays, adaptations or translations. We accept only one script per playwright per year. Residents of states served by US West (AZ, CO, MN, MT, NE, ND, OR, SD, UT, WA and WY) may submit scripts directly. An SASE must accompany the script. Residents of other states should send a cover letter, resume, synopsis, ten pages of dialogue, a description of any workshops or amateur productions the script has received and an SASE."

DETROIT REPERTORY THEATRE, 13103 Woodrow Wilson, Detroit MI 48238-3686. (313)868-1347. Fax: (313)868-1705. Contact: Barbara Busby, literary manager. Estab. 1957. Produces 4 plays/year. Professional theater, 194 seats operatinge on A.E.A. SPT contract Detroit metropolitan area. Submit complete ms in bound folder, cast list and description with SASE. Reports in 3-6 months. Pays royalty.
Needs: Wants issue-oriented works. Cast limited to no more than 7 characters.
Tips: No musicals or one-act plays.

DINER THEATRE, 2015 S. 60th St., Omaha NE 68106. (402)553-4715. Fax: (402)553-4715. E-mail: dmarr@aol.com. Artistic Director: Doug Marr. Estab. 1983. Produces 5 plays/year. Professional productions, general audience. Query with synopsis. Reports in 2 months on submissions. Pays $15-30/performance.
Needs: Comedies, dramas, musicals—original unproduced works. Full length, all styles/topics.

N DIXON PLACE, 258 Bowery, New York NY 10012-3501. (212)219-3088. Fax: (212)274-9114. Executive Director: Ellie Covan. Estab. 1986. Produces 12 plays/year. "We present play readings at our downtown, off-off Broadway performance venue. The audience is usually made up of supporters of the writer, and other artists. Submit 10-page script sample with synopsis. Reports in 6 months. Pays flat fee.
Needs: Musicals, one-acts, full-length plays, not already read or workshopped in New York. Particularly interested in non-traditional, either in character, content, structure and/or themes. "We almost never produce kitchen sink, soap opera-style plays about AIDS, coming out, unhappy love affairs, getting sober or lesbian parenting. We regularly present new works, plays with innovative structure, multi-ethnic content, non-naturalistic dialogue, irreverent musicals and the elegantly bizarre. We are an established performance venue with a very diverse audience. We have a reputation for bringing our audience the unexpected."

N STEVE DOBBINS PRODUCTIONS, 650 Geary St., San Francisco CA 94102. (415)441-6655. Fax: (415)441-9567. Artistic Director: Steve Dobbins. Estab. 1992. Produces 5 plays/year. Produces professional plays for all audiences. Query with synopsis, include sample of dialogue. Reports in 4 months. Pays 4-6% royalty.
Needs: Political and musicals. Limit cast size to 16.

A DORSET THEATRE FESTIVAL, Box 510, Dorset VT 05251-0510. (802)867-2223. Fax: (802)867-0144. E-mail: theatre@sover.net. Website: http://www.theatredirectories.com. Contact: Jill Charles, artistic director. Estab. 1976. Produces 5 plays/year, 1 a new work. "Our plays will be performed in our Equity summer stock theatre and are intended for a sophisticated community." *Agented submissions only.* Reports in 3-6 months. Rights and compensation arranged on an individual basis.
Needs: "Looking for full-length contemporary American comedy or drama. Limited to a cast of six."
Tips: "Language and subject matter appropriate to general audience."

DRAMATIC PUBLISHING, 311 Washington, Woodstock IL 60098. (815)338-7170. Fax: (815)338-8981. E-mail: 75712.3621@compuserve.com. Website: http://www.dramaticpublishing.com. Editor: Linda Habjan. Publishes paperback acting editions of original plays, adaptations and translations. Publishes 50-70 titles/year. Receives 500-1,000 queries and 500-1,000 mss/year. Pays 10% royalty on scripts; performance royalty varies. Publishes play 12-18 months after acceptance of ms. Accepts simultaneous submissions. Reports in 1 month on queries, 2 months on proposals, 6 months on mss. Catalog and ms guidelines free.

- Dramatic Publishing is seeking more material for the high school market and community theater.

Needs: Interested in playscripts appropriate for children, middle and high schools, colleges, community, stock and professional theaters. Send full ms.

DRAMATICS MAGAZINE, 3368 Central Pkwy., Cincinnati OH 45225. (513)559-1996. Fax: (513)559-0012. E-mail: pubs@one.net. Website: http://www.etassoc.org. Editor: Don Corathers. Estab. 1929. Publishes 5 plays/year. For high school theater students and teachers. Submit complete ms. Reports in 3 months. Buys first North American serial rights only. Accepts previously published plays. Send tearsheet, photocopy or typed ms with rights for sale noted and information about when and where the work previously appeared. For reprints, pays 50% of the amount paid for an original piece. Purchases one-time publication rights only for $100-400.
Needs: "We are seeking one-acts to full-lengths that can be produced in an educational theater setting. No musicals."
Tips: "No melodrama, farce, children's theater, or cheap knock-offs of TV sitcoms or movies. Fewer writers are taking the time to learn the conventions of theater—what makes a piece work on stage, as opposed to film and television—

and their scripts show it. We're always looking for good interviews with working theatre professionals."

EAST WEST PLAYERS, 244 S. San Pedro St., Suite 301, Los Angeles CA 980012-3832. Fax: (213)625-7111. E-mail: ewplayers@earthlink.net. Website: http://www.earthlink.net/~ewplayers. Contact: Ken Narasaki, literary manager. Artistic Director: Tim Dang. Estab. 1965. Produces 5 plays/year. Professional theater performing under Equity 99-seat contract, presenting plays which explore the Asian-Pacific or Asian-American experience. Query with synopsis. Reports in 3 months on submissions. Pays royalty against percentage of box office.
Needs: "Whether dramas, comedies or performance art or musicals, all plays must either address the Asian-American experience or have a special resonance when cast with Asian-American actors."

- East West Players also holds a competition from January 1 through April 1. Send SASE for guidelines.

ELDRIDGE PUBLISHING CO., P.O. Box 1595, Venice FL 34284. (941)496-4679. Fax: (941)493-9680. E-mail: info@histage.com. Website: http://www.histage.com (general) and http://www.95church.com (religious). Editor: Susan Shore. Estab. 1906. Publishes 50-60 new plays/year for junior high, senior high, church and community audience. Query with synopsis (acceptable) or submit complete ms (preferred). Please send cassette tapes with any musicals. Reports in 2 months. Buys all rights. Pays 50% royalties and 10% copy sales. Makes outright purchase of $200-500. Writer's guidelines for #10 SASE.
Needs: "We are most interested in full-length plays and musicals for our school and community theater market. Nothing lower than junior high level, please. We always love comedies but also look for serious, high caliber plays reflective of today's sophisticated students. We also need one-acts and plays for children's theater. In addition, in our religious market we're always searching for holiday or any time plays."
Tips: "Submissions are welcomed at any time. Authors are paid royalties twice a year. They receive complimentary copies of their published plays, the annual catalog and 50% discount if buying additional copies."

N **ENCORE PERFORMANCE PUBLISHING**, P.O. Box 692, Orem UT 84059-4554. (801)225-0605. Fax: (801)765-0489. E-mail: Encoreplay@aol.com. Contact: Michael C. Perry, editor. Estab. 1979. Publishes 20-50 plays/year. "Our audience consists of all ages with emphasis on the family; educational institutions from elementary through college/university, community theaters and professional theaters." No unsolicited mss. Query with synopsis. Reports in 1 month on queries; 3 months on scripts. Pays 50% performance royalty; 10% book royalty. Submit from May-August.
Needs: "We are looking for plays with strong message about or for families, plays with young actors among cast, any length, all genres. We prefer scripts with at least close or equal male/female roles, could lean to more female roles." Plays must have had at least 2 fully staged productions. Unproduced plays can be read with letter of recommendation accompanying the query.
Tips: "No performance art pieces or plays with overtly sexual themes or language. Looking for adaptations of Twain and other American authors."

THE ENSEMBLE STUDIO THEATRE, 549 W. 52nd St., New York NY 10019. (212)247-4982. Fax: (212)664-0041. Artistic Director: Curt Dempster. Contact: Derek McKinney, literary associate. Estab. 1971. Produces 250 projects/year for off-off Broadway developmental theater. 100-seat house, 60-seat workshop space. Do not fax mss or résumés. Submit complete ms. Reports in 3 months. Standard production contract: mini contract with Actors' Equity Association or letter of agreement. Pays $80-1,000.
Needs: Full-length plays with strong dramatic actions and situations and solid one-acts, humorous and dramatic, which can stand on their own. Musicals also accepted; send tape of music. No verse-dramas or elaborate costume dramas.
Tips: Submit work September-April. "We are dedicated to developing new American plays."

ENSEMBLE THEATRE OF CINCINNATI, 1127 Vine St., Cincinnati OH 45248. (513)421-3555. Fax: (513)421-8002. Contact: D. Lynn Meyers, producing artistic director. Produces 14 plays/year. Professional-year round theater. Query and sysnopsis, submit complete ms or submit through agent. Reports in 5 months. Pays 5-10% royalty.
Needs: Dedicated to good writing, any style.

EUREKA THEATRE COMPANY, 330 Townsend, Suite 210, San Francisco CA 94107. (415)243-9899. Fax: (415)243-0789. Contact: Joe DeGuglielmo, associate artistic director. Estab. 1972. Produces 3-5 fully-staged plays/year. Plays performed in professional-AEA, year-round for socially involved adult audiences. Query with letter of inquiry, synopsis, scene sample (15 pages maximum) and résumé. Reports in 6 months. Rights negotiated. Pays 4-8% royalty.
Needs: Intelligent, provocative plays for adult general audiences. Plays with fewer production complexities preferred. Smaller casts (less than 8) preferred.
Tips: "No one-acts (although we would consider a collection and short works by a single writer or collective); no light-hearted musicals. We are tired of being told 'this is the next *Angels in America*.' We want plays which reflect the cultural diversity of the area in which we live and work. Remember, you are writing for the live stage, *not* for film or TV."

N **FIRST STAGE**, P.O. Box 38280, Los Angeles CA 90038. (213)850-6271. Fax: (213)850-6295. Contact: Dennis Safren, literary manager. Estab. 1983. First Stage is a non-profit organization dedicated to bringing together writers, actors and directors in the development of new material for stage and screen. Produces 50 plays/year. Submit complete ms. Reports in 6 months.
Needs: Original non-produced plays in any genre.

Tips: No TV sitcoms. "We are a development organization."

[A] **FLORIDA STAGE**, (formerly Pope Theatre Company), 262 S. Ocean Blvd., Manalapan FL 33462. (561)585-3404. Fax: (561)588-4708. Producing Artistic Director: Louis Tyrrell. Estab. 1987. Produces 6 plays/year (5 during the regular season, 1 in the summer). "We are a fully professional (LOA) theater. We attract an audience comprised of both local residents and seasonal visitors. Many, but by no means all, of our subscribers are retirees." *Agented submissions only.* Reports in 6 months. Buys production rights only. Pays 6-10% royalty. "A SASE is required if a playwright wants a script returned."
Needs: "We produce new American plays. We prefer to do Florida premieres of thought-provoking, socially-conscious, challenging plays. Our stage is relatively small, which prevents us from producing works with a large cast."

FLORIDA STUDIO THEATRE, 1241 N. Palm Ave., Sarasota FL 34236. (941)366-9017. Fax: (941)955-4137. E-mail: fst.cangermann@juno.com. Contact: Chris Angermann, associate director. Produces 7 established and 6 new plays/year. FST is a professional, not-for-profit theater. Plays are produced in 170-seat mainstage and 100-seat cabaret theater for subscription audiences. FST operates under a small professional theater contract of Actor's Equity. Query with synopsis. Reports in 2 months on queries; 6 months on mss. Pays $200 for workshop production of new script.
Needs: Contemporary plays, musical reviews, character plays. Prefer casts of no more than 8 and single sets on mainstage, 3-4 in cabaret.
Tips: "We are looking for material for our Cabaret Theatre—musical revues, one-two character musicals, one-character shows. All should be in two acts and run no longer than 90 minutes, including a 10- 15-minute intermission."

THE FOOTHILL THEATRE COMPANY, P.O. Box 1812, Nevada City CA 95959. (530)265-9320. Fax: (530)265-9325. E-mail: ftc@foothilltheatre.org. Website: http://www.foothilltheatre.org. Contact: Philip Charles Sneed, artistic director. Estab. 1977. Produces 6-9 plays/year. "We are a professional theater company operating under an Actors' Equity Association contract for part of the year, and performing in the historic 246-seat Nevada Theatre (built in 1865) and at an outdoor amphitheatre on the north shore of Lake Tahoe. The audience is a mix of locals and tourists." Query with synopsis or submit complete script. Reports in 6 months or less. Buys negotiable rights. Pay varies.
Needs: "We are most interested in plays which speak to the region and its history, as well as to its current concerns. No melodramas. Theatrical, above all." No limitations.
Tips: "Avoid the cliché at all costs, and don't be derivative; we're interested in a unique and unassailable vision."

FOUNTAIN THEATRE, 5060 Fountain Ave., Los Angeles CA 90029. (213)663-2235. Fax: (213)663-1629. Artistic Directors: Deborah Lawlor, Stephen Sachs. Contact: Simon Levy, dramaturg. Estab. 1990. Produces both a theater and dance season. Produced at Fountain Theatre (99-seat equity plan). Query through agent or recommendation of theater professional. Query with synopsis to: Simon Levy, producing director/dramaturg. Reports in 6 months. Rights acquired vary. Pays royalty.
Needs: Original plays, adaptations of American literature, "material that incorporates dance or language into text with unique use and vision."

THE FREELANCE PRESS, P.O. Box 548, Dover MA 02030-2207. (508)785-8250. Managing Editor: Narcissa Campion. Estab. 1984. Publishes 4 plays/year for children/young adults. Submit complete ms with SASE. Reports in 4 months. Pays 2-3% royalty. Pays 10% of the price of each script and score.
Needs: "We publish original musical theater to be performed by young people, dealing with issues of importance to them. Also adapt 'classics' into musicals for 8- to 16-year-old age groups to perform." Large cast; flexible.

SAMUEL FRENCH, INC., 45 W. 25th St., New York NY 10010. (212)206-8990. Fax: (212)206-1429. Contact: William Talbot, editor. Estab. 1830. Publishes paperback acting editions of plays. Averages 50-70 titles/year. Receives 1,500 submissions/year, mostly from unagented playwrights. 10% of publications are from first-time authors; 20% from unagented writers. Pays 10% royalty on retail price. Publishes play an average of 6 months after acceptance. Accepts simultaneous submissions. Allow *minimum* of 4 months for reply. Catalog for $4.50.
Needs: Acting editions of plays.
Tips: "Broadway and Off-Broadway hit plays, light comedies and mysteries have the best chance of selling to our firm. Our market is comprised of theater producers—both professional and amateur—actors and students. Read as many plays as possible of recent vintage to keep apprised of today's market; write plays with good female roles; and be one hundred percent professional in approaching publishers and producers."

[N] **THE GLINES**, 240 West 44th St., New York NY 10036. (212)354-8899. Artisitic Director: John Glines. Estab. 1976. Produces 2-3 plays/year. Off-off broadway for a general audience. Query and synopsis. Reports in 2 months. Pays negotiable.
Needs: Plays must deal with the gay experience. Prefer full-length. Prefer small cast, few props, simple staging.
Tips: Think "two boards and a passion."

GRETNA THEATRE, P.O. Box 578, Mt. Gretna PA 17064. (717)964-3322. Fax: (717)964-2189. **Contact:** Pat Julian, producing director. Estab. 1977. "Plays are performed at a professional equity theater during summer." Query with

synopsis. "Include character breakdown with script's production history, plus five pages." Reports in 4-6 weeks. Rights negotiated. Royalty negotiated (6-12%).
Needs: "We produce full-length plays for a summer audience—subject, language and content are important."
Tips: "No one-acts." Special interest in new musicals; comedy is popular.

THE GROUP (Seattle Group Theatre), 305 Harrison St., Seattle WA 98109. (206)441-9480. Fax: (206)441-9839. Artistic Director: José Carrasquillo. Contact: Literary Department. Estab. 1978. Produces 5 plays/year. "Plays are performed in our 197-seat theater—The Carlton Playhouse. Intended for a multiethnic audience. Professional, year-round theater." Query with synopsis, sample pages of dialogue and SASE for reply. No phone calls. Reports in 6-8 weeks. Rights obtained varies per production. Royalty varies.
Needs: "We look for scripts suitable for multiethnic casting that deal with social, cultural and political issues relevant to the world today."

HEUER PUBLISHING CO., 233 Dows Bldg., Box 248, Cedar Rapids IA 52406-0248. (319)364-6311. Fax: (319)364-1771. E-mail: editor@hitplays.com. Website: http://www.hitplays.com. Owner/Editor: C. Emmett McMullen. Estab. 1928. Publishes plays and musicals for junior and senior high school and church groups. Query with synopsis or submit complete script. Reports in 2 months. Purchases amateur rights only. Pays royalty or makes outright purchase.
Needs: "One-, two- and three-act plays and musicals suitable for middle, junior and senior high school productions. Preferably comedy or mystery/comedy with a large number of characters and minimal set requirements. Please avoid controversial or offensive subject matter."

HIPPODROME STATE THEATRE, 25 SE Second Place, Gainesville FL 32601. (352)373-5968. Website: http://hipp.gator.net. Contact: Tamerin Dygert, dramaturg. Estab. 1973. 7 productions per season. Plays are performed on one main thrust stage (266 seats). Query with synopsis, résumé and SASE; professional recommendation and agent submission preferred. No unsolicited scripts. Response: 3 months.
Needs: "We accept plays of any genre or subject matter. We are in need of more multi-cultural plays (anything that is outside the genre of white middle-class lives). We're looking for writers with fresh, original voices whose résumés reflect their professional work." Cast should not exceed 8; staging flexible, but should be appropriate for thrust stage. "We do not accept unsolicited scripts and usually produce only one or two new works per season. Please send query letter, résumé and synopsis only—*no* scripts until we request them (it helps us respond more efficiently)." Prefer professional references. Please include a SASE for reply.
Tips: "We have a need for multi-cultural plays although our audiences also enjoy adaptations of classics. We enjoy comedies but are not interested in the sit-com style of writing. Please note that we also don't have a huge need for children's shows or musicals. For more information on our season, please visit our award-winning website."

N **HOLVOE BOOKS, LTD.**, P.O. Box 62, Hewlett NY 11557-0062. (800)536-0099. E-mail: dlonstage@aol.com. Assistant Editor: Steven Fisch. Publishes hardcover and trade paperback originals. Publishes 2-4 titles/year. Receives 30 queries and 200 mss/year. 25% of plays from first-time authors; 60% unagented writers. Pays royalty and/or makes outright purchase. Advance varies. Publishes play 1-2 years after acceptance of ms. Accepts simultaneous submissions. Reports in 1 month on queries, 1-2 years on mss. Manuscript guidelines for #10 SASE.
Needs: Any length, any style, but should read well on the stage. Submit entire ms with SASE.
Recent Title: *Florida Bound*, by William S. Leavengood.
Tips: Audience is educators, theater professionals and theater lovers. "If accepted, playwright *must* be able to send manuscripts via electronic (disk, e-mail) form."

HORIZON THEATRE COMPANY, P.O. Box 5376, Atlanta GA 31107. (404)523-1477. E-mail: horizonco@mindspring.com. Website: http://www.mindspring.com/~horizonco/. Contact: Sarah Raskin, literary manager. Artistic Director: Lisa Adler. Estab. 1983. Produces 4 plays/year. Professional productions. Query with synopsis and résumé. Reports in 1-2 years. Buys rights to produce in Atlanta area. Pays 6-8% royalty or $50-75/performance.
Needs: "We produce contemporary plays with realistic base, but which utilize heightened visual or language elements. Interested in comedy, satire, plays that are entertaining and topical, but also thought provoking. Also particular interest in plays by women or with Southern themes." No more than 10 in cast.
Tips: "No plays about being in theater or film; no plays without hope; no plays that include playwrights as leading characters; no all-male casts; no plays with all older (50 plus) characters."

ILLINOIS THEATRE CENTRE, 400A Lakewood Blvd., Park Forest IL 60466. (708)481-3510. Fax: (708)481-3693. Artistic Director: Etel Billig. Literary Manager: Barbara Mitchell. Estab. 1976. Produces 8 plays/year. Professional Resident Theatre Company in our own space for a subscription-based audience. Query with synopsis or agented submission. Reports in 2 months. Buys casting and directing and designer selection rights. Pays 7-10% royalty.
Needs: Wants all types of 2-act plays, musicals, dramas. Prefers cast size of 6-10.
Tips: Always looking for mysteries and comedies.

INTERACT THEATRE COMPANY, The Adrienne, 2030 Sansom St., Philadelphia PA 19103. (215)568-8077. Fax: (215)568-8095. Contact: Seth Rozin, artistic director. Estab. 1988. Produces 3 plays/year. Produces professional productions for adult audience. Query with synopsis. Reports in 2 months. Pays 2-8% royalty or $25-100/performance.
Needs: Contemporary dramas and comedies that explore issues of political, social, cultural or historical significance. Prefer plays that raise interesting questions without giving easy, predictable answers. Limit cast to 10.
Tips: No romantic comedies, family dramas, agit prop.

INTIMAN THEATRE, P.O. Box 19760, Seattle WA 98119. (206)269-1901. Fax: (206)269-1928. E-mail: intiman@scn.org. Website: http://www.seattlesquare.com/Intiman. Artistic Director: Warner Shook. Contact: Literary Manager. Estab. 1972. Produces 6 plays/year. LORT C Regional Theater in Seattle. Best submission time is December through May. *Agented submissions only.* Submissions accompanied by professional recommendation are also accepted.
Needs: Well-crafted dramas and comedies by playwrights who fully utilize the power of language and character relationships to explore enduring themes. Prefers character-driven plays.
Tips: "Our play development program conducts four readings per year of previously unproduced plays.

INVISIBLE THEATRE, 1400 N. First Ave., Tucson AZ 85719. (520)882-9721. Fax: (520)884-0672. Contact: Susan Claassen, managing artistic director. Query first. No unsolicited submissions.

JEWEL BOX THEATRE, 3700 N. Walker, Oklahoma City OK 73118-7099. (405)521-1786. Fax: (405)525-6562. Contact: Charles Tweed, production director. Estab. 1986. Produces 6 plays/year. Amateur productions. For 3,000 season subscribers and general public. Submit complete script. Reports in 4 months. Pays $500 contest prize.
Needs: Send SASE for entry form during September-October. We produce dramas and comedies. Only two- or three-act plays can be accepted. Our theater is in-the-round, so we adapt plays accordingly." Deadline: mid-January.

JEWISH REPERTORY THEATRE, 1395 Lexington Ave., New York NY 10128. (212)415-5550. Fax: (212)415-5575. E-mail: jrep@echonyc.com. Website: http://www.jrt.org. Contact: Ran Avni, artistic director. Estab. 1974. Produces 4 plays, 15 readings/year. New York City professional off-Broadway production. Submit complete script with SASE. Reports in 1 month. First production/option to move to Broadway or off-Broadway. Pays royalty.
Needs: Full-length only. Straight plays, musicals. Must have some connection to Jewish life, characters, history. Maximum 7 characters. Limited technical facilities.
Tips: No biblical plays.

KUMU KAHUA, 46 Merchant St., Honolulu HI 96813. (808)536-4222. Fax: (808)536-4226. Artistic Director: Harry Wong. Estab. 1971. Produces 5 productions, 3-4 public readings/year. "Plays performed at new Kumu Kahua Theatre, flexible 120-seat theater, for community audiences." Submit complete script. Reports in 4 months. Pays royalty of $50/performance; usually 12 performances of each production.
Needs: "Plays must have some interest for local Hawai'i audiences, preferably by being set in Hawai'i or dealing with some aspect of the Hawaiian experience. Prefer small cast, with simple staging demands."
Tips: "We need time to evaluate scripts (our response time is four months)."

LARK THEATRE COMPANY/PLAYWRIGHTS WEEK, 939 Eighth Ave., New York NY 10019. (212)246-2609. Producing Director: John C. Eisner, producing director. Estab. 1994. Produces 4 productions/year, 8 during Playwrights Week. "Our mission is to 'ready new plays for production.' Hence, we are a play development organization. We offer readings and developmental workshops, sometimes in limited runs off-Broadway." Submit complete manuscript. Reports in 8 months. No rights purchased at outset for Playwrights Week. Usually an off-Broadway option at next level of developmental production." Pays 5½-7½% royalty (off-Broadway) or per performance (workshops). Sometimes pays travel per diem for Playwrights Week.
Needs: "We focus on the language of live theatre. Although we have no specific restrictions, we like to see creative use of language and theatrical innovation. Our taste for simple staging and resonant, truthful language."
Tips: No television scripts or screenplays. "It is time to reinvent an intimate, simple theater that can compete in a technological world according to its own terms. We seek long-term developmental relationships with playwrights. Sometimes we choose a play because we are interested in the writer's voice as much as the work in question."

LILLENAS PUBLISHING CO., P.O. Box 419527, Kansas City MO 64141-6527. (816)931-1900. Fax: (816)753-4071. E-mail: drama@lillenas.com. Contact: Kim Messer, assistant. Estab. 1926. "We publish on two levels: (1) Program Builders—seasonal and topical collections of recitations, sketches, dialogues and short plays; (2) Drama Resources. These assume more than one format: (a) full-length scripts, (b) one-acts, shorter plays and sketches all by one author, (c) collection of short plays and sketches by various authors. All program and play resources are produced with local church and Christian school in mind. Therefore there are taboos." Queries are encouraged, but synopses and complete scripts are read. "First rights are purchased for Program Builder scripts. For our line of Drama Resources, we purchase all print rights, but this is negotiable." Writer's guidelines for #10 SASE. Reports in 3 months.

- This publisher is more interested in one-act and full-length scripts—both religious and secular. Monologs are of lesser interest than previously. There is more interest in Readers' Theatre.

Needs: 98% of Program Builder materials are freelance written. Scripts selected for these publications are outright purchases; verse is minimum of 25¢/line, prose (play scripts) are minimum of $5/double-spaced page. "Lillenas Drama Resources is a line of play scripts that are, for the most part, written by professionals with experience in production as well as writing. However, while we do read unsolicited scripts, more than half of what we publish is written by experienced authors whom we have already published." Drama Resources (whether full-length scripts, one-acts, or sketches) are paid on a 10% royalty. There are no advances.

Tips: "All plays need to be presented in standard play script format. We welcome a summary statement of each play. Purpose statements are always desirable. Approximate playing time, cast and prop lists, etc. are important to include. We are interested in fully scripted traditional plays, reader's theater scripts, choral speaking pieces. Contemporary settings generally have it over Biblical settings. Christmas and Easter scripts must have a bit of a twist. Secular approaches to these seasons (Santas, Easter bunnies, and so on), are not considered. We sell our product in 10,000 Christian bookstores and by catalog. We are probably in the forefront as a publisher of religious drama resources." Request a copy of our newsletter and/or catalog.

MAGIC THEATRE, INC., Bldg. D, Fort Mason, San Francisco CA 94123. (415)441-8001. Fax: (415)771-5505. E-mail: magicthtre@aol.com. Website: http://www.members.aol.com/magicthtre. Contact: Kent Nicholson, literary manager. Artistic Director: Mame Hunt. Estab. 1967. Produces 6 plays/year plus numerous co-productions. Regional theater. Query with synopsis. Reports in 4 months. Pays royalty or per performance fee."

Needs: "Plays that are innovative in theme and/or craft, cutting-edge political concerns, intelligent comedy. Full-length only, strong commitment to multicultural work

Tips: "Not interested in classics, conventional approaches and cannot produce large-cast plays. Send query to Kent Nicholson, literary manager."

MANHATTAN THEATRE CLUB, 311 W. 43rd St., 8th Floor, New York NY 10036. Director of Play Development: Kate Loewald. Produces 8 plays/year. Two-theater performing arts complex classified as off-Broadway, using professional actors. No unsolicited scripts. No queries. Reports in 6 months.

Needs: "We present a wide range of new work, from this country and abroad, to a subscription audience. We want plays about contemporary concerns and people. Comedies are welcome. Multiple set shows are discouraged. Average cast is eight."

N A **McCARTER THEATRE**, 91 University Place, Princeton NJ 08540. (609)683-9100. Fax: (609)497-0369. Contact: Janice Paian, literary manager. Produces 5 plays/year; 1 second stage play/year. Produces professional productions for a 1,077-seat theater. Query with synopsis; *agented submissions only.* Reports in 1 month; agent submissions 3 months. Payment negotiable.

Needs: Full length plays, musicals, translations.

MERIWETHER PUBLISHING LTD. (Contemporary Drama Service), Dept. WM, 885 Elkton Dr., Colorado Springs CO 80907-3557. President: Mark Zapel. Executive Editor: Arthur L. Zapel. Estab. 1969. "We publish how-to materials in book and video formats. We are interested in materials for middle school, high-school and college level students only. Our Contemporary Drama Service division publishes 60-70 plays/year." 80% written by unpublished writers. Buys 40-60 scripts/year from unpublished/unproduced writers. 90% of scripts are unagented submissions. Reports in 1 month on queries; 2 months on full-length mss. Query with synopsis/outline, résumé of credits, sample of style and SASE. Catalog available for $2 postage. Offers 10% royalty or makes outright purchase.

Needs: Book mss on theatrical arts subjects, especially books of short scenes for amateur and professional actors. "We are now looking for scenebooks with special themes: 'scenes for young women,' 'comedy scenes for two actors', etc. These need not be original, provided the compiler can get letters of permission from the original copyright owner. We are interested in all textbook candidates for theater arts subjects. Christian children's activity book mss also accepted. We will consider elementary level religious materials and plays, but no elementary level children's secular plays. Query. Pays royalty; sometimes makes outright purchase.

Tips: "We publish a wide variety of speech contest materials for high-school students. We are publishing more full length play scripts and musicals based on classic literature or popular TV shows, provided the writer includes letter of clearance from the copyright owner. Our educational books are sold to teachers and students at college and high-school levels. Our religious books are sold to youth activity directors, pastors and choir directors. Our trade books are directed at the public with a sense of humor. Another group of buyers is the professional theater, radio and TV category. We will be especially interested in full length (two- or three-act) plays with name recognition, either the playwright or the adaptation source."

MERRIMACK REPERTORY THEATRE, Dept. WM, 50 E. Merrimack St., Lowell MA 01852-1205. (978)454-6324. Fax: (978)934-0166. Producing Artistic Director: David G. Kent. Contact: Emma Fried. Estab. 1979. Produces 7 plays/year. Professional LORT D. *Agented submissions* and letters of inquiry only. Reports in 6 months.

Needs: All styles and genres. "We are a small 372-seat theater—with a modest budget. Plays should be good stories, with strong dialogue, real situations and human concerns. Especially interested in plays about American life and culture."

MILL MOUNTAIN THEATRE, Market Square, Center in Square, Roanoke VA 24011-1437. (703)342-5730. Fax: (540)342-5745. E-mail: mmtmail@intrlink.com. Website: http://www.intrlink.com/MMT. Executive Director: Jere Lee Hodgin. Literary Manager: Jack Parrish. Produces 8 established plays, 10 new one-acts and 2 new full-length plays/year. "Some of the professional productions will be on the main stage and some in our alternative Theater B." Send letter with SASE. Reports in 8 months. Payment negotiable on individual play. Send SASE for play contest guidelines; cast limit 15 for play and 24 for musicals. Do not include loose stamps or money.
Needs: "We are interested in plays with racially mixed casts, but not to the exclusion of others. We are constantly seeking one-act plays for 'Centerpieces', our lunch time program of script-in-hand productions. Playing time should be between 25-35 minutes. Cast limit 6."
Tips: "Subject matter and character variations are open, but gratuitous language and acts are not acceptable unless they are artistically supported. A play based on large amounts of topical reference or humor has a very short life. Be sure you have written a play and not a film script."

[N] **MISSOURI REPERTORY THEATRE**, 4949 Cherry, Kansas City MO 64110. (816)235-2727. Fax: (816)235-5367. Contact: George Keathley, artistic director. Query first. No unsolicited submissions.

THE NATIONAL PLAYWRIGHTS CONFERENCE/NEW DRAMA FOR MEDIA PROJECT AT THE EUGENE O'NEILL THEATER CENTER, 234 W. 44th St., Suite 901, New York NY 10036-3909. (212)382-2790. Fax: (212)921-5538. E-mail: acthuman@aol.com. Artistic Director: Lloyd Richards. Contact: Mary F. McCabe, managing director. Estab. 1965. Develops staged readings of 9-12 stage plays, 2-3 screenplays or teleplays/year. "We accept unsolicited scripts with no prejudice toward either represented or unrepresented writers. Our theater is located in Waterford, Connecticut, and we operate under an Equity LORT contract. We have three theaters: Barn—250 seats, Amphitheater—300 seats, Instant Theater—150 seats. Submission guidelines for #10 SASE with 2 first-class stamps in the fall. Complete bound, professionally unproduced, original plays are eligible (no adaptations). Decision by late April. Pays stipend plus room, board and transportation. We accept script submissions September 15-December 1 of each year. Conference takes place during July each summer."

- Scripts are selected on the basis of talent, not commercial potential.

Needs: "We use modular sets for all plays, minimal lighting, minimal props and no costumes. We do script-in-hand readings with professional actors and directors. Our focus is on new play/playwright development."

THE NEW AMERICAN THEATER CENTER, 118 N. Main St., Rockford IL 61101. (815)963-9454. Fax: (815)963-7215. Contact: Richard Raether, associate artistic director: Produces a spectrum of American and international work in 10-month season. "The New American Theater Center is a professional equity theater company performing on two stages, a thrust stage with 282-seat house and a 100-seat house theater in the round, in a predominantly middle-class Midwestern town." Submit synopsis with SASE. *No* full scripts. Pays royalty based on number of performances.
Needs: No limitations, prefer contemporary pieces. Open to format, etc. No opera.
Tips: "We look for new work that addresses contemporary issues; we do not look for work of any one genre or production style."

NEW PLAYS INCORPORATED, P.O. Box 5074, Charlottesville VA 22905. (804)979-2777. E-mail: patwhitton@aol.com. Website: http://www.newplaysforchildren.com. Contact: Patricia Whitton, artistic director. Estab. 1964. Publishes 3-6 plays/year. Publishes for children's or youth theaters. Submit complete ms or for adaptations, query first. Reports in 2 months or longer. Buys all semi-professional and amateur rights in U.S. and Canada. Pays 50% royalty.
Needs: I have eclectic taste—plays must have quality and originality in whatever genres, topics, styles or lengths the playwright chooses."
Tips: "No adaptations of stuff that has already been adapted a million times, e.g., *Tom Sawyer*, *A Christmas Carol*, or plays that sound like they've been written by the guidance counselor. There will be more interest in youth theater productions with moderate to large casts (15+). Plays must have been produced, directed by someone other than the author or author's spouse. People keep sending us material suitable for adults. This is not our market!"

NEW PLAYWRIGHTS' PROGRAM, The University of Alabama, P.O. Box 870239, Tuscaloosa AL 35487-0239. (205)348-9032. Fax: (205)348-9048. E-mail: pcastagn@woodsquad.as.ua.edu. Website: http://www.as.ua.edu/theatre/npp.htm. Director/Dramaturg: Dr. Paul C. Castagno. Endowed by Gallaway Fund, estab. 1982. Produces at least 1 new play/year. Mainstage and second stage, University Theatre, The University of Alabama. Submit synopsis or complete ms, August-March. Playwrights may submit potential workshop ideas for consideration. Reports in 6 months. Accepts scripts in various forms: new dramaturgy to traditional. Recent MFA playwriting graduates (within 1 year) may be given consideration for ACTF productions. Send SASE. Stipends competitive with or exceed most contests.
Needs: Southern themes; mainstage material.

[N] **NEW REPERTORY THEATRE**, P.O. Box 610418, Newton Highlands MA 02161-0418. (617)332-7058. Fax: (617)527-5217. Producing Artistic Director: Rick Lombardo. Estab. 1984. Produces 5 plays/year. Professional theater, general audience. Query with synopsis. Production, subsidiary. Pays 5-10% royalty.

Needs: Idea laden, all styles, full-length only. Small cast, unit set.
Tips: No sit-coms like comedies. Incorporating and exploring styles other than naturalism.

NEW STAGE THEATRE, 1100 Carlisle, Jackson MS 39202. (601)948-0143. Fax: (601)948-3538. Contact: John Maxwell, artistic director. Estab. 1965. Produces 9 plays/year. "Professional productions, 8 mainstage, 1 in our 'second space.' We play to an audience comprised of Jackson, the state of Mississippi and the Southeast." Query with synopsis. Reports in 6 weeks. Exclusive premiere contract upon acceptance of play for mainstage production. Pays royalty of 5-8% or $25-60/performance.
Needs: Southern themes, contemporary issues, small casts (5-8), single set plays.
- The New Stage no longer accepts children's theater.

NEW YORK STATE THEATRE INSTITUTE, 155 River St., Troy NY 12180. (518)274-3200. Fax: (518)274-3815. E-mail: nysti@crisny.org. Website: http://www.crisny.org/not-for-profit/nysti. Contact: Patricia Di Benedetto Snyder, producing artistic director. Produces 5 plays/year. Professional regional productions for adult and family audiences. "We are not interested in material for 'mature' audiences." Submit query with synopsis. Reports in 1 month on synopsis. Pay varies.

NEW YORK THEATRE WORKSHOP, 83 E. Fourth St., New York NY 10003. (212)780-9037. Fax: (212)460-8996. Artistic Director: James C. Nicola. Contact: Mandy Mishell Hackett, literary manager. Estab. 1979. Produces 4-6 full productions; approximately 50 readings/year. Plays are performed off-Broadway, Equity LOA contract theater. Audience is New York theater-going audience and theater professionals. Query with synopsis and 10-page sample scene. Reports in 5 months. Option to produce commercially; percentage of box office gross from commercial and percentage of author's net subsidiary rights within specified time limit from our original production. Pays fee because of limited run, with additional royalty payments; for extensions; $1,500-2,000 fee range.
- The New York Theatre Workshop offers Van Lier Playwrighting Fellowships for emerging writers of color based in New York City. Address inquiries to Chion Miyagawa, Artistic Associate.

Needs: Full-length plays, one acts, translations/adaptations, music theater pieces; proposals for performance projects. Socially relevant issues, innovative form and language. Plays utilizing more than 8 actors usually require outside funding.
Tips: "No overtly commercial and conventional musicals or plays."

N **THE NEXT THEATRE CO.**, 927 Noyes, Evanston IL 60201. (847)475-6763. Fax: (847)475-6767. Contact: Steve Pickering, artistic director. Estab. 1981. Produces 4 plays/year. Produces professional theater for adult audiences. Query with synopsis; include 10-page sample. Reports in 2-3 months. Rights negotiable. Pays 5% royalty.
Needs: "Plays and playwrights who create imaginative worlds and people with fascinating characters; with a rich sense of history and/or mythology; and with a unique or inventive use of language." Prefers small cast and simple sets, but not a requirement.
Tips: No musicals, realism or television. "Be mindful of the potential of the medium. Engage the audience's imagination, for that is the way to their minds and hearts."

NINE O'CLOCK PLAYERS, 1367 N. St. Andrews Place, Los Angeles CA 90028-8592. (213)469-1973. Estab. 1928. Contact: Play Reading Chairman. Produces 2 plays/year. "Plays produced at Assistance League Playhouse by resident amateur and semi-professional company. All plays are musical adaptations of classical children's literature appropriate for children ages 4-12." Query with synopsis. Reports in 1 month. Pays negotiable royalty or per performance.
Needs: "Plays must have at least 9-15 characters and be 75 minutes long. Productions are done on a proscenium stage in classical theater style. All plays must have humor, music and good moral values. No audience participation improvisational plays."

NORTHLIGHT THEATRE, 9501 Skokie Blvd., Skokie IL 60077. (847)679-9501. Contact: Russell Vandenbroucke, artistic director:. Estab. 1975. Produces 5 plays/year. "We are a professional, Equity theater, LORT D. We have a subscription base of over 6,000, and have a significant number of single ticket buyers." Query with synopsis and SASE. Reports in 3 months. Buys production rights plus royalty on future mountings. Pays royalty.
Needs: "Full-length plays, translations, adaptations, musicals. Interested in plays of 'ideas,' plays that are passionate and/or hilarious, stylistic exploration, intelligence and complexity. Generally looking for cast size of eight or less, but there are always exceptions made for the right play."
Tips: "Please, do not try to do what television and film do better! Also, no domestic realism."

ODYSSEY THEATRE ENSEMBLE, 2055 S. Sepulveda Blvd., Los Angeles CA 90025. (310)477-2055. Fax: (310)444-0455. Contact: Sally Essex-Lopresti, director of Literary Programs. Estab. 1965. Produces 9 plays/year. Plays performed in a 3-theater facility. "All three theaters are Equity 99-seat theater plan. We have a subscription audience of 4,000 for a nine-play main season, and they are offered a discount on our rentals and co-productions. Remaining seats are sold to the general public." Query with résumé, synopsis, cast breakdown and 8-10 pages of sample dialogue and cassette if a musical. Scripts must be securely bound. Reports in 1 month on queries; 6 months on scripts. Buys negotiable rights. Pays 5-7% royalty. Does *not* return scripts without SASE.
Needs: "Full-length plays only with either an innovative form and/or provocative subject matter. We desire highly theatrical pieces that explore possibilities of the live theater experience. We are seeking full-length musicals and some

plays with smaller casts (2-4). We are not reading one-act plays or light situation comedies. We are seeking Hispanic material for our resident Hispanic unit as well as plays from all cultures and ethnicities."

OLDCASTLE THEATRE COMPANY, Box 1555, Bennington VT 05201-1555. (802)447-0564. Fax: (802)442-3704. Contact: Daryl Kenny, marketing director. Artistic Director: Eric Peterson. Produces 6 plays/year. Plays are performed in the new Bennington Center for the Arts, by a professional Equity theater company (in a May-October season) for general audiences, including residents of a three-state area and tourists during the vacation season. Submit complete ms. Reports in 6 months. Pays by negotiation with the playwright. A not-for-profit theater company.
Needs: Produces classics, musicals, comedy, drama, most frequently American works. Usual performance time is 2 hours.

OMAHA THEATER COMPANY FOR YOUNG PEOPLE, (formerly Emmy Gifford Children's Theater), 3504 Center St., Omaha NE 68105. (402)345-4849. Artistic Director: James Larson. Produces 6 plays/year. "Our target audience is children, preschool-high school and their parents." Query with synopsis and SASE. Reports in 9 months. Royalty negotiable.
Needs: "Plays must be geared to children and parents (PG rating). Titles recognized by the general public have a stronger chance of being produced." Cast limit: 25 (8-10 adults). No adult scripts.
Tips: "Unproduced plays may be accepted only after a letter of inquiry (familiar titles only!)."

THE OPEN EYE THEATER, P.O. Box 959, Margaretville NY 12455. Phone/fax: (914)586-1660. E-mail: openeye@catskill.net. Website: http://www.tchouse.com. Select Arts Centers. Contact: Amie Brockway, producing artistic director. The Open Eye is a not-for-profit professional theater company working in New York City since 1972, in the rural villages of Delaware County, NY since 1991, and on tour. The theater specializes in the development of new plays for multi-generational audiences (children ages 8 and up, and adults of all ages). Ensemble plays with music and dance, culturally diverse and historical material, myth, folklore, and stories with universal themes are of interest. Program includes readings, developmental workshops, and fully staged productions.
Tips: Send one-page letter with one-paragraph plot synopsis, cast breakdown and setting, résumé and SAE. "We will provide the stamp and contact you *if we want to see the script.*"

N **PEGASUS THEATRE**, 3916 Main St., Dallas TX 75226-1228. (214)821-6005. Fax: (214)826-1671. Contact: Kurt Kleinmann, artistic director. Estab. 1985. Produces 4 full productions, 4-6 readings/year. Produces plays under an Umbrella Agreement with AEA. "Our productions are presented for the general public to attend." Query with synopsis; include 10 sample pages. Reports in 6 months. Pays 5-8% royalty.
Needs: New and original comedies with a satiric slant. Limit cast size to under 10, single set.
Tips: "No murder-mysteries, please. We'd rather not look at one-acts that don't have companion pieces or at plays that read and play like extended-length sitcoms. Neatness and proper formatting always make a better impression—even with the best of scripts."

N A **PHILADELPHIA THEATRE COMPANY**, 1811 Chestnut St., Suite 300, Philadelphia PA 19103. (215)568-1920. Fax: (215)568-1944. Contact: Sara Garonzik, producing artistic director. Estab. 1974. Produces 4 plays/year. *Agented submissions only.*

PIER ONE THEATRE, P.O. Box 894, Homer AK 99603. (907)235-7333. Website: http://www.alaska.net/~wmbell. Contact: Lance Petersen, artistic director:. Estab. 1973. Produces 5-8 plays/year. "Plays to various audiences for various plays—e.g. children's, senior citizens, adult, family, etc. Plays are produced on Kemai Peninsula." Submit complete script. Reports in 3 months. Pays $25-125/performance.
Needs: "No restrictions—willing to read *all* genres. However, for the near future, our New Works program will present work by Alaskan playwrights and work of specific Alaskan interest."
Tips: "We prefer to have the whole script to evaluate."

PIONEER DRAMA SERVICE, INC., P.O. Box 4267, Englewood CO 80155-4267. (303)779-4035. Fax: (303)779-4315. E-mail: piodrama@aol.com. Website: www.pioneerdrama.com. Publisher: Steven Fendrich, Contact: Lynne Zborowski, submissions editor. Estab. 1963. Publishes approximately 30 new plays/year. Plays are performed by schools, colleges, community theaters, recreation programs, churches and professional children's theaters for audiences of all ages. Query preferred; unsolicited scripts with proof of production accepted. Reports in 2 weeks on queries, in 4-6 months on scripts. Retains all rights. Pays on royalty basis. All submissions automatically entered in Shubert Fendrich Memorial Playwriting Contest. Guidelines for SASE.
Needs: "Musicals, comedies, mysteries, dramas, melodramas and children's theater. Two-acts up to 90 minutes; children's theater, 1 hour. Prefers many female roles, simple sets. "Plays need to be appropriate for amateur groups." Prefers secular plays.
Tips: Interested in adaptations of classics of public domain works appropriate for children and teens. Also plays that deal with social issues for teens and preteens.

PLAYERS PRESS, INC., P.O. Box 1132, Studio City CA 91614-0132. Contact: Robert W. Gordon, editorial vice president:. "We deal in all entertainment areas and handle publishable works for film and television as well as theater.

Performing arts books, plays and musicals. All plays must be in stage format for publication." Also produces scripts for video and material for cable television. 80% freelance written. 20-30 scripts/year unagented submissions; 5-15 books also unagented. Works with 1-10 unpublished/unproduced writers annually. Query. "Include #10 SASE, reviews and proof of production. All play submissions must have been produced and should include a flier and/or program with dates of performance." Reports in 1 month on queries; 1 year on mss. Buys negotiable rights. "We prefer all area rights." Pays variable royalty according to area; approximately 10-75% of gross receipts. Also makes outright purchase of $100-25,000 or $5-5,000/performance.

Needs: "We prefer comedies, musicals and children's theater, but are open to all genres. We will rework the script after acceptance. We are interested in the quality, not the format. Performing Arts Books that deal with theater how-to are of strong interest."

Tips: "Send only material requested. Do not telephone."

PLAYS, The Drama Magazine for Young People, 120 Boylston St., Boston MA 02116-4615. Editor: Sylvia K. Burack. Contact: Elizabeth Preston, managing editor. Estab. 1941. Publishes approximately 75 one-act plays and dramatic program material each school year to be performed by junior and senior high, middle grades, lower grades. "Scripts should follow the general style of *Plays*. Stage directions should not be typed in capital letters or underlined. No incorrect grammar or dialect." Desired lengths are: junior and senior high—15-18 double-spaced pages (20-30 minutes playing time); middle grades—10-12 pages (15-20 minutes playing time); lower grades—6-10 pages (8-15 minutes playing time). Buys all rights. Pays "good rates on acceptance." Query first for adaptations. Reports in 2-3 weeks. Sample copy $3.50. Send SASE for specification sheet.

Needs: "Can use comedies, farces, melodramas, skits, mysteries and dramas, plays for holidays and other special occasions, such as Book Week; adaptations of classic stories and fables; historical plays; plays about black history and heroes; puppet plays; folk and fairy tales; creative dramatics; and plays for conservation, ecology or human rights programs."

N **PLAYS ON TAPE**, P.O. Box 5789, Bend OR 97708. (541)923-6246. Literary Manager: Silvia Gonzales S. Estab. 1997. All audiences. Buys 5 scripts/year. Works with 5 writers/year. Buys audio rights only. Accepts previously produced material. No submissions will be returned. Reports in 3 months on queries; 4 months on submissions. Catalog free. Query with synopsis. Pays advance and small royalty.

Needs: Tapes and CDs. "We are interested in off-beat, on-the-edge, contemporary works by all writers. You can be green with purple polka dots and we will read your submission."

N **PLAYS-IN-PROGRESS**, 615 4th St., Eureka CA 95501. (707)443-3724. Artistic Director: Susan Bigelow-Marsh. Estab. 1988. Produces 5 plays/year. Non-profit, with adult audiences. Submit complete manuscript. Reports in 6 months. Pays maximum of 10% royalty.

Needs: Innovative, socially relevant, full-length drama and comedies. Simple scenes; cast limit 8.

Tips: Do not want to see musicals, children plays. "Bound scripts only. All must contain SASE."

N **THE PLAYWRIGHTS' CENTER'S PLAYLABS**, 2301 Franklin Ave. E., Minneapolis MN 55406. (612)332-7481. Fax: (612)332-6037. E-mail: pwcenter@mtn.org. Website: http://www.pwcenter.org. Lab Director: Elissa Adams. Estab. 1971. "Playlabs is a 2-week developmental workshop for new plays. The program is held in Minneapolis and is open by script competition. It is an intensive two-week workshop focusing on the development of a script and the playwright. Four to six new plays are given rehearsed public readings at the site of the workshop." Announcements of playwrights by May 1, 1999. Playwrights receive honoraria, travel expenses, room and board.

Needs: "We are interested in playwrights with talent, ambitions for a sustained career in theater and scripts which could benefit from an intensive developmental process involving professional dramaturgs, directors and actors. US citizens or permanent residents, only. Participants must attend all or part of conference, depending on the length of their workshop. No previously produced or published materials. Send SASE after October 15, 1998 for application. Submission deadline: December 15, 1998.

Tips: "We do not buy scripts or produce them. We are a service organization that provides programs for developmental work on scripts for members."

PLAYWRIGHTS HORIZONS, 416 W. 42nd St., New York NY 10036. (212)564-1235. Contact: Sonya Sobieski; literary director (plays); send musicals Attn: Musical Theatre Program. Artistic Director: Tim Sanford. Estab. 1971. Produces 6 plays/year plus a reading series. Plays performed "off-Broadway for a literate, urban, subscription audience." Send complete ms with author bio. Response: 6 months. Negotiates for future rights. Pays outright sum, and then percentage after a certain run.

Needs: "We are looking for new, full-length plays and musicals by American authors."

Tips: "No adaptations, children's theater, biographical or historical plays. We look for plays with a strong sense of language and a clear dramatic action that truly use the resources of the theater."

PLAYWRIGHTS THEATRE OF NEW JERSEY, 33 Green Village Rd., Madison NJ 07940. (201)514-1787. Website: http://www.ptnj.org. Producing Artistic Director: John Pietrowski. Artistic Director: Joseph Megel. Contact: Peter Hays, literary manager. Estab. 1986. Produces 1-3 productions, 8 staged readings and sit-down readings/year. "We operate under a letter of agreement (LOA with LORT Rules) with Actors' Equity Association for all productions. Readings are held under a staged reading code." Submit complete ms. Short bio and production history required. Reports in 6-12 months. "For productions we ask the playwright to sign an agreement that gives us exclusive rights to the play for the production period and for 30 days following. After the 30 days we give the rights back with no strings attached, except for commercial productions. We ask that our developmental work be acknowledged in any other professional productions." Pays $500 for productions, $125 for staged readings. Scripts accepted September 1-April 30 only.

- "We no longer accept unsolicited work. Playwrights however can submit the first 10 pages, a synopsis, bio and history of play, if any. Playwrights should write to us for guidelines first."

Needs: Any style or length; full length, one acts, musicals.

Tips: "We are looking for American plays in the early stages of development—plays of substance, passion, and light (comedies and dramas) that raise challenging questions about ourselves and our communities. We prefer *that can work only on the stage* in the most theatrical way possible—plays that are not necessarily 'straight-on' realistic, but rather ones that use imagery, metaphor, poetry and musicality in new and interesting ways. Plays go through a three-step development process: a roundtable (inhouse reading), a public concert reading and then a workshop production."

[A] **PRIMARY STAGES COMPANY, INC.**, 584 Ninth Ave., New York NY 10036. (212)333-7471. Fax: (212)333-2025. Contact: Tricia McDermott, literary manager. Artistic Director: Casey Childs. Estab. 1983. Produces 4 plays, several readings and workshops/year. All plays are produced professionally off-Broadway at Primary Stages Theatre, 354 W. 45th St. *Agented submissions only.* Reports in 6 months. "If Primary Stages produces the play, we ask for the right to move it for up to six months after the closing performance." Writers paid $1,800 for production. "No unsolicited scripts accepted! Write for guidelines and enclose SASE."

Needs: "We are looking for highly theatrical works that were written exclusively with the stage in mind. We do not want TV scripts or strictly realistic plays. Looking for small cast musicals never produced in the New York City area."

Tips: No "living room plays, disease-of-the-week plays, back-porch plays, father/son work-it-all-out-plays, etc."

[N] **PUERTO RICAN TRAVELING THEATRE**, 141 West 94th St., New York NY 10036. (212)354-1293. Fax: (212)307-6769. Founder/Artistic Director: Miriam Colon Valle. Estab. 1967. Produces 3 plays/year. Two plays in our theater, one during the summer in the streets, parks, playgrounds. Professional Theatre, Actors Equity LOA contract. Query and synopsis. Contract negotiable. Retain some subsidiary rights. Fee negotiable, but we are a small theater.

Needs: Primarily plays by Latinos or Spaniard. Prefer strong story lines. Limit 8 characters. No fly space, little wing space. The stage is 21′×19′.

Tips: No sitcoms or revues. "Make certain the play is for the stage, not for TV or films. That means larger than life characters, heightened language."

[N] **THE PURPLE ROSE THEATRE CO.**, P.O. Box 220, Chelsea MI 48118. (313)475-5817. Fax: (313)475-0802. Contact: Guy Sanville, artistic director. Estab. 1990. Produces 4 plays/year. PRTC is a regional theater with an S.P.T. Equity contract which produces plays intended for Midwest/Middle American audience. Query with synopsis, character breakdown, and 10-page dialogue sample. Expect replies in 3-4 months. Pays 5-10% royalty.

Needs: Modern, topical 2 acts, 90-120 minutes. Will also accept 1 acts and children's plays. Prefer scripts that use comedy to deal with serious subjects. 8 cast maximum. No fly space, unit set preferable but not required. Intimate 119 seat ¾ thrust house.

[A] **JONATHAN REINIS PRODUCTIONS, THEATRE ON THE SQUARE**, 450 Post St., San Francisco CA 94102. (415)433-6461. Estab. 1982. Produces 3 plays/year. Professional productions. 700-3,000 seats. All Equity or union actors. General audience. *Agented submissions only.* Reports in 2 months. Subsidiary rights negotiable. Pays 6% royalty for musicals, 8-10% for plays.

Needs: Musicals, dramas, comedies.

Tips: "No dreary, depressing ideological plays. Dance has become much more important. Younger generations (stomp, etc.) are leaning to performance art. Be flexible."

[N] **SAN JOSÉ REPERTORY THEATRE**, P.O. Box 2399, San Jose CA 95109. (408)291-2266. Website: http://www.sjrep.com. Artistic Director: Ms. Timothy Near. Contact: J.R. Orlando, artistic assistant. Estab. 1980. Produces 6 plays/year. Professional Lort C theater. Query with synopsis. Reports in 6 months. Pays royalty.

Needs: Small cast musicals (no more than 8 including musicians) multicultural plays.

Tips: "San Jose Rep is unlikely to produce playwrights without *some* kind of track record. Generally they must have had at least one play produced professionally."

[N] **SYL SCHERER**, P.O. Box 5789, Bend OR 97708. (541)923-6246. Literary Manager: Silvia Gonzalez S. Estab. 1996. Publishes 3-4 plays/year. "Audio theatre. We produce/publish offbeat contemporary stage plays for audio cassette and compact disc. Our audience is anyone: audio book listeners, etc." Query with synopsis or submit complete ms with SASE (if return is desired). Reports in 4 months. Buys audio rights only. Pays royalty (negotiable). Offers advance of $1,000 with small royalty.

Needs: Offbeat contemporary stage plays that won't diminish in quality when placed on audio. "Right now we are focusing on 2-5 characters."

Tips: "No historical material, kitchen soaps, one-person shows or plays with too many locations. We like bizarre works, or extremely thought-provoking. We are not afraid of street language (we don't censure). Send 10-20 pages on recycled paper, send 4th class; you don't need to impress us (we are playwrights). Not that interested in resumes. We like good quotes if play has been reviewed. Don't care if play has been produced. Just make sure play can be brilliant if on audio."

SHAW FESTIVAL THEATRE, P.O. Box 774, Niagara-on-the-Lake, Ontario L0S 1J0 Canada. Fax: (905)468-5438. E-mail: systems@shawfest.com. Website: http://shawfest.sympatico.ca. Contact: Christopher Newton, artistic director. Estab. 1962. Produces 10 plays/year. "Professional summer festival operating three theaters (Festival: 861 seats; Court House: 324 seats; Royal George: 328 seats). We also host some music and some winter rentals. Mandate is based on the works of G.B. Shaw and his contemporaries. We prefer to hold rights for Canada and northeastern US, also potential to tour." Pays 5-6% royalty. Submit with SASE or SAE and IRCs, depending on country of origin.
Needs: "We operate an acting ensemble of up to 75 actors; this includes 14 actor/singers and we have sophisticated production facilities. During the summer season (April-October) the Academy of the Shaw Festival sometimes organizes workshops of new plays."

SOUTH COAST REPERTORY, P.O. Box 2197, Costa Mesa CA 92628-1197. (714)708-5500. Fax: (714)545-0391. Website: http://www.ocartsnet.org/scr/. Dramaturg: Jerry Patch. Literary Manager: John Glore. Estab. 1964. Produces 6 plays/year on mainstage, 5 on second stage. Professional nonprofit theater; a member of LORT and TCG. "We operate in our own facility which houses a 507-seat mainstage theater and a 161-seat second stage theater. We have a combined subscription audience of 21,000." Query with synopsis; scripts considered if submitted by agent. Reports in 4 months. Acquires negotiable rights. Pays negotiable royalty.
Needs: "We produce full lengths. We prefer plays that address contemporary concerns and are dramaturgically innovative. A play whose cast is larger than 15-20 will need to be extremely compelling, and its cast size must be justifiable."
Tips: "We don't look for a writer to write for us—he or she should write for him or herself. We look for honesty and a fresh voice. We're not likely to be interested in writers who are mindful of *any* trends. Originality and craftsmanship are the most important qualities we look for."

[N] **SOUTH COAST REPERTORY'S HISPANIC PLAYWRIGHT'S PROJECT**, P.O. Box 2197, Costa Mesa CA 92628-2797. (714)708-5500, ext. 5405. Director of HPP: Juliette Carrillo. Estab. 1985. Produces 3 plays/year. "Professional regional theatre, workshops format, general audience." Submit complete manuscript during submission period only Nov. 1998-Jan. 1999. Report in 2 months. Hold rights to do production for 30 days after reading. Pays per diem, travel & lodging for workshop.
Needs: Writers must be of Latino heritage. No plays entirely in Spanish (must be mostly English). No musicals.

STAGE ONE: The Louisville Children's Theatre, 5 Riverfront Plaza, Louisville KY 40202-3300. (502)589-5946. Fax: (502)588-5910. E-mail: kystageone@aol.com. Website: http://www.stageone.org. Contact: Moses Goldberg, producing director. Estab. 1946. Produces 6-7 plays/year. 20% freelance written; 15-20% unagented submissions (excluding work of playwright-in-residence). Plays performed by an Equity company for young audiences ages 4-18; usually does different plays for different age groups within that range. Submit complete script. Reports in 4 months. Pays negotiable royalty or $25-75/performance.
Needs: "Good plays for young audiences of all types: adventure, fantasy, realism, serious problem plays about growing up or family entertainment. Cast: ideally, twelve or less. Honest, visual potentiality, worthwhile story and characters are necessary. An awareness of children and their schooling is a plus. No campy material or anything condescending to children. Musicals if they are fairly limited in orchestration."

STAGE WEST, P.O. Box 2587, Fort Worth TX 76113. (817)924-9454. Fax: (817)926-8650. Contact: Jim Covault, artistic director. Estab. 1979. Produces 9 plays/year. "We stage professional productions at our own theater for a mixed general audience." Query with synopsis. Reports in 6 months. Rights are negotiable. Pays 7% royalty.
Needs: "We want full-length plays that are accessible to a mainstream audience but possess traits that are highly theatrical. Cast size of ten or less and single or unit set are desired."

STEPPENWOLF THEATRE COMPANY, 1650 N. Halsted, Chicago IL 60614. (312)335-1888. Artistic Director: Martha Lavey. Contact: Michele Volansky, dramaturg/literary manager. Estab. 1976. Produces 9 plays/year. 500 + 300 seat subscriber audience. Many plays produced by Steppenwolf have gone to Broadway. "We currently have 18,000 savvy subscribers." Query with synopsis, 10 pages sample dialogue. Agented submissions only or letter of recommendation from theater professional. Reports in 6 months. Buys first, second class and regional rights. Pays 6-8% royalty.
Needs: Wants all sorts of full-lengths with strong ensemble acting possibilities. "However, musicals are not our forté. Also, we've rarely produced one-acts and a 28-character play may be pushing it."
Tips: "Look to our history to know if your play is 'Steppenwolf material.' "

[A] **STUDIO ARENA THEATRE**, 710 Main St., Buffalo NY 14202. (716)856-8025. Fax: (716)856-3415. Website: http://www.studioarena.org. Contact: Gavin Cameron-Webb, artistic director. Estab. 1965. Produces 9 plays/year. Professional productions. *Agented submissions only.*
Needs: Full-length plays. No fly space.

[N] **SYRACUSE STAGE**, 820 E. Genesee, Syracuse NY 13210-1508. (315)443-4008. Fax: (315)443-9846. E-mail: syrstage@syr.edu. Website: http://www.syracusestage.org. Contact: Artistic Director. Estab. 1974. Produces 7 plays/

year, plus one children's play. Professional LORT productions. Query with synopsis, résumé, character breakdown and an excerpt of 10 pages (cassette for musicals). Rights defined in contracts.
Needs: Full-length plays—one-person shows. Translations and adaptations accepted. All styles of theater.
Tips: No sitcom-like plays.

THE TEN-MINUTE MUSICALS PROJECT, P.O. Box 461194, West Hollywood CA 90046. (213)656-8751. Producer: Michael Koppy. Estab. 1987. Produces 1-10 plays/year. "Plays performed in Equity regional theaters in the US and Canada." Submit complete script, lead sheets and cassette. Deadline August 31; notification by December 15. Buys performance rights. Pays $250 royalty advance upon selection, against equal share of performance royalties when produced. Submission guidelines for #10 SASE.
Needs: Looking for complete short stage musicals playing between 7-14 minutes. Limit cast to 10 (5 women, 5 men).

N **THEATER BY THE BLIND**, 306 W. 18 St., New York NY 10011. (212)243-4337. Artistic Director: Ike Schambelan. Estab. 1979. Produces 20 plays/year. "Off-off Broadway, Theater Row, general audiences, seniors, students, disabled." Submit complete ms. Reports in 3 months. "If rights transfer, we'll like a piece." Pays outright purchase $250-500.
Needs: Genres about blindness.

THE THEATER OF NECESSITY, 11702 Webercrest, Houston TX 77048. (713)733-6042. Artistic Director: Philbert Plumb. Estab. 1981. Produces 4 plays/year. Plays are produced in a small professional theater. Submit complete script. Reports in 1 year. Buys performance rights. Pays standard royalties based on size of house for small productions or individual contracts for large productions (average $500/run). "We usually keep script on file unless we are certain we will never use it." Send SASE with script and #10 SASE for response.
Needs: "Any play in a recognizable genre must be superlative in form and intensity. Experimental plays are given an easier read. We move to larger venue if the play warrants the expense."

N **THEATER OF THE FIRST AMENDMENT**, George Mason University MS 3E6, Fairfax VA 22030. (703)993-1122. Contact: Kristin Johnsen-Neshati, dramaturg. Estab. 1990. Produces 3 plays/year. Professional productions performed in an Equity LOA 150-seat theater. Query with synopsis. Reports in 3 months. Pays combination of percentage of box office gross against a guaranteed minimum royalty.

THEATRE & COMPANY, 20 Queen St. N., Kitchener, Ontario N2H 2G8 Canada. Fax: (519)571-9051. E-mail: stuartsw@wchat.on.ca. Website: http://www.stage-door.org/the&co.html. Artistic Director: Stuart Scadron-Wattles. Contact: Henry Bakker, literary manager. Estab. 1988. Produces 5 plays/year. Professional (non-equity) productions for a general audience. Query with synopsis and SAE with IRCs. Reports in 3 months. Pays $50-100/performance.
Needs: "One act or full length; comedy or drama; musical or straight; written from or compatible with a biblical world view." No cast above 10; prefers unit staging. Looking for small cast (less than 8) ensemble comedies.

- Theatre & Company is particularly interested in work by Canadians.

Tips: Looks for "non-religious writing from a biblical world view for an audience which loves the theater. Avoid current trends toward shorter scenes. Playwrights should be aware that they are writing for the stage—not television. We encourage audience interaction, using an acting ensemble trained in improvisation."

THEATREVIRGINIA, 2800 Grove Ave., Richmond VA 23221-2466. Contact: George Black, producing artistic director. Estab. 1955. Produces 5-8, publishes 0-1 new play/year. Query with synopsis and 15 page sample. Accepts agented submissions. Solicitations in 1 month for initial query, 3-8 months for script. Rights negotiated. Payment negotiated.
Needs: No one-acts; no children's theater.

THEATREWORKS/USA, 151 W. 26th St., New York NY 10001. (212)647-1100. Artistic Director: Jay Harnick. Estab. 1961. Produces 3-6 new productions/year. Professional Equity productions for young audiences. Query and synopsis or submit complete ms. Reports in 6 months. Pays 6% royalty.
Needs: "One-hour musicals or plays with music written for K-3rd or 3rd-7th grade age groups. Subjects: historical, biography, classic literature, fairy tales with specific point of view, contemporary literature. Limited to 5-6 actors and a portable set. Do not rely on lighting or special effects."
Tips: "No campy, 'fractured' fairy tales, shows specifically written to teach or preach, shows relying heavily on narrators or 'kiddy theater' filled with pratfalls, bad jokes and audience participation. Write smart. Kids see a lot these days, and they are sophisticated. Don't write down to them. They deserve a good, well-told story. Seeing one of our shows will provide the best description."

N **UBU REPERTORY THEATER PUBLICATIONS**, 151 W. 28th St., New York NY 10001. (212)679-7540. Fax: (212)679-2033. Contact: Françoise Kourilsky, also Robin Gillette, general manager. Estab. 1982. Produces 3-4 plays/year; 1-2 books/year. Publishes for general academic and Francophile/Francophone audience. Query with synopsis or submit complete ms. Reports in 3-6 months. Buys performance, publication and translation rights. Pays 2-4% royalty (writers usually 4%, translators 2%).
Needs: Contemporary French-language plays in translation as well as "modern classics" of the French theater. "We publish only contemporary French-language plays in translation." Limit cast to 5-6 actors.

Tips: "No plays originally written in any language other than French! English translations of French-language plays may be submitted, provided translation rights have been obtained."

URBAN STAGE, (formerly Playwrights Preview Productions), 17 E. 47th St., New York NY 10017. (212)421-1380. Fax: (212)421-1387. E-mail: UrbanStage@aol.com. Website: http://www.mint.net/urbanstages.com. Contact: Ella Smith, literary consultant. Artistic Director: Frances Hill. Literary Manager: David Sheppard. Estab. 1983. Produces 2-3 plays/year. Professional productions off or off off-Broadway—throughout the year. General audience. Submit complete script, one play only. Reports in 4 months. If produced, option for 6 months. Pays royalty.
Needs: Both one-act and full-length; generally 1 set or styled playing dual. Good imaginative, creative writing. Cast limited to 3-7.
Tips: "We tend to reject 'living-room' plays. We look for imaginative settings. Be creative and interesting with intellectual content. All submissions should be bound. Send SASE. We are looking for plays with ethnic backgrounds."

VIGILANTE THEATRE CO., P.O. Box 507, Bozeman MT 59771-0507. (406)586-3897. Artistic Director: Brian V. Massman. Estab. 1982. Produces 1-2 plays/year. Plays by professional touring company that does productions by or about people and themes of the Northwest. "Past productions were concerned with homeless people, agriculture, literature by Northwest writers, one-company towns and spouse abuse in rural areas." Submit complete ms. Reports in 6 months. Pays $10-50/performance.
Needs: Produces full-length plays, small musicals and some one-acts. "Staging suitable for a small touring company and cast limited to four actors (two men, two women). Double casting actors for more play characters is also an option."
Tips: "No large musicals requiring orchestras and a chorus line. Although we prefer a script of some thematic substance, the company is very adept at comedy and would prefer the topic to include humor."

WALNUT STREET THEATRE, Ninth and Walnut Streets, Philadelphia PA 19107. (215)574-3550. Fax: (215)574-3598. Producing Artistic Director: Bernard Havard. Contact: Beverly Elliott, literary manager. Estab. 1809. Produces 5 mainstage and 5 studio plays/year. "Our plays are performed in our own space. WST has 3 theaters—a proscenium (mainstage), 1,052 seats; 2 studios, 79-99 seats. We have a subscription audience, largest in the nation." Query with synopsis and 10-20 pages. Writer's must be members of the Dramatists' Guild. Reports in 5 months. Rights negotiated per project. Pays royalty (negotiated per project) or outright purchase.
Needs: "Full-length dramas and comedies, musicals, translations, adaptations and revues. The studio plays must have a cast of no more than four, simple sets."
Tips: "Bear in mind that on the mainstage we look for plays with mass appeal, Broadway-style. The studio spaces are our off-Broadway. No children's plays. Our mainstage audience goes for work that is entertaining and light. Our studio season is where we look for plays that have bite and are more provocative." Include SASE for return of materials.

WATERLOO COMMUNITY PLAYHOUSE, P.O. Box 433, Waterloo IA 50704-0433. (319)235-0367. Fax: (319)235-7489. Contact: Charles Stilwill, managing artistic director. Estab. 1917. Plays performed by Waterloo Community Playhouse with a volunteer cast. Produces 11 plays (7 adult, 4 children's); 1-2 musicals and 9-10 nonmusicals/year; 1-3 originals. 17% freelance written; most unagented submissions. Works with 1-3 unpublished/unproduced writers annually. "We are one of few theaters with a commitment to new scripts. We do at least one and have done as many as four a year. We have 4,300 season members. Average attendance is 3,300. We do a wide variety of plays. Our public isn't going to accept nudity, too much sex, too much strong language. We don't have enough Black actors to do all-Black shows. Theater has done plays with as few as 2 characters, and as many as 98. On the main stage, we usually pay between $400 and $500. We also produce children's theater. Submit complete script. Please, no loose pages. Reports negatively within 1 year, but acceptance sometimes takes longer because we try to fit a wanted script into the balanced season. We sometimes hold a script longer than a year if we like it but cannot immediately find the right slot for it. In 1998 we did the midwest premiere of *The Moving of Lilla Barton* which was written in 1993 and the year before we did the midwest premiere of *Three to Get Ready*, written in 1991. We did the world premiere of *A Tradition of Service* written in 1995."
Needs: "For our Children's Theater and our Adult Annual Holiday (Christmas) show, we are looking for good adaptations of name stories. Most recently: *Miacle on 34th Street*, *Best Christmas Pageant Ever* and *It's A Wonderful Life*."

WEST COAST ENSEMBLE, P.O. Box 38728, Los Angeles CA 90038. (310)449-1447. Fax: (310)453-2254. Contact: Les Hanson, artistic director. Estab. 1982. Produces 6 plays/year. Plays performed at a theater in Hollywood. Submit complete script. Reports in 6-9 months. Obtains exclusive rights in southern California to present the play for the period specified. All ownership and rights remain with the playwright. Pays $25-45/performance.
Needs: Prefers a cast of 6-12.
Tips: "Submit the script in acceptable dramatic script format."

WESTBETH THEATRE CENTER, INC., 151 Bank St., New York NY 10014-2049. (212)691-2272. Fax: (212)924-7185. Producing Director: Arnold Engelman. Associate Producer: Donna DuCarme. Estab. 1977. Professional off-Broadway theater. Obtains rights to produce as showcase with option to enter into full option agreement. Extensive development program.
Needs: "Contemporary full-length plays. Production values (i.e., set, costumes, etc.) should be kept to a minimum." No period pieces. Limit 10 actors; doubling explained.

WILLOWS THEATRE COMPANY, 1975 Diamond Blvd., #A-20, Concord CA 94520. (510)798-1300. Fax: (510)676-5726. E-mail: willowsth@aol.com. Producing Artistic Director: Richard Elliott. "Professional productions for a suburban audience." Query and synopsis with SASE or agented submissions. Accepts new mss in April and May only. Queries year-round. Reports in 2 weeks on queries; 6 months on scripts. Pays royalty.
Needs: "Commercially viable, small-medium size musicals or comedies *only*. No more than 15 actors. Unit or simple sets with no fly space, do more than seven pieces."

THE WOMEN'S PROJECT AND PRODUCTIONS, 55 West End Ave., New York NY 10023. (212)765-1706. Fax: (212)765-2024. Website: http://www.womensproject.org. Contact: Lisa McNulty, literary manager. Artistic Director: Julia Miles. Estab. 1978. Produces 3 plays/year. Professional Off-Broadway productions. Query with synopsis and 10 sample pages of dialogue. Reports in 1 month on queries.
Needs: "We are looking for full-length plays, written by women."

WORCESTER FOOTHILLS THEATRE COMPANY, 100 Front St., Suite 137, Worcester MA 01608. (508)754-3314. Artistic Director: Marc P. Smith. Estab. 1974. Produces 7 plays/year. Full time professional theater, general audience. Query with synopsis. Reports in 3 weeks. Pays royalty.
Needs: "Produce plays for general audience. No gratuitous violence, sex or language. Prefer cast under 10 and single set. 30′ proscenium with apron but no fly space."

SCREENWRITING

Practically everyone you meet in Los Angeles, from your airport cabbie on, is writing a script. It might be a feature film, movie of the week, TV series or documentary, but the sheer amount of competition can seem overwhelming. Some will never make a sale, while others make a decent living on sales and options without ever having any of their work produced. But there are those writers who make a living doing what they love and see their names roll by on the credits. How do they get there? How do *you* get there?

First, work on your writing. You'll improve with each script, so there is no way of getting around the need to write and write some more. It's a good idea to read as many scripts as you can get your hands on. Check your local bookstores and libraries. Script City (8033 Sunset Blvd., Suite 1500, Hollywood CA 90046, (800)676-2522) carries thousands of movie and TV scripts, classics to current releases, as well as books, audio/video seminars and software in their $2 catalog. Book City (6631 Hollywood Blvd., Hollywood CA 90028, (800)4-CINEMA) has film and TV scripts in all genres and a large selection of movie books in their $2.50 catalog.

There are lots of books that will give you the "rules" of format and structure for writing for TV or film. Samuel French (7623 Sunset Blvd., Hollywood CA 90046 (213)876-0570) carries a number of how-to books and reference materials on these subjects. The correct format marks your script as a professional submission. Most successful scriptwriters will tell you to learn the correct structure, internalize those rules—and then throw them away and write intuitively.

Writing for TV

To break into TV you must have spec scripts—work written for free that serves as a calling card and gets you in the door. A spec script showcases your writing abilities and gets your name in front of influential people. Whether a network has invited you in to pitch some ideas, or a movie producer has contacted you to write a first draft for a feature film, the quality of writing in your spec script got their attention and that may get you the job.

It's a good idea to have several spec scripts, perhaps one each for three of the top five shows in the format you prefer to work in, whether it's sitcom (half-hour comedies), episodic (one hour series) or movie of the week (two hour dramatic movies). Perhaps you want to showcase the breadth of your writing ability; some writers have a portfolio of a few eight o'clock type shows (i.e., *Friends*, *Mad About You*, *Home Improvement*), a few nine-o'clock shows (i.e., *Ellen*, *Seinfeld*, *The X Files*) and one or two episodics (i.e., *Homicide*, *Law and Order*, *NYPD Blue*). These are all "hot" shows for writers and can demonstrate your abilities to create believable dialogue for characters already familiar to your intended readers. For TV and cable movies you should have completed original scripts (not sequels to existing movies) and you might also have a few for episodic TV shows.

In choosing the shows you write spec scripts for you must remember one thing: don't write a script for a show you want to work on. If you want to write for *NYPD Blue*, for example, you'll send a *Law and Order* script and vice versa. It may seem contradictory, but it is standard practice. It reduces the chances of lawsuits, and writers and producers can feel very proprietary about their show and their stories. They may not be objective enough to fairly evaluate your writing. In submitting another similar type of show you'll avoid those problems while demonstrating comparable skills.

In writing your TV script you must get *inside* the show and understand the characters' internal motivations. You must immerse yourself in how the characters speak, think and interact. Don't introduce new characters in a spec script for an existing show—write believable dialogue for the characters as they are portrayed. Be sure to choose a show that you like—you'll be better able to demonstrate your writing ability through characters you respond to.

You must also understand the external factors. How the show is filmed bears on how you write. Most sitcoms are shot on videotape with three cameras, on a sound stage with a studio audience. Episodics are often shot on film with one camera and include on-location shots. *Mad About You* has a flat, evenly-lit look and takes place in a limited number of locations. *Law and Order* has a gritty realism with varying lighting and a variety of settings from McCord's office to outside a bodega on East 135th.

Another important external influence in writing for TV is the timing of commercials in conjunction with the act structure. There are lots of sources detailing the suggested content and length of acts, but generally a sitcom has a teaser (short opening scene), two acts and a tag (short closing scene), and an episodic has a teaser, four acts and a tag. Each act closes with a turning point. Watching TV analytically and keeping a log of events will reveal some elements of basic structure. *Successful Scriptwriting*, by Wolff & Cox (Writer's Digest Books), offers detailed discussions of various types of shows.

Writing for the movies

With feature films you may feel at once more liberated and more bound by structure. An original movie script contains characters you have created, with storylines you design, allowing you more freedom than you have in TV. However, your writing must still convey believable dialogue and realistic characters, with a plausible plot and high-quality writing carried through the roughly 120 pages. The characters must have a problem that involves the audience. When you go to a movie you don't want to spend time watching the *second* worst night of a character's life. You're looking for the big issue that crystallizes a character, that portrays a journey with important consequences.

At the same time you are creating, you should also be constructing. Be aware of the basic three act structure for feature films. Scenes can be of varying lengths, but are usually no longer than three to three and a half pages. Some writers list scenes that must occur, then flesh them out from beginning to end, writing with the structure of events in mind. The beginning and climactic scenes are the easiest; it's how they get there from here that's difficult.

Many novice screenwriters tend to write too many visual cues and camera directions into their scripts. Your goal should be to write something readable, like a "compressed novella." Write succinct resonant scenes and leave the camera technique to the director and producer. In action/adventure movies, however, there needs to be a balance since the script demands more visual direction.

It seems to be easier for TV writers to cross over to movies. Cable movies bridge the two, and are generally less derivative and more willing to take chances with a higher quality show designed to attract an audience not interested in network offerings. Cable is also less susceptible to advertiser pullout, which means it can tackle more controversial topics.

Feature films and TV are very different and writers occupy different positions. TV is a medium for writers and producers; directors work for them. Many TV writers are also producers. In feature films the writers and producers work for the director and often have little or no say about what happens to the work once the script has been sold. For TV the writer pitches the idea; for feature films generally the producer pitches the idea and then finds a writer.

Marketing your scripts

If you intend to make writing your profession you must act professionally. Accepted submission practices should become second nature.

- The initial pitch is made through a query letter, which is no longer than one page with a one paragraph synopsis and brief summary of your credits if they are relevant to the subject of your script.
- Never send a complete manuscript until it is requested.
- Almost every script sent to a producer, studio or agent must be accompanied by a release form. Ask for that company's form when you receive an invitation to submit the whole script. Mark your envelope "release form enclosed" to prevent it being returned unread.
- Always include a self-addressed stamped envelope (SASE) if you want your work returned; a disposable copy may be accompanied by a self-addressed stamped postcard for reply.
- Allow four to six weeks from receipt of your manuscript before writing a follow-up letter.

When your script is requested, be sure it's written in the appropriate format. Unusual binding, fancy covers or illustrations mark an amateur. Three brass brads with a plain or black cover indicate a pro.

There are a limited number of ideas in the world, so it's inevitable that similar ideas occur to more than one person. Hollywood is a buyer's market and a release form states that pretty clearly. An idea is not copyrightable, so be careful about sharing premises. The written expression of that idea, however, can be protected and it's a good idea to do so. The Writers Guild of America can register scripts for television and theatrical motion pictures, series formats, storylines and step outlines. You need not be a member of the WGA to use this service. Copyrighting your work with the Copyright Office of the Library of Congress also protects your work from infringement. Contact either agency for more information and an application form.

If you are a writer, you should write—all the time. When you're not writing, read. There are numerous books on the art, craft and business of screenwriting. See the Publications of Interest at the end of *Writer's Market* for a few or check the catalogs of companies previously mentioned. The different industry trade papers such as *Daily Variety* and *Hollywood Reporter* can keep you in touch with the day to day news and upcoming events. Specialty newsletters such as *Hollywood Scriptwriter* (P.O. Box 10277, Burbank CA 91510, (818)845-5525, http://www.hollywoodscriptwriter.com) offer tips from successful scriptwriters and agents. The *Hollywood Creative Directory* is an extensive list of production companies, studios and networks that also lists companies and talent with studio deals.

Computer services have various bulletin boards and chat hours for scriptwriters that provide contact with other writers and a chance to share information and encouragement.

It may take years of work before you come up with a script someone is willing to take a chance on. Those years need to be spent learning your craft and understanding the business. Polishing scripts, writing new material, keeping current with the industry and networking constantly will keep you busy. When you do get that call you'll be confident in your abilities and know that your hard work is beginning to pay off.

Information on screenwriting markets listed in the previous edition of *Writer's Market* but not included in this edition can be found in the the General Index.

N ALEXANDER/ENRIGHT AND ASSOCIATES, 201 Wilshire Blvd., 3rd Floor, Santa Monica CA 90401. Contact: Sarah Koepple, development associate. Produces for a general television audience. Buys 3 scripts/year. Works with many writers/year. Buys TV and film rights only. Accepts previously produced material. Reports in 1 month on queries; 6 weeks on submissions. Query with synopsis. Pays in accordance with Writer's Guild standards.
Needs: Women driven dramas, but will accept others. No extreme violence, horror or stalkers.

N ALPHAVILLE, 555 Melrose Ave., Los Angeles CA 90038. Director of Development: Ray Lee. Estab. 1987. General audience. Buys 5-10 scripts/year. Buys all rights. Accepts previously produced material. Reports in 1-2 months on queries. "I'd like to read a catalog without having to contact writer unless I like an idea." Pays in accordance with Wrtier's Guild standards.
Needs: Films. Adventure/action, thrillers.

THE AMERICAN MOVING PICTURE COMPANY INC., 838 N. Doheny Dr., #904, Los Angeles CA 90069. (310)276-0750. Contact: Isabel Casper, vice president, creative affairs. Estab. 1979. Theatrical motion picture audience. Buys screenplay rights and ancillaries. Produced four theatrical motion pictures. Does not return submissions. Reports in 1 month. Query with synopsis. Pays in accordance with Writers Guild standards or more.
Needs: Films (35mm), commercial. "We want commercial and unique material."

N ☐ AMERICAN WORLD PICTURES INC., 21800 Oxnard St., Suite 480, Studio City CA 91367. Development/Acquisitions: Brian Etting/Terese Linden. Estab. 1991. Video/television market-Adults. Buys 4 scripts/year. Works with 5 writers/year. Buys all rights. Accepts previously produced material. Reports in 1-2 months on queries; 2-3 months on submissions. Query.
Needs: Films (35mm). Action, suspense, thriller genres only.
Tips: Strong characters, strong dialogue.

ANGEL FILMS, 967 Highway 40, New Franklin MO 65274-9778. (573)698-3900. Fax: (573)698-3900. E-mail: angelfilm@aol.com. Vice President Production: Matthew Eastman. Estab. 1980. Produces material for feature films, television. Buys 10 scripts/year. Works with 20 writers/year. Buys all rights. Accepts previously published material (if rights available). Reports in 1 months on queries; 1-2 months on scripts. Query with synopsis. Makes outright purchase. Our company is a low-budget producer, which means people get paid fairly, but don't get rich."
Needs: Films (35mm), videotapes. "We are looking for projects that can be used to produce feature film and television feature film and series work. These would be in the areas of action adventure, comedy, horror, thriller, science fiction, animation for children." Also looking for direct to video materials.
Tips: "Don't copy others. Try to be original. Don't overwork your idea. As far as trends are concerned, don't pay attention to what is 'in.' By the time it gets to us it will most likely be on the way 'out.' And if you can't let your own grandmother read it, don't send it. Slow down on western submissions. They are not selling. If you wish material returned, enclose proper postage with all submissions. Send SASE for response to queries and return of scripts."

ANGEL'S TOUCH PRODUCTIONS, 22906 Calabash St., Woodland Hills CA 91364. Contact: Phil Nemy, director of development. Estab. 1986. Professional screenplays and teleplays. Send synopsis. Reports in 8 months. Rights negotiated between production company and author. Payment negotiated.
Needs: All types, all genres, only full-length teleplays and screenplays—no one-acts.
Tips: "We only seek feature film screenplays, television screenplays, and episodic teleplays. No phone calls!"

N THE BADHAM COMPANY, 4035 Goodland Ave., Studio City CA 91604. (818)623-2929. Estab. 1991. Theatrical audience. Buys 1 script/year. Works with 2-3 writers/year. Buys first rights. Accepts previously produced material. Reports in 1 month. Query with synopsis. We go to studio and they purchase option.
Needs: Films (35mm).
Tips: "It's too easy to write action and ignore characters."

BARNSTORM FILMS, 73 Market St., Venice CA 90291. (310)396-5937. Estab. 1969. Produces feature films. Buys 2-3 scripts/year. Works with 4-5 writers/year.
Tips: Looking for strong, character-based commercial scripts. Not interested in science fiction or fantasy. Must send SASE with query letter. Query first, do not send script unless we request it!"

☐ BIG EVENT PICTURES, (formerly StoneRoad Production, Inc.), 11288 Ventura Blvd., #909, Studio City CA 91604. E-mail: stoweroad1@aol.com. Contact: Michael Cargile, president. Produces feature films for theaters, cable TV and home video. PG, R, and G-rated films. Buys/options 10 scripts/year. Reports in 1 month on queries if interested; 2 months requested on submissions. Query with SASE and synopsis. Pay varies greatly.
Needs: Films. All genres. Looking for good material from writers who have taken the time to learn the unique and difficult craft of scriptwriting.
Tips: "Interesting query letters intrigue us—and tell us something about the writer. Query letter should include a short 'log line' or 'pitch' encapsulating 'what this story is about'. We look for unique stories and strong characters. We would like to see more action and science fiction submissions. We make movies that we would like to see. Producers are known for encouraging new (e.g. unproduced) screenwriters and giving real consideration to their scripts."

BIG STAR MOTION PICTURES LTD., 13025 Yonge St., #201, Richmond Hill, Ontario L4E 1Z5 Canada. (416)720-9825. Fax: (905)773-3153. E-mail: bigstar@pathcom.com. Contact: Frank A. Deluca. Estab. 1991. Buys 5 scripts/year. Works with 5-10 writers/year. Reports in 3 months on queries; 3 months on scripts. Submit synopsis first. Scripts should be submitted by agent or lawyer.
Needs: Films (35mm). "We are very active in all medias, but are primarily looking for television projects, cable, network, etc. Family Films are of special interest."

BOZ PRODUCTIONS, 10960 Wilshire Blvd., Suite 734, Los Angeles CA 90024. (310)235-5401. Fax: (310)235-5766. E-mail: boz51@aol.com. Director of Development: Jeff Monarch. Estab. 1987. All audiences. Buys 3-5 scripts/year. Works with several writers/year. Buys all rights. Accepts previously produced material. Reports in 1 month on queries; 1-2 months on scripts. Query with synopsis and résumé. Pay varies.
Needs: Films (35mm). Feature-length film scripts or rights to real stories for MOW's.

CANVAS HOUSE FILMS, 3671 Bear St., #E, Santa Ana CA 92704. Contact: Mitch Teemley, producer. Estab. 1994. General audience. Buys 2-3 scripts/year. Works with 10-15 writers/year. Buys first rights, all rights. Accepts previously produced material. Reports in 1 month on queries; 4 months on submissions. Query with detailed (2-4 page) synopsis and résumé or list of credits. Pays in accordance with Writers Guild standards.
Needs: Films (35mm). "Quality feature-length filmscripts—all types, but no lurid, 'hard-R'-rated material."
Tips: "Know proper formatting and story structure. There is a need for 'family' material that can appeal to *grown-ups* as well as children."

CAPITAL ARTS ENTERTAINMENT, INC., 23315 Clifton, Valencia CA 91354. President of Development: Rob Kerchner. Estab. 1994. Family audiences. Buys 5 scripts/year. Works with 20 writers/year. Buys all rights. No previously produced material. No submissions will be returned. Reports in 1 month on queries; 1-24 months on submission. Query with synopsis only. No scripts or they will be destroyed. Pay outright purchase $1,000-15,000.
Tips: Send only family pitches (especially high concept) for completed spec scripts.

ALLAN CARR ENTERPRISES, P.O. Box 15568, Beverly Hills CA 90209-1568. (310)278-2490. Producer: Rob Bonet. Estab. 1977. Buys 15-20 scripts/year. Works with 10 writers/year. Buys rights depending on film or theater. Accepts previously produced material. Reports in 1 month. Catalog for #10 SASE. Query with synopsis. Pays in accordance with Writer's Guild standards.
Needs: Films (35mm, 70mm), VHS tapes 20 minutes or less. Romantic comedy, adventure, dramantic black comedy.

CINE/DESIGN FILMS, INC., P.O. Box 6495, Denver CO 80206. (303)777-4222. E-mail: jghusband@aol.com. Producer/Director: Jon Husband. Produces educational material for general, sales-training and theatrical audiences. 75% freelance written; 90% unagented submissions. "Original, solid ideas are encouraged." Rights purchased vary.
Needs: Films (16, 35mm). "Motion picture outlines in the theatrical and documentary areas. We are seeking theatrical scripts in the low-budget area that are possible to produce for under $2 to 3 million. We seek flexibility and personalities who can work well with our clients." Send 8-10-page outline before submitting ms. Pays $100-200/screen minute on 16mm productions. Theatrical scripts negotiable.
Tips: "Understand the marketing needs of film production today. Materials will not be returned."

CLARK FILM PRODUCTION CHARITY, INC., P.O. Box 773, Balboa CA 92661. Contact: Mr. Steven Clark, president. Estab. 1987. General audience. Buys 1 script/year. Works with 4 writers/year. Buys first rights. Accepts previously produced material. Reports in 6 months. Submit synopsis/outline. Pays in accordance with Writers Guild of America west standards.
Needs: Family-oriented, general audience materials, with universal appeal.
Recent Production: "Currently working with King Kigel V, His Majesty the King of Rwanda, Africa, on a public service announcement through United Nations UNICEF for His Majesty's children and orphans with relief. Although now accepting general audience material, as always."

CLC PRODUCTIONS, 1223 Wilshire Blvd., Suite 404, Santa Monica CA 90403. (310)454-0664. Contact: Susan Roberts. Estab. 1984. T.V. and film. "We are interested in suspense, comedy. Action/adventure with a strong female role age 35-45." Buys 4-5 scripts/year. Works with 5-10 writers/year. Buys all rights. Accepts previously produced materials. Reports in 1 month on submissions.

CODIKOW FILMS, 8899 Beverly Blvd., #719, Los Angeles CA 90048. (310)246-9388. Fax: (310)246-9877. Website: http://www.codikowfilms.com. Director of Development: Diana Williams. Estab. 1990. Buys 6 scripts/year. Works with

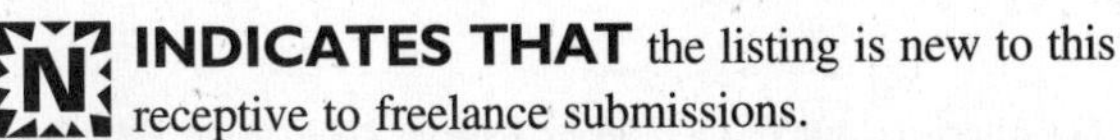
INDICATES THAT the listing is new to this edition. New markets are often more receptive to freelance submissions.

12 writers/year. Buys all rights. Reports in 2 months on submissions. Query or résumé. Pays in accordance with Writer's Guild standards.
Needs: Films (35mm). Commercial and independent screenplays; good writing—all subjects.

CPC ENTERTAINMENT, 840 N. Larrabee St., #2322, Los Angeles CA 90069. (310)652-8194. Fax: (310)652-4998. E-mail: 74151.1117@compuserve.com. Producer/Director: Peggy Chene. Vice President, Creative Affairs: Meri Howard. Development Associate: Eileen Aronas. Feature and TV. Buys 15 scripts/year. Works with 24 writers/year. Buys all rights. Recent production: "In the Eyes of a Stranger," CBS-TV thriller starring Richard Dean Anderson, CBS-TV. Reports in 2 months on queries; 3 months on submissions. Query with 1 sentence premise, 3 sentence synopsis and résumé. Outright purchase WGA minimum; and up.

- CPC Entertainment is looking for scripts of wider budget range, from low independent to high studio.

Needs: Needs feature and TV movie screenplays: small independent, or any budget for thrillers, true stories, action/adventure, character driven stories of any genre.

DAYDREAM PRODS., INC., 8969 Sunset Blvd., Los Angeles CA 90069. (310)285-9677. E-mail: dydream@earthlink.net. Contact: Sheryl Schwartz. Estab. 1995. Buys 2 scripts/year. Works with 3-4 writers/year. Buys all rights. Previously produced material OK. Reports in 4 months on submissions. Query with synopsis. Pays in accordance with Writer's Guild standards.
Needs: Films (35mm).
Tips: "Looking for television projects, MOW's sitcoms and children's programming."

EARTH TRACKS PRODUCTIONS, 4809 Avenue N, Suite 286, Brooklyn NY 11234. Contact: David Krinsky. Estab. 1985. Produces material for independent studios. Buys 1-3 scripts/year. Buys all rights. No books, no treatments, no plays, no articles. *Only* completed movie scripts. Reports in 6 weeks on queries.

- This producer notes a high rate of inappropriate submissions. Please read and follow guidelines carefully.

Needs: Commercial, well-written, low budget, high concept scripts in the drama, dark comedy and thriller genres. No other genre scripts. Query with 1-page synopsis and SASE. No treatments. *Do not send any scripts unless requested.* Also looking for writers to script existing projects in development.
Tips: "Writers should be flexible and open to suggestions. Material with interest (in writing) from a known actor is a *major plus* in the consideration of the material. Any submissions of more than two pages will *not* be read or returned. We have recently reorganized and are only seeking quality, *low budget* scripts for inhouse production. Controversial, with strong lead characters (dialogue), are preferred." (Examples: 'Natural Born Killers,' 'From Dusk Till Dawn,' 'Pulp Fiction.') Do not send queries by certified/registered mail. They will be rejected. Note: Due to new postal regulations requested scripts are no longer returned. We do not have personnel to send to post office to wait on line to return your scripts. Sorry. They can no longer be dropped in mailboxes for return. Writers who insist their scripts be returned must pay a fee for our time and labor of $15 per script. No exceptions. There is no fee to read requested material. Writers must submit signed release forms with submission."

N **EAST EL LAY FILMS**, 12041 Hoffman St., Studio City CA 91604. (818)769-4565. (818)769-1917. Contact: Daniel Kuhn, president. Co-President: Susan Coppola (director). Estab. 1992. Low-budget feature films for television markets. Buys 2 scripts/year. Works with many writers/year. Buys first rights and options for at least 1 year with refusal rights. Reports in 3-4 weeks on queries. Query with synopsis and résumé. Pays royalty, makes outright purchase or option fee.
Needs: Film loops (35mm), videotapes.

ENTERTAINMENT PRODUCTIONS, INC., 2118 Wilshire Blvd., Suite 744, Santa Monica CA 90403. (310)456-3143. Fax: (310)456-8950. Producer: Edward Coe. Contact: Story Editor. Estab. 1971. Produces films for theatrical and television (worldwide) distribution. Reports in 1 month only if SASE enclosed.
Needs: Screenplay originals. Query with synopsis and SASE. Price negotiated on a project-by-project basis. Writer's release in any form will be acceptable.
Tips: "State why script has great potential."

EPIPHANY PRODUCTIONS INC., 10625 Esther Ave., Los Angeles CA 90064. Fax: (310)815-1269. E-mail: roadog@concentric.net. Contact: Scott Frank, president. Estab. 1983. Film and TV audiences. Buys 12 scripts/year. Works with 18 writers/year. Reports in 3 months on submissions. Query with synopsis. Produced 2 Showtime movies in 1995. Produced feature, *Roaddogs* in 1997.
Tips: We are seeking compelling human stories with rich characters that can be shot on a modest budget, 3-10 million."

N **JOSEPH FEVRY ENTERTAINMENT**, 230 West 41st St., Suite 1400, New York NY 10036. (212)221-9090. Executive Producer: Joseph Fevry. Estab. 1982. Buys all rights. Accepts previously produced material. Reports in 1 month. Query with synopsis or completed script. Pays negotiated option.
Needs: Films.

N **FORRESTER FILMS**, 2803 Forrester Dr., Los Angeles CA 90064. President: Barbara Klein. Estab. 1992. Theatrical audience. Buys 2 scripts/year. Works with 20 writers/year. Buys all rights. Accepts previously produced material.

No submissions will be returned. Reports in 1 month on queries; 3 months on submissions. Query with synopsis. Pays in accordance with Writer's Guild standard.
Needs: Films (35mm).
Tips: "Individual market getting tougher and tougher. So material has to be better and better."

BETH GROSSBARD PRODUCTIONS, 5168 Otis Ave., Tarzana CA 91356. Contact: Beth Grossbard, producer. Estab. 1994. Buys 6 scripts/year. Works with 20 writers/year. First rights and true life story rights. Reports in 3 months on queries; 4 months on submissions. Query with synopsis, treatment/outline and completed script. Pays in accordance with Writer's Guild standards.
Needs: Films (35mm).
Tips: "Looking for unique, high-concept stories; family dramas; personal accounts; true stories; social issues."

N **HANDPRINT ENTERTAINMENT**, 8436 W. 3rd St., Suite #650, Los Angeles CA 90036. Estab. 1997. Young adult to adult 18-40. Buys 10 scripts/year. Works with 40 writers/year. Buys first or all rights. "We are submit to 20th Century Fox to buy or seek our own means." Accepts previously produced material. Reports in 1 month. Query with synopsis. Pays in accordance with Writer's Guild standards.
Needs: Television films.
Tips: "Commerically-minded material with an edge—thrillers, dramas, action. Push the envelope of your genre."

N **NICHOLAS HASSITT FILMS**, 1345 N. Hayworth Ave., Suite 210, West Hollywood CA 90046. Contact: Simon Ledworth, director of development. Estab. 1994. Material intended for general audience. Buys 4 scripts/year. Works with 15 writers/year. Buys all rights. Accepts previously produced material. Reports in 1 month. Query with synopsis. Pays in accordance with Writer's Guild standards.
Needs: Films (35mm). "Looking for screenplays and novels that can be developed in feature film."

HBO PICTURES, 2049 Century Park E., Suite 3600, Los Angeles CA 90067. (310)201-9302. Fax: (310)201-9552. Contact: Bettina Moss, story editor. Reports in 1 month. Query with synopsis one page or shorter. Payment varies.
Needs: Features for TV. Looks at all genres except family films or films with children as main protagonists. Focus on socially relevant material.

N ☐ **HELIOS PRODUCTIONS**, 5514 Wilshire Blvd., 11th Floor, Los Angeles CA 90036. (213)934-5454. Contact: Tyler Steele. Estab. 1984. Television (network & cable). Buys 12-15 scripts/year. Works with 6-10 writers/year. Buys all rights, film rights & serial. Accepts previously produced material. Reports in 1 month on queries; 1-2 months on submissions. Catalog for SAE with 2 first-class stamps. Query or phone query/pitch. Pays outright in accordance with Writer's Guild standards.
Needs: Films, movies for television.

N ☐ **IFM FILM ASSOCIATES INC.**, 1541 N. Gardner St., Los Angeles CA 90046. (213)874-4249. Executive Vice President: Ann Lyons. Estab. 1994. Film and television all media world wide. Buys 10 scripts/year. Works with 30 writers/year. Buys all rights. No previously produced material. No submissions will be returned. Reports in 1 month on queries; 1-3 months on submissions. Catalog for SAE with $3. Query with synopsis. Pays in accordance with Writer's Guild standards, or so otherwise negotiated.
Needs: Film (35mm). Thrillers, family, action.

INTERNATIONAL HOME ENTERTAINMENT, 1440 Veteran Ave., Suite 650, Los Angeles CA 90024. (213)460-4545. Contact: Jed Leland, Jr., assistant to the president. Estab. 1976. Buys first rights. Reports in 2 months. Query. Pays in accordance with Writers Guild standards.

- Looking for material that is international in scope.

Tips: "Our response time is faster on average now (3-6 weeks), but no replies without a SASE. *No unsolicited scripts*.We do not respond to unsolicited phone calls."

N **MARTY KATZ PRODUCTIONS**, 1250 6th St., Suite 205, Santa Monica CA 90401. (310)260-8501. Contact: Fred Levy. Estab. 1992. Produces material for all audiences. Buys first, all and film rights. Accepts previously produced material. Reports in 1 month.
Needs: Films (35mm).

KJD TELEPRODUCTIONS, 30 Whyte Dr., Voorhees NJ 08043. (609)751-3500. Fax: (609)751-7729. E-mail: mactod ay@ios.com. President: Larry Scott. Estab. 1989. Broadcast audience. Buys 6 scripts/year. Works with 3 writers/year. Buys all rights. No previously produced material. Reports in 1 month. Catalog free. Query. Makes outright purchase.
Needs: Films, videotapes, multimedia kits.

N **ADAM KLINE PRODUCTIONS**, 11925 Wilshire Blvd., 3rd Floor, Los Angeles CA 90025. (310)312-4814. Producer: Adam Kline. Estab. 1994. Features. Buys 20 scripts/year. Works with 200+ writers/year. Buys all rights. Accepts previously produced material. Report in 1 week on queries; 1-2 months on submissions. Query with synopsis

or 5-7 sentence summary of finished feature length screenplay(s) of any genre or budget. All negotiable in all types of options or purchases.
Needs: "I needs scripts. I look for commercial mainstream material."

N **KN'K PRODUCTIONS INC.**, 5230 Shira Dr., Valley Village CA 91607-2300. (818)760-3106. Fax: (818)760-2478 or (818)760-3106. Creative Director: Katharine Kramer. Estab. 1992. "Looking for film material with strong roles for mature women (ages 40-55 etc.). Also roles for young women and potential movie musicals, message movies." Buys 3 scripts/year. Works with 5 writers/year. Buys all rights. No previously produced material. Reports in 2-3 months. Catalog for #10 SASE. Submit synopsis, complete script and résumé. Pays in accordance with Writers Guild standards or partnership.
Needs: Multimedia kits. "Doing more partnerships with writers as opposed to just Writers Guild minimum. Concentration on original vehicles for the mature actress to fill the gap that's missing from mainstream cinema."
Tips: "We are primarily looking for women's projects, for female-driven vehicles for mature actresses, 45-55, but we are emphasizing music-driven projects more and more. We are also looking for strong male-driven vehicles (emphasis on mature actors.) We are focusing on character-driven, original material."

N **THE JONATHON KRANE GROUP**, 9255 Sunset Blvd., #1111, Los Angeles CA 90069. Contact: Kimberlyn Lucken. Estab. 1981. Produces material for all audiences. Works with 15 writers/year. Have first look with Fox 2000. Accepts previously produced material. Reports in 1 month on queries; 2 months on submissions. Query with synopsis.
Needs: Films (35mm). "All genre and budget ranges."

LANCASTER GATE ENTERTAINMENT, 4702 Hayvenhurst Ave., Encino CA 91436. (818)995-6000. Contact: Brian K. Schlichter, director of development. Estab. 1989. Theatrical and television. Works with dozens of writers/year. Rights purchased negotiable. Recently produced projects: *Grumpy Old Men*, *Grumpier Old Men*, *Angel Flight Down*, *Deadly Web*, *December*. Reports in 1 month on queries. Query. Pays in accordance with Writer's Guild standards.
Needs: Films (35mm-70mm). Feature and long form television scripts.

N **THE LANDSBURG COMPANY**, 11811 W. Olympic Blvd., Los Angeles CA 90064-1113. (310)478-7878. Contact: Gloria Morris, development manager. Estab. 1972. Produces for a general television audience. Options 5 scripts/year. Works with 20 writers/year. Buys first, book and life rights. Accepts previously produced work. Reports in 2 weeks on queries; 2 months on submissions. Query with synopsis. Pays in accordance with Writer's Guild standards.
Tips: "We concentrate on long form projects for network and cable television. Stories that follow trends, that have a feature feel and that have a universal appeal."

N **ANDREW LAUREN PRODUCTIONS**, 114 E. 70th St., Suite #3, New York City NY 10021. (212)639-1975. Director of Development: Jordon Hoffman. Estab. 1996. Produces for theatrical audiences. Buys all rights. Reports in 1 month on queries; 4 months on submissions. Query. Pays in accordance with Writer's Guild standards.
Needs: Films (35mm). "We are looking for original feature length screenplays or a writer who can adapt one."

N **LICHT/MUELLER FILM CORP.**, 132A S. Lasky Dr., Suite #200, Beverly Hills CA 90212. Creative Assistant: David Blackman. Estab. 1983. Produces material for all audiences. Accepts previously produced material. Reports in 1 month on queries; 3 months on submissions. Query with synopsis.
Needs: Films (35mm). "Scripts for feature films."

N **LOCKWOOD FILMS (LONDON) INC.**, 2569 Boston Dr., RR #41, London, Ontario N6H 5L2 Canada. (519)434-6006. Fax: (519)645-0507. E-mail: mark.mccurdy@odyssey.on.ca. President: Nancy Johnson. Estab. 1974. Audience is entertainment and general broadcast for kids 9-12 and family viewing. Works with 5-6 writers/year. Submit query with synopsis, résumé or sample scripts. "Submissions will not be considered unless a proposal submission agreement is signed. We will send one upon receiving submissions." Negotiated fee.
Needs: Family entertainment: series, seasonal specials, mini-series, and movies of the week. Also feature films, documentaries.
Tips: "Potential contributors should have a fax machine and should be prepared to sign a 'proposal submission agreement.' We are in development with national broadcaster on live-action family drama series. Looking for international co-production opportunities."

N **LONGFELLOW PICTURES**, 145 Hudson St., 12th Floor, New York NY 10013. (212)431-5550. Fax: (212)431-5822. E-mail: longpics@aol.com. Contact: Tara Connaughton, director of creative development. All audiences. Buys 4-8 scripts/year. Works with 4-6 writers/year. Buys all rights. Accepts previously produced material. Reports in 1 month on queries, 8 months on submissions. Query with synopsis.
Needs: Films.

N **LOIS LUGER PRODUCTIONS**, 800 South Carson Ave., Los Angeles CA 90036. (213)937-8996. Vice President Current Affairs: Wendy Arthur. Estab. 1986. Buys 6 scripts/year. Works with 20 writers/year. Buys all rights, excluding book publishing rights. Accepts previously produced material. Reports in 1 month on queries; 2-3 months on submissions. Query with synopsis. Pays in accordance with Writer's Guild standards.

Needs: Films.

N A **LUMIERE**, 8442 Melrose Place, Los Angeles CA 90069. (213)653-7878. Chief Executive Officer: Randolph Pitts. Estab. 1984. Produces material for the general audience. Buys 5 scripts/year. Works with 10 writers/year. Accepts previously produced material. Reports in 2 months. Query through known agent or attorney. Pays negotiated on case by case bases.
Needs: Films (35mm). "Screenplays which will attract major directing and acting talent, regardless of genre or perceived commerciality."

LEE MAGID PRODUCTIONS, P.O. Box 532, Malibu CA 90265. (213)463-5998. President: Lee Magid. Produces material for all markets: adult, commercial—even musicals. 90% freelance written. 70% of scripts produced are unagented submissions. Works with many unpublished/unproduced writers. Buys all rights or will negotiate. No previously produced material. Does not return unsolicited material.
Needs: Films, sound filmstrips, phonograph records, television shows/series and videotape presentations. Currently interested in film material, either for video (television) or theatrical. "We deal with cable networks, producers, live-stage productions, etc." Works with musicals for cable TV. Prefers musical forms for video comedy. "We're interested in comedy material. Forget drug-related scripts." Submit synopsis/outline and résumé. Pays royalty, in accordance with Writers Guild standards, makes outright purchase or individual arrangement depending on author.

MEDIACOM DEVELOPMENT CORP., P.O. Box 6331, Burbank CA 91510-6331. (818)594-4089. Contact: Felix Girard, director/program development. Estab. 1978. 80% freelance written. Buys 8-12 scripts/year from unpublished/unproduced writers. 50% of scripts produced are unagented submissions. Query with samples. Reports in 1 month. Buys all rights or first rights. Written query only. Please do not call.
Needs: Produces films, multimedia kits, tapes and cassettes, slides and videotape with programmed instructional print materials, broadcast and cable television programs. Publishes software ("programmed instruction training courses"). Negotiates payment depending on project. Looking for new ideas for CD-ROM titles.
Tips: "Send short samples of work. Especially interested in flexibility to meet clients' demands, creativity in treatment of precise subject matter. We are looking for good, fresh projects (both special and series) for cable and pay television markets. A trend in the audiovisual field that freelance writers should be aware of is the move toward more interactive video disc/computer CRT delivery of training materials for corporate markets."

MILWAUKEE FILMWORKS, 4218 Whitsett Ave., Suite 4, Studio City CA 91604. (818)762-9080. Fax: (310)278-2632. Contact: Douglas Gardner. Estab. 1991. Film and TV audience. Works with 6 writers/year. Buys screenplays-option. *Feature scripts only.* Returns submissions on a case to case basis. Reports in 3 months. Query with complete script. Pay varies in accordance with Writers Guild standards.
Tips: "Looking for good action scripts to be submitted."

MNC FILMS, P.O. Box 16195, Beverly Hills CA 90209-2195. E-mail: mncfilms@aol.com. Contact: Mark Cohen, producer. Estab. 1991. Feature film audience. Buys 2 scripts/year. Works with 3 writers/year. Buys all rights or purchases option on screenplay. Accepts previously produced material. Reports in 2 months. Query with synopsis. Pays in accordance with Writers Guild standards (work for hire) or variable fee for option of material.
Needs: Film (35mm). Feature length films. "I'm looking for story-driven films with well-developed characters. Screenplays or books easily adaptable for lower budget (few locations, stunts, special effects)."
Tips: "In the past I have received many submissions from writers who do not pay attention to the type of material that I am looking for. I am looking for character-driven stories with an emphasis on individuals and relationships."

MONAREX HOLLYWOOD CORPORATION, 9421½ W. Pico Blvd., Los Angeles CA 90035. (310)552-1069. Contact: Chris D. Nebe, president. Estab. 1978. Award-winning producers of theatrical and television motion pictures and miniseries; also international distributors. Buys 5-6 scripts/year. Buys all rights. Reports in 2 months.
Needs: "We are seeking action, adventure, comedy and character-oriented love stories, dance, horror and dramatic screenplays." First submit synopsis/outline with SASE. After review of the synopsis/outline, the screenplay will be requested. Pays in accordance with Writers Guild standards.
Tips: "We look for exciting visuals with strong characters and a unique plot."

MONTIVAGUS PRODUCTIONS, 13930 Burbank Blvd., Suite 100, Sherman Oaks CA 91401-5003. (818)782-1212. Fax: (818)782-1931. Contact: Douglas Coler, VP Creative Affairs. Estab. 1990. Buys 3 scripts/year. Works with 3-4 writers/year. Buys all rights. Query with synopsis only. Responds if interested in synopsis; 1 month on scripts. Encourages submissions from new and emerging writers. Also interested in novels, short stories and plays for adaptation to the big screen. Pays in accordance with Writers Guild standards. Also accepts plays for theatrical staging under it's stageWorks! program.
Needs: Films (35mm).
Tips: Looking for character-driven scripts; no big budget action films. Keep query short and to the point. Synopsis should be a half to three-quarters of a page. No longer. "Please don't tell me how funny, or how good or how exciting your script is. I'll find out. It's the story I want to know first." Unsolicited scripts will be returned unread. Proper script format a must. Coverage will be shared with the writer.

MORROW-HEUS PRODUCTIONS, 8800 Venice Blvd., #209, Los Angeles CA 90034. (310)815-9973. Website: http://www.members.aol.com/MorrowHeus/pagel.html.Contact: Paul Shrater, director of development. Estab. 1989. Intended for the worldwide film and television audience. Buys film and television option. Accepts previously produced material. Reports in 1 month. Send query with synopsis. Pays negotiated option (standard industry practice).
Needs: Films (35mm). Feature film, television mow, drama, comedy, romance, adventure, action, thriller, family.

N **MOUNTAIN DRIVE**, 625 Arizona Ave., Santa Monica CA 90401. (310)395-6200. Development Director: John G. Otto. Estab. 1980. Film and TV audience. Works with 10-15 writers/year. Buys all rights. Accept previously produced material. Reports in 1-2 months on queries; 1 month on submissions. Catalog for #10 SASE. Query with synopsis or completed script. Pays by royalty, outright purchase or in accordance with Writer's Guild standards.
Needs: Films (35mm), videotapes. "Mini-series-historical, contemporary dramas. Children's programming, family films, as well as Satuday morning. Sci-fi stories. Action-adventure-syndication."
Tips: "Please ensure that script/treatment is registered. Receive thousands of scripts each year with no return information. Trends seem to go with character-driven material. Effects important in some respect, but good story is what counts."

MOVIE REPS INTERNATIONAL, 7135 Hollywood Blvd., #104, Los Angeles CA 90046. (213)876-4052. Contact: Krishna Shah, president/CEO. Fax: (213)876-4052. Estab. 1989. US and foreign audiences. Buys 4 scripts/year. Works with 2 writers/year. Buys first or all rights. No previously produced material. Reports in 1 month on queries. Free catalog. Query with synopsis. Pays royalty or makes outright purchase.
Needs: Films (35mm). Feature film script, minimum 100 pages. Genres: action/thriller, romantic comedy, adventure, art type of film. Looking for: fresh ideas, no holds bar kind of script, extremely original.
Tips: Originality is key; and combine it with high concept.

N **MWG PRODUCTIONS**, 2317 Vasanta Way, Los Angeles CA 90068. (213)469-8290. Contact: Max Goldenson, executive producer. Estab. 1981. Buys 3 scripts/year. Works with 10 writers/year. Buys all rights. Accepts previously produced material. Reports in 1 month on queries; 3 months on submissions. Query with synopsis and résumé. Pays in accordance with Writer's Guild standards.
Needs: Films, multimedia kits and videotapes.

NEW & UNIQUE VIDEOS, 2336 Sumac Dr., San Diego CA 92105. (619)282-6126. E-mail: videos@concentric.net. Website: http://www.concentric.net/~videos. Contact: Candace Love, creative director. Estab. 1982. General TV and videotape audiences. Buys 10-15 scripts/year. Buys first rights, all rights. No previously produced material. Reports in 1-2 months. Catalog for #10 SASE. Query with synopsis. Makes outright purchase, negotiable.
Needs: Videotapes.
Tips: "First and foremost, read these tips very carefully. We are seeking unique slants on interesting topics in 60-90 minute special-interest videotape format, preferably already produced, packaged and ready for distribution. Currently distributed titles include 'Massage for Relaxation'; 'Ultimate Mountain Biking' and 'Full Cycle: World Odyssey.' No movies or movie treatments. We concentrate on sports, health and other educational home-video titles. Please study the genre and get an understanding of what 'special interest' means. Send a SASE for our catalog to see what kinds of titles we produce. This will save you time and resources. Video distribution has become highly competitive. Doing adequate homework at the beginning will prevent heartache down the road. Study your market. Determine the need for (yet another?) video on your topic. The elements for success are: intensive market research, passion, humor, imagination and a timely or timeless quality."

N **OMEGA ENTERTAINMENT**, 8760 Shoreham Dr., Los Angeles CA 90069. Vice President: Christy L. Pokarney. Estab. 1979. Produces material for film (worldwide). Buys 1 scripts/year. Works with 4 writers/year. Buys all rights. Accepts previously produced material. Query with synopsis. Pays royalty or outright purchase.
Needs: Films (35mm).

N **OPEN DOOR ENTERTAINMENT**, 1519 Glencoe Ave., Venice CA 90291. (310)664-9876. President: Kai Schoenhals. Estab. 1997. Feature films. Global distribution all ages. Buys 4-7 scripts/year. Works with 15-20 writers/year. Buys first rights, all rights and film rights, limited options. Accept previously produced material. Reports in 1 month, depending on where we are in terms of production and travel. Query with synopsis, completed script or resume. Pays 2-5% dependent, once we begin principle photography.
Needs: Films (35mm).
Tips: "We have offices in LA, NYC, London, Copenhagen and Warsaw. We are interested in crossing the Atlantic gap. We are most interested in bringing projects to Poland to be put into production there. (i.e., genre, sci-fi, fantasy, horror, epic, comedy, drama, action)."

TOM PARKER MOTION PICTURES, 3941 S. Bristol, #285, Santa Ana CA 92704. (714)545-2887. Fax: (714)545-9775. President: Tom Parker. Contact: Yvonne Ortega, script/development. Produces and distributes feature-length motion pictures worldwide for theatrical, home video, pay and free TV. Also produces short subject special interest films (30, 45, 60 minutes). Works with 5-10 scripts/year. Previously produced and distributed "Amazing Love Secret" (R), and "The Sturgis Story" (R). Reports in 6 months. "Follow the instructions herein and do not phone for info or to inquire about your script."

Needs: "Complete script *only* for low budget (under $1 million) "R" or "PG" rated action/thriller, action/adventure, comedy, adult romance (R), sex comedy (R), family action/adventure to be filmed in 35mm film for the theatrical and home video market. (Do not send TV movie scripts, series, teleplays, stage plays). *Very limited dialogue.* Scripts should be action-oriented and fully described. Screen stories or scripts OK, but no camera angles please. No heavy drama, documentaries, social commentaries, dope stories, weird or horror. Violence or sex OK, but must be well motivated with strong story line." Submit synopsis and description of characters with finished scripts. Makes outright purchase: $5,000-25,000. Will consider participation, co-production.
Tips: "Absolutely will not return scripts or report on rejected scripts unless accompanied by SASE."

PAULIST PRODUCTION, 17575 Pacific Coast Hwy., P.O. Box 1057, Pacific Palisades CA 90272-4148. (310)454-0688. Director of Development: Barbara R. Nicolos. Estab. 1964. General public-domestic and international audiences. Buys 2-3 scripts/year. Buys all rights or film/tv rights for published works. Accepts previously produced material. Report in 1 month on queries; 2 months on submissions. Query with synopsis. Pays in accordance with Writer's Guild standards.
Needs: Films (35mm). "We are looking for material to develop into television/cable movies. Our criterion are powerful narratives with well-drawn characters which shed light on man's search for meaning and personal growth. We want spiritual themes which are not necessarily overtly Christian, but which do not reject traditional Christian values."
Tips: "Would be screenwriters should be very careful to adhere to the industry standards for formatting a screenplay. A brilliant narrative is no substitute for the wrong margins or typeface. Synopsis should be more about the theme of the work and why it should be made than all the details of the story. . . . If a script is ailing violence and gratuitous sex aren't going to cure it. Don't add artificial sub plots just because it seems to be what sells."

PHASE I PRODUCTIONS, 429 Santa Monica Blvd., Suite #610, Santa Monica CA 90401. Vice President: Kristin Schwarz. Estab. 1995. Film and TV audiences. Buys 12 scripts/year. Works with 3 dozen scripts in-house. Buys all rights. No previously produced material. Reports in 1-2 weeks on queries; 1-2 months on submissions. Submissions must not be unsolicited. Must come through agent or attorney or will be returned. Pays in accordance with Writer's Guild standards.
Needs: Films. Feature film and television and cable movies.

POP/ART FILM FACTORY, 513 Wilshire Blvd., #215, Santa Monica CA 90401. Contact: Daniel Zirilli. Estab. 1990. Produces material for "all audiences/features films." Query with synopsis. Pays on per project basis.
Needs: Film (35mm), documentaries, multimedia kits. "Looking for interesting productions of all kinds. We are producing 3 feature films per year, and 15-20 music-oriented projects. Also looking for exercise and other special interest videos."
Tips: "Be original. Do not play it safe. If you don't receive a response from anyone you have ever sent your ideas to, or you continually get rejected, don't give up if you believe in yourself. Good luck and keep writing!"

PORTAGE ROAD ENTERTAINMENT INC., 4040 Alta Mesa Dr., Studio City CA 91604. President: Jeff Wollnough. Estab. 1994. Film and television features. Buys 3-7 scripts/year. Works with 3-7 writers/year. Buys all rights. Accept previously produced material. Reports in 1 month on queries; 3 months on submissions. Query with synopsis or completed script.
Needs: Films (35mm). We are seeking viable feature film and movie of the week television. Properties—all genres.

PROMARK ENTERTAINMENT GROUP, 3599 Cahuenga Blvd. W., Los Angeles CA 90026. (213)878-0404. Fax: (213)878-0486. Contact: Gil Adrienne Wishnick, vice president Creative Affairs. Promark is a foreign sales company, producing theatrical films for the foreign market, domestic theatrical and cable as well as for video. Buys 8-10 scripts/year. Works with 8-10 writers/year. Buys all rights. Reports in 1 month on queries, 2 months on submissions. Query with synopsis. Makes outright purchase.

- Promark is concentrating on action-thrillers in the vein of *The Net* or *Marathon Man*. They are not looking for science fiction/action as much this year, as they have a rather full production slate with many sci-fi and techno-thrillers.

Needs: Film (35mm). "We are looking for screenplays in the action, action-adventure, thriller and science fiction/action genres. Our aim is to produce lower budget (3 million and under) films that have a solid, novel premise—a smart but smaller scale independent film. Our films are male-oriented, urban in setting and hopefully smart. We try to find projects with a fresh premise, a clever hook and strong characters. We will also consider a family film, but not a drama or a comedy. Again, these family films need to have an element of action or suspense. We are not interested in comedies, dramas or erotic thrillers. Our budgets are lower, approximately three million and under. Among the films we produced are: *A Breed Apart*, a psychological thriller with Andrew McCarthy; *The Invader*, a sci-fiction action/drama, starring Sean Young, Ben Cross and Nick Mancuso; *The Shadowmen* with Eric Roberts, Sherilyn Fenn and Dean Stockwell; and a sci-fi thriller about cloning entitled *Johnny 2.0*, which stars Jeff Fahey."
Tips: "Check on the genres any potential production company accepts and slant your submissions accordingly. Do your homework before you send a query or call. Find out who to contact, what their title is and what the production company tends to make in terms of genre, budget and style. Find the address yourself—don't ask the production executive for it, for example. It's insulting to the executive to have to inform a caller of the company name or address. We are currently looking for suspenseful thrillers with interesting, even quirky characters. We are also looking for family films, specifically

adventure yarns for and about kids (ages 8-13) in which the kids are the action heroes. The budgets are low (750,000), so special effects are out. Otherwise, our needs remain roughly the same."

THE PUPPETOON STUDIOS, P.O. Box 80141, Las Vegas NV 89180. Website: http://www.scifistation.com. Contact: Arnold Leibovit, vice president of production. Estab. 1987. "Broad audience." Works with 2 writers/year. Reports in 1 month on queries; 2 months on scripts. Query with synopsis. Submit complete script. A Submission Release *must* be included with all queries. Currently producing the animated feature, "Moby Dick: The Whale's Tale." SASE required for return of all materials. Pays in accordance with Writers Guild standards. No novels, plays, poems, treatments; no submissions on computer disk. Unsolicited scripts must have release. Must include release form.
Needs: Films (35mm). "We are seeking animation properties including presentation drawings and character designs. The more detailed drawings with animation scripts the better. Always looking for fresh broad audience material."

N □ **REEL LIFE WOMEN**, 10158 Hollow Glew Cir., Bel Air CA 90077. (310)271-4722. Co-President: Joanne Parrent. Estab. 1997. Mass audiences. Buys 3-4 scripts/year. Accepts previously produced material. Reports in 1 month on queries; 2 months on submissions. Query with synopsis, resume or SASE for response to query. Pays in accordance with Writer's Guild standards.
Needs: Films. Looking for full-length scripts for feature films or television movies only. (No series or episode TV scripts.) Must be professionally formatted (courier 12pt.) and under 130 pages. All genres considered particularly drama, comedy, action, suspense.
Tips: "We are particularly interested in stories with strong female main characters."

N **RICHULCO, INC.**, 11041 Santa Monica Blvd., Suite 511, Los Angeles CA 90025. Contact: Richard Hull. Estab. 1993. All audiences. Buys 2 scripts/year. Works with 10-15 writers/year. Buys all rights. Accepts previously produced material. Reports in 1 month on queries; 3 month on submissions. Query with synopsis or resume.
Needs: Films (35mm), videotapes. High concept, excellent dialogue, screenplays.

N **ROBERT SCHAFFEL/SHARON ROESLER**, (formerly Eclectic Films, Inc.), 5750 Wilshire Blvd., Suite 580, Los Angeles CA 90036. Producers: Robert Schaffel/Sharon Roesler. Feature film audience—worldwide. Reports in 2 months on script. Call or write to request permission to submit completed screenplays.

THE SHELDON/POST COMPANY, 1437 Rising Glen Rd., Los Angeles CA 90069. Contact: Mark Wright, director of development. Producers: David Sheldon, Ira Post. Estab. 1989. Produces theatrical motion pictures, movies and series for television. Options and acquires all rights. Reports in 2 months. Query with 1-2 page synopsis, 2-3 sample pages and SASE. "Do not send scripts or books until requested. If the synopsis is of interest, you will be sent a release form to return with your manuscript. No phone inquiries." Pays in accordance with Writers Guild standards.
Needs: "We look for all types of material, including women's stories, children's and family stories, suspense dramas, horror, sci-fi, thrillers, action-adventure." True stories should include news articles or other documentation.
Tips: "A synopsis should tell the entire story with the entire plot—including a beginning, a middle and an end. During the past three years, the producers have been in business with 20th Century Fox, Paramount Pictures, Columbia Pictures and currently have contracts with Dick Clark Productions. Most recent productions: "Grizzly Adams and the Legend of Dark Mountain" and "Secrets of a Small Town."

DARRYL SILVER, 8050-4 Canby, Reseda CA 91335. Contact: Darryl Silver. Estab. 1995. Feature and TV. Buys 7 scripts/year. Works with 15-25 writers/year. Buys all rights. No previously produced material. Reports in 1 month. Query with synopsis. Buys option first.
Needs: Films (35mm) and TV.

SKYLARK FILMS, 1123 Pacific St., Santa Monica CA 90405. (310)396-5753. Fax: (310)396-5753. E-mail: skyfilm@aol.com. Contact: Brad Pollack, producer. Estab. 1990. Buys 6 scripts/year. Buys first or all rights. Accepts previously produced material. Reports in 2-4 weeks on queries; 1-2 months on submissions. Query with synopsis. Option or other structures depending on circumstances. Pays in accordance with Writer's Guild standards.
Needs: Films (TV, cable, feature).

- Skylark Films is now seeking action, suspense, thrillers and science fiction.

Tips: "Generally, we look for the best material we can find, other than the horror genre. Particular new areas of focus are romantic comedy, true stories for TV mow's and low-budget quirky material. No response unless we want to see material. Will also look at material for ½ weekly television syndication possibilities."

N **SKYLINE PARTNERS**, 10550 Wilshire Blvd., #304, Los Angeles CA 90024. Contact: Fred Kuehuert. Estab. 1990. Produces material for theatrical, television, video audiences. Buys 3 scripts/year. Buys all rights. Accepts previously produced material. Reports in 2 months on queries. Buys all rights. Accepts previously produced material. Reports in 2 months on queries. Query with synopsis. Pays per negotiation.
Needs: Films (35mm).

N □ **ALAN SMITHEE FILMS**, 7510 Sunset Blvd., Suite #525, Hollywood CA 90046. Director: Fred Smythe. Estab. 1990. Mass, cable television and theatrical releases. Buys 2 scripts/year. Works with 10 writers/year. Buys first

time rights, all rights or options short-term. No previously produced material. No submissions will be returned. Reports in 2 months. Query with synopsis. Pays in accordance with Writer's Guild standards.
Needs: Films (35mm), videotapes. No specific needs. Varies constantly with market.
Tips: "Strong dialogue. Fresh angles in storylines. It's all been told before, so tell it well."

N **SPECTACOR FILMS**, 9000 Sunset Blvd., #1550, West Hollywood CA 90069. Director of Development: Jonathan Mundale. Estab. 1988. HBO audiences. Buys 3-4 scripts/year. Works with 10-12 writers/year. Buys all rights. No previously produced material. Reports in 1 month on queries; 3 months on submissions. Query with synopsis or completed script. Pays small option money applicable to $40-50,000 purchase price.
Needs: Films. Low budget action scripts. Should be 105 pages or less. Cop/action stories, buddy action stories. Unique hook or idea. Hero should be male in his 30's.
Tips: "Don't think you are the only one writing the great 'millenium' script or the great 'cloning' script. There are thousands of them."

STARMIST DEVELOPMENT, INC., P.O. Box 6006, Torrance CA 90504-0006. Contact: Arnold Lütz, CEO. Estab. 1995. Film, video and television audience. Buys 5-6 scripts/year. Buys all rights. Reports in 6 months. Completed script and treatment. Pays $1,000-100,000.
Needs: Also accepting original 35mm films and videotapes for distributor. Pays $100,000-300,000.
Tips: "Be patient. The movie industry is a slow beast, but the rewards are beautiful. Take your time writing your treatment and screenplay. We're looking for all types of material, including women's stories, suspense dramas, family stories, horror, sci-fi, thrillers, action-adventure and more. Enclose postage if you want your script returned."

N **STEVENS & ASSOCIATES**, 9454 Wilshire Blvd., Beverly Hills CA 90212. (310)275-7541. President: Neal Stevens. Estab. 1995. All demographics. Buys 15 scripts/year. Works with 75 writers/year. Accepts previously produced material. Sometimes returns submissions with SASE. "Everything has to come through letter." Reports in 3-4 weeks on queries; 2-3 weeks on submissions. Query or query with synopsis. Pays varies depending on the project.
Needs: Films.
Tips: "Looking for 'splashy' material that jumps off the page. Good stay, dialogue and plot. We're very particular. Company is two years old and about to make third film."

N **STORY BROOKE FILMS**, 10380 Tennessee Ave., Los Angeles CA 90064. (310)553-9642. Owner: James Brooke. Estab. 1990. Buys 5 scripts/year. Works with 20 writers/year. Buys all rights. Accepts previously produced material. Reports in 1 month. Query with synopsis. Pays in accordance with Writer's Guild standards.
Needs: Films. Feature length screenplays.

STORYOPOLIS PRODUCTIONS, 116 N. Robertson, #A, Los Angeles CA 90048. (310)358-2525. Contact: Janet Salas, creative executive. Estab. 1994. Film/TV producer. Query and synopsis. Reports in 3 months. Options film/TV rights. Pay varies. Whole family entertainment, skewed sensibility or stories based on myth, fable, fairy tale.

N **STRATUM ENTERTAINMENT**, 747 Tearwood Rd., Los Angeles CA 90049. (310)472-4217. President: Dianne Mandell. Estab. 1995. Buys 2-3 scripts/year. Works with 20 writers/year. Buys first and all rights. Accepts previously produced material. Reports immediately on queries; 1 month on submissions. Complete script. Pays in accordance with Writer's Guild standards.
Needs: Films.

A **STUDIO MERRYWOOD**, 85 Putnam Ave., Hamden CT 06517-2827. Phone/fax: (203)407-1834. E-mail: merrywood@compuserve.com. Website: http://ourworld.compuserve.com/homepages/Merrywood. Contact: Raul daSilva, creative director. Estab. 1984. Produces animated motion pictures for entertainment audiences. "We are planning to severely limit but not close out freelance input. Will be taking roughly 5-7%. We will accept only material which we request from agent. Cannot return material or respond to direct queries."

- The Merrywood Studio is no longer producing children's animation of any kind.

Needs: Proprietary material only. Human potential themes woven into highly entertaining drama, high adventure, comedy. This is a new market for animation with only precedent in the illustrated novels published in France and Japan. Cannot handle unsolicited mail/scripts and will not return mail. Open to *agented* submissions of credit sheets, concepts and synopses only. Profit sharing depending upon value of concept and writer's following. Pays at least Writers Guild levels or better, plus expenses.
Tips: "This is *not a market for beginning writers*. Established, professional work with highly unusual and original themes is sought. If you love writing, it will show and we will recognize it and reward it in every way you can imagine. We are not a 'factory' and work on a very high level of excellence."

TALKING RINGS ENTERTAINMENT, P.O. Box 80141, Las Vegas NV 89180. E-mail: director@scifistation.com. Website: http://www.scifistation.com. President/Artistic Director: Arnold Leibovit. Contact: Barbara Schimpf, vice president, production. Estab. 1988. "Produces material for motion pictures and television. Works with 5 writers/year. Reports on submissions in 2 months. No treatments, novels, poems or plays, no submissions on computer disk. Query with logline and synopsis. A Submission Release *must* be included with all queries. Produced and directed "The Fantasy

Film Worlds of George Pal," "The Puppetoon Movie." Currently producing a remake of "The Time Machine," "7 Faces of Dr. Lao." SASE required for return of all materials. Pays in accordance with Writers Guild Standards.
Needs: "Prefers high concept, mixed genres, comedy, adventure, sci-fi/fantasy, as well as unusual visually rich character driven smaller works with unusual twists, comic sensibility, pathos and always always the unexpected." Films (35mm), videotapes. No unsolicited unagented material. Must include release form.
Tips: "New policy: submission of logline and synopsis for evaluation first. Do not send scripts until we ask for them. A Talking Rings Entertainment release form must be completed and returned with material. Accepting loglines via e-mail at director@scifistation.com."

N **THREE GUYS FROM VERONA INC.**, 12423 Ventura Ct., Studio City CA 91604. (818)509-2288. Partner: Clancy Grass. Estab. 1993. Buys 3 scripts/year. Works with 7-8 writers/year. Buys first and all rights. Accepts previously produced material. Reports in 1 month on queries; 3 months on submissions. Catalog for #10 SASE. Query with synopsis. Pays in accordance with Writer's Guild standards excluding synopsis.
Needs: Films (16 & 35mm), videotapes. Looking for great idea, nothing specific.

U.S. FILM CORP., 2029 Century Park E., #1260, Los Angeles CA 90067. (310)475-4547. Contact: Robert Nau, president. Estab. 1993. Action audience. Buys 5 scripts/year. Works with 10 writers/year. Buys all rights. Reports in 1 month. Query with synopsis. Pays per negotiation.
Needs Films (35mm). Action adventure, thrillers—feature length.

N ☐ **RONI WEISBERG PRODUCTIONS,** 10960 Wilshire Blvd., 7th Floor, Los Angeles CA 90024. (310)235-5478. Executive Producer: Roni Weisberg. Estab. 1985. Television, film and cable. Buys 4 scripts/year. Works with 20 writers/year. Buys rights as necessary. Accepts previously produced material. Reports in 1 month. Query with synopsis. Pays in accordance with Writer's Guild standards.
Needs: Films (35mm), videotapes. Female appeal/drama, thrillers, contoversial subject, kid/family comedy.
Tips: "Promotable concept driven material regardless of genre."

WONDERLAND ENTERTAINMENT GROUP, 1712 Anacapa St., Santa Barbara CA 93101. (805)569-0733. Fax: (818)769-5391. E-mail: wl1@gte.net. Contact: Emmanuel Itier, president. Estab. 1989. Produces material for any audience. Buys 5 scripts/year. Works with 4 writers/year. Buys all rights. Accepts previously produced material. Reports in 1 month. Submit complete script and résumé. Pays in accordance with Writers Guild standards.
Needs: Films. "We are seeking any screenplay for full-length motion pictures."
Tips: "Be patient but aggressive enough to keep people interested in your screenplay."

N **WORLD FILM SERVICES**, 630 Fifth Ave., Suite 1505, New York NY 10111. (212)632-3456. Director of Development: David Laserson. Estab. 1963. Mainstream, family, adult. Buys 5 scripts/year. Works with 5-20 writers/year. Buys all rights. No previously produced material. Reports in 1 month on queries; 2 months on submissions. Query. Pays in accordance with Writer's Guild standards.
Needs: Films (35mm). "We are looking for beautifully written, character-driven screenplays that can play big. Scripts A-list talent would give their *** to star in."
Tips: "Never assume the director will ameliorate the weak spots in your script. Try to really write a film on paper, to the tiniest detail. Leave the reader reeling from your VISION."

N **ZANIMO PRODUCTIONS USA, INC.**, 6308 W. 89th St., Suite 211, Los Angeles CA 90045. Contact: Tambre Hemstreet, president. Estab. 1991. Produces for a feature film or cable audience. Options 5-10 scripts/year. Works with 10 writers/year. Reports in 1 month on queries; 2 months on submissions. Query with synopsis. Payment depends entirely on each individual submission.
Needs: Films (35mm). Action, dramatic or thrillers—feature screenplays (like "The Grifters"). No period pieces. Length: under 120 pages.
Tips: High concept is not enough. There must be depth to the story and the characters. Must send query letter with synopsis first. Scripts by request only please."

N **ZIDE ENTERTAINMENT/ZIDE/PERRY FILMS**, 9100 Wilshire Blvd., Suite 615E, Beverly Hills CA 90212. (310)887-2990. Contact: J.C. Spink. Estab. 1994. All audiences. "We set up about 20 projects a year, 1998 should be even bigger." Works with 50 writers/year. Buys management/production company rights. Reports in 1 month. Query with synopsis. We keep a management percentage.
Needs: Films (35mm). Scripts, books, comic books, treatments.

MARKETS THAT WERE listed in the 1998 edition of *Writer's Market* but do not appear this year are listed in the General Index with a notation explaining why they were omitted.

Syndicates

Newspaper syndicates distribute columns, cartoons and other written material to newspapers around the country—and sometimes around the world. Competition for syndication slots is stiff. The number and readership of newspapers are dropping. With paper costs high, there are fewer pages and less money to spend in filling them. Coveted spots in general interest, humor and political commentary are held by big-name columnists such as Ellen Goodman, Bob Herbert and Cal Thomas. And multitudes of aspiring writers wait in the wings, hoping one of these heavy hitters will move on to something else and leave the spotlight open.

Although this may seem discouraging, there are in fact many areas in which less-known writers are syndicated. Syndicates are not looking for general interest or essay columns. What they are looking for are fresh voices that will attract readers. As consumer interests and lifestyles change, new doors are being opened for innovative writers capable of covering emerging trends.

Most syndicates distribute a variety of columns, cartoons and features. Although the larger ones are usually only interested in running ongoing material, smaller ones often accept short features and one-shots in addition to continuous columns. Specialized syndicates—those that deal with a single area such as business—often sell to magazines, trade journals and other business publications as well as to newspapers.

THE WINNING COMBINATION

In presenting yourself and your work, note that most syndicated columnists start out writing for local newspapers. Many begin as staff writers, develop a following in a particular area, and are then picked up by a syndicate. Before approaching a syndicate, write for a paper in your area. Develop a good collection of clips that you feel is representative of your best writing.

New ideas are paramount to syndication. Sure, you'll want to study the popular columnists to see how their pieces are structured (most are short—from 500-750 words—and really pack a punch), but don't make the mistake of imitating a well-known columnist. Syndicates are looking for original material that is timely, saleable and original. Do not submit a column to a syndicate on a subject it already covers. The more unique the topic, the greater your chances. Most importantly, be sure to choose a topic that interests you and one you know well.

APPROACHING MARKETS

Request a copy of a syndicate's writer's guidelines. It will give you information on current needs, submission standards and response times. Most syndicates prefer a query letter and about six sample columns or writing samples and a SASE. You may also want to include a client list and business card if available. If you have a particular area of expertise pertinent to your submission, mention this in your letter and back it up by sending related material. For highly specialized or technical matter, provide credentials to show you are qualified to handle the topic.

In essence, syndicates act as agents or brokers for the material they handle. Writing material is usually sold as a package. The syndicate will promote and market the work to newspapers (and sometimes to magazines) and keep careful records of sales. Writers receive 40-60% of gross receipts. Some syndicates may also pay a small salary or flat fee for one-shot items.

Syndicates usually acquire all rights to accepted material, although a few are now offering writers and artists the option of retaining ownership. In selling all rights, writers give up ownership and future use of their creations. Consequently, sale of all rights is not the best deal for writers, and has been the reason many choose to work with syndicates that buy less restrictive rights. Before signing a contract with a syndicate, you may want to go over the terms with an attorney or with an agent who has a background in law. The best contracts will usually offer the writer a percentage of gross receipts (as opposed to net receipts) and will not bind the writer for longer than five years.

THE SELF-SYNDICATION OPTION

Many writers choose to self-syndicate. This route allows you to retain all rights, and gives you the freedom of a business owner. But as a self-syndicated writer, you must also act as your own manager, marketing team and sales force. You must develop mailing lists, and a pricing, billing and collections structure.

Payment is usually negotiated on a case-by-case basis. Small newspapers may offer only $10-20 per column, but larger papers may pay much more (for more information on pay rates, see How Much Should I Charge? on page 72). The number of papers you deal with is only limited by your marketing budget and your tenacity.

If you self-syndicate, be aware that some newspapers are not copyrighted, so you should copyright your own material. It's less expensive to copyright columns as a collection than individually. For more information on copyright procedures, see Copyrighting Your Writing in the Business of Writing section.

FOR MORE INFORMATION . . .

A complete listing of syndicates with contact names and the features they represent can be found in the *Editor & Publisher Syndicate Directory* (11 W. 19th St., New York NY 10011). The weekly magazine, *Editor & Publisher*, also has news articles about syndicates and can provide you with information about changes and events in the industry.

Information on syndicates listed in the previous edition of *Writer's Market* but not included in this edition can be found in the General Index.

[N] **THE AMERICAN NEWS SERVICE**, 289 Fox Farm Rd., Brattleboro VT 05301. (802)254-6167. Contact: Peter Sears, managing editor. Estab. 1995. 80% freelance written on a one-time basis. Buys 166 features/year. Works with 20 writers/year. Works with 0 previously unpublished writers/year. Syndicates to newspapers and radio. Reports in 1 month. Buys first North American serial rights. Free writer's guidelines. Submit complete ms.
Needs: Newspaper features. Buys features (800-1,000 words) covering innovations in community development, economics, education, community arts, environmental protection, healthcare, criminal justice, etc. Pays minimum guarantee $250-400.
Tips: "To enhance your chances, please review our stories on our website: americannews.com. Look for little-known developments of solution-oriented action at the community level. Look for local examples with national impact."

[N] **ARTHUR'S INTERNATIONAL**, 2613 High Range Dr., Las Vegas NV 89134. (702)228-3731. Editor: Marvin C. Arthur. Syndicates to newspapers and magazines. Reports in 1 week. "SASE must be enclosed." Buys all rights.
Needs: Fillers, magazine columns, magazine features, newspaper columns, newspaper features and news items. "We specialize in timely nonfiction and historical stories, and columns, preferably the unusual. We utilize humor. Travel stories utilized in 'World Traveler.' " Buys one-shot features and article series. "Since the majority of what we utilize is column or short story length, it is better to submit the article so as to expedite consideration and reply. Do not send any lengthy manuscripts." Pays 50% of net sales, salary on some contracted work and flat rate on commissioned work. Currently syndicates "Marv," by Marvin C. Arthur (informative, humorous, commentary); "Humoresque," by Don Alexander (humorous); and "World Spotlight," by Don Kampel (commentary).
Tips: "We do not use cartoons but we are open for fine illustrators."

[N] **AUTO DIGEST**, P.O. Box 459, Prineville OR 97754-0459. (541)923-3936. E-mail: adigest@transport.com. Estab. 1992. 17% written by writers on contract. Buys 100 features/year. Works with 3-4 writers/year. Syndicates to newspapers and internet. Reports in 2 months. Buys first North American serial rights. Pays when paid by publication. Query only.
Needs: Uses newspaper columns and news items. All writers equally split fee after expenses. Currently syndicates New car reviews, by Bill and Barbara Schaffer (800-1,000 words plus photo); Auto Update, by Bill and Barbara Schaffer (400-500 words); Auto Forum, by Chip Keen (400-500 words).

N **BLACK PRESS SERVICE, INC.**, 166 Madison Ave., New York NY 10016. (212)686-6850. Fax: (212)686-7308. Contact: Roy Thompson, editor. Estab. 1966. 10% written on contract; 10% freelance written on a one-time basis. Buys hundreds of features/year. Works with hundreds of writers/year. Syndicates to magazines, newspapers and radio. Reports in 2 months. Buys all rights. Submit complete ms.

Needs: Magazine and newspaper columns; news items; magazine and newspaper features; radio broadcast material. Purchases single (one shot) features and articles series (current events oriented). Pays variable flat rate. Currently syndicates Bimonthly Report, by staff (roundup of minority-oriented news).

N **BOOTSTRAPS**, 249 W. 21st St., New York NY 10011. Editor: William Neal. Estab. 1979. 100% freelance written by writers on a one-time basis. Buys 52 features/year. Works with any number of writers/year. Works with new, previously unpublished writers. Syndicates to newspapers. Reports in 1 month. Buys first North American serial rights. Writer's guidelines for #10 SASE. Query only.

Needs: Newspaper columns. Purchases single (one shot) and continuing features. Pays 50% author's percentage.

Tips: "We are looking for solutions to national problems—state the problem and state your solution—that are not being adequately addressed in legislatures or in the media. This search calls for original ideas, or old ideas, with rational, feasible, solutions on topics involving and/or affecting individuals or people in general. We will consider—but not limit our interests to—such topics as crime, prisons, illegal drug traffic and use, education drop-outs, innovative education systems and standards, etc. We will not consider strictly partisan issues such as race, religion, discrimination, or political issues such as term limits, fund raising, etc. Restrict your article to 750 words, one topic per article, typed, double-spaced on one side of 8½×11″ paper, with your name and complete address on the top left-hand corner. Include postage on SAE."

N **COMPUTERUSER MAGAZINE**, 220 S. Sixth St., Suite 500, Minneapolis MN 55402. (612)336-9286. E-mail: cueditor@usinternet.com or twahman@mspcommunications.com. Website: http://www.computeruser.com. Contact: Tyra Novic Wahman. Estab. 1982. 100% written by writers on contract. Buys 36-50 features/year. Works with 40 writers/year. Syndicates to magazines, newspapers. Reports in 4 months. Buys all rights. No writer's guidelines. Submit complete ms or query with clips of published work.

Needs: Magazine features (high technology/computing only, business end-user orientation). Pays 10% author's percentage or minimum guarantee of $50-300. Currently syndicates Computer Pursuits, by Nelson King (industry observation and predictions); Insights, by James Mathewson (industry and Human-factors observations); CD-ROM, by various authors (CD-ROM reviews), Diversions, by Michael Finley.

Tips: "We cover the whole computer industry, all platforms from a business user perspective. We take 90% of our material from a longstanding board of contributing editors. Spots are limited and often winnowed for contributing writers. We are journalists, not technical writers or PC hacks. Send samples or finished piece with SASE. We will respond."

N **CONTINENTAL FEATURES/CONTINENTAL NEWS SERVICE**, 501 W. Broadway, Suite 265, Plaza A, San Diego CA 92101-3802. (619)492-8696. Website: http://www.mediafinder.com (under online store). Editor-in-Chief: Gary Salamone. Estab. 1981. 100% writers on contract. "Writers who offer the kind and quality of writing we seek stand an equal chance regardless of experience." Syndicates to print media. Reports in 1 month with SASE. Writer's guidelines for #10 SASE.

Needs: Magazine and newspaper features. "Feature material should fit the equivalent of one-quarter to one-half standard newspaper page, and Continental News considers an ultra-liberal or ultra-conservative slant inappropriate." Query with SASE. Pays 70% author's percentage. Currently syndicates News and Comment, by Charles Hampton Savage (general news commentary/analysis); Continental Viewpoint, by staff; Portfolio, (cartoon/caricature art); Travelers' Checks, by Ann Hattes; and OnVideo, by Harley Lond; over 50 features in all.

- This syndicate is considering fewer proposals for one-time projects. Virtually all of their new feature creators are signed to work on a continuing basis.

Tips: "*CF/CNS* is working to develop a feature package of greater interest and value to an English-speaking international audience. That is, those writers who can accompany their economic-social-political analyses (of foreign countries) with photo(s) of the key public figure(s) involved are particularly in demand. Official photos (8×10 down to 3×5) of key government leaders available from the information ministry/press office/embassy will be acceptable. *CF/CNS* emphasizes analytical/explanatory articles, but muckraking articles (where official-photo requests are inopportune) are also encouraged."

N **DEMKO'S AGEVENTURE SYNDICATED NEWS SERVICE**, 21946 Pine Trace, Boca Raton FL 33428-3057 (561)482-6271. E-mail: demko@demko.com. Estab. 1983. 25% written by writers on contracts; 25% freelance written on a one-time basis. Buys 52 feautres/year. Works with 27 writers/year. Syndicates to magazines, radio, newspapers and internet-zines. Reports back 10-30 days. **Pays on acceptance.** Send writer's guidelines via e-mail only. Query via e-mail.

Needs: Uses news items. Purchases single (one shot) features and article series (250-500 words). Pays flat rate. Currently syndicates *Senior Living (500-750 words) lifestyle feature columns—staff writer; Sonic Boomers* (150-2,00 words and photo) personal profiles (age 40-50); *Aging America* (50-75 words) mature market news items.

Tips: Stick with what you know in order to avoid superficial content. Query via e-mail and limit work samples (2-3). Be assertive and upfront—specify your product and costs/prices in advance.

EDITORIAL CONSULTANT SERVICE, P.O. Box 524, West Hempstead NY 11552-1206. Phone/fax: (516)481-5487. Contact: Arthur A. Ingoglia, editorial director. Estab. 1964. 40% written on contract; 25% freelance written on a one-time basis. "We work with 75 writers in the US and Canada." Adds about 10 new columnists/year. Syndicates material to an average of 60 newspapers, magazines, automotive trade and consumer publications, and radio stations with circulation of 50,000-575,000. Buys all rights. Writer's guidelines for #10 SASE. Reports in 1-2 months.
Needs: Magazine and newspaper columns and features, news items, radio broadcast material. Prefers carefully documented material with automotive slant. Also considers automotive trade features. Will consider article series. No horoscope, child care, lovelorn or pet care. Query. Author's percentage varies; usually averages 50%. Additional payment for 8×10 b&w and color photos accepted with ms. Submit 2-3 columns. Currently syndicates Let's Talk About Your Car, by R. Hite.
Tips: "Emphasis is placed on articles and columns with an automotive slant. We prefer consumer-oriented features, how to save money on your car, what every woman should know about her car, how to get more miles per gallon, etc."

INFINITY FEATURES, 313 Heathcote Rd., Scarsdale NY 10583-7154. (914)472-9459. E-mail: infinityf@aol.com. Estab. 1982. 100% freelance written on a one-time basis. Buys 25 features/year. Works with 15 writers/year. Syndicates to magazines and newspapers, all overseas. Reports in 2 weeks only if interested. Buys one-time rights for a single country. Pays on publication. "We ask for 'story suggestions' in a brief quarter page paragraph form faxed or mailed to us." Query with published clips.
Needs: Magazine columns and features; newspaper columns and features; news items. Purchases single features and article series. Pays author's percentage 50; minimum guarantee $250. Pays $100-3,000. "We don't have regular material however we market a very wide range of articles whose subjects vary from womens issues to science and technology; politics; parenting; travel; fitness and health and more."
Tips: Needs "Text that is news oriented is in demand as well as enlightening material that will educate an overseas audience."

INTERPRESS OF LONDON AND NEW YORK, 400 Madison Ave., New York NY 10017. (212)832-2839. Contact: Jeffrey Blyth, editor-in-chief. Estab. 1971. 10% freelance written on a one-time basis. Buys 10-12 features/year. Works with 4-5 writers/year. Works with 1-2 new previously unpublished writers/year. Syndicates to newspapers and radio. Reports in 1 week. Buys all rights. Writer's guidelines for #10 SASE. Query only.
Needs: Magazine features, newspaper features and off-beat feature stories. Purchases one shot features. Pays 60% author's percentage. Additional payment for photos. Currently syndicates Destination America, by various writers (travel) series; Book World, by Myran Grier (book news/reviews); Dateline NY, by various writers (show biz news/features).

MEGALO MEDIA, P.O. Box 678, Syosset NY 11791. (212)535-6811. Editor: J. Baxter Newgate. Estab. 1972. 50% written on contract; 50% freelance written on a one-time basis. Works with 5 previously unpublished writers/year. Syndicates to newspapers. Reports in 1 month. Buys all rights. Free writer's guidelines.
Needs: Crossword puzzles. Buys one-shot features. Submit complete ms. Pays flat rate of $150 for Sunday puzzle. Currently syndicates National Challenge, by J. Baxter Newgate (crossword puzzle); Crossword Puzzle, by J. Baxter Newgate.

MORTGAGE MARKET INFORMATION SERVICES, 53 E. St. Charles Rd., Villa Park IL 60181. (630)782-4387. E-mail: editorial@banking.interest.com. Estab. 1987. 75% written by writers on contract; 25% freelance written on a one-time basis. Buys 50 features/year. Works with 2 writers/year. Syndicates to newspapers, Internet. Does not return submissions. Reports in 2 weeks. Rights purchsed vary based on content usage. **Pays on acceptance.** Writer's guidelines for #10 SASE. Query with published clips.
Needs: Newspaper columns, news items of interest to mortgage lending professionals. Purchases single (one shot) features and article series. Pays per target word range set per assignment (about 25¢/word). Additional payment for photos accepted with the ms. Mortgages, by Jim DeBoth (consumer home finance information); Daily Mortgage News, by Bill Steele (daily mortgage rate review and forecast); Fax Weekly Report, by Bill Steele various contributors (industry newsletter for mortgage lending professionals).
Tips: "If you are knowledgeable of a particular topic, you should be able to get a lot of mileage out of a story by submitting it to several related trade publications. Some trade publications will forego exclusivity rights in exchange for a lower fee."

NATIONAL NEWS BUREAU, P.O. Box 43039, Philadelphia PA 19129-0628. (215)849-9016. Contact: Harry Jay Katz, editor. 20% written by writers on contract; 35-40 freelance written on a one-time basis. Buys 100 features/year. Works with 200 writers/year. Works with 50% new previously unpublished writers/year. Syndicates to magazines and newspaper. Reports in 2 weeks. Buys all rights. Pays on publication. Writer's guidelines for 9×12 SAE with 3 first-class stamps.
Needs: Magazine features; newspaper columns and features. "We do many reviews and celebrity interviews. Only original, assigned material." One-shot features and article series; film reviews, etc. Query with clips. Pays $5-200 flat rate or 50% author's percentage. Offers $5-200 additional payment for photos accompanying ms.

NEW LIVING, P.O. Box 1519, Stony Brook NY 11790. (516)751-8819. Fax: (516)751-8910. E-mail: newliving@aol.com. Website: http://www.newliving.com. Contact: Mark Kalaygian, editor. Publisher: Christine Lynn Harvey. Estab. 1991. 20% written under contract; 5% freelance written on one-time basis. Buys 20 features/year. Works with 20 writers/year. Works with 5 previously unpublished writers/year. Syndicates to magazines, newspapers, radio, 900 phone lines. Reports in 6 months. Buys all rights. Query with clips of published work. Writer's guidelines for #10 SASE.
Needs: Magazine and newspaper columns and features, news items, fillers, radio broadcast material. Purchases single (one shot) features and articles series. "Looking for articles on health and fitness (nutrition, healthy recipes, sports medicine, exercise tips, running, tennis, golf, bowling, aerobics, cycling, swimming, cross-training, watersports, travel, medical advice)." Also offers to list author's business affiliation, address, and phone number in article.
Photos: Offers $25-100 for photos accepted with ms.
Tips: "Be highly qualified in the area that you are writing about. If you are going to write a medical column, you must be a doctor, or at least affiliated with a nationally recognized medical organization."

PRESS ASSOCIATES, INC., 815 15th St. N.W., Washington DC 20005. (202)638-0444. Fax: (202)638-0955. President/Editor: Mark Gruenberg. Estab. 1957. 10% written by writers on contract. Buys 100 features/year. Works with 2 writers/year. Syndicates to union newspapers and publications.
Needs: "We will now consider but not necessarily accept, 400- to 800-word news stories at 10-15¢/word on worker-related issues—from worker's viewpoint. Query only." Currently syndicates Work & Health, by Phillip L. Polakoff, M.D. (medical column); How To Buy, by Esther Margolus (consumer column); Washington Window, by staff (political comment/analysis).

SPECIALTY FEATURES SYNDICATE, 17255 Redford Ave., Detroit MI 48219. Contact: L. E. Crandall, managing editor. Estab. 1952. Buys 40-50 features/year. Syndicates to magazines (occasionally) and newspapers (currently serving 480 newspapers). Reports in 2-3 months. Buys all rights. Query with brief outlines.
Needs: Magazine and newspaper features, single features, articles series. "We specialize in 'how-to' material with emphasis on health, food, nutrition, self-improvement and book condensations of subjects with wide appeal. **Pays on acceptance** and is negotiable.

THE SPORTS NETWORK, 95 James Way, Southampton PA 18966. (215)942-7890. Fax: (215)942-7647. E-mail: kcastro@sportsnetwork.com. Website: http://www.sportsnetwork.com. Contact: Kate Castronuovo, syndication editor. Estab. 1980. 30% written on contract; 10-15% freelance written on one-time basis; balance by in-house personnel. Buys 200-250 features/year. Works with 50-60 writers/year and 10-15 new previously unpublished writers/year. Syndicates to magazines, newspapers, radio and has the additional benefit of being an international sports wire service with established awareness globally furnishing exposure world-wide for its writers/clients. Reports immediately. Buys all rights. Free writer's guidelines. Query with clips of published and/or sample works and SASE.
Needs: Fillers, magazine and newspaper columns and features, news items, radio and broadcast material, single features (timely sports pieces, from 700-1,000 words). Seeking ongoing coverage pieces of teams (professional) leagues (professional), conferences (college) and sports, 1-2 times weekly. Payments variable. Currently syndicates The Sandlot Shrink, by Dennis LePore; Infosport, by Julie Lanzillo; The Women's Basketball Journal, Bball Stats, by Robert Chaikin; Inside The Ring, by Max Hammer; John Iovino's Sportfolio (boxing).
Tips: "The competition for sports is fast and furious, so right time and place, with a pinch of luck, are ingredients that complement talent. Making inroads to one syndicate for even one feature is an amazing door opener. Focus on the needs of that syndicate or wire service (as is the case with TSN) and use that as a springboard to establish a proven track record with quality work that suits specific needs. Don't give up and don't abandon the day job. This takes commitment, desire, knowledge of the topic and willingness to work at it while being able to handle rejection. No one who reads submissions really 'knows' and the history of great rejections would fill volumes, from *Gone With The Wind* to Snoopy and Garfield. We are different in that we are looking for specific items and not a magical cartoon (although sports cartoons will work), feature or story. Give us your best in sports and make certain that it is in tune with what is happening right now or is able to stand the test of time, be an evergreen and everlasting if it is a special feature."

TEENAGE CORNER, INC., 70-540 Gardenia Ct., Rancho Mirage CA 92270. President: Mrs. David J. Lavin. Buys 122 items/year for use in newspapers. Submit complete ms. Reports in 1 week. Material is not copyrighted.
Needs: 500-word newspaper features. Pays $25.

TV DATA, Northway Plaza, Queensbury NY 12804. (518)792-9914. E-mail: gsacks@tvda.com. 25% written by writers on contract; 50% freelance written on a one-time basis. Buys 100 features/year. Works with 20 writers/year. Syndicates to newspapers and internet. Does not return submissions. Reports in 1 month. Buys all rights. Pays on publication. Query with published clips.
Needs: Uses newspaper columns and features and fillers.

Greeting Cards & Gift Ideas

How many greeting cards did you buy last year? Americans bought nearly seven and a half billion cards last year. That's according to figures published by The Greeting Card Association, a national trade organization representing the multi-billion dollar greeting card industry.

In fact, nearly 50% of all first class mail now consists of greeting cards. And, of course, card manufacturers rely on writers to supply them with enough skillfully crafted sentiments to meet the demand. The perfect greeting card verse is one that will appeal to a large audience, yet will make each buyer feel that the card was written exclusively for him or her.

Three greeting card companies dominate this industry; together, American Greetings, Hallmark and Gibson Greetings supply 85% of all cards sold. The other 15% are published by approximately 1,500 companies who have found success mainly by not competing head to head with the big three but by choosing instead to pursue niche markets—regional and special-interest markets that the big three either cannot or do not supply.

A PROFESSIONAL APPROACH TO MARKETS

As markets become more focused, it's important to keep current on specific company needs. Familiarize yourself with the differences among lines of cards by visiting card racks. Ask retailers which lines are selling best. You may also find it helpful to read trade magazines such as *Gifts and Decorative Accessories* and *Party and Paper Retailer*. These publications will keep you apprised of changes and events within the field, including seminars and trade shows.

Once you find a card line that appeals to you, write to the company and request its market list, catalog or submission guidelines (usually available for a SASE or a small fee). This information will help you determine whether or not your ideas are appropriate for that market.

Submission procedures vary among greeting card publishers, depending on the size and nature of the company. Keep in mind that many companies (especially the large ones) will not review your writing samples until you've signed and returned their disclosure contract or submission agreement, assuring them that your material is original and has not been submitted elsewhere.

Some editors prefer to see individual card ideas on 3×5 cards, while others prefer to receive a number of complete ideas on 8½×11 bond paper. Be sure to put your best pieces at the top of the stack. Most editors do not want to see artwork unless it is professional, but they do appreciate conceptual suggestions for design elements. If your verse depends on an illustration to make its point or if you have an idea for a unique card shape or foldout, include a dummy card with your writing samples.

The usual submission includes from 5 to 15 card ideas and an accompanying cover letter, plus mechanical dummy cards, if necessary. Some editors also like to receive a résumé, client list and business card. Some do not. Be sure to check the listings and the company's writer's guidelines for such specifications before submitting material.

Payment for greeting card verse varies, but most firms pay per card or per idea; a handful pay small royalties. Some companies prefer to test a card first and will pay a small fee for a test card idea. In some instances, a company may even purchase an idea and never use it.

Greeting card companies will also buy ideas for gift products and may use card material for a number of subsequent items. Licensing—the sale of rights to a particular character for a variety of products from mugs to T-shirts—is a growing part of the industry. Because of this, however, note that most card companies buy all rights. We now include in this section markets for licensed product lines such as mugs, bumper stickers, buttons, posters and the like.

Information of interest to writers wishing to know more about working with the greeting card industry is available from the Greeting Card Association (1200 G Street NW, Suite 760, Washington, DC 20005).

MANAGING YOUR SUBMISSIONS

Because you will be sending out many samples, you may want to label each sample. Establish a master card for each verse idea and record where and when each was sent and whether it was rejected or purchased. Keep all cards sent to one company in a batch and give each batch a number. Write this number on the back of your return SASE to help you match up your verses as they are returned.

Information on greeting card companies listed in the previous edition of *Writer's Market* but not included in this edition can be found in the General Index.

AMBERLEY GREETING CARD CO., 11510 Goldcoast Dr., Cincinnati OH 45249-1695. (513)489-2775. Editor: Dave McPeek. Estab. 1966. 90% freelance written. Bought 200 freelance ideas last year. Reports in 1 month. Material copyrighted. Buys all rights. **Pays on acceptance.** Writer's guidelines for #10 SASE. Market list regularly revised.

- This company is now accepting alternative humor.

Needs: "Original, easy to understand, belly-laugh or outrageous humor. We sell to the 'masses, not the classes,' so keep it simple and to the point. Humor accepted in all captions, including general birthday, family birthday, get well, anniversary, thank you, friendship, etc. No non-humorous material needed or considered this year." Pays $150/card idea. Submit maximum 10 ideas/batch.

Tips: "Send SASE for our writer's guidelines before submitting. Amberley publishes humorous specialty lines in addition to a complete conventional line that is accented with humor. Since humor is our specialty, we are highly selective. Be sure your SASE has correct U.S. postage. Otherwise it will not be returned."

bePUZZLED, Mystery Jigsaw Puzzles, 1001 Farmington Ave., Suite 205, W. Hartford CT 06107. (860)561-9600. Fax: (860)561-9552. E-mail: malbepuzzd@aol.com. Contact: Mary Ann Lombard, founder. Creative Director: Richard DeZinno. 100% freelance written. Estab. 1987. Pays on completion. Publishes ms 9 months after acceptance. Byline given (sometimes pen name required). Buys all rights. Submit seasonal/holiday material 9 months in advance. Accepts simultaneous submissions. Reports in 2 weeks on queries, 3 months on mss. Writer's guidelines for SASE.

Needs: Mystery jigsaw puzzle using short mystery stories for children and adults. Adventure, humorous, mainstream, mystery, suspense (*exact* subject within genre above is released to writers as available.) Buys 10 mss/year. Query. Length: 3,500-5,500 words. Pays $250-2,000.

Tips: "Writers must follow submission format as outlined in writer's guidelines. We incorporate short mystery stories and jigsaw puzzles into a game where the clues to solve the mystery are cleverly hidden in both the short story and the puzzle picture. Writer must be able to integrate the clues in the written piece to these to appear in puzzle picture. Playing one of our games helps to clarify how we like to 'marry' the story clues and the visual clues in the puzzle." Manuscripts may not be returned.

BLUE MOUNTAIN ARTS, INC., Dept. WM, P.O. Box 1007, Boulder CO 80306-1007. E-mail: bma@rmi.net. Website: http://www.bluemountainarts.com. Contact: Editorial Department. Estab. 1971. Buys 100 items/year. Reports in 3 months. Pays on publication. Writer's guidelines for #10 SASE. Enclose SASE with submission.

Needs: "We are interested in reviewing poetry and writings that would be appropriate for greeting cards, which means that they should reflect a message, feeling, or sentiment that one person would want to share with another. We'd like to receive sensitive, original submissions about love relationships, family members, friendships, philosophies, and any other aspect of life. Poems and writings for specific holidays (Christmas, Valentine's Day, etc.) and special occasions, such as graduation, birthdays, anniversary, and get well are also considered." Submit seasonal material at least 4 months in advance. Buys worldwide, exclusive rights, $200/poem; anthology rights $25.

Other Product Lines: Calendars, gift books, prints, mugs.

Tips: "We strongly suggest that you familiarize yourself with our products before submitting material, although we caution you not to study them too hard. We do *not* need more poems that sound like something we've already published. We're looking for poetry that expresses real emotions and feelings, so we suggest that you have someone specific in mind (a friend, relative, etc.) as you write. The majority of the poetry we publish *does not rhyme*. We do not wish to receive books, unless you are interested in having portions excerpted for greeting cards; nor do we wish to receive artwork or photography. We prefer that submissions be typewritten, one poem per page, with name and address on every page. Only a small portion of the freelance material we receive is selected each year, either for publication on a notecard or in a gift anthology, and the review process can also be lengthy, but please be assured that every manuscript is given serious consideration."

BRILLIANT ENTERPRISES, 117 W. Valerio St., Santa Barbara CA 93101-2927. Contact: Ashleigh Brilliant, president. Estab. 1967. Buys all rights. Submit words and art in black on 3½×3½ horizontal, thin white paper in batches of no more than 15. Reports "usually in 2 weeks." Catalog and sample set for $2.
Needs: Postcards. Messages should be "of a highly original nature, emphasizing subtlety, simplicity, insight, wit, profundity, beauty and felicity of expression. Accompanying art should be in the nature of oblique commentary or decoration rather than direct illustration. Messages should be of universal appeal, capable of being appreciated by all types of people and of being easily translated into other languages. Because our line of cards is highly unconventional, it is essential that freelancers study it before submitting. No topical references or subjects limited to American culture or puns." Limit of 17 words/card. Pays $50 for "complete ready-to-print word and picture design."

THE CALLIGRAPHY COLLECTION INC., 2604 NW 74th Place, Gainesville FL 32653. (352)375-8530. Fax: (352)374-9957. E-mail: artistkaty@aol.com. Owner: Katy Fischer. Reports in 6 months. Buys all rights. Pays on publication.
Needs: "A line of framed prints of watercolors with calligraphy." Conventional, humorous, inspirational, sensitivity, soft line. Prefers unrhymed verse, but will consider rhymed. Submit 3 ideas/batch. Pays $75-200/framed print idea.
- The Calligraphy Collection has increased their payment rates.

Other Product Lines: Gift books, plaques, musical picture frames.
Tips: "We are looking for sentimental and inspirational sayings such as can be given to friends or family, or used as a wedding or graduation gift, but that do not mention specific occasions as such. For example, Mother saying that could be given all year as well as on Mother's Day. Our main markets are women 20 to 50 years of age. We are looking for verses that tell someone significant how much they mean to you, how important their friendship is or what is special about knowing them. All that in 35 words or less. We are looking for sayings to incorporate into items that caring people would like to give as lasting gifts."

N **CARDMAKERS**, P.O. Box 236, 66 High Bridge Rd., Lyme NH 03768. (603)795-4422. Contact: Peter D. Diebold. Estab. 1978. Receives very few submissions/year. Submit seasonal/holiday material 10 months in advance. Reports in 3 months. Buys all greeting cards rights. **Pays on acceptance**. Writer's guidelines/market list for free or for SAE.
Needs: Holiday (mostly) & everyday, humorous. "We like upbeat humor, skip sick or raunchy. Our customers use our cards to greet their customers so a positive approach/result is desirable." Prefers unrhymed verse.
Tips: "We are primarily a direct marketer of business to business greetings targeted to specific interest groups—i.e. Stockbrokers, Boaters, etc . . . We also publish everday cards for those same specific interests. So far, all our ideas and captions have been generated internally. We work with many free-lancers on design and have recently decided to solicit ideas from writers. Please don't call. Send us a simple bio, samples if possible & SASE and we'll get in touch."

COMSTOCK CARDS, 600 S. Rock, Suite 15, Reno NV 89502-4115. Fax: (702)856-9406. E-mail: comstock@intercomm.com. Contact: David Delacroix, production manager. Estab. 1986. 35% freelance written. Receives 2,000 submissions/year; bought 150 freelance ideas/samples last year. Submit seasonal/holiday material 1 year in advance. Reports in 5 weeks. Buys all rights. **Pays on acceptance.** Writer's guidelines/market list for SASE. Market list issued once.
Needs: Humorous, informal, invitations, "puns, put-downs, put-ons, outrageous humor aimed at a sophisticated, adult female audience. Also risqué cartoon cards. No conventional, soft line or sensitivity hearts and flowers, etc." Pays $50-75/card idea, cartoons negotiable.
Other Product Lines: Notepads, cartoon cards, invitations.
Tips: "Always keep holiday occasions in mind and personal me-to-you expressions that relate to today's occurrences. Ideas must be simple and concisely delivered. A combination of strong image and strong gag line make a successful greeting card. Consumers relate to themes of work, sex and friendship combined with current social, political and economic issues."

CURRENT, INC., Box 2559, Colorado Springs CO 80901-2559. (719)594-4100. Submit to: Freelance Editors. Estab. 1950. 10-15% freelance written. Receives an estimated 2,000 submissions/year; bought 250 ideas/samples last year. Submit best humor ideas *only* for birthday, friendship, get well. Reports in 6 weeks. Buys all rights. **Pays on acceptance**, "flat fee only; no royalty." Writer's guidelines for #10 SASE.
Needs: Humorous, religious, conventional, seasonal, cute. Avoid overly risqué. Accepts submissions for all categories of conventional greeting card sentiments. All occasion and woman-to-woman cards; short 1-2 line puns and prose not too risque. Pays $100/sentiment.
Tips: "We're always eager to find talented writers with fresh ideas. Our customers are 97% women and 80% of them are married with children under 18. Writers need to keep in mind the audience we're trying to reach. It's helpful to review our direct mail catalog. Before submitting your work to us, ask yourself if your writing stands apart for one or more of these reasons: fresh insight; new twist to old idea; untapped, but common sending situation; clever language, word play, or visual image; unusual rhyme scheme or rhyme words; new twist to non-card product ideas."

N **DCI STUDIOS**, 4006 Central, Kansas City MO 64111. Freelance Coordinator: Scott Oppenheimer. Estab. 1992. Submit seasonal/holiday material 6 months in advance. Reports in 3 months. Buys greeting card rights. **Pays on acceptance**. Writers guidelines/market list for free. Market list issued one time only.
Needs: Inspirational, humorous, soft line. Prefers unrhymed verse. Submit 25-50 ideas/batch.
Tips: "We are looking for fresh, new, innovative humor. We divide our humor needs into general jokes and woman's

humor. The only thing we remind writers of is that our market is mostly womaen between 19 and 55. So we need to create a product that will appeal to them."

N **DESIGN DESIGN INC.**, P.O. Box 2266, Grand Rapids MI 49501-2266. Fax: (616)774-2448. Creative Director: Tom Vituj. Estab. 1985. Submit seasonal/holiday/everyday material 1 year in advance. Buys all rights. Pays on publication. Writer's guidelines for SASE.
Needs: Prefers unrhymed verse; conventional, informal, sensitive, humorous, juvenile submissions. Submit 12 concepts.

DUCK AND COVER PRODUCTIONS, P.O. Box 21640, Oakland CA 94620. Contact: Jim Buser. Estab. 1990. 50% freelance written. Receives 1,000 submissions/year. Bought 120 ideas/samples last year. Reports in 3 weeks. Buys all rights on novelty products. Pays on publication. Guidelines for #10 SAE with 2 first-class stamps.
Other Product Lines: Novelty buttons and magnets *only*. "We do *not* make greeting cards." Pays $25/idea.
Tips: "We do best with original, intelligent statements that make fun of life in the neurotic 90s. Our target audience would be educated, aware, yet skeptical and anxious young adults; however, anyone with an offbeat sense of humor can enjoy our line. We sell to novelty stores, head shops, record stores, bookstores, sex shops, comic stores, etc. There are no taboos for our writers; we encourage them to be as weird and/or rude as possible. We feel buttons and magnets are commercial cousins to graffiti. Let your inner child thumb his nose at society. Cerebral material that makes use of contemporary pop vocabulary is a plus. We do *not* want to see old clichés or slogans already in the market."

ENCORE STUDIOS, 17 Industrial West, Clifton NJ 07012. (201)472-1800, ext. 505. Fax: (201)472-3264. E-mail: encore17@aol.com. Website: http://www.encorestudios.com. Contact: Ceil Benjamin, art director. Estab. 1979. 75% of material freelance written. Receives 300 submissions/year. Submit seasonal/holiday material 8 months in advance. Reports in 3 months. **Pays on acceptance.** Market list regularly revised.
Needs: Personalized announcements, wedding, party, bar/bat mitzvah, birth announcements and holiday cards.
Tips: Looking for cards with a classy, sophisticated style and a clever saying for an upscale audience.

EPCONCEPTS, P.O. Box 363, Piermont NY 10968. Contact: Steve Epstein, owner. Estab. 1983. 95% freelance written. Receives 1,200 submissions/year; bought 25 ideas/samples last year. Submit seasonal/holiday material 2 months in advance. Reports in 3 months. Buys one-time greeting card rights. Pays ½ on acceptance; ½ on publication. Writer's guidelines for #10 SASE.
Needs: Announcements, conventional, humorous, informal, inspirational, invitations, juvenile, studio, all holidays. Prefers unrhymed verse ideas. Submit 20 ideas/batch on 8½×11 paper; no index cards. Include #10 SASE with submissions for reply.
Other Product Lines: Buttons, mugs.
Tips: "Humorous sells best; especially birthdays, anniversaries, friendship/love and light risqué. Target audience is ages 20-50, upscale and appreciative of photography, antiques, illustrations and cartoons. Trends can always include certain social and political phenomenons, e.g., Presidents, first ladies, etc."

EPHEMERA, INC., P.O. Box 490, Phoenix OR 97535. E-mail: ephemera@mind.net. Website: http://www.mind.net/ephemera. Contact: Editor. Estab. 1979. 90% freelance written. Receives 2,000 submissions/year; bought 300 slogans for novelty buttons and magnets last year. Reports in 6 weeks. Buys all rights. Pays on publication. Writer's guidelines for self addressed stamped envelope. Complete full color catalog available for $4.
Needs: Provocative, irreverent and outrageously funny slogans for novelty buttons, magnets and stickers. "We want concise, high impact gems of wit that would sell in trendy card and gift shops, bookstores, record shops, political and gay shops, head shops, adult stores, amusement parks, etc! We've been in business for over 20 years and we have a reputation as *the* publisher of the wackiest slogans." Pays $35/slogan.
Tips: "We're looking for satirical slogans about current events, pop culture, political causes, the president, job attitudes, coffee, booze, pot, drugs, sexual come-ons and put-downs, aging, slacker angst, gays and lesbians. But please don't limit yourself to these topics! Make us laugh out loud!"

GALLANT GREETINGS, Dept. WM, P.O. Box 308, Franklin Park IL 60131. E-mail: chrisa@gallantgreetings.com. Website: http://www.gallantgreetings.com. Contact: Chris Allen, vice president, sales and marketing. 90% freelance written. Bought 500 freelance ideas/samples last year. Reports in 3 months. Buys world greeting card rights.
Needs: Traditional and humorous greeting card verse. Submit 20 cards/batch. Include SASE for return.

KATE HARPER DESIGNS, P.O. Box 2112, Berkeley CA 94702. Contact: Editor. Estab. 1993. 100% freelance written. Submit seasonal/holiday material 1 year in advance. Reports in 3 months. Pays flat fee for usage, not exclusive, $25-50 plus author's name credit. **Pays on acceptance**. Writer's guidelines/market list for SASE.
Needs: Humorous, informal, inspirational, sensitivity, everyday cards. Prefers unrhymed verse ideas. Submit 10 ideas/batch. We are looking for more seasonal and occasional themes: birthday, valentine and love, thank you, Christmas, Mother's Day. Please be "indirect" about season themes. For example instead of using words "Mother's Day" on a Mother's Day card, use themes of caring or closeness. Instead of using the word birthday—use themes of aging and growth. Valentines could be love and romance, etc.

- Ms. Harper notes she wants to see "more topics on current events—sophisticated themes that working parents or adults deal with on a day-to-day basis."

Tips: "Quotes needed about work, family, love, kids, career, technology and marriage with a twist of humor. Something a working mom would laugh at and/or tips on how to have it all and still live to tell about it. Be adventurous and say what you really think in first person. What is ironic about this world we live in? What is the message you want to put out in the world? Don't be afraid to take risks and push beyond greeting card stereotypes. Nothing cute or sweet. Avoid quotes about women and weight, PMS, chocolate, diet, sex. Write as if you were talking to your best friend at the kitchen table. Be personal, and speak in an 'I' voice, like you've been there. We seek out new and unknown writers with a zing. Avoid traditional ideas of card quotes. Serious quotes also considered. Quotes must be 20 words or less. For front of card only. Do not send quotes for inside of card."

N **HERITAGE COLLECTION**, 79 Fifth Ave., New York NY 10003. (212)647-1000. Contact: Allison Powe, creative director. Estab. 1992. 30% of material freelance written. Receives 300 submissions/year; bought 50 ideas/samples last year. Submit seasonal/holiday material 6 months in advance. Reports in 2 months. Buys greeting publishing rights only. Pays on publication. Writer's guidelines/market list for SAE.
Needs: Inspirational, juvenile. Prefers unrhymed verse. Submit 12 ideas/batch.
Tips: Audience is African-American, ages 25-45. Sees a trend toward more ethnic, inspirational and spiritual cards.

J-MAR, P.O. Box 23149, Waco TX 76702. (817)751-0100. Fax: (817)751-0054. Assistant Product Marketing Manager: C.M. Nevill. Estab. 1984. 25% freelance written. Receives 200 submissions/year; bought 7 ideas/samples last year. Submit seasonal/holiday material 10 months in advance. All submissions filed. Reports in 2 months. Buys all rights. **Pays on acceptance**.
Needs: Inspirational, soft line, friendship, birthdays, motivational, family, get well, sympathy, encouragement, humor, juvenile, seasonal, christenings, pastor/church thank you. Prefers either rhymed or unrhymed verse ideas.
Other Product Lines: Bookmarks, gift books, greeting books, calendars, puzzles.
Tips: "J-Mar's target audience is the Christian market. J-Mar appreciates submissions focused on core inspirational Christian values, verses and themes. Submissions can include biblical references or verses, poems and/or text.

KOGLE CARDS, INC., 1498 S. Lipan St., Denver CO 80223. (303)698-9007. President: Patricia Koller. Contact: Ace Van Wanseele, art director. Estab. 1982. 40% freelance written. Receives 100 submissions/year; bought 80 ideas/samples last year. Submit seasonal/holiday material 18 months in advance. Reports in 1 month. Buys all rights. Pays on publication.
Needs: Humorous, business related. Rhymed or unrhymed verse ideas.
Tips: "We produce cards designed for the business community, in particular salespeople, real estate, travel, hairdresser, insurance and chiropractic."

LAURA LEIDEN CALLIGRAPHY, INC., P.O. Box 141-WM, Watkinsville GA 30677. Contact: Jennifer. Estab. 1978. 99% freelance written. Receives 150 submissions/year; bought 45 ideas/samples last year. Submit seasonal/holiday material 1 year in advance. Returns submissions if requested, but frequently keeps for later consideration. Reports in 1-6 months. Buys all rights. **Pays on acceptance**. After first purchase, they notify writers of current needs.
Needs: Traditional, inspirational, poems for family members and about the joys and trials of raising kids. Prefers rhymed verse. "Tear Jerkers" preferred. Verses to be no shorter than three stanzas. Submit 6 ideas/batch.
Other Product Lines: Plaques.
Tips: "Trends now are heavily leaning on sentimental and nostalgic verses about and for family."

LOVE GREETING CARDS, INC., 1717 Opa Loca Blvd., Opa-Locka FL 33054. (305)685-5683. Fax: (305)685-8473. Contact: Norman Drittel. Estab. 1984. 75% freelance written. Receives 200-300 submissions/year; bought 400 ideas/samples last year. Submit seasonal/holiday material 6 months in advance. Reports in 1 month. Buys all rights. **Pays on acceptance**. Market list regularly revised.
Needs: Informal, juvenile, humorous, general.

- Love Greeting Cards is expanding and looking for more freelance material this year.

Other Product Lines: Greeting cards, posters, books ($100-300), posters ($200-500).
Tips: "There's a great demand for animal cards, flowers and computer art for greeting cards."

OATMEAL STUDIOS, P.O. Box 138W3, Rochester VT 05767. (802)767-3171. Creative Director: Helene Lehrer. Estab. 1979. 85% freelance written. Buys 200-300 greeting card lines/year. **Pays on acceptance.** Reports within 6 weeks. Current market list for #10 SASE.
Needs: Birthday, friendship, anniversary, get well cards, etc. Also Christmas, Hanukkah, Mother's Day, Father's Day, Easter, Valentine's Day, etc. Will review concepts. Humorous material (clever and *very* funny) year-round. "Humor, conversational in tone and format, sells best for us." Prefers unrhymed contemporary humor. Current pay schedule available with guidelines.
Other Product Lines: Notepads, stick-on notes.
Tips: "The greeting card market has become more competitive with a greater need for creative and original ideas. We are looking for writers who can communicate situations, thoughts, and relationships in a funny way and apply them to a birthday, get well, etc., greeting and we are willing to work with them in targeting our style. We will be looking for material that says something funny about life in a new way."

PANDA INK GREETING CARDS, P.O. Box 5129, West Hills CA 91308-5129. (818)340-8061. Fax: (818)883-6193. Contact: Ruth Ann Epstein. Estab. 1981. 10-20% freelance written. Receives 100 submissions/year; bought 50 ideas/samples last year. Submit seasonal/holiday material 6 months in advance. Reports in 1 month. Buys first rights. **Pays on acceptance**. Writer's guidelines for SASE.
Needs: Conventional, humorous, juvenile, soft line, Judaic, ethnic. Prefers rhymed verse ideas. Submit 10 ideas/batch.
Tips: "No risqué, sarcasm, insulting. Need Jewish/Yiddish language in most cases. We now have a metaphysical line of cards."

N **PARAMOUNT CARDS, INC.**, 400 Pine St., Pawtucket RI 02860. (401)726-0800. Contact: Editorial Department. Estab. 1906. 15% of material freelance written. Receives 5,000-10,000 submissions/year; bought 200 ideas/samples last year. Submit seasonal/holiday material 11 months in advance. Reports in 6 weeks. Buys all rights. **Pays on acceptance**. Market list issued one time only.
Needs: Conventional, humorous, inspirational, juvenile. Prefers either rhymed or unrhymed verse ideas. Submit 10-12 ideas/batch.

C.M. PAULA COMPANY, 6049 Hi-Tek Court, Mason OH 45040. Contact: Editorial Supervisor. Estab. 1958. 10% freelance written. "Looking for humor *only* from previously published social-expression writers. Seasoned writers should submit published writing samples. If there is a match in style, we will then contact writers with assignments." Reports in 2-3 months. Buys all rights. **Pays on acceptance**.
Product Lines: Key rings, stationery pads, magnets, dimensional statues and awards.
Tips: "Our needs are light humor. A writer can get a quick idea of the copy we use by looking over our store displays. Please note—we do not publish greeting cards."

PLUM GRAPHICS INC., P.O. Box 136, Prince Station, New York NY 10012. (212)337-0999. Contact: Michelle Ingram. President: Yvette Cohen. Estab. 1983. 100% freelance written. Bought 21 samples last year. Does not return samples unless accompanied by SASE. Reports in 4 months. Buys greeting card and stationery rights. Pays on publication. Guidelines sheet for SASE, "sent out about twice a year in conjunction with the development of new cards."
Needs: Humorous. "We don't want general submissions. We want them to relate to our next line." Prefers unrhymed verse. Greeting cards pay $40-50.
Tips: "Humor is always appreciated. We want short, to-the-point lines."

N **PORTAL PUBLICATIONS**, 201 Alameda Del Prado, Novato CA 94941. (415)924-5652. Attention: Editorial Department. Estab. 1954. 50% freelance written. Receives 200 submissions/year; bought 40 freelance ideas/samples last year. Reports in 3 months. Pays on publication. "Please send an example of your work so that we may keep it on file. If in the future, we have a need for writers for our greeting cards or other products we will contact you."
Needs: Conventional, humorous, informal, soft line, studio. Also copy for humorous and inspirational posters. Prefers unrhymed verse. Submit 12 ideas/batch.
Other Product Lines: Calendars, posters.
Tips: "Upscale, cute, soft, humorous cards for bookstores and college bookstores."

RESTAURANT GREETING CARDS, 8440 Runford Dr., Boynton Beach FL 33437-2723. (561)392-8985. Fax: (561)392-4174. E-mail: mito@emi.net. Contact: Michael Tomasso. Estab. 1975. 75% freelance written. Receives 100 submissions/year; bought 10 ideas/samples last year. Submit seasonal/holiday material 8 months in advance. Reports in 3 months. Pays on publication. Market list available on mailing list basis.
Needs: Humorous (must be restaurant related). Prefers unrhymed verse.
Tips: "Target market is restaurants. Humorous greeting, birthday, thank you, sells well. Pizza delivery, Chinese delivery, bagel, bakery, deli. Be sure not to offend ethnicity of card subject."

ROCKSHOTS, INC., 632 Broadway, New York NY 10012. (212)420-1400. Fax: (212)353-8756. Contact: Bob Vesce, editor. Estab. 1979. Buys 75 greeting card verse (or gag) lines/year. Reports in 2 months. Buys rights for greeting-card use. Writer's guidelines for SASE.
Needs: Humorous ("should be off-the-wall, as outrageous as possible, preferably for sophisticated buyer"); soft line; combination of sexy and humorous come-on type greeting ("sentimental is not our style"); and insult cards ("looking for cute insults"). No sentimental or conventional material. "Card gag can adopt a sentimental style, then take an ironic twist and end on an off-beat note." Submit no more than 10 card ideas/samples per batch. Send to Attention: Submissions. Pays $50/gag line. Prefers gag lines on 8×11 paper with name, address, and phone and social security numbers in right corner, or individually on 3×5 cards.
Tips: "Think of a concept that would normally be too outrageous to use, give it a cute and clever wording to make it drop-dead funny, and you will have commercialized a non-commercial message. It's always good to mix sex and humor. Our emphasis is definitely on the erotic. The trend is toward 'light' sexy humor, even cute sexy humor. 'Cute' has always sold cards, and it's a good word to think of even with the most sophisticated, crazy ideas. 80% of our audience is female. Remember that your gag line will be illustrated by a photographer, so try to think visually. If no visual is needed, the gag line *can* stand alone, but we generally prefer some visual representation. It is a very good idea to preview our cards at your local store if this is possible to give you a feeling of our style."

SECOND NATURE LTD., 10 Malton Rd., London W10 5UP England. 011-44-181-960-0212. Fax: (011-44-181-960-8700. E-mail: sales@secondnature.co.uk. Website: http://secondnature.co.uk. Editor: Rod Shrager. Estab. 1980. Submit seasonal material 18 months in advance. Reports in 6 weeks. **Pays on acceptance.** Market list is regularly revised.
Needs: Humorous, informal, inspirational and soft line. Rhymed and unrhymed verse OK.

N **SILVER VISIONS**, P.O. Box 415, Newton Highlands MA 02161. (617)244-9504. Contact: B. Kaufman, editor. Estab. 1981. Submit seasonal/holiday material 9-12 months in advance. Reports in 6 months. Pays on publication. Guidelines for SASE.
Needs: Humorous, humorous Jewish, contemporary occasion for photography line. "Copy must work with a photograph; in other words, submit copy that can be illustrated photographically." Send 10-16 card ideas/batch.

SUNRISE PUBLICATIONS, INC., P.O. Box 4699, Bloomington IN 47402-4699. (812)336-9900. E-mail: info@interart.com. Website: http://www.interart.com. Contact: Kevin Kleine, creative writer. Estab. 1974. 5% freelance written. Receives 600 submissions/year. Bought 15 ideas/samples last year. Reports in 3 months. Buys worldwide exclusive license in all commercial formats. **Pays on acceptance.** Writer's guidelines for #10 SASE. Market list issued one-time only. Submissions accepted via e-mail.
Needs: Contemporary, humorous, informal, soft line. No "off-color humor or lengthy poetry. Generally, we like short one- or two-line captions, sincere or clever. Our customers prefer this to lengthy rhymed verse. Longer copy is used but should be conversational. Submit ideas for birthday, get well, friendship, wedding, baby congrats, sympathy, thinking of you, anniversary, belated birthday, thank you, fun and love. We also have strong seasonal lines that use traditional, humorous and inspirational verses. These seasons include Christmas, Valentine's Day, Easter, Mother's Day, Father's Day, Graduation, Halloween and Thanksgiving." Payment varies.
Tips: "Think always of the sending situation and both the person buying the card and its intended recipient. Most of our traditional versing is done inhouse. We continue to look for exceptionally fresh and lively or emotionally compelling ideas. We avoid any put-downs or age slams, anything mean-spirited or lewd."

UNIQUE GREETINGS, INC., P.O. Box 5783, Manchester NH 03108. Estab. 1988. 10% freelance written. Receives 15 submissions/year. Submit seasonal/holiday material 1 year in advance. Reports in 6 weeks. Buys all rights. Writer's guidelines/market list for SASE. Market list regularly revised.
Needs: Watercolors, cute animals, flower scenes, etc. Prefers unrhymed verse. Submit 12 ideas/batch.
Tips: "General and Happy Birthday sell the best."

VAGABOND CREATIONS, INC., 2560 Lance Dr., Dayton OH 45409. (937)298-1124. Contact: George F. Stanley, Jr., editor. 10% freelance written. Bought 10-15 ideas/samples last year. Submit seasonal/holiday material 6 months in advance. Reports in 1 week. Buys all rights. Ideas sometimes copyrighted. **Pays on acceptance.** Writer's guidelines for #10 SASE. Market list issued one time only.
Needs: Cute, humorous greeting cards (illustrations and copy) often with animated animals or objects in people-situations with short, subtle tie-in message on inside page only. No poetry. Pays $15-25/card idea.

WARNER PRESS, PUBLISHERS, 1200 E. Fifth St., P.O. Box 2499, Anderson IN 46018-9988. Contact: Robin Fogle, communications editor. Estab. 1880. 50% freelance written. Reports in 2 months. Buys all rights. **Pays on acceptance.** Must send #10 SASE for guidelines before submitting.
Needs: Religious themes; sensitive prose and inspirational verse for Sunday bulletins. Pays $20-35. Also accepts ideas for coloring and activity books. Submit 5 pieces/batch with SASE. Include words "Freelance Approval" below return address on submission.

- Warner Press has restructured and no longer buys material for boxed cards, posters, or calendars. It still purchases longer poetry and devotional material for use on Sunday bulletins.

WEST GRAPHICS, 1117 California Dr., Burlingame CA 94010. (800)648-9378. Website: http://www.west-graphics.com. Contact: Production Department. Estab. 1980. 80% freelance written. Receives 20,000 submissions/year; bought 100 freelance ideas/samples last year. Reports in 6 weeks. Buys greeting card rights. Pays 30 days after publication. Writer's guidelines/market list for #10 SASE.
Needs: "We are looking for outrageous adult humor that is on the cutting edge." Prefers unrhymed verse. Submit 20-30 ideas/batch. Pays $60-100.
Tips: "West Graphics is an alternative greeting card company which offers a diversity of humor from 'off the wall' to 'tastefully tasteless'. Our goal is to publish cards that challenge the limits of taste and keep people laughing. The majority of our audience is women in their 30s and 40s, ideas should be targeted to birthday sentiment."

MARKETS THAT WERE listed in the 1998 edition of *Writer's Market* but do not appear this year are listed in the General Index with a notation explaining why they were omitted.

Contests & Awards

The contests and awards listed in this section are arranged by subject. Nonfiction writers can turn immediately to nonfiction awards listed alphabetically by the name of the contest or award. The same is true for fiction writers, poets, playwrights and screenwriters, journalists, children's writers and translators. You'll also find general book awards, miscellaneous awards, arts council and foundation fellowships, and multiple category contests.

New contests and awards are announced in various writer's publications nearly every day. However, many lose their funding or fold—and sponsoring magazines go out of business just as often. We have contacted the organizations whose contests and awards are listed here with the understanding that they are valid through 1998-1999. If you are using this section in 2000 or later, keep in mind that much of the contest information listed here will not be current. Requirements such as entry fees change, as do deadlines, addresses and contact names.

To make sure you have all the information you need about a particular contest, always send a self-addressed, stamped, business-sized envelope (#10 SASE) to the contact person in the listing before entering a contest. The listings in this section are brief, and many contests have lengthy, specific rules and requirements that we could not include in our limited space. Often a specific entry form must accompany your submission. A response with rules and guidelines will not only provide specific instructions, it will also confirm that the award is still being offered.

When you receive a set of guidelines, you will see that some contests are not for some writers. The writer's age, previous publication, geographic location and the length of the work are common matters of eligibility. Read the requirements carefully to ensure you don't enter a contest for which you are not qualified. You should also be aware that every year, more and more contests, especially those sponsored by "little" literary magazines, are charging entry fees.

Contest and award competition is very strong. While a literary magazine may publish ten short stories in an issue, only one will win the prize in a contest. Give yourself the best chance of winning by sending only your best work. There is always a percentage of manuscripts cast off immediately as unpolished, amateurish or wholly unsuitable for the competition.

To avoid first-round rejection, make certain that you and your work qualify in every way for the award. Some contests are more specific than others. There are many contests and awards for a "best poem," but some award only the best lyric poem, sonnet or haiku.

Winning a contest or award can launch a successful writing career. Take a professional approach by doing a little extra research. Find out who the previous winner of the award was by investing in a sample copy of the magazine in which the prize-winning article, poem or short story appeared. Attend the staged reading of an award-winning play. Your extra effort will be to your advantage in competing with writers who simply submit blindly.

If a contest or award requires nomination by your publisher, ask your publisher to nominate you. Many welcome the opportunity to promote a work (beyond their own, conventional means). Just be sure the publisher has plenty of time before the deadline to nominate your work.

Further information on funding for writers is available at most large public libraries. See the *Annual Register of Grant Support* (National Register Publishing Co., a division of Reed-Elsevier, *Foundations and Grants to Individuals* (Foundation Center, 79 Fifth Ave., New York NY 10003) and *Grants and Awards Available to American Writers* (PEN American Center, 568 Broadway, New York NY 10012). For more listings of contests and awards for fiction writers, see *Novel & Short Story Writer's Market* (Writer's Digest Books). *Poet's Market* (Writer's Digest Books) lists contests and awards available to poets. *Children's Writer's & Illustrator's Market* (Writer's

Digest Books) has a section of contests and awards, as well. Two more good sources for literary contests are *Poets & Writers* (72 Spring St., New York NY 10012), and the *Associated Writing Programs Newsletter* (Old Dominion University, Norfolk VA 23529). Journalists should look into the annual Journalism Awards Issue of *Editor & Publisher* magazine (11 W. 19th St., New York NY 10011), published in the last week of December. Playwrights should be aware of the newsletter put out by The Dramatists Guild, (234 W. 44th St., New York NY 10036).

Information on contests and awards listed in the previous edition of *Writer's Market* but not included in this edition can be found in the General Index.

General

AMERICAN BOOKSELLERS BOOK OF THE YEAR (ABBY), American Booksellers Association, 828 S. Broadway, Tarrytown NY 10591. (914)591-2665. Fax: (914)591-2720. E-mail: jperlst@bookweb.org. Website: http://www.-bookweb.org. Award Director: Jill Perlstein. Offered annually to previously published adult and children's titles that booksellers (members of the ABA) most enjoyed handselling (recommending) to their customers. Nominations and winners are selected by ABA members. Awards are presented at the annual ABA convention and BookExpo America. Prizes: $5,000 to each author (adult and children's), an engraved Tiffany glass prism; four books in each category are awarded with the title "Honor Book."

BANTA AWARD, Wisconsin Library Association, % Literary Awards Comm., 5250 E. Terrace Dr., Suite A-1, Madison WI 53718-8345. (608)245-3640. Website: http://www.bratshb.uwc.edu/nwla/. Contact: Chair, Literary Award Committee. Offered annually to books published during the year preceding the award. The Literary Awards Committee reviews all works by Wisconsin authors that are not edited, revised editions, textbooks or written in foreign languages. Review copies or notification of books, along with verification of the author's ties to Wisconsin, may be submitted to the Committee by the publisher or author. Deadline: March of calendar year following publication. Prize: $500, a plaque given by the Banta Corporation Foundation, and presentation at the Annual Conference of the Wisconsin Library Association between late October and early November. Only open to writers born, raised, or currently living in the state.

BUNTING FELLOWSHIP, Radcliffe College, 34 Concord Ave., Cambridge MA 02138. (617)495-8212. Fax:(617)495-8136. E-mail: bunting_fellowships@radcliffe.harvard.edu. or soares@radmail.harvard.edit. Website: http://www.radcliffe.edu/bunting. Contact: Paula Soares, fellowships coordinator. "To support women of exceptional promise and demonstrated accomplishment who wish to pursue independent work in academic and professional fields and in the creative arts. Projects with public policy applications are especially encouraged. Applications will be judged on the quality and significance of the proposed project, the applicant's record of accomplishment, and on the difference the fellowship might make in advancing the applicant's career." Deadline varies. Call or write for application. Award is $36,500 stipend, plus office space and access to most resources at Harvard University and Radcliffe College. "The competition for writers is very high. We discourage writers who have not had publications or demonstrated a high level of accomplishment."

DWAA ANNUAL WRITING COMPETITION, Dog Writers Association of America, 3809 Plaza Dr., No. 107-309 Oceanside CA 92056. (760)630-3828. Contest Director: Liz Palika. Entries must have appeared in print September 1-August 31. "Various categories and special awards are designed to reward excellence annually in the ever-growing field of dog writing." Deadline: September 1. Guidelines and entry forms available for SASE. Charges $12/submission, plus $1/each special award consideration. "The award for the various regular categories is the Maxwell Medallion. In addition, we offer several corporate-sponsored special awards consisting of cash grants and certificates, plaques or trophies." The authors retain all rights to their work, yet their signatures on the entry forms grant the association the right to reprint the material for publicity and anthology purposes.

EDITORS' BOOK AWARD, Pushcart Press, P.O. Box 380, Wainscott NY 11975. (516)324-9300. President: Bill Henderson. Unpublished books. Deadline: October 15. "All manuscripts must be nominated by an editor in a publishing house."

N **MARGARET A. EDWARDS AWARD**, Young Adult Library Services Association, a division of the American Library Association, 50 E. Huron St., Chicago IL 60611. Fax: (312)664-7459. E-mail: yalsa@ala.org. Website: http://www.ala.org\yalsa. Contact: Linda Waddle, deputy executive director, Young Adult Library Association. Offered annually to "an author whose book or books have provided young adults with a window through which they can view their world and which will help them to grow and to understand themselves and their role in society." Author is recognized for books published at least 5 years before the award year. Guidelines for SASE. Prize: Citation and $1,000.

FRIENDS OF THE DALLAS PUBLIC LIBRARY AWARD, The Texas Institute of Letters, P.O. Box 298300, Fort Worth TX 76129. (Must be marked Attn: TCU Press). (817)257-7822. Fax: (817)257-5075. Website: http://wwwprs.tcu.edu/prs/TIL. Contact: Judy Alter, award director. Offered annually for submissions published January 1-December 31 of previous year to recognize the writer of the book making the most important contribution to knowledge. Deadline: January 4. Guidelines for SASE. Prize: $1,000. Writer must have been born in Texas, have lived in the state at least 2 consecutive years at some time, or the subject matter of the book should be associated with the state.

HAWAI'I AWARD FOR LITERATURE, State Foundation on Culture and the Arts, 44 Merchant St., Honolulu HI 96813. (808)586-0306. Fax: (808)586-0308. E-mail: sfca@sfca.state.hi.us. Website: http://www.state.hi.us/sfca. Contest/Award Director: Hawai'i Literary Arts Council (Box 11213, Honolulu HI 96828-0213). "The annual award honors the lifetime achievement of a writer whose work is important to Hawai'i and/or Hawai'i's people." Deadline: November. Nominations are a public process; inquiries should be directed to the Hawai'i Literary Arts Council at address listed. Prize: a governor's reception and cash award. "Cumulative work is considered. Self nominations are allowed, but not usual. Fiction, poetry, drama, certain types of nonfiction, screenwriting and song lyrics are considered. The award is not intended to recognize conventional academic writing and reportage, nor is it intended to recognize more commercial types of writing, e.g., advertising copy, tourist guides, and how-to manuals."

N **MINNESOTA VOICES PROJECT COMPETITION**, New Rivers Press, 420 N. Fifth St., #910, Minneapolis MN 55401. (612)339-7114. E-mail: newrivpr@mtn.org. Website: http://www.mtn.org/~newrivpr. Contact: C.W. Truesdale, editor/publisher. Offered annually for new and emerging writers of poetry, prose, essays, and memoirs (as well as other forms of creative prose) from Wisconsin, Minnesota, Iowa and the Dakotas, to be published in book form for the first time. Deadline: April 1. Guidelines for SASE.

MISSISSIPPI REVIEW PRIZE, Mississippi Review, U.S.M. Box 5144, Hattiesburg MS 39406. (601)266-4321. Fax: (601)266-5757. E-mail: fb@netdoor.com. Contact: Frederick Barthelme, contest director. Offered annually for unpublished literary, short fiction and poetry. Charges $10/story, 2 stories maximum. Maximum 6,500 words (25 pages). $5/poem, limit 4 entries/author ($20). Prize: $750 each for fiction and poetry. Mississippi Review keeps first rights to publication.

N **NEW WRITING AWARD**, New Writing, Box 1812, Amherst NY 14226-7812. E-mail: newwriting@aol.com. Website: http://members.aol.com/newwriting/. Contact: Sam Meade. Offered annually for unpublished work "to award the best of *new* writing. We accept short stories, poems, plays, novels, essays, films and emerging forms. All entries are considered for the award based on originality." Charges $10 + 10¢ per page reading fee for first entry; $5 + 10¢ per page per additional entry—no limit. Guidelines and form for SASE. Prize: Monetary award (up to $3,000 in cash and prizes) and possible publication. Judged by editors. "We are looking for new, interesting or experimental work."

PEN CENTER WEST LITERARY AWARDS, PEN Center West, 672 S. Lafayette Park Place, #41, Los Angeles CA 90057. (213)365-8500. Fax: (213)365-9616. E-mail: rit2writ@ix.netcom.com. Contact: Rachel J. Hall, administrative coordinator. Estab. 1952. Awards and $500 cash prizes offered for work published in previous calendar year. Deadline: 4 copies must be received by December 31. Open to writers living west of the Mississippi River. Award categories: fiction, nonfiction, poetry, drama, children's literature, screenplay, teleplay, journalism, criticism, translation.

PULITZER PRIZES, The Pulitzer Prize Board, 709 Journalism, Columbia University, New York NY 10027. (212)854-3841. Website: http://www.pulitzer.org. Contact: Seymour Topping, administrator. Estab. 1917. Journalism in US newspapers (published daily or weekly), and in letters, drama and music by Americans. Deadline: February 1 (journalism); March 1 (music and drama); July 1 and November 1 (letters).

ROCKY MOUNTAIN ARTISTS' BOOK COMPETITION, Hemingway Western Studies Center, Boise State University, 1910 University Dr., Boise ID 83725. (208)385-1999. Fax: (208)385-4373. E-mail: ttrusky@bsu.idbsu.edu. Website: http://www.idbsu.edu/hemingway.com. Contest Director: Tom Trusky. Offered annually "to publish multiple edition artist's books of special interest to Rocky Mountain readers. Topics must be public issues (race, gender, environment, etc.). Authors may hail from Topeka or Ulan Bator, but their books must initially have regional appeal." Deadline: September 1-December 1. Guidelines for SASE. Prize: $500, publication, standard royalties. First rights to Hemingway Center. Open to any writer/artist.

THE CARL SANDBURG LITERARY AWARDS, The Friends of the Chicago Public Library, 400 S. State St., 10S-7, Chicago IL 60605. (312)747-4907. Fax: (312)747-4077. E-mail: friendscpl@aol.com. Contact: Tina M. Garepis, program manager. Estab. 1979. Chicago (and metropolitan area) writers of published fiction, nonfiction, poetry and children's literature. Book must be published between June 1, 1997 and May 31, 1998. Deadline for submission: July 1. Charges $25 fee.

TOWSON UNIVERSITY PRIZE FOR LITERATURE, College of Liberal Arts, Towson University, Towson MD 21252. (410)830-2128. Award Director: Dean, College of Liberal Arts. Contact: Dan. L. Jones, dean. Estab. 1979. Book or book-length ms that has been accepted for publication, written by a Maryland author of no more than 40 years of age. Deadline: May 15. Guideline for SASE. Prize: $1,000.

WHITING WRITERS' AWARDS, Mrs. Giles Whiting Foundation, 1133 Avenue of the Americas, 22nd fl., New York NY 10036. Contact: Barbara K. Bristol, director. "The Foundation gives annually $30,000 each to up to ten writers of poetry, fiction, nonfiction and plays. The awards place special emphasis on exceptionally promising emerging talent." Direct applications and informal nominations are not accepted by the Foundation.

WORLD FANTASY AWARDS ASSOCIATION, P.O. Box 1666, Lynnwood, WA 98046. Website: http://farrsite.com/wfc/wfc6.htm. President: Peter Dennis Pautz. Estab. 1975. Previously published work recommended by previous convention attendees in several categories, including life achievement, novel, novella, short story, anthology, collection, artist, special award-pro and special award non-pro. Deadline: July 1. Works are recommended by attendees of current and previous 2 years' conventions, and a panel of judges. Winners determined by vote of panel.

Nonfiction

ABC-CLIO AMERICA: HISTORY AND LIFE AWARD, Organization of American Historians. (812)855-9852. Fax: (812)855-0696. E-mail: kana@oah.indiana.edu. Website: http://www.indiana.edu/~oah. Contact: Award and Prize Committee Coordinator. Offered every two years for a previously published article to recognize and encourage scholarship in American history in the journal literature advancing new perspectives on accepted interpretations or previously unconsidered topics. Deadline: November 15 of even-numbered years. Prize: $750 and certificate. Before submitting a nomination, a listing of current committee members and details about individual prizes must be obtained by sending SASE to: Award and Prize Committee Coordinator, Organization of American Historians, 112 N.Bryan St. Bloomington IN 47408-4199.

N **HERBERT BAXTER ADAMS PRIZE**, American Historical Association, 400 A St. SE, Washington DC 20003. Fax: (202)544-8307. Contact: Book Prize Coordinator. Offered annually for a US or Canadian author's first substantial book in the field of European history. In odd years, books focusing on topics after 1815 are eligible. In even years, books focusing on topics prior to 1815 are eligible. Guidelines for #10 SASE. Prize: amount varies. Deadline: May 15.

AIP SCIENCE WRITING AWARDS IN PHYSICS & ASTRONOMY, American Institute of Physics, One Physics Ellipse, College Park MD 20740. (301)209-3090. Fax: (301)209-0846. E-mail: jwrather@aip.acp.org. Website: http://www.aip.org. Contact: Joan Wrather, manager Public Information Division. Offered annually for previously published work "to recognize and stimulate distinguished writing that improves the general public's understanding and appreciation of physics and astronomy." Deadlines: articles, booklets or books by professional journalists published between January 1-December 31 due February 6; articles, booklets or books intended for children up to 15 years published between July 1-June 30 due July 24; articles, booklets or books by physicists or astronomers published between May 1-April 30 due May 19. Guidelines for SASE. Prize: $3,000, inscribed Windsor chair, certificate and certificate to publisher.

N **ASCAP-DEEMS TAYLOR AWARD**, American Society of Composers, Authors & Publishers, One Lincoln Plaza, New York NY 10023. (212)621-6323. Director: Esther San Saurus. Offered annually for previously published work in the preceding year to authors and journalists having books and articles on the subject of music. Subject matter may be biographical or critical, repertorial or historical—any form of nonfiction prose about music and/or its creators—not an instructional textbook, how-to guide or work of fiction. Reprints or translations of works previously published outside the US are eligible. Program notes or lincr notes are eligible. Deadline: April 30. Guidelines for SASE. Prize: $500 for the best book; $250 for the best newspaper, journal or magazine article; and a plaque to author or journalist and respective publisher.

N **MRS. SIMON BARUCH UNIVERSITY AWARD**, United Daughters of the Confederacy, 328 N. Boulevard, Richmond VA 23220-4057. (804)355-1636. Fax: (804)353-1396. Offered biannially in even-numbered years for unpublished work for the purpose of encouraging research in Southern history, the United Daughters of the Confederacy offers as a grant-aid of publication the Mrs. Simon Baruch University Award of $2,000. Deadline: May 1. Authors and publishers interested in the Baruch Award contest should ask for a copy of these rules. All inquiries should be addressed to the Chairman of the Mrs. Simon Baruch University Award Committee at the above address. Award: $2,000 and $500 author's award. Invitation to participate in the contest is extended (1) to anyone who has received a Master's, Doctoral, or other advanced degree within the past fifteen years, from a university in the United States; and (2) to any graduate student whose thesis or dissertation has been accepted by such an institution. Manuscripts must be accompanied by a statement from the registrar giving dates of attendance, and by full biographical data together with passport photograph of the authors.

N **GEORGE LOUIS BEER PRIZE**, American Historical Association, 400 A St. SE, Washington DC 20003. Fax: (202)544-8307. Contact: Book Prize Coordinator. Offered annually for the best work on European international history since 1895 that is submitted by a scholar who is a United States citizen. Prize: amount varies. Deadline: May 15.

RAY ALLEN BILLINGTON PRIZE, Organization of American Historians. (812)855-9852. Fax: (812)855-0696. Contact: Award and Prize Committee Coordinator. E-mail: kara@oah.indiana.edu. Website: http://www.indiana.edu/

~oah. Offered every two years for the best book in American frontier history, defined broadly so as to include the pioneer periods of all geographical areas and comparisons between American frontiers and others. Deadline: October 1 of even-numbered years. Prize: $1,000, certificate and medal. Before submitting a nomination, a listing of current committee members and details about individual prizes must be obtained by sending SASE to: Award and Prize Committee Coordinator, Organization of American Historians, 112 N. Bryan St., Bloomington IN 47408-4199.

N **THE PAUL BIRDSALL PRIZE IN EUROPEAN MILITARY & STRATEGIC HISTORY**, American Historical Association, 400 A. St. SE, Washington DC 20003. Fax: (202)544-8307. Contact: Book Prize Coordinator. Offered biannually for a major work in European military and strategic history. Guidelines for SASE. Prize: amount varies. Deadline: May 15. Next award year is 2000.

N **JAMES HENRY BREASTED PRIZE**, American Historical Association, 400 A St. SE, Washington DC 20003. Fax: (202)544-8307. Contact: Book Prize Coordinator. Offered annually in a 4-year chronological cycle for an outstanding book in any field of history prior to 1000 A.D. Prize: amount varies. Deadline: May 15. In 1999, books in African, North American and Latin American history will be eligible.

N **BRITISH COUNCIL PRIZE**, North American Conference on British Studies, Dept. of History, Reed College, Portland OR 97202-8199. (503)771-1112 ext. 7334. Fax: (503)777-7769. E-mail: dsacks@reed.edu. Contact: David Harris Sacks, executive secretary. Offered annually for best books in any field of British Studies after publication by a North American in previous year. Previously published submissions. Deadline: May 1. Guidelines for SASE. Prize: $1,000. Open to American or Canadian writers.

THE BROSS PRIZE, Lake Forest College, 555 N. Sheridan, Lake Forest IL 60045. (847)735-5169. Fax: (847)735-6192. Contact: Professor Ron Miller. Offered every 10 years for unpublished work "to award the best book or treatise on the relation between any discipline or topic of investigation and the Christian religion." Deadline: September 1, 2000. Guidelines for SASE. Prize: Award varies depending on interest earned. Manuscripts awarded prizes become property of the college. Open to any writer.

CANADIAN LIBRARY ASSOCIATION STUDENT ARTICLE CONTEST, Canadian Library Association, 200 Elgin St., Suite 602, Ottawa, Ontario K2P 1L5 Canada. (613)232-9625, ext. 318. Fax: (613)563-9895. Contest Director: Brenda Shields. Offered annually to "unpublished articles discussing, analyzing or evaluating timely issues in librarianship or information science." Deadline: March 15. Guidelines for SASE. Prizes: 1st-$150, publication in *Feliciter*, trip to CLA's annual conference; Runners-Up: $75 choice of CLA publications. Judged by a CLA panel. "Open to all students registered in or recently graduated from a Canadian library school, a library techniques program or faculty of education library program. Submissions may be in English or French."

MORTON N. COHEN AWARD, Modern Language Association of America, 10 Astor Place, New York NY 10003-6981. (212)614-6406. Fax: (212)533-0680. E-mail: awards@mla.org. Website: http://www.mla.org. Contact: Richard Brod. Estab. 1989. Awarded in odd-numbered years for a previously published distinguished edition of letters. At least 1 volume of the edition must have been published during the previous 2 years. Prize: $1,000. Guidelines for #10 SASE. Deadline: May 1.

THE NATHAN COHEN AWARD FOR EXCELLENCE IN THEATRE CRITICISM, The Canadian Theatre Critics Association, 250 Dundas St. W., Suite 700, Toronto, Ontario M5T 2Z5 Canada. (416)537-0647. Fax: (416)537-2075. E-mail: artemis@adeo.comm. Contact: Jeniva Berger. Offered annually to previously published theater criticism published between January 1-December 31. "The national award is presented annually to help recognize high critical standards and to give encouragement to those working professionally in the field of theater criticism. There are two categories: Long Review for reviews, profiles and other theatrical features of 1,000 words to a maximum of 4,000 words; and Short Review for reviews of up to 1,000 words." Deadline: April 1. Guidelines for SASE. Charges $10 fee. Prize: $500 and a framed certificate. "There is a different judge each year. Our judges have been renowned Canadian theater people—writers such as Timothy Findley, playwrights such as Sharon Pollock, and performers such as R.H. Thomson." Entrants must be Canadian or Canadian residents.

CARR P. COLLINS AWARD, The Texas Institute of Letters, P.O. Box 298300, Fort Worth TX 76129. (817)921-7822. Fax: (817)257-5075. E-mail: jalter@gamma.is.tcu.edu. Website: http://www.gamma.is.tcu.edu/prs/til. Contact: Judy Alter. Offered annually for work published January 1-December 31 of the previous year to recognize the best nonfiction book by a writer who was born in Texas or who has lived in the state for at least 2 consecutive years at 1 point or a writer whose work has some notable connection with Texas. Deadline: January 2. Guidelines for SASE. Prize: $5,000.

COLORADO PRIZE, Colorado Review/Center for Literary Publishing, Department of English, Colorado State University, Ft. Collins CO 80523. (970)491-5449. E-mail: creview@vines.colostate.edu. Website: http://www.colostate.edu/Depts/English/pubs/colrev/colrev.htm. General Editor: David Milofsky. Offered annually to an unpublished collection. Deadline: January 11. Guidelines for SASE. Charges $20 fee. Prize: $1,500 and publication of book.

COMPETITION FOR WRITERS OF B.C. (BRITISH COLUMBIA) HISTORY, B.C. Historical Federation, 7953 Rosewood St., Burnaby, British Columbia V5E 2H4 Canada. (604)522-2062. Contest Director: Mrs. Pixie McGeachie. Offered annually to books published during contest year "to promote the history of British Columbia." Book must contain any facet of B.C. history. Submit 2 copies to the contest and they become the property of the B.C. Historical Federation.Deadline: December 31. Guidelines for SASE. Prizes: 1st-The Lieutenant Governor's Medal for Historical Writing and $300, 2nd-$200, 3rd-$100. Open to any writer.

AVERY O. CRAVEN AWARD, Organization of American Historians. (812)855-9852. Fax: (812)855 0696. E-mail: kara@oah.indiana.edu. Website: http://www.indiana.edu/~oah. Contact: Award and Prize Committee Coordinator. Offered annually for the most original book on the coming of the Civil War, the Civil War years, or the Era of Reconstruction, with the exception of works of purely military history. Deadline: October 1. Prize: $500 and certificate. Before submitting a nomination, a listing of current committee members and details about individual prizes must be obtained by sending SASE to: Award and Prize Committee Coordinator, Organization of American Historians, 112 N. Bryan St., Bloomington IN 47408-4199.

MERLE CURTI AWARDS IN AMERICAN SOCIAL AND INTELLECTUAL HISTORY, Organization of American Historians. (812)855-9852. Fax: (812)855-0696. E-mail: kara@oah.indiana.edu. Website: http://www.indiana.edu/~oah. Contact: Award and Prize Committee Coordinator. Offered annually for books in the field of American social history (even-numbered years) and intellectual history (odd-numbered years). Deadline: October 1. Prize: $1,000, certificate and medal. Before submitting a nomination, a listing of current committee members and details about individual prizes must be obtained by sending SASE to: Award and Prize Committee Coordinator, Organization of American Historians, 112 N. Bryan St., Bloomington IN 47408-4199.

N **DE LA TORRE BUENO PRIZE**, Dance Perspectives Foundation, 150 Claremont Ave., Ste. 2C., New York NY 10027-4672. (212)662-6515. Contact: Donald F. McDouggh. Estab. 1973. Open to writers or their publishers who have published an original book of dance scholarship within the previous year. Deadline: February 15.

N **THE PREMIO DEL REY PRIZE**, American Historical Association, 400 A St. SE, Washington DC 20003. Fax: (202)544-8307. Contact: Book Prize Coordinator. Offered biannually for a distinguished book in English in the field of early Spanish and Hispanic history and culture (prior to 1516). Guidelines for SASE. Prize: amount varies. Deadline: May 15. Next award year is 2000.

DEXTER PRIZE, Society for the History of Technology, History Dept., Auburn University, 310 Thach Hall, Auburn AL 36849. (334)844-6645. Fax: (334)844-6673. Contact: Society Secretary. Estab. 1968. For work published in the previous 3 years: for 1998—1995 to 97. "Award given to the best book in the history of technology." Deadline: April 15. Guidelines for SASE. Prize: $2,000 and a plaque from the Dexter Chemical Company.

ANNIE DILLARD AWARD IN NONFICTION, The Bellingham Review, M.S. 9053, Western Washington University, Bellingham WA 98225. Website: http://www.wwu.edu/~bhreview/. Contact: Mr. Robin Hemley. Unpublished essay on any subject and in any style. Submissions from January 2-March 1. Guidelines and entry fees for SASE. Prize: 1st-$500; 2nd-$250; 3rd-$100, plus publication and copies.

N **GORDON W. DILLON/RICHARD C. PETERSON MEMORIAL ESSAY PRIZE**, American Orchid Society, Inc., 6000 S. Olive Ave., West Palm Beach FL 33405-9974. (561)585-8666. Fax: (561)585-0654. E-mail: TheAOS@compuserve.com. Website: http://www.pathfinder.com/vg/Gardens/AOS. Contact: Jane Mengel. Estab. 1985. "An annual contest open to all writers. The theme is announced each May in the *Orchids* magazine. All themes deal with aspect of orchids, such as repotting, growing, hybridizing, etc. Unpublished submissions only." Themes in past years have included Orchid Culture, Orchids in Nature and Orchids in Use. Deadline: November 30. Guidelines for SASE. Prize: $1,000 and certificate. Winning entry published in the May issue of *Orchids* magazine. Buys one-time rights.

N **JOHN H. DUNNING PRIZE IN AMERICAN HISTORY**, American Historical Association, 400 A St. SE, Washington DC 20003. Fax: (202)544-8307. Contact: Book Prize Coordinator. Offered biannually in odd-numbered years for any topic in US history; must be the author's first or second book. Prize: amount varies. Deadline: May 15.

EDUCATOR'S AWARD, The Delta Kappa Gamma Society, P.O. Box 1589, Austin TX 78767. (512)478-5748. Fax: (512)478-3961. E-mail: societyd@deltakappagamma.org. Executive Coordinator: Dr. Theresa Fechek. Offered annually for quality fiction published January-December of previous year. This award recognizes educational research and writings of women authors whose book may influence the direction of thought and action necessary to meet the needs to today's complex society. Deadline: February 1. Guidelines for SASE. Prize: $1,500. The book must be written by one woman or by two women who are citizens of any country in which The Delta Kappa Gamma Society International is organized: Canada, Costa Rica, El Salvador, Finland, Germany, Great Britain, Guatemala, Iceland, Mexico, The Netherlands, Norway, Puerto Rico, Sweden, United States.

EVERETT E. EDWARDS AWARD, Agricultural History Center for Agricultural History, Iowa State University, 618 Ross Hall, Ames IA 50011-1202. (515)294-1596. Fax: (515)294-6390. E-mail: rdhurt@iastate.edu. Website: http://

www.iastate.edu/~history_info/aghistory.htm. Contact: Douglas Hurt, Dept. of History, Iowa State University, Ames, Iowa 50011. Offered annually for best article on any aspect of agricultural and rural history, broadly interpreted, submitted by a graduate student. Deadline: December 31. Guidelines for SASE. Prize: Monetary award to the author and publication in the journal. Award made at OAH annual meeting. Judged by committees composed of members of the Agricultural History Society. Open to submission by any graduate student.

WILFRED EGGLESTON AWARD FOR NONFICTION, Writers Guild of Alberta, 11759 Great Rd., Edmonton Alberta T5M 3K6 Canada. (403)422-8174. Fax: (403)422-2663. E-mail: writers@compusmart.ab.ca. Assistant Director: Darlene Diver. Nonfiction book published in current year. Must be an Alberta author.

THE ALFRED EINSTEIN AWARD, American Musicological Society, 201 S. 34th St., Philadelphia PA 19104. (215)898-8698. Fax: (216)573-3673. Offered annually for material previously published from June 1-May 31 of the previous year. "The Alfred Einstein Award will honor each year a musicological article of exceptional merit by a scholar in the early stages of his or her career who is a citizen or permanent resident of Canada or the U.S." Deadline: June 1. No entry form. "The committee will entertain nomination from any individual, including eligible authors, who are encouraged to nominate their own articles. Nominations should include: author's name, title of article, name and year of periodical where published." Prize: $400 and certificate. "The article must have been published during the preceding calendar year, in any country and in any language. The article must be written by a scholar in the early stages of his or her career, 'early stages' typically indicated by time from completion of Ph.D. degree or academic appointment at non-tenured level."

RALPH WALDO EMERSON AWARD, Phi Beta Kappa Society, 1811 Q St., N.W., Washington DC 20009. (202)265-3808. Fax: (202)986-1601. E-mail: lsurles@pbk.org. Contact: Linda D. Surles, award director. Offered annually for scholarly studies of the intellectual and cultural condition of man. Submissions are required to be published between May 1, 1997 and April 30, 1998. Deadline: April 30. Guidelines for SASE. Prize: $2,500. Judged by the Committee for the Ralph Waldo Emerson Award (seven members).

N **DAVID W. AND BEATRICE C. EVANS BIOGRAPHY AWARD**, Mountain West Center for Regional Studies, Utah State University, 0735 University Blvd., Logan UT 84322-0735. (435)797-3630. Fax: (435)797-3899. E-mail: jreilly@cc.usu.edu. Contact: Clyde A. Milner II or Jane Reilly. Estab. 1983. Offered to encourage the writing of biography about people who have played a role in Mormon Country. (Not the religion, the country: Intermountain West with parts of Southwestern Canada and Northwestern Mexico.) Deadline: December 1. Prize: in excess of $5,000. Publishers or author may nominate book. Criteria for consideration: Work must be a biography or autobiography on "Mormon Country"; must be submitted for consideration for publication year's award; new editions or reprints are not eligible; mss are accepted. Submit 6 copies.

N **JOHN K. FAIRBANK PRIZE IN EAST ASIAN HISTORY**, American Historical Association, 400 A St. SE, Washington DC 20003. Fax: (202)544-8307. Contact: Book Prize Coordinator. Offered annually for an outstanding book on the history of China proper, Vietnam, Chinese central Asia, Mongolia, Manchuria, Korea or Japan since the year 1800. Guidelines for #10 SASE. Prize: amount varies. Deadline: May 15.

N **HERBERT FEIS AWARD FOR NONACADEMICALLY-AFFILIATED HISTORIANS**, American Historical Association, 400 A St. SE, Washington DC 20003. Contact: Book Prize Coordinator. Estab. 1984. Offered annually for the best book, article/articles, or policy paper by an historian not affiliated with academe. Prize: amount varies. Funded by a grant from the Rockefeller Foundation. Deadline: May 15.

FOREIGN LANGUAGE BOOK AND FOREIGN LANGUAGE ARTICLE PRIZES, Organization of American Historians. (812)855-9852. Fax: (812)855-0696. E-mail: kara@oah.indiana.edu. Website: http://www.indiana.edu/~oah. Contact: Award and Prize Committee Coordinator. Offered biannually for the best book and annually for the best article on American history that have been published in languages other than English. Eligible books or articles should be concerned with the past (recent or distant) or with issues of continuity and change. Entries should also be concerned with events or processes that began, developed, or ended in what is now the United States. Deadline: May 1. Prize: English translation and publication. Winning article will be printed in the *Journal of American History* and its author awarded a certificate and a $500 subvention for refining the article's English translation; winning book will receive $1,000 toward translation for publication in English, and the author will receive a certificate. Before submitting a nomination, a listing of current committee members and details about individual prizes must be obtained by sending SASE to: Award and Prize Committee Coordinator, Organization of American Historians, 112 N. Bryan St., Bloomington IN 47408-4199.

GEORGE FREEDLEY MEMORIAL AWARD, Theatre Library Association, Benjamin Rosenthal Library, Queens College, C.U.N.Y., 65-30 Kissena Blvd., Flushing NY 11367. (718)997-3799. Fax: (718)997-3753. E-mail: rlwqc@cunyvm.cuny.edu. Contact: Richard Wall, Book Awards Committee Chair. Estab. 1968. Book published in the United States within the previous calendar year on a subject related to live theatrical performance (including cabaret, circus, pantomime, puppetry, vaudeville, etc.). Eligible books may include biography, history, theory, criticism, reference or related fields. Prize: $250 and certificate to the winner; $100 and certificate for Honorable Mention. Submissions and deadline:

Nominated books are requested from publishers; one copy should be received by each of three award jurors as well as the Chairperson by February 15 of the year following eligibility.

THE CHRISTIAN GAUSS AWARD, The Phi Beta Kappa Society, 1811 Q St. NW, Washington DC 20009-1696. (202)265-3808. Fax: (202)986-1601. E-mail: lsurles@pbk.org. Contact: Administrator, Phi Beta Kappa Book Awards. Estab. 1950. Works of literary criticism or scholarship published in the US during the 12-month period preceding the entry deadline, and submitted by the publisher. Books must have been published May 1, 1997-April 30, 1998. Deadline: April 30. Author must be a US citizen or resident. Prize: $2,500.

LIONEL GELBER PRIZE, Lionel Gelber Foundation, 112 Braemore Gardens, Toronto Ontario M6G 2C8 Canada. (416)652-1947 or (416)656-3722. Fax: (416)658-5205. E-mail: meisner@interlog.com. Prize Manager: Susan Meisner. The largest juried prize of its kind, the international Lionel Gelber Prize is awarded annually in Canada to the author of the year's most outstanding work of nonfiction in the field of international relations. Books must be published in English or English translation between September 1, 1997 and August 31. Deadline: May 31. Guidelines for SASE; however, the publisher must submit the title on behalf of the author. Prize: $50,000 (Canadian funds).

N **LEO GERSHOY AWARD**, American Historical Association, 400 A St. SE, Washington DC 20003. Fax: (202)544-8307. Contact: Book Prize Coordinator. Offered annually to the author of the most outstanding work in English on any aspect of the field of 17th and 18th-century Western European history. Prize: amount varies. Deadline: May 15.

LOUIS GOTTSCHALK PRIZE, American Society for 18th Century Studies, Wake Forest University, P.O. Box 7867, Winston-Salem NC 27109. (336)727-4694. Fax: (336)727-4697. E-mail: asecs@wfu.edu. Website: http://www.direct.press.jhu.edu/Associations/Asecs. Executive Secretary: Byron R. Wells. Offered annually for previously published (between January 1997 and December 1998) work. Purpose is to award outstanding historical or critical study on the 18th century. Deadline: November 15, 1998. Guidelines and form available for SASE. Publisher must send 5 copies for contest. Prize: $1,000 and certificate from ASECS. Winners must be society members ($25-65 dues).

N **JOAN KELLY MEMORIAL PRIZE IN WOMEN'S HISTORY**, American Historical Association, 400 A St. SE, Washington DC 20003. Fax: (202)544-8307. Contact: Book Prize Coordinator. Estab. 1984. Offered annually for the best work in women's history and/or feminist theory. Prize: amount varies. Deadline: May 15.

THE OTTO KENKELDEY AWARD, American Musicological Society, 201 S. 34th St., Philadelphia PA 19104. (215)898-8698. Fax: (215)573-3673. E-mail: ams@sas.upenn.edu. Website: http://www.musdra.ucdavis.edu/Documents/AMS/AMS.html. Offered annually for material published during the previous year. "The Otto Kenkeldey Award will honor each year the work of musicological scholarship deemed to be the most distinguished of those published during the previous year in any language in any country by a scholar who is a citizen or permanent resident of Canada or the U.S. Nominations, including self-nominations and publications may be submitted to the chair of the committee. Nominations and submissions are not requested, but neither are they discouraged." Prize: $400 and certificate. "Works should be a major book, edition, or other piece of scholarship that best exemplifies the highest qualities of originality of interpretation, clarity of though, and communication. It should be a work of musicological scholarship."

THE KIRIYAMA PACIFIC RIM BOOK PRIZE, Kiriyama Pacific Rim Foundation and University of San Francisco Center for the Pacific Rim, University of San Francisco Center for the Pacific Rim, 2130 Fulton St., San Francisco CA 94117-1080. (415)422-5984. Fax: (415)422-5933. E-mail: cuevas@usfca.edu. Website: http://www.usfca.edu/pac_rim/kiriyama.html. Contest Director: Dr. Barbara Bundy. Offered for work published November 1-October 31 of the award year to promote books that will contribute to better understanding and increased cooperation throughout all areas of the Pacific Rim. Deadline: July 1. Prize: $30,000 to be divided equally between the publisher and author. Books must be submitted for entry by the publisher. Proper entry forms must be submitted. "Rules and award amount subject to change in 1999."

KATHERINE SINGER KOVACS PRIZE, Modern Language Association of America, 10 Astor Place, New York NY 10003-6981. (212)614-6406. Fax: (212)533-0680. E-mail: awards@mla.org. Website: http://www.mla.org. Contact: Richard Brod. Estab. 1990. Offered annually for book in English on Latin American or Spanish literatures or cultures published in previous year. Authors need not be members of the MLA. Guidelines for #10 SASE. Prize: $1,000. Deadline: May 1.

RICHARD W. LEOPOLD PRIZE, Organization of American Historians. (812)855-9852. Fax: (812)855-0696. E-mail: kara@oah.indiana.edu. Website: http://www.indiana.edu/~oah. Contact: Award and Prize Committee Coordinator. Offered every 2 years for the best book written by a historian connected with federal, state, or municipal government, in the areas of foreign policy, military affairs broadly construed, the historical activities of the federal government, or biography in one of the foregoing areas. The winner must have been employed in a government position for at least 5 years, and the publisher should include verification of this fact when a book is submitted. Deadline: September 1 of odd-numbered years. Prize: $1,500 and certificate. Before submitting a nomination, a listing of current committee members and details about individual prizes must be obtained by sending SASE to: Award and Prize Committee Coordinator, Organization of American Historians, 112 N. Bryan St., Bloomington IN 47408-4199.

N **LERNER-SCOTT PRIZE**, Organization of American Historians. (812)855-9852. Fax: (812)855-0696. E-mail: kara@oah.indiana.edu. Website: http://www.indiana.edu/~oah. Contact: Award and Prize Committee Coordinator. Offered annually for the best doctoral dissertation in US women's history. Each application must contain a letter of support from a faculty member at the degree-granting institution, along with an abstract, table of contents, and sample chapter from the dissertation. Finalists will be asked to submit a complete copy of the dissertation to each committee member at a later date. Deadline: November 1. Prize: $1,000 and certificate. Before submitting a nomination, a listing of current committee members and details about individual prizes must be obtained by sending SASE to: Award and Prize Committee Coordinator, Organization of American Historians, 112 N. Bryan St., Bloomington IN 47408-4199.

N **LITTLETON-GRISWOLD PRIZE**, American Historical Association, 400 A St. SE, Washington DC 20003. Fax: (202)544-8307. Contact: Book Prize Coordinator. Estab. 1985. Offered annually for the best book in any subject on the history of American law and society. Deadline: May 15. Prize: amount varies.

N **WALTER D. LOVE PRIZE**, North American Conference on British Studies, Dept. of History, Reed College, Portland OR 97202-8199. (503)771-1112 ext. 7334. Fax: (503)777-7769. E-mail: dsacks@reed.edu. Contact: David Harris Sacks, executive secretary. Offered annually for best article in any field of British Studies. Previously published submissions. Deadline: Dec. 31. Guidelines for SASE. Prize: $150. Open to American or Canadian writers.

JAMES RUSSELL LOWELL PRIZE, Modern Language Association of America, 10 Astor Place, New York NY 10003-6981. (212)614-6406. Fax: (212)533-6080. E-mail: awards@mla.org. Website: http://www.mla.org. Contact: Richard Brod. Offered annually for literary or linguistic study, or critical edition or biography published in previous year. Open to MLA members only. Guidelines for #10 SASE. Prize: $1,000. Deadline: March 1.

MACPHERSON PRIZE, Canadian Political Science Association, 1 Stewart St., #205, Ottawa, Ontario K1N 6H7 Canada. (613)564-4026. Fax: (613)230-2746. E-mail: cpsa@csse.ca. Contact: Michelle Hopkins. Contest offered every 2 years (even years) for the best book published in English or in French, in the field of political theory. Deadline: December 10. Prize: $750 and a set of the books submitted. Canadian citizen or a permanent resident (landed immigrant) who resides in Canada. Single-authored books only.

N **HOWARD R. MARRARO PRIZE**, American Historical Association, 400 A St. SE, Washington DC 20003. Fax: (202)544-8307. E-mail: aha@theaha.org. Website: http://www.chnm.gmu.edu/aha. Contact: Book Prize Coordinator. Offered annually for the best work in any epoch of Italian history, Italian cultural history, or Italian-American relations. Prize: amount varies. Deadline: May 15.

HOWARD R. MARRARO PRIZE and SCAGLIONE PRIZE FOR ITALIAN LITERARY STUDIES, Modern Language Association of America, 10 Astor Place, New York NY 10003-6981. (212)614-6406. Fax: (212)533-0680. E-mail: awards@mla.org. Website: http://www.mla.org. Contact: Richard Brod. Joint prize offered in even-numbered years for books or essays on any phase of Italian literature or comparative literature involving Italian, published in previous 2 years. Open to MLA members only. Guidelines for #10 SASE. Prize: $1,000. Deadline: May 1.

THE MAYFLOWER SOCIETY CUP COMPETITION, North Carolina Literary and Historical Association, 109 E. Jones St., Room 23, Raleigh NC 27601-2807. (919)733-9375. Contact: Jerry C. Cashion, awards coordinator. Offered annually for previously published nonfiction by a North Carolina resident. Deadline: July 15.

McLEMORE PRIZE, Mississippi Historical Society, P.O. Box 571, Jackson MS 39205-0571. (601)359-6850. Fax: (601)359-6975. Secretary: Elbert R. Hilliard. Estab. 1902. Scholarly book on a topic in Mississippi history/biography published in the year of competition (year previous to January 1 deadline). Deadline: November 1.

N **MID-LIST PRESS FIRST SERIES AWARD FOR CREATIVE NONFICTION**, Mid-List Press, 4324 12th Ave. S., Minneapolis MN 55407-3218. Fax: (612)823-8387. E-mail: guide@midlist.org. Website: http://www.midlist.org. Contact: Lane Stiles, senior editor. Open to any writer who has never published a book of creative nonfiction. Submit either a collection of essays or a single book-length work; minimum length 50,000 words. Charges $15 fee. Submit entire ms beginning after March 31; must be postmarked by July 1. Accepts simultaneous submissions. Guidelines and entry form for SASE or from website at http://www.midlist.org. Awards include publication and an advance against royalties.

KENNETH W. MILDENBERGER PRIZE, Modern Language Association of America, 10 Astor Place, New York NY 10003-6981. (212)614-6406. Fax: (212)533-0680. E-mail: awards@mla.org. Website: http://www.mla.org. Contact: Richard Brod. Offered annually for a research publication from the previous year in the field of teaching foreign languages and literatures. Guidelines for #10 SASE. Prize: $500 and a year's membership in the MLA. Deadline: May 1. Author need not be member.

MLA PRIZE FOR A DISTINGUISHED SCHOLARLY EDITION, Modern Language Association of America, 10 Astor Place, New York NY 10003-6981. (212)614-6406. Fax: (212)533-0680. E-mail: awards@mla.org. Website: http://www.mla.org. Contact: Richard Brod, director of special projects. Offered in odd-numbered years. Work published between 1997 and 1998 qualifies for the 1999 competition. To qualify for the award, an edition should be based on an examination of all available relevant textual sources; the source texts and the edited text's deviations from them should by fully described; the edition should employ editorial principles appropriate to the materials edited, and those principles should be clearly articulated in the volume; the text should be accompanied by appropriate textual and other historical contextual information; the edition should exhibit the highest standards of accuracy in the presentation of its text and apparatus; and the text and apparatus should be presented as accessibly and elegantly as possible. Deadline: May 1. Guidelines for SASE. Prize: $1,000 and certificate. Editor need not be a member of the MLA.

MLA PRIZE FOR A FIRST BOOK, Modern Language Association, 10 Astor Place, New York NY 10003-6981. (212)614-6406. Fax: (212)533-0680. E-mail: awards@mla.org. Website: http://www.mla.org. Contact: Richard Brod. Offered annually for the first book-length scholarly publication by a current member of the association. To qualify, a book must be a literary or linguistic study, a critical edition of an important work, or a critical biography. Studies dealing with literary theory, media, cultural history and interdisciplinary topics are eligible; books that are primarily translations will not be considered. Deadline: May 1. Guidelines for SASE. Prize: $1,000 and certificate.

MLA PRIZE FOR INDEPENDENT SCHOLARS, Modern Language Association of America, 10 Astor Place, New York NY 10003-6981. (212)614-6406. Fax: (212)533-0680. E-mail: awards@mla.org. Website: http://www.mla.org. Contact: Richard Brod. Offered annually for book in the field of English or another modern language or literature published in previous year. Authors who hold tenured or tenured-track positions in higher education are not eligible. Authors do not need to be members of MLA to compete for this prize. Guidelines and application form for SASE. Prize: $1,000 and a year's membership in the MLA. Deadline: May 1.

N **GEORGE JEAN NATHAN AWARD FOR DRAMATIC CRITICISM**, Cornell University, Department of English, Goldwin Smith Hall, Ithaca NY 14853. (607)255-6801. Fax: (607)255-6661. E-mail: english_chair@cornell.edu. Contact: Chair, Dept. of English. Offered annually to the American "who has written the best piece of drama criticism during the theatrical year (July 1-June 30), whether it is an article, an essay, treatise or book." Guidelines for SASE. Prize: $10,000 and a trophy. Only published work may be submitted; author must be an American citizen.

NATIONAL JEWISH BOOK AWARD—CONTEMPORARY JEWISH LIFE, The Jewish Book Council, 15 E. 26th St., New York NY 10010. (212)532-4949. Contact: Carolyn Starman Hessel. Offered annually for a nonfiction work dealing with the sociology of modern Jewish life.

NATIONAL JEWISH BOOK AWARD—HOLOCAUST, Leon Jolson Award, Jewish Book Council, 15 E. 26th St., New York NY 10010. (212)532-4949. Contact: Carolyn Starman Hessel. Offered annually for a nonfiction book concerning the Holocaust. Deadline: September 1.

N **NATIONAL JEWISH BOOK AWARD—ISRAEL**, Morris J. and Betty Kaplun Memorial Award, Jewish Book Council, 15 E. 26th St., New York NY 10010. (212)532-4949 ext. 297. Contact: Sharon Friedman, president. Executive Director: Carolyn Starman Hessel. Offered annually for a nonfiction work about Zionism and/or the State of Israel. Deadline: September.

NATIONAL JEWISH BOOK AWARD—JEWISH CHRISTIAN RELATIONS, Chas. H. Revson Foundation Award, Jewish Book Council, 15 E. 26th St., New York NY 10010. (212)532-4949, ext. 297. Fax: (212)481-4174. Contact: Sharon Friedman, president. Executive Director: Carolyn Starman Hessel. Offered for a nonfiction work detailing some aspect of Jewish-Christian relations.

NATIONAL JEWISH BOOK AWARD—JEWISH HISTORY, Gerrard and Ella Berman Award, Jewish Book Council, 15 E. 26th St., New York NY 10010. (212)532-4949 ext. 297. Contact: Carolyn Starman Hessel, director. Offered annually for a book of Jewish history. Deadline: September 1.

NATIONAL JEWISH BOOK AWARD—JEWISH THOUGHT, Dorot Foundation Award, Jewish Book Council, 15 E. 26th St., New York NY 10010. (212)532-4949. Contact: Carolyn Starman Hessel, director. Offered annually for a book dealing with some aspect of Jewish thought, past or present. Deadline: September 1.

NATIONAL JEWISH BOOK AWARD—SCHOLARSHIP, Sarah H. and Julius Kushner Memorial Award, Jewish Book Council, 15 E. 26th St., New York NY 10010. (212)532-4949. Contact: Carolyn Starman Hessel, director. Offered annually for a book which makes an original contribution to Jewish learning. Deadline: September 1.

NATIONAL JEWISH BOOK AWARD—VISUAL ARTS, Anonymous Award, Jewish Book Council, 15 E. 26th St., New York NY 10010. (212)532-4949. Contact: Carolyn Starman Hessel, director. Offered annually for a book about Jewish art. Deadline: September 1.

NATIONAL WRITERS ASSOCIATION NONFICTION CONTEST, The National Writers Association, Suite 424, 1450 S. Havana, Aurora CO 80012. (303)751-7844. Fax: (303)751-8593. E-mail: sandywrter@aol.com. Director: Sandy Whelchel. Annual contest "to encourage writers in this creative form and to recognize those who excel in nonfiction writing." Charges $18 fee. Deadline: December 31. Prizes: $200, $100, $50. Guidelines for #10 SASE.

THE FREDERIC W. NESS BOOK AWARD, Association of American Colleges and Universities, 1818 R St. NW, Washington DC 20009. (202)387-3760. Fax: (202)265-9532. E-mail: info@aacu.nw.dc.us. Website: http://www.aacuedu.org. Contact: Peggy Neal, director for membership. Offered annually for work previously published July 1-June 30 of the year in which it is being considered. "Each year the Frederic W. Ness Book Award Committee of the Association of American Colleges and Universities recognizes books which contribute to the understanding and improvement of liberal education." Deadline: August 15. Guidelines for SASE and on Website. "Writers may nominate their own work; however, we send letters of invitation to publishers to nominate qualified books." Prize: Presentation at the association's annual meeting and $1,000. Transportation and one night hotel for meeting are also provided.

NORTH AMERICAN INDIAN PROSE AWARD, University of Nebraska Press, 312 N. 14th St., Lincoln NE 68588-0484. Fax: (402)472-0308. E-mail: gdunham@unlinfo.unl.edu. Editor, Native American Studies: Gary H. Dunham. Offered for the best new work by an American Indian writer. Prize: publication by the University of Nebraska Press with $1,000 advance. Guidelines for #10 SASE. Deadline: July 1.

ELI M. OBOLER MEMORIAL AWARD, American Library Association's Intellectual Freedom Round Table, 50 E. Huron St., Chicago IL 60611. (312)280-4223. Fax: (312)280-4227. E-mail: IFRT@ALA.ORG. Website: http://www.ala.org/IFRT. Contact: Cynthia Robinson, associate director. Offered every 2 years "to the author of an article (including a review), a series of thematically connected articles, a book, or a manual published on the local, state or national level, in English or in English translation. The works to be considered must have as their central concern one or more issues, events, questions or controversies in the area of intellectual freedom, including matters of ethical, political, or social concern related to intellectual freedom. The work for which the award is granted must have been published within the *two-year* period ending the December prior to the ALA Annual Conference at which it is granted." Deadline: December 1, 1999.

FRANK LAWRENCE AND HARRIET CHAPPELL OWSLEY AWARD, Southern Historical Association, Department of History, University of Georgia, Athens GA 30602-1602. (706)542-8848. Fax: (706)542-2455. Website: http://www.uga.edu/~sha. Managing Editor: John B. Boles. Contact: Secretary-Treasurer. Estab. 1934. Offered in odd-numbered years for recognition of a distinguished book in Southern history published in even-numbered years. Publishers usually submit the books. Deadline: March 1.

LOUIS PELZER MEMORIAL AWARD, Organization of American Historians. (812)855-9852. Fax: (812)855-0696. E-mail: kara@oah.indiana.edu. Website: http://www.indiana.edu/~oah. Contact: Award and Prize Committee Coordinator. Offered annually for the best essay in American history by a graduate student. The essay may be about any period or topic in the history of the United States, and the author must be enrolled in a graduate program at any level, in any field. Entries should not exceed 7,000 words. Deadline: November 30. Prize: $500, medal, certificate and publication in the *Journal of American History*. Before submitting a nomination, a listing of current committee members and details about individual prizes must be obtained by sending SASE to: Award and Prize Committee Coordinator, Organization of American Historians, 112 N. Bryan St., Bloomington IN 47408-4199.

PEN/JERARD FUND, PEN American Center, 568 Broadway, New York NY 10012. (212)334-1660. Fax: (212)334-2181. E-mail: jm@pen.org. Contact: John Morrone. Estab. 1986. Biennial grant of $4,000 for American woman writer of nonfiction for a booklength work in progress in odd-numbered years. Guidelines for #10 SASE. Next award: 1999. Deadline: January 2.

PEN/MARTHA ALBRAND AWARD FOR FIRST NONFICTION, PEN American Center, 568 Broadway, New York NY 10012. (212)334-1660. Fax: (212)334-2181. E-mail: jm@pen.org. Coordinator: John Morrone. Offered annually for a first-published book of general nonfiction distinguished by qualities of literary and stylistic excellence. Eligible books must have been published in the calendar year under consideration. Authors must be American citizens or permanent residents. Although there are no restrictions on the subject matter of titles submitted, non-literary books will not be considered. Books should be of adult nonfiction for the general or academic reader. Deadline: December 15. Publishers, agents and authors themselves must submit *3* copies of each eligible title. Prize: $1,000 and a residence at the Johnson Studio Center, Johnson, Vermont.

PEN/SPIELVOGEL-DIAMONSTEIN AWARD, PEN American Center, 568 Broadway, New York NY 10012. (212)334-1660. Fax: (212)334-2181. E-mail: jm@pen.org. Coordinator: John Morrone. Offered for the best previously unpublished collection of essays on any subject by an American writer. "The $5,000 prize is awarded to preserve the dignity and esteem that the essay form imparts to literature." Authors must be American citizens or permanent residents. The essays included in books submitted may have been previously published in magazines, journals or anthologies, but must not have collectively appeared before in book form. Books will be judged on literary character and distinction of the writing. Publishers, agents, or the authors must submit 4 copies of each eligible title. Deadline: December 15.

PHI BETA KAPPA BOOK AWARDS, The Phi Beta Kappa Society, 1811 Q St. NW, Washington DC 20009-1696. (202)265-3808. Fax: (202)986-1601. E-mail: lsurles@pbk.org. Website: http://www.pbk.org. Contact: Linda D. Surles.

Offered annually to recognize and honor outstanding scholarly books published in the US May 1, 1997-April 30, 1998 in the fields of the humanities, the social sciences, and the natural sciences and mathematics. Deadline: April 30. Guidelines for SASE. Prize: $2,500. "Authors may request information, however books must be submitted by the publisher." Entrants must be US citizens or residents.

JAMES A. RAWLEY PRIZE, Organization of American Historians. (812)855-9852. Fax: (812)855-0696. E-mail: kara@oah.indiana.edu. Website: http://www.indiana.edu/~oah. Contact: Award and Prize Committee Coordinator. Offered annually for a book dealing with the history of race relations in the US. Deadline: October 1. Prize: $750 and certificate. Before submitting a nomination, a listing of current committee members and details about individual prizes must be obtained by sending SASE to: Award and Prize Committee Coordinator, Organization of American Historians, 112 N. Bryan St., Bloomington IN 47408-4199.

PHILLIP D. REED MEMORIAL AWARD FOR OUTSTANDING WRITING ON THE SOUTHERN ENVIRONMENT, Southern Environmental Law Center, 201 W. Main St., Charlottesville VA 22902. (804)977-4090. Fax: (804)977-1483. E-mail: cmccue@selcva.org. Contact: Cathryn McCue, award director. Offered annually for pieces published in the previous calendar year "to encourage and promote writing about natural resources in the South as a way to focus attention on these environmental issues." Deadline: March. Guidelines for SASE. Prize: $1,000. Judged by "prominent writers (not necessarily nature writers) and members of our board of trustees."

N **EVELYN RICHARDSON MEMORIAL LITERARY AWARD**, Writers' Federation of Nova Scotia, 1809 Barrington St., Suite 901, Halifax, Nova Scotia B3J 3K8 Canada. (902)423-8116. Fax: (902)422-0881. E-mail: writers1@fox.nstn.ca. Contact: Awards committee. Contest is offered annually for best nonfiction book by Nova Scotian published during the previous calendar year. Deadline: January 30. Send 4 copies with letter. Prize: cash award and prize ceremony. Open to writers who were born, or have lived for the past year in Nova Scotia.

ELLIOTT RUDWICK PRIZE, Organization of American Historians. (812)855-9852. Fax: (812)855-0696. E-mail: kara@oah.indiana.edu. Website: http://www.indiana.edu/~oah. Contact: Award and Prize Committee Coordinator. Offered every 2 years for a book on the experience of racial and ethnic minorities in the United States. Books on interactions between 2 or more minority groups, or comparing the experience of 2 or more minority groups are especially welcome. Deadline: September 1 of even-numbered years. Prize: $2,000 and certificate. No book that has won the James A. Rawley Prize will be eligible for the Elliott Rudwick Prize. Before submitting a nomination, a listing of current committee members and details about individual prizes must be obtained by sending SASE to: Award and Prize Committee Coordinator, Organization of American Historians, 112 N. Bryan St., Bloomington IN 47408-4199.

THE CORNELIUS RYAN AWARD, The Overseas Press Club of America, 320 East 42 St., New York NY 10017. (212)983-4655. Fax: (212)983-4692. Manager: Sonya Fry. Offered annually for excellence in a nonfiction book on foreign affairs. Deadline: January 31. Guidelines for SASE. Generally publishers nominate the work, but writers may also submit in their own name. Charges $100 fee. Prize: certificate and $1,000. The work must be published and on the subject of foreign affairs.

THEODORE SALOUTOS AWARD, Agricultural History, Iowa State University, Ames IA 50011-1202. (515)294-1596. Fax: (515)294-6390. E-mail: aghistory@iastate.edu. Website: http://www.public.iastate.edu/~history_info/homepage.htm. Contact: R. Douglas Hurt, Center for Agricultural History, Iowa State University, Ames, Iowa, 50011-1202. Offered annually for best graduate paper submitted to Agricultural History. Deadline: December 31. Prize: Monetary award and publication in the journal. Award made at OAH annual meeting. Nominations can be made by authors, publishers or anyone else.

THE BARBARA SAVAGE "MILES FROM NOWHERE" MEMORIAL AWARD, The Mountaineers Books, 1001 SW Klickitat Way, Suite 201, Seattle WA 98134. (206)223-6303. Fax: (206)223-6306. E-mail: mbooks@mountaineers.org. Website: http://www.mountaineers.org. Award Director: Margaret Foster, editor-in-chief. Offered in even-numbered years for previously unpublished book-length nonfiction personal adventure narrative. Narrative must be based on an outdoor adventure involving hiking, mountain climbing, bicycling, paddle sports, skiing, snowshoeing, nature, conservation, ecology, or adventure travel not dependent upon motorized transport. Subjects *not* acceptable include hunting, fishing, or motorized or competitive sports. Guidelines for #10 SASE. Prize: $3,000 cash award, a $12,000 guaranteed advance against royalties and publication by The Mountaineers. Deadline: October 1, 1998.

- More regional and conservation-oriented titles are preferred.

ALDO AND JEANNE SCAGLIONE PRIZE FOR STUDIES IN GERMANIC LANGUAGES, Modern Language Association of America, 10 Astor Place, New York NY 10003-6981. (212)614-6406. Fax: (212)533-0680. E-mail: awards@mla.org. Website: http://www.mla.org. Contact: Richard Brod. Offered in even-numbered years for outstanding scholarly work appearing in print in the previous two years and written by a member of the MLA, on the linguistics or literatures of the Germanic languages. Deadline: May 1. Guidelines for SASE. Prize: $1,000 and certificate presented at association's annual convention in December. Works of literary history, literary criticism, and literary theory are eligible; books that are primarily translations are not.

ALDO AND JEANNE SCAGLIONE PRIZE FOR STUDIES IN SLAVIC LANGUAGES AND LITERATURES, Modern Language Association, 10 Astor Place, New York NY 10003-6981. (212)614-6406. Fax: (212)533-0680. E-mail: awards@mla.org. Website: http://www.mla.org. Contact: Richard Brod. Offered each odd-numbered year for books published in the previous 2 years. Books published in 1997 or 1998 are eligible for the 1999 award. Membership in the MLA is not required. Works of literary history, literary criticism, philology and literary theory are eligible, books that are primarily translations are not. Deadline: May 1. Guidelines for SASE. Prize: $1,000 and a certificate.

ALDO AND JEANNE SCAGLIONE PRIZE IN COMPARATIVE LITERARY STUDIES, Modern Language Association of America, 10 Astor Place, New York NY 10003-6981. (212)614-6406. Fax: (212)533-0680. E-mail: awards@mla.org. Website: http://www.mla.org. Contact: Richard Brod. Offered annually for outstanding scholarly work published in the preceding year in the field of comparative literary studies involving at least 2 literatures. Deadline: May 1. Prize: $1,000 and certificate. Writer must be a member of the MLA. Works of scholarship, literary history, literary criticism and literary theory are eligible. Books that are primarily translations are not.

ALDO AND JEANNE SCAGLIONE PRIZE IN FRENCH AND FRANCOPHONE STUDIES, 10 Astor Place, New York NY 10003-6981. (212)614-6406. Fax: (212)533-0680. E-mail: awards@mla.org. Website: http://www.-mla.org. Contact: Richard Brod. Offered annually for work published in the preceding year that is an outstanding scholarly work in the field of French or francophone linguistic or literary studies. Prize: $1,000 and certificate. Writer must be a member of the MLA. Works of scholarship, literary history, literary criticism and literary theory are eligible; books that are primarily translations are not. Deadline: May 1.

N **SCIENCE IN SOCIETY AWARD**, National Association of Science Writers, Inc., P.O. Box 294, Greenlawn NY 11740. (516)757-5664. E-mail: diane@nasw.org. Website: http://www.nasw.org. Contact: Diane McGurgan. Offered annually to articles/broadcasts published between June 1 and May 31 in the categories: newspapers, magazines, television and radio. Deadline: July 1. Guidelines and entry form available for SASE. Prize: $1,000 and Certificate of Recognition. Material may be a single article or broadcast or a series.

SCIENCE IN SOCIETY BOOK AWARDS, Canadian Science Writers' Association, P.O. Box 75, Station A, Toronto, Ontario M5W 1A2 Canada. (416)928-9624. Fax: (416)924-6715. E-mail: cswa@interlog.com. Website: http://www.interlog.com/~cswa. Director: Andy F. Visser-deVries. Offered annually for a first edition work published in Canada from Jan 1-Dec 31 of that year. Two awards: Children's Book Award and General Science Book Award, available for and to the general public with value in promoting greater understanding of science. Deadline: December 15. Guidelines for SASE. Prize: $1,000 and a plaque. Works entered become property of CSWA. Open to Canadian citizens or residents.

SCIENCE WRITING AWARD IN PHYSICS AND ASTRONOMY BY SCIENTISTS, American Institute of Physics, One Physics Ellipse, College Park MD 20740. (301)209-3090. Fax: (301)209-0846. E-mail: jwrather@aip.acp.org. Contest/Award Director: Joan Wrather. Offered annually to previously published entries appearing in print between May 1, 1997 and April 30, 1998 "to recognize and stimulate distinguished writing that improves the general public's understanding and appreciation of physics and astronomy." Deadline: May 19 (unless it falls on a Saturday or Sunday). Guidelines available, SASE is not necessary. Prize: $3,000, a Windsor Chair and a certificate. Judged by a committee of distinguished scientists and journalists. Articles, booklets, or books must be intended for the general public by physicists, astronomers or members of AIP Member and Affiliated Societies.

SCIENCE-WRITING AWARD IN PHYSICS AND ASTRONOMY, American Institute of Physics, 1 Physics Ellipse, College Park MD 20740-3843. (301)209-3090. E-mail: jwrather@aip.acp.org. Website: http://www.aip.org. Contact: Joan Wrather. Previously published articles, booklets or books "that improve public understanding of physics and astronomy." Deadline: February 3 for professional writers; May 19 for physicists, astronomers or members of AIP member and affililated societies; July 25 for articles or books intended for children, preschool-15 years old.

N **SERGEANT KIRKLAND'S PRIZE IN CONFEDERATE HISTORY**, Sergeant Kirkland's Museum and Historical Society, Inc., 912 Lafayette Blvd., Fredericksburg VA 22401-5617. (540)899-5565. Fax: (540)899-7643. E-mail: civil-war@msn.com. Offered annually for the best research work focusing on an individual Confederate soldier or regimental unit. Text must have been in publication during the 12 months prior to the June 1 deadline. Studies should be in scholarly form and based, in part, on primary sources, with the usual documentation and bibliography. Must be at least 65,000 words. Prize: $500 and engraved plaque.

MINA P. SHAUGHNESSY PRIZE, Modern Language Association of America, 10 Astor Place, New York NY 10003-6981. (212)614-6406. Fax: (212)533-0680. E-mail: awards@mla.org. Website: http://www.mla.org. Contact: Richard Brod. Offered annually for research publication (book or article) in the field of teaching English language, literature, rhetoric and composition published during preceding year. Guidelines for #10 SASE. Prize: $1,000 and a year's membership in the MLA. Deadline: May 1.

FRANCIS B. SIMKINS AWARD, Southern Historical Association, Department of History, University of Georgia, Athens GA 30602-1602. (706)542-8848. Fax: (706)542-2455. Managing Editor: John B. Boles. Contact: Secretary-

Treasurer. Estab. 1934. Offered in odd-numbered years for recognition of the best first book by an author in the field of Southern history over a 2-year period. Deadline: March 1.

SMILEY PRIZE, Canadian Political Science Association, 1 Stewart St., #205, Ottawa, Ontario K1N 6H7 Canada. (613)564-4026. Fax: (613)230-2746. E-mail: cpsa@csse.ca. Contact: Michelle Hopkins. Offered every 2 years (even years) for the best book, in English or French, published in a field relating to the study of government and politics in Canada. Deadline: December 10. Prize: $750 and a set of the books submitted. No textbooks, edited texts or collections of essays.

N **THE JOHN BEN SNOW PRIZE**, Syracuse University Press, 1600 Jamesville Ave., Syracuse NY 13244. (315)443-5534. Fax: (315)443-5545. Contact: Dr. Robert Mandel. Offered annually for unpublished submissions. The John Ben Snow Prize, inaugurated in 1978, is given annually by Syracuse University Press to the author of a book-length nonfiction manuscript dealing with some aspect of New York State. The purpose of the award is to encourage the writing of books of genuine significance and literary distinction that will augment knowledge of New York State and appreciation for its unique physical, historical and cultural characteristics. A manuscript based on direct, personal experience will receive the same consideration as one relying on scholarly research. The criteria are authenticity, accuracy, readability and importance. Deadline: December 31. Prize: $1,500 to the author as advance against royalties and publication by Syracuse University Press. Guidelines for SASE.

N **BRYANT SPANN MEMORIAL PRIZE**, Eugene V. Debs Foundation, History Department, Indiana State University, Terre Haute IN 47809. Estab. 1980. Contact: Edwin Spear. Offered annually "to promote the cause of social justice in the tradition of Eugene V. Debs." Deadline: April 30. Guidelines for SASE. SASE also required with submissions. Prize: $1,000 and recognition at the annual Debs dinner. Open to any writer.

CHARLES S. SYDNOR AWARD, Southern Historical Association, Department of History, University of Georgia, Athens GA 30602. (706)542-8848. Fax: (706)542-2455. Contact: Secretary-Treasurer. Offered in even-numbered years for recognition of a distinguished book in Southern history published in odd-numbered years. Deadline: March 1.

THE THEATRE LIBRARY ASSOCIATION AWARD, Theatre Library Association, Benjamin Rosenthal Library, Queens College, C.U.N.Y., 65-30 Kissena Blvd., Flushing NY 11367. (718)997-3799. Fax: (718)997-3753. E-mail: rlwqc@cunyvm.cuny.edu. Contact: Richard Wall, book awards committee chair. Estab. 1973. Book published in the United States within the previous calendar year on a subject related to recorded or broadcast performance (including motion pictures, television and radio). Eligible books may include biography, history, theory, criticism, reference or related fields. Prize: $250 and certificate to the winner; $100 and certificate for Honorable Mention. Submissions and deadline: Nominated books are requested from publishers; one copy should be received by each of three award jurors as well as the Chairperson by February 15 of the year following eligibility.

N **TRAVEL WRITING CONTEST**, Val-Tech Publishing, Inc., P.O. Box 25376, St. Paul MN 55125. (612)730-4280. Website: http://www.sowashco.com/writersjournal. Contact: Valerie Hockert. Offered annually "to help writers in this genre." Deadline: November 30. Guidelines for SASE. Charges $5 fee. Prizes: 1st-$50, 2nd-$25, 3rd-$15. Buys one-time rights. Open to any writer.

FREDERICK JACKSON TURNER AWARD, Organization of American Historians. (812)855-9852. Fax: (812)855-0696. E-mail: kara@oah.indiana.edu. Website: http://www.indiana.edu/~oah. Contact: Award and Prize Committee Coordinator. Offered annually for an author's first book on some significant phase of American history and also to the press that submits and publishes it. The entry must comply with the following rules: 1) the work must be the first book-length study of history published by the author; 2) if the author has a Ph.D., he/she must have received it no earlier than seven years prior to submission of the manuscript for publication; 3) the work must be published in the calendar year before the award is given; 4) the work must deal with some significant phase of American history. Deadline: September 1. Prize: $1,000, certificate and medal. Before submitting a nomination, a listing of current committee members and details about individual prizes must be obtained by sending SASE to: Award and Prize Committee Coordinator, Organization of American Historians, 112 N. Bryan St., Bloomington IN 47408-4199.

N **UNDERGRADUATE ANNUAL PAPER COMPETITION IN CRYPTOLOGY**, *Cryptologia*, United States Military Academy, West Point MD 10996. Contact: Editor. Unpublished papers on cryptology from undergraduates only. Deadline: January 1.

WEATHERFORD AWARD, Berea College Appalachian Center and Hutchins Library, C.P.O. 2336, Berea KY 40404. (606)986-9341 ext 5140. Contact: Gordon B. McKinney, director, Appalachian center. Offered annually for outstanding published writing which best illustrates the problems, personalities and unique qualities of the Appalachian South between January 1-December 31. Deadline: December 31. Guidelines for SASE. Prize: $500. Judged by an independent committee from various parts of the Appalachian South. Entries must have been first published during the year for which the award is made and may be nominated by its publisher, a member of the award committee or any reader.

JON WHYTE ESSAY COMPETITION, Writers Guild of Alberta, 11759 Groat Rd., Edmonton, Alberta T5M 3K6 Canada. (403)422-8174. Fax: (403)422-2663. E-mail: writers@compusmart.ab.cq. Assistant Director: Darlene Diver. Offered annually for unpublished work. Essay competition on announced theme. Theme is announced May 1. Winner announced October 15. 2,800 words. Deadline: September 1. Guidelines for SASE. Charges $10 fee Canadian. Prize: $2,000 plus publication in 2 newspapers and radio readings. Must be Alberta resident.

THE ELIE WIESEL ETHICS ESSAY CONTEST, 450 Lexington Ave., Ste. 1920, New York NY 10017. Contest Director: Cicily Wilson. Offered annually to unpublished full-time college undergraduate juniors and seniors. Deadline: January 22. SASE for entry form and guidelines required. Prizes: 1st-$5,000; 2nd-$2,500; 3rd-$1,500; two honorable mentions-$500 each. Judged by Mr. Elie Wiesel and a committee drawn from the world of academe. "The Elie Wiesel Foundation for Humanity reserves the right to publish the winning essays in whole or in part. These essays may not be published elsewhere without written permission from the Foundation." Open to any student registered during the fall semester 1998 as a full-time junior or senior at an accredited 4-year college or university.

L. KEMPER AND LEILA WILLIAMS PRIZE, The Historic New Orleans Collection and Louisiana Historical Association, 533 Royal St., New Orleans LA 70130-2179. Fax: (504)598-7108. Website: http://www.hnoc.org. Contact: Chair, Williams Prize Committee. Director: Dr. Jon Kukla. Offered annually for the best published work on Louisiana history. Deadline: January 15. Prize: $1,500 and a plaque.

Fiction

AIM MAGAZINE SHORT STORY CONTEST, P.O. Box 1174, Maywood IL 60153-8174. (773)874-6184. Managing Editor: Dr. Myron Apilado. Contact: Ruth Apilado, associate editor. Estab. 1974. Unpublished short stories (4,000 words maximum) "promoting brotherhood among people and cultures." Deadline: August 15.

ANNUAL SHORT STORY CONTEST, (formerly Penny Dreadful Short Story Contest), sub-TERRAIN Magazine, P.O. Box 1575, Bentall Centre, Vancouver, British Columbia V6C 2P7 Canada. (604)876-8710. Fax: (604)879-2667. E-mail: subter@plnc.com. Offered annually to foster new and upcoming writers. Deadline May 15. Guidelines for SASE. Charges $15 fee for first story, $5 for additional entries. Prize: $250 (Canadian), publication in summer issue and 4-issue subscription to sub-TERRAIN.

ANVIL PRESS INTERNATIONAL 3-DAY NOVEL WRITING CONTEST, Anvil Press, 204-A 175 E. Broadway, Vancouver, British Columbia V5T 1W2 Canada. (604)876-8710. Fax: (604)879-2667. E-mail: subter@pinc.com. Website: http://www.bc.books.ca. Contact: Brian Kaufman. Estab. 1988. Offered annually for the best novel written in 3 days (Labor Day weekend). Entrants return finished novels to Anvil Press for judging. Registration deadline: Friday before Labor Day weekend. Send SASE (IRC if from the US) for details. Charges $25 fee.

B&A FICTION CONTEST, P.O. Box 702, Station P, Toronto, Ontario M5S 2Y4 Canada. (416)535-1233. E-mail: timnancy@ica.net. Publisher: Tim Paleczny. Asards "to discover new writers and generate more excitement for their work in the literary community." Annual competition for short stories from any genre. Guidelines for SASE or IRC. Charges $18 (US) for entries from outside Canada; $18 (Canadian) from inside. Entrant receives a 1-year subscription to *B&A*. Prize: The Humber School for Writers Prize (writing course, value up to $1,000); The Random House/Knopf/Vintage Canada Prize (books, value $1,000); The B&A Prize ($500 cash). Contest prizes are valued in Canadian currency.

BOSTON REVIEW SHORT STORY CONTEST, *Boston Review*, E-53-407 MIT, Cambridge MA 02139. (617)494-0708. Stories should not exceed four thousand words and must be previously unpublished. Deadline: September 1. Charges $10 fee, payable to *Boston Review*, check or money order. Prize: $1,000 and publication in the December/January issue of *Boston Review*.

BRAZOS BOOKSTORE (HOUSTON) SHORT STORY AWARD, The Texas Institute of Letters, P.O. Box 298300, Fort Worth TX 76129. (817)921-7822. Fax: (817)257-5075. E-mail: jalter@gamma.is.tcu.edu. Website: http://www.gamma.is.tcu.edu/prs/til. Contact: Judy Alter, director. Offered annually for previously published work between January 1 and December 31 of year before award is given to recognize the best short story submitted to the competition. The story submitted must have appeared in print for the first time to be eligible. Deadline: January 4. Guidelines for SASE. Prize: $750. Writers must have been born in Texas, must have lived in Texas for at least two consecutive years or the subject matter of the work must be associated with Texas.

GEORGES BUGNET AWARD FOR FICTION (NOVEL), Writers Guild of Alberta, 11759 Groat Rd., Edmonton Alberta T5M 3K6 Canada. (403)422-8179. Fax: (403)422-2663. E-mail: writers@compusmart.ab.ca. Assistant Director: Darlene Diver. Offered annually for work previously published January 1-December 31 of the past year. Deadline: December 31. Guidelines for SASE. Prize: $500 and leatherbound copy of book. Must be an Alberta author.

RAYMOND CARVER SHORT STORY CONTEST, English Department, Humboldt State University, Arcata CA 95521. Contact: Student Coordinator. Offered annually for unpublished work. Deadline: December 1. Guidelines available for SASE. Charges $10/story fee. Prizes: 1st-$500 plus publication in *Toyon*, Humboldt State University's literary magazine; 2nd-$250; 3rd-honorable mention. Open to any US writer.

DAVID DORNSTEIN MEMORIAL CREATIVE WRITING CONTEST FOR YOUNG ADULT WRITERS, The Coalition for the Advancement of Jewish Education, 261 W. 35th St., Floor 12A, New York NY 10001. (212)268-4210. Fax: (212)268-4214. E-mail: 500-8447@mcimail.com. Website: http://www.caje.org. Executive Director: Eliot Spack. Contest offered annually for unpublished short story based on a Jewish theme or topic. Deadline: December 31. Guidelines for SASE. Prize: 1st-$700; 2nd-$200; 3rd-$100, and pubulication in the *Jewish Education News*. Writer must prove age of 18-35 years old. Story must be based on Jewish theme, topic. Submit only 1 story each year.

N **ARTHUR ELLIS AWARDS**, Crime Writers of Canada, 3007 Kingston Rd., Box 113, Scarborough, Ontario M1M 1P1 Canada. (416)466-9826. Fax: (416)406-6141. E-mail: ap113@torfree.net. Website: http://www.swifty.com/cwc/cwehome.htm. Contact: James Dubro. Annual award for crime literature published during the year of the award. Categories: Best Crime Novel, True Crime Novel, Crime Short Story, Crime Genre Criticism/Reference/Anthology, Play, Juvenile Crime Fiction. Deadline: January 31. Prize: a symbolic hanged person, cash prizes from year to year in certain categories. Open to Canadian writers.

THE EVERGREEN CHRONICLES NOVELLA CONTEST, The Evergreen Chronicles, P.O. Box 8939, Minneapolis MN 55408. (612)823-6638. E-mail: cynatecoff@aol.com. Contest Director: Jim Berg. Offered annually. Looking for an original novella by an emerging, unpublished gay, lesbian, bisexual, straight or transgendered writer. Deadline: September 30. Guidelines for SASE. Prizes: 1st-$500 and publication in special issue of *The Evergreen Chronicles*, 2nd-$100 and possible publication. Finalists are selected by *Evergreen* editorial staff, and guest judges select winners. First and second rights for winners are retained. Open to writers who have had no more than one novel or novella published. Manuscripts must in some way address the gay, lesbian, bisexual or transgender experience.

THE WILLIAM FAULKNER CREATIVE WRITING COMPETITION, The Pirate's Alley Faulkner Society, 632 Pirate's Alley, New Orleans LA 70116-3254. (504)586-1609. Contest Director: Joseph J. DeSalvo, Jr. Contact: Rosemary James, editor. Offered annually for unpublished mss to encourage publisher interest in a promising writer's novel, novella, short story, personal essay, poem or short story by a Louisiana high school student. Deadline: April 15. Guidelines for SASE. Charges entry fee: novel-$35; novella-$30; short story $25; personal essay-$25; individual poem-$25; high school short story $10. Prize: novel-$7,500; novella-$2,500; short story-$1,500; personal essay-$1,000; individual poem-$750; high school-$750 for student and $250 for sponsoring teacher; and expenses for trip to New Orleans for Faulkner Celebration. Excerpts published in Society's Literary Quarterly, *The Double Dealer Redux*. The Society retains the right to publish excerpts of longer fiction; short stories in toto. Judges are well known authors. Open to all US residents.

ROBERT L. FISH MEMORIAL AWARD, Mystery Writers of America, Inc., 17 E. 47th St., 6th Floor, New York NY 10017. (212)888-8171. Fax: (212)888-8107. Website: http://www.mysterywriters.org/. Contact: Priscilla Ridgway. Offered annually for the best first mystery or suspense short story published during the previous year. Deadline: December 1.

H.E. FRANCIS SHORT STORY AWARD, University of Alabama in Huntsville & Ruth Hindman Foundation, 2007 Gallatin St., Huntsville AL 35801. Fax: (205)533-6893. E-mail: HTP@aol.com. Contact: Mary Hindman, editor. Offered annually for unpublished work. Deadline: December 31. Guidelines for SASE. Charges $15 reading fee. Prize: $1,000. Acquires first time publication rights.

N **THE GILLER PRIZE**, 21 Steepleview Cres., Richmond Hill, Ontario L4C 9R1 Canada. (905)508-5146. Fax: (905)508-4469. Offered annually to the author of the best Canadian novel or short story collection published in English between October 31 of the year previous and November 1 of the current year. Deadline: August 15. Guidelines for SASE. Prize: $25,000 (Canadian). Works must be submitted by publishers. Authors must be Canadian citizens or permanent residents of Canada.

DRUE HEINZ LITERATURE PRIZE, University of Pittsburgh Press, 3347 Forbes Ave., Pittsburgh PA 15261. Contact: Ed Ochester, series editor. Estab. 1936. Collection of short fiction. Offered annually to writers who have published a book-length collection of fiction or a minimum of 3 short stories or novellas in commercial magazines or literary journals of national distribution. Does not return manuscripts. Guidelines for SASE (essential). Submit: May-June. Prize: $10,000.

N **ERNEST HEMINGWAY FIRST NOVEL CONTEST**, International Hemingway Festival, 2323 Del Prado Blvd., Cape Coral FL 33990. (941)945-6308. Website: http://www.hemingwayfestival.com. Contact: Mina Hemingway. Offered annually for unpublished work to help an aspiring novelist become published. Deadline: May 1. Guidelines for SASE. Charges $45 fee. Prize: $1,000 plus literary representation for one year; plus roundtrip airfare to and admittance to the following year's Earnest Hemingway Literary Conference. Restricted to writers who have not had a novel published. All finalists receive the judges' critiques of their submission. Winner announced at end of festival.

ERNEST HEMINGWAY FOUNDATION PEN AWARD FOR FIRST FICTION, PEN New England, P.O. Box 725, North Cambridge MA 02140. First-published novel or short story collection by an American author. Submit 3 copies. Deadline: December 15.

N **ERNEST HEMINGWAY SHORT STORY COMPETITION**, International Hemingway Festival, 2323 Del Prado Blvd., Cape Coral FL 33990. (941)945-0308. Website: http://www.hemingwayfestival.com. Contact: Mina Hemingway. Offered annually to recognize quality short story writing. For unpublished short stories. Does not return submissions. Deadline: May 1. Guidelines and entry form for SASE. Charges $20 entry fee. Prize: $1,000, publication in *Sanibal Captiva Review* and entry to Ernest Hemingway Literary Conference. Winner announced at end of conference.

LORIAN HEMINGWAY SHORT STORY COMPETITION, Hemingway Days Festival, P.O. Box 993, Key West FL 33041-0993. (305)294-0320. Fax: (305)292-3653. E-mail: calico2419@aol.com. Fax and e-mail for guideline requests only. Coordinators: Lorian Hemingway and Carol Shaughnessy. Estab. 1981. Unpublished short stories. Deadline: June 15. Charges $10 fee for each story postmarked by June 1, $15 for each story postmarked by June 15; no stories accepted after June 15. Guidelines for SASE. Prize: 1st-$1,000; 2nd and 3rd-$500 runner-up awards; up to 10 honorable mentions.

N **L. RON HUBBARD'S WRITERS OF THE FUTURE CONTEST**, P.O. Box 1630C, Los Angeles CA 90078. (213)466-3310. Fax: (213)466-6474. Website: http://www.theta.com/asi. Contest Administrator: Leslie Potter. Unpublished science fiction, fantasy and horror. Guidelines for #10 SASE. Prize: $2,250 quarterly prizes; $4,000 annual Grand Prize, with 5-day workshop and publication in major anthology. Authors retain all rights.

INTERNATIONAL IMITATION HEMINGWAY COMPETITION, PEN Center West, 672 S. La Fayette Park Place, Suite 41, Los Angeles CA 90057. (213)365-8500. Fax: (213)365-9616. E-mail: rit2writ@ix.netcom.com. Contact: Rachel Hall. Offered annually for unpublished one-page (500 words) parody of Hemingway. Must mention Harry's Bar and must be funny. Deadline: March 15. Winner receives round trip transportation for two to Florence, Italy and dinner at Harry's Bar & American Grill in Florence.

JAMES FELLOWSHIP FOR THE NOVEL IN PROGRESS, The Heekin Group Writers' & Education Fund, P.O. Box 1534, Sisters OR 97759. Phone/fax: (541)548-4147. E-mail: Hgfhl@aol.com. Director: Sarah Heekin Redfield. Offered annually for unpublished work. "Our writing fellowships program is designed to support the community of new and emerging writers." Deadline: December. Guidelines for SASE. Charges $25 fee. Prize: 2 awards of $3,000.

JAPANOPHILE ANNUAL SHORT STORY CONTEST, *Japanophile*, P.O. Box 7977, 415 N. Main St., Ann Arbor MI 48107. (517)669-2109. E-mail: japanlove@aol.com. Website: http://www.voyager.net/japanophile. Director: Susan Lapp. Offered annually for unpublished work to encourage good fiction-writing that contributes to understanding of Japan and Japanese culture. Deadline: December 31. Guidelines for SASE. Charges $5 fee. Prize: $100, a certificate, and usually publication.

JAMES JONES FIRST NOVEL FELLOWSHIP, Wilkes University, English Department, Kirby Hall, Wilkes-Barre PA 18766. (717)408-4530. Fax: (717)408-7829. E-mail: shaffer@wilkesl.wilkes.edu. Website: http://wilkes.edu/~english/jones.html. Contest Director: Patricia B. Heaman. Offered annually for unpublished novels, novellas and closely-linked short stories (all works-in-progress). "The award is intended to honor the spirit of unblinking honesty, determination and insight into modern culture exemplified by the late James Jones." Deadline: March 1. Guidelines for SASE. Charges $15 fee. Prize: $2,500. The competition is open to all American writers who have not previously published novels.

JESSE H. JONES AWARD, The Texas Institute of Letters, P.O. Box 298300, Fort Worth TX 76129. (817)921-7822. Fax: (817)257-5075. E-mail: jalter@gamma.is.tcu.edu. Website: http://www.gamma.is.tcu.edu/prs/til. Contact: Judy Alter, director. Offered annually for work previously published January 1-December 31 of year before award is given to recognize the writer of the best book of fiction entered in the competition. Deadline: January 4. Guidelines for SASE. Prize: $6,000. Writers must have been born in Texas, or have lived in the state for at least two consecutive years at some time, or the subject matter of the work should be associated with the state.

LIBIDO SHORT FICTION CONTEST, *Libido*, 5318 N. Paulina St., Chicago IL 60640. Fax: (773)275-0752. E-mail: rune@mcs.com. Website: http://www.sensualsource.com. Contact: J.L. Beck, submissions editor. Erotic short fiction, 1,000-4,000 words. Deadline: Entries must be postmarked by no later than September 1. Only entries with SASE will be returned. Entries must clearly say "contest" on the envelope. Charges $15 fee. Prizes: 1st-$1,000 and publication in *Libido*; 2nd-$200; 3rd through 5th-1-year subscriptions to *Libido*. "Open to all sexual orientations, but winning stories will fit the general tone and style of *Libido*. Bonus points are awarded for accuracy of characterization, sense of style and humor, particularly the darker side." For issue with last year's winner, send $8.

LINES IN THE SAND SHORT FICTION CONTEST, LeSand Publications, 1252 Terra Nova Blvd., Pacifica CA 94044. (415)355-9069. Contact: Barbara J. Less, associate editor. Estab. 1992. Offered annually to encourage the writing of good, short fiction. Deadline: November 30. Guidelines for #10 SASE. Charges $5 fee. Prizes: 1st-$50; 2nd-$25; 3rd-$10; plus publication in January/February Awards edition.

LONG FICTION CONTEST, White Eagle Coffee Store Press, P.O. Box 383, Fox River Grove IL 60021. (708)639-9200. E-mail: wecspress@aol.com. Website: http://www.members.aol.com/wecspress. Contact: Frank E. Smith, publisher. Offered annually since 1993 for unpublished work to recognize and promote long short stories of 8,000-14,000 words (about 30-50 pages). Deadline: December 15. Guidelines for SASE. Charges $12 fee. $8 for second story in same envelope. A.E. Coppard Prize: $500 and publication plus 25 copies of chapbook. Open to any writer, no restrictions on materials. Sample of previous winner: $5.95, including postage.

THE MALAHAT REVIEW NOVELLA PRIZE, The Malahat Review, Box 1700 STN CSC, Victoria, British Columbia V8W 2Y2 Canada. (250)721-8524. E-mail: malahat@uvic.ca. Contest Director: Derk Wynand. Offered every 2 years (even years) to promote unpublished novellas. Deadline: March 1. Guidelines for SASE. Charges $25 fee (includes a one-year subscription to *Malahat*, published quarterly). Prize: $400, plus payment for publication. ($25/page). Obtains first world rights. After publication rights revert to the author. Open to any writer.

MALICE DOMESTIC AWARD, Malice Domestic, % Pam Reed Bookstore, etc., 27 W. Washington St., Hagerstown MD 21740. (201)797-8896. Fax: (301)797-9453. Website: http://www.erols.com/malice. Contact: Pamela Reed, director. Offered annually for unpublished work. MALICE will award two grants to unpublished writers in the Malice Domestic genre at MALICE VIII in April '99. The competition is designed to help the next generation of Malice authors get their first work published and to foster quality Malice literature. Deadline: December 15. Guidelines for SASE. Prize: $500. Writers must not have published a book in any field. Members of the Malice Domestic Board of Directors and their families are ineligible to apply. MALICE encourages applications from minority candidates.

MARY MCCARTHY PRIZE IN SHORT FICTION, Sarabande Books, 2234 Dundee Rd., #200, Louisville KY 40205. (502)458-4028. Fax: (502)458-4065. E-mail: sarabandeb@aol.com. Website: http://www.SarabandeBooks.org. Contact: Sarah Gorham, contest director. Offered annually to award publication to an outstanding collection of stories or novellas. Submissions accepted January 1-February 15. Guidelines for SASE. Charges $15 fee. Prize: $2,000 publication (paper and cloth), standard royalty contract. All finalists considered for publication. Judged by nationally prominent writers.

MID-LIST PRESS FIRST SERIES AWARD FOR SHORT FICTION, Mid-List Press, 4324 12th Ave. S., Minneapolis MN 55407-3218. Fax: (612)823-8387. E-mail: guide@midlist.org. Website: http://www.midlist.org. Contact: Lane Stiles, senior editor. Open to any writer who has never published a book-length collection of short fiction (short stories, novellas); minimum 50,000 words. Submit entire ms beginning *after* March 31, and must be postmarked by July 1. Accepts simultaneous submissions. Charges $15 fee. Enclose SAS postcard for acknowledgment of receipt of ms. Guidelines and entry form for SASE or from website. Awards include publication and an advance against royalties.

MID-LIST PRESS FIRST SERIES AWARD FOR THE NOVEL, Mid-List Press, 4324-12th Ave. S., Minneapolis MN 55407-3218. Fax: (612)823-8387. E-mail: guide@midlist.org. Website: http://www.midlist.org. Contact: Lane Stil es, senior editor. Offered annually for unpublished novels to locate and publish quality manuscripts by first-time writers, particularly those mid-list titles that major publishers may be rejecting. Deadline: February 1. Guidelines for SASE or from website. Charges $15 fee. Prize: $1,000 advance against royalties, plus publication. Open to any writer who has never published a novel.

MILKWEED NATIONAL FICTION PRIZE, Milkweed Editions, 430 First Ave. N., Suite 400, Minneapolis MN 55401. (612)332-3192. Fax: (612)332-6248. Contact: Elisabeth Fitz, first reader. Estab. 1986. Annual award for unpublis hed works. "Milkweed is looking for a novel, novella, or a collection of short stories. Manuscripts should be of high literary quality and must be double-spaced and between 150-400 pages in length." *Must* request contest guidelines, send SASE. "SAS mailer large enough to hold your manuscript must accompany submission for manuscript to be returned. If no SAS mailer is sent along, manuscript will be recycled." Prize: Publication by Milkweed Editions and a cash advance of $2,000 against any royalties or other payment agreed upon in the contractual arrangement negotiated at the time of acceptance. Winner will be chosen from the manuscripts Milkweed accepts for publication each year. All manuscripts submitted to Milkweed will automatically be considered for the prize. Submission directly to the contest is no longer necessary. "Manuscript must be written in English. Writers should have previously published a book of fiction or three short stories (or novellas) in magazines/journals with national distribution." Catalog available on request for $1.50.

NATIONAL WRITERS ASSOCIATION NOVEL WRITING CONTEST, The National Writers Association, Suite 424, 1450 S. Havana, Aurora CO 80012. (303)751-7844. Fax:(303)751-8593. E-mail: sandywrter@aol.com. Director: Sandy Whelchel. Annual contest "to help develop creative skills, to recognize and reward outstanding ability and to increase the opportunity for the marketing and subsequent publication of novel manuscripts." Deadline: April 1. Guidelines for #10 SASE. Charges $35 fee. Prizes: 1st-$500; 2nd-$300; 3rd-$200.

NATIONAL WRITERS ASSOCIATION SHORT STORY CONTEST, The National Writers Association, Suite 424, 1450 S. Havana, Aurora CO 80012. (303)751-7844. Fax:(303)751-8593. E-mail: sandywrter@aol.com. Director: Sandy Whelchel. Annual contest "to encourage writers in this creative form and to recognize those who excel in fiction writing." Deadline: July 1. Guidelines for #10 SASE. Charges $15 fee. Prizes: $200, $100, $50, copy of *Writer's Market*.

NEPEAN PUBLIC LIBRARY ANNUAL SHORT STORY CONTEST, Nepean Public Library, 101 Centrepointe Dr., Nepean, Ontario K2G 5K7 Canada. E-mail: steasdal@library.on.ca. Contest Director: Marlene McCausland. Offered annually for unpublished short stories to encourage writing in the community." Deadline: March 2. Guidelines for SASE. Charges $5/story fee. Prizes: 1st-$500; 2nd-$250; 3rd-$100. "We retain the right to display and publish them at a later date. All other rights remain with the author." Open to residents of Ottawa-Carleton Regional Municipality, Ontario, age 18 and over.

NEW MUSE AWARD, Broken Jaw Press/M.A.P. Productions, Box 596 Station A, Fredericton, New Brunswick E3B 5A6 Canada. Contact: Joe Blades. Offered annually for unpublished fiction book mss of 120 maximum pages to encourage development of booklength mss by writers without a first book published. Deadline: February 28. Guidelines for SASE (with Canadian postage or IRC). Charges $20 fee (all entrants receive copy of winning book upon publication). Prize: book publication on trade terms.

N NORTHWOODS JOURNAL'S ANNUAL NATIONAL SHORT FICTION CONTEST, Conservatory of American Letters, P.O. Box 298, Thomaston ME 04861. (207)354-0998. Fax: (207)354-8953. E-mail: cal@lme.net. Contact: Dr. Ken Sieben. Offered annually "find the best short fiction of the year." Deadline: February 15. Guidelines for SASE. Charges $7 fee per 2,500 words or any part. Prize: 1st-$100 plus publication and further payment, 2nd-$50 and possible publication, 3rd-$25 and possible publication. Open to all writers.

THE FLANNERY O'CONNOR AWARD FOR SHORT FICTION, The University of Georgia Press, 330 Research Dr., Athens GA 30602-4901. (706)369-6140. Fax: (706)369-6131. E-mail: jkobres@ugapress.uga.edu. Contact: Jane Kobres, competition coordinator. Estab. 1981. Submission period: April-May 31. Charges $15 fee. Does not return mss. Manuscripts must be 200-275 pages long. Authors do not have to be previously published. Guidelines for SASE. Prize: $1,000 and publication by Press under standard book contract.

HOWARD O'HAGAN AWARD FOR SHORT FICTION, Writers Guild of Alberta, 11759 Groat Rd., Edmonton Alberta T5M 3K6 Canada. (403)422-8174. Fax: (403)422-2663. E-mail: writers@compusmart.ab.ca. Assistant Director: Darlene Diver. Short fiction book published in current year. Must be an Alberta author.

CHRIS O'MALLEY PRIZE IN FICTION, *The Madison Review*, Dept. of English, 600 N. Park St., Madison WI 53706. (608)263-3374. Contest Director: Ronald Kuka. Offered annually for previously unpublished work. Awarded to the best piece of fiction. Deadline: September 30. Prize: $500, plus publication in the spring issue of *The Madison Review*. All contest entries are considered as submissions to *The Madison Review*, the literary journal sponsoring the contest. No simultaneous submissions to other publications. Charges $3 fee.

N WILLIAM PEDEN PRIZE IN FICTION, The Missouri Review, 1507 Hillcrest Hall, Columbia MO 65211. (573)882-4474. Fax: (573)884-4671. E-mail: moreview@shawme.missouri.edu. Website: http://www.missouri.edu/~moreview. Contact: Greg Michalson, managing editor. Offered annually "for the best story published in the past volume year of the magazine. All stories published in *MR* are automatically considered." Prize: $1,000 cash prize; the winner is honored at a reading/reception in November.

PEN/FAULKNER AWARDS FOR FICTION, PEN/Faulkner Foundation, 201 East Capitol St., Washington DC 20003. (202)675-0345. Fax: (202)608-1719. E-mail: delaney@folger.edu. Website: http://www.folger.edu. Contact: Janice F. Delaney, executive director:. Offered annually for published work in a calendar year for best book-length work of fiction by American citizen. Deadline: October 31. Prize: $15,000—one winner, 5,000—4 nominees. Judged by 3 writers of fiction (published); different each year.

PLAYBOY COLLEGE FICTION CONTEST, *Playboy*, 680 N. Lake Shore Dr., Chicago IL 60611. (312)751-8000. Website: http://www.playboy.com. Fiction Editor: Alice Turner. Annual award for unpublished short stories by registered students at a college or university. Submissions accepted September 1-January 1. Information in October issue or send SASE to College Fiction Contest, 730 Fifth Ave., New York NY 10019. Prizes: 1st-$3,000 and publication in *Playboy*; 2nd-$500; four runners-up-$200.

PROMETHEUS AWARD/HALL OF FAME, Libertarian Futurist Society, 89 Gebhardt Rd., Penfield NY 14526. (716)248-5646. E-mail: VVARGA@compuserv.com Website: http://www.libertarian.com/LFS/. Contact: Victoria Varga, director. Estab. 1979. Prometheus Award: pro-freedom, anti-authoritarian novel published during previous year. Hall of Fame: one classic libertarian novel at least 5 years old. Deadline: March 1.

QUARTERLY WEST NOVELLA COMPETITION, *Quarterly West*, 317 Olpin Union, University of Utah, Salt Lake City UT 84112. (801)581-3938. Contact: Margot Schilpp, editor. Estab. 1976. Offered biennially for 2 unpublished novellas of 50-125 pages. Charges $20 fee. Guidelines for SASE. Deadline: December 31 of even-numbered years. Prize: 2 winning writers receive $500 and publication in *Quarterly West*.

THOMAS H. RADDALL ATLANTIC FICTION PRIZE, Writers' Federation of Nova Scotia, 1809 Barrington St., #901, Halifax, Nova Scotia B3J 3K8 Canada. (902)423-8116. Fax: (902)422-0881. E-mail: writersl@fox.nstn.ca. Website: http://www.chebucto.ns.ca/Culture/WFNS/index.html. Award Director: Jane Buss. Offered annually to fiction published during the year preceding the competition. The Prize "honors the best fiction writing by an Atlantic born (Nova Scotia, New Brunswick, Newfoundland, Prince Edward Island) or resident (1 year) writer. Deadline: January 30. Forward 4 copies of published book of fiction to the Writers' Federation of Nova Scotia. Prize: $5,000 (Canadian funds) and medal.

SIR WALTER RALEIGH AWARD, North Carolina Literary and Historical Association, 109 E. Jones St., Raleigh NC 27601-2807. (919)733-9375. Awards Coordinator: Jerry C. Cashion. Offered annually for previously published fiction by a North Carolina resident. Deadline: July 15.

HAROLD U. RIBALOW AWARD, Hadassah WZOA, 50 W. 58th St., New York NY 10019. Fax: (212)446-9521. Editor: Alan Tigay. Offered annually for an English-language book of fiction on a Jewish theme published January 1-December 31 in a calendar year. Deadline: April. Prize: $1,000. Books should be submitted by the publisher.

N **RIVER CITY WRITING AWARDS IN FICTION**, The University of Memphis/Hohenberg Foundation, Dept. of English, Memphis TN 38152. (901)678-4591. Fax: (901)678-2226. Director: Dr. Thomas Russell. Offered annually for unpublished short stories of 7,500 words maximum. Deadline: January 20. Guidelines for SASE. Charges $9.50, which is put toward a one year subscription for *River City*. Prize: First place $2,000; second $500; third $300. 15 finalists are chosen by The University of Memphis Creative Writing faculty. Prize winners are chosen by a nationally-known author. Open to any writer.

THE IAN ST. JAMES AWARDS, P.O. Box 60, Cranbrook, Kent TN17 2ZR United Kingdom (01580)212626. Fax: (01580)212041. Contact: Merric Davidson. Offered annually to unpublished short stories. Deadline: April 30. Guidelines for SASE with IRCs. Charges £5 fee or *additional* £10 if *detailed* critique is required. Prizes: 1st-£2,000, 2nd-£1,000, 3rd-£500, seven honorable mentions-£200. Winning stories published in annual book. Runners-up (approximately 40) published in *The New Writer* magazine. Open to writers over 18 without a novel or novella published.

THE SANDSTONE PRIZE IN SHORT FICTION, (formerly Ohio State University Press Prize in Short Fiction), Ohio State University Press and the MFA Program in Creative Writing at The Ohio State University, 1070 Carmack Rd., Columbus OH 43210-1002. (614)292-6930. Fax: (614)292-2065. E-mail: ohiostatepress@osu.edu. Director: William Roorbach. Offered annually to published and unpublished writers. Accepts submissions in January only. Charges $20 fee. Prize: $1,500, publication under a standard book contract, an invitation to Ohio State University to give a public reading and direct a creative writing workshop. Submissions may include short stories, novellas or a combination of both. Manuscripts must be 150-300 typed pagees. Novellas must not exceed 125 pages. No employee or student of Ohio State University is eligible.

SEVENTEEN MAGAZINE FICTION CONTEST, 850 Third Ave., New York NY 10022. E-mail: seventeen@aol.com. Estab. 1948. Contact: Ben Schrank, fiction editor. Previously unpublished short stories from writers 13-21 years old. Deadline: April 30. Guidelines for SASE, or check the November issue. Prize: 1st-$1,000 and publication in the magazine; 2nd-$500; 3rd-$250; five honorable mentions-$50.

N **JOHN SIMMONS SHORT FICTION AWARD and IOWA SHORT FICTION AWARDS**, Iowa Short Fiction Award, Iowa Writers' Workshop, 102 Dey House, Iowa City IA 52242-1000. Offered annually for previously unpublished fiction. Prize: publication by the University of Iowa Press. Guidelines for #10 SASE. Submissions: August 1-September 30 only.

N **KAY SNOW WRITING AWARDS**, Willamette Writers, 9045 SW Barbur Blvd., Suite 5a, Portland OR 97219. (503)452-1592. Fax: (503)452-0372. E-mail: wilwrite@teleport.com. Website: http://www.teleport.com/wilwrite/. Contact: Martha Miller. Annual contest to "offer encouragement and recognition to writers with unpublished submissions." Deadline: May 15. Guidelines for SASE. Charges $15 fee. Prize: 1st-$200, 2nd-$100, 3rd-$50, excerpts published in Willamette Writers newsletter, and winners acknowledged at banquet during writing conference. Acquires right to publish excerpts from winning pieces one time in their newsletter.

SOUTH CAROLINA FICTION PROJECT, South Carolina Arts Commission, 1800 Gervais St., Columbia SC 29201. (803)734-8696. Fax: (803)734-8526. Contest Director: Sara June Goldstein. Offered annually for unpublished fiction. Deadline: January 15. Guidelines for SASE. Prize: $500. Judged by a panel of professional writers. *The Post and Courier* newspaper (Charleston SC) purchases first publication rights. Open to any writer who is a legal resident of South Carolina, as well as writers residing in the state. 12 stories are selected for monthly publication.

N **CARL STENTNER SHORT STORY AWARD**, P.E.I. Council of the Arts, 115 Richmond St., Charlestown PEI C1A 1H7 Canada. (902)368-4410. Fax: (902)368-4418. Contact: Judy MacDonald. Contest offered annually for unpublished short stories; 1 story per entry. Deadline: February 15. Guidelines for SASE. Charges $8 fee. Prize: Monetary. Open to individuals who have been resident of Prince Edward Island at least 6-12 months preceeding the deadline for entries.

N **STORY'S CARSON MCCULLERS PRIZE FOR THE SHORT STORY**, STORY, 1507 Dana Ave., Cincinnati OH 45207-9996. (513)531-2690, ext. 268. Fax: (513)531-1843. E-mail: competitions@fwpubs.com. Contact: Sandi Luppert, promotion manager. Competition open to literary work of all styles and subjects. Offered annually for unpublished work not under consideration at other publications. Charges $10 fee. Prize: 1st-$2,500; 3 finalists-$1,000; 20 honorable mentions-Citations of Merit. STORY reserves the right to publish selected winners. Buys first North American serial rights. Guidelines for SASE. Deadline: May 1.

STORY'S SHORT STORY COMPETITION, STORY, 1507 Dana Ave., Cincinnati OH 45207. (513)531-2690, ext. 268. Fax: (513)531-1843. E-mail: competitions@fwpubs.com. Contact: Sandi Luppert, promotion manager. Offered annually for unpublished work. Deadline: October 31. Guidelines for SASE. Charges $10 fee. Prize: 1st-$1,500; 2nd-$750; 3rd-$500; 4th-10th-$100; 11th-25th-$50 worth of Story Press books. On occasion, awards merchandise prizes from additional sponsors. Entries must not be under consideration at other publications. Writers are free to market them elsewhere after winners are announced. STORY reserves the right to publish selected winners. Buys first North American rights.

N **SUDDEN FICTION CONTEST**, *Berkeley Fiction Review*, % Eshleman Library, 201 Heller Lounge, University of California, Berkeley CA 94720-4500. Offered annually for unpublished short stories under 1,000 words to showcase the relatively new genre of sudden fiction. Deadline: Feb. 9. Charges $6 fee/first entry, $4/subsequent entries. Prize: 1st-$200 and publication, 2nd, 3rd-publication.

TARA FELLOWSHIP FOR SHORT FICTION, The Heekin Group Writers' & Education Fund, P.O. Box 1534, Sisters OR 97759. Phone/fax: (541)548-4147. E-mail: Hgfh1@aol.com. Director: Sarah Heekin Redfield. Offered annually for unpublished work. "Our writing fellowships program is designed to support the community of new and emerging writers." Deadline: December 1. Guidelines for SASE. Charges $25 fee. Prize: 2 for Tara Fellowship, $1,500.

SYDNEY TAYLOR MANUSCRIPT COMPETITION, Association of Jewish Libraries, 1327 Wyntercreek Lane, Dunwoody GA 30338. Fax: (770)671-8380. E-mail: m-psand@mindspring.com. Website: http://www.aleph.lib.ohio-state.edu/www/awl.html. Coordinator: Paula Sandfelder. Offered annually for unpublished authors of books only. "Material should be a work of fiction in English, with universal appeal of Jewish content for readers aged 8-11 years. It should deepen the understanding of Judaism for all children, Jewish and non-Jewish, and reveal positive aspects of Jewish life. No short stories. Length: 64-200 pages." Deadline: January 15. Guidelines for SASE. Prize: $1,000. Judged by 5 AJL member librarians. Open to any unpublished writer of books.

STEVEN TURNER AWARD, The Texas Institute of Letters, P.O. Box 298300, Fort Worth TX 76129. (817)921-7822. Fax: (817)257-5075. E-mail: jalter@gamma.is.tcu.edu. Website: http://www.gamma.is.tcu.edu/prs/til. Submissions must be marked Attn: TCU Press. Contact: Judy Alter, director. Offered annually for previously published work between January 1 and December 31 of year before. The award is given to recognize the writer of the best first book of fiction submitted. Deadline: January 4. Guidelines for SASE. Prize: $1,000. To be eligible, a writer must have been born in Texas, or have lived in the state for at least two consecutive years at some time, or the subject matter of the work should be associated with the state.

N **VERY SHORT FICTION AWARD**, Glimmer Train Press, Inc. 710 SW Madison St., Suite 504, Portland OR 97205-2900. (503)221-0836. Fax: (503)221-0837. Contact: Linda Burmeister Davies. Website: http://www.glimmertrain.com. Offered twice yearly to encourage the art of the very short story. "Send your unpublished very short story with $10 reading fee/story. Word count: 2,000 max. Must be postmarked April 1-July 31 or November 1-January 31. Cover letter optional. First page of story to include name, address, phone, word count, and 'VSF'. 'VSF' must also be written on the outside of the envelope. Winners will be called by November 1 or May 1. For a list of winners, include SASE with your story." Prizes: First place is $1,200, publication in *Glimmer Train Stories* (circulation 13,000), and 20 copies of that issue. First/second runners-up receive $500/300, respectively and consideration for publication.

EDWARD LEWIS WALLANT BOOK AWARD, Department of English, Franklin & Marshall College, P.O. Box 3003, Lancaster PA 17604-3003. Contact: Dr. Sanford Pinsller. Estab. 1963. Offered for fiction with significance for the American Jew (novel or short stories) by an American writer (one who was born or educated in the United States) published during current year. Deadline: December 31.

WELLSPRING'S SHORT FICTION CONTEST, 4080 83rd Ave. N., Suite A, Brooklyn Park MN 55443. Phone/fax: (612)566-6663. Contest Director: Meg Miller. Estab. 1988. Offered 2 times/year for previously unpublished short fiction to encourage the writing of well-crafted and plotted, meaningful short fiction. Deadlines: January 1, July 1. Guidelines for #10 SASE. Charges adults $10 fee; teens $5 fee. Prize: 1st-$50; 2nd-$30; 3rd-$20. $6 for sample copy.

THOMAS WOLFE FICTION PRIZE, North Carolina Writers' Network, 3501 Hwy. 54 W., Studio C, Chapel Hill NC 27516. Fax: (919)929-0535. E-mail: nc_writers@unc.edu. Contact: Frances O. Dowell, program coordinator. Offered annually for unpublished work "to recognize a notable work of fiction—either short story or novel excerpt—while honoring one of North Carolina's best writers—Thomas Wolfe." Deadline: August 31. Guidelines for SASE. Charges $7 fee. Prize: $500 and potential publication. Past judges have included Anne Tyler, Barbara Kingsolver, C. Michael Curtis and Randall Kenan.

TOBIAS WOLFF AWARD IN FICTION, The Bellingham Review, M.S.9053, Western Washington University, Bellingham WA 98225. Website: http://www.wwu.edu/~bhreview/. Contact: Mr. Robin Hemley. Offered annually for unpublished short stories or novel excerpts. Submissions from January 2-March 1. Guidelines for SASE. Charges $10 fee/first entry; $5 for subsequent entries. Prize: 1st-$1,000; 2nd-$250; 3rd-$100, plus publication and copies.

WRITERS' JOURNAL ANNUAL SHORT STORY CONTEST, Val-Tech Publishing, Inc., P.O. Box 25376, St. Paul MN 55125. (612)730-4280. Website: http://www.sowashco.com/writersjournal. Contact: Valerie Hockert. Estab. 1987. Previously unpublished short stories. Deadline: May 31. Charges $5 fee.

WRITERS' JOURNAL FICTION CONTEST, Val-Tech Publishing, P.O. Box 25376, St. Paul MN 55125. (612)730-4280. Website: http://www.sowashco.com/writersjournal. Contact: Valerie Hockert. Offered annually for previously unpublished fiction. Deadline: December 31. Charges $5 fee.

Poetry

N **MILTON ACORN POETRY AWARD**, P.E.I. Council of the Arts, 115 Richmond St., Charlestown PE C1A 1H7 Canada. (902)368-4410. Fax: (902)368-4418. Contact: Judy MacDonald. Contest offered annually for unpublished poetry; 10 pages per entry maximum, either one poem or a collection. Deadline: February 15. Guidelines for SASE. Charges $8 fee. Prize: Monetary. Open to individuals who have been resident of Prince Edward Island at least 6-12 months proceeding the deadline for entries.

N **ADAPTABLES ANNUAL POETRY AWARD**, The Adaptables, Inc., P.O. Box 30246, Winston-Salem NC 27130-0246. (336)896-0779. Fax: (336)759-2677. Contact: Mike Phillips. Offered annually "to increase awareness of the abilities of people with disabilities. Deadline: September 15. Guidelines for SASE. Charges $10/poem. Prizes: 1st-$200, 2nd-$100, 3rd-$50, poems of merit-publication plus copies. Writer must have a disability as defined by The Americans with Disabilities Act.

AKRON POETRY PRIZE, University of Akron Press, 374B Bierce Library, Akron OH 44325-1703. (330)972-5342. Fax: (330)972-5132. E-mail: press@uakron.edu. Website: http://www.uakron.edu/uapress. Contest Director: Elton Glaser. Annual contest for unpublished poetry. "The Akron Poetry Prize brings the public writers with original and compelling voices. Books must exhibit three essential qualities: mastery of language, maturity of feeling and complexity of thought." Deadline: Entries must be postmarked between May 15-June 30. Guidelines available online or for SASE. Charges $20. Winning poet receives $500 and publication of book. The final selection will be made by a nationally prominent poet. The University of Akron Press has the right to publish the winning manuscript, inherent with winning the Poetry Prize. Open to all poets writing in English.

ANHINGA PRIZE FOR POETRY, Anhinga Press, P.O. Box 10595, Tallahassee FL 32302. Phone/fax: (904)442-6323. Website: http://www.anhinga.org. Contact: Rick Campbell. Offered annually for a book-length collection of poetry by an author who has not published more than one book of poetry. "We use a well-known independent judge." Submit January 1-March 15. Guidelines for #10 SASE. Charges $20 fee. Prize: $2,000 and publication. Open to any writer writing in English.

ANNUAL INTERNATIONAL POETRY CONTEST, Poet's Study Club of Terre Haute, Indiana, 826 S. Center St., Terre Haute IN 47807. (812)234-0819. Contact: Esthre Alman, president of Poet's Study Club. Offered annually in 3 categories: Serious Poems, Light Verse, Haiku. Deadline: February 1. Guidelines for SASE. Prizes: 1st-$25 and 2nd-$15 in each category. Judged by competent writers who also often judge for our State Poetry Societies, etc. Open to any writer.

ANNUAL POETRY CONTEST, National Federation of State Poetry Societies, 1206 13th Ave., SE, St. Cloud MN 56304. Chairperson: Claire van Breemen Downes. Estab. 1959. Previously unpublished poetry. "Fifty categories. Flier lists them all." Deadline: March 15. Guidelines for #10 SASE. Charges fees. See guidelines for fees and prizes. All awards are announced in June. Top awards only (not honorable mentions) published the following June.

ATLANTIC CANADIAN POETRY PRIZE, Writers' Federation of Nova Scotia, 1809 Barrington St., Suite 901, Halifax, Nova Scotia B3J 3K8 Canada. (902)423-8116. Fax: (902)422-0881. E-mail: writers1@fox.nstn.ca. Contact: Awards committee. Offered annually to the best book of poetry by Atlantic Canadian published during previous calendar, except 1998 prize which must have appeared in previous 2 calendar years. Deadline: January 30. Send 4 copies of book with letter. Prize: Cash and prize ceremony. Judged by a committee. Open to Atlantic Canadians only.

THE FREDERICK BOCK PRIZE, *Poetry*, 60 W. Walton St., Chicago IL 60610. (312)255-3703. Editor: Joseph Parisi. Offered annually for poems published in *Poetry* during the preceding twelve months (October through September). Guidelines for SASE. Prize: $300. Judged by the editors of *Poetry*. *Poetry* buys all rights to the poems published in the magazine. Copyrights are returned to the authors on request. Any writer may submit poems to *Poetry*. Only poems published in *Poetry* during the preceding year are considered for the annual prizes.

GEORGE BOGIN MEMORIAL AWARD, Poetry Society of America, 15 Gramercy Park S., New York NY 10003. (212) 254-9628. E-mail: timothyd@poetrysociety.org. Website: http://www.poetrysociety.org. Contact: Award Director. Offered for a selection of 4-5 poems that reflects the encounter of the ordinary and the extraordinary, uses language in an original way, and takes a stand against oppression in any of its forms. Guidelines for #10 SASE. Guidelines subject to change. Deadline: December 19. Charges $5 fee for nonmembers. Prize: $500.

BOSTON REVIEW POETRY CONTEST, *Boston Review*, E-53-407 MIT, Cambridge MA 02139. (617)494-0708. Submit up to five unpublished poems, no more than ten pages total. Deadline: June 15, 1999. Charges $10 fee, payable to *Boston Review*, check or money order. Prize: $1,000 and publication in the October/November 1998-99 issue of *Boston Review*.

BARBARA BRADLEY AWARD, New England Poetry Club, 11 Puritan Rd., Arlington MA 02174-7710. Contact: Virginia Thayer. Offered annually for a lyric poem under 21 lines, written by a woman. Deadline: June 30. Guidelines for SASE. Charges $3 entry fee for nonmembers. Prize: $200.

BRITTINGHAM PRIZE IN POETRY/FELIX POLLAK PRIZE IN POETRY, University of Wisconsin Press, 2537 Daniels St., Madison WI 53718-6772. Contest Director: Ronald Wallace. Estab. 1985. Unpublished book-length mss of original poetry. Submissions must be *received* by the press *during* the month of September accompanied by a SASE for contest results. Prizes: $1,000 and publication of the *2 winning mss*. Guidelines for #10 SASE. Manuscripts will *not* be returned. Charges $20 fee, payable to University of Wisconsin Press. One entry fee covers both prizes.

BUCKNELL SEMINAR FOR YOUNGER POETS, Stadler Center for Poetry, Bucknell University, Lewisburg PA 17837. (717)524-1853. E-mail: sstyers@bucknell.edu. Website: http://www.bucknell.edu/departments/english/poetry_center/. Director: Cynthia Hogue. Contact: Steven Styers, assistant to the director. Offered annually. "The Seminar provides an extended opportunity for undergraduates to write and to be guided by established poets. It balances private time for writing, disciplined learning, and camaraderie among the 10 Fellows selected." Deadline: March 1. Guidelines for SASE. Prize: 10 fellowships provide tuition, room, board and spaces for writing during 4-week long seminar. Fellows are responsible for their own transportation. Only students from American colleges who have completed their sophomore, junior or senior years are eligible to apply.

CANADIAN CHAPBOOK MANUSCRIPT CONTEST, League of Canadian Poets, 54 Wolseley St., Toronto Ontario M5T 1A5 Canada. (416)504-1657. (416)504-0096. E-mail: league@ican.net. Website: http://www.swifty.com. Offered annually for unpublished work to seek and encourage new poetic talent. Deadline: March 1. Guidelines for SASE. Charges $5 fee for ms. Prize: $1000 plus publication. Canadian citizens or landed immigrants only.

CANADIAN YOUTH POETRY CONTEST, League of Canadian Poets, 54 Wolseley St., Toronto Ontario M5T 1A5 Canada. (416)504-1657. (416)504-0096. E-mail: league@ican.net. Website: http://www.swifty.com. Offered annually for unpublished work to seek and encourage new poetic talent. Deadline: March 1. Guidelines for SASE. Charges $5 fee for poem. Prize: 1st -$500; 2nd-$350; 3rd-$250. Canadian citizens or landed immigrants only.

CLEVELAND STATE UNIVERSITY POETRY CENTER PRIZE, Cleveland State University Poetry Center, 1983 E. 24 St., Cleveland OH 44115-2440. (216)687-3986. Fax: (216)687-6943. E-mail: poetrycenter@popmail.csuohio.edu. Website: http://www.ims.csuohio.edu/poetry/poetrycenter.html. Contact: Poetry Center Coordinator. Estab. 1962. Offered to identify, reward and publish the best unpublished book-length poetry ms submitted. Submissions accepted only December-February. Deadline: Postmarked on or before March 1. Charges $15 fee. "Submission implies willingness to sign contract for publication if manuscript wins." $1,000 prize for best ms. One or more of the other finalist mss may be published for standard royalty (no prize). Guidelines for SASE. Manuscripts are not returned.

CONTEMPORARY POETRY SERIES, University of Georgia Press, 330 Research Dr., Athens GA 30602. (706)369-6140. Fax: (706)369-6131. E-mail: jkobres@ugapress.uga.edu. Coordinator: Jane Kobres. Offered 2 times/year. Two awards: for poets who have not had a full-length book of poems published (deadline in September), and poets with at least one full-length publication (deadline in January). Guidelines for SASE. Charges $15 fee.

BILLEE MURRAY DENNY POETRY AWARD, Lincoln College, 300 Keokuk St., Lincoln IL 62656. Contact: Janet Overton, contest administrator. Estab. 1981. Unpublished poetry. Deadline: May 31. Prizes: $1,000, $500, $250. Charges $10/poem fee (limit 3-$30). Send SASE for entry form.

ALICE FAY DI CASTAGNOLA AWARD, Poetry Society of America, 15 Gramercy Park S., New York NY 10003. (212)254-9628. E-mail: timothyD@poetrysociety.org. Website: http://www.poetrysociety.org. Contact: Award Director. Manuscript in progress: poetry, prose or verse-drama. Guidelines for #10 SASE. Guidelines subject to change. Deadline: December 19. Prize: $1,000. Members only.

"DISCOVERY"/THE NATION, The Joan Leiman Jacobson Poetry Prizes, The Unterberg Poetry Center of the 92nd Street YM-YWHA, 1395 Lexington Ave., New York NY 10128. Contact: Kelli Rae Patton, assistant to the director. Estab. 1973. Open to poets who have not published a book of poems (chapbooks, self-published books included). Deadline: late January. Charges $5 fee. Write for complete competition guidelines, or call (212)415-5759.

MILTON DORFMAN POETRY PRIZE, Rome Art & Community Center, 308 W. Bloomfield St., Rome NY 13440. Fax: (315)339-1090. Contact: Maureen Murphy. Estab. 1990. "The purpose of the Milton Dorfman Poetry Prize is to offer poets an outlet for their craft. All submissions must be previously unpublished." Entries accepted: July 1-November 1. Guidelines for #10 SASE. Charges $5 fee per poem. Make checks payable to: Rome Art & Community Center. Prize: 1st-$500; 2nd-$200; 3rd-$100. Open to any writer. Include name, address and phone number.

EDITORS' PRIZE, Spoon River Poetry Review, Campus Box 4240, English Dept., Illinois State University, Normal IL 61790-4240. (309)438-7906. Fax: (309)438-5414. Website: http://www.litline.org. Contest Director: Lucia Cordell Getsi, editor. Offered annually to unpublished poetry "to identify and reward excellence." Deadline: May 1. Guidelines for SASE. Charges $15/3 poem fee (entitles entrant to a year's subscription valued at $14). Prizes: 1st-$500, two $100 runner-up prizes, publication of first place, runners-up, honorable mention and selected finalist poems. Judged by a nationally-known poet. Open to all writers.

N **ROBERT G. ENGLISH/POETRY IN PRINT**, P.O. Box 30981, Albuquerque NM 87190-0981. Phone/fax: (505)888-3937. Contact: Robert G. English. Offered annually "to help a poetry writer accomplish their own personal endeavors. Hopefully the prize amount of the Poetry in Print award will grow to a higher significance." Deadline: August 1. Charges $5/poem. Prize: $500. "The contest is open to any writer of any age. Hopefully to prepare writers other than just journalists with a stronger desire to always tell the truth."

N **EYE SCRY POETRY CHAPBOOK CONTEST**, Eye Scry Publications (MKASHEF Enterprises), P.O. Box 688, Yucca Valley CA 92286-0688. Contact: Wendy Rathbone. "Biannual contest to find short poetry chapbooks that are exceptional and deserve to be published." Deadlines: January 1 and July 1. Guidelines for SASE. Charges $10 fee. Prizes: 1st-$100, 2nd-$50, 3rd-$25. "All poets, all themes welcomed. Manuscripts should be 20-30 pages. Send SASE for winners list."

NORMA FARBER FIRST BOOK AWARD, Poetry Society of America, 15 Gramercy Park S., New York NY 10003. (212)254-9628. E-mail: timothyD@poetrysociety.org. Website: http://www.poetrysociety.org. Contact: Award Director. First book of original poetry submitted by the publisher. Deadline: December 19. Charges $10/book fee. Guidelines for #10 SASE. Guidelines subject to change. Prize: $500.

THE 49th PARALLEL POETRY AWARD, The Bellingham Review, M.S. 9053, Western Washington University, Bellingham WA 98225. Website: http://www.wwu.edu/~bhreview. Contest Director: Robin Hemley. Estab. 1977. Offered annually for unpublished poetry. Submit October 1-December 31. Send SASE for new guidelines. Charges $5 fee/poem; checks payable to The Western Foundation/Bellingham Review. Awards: 1st-$500, 2nd-$250, 3rd-$100, plus publication and copies.

N **THE FOUR WAY BOOKS INTRO SERIES**, Four Way Books, P.O. Box 535, Village Station, New York NY 10014. Phone/fax: (781)837-4887. Submissions accepted January 1, 1999 through March 31, 1999. Guidelines for SASE. Charges $18 fee/submissions. Prize: $2,000 honorarium, $1,500 author tour money and publication of winning ms. Judge: to be announced.

GREEN LAKE CHAPBOOK PRIZE, Owl Creek Press, 2693 SW Camano Dr., Camano Island WA 98292. Contact: Rich Ives. Any combination of published and unpublished poems under 40 pages in length as long as the work has not previously appeared in book form (except anthologies). Guidelines for SASE. Include SASE for return of ms. Deadline: August 15. Charges $10 fee. Prize: Publication and $500 advance against royalties.

N **GROLIER POETRY PRIZE**, Grolier Poetry Book Shop, Inc. & Ellen LaForge Memorial Poetry Foundation, Inc., 6 Plympton St., Cambridge MA 02138. (617)547-4648. Website: http://www.boston.com. Contact: Ms. Louisa Solano. Estab. 1973. For previously unpublished work to encourage and recognize developing writers. Open to all poets who have not published with either a vanity, small press, trade, or chapbook of poetry. Opens January 15; deadline: May 1. Guidelines must be followed; send SASE. Charges $6 fee. Prize: honorarium of $150 for two poets. Also poems of each winner and 4 runners-up will be published in the Grolier Poetry Prize Annual.

N **ERNEST HEMINGWAY POETRY COMPETITION**, International Hemingway Festival, 2323 Del Prado Blvd., Cape Coral FL 33990. (941)945-0308. Website: http://www.hemingwayfestival.com. Contact: Mina Hemingway. Offered annually for unpublished poets. Deadline: May 1. Guidelines and entry form for SASE. Charges $10 fee. Prize: $250, publication in *Sanibel Captiva Review* and entry to Ernest Hemingway Literary Conference. Winner announced last day of festival.

CECIL HEMLEY MEMORIAL AWARD, Poetry Society of America, 15 Gramercy Park S., New York NY 10003. (212)254-9628. E-mail: timothyd@poetrysociety.org. Website: http://www.poetrysociety.org. Contact: Award Director. Unpublished lyric poem on a philosophical theme. Guidelines for #10 SASE. Deadline: December 19. Members only. Prize: $300.

THE BESS HOKIN PRIZE, *Poetry*, 60 W. Walton St., Chicago IL 60610. (312)255-3703. Editor, *Poetry*: Joseph Parisi. Offered annually for poems published in *Poetry* during the preceding twelve months (October through September). Guidelines for SASE. Prize: $500. Judged by the editors of *Poetry. Poetry* buys all rights to the poems published in the magazine. Copyrights are returned to the authors on request. Any writer may submit poems to *Poetry.* Only poems published in *Poetry* during the preceding year are considered for the annual prizes.

N **FIRMAN HOUGHTON AWARD**, New England Poetry Club, 11 Puritan Rd., Arlington MA 02174-7710. Contest Director: Virginia Thayer. Offered annually for a lyric poem worthy of the former NEPC president. Deadline: June 30. Guidelines for SASE. Charges $5 or 3 poems for $10 entry fee for nonmembers. Prize: $250.

IOWA POETRY PRIZES, University of Iowa Press, 119 W. Park Rd., Iowa City IA 52242. Fax: (319)335-2055. Website: http://www.uiowa.edu/~uipress. Contact: Holly Carver, interim director. "The awards were initiated to encourage mature poets and their work." Manuscripts received in May. Send SASE. No reader's fee. Two $1,000 prizes are awarded annually. Competition open to writers of English (whether citizens of US or not) who have published at least 1 previous book. No member of the faculty, staff or student body of University of Iowa is eligible.

RANDALL JARRELL POETRY PRIZE, North Carolina Writers' Network, 3501 Highway 54 West, Studio C, Chapel Hill NC 27516. E-mail: ncwriters@unc.sunsite.edu. Website: http://sunsite.unc.edu/ncwriters. Contact: Frances O. Dowell, program coordinator. Offered annually for unpublished work "to honor Randall Jarrell and his life at UNC-Greensboro by recognizing the best poetry submitted." Deadline: November 1. Guidelines for SASE. Charges $7 fee. Prize: $500, a public reading and reception and publication in *Parnassus: Poetry in Review.*

THE CHESTER H. JONES FOUNDATION NATIONAL POETRY COMPETITION, P.O. Box 498, Chardon OH 44024-9996. Estab. 1982. Contact: Mary J. Ferris, manager. Offered annually to encourage unpublished poets. Winning poems plus others, called "commendations," are published in a chapbook available from the foundation. Deadline: March 31. Charges $2 fee for first poem, $1 for each succeeding poem up to 10. Maximum 10 entries, no more than 32 lines each; must be unpublished. Prize: 1st-$1,000; 2nd-$750; 3rd-$500; 4th-$250; 5th-$100; several honorable mentions-$50. All commendations which are printed in the winners book receive $10. Winners receive the book free. "We require the right to publish the poems first."

THE JUNIPER PRIZE, University of Massachusetts, Amherst MA 01003. (413)545-2217. Fax: (413)545-1226. Website: http://www.umass.edu/umpress. Contact: Chris Hammel, assistant editor. Estab. 1964. Subsequent book of poetry. Deadline: September 30. Charges $10 fee.

KALLIOPE'S ANNUAL SUE SANIEL ELKIND POETRY CONTEST, *Kalliope, a journal of women's art*, 3939 Roosevelt Blvd., Jacksonville FL 32205. (904)381-3511. Contact: Mary Sue Koeppel. Offered annually for unpublished work. "Poetry may be in any style and on any subject. Maximum poem length is 50 lines. Only unpublished poems and poems not submitted elsewhere are eligible." Deadline: November 1. Guidelines for SASE. Charges entry fee: $4/poem or 3 poems for $10. No limit on number of poems entered by any one poet. Prize: $1,000, publication of poem in *Kalliope*. The winning poem is published as are the finalists' poems. Copyright then returns to the authors.

BARBARA MANDIGO KELLY PEACE POETRY AWARDS, Nuclear Age Peace Foundation, 1187 Coast Village Rd., Suite 123, Santa Barbara CA 93108. Fax: (805)568-0466. E-mail: wagingpeace@napf.org. Website: http://www.napf.org. Contact: Chris Pizzinat and Ruth Floyd. Offered annually for unpublished poems "to encourage poets to explore and illuminate some aspect of peace and the human spirit." Deadline: Postmarked by July 1. Guidelines for SASE. Charges $5 fee for 1-3 poems. No fee for youth entries. Prizes: Adult-$500, youth (13-18)-$250, youth (12 and under)-$250. Judged by a committee of poets chosen by the Nuclear Age Peace Foundation. The Nuclear Age Peace Foundation reserves the right to publish and distribute the award-winning poems. Open to any writer.

THE GEORGE KENT PRIZE, *Poetry*, 60 W. Walton St., Chicago IL 60610. (312)255-3703. Editor, *Poetry*: Joseph Parisi. Offered annually for poems by an Illinois author published in *Poetry* during the preceding twelve months (October through September). Guidelines for SASE. Prize: $500. Judged by the editors of *Poetry*. *Poetry* buys all rights to the poems published in the magazine. Copyrights are returned to the authors on request. Any writer may submit poems to *Poetry*. Only poems published in *Poetry* during the preceding year are considered for the annual prizes. This contest is open only to any resident of Illinois.

(HELEN AND LAURA KROUT MEMORIAL) OHIOANA POETRY AWARD, Ohioana Library Association, 65 S. Front St., Suite 1105, Columbus OH 43215. (614)466-3831. Fax: (614)728-6974. E-mail: ohioana@winslo.ohio.gov. Website: http://www.oplin.lib.oh.us/OHIOANA/. Contact: Linda R. Hengst. Offered annually "to an individual whose body of work has made, and continues to make, a significant contribution to the poetry and through whose work, interest in poetry has been developed." Deadline: December 31. Guidelines for SASE. Prize: $1,000. Recipient must have been born in Ohio or lived in Ohio at least 5 years.

LAST POEMS POETRY CONTEST, sub-TERRAIN Magazine, P.O. Box 1575, Bentall Centre, Vancouver, British Columbia V6C 2P7 Canada. (604)876-8710. Fax: (604)879-2667. E-mail: subter@pinc.com. Offered annually for unpublished poetry that encapsulates the North American experience at the close of the 20th Century. Deadline: January 31. Guidelines for SASE. Charges $15 fee, 4 poem limit. Prize: $200, publication in spring issue and 4-issue subscription to sub-TERRAIN.

THE JAMES LAUGHLIN AWARD, The Academy of American Poets, 584 Broadway, Suite 1208, New York NY 10012-3250. (212)274-0343 Ext. 14. Fax: (212)274-9427. E-mail: poets@artswire.org. Website: http://www.poets.org. Contact: India Amos. Offered annually to submissions under contract with publishers. Previously published entries must have come under contract during the 12 months preceding the deadline. The purpose of the award is to recognize and support a poet's second book. Deadline: April 30. Guideline for SASE. Prize: $5,000 and the Academy will purchase at least 6,000 hardcover copies for distribution. Judged by a panel of three poets. Submissions must be in English by one poet, and it must be the poet's second book.

LEAGUE OF CANADIAN POETS AWARDS, National Poetry Contest, Canadian Poetry Chapbook Manuscript Contest, Canadian Youth Poetry Contest, Gerald Lampert Memorial Award, and Pat Lowther Memorial Award, 54 Wolseley St., 3rd Floor, Toronto, Ontario M5T 1A5 Canada. (416)504-1657. Fax: (416)504-0096. E-mail: league@ican.net. Website: http://www.swifty.com/lc/. Estab. 1966. Offered annually to promote new Canadian poetry/poets and also to recognize exceptional work in each category. Submissions to be published in the preceding year (awards), or previously unpublished (poetry contest, chapbook contest, youth contest). Deadline: January 31. Deadline for chapbook contest: March 1. Enquiries from publishers welcome. Charge: $6/poem fee for contest, $15 for chapbook contest; $5/poem for youth poetry contest and $15 fee/title for each award. Open to Canadians living at home and abroad. The candidate must be a Canadian citizen or landed immigrant, although publisher need not be Canadian. For complete contest and awards rules, contact Edita Petrauskaite at address above.

THE LEVINSON PRIZE, *Poetry*, 60 W. Walton St., Chicago IL 60610. (312)255-3703. Editor, *Poetry*: Joseph Parisi. Offered annually for poems published in *Poetry* during the preceding twelve months (October through September). Guidelines for SASE. Prize: $500. Judged by the editors of *Poetry*. *Poetry* buys all rights to the poems published in the magazine. Copyrights are returned to the authors on request. Any writer may submit poems to *Poetry*. Only poems published in *Poetry* during the preceding year are considered for the annual prizes.

THE RUTH LILLY POETRY PRIZE, The Modern Poetry Association, 60 W. Walton St., Chicago IL 60610-3305. Contact: Joseph Parisi. Estab. 1986. Offered annually to poet whose accomplishments in the field of poetry warrant extraordinary recognition. No applicants or nominations are accepted. Deadline varies. Prize: $75,000.

LOCAL 7's ANNUAL NATIONAL POETRY COMPETITION, Santa Cruz/Monterey Local 7, National Writers Union, P.O. Box 2409, Aptos CA 95001-2409. Website: http://www.mbay.net/~nwu. Contact: Contest Coordinator. Offered annually for previously unpublished poetry to encourage the writing of poetry and to showcase unpublished work of high quality. Proceeds support the work of Local 7 of the National Writers Union. Deadline varies. Guidelines for #10 SASE. Charges $3/poem fee. Prize: 1st-$200; 2nd-$100; 3rd-$50.

N **LOUISE LOUIS/EMILY F. BOURNE STUDENT POETRY AWARD**, Poetry Society of America, 15 Gramercy Park NY 10003. (212)254-9628. Fax: (212)673-2352. E-mail: timothyd@poetrysociety.org. Website: http://www.poetrysociety.org. Director: Timothy Donnelly. Offered annually for published work to promote excellence in student poetry. Deadline: December 22. Guidelines for SASE. Charges $1 per students submitting single entries. $10 per high school submitting unlimited number of their students' poems. Prize: $100. Judged by prominent established poets. Open to American high school or preparatory school students (grades 9 to 12).

LYRIC POETRY AWARD, Poetry Society of America, 15 Gramercy Park, New York NY 10003. (212)254-9628. Fax: (212)673-2352. E-mail: timothyD@poetrysociety.org. Website: http://www.poetrysociety.org. Director: Timothy Donnelly. Offered annually for unpublished work to promote excellence in the lyric poetry field. Deadline: December 19. Guidelines for SASE. Prize: $500.

NAOMI LONG MADGETT POETRY AWARD, Lotus Press, Inc., P.O. Box 21607, Detroit MI 48221. (313)861-1280. Fax: (313)861-4740. E-mail: lotuspress@aol.com. Contact: Constance Withers. Offered annually to recognize an outstanding unpublished poetry ms by an African-American. Entries accepted from February 1-April 1. Guidelines for SASE. Charges $15 fee. Prize: $500 and publication by Lotus Press. Open to any African-American poet.

THE MALAHAT REVIEW LONG POEM PRIZE, The Malahat Review, Box 1700 STNCSC, Victoria, British Columbia V8W 2Y2 Canada. E-mail: malahat@uvic.ca. Contact: Derk Wynand. Offered every 2 years to unpublished long poems. Deadline: March 1. Guidelines for SASE. Charges $25 fee (includes a one-year subscription to the *Malahat*, published quarterly.) Prize: $400, plus payment from publication ($25/page). Preliminary reading by editorial board; final judging by the editor and 2 recognized poets. Obtains first world rights. After publication rights revert to the author. Open to any writer.

THE LENORE MARSHALL POETRY PRIZE, (formerly The Lenore Marshall Prize), *The Nation* and The Academy of American Poets, 584 Broadway, Suite 1208, New York NY 10012. (212)274-0343, ext. 14. E-mail: poets@artswire.org. Website: http://www.poets.org. Awards Administrator: India Amos. Book of poems published in US during previous year and nominated by the publisher. Prize: $10,000. Deadline: June 1. Send SASE to the Academy of American Poets for details.

LUCILLE MEDWICK MEMORIAL AWARD, Poetry Society of America, 15 Gramercy Park S., New York NY 10003. (212)254-9628. E-mail: timothyD@poetrysociety.org. Website: http://www.poetrysociety.org. Contact: Award Director. Original poem in any form or freedom on a humanitarian theme. Guidelines for #10 SASE. Guidelines subject to change. Prize: $500. Deadline: December 19. Members only.

MID-LIST PRESS FIRST SERIES AWARD FOR POETRY, Mid-List Press, 4324 12th Ave. S., Minneapolis MN 55407-3218. Fax: (612)823-8387. E-mail: guide@midlist.org. Website: http://www.midlist.org. Contact: Lane Stiles, senior editor. Estab. 1990. Offered annually for unpublished book of poetry to encourage new poets. Deadline: February 1. Guidelines for SASE or from website. Charges $15 fee. Prize: publication and an advance against royalties. Judged by Mid-List's editors and ms readers. Winners are offered a contract at the conclusion of the judging. Contest is open to any writer who has never published a book of poetry. ("We do not consider a chapbook to be a book of poetry.")

VASSAR MILLER PRIZE IN POETRY, University of North Texas Press, % Scott Cairns, English Dept., Old Dominion University, Norfolk VA 23529. (757)683-4042. Fax: (757)683-5746. E-mail: scairns@odu.edu. Series Editor: Scott Cairns. Offered annually for 50-80 p.p., original, unpublished poetry ms. Deadline: November 30. Guidelines for SASE. Charges $16 fee, payable to UNT Press. Prize: $500 and standard publication contract with UNT Press. A different final judge each year; past judges include Richard Howard, Cynthia MacDonald, Sydney Lea, Yusef Komunyakaa and Heather McHugh. Standard copyright in author's name when published.

N **MISSISSIPPI VALLEY NON-PROFIT POETRY CONTEST**, P.O. Box 3188, Rock Island IL 61204-3188. (309)259-1057. President: Max Molleston. Estab. 1972. Unpublished poetry: adult general, student division, Mississippi Valley, senior citizen, religious, rhyming, jazz, humorous, haiku, history and ethnic. Deadline: September 1, 1998. Charges $5 fee, $3 for students. Up to 5 poems may be submitted with a limit of 50 lines/poem.

MORSE POETRY PRIZE, Northeastern University English Deptment, 406 Holmes Hall, Boston MA 02115. (617)437-2512. Website: http://www.casdn.neu.edu/~english/morse.htm. Contact: Guy Rotella. Previously published poetry, book-length mss of first or second books. Charges $10/fee. Prize: Publication by Northeastern University Press and a $500 cash award. Deadline: September 15.

KATHRYN A. MORTON PRIZE IN POETRY, Sarabande Books, 2234 Dundee Rd., Suite 200, Louisville KY 40205. (502)458-4028. Fax: (502)458-4065. E-mail: sarabandeb@aol.com. Website: http://www.SarabandeBooks.org. Contact: Sarah Gorham, editor-in-chief. Offered annually to award publication to an outstanding collection of poetry. Submissions accepted January 1-February 15. Guidelines for SASE. Charges $15 fee. Prize: $2,000, publication (paper and cloth), standard royalty contract. All finalists considered for publication. Judged by nationally prominent writers.

N **ERIKA MUMFORD PRIZE**, New England Poetry Club, 11 Puritan Rd., Arlington MA 02174-7710. Contact: Virginia Thayer. Offered annually for a poem in any form about foreign culture or travel. Deadline: June 30. Guidelines for SASE. Charges $5 or 3 poems for $10 entry fee for nonmembers. Prize: $250.

NATIONAL LOOKING GLASS POETRY CHAPBOOK COMPETITION, *Pudding Magazine: The International Journal of Applied Poetry*, 60 N. Main St., Johnstown OH 43031. (740)967-6060. Contact: Jennifer Bosveld, contest director. "To publish a collection of poems that represents our magazine's editorial slant: popular culture, social justice, psychological, etc. Poems might be themed or not." Two opportunities annually. Deadlines: June 30 and September 30. Guidelines for #10 SASE. Charges $10 fee. Prize: $100, 20 free books, 10 more to the reviewer of the poet's choice.

NATIONAL POETRY BOOK AWARD, Salmon Run Press, P.O. Box 672130, Chugiak AK 99567-2130. (907)688-4268. E-mail: jpsmeker@aol.com. Contact: John Smelcer. Offered annually to previously published or unpublished poetry. "Each year we invite poets nationwide to send their 48-96 page poetry ms. After the deadline, our judge/staff selects one ms to become published in a run of no fewer than 500 copies." Deadline: December 30. Guidelines for SASE. Charges $10 fee. Prize: $1,000, publication of ms (minimum 500 copies), advertising in national literary magazines (*Poets & Writer*, etc.), arrangements for national reviews with approximately 50-100 promotional copies sent. Author maintains all rights.

NATIONAL POETRY CONTEST, League of Canadian Poets, 54 Wolseley St., Toronto Ontario M5T 1A5 Canada. (416)504-1657. (416)504-0096. E-mail: league@ican.net. Website: http://www.swifty.com. Offered annually for unpublished work to seek plus encourage new poetic talent. Deadline: January 31. Guidelines for SASE. Charges $6 fee for poem. Prize: 1st-$1,000; 2nd-$750; 3rd-$500. Canadian citizens or landed immigrants only.

THE NATIONAL POETRY SERIES, P.O. Box G, Hopewell NJ 08525. (609)466-9712. Fax: (609)466-4706. Director: Daniel Halpern. The National Poetry Series was established to ensure the publication of five new books of poetry in America each year. "Manuscripts should be 48-64 pages in length and previously unpublished." Deadline: January 1-February 15. For guidelines send SASE. Charges $25 fee. Prize: Book publication and $1,000 award. Judged by five different judges, each a poet of national reputation. Judges are different each year. Open to US citizens only.

NATIONAL WRITERS ASSOCIATION POETRY CONTEST, The National Writers Association, Suite 424, 1450 S. Havana, Aurora CO 80012. (303)751-7844. Fax:(303)751-8593. E-mail: sandywrter@aol.com. Director: Sandy Whelchel. Annual contest "to encourage the writing of poetry, an important form of individual expression but with a limited commercial market." Charges $10 fee. Prizes: $100, $50, $25. Guidelines for #10 SASE.

HOWARD NEMEROV SONNET AWARD, *The Formalist: A Journal of Metrical Poetry*, 320 Hunter Dr., Evansville IN 47711. Contact: Mona Baer. Offered annually for an unpublished sonnet to encourage poetic craftsmanship and to honor the memory of the late Howard Nemerov, third US Poet Laureate and a masterful writer of sonnets. Deadline: June 15. Guidelines for SASE. Entry fee: $3/sonnet. Prize: $1,000 cash and publication in *The Formalist*; 11 other finalists also published. Acquires first North American serial rights for those sonnets chosen for publication. Upon publication all rights revert to the author. Open to the international community of writers.

NEW ENGLAND POETRY CLUB CONTESTS, New England Poetry Club, 11 Puritan Rd., Arlington MA 02174-7710. Contact: Virginia Thayer. Offered annually to multiple categories of unpublished poetry. Deadline: June 30. Guidelines for SASE. No entry fee for club members. Charges $5 or three poems for $10. Prizes: $100-500, varies for each award. Judged by well-known poets and/or previous winners of Poetry Club awards. Some contests are only available to club members. No poem may be entered in more than one contest.

bp NICHOL CHAPBOOK AWARD, Phoenix Community Works Foundation, 316 Dupont St., Toronto, Ontario M5R 1V9 Canada. (416)964-7919. Fax: (416)964-6941. Award Director: Philip McKenna. Offered annually to a previously published chapbook (10-48 pp) of poetry in English, published in Canada during the year prior to the year of the award. Deadline: March 30. Prize: $1,000 (Canadian). Judged by two writers appointed by the Foundation. Open to any writer. Author or publisher may make submissions. Send 3 copies (nonreturnable), plus a short c.v. of the author.

NORTHWOODS JOURNAL'S ANNUAL NATIONAL POETRY COMPETITION, Conservatory of American Letters, P.O. Box 298, Thomaston ME 04861. (207)354-0998. Fax: (207)354-8953. E-mail: cal@lme.net. Contact: Dr. Roy Schwartzman. Offered annually for unpublished poetry "to try and find the best poetry book of the year." Deadline: January 15. Guidelines for SASE. Charges $12 per 128 pages or any part. Prize: $250 cash award plus publication with $250 or more advance ($500 minimum).

THE FRANK O'HARA AWARD CHAPBOOK COMPETITION, Thorngate Road, Campus Box 4240, English Dept., Illinois State University, Normal IL 61790-4240. (309)438-7705. Fax: (309)438-5414. E-mail: jmelled@ilstu.edu. Website: http://www.litline.org/html/thorngate.html. Director: Jim Elledge. Offered annually to published or unpublished poetry. "To recognize excellence in poetry by gays, lesbians and bisexuals. Entrants may be beginners, emerging poets or those with a national reputation. Poems may be formal, free verse, post-modern, prose poems, etc." Deadline: February 1. Guidelines for SASE. Charges $15/ms fee. Prize: $500 and publication of the winning ms; author also receives 25 copies of the chapbook.

THE OHIO STATE UNIVERSITY PRESS/THE JOURNAL AWARD IN POETRY, The Ohio State University Press and *The Journal*, 1070 Carmack, Columbus OH 43210. (614)292-6930. Fax: (614)292-2065. E-mail: ohiostatepress@osu.edu. Director: David Citino. Offered annually for unpublished work. Minimum of 48 pages of original poetry. Entries accepted September 1-30. Charges $15 fee. Prize: $1,000 and publication royalties.

NATALIE ORNISH POETRY AWARD IN MEMORY OF WAYNE GARD, The Texas Institute of Letters, P.O. Box 298300, Fort Worth TX 76129. (817)921-7822. Fax: (817)257-5075. E-mail: jalter@gamma.is.tcu.edu. Website: http://www.gamma.is.tcu.edu/prs/til. Submissions must be marked Attn: TCU Press. Contact: Judy Alter. Offered annually for previously published work between January 1 and December 31 of year before award is given to honor the writer of the best book of poems published during the previous year. Deadline: January 4. Guidelines for SASE. Prize: $1,000. Judged by a panel of three. Poet must have been born in Texas, have lived in the state at some time for at least two consecutive years, or subject matter is associated with the state.

GUY OWEN POETRY PRIZE, *Southern Poetry Review*, Advancement Studies, CPCC, Charlotte NC 28235. (704)330-6002. Contact: Ken McLaurin, award director:. Estab. 1985. Offered annually for the best unpublished poem submitted in an open competition. Given in memory of Guy Owen, a poet, fiction writer and founder of *Southern Poetry Review*. Submit in April only—3-5 previously unpublished poems and SASE. Charges $8 fee that includes one year subscription to *SPR* to begin with the Winter issue, containing the winning poem. Prize: $500 and publication in *SPR*. All submissions considered for publication.

OWL CREEK POETRY PRIZE, Owl Creek Press, 2693 SW Camano Dr., Camano Island WA 98292.
- At press time we were notified that this prize, along with the Owl Creek Press Prize for Fiction and the Green Lake Chapbook Prize, have been discontinued.

N **PANHANDLER POETRY CHAPBOOK COMPETITION**, *The Panhandler*, English Dept., University of West Florida, 11000 University Parkway, Pensacola FL 32514-5751. (904)474-2923. Editor: Laurie O'Brien. Estab. 1979. Individual poems may have been published. To honor excellence in the writing of short collections of poetry. Two winning mss are published each year between 24-32 pages. Deadline: December 1. Charges $15 fee (includes copy of winning chapbooks).

PAUMANOK POETRY AWARD, Visiting Writers Program, SUNY Farmingdale, Knapp Hall Farmingdale NY 11735. E-mail: brownml@farmingdale.edu. Website: http://www.farmingdale.edu/CampusPages/ArtsSciences/EnglishHumanities/paward.html. Contact: Margery L. Brown, director, visiting writers program. Offered annually for published or unpublished poems. Send cover letter, 1-paragraph bio, 1-5 poems (name and address on each poem). Include SASE for notification of winners. (Send photocopies only; mss will not be returned.) Deadline: September 15. Charges $12 fee, payable to SUNY Farmingdale VWP. Prize: 1st-$1,000 plus expenses for a reading in 1999-2000 series; 2 runners-up—$500 plus expenses for a reading in series.

THE RICHARD PHILLIPS POETRY PRIZE, The Phillips Publishing Co., P.O. Box 121, Watts OK 74964. Contact: Richard Phillips, Jr. Offered annually to give a modest financial reward to emerging poets who have not yet established themselves sufficiently to generate appropriate compensation for their work. Deadline: Postmarked by January 31. Guidelines for SASE. Charges $15 fee. Prize: $1,000 and publication. Open to all poets. "There are no anthologies to buy. No strings attached. Simply put, the poet who enters the best manuscript will win the prize of $1,000 and will receive a check in that amount within 60 days of the deadline." Recent winners: Deborah Vallet (Atlanta GA) 1996; Kathryn Presley (Somerville TX) 1997; Jana Klenburg (New York, NY) 1998.

POET LORE NARRATIVE POETRY CONTEST, *Poet Lore*, The Writer's Center, 4508 Walsh St., Bethesda MD 20815. (301)654-8664. E-mail: postmaster@writer.org. Website: http://www.writer.org. Contact: Phillip Jason. Estab. 1889. Offered annually for unpublished narrative poems of 100 lines or more. Deadline: November 30. Prize: $350 and publication in *Poet Lore*. "*Poet Lore* has first publication rights for poems submitted. All rights revert to the author after publication in *Poet Lore*."

N **POETIC LICENSE**, Eye Scry Publications (MKASHEF Enterprises), P.O. Box 688, Yucca Valley CA 92286-0688. Contact: Alayne Gelfand. Biannual. "We sponsor thematic contests. Each contest hopes to feature excellent depictions of that particular theme." Deadlines: February 1 and August 1. Prizes: 1st-$500, 2nd-$100, 3rd-$50, five honorable mentions. All winners receive publication and 1 copy. Judged by Alayne Gelfand, Wendy Rathbone, Della Van Hise—all published writers/poets. Ms. Gelfand is also editor of the erotic vampire anthology *Prisoners of the Night*. "All writers are invited to enter with a limit of three poems per entrant. A SASE should be included with submission. Also, if you do not wish to be published, if you do not win a cash prize, please state so with your entry. Please SASE for the theme of our current contest before entering."

N **POETRY PUBLICATION**, The PEN (Poetry Explosion Newsletter), The Poet Band Co., P.O. Box 4725, Pittsburgh PA 15206. E-mail: aford@hillhouse.ckp.edu. Editor/owner: Arthur C. Ford. Estab. 1984. Send maximum of 5 poems. Enclose $1 for reading fee. Use rhyme and non-rhyming verse. Maximum lines: 40. Prose maximum: 200-300 words. Allow 1 month for response. Sample copy $5. Send SASE for more information. Quarterly newsletter (*The Pen*) issued March, June, September and December. Subscriptions are $20 (yearly) or $35 for 2 years.

POETS CLUB OF CHICAGO INTERNATIONAL SHAKESPEAREAN/PETRARCHAN SONNET CONTEST, 130 Windsor Park Dr. C-323, Carol Stream IL 60188. Chairman: LaVone Holt. Annual contest for original and unpublished sonnets. Estab. 1954. Deadline: August 1. Guidelines for SASE after March 1. Prizes: 1st-$50, 2nd-$35, 3rd-$15; two honorable mentions.

FELIX POLLAK PRIZE IN POETRY/BRITTINGHAM PRIZE IN POETRY, University of Wisconsin Press, 2537 Daniels St., Madison WI 53718-6772. Contest Director: Ronald Wallace. Estab. 1994. Unpublished book length ms of original poetry. Submissions must be received by the press during the month of September (postmark is irrelevant) and must be accompanied by SASE for contest results. Prize: $1,000 and publication to the 2 best submissions. Guidelines for #10 SASE. Does not return mss. Charges $20 fee, payable to University of Wisconsin Press. One fee covers both competitions. Notification in February.

QUARTERLY REVIEW OF LITERATURE POETRY SERIES, 26 Haslet Ave., Princeton NJ 08540. (609)921-6976. Website: http://www.princeton.edu/~qrl. "QRL Poetry Series is a book publishing series chosen from an open competition." Publishes 4-6 titles/year. Prize: $1,000, publication and 100 copies to each winner for a book of miscellaneous poems, a single long poem, a poetic play or a book of translations. Guidelines for SASE.

ROANOKE-CHOWAN AWARD FOR POETRY, North Carolina Literary and Historical Association, 109 E. Jones St., Room 23, Raleigh NC 27601-2807. (919)733-9375. Fax: (919)733-8807. Awards Coordinator: Jerry C. Cashion. Previously published poetry by a resident of North Carolina. Deadline: July 15.

NICHOLAS ROERICH POETRY PRIZE, Story Line Press, Three Oaks Farm, Brownsville OR 97327-9718. (541)466-5352. Fax: (541)466-3200. E-mail: slp@ptinet.net. Contact: Jenny Root or Robert McDowell. Estab. 1988. Full-length book of poetry. Any writer who has not previously published a full-length collection of poetry (48 pages or more) in English is eligible to apply. Deadline: May 1-October 15. Guidelines for SASE. Charges $20 fee. Prize: winner—$1,000, publication, a reading at the Nicholas Roerich Museum in New York. Runner-up—scholarship to Wesleyan Writers Workshop.

ANNA DAVIDSON ROSENBERG AWARD FOR POEMS ON THE JEWISH EXPERIENCE, Judah L. Magnes Museum, 2911 Russell St., Berkeley CA 94705. (510)549-6950. Contact: Paula Friedman. Offered annually for unpublished work to encourage poetry of/on/from the Jewish experience. Deadline for requesting mandatory entry forms is July 15; deadline for receipt of poems is August 31. Guidelines and entry form for SASE. Submissions must include entry form. Charges $2 fee for up to 3 poems. Prize: 1st-$100; 2nd-$50; 3rd-$25; $25-New/Emerging Poet Prize; $25-Youth Award; also, Senior Award and Honorable Mentions. All winners receive certificate, and winning poems are read in an Awards Reading here.

SHELLEY MEMORIAL AWARD, Poetry Society of America, 15 Gramercy Park S., New York NY 10003. (212)254-9628. E-mail: timothyd@poetrysociety.org. Website: http://www.poetrysociety.org. Contact: Award Director. Deadline: December 19. By nomination only to a living American poet. Prize: $2,000-6,000.

SLIPSTREAM ANNUAL POETRY CHAPBOOK COMPETITION, *Slipstream*, Box 2071, Niagara Falls NY 14301. (716)282-2616 after 5P.M. EST. Website: http://wings.buffalo.edu/libraries/units/pl/slipstream. Contact: Dan Sicoli, director. Offered annually to help promote a poet whose work is often overlooked or ignored. Deadline: December 1. Guidelines for SASE. Charges $10 fee. Prize: $500 and 50 copies of published chapbook. Judged by editors of Slipstream magazine. Open to any writer. Past winners have included Gerald Locklin, David Chorlton, Serena Fusek, Robert Cooperman, Sherman Alexie, Kurt Nimmo, Katharine Harer, Richard Amidon, Matt Buys and Leslie Anne Mcilroy.

PEREGRINE SMITH POETRY CONTEST, Gibbs Smith, Publisher, P.O. Box 667, Layton UT 84041. (801)544-2958. Fax: (801)544-5582. Poetry Editor: Gail Yngve. Offered annually for unpublished work. The purpose of this award is to recognize and publish a previously unpublished work. Deadline: April 30. "We only accept submissions during the month of April each year." Guidelines for SASE. Charges $15 fee. Prize: $500 and publication of the winning entry. Judged by Christopher Merrill.

SNAKE NATION PRESS'S ANNUAL POETRY CONTEST, Snake Nation Press, 110 #2 W. Force St., Valdosta GA 31601. (912)219-8334. Nancy Phillips, editor. Contact: Roberta George, contest director: . Estab. 1989. Annual contest to give a wider audience to readable, understandable poetry. Deadline: March 15. Guidelines for #10 SASE. Charges $10 fee. Prize consists of $500, 50 copies and distribution.

THE SOW'S EAR CHAPBOOK PRIZE, *The Sow's Ear Poetry Review*, 19535 Pleasant View Dr., Abingdon VA 24211-6827. (540)628-2651. E-mail: richman@preferred.com. Contest Director: Larry K. Richman. Estab. 1988. 24-26 pages of poetry. Submit March-April. Guidelines for #10 SASE or request by e-mail. Charges $10 fee. Prize: 1st-$500, 50 copies and distribution to subscribers; 2nd-$100; 3rd-$100.

THE SOW'S EAR POETRY PRIZE, The Sow's Ear Poetry Review, 19535 Pleasant View Dr., Abingdon VA 24211-6827. (540)628-2651. E-mail: richman@preferred.com. Contest Director: Larry K. Richman. Estab. 1988. Previously unpublished poetry. Submit September-October. Guidelines for #10 SASE or request by e-mail. Charges $2 fee/poem.

Prizes: $500, $100, $50 and publication, plus publication for 20-25 finalists. All submissions considered for publication.

SPRING AND FALL POETRY CHAPBOOK CONTESTS, White Eagle Coffee Store Press, P.O. Box 383, Fox River Grove IL 60021-0383. (847)639-9200. E-mail: wecspress@aol.com. Website: http://members.aol.com/~ecspress. Contact: Frank E. Smith, publisher. Offered 2 times/year since 1991 to unpublished poetry chapbooks. Length: 20-24 pages. Deadlines: March 30 and September 30. Guidelines for SASE. Charges $10 fee. Prize: $200, publication and 25 copies of chapbook. Open to any writer. Previous winners include Timothy Russell, Becky Gould Gibson, Leilani Wright, Robert Joe Stout, L.L. Harper, Luisa Villani.

ANN STANFORD POETRY PRIZE, The Southern California Anthology, % Master of Professional Writing Program, WPH 404, U.S.C., Los Angeles CA 90089-4034. (213)740-3252. Website: http://www.usc.edu/dept/LAS/mpw. Contest Director: James Ragan. Estab. 1988. Previously unpublished poetry to honor excellence in poetry in memory of poet and teacher Ann Stanford. Include cover sheet with name, address and titles of the 5 poems entered. Deadline: April 15. Guidelines for #10 SASE. Charges $10 fee. Prize: 1st-$750; 2nd-$250; 3rd-$100. Winning poems are published in *The Southern California Anthology* and all entrants receive a free issue.

THE AGNES LYNCH STARRETT POETRY PRIZE, University of Pittsburgh Press, 3347 Forbes Ave., Pittsburgh PA 15261. (412)383-2456. Fax: (412)383-2466. Series Editor: Ed Ochester. Estab. 1936. First book of poetry for poets who have not had a full-length book published. Deadline: March and April only. Guidelines for SASE (essential). Prize: $3,000.

STEPHAN G. STEPHANSSON AWARD FOR POETRY, Writers Guild of Alberta, 11759 Groat Rd., Edmonton Alberta T5M 3K6 Canada. (403)422-8174. Fax: (403)422-2663. E-mail: writers@compusmart.ab.ca. Assistant Director: Darlene Diver. Poetry book published in current year. Must be an Alberta poet.

STILL WATERS PRESS POETRY CHAPBOOK COMPETITIONS, 459 S. Willow Ave., Galloway Township NJ 08201-4633. E-mail: salake@ix.netcom.com. Website: http://www2.netcom.com/~salake/StillWatersPoetry.html. Contact: Shirley Lake, founding editor. Two contests offered annually to unpublished chapbooks or previously published poems in chapbooks. Deadlines: February 28 (Women's Words) and September 30 (Winter). Guidelines for SASE. Charges $10 fee. Prizes: Publication with review distribution and publicity package, plus copies. Simultaneous submissions prohibited. Previous publication history and copyright permission required, if applicable. The Women's Words Competition is open to women only. The Winter Competition is open to women and men.

THE EUNICE TIETJENS MEMORIAL PRIZE, *Poetry*, 60 W. Walton St., Chicago IL 60610. (312)255-3703. Editor, *Poetry*: Joseph Parisi. Offered annually for poems published in *Poetry* during the preceding twelve months (October through September). Guidelines for SASE. Prize: $200. Judged by the editors of *Poetry*. *Poetry* buys all rights to the poems published in the magazine. Copyrights are returned to the authors on request. Any writer may submit poems to *Poetry*. Only poems published in *Poetry* during the preceding year are considered for the annual prizes.

KATE TUFTS DISCOVERY AWARD FOR POETRY, The Claremont Graduate School, 160 E. Tenth St., Claremont CA 91711-6165. (909)621-8974. Website: http://www.cgs.edu/common/tuftsent.html. Award Director: Jack Miles. Offered annually for poetry published in a first or very early book in English during the previous year. Guidelines and form for SASE. Entry form must accompany submission. Deadline: September 15. Prize: $5,000. Entrants must agree to reproduction rights and to be present at award ceremony.

KINGSLEY TUFTS POETRY AWARD AT THE CLAREMONT GRADUATE SCHOOL, The Claremont Graduate School, 160 E. Tenth St., Claremont CA 91711-6165. (909)621-8974. Website: http://www.egs.edu/common/tuftsent.html. Award Director: Jack Miles. Offered annually for poetry published in book form in English during the previous year. Also open to book-length mss that have not been published but were created in the year prior to the award. In that case, poet must have publication credits. Guidelines and form for SASE. Entry form must accompany submission. Deadline: September 15. Prize: $50,000. Entrants must agree to reproduction rights and to be present at award ceremony and week's residency the Claremont Graduate School.

UNION LEAGUE CIVIC AND ARTS POETRY PRIZE, *Poetry*, 60 W. Walton St., Chicago IL 60610. (312)255-3703. Editor, *Poetry*, Joseph Parisi. Offered annually for poems published in *Poetry* during the preceding twelve months (October through September). Guidelines for SASE. Prize: $1,000. Judged by the editors of *Poetry*. *Poetry* buys all rights to the poems published in the magazine. Copyrights are returned to the authors on request. Any writer may submit poems to *Poetry*. Only poems published in *Poetry* during the preceding year are considered for the annual prizes.

DANIEL VAROUJAN AWARD, New England Poetry Club, 11 Puritan Rd., Arlington MA 02174-7710. Contact: Virginia Thayer. Offered annually for "an unpublished poem worthy of Daniel Varoujan, a poet killed by the Turks at the onset of the first genocide of this century which decimated three-fourths of the Armenian population." Send poems in duplicate. Charges $5 per poem or 3 poems for $10. Deadline: June 30. Guidelines for SASE. Prize: $500. Open to any writer.

VERVE POETRY CONTEST, *VERVE* Magazine, P.O. Box 3205, Simi Valley CA 93093. Contest Director: Ron Reichick. Estab. 1989. Offered 2 times/year for previously unpublished poetry. "Fund raiser for *VERVE* Magazine which receives no grants and has no ties with any institutions." Deadlines: April 1 and October 1. Guidelines for #10 SASE. Charges $2/poem. Prizes: 1st-$100 and publication in *Verve*; 2nd-$50; 3rd-$25.

THE WASHINGTON PRIZE, The Word Works, Inc., P.O. Box 42164, Washington DC 20015. E-mail: wordworks@shirenet.com. Website: http://www.writer.org/wordwork/wordwrk1.htm. Contact: Miles David Moore. Offered annually "honoring the best full-length poetry manuscript (48-64 pp.) submitted to the Word Works each year. The Washington Prize contest is the only forum in which we consider unsolicited manuscripts." Deadline: March 1 (postmark). Guidelines for SASE. Charges $20 fee. Prizes: $1,000 and book publication; all entrants will receive a copy of the winning book. The Word Works acquires first and subsequent English-language publication rights. "The contest is open to any writer with an unpublished, full-length poetry manuscript. Individual poems in the manuscript may have been published elsewhere. All manuscripts shuold include a signed title page with address and phone number, a table of contents, an acknowledgments page and a short biography. For contest results, include a business-sized SASE. No manuscripts will be returned."

WHITE PINE PRESS POETRY PRIZE, White Pine Press, 10 Village Square, Fredonia NY 14063. (716)672-5743. Website: http://www.bluemoon.net/~pine/. Contact: Elaine LaMattina, managing director. Offered annually for previously published or unpublished poets. Deadline: October 31. Guidelines for SASE. Charges $15 fee. Prize: $500 plus publication. "Initial screening is done by our in-house editorial staff. Finalists are judged by a poet of national reputation. If the winner is published by White Pine Press, we hold rights until the book is out of print; then rights revert to the author. With previously published work, the author is responsible for obtaining permission for publication by White Pine Press." Open to any writer who is a US citizen.

THE WALT WHITMAN AWARD, The Academy of American Poets, 584 Broadway, Suite 1208, New York NY 10012-3250. (212)274-0343. Fax: (212)274-9427. E-mail: poets@artswire.com. Website: http://www.poets.org. Contact: India Amos. Offered annually to publish and support a poet's first book. Entries accepted from September 15-November 15. Guidelines for SASE. Charges $20 fee. Prize: $5,000, a residency for one month at the Vermont Studio Center, publication by Louisiana State University Press. Judged by an eminent poet. Submissions must be in English by a single poet. Translations are not eligible. Contestants must be living citizens of the US and have neither published nor committed to publish a volume of poetry 40 pages or more in length in an edition of 500 or more copies.

WICK POETRY CHAPBOOK SERIES "OPEN" COMPETITION, Wick Poetry Program Dept. of English, Kent State University, P.O. Box 5190, Kent OH 44242-0001. (330)672-2067. Fax: (330)672-3152. Website: http://www.kent.edu/english/wick.htm. Director: Maggie Anderson. Publication of a chapbook of poems by a poet currently living in Ohio. Deadline: October 31. Guidelines for SASE. Charges $5 entry fee. Prize: Publication of the chapbook by the Kent State University Press.

WICK POETRY CHAPBOOK SERIES "STUDENT" COMPETITION, Wick Poetry Program, Dept. of English, Kent State University, P.O. Box 5190, Kent OH 44242-0001. (330)672-2067. Fax: (330)672-3152. Website: http://www.kent.edu/english/wick.htm. Director: Maggie Anderson. Publication of a chapbook of poems by a poet currently enrolled in an Ohio college or university. Deadline: October 31. Guidelines for SASE. Prize: Publication of the chapbook by the Kent State University Press.

STAN AND TOM WICK POETRY PRIZE, Wick Poetry Program, Dept. of English, Kent State University, P.O. Box 5190, Kent OH 44242-0001. (330)672-2067. Website: http://www.kent.edu/english/wick.htm. Director: Maggie Anderson. First Book Prize open to anyone writing in English who has not previously published a full-length book of poems (a volume of 48 pages or more published in an edition of 500 or more copies). Deadline: May 1. Guidelines for SASE. Charges $15 entry fee. Prize: $2,000 prize and book publication by the Kent State University Press.

N **WILLIAM CARLOS WILLIAMS AWARD**, Poetry Society of America, 15 Gramercy Park S, New York NY 10003. (212)254-9628. E-mail: timothyd@poetrysociety.org. Website: http://www.poetrysociety.org. Award Director: Timothy Donnelly. Offered annually for a book of poetry published by a small press, non-profit or university press between October 1 and December 21. Deadline: December 20. Guidelines for SASE. Charges $10 fee. Prize: between $500 and $1,000. Winning books are distributed to PSA members upon request and while supplies last. Judged by renowned poets of diverse styles and backgrounds. Open to any writer.

ROBERT H. WINNER MEMORIAL AWARD, Poetry Society of America, 15 Gramercy Park S., New York NY 10003. (212)254-9628. E-mail: timothyd@poetrysociety.org. Website: http://www.poetrysociety.org. Contact: Award Director. "For a poet whose first book appeared when he was almost 50, recognizing and rewarding the work of someone in midlife. Open to poets over 40, still unpublished or with one book." Guidelines for #10 SASE. Guidelines subject to change. Charges $5 fee for nonmembers. Deadline: December 19. Prize: $2,500.

THE J. HOWARD AND BARBARA M.J. WOOD PRIZE, *Poetry*, 60 W. Walton St., Chicago IL 60610. (312)255-3703. Editor, *Poetry*: Joseph Parisi. Offered annually for poems published in *Poetry* during the preceding twelve months

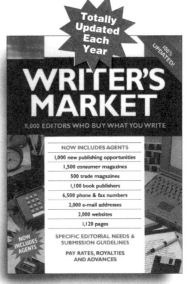

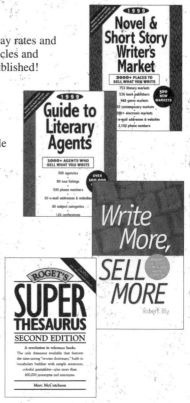

(October through September). Guidelines for SASE. Prize: $3,000. Judged by the editors of *Poetry. Poetry* buys all rights to the poems published in the magazine. Copyrights are returned to the authors on request. Any writer may submit poems to *Poetry.* Only poems published in *Poetry* during the preceding year are considered for the annual prizes.

THE WRITER MAGAZINE/EMILY DICKINSON AWARD, Poetry Society of America, 15 Gramercy Park S., New York NY 10003. (212)254-9628. E-mail: timothyd@poetrysociety.org. Website: http://www.poetrysociety.org. Contact: Award Director. Poem inspired by Emily Dickinson, though not necessarily in her style. Guidelines for #10 SASE. Guidelines subject to change. Deadline: December 19. Members only. Prize: $100.

WRITERS' JOURNAL QUARTERLY POETRY CONTEST, Val-Tech Publishing, Inc., P.O. Box 25376, St. Paul MN 55125. (612)730-4280. Website: http://www.sowashco.com/writersjournal. Contact: Esther M. Leiper. Previously unpublished poetry. Deadlines: February 28, April 15, August 15, November 30. Charges $2 fee first poem; $1 each thereafter.

YALE SERIES OF YOUNGER POETS, Yale University Press, P.O. Box 209040, New Haven CT 06520-9040. Website: http://www.yale.edu/yup/. Contact: Richard Miller. First book of poetry by poet under the age of 40. Submit during February. Guidelines for SASE. Charges $15 fee. Winning manuscript is published by Yale University Press. The author receives royalties.

PHYLLIS SMART YOUNG PRIZES IN POETRY, *The Madison Review*, Dept. of English, 600 N. Park St., Madison WI 53706. (608)263-3374. Director: Ronald Kuka. Contact: Michelle Ephraim or Christine Grimando. Offered annually for previously unpublished work. "Awarded to the best poems submitted, out of a field of around 500 submissions yearly. The purpose of the prize is to award good poets." Submissions must consist of 3 poems. Deadline: September 30. Prize: $500; plus publication in the spring issue of *The Madison Review.* All contest entries are considered as submissions to *The Madison Review*, the literary journal sponsoring the contest. No simultaneous submissions to other publications. Charges $3 fee.

N **ZUZU'S PETALS POETRY CONTEST**, *Zuzu's Petals Quarterly Online*, P.O. Box 156, Whitehall PA 18052. E-mail: zuzu@lehigh.net. Website: http://www.lehigh.net/zuzu/. Contact: T. Dunn, editor. Offered 2 times/year for previously unpublished poetry. Deadline: March 1, September 1. Guidelines for #10 SASE. Charges $2 fee/poem. Prize: top 3 winners share 40% of the contest's proceeds. All entries automatically considered for publication.

Playwriting & Scriptwriting

ALASKA NATIVE PLAYS CONTEST, University of Alaska Anchorage, 3211 Providence Dr., Anchorage AK 99508. (907)786-1794. Fax: (907)786-1799. E-mail: afdpe@uaa.alaska.edu. Website: http://www.uaa.alaska.edu. (Click Theatre; Click Native Plays). Contest Director: Dr. David Edgecombe. Offered annually for unpublished works "to encourage the writing, reading and production of plays with American Native (Indian) issues, themes and characters." Deadline: March 20. Guidelines for SASE. Prize: 1st-$500; 2nd-$200; 3rd-$100. "Any writer may enter—Native American writers are strongly encouraged."

N **AMERICAN COLLEGE THEATER FESTIVAL: MICHAEL KANIN PLAYWRITING AWARDS PROGRAM**, The John F. Kennedy Center for the Performing Arts, JFK Center, Washington DC 20566-0001. (202)416-8857. Fax: (202)416-8802. Website: http://www.kennedy-center.org. Award Director: John Lion. Includes "a series of awards to encourage student writers." Deadline is rolling. Guidelines for SASE. Charges $200-250 fee. Prizes vary for each award in the series up to $2,500 and production. Entries must be plays fully produced at a college or university and can only come from a sponsoring college or university department.

AMERICAN SKETCHES, Florida Studio Theater, (formerly American Shorts), 1241 N. Palm Ave., Sarasota FL 34236. (941)366-9017. Fax: (941)955-4137. Offered annually for unpublished plays no more than 5 pages long on a theme that changes every year. Deadline varies. Query or call Chril Angermann. Prize: $500.

N **ANNUAL INTERNATIONAL ONE PAGE PLAY COMPETITION**, Lamia Ink!, P.O. Box 202, Prince Street Station, New York NY 10012. (212)978-4413. Fax: (212)598-4629. Award Director: Cortland Jessup. Offered annually for previously published or unpublished one page plays. Deadline: March 15. Guidelines for SASE. Charges $1/play (maximum of 3 entries per author). Prize: $200 and staged reading and publication of 12 finalists. Acquires "the rights to publish in our magazine and to be read or performed at the prize awarding festival."

N **ANNUAL KEY WEST THEATRE FESTIVAL**, P.O. Box 992, Key West FL 33041. (305)292-3725 or (800)741-6945. Fax: (305)293-0845. Contact: Joan McGillis. E-mail: theatrekw@aol.com. Offered annually for unpublished submissions to develop new plays from either new or established playwrights. Deadline: March 31. Guidelines for SASE. Award: Round trip airfare to Key West and lodging in Key West for a minimum of one week. Open to any writer when submitted by agent or by professional recommendation.

ANNUAL ONE-ACT PLAY COMPETITION, TADA!, 120 W. 28th St., New York NY 10001. (212)627-1732. Fax: (212)243-6736. E-mail: tada@tadatheater.com. Website: http://www.tadatheater.com. Contact: Victoria Connolly, community development. Offered annually for unpublished work to encourage playwrights, composers and lyricists to develop new plays for young audiences. Deadline: varies each year, usually in early spring/late winter. For guidelines call Jessica Maccario at (212)627-1732. Prize: cash prize and staged readings of winners. Must be material with a cast composed predominantly of children.

N AUSTIN HEART OF FILM FESTIVAL FEATURE LENGTH SCREENPLAY AWARD, 1600 Nueces, Austin TX 78701. (512)478-4795. Fax: (512)478-6205. E-mail: ausfilm@aol.com. Website: http://www.austinfilmfestival.org. Award Director: Darrell Kreitz. Offered annually for unpublished screenplays. The Austin Film Festival is looking for quality screenplays which will be read by industry professionals. The contest hopes to give unknown writers exposure to producers and other industry executives. Two competitions: (Adult/Mature Category, Children/Family Category) and Best Feature Film Award. Deadline: screenplay: May 15th; film: August 7. Guidelines for SASE or call 1-800-310-3378. Charges $35 entry fee. Prize: Feature Length, both categories are $3,500 each plus airfare and accomodations to conference in Austin (October 1-8). The writer must hold the rights when submitted. It must be original work. The screenplay must be between 90 and 130 pages. It must be in standard screenplay format (industry standard).

THE MARGARET BARTLE PLAYWRITING AWARD, Community Children's Theatre of Kansas City, 8021 E. 129th Terrace, Grandview MO 64030-2114. (816)761-5775. Award Director: E. Blanche Sellens. Chairman: Margaret Bartle (playwriting award). Estab. 1951. Offered annually for unpublished plays for elementary school audiences. "Our purpose is two-fold: to award a deserving author of a good, well-written play, and to produce the play royalty-free by one of our trouping units." Deadline: January 31. Guidelines for SASE. Prize: $500.

N GEORGE HOUSTON BASS MEMORIAL AWARD, Rites and Reason Theatre, Box 1148, Providence RI 02912. E-mail: sheila-grant@brown.edu. Contact: Elmo Terry-Morgan. Offered annually for unpublished work. "Unproduced one act plays reflecting experiences in the African diaspora. Synopsis submitted first to the George Houston Bass Play-Rites Festival." Deadline: April. Guidelines for SASE. Prize: Cash award and staged reading as part of the George Houston Bass Play-Rites Festival.

BAY AREA PLAYWRIGHTS FESTIVAL, The Playwrights Foundation, P.O. Box 460357, San Francisco CA 94146. (415)263-3986. E-mail: kentnich@aol.com. Contact: Jayne Wenger, artistic director. Offered annually to unpublished plays to encourage development of a new work. Deadline: February 1. Prize: small stipend and a professionally staged reading. Judged by a committee of 7 theater professionals. Unproduced full-length plays only.

THE BEVERLY HILLS THEATRE GUILD-JULIE HARRIS PLAYWRIGHT AWARD COMPETITION, 2815 N. Beachwood Drive, Los Angeles CA 90068. (213)465-2703. Contact: Marcella Meharg, playwright award coordinator. Estab. 1978. "Annual contest to discover new dramatists and to encourage established and aspiring playwrights to develop quality plays for the theatre." Original full-length plays, unpublished, unproduced and not currently under option. "We will be establishing an additional competition to open 1/99 for plays written for children's theatre." Application and guidelines required, available upon request with SASE. Submissions accepted with applications from August 1-November 1. Prizes: 1st - $5,000, 2nd - $2,000, 3rd - $1,000.

CALIFORNIA YOUNG PLAYWRIGHTS CONTEST, Playwright Project, 450 B St., Suite 480, San Diego CA 92101. (619)239-7483. Fax: (619)239-1558. Contest Director: Deborah Salzer. Offered annually for previously unpublished plays by young writers to stimulate young people to create dramatic works, and to nurture promising young writers (under age 19). Deadline: April 1. Guidelines for SASE. Prize: professional production of 3-5 winning plays at the Old Globe Theatre in San Diego, plus royalty. All entrants receive detailed evaluation letter." Scripts must be a minimum of 10 standard typewritten pages; send 2 copies. Writers must be California residents under age 19 as of the deadline date.

CEC JACKIE WHITE MEMORIAL NATIONAL CHILDREN'S PLAYWRITING CONTEST, Columbia Entertainment Company, 309 Parkade Blvd., Columbia MO 65202. (573)874-5628. Contact: Betsy Phillips. Estab. 1988. Offered annually for "top notch unpublished scripts for theater school use, to challenge and expand the talents of our students, ages 10-15. Should be a full length play with speaking roles for 20-30 characters of all ages with at least 10 roles developed in some detail." Deadline: June 1. Prize: $250 cash award for 1st place. "Production is usual, but the company reserves the right to grant the 1st place prize money without production. When produced, travel money is available for playwright." Guidelines for SASE. Entrants receive written evaluation of work. Charges $10 fee.

N CHARLOTTE FESTIVAL/NEW PLAYS IN AMERICA, Charlotte Repertory Theatre, 2040 Charlotte Plaza, Charlotte NC 28244. Literary Associate: Carol Bellamy. Four plays selected for each festival. Must be full scripts—no one acts or musicals. Must not have had any previous professional production. Accepted all year. Prize: staged reading of script, transportation to festival, small honorarium for expenses. Scripts *must be bound* and include SASE if need to be returned. No cassettes, international reply coupons or videos accepted.

N **CLEVELAND PUBLIC THEATRE NEW PLAYS FESTIVAL**, Cleveland Public Theatre, 6415 Detroit Ave., Cleveland OH 44102. (216)631-2727. Fax: (216)631-2575. E-mail: cpt@en.com. Website: http://www.en.com/cpt. Contact: Terence Cranendonk, festival director. Estab. 1983. Annual festival of staged readings of 10-15 alternative, experimental, poetic, political work, and plays by women, people of color, gays/lesbians. Deadline: September 1. Guidelines for SASE. Charges $10 fee. "We accept both full-length and one-acts, but emphasize shorter works, simple set, 10 actor cast maximum. Generally, half of the works in the New Plays Festival are by Ohio playwrights."

N **COE COLLEGE PLAYWRITING FESTIVAL**, Coe College, 1220 First Ave. NE., Cedar Rapids IA 52402-5092. (319)399-8689. Fax: (319)399-8557. E-mail: swolvert@coe.edu. Contact: Susan Wolverton. Estab. 1993. Offered biennially for unpublished work to provide a venue for new works for the stage. "There is usually a theme for the festival. We are interested in full-length productions, *not* one acts or musicals." Guidelines for SASE. Prize: $325, plus 1-week residency as guest artist with airfare, room and board provided. "There are no specific criteria although a current résumé and synopsis is requested."

THE COLUMBUS SCREENPLAY DISCOVERY AWARDS, 433 N. Camden Dr., #600, Beverly Hills CA 90210. (310)288-1882. Fax: (310)475-0193. E-mail: awards@hollywoodawards.com. Website: http://www.HollywoodAwards.com. Monthly and annual contest "to discover new screenplay writers." Deadline: November 1. Charges $55 fee. Prize: options up to $10,000, plus professional development guidance and access to agents, producers, and studios. Judged by reputable industry professionals (producers, development executives, story analysts). Writer must give option to purchase if selected.

CUNNINGHAM PRIZE FOR PLAYWRITING, The Theatre School, DePaul University, 2135 N. Kenmore, Chicago IL 60614. (773)325-7938. Fax: (773)325-7920. E-mail: lgoetsch@wppost.depaul.edu. Website: http://www.theatreschool.depaul.edu. Contact: Lara Goetsch. Offered annually for published or unpublished work "to recognize and encourage the writing of dramatic works which affirm the centrality of religion, broadly defined, and the human quest for meaning, truth and community." Deadline: December 1. Guidelines for SASE. Prize: $5,000. Open to Chicago residents, defined as within 100 miles of the Loop.

DAYTON PLAYHOUSE FUTUREFEST, The Dayton Playhouse, 1301 E. Siebenthaler Ave., Box 1957, Dayton OH 45414-5357. (937)277-0144. Fax: (937)227-9539. Managing Director: Tina McPhearson. Estab. 1983. "Three plays selected for full productions, three for readings at July 1998 FutureFest weekend; the six authors will be given travel and lodging to attend the festival." Prizes: $1,000 and $100 to the other 5 playwrights. Guidelines for SASE. Guidelines can also be faxed. Deadline: September 30.

WALT DISNEY STUDIOS FELLOWSHIP PROGRAM, Walt Disney Studios, 500 S. Buena Vista St., Burbank CA 91521. (818)560-6894. Contact: Troy Nethercott. Offering up to 9 positions for writers to work full-time developing their craft at Disney in feature film and television writing. Deadline: April 1-17, 1998. "Writing samples are required, as well as a résumé, completed application form and notarized standard letter agreement (available from the Program Administrator.)" A $33,000 salary for 1 year period beginning mid-October. Fellows outside of LA area will be provided with airfare and 1 month's accommodations. Members of the WGA should apply through the Guild's Employment Access Department at (213)782-4648.

DRURY COLLEGE ONE-ACT PLAY CONTEST, Drury College, 900 N. Benton Ave., Springfield MO 65802-3344. (417)873-7430. Contact: Sandy Asher. Estab. 1986. Offered in even-numbered years for unpublished and professionally unproduced plays. One play per playwright. Deadline: December 1. Guidelines for SASE.

DUBUQUE FINE ARTS PLAYERS ANNUAL ONE-ACT PLAYWRITING CONTEST, 1321 Tomahawk Dr., Dubuque IA 52003. (319)583-6748. Website: http://www.dubuque.lib.ia_us/nonprofits//dfap/rules.htm. Contact: Jennie G. Stabenow, contest coordinator. Annual competition since 1977 for previously unpublished, unproduced plays. Adaptations must be of playwright's own work or of a work in the public domain. No children's plays or musicals. No scripts over 35 pages or 40 minutes performance time. Two copies of ms required. Script Readers' review sheets available. "Concentrate on character, relationships, and a good story." Deadline: January 31. Guidelines for #10 SASE. Charges $10 fee for each play submitted. Prizes: $600, $300, $200, plus possible full production of play. Buys rights to first full-stage production and subsequent local video rights. Reports by June 30.

DAVID JAMES ELLIS MEMORIAL AWARD, Theatre Americana, Box 245, Altadena CA 91003-0245. (626)683-1740. Contact: Playreading Committee. Offered annually for previously unpublished work to produce original plays of Americana background and history or by American authors. Deadline: January 31. "No entry necessary but we will send guidelines on request with SASE." Prize: $500.

EMERGING PLAYWRIGHT AWARD, Urban Stages, 17 E. 47th St., New York NY 10017. (212)421-1380. Fax: (212)421-1387. E-mail: urbanstages@aol.com. Website: http://www.mint.net/urbanstages. Contact: David Sheppard, Jr. Submissions required to be unpublished and unproduced in New York City. Send script, letter of introduction, production history, author's name résumé and SASE. Submissions accepted year-round. Plays selected in August and January for award consideration. Estab. 1983. Prize: $500 and New York showcase production. One play submission per person.

SHUBERT FENDRICH MEMORIAL PLAYWRITING CONTEST, Pioneer Drama Service, Inc., P.O. Box 4267, Englewood CO 80155. (303)779-4035. Fax: (303)779-4315. E-mail: piodrama@aol.com. Website: http://www.pioneerdrama.com. Contact: Editorial Staff. Offered annually for unpublished but previously produced submissions to encourage the development of quality theatrical material for educational and community theater. Deadline: March 1. Guidelines for SASE. Prize: $1,000 royalty advance, publication. Rights acquired only if published. People already published by Pioneer Drama are not eligible.

THE FESTIVAL OF EMERGING AMERICAN THEATRE, The Phoenix Theatre, 749 N. Park Ave., Indianapolis IN 46202. (317)635-7529. Fax: (317)635-0010. Website: http://www.phoenixtheatre.org. Contact: Bryan Fonseca. Annual playwriting competition for previously unproduced full-length and one-act works. Submit script, 1-2 page synopsis, production history of play and author's bio/résumé. Include 9×12 SASE for return of script; #10 SASE if judge's critique desired. Guidelines for SASE. Charges $5 entry fee. Deadline: February 28. Announcement and notification of winners in May. First prize: $750 honorarium for full-length play, $325 for one-act.

[N] **FESTIVAL OF FIRSTS**, City of Carmel-by-the-Sea-Community and Cultural Dept., P.O. Box 1950, Carmel CA 93921-1950. (408)624-3996. Fax: (408)624-0147. Award Director: Brian Donoghue. Offered annually for unpublished plays to recognize and foster the art of playwriting. Deadline: June 15 through August 31. Guidelines for SASE. Charges $15/script. Prize: up to $1,000.

FESTIVAL OF NEW WORKS, Plays-In-Progress, 615 Fourth St., Eureka CA 95501. (707)443-3724. Contact: Susan Bigelow-Marsh. Offered fall and spring for unpublished/unproduced submissions to give playwrights an opportunity to hear their work and receive audience feedback. "We also produce a full season of new unproduced plays—submission deadline is June 1." Deadlines: August 1 and March 1. Guidelines for SASE. Award: staged reading.

FMCT'S BIENNIAL PLAYWRIGHTS COMPETITION (MID-WEST), Fargo-Moorhead Community Theatre, 333 S. Fourth St., Fargo ND 58103-1913. (701)235-1901. Fax: (701)235-2685. E-mail: fmct@pol.org. Website: http://www.fargoweb.com/fmct. Contact: Cindy Snelling, director of education. Estab. 1988. Biennial contest (next contest will be held 1999). Submissions required to be unpublished, unproduced one-acts 30-50 minutes in length. Send SASE for contest rules. Deadline: July 1, 1999.

FULL-LENGTH PLAY COMPETITION, West Coast Ensemble, P.O. Box 38728, Los Angeles CA 90038. (310)449-1447. Fax: (310)453-2254. Contact: Les Hanson. Offered annually "to nurture, support and encourage" unpublished playwrights. Deadline: December 31. Guidelines for SASE. Prize: $500 and presentation of play. Permission to present the play is granted if work is selected as finalist.

JOHN GASSNER MEMORIAL PLAYWRITING COMPETITION, New England Theatre Conference, Inc., Department of Theatre, Northeastern University, 360 Huntington Ave., Boston MA 02115. E-mail: netc@world.std.com. Website: http://world.std.com/~netc/. Offered annually to unpublished full-length plays and scripts for youth theater. Deadline: April 15. Guidelines for SASE. Charges $10 fee. Prizes: 1st-$1,000; 2nd-$500. Open to New England residents NETC members. Playwrights living outside New England may participate by joining NETC.

[N] **GREAT PLAINS PLAY CONTEST**, University Theatre of the University of Kansas, 317 Murphy Hall, Lawrence KS 66045-2176. (785)864-3381. Fax: (785)864-5251. E-mail: dunruh@falcon.cc.ukans.edu. Contact: Delbert Unruh. Offered annually to encourage development and production of full-length dramatic works or musicals about life on the Great Plains. Plays must be full-length, original work or original adaptation that has not been professionally produced or not been produced more than twice by amateur or educational compnies. Deadline: September 1. Prize: $500 Development Award, $2,000 Production Award (production at Univ. Theatre and $500 for travel and housing during production). Acquires right to publish winning works in anthology.

GREAT PLATTE RIVER PLAYWRIGHTS FESTIVAL, University of Nebraska at Kearney, Theatre Department, 905 W. 25th St., Kearney NE 68849. (308)865-8406. Fax: (308)865-8157. E-mail: greenj@platte.unk.edu. Contact: Jeffrey Green. Estab. 1988. Unpublished submissions. "Purpose of award is to develop original dramas and encourage playwrights to work in regional settings. There are five catagories: 1) Adult; 2) Youth (Adolescent); 3) Children's; 4) Musical Theater; 5) Native American. Entries may be drama or comedy." Deadline: April 1. Awards: 1st-$500; 2nd-$300; 3rd-$200; plus free lodging and a travel stipend. "The Festival reserves the rights to development and premiere production of the winning plays without payment of royalties." Contest open to entry by any writer "provided that the writer submits playscripts to be performed on stage—works in progress also acceptable. Works involving the Great Plains will be most favored. More than one entry may be submitted." SASE required for return of scripts. Selection announcement by July 31 only to writers who provide prepaid postcard or SASE.

PAUL GREEN PLAYWRIGHTS PRIZE, North Carolina Writers' Network, 3501 Hwy. 54 W., Studio C, Chapel Hill NC 27516. Fax: (919)929-0535. E-mail: nc_writers@unc.edu. Contact: Frances O. Dowell, program coordinator. Offered annually for unpublished submissions to honor a playwright, held in recognition of Paul Green, North Carolina's dramatist laureate and Pulitzer Prize-winning playwright. Deadline: September 30. Guidelines for SASE. Charges $10 ($7.50 for NCWN members). Prize: $500 and potential production of play. Open to any writer.

HEART OF FILM FEATURE LENGTH SCREENPLAY AWARD, 1600 Nueces, Austin TX 78701. (512)478-4795. Fax: (512)478-6205. E-mail: http://www.austinfilm@aol.com. Website: http://www.austinfilmfestival.org. Contact: Darnell Kreitz, screenplay competition coordinator. Offered annually for unproduced screenplays. Sponsored by the Austin Film Festival and Heart of Film Screenwriters Conference, the competition is looking for quality screenplays to be read, at the finalist and semi-finalist levels, by a jury of producers, development executives and writers in order to offer unknown writers industry exposure. Two categories: Adults/Mature and Children/Family. Prizes: $3,500 for the winner of each category plus air fare and accommodations to attend the Austin Film Festival and Heart of Film Screenwriters Conference in October and participation in the Festival's Mentorship Program. Deadline: May 15. Entry fee: $35. Winners are announced October 3 during the AFF Awards Luncheon. The writer must hold rights when submitted. The script must be original work and must be 90-130 pages. Guidelines for SASE or call 1(800)310-FEST for more info.

N **ERNEST HEMINGWAY PLAY WRITING COMPETITION**, International Hemingway Festival, 2323 Del Prado Blvd., Cape Coral FL 33990. (941)945-0308. Website: http://www.hemingwayfestival.com. Contact: Mina Hemingway. Offered annually for unpublished plays. Deadline: May 1. Submissions not returned. Guidelines and entry form for SASE. Charges $35/entry. Prize: $500 and admittance to the following year's Ernest Hemingway Literary Conference. Winner announced at end of festival.

HENRICO THEATRE COMPANY ONE-ACT PLAYWRITING COMPETITION, Henrico Recreation & Parks, P.O. Box 27032, Richmond VA 23273. (804)501-5115. Fax: (804)501-5284. Contest/Award Director: Amy A. Perdue. Offered annually for previously unpublished or unproduced plays or musicals to produce new dramatic works in 1-act form. Deadline: July 1. Guidelines for SASE. Prize: winner $250; runner-up $125; Winning entries may be produced; videotape sent to author. "Scripts with small casts and simpler sets given preference. Controversial themes should be avoided."

HIGH SCHOOL PLAYWRITING CONTEST, Baker's Plays, 100 Chauncy St., Boston MA 02111-1783. (617)482-1280. Fax: (617)482-7613. Contact: Ray Pape, contest director. Offered annually for previously unpublished plays. "Open to any high school student. Plays must be accompanied by the signature of a sponsoring high school drama or English teacher, and it is recommended that the play receive a production or a public reading prior to the submission." Deadline: postmarked by January 31. Guidelines for #10 SASE. Prize: 1st-$500 and the play published by Baker's Plays; 2nd-$250 and Honorable Mention; 3rd-$100 and Honorable Mention. Write for more information.

HUDSON RIVER CLASSICS ANNUAL CONTEST, Hudson River Classics, Inc., P.O. Box 940, Hudson NY 12534. Phone/fax: (518)828-1329. Contact: W. Keith Hedrick. Offered annually for unpublished playwrights. Submit entries between March 1-June 1. Guidelines for SASE. Charges $5 fee. Prize: $500 and concert reading of winning play. Judges vary. Writers must be from the Northeastern US.

INTERNATIONAL ONE-PAGE PLAY COMPETITION, *Lamia Ink!*, P.O. Box 202, Prince St. Station, New York NY 10012. Contact: Cortland Jessup, founder. Offered annually to encourage and promote performance writers and to challenge all interested writers. Interested in all forms of theater and performance writing in one page format. Deadline: March 15. No phone calls. Guidelines for SASE. Charges $1/one-page play. Maximum of 3 plays per author per competition. Prize: 1st-$200. Public reading given for top 12 in NYC. Publication in *Lamia Ink!*. If play has been previously published, playwright must have retained copyright. Prize: 1st-$200.

JEWEL BOX THEATRE PLAYWRIGHTING COMPETITION, Jewel Box Theatre, 3700 N. Walker, Oklahoma City OK 73118-7099. (405)521-1786. Contact: Charles Tweed, production director. Estab. 1982. Two- or three-acts accepted or one-acts comprising an evening of theater. Deadline: January 15. Send SASE in October for guidelines. Prize: $500.

THE KENNEDY CENTER FUND FOR NEW AMERICAN PLAYS, J.F. Kennedy Center for the Performing Arts, Washington DC 20566. (202)416-8024. Fax: (202)416-8205. Website: http://kennedy-center.org. Contact: Rebecca Foster, manager, theater programming. Estab. 1988. Previously unproduced work. "Program objectives: to encourage playwrights to write, and nonprofit professional theaters to produce new American plays; to ease the financial burdens of nonprofit professional theater organizations producing new plays; to provide a playwright with a better production of the play than the producing theater would normally be able to accomplish." Deadline: May 1 (date changes from year to year). "Nonprofit theater organizations can mail in name and address to be placed on the mailing list or check website." Prize: $10,000 for playwrights plus grants to theaters based on scripts submitted by producing theaters. A few encouragement grants of $2,500 and a new comedy grant of $5,000 are given to promising playwrights chosen from the submitted proposals. Submissions and funding proposals only through the producing theater.

N **LEE KORF PLAYWRITING AWARDS**, The Original Theatre Works, Cerritos College, 11110 Alondra Blvd., Norwalk CA 90650. (562)860-2451, ext. 2638. Fax: (562)467-5005. Contact: Gloria Manriquez. Estab. 1984. Previously unproduced plays. "All plays—special attention paid to plays with multicultural theme." Deadline: September 1. Send for application and guidelines. Charges $5 entry fee. Prize: $750 royalty plus full-scale production of winning entry.

KUMU KAHUA/UHM THEATRE DEPARTMENT PLAYWRITING CONTEST, Kumu Kahua Theatre Inc./ University of Hawaii at Manoa, Department of Theatre and Dance, 1770 East-West Rd., Honolulu HI 96822. (808)956-2588. Fax: (808)956-4234. Website: http://www2.hawaii.edu/~theatre. Contact: Dennis Carroll. Offered annually for unpublished work to honor full-length and short plays. Deadline: January 1. Guidelines available every September. Prize: $500 (Hawaii Prize); $400 (Pacific Rim); $200 (Resident). First 2 categories open to residents and nonresidents. For Hawaii Prize, plays must be set in Hawaii or deal with some aspect of the Hawaiian experience. For Pacific Rim prize, plays must deal with Hawaii or the Pacific Islands, Pacific Rim or Pacific/Asian/American experience—short plays only considered in 3rd category!

L.A. DESIGNERS' THEATRE-COMMISSIONS, L.A. Designers' Theatre, P.O. Box 1883, Studio City CA 91614-0883. (213)650-9600. Fax: (818)985-9200. (818)769-9000 T.D.D. E-mail: ladesigners@juno.com. Contact: Richard Niederberg, director. Quarterly contest "to promote new work and push it onto the conveyor belt to filmed or videotaped entertainment." All submissions must be registered with copyright office and be unpublished by "major" publishers. Material will *not* be returned. Deadline: March 15, June 15, September 15, December 15. "No rules, no fees, no entry forms. Just present an idea that can be commissioned into a full work." Prize: Production or publication of the work in the Los Angeles market. "We only want 'first refusal.' If you are picked, we negotiate royalties with the writer." Proposals for works not yet completed are encouraged.

N **LITTLE THEATRE OF ALEXANDRIA ANNUAL ONE-ACT PLAYWRITING CONTEST**, Little Theatre of Alexandria, 600 Wolfe St., Alexandria VA 22314. (703)683-5778. Chairman, One Act Play Reading Committee: Bonnie Jourdan. Offered annually for unpublished and unproduced plays. Deadline: February 28. Charges $5 fee. Prizes: 1st-$350; 2nd-$250; 3rd-$150. Judged by a committee of 14 people.

LOVE CREEK ANNUAL SHORT PLAY FESTIVAL, Love Creek Productions, % Granville, 162 Nesbit St., Weehawken NJ 07087-6817. E-mail: creekread@aol.com. Festival Manager: Cynthia Granville-Callahan. Estab. 1985. Annual festival for unpublished plays, unproduced in New York in the previous year, under 40 minutes, at least 2 characters, larger casts preferred. "We established the Festival as a playwriting competition in which scripts are judged on their merits in performance." Deadline: ongoing. Guidelines for #10 SASE. All entries must specify "festival" on envelope and must include letter giving permission to produce script, if chosen and stating whether equity showcase is acceptable. Cash price awarded to winner. "For 1998-99 we are giving strong preference to scripts featuring females in major roles in casts which are predominantly female."

LOVE CREEK MINI FESTIVALS, Love Creek Productions, % Granville, 162 Nesbit St., Weehawken NJ 07087-6817. Festival Literary Manager: Cynthia Granville-Callahan. "The Mini Festivals are an outgrowth of our annual Short Play Festival in which we produce scripts concerning a particular issue or theme which our artistic staff selects according to current needs, interests and concerns of our members, audiences and playwrights submitting to our Short Play Festival throughout the year." Considers scripts unpublished, unproduced in New York City in past year, under 40 minutes, at least 2 characters, larger casts preferred. Guidelines for #10 SASE. Submissions must list name of festival on envelope and must include letter giving permission to produce script, if chosen, and stating whether equity showcase is acceptable. Finalists receive a mini-showcase production in New York City. Winner receives a cash prize. Write for upcoming themes, deadlines ongoing. Fear of God: Religion in the 90s, Gay and Lesbian Festival will be presented again in 1998 along with others TBA. "For 1998-99 we are giving strong preference to scripts featuring females in major roles in casts which are predominantly female."

THE LOW-BUDGET FEATURE PROJECT, Cyclone Entertainment Group/Cyclone Productions, 3412 Milwaukee, Suite 485, Northbrook IL 60062. (847)657-0446. Fax: (847)657-0446. Contact: Lee Alan. Offered annually. The Low-Budget Feature Project is a program designed to establish an avenue by which screenwriter's may obtain a feature film writing credit. The selected script is produced as a feature film. Deadline: April 1. Guidelines for SASE. Charges $50 entry fee. Prize: The winning applicant will be eligible to receive 5% of the film's profits, if any, until the films' copyright has expired or the film is sold. Judged by the production team and director-Lee Alan. Only after winner is selected do we enter into an additional rights agreement. Open to any writer.

MAXIM MAZUMDAR NEW PLAY COMPETITION, Alleyway Theatre, One Curtain Up Alley, Buffalo NY 14202-1911. (716)852-2600. Fax: (716)852-2266. E-mail: alleywayth.com. Website: http://www.alleyway.com. Dramaturg: Kevin Stevens. Estab. 1990. Annual competition. Full Length: not less than 90 minutes, no more than 10 performers. One-Act: less than 60 minutes, no more than 6 performers. Musicals must be accompanied by audio tape. Deadline: July 1. Finalists announced January 1. "Playwrights may submit work directly. There is no entry form. Annual playwright's fee $5; may submit one in each category, but pay only one fee. Please specify if submission is to be included in competition." Prize: full length—$400, travel plus lodging, production and royalties; one-act—$100, production plus royalties. "Alleyway Theatre must receive first production credit in subsequent printings and productions."

MIDWESTERN PLAYWRIGHTS FESTIVAL, University of Toledo and Toledo Rep Theatre, University of Toledo, Toledo OH 43606. (419)530-2202. Fax: (419)530-8439. Contact: John S. Kuhn. Offered annually for unpublished submissions to celebrate regional theater. Deadline: June 1. Guidelines for SASE. Prize: The winning playwright will receive $1,000, a staged reading and full production of the winning play in the Spring at the Toledo Repertoire Theatre.

A stipend will also be provided for travel, room and board for the readings and for a two-week residency during production. Two other finalists will receive $350 and $150 and staged readings. Judged by members from both sponsoring organizations. Playwright must be an Ohio, Michigan, Illinois or Indiana resident. Submission must be an unpublished, full-length, two-act play, not produced professionally. Cast limit of ten, prefer one set, commercially producible.

MILL MOUNTAIN THEATRE NEW PLAY COMPETITION, Mill Mountain Theatre, Center in the Square, 1 Market Square, 2nd Floor, Roanoke VA 24011-1437. (703)342-5730. Fax: (540)342-5745. E-mail: mmtmail@intrlink.com. Website: http://www.intrlink.com/MMT. Literary Manager: Jack Parrish. Estab. 1985. Previously unpublished and unproduced plays for up to 10 cast members. Plays must be agent submitted—or have the recommendation of a director, literary manager or dramaturg. Deadline: January 1. Guidelines for SASE.

N **MOVING ARTS PREMIERE ONE-ACT COMPETITION**, Moving Arts, 1822 Hyperion, Los Angeles CA 90027. (213)665-8961. Fax: (213)665-1816. E-mail: movnarts@primenet.com. Website: http://www.primenetcom/~movnarts. Award Director: Rebecca Rasmussen. Offered annually for unpublished one-act plays and "is designed to foster the continued development of one-act plays." Deadline: February 28. Guidelines for SASE. Charges $8 fee/script. Prizes: 1st-$200 plus a full production with a 4-8 week run. 2nd and 3rd-program mention and possible production. All playwrights are eligible except Moving Arts company members.

MRTW ANNUAL RADIO SCRIPT CONTEST, Midwest Radio Theatre Workshop, 915 E. Broadway, Columbia MO 65201. (573)874-5676. Contact: Sue Zizza. Estab. 1979. "To encourage the writing of radio scripts and to showcase both established and emerging radio playwrights. Some winning works are produced for radio and all winning works are published in the annual MRTW Scriptbook, the only one of its kind in this country." Deadline: November 15. Guidelines for SASE. "A cash award of $800 is split among the top 2-4 entries, depending on recommendation of the jurors. Winners receive free workshop registration. Those who receive honorable mention, as well as award-winning plays, are included in the scriptbook; a total of 10-16 are published annually. We acquire the right to publish the script in the scriptbook, which is distributed at cost, and the right to produce the script for air; all other rights retained by the author."

MUSICAL STAIRS, West Coast Ensemble, P.O. Box 38728, Los Angeles CA 90038. (310)449-1447. Fax: (310)453-2254. **Contact**: Les Hanson. Offered annually for unpublished writers "to nurture, support and encourage musical creators." Deadline: June 30. Prize: $500 and presentation of musical. Permission to present the musical is granted if work is selected as finalist.

NANTUCKET SHORT PLAY COMPETITION AND FESTIVAL, Nantucket Theatrical Productions, Box 2177, Nantucket MA 02584. (508)228-5002. Contest Director: Jim Patrick. Offered annually for unpublished plays to "seek the highest quality of playwriting distilled into a short play format." Deadline: January 1. Charges $6 fee. Prize: $200 plus staged readings. Selected plays also receive staged readings. "We acquire the right to give up to four staged readings within one calendar year of submission deadline. Would like to see a wider range of works featuring kids, adolescents or multicultural casts." Plays must be less than 40 pages.

NATIONAL HISPANIC PLAYWRITING AWARD, Arizona Theatre Co. in affiliation with Centro Cultural Mexicano, P.O. Box 1631, Tucson AZ 85702. (520)884-8210. Fax: (520)628-9129. Contest Director: Elaine Romero. Offered annually for unproduced, unpublished plays. "The plays may be in English, bilingual or in Spanish (with English translation). The award recognizes exceptional full-length plays by Hispanic playwrights." Deadline: October 31. Guidelines for SASE. Prize: $1,000 and possible inclusion in ATC's Genesis New Play Reading Series. Open to Hispanic playwrights currently residing in the United States, its territories, and/or Mexico.

N **NATIONAL ONE-ACT PLAYWRITING COMPETITION**, Little Theatre of Alexandria, 600 Wolfe St., Alexandria VA 22314. (703)683-5778. Fax: (703)683-1378. E-mail: ltlthtre@erols. Contact: Chairman Playwriting Competition. Estab. 1978. To encourage original writing for theatre. Submissions must be original, unpublished, unproduced one-act stage plays. Deadline: February 28. Guidelines for SASE. Submit scripts after October 1. Charges $5 fee. Prize: 1st-$350; 2nd-$250; 3rd-$150. "We usually produce top two or three winners."

N **NATIONAL PLAY AWARD**, National Repertory Theatre Foundation, P.O. Box 286, Los Angeles CA 90078. (213)465-9517. Fax: (310)652-2543. Contact: Ann Farthing, literary manager. Offered annually for unpublished full-length original plays. Deadline: January 1 through March 30. Guidelines for SASE. Charges $25 fee. Prizes: 1st-$5,000 and production; 4 runners up receive staged readings.

NATIONAL PLAYWRIGHTS' AWARD, Unicorn Theatre, 3820 Main St., Kansas City MO 64111. (816)531-7529. Fax: (816)531-0421. Contact: Herman Wilson, literary assistant. Offered annually for previously unproduced work. "We produce contemporary original scripts, preferring scripts that deal with social concerns. However, we accept (and have produced) comedies." Guidelines for SASE. Prize: $1,000 in royalty/prize fee and mainstage production at the Unicorn as part of its regular season.

NATIONAL TEN-MINUTE PLAY CONTEST, Actors Theatre of Louisville, 316 W. Main St., Louisville KY 40202-4218. (502)584-1265. Fax: (502)561-3300. Contact: Michael Bigelow Dixon, literary manager. Estab. 1964. Previously unproduced (professionally) ten-minute plays (10 pages or less). "Entries must *not* have had an Equity or Equity-waiver production." Postmark deadline: December 1. Prize: $1,000. Please write or call for submission guidelines.

NEW AMERICAN COMEDY SHOWCASE, Ukiah Players Theatre, 1041 Low Gap Rd., Ukiah CA 95482. (707)462-1210. Contact: Doug Hundley. Offered every 2 years for unpublished work to help playwrights develop their full-length comedies into funnier, stronger scripts. Deadline: November 30 of odd-numbered years. Guidelines for SASE. Two scripts chosen for staged readings the following year. One of those chosen for full production the year after that. $25 per performance royalty for readings (2); $50 per performance royalty for full productions (6-8). Travel paid for winning playwright (up to $400) to Ukiah for two-week workshop and rehearsal. Lodging and per diem also provided.

THE NEW HARMONY PROJECT CONFERENCE/LABORATORY, The New Harmony Project, 613 N. East St., Indianapolis IN 46202. (317)464-9405. Fax: (317)635-4201. Contact: Jeffrey L. Sparks, executive director. Offered annually for previously published or unpublished scripts. "The purpose is to identify new theater and film scripts that emphasize the dignity of the human spirit and celebrate the worth of the human experience." Deadline: Mid-November. "Writers of selected scripts, along with writers-in-residence and a company of actors, directors and dramaturges, are brought to New Harmony, Indiana for two and one-half weeks in May. During this time, scripts are put through a series of rehearsals with actors and directors. Critique sessions are held with writers, actors and directors. Each fully-developed script is given a final reading with an audience of conference participants and special invited guests on the final weekend. We look for writers whose work reflects our philosophy and who we think would benefit from development at The New Harmony Project. We accept proposals on an open-call basis (with specified guidelines), then request scripts from selected writers. Of those scripts submitted, up to four are selected for full development, and up to three for limited development."

N **NEW PLAYS FESTIVAL/CHILCOTE AWARD**, Cleveland Public Theatre, 6415 Detroit Ave., Cleveland OH 44102. (216)631-2727. Fax: (216)631-2575. E-mail: cpt@en.com. Website: http://www.en.com/cpt. Award Director: Terence Cranendonk. Offered annually for unproduced stage plays "to workshop and develop alternative theatre scripts regionally, nationally and worldwide by culturally diverse playwrights and present staged readings to the public." Deadline: September 1. Guidelines for SASE. Charges $10 fee. Prize: one week rehearsal in Cleveland, two staged readings in January New Plays Festival, travel stipend. Two plays included in the Festival receive $2,000 award and one is guaranteed full production in following season.

NEW VOICE SERIES, Remembrance Through the Performing Arts, 3300 Bee Caves Rd., Suite 650, Austin TX 78746. (512)329-9118. Award Director: Marla Macdonald. Offered annually "to find talented central Texas playwrights who are in the early stages of script development. We develop these scripts on the page through a Work In Progress production." Deadline: December 1. Playwrights need to send script, bio and a script size SASE. Prize: free development of their play with our company plus free representation of their plays to theaters nationally for world premieres. Open to Texas playwrights only.

N **NEW WORKS FOR THE STAGE**, COE College Theatre Arts Department, 1220 First Ave. NE, Cedar Rapids IA 52402. (319)399-8689. Fax: (319)399-8557. E-mail: swolvert@coe.edu. Contact: Susan Wolv. Offered every 2 years (odd years) "to encourage new work, to provide an interdisciplinary forum for the discussion of issues found in new work, to offer playwright contact with theater professionals who can provide response to new work." Deadline: June 1. Prize: $325 plus travel, room and board for residency at the college. Full-length, original unpublished and unproduced scripts only. No musicals, adaptations, translations or collaborations. Include one-page synopsis, résumé and SASE if the script is to be returned.

OFF-OFF-BROADWAY ORIGINAL SHORT PLAY FESTIVAL, 45 W. 25th St., New York NY 10010. Fax: (212)206-1429. Contact: William Talbot. Offered annually for unpublished work. "The Festival was developed in 1976 to bolster those theater companies and schools offering workshops, programs and instruction in playwriting. It proposes to encourage them by offering them and their playwrights the opportunity of having their plays seen by new audiences and critics, and of having them reviewed for publication." Deadline: early spring. Guidelines for SASE. Prize: "Presentation on NY stage before NY audiences and critics. Publication of selected plays by Samuel French, Inc." "No individual writer may enter on his/her own initiative. Entries must come from theater companies, professional schools or colleges which foster playwriting by conducting classes, workshops or similar programs of assistance to playwrights."

OGLEBAY INSTITUTE TOWNGATE THEATRE PLAYWRITING CONTEST, Oglebay Institute, Stifel Fine Arts Center, 1330 National Rd., Wheeling WV 26003. (304)242-7700. Fax: (304)242-7747. Contact: Director, Performing Arts Dept. Estab. 1976. Offered annually for unpublished works. Deadline: December 31. Guidelines for SASE. Prize: $300, limited-run production of play. "All full-length *non-musical* plays that have never been professionally produced or published are eligible." Winner announced May 31.

N **ONE-ACT PLAYWRITING COMPETITION**, Warehouse Theatre Company, Stephens College, Box 2007, Columbia MO 65215. "The entry must be a one-act play. Full-lengths, musicals, and children's plays will not be accepted. The playwright must be a student of graduate, undergraduate, or high school level. Playwrights are encouraged to submit plays which are by, for, and about women. The entry should be an original work and should not have been previously produced or published." Deadline: Postmarked Jan. 31. Scripts returned with proper SASE. Charges $10 fee. Checks or money orders should be made payable to Warehouse Theatre Company. Prize: $200 for playwright and production by the Warehouse Theatre Company.

OPUS MAGNUM DISCOVERY AWARD, Christopher Columbus Society, 433 N. Camden Dr., #600, Beverly Hills CA 90210. (310)288-1881. Fax: (310)288-0257. E-mail: awards@hollywoodawards.com. Website: http://screenwriters.com. Contact: Carlos de Abreu, president. Annual award to discover new authors with books/manuscripts that can be optioned for features or TV movies. Deadline: December 1. Guidelines for SASE. Charges $75 fee. Prize: Option moneys to winner, up to $10,000. Judged by entertainment industry story analysts and producers.

MILDRED & ALBERT PANOWSKI PLAYWRITING AWARD, Forest A. Roberts Theatre, Northern Michigan University, Marquette MI 49855-5364. (906)227-2553. Fax: (906)227-2567. Website: http://www.nmu.edu/theatre. Award Director: Dr. James A. Panowski. Contact: E. Milkovich, award coordinator. Estab. 1978. Unpublished, unproduced, full-length plays. Scripts must be *received* on or before the Friday before Thanksgiving. Guidelines and application for SASE. Prize: $2,000. Judged by members of a university-wide screening committee.

PERISHABLE THEATRE'S WOMEN'S PLAYWRITING FESTIVAL, P.O. Box 23132, Providence RI 02903. (401)331-2695. Fax: (401)331-7811. Website: http://www/AS220.Org/Perishable or www.Perishable.Org. Festival Directors: Kathleen Jenkins and Vanessa Gilbert. Offered annually for unpublished plays to encourage women playwrights. Deadline: December 31. Guidelines for SASE. Charges $5 fee. Prize: 3 winners $250 each. Judged by the co-directors and the artistic director of the theater. Open to women playwrights exclusively.

N **PILGRIM PROJECT GRANTS**, 156 Fifth, #400, New York NY 10010. (212)627-2288. Fax: (212)627-2184. Contact: Davida Goldman. Grants for a reading, workshop production or full production of plays that deal with questions of moral significance. Deadline: ongoing. Guidelines for SASE. Grants: $1,000-7,000.

PLAYHOUSE ON THE SQUARE NEW PLAY COMPETITION, Playhouse on the Square, 51 S. Cooper, Memphis TN 38104. Contact: Jackie Nichols. Submissions required to be unproduced. Deadline: April 1. Guidelines for SASE. Prize: $500 plus production.

THE PLAYWORKS FESTIVAL, University of Texas at El Paso, Theatre Arts Department, 500 W. University, El Paso TX 79968-0549. (915)747-7854. Fax: (915)747-5438. E-mail: mwright@utep.edu. Website: http://www.utep.edu/theatre. Director: Michael Wright. Offered annually for 3 residencies in the program. Each writer-in-residence is expected to develop a new play during the 3-week residency through daily workshops. "We are especially interested in students of Hispanic-American or Native American origin." Deadline: January 31. Guidelines for SASE. Prize: "We provide support for travel and per diem, plus an honorarium." Open to undergraduate or graduate students only.

PLAYWRIGHTS' CENTER JEROME PLAYWRIGHT-IN-RESIDENCE FELLOWSHIP, The Playwrights' Center, 2301 Franklin Ave. E, Minneapolis MN 55406. (612)332-7481. Fax: (612)332-6037. E-mail: pwcenter@mtn.org. Website: http://www.pwcenter.org. Lab Director: Elissa Adams. Estab. 1976. To provide emerging playwrights with funds and services to aid them in the development of their craft. Deadline: September 15. Open to playwrights only—may not have had more than 2 different fully staged productions of their works by professional theaters. Must spend fellowship year in Minnesota at Playwrights' Center.

PLAYWRIGHTS' CENTER McKNIGHT FELLOWSHIP, The Playwrights' Center, 2301 Franklin Ave. E, Minneapolis MN 55406. (612)332-7481. Fax: (612)332-6037. E-mail: pwcenter@mtn.org. Website: http://www.pwcenter.org. Lab Director: Elissa Adams. Estab. 1982. Recognition of playwrights whose work has made a significant impact on the contemporary theater. Deadline: January 15. Open to playwrights only. Must have had a minimum of two different fully staged productions by professional theaters. Must spend 1 month at Playwrights' Center. US citizens or permanent residents only. Prize: two $10,000 fellowship awards.

N **PLAYWRIGHTS' THEATER OF DENTON NEW PLAY COMPETITION**, Playwrights' Theater of Denton, P.O. Box 732, Denton TX 76202-0732. Contact: Mark Pearce. Offered annually for stage plays of any length. Deadline: December 15. Guidelines for SASE. Charges $15 fee, payable to Sigma Corporation. Prize: $500. Open to any writer.

PRINCESS GRACE AWARDS PLAYWRIGHT FELLOWSHIP, Princess Grace Foundation—USA, 150 E. 58th St., 21st Floor, New York NY 10155. (212)317-1470. Fax: (212)317-1473. E-mail: PGFUSA@PGFUSA.COM. Website: http://www.pgfusa.com. Contact: Ms. Toby E. Boshak. Offered annually for unpublished submissions to support playwright through residency program with New Dramatists, Inc. located in New York City. A ten-week residence. Deadline: March 31. Guidelines for SASE. Award: $7,500 plus ten-week residency with New Dramatists, Inc. in New York City.

Must be a US citizen or have US status; candidate should be under 30 at time of application.

PROMISING PLAYWRIGHT AWARD, Colonial Players, Inc. 98 Tower Dr., Stevensville MD 21666. Also: P.O. Box 2167, Annapolis MD 21401. (410)263-0533. Coordinator: Fran Marchand. Offered every 2 years for unpublished plays by residents of Maryland, Virginia, West Virginia, Pennsylvania, Delaware and Distrit of Columbia "to encourage aspiring playwrights." Submissions accepted September 1-December 31 of even-numbered years. Guidelines for #10 SASE. Prize: $750 plus possible production of play.

PUTTIN' ON THE RITZ, ONE-ACT PLAY CONTEST, Puttin' On the Ritz, Inc., 915 White Horse Pike, Oaklyn NJ 08107. (609)858-5230. Fax: (609)858-0812. E-mail: forrest37@aol.com. Contest Director: Alex Wilkie. Offered annually "to encourage playwrights by the production of their new works. We especially encourage playwrights from the New Jersey/Philadelphia region." Deadline: January 31. Prize: production of those works selected by the One-Act Play contest committee. "We receive about 125 plays, and of those, produce three or four." Plays that have been professionally produced will not be considered. "Plays that run 40 minutes or less preferred. Plays without a SASE will not be returned."

GWEN PHARIS RINGWOOD AWARD FOR DRAMA, Writers Guild of Alberta, 11759 Great Rd., Edmonton, Alberta T5M 3K6 Canada. (403)422-8174. Fax: (403)422-2663. E-mail: writers@compusmart.ab.ca. Contact: Darlene Diver. Drama book published in current year or script of play produced three times in current year in a community theater. Must be an Alberta playwright. Eligible plays must be registered with the WGA-APN Drama Award Production Registry. Contact either the WGA head office, or the Alberta Playwrights' Network for registry forms.

ROCHESTER PLAYWRIGHT FESTIVAL, Midwest Theatre Network, 5031 Tongen Ave. NW, Rochester MN 55901. (507)281-1472. Executive Director: Joan Sween. Offered for unpublished submissions to support emerging playwrights. No categories, but entries are considered for production by various types of theaters: community theater, dinner theater, issues theater, satiric/new format theater, children's theater, musical theater. Entry form required. Guidelines and entry form for SASE. No fee for first entry. Subsequent entries by same author, $10 fee. Prize: full production, travel stipend, accomodations, cash prize.

RICHARD RODGERS AWARDS IN MUSICAL THEATER, American Academy of Arts and Letters, 633 W. 155th St., New York NY 10032-7599. (212)368-5900. Fax: (212)491-4615. Executive Director: Virginia Dajani. Estab. 1978. The Richard Rodgers Awards subsidize full productions, studio productions and staged readings by nonprofit theaters in New York City of works by composers and writers who are not already established in the field of musical theater. Deadline: November 2. SASE for guidelines and application.

THE LOIS AND RICHARD ROSENTHAL NEW PLAY PRIZE, Cincinnati Playhouse in the Park, Box 6537, Cincinnati OH 45206-0537. (513)345-2242. Website: http://www.cincyplay.com. Contact: Associate Artistic Director. For playwrights and musical playwrights. Annual award. "The Lois and Richard Rosenthal New Play Prize was established in 1987 to encourage the development of new plays that are original, thearical, strong in character and dialgoue, and make a significant contribution to the literature of American theatre. Residents of Cincinnati, the Rosenthals are committed to supporting arts organizations and social agencies that are innovative and that foster social change."
Needs: Plays must be full-length in any style: comedy, drama, musical, etc. Translations, adaptations, individual one-acts and any play previously submitted for the Rosenthal Prize are not eligible. Collaborations are welcome, in which case prize benefits are shared. Plays must be unpublished prior to submission and may not have received a full-scale professional production. Plays that have had a workshop, reading or non-professional production are still eligible. Playwrights with past production experience are especially encouraged to submit new work. Submit a two-page maximum abstract of the play including title, character breakdown, story synopsis and playwright information (bio or resume). Also include up to five pages of sample dialogue. If sumbitting a musical, please include a tape of selections from the score. All abstracts and dialogue samples will be read. From these, selected manuscripts will be solicited. Do not send a manuscript with or instead of the abstract. All unsolicited manuscripts will be returned unread. Submitted materials, including tapes,will be returned only if a SASE with adequate postage is provided. The Rosenthal Prize is open for submission from July 1st to December 31st. Only one submission per playwright each year. Prize: The Rosenthal Prize play receives a full production at Cincinnati Playhouse in the Park as part of the theatre's annual season and is given regional and national promotion. The playwright receives a $10,000 award plus travel and residency expenses for the Cincinnati rehearsal period.

THE SCREENWRITER'S PROJECT, Cyclone Entertainment Group/Cyclone Productions, 3412 Milwaukee, Suite 485, Northbrook IL 60062. (847)657-0446. Fax: (847)657-0446. E-mail: cycprod@aol.com. Website: http://www.cyclone-entertainment.com. Contact: Lee Alan, director. Offered annually to give both experienced and first-time writers the opportunity to begin a career as a screenwriter. Deadline: August 1. Guidelines for SASE. Charges $35 fee for August 1 deadline; $40 fee for September 1 deadline. Prizes: three $5,000 grants.

SIENA COLLEGE INTERNATIONAL PLAYWRIGHTS COMPETITION, Siena College Theatre Program, 515 Loudon Rd., Loudonville NY 12211-1462. (518)783-2381. Fax: (518)783-4293. E-mail: maciag@siena.edu. Website: http://www.siena.edu. Contact: Gary Maciag, director of theatre. Offered every 2 years for unpublished plays "to allow students to explore production collaboration with the playwright. In addition, it provides the playwright an important development opportunity. Plays should be previously unproduced, unpublished, full-length, non-musicals and free of copyright and royalty restrictions. Plays should require unit set or minimal changes and be suitable for a college-age cast of 3-10. There is a required 6-week residency." Deadline: June 30 even-numbered years. Guidelines for SASE. Guidelines are available after November 1 in odd-numbered years. Prize: $2,000 honorarium; up to $1,000 to cover expenses for required residency; full production of winning script. Winning playwright must agree that the Siena production will be the world premiere of the play.

DOROTHY SILVER PLAYWRITING COMPETITION, Jewish Community Center, 3505 Mayfield Rd., Cleveland Heights OH 44118. (216)382-4000, ext. 275. Fax: (216)382-5401. Contact: Elaine Rembrandt. Estab. 1948. All entries must be original works, not previously produced, suitable for a full-length presentation; directly concerned with the Jewish experience. Deadline: December 15. Cash award plus staged reading.

SOUTH CAROLINA PLAYWRIGHTS' FESTIVAL, Trustus Theatre, P.O. Box 11721, Columbia SC 29211. (803)771-9153. Contact: Tim Gardner, literary manager. Estab. 1989. Offered annually for professionally unproduced work. Full-length plays. No musicals, children's shows, translations or adaptations. Cast limit 8, 1 set preferred. Submit January 1-March 1. Guidelines for SASE. Prize: 1st-$500, full production, travel and housing for opening; 2nd-$250 plus staged reading; one acts $50 and late night readings. Submission procedure: application (available after September 1, 1999), 1 copy of synopsis, 1 copy of résumé, SASE. "Unsolicited scripts will be recycled."

SOUTHEASTERN THEATRE CONFERENCE NEW PLAY PROJECT, 461 King Richard Dr,. Murray KY 42701-9061. (502)762-5487. E-mail: jamesaye@aol.com. Contact: James I. Schempp. Offered annually for the discovery, development and publicizing of worthy new unproduced plays and playwrights. Eligibility limited to members of 10 state SETC Region: AL, FL, GA, KY, MS, NC, SC, TN, VA, WV. Submit March 1-June 1. Bound full-length or related one acts under single cover (one submission only). Send SASE with scripts for return. Guidelines available upon request. Prize: $1,000, staged reading at SETC Convention, expenses paid trip to convention and preferred consideration for National Playwrights Conference.

SOUTHWEST THEATRE ASSOCIATION NEW PLAY CONTEST, Southwest Theatre Association, Department of Theatre Arts, University of Texas at El Paso, 500 W. University, El Paso TX 79968-0549. (915)747-7854. Fax: (915)747-5438. E-mail: mwright@utep.edu. Contact: Michael Wright, head of playwrighting and directing. Annual contest for unpublished, unproduced work to promote the writing and production of new plays in the Southwest region. Deadline: March 16. Guidelines for SASE. Charges $10. Prize: $200 honorarium, a reading at the annual SWTA convention, publication in *Theatre Southwest*. No musicals or children's plays. Letter of recommendation suggested.

STANLEY DRAMA AWARD, Dept. of Theatre, Wagner College, Staten Island NY 10301. Fax: (718)390-3323. Contact: Elizabeth Terry, director. Offered for original full-length plays, musicals or one-act play sequences that have not been professionally produced or received trade book publication. Presented as a memorial to Alma Timolat Stanley (Mrs. Robert C. Stanley). Deadline: October 1. Guidelines for SASE. Award: $2,000. Stage plays only.

MARVIN TAYLOR PLAYWRITING AWARD, Sierra Repertory Theatre, P.O. Box 3030, Sonora CA 95370-3030. (209)532-3120. Fax: (209)532-7270. E-mail: srt@mlode.com. Website: http://www.mlode.com/~nsierra/srt. Producing Director: Dennis Jones. Estab. 1981. Full-length plays. Deadline: August 31, 1999.

TEXAS PLAYWRIGHT FESTIVAL, Stages Repertory Theatre, 3201 Allen Pkwy., Suite 101, Houston TX 77019. (713)527-0240. Fax: (713)527-8669. Contact: Rob Bundy, artistic director. Offered annually to provide an outlet for unpublished Texas playwrights. Entries received from October 1-February 14. Guidelines for SASE. Prize: A reading by professional actors and a small stipend is awarded if available. Writer must be a current or previous resident of Texas, or the play must be set in Texas or have a Texas theme.

THEATRE BC'S ANNUAL CANADIAN NATIONAL PLAYWRITING COMPETITION, Theatre BC, 1005 Broad St., #307, Victoria, British Columbia V8W 2A1 Canada. (250)381-2443. Fax: (250)381-4419. E-mail: theatrebc@pacificcoast.net. Website: http://www.culturenet.ca/theatrebc/. Executive Director: Jim Harding. Offered annually to unpublished plays "to promote the development and production of new plays (previously unproduced) at all levels of theater. Categories: Full-Length (2 acts or longer); One Act (less than 60 minutes) and an open Special Merit (juror's discretion). Deadline: June. Guidelines for SASE or check Theatre BC's website. Charges $35/entry and $25 (optional) for written critique. Prize: Full-Length-$1,500; One Act-$1,000; Special Merit-$750. Winners are also invited to new play workshops: 18 hours with a professional dramaturge, registrant actors and a public readings at provincial "Backstage" workshop (every November). Production and publishing rights remain with the playwright. Any resident in Canada is eligible. All submissions are made under pseudonyms. E-mail inquiries welcome.

N **THEATRE CONSPIRACY ANNUAL NEW PLAY CONTEST**, Theatre Conspiracy, 10091 McGregor Blvd., Ft. Myers FL 33919. (941)936-3239. Fax: (941)936-0510. Award Director: Bill Taylor. Offered annually for unpublished full length plays with 6 or less characters and simple production demands." Deadline: January 10. Guidelines for SASE. Charges $10 fee. Prize: $500 and full production.

THEATRE PEI NEW VOICES PLAYWRITING AWARDS, P.E.I. Council of the Arts, 115 Richmond St., Charlestown PE C1A 1H7 Canada. (902)368-4410. Fax: (902)368-4418. Contact: Judy MacDonald. Contest offered annually. Deadline: February 15. Guidelines for SASE. Charges $8 fee. Prize: Monetary. Open to individuals who have been resident of Prince Edward Island at least 6-12 months proceeding the deadline for entries.

UNICORN THEATRE NATIONAL PLAYWRIGHTS' AWARD, Unicorn Theatre, 3828 Main St., Kansas City MO 64111. (816)531-7529. Fax: (816)531-0421. Award Director: Herman Wilson. Offered annually to "encourage and assist the development of an unpublished and unproduced play." Deadline: April 30. Guidelines for SASE. Prize: $1,000 and production. Acquires 2% subsidiary rights of future productions for a 5 year period.

UNIVERSITY OF ALABAMA NEW PLAYWRIGHTS PROGRAM, P.O. Box 870239, Tuscaloosa AL 35487-0239. (205)348-9032. Fax: (205)348-9048. E-mail: pcastagn@woodsquad.as.ua.edu. Website: http://www.as.ua.edu/theatre/npp.htm (includes guidelines). Director/Dramaturg: Dr. Paul C. Castagno. Estab. 1982. Full-length plays for mainstage; experimental plays for B stage. Workshops and small musicals can be proposed. Queries responded to quickly. Competitive stipend. Development process includes readings, visitations, and possible complete productions with faculty director and dramaturg. Guidelines for SASE. Up to 6 months assessment time. Submit August-March.

URBAN STAGES AWARD, 17 E. 47th St., New York NY 10017. (212)289-2168. Fax: (212)380-1387. E-mail: urbanstage@aol.com. Website: http://www.mint.net/urabanstages. Contact: Ella Smith. Audience development program of radio-style staged readings that tour the libraries throughout the boroughs of New York City. Ethnically diverse encouraged. Plays between 30-60 minutes. Cast maximum of 5 (doubling encouraged). Submissions must be unpublished and unproduced in New York City. Send script, letter of introduction, production or reading history, author's résumé and SASE. Submissions accepted February 1-June 15. Prize: $200; air fare for out-of-town playwrights.

VERMONT PLAYWRIGHT'S AWARD, The Valley Players, P.O. Box 441, Waitsfield VT 05673. Website: http://www.floydianslip.com/ph/val_play.htm. Award Director: Jennifer Howard. Offered annually for unpublished nonmusical, full-length play suitable for production by a community theater group to encourage development of playwrights in Vermont, New Hampshire and Maine. Deadline: February 1. Prize: $1,000. Open to residents of VT, NH or ME.

VERY SPECIAL ARTS PLAYWRIGHT DISCOVERY PROGRAM, Very Special Arts, 1300 Connecticut Ave. NW, Suite 700, Washington DC 20036. (800)933-8721. Fax: (202)737-0645. E-mail: playwright@vsarts.org. Website: http://www.vsarts.org. Invites individuals with disabilities to submit a play that documents the experience of living with a disability. One play in each age category—age 18 and under; age 19 and up—will be selected for production at the John F. Kennedy Center for the Performing Arts. Prize: monetary award and a trip to Washington D.C. to view the production. Deadline: late April. Guidelines for SASE.

THEODORE WARD PRIZE FOR PLAYWRITING, Columbia College Theater/Music Center, 72 E. 11th St., Chicago IL 60605-1996. Fax: (312)663-9591. E-mail: chigochuck@aol.com. Contact: Chuck Smith. Estab. 1985. "To uncover and identify new unpublished African-American plays that are promising and produceable." Deadline: July 1. All rights for music or biographies must be secured prior to submission. All entrants must be of African-American descent and residing within the US. Only 1 complete script per playwright will be accepted.

WE DON'T NEED NO STINKIN' DRAMAS, (formerly Mixed Blood Versus America), Mixed Blood Theatre Company, 1501 S 4th St., Minneapolis, MN 55454. E-mail: mixedblood@wavetech.net. Contact: Dave Kunz. Offered for full-length, contemporary comedies; particularly comedies about race, sports or containing political edge (or similarly themed musical comedies). Must remain unproduced as of October 1, 1998. No one-acts. Scripts must be 65 pages long. Guidelines for SASE. Deadline: March 15. Prize: Winner will receive a cash prize of $2,000 if Mixed Blood chooses to produce the winning script, or $1,000 if Mixed Blood declines production. Open to American citizens.

L. ARNOLD WEISSBERGER PLAYWRITING COMPETITION, New Dramatists, Inc., 424 W. 44th St., New York NY 10036-5205. (212)757-6960. Fax: (212)265-4738. Website: http://www.itp.tsoa.nyu.edu/-diana/ndintro.html. Contact: Ron Riley. Estab. 1984. "The L. Arnold Weissberger Award is a cash prize offered annually that recognizes a previously unproduced new play by a playwright with any level of experience. The selection criteria was established by L. Arnold Weissberger, a theatrical attorney, who sought to discover a 'well-made play.' " Deadline: applications accepted December 31-May 31, the deadline, for an award announcement the following May. Guidelines for SASE. Prize: $5,000 and a public staged reading of the prize-winning play. Plays must be submitted by nomination only. Nominators may include artistic directors or literary managers of nonprofit theaters; literary agents; dramaturgs affiliated with university drama departments or professional producing theater companies; chairpersons and accredited university theater or playwriting programs. Nominations will be limited to one script per nominator. Nomination letters are recommended but not required. All scripts must include name, address, phone number and title of nominator, in addition to playwright.

WEST COAST ENSEMBLE FULL-PLAY COMPETITION, West Coast Ensemble, P.O. Box 38728, Los Angeles CA 90038. Contact: Les Hanson, artistic director. Estab. 1982. Unpublished (in Southern California) plays. No musicals or children's plays for full-play competition. No restrictions on subject matter. Deadline: December 31.

JACKIE WHITE MEMORIAL NATIONAL CHILDREN'S PLAYWRITING CONTEST, Columbia Entertainment Co., 309 Parkade, Columbia MO 65202. (573)874-5628. Contest Director: Betsy Phillips. Offered annually for unpublished plays. "Searching for good scripts suitable for audiences of all ages to be performed by the 35-40 students, grade 6-9, in our theater school." Deadline: June 1. Guidelines for SASE. Charges $10 fee. Prize: $250. Full production, plus travel expenses to come see production is probable but company reserves the right to grant prize money without production."

WICHITA STATE UNIVERSITY PLAYWRITING CONTEST, University Theatre, Wichita State University, Wichita KS 67260-0153. (316)689-3185. Fax: (316)689-3951. E-mail: lclark@twsuvm.uc.twsu.edu. Contest Director: Professor Leroy Clark, chair, school of performing arts. Estab. 1974. Unpublished, unproduced full-length or 2-3 short plays of at least 90 minutes playing time. No musicals or children's plays. Deadline: February 15. Guidelines for SASE. Prize: production of winning play (ACTF) and expenses paid trip for playwright to see final rehearsals and/or performances. Contestants must be graduate or undergraduate students in a US college or university.

TENNESSEE WILLIAMS/NEW ORLEANS LITERARY FESTIVAL ONE-ACT CONTEST, The Creative Writing Workshop at the University of New Orleans, 5500 Prytania St., Suite 217, New Orleans LA 70115. (504)581-1144. Fax: (504)529-2430. E-mail: twtest@gnofn.org. Website: http://www.gnofn.org/~twfest. Contact: Creative Writing Program and Drama Department. Offered annually to unpublished and unproduced plays "to foster continuing interest in the playwriting field and to honor the creative spirit of America's greatest playwright, Tennessee Williams." Deadline: December 1. Guidelines for SASE or call the festival office. Charges $15 fee. Prize: $1,000, a staged reading at festival the year the prize is won and a full production the following year. Length: 1 hour maximum.

WOMEN'S PLAYWRITING FESTIVAL, Perishable Theatre, P.O. Box 23132, Providence RI 02903. (401)331-2695. Fax: (401)331-7811. Contact: Kathleen Jenkins. SASE for guidelines.

N **YEAR END SERIES (YES) NEW PLAY FESTIVAL**, Northern Kentucky University Department of Theatre, Nunn Dr., Highland Heights KY 41099-1007. (606)572-6362. Fax: (606)572-6057. E-mail: forman@nku.edu. Award Director: Sandra Forman. Offered every 2 years for unpublished full-length plays and musicals. Deadline: October 31 (even years). Guidelines for SASE. Prize: $400 and an expense-paid visit to Northern Kentucky University to see the play produced. Judged by the Department of Theatre Faculty. Open to all writers.

YOUNG CONNECTICUT PLAYWRIGHTS FESTIVAL, Maxwell Anderson Playwrights Series, P.O. Box 671, West. Redding CT 06896. (203)938-2770. Contact: Bruce Post. Offered annually for unpublished plays to offer recognition and encouragement to young playwrights. Deadline: April 3. Guidelines for SASE. Prize: Awards ceremony, professionally staged reading for 4 finalists. Open to Connecticut resident aged 12-19.

YOUNG PLAYWRIGHTS FESTIVAL, Young Playwrights Inc., Suite 906, 321 W. 44th St., New York NY 10036. (212)307-1140. Fax: (212)307-1454. E-mail: writeaplay@aol.com. Contact: Sheri M. Goldhirsch, artistic director. Offered annually. Only stage plays accepted for submission (no musicals, screenplays or adaptations). "Writers aged 18 or younger are invited to send scripts for consideration in the annual Young Playwrights Festival. Winning plays will be performed in professional Off Broadway production." Deadline: December 1. Contest/award rules for #10 SASE. Entrants must be 18 or younger as of the annual deadline.

Journalism

AMY WRITING AWARDS, The Amy Foundation, P.O. Box 16091, Lansing MI 48901. (517)323-6233. Fax: (517)323-7293. Website: http://www.amyfound.org. Contact: James Russell, president. Estab. 1985. Nonfiction articles containing scripture published in the secular media. Deadline: January 31, for those from previous calendar year. Prize: $10,000, $5,000, $4,000, $3,000, $2,000 and 10 prizes of $1,000.

THE WHITMAN BASSOW AWARD, Overseas Press Club of America and AT&T, 320 East 42 St., Mezzanine, New York NY 10017. (212)983-4655. Fax: (212)983-4692. Manager: Sonya Fry. Offered annually for previously published best reporting in any medium on international environmental issues. Deadline: January 31. Charges $100 fee. Prize: certificate and $1,000. Work must be published by US-based publications or broadcast.

MIKE BERGER AWARD, Columbia University Graduate School of Journalism, 2950 Broadway, New York NY 10027-7004. (212)854-5984. Fax: (212)854-7837. Website: http://www.jrn.columbia.edu. Contact: Pilar Alayo. Offered annually honoring "human interest reporting about the daily life of New York City in the traditions of the late Meyer 'Mike' Berger." Deadline: February 15. Guidelines for SASE. Cash prize.

THE WORTH BINGHAM PRIZE, The Worth Bingham Memorial Fund, 1616 H Street, N.W., 3rd Floor, Washington DC 20006. (202)737-3700. Fax: (202)737-0530. E-mail: susan@icfj.org. Award Director: Susan Talalay. Offered annually to articles published during the year of the award. "The Prize honors newspaper or magazine investigative reporting of stories of national significance where the public interest is being ill-served. Entries may include a single story, a related series of stories or up to three unrelated stories." Deadline: February 15. Award rules for SASE. Prize: $10,000. Judged by a three-person panel.

THE ERIC AND AMY BURGER AWARD, Overseas Press Club of America, 320 East 42 St., Mezzanine, New York NY 10017. (212)983-4655. Fax: (212)983-4692. Manager: Sonya Fry. Offered annually for previously published best reporting in any medium dealing with human rights. Deadline: January 31. Charges $100 fee. Prize: certificate and $1,000. Work must be published by US-based publications or broadcast.

CANADIAN FOREST SERVICE-SAULT STE. MARIE JOURNALISM AWARD, Canadian Forest Service-Sault Ste. Marie/Natural Resources Canada, % CSWA, P.O. Box 75, Station A, Toronto, Ontario M5W 1A2 Canada. (416)928-9624. Fax: (416)924-6715. E-mail: cswa@interlog.com. Website: http://www.interlog.com/~cswa. Contact: Andy F. Visser-deVries. Offered annually for work published January 1-December 31 of the previous year to recognize outstanding journalism that promotes public awareness of forests and issues surrounding forests in Ontario. Deadline: February 15. Guidelines for SASE. Prize: for 1 newspaper and for 1 magazine $750 and plaque each. Material becomes property of Canadian Forest Service. Does not return mss. Open to writers who have published in an Ontario publication.

RUSSELL L. CECIL ARTHRITIS MEDICAL JOURNALISM AWARDS, Arthritis Foundation, 1330 West Peachtree St. NW, Atlanta GA 30309-9901. (404)872-7100. Fax: (404)872-0457. E-mail: lnewbern@arthritis.org. Website: http://www.arthritis.org. Contact: Lisa M. Newbern. Estab. 1956. News stories, articles and radio/TV scripts on the subject of arthritis and the Arthritis Foundation published or broadcast for general circulation during the previous calendar year. Deadline: February 15.

HARRY CHAPIN MEDIA AWARDS, World Hunger Year, 505 Eighth Ave., 21st Floor, New York NY 10018-6582. (212)629-8850 ext. 137. Fax: (212)465-9274. E-mail: whyawards@aol.com. Website: http://www.iglou.com/why. Contact: Jessica Keith. Estab. 1982. Critical issues of domestic and world hunger, poverty and development (newspaper, periodical, TV, radio, photojournalism, books). Prizes: $1,000-2,500. Deadline: February 18.

CORPORATE COVER-UP CONSPIRACY CONTEST, *Whistleblower Magazine* and Truth, Justice & American Way Society, P.O. Box 383, Cookeville TN 38503. (615)432-6046. Award Director: G.W. Brown. Offered annually "to expose stories such as nuclear plant conspiracies that mainstream media fear to touch." Deadline: May 1. "Sample issue with the type of story we are seeking: $4. Prize: $500, plus best of contest will be published in the April 1998 issue of the *Whistleblower*. "We claim the rights to published winning entries. Supporting documentation for any event is required."

DART AWARD, Dart Foundation through Michigan State University's Victims and the Media Program, MSU School of Journalism, East Lansing MI 48824-1212. (511)432-2171. Fax: (517)355-7710. E-mail: bucquero@pilot.msu.edu. Website: http://www.journalism.msu.edu/victims.html. Asstistant Director: Bonnie Bucqueroux. Offered annually for previously published work to encourage treatment of victims and victim issues with compassion, dignity, and respect. Awarded for best newspaper feature on victim(s) of violence each year. Deadline: March 1. Guidelines for SASE. Prize: $10,000 to winning newspaper, shared with team. Open to all daily and weekly newspapers.

FEATURE ARTICLE AWARD, P.E.I. Council of the Arts, 115 Richmond St., Charlestown PE C1A 1H7 Canada. (902)368-4410. Fax: (902)368-4418. Contact: Judy MacDonald. Offered annually for 1 feature article (intended for print, not broadcast), published or unpublished. Deadline: February 15. Guidelines for SASE. Charges $8 fee. Prize: Monetary. Open to individuals who have been resident of Prince Edward Island at least 6-12 months proceeding the deadline for entries.

FOURTH ESTATE AWARD, American Legion National Headquarters, 700 N. Pennsylvania, Indianapolis IN 46206. (317)630-1253. Fax: (317)630-1368. E-mail: pr@legion.org. Website: http://www.legion.org. Contact: Joe March. Estab. 1919. Offered annually for excellence in journalism in a published or broadcast piece on an issue of national concern during the previous calendar year. Deadline: January 31. Prize: $2,000 stipend.

THE GREAT AMERICAN TENNIS WRITING AWARDS, *Tennis Week*, 341 Madison Ave., New York NY 10017. (212)808-4750. Fax: (212)983-6302. E-mail: tennisweek@tennisweek.com. Publisher: Eugene L. Scott. Contact: Heather Holland or Kim Kodl, managing editors. Estab. 1974. Category 1: unpublished ms by an aspiring journalist with no previous national byline. Category 2: unpublished ms by a non-tennis journalist. Category 3: unpublished ms by a tennis journalist. Categories 4-6: published tennis-related articles and book award. Deadline: December 15.

O. HENRY AWARD, The Texas Institute of Letters, P.O. Box 298300, Fort Worth TX 76129. (817)921-7822. Fax: (817)257-5075. E-mail: jalter@gamma.is.tcu.edu. Website: http://www.gamma.is.tcu.edu/prs/til. Submissions must be marked Attn: TCU Press. Contact: Judy Alter, director. Offered annually for previously published work between January 1-December 31 of previous year to recognize the best-written work of journalism appearing in a magazine or weekly newspaper. Deadline: January 4. Guidelines for SASE. Prize: $1,000. Judged by a panel chosen by the TIL Council.

Writer must have been born in Texas, have lived in Texas for at least two consecutive years at some time, or the subject matter of the work should be associated with Texas.

SIDNEY HILLMAN FOUNDATION, Unite, 1710 Broadway, New York NY 10019. (212)265-7000 ext 725. Fax: (212)582-3175. E-mail: jmort@uniteunion.org. Website: http://www.uniteunion.org. Executive Director: Jo-Ann Mort. Offered annually to recognize outstanding contributions dealing with social/economic themes and the advancement of social welfare. Contributions may be in the form of published daily or periodical journalism, nonfiction, radio and television. Deadline: January 17. Guidelines for SASE. Prize: $2,000 plus plaque. Judges: Hendrick Hertzberg, *The New Yorker*, Sara Fritz, *The Los Angeles Times*, Frank Snobuda, *The Washington Post*. Open to any writer.

N **THE ROY W. HOWARD AWARDS, FOR PUBLIC SERVICE REPORTING**, Scripps Howard Foundation, P.O. Box 5380, Cincinnati OH 45201-5380. (513)977-3035. E-mail: cottingham@scripps.com. Website: http://www.scripps.com/foundation. Contact: Patty Cottingham, executive director. Open to any daily newspaper or wire service in the US or its territories for work published in a newspaper. Visit the foundation's website for official rules and entry form.

INTERNATIONAL READING ASSOCIATION PRINT MEDIA AWARD, International Reading Association, P.O. Box 8139, Newark DE 19714-8139. (302)731-1600 ext. 215. Fax: (302)731-1057. Contact: Janet Butler. Estab. 1956. Recognizes outstanding reporting on reading and literacy by professional journalists. Deadline: January 15.

N **ROBERT F. KENNEDY JOURNALISM AWARDS**, 1367 Connecticut Ave. NW, Suite 200, Washington DC 20036. (202)463-7575. Fax: (202)463-6606. E-mail: info@rfkmemorial.org. Website: http://www.rfkmemorial.org. Director: Laura H. Gross. Estab. 1968. Articles published in current year entries on problems of the disadvantaged. Entries may include accounts of the lifestyles, challenges and potentials of the disadvantaged in the United States; insights into the causes, conditions and remedies of their plight, and critical analyses of public policies, programs, attitudes and private endeavors relevant to their lives. Deadline: last Friday of January. Charges $20 fee; free to students. Prize: $1,000.

DONALD E. KEYHOE JOURNALISM AWARD, Fund for UFO Research, P.O. Box 277, Mt. Rainier MD 20712. (703)684-6032. Fax: (703)684-6032. Website: http://www.fufor.org. Contact: Don Berliner, chairman. Estab. 1979. Offered annually for the best article or story published or broadcast in a newspaper, magazine, TV or radio news outlet during the previous calendar year. Separate awards for print and broadcast media. Also makes unscheduled cash awards for published works on UFO phenomena research or public education.

HERB LAMPERT STUDENT WRITING AWARD, Canadian Science Writers' Association, P.O. Box 75, Station A, Toronto, Ontario M5W 1A2 Canada. (416)928-9624. E-mail: cswa@interlog.com. Contest/Award Director: Andy F. Visser-deVries. Offered annually to any student science writer who has an article published in a student or other newspaper or aired on a radio or TV station in Canada. Deadline: February 15. Guidelines for SASE. Prize: $750 for print and broadcast winners. Open to any Canadian resident or citizen.

N **THE EDWARD J. MEEMAN AWARDS, FOR ENVIRONMENTAL REPORTING**, Scripps Howard Foundation, P.O. Box 5380, Cincinnati OH 45201-5380. (513)977-3035. E-mail: cottingham@scripps.com. Website: http://www.scripps.com/foundation. Contact: Patty Cottingham, executive director. Open to any daily newspaper or wire service in the US or its territories for work published in a newspaper. Visit the foundation's website for official rules and entry form.

ROBERT T. MORSE WRITER'S AWARD, American Psychiatric Association, 1400 K St. NW, Washington DC 20005. (202)682-6324. Fax: (202)682-6255. E-mail: emurphy@psych.org. Website: http://www.psych.org. Media Assistant: Erin Murphy. Offered annually for articles previously published August 1-July 31. Deadline: July 31. Send name and address—no envelope required. Prizes: $1,000 Honorarium and plaque to be presented at APA's Annual Meeting. Judges: 4 psychiatrists and 3 mental health professional communicators. "Anyone can be nominated, but no books! Just articles."

FRANK LUTHER MOTT-KAPPA TAU ALPHA RESEARCH AWARD IN JOURNALISM, University of Missouri, School of Journalism, Columbia MO 65211. (573)882-7685. E-mail: ktahq@showme.missouri.edu. Contact: Dr. Keith Sanders, executive director, Kappa Tau Alpha. For "best researched book in mass communication." Requires 6 copies. No forms required. Deadline: December 1. Award: $1,000.

NATIONAL AWARDS FOR EDUCATION REPORTING, Education Writers Association, 1331 H St. NW, #307, Washington DC 20005. (202)637-9700. Website: http://www.ewa.org. Contact: Lisa Walker, executive director. Estab. 1960. Offered annually for submissions published during the previous year. Categories are: 1) newspapers under 100,000 circulation; 2) newspapers over 100,000 circulation; 3) magazines excluding trade and institutional journals that are circulated to the general public; 4) special interest, institutional and trade publications; 5) television; and 6) radio. Write for more information. Deadline: mid-January. Charges $35 fee.

ALICIA PATTERSON JOURNALISM FELLOWSHIP, Alicia Patterson Foundation, 1730 Pennsylvania Ave. NW, Suite 850, Washington DC 20006. (202)393-5995. Fax: (301)951-8512. E-mail: apfengel@charm.net. Website: http://www.aliciapatterson.org. Contact: Margaret Engel. Offered annually for previously published submissions to give 8-10 print ,JOUjournalists or photojournalists a year of in-depth research and reporting. Applicants must have 5 years of professional print journalism experience and be US citizens. Fellows write 4 magazine-length pieces for the *Alicia Patterson Reporter*, a quarterly magazine, during their fellowship year. Fellows must take a year's leave from their jobs, but may do other freelance articles during the year. Deadline: October 1. Write, call, fax or check website for applications. Prize: $30,000 stipend for calendar year.

THE POPE AWARD FOR INVESTIGATIVE JOURNALISM, The Pope Foundation, 211 W. 56 St., Suite 5H, New York NY 10019. Director: Catherine E. Pope. Offered annually to journalists who have been working for a minimum of 10 years. Deadline: November 1. Guidelines for SASE. Prize: 3 awards of $15,000 each.

N **ERNIE PYLE AWARD FOR HUMAN INTEREST WRITING**, Scripps Howard Foundation, P.O. Box 5380, Cincinnati OH 45201-5380. (513)977-3035. E-mail: cottingham@scripps.com. Website: http://www.scripps.com/foundation. Contact: Patty Cottingham, executive director. Open to any newspaper or wire service journalist for work published in a daily newspaper in the US or its territories. Visit the foundation's website for official rules and entry form.

THE MADELINE DANE ROSS AWARD, Overseas Press Club of America, 320 East 42 St., Mezzanine, New York NY 10017. (212)983-4655. Fax: (212)983-4692. Manager: Sonya Fry. Offered annually for previously published best foreign correspondent in any medium showing a concern for the human condition. Deadline: January 31. Charges $100 fee. Prize: certificate and $1,000. Work must be published by US-based publications or broadcast.

N **THE CHARLES M. SCHULZ AWARD**, Scripps Howard Foundation, P.O. Box 5380, Cincinnati OH 45201-5380. (513)977-3035. E-mail: cottingham@scripps.com. Website: http://www.scripps.com/foundation. Contact: Patty Cottingham, executive director. Open to any student cartoonist at a college newspaper or college magazine in the US or its territories. Visit the foundation's website for official rules and entry form.

SCIENCE IN SOCIETY JOURNALISM AWARDS, Canadian Science Writers' Association, P.O. Box 75, Station A, Toronto, Ontario M5W 1A2 Canada. Phone: (416)960-9624. Fax: (416)924-6715. E-mail: cswa@interlog.com. Website: http://www.interlog.com/~cswa. Contact: Andy F. Visser-deVries. Offered annually for work published/aired January 1-December 31 of previous year to recognize outstanding contributions to science journalism in all media. Two newspaper, 2 magazine, 2 TV, 2 radio, 1 trade publication, student science writing award (Herb Lampert Student Writing Award). Deadline: January 31. Guidelines for SASE. Prize: $1,000 and a plaque. Material becomes property of CSWA. Does not return mss. Open to Canadian citizens or residents of Canada.

SCIENCE WRITING AWARD IN PHYSICS AND ASTRONOMY FOR JOURNALISTS, American Institute of Physics, One Physics Ellipse, College Park MD 20740. (301)209-3090. Fax: (301)209-0846. E-mail: jwrather@aip.acp.org. Contest/Award Director: Joan Wrather. Offered annually to previously published work appearing in print in 1997 "to recognize and stimulate distinguished writing that improves the general public's understanding and appreciation of physics and astronomy." Deadline: February 6 (unless it falls on Saturday or Sunday). Guidelines available, SASE is not necessary. Prize: $3,000, a Windsor Chair and a certificat. Entrants must be a journalist, and articles, booklets or books must be intended for the general public.

N **CHARLES E. SCRIPPS AWARD FOR DISTINGUISHED SERVICE TO LITERACY**, Scripps Howard Foundation, P.O. Box 5380, Cincinnati OH 45201-5380. (513)977-3035. E-mail: cottingham@scripps.com. Website: http://www.scripps.com/foundation. Contact: Patty Cottingham, executive director. Open to any individual or organization in the US or its territories. Nominations may be made by individuals, news organizations or literary groups or any interested party. Visit the foundation's website for official rules and entry form.

N **THE EDWARD WILLIS SCRIPPS AWARD FOR DISTINGUISHED SERVICE TO THE FIRST AMENDMENT**, Scripps Howard Foundation, P.O. Box 5380, Cincinnati OH 45201-5380. (513)977-3035. E-mail: cottingham@scripps.com. Website: http://www.scripps.com/foundation. Contact: Patty Cottingham, executive director. Open to any individual or organization in the US or its territories. Visit the foundation's website for official rules and entry form.

N **SOVEREIGN AWARD OUTSTANDING NEWSPAPER STORY, OUTSTANDING FEATURE STORY**, The Jockey Club of Canada, P.O. Box 156, Rexdale, Ontario M9W 5L2 Canada. (416)675-7756. Fax: (416)675-6378. E-mail: tjcc@ftn.net. Contact: Bridget Bimm, executive director. Estab. 1973. Offered annually to recognize outstanding achievement in the area of Canadian thoroughbred racing journalism published November 1-October 31 of the previous year. Newspaper Story: Appeared in a newspaper by a racing columnist on Canadian Racing subject matter. Outstanding Feature Story: Appeared in a magazine book or newspaper, written as feature story on Canadian Racing subject matter. Deadline: October 31. There is no nominating process other than the writer submit no more than 1 entry per category. Special Criteria: Must be of Canadian racing content. A copy of the newspaper article or magazine story must be provided along with a 3¼″ disk containing the story in an ASCII style format.

I.F. STONE AWARD FOR STUDENT JOURNALISM, The Nation Institute, 72 Fifth Ave., New York NY 10011. (212)242-8400. Director: Peter Meyer. **Contact**: Richard Kim, assistant director. Offered annually to recognize excellence in student journalism. Open to undergraduate students in US colleges. Prize: $1,000, plus publication. Deadline: June 30.

THE WALKER STONE AWARD FOR EDITORIAL WRITING, Scripps Howard Foundation, P.O. Box 5380, Cincinnati OH 45201-5380. (513)977-3035. E-mail: cottingham@scripps.com. Website: http://www.scripps.com/foundation. Contact: Patty Cottingham, executive director. Open to any newspaper or wire service journalist for work published in a daily newspaper in the US or its territories. Visit website for official rules and entry form.

STUDENT MAGAZINE CONTEST, Magazine Division, Association for Education in Journalism and Mass Communication, The Medill School of Journalism, Northwestern University, Evanston IL 60208-2101. (847)491-2085. Fax: (847)491-5907. E-mail: c-kitch@nwu.edu. Contact: Prof. Carolyn Kitch. Offered annually for articles published or written between April 30 and April 30 of previous year. Two categories: Consumer Magazine Article for nonfiction articles written for a general or special interest magazine available to the public either through newsstand sales or subscription; Trade Magazine Article (graduate category and undergraduate category) is for nonfiction articles written for a specialized business magazine covering a specific industry or occupation. "Emphasis is on useful information readers need to get ahead professionally and make their business successful; articles may also focus on trends or projections in a certain industry or profile an industry leader. For each entry: Form (1 per entry) signed by a faculty member attesting to the accuracy of the information provided; Target magazine written in the appropriate place on the entry form; Correct category checked on the entry form; (2) copies of the article manuscript or tearsheet with the author's name and school eliminated; (2) blind title pages that include article title, category and target magazine. Entries are not returned. Deadline: May 1. Guidelines for SASE. Charges $5 fee. Prizes: $100. This is a contest for students in journalism and English programs. Entrants must be sponsored by a faculty member and work must be produced in a class. In other words, a student working on an internship can't enter work produced on the job."

THE TEN BEST "CENSORED" STORIES OF 1998, Project Censored—Sonoma State University, Rohnert Park CA 94928. (707)664-2500. Fax: (707)664-2108. E-mail: project.censored@sonoma.edu. Website: http://www.censored.sonoma.edu/projectcensored/. Contact: Peter Philip, director. Estab. 1976. Current published, nonfiction stories of national social significance that have been overlooked or under-reported by the news media. Deadline: November 1.

- Peter Phillips and Project Censored choose 25 stories that have been underreported to make up *Censored: The News That Didn't Make the News and Why*, published by Seven Stories Press.

PAUL TOBENKIN MEMORIAL AWARD, Columbia University Graduate School of Journalism, 2950 Broadway, New York NY 10027-7004. (212)854-5984. Fax: (212)854-7837. Website: http://www.jrn.journalism.edu/. Contact: Pilar Alayo. Offered annually honoring "outstanding achievement in the field of newspaper writing in the fight against racial and religious hatred, intolerance, discrimination and every form of bigotry, reflecting the spirit of Paul Tobenkin. Deadline: February 15. Guidelines for SASE. Cash prize.

STANLEY WALKER JOURNALISM AWARD, The Texas Institute of Letters, P.O. Box 298300, Fort Worth TX 76129. (817)921-7822. Fax: (817)257-5075. E-mail: jalter@gamma.is.tcu.edu. Website: http://www.gamma.is.tcu.edu/prs/til. Contact: Judy Alter, director. Offered annually for work published January 1-December 31 of previous year to recognize the best writing appearing in a daily newspaper. Deadline: January 4. Guidelines for SASE. Prize: $1,000. Writer must have been born in Texas, or must have lived in the state for 2 consecutive years at some time, or the subject matter of the article must be associated with the state.

Writing for Children & Young Adults

AMERICAN ASSOCIATION OF UNIVERSITY WOMEN AWARD, NORTH CAROLINA DIVISION, North Carolina Literary and Historical Association, 109 E. Jones St., Raleigh NC 27601-2807. (919)733-9375. Awards Coordinator: Jerry C. Cashion. Previously published juvenile literature by a North Carolina resident. Deadline: July 15.

R. ROSS ANNETT AWARD FOR CHILDREN'S LITERATURE, Writers Guild of Alberta, 11759 Groat Rd., Edmonton, Alberta T5M 3K6 Canada. (403)422-8174. Fax: (403)422-2663. E-mail: writers@compusmart.ab.ca. Director: Darlene Diver. Children's book published in current year. Must be an Alberta author.

ARROZ CON LECHE, Hispanic Books Distributors, Inc., 1328 W. Prince Rd., Tucson AZ 85705. Fax: (520)690-6574. E-mail: hbdusa@azstamet.com. Contact: Dr. Arnulfo D. Trejo, president. Offered annually for unpublished works of fiction for ages k-4 to encourage more Hispanic authors to write for children. Deadline: April 24. Guidelines for SASE. Prize: $1,000. Open to adult authors of Latino heritage, born, raised or residing permanently in this country, including Puerto Rico.

IRMA S. AND JAMES H. BLACK AWARD, Bank Street College of Education, 610 W. 112th St., New York NY 10025. (212)875-4452. Fax: (212)875-4558. E-mail: lindag@bnkst.edu. Website: http://www.bnkst.edu/library/isb.html. Award Director: Linda Greengrass. Estab. 1972. Offered annually for a book for young children, for excellence of both text and illustrations. Entries must have been published during the previous calendar year. Deadline for entries: January 1st after book is published.

BOOK PUBLISHERS OF TEXAS AWARD FOR CHILDREN'S OR YOUNG PEOPLE'S BOOK, The Texas Institute of Letters, P.O. Box 298300 Fort Worth TX 76129. (817)921-7822. Fax: (817)257-5075. E-mail: jalter@gamma.is.tcu.edu. Website: http://www.gamma.is.tcu.edu/prs/til. Materials must be marked Attn: TCU Press. Contact: Judy Alter, director. Offered annually for work published January 1-December 31 of previous year to recognize the best book for children or young people. Deadline: January 4. Guidelines for SASE. Prize: $250. Writer must have been born in Texas or have lived in the state for at least 2 consecutive years at 1 time, or the subject matter is associated with the state.

BOSTON GLOBE-HORN BOOK AWARD, *The Boston Globe*, 135 Morrissey Blvd, P.O. Box 2378, Boston MA 02107. Also: The Horn Book Magazine, 11 Beacon St., Suite 1000, Boston MA 02108. Offered annually for previously published work in children's literature. Awards for original fiction or poetry, picture book, and nonfiction. Publisher submits entry. Deadline: May 15. Prize: $500 in each category.

N **MARGUERITE DE ANGELI PRIZE**, Bantam Doubleday Dell Books for Young Readers, 1540 Broadway, New York NY 10036. (212)354-6500. Fax: (212)782-9698. Contact: Wendy Lamb, executive editor. Offered annually for unpublished fiction manuscript suitable for readers 7-10 years of age that concerns the diversity of the American experience, either contemporary or historical. Deadline: manuscripts must be postmarked after April 1, but no later than June 30. Send manuscripts to Marguerite de Angeli Contest Bantam Doubleday Dell. Guidelines for SASE. Prize includes a book contract with a cash advance.

DELACORTE PRESS PRIZE FOR A FIRST YOUNG ADULT NOVEL, Delacorte Press, 1540 Broadway, New York NY 10036. (212)354-6500. Executive Editor: Wendy Lamb. Estab. 1983. Previously unpublished young adult fiction. Submissions: October 1-December 31. Guidelines for SASE. Prize: $1,500 cash, publication and $6,000 advance against royalties.

N **FRIENDS OF AMERICAN WRITERS YOUNG PEOPLE'S LITERATURE AWARDS**, 680 Lake Shore Dr., Chicago IL 60611. (312)664-5628. Contact: Ms. Minnie Orfanos. Estab. 1960. "Annual awards for children's books that were published in the past year. Entry must be first, second or third children's book published by the author. The author must be a resident or native of AR, IL, IN, IA, KS, MI, MN, MO, NE, ND, OH, SD or WI or story can be *set* in one of these states. No poetry." Prize consists of cash (no less than $400 each) to 2 writers; certificates to publishers. Send SASE for guidelines. Deadline: Dec. 31.

GOLDEN KITE AWARDS, Society of Children's Book Writers and Illustrators (SCBWI), 345 N. Maple Dr., Suite 296, Beverly Hills CA 90210. (310)859-9887. E-mail: scbwi@juno.com. Website: www.scbwi.org. Coordinator: Sue Alexander. Estab. 1973. Calendar year published children's fiction, nonfiction and picture illustration books by a SCBWI members only. Deadline: December 15.

N **GUIDEPOSTS YOUNG WRITERS CONTEST**, *Guideposts*, 16 E. 34th St., New York NY 10016. (212)251-8100. Fax: (212)684-0679. Website: http://www.guideposts.org. Contact: James McDermont. Offered annually for unpublished high school juniors and seniors. "We accept submissions after announcement is placed in the October issue each year." Deadline: Monday after Thanksgiving. Guidelines in October issue and online. Prizes: 1st-$8,000, 2nd-$7,000, 3rd-$5,000, 4th-8th: $1,000, 9th-25th: portable electronic typewriter. Judged by the editors of *Guideposts*. "If the manuscript is placed, we require all rights to the story in that version." Open only to high school juniors or seniors.

HIGHLIGHTS FOR CHILDREN FICTION CONTEST, *Highlights for Children*, 803 Church St., Honesdale PA 18431-1824. Contact: Marileta Robinson, senior editor. Manuscript Coordinator: Beth Troop. Estab. 1946. Stories for children ages 2-12; category varies each year. Guidelines for SASE. Stories should be limited to 900 words for older readers, 500 words for younger readers. No crime or violence, please. Specify that ms is a contest entry. All entries must be postmarked January 1-February 28.

INTERNATIONAL READING ASSOCIATION CHILDREN'S BOOK AWARD, International Reading Association, P.O. Box 8139, 800 Barksdale Rd., Newark DE 19714-8139. (302)731-1600 ext. 221. Fax: (302)731-1057. E-mail: 75141.2005@compuserve.com. First or second book by an author who shows unusual promise in the children's book field. Categories: younger readers, ages 4-10; older readers, ages 10-16+, and informational book (ages 4-16+). Deadline: December 1.

MILKWEED PRIZE FOR CHILDREN'S LITERATURE, Milkweed Editions, First Ave. N., Suite 400, Minneapolis MN 55401. (612)332-3192. E-mail: books@milkweed.org. Website: http://www.milkweed.org. Contact: Elisabeth Fitz, first reader. Annual prize for unpublished works. Estab. 1993. "Milkweed is looking for a novel or biography intended for readers aged 8-14. Manuscripts should be of high literary quality and must be double-spaced, 90-200 pages in length. The Milkweed Prize for Children's Literature will be awarded to the best manuscript for children ages 8-14 that Milkweed accepts for publication during each calendar year by a writer not previously published by Milkweed Editions." Prize: $2,000 advance on any royalties agreed upon at the time of acceptance. Must SASE for guidelines, both for regular children's submission policies and for the announcement of the restructured contest. Catalog for $1.50 postage.

LUCY MAUD MONTGOMERY PEI CHILDREN'S LITERATURE AWARD, P.E.I. Council of the Arts, 115 Richmond St., Charlestown PE C1A 1H7 Canada. (902)368-4410. Fax: (902)368-4418. Contact: Judy MacDonald. Offered annually for a story written for children ages 5-12. Deadline: February 15. Guidelines for SASE. Charges $8 fee. Prize: Monetary. Open to individuals who have been resident of Prince Edward Island at least 6-12 months proceeding the deadline for entries.

THE NATIONAL CHAPTER OF CANADA IODE VIOLET DOWNEY BOOK AWARD, National Chapter of Canada IODE, 40 Orchard View Blvd., Suite 254, Toronto, Ontario M4R 1B9 Canada. (416)487-4416. Fax: (416)487-4417. Contest/Award Director: Mrs. Marty Dalton. Offered annually for children's books of at least 500 words. Entries must have appeared in print between January 1 and December 31. Deadline: January 31 of following year. Guidelines for SASE. Prize: $3,000 (Canadian funds). Judged by members of IODE. Entrants must be Canadian citizens.

NATIONAL JEWISH BOOK AWARD—CHILDREN'S LITERATURE, Jewish Book Council, 15 E. 26th St., New York NY 10010. (212)532-4949. Director: Carolyn Starman Hessel. Children's book on Jewish theme. Deadline: September 1.

NATIONAL JEWISH BOOK AWARD—CHILDREN'S PICTURE BOOK, Marcia and Louis Posner Award, Jewish Book Council, 15 E. 26th St., New York NY 10010. (212)532-4949, ext. 297. Director: Carolyn Starman Hessel. Author and illustrator of a children's book on a Jewish theme. Deadline: September 1.

SCOTT O'DELL AWARD FOR HISTORICAL FICTION, 1700 E. 56th St., #3906, Chicago IL 60637. (773)752-7880. Contact: Zena Sutherland, director. Estab. 1981. Historical fiction book for children set in the Americas. Entries must have been published during previous year. Deadline: December 31.

PEN/NORMA KLEIN AWARD, PEN American Center, 568 Broadway, New York NY 10012. (212)334-1660. Fax: (212)334-2181. E-mail: jm@pen.org. Contact: John Morrone. Offered in odd-numbered years to recognize an emerging voice of literary merit among American writers of children's fiction. *Candidates may not nominate themselves*. Next award is 1999. Deadline: December 15. Guidelines for #10 SASE. Award: $3,000.

PRIX ALVINE-BÉLISLE, Association pour L'avancement des sciences et des techniques de la documentation, ASTED Inc., 3414 av. Parc #202, Montreal, Quebec, Canada. (514)281-5012. Fax: (514)281-8219. E-mail: info@asted.org. Website: http://www.asted.org. Contact: Josée Valiquette, director. Offered annually for work published the previous year before the award to promote authors of French youth literature in Canada. Deadline: April 1. Prize: $500. "It is not the writers but the editors who send their books to us."

SCIENCE WRITING AWARD IN PHYSICS AND ASTRONOMY FOR CHILDREN, American Institute of Physics, One Physics Ellipse, College Park MD 20740. (301)209-3090. Fax: (301)209-0846. E-mail: jwrather@aip.acp.org. Contest/Award Director: Joan Wrather. Offered annually to previously published entries appearing in print between July 1, 1998 and June 30, 1999, "to recognize and stimulate distinguished writing that improves the children's understanding and appreciation of physics and astronomy." Deadline: July 24 (unless it falls on a Saturday or Sunday). Guidelines available; SASE is not necessary. Prize: $3,000, a Windsor Chair and a certificate. Articles booklets or books must be intended for children ages preschool to fifteen years old.

SILVER BAY AWARDS FOR CHILDREN'S LITERATURE, The Writer's Voice of the Silver Bay Association, Silver Bay NY 12874. (518)543-8833. Fax: (518)543-6733. Contact: Sharon Ofner. Offered annually for best unpublished children's manuscript set in the Adirondack Mountains, illustrated or non-illustrated. Deadline: February 1. Charges $25 fee. Prize: $1,000.

(ALICE WOOD MEMORIAL) OHIOANA AWARD FOR CHILDREN'S LITERATURE, Ohioana Library Association, 65 Front St., Suite 1105, Columbus OH 43215. (614)466-3831. Fax: (614)728-6974. E-mail: ohioana@winslo.ohio.gov. Website: http://www.oplin.lib.oh.us/OHIOANA/. Contact: Linda R. Hengst. Offered "to an author whose body of work has made, and continues to make, a significant contribution to literature for children or young adults." Prize: $1,000. Deadline: December 31. Nomination forms available for SASE. Recipient must have been born in Ohio or lived in Ohio at least 5 years.

WORK-IN-PROGRESS GRANT, Society of Children's Book Writers and Illustrators (SCBWI) and Judy Blume, 345 N. Maple Dr., #296, Beverly Hills CA 90210. E-mail: scbwi@juno.com. Website: http://www.scbwi.org. Two grants—one designated specifically for a contemporary novel for young people—to assist SCBWI members in the completion of a specific project. Deadline: March 1. Guidelines for SASE. Members only.

WRITING FOR CHILDREN COMPETITION, The Writers' Union of Canada, 24 Ryerson Ave., Toronto, Ontario M5T 2P3. (416)703-8982. E-mail: twuc@the-wire.com. Website: http://www.swifty.com/twuc. Offered annually "to discover developing Canadian writers of unpublished children's/young-adult works." Deadline: April 23. Charges $15/entry fee. Prize: $1,500. The winner and 11 finalist's pieces will be submittd to a Canadian publisher of children's books. Open to Canadian citizens or landed immigrants who have not been published in book format and who do not currently have a contract with a publisher.

Translation

AMERICAN TRANSLATORS ASSOCIATION HONORS AND AWARDS, American Translators Association, 1800 Diagonal Rd., Suite 220, Alexandria VA 22314. (703)683-6100. Fax: (703)683-6122. E-mail: ata@atanet.org. Website: http://www.atanet.org. Contact: Walter Bacak, executive director. Student award offered annually; other awards offered every 2 years. Categories: best student translation; best literary translation in German; and best literary translation in any language but German. Guidelines for SASE. Prize varies—usually $500-1,000 and a trip to annual conference.

ASF TRANSLATION PRIZE, The American-Scandinavian Foundation, 725 Park Ave., New York NY 10021. (212)879-9779. Fax: (212)569-5385. Offered annually to a "translation of Scandinavian literature into English of a Nordic author born within last 200 years." Deadline: June 1, 1998. Guidelines for SASE. Prizes: $2,000, publication of an excerpt in an issue of Scandinavian Review and a commemorative bronze medallion; the Inger Sjöberg Prize of $500. "The Prize is for an outstanding English translation of poetry, fiction, drama or literary prose originally written in Danish, Finnish, Icelandic, Norwegian or Swedish that has not been previously published in the English language."

FELLOWSHIPS FOR TRANSLATORS, National Endowment for the Arts Literature Program, 1100 Pennsylvania Ave. NW, Washington DC 20506. (202)682-5428. Website: http://arts.endow.gov. Contact: Heritage and Preservation Division. Published translators of exceptional talent.

SOEURETTE DIEHL FRASER TRANSLATION AWARD, The Texas Institute of Letters, P.O. Box 298300, Fort Worth TX 76129. (817)921-7822. Fax: (817)257-5075. E-mail: jalter@gamma.is.tcu.edu. Website: http://www.gamma.is.tcu.edu/prs/til. Contact: Judy Alter, director. Offered annually for work published January 1-December 31 of previous year to recognize the best translation of a literary book into English. Deadline: January 4. Guidelines for SASE. Prize: $1,000. Translator must have been born in Texas or have lived in the state for at least two consecutive years at some time.

GERMAN PRIZE FOR LITERARY TRANSLATION, American Translators Association, 1800 Diagonal Rd., Suite 220, Alexandria VA 22314. Phone/fax: (703)683-6100. Website: http://www.atanet.org. Chair: Eric McMillan. Contact: Walter Bacak, executive director. Offered in odd-numbered years for previously published book translated from German to English. In even-numbered years, the Lewis Galentière Prize is awarded for translations other than German to English. Deadline April 15. Prize: $1,000, a certificate of recognition, and up to $500 toward expenses for attending the ATA Annual Conference.

JOHN GLASSCO TRANSLATION PRIZE, Literary Translators' Association of Canada, Association des traducteurs et traductrices littéraires du Canada, 3492, av. Laval, Montreal, Quebec H2X 3C8 Canada. E-mail: alterego@rocler.qc.ca. Estab. 1981. Offered annually for a translator's *first* book-length literary translation into French or English, published in Canada during the previous calendar year. The translator must be a Canadian citizen or landed immigrant. Eligible genres include fiction, creative nonfiction, poetry, published plays, children's books. Deadline: January 15. Write for application form. Award: $500.

THE HAROLD MORTON LANDON TRANSLATION AWARD, The Academy of American Poets, 584 Broadway, Suite 1208, New York NY 10012-3250. (212)274-0343, Ext. 14. Fax: (212)274-9427. E-mail: poets@artswire.com. Website: http://www.poets.org. Contact: India Amos. Offered annually to recognize a published translation of poetry from any language into English. Deadline: December 31. Guidelines for SASE. Prize: $1,000. Judged by a noted translator. Translators must be living US citizens. Anthologies by a number of translators are ineligible.

PEN/BOOK-OF-THE-MONTH CLUB TRANSLATION PRIZE, PEN American Center, 568 Broadway, New York NY 10012. (212)334-1660. Fax: (212)334-2181. E-mail: jm@pen.org. Contact: John Morrone. One award of $3,000 to a literary book-length translation into English published in the calendar year under consideration. (No technical, scientific or reference.) Deadline: December 15. Publishers, agents or translators may submit 3 copies of each eligible title.

THE RAIZISS/DE PALCHI TRANSLATION FELLOWSHIP, The Academy of American Poets, 584 Broadway, Suite 1208, New York NY 10012-3250. (212)274-0343. Fax: (212)274-9427. E-mail: poets@artswire.org. Website: http://www.poets.org. Contact: Matthew Brogan. Offered every 2 years to recognize outstanding unpublished translations of modern Italian poetry into English. Accepts entries from September 1-November 1, 1998. Guidelines for SASE.

Prize: $20,000 and a one-month residency at the American Academy in Rome. Applicants must verify permission to translate the poems or that the poems are in the public domain. Open to any US citizen.

ALDO AND JEANNE SCAGLIONE PRIZE FOR TRANSLATION OF A LITERARY WORK, Modern Language Association of America, 10 Astor Place, New York NY 10003-6981. (212)614-6406. Fax: (212)533-0680. E-mail: awards@mla.org. Website: http://www.mla.org. Contact: Richard Brod, director of special projects. Offered in even-numbered years for the translation of a book-length literary work appearing in print during the previous two years. Deadline: May 1. Guidelines for SASE. Prize: $1,000 and a certificate presented at the association's annual convention in December. Translators need not be members of the MLA.

N **STUDENT TRANSLATION PRIZE**, American Translators Association, % Eric McMillen, 1800 Diagonal Rd., Suite 220, Alexandria VA 22314 (703)683-6100. Fax: (703)683-6122. Support is granted for a promising project to an unpublished student enrolled in a translation program at a US college or university. Deadline: April 15. Must be sponsored by a faculty member.

N **TRANSLATION PRIZE**, French-American Foundation, 41 E. 72nd St., New York NY 10021. (212)288-4400. Fax: (202)288-4769. E-mail: french_amerfdn@msn.com. Contact: Violaine Lenoir. "The prize is awarded annually for the best translation of a prose work from French to English published the previous year or scheduled to be published. All categories of prose work are eligible with the exception of poetry, technical, scientific and reference works and children's literature." Deadline: July 3. Prize: $5,000. Judged by a review panel of 7 editors, writers or translators. "Books or galleys must be submitted in duplicate and accompanied by the French original work. The translation must have been published in the United States. The French work must have been published in France."

Multiple Writing Areas

AKRON MANUSCRIPT CLUB WRITER'S CONTEST, Akron Manuscript Club, Akron University, Falls Writer's Workshop & Taylor Memorial Library, P.O. Box 1101, Cuyahoga Falls OH 44223-0101. (216)923-2094. E-mail: mmlop @aol.com. Contact: M.M. LoPiccolo. Estab. 1929. Offered annually for previously unpublished stories to provide critique, encouragement and some financial help to authors in 3 categories. Deadline is always sometime in March. Guidelines for #10 SASE. Charges $25 entry/critique fee. Prize: 1st-certificate to $50, according to funding; 2nd and 3rd-certificates. Send no entry until you get current guidelines.

AMELIA STUDENT AWARD, *Amelia Magazine*, 329 E St., Bakersfield CA 93304. (805)323-4064. Editor: Frederick A. Raborg, Jr. Previously unpublished poems, essays and short stories by high school students, 1 entry per student; each entry should be signed by parent, guardian *or* teacher to verify originality. Deadline: May 15. No entry fee; however, if guidelines and sample are required, please send SASE with $3 handling charge.

ANTIETAM REVIEW LITERARY AWARD, *Antietam Review*, 41 S. Potomac, Hagerstown MD 21740-5512. Short fiction (up to 5,000 words) and poetry (up to 30 lines). Submissions accepted from June 1-September 1. Guidelines for SASE. Charges $10 reading fee/short story, $3/poem. Up to 5 entries at a time are permitted. First prize (fiction): $100, publication in *AR*, 2 copies of the magazine. First prize (poetry): $50, publication, plus 2 copies. ALL entries considered for publication. Open to natives or residents of MD, PA, VA, WV, DE and DC.

ARTS AND LETTERS COMPETITION, Government of Newfoundland and Labrador Culture and Heritage Division, Box 1854, St. John's, Newfoundland A1C 5P9 Canada. (709)729-5253. Fax: (709)729-5952. Secretary: Regina Best. Offered annually "to encourage creative talent of the residents of Newfoundland and Labrador. Senior Divison (19 years and older): poetry, fiction, nonfiction and dramatic scripts. Junior (E.J. Pratt) Division (12-18 years old): prose and poetry. All work submitted must be unpublished. Guidelines for SASE or call the Arts and Letters Competition office at (709)729-5253 (must have application form accompanying entry). Prizes, Senior Division: 1st-$600, 2nd-$300, 3rd-$150 for each category; Junior Division: 1st-$300, 2nd-$200, 3rd-$100 for each category. Rights remain with the author, but the first place winner is usually published in an annual booklet. Open to residents of province of Newfoundland and Labrador.

N **ATLANTIC WRITING COMPETITION**, Wrtiers Federation of Nova Scotia, 1809 Barrington St., Suite 901, Halifax, Nova Scotia B3J 3K8 Canada. Contact: Awards committee. Offered annually for unpublished work in 6 categories: novel, nonfiction book, short story, poetry, writing for children or magazine article. Deadline: August 7. Guidelines for SASE. Charges $15 fee; ($10 for WFNS members). Prizes for nonfiction book: 1st-$200, 2nd-$150, 3rd-$100; novel: 1st-$200, 2nd-$150, 3rd-$100; short story: 1st-$100, 2nd-$75, 3rd-$50; poetry: 1st-$100, 2nd-$150, 3rd-$50; writing for children: 1st-$150, 2nd-$75, 3rd-$50; magazine article: 1st-$150, 2nd-$75, 3rd-$50. Judged by a committee. Open to Atlantic Canadians only.

AWP AWARD SERIES, Associated Writing Programs, Tallwood House, Mail Stop 1E3, George Mason University, Fairfax VA 22030. (703)993-4301. Fax: (703)993-4302. E-mail: awp@gmu.edu. Website: http://web.gmu.edu/departme

nts/AWP. Contact: David Sherwin. Offered annually to foster new literary talent. Categories: poetry, short fiction, creative nonfiction, novel. Entries must be postmarked between January 1 and February 28. Guidelines for SASE. Charges $20-nonmembers, $10 for members. Winners receive a cash honorarium (novel-$10,000; other categories-$2,000) and publication by a participating press. Open to all writers.

BAKELESS LITERARY PUBLICATION PRIZES, Bread Loaf Writers' Conference/Middlebury College, Middlebury College, Middleburg VT 05753. (802)443-5286. Fax: (802)443-2087. Contest Director: Michael Collier. Offered annually for unpublished authors of poetry, fiction and creative nonfiction. Submissions accepted January 1-March 1. Guidelines for SASE. Charges $10 fee. Prize: Publication of book length ms by University Press of New England and a Fellowship to attend the Bread Loaf Writers' Conference. Open to all writing in English who have not yet published a book in their entry's genre.

EMILY CLARK BALCH AWARD, *Virginia Quarterly Review*, 1 West Range, Charlottesville VA 22903. (804)924-3124. Fax:(804)924-1397. Contact: Staige D. Blackford, editor. Best short story/poetry accepted and published by the *Virginia Quarterly Review* during a calendar year. No deadline.

N **BYLINE MAGAZINE AWARDS**, P.O. Box 130596, Edmond OK 73013-0001. (405)348-5591. Fax: (405)348-5591. E-mail: bylinemp@aol.com. Website: http://www.bylinemag.com. Award Director: Marcia Preston. Contest includes several monthly contests, open to anyone, in various categories that include fiction, nonfiction, poetry and children's literature, an annual poetry chapbook award which is open to any poet and an annual ByLine Literary Awards in short story and poetry, open only to our subscribers. Deadlines: chapbook—March 1; ByLine Literary Award—November 1; monthly contests have various deadlines. Guidelines for SASE. Charges $3-5 monthly contests and ByLine Literary Award and $12 chapbook. Prizes: monthly contests—cash and listing in magazine; chapbook award—publication of chapbook, 50 copies and $100; ByLine Literary Award—$250 in each category, plus publication in the magazine. Judged by various professional poets, fiction writers and editors. For chapbook award and ByLine Literary Awards, publication constitutes part of the prize, and winners grant first NA rights to ByLine. Monthly contests and poetry chapbook competition are open to any writer. BLA's are open to subscribers only.

N **CALIFORNIA WRITERS' CLUB CONFERENCE AND CONTEST**, P.O. Box 1281, Berkeley CA 94701. Website: http://calwriters@ndti.net. Unpublished adult fiction (short stories), adult fiction (novels), adult nonfiction, juvenile fiction, poetry and scripts. Next: at Asilomar, CA, June 1999. Guidelines available to all writers with SASE only to address above.

CANADIAN AUTHORS ASSOCIATION ANNUAL CREATIVE WRITING AWARDS FOR HIGH SCHOOL, COLLEGE AND UNIVERSITY STUDENTS, Canadian Authors Association, Box 32219, 250 Harding Blvd. W, Richmond Hill, Ontario L4C 9R0 Canada. (905)737-2961. E-mail: bfarrar@gta.igs.net. Website: http://www.canauthors.org/studentform.html (includes entry form and guidelines). To encourage creative writing of unpublished fiction and poetry by writers between ages 12-21. Deadline: postmarked by March 31, 1999. Must be secondary school, college or university student. Prizes of $500 and 4 honorable mentions in each category (best poem, best story). Top 10 published (5 per genre) $5 entry. Send SAE and 1 IRC, or SASE in Canada for guidelines.

THE CHELSEA AWARDS FOR POETRY AND SHORT FICTION, % Richard Foerster, Editor, P.O. Box 1040, York Beach ME 03910. Estab. 1958. Previously unpublished submissions. "Two prizes awarded for the best work of short fiction and for the best group of 4-6 poems selected by the editors in anonymous competitions." Deadline: June 15 for fiction; December 15 for poetry. Guidelines for SASE. Charges $10 fee (includes free subscription to *Chelsea*). Checks made payable to Chelsea Associates, Inc. Prize: $1,000, winning entries published in *Chelsea*. Include SASE for notification of competition results. Does not return mss. *Note:* General submissions and other business should be addressed to the editor at *Chelsea*, P.O. Box 773, Cooper Station, New York, NY 10276.

N **CHICANO/LATINO LITERARY CONTEST**, Department of Spanish and Portuguese, University of California-Irvine, Irvine CA 92717. (714)824-6901. Contact: Alejandro Morales or Ruby Trejo. Estab. 1974. "To promote the dissemination of unpublished Chicano/Latino literature in Spanish or English, and to encourage its development. The call for entries will be genre specific, rotating through four categories: short story (1996), poetry (1997), drama (1998) and novel (1999)." Deadline: April 30. Prize: 1st-$1,000; 2nd-$500; 3rd-$250. "Interested parties may write for entry procedures." The contest is open to all citizens or permanent residents of the US.

CITY OF TORONTO BOOK AWARD, City of Toronto, Corporate Communications, Toronto City Hall, Toronto, Ontario M5H 2N2 Canada. (416)392-0468. Fax: (416)392-7999. Offered annually for work published January 1-December 31 of previous year to honor authors of books of literary or artistic merit that are evocative of Toronto. Deadline: January 31. Guidelines for SASE. Prize: Total of $15,000 in prize money. Each finalist (usually 4-6) receives $1,000 and the winning author receives the remainder ($9,000-11,000). Fiction and nonfiction books for adults and/or children are eligible. Textbooks, reprints and mss are not eligible.

CNW/FLORIDA STATE WRITING COMPETITION, Florida Freelance Writers Association, P.O. Box A, North Stratford NH 03590-0167. (603)922-8338. Fax: (603)922-8339. E-mail: danakcnw@ncia.net. Contact: Dana Cassell, executive director. Deadline: March 15. Subject areas include: adult articles, adult short stories, writing for children, novels, nonfiction books (may add poetry in 1999); categories within these areas vary from year to year. Guidelines for #10 SASE. Entry fees vary from year to year; in 1998 were $5-20. Prizes: cash, books, membership, certificates.

THE DANCING JESTER PRESS "ONE NIGHT IN PARIS SHOULD BE ENOUGH" CONTEST, The Danc ing Jester Press, 3411 Garth Rd., Suite 208, Baytown TX 77521. E-mail: djpress@aol.com. Contact: (Ms.) Shiloh Daniel. Offered annually for unpublished work to recognize excellence in poetics. Prize: 1st-the night of April 1, 1999 in Paris, France, all expenses paid; 2nd-chapbook publication; 3rd-a pair of "One Night in Paris Should Be Enough" T-shirts.

N **EYSTER PRIZE**, *New Delta Review*, % Department of English, Louisiana State University, Baton Rouge LA 70803-5001. (504)388-4079. Contact: Fiction Editor and Poetry Editor. Estab. 1983. Semiannual award for best works of poetry and fiction in each issue. Deadlines: March 1 (spring/summer issue); September 1 (fall/winter issue).

FEMINIST WRITERS' CONTEST, Dept WM, Des Plaines/Park Ridge NOW, P.O. Box 2440, Des Plaines IL 60018. Contact: Contest Director. Estab. 1990. Categories: Fiction and nonfiction (3,000 or fewer words). Work should reflect feminist perspectives (should not endorse or promote sexism, racism, ageism, anti-lesbianism, etc.) Guidelines for SASE. Deadline: August 31. Charges $10 fee. Cash awards.

GEORGETOWN REVIEW FICTION AND POETRY CONTEST, P.O. Box 6309, Southern Station, Hattiesburg MS 39406-6309. (601)544-0639. E-mail: gr@georgetownreview.com. Website: http://www.georgetownreview.com. Contact: Victoria Lancelotta, fiction editor. Steven Conti, managing editor. Deadline: October 1. Guidelines for SASE. Entry fee: $10/short story; $5/poem, $2 each additional poem. Prize: $1,000 for winning story; $500 for winning poem. Nine finalists receive publication and 1 year's subscription. Maximum length: 25 pages or 6,500 words. Previously published or accepted work ineligible. No mss returned.

GEORGIA STATE UNIVERSITY REVIEW WRITING CONTEST, Georgia State University Review, Georgia State University Plaza, Campus Box 1894, Atlanta GA 30303-3083. (404)651-4804. Fax: (404)651-1710. Contact: Cindy Cunningham, editor. Offered annually "to publish the most promising work of up-and-coming writers of poetry (3-5 poems. None over 100 lines.) Fiction (10,000 word limit). Deadline: January 31. Guidelines for SASE. Charges $10 fee. Prize: $1,000 to winner of each category, plus a copy of winning issue to each paid submission. Fiction and poetry editors subject to change annually. Rights revert to writer upon publication.

THE GREENSBORO REVIEW LITERARY AWARD IN FICTION AND POETRY, *The Greensboro Review*, English Department, 134 McIver, UNCG. P.O. Box 26170, University of North Carolina-Greensboro, Greensboro NC 27402-6170. (336)334-5459. Fax: (336)334-3281. E-mail: clarkj@fagan.uncg.edu/eng/mfg. Website: http://www.uncg.edu/eng/mfa. Contact: Fiction or Poetry Editor. Estab. 1984. Annual award for fiction and poetry recognizing the best work published in the winter issue of *The Greensboro Review*. Deadline: September 15. Sample copy for $5.

HACKNEY LITERARY AWARDS, *Writing Today*, Box 549003/Birmingham-Southern College, Birmingham AL 35254. (205)226-4921. Fax: (205)226-3072. E-mail: Mhamner@bsc.edu. Website: http://www.bsc.edu/. Contact: Dr. Myra Crawford. Estab. 1969. Offered annually for unpublished novel, short story (maximum 5,000 words) and poetry (50 line limit). Deadline: September 30 (novels), December 31 (short stories and poetry). Guidelines on website or for SASE. Charges $25 entry fee for novels, $10 for short story and poetry. Prize: $5,000 for each category.

CHARLES JOHNSON AWARD FOR FICTION AND POETRY, Charles Johnson, Ricardo Cortez Cruz, Southern Illinois University, English Dept. 4503, Carbondale IL 62901-4503. (618)453-5321. E-mail: cruz@siu.edu. Website: http://www.siu.edu/~johnson. Award Director: Ricardo Cortez Cruz. Offered annually for unpublished poets and fiction writers. "The contest seeks to support increased artistic and intellectual growth and encourage excellence and diversity in creative writing." Deadline: January 28. Guidelines for SASE. Prizes: $500 and a signed copy of a book by Charles Johnson. "Open to all U.S. college students exploring issues relevant to minority and/or marginalized culture."

N **ROBERT F. KENNEDY BOOK AWARDS**, 1367 Connecticut Ave., NW, Suite 200, Washington DC 20036. (202)463-7575, ext. 244. Fax: (202)463-6606. E-mail: hdunn@rfkmemorial.org. Website: http://www.rfkmemorial.org. Director: Holly Dunn. Offered annually for work published the previous year which most faithfully and forcefully reflects Robert Kennedy's purposes—"his concern for the poor and the powerless, his struggle for honest and even-handed justice, his conviction that a decent society must assure all young people a fair chance, and his faith that a free democracy can act to remedy disparities of power and opportunity." Deadline: January 2. Charges $25 fee. Prize: grand-prize winner-$2,500 and a bust of Robert F. Kennedy.

N **JACK KEROUAC LITERARY PRIZE**, Lowell Celebrates Kerouac!, P.O. Box 8788, Lowell MA 01953-8488. Contact: contest coordinator. Offered annually for unpublished fiction, nonfiction and poetry. Deadline: May 15 through August 15. Guidelines for SASE. Charges $5 fee. Prize: $500 for each category and invitation to read at festival. Judged by an outside judge. Open to any writer.

HENRY KREISEL AWARD FOR BEST FIRST BOOK, Writers Guild of Alberta, 11759 Groat Rd., Edmonton Alberta T5M 3K6 Canada. (403)422-8174. Fax: (403)422-2663. E-mail: writers@compusmart.ab.ca. Assistant Director: Darlene Diver. Book can be of any genre published in current year. It must be an Alberta author's first book.

LARRY LEVIS EDITORS' PRIZE IN POETRY, FICTION, ESSAY, The Missouri Review, 1507 Hillcrest Hall, Columbia MO 65211. (573)882-4474. Fax: (573)884-4671. E-mail: moreview@showme.missouri.edu. Website: http://www.missouri.edu/~moreview. Contact: Greg Michalson. Offered annually for unpublished work in 3 categories: Fiction, essay and poetry. Deadline: Dec. 31. Guidelines for SASE after June. Charges $15 fee (includes a 1 year subscription). Prize: fiction and poetry winner-$1,500 and publication in the spring issue; essay winner-$1,000 and publication.

LITERARY COMPETITION, Writers' Federation of New Brunswick, P.O. Box 37, Station A, Fredericton, New Brunswick E3B 4Y2 Canada. Phone/fax: (506)459-7228. E-mail: aa821@fan.nb.ca. Website: http://www.sjfn.nb.ca/community_hall/w/writers_Federation_NB/index.htm. Project Coordinator: Anna Mae Snider. Offered annually for unpublished fiction, nonfiction, poetry and children's literature. Also awarded: the Alfred Bailey Prize (for poetry ms), The Richards Prize (short novel, collection of short stories) and The Sheree Fitch Prize (writers 14-18 years old). Deadline: February 14. Guidelines for SASE. Charges $10 for members/students, $15 for nonmembers. Prizes: fiction, nonfiction, poetry, children's literature, 1st-$150, 2nd-$75, 3rd-$30; the Alfred Bailey Prize and the Richards Prize-$400 each; the Sheree Fitch Prize, 1st-$150, 2nd-$100, 3rd-$50. Judged by published writers from outside New Brunswick. The contest is open to New Brunswick residents only.

MANITOBA LITERARY AWARDS, Manitoba Writers Guild, 206-100 Arthur St., Winnipeg, Manitoba R3B 1H3 Canada. (204)942-6134. Fax: (204)942-5754. E-mail: mbwriter@escape.ca. Website: http://www.mbwriter.mb.ca. Contact: Robyn Maharaj. Awards offered annually include: the McNally Robinson Book of Year Award (adult), the McNally Robinson Book for Young People (8 and under and 9 and older). the John Hirsch Award for Most Promising Manitoba Writer, and two Book Publishers Awards. Awards offered biennially include: the Heaven Chapbook Prize and les Prix des caisse populaires. Deadline for books is December 1st. Books published between December 1-31 will be accepted until mid-January. Prizes: $250-3,000. Guidelines and submission forms available upon request. Open to Manitoba writers only.

MASTERS LITERARY AWARDS, Center Press, P.O. Box 16452, Encino CA 91416-6452. E-mail: tr22@usa.net. Website: http://www.concentric.net/~medianet/index.html. Contact: Gabriella Stone, managing editor. Offered annually and quarterly for work published within 2 years (preferred) and unpublished work (accepted). Fiction: 15 page, maximum; Poetry: 5 pages or 150 lines, maximum; Nonfiction: 10 page, maximum. Deadlines: March 15, June 15th, August 15th, December 15. Guidelines for SASE. Charges $15 reading/administration fee. Prizes: 4 quarterly honorable mentions from which is selected one yearly Grand Prize of $1,000. "A selection of winning entries will appear in our national literary publication." Center Press retains one time publishing rights to selected winners.

THE MILTON CENTER POST-GRADUATE FELLOWSHIP, The Milton Center, 3100 McCormick Ave., Wichita KS 67213. (316)942-4291, ext. 326. Contact: Virginia Stem Owens. Offered annually for unpublished submissions "to provide new writers of Christian commitment with the opportunity to complete their first book-length manuscript of fiction or poetry with a supportive community of writers." Deadline: January 31. Guidelines for SASE. Charges $15 fee. Award: $11,000 stipend, plus living expenses for one (married applicants welcome, although expenses are only provided for one). Judged by The Fellows of the Milton Center. Two fellowships are awarded/year.

THE NEBRASKA REVIEW AWARDS IN FICTION AND POETRY, *The Nebraska Review*, FAB 212, University of Nebraska-Omaha, Omaha NE 68182-0324. (402)554-2880. (402)554-3436. E-mail: nereview@fa-cpacs.unomaha.edu. Contact: Susan Aizenberg (poetry), James Reed (fiction). Estab. 1973. Offered annually for previously unpublished fiction and a poem or group of poems. Deadline: November 30. Charges $9 fee (includes a subscription to *The Nebraska Review*). Prize: $500 for each category.

NEW MILLENNIUM WRITINGS AWARD, New Millennium Writings Journal, P.O. Box 2463, Knoxville TN 37901. (423)428-0389. Website: http://www.mach2.com/books or http://www.magamall.com. Contact: Don Williams, director. Offered twice annually for unpublished fiction, poetry, essays or nonfiction prose, to encourage new fiction writers, poets and essaysists and bring them to attention of publishing industry. Deadline: January 31, June 15. Guidelines for SASE. Charges $10 fee. Entrants receive an issue of *NMW* in which winners appear. Prize: Fiction-$1,000; Poetry-$1,000; Essay or nonfiction prose-$500 and publication of winners and runners-up, 25 honorable mentions listed.

NEW WRITERS AWARDS, Great Lakes Colleges Association, The Philadelphia Center, North American Building, 7th Floor, 121 S. Broad St., Philadephia PA 19107. Fax: (215)735-7373. E-mail: clark@philactr.edu. Contact: Prof. Mark Andrew Clark, award director. Offered annually to the best first book of poetry and the best first book of fiction among those submitted by publishers. Deadline: February 28. Guidelines for SASE. Prizes: Winning authors will be invited to tour the GLCA colleges, where they will participate in whatever activities they and the college deem appropriate. An honorarium of at least $300 will be guaranteed the author by each of the colleges they visit. Open to any first book of poetry or fiction submitted by a publisher.

NIMROD, (formerly Nimrod, Arts and Humanities Council of Tulsa Prizes), The University of Tulsa, 600 S. College, Tulsa OK 74104-3189. (918)631-3080. Fax: (918)631-3033. E-mail: ringoldfl@centum.utulsa.edu. Website: http://www.utulsa.edu/NIMROD/nimrod.html. Contact: Francine Ringold, editor. Unpublished fiction and poetry. Theme issue in the spring. *Nimrod*/Hardman Awards issue in the fall. For contest or theme issue guidelines send SASE. Deadline: April 18. Charges $20 fee, $20 includes two issues. Sample copies $10.

NORTH AMERICAN NATIVE AUTHORS FIRST BOOK AWARDS, The Greenfield Review Literary Center, P.O. Box 308, Greenfield Center NY 12833. (518)583-1440. Fax: (518)583-9741. Website: http://nativeauthors.com. or http://www.greenfieldreview.com. Contact: Joseph Bruchac. Offered annually for unpublished work in book form to recognize literary achievement in prose and in poetry by Native North American writers who have not yet published a book. Deadline: March 15. Guidelines for SASE. Prize: $500 plus publication by The Greenfield Review Press with a standard contract for royalties. Open to American Indian, Inuit, Aleut or Metis writers who have not yet published a book.

OHIOANA BOOK AWARDS, Ohioana Library Association, 65 S. Front St., Room 1105, Columbus OH 43215. (614)466-3831. Fax: (614)728-6974. E-mail: ohioana@winslo.ohio.gov. Website: http://www.oplin.lib.oh.us/OHIOANA. Contact: Linda Hengst, director. Annual contest "to bring national attention to Ohio authors and their books." Categories: fiction, nonfiction, juvenile, poetry, and books about Ohio or an Ohioan. Deadline: December 31. Guidelines for SASE. Writers must have been born in Ohio or lived in Ohio for at least 5 years.

KENNETH PATCHEN COMPETITION, Pig Iron Press, P.O. Box 237, Youngstown OH 44501. (330)747-6932. Fax: (330)747-0599. Contact: Bill Koch. Offered biannually for unpublished poetry or fiction (except for individual works published in magazines/journals). Alternates between poetry and fiction. Deadline: December 31. Guidelines for SASE. Charges $10 fee. Prize: trade Paperback publication in an edition of 800 copies, and $500.

N **QSPELL LITERARY AWARDS**, QSPELL-Quebec Society for the Promotion of English Language Literature, 1200 Atwater Ave., Montreal, Quebec H3Z 1X4 Canada. Fax: (514)933-0878. E-mail: qspell@total.net. Website: http://www.qspell.org. Offered annually for work published May 16, 1997-May 15, 1998 to honor excellence in English-language writing in Quebec. Categories—fiction, nonfiction, poetry and QSPELL/FEWQ Best First Book (by an author who has not been previously published in book form). Deadline: May 31. Guidelines for SASE. Charges $10/title. Prize: $2,000 in each category. Author must have resided in Quebec for 3 of the past 5 years.

QUINCY WRITER'S GUILD ANNUAL CREATIVE WRITING CONTEST, Quincy Writer's Guild, c/o Rev. Michael Barrett, P.O. Box 433, Quincy IL 62306-0433. Categories include serious poetry, light poetry, short story, fiction. Deadline: January 1-April 15. Charges $2/poem; $4/short story or article. "No identification should appear on manuscripts, but send a separate 3×5 card attached to each entry with name, address, phone number, word count, and title of work. Entries must be submitted in triplicate." Previously unpublished work. Deadline: January 1-April 1. Guidelines for SASE. Cash prizes.

RHYME TIME CREATIVE WRITING COMPETITION, *Rhyme Time*, P.O. Box 2907, Decatur IL 62524. Award Director: Linda Hutton. Estab. 1981. Annual no-fee contest. Submit 1 typed poem, any style, any length. One winner will receive $25; one runner-up will receive a year's subscription to *Rhyme Time*. No poems will be published. Include SASE. Deadline: November 1.

MARY ROBERTS RINEHART FUND, MSN 3E4 English Department, George Mason University, 4400 University Dr., Fairfax VA 22030-4444. (703)993-1180. Contact: William Miller. Offered annually for unpublished authors. Grants by nomination to unpublished creative writers for fiction, poetry, drama, biography, autobiography or history with a strong narrative quality. Submissions are accepted for fiction and poetry in odd years, and nonfiction and drama in even years. Deadline: Nov. 30. Prize: varies, approximately $1,000. Submissions must include nominating letter from person in appropriate field.

BRUCE P. ROSSLEY LITERARY AWARD, 96 Inc., P.O. Box 15558, Boston MA 02215. (617) 267-0543. Fax: (617)262-3568. Director: Vera Gold. Offered biennially, in even years, to give greater recognition to a writer of merit. In addition to writing, accomplishments in the fields of teaching and community service are considered. Deadline: September 30. Nominations are accepted from August 1 to September 30. Guidelines for SASE. Charges $10 fee. Prize: $1,000. Any writer in New England may be nominated, but the focus is merit and those writers who have been under-recognized.

SHORT GRAIN WRITING CONTEST, Grain Magazine, P.O. Box 1154, Regina Saskatchewan S4P 3B4 Canada. (306)244-2828. Fax: (306)244-0255. E-mail: grain.mag@sk.sympatico.ca. Website: http://www.skwriter.com. Contest Director: J. Jill Robinson. Offered annually for unpublished dramatic monologues, postcard stories (narrative fiction) and prose (lyric) poetry. Maximum length for all entries: 500 words. Deadline: January 31. Guidelines for SAE and International Reply Coupons or Canadian stamps. Charges $20 fee for 2 entries, plus $5 for additional entries; US and International entries: $20, plus $4 postage in US funds (non-Canadian). Prizes: 1st-$500, 2nd-$300, 3rd-$200. All entrants receive a one year subscription to *Grain*. *Grain* purchases first Canadian serial rights only. Copyright remains with the author. Open to any writer. No fax or e-mail submissions.

SHORT PROSE COMPETITION FOR DEVELOPING WRITERS, The Writers' Union of Canada, 24 Ryerson Ave., Toronto, Ontario M5T 2P3 Canada. (416)703-8982. E-mail: twuc@the-wire.com. Competition Administrator: Kerry Lamond. Offered annually "to discover developing Canadian writers of unpublished prose fiction and nonfiction." Deadline: November 3. "Visit our website at http://www.swifty.com/twuc." Length: 2,500 words max. Charges $25/entry fee. Prize: $2,500 and publication in *Books in Canada* (a Canadian literary journal). Open to Canadian citizens or landed immigrants who have not been published in book format and who do not currently have a contract with a publisher.

SONORA REVIEW ANNUAL LITERARY AWARDS, *Sonora Review*, English Department, University of Arizona, Tucson AZ 85721. E-mail: sonora@u.Arizona.edu. Contact: poetry, fiction or nonfiction editor. $500 Fiction Award given each Spring to the best previously unpublished short story. Deadline: December 1. Charges $10 or $12 one-year subscription fee. $500 Poetry Award given each Fall to the best previously unpublished poem. Four poems/5 page maximum submission. Deadline: July 1. Charges $10 or $12 one-year subscription fee. $150 nonfiction award given each fall to the best previously unpublished essay. Deadline: July 1. Charges $10 reading fee or $12 one-year subscription. For all awards, all entrants receive a copy of the issue in which the winning entry appears. No formal application form is required; regular submission guidelines apply. SASE required for return of ms. Guidelines for #10 SASE. For samples, send $6.

SOUTHWEST REVIEW AWARDS, Southern Methodist University, 307 Fondren Library West, P.O. Box 750374, Dallas TX 75275-0374. (214)768-1036. Fax: (214)768-1408. E-mail: swr@mail.smu.edu. Contact: Elizabeth Mills. "The $1,000 John H. McGinnis Memorial Award is given each year for fiction and nonfiction that has been published in the *Southwest Review* in the previous year. Stories or articles are not submitted directly for the award, but simply for publication in the magazine. The Elizabeth Matchett Stover Award, an annual prize of $150, is awarded to the author of the best poem or group of poems published in the magazine during the preceding year."

N **WALLACE STEGNER FELLOWSHIPS**, Creative Writing Program, Stanford University, Dept. of English, Stanford CA 94305-2087. (650)723-2647. Fax: (650)723-3679. E-mail: gay.pierce@forsythe.stanford.edu. Website: http://www-leland.stanford.edu/dept/english/cw. Program Administrator: Gay Pierce. Offered annually for a two-year residency at Stanford for emerging writers to attend the Stegner workshop and writer under guidance of the creative writing faculty. Deadline: December 1. Guidelines available. Charges $40 fee. Prize: living stipend (currently $15,000/year) and required workshop tuition of $5,000/year.

SUB-TERRAIN MAGAZINE AWARDS, *Sub-Terrain Magazine*, 175 E. Broadway, #204A, Vancouver, British Columbia V5T 1W2 Canada. (604)876-8710. Fax: (604)879-2667. E-mail: subter@pinc.com. Website: http://www.anvilpress.com. Contest/Award Director: Brian Kaufman. Offered annually to unpublished novels, nonfiction, poems, short stories and photography. Contests include the Anvil Press International 3-Day Novel Writing Contest, Sub-Terrain Creative Nonfiction Writing Contest, The Not Quite the Cover of the Rolling Stone Award, Last Poems Poetry Contest and Moonless Night Short Story Contest. Deadlines vary. Charges $15 fee including a subscription to magazine; $25 for 3-Day-Novel Contest. Prizes: cash prize and publication. The winner of The 3-Day Novel Contest receives a cash prize and royalties. The magazine acquires one-time rights only; after publication rights revert to the author.

TENNESSEE WRITERS ALLIANCE LITERARY COMPETITION, Tennessee Writers Alliance, P.O. Box 120396, Nashville TN 37212. (615)385-3163. Website: http://www.concerthall.com/t-w-a.html. Contact: Sallie Bissell, executive director. Offered annually on rotating basis for unpublished short fiction, poetry, nonfiction (personal essay). Deadline varies. Guidelines for SASE. Charges $10 fee for members, $15 fee for non-member Tennessee residents. Prize: 1st-$500; 2nd-$250; 3rd-$100 and publication. Acquires right to publish once. Open to any member of Tennessee Writers Alliance and Tennessee residents. Membership open to all, regardless of residence, for $25/year, $15/year for students.

N **"TO GET INK" WRITER'S CONTEST**, Writers of Kern, P.O. Box 6694, Bakersfield CA 93386-6694. (805)871-5834. E-mail: wgable@kern.com. Award Director: Barbara Gabel. Offered annually for unpublished fiction (short story and novel), nonfiction and poetry. Deadline: July 15. Guidelines for SASE. Charges $10 fee. Prizes: 1st-$35 per category, 2nd-3rd-receive certificates. Judged by authors, editors and agents. Open to any writer.

WINNERS' CIRCLE SHORT STORY CONTEST, Canadian Authors Association, Metropolitan Toronto Branch, 33 Springbank Ave., Scarborough, Ontario M1N 1G2 Canada. (416)698-8687. Fax: (416)698-8687. E-mail: caamtb@inforamp.ca. Contact: Bill Belfontaine. Contest to encourage new short stories and personal essays which help authors to get published. Charges $20, $10 from each entry can be used to discount cost of $115 plus GST for new memberships in the Canadian Authors Association. Prizes: Grand Prize-$1,000, 1st-$250, 2nd-$100, 3rd $50 and 5 honorary mention winners. Winners of cash prizes and honorary mentions published in Winners' Circle Anthology. Deadline: July 1-November 30. Acquires first publishing rights required but copyright owned by writer. SAE plus 90 cents postage or IRC for guidelines.

WRITER'S DIGEST NATIONAL SELF-PUBLISHED BOOK AWARDS, *Writer's Digest*, 1507 Dana Ave., Cincinnati OH 45207-9966. (513)531-2690, ext. 268. Fax: (513)531-1843. E-mail: competitions@fwpubs.com. Contact: Sandi Luppert, promotions manager. Offered annually for self-publishers to bring their books to the attention of publishers and editors. Categories: life stories, cookbooks, children's and young adult books, fiction, nonfiction and poetry. Charges entry fee. Guidelines for #10 SASE. Deadline: December 15.

WRITER'S DIGEST WRITING COMPETITION, *Writer's Digest*, 1507 Dana Ave., Cincinnati OH 45207-9966. (513)531-2690, ext. 268. Fax: (513)531-1843. E-mail: competitions@fwpubs.com. Contact: Sandi Luppert. Contest in 68th year. Categories: Personal Essays, Feature Articles, Mainstream/Literary Short Stories, Genre Short Stories, Rhyming Poems, Non-Rhyming Poems, Stage Plays, Television/Movie Scripts and Children's Fiction and Nonfiction. Submissions must be unpublished. For guidelines send #10 SASE. Charges entry fee. Deadline: May 31.

Arts Councils & Foundations

ARTIST FELLOWSHIP, Alabama State Council on the Arts, 201 Monroe St., Montgomery AL 36130. (334)242-4076, ext. 226. Fax: (334)240-3269. E-mail: becky@arts.state.al.us. Literature Programs Manager: Becky Mullen. Offered every 2 years for previously published work based on achievement and quality of work. Artists may use funds to set aside time to create their art, improve their skills, or do what they consider most advantageous to enhance their artistic careers. Deadline: May 1. Call or write to request guidelines. Prize: $5,000 (2) or $10,000 (1) (most often 2 artists are chosen). Open to residents of Alabama who have lived in state for 2 years prior to application.

N **ARTIST FELLOWSHIP**, Connecticut Commission on the Arts, 755 Main St., Hartford CT 06103. (860)566-4770. Fax: (860)566-6462. Website: http://www.cs/net/ctstateu.edu/cca/. Contact: Linda Dente, senior program manager. Previously published or unpublished work to assist in the development and encouragement of Connecticut writers of substantial talent. Deadline: September 14, 1998. Awards are biennial. Guidelines for SASE. Prize: $2,500 or $5,000. Must be residents of the State of Connecticut for 4 years or more. Cannot be a student.

ARTIST FELLOWSHIP AWARDS, Wisconsin Arts Board, 101 E. Wilson St. 1st Floor, Madison WI 53702. (608)264-8191. Fax: (608)267-0380. E-mail: mfraire@arts.state.wi.us. Director: Mark Fraire. Offered every 2 years to recognize the significant contributions of professional artists in Wisconsin, and intended to support continued artistic and professional development, enabling artists to create new work, complete work in progress, and pursue activities which contribute to their artistic growth. Deadline: September 15. SASE is not necessary. Contact WAB at (608)266-0190 to receive application materials. Applicants must reside in Wisconsin a minimum of 1 year prior to application and may not be full-time students pursuing a degree in the fine arts.

ARTISTS FELLOWSHIP, Japan Foundation, 39th Floor, 152 W. 57th St., New York NY 10019. (212)489-0299. Fax: (212)489-0409. E-mail: chris_watanabe@jfny.org. Website: http://www.jfny.org/. Contact: Chris Watanabe. Offered annually. Deadline: December 1. "Contact us in September. Write or fax. Judged by committee at the Japan Foundation headquarters in Tokyo. Keep in mind that this is an international competition. Due to the breadth of the application pool only four artists are selected for awards in the U.S. Applicants need not submit a writing sample, but if one is submitted it must be brief. Three letters of recommendation must be submitted from peers. One letter will double as a letter of affiliation, which must be submitted by a *Japan-based* (not necessarily an ethnic Japanese) peer artist. The applicant must present a concise and cogent project objective and must be a professional writer/artist with accessible qualifications, i.e., a list of major works or publications."

ARTS RECOGNITION AND TALENT SEARCH, National Foundation for Advancement in the Arts, 800 Brickell Ave., Suite 500, Miami FL 33131. (305)377-1140 or (800)970-ARTS. Fax: (305)377-1149. E-mail: nfaa@nfaa.org. Website: http://www.nfaa.org. Programs Administration Director: Laura Padron. Contact: Karla V. Hernandez, communications coordinator. Estab. 1981. For achievements in dance, music (classical, jazz and vocal), photography, theater, visual arts and writing. Students fill in and return the application, available at every public and private high school around the nation, for cash awards of up to $3,000 each and scholarship opportunities worth more than $3 million. Deadline: early—June 1, regular—October 1. Charges $25 registration fee for June; $35 for October.

GEORGE BENNETT FELLOWSHIP, Phillips Exeter Academy, 20 Main St., Exeter NH 03833-2460. Coordinator, Selection Committee: Charles Pratt. Estab. 1968. Annual award of stipend, room and board "to provide time and freedom from material considerations to a person seriously contemplating or pursuing a career as a writer. Applicants should have a manuscript in progress which they intend to complete during the fellowship period." Guidelines for SASE. The committee favors writers who have not yet published a book with a major publisher. Deadline: December 1. Charges $5 fee. Residence at the Academy during the Fellowship period required.

BUSH ARTIST FELLOWSHIPS, The Bush Foundation, E-900 First National Bank Bldg., 332 Minnesota St., St. Paul MN 55101. (612)227-5222. Contact: Kathi Polley. Estab. 1976. Award for Minnesota, North Dakota, South Dakota, and western Wisconsin residents 25 years or older (students are not eligible) "to buy 12-18 months of time for the applicant to further his/her own work." Up to 15 fellowships/year, $40,000 each. Deadline: October. All application categories rotate on a two year cycle. Literature (fiction, creative nonfiction, poetry) and scriptworks (playwriting, screenwriting) will be offered next for the 1999 fellowships. Publishing, performance and/or option requirements for eligibility. Applications available August 1998.

N **CHLA RESEARCH FELLOWSHIPS & SCHOLARSHIPS**, Children's Literature Association, P.O. Box 138, Battle Creek MI 49016-0138. (616)965-8180. Fax: (616)965-3568. E-mail: chla@mlc.lib.mi.us. Website: http://ebbs.english.vt.edu/chla. Contact: CHLA Scholarship Chair. Offered annually. "The fellowships are available for proposals dealing with criticism or original scholarship with the expectation that the undertaking will lead to publication and make a significant contribution to the field of children's literature in the area of scholarship or criticism." Deadline: February 1. Guidelines for SASE. Prize: awards range from $250-1,000. Funds are not intended for work leading to the completion of a professional degree.

DOCTORAL DISSERTATION FELLOWSHIPS IN JEWISH STUDIES, National Foundation for Jewish Culture, 330 7th Ave., 21st Floor, New York NY 10001. (212)629-0500. Fax: (212)629-0508. E-mail: nfjc@jewishculture.org. Website: http://www.jewishculture.org. Offered annually to students. Deadline varies, usually early January. Guidelines for SASE. Prize: a $6,000-$9,000 grant. Open to students who have completed their course work and need funding for research in order to write their dissertation thesis or a Ph.D. in a Jewish field of study.

N **FELLOWSHIP**, William Morris Society in the U.S., P.O. Box 53263, Washington DC 20009. E-mail: biblio@aol.com. Website: http://www.ccny.cuny.edu/wmorris/morris.html. Contact: Mark Samuels Lasner. Offered annually "to promote study of the life and work of William Morris (1834-96), British poet, designer and socialist. Award may be for research or a creative project." Deadline: December 1. CV, 1 page proposal and 2 letters of recommendation required for application. Prize: up to $1,000, multiple, partial awards possible. Applicants must be US citizens or permanent residents.

FELLOWSHIP-LITERATURE, Alabama State Council on the Arts, 201 Monroe St., Montgomery AL 36130. (334)242-4076, ext. 226. Fax: (334)240-3269. Contact: Becky Mullen. Literature Fellowship offered on alternate, even-numbered years for previously published or unpublished work to set aside time to create and to improve skills. Two year Alabama residency requirement. Deadline: May 1. Guidelines available. Prize: $10,000 or $5,000.

FELLOWSHIPS (LITERATURE), RI State Council on the Arts, 95 Cedar St., Suite 103, Providence RI 02903. (401)277-3880. Fax: (401)521-1351. E-mail: ride0600@ride.ri.net. Website: http://www.modcult.brown.edu/RISCA/. Director: Randall Rosenbaum. Offered every two years for previously published or unpublished work. Deadline: April 1, 1999. Guidelines for SASE. Prize: $5,000 fellowship; $1,000 runner-up. Open to Rhode Island residents only.

N **WILLIAM FLANAGAN MEMORIAL CREATIVE PERSONS CENTER**, Edward F. Albee Foundation, 14 Harrison St., New York NY 10013. (212)226-2020. Contact: David Briggs, foundation secretary. Annual one-month residency at "The Barn" in Montauk, New York offers writers privacy and a peaceful atmosphere in which to work. Deadline: April 1. Prize: room only, writers pay for food and travel expenses.

FLORIDA INDIVIDUAL ARTIST FELLOWSHIPS, Florida Department of State, Division of Cultural Affairs, The Capitol, Tallahassee FL 32399-0250. (904)487-2980. Fax: (904)922-5259. Website: http://www.dos.state.fl.us. Contact: Valerie Ohlsson, arts consultant. Open to Florida writers only. Prize: $5,000 each for fiction, poetry and children's literature. Deadline: January.

GAP (GRANTS FOR ARTIST PROJECTS); FELLOWSHIP, Artist Trust, 1402 Third Ave, Suite 404, Seattle WA 98101-2118. (206)467-8734. Fax: (206)467-9633. E-mail: arttrust@eskimo.com. Website: http://www.halcyon.com/cglew/. Contact: Barbara Courtney, executive director. "The GAP is awarded to 30-50 artists, including writers, per year. The award is meant to help finance a specific project, which can be in very early stages or near completion. Literature fellowships are offered every other year, and approximately six literature fellowships are awarded. The award is made on the basis of work of the past five years. It is 'no-strings-attached' funding." Artist Trust's Fellowship Awards are funded in part, through a partnership with the Washington State Arts Commission. Guidelines for SASE. Prize: GAP: up to $1,200. Fellowship: $5,000. Fulltime students not eligible. Open to *Washington state residents only.*

HEEKIN GROUP FOUNDATION WRITING FELLOWSHIPS PROGRAM, The Heekin Group Writers' and Education Fund, P.O. Box 1534, Sisters OR 97759. (541)548-4147. E-mail: ltgfh1@aol.com. Contest/Award Director: Sarah Heekin Redfield. Offered annually for unpublished works. James Fellowship for the Novel in Progress (2), Tara Fellowship for Short Fiction (2); Mary Molloy Fellowship for Children's Working Novel (1); The Cuchulain Fellowship for Rhetoric (1). These 6 fellowships are awarded to beginning career writers for assistance in their literary pursuits. Deadline: December 1. Guidelines for SASE. Charges $25 fellowship application fee. Prize: James Fellowship: $3,000; Tara Fellowship: $1,500; Mary Molloy Fellowship: $2,000; Siobhan Fellowship: $2,000. Fellowships are available to those writers who are unpublished in the novel, short fiction, juvenile novel and essay.

THE HODDER FELLOWSHIP, Princeton University Humanities Council, 122 E. Pyne, Princeton NJ 08544. (609)258-4713. E-mail: humcounc@princeton.edu. Website: http://www.princeton.edu/~humcounc/. The Hodder Fellowship is awarded to a humanist in the early stages of a career for the pursuit of independent work in the humanities. The recipient has usually written one book and is working on a second. Preference is given to applicants outside of academia. "The Fellowship is designed specifically to identify and nurture extraordinary potential rather than to honor distinguished achievement." Candidates for the Ph.D. are not eligible. Prize: $45,000 stipend and a year residence at Princeton. SASE for guidelines or request via e-mail. Deadline: November 1.

IDAHO WRITER-IN-RESIDENCE, Idaho Commission on the Arts, Box 83720, Boise ID 83720-0008. (208)334-2119. 1·800·ART·FUND (in Idaho) Fax: (208)334-2488. Website: http://www.state.id.us/arts/. Contact: Literature director. Estab. 1982. Offered every 3 years. Award of $8,000 for an Idaho writer, who over the three-year period reads his/her work throughout the state to increase the appreciation for literature. Deadline: January, 2001. Guidelines for SASE. Open to any Idaho writer.

INDIVIDUAL ARTIST FELLOWSHIP, Oregon Arts Commission, 775 Summer St. NE, Salem OR 97310. (503)986-0086. Fax: (503)986-0260. E-mail: michael.b.faison@state.or.us. Website: http://www.das.state.or.us/OAC/. Contact: Michael Faison, assistant director. Offered in even-numbered years to reward achievement in the field of literature. Deadline: September 1. Guidelines for SASE. Prize: $3,000. "Writers must be Oregon residents 18 years and older. Degree candidate students not eligible."

INDIVIDUAL ARTIST FELLOWSHIP, Tennessee Arts Commission, 401 Charlotte Ave., Nashville TN 37243-0780. (615)741-1701. Fax: (615)741-8559. E-mail: aswanson@mail.state.tn.us. Website: http://www.arts.state.tn.us. Director: Alice Swanson. Offered annually for recognition for emerging literary artists. Deadline: First or 2nd Monday in January. Write to above address or call—guidelines too large for SASE—we will mail. Prize: $2,000 or more. Must be resident of Tennessee. 1999 prose, 2000 poetry, etc. Must have publication history.

INDIVIDUAL ARTIST FELLOWSHIP AWARD, Montana Arts Council, 316 N. Park Ave., Suite 252, Helena MT 59620. (406)444-6430. Contact: Arlynn Fishbaugh. Offered annually to *Montana residents only*. Deadline: Fall.

INDIVIDUAL ARTISTS FELLOWSHIPS, Nebraska Arts Council, 3838 Davenport St., Omaha NE 68131-2329. (402)595-2122. Fax: (402)595-2334. Website: http://www.gps.k12.ne.us/nac_web_site/nac.htm. Contact: Suzanne Wise. Estab. 1991. Offered every 3 years (literature alternates with other disciplines) to recognize exemplary achievements by originating artists in their fields of endeavor and supports the contributions made by Nebraska artists to the quality of life in this state. Deadline: November 15, 2000. "Generally, distinguished achievement awards are $5,000 and merit awards are $1,000-2,000. Funds available are announced in September prior to the deadline." Must be a resident of Nebraska for at least 2 years prior to submission date; 18 years of age; not enrolled in an undergraduate, graduate or certificate-granting program in English, creative writing, literature, or related field.

JOSEPH HENRY JACKSON AWARD, The San Francisco Foundation, Administered by Intersection for the Arts, 446 Valencia St., San Francisco CA 94103. (415)626-2787. Fax: (415)626-1636. E-mail: intrsect@wenet.net. Contact: Charles Wilmoth, program director. Estab. 1965. Offered annually for unpublished, work-in-progress fiction (novel or short story), nonfiction or poetry by author age 20-35, with 3-year consecutive residency in northern California or Nevada prior to submission. Deadline: November 15-January 31. Guidelines for SASE.

EZRA JACK KEATS MEMORIAL FELLOWSHIP, Ezra Jack Keats Foundation (funding) awarded through Kerlan Collection, University of Minnesota, 109 Walter Library, 117 Pleasant St. SE., Minneapolis MN 55455. (612)624-4576. Fax: (612)625-5525. E-mail: CLRC@tc.umn.edu. Website: www.lib.umn.edu/special/Kerlan. Curator, Kerlan Collection: Karen Hoyle. Contact: Carrie Tahtamouni, library assistant. "To award a talented writer and/or illustrator of children's books who wishes to use Kerlan Collection for the furtherance of his or her artistic development." Deadline: May 1. Guidelines for SASE. Prize: $1,500 for travel to study at Kerlan Collection. "Special consideration will be given to someone who would find it difficult to finance the visit to the Kerlan Collection."

THE GERALD LOEB AWARDS, The John E. Anderson Graduate School of Management at UCLA, 110 Westwood Plaza, Suite F315, Box 951481, Los Angeles CA 90095-1481. (310)206-1877. Fax: (310)206-9856. E-mail: loeb@anderson.ucla.edu. Website: http://www.anderson.ucla.edu/media/loeb. Contact: Office of Communications. Consideration is limited to articles published in the previous calendar year. "To recognize writers who make significant contributions to the understanding of business, finance and the economy." Open for print and broadcast media. Deadline: February 6. Charges $50 fee ($25 for small newspapers) Prize: $2,000 in each category. Honorable mentions, when awarded, receive $500.

N **LOFT MENTOR SERIES**, The Loft, Pratt Community Center, 66 Malcolm Ave. SE, Minneapolis MN 55414-3551. E-mail: loft@loft.org. Website: http://www.loft.org. Contact: Program Coordinator. Estab. 1974. Opportunity to work with 4 nationally known writers and small stipend available to 8 winning poets and fiction writers. "Must live close enough to Minneapolis to participate fully in the series." Deadline: May. Guidelines for SASE. Charges $10 fee for nonmembers. Prize: $500.

N WALTER RUMSEY MARVIN GRANT, Ohioana Library Association, 65 S. Front St., Suite 1105, Columbus OH 43215. (614)466-3831. Fax: (614)728-6974. E-mail: ohioana@winslo.ohio.gov. Website: http://www.oplin.lib.oh.us/OHIOANA. Contact: Linda Hengst, director. Offered annually. Applicant must have been born in Ohio or have lived in Ohio for 5 years or more, must be 30 years of age or younger, and not have published a book. Deadline: January 31. Entries submitted may consist of up to 6 pieces of prose. No submission may total more than 60 pages or less than 10. No entries will be returned.

McKNIGHT ARTIST FELLOWSHIPS FOR WRITERS, (formerly Loft-McKnight Writers Award), administered by The Loft, 66 Malcolm Ave. SE, Minneapolis MN 55414-3551. Website: http://www.loft.org. Contact: Deidre Pope. Five awards of $10,000 and two awards of distinction at $20,000 each for *Minnesota* writers of poetry and creative prose. Deadline: November. Guidelines for SASE. Charges $10 fee.

MONEY FOR WOMEN, Barbara Deming Memorial Fund, Inc., P.O. Box 630125, The Bronx NY 10463. Contact: Susan Pliner. "Small grants to individual feminists in art, fiction, nonfiction and poetry, whose work addresses women's concerns and/or speaks for peace and justice from a feminist perspective." Deadlines: December 31 and June 30. Guidelines for SASE. Prize: grants up to $1,000: "The Fund does *not* give educational assistance, monies for personal study or loans, monies for dissertation or research projects, grants for group projects, business ventures, or emergency funds for hardships." Open to citizens of the US or Canada.

- The fund also offers two awards, the "Gerty, Gerty, Gerty in the Arts, Arts, Arts" for outstanding works by a lesbian and the "Fannie Lou Hamer Award" for work which combats racism and celebrates women of color.

N NANTUCKET SHORT STORY COMPETITION & FESTIVAL, Nantucket Theatrical Productions, Box 2177, Nantucket MA 02584. (508)228-5002. Literary Manager: Jim Patrick. Deadline: January 1, 1999. Charges $6 fee per play. Guidelines for SASE. Open subjects but would like to see more adolescent and kids plays; multicultural works. Length should be 70 pages or less.

NATIONAL MUSIC THEATER CONFERENCE, Eugene O'Neill Center, 234 W. 44th St., #901, New York NY 10036. (212)382-2790. Fax: (212)921-5538. Contest Director: Paulette Haupt. Contact: Michael Nassar, associate director. Offered annually to unpublished musicals or operas. "The O'Neill Theater Center is a developmental theater in which visions can be explored and risks can be taken that are not possible during production deadlines. The focus of the conference is on the creative process while a work is still in progress." Deadline: March 1. Application and guidelines for SASE. Charges $10 entry fee. Prize: Artists selected receive a stipend, room and board, and round trip transportation from New York to Connecticut, in addition to the developmental process provided by the O'Neill Theater Center. Open to any writer.

N NEW YORK STATE WRITER-IN-RESIDENCE PROGRAM, New York State Council on the Arts, 915 Broadway, New York NY 10010. (212)387-7022. Fax: (212)387-7164. E-mail: kmasterson@nysca.org. Website: http://www.artswire.org/artswire/nysca/nysca. Contact: Kathleen Masterson, literature program director. Offered in odd-numbered years to support writers' work and give writers a chance to work with a nonprofit organization in a community setting." Deadline: March 1. Award: $8,500 stipend for a 3 month residency. Applicant must be nominated by a New York state nonprofit organization.

JAMES D. PHELAN LITERARY AWARD, The San Francisco Foundation, Administered by Intersection for the Arts, 446 Valencia St., San Francisco CA 94103. (415)626-2787. Fax: (415)626-1636. E-mail: intrsect@wenet.net. Contact: Charles Wilmoth, program director. Estab. 1965. Offered annually for unpublished, work-in-progress fiction, nonfiction, short story, poetry or drama by California-born author age 20-35. Deadline: November 15-January 31. Guidelines for SASE.

N TRILLIUM BOOK AWARD/PRIX TRILLIUM, Ontario Ministry of Citizenship, Culture and Recreation, 77 Bloor St. W., 3rd Floor, Toronto, Ontario M7A 2R9 Canada. (416)314-7745. Website: http://www.gov.on.ca/MCZCR. Director: Jim Polk. Offered annually for work previously published between January 1 and December 31. This is the Ontario government's annual literary award. There are 2 categories—an English language category and a French language category. Deadline: mid-December. Guidelines for SASE. Publishers submit books on behalf of authors. Prize: the winning author in each category receives $12,000; the winning publisher is each category receives $2,500. Authors must be an Ontario resident three of the last five years.

UCROSS FOUNDATION RESIDENCY, 2836 US Highway 14-16E, Clearmont WY 82835. (307)737-2291. Fax: (307)737-2322. Contact: Sharon Dynak, executive director. Eight concurrent positions open for artists-in-residence in various disciplines (includes writers, visual artists, music, humanities) extending from 2 weeks-2 months. No charge for room, board or studio space. Deadline: March 1 for August-December program; October 1 for February-June program.

N VERMONT ARTS COUNCIL, 136 State St., Drawer 33, Montpelier VT 05633-6001. (802)828-3291. Fax: (802)828-3363. E-mail: info@arts.vca.state.vt.us. Website: http://www.state.vt.us/vermont-arts. Artist Grants Coordinator: Michele Bailey. Offered quarterly for previously published or unpublished works. Opportunity Grants are for specific projects of writers (poetry, playwriters, fiction, nonfiction) as well as not-for-profit presses. Also available are Artist Development funds to provide technical assistance for Vermont Writers. Write or call for entry information. Prize: $250-5,000. Open to VT residents only.

WRITERS FELLOWSHIPS, NC Arts Council, Dept. of Cultural Resources, Raleigh NC 27601-2807. (919)733-2111, ext. 22. E-mail: dmcgill@ncacmail.dcr.state.nc.us. Website: http://www.ncarts.org. Literature Director: Deborah McGill. Offered every two years. "To serve writers of fiction, poetry, literary nonfiction and literary translation in North Carolina and to recognize the contribution they make to this state's creative environment." Deadline: November 1, 1998. Write for guidelines. We offer eleven $8,000 grants every two years. Writer must have been a resident of NC for at least a year and may not be enrolled in any degree-granting program at the time of application.

Miscellaneous

BOWLING WRITING COMPETITION, American Bowling Congress Publications, 5301 S. 76th St., Greendale WI 53129-1127. Fax: (414)421-3013. Editor: Bill Vint. Contact: Mark Miller, assistant editor. Estab. 1935. Feature, editorial and news all relating to the sport of bowling. Deadline: December 1. Prize: First place in each division will carry a $300 award. In addition to the first place awards, others will be: News and Editorial-$225, $200, $175, $150, $75 and $50; Feature-$225, $200, $175, $150, $125, $100, $75, $50 and $50. There also will be five honorable mention certificates awarded in each category.

N **LANDMARK EDITIONS NATIONAL WRITTEN & ILLUSTRATED BY AWARDS CONTEST FOR STUDENTS**, Landmark Editions, Inc., P.O. Box 270169, Kansas City MO 64127. (816)241-4919. Editorial Director: Nan Thatch. Annual awards for students aged 6-19. Each ms must be written and illustrated by the same student and submitted only via the contest. Free guidelines for SASE. Charges $1 book entry fee.

STEPHEN LEACOCK MEMORIAL AWARD FOR HUMOUR, Stephen Leacock Associates, P.O. Box 854, Orillia, Ontario L3V 6K8 Canada. (705)325-6546. Contest Director: Jean Dickson. Estab. 1947. For a book of humor published in previous year by a Canadian author. Include 10 copies of each entry and a b&w photo with bio. Deadline: December 31. Charges $25 fee. Prize: Stephen Leacock Memorial Medal and Laurentian Bank of Canada Award of $5,000.

N **NMMA DIRECTORS AWARD**, National Marine Manufacturers Association, 600 Third Ave., New York NY 10016. (212)922-1212. Fax: (212)922-9581. Contribution to boating and allied water sports through newspaper, magazine, radio, television, film or book as a writer, artist, broadcaster, editor or photographer. Nomination must be submitted by a representative of a member company of National Marine Manufacturers Association. Deadline: Nov. 30.

N **PEN WRITING AWARDS FOR PRISONERS**, PEN American Center, 568 Broadway, New York NY 10012. Fax: (212)334-2181. E-mail: pen@echonyc.com. Website: http://www.pen.org. Contact: Jackson Taylor, coordinator. "Awarded to the authors of the best poetry, plays, short fiction and nonfiction received from prison writers in the U.S." SASE. Deadline September 1. Prizes: 1st-$100; 2nd-$50; 3rd-$25 (in each category).

CONTESTS AND AWARDS that were listed in the 1998 edition of *Writer's Market* but do not appear this year are listed in the General Index with a notation explaining why they were omitted.

Resources

Publications of Interest

In addition to newsletters and publications from local and national organizations, there are trade publications, books, and directories which offer valuable information about writing and about marketing your manuscripts and understanding the business side of publishing. Some also list employment agencies that specialize in placing publishing professionals, and some announce actual freelance opportunities.

TRADE MAGAZINES

ADVERTISING AGE, Crain Communications Inc., 740 N. Rush St., Chicago IL 60611. (312)649-5200. *Weekly magazine covering advertising in magazines, trade journals and business.*

AMERICAN JOURNALISM REVIEW, 8701 Adelphi Rd., Adelphi MD 20783. (301)431-4771. *10 issues/year magazine for journalists and communications professionals.*

DAILY VARIETY, Daily Variety Ltd./Cahners Publishing Co., 5700 Wilshire Blvd., Suite 120, Los Angeles CA 90036. (213)857-6600. *Trade publication on the entertainment industry, with helpful information for screenwriters.*

EDITOR & PUBLISHER, The Editor & Publisher Co., 11 W. 19th St., New York NY 10011. (212)675-4380. *Weekly magazine covering the newspaper publishing industry.*

FOLIO, Cowles Business Media, 11 Riverbend Dr. South, P.O. Box 4272, Stamford CT 06907-0272. (203)358-9900. *Monthly magazine covering the magazine publishing industry.*

GIFTS & DECORATIVE ACCESSORIES, Geyer-McAllister Publications, Inc., 51 Madison Ave., New York NY 10010-1675. (212)689-4411. Monthly magazine covering greeting cards among other subjects, with an annual buyer's directory in September.

HORN BOOK MAGAZINE, 11 Beacon St., Boston MA 02108. (617)227-1555. *Bimonthly magazine covering children's literature.*

PARTY & PAPER RETAILER, 4 Ward Corp., 70 New Canaan Ave., Norwalk CT 06850. (203)845-8020. *Monthly magazine covering the greeting card and gift industry.*

POETS & WRITERS INC., 72 Spring St., New York NY 10012. (212)226-3586. *Bimonthly magazine, primarily for literary writers and poets.*

PUBLISHERS WEEKLY, Bowker Magazine Group, Cahners Publishing Co., 245 W. 17th St., New York NY 10011. (212)645-0067. *Weekly magazine covering the book publishing industry.*

SCIENCE FICTION CHRONICLE, P.O. Box 022730, Brooklyn NY 11202-0056. (718)643-9011. *Monthly magazine for science fiction, fantasy and horror writers.*

TRAVELWRITER MARKETLETTER, The Waldorf-Astoria, 301 Park Ave., Suite 1880, New York NY 10022. *Monthly newsletter for travel writers with market listings as well as trip information.*

THE WRITER, 120 Boylston St., Boston MA 02116. (617)423-3157. *Monthly writers' magazine.*

WRITER'S DIGEST, 1507 Dana Ave., Cincinnati OH 45207. (513)531-2690. *Monthly writers' magazine.*

WRITING FOR MONEY, Blue Dolphin Communications, Inc., 83 Boston Post Rd., Sudbury MA 01776. *Bimonthly freelance market reports.*

BOOKS AND DIRECTORIES

AV MARKET PLACE, R.R. Bowker, A Reed Reference Publishing Co., 121 Chanlon Rd., New Providence NJ 07974. (908)464-6800.

THE COMPLETE BOOK OF SCRIPTWRITING, by J. Michael Straczynski, Writer's Digest Books, 1507 Dana Ave., Cincinnati OH 45207. (513)531-2690.

THE COMPLETE GUIDE TO SELF PUBLISHING, by Marilyn and Tom Ross, Writer's Digest Books, 1507 Dana Ave., Cincinnati OH 45207. (513)531-2690.

COPYRIGHT HANDBOOK, R.R. Bowker, A Reed Reference Publishing Co., 121 Chanlon Rd., New Providence NJ 07974. (908)464-6800.

DRAMATISTS SOURCEBOOK, edited by Kathy Sova, Theatre Communications Group, Inc., 355 Lexington Ave., New York NY 10017. (212)697-5230.

EDITORS ON EDITING: What Writers Need to Know About What Editors Do, edited by Gerald Gross, Grove/Atlantic Press, 841 Broadway, New York NY 10003. *Forty essays by America's most distinguished trade book editors on the art and craft of editing*

GRANTS AND AWARDS AVAILABLE TO AMERICAN WRITERS, *19th Ed., PEN American Center, 568 Broadway, New York NY 10012. (212)334-1660.*

GUIDE TO LITERARY AGENTS, edited by Donya Dickerson. Writer's Digest Books, 1507 Dana Ave., Cincinnati OH 45207. (513)531-2690.

THE GUIDE TO WRITERS CONFERENCES, ShawGuides, Inc. Educational Publishers, Box 1295, New York NY 10023. (212)799-6464. http://www.shawguides.com.

HOW TO WRITE IRRESISTIBLE QUERY LETTERS, by Lisa Collier Cool, Writer's Digest Books, 1507 Dana Ave., Cincinnati OH 45207. (513)531-2690.

INTERNATIONAL DIRECTORY OF LITTLE MAGAZINES & SMALL PRESSES, edited by Len Fulton, Dustbooks, P.O. Box 100, Paradise CA 95967. (530)877-6110.

LITERARY MARKET PLACE and INTERNATIONAL LITERARY MARKET PLACE, R.R. Bowker, A Reed Reference Publishing Co., 121 Chanlon Rd., New Providence NJ 07974. (908)464-6800.

MAGAZINE WRITING THAT SELLS, by Don McKinney, Writer's Digest Books, 1507 Dana Ave., Cincinnati OH 45207. (513)531-2690.

MY BIG SOURCEBOOK, 66 Canal Center Plaza, Suite 200, Alexandria VA 22314-5507. (703)683-0683.

NATIONAL WRITERS UNION GUIDE TO FREELANCE RATES & STANDARD PRACTICE, by Alexander Kopelman, distributed by Writer's Digest Books, 1507 Dana Ave., Cincinnati OH 45207, (513)531-2690.

PROFESSIONAL WRITER'S GUIDE, edited by Donald Bower and James Lee Young, National Writers Press, Suite 424, 1450 S. Havana, Aurora CO 80012. (303)751-7844.

STANDARD DIRECTORY OF ADVERTISING AGENCIES, National Register Publishing, A Reed Reference Publishing Co., 121 Chanlon Rd., New Providence NJ 07974. (908)464-6800.

SUCCESSFUL SCRIPTWRITING, by Jurgen Wolff and Kerry Cox, Writer's Digest Books, 1507 Dana Ave., Cincinnati OH 45207. (513)531-2690.

THE WRITER'S GUIDE TO BOOK EDITORS, PUBLISHERS & LITERARY AGENTS, by Jeff Herman, Prima Publishing, Box 1260, 3875 Atherton Rd., Rocklin CA 95765. (916)632-4400 .

Websites of Interest

The Internet provides a wealth of information for writers. The number of websites devoted to writing and publishing is vast and will continue to expand as the year progresses. Below is a short—and thus incomplete—list of websites that offer information and hypertext links to other pertinent sites relating to writing and publishing. Because the Internet is such an amorphous, evolving, mutable entity with website addresses launching, crashing and changing daily, some of these addresses may be obsolete by the time this book goes to print. But this list does give you a few starting points for your online journey. If, in the course of your electronic ventures, you find additional websites of interest, please let us know by e-mailing us at writersmarket@fwpubs.com.

AcqWeb: http://www.library.vanderbilt.edu/law/acqs/acqs.html

Although geared toward librarians and researchers, AcqWeb provides reference information useful to writers, such as library catalogs, bibliographic services, Books in Print, and other Web reference resources.

Amazon.com: http://www.amazon.com

Calling itself "A bookstore too big for the physical world," Amazon.com has more than 3 million books available on their website at discounted prices, plus a personal notification service of new releases, reader reviews, bestseller and suggested book information.

Authorlink: http://www.authorlink.com

An information and news service for editors, literary agents and writers. Showcasing and matching quality manuscripts to publishers' needs, this site also contains interviews with editors and agents, publishing industry news, links and writer's guidelines.

Barnes and Noble Online: http://www.barnesandnoble.com

The world's largest bookstore chain's website contains 600,000 in-stock titles at discount prices as well as personalized recommendations, online events with authors and book forum access for members.

Book Zone: http://www.bookzone.com

A catalog source for books, audio books, and more, with links to other publishing opportunities, diversions and distractions, such as news, classifieds, contests, magazines, and trade groups.

Books A to Z: http://www.booksatoz.com

Information on publications services and leads to other useful websites, including areas for book research, production services, self-publishing, bookstores, organizations, and publishers.

Books and Writing Online: http://www.interzone.com/Books/books.html

A collection of sources directing you to other sites on the net, this is a good place to jump to other areas on the Web with information pertaining to writing, literature and publishing.

BookWeb: http://www.ambook.org

This ABA site offers books news, markets, discussions groups, events, resources and other book-related information.

Bookwire: http://www.bookwire.com

A gateway to finding information about publishers, booksellers, libraries, authors, reviews and awards. Also offers information about frequently asked publishing questions and answers, a calendar of events, a mailing list, and other helpful resources.

Children's Writing Resource Center: http://www.write4kids.com

Presented by Children's Book Insider, The Newsletter for Children's Writers. Offers information on numerous aspects of publishing and children's literature, such as an InfoCenter, a Research Center, results of various surveys, and secrets on getting published.

Crisp: http://www.crispzine.com

Award-winning Bibliotech section features established fiction and poetry editors volunteering their creative and connective assistance to new "under35" writers, as well as multi-genre excerpts, interviews, information and inspiration for—and from—writers of all ages.

Editor & Publisher: http://www.mediainfo.com

The Internet source for Editor & Publisher, *this site provides up-to-date industry news, with other opportunities such as a research area and bookstore, a calendar of events and classifieds.*

The Electronic Newsstand: http://www.enews.com

One of the largest directories of magazines on the Web. The Electronic Newsstand not only provides links to their magazines, but also tracks the content of many major magazines on a continually updating basis. It also allows the user to customize their own newsstand to view only the magazines of their choice.

Inkspot: http://www.inkspot.com

An elaborate site that provides information about workshops, how-to information, copyright, quotations, writing tips, resources, contests, market information, publishers, booksellers, associations, mailing lists, newsletters, conferences, and more.

Internet Entertainment Network: http://HollywoodNetwork.com

This site covers everything in Hollywood whether its dealmaking, music, screenwriting, or profiles of agents and Hollywood executives.

Internet Road Map to Books: http://www.bookport.com/b_roadmap.html

Leads to publishers' websites, resources for writers, book reviews, online editing, and other helpful areas.

John Labovitz's E-zine List: http://www.meer.net/~john1/e-zine-list

Searchable database of nearly 2,500 e-zines updated monthly, browsable by title or by a list of key words, such as fiction, literary, essays, fantasy, travel, etc.

Publishers' Catalogues Home Page: http://www.lights.com/publisher/index.html

A mammoth link collection of publishers around the world arranged geographically. This site is one of the most comprehensive directories on the Internet of publishers.

United States Postal Service: http://www.usps.gov/welcome.htm

Domestic and International postage rate calculator, stamp ordering, zip code look up, express mail tracking, etc.

The Write Page: http://www.writepage.com

Online newsletter for readers and writers of genre fiction, featuring information on authors, books about writing, new releases, organizations, conferences, websites, research, public service efforts writers can partake in, and writer's rights.

Organizations of Interest

BY ANDREW LUCYSZYN

Writing is a solitary exercise—it often leaves writers shut away by themselves. Writers' organizations can provide contact to the outside world, allowing you to connect with thousands of others who share the same goals, struggle with the same challenges and ask the same questions about editors, publishers and agents.

An organization's function varies according to its size and goals. Local groups tend to focus on assisting with the craft of writing through critique or reading sessions. National organizations often pursue goals that are wider in scope, such as negotiating collective bargaining agreements or health insurance coverage for members. Organizations offer diverse benefits, from helpful newsletters and workshops, to dependable databases of other writers' experiences in different markets, to highly prestigious awards. Members' contributions differ as well, ranging from who brings the doughnuts next week to hundreds of dollars in dues and meeting professional membership qualifications.

The Internet has given discussion groups a new platform on which to meet, and writers have taken full advantage of this common meeting ground. Some organizations operate only online with moderated forums, vast information resources and members from around the world. These groups have the advantage of instant communication and a wide array of opinions. However, they leave you staring at the computer in your den.

Whether you write nonfiction or science fiction, self-help or short stories, there are national organizations representing your field as a whole or representing their members in court. Hundreds more smaller, local groups are providing assistance from paragraph to paragraph. There is an organization—probably several—to suit your needs.

ACADEMY OF AMERICAN POETS, 584 Broadway, Suite 1208, New York NY 10012-3250. (212)274-0343. Fax: (212)274-9427. Website: http://www.poets.org. Contact: David Killeen.

AMERICAN BOOK PRODUCERS ASSOCIATION, 160 Fifth Ave., Suite 625, New York NY 10010-7000. (212)645-2368.

AMERICAN MEDICAL WRITERS ASSOCIATION, 9650 Rockville Pike, Bethesda MD 20814-3998. (301)493-0003.

AMERICAN SOCIETY OF JOURNALISTS AND AUTHORS (ASJA), 1501 Broadway, Suite 302, New York NY 10036. (212)997-0947. Fax: (212)768-7414. E-mail: asja@compuserve.com. Website: http://www.asja.org. Executive Director: Alexandra Owens.

AMERICAN TRANSLATORS ASSOCIATION, 1800 Diagonal Rd., Suite 220, Alexandria VA 22314-0214. (703)683-6100.

ASIAN AMERICAN WRITERS' WORKSHOP, 37 St. Mark's Place, New York NY 10003. (212)228-6718. Fax: (212)228-7718. Website: http://www.panix.com/~aaww/.

ASSOCIATED WRITING PROGRAMS, Tallwood House MS1E3, George Mason University, Fairfax VA 22030.

ASSOCIATION OF AUTHORS' REPRESENTATIVES, 10 Astor Pl., 3rd Floor, New York NY 10003. (212)353-3709.

ASSOCIATION OF DESK-TOP PUBLISHERS, 3401-A800 Adams Ave., San Diego CA 92116-2490. (619)563-9714.

THE AUTHORS GUILD, 330 W. 42nd St., 29th Floor, New York NY 10036. (212)563-5904.

THE AUTHORS LEAGUE OF AMERICA, INC., 330 W. 42nd St., New York NY 10036. (212)564-8350.

CANADIAN AUTHORS ASSOCIATION, 320 S. Shores Rd., P.O. Box 419, Campbellford, Ontario, K0L 1L0, Canada. (705)653-0323. Fax: (705)653-0593. E-mail: canauthedden.on.ca. Website: http://www.Canauthors.org/national .html. Contact: Alec McEachern.

THE DRAMATISTS GUILD, 1501 Broadway, Suite 701, New York NY 10036-5601. (212)398-9366. Fax: (212)944-0420.

EDITORIAL FREELANCERS ASSOCIATION, 71 W. 23rd St., Suite 1900, New York NY 10010. (212)929-5400. Fax: (212)929-5439. Website: http://www.THE-EFA.org.

EDUCATION WRITERS ASSOCIATION, 1331 H. NW, Suite 307, Washington DC 20036. (202)637-9700. Fax:(202)637-9707. E-mail: ewaoffice@aol.com. Website: http://www.ewa/org.

FREELANCE EDITORIAL ASSOCIATION, P.O. Box 380835, Cambridge MA 02238-0835. (617)576-8797.

INTERNATIONAL ASSOCIATION OF BUSINESS COMMUNICATORS, 1 Hallidie Plaza, Suite 600, San Francisco CA 94102. (415)433-3400. Website: http://www.iabc.com.

INTERNATIONAL ASSOCIATION OF CRIME WRITERS INC., North American Branch, JAF Box 1500, New York NY 10116. (212)243-8966.

INTERNATIONAL ONLINE WRITERS ASSOCIATION (IOWA), Website: http://www.best.com/~kali/iowa/.

INTERNATIONAL TELEVISION ASSOCIATION, 6311 N. O'Connor Rd., Suite 230, Irving TX 75039. (972)869-1112. E-mail: itvahq@worldnet.att.net. Website: http://www.itva.org.

INTERNATIONAL WOMEN'S WRITING GUILD, Box 810, Gracie Station, New York NY 10028-0082. (212)737-7536. Website: http://www/iwwg.com. Executive Director: Hannelore Hahn.

MYSTERY WRITERS OF AMERICA, INC., 17 E. 47th St., 6th Floor, New York NY 10017. Website: http://www.bookwire.com/mwa/. President: Donald E. Westlake. Executive Director: Priscilla Ridgeway.

NATIONAL ASSOCIATION OF SCIENCE WRITERS, Box 294, Greenlawn NY 11740. (516)757-5664.

NATIONAL WRITERS ASSOCIATION, 1450 S. Havana, Suite 424, Aurora CO 80012. (303)751-7844.

NATIONAL WRITERS UNION, 113 University Pl., 6th Floor, New York NY 10003. (212) 254-0279. Fax: (212) 254-0673. E-mail: nwu wu.org. Website: http://www.nwu.org/nwu. Contact: Bruce Hartford.

NEW DRAMATISTS, 424 W. 44th St., New York NY 10036. (212)757-6060.

PEN AMERICAN CENTER, 568 Broadway, New York NY 10012. (212)334-1660.

POETRY SOCIETY OF AMERICA, 15 Grammercy Park, New York NY 10003. (212)254-9628. Website: http://www.bookwire.com/psa/psa.html.

POETS & WRITERS, 72 Spring St., New York NY 10012. (212)226-3586. Fax: (212) 226-3963. Website: http://www.pw.org.

PUBLIC RELATIONS SOCIETY OF AMERICA, 33 Irving Pl., New York NY 10003. (212)995-2230.

ROMANCE WRITERS OF AMERICA, 13700 Veterans Memorial, Suite 315, Houston TX 77014-1073. (281) 440-6885. Fax: (281) 440-7510. Website: http://www. rwanational.com. President: Libby Hall.

SCIENCE FICTION AND FANTASY WRITERS OF AMERICA, INC., 532 La Guardia Pl., #632, New York NY 10012-1428. Website: http://www.sfwa.org/org/sfwa_info.htm. President: Michael Capobianco.

SOCIETY OF AMERICAN BUSINESS EDITORS & WRITERS, University of Missouri, School of Journalism, 76 Gannett Hall, Columbia MO 65211. (573)882-7862. Fax: (573)884-1372. Website: http://www.sabew.org. Contact: Doris Barnhart, executive assistant.

SOCIETY OF AMERICAN TRAVEL WRITERS, 4101 Lake Boone Trail, Suite 201, Raleigh NC 27607. (919)787-5181.

SOCIETY OF CHILDREN'S BOOK WRITERS AND ILLUSTRATORS, 345 N. Maple Dr., Suite 296, Beverly Hills CA 90210. (310)859-9887. Website: http://www.scbwi.org. President: Stephen Mooser. Executive Director: Lin Oliver.

SOCIETY OF PROFESSIONAL JOURNALISTS, 16 S. Jackson, Greencastle IN 46135-1514. (765)653-3333. Website: http://www.spj.org.

VOLUNTEER LAWYERS FOR THE ARTS, One E. 53rd St., 6th Floor, New York NY 10022. (212)319-2787.

WRITERS GUILD OF ALBERTA, 11759 Groat Rd., Edmonton, Alberta, T5M 3K6, Canada. (403)422-8174.

WRITERS GUILD OF AMERICA, East Chapter: 555 W. 57th St., New York NY 10019, (212)767-7800; West Chapter: 8955 Beverly Blvd., West Hollywood CA 90048, (310)550-1000. Website: http://www.wga.org.

Glossary

Key to symbols and abbreviations appears on the front and back inside covers.

Advance. A sum of money a publisher pays a writer prior to the publication of a book. It is usually paid in installments, such as one-half on signing the contract; one-half on delivery of a complete and satisfactory manuscript. The advance is paid against the royalty money that will be earned by the book.

Advertorial. Advertising presented in such a way as to resemble editorial material. Information may be the same as that contained in an editorial feature, but it is paid for or supplied by an advertiser and the word "advertisement" appears at the top of the page.

All rights. See Rights and the Writer in the Minding the Details article.

Anthology A collection of selected writings by various authors or a gathering of works by one author.

Assignment. Editor asks a writer to produce a specific article for an agreed-upon fee.

Auction. Publishers sometimes bid for the acquisition of a book manuscript that has excellent sales prospects. The bids are for the amount of the author's advance, advertising and promotional expenses, royalty percentage, etc. Auctions are conducted by agents.

Avant-garde. Writing that is innovative in form, style or subject matter. Avant-garde works often are considered difficult and challenging.

B&W. Abbreviation for black and white photographs.

Backlist. A publisher's list of its books that were not published during the current season, but that are still in print.

Belles lettres. A term used to describe fine or literary writing—writing more to entertain than to inform or instruct.

Bimonthly. Every two months. See also *semimonthly.*

Bio. A sentence or brief paragraph about the writer. It can appear at the bottom of the first or last page of a writer's article or short story or on a contributor's page.

Biweekly. Every two weeks.

Boilerplate. A standardized contract. When an editor says "our standard contract," he means the boilerplate with no changes. Writers should be aware that most authors and/or agents make many changes on the boilerplate.

Book packager. Draws all elements of a book together, from the initial concept to writing and marketing strategies, then sells the book package to a book publisher and/or movie producer. Also known as book producer or book developer.

Business size envelope. Also known as a #10 envelope, it is the standard size used in sending business correspondence.

Byline. Name of the author appearing with the published piece.

Category fiction. A term used to include all various labels attached to types of fiction. See also *genre.*

CD-ROM. Compact Disc-Read Only Memory. A computer information storage medium capable of holding enormous amounts of data. Information on a CD-ROM cannot be deleted. A computer user must have a CD-ROM drive to access a CD-ROM.

Chapbook. A small booklet, usually paperback, of poetry, ballads or tales.

Clean copy. A manuscript free of errors, cross-outs, wrinkles or smudges.

Clips Samples, usually from newspapers or magazines, of your *published* work.

Coffee table book. An oversize book, heavily illustrated.

Column inch. The amount of space contained in one inch of a typeset column.

Commercial novels. Novels designed to appeal to a broad audience. These are often broken down into categories such as western, mystery and romance. See also *genre.*

Commissioned work. See *assignment.*

Concept. A statement that summarizes a screenplay or teleplay—before the outline or treatment is written.

Contact sheet. A sheet of photographic paper on which negatives are transferred so you can see the entire roll of shots placed together on one sheet of paper without making separate, individual prints.

Contributor's copies. Copies of the issues of magazines sent to the author in which the author's work appears.

Cooperative publishing. See *co-publishing.*

Co-publishing. Arrangement where author and publisher share publication costs and profits of a book. Also known as *cooperative publishing*. See also *subsidy publisher.*

Copyediting. Editing a manuscript for grammar, punctuation and printing style, not subject content.

Copyright. A means to protect an author's work. See Copyright in the Minding the Details section.

Cover letter. A brief letter, accompanying a complete manuscript, especially useful if responding to an editor's request for a manuscript. A cover letter may also accompany a book proposal. A cover letter is *not* a query letter; see Targeting Your Ideas in the Getting Published section.

CV. Curriculum vita. A brief listing of qualifications and career accomplishments.

Derivative works. A work that has been translated, adapted, abridged, condensed, annotated or otherwise produced by altering a previously created work. Before producing a derivative work, it is necessary to secure the written permission of the copyright owner of the original piece.

Desktop publishing. A publishing system designed for a personal computer. The system is capable of typesetting, some illustration, layout, design and printing—so that the final piece can be distributed and/or sold.

Disk. A round, flat magnetic plate on which computer data may be stored.

Docudrama. A fictional film rendition of recent newsmaking events and people.

Dot-matrix. Printed type where individual characters are composed of a matrix or pattern of tiny dots. Near letter quality (see *NLQ*) dot-matrix submissions are generally acceptable to editors.

Electronic submission. A submission made by modem or on computer disk.

El-hi. Elementary to high school.

E-mail. Electronic mail. Mail generated on a computer and delivered over a computer network to a specific individual or group of individuals. To send or receive e-mail, a user must have an account with an online service, which provides an e-mail address and electronic mailbox.

Epigram. A short, witty sometimes paradoxical saying.

Erotica. Fiction or art that is sexually oriented.

Experimental. See *avant-garde*.

Fair use. A provision of the copyright law that says short passages from copyrighted material may be used without infringing on the owner's rights.

Fax (facsimile machine). A communication system used to transmit documents over telephone lines.

Feature. An article giving the reader information of human interest rather than news. Also used by magazines to indicate a lead article or distinctive department.

Filler. A short item used by an editor to "fill" out a newspaper column or magazine page. It could be a timeless news item, a joke, an anecdote, some light verse or short humor, puzzle, etc.

First North American serial rights. See Rights and the Writer in the Minding the Details article.

Formula story. Familiar theme treated in a predictable plot structure—such as boy meets girl, boy loses girl, boy gets girl.

Frontlist. A publisher's list of its books that are new to the current season.

Galleys. The first typeset version of a manuscript that has not yet been divided into pages.

Genre. Refers either to a general classification of writing, such as the novel or the poem, or to the categories within those classifications, such as the problem novel or the sonnet. Genre fiction describes commercial novels, such as mysteries, romances and science fiction. Also called category fiction.

Ghostwriter. A writer who puts into literary form an article, speech, story or book based on another person's ideas or knowledge.

Gift book. A book designed as a gift item. Often small in size with few illustrations and placed close to a bookstore's checkout as an "impulse" buy, gift books tend to be written to a specific niche, such as golfers, mothers, etc.

Glossy. A black and white photograph with a shiny surface as opposed to one with a non-shiny matte finish.

Gothic novel. A fiction category or genre in which the central character is usually a beautiful young girl, the setting an old mansion or castle, and there is a handsome hero and a real menace, either natural or supernatural.

Graphic novel. An adaptation of a novel in graphic form, long comic strip or heavily illustrated story, of 40 pages or more, produced in paperback form.

Hard copy. The printed copy of a computer's output.

Hardware. All the mechanically-integrated components of a computer that are not software. Circuit boards, transistors and the machines that are the actual computer are the hardware.

High-lo. Material written for newer readers, generally adults, with a *high* interest level and *low* reading ability.

Home page. The first page of a World Wide Web document.

Honorarium. Token payment—small amount of money, or a byline and copies of the publication.

How-to. Books and magazine articles offering a combination of information and advice in describing how something can be accomplished. Subjects range widely from hobbies to psychology.

Hypertext. Words or groups of words in an electronic document that are linked to other text, such as a definition or a related document. Hypertext can also be linked to illustrations.

Illustrations. May be photographs, old engravings, artwork. Usually paid for separately from the manuscript. See also *package sale*.

Imprint. Name applied to a publisher's specific line or lines of books (e.g., Anchor Books is an imprint of Doubleday).

Interactive. A type of computer interface that takes user input, such as answers to computer-generated questions, and then acts upon that input.

Interactive fiction. Works of fiction in book or computer software format in which the reader determines the path the story will take. The reader chooses from several alternatives at the end of a "chapter," and thus determines the structure of the story. Interactive fiction features multiple plots and endings.

Internet. A worldwide network of computers that offers access to a wide variety of electronic resources. Originally a US Department of Defense project, begun in 1969.

Invasion of privacy. Writing about persons (even though truthfully) without their consent.

Kill fee. Fee for a complete article that was assigned but which was subsequently cancelled.

Lead time. The time between the acquisition of a manuscript by an editor and its actual publication.

Letter-quality submission Computer printout that looks typewritten.

Libel. A false accusation or any published statement or presentation that tends to expose another to public contempt, ridicule, etc. Defenses are truth; fair comment on a matter of public interest; and privileged communication—such as a report of legal proceedings or client's communication to a lawyer.

List royalty. A royalty payment based on a percentage of a book's retail (or "list") price. Compare *net royalty.*

Literary fiction. The general category of serious, non-formulaic, intelligent fiction.

Little magazine. Publications of limited circulation, usually on literary or political subject matter.

LORT. An acronym for League of Resident Theatres. Letters from A to D follow LORT and designate the size of the theater.

Magalog. Mail order catalog with how-to articles pertaining to the items for sale.

Mainstream fiction. Fiction that transcends popular novel categories such as mystery, romance and science fiction. Using conventional methods, this kind of fiction tells stories about people and their conflicts with greater depth of characterization, background, etc., than the more narrowly focused genre novels.

Mass market. Nonspecialized books of wide appeal directed toward a large audience. Smaller and more cheaply produced than trade paperbacks, they are found in many non-bookstore outlets, such as drug stores, supermarkets, etc.

Microcomputer A small computer system capable of performing various specific tasks with data it receives. Personal computers are microcomputers.

Midlist. Those titles on a publisher's list that are not expected to be big sellers, but are expected to have limited sales. Midlist books are mainstream, not literary, scholarly or genre, and are usually written by new or unknown writers.

Model release. A paper signed by the subject of a photograph (or the subject's guardian, if a juvenile) giving the photographer permission to use the photograph, editorially or for advertising purposes or for some specific purpose as stated.

Modem. A device used to transmit data from one computer to another via telephone lines.

Monograph. A detailed and documented scholarly study concerning a single subject.

Multimedia. Computers and software capable of integrating text, sound, photographic-quality images, animation and video.

Multiple submissions Sending more than one poem, gag or greeting card idea at the same time. This term is often used synonymously with simultaneous submission.

Narrative nonfiction. A narrative presentation of actual events.

Narrative poem. Poetry that tells a story. One of the three main genres of poetry (the others being dramatic poetry and lyric poetry).

Net royalty. A royalty payment based on the amount of money a book publisher receives on the sale of a book after booksellers' discounts, special sales discounts and returns. Compare list royalty.

Network. A group of computers electronically linked to share information and resources.

New Age. A "fringe" topic that has become increasingly mainstream. Formerly New Age included UFOs and occult phenomena. The term has evolved to include more general topics such as psychology, religion and health, but emphasizing the mystical, spiritual or alternative aspects.

Newsbreak. A brief, late-breaking news story added to the front page of a newspaper at press time or a magazine news item of importance to readers.

NLQ. Near letter-quality print required by some editors for computer printout submissions. See also *dot-matrix*

Novelette. A short novel, or a long short story; 7,000 to 15,000 words approximately. Also known as a novella.

Novelization. A novel created from the script of a popular movie, usually called a movie "tie-in" and published in paperback.

Offprint. Copies of an author's article taken "out of issue" before a magazine is bound and given to the author in lieu of monetary payment. An offprint could be used by the writer as a published writing sample.

On spec. An editor expresses an interest in a proposed article idea and agrees to consider the finished piece for publication "on speculation." The editor is under no obligation to buy the finished manuscript.

One-shot feature. As applies to syndicates, single feature article for syndicate to sell; as contrasted with article series or regular columns syndicated.

One-time rights. See Rights and the Writer in the Minding the Details article.

Online Service. Computer networks accessed via modem. These services provide users with various resources, such as electronic mail, news, weather, special interest groups and shopping. Examples of such providers include America Online and CompuServe.

Outline. A summary of a book's contents in five to 15 double-spaced pages; often in the form of chapter headings with a descriptive sentence or two under each one to show the scope of the book. A screenplay's or teleplay's outline is a scene-by-scene narrative description of the story (10-15 pages for a ½-hour teleplay; 15-25 pages for a 1-hour teleplay; 25-40 pages for a 90-minute teleplay; 40-60 pages for a 2-hour feature film or teleplay).

Over-the-transom. Describes the submission of unsolicited material by a freelance writer.

Package sale. The editor buys manuscript and photos as a "package" and pays for them with one check.

Page rate. Some magazines pay for material at a fixed rate per published page, rather than per word

Parallel submission. A strategy of developing several articles from one unit of research for submission to similar magazines. This strategy differs from simultaneous or multiple submission, where the same article is marketed to several magazines at the same time.

Payment on acceptance. The editor sends you a check for your article, story or poem as soon as he decides to publish it.

Payment on publication. The editor doesn't send you a check for your material until it is published.

Pen name. The use of a name other than your legal name on articles, stories or books when you wish to remain anonymous. Simply notify your post office and bank that you are using the name so that you'll receive mail and/or checks in that name. Also called a pseudonym.

Photo feature. Feature in which the emphasis is on the photographs rather than on accompanying written material.

Plagiarism. Passing off as one's own the expression of ideas and words of another writer.

Potboiler. Refers to writing projects a freelance writer does to "keep the pot boiling" while working on major articles—quick projects to bring in money with little time or effort. These may be fillers such as anecdotes or how-to tips, but could be short articles or stories.

Proofreading. Close reading and correction of a manuscript's typographical errors.

Proposal. A summary of a proposed book submitted to a publisher, particularly used for nonfiction manuscripts. A proposal often contains an individualized cover letter, one-page overview of the book, marketing information, competitive books, author information, chapter-by-chapter outline, 2-3 sample chapters and attachments (if relevant) such as magazine articles about the topic and articles you have written (particularly on the proposed topic).

Proscenium. The area of the stage in front of the curtain

Prospectus. A preliminary written description of a book or article, usually one page in length.

Pseudonym. See *pen name.*

Public domain. Material that was either never copyrighted or whose copyright term has expired.

Query. A letter to an editor intended to raise interest in an article you propose to write.

Release. A statement that your idea is original, has never been sold to anyone else and that you are selling the negotiated rights to the idea upon payment.

Remainders. Copies of a book that are slow to sell and can be purchased from the publisher at a reduced price. Depending on the author's book contract, a reduced royalty or no royalty is paid on remainder books.

Reporting time. The time it takes for an editor to report to the author on his/her query or manuscript.

Reprint rights. See Rights and the Writer in the Minding the Details article.

Round-up article. Comments from, or interviews with, a number of celebrities or experts on a single theme.

Royalties, standard hardcover book. 10% of the retail price on the first 5,000 copies sold; 12½% on the next 5,000; 15% thereafter.

Royalties, standard mass paperback book. 4 to 8% of the retail price on the first 150,000 copies sold.

Royalties, standard trade paperback book. No less than 6% of list price on the first 20,000 copies; 7½% thereafter.

Scanning. A process through which letter-quality printed text (see *NLQ*) or artwork is read by a computer scanner and converted into workable data.

Screenplay. Script for a film intended to be shown in theaters.

Self-publishing. In this arrangement, the author keeps all income derived from the book, but he pays for its manufacturing, production and marketing.

Semimonthly. Twice per month.

Semiweekly. Twice per week.

Serial. Published periodically, such as a newspaper or magazine.

Sidebar. A feature presented as a companion to a straight news report (or main magazine article) giving sidelights on human-interest aspects or sometimes elucidating just one aspect of the story.

Similar submission. See *parallel submission.*

Simultaneous submissions. Sending the same article, story or poem to several publishers at the same time. Some publishers refuse to consider such submissions. No simultaneous submissions should be made without stating the fact in your letter.

Slant. The approach or style of a story or article that will appeal to readers of a specific magazine. For example, a magazine may always use stories with an upbeat ending.

Slice-of-life vignette. A short fiction piece intended to realistically depict an interesting moment of everyday living.

Slides. Usually called transparencies by editors looking for color photographs.

Slush pile. The stack of unsolicited or misdirected manuscripts received by an editor or book publisher.

Software. The computer programs that control computer hardware, usually run from a disk drive of some sort. Computers need software in order to run. These can be word processors, games, spreadsheets, etc.

Speculation. The editor agrees to look at the author's manuscript with no assurance that it will be bought.

Style. The way in which something is written—for example, short, punchy sentences or flowing narrative.

Subsidiary rights. All those rights, other than book publishing rights included in a book contract—such as paperback, book club, movie rights, etc.

Subsidy publisher. A book publisher who charges the author for the cost to typeset and print his book, the jacket, etc. as opposed to a royalty publisher who pays the author.

Synopsis. A brief summary of a story, novel or play. As part of a book proposal, it is a comprehensive summary condensed in a page or page and a half, single-spaced. See also *outline.*

Tabloid Newspaper format publication on about half the size of the regular newspaper page, such as the *National Enquirer.*

Tagline. A caption for a photo or a comment added to a filler.

Tearsheet Page from a magazine or newspaper containing your printed story, article, poem or ad.

TOC. Table of Contents.

Trade. Either a hardcover or paperback book; subject matter frequently concerns a special interest. Books are directed toward the layperson rather than the professional.

Transparencies. Positive color slides; not color prints.

Treatment. Synopsis of a television or film script (40-60 pages for a 2-hour feature film or teleplay).

Unsolicited manuscript. A story, article, poem or book that an editor did not specifically ask to see.

User friendly. Easy to handle and use. Refers to computer hardware and software designed with the user in mind.

Vanity publisher. See *subsidy publisher.*

Word processor. A computer program, used in lieu of a typewriter, that allows for easy, flexible manipulation and output of printed copy.

World Wide Web (WWW). An Internet resource that utilizes hypertext to access information. It also supports formatted text, illustrations and sounds, depending on the user's computer capabilities.

Work-for-hire. See Copyright in the Minding the Details article.

YA. Young adult books.

Book Publishers Subject Index

This index will help you find publishers that consider books on specific subjects—the subjects you choose to write about. Remember that a publisher may be listed here under a general subject category such as Art and Architecture, while the company publishes *only* art history or how-to books. Be sure to consult each company's detailed individual listing, its book catalog and several of its books before you send your query or proposal. The page number of the detailed listing is provided for your convenience.

FICTION

NONFICTION

BOOK PUBLISHERS SUBJECT INDEX

BOOK PUBLISHERS SUBJECT INDEX

NO POSTAGE
NECESSARY
IF MAILED
IN THE
UNITED STATES

BUSINESS REPLY MAIL
FIRST-CLASS MAIL PERMIT NO. 17 CINCINNATI OH

General Index

This index lists every market appearing in the book; use it to find specific companies you wish to approach. Markets that appeared in the 1998 edition of *Writer's Market* but are not included in this edition are identified by a two-letter code explaining why the market was omitted: (**ED**)—Editorial Decision, (**NS**)—Not Accepting Submissions, (**NR**)—No or Late Response to Listing Request, (**OB**)—Out of Business, (**RR**)—Removed by Market's Request, (**UC**)—Unable to Contact, (**RP**)—Business Restructed or Purchased, (**NP**)—No longer pays or Pays in copies only, (**SR**)—Subsidy/Royalty Publisher, (**UF**)—Uncertain Future.

A

B

F

G

H

I

J

M

N

O

P

Q

R

S

U

V

W

X

Y

Z